# Proceedings of the
# Indian National Congress
## Vol. 2:1890-1894

Edited and Introduced by

**Mushirul Hasan**

Published by

NIYOGI BOOKS

D-78, Okhla Industrial Area, Phase-I
New Delhi-110 020, India
Tel: 91-11-26816301, 49327000
Fax: 91-11-26810483, 26813830
email: niyogibooks@gmail.com
www.niyogibooksindia.com



ISBN: 978-93-81523-87-2
Year of Publication: 2014



Printed at: Niyogi Offset Pvt. Ltd., New Delhi, India

# Introduction

## Indian National Congress: Early Aspirations to Freedom

### Mushirul Hasan

The Indian National Congress had changed a great deal since its birth in December 1885. Without acquiring a 'national' status, it wielded a fair degree of political influence through the affiliated societies, political as well as social. It was no longer a mere pressure group on authorities, but could take its own line over policy without fear of embarrassing them. For an ordinary member, it was the path to influence and honour. For the intelligentsia, new ideas were beginning to break on to public consciousness. Hence, the years covered in this volume give the appearance of a 'new' India.

*Eh larka tarahdar paida hua hai.*

'This boy is smart at birth,' 9 January 1890. On the Indian National Congress.

The associations were held together by certain common principles, but they languished by the end of the nineteenth century. A closer look at the Congress (1890-94) shows how very different it was from the associations. These years saw a new start, a much more promising trend towards achieving some measure of practical reforms. At the same time, it would be misleading to picture the Congress growing by leaps and bounds. What can be said with certainty is that its membership is difficult to ascertain as individual members were sometimes more, sometimes less. Not all of them were active. The venue made a difference: in big cities, the Congress could call on a couple of hundred more members, including recognised figures or members of the urban gentry. They were nearly always on the Congress side. Most of the vernacular newspapers were supportive. In day-to-day affairs, therefore, the Congress was slowly and steadily becoming part of an expanded political community.

Although these possibilities of expansion offered many choices, there were glaring inconsistencies and contradictions in the pursuit of certain policies and programmes. Until

1899, the Congress did not have a written constitution. Many of the founders expressed their apprehension about the future. There was, consequently, divergence of outlook, with the proponents of a virulent form of nationalism finding it difficult to grasp the ideas underlying the approaches of Dadabhai Naoroji and Gopal Krishna Gokhale. With their patience running out, their doubts increased about their continuing cooperation with the government. This said, the moderates had more to offer, at any rate on paper, and their moderation turned out to be their principal asset in future years. At the time, they represented what their supporters wanted.

Nevertheless, the Congress had to overcome the opposition of Syed Ahmad Khan, the Aligarh reformer. He was a product of the 'Delhi Renaissance', proud and privileged. But he was too elitist in his background to sympathise with the masses or share their aspirations. Once he moved from Delhi, his birthplace, to fulfil his dream of starting a college in Aligarh, he became more and more distant from the people. He could only think of the well-to-do Muslims, i.e., the emerging middle class or the landowning aristocracy, and the impact of Congress policies on their fortunes. Badruddin Tyabji pointed out that there was room for compromise, but Syed Ahmad was not convinced. He was strong in resistance and somewhat crude in raising the spectre of Bengali domination. Contemporaries thought that the bureaucracy set him up to pursue its 'divide and rule' policies.

Going by such examples, it appeared as if 'unity' existed more on paper than in reality. Allan Octavian Hume, one of the founders, realised that the cleavage existed in many other areas. This was in part because ordinary men and women did not understand the theories. They were interested in action, not in theory. They desired remedial measures and not improvised action. The leaders, on the other hand, had to work, more or less unitedly, to overcome their shortcomings. They had to. They wanted power to spring back into effective political action. They wanted to gain a popular-based following, and not just men of middle-class origin.

Let us pause to mention the class background of the leaders. Generally speaking, officials described them as lawyers and professional lawyers of high caste elites, such as the bhadralok in Bengal and the Chitpavan Brahmans in Maharashtra, and portrayed them as shrewd manipulators, who exploited the gullible masses to promote their own ends. Nowadays, this cut-and-dried explanation has been replaced by a more sophisticated approach to the rise of Congress nationalism. It is increasingly clear that what transformed Indian politics was the spirit of cool calculation, and the significant moves towards the politics of the masses, away from those of privilege alone.

In this respect, some of the prominent Congress leaders enhanced their standing and importance. Beneficiaries of the Western system of education, which also produced ultra-conservatives, believed that the future of the nation depended on revitalising and drawing together the people's strength. Only in this way, they thought, could the various castes and communities be welded into a coherent whole. They also reached out to the political classes in Great Britain, a strategy that worked for a while. Back home, they were prepared to collaborate with Dufferin and his successors and accept the monarchy. But they were disillusioned. They could not convince him to appreciate their point of view. They couldn't convince him that reform was a better alternative to repression or political conservatism. As a matter of fact, Dufferin expressed no interest even in a cautious beginning of collaboration. He wanted to ensure that this great new force ('microscopic minority') was not harnessed to contribute to the strength and prosperity of the citizens of the Indian Empire. This being the case, the Congress leaders, with all their good intentions, could not narrow the gulf separating the rulers and the ruled. This led them to follow the political and social path of evolution, not revolution.

On the credit side, prominent Congress leaders were wedded to social reform and representative government. In a country of uneven development, their concern for the poor and the minorities was genuine. In this respect they followed broad and consistent aims. What is more, they consistently proclaimed their faith in building an inclusive society in a sharply differentiated society. In a country so rent by caste and communal disputes and by faction and regional particularism, this was itself a notable success. Thus Pandit Bishan Narayan Dar proclaimed at the Calcutta Congress, 'what are called Hindu interests and Mahomedan interests have really no existence in political matters'. He was cheered by the delegates.

On the debit side, the Congress' dependence on the government's 'goodwill' diminished its standing. This is illustrated by the opening speech of the Chairman of the Reception Committee of the Calcutta Congress in 1890, and the reference to Pherozeshah Mehta who welcomed the delegates in Bombay, as 'the grandest outcome of British Rule in India'. Notice, too, that the 1890 session of the Congress dissolved with the 'constitutional cheers', 'Long Live our Queen-Empress'. The proceedings (see below, p. 92) conclude with the following: 'Loud and prolonged cheers for the Queen-Empress were then given, and repeated many times, and then, as dusk closed in, the assembly dissolved'. The ordinary member who took the trouble of attending the annual session could scarcely be aroused by all this.

The Congress support structure was too much based on personal, regional and caste loyalties. As a result, the bosses represented not so much their party but specific interests to secure benefits for their constituency. Moreover, the Congress followed cautious socio-political policies, and moved lazily in the contested terrain of constitutional reforms. Hence, it was conceived to be an assembly only for the benefit of politicians and special-interest groups. Soon enough, the annual sessions turned into a big mela or a tamasha. Popular enthusiasm began to wane. Funds dried up. Not many heeded the high-pitched rhetoric. The leaders were earnest and well-intentioned, but they did little beyond renewing their pledges. They were, moreover, divided over future strategy and tactics. The internal feuds weakened the Congress.

Just when the morale was down, a silver lining appeared in an otherwise dismal picture. During the years covered by this volume, the leaders saw the involvement of the masses in politics as inevitable and so, sought to work with the new forces and to draw them into their fold. Owing to this noticeable shift in emphasis, India's poverty and impoverishment, compared with Britain's wealth and prosperity, became a common theme of discussion. Thus a major resolution on 'poverty' was adopted at the Madras Congress in 1894 (appended to the Report of the Tenth INC). Public discourses took a shift to, what in the latter-day parlance, was described as the 'left of centre'. Why, it was asked, was the empire so powerful and the colony caught in the poverty trap of a backward agrarian economy? Why were the masses exploited in the interests of the empire? The burgeoning vernacular press thirsted for action so that the drain of wealth could be stopped, expenditure on defence curtailed, taxation lowered, and the nation's wealth be distributed among the disadvantaged groups. The litany of complaints ran into numerous pages.

In 1892, the Congress met in Allahabad. It rejected the Indian Councils Act as well as the government of India resolution on the report of the Public Service Commission. It took up other issues as well, including taxation, the currency question, reduction of salt duty, judicial and police reforms, etc. W.C. Bonnerjee talked of agitation without stopping 'until we get what we all think and we all believe (Allahabad, 1892)'. A year later, the Madras Congress

*Sun to sahi jahaan me hai tera fasana kya; kehti hai tujhko khalq-i khuda ghaibana kya.*

'Do listen to what tales are being told about you; by what various names people call you behind your back,' 25 June 1891. The story of poverty-stricken Indians pleading for relief from the government. The man in boots and bow-tie symbolizes British colonialism. In this picture, a woman—'Hind'—draws his attention to the poverty-stricken child. The artist manages to bring out the disdain and indifference of the man marked 'England'; if equal interest is the clothing of the seven Indian figures. The Urdu verse is by the poet Insha.

claimed that it had 'amid scenes of enthusiasm' placed before 'an increasingly attentive public' the need for reform and the need for redress of grievances in the Indian Empire.

The Congress has lived through the vicissitudes of history for well over a century: it is a monumental achievement. It has worked with different combinations and forged coalitions to leave its imprint on India's political histories. It has committed countless errors, some knowingly but most unwittingly; the appeasement of caste and community leaders misfired; so did the readiness to trim the ideological sails to court the powerful and the wealthy. Yet the Congress showed extraordinary resilience. By the closing year of 1890, the assertion of caste and community identities became a source of embarrassment to all those Congressmen who proclaimed nationalist ideals. Under the circumstances, it was no mean achievement to keep the flock together.

It would be facile to judge the Congress performance in this short introduction, but it may be appropriate to conclude that it is not helpful to look upon Naoroji or Gokhale as precursors of Mohandas Karamchand Gandhi. These men and their policies must be examined in the context of the conditions of their times.

# REPORT

OF

# THE SIXTH

# INDIAN

# NATIONAL CONGRESS,

HELD AT

# CALCUTTA,

*On the 26th, 27th, 29th & 30th December,*

1890.

# In Memoriam.

# CHARLES BRADLAUGH,

THE

***FRIEND AND CHAMPION***

OF

# INDIA.

Born 26th September 1833.

Died 30th January 1891.

**He was one, who never turned his back but strode breastforwards,**
**Never doubted, clouds would break,**
**Never dreamed, though right *were* worsted, wrong *could* triumph,**
**Held—we fall to rise, are baffled to fight better, sleep to wake !**

# CONTENTS.

# THE SIXTH INDIAN NATIONAL CONGRESS.

**"Of course we have to submit resignedly to this ruinous, this unprincipled trans-frontier policy of the Government until we succeed in awakening the conscience of our British fellow-subjects. We are British subjects now of our own free choice; we have thrown in our lot with England for better and for worse, and it is this which enhances England's sin in permitting the continuance of this hateful policy. Will our British brethren never awake?"**

(*Speech of Mr. Dinshaw E. Wacha.**)

THE SIXTH CONGRESS assembled, for its first sitting, early in the afternoon of the 26th December, 1890. It met in a vast hall or pavilion, 250 feet in length by 150 in breadth, erected for the purpose in the Tivoli Gardens, a place of public resort at other times (most kindly lent by the Proprietors), a sort of minor Vauxhall, where switchback railways, balloons, swimming bath and other attractions have, from time to time, in the past, rendered it well known to the public.

The huge hall, with its multitudinous platforms rising terrace above terrace, elaborated throughout—ceilings, pillars and curtains—with the national colours, Red, Green and White, presented, perhaps, a more striking appearance than any of its predecessors. It nominally provided seats for only some 5,200 persons, but at one time during the first day accommodated very nearly 8,000. Yet, despite its great size, as in the case of all previous Congress Halls, its acoustic properties were such that every word spoken by the vast majority of the speakers (who all spoke from a raised tribune at the back of the President's platform) was distinctly heard even in the furthest corners. A new and pleasing feature was the approach; a covered passage 300 feet long, 50 wide and 30 high, open at the sides (though shaded here by rows of huge and gaily variegated crotons), leading straight from the outer gate to the centre of the hall. It was divided by the posts, or pillars, that supported the embroidered crimson cloth roofing, into three aisles, the central one for passers to and fro, and the lateral ones furnished luxuriously to serve as waiting and drawing rooms.

The Chair was taken at 2 P.M. by Mr. Mano Mohan Ghose, an eminent Calcutta Barrister, whose duty it was, as Chairman of the Reception Committee, to welcome all the delegates and call upon them to elect a President. It is needless, for those who know Mr. Mano Mohan Ghose, to say that both these duties were gracefully and effectively performed. The whole speech should be read, but one important passage, lengthy though it be, may be appropriately reproduced here †:—

"Our proceedings have been subjected to much and varied criticism, and for my part I am glad that such should have been the case. All our proceedings, our discussions,

* *Vide* Detailed Report, p. 48.

† Detailed Report, pp. 6, 7.

and our resolutions are public property, and it is only right thatthey should be subjected to public scrutiny, for I believe we have everything to gain and nothing to lose from honest criticism (*cheers*), however unfavourable such criticism may be. That besides legitimate criticism, the proceedings of such a body as ours should be subjected to unworthy attacks and our aims misrepresented and distorted is a matter which, however painful to us all, ought not to discourage and dishearten us. For what great cause in the history of this world has ever triumphed without, in the first instance, having met with unworthy and even rancorous opposition? Our opponents have not even hesitated to accuse the promoters of this movement of disloyalty to the British Government. If I could bring myself to believe that the accusation, however unfounded, had been honestly preferred by those who are responsible for starting it, I should have felt myself called upon to deal with it seriously; but the charge has always seemed to me so preposterous and so dishonest on the part, at any rate, of a large portion of our detractors, that I think every speaker in this hall ought to treat it with silent contempt.

"There is, I believe, no one present here, who, in his heart of hearts, does not feel that at no period in the history of India were life and property more secure than they are at the present day. If English rule in India had done nothing more than that, we should, even then, have had ample reason to be grateful to England, for, as you know, the establishment of peace and the maintenance of law and order are the first requisites for the happiness of a people. To my mind, our allegiance to the British Government is based, not only on the feeling of gratitude which the benefits conferred upon us must evoke in our hearts, but also upon the highest grounds of expediency; for every sane man in India, who is capable of thinking, must feel that any change of Government at the present time would be the greatest calamity that could befall the people of this country. (*Cheers*). That we should have been better pleased if we could have governed ourselves, as well as we are governed by England, is a sentiment which we need not in the least shrink from avowing, because not only is such a feeling natural, but it is perfectly consistent to my mind with true loyalty to England. (*Hear, hear*). The National Congress movement was fittingly described last year by my friend Mr. Pherozshah Mehta, while welcoming the Delegates in Bombay, as 'the grandest outcome of British Rule in India.' To that description I will venture to add that it is also the natural and, indeed, the inevitable outcome of the generous policy pursued by England in this country. The fact which we all gratefully acknowledge, namely, that India is now better governed than before, or the fact that no other Asiatic country is, at the present time, better governed, furnishes no argument whatever against the demands made by us with the sole object of improving the administration of the country. The English people have no right to complain if we refuse to judge of their acts and professions as rulers of this country, by any standard lower than what they themselves have taught us to respect and admire. If England has been instrumental in teaching an Asiatic people a higher code of political morality she can scarcely complain, with any show of reason, if we expect her strictly to adhere to that code in the government of her own dependencies, and to carry out the professions and declarations which have from time to time been made in her name and on her behalf. The great demonstration of to-day, I think, we are all agreed, implies nothing more than this, *viz.*, that much as England has done for us, she has yet a great deal more to do, or, in other words, that the administration of India is not perfect, but that there is still considerable room for its improvement and reform. This, I believe, to be the keystone of this great national movement. It is not a movement intended in the slightest degree to embarrass or hamper the Government of the country, but to assist that Government by every means in the great and difficult task in which it is engaged. Viewed in this light—and I am sure you all agree with me that it is our most anxious desire that it should be viewed in no other light—I fail to understand how it is that we have not yet met with a sympathetic recognition at the hands of those who are responsible for the good government of this country. It is impossible in any country to carry on the work of government for any length of time, without consulting the wishes and wants of those who are governed, and it is obvious that when the government of a country is practically in the hands of a foreign people, it is all the more necessary for that Government, and, indeed, it is its duty, if it is to exist for any good purpose, to ascertain the wishes and even the aspirations of those who are governed. If such is the duty cast upon those who are called upon to govern, it is equally the duty of the people themselves to acquaint the Government by all constitutional means with their own wishes and their requirements. We are not so unreasonable as to expect that all our suggestions should be at once carried out, or that all our demands should be at once granted without due consideration. All that we desire is that our suggestions should be honestly and sympathetically considered, and that if difficulties, which we ourselves may fail to perceive, should deter the Government of the day from acceding to any of our wishes, we may be taken into the confidence of the Government, so to speak, in order that we may be in a position to help it, if we can, in grappling with those difficulties. (*Hear, hear*). This, I believe, is the true position which the National Congress in India desires to occupy.

"An idea is said to prevail among certain officials in the vicinity of Whitehall as well as in this country, to the effect that the supremacy of England in India is mainly based upon the disunion of the different races existing in this country, and that any attempt to unite them, even to a limited extent, upon a common political platform, is fraught with ultimate danger to the safety of the British Empire. I cannot for a moment believe that any Englishman, having any claim to statesmanship, can seriously entertain such an idea, based as it is altogether upon a superficial, and, I venture to think, an erroneous conception of fact.

"'To divide and rule' is a wicked policy as unworthy of the great English people as it is practically impossible after what they have themselves done for us; because you can no more now keep the different races of this country disunited in feelings and sentiments, for any length of time, than you can abolish your schools and colleges, your railroads and telegraphs.

"But then it is asked: 'Whom does the National Congress represent? What right has it to speak on behalf of the masses of the people who know nothing about the Congress?' My answer is, the National Congress represents the thinking portion of the people of India. (*Cheers*). The Delegates present here to-day are the chosen representatives of that section of the Indian people who have learnt to think and whose number is daily increasing with marvellous rapidity. It is perfectly correct that the ignorant masses whom we seek to represent are still unable, in many provinces, to take an active interest in the great social and administrative problems which are now engaging the attention of the educated classes; but history teaches that, in all countries and in all ages, it is the thinking classes who lead the unthinking, and in the present state of our own society we are bound, not only to think for ourselves, but also to think for those who are still too ignorant to exercise that important function. (*Cheers*). If by reason of the peculiar intellectual condition of the people of India whom we are seeking to represent, not only some of those who have actually chosen us as their delegates, but also many others are still incapable of exercising any choice in the matter, I am sure we are not insensible of the grave responsibilities which we are incurring in speaking and acting on their behalf. Our duty to our less favoured countrymen requires that we should not shrink from incurring those responsibilities. I believe we are all agreed that it is our duty to educate our ignorant countrymen not only to think, but to think rightly, and to instil into their minds the fundamental doctrine that the happiness of a people primarily depends upon the maintenance of law and order in the country, and that if they have any grievances the only way to obtain redress is to agitate by peaceable and lawful methods. In trying to discharge so obvious a duty we can well afford to be ridiculed as self-styled delegates or as belonging only to 'a microscopic minority.' (*Cheers and laughter*).

"Gentlemen, I feel I ought not to trespass much longer on your patience, but there is one other accusation to which I cannot help alluding, although it has been satisfactorily answered at more than one of our previous gatherings—I refer to the charge, so often repeated, that the National Congress as a body is opposed to social reforms. Such an accusation is based upon an entire misapprehension of the scope and functions of the National Congress, whose object, as I have already explained, is to point out to the Government what we conceive to be the defects in the administration of the country, and to ask only for such reforms as we are ourselves absolutely incapable of introducing without the aid of the Government, and in regard to the necessity of which we are all practically of one mind. Now, the many questions of social reform which are at present engaging the attention of the educated classes throughout India are questions, the solution of which is entirely in the hands of the people themselves. It is open to all of us to live as we like, or to eschew or alter at any time any custom which we may consider inconvenient or mischievous. The remedy being entirely in our own hands we can apply it whenever we choose, and on the majority of points we are, unfortunately, by no means all of one mind yet. Besides, it should be borne in mind that the Congress is composed of diverse communities, each having its own religion and its peculiar usages, and it would be impossible for such a body to discuss the social customs of a particular community, based as they often are upon religious ideas, regarding which the members of another community professing a different religion have no adequate knowledge or information. (*Hear hear*). But it by no means follows that the promoters of the National Congress are not as keenly alive to the importance of social as they are to that of political reforms. The same educational agency which has given life to the National Congress has already helped to bring about enormous social changes throughout India. Half a century is but a day in the life of a nation, and any one who compares the state of Indian society of the present day with what was the case even 30 years ago, cannot but be surprised at the rapidity with which we have moved in social matters during that period. If there are some who think we ought to have moved still faster, they, in my opinion, ignore altogether the enormous difficulties against which we have to contend in this matter. There are movements of a very important character already on foot amongst the different communities of our people, to promote the cause of social and religious reform, and in my humble judgment we should be travelling out of our legitimate province if we were to deal with such questions in this assembly. Those who know my own views will readily believe that I yield to none in the country in attaching importance to the question of social reform ; but at the same time I cannot but feel that it is our duty, however keenly we may feel on the subject, to remember that any precipitate or inconsiderate action, before the creation of a healthy public opinion in a community, is often apt to retard progress and to defeat the very object we have in view. (*Hear, hear*). We ought to be thankful to our English friends for any suggestions they may be disposed to make to us on the question of social reform, so long as those suggestions are made in a sympathetic spirit ; but at the same time we must ask them to bear in mind that it is impossible for an outsider or foreigner to realize adequately the difficulties which the different Indian communities have to contend against in matters of social reform. Our English friends, whose kind sympathy and advice our social reformers are always delighted to have, may also be asked to remember that the decision of the question as to what reforms should or should not be introduced must, from the very nature of the case, rest with the Indian people themselves, and that therefore the true remedy lies in educating the people and creating a healthy public opinion on questions of social reform. To my mind, this gathering itself must have, and indeed already *has* had, the effect, directly and indirectly, of giving a great impetus to the cause of social reform. It is true that there are social problems connected with our domestic life of so important and pressing a character that, in my opinion, the sooner we direct our attention to them, and deal vigorously with them, the better for our country ; but all I say is, that those are questions with which the Congress, composed as it is of different communities, ought not at present to have any direct concern. (*Cheers.*) "

Sir Romesh Chunder Mitter, a well-known Judge of the High Court, (from which he has only recently retired, and of which he at one time acted as Chief Justice,) and now a Member of the Viceroy's Council, then proposed Mr. Pherozshah Mehta (a Parsi) of Bombay as President of the Congress, and the proposal having been duly seconded, supported and unanimously carried, this gentleman was formally installed.

In commencing his inaugural address, the whole of which should be perused,* he referred to the futile attempt that has been made, by a "micros copic minority" of the Parsis, acting under Anglo-Indian inspiration, to detach their co-religionists from the Congress movement. He said † :—

"In speaking of myself as a native of this country, I am not unaware that, incredible as it may seem, Parsis have been both called, and invited and allured to call themselves foreigners. If twelve centuries, however, entitle Angles and Saxons, and Normans and Danes, to call themselves natives of England, if a lesser period entitles the Indian Mahomedans to call themselves natives of India, surely *we* are born children of the soil, in which our lot has been cast for a period of over thirteen centuries, and where, ever since the advent of the British power, we have lived and worked, with our Hindu and Mohamedan neighbours, for common aims, common aspirations, and common interests. To my mind a Parsi is a better and a truer Parsi, as a Mahomedan or a Hindu is a better and truer Mahomedan or Hindu, the more he is attached to the land which gave him birth, the more he is bound in brotherly relations and affection to all the children of the soil, the more he recognizes the fraternity of all the native communities of the country, and the immutable bond which binds them together in the pursuit of common aims and objects, under a common Government."

* * * * *

"The birthright, therefore, gentlemen, which the Parsis thus possess of so indefeasible and glorious a character, they have refused and will always refuse to sell for any mess of pottage, however fragrant and tempting. (*Loud Cheers.*)"

Then congratulating the Congress on the progress it had effected he remarked ‡ :—

"We have survived the ridicule, the abuse, and the misrepresentation. We have survived the charge of sedition and disloyalty. We have survived the charge of being

* Detailed Report, pp. 10—17.
† Detailed Report, p. 10.
‡ Idem.

a microscopic minority. We have also survived the charge of being guilty of the atrocious crime of being educated, and we have even managed to survive the grievous charge of being all Babus in disguise. (*Laughter and Cheers.*) "

* * * * *

" The question of our loyalty is set at rest for ever. In the debate on Lord Cross's India Reform Bill in the House of Lords, Viceroy after Viceroy bore emphatic testimony to the loyal and peaceful character of our aims and efforts. Within the last few days the voice of no less a personage than one of our former Secretaries of State has confirmed this testimony. Lord R. Churchill—it is to no less distinguished a public man that I refer—has publicly declared that 'he could sincerely remark that no one will rejoice more than himself if the deliberations of the Indian National Congress shortly to be resumed were to contribute effectually to the progress and the welfare of the Indian people.' Then, Gentlemen, it is made clear that we have not learnt the lessons of history so badly, as to demand the introduction of the full-blown representative institutions which, in England, have been the growth of centuries. It is made clear that we have not asked for even such a modicum as was enjoyed by the English people even before the time of Simon de Montfort, more than five centuries ago, nay, that we have not asked even for representative institutions of a governing or ruling character at all. Indeed, so far as this historical argument is concerned, we have not alone proved that we have *not* been guilty of disregarding it, but we have been successful in turning the tables upon our adversaries. We have shown that it is they who defy the lessons of history and experience when they talk of waiting to make a beginning, till the masses of the people are fully equipped with all the virtues and all the qualifications which adorn the citizens of Utopia, in fact till a millennium has set in, when we should hardly require such institutions at all. We have shown that people who indulge in such vain talk have never understood the laws of human progress, which, after all is a series of experiments, in which men and institutions re-act upon each other for their mutual improvement and perfection. We have also proved that, in spite of our education, and even with our racial and religious differences, the microscopic minority can far better and far more intuitively represent the needs and the aspirations of their own countrymen than the still more microscopic minority of the omniscient District Officers, whose, colloquial knowledge of the Indian languages seldom rises above the knowledge of English possessed, for instance, by French waiters at Paris Hotels which proudly blazon forth the legend—'Ici on parle Anglais;' and whose knowledge of native domestic and social life and ways and habits of thought seldom extends beyond a familiarity with flattering expressions of the Saheb's greatness and paternal care, sometimes inspired by courtesy and sometimes by interest.

"Then, Gentlemen, our right to the designation of a National body has been vindicated. It is so admirably set forth in an article which appeared in a Conservative Review—*The National*—from the pen of a Conservative, who, however, speaks from the fulness of intimate knowledge, that I cannot resist the temptation of borrowing from it: 'The supposed rivalry,' says the writer, 'between Mussulmans and Hindus is a convenient decoy to distract attention and to defer the day of reform. I do not wish to affirm that there is no antagonism between the adherents of the two faiths; but I do most positively assert that the antagonism has been grossly exaggerated. Every municipal improvement and charitable work finds members of the two faiths working together and subscribing funds to carry it out. Every political paper in the country finds supporters from believers in both creeds. Just the same is witnessed in the proceedings of the Congress. The members of the Congress meet together as men, on the common basis of the nationality, being citizens of one country, subjects of one power, amenable to one code of laws, taxed by one authority, influenced for weal or woe by one system of administration, urged by like impulses to secure like rights and to be relieved of like burdens. If these are not sufficient causes to weld a people together into one common alliance of nationality, it is difficult to conceive what would be sufficient. It is for this reason the organization has been called the Indian National Congress; not because, as many, besides Mr. Keane, have assumed, that it claims a non-existent unity of race, but because it deals with rights and interests which are national in character, and matters in which all the inhabitants of the Indian peninsula are equally concerned.'

"I think we may take it, Gentlemen, that we have passed through the first two stages, and that the loyalty, the moderation, the propriety, and the constitutional and national character of our mission are now established beyond a doubt. But, however arduous and however provoking some of the experiences of the trial through which we have passed, they should not leave any trace of bitterness behind. For let us not imagine that they were devoid of chastening and beneficial effects upon ourselves. Let us frankly acknowledge that they also must have had their share in contributing to add clearness to our thoughts, sobriety to our methods, and moderation to our proposals. If I might use a proscribed, but not unscriptural, phrase we must give even the devil his due. *(Laughter.)*"

Gratefully acknowledging the services rendered to India by Mr. Caine and other English friends, and specially by our late deeply lamented member Mr. Bradlaugh, not then, yet, lost to us, he turned to Mr. Bradlaugh's last year's Bill and Lord Cross's Bill, and fully exposed the feebleness of the arguments on which the omission from this latter of any recognition of the elective principle was vainly sought, at the time, to be justified. He said * :—

"But the next result, which the introduction of Mr. Bradlaugh's Bill achieved, was gratifying in the highest degree. It at once dispelled the fit of profound cogitation, in which men at the head of Indian affairs are so apt to be lost, that they can never spontaneously recover from it. Lord Cross's Indian Council's Bill promptly saw the light of day in the House of Lords. It was at once the official recognition of the *raison d'être* of the Congress, and the first fruits of its labours. In itself, however, it was a most halting and unsatisfactory measure."

* * * * * * *

"The omission of the elective principle from the Bill was boldly justified by Lord Salisbury on the gound that 'the principle of election or government by representation was not an Eastern idea, and that it did not fit Eastern traditions or Eastern minds.' I wish to speak of his Lordship with all the respect to which his high talents and great intellectual attainments justly entitle him ; but it is not a little surprising as well as disappointing to find the Prime Minister of England, a statesman who, as Lord Cranborne, was once Secretary of State for India, displaying such profound ignorance of the history of the Indian people and the genius of the Indian mind. The late Mr. Chisolm Anstey, a man of immense erudition, once pointed out at a meeting of the East India Association in London, that 'we are apt to forget in this country when we talk of preparing people in the East by education, and all that sort of thing, for Municipal Government and Parliamentary Government, that the East is the parent of Municipalities. Local Self-Government, in the widest acceptation of the term, is as old as the East itself. No matter what may be the religion of the people who inhabit what we call the East, there is not a portion of the country from west to east, from north to south, which is not swarming with municipalities ; and not only so, but like to our municipalities of old, they are all bound together as in a species of network so that you have ready made to your hand the framework of the great system of representation.' Sir H. Maine has shown that the Teutonic Mark was hardly so well organized or so essentially representative as an Indian village communitiy, until the precise technical Roman form was engrafted upon it *(Cheers.)*

"But leaving village communities alone, what do we find at the present day over the whole country but all sorts and conditions of people, from the highest to the lowest, meeting together and transacting the business of their numberless castes, in assemblies which, in their constitution and their mode of working, are the exact prototypes of the Saxon Witans, from which the English parliamentary institutions have sprung. It is true that circumstances never allowed the representative genius of the people to develop forms and organizations for higher political functions. But it is no less true that the seed and the soil are there, waiting only for the skilful hand, and the watchful mind, which we of the Congress firmly believe we have secured in the presence of Englishmen in this country."

Pursuing the question of the introduction of the elective element into the Government of India, he advocated the acceptance by the Congress of the New Bill then recently introduced by Mr. Bradlaugh into the House of Commons, showed that Lords Northbrook, Ripon and Dufferin, the three most capable living Ex-Viceroys, were in favour of some step in this direction, and gracefully expressed the hope that the present Viceroy would prove not less liberal in his views regarding this question than his illustrious grandsire. He touched upon

* Detailed Report, p. 13.

the growing feeling amongst the British public in favour of reform for India, and concluded his address with the following* remarks :—

"It seems to me that success is well within our reach, if we resolutely apply ourselves to obtain, in the first instance at least, the recognition and application of the principle of election in the organization of our Legislative Councils. Let us then strive for it with the sagacity of practical men, who have not learnt in vain the lessons taught by English political history, and who know the value of moderate, gradual, and substantial gain.

"To the many reasons which have been set forth in Congress after Congress, proving the imperative need of reformed Councils, another has been now added. The discussion of the Indian Budget in the House of Commons was always more or less of a sham ; but it was a sham for which the officials of the India Office thought it at least a matter of decency to shed a tear of remorse. But now Sir John Gorst has boldly and candidly declared in his place in the House that there need be no sham regret at all ; that if anything, it was rather to be hoped and wished for, that the House of Commons should not waste its time over the weary farce. (*Shame, Shame.*) It is now officially declared that it is right and proper that Parliament should,—to use Mr. Yule's happy way of putting it,—throw 'the great and solemn trust of an inscrutable Providence' back into the hands of Providence to be looked after as Providence itself thinks best, with such grace as Providence may choose to pour on the heads of Sir John Gorst, his heirs, successors, and assigns. I think you will agree with me that when the responsible advisers of the Crown, on Indian matters, propound doctrines of such a character it is high time that we should raise our united voice to demand Local Councils possessing some guarantees for energy and efficiency. (*Cheers.*)

"It has been said that our united voice is the voice only of a certain portion of the people and not of the masses ; and that it is even then the voice of indifference, and not of urgency and excitement. These remarks are intended to be cast as matters of reproach against the Congress ; properly understood they constitute its chief glory. If the masses were capable of giving articulate expression to definite political demands, then the time would have arrived, not for consultative Councils but for representative institutions. It is because they are still unable to do so that the function and the duty devolve upon their educated and enlightened compatriots to feel, to understand and to interpret their grievances and requirements, and to suggest and indicate how these can best be redressed and met. History teaches us that such has been the law of widening progress in all ages and all countries, notably in England itself. That function and that duty, which thus devolve upon us, are best discharged, not in times of alarm and uneasiness, of anger and excitement, but when the heart is loyal and clear, and the reason unclouded. It is, I repeat, the glory of the Congress that the educated and enlightened people of the country seek to repay the debt of gratitude, which they owe for the priceless boon of education, by pleading, and pleading temperately, for timely and provident statesmanship. (*Cheers.*)

"I have no fears but that English statesmanship will ultimately respond to the call. I have unbounded faith in the living and fertilizing principles of English culture and English civilization. It may be that, at times, the prospect may look dark and gloomy. Anglo-Indian opposition may look fierce and uncompromising. But my faith is large, even in Anglo-Indians. As in the whole universe, so in individuals, in communities, there is a perpetual conflict going on between the higher and lower passions and impulses of our nature. Perhaps some of you have read a little novel, called Dr. Jekyll and Mr. Hyde, the plot of which hinges on the conflict between the two sides of a man's nature, the higher and the lower, embodied each, for the time being, in a separate and distinct individuality. If the lower tendencies are sometimes paramount in the Hydes of Anglo-Indian Society, if as our last President, Sir W. Wedderburn, said, the interests of the services are antagonistic to and prevail over the interests of the Indian people, it is still the oscillation of the struggle ; it is still only one side of the shield. They cannot permanently divest themselves of the higher and nobler nature, which, in the end, must prevail, and which has prevailed in so many honorable, distinguished and illustrious instances. They are after all a part and parcel of the great English nation, bone of their bone, and flesh of their flesh, and they must even work along the main lines of that noble policy which Great Britain has deliberately adopted for the government of this country. When in the inscrutable dispensation of Providence, India was assigned to the care of England, one can almost imagine that the choice was offered to her as to Israel of old : 'Behold, I have placed before you a blessing and a curse ; a blessing, if ye will obey the commandments of the Lord your God : a curse, if ye will not obey the commandments of the Lord your God, but go after other gods whom ye have not known.'

* Detailed Report, pp. 16, 17.

"All the great forces of English life and society, moral, social, intellectual, political, are, if slowly, yet steadily and irresistibly, declaring themselves for the choice which will make the connection of England and India a blessing to themselves, and to the whole world, for countless generations. Our Congress asks but to serve as a modest handmaid to that movement, asks but to be allowed to show the pits and the falls, asks but to be allowed to join in the blessing which England will as surely earn as there is an 'Eternal that maketh for righteousness.' (*Cheers*)

"I appeal to all true Englishmen—to candid friends as to generous foes—not to let this prayer go in vain. It may be that we sometimes speak in uncouth and outlandish ways, it may be that we sometimes stray in some confusion of thought and language ; still it is the prayer of a rising, growing and hopeful nation. I will appeal to them to listen to the sage counsels of one of the most careful and observant of their modern politicians, who, like the prophet Balaam, called, I will not say, exactly to curse us, has however, blessed us utterly. In his 'Problems of Greater Britain,' Sir Charles Dilke thus sums up his views on the Congress : 'Argument upon the matter is to be desired, but not invective, and there is so much reason to think that the Congress movement really represents the cultivated intelligence of the country that those who ridicule it do harm to the imperial interests of Great Britain, bitterly wounding and alienating men who are justified in what they do, who do it in reasonable and cautious form, and who ought to be conciliated by being met half-way. (*Cheers*). The official class themselves admit that many of the natives who attack the Congress do so to ingratiate themselves with their British rulers and to push their claims for decorations. (*Hear, hear*). Our first duty in India is that of defending the country against anarchy and invasion, but our other greatest duty is to learn how to live with what is commonly called the Congress movement, namely, with the development of that new India which we have ourselves created. Our past work in India has been a splendid task, splendidly performed, but there is a still nobler one before us, and one larger even than that labour on the Irish problem to which our public men on both sides seem too much inclined to give their whole attention.' So careful an estimate of the work and spirit of the Congress movement cannot but commend itself to all thoughtful minds.

"However that may be, our duty lies clear before us, to go on with our work firmly and fearlessly, but with moderation, and above all with humility. If we might be permitted to adopt those noble words of Cardinal Newman, we may say :—

Lead kindly light amid the encircling gloom,
  Lead thou me on !
The night is dark and I am far from home,
  Lead thou me on !
Keep thou my feet, I do not ask to see
  The distant path, one step's enough for me." (*Long and enthusiastic cheering*).

The assembly then proceeded to elect its Subjects Committee. The functions of this Committee are very important and are not, even yet, generally understood by the public. Months before the Congress meets, the Committee of the circle in which it is to assemble calls upon all the Standing Committees, (of which there is one to each circle) to submit, after consultation with their divisional and sub-divisional Committees, a list of the subjects which they suggest for the consideration of the coming assembly. Their replies are compiled by the Committee first mentioned ; subjects proposed by a majority of the Committees are accepted and embodied in a circular to all the Standing or Circle Committees, notifying that these are the subjects which will be submitted by the Reception Committee to the Subjects Committee when it is formed. Subjects proposed by less than half of the committees are not included. Every delegate, therefore, now-a-days, knows; or *can* know if he chooses, and ought to know, before he leaves his Province, what the subjects are which will primarily engage the attention of the Congress.

As soon as the President's inaugural address has been delivered the assembled delegates of each circle proceed to elect from amongst themselves the men whom they desire to represent them on the Subjects Committee. This is always a large body; this year it included about 110 gentlemen, of all races and castes, residents of 70 of the largest towns in the Empire and belonging to every Province therein, except Sind. To this Committee is submitted, as a basis of discussion, the list of subjects compiled by the Reception Committee from the replies of *all* the Standing Committees, and it is this Committee who decide which of these shall be taken up, who frame the resolutions in regard to those that they decide to lay before the assembly, and who select the speakers who are to propose and second these resolutions. Reporters and spectators are excluded from the sittings of this Committee so as to give the utmost freedom of debate, and it is impossible to deny that in this Committee every subject is more effectively and completely threshed out, by rapid questions and answers and tiny speeches lasting two or three minutes only, by committee proceedings, in fact, in which every man present takes an active part, than they can be in the formal speeches of half a dozen members in the Congress itself. Matters are always rapidly and satisfactorily disposed of It is hardly ever necessary to vote, because, according to one of the basal principles of the Congress, subjects in regard to which, after full discussion, considerable difference of opinion continues to exist, are *ipso facto* thrown out. The main object of the Congress is to press upon the attention of the Government of India and the people and Government of England those reforms, and those reforms only, in regard to which the whole country has come to a substantial agreement; in regard to which the people of all provinces, of all races, castes and creeds, are practically of one mind.

This is the explanation of that marvellous unanimity, often suspiciously commented on by European critics, that characterizes, as a rule, the Congress debates. The Congress itself, through its elected representatives, weeds out all subjects in regard to which a practical agreement, in all parts of the country and by all parties, has not been arrived at. It is this, too, which ought to give such weight to the formal recommendations of the Congress, since these are not proposals advocated by this or that body, this or that province, but only such as are concurred in by the educated and semi-educated classes throughout the Empire.

Of course, besides the subjects embodied in the Reception Committee's list many others are brought forward in the Subjects Committee, by one or more province, or even by individual members, and duly discussed; but these rarely secure a sufficient unanimity of assent to permit of their being then submitted to the Congress, though, having thus been brought within the sphere of practical politics, and hence being during the year talked of all over the country, they, not unfrequently, are sent up next year from a majority of the committees, and so find a place in the next year's Reception Committee's list.

This year the Subjects Committee held six sittings extending in the aggregate over fully eighteen hours, not one minute of which was wasted in oratory or useless talk, and it is really to be regretted that neither the Government nor the public can fully realize the care and acuteness, with which not only the subjects which actually came before the Congress, but fully a dozen others, were canvassed and criticised by this most truly representative body, representative to an extent not yet fully realized, except in Congress circles, of the entire culture and intelligence of the nation.

As soon as the election of the Subjects Committee had been formally completed and ratified, all the names being read out, by the entire assembly, the President adjourned the meeting till the next day at 1-30 P.M., so as to allow time for the Committee at an evening and morning session to prepare the work for the next day.

On Saturday, when the Congress re-assembled, the first subject taken up was the expansion and reform of the Legislative Councils, and a resolution was proposed by Mr. Lal Mohan Ghose* (whilom candidate for Deptford) approving the Bill then recently introduced into the House of Commons, by the late Mr. Bradlaugh, to amend the Indian Councils Act of 1861, "*as calculated to secure a substantial instalment of that reform, in the Administration of India, for which it* (the Congress) *has been agitating*," and praying both Houses of Parliament to pass the same into law.

The reform embodied in this Bill—the introduction of a true, elected, representative element into the Government of India—is, in the opinion of the people of India, the one fundamental reform, on which all other reforms hinge, and the only reform which can pave the way for the real prosperity of the country and secure the permanence of the union of England and India. Necessarily this being so, the discussions, although absolute unanimity prevailed, were somewhat protracted, but the matter has been so exhaustively threshed out at former Congresses that it will only be needful here to reproduce a few passages from the many speeches delivered on this occasion.

Mr. Lal Mohan Ghose remarked † :—

"There are, I believe, certain points on which there prevails an almost absolute unanimity of opinion amongst the thinking and educated classes of our countrymen. We are all united in demanding that there should be some substantial expansion of our Supreme and Local Legislative Councils ; and this Bill provides for that expansion by proposing to raise the number of members of the Governor-General's Council to something between 40 and 60, and that of the Council of the various Lieutenant-Governors and Governors of Provinces to something between 36 and 48. Now there is no particular magic in any given number, but it seems to me that this proposal is so reasonable and modest that no honest or candid critic can accuse us of desiring suddenly to revolutionize the Government of this country. (*Cheers*). On the other hand, if there be any amongst us who think that the Bill does not go as far as it might have done, in this direction, I would beg of them to remember that it is impossible for us to err on the side of moderation (*hear, hear*) ; and that the more cautiously these changes and reforms are introduced, the greater is the chance of their ultimate success. (*Cheers*).

"The other point upon which we are also agreed is this, that there should be some fair share of popular representation in these councils, and, further, that this popular representation should be based upon some application of the principle of election. Now I have always been

* Detailed Report, pp. 20—22.
† Detailed Report, pp. 20, 21.

of opinion that, wholly irrespective of the capacities or qualifications of the persons whom the Government might nominate under the present system, even when the choice of the Government happens to fall, as I admit it does frequently fall, upon the very men whom we would ourselves be the first to elect—take, for example, the latest instance before us—the nomination by the Viceroy of our distinguished friend Sir Romesh Chunder Mitter—(*Cheers*), even in such cases I have always felt that it would greatly improve and strengthen the position of our members of Council if they held their seats by the suffrages of their fellow-countrymen rather than by the grace and favour of the Government. With your permission, Sir, I will read one short sentence from a memorial that was presented to Lord Hartington by a large deputation of English and Indian gentlemen, of whom I had the honor to be one, ten years ago, just after the great Liberal victory of 1880: 'Although some of these members' (alluding to the nominated members of Council) 'render useful services to the State, it is obvious that so long as all the members are nominated by the Government, however carefully the selection may be made, the members so appointed cannot feel or be credited with that independence, which it is essential they should enjoy, nor can their opinions possess the weight and authority which belongs to the voice of representatives elected by the people.' That short sentence, I believe, expresses the unanimous opinion of us all (*Cheers*); and for my part I am unable to conceive the possibility, even, of any differences of opinion, upon this great question of principle. (*Cheers.*)"

After counselling the acceptance of Mr. Bradlaugh's Bill, although not going nearly so far as many here consider desirable, and advocating moderation, mutual toleration and a liberal give-and-take attitude, he concluded* with these remarks :—

"I think if you approach this great question in that generous spirit there is nothing that can prevent the ultimate triumph of the great cause we have at heart. All the signs of the times seem to be entirely favourable. I find gathered together under this great pavilion representatives of all nations, of all communities inhabiting this great country—a sight which, only a few years ago, nobody would have dreamed of as being possible. We have across the seas in England a British people willing and anxious to extend to us the right hand of fellowship. Of late they have given us the sincerest, the strongest, the most convincing proofs of their sympathy. British constituencies have emphatically endorsed the great doctrine of the Queen's Proclamation, the doctrine of the equal rights of all Her Majesty's subjects. They have endorsed them by going so far as even to invite some of your own fellow-countrymen to stand as their Parliamentary representatives. Who among us would have thought twenty, or even ten years ago, that such a thing was within the bounds of possibility? I ask you, Gentlemen, if these things are not sufficient to cheer us, to encourage us to go on labouring firmly, generously and steadfastly, through good report and through evil report, until we have at last succeeded in convincing the people and Parliament of England that the reforms we ask for are just, moderate and legitimate and calculated greatly to improve the administration of this country and to broaden and strengthen the foundations of the British Empire in India. (*Cheers*). Gentlemen, our motto is reform and not revolution (*hear, hear*), and my own experience of the just and generous instincts of the English people convinces me that a measure which, like this Bill of Mr. Bradlaugh's, proposes to concede to us some share in the management of our own affairs and some voice in the administration of our own country, some representation in our councils, cannot fail to commend itself to the approval of the English nation. (*Cheers.*)"

Pandit Madan Mohan Malaviya spoke at considerable length.† He said:—

"The one consideration that has induced us to accept Mr. Bradlaugh's Bill is a desire to conciliate, so far as may be in our power, without, of course, sacrificing the principle we have been contending for, those of our opponents who think the reform we have been seeking might lead to undesirable results. I hope that no reasonable man will any longer hesitate in giving the Bill his best support, and that Parliament will soon pass it into law. (*Cheers.*)

"If it be otherwise, Gentlemen, we shall al l, we and other civilized countries, be greatly surprised and disappointed, for, Gentlemen, what is it that we ask for? Is it not for a limited and qualified—an extremely limited and qualified—application of that principle of representation in the administration of this country, which the genius of the English nation has for 600 long years recognized as best calculated to make Governments good and the governed happy and prosperous?"

* * * * * * * * *

* Detailed Report, pp. 21, 22.
† Detailed Report, pp. 24—27.

Ever since the time of Simon de Montfort—he went on to say—

"This has been the guiding principle of English political existence. Englishmen have extolled it in theory and maintained it in practice at the sacrifice of a large amount of treasure and life. They have carried it with them wherever they have gone, and the nations of Europe, long held in bondage by their despots, have learnt it at the feet of England and thrived under it. (*Cheers.*) Englishmen rightly feel a pride in having been the apostles of this political Christianity, and Mr. Gladstone expressed a widely-prevalent belief when speaking at the Piccadilly Hall in May last, he said : * * * *
'In the adoption of that system (the system of representation) we long stood alone, but one after another the great countries of the world have come in, and the nations sprung from our loins have given further countenance and currency to our example, and now the man would be deemed mad who should denounce the system of popular representation.' (*Cheers*). But I need not dilate further on this point. Everyone, if, as Mr. Gladstone says, he is not mad, or (permit me to add) if he has not degenerated by contact with the worst phases of Oriental thought, will admit the soundness of the principle. And it is only for a partial introduction of this principle into the administration of our country that we have been so long, and hitherto vainly, praying. (*Cheers.*)"

He pointed out the rottenness of any system of representation such as was contemplated by Lord Cross's Bill as introduced, under which all the so-called representatives of the *people* were to be nominated by the *Government.* He refuted, as, indeed, the President had already done in his inaugural address, the absurd statements of the Marquess of Salisbury and Lord Cross that representative institutions were foreign to India, and that India did not possess the elements of good constituencies ; and, referring to the close and rotten boroughs that subsisted in England, even up to 1830, he said, and said truly, amidst loud applause—

"You will, I am sure, agree with me when I say that no electorates that might be formed here could be half as bad as those which existed in the Anti-Reform days in England before the period of the passing of the Reform Bill. You have all heard of the close and rotten boroughs."

He went on to show that even these—infinitely worse as they were than any constituencies that could now-a-days be created in India—had yet done good service to the State by introducing into public life innumerable great men, who would certainly never have been selected by Government under any pure nomination system. He concluded thus :—

"I have already received, Gentlemen, a note* of warning from the President that I should not go further ; but I hope he will permit me to say one word with regard to another objection put forth by Viscount Cross and Lord Salisbury in their speeches on the second reading of the Official Indian Reform Bill. Said the Secretary of State for India : "As was well said by the late Mr. Henry Maine in speaking of India : 'There is no more resemblance between a Punjabee and a Bengalee, between an Indian of Hindustan and an Indian of Malabar, than there is between an Englishman and a Roumanian, or between a Spaniard and a Swede.'" The Marquess of Salisbury added : 'The difficulty of introducing the elective principle, largely dependent upon the peculiarities of Eastern minds, is also, to a great extent, as the noble Lord pointed out, due to the fact that we have to deal with a deeply-divided population. Representative government answers admirably so long as all those who are represented desire much the same thing and have interests tolerably analogous ; but it is put to an intolerable strain when it rests upon a community divided into two sections, † one of which is bitterly hostile to the other and desirous of opposing it upon all occasions.' I think, Gentlemen, this grand assembly,

---

* Speakers are nominally limited, proposers of resolutions to ten minutes, others to five. Where a man speaks well and is carrying the audience with him the rule is not very rigidly enforced, but the Pandit had been speaking for nearly a quarter of an hour, and hence the stroke upon the President's gong.

† We should very much like to know whether Great Britain, herself, is not divided into two sections, one of which is bitterly hostile to the other, and desirous of opposing it on all occasions!

composed of men of all the different provinces of India, is a living refutation of their Lordships' objection. (*Cheers*). It is absolutely untrue to say that the two great sections of our community are utterly hostile to each other and desirous of opposing each other on all occasions. Their interests are not only 'tolerably analogous,' but identical in nine hundred and ninety-nine cases out of every thousand that could come before the councils. The absence of a common faith, which Lords Cross and Salisbury considered a valid excuse for not introducing the elective principle here, is purely imaginary. They, no doubt, follow different religious persuasions, but there exists amongst them a common faith which is—

"Taught by no priest, but by their beating hearts :
Faith to each other : the fidelity
Of fellow-wanderers in a desert place
Who share the same dire thirst, and, therefore share
The scanty water: the fidelity
Of men whose pulses leap with kindred fire,
Who, in the flash of eyes, the clasp of hands,
The speech that even in lying tells the truth
Of heritage inevitable as past deeds,
Nay, in the silent bodily presence feel
The mystic stirring of a common life
Which makes the many one. (*Loud Cheers*)."

Pandit Bishan Narayan Dhar, who followed, pursued this question of the supposed diversity of Hindu and Mahomedan interests further. He said : * "What are called Hindu interests and Mahomedan interests have really no existence in political matters (*cheers*)," and he continued :—

"I feel deeply the responsibility of my words, and I do not hesitate to say, from what I know in my experience in the United Provinces, that whatever we hear about Mahomedan opposition to political reform and about the antagonism of Hindu interests and Mahomedan interests, is due to the deliberate policy adopted by certain members, at any rate, of the governing classes. (*Cheers*).

"It is a serious charge to bring against officers of Government that they want to keep the people disunited, and seek to follow the low, evil maxim 'divide and rule.' But I am prepared to show from the writings of Anglo-Indian statesmen, who have held high positions in this country, that some of them, at any rate, do believe that race antagonisms and religious rivalries are the chief factors that contribute to the strength and permanence of British rule in this country. (*Cheers and cries of 'shame!'*)"

Then he quoted a passage from a quite recent lecture by Sir John Strachey, showing clearly that, like many of our typical Bureaucrats, that gentleman really holds that the existence side by side of two hostile races in India would be a source of strength to the British Government and ought to be taken advantage of by it.

"I call that," he went on to say, "an immoral doctrine. (*Cheers.*) I call it a shameful policy for those who have faith in the teachings of Christianity. At the same time it cannot be denied that that is the deliberate policy of some sections of our Indian bureaucracy. In the United Provinces we see the fruit of the seed that has thus been sown. This fruit is bloodshed and bitterness in the United Provinces ; and in recent years the religious disputes between Mahomedans and Hindus are, in the mind of every well-wisher of his country, a cause of regret or shame. For my part I attribute them entirely to the policy which the Government, or at any rate some of its component parts, have adopted towards this country."

* * * * * * * *

"We all know that those disputes, in any aggravated form, are of recent origin. Ten years ago they hardly existed. Even in Mahomedan times Hindus and Mahomedans lived together peaceably. Even in times when, according to Sir James Stephen, the Mahomedans proposed to everybody the alternative of the Koran or the sword, Hindus enjoyed equal rights with Mahomedans, held the highest posts, and governed large sections of Mahomedans. But it appears to me that the Government of India, for it is, in the last analysis, this Government which must be held responsible for the acts of its subordinates, the Government of India, I say, has adopted a different policy. I think that Government

* Detailed Report, pp. 27, 28.

may be reminded of a certain fact in the history of India. There was a time when India v divided into small sects, when the Mahomedans stood aloof from the conquered people when the doctrines of religious toleration and free discussion were unknown. Enough time had not elapsed to mitigate the existing differences. At that stage there appeared a man who was destined to be the greatest Mahomedan ruler that India ever had. He adopted a new policy, he tried the grand and successful experiment of basing his rule, not upon the fears of the people, but upon their affections. (*Cheers.*) He ignored all class and religious differences, and proclaimed, for the first time in this country, the doctrine of universal toleration ; and by his wise, noble, and far-seeing policy he raised the Mogul Empire to a power and a glory that excited the envy and admiration of the world. Is that noble policy of Akbar going to be reversed by the British Government ? Are the British people, who are 'the heirs of all the ages,' and 'in the foremost files of time,' going to reverse that policy and adopt a different one ? 'Divide and rule' may be a good principle for a time but when a higher and a purer moral consciousness dawns upon the minds of our rulers, I believe they will see that that power alone is secure which rests upon the affections and the will of the nation. (*Cheers.*)"

Mr. V. Krishnaswami Iyer, after pointing out certain minor verbal alterations that he and many of his friends considered necessary in Mr. Bradlaugh's Bill, went on to make certain remarks in regard to the Native State of Mysore that are well worthy of notice. "That State," he remarked : *—

"Has had a Representative Assembly for the last ten years. In the year 1881 the Dewan of Mysore created the nucleus of a representative assembly. It did not possess political privileges, but it had the right of stating grievances to the Maharaja. Last year, I believe, the Dewan of Mysore made a new and important departure with regard to the constitution of that assembly. As the arrangement now stands the franchise is restricted to persons having a certain property qualification—the payment of 100 rupees to the Government ; but Local Boards and Municipalities are also entitled to elect a certain number of members. The persons elected in each district meet in the district itself, and they elect representatives to attend the representative assembly in Mysore, and that assembly has a right to put any question it likes to the Dewan and the Maharaja, and is entitled to receive an answer. That assembly has been created in a province which has not received the benefit of liberal education to the same extent as the provinces directly under the control of England, and has enjoyed this privilege in its original form for a considerable time, and statesmen ruling over that country have testified to the wisdom of the further advance made by the present Dewan.

"I should like to read one short paragraph from the speech of the late Dewan, Mr. C. Ranga Charlu, C.I.E., delivered on the 26th of October 1882, to the Mysore Representative Assembly.

"He said : 'If the spread of any high degree of education among the great mass of the people were to be insisted upon as a *sine qua non*, we may have to wait for ever ; meanwhile every year under an autocratic system of Government will find the people less fit for representative institutions. The sprinkling of educated men who are sure to be found in these representative bodies will serve for all purposes of leading and guiding ; but what is required in the great body of the representatives is common sense and practical views, which are sure to be possessed by men of ordinary knowledge engaged in industrial and other useful occupations.'

"It was not, you see, that the people should all of them be educated ; it was not that there should be a large proportion of the people educated before they were entitled to have conferred upon them the privilege of electing members to the Legislative Council ; the mere fact that there is a considerable body of the people, not necessarily a large percentage, but a large body of educated people, who are qualified to take an intelligent interest in the proceedings of the Government, entitles them, according to the late Prime Minister of Mysore, to a voice in the administration. The fact that they are a 'microscopic minority,' or that they are not a large percentage of the people, is not to form a reason for their being debarred from enjoying the privilege of electing members or discussing Budgets. (*Cheers*). How so infinitely superior a man, as Mr. Ranga Charlu, was only utilized by Providence as Prime Minister of a little state like Mysore, and so infinitely inferior a man, as the Marquess of Salisbury, is tolerated as a Prime Minister of a vast Empire like Great Britain, is one of those matters that fairly bewilder those who, like myself, believe in a righteous over-ruling power that guides and governs the affairs of mankind. (*Loud cheers and laughter.*)"

* Detailed Report, p. 30.

Syed Sharfuddeen, a Mahomedan Barrister from Patna, said that he was glad Mr. Bradlaugh's new Bill laid less stress upon the Minorities Clause. He put the question thus*:—

"Let me say at once that from the first I was opposed to this clause, although I am a Mussalman, and so belong to a class, which, in this country, no doubt, is in the minority. My reason is this. We have municipal laws in this country, and we have district boards; but neither in the Municipal Act nor in the Local Self-Government Act is there any clause for the protection of minorities, nor has the absence of any such clause ever, anywhere, caused the slightest inconvenience. This, I think, you will take as a sufficient proof of the good-will of the Mahomedans towards Hindus and of Hindus towards Mahomedans. (*Cheers.*) I am a delegate from a place which now and then gets a westerly breeze from Aligarh.† (*Laughter.*) I come from Patna, where, in the second week of this month, there was a general election of the municipality, twenty members being elected under the Act, and, out of those 20 members, you will be surprised to learn that 13 were Mahomedans, and that these 13 were not elected by Mahomedans only, but also by Hindus. You will find, therefore, that my position in opposing the Protection-of-Minorities Clause is not without due warrant."

Precisely similar testimony was borne ‡ by the President, himself the representative of one of the smallest minorities in the country, that of the Parsis, who constitute less than one two-thousandth of the population. He remarked:—

"Experience has shown that even in a preponderating Hindu electorate it does not happen that Hindus only are elected, as so many other, besides racial, forces and interests concur in influencing the selection. If we may apply the lessons learnt from experience in municipal elections, I may mention the remarkable fact that in the Town Council or, what is now called the Standing Committee of the Bombay Corporation, composed of 12 members, there have been frequently 5 Parsis, 3 Europeans, 2 Hindus and 2 Mahomedans."

Syed Sharfuddeen went on to say—

"My second point relates to the Bill of Lord Cross. You will understand that Lord Cross is, no doubt, technically responsible for the introduction of this Bill into the House; but you will also understand that he is, or ought to be, guided by his Council. Lord Cross is nobody, and cannot possibly know anything of Indian matters, except in so far as he represents his Council in the India Office. His advisers are mostly those who have served in India a good many years, but who retired long before the existence of this Congress, and who, therefore, possess no knowledge of that new India which has grown up in this country. (*Hear, Hear.*) So that to blame Lord Cross for the introduction of this futile Bill would be rather unjust. The councillors he needs are men of a different class, and we in this assembly would advise the Government in England to select, as councillors of the Secretary of State for India, men who have full experience of the present state of the country (*cheers*), and who are not hampered by class traditions and prejudices. (*Loud cheers*)."

Mr. Nasir Ali Shohrat, who spoke next, a Mussalman from Delhi, worked out this idea further. He remarked §:—

"Of course, many of the members of the Secretary of State's Council are opposed to this as to every other reform; but this does not surprise us in the case of such antiquated personages. The wonder is not that they oppose this measure, but that the English nation still allows such fossils to fill these important posts instead of replacing them by modern-living men. (*Cheers and laughter*). You can all understand that in choosing a pleader we select one in active practice in the Courts, thoroughly up in the law of the present day, not some old fogey who has not read a new law for the last quarter of a century, and whose knowledge of the practice of the Courts is confined to that of fifty years ago! These councillors are absolutely ignorant of our Modern India of to-day. (*Cheers.*) During the

---

* Detailed Report, p. 30.

† Aligarh is the head quarters of Sir Syed Ahmed Khan who, though formerly an enthusiastic advocate for an advanced system of Representative Government, of recent years, under official guidance, has more than once denounced vehemently that very small tentative step in the direction of such institutions that the Congress has advocated.

‡ Detailed Report, pp. 12, 13.

§ Idem, p. 31.

the last ten years, even, the entire country has been so metamorphosed as to be barely the same place it was. (*Loud cheers*). Why do these worthy old gentlemen remain to clog the wheels of progress? And why do they oppose our modest demands for representation? Because, say they, of the disunion of Mahomedans and Hindus. But there is no sort of disunion amongst Mahomedans and Hindus on these political matters. (*Cheers.*) All are of one mind. (*Loud cheers*). No doubt Sir Syed Ahmed and his now microscopic following tried to create such disunion; but all see now with what conspicuous failure. I fear I cannot give him credit for good faith. Had his motives been good he would have given expression to his new views on the Congress platform, and have explained how it came about that he was now denouncing the very proposals that a few years back he had himself most strongly urged. Had he done this the whole matter would have been fully discussed and a fair decision arrived at. He did not do so, and from this the only possible conclusion is that he was not actuated by a pure desire for the public welfare but by other motives. By his influence and vehemence he did in some places and instances succeed in creating some unpleasantness between Hindus and Mahomedans, and, perhaps, here and there, evil traces of his unpatriotic work may yet linger. Yet, despite this, despite all he and his masters amongst the officials could do, there is practically at this present time absolutely no disunion as regards Congress questions between Mussalmans and Hindus. (*Prolonged cheering.*)"

This subject, of the Legislative Councils, disposed of, the assembly passed on to re-affirm, in an omnibus resolution, a whole group of resolutions which, having been threshed out in many past Congresses and discussed at thousands of public meetings and in thousands of newspaper articles and pamphlets, now constitute, *nemine dissentiente*, accepted planks in the Congress platform.

We may well leave Mr. Kali Charan Bannerjee to state the case in his own words * :—

MR. PRESIDENT, LADIES AND GENTLEMEN,—As an old driver of your omnibus (*laughter*,) in regard to which, by-the-bye, it may soon be necessary to legislate as to how many it should be allowed to carry, I may be permitted to drive it once more. There will be no detention with a view to check the passengers; they are all familiar faces, and you would know them at a glance. The resolution I have to propose is—

*That this present Congress does hereby ratify and confirm the resolutions passed by previous Congresses as to—*

(a) *the urgent necessity for the complete separation of executive and judicial functions, such that in no case shall the two functions be combined in the same officer;*

(b) *the expediency of extending into many parts of the country, where it is not at present in force, the system of trial by jury;*

(c) *the necessity of withdrawing from the High Courts the powers, first vested in them in 1872, of setting aside verdicts of acquittal by juries;*

(d) *the necessity of introducing, into the Code of Criminal Procedure, a provision enabling accused persons, in warrant cases, to demand that instead of being tried by the Magistrate they be committed to the Court of Sessions;*

(e) *the highly unsatisfactory character of the existing system of Police Administration in India, and the absolute necessity of a fundamental reform therein;*

(f) *the expediency of both establishing Military Colleges, in India, whereat the Natives of India, as defined by Statute, may be educated and trained for a military career as officers of the Indian Army, and of authorising, under such rules and restrictions as may seem necessary, such a system of volunteering, for the Indian inhabitants of the country, as may qualify them to support the Government in any crisis;*

(g) *the extremely unsatisfactory character of the Income Tax Administration, especially as regards incomes below rupees one thousand, and the expediency of raising the taxable minimum to this amount;*

(h) *the extreme importance of increasing, instead of diminishing, as the present tendency appears to be, the public expenditure on education in all its branches, and the necessity, in view to the promotion of one of the most essential of these*

* Detailed Report, pp. 32, 33.

*branches, the technical, of the appointment of a mixed commission to enquire into the present industrial condition of the country ;*

(i) *the necessity for the reduction of, instead of the continual increase to, the military expenditure of the country ;*

(j) *the necessity, if any real justice is to be done to the people of India, of holding, simultaneously in India and England, examinations, at present held only in England, for the Civil branches of the Public Service in India ;*

(k) *the expediency of so modifying the rules made under Act XI of 1878 (the Arms Act) that all restrictions as to the possession and bearing of arms shall apply equally to all persons residing in or visiting India ; that licenses to possess and bear arms shall be liberally and generally distributed wherever wild animals habitually destroy human life, cattle or crops ; and that these and all licenses issued under the rules shall be granted once for all, shall operate throughout the Provincial jurisdiction within which they are issued, be only revocable on proof of misuse, and shall not require yearly or half yearly renewals.*

"Let me remind you that these resolutions were passed by previous Congresses, and you are now called upon simply to ratify and confirm them. In other words, you are called upon simply to be loyal to your traditions (*cheers*), for I take it that the Congress is old enough to have traditions of its own. In order to help your memories let me briefly describe to you the eleven passengers that I carry in my omnibus. I will begin with the last resolution (*k*). We are grateful to our Government for the security that we enjoy as to life and property from human invasions ; what we seek is that we should have security also, as far as wild animals are concerned. (*Hear, hear*). And in that connection we desire it to be remembered that wild animals make no distinction between the European and the Indian. (*Laughter.*) I have spoken of wild animals ; what as to the wild men ? We are grateful to our Government for the machinery that exists for the prevention and suppression of crime ; at the same time we cannot shut our eyes to the fact that the administration of justice in this country admits of improvement, and that it ought to be elevated to a footing in which it might be spoken of as self-justifying in its character. We desire, therefore, that the police should be reformed so that it may not be possible for them to place, habitually, innocent men in the dock. We desire further to secure that when Magistrates hold a trial in any case, they should bring to the trial a mind which should be, as far as the *facts* of the case are concerned, a *tabula rasa.* I do not mean that they should bring to the trial of cases a mind that should be a *tabula rasa* as far as the *law* of the case is concerned. (*Laughter*). We desire further that in the administration of justice in this country the people should be allowed the benefit of the judgment of their peers, that this privilege should not be confined to a few favoured spots, but that it should be extended to all parts of the country to which it may be extended with advantage. We desire further that this privilege of having the judgment of one's peers in any case should not be allowed to become a farce and a nullity by being in danger of being set aside even by the highest Court in the country. I may describe these six resolutions as being on a certain level, that is, the level of protection. I now pass on to another class of resolutions that we have in this omnibus, and in order to help your memories I will mention a word which begins with the same letter—P. I am going to place before you four P.'s. Following protection I will give you the watch-word : plenty. We desire that the poor of the country should be enabled to live, at any rate, from hand to mouth ; that thay may be in no danger of having what little they may possess for their sustenance diminished by the imposition of any species of taxation which is likely to press hard upon them, whether as regards the nature of the tax itself or as regards the administration of the tax. Then after plenty let me give you the word peace, and here I take it that I am not wrong in regarding the British nation as under an inspiration which ought to enable it to usher in a reign of peace which is prophesied as part of the faith which inspires that country—a reign which, when it is once inaugurated, shall lead men to beat their swords into ploughshares and their spears into pruning hooks. A nation that lives and moves under such an inspiration is surely destined to usher in this reign of peace rather than to go on in a direction which indicates the permanence of war. We desire, then, that the military expenditure of the country should be reduced rather than allowed continually to increase. But if the British nation happens to be lacking in faith so that thay are not in a position to lay hold of the sure word of prophecy we make to them a certain offer, by way of an earthly support. That is, we invite them to allow us to train ourselves in that same art of war so that when they do need earthly help we shall be prepared, all of us, to render it. I now come to the last, which I describe as the *panacea ;* because after all when we seek to introduce reforms into our country it is not possible for any of them to take root unless the people are educated to help in the cause of reform. (*Cheers.*) So it is that we desire to secure that the expenditure in aid of education in all its branches should not be diminished. And here I ought to draw your attention to what is prominently brought out in one of the resolutions, that there should be no distinction ever suggested between high education and low education. An educated carpenter stands on the same footing exactly as an educated lawyer. There is no such thing as high and low in the matter of education. If education is to be a passport to the various services of the country, we desire that those passports should not be hampered by conditions which may render them simply inaccessible to certain persons who cannot fulfil those conditions. Gentlemen, the omnibus has now reached its destination, and the ocupation of the driver is gone. (*Laughter and cheers.*)"

Mr. G. S. Khaparde, in supporting the resolution, gave expression to a feeling very general now amongst the rising educated generation. "I would not," he said, "compare this resolution to an omnibus, but rather to a casket of jewels," jewels that the well-wishers of both India and England have dug out of the matrix of popular sentiment, have laboriously polished, and now present to the Viceroy asking him to decorate with them British rule and India's people. He went* on:—

"There is one jewel that some of us especially desire to possess. Some of us would like to hold office in Her Majesty's army. We live, I joyfully admit, under the protection of the British Crown and flag, and we desire that we should be allowed to fight under that flag. We fight as soldiers; I should like to fight as an officer; I want to command a few hundreds. That is all we ask—not much. One would think that to give me the command of a hundred sepoys or a few cavalry soldiers would not be very dangerous, the Commander-in-Chief and the General and the Brigadier and the Colonel being all above me. Yet they say: "No, you are not fit." I ask have I been examined and found wanting? They will not answer that question, and they will not send me to school. They are just like a stepmother to us! (*Laughter*.)"

Even the Russian Government with all its despotic traditions is not so exclusive, and, we fear we must add, so senseless in this one matter, at any rate, as is our own. There are hundreds of fine young men now growing up, the inclusion of whom as officers in India's armies would strengthen Britain's hold on her Indian Empire far more than any possible quarrels the officials can succeed in fostering between different classes of their subjects; but, although the Punjab and Bombay Governments, H. R. H. the Duke of Connaught and others have strongly recommended the creation of Military Colleges in view to this, some authorities, (alas that we do not know who, and so cannot characterize them as their folly merits) always block the way to this, as to all the other needful reforms, so persistently, but hitherto vainly, advocated by the Congress.

It is a part and parcel of this jealous, suspicious policy that they will not allow Indians to volunteer, and that by their indiscriminate disarmament they are doing their utmost to emasculate the people and so render them helpless to support Government in any time of trial. Had this same idiotic policy been pursued for the 25 years prior to the Mutiny, 1857 would have seen the end of British rule here. It was the people—the armed people accustomed to handle weapons—who rallied to the British Standards in those dark days of danger and distress and saved the British Empire in the East. Well said †Mr. Sadur-uddeen Ahmed, a Mussalman from Allahabad:—

"The taking of arms from the natives and the enforcement of, practically, prohibitive rules regarding the grant of license is not only prejudicial to the natives of India, but is equally calculated to weaken and cripple the Government itself. Hundreds of millions

* Detailed Report, p. 34.

† Detailed Report, pp. 35, 36.

of people are now under the sway of the British Government in India, none of whom can possibly entertain the remotest feeling of hostility to the Government. On the other hand, they are loyal and faithful subjects, and as the Indian Mutiny of 1857 amply proved, their attachment did not waver even in those troublous times when every stupid and faithless sepoy broke into open rebellion. Is it under the circumstances advisable to render powerless and emasculate, on mere suspicion, a nation whose loyalty has been tested and tried during the last hundred years, by depriving them of the privilege of carrying arms and keeping themselves in touch with the methods of modern warfare? (*Cheers*). If out of the hundreds of millions that inhabit this vast empire, only a few lakhs were allowed the privilege of carrying arms, the Government would have beside it, without incurring any additional expenditure, a vast array of armed men to support and to assist it in times of need. (*Loud Cheers.*)

"The Emperors of old had confidence in the bravery and faithfulness of the people and never deprived them of arms, and derived considerable assistance from the people in return. The martial spirit of the people of the country raised the descendants of Taimur, Akbar in particular, to the highest pitch of supremacy and power. If the people of India with arms in their hands and bullets in their pockets could remain subject to the Mahomedan's empire and accepted its supremacy, does it stand to reason that they would rebel against so just and civilized a Government as that of the British people? (*Loud Cheers*)."

* * * * *

"No Emperor ever feared the sword of his subject, nor ever emasculated a brave nation by force. The natives of India belong to a race which opposed Alexander and turned him back beyond the Indus. They are descendants of those brave people who, in the battle of Telaveri, made Shahabuddeen Ghori taste the efficacy of a sword, and made him retreat headlong with his army for upwards of forty miles. To convert such brave and faithful people into protectors of the Throne and guards of the State is to invigorate and strengthen the foundations of the Government. You must have read in history that when Nadir Shah once summoned the Nawab of Furrukabad to Delhi for an interview, and the Nawab replied that he could not come without his armour and weapons, Nadir said: 'Go and tell him he may come with his artillery' (*Cheers*). What a revolution! There was a time when the Emperors of old were not afraid of the arms of their enemies; a time has now come when we unfortunate, though loyal and faithful subjects, are distrusted even by our own Government. (*Loud cheers.*)"

A very strong feeling too exists as to the refusal of Government to grant simultaneous examinations in India and England for the civil branches of the service.

A Panjabi, Lala Dharam Dass, remarked * :—

"It is a matter of regret that our demands have so far been, save in some small matters, practically ignored. It is the educated alone who can fully appreciate the blessings of good government, and who are able to point out its defects. No doubt educated persons do demand a share in the administration of the Government, and have not noble and just British statesmen admitted from time to time the justice of such demands? The people of India want justice—real justice, not sham. The resolution declares the necessity of holding Civil Service examinations simultaneously in England and in India. The Government have practically closed the Civil Service against natives by holding competitive examinations in England only, and there are but very few of the qualified Indian candidates who can succeed in going to England."

Another gentleman said † :—

"I have a great fancy for one of the passengers in the omnibus, namely (J) 'the necessity, if any real justice is to be done to the people of India, of holding simultaneously, in England and India examinations, at present held only in England, for the civil branches of the Public Service in India.' I am not going to give facts, and figures; that has often been done. I will only quote a line from the despatch: 'They have no desire to extend the practical application of this principle further than political necessity requires.' Now we say that political necessity requires that the Government of a country should at any rate be *largely* composed of the people of that country, of persons thoroughly conversant with the habits, customs, views, wishes, wants of the people, of persons whose interest are to a great degree identical with those of the people.

* Detailed Report, p. 35.
† Detailed Report, p. 36.

Whereas under the existing system the Government is exclusively composed of foreigners ignorant alike of everything that really concerns the people, and whose interests are distinctly, in most cases, antagonistic to those of the country. Having regard to these anomalies, I say it is absolutely necessary that there should be simultaneous examinations in India and England (*cheers*), so that gradually the Government may come to be largely composed of Indians (*Cheers*)."

But these, and indeed all the other questions referred to in the omnibus resolution, have been so exhaustively discussed and so unanswerably reasoned out, that the neglect of the Government to introduce these pressingly needful reforms can only be due either to sheer perversity, or to an unwillingness to face the laborious tasks that the inception of this new departure would, admittedly, involve. Under either alternative no intelligent, unbiased and conscientious Ruler in India can contemplate the attitude of our existing bureaucracy, busied about tithes of mint and cummin, heedless of weightier matters—*operose nihil agendo*—without some sense of shame and self-reproach; not one, if true to his own better instincts, can escape the humiliating confession, *Video meliora, proboque, deteriora sequor.*

The next resolution prayed for the restoration, by the House of Commons, of the old privilege, until recently possessed by India's friends in Parliament, of bringing forward Indian grievances before the Indian Budget was introduced, and protested against the shameless way in which that Budget, involving all the best interests of 250 millions of people, is disposed of, year by year, at a single sitting, at the fag end of the season, in a House in which, often, not even half a dozen members are continuously present.

"This Sir," said* Mr. W. S. Caine, "is a resolution which has been submitted at previous Congresses, but which has not had the effect that the Congress desire; for the House of Commons has taken no notice of the petition which was sent from Bombay, and it is, therefore, important that the resolution should be re-affirmed, not in an omnibus, but in a carriage of its own (*cheers and laughter*), so that, if possible, we may secure the restoration of one of the most important rights which India previously possessed. The old principle, which is almost as old as Parliamentary institutions in England, that grievance should come before supply, is one of the rights which are held to more tenaciously by members of Parliament than perhaps any other parliamentary right. This resolution craves the restoration of a privilege which is the equivalent, so far as the Indian people are concerned, of that ancient charter of our liberty that grievance shall come before supply. It is also, no doubt, a distinct grievance, and one felt throughout India, that the Budget dealing with the whole finances of the British Empire should be discussed on a single evening at the hottest time of the year at a period when members of Parliament are weary with six months hard work, and when the bulk of them have left London for their holidays. (*Shame!*) It has long been the custom to treat what I consider one of the most important subjects that come before Parliament with such scant courtesy as that which I have now described. There is no doubt that all Indian questions, with the exception of the Budget itself, are shut out from discussion, except under the chances of a ballot. The only mode by which members of Parliament interested in Indian questions can bring them before the House is by balloting for an opportunity of moving a resolution, on what are called private member's nights—Tuesday and Friday. When you remember that every Tuesday and Friday, while the House sits, from 150 to 200 members of Parliament place down different subjects, in which they are interested, to be ballotted upon, you will see that the chances of an Indian question coming on, there being perhaps only three or four members to put such questions down, are about one in fifty."

* * * *

"In the old times before 1888, when this privilege was taken away, if we missed our opportunities of bringing Indian grievances before Parliament by resolution on a private

* Detailed Report, pp. 57, 58.

member's night, we had the privilege of grievance before supply on the Budget night to fall back upon. That is now gone, and we wish to have it restored. You must remember that the responsibilities of Parliament towards India are increasing every year. More and more India is being brought into touch with England. (*Cheers.*) During the last five years the interest which has been taken by all politicians, especially by Liberal politicians, in the action of the Indian National Congress, has done much to stimulate the interest of English people in India. But, as our responsibility increases, we find that our powers decrease."

The question need not be pursued further here. The justice of the reclamations of the Congress on these heads is so manifest that, whenever any considerable number of members of Parliament can be induced to look into the subject, the matter will assuredly be put right. Already motions on this point are before the House, which will doubtless be repeated every season, until the desired result is attained.

Mr. D. E. Wacha moved* the fourth resolution, which may be quoted in its entirety as fully telling its own story. It ran thus : Resolved—

" *That while recognizing the action taken in response to its previous prayers in the matter of excise reform by H. M.'s Secretary of State for India and the Supreme Government here, and noting with pleasure the increase to the import duty on spirits, the taxation imposed on Indian-brewed malt liquors, the decision of the Bengal Government to abolish the outstill system, and the closing of over 7,000 liquor shops by the Madras Grovernment in 1889-90, this Congress regrets that it is still necessary to urge the Government of India to insist on all Provincial Administrations carrying out in their integrity, the policy, in matters of excise, enunciated in Clauses 103, 104 and 105 of the despatch published in the Gazette of India of March 1st, 1890, especially as to sub-section 4 of Clause 103, viz.,* "*That efforts should be made to ascertain the existence of the local public sentiment, and that a reasonable amount of deference should be paid to such opinion when ascertained.*"

Both Bengal and Madras have moved, to a certain extent, in the right direction, but Lord Reay, though a most liberal-minded man, and, in almost every other respect, one of the most popular Governors an Indian Presidency has ever had, allowed himself to be misled by a very clever, but as regards the fundamental principles of excise administration, a wholly wrong-headed civilian. Thus it happens that it is chiefly against the Bombay Government that Mr. Wacha directs his remarks. After acknowledging the good work done elsewhere, he says :—

" I regret that I cannot speak similarly of my own Province ; the Bombay Government has done absolutely nothing. Nay, the Bombay Government, instead of reforming its ways, has become a worse sinner since the date of the orders of the House of Commons. That is to me a matter of great regret, because, after all our efforts, we are no better off than we were three years ago. Indeed, instead of the Government of Bombay taking the lesson to heart, as given in the resolution of the House of Commons, and by the Government of India itself, it has been going in the wrong direction and increasing the consumption and increasing the revenue. (*Shame !*) For your information I beg in a very short compass to put some statistics before you from which you will see that the statement I have made is not a mere haphazard statement, but a statement borne out by official statistics. The revenue in 1881-82 was 38 lakhs ; in 1889-90 it had reached 74 lakhs—an increase of 95 per cent. The consumption has also increased from 18 lakhs of gallons to 27 lakhs, an increase of 50 per cent. Then, again, while Madras justly takes credit for having closed 7,000 liquor shops in a single year, what do we find in Bombay ? This : That in 1887-88 we had 4,443 shops, and in 1888-89 we had 4,739 shops, an increase of about 300. This, let me say, has reference more to country spirits than to toddy or other liquor. One of the strongest grievances involved in the abkari administration is that regarding new toddy. Toddy in Bombay, as in other parts of the country, is drunk by the labouring classes

* Detailed Report, pp. 39—45.

for whom Manchester philanthropists have been exerting themselves with so much solicitude. (*Laughter.*) It is comparatively innocuous, not having the strength of ordinary alcoholic beverages ; but it is boycotted in Bombay in order that the consumption of ardent spirits may be stimulated. What is the result ? Ten years ago there were lakhs of palm trees tapped in different directions, but now the trees stand yielding nothing from the soil they occupy ; not a single tree is allowed to be tapped by its owners. The fact is that the original drawers of toddy have lost their industry, and they are now eking out a miserable subsistence in all sorts of miscellaneous and possibly, some of them, questionable ways ; and I should not be surprised if many of them have gone to swell the large number of people of whom Sir William Hunter speaks as going with half a meal a day in India. This is a sad picture of the disastrous results of the Bombay abkari administration. Under these circumstances I think you will agree with the statement in the resolution that it is necessary, at this stage, that the Government of India should actually call upon those provincial administrations, which have not carried out this reform, to do so without delay. The farming system is still flourishing in Bombay ; the traffic has been stimulated, and it has brought shops to many villages where there were none. The result has been that intemperance has increased.

"With regard to the last and most important part of the resolution I believe there is no one who has given two minutes consideration to this subject who would not say that, in a country like India, sober from ancient times (whatever may be said to the contrary), it is absolutely necessary that the principle inculcated by the House of Commons, as far as local option for India is concerned, should be carried out, even though in some localities it may be necessary to do this slowly and gradually. I cannot better impress you with the importance of this than by a quotation from a statement of the Government of India. They say 'that efforts should be made to ascertain the existence of local public sentiment, and that a reasonable amount of deference should be paid to such opinion when ascertained.' I will give you an instance of the reasonable amount of deference paid to such opinion in Bombay. In the centre of the mill district at Ahmedabad the Collector lately gave a license to open a liquor shop. All the owners of the mills asked to have it closed, but the request was not granted. Then, again, these same people at Ahmedabad, fully aware of the evil of intemperance, requested Lord Harris, when on a visit to the town, that local option might be introduced, but this also was refused. This refusal is a matter of regret, firstly, because it was a disobedience of the instructions of the Government of India ; and, secondly, because the introduction of the system there—when the people voluntarily asked for it—was an experiment worthy of trial, if only to prove the goodness and sincerity of the intentions of Government. Lord Harris is, no doubt, new to this country, but I do hope and believe that when he has studied the whole question in all its aspects he will at least try to do his best to introduce this system of local option in Bombay, because I believe that on this question the salvation of India, so far as drinking is concerned, mainly rests." (*Cheers*).

It is well to give prominence to this to enable people in England to realize how a single, clever, wrongheaded civilian can nullify the distinct orders alike of the House of Commons and the Government of India. This question of reform in the Excise Administration is exciting the greatest attention throughout the country, in a great measure in consequence of Mr. Caine's and his fellow labourers' strenuous personal exertions. Hundreds of temperance associations are springing up, and now that we have friends and supporters in Great Britain, it is certain that Government will get no peace until it thoroughly reforms its liquor department. The debate was marked by much earnestness. Mr. Kashinath Natu from the Deccan said*:—

"If one of our forefathers, who lived 150 years ago, were to stand here and see this august assembly, with what wonder would he regard a sight which, in his own day, would have been an absolute impossibility ? But he would be still more wonder-struck to find a proposition being made for which there was no necessity whatever in his day. In the elevated sanctuaries of the Himalayas he devoted his time and thoughts to the contemplation of the infinite and absolute ; but the entire devotion of too many of his descendants seems to centre nowadays on a cupboard full of bottles, and he would be astonished to find not a few outcastes here and there, but legions of the highest caste men slaves to the grossest of all vices, intemperance. If we are slow in other matters, we have made

* Detailed Report, p. 41.

almost incredible progress in this. Not long ago in our province the income from this source was only Rs. 10,000, but it is now no less than ten lakhs. (*Shame !*) Where there was no man seen drunk in the streets, there are now hundreds.

"I have come here to support a proposition that ought, I think, to be self-supporting: certainly it needs no support from one so little known as myself. But I speak from the natural impulses of my own heart, and I have a very strong hope that the day will come when, to adapt the Englishman's saying, 'we shall not have a single slave to contaminate our soil,' we shall not have a single drop of spirit to contaminate our sons. Some gentlemen who are otherwise kindly disposed say that this is all the result of education. And who has given us that education? I am inclined to allow the Government to stand *in loco parentis*. 'You are our kind parents and, occupying that position, are you going to open grogshops in every town and street?' It is a thing about which there can be no two opinions even in the House of Parliament. We earnestly ask the Government to do what? To lessen that vice, the prevalence of which is owing in great measure to their own policy. They gave us education, no doubt, but they also made us acquainted with the drink bottle. 'It is you,' we can truly say to them, 'who have brought the evil into our country, and to whom, if not to you, shall we go to find a remedy? You cannot say no to us. You *must* close the grogshops. It is said we are not fit to govern ourselves. You have given us the municipal franchise and empowered us to deal with sanitation and other matters; and yet in the same breath you say that we are not fit to regulate our grogshops, to decide on the numbers we will have, or to resolve that we will have none at all.' I cordially support this proposition, and I hope the day will come when India will say, 'No liquor, no brandy here, but only Adam's ale—pure water!' (*Cheers*)."

No less earnest, though in his own quaint way, was Lalla Murlidhur from the Panjab, well known as one of the staunchest Congressmen in India, and abundantly persecuted in consequence, in past times, by the officials. He remarked *:—

Now I come to the point. I do not know why you blame these grogshops and grogsellers, and those who promote the drink traffic. There is more philosophy in a bottle of wine than in all the schools, because it proves in a minute what sages have taken long ages to solve—the problem of the transmigration of souls. (*Cheers and laughter*). It proves how a human being passes into a brute, and can assume the form of a donkey at will. (*Laughter*). Yes, even the Theosophists will be puzzled to solve this problem. While the East has taught the West mathematics, astronomy and other sciences, in exchange the West has given us liquor—damnation instead of salvation. That really is a very good barter. We have bargained away our souls, and what have we in exchange? A bottle of gin or a glass of whiskey."

In the Panjab he said some reforms were being carried out:—

"But, in spite of all this, people have become more addicted to drink because it has been thought to be an adjunct of Western civilization. It is thought that a man cannot become a perfect gentleman unless he drinks a glass of wine. Now another Governor has come to the rescue of the present generation, and he says that if a person indulges in a glass of whiskey there is no harm in it. Is there no harm? Is that the idea of the Governor of millions of people that there is no harm in throwing temptation in the way of the poor wretched creatures who live on one meal a day? They have their children living in misery—clad in rags.........lying in the mud; but all this is not enough, there must be these foul liquor shops to tempt them to make things even worse! (*Shame, shame*).

"Even our Mahomedan rulers hated and held the liquor traffic accursed. It has been left for our Christian rulers to love it, pet it, stimulate it, and make money by crores out of it! (*Hear, hear*).

"Now we find, even in Burmah, a newly conquered Province, we find that liquor shops have been started. And for whose benefit? Not certainly for the benefit of the Burmese, whose creed forbids strong drink, and who are only now, under British tuition, learning how to grow into drunkards and beasts? (*Hear.*) For whose benefit then? The benefit of the British Government, and I marvel equally at the folly and the wickedness of the course adopted. Will a drunken population serve them as well; will it, even in the long run, fill their exchequer as full as a sober one? (*Cheers*). How too can men, who pretend to believe in God and a

* Detailed Report. pp. 41, 42.

future state, thus set to work coldly, cruelly, systematically to seduce the people committed to their charge by Him into all kinds of sin and misery. And what wickedness does not the habit of drinking lead to? It is not forme to speak much about the evils of drinking. You who have been born in this country and have never tasted liquor have always held it to be only another name for—damnation. (*Laughter*). With those few words I support the resolution. (*Cheers*). I will only add one word. You laugh at me and think that I am a fool. (*No, no*). Really I am a fool (*laughter*), and you must thank the Punjab people, because the representative character of this National Congress would not have been perfect without the presence of one fool, at least, tc represent the many. (*Laughter and prolonged cheers*).

Guru Pratab Singh, one of the spiritual leaders of the Sikhs, made* a really very remarkable speech which we reproduce :—

"FRIENDS,—With great respect I beg to state that we Sikhs heartily sympathize with the National Congress; for the national blessings which it is conferring, and will confer, cannot be looked for from any other organization or institution.

"I belong to the family of Sikh Gurus known as Sodhi. I, with my followers, am a supporter of the Congress with body and wealth. My followers are about 25,000 men, and range from Lahore to Candahar.

"Drinking is positively prohibited in our creed as it is in others. No one dare speak in favour of drink. I am much struck that now-a-days it should be needful to warn people against drinking. There was a time when a drunkard would have tried in vain to force his vile liquor on his neighbours; in vain, for people avoided drink, with very rare exceptions, out of respect for their creeds. Now, alas, it is quite common to find men lying naked, and insensible from drink, about our streets.

"What are the best loved things in the world for which all people toil? Is it not wife and children? But those given to drinking do not spare even these, but despoil them of their jewels, nay of their very food, to satisfy their accursed craving.

"The hapless wives and children of this legion of beasts addressed their prayers for succour to God, who listened mercifully and moved the hearts of Mr. Caine and the Congress leaders to espouse their cause and endeavour to rescue the people of India from this great sin and misery that the Government has unwittingly brought upon them.

"This Congress, bent upon this and other good works for our suffering brethren, is not an assembly of men, but of Devas.† It is a place of pilgrimage which purifies the heart choked by the impurities of a lifetime.

"The ruler for the time being is the Vicegerent of God on earth. Our Gracious Empress now occupies such a place. It is in Her name and encouraged by the sacredness of Her position that we of the Congress lift up our voices against this and other great evils from which India is now suffering. May God incline Her heart to listen to our prayers.

"Since this work of the National Congress has begun, educated men have commenced to labour for the good of their fellows, and especially to devote their energies to rooting out this drink evil.

"More than one local Government has taken steps in the right direction, and for this we have to thank both Englishmen like Mr. Caine and his supporters in England, and our National Congress here in India.

"Government revenue will decrease, and some think this will harm Government; but when the people benefit, as in this case, any wise Government counts all such losses a gain Nay, where Government got one rupee by the drunkenness of its subjects, it will gain ten by their sobriety.

"It is very strange that though education has so widely spread, drink seems to have done so equally. Either education has not produced the expected results, or there has not been enough of it, or it is not the right sort, not sufficiently embodying a moral element. I do not rightly understand, but I pray God Almighty to crown the efforts of this Congress, and of all

* Detailed Report, pp. 42, 43.
† *Viz.*, Semi-divine beings.

who side with them in endeavouring to save the people from this evil of drunkenness, and may He crown our Queen Empress with the choicest blessings and incline her heart to decree the rescue of her people from this grim monster."

The good Guru's perplexity at the untoward results of the education now being diffused amongst us is not unnatural; but the fact is that Western culture is destroying the moral sanctions of the indigenous creeds, and as yet replacing them by no higher law. Social reformers, almost all of them, save those who as Government servants are debarred from this, good Congressmen as well, and pious votaries of many creeds are trying, everywhere, to stem the growing evil; but it is to be feared that, unless some new and vivifying faith grows up in the heart of the nation, the almost wholly foreign and purely secular education, now being poured into the country, will give rise, not only to the expected good fruit, but also to a dire and unexpected crop of noxious weeds. No doubt political responsibility, if the Government could be induced to concede it, and other reforms that we have advocated, would do a good deal towards raising the moral as well as the physical status of the people, but even the most sanguine cannot flatter themselves that these will adequately fill the void left by the extraordinarily rapid decay of religious belief.

The resolution was passed unanimously, and then the Congress adjourned until 11 A.M of the following Monday.

On Sunday the Social Conference assembled in the Congress Pavilion, and passed, after much discussion, various important resolutions in regard to matters of Social Reform. But the Social Conference will, as in former years, publish its own separate Report, and nothing further need be said of it here. The matter is only mentioned because this year, for the first time, some few persons, belonging to the old conservative party, addressed a number of representations to the President and General Secretary and to the delegates as a body, urging them not to permit the Social Conference to use the Congress Hall, and it is satisfactory to be able to record that not one single delegate was found willing to support this intolerant proposition.

On Monday, when the Congress re-assembled, the first resolution brought forward prayed for a reduction of the salt tax. Year by year, as the popular element grows stronger and stronger in the Congress party, the delegates find themselves, compelled by their constituencies, to lay more and more stress upon this subject. The resolution ran as follows:—

" *RESOLVED—That the condition of the finances of India having materially improved, and those special circumstances on which the Government relied to justify the recent enhancement of the salt tax having, practically, ceased to exist, this Congress considers it essential that the enhancement referred to should be remitted at an early date, and empowers its President to submit a special memorial on the subject, in its name and on its behalf, to H. E. the Viceroy in Council.*

It was proposed by Mr. Pringle Kennedy, and the subject is of such vital importance to our poorer classes, *viz.*, to four-fifths of the population, that no apology seems necessary for quoting at great length, alike from his speech and from those of other delegates who supported the proposal. Mr. Kennedy said :*—

"Not everybody in India is a contributor to the abkari revenue, and, if Mr. Caine has his way, the number of such contributors will dwindle by shrinkage to a vanishing quantity. All the inhabitants of India are not fortunate enough to possess Rs. 500 a year, and to have in consequence the pleasure of submitting to the income-tax. But every man, woman and child in this country must eat salt, and thus be a feeder of the Imperial Treasury. (*Hear, hear*).

"The salt-tax is an income-tax on all incomes down to the lowest. The poorer a man is, the heavier is its incidence. What that incidence is I shall hereafter show. In England a labourer who drinks neither alcoholic beverages nor tea nor yet smokes tobacco, pays nothing to the State. In India the lowliest peasant, the poorest coolie, nay the very beggar widow in the street, has to drop her mite into the Imperial Treasury. (*Hear, hear*). Such a tax needs very cogent reasons to defend it."

* * * * * * * *

"When I hear that the people do not mind it, the only meaning that I can put to this expression is that people do not speak of it. Gentlemen, an eel is said not to mind skinning. It is used to it. I suppose it seems to them a visitation of an inscrutable providence ; and hence, no doubt; our people, unless questioned, do not, in many parts of the country, speak much about it. But when I think of the salt tax, my thought takes me to Feudal France, when that existed under the name of the Gabelle. They did not mind it, so the rulers said : and, no doubt, even if they did, they rather hesitated to press the point, for, in those days, a gallows was found to be even more disagreeable than a poll tax, and their rulers were quite handy at hanging all who differed from them on such political questions. But, Gentlemen, if the wheels of God grind slowly, yet they grind exceeding small, and the end came, I need not say how.

"Now I come to the incidence of the Indian salt tax. Bear with me while I give you a few figures. I shall try to make them as round and simple as I can. First of all, from enquiry, amongst other places at Her Majesty's jails where luxuriesare not likely to be given, I find that nine or ten chittacks a month, or seven seers and a little over—we will drop the little over—are necessary to keep an adult in health. Now, there are more than twenty-five tens of millions of people in India, and making a deduction for children and others, who need a less quantity of salt than adults, we may take it that 20 tens of millions rations of salt at the rate, above mentioned, or something over 3½ tens of millions of maunds of salt, are necessary to keep the people in health. And this quantity at Rs. 2-8 per maund, the present rate of duty, should yield $8\frac{7}{10}$ tens of millions of rupees. But if I turn to the latest revenue returns, I find that 7¼ tens of millions of rupees roughly was the last year's salt revenue. This gives 6 annas a head : and it shows, since the tax is one anna a seer, the fact that each person has 6 and not 7 seers of salt a year, as he ought to have at the least. (*Hear, hear.*) As a matter of fact in British territory, (they are better off in some of the native states) the Government itself calculates the consumption at not more than 10lbs. or a little less than 5 seers per head. There is doubtless considerable smuggling on the one side, but on the other it must be mentioned that human consumption is not the sole, though the chief, use of salt, and that many of the people consume a far greater quantity than the minimum we have given. I know perfectly well that many of the people have not sufficient bread either, but the price of that is not artificially raised by Government.

"Let us look at the subject from a different point of view. In an article in the *Pioneer*, some months ago, by Mr. Robertson, it was stated that a Madras official, who made a careful study of the question, had ascertained that the average monthly income of the agriculturists in the district of Karnool was 12 annas per head, say Rs. 4 for a family of five. Very rough calculations on my part give me similar results for the districts of Durbhangah and Mozufferpore. The *Gazetteer* published several years ago, gives the expenditure of a well-to-do Tirhoot peasant, and therefore I presume the income at about Rs. 11 per month. This was for a family of five. The poorer, it is said, have to reduce their expenditure to about half of this. Let us say Rs. 5 for a family of five. Now if these five ate 24 seers of salt in the year, as in accordance with the official calculations already stated, they would do, this would be (leaving out any calculation for the increased price, which, as all economists know, considerably exceeds the amount of the tax itself), at one anna a seer, Rs. 1-8, and so a family having Rs. 60 a year would have to pay Rs. 1-8 as their salt duty. This is a tax of nearer five than four pies a month and this too on incomes not over Rs. 500 a year, but of only Rs. 5 a month. If mine, and a Madras civilian's figures be taken, the people of these districts would be paying over 6 pies in the rupee, and if they ate 7 instead of 6 seers,

* Detailed Report, pp. 44, 45.

the tax would be nearly 7 pies in the rupee, and that on incomes of less than Rs. 50 a year. Think of these facts, ye Gentlemen, who have incomes over Rs. 500 a year, and grumble at the payment of 4 pies in the rupee! Meditate over them those of you who possess an income of over Rs. 2,000 a year and whine * at the payment of 5 pies in the rupee!

"Now, Sir, only one word more about figures. If the tax were reduced to Rs. 2, salt would sell at about 13 seers instead of 10 seers for the rupee as it now does. If the duty were reduced to one rupee, as Lord Mayo, Sir J. Strachey, and subsequently Sir Evelyn Baring desired, salt would sell for 20 seers for the rupee, and if salt were duty free, a blessed day, but I am afraid far away in the millennium, salt would sell at 40 seers for the rupee in those places even where it is now dearest, and in many provinces it would be far cheaper. Why the actual cost of producing one maund of salt at the Mayo mines, the Sambhur lake, the Kareghora works and the Madras coast works, is under *two annas!* But, Gentlemen, Government, like other people, must live. We do not ask for he abolition of the whole tax. Mr. Caine is for doing away with the abkari revenue, others for reducing the income-tax. We say that already the financial situation is so improved—on this point, I believe, a speaker after me will dilate—that a part of the salt tax may be remitted, and, by judicious economy and reduction of military expenditure and home charges, the tax may be still further lowered.

"When you get your Representative Councils, you may be sure that the Government will listen to you, when you propose to tax yourselves, if in no other matter. If then this burden is still too heavy for the millions of the land after all economy is made, the only way whereby you can alleviate its weight is by taking some of it on yourselves. Gentlemen, when some fifty years ago, John Bright lay prostrate under one of the greatest afflictions that can befall mortal man, Cobden came to him and said: 'Your grief is great, but remember that there are millions of widows and widows' sons who perish this day in England from lack of cheap bread.' In this great land of India there are millions of men and women and children this day who have their lives shortened, their physique stunted, and with their physique, their moral and intellectual faculties blunted, by lack of cheap salt. (*Hear, hear*). I address many of the great of this land. Will they use all their influence to make this precious necessary of life cheaper? Fellow Delegates, will you show that they accuse you falsely, who say your care is all for yourselves and that this movement is simply one for the substitution of Indian dark-skinned for European fair-skinned Brahmins, by saying: 'If in no other way can this yoke be made less grievous, tax us, tax the rich but let the poor go!' I appeal to you, one and all in this Hall, to show that Western education has brought with it an increase of sympathy and charity for your poorer brethren, for the dumb millions of the land, without which sympathy and charity, all the knowledge of this earth is but as sounding brass and a tinkling cymbal." (*Loud cheers*).

To him followed Mr. Dinshaw E. Wacha of Bombay in a closely reasoned speech which does not admit of condensation. He said:—†

"You have already heard Mr. Kennedy on the question of the consumption of salt and the oppressive incidence of the salt tax on the people. I will, however, make a few further observations on this part of the subject, before I dwell at some length on the financial condition of the country, which is the ground on which we propose to memorialise the Government of India to reduce the tax. The principal object of the Resolution before you is to urge upon the Government the justice of remitting the enhanced salt duty of 8 annas per maund, which is no longer imperative on account of the material improvement which the finances of the Empire have undergone since the date of its imposition. It is needless for me to recall to your memory the pretext under which the enhancement was justified in the early part of 1888, despite the fact that well-informed critics in the press and responsible associations, at the time, conclusively showed that it was uncalled for.

"Previous to the imposition of the augmented duty, the Government of India had absorbed in two years 8¾ crores of rupees, *viz.:*—

| | |
|---|---|
| By Income Tax ... ... ... ... ... | Rs. 2,75,00,000 |
| Improvements and Economies ... ... ... ... ... | „ 2,00,00,000 |
| Curtailment of Provincial Allotment ... ... ... ... | „ 1,00,00,000 |
| Appropriation of Famine and Railway Fund ... ... ... ... | „ 3,00,00,000 |

* Great indignation is felt, as a rule, by Indians, at the selfish outcry of many Europeans, especially in Calcutta, against the Income-tax. If they only asked, as the Congress does, that incomes below £70 a year should be exempt from the Tax, all would sympathize with them. As it is, all they want is to save their own pockets and get rid of the Tax altogether; already the poor pay far too much, the rich far too little; and instead of abolishing the tax, Government should raise it to 6 pie per rupee on all incomes exceeding Rs. 10,000 per annum.

† Detailed Report, pp. 46—49.

This colossal amount of nearly 9 crores was wasted on the following questionable and hazardous enterprises :—

| | | |
|---|---|---|
| Upper Burmah acquisition ... ... ... ... ... | Rs. | 3,51,00,000 |
| Penjdeh Field Force ... ... ... ... ... ... | „ | 2,11,60,000 |
| Transfrontier Defences and Railways ... ... ... ... | „ | 2,00,00,000 |
| Additional Military Expenditure ... ... ... ... ... | „ | 98,00,000 |

" But even after the absorption of such a vast amount there was a heavy deficiency which, the Government regretfully urged, necessitated a recourse to additional taxation in the shape of an enhanced duty of 8 annas per maund on such a necessary of life as salt. The deficiency was chiefly attributable, according to Lord Dufferin's statement, to the fall in the value of silver.

" We need not, however, trouble ourselves much with the past. We are now here to remind the Government that our finances are in a condition to justify the remission of the enhanced duty. For that purpose let me put some statistics before you. I know that statistics are very dry, and that blue books of a dry-as-dust character are never looked at by the public; but, considering the importance of the resolution before you, I hope you will give your attention to the figures I am going to place before you.

"Previous Finance Ministers, particularly Sir John Strachey and Sir Evelyn Baring, two of the ablest ministers since the days of the late Mr. Wilson and Mr. S. Laing, repeatedly declared that the lower the salt duty the better for the country and the better for the Imperial revenue, because a lower duty stimulates consumption and a higher one restricts it. Government itself has admitted the soundness of this doctrine, and I will now proceed to show by figures how a lower or higher duty affects consumption. In 1876-77, when various rates of duty were enforced in the different provinces of the Empire, the total recorded amount which paid the salt-tax was 25,847,830 maunds. In 1878, Sir John Strachey brought about an equalization of the duty, everywhere, by fixing the uniform rate of Rs. 2-8 per maund. It remained in force till 1882. During this period the annual quantity of salt which paid the duty of Rs. 2-8 per maund averaged 27,288,569 maunds. This annual average, compared with the consumption recorded in 1876-77, showed a growth of 5·5 per cent. In 1882, the government of Lord Ripon reduced the duty to Rs. 2 per maund, at which it remained till it was again raised to Rs. 2-8 by Lord Dufferin in 1888. The quantity which paid the reduced duty of Rs. 2 averaged during the five years 30,830,847 maunds per annum.

" The increase during this quinquennial period, compared with the average of the previous four years, was 3,542,278 maunds, equal to a percentage of 13. Thus, while in the period when the duty was Rs. 2-8, the increase equalled 1·37 per cent per annum ; in the period when it was Rs. 2 the growth equalled 2·6 per cent per annum. (*Cheers*). It is obvious that, had there been no enhancement, the progress in consumption up to date would have been maintained at that or even a higher rate. But just as this progress was perceptible all throughout the country, the financial embarrassments of the Government led, as they asserted, to the augmentation of the duty and with it to a restricted consumption. In his last financial statement Sir David Barbour has tried to show that the progress of consumption has received no check. According to his own figures, however, as given in the 23rd paragraph of that statement, it is clear that consumption in 1890-91 is estimated at about 31,930,000 maunds, which is less by 900,000 maunds than the recorded figures of 1886-87.

" Sir David attempts to demonstrate that, in spite of the increased duty, consumption, which had evidently fallen, is again creeping to the old level. But Sir David forgets two important factors : Firstly, that population is increasing at the rate of one per cent. per annum ; and, secondly, that but for the enhancement, the percentage of progress observable till 1887 might have been better in 1890-91. Indeed, it is a question whether the consumption per head has not fallen below the average of 10lb. per annum. That average is considered everywhere, but in India, to be quite inadequate, especially as we allow nothing in our computation for the consumption of cattle, hundreds of thousands of whom annually lose condition for want of salt and die off consequently on the smallest failure of pasturage, and thus cripple to a serious extent the means which mainly contribute to the production of our national wealth."

" I will give you some figures of the consumption of salt in Europe and America, from which it will be easily perceived how much India falls short of what may be called an adequate consumption of salt. In the United Kingdom there is no duty, and the consumption is 80lb. per head, but of course this includes much salt for manufacturing purposes. In France it is 50lb.; in Germany 25 ; in Russia 19—Russia, whose economic conditions are in some respects, identical with those of India ; in Austria 14, in Italy 18, in Spain and Portugal, poor as they are, 17lb. The consumption in the United States is 39lbs., the average in Europe is 26lbs.

"Then look at the incidence of the duty. The average income per head of the European population is £15 4*s.* 7¼*d.* per head, while the salt duty per head averages 11*d.* Now taking the rupee at 1*s.* 6*d.* the average income of the population in India is £2, while the salt duty per head averages 5*d.* and 1½ farthings. Therefore, in Europe, the salt duty is 0·3 per cent. on the income, while in India it is over 1 1 per cent—or, in other words, the incidence of the salt tax is now nearly four times as heavy in India as in Europe. Formulated in other terms it means that India, with an income hardly more than ⅛th that of Europe, pays nearly half as much as a tax on a necessity of life like salt. Thus the duty operates as a real hardship on the poorest people, who constitute the large majority of our population. How great is the hardship may be realised by taking a concrete example. A family of five consumes on an average, say, 50lbs. of salt annually. But there are only two bread-winners, man and wife, the rest being young persons or children. Taking the average income of each *earner* at the official computation, *viz.*, Rs. 27 per head, and calculating the lowest retail bazar price at Rs. 3 per maund, it will be found that there is a burden of nearly 4 per cent. on the combined income per annum merely for salt. Imagine an income-tax of 4 per cent on a poor family of 5, and nearly one-sixth of this is due to the extra 8 annas. Thus the enhancement of the duty, however small, operates with great hardship on the masses.

"Under these circumstances it is a matter of deep regret to us all that the two* native gentlemen who were present at the meeting at the Viceregal Council when this enhancement Bill was passed, should have observed that increased duty would not be felt by the people! I believe that statement was directly opposed to the all but absolutely universal opinion outside the Council Chamber. The statement was more to be regretted because it misled Lord Dufferin into observing, later on in his speech, that the Council were 'glad to hear' that the enhancement of the duty would not be considered a hardship. This is the way in which nominated members of the Viceregal Council fulfil their trust. It is evident that had there been elected representatives of the people, as proposed by us for the reformed Legislative Councils, no such opinion would have been allowed to prevail and mislead the Government. (*Cheers*). Eight annas may appear trifling to most of us; but they mean a great deal to the poorest. What they signify may be best stated in the substance of the words of Sir Evelyn Baring: 'Eight annas to the poor ryot means the purchase of either 3 yards of cloth or a little *lota*.'

"Gentlemen, all through the history of the salt tax it has been said that it is a poll-tax and that it falls heavily on the poor. My personal opinion is that it should have no place in our fiscal system, for it is a tax on a necessary of life, and is, moreover, at its present rate fully 25 times the actual cost of production. Eminent statesmen, from Sir John Lawrence to Lord Ripon, have disapproved of it. But it is now too late to abolish it altogether. It is of no use contending with existing facts. All that we should strive for is a low duty, on the sound principle that it is conducive to greater consumption both for men and cattle.

"I now pass to the second part of the resolution. I hold in my hand a copy of the explanatory memorandum by the Under Secretary of State for India, presented to Parliament in August last. At page 50 there is a table of *Net* Revenue and Expenditure for the three years ending 1889-90, and also budget estimates for the current official year. Comparing the complete accounts of 1887-88 with the estimates of this year what do we find! This only, that there is a satisfactory growth of revenue under all the principal heads. Leaving alone opium, salt and provincial rates I find that the increase under the other heads amounts to 143 lakhs of rupees as under:—

| | | Accounts. 1887-88. | Budget Estimates. 1890-91. | Increase. 1890-91 |
|---|---|---|---|---|
| Land Revenue .Rx. | ... | 19,653,000 | 20,119,000 | 466,000 |
| Stamps ,, | ... | 3,669,000 | 3,846,000 | 177,000 |
| Excise ,, | ... | 4,374,000 | 4,645,000 | 271,000 |
| Customs ,, | ... | 1,182,000 | 1,378,000 | 196,000 |
| Assessed Taxes ,, | ... | 1,383,000 | 1,514,000 | 131,000 |
| Forest ,, | ... | 402,000 | 565,000 | 163,000 |
| Registration ,, | ... | 123,000 | 150,000 | 27,000 |

"Thus, apart from salt, which now yields a larger revenue on account of a higher duty, apart from opium which is precarious in its yield, and apart from provincial rates which are mere transfer receipts, there is a growth in four years of 143 lakhs. But beyond this improvement on the revenue side there is, gentlemen, a material saving in one item of Imperial expenditure. I refer to the interest charge on the ordinary debt. In 1887-88, the net charge under this head was Rs. 46,950,000. In the estimates of expenditure for 1890-91 it is put down at Rs. 35,060,000. The saving in four years amounts to 118 lakhs. While we

* Rajah Peary Mohan Mookerjee, one of the two gentlemen referred to, was on the platform.

note this improvement in our national expenditure with great satisfaction, we cannot but feel aghast when we discover that expenditure under other heads had risen by leaps and bounds by no less than 308 lakhs.

| | | Accounts. 1887-88. | Budget Estimates. 1890-91. | Increases. |
|---|---|---|---|---|
| Civil Department | Rx. ... | 11,410,000 | 12,075,000 | 665,000 |
| Miscellaneous Charges | „ ... | 3,155,000 | 3,702,000 | 547,000 |
| Buildings and Roads | „ ... | 4,859,000 | 5,128,000 | 269,000 |
| Army Services | „ ... | 19,357,000 | 20,522,000 | 1,165,000 |
| Special Defence Works | „ ... | 456,000 | 892,000 | 436,000 |

"Thus in four years they have managed to run up Civil and Military charges, including defence works, by the enormous extent of 3 crores. The army services alone have increased by a crore and sixteen lakhs! not to speak of defence works having been run up 100 per cent! *It is these stupendous charges which eat up your growing revenue. It is the so-called defence policy, the safeguarding of our frontiers and transfrontiers from a bugbear of their own creation, created to find staff appointments, and employments to the already monied European classes, which is at the root of the financial embarrassments of the Government and at the root of the starvation and misery which are eating away the lives of tens of millions of our pauper Indians.** There are military and other critics who disapprove of that policy. Our late lamented friend Mr. Slagg characterised it two years ago, as you may remember, as a 'mad' policy, when speaking on the subject in the House of Commons. *I believe that it is a 'mad' policy. I know that it is a wicked policy, and, as long as it is pursued headlong, it will continue to embarrass the finances and add millions yearly to our already alarmingly heavy death roll.* The embarrassments arising from the fall in the value of silver are in my opinion nothing—a mere fleabite—compared with the financial difficulties in which the Government of India is plunged by this insane military policy. *I repeat; that unless a great effort is made at future Congresses to force the Government to desist from these reckless and indefensible operations beyond the natural lines of Indian defence, there can be scarcely any hope of pecuniary relief to the tax payer—scarcely any hope for the amelioration of the miserable condition of our starving millions.* Since the Panjdeh scare they have spent, according to the official statements, full 13 crores on the so-called trans-frontier defences; but we have not yet seen the last of them, for in the last financial statement reference is made to a further probable expenditure of a crore!

"I now come to the practical part of the resolution. *Of course, we have to submit resignedly to this ruinous, this unprincipled trans-frontier policy of the Government until we succeed in awakening the consciences of our British fellow-subjects. We are British subjects, now, of our own free choice; we have thrown in our lot with England for better and for worse, and it is this which enhances England's sin in permitting the continuance of this hateful policy.* Will our British brethren never awake? Meanwhile more ammunition, more explosives, more fireworks and even more troops are being requisitioned. These costly pastimes, amusements to our rulers, death to our people, may deter the authorities from giving ear to our prayers and protests. But it is well, none the less, to remind them of their own declaration that the enhanced duty 'must go' as soon as the finances permit.

"One of the principal grounds on which Lord Dufferin stated that he was obliged, '*with the greatest reluctance*,' to increase the duty, was the loss by exchange. I quote from the speech he made about the beginning of 1888: 'Unfortunately, it has become my lot on several occasions to add to the taxation of the country, but in justification of this hard necessity, it is sufficient for me to remark that since my arrival in India, owing to the depreciation in the price of silver, the annual accumulation of loss to the Government has progressively increased yearly by a million.' He goes on to say: 'The loss in 1884-85, when I first took up the reins of Government, stood at 3·40 crores; in 1885-86 at 4·40 crores; in 1886 at 5·40 crores, and in 1887-88 at 6·60 crores.' The latest financial statement gives the loss on exchange at 7 crores. It was, however, promised by both Lord Dufferin and Mr. Westland that the duty should be remitted on the first opportunity that the finances were relieved of this embarrassment. That opportunity has now arrived. Since the publication of the last budget you are all aware that exchange has greatly improved, partly in consequence, possibly, of the action taken in regard to silver in the United States. Though we had violent fluctuations in August and September last, exchange still stands to-day at about 1*s.* 6½*d.* The amount to be remitted this year to the Secretary of State is nearly 15 millions sterling. The rate of exchange was estimated in March last at 1*s.* 4½*d.*, and the probable loss at that rate was computed to be 7 crores. But already 11 millions have been remitted at an average rate of 1*s.* 6½*d.*, and there is no reason to doubt that the balance of the remittance will be made at or about the same rate: Sir John Gorst himself

* The italics are of course, ours, but it is impossible to emphasize too strongly these pregnant words which embody the convictions of all the best and most earnest of our Indian thinkers.

stated when presenting the budget in August last that the rate would probably be maintained at 1*s.* 6½*d.*, so that it may be taken for granted that the loss by exchange will be very much less than the budget estimate of 7 crores. I compute it at only about 4·66 crores. Thus, apart from all other fluctuations of revenue and expenditure, there would be a saving under this head alone of nearly 2½ crores. Sir John Gorst counts on a surplus of 1·87 crores. Taking his figures and the actual surplus of 2 crores of last year, it may be reasonably expected that there will be available a surplus of not less than 4 crores in all. And, unless the authorities persevere in muddling it away on military mischief, that surplus should suffice, not only for the remission of the enhanced duty, but for reduction of this latter to Re. 1-8. (*Loud cheers*).

"But I beg to bring to your notice two more facts which will convince you that, *even apart from these surpluses*, the financial condition of the Imperial Treasury has so far improved as to justify our demand for a remission. The additional duty yields, it is asserted, 1½ crores (it is not really so much), and I say that that 1½ crores could be dispensed with easily for some years to come. According to Sir David Barbour's statement, there has been a permanent growth in the principal heads of revenue of ¾ of a crore per annum; exchange, again, is unlikely to go back to 1*s.* 4½*d.* for some time to come. Looking at current events and the further agitation on silver in America, it seems that a rate of 1*s.* 6½*d.*, or even 1*s.* 6*d.*, will be fairly maintained. But even if exchange could be maintained at 1*s.* 5½*d.* that would diminish the loss on the Secretary of State's bills in future to the extent of 1 crore roughly speaking, for an improvement of a penny in exchange gives a saving, according to official estimates, of just that amount. This saving, plus the permanent increase of ¾ crore in the principal sources of revenue, make up 1¾ crores, so that the Government is in a position to safely give up the 1½ crore now supposed to be derived from the additional duty of 8 annas per maund; as a matter of fact the loss, owing to increased consumption, would, after the first year, be less than one crore. Both financial conditions and the justice of the case demand, imperatively, that a remission should be made. I think, Gentlemen, I have now shown substantial reasons for the remission. And if you think I have made out a substantial case on which to base our representation to Government to remit the duty, I am sure that that representation will, at any rate, *deserve* an attentive and favorable consideration at the hands of the authorities. (*Loud and prolonged cheers*)."

Then followed Mr. G. K. Gokhale, who spoke* as follows:—

I have been asked to support this proposition that has been ably proposed, seconded and explained by previous speakers. My predecessors have dealt with certain aspects of the question, and I will with your permission deal with one or two others. I say that the measures for the enhancement of the duty on salt in January 1888 by a mere executive order of the Government of India was a cruel departure—I might almost say a criminal departure—from the wise policy long since laid down by the Government of India and re-affirmed, strange as it may seem, when Lord Lytton was our Viceroy and Sir John Strachey our Finance Minister, namely the policy of raising a revenue from salt by a low rate of duty and unrestricted consumption instead of by a high rate of duty and restricted consumption. I say that this new departure was extremely unjust, that as a measure of statesmanship it was extremely impolitic, and that its consequences have been simply disastrous. I know these are serious charges, but I think I can substantiate them. First, with regard to the charge of injustice. When Lord Dufferin's government passed the Income Tax Act of 1886 his Lordship said that the measure was not brought forward in any spirit of apology; that the masses of the country were already contributing more than their proper share to the expenses of the country, and that the income-tax would only equalize the burdens on the various classes. Well, the burdens being thus equalised in 1886, I ask on what principle of justice and equity was it that when two years afterwards a new emergency, as Government were pleased to call it, arose for additional taxation, it was the poor masses who were selected? How was it that when it was found necessary to create a fresh inequality in the taxation of the country matters were so arranged that the inequality was again prejudicial to the toiling masses? I do not know whether it was because the masses were almost certain to suffer silently without protest—I would even say without complaint—whereas their wealthier brethren were as certain to denounce any taxation on them in the public press and at St. Andrew's dinner speeches. So much with regard to the injustice of the measure: now with regard to its impolicy. We have on our side an authority not only infinitely greater than myself but one to which the Government of India ought to bow—I mean the authority of the Secretary of State for India, Lord Cross himself. Three months after the measure of

* Detailed Report, pp. 49—51.

enhancement his Lordship wrcte a Despatch to the Government on the subject. It was dated April 12th, 1888, and in it he expresses his great regret at the enhancement of the salt duty, and directed the Government of India in very distinct, unequivocal, and I would say peremptory, terms to take off the additional eight annas on thefirst opportunity afforded by the finances. He then went on to say that even from the point of view of expediency the enhancement was extremely undesirable, because in the case of so vast an empire as India it was absolutely essential for the Government always to hold in hand some financial reserve which they might utilize on occasions of any sudden and dangerous crisis. So much with regard to impolicy : now, with regard to consequences, I am going to show that consumption has actually been restricted by this measure. In 1888 Mr. Westland, our Finance Minister, said that the enhancement would not affect the consumption of the country. The figures supplied by Sir David Barbour himself belied that prediction. The last year unaffected was 1886-87, and then the consumption stood at 3 crores and 10 lakhs of maunds. The next year, 1887-88, the first year affected by the measure, there was a fall of 6 lakhs of maunds, the figures being 3 crores 4 lakhs. The next year there was a further fall of 6 lakhs, the figures being 2 crores 98 lakhs. It is true that the figures have now gone up to those of 1886-87, but that does not show that the restrictive operation of that enhancement has ceased, because we have to take into consideration the important factor of the increase in the consumption of salt owing to the normal growth of the population. That normal growth is one per cent per annum, and taking the consumption at 10lbs. per head, you find that every year there ought to be an increase of fully 3 lakhs of maunds in the consumption of salt.

"Taking this into account you will see that in the first year affected by the enhancement there was a fall of 9 lakhs, in the second of 18, and in the third of 9. Altogether in the last three years 36 lakhs of maunds less have been consumed by the people than they would have consumed if there had not been the enhancement. (*Cheers*). Sir John Gorst speaking the other day in the House of Commons said that the diminution in the consumption of salt was not appreciable—that was the term he used. I do not know what dictionaries would justify the use of the term, but Sir John Gorst is welcome to usethe word in this connection. But I ask him, and those who think with him, who are the persons affected by this diminishing consumption? I dare say there is not a single person present, not a single member of those who are called the middle and upperclasses, who have consumed, during the last three years, one grain of salt less than he would have done if there had been no enhancement. Who are the persons affected? They are those who have been estimated by Sir William Hunter at 40 millions, and by Sir Charles Elliott at 70 millions, who always exist on the borderland of famine, so that, directly there is the least failure, down the precipice they go. The persons affected by this enhancement are they to whom the lines of the Corn Law poet might aptly be applied :—

'Landless, joyless, helpless, hopeless,
Gasping still for bread and breath
To their graves by trouble hunted
India's helots toil till death.' (*Loud cheers.*)

"When you call to mind the thin emaciated figures of these unhappy, miserable, brethren, who have as much right to the comforts of this, God's, earth as you or I or any one else ; when you remember that the lives of these brethren are so uniformly dark and miserable, that they are hardly cheered by a single ray of hope, or relieved by a single day of rest ; when, further, you remember that a person does not generally trench upon his stock of necessaries before he has parted with every luxury, every single comfort that he may allow himself ; when you recall all these things, you will clearly understand what grievous and terrible hardship and suffering and privation this measure of enhancement, which has curtailed the poor man's consumption of salt by thirty-six lakhs of maunds, has really entailed. (*Cheers.*)"

Space will not allow us to reproduce much more of these earnest and eloquent appeals on behalf of our suffering masses. We will therefore only quote further one short passage from Lala Murlidhur's speech* :—

"If you deny," he said, "salt to these poor people, you may as well deny them air to breathe, light to see, and water to drink. What does the salt duty mean? It is a tax on hunger and on thirst ; it is a tax on one's life. It is a wrong which presses hard on these people. Place yourselves in the position of these poor men ; go to their homes and see for yourselves what sort of life they lead ; and then say if you will deny them the last thing

* Detailed Report, pp. 52, 53.

which makes the scanty insipid scraps of food, which is all they can ever compass, at all palatable to these wretched creatures. (*Cheers.*) For God's sake, I say, do not deny them this one luxury which they stand much in need of. Do any of us approve this cruel grinding of our pauper brethren? Do I, do any of us?"

No! Certainly *no one* then present, unless indeed it might be Rajah Peary Mohun Mookerjee, who in the Viceroy's Council supported this cruel enhancement in 1888. But to him doubtless these vehement and unanswerable condemnations of the policy he had supported were unpalatable, and it happened that, at this juncture, a gentleman rose to propose an amendment, which, if entertained seriously by any appreciable section of the assembly would, to a certain extent, have excused his action.

The purport of the amendment * was that there was no necessity for reducing the tax, but that Government ought to make special rules for special localities regarding the preparation and consumption of salt for the preservation of cattle and industrial purposes. Mr. Deva Prasad Sarvadhikari's speech † which may be read, was not devoid of cleverness; he had a bad case and was absolutely ignorant of the salt question, and yet he spoke fluently for a quarter of an hour, making at least some semblance of defending his amendment. To his head as a lawyer his address may not do discredit, but where his heart as a citizen is concerned the verdict must be different.

To the astonishment of all present, Mr. R. D. Mehta of Calcutta rose to second the amendment. He clearly had never considered the subject, and his main point ‡ was that there was *no* substantial difference between the original proposition and the amendment! He appears to have been actuated by a chivalrous feeling that every opinion ought to have a hearing, and that as no one *else* would second the amendment, he would.

He was followed by Mr. Mohini Mohan Chatterjee who took him and his leader, and Rajah Peary Mohun Mookerjee properly to task. Some passages § from his speech we may usefully reproduce :—

"Mr. Mehta asks what is the substantial difference between the original proposition and this so-called amendment. (*Cheers.*) They are utterly different and distinct. (*Cheers.*) We say that the salt-tax generally should be reduced, so that all our pauper millions, who chiefly feel the tax, throughout the Empire, should be relieved *pro tanto*. He says, make special rules for special localities, so that some small isolated communities may be benefited. Our proposition is simple and practical—his absolutely impracticable. (*Cheers.*)

"Of course, he has not studied the question. Of course he does not know that differential rates of duty involving cordons to keep the cheaper salt out of localities where it is not intended to be used, are absolutely indefensible; that from Lord Mayo's time the whole aim of every reformer has been to get rid of these cordons by having one uniform invariable rate of duty throughout Hindustan; that this by infinite pains has been accomplished; and that his resolution proposes to resuscitate all the evils inseparable from differential rates. Our resolution asks for a practical reform—his for an impracticable retrograde movement; that is the substantial difference! (*Loud cheers.*)

"As far as I can understand its scope the amendment proposed, with the exception of the verbal alteration suggested, comes to this: Let rules be made enabling particular communities of

---

* *Vide* Detailed Report, p. 53.
† Detailed Report, pp. 53—55.
‡ Detailed Report, p. 55.
§ Detailed Report, pp. 55—57.

men in particular localities—I don't think it can mean the country generally, or there would be an end of salt taxation—to make their own salt, never mind how unwholesome it may be. Rules it seems are to be made with reference to local peculiarities, which, to my mind, only means, let those who are living on the sea coast make their own salt ; and how is this salt to be prevented from going inland ? But if these rules are to be general, then every man living anywhere where there is even salt earth may make his own salt cheap and nasty ; and we do not want that ; and, moreover, nothing short of millions of preventive officials can prevent this cheap and nasty salt, once made, from circulating over the entire country ; and we don't want a new army of licensed blackmailers ; and without this army the cheap salt will circulate and salt taxation come to an end ; and we don't want that even, as yet ; we can't afford it, though we can afford to reduce the rate by eight annas, and thus no doubt sacrifice about one million sterling of revenue which Mr. Watcha has shown that we can well spare if there be no new frontier extravagances. (*Loud cheers.*)

"The salt-tax is objectionable because it is a tax on life. It is not an income-tax, but a tax on life itself. (*Cheers*). As to the remedy proposed by the amendment, it is worse even than the malady. (*Hear, hear.*) Independent of the army of blackmailers, the salt thus made will be bad salt, full of sulphates and nitrates, not only of sodium, but also of lime and magnesium. It is really better that the people should have no salt than have salt which will introduce disease into the system.

"There is one other point in connection with the amendment to which I wish to make reference. If it were practically carried into effect in the manner in which I believe it to be intended, the result will be great inequality in the taxation levied upon salt in different *parts* of the country. If we could *exempt classes* and so arrange that the poor should get their salt free, there would be something in it. But that is impossible ; even with differential rates they can only be applied to localities ; all in which, rich or poor, must enjoy the cheaper salt—to me an absurd proposition. I do not know what you think, but certainly I should think that this would be a great evil. Why should one locality pay Re. 1 and another Rs. 3 duty per maund on its salt ? This was the old vicious exploded system. Are we to go back to this ? We do not want that some parts should have a plentiful and cheap supply, while in others salt should be scarcer and dearer even than at present. What we want is wholesome salt, cheap, and plenty of it ; and that, as I have tried to show, the amendment does not provide for."

* * * * * * * *

"When, gentlemen occupying high positions, coddled in the lap of luxury, say, 'Oh the poor won't feel it,' there is something so chilling, so discouraging, so sickening in this cynicism that the power of adjectives is quite unable to properly characterize such base and selfish utterances."

Other speakers followed exposing the fallacy of Mr. D. P. Sarvadhikari's verbal meanderings (they really cannot be called *arguments*) ; then the amendment was put, no one but the proposer and seconder voting for it, and finally the resolution was carried unanimously, not even Messrs. Mehta and Sarvadhikari seeing their way to oppose it.

The next resolution referred to a question, the Permanent Settlement, in which the entire population of India is almost as deeply and actively interested as in the reduction of the Salt Tax. No doubt the idea is very prevalent that this question only interests the Zemindars and Taluqdars and other wealthy people, and hence outsiders speak of this as a mere class question. But no greater misconception could exist. In the first place the great bulk of the agriculturists throughout the Bombay and Madras Presidencies are peasant proprietors, and elsewhere the cultivators are strongly of opinion, and we believe rightly so, that were the Government to leave off screwing the Zemindars, these would, for the most part, deal more liberally with their cultivators. All classes know well that, once a permanent settlement is secured, a much larger yield can be obtained from the soil, and all classes reckon on sharing in the enhanced profits.

The resolution was thus worded :—

*RESOLVED*—"*That having reference to the expectations created throughout the country by the despatch of Her Majesty's Secretary of State in 1862, the principles of which were re-affirmed in a subsequent despatch of 1865, promising the extension of a permanent settlement to all temporarily settled tracts in which certain conditions were fulfilled, and to the fact that throughout large portions of the country those conditions have long since been fulfilled, this Congress respectfully submits that the Government of India is, now, in honour bound to take up this question of permanent settlement without further delay, in view to practical action thereon, such that fixity and permanence may be given to the Government land revenue demand as explicitly promised, by Her Majesty's Secretary of State, more than quarter of a century ago.*"

This was proposed by Mr. R. N. Mudholkar in an admirable speech. He said* :—

"I confess that the question with which this resolution deals is one of vast importance, and at the same time one of considerable perplexity, and the time allotted to a speaker by the rules will not enable me to do full justice to it. I will, however, lay before you, as briefly as I can, certain considerations which go far to justify and support the demand we make. As I have said, India is an agricultural country. 'The wealth of India' of which the poet speaks has vanished. The gorgeous fabrics which India produced are now reduced to an almost inappreciable quantity. Wherever you go you find that the people are being thrown on the soil. Take the estimates framed by the Famine Commission, and you find that 90 per cent. of the rural population is closely connected with the soil, and 80 per cent. of the whole population is wholly dependent upon the soil. Taking later calculations, you will find that the proportion has risen to as much as 86 per cent., and, with our indigenous industries dying out, this pressure of the population upon the land is growing every day, and you find that vast tracts which were at one time considered as not being fit for cultivation are being taken up for this purpose. The arable area under cultivation has increased vastly ; and though this industry is not in many places paying, through sheer necessity people are compelled to have recourse to poorer and poorer soils. The effect of this has been that land which was required for grazing purposes is now taken up for agricultural purposes, and the result of that you see in the deterioration of your agricultural stock. If you compare this area with the amount of population, you will find a state of things which must make us really very anxious ; that is, that while the area under cultivation is estimated to be a little less than 190 million acres, the population which it has to support is nearly 197 millions. I take my figures from the latest Government statistics. This means less than an acre per head, and, according to Sir William Hunter, at least an acre per head is required to maintain a man sufficiently. Here, therefore, is this one great problem before you. You find that the only industry by which you can maintain your people is in a very unsatisfactory condition. You may almost say that the widest limit of cultivation has been reached, and the question is, what are we to do ? The only solution is improvement in cultivation itself, and here it is that the question of permanent settlement becomes of the greatest importance.

"If the oldest industry we have is to be maintained, in a state of prosperity, it is necessary that that industry should be improved. But here, throughout the major part of the country, you find that there is an almost insuperable obstacle to all improvement interposed, and that is on account of the temporary settlement and the fatal discouragement of improvements which this involves. The policy with regard to land tenure followed by the Government for nearly 100 years has been one of violent oscillation. Whenever there is a crisis in the agricultural history of the country you find that the heads of the Government are quite willing to accept statesmanlike and broad views ; but when the crisis is past and the danger is over, for a time, there is a return to a huckstering policy,—a policy of trying to make as much money out of the landholder as possible. The famine in Bengal in 1770 secured to Bengal the permanent settlement. In 1860 there was a famine in the N. W. Provinces, and the gravity of the famine and the danger which the Government saw in the recurrence of such famines led to the appointment of a Commission. That Commission took evidence and went carefully into the matter, and came deliberately to the conclusion that in the interests of the country it was absolutely necessary that fixity and permanency of tenure should be granted.

* Detailed Report, pp. 59—61.

"This is what the Commission say in the Report submitted by their President: 'Entertaining the most earnest conviction that the State interests and popular interests will be alike strengthened in an increasing ratio by the step, the first and, as I believe, most important measure, I have respectfully to submit, for consideration, is the expediency of fixing for ever the public demand on the land, and thus converting the existing settlement into a settlement for perpetuity.'

"This recommendation of the Commission was endorsed by the Lieutenant-Governor and Council, and it met with the approval of the Viceroy, that great man, Lord Canning.

"The Governor-General said: 'His Excellency believes that increased security of fixed property and comparative freedom from the interference of fiscal officers of the Government, will tend to create a class which, although composed of various races and creeds, will be peculiarly bound to the British rule; while, under proper regulations, the measure will conduce materially to the improvement of the general revenue of the Empire.'

"This report of the Commission, with the recommendation of the Viceroy, was sent to the Secretary of State, and this was what Lord Halifax laid down in his famous despatch of 1862: 'After the most careful review of all these considerations Her Majesty's Government are of opinion that the advantages which may reasonably be expected to accrue not only to those immediately connected with the land, but to the community generally, are sufficiently great to justify them in incurring the risk of some prospective loss of revenue in order to attain them, and that a settlement in perpetuity in the districts in which the conditions required are, or may hereafter be fulfilled, is a measure dictated by sound policy, and calculated to accelerate the development of the resources of India, and to ensure in the highest degree the welfare and contentment of all classes of Her Majesty's subjects in the country.'

"A more satisfactory resolution, a more statesmanlike wish, a more just and humane conclusion could not have been arrived at. But it has been our misfortune that, when a thing has been offered by one hand, the other hand has always been ready to snatch it away. There was a change of government in England, and pressure was brought to bear by the members of the India Council to prevent the carrying out of the recommendations in the despatch of 1862. The clear promise, however, and the generous principles laid down in that despatch were such that they could not be abrogated: and what was sought to be done was to saddle those recommendations with further conditions. The only condition laid down in the despatch of 1862 was that its terms were to be extended to those provinces where four-fifths of the land was brought under cultivation. It was found that this condition was satisfied by a number of estates, and it was also found that other persons were willing to carry out the terms of the resolution. Here it was that mischief was done. A new condition was imposed in the despatch of 1865, and that was that the recommendations in the despatch of 1862 should be extended to estates only if, in the opinion of the executive authorities, the public works of the Government were not likely to be so extended within the next 20 years as to benefit the estates to the extent of 20 per cent. Well, you will find that those conditions have been satisfied; nearly 27 years (certainly 25 years) have elapsed, and as to public works you find that all the main lines and feeder lines of railways have been constructed, and the main irrigation works have also been completed."

*　　*　　*　　*　　*　　*

"You see, therefore, that the conditions have been carried out, and yet the same system continues—that system which has been stigmatized by Government itself as one which is harassing to the people, as one which unsettles all relations between landlord and tenant, and as one which causes the greatest uneasiness. I am not using my own expressions, but the words used in the resolution of Lord Ripon in 1883. The view which was laid down in 1862 was, as I told you, opposed by Government officials in India and England; but a justification of those recommendations was supplied by stern facts which happened later on. In 1874 the riots in Bombay resulted in considerable loss of property and damage to person. Then there was the famine of 1877, and the Government officials were obliged to admit that nearly 40 millions of people belonging to the agricultural population were on the brink of starvation. Still you find that there was a disinclination to carry out the principles laid down over and over again, and the justice of which was admitted. I will only refer to two authorities, whose eminence in these matters is not disputed, Sir Louis Malet and Sir James Caird, both of whom stigmatize the present system. Sir James Caird moreover distinctly says that a thirty years' settlement cannot be expected to produce sufficient stimulus to ensure improvement in the agriculture of the country; that is the deliberate opinion of the President of the Famine Commission. In spite of these things we find that the system is continued. The evil is to be deplored in more respects than one. In the first place rent in India, or revenue, has nothing like it anywhere. Take the proportion of rent to gross produce in any country in Europe, and you will find that India is placed on a basis of its own. In Great Britain the proportion of gross produce to rent is 1 to 33; in Europe generally 1 to 50. The lowest in Europe, Denmark, is 1 to 27. In India it is 1 to 3 or 1 to 4. That is, for every four rupees you get from the land you give one rupee to the Government; whereas in Europe, out of 50 rupees coming from the soil, only one goes to the landlord. Then it is not only the high rate, but the uncertainty of the enhancement. You do not know in what way the enhancement may come. There is the re-classification of soils, which means raising the soil of an estate from the third class to the second or the second to the first, and so on, and the consequent raising of the land revenue itself, and there is the enhancement of the revenue independent of any such supposed change in the status of the soil. All these operations have been productive of the great mischief of putting an end to all improvements.

" These are facts that require serious consideration. I admit that there are grave difficulties in the way of Government from the rupee going down. Of course, it would be difficult to settle the question in an off-hand manner; but I do not think the difficulty is such as to baffle the resources of statesmanship, nor do I think that our administrators are so devoid of statesmanship as to be unable to grapple with it. What we ask is that there should be some fixity. That fixity need only be as regards production. *If the proportion of produce to rent were fixed; if it were laid down once for all that each plot should pay yearly the money value, settled quinquennially, on the basis of the preceding five years local prices, of so many maunds of jowar, bajra, wheat, barley, cotton, sessamum, as the case might be, due reference being had to the culture prevalent in each village, I suppose that would satisfy the requirements of the people.** It is a problem which can be solved. I appeal to Great Britain and to our administrators here to make a real effort to solve it, and thus carry out the principles laid down by successive Governments in England—principles which have their greatest justification in justice and in humanity. *(Cheers.)*

Mr. Boikantha Nath Sen followed in another excellent speech, † which we reproduce *in extenso* :—

" This is a resolution in which there is no question of sentiment. It is a question which affects materially the prosperity of the country and which affects the Government also in a very material way. It has been observed that this is a resolution not for the benefit of the delegates, but for the benefit of the people. I go further and say that it is a resolution which, if carried, and accepted loyally by the Government, will bring benefits to the Government itself. *(Cheers)*. Let me notice the way in which the resolution has been divided. It refers, you see, to the despatch of 1862, confirmed by that of 1865. It says that the Government is 'now in honor bound.' Observe the force of the word 'now.' Let me place before you another fact, that a permanent settlement was accorded to Bengal in 1793, when you will find a minute by the Board of Revenue at Fort St. George, delivered by Mr. White, and approved of by a Select Committee which was appointed to investigate the affairs of the East India Company. That approval was made in 1812; that principle was recognised, and emphasized, and a line of action was formulated 50 years afterwards in 1862, in the despatch of the Secretary of State. Twenty-seven years have now passed, and we are

* We italicize this passage because we believe that it affords a solution of one of the greatest difficulties that Government recognizes to dealing with this question. This question was strongly urged at the Allahabad Congress (*vide* p. 89 of the Detailed Report of the Fourth Congress) by Sheikh Raza Hoossein Khan.

This is what he said: " When I say a permanent settlement, I do not necessarily mean a permanent settlement precisely similar to that in Bengal. In the first place, we are wiser now than we then were. The experience of eighty years has shown us how we can improve on that settlement in many particulars. In the second place landed tenures vary all over the country, and in each place the permanent settlement must vary accordingly. And again when I say a permanent settlement and speak of a fixity of the Government demand, I do not necessarily mean that that demand should be settled in Rupees. On the contrary, I am disposed to believe that it would have to be fixed in terms of quantities of the three or four chief local staples of produce, in regard to which a cash revaluation might be made at intervals of, say, every three, five or seven years, based upon the average local prices of those staples during the preceding period. Thus, if the Government demand in any village were fixed at 50 maunds of wheat, 100 maunds of jowar, 100 maunds of bajra, 50 maunds of gram, and 50 maunds of urhar, this would remain the demand for all time, but every three, five, or seven years the actual member of rupees would be fixed by a calculation based on the average *local* price of these articles during the past three, five or seven years. I can only say that, unless some such fixity is given to the Government demand in our province, cultivation will never keep up with the growth of population. Grant it, and hundreds of thousands of wells will be dug within the first five years, and millions of acres that now yield only small unirrigated crops would yield double and treble the amounts of far more valuable staples. By one way or another people would manage to put double the amount of manure they now do into the ground. But no great improvement can take place so long as the people are for ever on the look-out for the recurring swoop of the settlement officer to sweep the fruits of their labours into the official net. Mr. Howard spoke of the 'unearned increment,' which is explained to me to mean, profits that a person has not made for himself, and he tells us that a great political economist tells us this should belong to Government. Well, if this is political economy, our system must be perfection, for at every revision Government appropriates the profits that it never earned, but which the cultivators of the soil have earned *(Laughter.)*"

† Detailed Report, pp. 62, 63.

where we were in 1812, because there is no indication of a permanent settlement being carried out in those provinces where it was not conceded very nearly a century ago.

"Why is it so? We all know that land revenue forms the central figure in the group of English taxation, and there is an apprehension of a loss of prospective increment in the Government revenue, based on what is supposed, in a mistaken way, to be the results of the permanent settlement in Bengal, and what is still erroneously considered to be a wanton sacrifice, as it were, of the resources of the State by Lord Cornwallis, for the sole purpose of giving satisfaction to the landed proprietors. Now it is on account of apprehensions and misapprehensions like these that effect has not been given to the despatch of 1862. Before I proceed further let me place before you further statistics. The territories which are under the administration of the Lieutenant-Governor of Bengal extend over an area of 140,000 square miles, of which 120,000 enjoy the benefits of the permanent settlement. But at the time when the permanent settlement was granted to Bengal only one-third had been brought under cultivation. The land revenue from Bengal is about four crores and the gross rental is about 20 crores (I make a technical distinction between revenue and rental.) Then the incidence of the land revenue in Bengal is Rs. 55 to 100 persons of the population ; in the Punjab, Rs. 109 to 100 persons ; in the North-Western Provinces, Rs. 129 to 100 persons ; in the Madras Presidency, Rs. 134 to 100 persons ; and in Bombay, Rs. 234 to 100 persons. Now, apart from other questions which are undoubtedly of a very weighty nature, and which, in summing up, I shall have occasion to refer to, I venture to think that the high standard of revenue which has been attained ought of itself to be considered a sufficient reason for the Government according a permanent settlement to those provinces where it has not been extended.

"You have heard from the able mover of the resolution what area has been actually brought under cultivation, and what little, and that of the poorest quality as a rule, yet remains to be cultivated ; so that the time has surely arrived when, apart from other questions, this high ratio of cultivation would justify the Government in giving fixity to their demands. Let us see a little further how the matter stands. There is much more to be said. The experiment of 100 years in Bengal furnishes us with certain data which will enable you to solve the problem in a satisfactory way. This permanent settlement must be considered as the very best manure you can give to the land : for shortly after the permanent settlement of Bengal there was a wonderful increase in the cultivation. Before the permanent settlement only a third was under cultivation, but now you will scarcely find one-thirtieth uncultivated.

"Then you may look upon this permanent settlement as a very important agent in the distribution of the proprietary interest in the soil among the various classes. It has also been a very important factor in bringing about social reform. Who ever had an idea of a middle class? I say, this middle class is to a great extent the growth of the permanent settlement. Where is it anything like so strong in numbers and in wealth as in Bengal, (*cheers*) although now the example of Bengal has more or less pervaded the entire Empire? But, for that permanent settlement, India would have had, as in Russia, the poor and the rich, but no middle class such as you find crowding this great hall. These, then, have been the direct benefits of the permanent settlement. Now let us see what can the Government expect more. Would it be a sufferer in the long run? Look at the case of Orissa. Orissa was temporarily settled for 30 years, and the lease expired in 1866. There was then, as you all know, a famine, and the Government could not possibly on that occasion think of enhancing the revenue by making a re-settlement, so that it had to renew the settlement for another 30 years. That settlement is still going on, and it will expire in 1895. Progress has been kept in abeyance for 60 years. No capitalist would venture to invest his money in land in Orissa. For 60 years progress has been retarded by the inactivity (if nothing else) of the Government.

"We find that from that portion of Bengal which has not received this boon Government does not expect much. There are authoritative reports to Government that if a permanent settlement be withheld from those other provinces, there would be at *best* (as I had occasion to remark on the last occasion) a gain to the Government of 30 lakhs of rupees. Now let us see how we fare in Bengal. In the Civil administration alone, in the whole of India, there is a loss of 12 lakhs, the expenditure exceeding the receipts by that amount. But in Bengal there is a surplus of 14 lakhs, and what is this owing to? In education, in Bengal, 83 lakhs are spent, out of which only 21 lakhs are spent by the State, the balance being spent by private individuals who are able to pay on account of the permanent settlement. See how the Government has been gaining in this way. If, then, the permanent settlement be extended to other provinces, I venture to submit that there is not the least reason for the Government suffering in any way in its finances. Whatever it may apparently suffer, from a purely treasury point of view, in the matter of direct loss of future enhancements of land revenue, will be more than compensated by gains from other sources through new channels which will be created by this permanent settlement of its own force. Now, while the Government has pledged itself by its despatch of 1862, confirmed by the despatch of 1865, it is undoubtedly in honor bound to redeem its pledge. By according this concession the Government will derive benefit in two ways: in the first place by saving its honor by the redemption of its solemn pledges; in the second, even financially, as sharing the enhanced prosperity of its people.

"Its good deed may directly diminish by a few lakhs the land revenue of fifty years hence; but crores to replace these will have poured down from the happy consequences of that honest policy. As Kalidasa says:—

"The sun draws the water from the soil, but this is returned a thousandfold in the shape of rain." (*Cheers.*)

Mr. Janoki Nath Bose from Orissa next spoke:—

"What do we see," he urged,* "in the province of which I am a representative? The zemindars are almost all deeply involved in debt; they cannot pay the Government revenue at the proper time; often you see their properties being sold at public auction to meet the demands made upon them; they have no resource but to incur debts at a very high rate of interest. If we look at the condition of the ryots what do we see? That they are being rack-rented; they cannot get a full meal in two days; they cannot get a waistcloth even once a year. Such is the condition to which Government has reduced the zemindars and ryots through their unwillingness to introduce a permanent settlement, and through the consequent impossibility of the vivification of this national industry by capital. Contrast the state of Bengal with that of other provinces where there is no permanent settlement. Here we find the zemindars occupying a high place, but in other parts they are poor men and cannot take part in any national undertaking that requires money. Look at the ryots. We have some poor, no doubt, but look at the millions of well-to-do tenants of all grades. In what other province do you find any large proportion of such? For 50 years, at least six millions sterling have yearly gone into the pockets of the people that would, under the temporary settlement system, have gone into those of the Government, to be wasted doubtless in frontier defences (*cheers*), and I venture to say that those six millions have profited the country ten times more than they would have done had they gone into the coffers of the State. (*Cheers*). The temporary settlement system is everywhere ruining the zemindars. It has been said, let the zemindars be ruined, we do not care, provided we have got peasant proprietors. But that is a very idiotic and narrow policy. In the first place the zemindars, the landed aristocracy of our country, constitute, in many provinces, a definite and important institution which has taken deep root and cannot hastily be done away with, and in the second place the same cause that wrecks the zemindars will, as time runs on, ruin even peasant proprietors. There are many who say 'if the permanent settlement can give rise to peasant proprietors it is all right, but if it will only enrich the zemindars we are not for it.' I submit that that is a ridiculous view of the case. In the first place all through Bombay and Madras, it is just with peasant proprietors that we desire to see a permanent settlement. Again where we have zemindars they are none the less a portion of the people, and from their position whatever affects them injuriously affects all subordinate classes of agriculturists equally injuriously, while what benefits them, benefits equally directly and indirectly, not only all subordinate holders of land but, in a country like this where everything hinges on the land, the entire community.

"Now, what do we see in Orissa? We see that the zemindars are mostly over head and ears in debt, and that what with their irrigation tax and the rent the poor ryots are being trodden under foot; their condition is most deplorable; they have not a full meal every two days, they have nothing in times of scarcity to fall back upon, they are perpetually on the verge of starvation. I am sure that if the permanent settlement is introduced into that province, if there is no more Government rack-renting, if the Government ceases to threaten them with periodical re-assessments, you will find that capital will flow into the land, that cultivation will improve, and that in 30 years the condition of the zemindars and ryots will be so much improved that no one in that flourishing land will be able to recognize this now backward, miserable, poverty-stricken region.

"Moreover, apart from the consequences, on abstract principles only, the action of the Government in increasing the land revenue every 25 and 30 years is not just. It is a case of reaping where they have not sowed, of greedily grasping the fruits of the tiller of the soil's persistent labour, of arbitrarily confiscating the fruits of its subjects industry, it is unjust I say in principle, and like all injustice it is thoroughly bad policy in the long run."

* Detailed Report, pp. 63, 64.

Lala Jaisee Ram from the Panjab declared equally strongly the urgent necessity for a permanent settlement in his province, and concluded his speech in words that deserve the most careful consideration :—

"It may be said," he remarked,* "that the finances of the Government will suffer by conceding a permanent settlement. But this argument can be at once overthrown by the long experience of a hundred years in Bengal. Has the Government of India, has the country at large, suffered in consequence of even this badly arranged and prematurely conceded permanent settlement in Bengal? Look to the commerce of Calcutta; look to the density of the population; look to the great spread of education and the enormous masses of well-to-do people, the like of all of which is to be seen nowhere else, and then let any man dare to deny that even this crude, imperfectly carried out settlement, conceded before more than one-third of the culturable area was under culture, has been, solely in virtue of the one attribute of permanence, an immense boon to the people and a gigantic source of strength to the Empire. (*Prolonged cheers.*)"

The next speaker reiterated the expediency of extending the permanent settlement, now confined to Bengal, to other Provinces. In the course of his speech he remarked †—

"I should like to be permitted to read one or two passages from a paper read some time ago by a very high official of the Revenue Board of this province in England : 'An examination of those results (of permanent settlement) will, perhaps, lead us to the conclusion that the permanent settlement was a wise and statesmanlike measure; that politically it has been a tower of strength to the Empire; that, from a social and economic point of view, it has stimulated the prosperity and fostered the intelligence of the province; and that, even from a strictly financial stand point, the surrender of an increased land tax has been in some measure compensated by the steady development of other branches of the public revenue.' He has given some figures, which one of my predecessors has referred to, showing how the province of Bengal has been benefited financially by the permanent settlement. I will not, therefore, read any more passages. The same gentleman lays down that the creation of an independent middle class is not an evil, but a blessing (*Cheers.*) It is the middle class that has taken advantage of all the reforms introduced by British rule in India. It is that middle class which mainly fills this pavilion, and the authority I have quoted says further that it is a fruitful source of strength to the State. The creation of that class is not to be deplored. Suppose, for instance, though this can never be generally true, that the permanent settlement does not benefit the ryots, or say some classes of the ryots in a poor agricultural district. What is the practical effect? Is it undesirable that the land should be held mainly by those who can afford to improve it? Is it desirable that the land should be generally cultivated by poor hand-to-mouth cultivators? Is it not better that those agriculturists, who are so poor that they can give nothing to the land, should be labourers rather than holders of the land? Is this not better for these men themselves,—better for the land, better for the country? If the permanent settlement has the effect of converting in some places starving tenants into well-fed labourers, of creating a strong middle class, is this any argument against a permanent settlement? Is it not desirable that the material wealth of the country, for the increase of which our British Government is so anxious, *should* be increased? And how can that material wealth be more certainly increased than by the creation of a class of small capitalists—a middle class in fact.

"These two objections then are invalid. All we ask is that the Government should open a discussion on the subject We say to them : 'You have closed discussion for a quarter of a century, don't close it any more.' I come from Berar. You know it is by an official fiction, not under British rule; but all the same it has British rulers, British missionaries, British laws, and the advantages and disadvantages of British rule. We have no legislation for ourselves, nothing like it. If a permanent settlement is granted to other provinces, we know, of course, that we shall not get it as soon as you do, if at all; my friends, we shall be left behind lamenting, I fear. But that is no reason why we should hesitate to join you in reasonable demands. We Berarese are first of all Indians, and we have joined the Congress not because, perhaps, any direct benefit will be gained by Berar even when the Congress triumphs, but because this triumph will benefit our country; because we are all one; because your happiness, your prosperity, means the advancement of our native land, and a source of perennial rejoicing to us; even though we poor Berarese have to sit in darkness outside the banquet hall. (*Loud cheers.*)"

---

* Detailed Report, pp. 64, 65.
† Detailed Report, pp. 65, 66.

The pathetic earnestness of Mr. Devarao Vinayek's concluding words should not pass unnoticed. They embody those noble sentiments of national unity which it has been one function of the Congress, not indeed to generate, but to crystallize into practical life.

Many other excellent speeches followed, notably one * by Mr. R. P. Karandakar (which should be read) showing how disastrously the temporary settlement is working in the Bombay Presidency, but we shall only reproduce one more extract, and that from a speech by Mr. A. Nundy, a Barrister, of Jubbulpore, which, though delivered in connection with the salt question, more properly pertains to the present one.

"You are all aware, Gentlemen," he remarked, † "that the temporary settlement prevails in the Central Provinces. I am not going to speak on the advantages of a permanent settlement, for I should thereby be encroaching on the duties of the speakers on the resolution which follows this; but I wish merely to point out that, owing to the new settlement, which is now in progress, a state of things is being brought about, which demands that relief, of some kind at least, should be given to the impoverished masses of the Central Provinces, and that this relief can, to some extent, be obtained by a partial reduction of the salt-tax. As most of you are aware, the periodical settlement took place in 1864-65, and it shortly expires. For the last three years survey and settlement officers are traversing the country, and what has been the result?

"The Government revenue has been increased as regards some villages 40 per cent., 50 per cent., and even 100 per cent. This, Gentlemen, let me assure you, I say on the highest authority possible. Now, who is to pay this increased revenue? I shall show you that eventually it is the poor ryot who will have to pay it. I ought here to remind you that besides the Government revenue, the Malguzar, that is the owner of the village, has to meet a variety of other demands. He has to pay the education-cess; he has to pay the putwari-cess; he has to pay for the maintenance of the hospitals; and, lastly, he has to pay the road-cess. The Imperial Government requires him to pay these cesses; but there are other local demands which he has to satisfy. The District Officer proceeds on tour, the unfortunate Malguzar has not only to see that the road is carefully prepared for his progress, but he has to meet the hundred and one demands of his camp-followers, whose requirements it is not easy to satisfy. So great does this evil become sometimes that the Malguzar dreads nothing more than the dubious honour of a District Officer passing through his village.

"Having met these Government and other demands, what is the financial position of the Malguzar? I have been assured not by one, but by a number of these Malguzars, that after paying up these demands they find that sometimes there is hardly any surplus left for themselves—and they too must live—and if any, a very small one indeed. And now the Government steps in and increases the revenue by 40, 50 and 100 per cent.

"When this last settlement took place it was declared that the revenue then assessed would not be increased for at least a period of 30 years; but what did the Government do? It did not directly increase the revenue; it dared not be guilty of such a shameless and open breach of faith, but by means of incidental charges and cesses it has indirectly increased the charge by 25 per cent. Besides there are a number of other indirect demands which the Malguzars have to meet; there is the imperial road-cess of which I have spoken, but besides this there is another road-cess, the District Officers' road-cess. When a District Officer goes on a tour through the country, or goes on a *shikar* (or shooting) expedition, they have to prepare the road for him and have to provide the incidental expenses which the followers of the camp are put to. There are also other demands. Last year I asked one of the Malguzars for a subscription to the National Congress Fund; but he said it was a very inconvenient time, for shortly before he had been giving a sum of money for a memorial to one of the officials. I asked the official's name, and he said—let us say—'John Smith.' I asked 'Of what service?' and he mentioned the service. 'Why did you give it?' I asked. 'Well,' he said, 'I never had the pleasure of meeting the officer, but I gave the money at the instance of the tahsildar, who had been asked by the officials to get contributions towards the memorial. Now I put it to you, was that a voluntary contribution, or was it not a species of tax? This then being the case with the Malguzars, the question arises, are

* *Vide* Detailed Report, pp. 66, 67.
† Detailed Report, pp. 51, 25.

they in a position to meet any extra revenue which the Government imposes? Many of them have proved to me that after all these demands are paid there is scarcely any surplus left to them; if there is any it is very small. To what then will the Malguzar be reduced? To either one of two alternatives: either to quit their villages or to increase the rent of their tenants. It is impossible to expect them to quit, and the necessary consequence is that the poor will have their rents raised. And who are these? Not the well-to-do ryots, but those who have small holdings and live from hand to mouth—these will have to pay the enhanced revenue, and will have starvation facing them. I therefore put it to you whether the position of the Central Provinces does not demand that this resolution should be carried, and that some response should be made to it by the Government. The Government has the right, as the law stands, to arrange periodically the revenue imposed on each village, and they are not likely to give up exercising that right so long as a permanent settlement is not conceded. So long as they exercise that right, the landholder already pressed for means will accept no share of the new burthen. The well-to-do cultivators, with occupancy rights and means to defend these rights in the Courts, will allow no portion of it to be laid upon their shoulders, and all enhancements will have to come from those who have only small holdings, who have no fixed tenures and no means, from the very poor in fact, the members of that army of martyrs, our starving fifty millions, on whom it is that this heavy salt tax presses heaviest."

The resolution was, it is almost needless to say, carried unanimously and with great enthusiasm, but if any of our English readers, realising the justice and the wisdom of the people's demands in this matter, conceive that the result of these discussions will be that Government will take the subject in hand, they wholly misunderstand the temper and character of the Indian official classes of the present day. For many years now the Covenanted Civil Service, as a body, appear to have utterly lost that noble desire to raise, and advance the prosperity of, the people (committed, alike by England and by Divine Providence, to their charge) that once characterized their predecessors. To draw their handsome salaries, the largest enjoyed by any body of civil officers in the world, to save money, keep things quiet on the surface, do as little as possible outside their ordinary routine work, and get away to England to spend, there, the money of the people of India, appear to be the most cherished objects of the great majority. They are not now, with rare exceptions here and there, the men that civilians once were—men who were completely in sympathy and touch with India's people, and freely gave for them their time, their money, their brains and even their lives; it may be that many of them are disappointed men, whose careers in India have not furnished them with those openings for advancement, that they believe that they would have been able to secure in England; it may be that the increased facilities for visiting England and the startling contrast between the happy homes they revisit and the squalid misery of their surroundings in the outstations at which so much of their service has to be passed, disgusts them both with the country and with their work; but be the cause what it may, too many of them seem, unfortunately, to degenerate into mere hirelings, as the Christian Scriptures put it, caring nought for the flock. *Super antiquas vias stare*, wherever the real interests of the people demand an advance (there is abundant mischievous activity where patience only is really needed); *quieta non movere*, no matter what lies hidden beneath, so long as there are hopes of its continuing hidden for *their* time. These are their mottoes, and wrapped in an impenetrable mantle of self-sufficient ignorance (for there is no class in the country, whether missionaries, merchants or military men, who know so little of the real wants and wishes of the people), nothing can move them from their ignoble apathy and fixed determination to cling, limpet-like, to the dreary *non-possumus* cliffs of officialism, but the trumpet call of a debate in, or better still a resolution of, the House of Commons.

It is the conviction of this fact, coupled with the underhand persecution, that the Congress party have been subjected to by so many of the officials, that has hitherto embittered the struggle for reform. To that persecution Lord Lansdowne has now, as we shall see directly, authoritatively put a stop, and if he can also infuse a little of the old spirit into the officials, if he can awaken something of the old unselfish desire and resolve to help, befriend and raise our people, no matter at what sacrifice of personal interests and comfort, which once made the Indian Covenanted Civil Service the noblest in the world, he will merit and earn a place in the affections and respect of India second to that of no other Viceroy.

The next resolution tells its own story. It ran thus* :—

*RESOLVED—That this Congress having observed with surprise a notice, apparently official, in various Calcutta newspapers, which runs as follows :—*

*" THE CONGRESS.*

*" The Bengal Government having learnt that tickets of admission to the visitors' enclosure in the Congress pavilion have been sent to various Government officers residing in Calcutta, has issued a circular to all Secretaries and heads of departments subordinate to it, pointing out, that, under the orders of the Government of India, the presence of Government officials, even as visitors at such meetings, is not advisable, and that their taking part in the proceedings of any such meetings is absolutely prohibited ;"*

*and having also considered a letter addressed by the Private Secretary of His Honor the Lieutenant-Governor of Bengal to the Secretary of the Reception Committee of which the following is an exact copy :—*

*" Belvedere, 26th December 1890.*

*" Dear Sir,—In returning herewith the seven cards of admission to the visitor's enclosure of the Congress pavilion which were kindly sent by you to my address yesterday afternoon, I am desired to say that the Lieutenant-Governor and the members of his household could not possibly avail themselves of these tickets, since the Orders of the Government of India definitely prohibit the presence of Government officials at such meetings.*

*" Yours faithfully,*
*" P. C. LYON,*
*" Private Secretary."*

*" To*
*" J. GHOSAL, Esq.,*
*" Secretary, Congress Reception Committee."*

*authorizes and instructs its President, Mr. Pherozshah Mehta, to draw the attention of His Excellency the Viceroy to the declaration embodied in these papers, that Government servants are prohibited from attending any meetings of this Congress even as spectators, and to enquire, most respectfully, whether His Honor the Lieutenant-Governor of Bengal has, or has not, correctly interpreted the orders of the Government of India.*

Naturally the Congress party viewed these manifestos with considerable indignation, and after two speeches, which may be read, the † one by Mr. Mano Mohan Ghose, the other ‡ by Mr. George Yule, the resolution was carried by acclamation. The Anglo-Indian journals were of course jubilant at the emphatic snub that had, they conceived, been administered to the Congress people, but they were not *quite* so jubilant over the reply that our reference elicited from H. E. the Viceroy. The following is the text of the letter addressed by H. E.'s Private Secretary to the General Secretary of the Congress :—

" With reference to the communications which have recently taken place, first, between Mr. Mehta and the Viceroy, and, after Mr. Mehta's departure from Calcutta, between yourself and His Excellency, upon the subject of the letter received by the Secretary of the Reception Committee from the Private Secretary of the Lieutenant-Governor of Bengal, in reference to the attendance of Government servants at meetings of the Congress, I am authorized by His Excellency to say that Mr. Lyon's letter of December 26th, in which it was stated that ' the orders of the Government of India definitely prohibit the presence of Government officials at such meetings,' and the Circular in which that letter was communicated to the heads of departments under the Bengal Government, were issued under a misapprehension as to the purport of the orders of the Government of India. It was at once recognised both by the Government of

* Detailed Report, p 70.
† Detailed Report, pp. 69, 70.
‡ Detailed Report, pp. 70, 71.

Bengal, of its own motion, and by the Government of India, that the letter in question went beyond those orders, and an amended Circular, in which it was pointed out that the expression 'absolute prohibition' had reference only to the participation of Government officials in the proceedings of a political meeting, was subsequently issued by the Bengal Government to the heads of departments. I enclose herewith a copy of the orders of the Government of India.

"These orders, which arose out of a totally different matter, had no special reference to the Congress movement, and were certainly not framed in a spirit of hostility to it. The publications of some of the supporters of the Congress have, in the opinion of the Government of India, been open to serious question ; but, apart from this, the movement is regarded as one of those which, in the words of the Circular, are 'perfectly legitimate in themselves, and which private persons are free to promote,' but from participation in which Government officials are, for the reasons specified in the orders, necessarily debarred.

"The Government of India recognise that the Congress movement is regarded as representing in India what in Europe would be called the more advanced Liberal party, as distinguished from the great body of Conservative opinion which exists side by side with it. They desire themselves to maintain an attitude of neutrality in their relations with both parties, so long as these act strictly within constitutional limits.

"They intend that all Government servants shall preserve a similar attitude of neutrality, and shall abstain from active participation in political or *quasi*-political movements of all kinds; and also from putting pressure upon others in order to induce them to take part, or not to take part, in any movement which is legitimate in itself. It was with the above objects that the orders of March 1890 were issued.

"In reference to a specific question which you addressed to His Excellency, I am to say that the orders apply only to those who are actually, at the time being, Government servants, but not to pensioners and others who have quitted the service of the Government for good."

Nothing could be more satisfactory. The Viceroy has formally declared that the Congress is a perfectly legitimate movement ; that every one not a Government official is perfectly free to join it ; and that all officials are explicitly enjoined not to impede the movement in any way, and not to put any pressure on any one to induce them to abstain from aiding or joining it. The most enthusiastic Congressman never desired any thing better ; and widespread indeed has been the satisfaction engendered by Lord Lansdowne's straightforward and manly vindication of popular liberty of speech and action in political matters. As has been happily said :—

"Under any circumstance this candid and characteristically British declaration in favour of freedom of opinion and action in political matters in the case of *all* private persons (no less important in its way than Lord Metcalfe's in favour of freedom of the press) ought to go far to bridge the gulf which for years, unhappily, has been widening between the European official classes and the Indian public."

And so it assuredly might, if Lord Lansdowne can persuade the officials, besides ceasing to persecute us, to set to work in hearty earnest, forgetting their recently evolved dogma of apathy, to ameliorate the hapless lots of the fifty odd millions of our half-starving brethren, in whose interests, and on whose behalf, the Congress has been ceaselessly, but thus far almost unavailingly, pleading and labouring, from its very inception.

This resolution disposed of—of course, although we have anticipated results to make the case complete, the letter did not come to hand until long after the Congress closed—the Congress adjourned until the next day, Tuesday, the 30th.

The first business dealt with when the Congress re-assembled was a vote of thanks to Mr. Bradlaugh, to the members of our British Committee and to others who, during 1890, have rendered good service to the Congress cause not forgetting "*all those members of the British Public, who so kindly welcomed and so sympathetically gave audience, in over fifty public and a far larger number of private meetings, to one or more of our delegates.*"

The delegates to England, of course, were not forgotten. Said* the Hon. Pandit Ajoodhia Nath—

" Our delegates met with a splendid reception in England, not only from the constituency of Mr. Bradlaugh, whom I have recommended to you for your warm acknowledgments, but also from Glasgow, Aberdeen, Newcastle, Manchester, Birmingham, Bristol, Exeter, Plymouth and a great many other communities. These delegates have done us good service, and indeed it could not be otherwise when you think who they were."

Mr. Hamid Ali, a Mahomedan Barrister from Lucknow, added† :—

" To serve, is a far higher and nobler law of life than even to rule (*hear, hear*), and this principle has been well expressed in the lives of those gentlemen who have done so much for our country. In the words of the Poet Laureate :

" Not he who breaks the dams, but he
Who through the Channels of the State
Convoys the people's wish, is great,
His name is pure, his fame is free." (*Cheers.*)

" I have not the slightest doubt that their names and fame, inscribed on the page of time in deathless characters of gold, with this noble inscription, 'these were the workers who knew how to serve,' will be handed down to a far distant posterity. (*Cheers*)."

Said‡ Mr. Hem Chunder Rai—

" Nor, in making this public acknowledgment of the services of our English benefactors, must we omit to couple the names of, and pay our humble tribute to, those distinguished countrymen of ours who, at considerable sacrifice of time, money, and energy, undertook a trip to England to enlighten the British public as to our wrongs and disabilities, our needs and aspirations. Doubtless they—

Have sown some generous seed
Fruitful of further thought and deed.

" But their work needs a healthy continuity, and we only hope that the work so auspiciously commenced will evoke widespread response, and that round this little group of Indian patriots there will be formed a large company of patriotic gentlemen ready to undergo similar sacrifices on similar errands. And, in return for their noble services, let us offer them our humble, yet heartfelt thanks, and that which is, indeed, the highest reward that a public man can aspire to—the deep and lasting gratitude of a United People."

There was a good deal of speaking, § but further quotations are needless and the resolution was passed by acclamation.

Next followed a vote ¶ of thanks to house proprietors, including Sir Romesh Chunder Mitter, who had kindly lent to the Congress, houses and grounds, both for the erection of the pavilion and the accommodation of the delegates, no easy matter in a city like Calcutta.

Then the holding of the 7th Congress at Christmas 1891, at either Nagpore or Madras (the former has subsequently been definitely fixed upon) was resolved** and then a quite new departure was taken in the following resolution.

*That provisional arrangements be made to hold a Congress, of not less than 100 delegates, in England, all things being convenient, in 1892, and that the several Standing Congress*

* Detailed report, p. 73.
† Detailed Report, p. 74.
‡ Detailed Report, p. 77.
§ *Vide* Detailed Report, pp. 72—78.
¶ Detailed Report, p. 78.
** Detailed Report, p. 79.

*Committees be directed to report, at the coming Congress, the names of the delegates that it is proposed to depute from their respective circles.*

Only six years ago, before the first Congress met, such a proposal would have been indignantly repudiated, so strong was the religious objection to crossing the seas by a majority, of even the educated classes. Now, such has been the educational effect of these gatherings that not one single man present had one word to say against the suggestion ; on the contrary it was received with enthusiasm, and besides one European, one Sikh, and one Mahomedan who spoke for their respective communities, eleven * orthodox Hindus, all leading and representative men, so far from banning, altogether blessed the idea.

In moving the resolution Babu Norendro Nath Sen said :—

"I have only to remind you that, after all, it is Englaud that is the last resort for appeal on all Indian questions. Our ultimate judges are the British Public, the British Press, and the British Parliament."

Mr. Viraraghava Chariar, a Madras Brahmin, remarked in the course of his speech :—

"Had it not been for this Congress, Madras would have been nowhere. It has been greatly helping the people in Madras. Before that time Madras was called benighted. Now we have, all throughout the Presidency, Standing Congress Committees to help the Central Committee at Madras. Much has been said about the orthodox opinions that would prevent our undertaking a sea voyage to England. On behalf of my province I venture to say that we have never allowed and never shall allow orthodoxy, or any other doxy, to stand in the way of our political advancement. (*Cheers*)."

That is the true doctrine of caste. When one is in for a real fight, caste *must* give way to the cause. Many years ago, late in May 1858, a long line of native soldiers lay, under a heavy but ill-directed fire, sheltered behind a low mud bank that stretched far away to the right down to a huge many flighted well. On the extreme left knelt an European officer, beside him lay an old Brahmin Subedar. Some 150 yards in front, on the other side of a narrow plain, hidden by dense bushes and clouds of smoke, cowered a large force of the enemy. Sporadic pops danced along the line as from moment to moment glimpses of glittering bayonets or brightly colored turbans gleamed out in the jungle, from time to time swelling, for a brief space, into musketry tempests, when bodies of men suddenly emerged for a few seconds in the open, which they lacked the pluck to cross. It was past noonday ; the scorching wind tore in gusts along the line ; above the little plain, the air twisted and quivered, glazed and glassy ; the barrels, all metal equipments, even the black leather belts, burnt fingers that strayed heedlessly on them, and the old muskets (Enfields were only just then coming up and not even all European Regiments yet had them) rung out, as they only could when the powder was nearly red hot ; water vessels were being continually passed along the line, but at last one man crawled up bringing a large lota of cold clear water for the Subedar. "Subedar Sahib," said the European, "if you can spare any of that water, I am just dying of thirst." "Drink Sahib," said the Subedar, and the officer placed his joined hands beneath his mouth, so that the water might be poured into them, and he drink without touching

* *Vide* Detailed Report, pp. 79—88.

the vessel. "No, Sahib, take the lota." "But I shall spoil your caste if I touch it." "Drink Sahib," the old Brahmin repeated, handing the lota. "In war there is no distinction of caste—we are all caste brothers that fight for the same cause." So the European officer and the Brahmin Subedar both drank freely out of that selfsame lota, and the Subedar was none the worse for it and the officer much the better, and thereby was forged one more link of that golden chain which for ever binds the heart of that European officer to the cause of the people of India.

To return. The debate, if such this long discussion without a difference can be called, lasted for some time, but it seems scarcely needful to reproduce much of it. Said Devarao Vinayek * :—

"Socially speaking there is no difficulty. No duty is superior to our duty to the country in which we were born. We have all of us duties to discharge to our countrymen and friends, and if we do not discharge them we do not fulfil the noble purposo by which alone our existence is justified. Some social objections there may be. If you want to go to England for your profit, for pecuniary purposes, your people may or may not object to take you on your return back into your own caste ; but, when you take a nobler duty in hand, when you have gone forth and crossed the stormy ocean solely to serve your country, even the old people, let alone younger generations, are not so blind as to think of putting an obstacle in their patriot brethren's noble course, and they will not only receive you on your return into the bosom of your caste, but receive you with open arms, with rejoicings, praise and gratitude. *(Loud cheers.)*"

Most of the speeches re-echo in different keys these sentiments, but Pandit Shyam Narayan Masaldan's address, as coming from a purely orientally educated and entirely orthodox man, deserves special attention.

I come before you," he explained, "not only to give a formal support to the resolution which is now before you, but because I think that it is really a useful resolution. We, the delegates of the Congress, enjoy perfect freedom of thought and speech, and when we give our opinion upon any subject, we do so after much careful consideration. We are not like the members of the Viceroy's Council, who would support any measure that is introduced by the Government. *(Cheers.)*

"And this is not a mere opinion which may or may not be true, but the statement of a fact which rests upon the authority of some of the highest statesmen who have been in charge of Indian affairs, and which is one of the principal reasons why we are desirous of passing the present resolution. Some twenty years ago, the Duke of Argyle, who was then our Secretary of State, wrote to the Viceroy to the effect that 'the Government in India were merely Executive Officers of the Home Government, who hold the ultimate power of requiring the Governor-General to introduce a measure, and of requiring also all the official members to vote for it.' Some fifteen years later this doctrine was emphasised by Lord Dufferin in words of wider and clearer significance. In his Minute on Council Reform, which, fortunately, saw the light, before the Official Secrets Act came into existence, the following remarkable words occur : 'The executive that represents her (the Queen's) *Imperium* in India is an executive directly responsible, not to any local authority, but to the Sovereign and to the British Parliament. Nor could its members divest themselves of this responsibility as long as Great Britain remains the paramount administration in India.

Now without wishing to say one word as to the morality of the doctrine which has been so authoritatively propounded, and which divests the Government of all responsibility to the people whom it governs, I may invite your attention to the position in which this theory of the British Government places us. The fountain-head of our legislation is the Supreme Council. Every measure that is introduced therein is passed by the vote of the appointed members who form the majority. But their vote is controlled by the Secretary of State,

* Detailed Report, p. 82.

who in his turn is controlled by Parliament, and Parliament reflects the opinion of the British nation.

"In the last resort then the responsibility rests upon the British nation, who know little about Indian affairs, and whose knowledge of India is confined to purely official sources. Now, the principal source of such knowledge is, of course, the Secretary of State, but he himself has to rely upon the India Council ; and yet what is this India Couucil ? It is composed of Anglo-Indian Officials who are at least thirty years behind the age, whose knowledge of Indian matters consists of things which existed a generation ago, but which have entirely changed now, and who, therefore, have little sympathy with the hopes and aspirations of New India. These, gentlemen, are the Secretary of State's Councillors, and they have to sit in judgment upon their own past acts. It is not likely that these old officials would take an unfavourable view of things of which they themselves were the authors, or of the system under which they have passed the best years of their lives. Thus, then, the knowledge of Indian matters which the Secretary of State derives from them is such as is allowed to pass through the hands of his Councillors who, of course, on all occasions rely on official blue books which give a purely imaginary and rose-colored view of Anglo-Indian administration.

"The value of even this one-sided information and advice is very much diminished when we remember that the India Council gives its advice to the Secretary of State under no sense of responsibility to the public or the Government, since their minutes are not published, nor the Secretary of State bound to follow them.

"But, nevertheless, they exercise a decisive influence upon his judgment, even in their irresponsible position, because, although not bound to follow their advice, yet, as a matter of course, the Secretary of State, having no better guides and assistants upon whom he may rely for Indian experience, has to follow them and shape his Indian policy, as a rule, in accordance with their suggestions.

"Thus, the position of Indian politics is this : The Viceroy cannot do anything without the sanction of the Secretary of State. The Secretary of State either will not move unless some Parliamentary pressure is brought to bear upon him, or, if he moves at all, it will be in the direction of Anglo-Indian opinion. Parliament won't move unless the nation compels it do so ; and the British nation won't move unless it is made alive to the real grievances of the Indian people, and its mind is disabused of the delusive accounts it has heard through official sources of the so-called peace and prosperity of this country.

"At present Parliament is not much interested in Indian matters. Our Budget is placed before it at the fag-end of the session, and those who speak upon it have to address empty benches. And yet it was the Duke of Argyle who, in a remarkable pamphlet on the Administrations of Lord Dalhousie and Lord Canning, which he published some thirty years ago, said that at a time when the Indians had no representatives of their own in the Council, and when there was no strong public opinion to check the despotism of the ruling class, it was the duty of Parliament to keep a vigilant eye over Indian matters, and to act as the protector of the people against the aggressions of the Anglo-Indian community. (*Hear, hear.*)

"Thus, it is our first duty to acquaint Parliament and the British people with that side of the picture which is generally concealed by the official class, and to remind them of the sacred and solemn task which God, in his inscrutable wisdom, has imposed upon them of governing two hundred and fifty millions of human beings. Therefore the step which you propose to take by holding a future session of the Congress in London is dictated alike by our present political necessity and by the constitution of our Government. It will be indeed a grand day in the history of this country when the representatives stand face-to-face with the great British Nation, not as State prisoners used to stand before Oriental despots with halters round their necks, but as fellow-subjects and fellow-citizens with the charter of liberty in their hands, able to state their grievance before it and entreat it to extend to them the same principles of justice and generosity which it has extended to the Colonies. (*Cheers.*)

"It is said that the people are not fit for the reforms they advocate ; that the desire for political progress is confined only to the educated classes who form but a mere fringe of the whole society, and that the vast bulk of the people are perfectly satisfied with their present lot. Now this is I submit a mistake. Whatever may be the aspirations of the English-knowing classes, I stand before you as a specimen of that vast body of Indians who have not received the light of Western knowledge, but, while speaking on behalf of such men, I can assure you that, call them what our critics may—ignorant, bigotted, semi-civilized, old-fashioned 'black men'—they are as ardent advocates of reform as the educated classes themselves, and possess among them materials of political knowledge, which can never fail to be of use to the Government and the country. (*Cheers.*)"

Note specially this concluding para. It is a fatal misconception of our Anglo-Indian opponents that the desire for justice and freedom, of which the Congress is the mouthpiece, exists only amongst those conversant with the English language. But it is not so ; the sacred fire burns brightly in the hearts of millions on millions of thoughtful men like our Pundit, who, like him, know next to nothing of English, and it is this vast body of thinking Indians on whom, as a broad and adamantine base, securely rests that, as yet, comparatively miniature work of art, the English-educated class.

This resolution unanimously passed ; *others relating to the financial arrangements of the Congress, the reappointment of the General and Joint General Secretaries, and the appointment of delegates to England, merely formal matters, were duly disposed of. It is needless to reproduce any of the speeches *á propos* of these, but the Rev. Ram Chander Bose's thoughtful remarks in regard to things in general, rather than upon the particular resolution he was called to support, may be quoted. He remarked† :—

"The resolution I have to second is not a source of such great pleasure to me as the resolution you have just passed. The idea of holding a Congress in London is, I believe, the grandest that has flashed on the collective intellect of the National Congress. (*Hear, hear.*) Why? Because we are sure to have in England the sympathy, the encouragement, and the co-operation which we have failed to elicit in this land.

"There is between England and ourselves and this National Congress what may be called a community of aim. To explain this I must go down to one of the fundamental principles of political science. Several accusations have been preferred against us, and these are obviously ridiculous. If we were accused of idealism, I might be disposed to plead guilty to the soft impeachment. There can be no realism without pre-existing or precedent idealism. All our demands are realistic, but I have not the slightest hesitation in admitting that they have all emanated from an ideal. A great writer in view of the common saying 'man is metaphysical *nolens volens*,' says that 'man is a politician *nolens volens*." Sensible thoughtful men have before their mental vision an ideal of political development. What is that ideal? The ideal is government of the people by the people and for the people, not government by a monopoly and for a monopoly. Towards this ideal all the best Governments and most enlightened countries of the world are working, and especially England. In the home of constitutional liberty all the foremost thinkers are working up towards this great ideal ; and my friends, we aspire to see *our* Government working up to it also. England is taking grand steps towards this ideal. We ask our Government to take incipient steps towards it. But the step, whether incipient or matured, is one and the same, or has one and the same object in view. The goal is one, and therefore the aim of England and the aim of this Congress are one and the same. (*Cheers*).

"But there is between England and this National Congres snot only a community of aim but community of interest. The destinies of this country are inseparably bound up with the destinies of England. A prosperous India is to England a source of strength ; a weakened, debilitated, impoverished India is to England a weakness. What will be the upshot of the Congress? The National Congress is the great lever, and is fitted, eminently fitted, to raise this country in intelligence, in wealth, in prosperity and in glory. (*Cheers*). And when the country is raised in glory, in strength and prosperity, it will be a source of strength to England. Therefore between England and the National Congress there is a community of interest and therefore a community of method, if you will allow me the expression. The methods utilised by us are the very methods that have been utlised in England by its great political agitators. I do not for a moment maintain that English political agitators have never gone beyond the hallowed line of legitimate

* *Vide* Detailed Report, pp. 88—91.
† Detailed Report, pp. 88, 89.

and constitutional methods. I am aware that at times these agitators have broken windows and smashed chandeliers (*laughter*), and these are vagaries that *we* could never tolerate. (*Cheers*). But the methods utilised there are on the whole constitutional ; and our methods are constitutional. There is then a harmony between the methods employed there and the methods employed by us. (*Cheers*).

" And, lastly, between this Congress and England there is a community of hope. What is England's grand mission in the world ? It is to spread constitutionalism, and the glory of civilization that has evolved from it, throughout the world. And when the National Congress shall have done its work in India, India's glorious mission will be to spread constitutionalism and the civilization emanating from it, throughout Asia, throughout Africa, nay, throughout the whole world."

* * * * * * *

" These remarks of course are not on the subject of the resolution. (*Laughter*). When I was in America a gentleman was going to a meeting and a friend of his met him and said ' are you going to speak on the subject ?' No, he said, I am not going to speak on *the* subject, but I am going to speak on *some* subject Now I have spoken on some subject, if not on *the* subject. (*Laughter and cheers*)."

Then followed the usual vote of thanks to the President, proposed* this year by one of the lady delegates, Mrs. Kadumbini Gangooly, B. A. and L. M. S., a Lady Doctor, and acknowledged in a few felicitous words† by Mr. Mehta, and then with its wonted hearty and oft-repeated cheers for our Queen Empress, the Sixth National Indian Congress dissolved.

Having thus sketched the proceedings of the Congress we may now say a few words about its composition. This year the Congress was a very small one ; last year the Congress, by a special resolution, restricted the number of delegates to be elected this year to five per million of the population (199 millions) represented. Rather more however than 1,000 (the proper number was 995) were elected, but only 702 actually attended, of whom only 677 were properly registered under the special certificates now required. The three hundred odd elected delegates who failed to appear were deterred, some, as in the case of Sindh, (the only district that did not send a single delegate) by the great expense and great length of the journey ; by sickness and, in three cases, death ; by the death of relatives and the consequent inability (in the case of Hindoos) to participate in public business and by pressing personal business. Next year different arrangements will be made, by electing subsidiary delegates to insure the attendance of the full 1,000, but this year the gathering itself was not much larger than a very full House of Commons, which has, we believe, on one occasion mustered 650. On the other hand the number of spectators, though all had to pay for admission, exceeded that at any previous Congress, more than 7,000 being present on the first day and the number never falling at any time below 4,000. Indeed, a very large number of these latter came from other provinces and would have been delegates had our last year's rule not been strictly enforced.

Of the 677 registered delegates 505 were Hindoos, 116 (or rather over 17%, against 18% at Allahabad, and 13½% at Bombay last year) were Mussalmans, three Jains, seven Parsis, three Sikhs, 18 Brahmos, 15 Native, 1 Armenian and 7 European Christians.

---

* Detailed Report, p. 91.
† Detailed Report, pp. 91, 92.

As regards occupations some 250 were Zemindars, Talookdars, Landholders of various kinds and cultivators ; some 30 were Bankers, 70 Merchants and Traders ; nearly 300 Barristers, Advocates, Solicitors, Pleaders and Mukhtears; 41 Principals, Professors and Masters of Colleges and Schools ; the same number of Journalists and Newspaper proprietors ; 31 Medical men, 6 Engineers, a few Mill-owners, Contractors, Indigo and Tea Planters, &c., and 16 Missionaries and religious teachers of various creeds.

More than two hundred of these gentlemen were Chairmen, Vice-Chairmen or Members of District and Local Boards or Municipalities ; showing that, despite the widespread, though not universal, local official opposition to, and discountenance of, Lord Ripon's noble scheme of local self-government, these bodies do yet manage to secure the services of a considerable number of our most enlightened citizens; nearly one hundred were Honorary Magistrates, a position akin to that of Justices of the Peace in England, further confirming what Lord Lansdowne's letter has gone far to establish, *viz.*, that, however great the hostility of certain sections of the rank and file of the service, the more enlightened officials have no wish, actually, to boycott the Congress party.

There were several members of the Viceroy's and other Legislative Councils, many Fellows of Universities, ten Nawabs, two or three Rajahs, and so forth. This year only 160 were graduates, against 250 last year, but then they were 160 out of 677, or over 23% against 250 out of 1889, which is less than 14%. On the whole Law and the learned professions mustered more strongly, proportionally, than at Bombay, and the mercantile classes markedly less strongly, and this was only what might have been expected, seeing that this year Bengal, alone, sent its full quota, while last year the majority of the delegates were from Bombay and Madras.

Looking back at the proceedings of the late Congress the fact that chiefly strikes us, is, that the most important advances made this year were in the direction, *not* of Political but of Social Reform. Times without number we have urged that, although not directly concerning ourselves with Social questions, indirectly the Congress must prove the most important of all factors in the Social Regeneration of the country.

This last Congress must have convinced all impartial judges that the claims thus made on behalf of the movement are not unfounded.

Last year we had many lady delegates, but it need no longer be a secret, that, at the time, although a large majority of the delegates approved the measure, a considerable section of the more conservative members viewed the prospect of the intermingling of the sweet voices of women in the debates, with the manly accents of the robuster sex, with considerable repugnance. Accordingly, as one of the basal principles of the Congress is to take no important step until practical unanimity in its favour has been secured, a covenant was entered into with the ladies, that they should be seen, but not heard. This year the innovation has become so thoroughly familiarized to the mind of the country that any number of lady delegates might have attended, in full confidence of receiving the warmest welcome from all sections of the delegates. But the dear ladies resented, and we think justly, the silence imposed upon them ; they refused to recognize, as having any practical value, the æsthetic charm which their presence on the platform conferred on the entire gathering ; they said, "we have no '*cacoethes loquendi*,' that is merely one of your unmanly male slanders on our sex, but if we are not allowed to speak, in case we so desire, as several of us did on one occasion at the last Congress, what is the use of our attending ? Better have some pretty wax figures, nicely dressed on the platform ; they will serve your purpose equally well ! " Consequently since, until the Congress met, no assurance could be given as to what its views on this point might prove to be, only four lady delegates honoured the assembly with their presence. But this year, thanks, primarily, to our President, to Mr. Mano Mohan Ghose and to Sir Romesh Chunder Mitter, the remaining step towards the political enfranchisement of the women of the Congress party was taken, and a woman was not only allowed to speak, but was selected for the honorable post of proposing the vote of thanks to the President, and was rapturously received by the entire gathering. Thus was initiated, without one single dissentient voice, a reform, which in its ultimate consequences will greatly facilitate the labours of our Social Reformers in their efforts to raise the status of our Indian women ; and if the Congress had never done anything beyond bringing about, with the full consent of all parties, this one reform, it would have deserved well of the country.

But it did more, and achieved another equally important step, also in the direction of Social Reform. A few years back the few men who visited England returned in fear and trembling to their native land. The religious or socio-religious prejudice against crossing the black waters of the ocean was so strong that most of these were virtually outcasted, or had to become Brahmos, or join some other sect to avoid this. Some few performed expiatory penances and were re-admitted to caste, while a very few, by judicious silence and by keeping carefully in the background, aided by influential fellow-castemen, crept back unchallenged into their old places. When, however, our troops returned from Abyssinia, Malta and Egypt, the people who, whatever their feelings towards the local bureaucracy (and there are individual members even of this body whom they greatly respect and like) are intensely loyal to the Crown, felt that they could not outcaste brave men who had been abroad to fight for their Sovereign, and with very rare exceptions the native officers and men of these regiments were welcomed back in their homes as if nothing had happened. But the prejudice remained, and private persons still felt that a voyage to England involved a very serious risk of a practical forfeiture of caste status. When our delegates, however, returned last year from England, common sense taught even the most orthodox that a grateful recognition of the spirit of self-sacrifice in which these men had gone forth to plead India's cause before the British public, was a necessity, and that any talk, even, of outcasting them, would be treason to their own and their country's best interests.

Taking advantage of this feeling, now grown general, the resolution for an English Session of the Congress in 1892 was brought forward and received with unanimous approval, and, whether that Session ever takes place or not, a formal public enunciation has been made, once and for ever, by orthodox leaders from all parts of the country; that no penalties of caste are necessarily incurred by a visit to England; and that taking proper precautions the most orthodox may safely proceed thither. Five years ago any such unanimous verdict would have been impossible, and that it has now become an accomplished fact is mainly due to the indirect influence exerted by the Congress movement.

Nothing, nowadays, is more desirable than that numbers of educated Indians should visit Great Britain, and there learn for themselves what good, English, middle class, home and family life really are. As it is, the great majority of the young Indians who have visited England, and become familiar with only one side, and that a sadly seamy side, of London life, return to India, impressed, and not without good cause, with a conviction of the superiority of Indian domestic customs and Indian social morality. So it may not be out of place to suggest to those philanthropic English ladies and gentlemen, who are importuning our Government to legislate rashly in regard to the social customs, (of the real character of which they are ignorant) of a foreign people (of whom they know nothing), that they might employ their time, money and superfluous energies far more profitably, even to the cause they have at heart, by welcoming kindly and cordially all Indian gentlemen who visit England, receiving them at their houses, not once in a way and formally, but habitually, as real friends, and thus providing them with object lessons of that higher, freer, domestic life, which is alike the strength and glory of Great Britain.

But we are trespassing on the province of our colleagues, the social reformers, and must revert to the even more vital questions with which the Congress, as such, has to deal directly.

Although our present Viceroy seems not only desirous of seeing and judging for himself, but thoroughly imbued with the true spirit of Liberalism; although in every province there remain still some faithful few, who deprecate and deplore all the evil that is on foot; although throughout Great Britain signs appear that, here and there, her people are commencing to realize the grave responsibility in regard to India which has devolved upon them, the administration of India still remains, alas! as a whole, "linked with some virtues but a thousand crimes." Millions of educated and patriotic men (than whom no more loyal or loving subjects are numbered in the vast Empire that owns the sway of our beloved Queen Empress) are treated as political helots to gratify the class prejudices and *amour propre* and fill the pockets of a handful of bureaucrats, the average men amongst whom are, positively, less qualified for rule, *in India*,* than a very considerable proportion of those whom England permits them to misgovern.

India's people, free born British subjects, are denied the smallest fraction of those fundamental political privileges which, as British citizens, are their inherent birthright.

Ninety-five per cent of all the most important and responsible offices in the country are monopolized by Europeans, on salaries fully double of those that would secure quite as, in many cases far more, competent Indians for the majority of these posts.

One-fifth of the entire population tremble on the verge of starvation, to perish by millions whenever the smallest natural calamity of drought or flood increases by one iota the insecurity of their position, and the money wrung from our pauper population, by the cruel taxation of the first necessaries of life— the money which is all our Government has had to show for the 20 odd millions who in recent years have succumbed to famine and its consequences,—is ruthlessly squandered in bloodshed, and in wicked, and idiotically mismanaged, aggressions on feebler neighbours, to gratify the ignoble cravings for personal distinctions † and titles, of individual members of a Simla cabal.

---

*Pay, promotion and polyliteral affixes appear to be the sole things in which most of our modern civilians take any real interest. They are mere professional administrators, who take up the work simply as a matter of business and as a means of making money. They are consequently wholly out of touch with the people to whom, with rare exceptions, they are bound by no earnest unselfish desire to do good, no real heartfelt interest in their welfare and progress. How is it that, while the civilians are comparatively well-to-do and very powerful, and the missionaries poor and powerless, while the missionaries fearlessly attack the indigenous faiths with which the civilians never meddle, the people yet look up to so many of these missionaries with gratitude and respect, while we can number on our fingers the civilians of whom this can be said? Simply because in the missionaries the people recognize an earnest, unselfish (even if, in their opinion, misdirected) desire to help, raise, comfort and befriend them, while in the majority of the civilians they can only discover dislike of themselves, hatred of their country, and a purely selfish eagerness to "*get on*" in the service! Thus represented how long can Great Britain expect to maintain, unshaken, the vital hold she still, by God's blessing, retains upon the hearts of the people of India? The competitive system has failed; it has brought us shoals of well-educated men, no doubt, scarcely, in all these years, a score of faithful friends. The moral standard amongst politicians in England is so low that we can suggest no better system for appointing men there, and the only remedy, therefore, is so to work this system by granting examinations in India as well as in England, that all those offices, directly in touch with the people, shall soon be mainly filled by Indians, who not only love England far more truly than most of her perpetually grumbling children here, but sympathize with every emotion of the hearts of their fellow-countrymen, as even the very best of foreigners never can nor could.

† All this is fully exposed in the naive revelations, contained in Sir C. Macgregor's memoirs. No wonder the *officials* waxed indignant at this ruthless, though wholly unintentional expose of that iniquitous Afghan campaign. Nothing more damnatory of any Government ever appeared than these cruel revelations of the Lytton administration. As to Macgregor himself a couple of passages, culled almost at random, will show the spirit in which, with light hearts, some of our modern Indian Military heroes enter on the work of slaughter.

"I do hope we shall make a good thing of it, as it will be the making of me. I should like to get one or two not very bad wounds, which would necessitate my going home. I think it is a great shame they have not brought out some honours before this. We all lose by it, and it shows a great want of appreciation of the way to manage soldiers, who should get frequent fillips during a campaign, especially a long one." Much in the same strain he writes on the 5th August: "Oh that I may get it (the vacant Brigade)! I feel sure I shall succeed, as I will anywhere on my own resources. This staff work does not suit me; it cramps and cabins one's energies and leaves me no initiative. It has played the devil with me, and if I can only escape I shall do; so if we go to Candahar and on to Herat I might possibly end by getting a V.C. after all."

Here was no thought of the starving millions in India, of the honest British and Indian soldiers sent up to die at a cost that would have fed those millions: of the Afghan homesteads ravaged and burnt, and honest Afghan peasants butchered, because they fought to defend their country against utterly unprovoked foreign aggression. No. the only thought in Macgregor's mind was "*I might possibly end by getting a V.C. after all.*"

What some of our nobler soldiers thought of the matter may be gathered from what another writer tells us of Sir F. Maude: "Well, one day he (Sir F. Maude) came in a state of evident irritation; he was shocked and very angry at the barbarous order which he said he was compelled to issue. 'I never thought it possible,' he said, 'that the General in command of an English force would have had to do this sort of thing; but though I must promulgate the orders I shall take care that no one is shot or hanged by me or by my order, merely because he is found with arms in his hands.' He went on to say that, so far from regarding the Afghans as criminals, he considered that the Afghans had every right to repel by force of arms 'the invaders of their country.' He was so angry—so utterly disgusted (and I could see that, though he did not mention them, he had in his mind the various barbarities of burning villages, etc.) with these practices which no civilised nation would tolerate in Europe for an instant—that he went on to say 'they would never dare' to do this sort of thing in Europe.' 'Even the Russians would not resort to practices of this kind, he said; and he then went on to add sadly that it was perfectly useless his pointing out the barbarity of these things, for the 'Mutual Admiration Society' at Simla would never listen to him: and he did not belong to it, and they would pay no heed to anything he (Maude) might say. Colonel Limmond, whom I had had the honor of serving under, years ago, when I was an Assistant Engineer, also spoke to me of this order in terms of the utmost indignation."

Almost every indigenous art and industry has been crushed, and agriculture the one art, on which now depend nearly 90% of the population, is slowly deteriorating under a grasping rack-renting system of temporary settlements and, with it, our crops and our cattle.

The masses are being persistently demoralized; despite the distinct orders of the House of Commons, an iniquitous system of excise, calculated to stimulate drunkenness and all its attendant crimes and vices, is still retained, only slightly and superficially reformed in some provinces, in all its original iniquity in others.

Under a barbarous and obsolete system, miscalled, of Justice, Executive and Judicial, Fiscal and Police powers are so combined in one functionary, that powers professedly granted for one purpose are practically utilized in furtherance of others, for which no civilized Government in the world would, now-a-days, dare to confer them.

There is practically no justice in India for the poor against the rich, or the non-official against the official, and the Police, who should be the protectors of the poor and the honest, are their terror and their worst oppressors.

What wonder, if some of us, who come of sterner sires, at times, despairing of justice at the hands of man, cry out in bitterness of heart: "How long, Oh Lord, how long ?" But the patient East, sublime in its resignation and charity, longs only to forgive and to forget the *past*, and prays only for justice, however tardy, in the *present*; and wrongs that long since would have roused Teutonic or Gallic nations to frenzy, tolerated in remembrance of the civic peace and order, education and other benefits, unquestionably conferred by England, awaken in the mind of India's people (far truer Christians, though they know it not, than that proud nation which permits all this evil, and is answerable for it, before God and man) only the mild reproaches embodied in the words with which we headed this article,

> "Of course we have to submit resignedly to this ruinous, this unprincipled trans-frontier policy of the Government until we succeed in awakening the conscience of our British fellow-subjects. We are British subjects, now, of our own free choice; we have thrown in our lot with England for better and for worse, and it is this which enhances England's sin in permitting the continuance of this hateful policy. Will our British brethren never awake ?"

Alas! No mortal can reply—their slumber has been long—but they may yet awake.

# SUMMARY OF RESOLUTIONS

PASSED AT THE

# SIXTH INDIAN NATIONAL CONGRESS,

**Held at Calcutta on the 26th, 27th, 29th and 30th December 1890.**

## RESOLUTION I.

**Resolved**—That this Congress, having considered the draft Bill recently introduced into Parliament by Mr. Charles Bradlaugh, entitled " an Act to amend the Indian Councils Act of 1861," approves the same as calculated to secure a substantial instalment of that reform, in the Administration of India, for which it has been agitating, and humbly prays the Houses of Parliament of the United Kingdom of Great Britain and Ireland to pass the same into law; and further that its President, Mr. Pherozshah Mehta, is hereby empowered to draw up and sign, on behalf of this assembly, a petition to the House of Commons to the foregoing effect, and to transmit the same to Mr. Charles Bradlaugh for presentation, thereto, in due course.

## RESOLUTION II.

**Resolved**—That this present Congress does hereby ratify and confirm the resolutions passed by previous Congresses as to—

(*a*) the urgent necessity for the complete separation of executive and judicial functions, such that, in no case, shall the two functions be combined in the same officer ;

(*b*) the expediency of extending into many parts of the country, where it is not at present in force, the system of trial by jury ;

(*c*) the necessity of withdrawing from the High Courts the powers, first vested in them in 1872, of setting aside verdicts of acquittal by juries ;

(*d*) the necessity of introducing, into the Code of Criminal Procedure, a provision enabling accused persons, in warrant cases, to demand that instead of being tried by the Magistrate they be committed to the Court of Sessions ;

(*e*) the highly unsatisfactory character of the existing system of Police Administration in India, and the absolute necessity of a fundamental reform therein ;

(*f*) the expediency of both, establishing Military Colleges in India, whereat the Natives of India, as defined by Statute, may be educated and trained for a military career as officers of the Indian Army, and of authorising, under such rules and restrictions as may seem necessary, such a system of volunteering, for the Indian inhabitants of the country, as may qualify them to support the Government in any crisis ;

(*g*) the extremely unsatisfactory character of the Income Tax Administration, especially as regards incomes below rupees one thousand, and the expediency of raising the taxable minimum to this amount;

(*h*) the extreme importance of increasing, instead of diminishing, as the present tendency appears to be, the public expenditure on education in all its branches, and the necessity, in view to the promotion of one of the most essential of these branches, the technical, of the appointment of a mixed commission to enquire into the present industrial condition of the country ;

(*i*) the necessity for the reduction of, instead of the continual increase to, the military expenditure of the country ;

(*j*) the necessity, if any real justice is to be done to the people of India, of holding, simultaneously in India and England, examinations, at present held only in England, for the Civil branches of the Public Service in India ;

(*k*) the expediency of so modifying the rules made under Act XI of 1878 (the Arms Act) that all restrictions as to the possession and bearing of arms shall apply equally to all persons residing in or visiting India ; that licenses to possess and bear arms shall be liberally and generally distributed wherever wild animals habitually destroy human life, cattle or crops ; and that these and all licenses issued under the rules shall be granted once for all, shall operate throughout the Provincial jurisdiction within which they are issued, be only revocable on proof of misuse, and shall not require yearly or half-yearly renewals.

## RESOLUTION III.

**Resolved**—That this Congress respectfully expresses the earnest hope that in the interest of the people of India, the House of Commons will forthwith restore the right, formerly possessed by members of that Honourable House, of stating to Parliament any matter of grievance of the natives of India before Mr. Speaker leaves the Chair, for the presentation in Committee of the Indian Budget statement, and earnestly trusts that the House of Commons will, in future, take into consideration the Annual Indian Budget statement at such a date as will ensure its full and adequate discussion, and further authorizes its President to sign a Petition, in the name and on behalf of this Congress, for presentation to the House of Commons, in accordance with the terms of this Resolution.

## RESOLUTION IV.

**Resolved**—That, while recognizing the action taken, in response to its previous prayers, in the matter of Excise Reform by H. M.'s Secretary of State for India and the Supreme Government here, and noting with pleasure the increase to the import duty on Spirits, the taxation imposed on Indian-brewed malt liquors, the decision of the Bengal Government to abolish the outstill system, and the closing of over 7,000 liquor shops by the Madras Government in 1889-90, this Congress regrets that it is still necessary to urge the Government of India to insist on *all* Provincial administrations carrying out in their integrity the policy in matters of Excise enunciated in paras. 103, 104 and 105 of the despatch published in the *Gazette of India* of March 1st, 1890, especially as to subsection 4 of para. 103, *viz.*—

"That efforts should be made to ascertain the existence of local public sentiment, and that a reasonable amount of deference should be paid to such opinion when ascertained."

## RESOLUTION V.

**Resolved**—That the condition of the Finances of India having materially improved, and those special circumstances on which the Government relied to justify the recent enhancement of the Salt Tax having practically ceased to exist, this Congress considers it essential that the enhancement referred to should be remitted at an early date, and empowers its President to submit a special memorial on the subject in its name and on its behalf to H. E. the Viceroy in Council.

## RESOLUTION VI.

**Resolved**—That having reference to the expectations created throughout the country by the Despatch of Her Majesty's Secretary of State in 1862, the principles of which were re-affirmed in a subsequent Despatch of 1865, promising the extension of a Permanent Settlement to all temporarily settled tracts in which certain conditions were fulfilled, and to the fact that throughout large portions of the country those conditions have long since been fulfilled, this Congress respectfully submits that the Government of India is now in honour bound to take up this question of Permanent Settlement, without further delay, in view to practical action thereon such that fixity and permanency may be given to the Government Land Revenue demand as explicitly promised, by Her Majesty's Secretary of State, more than a quarter of a century ago.

## RESOLUTION VII.

**Resolved**—That this Congress, having observed with surprise a notice, apparently official, in various Calcutta newspapers which runs as follows :—

THE CONGRESS.

"The Bengal Government having learnt that tickets of admission to the visitors' enclosure in the Congress pavilion have been sent to various Government officers residing in Calcutta, has issued a circular to all Secretaries, and heads of departments subordinate to it, pointing out that under the orders of the Government of India the presence of Government officials, even as visitors at such meetings, is not advisable, and that their taking part in the proceedings of any such meetings is absolutely prohibited :"

and having also considered a letter addressed by the Private Secretary of His Honor the Lieutenant-Governor of Bengal to the Secretary of the Reception Committee, of which the following is an exact copy :—

BELVEDERE, *26th December* 1890.

"DEAR SIR,—In returning herewith the seven cards of admission to the visitors' enclosure of the Congress pavilion, which were kindly sent by you to my address yesterday afternoon, I am desired to say that the Lieutenant-Governor and the members of his household could not possibly avail themselves of these tickets, since the orders of the Government of India definitely prohibit the presence of Government officials at such meetings.

Yours faithfully,
P. C. LYON,
*Private Secretary.*"

"To
J. GHOSAL, ESQ.,
*Secretary, Congress Reception Committee.*"

authorizes and instructs its President to draw the attention of His Excellency the Viceroy to the declaration embodied in these papers that Government servants are prohibited from attending any meetings of this Congress even as spectators, and to enquire, most respectfully, whether His Honor the Lieutenant-Governor of Bengal has, or has not, correctly interpreted the orders of the Government of India.

## RESOLUTION VIII.

**Resolved**—That the best thanks of this Congress be tendered to Mr. Charles Bradlaugh, M.P., for the invaluable services rendered by him during the past year, as also to Sir W. Wedderburn, Mr. W. S. Caine, Mr. J. Bright Maclaren, M.P., Mr. J. Ellis, M.P., Mr. George Yule, and Mr. Dadabhai Naorojee for the unselfish zeal and ability with which they have presided over the British Agency of the Congress ; further that they put on record an expression of their high appreciation of the manner in which Mr. Digby, C.I.E., Secretary of the Agency, and Messrs. Surendra Nath Banerjee, R. N. Mudholkar, W. C. Bonnerjee, Eardly Norton, and A. O. Hume, delegates to England, respectively, discharged the onerous duties imposed upon them, and of their gratitude to all those members of the British public who so kindly welcomed and so sympathetically gave audience, in over fifty public and a far larger number of private meetings, to one or more of these delegates.

## RESOLUTION IX.

**Resolved**—That a vote of thanks be recorded to Kumar Debendra Mullick and Brothers, Proprietors of the Tivoli Gardens, Mr. N. C. Bose and Babu Bhupendra Nath Bose, Proprietors of Mohan Bagan Villa, and to the Hon'ble Sir Romesh Chandra Mitra, Mr. T. N. Palit, Babus Janokee Nath Roy, Gopee Mohan Roy, Harendra Nath Roy, Kissory Mohan Roy, Ramanath Ghose, and Jamadar Ghasiram, owners of houses kindly lent for the use of delegates.

## RESOLUTION X.

**Resolved**—That the Seventh Indian National Congress do assemble on the 26th December, 1891, at either Madras or Nagpore, as may be hereafter settled, in consultation between the Madras, Central Provinces and Berar Committees, and the Joint General Secretary.

## RESOLUTION XI.

**Resolved**—That provisional arrangements be made to hold a Congress, of not less than 100 delegates, in England, all things being convenient, in 1892, and that the several standing Congress Committees be directed to report, at the coming Congress, the names of the delegates that it is proposed to depute from their respective circles.

## RESOLUTION XII.

**Resolved**—That of the Funds now in the Joint General Secretary's hands and about to be received, a further sum of twenty thousand rupees be added to the Permanent Fund and placed in fixed deposits, and that the rest of the funds accruing on account of this current year, 1890, be held by him available for the immediate purposes of the British Committee of the Indian National Congress, but to be replaced as the subscriptions for 1891 are received, and, ultimately, also added to the Permanent Fund.

## RESOLUTION XIII.

**Resolved**—That a sum of Rs. 40,000, exclusive of individual donations, is assigned for the expenses of the British Committee of the Congress and Rs. 6,000 for the General Secretary's Office and Establishment, and that the several circles and districts do contribute as arranged in Committee.

## RESOLUTION XIV.

**Resolved**—That Mr. A. O. Hume and Pandit Ajoodhia Nath are re-elected General and Joint-General Secretaries for the ensuing year.

## RESOLUTION XV.

**Resolved**—That this Congress does formally appoint Messrs. G. Yule, Pherozshah Mehta, W. C. Bonnerjee, J. Adam, Mono Mohan Ghose, A. O. Hume, Kali Charan Banerjee, Dadabhai Naorojee, D. A. Khare, and such other gentlemen as may volunteer for the duty with the sanction and approval of the standing Congress Committees of their respective circles, to represent its views in England, and press upon the consideration of the British Public the political reforms which the Congress has advocated.

CALCUTTA:
*December 31st, 1890.*

PHEROZSHAH MEHTA,
*President of the Sixth Indian National Congress.*

# DETAILED
# REPORT OF THE PROCEEDINGS
OF THE
# SIXTH INDIAN NATIONAL CONGRESS,
HELD AT
# CALCUTTA,
## *ON THE 26th, 27th, 29th & 30th OF DECEMBER, 1890.*

## FIRST DAY'S PROCEEDINGS.

**1st Day.**

THE SIXTH INDIAN NATIONAL CONGRESS assembled for its first sitting early in the afternoon of the 26th of December, in a vast pavilion, erected for the purpose in the Tivoli Gardens, Calcutta, a well-known place of amusement, most generously placed by the proprietors (together with a large two-storied house standing in the gardens) at the local Committee's disposal.

The pavilion, the largest yet constructed for the Congress, measured 250 feet by 150 feet, and provided ample sitting-room for over 5,000 visitors and delegates, but as a matter of fact, on the opening day, nearly 8,000 persons were gathered together in the Congress Hall.

At 2 P.M. the Chair was taken by Mr. Mono Mohan Ghose, the Chairman of the Reception Committee, on whom, in accordance with precedent, it devolved to open the Congress, welcome the delegates from other provinces, and call upon the assembly to elect a President.

MR. MONO MOHAN GHOSE (*Calcutta, No. 8, in list*) rose and said :—

**Chairman of Reception Committee's Address.**

DELEGATES TO THE NATIONAL CONGRESS,—It has devolved upon me to offer you our most hearty welcome on this great occasion. It has been impossible for me to decline the honor which the Reception Committee have thought fit to confer on me by asking me to be their Chairman, and in that capacity to welcome you in their name and on their behalf. That honor, you will I am sure all agree with me, could not have been possibly conferred, in the first instance, upon any abler or worthier member of the Bengali Community than my esteemed friend the Hon'ble Sir Romesh Chander Mitter. (*Cheers*). It is a matter of congratulation to all of us that, although the cause of the administration of justice in these provinces has suffered by his retirement from the high office which he lately held, he is now in a position to take an active interest in the proceedings of this great national demonstration, and to guide us by his varied experience and by his sound judgment. When I learnt that the state of his health precluded him from occupying the position which legitimately belongs to him, and that it was his especial desire that I should perform that duty, which of all men in our community no one could have performed more gracefully or fittingly than he, I felt that I had no right, by reason of my own incompetency and unworthiness, to decline the high honor which my colleagues had decided to bestow on me. I conceive

1st Day.

Chairman of Reception Committee's Address.

it is not only an honor, but a duty, which every citizen owes to his country, to respond cordially to any call which may be made upon him to assist in an undertaking which has for its object the welfare and the happiness of one's fellow-countrymen. (*Cheers*).

On the last occasion when you assembled in this city you were welcomed by one of the most distinguished citizens of Calcutta, who, by reason of his profound scholarship and wide reputation, was eminently fitted to be the spokesman on behalf of the people of these provinces. It is a matter of sincere regret to us all that long-continued illness should have prostrated our distinguished friend Raja Rajendra Lala Mitra, but it will be a source of gratification to you all to be assured that, though tied down to his sick bed and therefore unable to greet you once more on behalf of the people of Bengal, his heart is entirely with us (*loud cheers*), and that he continues to be as staunch a supporter of this great movement as ever. (*Cheers*). It is my painful duty to express to you on behalf of the Reception Committee our sorrow at the irreparable loss we have sustained in the course of the year by the death of one of our ablest and most zealous workers—I mean the late Babu Mohesh Chander Choudhry. (*Loud cheers*). In him Bengal has lost one of her truest patriots, and the National Congress one of its most earnest supporters and active workers. I had the high privilege of enjoying his friendship for many years, and I can unhesitatingly assert that this presidency has not yet produced a man whose memory ought to be more dearly cherished by us than that of my lamented friend Mohesh Chander Choudhry. (*Cheers.*) In simplicity of habits and purity of life he was essentially what a pious Hindu ought to be, while in breadth of views, in honesty of purpose, and in general culture few men excelled him even among the more favored races of the West. Such a man the hand of death has somewhat prematurely removed from us, and, before we had quite time to recover from the shock, we found ourselves deprived, though temporarily, of the valuable assistance and co-operation of two of our most energetic workers, one of whom, I regret to say, is unable, by reason of continued ill health and domestic affliction, to be present to-day—I mean our distinguished friend Mr. W. C. Bonnerjee (*loud and continued cheers*), while the other, after suffering from severe illness for some time, is, I am glad to find, able, at any rate, to encourage us by his presence though still too weak to cheer us by his eloquence—I refer to my friend Mr. Surendra Nath Bannerjee. (*Loud Cheers*).

It is now four years since the National Congress met in this city; since then you have assembled in the great cities of Madras, Allahabad and Bombay, in every one of which places the reception accorded to the Delegates has been of such a character as to make us in Calcutta feel that, after all, we are able to do very little in connection with the Congress of 1890 to deserve the high rank which is popularly assigned to Bengal as the most advanced and the wealthiest province in India. I am afraid, that, with all our efforts this year to give you a fitting reception, our arrangements are defective in many respects; but this I can assure you, on behalf of the people of Bengal, that they yield to no other Presidency in the heartiness and the cordiality of the welcome which they wish to offer to the distinguished representatives of the different parts of this great country, who have honored us with their presence to-day.

It is not within my province to discuss any of the topics which are likely to engage your attention this session; but it is I think fitting that I should not sit down without making some general observations as regards the real aims and objects of the National Congress and our course of action in the future. Our proceedings have been subjected to much and varied criticism, and for my part I am glad that such should have been the case. All our proceedings, our discussions, and our resolutions are public property, and it is only right that they should be subjected to public scrutiny, for I believe we have everything to gain and nothing to lose from honest criticism (*cheers*), however unfavorable such criticism may be. That, besides legitimate criticism, the proceedings of such a body as ours should be subjected to unworthy attacks and our aims misrepresented and distorted is a matter which, however painful to us all, ought not to discourage and dishearten us. For what great cause in the history of this world has ever triumphed without, in the first instance, having met with unworthy and even rancorous opposition? Our opponents have not even hesitated to accuse the promoters of this movement of disloyalty to the British Government. If I could bring myself to believe that the accusation, however unfounded, had been honestly preferred by those who are responsible for starting it, I should have felt myself called upon to deal with it seriously; but the charge has always seemed to me so preposterous and so dishonest on the part, at any rate, of a large portion of our detractors, that I think every speaker in this hall ought to treat it with silent contempt.

There is, I believe, no one present here who in his heart of hearts does not feel that at no period in the history of India were life and property more secure than they are at the present day. If English rule in India had done nothing more than that, we should, even then, have had ample reason to be grateful to England, for, as you know, the establishment of peace and the maintenance of law and order are the first requisites for the happiness of a people. To my mind, our allegiance to the British Government is based, not only on the feeling of gratitude which the benefits conferred upon us must evoke in our hearts, but also upon the highest grounds of expediency; for every sane man in India, who is capable of thinking, must feel that any change of Government at the present time would be the greatest calamity that could befall the people of this country. (*Cheers*). That we should have been better pleased if we could have governed ourselves as well as we are governed by England, is a sentiment which we need not in the least shrink from avowing, because not only is such a feeling natural, but it is perfectly consistent to my mind with true loyalty to England. (*Hear, hear*). The National Congress movement was fittingly described last year by my friend Mr. Pherozshah Mehta, while welcoming the Delegates in Bombay, as "the grandest outcome of British Rule in India." To that description I will venture to add that it is also the natural and, indeed, the inevitable outcome of the generous policy pursued by England in this country. The fact which we all gratefully acknowledge, namely, that India is now better governed than before, or the fact that no other Asiatic country is at the present time better governed, furnishes no argument whatever against the demands made by us with the sole object of improving the administration of the couutry. The English people have no right to complain if we refuse to judge of their acts and professions as rulers of this country by any standard lower than what they themselves have taught us to respect and admire. If England has been instrumental in teaching an Asiatic people a higher code of political morality she can scarcely complain, with any show of reason, if we expect her strictly to adhere to that code in the government of her own dependencies, and to carry out the professions and declarations which have from time to time been made in her name and on her behalf The great demonstration of to-day, I think, we are all agreed, implies nothing more than this, *viz.*, that, much as England has done for us, she has yet a great deal more to do, or, in other words, that the administration of India is not perfect, but that there is still considerable room for its improvement and reform. This, I believe, to be the keystone of this great national movement. It is not a movement intended in the slightest degree to embarrass or hamper the Government of the country, but to assist that Government by every means in the great and difficult task in which it is engaged. Viewed in this light—and I am sure you all agree with me that it is our most anxious desire that it should be viewed in no other light—I fail to understand how it is that we have not yet met with a sympathetic recognition at the hands of those who are responsible for the good government of this country. It is impossible in any country to carry on the work of government for any length of time, without consulting the wishes and wants of those who are governed, and it is obvious that when the Government of a country is practically in the hands of a foreign people, it is all the more necessary for that Government, and, indeed, it is its duty, if it is to exist for any good purpose, to ascertain the wishes and even the aspirations of those who are governed. If such is the duty cast upon those who are called upon to govern, it is equally the duty of the people themselves to acquaint the Government by all constitutional means with their own wishes and their requirements. We are not so unreasonable as to expect that all our suggestions should be at once carried out, or that all our demands should be at once granted without due consideration. All that we desire is that our suggestions should be honestly and sympathetically considered, and that if difficulties, which we ourselves may fail to perceive, should deter the Government of the day from acceding to any of our wishes, we may be taken into the confidence of the Government, so to speak, in order that we may be in a position to help it, if we can, in grappling with those difficulties. (*Hear, hear*). This, I believe, is the true position which the National Congress in India desires to occupy.

An idea is said to prevail among certain officials in the vicinity of Whitehall as well as in this country, to the effect that the supremacy of England in India is mainly based upon the disunion of the different races existing in this country, and that any attempt to unite them, even to a limited extent upon a common political platform, is fraught with ultimate danger to the safety of the British Empire. I cannot for a moment believe that any Englishman, having any claims to Statesmanship, can seriously entertain such an idea, based as as it is altogether upon a superficial, and, I venture to think, an erroneous conception of facts.

"To divide and rule" is a wicked policy as unworthy of the great English people as it is practically impossible after what they have themselves done for us; because you can no more, now, keep the different races of this country disunited in feelings and sentiments for any length of time than you can abolish your schools and colleges, your railroads and telegraphs.

But then it is asked, 'Whom does the National Congress represent? What right has it to speak on behalf of the masses of the people who know nothing about the Congress?" My answer is, the National Congress represents the thinking portion of the people of India. (*Cheers*). The Delegates present here to-day are the chosen representatives of that section of the Indian people who have learnt to think and whose number is daily increasing with marvellous rapidity. It is perfectly correct that the ignorant masses whom we seek to represent are still unable, in many Provinces, to take an active interest in the great social and administrative problems which are now engaging the attention of the educated classes; but history teaches that, in all countries and in all ages, it is the thinking classes who lead the unthinking

1st Day.

Chairman of Reception Committee's Address.

and in the present state of our own society we are bound, not only to think for ouselves, but also to think for those who are still too ignorant to exercise that important function. (*Cheers*). If by reason of the peculiar intellectual condition of the people of India whom we are seeking to represent, not only some of those who have actually chosen us as their delegates, but also many others are still incapable of exercising any choice in the matter, I am sure we are not insensible of the grave responsibilities which we are incurring in speaking and acting on their behalf. Our duty to our less favoured countrymen requires that we should not shrink from incurring those responsibilities. I believe we are all agreed that it is our duty to educate our ignorant countrymen not only to think, but to think rightly, and to instil into their minds the fundamental doctrine that the happiness of a people primarily depends upon the maintenance of law and order in the country, and that if they have any grievances the only way to obtain redress is to agitate by peaceable and lawful methods. In trying to discharge so obvious a duty we can well afford to be ridiculed as self-styled delegates or as belonging only to "a microscopic minority." (*Cheers and laughter*).

Gentlemen, I feel I ought not to trespass mnch longer on your patience, but there is one other accusation to which I cannot help alluding although it has been satisfactorily answered at more than one of our previous gatherings—I refer to the charge, so often repeated, that the National Congress as a body is opposed to social reforms. Such an accusation is based upon an entire misapprehension of the scope and functions of the National Congress, whose object, as I have already explained, is to point out to the Government what we conceive to be the defects in the administration of the country, and to ask only for such reforms as we are ourselves absolutely incapable of introducing without the aid of the Government, and in regard to the necessity of which we are all practically of one mind. Now, the many questions of social reform which are at present engaging the attention of the educated classes throughout India are questions the solution of which is entirely in the hands of the people themselves. It is open to all of us to live as we like, or to eschew or alter at any time any custom which we may consider inconvenient or mischievous. The remedy being entirely in our own hands we can apply it whenever we choose, and on the majority of points we are unfortunately by no means all of one mind yet. Besides, it should be borne in mind that the Congress is composed of diverse communities, each having its own religion and its peculiar usages, and it would be impossible for such a body to discuss the social customs of a particular community, based as they often are upon religious ideas, regarding which the members of another community professing a different religion have no adequate knowledge or information. (*Hear, hear*). But it by no means follows that the promoters of the National Congress are not as keenly alive to the importance of social as they are to that of political reforms. The same educational agency which has given life to the National Congress has already helped to bring about enormous social changes throughout India. Half a century is but a day in the life of a nation, and any one who compares the state of Indian society of the present day with what was the case even 30 years ago, cannot but be surprised at the rapidity with which we have moved in social matters during that period. If there are some who think we ought to have moved still faster, they, in my opinion, ignore altogether the enormous difficulties against which we have to contend in this matter. There are movements of a very important character already on foot amongst the different communities of our people, to promote the cause of social and religious reform, and in my humble judgment we should be travelling out of our legitimate province if we were to deal with such questions in this assembly. Those who know my own views will readily believe that I yield to none in the country in attaching importance to the question of social reform; but at the same time I cannot but feel that it is our duty, however keenly we may feel on the subject, to remember that any precipitate or inconsiderate action before the creation of a healthy public opinion in a community is often apt to retard progress and to defeat the very object we have in view (*Hear, hear*). We ought to be thankful to our English friends for any suggestions they may be disposed to make to us on the question of social reform, so long as those suggestions are made in a sympathetic spirit; but at the same time we must ask them to bear in mind that it is impossible fo an outsider or foreigner to realize adequately the difficulties which the different Indian communities have to contend against in matters of social reform. Our English friends, whose kind sympathy and advice our social reformers are always delighted to have, may also be asked to remember that the decision of the question as to what reforms should or should not be introduced must, from the very nature of the case, rest with the Indian people themselves, and that therefore the true remedy lies in educating the people and creating a healthy public opinion on questions of social reform. To my mind, this gathering itself must have, and indeed already *has* had, the effect, directly and indirectly, of giving a great impetus to the cause of social reform. It is true that there are social problems connected with our domestic life of so important and pressing a character that, in my opinion, the sooner we direct our attention to them, and deal vigorously with them, the better for our country; but all I say is, that those are questions with which the Congress, composed as it is of different communities, ought not at present to have any direct concern. (*Cheers*).

I have thus far dealt with criticisms which have emanated chiefly from members of the

Chairman of Reception Committee's Address.

Anglo-Indian community and the English press; but, before I conclude, I may be permitted to allude to one argument which I have sometimes heard used by some of our own people who are in sympathy with the Congress. I have heard it asked: "What good result has the Congress secured to us?" To those desponding spirits among us who are apt to indulge in such an argument I cannot do better than reply in the words of one who spent his noble life in agitating for the good of his own country, and of mankind in general, and whose name is deservedly cherished by us all in India.

In 1885, when I had the honor of a long interview with the late Mr. John Bright (*loud cheers*) at Birmingham, he told me, as I was coming away: "Tell your people on your return home that they must not expect immediate results, nor must they lose heart if they do not get what they want. The English people themselves have not obtained any concession from their own Government without long and persistent agitation. It took Cobden and myself 30 years to get the Corn Laws repealed. Tell your people, as coming from me, that they do not deserve to succeed if they expect immediate results." I trust that this message, sent to us by that great champion of our rights a few years before his death, will encourage you all to persevere in the great cause which you have taken up. Remember that this is only a beginning of a great struggle, and that these annual gatherings of ours are but physical representations of that great and wonderful national awakening which is taking place everywhere in India. (*Cheers*). The sight that we witness to-day may well justify any one of us indulging in the reverie of the great English poet when he exclaimed: "Methinks I see in my mind's eye a noble and puissant nation rousing herself like a strong man after sleep and shaking her invincible locks. Methinks I see her as an eagle mewing her mighty youth and kindling her undazl'd eyes at the full midday beam, purging and unscaling her long abused sight at the fountain itself of heavenly radiance, while the whole noise of timorous and flocking birds, with those also that love the twilight, flutter about, amazed at what this means, and in their envious gabble would prognosticate a year of sects and schisms." Gentlemen, I once more beg to offer you a hearty welcome, and I ask you to proceed to the business of the day by electing a President for this the Sixth Indian National Congress. (*Loud and prolonged cheers*).

**Election of a President.**

**Sir Romesh Chunder Mitter proposes Mr. Pherozshah Mehta.**

Sir Romesh Chunder Mitter (*Calcutta, No. 1, in list*) (late acting Chief Justice of the High Court, Calcutta) rose and said:—Mr. Chairman of the Reception Committee, Ladies and Gentlemen,—I feel great pleasure in being called upon to move the first resolution, and probably the only resolution that will be placed before you this day, *viz.*, that in regard to the election of a President for this great national gathering, here this day assembled. I am extremely thankful to the Reception Committee and its Chairman for having assigned to me this duty—a very agreeable duty to myself, and one that will involve very little labour on my part. It affords me great pleasure to be allowed an opportunity of taking a very small part in the proceedings of this great national gathering. The duty assigned to me, though, as I have said, involving very little labour, is an important one, because it will secure to you a leader who will guide your deliberations; and when I simply mention the name which I have to propose I feel assured that it will be received with general acclamation. By his distinguished career at the Bar of the Bombay High Court, and the conspicuous part which he has borne in so many important movements and questions, the name of Mr. Pherozshah Mehta (*loud cheers*) has become almost a household word to all educated persons in India. He enjoys the full confidence, not only of the province to which he belongs, but also of the sister provinces. With these few words I beg to propose that Mr. Pherozshah Mehta be elected President of the Indian National Congress for the year 1890. (*Cheers*).

**Nawab Shamshoodowla seconds.**

Nawab Shamshoodowla (*Lucknow, No. 472, in list*) seconded the motion.

**Mr. Ananda Charlu supports.**

Mr. Ananda Charlu (*Madras, No. 611, in list*)—I beg to support the motion. Were I to fulfil the ordinarily understood duties of my position as a supporter I should have to set to work on the proverbially thankless task of painting the lily white. But that is quite unnecessary, you will all I think agree. If Mr. Pherozshah were not well known to all of you—and to all India equally—having myself known him pretty intimately for a long time, I might be able to say something worth listening to; but as he is so well known to you all, I will do no more than ask permission to support the proposition that has been made, that he be elected President of the Sixth Indian National Congress. (*Cheers.*)

**Nawab Goulam Rubbani also supports.**

Nawab Goulam Rubbani (*Calcutta, No. 672, in list*) also supported the motion, which was unanimously adopted with loud acclamations.

1st Day.

Mr. Pherozshah declared duly elected.

Mr. Mono Mohan Ghose (*Calcutta, No. 8, in list*)—I now declare Mr. Mehta to have been duly elected.

The President's Inaugural Address.

Mr. Pherozshah Mehta (*Bombay, No. 542, in list*) then took the Chair and delivered the following address :—

Ladies and Gentlemen,—I beg to tender to you my most sincere thanks for the honor you have done me in calling me to preside over your deliberations this year. I cannot imagine a greater honor for a native of this country than to be elected, by your free and spontaneous suffrages, President of an assembly which is now one of the recognized institutions of the country—an unconventional Convention of the Empire which, we may say without undue ostentation, has already earned a place in history,—not less surely, let us trust, than the famous St. Andrew's Dinners of this city,—as making an epoch in the march of events moulding the lofty destinies of this magnificent land. In speaking of myself as a native of this country, I am not unaware that, incredible as it may seem, Parsis have been both called, and invited and allured to call themselves, foreigners. If twelve centuries, however, entitle Angles and Saxons, and Normans and Danes, to call themselves natives of England, if a lesser period entitles the Indian Mahomedans to call themselves natives of India, surely we are born children of the soil, in which our lot has been cast for a period of over thirteen centuries, and where, ever since the advent of the British power, we have lived and worked, with our Hindu and Mahomedan neighbours, for common aims, common aspirations, and common interests. To my mind, a Parsi is a better and a truer Parsi, as a Mahomedan or a Hindu is a better and truer Mahomedan or Hindu ; the more he is attached to the land which gave him birth, the more he is bound in brotherly relations and affection to all the children of the soil, the more he recognizes the fraternity of all the native communities of the country, and the immutable bond which binds them together in the pursuit of common aims and objects under a common Government. Is it possible to imagine that Dadabhai Naorojee, for instance, true Parsi that he is, is anything but an Indian, living and working all his life for all India, with the true and tender loyalty of a son ? Can any one doubt, if I may be allowed to take another illustration, that Sir Syed Ahmed Khan was greater and nobler when he was devoting the great energies and talents with which he is is endowed,—if, for the benefit of Mahomedans in particular,—for the benefit of all Indians in general, than when, as of late, he was preaching a gospel of selfishness and isolation? The birthright, therefore, gentlemen, which the Parsis thus possess of so indefeasible and glorious a character, they have refused and will always refuse to sell for any mess of pottage, however fragrant and tempting (*Loud cheers*). More especially, therefore, as an Indian it is that I return to you my grateful thanks for the honor you have done me.

I have ventured, Gentlemen, to ascribe to the Congress the credit of making an epoch in Indian political progress. A very brief survey of the incidents of the twelve months that have elapsed since we last met will amply justify our title to that distinction. In the admirable address which was delivered by my predecessor in this chair at Allahabad, Mr. Yule pointed out that all movements of the kind in which we are concerned pass through several phases as they run their course. The first is one of ridicule. That is followed, as the movement progresses, by one of abuse, which is usually succeeded by partial concession, and misapprehension of aim, accompanied by warnings against taking big jumps into the unknown. The final stage of all is a substantial adoption of the object of the movement, with some expression of surprise that it was not adopted before. Well, Gentlemen, we have pretty well passed the first two stages. We have survived the ridicule, the abuse, and the misrepresentation. We have survived the charge of sedition and disloyalty. We have survived the charge of being a microscopic minority. We have also survived the charge of being guilty of the atrocious crime of being educated, and we have even managed to survive the grievous charge of being all Babus in disguise. (*Laughter and cheers*).

The question of our loyalty is set at rest for ever. In the debate on Lord Cross's India Reform Bill in the House of Lords, Viceroy after Viceroy bore emphatic testimony to the loyal and peaceful character of our aims and efforts. Within the last few days the voice of no less a personage than one of our former Secretaries of State has confirmed this testimony. Lord R Churchill—it is to no less distinguished a public man that I refer—has publicly declared that "he could sincerely remark that no one will rejoice more than himself if the deliberations of the Indian National Congress shortly to be resumed were to contribute effectually to the progress and the welfare of the Indian people." Then, Gentlemen, it is made clear that we have not learnt the lessons of history so badly, as to demand the introduction of the full-blown representative institutions which, in England, have been the growth of centuries. It is made clear that we have not asked for even such a modicum, as was enjoyed by the English people even before the time of Simon de Montfort, more than five centuries ago, nay, that we have not asked even for representative institutions of a governing or ruling character at all. Indeed, so far as this historical argument is concerned, we have not alone proved that we have *not* been guilty of disregarding it, but we have been successful in turning the tables upon our adversaries. We have shown that it is they who defy the lessons of history and experience when they talk of waiting to make a beginning, till the masses of the people are fully equipped with all the virtues and all the qualifications which adorn the citizens of Utopia, in fact, till a millennium has set in, when we should hardly require such institutions at all. We have shown that people who indulge in such vain talk have never understood the laws of human progress, which, after all, is a series of experiments, in which men and institutions re-act upon each other for their mutual improvement and perfection. We have also proved that, in spite of our education, and even with our racial and religious differences, the microscopic minority can far better and far more intuitively represent the needs and the aspirations of their own countrymen than the still more microscopic minority of the omniscient District Officers, whose colloquial knowledge of the Indian languages seldom rises above the knowledge of English possessed, for instance, by French waiters at Paris Hotels which proudly blazon forth the legend—'Ici on parle Anglais ;' and whose knowledge of native domestic and social life aud ways and habits of thought seldom extends beyond a familiarity with flattering expressions of the Saheb's greatness and paternal care, sometimes inspired by courtesy and sometimes by interest. An amusing story was related to me of a little incident that occurred only the other day which is not without instruction as illustrating the amount of knowledge possessed by Anglo-Indians of the people among whom they have moved for years. The wife of a member of Parliament, who has come out on a visit to India this year—herself as distinguished as her husband for her kindly sympathy in Indian welfare—was sitting at dinner next to a learned member of my profession, who, in the course of conversation, grew humorous and sarcastic by turns, in the fashion of M. Rudyard Kipling, on the ridiculous and outrageous pretensions of globe-trotters to know the country and its people better than Anglo-Indians who had lived in it for years. He was rattling away, well satisfied with himself and the impression he thought he was producing on the lady, when, with the sweetest of smiles, she gently asked him how long he had been himself in India. Fifteen years —more or less—was the answer. I suppose you know well Mr.—— naming a gentleman whose recent elevation to the Bench of one of our High Courts was received everywhere with pleasure and approbation. Of course, I do, said his brother in the same profession. Can you tell me if he has only one wife or more than one ? Slowly came the answer, No I fear I can't. Well I can tell *you* ; you see I have been only a few days in the country, said the lady quietly, and yet I think I know a thing or two which you don't. I trust my learned friend, who is the hero of this story, was properly grateful to the lady for giving him some serious food for reflection.

Then, Gentlemen, our right to the designation of a National body has been vindicated. It is so admirably set forth in an article which appeared in a Conservative Review—*The National*—from the pen of a Conservative who, however, speaks from the fulness of intimate knowledge, that I cannot resist the temptation of borrowing from it. "The supposed rivalry," says the writer, "between Mussulmans and Hindus is a convenient decoy to distract attention and to defer the day of reform. I do not wish to affirm that there is no antagonism between the adherents of the two faiths; but I do most positively assert that the antagonism has been grossly exaggerated. Every municipal improvement and charitable work finds members of the two faiths working together and subscribing funds to carry it out. Every political paper in the country finds supporters from believers in both creeds. Just the same is witnessed in the proceedings of the Congress. The members of the Congress met together as men, on the common basis of nationality, being citizens of one country, subjects of one power, amenable to one code of laws, taxed by one authority, influenced for weal or woe by one system of administration, urged by like impulses to secure like rights and to be relieved of like burdens. If these are not sufficient causes to weld a people together into one common alliance of nationality, it is difficult to conceive what would be sufficient. It is for this reason the organization has been called the Indian National Congress ; not because, as many besides Mr. Keane have assumed, that it claims a non-existent unity of race, but because it deals with rights and interests which are national in character, and matters in which all the inhabitants of the Indian peninsula are equally concerned."

I think we may take it, Gentlemen, that we have passed through the first two stages, and that the loyalty, the moderation, the propriety, and the constitutional and national character of our mission are now established beyond a doubt. But, however arduous and however provoking some of the experiences of the trial through which we have passed, they should not leave any trace of bitterness behind. For let us not imagine that they were devoid of chastening and beneficial effects upon ourselves. Let us frankly acknowledge that they also must have had their share in contributing to add clearness to our thoughts, sobriety to our methods, and moderation to our proposals. If I might use a proscribed, but not unscriptural, phrase we must, give even the devil, his due. (*Laughter.*)

It is on the third stage—the era of achievement—that we have now entered. It is true that a majority of the Congress proposals do not still seem to have made much headway. Even as regards the proposal to separate the Executive and the Judicial functions, lauded by Lord Dufferin "as a counsel of perfection to which the Government were ready to subscribe," Government are yet so absorbed in admiration of it that they have not recovered themselves sufficiently to take action. There is, however, no reason to despair. It was once proved upon sworn testimony in the Bombay High Court, before the late Chief Justice Sir M. Westropp that a woman required 22 months for parturition in the air of the province of Kattyawar. It is not impossible, Gentlemen, that the air of Simla may similarly necessitate a more than ordinarily long period of gestation to perfect even counsels of perfection; and therefore we must possess our souls in more than ordinary patience, lest any precipitate pressure might occasion a miscarriage. (*Laughter*). In one little matter, complete success has attended our efforts, *viz.*, as regards the duty on silver-plate. The Abkari cause is also safe in the custody of that redoubtable champion, of whose formidable prowess you can form some idea, when you remember that it was he who so completely put to rout Mr. Goschen's Compensation clauses. It is a matter of no small congratulation to us to welcome Mr. Caine as one of our own Delegates. He first came out to this country with a free and open mind on the Congress question; with that fearless independence which characterizes him, and which always when I see him recalls to my mind those famous lines of Burns—"The man of independent mind is king of men for a' that," he went for his education to Aligarh. Thanks to Mr. Th. Beck and Sir Syed Ahmed, he has come to us, not only a staunch Congressman in principles, but, as one of the Indian Political Agency, he has thrown his indomitable energy and his high-souled advocacy into active support of the movement. Mr. Caine can truly boast that, if he has not succeeded in extorting from Mr. Pritchard and all the most zealons Abkari officers the confession that they are Bacchus and his crew in disguise, they dare not, at least, throw off their masks, while his watchful eye is upon hem, but must continue to do penance in the assumed garb of uncomfortable and uncongenial principles. Leaving Christian to continue his combat with Apollyon, it is when we come to the central proposal of the Congress regarding the Legislative Councils, for the purpose of expanding and putting life in them, that we can congratulate ourselves on being on the verge of an important step. Many have been the circumstances, and many the forces and influences, that have contributed to this result. First and foremost among them is the circumstance that, without legal votes and legal qualifications, we have had the good fortune to become possessed of a member of our own in Parliament. Do not imagine, Gentlemen, that Dadabhai Naoroji or Lalmohan Ghose has at length been returned. But what member, even if we had the direct franchise, could have served us as Mr. Bradlaugh has done during the last twelve months? To say that the whole country is grateful to him for the untiring energy, the indefatigable care, the remarkable ability with which he has watched and worked for its best interests in that House, where he has achieved so honorable a position for himself, can only most imperfectly express the depth and extent of the sentiments that are felt for him throughout the length and breadth of the land. His name has literally become a household word. He is raising up to himself a memorial in the hearts of the people of India, which will reflect more lustre on his name than titles and orders, and endure longer than monuments of brass or marble. (*Loud cheers.*)

We have been fortunate indeed in securing the sympathies of such a champion. No sooner did he return to England than he at once proceeded to redeem the promise he had made on that behalf, by introducing in the House of Commons his India Councils Reform Bill, drawn on the lines which were sketched and formulated at the last Congress, and with which you are all familiar under its justly deserved brief designation of the Madras Scheme. Two important results were the immediate outcome of this step. The scheme which was thus propounded was in its nature a tentative measure, so far as its details were concerned; and it at once drew forth useful and guiding criticism. In several respects its scope was misunderstood, especially as regards its supposed sweeping character which might have been avoided, had we specified in the Congress skeleton sketch the restrictive limitations hedging the qualifications of the electorate. The criticisms of men like Sir W. Hunter and Sir R. Garth, for whose thoughtful, sympathetic and friendly attitude towards Indian progress we are always so deeply grateful, exposed, however, one defect demanding serious consideration, *viz.*, that the scheme was laid on new lines, and had a somewhat theoretical air, which Englishmen rather fight shy of in practical politics. In justice to the scheme, however, it should be said that Sir Richard Garth put his finger on a possible, rather than a probable, result when he thought that it would enable the Hindus to submerge the other Indian communities. Experience has shown that even in a preponderating Hindu electorate it does not happen that Hindus only are elected, as so many other, besides racial, forces and interests concur in influencing the selection. If we may apply the lessons learnt from experience in municipal elections, I may mention the remarkable fact that in the Town Council or, what is now called the Standing Committee of the Bombay Corporation, composed of 12 members, there have been frequently 5 Parsis, 3 Europeans, 2 Hindus and 2 Mahomedans. Sir R. Garth's criticism on this point, however, throws out a warning which should not be hastily disregarded.

But the next result, which the introduction of Mr. Bradlaugh's bill achieved, was gratifying in the highest degree. It at once dispelled the fit of profound cogitation, in which men at the head of Indian affairs are so apt to be lost, that they can never spontaneously recover from it. Lord Cross's Indian Council's Bill promptly saw the light of day in the House of Lords. It was at once the official recognition of the *raison-d-être* of the Congress, and the first fruits of its labours. In itself, however, it was a most halting and unsatisfactory measure. In framing it, the Prime Minister and the Indian Secretary of State, seem to have been pervaded with a conception of the Indian people as a sort of Oliver Twist, always asking for more, to whom it would be therefore a piece of prudent policy to begin with offering as little as possible. The Government Bill may be aptly described as a most superb steam-engine in which the necessary material to generate steam was carefully excluded, substituting in its place colored shams to look like it. The rights of interpellation and of the discussion of the Budget were granted, but the living forces of the elective principle, which alone could properly work them, were not breathed into the organization of the enlarged councils. The omission of the elective principle from the bill was boldly justified by Lord Salisbury on the ground that "the principle of election or government by representation was not an Eastern idea, and that it did not fit Eastern traditions or Eastern minds." I wish to speak of his Lordship with all the respect to which his high talents and great intellectual attainments justly entitle him ; but it is not a little surprising as well as disappointing to find the Prime Minister of England, a statesman who, as Lord Cranborne, was once Secretary of State for India, displaying such profound ignorance of the history of the Indian people and the genius of the Indian mind. The late Mr. Chisolm Anstey, a man of immense erudition, once pointed out at a meeting of the East India Association in London, that "we are apt to forget in this country when we talk of preparing people in the East by education, and all that sort of thing, for Municipal Government and Parliamentary Government, that the East is the parent of Municipalities. Local Self Government in the widest acceptation of the term, is as old as the East itself. No matter what may be the religion of the people who inhabit what we call the East, there is not a portion of the country from west to east, from north to south, which is not swarming with municipalities ; and not only so, but like to our municipalities of old, they are all bound together as in a species of network so that you have ready made to your hand the framework of a great system of representation." Sir H. Maine has shown that the Teutonic Mark was hardly so well organized or so essentially representative as an Indian village community, until the precise technical Roman form was engrafted upon it. (*Cheers.*)

But leaving village communities alone, what do we find at the present day over the whole country but all sorts and conditions of people, from the highest to the lowest, meeting together and transacting the business of their numberless castes, in assemblies which, in their constitution and their mode of working, are the exact prototypes of the Saxon Witans,. from which the English parliamentary institutions have sprung. It is true that circumstances never allowed the representative genius of the people to develop forms and organizations for higher political functions. But it is no less true, that the seed and the soil are there, waiting only for the skilful hand, and the watchful mind, which we of the Congress firmly believe we have secured in the presence of Englishmen in this country. The disdainful attitude of Lord Salisbury as to our aptitude for representative institutions need, however, bring no despair to our minds. His late Chief, Lord Beaconsfield, once said of him on a memorable occasion that he was a man who never measured his phrases or his sweeping assertions. On the contrary, I draw an augury of good hope from his pronouncement and that made by his son Lord Hugh Cecil that "the Indian was not only a good Government, but it was probably the best conceivable Government that the population could possibly live under." On the eve of the passing of the great English Reform Bill, the Duke of Wellington, then the Tory Prime Minister, proclaimed in the same House of Lords that the existing constitution of the House of Commons was perfect, and that the wit of man could not *a priori* have devised anything so perfect. The declaration was received by the Liberals as a sure portent of victory ; and the Reform Bill was passed within little more than a year after. I trust that the Salisbury pronouncement may prove prophetic in the same way. (*Cheers*).

It is needless to discuss Lord Cross's perfunctory measure any further ; even with the amendment which Lord Northbrook succeeded in getting accepted, it left the House of Lords in the same lifeless condition in which it entered. As soon as it reached the House of Commons, Mr. Bradlaugh fastened on it at once. It was true that he had got there his own bill, but Mr. Bradlaugh is a master of parliamentary tactics inferior, if to any, only to Mr. Gladstone. He at once perceived that the supreme struggle was to be no more between one scheme and another, between territorial electorates or local Boards, but that every nerve would have to be strained and every resource husbanded, to obtain in the first place recognition of the elective principle. That secured, everything else would follow in its own good time. With a masterly comprehension of the situation, he placed before the House amendments to the Bill, directed to substitute the process of election for that of nomination. The Bill and the amendments have however all gone the way of the majority, and the session closed without the opportunity of discussing them. Profiting, however, by the lessons in which the experience of the last twelve months was prolific, both without and within the walls of Parliament, Mr Bradlaugh has hit upon the notable expedient of ploughing with Lord Cross's heifer. He has already introduced a new Bill, based on the same lines as Lord Cross's Bill, but vivifying it by the affirmation of the principle for which we are fighting. That Bill will be laid before you for your consideration. It will be for you to deal with it in your wisdom. However you may decide, of one thing I am certain, that you will maintain the character for moderation, sagacity, and practical good sense which you have so arduously acquired by your self-sacrificing and noble labours during the five years of the existence of the Congress. It is not for me to anticipate your verdict. But I am sure you will allow me, out of my anxious solicitude for the triumph of the cause we have all so earnestly at heart, to state the reasons which to my mind make so imperatively for the acceptance of the new draft, in which I cannot but recognize the statesmanlike craft and thorough knowledge of the shifting phases of English politics which Mr. Bradlaugh so eminently possesses, and which, as we all earnestly pray, promises to place him at no distant date in the front ranks of politicians in office, as he already is in the front ranks of those not in office. The old draft, admirably devised in some respects,—with many virtues, and a few faults,—has not proved congenial to the English political mind, averse to new departures, and looking askance at theoretical airs of perfection. The new Bill has, on the other hand, all the elements of success in its favour. Its most striking merit is that it gathers round it the cautious, the carefully weighed, and responsible opinions of some of the best Viceroys we have ever had. Lord Northbrook has pronounced in favour of a properly safe-guarded application of some mode of election. The righteous sympathies of the Marquis of Ripon are as warmly with us as ever, and his great authority weighs on the same side. Still more valuable, as coming from a Viceroy who left only the other day, is the measured and calculated approval which Lord Dufferin has recorded in a despatch, in referring to which I hope I am not making myself liable to the terrors of the Official Secret's Act. In mentioning Lord Dufferin, I will frankly say that we have not sufficiently recognised the great debt of gratitude which we owe to him in this respect. partly, I believe, through ignorance, and partly through misappreciation of the course he adopted, to neutralize opposition against the measures he recommended. An unrivalled diplomatist, his wary statesmanship was apt to assume the hues of the craft of which he is so accomplished a master. He sought an occasion when he could launch his proposals without provoking disagreement, endeavouring rather to conciliate it The epoch-making St. Andrew's Dinner of 1888 offered him the needful opportunity. He knew Scotchmen, and their matter-of-fact character, so inimitably delineated by Charles Lamb. He knew, as that charming essayist tells us, that "surmises, guesses, misgivings, half intuitions, partial illuminations, dim instincts, embryo conceptions had no place in their brain or vocabulary." He drew before his hosts a vivid and alarming picture of imaginary Congress proposals—of "an ideal authoritatively suggested of the creation of a representative body or bodies, in which the official element shall be in a minority, who shall have what is called the power of the purse, and who, through this instrumentality, shall be able to bring the British executive into subjection to their will." But while his excited and valiant hosts rushed off, crying Scotchmen to the rescue, to tilt at windmills, he quietly threw in a sympathetic recognition of our just and legitimate aspirations, and proceeded to record a minute in which he substantially backed up the veritable Congress proposals. In this Despatch Lord Dufferin has briefly described his scheme as a plan for the enlargement of the Provincial Councils, for the enhancement of their status, the multiplication of their functions, the partial introduction into them of the elective principle, and the liberalization of their general character as political institutions. At this year's St. Andrew's dinner, Sir Charles Elliott eulogized Lord Dufferin's speech as epoch-making and fixing the bounds and limits of our demands--'so far and no further.' We are quite content to go as far ; we have never asked to go very much further. We may therefore fairly infer from Sir Charles Elliott's speech that he is in accord and sympathy with the main underlying principles of Lord Dufferin's scheme, and we can therefore congratulate the people of Bengal on their good fortune in possessing a ruler whom we can justly claim to be a true Congresswalla at heart. (*Laughter and cries of Oh! Oh!*)

I will not speculate without official sanction on the views of the present Viceroy. But I may permit myself to remind you that it was to Henry Marquis of Lansdowne that

Macaulay dedicated those speeches, in one of which, dipping far into the future, he spoke about the future Government of India in that noble passage with which we are all familiar: "The destinies of our Indian Empire are covered with thick darkness. It is difficult to form any conjecture as to the fate reserved for a state which resembles no other in history, and which forms by itself a separate class of political phenomena. The laws which regulate its growth and decay are still unknown to us. It may be that the public mind of India may expand under our system till it has outgrown that system; that by good Government we may educate our subjects into a capacity for better government; that having become instructed in European knowledge they may in some future age demand European institutions. Whether such a day will ever come I know not. But never will I attempt to avert or retard it. Whenever it comes, it will be the proudest day in English history. To have found a great people sunk in the lowest depths of slavery and superstition, to have so ruled them as to have made them desirous and capable of all the privileges of citizens, would indeed be a title to glory all our own." The dawn of that day which Macaulay foresaw, in dim, but prophetic, vision, is now breaking on the horizon; the curtain is rising on the drama which unfolds the vista to that title to glory. Let us earnestly hope that the present illustrious bearer of the great historic name of Lansdowne, who, by a wonderful ordering of events, has now come to rule over us, may watch the glowing streaks of light with generous sympathy, and may preside over the march of events with timely and provident statesmanship. *(Loud cheers).*

This weighty concensus of the best viceregal opinion which I have placed before you, in favour of the principle of the new draft, we may expect to be backed up by the potent voice of that Grand Old Man, whom we reverence, not only as the greatest parliamentary leader of modern times, but as the individual embodiment of the highest conception of moral and political duty which English statesmanship has reached in the 19th century. You are aware that Mr. Bradlaugh has recently declared that he was authorized to say that the course pursued by him in reference to the Government Bill, in endeavouring to obtain a recognition of the elective principle, was approved by Mr. Gladstone, who intended to have supported him by speech. It would require considerations of overpowering force, indeed, to persuade us to any course by which we might run the risk of losing such an almost certain pledge of ultimate victory. *(Cheers).*

Another potent factor has come into existence within this year, which is calculated to help us materially—if we confine our efforts to the simple issue of election *versus* nomination—in the force of English public opinion which, without undertaking to pronounce on questions of detail, has now declared itself to a very considerable extent emphatically in favour of the vital principle of election. The credit of informing the English mind and stirring the English conscience on this momentous question belongs to that small band of noble workers who were appointed at the last Congress to plead the cause of India before the great English people in their own country, and who cheerfully crossed the seas in obedience to such a call of duty, without counting the inevitable cost and sacrifice. The task which they undertook was a formidable one; they have discharged it in a manner of which it is difficult to speak too highly. Of the leader of that band I cannot trust myself to speak with sober moderation, when I remember that it is to his genius we owe that flash of light which pointed out the creation of a body like the Congress, as fraught with the promotion of the best interests of English rule in India. I know there are numerous claimants for the credit of the idea, but if I may be pardoned for employing the rudely forcible language of Carlyle, "the firepan, the kindling, the bitumen were his own; but the lumber of rags, old wood, and nameless combustible rubbish (for all is fuel to him) was gathered from hucksters and of every description under Heaven. Whereby indeed hucksters enough have been heard to exclaim: Out upon it, the fire is *mine.*" He brought to bear upon his new enterprise the same zeal and fervour, combined with thoughtful judgment, that he has unsparingly bestowed for so many years upon the cause to which he has devoted his life. His presence on the Congress Deputation entailed a further sacrifice and affliction, for which we can offer no consolation or reparation except our deepest and most respectful sympathy. In his great and noble mission, Mr. Hume *(loud cheers)* had the entire co-operation of a man of no ordinary powers and capacity. The rare and unrivalled powers of oratory which we have learned to admire in Mr. Surendranath Bannerji *(cheers)*—for it is of him I speak—never shone with more brilliant effect than when he was pleading the cause of his countrymen at the bar of the English people, with a fire and energy that extorted universal respect and admiration. They had a powerful coadjutor in my friend Mr. Eardley Norton, who has known so well how to make *splendid* use of the heritage of great thoughts and noble deeds which he received from his distinguished father. Mr. Mudholkar from the Central Provinces did yeoman's service in the same cause and his sober and thoughtful eloquence did not carry less weight than that of his brilliant colleagues. There is no need for me to say anything of the services of Sir William Wedderburn, Mr. Dadabhai Naoroji, and our other friends in England. But I cannot allow this opportunity to pass without grateful acknowledgment of the unceasing toil, the prodigious energy, and the organizing capacity contributed by Mr. William Digby. The delegates assembled here might render no inconsiderable service to our cause if they exerted themselves to stimulate by thousands and tens of thousands the circulation of the Congress paper entitled 'India,' started under the auspices of our British committee and conducted with such marked ability by him, and which has done, and promises to do, more and more, such incalculable benefit to the object we have at heart. The result of the English campaign clearly shows the wisdom of the new plan of operations suggested by Mr. Bradlaugh. It seems to me that success is well within our reach, if we resolutely apply ourselves to obtain, in the first instance at least, the recognition and application of the principle of election in the organization of our Legislative Councils. Let us then strive for it with the sagacity of practical men, who have not learnt in vain the lessons taught by English political history, and who know the value of moderate, gradual, and substantial gain.

To the many reasons which have been set forth in Congress after Congress, proving the imperative need of reformed Councils, another has been now added. The discussion of the Indian Budget in the House of Commons was always more or less of a sham; but it was a sham for which the officials of the India Office thought it at least a matter of decency to shed a tear of remorse. But now Sir John Gorst has boldly and candidly declared in his place in the House that there need be no sham regret at all; that if anything, it was rather to be hoped and wished for, that the House of Commons should not waste its time over the weary farce. (*Shame, Shame*). It is now officially declared that it is right and proper that Parliament should,—to use Mr. Yule's happy way of putting it,—throw "the great and solemn trust of an inscrutable Providence" back into the hands of Providence to be looked after as Providence itself thinks best, with such grace as Providence may choose to pour on the heads of Sir John Gorst, his heirs, successors, and assigns. I think you will agree with me that, when the responsible advisers of the Crown on Indian matters propound doctrines of such a character, it is high time that we should raise our united voice to demand Local Councils posesssing some guarantees for energy and efficiency. (*Cheers*).

It has been said that our united voice is the voice only of a certain portion of the people and not of the masses; and that it is even then the voice of indifference, and not of urgency and excitement. These remarks are intended to be cast as matters of reproach against the Congress; properly understood they constitute its chief glory. If the masses were capable of giving articulate expression to definite political demands, then the time would have arrived, not for consultative Councils but for representative institutions. It is because they are still unable to do so that the function and the duty devolve upon their educated and enlightened compatriots to feel, to understand and to interpret their grievances and requirements, and to suggest and indicate how these can best be redressed and met. History teaches us that such has been the law of widening progress in all ages and all countries, notably in England itself. That function and that duty, which thus devolve upon us, is best discharged, not in times of alarm and uneasiness, of anger and excitement, but when the heart is loyal and clear and reason unclouded. It is, I repeat, the glory of the Congress that the educated and enlightened people of the country seek to repay the debt of gratitude, which they owe for the priceless boon of education, by pleading, and pleading temperately, for timely and provident statesmanship. (*Cheers*).

I have no fears but that English statesmanship will ultimately respond to the call. I have unbounded faith in the living and fertilizing principles of English culture and English civilization. It may be that, at times, the prospect may look dark and gloomy. Anglo-Indian opposition may look fierce and uncompromising. But my faith is large, even in Anglo-Indians. As in the whole universe, so in individuals, in communities, there is a perpetual conflict going on between the higher and lower passions and impulses of our nature. Perhaps some of you have read a little novel, called Dr. Jekyll and Mr. Hyde, the plot of which hinges on the conflict between the two sides of a man's nature, the higher and the lower, embodied each, for the time being, in a separate and distinct individuality. If the lower tendencies are sometimes paramount in the Hydes of Anglo-Indian society, if as our last President, Sir W. Wedderburn said, the interests of the services are antagonistic to and prevail over the interests of the Indian people, it is still the oscillation of the struggle; it is still only one side of the shield. They cannot permanently divest themselves of the higher and nobler nature, which, in the end, must prevail, and which has prevailed in so many honorable, distinguished and illustrious instances. They are after all a part and parcel of the great English nation, bone of their bone, and flesh of their flesh, and they must even work along the main lines of that noble policy which Great Britain has deliberately adopted for the government of this country. When, in the inscrutable dispensation of Providence, India was assigned to the care of England, one can almost imagine that the choice was offered to her as to Israel of old: "Behold, I have placed before you a blessing and a curse; a blessing, if ye will obey the commandments of the Lord your God: a curse, if ye will not obey the commandments of the Lord your God, but go after other gods whom ye have not known."

**1st Day.**

**The President's Inaugural Address.**

All the great forces of English life and society, moral social, intellectual, political, are, if slowly, yet steadily and irresistibly, declaring themselves for the choice which will make the connection of England and India a blessing to themselves, and to the whole world, for countless generations. Our Congress asks but to serve as a modest hand-maid to that movement, asks but to be allowed to show the pits and the falls, asks but to be allowed to join in the blessing which England will as surely earn as there is an " Eternal that maketh for righteousness. " (*Cheers*).

I appeal to all true Englishmen—to candid friends as to generous foes—not to let this prayer go in vain. It may be that we sometimes speak in uncouth and outlandish ways, it may be that we sometimes stray in some confusion of thought and language ; still it is the prayer of a rising, growing and hopeful nation. I will appeal to them to listen to the sage counsels of one of the most careful and observant of their modern politicians, who, like the prophet Balaam, called, I will not say, exactly to curse us, has however blessed us utterly. In his " Problems of Greater Britain, " Sir Charles Dilke thus sums up his views on the Congress : "Argument upon the matter is to be desired, but not invective, and there is so much reason to think that the Congress movement really represents the cultivated intelligence of the country, that those who ridicule it do harm to the imperial interests of Great Britain, bitterly wounding and alienating men who a e justified in what they do, who do it in reasonable and cautious form, and who ought to be conciliated by being met half-way. (*Cheers*). The official class themselves admit that many of the natives who attack the Congress do so to ingratiate themselves with their British rulers and to push their claims for decorations. (*Hear, hear*). Our first duty in India is that of defending the country against anarchy and invasion, but our other greatest duty is to learn how to live with what is commonly called the Congress movement, namely, with the development of that new India which we have ourselves created. Our past work in India has been a splendid task, splendidly performed, but there is a still nobler one before us, and one larger even than that labour on the Irish problem to which our public men on both sides seem too much inclined to give their whole attention." So careful an estimate of the work and spirit of the Congress movement cannot but commend itself to all thoughtful minds.

However that may be, our duty lies clear before us to go on with our work firmly and fearlessly, but with moderation, and above all with humility. If we might be permitted to adopt those noble words of Cardinal Newman, we may say—

Lead kindly light amid the encircling gloom,
    Lead thou me on !
The night is dark and I am far from home,
    Lead thou me on !
Keep thou my feet, I do not ask to see
    The distant path, one step's enough for me. (*Long and enthusiastic cheering*).

I will now ask you to elect the Subjects Committee.

*After some discussion and the reading out of all the names proposed by the several circles and their acceptance by the Congress as a body, the following Subjects Committee was declared to have been duly constituted :—*

**Election of a Subjects Committee.**

CALCUTTA CIRCLE (*includes the presidency and Burdwan Divisions, Orissa, Assam, Sylhet and Cachar*).

1. GEORGE YULE, ESQ. (Calcutta.)
2. C. SWINHOE, ESQ. ( do. )
3. R. D. MEHTA, ESQ. ( do. )
4. A. CHOWDHRY, ESQ. ( do )
5. THE REVD. KALI CHARAN BANERJI ( do. )
6. DR. TROILOKYA NATH MITTER ( do. )
7. PANDIT PRAN NATH SARASVATI ( do. )
8. BABU NORENDRO NATH SEN ( do. )
9. " BHUPENDRA NATH BOSE ( do. )
10. " DEVENDRA CHANDRA GHOSE ( do. )
11. " MOHINI MOHAN CHATTERJI ( do. )
12. " MOTI LALL GHOSE (Jessore).
13. " KALI SHANKAR SUKUL (Narail).
14. " NAFAR CHANDRA PAL CHOUDHRY (Nuddea).
15. " HEERUMBA CHANDRA MOITRO ( do. )
16. " BOIKANTHA NATH SEN (Murshidabad).
17. " TARA PROSONNO MUKHERJI (Burdwan).
18. " BISHNU PODO CHATTERJI (Hooghly).
19. " NURSING CHANDRA DUTT (Howrah).
20. " JOGENDRA CHANDRA ROY (Midnapur).
21. " DHONE KRISTO GHOSE (Birbhum).
22. " GOVIND CHARAN DASS (Tipperah).

**1st Day.**

**Election of a Subjects Committee.**

| Circle | No. | Name | Place |
|---|---|---|---|
| CALCUTTA CIRCLE—(*contd.*) | 23. | BABU BEPIN CHUNDER PAL | (Sylhet). |
| | 24. | „ BARODA CHANDRA HALDAR | (Assam). |
| | 25. | „ JANOKI NATH BOSE | (Orissa). |
| DACCA CIRCLE (*includes the Dacca and Chittagong Divisions*). | 1. | BABU KOILASH CHANDRA SEN | (Dacca). |
| | 2. | „ KISHORILAL SIRKAR | ( do. ) |
| | 3. | „ DWARKANATH GANGULI | ( do. ) |
| | 4. | „ PEARY LAL ROY | (Bakergunge). |
| | 5. | „ RADHA BALLABH CHOWDHRY | (Mymensingh). |
| | 6. | „ PROSONNO KUMAR BOSE | (Tangail). |
| RAJSHAHYE CIRCLE (*includes the Rajshahye Division*). | 1. | BABU RAJKUMAR SIRKAR | (Rajshahye). |
| | 2. | „ KALI KISHORE MUNSHI | (Bogra). |
| | 3. | „ GIRISH CHUNDER ROY | (Pubna.) |
| BHAGALPUR CIRCLE (*includes the Bhagulpur Division.*) | 1. | RAI SURYA NARAIN SING BAHADUR | (Bhagalpur.) |
| | 2. | „ TEJ NARAIN SING BAHADUR | ( do. ) |
| | 3. | DR. LADLI MOHUN GHOSH | ( do. ) |
| | 4. | BABU PARVATI CHARAN DASS | (Purnea.) |
| | 5. | „ AKHILESHVAR PRASAD | (Monghyr) |
| CHOTA NAGPUR CIRCLE (*includes the Chota Nagpur Division.*) | 1. | RAI JADUNATH MUKHERJI | (Hazaribagh.) |
| BEHAR CIRCLE (*includes the Patna Division.*) | 1. | MOULVIE SHURFUDDIN | (Bankipur.) |
| | 2. | „ ABDUL HAMID | ( do. ) |
| | 3. | BABU SALIGRAM SING | ( do. ) |
| | 4. | PANDIT SHAMLAL NARAIN | (Patna.) |
| | 5. | BABU RAGHUBUNS SAHAI | ( do. ) |
| | 6. | PRINGLE KENNEDY, ESQ. | (Mozufferpur.) |
| | 7. | BABU RAMDHAN SAHAI | ( do. ) |
| BENARES CIRCLE (*includes the Benares Division.*) | 1. | SHEIKH NUSSEEROODEEN | (Benares.) |
| | 2. | BABU GOVIND DASS | ( do. ) |
| | 3. | BABU UPENDRANATH BOSE | ( do. ) |
| | 4. | LALA SREE RAM | (Mirzapur.) |
| | 5. | LALA BENI PERSHAD | ( do. ) |
| N. W. P. CIRCLE (*includes the whole N. W. P. except the Benares Division.*) | 1. | PUNDIT MADAN MOHAN MALAVIYA | (Allahabad.) |
| | 2. | „ BULDEO RAM DAVE | ( do. ) |
| | 3. | MUNSHI MADHAVAPRASAD | ( do. ) |
| | 4. | „ SADRUDDIN AHMED | ( do. ) |
| | 5. | BABU CHAROO CHANDER MITTER | ( do. ) |
| | 6. | HAFIZ ABDUL RAHIM | (Allygurh.) |
| | 7. | PUNDIT PRITHI NATH | (Cawnpore.) |
| | 8. | HAKIM FAKRUDDIN | ( do. ) |
| | 9. | LALA DWARKA DASS | (Agra.) |
| | 10. | PUNDIT DAMMI LAL | (Mainpuri.) |
| | 11. | „ RAGHUBEER SARAN | (Meerut.) |
| | 12. | „ HARI RAM PANDE | (Almora.) |
| OUDH CIRCLE (*includes the whole Province of Oudh.*) | 1. | SYED HAMID ALI KHAN | (Lucknow.) |
| | 2. | MUNSHI GUNGAPERSHAD VARMA | ( do. ) |
| | 3. | PUNDIT BISHAN NARAYAN DHAR | ( do. ) |
| | 4. | RAI KAKU MULL BAHADUR | (Fyzabad.) |
| | 5. | LALA GOKAL CHAND | ( do. ) |
| | 6. | BABU PITAM ROY | (Sitapur.) |
| PUNJAB CIRCLE (*incudes the whole Punjab except the Delhi Division*). | 1. | LALA DHURM DAS SURI | (Lahore.) |
| | 2. | DR. PRAMANAND | ( do. ) |
| | 3. | BABU JOGENDRO CHANDRA BOSE | ( do. ) |
| | 4. | BABA NARAYAN SING SODHI | (Amritsar.) |
| | 5. | DR. GUNGADIN | ( do. ) |
| | 6. | CAPTAIN A. BANON | (Kangra.) |
| | 7. | LALA MURLIDHUR | (Umballa.) |
| | 8. | BAKSHI JAISHI RAM | (Julundur.) |

| Circle | No. | Name | Place |
|---|---|---|---|
| Delhi Circle (*includes the Delhi Division*). | 1. | Moulvie M. Rukunuddin Jadoo | (Delhi.) |
| | 2. | „ Shahabudin Sakel | ( do. ) |
| | 3. | „ Nisar Ali Shohrat | ( do. ) |
| Guzerat Circle (*includes Guzerat, Cutch, Kathyawar and Panch Mahals*). | 1. | H. Nanabhai Haridas, Esq. | (Surat.) |
| Bombay Circle (*includes Bombay City and Tanna, Colaba and Ratnagiri districts*). | 1. | D. E. Wacha, Esq. | (Bombay.) |
| | 2. | Daji Abaji Khare, Esq. | ( do. ) |
| | 3. | Narain Vishnu Gokhale, Esq. | ( do. ) |
| Deccan Circle (*includes entire Deccan—(except the Sholapore district)—N. Canara and Khandeish*). | 1. | M. B. Namjoshi, Esq. | (Poona.) |
| | 2. | B. G. Tilak, Esq. | ( do. ) |
| | 3. | S. B. Bhate, Esq. | ( do. ) |
| | 4. | R. P. Karandikar, Esq. | (Satara.) |
| Sholapore Circle (*includes only the Sholapore district*). | 1. | W. S. Caine, Esq. | (Sholapore.) |
| Berar Circle (*includes the whole of Berar.*) | 1. | Deorao Vinayek, Esq. | (Akola.) |
| | 2. | R. N. Mudholkar, Esq. | (Amraoti.) |
| | 3. | G. S. Khaparde, Esq. | (Ellichpur.) |
| Central Provinces Circle (*includes the whole of the C. Pces.*) | 1. | A. Nundy, Esq. | (Jubbulpore.) |
| | 2. | C. V. Nayadu, Esq. | (Nagpur.) |
| | 3. | Lakshman Govind Rao, Esq. | (Wardha.) |
| Madras Circle (*includes the entire Madras Presidency.*) | 1. | P. Ananda Charlu, Esq. | (Madras.) |
| | 2. | V. Sundaram Shastri, Esq. | ( do. ) |
| | 3. | M. Ramaswami Naidu, Esq. | ( do. ) |
| | 4. | M. Viraraghava Chariar, Esq. | ( do. ) |
| | 5. | K. P. Viswanada Iyer, Esq. | (Madura.) |
| | 6. | Tirumalai Mudeliar, Esq. | ( do. ) |
| | 7. | V. Krisnaswami Iyer, Esq. | (Tanjore.) |
| | 8. | P. Rathna Sabapathi Pillai, Esq. | ( do. ) |
| | 9. | R. Sundaram Iyer, Esq. | (Dindigul.) |
| | 10. | S. Kasturiranga Iyengar, Esq. | (Coimbatore.) |
| | 11. | C. Vijiaraghava Chariar, Esq. | (Salem.) |
| | 12. | C. Jambulinga Mudeliar, Esq. | (Cuddapah.) |
| | 13. | C. Chidambara Row, Esq. | (Kurnool.) |
| | 14. | Madhava Row Naidu, Esq. | (Vizianagram.) |
| | 15. | K. Vencanna Pantulu, Esq. | ( do. ) |
| | 16. | J. P. Kotalingam, Esq. | (Cuddalore.) |
| Ex-Officio. | 1. | Pherozshah M. Mehta, Esq. | (President, Bombay.) |
| „ | 2. | Mono Mohun Ghosh, Esq. | (Chairman, Reception Committee, Bengal.) |
| „ | 3. | Sir Romesh Chunder Mitter, Kt. | (Proposer of President. Bengal.) |
| „ | 4. | A. O. Hume, Esq., C. B. | (General Secretary, Punjab.) |
| „ | 5. | The Hon'ble Pundit Ajoodhianath | (Joint-General Secretary, N. W. P.) |
| „ | 6. | J. Ghosal, Esq. | (Joint Secretary, Reception Committee, Bengal.) |
| „ | 7. | Rai Rajkoomar Sarvadhikari Bahadur | ( do. ) |

**1st Day.**

**Election of a Subjects Committee.**

The President.—The Subjects Committee will now proceed to perform their proper functions ; and I therefore adjourn this meeting to-morrow, at 1 o'clock.

**Adjournment of the Assembly.**

Half an hour later, when the Hall had been cleared, and the lamps lighted, the Subjects Committee met and sat until late. Next morning it re-assembled at 10 A.M., and sat until shortly before the re-assembling of the Congress.

# SECOND DAY'S PROCEEDINGS.

## Saturday, 27th December, 1890.

THE Congress reassembled at 1-30 P.M.

**2nd Day.**

THE PRESIDENT.—Gentlemen, in appointing the members of the Subjects Committee, yesterday, two names were inadvertently omitted—the names of two delegates from Assam—Mr. Bipin Chunder Pal and Mr. Majumdar. I beg to propose that these gentlemen's names should, now, be duly entered in the list of the Subjects Committee.

The motion was unanimously agreed to.

THE PRESIDENT.—In commencing the proceedings of to-day I have to make the announcement customary at all our Congresses as to certain rules to be observed in our procedure. It is absolutely necessary that some definite time should be allowed to the speakers, or the Congress might go on for ever. According to our established usage every mover of a resolution will be allowed ten minutes, and the seconders and supporters five minutes; and if speakers will only go straight to the point I am sure they will find that time sufficient. I will now call upon Mr. Lal Mohan Ghose to move the first resolution.

**Res. I. Expansion and Reform of Legislative**

MR. LAL MOHAN GHOSE (*Calcutta, No. 12, in list*).—MR. PRESIDENT AND GENTLEMEN,—I have much pleasure in proposing for your acceptance the following resolution:—

*That this Congress, having considered the draft Bill recently introduced into Parliament by Mr. Charles Bradlaugh, entitled "An Act to amend the Indian Councils Act of 1861," approves the same as calculated to secure a substantial instalment of that reform, in the Administration of India, for which it has been agitating, and humbly prays the Houses of Parliament of the United Kingdom, of Great Britain and Ireland, to pass the same into law; and further that its President, Mr. Pherozshah Mehta, is hereby empowered to draw up and sign on behalf of this assembly, a petition to the House of Commons to the foregoing effect, and to transmit the same to Mr. Charles Bradlaugh for presentation, thereto, in due course.*

It seems to me, Sir, that this new and modified Bill affirms all the great questions of principle upon which we are all agreed, and I venture to think that it stands a much better chance of receiving a favourable consideration at the hands of Parliament than the scheme embodied in Mr. Bradlaugh's original Bill. There are, I believe, certain points on which there prevails an almost absolute unanimity of opinion amongst the thinking and educated classes of our countrymen. We are all united in demanding that there should be some substantial expansion of our Supreme and Local Legislative Councils; and this Bill provides for that expansion by proposing to raise the number of members of the Governor-General's Council to something between 40 and 60, and that of the Council of the various Lieutenant-Governors and Governors of Provinces to something between 36 and 48. Now there is no particular magic in any given number; but it seems to me that this proposal is so reasonable and modest that no honest or candid critic can accuse us of desiring suddenly to revolutionize the Government of this country. (*Cheers*). On the other hand, if there be any amongst us who think that the Bill does not go as far as it might have done in this direction, I would beg of them to remember that it is impossible for us to err on the side of moderation (*hear, hear*); and that the more cautiously these changes and reforms are introduced, the greater is the chance of their ultimate success. (*Cheers*).

The other point upon which we are also agreed is this, that there should be some fair share of popular representation in these councils, and, further, that this popular representation should be based upon some application of the principle of election. Now I have always been of opinion that, wholly irrespective of the capacities or qualifications of the persons whom the Government might nominate under the present system, even when the choice of the Governmemt happens to fall, as I admit it does frequently fall, upon the very men whom we would ourselves be the first to elect—take, for example, the latest instance before us—the nomination by the Viceroy of our distinguished friend Sir Romesh Chander Mitter—(*Cheers*) even in such cases I have always felt that it would greatly improve and strengthen the position of our members of Council if they held their seats by the suffrages of their fellow-countrymen rather than by the grace and favour of the Government. With your permission, Sir, I will read one short sentence from a memorial that was presented to Lord Hartington by a large deputation of English and Indian gentlemen of whom I had the honor to be one, ten years ago, just after the great Liberal victory of 1880 : "Although some of these members" (alluding to the nominated members of Council) "render useful services to the State, it is obvious that so long as all the members are nominated by the Government, however carefully the selection may be made, the members so appointed cannot feel or be credited with that independence, which it is essential they should enjoy, nor can their opinions possess the weight and authority which belongs to the voice of representatives elected by the people." That short sentence, I believe, expresses the unanimous opinion of us all (*cheers*) ; and for my part I am unable to conceive the possibility, even, of any differences of opinion, upon this great question of principle. (*Cheers.*)

But, Gentlemen, the question of representation is such a large one, and it is, moreover, so complicated by the existence among us of a variety of interests apparently conflicting with each other, which nevertheless have to be reconciled and safeguarded, that we must all be prepared to admit that there is very considerable room for honest differences of opinion when you come to discuss any particular method or scheme whereby effect is to be given to those principles to which I have referred. We must bear in mind that in a matter like this we should be prepared to make large and generous concessions to each other. We should be prepared to give and take. We should be ready, even, to make large allowances for the unreasonable prejudices of our political opponents whom we should constantly endeavour to conciliate and win over. Speaking for myself, and having regard to these considerations, to which I have briefly adverted, I must, frankly, tell you that I venture to think that the present modified Bill is a great improvement upon its predecessor. As I said the other day at the Town Hall at one of our meetings, I thought it my duty to abstain from any public criticism of that old Bill so long as it held the field ; but now I am free to admit to you that the scheme of creating an electoral college never commended itself to my judgment. I may be right or I may be wrong. I desire to speak with the utmost respect for those who may have been the authors of that scheme, and also for those who may still cherish some preference for it ; but in my humble judgment it seemed to me to be neither a practicable nor a workable measure. I found no precedent for it in the country whose political institutions seemed to me to furnish the worthiest models for imitation —the country with which our own political destinies are inseparably intertwined. But, Gentlemen, what is of much greater importance is this. That scheme was adversely criticised, not only by leading influential and friendly newspapers in this country, such as the *Statesman* and the *Indian Daily News*, but we have the authority of Mr. Bradlaugh himself, who, in his letter to the British Committee of the Congress, tells us that in England the Bill as read a first time has, with some exceptions, been disapproved by the press of all shades of opinion, and has not been very warmly supported by any considerable number of members of the House. Under these circumstances I myself believe, and sincerely hope and trust, that you will all be of opinion, in spite of any private predilections of your own (because we must be prepared to accept what there is anything like a prospect of getting), that Mr. Bradlaugh has exercised a very wise discretion in recasting the Bill in its present shape, so as to make it more acceptable to the press, to the people and to the Parliament of England. (*Cheers*).

Gentlemen, if this Bill passes into law, as I hope it may, the duty will be cast upon the Government of India of framing a scheme for election subject to the final control and approval of Parliament. And it seems to me that there is at least one great advantage in thus casting this duty upon the Government itself. We have in our midst, as you are aware, a variety of communities who, being in a minority in point of numbers, are, or at least some few members of these profess themselves to be, greatly alarmed at any proposal to introduce the elective principle into the institutions of this country. Well, Gentlemen, these communities, or, more properly speaking, such of the leaders of those communities as have been sounding the note of alarm, can hardly profess to apprehend anything like these dangers from a scheme to be drawn up by the Government of India itself, who surely may be trusted to safe-guard to the fullest extent all the legitimate rights and interests of all the minorities in this country. (*Cheers*). On the other hand, the Hindoo community all over India, who form the great majority in the population of this country, ought to be prepared to make very large and generous concessions : they ought to be prepared to have the largest amount of toleration for those of their brethren, for those of their Mohamedan or Parsee or European fellow subjects, who may fancy that their own special interests are in any way likely to be threatened or invaded. Let us have a spirit of entire toleration; let there be no attempt whatever at dictation; and, above all, let there be no abuse or condemnation, whether of individuals or of classes simply because, as yet, they are unable to agree with us upon every point of our political programme. (*Cheers*).

I think if you approach this great question in that generous spirit there is nothing that can prevent the ultimate triumph of the great cause we have at heart. All the signs of the times seem to be entirely favorable. I find gathered together under this great pavilion representatives of all nations, of all communities inhabiting this great country—a sight which, only a few years ago, nobody would have dreamed of as being possible. We have across the seas in England a British people willing and anxious to extend to us the right hand of fellowship Of late they have given us the sincerest, the strongest, the most convincing proofs of their sympathy. British contituencies have emphatically endorsed the great doctrine of the Queen's Proclamation, the doctrine of the equal rights of all Her Majesty's subjects; they have endorsed them by going so far as even to invite some of your own fellow-countrymen to stand as their Parliamentary representatives. Who among us would have thought, twenty or, even ten years ago, that such a thing was within the bounds of possibility? I ask you, Gentlemen, if these things are not sufficient to cheer us, to encourage us to go on labouring firmly, generously and steadfastly, through good report and through evil report, until we have at last succeeded in convincing the people and Parliament of England that the reforms we ask for are just, moderate and legitimate, and calculated greatly to improve the administration of this country and to broaden and strengthen the foundations of the British Empire in India. (*Cheers*). Gentlemen, our motto is Reform, and not Revolution (*hear, hear*), and my own experience of the just and generous instincts of the English people convinces me that a measure which, like this Bill of Mr. Bradlaugh's, proposes to concede to us some share in the management of our own affairs and some voice in the administration of our own country, some representation in our councils, cannot fail to commend itself to the approval of the English nation. (*Cheers.*)

Mr. Ananda Charlu (*Madras, No. 611, in list*) seconded the motion. He said: Mr. President and Gentlemen,—Within the five minutes allotted to me I propose to undertake the task, not of amplifying, but of abridging and bringing to a focus the position to which this question has advanced. It is said that a poet's best thoughts are his first thoughts; and it so happens that the first thoughts of the Congress, on this question, appear to have been its best thoughts. If you will look at the Bill, which is submitted to our consideration, and compare its provisions with the resolution adopted at the First Congress, you will agree with me that the Congress deserves the praise bestowed upon the poet. The Bill before us is thus briefly described in a report which has been drawn up: "The electorate to be constituted for the purposes of representation is not defined. Mr. Bradlaugh has merely indicated in the Bill that the franchise should be conferred on at least two per cent. of the population of this country. Whether those who possess the franchise are to elect directly the members of Council or are to have immediate representation through an electoral college or colleges, or municipal bodies, or in any other manner, is left undetermined by the Bill itself. The Government of this country will frame the rules, and they will be subject to the sanction of Parliament. The people of India will have the opportunity of expressing their opinions upon the rules so framed, and we may well hope that the sanction of Parliament will not be given to rules that do not command the general assent of the people here." That, in brief, is the position of the Bill. If you will look at the resolution adopted on this subject by the First Congress you will find that it only advocated and emphasized the admission of a considerable number of elected members into the various Councils. But after the First Congress it so happened that there was a howl raised, that the proposition was vague, that there was no system propounded by it, that it was very easy to assert that a certain principle ought to be given effect to, but that the task of systematizing the method and giving effect to it was the real difficulty. (*Hear, hear.*)

Therefore, it was that the Congress did what was really not of much immediate practical use. We were tempted to go into particulars. At the Second Congress by resolution we, no doubt, affirmed and emphasized the resolutions arrived at, at the previous Congress, but we went further and set forth in what manner the electorate might be constituted and we went even further for the purpose of making clear what, in our opinion, the various powers of the Councils ought to be, and so on. That I considered at the time, and I still consider, and am glad to say we shall all now consider, was a work of supererogation. We abdicated a perfectly impregnable position for the purpose of satisfying an unreasoning howl; though, inasmuch as no notice was taken of the resolution first adopted, probably we were not far wrong in considering that we might make a move to attract attention on the part of those who were apparently unwilling to hear. With that view it was that at the Second Congress an amplified system was submitted and adopted. In the Third and Fourth Congresses we proceeded no further. We merely contented ourselves with re-affirming the resolution adopted at the Second Congress. But at the First, Second, Third and Fourth Congresses we equally enunciated the principles on which we relied; and, though we endeavoured to gratify the demand for practical suggestions that was raised, still our voice was as a cry in the wilderness — we were, as it seemed, only beating the air.

At that juncture Mr. Bradlaugh came to our help. No question, be it ever so good, will be taken up by persons in authority until it is brought within the domain of practical politics. That was our position before Mr. Bradlaugh came to our help. Before the last Congress came off however, Mr. Bradlaugh drew up a Bill on the basis of the Calcutta, Madras and Allahabad resolutions, which were practically one, and it became pretty clear that before long the Bill would be introduced into Parliament. That was an immense step, and a very useful step, in bringing the question within the domain of practical, politics, for as we saw, later, as soon as that step *was* actually taken, in came the Government with a Bill of its own—the Bill known as Lord Cross's Bill. To return, Mr. Bradlaugh drew up a Bill in accordance with the resolutions arrived at by the Congress in previous years. Before the last Congress was held that Bill was widely circulated, and it was sent to the various Congress Committees in this country. It was carefully looked into, and a scheme was submitted going into further particulars. Now that there was somebody to listen to us, now that there was somebody to give the matter a push in the proper direction, it was felt that, having gone so far, we must complete our work: and the last Congress adopted a resolution still further amplifying previous resolutions. Then Mr. Bradlaugh drew up and introduced a Bill in accordance with this our latest resolution; Lord Cross then at once came forward with his Bill and blocked this Bill, while our supporters in Parliament blocked Lord Cross's Bill, and nothing came of either.

Now a fresh start had to be made, and it became necessary to pause and consider whether it was worth our while, whether it was wise, to adhere to the position we had taken up by the Bombay resolution. That resolution set forth in some detail a definite scheme for giving effect to the principles in regard to which we were all agreed, and, though, as a matter of fact, we only offered this as a suggestion, those opposed to us seemed to fancy that the principles were dependent on the appropriateness of the details suggested, and everybody began to pick holes in these. Destructive criticism was to be found in abundance, but unfortunately no *practical* suggestions, for improving our avowedly tentative and suggestive scheme. The great merit of the present Bill is that there can be no longer any more destructive criticism upon it. It erects an independent platform, on which every one, who wishes to be heard, must come with some constructive criticism, and it is on that platform that the question will have to be fought out. The question is between Governmental selection and popular election. If election by the people be accepted, then there arises the further question whether the election is to be direc or indirect. And next, if it is to be indirect, is it to be by the bodies already existing in the municipalities or in any other way? All these are questions which remain to be discussed in the future, when this present Bill establishing our main principles has passed the two houses of Parliament. Therefore, Gentlemen, in adopting this proposition we give up no principle that we have enunciated in the past. We only abstain from reiterating former suggestions as to the methods in which effect might be given to those principles.

One word more before I retire. This is the year 1891. Lord Ripon's scheme of Local Self-Government was introduced in 1882. A year before that Mysore witnessed the birth of the germ of a system of Local Self-Government, called by courtesy a representative assembly. That so-called representative assembly has been greatly modified and improved during the past year, has in fact become, now, a reality; and I hope that this coming year will witness a similar advance, where we are concerned, to that which took place in 1882 in India over what had been done in Mysore in 1881. *(Cheers)*.

MR. C. V. NAYADU (*Central Provinces, No. 604, in list*) —MR. CHAIRMAN AND BROTHER DELEGATES,—It is a great pleasure to me to attend this huge gathering and grand assembly, consisting of various castes, creeds and colours, hailing from all parts of the country, to discuss the political grievances of this vast Empire, and to submit its deliberations to the Imperial Parliament, which is the home of freedom and the abode of justice. This gathering is an indication of the tendency of the public mind to appreciate the importance of this national movement, which is the surest guarantee of the progress and libertyof the Indian people, and Progress and Liberty are, as you know, the great characteristics of the British nation, and the means of satisfying in the purest form the cravings of the Indian mind. Sir, I come as a humble delegate from the Central Provinces, and I hope I shall be able to do my duty honestly as a delegate by truly representing the views of my electors in those Provinces. In fulfilment of this duty I have come here to support the resolution, which embodies the adoption of Mr. Bradlaugh's Bill, and I do so most heartily. During my sojourn in England, where I remained for three years, studying at the Cambridge University, I had the pleasure of submitting a similar resolution to the Indian Civil Service Society at Cambridge, by whom it was carried by a good majority. (*Cheers*). I also submitted and succeeded in carrying a proposal of a like nature in the Hardwick Society, consisting of lawyers, in London, where our esteemed friend and orator Mr. Surendra Nath Banerji lately delivered an address. I may further state that I had the pleasure of submitting a Bill, embodying the same principles to the Paddington Parliament. Perhaps, some members present do not know what the Paddington Parliament is. Let me inform them that London boasts of local imitation Parliaments of its own, which are formed on the model of the Imperial Parliament. It was my good fortune to represent at the Paddington Parliament the highest Indian official, the Secretary of State for India (*Cheers and laughter*), and in that capacity I had the satisfaction of carrying the Bill through the various readings, after a strong opposition from the Conservative party, without, at the latest stage, a single dissentient voice; and I earnestly hope that this (Mr. Bradlaugh's) Bill will be carried with the same enthusiasm and unanimity in the Imperial Parliament of Great Britain. (*Cheers*). I am sorry my limited time of five minutes prevents me from entering into the details of the resolution, but I hear the warning bell of the President, and as it has been fully and ably dealt with by my predecessors, the proposer and the seconder, it will suffice if I content myself with very heartily supporting it. (*Cheers.*)

MR. DAJI ABAJI KHARE (*Bombay, No. 555, in list*).—MR. PRESIDENT and GENTLEMEN,—You have all no doubt come to the conclusion that the Bill which is at present proposed is a very good one and that we were, perhaps, not quite right in giving support to the elaborate scheme agreed upon at the last Congress. But I think that scheme has done us very good service, and that service is this. We have been blamed for being led by the nose, as it were, by the people of Bengal; but it appeared by our procedure last year that Madras was to prevail over all others. In giving our support to the principle of this Bill we of course admit that there may arise a variety of opinions as to the details of the scheme that will have to be worked out in giving effect to its provisions. What we all insist upon is this, that the rules and regulations which the Bill says the Government of India will frame shall be published before hand in this country so as to give us the advantage of being able to criticize them before the Government of India passes them and sends them for the approval of the Secretary of State in England and the Houses of Parliament. Substantially, of all that we wanted, we have the germs in this Bill. We accept it confessedly as only an instalment, but an instalment which we should gratefully receive. The Bill as it stands may be open to those general objections which have been taken from time to time to the introduction of representative institutions into this country; but I can assert without fear of contradiction that this Bill offers to us no big jump in the dark. It demands no Parliamentary institutions. No doubt it will bring into the Council some educated people elected by the masses at large, or by those on whom the franchise will be conferred; but the charge that the Congress is worked in the interests of educated people only is quite unfounded. We see that the present nominations that the Government is making are chiefly from the educated people in India; and if we choose from the educated people we think we can do it better than the Government themselves. (*Hear, hear*).

PUNDIT MADAN MOHAN MALAVIYA (*N.-W. Provinces, No. 394, in list*)—MR. CHAIRMAN, LADIES AND GENTLEMEN,—It gives me very great pleasure to be allowed to speak in support of this resolution, not only because it is the most important of all the resolutions before the Congress, but also because I have always taken the keenest interest in the discussion of the subject of the resolution. You very well know that it is the position created by Lord Cross's Bill that has necessitated the introduction of the new Bill by Mr. Bradlaugh, and all that you are now required to do is to express your approval and record your support of that new Bill. There is, no doubt, a good deal of difference between this Bill and the previous one; but, as has been pointed out by other speakers, the difference lies, not in principle, but in matters of detail, and so long as the principle is assured, we should be satisfied with any, though a very modest, instalment of reform. (*Cheers*). Let us hope, however, Gentlemen, that while we are thus willing to be satisfied with even so modest a measure of reform as that embodied in Mr. Bradlaugh's Bill, those with whom it lies to accept or reject our proposals will lend a more willing and kindly ear to our representations of this year than they have hitherto done. (*Cheers.*)

It must at the same time be clearly understood that it is not because we think that our demands in previous years were immoderate or unreasonable that we accept Mr. Bradlaugh's Bill. We have ever been moderate in our demands, as moderate as the circumstances of the country and the situation we were in required us to be. The one consideration that has induced us to accept Mr. Bradlaugh's Bill is a desire to conciliate, so far as may be in our power, without, of course, sacrificing the principle we have been contending for, those of our opponents who think the reform we have been seeking might lead to undesirable results. I hope that no reasonable man will any longer hesitate in giving the Bill his best support, and that Parliament will soon pass it into law. (*Cheers.*)

If it be otherwise, Gentlemen, we shall all, we and other civilized countries, be greatly surprised and disappointed; for, Gentlemen, what is it that we ask for? Is it not for a limited and qualified—an extremely limited and qualified—application of that principle of representation in the administration of this country, which the genius of the English nation has for 600 long years recognised to be that best calculated to make governments good and the governed happy and prosperous? Six hundred years ago, when the victory of Lewes had laid the despotism of King John low, and England breathed the air of liberty under Earl Simon de Monfort, an English poet well expressed the theory of governments. Said he: "Let the community of the realm advise, and let it be known what the generality, to whom their own laws are best known, think on the matter. They who are ruled by the laws know those laws best. They who make daily trial of them are best acquainted with them, and since it is their own affairs which are at stake, they will take more care and will act with an eye to their own peace. It concerns the community to see what sort of men ought justly to be chosen for the weal of the realm." Ever since that time this has been the guiding principle of English political existence. Englishmen have extolled it in theory and maintained it in practice at the sacrifice of a large amount of treasure and life. They have carried it with them wherever they have gone, and the nations of Europe, long held in bondage by their despots, have learnt it at the feet of England and thrived under it. (*Cheers.*) Englishmen rightly feel a pride in having been the apostles of this political christianity, and Mr. Gladstone expressed a widely prevalent belief, when speaking at the Piccadilly Hall in May last. He said: "It often happens in the counsels of Providence that each nation, or some particular nation, is appointed to work out great social, political or economical problems for the world at large. It has been given to this country, almost exclusively, to work out for the benefit of the world at large enormous advantages. In the adoption of that system (the system of representation) we long stood alone, but one after another the great countries of the world have come in, and the nations sprung from our loins have given further countenance and currency to our example, and now the man would be deemed mad who should denounce the system of popular representation." (*Cheers*). But I need not dilate further on this point. Everyone, if, as Mr. Gladstone says, he is not mad, or (permit me to add) if he has not been degenerated by contact with the worst phases of Oriental thought, will admit the soundness of the principle. And it is only for a partial introduction of this principle into the administration of our country that we have been so long, and hitherto vainly, praying. (*Cheers*).

I will now briefly deal with those objections which have been brought against the introduction of that principle here. The principal point of difference between ourselves and the Government in the matter of the reform of the Councils is as regards the manner of appointing the members of the Councils. The Government seem determined to retain the power of appointing *all* the members in their own hands exclusively. We think it absolutely necessary for the cause of good government that the people should have the privilege of electing at least *some* of the members. We discussed, most of you might remember, this question very fully last year, and I did hope that nothing further need be said to prove the grave disadvantages of leaving the power of nominating *all* the members of the Councils entirely in the hands of Government, and the necessity and expediency of allowing the people some voice in the appointment of *some* at least of those who are officially described as the representatives of the people. But I am sorry to find that there are still people who fail to understand the question. Possibly Gentleman, it will be enough for me to mention, in this connection, that even the *Times* of London—perhaps, at *present*,—for if the Radicals get into power it will be Radical forthwith—the most conservative of papers in existence—has denounced the system of nomination. In commenting on Lord Cross's Bill the *Times* said: "There is no doubt force in the argument that nomination is not calculated to give the Government the advantage of contact with some highly important factors in Indian society; no Government is likely to select as its advisers persons conspicuous for their political opposition, and thus the Viceroy's choice is almost certain to be hampered on the side where, perhaps, information at first hand is most needed." But that is not all. If the Government in England can seldom be expected to choose men conspicuous for their political opposition as councillors, the Government in India are even more unfavourably situated here in this respect. Our Government officials,—the district officials, for it is through them that the Government chooses here members for the Council—are much less in touch with the people here than the officials in England. How—here where, Gentlemen, the great majority of respectable people abstain from visiting officials because they have to leave their shoes outside the bungalow and their carriages outside the compound—can we expect the Government officials, the chief authorities through whom recommendations for councillorships are made, to know and select those persons best fitted to help the Government in the work of legislation, and good government?

If, therefore, Gentlemen, Government wish to increase the number of members of the Council without giving us the right of electing some of them, let them not extend that cruel mercy to us. It will be the unkindest service the Government could render to the people. Is it necessary for me to tell you why? We have been complaining, as it were, that our homes and hearths are not properly protected, and that with the present chowkidars our homes and property are not safe. We have prayed for an increase of their number and for some voice in their appointment, that we may have some control over them, and how does the Government respond to our prayer? It wishes to increase the number of chowkidars without giving us even a shadow of control ever them. It proposes to arm them with very fine weapons, the weapons of interpellation and the right of discussing the budget; but

2nd Day.

Res. I. Expansion and Reform of Legislative Councils.

it gives us no guarantee as to how those weapons will be used. When you wanted those weapons to be placed in the hands of persons whom you could trust, Government wishes to place them in the hands of men on whom you have no reliance, and who, for all that we know, might turn those weapons against us to do us injury thereby. (*Cheers*).

It is all very well for the Government to wish to nominate half a dozen more members into the Council, so that wherever any measure is brought forward, wherever any fresh tax is to be imposed, and the organs of public opinion loudly protest that the country is poor and unable to bear further burthens, these nominees of the Government may be trotted forth in Council to say that the country was never so happy and prosperous. It would be like those chowkidars saying, when we complain of our property being robbed: "You prefer this complaint so that you may escape taxation. You have not lost your property. It has not been stolen. You have yourself removed it to some other place to make a plea for escaping rightful taxation." The additional nominated members will be very much like those additional chowkidars over whom we shall have no control whatever (*hear, hear*), who will in no way be accountable to us for their conduct. Do you think, under these circumstances, there was no justification for the remark of one whom we highly respect, the greatest friend of India and England yet born, need I name Mr. Hume (*loud cheers*) when he said regarding the proposals of Government that when we asked for bread the Government cast a stone in our faces?

I am afraid I have taken up too much of your time (*cries of "go on"*) I thank you for the concession, which I hope will be confirmed by the President. I will not dwell further on the disadvantages of the system of nomination. I will now briefly deal with another important point, namely, what some of the Viceroys and the Secretary of State, and particularly the Marquis of Salisbury, have said to be the chief obstacle in the way of introducing the principle of representation in the administration of this country. They have said that no constituency could be found in India to which the privilege of electing members could be extended. It seems to me that nothing could be sadder than to see the Premier of England occupying the high position that he does, and the Secretary of State for India, putting forth such an utterly false and groundless plea against the introduction of the principle of representation in this country It was to be expected that having had such long parliamentary careers, and having lived the greater part of their lives in England, the home of parliamentary institutions, they would know that constituencies are created not by the people but by the Government. The elements which go to make up a constituency no doubt exist; but until the Government chooses to confer the franchise on those elements, no constituency can possibly be created. But then they have the hardihood, I had almost said the audacity, to deny that there exist elements in India sufficient to form constituencies in this country. There also they show their utter ignorance—ignorance which, at any rate, is not pardonable in such men when they discuss political questions of grave importance—of the history of their own country and Parliament. You will, I am sure, agree with me when I say that no electorates that might be formed here could be half as bad as those which existed in the Anti-Reform days in England before the period of the passing of the Reform Bill. You have all heard of the close and rotten boroughs. But close and rotten as they were, even they did excellent service to the English nation by returning some of the brightest and most illustrious men of England to Parliament. Lord North, Mr. Burke, Mr. Pitt, Mr. Fox, Lord Granville, the Marquis of Wellesley, Mr. Canning, Lord Brougham, Lord Grey, and a host of others like them, were first elected by close and rotten boroughs. Mr. Sheridan was returned by a constituency of only 70 electors, and Mr. Wyndham by 145 electors. The great Lord Chatham was first returned by old Sarum, and his son, the renowned Mr. Pitt, the great parliamentary leader and minister, was returned by a constituency numbering only 100 electors. These close and rotten boroughs, therefore, rendered very good service to the country. It is anything but probable that these men would have found their way to Parliament, and their valuable services have been secured to their country if the only entrance to it had been in the hands of Government. How could the Government have known their talents and abilities, and would it have been so saintly as to select men who were noted for their independence and their hatred for all but what was righteous and just? (*Cheers*).

I have already received, Gentlemen, a note of warning from the President that I should not go further; but I hope he will permit me to say one word with regard to another objection put forth by Viscount Cross and Lord Salisbury in their speeches on the second reading of the Official Indian Reform Bill. Said the Secretary of State for India, "as was well said by the late Mr. Henry Maine in speaking of India: 'There is no more resemblance between a Punjabee and a Bengalee, between an Indian of Hindustan and an Indian of Malabar, than there is between an Englishman and a Roumanian, or between a Spaniard and a Swede.'" The Marquis of Salisbury added: "The difficulty of introducing the elective principle, largely dependent upon the peculiarities of Eastern minds, is also, to a great extent, as the noble Lord pointed out, due to the fact that we have to deal with a deeply divided population. Representative government answers admirably so long as all those who are represented desire much the same thing and have interests tolerably analogous; but it is put to an intolerable strain when it rests upon a community divided into two sections, one of which is bitterly hostile to the other and desirous of opposing it upon all occasions." I think, Gentlemen, this grand assembly, composed of men of all the different provinces of India, is a living refutation of their Lordships objection. (*Cheers*). It is absolutely untrue to say that the two great sections of our community are utterly hostile to each other and desirous of opposing each other on all occasions. Their interests are not only "tolerably analogous," but identical in nine hundred and ninety-nine cases out of every thousand that could come before the councils. The absence of a common faith, which Lords Cross and Salisbury considered a valid excuse for not introducing the elective principle here, is purely imaginary. They, no doubt, follow different religious persuasions, but there exists amongst them a common faith which is—

> "Taught by no priest, but by their beating hearts,
> Faith to each other; the fidelity
> Of fellow-wanderers in a desert place,
> Who share the same dire thirst and therefore share
> The scanty water; the fidelity
> Of men whose pulses leap with kindred fire,
> Who in the flash of eyes, the clasp of hands,
> The speech that even in lying tells the truth
> Of heritage, inevitable as past deeds,
> Nay, in the silent bodily presence feel
> The mystic stirring of a common life,
> Which makes the many one." (*Loud Cheers*).

I think, Gentlemen, we have shown all the most important objections brought forward by Lords Cross and Salisbury, and their like, to be untenable, and I earnestly hope that even they will lend their support to the new Bill introduced by Mr. Bradlaugh. (*Cheers*).

PUNDIT BISHEN NARAYAN DHAR (*Oudh, No. 483, in list*)—MR. CHAIRMAN, LADIES AND GENTLEMEN,—The discussion has hitherto been confined to the matter of principle involved in the resolution; but I think it is well, after the discussion of the principle of representation, that the delegates should also give their opinion upon the different points of detail, which are nearly as important as the principle itself. It was well said by Mr. Caine last evening that to-day's debate will be read with great interest by the Houses of Parliament, and I think Parliament should know the opinions of the delegates not only upon the principle of election, but also upon certain matters of detail. That portion of the Bombay scheme, which has excited the greatest amount of attention and public criticism in my part of India, is the clause providing for the representation of minorities—meaning, of course, Mohammedan minorities—upon the Legislative Councils. I wish that this portion of the subject had been discussed by my friend Mr. Hamid Ali, who is absent to-day. I think it is as well that the Congress and also the Houses of Parliament should be in a position to know the sentiments of at least most of my friends in Oudh and the N.-W. P. on the subject. I rejoice that the Congress has this year omitted the details; and that even the clause for the representation of minorities which does appear in the present Bill is in a very mild form as compared with that embodied in the previous Bill. I always thought that that minorities clause was a mistake. I object to the principle of it on two grounds. I object to it because I think that what are called Hindu interests and Mohammedan interests have really no existence in political matters. (*Cheers*). The provision in the Bombay scheme was simply to give satisfaction to those of our critics who thought that the interests of minorities would be sacrificed unless there was some express provision in the scheme itself. But besides that I think that the Legislative Council is a body where national interests ought to be represented, and where all sectarian interests and class bias should be excluded. The object of a National Assembly is only to discuss those matters which are common to the whole Indian nation. On principle, therefore, I object to any clause for the representation of minorities. But I object on another ground also. I am glad that the Congress has left these matters of detail in the hands of Government, because it will save the Congress from a good deal of odium, and throw upon the Government the entire responsibility of adjusting the conflicting interests, so-called, of the Hindu and Mohammedan communities. But, Gentlemen, from this change of front, if I may so call it, in the National Congress, we must not expect too much. We must not think that it will conciliate our official opponents, or that it will in any measure soften the hearts of Sir Syed Ahmed and his friends. There was a time when Sir Syed Ahmed talked unceasingly on the unity of Hindus and Mohammedans; but now, like Timon of Athens, he has nothing but curses and imprecations on his lips for those who, in the political sphere at least, are trying to remove all invidious distinctions of colour and creed. I do not blame him because I think he and his friends are in this matter mere

2nd Day.

Res. I. Expansio and Reform of Legislative Councils.

tools with which a certain section of the official class works out its own designs. I feel deeply the responsibility of my words, and I do not hesitate to say, from what I know in my experience in the United Provinces, that whatever we hear about Mohammedan opposition to political reform and about the antagonism of Hindu interests and Mohammedan interests, is due to the deliberate policy adopted by certain members, at any rate, of the governing classes. (*Cheers*).

It is a serious charge to bring against officers of Government, that they want to keep the people disunited, and seek to follow the low, evil maxim ".divide and rule." But I am prepared to show from the writings of Anglo-Indian statesmen, who have held high position in this country, that some of them, at any rate, do believe that race antagonisms and religious rivalries are the chief factors that contribute to the strength and permanence of British rule in this country. (*Cheers and cries of " shame !"*). On this point I will quote the words of Sir John Strachey in a recent lecture on India: " So far as any elements of political danger from Mohammedans exist they are completely nullified by the fact that the feelings of all true Mohammedans towards idolatrous Hindus are far more hostile than towards Christians; and any religious outburst on their part would be met by Hindus with equal animosity and greater strength. The truth plainly is that the existence side by side of these hostile creeds is one of the strong points in our political position in India. The better class of Mohammedans are already a source of strength and not of weakness, and a continuously wise policy might, I believe, make them strong and important supporters of our power. They constitute a small but energetic minority of the population whose political interests are identical with ours, and who under no conceivable circumstances, would prefer Hindu dominion to our own." I think these words very clearly show what Sir John Strachey means. He means that the existence side by side of two hostile races in India is a strong point in its Government, and it follows, as a matter of course, that the strong point ought to be taken advantage of by the government, and that these animosities ought to be kept up, and kindled, if need be, to make the British rule more secure. (*Loud cries of " shame, shame "*).

I call that an immoral doctrine (*Cheers.*) I call it a shameful policy for those who have faith in the teachings of Christianity. At the same time it cannot be denied that that is the deliberate policy of some sections of our Indian bureaucracy. In the United Provinces we see the fruit of the seed that has thus been sown. This fruit is bloodshed and bitterness in the United Provinces; and in recent years the religious disputes between Mohammedans and Hindus, are, in the mind of every well-wisher of his country, a cause of regret or shame. For my part I attribute them entirely to the policy which the Government, or at any rate some of its component parts, have adopted towards this country. I know that Lord Lansdowne has administered a gentle rebuke to the contending parties, and Sir A. Colvin has also said something to the same effect; but can you believe that those words can have any effect upon the public mind so long as the policy of numbers of the local representatives of the Government is to maintain these differences as among the chief factors which contribute to its permanence?

We all know that those disputes in any aggravated form are of recent origin. Ten years ago they hardly existed. Even in Mohammedan times, Hindus and Mohammedans lived togther peaceably. Even in times when, according to Sir James Stephen, the Mohammedans proposed to everybody the alternative of the Koran or the sword, Hindus enjoyed equal rights with Mohammedans, held the highest posts, and governed large sections of Mohammedans. But it appears to me that the Government of India, for it is, in the last analysis, this Government which must be held responsible for the acts of its subordinates, the Government of India, I say, has adopted a different policy. I think that Government may be reminded of a certain fact in the history of India. There was a time when India was divided into small sects., when the Mohammedans stood aloof from the conquered people, when the doctrines of religious toleration and free discussion were unknown. Enough time had not elapsed to mitigate the existing differences. At that stage there appeared a man who was destined to be the greatest Mohammedan ruler that India ever had. He adopted a new policy, he tried the grand and successful experiment of basing his rule not upon the fears of the people, but upon their affections. (*Cheers.*) He ignored all class and religious differences, and proclaimed for the first time, in this country, the doctrine of universal toleration; and by his wise, noble, and far-seeing policy, he raised the Mogul Empire to a power and a glory that excited the envy and admiration of the world. Is that noble policy of Akbar going to be reversed by the British Government? Are the British people, who are "the heirs of all the ages," and "in the foremost files of time," going to reverse that policy and adopt a different one? " Divide and rule" may be a good principle for a time; but when a higher and a purer moral consciousness dawns upon the minds of our rulers, I believe they will see that that power alone is secure which rests upon the affections and the will of the nation. (*Cheers.*)

LALA HUKUM CHAND (*Panjab, No. 525, in list*)—BROTHERS!—I have purposely used the term brothers, because we *are* all brothers; whatever religion we may follow, whatever calling we may pursue, whatever part of the world we may inhabit, we are all brothers ; our political interests are united, and we should be one (*cheers*)—one in the interests of the public and in the welfare of the country. I thank the President for permitting me to speak in support of this resolution already proposed, seconded and supported by eminent speakers of this learned country. It will be well if the Bill in its present form should pass. The proverb says that something is better than nothing. We shall not gain all we want by the adoption of this Bill, but in the end our object will be achieved. It is said that India is not a nation. I maintain that India is a nation, and this assembly is a proof of my assertion. Men have gathered together here from all the different parts of the Empire ; men, adherents of all the different religions and creeds of this vast Empire, and why ? To promote the welfare of their country, and to ask the Government to do something for the prosperity of their nation. We make no distinction of province, creed, or people on this our national platform. All are one. (*Cheers.*) I gladly support this resolution. (*Cheers*).

Mr. V. Krishna Swami Iyer (*Madras, No. 642, in list*)—Mr. President, Ladies and Gentlemen,—I make no preface and offer no apology for my presence here. I will simply state a few facts in connection with Mr. Bradlaugh's Bill and then retire. The Congress has been frequently charged with being immoderate in its demands. I will show you that that charge is absolutely without foundation. Take the first point. Mr. Bradlaugh's Bill says that one-third of the members of the Legislative Councils, at least, ought to be elected. Let me ask you to remember what the resolution was that you passed at the Congress in Calcutta four years ago. You then said that you would have not less than one-half of the members elected, and Mr. Bradlaugh in his Bill, presented at the beginning of this year, said that out of the 80 members he wanted that 40 should be elected—a proportion of one-half. In the present Bill the proportion insisted on is only one-third. Is not that a proof of the moderation of the Congress ? Take another instance. Mr. Bradlaugh first asked that the Viceroy's Council should consist of 80 members and the Lieutenant-Governor's 76 members ; but in the present Bill it is said that the Viceroy's Council should consist of between 40 and 60 members, and the Lieutenant-Governor's of 36. Is not that again a proof of the moderation of the Congress. ? In the first Bill it was provided that whenever there was a difference of opinion between the Executive and the Legislative Council, when the Legislative Council carried a measure against the wishes of the Executive Council, the Viceroy might veto it ; but he was bound to state the reasons, which were to be submitted to a Standing Committee of the House of Commons. There is no mention of that in the present Bill : there is no necessity for the Viceroy to state the reasons for overruling the decision of the majority of the Legislative Council. This abandonment of that portion of the scheme, justified by political prudence as one means, in Mr. Bradlaugh's opinion, of recommending the measure to the British electorate, is, I claim, a further and signal proof of the moderation of the Congress. (*Cheers*).

But I do not wish it to go forth and be understood in England that we accept every proposition of this Bill. There are some portions to which we cannot give acceptance, and to which we desire to draw the attention of Mr. Bradlaugh and of the British electors. It is said in the Bill that one-third of the members of Councils, Provincial or Imperial, at least, shall be elected, and not more than one-half. I think, and my friends who agree with me upon the matter think, that there should be no maximum limit imposed. Not that we claim that more than one-half, say three-fourths or four-fifths, should be elected, but that it should be left to the discretion of the Government of India, the minimum being fixed, to extend the number from time to time as they might desire. (*Cheers*). That is a matter upon which I should like to have a distinct pronouncement before the resolution is passed. Then there is another point. The original Bill stated that the tenure of office of every member of Council should be three years. In the present Bill, although three years is the term of office of a member of the Local Councils, the tenure of office of the Viceroy's and Lieutenant-Governor's Council is only two years. (*Cries of "no, no, you misunderstand the Bill."*) Well, that is how I interpret the draft, and I ask you to consider whether it is not desirable that a member of the Viceroy's Council, not merely for the sake of uniformity with local Councils, but on the score of principle, should hold his seat for three years in order that he may be able to render good service by means of the experience he has acquired in the Council. Is two years a sufficient period ? (*Cries of "But you are wrong, the Bill provides three years for all."*) If it be so I am satisfied, but that is not how I read it. Then it is provided in one of the clauses that the sanction of Parliament has to be obtained to any rules passed by the Viceroy with reference to interpellation and the discussion of the Budget in his own Council ; but Local Councils may make rules subject to the sanction of the Viceroy, and it is not necessary that they should be brought before Parliament for its sanction. I do not think you would allow such a statement to remain in the Bill. (*Cries of "There is no such statement."*) I think it would be the unanimous sense of the meeting that there ought to be no difference in the matter of interpellation and the discussion of the Budget as between the Viceroy's Council and the Local and Legislative Councils. (*Hear, hear, but you are wrong.*) Well, if that is not the intention of the Bill, then in Section 2, after the words "and any rule made" you must insert the words "or sanctioned."

To return to the charge of want of moderation. Look at a province which is directly under the control of the Government of India—the province of Mysore. That province has had a representative assembly for the last ten years. In the year 1881 the Dewan of Mysore created the nucleus of a representative assembly. It did not possess political privileges, but it had the right of stating grievances to the Maharaja. Last year, I believe, the Dewan of Mysore made a new and important departure with regard to the constitution of that assembly. As the arrangement now stands the franchise is restricted to persons having a certain property qualification—the payment of 100 rupees to the Government; but Local Boards and Municipalities are also entitled to elect a certain number of members. The persons elected in each district meet in the district itself, and they elect representatives to attend the representative assembly in Mysore, and that assembly has a right to put any question it likes to the Dewan and the Maharaja, and is entitled to receive an answer. That assembly has been created in a province which has not received the benefit of liberal education to the same extent as the provinces directly under the control of England, and has enjoyed this privilege in its original form for a considerable time, and statesmen ruling over that country have testified to the wisdom of the further advance made by the present Dewan.

I should like to read one short paragraph from the speech of the late Dewan, Mr. C. Ranga Charlu, C. I. E., delivered on the 26th of October 1882 to the Mysore Representative assembly.

He said: "If the spread of any high degree of education among the great mass of the people were to be insisted upon as a *sine qua non*, we may have to wait for ever; meanwhile every year under an autocratic system of Government will find the people less fit for representative institutions. The sprinkling of educated men who are sure to be found in these representative bodies will serve for all purposes of leading and guiding, but what is required in the great body of the representatives is common sense and practical views, which are sure to be possessed by men of ordinary knowledge engaged in industrial and other useful occupations."

It was not, you see, that the people should all of them be educated: it was not that there should be a large proportion of the people educated before they were entitled to have conferred upon them the privilege of electing members to the Legislative Council; the mere fact that there is a considerable body of the people, not necessarily a large percentage but a large body of educated people, who are qualified to take an intelligent interest in the proceedings of the Government, entitles them, according to the late Prime Minister of Mysore, to a voice in the administration. The fact that they are a "microscopic minority," or that they are not a large percentage of the people, is not to form a reason for their being debarred from enjoying the privilege of electing members or discussing Budgets. (*Cheers*). How so infinitely superior a man, as Mr. Ranga Charlu, was only utilized by Providence as Prime Minister of a little state like Mysore, and so infinitely inferior a man, as the Marquess of Salisbury, is tolerated as Prime Minister of a vast empire like Great Britain, is one of those matters that fairly bewilder those who, like myself, believe in a righteous overruling power that guides and governs the affairs of mankind. (*Loud cheers and laughter.*)

MR. SHARFUDDIN (*Patna, No. 323, in list*)—MR. PRESIDENT AND BROTHER DELEGATES,—The resolution before you has, I think, already been discussed in almost all its bearings, and I will confine myself to two questions. The first is the clause for the protection of minorities. Let me say at once that from the first I was opposed to this clause, although I am a Mussleman, and so belong to a class, which, in this country, no doubt, is in the minority. My reason is this. We have municipal laws in this country, and we have district boards; but neither in the municipal Act nor in the Local self-Government Act is there any clause for the protection of minorities, nor has the absence of any such clause ever, anywhere, caused the slightest inconvenience. This, I think, you will take as a sufficient proof of the goodwill of the Mohammedans towards Hindus and of Hindus towards Mohammedans. (*Cheers*). I am a delegate from a place, which now and then gets a westerly breeze from Aligarh (*laughter.*) I come from Patna, where in the second week of this month there was a general election of the municipality, twenty members being elected under the Act, and out of those 20 members you will be surprised to learn that 13 were Mohammedans, and that these 13 were not elected by Mohammedans only, but also by Hindus. You will find, therefore, that my position in opposing the protection of minorities clause is not without due warrant. My second point relates to the Bill of Lord Cross. You will understand that Lord Cross is, no doubt, technically responsible for the introduction of this Bill into the House; but you will also understand that he is, or ought to be, guided by his Council. Lord Cross is nobody, and cannot possibly know anything of Indian matters, except in so far as he represents his Council in the Indian office. His advisers are mostly those who have served in India a good many years, but who retired long before the existence of this Congress, and who, therefore, possess no knowledge of that new India which has grown up in this country. (*Hear, hear.*) So that to blame Lord Cross for the introduction of this futile Bill would be rather unjust. The counsellors he needs are men of a different class, and we in this assembly would advise the Government in England to select as counsellors of the Secretary of State for India, men who have full experience of the present state of the country (*cheers*), and who are not hampered by class traditions and prejudices. (*Loud cheers*).

Mr. Nasir Ali Shohrat (*Delhi, No. 534, in list*), speaking in Urdu, said: Mr. President and Gentlemen,—I rise to support in a few words the remarks of my esteemed friend Mr. Sharfuddin of Patna in regard to Mr. Bradlaugh's New Indian Councils Reform Bill. It does not give us all we want, but we shall all none the less be grateful if we get, soon, even as much as it provides for. Why should we not get it? Is there any class of people in England who disapprove the elective and representative system? To any free and constitutional Government such a system is essential. I would even say that E gland is what she is, and her system of Government, justly lauded throughout the world, what it is, almost mainly in virtue of this system. How can the English, who have given us so many other good things, now refuse to extend to us gradually, and this is all we ask for, this greatest blessing also? (*Cheers*).

Of course many of the members of the Secretary of State's Council are opposed to this as to every other reform; but this does not suprise us in the case of such antiquated personages. The wonder is not that they oppose this measure, but that the English nation still allows such fossils to fill these important posts instead of replacing them by modern living men. (*Cheers and laughter*). You can all understand that in choosing a pleader, we select one in active practice in the Courts, thoroughly up in the law of the present day, not some old fogy who has not read a new law for the last quarter of a century, and whose knowledge of the practice of the Courts is confined to that of fifty years ago! These counsellers are absolutely ignorant of our Modern India of to-day. (*Cheers.*) During the last ten years, even, the entire country has been so metamorphized as to be barely the same place it was. (*Loud cheers*). Why do these worthy old gentlemen remain to clog the wheels of progress? And why do they oppose our modest demands for representation? Because, say they, of the disunion of Mohammedans and Hindus. But there is no sort of disunion amongst Mohammedans and Hindus on these political matters. (*Cheers.*) All are of one mind. (*Loud cheers*). No doubt Sir Syed Ahmed and his now microscopic following tried to create such disunion, but all see now with what conspicuous failure. I fear I cannot give him credit for good faith. Had his motives been good he would have given expression to his new views on the Congress platform, and have explained how it came about that he was now denouncing the very proposals that a few years back he had himself most strongly urged. Had he done this the whole matter would have been fully discussed and a fair decision arrived at. He did not do so, and from this the only possible conclusion is that he was not actuated by a pure desire for the public welfare, but by other motives. By his influence and vehemence he did in some places and instances succeed in creating some unpleasantness between Hindus and Mohammedans, and, perhaps, here and there evil traces of his unpatriotic work may yet linger. Yet, despite this, despite all he and his masters amongst the officials could do, there is practically at this present time absolutely no disunion as regards Congress questions between Musalmans and Hindus. (*Prolonged cheering*).

Mr. Biprodas Banerjee (*Calcutta, No. 38, in list*)—Mr. President and Brother Delegates, Ladies and Gentlemen,—The matter now before you is very important, and we have been fighting for it for the last six or seven years. It has been discussed not only here, but also by the people and the press in England, and even by the Continental press. It is, in short, the very turning point of our political career as a nation. The proposition before you is to affirm the Bill introduced into Parliament by Mr. Bradlaugh. It is our duty to see if we can get not only the native inhabitants of the country to our side, but also the non-official Europeans. For that reason I beg to propose that we postpone this question till Monday ("*No, no.*") I propose it for this reason. (A voice: "*Support the proposition.*") If you do you will support a fiction. The Bill is not before the members, and the printed paper was not placed in the hands of the members until past 2 o'clock. I do not wish to blame anyone. I desire that before coming to a final decision an opportunity may be afforded for seriously considering this Bill.

The President: I am afraid that Mr. Biprodas Banerjee has not quite understood two things. I am sure if he had he would not have made this proposition for adjournment. I think you will bear me out when I say that the Bill has not only been before this Congress,

2nd Day.

Res. I. Expansion and Reform of Legislative Councils.

but before the country for a long time (*hear, hear*); and secondly, he will be good enough to remember what is the function of the Subjects Committee with regard to the Congress. That Committee was appointed last evening for the purpose of drawing up the propositions to be laid before the Congress. They have performed their duty; the resolution has been moved, the subject fully discussed, and I ask you whether, having heard eleven speakers, you do not think that enough has been said in the way of discussion. ("*Yes, yes.*") If that is your view, I will at once put the first resolution ("*vote, vote*"), which will stand as follows :—

RESOLVED—*That this Congress, having considered the draft Bill recently introduced into Parliament by Mr. Charles Bradlaugh, entitled "An Act to amend the Indian Councils Act of 1861," approves the same as calculated to secure a substantial instalment of that reform in the Administration of India, for which it has been agitating, and humbly prays the Houses of Parliament of the United Kingdom of Great Britain and Ireland to pass the same into law; and further that its President, Mr. Pherozshah Mehta, is hereby empowered to draw up and sign, on behalf of this assembly, a petition to the House of Commons to the foregoing effect, and to transmit the same to Mr. Charles Bradlaugh for presentation thereto in due course.*

The resolution was then put and carried unanimously.

Res. II.—Confirmation of Resolutions passed at previous Congresses *in re* Judicial and Police Reforms, Military Colleges, Volunteering, Income Tax, Education, Reduction of Expenditure, Simultaneous examinations in India and England, and the Modification of the Arms Act Rules.

MR. KALI CHARAN BANERJEE (*Calcutta, No. 66, in list*)—MR PRESIDENT, LADIES AND GENTLEMEN,—As an old driver of your omnibus (*laughter*) in regard to which, by-the-bye, it may soon be necessary to legislate as to how many it should be allowed to carry, I may be permitted to drive it once more. There will be no detention with a view to check the passengers; they are all familiar faces, and you would know them at a glance. The resolution I have to propose is—

*That this present Congress does hereby ratify and confirm the resolutions passed by previous Congresses as to—*

(*a*) *the urgent necessity for the complete separation of executive and judicial functions, such that in no case shall the two functions be combined in the same officer;*

(*b*) *the expediency of extending into many parts of the country, where it is not at present in force, the system of trial by jury;*

(*c*) *the necessity of withdrawing from the High Courts the powers, first vested in them in 1872, of setting aside verdicts of acquittal by juries;*

(*d*) *the necessity of introducing, into the Code of Criminal Procedure, a provision enabling accused persons, in warrant cases, to demand that instead of being tried by the Magistrate they be committed to the Court of Sessions;*

(*e*) *the highly unsatisfactory character of the existing system of Police Administration in India, and the absolute necessity of a fundamental reform therein;*

(*f*) *the expediency of both establishing Military Colleges in India, whereat the Natives of India, as defined by Statute, may be educated and trained for a military career as officers of the Indian Army, and of authorising, under such rules and restrictions as may seem necessary, such a system of volunteering for the Indian inhabitants of the country as may qualify them to support the Government in any crisis;*

(*g*) *the extremely unsatisfactory character of the Income Tax Administration, especially as regards incomes below rupees one thousand, and the expediency of raising the taxable minimum to this amount;*

(*h*) *the extreme importance of increasing, instead of diminishing, as the present tendency appears to be, the public expenditure on education in all its branches, and the necessity, in view to the promotion of one of the most essential of these branches, the technical, of the appointment of a mixed commission to enquire into the present industrial condition of the country;*

(*i*) *the necessity for the reduction of, instead of the continual increase to, the military expenditure of the country;*

(*j*) *the necessity, if any real justice is to be done to the people of India, of holding, simultaneously in India and England, examinations, at present held only in England, for the Civil branches of the Public Service in India;*

(*k*) *the expediency of so modifying the rules made under Act XI of 1878 (the Arms Act) that all restrictions as to the possession and bearing of arms shall apply equally to all persons residing in or visiting India; that licenses to possess and bear arms shall be liberally and generally distributed wherever wild animals habitually destroy human life, cattle or crops; and that these and all licenses issued under the rules shall be granted once for all, shall operate throughout the Provincial jurisdiction within which they are issued, be only revocable on proof of misuse, and shall not require yearly or half-yearly renewals.*

**2nd Day,**

**Res. II. Confirmation of Resolutions passed at previous Congresses *in re* Judicial and Police Reforms Military Colleges, Volunteering, Income Tax, Education, Reduction of Expenditure, Simultaneous examinations in India and England, and the Modification of the Arms Act Rules.**

Let me remind you that these resolutions were passed by previous Congresses, and you are now called upon simply to ratify and confirm them. In other words, you are called upon simply to be loyal to your traditions (*cheers*), for I take it that the Congress is old enough to have traditions of its own. In order to help your memories let me briefly describe to you the eleven passengers that I carry in my omnibus. I will begin with the last resolution (*l*). We are grateful to our Government for the security that we enjoy as to life and property from human invasions ; what we seek is that we should have security, also, as far as wild animals are concerned. (*Hear, hear*). And in that connection we desire it to be remembered that wild animals make no distinction between the European and the Indian. (*Laughter*). I have spoken of wild animals ; what as to the wild men ? We are grateful to our Government for the machinery that exists for the prevention and suppression of crime ; at the same time we cannot shut our eyes to the fact that the administration of justice in this country admits of improvement, and that it ought to be elevated to a footing in which it might be spoken of as self-justifying in its character. We desire, therefore, that the police should be reformed, so that it may not be possible for them to place, habitually, innocent men in the dock. We desire further to secure that when Magistrates hold a trial in any case, they should bring to the trial a mind which should be, as far as the *facts* of the case are concerned, a *tabula rasa*. I do not mean that they should bring to the trial of cases a mind that should be a *tabula rasa* as far as the *law* of the case is concerned. (*Laughter*). We desire further that in the administration of justice in this country, the people should be allowed the benefit of the judgment of their peers, that this privilege should not be confined to a few favoured spots, but that it should be extended to all parts of the country to which it may be extended with advantage. We desire further that this privilege of having the judgment of one's peers in any case should not be allowed to become a farce and a nullity by being in danger of being set aside even by the highest court in the country. I may describe these six resolutions as being on a certain level, that is, the level of protection. I now pass on to another class of resolutions that we have in this omnibus, and in order to help your memories I will mention a word which begins with the same letter—P. I am going to place before you four P's. Following protection I will give you the watch-word: plenty. We desire that the poor of the country should be enabled to live, at any rate, from hand to mouth ; that they may be in no danger of having what little they may posssess for their sustenance diminished by the imposition of any species of taxation which is likely to press hard upon them, whether as regards the nature of the tax itself or as regards the administration of the tax. Then after plenty let me give you the word peace, and here I take it that I am not wrong in regarding the British nation as under an inspiration which ought to enable it to usher in a reign of peace which is prophesied as part of the faith which inspires that country—a reign which when it is once inaugurated shall lead men to beat their swords into ploughshares and their spears into pruning hooks. A nation that lives and moves under such an inspiration is surely destined to usher in this reign of peace rather than to go on in a direction which indicates the permanence of war. We desire, then, that the military expenditure of the country should be reduced rather than allowed continually to increase. But if the British nation happens to be lacking in faith so that they are not in a position to lay hold of the "sure word of prophecy," we make to them a certain offer, by way of an earthly support. That is, we invite them to allow us to train ourselves in that same art of war so that when they do need earthly help we shall be prepared, all of us, to render it. I now come to the last, which I describe as the *panacea* ; because after all when we seek to introduce reforms into our country it is not possible for any of them to take root unless the people are educated to help in the cause of reform. (*Cheers*). So it is that we desire to secure that the expenditure in aid of education in all its branches should not be diminished. And here I ought to draw your attention to what is prominently brought out in one of the resolutions, that there should be no distinction ever suggested between high education and low education. An educated carpenter stands on the same footing exactly as an educated lawyer. There is no such thing as high and low in the matter of education. If education is to be a passport to the various services of the country, we desire that those passports should not be hampered by conditions which may render them simply inaccessible to certain persons who cannot fulfil those conditions. Gentlemen, the omnibus has now reached its destination, and the occupation of the driver is gone. (*Laughter and cheers.*)

Mr. K. P. Vishwanadha Iyer (*Madras, No. 613, in list*), in seconding the resolution, said : Mr. President, Ladies and Gentlemen,—In the first place the necessity for reform on the lines suggested in some of the clauses that make up this omnibus resolution has been admitted by the Government itself ; for instance with respect to the separation of the judicial from the

**2nd Day.**

**Res. II. Confirmation of Resolutions passed at previous Congresses *in re* Judicial and Police Reforms, Military Colleges, Volunteering, Income Tax, Education, Reduction of expenditure, Simultaneous examinations in India and England, and the Modification of the Arms Act Rules.**

executive functions, with respect to police administration, and with respect to technical education. Yet what has the Government *done* with regard to these very necessary reforms? As to the separation of the executive and judicial functions it has done absolutely nothing, and as to technical education nothing worthy of the name. The question then arises, why this inactivity? On the other hand, look at the mischievous activity with respect to the Uncovenanted Civil Service. I ask you will there be this inactivity if we have our own representatives in the Legislative Council with respect to these important matters of reform? It appears to me that all this covert opposition of the Local Governments and their unwillingness to legislate according to our prayer, even when they admit that our prayers are just, arises in this way: They seem to say to themselves: "Have we not done and are we not still doing a good deal for these people? Why do they still speak of wrongs and grievances? They do not simply come to us for redress of any grievances they have, but they meet and discuss and say they will go to Parliament and to the British nation, which know nothing of them, while we know everything. So long as they do so they shall not have what they want, or, at least, they shall not have it soon." But if we petition what is it they say? "Ah! these B.A.'s, these seditionists!" We have been called by our opponents mere place-hunters and self-seekers. This omnibus resolution gives the lie to it. Look at the resolution relating to the police, to accused persons, and particularly to the income tax. And, looking out of our omnibus, look at the resolution relating to the salt tax, which will soon be before us. Considering these particular matters the present resolution may be called, as it has been called, the poor man's resolution. Our opponents, while they are kind enough to call us by all sorts of names, do not protest against the salt tax or against the abolition of import duties; but they want to do away with the income tax, the only tax that touches them. Under these circumstnces well may we say, save us from our friends. As to education, while we are twitted with being half-educated B. A.'s, do they want us to be better men, to be better educated? No We are not to have even our higher education as it stands; we shall have none of it, no higher education at all. Education makes us seditious. If we want it let us pay for the whole of it. This is their opinion; it is an open secret; but who will say that they are right? With these few remarks I beg to second the resolution. (*Cheers*).

Mr. G. S. Khaparde (*Berar, No. 584, in list*)—Ladies and Gentlemen,—I rise nominally to support this proposition, which, however, in reality needs no support of mine or of any one else. It has already been before you, piecemeal, and to its various component parts you have devoted much time, and your closest attention in the past, and have come to certain conclusions which are now embodied in these eleven clauses. I have only to support them as a sort of supernumerary on the omnibus, to employ my leader's phraseology. But I would not compare this resolution to an omnibus, but rather to a casket of jewels. We have formed, after due deliberation, certain ideas, and I call those ideas jewels, and we offer them to the Viceroy and ask him to decorate the people of India with them. Let us see how far they have been given. One of them has been given very reluctantly and with a very grudging spirit indeed to a few districts in the Madras Presidency; the rest of us have to look and ask for some of them. I hope we are not envious, but we sincerely desire that some of these jewels may be given to us also. I am speaking of the first part of the resolution regarding the separation of the judicial function from the executive. Ten of these jewels have not even partially been given to anybody, not even lent on a holiday, or for a drive, or an airing. (*Laughter and cheers*). There is one jewel that some of us especially desire to possess. Some of us would like to hold office in her Majesty's army. We live, I joyfully admit, under the protection of the British Crown and flag, and we desire that we should be allowed to fight under that flag. We fight as soldiers; I should like to fight as an officer; I want to command a few hundreds. That is all we ask—not much. One would think that to give me the command of a hundred sepoys or a few cavalry soldiers would not be very dangerous, the Commander-in-Chief and the General and the Brigadier and the Colonel being all above me. Yet, they say "No, you are not fit." I ask, Have I been examined and found wanting? They will not answer that question, and they will not send me to school. They are just like a stepmother to us! (*Laughter*). I think I have now done my part as a supernumerary, and I retire. (*Cheers*).

Lala Dharam Das (*Punjab, No. 521, in list*)—Mr. President, Ladies and Gentlemen,—I also beg to support the resolution that has been so neatly proposed. We all know that Government should be prepared to defend the country against foreign invasion, and consequently we admit that great expenses must be borne by the people to help the Government to carry out the necessary plans of defence. We do not complain that we are taxed, but that we are injudiciously and inequitably taxed. Persons whose incomes are below Rs. 85 a month are hardly able to bear anything in the shape of income tax, and the resolution says it is expedient that the taxable minimum should be raised so that the tax may not press upon such persons. We have read the disappointing and disheartening communication received from the Government by the Calcutta Chamber of Commerce; but after the speeches delivered on the occasion of the St. Andrew's Dinner, we may now hope that the Government will again consider the question, not of the abolition, but of the readjustment of this tax. We are grateful to the Government for the many benefits we enjoy under their paternal care. It is painful, however, to find the sympathies of the lower classes alienated from the Government because of the extremely unsatisfactory manner in which this tax is collected. Government ought to be aware of this. We ask for a readjustment, and so possibly a reduction in the gross proceeds of the tax, and at the same time we ask for a reduction of unnecessary expenditure. For some years past the military expenditure of the country has been increasing by leaps and bounds, and it is absolutely necessary that there should be a check placed upon this wicked waste. It is a matter of regret that our demands have so far been, save in some small matters, practically ignored. It is the educated alone who can fully appreciate the blessings of good government, and who are able to point out its defects No doubt educated persons do demand a share in the administration of the Government; and have not noble and just British statesmen admitted from time to time the justice of such demands? The people of India want justice—real justice, not sham. The resolution declares the necessity of holding Civil Service examinations simultaneously in England and in India. The Government have practically closed the Civil Service against natives by holding competitive examinations in England only, and there are but very few of the qualified Indian candidates who can succeed in going to England. It is absolutely necessary that the Government should appoint a mixed Commission to enquire into the industrial condition of the country. As to military appointments, even the chiefs, who are thoroughly loyal, cannot get real commissions, they now and then get honorary ones), nor is it possible for them actually to serve in the army except by entering as private soldiers. There are no colleges in the country for their training. The Punjab and Bombay Governments recommended the establishment of such colleges, and it was hoped that their recommendation would be favourably considered, especially as H. R. H. the Duke of Connaught had been pleased to attest the expediency of the proposal. But with one stroke of the pen the Secretary of State decided the other way. Let us once more bring to the notice of the Government what the country feels about the unsatisfactory character of the system of police administration, and let us at the same time hope that the necessary reforms will be effected at no distant date now that the Police Commission has been appointed by the Government. You must all have read of the sufferings of the people at Amritsar, due to the conduct of a police officer brought to light by our local paper, *The Tribune.* The people all over the Punjab are anxiously waiting to see what redress can be obtained from the House of Commons in this matter. (*Cheers*).

MUNSHI SADRUDDEEN AHMED (*Allahabad, No. 382, in list*) then spoke in Urdu, and said. Glory in the first place to Sir Syed Ahmad Khan, the leader of disunion, the patriarch of jealousy, the parent of obstinacy, the ancestor of doggedness, and the living saint of Anti-Congressists! (*Loud laughter and cheers*).

Gentlemen, I stand here to support some of the clauses of the resolution; but by. far the most important clause to which I shall refer relates to the Arms Act Rules.

The taking of arms from the natives and the enforcement of, practically, prohibitive rules regarding the grant of licenses is not only prejudicial to the natives of India, but is equally calculated to weaken and cripple the Government itself. Hundreds of millions of people are now under the sway of the British Government in India, none of whom can possibly entertain the remotest feeling of hostility to the Government. On the other hand, they are loyal and faithful subjects, and, as the Indian Mutiny of 1857 amply proved, their attachment did not waver even in those troublous times when every stupid and faithless sepoy broke into open rebellion. Is it under.the circumstances advisable to render powerless and emasculate, on mere suspicion, a nation whose loyalty has been tested and tried during the last hundred years, by depriving them of the privilege of carrying arms and keeping themselves in touch with the methods of modern warfare? (*Cheers*). If out of the hundreds of millions that inhabit this vast empire, only a few lakhs were allowed the privilege of carrying arms, the Government would have beside it, without incurring any additional expenditure, a vast array of armed men to support and to assist it in times of need. (*Loud cheers.*)

The Emperors of old had confidence in the bravery and faithfulness of the people, and never deprived them of arms, and derived considerable assistance from the people in return. The martial spirit of the people of the country raised the descendants of Taimur, Akbar in particular, to the highest pitch of supremacy and power. If the people of India with arms in their hands and bullets in their pockets could remain subject to the Mohammedan's empire and accepted its supremacy, does it stand to reason that they would rebel against so just and civilized a Government as that of the British people? (*Loud cheers*). The peace and prosperity of a people are among the first requisites of sovereignty, and these cannot be secured unless the rulers and the ruled repose mutual confidence in each other. The confidence of the people is dependent on the non-interference of the sovereign with the privileges of the people and their right to do such lawful acts as they please. At any rate

2nd Day.

Res. II. Confirmation of Resolutions passed at previous Congresses *in re* Judicial and Police Reforms, Military Colleges, Volunteering, Income Tax, Education, Reduction of Expenditure, Simultaneous examinations in India and England, and the Modification of the Arms Act Rules.

arms are the sole protectors of life and property; and their deprivation causes disappointment and dejection which knows no bounds.

If, God forbid, India were to be pounced upon by any enemy from the West, women with their curses, and unarmed men with empty abuses, will face the enemy, and the enemy will laugh and say :—

Is sadgi se kaun na marjai ai Khuda,
Larti hain our hathmen talwar bhi nahin.

Oh, God! who would not die at this simplicity,
They dare to fight though they have not a sword in their hands. (*Cheers.*)

No Emperor ever feared the sword of his subject, nor ever emasculated a brave nation by force. The natives of India belong to a race which opposed Alexander and turned him back beyond the Indus. They are descendants of those brave people who, in the battle of Telaveri, made Shahabuddeen Ghori taste the efficacy of a sword, and made him retreat headlong with his army for upwards of forty miles. To convert such brave and faithful people into protectors of the Throne and guards of the State is to invigorate and strengthen the foundations of the Government. You must have read in history that when Nadir Shah once summoned the Nawab of Furrukabad to Delhi for an interview, and the Nawab replied that he could not come without his armour and weapons, Nadir said : "Go and tell him he may come with his artillery." (*Cheers*). What a revolution ! There was a time when the Emperors of old were not afraid of the arms of their enemies ; a time has now come when we unfortunate, though loyal and faithful subjects, are distrusted even by our own Government. (*Loud cheers*).

In regard to the police system it is sufficient to say that the police, if they do not consider their powers more extensive than those of God himself, at least do consider them to be co-equal with His. (*Cheers.*)

This should be considered and the people should be relieved of their oppression. (*Hear.*)

One word more about the income tax. It is on all hands admitted that both the black and the white are the progeny of Adam and the subjects of Her Majesty the Queen. Then why should one be favoured more than the other? As persons possessing an income below one thousand rupees are exempted in England from the income tax, the people of India, who are far poorer, possessing an income below rupees one thousand should be similarly exempted. (*Loud and prolonged cheers*).

Babu Bishnupada Chatterjee (*Hoogly, No. 161, in list*).—I rise, Sir, to support this resolution. I do not know how many horses are needed to drag an omnibus in England. On the occasion of the last Congress this proposition was ably moved by Mr. Kalicharan Banerjee and seconded by Mr. Chandavarkar, and it was carried unanimously. You may ask me why it is brought forward again. The answer is that the disease is still prevalent, the doctors are not forthcoming with their medicine, much less their advice. But I can assure you the case is not hopeless. Everything depends upon united action and constant agitation. I have a great fancy for one of the passengers in the omnibus, namely (J) " the necessity, if any real justice is to be done to the people of India, of holding simultaneously, in England and India, examinations, at present held only in England, for the civil branches of the Public Service in India." I am not going to give facts and figures ; that has often been done. I will only quote a line from the despatch : "They have no desire to extend the practical application of this principle further then political necessity requires." Now we say that political necessity requires that the Government of a country should at any rate be *largely* composed of the people of that country, of persons thoroughly conversant with the habits, customs, views, wishes, wants of the people, of persons whose interests are to a great degree identical with those of the people. Whereas under the existing system the Government is exclusively composed of foreigners ignorant alike of everything that really concerns the people, and whose interests are distinctly, in most cases, antagonistic to those of the country. Having regard to these anomalies, I say it is absolutely necessary that there should be simultaneous examinations in India and England (*cheers*), so that gradually the Government may come to be largely composed of Indians (*Cheers*).

The President : Several names of speakers have been sent up (" *vote.*") If you think that the matter has been sufficiently discussed, I will not give these gentlemen the trouble of coming up (" *vote, vote.*)"

Then our second resolution will stand thus :—

Resolved—*That this present Congress does hereby ratify and confirm the resolutions passed by previous Congresses as to—*

(*a*) *the urgent necessity for the complete separation of executive and judicial functions, such that in no case shall the two functions be combined in the same officer ;*

(b) *the expediency of extending into many parts of the country, where it is not at present in force, the system of trial by jury ;*

(c) *the necessity of withdrawing from the High Courts the powers, first vested in them in 1872, of setting aside verdicts of acquittal by juries ;*

(d) *the necessity of introducing, into the Code of Criminal Procedure, a provision enabling accused persons, in warrant cases, to demand that instead of being tried by the Magistrate they be committed to the Court of Sessions ;*

(e) *the highly unsatisfactory character of the existing system of Police Administration in India, and the absolute necessity of a fundamental reform therein ;*

(f) *the expediency of both establishing Military Colleges in India, whereat the Natives of India, as defined by Statute, may be educated and trained for a military career as officers of the Indian Army, and of authorising, under such rules and restrictions as may seem necessary, such a system of volunteering for the Indian inhabitants of the country as may qualify them to support the Government in any crisis ;*

(g) *the extremely unsatisfactory character of the Income Tax Administration, especially as regards incomes below rupees one thousand, and the expediency of raising the taxable minimum to this amount ;*

(h) *the extreme importance of increasing, instead of diminishing, as the present tendency appears to be, the public expenditure on education in all its branches, and the necessity, in view to the promotion of one of the most essential of these branches, the technical, of the appointment of a mixed commission to enquire into the present industrial condition of the country ;*

(i) *the necessity for the reduction of, instead of the continual increase to, the military expenditure of the country ;*

(j) *the necessity, if any real justice is to be done to the people of India, of holding, simultaneously in India and England, examinations, at present held only in England, for the Civil branches of the Public Service in India ;*

(k) *the expediency of so modifying the rules made under Act XI of 1878 (the Arms Act) that all restrictions as to the possession and bearing of arms shall apply equally to all persons residing in or visiting India ; that licenses to possess and bear arms shall be liberally and generally distributed wherever wild animals habitually destroy human life, cattle or crops ; and that these, and all licenses issued under the rules, shall be granted once for all, shall operate throughout the Provincial jurisdiction within which they are issued, be only revocable on proof of misuse, and shall not require yearly or half-yearly renewals.*

**2nd Day.**

**Res. II. Confirmation of Resolutions passed at previous Congresses *in re* Judicial and Police Reforms, Military Colleges, Volunteering, Income Tax, Education, Reduction of Expenditure, Simultaneous examinations in India and England, and the Modification of the Arms Act Rules.**

The resolution was then put to the vote and carried unanimously.

**Res. III. Modifications of the Rules and practice of the House of Commons in regard to Indian Budgets.**

MR. W. S. CAINE (*Sholapore, No. 582, in list*)—MR. PRESIDENT, LADIES AND GENTLEMEN,—The resolution which I have to submit is as follows :—

*That this Congress respectfully expresses the earnest hope that in the interest of the people of India, the House of Commons will forthwith restore the right, formerly possessed by members of that Honourable House, of stating to Parliament any matter of grievance of the natives of India before Mr. Speaker leaves the Chair, for the presentation in Committee of the Indian Budget statement, and earnestly trusts that the House of Commons will in future take into consideration the Annual Indian Budget statement at such a date as will ensure its full and adequate discussion, and further authorizes its President to sign a petition, in the name and on behalf of this Congress, for presentation to the House of Commons, in accordance with the terms of this resolution*

This, Sir, is a resolution which has been submitted at previous Congresses, but which has not had the effect that the Congress desire ; for the House of Commons has taken no notice of the petition which was sent from Bombay, and it is, therefore, important that the resolution should be re-affirmed, not in an omnibus, but in a carriage of it own (*cheers and laughter*), so that, if possible, we may secure the restoration of one of the most important rights which India previously possessed. The old principle, which is almost as old as Parliamentary institutions in England, that grievance should come before supply, is one of the rights which are held to more tenaciously by members of Parliament than perhaps any other parliamentary rights. This resolution craves the restoration of a privilege which is the equivalent, so far as the Indian people are concerned, of that ancient charter of our liberty that grievance shall come before supply. It is, also, no doubt, a distinct grievance, and one felt throughout India, that the Budget dealing with the whole finances of the British Empire should be discussed on a single evening at the hottest time of the year at a period when members of Parliament are weary with six months hard work, and when the bulk of them have left London for their holidays. ("*Shame !*") It has long been the

2nd Day.

Res III. Modifications of the Rules and practice of the House of Commons in regard to Indian Budgets.

custom to treat what I consider one of the most important subjects that come before Parliament with such scant courtesy as that which I have now described. There is no doubt that all Indian questions, with the exception of the Budget itself, are shut out from discussion, except under the chances of a ballot. The only mode by which members of Parliament interested in Indian questions can bring them before the House is by balloting for an opportunity of moving a resolution on what is called private member's nights—Tuesday and Friday. When you remember that every Tuesday and Friday, while the House sits, from 150 to 200 members of Parliament place down different subjects in which they are interested to be balloted upon, you will see that the chances of an Indian question coming on, there being perhaps only three or four members to put such questions down, are about one in fifty. The Bill you have been considering in the first resolution I am afraid has no chance of being discussed in the present Parliament, because Mr. Bradlaugh had no good luck with his ballot and all sorts of questions of the highest importance brought in by Bill and by Resolution have constantly to give way to questions of minor importance, the movers of which find it impossible to bring down 40 men to the House to discuss them. In the old times before 1888, when this privilege was taken away, if we missed our opportunities of bringing Indian grievances before Parliament by resolution on a private member's night, we had the privilege of grievance before supply on the Budget night to fall back upon. That is now gone, and we wish to have it restored. You must remember that the responsibilities of Parliament towards India are increasing every year. More and more India is being brought into touch with England. (*Cheers*). During the last five years the interest which has been taken by all politicians, especially by Liberal politicians, in the action of the Indian National Congress, has done much to stimulate the interest of English people in India. But, as our responsibility increases, we find that our powers decrease. There is no doubt that, as time goes on, every year will bring about an increased interest in India. If it had not been for the early meeting of Parliament during the current year, I believe between 30 and 40 members of the House of Commons would have been in India, at the present moment, studying your questions for themselves and realizing their responsibilities. (*Cheers*). I am glad to say that we have one member of Parliament present, but he is the only one, so far as I know, who is now in the country. Now, the only way by which Indian grievances can be discussed in public and opinion taken upon them in India is before the National Congress, and in England before the House of Commons. You, when you get members of Parliament, receive them with hospitality, treat them with rare courtesy and kindness, and do the utmost in your power to make them familiar with the wants and aspirations of the Indian people. These "travelling members of Parliament" are not so popular with the governing class as I should like to see them. (*Laughter*). We come here to do what we can to help the authorities of India to govern this country wisely and well; and our good intentions are called in question, and our services are not welcomed. We are constantly enabling them to improve their own administration, as you will find affirmed in the resolution which follows the present one. We instructed them two years ago with regard to the administration of one of the most important departments, and they have carried out those instructions with a reasonable amount of fidelity. These travelling members of Parliament will go back to their country, and you will have presently an army in Parliament, an increasing army anxious to discuss what you yourselves cannot discuss in your Parliament and legislate upon for yourselves. Now there is only one way by which the Government of India can get rid of the nuisance of travelling M. P.'s who come and poke their noses into their affairs. We in Parliament do not particularly want to be troubled with Indian affairs. We have affairs of our own in which we are deeply interested, and it is only under compulsion that we take your matters in hand at all. I simply look upon Parliament as holding Indian affairs in trust until this promising child, which is present in this building, arrives at the age of maturity; and then we shall be glad to give up our trust to our ward. Then if the Government of India dislike, as I believe they dislike, the interference of Parliament, and of members of Parliament, they can get rid of that interference by acting up to the spirit of the first resolution which you have carried, and by admitting you to some share in a representative Government of your own. (*Cheers*). When that comes our functions will have gone; we shall be no longer required; you will then be able to deal with your own affairs without our help; you will be permitted, I should hope, to vote your own Budget, and we shall be relieved of a considerable responsibility and a considerable burden. I have great pleasure in moving this resolution. (*Cheers*).

Mr. R. D. Mehta (*Calcutta, No. 670, in list*)—Mr. President, Brother Delegates and Sister Delegates,—I find that coming after so distinguished a speaker as Mr. Caine, who has also proved himself to be *able* (*laughter*), I have very little to add. In former years, when the House went into Committee upon the Indian Budget, any member of the House had the privilege of laying before the House any question affecting the Indian People. The new rule, however, disallowed this privilege, and, I need not say, with most prejudicial results to India. But this is not all. Our Budget statements, as Mr. Caine has pointed out, are brought forward for discussion in the dog days of August, before a row of empty benches, and the Under-Secretary finds himself addressing perhaps a couple of Anglo-Indian members. I should like to know how the

English people would tolerate a farce of this kind with regard to their own Budget. If the Chancellor of the Exchequer were to discuss the English Budget before empty benches, there would be such a howl of indignation that absent members would know how to conduct themselves next time. But we, the inhabitants of an unrepresented Empire, may cry at the top of our voices, and no one listens to the protests of a people who have no share, no part, no vote in the Government of their country. I will not detain you longer, but I have great pleasure in seconding the resolution so ably and eloquently proposed by Mr. Caine. (*Cheers*).

**2nd Day.**

**Res. III. Modifications of the Rules and practice of the House of Commons in regard to Indian Budgets.**

Mr. G. Yule (*Calcutta, No. 13, in list* ) (in response to repeated calls) said : I thought I should have been allowed to escape, even showing myself at a higher altitude * than alongside the President. (*No, no*). I sympathize most cordially with the resolution which is at present before you, and I am quite convinced that if we had the opportunity of discussing the Budget in Parliament, I could undertake, in the question of stores alone, to save as much, at all events, as would enable the Government to raise the taxable minimum for income tax to Rs. 1,000. (*Cheers.*) I do not know any commercial undertaking, and I am certain that there is no Government undertaking of a commercial character, which is carried on as the Store Department is, without knowledge on the part of superiors, and with insuffícent payment on the part of those who are entrusted with the purchasing of stores for us. I say that there are no commercial men who would not come to the conclusion that, after twenty years of such a mode of carrying on business without check, there must be a great amount of bribery and corruption. On that account alone if this resolution were to have the ear of the House of Commons and to be passed, I confidently assert that we should be able to save the people of India at least one-half of the present amount of income tax. (*Hear, hear.*) I support the resolution most cordially, and I hope you will see it passed in the House of Commons as soon as you expect it. (*Cheers.*) (*Cries of "vote, vote"*).

The President : Shall I now put the resolution (*Yes, yes*). Very well, then the third resolution will stand :—

Resolved—*That this Congress respectfully expresses the earnest hope that, in the interest of the people of India, the House of Commons will forthwith restore the right, formerly possessed by members of that Honourable House, of stating to Parliament any matter of grievance of the natives of India before Mr. Speaker leaves the Chair, for the presentation in Committee of the Indian Budget statement, and earnestly trusts that the House of Commons will, in future, take into consideration the Annual Indian Budget statement at such a date as will ensure its full and adequate discussion, and further authorizes its President to sign a petition, in the name and on behalf of this Congress, for presentation to the House of Commons, in accordance with the terms of this resolution.*

The resolution was then carried by acclamation.

Mr. D. E Wacha (*Bombay, No. 543, in list*), in proposing the fourth resolution, said : The resolution entrusted to me is this :—

**Res. IV. Necessity for further Reform in the Excise Administration.**

*That while recognizing the action taken in response to its previous prayers in the matter of excise reform by H. M.'s Secretary of State for India and the Supreme Government here, and noting with pleasure the increase to the import duty on spirits, the taxation imposed on Indian-brewed malt liquors, the decision of the Bengal Government to abolish the outstill system, and the closing of over 7,000 liquor shops by the Madras Government in 1889-90, this Congress regrets that it is still necessary to urge the Government of India to insist on all Provincial Administrations carrying out, in their integrity, the policy in matters of excise, enunciated in clauses 103, 104 and 105 of the despatch published in the Gazette of India of March 1st, 1890, especially as to subsection 4 of clause 103, viz.: "That efforts should be made to ascertain the existence of the local public sentiment, and that a reasonable amount of deference should be paid to such opinion when ascertained."*

This is the third time in the history of the Congress that I have been asked to propose a resolution on excise reform. It was at the Allahabad Congress that the question of abkari administration was first brought forward, partly as a political and partly as a social question. But at the time it took the form of a prayer, that in view of the increasing intemperance in the country the Government might be moved to appoint a Commission to enquire generally into the abkari administration. The first fruit of that resolution was that the matter was earnestly taken up by the redoubtable Mr. Caine in the House of Commons. With his assistance and that of his colleague, Mr. Samuel Smith, the House of Commons passed the famous resolution of 30th April 1889, with which we are all familiar. It was the first step taken towards practical reform. In fact, as the President very properly observed in his eloquent address yesterday, the abkari question is one of the two questions out of the many which the Congress has discussed on which some practical action has been taken. The other

* The speaker's tribune was elevated above all the other seats and places.

2nd Day.

Res. IV. Necessity for further Reform in the Excise Administration.

question related to the abolition of the silver plate duty, on which also I had the honour to speak at the last Congress at Bombay. From the tenor of the resolution which I have just read out to you, you will have observed that it comprises three distinct matters. Firstly, that we recognize the practical action the authorities have taken in the matter of the reform of our excise administration; secondly, that we also recognize efforts which at least two of the Provincial Governments have already made to check the consumption of liquor; and thirdly, that we still require other Provincial Administrations to carry out in their full integrity the instructions laid down in the excise despatch of March 1890.

It is, indeed, a source of gratification to us that our agitation on abkari matters has so far borne fruit, that we have not only elicited a practical resolution from the House of Commons, but also from the Government of India in that ponderous despatch of March 1890. In consequence of the despatch, be it said to the credit of the Bengal Government, and especially of Sir Steuart Bayley, the consumption of liquor in Bengal has decreased, and also the revenue. That is exactly the thing we want. There ought to be, as far as possible, a minimum of consumption, never mind what the revenue may be, because the reform is in a great measure a moral one. It must also be said, to the credit of Lord Connemara and the Madras Government, that they have been able in one year to close 7,000 liquor shops in a population of 35 millions. This is an augury, that, so far as the Madras Presidency is concerned, we are entering upon an era of social reform. (*Cheers*).

I regret that I cannot speak similarly of my own Province; the Bombay Government has done absolutely nothing. Nay, the Bombay Government, instead of reforming its ways, has become a worse sinner since the date of the orders of the House of Commons That is to me a matter of great regret, because, after all our efforts, we are no better off than we were three years ago. Indeed, instead of the Government of Bombay taking the lesson to heart, as given in the resolution of the House of Commons, and by the Government of India itself, it has been going in the wrong direction and increasing the consumption and increasing the revenue. ("*Shame!*") For your information I beg in a very short compass to put some statistics before you from which you will see that the statement I have made is not a mere haphazard statement, but a statement borne out by official statistics. The revenue in 1881-82 was 38 lakhs; in 1889-90 it had reached 74 lakhs—an increase of 95 per cent. The consumption has also increased from 18 lakhs of gallons to 27 lakhs, an increase of 50 per cent. Then, again, while Madras justly takes credit for having closed 7,000 liquor shops in a single year, what do we find in Bombay? This: That in 1887-88 we had 4,443 shops, and in 1888-89 we had 4,739 shops, an increase of about 300. This, let me say, has reference more to country spirits than to toddy or other liquor. One of the strongest grievances involved in the abkari administration is that regarding new toddy. Toddy in Bombay, as in other parts of the country, is drunk by the labouring classes, for whom Manchester philanthropists have been exerting themselves with so much solicitude. (*Laughter.*) It is comparatively innocuous, not having the strength of ordinary alcoholic beverages; but it is boycotted in Bombay in order that the consumption of ardent spirits may be stimulated. What is the result? Ten years ago there were lakhs of palm trees tapped in different directions, but now the trees stand yielding nothing from the soil they occupy; not a single tree is allowed to be tapped by its owners. The fact is that the original drawers of toddy have lost their industry, and they are now eking out a miserable subsistence in all sorts of miscellaneous and possibly some of them questionable ways; and I should not be surprised if many of them have gone to swell the large number of people of whom Sir William Hunter speaks as going with half a meal a day in India. This is a sad picture of the disastrous results of the Bombay àbkari administration. Under these circumstances I think you will agree with the statement in the resolution that it is necessary, at this stage, that the Government of India should actually call upon those provincial administrations, which have not carried out this reform, to do so without delay. The farming system is still flourishing in Bombay; the traffic has been stimulated, and it has brought shops to many villages where there were none. The result has been that intemperance has increased.

With regard to the last and most important part of the resolution I believe there is no one who has given two minutes consideration to this subject who would not say that, in a country like India, sober from ancient times (whatever may be said to the contrary), it is absolutely necessary that the principle inculcated by the House of Commons, as far as local option for India is concerned, should be carried out, even though in some localities it may be necessary to do this slowly and gradually. I cannot better impress you with the importance of this than by a quotation from a statement of the Government of India. They say "that efforts should be made to ascertain the existence of local public sentiment, and that a reasonable amount of deference should be paid to such opinion when ascertained." I will give you an instance of "the reasonable amount of deference paid to such opinion" in Bombay! In the centre of the mill district at Ahmedabad the Collector lately gave a license to open a liquor shop. All the owners of the mills asked to have it closed, but the request was not granted. Then again these same people at Ahmedabad, fully aware of the evil of intemperance, requested Lord Harris when on a visit to the town, that local option might be introduced, but this also was refused. This refusal is a matter of regret, firstly, because it was a disobedience of the instructions, of the Government of India; and, secondly, because the introduction of the system there—when the people voluntarily asked for it—was an experiment worthy of trial, if only to prove the goodness and sincerity of the intentions of Government. Lord Harris is, no doubt, new to this country, but I do hope and believe that when he has studied the whole question in all its aspects, he will at least try to do his best to introduce this system of local option in Bombay, because I believe that on this question the salvation of India, so far as drinking is concerned, mainly rests. (*Cheers*).

MR. KASHINATH NATU (*Poona, No. 557, in list*), in seconding the resolution, said,—If one of our forefathers, who lived 150 years ago, were to stand here and see this august assembly, with what wonder would he regard a sight which, in his own day, would have been an absolute impossibility! But he would be still more wonder-struck to find a proposition being made for which there was no necessity whatever in his day. In the elevated sanctuaries of the Himalayas he devoted his time and thoughts to the contemplation of the infinite and absolute; but the entire devotion of too many of his descendants seems to centre nowadays on a cupboard full of bottles, and he would be astonished to find not a few out castes, here and there, but legions of the highest caste men slaves to the grossest of all vices, intemperance. If we are slow in other matters, we have made almost incredible progress in this. Not long ago in our province the income from this source was only Rs. 10,000, but it is now no less than ten lakhs. ("*Shame!*") Where there was no man seen drunk in the streets, there are now hundreds.

I have come here to support a proposition that ought, I think, to be self-supporting: certainly it needs no support from one so little known as myself. But I speak from the natural impulses of my own heart, and I have a very strong hope that the day will come when, to adapt the Englishman's saying, "we shall not have a single slave to contaminate our soil," we shall not have a single drop of spirit to contaminate our sons. Some gentlemen who are otherwise kindly disposed say that this is all the result of education. And who has given us that education? I am inclined to allow the Government to stand *in loco parentis*. "You are our kind parents and, occupying that position, are you going to open grogshops in every town and street?" It is a thing about which there can be no two opinions even in the House of Parliament. We earnestly ask the Government to do what? To lessen that vice, the prevalence of which is owing in great measure to their own policy. They gave us education, no doubt, but they also made us acquainted with the drink bottle. "It is you," we can truly say to them, "who have brought the evil into our country, and to whom, if not to you, shall we go to find a remedy? You cannot say no to us. You *must* close the grogshops. It is said we are not fit to govern ourselves. You have given us the municipal franchise and empowered us to deal with sanitation and other matters; and yet in the same breath you say that we are not fit to regulate our grogshops, to decide on the numbers we will have, or to resolve that we will have none at all." I cordially support this proposition, and I hope the day will come when India will say, "No liquor, no brandy here, but only Adam's ale—pure water!" (*Cheers*).

LALA MURLIDHAR (*Punjab, No. 531, in list*)—MR. PRESIDENT, BROTHER DELEGATES AND LADY DELEGATES,—You do not expect a mouse to roar like a lion; and you do not expect from me an eloquent speech such as you have had from our friends who have preceded me. At the first Congress I confessed that I was a murderer—of the Queen's English,—but then I escaped punishment. But the President of the present Congress has doomed me to death. He gives me but five minutes to live. (*Laughter.*) Now that I stand on this platform I feel like the unhappy man who has been sentenced to be hanged. (*Laughter*). In the presence of so many spectators, and at the sight of this august assembly and of so many learned scholars, I feel as if I had lost the faculty of speech; in four minutes more the President will sound the gong—the drop will fall—or at least I shall drop out of the tribune—now can you wonder that I feel just like the man about to be hanged? (*Laughter.*)

Now I come to the point. I do not know why you blame these grogshops and grogsellers, and those who promote the drink traffic. There is more philosophy in a bottle of wine than in all the schools, because it proves in a minute what sages have taken long ages to solve—the problem of the transmigration of souls. (*Cheers and laughter.*) It proves how a human being passes into a brute, and can assume the form of a donkey at will. (*Laughter*). Yes, even the Theosophists will be puzzled to solve this problem. While the East has taught the West mathematics, astronomy and other sciences, in exchange the West has given us liquor—damnation instead of salvation. That really is a very good barter! We have bargained away our souls, and what have we in enchange? A bottle of gin or a glass of whiskey. A very good exchange indeed! We have proved very wise in our generation—very wise, indeed, to permit the growth of such a traffic. I feel sincerely thankful to the Punjab Government that

2nd Day.

Res. IV. Necessity for further Reform in the Excise Administration.

it has really tried to give effect to the resolution passed by the Secretary of State and the Government of India. All the *chandoo** shops in the Punjab Province have been closed; there are now none in the Amballa district; while there are thousands in other provinces. But, in spite of all this, people have become more addicted to drink, because it has been thought to be an adjunct of Western civilization. It is thought that a man cannot become a perfect gentleman unless he drinks a glass of wine. Now another Governor has come to the rescue of the present generation, and he says that if a person indulges in a glass of whiskey there is no harm in it. Is there no harm? Is that the idea of the Governor of millions of people, that there is no harm in throwing temptation in the way of the poor wretched creatures who live on one meal a day? They have their children living in misery—clad in rags............lying in the mud; but all this is not enough, there must be these foul liquor shops to tempt them to make things even worse! (*Shame, shame.*)

Even our Mohammedan rulers hated and held the liquor traffic accursed. It has been left for our Christian rulers to love it, pet it, stimulate it, and make money by crores out of it! (*Hear, hear.*)

Now we find, even in Burmah, a newly conquered Province, we find that liquor shops have been started. And for whose benefit? Not certainly for the benefit of the Burmese, whose creed forbids strong drink, and who are only now, under British tuition, learning how to grow into drunkards and beasts? (*Hear.*) For whose benefit then? The benefit of the British Government, and I marvel equally at the folly and the wickedness of the course adopted. Will a drunken population serve them as well, will it, in the long run, even fill their exchequer as full as a sober one? (*Cheers*). How too can men, who pretend to believe in God and a future state, thus set to work coldly, cruelly, systematically to seduce the people committed to their charge by Him into all kinds of sin and misery? And what wickedness does not the habit of drinking lead to? It is not for me to speak much about the evils of drinking. You who have been born in this country and have never tasted liquor have always held it to be only another name for—damnation. (*Laughter.*) With these few words I support the resolution. (*Cheers*). I will only add one word. You laugh at me and think that I am a fool. (*"No, no"*). Really I am a fool (*laughter*), and you must thank the Punjab people, because the representative character of this National Congress would not have been perfect without the presence of one fool at least to represent the many. (*Laughter and prolonged cheers.*)

Guru Pratap Singh Sodhi (*Lahore, No. 526, in list*), speaking in Panjabi, said: Friends,—With great respect I beg to state that we Sikhs heartily sympathize with the National Congress; for the national blessings which it is conferring, and will confer, cannot be looked for from any other organization or institution.

I belong to the family of Sikh Gurus known as Sodhi. I, with my followers, am a supporter of the Congress with body and wealth. My followers are about 25,000 men, and range from Lahore to Candahar.

Drinking is positively prohibited in our creed as it is in others. No one dare speak in favour of drink. I am much struck that nowadays it should be needful to warn people against drinking. There was a time when a drunkard would have tried in vain to force his vile liquor on his neighbours; in vain, for people avoided drink, with very rare exceptions, out of respect for their creeds. Now, alas, it is quite common to find men lying naked, and insensible from drink, about our streets.

What are the best loved things in the world for which all people toil? Is it not wife and children? But those given to drinking do not spare even these, but despoil them of their jewels, clothes, nay of their very food, to satisfy their accursed craving.

The helpless wives and children of this legion of beasts addressed their prayers for succour to God, who listened mercifully and moved the hearts of Mr. Caine and the Congress leaders to espouse their cause and endeavour to rescue the people of India from this great sin and misery that the Government has unwittingly brought upon them.

This Congress, bent upon this and other good works for our suffering brethern, is not an assembly of men, but of Devas.† It is a place of pilgrimage which purifies the heart choked by the impurities of a life time.

The ruler for the time being is the Vicegerent of God on earth. Our Gracious Empress now occupies such a place. It is in Her name and encouraged by the sacredness of Her position,

* *Chandoo* is a very deleterious preparation of opium.

† *Vis.*, Semi-divine beings.

that we of the Congress lift up our voices against this and other great evils from which India is now suffering. May God incline Her heart to listen to our prayers.

**2nd Day.**

**Res. IV. Necessity for further Reform in the Excise Administration.**

Since this work of the National Congress has begun, educated men have commenced to labour for the good of their fellows, and especially to devote their energies to rooting out this drink evil.

More than one local Government has taken steps in the right direction, and for this we have to thank both Englishmen like Mr. Caine and his supporters in England, and our National Congress here in India.

Government revenue will decrease, and some think this will harm Government; but when the people benefit, as in this case, any wise Government counts all such losses a gain. Nay where Government got one rupee by the drunkenness of its subjects, it will gain ten by their sobriety.

It is very strange that though education has so widely spread, drink seems to have done so equally. Either education has not produced the expected results, or there has not been enough of it, or it is not the right sort, not sufficiently embodying a moral element. I do not rightly understand, but I pray God Almighty to crown the efforts of this Congress, and of all who side with them in endeavouring to save the people from this evil of drunkenness, and may he crown our Queen Empress with the choicest blessings and incline her heart to decree the rescue of her people from this grim monster.

I altogether go with this resolution. May it triumph.

Mr. W. S. Caine (*Sholapore, No. 582, in list*) in response to repeated calls, rose and said: I have much pleasure in supporting this resolution. (*Cheers*).

The President: You have just heard one of the shortest and sweetest speeches that we have yet had (*laughter*) and are no one doubt prepared to vote. (*Cries of yes, yes, vote, vote.*)

Our fourth resolution then will stand thus :—

Resolved—*That, while recognizing the action taken, in response to its previous prayers, in the matter of excise reform, by H. M.'s Secretary of State for India and the Supreme Government here, and noting with pleasure the increase to the import duty on spirits, the taxation imposed on Indian-brewed malt liquors, the decision of the Bengal Government to abolish the outstill system, and the closing of over 7,000 liquor shops by the Madras Government in 1889-90, this Congress regrets that it is still necessary to urge the Government of India to insist on all Provincial administrations carrying out in their integrity the policy, in matters of excise, enunciated in paras 103, 104 and 105 of the despatch published in the "Gazette of India of March 1st, 1890" especially as to subsection 4 of para. 103, viz.—*

*"That efforts should be made to ascertain the existence of local public sentiment, and that a reasonable amount of deference should be paid to such opinion when ascertained."*

The resolution was put and carried unanimously.

The President: I now adjourn this assembly to 11 A. M. on Monday.

The Subjects Committee then resumed its sittings.

---

On the Sunday, the Social Conference assembled in the Congress Pavilion, and passed, after much discussion, various important resolutions in regard to matters of Social Reform. But the Social Conference will, as in former years, publish its own separate Report, and nothing further need be said of it here. The matter is only mentioned because this year, for the first time, some few persons belonging to the old conservative party, addressed a number of representations to the President and General Secretary, and to the Delegates as a body, urging them not to permit the Social Conference to use the Congress Hall, and it is satisfactory to be able to record that not one single Delegate was found willing to support this intolerant proposition.

---

# THIRD DAY'S PROCEEDINGS.

## Monday, 29th December, 1890.

---

The Congress re-assembled at 11-30 A.M.

**3rd Day.**

THE PRESIDENT : GENTLEMEN,—We have an extensive bill of fare before us, and must fall to with good appetites. (*Laughter*). There is no time to be lost, and I will call upon Mr. Kennedy to hand round the first dish, which at any rate will not be wanting in *salt.* (*Cheers*).

**Res. V. Reduction of the Salt Duty.**

MR. PRINGLE KENNEDY (*Behar, No. 352, in list*) in addressing the assembly, said: MR. PRESIDENT AND FELLOW DELEGATES,—The resolution I have the honour to propose is as follows :—

RESOLVED—*That the condition of the finances of India having materially improved, and those special circumstances on which the Government relied to justify the recent enhancement of the salt-tax having, practically, ceased to exist, this Congress considers it essential that the enhancement referred to should be remitted at an early date, and empowers its President to submit a special memorial on the subject, in its name and on its behalf, to H. E. the Viceroy in Council.*

Not everybody in India is a contributor to the abkari revenue, and, if Mr. Caine has his way, the number of such contributors will dwindle by shrinkage to a vanishing quantity. All the inhabitants of India are not fortunate enough to possess Rs. 500 a year, and to have in consequence the pleasure of submitting to the income-tax. But every man, woman and child in this country must eat salt, and thus be a feeder of the Imperial treasury. (*Hear, hear*).

The salt-tax is an income-tax on all incomes down to the lowest. The poorer a man is, the heavier is its incidence. What that incidence is I shall hereafter show. In England a labourer who drinks neither alcoholic beverages, nor tea, nor yet smokes tobacco, pays nothing to the State. In India the lowliest peasant, the poorest coolie, nay the very beggar widow in the street, has to drop her mite into the Imperial Treasury. (*Hear, hear*). Such a tax needs very cogent reasons to defend it. Those ordinarily given are—first antiquity, second facility of collection, third that the people do not mind it, fourth lightness of assessment, fifth financial necessity. As to the first, all that I have to say is that other things, such as human sin and human misery, are old, older than even the salt-tax. As to the second, facility of collection, I must remind you that the working of every revenue department in India eventually rests with red-turbaned gentlemen, in whom the predatory instinct is, I am afraid, generally too strong for any curb of conscience. As to the third point, when I hear that the people do not mind it, the only meaning that I can put to this expression is that people do not speak of it. Gentlemen, an eel is said not to mind skinning. It is used to it. I suppose it seems to them a visitation of an inscrutable providence ; and hence, no doubt, our people, unless questioned, do not, in many parts of the country, speak much about it. But when I think of the salt-tax, my thought takes me to Feudal France, when that existed under the name of the Gabelle. They did not mind it, so the rulers said: and no doubt, even if they did, they rather hesitated to press the point, for, in those days, a gallows was found to be even more disagreeable than a poll tax, and their rulers were quite handy at hanging all who differed from them on such political questions. But, Gentlemen, if the wheels of God grind slowly, yet they grind exceeding small, and the end came, I need not say how.

Now I come to the incidence of the Indian salt-tax. Bear with me while I give you a few figures. I shall try to make them as round and simple as I can. First of all, from enquiry, amongst other places, at Her Majesty's jails where luxuries are not likely to be given, I find that nine or ten chittacks a month, or seven seers and a little over—we will drop the little over—are necessary to keep an adult in health. Now, there are more than twenty-five tens of millions of people in India, and making a deduction for children and others, who need a less quantity of salt than adults, we may take it that 20 tens of millions rations of salt at the rate above mentioned or something over $3\frac{1}{2}$ tens of millions of maunds of salt are necessary to keep the people in health. And this quantity at Rs. 2-8 per maund, the

3rd Day.

Res. V. Reduction of the Salt Duty.

present rate of duty, should yield $8\frac{7}{10}$ tens of millions of rupees. But if I turn to the latest revenue returns, I find that $7\frac{1}{4}$ tens of millions of rupees roughly was the last year's salt revenue. This gives 6 annas a head, and it shows since the tax is one anna a seer, the fact that each person has 6 and not 7 seers of salt a year, as he ought to have at the least. (*Hear, hear*). As a matter of fact in British territory, (they are better off in some of the native states,) the Government itself calculates the consumption at, not more than 10lbs or a little less than 5 seers, per head. There is doubtless considerable smuggling on the one side, but on the other it must be mentioned that human consumption is not the sole, though the chief, use of salt, and that many of the people consume a far greater quantity than the minimum we have given. I know perfectly well that many of the people have not sufficient bread either, but the price of that is not artificially raised by Government.

Let us look at the subject from a different view. In an article in the *Pioneer*, some months ago, by Mr. Robertson, it was stated that a Madras official, who had made a careful study of the question, had ascertained that the average monthly income of the agriculturists in the district of Karnal was 12 annas per head, say Rs. 4 for a family of five. Very rough calculations on my part give me similar results for the districts of Durbhangah and Mozufferpore. The *Gazetteer* published several years ago gives the expenditure of a well-to-do Tirhoot peasant, and therefore I presume the income, at about Rs. 11 per month. This was for a family of five. The poorer, it is said, have to reduce their expenditure to about half of this. Let us say Rs. 5 for a family of five. Now if these five ate 24 seers of salt in the year, as in accordance with the official calculations already stated, they would do, this would be (leaving out any calculation for the increased price, which, as all economists know, considerably exceeds the amount of the tax itself), at 1 anna a seer Rs. 1-8, and so a family having Rs. 60 a year would have to pay Rs. 1-8 as their salt duty. This is a tax of nearer five than four pies a month and this too on incomes not over Rs. 500 a year, but of only Rs. 5 a month. If mine and the Madras civilian's figures be taken, the people of these districts would be paying over 6 pies in the rupee, and if they ate 7 instead of 6 seers, the tax would be nearly 7 pies in the rupee, and that on incomes of less than Rs. 50 a year. Think of these facts, ye Gentlemen, who have incomes over Rs. 500 a year and grumble at the payment of 4 pies in the rupee! Meditate over them those of you who possess an income of over Rs. 2,000 a year and whine at the payment of 5 pies in the rupee!

Now, Sir, only one word more about figures. If the tax were reduced to Rs. 2, salt would sell at about 13 seers instead of 10 seers as it now does. If the duty were reduced to one rupee, as Lord Mayo, Sir J. Strachey, and subsequently Sir Evelyn Baring desired, salt would sell for 20 seers for the rupee, and if salt were duty free, a blessed day, but I am afraid far away in the millennium, salt would sell at 40 seers for the rupee in those places even where it is now dearest, and in many provinces it would be far cheaper. Why the actual cost of producing one maund of salt at the Mayo mines, the Sambhur lake, the Kareghora works and the Madras coast works is under *two annas!* But, Gentlemen, Government, like other people, must live. We do not ask for the abolition of the whole tax. Mr. Caine is for doing away with the abkari revenue, others for reducing the income-tax. We say that already the financial situation is so improved—on this point, I believe, a speaker after me will dilate—that a part of the salt tax may be remitted, and by judicious economy and reduction of military expenditure and home charges the tax may be still further lowered.

When you get your Representative Councils, you may be sure that the Government will listen to you, when you propose to tax yourselves, if in no other matter. If then this burden is still too heavy for the millions of the land after all economy is made, the only way whereby you can alleviate its weight is by taking some of it on yourselves. Gentlemen, when some fifty years ago John Bright lay prostrate under one of the greatest afflictions that can befall mortal man, Cobden came to him and said: "Your grief is great, but remember that there are millions of widows and widows' sons who perish this day in England from lack of cheap bread." In this great land of India there are millions of men and women and children this day who have their lives shortened, their physique stunted, and with their physique, their moral and intellectual faculties blunted, by lack of cheap salt. (*Hear, hear*). I address many of the great of this land. Will they use all their influence to make this precious necessary of life cheaper? Fellow Delegates, will you show that they accuse you falsely, who say your care is all for yourselves and that this movement is simply one for the substitution of Indian dark-skinned for European fair-skinned Brahmins, by saying: "If in no other way can this yoke be made less grievous, tax us, tax the rich but let the poor go! I appeal to you, one and all in this Hall, to show that Western education has brought with it an increase of sympathy and charity for your

3rd Day.

Res. V. Reduction of the Salt Duty.

poorer brethren, for the dumb millions of the land, without which sympathy and charity, all the knowledge of this earth is but as sounding brass and a tinkling cymbal." (*Loud cheers*).

DINSHAW EDULJEE WACHA (*Bombay, No. 543, in list*)—MR. PRESIDENT AND FELLOW DELEGATES,—You have already heard Mr. Kennedy on the question of the consumption of salt and the oppressive incidence of the salt tax on the people. I will, however, make a few further observations on this part of the subject, before I dwell at some length on the financial condition of the country, which is the ground on which we propose to memorialise the Government of India to reduce the tax. The principal object of the Resolution before you is to urge upon the Government the justice of remitting the enhanced salt duty of 8 annas per maund which is no longer imperative on account of the material improvement which the finances of the Empire have undergone since the date of its imposition. It is needless for me to recall to your memory the pretext under which the enhancement was justified in the early part of 1888, despite the fact that well-informed critics in the press and responsible associations at the time conclusively showed that it was uncalled for.

Previous to the imposition of the augmented duty, the Government of India had absorbed in two years 8¾ crores of rupees, *viz.:*—

| | |
|---|---|
| By Income Tax ... ... ... ... ... ... | Rs. 2,75,00,000 |
| Improvements and Economies ... ... ... ... ... | „ 2,00,00,000 |
| Curtailment of Provincial Allotment ... ... ... ... | „ 1,00,00,000 |
| Appropriation of Famine and Railway Fund ... ... ... ... | „ 3,00,00,000 |

This colossal amount of nearly 9 crores was wasted on the following questionable and hazardous enterprises :—

| | |
|---|---|
| Upper Burmah acquisition ... ... ... ... ... | Rs. 3,51,00,000 |
| Penjdeh Field Force ... ... ... ... ... ... | „ 2,11,60,000 |
| Transfrontier Defences and Railways ... ... ... ... | „ 2,00,00,000 |
| Additional Military Expenditure ... ... ... ... ... | „ 98,00,000 |

But even after the absorption of such a vast amount there was a heavy deficiency which, the Government regretfully urged, necessitated a recourse to additional taxation in the shape of an enhanced duty of 8 annas per maund on such a necessary of life as salt. The deficiency was chiefly attributable, according to Lord Dufferin's statement, to the fall in the value of silver.

We need not, however, trouble ourselves much with the past. We are now here to remind the Government that our finances are in a condition to justify the remission of the enhanced duty. For that purpose let me put some statistics before you. I know that statistics are very dry, and that blue books of a dry-as-dust character are never looked at by the public; but considering the importance of the Resolution before you, I hope you will give your attention to the figures I am going to place before you.

Previous Finance Ministers, particularly Sir John Strachey and Sir Evelyn Baring, two of the ablest ministers since the days of the late Mr. Wilson and Mr. S. Laing, repeatedly declared that the lower the salt duty the better for the country and the better for the Imperial revenue, because a lower duty stimulates consumption and a higher one restricts it. Government itself has admitted the soundness of this doctrine, and I will now proceed to show by figures how a lower or higher duty affects consumption. In 1876-77, when various rates of duty were enforced in the different provinces of the Empire, the total recorded amount which paid the salt-tax was 25,847,830 maunds. In 1878, Sir John Strachey brought about an equalization of the duty everywhere by fixing the uniform rate of Rs. 2-8 per maund. It remained in force till 1882. During this period the annual quantity of salt which paid the duty of Rs. 2-8 per maund averaged 27,288,569 maunds. This annual average, compared with the consumption recorded in 1876-77, showed a growth 5·5 per cent. In 1882, the government of Lord Ripon reduced the duty to Rs. 2 per maund, at which it remained till it was again raised to 2-8 by Lord Dufferin in 1888. The quantity which paid the reduced duty of Rs. 2 averaged during the five years 30,830,847 maunds per annum.

The increase during this quinquennial period, compared with the average of the previous four years, was 3,542,278 maunds, equal to a percentage of 13. Thus, while in the period when the duty was Rs 2-8, the increase equalled 1·37 per cent per annum ; in the period when it was Rs. 2 the growth equalled 2·6 per cent per annum. (*Cheers*). It is obvious that, had there been no enhancement, the progress in consumption up to date would have been maintained at that or even a higher rate. But just as this progress was perceptible all throughout the country, the financial embarrassments of the Government led, as they asserted, to the augmentation of the duty and with it to a restricted consumption. In his last financial statement Sir David Barbour has tried to show that the progress of consumption has received no check. According to his own figures, however, as given in the 23rd paragraph of that statement, it is clear that consumption in 1890-91 is estimated at about 31,930,000 maunds, which is less, by 900,000 maunds, than the recorded figures of 1886-87.

Sir David attempts to demonstrate that, in spite of the increased duty, consumption, which had evidently fallen, is again creeping to the old level. But Sir David forgets two important factors: Firstly, that population is increasing at the rate of one per cent per annum; and, secondly, that but for the enhancement, the percentage of progress observable till 1887 might have been better in 1890-91. Indeed, it is a question whether the consumption per head has not fallen below the average of 10lbs. per annum. That average is considered everywhere, but in India, to be quite inadequate, especially as we allow nothing in our computation for the consumption of cattle, hundreds of thousands of whom annually lose condition for want of salt and die off consequently on the smallest failure of pasturage, and thus cripple to a serious extent the means which mainly contribute to the production of our national wealth.

I will give you some figures of the consumption of salt in Europe and America, from which it will be easily perceived how much India falls short of what may be called an adequate consumption of salt. In the United Kingdom there is no duty, and the consumption is 80lbs. per head, but of course this includes much salt for manufacturing purposes. In France it is 50lbs; in Germany 25, in Russia 19—Russia whose economic conditions are in some respects identical with those of India; in Austria 14, in Italy 18, in Spain and Portugal, poor as they are, 17lbs. The consumption in the United States is 39lbs. the average in Europe is 26lbs.

Then look at the incidence of the duty. The average income per head of the European population is £15 4*s.* 7½*d.* per head, while the salt duty per head averages 11*d.* Now, taking the rupee at 1*s.* 6*d.* the average income of the population in India is £2, while the salt duty per head averages 5*d.* and 1½ farthings. Therefore in Europe the salt duty is 0·3 per cent on the income, while in India it is over 1·1 per cent—or, in other words, the incidence of the salt tax is now nearly four times as heavy in India as in Europe. Formulated in other terms it means that India, with an income hardly more than ⅛th that of Europe, pays nearly half as much as a tax on a necessity of life like salt. Thus the duty operates as a real hardship on the poorest people, who constitute the large majority of our population. How great is the hardship may be realised by taking a concrete example. A family of five consumes on an average, say, 50lbs. of salt annually. But there are only two bread-winners, man and wife, the rest being young persons or children. Taking the average income of each *earner* at the official computation, *viz.*, Rs. 27 per head, and calculating the lowest retail bazar price at Rs 3¼ per maund it will be found that there is a burden of nearly 4 per cent. on the combined income per annum merely for salt. Imagine an income-tax of 4 per cent. on a poor family of 5 and nearly one-sixth of this is due to the extra 8 annas. Thus the enhancement of the duty, however small, operates with great hardship on the masses.

Under these circumstances it is a matter of deep regret to us all that the two native gentlemen, who were present at the meeting of the Viceregal Council when this enhancement Bill was passed, should have observed that the increased duty would not be felt by the people! I believe that statement was directly opposed to the, all but absolutely, universal opinion outside the Council Chamber. The statement was more to be regretted because it misled Lord Dufferin into observing later on in his speech that the Council were "glad to hear that the enhancement of the duty would not be considered a hardship." This is the way in which nominated members of the Viceregal Council fulfil their trust. It is evident that had there been elected representatives of the people, as proposed by us for the reformed Legislative Councils, no such opinion would have been allowed to prevail and mislead the Government. (*Cheers*). Eight annas may appear trifling to most of us; but they mean a great deal to the poorest. What they signify may be best stated in the substance of the words of Sir Evelyn Baring: "Eight annas to the poor ryot means the purchase of either 3 yards of cloth or a little *lota*."

Gentlemen, all through the history of the salt tax it has been said that it is a poll-tax, and that it falls heavily on the poor. My personal opinion is that it should have no place in our fiscal system, for it is a tax on a necessary of life, and is, moreover, at its present rate fully 25 times the actual cost of production. Eminent statesmen, from Sir John Lawrence to Lord Ripon, have disapproved of it. But it is now too late to abolish it altogether. It is of no use contending with existing facts. All that we should strive for is a low duty on the sound principle that it is conducive to greater consumption both for men and cattle.

**3rd Day.**

**Res. V. Reduction of the Salt Duty.**

I now pass to the second part of the Resolution. I hold in my hand a copy of the explanatory memorandum by the Under Secretary of State for India, presented to Parliament in August last. At page 50 there is a table of *Net* Revenue and Expenditure for the three years ending 1889-90, and also budget estimates for the current official year. Comparing the complete accounts of 1887-88 with the estimates of this year what do we find ! This only, that there is a satisfactory growth of revenue under all the principal heads. Leaving alone opium, salt and provincial rates I find that the increase under the other heads amounts to 143 lakhs of rupees as under :

| | | Accounts. 1887-88. | Budget Estimates. 1890-91. | Increase. 1890-91. |
|---|---|---|---|---|
| Land Revenue | Rx. ... | 19,653,000 | 20,119,000 | 466,000 |
| Stamps | " ... | 3,669,000 | 3,846,000 | 177,000 |
| Excess | " ... | 4,374,000 | 4,645,000 | 271,000 |
| Customs | " ... | 1,182,000 | 1,378,000 | 196,000 |
| Assessed Taxes | " ... | 1,383,000 | 1,514,000 | 131,000 |
| Forest | " ... | 402,000 | 565,000 | 163,000 |
| Registration | " ... | 123,000 | 150,000 | 27,000 |

Thus, apart from salt, which now yields a larger revenue on account of a higher duty, apart from opium which is precarious in its yield, and apart from provincial rates which are mere transfer receipts, there is a growth in four years of 143 lakhs. But beyond this improvement on the revenue side there is, gentlemen, a material saving in one item of Imperial expenditure. I refer to the interest charge on the ordinary debt. In 1887-88, the net charge under this head was Rs. 46,950,000. In the estimates of expenditure for 1890-91 it is put down at Rs. 35,060,000. The saving in four years amounts to 118 lakhs. While we note this improvement in our national expenditure with great satisfaction, we cannot but feel aghast when we discover that expenditure under other heads had risen by leaps and bounds by no less than 308 lakhs.

| | | Accounts. 1887-88. | Budget Estimate. 1890-91. | Increases. |
|---|---|---|---|---|
| Civil Department | Rx. ... | 11,410,000 | 12,075,000 | 665,000 |
| Miscellaneous Charges | " ... | 3,155,000 | 3,702,000 | 547,000 |
| Buildings and Roads | " ... | 4,859,000 | 5,128,000 | 269,000 |
| Army Services | " ... | 19,357,000 | 20,522,000 | 1,165,000 |
| Special Defence Works | " ... | 456,000 | 892,000 | 436,000 |

Thus in four years they have managed to run up Civil and Military charges, including defence works, by the enormous extent of 3 crores. The army services alone have increased by a crore and sixteen lakhs ! not to speak of defence works having been run up 100 per cent ! It is these stupendous charges which eat up your growing revenue. It is the so-called defence policy, the safeguarding of our frontiers and transfrontiers from a bugbear of their own creation, created to find staff appointments, and employment to the already monied European classes which is at the root of the financial embarrassments of the Government and at the root of the starvation and misery which are eating away the lives of tens of millions of our pauper Indians. There are military and other critics who disapprove of that policy. Our late lamented friend Mr. Slagg characterised it two years ago, as you may remember, as a "mad" policy, when speaking on the subject in the House of Commons. I believe that it is a "mad" policy I know that it is a wicked policy and as long as it is pursued headlong it will continue to embarrass the finances and add millions yearly to our already alarmingly heavy death roll. The embarrassments arising from the fall in the value of silver are in my opinion nothing—a mere fleabite compared with the financial difficulties in which the Government of India is plunged by this insane military policy. I repeat ; that unless a great effort is made at future Congresses to force the Government to desist from these reckless and indefensible operations beyond the natural lines of Indian defence, there can be scarcely any hope of pecuniary relief to the taxpayer—scarcely any hope for the amelioration of the miserable condition of our starving millions. Since the Panjdeh scare they have spent, according to the official statements, full 13 crores on the so-called trans-frontier defences ; but we have not yet seen the last of them, for in the last financial statement reference is made to a further probable expenditure of a crore !

I now come to the practical part of the resolution. Of course we have to submit resignedly to this ruinous, this unprincipled trans-frontier policy of the Government until we succeed in awakening the consciences of our British fellow-subjects. We are British subjects now of our own free choice ; we have thrown in our lot with England for better and for worse, and it is this which enhances England's sin in permitting the continuance of this hateful policy. Will our British brethren never awake ? Meanwhile more ammunition, more explosives, more fireworks and even more troops are being requisitioned. These costly pastimes, amusements to our rulers, death to our people, may deter the authorities from giving ear to our prayers and protests. But it is well, none the less, to remind them of their own declaration that the enhanced duty "must go" as soon as the finances permit.

3rd Day.

Res. V. Reduction of the Salt Duty.

One of the principal grounds on which Lord Dufferin stated that he was obliged, "*with the greatest reluctance*," to increase the duty, was the loss by exchange. I quote from the speech he made about the beginning of 1888. "Unfortunately, it has become my lot on several occasions to add to the taxation of the country, but in justification of this hard necessity, it is sufficient for me to remark that since my arrival in India, owing to the depreciation in the price of silver, the annual accumulation of loss to the Government has progressively increased yearly by a million." He goes on to say: "The loss in 1884-85, when I first took up the reins of Government, stood at 3·40 crores; in 1885-86 at 4·40 crores; in 1886 at 5·40 crores, and in 1887-88 at 6 60 crores." The latest financial statement gives the loss on exchange at 7 crores. It was, however, promised by both Lord Dufferin and Mr. Westland that the duty should be remitted on the first opportunity that the finances were relieved of this embarrassment. That opportunity has now arrived. Since the publication of the last budget you are all aware that exchange has greatly improved, partly in consequence, possibly, of the action taken in regard to silver in the United States. Though we had violent fluctuations in August and September last, exchange still stands to-day at about 1*s.* 6½*d.* The amount to be remitted this year to the Secretary of State is nearly 15 millions sterling. The rate of exchange was estimated in March last at 1*s.* 4⅓*d.* and the probable loss at that rate was computed to be 7 crores. But already 11 millions have been remitted at an average rate of 1*s.* 6½*d.*, and there is no reason to doubt that the balance of the remittance will be made at or about the same rate. Sir John Gorst himself stated when presenting the budget in August last that the rate would probably be maintained at 1*s.* 6½*d.* So that it may be taken for granted that the loss by exchange will be very much less than the budget estimate of 7 crores. I compute it at only about 4·66 crores. Thus, apart from all other fluctuations of revenue and expenditure, there would be a saving under this head alone of nearly 2½ crores. Sir John Gorst counts on a surplus 1·87 crores. Taking his figures and the actual surplus of 2 crores of last year, it may be reasonably expected that there will be available a surplus of not less than 4 crores in all And unless the authorities persevere in muddling it away on military mischief that surplus should suffice, not only for the remission of the enhanced duty, but for reduction of this latter to Rs. 1-8. (*Loud cheers*).

But I beg to bring to your notice two more facts which will convince you that *even apart from these surpluses*, the financial condition of the Imperial Treasury has so far improved as to justify our demand for a remission. The additional duty yields, it is asserted, 1½ crores (it is not really so much), and, I say that that 1½ crores could be dispensed with easily for some years to come. According to Sir David Barbour's statement, there has been a permanent growth in the principal heads of revenue of ¾ of a crore per annum; exchange, again, is unlikely to go back to 1*s.* 4½*d.* for some time to come. Looking at current events and the further agitation on silver in America, it seems that a rate of 1*s.* 6½*d.* or even 1*s.* 6*d.* will be fairly maintained. But even if exchange could be maintained at 1*s.* 5½*d.* that would diminish the loss on the Secretary of State's bills in future to the extent of 1 crore roughly speaking, for an improvement of a penny in exchange gives a saving, according to official estimates, of just that amount. This saving, plus the permanent increase of ¾ crore in the principal sources of revenue, make up 1¾ crores, so that the Government is in a position to safely give up the 1½ crore now supposed to be derived from the additional duty of 8 annas per maund; as a matter of fact the loss, owing to increased consumption, would, after the first year, be less than one crore. Both financial conditions and the justice of the case demand, imperatively, that a remission should be made. I think, Gentlemen, I have now shewn substantial reasons for the remission. And if you think I have made out a substantial case on which to base our representation to Government to remit the duty, I am sure that that representation will at any rate *deserve* an attentive and favorable consideration at the hands of the authorities. (*Loud and prolonged cheers*).

Mr. G. K. Gokhale (*Bombay, No. 560, in list*)—Mr. President, Ladies, and Gentlemen,—I have been asked to support this proposition that has been ably proposed, seconded and explained by previous speakers My predecessors have dealt with certain aspects of the question, and I will with your permission deal with one or two others. I say that the measures for the enhancement of the duty on salt in January 1888 by a mere executive order of the Government of India was a cruel departure—I might almost say a criminal departure—from the wise policy long since laid down by the Government of India and re-affirmed, strange as it may seem, when Lord Lytton was our Viceroy and Sir John Strachey our Finance Minister, namely the policy of raising a revenue from salt by a low rate of duty and unrestricted consumption instead of by a high rate of duty and restricted consumption. I say that this new departure was extremely unjust, that as a measure of statesmanship it was extremely impolitic, and that its consequences have been simply disastrous. I know these are serious charges, but I think I can substantiate them. First, with regard to the charge of injustice. When Lord

3rd Day.

Res. V. Reduction of the Salt Duty.

Dufferin's government passed the Income Tax Act of 1886 his Lordship said that the measure was not brought forward in any spirit of apology, that the masses of the country were already contributing more than their proper share to the expenses of the country, and that the income-tax would only equalize the burdens on the various classes. Well, the burdens being thus equalised in 1886, I ask on what principle of justice and equity was it that when two years afterwards a new emergency, as Government were pleased to call it, arose for additional taxation, it was the poor masses who were selected? How was it that when it was found necessary to create a fresh inequality in the taxation of the country matters were so arranged that the inequality was again prejudicial to the toiling masses? I do not know whether it was because the masses were almost certain to suffer silently without protest—I would even say without complaint—whereas their wealthier brethren were as certain to denounce any taxation on them in the public press and at St. Andrew's dinner speeches. So much with regard to the injustice of the measure: now with regard to its impolicy. We have on our side an authority not only infinitely greater than myself but one to which the Government of India ought to bow—I mean the authority of the Secretary of State for India, Lord Cross himself. Three months after the measure of enhancement his Lordship wrote a Despatch to the Government on the subject. It was dated April 12th, 1888, and in it he expresses his great regret at the enhancement of the salt duty, and directed the Government of India in very distinct, unequivocal, and I would say peremptory terms to take off the additional eight annas on the first opportunity afforded by the finances. He then went on to say that even from the point of view of expediency the enhancement was extremely undesirable, because in the case of so vast an empire as India it was absolutely essential for the Government always to hold in hand some financial reserve which they might utilize on occasions of any sudden and dangerous crisis. So much with regard to impolicy: now, with regard to consequences, I am going to show that consumption has actually been restricted by this measure. In 1888 Mr. Westland, our Finance Minister, said that the enhancement would not affect the consumption of the country. The figures supplied by Sir. David Barbour himself belied that prediction. The last year unaffected was 1886-87, and then the consumption stood at 3 crores and 10 lakhs of maunds. The next year, 1887-88, the first year affected by the measure, there was a fall of 6 lakhs of maunds, the figures being 3 crores 4 lakhs. The next year there was a further fall of 6 lakhs, the figures being 2 crores 98 lakhs. It is true that the figures have now gone up to those of 1886-87, but that does not show that the restrictive operation of that enhancement has ceased, because we have to take into consideration the important factor of the increase in the consumption of salt owing to the normal growth of the population. That normal growth is one per cent per annum, and taking the consumption at 10lbs. per head, you find that every year there ought to be an increase of fully 3 lakhs of maunds in the consumption of salt.

Taking this into account you will see that in the first year affected by the enhancement there was a fall of 9 lakhs, in the second of 18, and in the third of 9. Altogether in the last three years 36 lakhs of maunds less have been consumed by the people than they would have consumed if there had not been the enhancement. (*Cheers*). Sir John Gorst speaking the other day in the House of Commons, said that the diminution in the consumption of salt was not appreciable—that was the term he used. I do not know what dictionaries would justify the use of the term, but Sir John Gorst is welcome to use the word in this connection. But I ask him, and those who think with him, who are the persons affected by this diminishing consumption? I dare say there is not a single person present, not a single member of those who are called the middle and upper classes, who have consumed, during the last three years, one grain of salt less than he would have done if there had been no enhancement. Who are the persons affected? They are those who have been estimated by Sir William Hunter at 40 millions, and by Sir Charles Elliott at 70 millions, who always exist on the borderland of famine, so that, directly there is the least failure, down the precipice they go. The persons affected by this enhancement are they to whom the lines of the Corn Law poet might aptly be applied:—

> "Landless, joyless, helpless, hopeless,
> Gasping still for bread and breath
> To their graves by trouble hunted
> India's helots toil till death." (*Loud cheers.*)

When you call to mind the thin emaciated figures of these unhappy, miserable, brethren, who have as much right to the comforts of this, God's, earth as you or I or any one else; when you remember that the lives of these brethren are so uniformly dark and miserable, that they are hardly cheered by a single ray of hope, or relieved by a single day of rest; when, further, you remember that a person does not generally trench upon his stock of necessaries before he has parted with every luxury, every single comfort that he may allow himself; when you recall all these things, you will clearly understand what grievous and terrible hardship and suffering and privation, this measure of enhancement which has curtailed the poor man's consumption of salt by thirty-six lakhs of maunds has really entailed. (*Cheers*). We are appealing in the present instance to the Government of India to reduce the duty on salt from two rupees eight annas to two rupees per maund. My friend Mr. Watcha has shown that the state of the finances permits of such reduction. We are appealing to the sense of justice of the Government of India. We are appealing to their statesmanship, to their righteousness, and I will even go further and say to their mercy. The past is in the past and no one can recall it ; but this much can surely be done—further evil and misery from this source can be averted. It is with this hope that I support this proposition, and in this hope I ask you to carry it with acclamation. (*Cheers.*)

Mr. Jamietram Nanabhai Haridas (*Bombay, No. 545, in list*)—Mr. President, Ladies and Gentlemen,—I most cordially support this proposition. My support, however, is really superfluous after the able speeches we have heard. It was previously adopted by the Congress ; what we now do is to confirm, ratify and reiterate it with emphasis. Its very importance obliges us,—nay it is our sacred duty—to protest strongly against the continuation of an enhancement, which tells so much upon the fifty millions of paupers over which India now mourns. Let "united, strenuous and continuous efforts, combined with willing and resolute determination, till success is achieved," be our motto. We are under a greater obligation to try again and again till we are heard, for we do so on behalf of the poor dumb masses. Need I remind you of their extreme poverty ? Need I prove it before you—you of the Congress who are of the people, and who mix among them so frequently—you who every day personally witness it ? Need I labour to establish the very apparent proposition that salt is one of the necessaries of life ? Need I tell you that the price of salt has been artificially raised by the action of Government to many times, 30, even 40 times, the actual cost of production ? So we have these facts before us : salt is necessary for life, salt is very dear, and the people are extremely poor. This is hard, very hard, and exceedingly cruel. Good men exult over the successes achieved in the prevention of cruelty to animals ; but I fail to see why we should not have a *society* systematically working to prevent cruelty to higher animals, *viz.* human beings ! Cruel, indeed, is the working of the salt-tax laws. The proposition before us goes not far enough. For not only is this taxation itself radically bad and wrong—a tyranny of the rich over the poor which, instead of being reduced by only eight annas as we are asking, should be reduced, except in times of war and sudden financial crisis, by two rupees, or at any rate by Re. 1-8, but the law imposing the taxation is so framed as to involve almost a maximum of annoyance to the people. Every one knows this, but day by day the law reveals new grounds for detesting the whole system. One very harsh provision was only recently brought to light in two cases, both of a similar character. You will find from these, that if accidently you happen to pour water over your salt, and so dissolve it, you will be guilty of an offence as soon as you apply heat to recover the salt. Thus has been created an artificial and technical offence out of an act which is both religiously and morally innocent. I am afraid that if the next rainy season turns your salt into water, you must throw it away. You cannot, without committing a crime, recover it by applying heat, artificial or natural. How long is the country to endure this systematised oppression ? Well, every little helps and I cordially support this present resolution as going, at any rate, a single step along the right road. (*Loud cheers.*)

Mr. A. Nandy (*Central Provinces, No. 607, in list*)—Mr. President, Ladies and Gentlemen,—I rise with great pleasure to support this resolution, and to add my testimony to the great pressure of this salt taxation on the masses of India. Previous speakers have adequately referred to the special reasons which led to the increase of the duty on salt ; they have graphically described the evils attending on this iniquitous impost ; and they have further established, beyond a shadow of doubt, that the time has now arrived when this heavy duty on salt should be reduced. I have no desire to dilate further on these points ; but I wish to bring home to your minds, Gentlemen, that the Central Provinces, from which I have the honour of being sent as a delegate, has a special interest in this question. It has been shown that it is a matter of grave necessity that this duty on salt should be reduced all over India ; but I say, Sir, that it is not only a matter of necessity, but of great urgency that this reduction should be carried out in the Central Provinces, and that this should be done promptly and without delay.

You are all aware, Gentlemen, that the temporary settlement prevails in the Central Provinces. I am not going to speak on the advantages of a permanent settlement, for I should thereby be encroaching on the duties of the speakers on the resolution which follows this ; but I wish merely to point out that, owing to the new settlement, which is now in progress, a state of things is being brought about, which demands that relief of some kind, at least, should be given to the impoverished masses of the Central Provinces, and that this relief can, to some extent, be obtained by a partial reduction of the salt-tax. As most of you are aware, the periodical settlement took place in 1864-65, and it shortly expires. For the last three years survey and settlement officers are traversing the country, and what has been the result ?

3rd Day.

Res. V. Reduction of the Salt Duty.

The Government revenue has been increased as regards some villages 40 per cent., 50 per cent., and even 100 per cent. This, Gentlemen, let me assure you, I say on the highest authority possible. Now, who is to pay this increased revenue? I shall show you that eventually it is the poor ryot who will have to pay it. I ought here to remind you that besides the Government revenue, the malguzar, that is the owner of the village, has to meet a variety of other demands. He has to pay the education-cess; he has to pay the putwari-cess; he has to pay for the maintenance of the hospitals; and, lastly, he has to pay the road-cess. The Imperial Government requires him to pay these cesses; but there are other local demands which he has to satisfy. The District Officer proceeds on tour, the unfortunate malguzar has not only to see that the road is carefully prepared for his progress; but he has to meet the hundred and one demands of his camp-followers, whose requirements it is not easy to satisfy. So great does this evil become sometimes that the malguzar dreads nothing more than the dubious honour of a District Officer passing through his village.

Having met these Government and other demands, what is the financial position of the Malguzar? I have been assured not by one, but by a number of these malguzars, that after paying up these demands, they find that sometimes there is hardly any surplus left for themselves—and they too must live—and if any, a very small one indeed. And now the Government steps in and increases the revenue by 40, 50 and 100 per cent.

When this last settlement took place it was declared that the revenue then assessed would not be increased for at least a period of 30 years; but what did the Government do? It did not directly increase the revenue; it dared not be guilty of such a shameless and open breach of faith, but by means of incidental charges and cesses it has indirectly increased the charge by 25 per cent. Besides these there are a number of other indirect demands which the malguzars have to meet; there is the imperial road-cess of which I have spoken, but besides this there is another road cess, the District Officers' road-cess. When a District Officer goes on a tour through the country, or goes on a *shikar* (or shooting) expedition, they have to prepare the road for him and have to provide the incidental expenses which the followers of the camp are put to. There are also other demands. Last year I asked one of the malguzars for a subscription to the National Congress Fund; but he said it was a very inconvenient time, for shortly before he had been giving a sum of money for a memorial to one of the officials. I asked the official's name, and he said—let us say—"John Smith." I asked "Of what service?" and he mentioned " the service. "Why did you give it?" I asked. "Well," he said, "I never had the pleasure of meeting the officer, but I gave the money at the instance of the tahsildar, who had been asked by the officials to get contributions towards the memorial." Now I put it to you, was that a voluntary contribution, or was it not a species of tax? This then being the case with the malguzars, the question arises, are they in a position to meet any extra revenue which the Government imposes? Many of them have proved to me that after all these demands are paid there is scarcely any surplus left to them; if there is any it is very small. To what then will the malguzars be reduced? To either one of two alternatives: either to quit their villages or to increase the rent of their tenants. It is impossible to expect them to quit, and the necessary consequence is that the poor will have their rents raised. And who are these? Not the well-to-do ryots, but those who have small holdings and live from hand to mouth—these will have to pay the enhanced revenue, and will have starvation facing them. I therefore put it to you whether the position of the Central Provinces does not demand that this resolution should be carried and that some response should be made to it by the Government. The Government has the right, as the law stands, to arrrange periodically the revenue imposed on each village, and they are not likely to give up exercising that right so long as a permanent settlement is not conceded. So long as they exercise that right, the landholder already pressed for means will accept no share of the new burthen. The well-to-do cultivators, with occupancy rights and means to defend these rights in the Courts, will allow no portion of it to be laid upon their shoulders, and all enhancements will have to come from those who have only small holdings, who have no fixed tenures and no means, from the very poor in fact, the members of that army of martyrs, our starving fifty millions, on whom it is that this heavy salt tax presses heaviest—one small relief for these this resolution advocates, and I therefore most cordially support it, small and insignificant, comparatively speaking, as that relief is. *(Prolonged cheers)*.

LALA MURLIDHUR (*Panjab, No. 531, in list*)—MR. PRESIDENT AND GENTLEMEN,—In bygone days our time was divided into three great divisions—youth, manhood, old age,—each spread over more than a score of years. But now the angel of death has prescribed a period of five minutes for a speaker to exist in this Tribune. (*Laughter.*) Having wasted so many years of my life, I will not waste these precious minutes which have been allotted to me, and therefore I will at once proceed to make my last will and testament. Mr. Watcha has said that this is a dry subject. I do not see why people should dislike a dry subject. They do not dislike a dry dress, a dry room, dry weather, or dry salt; but they do not like a dry subject. (*Laughter*). It is strange indeed. Now I take it that it is the duty of every man who eats the salt of another to prove true to the salt, to be faithful to him. And Government being in the position of a public servant, it is the duty of the public servant to be true to the public. But has it been faithful to the public? I submit it has not. I have to deal with the subject of salt. What does the salt duty mean? Do those who adorn the benches of the Legislative Councils stand in need of salt? Of course they do; they like it very much. But then they say, "It is not liked by the poorer classes; it is a necessity for us, but not for them." Is that just or reasonable? If there are any people whose only luxury in life is salt, and who are denied the blessings which God has conferred upon others, they are the famine-stricken people who live in huts. The rich people, it is said, require salt, but the poor do not. Of course they do not. They live on sufferance; life is a long misery to them; and it would have been better had they not been born in this miserable world than be denied this, their sole luxury, which is a necessity to other people. Shame, gentlemen, why does this state of things prevail! Because you have not proper representatives of these poor classes who stand in need of salt on the Legislative Council. It is only Sir Syed Ahmed who is a fit representative of these poor classes. I ask, is he a proper person to understand their needs? If you deny salt to these poor people, you may as well deny them air to breathe, light to see, and water to drink. What does the salt duty mean? It is a tax on hunger and on thirst; it is a tax on one's life. It is a wrong which presses hard on these people. Place yourselves in the position of these poor men; go to their homes and see for yourselves what sort of life they lead; and then say if you will deny them the last thing which makes the scanty insipid scraps of food, which is all they can ever compass, at all palatable to these wretched creatures. (*Cheers.*) For God's sake, I say, do not deny them this one luxury which they stand much in need of. Do any of us approve this cruel grinding of our pauper brethren? Do I, do any of us? No, I at any rate will that henceforth there should be some mitigation of their sufferings in this respect at least, and this being my last *will* and testament, I would ask, as it is nuncupative, some gentlemen here, either the reporters for the press or some registrar or magistrate in this august assembly, to go and register, after my death, this last will and testament of mine in the Government Office; and as the time of my dissolution is fast approaching, I make this last appeal to the Government to reduce the tax and make the poor people a little less miserable. (*Cheers*).

Mr. Deva Prasad Sarvadhikari (*Calcutta, No. 57, in list*)--I have listened, Sir, with great care and attention to the interesting and able speeches in support of this resolution, but you will excuse me if I confess that I am by no means persuaded that the resolution as it now stands is fit for your adoption. Facts and figures, no doubt, have been quoted which tend to a conclusion with which no one would quarrel; but we must not forget that that conclusion being conceded, the other things which we demand do not necessarily follow. I know it is a difficult task for one like myself to address so large and mixed a gathering in opposition to the prevailing sense of the meeting. But I feel it my duty to speak; and permit me to remind you that in a deliberative assembly like this one is apt to be led, unconsciously, no doubt, into the adoption of views and opinions which are not likely to commend themselves to their better judgment.

(*A voice*: "*Move your amendment.*") I will bring it in at the proper time. ("*Read it.*") I will read it presently.

The President: If it is the wish of the meeting that the amendment should be read, I think it *should* be read.

Mr. Sarvadhikari: I will obey the Chair and read it. You will see that it does not materially alter the resolution, but to a certain extent it goes counter to it. It is to the following effect:—

"*That the condition of the finances of India having improved, and those special circumstances, on which the Government relied to justify the recent enhancement of the salt-tax; having partially ceased to exist, this Congress considers that the provisions of the Salt Act, regarding the preparation and consumption of salt for the preservation of cattle and industrial purposes, should be modified according to special circumstances prevailing in different localities, and empowers its President to submit a special memorial on the subject in its name and on its behalf to His Excellency the Viceroy in Council.*"

3rd Day.

Res. V. Reduction of the Salt Duty.

You will observe that I only suggest such an alteration as would be consistent with the former part of the programme that you have already adopted. It behoves you to give special care and consideration before you commit yourselves to the adoption of the original resolution. I am aware that it has received the sanction of a previous Congress ; but that to my mind does not go for much. A lawyer by profession, and perhaps by instinct and tradition, I should be inclined to attach due importance to case law ; but I ask you on a question of national importance not to be solely guided by precedents that are by no means sound. I take the liberty of pointing out to you that the resolution as it stands is not fit for your adoption (*cries of "it is, it is*)" : first, because it is based upon an insufficient conception of facts, and, secondly, because it involves the acceptance of principles which are unsound at bottom notwithstanding their specious appearance. The resolution alludes to the great improvements which have taken place in the finances of India. We have had a formidable array of facts and figures, which, however, appear to be an illusory dream, having nothing more than a paper existence. Upon the supposition of this surplus numerous demands have been made upon the Government which Government has not been able to accede to, partly because of its notorious disinclination to reduce any existing burden the renewal of which would be objected to in time of need, but especially because it has never had any tangible and real surplus with which honestly to meet those demands. Taking, however, the surplus to be real, and not supposititious, what should be the first demand for relief ? Surely not this indirect burden which they, perhaps, do not perceive in the long run, which, though objectionable in principle, is lightly felt because of its pretty even distribution and pretty equitable incidence. I think your first demand should be with regard to those obnoxious imposts of an inquisitorial character ("*no, no*"), "those little premia for safety and security," in the felicitous language of Lord Dufferin in announcing to the tax-paying world at Agra the resuscitation of a monster whom we had taken to be dead for good, under the fostering care of Lord Northbrook. You have been crying "*no, no,*" and I perfectly sympathize with you ; but, in carrying out the omnibus resolution, you ought to have remembered that you are giving effect to a demand for a partial abolition at any rate of the income-tax. You are responsible members of a national assembly which, though not "endowed with power," should so act and deliberate as to make the rulers of our destinies think that we are well fitted for the exercise of any powers that may be conceded to us. Having adopted one part of the programme, it remains for you to be consistent. I am sorry that I have had to diverge. I will now come to the point. You have been crying out against the income-tax with commendable loudness and constancy (*A voice*: "*No, never ; only against its low incidence ; loud cheers*)' although with not much appreciable result so far. In the course of your present deliberations, as I have pointed out, you have accepted this principle of indirect taxation. You did the same thing in former years by asking for the reimposition of those import duties, which were abandoned in a fashion which it would not be prudent to characterize in the presence of the honorable member for Manchester. Well, your representatives in the press and on the platform have repeatedly emphasized that principle, and some of you are clearly of opinion (*no, no*) that the octroi should replace all other forms of municipal taxation, though thereby the food and clothes of the meanest and poorest citizens should be taxed. Those of you who are acquainted with the working of the octroi in the North-Western Provinces and elsewhere will know that the burden is not very heavily felt, and yet the municipal finances flourish ("*Question, to the point*"). Evils, no doubt, there are concomitant with a system like that, but they are evils of detail which it is for the executive to rectify. I do not deny that evils exist in connection with the salt-tax also, but they are evils to be rectified. Those who are acquainted with the hardships felt by seaside people who have been so long accustomed to make their own salt, which they are now precluded from doing, will no doubt sympathize with the resolution at the first glance ; and I myself sympathize with it. All I ask you is to consider whether you will allow your sympathies to go counter to reason and common sense. Sentiment has, no doubt, its place in the counsels of the Empire ; but sentiment alone cannot shape a nation's laws. They should be founded upon the sure basis of facts ; and if some details are oppressive let them be remedied.

Ask the Government to allow people to make their own salt for the preservation of cattle and for industrial purposes. Let there be an amendment of the local and imperial laws in that behalf. Bombay or Madras cases of hardship and severity alone cannot control legislation. There are no doubt extreme cases, and I should have been glad if this resolution had been pertinently addressed to the rectification of those evils. If you wish to hear the last of these complaints you will have to abolish the tax altogether, and that you cannot do I am no apologist for taxation ; no one is. But the millennium is not so near at hand ; you have to grapple with the situation as you find it, and under existing circumstances neither the total abolition nor the material reduction of the salt tax would be possible. Therefore you ought to accept it with the best grace. I know that my amendment will be lost, but I feel it my duty to move it. Some of you go so far as to ask for the total abolition of this tax (*no, no*) ; you ask very properly that a portion of the excise duties should be abandoned ; you ask for a large expenditure on education ; you ask for a separation of the judicial and executive functions ; and you ask for other improvements for which there must be money. Government must have money, and it is one of the duties of loyal citizens to find money, and, if that is so we must find it in the least objectionable way. It is for you to consider whether indirect taxation is not what will suit the country best ( *no, no* ). I appeal to you not to be led away by hasty impulses and first impressions. You should look coolly at the matter and decide as responsible members of a responsible assembly to which powers may come in due time. I am sorry to go counter to the prevailing sense of the meeting, but I ask you to give the matter your careful deliberation. Bombay has conferred great obligations upon us ; no abler man than Dadabhai Naorojee could be found ; but I appeal to them not to mar the generosity shown to us by forcing upon us propositions which are at war with reason and common sense, and, above all, with the spirit of moderation. (*No, no, bosh !* )

Mr. R. D. Mehta (*Calcutta, No. 670, in list*), who was received with cheers, said : Mr. President and Gentlemen,—Let me first of all thank you for your plaudits, and, secondly, let me beg the favour of your not hurling me down from this exalted pulpit by your cries of "no no." I am sure, addressing as I am practical and sensible men who have come from such great distances to deliberate on the wants of the country, that I shall be able to carry my point and convince you. We have had the good fortune of listening to facts and figures cited by my esteemed fellow-countryman Mr. Watcha, who has no doubt made a great study of them ; but are you wiser than you were when you entered this pavilion ? (*yes, yes*). There may be a few exceptional cases, but I say no ( *and we say yes, yes.*) Suppose the eight annas reduction is brought into effect, what would be the saving per head ? That is a point to be carefully considered. Shall we put forward a resolution like this which will meet with nothing but a rebuff from the Government of India ? ( *Shame !*). If Mr. Watcha had told us what would be the saving per head, I would not have come before you. ( "*He has—sit down.*") The able seconder of the motion has brought forward for your sympathy the question of the preservation of our cattle. Are we not all agreed that the preservation of cattle should be the chief care of every civilized man ? It is on behalf of those dumb creatures that my friend has moved his amendment (*no.*) I think you have not quite understood the terms of it. Neither the mover nor myself desires to go against the resolution, but we propose something in the nature of an addition which we think cannot but carry great weight with the Government. When you say " reduce the duty by eight annas per maund," do you know the amount you ask ? (*Yes, a million sterling.*) And do you offer anything to compensate it ? (*No, because Government can now afford it.*) You do not know anything of the kind. Let us be moderate in our demands. Let the Government understand what we are craving for—the preservation of our cattle—in that we are all unanimous. The amendment is not contrary to the resolution (*it is, it is*) ; and if you will permit the insertion of the words proposed in the amendment, it will meet our wishes and the wishes of the general mass of the people whose representatives we are (*no, no.*) What is the alteration we propose ? The resolution says : " The condition of the finances of India having materially improved." We propose to expunge the word " materially," and we also propose to say " those special circumstances, &c., having *partially* ceased to exist, " not practically ceased to exist. Then the amendment proceeds : " *This Congress considers that the provisions of the Salt Act regarding the preparation and consumption of salt for the preservation of cattle and industries should be modified according to special circumstances prevailing in different localities, and empowers its President to submit a memorial on the subject in its name and on its behalf to H. E. the Viceroy in Council.*" Wherein lies the substantial difference between the original resolution and the amendment ? What we all want is to see that one great point is gained—the preservation of our cattle, on which the proposer and seconder of the resolution have laid so much stress. ("*First preserve the people.*")

Mr. Mohini Mohun Chatterjee (*Calcutta, No. 24, in list*)—Mr. President and Brother Delegates,—In coming here this morning I thought I should not have to speak, because a multiplicity of words is not necessary to recommend what I may call the people's resolution to the people's Congress. ( *Cheers.*) In one way I am glad that this amendment is before you, for it allows us an opportunity of considering our position, though I believe that there has never been at any time any misconception about it. Mr. Mehta asks what is the substantial difference between the original proposition and this so-called amendment. (*Cheers.*) They are utterly different and distinct. (*Cheers*). We say that the salt-tax generally should be reduced, so that all our pauper millions who chiefly feel the tax, throughout the Empire, should be relieved *pro tanto.* He says make special rules for special localities, so that some small isolated communities may be benefited.

Our proposition is simple and practical—his absolutely impracticable ( *Cheers*). Of course he has not studied the question. Of course he does not know that differential rates of duty involving cordons to keep the cheaper salt out of localities where it is not intended to be used are

3rd Day.

Res. V. Reduction of the Salt Duty.

absolutely indefensible; that from Lord Mayo's time the whole aim of every reformer has been to get rid of these cordons by having one uniform invariable rate of duty throughout Hindustan; that this by infinite pains has been accomplished; and that his resolution proposes to resuscitate all the evils inseparable from differential rates. Our resolution asks for a practical reform,—his for an impracticable retrograde movement: that is the substantial difference! (*Loud cheers.*)

As far as I can understand its scope the amendment proposed, with the exception of the verbal alteration suggested, comes to this: Let rules be made enabling particular communities of men in particular localities—I don't think it can mean the country generally or there would be an end of salt taxation—to make their own salt, never mind how unwholesome it may be. Rules it seems are to be made with reference to local peculiarities, which, to my mind, only means, let those who are living on the sea coast make their own salt; and how is this salt to be prevented from going inland? But if these rules are to be general, then every man living anywhere where there is even salt earth may make his own salt, cheap and nasty; and we do not want that; and, moreover, nothing short of millions of preventive officials can prevent this cheap and nasty salt, once made, from circulating over the entire country; and we don't want a new army of licensed blackmailers; and without this army the cheap salt will circulate and salt taxation come to an end; and we don't want that even, as yet; we can't afford it, though we can afford to reduce the rate by eight annas, and thus no doubt sacrifice about one million sterling of revenue which Mr. Watcha has shown that we can well spare if there be no new frontier extravagances. (*Loud cheers.*)

The salt-tax is objectionable because it is a tax on life. It is not an income-tax, but a tax on life itself. (*Cheers*). As to the remedy proposed by the amendment, it is worse even than the malady. (*Hear, hear.*) Independent of the army of blackmailers, the salt thus made will be bad salt, full of sulphates and nitrates, not only of sodium, but also of lime and magnesium. It is really better that the people should have no salt than have salt which will introduce disease into the system.

There is one other point in connection with the amendment to which I wish to make reference. If it were practically carried into effect in the manner in which I believe it to be intended, the result will be great inequality in the taxation levied upon salt in different *parts* of the country. If we could *exempt classes* and so arrange that the poor should get their salt free, there would be something in it. But that is impossible; even with differential rates they can only be applied to localities.; all in which, rich or poor, must enjoy the cheaper salt—to me an absurd proposition. I do not know what you think, but certainly I should think that this would be a great evil. Why should one locality pay Re. 1 and another Rs. 3 duty per maund on its salt? This was the old vicious exploded system. Are we to go back to this? We do not want that some parts should have a plentiful and cheap supply, while in others salt should be scarcer and dearer even than at present. What we want is wholesome salt, cheap, and plenty of it; and that, as I have tried to show, the amendment does not provide for.

The argument advanced in support of it is: if you do away with the salt-tax where are you to get the money to keep the Government going? The answer is, firstly, that by the arrangements hinted at by the very vague amendment, an even greater amount of revenue would be sacrificed; either by the free circulation of the home-made salt, or by the prodigious establishments needed to prevent this, than by the reform that we have suggested; secondly, that this latter involves at most a reduction of one million in the revenue, and this our finances can now bear. The proposer of the amendment did not omit to mention the remission of import duties. If the question suggested were ever addressed to us; if it were said, "We having remitted the import duties, where will you now find the money to pay our way if you reduce the salt-tax?" I only should reply in the language of the proverb: "Having put your finger into my eye, do you ask me why I shed tears? (*Loud cheers*). But the fact is our resolution cannot call for any such question. We are now paying our way—far more than paying our way; there will be a surplus if the finances are honestly administered, and we ask that a portion of this should be assigned for this reduction.

Then, again, I am surprised that neither the mover nor the seconder of the amendment has taken the slightest notice of the fact brought before you very clearly by the able seconder of the resolution that a low tax on salt always increases consumption. So, therefore, though the loss might be a million sterling in the first year, there is every reason to believe that increased consumption and increased population would soon make up even this large amount, thus balancing both sides, and that is a another strong argument for the reduction.

In the next place, I think the proposer of the amendment was hardly correct when he characterized the improvement in the finances of the country as somewhat illusory and suppositious. Our Finance Minister, I believe, has himself declared that there has been a permanent improvement in the finances of the country ; that he expects out of the general revenue there will be a surplus of three-quarters of a million, not this year alone, but from year to year. As the able seconder of the resolution has shown, upon exchange there will be a saving of another three-quarters of a million on the least sanguine estimate, altogether one and a half millions ; and if the tax were reduced by eight annas the loss would only be about a million. So that if there is no compensation by increased consumption, at all events the surplus will be able to meet the loss. Now, the question we have to consider is whether or not, under the present circumstances of the country, this—to the very poor—bitterly oppressive tax is not on the whole the most important to be dealt with, and whether it should not be brought at once within more moderate proportions. We can imagine upon the occasion of some great festivity at Government House a poor widow coming with her helpless orphans and saying : " By reducing this tax on salt you will give me and my orphan children at least six extra meals in a year." In order to appreciate the full significance of that, let me remind you of the fact that more than one-fifth of the population of this great country gets from year's end to year's end scarcely one full meal a day. Six annas saved to every family means six additional meals during the year ; and I say, considering the expensive scale upon which the Government of this country is conducted, we ought to put aside all other considerations, and we ought first to try and find those six additional meals a year for the poverty-stricken, disease-stricken, helpless poor of this country. (*Cheers*).

When gentlemen occupying high positions, coddled in the lap of luxury, say, " Oh, the poor won't feel it," there is something so chilling, so discouraging, so sickening in this cynicism that the power of adjectives is quite unable to properly characterize such base and selfish utterances. Well might the poor of the country say :—

> " Nay, take my life and all · · · · · ·
> " You take my life when you thus take the means,
> " Whereby I live ! " (*Cheers*).

Mr. Jambulingam Mudliar (*Madras, No. 645, in list*)—Mr. President and Gentlemen,—When I saw my name in the list, almost at the end, I thought I should have very little to say, and that I might depart from this pulpit simply remarking that I supported the proposition, and as I listened to the force and completeness with which the able mover and seconder of the resolution put the facts and figures of the case, I felt that it would be superfluous and almost impertinent to try to add anything to what they have said.

Now, however, if I occupy the five minutes allowed me, it is because of the amendment that has just been moved and seconded. I will, however, confine myself to one point. The mover of the amendment argued that the salt-tax, being an indirect tax, and even and equitable in its distribution, is an excellent one. Now I cannot understand how he makes out the even and equitable distribution. If he simply means that it pecuniarily affects all people, poor and rich, to an equal extent that may be so ; but if he also means that the incidence, the real *quantum* of taxation, is equal as between the poor and the rich, then I differ from him. As far as the human consumption of salt is concerned, the poor man does not eat much less than the rich man ; but the necessities of the agriculturist, the necessities of the ryot, require that they should purchase an infinitely larger quantity of salt for their own and their cattle's use than is required by the rich man. I believe it may be taken at ten or twenty times as much. If you consider that aspect of the case, you will see at once that, independent of the difference in size of the funds from which it is disbursed, the tax, actually, and not merely relatively, falls much more heavily on the poor man than upon the rich man. (*Cheers*). What then becomes of the statement that the salt-tax, being indirect, and evenly and equitably distributed, is a good tax ?

With regard to the income-tax, the mover of the amendment has been under an entire misapprehension as to the scope of our prayer. He appeared to think that we asked for the abolition of the tax. Certainly not. If we have a prayer with reference to the income-tax, its scope is the same as that with reference to the salt-tax. We want to reduce the salt-tax to help the masses, not to benefit ourselves. We want the taxable minimum to be raised to Rs. 1,000, and that not to help ourselves, pleaders, medical men, merchants, and men of that kind, but to help the masses. Then we are assured that if we went for a reduction of the salt-tax we should meet with a rebuff from the Government. That point has been referred to by Mr. Wacha, who has distinctly shown us that the enhancement of the salt-tax was greatly against the inclination of the Government, and that the Secretary of State sent his mandate that a reduction should be effected at the earliest opportunity that presented itself. I do not, therefore, understand why we should get a rebuff from the Government if we ask a reduction to the former limit. If we should get a rebuff, then all I can say is more shame to the Government. (*Loud cheers.*) We, at any rate, shall have no cause for shame.

3rd Day.

Res. V. Reduction of the Salt Duty.

As to the amendment itself. I ask you to consider whether, consistently with the monopoly of salt by the Government, it is possible to frame acts or rules in the manner proposed. Is it possible to separate the salt required for agricultural purposes from that required for home consumption, and yet to maintain the monopoly? I submit it is utterly unworkable. I am informed that a system of the same kind was tried at Madras, and, being found to be a thorough failure, was given up. Indeed, common sense is enough to show that it must be a failure, and that it is not possible to maintain the monopoly consistently with giving indulgences for other purposes. I trust, therefore, that the amendment will be unanimously rejected. (*Cheers.*)

SWAMI ALARAM (*N. W. P., No. 433, in list*) then spoke in Hindi and said: FRIENDS!—God, who himself is neither a Hindu, nor a Mussulman, nor a Christian, nor a Parsi, sees all sorts of religion with an equal eye. That impartial God has entrusted Her Majesty the Maharani Victoria with this special function of seeing with an equal eye; for in the year 1858 Her Majesty has promised that she would equally deal with the Hindus, Mussulmans, Christians, Parsis, and believers in other religions. Similarly in the year 1833, some six hundred and fifty members of the Parliament and several lords made the same promise. Therefore it is our duty that, leaving aside animosity, we should ourselves unite, and beg from Her Majesty our rights. The Government has framed the Penal Code to put an end to quarrels amongst us. If we do not unite, we shall be criminals in the sight of Government.

You see that the duty on salt has increased so much that the poor cannot procure salt to cook their pulses with. Lord Ripon reduced the duty to Rs. 2 per maund, and expressed a hope of gradually reducing it to only one rupee; but Lord Dufferin, on the contrary, has enhanced the duty to Rs. 2-8 per maund, and for this the poor are suffering much. This action is improper.

It is the wish of the National Congress that as the son lodges his complaints before his father so the complaints of the poor and destitute should be made known to Her Majesty the Maharani. Friends, the National Congress does not ask for sovereign power, but the National Congress desires that the supremacy of the British Government might remain so long as the sun and the moon are not destroyed. The National Congress does not want to form a Parliament, but it wishes that the English Parliament might remain intact all along. Without any bias, I am speaking out the truth that the National Congress wants this, that the amount of duty on salt, which has become an instrument of oppression to the poor, might be reduced. Victory be to Her Majesty the Maharani and the Indian National Congress!

THE PRESIDENT: I will now put the amendment, and then the resolution, which, you will observe, asks for the remission of the recent enhancement to the salt duty, not the total abolition of that duty. The amendment differs from the resolution in this essential particular, that it wishes to retain the enhanced salt tax, and only asks that, though the circumstances that justified the enhancement have to a considerable extent ceased to exist, the tax should still remain, but that the provisions with regard to the preparation and consumption of salt should be modified according to local circumstances. You see, therefore, that there is an essential difference between the original resolution and the amendment.

*The amendment was then put, but only two hands, those of the proposer and seconder, were held up in its favor, nearly all hands being held up against it. The resolution was afterwards put and carried without a dissentient voice.*

THE PRESIDENT: Then I declare that this, our fifth resolution,

RESOLVED—*That the condition of the Finances of India having materially improved, and those special circumstances on which the Government relied to justify the recent enhancement of the salt-tax having practically ceased to exist, this Congress considers it essential that the enhancement referred to should be remitted at an early date, and empowers its President to submit a special memorial on the subject, in its name and on its behalf, to H. E. the Viceroy in Council.*

has been unanimously carried, and I call upon Mr. Mudholkar to move the sixth resolution.

Res. VI. Extension of the Permanent Settlement.

MR. R. N. MUDHOLKAR (*Berar, No. 585, in list*), who was loudly cheered, on rising, said: I am very grateful to you, my friends, for the cheers you have given me; but, as the time allotted to me is very short, I will directly address myself to the subject. Mr. President, Ladies and Gentlemen, the resolution with which I am entrusted is one, like its predecessor, entitled to be called a people's question. Like the salt-tax, the question of a permanent settlement is one with which the comfort, the very existence of the masses, is intimately connected.

**3rd Day.**

**Res. VI. Extension of the Permanent Settlement.**

Throughout the length and breadth of the land you find that the staple industry of the country is agriculture, and that being so, the system of tenure under which our agricultural operations are carried on, is one of the greatest importance to us. Resolution No. VI., with which I am entrusted, runs thus :—

*That having reference to the expectations created throughout the country by the despatch of Her Majesty's Secretary of State in 1862, the principles of which were re-affirmed in a subsequent despatch of 1865, promising the extension of a permanent settlement to all temporarily settled tracts in which certain conditions were fulfilled, and to the fact that throughout large portions of the country those conditions have long since been fulfilled, this Congress respectfully submits that the Government of India is, now, in honour bound to take up this question of permanent settlement without further delay, in view to practical action thereon, such that fixity and permanence may be given to the Government land revenue demand as explicitly promised, by Her Majesty's Secretary of State, more than a quarter of a century ago.*

I confess that the question with which this resolution deals is one of vast importance, and at the same time one of considerable perplexity, and the time allotted to a speaker by the rules will not enable me to do full justice to it. I will, however, lay before you, as briefly as I can, certain considerations which go far to justify and support the demand we make. As I have said, India is an agricultural country. "The wealth of India" of which the poet speaks has vanished. The gorgeous fabrics which India produced are now reduced to an almost inappreciable quantity. Wherever you go you find that the people are being thrown on the soil. Take the estimates framed by the Famine Commission, and you find that 90 per cent. of the rural population is closely connected with the soil, and 80 per cent. of the whole population is wholly dependent upon the soil. Taking later calculations, you will find that the proportion has risen to as much as 86 per cent. and, with our indigenous industries dying out, this pressure of the population upon the land is growing every day, and you find that vast tracts which were at one time considered as not being fit for cultivation are being taken up for this purpose. The arable area under cultivation has increased vastly ; and though this industry is not in many places paying, through sheer necessity people are compelled to have recourse to poorer and poorer soils. The effect of this has been that land which was required for grazing purposes is now taken up for agricultural purposes, and the result of that you see in the deterioration of your agricultural stock. If you compare this area with the amount of population, you will find a state of things which must make us really very anxious ; that is, that while the area under cultivation is estimated to be a little less than 190 million acres, the population which it has to support is nearly 197 millions. I take my figures from the latest Government statistics. This means less than an acre per head, and, according to Sir William Hunter, at least an acre per head is required to maintain a man sufficiently. Here, therefore, is this one great problem before you. You find that the only industry by which you can maintain your people is in a very unsatisfactory condition. You may almost say that the widest limit of cultivation has been reached, and the question is, what are we to do ? The only solution is improvement in cultivation itself, and here it is that the question of permanent settlement becomes of the greatest importance.

If the oldest industry we have is to be maintained in a state of prosperity it is necessary that that industry should be improved. But here, throughout the major part of the country, you find that there is an almost insuperable obstacle to all improvement interposed, and that is on account of the temporary settlement and the fatal discouragement of improvements which this involves. The policy with regard to land tenure followed by the Government for nearly 100 years has been one of violent oscillation. Whenever there is a crisis in the agricultural history of the country you find that the heads of the Government are quite willing to accept statesmanlike and broad views ; but when the crisis is past and the danger is over, for a time, there is a return to a huckstering policy,—a policy of trying to make as much money out of the landholder as possible. The famine in Bengal in 1770 secured to Bengal the permanent settlement. In 1860 there was a famine in the N. W. Provinces, and the gravity of the famine and the danger which the Government saw in the recurrence of such famines led to the appointment of a Commission. That Commission took evidence and went carefully into the matter, and came deliberately to the conclusion that in the interests of the country it was absolutely necessary that fixity and permanency of tenure should be granted.

This is what the Commission say in the Report submitted by their Presidents : "Entertaining the most earnest conviction that the State interests and popular interests will be alike strengthened in an increasing ratio by the step, the first and, as I believe, most important measure, I have respectfully to submit, for consideration, is the expediency of fixing for ever the public demand on the land, and thus converting the existing settlement into a settlement for perpetuity."

3rd Day.

Res. VI. Extension of the Permanent Settlement

This recommendation of the Commission was endorsed by the Lieutenant-Governor and Council, and it met with the approval of the Viceroy, that great man, Lord Canning.

The Governor-General said : " His Excellency believes that increased security of fixed property and comparative freedom from the interference of fiscal officers of the Government, will tend to create a class which, although composed of various races and creeds, will be peculiarly bound to the British rule ; while, under proper regulations, the measure will conduce materially to the improvement of the general revenue of the Empire."

This report of the Commission, with the recommendation of the Viceroy, was sent to the Secretary of State, and this was what Lord Halifax laid down in his famous despatch of 1862 : " After the most careful review of all these considerations Her Majesty's Government are of opinion that the advantages which may reasonably be expected to accrue not only to those immediately connected with the land, but to the community generally, are sufficiently great to justify them in incurring the risk of some prospective loss of revenue in order to attain them, and that a settlement in perpetuity in the districts in which the conditions required are, or may hereafter be fulfilled, is a measure dictated by sound policy, and calculated to accelerate the development of the resources of India, and to ensure in the highest degree the welfare and contentment of all classes of Her Majesty's subjects in the country."

A more satisfactory resolution, a more statesmanlike wish, a more just and humane conclusion could not have been arrived at. But it has been our misfortune that, when a thing has been offered by one hand, the other hand has always been ready to snatch it away. There was a change of government in England, and pressure was brought to bear by the members of the India Council to prevent the carrying out of the recommendations in the despatch of 1862. The clear promise, however, and the generous principles laid down in that despatch were such that they could not be abrogated ; and what was sought to be done was to saddle those recommendations with further conditions. The only condition laid down in the despatch of 1862 was that its terms were to be extended to those provinces where four-fifths of the land was brought under cultivation. It was found that this condition was satisfied by a number of estates, and it was also found that other persons were willing to carry out the terms of the resolution. Here it was that mischief was done. A new condition was imposed in the despatch of 1865, and that was that the recommendations in the despatch of 1862 should be extended to estates only if, in the opinion of the executive authorities, the public works of the Government were not likely to be so extended within the next 20 years as to benefit the estates to the extent of 20 per cent. Well, you will find that those conditions have been satisfied ; nearly 27 years (certainly 25 years) have elapsed, and as to public works you find that all the main lines and feeder lines of railways have been constructed, and the main irrigation works have also been completed. And as far as cultivation itself is concerned, a few facts, taken from the latest statistical abstract published by the Government in England, will show that all those conditions have been practically carried out in the greater part of the country except in parts of the Punjab and the Central Provinces.

In Madras you find that 28 millions of acres have been cultivated, and only 8 millions are available for cultivation. In Bombay more than 36 millions have been under cultivation, and only 8 millions are available for cultivation. In both cases, of course, these 8 millions are of the lowest quality, and much of it really not worth cultivation. In Berar more than 7 million acres are under cultivation, and only 700,000 are available for cultivation. In the North-West Provinces over 27½ millions are under cultivation, and only 7 millions are available for cultivation. In Oudh over 9 millions are under cultivation, and only 3 millions are available for cultivation. You see, therefore, that the conditions have been carried out, and yet the same system continues—that system which has been stigmatized by Government itself as one which is harassing to the people, as one which unsettles all relations between landlord and tenant, and as one which causes the greatest uneasiness. I am not using my own expressions, but the words used in the resolution of Lord Ripon in 1883. The view which was laid down in 1862 was, as I told you, opposed by Government officials in India and England ; but a justification of those recommendations was supplied by stern facts which happened later on. In 1874 the riots in Bombay resulted in considerable loss of property and damage to person. Then there was the famine of 1877, and the Government officials were obliged to admit that nearly 40 millions of people belonging to the agricultural population were on the brink of starvation. Still you find that there was a disinclination to carry out the principles laid down over and over again, and the justice of which was admitted. I will only refer to two authorities, whose eminence in these matters is not disputed, Sir Louis Malet and Sir James Caird, both of whom stigmatize the present system. Sir James Caird moreover distinctly says that a thirty years' settlement cannot be expected to produce sufficient stimulus to ensure improvement in the agriculture of the country ; that is the deliberate opinion of the President of the Famine Commission. In spite of these things we find that the system is continued. The evil is to be deplored in more respects than one. In the first place rent in India, or revenue, has nothing like it anywhere. Take the proportion of rent to gross produce in any country in Europe, and you will find that India is placed on a basis of its own. In Great Britain the proportion of gross produce to rent is 1 to 33; in Europe generally 1 to 50. The lowest in Europe, Denmark, is 1 to 27. In India it is 1 to 3 or 1 to 4. That is, for every four rupees you get from the land you give one rupee to the Government; whereas in Europe, out of 50 rupees coming from the soil, only one goes to the landlord. Then it is not only the high rate, but the uncertainty of the enhancement. You do not know in what way the enhancement may come. There is the re-classification of soils, which means raising the soil of an estate from the third class to the second or the second to the first, and so on, and the consequent raising of the land revenue itself, and there is the enhancement of the revenue independent of any such supposed change in the status of the soil. All these operations have been productive of the great mischief of putting an end to all improvements.

These are facts that require serious consideration. I admit that there are grave difficulties in the way of Government from the rupee going down. Of course it would be difficult to settle the question in an off-hand manner; but I do not think the difficulty is such as to baffle the resources of statesmanship, nor do I think that our administrators are so devoid of statesmanship as to be unable to grapple with it. What we ask is that there should be some fixity. That fixity need only be as regards production. If the proportion of produce to rent were fixed; if it were laid down once for all that each plot should pay yearly the money value, settled quinquennially, on the basis of the preceding five years local prices, of so many maunds of jowar, bajra, wheat, barley, cotton, sessamum, as the case might be, due reference being had to the culture prevalent in each village, I suppose that would satisfy the requirements of the people. It is a problem which *can* be solved. I appeal to Great Britain and to our administrators here to make a real effort to solve it, and thus carry out the principles laid down by successive Governments in England—principles which have their greatest justification in justice and in humanity. (*Cheers.*)

*It being 2* P.M. *the Congress then adjourned for half an hour.*

On the re-assembly of the Congress—

MR. RATNA SABAPATHI PILAI (*Madras, No. 646, in list*), resuming the debate, said: I beg to support this resolution. I come from the district of Tanjore in the Presidency of Madras, where re-settlement operations are at this moment in full swing. I am a landholder myself; I know the ins and the outs of this question as it affects the ryots of Southern India; and I can assure you that there is at the present moment a reign of terror in my district: there is not a ryot who is not filled with alarm as to the expected results of the settlement operations. Security of property is no less a function of Government than security of person. We are all thankful to Government for the security of person and property that we enjoy. The protection we enjoy is from robbers, dacoits and lawless subjects; but we want the protection of our property from the Government itself (*loud cheers*); we want to be saved from our own friends.

The Bengal Presidency, or part of it, has had the blessing of a permanent settlement conferred on it; and I ask, why not extend the same to other parts of the Empire? The wealth of the nation is the wealth of the Government itself. What ryot will dare to invest his savings, if any, in his holding with the periodical visitations of the Settlement Department before his mind's eye? This unsettled state of mind has a most demoralizing effect upon landholders, who are already living from hand to mouth; it is destructive of all agricultural progress, nay decent well-being. Seventy-five per cent. of the landlords in the district of Tanjore, which is commonly talked of as the garden of Southern India, are involved in debt. I dare not look into the future. Already rumours are afloat that the assessment will be increased by 50 per cent. Even if it is increased by 30 per cent the result, I fear, will be simply disastrous. But Government may say, "We must move; we cannot afford to stand still; we must obey the law of nature: the world itself moves." But I should be glad if the Government would apply this law of nature to the administrative machinery of the country, and grant us the voice that we demand in the affairs of our own country. (*Cheers*). The change is necessitated by the changed circumstances of the Empire. The Government are eager to obey this law of change whenever the changes tend to fill their own exchequer; but they are exceeding loth to move in any matter if the change touches their prerogatives or privileges. Only last year a friend of mine, a landholder in the district of Tanjore, suffered by speaking out his mind, by writing to the papers complaining of the threats of illegal exactions on the part of the subordinate officials of the Settlement Department. Although he was a landlord he happened to be a servant of the Government as well. He was a Professor in a Government College and also M. A. of the University of Madras. Government, taking advantage of his position, suspended him for a period of six months, because, in the *bonâ fide* protection of his own interests, and the interests of his co-landholders, he wrote to the press bringing to the notice of the public the threats of exaction on the part of subordinates of the Settlement Department. I am glad to tell you that the Government of Madras which took this unprecedented step felt it to be such on reconsideration, and by way of amends elevated my friend to a position of greater trust and responsibility. (*Cheers*). I trust that the Government of India will make an equally edifying repentance, and having first tried to crush our movement, and allowed its officers in many places virtually to persecute our members, will now hasten to accede to the reasonable demands of this assembly, and, amongst other things, take steps to secure to us a permanent settlement and fixity of tenure. (*Cheers.*)

MR. BOIKANTHA NATH SEN (*Bengal, No. 107, in list*)—MR. PRESIDENT, FELLOW DELEGATES, LADIES AND GENTLEMEN,—I have much pleasure in supporting this resolution, the more so that I had the honor to support a similar one at Bombay. The time allotted to me does not permit of any lengthened discussion. The observations which have been made may be considered as the principal arguments put forward. Those I now propose to place before you may be tacked on to them, and the whole may be regarded as one series of arguments placed before the public for the due consideration of the Government.

This is a resolution in which there is no question of sentiment. It is a question which affects materially the prosperity of the country and which affects the Government also in a very material way. It has been observed that this is a resolution not for the benefit of the delegates, but for the benefit of the people. I go further and say that it is a resolution which, if carried, and accepted loyally by the Government, will bring benefits to the Government itself. (*Cheers*). Let me notice the way in which the resolution has been divided. It refers, you see, to the despatch of 1862, confirmed by that of 1865. It says that the Government is "now in honor bound." Observe the force of the word "now." Let me place before you another fact, that a permanent settlement was accorded to Bengal in 1793, when you will find a minute by the Board of Revenue at Fort St. George, delivered by Mr. White, and approved of by a Select Committee which was appointed to investigate the affairs of the East India Company. That approval was made in 1812; that principle was recognised, and emphasized and a line of action was formulated 50 years afterwards in 1862, in the despatch of the Secretary of State. Twenty-seven years have now passed, and we are where we were in 1812, because there is no indication of a permanent settlement being carried out in those provinces where it was not conceded very nearly a century ago.

Why is it so? We all know that land revenue forms the central figure in the group of English taxation, and there is an apprehension of a loss of prospective increment in the Government revenue, based on what is supposed in a mistaken way to be the results of the permanent settlement in Bengal, and what is still erroneously considered to be a wanton sacrifice, as it were, of the resources of the State by Lord Cornwallis, for the sole purpose of giving satisfaction to the landed proprietors. Now it is on account of apprehensions and misapprehensions like these that effect has not been given to the despatch of 1862. Before I proceed further let me place before you further statistics. The territories which are under the administration of the Lieutenant-Governor of Bengal extend over an area of 140,000 square miles, of which 120,000 enjoy the benefits of the permanent settlement. But at the time when the permanent settlement was granted to Bengal only one-third had been brought under cultivation. The land revenue from Bengal is about four crores and the gross rental is about 20 crores (I make a technical distinction between revenue and rental.) Then the incidence of the land revenue in Bengal is Rs. 55 to 100 persons of the population; in the Punjab, Rs. 109 to 100 persons; in the North-Western Provinces, Rs. 129 to 100 persons; in the Madras Presidency, Rs. 134 to 100 persons; and in Bombay, Rs. 234 to 100 persons. Now, apart from other questions which are undoubtedly of a very weighty nature, and which, in summing up, I shall have occasion to refer to, I venture to think that the high standard of revenue which has been attained ought of itself to be considered a sufficient reason for the Government according a permanent settlement to those provinces where it has not been extended.

You have heard from the able mover of the resolution what area has been actually brought under cultivation, and what little, and that of the poorest quality as a rule, yet remains to be cultivated; so that the time has surely arrived when, apart from other questions, this high ratio of cultivation would justify the Government in giving fixity to their demands. Let us see a little further how the matter stands. There is much more to be said. The experiment of 100 years in Bengal furnishes us with certain data which will enable you to solve the problem in a satisfactory way. This permanent settlement must be considered as the very best manure you can give to the land: for shortly after the permanent settlement of Bengal there was a wonderful increase in the cultivation. Before the permanent settlement only a third was under cultivation, but now you will scarcely find one-thirtieth uncultivated.

Then you may look upon this permanent settlement as a very important agent in the distribution of the proprietary interest in the soil among the various classes. It has also been a very important factor in bringing about social reform. Who ever had an idea of a middle class? I say, this middle class is to a great extent the growth of the permanent settlement. Where is it anything like so strong in numbers and in wealth as in Bengal? (*Cheers.*) Although now the example of Bengal has more or less pervaded the entire Empire. But, for that permanent settlement India would have had, as in Russia, the poor and the rich' but no middle class such as you find crowding this great hall. These, then, have been the direct benefits of the permanent settlement. Now let us see what can the Government expect more. Would it be a sufferer in the long run? Look at the case of Orissa. Orissa was temporarily settled for 30 years, and the lease expired in 1866. There was then, as you all know, a famine, and the Government could not possibly on that occasion think of enhancing the revenue by making a re-settlement, so that it had to renew the settlement for another 30 years. That settlement is still going on, and it will expire in 1895. Progress has been kept in abeyance for 60 years. No capitalist would venture to invest his money in land in Orissa. For 60 years progress has been retarded by the inactivity (if nothing else) of the Government.

We find that from that portion of Bengal which has not received this boon Government does not expect much. There are authoritative reports to Government that if a permanent settlement be withheld from those other provinces, there would be at *best* (as I had occasion to remark on the last occasion) a gain to the Government of 30 lakhs of rupees. Now let us see how we fare in Bengal. In the Civil administration alone in the whole of India there is a loss of 12 lakhs, the expenditure exceeding the receipts by that amount. But in Bengal there is a surplus of 14 lakhs, and what is this owing to? In education, in Bengal, 83 lakhs are spent, out of which only 21 lakhs are spent by the State, the balance being spent by private individuals who are able to pay on account of the permanent settlement. See how the Government has been gaining in this way. If, then, the permanent settlement be extended to other provinces, I venture to submit that there is not the least reason for the Government suffering in any way in its finances. Whatever it may apparently suffer, from a purely treasury point of view, in the matter of direct loss of future enhancements of land revenue, will be more than compensated by gains from other sources through new channels which will be created by this permanent settlement of its own force. Now, while the Government has pledged itself by its despatch of 1862, confirmed by the despatch of 1865, it is undoubtedly in honor bound to redeem its pledge. By according this concession the Government will derive benefit in two ways: in the first place by saving its honor by the redemption of its solemn pledges; in the second, even financially as sharing the enhanced prosperity of its people.

Its good deed may directly diminish by a few lakhs the land revenue of fifty years hence; but crores to replace these will have poured down from the happy consequences of that honest policy. As Kalidasa says:—

"The sun draws the water from the soil, but this is returned a thousandfold in the shape of rain." (*Cheers.*)

BABU JANOKI NATH BOSE (*Orissa, No. 190, in list*)—MR. PRESIDENT, LADIES AND GENTLEMEN,—I have much pleasure in giving my cordial support to this resolution. My simple desire is to let this august assembly know what are the feelings of the people of the province, which I have the honor to represent, with regard to this very important question. You have been told that a permanent settlement has not been introduced into the backward province of Orissa. I happen to work there as a lawyer though I am not a permanent resident of the province. During the years I have been practising there I have acquired some knowledge as to the condition in which the agriculturists of the province are placed. It has been said in very high quarters that India's land revenue is very flexible; that it can be compared to India-rubber and drawn to any length to meet emergencies that it is a source of income which can be increased to any extent. But as India-rubber being drawn beyond certain limits will break, so this source of revenue, if strained to extremes, would certainly fail and with disastrous results. If continued to be carried to extremes, as has been hitherto too often the fashion, the temporary land revenue system must produce rack-renting, which already exists in many provinces, which has already led to dire famines, which, as it grows, must mean direr famines still in even closer succession.

This question affects not only zemindars but all of every grade who draw subsistence from the soil, and a permanent settlement would prove not only a blessing to agriculturists but even, in the long run, to the Government itself. In the case of land revenue it should be borne in mind that it is really not nearly so flexible as it is thought; that there is a limit to its capacity for expansion;

3rd Day.

Res. VI. Extension of the Permanent Settlement.

and that if you strain it beyond those limits the whole system will collapse. There are provinces where this is even now imminent. What do we see in the province of which I am a representative? The zemindars are almost all deeply involved in debt; they cannot pay the Government revenue at the proper time; often you see their properties being sold at public auction to meet the demands made upon them; they have no resource but to incur debts at a very high rate of interest. If we look at the condition of the ryots what do we see? That they are being rack-rented; they cannot get a full meal in two days; they cannot get a waistcloth even once a year. Such is the condition to which Government has reduced the zemindars and ryots through their unwillingness to introduce a permanent settlement, and through the consequent impossibility of the vivification of this national industry by capital. Contrast the state of Bengal with that of other provinces where there is no permanent settlement. Here we find the zemindars occupying a high place, but in other parts they are poor men and cannot take part in any national undertaking that requires money. Look at the ryots. We have some poor, no doubt, but look at the millions of well-to-do tenants of all grades. In what other province do you find any large proportion of such? For 50 years at least six millions sterling have yearly gone into the pockets of the people that would, under the temporary settlement system, have gone into those of the Government, to be wasted doubtless in frontier defences (*cheers*), and I venture to say that those six millions have profited the country ten times more than they would have done had they gone into the coffers of the State. (*Cheers*). The temporary settlement system is everywhere ruining the zemindars. It has been said, let the zemindars be ruined, we do not care, provided we have got peasant proprietors. But that is a very idiotic and narrow policy. In the first place the zemindars, the landed aristocracy of our country, constitute, in many provinces, a definite and important institution which has taken deep root and cannot hastily be done away with, and in the second place the same cause that wrecks the zemindars will, as time runs on, ruin even peasant proprietors. There are many who say "if the permanent settlement can give rise to peasant proprietors it is all right, but if it will only enrich the zemindars we are not for it." I submit that that is a ridiculous view of the case. In the first place all through Bombay and Madras, it is just with peasant proprietors that we desire to see a permanent settlement. Again where we have zemindars they are none the less a portion of the people, and from their position whatever affects them injuriously affects all subordinate classes of agriculturists equally injuriously, while what benefits them, benefits equally directly and indirectly not only all subordinate holders of land but, in a country like this where everything hinges on the land, the entire community.

Now, what do we see in Orissa? We see that the zemindars are mostly over head and ears in debt, and that what with their irrigation tax and the rent the poor ryots are being trodden under foot; their condition is most deplorable; they have not a full meal every two days, they have nothing in times of scarcity to fall back upon, they are perpetually on the verge of starvation. I am sure that if the permanent settlement is introduced into that province, if there is no more Government rack-renting, if the Government ceases to threaten them with periodical re-assessments, you will find that capital will flow into the land, that cultivation will improve, and that in 30 years the condition of the zemindars and ryots will be so much improved that no one in that flourishing land will be able to recognize this now backward, miserable, poverty-stricken region. Moreover, apart from the consequences, on abstract principles only, the action of the Government in increasing the land revenue every 25 and 30 years is not just.

It is a case of reaping where they have not sowed, of greedily grasping the fruits of the tiller of the soil's persistent labour, of arbitrarily confiscating the fruits of its subjects industry, it is unjust I say in principle, and like all injustice it is thoroughly bad policy in the long run. From every point of view, therefore, a permanent settlement is desirable, and holding this I most strongly support the resolution now before you.

LALA JAISEE RAM (*Panjab, No. 532, in list*)—MR. PRESIDENT, LADIES AND GENTLEMEN,—The resolution I have been called upon to support is one of the greatest importance. I come from the Punjab, and I shall speak from a Punjabi's point of view. Our province is the poorest province, I fear, in the whole British empire. As elsewhere, so in the Punjab, the enterprise of British merchants has almost brought about the complete extinction of all native indigenous arts and industries. Past history shows us that the Punjab has produced but very few enterprising merchants, and it is so circumstanced that its physical situation will never bring it on a level with its sister provinces in regard to trade. The Punjab is essentially an agricultural province. Its prosperity depends on the prosperity of the holders and tillers of the soil, and nowhere is the necessity of a permanent settlement more felt than in the Punjab. Our existing temporary settlements seem mere embodiments of that leading principle of the old Sikha Shahi rule, that Government should get, or in other words extort, the utmost possible pie from the people. The fluctuating nature of the settlement and the perpetual liability to an increased demand on the part of the State, takes all heart out of even the hardworking Jât and keeps him ever in poverty. Our present system is a tax on—nay a confiscation of—the values of improvements, and thus deters the agriculturist from ever making the best of his land. (*Hear, hear*). The settlement itself, so long as it is in progress, and it lasts for years, is always a curse to the zemindars. The heavy expenses unnecessarily incurred by Government are in this matter payable by the people—aye ! and much more, as black mail, in one shape or other. It is not uncommon too for the greedy subordinate officials to stir up strife by making false entries, and this adds to the fast increasing litigation which has already proved so ruinous to the zemindars. The anxiety we feel for a permanent settlement is not altogether novel, nor one that originated wholly with us. Thirty years ago the local Government declared the expediency of commencing a register of permanent settlements for fully cultivated tracts, but it was not allowed to give practical effect to its views then for reasons which it is needless now to discuss, for time has brought forth happy changes, and there is nothing now which stands in the way. The chief condition laid down in the despatch was that at least four-fifths of the culturable area should be redeemed and brought into cultivation. If any other province has not fulfilled this condition the Punjab has. Take a trip from Delhi to Peshawar, exclude the hilly barren tracts from consideration, and you will find the whole of the land under cultivation. It may be said that the finances of the Government will suffer by conceding a permanent settlement. But this argument can be at once overthrown by the long experience of a hundred years in Bengal.

Has the Government of India, has the country at large suffered in consequence of even this badly arranged and prematurely conceded permanent settlement in Bengal ? Look to the commerce of Calcutta ; look to the density of the population ; look to the great spread of education and the enormous masses of well-to-do people, the like of all of which is to be seen nowhere else, and then let any man dare to deny that even this crude, imperfectly carried out settlement, conceded before more than one-third of the culturable area was under culture, has been, solely in virtue of the one attribute of permanence, an immense boon to the people and a gigantic source of strength to the Empire. (*Prolonged cheers.*)

MR. DEORAO VINAYEK (*Berar, No. 590, in list*)—MR. PRESIDENT, BROTHER DELEGATES, LADIES AND GENTLEMEN,—I have great pleasure in supporting the resolution which is now before you, coming as I do from the same quarter as the delegate who proposed it. The resolution simply asks the Government to fulfil their noble and benevolent promise made more than a quarter of a century ago. Some may say that Government has made the promise, and is capable of fulfilling it unrequested. It may be so or it may not ; but the time is such that we cannot get anything unless we seek it. Demand ought to precede supply, as the saying goes. My predecessors have read you the despatches and some figures in regard to the satisfying of the required conditions for the bestowal of permanent settlement on nearly the whole of India. They have shown you that Government is in honor bound to fulfil their promises, and they have shown by certain experience in Bengal that the permanent settlement, if given at all, will not disappoint the Government. I will not take up your time unnecessarily by reading those notable despatches again. I will simply refer to one or two questions which, in my humble opinion, it is very important to have discussed in this assembly.

I come from Berar, and I had the honor of discussing this question with some high revenue officials there. They discussed them with a free mind, always open to reason. Their views may be against permanent settlement, and they may have reasons to substantiate those views ; but they listen to what we say with open minds. When we convince them that what we claim is not unreasonable they admit it, and I hope that they will assist us if we prove our case to be a strong one, at all events that they will not bring forward any opposition. Amongst their objections to a permanent settlement are these : First, they say that by a permanent settlement Government will be bound down to a certain fixed revenue, and that with ever increasing administrative charges there will be no corresponding increase of revenue. They also say that the boon of a permanent settlement, if granted at all, will not benefit those in whose interest that boon is claimed—that is the cultivators. These are very grave questions now, and to answer them in the time allotted is impossible. I should like to be permitted to read one or two passages from a paper read some time ago by a very high official of the Revenue Board of this province in England : "An examination of those results (of permanent settlement) will, perhaps, lead us to the conclusion that the permanent settlement was a wise and statesmanlike measure ; that politically it has been a tower of strength to the Empire ; that, from a social and economic point of view, it has stimulated the prosperity and fostered the intelligence of the province ; and that, even from a strictly financial stand point, the surrender of an increased land tax has been in some measure compensated by the steady development of other branches of the public revenue." He has given some figures, which one of my predecessors has referred to, showing

3rd Day.

Res. VI. Extension of the Permanent Settlement.

how the province of Bengal has been benefited financially by the permanent settlement. I will not, therefore, read any more passages. The same gentleman lays down that the creation of an independent middle class is not an evil, but a blessing. (*Cheers.*) It is the middle class that has taken advantage of all the reforms introduced by British rule in India. It is that middle class which mainly fills this pavilion, and the authority I have quoted says further that it is a fruitful source of strength to the State. The creation of that class is not to be deplored. Suppose, for instance, though this can never be generally true, that the permanent settlement does not benefit the ryots, or say some classes of the ryots in a poor agricultural district. What is the practical effect? Is it undesirable that the land should be held mainly by those who can afford to improve it? Is it desirable that the land should be generally cultivated by poor hand-to-mouth cultivators? Is it not better that those agriculturists, who are so poor that they can give nothing to the land, should be labourers rather than holders of the land? Is this not better for these men themselves,—better for the land, better for the country? If the permanent settlement has the effect of converting in some places starving tenants into well-fed labourers, of creating a strong middle class, is this any argument against a permanent settlement? Is it not desirable that the material wealth of the country, for the increase of which our British Government is so anxious, *should* be increased? And how can that material wealth be more certainly increased than by the creation of a class of small capitalists—a middle class in fact?

These two objections then are invalid. All we ask is that the Government should open a discussion on the subject. We say to them: "You have closed discussion for a quarter of a century, don't close it any more." I come from Berar. You know it is, by an official fiction, not under British rule; but all the same it has British rulers, British missionaries, British laws, and the advantages and disadvantages of British rule. We have no legislation for ourselves, nothing like it. If a permanent settlement is granted to other provinces we know, of course, that we shall not get it as soon as you do, if at all, my friends. We shall be left behind lamenting, I fear. But that is no reason why we should hesitate to join you in reasonable demands. We Berarese are first of all Indians, and we have joined the Congress, not because, perhaps, any direct benefit will be gained by Berar even when the Congress triumphs, but because this triumph will benefit our country; because we are all one; because your happiness, your prosperity, means the advancement of our native land, and a source of perennial rejoicing to us; even though we poor Berarese have to sit in darkness outside the banquet hall. (*Loud cheers.*)

MR. R. P. KARANDIKAR (*Poona, No. 575, in list*)—MR. PRESIDENT, LADIES AND GENTLEMEN,—Allow me to thank you on behalf of the persons who have sent me here for enabling a humble delegate like myself to bring their difficulties before you. They have asked me not to make a long speech, but to place before you the practical side of the question as viewed by the Bombay people themselves.

Directly after the despatch was received every local Government applied to bring into operation the recommendations made by the Secretary of State, but for the time the matter lapsed. Twenty years or so later, by the influence exercised on the Bombay Government from various directions, it was induced to take up this subject in the form of a small legislative enactment by the Act of 1888. That is not an enactment which deals directly with the permanent settlement question, but it tries in its own way to allay the fears of the cultivators in regard to enhanced taxation on the land. We, Bombay people, cannot sufficiently thank the gentlemen who represented them in the Bombay Legislative Council, nor the Government that appointed those members. I need hardly refer to such distinguished personages as the Hon. Mr. Ranade, and also to one whose recent elevation to the Bench has deprived the Congress of one of its most modest and moderate supporters, Mr. Justice Telang. I mention these two names, not to magnify the matter, but to tell you that, despite the assistance of these gentlemen and others (I include European officers and gentlemen on the Council), very little could be done in that direction. I will tell you why. In Bill No. 5 of 1885, which assumed the form of law in the Act of 1888—a pretty long time for a measure to be hung up—three points were intended to be secured: First, all improvements made by the cultivator out of his own pocket and by his own labors were to be free from enhanced taxation; second, after 1892 there was to be no re-survey; and, third, the assessment was never to be increased by more than a certain maximum ratio fixed by the Act. These were the three important features of the Bill. But let me point out that all this practically goes for nothing. There has been going on a re-survey now, for no one knows how many years. The survey officers have authority to re-classify the land under the cultivation of a particular cultivator. The point suggested was: "If you have classified the land in the year 1862, what is the necessity for allowing the Survey Department to exercise its functions in re-classifying it after the lapse of 30 years?" The true answer was: "In order that there may be oppression upon the people." Of course that would not be the official answer at the time, but it is the only true one. It was pointed out how impossible it was for the Survey Department officers to distinguish between land brought to a superior quality by the exertion and the money of the cultivators, and the land which was, on their own supposition, included in an inferior class owing to a mistake on their own part. In that case it was suggested that it was absurd to expect the cultivator to prove that the land was brought to a superior quality by his own particular exertions. The burden was thrown entirely by the Act upon the cultivator, which is a simple absurdity. This was pointed out to the Council, but His Excellency, as far as my knowledge goes, said it was for the cultivator to prove that he has brought the land up to a superior quality. I ask you as sensible men whether, after the lapse of 30 years patient toil, gradually improving his holding by sheer hard work, a cultivator can possibly be in a position to point out that it is by such and such a process that he has brought his land to a superior quality. It is elbow grease that has done it—and how can he prove that except by pointing to the land? But the Government say no; looking to the land we think we made a mistake and under assessed it 30 years ago—you prove that we did not. Would it not be reasonable to expect that the survey department officers who first assessed the land as of a particular quality should prove that they *had* committed a mistake in the first instance! Consequently the burden of proof was, in my humble opinion, mislaid. That touches too the question about not enhancing the revenue in consequence of improvements made by the cultivator. As there is nothing to distinguish between the improvements made by the long persistent labour of the cultivators and mistakes made by survey officers, naturally this enactment had not the effect of assuring people of the good faith of the Government. Then comes the second question about the maximum limit fixed by the Act. As you all know this was placed at so high a figure, that having regard to the circumstances under which the country is labouring, any enhancement at all approaching this maximum would absolutely ruin nine-tenths of our Bombay landholders, whose land, as pointed out by abler speakers, is already much more highly taxed than that of any other province. This enactment is, therefore, a mere sham, utterly ineffective and insufficient; and anything short of permanent settlement will entirely fail to improve the wretched condition of ryots, an object which one must needs think should be cherished by all generous-minded Governments in all countries. (*Cheers*). Having this re-classification sword still hanging over their heads, you will see that our cultivators are dissuaded, discouraged, I may say practically debarred from putting any money into the land, from even giving it one particle more labour than is necessary to extract its present scanty crops, and all capitalists are prevented from interfering to aid the improvement either of the land itself or of the staples it now produces. This want of security, of permanence of tenure, it is which has retarded the progress of agriculture in India, which, you know, is mainly an agricultural country—nay which has brought about a gradual deterioration in our lands as a whole, and in our own old careful system of tillage. That is bad, and not less so that the people should hoard or bury their little savings, or even place them in Savings Banks, and should not be able to put any of them into the land.

One point more: The function of the Government is to frame the assessment and that is done quite *ex parte* and without a hearing of the assessee! It is said: "You have a right of appeal—any cultivator that thinks himself aggrieved may petition the Government." But you all know what giving such right of appeal means—a poor ignorant villager appealing against a great Government Department. That is a position that the cultivator is unable to occupy, and it is simply adding insult to injustice to ask him to take it. I say then, that the required conditions have long been fulfilled, and the Government is in honor bound to take up this question of a permanent settlement, and I support most energetically on behalf of the people of the Bombay Presidency the resolution now before the Congress. (*Cheers*).

BAWA NARAYAN SING (*Punjab, No. 527, in list*) spoke in Punjabi and said: Gentlemen and well-wishers of the country and of the British Government,—Permanent settlement of land is as much beneficial to the Government as it is to the natives of the country. A person does not make permanent arrangements for a particular place until he is sure of permanently settling there. When an officer goes to a new district he generally first stops at some hotel and afterwards he makes other arrangements for his stay in the place, but he makes permanent arrangements when he knows that he is pucca, and that he will stay there permanently. It is our desire that the British Government may remain as our rulers permanently, and therefore we pray for a permanent settlement from them now that the country has, under the fostering care of the Government, sufficiently improved as far as cultivation is concerned. It is well known that prosperity has followed the permanent settlement of Bengal, and the people of that Province on the whole have enjoyed great advantages. The permanent settlement was made nearly 100 years ago by order of the then Government as calculated to improve the condition of the soil and the people, and as a matter of fact that result has followed. But in later times other high officials have entertained the opinion, which is by no means sound, but on the contrary shallow and one-sided, that the Government has suffered a great loss owing to the permanent settlement of Bengal. It should be considered that no such vast improvements as we witness here this day would have been at all possible if the permanent settlement had been denied to the people of the Province. Now we cannot expect any similar great improvements in the other Provinces if permanent settlements are not granted to these also in good time. Government may look for an increase of revenue with the increased produce of the soil no doubt, but people make no efforts to increase, as they could if they chose, the produce of the soil, when they know they will not get the benefits, as the next settlement will swallow up the fruit of their labours. Therefore Government should consider it a sufficient gain to increase the prosperity of the country and secure the affection of the people. And the Government will be liked by the people more and more if they conclude a permanent settlement. That Government is I hold fortunate whose subjects ask the Government for a permanent settlement, because with this prayer there is involved a desire for, and belief in, the permanency of the Government. When we ask the Government to grant us permanent settlements we at the same time virtually pledge ourselves to the permanency of the British rule over India, or what would avail *their* permanent settlement, and our rulers should congratulate themselves that they are sufficiently approved by the people for this. If the Government will not sanction permanent settlements now when it is needed and is thus pressed for, it will be the Government itself that will suffer more than even the people. (*Cheers*).

Mr. Hamid Ali Khan (*Lucknow, No. 481, in list*)—Mr. President, Ladies and Gentlemen,—In the first place let me express my sincere regret that owing to many engagements which it was impossible to postpone I was not present when my name was called out on Saturday to support the resolution. It has been often remarked in my part of the country that this resolution is a resolution of the rich people, the zemindars and the talukdars ; but in my opinion it is a resolution of those about whom the poet sang nearly a century ago in words somewhat to this effect :—

"Princes may flourish, or Princes may fade ;
A breath can make them, as a breath has made :
But the poor peasantry, their country's pride,
When once destroyed can never be supplied."

It gives me sincere pleasure that this resolution embodies the views of a friend of mine, Sir A. Colvin, because in 1874, when he was Secretary to the Board of Revenue, he wrote a very important memorandum condemning the re-settlement in the N. W. P. and other parts of India. It has been well remarked that India is an agricultural country, and as such must continue for centuries to come. You know that the zemindars take only a 30 years interest in the land, because they know that if they spend anything upon the land, and if the profits increase, these will not go into their pockets, but into the pockets, at least in great measure, of the Government.

I wish to say a few words with regard to the provinces from which I come. About 25 years ago the settlement of Oude was made, and the condition of the talukdars is now such a deplorable one that they have not yet forgotten the misfortunes and troubles which they suffered in that settlement. The debts they then incurred in greasing the palms of all and sundry have not yet in many cases been cleared off. The period is again approaching ; and there is not a single talukdar or landholder, big or little, in our province who is not trembling in his shoes, and who is not praying day and night for the blessing of a permanent settlement. The expenses, you know, of all that great body of the talukdars continually increase, and as they have not yet benefited by English education, and the Government always exacts larger and larger contributions from them, their ryots suffer and the condition alike of talukdar, zemindar and ryot will be still more deplorable before this coming settlement is accomplished. Before I conclude let me say, apart from the question we are discussing, that my co-religionists must bear in mind that they are Indians first and Mahomedans next. (*Cheers*).

Hafiz Abdur Raheem (*Aligarh, No. 446, in list*) spoke in Urdu and said: Mr. President, Ladies and Gentlemen,—After hearing the able speeches of Mr. Madholkar and Babu Bykantha Nath Sen and others I hesitated to rise ; but in obedience to the order of the President I have no other alternative than to speak a few words. The resolution which is before us just now is based on two Despatches of the Secretary of State for India ; but I shall support it on a ground quite independent of the Despatches. Mr. Fawcett, in his Political Economy, observes that in countries where labour is done by slaves the people never thrive, for since the slaves know that what they earn is not their own they do not care to work as hard as they would otherwise do. This is the case with those districts where the settlement is temporary. No zemindar or tenant tries to improve or to be diligent for fear the revenue or the rent may be enhanced.

**3rd Day.**

**Res. VI. Extension of the Permanent Settlement.**

Some people think that the permanent settlement is only advantageous to the zemindar. This is a mistake. At a permanent settlement the rights and privileges of the tenants ought to be distinctly defined and provisions made for their protection. I am a resident of Zillah Jounpur, where the permanent settlement prevails, and practise as a pleader in Aligarh, which is temporarily settled. I am therefore in a position to express an opinion as to the effects of both these forms of settlement. In Jounpur landed property is very rarely put up to sale, and there is always a large number of purchasers at public auctions, whereas in Aligarh sale of land is very common and sales are very frequently put off for want of bidders ; and it often happens that decree holders themselves are compelled to purchase the lands they have put up for sale. In Jounpur the price of land is nearly double that in Aligarh ; and this fact is even recognized by the legislature. Under the Court Fees Act the valuation of land in permanently settled districts is ten times the revenue ; whereas it is only five times the revenue in districts not permanently settled.

There is another point which is fit to be taken into consideration. It would seem from the Despatches that the Government is of opinion that a country should be permanently settled after it has been fully cultivated, whereas zemindars think that they should wait to make improvements till the land is permanently settled. So that the Government is waiting for the zemindars to improve, whereas the zemindars are waiting for the permanent settlement. But the Government cannot compel any one to make improvements, so that, under the circumstances, there is no other course but that the Government should be the first to move in the matter. If it is wished that the country should be prosperous a permanent settlement is an absolute necessity ; otherwise those parts of Hindustan which are not permanently settled will remain in the backward condition of those countries where labour is done by slaves. I have therefore great pleasure in supporting the resolution that is before us.

MR. SAJJAD HUSSAIN (*Lucknow, No. 480, in list*) then spoke in Urdu :

(*It has been impossible to procure any report of this gentleman's speech.*)

THE PRESIDENT : I really think, Gentlemen, that we must finish this discussion. Do you desire any more speeches on this question (*No, no. Vote, vote.*)

Then I put our sixth resolution which runs thus—

RESOLVED—*That having reference to the expectations created throughout the country by the Despatch of Her Majesty's Secretary of State in 1862, the principles of which were re-affirmed in a subsequent Despatch of 1865, promising the extension of a Permanent Settlement to all temporarily settled tracts, in which certain conditions were fulfilled, and to the fact that throughout large portions of the country those conditions have long since been fulfilled, this Congress respectfully submits that the Government of India is now in honour bound to take up this question of Permanent Settlement without further delay, in view to practical action thereon such that fixity and permanency may be given to the Government Land Revenue demand as explicitly promised, by Her Majesty's Secretary of State, more than a quarter of a century ago.*

The resolution was then put and carried unanimously.

THE PRESIDENT : I will now ask Mr. Manomohun Ghose to propose the seventh resolution.

**Res. VII. Protesting against orders prohibiting Government officials from attending the Congress even as spectators.**

MR. MANOMOHUN GHOSE (*Calcutta, No. 8, in list*) said : MR. PRESIDENT, LADIES AND GENTLEMEN,—The Subjects Committee have decided that it is the duty of the Chairman of the Reception Committee to move the next resolution, and I have, therefore, no option but to rise and discharge that duty to the best of my power. It will, however, not be necessary for me in discharging that duty to detain you more than the minimum period which the President has prescribed for speakers in this assembly. Your attention has probably been drawn to a very remarkable advertisement, which has been appearing in the public papers of Calcutta, whereby, apparently officially, the Government of Bengal directs, or rather professes to advise, that its officers should not attend the Congress even as visitors. (*Shame, shame.*) I am not surprised at this display of feeling on your part, because speaking for myself, ever since I saw that resolution, it has filled me with grief and amazement, and it must have had the same effect upon every one of you. Gentlemen, it strikes me that a more short-sighted policy could not be conceived than that which is the cause of this strange action on the part of the Government. To my mind it displays a want of statesmanship for which I confess I was not prepared. The Government of a country may have a right, I am not prepared to say that it has ; it may claim to itself the right that its officers should not take any part in any

3rd Day.

Res. VII. Protesting against orders prohibiting Government officials from attending the Congress even as spectators.

political meetings or political discussions. Such a course may be open to a Government to take, although I myself should consider it to be almost amounting to a confession of weakness. But the Government, if we rightly interpret its action, professes to go further. It says not only shall its officers not take any part in any public meeting, but they shall not attend even as silent spectators or visitors. (*Shame, shame.*) To my judgment this amounts to a sad confession of weakness (*cheers*)—a confession of weakness which I do not think the Government of this country has any need to make. It must imply one of two things; and, looked at from either point of view, the action of the Government is one which we cannot but deplore. It must imply either that the Government has so little confidence in its own officers that it cannot trust them to resist being contaminated by the discussions in the Congress, or it must imply that the Government is really hostile to our constitutional method of public agitation. Looking at it from either point of view, the action of the Government is exceedingly to be deplored. So far as it implies a confession of weakness, I consider that the Government of India is much too strong to justify its making such a confession. I consider it to be a very strong Government, not because, as it is sometimes supposed, it is based upon the fears of the people, nor, as it is said, because it is based upon the disunion and discord which are said to exist between the different races of India, but, it is strong, because it is based upon the willing allegiance of a loyal people. (*Cheers*). Looked at therefore from any point of view, it is an action which is wholly unintelligible to me, and I believe to most of you. (*All, all*). We are, however, in this predicament; we have not before us any authoritative declaration, certainly not in the words of the Government of India, as to what its orders are on the subject, except an advertisement, which is not altogether consistent with another document, written by the Secretary of the Lieutenant-Governor to our Secretary of the Reception Committee. In the advertisement we are told that the Government considers it not advisable for its officers to attend such meetings. In a letter, which is placed before us and printed, and which I shall presently read, we are told that the orders of the Government of India definitely prohibit the presence of any officials, or indeed by implication, of any members of their household. (*Cheers and laughter*). For my own part, not knowing what the exact terms of the orders of the Government are, I think, we cannot do better than adopt a course which the resolution, which I am about to move, suggests should be adopted. We cannot take any action in the matter until we know what are the exact terms, and what the intentions of the Government of India are. We desire, therefore, that the Government of India should be respectfully moved to place us in possession of such information as it thinks fit to disclose on the subject. It is for these reasons, therefore, that I move this resolution in the paper before you. (*Cheers*). It runs thus:—

*That this Congress having observed with surprise a notice, apparently official, in various Calcutta newspapers, which runs as follows:—*

*" THE CONGRESS.*

*" The Bengal Government having learnt that tickets of admission to the visitors' enclosure in the Congress pavilion have been sent to various Government Officers, residing in Calcutta, has issued a Circular to all Secretaries and Heads of Departments subordinate to it, pointing out that, under the orders of the Government of India, the presence of Government officials, even as visitors at such meetings, is not advisable and that their taking part in the proceedings of any such meetings is absolutely prohibited."*

*and having also considered a letter addressed by the Private Secretary of His Honor the Lieutenant-Governor of Bengal to the Secretary of the Reception Committee of which the following is an exact copy:—*

*" Belvedere, 26th December, 1890.*

*" Dear Sir,—In returning herewith the seven cards of admission to the visitors' enclosure of the Congress pavilion, which were kindly sent by you to my address yesterday afternoon, I am desired to say that the Lieutenant-Governor and the members of his household could not possibly avail themselves of these tickets since the orders of the Government of India definitely prohibit the presence of Government officials at such meetings.*

*" Yours faithfully,*
*" P. C. LYON,*
*" Private Secretary."*

*" To J. Ghosal, Esq., Secretary, Congress Reception Committee."*

*authorizes and instructs its President, Mr. Pherozshah Mehta, to draw the attention of His Excellency the Viceroy to the declaration embodied in these papers, that Government servants are prohibited from attending any meetings of this Congress even as spectators, and to enquire most respectfully whether His Honor the Lieutenant-Governor of Bengal has, or has not, correctly interpreted the orders of the Government of India.*

MR. GEORGE YULE (*Calcutta, No. 13, in list*), in seconding the resolution, said: I have given some study to the instructions that have been issued by the Government, and also to the letter, which has been written by Sir Charles Elliott, and I must say that

**3rd Day.**

**Res. VII. Protesting against orders prohibiting Government officials from attending the Congress even as spectators.**

I am unable to comprehend their meaning or their purport. (*Hear, hear*). If their objection lies in the fact that we are a Congress of people, I want to know what is a Congress. It is an assemblage of persons of indefinite size. If that is so, then I wish to ask is the St. Andrew's Dinner not an assemblage of persons ! Is that too not a Congress. (*Cheers*). Are political subjects not talked of there ? (*Hear, hear*). Of late years, in fact, the St. Andrew's Dinner has been made the platform from which political spouting might be made. (*Cheers*). Yet that is not only patronized by Government Officials, but it is availed of by the highest Government Officials to propound their views. I take it, therefore, Gentlemen, that there has been some great mistake about this instruction, that it has been issued by some Dogberry "clothed in a little brief authority." If it has been issued with the sanction of a higher authority, then I state as a positive conviction, that it is a great and serious mistake. (*Cheers*). But if it has received the sanction of the highest authority, if that instruction has been published, and that letter written with the highest authority of the land, deliberately, then I also deliberately say that it is a piece of gross insolence offered to a body of men, whose chief public characteristics are, firstly, devotion to the Queen (*cheers*), and, secondly, devotion to the true interest of the country (*cheers*), and who are animated with as true and as honest a purpose as any official in the land. (*Renewed cheers*). Any instructions, therefore, which carry on their face, as these instructions do in my judgment, an insinuation that we are unworthy to be visited by Government officials, I resent as an insult, and I retort that in all the qualities of manhood we are as good as they. (*Loud cheers.*) I think, however, Gentlemen, that we may charitably conclude that this piece of business is simply a mistake on the part of a subordinate official, and in that spirit I cordially second the motion that is now before the Congress. (*Cheers.*)

THE PRESIDENT : I think, gentlemen, I may now put this resolution. I think you will all agree with me, that whether Mr. Yule's charitable hypothesis be correct or not, the matter is one of very little importance to us. (*Laughter.*) It may involve the gravest discredit to Government (*hear, hear*), and we are bound to give them an opportunity of extricating themselves from the undignified and ludicrous position, if not worse, in which these precious orders apparently place them ; but beyond this, so far as we are concerned, the matter having served to amuse us for an hour, may be dropped. (*Loud cheers and laughter.*) Shall I put the resolution ? (*Yes, yes, vote*).

Then our seventh resolution stands :—

RESOLVED—*That this Congress having observed with surprise a notice, apparently official, in various Calcutta newspapers, which runs as follows :—*

*"THE CONGRESS.*

*"The Bengal Goverment having learnt that tickets of admission to the visitors' enclosure in the Congress pavilion have been sent to various Government officers residing in Calcutta, has issued a circular to all Secretaries and heads of departments subordinate to it, pointing out, that, under the orders of the Government of India, the presence of Government officials, even as visitors at such meetings, is not advisable, and that their taking part in the proceedings of any such meetings is absolutely prohibited."*

*and having also considered a letter addressed by the Private Secretary of His Honor the Lieutenant-Governor of Bengal to the Secretary of the Reception Committee, of which the following is an exact copy :—*

*"Belvedere, 26th December 1890.*

*"Dear Sir,—In returning herewith the seven cards of admission to the visitor's enclosure of the Congress pavilion which were kindly sent by you to my address yesterday afternoon, I am desired to say that the Lieutenant-Governor and the members of his household could not possibly avail themselves of these tickets, since the orders of the Government of India definitely prohibit the presence of Government officials at such meetings.*

*"Yours faithfully,*

*"P. C. LYON,*

*"Private Secretary."*

*"To*

*"J. GHOSAL, Esq.,*

*"Secretary, Congress Reception Committee."*

*authorizes and instructs its President to draw the attention of His Excellency the Viceroy to the declaration embodied in these papers that Government servants are prohibited from attending any meetings of this Congress even as spectators, and to enquire, most respectfully, whether His Honor the Lieutenant-Governor of Bengal has, or has not, correctly interpreted the orders of the Government of India.*

The resolution was then carried by acclamation.

THE PRESIDENT : It is getting very late, and I therefore adjourn the Congress until tomorrow at 12 noon. The meeting then broke up with loud cheers.

# FOURTH DAY'S PROCEEDINGS.

## Tuesday, the 30th December 1890.

---

**4th Day.**

**Res. VIII. Thanking Mr. Bradlaugh, the British Committee & others for services rendered to the Congress and the country during 1890.**

THE PRESIDENT said: I shall now call upon the Hon'ble Pundit Ajoodhia Nath to move the eighth resolution, which runs thus :—

*That the best thanks of this Congress be tendered to Mr. Charles Bradlaugh, M.P., for the invaluable services rendered by him during the past year, as also to Sir W. Wedderburn, Mr. W. S. Caine, Mr. J. Bright Maclaren, M.P., Mr. J. Ellis, M.P., Mr. George Yule, and Mr. Dadabhai Naoroji for the unselfish zeal and ability with which they have presided over the British Agency of the Congress; further that they put on record an expression of their high appreciation of the manner in which Mr. Digby, C.I.E., Secretary of the Agency, and Messrs. Surendra Nath Banerji, R. N. Mudholkar, W. C. Bonnerji, Eardley Norton and A. O. Hume, delegates to England, respectively, discharged the onerous duties imposed upon them and of their gratitude to all those members of the British public, who so kindly welcomed and so sympathetically gave audience, in over fifty public and a far larger number of private meetings, to one or more of these delegates.*

PUNDIT AJOODHIA NATH (*N.-W. Provinces, No. 339, in list*) said: MR. PRESIDENT, LADIES AND GENTLEMEN,—Many of you have performed with conspicuous ability the duty of moving, seconding, or supporting the resolutions that have already been passed, but it was left to me to undertake the nobler and more pleasant task of asking you to express some little measure of your gratitude to those friends who have helped us at a time when we needed that help most. (*Cheers*). A friend in need is a friend indeed, and we must endeavour to repay our obligations. (*Loud cheers*).

I am afraid I spoke too hastily. We are so much in debt that we cannot lift our head even under that load of obligations, let alone repay them; but by passing this resolution you may at any rate prevent *interest* from accumulating. The kindness of those friends who helped the Congress in its infancy cannot be too highly eulogized. This child, which, only a few years ago, was simply a baby in arms, is now able to walk, but it has not learned to walk intuitively. It has been most affectionately and most carefully taught walking by fathers and uncles, by brothers and cousins. (*Cheers*). And it is nothing but fair that we should acknowledge the support which they have all along most readily accorded to us. But when a family is about to thank its supporters, it does not name the parents first. And leaving alone for the present, the Father of the Congress, first and foremost amongst those who are entitled to our acknowledgments is Mr. Charles Bradlaugh with his constituents. (*Cheers*). The services of Mr. Bradlaugh have been simply invaluable. (*Cheers*). You all know that last year, when the Congress was held at Bombay, he came to India to see this august assembly for himself, although he was not in a fit state of health to do much work. But that is not all; he has drafted several Bills, and two he has introduced already into Parliament, for the reform and expansion of our Councils. He has also, in many respects, helped us and our British Committee with his valuable advice. It is partly by his exertions that the duty on silver in England has been abolished, and he has put a great many questions relating to India to the ministry—questions which have instilled a wholesome sense of their responsibilities into the hearts of numbers of officials heretofore practically irresponsible and, in their own eyes, infallible. He could not have done all this without the permission of his constituents. These constituents also are, therefore, entitled to our best thanks. (*Cheers*). Let me assure Mr. Bradlaugh and all our English friends who have lent us a helping hand that their kindness and confidence has not been misplaced or thrown away. They have helped a nation, which is devoted to its Sovereign and its country, (*cheers*) whose claims are most moderate and reasonable, whose methods are always legal and constitutional, who know how to appreciate kindness, and who are ever ready to do all that lies in their power to secure the permanency of British rule. (*Cheers*).

I may further be permitted to say that England in helping India helps herself. (*Cheers*). If we are truly grateful to Great Britain for the many blessings conferred upon us, England may well be proud of this dependency. India is the brightest gem in the English Crown, and sheds upon it, its greatest lustre. To increase the brilliancy of this gem is to add to the lustre shed upon that Crown. (*Cheers*)

4th Day.

Res. VIII. Thanking Mr. Bradlaugh, the British Committee and others for services rendered to the Congress and the country during 1890.

The next claimants to our gratitude are our British Committee, and their claims are, indeed, well founded. That the Chairman of the Committee, Sir William Wedderburn (*cheers*), presided last year at the Congress, is already well known to you. Another member of that Committee is now amongst you, and his services to our cause, his kindly feelings towards our countrymen, require no commendation from me. You can easily understand whom I mean—Mr. W. S. Caine. (*Cheers.*) Another member of that Committee is the old veteran champion of our cause, Mr. Dadabhai Naoroji. (*Cheers.*) Another of our esteemed friends is Mr. George Yule. (*Cheers.*) I will not take up your time by enlarging upon the valuable assistance you have received from them. This is too well known to be mentioned again here. (*Cheers.*) The other members of the Committee are Mr. J. Bright McLaren, M.P., and Mr. J. Ellis, M.P., and they, *and the entire Committee*, have one and all rendered conspicuous services to us.

We must not also forget the claims of the indefatigable Secretary of that Committee, Mr. William Digby. (*Cheers.*) The zeal and energy with which he has discharged his duties deserve the highest commendation. I refer to his exertions on behalf of the British Committee of the Indian National Congress, not to his work in his Private Political Agency, of which we in the Congress know nothing officially. The Indian National Congress does not officially recognize the so-called Political Agency, though we all privately wish it success for Mr. Digby's sake. The Congress is in no way connected with this Agency, nor is it in any manner cognizant of or responsible for its proceedings. It must be clearly understood that those who support that Agency do not, in the least, contribute to the funds of the Indian National Congress. Our leaders have not the remotest connection with that Political Agency. I am commending the exertions of Mr. Digby as our Secretary, as the Secretary of the British Committee of the Indian National Congress. (*Cheers.*)

While I am introducing these distinguished men to your notice, I see before me those excellent friends who did us excellent service in England this year as our delegates: Their countenances seem to betray a feeling that I had forgotten them ; but I am not so ungrateful as to forget their services. We know that it is due to their wise and strong advocacy that a very important section of the English community take such a lively interest in the affairs of this Congress. (*Hear, hear.*) It was through their exertions that that glory of England and the blessing of India, the Right Honorable William Gladstone (*hear, hear*), promised to support Mr. Bradlaugh's motion before the House of Commons this year. If we receive no hearing from the Conservative party, it is no fault of ours. If they do not wish even to give us an impartial hearing and condemn us, we cannot help it. We have always been anxious, and are still so, that Indian questions should not form part of the English Political programme.

We value the help and co-operation of one party as much as the other. But I am sorry to say that the course we desired to take is impracticable. I must not conceal from our English and Indian friends that many of my countrymen believe that they have very little to expect from a party who have for their leader a statesman who, as far India is concerned, does not hesitate to call white, black. ("*Shame.*") Do not run away with the idea that I refer to the incident between Lord Salisbury and Dadabhai Naoroji. There is, however, a point in that incident which, to the best of my knowledge, has not been publicly noticed. Lord Salisbury had in his public speech called Mr. Dadabhai Naoroji a black man. There arose then a storm of adverse criticism against which even the premiership of England did not afford sufficient protection, and Lord Salisbury was obliged to offer an explanation. But what did the noble lord say? That he meant nothing except that Mr. Dadabhai Naoroji belonged to a different race and could not represent the interests of Englishmen in Parliament. To offer such an explanation was really to plead guilty to the charge ; the whole sting of the remark lay in the so-called apology. You all know that the phrase " black man " is a contemptuous, contumelious expression applied to us by our Anglo-Indian detractors. It means to imply inferiority of race and our disqualification to hold any office of trust and honer. And little did I think that this infection had reached England. But I admire the candour of Lord Salisbury. I now find that this contamination has reached, through the India Office, the English Cabinet. Be that as it may, I hope the better classes of the Conservative party will give us a hearing when our friends go to England, and will not allow it to be said that the Conservatives of England are affected by political bigotry and superstition.

Our delegates met with a splendid reception in England, not only from the constituency of Mr. Bradlaugh, whom I have recommended to you for your warm acknowledgments, but also from Glasgow, Aberdeen, Newcastle, Manchester, Birmingham, Bristol, Exeter, Plymouth and a great many other communities. These delegates have done us good service, and indeed it could not be otherwise when you think who they were. I have only to mention their names, and you will see that after that selection had been made the result achieved was a foregone conclusion.

4th Day.

Res. VIII. Thanking Mr. Bradlaugh, the British Committee and others for services rendered to the Congress and the country during 1890.

Among the delegates were Mr. Surendra Nath Banerji (*cheers*), Mr. R. N. Mudholkar (*cheers*), our valued friend Mr. W. C. Bonnerjee, Mr. Eardley Norton of Madras, and last, but not least, one who is the pride of England and the lover of India, one who is the soul of this Congress, Mr. Hume. (*Enthusiastic cheers.*) Mr. Hume has been truly described as the " father of the Indian National Congress." He retired from the public service much earlier than he need have done, and he denied himself the honor of being the ruler of a province, and ever since that time has spared neither time nor money nor energy to make the Congress a complete success. He has worked day and night for us, neglecting his own private affairs, and when he knew that we could not help ourselves, he opened his purse most generously. (*Hear, hear.*) He has been working for us on his sick-bed. If any body knows that by working in that way for us he has ruined his health it is I. In doing that, he has been only following the noble traditions of his family. (*Cheers.*) His father had worked hard for the good of the land of his birth (*hear, hear*), and to introduce reforms into Parliament, and this worthy son of the worthy father has laboured for the good of the land of his adoption. (*Cheers.*) But alas ! in the midst of all that kindness, he is inclined to be not only unkind but cruel. He, at times, says that the time has arrived that he should retire from the office of General Secretary. (*No, no.*) The reply to this question by the Congress is one and one only. The Congress says, do not be cruel. Do not leave your most beloved infant child an orphan while you are still living. His connection as General Secretary is too sacred to be broken while he and we are alive, and when we are gone the coming generations of India will cherish his memory with feelings of the deepest gratitude. (*Cheers.*) Gentlemen, I hope and trust that, long before I die, I shall have the pleasure and gratification of seeing his statue erected by the people he has helped. I now move the resolution for adoption, and I hope you will carry it with acclamation. (*Loud cheers.*)

MR. HAMID ALI (*Lucknow, No. 481, in list*)—MR. PRESIDENT, LADIES, AND GENTLEMEN I have much pleasure in seconding the resolution. The services of the gentlemen enumerated in the resolution are too well known to require any mention or even allusion from me. I believe I express the sense of the entire assembly when I say that language is too poor to give us words strong enough to express our heartfelt gratitude and obligations to them. Besides, I think it is not in the power of this Congress to convey sufficiently our obligations and gratitude, and, therefore, I am satisfied to leave this task to posterity, who will thank them from the bottom of their heart. To serve, is a far higher and nobler law of life than even to rule (*hear, hear*), and this principle has been well expressed in the lives of those gentlemen who have done so much for our country. In the words of the Poet Laureate :

> " Not he who breaks, the dams, but he
> Who through the Channels of the State
> Convoys the people's wish, is great,
> His name is pure, his fame is free." (*Cheers.*)

I have not the slightest doubt that their names and fame, inscribed on the page of time in deathless characters of gold, with this noble inscription, " these were the workers who knew how to serve, " will be handed down to a far distant posterity. (*Cheers*).

BABU NORENDRA NATH SEN (*Calcutta, No. 671, in list*)—I have been asked to support this resolution, and a more agreeable duty it has seldom fallen to my lot to perform. Differences of opinion might exist in regard to some of the other matters which have come up here for our consideration, but there can be none in regard to the subject of this resolution. There is not another man who has earned our gratitude more deservedly, by his persistent and wholly disinterested advocacy of the cause of India, in Parliament, than Mr. Charles Bradlaugh (*cheers*), the Junior Member for Northampton, but more familiarly known to us all as the Member for India. This last title formerly belonged to that devoted friend of this country, the late lamented Mr. Henry Fawcett. It has now worthily descended to Mr. Bradlaugh, whose good services in our behalf are even much greater than those of Mr. Fawcett, great as those services undoubtedly were. In fact, it has been our good fortune to secure in Mr. Bradlaugh a friend in Parliament, whose powerful advocacy is proving simply invaluable to us. In this rare acquisition I, for one, see the hand of Providence. God has, I believe in his good time, prepared Mr. Bradlaugh to write and work for India, and this overpowering thought ought to stimulate all the more our future efforts. I am sure that we shall find more friends in Parliament like Mr. Bradlaugh, if we only can prove that we deserve to have them. Everything depends on ourselves. I have often and often heard the question asked—what good has come of the Congress movement ? Well, if the reply was to come from me, I should say that the Congress has brought to us Charles Bradlaugh, our staunchest friend, our redoubtable champion in the British Parliament. The Congress may have done nothing more—but because it has been able to secure such a friend as Mr. Bradlaugh it has deserved well of the country, and all our labours and pecuniary

4th Day.

Res. VIII. Thanking Mr. Bradlaugh, the British Committee and others for services rendered to the Congress and the country during 1890.

sacrifices have not been put forth in vain. We have now, thanks to the Congress, at least one man in Parliament, to whom we can turn in the hour of trial, to whom we can apply hopefully in an emergency, and for the redress of our grievances. The great English Tribune has, by his unceasing efforts in furtherance of our cause, infused a most wholesome terror into the dual Government of this country, and has at least succeeded to some extent in keeping Anglo-Indian officials on the alert. He has evidently made them uncomfortable ; and herein lies the secret of so much official opposition to the Congress in this country. No earthly gifts in our power can repay our debt to Mr. Bradlaugh. We can only make him our heart's offering of love and gratitude. (*Loud cheers.*)

But if he has rendered invaluable services, the services of the British Congress Committee have been none the less valuable. Such a Committee of influential Englishmen was very much needed for a long time, and in this Committee, which we have now got in London, under the leadership of Sir William Wedderburn, we have at last got what we so long wanted. With a powerful Committee in London to help our cause, and with Mr. Bradlaugh and other friends to take care of our interests in Parliament, we can surely calculate upon achieving a great deal. It is said that Mr. Digby is a paid agent of ours, and that a paid agent cannot carry much weight in England ; but Mr Digby is entirely in the hands of the English Committee, who are working most disinterestedly and unselfishly for us. The Committee are only adding to the load of obligations to England, under which India is placed on various grounds. It is an article of faith that Englishmen are unconscious instruments in the hands of God for the complete uplifting of our countrymen. When they choose to take us by the hand, we cannot have more sincere and staunch friends than they in the whole world. (*Cheers.*)

And how shall we thank our own delegates whom we sent to England to plead our cause? How can we sufficiently thank Mr. Hume, Babu Surendra Nath Bannerji, Mr. Norton, Mr. Joshi, and Mr. Mudholkar? They showed a self-sacrificing spirit which others of us would do well to imitate. It is this spirit, which is very much wanting in us, which we most need to advance us as a nation. In the proportion in which every one of us gives proof of such personal sacrifices, in the same proportion will India progress. All our delegates discharged their duty most nobly and manfully. But the gentleman who, from all accounts, created the greatest impression in England by his eloquence was my esteemed friend, Babu Surendra Nath Bannerji. (*Cheers*). He has quite won the hearts of the Indian people by the great service he has rendered to them. (*Cheers.*)

Before I sit down, I have one word to add, and that is that our venerable friend, Mr. Dadabhai Naoroji, has practically become our standing delegate in England, and by his presence there he is doing all he can to protect the interests of this country. He deserves our warmest thanks, and so do the Liberals of the Finsbury constituency, who are trying to provide him with a seat in Parliament. I will not take up more of your time. I am sure that you will most gladly and enthusiastically adopt the resolution which I have had the pleasure of supporting. (*Cheers.*)

MR. J. K. CAMA (*Bombay, No. 544, in list*)—MR. PRESIDENT, LADIES AND GENTLEMEN,— It is with peculiar pleasure that I am here in response to the President's call to support this resolution, not because it is a resolution that requires any support, for I know full well that the names before you belong to gentlemen whose praises it requires no bard or songster to sing; that they are names which are cherished as amongst the richest and choicest gems of the land ; but because it is a matter of peculiar gratification to me to be in a position to tell you that it has been my good fortune to have had the opportunity of taking an active share in the candidature of one of these gentlemen, a true and noble son of India, whom you did the honor of electing as your President some four years ago in this very city. I refer to our esteemed countryman Mr. Dadabhai Naoroji, who stood as a candidate for the Holborn division of Finsbury at the General Election of 1886.

Knowing as I do the keen interest you have always taken in the candidature of natives of India in the British Constituencies, and the very close and lively interest with which you have followed Mr. Dadabhai Naoroji s campaign, I cannot help thinking that a short sketch of that campaign will not be without some interest to your active and energetic minds. For it was in that campaign that it was pre-eminently shown what a true born native of India could achieve under the most adverse and trying circumstances. It was then that Mr. Dadabhai's indefatigable industry, his indomitable courage, his great erudition and his supreme sacrifice were most markedly shown. I will at once take you into the thick of that campaign. It was on the 12th of April 1886 that our friend set foot in Great Britain with the object of finding a constituency in which to stand. It was in the midsummer of that memorable year that Mr. Gladstone's Parliament was dissolved

4th Day.

Res. VIII. Thanking Mr. Bradlaugh, the British Committee and others for services rendered to the Congress and the country during 1890.

and Great Britain was threatened with one of the gravest crises that have stirred it for some time. It was in the midst of all this trouble and turmoil that Mr. Dadabhai Naoroji had the good fortune to secure a constituency, but only three weeks before the day of the poll—a constituency in the very heart of the great metropolis, a constituency essentially Conservative in its elements. And what was his situation? He found that the Liberal cause in the Holborn Division of Finsbury was lying idle; it was asleep, and it wanted a man with Herculean power to awaken it. There was no Liberal organized committee there; and what did Mr. Dadabhai Naoroji do? Did he shrink or flinch from this Herculean task? No, Gentlemen, he went bravely to work and organized a Liberal committee; meetings were called in various halls, open-air gatherings were summoned, addresses were delivered and the campaign was fairly begun. The shrewdness of his speech, the soundness of his arguments, and his incontestable statistical statements, won for him the applause and the good graces of his hearers. When he placed before the British public the grievances and the just claims of the teeming millions of India, when he reached the heart of John Bull through the prayers of the bleeding lambs of India, it was then that the sympathy and support of his hearers were strong and loud. What was the end of the campaign? Rome was not built in a day, and a seat in Parliament cannot be gained in three weeks. His was a victory unparalleled in history. The victory was his because he obtained, in the first place, a constituency; the victory was his because he was nominated as a candidate; the victory was his because he went to the poll; and, more than all, the victory was his because he succeeded in reducing the majority of his Conservative opponent who was returned. But, Gentlemen, although he was not returned to Parliament, his voice commenced to be heard, and is now heard in Parliament through those English members who are sitting there, ready and willing to seek information from, and take council with him. At present he is the accepted Liberal candidate for Clerkenwell, and there he works ardently and incessantly for the good of India; and great will be the day for India—and I think the day must come, and I hope it is not far distant—when Mr. Dadabhai Naoroji is returned to Parliament to the glory and honour of this great Empire. (*Cheers*).

Mr. Beglar (*Calcutta, No. 150, in list*)—Mr. President,—It is a great pleasure to be one of the supporters of this resolution. It is only natural that the Congress should be grateful to its teacher, its "*gooroo*," (for that is the relation to the Congress in which our worthy secretary, Mr. A. O. Hume stands), to Mr. Charles Bradlaugh, its champion, and Sir William Wedderburn, its leading advocate, a man who has exerted himself in the good cause, not only in India but everywhere else. I am only sorry that there are not more to be thankful to and to include in our resolution. It appears to me that those men, who have supported us at a time when all kinds of insinuation and opposition prevailed against the Congress, deserve our thanks in a way quite exceptional; in a way in which those who come after them will certainly not merit.

We have heard it said that the Congress people are only for themselves; that the Congress demands are excessive; that the Congress is seditious; that it only thinks of itself and would be tyrannical over minorities; that it does not care to look to the other side of the question. It appears to me that all these objections have already vanished. It is how indisputable that the Congress delegates are not sham delegates, but are really elected by large sections of the people, not only the learned and educated, but the masses of the people earning their 5 or 10 rupees a month. Our resolutions have shown that the Congress cares for other people, that it cares for the poor. The resolution as to the salt tax is distinctly intended for the relief of the poor. It is said that we might get a larger number of supporters if our methods were a little more moderate. Our demands are certainly moderate,—there is nothing immoderate in these, but—perhaps they mean that we might adopt a more moderate tone,

The President: That is not the question.

Mr. Beglar: I am trying to show that there are possibly means by which the number whom we have to thank may be increased year by year.

The President: That is not the proposition before the Congress.

Mr. Beglar: I need only add, then, that I for one am deeply grateful to all these gentlemen named in the resolution (*cheers.*) and support this latter from the bottom of my heart. (*Cheers.*)

4th Day.

Res. VIII. Thanking Mr. Bradlaugh, the British Committee and others for services rendered to the Congress and the country during 1890.

Mr. Hem Chandra Rai (*Calcutta, No. 201, in list*) in supporting the resolution said: Mr. President, Brother Delegates, Ladies and Gentlemen,—I am extremely grateful to you for the opportunity you give me of taking part in the deliberations of this great national gathering, the more so because I need not add any words of my own to what has fallen from the previous speakers in commending the resolution under discussion to your acceptance and approval, for there cannot possibly be any two opinions, as to the propriety and, what is more, the extreme necessity of acknowledging, however humbly, the great services rendered to our cause by the distinguished gentlemen, whose names figure in the resolution which I have the honour to support.

No words can be adequate to describe the priceless services rendered by Mr. Bradlaugh, and I will not mar the intense, if silent, feeling of national gratitude which pervades the Indian continent, from one end to the other, towards that remarkable personage by attempting to delineate it by any feeble words of my own. And Mr. Bradlaugh has been ably seconded in his great undertaking by some other English philanthropists, whose unselfish devotion to India, the language of panegyric, however you may strain it, would be inadequate to express. One of these, Mr. Caine, we have been able to welcome in our midst. Last time when he was here his outspoken denunciations of the excise policy of the Indian Government brought down upon him fierce attacks by the Anglo-Indian Journals, one of which went so far as to make the silly proposal to deport him out of India. (*cries of 'shame.'*) I am not at all surprised, Gentlemen, that you respond to my mention of that un-English suggestion by cries of shame, for that is the only term which expresses the intense feeling of indignation that we all experienced on the occasion. Happily, however, the threatened deportation did not take place. Mr. Caine has managed to survive those invectives, and there he sits to-day, honoured and applauded by all, and ready to help us by his wise counsels and weighty support. Ladies and Gentlemen, attacks like the above only indicate the difficulties which beset the path of our English friends; all the more necessary, therefore, that we should, in unmistakable terms, give public expression to our feelings of thankfulness, for their human efforts on our behalf. Not that they themselves desire such an acknowledgment for who can imagine, much less believe, that any but the purest motives actuate Mr. Hume, also now bereft of his dear partner in life, in the noble example of self-sacrifice which he displays—an example equalled only by that of John Howard of immortal name—not that they themselves desire such an acknowledgment, but because we have a duty to discharge, which we cannot possibly shirk. Nor, in making this public acknowedgment of the services of our English benefactors, must we omit to couple the names of, and pay our humble tribute to, those distinguished countrymen of ours who, at considerable sacrifice of time, money, and energy, undertook a trip to England to enlighten the British public as to our wrongs and disabilities, our needs and aspirations. Doubtless they

> Have sown some generous seed
> Fruitful of further thought and deed.

But their work needs a healthy continuity, and we only hope that the work so auspiciously commenced will evoke widespread response, and that round this little group of Indian patriots there will be formed a large company of patriotic gentlemen ready to undergo similar sacrifices on similar errands. And, in return for their noble services, let us offer them our humble, yet heartfelt thanks, and that which is, indeed, the highest reward that a public man can aspire to—the deep and the lasting gratitude of a United People.

Moulvie Rukunuddin (*Delhi, No. 533, in list*) spoke in Urdu and said: Gentlemen,—This great gathering which has drawn us all here to Calcutta from every Province and City of Hindustan is the sixth sitting of the Indian National Congress. Throughout the years over which these sittings have extended, the aims, the objects of the Congress have been day by day growing more and more familiar with the entire population and more and more accepted by all as indicating the true road of progress for our country. Look back at what India was six years ago—look at it now. If the Congress has no other merits, all, even our adversaries, must admit that it has proved itself an unexampled organization for the political education of our people. (*cheers.*) They who were so lately sunk in hopeless ignorance of their natural rights, those whose hearts seven years ago knew neither hope nor longing for better things—now *know*, and, do not forget that if union be strength, knowledge is power. (*loud cheers*) I am a Delegate from Delhi—a Musulman, and I am glad now even at this sixth sitting to have the chance of publicly avowing the gratitude that, for my country's sake, I feel for the Congress and its past labours. I have been rather suddenly called upon to support this resolution of thanks to those English and Indian gentlemen, who during this year, now almost past, have rendered conspicuous services to the Congress, in other words to India's cause. I support it with all my heart; the names of Bradlaugh and Hume, of Caine and Digby are becoming household words

4th Day.

Res. VIII. Thanking Mr. Bradlaugh, the British Committee and others for services rendered to the Congress and the country during 1890.

throughout the land, but all this has been already well said by other speakers: it is useless to prolong the debate, and I will therefore only ask you now to pass this resolution with acclamation. (*Yes, vote, vote*).

THE PRESIDENT: Then, I put this 8th resolution :—

RESOLVED.—*That the best thanks of this Congress be tendered to Mr. Charles Bradlaugh, M.P., for the invaluable services rendered by him during the past year, as also to Sir W. Wedderburn, Mr. W. S. Caine, Mr. J. Bright Maclaren, M.P., Mr. J. Ellis, M.P., Mr. George Yule, and Mr. Dadabhai Naorojee for the unselfish zeal and ability with which they have presided over the British Agency of the Congress; further that they put on record an expression of their high appreciation of the manner in which Mr. Digby, C.I.E., Secretary of the Agency and Messrs. Surendro Nath Banerjee, R. N. Mudholkar, W. C. Bonerjee, Eardley Norton, and A. O. Hume, delegates to England, respectively, discharged the onerous duties imposed upon them, and of their gratitude to all those members of the British public who so kindly welcomed and so sympathetically gave audience, in over fifty public and a far larger number of private meetings, to one or more of these Delegates.*

THE PRESIDENT: The resolution has been carried by acclamation. I will now call upon Mr. Monomohun Ghose to propose the 9th Resolution.

Res. IX. Vote of thanks to house proprietors who lent their houses and grounds for the erection of the Pavilion, or the reception of Delegates.

MR. MONOMOHUN GHOSE (*Calcutta, No. 8, in list*)—It is unnecessary for me to make another speech. My only excuse for intruding upon your attention once more is that it is appropriate that the pleasant and agreeable duty involved in moving the Ninth Resolution should devolve upon the Chairman of the Reception Committee. This is the Resolution :—

*That a vote of thanks be recorded to Kumar Debendra Mullick and Brothers, Proprietors of the Tivoli Gardens; Mr. N. C. Bose and Babu Bhupendra Nath Bose, Proprietors of Mohan Bagan Villa; and to the Hon'ble Sir Romesh Chandra Mitra, Mr. T. N. Palit, Babus Janokee Nath Roy, Gopee Mohan Roy, Harendra Nath Roy, Kissory Mohan Roy, Ramanath Ghose, and Jamadar Ghasiram, owners of houses kindly lent for the use of delegates.*

I am sure that in the city of Calcutta no better place could have been selected than the one in which we are assembled to-day. Calcutta is an exceedingly difficult place for the reception of such a large assembly, and the Reception Committee have had great difficulty in selecting an appropriate place for this occasion, and had it not been for the kindness of the proprietors of these gardens and of the palatial residence, in which some 200 of you are luxuriously lodged, it would have been extremely difficult, if not impossible, for us to have received and accommodated you in the way we have been able to do (*Cheers*); and I am sure you will all agree with me that the necessity of thanking the friends who have thus aided us devolves not only on the reception Committee but also on yourselves, and that the thanks of the entire Congress are due to the proprietors of these fine gardens and that princely residence. (*Cheers.*) I may add as regards one of these Babu Bhupendro Nath Bose (*cheers*) that, independent of his and his partner's liberality in the matter of placing that great palace the Mohan Bagan Villa at our disposal, no man connected with the Reception Committee has worked harder or with greater zeal. (*Loud cheers*) I must not forget to mention also in this connection the cordiality with which several other public spirited gentlemen of the city have come forward to place at our disposal their own residences for the reception of some of the delegates who have come to Calcutta. (*Cheers*). prominent amongst them is our distinguished friend Sir Romesh Chandra Mitra (*Cheers*); there is also Mr. T. Palit who has placed his beautiful residence at the disposal of the Reception Committee; ant there are gentlemen whose names are embodied in the resolution, Babus Janokee Nath Roy, Gopee Mohan Roy, Harendra Nath Roy, Kissory Mohan Roy, Ramanath Ghose and Jamadar Ghasiram, owners of houses lent for the use of the delegates, all of whom have voluntarily come forward to help the Reception Committee in a public spirited manner. (*Cheers*). I am sure no words of mine are necessary to commend the resolution to your approval, and that you will carry it by acclamation.

BABU NAFFER CHANDER PAL CHOWDHUREE (*Bengal, No. 139, in list*)—I have great pleasure in seconding the resolution. If you adopt it you will only be giving these gentlemen what is justly due to them. I am rather surprised that it has been considered necessary to have a seconder, as I think the resolution ought to have been carried by acclamation as soon as it was proposed by my predecessor.

4th Day.

Res IX. Vote of thanks to house proprietors who lent their houses and grounds for the erection of the Pavilion, or the reception of Delegates.

THE PRESIDENT : I accept the suggestion made by the seconder, and will ask you to carry it by acclamation ; it is our Ninth Resolution and is thus worded :—

RESOLVED—*That a vote of thanks be recorded to Kumar Debendra Mullick and Brothers, Proprietors of the Tivoli Gadrens, Mr. N. C. Bose and Babu Bhupendra Nath Bose, Proprietors of Mohan Bagan Villa, and to the Hon'ble Sir Romesh Chandra Mitra, Mr. T. N. Palit, Babus Janokee Nath Roy, Gopee Mohan Roy, Harendra Nath Roy, Kissory Mohan Roy, Ramanath Ghose, and Jamadar Ghasiram, owners of houses kindly lent for the use of delegates.*

Carried by acclamation.

Res. X. Next Congress to be held a Nagpore or Madras.

MR. A. O. HUME (*Punjab, No. 519, in list*), who, on rising, was received with vociferous applause, the entire Congress standing, said: GENTLEMEN, I do not know whether I shall be able to make myself heard. I have such a terrible cold that I am afraid my voice will hardly travel over this vast assembly (*cries of we can hear every word*). All right! Then, allow me, in the first place, to thank you for the very, very kind reception you have just given me. It is far more warm and enthusiastic than I have deserved. ("*No, No*"). But then it is the nature of the people of India to be extremely, excessively, I may almost say, exaggeratedly, grateful for everything done for them ("*No, No.*") Knowing then your grateful and generous hearts, I accept your enthusiastic reception of me not as a just tribute to any merits of mine, but as the necessary outcome of your own kindly, loving natures.

And now I ask you to allow me to propose to you the little formal resolution which, as in past years, it falls to my lot to bring before you. There is only one little difficulty about it. I am going to ask you to say that the next Congress shall be held......... where? It is not quite settled, and we are obliged, therefore to lay before you two alternative names. The Madras Committee have very kindly and liberally offered to have the Congress there. We all like the Madras people, and many of us would prefer going these to anywhere else, but we feel that it would be very far for the delegates of many circles to travel. It would be very difficult to get a reasonably good attendance of delegates from the Punjab, from Oude, the North-West Provinces, Behar, and even Bengal, unless gentlemen were prepared to go by sea, and all our delegates are not prepared to do this, and 96 hours journey by rail is no joke. We have therefore all thought that, if possible, we ought to have the Congress at a more central situation—Nagpore is the capital of the Central Provinces and about the most central spot in the Empire, and it is a place at which the Congress has never before met, and we have hopes of being able to arrange for the Congress being held at Nagpore next year. Unfortunately, owing to sickness and other circumstances, the real leaders of our party in Nagpore are not present at the Congress this year, and until we consult them no positive decision on this point can be arrived at. You are now in a position to understand the wording of the resolution which I shall read to you:—

RESOLVED.—*That the Seventh Indian National Congress do assemble on the 26th December, 1891, at either Madras or Nagpore, as may be hereafter settled, in consultation between the Madras, Central Provinces and Berar Committees, and the Joint-General Secretary.*

If you all agree to this, and I am sure you will, as you are all reasonable and sensible men, you will please carry it at once; and do not let us waste the time of the Congress by requiring any one to second it. (*Loud and prolonged cheering.*)

THE PRESIDENT: The tenth resolution has been carried by acclamation.

Res. XI. Provisonal arrangements for holding a Congress in London in 1892.

BABU NORENDRO NATH SEN (*Calcutta, No. 671, in list*) then moved the Eleventh Resolution, *viz.* :—

*That provisional arrangements be made to hold a Congress, of not less than hundred delegates, in England, all things being convenient, in 1892, and that the several Standing Congress Committees be directed to report at the coming Congress, the names of the delegates, that it is proposed to depute from their respective circles.*

He said: MR. PRESIDENT, LADIES AND GENTLEMEN,—In moving this resolution, I have only to remind you that, after all, it is England that is the last resort for appeal on all India questions. Our ultimate judges are the British Public, the British Press, and the British

4th Day.

Res. XI. Provisonal arrangements for holding a Congress in London in 1892.

Parliament. The Government of this country is not now what it was of old, and our affairs are administered more from the India Office in London than from Calcutta or Simla. The Government of this country is carried on by constant reference to the Secretary of State and his Council. The real seat of our Government is not now Calcutta or Simla but it is London, and our real rulers reside in the Metropolis of the United Kingdom of Great Britain and Ireland. Sir we have held already six annual sessions of the National Congress in India. I think, and many others think with me, that since London is the *de facto* seat of our Government and our real rulers reside there, the Indian National Congress may not now unfitly hold a sesion in that great city, The assemblage of the Congress in London will create an impression in England, such as the six sessions of the Congress have not together produced. Our delegates, who visited England last year, incline to this view, and they urge on us the importance of the Congress meeting in London some time in April or May 1892. You need not be reminded what good the visits of our delegates to England from time to time have brought forth. Whatever interest Englishmen take in the affairs of this country to-day has resulted, mainly, from the periodical visits of our delegates. If, then, the stray visits of a few delegates have done so much good how much more may we not expect from the meeting of the delegates to tho National Congress in London? It is impossible to exaggerate the importance of holding a session of the Congress, say, at Exeter Hall or St. James' Hall, in London. My friend, Babu Surendra Nath Banneiji, from his late experience as one of our delegates to England, is particularly anxious that we should adopt this course. Mr. Caine decidedly shares this opinion. I myself have long been convinced of the wisdom of such a step, and have, in fact, been advocating the adoption of this course for the last three years or more. Sir, hitherto we have been crying more or less in the wilderness. Let the Congress cry be now heard in England itself from the mouths of its assembled delegates, and then the cry may be heeded. I cannot too strongly recommend you to adopt this resolution, which I believe to be the most important resolution that has been brought before the Congress this year. We need not bold a very crowded Congress in London. A minimum of, say, a hundred delegates will be sufficient for all purposes. If we can find more delegates to go, why so much the better. We do not force the delegation upon any body. It is proposed to make such arrangements for the voyage and back, and during the time of the stay of the delegates in England, as shall be in consonance with the habits and religious feelings of even the most rigidly o thodox Hindus. The presence of a hundred Indian delegates, or more, in London, in Congress assembled, appealing to Englishmen in their very homes, must, let us hope, result in the appeal being granted. But apart from the political effect of such a Congress, the social effect on us all will be great and all-permeating, and besides, in the present state of public feeling in England, the cause of India cannot fail to be very much advanced. I am glad to be able to say that each of the Presidencies and Provinces in India undertakes to send a number of delegates to make, up the full complement of the minimum number wanted.

In commending this resolution to your approval, I have only to tell you that thirty-eight years ago, in this great city, when the Indian legislature passed the Lex Loci Act by which a Hindu, who renounced his religion, was declared qualified to inherit his ancestral property, the orthodox Hindu community, with Rajah Sir Radhakanta Deb at their head, appealed to Parliament for its repeal. Mr. John Farley Leith, the eminent Barrister, was retained as agent in London for the Calcutta Hindu community. Mr. Leith urged the necessity of a deputation from among the orthodox Hindus proceeding to England, and seeking justice personally at the hands of Parliament, in order to convince that body of the depth of Hindu feeling which the passing of the Lex Loci Act had roused. The orthodox Calcutta Hindus then seriously thought of acting upon Mr. Leith's suggestion, and I know it for a fact that preparations were actually in progress for that purpose. But some causes, other than social, led to the abandonment of the idea. I strongly feel that if the idea had been then carried out, and followed largely throughout India, we should have been better governed during the interval between then and now, and the progress of India would not have been hindered for such a length of years. Ladies and gentlemen, I have much pleasure in moving the resolution and recommending it for your acceptance. (*Cheers.*)

Babu Saligram Singh (*Calcutta, No. 60, in list*)—Mr. President, Ladies and Gentlemen,—The manifold advantages which would accrue to the cause of the Congress by holding a meeting in England I need not dwell on, because they have been so clearly stated by the speaker who preceded me. There is, however, one matter in connection with this resolution to which I beg to draw your attention. It is apprehended that there may be some difficulty in the case of orthodox delegates in proceeding to Europe; but I may mention that I had an opportunity of speaking to some of the leading delegates of Behar and Oudh last evening, and I am assured by them that there would be no such difficulty if suitable arrangements could be made for the voyage. Further, I am hopeful that there may be no difficulty, because I know that there have been precedents and that orthodox Hindus have gone beyond the seas—I refer to the soldiers who went to Abyssinia and Egypt—(*cheers*) who, on their return, were received, without any loss of caste status, by their people. Their cause was a noble one, namely, to fight for the Crown and for the Government under whom they lived; and that was one of the considerations which led their people to receive them on their return. The cause for which we are contending is equally laudable. We are fighting for the cause of our people, and there is no reason to doubt that the delegates, when they come from England, will be received with acclamation by their own people, without any dissentient voices. (*Cheers*).

MR. VIRARAGHAVA CHARIAR (*Madras, No. 620, in list*)—MR. PRESIDENT AND FELLOW DELEGATES,—I have much pleasure in supporting the resolution. This question is not new to us. It has been before the country for the last two years. A certain gentleman from Bombay addressed a letter and submitted his proposals for an English session of the Congress to the various Standing Congress Committees, and they were received with great attention and approval. Moreover, you will remember that some years ago, when there was a rumour that Government had an idea of suppressing the Congress, we had almost made up our minds to hold it in London, as also that many offers and promises of funds were made in case such a measure proved necessary.

You will, no doubt, be surprised to find me speaking as one of the supporters of the proposition, coming, as I do, from Madras, where a sea voyage is actually prohibited, especially among the Brahmins; and not only this, but where there is a difficulty as to dining together, even among the Brahmins themselves. But this great national movement, though ostensibly a political one, is still a social one. Ever since it had its origin in the Great Hall at Bombay it has been spreading its wholesome influence in all directions. It has been bringing us together and making for us friends all over the country who are helping each other in a thousand and one ways. But, Gentlemen, after two years existence it brought forth in Madras a social conference to work equally in other directions, and if next the Congress be held in Madras it will bring forth another child—the British Congress to be held in London. Had it not been for this Congress, Madras would have been nowhere. It has been greatly helping the people in Madras. Before that time Madras was called benighted. Now we have all throughout the Presidency Standing Congress Committees to help the Central Committee at Madras. Much has been said about the orthodox opinions that would prevent our undertakng a sea voyage to England. On behalf of my province I venture to say that we have never allowed and never shall allow orthodoxy, or any other doxy, to stand in the way of our political advancement. (*Cheers*).

It was in the highest days of orthodoxy in Poona that we ventured to cross the barriers of the Indus and the Sulieman range and establish our forces in Afghanistan, and it was in those days that the first diplomatic deputation was sent to the English court. I think, therefore, that every one of you will say that, as it is necessary in these days to send a delegation to England and hold a session in the very heart of London, the proposal should meet, as I am sure it will in my province, the cordial support of the public. I have not the least doubt that you have considered that an English agitation is very essential to the success of our undertaking. It is no use breaking one's head against the stone or *wooden* walls here. You have already considered it necessary to have an English agency in England. Then you have sent pioneers to clear the ground for us. I mean the delegates appointed last year whose good work you have so heartily recognized. What then remains? To remove your battle-fields to England, to the very heart of London. That is the logical sequence of the delegation sent last year to England. (*Cheers*).

Then, speaking from a business point of view, you have an English Agency, and, although you may recognize its services, it is a good commercial principle, not to depend entirely upon agents, but to do part of the business yourself. Consequently, from a business point of view, it is necessary that you should hold a sitting of the Congress in London, if not this year or next year—sooner or later. This resolution, therefore, comes in as a sequence to what you have done. All things being convenient (by which it is understood the political situation in England being favourable to our aspirations at the time) we propose in the summer of 1892 holding a Congress in London, and thus driving this national agitation *home* in every sense of the word. (*Cheers*).

MR. DEORAO VINAYEK (*Berar, No. 590, in list*)—MR. PRESIDENT, LADIES AND GENTLEMEN,—I have not been called upon to support this resolution because my predecessors have left anything unsaid, but because I come from a province from which no one else has been called upon to speak to this point. The proposition is such that very little need be said upon it. We have held our six meetings of the Congress in

4th Day,

Res. XI. Provisional arrangements for holding a Congress in London in 1892.

this country, and the seventh we hope to hold in Madras. We have fought our battle here, and the time has nearly come when we should move our camp to a stronger and more commanding position where we shall have a greater chance of success. Here, in India, we have been misrepresented, our objects and aims misreported, our methods misconstrued and all Congresswallahs denounced as bad men! But we prove by our actions that we are not so bad as we are represented to be. Our Government ought to know this. It is our duty to show them that we are not bad men. From a political point of view we think we must go to London, where we shall show our true rulers, the people of Great Britain, that we are not bad men. We do our duty not only to our country but to our Government as well. Remembering the difficulties of the Government we make our representations absolutely moderate and quite practical. I support the resolution with pleasure.

Socially speaking, there is no difficulty. No duty is superior to our duty to the country in which we were born. We have all of us duties to discharge to our countrymen and friends, and if we do not discharge them we do not fulfil the noble purpose by which alone our existence is justified. Some social objections there may be. If you want to go to England for your profit, for pecuniary purposes, your people may or may not object to take you on your return back into your own caste ; but, when you take a nobler duty in hand, when you have gone forth and crossed the stormy ocean solely to serve your country, even the old people, let alone younger generations, are not so blind as to think of putting an obstacle in their patriot brethren's noble course, and they will not only receive you on your return into the bosom of your caste, but receive you with open arms, with rejoicings, praise and gratitude. ( *Loud cheers.* )

MR. DHONDO SHAMRAO GARUD (*Bombay, No. 548, in list*)—MR. PRESIDENT, LADIES AND GENTLEMEN,—In supporting this resolution I feel my task very much lightened by what the able speakers who have preceded me have said. The grateful acknowledgments which you felt it your duty to make, only a short time ago, of our obligations to the delegates who, at no small sacrifice of time and money, went across the seas to represent our cause before the people of England, will prepare you to admit freely that the scheme of holding a special session of this Congress in England is by no means a visionary one. If three or four men only benefited our cause so markedly, surely a deputation of a large body of earnest men, such as it is proposed to send, is calculated still more largely to conduce to the national benefit. If we thereby secure the sympathies of a larger number of members of Parliament irrespective of parties, that is in itself a service which cannot be over-rated. But over and above that there are the sympathies of English electors themselves, which a larger diffusion of a correct knowledge of Indian subjects and of the loyal aims and aspirations of this assembly, will not fail to win over to our side. (*Cheers*).

It must be admitted that there are at the outset great difficulties, both pecuniary and social, to contend with in such an undertaking. But I do hope and trust that the patriotism of our countrymen will rise superior to other minor considerations, and that if we but give " a long pull, a strong pull and a pull altogether," it will not be difficult for us to achieve our object. ( *Cheers.*) It cannot be denied that if we succeed in carrying it out we shall have an ample return in the advantages it will bring back to us in every shape, whether political, social, moral or educational. Of the necessity of such an undertaking there can also, I think, be no two opinions. Gentlemen, the uncovenanted services lately had a Parliamentary Committee to inquire into their grievances, and it cannot be denied that it brought to them a large measure of relief. But, although we have for a long time been asking for a Royal Commission to inquire into the material condition of India, we have not yet succeeded in obtaining it. In the good old days of the East India Co., Royal Commissions were a settled institution ; but there has been no Royal Commission since the direct assumption of the Government by the Crown, that is to say for more than thirty years past. So long, therefore, as there is no Royal Commission the next best thing we can do is to select picked and typical representatives, people from all parts of the country, who will go to England and lay our case before the English people, the very persons who hold the political destinies of our country in their hands. ( *Cheers.*)

MR. HARDEO RAM NANABHAI HARIDAS (*Guzerat, No. 538, in list*)—LADIES AND GENTLEMEN,—The subject before you is a very important one and deserves your serious consideration. There is no question as to its political utility, since the British are ever ready to come to the assistance of oppressed nations. Those who emancipated the negro slaves will surely come to your assistance, you who are Aryans like themselves, and give you a political franchise and political salvation. A suggestion like the present one was made a year or two ago, but serious difficulties were raised, and the suggestion could not readily be accepted. But after all a compromise was effected, and instead of holding a Congress in England it was decided to send a few delegates to London to try the experiment of the political utility of such a step. But, Gentlemen, when our leaders went there, when they were fighting hard for the benefit of their country, engaged in a noble service, our enemies taunted them with being representatives of themselves and not of the dumb millions of India. Last year, being excited by this taunt, our Congress decided that the delegates for this year should not go without holding in their hands credentials of representation, and therefore certain gentlemen were appointed to go to England as representatives of the Congress and plead before our large-hearted British fellow subjects in their own homes. But this year we go a step further in the process of evolution. From being representatives of a few people assembled in the National Congress, our representatives will be elected by the dumb millions themselves to plead before the British Nation and to tell them what our grievances, our disabilities and our aspirations are. You all know the success with which the batch of noble political pilgrims, headed by their venerable chief, and Mr. Surrendra Nath Banerjea, pleaded our cause, and with what devotion they smoothed the way for our political salvation. They did a credit to themselves and to the poor country that sent them. At the same time we should be cautious ; we should not be overborne by too much zeal and enthusiasm. Of course hold the Congress, but in selecting delegates the greatest care should be exercised. Select your very best men and send them by all means. If such a deputation from us hold sittings in London the greatest political good may be expected : the British Nation will then be in a position to judge how far the accusation that we Congresswallahs are a set of sedition-mongers, place-seekers discontented do-nothings, holds water. The London session of Congress will also be an epoch in the history of the world ; and if we but succeed in educating British opinion in our favor, the work of the Congress will be done. But, Gentlemen, in our flights of enthusiasm we should not be blind to other considerations. Care should be taken that the susceptibilities of the orthodox party should not be roughly overridden in our Oriental enthusiasm. No pressure, however little, should be used to induce delegates to go to the London Congress. I do not object to the London Congress, I am entirely in favour of it, but I give you this warning, and resume my seat. (*Cheers*).

Mr. Luchman Row Govind (*Central Provinces, No. 609, in list*)—Mr. President and Brother Delegates,—This is the first time that I have stood before you, and I will be as brief as I can. After the able, vigorous and energetic support which this resolution has received at the hands of several preceding speakers, it would be superfluous in me to add anything more to prove its importance and necessity. Nor need I dwell upon the advantages and benefits that will follow from it. I have much pleasure in supporting the resolution. (*Cheers*).

Sodhi Pratap Singh (*Amritsar, No. 526, in list*) then spoke in Punjabi and said: Mr. President and Gentlemen,—It is with great pleasure that I support the proposal that some hundred or so of our best men should meet as a Congress in London in 1892. London is the capital of our royal mother Queen Victoria, at whose footstool all aggrieved seek redress. There we shall have a chance of informing our mother of all we suffer and all we want. Though the papers and our reports convey to her some idea of our needs, yet that is not the same thing as it will be when we appeal to her, as it were, at her Palace gates. Surely she will bring about a granting of our prayers, and see that we return back rejoicing, our wishes realized and crowned with fruition.

There also we shall have an opportunity of stating our case fully and clearly before British audiences all over the United Kingdom, and the more good men we send, the greater number of meetings we shall be able to address. That we should have come so far and have made such sacrifices to lay our grievances before the public there, will in itself be no little guarantee of their reality. I come from the Punjab and no one there is opposed to the idea of holding a session of the Congress in England. In the Punjab none now a days object to a man's going to England, on the contrary many desire to go there. I held a commission. in the 12th Bengal Cavalry and have been to Abyssinia, Malta and other places over the sea, but neither I nor any of my comrades have ever been outcasted. Thousands of other Panjabi soldiers have similarly crossed the black waters without incurring any social penalties. If no one objected when we went merely to fight for the British Government is it possible that any one should object when we go to England to serve our own country and our own countrymen? In the days of Maharajah Ranjit Singh, Sikh forces fought in Afghanistan, they were never outcasted and no one will be outcasted in my province who goes now to London on this public service. By going we shall all be able to get a clearer idea of the British constitution, and how it works, and how best we may under its shadow obtain our rights and our wishes. We shall do something towards securing a more widespread sympathy amongst our British fellow-subjects and it may even be that they, under our Maharani's favouring glances, may send us back

4th Day.

Res. XI. Provisional arrangements for holding a Congress in London in 1892.

with our political mission to some extent crowned with success. Even if it be not so we shall have taken a new and important step in that direction. So I cordially support the resolution. (*Cheers.*)

PANDIT SHAYAM NARAYAN MASALDAN (*Lucknow, No. 484, in list*), then spoke in Urdu and said :—

MR. PRESIDENT, LADIES AND GENTLEMEN,—I come before you not only to give a formal support to the resolution which is now before you, but because I think that it is really a useful resolution. We, the delegates of the Congress, enjoy perfect freedom of thought and speech, and when we give our opinion upon any subject, we do so after much careful consideration. We are not like the members of the Viceroy's Council, who would support any measure that is introduced by the Government. (*Cheers.*)

And this is not a mere opinion which may or may not be true, but the statement of a fact which rests upon the authority of some of the highest statesmen who have been in charge of Indian affairs, and which is one of the principal reasons why we are desirous of passing the present resolution. Some twenty years ago, the Duke of Argyle, who was then our Secretary of State, wrote to the Viceroy to the effect that "the Government in India were merely Executive Officers of the Home Government, who hold the ultimate power of requiring the Governor-General to introduce a measure, and of requiring also all the official members to vote for it." Some 15 years later this doctrine was emphasised by Lord Dufferin in words of wider and clearer significance. In his Minute on Council Reform, which fortunately saw the light, before the Official Secrets Act came into existence the following remarkable words occur : "The executive that represents her (the Queen's) *Imperium* in India is an executive directly responsible, not to any local authority, but to the Sovereign and to the British Parliament. Nor could its members divest themselves of this responsibility as long as Great Britain remains the paramount administration in India.

Now without wishing to say one word as to the morality of the doctrine which has been so authoritatively propounded, and which divests the Government of all responsibility to the people whom it governs, I may invite your attention to the position in which this theory of the British Government places us. The fountain-head of our legislation is the Supreme Council. Every measure that is introduced therein is passed by the vote of the appointed members who form the majority. But their vote is controlled by the Secretary of State, who in his turn is controlled by Parliament, and Parliament reflects the opinion of the British nation.

In the last resort then the responsibility rests upon the British nation, who know little about Indian affairs, and whose knowledge of India is confined to purely official sources. Now, the principal source of such knowledge is, of course, the Secretary of State, but he himself has to rely upon the India Council ; and yet what is this India Council ? It is composed of Anglo-Indian Officials who are at least thirty years behind the age, whose knowledge of Indian matters consists of things which existed a generation ago, but which have entirely changed now, and who, therefore, have little sympathy with the hopes and aspirations of New India. These, gentlemen, are the Secretary of State's Councillors, and they have to sit in judgment upon their own past acts. It is not likely that these old officials would take an unfavourable view of things of which they themselves were the authors, or of the system under which they have passed the best years of their lives. Thus, then, the knowledge of Indian matters which the Secretary of State derives from them is such as is allowed to pass through the hands of his Councillors who, of course, on all occasions rely on official blue books which give a purely imaginary and rose-colored view of Anglo-Indian administration.

The value of even this one-sided information and advice is very much diminished when we remember that the Indian Council gives its advice to the Secretary of State under no sense of responsibility to the public or the Government since their minutes are not published, nor the Secretary of State bound to follow them.

But, nevertheless, they exercise a decisive influence upon his judgment, even in their irresponsible position, because, although not bound to follow their advice, yet, as a matter of course, the Secretary of State, having no better guides and assistants upon whom he may rely for Indian experience, has to follow them and shape his Indian policy, as a rule, in accordance with their suggestions.

Thus, the position of Indian politics is this : The Viceroy cannot do anything without the sanction of the Secretary of State. The Secretary of State either will not move unless some Parliamentary pressure is brought to bear upon him, or, if he moves at all, it will be in the direction of Anglo-Indian opinion. Parliament won't move unless the nation compels it do so; and the British nation won't move unless it is made alive to the real grievances of the Indian people, and its mind is disabused of the delusive accounts it has heard through official sources of the so-called peace and prosperity of this country.

At present Parliament is not much interested in Indian matters. Our Budget is placed before it at the fag-end of the session, and those who speak upon it have to address empty benches. And yet it was the Duke of Argyle who, in a remarkable pamphlet on the Administrations of Lord Dalhousie and Lord Canning, which he published some thirty years ago, said that at a time when the Indians had no representatives of their own in the Council, and when there was no strong public opinion to check the despotism of the ruling class, it was the duty of Parliament to keep a vigilant eye over Indian matters, and to act as the protector of the people against the aggressions of the Anglo-Indian community. (*Hear, hear.*)

Thus, it is our first duty to acquaint Parliament and the British people with that side of the picture which is generally concealed by the official class, and to remind them of the sacred and solemn task which God, in his inscrutable wisdom has imposed upon them of governing wo hundred and fifty millions of human beings. Therefore the step which you propose to take by holding a future session of the Congress in London is dictated alike by our present political necessity and by the constitution of our Government. It indeed will be a grand day in the history of this country when the representatives stand face-to-face with the great British Nation, not as State prisoners used to stand before Oriental despots with halters round their necks, but as fellow-subjects and fellow-citizens with the charter of liberty in their hands, able to state their grievances before it and entreat it to extend to them the same principles of justice and generosity which it has extended to the Colonies. (*Cheers.*)

It is said that the people are not fit for the reforms they advocate; that the desire for political progress is confined only to the educated classes who form but a mere fringe of the whole society, and that the vast bulk of the people are perfectly satisfied with their present lot Now this is I submit a mistake. Whatever may be the aspirations of the English-knowing Classes, I stand before you as a specimen of that vast body of Indians who have not received the light of Western knowledge, but, while speaking on behalf of such men, I can assure you that, call them what our critics may—ignorant, bigotted, semi-civilized, old-fashioned "black men"—they are as ardent advocates of reform as the educated classes themselves, and possess among them materials of political knowledge, which can never fail to be of use to the Government and the country. (*Cheers.*)

It is, however, a happy augury for the future of this country that Parliament has of late begun to manifest some increasing interest in her affairs, and I doubt not that, if you succeed in carrying into practice the resolution which you are about to pass, you will open to England a new world of knowledge and information upon Indian matters, in the light of which she will be able to see the wrongs and injustice which her servants have done to us in her name; and as soon as she sees them she will remove them and will satisfy our just aspirations, which are the fruit of the civilization she has spread amongst us. (*Cheers.*)

PANDIT MADAN MOHAN MALAVIYA (*N. W. Provinces, No. 394, in list*)—MR. PRESIDENT, LADIES AND GENTLEMEN,—I should have very much liked to be excused from supporting this resolution for two reasons: in the first place, because I think the resolution is sufficient in itself, and, in the second place, because I am far from well. It has, however, been thought desirable that speakers from every part of the conntry should testify to the feeling likely to be entertained by the people at large when this proposal is made public. In trying to do this I will venture to point out that if this proposal is accepted by a very considerable proportion of our countrymen who, either through ignorance or misapprehension or some other cause, are opposed to the idea of going to England, or think that a voyage to England disqualifies men in certain respects, the sole consideration which will reconcile them to the proposal will be that they will realize that, thereby, good will be done to this country. I wish you clearly to understand that it is wholly a political mission, with nothing whatever of a social character attached to it, and that if we venture to think of holding a Congress in England, while a considerable portion of our countrymen are, for some reason or other, opposed to that idea, it is simply because we are prompted by the best of motives to do good to our fellows. It is not a matter of choice, but a matter of clear, and I would say, sheer necessity. I should be happy if the necessity did not arise. I should rejoice if before 1892 comes Parliament has passed Mr. Bradlaugh's Bill, and made us those other concessions which we have been claiming, so that we may then have no necessity for holding a Congress in England. Not that I undervalue the great social, literary and other advantages which will accrue from a voyage to England, I covet and value them as highly as any person present, but I confess I covet and value

**4th Day.**

**Res. XI. Provisional arrangements for holding a Congress in London in 1892.**

the affections of those near and dear to me a good deal more. I value the sympathy of those in whose midst my lot has been cast, and for whose benefit I wish to labor to the extent of my power ; and if any act of mine could alienate their sympathy I would abstain from it. But one consideration which will reconcile them to the idea is that we shall be going to England, not for any social or private personal advantages, but simply for the sake of securing for them concessions which will promote their happiness and welfare. I wish also to point out that our belief is that we shall not have to do anything but what we may desire, and what our religious precepts enjoin, in going to England, and that those of us who want to be true orthodox people, and are really so, can be as orthodox by going to England as by remaining here. No one will force you to do anything you think to be against your religion or the teachings of your ancestors ; only make up your minds to make the sacrifice that is necessary. Of course, the sacrifice is very great. It is a greater sacrifice than anything I can think of for a man to run the risk of alienating the sympathy of his people, or diminishing the warmth of the affections of those near and dear to him. But many great and heavy sacrifices have to be made when you want to benefit your country. Do you not, when there is a distinct call to fight for your country and your sovereign, go into the battle and try to do the best you can? You lay aside all personal and private considerations. You may to a certain extent injure the feelings of your people, but you do it simply because you think it a clear call of duty. So it will be in this respect. If we go to England it will be in response to the clear call of duty, and I hope that all our countrymen, the most orthodox even, will be reconciled to the idea when they look at it in that light, and that no one will try to put it in any other light. (*Cheers.*)

MR. PRAN NATH SARASWATI (*Calcutta, No. 42, in list*)—MR. PRESIDENT AND FELLOW DELEGATES,—If I were to consult my personal inclinations I should not be here at this time of the day. I know full well the value of time, and I am fully conscious of the absence on my part of those gifts of oratory which are calculated to reach the ears and hearts of a large body of men like this. If, therefore, I stand here to-day, it is more in the position of a witness than of an advocate, because, I take it, this duty has been imposed upon me so that I may disclose the attitude of the conservative party, so to speak, in Upper India. Gentlemen, belonging as I do to a race whose limits are the snow-clad Himalayas and the dark waters of the ocean, and claiming as I do some acquaintance with our ancient Brahman literature, I can truly testify that there is nothing in the tenets of our religion which prohibits sea voyages *as such* ; that, I am confident, is the better opinion, and I can also testify, as being in touch with the true orthodox opinion in Upper India, that if it should please the country to endorse the mandate of the Congress, with regard to the meeting in London in 1892, which I hope will be endoresd at our next Congress meeting in India, and if you will take care to meet to the best of your power the special requirements of orthodox Hindu gentlemen—and I have no doubt the best endeavours will be made—if these wants are met I can assure you there will be no difficulty in getting representative orthodox Hindu gentlemen from Upper India to represent your country. (*Cheers*).

RAJ KUMAR NILKRISHNA BAHADUR (*Calcutta, No. 10, in list*)—LADIES AND GENTLEMEN,—The cheers that you haye accorded to the various speakers are a clear indication of your views as to the necessity of a mission to England. I never could have thought that so many gentlemen would be required to support this resolution, believing that you would at once adopt it when it was proposed. We stand before the British public as complainants and the Indian Government is the defendant. The British Parliament should be considered as the real jury before whom we are to lay our case. Under the circumstances I think it is only proper and necessary that we should send this our proposed grand mission to England as you have already sent a few individuals to feel the way for them. I trust that you will carry this resolution by acclamation. (*Cheers*).

RAI KAKUMAL (*Oudh, No. 513, in list*)—MR. PRESIDENT AND BROTHER DELEGATES,—I ask permission to speak on this subject, not because I am an orator or that I have anything to add, or that anything has been left unsaid that ought to be said, but because there have been none of my caste among the supporters of this resolution, and, if I did not speak, it might be understood that my community is keeping aloof from this question. I have great pleasure in supporting the resolution on behalf of my community ; and I think that by so many of us going so far across the sea, at our own expense, we shall prove to the Great English Nation that we are in earnest, and that our grievances are real and not imaginary. (*Cheers*)

MR. SHARFUDDEEN (*Patna, No. 323, in list*)—MR. PRESIDENT, LADIES AND GENTLEMEN,—I think I have been called upon to say a word with regard to the feelings of Mohammedans in general with reference to this resolution. Although I cannot claim to be a very orthodox

Mohammedan, I am in a position to inform you that Mohammedans, as a religious body, have not the least objection to crossing the seas, for the best of reasons that they came to India by crossing the seas. I believe I am to be the last speaker, and I will ask the President to put the matter to the vote.

THE PRESIDENT: Before I put the resolution perhaps you may like to hear what Mr. Caine may have to say upon the subject. (*Loud cheers*).

MR. W. S. CAINE (*Sholapur, No. 582, in list*)—MR. PRESIDENT, LADIES AND GENTLEMEN,—It has always been the custom, I believe, at previous Congresses, when a place has been finally decided upon at which the next Congress should meet, for some one from that place to get into the tribune and say how pleased he and his friends are that that particular place has been chosen for the next meeting. Now, you have not finally decided upon where the next Congress is to meet, but I hope when I have finished, what I have to say, you will settle definitely where the one after that is to meet, and I sincerely trust that that will be London (*Cheers*). I have been greatly impressed by the debate that has just taken place, and so I trust will be the general public, from the fact that out of fifteen speeches thirteen have come from orthodox Hindus, one being a Sikh and one a Moslem. That, I think, is a most important fact, for it demonstrates completely that orthodox Hinduism has no objection whatever to crossing the sea if Hindustan is to be served thereby, and does not fear any evil consequences from taking that particular course in a good cause. (*Cheers*). The resolution says that the Congress is to be held in England, "all things being convenient." That is a very considerable proviso. I can only say on behalf of your friends in England, who are many more than you think, that it will not be in the least inconvenient to us to welcome you and entertain you when you get there. (*Cheers*). The only risk of inconvenience is that some of your friends may be engaged in fighting for positions in Parliament, from which, in time to come, they may fight your battles. (*Cheers*). The only thing I think that can prevent the success of the Congress meeting in London in 1892 will be that the present government, which has great tenacity, will be hanging on by tooth and claw till that particular year (*laughter*); but if public opinion can succeed in turning them out, next year, then I think there will be nothing, so far as we are concerned, that need in the least degree interfere with the convenience of your meeting in London. One thing, at any rate, I can promise you, that, if you meet in London, no manifesto will be issued forbidding Secretaries of State or even penny-post men (*laughter*) from listening to what you have to say. I think that Her Majesty the Queen is much more likely to invite you all to Buckingham Palace than to forbid any of her faithful servants from taking seats in the galleries, that I am sure will be thronged at every meeting of the Congress in London. (*Cheers.*) The time has gone by for making speeches on this occasion ("*Go on*") Well, I look forward to the time when a hundred, or it may be a thousand Indian gentlemen will find their way across the ocean to hold a Congress meeting in London. It is not always easy for the members of the political agency at home, and those of us whose business it is to advocate your cause at public meetings, and in the press, to bring home to the minds of the English people what this great assemblage really means. I endeavour, when I am in India and attending your Congress meetings to write home to the press some feeble scription of the marvellous scenes and the fascinating debate, within your halls; but no pen can describe and no artist depict satisfactorily either to the eye or the mind of English people what the Indian National Congress really means. It will then be a great object lesson to the English people if we can gather together in Exeter Hall or the Crystal Palace or some other building of great dimensions, the Indian National Congress, that men may hear for themselves and have reported verbatim in every newspaper in the land the reasonable, sensible, statesmanlike aud truly patriotic speeches which are delivered here. If the authors of that manifesto, which was so justly censured yesterday, will take the trouble, when the verbatim report of the proceedings of this Congress is published, to read it through from beginning to end, I think they can only lay the volume down with a feeling of profound shame (*hear, hear*), that they have interdicted Government servants from even listening to the loyal speeches that have been delivered. I have sat here throughout the whole of these proceedings, and not one single word have I heard that could give the slightest justification for the disgraceful manifesto which appeared in the papers yesterday. (*Cheers.*) At all events, when you come to England you will be listened to, your meetings will be free and open, and I venture to prophesy that there will be hardly a single member of either the upper or lower Houses of Parliament who will not seize the opportunity of seeing and hearing for himself what are the true aspirations of educated Indians. I can only promise on my own behalf, and I think on behalf of all your friends, that when you come you shall have a right royal welcome. (*Cheers*). Everything we can do to make your visit pleasant, to make it useful to the cause you have at heart, and to make it tend *to* the binding together of the Great British Empire of which we are, all, so justly proud, shall be done; and if any of you are still bound by caste rules to any rigid extent, we will do every

4th Day.

Res. XI. Provisional arrangements for holding a Congress in London in 1892.

thing we can, if you will only tell us how to do it, to make it perfectly easy for the most orthodox of Hindus, from the Himalayas to Cape Comorin, to visit England without the slightest chance of breaking caste or breaking any of the rules of their religion which they are endeavouring to carry out, and in which every good man must encourage and support them. In the name of all your friends in England—and I will go further and say, in the name of the great English people—I promise you that when you come you will receive such a welcome as will make your hearts rejoice. (*Loud Cheers*).

THE PRESIDENT: I now propose that we pass the Eleventh Resolution, but so many speeches have intervened since you heard it that I will read it to you again.

RESOLVED.—*That provisional arrangements be made to hold a Congress, of not less than 100. delegates, in England, all things being convenient, in 1892, and that the several Standing Congress Committees be directed to report, at the coming Congress, the names of the delegates that it is proposed to depute from their respective circles.*

Now those of you who are in favour of this resolution hold up your hands. (*Cries of all, all.*) Now those who are of the contrary opinion. (*None, none*).

Then this resolution has been unanimously carried, and I call on Mr. Watcha to propose the Twelfth Resolution.

Res. XII. Additions to the permanent fund of the Congress.

MR. D. E. WATCHA (*Bombay, No. 543, in list*)—MR. PRESIDENT, LADIES AND GENTLEMEN,—The resolution entrusted to me is a formal one and I do not think it need detain you more than a minute. The resolution is:

*That of the Funds now in the Joint General Secretary's hands and about to be received, a further sum of twenty thousand rupees be added to the permanent fund and placed in fixed deposits, and that the rest of the funds accruing on account of this current year 1890, be held by him available for the immediate purposes of the British Committee of the Indian National Congress, but to be replaced as the subscriptions for 1891 are received, and ultimately also added to the permanent fund.*

This Resolution requires no speech from me to commend it to your approval, for really it is a resolution concerning our own domestic economy. The last two days we have been busily engaged with external politics, this is a mere matter of detail of domestic politics, putting our household together, husbanding our resources, and seeing how we can make the Congress stronger and stronger by conserving the sinews of war. You will rejoice to hear that there is a nucleus of a permanent fund which we owe in no small degree to the eloquent appeal which our friend Mr. Banerjee made last year at the Congress. We are now in a position to add to that fund another twenty thousand rupees. You will rejoice to hear that the Congress fund is progressing with the Congress. Gentlemen, we hope now that a good foundation has been laid, that, year by year, as the Congress progresses we shall also progress with our funds, and that our permanent fund will reach twenty lakhs of rupees. (*Hear, hear*). Twenty lakhs of rupees is nothing in a population of twenty crores. It means the per cent. You are paying two and a half per cent income tax, and this one per cent. for a patriotic object will not be serious. With these observations I beg to propose this resolution (*Cheers*).

THE REVEREND RAM CHUNDER BOSE (*Lucknow, No. 505, in list*)—MR. PRESIDENT AND FELLOW DELEGATES,—I represent among you the garrulity of age and you will not be surprised if I fly off at a tangent from my text, and make an observation or two on what I have seen during this Congress session.

The resolution I have to second is not a souree of such great pleasure to me as the resolution you have just passed. The idea of holding a Congress in London is, I believe, the grandest that has flashed on the collective intellect of the National Congress. (*Hear, hear.*) Why? Because we are sure to have in England the sympathy, the encouragement and the co-operation which we have failed to elicit in this land.

There is between England and ourselves and this National Congress what may be called a community of aim. To explain this I must go down to one of the fundamental principles of political science. Several accusations have been preferred against us, and these. are obviously ridiculous. If we were accused of idealism, I might be disposed to plead guilty to the soft impeachment. There can be no realism without pre-existing or precedent idealism. All our demands are realistic, but I have not the slightest hesitation in admitting that they have all emanated from an ideal. A great writer in view of the common saying "man is metaphysical *nolens volens*," says that "man

4th Day.

Res. XII. Additions to the permanent fund of the Congress.

is a politician *nolens volens.*" Sensible thoughtful men have before their mental vision an ideal of political development. What is that ideal? The ideal is government of the people by the people and for the people, not government by a monopoly and for a monopoly. Towards this ideal all the best Governments and most enlightened countries of the world are working, and especially England. In the home of constitutional liberty all the foremost thinkers are working up towards this great ideal; and my friends, we aspire to see *our* Government working up to it also. England is taking grand steps towards this ideal. We ask our Government to take incipient steps towards it. But the step, whether incipient or matured, is one and the same, or has one and the same object in view. The goal is one, and therefore the aim of England and the aim of this Congress are one and the same. (*Cheers*).

But there is between England and this National Congress not only a community of aim but community of interest. The destinies of this country are inseparably bound up with the destinies of England. A prosperous India is to England a source of strength; a weakened, debilitated, impoverished India is to England a weakness. What will be the upshot of the Congress! The National Congress is the great lever, and is fitted, eminently fitted, to raise this country in intelligence, in wealth, in prosperity and in glory. (*Cheers.*) And when the country is raised in glory, in strength and prosperity, it will be a source of strength to England. Therefore between England and the National Congress there is a community of interest and therefore a community of method, if you will allow me the expression. The methods utilised by us are the very methods that have been utilised in England by its great political agitators. I do not for a moment maintain that English political agitators have never gone beyond the hallowed line of legitimate and constitutional methods. I am aware that at times these agitators have broken windows and smashed chandeliers, (*laughter*), and these are vagaries that *we* could never tolerate. (*Cheers*). But the methods utilised there are on the whole constitutional; and our methods are constitutional. There is then a harmony between the methods employed there and the methods employed by us. (*Cheers*).

And, lastly, between this Congress and England there is a community of hope. What is England's grand mission in the world? It is to spread constitutionalism, and the glory of civilization that has evolved from it, throughout the world. And when the National Congress shall have done its work in India, India's glorious mission will be to spread constitutionalism and the civilization emanating from it, throughout Asia, throughout Africa, nay, throughout the whole world.

Two remarks more, and I shall have done. Our English friends, and especially Mr. Hume (*cheers*), who has justly been described as the father of the National Congress, have been represented by the Anglo-Indian Press almost universally as denationalized. They are not denationalized, they are de-Anglo-indianized, and re-nationalized. (*Cheers*). The great heart of Great Britain beats in unison with the heart of this Congress. Their aspirations are in union with our aspirations, and those who deny our aspirations, and who stand in the way of Government making progress when it ought to make progress, are guilty of the highest sedition against the highest principles of Government. *They* are denationalized: our friends are anglicized. (*Loud cheers*).

These remarks of course are not on the subject of the resolution. (*Laughter*). When I was in America a gentleman was going to a meeting and a friend of his met him and said "are you going to speak on the subject?" No, he said, I am not going to speak on *the* subject but I am going to speak on *some* subject. Now I have spoken on some subject, if not on *the* subject. (*Laughter and Cheers.*)

THE PRESIDENT: Now we will come to *the* subject, and I will ask you to vote for the Resolution No. 12.

RESOLVED.—*That of the Funds now in the Joint General Secretary's hands and about to be received, a further sum of twenty thousand rupees be added to the permanent Fund and placed in fixed deposits, and that the rest of the funds accruing on account of this current year, 1890, be held by him available for the immediate purposes of the British Committee of the Indian National Congress, but to be replaced as the subscriptions for 1891 are received, and ultimately also added to the permanent Fund.*

The resolution was carried unanimously.

4th Day.

Res. XIII. Expenses of the British Committee and General Secretary's Office.

MR. MUDHOLKAR (*Berar, No. 585, in list*)—MR. PRESIDENT, LADIES AND GENTLEMEN,—This again is purely formal matter which requires the sanction of the Congress. Only an hour ago you passed a resolution approving of the action of the Delegates whom you deputed to England last summer. The proposition with which I am entrusted is one which is closely connected with the carrying on of the work which was begun by you in December last, namely, that of sending deputations to England. Resolution 13, of which I am in charge, deals with the question of ways and means for carrying out that object and others connected with our British Committees' work. It runs thus :—

*That a sum of Rs. 40,000, exclusive of individual donations, is assigned for the expenses of the British Committee of the Congress and Rs. 6,000 for the General Secretary's Office and Establishment, and that the several circles and districts do contribute as arranged in Committee.*

When I was in England every week there were telegrams sent by your friends here to apprize the British public that the Congress movement in India was dying of inanition, that the funds of which such promises were held out in December last were not forthcoming, and that the Congress cause was in danger of extinction. Those of us who knew how the facts really stood were in no way afraid of what the consequences would be. We knew that sooner or later the money would be forthcoming ; and even at the time the telegrams were being sent, money was found for the purposes for which it was promised. I hope that the spirit shown by our people last year will still be manifested as long as it is necessary, as long as we live as a nation, aye, as long as one individual is left among us. (*Cheers*). Only a very small sum, 40,000 rupees, is wanted for the English expenses, and only 6,000 rupees for the expenses here, and I am sure the generosity of the public is not so dead that we shall not be able to find this sum. (*Cheers.*)

MR. A. CHOWDREE (*Calcutta, No. 62, in list*)—MR. PRESIDENT AND BROTHER DELEGATES,—I have great pleasure in seconding the resolution. I will not add another word. (*Cheers.*)

MUNSHI SAJJAD HUSSEIN : (*Lucknow, No. 480, in list*) then spoke in Urdu.

(*It has been found impossible to procure any report of this gentleman's speech.*)

THE PRESIDENT : I may now, I think, put this 13th Resolution.

RESOLVED.—*That a sum of Rs. 40,000, exclusive of individual donations, is assigned for the expenses of the British Committee of the Congress, and Rs. 6,000 for the General Secretary's Office and Establishment, and that the several circles and districts do contribute as arranged in Committee.*

The resolution is carried unanimously.

Res. XIV. Reappointment of General and Joint General Secretaries

THE PRESIDENT : The next resolution is one which at all previous meetings of the Congress, which I have attended, has been moved by my friend Mr. W. C. Bonnerjee, and it is a matter of the greatest regret to me that he is not able to attend to-day and move it in this Congress. I have asked another delegate to take his place. I hope he will not consider me imperious or dictatorial ; but with deference even to my friend Sir Romesh Chander Mitter, I am going to issue a writ of prohibition both on the speaker not to speak one word more than to move the resolution, and on you gentlemen not to call upon him to say a word more. I know of course that in your heart of hearts you would wish to hear not only his one word, but a long speech from him ; but he has only with difficulty just left a sick bed and he must positively not be asked to exert himself.

MR. SURENDRA NATH BANERJEE (*Calcutta, No. 52. in list*) who was received with prolonged and enthusiastic cheering, said : BROTHER DELEGATES,—I am not going to transgress the writ which has been issued against me and against you by my friend the President. Physically I feel unequal to reply to that demonstration of enthusiasm which has been displayed on my behalf. I feel truly grateful for it, and it will be an incentive to me to exert myself still more in furtherance of those patriotic duties which I hold dearer than life itself. (*Cheers.*) I have now to move a formal Resolution, which I think you will carry by acclamation.

RESOLVED.—*That Mr. A. O. Hume and Pandit Ajoodhia Nath are re-elected General and Joint-General Secretaries for the ensuing year.*

I am sure it does not need a seconder. (*Cheers.*)

The resolution was carried by acclamation

THE HONORABLE PUNDIT AJOODHIA NATH (*N. W. Pces. No. 399, in list*)—Mr. President and Fellow Delegates,—I have not come upon this scaffold (*laughter*) a second time to trouble you with another speech. I have to move a formal resolution though a very important one. It requires only to be read to commend it to you.

**4th Day.**

**Res XV. Appointment of Delegates to England.**

RESOLVED—*That this Congress does formally appoint Messrs. G. Yule, Pherozshah Mehta, W. C. Bonnerjee, J. Adam, Mono Mohan Ghose, A. O. Hume, Kali Charn Banerjee, Dadabhai Naorojee, D. A. Khare, and such other gentlemen as may volunteer for the duty with the sanction and approval of the Standing Congress Committees of their respective circles, to represent its views in England, and press upon the consideration of the British Public the political reforms which the Congress has advocated.*

In accepting this resolution you will only be following the precedent of last year.

THE PRESIDENT : I do not think that this Resolution needs a *seconder*.

The Resolution was carried by acclamation.

THE PRESIDENT : And now, Gentlemen, our long list of resolutions has come to an end—the dishes have all been handed round and the banquet is over. (*Laughter*)

MR. MONMOHUN GHOSE (*Calcutta, No. 8, in list*)—Not quite yet (*laughter*), but the time has now come when I must ask permission to usurp the functions of the President, and to call upon some one to move a vote of thanks to the chair. I have been considering who the person ought to be, and my choice has fallen upon one whom I trust you will also, by general consent, approve of. One of the most notable features of the last Congress in Bombay was the presence of lady delegates. The same interesting feature exists at this Congress also. And if lady delegates are to appear amongst us, it is right that we should recognize their presence and assign to them such part as they may wish to take. I think from what I know of the views and feelings of my friend Mr. Pherozshah Mehta (*laughter*) that he will take it as a compliment if I ask one of the lady delegates, Mrs. Kadumbini Gangooly to propose the resolution. (*Prolonged cheers*).

**Vote of Thanks to the President.**

MRS. KADUMBINI GANGOOLY (*Calcutta, No. 78, in list*) (who was received with loud applause) said : MR. PRESIDENT, LADIES AND GENTLEMEN,—I thank you for your kindness and for the honour you have done me by placing me at this high altitude. I am not going to make a long speech, as a woman's voice is not strong enough to make itself audible in this enormous mall. But the resolution which I am going to move does not require much speechifying. It has always been usual for the Congress to select its President, not from the Province in which it is held but from a sister Province. Bengal has followed that example. It called upon a sister Province to send a president whom it would select, and Bombay came forward with its true and noble son Mr. Pherozshah Mehta (*Cheers*) in order that we might elect him as our President. We are rejoiced to have him, and I think you will all agree with me that we could not have found a better man. (*Cheers*). There could be no truer heart than that of Mr. Pherozshah Mehta. Manfully and nobly he has discharged his duties, and we are deeply indebted to him for his services. With these few remarks I will retire, asking Mr. Monmohun Ghose to come forward, and with his powerful voice call upon you to carry this vote of thanks by acclamation. (*Cheers*)

MR. MONMOHUN GHOSE (*Calcutta, No. 8, in list*)—I am sure you do not require me to put the vote of thanks formally. It is but the outward and visible sign of the feelings which fill every heart here. (*Cheers*).

The vote of thanks was then carried amidst prolonged and reiterated cheers.

THE PRESIDENT : Mrs. Kadumbini Gangooly, Ladies and Gentlemen,—I am quite sure that I must be an object of envy to all my predecessors in this chair, including Mr. Yule whom I see before me, because my Presidency has been rendered illustrious by the circumstance that it is a lady delegate whom you have asked and who has been kind enough to propose this vote of thanks to me. My thanks are doubly due to you for this act of kindness : they are due to you for the cordial manner in which you have received this vote of thanks and for the way in which you have enabled me to earn it by the steady and unanimous support which all of you have given me during these four long days' proceedings. I am really grateful to you for the way in which you have assisted me in carrying these proceeding to so successful a close.

**President's concluding address.**

**4th Day.**

**President's concluding address.**

And now the very pleasant task devolves upon me of proposing in my turn a vote of thanks to those who have laboured to make this Congress the great success it has been. Gentlemen, I move a cordial vote of thanks to the Chairman and the members of the Reception Committee who have given us so hearty a welcome in the principal city of Bengal. It is not necessary for me to say one word with regard to its Chairman Mr. Monomohun Ghose. All who knew him, knew well how he would carry himself in the important position in which you have placed him. Gentlemen, it would be invidious to name the different members of the Reception Committee who have worked for the purpose of making this Congress all it has been. But I do not think I should be discharging my duty properly if I did not name one who has been working all along with heart and soul to make our reception so splendid—I mean my friend Mr. Ghosal. (*Loud cheers*). I have seen him labouring with my own eyes day and night, and I think that the success of this Congress is in no small measure due to his untiring exertions. (*Hear, hear.*) Then there are other members of the Reception Committee whom I am bound to mention, though I will name them briefly for fear of doing injustice to those whom in justice I might name, and who have worked with great assiduity. I must mention the name of my friend Mr. Charoo Chunder Mitter (*cheers*), who has been working, though for a brief period, as earnestly, as indefatigably and zealously as we remember that he worked at the Congress at Allahabad. I think you will also expect me to name Raj Kumar Sarvadhikari, who also has devoted a great deal of time and labor to the matter. Then I cannot forget the name of Baboo Bhupendra Nath Bose (*cheers*), and I must of all things not forget the name of our friend Captain Banon who has worked for the success of this Congress, as he has worked for the success of all previous Congresses. (*Loud cheers.*) Then I will briefly mention our friends Baboos Dwarka Nath Gangooly and Poshuputti Bose, who have also laboured hard to make our reception as charming as it has proved. But, Gentlemen, having named the members of the Reception Committee I must not forget that our thanks are due to those, of whose names, some 400 in number, I cannot give you a list; but whom I must mention as having come forward to assist the Reception Committee—I refer to the volunteers. (*Cheers.*) It was perhaps a humble task to perform, but unless that task had been performed in the manner in which they did it, it would have been impossible to preserve order and make our deliberations as orderly as they have been; impossible for any of the delegates to have enjoyed those comforts which have made our sojourn here a real pleasure. I must not forget either the members of those Committees who have also aided in the good work—the members of the Engineering Committee, the Medical Committee and Sanitary Committee. If I were to specify all the names I ought to specify I might go on for ever. I will only ask you to say that all these gentlemen and all these committees, whom I have named, deserve our warmest thanks for the great exertions that they have put forth in making our reception as complete and cordial as it has been. I think I am entitled in the name of the whole Congress (*cries of yes, yes*), and I hasten to do so, to thank Mr. Monomohun Ghose and the members of the Reception Committee and all the other gentlemen whoam I have named or referred to, for their kind co-operation in promoting the success of the Congress. *(Loud and prolonged cheers.)*

Nothing now remains but to dissolve the Congress with the constitutional cheers which we always give: "Long live our Queen-Empress."

Loud and prolonged cheers for the Queen-Empress were then given, and repeated many times, and then, as dusk closed in, the assembly dissolved.

---

# APPENDIX I.

# LIST OF DELEGATES

WHO ATTENDED THE

# SIXTH INDIAN NATIONAL CONGRESS,

## *HELD AT CALCUTTA, DECEMBER, 1890.*

| Number. | Presidency or Government. | Congress Circle. | Electoral Division. | Names in full of Delegates, with Honorary Titles, Scholastic Degrees, etc. | Race, Religious denomination, and Caste, if any. | Occupation and Address. | How and when elected. |
|---|---|---|---|---|---|---|---|
| 1 | Bengal | Calcutta | British Indian Association. | Hon'ble Sir Romesh Chunder Mitter, KT., B.A., B.L. | Hindu Kayestha. | Zemindar; Member, Viceroy's Legislative Council of India; late Chief-Justice, Bengal, High Court; and Fellow of the Calcutta University, Puddapukar Road, Bhowanipore, Calcutta. | At a Meeting of the British Indian Association held on the 24th December 1890, and at a General Meeting of the Committee of the Southern Metropolitan Electoral Division, Calcutta, December 10th, 1890. |
| 2 | „ | „ | „ | Babu Judu Lal Mullick ... | Hindu Suburnabanick. | Landholder and Honorary Magistrate and Justice of the Peace. | At a Meeting of the British Indian Association held on the 24th December 1890. |
| 3 | „ | „ | „ | „ Kunja Lall Banerjee | Hindu Brahmin. | Zemindar and late Judge, Calcutta Court of Small Causes. | do. |
| 4 | „ | „ | „ | Rajah Sasi Shekhareswar Roy. | do. | Zemindar ... ... | do. |
| 5 | „ | „ | „ | Kumar Rameswar Malia ... | Hindu Brahmin. | Zemindar, Merchant, Honorary Magistrate; Member, National Chamber of Commerce; President, Howrah People's Association; and Member, British Indian Association, 6, Cullen Place, Howrah. | do. and at a Public Meeting held at the Howrah Town Hall, December 6th, 1890. |
| 6 | „ | „ | „ | Rai Raj Kumar Sarvadhikari Bahadur, B.L. | Hindu Kayestha. | Honorary Presidency Magistate; Fellow, Calcutta University; Secretary, British Indian Association, and Editor, "Hindu Patriot," 27, Mott's Lane, Calcutta. | At a Meeting of the British Indian Association held on the 24th December 1890. |
| | „ | „ | „ | Mr. J. Ghosal ... | Hindu Brahmin. | Zemindar, Merchant, Mill-owner, Honorary Magistrate and Municipal Commissioner of Calcutta; Member of the Government Committee of Management of the Bethune Female College; Trustee, Adi-Brahmo Somaj, &c., &c., Secretary, Congress Committee, Calcutta, and of Bengal Provincial Conference, &c., &c., Kashiabagan Garden House, Upper Circular Road, Calcutta. | At a Meeting of the British Indian Association held on the 24th December 1890, at a Public Meeting at Town Hall, December 23rd, 1890, and at a Meeting of the Bengal National Chamber of Commerce, December 1st, 1890. |

| Number. | Presidency or Government. | Congress Circle. | Electoral Division. | Names in full of Delegates, with Honorary Titles, Scholastic Degrees, etc. | Race, Religious denomination, and Caste, if any. | Occupation and Address. | How and when elected. |
|---|---|---|---|---|---|---|---|
| 8 | Bengal | Calcutta. | Northern Metropolitan Electoral Division, Calcutta. | Mr. Mono Mohun Ghose ... | Hindu Kayestha. | Barrister-at-Law, 4, Theatre Road. | Public Meeting at Town Hall, 23rd December 1890. |
| 9 | " | " | " | Maharaj Kumar Benoy Krishna Deb. | do. | Zemindar, Honorary Magistrate, Municipal Commissioner, Raja Nobo Krishna's Street. | do. |
| 10 | " | " | " | Maharaj Kumar Nil Krishna Deb. | do. | Zemindar, Honorary Presidency Magistrate, Raja Nobo Krishna's St., Calcutta. | do. |
| 11 | " | " | " | The Honorable Dr. Rash Behari Ghose, M.A., B.L., LL.D. | do. | Vakil, High Court; Member, Bengal Legislative Council; Fellow, Calcutta University. | do. |
| 12 | " | " | " | Mr. Lal Mohun Ghose ... | do. | Barrister-at-Law, 11, Store Road, Ballygunge. | do. |
| 13 | " | " | " | Mr. George Yule ... | English Christian. | Merchant ... | do. |
| 14 | " | " | " | Babu Abhoy Kumar Bose | Hindu Kayestha. | Vakil, High Court, 117, Cornwallis Street. | do. |
| 15 | " | " | " | Babu Rajendra Nath Banerjee, L.M.S. | Hindu Brahmin. | Medical Practitioner, Bhim Ghose's Lane, Calcutta. | do. |
| 16 | " | " | " | Babu Sadananda Misser, B.L. | do. | Pleader; Editor, "Sarsudha Nidhi," Burrabazar, Calcutta. | do. |
| 17 | " | " | " | Babu Ram Lal Set ... | Hindu. | Zemindar, Bortola Street ... | do. |
| 18 | " | " | " | Dr. Troylokhya Nath Mitter, M.A., B.L., LL.D. | Kayestha. | Vakil, High Court; Fellow, Calcutta University. | do. |
| 19 | " | " | " | Babu Saroda Churn Mitter, M.A., B.L. | do. | do. | do. |
| 20 | " | " | " | Babu Poshupati Nath Bose | do. | Zemindar, Bagh Bazar Street | do. |
| 21 | " | " | " | Rai Bipin Behari Mitter ... | do. | Zemindar, Shambazar ... | do. |
| 22 | " | " | " | Babu Protap Chundra Muzoomdar, L.M.S. | Hindu Brahmin. | Medical Practitioner ... | do. |
| 23 | " | " | " | Babu Bhupendra Nath Bose, M.A., B.L. | Hindu Kayestha. | Attorney-at-Law; Vakil, High Court, 14, Bolaram Ghose's Street. | do. |
| 24 | " | " | " | Babu Mohini Mohun Chatterjee, M.A., B.L. | Hindu Brahmin. | Attorney-at-Law, 10, Old Post Office Street. | do. |
| 25 | " | " | " | Babu Umesh Chunder Dutt, B.A. | Brahmo. | Principal, City College, 13, Mirzapore Street, Calcutta. | do. |
| 26 | " | " | " | Babu Heera Lall Johury ... | Hindu Jain. | Merchant, Burra Bazar, Cross Street, Calcutta. | do. |
| 27 | " | " | " | Dr. U. Banerjee, M.R.C.P.... | Hindu Brahmin. | Medical Practitioner, Beadon Street, Calcutta. | do. |
| 28 | " | " | " | Babu Gopal Pathuck ... | do. | Merchant ... | do. |
| 29 | " | " | " | Babu Nobin Chunder Boral. | Hindu Subarnabanick. | Attorney-at-Law, Honorary Magistrate, Municipal Commissioner, 10, Old Post Office Street, Calcutta. | do. |
| 30 | " | " | " | Babu Kamini Kumar Guha, M.A., B.L. | Kayestha. | Attorney-at-Law, Bonomali Sircar's Street, Calcutta. | do. |
| 31 | " | " | " | Munshi Ferok Hossain ... | Mahomedan. | Pleader, Small Cause Court, Sealdah, Calcutta. | do. |
| 32 | " | " | " | Munshi Dasaretoolla ... | do. | Landholder ... | do. |
| 33 | " | " | " | Moulvi Enayat Huq ... | do. | Merchant ... | do. |
| 34 | " | " | The Southern Metropolitan Electoral Division. | Kumar Satya Badi Ghosal | Hindu Brahmin. | Zemindar, Municipal Commissioner, and Honorary Magistrate Bhookoilash, Kidderpore, Calcutta. | Elected at a General Meeting of the Southern Metropolitan Electoral Division, Calcutta, on the 10th December 1890. |
| 35 | " | " | " | Mr. William Swinhoe ... | European Christian. | Lawyer, Merchant and Municipal Commissioner, Calcutta, Ballygunge. | do. |
| 36 | " | " | " | Babu Ashutosh Bose, B.L. | Kayestha. | Pleader, Judge's Court, Alipore. | do. |
| 37 | " | " | " | Babu Mohendra Nath Sen | do. | Zemindar, Vice-Chairman, South Suburban Municipality, Calcutta, Russa Pagla, Tallygunge. | do. |
| 38 | " | " | " | Babu Bipro Dass Banerjee | Hindu Brahmin. | Editor, Lawyer, Honorary Magistrate, Municipal Commissioner, Gorpar, Calcutta. | |

| Number. | Presidency or Government. | Congress Circle. | Electoral Division. | Names in full of Delegates, with Honorary Titles, Scholastic Degrees, etc. | Race, Religious denomination, and Caste, if any. | Occupation and Address. | How and when elected. |
|---|---|---|---|---|---|---|---|
| 39 | Bengal | Calcutta | The Southern Metropolitan Electoral Division. | Revd. Nunda Lall Dass ... | Bengalee Christian. | Professor and Missionary, Bhowanipore, Calcutta. | Elected at a General Meeting at the Southern Metropoliton Electoral Division, Calcutta, on the 10th December 1890. |
| 40 | " | " | " | Moulvi Zabodur Rohim Zabid, M.A., B.L. | Mahomedan. | Zemindar and Pleader, Judge's Court, 62, Sankaripara Road, Bhowanipore. | do. |
| 41 | " | " | " | Moulvi Hazi Bussiruddin ... | do. | Muktear, Alipore, Magistrate's Court, and Landholder, Chetla. | do. |
| 42 | " | " | " | Babu Pran Nath Pundit (Sarasvati), M.A., B.L. | Hindu Brahmin. | Vakil, High Court, and Zemindar. | do. |
| 43 | " | " | " | Babu Umakally Mukherjee, B.L. | do | Lawyer, Kidderpore, Calcutta | do. |
| 44 | " | " | " | Babu Debendra Chundra Ghose, B.L. | Hindu Kayestha. | Government Pleader, District Court, Alipore, Bhowanipore, Calcutta. | do. |
| 45 | " | " | " | Revd. C. N. Banerjee, B.A. | Bengalee Christian. | Missionary, Bhowanipore, Calcutta. | do. |
| 46 | " | " | " | Babu Okhil Chunder Mookerjee. | Hindu Brahmin. | Zemindar and Municipal Commissioner, Kidderpore, Calcutta. | do. |
| 47 | " | " | " | Babu Jogendra Nath Sen, M.A., B.L. | Hindu Kayestha | Lawyer, Bhowanipore ... | do. |
| 48 | " | " | " | Babu Iswar Chunder Chuckrobutty, B.L. | Hindu Brahmin. | Lawyer and Zemindar, Bhowanipore, Calcutta. | do. |
| 49 | " | " | " | Babu Tara Podo Ghosh ... | Hindu Kayestha. | Zemindar, Kidderpore ... | do. |
| 50 | " | " | " | Babu Bosunto Kumar Bose, M.A., B.L. | do. | Lawyer ... | do. |
| 51 | " | " | The Indian Association. | Raja Rajendra Narayan Deb Bahadoor. | Hindu Kayestha. | Zemindar and President, Indian Association. | Elected by the Indian Association at a Meeting dated 22nd December 1890. |
| 52 | " | " | " | Babu Surendra Nath Banerjee, B.A. | Hindu Brahmin. | Honorary Presidency Magistrate, Barrackpore; Municipal Commissioner; Editor, "Bengalee." | do. |
| 53 | " | " | " | Babu Lal Behari Bysack ... | Hindu | Municipal Commissioner and Honorary Presidency Magistrate, Calcutta. | do. |
| 54 | " | " | " | Babu Tarini Das Banerjee, M.A. | Hindu Brahmin. | Zemindar, 17, Iswar Mitter's Lane, Goa Bagan. | do. |
| 55 | " | " | " | Babu Jadab Chundra Dutt, M.A. | Hindu Tanti | Attorney-at-Law, High Court, Calcutta. | do. |
| 56 | " | " | " | Babu Satya Prosad Surbadhikary. | Hindu Kayestha. | Medical Practitioner, 1, College Street, Calcutta. | do. |
| 57 | " | " | " | Babu Deviprosad Surbadhikary, M.A., B.L. | do. | Attorney-at-Law ... | do. |
| 58 | " | " | " | Dr. M. M. Bose, M.D., L.R.C.P., EDIN, &c. | Brahmo. | Physician; Zemindar, 64-1, Raja Bazar, Calcutta. | do. |
| 59 | " | " | " | Babu Tarapodo Choudhury, M.A., B.L. | Hindu Vaidya. | Pleader, High Court; Zemindar, Merchant, 5 Mohesh Chunder Choudhury's Lane, Bhowanipore. | do. |
| 60 | " | " | " | Babu Saligram Sing, B.A., B.L. | Hindu. | Zemindar, Vakil & Honorary Magistrate, 119, Ripon Street, Calcutta. | do. |
| 61 | " | " | " | Mr. S. J. Padshah ... | Parsi. | Journalist, "Indian Mirror," Dhurrumtolla. | do. |
| 62 | " | " | " | Mr. A. Chaudhuri, B.A., L.L., M. (Cantab) M.A., Calcutta. | Hindu. | Zemindar, Haripore, Pabna; Barrister-at-Law, High Court, Calcutta; Officiating Secretary to the Indian Association. | do. |
| 63 | " | " | " | Babu Surendra Nath Dass | Hindu Kayestha. | Attorney-at-Law, 10, Sreenath Das's Lane, Calcutta. | do. |
| 64 | " | " | " | Babu Upendra Nath Mukherjee, B.L. | Hindu Brahmin. | Vakil ... | do. |
| 65 | " | " | " | Dr. K. G. Sircar, M.B., L.R.C.P., Edin., L.F.P.S., Glasgow. | Bengalee Christian. | Medical Practitioner, 4, Wellington Square, Calcutta. | do. |
| 66 | " | " | " | Babu Kalli Churn Banerjee, M.A., B.L. | do. | Vakil, High Court, Calcutta; Fellow of the Calcutta University, 81, Baranasi Ghose's Street, Calcutta. | do. |

| Number. | Presidency or Government. | Congress Circle. | Electoral Division. | Names in full of Delegates, with Honorary Titles, Scholastic Degrees, etc. | Race, Religious denomination, and Caste, if any. | Occupation and Address. | How and when elected. |
|---|---|---|---|---|---|---|---|
| 67 | Bengal | Calcutta | The Indian Association | Babu Nilkomal Mukherjee | Hindu Brahmin. | Banian and Zemindar ... | Elected by the Indian Association at a Meeting dated 22nd December 1890. |
| 68 | " | " | " | Babu Bhubun Mohun Das | Brahmo. | Vakil and Attorney-at-Law, High Court, Calcutta, 48, Pepulputty Road. | do. |
| 69 | " | " | " | Babu Promotho Nath Sen, M.A., B.L. | Hindu Vaidya. | Vakil, High Court, Calcutta, 5, Kenderdine's Lane. | do. |
| 70 | " | " | " | Dr. Pran Dhun Bose, M.B. | Bengalee Christian. | Practice of Medicine, 24, Mirzapur Street. | Elected by the Bengalee Christian Conference on the 5th December 1890. |
| 71 | " | " | " | Revd. Peary Mohun Mukherjee, S.P.G. | Bengalee Christian. | Missionary ... | do. |
| 72 | " | " | B. National Chamber of Commerce. | Babu Hurrendra Lal Roy... | Hindu. | Merchant and Zemindar ... | Elected at a Meeting of the Executive Committee of the Chamber held on the 1st December 1890. |
| 73 | " | " | " | Babu Damodar Das Bormon | do. | Zemindar ... | do. |
| 74 | " | " | " | Babu Bhola Nath Dhur ... | do. | Merchant ... | do. |
| 75 | " | " | Calcutta. | Mrs. Hemanta Kumari Sukul. | Brahmo. | ...... | At a Ladies' Public Meeting held at 81, Barranosi Ghose's Street, Calcutta, on the 24th December 1890. |
| 76 | " | " | " | Mrs. Susila Mazumdar | do. | Lady Superintendent of Girls' Boarding School. | do. |
| 77 | " | " | " | Mrs. Hemanta Kumari Choudhurani. | do. | Editor of "Sugrihini," a monthly journal. | do. |
| 78 | " | " | " | Mrs. Kadumbini Gangooly, B A., G.M.C.B. | do. | Lady Doctor ... | At a Meeting o[illegible] ld[illegible]dies held at Calcutta 1[illegible] the 22nd December 18[illegible] |
| 79 | " | " | (24 Pergunnahs) Diamond Harbour. | Babu Ganendra Chandra Roy Chowdhury. | Hindu Kayestha. | Pleader, Diamond Harbour ... | At a Meeting of [illegible]anch Indian Associatio[illegible] [illegible]ld at Diamond Harbour [illegible] the 8th December 189[illegible] |
| 80 | " | " | " | Pandit Rakhal Chandra Tewary. | Brahmin. | Pleader, Diamond Harbour; Honorary Magistrate. | do. |
| 81 | " | " | " | Babu Upendra Nath Bose ... | Kayestha | Zemindar ... | do. |
| 82 | " | " | " | Babu Raj Kumar Sircar ... | do. | do. ... | do. |
| 83 | " | " | (District 24-Pergunnahs) Baranagar | Babu Mohit Chandra Bose, M.A., B.L. | do. | Vakil, High Court, Baranagar | At a Public Meeting held at Baranagar on the 14th December 1890. |
| 84 | " | " | " | Rai Jotindro Nath Chowdhry, M.A., B.L. | do. | Zemindar, Baranagar ... | do. |
| 85 | " | " | Ichapore. | Babu Rajendra Lall Mukerjee, M.A. | Hindu Brahmin. | Landholder, Ichapore, 21, Jhamapukur Lane. | Elected at a Public Meeting held at Ichapore under the auspices of the Reform and Young Men's Association on the 6th December 1890. |
| 86 | " | " | Shahapore. | Pundit Kali Prossonno Kavyabissarod. | Agnostic. | Editor, "Union," Allahabad; Editor, "Cosmopolitan," Calcutta; Proprietor, Sumlar Press, Bhowanipore, &c., &c., &c., 69-70, Bolaram Bose's Ghat Road, Bhowanipore, Calcutta. | Elected at a Public Meeting held at the Association Rooms on the 24th December 1890. |
| 87 | " | " | Barrackpore Sub-Division (24 Pergunnahs). | Babu Bhubonath Nath Banerjee. | Hindu Brahmin. | Chairman, South Barrackpore Municipality; Zemindar, Pleader, 26-4, Scott's Lane, Calcutta. | By a Public Meeting held in the Barrackpore Sub-Division in the month of November 1890; (23rd) held at Khurdah. |
| 88 | " | " | Howrah. | Babu Mohendra Nath Roy, M.A., B.L. | Hindu Sudra. | Vakil of the Calcutta High Court; Law Professor, City College, Calcutta; and Landholder, Honorary Magistate of Howrah, Member of the District Board. | Elected at a Public Meeting held at the Howrah Town Hall on the 6th of December. 1890. |
| 89 | " | " | " | Babu Akshoya Churn Dass, B.L. | Hindu Kaiburto. | Pleader, District Court, Howrah; Honorary Secretary, Howrah People's Association. | do. |

| Number. | Presidency or Government. | Congress Circle. | Electoral Division. | Names in full of Delegates, with Honorary Titles, Scholastic Degrees, etc. | Race, Religious denomination, and Caste, if any. | Occupation and Address. | How and when elected. |
|---|---|---|---|---|---|---|---|
| 90 | Bengal | Calcutta | Howrah | Babu Nuro Singha Dutta, B.L. | Hindu Suburnabanik. | Vakil, High Court; Honorary Magistrate and Municipal Commissioner, Howrah. | Elected at a Public Meeting held at the Howrah Town Hall on the 6th of December 1890. |
| 91 | " | " | " | Babu Kedar Nath Bhattacharjee. | Hindu Brahmin. | Zemindar and Merchant, Santragachi, Howrah. | do. |
| 92 | " | " | " | Babu Gurudass Kundu Chowdhuree. | Hindu Teli. | Zemindar and Merchant, Mohiaris, Howrah; Member, District Board and National Chamber of Commerce. | do. |
| 93 | " | " | Utterparah Union. (Howrah District) | Babu Sree Krishna Roy Chowdhuree. | Hindu | Secretary, Utterparah Union. | At a Public Meeting at Utterparah held on 25th December 1890. |
| 94 | " | " | " | Babu Kissori Mohun Banerjee. | Brahmin | ...... | do. |
| 95 | " | " | Bali (Howrah District). | Babu Abinash Chunder Banerjee. | do. | Merchant ... | Elected at a Meeting held at Balli Rivers Thompson School, on 30th November 1890. |
| 96 | " | " | Oolubaria (Howrah District). | Babu Moni Mohun Ghose... | Kayestha | Zemindar and Pleader, Oolubaria, District Howrah. | At a Meeting of the Oolubaria Branch Indian Association held on the 29th November 1890. |
| 97 | | " | Murshidabad. | Sheikh Kurrim Buksh ... | Mohamedan. | ...... | At a Public Meeting of the Murshidabad Association, held on the 29th November 1890. |
| 98 | | " | " | Meer Ekram Hossein ... | do. | ...... | do. |
| 99 | | " | " | Babu Jugger Nauth Prosad Gupta. | Hindu Vaishya. | Zemindar ... | do. |
| 100 | " | " | " | Babu Bijoy Krishna Moitra, B.L. | Hindu Brahmin | Honorary Magistrate; Pleader, Judge's Court, Murshidabad. | do. |
| 101 | " | " | " | Kumar Woomesh Chunder Roy. | Kayestha | Zemindar ... | do. |
| 102 | " | " | " | Babu Sirish Chunder Basu Surbadhikary. | do. | do. ... | do. |
| 103 | | " | " | Babu Gopal Chunder Mukhapadhaya, M.A., B.L. | Brahmin | Vakil, High Court, Calcutta... | do. |
| 104 | | " | " | Babu Nuffor Dass Roy ... | Kayestha | Secretary, Murshidabad Association; Municipal Commissioner, Honorary Magistrate. | do. |
| 105 | " | " | " | Babu Mukunda Lal Burman | Hindu Kshatriya. | Honorary Magistrate, Municipal Commissioner, Silk Merchant, Zemindar. | do. |
| 106 | " | " | " | Babu Bono Beharee Sen ... | Hindu Kayestha. | Zemindar | do. |
| 107 | " | " | " | Babu Boikunt Nauth Sen... | do. | Honorary Magistrate, Zeminder, Municipal Chairman, Burhampur; President, Murshidabad Association; Vakil, High Court, Calcutta. | do. |
| 108 | " | " | " | Babu Hemendra Nauth Sen, B.L. | Hindu Vaidya. | Pleader, Judge's Court ... | do. |
| 109 | " | " | " | Babu Krishna Ballobh Roy. | Hindu Kayestha. | Pleader, Zemindar; Chairman of the Municipality and Local Board, Jangipur; Member, Dist. Board, Murshidabad, Honorary Magistrate, Public Notary. | do. |
| 110 | " | " | " | Babu Mohendra Nath Mukhopadhaya. | Hindu Brahmin. | Honorary Magistrate, Municipal Commissioner, Pleader, Judge's Court, &c. | do. |
| 111 | " | " | " | Babu Gour Bullobh Sen, M.A., B.L. | Hindu Kayestha. | ......... | do. |
| 112 | " | " | " | Babu Mohesh Narain Roy. | Hindu Kshatriya. | Pleader ... | do. |

Y

| Number. | Presidency or Government. | Congress Circle. | Electoral Division. | Names in full of Delegates, with Honorary Titles, Scholastic Degrees, etc. | Race, Religious denomination, and Caste, if any. | Occupation and Address. | How and when elected. |
|---|---|---|---|---|---|---|---|
| 113 | Bengal | Calcutta | Kandi (Murshidabad.) | Babu Ramindra Sundar Trivedi, M.A., Premchand Raichand Student. | Hindu Brahmin. | Zemindar ... | At a Public Meeting held at Kandi, December 14th, 1890. |
| 114 | " | " | Burdwan. | Babu Tara Prasanna Mukherjee, B.A., B.L. | Hindu Brahmin. | Pleader and Zemindar, Burdwan. | At a Meeting of the inhabitants of Burdwan held on the 13th December 1890. |
| 115 | " | " | Cutwa (Dt. Burdwan). | Dr. Brajendra Nath Sen, L.M.S. | Hindu Vaidya. | Medical Practitioner, Honorary Magistrate, second class, and Chairman, Local Board, Cutwa. | At a Public Meeting held at Cutwa on the 30th November 1890. |
| 116 | " | " | Amadpur (Burdwan.) | Babu Sripada Chowdhuri. | do. | Zemindar and Agent, C. S. N. and Co., Ld. | At a Public Meeting held at Amadpur, Dec. 13th, 1890. |
| 117 | " | " | Birbhoom. | Babu Dhankrishna Ghose, M.A., B.L. | Hindu Kayestha | Pleader, Zemindar and Chairman, Suri Municipality. | By a Public Meeting held in the Bar Library, Suri, 7th December 1890. |
| 118 | " | " | " | Babu Chandragati Mustofi, B.L. | do. | Pleader, Zemindar and Member, District Board, Suri, Birbhoom. | do. |
| 119 | " | " | Rampurhat (Birbhoom) | Babu Ananta Deb Banerjee. | Hindu Brahmin. | Pleader, Munsiff's Court, Rampurhat. | At a Public Meeting held at Rampurhat, December 7th, 1890. |
| 120 | " | " | Bankura | Babu Ramanuuda Chatterjee, M.A. | do. | Professor, City College, Calcutta. | At a Meeting of the [illegible]kura Association, [illegible]er 22nd, 1890. |
| 121 | " | " | " | Babu Mahesh Chandra Banerjee, B.L. | do. | Pleader, Judge's Court and Member, District Board, Bankura. | do. |
| 122 | " | " | Noakhally | Babu Rajani Kanta Bose | Hindu Kayestha. | Pleader, Judge's Court, Noakhally. | Elected at a Genc[illegible]eeting of the People's [illegible]ciation of Noakhally, De-cember 1890. |
| 123 | " | " | " | Babu Radha Kanta Aich, B.L. | do. | Pleader, Judge's Court, Noakally; Chairman, Noakhally Municipality. | do. |
| 124 | " | " | " | Babu Koruna Kumar Dass, B.L. | Hindu. | Pleader, Judge's Court, Noakhally. | do. |
| 125 | " | " | " | Babu Rajani Kanta Bose ... | Hindu Kayestha. | do. | do. |
| 126 | " | " | " | Babu Girija Kishore Ghose. | do. | Teacher, R. K. Jubilee School, Noakhally. | do. |
| 127 | " | " | Khulna | Babu Beni Bhusan Roy, B.L. | Hindu Kayestha | Pleader, Khulna ... | At a Public Meeting he[illegible] at Khulna, on Frida[illegible], th[illegible]5th December 1890. |
| 128 | " | " | " | Babu Amrita Lala Raha ... | do. | Talukdar; Member, District Board, Khulna. | do. |
| 129 | " | " | " | Rev. Gagan Chundra Dutta | Christian. | Khulna Town Missionary, Municipal Commissioner; Member, District Board. | do. |
| 130 | " | " | Bagirhat, (Khulna District.) | Babu Behari Lal Guha Roy, B.A. | Hindu Kayestha. | Head Master, H. E. School ... | At a Public Meeting of the Bagirhat People's Association, on the 18th December 1890. |
| 131 | " | " | Moolghar (Khulna District). | Babu Surendra Nath Gupta | Brahmo. | Head Master, Naldha School | At a Public Meeting of the inhabitants of Moolghar, Naldha, Manbhoge, &c., held on the 21st December 1890. |
| 132 | " | " | Jessore. | Babu Jadu Nath Ghosh, M.A. | Hindu Kayestha. | Landholder, 65/1, Mirzapore Street, Calcutta. | Elected at a Public Meeting held on the 13th December 1890, Branch Indian Association, Jessore. |
| 133 | " | " | Sub-Dvn. Magurah (Jessore District). | Babu Basanta Kumar Bose | Hindu Kayestha. | Pleader, Sub. Dvn. ... | Elected at a Special Meeting of the Magurah Branch Indian Association, held on the 29th [illegible]vember 1890. |
| 134 | " | " | " | Babu Jogendra Chundra Dass, B.A., B.L. | Hindu Vaidya. | Pleader and Landholder, Magurah. | do. |
| 135 | " | " | " | Babu Ambica Churn Sirkar | Hindu. | Landholder, Sub. Dvn. Magurah; Honorary Magistrate and Member, Magurah Local and District Boards. | do. |

| Number. | Presidency or Government. | Congress Circle. | Electoral Division. | Names in full of Delegates, with Honorary Titles, Scholastic Degrees, etc. | Race, Religious denomination, and Caste, if any. | Occupation and Address. | How and when elected. |
|---|---|---|---|---|---|---|---|
| 136 | Bengal. | Calcutta | Narail (Jessore District.) | Babu Kali Sankar Sukul, M.A. | Hindu | Principal, Narail Victoria College. | At a Public Meeting held on the 12th December 1890. |
| 137 | " | " | Krishnagore (Nuddea District.) | Babu Tarapada Banerjee, B.A., B.L. | Hindu Brahmin. | Vakil, Judge's Court, Krishnagore. | At a Public Meeting held at Krisnagore, November 25th, 1890. |
| 138 | " | " | " | Babu Jadu Nath Chatterjee, B.A., B.L. | do. | do. | do. |
| 139 | " | " | " | Babu Nafur Chundra Paul Chowdhury. | Hindu. | Zemindar, Merchant, Tea and Indigo Planter ; Vice-Chairman, District Board, and Honorary Magistrate, Krishnagore. | do. |
| 140 | " | " | " | Babu Prasanna Kumar Bose, M.A., B.L. | Hindu Kayestha. | Vakil, High Court, Honorary Magistrate and Pleader, Krishnagore. | do. |
| 141 | " | " | " | Babu Banko Behari Sinha | Hindu | Zemindar, Merchant ; Vice-Chairman, Local Board, and Member, District Board, Krishnagore. | do. |
| 142 | " | " | " | Babu Akshoy Kumar Mukherjee. | Hindu Brahmin. | Pleader, Judge's Court, Krishnagore. | do. |
| 143 | " | " | " | Babu Bishambhur Roy, B.A., B.L. | Hindu. | Pleader, Judge's Court ; Member, Local Board and District Board. | do. |
| 144 | " | " | " | Babu Nunda Gopal Bhaduri | Hindu Brahmin. | Merchant and Landholder ... | do. |
| 145 | " | " | Kishengunge (Nuddea District.) | Babu Pulin Vihari Lahiri... | do. | Pleader, District Court ; Vice-Chairman, Local Board, and Member, District Board, Krishnagore. | By the Committee of the Mahajan Shabha, Kishengunge, December 15th, 1890. |
| 146 |  | " | " | Dr. Jogadish Chundra Lahiri. | do. | Medical Practitioner, 101, College Street, Calcutta. | do. |
| 147 |  | " | Santipore. (Nuddea District.) | Dr. Bepin Behari Maitra ... | do. | Medical Practitioner, 45-9, College Street, Calcutta. | At a Public Meeting held at Santipore, December 14th, 1890. |
| 148 | " | " | Ranaghat (Nuddea District.) | Babu Bacharam Ghuttuck... | do. | Broker ... | At a Public Meeting held on the 10th December 1890. |
| 149 | " | " | " | Babu Surendra Nath Pal Chowdhury. | Hindu | Zemindar, late Chairman, Municipality, and Honorary Magistrate with 1st class power, Ranaghat. | At a Public Meeting, December 14th, 1890. |
| 150 | " | " | Chogdah (Nuddea District.) | Mr. Joseph Daviditch Melik Beglar. | Armenian | Landholder, Civil Engineer, and Anthologist. | At a Public Meeting held at Chogdah, December 7th, 1890 |
| 151 | " | " | " | Babu Akshoy Kumar Mittra. | Hindu Kayestha. | Talukdar, Chogdah ... | do. |
| 152 | " | " | Meherpore (Nuddea District.) | Babu Nitya Saran Mukerjee. | Hindu Brahmin. | Zemindar, Meherpore ... | At a Public Meeting, December 13th, 1890. |
| 153 | " | " | " | Babu Ramani Mohan Mullick | Hindu Vaidya. | do. ... | do. |
| 154 | " | " | Kushtea (Nuddea District.) | Babu Durga Das Banerjee... | Hindu Brahmin. | Pleader and Zemindar ... | At a Public Meeting held at Bahadarkali, November 28th, 1890. |
| 155 | " | " | " | Babu Purna Chandra Roy... | do. | Zemindar, Mukhtear, and Chairman, Local Board, Kushtea. | do. |
| 156 | " | " | " | Babu Basanta Kumar Chatterjee, B.A., B.L. | do. | Pleader, Judge's Court, and Secretary to the Krishnagore Branch Indian Association. | do |
| 157 | " | " | Kumarkhali (Nuddea District.) | Babu Heramba Chandra Maitra, M.A. | Brahmo | Professor, City College, Calcutta, and Member, District Board Nuddea. | At a Public Meeting held at Kumarkhali, November 18th, 1890. |
| 158 | " | " | Chuadanga (Nuddea District.) | Babu Akshay Kumar Maitra, B.L. | Hindu Brahmin. | Pleader and Zemindar, Krishnagore. | At a Public Meeting held on the 30th November 1890. |
| 159 | " | " | " | Babu Upendra Nath Acharjya | do. | Mukhtear, Chuadanga ... | do. |
| 160 | " | " | " | Babu Prassanna Chandra Roy, M.A., B.L. | Hindu Kshatriya. | Pleader and Zemindar, Chandipur, Kuralgachi. | do. |
| 161 | " | " | Hughli. | Babu Bishnupada Chatterjee, M.A., B.L. | Hindu Brahmin. | Pleader, Judge's Court, and Municipal Commissioner, Hughli. | At a Public Meeting held at Chinsurah, December 21st, 1890. |
| 162 | " | " | " | Babu Bejoy Gopal Ghose ... | Hindu Kayestha. | Landholder, Banker, Honorary Magistrate and Assistant Secretary, Local Congress Committee. | do. |
| 163 | " | " | " | Babu Hari Mohan Soor ... | Hindu | Pleader, Judge's Court, Hughli, and Municipal Commissioner, Chandernagore. | do. |

| Number. | Presidency or Government. | Congress Circle. | Electoral Division. | Names in full of Delegates, with Honorary Titles, Scholastic Degrees, etc. | Race, Religious denomination, and Caste, if any. | Occupation and Address. | How and when elected. |
|---|---|---|---|---|---|---|---|
| 164 | Bengal | Calcutta | British Chandernagore (Hughli District.) | Babu Satyaprasanna Ghose | Hindu | Zemindar, Honorary Magistrate and Municipal Commissioner. | At a Public Meeting held at Chinsurah, December 21st, 1890. |
| 165 | " | " | " | Babu Keshub Chandra Shadhu. | do. | Merchant ... | dc. |
| 166 | " | " | Bansberia (Hughli District.) | Raja Purnendu Dev Roy ... | do. | Zemindar and Municipal Commissioner. | do. |
| 167 | " | " | Serampore (Hughli District.) | Babu Nunda Lal Goshain | Hindu Brahmin. | Zemindar and Municipal Commissioner, Serampore. | At a Public Meeting held at Serampore, December 7th, 1890. |
| 168 | " | " | " | Rai Kedar Nath Chatterjee Bahadoor, L.M.S. | do. | Medical Practitioner and Vice-Chairman, Serampore Municipality. | do. |
| 169 | " | " | " | Babu Mahendra Chandra Lahiri. | do. | Pleader and Municipal Commissioner, Serampore. | do. |
| 170 | " | " | " | Munshi Golam Rosul ... | Mahomedan. | Zemindar ... | At a Meeting of Serampore Mofussil Association, Jonai, October 24th, 1890. |
| 171 | " | " | Tamluk. (Midnapore District.) | Babu Durga Ram Bose, B.L. | Hindu Kayestha | Vakil, High Court ... | Elected at a Public Meeting held on the 1st December 1890. |
| 172 | " | " | " | Babu Surendra Nath Chatterjee. | Hindu Brahmin. | Legal Practitioner ... | do. |
| 173 | " | " | Ghatal (Midnapore District.) | Babu Radha Shyam Gui ... | Hindu Tanti. | Talukdar, Merchant ... | At a Public Meeting held at Ghatal on 16th December 1890. |
| 174 | " | " | " | Babu Naryan Prosad Dutt | Hindu. | Pleader and Municipal Chairman, Ghatal. | do. |
| 175 | " | " | Contai (Midnapore District.) | Babu Shiva Ram Bosu, B.L | Hindu Kayestha. | Chakdar and Pleader, Contai. | At a Public Meeting held at Contai, December 1890. |
| 176 | " | " | Midnapore | Babu Bhubuneshur Mitra. | Hindu Kayestha. | Zemindar and Medical Practitioner, Bibigunge, Midnapore. | At a Public Meeting held inhabitants of Midnapore held on the 29th November 1890. |
| 177 | " | " | " | Babu Jogendro Chundra Roy. | Hindu Brahmin. | Zemindar, Pleader and a Member of the District Board, Midnapore, Colonelgolah, Midnapore. | do. |
| 178 | " | " | " | Babu Saroda Prosad Chatterjee. | Hindu Brahman. | Pleader | do. |
| 179 | " | " | " | Babu Rughunath Dass, M.A., B.L. | Hindu Karan.. | Zemindar and Pleader, and Vice-Chairman of the Midnapore Municipality and of the Sudder Local Board, and a Member of the District Board, Midnapore, Colonelgolah. | do. |
| 180 | " | " | " | Babu Jogendra Nath Sen ... | Hindu Kayestha. | Talukdar and Pleader; Member District Board, Midnapore, Bibigunge, Midnapore. | do. |
| 181 | " | " | " | Babu Krishna Lal Majumdar. | Hindu Vaidya. | Zemindar and Pleader ... | do |
| 182 | " | " | Arbalia | Babu Upendra Chundra Bose. | Hindu Kayestha | Vakil, High Court, 59, Puddopukur Road, Bhowanipore and Arbalia; Zemindar, President, Arbalia Gyan Vikashiney Sabha. | At a Meeting of the Managing Committee of the Arbalia G. V. Sabha, held on 20th November 1890. |
| 183 | " | " | " | Babu Bejoy Lall Dutt ... | Hindu Kayestha | Zemindar; Assistant Secretary, Arbalia Gyan Vikashiney Sabha, Arbalia, 59, Puddopukur Road, Bhowanipore. | do. |
| 184 | " | " | Chittagong | Babu Suresh Chandra Singha, M.A. | Hindu Kayestha. | Professor of Science, General Assembly's Institution, Calcutta. | At a Meeting of the District Board Association held on the 18th December 1890. |
| 185 | " | " | Tipperah. | Babu Gobind Chandra Dass, M.A., B.L. | Vaidya. | Vakil, High Court, Calcutta... | At a Meeting of the District Board Association, Tipperah, held on the 18th December 1890. |
| 186 | " | " | Chandpore (Tipperah District.) | Babu Kritanta Kumar Rose, M.A., B.L. | Kayestha. | Lawyer ... | At a Public Meeting held at Chandpore on the 7th December 1890. |
| 187 | " | " | " | Babu Hardyal Nag ... | do. | do. .. | do. |
| 188 | " | " | Balasore. | Babu Umesh Chandra Mondle. | Hindu Suburnabanik. | Zemindar and Merchant, Honorary Magistrate and Municipal Commissioner, Chinsura. | Elected at a Public Meeting held on the 7th December and at a Public Meeting held at Chinsurah, December 21st, 1890. |

| Number. | Presidency or Government. | Congress Circle. | Electoral Division. | Names in full of Delegates, with Honorary Titles, Scholastic Degrees, etc. | Race, Religious denomination, and Caste, if any. | Occupation and Address. | How and when elected. |
|---|---|---|---|---|---|---|---|
| 189 | Bengal | Calcutta | Balasore | Babu Bhagwan Chandra Dass. | Brahmo Urya. | Zemindar and Merchant, Balasore. | At a Public Meeting held on the 7th December 1890. |
| 190 | " | " | Cuttack (Orissa Association.) | Babu Janaki Nath Basu, B.A., B.L. | Hindu Kayestha. | Pleader, District Court, Cuttack. | At a Meeting held at Cuttack on 3rd December 1890. |
| 191 | " | " | Assam | Babu Ghunesyam Burrooa | Brahmin. | Pleader ... | At a Public Meeting of Nowgunj Ryats' Association, Assam. |
| 192 | " | " | " | Babu Manick Chunder Borooa. | Hindu | Honorary Magistrate and Vice-Chairman, Local Board, Assam; Merchant, 135, Bowbazar Street. | At a Public Meeting of the Assami Gentlemen, &c., held in Calcutta. |
| 193 | " | " | Nowgong (Assam District.) | Babu Ram Durlova Mazumdar. | Hindu Kayestha. | Pleader, Deputy Commissioner's Court, Nowgong. | Elected at a Meeting at Nowgong on 3rd December 1890. |
| 194 | " | " | Dhubri (Assam District.) | Babu Boroda Nath Haldar | Hindu Brahmin. | Manager to the Estate of Rani Abhageswari Devi of Bejni, Goalpara. | Elected at a Public Meeting held at Dhubri on 22nd December 1890. |
| 195 | " | " | " | Babu Kali Kumar Sircar, B.L. | Hindu. | Pleader ... | At a Public Meeting, 21st December 1890. |
| 196 | " | " | Sylhet (Assam District.) | Babu Bepin Chandra Pal... | Brahmo. | Secretary, Calcutta Public Library, 161-1, Old Bytakhana Bazar Road. | Elected at a Public Meeting held at Karimgunge on 17th December 1890. |
| 197 | " | " | " | Babu Radha Nath Chowdhry. | Hindu. | President, Karimgunge Association; Vice-Chairman of the Karimgunge Local Board; Editor and Proprietor, Paridersa Newspaper; Proprietor and Manager, Sylhet National Institution; Municipal Commissioner, Sylhet. | do. |
| 198 | " | Dacca | Dacca | Babu Chundra Mohan Sen, M.A., B.L. | Hindu. | Zemindar, Vakil, High Court, practising at Dacca. | At a Public Meeting held at Dacca, 17th December 1890. |
| 199 | " | " | Manikgunge. (Dacca District.) | Babu Pramatha Nath Sen, M.A., B.L. | Hindu Vaidya. | Vakil, High Court, 5, Kenderdine's Lane, Calcutta. | At a Public Meeting held at Manikgunge, 10th December 1890. |
| 200 | " | " | " | Babu Sarat Chundra Rai, B.L. | do. | Zemindar, Vakil, High Court, & Assistant Secretary, Pashchim Dacca Hitakari Shabha, 12, Nebootola Street, Calcutta. | do. |
| 201 | " | " | " | Babu Hem Chundra Rai, M.A., B.L. | do. | Zemindar & Pleader, Judge's Court, 12, Nebootola Street, Calcutta. | do. |
| 202 | " | " | Munshigunj. (Dacca District.) | Babu Dwarika Nath Gupta. | do. | Banker and Hony Magistrate, Munshigunj. | At a Public Meeting held at the Munshigunj Bar Library, 11th December 1890. |
| 203 | " | " | " | Babu Satyanand Basu, M.A., B.L. | Hindu Kayestha | Vakil, High Court, Calcutta. | do. |
| 204 | " | " | " | Babu Jagat Chandra Roy | Hindu | Pleader, Hony. Magistrate and Member, Local Board, Munshigunj. | do. |
| 205 | " | " | " | Babu Kailash Chandra Sen. | do. | Pleader, Judge's Court, Barisal. | do. |
| 206 | " | " | " | Babu Dwarka Nath Ganguli. | Brahmo. | Asst. Secy., Indian Association and Journalist, Calcutta. | do. |
| 207 | " | " | Mymensingh. | Babu Parvati Sankar Roy | Hindu | Zemindar, Teota ... | At a Public Meeting held at Manikgunge, 10th December 1890. |
| 208 | " | " | " | Babu Upendra Nath Roy, B.L. | Hindu Kayestha. | Pleader, District Court, Mymensing | At a Public Meeting held at Mymensing, 7th December 1890. |
| 209 | " | " | " | Babu Devendra Kishore Acharjya. | Hindu Brahmin. | Zemindar and Honorary Magistrate, Mymensingh. | do. |
| 210 | " | " | " | Babu Mahima Chundra Rai Chowdhuri. | Hindu Kayestha. | Zemindar, Mymensingh ... | do. |
| 211 | " | " | " | Babu Barada Kanta Bose | do. | Talukdar, Medical Practitioner and Municipal Commissioner. | do |
|  | " | " | " | Babu Srikanta Sen, B.A., B.L | Hindu Vaidya. | Pleader, Judge's Court, Mymensingh. |  |

| Number. | Presidency or Government. | Congress Circle. | Electoral Division. | Names in full of Delegates, with Honorary Titles, Scholastic Degrees, etc. | Race, Religious denomination, and Caste, if any. | Occupation and Address. | How and when elected. |
|---|---|---|---|---|---|---|---|
| 213 | Bengal | Dacca | Mymensingh. | Mir Masharaf Hossien ... | Mahomedan. | Editor, "Hitakari," Honorary Magistrate and Manager of Karimmunesa Khanum Choudhurani, Mymensingh. | At a Meeting of the Executive Committee of the Mymensingh Association, held on the 16th December 1890. |
| 214 | " | " | " | Moulavi Abdul Hamid Khan Ahmadi Yusaffzai. | do. | Editor, "Ahmadi" & Talukdar, Mymensingh. | At a Meeting of the Mahomedan Assembly, held at Calcutta, 24th December 1890. |
| 215 | " | " | " | Moulavi Kazi Meshabuddin Ahmadi. | do. | Zemindar, Mymensingh ... | do. |
| 216 | " | " | " | Moulavi Kazi Abdul Latiff | do. | Religious Preacher ... | do. |
| 217 | " | " | " | Babu Gurudas Chatterjee... | Brahmo. | Municipal Commissioner & Teacher, City Collegiate School, Mymensingh Branch. | At a Public Meeting held on the 7th December 1890. |
| 218 | " | " | " | Babu Brajendra Kishore Roy Chowdhury. | Hindu Brahmin. | Zemindar, Gouripur, Mymensingh. | do. |
| 219 | " | " | " | Babu Jogendra Narain Acharja Chowdhary. | do. | Zemindar, Muktagachi, Mymensingh. | do. |
| 220 | " | " | Iswargunge (Mymensingh District.) | Babu Shyama Charan Bose, B.A. | Hindu Kayestha. | .................. | By a Public Meeting. |
| 221 | " | " | Jamalpore (Mymensingh District.) | Babu Amar Chandra Dutt | Brahmo | Editor, "Charuvarta" ... | At a Public Meeting held at Sherpore, Mymensingh 15th December 1890. |
| 222 | | " | Jamalpur (Mymensingh District.) | Babu Ram Ratan Dey ... | Hindu Kayestha. | Pleader, Municipal Commissioner and Member, District Board, Jamalpur (Mymensingh.) | At a Public Meeting held at Jamalpur, December 4th, 1890. |
| 223 | " | " | Netrakona (Mymensingh District.) | Babu Gagan Chandra Shome | Kayestha | Talukdar, 22, Sitaram Ghose's Street, Calcutta. | At a Public Meeting held 23rd November 1890. |
| 224 | " | " | " | Babu Broja Nath Goswami. | Hindu Brahmin. | Pleader, Vice-Chairman, Municipality, and Member, Local Board, Netrakona. | do |
| 225 | " | " | Pingna. (Mymensingh District.) | Babu Ishan Chandra Chakravarty. | Hindu Brahmin. | Pleader, Munsiff's Court, and Member, Local Board, Pingna. | At a Public Meeting held the 3rd December 1890. |
| 226 | " | " | Backergunge. | Babu Biraj Mohan Rai Chowdhury. | Hindu Kayestha. | Zemindar and Municipal Commissioner. | At a Meeting of t[illegible] [illegible]isal People's Association December 21st, 1890 [illegible]r at a meeting of the re[illegible]es of Barisal, December 1890. |
| 227 | " | " | " | Babu Pyari Lall Roy, B.L. | do. | Vakil, Zemindar, Honorary Magistrate and late Chairman, Barisal Municipality. | do. |
| 228 | " | " | " | Babu Tarak Nath Biswas ... | do. | Zemindar, Jalabari ... | do. |
| 229 | " | " | " | Babu Aswini Koomar Dutt, M.A., B.L. | do. | Landholder, Pleader, Vice-Chairman, Municipality, Member, District Board, Secretary Barisal People's Association and Member, Local Board, Barisal. | do. |
| 230 | " | " | " | Babu Kailash Chandra Sen | Hindu Vaidya. | Mukhtear ... | At a Meeting of the Ba[illegible]sal People's Association, [illegible]ecember 21st, 1890. |
| 231 | " | " | " | Babu Dino Bandhu Das ... | do. | Pleader ... | do. |
| 232 | " | " | " | Babu Shashi Kumar Rai Chowdhury. | do. | Zemindar and Member, Local Board, Barisal. | do. |
| 233 | " | " | " | Babu Hara Kanta Sen ... | do. | Secretary, Barisal Local Office, and Assistant Secretary, People's Association. | do. |
| 234 | " | " | " | Moulavi Asmatali Khan Chowdhury. | Mahomedan. | Zemindar and late Member, Local Board, Barisal. | do. |
| 235 | " | " | " | Moulavi Abdul Kader ... | do. | Lecturer on Arabic and Persian, B. M. Institution, Barisal. | do. |
| 236 | " | " | Madaripore (Fureedpore District.) | Babu Amritalal Roy Chowdhury. | Hindu Brahmin. | Zemindar ... | At a Public Meeting helbn the 24th November [illegible]90 by the Madaripore Brch Indian Association. |
| 237 | " | | " | Babu Syama Churn Rai Chowdhury, B.A. | do. | Zemindar and Teacher, F. C. Institution, Calcutta. | do. |
| 238 | " | " | Kishoregunj. (Fureedpore Dist.) | Babu Guru Prasad Chakravarty. | Hindu Brahmin. | Pleader; Hony. Magistrate, and Vice-Chairman, Municipality and Local Board, Kishoregunj. | At a Meeting of the Kis[illegible]gunj Branch Indian [illegible]ciation, 30th Dece[illegible] 1890. |

| Number. | Presidency or Government. | Congress Circle. | Electoral Division. | Names in full of Delegates, with Honorary Titles, Scholastic Degrees, etc. | Race, Religious denomination, and Caste, if any. | Occupation and Address. | How and when elected. |
|---|---|---|---|---|---|---|---|
| 239 | Bengal | Dacca | Fureedpore | Babu Ram Narayan Agasti, B.A. | Hindu Brahmin. | Head Master, Kishoregunj H. E. School; Manager, Dewan Saheb's Estate; Hony. Magistrate, Municipal Commissioner, Member, Local Board and President, Branch Indian Association, Kishoregunj. | At a Meeting of the Kishoregunj Branch Indian Association, 30th December 1890. |
| 240 | " | " | " | Babu Ambica Charan Mazumdar, M.A., B.L. | Hindu Vaidya. | Pleader, Zemindar and Chairman, Municipality, Fureedpore. | At a Public Meeting held at Fureedpore, 14th December 1890, and also by Fureedpore Surhitsabha. |
| 241 | " | " | " | Babu Girija Sankar Mazumdar. | do. | Vakil, High Court, and Zemindar, Banibaha, Fureedpore. | At a Public Meeting held at Fureedpore, 14th December 1890. |
| 242 | " | " | " | Babu Umesh Chandra Sen, L.L. | do. | Pleader, Judge's Court, and Talukdar, Batajore, Jessore. | do. |
| 243 | " | " | " | Babu Kishori Lall Sarkar. | Hindu Kayestha. | Vakil, High Court and Taluqdar. | do. |
| 244 | " | " | " | Babu Gora Chand Das, B.L. | Hindu. | Pleader, Barisal ... ... | do. |
| 245 | " | " | " | Babu Jageswar Ray Chowdhury, B.A., B.L. | Hindu Kayestha. | Pleader, Judge's Court, 24 Parganas. | At an Ordinary Meeting of the Fureedpore Surhitsabha, 7th December 1890 |
| 246 | " | " | Bhanga (Fureedpore District.) | Babu Rajkumar Dutt ... | do. | Zemindar ... ... | At a Public Meeting held at Bhanga, December 1890. |
| 247 | " | " | Alisakanda (Fureedpore District.) | Babu Prasanna Kumar Bose. | Brahmo. | Landholder and Superintendent, Sanjibani. | At a Public Meeting held at Alisakanda, 15th December 1890. |
| 248 | " | " | " | Babu Krishna Kumar Mitra, B.A. | do. | Landholder, Editor, Sanjibani and Superintendent, City College (School Dept). | do. And also at Tangail, 15th December, 1890. |
| 249 | " | " | Goalundo (Fureedpore District.) | Babu Janoki Nath Pal, B.L. | Hindu Baroe. | Pleader, Rajbari, E. B. S. Ry. Station. | At a Public Meeting held at Goalundo, 7th September 1890. |
| 250 | " | Rajshahye. | Rajshahye. | Babu Taran Krishna Bhaumik. | Hindu Sudra. | Talukdar, Jotedar, and Moneylender; Honorary Magistrate, Bangari, Rajshahye. | At a Meeting of the Rajshahye Association, on 22nd December 1890. |
| 251 | " | " | " | Babu Rakhal Charan Mandal. | do. | Zemindar and Banker, Rampore Beauleah. | do. |
| 252 | " | " | " | Babu Jogendra Nath Chowdhury. | do. | Zemindar and Medical Practitioner, Dhakdhar, Rajshahye | do. |
| 253 | " | " | " | Raja Ramani Kanta Roy, B.A. | Hindu Brahmin. | Zemindar, Chowgong, District Rajshahye. | do. |
| 254 | " | " | " | Babu Jadob Chandra Chowdhury, B.L. | do. | Pleader, Judge's Court, Rajshahye. | do. |
| 255 | " | " | " | Babu Suresh Chandra Maitra, B.A., B.L. | do. | Landholder; Pleader, Judge's Court, Rajshahye; Member, Rajshahye District Board; Municipal Commissioner, Rampore Beauleah, and Secretary, Rajshahye Association. | do. |
| 256 | " | " | " | Babu Hiralal Roy, B.A. ... | Brahmo. | Honorary Magistrate and Head Master, H. E. School, Naogaon, Rajshahye. | At a Meeting of the Rajshahye Association, on 22nd December 1890, and at a Public Meeting, at Naogaon, on 19th December 1890. |
| 257 | " | " | " | Babu Rajkumar Sarkar ... | Hindu Kayestha. | Zemindar and President, Rajshahye Association, Karachmaria, Rajshahye. | Public Meeting at Beauleah, 30th November 1890. |
| 258 | " | " | " | Babu Hari Charan Maitra, L.L. | Hindu Brahmin. | Pleader, Judge's Court, and Honorary Magistrate, Rajshahye. | do. |
| 259 | " | " | " | Babu Mukunda Mohan Maitra, B.L. | do. | Pleader, Judge's Court, Rajshahye. | Public Meeting at Rampore Beauleah, on 30th November 1890, and at a Meeting of the Rajshahye Association, on the 22nd December 1890. |
| 260 | " | " | | Babu Tara Nath Choudhuri | do. | Zemindar, Taherpur ... | do. |
| 261 | " | " | Pabna ... | Babu Pratap Chandra Roy, L.L. | do. | Pleader Chairman, Local Board; Member, District Board, and Municipal Commissioner, Pabna. | At a Public Meeting held on the 23rd November 1890. |
| 262 | " | " | " | Babu Girish Chandra Roy, B.L. | Hindu Kayestha. | Pleader, Honorary Magistrate, and Zemindar, Pabna. | do. |

| Number. | Presidency or Government. | Congress Circle. | Electoral Division. | Names in full of Delegates, with Honorary Titles, Scholastic Degrees, etc. | Race, Religious denomination, and Caste, if any. | Occupation and Address. | How and when elected. |
|---|---|---|---|---|---|---|---|
| 263 | Bengal | Raj-shahye. | Bogra ... | Babu Pyari Sankar Das Gupta. | Hindu Vaidya. | Medical Practitioner, Honorary Magistrate, and Municipal Commissioner, Bogra. | At a Public Meeting at Bogra, on the 27th November 1890. |
| 264 | " | " | Dinajpore | Babu Madhab Chundra Chatterjee, M.A., B.L. | Hindu Brahmin. | Pleader, District Court, Dinajpore. | At a Public Meeting, held on the 12th November 1890. |
| 265 | " | " | " | Babu Hari Mohun Singha, B.A. | Hindu Kayestha. | Zemindar ... | do. |
| 266 | " | " | " | Babu Michu Chundra Sarkar. | do. | Zemindar and Merchant, Dinajpore. | do. |
| 267 | " | " | " | Babu Gouranga Sundar Mazumdar. | do. | Zemindar, Dinajpore ... | do. |
| 268 | " | " | " | Babu Umesh Chandra Khasnavis. | do. | Mukhtear, Dinajpore ... | do. |
| 269 | " | " | Julpaiguri. | Kumar Jagadindra Deb ... | Hindu. | Jotedar, Municipal Commissioner and Vice-President, Julpaiguri Branch, Indian Association. | At a Public Meeting of the Branch Indian Association, Julpaiguri, 14th December 1890. |
| 270 | " | " | " | Babu Umagati Roy, B.L ... | Hindu Brahmin. | Pleader; Secretary to the Branch Indian Association, and Director to the Julpaiguri Banking and Trading Corporation, Limited. | do. |
| 271 | " | " | " | Babu Akhoy Kumar Bose ... | Hindu Kayestha. | Pleader, Julpaiguri ... | do. |
| 272 | " | " | " | Babu Tarini Prasad Roy, B.L. | do. | Pleader and Secretary to the Ratepayer's Association, Julpaiguri. | do. |
| 273 | " | " | Rungpore. | Babu Ramani Mohan Roy | do. | Zemindar, Kankina, Rungpore | At a Public Meeting held at Rungpore on the 7th December 1890. |
| 274 | " | " | " | Babu Hem Chandra Mitra, B.L. | do. | Pleader, Rungpore ... | do. |
| 275 | " | " | " | Babu Kailash Chandra Roy | Hindu Vaidya. | Mukhtear, Rungpore ... | do. |
| 276 | " | " | " | Babu Biseswar Sen ... | do. | Pleader, Rungpore ... | do. |
| 277 | " | " | " | Babu Baroda Prasad Bagchi | Hindu Brahmin. | do. ... | do. |
| 278 | " | " | " | Babu Prasanna Nath Chowdhury. | do. | do. | do. |
| 279 | " | " | Nilphamari (Rungpore District.) | Babu Rajkumar Bhattacharjya. | do. | Pleader, Nilphamari | At a Meeting of the Nilphamari, Sanmilani Sabha on the 24th August 1890. |
| 280 | " | " | " | Babu Gopal Chandra Chatterji, M.A., B.L. | do. | Pleader; Member, District and Local Board; and Honorary Magistrate, Nilphamari. | do. |
| 281 | " | " | Sherpore (Bogra District.) | Babu Kali Kishore Munshi | do. | Zemindar, Honorary Magistrate, and Chairman, Municipality, Sherpore. | At a Public Meeting held at Bogra 7th December 1890. |
| 282 | " | Bhagulpore. | Bhagulpore. | Babu Sharoda Prosad Mookerjee B.A., B.L. | Hindu Brahmin. | Pleader, Bhagulpore ... | At a Public Meeting held on the 28th November 1890 in the Bhagulpore Institution. |
| 283 | " | " | " | Babu Dinabandhu Banerjee, B A.; B.L. | do. | do. ... | do. |
| 284 | " | " | " | Babu Harendra Lal Roy, B.A., B.L. | do. | do. ... | do. |
| 285 | " | " | " | Babu Srikumar Choudhuri, M.A., B.L. | do. | Pleader, Madhepurah (N. Bhagulpore.) | do. |
| 286 | " | " | " | Babu Moti Lal Miser ... | do. | Pleader, Municipal Commissioner, Bhagulpore. | do. |
| 287 | " | " | " | Babu Shyama Pada Ghose, L.M.S | Hindu Satgopa. | Medical Practitioner, Madhepurah (North Bhagulpore.) | do. |
| 288 | " | " | " | Babu Punchum Narayan Singh. | Hindu Rajput. | Zemindar, Koiriaputty, Gamhari P. O., Madhupore (N. Bhagulpore.). | do. |
| 289 | " | " | " | Babu Lukshmi Narayan Singh. | Hindu Kshatrya. | Honorary Magistrate; Member, District and Local Boards; Zemindar Babhni Gamhari, P. O. Madhepurah (N. Bhagulpore.) | do. |
| 290 | " | " | " | Babu Kuldip Lal ... | Hindu Agarwalla. | Zemindar; Municipal Commissioner and Hony. Magistrate, Bhagulpore. | do. |
| 291 | " | " | " | Babu Mohabir Prasad | Hindu Jaiswar. | Assistant, Messrs. T. N. Singh and Son of Calcutta. Jalalabad (S. Bhagulpore.) | do. |
| 292 | " | " | | Rai Tejnarayan Singh Bahadur. | Hindu Jaiswar. | Zemindar, Banker, Indigo Planter and Honorary Magistrate, Bhagulpore. | do. |

| Number. | Presidency or Government. | Congress Circle. | Electoral Division. | Names in full of Delegates, with Honorary Titles, Scholastic Degrees, etc. | Race, Religious denomination, and Caste, if any. | Occupation and Address. | How and when elected. |
|---|---|---|---|---|---|---|---|
| 293 | Bengal | Bhagulpore | Bhagulpore | Babu Juggernath Prasad, M.A., B.L. | Hindu Kayestha. | Zemindar and Pleader, Bhagulpore. | At a Public Meeting held on the 28th November 1890 in the Bhagulpore Institution. |
| 294 | " | " | " | Babu Shiva Sankar Sahai. | do. | Pleader, Bhagulpore, Honorary Magistrate, Municipal Commissioner, Member District Board. | do. |
| 295 | " | " | " | Babu Abinash Chandar Basu, B.A., B.L. | Hindu Kayestha. | do. ... | do. |
| 296 | " | " | " | Babu Sunkata Charan Mitter. | do. | do. ... | do. |
| 297 | " | " | " | Rai Surya Narayan Singh Bahadur, B.L. | do. | Pleader, Banker, Zemindar, Vice-Chairman District Board, and Municipal Chairman, Bhagulpore. | do. |
| 298 | " | " | " | Dr. Ladly Mohun Ghose ... | do. | Medical Practitioner, Honorary Magistrate, and Secretary, T. N. Jubilee College, Bhagulpore. | do. |
| 299 | " | " | " | Babu Rashbehari Lal Mondle. | Hindu Gwala. | Zemindar and Member, Local Board. | do. |
| 300 | " | " | " | Babu Upendra Chandra Singh. | Hindu Kayestha. | Municipal Commissioner; Member, District Board; Honorary Magistrate and Zemindar, Naga, Champanagur P. O. (Bhagulpore.) | do. |
| 301 | " | " | Monghyr. | Babu Narayan Das B. L. ... | Hindu Agarwalla. | Pleader, Monghyr ... | At a Public Meeting held at Monghyr on the 20th December 1890. |
| 302 | " | " | " | Babu Akhileswar Prasad, M.A., B.L. | Hindu Kayestha. | Zemindar and Pleader, Monghyr. | do. |
| 303 | " | " | Purnea. | Babu Chetnarayan ... | Hindu Kayestha. | Landholder, Mukhtear and Municipal Commissioner, Purnea. | At a Public Meeting held at Purnea on the 2nd December 1890. |
| 304 | " | " | " | Babu Golabnarayan ... | do. | Landholder and Mukhtear. | do. |
| 305 | " | " | " | Babu Shiva Prasad ... | do. | do. ... | do. |
| 306 | " | " | " | Babu Nanuck Pershad ... | do. | Pleader, Landholder, Vice-Chairman, Purnea Municipality, Municipal Commissioner and Member, District Board, Purnea. | do. |
| 307 | " | " | " | Babu Newalkishore ... | Hindu Agarwalla. | Zemindar, Hony. Magistrate and Municipal Commissioner, Purnea. | do. |
| 308 | " | " | " | Babu Bishen Chand ... | do. | Landholder, Indigo Planter, Honorary Magistrate, and Member, District Board, Purnea. | do. |
| 309 | " | " | " | Babu Jogendra Nath Mukherjee, M.A., B.L. | Hindu Brahmin. | Pleader, Purnea ... | do. |
| 310 | " | " | " | Babu Parbutty Churn Das, B.A., B.L. | Brahmo. | Pleader, Landowner, Member, District Board, Purnea. | do. |
| 311 | " | " | " | Babu Kamakhya Nath Ghose, L.M.S. | Hindu Satgopa | Doctor, Municipal Commissioner, Honorary Magistrate, Member District Board, Purnea. | do. |
| 312 | " | " | " | Mir Jowhur Ali ... | Mahomedan. | Zemindar and Municipal Commissioner. | do. |
| 313 | " | Chota-Nagpore. | Hazaribagh. | Rai Jadu Nath Mookherjee, B.L. | Hindu Brahmin. | Vakil; Honorary Magistrate; Vice-Chairman, Municipality; Director, Chota-Nagpore Banking Association, Ld., President, Union Club; Secretary D. C. Public Institution; Member, District Committee, and President, Hazaribagh Association. | At a General Meeting of the Hazaribagh Association and the residents of the town of Hazaribagh and its suburbs, the 7th December 1890. |
| 314 | " | " | " | Malik Hossain Bux ... | Mahomedan. | Landholder and Private Service. | do. |
| 315 | " | " | " | Mirza Imdad Ali Beg ... | do. | Landholder, Honorary Magistrate and Municipal Commissioner. | do. |
| 316 | " | " | " | Babu Hari Charan Mitra, M.A., B.L. | Hindu Kayestha. | Pleader, Hazaribagh; Vice-Chairman, District Board; Municipal Commissioner, Honorary Magistrate, and Director, Chota-Nagpore Banking Association. | do. |

| Number. | Presidency or Government. | Congress Circle. | Electoral Division. | Names in full of Delegates, with Honorary Titles, Scholastic Degrees, etc. | Race, Religious denomination, and Caste, if any. | Occupation and Address. | How and when elected. |
|---|---|---|---|---|---|---|---|
| 317 | Bengal | Chota-Nagpore. | Hazari-bagh. | Babu Girindra Kumar Gupta, M.A., B.L. | Hindu Vaidya. | Pleader, Municipal Commissioner; Secretary, Chota Nagpore Carrying Company, Limited; Joint-Secretary, Hazaribagh Union Club; Assistant Secretary, Hazaribagh Girls' School, and Secretary, Hazaribagh Association. | At a General Meeting of the Hazaribagh Association and the residents of the town of Hazaribagh and its suburbs on the 7th December 1890. |
| 318 | " | " | Ranchi. | Babu Jagat Pal Sahay ... | Hindu Kayestha. | Pleader; Municipal Commissioner and Member, District Educational Committee, Lohardugga. | By a Public Meeting at Ranchi on the 18th December 1890. |
| 319 | " | " | " | Babu Banwari Lal ... | do. | Zemindar and Muktear, Ranchi. | do. |
| 320 | " | " | " | Babu Panch Courry Dey, B.L. | do. | Pleader, Lohardugga, Municipal Commissioner, Member, District Educational Committee. | do. |
| 321 | " | " | Purulia. | Babu Ram Chandra Sinha, B.L. | do. | Pleader, Purulia ... | Purulia Sub-Committee, on the 3rd December 1890. |
| 322 | " | " | " | Babu Baidya Nath Ghatak, B.L. | Hindu Brahmin. | Pleader, Purulia ... | do. |
| 323 | " | Behar. | Patna District. | Syed Sharfuddin ... | Mahomedan. | Barrister-at-Law and Zeminder, Bankipore; Vice-Chairman, Patna District Board; Chairman, Dinapore Local Board, and Municipal Commissioner, Patna. | At a General Meeting held at Bankipore, on the 6th December 1890. |
| 324 | " | " | " | Babu Guru Prasad Sen, M.A., B.L. | Hindu Vaidya. | Zemindar and Vakil, High Court, practising at Bankipur; Municipal Commissioner, Patna, and Editor of "The Behar Herald and Indian Chronicle." | do. |
| 325 | " | " | " | Babu Biseswar Sinha ... | Hindu Kshatryia. | Zemindar and Pleader, Bankipur; Honorary Magistrate, Patna, and Member, Arrah Local Board. | do. |
| 326 | " | " | " | Moulovi Abdul Hamid, B.A., B.L. | Mahomedan. | Zemindar and Pleader, Bankipur; Honorary Magistrate, Patna; Member, Patna District Board, and Vice Chairman, Dinapore Local Board. | do. |
| 327 | " | " | " | Moulovi Basharat Hossein. | do. | Zemindar, Bankipore ... | do. |
| 328 | " | " | " | Moulovi Syed Ali Rashid... | do. | Zemindar and Contractor, Bankipore. | do. |
| 329 | " | " | " | Moulovi Syed Nuruddin Ahmed Balkhi. | do. | Zemindar and Pleader, Doondibazar, Patna City; Municipal Commissioner, Patna. | do. |
| 330 | " | " | " | Babu Mahabir Sahay, B.A., B.L. | Hindu Kayestha. | Vakil, High Court and Zemindar, Bhowanipore, Calcutta. | do. |
| 331 | " | " | " | Babu Purnenda Narayan Sinha, M.A., B.L. | do. | Pleader, Bankipore ... | do. |
| 332 | " | " | " | Babu Sham Narain ... | do. | Zemindar and Pleader, Bankipore; Member, Dinapore Local Board. | do. |
| 333 | " | " | " | Babu Surja Kumar ... | do. | Zemindar and Pleader, Bankipore. | do. |
| 334 | " | " | " | Babu Hanuman Sahay ... | do. | Zemindar, Shorampore *via* Phulbari P.O. | do. |
| 335 | " | " | " | Babu Raja Ram ... | Hindu Vaisya. | Zemindar and Banker, Patna City, and Honorary Magistrate. | do. |
| 336 | " | " | " | Pundit Jainarain Bajpai ... | Hindu Brahmin. | Zemindar and Banker, Patna City. | do. |
| 337 | " | " | " | Babu Narain Prasad, B.A., B.L. | Hindu Kshetry. | Vakil, High Court, Patna City; Municipal Chairman, Patna. | do. |
| 338 | " | " | Shahabad. | Syamlal Nanda ... | Hindu Kayestha. | Pleader, Zemindar, Baboo Bazaar, Arrah (Shahabad); Municipal Commissioner, Member, District and Local Board. | At a General Meeting held at Arrah on the 14th December 1890. |

| Number. | Presidency or Government. | Congress Circle. | Electoral Division. | Names in full of Delegates, with Honorary Titles, Scholastic Degrees, etc. | Race, Religious denomination, and Caste, if any. | Occupation and Address. | How and when elected. |
|---|---|---|---|---|---|---|---|
| 339 | Bengal | Behar | Shahabad | Babu Raghunundan Pershad, B.A., B.L. | Hindu Kayestha. | Zemindar; Vakil, High Court, Bhowanipore, Calcutta. | At a General Meeting held at Arrah on the 14th December 1890. |
| 340 | " | " | " | Babu Ram Rajendra Deo Narayan. | do. | Zemindar, Matukpur, Shahabad; Member, Local Board. | do. |
| 341 | " | " | " | Babu Raghubans Sahay, B.A., B.L. | do. | Vakil, Calcutta High Court; and Zemindar, Arrah; President, Arrah Bar. | do. |
| 342 | " | " | " | Babu Koylash Chandra Banerjee M.A., B.L. | Hindu Brahmin. | Vakil and Zemindar, Arrah. | do. |
| 343 | " | " | Behar People's Association. | Moulavi Mahomed Ismail. | Mahomedan. | Pleader and Zemindar, Subzibag, Bankipore. | At a Meeting of the Association held on the 15th December 1890. |
| 344 | " | " | " | Babu Surat Lal ... | Hindu Kurmi. | Zemindar and Cultivator, Daryapore. | do. |
| 345 | " | " | " | Babu Thakur Singh ... | do. | Zemindar, Chainpura, Harnut P.O., District Patna. | do. |
| 346 | " | " | " | Babu Mohesh Narayan ... | Hindu Kayestha. | Editor, "Kayestha Gazette," Bankipore. | do. |
| 347 | " | " | " | Babu Nand Kumar Prasad *alias* Lalla Prasad. | Hindu. | Zemindar, Bilwargunj, Patna City. | do. |
| 348 | " | " | Mozufferpore. | Babu Narayan Das ... | Hindu Kshatriya. | Zemindar ... | At a Public Meeting held at Mozufferpore on the 14th December 1890. |
| 349 | " | " | " | Babu Rameswar Narain Mahtha. | do. | Zemindar. Banker, Indigo Planter, Municipal Commissioner and Honorary Magistrate. | do. |
| 350 | " | " | " | Babu Biswanath Prasad Mahtha. | do. | Zemindar, Banker and Indigo Planter. | do. |
| 351 | " | " | " | Babu Gajadhar Prasad Sahu. | Hindu Sahu. | Zemindar and Banker ... | do. |
| 352 | " | " | " | Mr. Pringle Kennedy, M.A., B.L., Premchand Roychand Scholar. | European Christian. | Pleader, District Court, Mozufferpore. | do. |
| 353 | " | " | " | Babu Purmeshwar Narain Mahtha. | Hindu Kshatriya. | Zemindar, Banker, Indigo Planter, Municipal Commissioner, and Vice-Chairman, Mozufferpore; Member, District Board; Chairman, Local Board, and Hon. Magistrate. | do. |
| 354 | " | " | " | Babu Kunjan Lal ... | Hindu Agarwala | Zemindar and Banker, Mozufferpore. | do. |
| 355 | " | " | " | Mirza Golam Hyder ... | Mahomedan. | Manager of a Banking Firm | do. |
| 356 | " | " | " | Moulavi Syed Ahmed Hosein, B.L. | Mahomedan Shiah. | Pleader and Zemindar, Mozufferpore. | do. |
| 357 | " | " | " | Babu Suruj Deo Narayan Singh. | Hindu Babhun. | Zemindar, Mozufferpore ... | do. |
| 358 | " | " | " | Mr. B. D. Bose ... | Hindu Kayestha. | Barrister-at-Law, Mozufferpore. | do. |
| 359 | " | " | " | Babu Sharashi Charan Mitra, B.L. | do. | Pleader, Mozufferpore ... | do. |
| 360 | " | " | " | Babu Trailokya Nath Bose, M.A., B.L. | do. | Vakil and Zemindar, Mozufferpore. | do. |
| 361 | " | " | " | Babu Ramdhan Sahai ... | do. | Zemindar and Vice-Chairman, District Board; Honorary Magistrate, Municipal Commissioner. | do. |
| 362 | " | " | Durbhunga. | Babu Kripa Nath Mazumdar, B.A. | Hindu Vaidya. | Asst. Hd. Master, Raj School, Durbhanga; Honorary Magistrate and Municipal Commissioner. | By the Standing Congress Committee on the 20th December 1890. |
| 363 | " | " | " | Munshi Maneerallum ... | | Mukhtear, Durbhanga ... | do. |

| Number. | Presidency or Government. | Congress Circle. | Electoral. Division. | Names in full of Delegates, with Honorary Titles, Scholastic Degrees, etc. | Race, Religious denomination, and Caste, if any. | Occupation and Address. | How and when elected. |
|---|---|---|---|---|---|---|---|
| 364 | Bengal | Behar | Gya | Hakim Syed Attuf Hosein. | Mahomedan. | Medical Practitioner, Gya ... | At a Public Meeting held at Gya, on the 9th December 1890. |
| 365 | " | " | " | Babu Isri Prasad ... | Hindu Kayestha. | Zemindar and Rais, Mahalla Chowk, Gya. | do. |
| 366 | " | " | Tikari (Gya District). | Babu Nand Kishore Lall, M.A., B.L. | do. | Zemindar and Vakil, Gya ... | do. |
| 367 | " | " | " | Babu Deoki Nandan, B.A. | do. | Zemindar, Tikari, Dist. Gya... | do. |
| 368 | " | " | " | Moulavi Syed Sakhawat Hussain. | Mahomedan. | Zemindar and Rais Tikari, Gya. | do. |
| 369 | " | " | Saran | Babu Jadunath Mitter, B.A., B. L. | Hindu Kayestha. | Pleader, Saran ... | By a Public Meeting held on the 6th December 1890 |
| 370 | " | " | " | Babu Sheo Bux Mull ... | Hindu Marwari Agarwala. | Banker and Zemindar; Honorary Magistrate, Chapra. | do. |
| 371 | " | | Dumraon | Babu Mathura Prasad ... | Hindu Kayestha. | Zemindar, 4, Kyd Street ... | By Dumraon Friends' Debating Club, 23rd December 1890. |
| 372 | N. W. Provinces. | Benares. | Benares | Pundit Chunnilal Pande. | Hindu Brahmin | Private Service Johori Bazar, Benares City. | At a Public Meeting held at Benares, December 14th, 1890. |
| 373 | " | " | do. | Pundit Uma Sanker Dubey. | do. | Tripura Bhairani, Benares City. | do. |
| 374 | " | " | do. | Babu Mokshada Das Mitra. | Hindu Kayestha. | Zemindar and Banker, Benares City. | do. |
| 375 | " | " | do. | Babu Govinda Das ... | Hindu Agarwala. | Banker, Benares ... | do. |
| 376 | " | " | do. | Babu Upendra Nath Basu, B.A., L.L.B. | Hindu Kayestha. | Pleader, District Court, Benares City. | do. |
| 377 | " | " | Azamgarh | Babu Hira Lal ... | do. | Mukhtear ... | By Public Meeting held on 14th December 1890. |
| 378 | " | " | do. | Babu Mookteshar Roy ... | Hindu Brahmin. | Pleader Judge's Court, Azamgarh. | do. |
| 379 | " | " | do. | Babu Gourishankar Singh. | Hindu Kshatriya. | Zemindar and Pleader, Azamgarh. | do. |
| 380 | " | " | Mirzapore | Babu Sriram ... | Khetree | Zemindar, Municipal Commissioner, Member, District Board. | At a Public Meeting held on 22nd December at Kalandar Gir's House. |
| 381 | " | " | " | Babu Bani Pershad ... | Bhargava | Zemindar, Contractor, Hony. Magistrate, Member, Municipality and District Board. | do. |
| 382 | " | Allahabad. | Allahabad. | Munshi Sadrudeen Ahmed | Mahommedan | Zemindar, Syed of Sannut Jama'at. | Elected at a Public Meeting held in the Kayestha Pathsala Hall on the 11th December 1890. |
| 383 | " | " | | Mirza Mohammed Mahdi ... | do. | do. ... | Elected at a Public Meeting held in Rani Mandi on 22nd December 1890. |
| 384 | " | " | " | Moulvie Ameer Ali ... | do. | Government Pensioner ... | do. |
| 385 | " | " | " | Mir Akhtar Hussain ... | Mahomedan Shia | do. ... | do. |
| 386 | " | " | " | Mir Anwar Hussain ... | do. | do. ... | do. |
| 387 | " | " | " | Sheikh Nabee Ashraf ... | Mahomedan Sannut Jam'at. | Teacher and Zemindar ... | Elected at a Public Meeting held in Village Ujehnee on 21st December 1890. |
| 388 | " | " | " | Sheikh Mohammed Sadik... | do. | Zemindar ... | Elected at a Public Meeting held in Janka Village on 20th December 1890. |
| 389 | " | " | " | Sheikh Hassan Ali ... | do. | Private Service ... | do. |
| 390 | " | " | " | Mir Musarraf Ali ... | Mahomedan Shia. | do | Elected at a Public Meeting held in Village Karrali on 21st December 1890. |
| 391 | " | " | " | Sheikh Sa'aadat Ali ... | Mahomedan Sannut Jam'at. | do. ... | Elected at a Public Meeting held in Johnstongunje, Allahabad, on 17th December, 1890. |

| Number. | Presidency or Government. | Congress Circle. | Electoral Division. | Names in full of Delegates, with Honorary Titles, Scholastic Degrees, etc. | Race, Religious denomination, and Caste, if any. | Occupation and Address. | How and when elected. |
|---|---|---|---|---|---|---|---|
| 392 | — P N.-lou 90 | Allahabad. | Allahabad | Mir Hatim Ali ... | Mohammedan Shia. | Zemindar ... | At a Public Meeting held at Johnstongunj, Allahabad, on 23rd December 1890. |
| 393 | | ,, | ,, | Pundit Baldeo Ram Dave... | Gujrati Nagar Brahmin. | Vakil, High Court, N.-W. P.; Joint Secretary, Standing Congress Committee, Allahabad. | Elected at a Public Meeting held at the Kayestha Pathsala, on the 11th December 1890. |
| 394 | , | ,, | ,, | Pundit Madan Mohun Malaviya, B.A. | Hindu Malaviya Brahmin. | Joint Secretary, Standing Congress Committee, Allahabad. | do. |
| 395 | ,, | ,, | ,, | Pundit Beni Madhav Bhattacharjya. | Hindu Brahmin. | Pensioner, Municipal Commissioner, Honorary Magistrate, Allahabad. | do. |
| 396 | ,, | ,, | ,, | Babu Charu Chunder Mittra. | Hindu Kayestha. | Pleader, Zemindar and Vice-Chairman, Municipal Board, Allahabad. | do. |
| 397 | ,, | ,, | ,, | Mr. T. N. Ghose ... | do. | Pleader, District Court, and Secretary, Jubilee Club, Municipal Commissioner, Allahabad. | do. |
| 398 | ,, | ,, | ,, | Munshi Madhava Prasad ... | do. | Vakil, High Court, N.-W. P.; Zemindar and Honorary Magistrate; Honorary Secretary, Standing Congress Committee, Allahabad. | do. |
| 399 | , ,, | ,, | ,, | Hon: Pandit Ajoodhia Nath | Hindu Cashmeri Brahmin. | Joint General Secretary; Member, Royal Asiatic Society of Bengal; Vakil, High-Court; Member, Legislative Council, N. W. P. and Oudh; Fellow of Calcutta and Allahabad University. | do. |
| 400 | | ,, | , | Mr. L. Tracey ... | European Christian. | Editor, "Morning Post" ... | do. |
| 401 | | ,, | ,, | Sheikh Sabir Hussain .. | Mohammedan. | Zemindar ... | do. |
| 402 | ,, | ,, | ,, | Mirza Tufail Ali-Beg ... | Mohammedan Shia. | do. ... | do. |
| 403 | | ,, | ,, | Syed Mir-Jan | do. | do ... | do. |
| 404 | ,, | ,, | ,, | Mir Nourauz Ali ... | do. | do. ... | Elected at a Public Meeting held in Village Karali on 21st December 1890. |
| 405 | ,, | ,, | ,, | Mir Nazim Hussain ... | do. | do. ... | do. |
| 406 | ,, | ,, | ,, | Shah Sajjad Hussain Hafiz | Mohammedan Sunnat Jama'at. | Priest ... | Elected at a Public Meeting held in Village Kunkara on 19th December 1890. |
| 407 | ,, | ,, | ,, | Hafiz Kamruddin ... | do. | Zemindar ... | Elected at a Public Meeting held in Midara Village on 15th December 1890 |
| 408 | ,, | ,, | ,, | Sheikh Raza Hussain ... | Mohammedan Shia. | do ... | do. |
| 409 | ,, | ,, | ,, | Sheikh Zahiruddin ... | Mohammedan Sunnat Jama'at. | do. ... | do. |
| 410 | ,, | ,, | ,, | Munshi Ahmed Hussain... | do. | do ... | do. |
| 411 | ,, | ,, | ,, | Sheikh Ashraf Ali ... | do. | do ... | do. |
| 412 | ,, | ,, | ,, | Syed Rahmat Ali ... | Mohammedan Sunni | do. ... | do. |
| 413 | ,, | , | ,, | Sheikh Ali Mohammed ... | do. | do. | At a Public Meeting held at Kara on 22nd December 1890. |
| 414 | ,, | ,, | ,, | Sheikh Abdul Guffur ... | do. | do. ... | do. |
| 415 | ,, | ,, | Cawnpore | Hakim Fukrul Hussein ... | Mohammedan. | Physician ... | By Public Meeting at Lala Gaya Pershad's house, on 17th December 1890. |
| 416 | ,, | ,, | ,, | Syed Mohammad Hadi ... | Mohammedan. | Rais and Zemindar ... | do. |

| Number. | Presidency or Government. | Congress Circle. | Electoral Division. | Names in full of Delegates, with Honorary Titles, Scholastic Degrees, etc. | Race, Religious denomination, and Caste, if any. | Occupation and Address. | How and when elected. |
|---|---|---|---|---|---|---|---|
| 417 | N. W. P. | Allahabad. | Cawnpore. | Hafiz Aboo Said Khan ... | Mohammedan Pathan. | Proprietor of a Printing Press | By Public Meeting ecemLala Gaya Pershad's held on 17th Deecmber 18 |
| 418 | " | " | " | Moulvi Mahomed Siddiq ... | Mohammedan Syed. | Principal of Faiz-am Arabic School. | do. |
| 419 | " | " | " | Babu Ram Sing Bhargava | Hindu Brahmin. | Pleader ... ... | do |
| 420 | " | " | " | Lala Madho Ram ... | Hindu Khetri. | Banker ... ... | do. |
| 421 | " | " | " | Maharaj Sheo Sahay ... | Hindu Gore Brahmin. | Lecturer of Arya Somaj, Cawnpore. | do. |
| 422 | " | " | " | Pundit Prithinath ... | Hindu Brahmin. | Pleader and Zemindar ... | do. |
| 423 | " | " | " | Babu Hurnam Singh ... | Sikh. | Proprietor, "Cawnpore Gazette," Urdu. | do. |
| 424 | " | " | " | Lala Madan Chand Khunna. | Hindu Khetri. | Cloth Merchant ... | do. |
| 425 | " | " | " | Lala Gobind Pershad | do. | Merchant and Contractor ... | do. |
| 426 | " | " | " | Babu Gunga Dayal ... | Hindu Kayestha. | Pleader ... ... | do. |
| 427 | " | " | " | Pundit Hirdey Narain Koul | Hindu Brahmin. | Pleader; Assistant Secretary, Divisional Congress Committee, Cawnpore, and Assistant Secretary, Anjuman Refah-i-am, Cawnpore, and Zemindar. | do. |
| 428 | " | " | " | Babu Shewnarain ... | Hindu Mahasari Kshatrya. | Banker and Contractor ... | do. |
| 429 | " | " | " | Babu Nundunpershad ... | Hindu Khetri. | Merchant ... ... | do. |
| 430 | " | " | " | Lala Hukum Chand ... | Hindu Vyasa. Agarwala. | Banker .. ... | do. |
| 431 | " | " | " | Babu Bansidhar ... | Hindu Mohesri Vaisya. | Banker ... ... | do. |
| 432 | " | " | " | Babu Troilokya Nath Bauerjee. | Hindu Brahmin. | Pleader and Secretary, Reform Association, Cawnpore. | do. |
| 433 | " | " | Prayag Hindu Somaj. | Swami Ala Ram ... | Hindu | Missionary, Sanyasi ... | By a Meeting of the Prayag Hindu Samaj, date 23rd December 1890. |
| 434 | " | " | " | Lala Gonesh Pershad ... | Hindu Agarwala. | Banker, Zemindar, &c. ... | do. |
| 435 | " | " | Dehra Dun | Rev. Bhoobun Mohun Bose | Christian. | Pleader ... ... | Public Meeting held at 7th December 1890. |
| 436 | " | " | Moradabad. | Babu Narendra Chundra Bose. | Hindu Kayestha. | Vakil ... ... | At a Public Meeting held at Moradabad, 14th December 1890. |
| 437 | " | " | Agra. | Thakur Zahir Singh ... | Kshatryia. | Zemindar, Agra ... | At a Public Meeting held at Sheo-ka-Bazar, Agra on 7th December 1890. |
| 438 | " | " | " | Rai Sohanlall ... | Kayestha Arya. | Rais, Banker, Ferozabad ... | do. |
| 439 | " | " | " | Mirza Mahomed Ibrahim Beg Chagtai. | Mohammedan. | Zemindar ... | do. |
| 440 | " | " | " | Sheikh Khwaja Bux ... | do. | Proprietor, Miftahutullam Press, Mundla | do. |
| 441 | " | " | " | Munshi Mahomed Munir Khan. | do. | Merchant, Agra | do. |

| Number. | Presidency or Government. | Congress Circle. | Electoral Division. | Names in full of Delegates, with Honorary Titles, Scholastic Degrees, etc. | Race, Religious denomination, and Caste, if any. | Occupation and Address. | How and when elected. |
|---|---|---|---|---|---|---|---|
| 442 | N.-W. P. | Allahabad. | Aligurh. | Syed Sarfaraz Ali ... | Mahomedan. | Pleader and Zemindar ... | At a Public Meeting held at Aligurh, 14th December 1890. |
| 443 | " | " | " | Mohamed Surfaraz Khan | do. Pathan. | Pleader ... ... | do. |
| 444 | " | " | " | Mohamed Zaferiyab Khan | do. | Pleader ... ... | do. |
| 445 | " | " | " | Mohamed Mustajabullah Khan. | do. | Zemindar and Indigo Merchant. | do. |
| 446 | " | " | " | Hafiz Abdurrahim ... | do. Sheikh. | Pleader, Judge's Court, Aligurh. | do. |
| 447 | " | " | Jhansi. | Pundit Pryag Dass ... | Arya Brahmin. | Mukhtear and Zemindar ... | Public Meeting held at Jhansi on 17th December 1890. |
| 448 | " | " | " | Babu Basanta Kumar Sanyal. | Hindu Brahmin. | Pleader ... ... | do. |
| 449 | " | " | Almora. | Sheikh Manullah ... | Mahomedan. | Merchant ... ... | do. |
| 450 | " | " | " | Pundit Hari Ram Pande, B.A. | Brahmin. | Vakil, High Court, N.-W. P. | do. |
| 451 | " | " | Furruckabad. | Lala Durgaprasad ... | Boishanali Rastagi. | Banker, Rais, Municipal Commissioner. | By a Public Meeting held at Furruckabad City on the 10th December 1890. |
| 452 | " | " | " | Lala Jowala Prashad ... | Boishanali Vasiya. | Shopkeeper ... ... | do. |
| 453 | " | " | Banda. | Lola Rughuber Dyal ... | Hindu Kayestha. | Mukhtear, Secretary, Kayesth Sabha. | By a Public Meeting held on the 12th December 1890. |
| 454 | " | " | | Babu Kali Prosonno Bannerji | Hindu Brahmin. | Vakil, High Court, N.-W. P., Member, District Board. | At a Public Meeting held at Bareilly on the 21st December 1890. |
| 455 | " | " | " | Babu Prio Nath Bannerji ... | do. | Vakil, High Court, N.-W. P., Municipal Commissioner. | do. |
| 456 | Oudh | Lucknow. | Lucknow | Babu Sree Ram, M.A., B.L. | Hindu Kayestha. | Vakil Municipal Commissioner, Zemindar. | By a Public Meeting held on the 12th December 1890. |
| 457 | " | " | " | Pandit Maharaj Kishen ... | Arya Brahmin. | Rais ... | do. |
| 458 | " | " | " | Pundit Janki Nath ... | Kashmiri Brahman. | Pleader ... | do. |
| 459 | " | " | " | Nawab Nadir Saheb ... | Mohamedan | Wasikdar ... | At a General Meeting of the Anjuman Mahomedai, 22nd December 1890. |
| 460 | " | " | " | Nawab Ali Saheb ... | do. | Merchant ... | do. |
| 461 | " | " | " | Syed Aga ... | do. | Wasikdar ... | do. |
| 462 | " | " | " | Syed Munay Saheb ... | do. | Moulavi ... | do. |
| 463 | " | " | " | Nawab Masum Ali Khan ... | do. | Wasikdar ... | do. |
| 464 | " | " | " | Manshi Asgar Ali Khan | do. | Private Service ... | do. |
| 465 | " | " | " | Munshi Mohamed Furhat Ali. | do. | do. ... | do. |
| 466 | " | " | " | Syed Ameer Hussain Khan | do. | do. ... | do. |
| 467 | " | " | " | Syed Yakub Hussain ... | do. | do. ... | do. |

| Number | Presidency or Government. | Congress Circle. | Electoral Division. | Names in full of Delegates, with Honorary Titles, Scholastic Degrees, etc. | Race, Religious denomination, and Caste, if any. | Occupation and Address. | How and when elected. |
|---|---|---|---|---|---|---|---|
| 468 | Oudh | Lucknow. | Lucknow | Mohamed Baker Ali Khan | Mohamedan. | Private Service ... | At a General Meeting of the Anjuman Mohamedai, 22nd December 1890. |
| 469 | " | " | " | Syed Amrad Hossain ... | do. | do. ... | do. |
| 470 | " | " | " | Moulvi Jamshed Mirza ... | do. | do. ... | do. |
| 471 | " | " | " | Sufdar Hussain Khan .. | do. | do. ... | do. |
| 472 | " | " | " | Nawab Shumeshuddowla Bahadur. | do. | Wasikdar ... | do. |
| 473 | " | " | " | Nawab Hussain Mirza ... | do. | do. ... | do. |
| 474 | " | " | " | Moulvi Mohamed Safi ... | do. | Private Service ... | do. |
| 475 | " | " | " | Nawab Asafali Khan ... | do. | Wasikdar ... | do. |
| 476 | " | " | " | Nawab Umroo Mirza Khan | do. | do. ... | do. |
| 477 | " | " | " | Munshi Amjad Ali ... | do. | Private Service ... | do. |
| 478 | " | " | " | Syed Sajjad Hussain ... | do. | do. ... | do. |
| 479 | " | " | " | Nawab Husmut Hussain Khan. | do. | Pensioner ... | do. |
| 480 | " | " | " | Munshi Sajjad Hussain ... | do. | Editor ... | do. |
| 481 | " | " | " | Mr. Hamid Ali Khan ... | do. | Barrister-at-law, Municipal Commissioner. | do. |
| 482 | " | " | " | Munshi Gangaprasad Varma | Hindu. | Journalist, Proprietor, Advocate, and Hindustani Municipal Commissioner, Secretary Congress Committee. | At a Public Meeting held on the 14th December 1890. |
| 483 | " | " | " | Bishan Narayan Dar ... | Hindu Brahmin. | Barrister-at-Law, Municipal Commissioner. | do. |
| 484 | " | " | " | Pandit Sham Narain Masuldan. | Hindu Brahmin. | Landholder. Journalist, Municipal Commissioner. | do. |
| 485 | " | " | Anjuman Mahomedi. | Syed Baker Hussain Taba Tabai. | Mohamedan. | Rais ... | General Meeting at the Anjuman Mahomadai held on the 18th December 1890. |
| 486 | " | " | " | Nawab Aga Mohamed Jaffer Hussain Khan. | do. | do. ... | do. |
| 487 | " | " | " | Mirza Raza Hossain | do. | do. ... | do. |
| 488 | " | " | " | Nawab Syed Ali Khan ... | do. | do. ... | do. |
| 489 | " | " | " | Syed Kazim Hussain ... | do. | do. ... | do. |
| 490 | " | " | " | Syed Murtaza Hussain ... | do. | do. ... | do. |
| 491 | " | " | " | Munshi Mirza Hussain ... | do. | do. ... | do. |
| 492 | " | " | " | Munshi Mohamed Mohassen | do. | do. ... | do. |
| 493 | " | " | " | Syed Mohamed Abid ... | do. | do. ... | do. |
| 494 | " | " | " | Munshi Sardar Mirza ... | do. | do. ... | do. |
| 495 | " | " | " | Munshi Yusuf Hossain ... | do. | do. ... | do. |
| 496 | " | " | " | Syed Mohamed Hadi ... | do. | do. ... | do. |
| 497 | " | " | " | Munshi Mohamed Fakhruddin. | do. | do. ... | do. |
| 498 | " | " | " | Mirza Ali Hussain ... | do. | do. ... | do. |
| 499 | " | " | " | Nawab Mohamed Hussain Khan. | do. | do. ... | do. |
| 500 | " | " | " | Syed Kazim Hussain ... | do. | do. ... | do. |
| 501 | " | " | " | Tassadaq Hussain Khan ... | do. | do. ... | do. |
| 502 | " | " | " | Syed Mohamed Ibrahim Khan. | do. | do. ... | do. |
| 503 | " | " | Anjuman Rafaiam. | Babu Bhuban Mohan Roy | Hindu. | Merchant Nazirabad, Lucknow. | At a Meeting of the Rafaiam Association, Lucknow, held on the 11th December 1890. |
| 504 | " | " | " | " Nobin Chunder Mitter | do. | Pensioner, Doctor, Hydurgunj, Lucknow. | do. |
| 505 | " | " | " | Revd. Ram Chandra Bose. | Christian | Missionary Makbara Amjad Ali Shah, Lucknow. | do. |
| 506 | " | " | " | Babu Bepin Beharee Bose, M.A. | Hindu. | Vakil, High Court, Pleader and Honorary Secretary, Rifa-i-am Association, Lucknow, Jhoo Lall Bridge, Lucknow. | do. |
| 507 | " | " | " | Babu Kali Das Sirkar ... | Hindu. | Pensioner, Ghasyari Mandi, Lucknow. | do. |
| 508 | " | " | " | Sheikh Asgar Ali ... | Mohamedan. | Merchant, Chowk, Lucknow. | do. |
| 509 | " | " | Khiree. | Babu Sheo Baksh Rai ... | Hindu Vaisya. | Pleader and Banker; Honorary Magistrate, Secretary of District Board and Member of Municipal Board, Lukhipoor Khiree. | By Public Meeting. |
| 510 | " | , | " | Seth Dwarka Dass ... | Khettree. | Banker and Zemindar; Honorary Magistrate, Member, District Board, Municipal Commissioner. | do. |
| 511 | " | " | Jalsai Tahzil. | Babu Bunsi Lall Singha ... | Hindu. | Pleader, Golagunge ... | At a General Meeting of the Members of the Jalsai Tahzil held on 7th December 1890. |

| Number. | Presidency or Government. | Congress Circle. | Electoral Division. | Names in full of Delegates, with Honorary Titles, Scholastic Degrees, etc. | Race, Religious denomination, and Caste, if any. | Occupation and Address. | How and when elected. |
|---|---|---|---|---|---|---|---|
| 512 | Oudh | Lucknow | Fyzabad | Sheikh Kadir Buksh ... | Mahomedan. | Merchant and Vice-Chairman, District Board. | At a Public Meeting of the residents of Fyzabad and Ayuddhia held on 8th December 1890. |
| 513 | " | " | " | Rai Kaccoomal Bahadur | Hindu Aror Bansi. | Hony. Magistrate, Chairman, Municipal Board, Zemindar and Pleader. | do. |
| 514 | " | " | " | Babu Charu Charan Ghose | Hindu | Private Medical Practitioner, Proprietor of Printing Press and Druggist Shop, also Member of District and Municipal Board. | do. |
| 515 | " | " | " | Babu Gokul Chand ... | Hindu Kayestha. | Zemindar, Pleader, Vice-Chairman of District and Municipal Board, Honorary Magistrate. | do. |
| 516 | " | " | Sitapore | Munshi Lalta Pershad ... | Hindu Kayestha. | Government Pensioner and Zemindar. | do. |
| 517 | " | " | " | Babu Pitam Rai ... | do. | Sitapur (Oudh), Vakil, Honorary Bench Magistrate, Zemindar, &c., &c. | By a Public Meeting on 23rd December 1890. |
| 518 | " | " | " | Thakur Ganj Singh ... | Chuttree. Hindu. | Zemindar, Mouza Kishapar, District (Sitapur.) | do. |
| 519 | Punjab | Lahore | Lahore | Mr. A. O. Hume, C.B. ... | English Christian. | Retired Civilian, Resident at Simla. | By a Public Meeting held at Lahore, December 14th, 1890. |
| 520 | " | " | " | Babu J. C. Bose, M.A., B.L.... | Hindu Kayestha. | Pleader, Chief Court, Lahore | do. |
| 521 | " | " | " | Lala Dharm Dass Suri ... | Hindu. | Pleader, High Court, N.W.P. | do. |
| 522 | " | " | " | Dr. Parmananda ... | do. Khatriya. | Surgeon Dentist, Lahore ... | do. |
| 523 | " | " | " | Mr. Ishan Chandra Sarkar | Bengalee Christian. | Retired Engineer ... | do. |
| 524 | " | " | " | Babu Megh Nath Banerjee | Hindu Brahmin. | Medical Practitioner, Lahore | do. |
| 525 | " | " | " | Mr. Hukm Chand ... | Hindu Khetry. | Pleader ... ... | do. |
| 526 | " | " | " | Guru Sodhi Pratap Singh. | Sikh. | Lahore ... ... | do. |
| 527 | " | " | Amritsar | Bawa Narain Singh ... | do. | Pleader ... ... | At a Public Meeting held at Amritsar, December 7th, 1890. |
| 528 | " | " | " | Dr. Gangadin ... | Behari Arya. | Medical Practitioner, Amritsar | At a Public Meeting held at Amritsar, November 30th, 1890. |
| 529 | " | " | " | Babu Balmokund | Hindu Kayestha. | Agent, Law Publication and Private Secretary. | do. |
| 530 | " | " | Kangra | Captain A. T. Banon ... | European Christian. | Zemindar, Kulu, late Bengal Staff Corps. | At a Public Meeting held at Dharmsala, December 7th, 1890. |
| 531 | " | " | Umballa | Lala Murlidhar ... | Hindu | Pleader ... ... | At a Public Meeting held at Umballa, December 21st, 1890. |
| 532 | " | " | Jullundur | Bakshi Jaishi Ram ... | Hindu Mahajan. | Pleader, Chief Court, and Landholder. | By a Public Meeting. |
| 533 | " | Delhi | Delhi | Munshi Mahomed Rukunuddin Jadoo. | Mohammedan. | Sheristadar ... | Elected at a General Meeting held on the 14th December 1890. |
| 534 | " | " | " | Moulvi Nisar Ali Shohrat | do. | Director of Public Instruction, Cashmere. | do. |
| 535 | " | " | " | Munshi Mahomed Shahabuddin Sakil. | Mogul Mohammedan. | Translator ... | do. |
| 536 | " | " | " | Dr. Hem Chander Sen ... | Hindu Vaidya. | Medical Practitioner, Delhi... | do. |
| 537 | Bombay | Guzerat | Surat | Mr. Hargovind Harnarayan Vyas. | Hindu Brahmin. | District Pleader, Vadifalia, Surat. | By the Praja Hitbardhak Sabha, Surat, 12th December 1890. |
| 538 | " | " | " | Mr. Hardeoram Nanabhai Haridas | Hindu Kayastha. | Landed Proprietor, Gopipura, Surat, and 161, Malabar Hill Bombay. | do. |
| 539 | " | " | " | Mr. Ratiram Dargaram Dave, B. A. | Hindu Nagar Brahmin. | Articled Clerk ... | do. |
| 540 | " | " | " | Mr. Jugmohandas Vrindavandas. | Hindu. | Mill-owner and Banker, Bombay. | do. |

| Number. | Presidency or Government. | Congress Circle. | Electoral Division. | Names in full of Delegates, with Honorary Titles, Scholastic Degrees, etc. | Race, Religious denomination, and Caste, if any. | Occupation and Address. | How and when elected. |
|---|---|---|---|---|---|---|---|
| 541 | Bombay. | Guzerat. | Broach. | Mr. Ramdas Keshavji ... | Hindu Brahmin. | Merchant, Bombay ... | At a meeting of the Loka-Hitechhu Sabha, Broach, 6th December 1890. |
| 542 | „ | Bombay | Bombay Presidency Association. | Mr. Pherozeshah M. Mehta, M.A. | Parsi | Barrister-at-Law, Bombay ... | At a Special General Meeting held on the 15th December, 1890. |
| 543 | „ | „ | „ | Mr. Dinshaw Edulji Wacha. | do. | Merchant; Honorary Secretary, Bombay Presidency Association; Secretary, Standing Congress Committee; Member of the Municipal Corporation. | do. |
| 544 | „ | „ | „ | Mr. Jehangir K. R. Cama. | Parsi. | Barrister-at-Law, 12, Malabar Hill, Bombay. | do. |
| 545 | „ | „ | „ | Mr. Jamiatram Nanabhai Haridas, B.A., L.L.B. | Hindu. | Advocate, High Court, Bombay. | do. |
| 546 | „ | „ | „ | Mr. V. N. Gokhle, B.A., L.L.B. | Konkanstha Brahmin. | Pleader, High Court ... | do. |
| 547 | „ | „ | „ | Mr. S. W. Kane, L.M.S. | do. | Medical Practitioner ... | do. |
| 548 | „ | „ | „ | Mr. D. S. Garud, B.A., L.L.B. | Hindu Brahmin. | Solicitor, High Court, 3, Eldon Road, Fort, Bombay. | do. |
| 549 | „ | „ | „ | Mr. Vinayek N. Bhagwat | Konkanstha Brahmin. | Pensioner, Native State, Bombay. | do. |
| 550 | „ | „ | „ | Mr. Mulraj Khatao Makanji. | Hindu Bhattia. | Merchant, Bombay. | do. |
| 551 | „ | „ | Bombay Arya Dnanavardhak Sabha. | Mr. Rupsing Mathuradas Lowjee. | do. | do. | By Arya Dnanavardhak Sabha, December, 1890. |
| 552 | „ | „ | Thana. | Mr. Shankar Damodar Gupte. | Hindu Prabhu Kayestha. | Pleader, District Court, Thana, residing at Bassein. | At a Meeting of the Thana Association, held on the 7th December 1890. |
| 553 | „ | „ | „ | Mr. Hari Luxman Patel ... | Hindu Brahmin. | Pleader, District Court, Thana. | do. |
| 554 | „ | „ | Ratnagiri. | Mr. Dhondo Mahadeo Barve. | do. | Pleader, Sub-Judge's Court Municipal Commissioner, and Member, Local Board. | At a Public Meeting held at Ratnagiri, 16th November 1890. |
| 555 | „ | „ | „ | Dhaji Abaji Khare, B.A., LL.B. | do. | Pleader, High Court, Bombay. | do. |
| 556 | „ | „ | Colaba. | Mr. Martand Sivarao Dharkar. | Hindu Prabhu Kayestha. | Zemindar and Merchant, Pen, Kolaba district. | At a Meeting held at Alibag, 12th December, 1890. |
| 557 | „ | Deccan | Poona | Mr. R. S. Kashinath Govind Natu. | Brahmin. | Pleader, District Court, and Municipal Commissioner. | At a Public Meeting held in Town Hall, Poona, 10th December 1890. |
| 558 | „ | „ | „ | Mr. Vinayek Narayan Apte | do. | Trader, Member, Mercantile Association, and Member, Sarvajanik Sabha, Poona. | do. |
| 559 | „ | „ | „ | Mr. Vasudeo Laxman Athavale. | do. | Trader, Joint Secretary, Congress Committee, and Member, Sarvajanik Sabha, Poona. | do. |
| 560 | „ | „ | „ | Professor Gopalkrishna Gokhale, B.A. | do. | Professor, Ferguson College; Secretary, Poona Union Club; Honorary Secretary, Poona Sarvajanik Sabha; and Editor, "Sudharak" and "Quarterly Journal," Sarvajanik Sabha. | do. |
| 561 | „ | „ | „ | Mr. Bal Gangadhar Tilak, B.A., L.L.B. | do. | Professor, Ferguson College; Secretary, Standing Congress Committee; and Member, Sarvajanik Sabha. Poona; Editor of "Kesari" and the "Mahratta." | do. |
| 562 | „ | „ | „ | Mr. Vasudeo Balkrishna Kelkar, B.A. | do. | Professor, Ferguson College, and Joint Editor, "Marhatta and Kesary." | do. |
| 563 | „ | „ | „ | Mr. Hari Narayan Apte ... | do. | Editor, "Karamanook" ... | do. |
| 564 | „ | „ | „ | Mr. Vasudeo Ganesh Joshi | do. | Manager, "Chitra Shala," and Member, Sarvajanik Sabha, Poona. | do. |
| 565 | „ | „ | „ | R. S. Mahadev Ballal Namjoshi. | do. | Municipal Commissioner and Secretary, Industrial Conference and Museum. | do. |
| 566 | „ | „ | „ | Hon. Krishnaji Laxman Nulkar, C.I.E. | do. | Member, Viceregal Council, late Dewan of Cutch, Poona. | do. |

| Number. | Presidency or Government. | Congress Circle. | Electoral Division. | Names in full of Delegates, with Honorary Titles, Scholastic Degrees, etc. | Race, Religious denomination, and Caste, if any. | Occupation and Address. | How and when elected. |
|---|---|---|---|---|---|---|---|
| 567 | Bombay. | Deccan. | Poona. | Mr. R. S. Raghunathrao Ramchandra Agasti. | Brahmin | Pensioned Sub-Engineer ... | Elected by the Arbitration Court, Poona, 20th December 1890. |
| 568 | " | " | Ahmednagar. | Rao Saheb Raghunath Daji Nagarkar. | do. | Jagirdar, Landholder, Pleader, Municipal Commissioner, Moneylender and Member, District and Local Board; Member, Sarvajanik Sabha. | At a Public Meeting, held at Ahmednagar, 14th December 1890. |
| 569 | " | " | " | Mr. Shahurao Ramkrishna Modak. | Christian. | Evangelist ... | do. |
| 570 | " | " | Nasik. | Rao Saheb Gangadhar Narsinh Ketkar. | Hindu Brahmin. | District Pleader and Municipal Commissioner, Nasik. | At a Meeting of Sarvajanik Sabha, held at Nasik, 30th November 1890. |
| 571 | " | " | " | Mr. Wamanrao Balkrishna Ranade. | Arya Brahmin. | Editor, "Dyan Chakshu," Poona. | do. |
| 572 | " | " | Khandesh. | Rao Saheb Chintaman Bapuji Morgankar. | Hindu Brahmin. | Pleader and Vice-President, Municipality, Bhusawal. | At a Public Meeting held on 27th November 1890. |
| 573 | " | " | " | Mr. Sakharam Ganesh Patankar. | do. | Pleader and Municipal Commissioner, Bhusawal. | do. |
| 574 | " | " | Jalgaon. (Khandesh.) | Mr. Abaji Ragho Mhalas. | do. | Pleader, Jalgaon, Khandesh. | At a Public Meeting held at Jalgaon, 3rd December 1890. |
| 575 | " | " | Satara. | Mr. Raghunath Pandurang Karandikar, B.A. LL.B. | do. | Pleader, District Court, Satara. | At Public Meetings at Shiralawai and Satara, 30th November and 7th December 1890. |
| 576 | " | " | " | Rao Saheb Balvant Shridhar Sahasrabuddhe. | do. | Pleader, District Court, and Municipal Commissioner, Satara. | do. |
| 577 | " | " | Belgaum. | Mr. Anandarao Bhagwant Mudgiri. | do. | Pleader ... | At a Public Meeting held at the Belgaum District Association, 14th December 1890. |
| 578 | " | " | " | Mr. Bhimrao Shrinivasrao Bhide. | do. | Landholder ... | do. |
| 579 | " | " | " | Rao Saheb Sadashiv Balkrishna Bhate. | do. | Pleader ... | do. |
| 580 | " | " | Dharwar. | Mr. Vishvanath Mahadev Herlekar, B.A., L.L.B. | Hindu Vedic Brahmin. | Pleader, District Court, Dharwar. | At a Public Meeting held on the 7th December 1890. |
| 581 | " | " | Ichalkaranji. | Mr. Ram Chundra Baladev Apte. | Hindu Brahmin. | Vakil, Member, Local A. V. School Committee, and in charge of the "Indian National Congress Hall," Ichalkaranji. | At a Public Meeting held at the "Indian National Congress Hall," Ichalkaranji, 20th December 1890. |
| 582 | " | Sholapore. | Sholapore | Mr. William Sprostan Caine. | English Christian. | Honorary Secretary, Anglo-Indian Temperance Association. | Public Meeting, Sholapore, 21st November, 1890. |
| 583 | " | " | Bijapur. | Rao Bahadoor S. R. Kirloskar, B.A. | Deccan Brahmin. | Vakil, Bombay High Court, Pleader, Sholapur, Bijapur District Court, and President, Sholapore Municipality. | do. and Public Meeting at Bijapur of 23rd December 1890. |
| 584 | Government of India. | Berar. | Berar Sarvajanik Sabha. | Mr. Ganesh Shrikrishna Khaparde, B.A., L.L.B. | Hindu Brahmin. | Pleader, High Court; Chairman, District Board and Malgujar in the Central Provinces. | At a Meeting of the General Committee of the Berar Sarvajanik Sabha, held on the 6th of December 1890. |
| 585 | " | " | " | Mr. Rangnath Narsinh Mudholkar, B A., L.L.B. | do. | Pleader, High Court; Municipal Commissioner and Honorary Secretary, Berar, Sarvajanik Sabha. | do. |
| 586 | " | " | Akola. | Mr. Vyankatesh Krishna Desai. | Mahratta Brahmin. | Pleader, Municipal Commissioner and Deshmukh of Jalwud in the Bijapur Collectorate. | At a Meeting of delegates at Akola on the 20th December, 1890. |
| 587 | " | " | " | Mr. Govind Vishvanath. | do. | Pleader, Municipal Commissioner, Deshpande, and Agriculturist. | At a Public Meeting held at Akola on the 13th December 1890. |
| 588 | " | " | " | Mr. Panachand Nathoosawat. | Gujarati Jain. | Banker and Agriculturist ... | do. |
| 589 | " | " | " | Mr. Gopaldas Naraindas. | Hindu Gajarati Vaishnau. | Merchant and Agriculturist... | do. |
| 590 | " | " | " | Rao Saheb Deorao Vinayck | Hindu Mahratta Brahmin. | Pleader, Banker, Municipal Commissioner, and Agriculturist. | do. |
| 591 | " | " | " | Mr. Popatlal Parasram. | Gujarati Jain. | Banker and Agriculturist ... | do. |

| Number. | Presidency or Government. | Congress Circle. | Electoral Division. | Names in full of Delegates, with Honorary Titles, Scholastic Degrees, etc. | Race, Religious denomination, and Caste, if any. | Occupation and Address. | How and when elected. |
|---|---|---|---|---|---|---|---|
| 592 | Government of India. | Berar. | Akola. | Mr. Vyankatesh Ramchandra Mudholkar. | Deccan Brahmin. | Editor, "Vaidarbha," and Municipal Member and Secretary. | At a Public Meeting held at Akola on the 13th December 1890. |
| 593 | " | " | Basim. | Mr. Lakshman Atmaram Mahajan. | Hindu Marhatta Brahmin. | Merchant, Mangrul Pir, Vice-Chairman, District and Taluq Board, Basim. | At a Public Meeting held at Basim on the 24th November 1890. |
| 594 | " | " | " | Mr. Shankar Govind ... | do. | Pleader and Municipal Commissioner, Akola. | do. |
| 595 | " | " | Wun. | Mr. Lakshman Chintaman Bapat. | Hindu Brahmin. | Pleader, Yeotmal ... | At a Public Meeting held at Yeotmal on the 3rd December 1890. |
| 596 | " | " | " | Mr. Sadasiv Moreshwar Deva. | do. | do. | do. |
| 597 | " | " | Amraoti. | Mr. Vishwanath Kashinath Kale. | do. | Pleader, Amraoti ... | At a Public Meeting held at Amraoti on the 7th December, 1890. |
| 598 | " | " | " | Mr. Govind Narayan Kane. | Christian. | do. | do. |
| 599 | " | " | Berar Agricultural Association. | Mr. Wasudeo Narayan Jog. | Hindu Brahmin. | Pleader ... ... | At a Meeting held at Amraoti of the Members of the Association on the 15th December 1890. |
| 600 | " | " | Ellichpur. | Mr. Ganesh Nagesh Sahasrabudhe. | Brahmin. | Pleader, High Court and Secretary, Native General Library. | At a Public Meeting held at Ellichpore on the 7th December 1890. |
| 601 | " | " | Buldana. | Gulam Ahmed Khan Soudagar. | Mahomedan. | Merchant and Landholder, Buldana. | At a Public Meeting held at Buldana on 24th November 1890. |
| 602 | Central Provinces. | Nagpur | Nagpur | Pundit Raghunath Rao, B.A. | Maharastra Brahmin. | Fellow and Junior Professor, Morris College, Nagpur. | At a Public Meeting held on the 30th November 1890. |
| 603 | " | " | do. | Professor Bhagiratha Prasada, B.A. | Hindu. | Professor of Mathematics, Hislop College; President, Young Men's Association; Municipal Commissioner; Secretary and Treasurer, Abstinence Association, and Member, Loka Sabha, Nagpur. | do. |
| 604 | " | " | do. | Mr. Cottari Vyankat Ramanna Nayadu. | Hindu Kshatrya. | Barrister-at-Law, Nagpur ... | do. |
| 605 | " | " | do. | Mr. Govardhan Bapoo ... | Brahmin. | Zemindar, Bhandara ... | do. |
| 606 | " | " | Jubbulpur | Mr. Ram Gopal Misra ... | do. | Merchant, Jubbulpur ... | At a Public Meeting, December 6th, 1890. |
| 607 | " | " | do. | Mr. Alfred Nundy .. | Christian. | Barrister-at-Law, Municipal Commissioner, Jubbulpore. | do. |
| 608 | " | " | Wardha. | Mr. Vasudev Vinayek Paranjpe. | Hindu Brahmin. | Pleader, Secretary, District Council, and Vice-President, Municipality, Wardha. | At a Public Meeting held at Wardha on the 10th December 1890. |
| 609 | " | " | do. | Mr. Laxman Govind Deoskar. | do. | Pleader and Member, District Council, Wardha. | do. |
| 610 | " | " | Saugor. | Babu Tara Prasanna Sen, B.A., B.L. | Hindu Vaidya. | Vakil, High Court, Calcutta, and Advocate, Central Provinces. | At a Public Meeting of the Saugor Hitsabha Association, 30th November 1890. |
| 611 | Madras. | Madras. | Madras. | Rai P. Ananda Charlu, Bahadur, B.L. | Hindu Brahmin. | Vakil, High Court, Madras ... | Public Meeting at Madras, dated 8th December 1890. |
| 612 | " | " | " | Mr. M. Vencata Row ... | do. | Landowner ... ... | do. |
| 613 | " | " | " | Mr. K. P. Viswanadha Iyer, B.A., B.L. | do. | Vakil, High Court, Madras ... | do. |
| 614 | " | " | " | Mr. M. Ramaswamy Naidu | Hindu Sudra. | Timber Merchant, Madras ... | do. |
| 615 | " | " | " | Mr. C. Krishnaswamy Pillay | Hindu. | Contractor, Madras ... | do. |
| 616 | " | " | " | Mr. C. V. Sundara Shastri, B.A., B.L. | Hindu Brahmin. | Vakil, High Court, Madras ... | do. |
| 617 | " | " | " | Mr. S. Viraraghava Chariar. | do. | Merchant, Triplicane ... | do. |
| 618 | " | " | " | Mr. S. Raghava Chariar ... | do. | Merchant, Madras ... | do. |
| 619 | " | " | " | Mr. R. Ananda Row ... | do. | Pleader, Madras ... ... | do. |
| 620 | " | " | " | Mr. M. Viraraghava Chariar | do. | Joint Editor, "Hindu," Madras | do. |
| 621 | " | " | " | Mr. V. Sarangapani, Iyengar, B.A., B.L. | do. | Mylapur, Madras ... | do. |
| 622 | " | " | " | Mr. C. R. Thiruvenkatachariar, B.L. | do. | Mirasdar, Madras ... | do. |
| 623 | " | " | " | Mr. V. C. Seshachariar, B.A., B.L. | do. | Vakil, High Court, Madras ... | do. |
| 624 | " | " | " | Mr. V. C. Desikachariar, B.L. | do. | do. ... | do. |

| Number. | Presidency or Government. | Congress Circle. | Electoral Division. | Names in full of Delegates, With Honorary Titles, Scholastic Degrees, etc. | Race, Religious denomination, and Caste, if any. | Occupation and Address. | How and when elected. |
|---|---|---|---|---|---|---|---|
| 625 | Madras. | Madras. | Madras. | Mr. M. Venugopaul Pillai | Hindu. | Lawndowner, Royapettah, Madras. | Public Meeting at Madras, dated 8th December 1890. |
| 626 | „ | „ | „ | Mr. K. Ethiraja Pillai avel | do. | Contractor, Madras ... | do. |
| 627 | „ | „ | „ | Mr. C. V. Viswanadha Sastri, B.A. | Brahmin. | Vakil's Assistant, Sondayarpet, Madras. | do. |
| 628 | „ | „ | Madura. | Mr. M. S. Sankara Iyer | do. | Head-master, Zemindary High School, Sivaganga. | Public Meeting at Paramagudi, dated 30th November 1890. |
| 629 | „ | „ | „ | Mr. J. M. Nala Sawmy Pillay, B.A., B.L. | do. | Vakil, High Court, practising at Madura. | do. |
| 630 | „ | „ | „ | Mr. T. Ponnambala Mudaliar. | Hindu. | Landowner, Madura ... | do. |
| 631 | „ | „ | „ | Mr. M. Thirumalai Mudaliar. | do. | do. ... | do. |
| 632 | „ | „ | „ | Mr. V. Kamakshiappa Mudaliar. | do. | do. ... | do. |
| 633 | „ | „ | „ | Mr. P. N. Muthuswami Iyer. | Hindu Brahmin. | Vakil, High Court, Madura ... | do. |
| 634 | „ | „ | „ | Mr. P. Sankara Subba ... | do. | First Grade Pleader ... | do. |
| 635 | „ | „ | Tinnevelly. | Mr. S. Desikachariar ... | do. | First Grade Pleader ... | Elected at a Public Meeting held on the 3rd December 1890. |
| 636 | „ | „ | „ | Mr. R. M. Chedambaram Iyer. | do. | 2nd Grade Pleader ... | do. |
| 637 | „ | „ | Cocanada, Godavery District. | Mr. R. L. Maitra, M.A. | Bengali Christian. | Principal, Petapur Rajah's College. | At a Public Meeting of the townsmen of Cocanada, held on the 14th December 1890. |
| 638 | „ | „ | Kistna District. | Mr. M. Parankusam Pillai Garu. | Sudra. | Merchant, Contractor, and Landed Proprietor, Bezwada. | At a Public Meeting in the Rajah Kand Varu's Hall on the 3rd December 1890. |
| 639 | „ | „ | „ | Mr. M. Lakshmi Narashimha Chariar. | Hindu Brahmin. | Pleader, District Moonsiff's Court, Bezwada. | do. |
| 640 | „ | „ | „ | Mr. M. Ethiraja Pillay ... | do. | Merchant, Municipal Councillor, Bezvada. | do. |
| 641 | „ | „ | Kunnakudy, Madura District. | Mr. P. K. A. Komarappa Chettyar, F.T.S. | Hindu. | Proprietor, Pana Kuna, Anamoney Trading Company, Rayapuram, P. N. S. and Secretary General Natukotai Chetty's Association. | Elected on the 25th November 1890, by a Public Meeting of General Natukotai Chetty's Association. |
| 642 | „ | „ | Calicut. | Mr. V. Krishnaswami Iyer, B.A., B.L. | Hindu Brahmin. | Vakil, High Court ... | By a public meeting at Calicut. |
| 643 | „ | „ | „ | Mr. P. R. Sundarm Aiyer, B.L. | do. | Vakil, High Court ... | do. |
| 644 | „ | „ | „ | Mr. Baskaven Pitchu Pattas | do. | Merchant, Calicut ... | do. |
| 645 | „ | „ | Cuddapah | Rai Bahadur C. Jambulinga Mudaliar, B.A., M.L. | | Vakil, High Court ... | Public Meeting held at Cuddapah, dated 5th December 1890. |
| 646 | „ | „ | Tanjore. | Mr. P. Ratnasabapathi Pillay. | Hindu | Landholder, Pleader, Chairman Municipal Council, Negapatam. | By a Public Meeting at Negapatam and Meeting of Tanjore People's Association held 14th December 1890. |
| 647 | „ | „ | Vizagapatam. | Mr. O. V. Jaganadha Sastri | Hindu Brahmin. | Pleader, Parvatipur ... | By a Public Meeting on the 29th November 1890. |
| 648 | „ | „ | Woriur. | Mr. S. Madura Nayagam Pillay. | Hindu | Cigar Merchant ... | By a Public Meeting. |
| 649 | „ | „ | „ | Mr. N. Sawminatho Pillay. | do. | do. | do. |
| 650 | „ | „ | Trichinopoly. | Mr. V. Srinivasa Iyer ... | Hindu Brahmin. | Professor, S.P.G. College, Trichinopoly. | do. |
| 651 | „ | „ | Coimbatore. | Mr. Kasturi Ranga Iyengar, B.A., B.L. | do. | Vakil, High Court ... | By a Public Meeting on the 30th November 1890. |
| 652 | „ | „ | Gooty. | Mr. K. Subba Row ... | do. | Sub-Editor, "Hindu" ... | By a Public Metting held at Gooty on the 11th November 1890. |
| 653 | „ | „ | Kurnool. | Rao Saheb T. Chidambara Row, B.A. | Hindu Brahmin | First Grade Pleader and Landholder, Municipal Councillor, Kurnaul. | At a Public Meeting held at Kurnool for the election of Delegates on the 7th of December 1890. |
| 654 | „ | „ | „ | B. Konari Row ... | do. | Second Grade Pleader, Nandyal, Member, Taluq Board Nandyal. | do. |

| Number. | Presidency or Government. | Congress Circle. | Electoral Division. | Names in full of Delegates, with Honorary Titles, Scholastic Degrees, etc. | Race, Religious denomination, and Caste, if any. | Occupation and Address. | How and when elected. |
|---|---|---|---|---|---|---|---|
| 655 | Madras | Madras | Kurnool. | Mr. Paramanchala Pocha Nagi-Reddy. | Hindu | Landholder, Parmanchala Nandikothur Taluq. | At a Public Meeting, held at Markapur on Sunday, 14th December 1890. |
| 656 | " | " | Palghat. | Mr. V. Parameswara Iyer | Hindu Brahmin. | Editor, "Palghat Times" ... | By a Public Meeting, 10th December 1890. |
| 657 | " | " | Raja-mundry | Mr. T. S. Muthuswamy Sastri. | Hindu Brahmin. | Professor, Rajamundry ... | Public Meeting on the 14th December 1890. |
| 658 | " | " | Nellore. | Mr. S. Kuppusawmy Sarma, B.A., B.L. | do. | Vakil, High Court, Nellore ... | By a Public Meeting at Nellore. |
| 659 | " | " | Vizianagram. | Mr. V. Madhava Row Naidu, M.A. | Hindu | Professor, Maharajah's College, Vizianagram. | Public Meeting, 9th December. |
| 660 | " | " | " | Mr. Rao Saheb Venkanna Pantulu. | Hindu Brahmin. | Pleader, Member, Municipal Council & District Board. | do. |
| 661 | " | " | " | Mr. N. V. Chellapati Sastri | do. | Assistant Master, Maharajah's College, Vizianagram, Secretary, Local Mohyen Sabha, &c. | do. |
| 662 | " | " | Salem. | Mr. C. Vijiaraghava Chariar, B.A. | Hindu Brahmin. | Pleader, Salem ... | Public Meeting at Salem. |
| 663 | " | " | " | Mr. C. Venkatachariar ... | do. | Landholder, Member, District Board. | do. |
| 664 | " | " | " | Mr. B. Krishna Row, B.A., B.L. | do. | District Court Pleader ... | do. |
| 665 | " | " | North Arcot. | Mr. K. R. Mudaliar ... | Behauni Kayestha. | Landholder and Contractor... | By a Public Meeting at Chittoor. |
| 666 | " | " | S. Arcot. | Mr. J. P. Cotilingam, M.A. | Christian. | Principal, Cuddalore College. | 9th December at a Public Meeting. |
| 667 | " | " | Mahjana Sabha. | Mr. Ahmed Abdul Rahiman Saib. | Mahomedan. | Merchant and Landowner ... | Elected by the Mahajana Sabha. |
| 668 | Govt. of India. | " | Secundrabad. | Manchersha Nasharwanjee Gheista. | Parsee. | Dental Surgeon ... | By a Public Meeting presided over by Charkanda Rungiah Sowcar in December 1890. |
| 669 | " | " | " | Bezonji Adirji ... | do. | Pleader, James Street, Secunderabad. | do. |

*Failed to deposit Certificates.*

| Number. | Presidency or Government. | Congress Circle. | Electoral Division. | Names | Race, etc. | Occupation and Address. | How and when elected. |
|---|---|---|---|---|---|---|---|
| 670 | Bengal. | Calcutta. | ... | Mr. R. D. Mehta ... | Parsee. | Merchant. | |
| 671 | " | " | ... | Babu Norendro Nath Sen | Hindu. | Journalist and Attorney. | |
| 672 | " | " | ... | Nawab Goulam Rubbani | Mahomedan. | Private Gentleman. | |
| 673 | " | " | National Chamber of Commerce. | Babu Sitanath Roy, B.A., B.L. | Hindu. | Merchant, Banker; Secretary, B. N. Chamber of Commerce; Port Commissioner. | By the Chamber Executive Committee Meeting, 1st December 1890. |
| 674 | Madras | Madras | Salem | Noon Jappa Iyer ... | Brahmin. | Landholder ... | Public Meeting at Salem. |
| 675 | N. W. P. | Ahahabad. | Alahabad | Syed Mahommed Saki ... | Mahomedan Sunni. | Zemindar ... | At a Public Meeting held at Kara on 22nd December 1890. |
| 676 | Bengal | Calcutta | The N. M. Electoral Division. | Mr. T. Palit ... | Hindu Kayestha | Barrister-at-Law, Ballygunge Circular Road. | At the Public Meeting, Calcutta Town Hall, 23rd December 1890. |
| 677 | " | " | " | Honorable Dr. Mahendralal Sarcar, M.D. | Hindu. | Member, Bengal Legislative Council; Honorary Presidency Magistrate, Municipal Commissioner, Secretary, Science Association and Medical Practitioner, 54, Sankaritollah, Calcutta. | do. |

[*Unfortunately the names of several Gentlemen, who attended the Congress as Delegates, have been omitted from the above list, partly in consequence of their failure to file their election certificates and partly in consequence of some certificates having been, it is feared, mislaid. This report cannot now be delayed to supply these omissions, and those whose names have been thus omitted, will kindly accept this explanation.*]

# APPENDIX II.

# SUMMARY OF RESOLUTIONS

PASSED AT THE

# FIRST, SECOND, THIRD, FOURTH AND FIFTH CONGRESSES.

## RESOLUTIONS PASSED AT THE FIRST CONGRESS.

### RESOLUTION I.

**Resolved**—That this Congress earnestly recommends that the promised inquiry into the working of the Indian Administration, here and in England, should be entrusted to a Royal Commission, the people of India being adequately represented thereon, and evidence taken both in India and in England.

### RESOLUTION II.

**Resolved**—That this Congress considers the abolition of the Council of the Secretary of State for India, as at present constituted, the necessary preliminary to all other reforms.

### RESOLUTION III.

**Resolved**—That this Congress considers the reform and expansion of the Supreme and existing Local Legislative Councils, by the admission of a considerable proportion of elected members (and the creation of similar Councils for the North-Western Provinces and Oudh and also for the Punjab) essential; and holds that all Budgets should be referred to these Councils for consideration, their members being moreover empowered to interpellate the Executive in regard to all branches of the administration; and that a Standing Committee of the House of Commons should be constituted to receive and consider any formal protests that may be recorded by majorities of such Councils against the exercise by the Executive of the power which would be vested in it, of overruling the decisions of such majorities.

### RESOLUTION IV.

**Resolved**—That in the opinion of this Congress the competitive examinations now held in England for first appointments in various civil departments of the public service should henceforth, in accordance with the views of the India Office Committee of 1860, "be held simultaneously, one in England and one in India, both being as far as practicable identical in their nature, and those who compete in both countries being finally classified in one list according to merit," and that the successful candidates in India should be sent to England for further study, and subjected there to such further examinations as may seem needful. Further, that all other first appointments (excluding peonships, and the like) should be filled by competitive examinations held in India, under conditions calculated to secure such intellectual, moral, and physical qualifications as may be decided by Government to be necessary. Lastly, that the maximum age of candidates for entrance into the Covenanted Civil Service be raised to not less than 23 years.

### RESOLUTION V.

**Resolved**—That in the opinion of this Congress the proposed increase in the military expenditure of the empire is unnecessary, and, regard being had to the revenues of the empire and the existing circumstances of the country, excessive.

### RESOLUTION VI.

**Resolved**—That in the opinion of this Congress, if the increased demands for military expenditure are not to be, as they ought to be, met by retrenchment, they ought to be met, firstly, by the re-imposition of the Customs duties ; and, secondly, by the extension of the license-tax to those classes of the community, official and non-official, at present exempted from it, care being taken that in the case of all classes a sufficiently high taxable minimum be maintained. And, further, that this Congress is of opinion that Great Britain should extend an imperial guarantee to the Indian debt.

### RESOLUTION VII.

**Resolved**—That this Congress deprecates the annexation of Upper Burmah, and considers that if the Government unfortunately decide on annexation, the entire country of Burmah should be separated from the Indian Viceroyalty and constituted a Crown Colony, as distinct in all matters from the Government of the country as is Ceylon.

### RESOLUTION VIII.

**Resolved**—That the resolutions passed by this Congress be communicated to the Political Associations in each province, and that these Associations be requested, with the help of similar bodies and other agencies within their respective provinces, to adopt such measures as they may consider calculated to advance the settlement of the various questions dealt with in these resolutions.

### RESOLUTION IX.

**Resolved**—That the Indian National Congress re-assemble next year in Calcutta and sit on Tuesday, the 28th of December, 1886, and the next succeeding days.

---

## RESOLUTIONS PASSED AT THE SECOND CONGRESS.

---

### RESOLUTION I.

**Resolved**—That this Congress of Delegates from all parts of India do humbly offer its dutiful and loyal congratulations to Her Most Gracious Majesty, the Queen-Empress, on the approaching completion of the first half century of her memorable, beneficent and glorious reign, and heartily wish her many, many more, and happy years of rule over the great British Empire.

### RESOLUTION II.

**Resolved**—That this Congress regards with the deepest sympathy, and views with grave apprehension, the increasing poverty of vast numbers of the population of India, and (although aware that the Government is not overlooking this matter and is contemplating certain palliatives) desires to record its fixed conviction that the introduction of Representative Institutions will prove one of the most important practical steps towards the amelioration of the condition of the people.

### RESOLUTION III.

**Resolved**—That this Congress do, emphatically, re-affirm the 3rd Resolution of the Congress of 1885, and distinctly declare its belief that the reform and expansion of the Council of the Governor-General for making laws and of the Provincial Legislative Councils, therein suggested, have now become essential alike in the interests of India and England.

### RESOLUTION IV.

**Resolved**—That this Congress is of opinion that, in giving practical effect to this essential reform, regard should be had (subject to such modifications as, on a more detailed examination of the question, may commend themselves to the Government) to the principles embodied in the following tentative suggestions :—

(1.)—The number of persons composing the Legislative Councils, both provincial and of the Governor-General, to be materially increased. Not less than one-half the Members of such enlarged Councils to be elected. Not more than one-fourth to be officials having seats *ex-officio* in such Councils, and not more than one-fourth to be Members, official or non-official, nominated by Government.

(2.)—The right to elect Members to the Provincial Councils to be conferred only on those classes and members of the community, *primâ facie*, capable of exercising it wisely and independently. In Bengal and Bombay the Councillors may be elected by the Members of Municipalities, District Boards, Chambers of Commerce and the Universities, or an electorate may be constituted of all persons possessing such qualifications, educational and pecuniary, as may be deemed necessary. In Madras the Councillors may be elected either by District Boards, Municipalities, Chambers of Commerce, and the University, or by Electoral Colleges composed of Members partly elected by these bodies and partly nominated by Government. In the North-West Provinces and Oudh and in the Punjab Councillors may be elected by an Electoral College composed of Members elected by Municipal and District Boards, and nominated, to an extent not exceeding one-sixth of the total number, by Government, it being understood that the same elective system now in force where Municipal Boards are concerned will be applied to District Boards and the right of electing Members to these latter extended to the cultivating class. But whatever system be adopted (and the details must be worked out separately for each province) care must be taken that all sections of the community and all great interests are adequately represented.

(3.)—The elected Members of the Council of the Governor-General for making laws to be elected by the elected Members of the several Provincial Councils.

(4.)—No elected or nominated Member of any Council to receive any salary or remuneration in virtue of such Membership, but any such Member, already in receipt of any Government salary or allowance, to continue to draw the same unchanged during Membership, and all Members to be entitled to be reimbursed any expenses incurred in travelling in connection with their Membership.

(5.)—All persons, resident in India, to be eligible for seats in Council, whether as electees or nominees, without distinction of race, creed, caste or colour.

(6.)—All legislative measures and all financial questions, including all budgets whether these involve new or enhanced taxation or not, to be necessarily submitted to and dealt with by these Councils. In the case of all other branches of the administration, any Member to be at liberty, after due notice, to put any question he sees fit to the *ex-officio* Members (or such one of these as may be specially charged with the supervision of the particular branch concerned) and to be entitled (except as hereinafter provided) to receive a reply to his question together with copies of any papers requisite for the thorough comprehension of the subject, and on this reply the Council to be at liberty to consider and discuss the question, and record thereon such resolution as may appear fitting to the majority. Provided that, if the subject in regard to which the inquiry is made involves matters of Foreign policy, Military dispositions or strategy, or is otherwise of such a nature that, in the opinion of the Executive, the public interests would be materially imperilled by the communication of the information asked for, it shall be competent for them to instruct the *ex-officio* Members, or one of them, to reply accordingly, and decline to furnish the information asked for.

(7)—The Executive Government shall possess the power of overruling the decision arrived at by the majority of the Council, in every case in which, in its opinion, the public interests would suffer by the acceptance of such decision; but whenever this power is exercised a full exposition of the grounds on which this has been considered necessary, shall be published within one month, and in the case of local Governments they shall report the circumstances and explain their action to the Government of India, and, in the case of this latter, it shall report and explain to the Secretary of State; and in any such case on a representation made through the Government of India and the Secretary of State by the overruled majority, it shall be competent to the Standing Committee of the House of Commons (recommended in the 3rd Resolution of last year's Congress which this present Congress has affirmed) to consider the matter, and call for any and all papers or information, and hear any persons on behalf of such majority or otherwise, and thereafter, if needful, report thereon to the full House.

## RESOLUTION V.

**Resolved**—That this Congress do invite all Public Bodies and all Associations throughout the Country, humbly and earnestly, to entreat His Excellency the Viceroy to obtain the sanction of Her Majesty's Secretary of State for India, to the appointment of a Commission, to enquire exhaustively into the best method of introducing such a tentative form of Representative Institutions into India, as has been indicated in Resolutions III. of the past, and IV. of the present year's Congress.

## RESOLUTION VI.

**Resolved**—That a Committee composed of the gentlemen named in the margin* be appointed to consider the Public Service Question and report thereon to this Congress.

* Hon'ble Dadabhai Naoroji (*Bombay*).
" S. Subramania Iyer (*Madras*).
" Peary Mohun Mookerjee (*Calcutta*).
Mr. G. Subramania Iyer (*Madras*).
Babu Motilal Ghose (*Calcutta*).
Mr. Surendra Nath Bannerjee (*Calcutta*).
" Gungapershad Varma (*Lucknow*).
" Ramkali Chaudhuri (*Benares*).
Mr. Guru Prasad Sen (*Patna.*)
Pundit Prannath (*Lucknow*).
Munshi Kashipershad (*Allahabad*)
Nawab Reza Ali Khan (*Lucknow.*)
Mr. Hamid Ali (*Lucknow*).
Lala Kanhyalal (*Amritsar*).
Rao Sahib Gungadhar Rao Madhaw Chitnavis (*Nagpur*).
Mr. Rahimatulla M. Sayani (*Bombay*).

## RESOLUTION VII.

**Resolved**—That this Congress approves and adopts the report * submitted by the Committee appointed by Resolution VI.

---

### * REPORT.

We, the Members of the Committee appointed by the Congress to submit a statement in connection with the Public Service Question, have the honor to report that the following resolutions were unanimously adopted by us at a meeting held yesterday :—

1.—That the open Competitive Examination be held simultaneously both in India and in England.

2.—That the simultaneous Examinations thus held be equally open to all classes of Her Majesty's subjects.

3.—That the classified lists be prepared according to merit.

4.—That the Congress express the hope that the Civil Service Commissioners will give fair consideration to Sanskrit and Arabic among the subjects of examination.

5.—That the age of candidates eligible for admission to the open Competitive Examination be not less than 19, nor, as recommended by Sir C. Aitchison, more than 23 years.

6.—That simultaneous examinations being granted, the Statutory Civil Service be closed for first appointments.

7.—That the appointments in the Statutory Civil Service, under the existing rules, be still left open to the Members of the Uncovenanted Service and to professional men of proved merit and ability.

8.—That all appointments requiring educational qualifications, other than covenanted first appointments, be filled by Competitive Examinations held in the different Provinces, and open in each Province to such natural-born subjects of H. M. only as are residents thereof.

These Resolutions, it is hoped, cover the main principles which underlie the questions set by the Public Service Commission. For a more detailed consideration there was no time.

(Sd.) DADABHAI NAOROJI,
*President of the Committee.*

*30th December, 1886.*

### RESOLUTION VIII.

**Resolved**—That, in the opinion of this Congress, the time has now arrived when the system of trial by jury may be safely extended into many parts of the country where it is not at present in force.

### RESOLUTION IX.

**Resolved**—That, in the opinion of this Congress, the innovation made in 1872 in the system of trial by jury, depriving the verdicts of juries of all finality, has proved injurious to the country, and that the powers then, for the first time, vested in Sessions Judges and High Courts, of setting aside verdicts of acquittal, should be at once withdrawn.

### RESOLUTION X.

**Resolved**—That, in the opinion of this Congress, a provision, similar to that contained in the Summary Jurisdiction Act of England (under which accused persons in serious cases have the option of demanding a committal to the Sessions Court), should be introduced into the Indian Code of Criminal Procedure, enabling accused persons, in warrant cases, to demand that, instead of being tried by the Magistrate, they be committed to the Court of Sessions.

### RESOLUTION XI.

**Resolved**—That this Congress do place on record an expression of the universal conviction that a complete separation of executive and judicial functions (such that in no case the two functions shall be combined in the same officer) has become an urgent necessity, and that, in its opinion, it behoves the Government to effect this separation without further delay, even though this should, in some Provinces, involve some extra expenditure.

### RESOLUTION XII.

**Resolved**—That, in view of the unsettled state of public affairs in Europe, and the immense assistance that the people of this country, if duly prepared therefor, is capable of rendering to Great Britain in the event of any serious complications arising, this Congress do earnestly appeal to the Government to authorise (under such rules and restrictions as may to it seem fitting) a system of Volunteering for the Indian inhabitants of the country, such as may qualify them to support the Government effectively in any crisis.

### RESOLUTION XIII.

**Resolved**—That Standing Congress Committees be constituted at all important centres.

### RESOLUTION XIV.

**Resolved**—That the Third Indian National Congress assemble at Madras on the 27th of December, 1887.

### RESOLUTION XV.

**Resolved**—That copies of these Resolutions be forwarded to His Excellency the Viceroy-in-Council, with the humble requests that he will cause the 1st Resolution to be submitted in due course to Her Majesty the Queen-Empress, that he will cause all the Resolutions to be laid before Her Majesty's Secretary of State for India, and that he himself will be graciously pleased, in consultation with his colleagues, to accord them his best consideration.

---

## RESOLUTIONS PASSED AT THE THIRD CONGRESS.

---

### RESOLUTION I.

**Resolved**—That a Committee is appointed, consisting of the gentlemen (marginally enumerated*), to consider what rules, if any, may now be usefully framed in regard to the constitution and working of the Congress, with instructions to report thereon to the Congress, on the 30th instant.

* Messrs. Namjoshi Chandavaker, Mir Humayun Jah Bahadur, Hajee Mahomed Abdul Shakoor Badshaw Sahib, S. Subramania Iyer, W. S. Gantz, Rangiah Naidu, Surendranath Bannerjee, Trailokhyanath Mitra, Kali Charan Bannerjee, Guru Prasad Sen, Saligram Singh, Ram Kali Chaudhuri, Hafiz Abdul Rahim, Rampal Singh, Pandit Madan Mohun, Ganga Prasad-Varma, Bishan Narayen Dar, Hamid Ali, Murlidhur, Satyanand Agnihotri, H. H. Dhruva, W. C. Bonnerjee, Norendranath Sen, Eardley Norton, Joy Govind Shome, Iswari Lal Sircar, G. Subramania Iyer, D. A. Khare, S. A. Saminada Iyer, Sabapathy Mudaliar, A. O. Hume, C. Vigiya Raghava Chariar, Govind Buksh, Karandikar.

## RESOLUTION II.

**Resolved**—That this Congress re-affirms the necessity for the expansion and reform of the Council of the Governor-General for making Laws, and the Provincial Legislative Councils, already set forth in Resolutions III. of the Congress of 1885 and 1886, and expresses the earnest hope that the Government will no longer delay action in the direction of this essential reform.

## RESOLUTION III.

**Resolved**—That this Congress once again places on record an expression of the universa conviction that a complete separation of the Executive and Judicial functions (such that in no case the two functions shall be combined in the same officer) has become an urgent necessity, and declares that, in its opinion, it behoves the Government to effect this separation, without further delay, even though this should, in some Provinces, involve some extra expenditure.

## RESOLUTION IV.

**Resolved**—That in view of the loyalty of Her Majesty's Indian subjects, this Congress considers it desirable that the Queen's Proclamation should be given effect to ; that the Military Service in its higher grades should be practically opened to the natives of this country ; and that the Government of India should establish Military Colleges in this country, whereat the natives of India, as defined by Statute, may be educated and trained for a military career as officers of the Indian Army.

## RESOLUTION V.

**Resolved**—That, in view of the unsettled state of public affairs in Europe, and the immense assistance that the people of this country, if duly prepared therefor, are capable of rendering to Great Britain in the event of any serious complications arising, this Congress once again earnestly appeals to the Government to authorize (under such rules and restrictions as may to it seem fitting,) a system of Volunteering for the Indian inhabitants of the country, such as may qualify them to support the Government, effectively, in any crisis.

## RESOLUTION VI.

**Resolved**—That, as the administration of the Income-Tax, especially as regards incomes below Rs. 1,000, has proved extremely unsatisfactory, it is essential, in the opinion of the Congress, that the taxable minimum be raised to Rs. 1,000, the loss of revenue thus involved being made good, and further financial difficulties, if any, met, by reductions in the existing public expenditure, or, should this prove impossible, by the re-imposition of an import duty on the finer classes of cotton goods.

## RESOLUTION VII.

**Resolved**—That, having regard to the poverty of the people, it is desirable that the Government be moved to elaborate a system of Technical Education, suitable to the condition of the country, to encourage indigenous manufactures by a more strict observance of the orders, already existing, in regard to utilizing such manufactures for State purposes, and to employ more extensively, than at present, the skill and talents of the people of the country,

## RESOLUTION VIII.

**Resolved**—That, in view of the loyalty of the people, the hardships which the present Arms' Act (XI of 1878) causes, and the unmerited slur which it casts upon the people of this country, the Government be moved so to modify the provisions of Chapter IV., and, if necessary, other portions of the said Act, as shall enable all persons to possess and wear arms, unless debarred therefrom, either as individuals or members of particular communities or classes, by the orders of the Government of India (or any local authority empowered by the Government of India on that behalf) for reasons to be recorded in writing and duly published.

## RESOLUTION IX.

**Resolved**—That the rules drafted by the Committee appointed under Resolution I. stand over for consideration till next Congress, but that, in the meantime, copies be circulated to all Standing Congress Committees, with the request that they will, during the coming year, act in accordance with these rules, so far as this may seem to them possible and desirable, and report thereon to the next Congress, with such further suggestions as to them may seem meet.

### RESOLUTION X.

**Resolved**—That the Fourth Indian National Congress assemble at Allahabad on the 26th December, 1888.

### RESOLUTION XI.

**Resolved**—That copies of these Resolutions be forwarded to His Excellency the Viceroy-in-Council, with the humble request that he will cause all the Resolutions to be laid before Her Majesty's Secretary of State for India, and that he himself will be graciously pleased, in consultation with his colleagues, to accord them his best consideration.

---

## RESOLUTIONS PASSED AT THE FOURTH CONGRESS.

---

### RESOLUTION I.

**Resolved**—That this Congress affirms the necessity for the expansion and reform of the Council of the Governor-General for making laws and regulations, and of the existing Provincial Legislative Councils, already set forth in Resolutions III. of the Congress of 1885 and 1886, and Resolution II. of the Congress of 1887 (a tentative scheme for which expansion and reform was suggested in Resolution IV. of the Congress of 1886); and further urges that a Legislative Council (of the same character as those which have been suggested for Provinces where Legislative Councils already exist) be established for the Punjab.

### RESOLUTION II.

**Resolved**—That this Congress, while appreciating the concessions proposed in the Report of the Public Service Commission, yet feels it necessary to put distinctly on record its opinion that full justice will never be done to the people of this country until the open competitive examination for the Civil Service of India is held simultaneously in England and in India.

### RESOLUTION III.

**Resolved**—That this Congress, having read and considered Resolution XI. of the Congress of 1886, to wit—

> "That this Congress do place on record an expression of the universal conviction that a complete separation of executive and judicial functions (such that in no case the two functions shall be combined in the same officer) has become an urgent necessity; and that, in its opinion, it behoves the Government to effect this separation without further delay, even though this should, in some provinces, involve some extra expenditure"—

and Resolution III. of the Congress of 1887, to the same effect, does now, hereby, affirm the same respectively.

### RESOLUTION IV.

**Resolved**—That this Congress, having read and considered Resolution VIII. of the Congress of 1886, to wit—

> "That, in the opinion of this Congress, the time has now arrived when the system of trial by jury may be safely extended into many parts of the country where it is not at present in force"—

Resolution IX. of the Congress of 1886, to wit—

> "That, in the opinion of this Congress, the innovation made in 1872 in the system of trial by jury, depriving the verdicts of juries of all finality, has proved injurious to the country, and the powers then for the first time vested in Sessions Judges and High Courts of setting aside verdicts of acquittal should be at once withdrawn"—

and Resolution X. of the Congress of 1886, to wit—

> "That, in the opinion of this Congress, a provision similar to that contained in the Summary Jurisdiction Act of England (under which accused persons in serious cases have the option of demanding a committal to the Sessions Court) should be introduced into the Indian Code of Criminal Procedure, enabling accused persons, in warrant cases, to demand that, instead of being tried by the Magistrate, they be committed to the Court of Sessions"—

does now, hereby, affirm the same respectively.

### RESOLUTION V.

**Resolved**—That, as it is the general belief of the people of this country that the existing system of police administration in India is highly unsatisfactory in itself and oppressive to them, the Government be respectfully urged to appoint a commission, consisting of official and non-official members, to investigate the entire question as speedily as possible.

## RESOLUTION VI.

**Resolved**—That this Congress having read and considered Resolution IV. o the Congress of 1887, to wit—

"That in view of the loyalty of Her Majesty's Indian subjects, the Congress considers it desirable that the "Queen's Proclamation should be given effect to; that the Military services in the higher grades should "be practically opened to the natives of this country; and that the Government should establish Military "Colleges in the country whereat the natives of India, as defined by Statute, may be educated and "trained for a Military career as officers of the Indian Army;"

Resolution XII. of the Congress of 1886, and Resolution V. of the Congress of 1887, to wit—

'That in view of the unsettled state of public affairs in Europe, and the immense assistance that the "people of this country, if duly prepared therefor, are capable of rendering to Great Britain in the "event of any serious complications arising, the Congress once again earnestly appeals to the Govern- "ment to authorize (under such rules and restrictions as to it may seem fitting) a system of "Volunteering for the Indian inhabitants of the country, such as may qualify them to support the "Government effectually in any crisis;"

and Resolution VIII. of the Congress of 1887, to wit—

"That in view of the loyalty of the people, the hardships which the present Arms Act (XI of 1878) causes, "and the unmerited slur which it casts upon the people of this country, the Government be moved "so to modify the provisions of Chapter IV., and, if necessary, other portions of the said Act, as shall "enable all persons to possess and wear Arms unless debarred therefrom, either as individuals, or "members of particular communities or classes, by the orders of the Government of India, (or any "local authority empowered by the Government of India on that behalf), for reasons to be recorded "in writing and duly published;"

does now, hereby, affirm the same respectively.

## RESOLUTION VII.

**Resolved**—That, having regard to the fact that a serious increase in the consumption of intoxicants has taken place under the systems of Abkari and Excise now prevailing in India, the Government be respectfully urged to adopt some such improved system as shall tend to discourage insobriety.

## RESOLUTION VIII.

**Resolved**—That, as the administration of the Income-Tax, especially as regards incomes below Rs. 1,000, has proved extremely unsatisfactory, it is essential, in the opinion of the Congress, that the taxable minimum be raised to Rs. 1,000.

## RESOLUTION. IX.

**Resolved**—That this Congress being of opinion that it is the first duty of the British Government in India to foster and encourage education, as well general as technical, in all its branches, and that the declaration made in the recent resolution of the Government of India on the subject of education is calculated to encourage the tendency to reduce imperial expenditure on education, and to withdraw from the control of it, respectfully urges upon Government the extreme importance of increasing, or at any rate of not decreasing, the present expenditure on education, and of the Government continuing to control the Educational Institutions of all kinds now existing.

## RESOLUTION X.

**Resolved**—That, having regard to the poverty of the people, the importance of encouraging indigenous manufactures, and the difficulty of practically introducing any general system of technical education with the present imperfect information, Government be moved to delay no longer the appointment of a mixed commission, to enquire into the present industrial condition of the country.

## RESOLUTION XI.

**Resolved**—That the foregoing Resolutions be submitted for the favourable consideration of His Excellency the Viceroy, and for transmission by him to Her Majesty's Government, with the humble request of this Congress that the reforms suggested in the said Resolutions (based as most of these are on Her Gracious Majesty's Proclamation of 1858) may now be effected; and that should it be deemed necessary first to institute any enquiry into any of the matters forming the subjects of these Resolutions, such enquiry may be made, as speedily as possible, by a Parliamentary Committee.

## RESOLUTION XII.

**Resolved**—That this Congress, having watched with interest and sympathy the exertions that are being made in England for the total abrogation of laws and rules relating to the regulation of prostitution by the State in India, places on record its appreciation of the services thus rendered to this country, and its desire to co-operate by all means in its power in the attainment of this laudable object.

### RESOLUTION XIII.

**Resolved**—That no subject shall be passed for discussion by the Subject Committee or allowed to be discussed at any Congress by the President thereof, to the introduction of which the Hindu or Mahomedan Delegates as a body object, unanimously or nearly unanimously ; and that if, after the discussion of any subject which has been admitted for discussion, it shall appear that all the Hindu or all the Mahomedan Delegates, as a body, are unanimously, or nearly unanimously, opposed to the Resolution which it is proposed to pass thereon, such Resolution shall be dropped ; provided that this rule shall refer only to subjects in regard to which the Congress has not already definitely pronounced an opinion.

### RESOLUTION XIV.

**Resolved**—That the question of the introduction of a Permanent Settlement of the Land Revenue Demand into the Madras and Bombay Presidencies and other provinces be referred to the several Standing Congress Committees, with instructions to report upon the same, in so far as it affects their respective circles, to the Congress of 1889.

### RESOLUTION XV.

**Resolved**—That this Congress puts on record its disapproval of the recent enhancement of the Salt Tax, as involving a perceptible increase to the burthens of the poorer classes, as also the partial absorption, in a time of peace and plenty, of the only Financial Reserve of the Empire.

### RESOLUTION XVI.

**Resolved**—That the Fifth Indian National Congress do assemble in the Bombay Presidency (either at Bombay itself or at Poona, as may be settled hereafter) on the 26th of December, 1889.

### RESOLUTION XVII.

**Resolved**—That Mr. A. O. Hume be re-appointed General Secretary for the ensuing year.

---

## RESOLUTIONS PASSED AT THE FIFTH CONGRESS.

### RESOLUTION I.

**Resolved**—That an address be presented to Mr. Charles Bradlaugh, M.P., on behalf of this Congress here assembled, and that Messrs. Adam, Pherozshah Mehta, and W. C. Bonnerjee are appointed a Committee to settle the wording of the said address.

### RESOLUTION II.

**Resolved**—That the following skeleton scheme for the reform and reconstitution of the Council of the Governor-General for making Laws and Regulations, and the Provincial Legislative Councils, is adopted, and that the President of this Congress do submit the same to Charles Bradlaugh, Esq., M.P., with the respectful request of this Congress that he may be pleased to cause a Bill to be drafted on the lines indicated in this skeleton scheme and introduce the same in the British House of Commons :—

## SCHEME.

(1) The Imperial and Provincial Legislative Councils to consist respectively of Members, not less than one half of whom are to be elected, not more than one-fourth to sit *ex-officio*, and the rest to be nominated by Government.

(2) Revenue districts to constitute ordinarily territorial units, for electoral purposes.

(3) All male British subjects above 21 years of age possessing certain qualifications and not subject to certain disqualifications (both of which will be settled later) to be voters.

(4) Voters in each district to elect representatives to one or more electoral bodies, according to local circumstances at the rate of 12 per million of the total population of the district, such representatives to possess certain qualifications and not to be subject to certain disqualifications, both of which will be settled later.

(5) All the representatives thus elected by all the districts included in the jurisdiction of each electoral body, to elect members to the Imperial Legislature at the rate of 1 per every five millions of the total population of the electoral jurisdiction, and to their own Provincial Legislature at the rate of 1 per million of the said total population, in such wise that whenever the Parsees. Christians, Mahomedans or Hindus are in a minority, the total number of Parsees, Christians, Mahomedans or Hindus, as the case may be, elected to the Provincial Legislature, shall not, so far as may be possible, bear a less proportion to the total number of members elected thereto, than the total number of Parsees, Christians, Hindus or Mahomedans, as the case may be, in such electoral jurisdiction, bears to its total population. Members of both legislatures to possess certain qualifications and not to be subject to certain disqualifications, both of which will be settled later.

(6) All elections to be by ballot.

## RESOLUTION III.

**Resolved**—That this present Congress does hereby ratify and confirm the resolutions passed by previous Congresses as to—

(a) the urgent necessity for the complete separation of executive and judicial functions, such that, in no case, shall the two functions be combined in the same officer;

(b) the expediency of extending into many parts of the country, where it is not at present in force, the system of trial by jury;

(c) the necessity of withdrawing from the High Courts, the powers, first vested in them in 1872, of setting aside verdicts of acquittal by juries;

(d) the necessity of introducing, into the Code of Criminal Procedure, a provision enabling accused persons, in warrant cases, to demand that, instead of being tried by the Magistrate, they be committed to the Court of Sessions;

(e) the highly unsatisfactory character of the existing system of Police Administration in India, and the absolute necessity of a fundamental reform therein;

(f) the expediency of both, establishing Military Colleges in India, whereat the Natives of India, as defined by Statute, may be educated and trained for a military career as officers of the Indian Army, and of authorising, under such rules and restrictions as may seem necessary, such a system of volunteering for the Indian inhabitants of the country as may qualify them to support the Government in any crisis;

(g) the extremely unsatisfactory character of the Income Tax Administration, especially as regards incomes below rupees one thousand, and the expediency of raising the taxable minimum to this amount;

(h) the extreme importance of increasing, instead of diminishing, as the present tendency appears to be, the public expenditure on education in all its branches, and the necessity, in view to the promotion of one of the most essential of these branches, the technical, of the appointment of a mixed commission to enquire into the present industrial condition of the country;

(i) the impolicy and injustice involved in the late increase of the Salt Tax in a time of profound peace, and the urgent necessity for an immediate reduction of this tax, and the reimposition, to balance the deficit thus caused, of light *ad valorem* import duties;

(j) the necessity for the reduction of, instead of the continual increase to, the military expenditure of the country.

## RESOLUTION IV.

**Resolved**—That this Congress hereby tenders its sincere thanks to Messrs. Caine and Smith, and the members who voted with them, in connection with the debate on the Indian Excise Question in the House of Commons; and, while fully appreciating what has been done by some of the local Governments towards the improvement of their systems of Excise and Abkari, desires to express the earnest hope that no further time may be lost in giving full effect to the Resolution of the House of Commons.

## RESOLUTION V.

**Resolved**—That this Congress, while thanking Her Majesty's Government for raising the age for the Indian Civil Service Competitive Examination from 19 to 23, does hereby put on record an emphatic expression of the universal disappointment which has been created by the rest of that Government's orders in regard to the Public Service Question, (the net result of which orders is to place the people of India in a worse position than they previously held), and reiterates the national conviction that no real justice will be done to India, in this matter, until the simultaneous holding in India, and in England, of all examinations, for all Civil branches of the Public Service in India, at present held only in England, be conceded.

## RESOLUTION VI.

**Resolved**—That, in view of the loyalty of the people, the hardships that the Arms Act (XI of 1878), as at present administered, entails, and the unmerited slur which it casts upon them, the Government be moved so to modify the rules made under this Act that all restrictions as to the possession and bearing of arms shall apply equally to all persons residing in or visiting India; that licenses to possess and bear arms shall be liberally and generally distributed wherever wild animals habitually destroy human life, cattle or crops; and that these and all licenses issued under the rules shall be granted once for all, shall operate throughout the Provincial jurisdiction within which they are issued, be only revocable on proof of misuse, and shall not require yearly or half-yearly renewals.

## RESOLUTION VII.

**Resolved**—That the Government be urged to take the subject of a Permanent Settlement once more under consideration in view to practical action thereon, such that fixity and permanency may be given to the Government Land Revenue demand without further delay, at any rate in all fully populated and well cultivated tracts of country.

## RESOLUTION VIII.

**Resolved**—That, in view of the fall that has already occurred in the price of silver and in the exchange value of the Indian Rupee, it is impolitic on the part of the British Government to maintain any hindrances whatever to the consumption of silver for manufacturing purposes; and that this Congress strongly urges upon Her Majesty's Government that, not only as an act of justice to India (a matter which has been repeatedly brought to the notice of Her Majesty's Ministers), but also as an act of expediency in the interests of Her Majesty's British as well as Indian subjects, the plate duties should be immediately abolished, and Hall marking be made a voluntary institution.

### RESOLUTION IX.

**Resolved**—That this Congress respectfully expresses the earnest hope that, in the interest of the people of India, the House of Commons will forthwith restore the right, formerly possessed by members of that Honourable House, of stating to Parliament any matter of grievance of the natives of India, before Mr. Speaker leaves the Chair, for the presentation in Committee of the Indian Budget statement, and earnestly trusts that the House of Commons will, in future, take into consideration the Annual Indian Budget statement at such a date as will ensure its full and adequate discussion; and further authorizes the President, Sir William Wedderburn, Bart., to sign a petition in the name and on behalf of this Congress for presentation to the House of Commons in accordance with the terms of this Resolution.

### RESOLUTION X.

**Resolved**—That, in view to his approaching departure, this Congress puts on record an expression of the high sense entertained, not only in the Bombay Presidency, but throughout India, of the ability, integrity and impartiality that have characterised Lord Reay's administration, as also of the gratitude which the whole country feels to be his due for the sympathy that he has ever extended to Indian aspirations and efforts.

### RESOLUTION XI.

**Resolved**—That the Subjects Committee be instructed to settle the question, (left open in the skeleton scheme for the reconstruction of the councils, embodied in Resolution II.), of the qualifications requisite for, and the disqualifications which should debar from, becoming—

(*a*) a Voter;
(*b*) a Representative;
(*c*) a Member of a Provincial Legislative Council, and
(*d*) a Member of the Imperial Legislative Council;

and to submit their Report thereon to Charles Bradlaugh, Esq., M.P., for the purposes of the Bill which he has been requested to have drawn.

### RESOLUTION XII.

**Resolved**—That Mr. A. O. Hume, C.B., be re-elected General Secretary of the National Indian Congress for the ensuing year.

### RESOLUTION XIII.

**Resolved**—

(*a*) That in view of the large number of delegates this year assembled, and the probability arising from past experience, of their number continuing to increase year by year, henceforth the number of delegates to be allowed from each Congress circle be limited to five per million of the total population of the circle: the Standing Committee of each circle allotting the number which their jurisdiction, as a whole, is entitled to elect, amongst their several electoral divisions, as may seem most expedient.

(*b*) That from the date of Mr. Hume's departure for England, the Hon'ble Pundit Ajoodhianath be appointed Joint General Secretary, and that Rs. 5,000 be assigned for the payment by him of such Assistant Secretaries as he may find it necessary to employ, clerical assistance, postage, telegraphs, and printing; and further that Mr. W. C. Bonnerjee be appointed Standing Counsel for Bengal, Mr. Pherozshah Mehta, Standing Counsel for Bombay, and Mr. Ananda Charlu, Standing Counsel for Madras, to the Joint General Secretary.

(*c*) That the tentative rules for the constitution and working of the Congress, which were first considered at Madras, and in regard to which various addenda have from time to time been circulated, be thoroughly considered during the coming year by the several Standing Congress Committees, and definitely dealt with by the Congress at its next session.

(*d*) That this Congress does hereby confirm the appointment of Sir W. Wedderburn, Bart., and Messrs. W. S. Caine, M.P., W. S. Bright Maclaren, M.P., J. E. Ellis, M.P., Dadabhai Naoroji and George Yule, as a Committee (with power to add to their number) to guide and direct the operations and control the expenditure of the National Congress Agency in England, and does further tender its sincere thanks to these gentlemen, and to Mr. W. Digby, C.I.E., the Secretary, for the service which they are rendering to India.

(*e*) That this Congress does formally appoint Mr. George Yule, Mr. A. O. Hume, Mr. Adam, Mr. Eardley Norton, Mr. J. E. Howard,* Mr. Pherozshah Mehta, Mr. Surendranath Banerjee, Mr. Mono Mohan Ghose, Mr. Shurfuddin, Mr. R. N. Mudholker, and Mr. W. C. Bonnerjee to represent its views in England and press upon the consideration of the British Public the political reforms which the Congress has advocated.

(*f*) That a sum of Rs. 45,000 be raised for the expenses of the Congress Work in this country and in England during the ensuing year, and that the different Standing Committees do send their respective apportioned amounts to the General Secretary, the one half in three, and the balance in six months.

### RESOLUTION XIV.

**Resolved**—That the Sixth Indian National Congress do assemble at some City in Bengal, the exact place to be fixed hereafter, on the 26th of December, 1890.

### RESOLUTION XV.

**Resolved**—That the Fifth Indian National Congress hereby tenders its heart-felt thanks to its President, Sir William Wedderburn, as well for his ready sacrifice of personal and political considerations involved by his journey from England to India, as for that courtesy, impartiality and never failing sympathy which, characteristics of his long and honourable career as an official of this country, have marked his control of the proceedings of this assembly.

* By some oversight, this gentleman's name was omitted, when the Resolution was read to the Congress; the error has been rectified with the consent of the several Standing Congress Committees.

# LIST OF THE CONGRESS PUBLICATIONS

## To be obtained at the

## OFFICE OF THE ADVOCATE LUCKNOW.

INDIAN POLITICS IN ENGLAND. This volume contains the weekly letters addressed by Mr. William Digby C. I. E. to "The Hindu" and "The Bengali" newspapers. These letters have been carefully revised by Mr. Digby and contain a complete record of one year's work in England. Every event of permanent importance and interest to the Indian reformers has been noticed. Following are the contents :—

SECTION A.—An Indian Official Reform Bill in Parliament ; Its progress and its delays.

SECTION B.—The Congress Council's Reform Bill ; The Member for India.

SECTION C.—The Congress of 1888 89 ; Some suggestions for consideration of the Congress ; The Congress at Bombay ; The misappropriation of famine taxation ; A general survey of Indian taxation ; The services of India ; Another cheating of the Indian people ; The Indian Budget Debate in August 1889 ; The Secretary of State's Council in 1890 ; Indian Ethnology and the Congress ; Lord Dufferin talking nonsense ; A lecture on India by Mr. Digby ; Reactionaries in the Secretary of State's Council ; Legislation in Calcutta and in Simla ; A lesson from London Strikes ; The Indian Budget Debate in August 1890 ; Mr. Bradlaugh on Indian Railway Finance ; Lord Cross's Indian Secretaryship ; Mr. Bradlaugh be-friending the India office ; Another broken official promise.

SECTION D.—The Congress Delegates in Britain.

SECTION E.—Disinterested work for India, John Bright, The Duke of Buckingham & Chandos, Messrs. Knight Kipling, John Slagg, M. P., Sir Lepel Griffin, K. C. S. I., Mr. W. S. Caine, The Marquis of Dufferin and Ava at the Mansion House London, Mr. W. T.Stead, Sir Richard Temple, Bart. G. C. S. I., M. P. H. H. Maharaja of Mysore Mr. James Bryce, M. P., Mr. Macgregor, Sir J. Stephen, K. C. S. I. Judge of the High Court of England, Lord Cross and Mr. W.Caine, Colonel G. B. Malleson, C. S. I. Personal Journalism, The Eurasian future, Lord Cross and India Office Administration, A compliment to Indian Local self-Government, Indian versus, Colonial expenditure in England, Unfamiliar view of Indian Administration, Twenty years more of Hinduism then the end, Indian Railway Finance, Lord Cross's indebtedness to Mr. Bradlaugh, An Anglo-Indian idea of sedition, A British "Black hole of Calcutta," Another unfamiliar view of India, The Queen Empress's promises recklessly broken, A British promise An interesting Trio,—which is the Blackman ? Bombay, an English Parliamentary Borough, A "Pentecost" for heathen Anglo-Indians, Some so-called marriage extravagancies in India, Hindu Hostel, The growth of Mr. Gladstone's head.

To make the publication of additional value, a nice portrait of Mr. Digby by an English Artist has also been attached to it. Price Re. 1 postage Annas 2

INDIA IN ENGLAND VOL. III.—A collection of speeches delivered and articles written on the Indian National Congress in 1890. Following are the contents :—

Mr. Bradlaugh's Bill ; Lord Cross's Bill ; Debate on Lord Cross's Bill ; Speeches of Viscount Cross ; Marquis of Ripon ; Earl of Northbrook, Marquis of Salisbury ; Earl of Kimberley, Earl Granvile ; Lord Stanley of Alderley Lord Dufferin's confidential minute in favour of election ; Sir Richard Temple on the reform of the Councils ; Sir William Hunter on Mr. Bradlaugh's Bill ; Sir Richard Garth on Mr. Bradlaugh's Bill ; Mr. A. O. Hume Sir Richard Garth's Letter, Sir Charles Dilke on the National Congress ; Mr. Fredrick Pincott on the Mahomedan opposition to the Congress ; The Right Hon. Hugh Childers, M. P., on the Congress, Mr. Goschen Indian Agitators ; Mr. Gladstone and the Congress delegates, The Congress Deputation in Great Britain ; Speeches of Sir William Wedderburn, BART, Mr. Dadabhai Nowroji ; Messrs. Hume ; Purser ; Cavington ; Alderman Derby, Bradlaugh ; Mr. Justin McCarthy, Mr. Martin-Wood ; Mr. F. Pincott ; John Meridith M. D., Rev. F. W. Aveling Mr. A. Barker, Mr. J. F. Keir, Professor Anthony, Mr. H. Whitefield ; Mr. R. N. Worth ; Mr. L. Latimer ; Mr. T. W. Crossman, Mr. E. R. Moxy Mr. Surredra Nath Bannerji ; Mr. F. Sonley Jonstone Mr. Padshaah ; Mr. Walten Hughes ; Mr. Bond ; Mr. Elliott ; Mr. D. M. Colah : Mr. Shaik Rahim ; Mr, A, C, Banerjee ; Mr, Surrendra Nath Banerjee at Hardvice Society Mr. Norton at Oxford Union ; Mr, J, F, W, Galbraith, Oriel ; Mr, H, E, A, Cotton, Mr. Surrendra Nath Banerjee at Oxford Union, Lord Hugh Cecil ; Mr, H. W. Liverside ; Mr, J, A, V, Magee ; Mr. Schwann ; Mr. Mudholkar ; Dr. Aubrey ; Mr. W. S. Caine ; Mr. Charles Bradlaugh at Croydon ; Rev. C. J, Streed ; Mr. W. C. Bannerjee ; Mrs. Grimwade, Pundit Bishun Narayan Dar on Lord Dufferin's Sir Anderw Dinner speech, Mr. Bradlaugh's Amended Indian Reform Bill, Mr. Bradlaugh's Indian Work in Parliament in 1890 Mr. Pincott's voting unit for India Mr. Bradlaugh on the Indian financial statement. Price Rs. 1 postage ans. 2.

INDIA IN ENGLAND, VOL II—(For 1889.) Contents :—

The introductory Essay.—Some Historial Analogies to the National Congress ; Reuter's Telegrams on the Congress ; Comments of the Press ; Sir Edward Watkin interviewed ; Mr. A. O. Hume on Sir Edward Watkins attack, Mr. Bradlaugh Libelled ; Mr. William Digby on Sir E. Watkin's attack, Memorandum of Indian Political Agency on the Reform of Councils ; Mr. Bradlaugh interviewed ; Two letters of Mr. William Digby to the Secretary of State on the report of the Public Service Commission ; Mr. William Digby's interview with Right H. William E. Gladstone ; Nottingham liberals and Indian Reform ; The Hull Radical Club and the Congress ; Mr. J. Dacosta's Notes on the Assesment and Collection of the Land Revenue in India ; Mr. C W. Whish on the Congress ; Mr. Frederic Pincott on the Congress ; Mr. Robert Brown on the Indian Financial Statement 1889-90 ; The Queen Empress's Promises : how they are broken ; Work of the Indian Political Agency ; India Awake ; Mr. Charles Bradlaugh at Newcastle ; Mr. Dadabhai Nowroji at Lough borough ; India neglected in the Queen's speech ; the Congress Catechism in Parliament ; Memo by Sir Willam Wedderburn ; Mr. C. Bradlaugh at Home ; Mr. Bradlaugh's Good Services for India ; Mr. Bradlaugh on the Indian Uncovenanted Service ; Mr. Bradlaugh on the Indian Budget ; The Liverpool demonstration ; Mr. W. S. B. MacLaren at Crew.

Price Re. 1. Postage 2 annas.

INDIA IN ENGLAND, VOL. 1.—(For 1888,) Contents :

Introduction ; Recent movements of India ; Mr. Dadabbai Naoroji at Islington Club ; Mr. Caine M. P. on the Congress ; The Indian Political and General Agency ; Circular letter ; Placards ; Sir W. W. Hunter's article in the *Times* ; Cuttings from the English Press ; Garth's "A few Plain Truths about India ;" Mr. W. C. Bonerji at Wainfleet ; Mr. Eardley Norton and Mr. W. C. Bonnerji at Bensham grove Gateshead ; Statement prepared by the English Agency for the information of the members of Parliament ; Indian Budget in the Parliament ; Great meeting in Northampton ; The present Problem in India ; Mr. W. C. Bonnerji at Wood Hall Spa, and Tetford Spalding and Lincoln ; Mr. Bradlaugh's speech on our Indian Empire ; Sir Willim Wedderburn's Lecture on our duty to India Sir J. B. Phear on the Congress ; Mr. William Digby on Sir Auckland Colvin ; Letters and Articles of the opponents ; Letters of Mr. Eardley Norton to the *Hindu* of Madaas. .

BIOGRAPHY OF MR. CAARLES BRADLAUGH M. P.—By Mr. Andelophe S. Headlingey with his Photo. Price with Postage Re. 1 -1

THE CAWNPORE ASSAULT CASE—Full record of the case official and othewise with an introduction, price 8 annas. Postage 2.

PUBLIC SERVICE COMMISSION AND ITS RESULT—Contains conclusions and suggestions of the Commission, Government of India and Lord Cross's despatches. Price 6½ annas.

LORD SALISBURY'S "BLACKMAN."—Contains cuttings from some 200 English papers bearing on the incident ; also speeches of the Mr. Nowrojee, Lord Ripon, Mr. W. Hunter M. P. and other English politicians at the National Liberal Club meeting, with full report of all other sympathetic public meetings held in Englad in honor of Mr. Nowroji with several woodcuts. Price 8 annas Postage. 0 0 6.

INDIA AS SEEN BY MR. CAINE.—Mr. W. S. Caine's ten letters, which he addressed to the English pepers from India in 1888. Price annas 8. Postage 0 0 6.

THE DRINK QUESTION IN PARLIAMENT.—Contains the full report of the speeches of Mr. S. Smith, Mr. W. S. Caine, Sir. R. Lethbridge, Sir Richard Temple, Sir John Gorst, Sir W. Harcourt, and other speakers. Price annas 2. Postage. 0 0 6.

MR. NORTON *versus* LORD DUFFERIN.—Lord Dufferin's St. Andrews Dinner speech, and Mr. E. Norton's Open letter to his Lordship. Price annas 2 Postage 0 0 6.

TWO MEMORABLE SPEECHES—Delivered by Mr. E. Norton at Pacheapaha's Hall, Madras, giving a full account of his English travels. Price 1½ anna. Postage 0 0 6.

REPORT OF THE FIRST NATIONAL CONGRESS.—Price 8 annas Postage 0 0 6.

FIFTH CONGRESS REPORT Rs, 1. Postage annas 3.

SIXTH CONGRESS REPORT. Rs. 1 postage annas 3.

MR. BRADLAUGH'S BILL by Pundit Bishen Narayan Dar ... 0 2 6

URDU

| | | | | Postage. | | |
|---|---|---|---|---|---|---|
| Second Congress Report ... ... ... | 1 | 0 | 0 | 0 | 2 | 0 |
| Third Congress Report ... ... ... | 1 | 0 | 0 | 0 | 2 | 0 |
| Fourth Congress Report ... ... ... | 1 | 0 | 0 | 0 | 2 | 0 |
| Fifth Congress Report ... ... ... | 1 | 0 | 0 | 0 | 2 | 0 |
| Sixth Congress Report ... ... ... | 1 | 0 | 0 | 0 | 2 | 6 |
| Conversation between Molvi Farid-ud-din-din and Ram Baksh ... | 0 | 0 | 6 | 0 | 0 | 6 |
| Catechism ... ... ... ... | 0 | 0 | 3 | 0 | 0 | 6 |
| Short History of English Constitution ... | 0 | 8 | 0 | 0 | 0 | 6 |
| Lord Dufferin's St. Andrew Dinner speech and Mr. Eardley Norton's Open letter ... ... ... | 0 | 1 | 6 | 0 | 0 | 6 |
| Letters of Mr. Hume and Sir Auckland Colvin ... ... | 0 | 3 | 0 | 0 | 0 | 6 |
| Lucknow speech of Hon'ble Pundt Ajodhia Nath ... | 0 | 1 | 0 | 0 | 0 | 6 |

HINDI

| | | | | | | |
|---|---|---|---|---|---|---|
| Fourth Congress Report ... ... ... | 1 | 0 | 0 | 0 | 2 | 6 |

CHROMO-LITHO PICTURES.

| | | | | | | |
|---|---|---|---|---|---|---|
| Presidents of the Congress from 1885 to 1889 with Mr. Hume.... | 0 | 4 | 0 | 0 | 0 | 6 |
| Chairmen of Reception Committees... ... ... | 0 | 4 | 0 | 0 | 0 | 6 |
| Lady Delegates—Congress 1889 ... ... ... | 0 | 4 | 0 | 0 | 0 | 6 |
| Indian Delegates to England with Messrs. Bradlaugh and Digby... | 0 | 4 | 0 | 0 | 0 | 6 |

# REPORT

OF

# THE SEVENTH INDIAN NATIONAL CONGRESS,

HELD AT

# NAGPUR,

*On the 28th, 29th and 30th December,*

1891.

# In Loving Remembrance

— OF —

# PUNDIT AJOODHIANATH,

VAKIL OF THE HIGH COURT, ALLAHABAD,
MEMBER OF THE LEGISLATIVE COUNCIL OF THE UNITED PROVINCES DURING THE YEARS 1886, 1887, 1888, 1889, 1890,
FELLOW OF BOTH THE CALCUTTA AND ALLAHABAD UNIVERSITIES,
AND
**Joint General Secretary of the Indian National Congress.**

**Appeared, 8th April 1840. Passed away, 11th January 1892.**

Death has no power, th' immortal soul to slay,
*That*, when its present body turns to clay,
Seeks a fresh home. and with unlessened might
Inspires another frame with life and light.
*Dryden.*

## TRIBUTES TO HIS MEMORY.

SIR JOHN EDGE, the CHIEF JUSTICE of the Allahabad High Court, said :—

"We feel that we ought not to allow this opportunity of our being assembled in Full Bench to pass without expressing our sorrow for the death and paying our tribute of respect to the memory of one who, for many years, has held a high position in this Court and in these Provinces as an advocate, and who was possessed of the highest legal and forensic attainments. On Monday last, we received the sad news that Pundit Ajudhya Nath had been removed by death from amongst us, and we of the Bench felt that we had lost in him not only a personal friend, but one of the best lawyers and ablest advocates of the Court. We felt that the members of the Bar and the vakils practising in this Court had lost in him also a friend, and that the profession at large of these Provinces had suffered a still greater loss in losing in him a bright and living example of what an honourable advocate should be. Pundit Ajudhya Nath * * * had that sound and rare judgment which enables a great advocate, as we think he was, to discriminate between the important and the unimportant facts and incidents in a case. * * * In his arguments before us he was most scrupulous in avoiding even the semblance of a misstatement of facts, and thereby secured in our Judges a thorough reliance upon his honour as an advocate. I need scarcely say that he was thoroughly independent. * * *

"This Court will be closed for the day, and also the office on account of the death of Pundit Ajudhya Nath."

At one of the largest public meetings ever held at ALLAHABAD it was resolved that—

"This meeting hereby puts on record its emphatic expression of the deep sorrow everywhere felt at the recent untimely death of Pundit Ajudhya Nath, who by his courageous, patriotic, and indefatigable labours in the cause of India's people had won the regard, esteem, and respect of all good men throughout the country."

At a great public meeting at MADRAS it was resolved—

"That this meeting desires to place upon record its high sense and appreciation of the splendid and disinterested services rendered by the late Hon. Pundit Ajudhya Nath, Pleader of the High Court of Allahabad, to the cause of the Indian National Congress, and to record its deep and lasting regret for the loss of a leader who, in his own person, combined so many and brilliant qualifications for command."

Again at NAGPORE it was—

"*Resolved*—That this General Public Meeting of the inhabitants of Nagpur does hereby put on record an expression of the universal sorrow with which all persons in these Central Provinces have received the sad intelligence of the untimely and deplorable death of Pundit Ajudhya Nath, late Joint General Secretary of the Indian National Congress. In Pundit Ajudhya Nath all felt that they had amongst them a most earnest, able and thoroughly upright champion of the people's cause, and one who commanded the unqualified respect of all classes of the community ; and they now feel that in losing him that cause has sustained a grievous and almost irreparable loss."

At a public meeting held in the Town Hall, CALCUTTA, it was resolved—

"That this Meeting desires to place on record its sense of the great and irreparable loss which the country has sustained by the death of Pundit Ajudhya Nath. His courage, devotion and self-sacrifice in the discharge of his public duties entitle his memory to the respectful gratitude of his countrymen."

At a public meeting at LAHORE it was resolved—

"That this meeting expresses its sense of deep and sincere sorrow at the untimely death of the Hon'ble Pundit Ajudhya Nath, Joint General Secretary, Indian National Congress, and of the great loss which the country has thereby sustained."

Speech of the Vice-Chancellor of the Calcutta University—

"In Pundit Ajudhya Nath we have lost another distinguished colleague, a man 'of whom,' as the Vice-Chancellor of the Allahabad University has justly remarked, 'any country and race might be proud.' His earnest exertions and immense self-sacrifice to promote the good of his country made him loved and respected by the educated classes all over India, and Bengal mourns his loss as deeply as his native province."

Resolutions similar in purport, to those above quoted, were passed at public meetings held at—

Aligarh,
Ahmednagger.
Amraoti.
Benares.,
Bombay.
Bankipore.
Bhusawal.
Bezwada.
Barisal.
Bogra.
Belaspur.
Bellary.
Berhampur.
Bhandara.
Cawnpur.
Chingleput.
Coconada.
Coimbatore.
Delhi.
Dhulea.
Durbhangah.
Ellichpur.
Fureedpore.
Farukhabad.
Guntur.
Gooty.
Gauhati.
Howrah.
Inchalkaranji.
Jalpaiguri.
Lucknow.
Meerut.
Multan.
Muzzufferpore.
Mangral Pir.
Mayavaram
Manickdaho.
Madura.
Masulipatam.
Moradabad.
Nasik.
Ongole.
Palghat.
Poona.
Rajnandgaon.
Sholapore.
Saharumpur.
Srivilliputur.
Secundrabad.
Tanjore.
Trichengode.
Triplicane.
Udumalpet.
Vizagapatam.
Wardha.
And many other places.

# CONTENTS.

# SUMMARY OF RESOLUTIONS

PASSED AT THE

# SEVENTH INDIAN NATIONAL CONGRESS,

**Held at Nagpur on the 28th, 29th and 30th December, 1891.**

## RESOLUTION I.

**Resolved**—That a Committee be appointed to consider and report, on or before the morning of the 30th instant, whether, or not, it is advisable to discontinue the Annual Sessions of the Indian National Congress until after the British Session, and, if not, under what regulations, as to numbers of delegates, localities for assemblage, and the like, future Congresses shall be held. The Committee to be composed as follows :—

EX-OFFICIO MEMBERS :

The President.
The Chairman of the Reception Committee.
The General Secretary.
The Joint General Secretary.
The Standing Counsels to the Congress.

ORDINARY MEMBERS :

Messrs. Surendranath Bannerjee.
Viraraghava Chariar.
Hafiz Abdul Raheem.
Gangapersad Varma.
Pringle Kennedy.
Guruprasad Sen.
D. E. Watcha.
M. B. Namjoshi.
Hamid Ali Khan.
Vishnu Moreshwar Bhide.

Messrs. Murlidhar.
Mudholkar.
Deo Rao Vinayak.
Gopal Rao Bhide.
Bipin Krishna Bose.
Dajee Abajee Khare.
Madan Mohan Malaviya.
Saligram Singh.
Sankara Nair.

## RESOLUTION II.

**Resolved**—That this Congress reaffirms the conclusion arrived at by all previous Congresses, *viz.*, that India can never be well or justly governed, nor her people prosperous or contented, until they are allowed, through their elected representatives, a potential voice in the Legislatures of their own country, and respectfully urges the people of Great Britain and Ireland, whose good will towards India it gratefully recognizes, to permit no further delay in the concession of this just and necessary reform.

## RESOLUTION III.

**Resolved**—That this Congress, concurring in the views set forth in previous Congresses, affirms—

That fully fifty millions of the population, a number yearly increasing, are dragging out a miserable existence on the verge of starvation, and that, in every decade, several millions actually perish by starvation.

That this unhappy condition of affairs is largely due to—

(*a*) the exclusion of the people of India from a due participation in the administration, and all control over the finances, of their own country, the remedy for which has been set forth in Resolution II ; to

(*b*) the extravagant cost of the present administration, Military and Civil, but especially the former ; and to

(*c*) a short-sighted system of Land Revenue Administration, whereby not only is all improvement in the agriculture of the country, on which nine-tenths of the population depend for subsistence, rendered impossible, but the gradual deterioration of that agriculture assured.

That hence it has become imperatively necessary—

that the cost of the administration be greatly reduced ; in the military branch, by a substantial reduction of the standing army, by the substitution of long term local European troops, like those of the Hon. E. I. Company, for the present short term Imperial regiments with their heavy cost of recruitment in England, in transport and of excessive mortality amongst non-acclimatized youths ; by the cessation of the gigantic waste of money that has gone on, now for several years, on so-called Frontier Defences, and by a strict economy in the Commissariat, Ordnance and Store Departments ; and in the Civil branch, by the wide substitution of a cheaper indigenous agency for the extremely costly imported Staff ; and

that measures be at once taken to give, as was promised by the British Government thirty years ago, fixity and permanence to the Land Revenue demand and thus permit capital and labour to combine to develop the agriculture of the country, which, under the existing system of temporary settlements, in recent times often lasting for short periods, in some cases only extending to 10 and 12 years, is found to be impossible ; and to establish agricultural banks.

That this Congress does most earnestly entreat the people of Great Britain and Ireland not to permit any further sacrifice of life by the shortcomings of the existing, doubtless well-intentioned, but none the less unsatisfactory, administration, but to insist, and speedily, on these reforms.

## RESOLUTION IV.

**Resolved**—That this Congress, concurring with previous Congresses, is of opinion that, to ensure the adequate protection and efficient defence of the country, it is desirable that the Government should conciliate Indian public opinion and encourage and qualify the Indians to defend their homes and their Government—

(*a*) by so modifying the rules under the Arms Act, as to make them equally applicable to all residents in, or visitors to, India, without distinction of creed, class or colour ; to ensure the liberal concession of licenses wherever wild animals habitually destroy human life, cattle or crops, and to make all licenses granted under the revised rules, of life-long tenure, revokable only on proof of misuse and valid throughout the Provincial Jurisdiction in which they are issued ;

(*b*) by establishing Military Colleges in India, whereat natives of India, as defined by Statute, may be educated and trained for a military career, as *commissioned or non-commissioned* officers (according to capacity and qualifications) of the Indian army;

(*c*) by organising, throughout the more warlike races of the Empire, a system of militia service; and

(*d*) by authorizing and stimulating a widespread system of volunteering, such as obtains in Great Britain, amongst the people of India.

## RESOLUTION V.

**Resolved**—That as one step towards ensuring the wider employment of Indians in the administration of the country, and as a matter of simple justice to the people of India, this Congress, agreeing with previous Congresses, declares it to be essential, that all examinations for any and all of the Civil Branches of the Public Service in India, which at present are held only in England, should henceforth be also held simultaneously in India.

## RESOLUTION VI.

**Resolved**—That this Congress concurs with its predecessors in strongly advocating—

(*a*) the reduction of the salt tax, by at least the amount of its latest enhancement;

(*b*) the raising of the income tax taxable minimum from Rs. 500 to Rs. 1,000;

(*c*) persistent pressure by the Government of India on all Provincial Administrations, to induce them to carry out, in its integrity, the excise policy enunciated in paras. 103, 104 and 105 of the despatch, published in the *Gazette of India*, of March 1st, 1890, and the introduction of a simple system of local option in the case of all villages.

## RESOLUTION VII.

**Resolved**—That having regard to the unsatisfactory character, in many respects, of the Judicial and Police Administration, this Congress concurs with its predecessors in strongly advocating—

(*a*) the complete separation of Executive and Judicial functions such that in no case shall the two functions be combined in the same officer;

(*b*) the extension into many parts of the country, where it is not at present in force, of the system of trial by jury;

(*c*) the withdrawal from High Courts of the powers, first vested in them in 1872, of setting aside verdicts of acquittals by juries;

(*d*) the introduction, into the Code of Criminal Procedure, of a provision enabling accused persons, in warrant cases, to demand that instead of being tried by the Magistrate they be committed to the court of sessions;

(*e*) the fundamental reform of the Police Administration, by a reduction in the numbers and an increase in the salaries, and in the qualifications of the lower grades, and their far more careful enlistment, and by the selection for the higher posts of gentlemen of higher capacities, more in touch with the respectable portions of the community, and less addicted to military pretensions, than the majority of the existing Deputy Inspectors General, Superintendents and Assistant Superintendents, of Police.

## RESOLUTION VIII.

**Resolved**—That this Congress, concurring with previous Congresses, affirms the importance of increasing (instead of diminishing, as appears to be the present policy of the Government) the public expenditure on all branches of education, and the expediency, in view to the promotion of one of the most essential of these branches, the technical, of appointing a mixed Commission to enquire into the present industrial condition of the country.

## RESOLUTION IX.

*Read the following telegram from General Booth :—*

"May I be allowed to commend, to the attention of the Congress, the claims of the millions of India's starving poor and to urge the consideration of some scheme by which these destitute multitudes can be placed upon the waste lands of the country, in such an organised and befriended manner, as will enable them to gain, for themselves, those necessaries of a healthy existence which, in their present circumstances, are denied ; praying for the blessing of God upon the labours of the Congress, yours in sympathy with every effort for the amelioration of the miseries of mankind."

**Resolved**—That the following telegram be despatched in reply to General Booth :—

"The Congress having received and considered your kindly message thank you cordially for the same. No possible scheme of internal immigration can perceptibly relieve the fifty to sixty millions of half-starving paupers, whose sad condition constitutes the primary *raison d'être* of the Congress. It is only by modifying the adverse conditions out of which this widespread misery arises, and by raising the moral standard of the people, that any real relief is possible. As regards the first, the Congress programme now embodies all primarily essential reforms ; as regards the second, in every province and in every caste, associations, public or private, are working with a yearly increasing earnestness. Many good missionaries are labouring in same field, and we have to thank you that your army too is now engaged in the good work of elevating our masses. May your efforts and ours, in both directions, be crowned with success. Congress, including men of many creeds, welcomes cordially all who seek to benefit our suffering brethren."

## RESOLUTION X.

*Read the Report of the Committee appointed, under Resolution (I.), which runs as follows :—*

"Your Committee have considered the matter referred to them and have also consulted, informally, various members of the Subjects Committee and other delegates. They are clearly of opinion that it is not advisable to discontinue the Annual Session of the Indian National Congress until after the British Session, and that future Congresses should be held under the same regulations as heretofore."

**Resolved**—That the Annual Sessions of the Congress in India continue to be held until all necessary reforms have been secured.

## RESOLUTION XI.

**Resolved**—That having regard to the very serious discontent created, especially in Peninsular India, by the practical administration of the Forest Laws, the Government of India be most respectfully, but earnestly, entreated to investigate this carefully, and endeavour to mitigate its harshness and render it less obnoxious to the poorer classes.

## RESOLUTION XII.

**Resolved**—That this Congress hereby tenders its most grateful acknowledgments to Sir W. Wedderburn, and the members of the British Congress Committee, for the services rendered by them to India during the past year, and respectfully urges them to widen henceforth the sphere of their usefulness, by interesting themselves, not only in those questions dealt with by the Congress here, but in all Indian matters submitted to them, and properly vouched for, in which any principle accepted by the Congress is involved.

## RESOLUTION XIII.

**Resolved**—That this Congress puts on record an expression of the gratitude felt, throughout India, for the signal services rendered by the late Mr. Charles Bradlaugh to that country's cause, and of the deep and universal sorrow which his untimely death has engendered ; and that a copy of this Resolution, signed by the President, be transmitted through the British Committee for presentation to Mrs. Bradlaugh Bonner.

## RESOLUTION XIV.

**Resolved**—That this Congress, hereby, puts formally on record its high estimate and deep appreciation of the great services which Mr. Dadabhai Naorojee has rendered, during more than a quarter of a century, to the cause of India ; that it expresses its unshaken confidence in him and its earnest hope that he may prove successful, at the coming elections, in his candidature for Central Finsbury, and, at the same time, tenders, on behalf of the vast population it represents, India's most cordial acknowledgments to all in England, whether in Central Finsbury or elsewhere, who have aided, or may aid him, to win a seat in the House of Commons.

## RESOLUTION XV.

**Resolved**—That in view of the General Election now impending in England, and in accordance with the recommendation of our British Committee, the provisional arrangements, set on foot in pursuance of the Resolution passed at the Calcutta Congress of 1890, for holding, all things being convenient, a Congress of not less than 100 Delegates in England in 1892, be now suspended until after such General Election.

## RESOLUTION XVI.

**Resolved**—That a sum of Rs. 40,000, exclusive of individual donations, is assigned for the expenses of the British Committee of the Congress, and Rs. 6,000 for the General Secretary's office and establishment, and that the several circles do contribute as arranged in Committee for the year 1892.

## RESOLUTION XVII.

**Resolved**—That Mr. A. O. Hume and Pandit Ajoodhianath are re-elected General and Joint-General Secretaries for the ensuing year.

## RESOLUTION XVIII.

**Resolved**—That the Eighth Indian National Congress do assemble on the 26th December 1892 at Allahabad.

P. ANANDA CHARLU,
*President of the Seventh Indian National Congress.*

# DETAILED
# REPORT OF THE PROCEEDINGS
OF THE
# SEVENTH INDIAN NATIONAL CONGRESS,
HELD AT
# NAGPORE,
*ON THE 28th, 29th, & 30th DECEMBER, 1891.*

## FIRST DAY'S PROCEEDINGS.

**1st Day.**

FOR THE SITTINGS of the SEVENTH INDIAN NATIONAL CONGRESS, a most beautiful Pavilion had been erected in the Lall Bagh, close to the Nagpore Railway Station. The Pavilion was small, only 180 by 120 feet, and since many passages and a central open space had to be left, it only afforded room for just 4,000 chairs, but it was certainly the best proportioned and most elegantly finished and decorated that the Congress has thus far enjoyed.

When the Congress assembled early in the afternoon of Monday, the 28th of December 1891, this Pavilion was filled to overflowing, and despite the remoteness of Nagpore, itself only a second rate city, the number of visitors fell little short of that recorded when the Congress met at Calcutta and Bombay.

At 2 P.M. precisely Mr. C. Narain Swami Nayadu, the Chairman of the Nagpore Municipality (the Mayor in fact of that city), who was also Chairman of the Congress Reception Committee, and whose duty, *ex-officio*, it was to welcome the delegates and invite them to elect a President, ascended the platform and took his seat.

MR. C. NARAIN SWAMI NAYADU (*Nagpore, No.* 432, *in list*) rose and said :—

**Chairman of Reception Committee's Address.**

SISTER AND BROTHER DELEGATES,—As Chairman of the Nagpore Reception Committee (an honor which I fear I have but ill-deserved), the most pleasant duty of welcoming you all to our Seventh Indian National Congress devolves upon me. The word "seven" awakens in me a strange sensation. It has a mysterious meaning. It has ever been considered by the best and wisest men of all ages as an auspicious number, carrying with it virtues of a peculiar character. It is a most auspicious sign, indeed, that the Congress, after its hard-fought battles on India's coasts, at Bombay, Madras and Calcutta, has at last been attracted by our *Arya Varta*, our mother country, to the very centre of the Empire, from whence I fully trust it will, by the grace of Providence, so develop and spread its vivifying life-giving influence, as to leave no corner of this great Empire uncheered by the gospel of good hope, that it bears to all India's children. (*Cheers*). May it be from Nagpur as a centre that our proposed mission issues to England, to impress upon our enlightened and ever-well-wishing Aryan brothers there, the necessity of enfranchising us, redressing our just grievances, and bringing us to the same level as themselves, as they have nobly pledged themselves before God and man to do. May it be from Nagpur, I say, as a centre, that this grand mission may start. (*Cheers*).

1st Day.

Chairman of Reception Committee's Address.

Ours is a humble province, a small city; our resources are very limited, and education here has, as yet, made no such great progress as in those parts of the country, which for far longer periods have enjoyed the privilege of British rule. But though we cannot for a moment pretend to vie with the splendid receptions accorded to you in the grander capitals of this great empire, we can at least honestly assure you—and I do so from the bottom of my heart—that in no other place have the people been more truly rejoiced at your presence, or more earnestly anxious to do all their little possible to make you welcome, happy and comfortable. (*Cheers*). Welcome, dear friends, welcome, welcome a thousand times! Forgive any shortcomings in our arrangements, and believe us that never were prouder or happier hosts, never guests that their hosts desired more to honor; that poor and humble as we are, our whole hearts are with you, our fellow-countrymen, and with the great cause which unites this day all India in one close brotherhood, seeking by all honorable and open means the good of our dear mother country, and all her countless millions of children. (*Loud cheers*).

At the very outset I desire, with your permission, to strike what I conceive to be the keynotes of this great, and, as many now feel, sacred movement. Loyalty to the British Crown have of the British people to whose advent, here, India owes its rebirth, a thorough and ungrudging appreciation of the excellence of the intentions of our Government in India, and a fixed desire and firm resolve to bring about, by loyal and constitutional means, such administrative reforms as shall permit of those good intentions, bearing still better fruit for India's people, than they have hitherto yielded. (*Cheers*).

Despite what some few people still seem to fancy, we are neither so inconsiderate nor so ungrateful as not to recognize fully and be deeply grateful for those good things that, under God's dispensing providence, have accrued to us through and by means of British Rule. But we clearly see that this Rule is still in many respects capable of improvement, and that year, by year, as time rolls on and the population increases and the natural and necessary consequences of widespread education evolve on a larger and ever larger scale, the necessity for that improvement becomes more and more urgent. Loyal and loving subjects of Great Britain as we are, desirous of the everlasting union of England and India, we *know*—let outsiders misjudge us as they may—that we can render no greater service to either country than by openly protesting against what we consider unsuitable and defective in the existing administration, and by insisting, by all proper and legitimate means, on those changes in this administration, which we, as children of the soil, and as knowing our own country and our countrymen in many respects better than our Rulers, see and feel to be a necessity of the times.

It is a great help and encouragement to us, after the unmerited abuse to which we were subjected in earlier years, to find that many of the ablest and greatest men, both in England and India, now commence to realize the great service that the Congress is performing, and to lend an ear to its counsels.

We remember with gratitude and satisfaction our present Viceroy's declaration last January, that the Congress was a perfectly legitimate movement, that every one, not a Government servant, was perfectly free to join it, and that all Government officials were prohibited from impeding it in any way or putting pressure on any one to induce them to abstain from aiding or joining it. (*Cheers.*)

Thus encouraged, and true to our first principles, true to England, true to our beloved country and our countrymen, let us persevere in the good work. One obstacle,—the cruel misconception, and, must I say it, the still more cruel misrepresentation of our aims and objects to which we were subjected,— has been practically overcome, but many others still remain. We have to get the rank and file of the European official community, as well as those of the higher ranks, not merely to tolerate us as harmless, well-intentioned enthusiasts, but to realize that we are earnest, practical men, who do really know our country and our countrymen, their wants and their aspirations, in many respects better than even the ablest amongst themselves. We have got to get them, in a word, to work along with us, realizing our capacities and usefulness, while we, on our part, cordially acknowledge their superiority in many points. We have got to bring home our exact position, the inequitable disabilities we labor under, our many grievances, the miserable condition of fully one-sixth of our poor population, to the Britishelectorate, and through them bring such pressure to bear on the overworked British House of Commons as will lead it to take up the legislation needful to permit the authorities here to effect the reforms we pray for. We have got to educate, each in our own province, district and town, those of our fellows, who as yet have failed to realize the purpose and true significance of our movement. We have to get the whole country solid behind us, and this we can do, and with God's help will do. (*Loud cheers.*) Lastly, remembering what our friend and General Secretary, India's "Grand old man," is never weary of telling us,

**1st Day.**

**Chairman of Reception Committee's Address.**

*viz.*, that in the long run every nation ever gets exactly as good a Government as it deserves, let us set our own houses in order, and make sure that we do really and truly deserve a better Government, in many respects, than is now ours ; let us aim at higher and nobler things than those which at present too absorbingly occupy most of us let us prove ourselves worthy, not only of a better Government, but of the great land that has borne us, and the illustrious ancestors from whom we have descended. (*Loud cheers*). But I occupy too much of your time (*no, no ; go on, go on*), and I must, without further preface, now call upon you to elect your President. (*Cheers.*)

Before you proceed to discharge this duty, however, there is one point which has escaped me, and to which I am bound to give every prominence, and that is the friendly and sympathetic attitude of our official chiefs here and in Berar. As to Berar I dare say my friend Rao Saheb Deo Rao Vinayek will have some mention to make of the kindly sympathy which Colonel Kenneth Mackenzie, the Commissioner of those Provinces, has ever displayed towards the Indian community and their aspirations. Here, I as a Central Provinces man, am chiefly concerned in acknowledging, publicly and gratefully, the liberal manner in which our respected Chief Commissioner, Mr. A. P. Macdonell, has dealt with the Congress question. Here in the Central Provinces we have had no official opposition to encounter. Our officials as a body are, it seems to me, certainly more in sympathy and touch with us Indians here than, if we are to believe half we hear, the officials in many other parts of the country seem to be. As regards the Congress, Mr. Macdonell has most unreservedly declared, both in words and in writing, that, so far as he was concerned, every official who wished it was at full liberty to attend the Congress as a visitor, and that all might rest assured that he should think no worse and no better of any officer because he did or did not attend the Congress ; it was a matter to be left entirely to their own discretion and in which they might just please themselves. To me in conversation he fully endorsed Lord Lansdowne's famous letter, which set forth that the Congress was a perfectly legitimate movement, and that the Congress party are analogous to the Liberal party in England, and he added : "Of course you Indian gentlemen, who think as you do, have a perfect right to agitate in a constitutional manner for those concessions to which you consider yourselves entitled." (*Cheers.*)

Gentlemen, if all the rulers and officials in India resembled the Chief Commissioner of the Central Provinces, and his officers, India would not now need, and would never have needed, a National Congress. But, alas ! they constitute exceptions and not the rule, and we are bound all of us to acknowledge in the most public manner such liberality and manly freedom from bureaucratic prejudice, and therefore before I go further I will ask you to give three cheers for Mr. A. P. Macdonell and the officers of the Central Provinces Commission. (*Loud and continued cheers.*)

And now this duty discharged, let me once more ask you to proceed to elect your President.

**Election of a President.**

**Pundit Ajoodhia Nath proposes Row Saheb P. Ananda Charlu.**

PUNDIT AJOODHIA NATH (*Allahabad, No.* 74, *in list*)—MR. CHAIRMAN AND FELLOW DELEGATES,—It is my privilege to ask you to elect Rai Bahadur Ananda Charlu as your President. (*Cheers.*) He is a leading Pleader in the Madras High Court and a leading citizen of Madras. He is a member of that small but illustrious band which originally founded the Congress at Bombay, and ever since then he has firmly stood by it. Whether Government officers declared themselves in favor of or against the movement, he has always openly proclaimed his adherence to the noble cause. He has not missed a single session of the Congress, and he has always taken a very deep interest in the movement. (*Cheers.*)

**Mr. Pherozshah Mehta seconds.**

MR. PHEROZSHAH M. MEHTA (*Bombay, No.* 256, *in list*)—MR. CHAIRMAN AND GENTLEMEN,—I have great pleasure in seconding the resolution which has just been placed before you by the Honorable Pundit Ajoodhia Nath. I have no doubt that the delegates present would have rejoiced if the Honorable Pundit himself had been voted to the chair this year. (*Cheers*). But we know that he is as modest and unselfish as he is public-spirited, patriotic and energetic. But while we should have been glad to see the Pundit in the chair, we are equally glad to hail, as President this year, a representative from that presidency which has done so much for the Congress. I have no doubt, gentlemen, that you will confirm the appointment of Mr. Ananda Charlu as President of the Congress with the most perfect unanimity. (*Cheers*).

The motion was then put to the assembly by the Chairman of the Reception Committee.

**Row Saheb P. Ananda Charlu declared duly elected.**

MR. C. NARAIN SWAMI NAYADU (*Madras, No.* 432, *in list*)—I now declare our friend Row Saheb P. Ananda Charlu, Bahadur, to have been duly elected President of this Seventh Indian National Congress, and on your behalf I invite him to take the Presidential Chair.

**1st Day.**

**The President's Inaugural Address.**

Row Saheb P. Ananda Charlu (*Madras, No.* 762, *in list*), then took his seat and, again rising, said:

Friends and Fellow Citizens,—I thank you most warmly for making me take the Presidential Chair on this occasion. That chair has narrowly missed a far higher honor than I can do to it, owing to two unforeseen occurrences. One of these occurrences is that the Hon'ble Pundit Ajoodhia Nath is unfortunately, for both you and me, not a Madrassee. Were it not that he genereusly abdicated the dignity in favour of Madras, I should gladly have avoided the danger of accepting a situation that would draw me into comparison with that unselfish. whole-hearted, intrepid, and outspoken apostle of this great national movement, (*Cheers*). But in this world of imperfections and of complex considerations, duty does not always fall on the fittest shoulders, and there is the additional reason that the unanimous mandate of the country compels my obedience.

The second occurrence I allude to, as the cause of my standing here to-day, is that my friend Dewan Bahadur Subramaniya Iyer* has been raised to a seat on the High Court Bench of Madras. At the first blush, this may seem a matter for regret ; but, from the point of view from which I regard it, it affords reason for congratulation, rather than for regret, and that, even *so far as the Congress is concerned* ; for does it not give us another and eloquent proof that, where other merits exist, active service in the cause of the public does, by no means, clash with the equally honourable ambition of obtaining high office as a public servant. Mr. Subramaniya Iyer's is the rare case of one who had not deliberately stood aloof from all public movements, with the possible prospect of entering Government service, and who, not lured away from the call of public duty by the first instalment of Government patronage, returned to that duty, as cheerfully and as actively as before, and who has been nevertheless again selected, to fill a high place in the official hierarchy of this country. With a scrupulous regard for the demands of both vocations, he took particular care that neither suffered by reason of the other, or on account of the other. Therefore, I assure you that, without meaning that I hope adequately to fill his place as the President of this great National Assembly, it should be a matter of rejoicing to the Congress that another of its prominent workers should have been elevated to the most dignified office, as yet open to indigonous talent, under the British administration of this country.

These personal considerations remind me of the loss—the irreparable loss—which the Congress has sustained, since its last sitting, by the lamented death of Mr. Charles Bradlaugh. *He* was the redoubtable champion who brought, within the domain of practical politics, one of the foremost subjects in the Congress programme. Till Mr. Bradlaugh, who may, without exaggeration, be described as an embodiment of universal benevolence, befriended our cause with his characteristic unselfishness, all our pathetic appeals for a forward step, in the direction of reforming our Legislative Councils, remained a veritable cry in the wilderness ; and the fact that, upon his death, even Lord Cross's halting measure was dropped, puts this beyond all doubt.

It is a matter for deep sorrow that Mr Charles Bradlaugh's useful career was cut short before he could redeem even his guarded promise to us, that he hoped to carve and shape a step or two in the up-hill work that lay in front of us—a work of such magnitude and importance as to make him weigh most scrupulously the words he used. There is little prospect of any *one* man proving to us the tower of strength that he unquestionably was, during the short time that we had the benefit of his lively sympathy and unremitting effort. We have indeed been slow to crect a memorial suited to his great merits and his unpurchased services in our cause ; and our unfriendly critics have *not* been slow to make capital out of this seeming apathy. In the Presidency from which I come, famine and its attendant evils are, within my personal knowledge, chiefly answerable for this seeming remissness in the fulfilment of our duty—a duty which, as we view it, consists in a recognition of the work of that unflinching advocate of the people's rights, not merely by the monied few, but also by that far larger class to which he belonged, and of which he was proud to declare that he reckoned himself as one. Our monsoons, gentlemen, have begun to give signs of improvement, though after a very long delay. May this improved state of things bring in thousands of small contributions which, tiny like the raindrops individually, may in the aggregate fill to overflowing the coffers of the many Bradlaugh Committees in the land. I have little doubt that this earnest appeal will meet with a ready, wide and adequate response before many months are over.

I shall next invite you, brethren, to join me in paying a similar loving, though mournful, tribute to the memories of two distinguished men who had figured as the Chairmen of Congress Reception Committees, and of whom death has robbed us since our last session—Raja Sir T. Madhava Rao, K.C.S.I., and Dr. Rejendra Lala Mitra, the latter of whom is, I think,

* This gentleman had been originally proposed by several committees for the Presidentship. His elevation to the Bench of the High Court rendered it impossible for him to take part in any Political movement.

**1st Day.**

**The President's Inaugural Address.**

better described and wider known under that title, which is a tribute to his profound scholarship and varied learning, than by the distinctions of Rai Bahadur and of Rajah—distinctions which came to him too late to add any lustre to his already brilliant fame. Our sincere gratitude is due to them for the eloquent exposition of the views of the Congress Party which their speeches as Chairmen embodied, and for the prominent part they took in the sittings of the Congress which they so heartily ushered in.

One more sincere friend of India, happily living and breathing in our midst and meriting our warmest acknowledgment, remains yet to be named—our General Secretary, Mr. A. O. Hume. (*Cheers*). Through good report and through evil report, and at the sacrifice of health, money, well-earned ease, and peace of mind, he has steadily and earnestly adhered to his labour of love in the progressive interests of the people of this country, and he has thus earned, not only *our* love and gratitude, but I hope also the love and gratitude of our children and children's children. (*Loud cheers.*)

He has recently given us warning that he contemplates an early retirement from his Indian field of labour—a retirement which involves the resignation of his office as the General Secretary of the Indian National Congress. This, we must confess, has come upon us as a surprise, though we had no business to be unprepared for it. This unpreparedness is, in the main, traceable to the habits generated in us by the monopolising character of British Indian rule which, taking upon itself all the solicitudes and almost all the responsibilities of the administration of the country, has given but little occasion for the development in us of the capacities and aptitudes necessary for facing with confidence a sudden emergency. If this were the second or third Session of the Congress, I should despond and shudder at the inevitable consequences. But thanks to his indefatigable exertions and his prophetic sagacity, he has coupled his warning with the inspiriting assurance that one great work of the Congress has been accomplished; that its programme has been built up and promulgated; that the present seventh session is needed, not so much to discuss new subjects, as to put the seal on all that its predecessors had done; and that it completes one distinct stage of our progress.

These are, without doubt, noble and encouraging words, and every syllable of them deserves our earnest attention. Let us look back on our career. What was our task at starting? In the words of our General Secretary, "a great work had to be done—we had to clear our own ideas and then make them clear to our opponents;—to thresh out by persistent discussion the wheat of our aspirations from the great body of chaff that must, in the very nature of things, have accompanied it. We had to find out exactly what those reforms were, which the country, as a whole, most desired; we had to evolve and formulate a clear and succinct programme—to erect a standard around which, now and for all time, until that programme is realized, all reformers and well-wishers of India could gather; and we had to place that programme on record in such a form that neither foreign autocrats nor domestic traitors could efface its pregnant lines," or read into those lines a meaning that they were not intended to convey.

Now, let us note how we were a mere handful, numbering less than four score when we started on our national mission; how at that moment it was little more than an untried, though cherished, idea that we should strive to mitigate, if not to eradicate, race-prejudices, to disarm creed-antipathies, and to remove provincial jealousies; and how, by that achievement as a means towards an end, we wished to develop and consolidate sentiments of national unity. Let us next note that, when under the impulse then given to our renovated national instincts, we met next year in Calcutta, that ripe scholar and sober antiquarian Dr. Rajendra Lala Mitra declared that he saw in the assembly before him the commencement of the realization of the dream of his life, *viz*, to witness the scattered units of his race come together, coalesce, and stand welded into one nation. Then came our session in Madras, and there we succeeded in blotting out the stigma that one part of our country was "benighted," and we exhibited the spectacle of a gathering, more considerable in numbers, more representative in composition, more adequate in the proportion of the Muhammadan contingent, more cordial in feeling, more in unison with the name of *this* institution, wider in basis and altogether a nearer approximation than had till then been attained to the conception of a nationality in that sense in which alone that word has a meaning in political parlance. On the impregnable basis which that gathering illustrated, the subsequent sessions of the Congress were constituted, and our success has been great and signal.

To detract from the worth and significance of the well-knit, ever-expanding phalanx known as the Indian National Congress, a desultory controversy was raised round the word *nationality*,—a controversy at once learned and unlearned, ingenious and stupid, etymological and ethnological. Now a common religion was put forward as the differentia; now a common language ; now a proved or provable common extraction ; and now the presence of the privileges of commensality and inter-conjugal kinship. These ill-considered and ill-intentioned hypotheses have, one and all, fallen to the ground, and no wonder: for the evident circumstance was lost sight of, that words might have divers acceptations—each most appropriate for one purpose, and, in a like degree, inappropriate for other purposes. In my view the word "nationality" should be taken to have the same meaning as the Sanscrit *Prajah*, which is the correlative of the term Rajah—the ruling power. Though, like the term *Prajah*, it may have various significations, it has but one obvious, unmistakable meaning in political language, *viz.*, the aggregate of those that are (to adapt and adopt the words of a writer in the *National Review*)—"citizens of one country, subordinate to one power, subject to one supreme Legislature, taxed by one authority, influenced, for weal or woe, by one system of administration, urged by like impulses to secure like rights and to be relieved of like burdens." It is in reality a potential class. In the first place it has for its central stock—like the trunk of a tree—the people who have for ages and generations settled and domiciled in a country, with more or less ethnic identity at bottom and more or less unified by being continually subjected to identical environments and to the inevitable process of assimilation. In the next place it gets added to, from time to time, by the accession of other peoples—like scions engrafted on the central stem, or like creepers attaching thereto—who settle in the country in a like manner, and come under the many unifying influences already referred to, though *still* exhibiting marks of separateness and distinctness. Affirm this standard, and you have an Indian nation. Deny it, and you have a nation *nowhere* on the face of the earth. (*Cheers.*)

A common language, a common religion, inter-dining, and inter-marriage are, without doubt, potent auxiliaries. These help, no doubt, by affording facilities for co-operation and by rendering easy the attainment of common objects. But, for all that, they are (at best) inseparable accidents, and it betrays a grievous obliquity of judgment to esteem them as constituting the very essence of what is understood by the term *nation.* We began, proceeded, and have persevered up to this day on the tacit assumption that such is the correct doctrine, and let us continue to exert ourselves on that principle at least as a working definition ; because, by pursuing such a course, and within the short period of seven years, we have accomplished *the great and palpable fact* that the Hindu and Mahomedan populations of this country—long separated from one another—long divided by parochial differences—long kept apart and estranged from one another by sectional and sectarian jealousies—have at last recognised one another as members of a single brotherhood, despite the many differences that still linger. This is a magnificent product of the Congress *as a mighty nationaliser.* The part it has already played in this direction is, indeed, glorious, and I am sure you will not charge me with holding Utopian views if, on the basis of what has been achieved and in view to the vital interests involved, I venture to predict that, through the agency of the Congress, far more intimate relations and far closer forms of kinship are in store for us in the not-remote future.

If this, brethren, is the subjective benefit, we, as the members of the Congress, have secured : what have we to show as its objective results ? I need not accumulate facts to make this clear. Let us first recall to our minds that, when we met at Bombay in the first year of our existence, we were referred to by the then head of the Indian Government only as an influential and intelligent body. Let us next remember that, when last year we assembled in the capital of this Empire, the present head of the Indian Government stamped and labelled us as an *established constitutional party,* carrying on a *legitimate* work with *legitimate* instruments and according to *acknowledged* methods. This is much for an Indian Viceroy to accept, though it is open to doubt whether we have received *all* our due, and whether we do not, correctly speaking, correspond to a more numerous, more influential, and more favoured party in England. Not only was there this change of opinion about ourselves, but there has been a distinct step taken by the authorities on the lines we had chalked out for reform. What was Lord Cross's India Bill but a confirmation of our views and a response—though a faltering response—to our chorus-voice. May we not also justly take credit for the labors (such as they were) of the Public Service Commission and the consequent raising of age for candidates to the Indian Covenanted Service, the inauguration of the policy of a larger recruitment of the Uncovenanted Service from the natives of this country, the creation of a Legislative Council for the N. W. Provinces, and a *marked improvement* in the class or quality of members selected for all the Legislative Councils in the country ever since. These are unmistakable evidences of our objective achievements, and I think, gentlemen, they are such as we may well be proud of.

But, notwithstanding all these grounds for congratulating ourselves, the lamentable fact remains that, *in regard to our higher claims,* little beyond lip-concession in this country and a half-hearted and halting measure (now shelved) in the imperial metropolis, has as yet fallen to our lot. We may work ever so long in this country, the prospect does not seem to brighten ; and the real cause may chiefly be that "the Government in India has no power ; the Council in London has no power ; the House of Commons *has* the power, but it refuses or neglects to exercise it," as Mr. Yule asserted from his place as the President of our session at Allahabad.

There is no doubt that Mr. Yule's last disjunctive sentence means more than he wished to convey. Nor did he intend all that is signified by his statement that six hundred and fifty odd members, who are bound to be the guardians and protectors of India's rights and liberties, "have thrown the great and solemn trust of an inscrutable Providence back upon the hands of Providence to be looked after as Providence itself thought best." Mr. Yule himself made this clear when he virtually told us, almost immediately after, that the members of the House of Commons had not time enough and information enough on the questions that came up before them, to be able to judge rightly.

What then is the remedy ? On whom is it incumbent to seek and secure the remedy ? The answer has been given, that the remedy lies in instructing the British public and in raising their level of information regarding Indian affairs to the standard of usefulness. The further answer has been given, that the duty of seeking and securing that remedy lies primarily on ourselves, secondarily on the British voting and thought-leading public, and finally on their accredited representatives who constitute the House of Commons. In partial discharge of these duties, we have maintained the British Congress Committee, composed of earnest and generous souls, working gratuitously for us, with a talented Secretary in Mr. Digby, whose well-informed, timely and earnest efforts in our behalf are the admiration of our friends and a thorn in the ribs of those of our foes, who endeavour to gain a point by deluding an uninstructed public with false and ill-founded representations. No words of mine are necessary to bring home to you the fact that a more capable, self-denying, and benevolent body of men never put their shoulders to a philanthropic work in our interests, and that a larger measure of success was never achieved than was accomplished by them, with their circumscribed opportunities and with many other demands on their time and attention. There are abundant signs that their numbers will increase, and that the sphere of their influence and usefulness will widen, provided we do, as I shall presently show, what is expected of us. A second agency which has come into being, and which is entirely due to British generosity, is the Indian party formed in the House of Commons itself. Mr. Charles Bradlaugh was its brilliant centre-piece, and since death filched that priceless jewel from us, the setting has remained with the socket still to be filled in. Here, again, it depends on ourselves whether *that* gap is to be adequately filled, and that body is to receive, in the requisite measure, accession of strength in numbers and influence ; or whether we are to be thrown back a quarter of a century, and find ourselves in the pre-Bradlaugh, pre-Congress, and pre-Ripon days of apathy, obscurity and inert resignation (*No, no*).

The anxious and well-considered advice of the British Congress Committee, and the mature opinion of the members of the Parliamentary Indian party, concur in urging us to change the *venue*—to transfer our operations to London itself. Members of our body, who have already rendered yeoman's service in England as our delegates before the British public, are of the same mind. Any doubt that may still linger must be dispelled by the fact that, although Lord Dufferin, as the head of the Indian Government, urged the wisdom and desirability of adopting some form of the elective principle in the constitution of our Legislative Councils, his recommendation, based—be it noted—on his personal grasp of local conditions, has been burked ; and that even the make-shift of a limping substitute for it, in the shape of Lord Cross's India Bill, has been shelved and pigeon-holed no one knows for how long, no one can tell with what motives. In the face of such a fate having overtaken the suggestions of the most cautious, diplomatic and wary Viceroy we have had, can we expect that either the present Viceroy, albeit he has put his seal of approval on us as a constitutional party, or any of his successors, will so far *discount their self-respect* as to court a similar summary and unceremonious treatment of their proposals ? It seems to me that the cumulative force of all these considerations points unmistakably to the absolute necessity of translating ourselves to London with the Congress banner over our heads, emblazoned with the figure of the Union Jack, as much for indicating our aims and objects as for fanning away from the delegates, assembled under its shade, all the noxious exhalations from those foul mouths which impute to us seditious intentions and anti-English proclivities,—as if, forsooth, the leaders of the Congress, who are the outcome of the British rule, and whose very existence depends on the maintenance of the British power in India, could be so irrational as to adopt the suicidal policy of lopping off the very branch on which they stand.

This momentous step of holding a meeting in London we can neither avoid nor postpone ; and I entreat you to revolve it earnestly in your minds, and to resolve right manfully to do what you finally find to be your plain duty. In regard to this step, I do not say that there are not serious difficulties to overcome. One great barrier—the dread of social ostracism—is not to be got rid of by mere rhetorical outbursts. The question deserves our most serious consideration.

It has to be soberly and dispassionately noted whether the restrictions as to the countries we could visit were not more stringent by far in the earliest times than ever after; whether many regions, originally tabooed in express terms in the Smrithis, were not in later days tacitly taken out of the category of forbidden land for an Aryan to enter; whether, in so far as a sea voyage is concerned, a distinction has not been drawn between the north and the south of India on the ground of custom; and whether, where the custom had existed, it was not allowed to be unobjectionable and perfectly compatible with being within the pale of Hinduism; and whether, lastly, and above all, there is not ground for the conclusion that the stringency of the rules in the Smrithis has been authoritatively declared to admit of relaxation in so far as the Grihasta is concerned, though not in the case of those who, vowing to consecrate themselves to a life of piety, practically release themselves from social and political duties and obligations, and are *therefore* denied the immunities held out to those who labour *for* and *in* such society.

If we decide in the affirmative, infinite will be our credit. If in so deciding it, we are forsaken by our kith and kin, it will still be considerably to our credit that we have made a heroic sacrifice for the sake of our country and in the interests of those very kith and kin who may be so cruel as to cast us off. But such social persecution and banishment cannot continue for ever. Our cause is so just and righteous, our principles and methods of action so loyal and upright, our opportunities of doing good so many and varied, that in the long run even our worst enemies will learn to find in us their best friends, and such of our kinsmen as estrange themselves from us will, I believe, gladly associate with us again and restore to us the social privileges that they temporarily withhold from us. Such is my belief, judging from precedents, in other, yet analogous, departures. But if the worst should happen, there is already the beginning of a Congress-caste fundamentally based on Hinduism and substantially in accord with its dictates, and such a visitation as a determined social banishment lasting for any length of time would only tend to cement that caste more closely together and to greater purpose. Thus would it be possible to form the nucleus of a daily multiplying and expansive fraternity, and it would soon be seen at large that by social union with it there is much to gain in matters mundane and little to lose in interests truly spiritual.

Should we succeed in holding a Session in London, and thereby secure seats for *elected* members in our Legislative Councils, that in itself would give us much indirect help in pushing on internal reform. A decent interment of rather moribund laws, virtually dead but lingering only to thwart, and the introduction of fresh laws to give an impulse to the betterment of our social condition, are now hopeless impossibilities. The Government fight shy of them, and nominated members, who take their cue from that Government, are equally timorous. If, however, this quiescence is departed from in any instance under the existing system, the Government and the members that lend themselves to the departure at once fall victims to calumnious abuse and unpopularity; for it is quite possible for a minority to raise a powerful cry and give it the character of a popular outburst of indignation. As matters stand, no means exist for gauging the popular feeling for or against the measure. Newspapers have too often given an uncertain sound, and commissions to take evidence cannot sit long enough and examine a large enough number of witnesses to be sure that a correct conclusion has been reached. If, as we propose, elected members should have seats among our legislators, the problem would be fairly solved. Men, seeking election, would find it necessary to present themselves with such proposals as, in their view, might be acceptable to the popular mind, and the fact of their being elected or rejected would, in many cases, afford conclusive proof whether the legislation proposed was well-timed or not, in harmony with popular feeling or at variance with it. Should any dispute arise as to whether a legislative measure proposed is popular or otherwise, the member in charge of it, and members in favour of it, might resign their seats and seek re-election on that very measure, while the Government, not identifying itself with the measure, would, without incurring any odium, be able to allow useful legislation to go on or to be tried, respecting matters which its solicitude, not to be misunderstood and not to incur unpopularity, might make it avoid.

Whatever may be our decision as to the duty of sending a gallant contingent to London to make up the Session of the Congress there, it is undoubtedly imperative on us to penetrate to the masses here more than hitherto, and deeply imbue them with the spirit of the Congress which is only another name for national sentiment. (*Cheers.*) The impression is still prevalent that as yet the effect of our efforts in this direction has been

**1st Day.**

**The President's Inaugural Address.**

only slight, and we have done little more than to scratch the outer skin and to awaken the spasmodic enthusiasm of our unanglicised brethren. Let us approach them, with all the energy and fervour that we have hitherto brought to the Congress platform, but which energy and fervour—so far as the Indian field is concerned—will not, on the present scale, be necessary for that purpose in future, quite apart from the question whether we should close our Congress labours in India for a time.

Whether we resolve to rest on our oars or not, it becomes our bounden duty all the same to go more amid the masses and to saturate their minds with the aspirations of a united nationality. There is another *very solid reason* for such effort. It involves the fulfilment of a trust; for, constituting the upper strata of the Indian society, we have first caught the light of the enlightened West—as mountain tops catch the first glimpses of the rising sun. But, unlike those glimpses, that light will not descend to the lower strata of our society, unless we actively transmit it from a sense of duty and a sense of honor.

Let us impart to our people, as we are in righteousness bound to do, our conviction that they should cease to look upon the British rule as the rule of a foreign people. We should ask them to look upon our British rulers as filling a gap that has existed in our national economy—as taking the place once held by the Kshatria, and as being therefore part and parcel of the traditional administrative mechanism of the land.

Let us not heed the sinister cry that we shall thereby drag the people of this country into discussing politics—into paths they are supposed never before to have trodden. For our part, *we* shall only act up to the undoubted right involved in the fact that we are England's subjects; and, as regards our countrymen at large, they will only be brought back to those privileges, which—unquestioned by authority and with the full knowledge of authority—our ancestors are recorded to have enjoyed in their Samsaths, Sabhas and Ootwaras, in the days treated of in that grand old epic—the Mahabharata.

Gentlemen, I am deeply thankful to you for the patient and indulgent attention you have accorded to me. Our British rulers have indeed withheld from us the privilege of demonstrating our love and loyalty towards our Sovereign Lady, the Empress Queen, by fighting her battles as volunteers under the British flag; but we have still some consolation left in the fact that "peace hath her victories no less renowned than those of war." The Congress platform is the field on which such bloodless triumphs are to be won, and though as yet we have had but a small measure of success, there is ground for hope in what the poet sings,—

> "For freedom's battle once begun,
> * * * *
> Though baffled oft, is ever won."

We, as the pioneers of the movement, may attain little more than the satisfaction of upholding what is right and protesting against what is wrong; but succeeding generations will reap the fruit of our labours, and will cherish with fond remembrance the names of those who had the courage and the humanity, the singleness of purpose and the self-sacrificing devotion to duty, to work for the benefit of posterity, in spite of calumny and persecution and great personal loss. Men, such as these, may attain no titles of distinction from Government, but they are "nobles by the right of an earlier creation." They may fail to win honour from their contemporaries as the truest apostles, but they are "priests by the imposition of a mightier hand;" and, when their life's work is done, they will have that highest of all earthly rewards,—the sense of having left their country better than they had found it,—the glory of having built up into a united and compact nation the divers races and classes of the Indian population, and the satisfaction of having led a people, sunk in political and social torpor, to think and act for themselves, and strive to work out their own wellbeing by constitutional and righteous methods. (*Loud and continued cheers*).

And now, gentlemen, I have to request you to elect your Subjects Committee.

**Election of the Subjects Committee.**

The delegates representing each of the Congress Circles then handed in slips bearing the names of those delegates chosen by them to represent their circle on the Subjects Committee:—

*The General Secretary then read out the names of the gentlemen thus elected, which were as follow:—*

| | | | |
|---|---|---|---|
| CALCUTTA CIRCLE. | 1. | J. GHOSAL, ESQ. | (Calcutta.) |
| | 2. | PANDIT PRAN NATH SARASVATI | ( do. ) |
| | 3. | REVD. C. N. BANERJI | ( do. ) |
| | 4. | BABU KALI CHARAN BANERJI | ( do. ) |
| | 5. | „ SURENDRA NATH BANERJI | ( do. ) |
| | 6. | „ BHUPENDRA NATH BOSE | ( do. ) |

**Election of the Subjects Committee.**

| Circle | No. | Name | Place |
|---|---|---|---|
| CALCUTTA CIRCLE. —(*contd.*) | 7. | BABU HERAMBO CHANDRA MOITRO | (Calcutta.) |
| | 8. | „ PREO NATH GHOSE | ( do. ) |
| | 9. | „ JAGADISH CHANDER LAHIRI | ( do. ) |
| | 10. | „ PULIN BIHARI SIRCAR | ( do. ) |
| | 11. | RAI JOTENDRO NATH CHOWDHRY | (24 Pergunnahs.) |
| | 12. | BABU AKSHAY CHARAN DASS | (Howrah.) |
| | 13. | „ JADU NATH CHATTERJEE | (Nuddeah.) |
| | 14. | „ BISWAMBHUR ROY | ( do. ) |
| | 15. | „ JAGADISH MUKERJEE | ( do. ) |
| | 16. | „ BASANTA KUMAR BOSE | ( Jessore. ) |
| | 17. | „ TRAILOKHYA NATH PAL | (Midnapur.) |
| | 18. | RAJAH SRINARAYAN PAL | ( do. ) |
| | 19. | BABU JADU BHUSHON MAZOOMDAR | ( Khulna. ) |
| DACCA CIRCLE. | 1. | BABU DHIRENDRA NATH KASTAGIR | (Chittagong.) |
| | 2. | „ PROSONNO KUMAR BOSE | (Mymensing.) |
| | 3. | DR. M. M. BOSE | ( do. ) |
| | 4. | BABU HARA KANTA SEN | ( Burrisal. ) |
| RAJSHAHYE CIRCLE. | 1. | BABU JADUB LAL ROY | ( Bogra. ) |
| | 2. | „ MADHUB CHUNDER CHATTERJEE | (Dinajpore. ) |
| | 3. | „ MOHINI MOHAN CHUCKERBUTTY | ( Pubna. ) |
| | 4. | „ MOHINI MOHUN LAHIRI | ( do. ) |
| | 5. | „ MUKUND MOHUN MOITRO | (Rajshahye. ) |
| BHAGALPUR CIRCLE. | 1. | BABU PARBUTTI CHARAN DASS | ( Bhagalpur. ) |
| CHOTA NAGPUR CIRCLE. | 1. | BABU JAGAT PAL SAHOY | (Hazaribagh.) |
| BEHAR CIRCLE. | 1. | BABU GURU PERSHAD SEN | (Bankipur.) |
| | 2. | „ SALIGRAM SINGH | ( do. ) |
| | 3. | MOULVIE ABDUL HAMID | ( do. ) |
| | 4. | MR. PRINGLE KENNEDY | (Mozufferpur.) |
| N. W. P. CIRCLE. | 1. | MUNSHI KASHI PRASAD | (Allahabad. ) |
| | 2. | PANDIT MADAN MOHAN MALAVIYA | ( do. ) |
| | 3. | „ MOTI LAL NEHRU | ( do. ) |
| | 4. | BABU CHARU CHANDAR MITTER | ( do. ) |
| | 5. | PANDIT BALDEO RAM DAVE | ( do. ) |
| | 6. | BABU KALIPROSSONO KAVIYA BISHARAD | ( do. ) |
| | 7. | MUNSHI SADRUDDEEN | ( do. ) |
| | 8. | PANDIT PRITHINATH | (Cawnpur.) |
| | 9. | HAFIZ ABDUR RAHIM | (Aligarh.) |
| | 10. | PANDIT JWALA DUTT JOSHI | (Almora.) |
| OUDH CIRCLE. | 1. | BABU BUNSHILAL SINGH | (Lucknow.) |
| | 2. | REVD. R. C. BOSE | ( do. ) |
| | 3. | BABU B. M. ROY | ( do. ) |
| | 4. | PANDIT SHYAM LAL MASLADAN | ( do. ) |
| | 5. | MUNSHI GUNGA PERSHAD VARMA | ( do. ) |
| PUNJAB CIRCLE. | 1. | LALA MURLIDHAR | (Umballa.) |
| | 2. | BABA NARAYAN SINGH | (Amritsar.) |
| | 3. | SODHI NUND KUMAR SINGH | ( do. ) |
| | 4. | CAPTAIN A. BANON | (Lahore.) |
| SCINDE CIRCLE. | 1. | MR. SHEWAKRAM AWATRAI | (Kurrachee.) |
| SURAT CIRCLE. | 1. | MR. HARDEORAM NANABHAI HARIDASS | (Surat.) |
| SHOLAPUR CIRCLE. | 1. | MR. G. K. GOKHALE | (Sholapur.) |
| | 2. | „ P. L. NAGPURKAR | ( do. ) |
| BELGAUM CIRCLE. | 1. | MR. M. B. NAMJOSHI | (Belgaum.) |
| | 2. | „ D. S. R. BHATE | ( do. ) |

**1st Day.**

**Election of the Subjects Committee.**

| | | | |
|---|---|---|---|
| Bhusawal Circle. | 1. | Mr. Vithul Govind Dastane | (Bhusawal.) |
| | 2. | „ Sakharam Ganesh | ( do. ) |
| Nugger Circle. | 1. | Mr. Sadashiv V. Jog | (Ahmednagar.) |
| | 2. | „ Shakkar Vinayek Vable | ( do. ) |
| Deccan Circle. | 1. | Rao Bahadur Vishnu Moreshvar Bhide | ( Poona. ) |
| | 2. | „ „ Gobind Ramchandra Garud | ( do. ) |
| | 3. | Rao Saheb Pandurang Ramchandra Karandikar | ( do. ) |
| | 4. | Mr. Pundlik Narayan | ( do. ) |
| Bombay Circle. | 1. | Mr. Dinshaw Eduljee Wacha | (Bombay.) |
| | 2. | „ Daji Abaji Khare | ( do. ) |
| | 3. | „ G. R. Kirloskar | ( do. ) |
| Berar Circle. | 1. | Mr. Rungnath N. Mudholkar | (Amraoti.) |
| | 2. | „ G. S. Khaparde | (Ellichpur.) |
| | 3. | Rao Saheb Deorao Vinayek | (Akola.) |
| Central Provinces (*including Nagpur and Jabalpur Circles.*) | 1. | Mr. Bhagirath Pershad | (Nagpur.) |
| | 2. | Babu Bipin Krishna Bose | ( do. ) |
| | 3. | Mr. Luxmon Govind Duraskar | (Arvi.) |
| | 4. | „ Bapurao Dada | (Nagpur.) |
| | 5. | „ Gopalrao Hari Bhide | ( do. ) |
| | 6. | Rao Saheb Chitnavis | ( do. ) |
| | 7. | Mr. Ganpatrao Ghatate | ( do. ) |
| | 8. | „ Sadaseo Rao Patwardhan | (Harda.) |
| | 9. | „ Alfred Nundy | (Jabalpur.) |
| Madras Circle. | 1. | Mr. M. Viraraghava Chariar | (Madras.) |
| | 2. | „ Viraswami Iyer | (Salem.) |
| | 3. | „ M. Krishna Chari | (Madras.) |
| | 4. | „ Ranga Chari | ( do. ) |
| | 5. | „ J. M. Nalaswami Pillai | (Madura.) |
| | 6. | „ K. Appiah Dikshitulu | (Guntur.) |
| | 7. | „ Paul Peter Pillai | (Madras.) |
| | 8. | „ P. Kesava Pillai | (Gooty.) |
| | 9. | „ K. Venkat Rao | (Bellary ) |
| | 10. | „ K. Venkata Chariar | (Salem.) |
| | 11. | „ N. Subarow Puntulu | (Coconada.) |
| | 12. | „ P. Rama Chandra Pillai | (Secunderabad.) |
| | 13. | Hon. C. Sankara Nair | (Calicut.) |
| | 14. | Rai Bahadur Sabapathi Mudliar | (Bellary.) |
| Ex-Officio. | 1. | Rai Bahadur P. Ananda Charlu | (President and Standing Counsel, Madras.) |
| | 2. | Mr. C. Narain Swami Nayudu | (Chairman, Reception Committee, Nagpore.) |
| | 3. | Mr. Pherozshah M. Mehta | (Standing Counsel, Bombay.) |
| | 4. | Mr. W. C. Bonnerjee | (Standing Counsel, Calcutta.) |
| | 5. | Mr. A. O. Hume, C. B. | (General Secretary, Punjab.) |
| | 6. | Hon. Pandit Ajudhianath | (Joint General Secretary, Allahabad.) |

Mr. Mullick (*Calcutta, No.* 34, *in list*)—I should like to ask by what process the names of the Bengal delegates, or rather the names of the Committee from Bengal, have been arrived at.

Mr. Surendra Nath Banerjee (*Calcutta, No.* 11, *in list*)—My friend may not know what has happened. There was a meeting of all the Bengal delegates.

1st Day.

Election of the Subjects Committee.

MR. MULLICK.—I am a Bengal delegate. I was not there.

MR. SURENDRA NATH BANERJEE.—It is unfortunate that you were not present. A circular was duly sent round and a formal meeting was held. We tried to reach everybody we could think of whose address we knew. At that meeting the names were submitted, and these gentlemen were elected. I think that is the formal, regular and constitutional way of electing members of the Subjects Committee, and that no objection can be taken to it.

A DELEGATE —All the delegates except that gentleman were present. It is to be regretted that our friend Mr. Mullick did not attend, but he surely could not expect seventy odd gentlemen to suspend their work because one of their number chanced to be absent. (*Cheers*).

THE PRESIDENT.—I do not think Mr. Mullick that your objection, if you intended your question as such, is sustainable. I will now ask the Congress as a whole whether they approve and ratify this election of the Subjects Committee.

*The President then put the question and the election was unanimously affirmed.*

THE PRESIDENT.—The Subjects Committee has now been duly elected, and I will ask all the members to meet me here on the *dais* as soon as this day's proceedings of the Congress has closed. But there is an important question that has been raised, and much discussed in certain quarters, *viz.*, as to whether the Congress as an Annual Meeting should continue as heretofore or be suspended for some time. To come to a satisfactory conclusion on that subject, it has been thought proper to propose the appointment of a small Sub-Committee to consider the question in all its bearings and bring up a report. Mr. Surendra Nath Banerjee will bring the proposition before you.

Res. I. Appointment of a Sub-Committee to report on the expediency of temporarily discontinuing the Annual Meetings of the Congress in India.

MR. SURENDRA NATH BANERJEE (*Calcutta, No.* 11, *in list*)—SISTER AND BROTHER DELEGATES,—I am called upon to move the following resolution, which, although a formal one, is one of the very gravest importance :—

RESOLVED—*That a Committee be appointed to consider and report, on or before the morning of the 30th instant, whether or not it is advisable to discontinue the Annual Sessions of the Indian National Congress until after the British Session, and, if not, under what regulations, as to numbers of delegates, localities for assemblage, and the like, future Congresses shall be held. The Committee to be composed as follows :—*

*Ex-Officio Members—*

The President.
The Chairman of the Reception Committee..
The General Secretary.
The Joint General Secretary.
The Standing Counsels to the Congress.

*Ordinary Members—*

Messrs. Surendranath Bannerjee.
Viraraghava Chariar.
Hafiz Abdul Raheem.
Gangapersad Varma.
Pringle Kennedy.
Guruprasad Sen.
D. E. Watcha.
M. B. Nam Joshi.
Hamid Ali Khan.
Vishnu Moreshwar Bhide.
Murlidhar.
Mudholkar.
Deo Rao Vinayek.
Gopal Rao Bhide.
Bipin Krishna Bose.
Dajee Abajee Khare.
Madana Mohan Malaviya.
Saligram Singh.
Sankara Nair.

To all outward appearance this is nothing more than a formal resolution, but the question which this Committee will be called upon to discuss is a question of the most vital

**1st Day.**

**Res. I. Appointment of a Sub-Committee to report on the expediency of temporarily discontinuing the Annual Meetings of the Congress in India.**

importance as far as this Congress is concerned. "To be or not to be," that is the question, which this Committee will be called upon to decide. Shall the Congress exist as it has existed in the past, or shall it pronounce its doom? That is the important, the vital, the pregnant question with which this Committee is charged. I do not wish to anticipate its verdict. Being on the Committee it would not be right for me to do so. But there are one or two considerations occurring to me at the present moment, which it is as well that I should bring before this meeting. Gentlemen, the spirit in which your opponents deal with any question which you take up is always one useful guide to the manner in which you should treat it It has, as you know, been suggested that we should not hold any more Annual Congresses until after the British Session. And what is the result? There is jubilation in the camp of the enemy. They say it is the beginning of the end. They say that you are about to abandon the Congress. The beginning of the end? The beginning rather of a new departure which I hope and trust will be memorable in our annals. Abandon the Congress? Much rather abandon life and all that we hold most dear. (*Loud cheers*). Abandon the Congress, the standard round which we have fought for the last eight years, the standard which we trust one day to carry proudly before us to victory? (*Cheers*) Abandon the Congress? No! We will do nothing of the kind. (*Cheers*). We mean to stick to the Congress. (*Cheers*). We mean to hold to it from year's end to year's end, until we have won for ourselves those rights and privileges to which (as natural born subjects of Her Majesty) we are indefeasibly entitled. (*Cheers*). But, gentlemen, let us look for a moment at the other side of the question. We must not blink the matter It is necessary to consider it in all its bearings. The financial aspect of the question is not to be overlooked. And when I refer to the financial aspect of the question I do so with assurance and confidence. I remember the days of the Bombay Congress. I remember our meeting one afternoon when I had the honour of making an appeal to you for the purpose of aiding the Congress with your funds, and you subscribed on the spot nearly sixty thousand rupees (*more*). Am I to understand that that enthusiasm has flagged, that that devotion has become weak, that the men of 1891 are not the men of 1889? (*No, no!*) I hope not. You are still the same! I am sure of it. Therefore I feel confident that if there is any difficulty with regard to this financial question the matter has only to be laid before you in order to evoke from you that enthusiastic response which you are accustomed to give when questions relating to your purse and connected with acts of self-sacrifice are brought before you. I have said that I do not wish to anticipate the verdict of this Committee. I am confident that it will discuss the question in all its bearings. We desire that the Congress should meet in London. I know nothing of greater importance. It means the culmination of our cherished hopes and aspirations. The Congress *must* be held in London. But if you desire this, it is necessary that we should keep up the fire, and maintain the national enthusiasm by continuing to hold the Congress sittings here. Therefore, having regard to all these considerations, but without attempting to anticipate the verdict of the Committee, I hope you will decide by an unanimous vote, by an emphatic and eloquent vote, by a vote which will carry with it a splendid money gift, to go on holding our Congresses in India, and that for the very same reasons that have decided you to hold the Congress in London, namely as essential steps to the realization of those national hopes and aspirations which we tenderly cherish, and the fruition of which we look forward to bequeathing as a priceless legacy to future generations of our beloved but now suffering country. (*Loud cheers.*)

PUNDIT PRANNATH SARASWATI (*Calcutta, No.* 15, *in list*)—I should have thought that it was a work of supererogation for any one to second a resolution so ably and eloquently proposed for our acceptance. I do it more as a matter of form than of necessity, and I am sure that you will unanimously accept the resolution. The subject is one of great importance involving the consideration of many details; and it is therefore only right and proper that a small and able Committee should sit to investigate the matter in all its bearings and to present to us a report which, by the weight of the names attached to it, will command unanimous acceptance.

The President then put the Resolution, which was carried unanimously.

THE PRESIDENT.—Before you leave I have the pleasure of inviting you, on behalf of the Reception Committee, to an evening party in this Pavilion, and trust that you will give us the honor of your presence at 9 o'clock.

---

**Adjournment of the Assembly.**

The Congress then adjourned until next day at 11-15 A.M. The Subjects Committee assembled and sat until 8-30 P.M.

---

# SECOND DAY'S PROCEEDINGS.

## Tuesday, December 29th, 1891.

THE Congress reassembled at 11-15 A.M.

**2nd Day.**

**Cheers for Mr. Gladstone on his commencement of his 83rd year.**

THE PRESIDENT.—Gentlemen,—Before we begin the proceedings of this day I must ask you to perform the agreeable duty of giving three cheers for William Ewart Gladstone, who to-day completes his 82nd and enters upon his 83rd year.

Three hearty cheers were given by the delegates and visitors, all rising in response to the President's suggestion.

THE PRESIDENT.—I will now call upon Mr. Bannerjee to move the 2nd Resolution.

**Res. II. Reform of the Legislative Councils.**

MR. SURENDRA NATH BANNERJEE (*Calcutta, No.* 11, *in list*)—MR. PRESIDENT, SISTER AND BROTHER DELEGATES,—I rise to move the following resolution :—

*That this Congress re-affirms the conclusion arrived at by all previous Congresses, viz., that India can never be well or justly governed, nor her people prosperous or contented, until they are allowed, through their elected representatives, a potential voice in the Legislatures of their own country, and respectfully urges the people of Great Britain and Ireland, whose good-will towards India it gratefully recognizes, to permit no further delay in the cnocession of this just and necessary reform.*

In moving this resolution you will permit me to observe that our present gathering is one of peculiar solemnity. Ordinarily speaking the meetings of the National Congress are sufficiently solemn. There is a dignity, a majesty about our proceedings which may be said to lie beyond what can attend gatherings convened at the fiat of official authority. It is no king, no priest nor prophet, who has brought us here on this occasion, unless it be that we have hied from the most distant parts of the empire in obedience to the summons of our illustrious friend behind me, the prophet of our race (*cheers*), who, emulating the sacrifice and the devotion of the *Rishis* of olden times, has consecrated the evening of his life to the service of the land of his adoption. (*Cheers*). Oh, no! We have come here under the irresistible pressure of an overwhelming impulse. It is the Spirit of patriotism that moves us and animates our being: it is this Spirit which is the presiding divinity of this place. Solemn, then, as our ordinary gatherings are, the circumstances of this meeting enhance its solemnity. We have met to confirm and ratify, by our seal and sanction, our deliberations in the past. Looking back to the past, we may well review it with hope and enthusiasm. I will not tread upon the ground which was so eloquently touched last night in that admirable discourse from the chair to which we listened with so much respect and attention. Nor will I seek to spoil the effect of that eloquence by expressing in language, less powerful than his, the toil-won achievements of this great national gathering. But this I will say without fear of challenge or contradiction, that there never has been a question taken up by this national gathering which we have not brought nearer to solution. Take, for instance, the question of the police. You took it up and discussed it, and recorded resolutions regarding it, and that is the question which is now being earnestly discussed and considered by the different Governments. You took up the question of the excise system, and the out-stills have been abolished throughout the districts of Bengal, with an exception here and there, while in the Madras Presidency the liquor shops have been closed by thousands. (*Cheers.*) You took up the question of the income-tax; and at the present moment I have reason to believe that the Government is considering the feasibility of raising the minimum of taxable income from Rs. 500 to Rs. 1,000. (*Cheers*).

You advocated the creation of councils for the N. W. Provinces and the Panjab. The N. W. Provinces have got their council, and that for the Panjab is being actively discussed. You pleaded for justice to the Indians in the matter of the public service, and they gave us, if nothing else, the Public Service Commission, and raised the age for the admission of candidates. You insisted on the separation of the judicial and executive functions, Lord Dufferin admitted that, in this matter, yours were counsels of perfection, and now I learn that in Madras, by next April, that separation will have become an accomplished fact. (*Loud cheers*). Then, again, you gave voice to the voiceless, heralded forth the cries of the poor by insisting upon the reduction of the salt duty. And what did the Viceroy of India say on the occasion of the

**2nd Day.**

**Res. II. Reform of the Legislative Councils.**

St. Andrew's Dinner, held about a fortnight ago? He said that if the financial position of the Government of India ever made it possible to consider the question of a reduction of taxes, the salt duties would be the first to be thought of. (*Cheers*). And, lastly, you took up the question, the question of all questions, which lies at the base of the Congress platform, the question of representative Government, and you have brought it within the range of practical politics. (*Cheers.*) When you took up that question seven or eight years ago, you were greeted with a burst of derisive laughter and scorn. That scorn and that laughter have now given place to respectful attention and recognition, and Lord Dufferin, no friend of the Congress movement, thought it necessary, pressed by circumstances over which he had no control, to recommend a reform of the Councils somewhat upon the lines indicated by the Congress. He recommended the reconstitution of the provincial councils upon an elective basis, and further, the expansion of the functions of the Legislative Councils, and, what is still more extraordinary, a Tory Government, with its re-actionary policy, with its traditions about the black-man, with its avowed policy (at least on the part of one responsible minister) to discourage talent and to encourage mediocrity. Such a Government has felt itself constrained to introduce a Bill with a view of giving effect to one portion of this reform. I think, gentlemen, looking at all this, that we have reason to be proud of what we have achieved. What is the position of the question at the present moment? It is as well that you should take a review of the situation. I think it may safely be said that the question has advanced by leagues! Circumstances have occurred, and evidence can be adduced within the last few months in support of the contention of the Congress leaders. Last Wednesday the Lieutenant-Governor of Bengal issued a resolution on the working of the municipalities in Bengal, in which he distinctly declared that he was on the whole well satisfied with the working of the Bengal municipalities. (*Cheers.*) Sir Charles Eliot is no respecter of persons or of institutions; he does not share in any of those sentiments which may be said to be peculiar to the Congress party; he is a matter-of-fact, business-like politician; and that is the opinion which he has placed on record. But that is not all. This is the opinion not only of Sir Charles Eliot but of a succession of Bengal Governors. Sir Ashley Eden, Sir Rivers Thomson, Sir Stewart Bayley have all expressed their deliberate opinion to the effect that the general results of local self-government have been satisfactory throughout Bengal. And I presume that similar testimony would be forthcoming from the other provinces. What then does all this imply? If it implies anything, it implies this: We go and tell the Government you have conferred upon us the boon of local self-government, you have tried us by conferring that privilege upon us, and you have found that we have been eminently successful in regard to that matter: therefore we claim, on the basis of our past achievements, that the principle should be extended to the wider concerns of the province and of the empire. (*Cheers.*) But that is not all. Take the case of the Mysore representative assembly. That assembly was not the creation of agitation; it was the product of the spontaneous beneficence of a far-seeing statesman whose memory ought to be cherished by the people of Southern India, C. Runga Charlu (*cheers*), and the labours of that assembly have been so singularly successful that the present Dewan, not the author of the original scheme but its watchful guardian, has found it necessary to reconstitute the present legislative assembly upon a partially representative and elective basis. It has been reserved—I say it with regret, but the fact must be stated—for a native State, supposed to be, in regard to culture, intelligence and the arts of progressive Government, behind Her Majesty's own dominions, to set an example to the British Government which that Government may do well to imitate. But, gentlemen, the most hopeful feature of the position lies in the attitude of the liberal party in England with regard to our progress. You are probably noting the tide of circumstances in England in connection with the Bill. The Government is playing a sort of hide-and-seek game in connection with the Bill. It introduces the Bill in the beginning of the year, it drops it towards the end of the year; and this process has been going on during the last two or three years. Can you solve the enigma? I think I can, at any rate, help you to a solution. In 1890 we had a conference (Mr. Hume and Mr. Mudholkar were there, and two or three others) with Mr. Gladstone, who gave us a sort of promise that he would speak in favour of Mr. Bradlaugh's amendment in support of the recognition of the elective element in the constitution of the Councils. The Government was alarmed; and well it might be. The fear has never since left them. They introduce the Bill as a matter of form, and drop it as a matter of necessity. (*Laughter and cheers*). That seems to be the explanation of the riddle. It is said in the resolution that, unless the people of this country, through their duly elected representatives, are allowed a substantial voice in the task of legislation, the country cannot be well or properly governed. Is the country well governed at the present moment? That is a very serious question. I have not the slightest hesitation in saying that it is not well governed. I mean no sort of reflection upon the official classes. There are very many honorable men amongst them, especially among the officials of this province, who are doing their very best in the arduous situations in which they find themselves. It is not the men who are to blame; it is the system; it is the bureaucracy, the autocratic despotism that has been established, that must be arraigned before the bar of public opinion in India and throughout the civilized world. To my mind it is a matter of astonishment that the system has been so successful as it has been. The reason is that it contains the leaven of popular institutions. It is a despotism tempered by a free press and by the right of public meeting. It is because of this element of popular institutions that the Government has been so far successful. But I say again the country is not properly governed. Finances form the backbone of an administration. John Bright, in one of his memorable speeches about India, said : "Tell me the financial position of a Government, and I will tell you all about the condition of the people, their prospects and their happiness." What is the financial position of the Government of India? It may be briefly summed up. It is a position of ever-recurring deficits diversified by ever-increasing debt. Do you call that a properly governed country? I say, no! Famines are of constant occurrence ; and millions of lives are lost every few years through starvation. Sir William Hunter said a dozen years ago that forty millions of our people live on one meal a day ; he would have alas! to raise the figure considerably now. The other day, when a great province was suffering from scarcity, and afflictions of a serious nature were impending, a provincial governor was indulging in a little devil-dancing in a summer retreat on the hills. Do you call that proper Government, righteous efficient Government? *I* do *not!* If *you* do, your conception of things and mine greatly differ, but I know well that *that* is *not* the conception of *Congress* men. The resolution also states that the people of this country cannot remain satisfied or contented unless, in the task of legislation, the assistance of properly elected men is secured by the Government. England has educated us, and has awakened in our minds ambitions which she is bound to satisfy. England has given us a free press, and has conferred upon us the inestimable boon of local self-government ; she has placed in our midst the marvels of Western civilization ; she has given us information and knowledge ; she has stimulated the intellect and ennobled the character ; and we should be less than human if, having lived under these influences, we were not fired with the lofty desire to transplant into our country some at least of those institutions which have contributed to uprear the fabric of English renown and greatness. (*Cheers*). Millions of money have been spent upon frontier defences, and God knows how many more millions will be spent upon those defences. But it seems to me amazing that the Government of the country should neglect to avail itself of those resources which lie near at hand, and which, if properly utilized, would afford the best safeguard against a Russian invasion. Could they by a process of justice and conciliation win the love and the enthusiastic gratitude of the people of India, that would be a barrier which would hurl back the multitudinous hordes of the Czar. But the policy of the Government is not a policy of conciliation I am sorry to say. At times it is an irritating policy. Take the case of the volunteers. We are excluded from enrolment as volunteers. Armenians, Negroes, West African mulattos, and nondescripts of humanity who infest the back slums of Calcutta—these are all elegible as volunteers, these are our martial heroes, these are the defenders of our hearths and homes. These are invidious distinctions ; and I am sure that they must disappear before the irresistible might of constitutional agitation. They are opposed to the spirit of British law ; they are opposed to the spirit of that law which is higher than all human laws, the law of nature, which is engraved on the hearts and consciences of the people of this country. Gentlemen, you are on the right track. Wisely have you resolved to hold a session of the Congress in London. If you care for the political amelioration of your people, if you care to win for them the inestimable boon of representative institutions, you cannot do better. England is the home of representative Government, the sanctuary of the free and brave. The history of England is, in the eloquent words of Mr. Gladstone, the history of the growth of representative institutions, a consecrated possession that in the counsels of Providence has been entrusted to the care and guardianship of the English people. To a people with such traditions and such instincts an appeal from the only great dependency where representative institutions do not exist can but elicit one reply ; and that reply will be in conformity with their noble traditions and in keeping with your legitimate aspirations. God grant that you may have strength of purpose to persevere in the effort to hold a session of Congress in London! God grant that you may overcome the obstacles, and they are legion, which lie in your path! God grant that you may be in a position to redeem the solemn word of honor which you have given in the eyes of the civilized world? Yes, your honor is pledged. You have entered into a solemn league and covenant before the eyes of man and God to hold a Congress in London. You may argue, you may philosophize, you may sophisticate ; you cannot get out of your position, you cannot wriggle out of it. There you stand ; your credit, your name, your reputation, the future of your country, the glory of your race, the possibilities of your advancement, are all staked upon the redemption of that solemn promise. I am sure you will rise to the height of the occasion. I have no misgivings, no doubts. I am sure the Congress will be held in London ; and when that is done you will not only have taken the most effective step towards the accomplishment of those aspirations which you have cherished for generations, but your Congress, political in its character, in its scope and in its tendencies, will have paved the way for the solution of a great social question which, in all its bearings upon distant posterity, will bring messages of unspeakable benefit and happiness to this country. (*Loud cheers*).

**2nd Day.**

**Res. II. Reform of the Legislative Councils.**

Rev. R. C. Bose (*Lucknow, No 126, in list*)—Coming, as I do, immediately after the most popular orator in India, I labour under peculiar disadvantages, and I am tempted to set forth my own unworthiness in a long preamble. But I resist the temptation and begin the business. In an able article which recently appeared in a well-known religious periodical an objection to the attitude of the Congress, which may be set aside as old, is reproduced, and an assertion made which cannot but strike us as very strange indeed. Some of the evils by which our social life is disfigured, and which peremptorily demand rectification, are dwelt upon in the article under notice, and it is triumphantly affirmed that we are wasting our time and attention in striving to form "the tail of the legislative council" rather than in removing evils which are admittedly demoralizing. It is an indisputable fact that by far the majority of those who would see our attention concentrated on social questions are animated by a very unworthy motive. They do not care a straw for the removal of our social maladies, and their aim, obviously, is to create a diversion in favour of the exclusive privileges with which they are blessed in this country. The latent sentiment of their hearts vocalized is "whether you remedy your social evils or not is a matter of very little consequence to us, only leave politics and our political ascendancy untouched." But, there are a few gentlemen who sincerely believe that in view of the magnitude of our social evils we are squandering away our energy in fruitless political discussions, and who, therefore, advise us to direct our attention from these discussions to the removal of those evils. We respect these persons, but we must be permitted to say that the advice they kindly give us involves a two-fold error. What right have they to draw a sharp line of demarcation between political evils and social evils? Are not political evils related to social evils as antecedents are related to their consequents, as causes are related to their effects? Does not political degradation often, if not invariably, bring about social degradation? The truth is the two classes of evils, political and social, act and re-act on each other, and if we begin reform in one region, the region in which it is practicable at present, and leave the other for a time untouched, we cannot reasonably be accused of wasting our energy. Again, political evils are surely as deplorable and demoralizing as social evils. In fact, political evils are to-day eating like cankerworms into the vitals of life in India as thoroughly and decidedly as social evils. What social evil is greater than the extravagant cost of the machinery of the State on account of which millions of our countrymen are not only ill-fed, ill-clothed and ill-roused, but brought to the borders, or rather the horrors, of starvation. Are not the taxes which fall most heavily on the classes least able to bear them as demoralizing as, say, early marriage? Is not that political death which is the inevitable result of our exclusion from the legislative councils of our own country and from its administration—is not that political death as great an evil as any social evil that can be named or imagined? Again, we do not by any means strive to "form the tail of the legislative council." On the contrary we oppose, with might and main, what may be called the tail system. The nominated members of, say, the Imperial Legislature, those who are nominated on account of their wealth rather than their intelligence and ability, are its tails, magnificent tails, tails in a blaze of purple and jewellery! But the members to be elected by the people are sure to form vital parts of its body, to complete its organism; they are to infuse new life into it; they are to cause new blood to rush through its veins; they are to effect in it, and through it, a revolution fraught with lasting good to the country. (*Loud cheers.*)

One word more, and I shall have done. The National Congress has been, during the last seven years, passing through its enthusiastic age. But its age of enthusiasm must give place to an era of cool calculation; its heroic age must be superseded by an age of calm statesmanship before it can be a source of permanent benefit to this country. In other words, its enthusiasm, which has been noisy, impetuous and dashing like the sources of a mighty river, must expand into a broad and tranquil stream ere it can fertilize the dreary wastes of Indian politics. (*Cheers*)

The President.—Gentlemen,—This resolution is one in regard to which no two opinions exist, or can exist, amongst us Indians. We have much to do, and therefore if you approve I will, without calling upon other speakers (and every man present is, I believe, ready to speak on *this* question), at once put the question. (*Cries of yes, yes. Vote, vote*).

Then, gentlemen, the 2nd Resolution—we passed the first, if you remember, yesterday in appointing that Sub-Committee—the 2nd Resolution, I say, will run as follows:—

"Resolved—*That this Congress reaffirms the conclusion arrived at by all previous Congresses, viz., that India can never be well or justly governed, nor her people prosperous or contented, until they are allowed, through their elected representatives, a potential voice in the Legislatures of their own country, and respectfully urges the people of Great Britain and Ireland, whose good-will towards India it gratefully recognizes, to permit no further delay in the concession of this just and necessary reform.*"

The Resolution was then put and carried by acclamation.

**2nd Day**

**Res. III. Grievous distress amongst people of India. The three prominent causes of this and the reforms needed for the removal of these.**

THE PRESIDENT.—I will now call on Mr. Pringle Kennedy to propose the 3rd Resolution.

MR. PRINGLE KENNEDY (*Mozufferpore, No. 73, in list*)—GENTLEMEN,—The proposition which I have the honor to move runs as follows :—

*That this Congress, concurring in the views set forth in previous Congresses, affirms—*

*That fully fifty millions of the population, a number yearly increasing, are dragging out a miserable existence on the verge of starvation, and that in every decade several millions actually perish by starvation.*

*That this unhappy condition of affairs is largely due to—*

(a) *the exclusion of the people of India from a due participation in the administration, and all control over the finances of their own country, the remedy for which has been set forth in Resolution II—to*

(b) *the extravagant cost of the present administration, Military and Civil, but especially the former; and to*

(c) *a short-sighted system of Land Revenue Administration whereby not only is all improvement in the agriculture of the country, on which nine-tenths of the population depend for subsistence, rendered impossible, but the gradual deterioration of that agriculture assured,*

*That hence it has become imperatively necessary—*

*that the cost of the administration be greatly reduced ; in the Military branch, by a substantial reduction of the standing army, by the substitution of long term local European troops, like those of the Hon. E. I. Company, for the present short term Imperial regiments with their heavy cost, of recruitment in England, in transport and of excessive mortality amongst non-acclimatized youths ; by the cessation of the gigantic waste of money that has gone on, now for several years, on so-called Frontier Defences, and by a strict economy in the Commissariat, Ordnance and Store Departments ; and in the Civil branch, by the wide substitution of a cheaper indigenous agency for the extremely costly imported Staff; and,*

*that measures be at once taken to give, as was promised by the British Government thirty years ago, fixity and permanence to the Land Revenue demand, and thus permit capital and labour to combine to develop the agriculture of the country, which, under the existing system of temporary settlements, in recent times often lasting for short periods, in some cases only extending to 10 and 12 years, is found to be impossible ; and to establish agricultural Banks.*

*That this Congress does most earnestly entreat the people of Great Britain and Ireland not to permit any further sacrifice of life by the shortcomings of the existing, doubtless well-intentioned, but none the less unsatisfactory, administration, but to insist, and speedily, on these reforms.*

"Peace, economy, reform :" the good old cause, the grand old cry—a cry, which to me, at least, and millions in Europe, comes like the sound of a trumpet. These are the three watchwords which we find in this resolution. You cannot have one without the others ; where one is not neither of the other two can flourish. First Peace : We ask that the army of India should be primarily armed for defence, not for offence, and we also ask that the waste from these so-called frontier defences may cease You all know that since the days when the good old policy of that good old man, Lord Lawrence, was abandoned, the Indian Government, under the lead of Lord Beaconsfield, went in search of a scientific frontier ; and you know that the scientific frontier has ever been pursued hither and thither and has never been found. Like a certain Japhet, who went in search of a father, we are still searching for it. Some time ago it was Kandahar, then it was Herat ; now we learn it is on the Pamirs ; and shortly I suppose we shall hear that it is in the Gobi desert or in the Great Sahara. We are told, and I believe told in all good faith, that this scientific frontier is needed for the purposes of defence. But it needs neither seer nor expert to say that, if it ever does become of any sort of use, it will not be used as an instrument of defence but of offence. England, by its geographical position happily, and India to a less extent, but still to a great extent (though I am afraid that the Government policy, which I do not like to characterize, is doing its best to do away with this insularity), needs not a militaryism similar to that which, like a night-mare, weighs down the nations of Europe. The other day the German Chancellor said : "Peace, peace, all is peace ; still I must have more troops." Now, Germany has an enemy on one side and an enemy on the other ; but we have no enemy or either side, unless we persistently go forward to seek him. My friend has already referred to the real defence of the country. Nobody will accuse the Earl of Derby of being an agitator. But it was he who said in the old debates of 1878 : „ A full treasury, a prosperous and contented people—these are the real defences of the country." If our rulers will not listen to the Earl of Derby, let them go a little further back and read the statement, which deserves to be remembered for all time, by Sir Thomas More : "Better rule a small territory and rule it well than rule a world and rule it

2nd Day.

Res. III. Grievous distress amongst people of India. The three prominent causes of this and the reforms needed for the removal of these.

badly." Next Economy. We ask for a reduction of both military and civil expenditure. Even for the best of Governments, for the ablest administrations, a nation may pay too highly; there must be some limit to expense. According to the old homely phrase, "you must cut your coat according to the cloth." The most obvious reform in civil expenditure would be the substitution, as far as practicable, of cheaper indigenous for more expensive imported agency. The home charges, which are really the greatest incubus on the Indian Treasury, consist in considerable part of charges connected with this more expensive European agency which we have to use. Then still more heavily figure in these home charges items with reference to military expenditure caused by the fact that the English Government, or the Secretary of State for India, regularly makes India the scape-goat for all experiments; it is the "vile body" on which experiments in military science and other matters of military administration may be tried; and, last of all, we ask for reform, first and chiefly, we ask for reform as regards the Councils. We ask that the people should have a potential voice in the making of the laws which they all have to obey, and in the settling of taxation which they will all have to pay. At present, to look at it in another way, the Government gets a great part of its knowledge of the feeling of the people from the newspapers. These are very valuable in many cases. But what we want is to have duly accredited representatives in the place of irresponsible newspaper editors (too often appointed by themselves). Then other reforms are asked for, prominent among which are fixity in our settlements, and also that the Government should help agriculturists by the establishment of banks. Let me ask your attention for a short time to the terms of the resolution. First, we make the statement, which I believe is nowhere doubted, that a great part of the people are in the deepest poverty. Millions, as we have been told, have not, from year's end to year's end, a sufficiency of food. From one day to another they do not know, what every one of us knows every day of his life, what it is to have their stomachs full. Actual starvation carries off a part; but who can tell the millions carried off by diseases which are engendered and fostered by insufficient nourishment? This mournful fact is acknowledged by all. Many responsible statesmen, in admitting it, argue that it is a law of nature—a huge population and an insufficient supply of food, and they come to the conclusion that nothing can be done. For my part, I will never accept what I may call the philosophy of despair. It seems to me very much as if a doctor who could not radically cure his patient should decline to treat him at all. We know that all the ills of mankind cannot be removed by the best Governments; but we know,—and history shows it in a thousand instances—that many ills can be thus removed. Then, having stated in our preamble that the people are very poor, we state what we believe to be three causes of the same. As regards the first, I need say nothing, as you have already heard enough from a more eloquent tongue than mine. As to the second point, the question of economy, we have already heard something, but I must add something more. Let no one think that we ask for an inferior army. We want as good an army as we can get. But we also want value for our money. A smaller army of veterans, hardy and inured to the climate, we are told on the highest military authority, would be better than a large army consisting of unacclimatized boys, a great number of whom die or have to go home every year on account of sickness, and who leave the army almost in every case just as they are beginning to be useful. As to the active army, as military authorities tell us, a great number of regiments are such that we could never think of putting them in line against the one enemy that we are told we have alone to fear—the Russians. In that case, what is the need for them at all? In another resolution we speak of the means whereby the internal peace of the country may be sufficiently kept. Some twelve years ago there was a commission headed by Sir Ashley Eden, in which certain recommendations were put forward. Those recommendations, I believe, were accepted by almost every responsible head of the army in India, the dissentients being very few. Yet those recommendations have never been carried out, simply for one reason, that the Secretary of State, and other persons around him, decline to part with their patronage. If one could get rid of a few useless general appointments it would do more good to the country than the disbanding of more than one regiment. As regards the civil administration I have already spoken. With reference to economy, all may be summed up by saying that if several of the millions, which now go into the coffers of the Government were left to fructify in the pockets of the people, much of the present poverty might disappear.

As regards the land settlement I will give you one instance.

In Gurgaon, in the Punjab, an assessment was made early in the Seventies, which was called a fair-weather settlement. About 1877 or 1878 came the years of famine. In 1881 or 1882 the people were numbered again; and, speaking from memory, I believe I am within the mark in saying that there was a diminution of 500,000 as compared with 1871. Now, where do you think I got this information? I have not got it from the railings of the native press. I have got it from the *Pioneer* itself, the organ of the Imperial Government, which, while the last Congress was sitting in Calcutta, actually published an article on the subject which, if

**2nd Day.**

**Res. III. Grievous Distress amongst people of India. The three prominent causes of this and the reforms needed for the removal of these.**

any of us on this platform had spoken, we should have been called liars, sedition-mongers, and I do not know what else. Well, Sir, we want to make future settlements on the Gurgaon principle impossible. Let me refer to Bengal. When the Permanent Settlement of 1796 took place there, two-thirds of it were calculated to be jungle ; now the greater part of it blossoms like a rose ; and, although the Government loses in regard to the land, it has a large revenue from other sources of income which have only become fruitful, because the people are prosperous. In Behar they are not so prosperous. The population is denser than in any other part of India, but, poor as the people are, they would be poorer still if they knew that at the end of 30 years the assessment was to be renewed. In the latter days of the old assessment they would make no wells and no improvements, knowing that they would ultimately be confiscated in great part (to use plain English) by the Government.

We also ask that the ryot should be able to get money in times of distress from agricultural banks. He now borrows from the village money-lender. What we want is that he should get his money at easier rates than at present. There is plenty of money in the country, and all that is wanted is to give the persons who lend abundant security, and let those that need it for the land have money at low rates of interest.

The last paragraph in the resolution deals with the British people. We appeal to them to help us in procuring these demands. It is desirable, not only for the sake of India, but for the sake of England herself. (*Cheers*). We appeal to the English Parliament, the mother of free parliaments, that she should confer on this country the great gift from which she herself has profited so much. We appeal to the great English nation to consolidate and complete the great work which has already commenced in India. We ask that the inestimable blessings which have resulted from free institutions in England may also be conferred on India. Light came from the East ; let it return to us from the West. If India gets from England what it has a right to demand there will be (in the language of the greatest Englishman living) a covenant between the two countries, not engraved on tablets of stone but in the hearts and consciences of men. Then in the words of the old motto, *quis separabit ?* Who will separate the two ? " Justice and Love—nay God himself—will have united them, and whom God hath joined together let no man put asunder." (*Cheers*).

Mr. Mudholkar (*Berar, No.* 273, *in list*)—Mr. President, Brother Delegates, Ladies and Gentlemen,—The 3rd Resolution which my friend Mr. Pringle Kennedy has proposed in so able and eloquent a manner is one which concerns the most vital interests of our people. It is a resolution which I may say affords the most convincing proof of the necessity that exists for what my friend has called the policy of peace, economy and reform. The resolution proposed by our great countryman Surendra Nath Bannerjee, which has been aptly called the main plank in our platform—the resolution about the reform of the Legislative Councils—is one which is brought forward, not on mere speculative grounds, but on the highest practical considerations. It is because we feel that the present system of Government is not productive of those benefits which were expected from the pure intentions of its founders that we have considered it necessary to advocate its reform. Every form of Government, like all human expedients, is only a means to an end ; and, if we find that this present form of Government is inadequate to secure the objects expected from it, it is necessary that it should be reformed. We say that, in spite of the noble and generous intentions of the British people and the British Government, the India of to-day presnets a most mournful and abnormal spectacle. Here is a country which poets have called the land of gold and pearls. The wealth of Ind is a simile familiar to all readers of literature. The mineral resources of the country are second to none in this world. And what do you find, and that under (so far as intentions go) one of the best Governments established by human agency ? There is peace (at any rate internally, on the ever-expanding frontiers, of course, Government has always some war on hand), there is order there are courts of justice, there is security of property ; and in a country with all these natural advantages what do we find ? We find that there is acute, widespread, growing poverty, that the masses are every day sinking lower and lower, that there is an utter absence of any economic staying power in them. It is natural that in face of results like these the minds of the people should be occupied with this unhappy state of affairs, and that they should ask for the reasons for this phenomenon. It may perhaps be said that our statement as to the people growing poorer is but the vapourings of the press or random assertions. What I say is not based on my knowledge, though I of course know it well ; I do not advance it on my own authority, but on the authority of the responsible officials of the Government. Here we have had Sir Wm. Hunter, Director General of Statistics for the Government of India, saying emphatically years ago, that fully 40 millions in India went through life with insufficient food. Then there is Sir Charles Eliot, the present Lieutenant-Governor of Bengal, writing as Chief Commissioner of Assam, who says : " I do not hesitate to say that half the agricultural population do not know from one year's end to another what

**2nd Day.**

**Res. III. Grievous Distress amongst people of India. The three prominent causes of this and the reforms needed for the removal of these.**

it is to have a full meal." Then there is another authority, Mr. Harrington, Commissioner of Lucknow, who says, that he has not the slightest hesitation in stating that the greater part of the population of India suffers from a daily insufficiency of food. Endless testimony to the same effect could be cited. That is the spectacle which is afforded you under this most beneficent of rules.

Take, again, the dismal record of famine. What do the Famine Commissioners themselves say? They say that there have been 17 great famines in this land of plenty in comparatively recent times. During the 12 years which preceded 1878, as many as 12 millions died. Most of these occurrences happened, not in the Native States, but in British India, in provinces directly under the Government of the British people (*Shame!*) Compare this heavy loss which the country has sustained with the deaths which occurred from what are called preventible causes in other countries. Take, for instance, the number who have died from war in Europe and in America. During the hundred years from 1793 to 1890, only four and a half million people died from war. Here, in India, you find that during some 12 years some 12 millions of people died from famine and starvation, the most miserable of deaths. Is this to be wondered at when you see how poor the people are, what their average income is, and how utterly impossible it is for them, in the best of times, to do more than just keep body and soul together? What is the average annual income of an Indian? From official statistics it is put down at Rs. 27; this is the estimate of Sir E. Baring, a responsible minister of Government. But Mr. Dadabhai Nowrojee's calculations show it to be nearer Rs. 20. In England the average income is £41, which, at the present rate of exchange, is Rs. 570. Taking the United Kingdom it is £35 per annum. For the poorest country in Europe it is £9; but for India it is less than £1 10*s*. Again, see from Government statistics what is necessary for the most frugal meals to be given even to the lowest people. The jail diet costs Rs. 23; the camp follower's diet costs the Government Rs. 30; the native sepoy's diet Rs. 42. According to the calculation of Sir James Peel, formerly member of the Bombay Legislative Council, and now a member of the Secretary of State's Council, it is necessary to have at least Rs. 40 for maintaining a Deccan agriculturist. Now, when you find that the average income per head in India is, even according to the officials, only Rs. 27, and that in all probability it does not exceed Rs. 21 for all purposes, and that for only feeding the criminals in jails, it is necessary to have Rs. 23, you can judge for yourselves what the condition of the masses must be. Especially if you bear in mind that this is an average, and that while several millions have immensely more, scores of millions have much less. If you require Rs. 30 for camp followers, people cannot maintain themselves for Rs. 21 and pay a lot of taxes besides. The result of this is that from one-fourth to one-fifth of our vast population are ever perilously near starvation. In normal years they manage with difficulty to keep themselves, but in years of scarcity, then comes the trial; and what happens? By hundreds of thousands, by millions, the people succumb, and there is an end of the whole thing, a large death-roll furnished by the dismal record of the history of the famine. On the other hand, what do you find in this the poorest of countries. You find that there is an administration which is perhaps the costliest in the world. It has been estimated that the gross income in India is about 540 millions of tens of rupees. Of this it is calculated that 450 millions are required for the most necessary expenses, so that there remain only 90 millions available. Out of this 90 millions let us see how much the Government requires from us. The gross revenue of the Government, according to the latest calculation, is slightly above 82 millions. From this we deduct the charges of the income from railways and opium (which are not taxation properly so called), and there remain 56 millions to be supplied out of the 90 millions; the balance being what is left for 250 millions of people for every purpose except the barest necessities, amounting to 4 annas per head of the population. When you find that the people are growing poorer day-by-day, and that the expenditure is not only so enormous but daily increasing, as the Secretary of State's memorandum admits, the subject is one requiring the most careful and anxious thought. It is one about which we have cried ourselves hoarse to the Government, but our voice is like "the voice of one crying in the wilderness." It is, therefore, necessary for us to carry our appeal to a higher, a more potent, and let us hope a more willing tribunal. The spectacle which India affords is one which civilized England ought not to look upon with equanimity. It is one which does not do credit to their administration. If these stern facts are brought to the notice of the people of England, we have great hopes that a nation which has spent millions upon millions in obtaining the emancipation of the Negroes will not fail to give a response to our appeal; and I feel sure that if we set to work in the right way with one accord and one heart, we shall obtain some redress, at any rate, of our cruel grievances. It is for you, gentlemen, to do the work. (*Cheers*).

MR. MURLIDHUR (*Panjab, No.* 132, *in list*), then spoke in Urdu. He said :—

BROTHERS,—I marvelled greatly that I was told off to speak on this question, seeing that much abler exponents of our grievances were already on the list, but I know, now; people

**2nd Day.**

**Res. III. Grievous Distress amongst people of India. The three prominent causes of this and the reforms needed for the removal of these.**

cannot listen so long to the sweet voices of the nightingales, the polished phrases of so many silver-tongued orators without longing, by way of contrast, for the hootings of the owl or the hoarse croak of the raven—in other words for the rough untutored speech of some uneducated man like myself. (*Laughter*). Ah you laugh ! but it is I who am to blame, for the tale I have to tell of the poverty of India's people is too sad, too hopeless for even a passing smile.

Alas, as a young and beautiful girl wedded to an old and decrepid husband, can enjoy no happiness, so India yoked to cruel poverty can know neither prosperity nor comfort. Look round you, you who rich and happy, have never known what it is to feel really the pangs of hunger, least of all to hear your children crying vainly for the food you cannot, cannot give them. Look round you in every *hamlet* in every *town*, and you will find scores or hundreds, who never, or very rarely, know what it is not to be pinched by hunger. who can reckon up child after child murdered by long-continued semi-starvation.

No doubt for nearly 1,000 years there has been Poverty in the land. She is an old hag, once a slave girl of Muhmud of Ghuzni, who, having robbed and ravaged India, left her behind him as a parting curse. But it needed the fostering influences of our well-intentioned but purblind Government to render that hag prolific, and now, lo ! she has brought forth a brood—wretchedness, misery, degradation, famine, pestilence and crime tenfold more evil than herself, which now hold millions and millions of our brethren and their hapless children tightly clutched in their cruel grip, and you ;—*you*, it seems, are content to join with these accursed monsters in battening on the heart's blood of your brethren (*cries of no, no.*) I say, yes, look round ; what are all these chandeliers and lamps, and European made chairs and tables, and smart clothes and hats, and English coats and bonnets and frocks, and silver-mounted canes, and all the luxurious fittings of your houses, but trophies of India's misery, mementoes of India's starvation ! Every rupee you have spent on Europe-made articles is a rupee of which you have robbed your poorer brethren, honest handicraftsmen, who can now no longer earn a living. Of course I know that it was pure philanthropy which flooded India with English-made goods, and surely, if slowly, killed out every indigenous industry—pure philanthropy which, to facilitate this, repealed the import duties and flung away three crores a year of a revenue which the rich paid, and to balance this wicked sacrifice raised the salt tax, which the poor pay ; which is now pressing factory regulations on us, to kill if possible the one tiny new industrial departure India could boast. Oh, yes, it is all philanthropy, but the result is that from this cause, amongst others, your brethren are starving. (*Shame, shame*)

Not 30 years ago wheat sold for $1\frac{1}{2}$ maunds and gram for 2 maunds for the rupee, for our grain was not exported to foreign lands. Now it is six times as dear, and six times as hard for the poor to fill their bellies, because our philanthropists have conjured up the phantasm of free trade to drain our granaries. Free trade, fair play between nations, how I hate the sham. What fair play in trade can there be between impoverished India and the bloated capitalist England ? As well talk of a fair fight between an infant and a strong man—a rabbit and a boa-constrictor. No doubt it is all in accordance with high economic science, but my friends remember this—this, too, is starving your brethren.

And our good Government is so grieved at the decay of all native industries, so anxious that we should once more be in a position to supply ourselves and find work here for our people, that they have established, I believe, nearly one dozen technical schools, amongst 300 millions of people. (*Hear, hear. Shame, shame.*)

Then there is an outrageously costly system of administration, civil and military ; our Government is anxious that we should have the very best article, and so imports all its officers, and while India's people starve, Europeans grow rich on India's money, and thousands of Indians are kept out of situations for which they are as fit, or fitter, than any of the Europeans we get now-a-days, and mere boys just fresh from school, because they have white faces, draw five times the salaries of old, experienced black-faced officers who knew their work before these boys were born, far better than these will ever know it. The bravest, ablest black man—men who have fought and shed their blood for England, in Afghanistan, Abyssinia, China and Egypt—English wars with which India had no concern, except that of paying or helping to pay for them—remain for life at the beck and call of the youngest English subaltern, and are never even promoted to a lieutenantcy, let alone any higher rank. This is no doubt true Christianity, and doing to others as you would be done to ; but alas ! even this true British Christianity is helping to starve your brethren. (*Shame*).

Then there is the costly, utterly unsuitable, foreign system (this too is imported, like so many of our other blessings) of civil and criminal, mis-called justice. I say our so-called courts of justice are too generally dens of injustice. Litigation, fostered and fomented by

2nd Day.

Res. III. Grievous Distress amongst people of India. The three prominent causes of this and the reforms needed for the removal of these.

this system—(*a voice*), "but you are a pleader yourself." (*Laughter.*) Yes, I am a pleader, and hence thoroughly know what I am speaking about. (*Cheers*). Litigation, I say, the necessary result of this unsuitable and alien system of judicature, has ruined large sections of the community morally and materially. Millions, who would otherwise have remained honest and truthful men, are now rogues and professional liars. In old days there was no tax on justice. You did not always get it, but when you did, it was free. Now I really think you never get it except by accident, and those foolish enough to go to courts to seek it, even if they go with full pockets, return as paupers, for fees and stamps and law charges of innumerable kinds, to say nothing of bribes, are now the order of the day. But this system of judicature is, also, helping to starve the people.

And then—again, of course, all a part of their philanthropy—for naturally they know so much more about our concerns and our interests than we do ourselves and can so much better feel where the yoke galls us than we foolish people can—they keep the whole management of our affairs in their own hands, and spend our money in their own ways, just as they know to be right. How should we know any thing about it? It is true that the greatest of the emperors always entrusted the management of the finances of the Empire to Hindu financiers, and that these managed passably well, and had always large surpluses and money to spare for wars and famines when these did, though the latter very rarely did, occur. But what was Akhbar when compared with Lords Lytton and Dufferin and the splendid deficits by which *they* immortalized themselves? (*Here the President sounded his gong*).

Gentlemen, the time of my dissolution is fast approaching, the angel of death has already sounded my doom. I will only say this; as a result of the causes, which I have touched upon and many others, which the President will not allow me to treat of, millions, millions of your countrymen, aye, and of their wives and children, are at this moment, have been any time this last 20 years and will, for all the Government of India seems inclined to do, remain forever, on the verge of starvation, in the depths of misery, and if you have the hearts of men, if you care for happiness in this world, if you would avoid misery in the next, you will persevere with redoubled and ever-growing energy and zeal in this glorious contest which the Congress is carrying on against despotic mismanagement and blundering philanthropy. You will persevere, regardless of the sneers of cynics, the frowns of authority and the base apathy of so many of your own people, until you wring from free England and free Britons, the reforms the Congress is fighting for and the political enfranchisement of our at present down-trodden and enslaved country. (*Loud and continued cheers.*)

MR. D. E. WACHA (*Bombay, No. 257, in list*)—I fear that, suffering as I am from a severe cold and sore throat, I may, perhaps, not be heard distinctly in every part of the pavilion, but I trust you will excuse me for any shortcomings, arising from this complaint, in the discharge of the duty that is entrusted to me. But for the fact that the question of the growing military expenditure of the country in all its branches, on which I am called upon to speak, is of the highest importance to our national well-being, I would have fain foregone the pleasure of addressing you

With this preliminary observation I now proceed with the subject in question. The speakers who preceded me have made you fairly acquainted, more or less, with the question of the prevailing poverty in India; and none, I think, has brought more vividly home to us the miserable condition of the masses, mostly the agricultural population, than our old friend Mr. Murlidhur, who has just left the tribune. The lifelike picture which he drew, and the object lesson he tried to convey to you thereby, were indeed most heartrending. They were such as might have moved even celestial hearts to pain. This, gentlemen, is the condition of the country to be witnessed from year to year, and if any person in India has devoted a lifetime to the study of the facts relating to this harrowing condition, and incessantly laboured to make us and our rulers understand the true causes of that poverty, it is our noble and patriotic countryman, Mr. Dadabhai Naoroji. (*Cheers*). It would be supererogatory for me, therefore, to refer to them at any length here. But if I may be briefly allowed to touch on the most salient causes of it, I would observe that two circumstances, above all others, have greatly contributed towards it. They are the system of land revenue assessments and land legislation. These have been mostly instrumental in bringing unnumbered woes on the peasantry. The impoverishment has so far increased and become general that the Government of India has thought it prudent and expedient to appoint a Land Indebtedness Commission and direct it to inquire minutely into the whole question connected with the debts of the peasantry and the impoverishment consequent thereon. Not only the condition of the ryots of the Deccan, but of the Punjab also, is to form the subject of its investigations. We all trust that the inquiries may be thorough, and that the sores may be probed to their innermost recesses, so that the necessary relief, if substantial relief come at all, be forthcoming. That the system of land revenue in vogue in all parts, save Bengal, has led the peasantry from

**2nd Day.**

**Res. III. Grievous Distress amongst people of India. The three prominent causes of this and the reforms needed for the removal of these.**

bad to worse is not denied. It has been officially admitted. Our rulers departed from the old system in vogue in the times prior to British occupation, which was really the sheet anchor of the agriculturists. It had the great merit of elasticity—elasticity in this sense, that in years of prosperity and abundance the ryot was able not only to pay his assessment to the State and maintain himself and his family, but lay by something against a rainy day or the inclemency of a bad season. The revenue, in fact, was paid in kind. But our rulers have changed all that, and introduced in its place the cast iron system of payment in hard cash at one invariable rate. It is unfortunately so rigid that there is no escape out of it for the ryot; while, to add to his misfortune, it has, more or less, to be paid in many provinces on two fixed dates during the year, when he is least able to pay it. In this aspect of the revenue system of British India there always lurks, I fear, great danger. The peasantry is the backbone of the country, and the land revenue derived by the State, is the backbone of Indian finance. You have only to conceive, and it is a possibility which is not remote, if things go on from bad to worse, as they do now, what may be the condition of the country, politically and financially, if, out of sheer poverty and starvation, the ryots refuse *en masse* to pay the State dues. The great danger, the great *internal* danger, infinitely more to be guarded and watched against than any external aggression, is, gentlemen, the possibility of a universal agrarian rising. (*Hear, hear*). Surely I need no further urge how grave and portentous is this condition of affairs, this growing poverty of the masses.

Then the second great evil, which in reality aggravates the first evil, is the land laws prevalent in the various provinces of the empire—the laws which Sir James Caird, when visiting this country fourteen years ago in his capacity as a member of the Famine Commission, characterised as "legal chicanery." You are all so well acquainted with the chicanery arising from the precious land revenue codes that I will not detain you with any description of the growing evils daily arising from them. Sir James has tersely referred to them in his separate report to the Secretary of State for India, dated 31st October 1879. Thus, in the words of that expert authority: "Having parted with the two sheet anchors, the native village organisation and the self-adjusting principle of land tenure, with produce rents, Indian State craft has fallen upon the quicksands of legal chicanery." I think, gentlemen, you will agree in that statement and not hesitate to attribute to these two causes a large measure of the present impoverishment of the Indian peasantry. There are a dozen other minor causes which I might rightly say would take twelve volumes and twelve years to acquaint you with. So that I would not even whisper them here. The problem presented to us is so perplexing that it would require a lifetime to study it; and I am afraid there are very few Indian gentlemen—they might be counted on your fingers—who have studied the question in the light in which it ought to be studied. Were it to be studied in the way it ought, I would entertain a hope that the next generation, if not ourselves, might witness a better and less oppressive and harsh system of land revenue assessments, suited to the circumstances and the ability of the ryot.

Coming now to the question of the growth of military expenditure I might remind you that at the first Bombay Congress I was entrusted with the task of seconding the resolution on it. Those of you who have taken the trouble to peruse the proceedings of that Congress will no doubt be able to follow me when I state that it is the amalgamation scheme of 1859, under which the organization of the India army was decreed to be uniform in all respects with that of the Queen's English army, which is at the root of all the woes and troubles and embarrassments to which the Indian treasury is subjected from time to time—troubles and embarrassments which have grown interminable as the interminable Indian jungles themselves since the days of the Second Afghan War—with but a brief respite of economy during the righteous administration of Lord Ripon. (*Cheers.*) The period embraced by the Viceroyalties of Lords Canning and Lawrence, say from 1859 to 1869, was one of consolidation,—consolidation consequent on the events which followed the dark days of 1857. The economical and sagacious statesmanship of those two excellent Viceroys (*cheers*) had really achieved a substantial reduction in our army expenditure. When Lord Lawrence left these shores the cost was 14 crores of rupees. His successor, Lord Mayo, loyally endeavoured to maintain it at that figure. But still, the amalgamation scheme, and the ruinous Staff Corps arrangements, were slowly making their inroads on the national treasury. It was virtually a partnership transaction, as was observed by the late Prof. Fawcett, (*hear, hear*) in which the stronger and the richer partner successfully managed to foist on the weaker and the poorer (*shame*) burdens which really did not belong to her. The Government of India itself has from time to time expressed the same sentiments in some of their important military despatches which may yet be read with profit. In my speech at the first Congress, I submitted ample evidence of the growth of the military expenditure as culled from official blue books and despatches. So I will not detain you by reciting them here,—suffice to say that, between 1864 and 1885, they had increased by

**2nd Day.**

**Res. III. Grievous Distress amongst people of India. The three prominent causes of this and the reforms needed for the removal of these.**

*five crores*. Since the days of the Second Afghan War of unhappy memory, there has been no limit to that growth. If you ask me the reason of it, I will say that it is the imperial policy of Great Britain which is annually entailing on the poor people of India sacrifices which they are absolutely unable to bear but which they do bear, all the same silently but with a sullen discontent. It is the policy of England in her relations with the politics of Central and Eastern Europe—the policy which leads to complications now and again with Turkey and Russia, and other great European powers—which unhappily leads to military activity or military "preparedness," so called in this country, entailing crores of wasteful expenditure. Of late, thanks to the Russophobists and the Imperialistic jingoes, at whose head is the veteran Sir Henry Rawlinson, our frontiers have remained constantly disturbed. It is all a game of cross purposes ever since poor Shere Ali was driven away from his throne to die in exile. The Russian game is to gain as far as possible a footing on the banks of the Bosphorus, while England tries to thwart her in that desire. As a consequence, the former tries, whenever occasion offers, to threaten England in Central Asia. But while Russia idly threatens us, the military taxeaters at Simla, who eagerly pant for promotions, decorations, and kudos besides, do not leave a stone unturned, under one pretext or another, to push forward what is euphemistically called the "scientific frontier" (*shame*)—a visionary frontier leading nowhere but ever plunging the country into greater and greater financial embarrassments. Scares are manufactured which could never be substantiated, and while this sort of manufactured panic is designedly created among us, they push on new schemes having for their object nothing but the conquest of wild border tribes, the despoiling them of their territories, the bribing of the recalcitratant with British rupees and so forth. They thus carry on a warfare of external aggression under the hollow pretence of defending India against so-called attacks from without. (*Shame*). From what I have stated you will no doubt be able to understand the import of the intense activity going on, on our N.-W. Frontier borders since 1885, and the rapid construction of forts, bridges and so-called strategical railways. There is a whole history of these scares and scientific frontiers, but which it is impossible for me to unfold before you on this occasion.

So I now pass on to the question of actual expenditure itself since 1885. That year was indeed a calamitous year for India. For it was the year which witnessed the forcible seizure of Upper Burmah, which brought an additional step in the Peerage to the Earl of Dufferin, the then Viceroy. At the first Congress we deprecated that seizure as iniquitous and unrighteous; and if you read between the lines all that has been stated in the blue books on this conquest, you will be fully convinced that the Congress was justified in condemning those proceedings. Thus our financial troubles recommenced with the Viceroyalty of Lord Dufferin, a well meaning and, so far as his private morals are concerned, virtuous Governor-General, but ignorant of the true facts and aspects of Indian problems. It was this ignorance which alone prompted him to precipitately rush into Upper Burmah. His ignorance could have been dispelled by the Foreign Office. But it is this Foreign Office of the Government of India which, more than all the Viceroys put together, since the days of Lord Lytton, is the real *fons et origo* of our woes and troubles on our frontiers East and West. The secret doings of that mischievous bureau will never be known, though, if disclosed, they might create such a revolution in opinion on the political history of India with Foreign States as to make us stand aghast. But on this subject, too, I will refrain from saying aught save this. Bring to bay the Foreign Office, and you at once bring military expenditure within reasonable bound and control. This is my humble conviction. At present the Foreign Department is more omnipotent than the Viceroy himself.

Well, gentlemen, it was the Viceroyalty of Lord Dufferin which led to the increase of 30,000 additional troops (10,000 English and 20,000 Native) saddling India with a permanent expenditure of another two crores. It was this Viceroyalty which laid the foundation of those financial embarrassments, the consequences of which are to be seen in the enhanced duty on salt and the reintroduction of the income-tax of nearly $6\frac{1}{4}d.$ in the pound. How fruitful are these embarrassments for evil may be further perceived in the larger amounts which India had annually to remit to England for the army services, effective and non-effective. When it is remembered that, on an average, we remit four millions sterling on this account, or just one-fourth of the whole amount of the bills annually sold by the Secretary of State for India, it will be evident how much heavier this loss becomes with every fall, even of one farthing, in the exchangeable value of the rupee.

But the increase is not only on account of additional troops; though it is a fact that, inclusive of the army services in Upper Burmah since 1885-86, the additional burden laid on the tax-payers is equal to twenty-four crores. There are again the expenses for special defence works, strategical railways, so-called punitive expeditions, mobilisation of the frontier army corps, transport service, new arms and ammunitions, and so forth. It would be tiresome to treat you to a formidable table of statistics; but if you would only

**Res. III. Grievous Distress amongst people of India. The three prominent causes of this and the reforms needed for the removal of these.**

turn to the pages of the current financial statement under the head of army, you would find all the details stated. I will, however, summarise these figur es for you. Thus :—

| | | Crores. |
|---|---|---|
| 1. | Increased Army Expenditure since 1885-86 ... ... ... | 24·22 |
| 2. | Special defence works to date ... ... ... ... | 3·77 |
| 3. | Strategic Railways to date ... ... ... ... ... | 7·50 |
| 4. | Frontier Expeditions to date ... ... ... ... ... | 1·32 |
| 5. | Upper Burmah Military Expenses ... ... ... ... | 10·02 |
| | Total ... ... ... ... | 48·83 |
| | *Add:* | |
| 6. | Special defence works, balance to complete ... ... ... | 1·23 |
| 7. | Strategic railways yet to be completed ... ... ... ... | 4·00 |
| | Grand Total ... ... ... | 54·06 |

I do not think, however, that the limit of the military expenditure will be reached when the special defences are completed and the additional railways, now under construction, are built; neither do I believe, gentlemen, that Upper Burmah will ever become a paying province. My fear is that there are many troubles still to be overcome there. But the Government is reckless. It is trying to heap on itself more troubles in that direction, while it is madly endeavouring to push the Eastern frontier to the very gates of Yunnan. You have but little idea of the difficulties beyond Bhamo; while the fixed intention of the Government is to penetrate the southernmost and fertile province of China, in obedience to the call of pious Manchester for the sale of the products of its spindles and looms. Remember, gentlemen, this may soon bring the Indian Government into collision with China. And I need not again describe to you what a Chinese war in that direction may mean. It will be as disastrous and sanguinary as the Second Afghan War or the war of the French with the natives of Tonquin a few short years ago.

You will thus perceive what possible embarrassments there loom in the near future for unhappy India. While your net land revenue is increasing during the last few years at the slow rate of twenty-five lakhs per annum, the *net* military expenditure is growing at the rate of 51 lakhs or at double the pace. The ryot is bled in order that the military taxeater may thrive and gain stars and medals (*shame*), but just think for a moment, gentlemen, how contented, how prosperous, how progressive India might have been to-day had she been saved this huge extraordinary extra expenditure of 54 crores in five years. How many productive commercial railways and irrigation canals, branch feeders and lines which are yet a crying want in almost every province of the empire, might have been built. And what blessings these might have brought to our unhappy countrymen. How many crores might have been easily spared to arrest the growth of that gaunt famine which is devastating parts of Southern India and the Deccan. Is there a doubt that all this expenditure is a pure waste—waste of the resources and the labour of the whole population? They might as well have dropped them to the bottom of the sea. (*Hear, hear.*)

You heard an hour ago from the lips of my eloquent friend on the right, Mr. Surendra Nath Banerjee, how the question of the reform of the Legislative Councils is closely connected with the entire policy—fiscal, political, and military—of the empire. No doubt this question of reform is the burning and pressing question of the day, and, of course, the Congress allows this question the first rank among its annual resolutions. It is right that it should be so, and I trust and hope we shall go on giving it that premier importance till we have obtained what we want. (*Hear, hear*). But permit me to say that no question presses on this country with such urgency as this question of the appalling growth of military expenditure. The saying of John Bright was quoted by my eloquent friend: "Tell me the finances of a country and I will tell you whether the Government is good or bad." Had that great friend of, and sympathiser with, the aspiration of Indians been living to-day, (*hear, hear*) I am quite sure that, looking at this appalling expenditure, he would not have failed to raise his powerful voice against and exert his influence to reduce it by denouncing it in the terms it deserved. Looking at the chronic impecunious condition of our finances he would have certainly observed that it was not one on which he could congratulate the rulers of India. In other words, that India was not wisely governed, or as she ought to be, and that she was not governed in the interests of the people. It is, gentlemen, recorded in black and white in the report of the Simla Army Commission, of which Sir Frederick Roberts was no inconspicuous a member, that the army seems to exist, not for the people of India, but that the people of India exist for the army. (*Shame*). Truer words were never recorded by an official Commission.

2nd Day.

Res. III. Grievous Distress amongst people of India. The three prominent causes of this and the reforms needed for the removal of these.

If then our finances are more or less embarrassed, and if military expenditure is the principal cause of that embarrassment, how are you to remedy this growing and uncontrolled evil? This is the practical question which it is our solemn duty to solve. For I repeat, gentlemen, and I repeat with emphasis, that on this question depend grave financial issues, aye, and the gravest political issues, in the near future. We must all endeavour, first, to realise the magnitude of this state of military finance. When you consider that the expenditure of a Government depends on the policy it pursues in its relations both to internal and external affairs, you will at once perceive that it is the present calamitous, nay culpable, foreign policy of the Government of India which dominates the whole condition of finance. And as the financial position of India in turn dominates all its other conditions, especially the material conditions, you will be further able to perceive how imperative is the urgency to agitate for a complete change of that policy. If our Government, therefore, adopts a wise policy you may depend on it that our finances in the near future can be more economically administered, and that the people will immensely advance in material prosperity. If, on the contrary, it persists, in spite of all remonstrances and representations, in adhering to its present fatal policy, it goes without saying that the material condition of our people will grow worse and worse till one day some appalling disaster (which God forbid) overtakes the Government. I think, therefore, you will agree with me that it is time for us all by our persistent agitation to bring about a healthy and wholesome change in the military policy of the Government. The military activity, which has been unceasing and restless since 1885, will never cease until we make it clear to the British electors at home that it needs to be altered. If we are only true to ourselves, we ought from this time forward to take every legitimate and constitutional means in our power to expose the utter wickedness, the absolute madness, of the course on which the Government are embarked. We must din it, not only into the ears of our rulers, for they seem to be of those who having ears hear not and having eyes see not, but into the ears of the public in Great Britain, that this growing military expenditure is eating away the vitals of the people, and can only lead to the ruin alike of India and of England. (*Hear, hear*).

Those who have followed the annual financial statements of recent years will have noted the tone in which this question of military expenditure is referred to by the Finance Minister. It is indeed satisfactory to note that following Sir Auckland Colvin and Mr. Ilbert, Sir David Barbour has not been unmindful of its great evils. I think in all fairness and justice it must be said that he has been a true friend of the people (*applause*) and has manfully endeavoured and is endeavouring, so far as he possibly could, to resist the uncontrolled and uncontrollable demand of the military advisers of the Viceroy for a larger and larger expenditure. And I beg you to specially mark the clear way in which he has given a warning in his latest financial statement. Finance Ministers and Viceroys have regretted the expenditure, but it is our great misfortune that they have hitherto done so little towards mitigating its appalling burden. A tone of helplessness pervades the financial statements whenever the question is referred to, as if a change in the policy could not bring about a better state of matters. In support of my statement allow me please to quote to you one or two short paragraphs. It is observed in the 23rd para of the financial statement of 1886-87 as follows: "By the events of late years, in Central Asia, India finds herself almost in contact with one of the greatest European powers, and she cannot hope to escape the necessity which the position imposes on her of increasing her military strength". The question here is this: *Who created the necessity!* Did the people of India create it? Did they appeal to their rulers to cross the natural but impregnable boundaries of the country on the north-west, and thoughtlessly rush into the open to meet the Russians half way? Did they say that benefit was to be derived from such a course; that India would be assured of greater external security and internal contentment? No. The people have all through condemned the procedure. They have still to be convinced of the "necessity" on which the Government grounds the increase in the military strength of the empire in a variety of ways. Gentlemen, it was the wise policy of the earlier generation of Viceroys, beginning with the ever sagacious John Lawrence, (than whom no other Viceroy has more fully grasped the true significance, of confining our line of defence within the natural boundaries of the Empire), and ending with Lord Northbrook, never to cross the Indus. The weighty reasons urged in favour of this line of policy may still be read with profit, in those ponderous Bluebooks on Central Asia which have been published since 1864, and which have been so well summarised in that book issued by Lord Lawrence and his coadjutors entitled "Causes of the Afghan War." To go beyond our natural line of defence, gentlemen, is to court defeat. We expose ourselves needlessly and fritter away the resources and strength which we ought to conserve for defence from within our impregnable boundaries whenever the dreaded external attack becomes a real one, which, I think, is still a remote contingency. At present we are creating an artificial ringfence in which to entrap ourselves. Just imagine what may be the result in case of a defeat. Let us assume the worst. Does it not stand to reason that the very lines of strategical railways, the very outposts and forts which we take to be our special defence works, would be in the hands of the enemies, and that these would be the very means whereby Russia would sooner become master of India than she could possibly have done had we left the natural physical difficulties of the country, untouched as Providence gave them to our hands? Ordinary common sense tells us that this policy is a most fatal one. It has not the merit of ordinary sagacity, let alone statesmanship. It is the maddest policy which a wise Government could be led or betrayed into adopting by its irresponsible military advisers. The late Mr. Slagr, whose memory we should always keep green, condemned it in that memorable debate he had in the House of Commons in the early part of 1889, as a "mad" policy. I go a step further and denounce this policy, this feverish military activity to checkmate Russia, halfway beyond the natural boundaries of India, as "epidemic lunacy," to quote the words of Professor Seeley. For verily, gentlemen, there seems to prevail a sort of epidemic, allied to madness, on this trans-frontier question at the head quarters of the Government.

But to pass on. Here is another statement from the speech of Mr. Westland, Acting Finance Minister, while introducing the Indian Tariff Act Amendment Bill in the Supreme Legislative Council on 27th January 1888.

"We might shut our eyes to events in Central Asia and refuse the increases of political and of military expenditure forced upon us by the approach of a great civilised power on our north-west frontier. In short, we might have refused to discharge the duties and responsibilities of a civilized Government, either with respect to our own subjects or to the nations which lie beyond our frontier; and those who think we should have observed this attitude are, to this limited extent, right in pointing to our increase of expenditure as evidence of want of financial control. With such people I do not care to argue, and the Legislative Council is not the place where such arguments are called for."

Here, gentlemen, it may be reasonable to ask again whether the Government of India is correct in observing that the increased expenditure is forced upon it by the progress of Russia in Central Asia? Can this statement be substantiated? Who is it that prompts Russia to approach nearer India? It is the Government of India which first takes a forward aggressive move under one pretext or another, supplied by the Foreign Office, a pretext which can never be verified because it is only an *ex parte* one. Russia only responds to the British move. Outpost answers outpost, and gun answers gun. Thus, is it not intelligible nay manifest to take the latest instance, that it is the occupation of Kashmir and Gilgit and other secret expeditions beyond that outpost which have brought the Russians on to the Pamirs? And yet a responsible official of the State complacently observed that it is not the business of his Government to argue with people who question the wisdom of its trans-frontier policy! The fact is, that Government is unwilling to argue with its critics, that is, the people of the country itself. Of course, we have a voice next to none in the present Legislative Councils, but if we had our reformed Councils, I dare say, my good friend Mr. Surendra Nath Bannerjee, and others might have risen in their place, and compelled the Government to listen to the arguments of those who condemn, and, in my opinion, justly condemn, this bloated army expenditure and this frantic trans-frontier policy. In such an eventuality India might have been better off to-day; for at least a greater portion of that wicked waste of 50 odd crores might have been saved to her. The whole question hinges on this: Are the trans-frontier defences required? Is it as wise policy to advance beyond the natural frontiers of India? They say it is a question for military experts. In the first place, I deny that proposition. *It is a question of policy and not of experts.* And on questions of policy those who have studied and given thought to them are as competent to pass an opinion as the Government itself.

But leaving this argument alone, may it be asked if even military experts are all agreed? Gentlemen, there are able military experts who have condemned the defences on which so many millions have been spent. They have demonstrated that in the long run these will prove a "death trap." There are experts like Colonels Maurice and Home who have written in the public journals on the question. And, if I am not misinformed, there is a very able minute of the former which is pigeon-holed in one of the secret bureaus of the India Office. It is stated therein that these strategical defences are entirely misconceived, and that the monies spent on them are a pure west of public monies. (*Hear, hear.*)

I will now pass on to other experts, though not military experts, who speak with authority from the position they occupied as the responsible members of the Executive Government of India during the Viceroyalty of Earl Dufferin in its earlier period. Their names are held in the highest respect. I allude to Sir Auckland Colvin and Mr. Ilbert, who have recorded a joint minute of dissent on the subject of increased troops and trans-frontier defences, which i as much remarkable for its independence as for its close reasoning and logic. It is not

**2nd Day.**

**Res. III. Grievous Distress amongst people of India. The three prominent causes of this and the reforms needed for the removal of these.**

possible to read the whole of that minute, but I will refer to some of the salient points—points which show conclusively the absence of any necessity for increased troops ; and, secondly, the aggressive character of the policy of the Government. They also direct attention to certain military despatches and show their apparent inconsistency. In fact the sum and substance of their argument is: That the increase of troops and other measures would "prove a weapon less of defence than of aggression." (*Hear hear.*)

This memorable statement, so forcibly and tersely put, changes the whole aspect of the policy pursued by Government. On the one side the military advisers say : "These are for your good ; we are going to make you secure against external attack." On the other hand, the two members, who have based their opinion on the strength of the opinions of various military critics themselves, observe : "No, do not believe what these military advisers say ; we have read the despatches, minutes and other papers on the subject, and we have come to the conclusion that the Government is pushing forward and extending its frontiers under the hollow pretence of repelling Russian invasion, and thus squandering away millions of monies of the tax-payers. (*Hear, hear*).

"The" Simla Army Commission had distinctly and categorically asserted that 50,000 troops would at any time suffice for repelling external attack. This was stated after mature deliberation and after the dire events and incidents connected with the disastrous Second Afghan War. The commission was fully aware of the nearer approach of the Russians, and, in spite of the knowledge of that fact, deliberately recorded that no increase of troops was at all necessary or even expedient. Sir Frederick Roberts was a member of that Commission and had signed that report. But within a few short years he has strangely changed his mind. It is a matter of deep regret that as the Commander-in-Chief of India he has wholly ignored his previous opinion as a member of the Simla Army Commission. But to proceed with the minute. In the very first paragraph, the dissentient members sound the keynote : "We have no desire to despute the claim of our military colleagues to speak on the point with greater authority than any to which we can pretend ; but we perceive that there is *a great divergence of opinion* on the subject among military *men* ; and we think that, in the consideration which has been now given to the subject, the obligation of the English Government to contribute towards the safety of the Indian Empire has been unduly minimised. The Indian Army Commission, who were appointed by and reported to Lord Lytton's Government, who wrote with perfect knowledge of the rapidity,and the direction of the Russian advance in Central Asia, and on whose recommendations are based some of the most important proposals of the despatch, summarised as follows, in their Reports of November 1879, the purpose for which the Army in India is maintained : (*a*) Preventing and repelling attacks or threatened aggression, from foreign enemies beyond the border ; (*b*) making successful or armed disturbance or rebellion within British India or its Feudatory States impossible ; and (*c*) watching and overawing the armies of native Feudatory States." "It appears indisputable from the report," proceed the dissentient members, "that, in their enumeration of these purposes, the Commission contemplated the contingency of operations beyond the frontier, not merely against Russia with Afghanistan as our ally, but against Russia assisted by Afghanistan." They say : "The external foes which the Indian Army may have to meet on its land frontier are Russia and Afghanistan on the North-West...............For operations against Russia or Afghanistan assisted by Russia, a force of two Army Corps, or 50,000 to 60,000 fighting men, might possibly be necessary. No one has ever suggested that the Army of India should be maintained at a strength necessary to put into the field a larger force than this." They were of opinion that the Army of India, if properly organised, was sufficient to provide for the purposes thus enumerated, without any addition to its numerical strength. They expressly made the reserve that in making this estimate they "did not take into consideration the contingency of a permanent or lengthened military occupation of Afghanistan."

So much, gentlemen, for the now-a-days alleged necessity of an increase in the Army But to add emphasis to their argument, Sir Auckland Colvin and Mr. Ilbert observe : "It is necessary, on the contrary, to remember that, since the Commission wrote, a large scheme of strategical frontier railways has been sanctioned, and is being vigorously pushed on ....... . Apart altogether from the immediate purpose which they serve, these works will add indirectly, but not inconsiderably, to the mobility and fighting strength of the force ?" Then, speaking of the frontier fortifications, they observe : "The frontier fortifications to which we refer cannot require, for their occupation, an increase to the Indian Army of 27,000 men. We fail to see why any force needed for this purpose should not be obtained in the mode contemplated by Lord Lytton's government, that is to say, by withdrawing the necessary troops from other parts of India." Then follows the most significant part of the minute, to which I beg to draw your special attention, as it is the kernel of the whole subject : "If the above reasoning is correct, there seems to us every reason to apprehend that the increases of our forces beyond the needs enumerated by the Army Commission may prove a weapon less of defence than of aggression. The presence in India of so strong a force as is desired may even suggest the permanent occupation of some part of Afghanistan. Against the policy of extending to a point beyond Kandahar, the frontier, formal or practical of British India, and the area which must be permanently held by British troops, weighty arguments, moral, political and financial, have been, and may still be, urged. But whatever may be the merits of such a proposal, it forms no part of the grounds on which an increase to our army is now advocated, and is foreign, we have every reason to believe, to the desires or intentions of our colleagues."

Here then, gentlemen, are some very important statements made and arguments urged from which you will no doubt be able to infer that the increased army strength adopted in 1885 was absolutely uncalled for, and that it is altogether unnecessary, even at this day, bearing in mind all that is going on on the frontier, and all the other military changes and organisations since brought into play. This being the situation, is not the following observation in the same minute prophetical? "We are further of opinion that the proposal is open to the objection that it may lead to the advocacy, and possibly to the adoption, of projects for the extension of our present frontier. The question then narrows itself to this: Is it the duty of the Government of India to maintain and charge to Indian revenues a permanent addition to its forces, not required for India, but available for the purpose of extending and securing its dominion beyond India?"

There are many other points which for want of time I must give up. But I cannot conclude this most important part of my observations without drawing your special attention to the caution and forethought displayed by the two members as far as the financial aspect of the question is concerned. In this respect they have rendered an invaluable service to India for which we must publicly acknowledge our warmest gratitude. *(Applause)* "We agree entirely with the opinion of those who hold that, as an alien people, our best claim to the regard of the natives of the country, and therefore one of our main sources of security lies in the fact that taxation is light. We believe that this is a principle which has been admitted by all Governments foreign to their subjects, and that it has been uniformly recognised and adopted by our predecessors in the administration of British India. It seems an axiom which at the present time it is singularly incumbent on the Government of India to bear in mind. If it was important when India had no European neighbour, it becomes much more so when she has at her frontier a power whose agents will make the most of all our mistakes, and will bid against us, by every means at their dsposal, for popularity. We are aware that it is easy to push this consideration too far, and that the Indian Government must be prepared to risk a certain unpopularity if it is convinced that the measures which it has in view, and for which the imposition of burdens is required, are of so urgent a character as to necessitate their adoption, all draw backs notwithstanding. But we have given in this minute our reasons for holding that in the present instance no sufficient case is made out for departing from the policy above indicated." *(Hear, hear.)*

Gentlemen, I have, I fear, taxed too much your patience already, and I am loth to tax it any more. But if you will kindly allow me the indulgence I would just read a short but pertinent extract from the pen of a German military critic on this trans-frontier defence question. It is meet that you should know what even Europeans, who are not Englishmen, think on the subject. "England may either await an aggressor on her Indian frontier or move against him across it. Political considerations plead in favour of the latter course, while on military grounds, the former might be preferable. An Anglo-Indian army which awaits the invader on the Indus is in close communication with its depôts, magazines, and its present sources of reinforcement. Above all, it would be nearer the sea, which is England's principal base in all her expeditions, and a numerically stronger English force could there be assembled than could be put forward to Kandahar or Herat. On the other hand, a Russian force, which had to advance to the Indus ere it could get within striking distance of the enemy, would be so far ahead of its base that it could with difficulty preserve its long line of communication. It would have to cross a wild monntain range after a long and weary march, part of which would be through barren desert, and on emerging from the passes it would find itself exposed to the fire of hostile forts, and the assaults of the fresh troops of the enemy." Here, gentlemen, is the opinion of a military foreign expert on the military aspect of the trans-frontier policy of the Government. Is it not in accord with the opinion of all common sense people? He plainly informs us that it is far better that the Indian Government should remain *within her line of defence* than rush forward beyond it and court defeat. In fact, that it can give a defeat to any aggressor coming from the other side if it only remains where it ought to remain.

You will thus be able to judge for yourselves from what I urged in my speech on the same subject at the first Congress, and from what I have adduced before you to-day how crushing is the growing burden of military expenditure and how uncalled for it is. It is fast increasing

**2nd Day.**

**Res. III. Grievous Distress amongst people of India. The three prominent causes of this and the reforms needed for the removal of these**

and it will go on increasing unless we are true to ourselves and legitimately and constitutionally resist further burdens in the same direction. We must agitate, firstly, for a complete change of the present unwise and aggressive policy—a policy which, under the hollow pretext of defending the Empire, secretly aims at extending its frontiers and is really courting untold disasters—in fact a policy of external aggression pure and simple. The pressure caused by the absorption of our resources, consequent on this mischievous policy, transcends in its cramping and distressing effects all other financial errors of the Government. And I repeat, we must earnestly agitate for either an outright reversal of that fatal policy or security against repetitions of similar disastrous sacrifices of our country's best and truest interests. If the policy is to be persisted in, then we must demand that England shall contribute a substantial share towards the cost entailed by that policy. I will not expatiate on this question, for I have taken up too much of your time. Moreover, I must leave many other points unsaid because they demand a greater occupation of the time of the Congress which, after all, is only very limited. I must therefore conclude with the earnest appeal to you to persist in raising and agitating this question in all places and on all occasions, if we are at all intent upon diminishing the present appalling burden on the shoulders of the Indian tax-payers. But before I sit down permit me to read a few verses from the pen of Dr. Pollen, a distinguished member of the Bombay Civil Service, who had stayed for some months in Russsia to study the language of the country. From his intimate contact with the people there he was of opinion that there was a great deal of exaggeration and misrepresentation as to the intentions of Russia. I believe there is a great deal of truth in his observations If Russia's political necessities goad her on forward in Central Asia, is it not true that the same necessities have in times past been alleged as compelling the British to annex, first to seize Sind, then the Punjab, then Lower Burmah, then Upper Burmah and so forth ? For my part, gentlemen, I believe that there is not in these respects a pin to choose between the practical political morality of the English and the Russians. (*Loud cheers*). Here then is Dr. Pollen's appeal to Englishmen which is indeed worth remembering. I am sure every right-minded Englishman who is not biassed, would admit the force of the observations which that liberal-minded and honest Bombay Civilian has embodied so eloquently in rhyme :—

Then, England, pause ! know friend from foe !
  Where, when, has Russia crossed thy path ?
That she doth ever greater grew
  Is this the only fault she hath ?
Thou callest her " a Giant Liar."
  Did Britain never stoop to lie ?
Is Prussia's moral standard higher ?
  Did Austria's ever range so high ?
Nay ! diplomatic lies have streamed
  Since first the Tower of Babel fell,
That Diplomat the best is deemed
  Who dexterous falsehoods best can tell.
In truth, the " Teuton " is thy foe !
  Thy rival he in every field ;
His power thy Court thy Councils know ;
  Thy Commerce nought from him can shield
His Princes lead thy Daughters forth
  Dowered deep in dowers of English gold
His merchant vesselsweep thy North ;
  Thy " silver streak" his warships hold.
He threatens thee on every side,
  While thou dost cringe to him and yield,
Surrendering to his armed pride
  The best of thy Colonial field.
He stirs the Russ against thy power,
  Pointing to plains of Hindustan,
Hoping to stay the dreaded hour
  When France will meet him, man to man.

But why should England cross the Russ ?
  We both have kindred work to do !
Asia is wide : for him, for us,
  There's space to spare, and high aims too.
Redeem the Cradle of our race,
  Let Commerce circle everywhere,
Let Love regain its pride of place,
  Let Eden once mo blossom there !
Let " great white Ts" let " great white Queen
  Stretch forth o'er Asia healing hands,
Touching the sere leaf into green,
  Blessing with bloom the barren lands.

England and Russia—friendly Powers,
  India secure, and ong and free,
Over the West no wacloud lowers,
  The East regains liberty !

(*Cheers.*)

2nd Day.

Res. III. Grievous Distress amongst people of India. The three prominent causes of this and the reforms needed for the removal of these.

PUNDIT MADAN MOHAN MALAVIYA (*Allahabad, No. 79, in list*)—MR. PRESIDENT, LADIES AND GENTLEMEN,—It is my duty to second the proposition, or part of the proposition which has been so ably moved by my friend Mr. Wacha. That duty is rendered easy by the exhaustive manner in which he has dealt with the subject; still I must ask your indulgence a few minutes in order to lay before you a few more ideas bearing on the same subject, and to show the extreme necessity and urgency of the reforms which we are advocating. It has often been said that we Congress people repeat from year to year the same old cries, the same demands, and then go back to our homes after completing this part of our work. But, gentlemen, who is to blame for this state of things! Are we to blame for repeating these old cries, or does not the blame rather pertain to the Government which turns from year to year a deaf ear to those our most earnest appeals? Numberless officers of the Government have said that the poverty of this country is unquestionably very great, and that poverty is growing from year to year. Sir W. Hunter, Sir Charles Eliot, Sir A. Colvin and a number of others have, from their seats in the Viceroy's Council, constantly repeated mournfully and sadly the fact that India is poor and is becoming poorer and poorer every day. And what do we find? Have any measures worthy of the name been adopted to ameliorate that condition, to check the growth of that poverty, and to stamp it out of the country? No, to our deep regret, and (I am extremely sorry to say it) to the shame of our Government, nothing, absolutely nothing, has been done. Ten or fifteen years ago Sir William Hunter said that nearly a fifth of the population of India, nearly 40 millions, go through life on insufficient food. Sir Charles Eliot, while Commissioner of Assam, said: "I do not hesitate to say that half our agricultural population do not know from year's end to year's end what it is to have their hunger satisfied." Sir E. Baring, Financial Minister in the Viceroy's Council, said." That the average income of the Indian people was Rs. 27 per head." Mr. Dadabhai Nowroji has proved, and Mr. Digby has also recently shown, that the amount is under Rs. 21 per head. But in view of these admitted and undeniable facts, what measures have the Government taken to check the growth of poverty and stamp it out of the land? They may no doubt have made efforts, now and then to show that they are willing to check the growth of this poverty. They now and then appoint a Commission to take evidence, here and there, and submit reports. But what is their treatment of these Commissions, and what do they do with these reports? They throw them aside for ever. There was the Simla Army Commission; there has been the Public Service Commission; there was the Finance Committee. What have their labors brought about? No doubt bulky reports ably written and printed; but nothing further has resulted from them. It is therefore no fault of ours. It gives us no pleasure to repeat these same old cries—cries prompted by the intense agony of our condition—cries which go out of our hearts and our lips, not because we desire to talk of these things, but because the pain we feel compels us to utter them, to make these appeals to the Government in the hope that their hearts may yet melt, that they may yet take pity on the condition of the people and make an honest, manly effort to cut down expenditure, and to save the people of this country from the misery they are suffering at the present moment.

Of course, we know that the causes of this poverty are manifold. No one can expect us, in the course of our debates here, much less in the short speeches made on any of these resolutions, to deal exhaustively with all the causes of that poverty. In this resolution we deal with the causes for which the Government is mainly responsible, and we point out the remedies which the Government can directly apply, if it chooses to do so, and which it is the plainest duty of the Government to apply, if it cares to call itself a civilized Government. What are those duties and those remedies? In the first three clauses you speak of the exclusion of the people of India from a due participation in the administration. That has been dealt with by my predecessors, and I will leave it. Those who follow me may well take up the question of revenue administration. My friend, Mr. Wacha, has spoken of the military expenditure of the country. It pains me deeply to think of that question. You know that in the gracious proclamation of Her Majesty she said that she held herself bound to her Indian people by the same ties and obligations as those which bind her to her subjects in Great Britain and Ireland; and, further that no Indian subject of Her Majesty will be excluded from any appointment by reason of birth, color or creed. And yet what do we find? Take the military branch of the service. Our countrymen have served the Government, and will continue to serve it with remarkable fidelity and unflinching courage; they have gone beyond the borders of India, wherever Her Majesty has desired them to go, and have fought and shed their blood. And what have been their rewards? They are confined to such subordinate positions as *Subedar* and *Resaldar* majorships; they are not allowed to go higher; after 25 years of valorous service, they remain subordinate to the sub-lieutenant, who joined yesterday. Is that carrying out the intentions of Her Most Gracious Majesty? Where is the justification, in reason or in fact, for not allowing Indian soldiers to be appointed as captains, as colonels, and as generals in Her Majesty's Army? Have they not faithfully

**2nd Day.**

**Res. III. Grievous Distress amongst people of India. The three prominent causes of this and the reforms needed for the removal of these.**

and bravely served Her Majesty in numberless battles? Can the most confirmed of our opponents point to one instance (setting aside the doubtful case of the sad Mutiny) in which Indian soldiers have not discharged their duties faithfully and honorably? Send Mahomedans to fight against the Afghan, they lay aside all considerations of religion aud fight against brethren of their own creed. Send Hindus to any part of the country beyond India; they fight for Her Majesty faithfully and honorably. Why then exclude these people from any participation in the reward of the higher branches of the military service? What is the result? That a large proportion of the income of this country goes to foreign lands in the shape of pension and pay. The same remark applies to Civil Administration. There is that gracious Proclamation, and there is the practice of Her Majesty's representatives here and in England. Is the practice in conformity with the Proclamation? You exclude Indian people almost entirely from the Covenanted Civil Service by saying that you will hold the examinations for it only in England. You do not employ children of the soil even in those positions which Secretaries of State for India have declared are reserved for children of the soil.—I mean employment in the Uncovenanted Service. You recruit officers for the Covenanted Civil Service. A hundred officers are needed; you recruit a hundred and fifty. The result is, in the first place, that you make the country pay for services which it does not require; and, in the second place, you make these covenanted officials encroach upon the grounds reserved for men in the Uncovenanted Service. For all matters, whatever branch you take up, forests or railways, or the P. W. D., the desire is not that Indians should be employed, not that fit men should be employed, but that places may be found (I am sorry to say so) for Englishmen in India, so that they may draw incomes far beyond their market value at their own homes, and take their savings and pensions hence to spend them in England. (*Cheers*). Let none think that I am prompted by any unkind feeling towards my English brethren in saying so. I have the same love, affection and esteem for them as I have for my other fellow human beings. What I say is that it is most improper, that it is unrighteous, that it is criminal and sinful to let people living in a distant country come here and enjoy all these advantages while you have a host of people starving at your door. You speak of the poverty of the country. What else can the country be but poor! The Marquis of Salisbury himself declared that much of the revenue of India is exported without any equitable equivalent in return. There are others who say that a large proportion of the revenue of India goes out in the shape of pay and pension to England and other places. The total expenditure of the Civil Service is about 14 millions. Of this nearly two-thirds go to Europeans, and only one-third to natives of this country. In the Military Service, again, all the loaves and fishes, all the best and most honored offices are given to Europeans, not because they are a whit fitter than their brother Indian soldiers, not because they are more courageous, more able to fight and to defeat the enemy, but because they happen to possess a fairer complexion. (*Shame*). Combining the Military and Civil Services, you will find, I cannot give the exact fignre, but it cannot be less than 15 millions sterling every year going in the shape of pay and pensions and home expenditure of various kinds to England from India never to return to it. The result has been well pointed out in the press and on the platform, but no one has put it more pithily than Mr. J. Wilson in the *Fortnightly Review* of March 1884, and his remarks are true now, with the necessary corrections. He says: "In one form or other we draw fully £30,000,000 a year from that unhappy country, and there the average wages of the natives is about £5 per annum, less rather than more, in many parts" (of course we know that it is nothing like £5; it is £1 and a few shillings.) "Our Indian tribute, therefore, represents the entire earnings of upwards of six (in reality twenty) million heads of families, say 30,000,000 (in reality 100 millions) of the people. It means the abstraction of more than one-tenth (really one-third) of the entire sustenance of India every year." I will not longer occupy your time. I have had my little say, and I hope that those who follow will make it clearer still that the Government, in excluding the children of the soil from employment in the higher branches of the service, are persisting, not only in a most unrighteous but a most suicidal policy. Gentlemen, Government cannot live without the people. Let the people continue to grow poorer and poorer, and the Government is nowhere, or at any rate it ceases to deserve the name of Government. We have hitherto appealed almost in vain; let us hope that our present appeals will not be entirely fruitless. It it true that we are interested, and, therefore, we speak with bitterness and warmth. Who else will speak but those who are interested. It is the man who is being flogged who cries out not the mere bystanders! We appeal to the English people who are our brethren to make their administration of this country more in conformity with reason, with justice and with common sense, with those high and noble principles, which have always been their pride and which have raised them to the proud position which they now occupy before the world. Then, and then alone, will British rule in India be the glory, as it should be of England. Let me quote, in conclusion, the words of Mr. Bright on this subject: "You must remember that all this great population has no voice in its own affairs. It is dumb before the power that has subjected it. It is never consulted upon any matter connected with its govern ment. It is subject to the power that rules over it, in a manner that cannot be said of the population of any Ccivilized or hristian people in the world." Let the English people make haste and take away this great reproach cast upon them by a man whom they revere, and then we shall all be happy in our mutual union and to own mutual benefit. (*Cheers*).

**2nd Day.**

**Res. III. Grievous Distress amongst people of India. The three prominent causes of this and the reforms needed for the removal of these.**

Mr. K. G. Deshpande (*Nagpore, No. 453, in list*)—Mr. President, Gentlemen and Brother Delegates,—Before addressing myself to the discharge of my proper duty as a supporter of the Resolution that has been so ably and eloquently proposed, seconded and supported by those who have preceded me allow me, as a humble representative of the chief city of these provinces, to tender to you a most hearty welcome to Nagpur, once one of the chief of Indian cities, of vast historical celebrity and importance, but now only the head-quarters of these backward provinces. I happen to be a landlord in these provinces, and my remarks will be confined to the special features of the settlement question as it affects us. There obtained in these provinces under the Bhonsala Raj a system of triennial farming leases to the patel on payment of a fixed premium. The patel was thus to all intents and purposes the head of the village community, with full powers to derive all profits from the possession of his villages, and with limited liability to pay the agreed revenues. Of course, he had no absolute ownership of the estate, but it rarely happened that property changed hands. On the contrary, in most cases, it was heritable and created customary rights in the lessee. When the British Government settled these provinces for the first time in 1867-68, the administration of Mr. (now Sir) Richard Temple, the author of the Settlement, now expiring, laid down three principles as the basis of the Land Settlement. I will discuss however, only one of them and leave the other two in the able hands of the speaker who follows me. The point I wish to deal with was the conferring of the private proprietory rights in the soil on the malguzars, with a promise to convert as soon as possible the temporary into a permanent settlement. Sir Richard observed at the time in support of the first principle that "another obvious and pressing need in these provinces is the recognition and determination of proprietory title and tenant right in the land. The matter lies deep at the root of all improvement in by far the largest portion of society. Until this shall be done the public mind will not be easy nor contented, capital will not be accumulated, and applied, and agriculture will not advance."

Besides a permanent limitation of the State demand was distinctly promised to the people of these provinces by Sir Richard Temple as the head of the administration. I read in support the following from one of his administration reports: "The period over which the limitation of the Government demand according to the new assessment is to extend, is thirty years for all districts alike; this has been sanctioned by Government. It has also been recommended that the boon of the Permanent Settlement, that is, the limitation of the Government demand in perpetuity, should be conceded to those landholders who might have brought their estates to a high state of cultivation. The Government have decided that after a lapse of three years from the commencement of the new settlement, those landholders who may be thought worthy of the concession, and who may desire a perpetual limitation of the Government demand, may have their assessments revised with a view a to such limitation in perpetuity being declared."

The advantages of the above policy cannot be better described than in the following words of Sir Richard Temple himself:—

"It would have an effect altogether beyond immediate calculation in stimulating the industry, enterprise, and, self-reliance of the agriculturists, the application of capital and the accumulation of wealth where the assessments were fair. It would be accepted as a great boon by the people; on the one hand the State no doubt will subject itself to prospective loss by surrendering all future rights to increase its land revenue. But on the other hand such loss would be more than compensated by the gradual, if not rapid, increase of all the other branches of revenue.

"These branches entirely depend on the growth of the wealth in the mass of the people. A Permanent Settlement will contribute more than any measure that could be devised to augment that wealth. It follows that a Permanent Settlement will cause all other heads of revenue, except the landtax, to increase. Now in these provinces more than one-third of the total revenue is derived from taxes other than that imposed upon the land. The other taxes are increasing, the landtax alone will remain stationary. In a fiscal point of view, then, there can be no fear for the success of a measure which would, while restricting the landtax, cause all other taxes to rise."

The evils of constant revisions of Settlement have been thus described by Sir Auckland Colvin in one of his minutes: "The value of the property depreciated until the exact amount of the new assessment is declared, credit affected, heart burning and irritation between landlord

**2nd Day.**

—

**Res. III. Grievous Distress amongst people of India. The three prominent causes of this and the reforms needed for the removal of these.**

and tenant, suspicion of the intention of the Government, a host of official underlings scattered broadcast over the vexed villages." The only rational ground on which the policy of short termed settlements can be defended is that the Government has a right to participate in any improvement in the condition of the country which is not the product of the people's personal labour and capital, but which results from changes in the extrinsic circumstances of the country, or in one word, "the unearned increment theory." Extension of cultivation and rise in prices of agricultural produce under the influence of general prosperity and the opening up of the empire, are the only causes which can operate to increase the profits of land independently of the efforts and exertions of the people themselves. As regards the first, Lord Lawrence said in his evidence before the Parliamentary Committee in 1873 that a margin must be kept in all villages for grazing purposes, and he fixed this margin at 20 per cent of the total average area. He further said that no revenue should be put on any but the cultivated land, and that the waste land including pasturage should be left untaxed. Now, as we ask for a permanent settlement only for such estates as have fulfilled the conditions laid down in the Secretary of State's well-known Despatch of1862, that at least four-fifths of the cultivable area should be redeemed and brought under plough, and, as according to the high authority of Lord Lawrence one-fifth of the total village area must be left unassessed for grazing purposes, it is clear that our prayer for a permanent settlement cannot be denied us on the ground of prospective loss of revenue to Government from extension of cultivation. As regards rise in prices it has to be borne in mind that along with it there is a corresponding rise in the cost of production and the prices of all the necessaries of life. Then, again, the major portion of the profits accruing from this source is intercepted by middle men leaving only a pittance for actual tillers of the soil. Rise in prices, stimulated by compulsory exports expanding every day with our growing liabilities, have little or no effect in increasing the real profits of cultivation for those with whom land is the only means of subsistence; for in a country where the people are too poor to effect any agricultural improvement, where the soil under an exhausting system of cultivation is fast deteriorating, and when more land has to be given to non-food crops year after year to respond to an ever-increasing export, and where at the same time with the increase of population the number of mouths to be fed is increasing, the local demand for food grows *pari passu*. Thus the main cause of the rise in price is decrease of production concurrently with a growing demand, both local and foreign. But what does this mean for the ryot? What else but that, while the exports bring him less and less returns, his home supply of food-grains diminishes. Again, those who have any experience of the Indian ryots know that with him the immediate object of cultivation is subsistence for himself and his family. He has little or no capital employed in his cultivation unless we include under this term his crude implements of husbandry. His seed-grain and his food-grain to maintain him till the next harvest, have all to be borrowed at a high rate of interest and are deducted by the money lender as soon as the harvest is cut and ready for the market. He has thus too little surplus left after meeting his own requirements and the claims of his creditor to be in a position to realize any profit from the high prices induced by foreign exports. Where a man's circumstances do not enable him to reserve enough food for himself and his family, and where he has no surplus to sell or, even if any is left, he is unable to sell it at the most advantageous time so as to secure the best price, no rise in the prices can have the effect of increasing his real profits of cultivation.

Again, agriculture in India is the most uncertain of industrial enterprises. It is subject to great vicissitudes. The least change in the weather may destroy the results of the most unwearied industry. This is specially the case in parts of the Central Provinces, like Bilaspur, where the population depend almost entirely on one solitary crop, and that crop is one which requires an abundant rainfall – I mean rice. Lastly, with a growing population, all depending on land, and a vanishing margin of culturable waste, the question how the people are to live and prosper is becoming every day one of the gravest moment. Land, which thirty years ago paid the Government dues and supported a community, say, averaging 150 per square mile, will now have to sustain the weight of enhanced State demands and at the same time to maintain a population twice as numerous. Thus a considerable portion of profits accruing from rise in prices will necessarily be absorbed in feeding the people, leaving a small margin for the Government to take in the shape of increased land revenue. It will thus be seen that the rise in prices will scarcely afford any room in the future for enhancement of assessment.

Admitting, however, that the Government cannot fix the land revenue in cash permanently, it is yet possible to give fixity to its demand by settling once for all the rate of land revenue in kind, for various classes of soil. If the Government follows the simple and broad classifications of soil known to the people, and does not introduce refinements of its own in the matter, if for each class of soil thus ascertained revenue in kind be fixed permanently and for ever, the Government will be in position to benefit by any future rise in price, and at the same time will give to the people that feeling of security which alone can induce them to spend their capital and put forth their strength in the cultivation of land. My friends who will follow me will give you practical illustrations of the evils of temporary settlements by putting before you certain facts and figures relating to the new settlement that is in progress among us. All I have to say as regards that is that, supposing a malguzar in those provinces, having strictly complied with the conditions laid down by Sir Richard Temple in his public declaration regarding the conferring of a permanent settlement, were to ask the Government to fulfil its promise in the matter, it could only refuse to do so by declining to be governed by those rules of equity and good conscience which, in the case of private individuals, it enforces through the agency of its Courts of Law. Instead of a permanent settlement, however, the period of the new settlement already made ranges from 10 to 12 years, and along with this are elaborate and complicated classifications of soil, while ingenious rules for revisions and enhancements of rents have been introduced and adopted with the result that the revenue has been immensely raised as you will be told later on. Whether justifiable or not such a sudden increase in their liabilities is sure to subject the people to the greatest difficulties. They have been accustomed for years past to regulate their expenditure on a certain scale. All of a sudden they are called upon to pay in the shape of tax on land double, treble, four times, five times, in one case sixteen times, the sum they were paying before. Before they can so re-adjust their domestic expenditure as to be able to live on a reduced scale some time must necessarily elapse, and in the interval they will for ever alienate from themselves all their other property to make good the inexorable State demand. Millions may be spent in opening up the communications of the country and developing its resources, but the people will remain as abjectly poor as ever. A single failure of harvest would be enough to depopulate whole tracts of the country and to drive the wretched agriculturists to flock like beggars to the relief works to earn their starvation wages. If then the whole population are not to be reduced into one dead level of poverty-stricken agriculturists to be decimated, in spite of all the aid the State in its bounty can give, by a single failure of harvest, the Government is bound to stay its hand and give the people an opportunity to accumulate wealth and property by conferring on them the boon of fixity and permanency of the revenue demand in some shape or form. Let this National Congress, therefore, in whose occurrence here, at this critical period of settlement operations in these provinces, there is, to my mind's eye, something providential, with one voice pray for the bestowal of this boon on these provinces. In the name of national good, justice and equity we beseech the Government, in the noble words of that generous and high-souled statesman Lord Cornwallis, "to endeavour to remedy evils by which the public interests are essentially injured, and by granting perpetual leases of land at fixed assessment to render their subjects the happiest people in India and to have reason to rejoice at the increase of their wealth and prosperity as it would infallibly add to the strength and resources of the State." We shall then invoke the Almighty and implore—

> " Full-uddered be the kine, the soil be fertile,
> May copious rains descend and balmy gales
> Breathe health and happiness on India's clime,
> And may the Monarchs, prosperous and just,
> Humble their foes and guard the world in peace."

With these remarks, gentlemen, I commend the Resolution to your approval and acceptance. (*Cheers*).

The Congress then adjourned for lunch. After a short adjournment, the Congress reassembled.

THE PRESIDENT.—GENTLEMEN,—In all previous sittings we had a rule as to the time that proposers of resolutions and other speakers should occupy. I have thought it my duty not to remind you of that rule, but considering the small progress that we have made, or rather the immense amount of work still remaining for us to do, and remembering that we have to close to-morrow evening, I now feel it my duty to remind you of the rule ; and I trust that no one will cavil if, in the discharge of my duty, I sound the gong and thus invite them to cease speaking. The rule is for movers of resolutions ten minutes, and for other speakers five minutes.

MR. GOPAL HARI BHIDE (*Nagpore, No.* 475, *in list*)—MR. PRESIDENT, LADIES AND GENTLEMEN,—India is essentially a country of agriculturists. This is specially the case with the Central Provinces. The people, mainly through necessity and force of circumstances, are compelled to depend solely on the produce of their lands for their livelihood. The question what share of such produce the Government should take as land revenue is therefore with us a question of life and death. The guiding principles of the old Settlement here were:—

**2nd Day.**

**Res. III. Grievous Distress amongst people of India. The three prominent causes of this and the reforms needed for the removal of these.**

(1.) Conferral of proprietory rights on the people.
(2.) Limitation of Government demand to 50 per cent. of the village profits.
(3.) Fixation of period of Settlement at 30 years.

Official records in support of this could have been quoted had time permitted.

As regards the first, the landholders or malguzars were everywhere recognized as proprietors. What was done under this head at the last Settlement has not been undone anywhere except in one district, Sambalpur. Here, in direct violation of the declarations of Sir Richard Temple in open Durbar, the Government now refuses to acknowledge the Gounteas, as the landlords are locally called, as proprietors of any but the bit of land actually cultivated by them. Not only that, but Maafi rights created by Sanads, granted by old native rulers and recognized at the last Settlement by the Settlement Officers, are now construed as amounting to a mere assignment of land revenue and not to a grant of the village itself, revenue free. These confiscatory measures have been petitioned against, and thanks are due to the present Chief Commissioner for having ordered enquiry into the subject.

As regards the second point, unfortunately the people were kept out of the benefits which the Government had resolved to confer on them, by the illegitimate action of the Settlement Officers. Sixty per cent. was the maximum fixed for the Nagpur Province, but the assessment as made swallowed up 80 per cent. of the profits. On the strength of this act of injustice and rack-renting the local administration has secured the sanction of the supreme Government for the abrogation of the 50 per cent. rule for the new Settlement that is now in progress, in order that Government Revenue may largely increase.

In my humble opinion, however, the right way to redress a wrong is not to perpetuate it, but to undo its effect by giving back to the people what has been unjustly withheld from them.

This shows that in India, for the sins both of omission and commission of Government officers, it is the people who have to suffer.

If the Settlement Officers at the last Settlement over-assessed in contravention of the express orders of Government, they ought to have been called upon to explain their irregular proceedings ; not only they were not so called upon, but were promoted to the highest posts and honors in the administration of these very provinces. However cruel was the conduct of these Settlement Officers towards the landholders in rack-renting them, the latter proved themselves more merciful towards their tenants. The Chief Commissioner in his address to the people of this division declared that the enhancement of rents payable by ryots in the Nagpur Division are moderate and fair. What is the reward for this moderation and fairness? Abrogation of the half assets rule and substitution in place thereof of 65 per cent. as the maximum limit.

If the Government cannot rise to the moral height of reducing the present assessment so as to make it 50 per cent. of the existing assets, it ought not to enhance it, unless it be to bring it up to that limit.

As regards the period, the new Settlement in Bilaspur and Raipur ranges from 10 to 12 years. In this district it is to be from 16 to 22 years. The reason given for the reduction in the period is that the Government intend to keep a small permanent settlement staff and to make new settlements by rotation district by district. This may be a justification for fixing a different period for different districts, but not for the reduction of the period. The principle of rotation could be given effect to equally well, if the period were to be from 26 to 34 years, or even greater. That there has been a radical change of policy under this head would appear from the fact that not merely long settlements, but a permanent limitation of the State demand on the fulfilment of certain conditions was publicly promised by the head of Government. I cannot give extracts from official records for fear of over-stepping the allotted time, but believe me my statement is so supported.

In other respects also the new Settlement is to differ from the old Settlement. The seer or homefarm of the proprietor was assessed before at half the prevailing rate. Now it is to be the full rate. With so high an assessment as 80 per cent. on an average and 100 or even 150 per cent. in individual instances, you will wonder how people lived under the weight of this crushing burden. The solution lies in the light assessment of the seer. By industry and expenditure of capital, prudent malguzars realized sufficient profits from these lands to enable them to meet the Government demand, and at the same time maintain themselves. The rest constituting the great majority are all sunk in poverty, and a Commission is now sitting to find out how to improve their condition. The remedy is, however, simple enough, if only the Government would see it and adopt it,—a light Settlement for a long period if not a permanent Settlement. Settlement profits from waste, or as they are called miscellaneous income, were either not taxed at all or only nominally so. Now they are to be fully taxed. What these precious miscellaneous profits are is a question which may well be asked. The possible yield from a tamarind, a mangoe, a mohwa and other similar trees is to be rated to revenue As a matter of fact, this income is so precarious and uncertain that speaking generally no permanant income is mado from it. Moreover, this is being done in violation of law which only allows such assessment under special previous sanction of the Supreme Government. No such sanction has been obtained. The cesses at the old Settlement were 4½ per cent. They have already from time to time been raised so that the total is now to stand at 13½ per cent. Moreover, at the new Settlement there are signs of more cesses coming into existence. Remuneration of mukudams at 5 per cent. and of lumbardars by sharers at the same rate is now payable by the malguzars. Imposition of a kotwal cess is, we hear, under contemplation. After meeting all these charges and the loss from uncertainties of season, unrealised rents and the failure of the so-called miscellaneous profits, the balance that will ultimately be left will be no adequate return for the capital spent in the acquisition and improvement of the village. There is no remedy for the state of unrest and anxiety which these constant changes of policy adopted in the supposed interest of the Government revenue create, except by giving effect to the principles embodied in the resolution which I have the honor to support. A persistence in the present policy will only substitute in place of the stimulus of hope the discouragement of utter despair, and this feeling is bound to paralyse all exertion and will lay the axe at the root of all progress and improvement.

Mr. Sadashiva Row (*Nagpore, No.* 685, *in list*) then spoke as follows in Mahratti :—

Mr. President and Brother Delegates,—I come from Bilaspur and am a landholder there. What revision of Settlement at short intervals of time means for the people is well illustrated by what has transpired in my district. A new Settlement has recently been made there, with the result that the land revenue has been enhanced 66, 99 and 116 per cent. in the three sub-divisions of the district respectively. The cesses were 4½ per cent. on the land revenue at the old Settlement ; but including some new cesses imposed subsequently, and the enhancement effected at the recent Settlement, they now stand at 13½ per cent., giving an increase of 9 per cent. These are general average results. In some individual villages, however, the revenue has been raised three to fifteen times or by 300 to 1,500 per cent. I admit their number is not many, but at the same time it is not inconsiderable. It has been authoritatively stated that, despite these heavy enhancements, the portion of the profits which the Government has now taken is less than the portion taken at the last Settlement. This is owing, it is said, to the large increase in the village profits since then. Assuming, for the present, the correctness of the figures upon which the new assessment is based, the case stands thus: At the last Settlement *seer* land (home farm) was assessed at half the prevailing rate of rent in my district. With this low valuation of *seer* the total assessable assets were put down at Rs. 4,43,361. But this concession regarding *seer* has now been withdrawn. In order that the comparison may be fair, assessable assets of the old Settlement must therefore be increased by the putting the full rate on *seer*. If this be done then the total assets come to Rs. 5,26,391. My authority for this is para. 302 of the Settlement Report. The Government demand being Rs. 2,51,934, the proportion it bore to the total assets was thus a little less than 48 per cent. The real burden of the demand was, however, even lighter than what this proportion indicates. For two sources of income were not taken into account or taxed, *viz.*, profit from waste lands and the prospective income from extension of cultivation and rise in rents. These were left untaxed for the people to enjoy. According to the figures of the new Settlement the profit under these heads have been about three and a quarter lakhs. Taking into consideration the fact that this income came into existence gradually and not at once, the average for the whole period of the Settlement may fairly be put down at half this sum. If this half be added to the assessable assets as given above, the proportion which the revenue bore to them would be 37 per cent. Now at the new Settlement the proportion is 54 per cent. for the whole district. Thus the Government has taken 6 per cent. more, if income from waste and extension of cultivation be left out of account, and 17 per cent more, if they be taken into consideration. The comparison is made to appear in favour of the new Settlement by ignoring the circumstance that there has been a change in the method of assessing *seer.*

If the Government had fixed the new assessment on the same percentage as was adopted at the old Settlement, *viz.*, 48, then the land revenue demand would have been about 87 thousand rupees less than what has actually been imposed. If the Settlement had been made on the basis of the fifty per cent. rule, then it would similarly have been about 60 thousand rupees less.

**2nd Day.**

**Res. III. Grievous Distress amongst people of India. The three prominent causes of this and the reforms needed for the removal of these.**

I have up till now assumed the correctness of the figures of assets of the new Settlement. In a petition which was recently presented to the Chief Commissioner by almost all the leading landholders in the district, their correctness has been challenged. In two of the sub-divisions the Settlement Officer has wrongly swelled the rental paid by the ryots by about Rs. 88,000 on the plea that there has been systematic and wholesale concealment of real rents in the village revenue papers submitted by the landholders to the Government. The Settlement Officer said that, under a combination between landlords and tenants, these village papers have year after year been falsified all throughout the district in order to show less income than what was actually made under the head of rent from ryots. It has been submitted that such perfect concord between two such classes of people having conflicting interests was impossible. It was further impossible that the fraud could have existed on such a large scale and for so many years without being detected by the local district officers. We also relied upon records prepared by the Imperial Survey party in view of the new Settlement. The difference between the rental as appearing in these records and the rental as assumed by the Settlement Officer, was about Rs. 88,000. The people preferred various other objections which it would be tedious to mention here. Their humble prayer was for an enquiry, but it has been refused. So that under the cover of this assumed rental, they have been wrongly charged with an excess of about Rs. 50,000 as land revenue besides cesses at 13½ per cent. These figures will give some idea of the heaviness of the burden which the new Settlement has imposed on the people. Already under its pressure transfers of land have considerably increased. Whereas in 1885-86 before the new Settlement, the total number of transfers by mortgage and sale was 66, it increased to 178 in 1890-91. It is to be hoped the Government will give some relief to the sorely stricken people of Bilaspur, and not turn a deaf-ear to their cry of despair.

Mr. Sabhapathi Moodliar (*Madras, No.* 791, *in list*)—Mr. President, Sisters and Brothers,—I am asked to support one of the minor propositions contained in this programme, *viz.*, that relating to the establishment and encouragement of agricultural banks. This is a matter in which I have some experience, and therefore I have ventured to come forward and give my humble opinion on this important subject. The establishment of agricultural banks is a great necessity from the fact that the ryots have now to pay at least 24 per cent. interest in the shape of money or in the shape of grain, for loans obtained from the so-called sowcar or other money-dealers. This is too well known to you, and therefore I will not say much on the subject. It is to prevent the ryot's position from becoming worse and worse every day that this proposition for establishing agricultural banks is brought forward. The Government of India have passed two Acts, one of which is called the Land Improvements Act, and the other the Agricultural Loans Act. These two Acts now remain in the Statute Book, under which the Government have authorized Collectors of districts to grant loan to ryots for the sinking of wells and for the improvement of lands in other ways, as well as to advance money to ryots in difficult times, such as times of famine, for the purchase of bullocks, seed-grain and other minor matters. But the procedure established by these Acts, or by the rules made under them, which have the force of law, is so circuitous that it takes two or three months before a ryot's application is complied with; and even then it is a matter of doubt whether the ryot will get half the amount he has applied for, the other half going as remuneration, not as a bribe, but as remuneration, for the people who have kindly interceded to get this loan for him. I have known cases recently in the district of Bellary which is now suffering from famine. People made applications about two months ago, and their requests have not been granted as yet. If such is the case in a famine district where the ryots wanted money immediately to enable them to carry on their avocations, to feed their cattle, to sow their land or to sink wells, what is likely to be the case where there is no such manifest pressing necessity for expedition? What, again, is likely to be the position of people in ordinary times who have to wait for months and months to get loans, and who then do not get the full sum of money applied for, but only a portion thereof, whereas they have to pay the whole amount by instalments? The fact is both Statutes were virtually dead letters. Every intended concession being so hedged round with red tape routine and official formalities, that no one practically obtains any benefit from them. It is, therefore, my duty to support this proposition for agricultural banks managed on ordinary business principles as strongly as my humble voice will enable me. I hope you will agree with me in thinking that this is one of the most important measures for relieving the ryots who are now in a very impoverished state (*cheers*), and it is not as if the thing was impracticable or difficult. The Government need not advance a rupee. There is plenty of money with the money-lenders which they would gladly put into these banks and receive thence a very moderate interest if only the investment is made safe for them. The best of these men might be directors, the Government nominating other men of repute, including, if it thought it desirable, some of it sown officers, as their co-directors. But you ask if they charge 24 per cent. now how would they consent to take 9 per cent. from the bank? They charge 24 per cent. now because of the terrible uncertainties and intolerable delays of the civil courts, in consequence of which it is often cheaper to let a fraudulent, and always cheaper to let a poor debtor, go than sue him, and so if they did not charge 24 per cent. they could not even keep up their capital intact, much less realize interest thereon. They would be glad to get regularly not 9 but even 6 per cent. All Government has to do is to frame rules for the banks, keep them to a certain extent under its control and authority, see that it is well represented on the direction, lay down the maximum rate of interest to be demanded from ryots who borrow, and the maximum interest ever to be paid to shareholders; then by law give all these loans, the second lien on the crops (just as by law the land revenue has the first lien), and make the instalments summarily recoverable, in the same way as, and along with, the Government revenue. Such a bank was actually organized at Poona, and approved by the Government of Bombay, but, as usual, disallowed without any reasons, worthy of the name, being advanced, by H. M. Secretary of State for India. Gentlemen, these banks have now become a necessity, and you will, I am sure, join me in insisting on them. (*Cheers.*)

**2nd Day.**

**Res. III. Grievous Distress amongst people of India. The three prominent causes of this and the reforms needed for the removal of these.**

MR. KALI CHARAN BANNERJEE (*Calcutta, No.* 10, *in list*)—GENTLEMEN,—In the matter of this resolution, after the consolidated findings of previous Congresses that have been quoted in your hearing, and the fresh evidence of experts that has been adduced before you, I am sure you do not need even a five minutes' summing up to determine what your verdict should be. If I were to sum up the resolution before you I should do it in four words, which ought to be words of authority to our Government "from death unto life." That is a transition which we may covet, and keenly covet, without a breach of the decalogue. It is a transition likewise which we may confidently expect a Christain Government to help us in securing for ourselves. If you consider the contents of this resolution you will be in a position to assert that it does not reflect the ambition of the Bengali Baboo or any of his aspirations. It embodies the response of humanity to the cry of helpless suffering. It is said that the attitude of our people towards the poor clashes with some of the principles of Western schools of political economy. We are told that in dealing with the poor we do not seek to secure that they help themselves. And that is why we seek such a regulation of the agricultural interests of the country as will make it possible for the poor to help themselves. Then, again, we seek the enforcement of economy. That you all know involves, in present circumstances, a good deal of retrenchment, and that this form of retrenchment may be secured we offer our services in order that the indigenous agencies and resources of the country may be utilized to the full. It is very often said of us that we make idle suggestions, and then do not come forward to help those who are expected to give effect to those suggestions. But here we offer our minds and our bodies, a reasonable sacrifice, to the service of the Government, in order that the Government and administration of the country may be worked in harmony with the well-being of the people. These are the two things that we seek to secure for the country, relief of the helpless poor through the enforcement of economy and the utilisation of indigenous resources and agencies. I am sure that I may, even at this stage, demand at your hands an unqualified verdict for the relief of the poor. (*Cheers*).

THE PRESIDENT.—GENTLEMEN,—Before I put this proposition to the vote I shall exercise one right, which I believe I possess, that of summing up in about half a dozen words the substance of the arguments hitherto brought forward. It seems to me that the result of the whole argument is that there are facts and figures of a very telling character impaling us on the horns of a dilemma: either, if we believe the authorities, to submit to Russian aggression, or, if we look to facts, to calmly look on when millions upon millions of our countrymen die of famine every decade. That is the sum and substance of the whole of what has been said. We call upon the Government to take away the one horn of that dilemma, which is based on undeniable facts, and is goring us even now, and leave us, if needs be, exposed to that other shadowy and still very distant horn, in which, sooth to say, we have no belief. I shall now call upon you to vote on this 3rd Resolution, which runs as follows:—

RESOLVED—*That this Congress, concurring in the views set forth in previous Congresses, affirms—*

*That fully fifty millions of the population, a number yearly increasing, are dragging out a miserable existence on the verge of starvation, and that in every decade several millions actually perish by starvation.*

*That this unhappy condition of affairs is largely due to—*

(*a*) *the exclusion of the people of India from a due participation in the administration, and all control over the finances, of their own country, the remedy for which has been set forth in Resolution II—to*

(*b*) *the extravagant cost of the present administration, Military and Civil, but especially the former; and to*

(*c*) *a short-sighted system of Land Revenue Administration whereby not only is all improvement in the agriculture of the country, on which nine-tenths of the population depend for subsistence, rendered impossible, but the gradual deterioration of that agriculture assured—*

**2nd Day.**

**Res. III. Grievous Distress amongst people of India. The three prominent causes of this and the reforms needed for the removal of these.**

*That hence it has become imperatively necessary—*

*that the cost of the administration be greatly reduced ; in the military branch, by a substantial reduction of the standing army, by the substitution of long term local European troops like those of the Hon E. I. Company, for the present short term Imperial regiments with their heavy cost of recruitment in England, in transport and of excessive mortality amongst non-acclimatized youths ; by the cessation of the gigantic waste of money that has gone on, now for several years, on so-called Frontier Defences, and by a strict economy in the Commissariat, Ordnance and Store Departments ; and in the Civil branch, by the wide substitution of a cheaper indigenous agency for the extremely costly, imported staff, and,*

*that measures be at once taken to give, as was promised by the British Government thirty years ago, fixity and permanence to the Land Revenue demand, and thus permit capital and labour to combine to develop the agriculture of the country, which under the existing system of temporary settlements, in recent times often lasting for short periods, in some cases only extending to 10 and 12 years, is found to be impossible, and to establish agricultural Banks.*

*That this Congress does most earnestly entreat the people of Great Britain and Ireland not to permit any further sacrifice of life by the shortcomings of the existing, doubtless well-intentioned but none the less, unsatisfactory administration, but, to insist, and speedily, on these reforms.*

The Resolution was then put and carried unanimously.

**Res. IV. Modification of the Rules under the Arms Acts and measures needful to qualify the people to defend their homes and Government.**

MR. B. G. TILAK (*Poona, No.* 164, *in list*)—LADIES AND GENTLEMEN,—Our worthy President observed yesterday that in this world of imperfections the burthen of duty often falls upon unworthy shoulders, and I stand before you as an illustration of his observations The proposition that has been entrusted to me ought to have been entrusted to strong hands. I can only say that I will try to do my duty.

The Resolution runs as follows :—

*That this Congress, concurring with previous Congresses, is of opinion that to ensure the adequate protection and efficient defence of the country, it is desirable that the Government should conciliate Indian public opinion and encourage and qualify the Indians to defend their homes and their Government—*

(*a*) *by so modifying the rules under the Arms Act as to make them equally applicable to all residents in, or visitors to, India, without distinction of creed, class or colour, to ensure the liberal concession of licenses wherever wild animals habitually destroy human life, cattle or crops, and to make all licenses granted under the revised rules, of life-long tenure, revocable only on proof of misuse and valid throughout the Provincial Jurisdiction in which they are issued ;*

(*b*) *by establishing Military Colleges in India whereat natives of India, as defined by Statute, may be educated and trained for a military career, as commissioned or non-commissioned officers (according to capacity and qualifications) of the Indian army ;*

(*c*) *by organising throughout the more warlike races of the Empire a system of militia service ; and*

(*d*) *by authorizing and stimulating a widespread system of volunteering, such as obtains in Great Britain, amongst the people of India.*

Shortly summed up the resolution comes to this : In the first place it relates to the military policy of the British Government. Hitherto it has been included in what was called the omnibus resolution. It has now been separated, and this year in laying down the programme we have given it as a separate item as distinct from the several other questions affecting the civil administration of the country. Our old writers and old Governments divided the Indian community into four parts : those whose business was, respectively, literature commerce, war, agriculture. The charge sometimes brought against the Congress that it is a mere gathering of place-hunting literati seems to have little weight when on examining the resolutions we find that the great bulk relate to measures requisite for the relief of the poverty of the masses, while one refers to agriculture, others to the military protection of the Empire, others to the reforms in the judicature and only one to education, and that mainly technical education. Here we have a resolution with which we—I mean those of us who do belong to the literary classes—have but little direct concern ; it is a resolution directly in the interests of the more warlike races and members of the community though indirectly, in so far as it will operate to diminish military expenditure, affecting us in common with the entire community of which we are a fractional component part.

2nd Day.

Res. IV. Modification of the Rules under the Arms Acts and measures needful to qualify the people to defend their homes and Government.

But when we ask for certain military privileges for our more warlike brethren, we are often told we are the only persons who want them, and when application is made for permission to start a military college, we are told that there are military difficulties in the way. That was the answer that the Government of India made last year in response to an application to start a military college in the Deccan to which His Royal Highness the Duke of Connaught had kindly consented to give his name. (*Cheers*). The principle involved in the resolution has been so far recognized in practice that we have made an appeal to the Government of India for granting us concessions, and their reply is that they do not dispute the principle, but there are administrative difficulties in the way. That is a very good excuse in its way, but the difficulty is not insurmountable. If we only keep on it may soon vanish. The principle has already been recognized by H. R. H. the Duke of Connaught, by Lord Reay, Governor of Bombay, and by Sir J. Dormer, C.-in-C. of Madras and other Commanders-in-Chief of Bombay before His Royal Highness. In all these cases the principle so recognized cannot be inconsistent with the best interests of Government. The question has often been put: "Has not the British Government undertaken to defend you from the attacks of a foreign power, to keep you in peace and prosperity? Then why do you want arms?" At first that appears sound, but a little consideration will show that the question can be answered satisfactorily. The responsibility that the British Government has undertaken is very great, almost terrible, to defend 250 millions against the attacks of wild animals in India and the wild bear of the north. As regards the wild beasts here, as a matter of fact, they wholly fail to defend us, and thousands of human lives, as their own returns show, and tens of thousands of cattle, are the victims of the present Arms Act Rules. As regards the other northern wild beast, no doubt, if the time ever comes, which we may venture to doubt, they will do their best. But in the meantime the cost of the preparations, which (as they will take no help from us) they feel bound to make, is simply crushing the life out of the country. Now we do not wish our people starved to death at this present time, because 25 years hence the Russians may venture on a raid into India. We want the cost of these military preparations largely reduced. But we do not desire to weaken the Government; on the contrary, we wish to strengthen it, to render it impregnable to all assaults, whether from Russia or other foe, and we ask the Government therefore to associate our people in the responsibility for the defence of our country, to take measures to train our people to fight for their homes and their Government, to keep alive the martial spirit where it still exists, to revive it where by their present short-sighted policy they have almost smothered it, and generally to realize that with the people, prosperous and contented and qualified to strike a good blow for hearth and home, it would be far more powerful for all good purposes than though it were able to create an army doubly as strong as the existing huge force. It is in this light that we have to consider this resolution. It is in this light that we ask that we should be provided with arms and taught their use, and that when we have been instructed we should not only get higher appointments in the military service but have the privilege of offering our voluntary services to the Government. We ask for these things from a desire to co-operate in the defences of the Empire and not from any other motive. You probably remember that the present Commander-in-Chief at Bombay, Sir G. Greaves, speaking of the military policy of India, said: "We rely upon you and you depend upon us." That surely means, in plain language, that the native Indian should stand shoulder to shoulder with British officers and troops on the battle-field and in office. If that is the ideal, is it to be realized? The argument usually put forward is that the Bengali Babus do not belong to the martial races. Take the argument for what it is worth. Here are millions who do belong to military races, who are asking for privileges that have been enjoyed by their forefathers, and the enjoyment of which had been shown to be consistent with the safety of the Empire; and the question is how far these privileges should now be granted. In the resolution some means are suggested, but I do not think this is the time to consider details or settle the programme definitely. It is at the outset at any rate a question of principle; it is not a question of details nor of expenditure, *that* can be settled when the time comes. I would add that the form in which, apparently for the sake of brevity, the clause relating to volunteering has this year been put, may possibly lead to misconceptions. When we speak of a widespread system of volunteering, we do not mean that everybody, indiscriminately, is to be permitted to volunteer. On previous occasions we have always laid down that volunteering is to be "*under such rules and restrictions as may be necessary*" or "*as to the Government may seem fitting*," and though this year the words are omitted, as needless to repeat, it is in no way intended to alter our standpoint. (*Hear, hear*). It has I believe always been the idea that volunteering should, practically, at present, be confined to those who are to a certain extent educated, and hence, necessarily, belong to the party of order, and certainly if this was our view in the past, this is not a restriction that the Congress could consent to forego in the present state on the country. (*Hear hear.*)

It has been said that the British Government will only allow the development of India on intellectual lines, not the development of the sinews of the country.

**2nd Day.**

**Res. IV. Modification of the Rules under the Arms Acts and measures needful to qualify the people to defend their homes and Government.**

On that question we are unanimously agreed that it is the duty of the Government to develop the nation in all its branches, and not allow it to be paralyzed in regard to one-half or one-quarter of its aspirations. That is exactly the point. There are four sides to the development, and they must all be looked to. When they are all developed we shall have time to consider what is to become of the united nation. As the matter stands at present, when there is a warlike chief, we are told that he ought to go to school and learn reading and writing. The result is that the whole nation is being demartialized and enervated, and deprived of men who could or would stand by the Government in times of difficulty. Already the Government is complaining of a difficulty in recruiting for the native army, and I fear that, unless they modify their present policy, that difficulty will increase—partly because they are, by their existing system, emasculating the more warlike tribes, and partly because a doubt is growing up as to serving as soldiers under a Government which treats its subjects with the distrust with which, judging from their policy in all these matters, they appear to regard us all. It will be a bad thing for India and a bad thing for Government if these obstacles to recruiting are allowed to develop further. It would lead to a state of things that I do not think we can permit to evolve, without a protest such as this Resolution embodies. (*Here the President touched his gong*). As the bell has rung I will only say further that as you have carried previous resolutions, so you will, I doubt not, carry this unanimously. (*Cheers.*)

MR. ALI MOHAMMED BHIMJI (*Bilaspore, No.* 687, *in list*)—MR. PRESIDENT AND FELLOW DELEGATES,—I have great pleasure in seconding this resolution, which, as you know, defines the military policy in certain matters that we desire to see adopted by the Indian Government. It has been said that the country is very poor, and that consequently our military expenses must be curtailed. But supposing, instead of being poor, it was rich, ought we to spend more than is necessary? Comparing the military expenses of European nations, you will see that with nations vastly richer than we are, their military expenses are small compared with ours. The German expenses man for man are one-fourth of the Indian expenses. The amount per soldier in Germany is Rs. 145, whereas in India it is Rs. 775. In France the amount is Rs. 185 and in England Rs. 285. Taking the average income in those countries, England stands at the top—£42 per head per annum; Germany £18; France £23; and India £1-10. Are we not then justified in asking the Government to reduce our expenditure? Why does England make poor India suffer for the wars she wants to carry on for the purposes of English trade and in the interests of the Manchester people? The Manchester people who have done so much for India—by repealing the cotton duties, if you please! It has been said that we want reform in the matters dealt with in this resolution to enable our warlike tribes to obtain a military education, but that the Babus are intellectually inclined and do not care about the question. But allow me to say that the Babus themselves have taken the initiative in this matter. Let me refer you to a petition lately presented to the Marquis of Lansdowne by the Babus of Bengal, containing the earnest request "that Your Excellency will be pleased to sanction our being formed into a corps of volunteers as a second or Bengal Battalion of the Presidency Volunteer Rifle Corps." And let me also recommend you to follow this example and send in petitions to the same effect. In regard to the question of volunteers, I do not see what objection there can be to our being enrolled. Are there not the armies of the Native States? If those in authority are afraid of natives carrying or being trained to arms, then I say there are plenty of natives in the Native States carrying arms. What harm are they doing? You are yourselves training armies for the Native States to supplement the Imperial defences. You are calling upon Europeans and Eurasians to come forward and enlist largely as volunteers; you give them inducements and exempt them from income-tax. Why then refuse the privilege to us, the natives of British India, who have been knocking at your door and calling until we have become hoarse. But let us go on knocking and knocking, and perhaps the door will, at last, be opened. (*Cheers.*)

MR. RAMA CHANDRA PILLAI (*Madras, No.* 811, *in list*)—BROTHER DELEGATES, LADIES AND GENTLEMEN,—I have been commanded by our esteemed President to support this resolution in consequence of the indisposition of the Hon'ble Mr. Sankara Nayar, who would have done ample justice to the subject. I will try and do my best to discharge the duty assigned to me, which is to support the sub-clause (*a*) of the resolution. Permit me, however, first to state that during the five years that I have been connected with the Congress I have taken great interest in this movement by convening meetings at the place from which I come. I may tell you that I do not belong to any presidency town or even to any of the regulation provinces in British India. I come from Secunderabad, which is the largest British military cantonment in India, in Hyderabad, Deccan, which state is ruled by a Prince called the Nizam. The reason why I mention the fact is that about four years ago, this Government—I mean H. H. the Nizam's—under the advice of certain British officers, who shall be nameless just now, issued a resolution in the *Official Gazette* strictly prohibiting, not only its own officers, but also it own subjects, from attending any meeting of, or relating to, the Congress (*Shame*)—the most severe penalties being laid down for any breach of these ridiculous orders. You may imagine then the difficulty we have to contend with, although Secunderabad itself is under British rule, in convening meetings. But with the co-operation of my friends I am glad to say I have succeeded in convening meetings year after year, and also in raising subscriptions for the Congress. (*Cheers*). I spoke on the subject to my brother pleaders and some of the leading Mahomedan vakils, and asked them to take part in the meetings. Of course they sympathized with the movement, and they promised to attend, but at the last moment they absented themselves. In spite of this disappointment we convened a large meeting, and it was attended by representative men of Secunderabad. I may say without egotism that the people of Secunderabad are nearly as well educated in matters relating to the National Congress as any other part of India. As a proof I may mention that I was authorized by my townsmen to promise a sum of Rs. 1,000 at the Congress held at Bombay, which I am glad to say has been paid in full. (*Cheers*). The town has a population of over 60,000, and how do you think we are treated. We had two English organs in Secunderabad—one was the *Deccan Times*, a respectable paper, but it was stopped four months ago. The other was the *Deccan Standard*, in my opinion a disreputable paper, subsidized by the Nizam's Government, but I am glad to say that this too has ceased to exist, though only last week. The Editor of the paper was appointed Superintendent of Education and of the Printing Establishment of the Nizam's Government. I interviewed our worthy General Secretary as to whether we delegates from Secunderabad might not be permitted to lay our grievance before the Congress; but he told me that this question was outside the Congress, and, therefore, it must be put off to some other occasion. The ground of our grievance was that a resolution was passed by the Government of India that no paper was to be started in places not coming under the category of British India without the special permission of the Political Agent; and we are therefore practically without a single paper in Secunderabad. With regard to the resolution I need not say much, as so much has been said by able speakers at previous Congresses. I am sure it will commend itself to you all. I do not see why there should not be more facilities for obtaining licenses for keeping arms in our homes. I think that the Government has fully satisfied itself of our loyalty. I do not believe that there is a single section of the nation so grateful to the British Government as ourselves. In Hyderabad there are turbulent races, Hindus and Mahomedans, Sikhs and Marathis, Turks, Arabs, Rohillas armed to the teeth; and it is a matter of great wonder that there never has been any rising against the Government. If, however, there have been no disturbances in a place like Hyderabad, notwithstanding the presence of all these professional swash-bucklers, there is no reason surely to fear any such in India on the part of the respectable and educated classes against our Government, which, with all its faults, may at any rate be truly said to be well meaning, and to have done India, in a great many ways, a great deal of good.

MR. C. S. NAYADU (*Nagpore, No.* 435, *in list*)—MR. PRESIDENT, SISTER AND BROTHER DELEGATES,—I rise to speak a few words on the resolution so ably proposed and seconded by my predecessors. In doing so, I have to keep two points in mind: first, to say what little I have to say within the space of five minutes; and, secondly, speak nothing but to the point. I rise to support the fourth resolution. Having been animated by the invincible warrior spirit for thousands of years, and having stood shoulder to shoulder as soldiers for our countries' sake on many a battle-field, I ask have we now, within the last quarter of a century, become so unfit that we are not to be allowed by our benign British rulers to wear weapons and qualify ourselves to defend our own sacred hearths and homes? (*Cheers*). The sacred promise, the solemn Proclamation of Her Majesty the Queen Empress of India, delivered to us by H. E. Lord Canning in 1857, put it very clearly before us that the rights and grievances of the Indian subjects of Her Majesty would be as fully considered as the rights and grievances of other subjects of our Sovereign, and that without any distinction of caste, color or creed. (*Hear, hear*). H. R. H. the Duke of Connaught says that the Indian people are brave and loyal, and he does not see any reason why a military institution like Sandhurst should not be opened in India. H. E. Sir George Greaves (the battered old soldier as he likes to call himself), while addressing the Kumars at Rajkot, asked them to become soldiers. He said he was a soldier, and that he was very fond of soldiery. I say, so are we. (*Cheers*). But how are we to be soldiers if we are denied the use of weapons, if we are debarred from becoming volunteers, and if we are prevented from joining any military institution, and that in the face of all these distinct promises? Oh! forgive me, dear Mr. President, don't look swords and daggers at me, although we are discussing the question of arms. I will soon join the majority. (*Laughter*). I ask what is the reason for this anomaly? All say, we are loyal, able and brave, and yet we are treated like children. When my distinguished friend, India's orator, Surendra Nath Banerjee (*loud cheers*), and India's grand old man, Mr. Hume (*loud cheers*) visited England, while addressing British audiences there, they said that the day was not far distant, they hoped, when young Indian gentlemen would be seen holding commissions in the army. I sincerely join in that hope, and I trust also that the day may soon come to revive a martial spirit in the breasts of all Indian's children,—the children of the mighty warriors of old and the descend-

2nd Day.

**Res. IV. Modification of the Rules under the Arms Acts and measures needful to qualify the people to defend their homes and Government.**

ants of heroes—so as to qualify all to fight side by side with our British brethren against the enemies of our common sovereign, our beloved Queen Empress. God bless her! (*Cheers*).

MR. NALA SWAMI PILLAI (*Madras, No.* 800, *in list*).—On the question of the arms rules I wish merely to press one or two points. Theoretically, those who are people of position can get licenses for arms, but in practice the obstacles are almost too vexatious. Applications have to be filed, we have to satisfy this, that and the other authority; we have to do many things that are not pleasant. You all know what I mean. I need not particularize. (*Laughter*). Then after a month or six weeks you do get the license, but that will only cover the arms in that one district. If you go shooting in the jungle, and cross the boundary and are caught, you are punished. You must take out a separate license in each district. Then these licenses have to be renewed before the close of each year, and to get them renewed you have to take your arms to the nearest Police Station and dance attendance there for, perhaps, a week and do other disagreeable things (*a laugh*), so that what with one thing and another, it is hardly to be expected that gentlemen will go through it all. As for poor men, who want arms to save their crops, why it may take them six months, or a year, to get a license and involve the loss of several weeks' work. Certainly the rules need amending as suggested in the Resolution, which I strongly support.

THE PRESIDENT.—I will now ask you to vote on the 4th Resolution which runs thus:—

RESOLVED—*That this Congress, concurring with previous Congresses, is of opinion that to ensure the adequate protection and efficient defence of the country, it is desirable that the Government should conciliate Indian public opinion and encourage and qualify the Indians to defend their homes and their Government—*

(*a*) *by so modifying the rules under the Arms Act, as to make them equally applicable to all residents in, or visitors to, India, without distinction of creed, class or colour, to ensure the liberal concession of licenses wherever wild animals habitually destroy human life, cattle or crops, and to make all licenses granted under the revised rules, of life-long tenure, revocable only on proof of misuse and valid throughout the provincial jurisdiction in which they are issued;*

(*b*) *by establishing Military Colleges in India whereat natives of India, as defined by Statute, may be educated and trained for a military career, as commissioned or non-commissioned officers (according to capacity and qualifications) of the Indian army;*

(*c*) *by organising throughout the more warlike races of the Empire a system of militia service; and*

(*d*) *by authorizing and stimulating a widespread system of Volunteering, such as obtains in Great Britain, amongst the people of India.*

The Resolution was then put and unanimously carried.

**Res. V. Simultaneous Examinations in India and England for all Civil Branches of the Indian Public Service.**

PUNDIT PRAN NATH SARASWATI (*Calcutta, No.* 15, *in list*)—MR. PRESIDENT AND FELLOW DELEGATES,—The Resolution which it has fallen to my lot to propose is this:—

*That as one step towards ensuring the wider employment of Indians in the administration of the country, and as a matter of simple justice to the people of India, this Congress, agreeing with previous Congresses, declares it to be essential that all examinations for any and all of the Civil Branches of the Public Service in India, which at present are held only in England, should henceforth be also held simultaneously in India.*

This resolution, like its predecessor, is only a further development of the 3rd Resolution already adopted. It embodies a demand which is no stranger to these meetings. I think the best plan for me will be to focus, as it were, the positive declarations of persons in authority upon the question at issue. From a very remote period every Government of India, I do not mean the Government of mere temporary invaders like that of Mahmud of Ghuznee, but every permanent and settled Government, has availed itself to the full of all the indigenous talent of the country as well in the Civil as in the Military Department of the Administration. At first the British Government, from the very nature of the case, also availed itself of such indigenous agency; but by a gradual process of elimination (for the most part owing to difficulties of linguistic attainments) it has now come to pass that every high post is rigidly entailed upon foreigners. But, although this is the practical result, declarations have not been wanting, from very early periods, as to the necessity, or the abstract propriety, of admitting the sons of the soil to a due share in the administration of the country. The first declaration, which I wish to place on record, is contained in the Statute 3 and 4, William IV, Cap. 85, sec. 87, well known as the Statute of 1833. It was then declared by the Lords and Commons of Parliament that "no native of the said territories" (meaning India) "nor any natural born subject of His Majesty resident therein, shall, by reason only of his religion, place of birth, descent, colour, or any of them, be disabled from holding any place, office or employment under the said Company" (meaning the East India Company, whose Charter was being renewed.) Twenty years after that Lord Monteagle in the House of Lords made the following declaration: "If the only door of admission to the Civil Service of India is a competitive examination carried on in London, what chance, or what possibility, is there of natives of India acquiring that fair share in the administration of their own country, which their education and abilities would enable them to fulfil, and therefore *entitles* them to possess?" Shortly afterwards. upon the pacification of the country after the mutiny, in 1858, on the occasion of the gracious Proclamation of Her Majesty, which the people of this country have always adhered to as the great charter of their liberties, the Sovereign was thus pleased to express herself: "We hold ourselves bound to the natives of our Indian territories by the same obligations of duty which bind us to all our other subjects, and those obligations, by the blessing of Almighty God, we shall faithfully and conscientiously fulfil. * * * * * And it is our further will that, so far as may be, our subjects, of whatever race or creed, be *freely* and *impartially* admitted to offices in our service, the duties of which they may be qualified, by their education, ability and integrity, duly to discharge." Gentlemen, in these late days the fashion has grown up in official circles (I am glad to say there are bright exceptions) of speaking disparagingly of this Proclamation. I need only remind you of the weighty words of Lord Ripon, who said that this document "is not a treaty or diplomatic instrument, but a declaration of principles of Government which, if it is obligatory at all, is obligatory in respect to all to whom it is addressed. The doctrine to which Sir James Stephen has given the sanction of his authority I feel bound to repudiate to the utmost of my power. It seems to me to be inconsistent with the character of my sovereign and with the honor of my country, and if it were once to be received and acted upon by the Government of England, it would do more than anything else could possibly do to strike at the root of our power and to destroy our just influence." After this we had an Official Committee of the India Office constituted of such experienced and honorable men as Sir James Willoughby, Mr. Mangles, Mr. Arbuthnot, Mr. Macnaghten and Sir Erskine Perry. That Committee were unanimously of opinion that, in order to redeem the pledges which former Governments had given to the people of India, it was necessary to hold simultaneous examinations in India and in England, classifying the candidates who pass the examination in one list, examining them by the same standards, and then giving appointments upon the amalgamated list. That was in 1860. Nine years afterwards the Duke of Argyll made this confession: "With regard, however to the employment of natives in the Government of this country, in the Covenanted Civil Service, formerly of the Company and now of the Crown, I must say that we have not fulfilled our duty, nor the promises and engagements which we have made." I take it that the Statute of 1870 was partly due to this confession, and it was thereby enacted that natives of India, of proved merit and ability, might be appointed to any office in the Indian Civil Service. The history of that Statute and of the Public Service Commission is too recent and too well known to require repetition. I will only draw your attention to the well known confidential despatch of Lord Lytton, in which he made the candid confession that whatever might be the declarations and promises of Parliament and the Crown, the Government of India had always tried to avoid the fulfilment of those pledges. The people of India endorse the opinion of Lord Lytton that those pledges have not been redeemed; but we are thankful to Lord Lytton for stating the dilemma, to which that non-fulfilment is due, so clearly. I have no doubt that if that dilemma is put to the people of England, to the House of Commons and to the Sovereign herself, in the form in which Lord Lytton has put it, *viz.*, whether the promises are to be kept or violated, there will come from our august Sovereign, from that august Assembly, and that august Nation, the unanimous assurance that the promises so often made were meant to be kept and not to be violated. And, gentlemen, the only practical way of enforcing those promises and making sure of their fulfilment is to insist upon the system of simultaneous examinations. (*Cheers*).

MR. N. SUBBA RAO (*Madras, No.* 788, *in list*)—MR. CHAIRMAN AND BROTHER DELEGATES,—The first thing that strikes one in reading the resolution is that we are making a royal road for our youths to become the rulers of the land. Our British critics have not been slow in charging us with being unfit to occupy such a position. The reason is not far to seek. They point to various disabilities under which we suffer in social matters. At the same time in making this charge, that we are unfit to enjoy the concession we claim, they lose sight of the fact that it is not the Hindus alone that ask for this concession, but Mahomedans, Christians and other races who are free from our prejudices, and they, therefore, make a grievous mistake. Moreover they do not take into consideration the fact that there are advanced sections among us already, powerful and numerous, who are slowly rising above these social prejudices.

**2nd Day.**

**Res. V. Simultaneous Examinations in India and England for all Civil Branches of the Indian Public Service.**

What we ask by this resolution is this : Devise such test to secure the highest talent, the largest conception of duty, and whatever else you may think proper, but only let these apply equitably and fairly to all, be they English or Indian. Do not let the best of us be handicapped; do not continue this policy of practical, even if unintentional, favoritism on the one hand and exclusion on the other, by which the best of the Indians cannot be utilized for consolidating your own rule. By the best of us, I mean not so much Hindus as Mahomedans, Eurasians, Christains and other races, whose traditions and habits leave them far more free to furnish the material necessary according to the approved Government standards. These races, as well as the advanced sections of the Hindu community, are at present grievously handicapped. I say it is these races just as much as the Hindus that feel the danger of sending their young people to England, possibly to fail, and their lives to be wasted in unknown lands. Therefore the Congress asks, on our behalf, for such examinations as may secure physical, moral and intellectual fitness, simultaneously in England and India, instead of as now only in England. It must not be understood by this that the Congress as a whole is pledged, in securing these examinations, to demand also that appointments shall be conferred without subsequent training in England. That is a question of detail which is left to the Government, whose duty it is to lay down what conditions shall combine to complete that fitness which, in its opinion, is needed to qualify the candidate for its service. I, for one, believe (and I know that this opinion is shared largely by a considerable body of Congress Members, men of "light and leading" in each province) that a training in England is essential before the candidate can enter on his duties in India and take his place, on an equal footing, with his brother civilians. There is no use in disguising this. We, at any rate several of us, are quite prepared for this. What the Congress as a whole asks is this : No matter what the tests, what the limitations may be, whether it be to go to England, America or Japan, whether it be to drop from a balloon, let those tests be the same to the English and Indian youths. We do not ask that English youths should come here to be examined, we ask only that our Indian youths be not compelled to go there to be examined. We ask that as English lads are examined in England, so Indian lads should be examined in India, and having passed and secured a lien, as it were, on an appointment, if Government so wishes it, let them go to England and go with hope, not anxiety, to go through the remaining tests. Such is briefly our request. Is this any new idea created by this Congress? No, gentlemen, we are charged with want of originality. I admit it freely in this instance, at any rate, since for the last 50 years or more we have been promised just this equality of treatment, first by the Parliament itself in 1833, and subsequently by our Queen Empress herself, to say nothing of other great authorities. On these promises rests our claim—"a claim" (in the words of Lord Lytton) "which has been repeatedly affirmed by British and Indian statesmen, and by the legislation of the Imperial Parliament, and which is recognised by the Government of India as binding on its honor and consistent with all the aims of its policy." (*Cheers*). Surely the time has come now to satisfy that claim. (*Loud cheers*).

THE PRESIDENT.—For seven years at least we have all been of one mind in regard to the subject-matter of this resolution, and so without further speaking I will ask you to vote on this 5th Resolution.

"RESOLVED—*That as one step towards ensuring the wider employment of Indians in the administration of the country, and as a matter of simple justice to the people of India, this Congress, agreeing with previous Congresses, declares it to be essential that all examinations, for any and all of the Civil Branches of the Public Service in India, which at present are held only in England, should, henceforth, be also held simultaneously in India.*"

The Resolution was then put and carried by acclamation.

**Res. VI.**

**Reduction in the Salt Tax. Raising of Income Tax taxable minimum. Honest adherence to Government's own declared Excise Policy.**

PANDIT AJOODHYA NATH (*Allahabad, No. 74, in list*)—MR. PRESIDENT AND FELLOW DELEGATES,—It is now my duty to propose the 6th Resolution for your acceptance. I proceed first to read it :—

*That this Congress concurs with its predecessors in strongly advocating —*

(*a*) *The reduction of the Salt tax, by at least the amount of its latest enhancement.*

(*b*) *The raising of the Income tax taxable minimum from Rs. 500 to Rs. 1,000.*

(*c*) *Persistent pressure by the Government of India on all provincial Administrations, to induce them to carry out, in its integrity, the excise policy enunciated in paras. 103, 104 and 105 of the Despatch, published in the "Gazette of India" of March 1st, 1890, and the introduction of a simple system of local option in the case of all villages.*

In other words, we propose to ask the Government to reduce the Salt tax, to raise the taxable minimum income to Rs. 1,000, and to compel its subordinates to carry out

**2nd Day.**

**Res. VI. Reduction in the Salt Tax. Raising of Income Tax taxable minimum. Honest adherence to Government's own declared Excise Policy.**

that policy in regard to excise which was sketched out by that Government itself. In defence of the enhancement of the Salt duty it is said, first, that it is an indirect tax, and that it entails upon each man so small contribution that it matters very little whether it is enhanced or not. But it is forgotten that this is a country where admittedly from 50 to 60 millions of people live on the verge of starvation, and that therefore even this light additional burden weighs heavily upon them. The Government, in dealing with questions between the landlord and money-lender on one side, and the ryot on the other, is profuse in its professions of sympathy and compassion; but in dealing with a tax by which its own coffers are to be filled to enable it to commit acts of extravagance, or worse, on the frontier and elsewhere, those humane feelings are entirely lost sight of.

I think I am entitled to speak of the evils of the income tax as it affects people whose income is small in my part of the country, and to speak with some authority. Many come to me for advice. I have a large number of acquaintances in the Public Service, many of whom are assessors of this income tax. It is a fact in Upper India that if any officer of Government in any particular year reduces the aggregate amount of the tax within his jurisdiction, he is called upon for an explanation, and a satisfactory explanation too. You know what is meant by satisfactory—an explanation which gives satisfaction to the superior authorities; but in almost every instance no explanation, however satisfactory in itself, is considered technically satisfactory. But if an income tax officer is so fortunate as to show an increase in the amount of tax levied by him in any particular year, so far from being called upon to give an explanation, he is commended to the notice of his superior officers. I remember that when the Act was passed in Mr. Wilson's time one Deputy Collector was actually recommended for promotion on that account. (*Shame*). Now, gentlemen, that being the case, on whom should the burden fall? Upon those whose incomes are small? In the first place, they do not keep very elaborate accounts, and it is difficult to prove what their exact income is. In the second place, even if they can prove it, it is very difficult for them to get a *bonâ-fide* hearing. It is obvious then that we ask you to adopt this resolution in the interests not of your wealthy countrymen, but of those who are comparatively poor.

The third and the last clause requires no argument from me to commend it to your notice. Government itself has laid down the policy, and we ask that Government should carry it out, and see it carried out by others, in its integrity. I am perhaps one of the fittest persons to ask you to adopt this part of the resolution, because in the North-West Provinces the local Government, to the best of my knowledge, has done nothing in that direction. Much has been done in Bengal and Madras, but the Government of the North-Western Provinces and Oudh has turned a deaf ear to the representations of the people and the recommendations of Parliament. One word, by the way, about local option. Whatever may be the difficulties in towns—and to me they do not seem serious, since each separate mohulla or ward can be treated as a separate hamlet—but I say whatever the difficulties, real or imaginary, in towns, no one can pretend that there would be the smallest difficulty in introducing the system of local option into all villages and hamlets, including populations not exceeding, say, 1,500 or 2,000 souls. The only thing necessary would be, on a day fixed and locally notified before hand, to poll all the adult males in each, as to whether they would or would not have a liquor shop within the limits of their mouza, or township, or parish, or whatever in English best describes the land area pertaining to each village. This done, we maintain that, wherever two-thirds of such adult males opposed the existence of a liquor shop within their limits, none should there be allowed. As Government is itself the proprietor of all these liquor shops (or public houses), and only lets them on competitive leases year by year to the highest bidders, no question of compensation can here complicate the question. Such a system would save annually millions and millions from drink, degradation and crime. (*Cheers*). Such a system can be introduced throughout the country in six months without the smallest difficulty, and the Government know this. (*Cheers*). Such a system would close nine-tenths of the rural liquor shops, and the Government know this well also (*cheers*); and this, it seems, is why they will have nothing to say to it. No, they will cling to their money, to the fruits of sin and misery, rather than act righteously and do justice. (*Loud cheers*). Individually our rulers are, I think, good men, many of them really religious men, but collectively they have neither conscience nor religion; their financial codes are their Shastras (*cheers*) and money, no matter how obtained, to spend on Frontier dacoities (*cheers*) on a grand scale, their *summum bonum*. None the less will we press this Resolution, until stung by shame, they realize that it is doing right, which constitutes the chief strength and glory of a Government. (*Loud cheers.*)

MR. M. V. JOSHI (*Berar, No. 278, in list*).—MR. PRESIDENT AND BROTHER DELEGATES,—I am taken by surprise in having to second this proposition. I expected that it would not come on for discussion so soon, but I do not think that any special preparation beyond what I

**2nd Day.**

**Res. VI. Reduction in the Salt Tax. Raising of Income Tax taxable minimum. Honest adherence to Government's own declared Excise Policy.**

know of the subject is necessary to introduce the subject to you, because it has been threshed out in all the previous Congresses; and we have simply to reiterate our former conclusions. I bring them forward for your confirmation and ratification. I need not tell you that this may be called especially a "people's" resolution. Every thing involved in it relates to the masses rather than to the richer classes. Referring to its various clauses it will be seen that we advocate first a reduction of the Salt tax. You know that salt is one of the prime necessaries of life in a country like this where the bulk of the inhabitants are vegetarians. In a country, too, which is essentially agricultural, we require salt for purposes of the most varied kind. We want it for human food, we want it for cattle and for the land. It is against every principle of political economy that such a necessary article of diet should be heavily taxed by the Government. It would not be justified in taxing an article like this except in the most dire necessity, say in time of war, or when the Treasury has to be replenished for some exigency which could not have been foreseen or provided against. But our bureaucratic Government cannot see this, and for this blindness there are two reasons. One reason is that there is not, as in England, the healthy stimulus of public opinion keeping a check upon the Government, and the other is that they, comparatively rich as they are, do not themselves in the smallest degree feel this tax, which yet presses so cruelly on our legions of paupers.

Now I might equally speak upon the other clauses of the resolution, but what would be the use of my thus wasting your time, the time of the assembly? I truly believe that there is no single delegate now present, no, nor one single intelligent Indian in the whole Empire, who does not this day, thanks to the labours of previous Congresses, understand all the questions involved in this resolution as well as I do myself, and who would not and does not endorse with unshakeable conviction all its proposals. You will carry it I know, unanimously.

Munshi Sheikh Husein, *v.* Sheikh Chand (*Bombay, No.* 260, *in list*) then spoke in Urdu to the following effect:—

The way the Government Forest Laws are worked is a scandal to a civilised administration, and in many parts of the Bombay Presidency, the peasantry call the Forest Department, Black Death. Even the dead leaves are taxed, and tens of thousands have been despotically shut off from rights of user that they and their forefathers have enjoyed from generation to generation. (*Question, question*).

The President.—We are not discussing Forest grievances at present.

Munshi Sheikh Husein.—Well then the absence of permanence in the land tenures, the want of a permanent settlement, is another crying evil. The fluctuations and continued increase in the land revenue demand leads to much misery and hardship and is the main cause of the ever-increasing indebtedness, misery and degradation of our ryots. Once grant a permanent settlement and the Deccan Ryots Relief Act will no longer be required, though it must be admitted that under existing conditions it operates somewhat favourably. (*Question, question*).

The President.—We are not now discussing the permanent settlement; will you please confine your remarks to the Resolution which is before the assembly.

Munshi Sheikh Husein.—Then I shall speak of the Salt tax. By making salt dear and greatly restricting its use, the health of the community and its herds is injuriously affected. If the Government want the ryots to be really *nimak halal* (faithful to their salt, *i.e.*, loyal to their rulers) it must reduce its tax on their *nimak* (*i.e.*, salt), and the tax is a bad one, not felt by the rich, pressing seriously on the very poorest. The Government cannot refuse this prayer, at any rate, of the Congress, since able medical men are unanimously of opinion that the want of salt engendered by the heavy duty and consequent heavy price brings about many diseases. (*Here there were interruptions and cries of time, time—vote, vote. The President touched his gong*).

The President.—I must ask you now to sit down; you have already spoken for five minutes, and the assembly wishes to dispose of the question.

Munshi Sheikh Husein.—But I have not said half I have to say, and I protest, after having been permitted to speak, against being thus interrupted. (*Cries of sit down, vote, vote*).

The President.—I am really very sorry, but it is your own fault. You would go on speaking on subjects not before the meeting. You have had the five minutes by rule allotted to speakers, and the meeting does not wish to hear you longer. (*Cries of vote, vote*). Very well, then I formally put to you our 6th Resolution, which stands thus :—

**2nd Day.**

**Res. VI. Reduction in the Salt Tax. Raising of Income Tax taxable minimum. Honest adherence to Government's own declared Excise Policy.**

RESOLVED—*That this Congress concurs with its predecessors in strongly advocating*—

(*a*) *The reduction of the Salt tax, by at least the amount of its latest enhancement.*

(*b*) *The raising of the Income tax taxable minimum from Rs. 500 to Rs. 1,000.*

(*c*) *Persistent pressure by the Government of India on all Provincial Administrations, to induce them to carry out, in its integrity, the excise policy enunciated in paras. 103, 104 and 105 of the Despatch, published in the "Gazette of India" of March 1st, 1890, and the introduction of a simple system of local option in the case of all villages.*

The Resolution was then carried unanimously.

**Res. VII. Reforms in the Judicial and Police Administration.**

MR. POORNENDU NARAYAN SINGH (*Behar, No. 64, in list*)—I beg to propose the following resolution :—

*That having regard to the unsatisfactory charactor, in many respects, of the Judicial and Police Administration, this Congress concurs with its predecessors in strongly advocating*—

( *a* ) *the complete separation of Executive and Judicial functions such that in no case shall the two functions be combined in the same officer ;*

( *b* ) *the extension into many parts of the country, where it is not at present in force, of the system of trial by jury ;*

( *c* ) *the withdrawal from High Courts of the powers, first vested in them in 1872, of setting aside verdicts of acquittals by juries ;*

( *d* ) *the introduction into the Code of Criminal Procedure of a provision enabling accused persons, in warrant cases, to demand that, instead of being tried by the Magistrate, they be committed to the Court of Sessions ;*

( *e* ) *the fundamental reform of the Police Administration, by a reduction in the numbers and an increase in the salaries, and in the qualifications of the lower grades, and their far more careful enlistment, and by the selection for the higher posts of gentlemen, of higher capacities, more in touch with the respectable portions of the community, and less addicted to military pretensions, than the majority of the existing Deputy Inspectors General, Superintendents and Assistant Superintendents of Police.*

With regard to the first clause ; the executive and judicial functions were united by the East India Company more on economical than on other grounds, but the great administrator, Lord Cornwallis, discovered that the result of that system was to sacrifice the administration of justice to the supposed fiscal interests of Government. It was he who made a beginning in the separation of executive and judicial functions by making a radical change in the codes for the administration of civil and criminal justice. In 1805 it was enacted that the Chief Justice was not to be a member of the Supreme Council, in order, as the preamble to the regulation says, that the separation of the judicial from the executive authority in all their gradation and branches, might, in form and practice, be carried into full operation. In 1831 Lord Auckland procured the sanction of the Court of Directors to the separation of the offices of Collector and Magistrate. You thus see that during the time of the East India Company, our position in this matter was far better than it is now. But the forward policy of Lord Cornwallis received a check in 1858, perhaps, on account of the darkness of the political atmosphere at that time. It was in that year that the offices of Collector and Magistrate were again united, and in 1872, when the matter again came before the Legislature, and when there was peace all over the country, the provisions were re-enacted in the code of that year, and the grounds set forth by Mr. FitzJames Stephen in a minute on the administration of civil and criminal justice in British India. He was of opinion that "the maintenance of the position of the district officers (Collector-Magistrates) is essential to the maintenance of our British rule ; and, in order to maintain that position, judicial power in criminal matters must be left in their hands. The exercise of criminal jurisdiction is both in theory and in fact the most distinctive and most easily and generally recognized mark of sovereign power. All the world over the man who can punish is the ruler." If this be the basic principle of the present anomalous union of the executive and judicial functions, the sooner its fallacy is exposed the better. I may tell you that Mr. Justice Phear, lately a Judge in the Calcutta High Court, made some very pertinent observations regarding this position of Mr. Stephen in his introduction to the Bengal Regulations. He says : "It may be well to consider that the District Magistrate does not in fact exercise the criminal jurisdiction. In the Lower Provinces he has not leisure to do so, and its exercise in practice devolves upon the Joint Magistrate. Again, the *nizamat*, or right to administer criminal justice, was not given to us at first, and it remained in the hands of the native, while we notwithstanding exercised the real sovereign power." Then the objection on financial grounds is equally futile. The existing staff of Assistant and Deputy Magistrates is quite sufficient, at any rate in Bengal and Behar, for the complete separation of the judicial and executive functions, if the staff be remodelled, and they be partially reinforced from the judicial service—I mean at head-quarters of the districts. But that is beside the question; we are not at present concerned with the financial aspect of the matter.

The next clause refers to the extension of the jury system in parts where it is not at present in vogue. The present jury districts in Bengal were created in 1862, in Madras also in the same year, and in Bombay in 1867. There are seven in Bengal, seven in Madras, and only one in Bombay. It is a calumny against the British rule to say that in the year 1862, more than a quarter of a century ago, we were where we are now. They speak of the abuses in jury trials in India. That is as much as to say that no human system is perfect. Human nature is the same in India as elsewhere, and it has been pointed out several times in these Congress meetings that many of the so-called abuses are due to the bad and wantonly, if not intentionally, careless selection of juries. And then what about the infinitely greater abuses in trials without juries by civilian Magistrates and Judges?

As to the withdrawal from the High Courts of the power invested in them in 1872, to set aside verdicts of acquittal by juries, I need only refer to some remarks made by those who have administered this law of 1872. Mr. Justice West, in a case in the Bombay High Court, said in distinct terms that the verdicts of juries ought not to be interfered with, first on the constitutional ground that it was not proper to take away powers from those in whose hands they were originally vested by the Legislature, and second that any undue interference might and must interfere with the jurymen's sense of responsibility.

The records of the High Courts, both of Bombay and Calcutta, sufficiently show their uneasiness in having to deal with cases already disposed of by juries. There is something inhuman in the suspense and mental torment to which an accused person is subjected after a protracted jury trial ending in a verdict of acquittal, simply because the element of finality is withdrawn from it. (*Cheers*). The point has been again and again pressed from the Congress platform, and in the interest of justice and humanity the British Government should not turn a deaf ear to our representations.

The next clause relates to the introduction into the Code of Criminal Procedure of a provision enabling accused persons, in warrant cases, to demand that, instead of being tried by the Magistrate, they be committed to the Court of Sessions. Now in Session cases the Magistrate inquires whether the accused can be committed to the Court of Sessions or not. If the accused himself requests to be committed to the Court of Sessions there is no reason why public time should be wasted, and the accused made to undergo the trouble and expense of magisterial proceedings. There are cases in which the Court of Sessions has a concurrent jurisdiction with the Magistrates. In such cases the accused ought to have the opportunity of having the benefit of going to the higher Court whenever he likes. Speaking of warrant cases, if the accused takes his trial at the Court of Sessions, a step will be taken in the separation of judicial and executive functions, without the addition of any public burden.

The next clause relates to police reform. That there is something radically wrong in the police administration is admitted on all hands. Sir Steuart Bayley's resolution on police reforms mentions that upwards of seventy per cent. of serious crimes in Bengal goes unpunished and ninety per cent. of dangerous offences against property remains undetected. In pursuance of this resolution, the Bengal Government appointed a Select Committee which submitted a report, and one must be thankful to Sir Charles Eliot for giving prompt effect to the recommendations of that Committee. Some of those suggestions covered the grievances pointed out by clause (*e*), but the recommendations do not cover the whole ground. As to the appointment of police officers the obvious necessity of the provision renders it needless for me to add any words of mine. As to the attitude of District Superintendents and Assistant Superintendents, I may be permitted to say that it is a notorious fact that these higher officers take a pleasure in making themselves mere uniformed satellites of the District Magistrates. Now I submit that by keeping themselves aloof from the people they are not in a position to inquire into the real grievances of the people, and also to discharge their duties properly. Without further remarks I will move the whole of the resolution, and recommend it to your acceptance. (*Cheers*).

MR. OKHOY CHUNDER DASS (*Calcutta, No.* 25, *in list*)—MR. PRESIDENT, SISTER AND BROTHER DELEGATES,—I have been greatly surprised at the announcement that I have to speak on this resolution, but as I am suddenly called upon as a delegate, it is my bounden duty to respond to the call of our honoured President. As regards the second and third questions referred to in the resolution, I think I need add nothing. My learned predecessor has already touched upon them at some length, and I will therefore confine my remarks to the last question, namely, the reform of the police administration. We are as anxious to get the police administration reformed as our benign British Government. We have the authority of no less a personage than Lord Dufferin as to the validity of our claim. In his memorable speech at St. Andrew's Dinner on the eve of his departure from India, His Excellency the Viceroy admitted the necessity of police reform ; in fact he said that the Congress resolution on this head was a "counsel of perfection," and that the consession should be granted ; but the promise of the noble Lord has not been redeemed. As regards the presidency police it is in a better state on account of the existence of public opinion and the constant vigilance of the press. The mofussil requires, I think, more reforming than the presidency police. The present District Superintendents are not well educated men. They enter the service by the back door of nomination, as they have not the slightest chance of getting any appointment through a competitive examination in any department of the State. They and the assistants are, as a rule, relatives of high officials who have been too backward to get into any other branch of the service. In regard to many of the present Assistant Superintendents of Police, their educational qualifications are absolutely nil. I have the authority of one in high position for this statement. An examination was held in Calcutta and the Assistant Superintendents of Police obtained only one, two, three, and four marks even in English, their own mother-tongue. Most of these Assistant Superintendents of Police are connected with officials enjoying the highest posts in the land. Some are sons and some are nephews, cousins, and so on. The police service has, to all intents and purposes, become a sort of family arrangement with these Anglo-Indian officials. These well-connected nonentities *do* not, because they *can*not, effectively discharge their duties. They are simply paid ; the police it seems to be thought existing only to provide for them. The Lieutenant-Governor of Bengal, Sir Steuart Bayley, announced that without passing a competitive examination no Assistant Superintendent of Police would be allowed to remain in the service. Even the *Pioneer*, the champion of these Europeans, remarked that hitherto examinations of officers were unknown in the police department, that it served as a refuge for incapables and asked if these places were taken from them what could they do. They would most probably, it was suggested, end their lives in England as members of some of the lower grades of the British Police Service. The whole matter lies in a nutshell ; broadly speaking the superior English officers are wholly unfit for their position. They are the flowers and fruit of an unchecked nepotism and intellectually the inferiors of many of their subordinates and many of the criminals whom they ought, but generally fail, to bring to justice. There are of course exceptions, and many wholly unfit for the very responsible positions they occupy are, as the phrase goes, "very good fellows," but they are wholly out of place in the positions into which their uncles and cousins have inducted them. As for the native subordinates rank and file, they are grievously under paid, selected in the most reckless way, often themselves worse criminals than the majority they have to arrest, to a great extent uneducated, and when in the Police taught chiefly to gabble by heart certain police regulations and attend to their uniform. What can you expect? With these remarks I beg to second the resolution. (*Cheers*).

The President.—Before putting this resolution to the vote I wish to say a word with regard to clause (*a*). For some time past the propensity to pass unappealable sentences and record findings of fact, on the part of the magistracy, has become great ; an immense injustice has in many instances resulted from that propensity. One instance which ought to be proclaimed from the Himalayas to the Cape Comorin is as follows : A magistrate was determined to convict a certain accused ; his predetermination was so manifest that the Government's power was invoked, and the magistrate's convicting hand was stayed. He was told to send the case up to the Sessions. He obeyed ; but the last sentence in his committing order ran thus : "I am perfectly satisfied as to the guilt of the accused ; I was prepared to convict him and pass sentence on him, but my hands have been tied." That case went before the Sessions Court which, after hearing the case for the prosecution, without even calling upon the accused for his defence, acquitted him honorably. That is a typical case ; and as I well know that many, if not all, of you can call to mind many cases of this nature, though none perhaps quite so atrocious, there will be no difficulty I apprehend in saying "Ay" to this, or indeed any section of this Resolution 7 which I will now read and formally put to you.

Resolved—*That having regard to the unsatisfactory character, in many respects, of the Judicial and Police Administration, this Congress concurs with its predecessors in strongly advocating—*

(*a*) *the complete separation of Executive and Judicial functions such that in no case shall the two functions be combined in the same officer ;*

(*b*) *the extension into many parts of the country, where it is not at present in force, of the system of trial by jury ;*

**2nd Day.**

**Res. VII. Reforms in the Judicial and Police Administration.**

( c ) *the withdrawal from High Courts of the powers, first vested in them in 1872, of setting aside verdicts of acquittals by juries ;*

( d ) *the introduction into the Code of Criminal Procedure of a provision enabling accused persons, in warrant cases, to demand that instead of being tried by the Magistrate, they be committed to the Court of Sessions ;*

( e ) *the fundamental reform of the Police Administration, by a reduction in the numbers and an increase in the salaries, and in the qualifications of the lower grades, and their far more careful enlistment, and by the selection for the higher posts of gentlemen, of higher capacities, more in touch with the respectable portions of the community, and less addicted to military pretensions, than the majority of existing Deputy Inspector-Generals, Superintendents and Assistant Superintendents of Police.*

The Resolution was carried unanimously.

**Res. VIII. Deprecates diminution of educational grants and in the interest of Technical Education advocates an enquiry into the industrial condition of the country.**

Herambo Chandra Moyitra (*Calcutta, No. 9, in list*)—Mr. President, Sister and Brother Delegates,—The resolution which has been entrusted to me runs as follows :—

*That this Congress, concurring with previous Congresses, affirms the importance of increasing (instead of diminishing, as appears to be the present policy of the Government) the public expenditure on all branches of education, and the expediency, in view to the promotion of one of the most essential of these branches, the technical, of appointing a mixed commission to enquire into the present industrial condition of the country.*

I will follow the example of my distinguished friend Babu Kali Charan Banerjee, who summed up the substance of the third resolution in four words. I will also sum up the substance and spirit of this resolution in four words—"from darkness unto light." We desire, as our friend said, certain great fundamental administrative changes which to India would be as the passing from death unto life, but we also simultaneously entreat our benign Government not by any mean economy in educational matters to impede the nation in its upward course from darkness unto light ; light without which life is miserable, nay, more miserable than death itself. This is a question of such magnitude and presenting to us so many aspects that I will only venture to glance at a few matters connected with it. The time has come when the Government is upon its trial with regard to its oft-repeated profession of anxiety to promote primary education. We see it gradually withdrawing itself from the sphere of higher education. Does it fear that we already know too much ? I am grieved to find that there is no longer anything new done by Government in that direction. The mouths that once were never weary of trumpeting the cause of higher education now maintain an inglorious silence, and yet in face of the fact that ampler resources have been placed at the disposal of Government by the contraction of its operations in the field of higher education, no new departure has been made in that of primary education. How can we account for this discrepancy between the professions of the Government and the manner in which it has been actually acting ? This is not the time to go into facts and figures, but it is a truth, which cannot be disputed by the most servile supporter of the official bureaucracy, that the Government of India spends a smaller amount proportionally upon education than the most backward countries in Europe. A Government, like ours, professing so loudly to be enlightened and Christian, priding itself on the nobility of its motives, ought to be a little ashamed, one would think, of such a state of affairs. (*Cheers*). I happen to be in possession of facts which have not yet found their way into public documents, and I will put you in possession of some of them. Some time ago the Director General of Public Instruction of Bengal happened to communicate with Sir Charles Eliot, his anxiety to promote primary education more largely and devote funds to that end. What was the reply ? That the Lieutenant-Governor had no funds to spare ; at the same time we believe it is in contemplation that all the district Schools of Bengal should be abolished, so far as the Government is concerned, and that the Colleges of Rajshaye and Hugli should be closed. That is the state of things. Let us resolve not to permit this scandal and barbarism. We will not allow tho Government to assert uncontradicted that it is anxious to promote primary education and yet remain doing nothing in that direction, while gradually withdrawing itself from all concern with higher education. It may be that higher education has made some little progress, but in comparison with the countries of Europe or America it cannot be said, as yet, to have taken a sufficiently deep root in the soil here. The Government that taunts us educated men with being a "microscopic minority" is at least bound, in decency, not to withdraw from us all sources of higher education. If the educated classes are a microscopic minority, who but the Government is to blame for this ? Perhaps at the root of this policy there may be some apprehensions, regarding the attitude of the educated classes towards the official class, apprehensions of hostility. Now, if hostility means hostility to unconstitutionalism, to despotism and to old and corrupt traditions, we are hostile ; but if hostility means reckless, inconsiderate, desperate enmity to constitutional Government, we are not the enemies of Government, we are its friends, the friends and supporters of order and justice and of the Crown of England. (*Cheers*).

**2nd Day.**

**Res. VIII. Deprecates diminution of educational grants and in the interests of Technical Education advocates an enquiry into the industrial condition of the country.**

As, in the sphere of religion, the human mind passes, if not rightly guided, in a single bound from grovelling superstition to defiant atheism, so in the sphere of intellectual culture the human mind, if not rightly guided, passes at a single bound from servile ignorance into defiant rebellion against the established order of things. Let Government beware of the fatal policy that would withdraw, just at this critical period, that rightful guidance which is essential to the peaceful evolution of the new order. It may be that the growth of education and of public opinion will be stronger and stronger, and will impose a check upon despotism, but it will at the same time strengthen the foundation of the British Empire. The true foundation of an Empire is righteousness—that righteousness that exalts the nations of the world. A truly constitutional Government has nothing to apprehend from the educated; they are its natural supporters, its necessary allies.

There is another cry that we often hear from officials, *viz.*, that they cannot provide bread, *i.e.*, official positions, for all the educated, and hence that they will stop educating. This resolution covers that ground. Education need not mean the casting of all minds in the same mould, and the turning out an unlimited supply of Clerks and Deputy Magistrates. Provide a many sided education, educate our people in such a manner that it may promote the development of the resources of the country, and show them how to earn their own bread. We do not want academic education merely; let us have a many-sided education, and the Government may be quite sure that its cry of inability to provide bread for the hungry literati will fast disappear before the expansion of the immense resources of this blessed land. It is they themselves who taunt us with being a "microscopic minority," who tacitly refuse to make any adequate efforts for the promotion of education. In reply to the charge of being a "microscopic minority," we say that it is a telescopic sort of benevolence which they manifest, and that it is so remote that it requires a most powerful political telescope to discover its wisdom. It is a telescopic sort of benevolence to be spending millions upon millions on frontier defences, and taking away money from the schools and colleges and technical institutes. Hence, it is one aim of this Congress to give prominence to this great question, and to force the Government to adopt a more liberal and righteous policy in this matter than has hitherto obtained. Even at the risk of being suspected to be a heterodox Congress-walla, I will declare my conviction that this resolution does not yield in importance to the great resolution with reference to the elective system. That is merely a weapon; education is to supply the power which is to wield that weapon righteously and efficiently. Be it then the glory of England to promote the interests of India by consecrating and vitalizing her exertions in the administration of this Empire, with a copious infusion of righteousness, so as to elevate this unhappy and still fallen country shorn of its glory and splendor, and teach our countrymen to regard the advent of the English as the great instrument, ordained by God Himself in his wisdom, for the revival of this down-trodden and unhappy land. (*Cheers*). It is hard upon three score years ago that this great problem formally forced itself on the consideration of the British nation. "Shall we for ever retain these Indians whose destinies God has confided to our charge, ignorant and as slaves, or shall we educate and raise them to be fit and anxious to join, as free men, in the administration of their own country?" Day after day in both Houses of Parliament, the great debate was carried on until the nation, through its peers and representatives, decided for the latter and nobler course. For years this decision was honestly acted up to, and Lord Derby's (then Lord Stanley's) despatch of 1859 and John Stuart Mill's famous despatch of 1854, remain proofs of the honesty of purpose of the British nation. But ever since the Congress arose to advocate and vindicate the cause of constitutional freedom, and threaten the autocratic powers and exclusive privileges of the great Indian bureaucracy, this latter, alarmed for these its cherished possessions, has begun to crave for a retrogade movement into the policy which their nobler countrymen, 60 years ago, indignantly repudiated. (*Shame, shame*).

It is too late, my friends—too late—the seed has been sown broadcast—has germinated, is germinating everywhere—in vain, you try now everywhere to repress and discourage higher education by every insidious means. You may delay, but you cannot destroy. You may earn hatred, you cannot secure the enslavement of those who now know that they are free British subjects. It is too late, put aside this folly, accept the inevitable and foreseen results of the policy your nobler predecessors deliberately adopted. Abstain from discouraging, as you now are discouraging, education, be true to the higher and better impulses of a Briton's heart, be true to the edicts of your senates, the orders of our Queen Empress, stimulate heart and soul, as in days gone by, education of all kinds and of every grade, and then, in lieu of a Frankenstein monster ever on the alert to destroy you, you will find in the educated generations that will rally round you, not indeed the servile sycophants that ignorance might have furnished you, but true, loyal and capable colleagues, whose foremost aim and chief glory it will be to labour on equal terms, side by side with you, to secure the safety, honour and welfare of our common sovereign and all her dominions. (*Loud cheers*).

MR. G. K. GOKHALE (*Poona, No. 172, in list*)—MR. PRESIDENT, LADIES AND GENTLEMEN,—

2nd Day.

Res. VIII. Deprecates diminution of educational grants and in the interests of Technical Education advocates an enquiry into the industrial condition of the country.

I have great pleasure in seconding the proposition which has just been so eloquently moved for your adoption by Mr. Moitra. As the time is very short I will do no more than put my points before you. My first point is that the Government has pledged itself in the most solemn and unreserved manner to regard the education of the people as its most sacred duty. In the despatch of 1854, which is believed to have emanated from Mr. John Stuart Mill, the Directors say that the education of the people is the most sacred and solemn duty of the Indian Government. After the transference of the Government of this country from the Company to the Crown in 1859, the Secretary of State for India, in a despatch to the Indian Government, reiterated the same thing. So far, therefore, as the promises of the Government are concerned there can be no doubt. My next point is, that taking all civilized countries into consideration. India is the least advanced in the matter of education. I have the statistics with me, but will not quote them. You will find that in the countries of Europe 90 per cent of the school-going population attend school; but in our own country the proportion is only 11 per cent. I have also statistics with regard to expenditure, but I will mention only a few. In Europe, in the most backward country as far as education is concerned, no less than 6·5 per cent. of the public revenues goes towards the expenses of education, whereas in India the proportion is about 1 per cent. The expenditure on education has not kept pace with the increase in the ordinary revenues of this country. About 20 years ago it was 1·4 per cent., and now it is only 1 per cent. The Education Commission appointed by Lord Ripon has exhaustively dealt with the question and recognized the necessity of increasing the educational expenditure. The most sympathetic of Governors-General in 1884 directed the local Governments to increase the outlay upon education as much as possible. Then came a change in the Government of the country, and in the policy of the Government. Lord Dufferin's Government issued a resolution in June 1888 distinctly stating that thereafter the expenditure on education should be reduced rather than increased. The policy of reducing the expenditure on education is only recent, coming into existence with the Government of Lord Dufferin. I was going to say something with regard to the picture presented by Lord Ripon's Government and Lord Dufferin's; but there is no time. The second part of the resolution asks the Government to appoint a commission of inquiry which is to report upon the industrial problems of the country. I am no great believer in these commissions. Their reports are submitted to Government, but nothing comes of them. There is, however, one distinct advantage about them, that they supply most exhaustive material for those who like to study the question. It is only in this light that I support the recommendntion on this subject. The Government cannot now hesitate. The time for hesitation has gone. In 1833, as my predecessor so eloquently explained, Government was at the parting of the ways, and if they wanted to hesitate should have hesitated then. But they, or rather the British nation, chose the policy that alone was consistent with the best traditions and the glory of England. Having entered upon that path, they cannot now go back, they cannot even halt; they must go on (*cheers*), and why in God's name should they halt? The spread of education in India means the glory of England, and an ever-growing guarantee for the peaceful continuance of her rule. For it involves a continuous expansion of that section of the community which labours to secure that happiness for and contentment amongst the masses, which are essential to the permanence of a foreign supremacy. Truly in the happiness and contentment of India's people lie England's glory and England's strength; and in England's sense of honour and justice lie, at this critical period all our hopes and all our aspirations. (*Cheers.*)

THE PRESIDENT.—Gentlemen, the shades of eve are falling fast. I am loath to stop this instructive and interesting debate, but as we are all agreed, and night is closing on us, I must do so. This then is our 8th Resolution.

RESOLVED -- *That this Congress, concurring with previous Congresses, affirms the importance of increasing (instead of diminishing, as appears to be the present policy of the Government) the public expenditure on all branches of education, and the expediency, in view to the promotion of one of the most essential of these branches, the technical, of appointing a mixed commission to inquire into the present industrial condition of the country."*

The Resolution was then put and carried with loud cheers.

THE PRESIDENT—Before we adjourn I want to say one word with regard to *our* "grand old man." I want all of you to go to Babu Bhupendra Nath Bose for Mr. Hume's photograph, an excellent picture, some thousand copies of which have been most generously supplied by Mr. Radha Raman Kar (*cheers*), a Calcutta gentleman, for gratuitous distribution to all Congress-wallahs (*continued cheering*). The Congress then adjourned to the next morning, Wednesday, the 30th, at 11 o'clock A.M.

# THIRD DAY'S PROCEEDINGS.

## Wednesday, December 30th 1891.

---

THE Congress re-assembled at 11 A.M.

**3rd Day.**

THE PRESIDENT.—GENTLEMEN,—You all know that this is the last day of the present Congress Meeting, and you also know that we have a good deal of work still to do. I need not remind you that there is a rule with regard to the time to be allowed to each speaker. That rule was not strictly enforced yesterday, but, considering that we must go through the work to-day, it will be my painful duty to exercise the authority which you have placed in my hands for the benefit of you all. Speaking to the point, and omitting all irrelevant and collateral discussion, is what we should all aim at.

**Large number of telegrams of sympathy and expressing regret at inability to attend.**

Before we proceed let me mention that we have had a very large number of telegrams expressive of sympathy in the Congress cause from different quarters, as well as telegrams expressive of their regret from a great number of delegates, who, in consequence of sickness or other causes, have been unable to attend; but there is one telegram which deserves special attention—I mean a telegram from General Booth—which I shall call on the General Secretary to read to you, together with the reply which your Subjects Committee has proposed to send, and which, I doubt not, you will adopt without a moment's hesitation.

**Res. IX. General Booth's Telegram and reply thereto.**

MR. A. O. HUME (*General Secretary*) (*Punjab, No.* 130, *in list*)—General Booth's telegram runs as follows: "May I be allowed to commend to the attention of the delegates the claims of the millions of India's starving poor, and to urge the consideration of some scheme by which these destitute multitudes can be placed upon the waste lands of the country, in such an organized and befriended manner, as will enable them to gain for themselves those necessities of healthy existence which, in their present circumstances, are denied to them. Praying for the blessing of God upon the labours of the Congress, yours in sympathy with every effort for the amelioration of mankind, William Booth, General of the Salvation Army."

To this it is proposed to send the following reply:—"The Congress having received and considered your kindly message, thank you cordially for the same. No possible scheme of internal immigration can perceptibly relieve the fifty to sixty millions of half-starving paupers, whose sad condition constitute the primary *raison d'être* of the Congress. It is only by modifying the adverse conditions out of which this widespread misery arises, and by raising the moral standard of the people that any real relief is possible. As regards the first, the Congress Programme now embodies all primarily essential reforms; as regards the second, in every province and in every caste, associations, public or private, are working with a yearly increasing earnestness. Many good missionaries are labouring in the same field, and we have to thank you that your army, too, is now engaged in the good work of elevating the masses. May your efforts and ours, in both directions, be crowned with success! Congress, including men of many faiths, welcomes cordially all who seek to benefit our suffering brethren."

THE PRESIDENT.— GENTLEMEN,—Does this reply of the Subjects Committee meet your approval? (*Cries of yes, yes, all right*). Very good then, to put every thing in form I shall submit the proposition as Resolution IX in the following form:—

*Read the following telegram from General Booth:—*

"May I be allowed to commend to the attention of the Congress the claims of the millions of India's starving poor, and to urge the consideration of some scheme by which these destitute multitudes can be placed upon the waste lands of the country, in such an organised and befriended manner, as will enable them to gain for themselves those necessaries of a healthy existence which in their present circumstances are denied. Praying for the blessing of God upon the labours of the Congress, yours in sympathy with every effort for the amelioration of the miseries of mankind.—WILLIAM BOOTH, *General of the Salvation Army.*"

RESOLVED—*That the following telegram be despatched in reply to General Booth:—*

"*The Congress having received and considered your kindly message thank you cordially for the same. No possible scheme of internal immigration can perceptibly relieve the fifty to*

**3rd Day.**

**Res. IX. General Booth's Telegram and reply thereto.**

*sixty millions of half-starving paupers, whose sad condition constitutes the primary* raison d'être *of the Congress. It is only by modifying the adverse conditions out of which this widespread misery arises, and by raising the moral standard of the people, that any real relief is possible. As regards the first, the Congress programme now embodies all primarily essential reforms; as regards the second, in every province and in every caste, associations, public or private, are working with a yearly increasing earnestness. Many good missionaries are labouring in same field, and we have to thank you that your army, too, is now engaged in the good work of elevating our masses. May your efforts and ours, in both directions, be crowned with success. Congress including men of many creeds, welcomes cordially all who seek to benefit our suffering brethern."*

The Resolution was then put and carried by acclamation.

**Res. X. The Annual Indian Sessions of the Congress to be continued until all necessary reforms are conceded.**

MR. W. C. BONNERJEE (*Calcutta, No.* 1, *in list*)—MR. PRESIDENT AND FELLOW DELEGATES,—I have a purely formal duty to perform and that is to present to you a report of the committee appointed under your first resolution. One word of introduction is necessary before I read the report. You will remember that the British Committee,—at a meeting held on the 13th October 1891, used these words: "At the same time the Committee, think it desirable that no other Session of Congress, after that of December of 1891, be held until the Congress has assembled in England." Out of deference to that opinion of the British Committee the General Secretary issued a notice to all standing Congress Committee asking them to consider this subject, and to come here prepared to say whether the Annual Indian Sessions should be discontinued or continued pending the British Session. We have all considered this matter, and it has been discussed, both formally and informally, all over the country, and as the result of that consideration and discussion, and in view to a formal settlement of the question, you appointed a committee whose report I am about to present to you. That report runs as follows:—

"*Your Committee have considered the matter referred to them, and have also consulted, informally, various members of the Subjects Committee and other delegates. They are clearly of opinion that it is not advisable to discontinue the Annual Session of the Indian National Congress until after the British Session, and that future Congresses should be held uuder the same regulations as heretofore.*" (*Loud and continued cheering*).

I have much pleasure in presenting that report to you, and from the way in which you have received it I have no doubt that it will be accepted unanimously. (*Cheers*). I move that it be accepted and filed amongst the records of the Congress.

PUNDIT AJOODHYA NATH (*Allahabad, No.* 74, *in list*)—It affords me sincere pleasure to second the adoption of this report. It is quite in accordance with my own feelings. (*Cheers*). I think we are all agreed that wherever else we may also hold Sessions of the Congress, we will go on holding our Annual Sessions in India until all needful reforms have been secured. (*Cries of yes, yes, yes*).

THE PRESIDENT.—Are you all agreed? (*yes, yes*). Shall I then put it formally as our tenth resolution! (*yes, yes*). Then it will run thus:—

*Read Report of the Committee appointed under Resolution (I.) which runs as follows:—*

"Your Committee have considered the matter referred to them, and have also consulted informally various members of the Subjects Committee and other delegates. They are clearly of opinion, that it is not advisable to discontinue the Annual Session of the Indian National Congress until after the British Session and that future Congresses should be held under the same regulations as heretofore."

RESOLVED—*That the Annual Sessions of the Congress in India continue to be held until all necessary reforms have been secured.*

The resolution was carried by acclamation.

**Res. XI. Necessity for mitigating the harshness of the practical administration of the Forest Laws.**

THE PRESIDENT.—GENTLEMEN,—Before I call upon the speaker who is in charge of the next resolution, I think it is necessary to make a few remarks to avoid future misconceptions. The proposition, as worded, might be construed to involve the admission that the Forest Laws in themselves are good enough, and that our complaint in regard to them is only as to the manner in which they are administered. I may tell you that it was never our intention, or the intention of those who framed the resolution, to make any such admission. The question of whether the laws themselves need amendment is left open, and the discussion to-day will be independent of that question, and without prejudice to any conclusions that a more minute investigation of all the sources of the present discontent may lead to.

**Res. XI. Necessity for mitigating the harshness of the practical administration of the Forest Laws.**

MR. PAUL PETER PILLAI (*Madras, No. 757, in list*)—I beg to move the following resolution :—

*That having regard to the very serious discontent created, especially in Peninsular India, by the practical administration of the Forest Laws, the Government of India be most respectfully, but earnestly, entreated to investigate this carefully and endeavour to mitigate its harshness and render it less obnoxious to the poorer classes.*

I am from Tinnevelly, the southernmost district in India. With the knowledge and experience of a small ryot owning a few acres, I have the good fortune to combine an intimate knowledge of the conditions and circumstances of landholders, of all grades and positions, among whom I move largely, and for whose benefit I am working, and I consequently know a good deal about the Forest Laws and their operation. I speak from personal knowledge and observation, and from careful study of the agricultural condition of the country. Some time ago I held and declared the opinion that the condition of agriculture was degenerating. Now I may venture to say that it is on the high road to a complete collapse. The indigenous arts and industries of the land have collapsed, or are collapsing. While this is the case with the arts and industries, agriculture, the only thing left for the people, may truly be said to be well on the way to a collapse. Alas ! if this goes on there will be an end of everything so far as India is concerned. The Forest Laws which I have now to discuss have, amongst other things, largely contributed to this unhappy result. I shall simply enumerate the various ways in which the Forest Laws exercise a disastrous influence on the agriculture of the country, at least as far as the Madras Presidency is concerned. With a single stroke of the legislators' pen the Forest Laws have extinguished the communal rights of the ryot—rights which have been enjoyed from time immemorial—rights recognised and respected by former Governments and even by the British Government in former times, which went so far as to issue *pottahs* to ryots for the enjoyment of such rights ; and several ryots showed me such *pottahs*. While the Government as a general rule reserved valuable timber forests, the ryots were allowed the enjoyment of minor forest produce, and of inferior wood necessary for every-day domestic use, free pasture, and the right of procuring vegetable manure, fuel, stone and gravel. Now all these rights and privileges have been taken away summarily by a single stroke of the legislators' pen. It is some thirty years since the Madras Government thought of developing and enlarging the Forest Administration. Since the passing of the Forest Act of 1882, the laws have been enforced rigorously with unhappy consequences to the ryot classes. By the extinction of these communal rights our peasant proprietors have ceased to possess that status and moral influence, as compared with non-land-owning classes, which so materially aided to reconcile them to their position. Any one acquainted with the village system of rural India, at any rate in the south, will agree with me in saying that the ryots have ever possessed unquestioned the gratuitous enjoyment of all waste lands, cultivable or uncultivable, the pottah lands under cultivation being answerable for the Government revenue and the waste lands under valuable timber forests being in the enjoyment of the State.

By the extinction of communal rights village society has been revolutionised. By the extinction of the rights and the privileges of the landholding community they are placed on the same dead level with the artizan and non-landholding inhabitants of villages. Not only that. Their condition has become inferior to these, for they are answerable for a heavy Government land tax though they have no longer the enjoyment of pasture for their cattle or the right of procuring wood for their houses and for agricultural implements, vegetable manure for their fields, thorns and prickly shrubs for fencing their fields, and the like. Under pressure of necessity they are driven to infringe the all-embracing Forest Laws and thus stand liable to criminal prosecution. For petty infringements of these vexatious forest ordinances thousands of criminal prosecutions take place in my district. The protecting wings of the Forest Laws have descended from the hills to the plains. The hills have been divided into reserved and unreserved forests. The plains also have been divided into reserved lands and unreserved. The ryots are often unable to find which are reserved and which are unreserved. The unreserved lands, if there be such, are let to the ryots with restrictions and prohibitory conditions. Unreserved lands are gradually dwindling to such an extent that in many a village there is hardly any room for cattle to move beyond fallow lands. In such places, if the pottah lands be under cultivation, the hardships are insuperable. Then I may refer to the loss of the privilege and status of the land-holding and cultivating community over mere artizans and labourers. The charges of labourers have risen enormously high without bringing any corresponding profit or benefit to the ryot. By the Forest Laws, which impose taxes on forest produce which was before exempt from taxation and Government interference, the land revenue is directly or more strictly speaking indirectly enhanced. The land is heavily taxed enough. Pasture for cattle necessary for agriculture is taxed. Vegetable manure is taxed. Wood, necessary for agricultural implements like the plough, is taxed. Even when the tax is paid the labourers

**3rd Day.**

**Res. XI. Necessity for mitigating the harshness of the practical administration of the Forest Laws.**

engaged in working out these forest products have to be paid heavily as they work subject to continual interference from forest subordinates, and this leads to worry and annoyance. Moreover, even when the ryot is willing to pay the tax, he experiences great difficulties in getting licenses. The social and economic revolution brought on by these changed conditions is most keenly felt in rural districts. The wages of the labourers engaged in procuring these articles, according to the laws of political economy, increase the wages of labour in other directions also. The abnormal disturbance of the labour market produced by this cause among others is a very serious subject for consideration. The Forest Laws are making great havoc with the live stock of the country so essential for its agriculture. I wrote to the leading paper in Madras, the *Madras Mail*, stating that by taking away pasture you destroy the British power in India, by taking away pasture you destroy cattle, and by destroying cattle you destroy the industry of agriculture in India. This is nothing but a truism. In consequence of the difficulties experienced in procuring food for cattle on the hills as well as on the plains there is heavy mortality among them. Cattle degenerate in every way, and accordingly there is a growing diminution of cattle power so essential for agriculture. There is a growing diminution in the supply of farm yard manure (animal dung and urine), in the supply of milk and its products, and in the supply of animal food. For want of nutrition and sufficient pasture cattle are degenerating in their procreative power. What a tremendous loss will these be to India, when all these things are put together. Whether there is pasture or not cattle must live. On account of the pasture difficulty cattle are liable to commit trespass upon prohibited lands reserved by the Government, or *pottah* lands under cultivation. Cattle are impounded wholesale in large numbers by 600 or 700 or 1,000 heads of cattle or sheep at a time. I have made a very strong protest against such wholesale impounding. In prosperous times even cattle degenerate and the live-stock declines rapidly in consequence of this iniquitous and blundering forest administration. Cattle-owners, in most instances, have not even half of what they had twenty years ago. In times of scarcity and distress they die in large numbers, which was not the case formerly, when the ryots had the right of free pasture and when they had the opportunity of economising and storing the fodder of the plentiful years for years of scarcity and drought. The Government realised last year one and a half lacs from pasture fees. While so much is realised from legal fees for pasture, the Government got three and a half lacs of rupees from penal fees by impounding cattle for trespass. The legal and penal fees amount to five hundred thousand rupees on account of pasture alone. You have heard of the controversy between Mr. Caine and Lord Wenlock about cattle mortality on account of the distress and famine in the Presidency of Madras. On the eve of my departure from Madras I read in the *Madras Times* (by no means friendly to Mr. Caine) that within the short period of eight months, from January to September this year, in the single district of North Arcot about three hundred thousand cattle perished from want of pasture and fodder over and above the normal mortality during the corresponding periods of previous years. The facts are from official reports obtained from tanneries. More than half of the cattle that died would have been useful for agricultural labour. Taking on an average that a bullock or draught ox is sufficient for cultivating six acres throughout a year, more than a million acres are without bullock power so necessary for agriculture in the district. I myself experienced just such a difficulty in 1886, when there was heavy mortality in my place on account of agricultural distress. The difficulty of procuring bullocks for ploughing was very great by the fall of rain out of season, and the ploughman's wages rose from three annas to a rupee and a half per day. On account of this difficulty I had to employ coolies to stir up the soil with mammoties and hoes according to the rude and primitive method of agriculture. There are a number of ryots who are driven to this primitive method of cultivation. This is one of the reasons why large areas of land, once under cultivation, are left lying waste.

There is a difficulty in procuring wood for agricultural implements like ploughs. The ryots are put to the hardships of buying timber, often of a valuable kind, from bazaars and markets far away from their places, while the wood in the village in the neighbourhood of their houses, and the use of which they have enjoyed from time immemorial, is closed against them.

There is difficulty also in procuring vegetable manure from Government forests and practically even from *pottah* lands, beyond forest thanas, by Government interference and taxation. How is it possible to carry on agriculture without vegetable manure and farm yard manure whose supply is growing more and more scanty every year? Land must necessarily deteriorate under such circumstances.

There are certain other hardships which the agricultural classes suffer equally with the non-land-owning classes. Fuel has become a State monopoly. The monopoly of fuel supply causes great hardships. The price of fuel has risen considerably. Often fuel is not procurable either for love or money. Fuel is as much a necessary of life as food

**Res. XI. Necessity for mitigating the harshness of the practical administration of the Forest Laws.**

itself. When there is a fuel famine the people suffer nearly as much as during the times of the worst famine and scarcity. I have heard of instances of ryots converting valuable teak and other timbers into fuel. I have heard of instances of even Government servants starving temporarily and delaying to attend to their office-work in consequence of the fuel difficulty. I have heard of people being driven to the necessity of soaking grain in water and eating it raw and fresh. While during ordinary times the price of fuel is high, in times of scarcity and distress the price becomes very low in consequence of too many of the coolie class and the poorest people, for want of better work, supplying fuel far in excess of the demand, the demand being lessened by the distress of the consumers. Thus in the district of Salem, while the coolie class sold their head loads of fuel for nine pice, the Government tax amounted to six pice, leaving a surplus of three pice only for the support of the labourer and his household. The matter was represented to the Collector and the Governor, but with no effect. The wild berries of trifling value, thatch grass, and inferior wood for constructing huts are taxed and are subject to prohibitory restraints. Even stones and gravel are taxed on pain of one month's imprisonment if removed from forest lands (plain and hill forests). My brother delegate, Mr. P. Kesara Pillai of Anantapoor, has told me to-day that there is a recent General Order of the Madras Government enjoining the revenue authorities to discourage the ryots from removing stones and gravel even from pottah lands. I believe fully in this strange treatment, because now and then there is such interference from the revenue authorities, and because we in our pottahs are requested or forced to declare the surrender of our claims over mineral produce and mining rights. I am unable to imagine how the removal of stones and gravel will injure forest conservancy. Any one who knows anything of our agriculture and forestry will tell you that the removal has only the contrary effect of improving the forests by improving the soil. By such restrictions the people suffer, especially in the Ceded Districts, where stones are largely used in house building.

When it was proposed to introduce forest legislation, it was done on the plea of making provision for posterity and following the scientific principle, of procuring more rain by increasing the foliage area. From philanthropic and scientific grounds it has in practice degenerated into a mere money-making and other people's property-grabbing arrangement. Everything within the forest limits has been taxed, except the atmosphere, without any rhyme or reason. Difficulties and ruinously prohibitory restrictions are raised with regard to the right of way for cattle and men even for drinking purposes. The Government seems to have some extraordinarily dismal idea about fires and cattle grazing. Forest fires are not caused by owners of cattle alone. They often arise from natural causes, like lightning and friction; under the influences of wind, dry sticks and bamboos rubbing against each other and igniting. But the economy of nature has so arranged things that pure grass hills will remain grass hills to eternity, unless the nature of the soil and topography of the ground are changed. Such hills which will remain useless for the growth of valuable timber are only slowly to be improved by the chemical action of the atmosphere on rocks and gravel, by the ashes of the grass burnt periodically and by the pasturage of cattle which give the hills the benefit of their manure. For the past ten years forests have been very rigorously conserved in my place, even from cattle trespass and protected from fire. But there is no progress in rainfall. There is less rainfall now in my parts than before. There has been a water famine in my place twice of the severest character unprecedented in the memory of living men, and that although the place is at the foot of the Western Ghats. Forests in Native States which have less scientific forestry, and in zemindaries which have no scientific forestry to boast of, are as good as Government forests and, in certain respects, even better in well managed States and estates, and in these there is none of the cruel rigour which characterises British territory, where the rulers do not seem to have realized the real reproductive and recuperative powers of nature. If the axe and saw be carefully watched and controlled within the forests, it is quite sufficient for the purposes of forest conservancy. These are some of the facts, and those who are well acquainted with the suffering of the ryots in consequence of all this absurd and useless so-called scientific forestry will feel that I have not overstated my case. Gentlemen, this is a very serious matter for the consideration of the Congress. Repeated memorials to the Government and protest in the press have been of no avail. If there be any institution that is to save India from its agricultural ruin resulting from the hardships inflicted by the forest laws, it is the National Congress. It is the highest duty of every one of the two hundred and eighty-five millions of India, princes and peasants, to support the grandest movement that history has ever seen. If we are not able or willing to support the movement we are not worthy of our existence and not fit to be called men and a nation. The grievances of the Forest Laws affecting millions of people are such as to require immediate redress. (*Cheers.*)

MR. R. P. KARANDIKAR (*Satara, No.* 197, *in list*)—MR. CHAIRMAN AND FELLOW DELEGATES,—I believe that the announcement made by our worthy President at the beginning of the discussion will dispel many of the fears that have been entertained by some of the delegates from the Bombay Presidency who wanted the Forest Laws themselves to be made the subject of dis-

**3rd Day.**

**Res. XI. Necessity for mitigating the harshness of the practical administration of the Forest Laws.**

cussion rather than tho administration thereof. I believe therefore that we need not waste time by going over that question, important as it is. I will refer to the serious inconveniences or, as the resolution puts it, the serious discontent created by the administration of these laws. In the first place, I would ask the favour of your walking with me out of this Pandal—I do not mean bodily, but mentally—and if you will go with me to a village situated somewhere in the western hills, you will find a small hut with a few persons consisting of a man, a female and some children. For the edification of those who are anxious to see what they are like I have their photographs here. (The photographs were distributed for inspection). We are now speaking in the interest, not of those who are rich, but of those who are really poor. Indeed this proposition may be called the poor man's proposition. If you look at the map of India you will see that the country has on the east and on the west mountainous ranges, and it is the people of these districts that are particularly affected by the Forest Laws. Here is the hut, there is the field, and you have the cattle outside the man's door ; there is also what is called the family. I want you to see on how many sides this family is encircled with difficulties consequent upon the introduction of the Forest Laws and their administration. I have here all the facts and materials with me, but I will simply draw your attention to the remarkable statements made in the speech by Sir Theodore Hope, who had charge of the forest measure in the Legislative Council, and who assured the people that the object of legislation was not to trespass on their rights, but merely to conserve and take better care of that part of the forest which was over and above the actual wants of the people who tilled and used the forests. Now you will see whether that promise, coming from so high an authority, has been kept, by the rules that profess to be framed under the regulation which was passed with this object in view. You will observe in the photograph that there is one bullock, a milch cow and a sheep. It is not expected that a cow is at all times giving milk. The rule is that as long as cattle give milk they are to be allowed free pasturage, provided that they belong to cultivators, and provided again that there is land belonging to the village in which the cultivator is resident included in the forest reserve. It cannot be supposed that at all times the cattle can be giving milk. You will see that the resolution has been cautiously worded, giving room for over-anxious officers to try their best and see that the interests of the Government are protected by increasing the revenue year by year. The cattle that are actually in use in agriculture are only not excluded. But all know what herds of cattle are, and we cannot suppose that all the herds can be used directly for the purpose of agriculture. With reference to the fields most complaints come from the western and eastern parts. In Peninsular India there is a cultivation known as shifting cultivation. As long as it goes on, and there are people who have lived by it for generations, it is necessary that the cultivator should have sufficient land at his disposal to make a living out of this kind of cultivation. I will give you a concrete instance because it is no use laying down general propositions. There are nine villages in my district in which the shifting cultivation area had been so restricted by the reserves that the only course open to the people was to cultivate portions of lands included in the reserves, and thus make themselves amenable to the law. Cases were actually prepared against the residents of all these villages, but fortunately common sense prevailed, and the matter was dropped. At every turn now-a-days the cultivator is harrassed and impeded by forest restrictions of one kind and another. Mr. P. P. Pillai has referred to many and universal grievances in regard to the forest administration, and I can confirm all he says. But besides these almost every place has some special grievance. Take the district of Tirwah and its grievances. It is a district in which more brushwood and foliage is required for agricultural purposes than in any other. There are hill slopes that are well watered, but to utilize these properly for rice and other crops, it is necessary to use quantities of vegetable ashes and refuse. But the privilege of collecting this needful manure, which has been enjoyed for centuries, is now denied to the villagers and complaints have been made to the Government which have not received a satisfactory answer. But the Forest Department with its aggrandizing policy is so powerful that the Government itself is almost powerless against it. I wish to say in conclusion that I have been specially sent here by a meeting, not attended by the cream of the educated natives of India, but by 8,000 people assembled from villages lying within a circle of some 50 miles, every man of whom would have told you, far better than I can do, how destructive of all prosperity and comfort to our ryots is the present system of forest administration. *(Cheers.)*

Mr. S. B. Bhate (*Belgaum, No.* 145, *in list*)—In rising to support this resolution, I must endeavour to remove a possible objection that may, with some show of reason, be raised to the discussion of the question involved in it. It is said, or felt, in certain quarters that this matter is provincial in its character, and that therefore the Congress has no concern with it. I desire to meet this objection. And the first consideration that I wish to urge is that in the present depressed condition of Indian industries, agriculture, upon which 86 per cent of the population depends for its means of sustenance, is inextricably bound up with forest laws and their administration. Various kinds of forest produce are required for agricultural purposes. It is from this standpoint that the question is to be regarded. And, if so, our grievances will be seen to be of universal application all over India. There

3rd Day.

Res. XI. Necessity for mitigating the harshness of the practical administration of the Forest Laws.

is within the district from which I come a large forest area; and, following the example of my leaders, I should like to place before you striking illustrations of the rigor of the administration of Forest Laws if it were necessary to do so. But really Mr. Pillai has gone over the whole ground, and I do not wish to trespass on your time, but I may mention that from 10 to 12 head of cattle can be purchased in my district for a rupee. Indeed, many cultivators of the soil are ready and willing to dispose of their-live stock as a gift. This because there is a fodder famine from which our cattle have been suffering, and were the rigor of the forest administration diminished, were the lands, into which, in such seasons, our cattle used to be driven to graze, once more, if only temporarily, thrown open to our starving herds, this deplorable state of things would be appreciably, yea immensely, ameliorated. (*Cheers*).

Mr. J. R. Nimbkar (*Nasik, No. 202, in list*) then spoke in Mahratti. The following is a translation :—

Gentlemen and Brother Delegates,—I have been permitted by our worthy President to support the 11th proposition, but in doing so I cannot, I feel, either satisfy myself as to the full discharge of my duty or do justice to the subject within the short time allowed to each speaker. You all know the subject in hand is a vast one and has numerous details; still I will try my best to put it before you in as explicit, but concise, a form as I can. Before proceeding, gentlemen, to touch the subject in hand I have to assure you here, that by finding fault with the forest administration of our Government we do not at all admit that our present Forest Law is in any wise agreeable to us. It requires substantial and numerous amendments which, however, do not fall within the scope of the present resolution, to make it compatible with the real interests and welfare of our masses. But we cannot have these greater changes all of a sudden. What we are now asking is that the law, bad, as we think it, may yet be fairly, righteously, and mercifully administered. To revert then, gentlemen, to the subject, I must first show you how injuriously the forest administration affects our poor ryots.

As a recognised principle throughout the civilized world, that country is prosperous whose peasantry is prosperous. The prosperity of the peasantry is the basis of the prosperity and material wealth of the country. It is the masses, or poorer classes, those illiterate, ignorant, suffering cultivators upon whom our daily existence depends. It is they whose better condition alone tends to the happiness of all other classes. It is they for whom the sovereign enjoys his sway. It is they for whom our hearts are most specially moved when we see their helpless condition. The poor who have not even rags to cover their persons, who have not even the means of living from hand to mouth, and who have no cultured mouths to plead their cause or expound their grievances—it is on behalf of these countless thousands of mute sufferers that we first and foremost attack the forest administration.

You all know, gentlemen, that forests, jungles, wilds, constitute one of the necessities of life. From birth to death, and even after it, we require all kinds of things that are derived from the forests and wilds. During our life we want fuel, we want wood, we want grass, stones, earth, leaves, bark, roots, and everything else, which being ours has been made to belong to others, not by Divine agency but by the avaricious desire on the part of men like ourselves. Nature has here in India provided us bountifully with all this without any request on our part, and for hundreds of generations we have enjoyed it unchallenged, but sad to say suddenly we have been deprived of it by man—by the Forest Administration—acting against nature.

If you look back and see what forests were in the times of the Hindu and Mohamedan rulers, you will find they were blessings, but under the present administration they are curses to all living in their neighbourhood. They existed solely for the real good of ryots, as all necessary rights of user were freely enjoyed by those—the inhabitants of the neighbourhood—for whom nature had manifestly designed them. Of recent years forest laws have been introduced, nominally, to protect the country from droughts, absence of rains, and famine, but practically they have been worked otherwise. To declare one policy and to work up to another, to the disadvantage of others, is not an honest act. If you desire a typical instance of that kind of thing it is before you in the present administration of forests.

I am an original inhabitant, rather a *Khot* and a *Dharekari* of a poor hilly village in a poor district, misnamed Ratnagiri. (I do not know who first named it the "Mountain of Jewels'). That district cannot maintain its residents for more than a quarter of a year upon its own produce. It has its peculiar hardships in connection with the Forest Administration, very different from any of yours. We have most of our "warkas," cultivation lands on the hills. We are the owners of them, but curiously and ridiculously enough we cannot take the least advantage of what may be upon them in the way of forest, brush, scrub, though

**3rd Day.**

**Res. XI. Necessity for mitigating the harshness of the practical administration of the Forest Laws.**

they are our own. Formerly sag, (teak), sesum, (black wood), and sandal trees were the only trees for the cutting of which permission was necessary from the immediate authorities.

We freely used the *rab* (fallen leaves, twigs, branches burnt for manure) from those trees, but now-a-days, under the most inconsiderate and harsh rules made by the Bombay Government, a cultivator is prohibited from gathering any fuel or *rab*, not only from the above named forbidden trees, but also from the trees called Ayan and Kinjal. What is the use of those trees then being our property, grown by us? Not only does the administration press this rule with the utmost stringency, but it further enhances our troubles under the new rules—so kindly framed to facilitate our exit from this world—by prohibiting a cultivator from burning *rab* or even cultivating any portions of his ground lying within the circumference of eight feet around any one of these his own trees. The "warkas" land in that district requires a fallow of at least four years, but owing to the operation of these rules there remains in some villages only half, and in some only one-third, of the cultivable lands, practically and legally, available for even this quadrennial agriculture. Thus, owing to this circumscribing scientific circumference rule, a large area of cultivable lands has to be left permanently uncultivated, and this is one of the ways in which the Forest Administration works as harshly and as mercilessly as a thirteenth month in a famine year.

Now with regard to cattle grazing: pasture lands have been almost swallowed up by the inordinate spread of reserved jungles. Where are the cattle to graze? The very means of husbandry, the cattle, have day by day diminished, owing to want of grass and hay. A few grazing grounds, out of so many ancient ones, have been kept, but to no purpose, as most of them can produce no grass and do not, and never can, suffice for the number of cattle in the neighbourhood. As we are not able to maintain sufficient cattle even for agricultural purposes, how can we expect to have them for milk and its products? Our people are, therefore, reduced to skeletons, being vegetarians as they are. In spite of the so-called spread of education our villagers, having no doctors, have to be their own physicians, but whence to bring the needful simples, the roots and leaves of plants or trees, as all these are now inside Government reserves? If to save his life from disease a man brings a chitak's weight of any thing medicinal out of the forest, he is fined under the forest produce definition section which, gentlemen, you must have specially studied, if only for the sake of curiosity.

Now with respect to the mortality of ryots from the spread of forests; instances are numerous in several districts, such as Sholapur and others, where the, to European sportsmen, greatly beloved tigers and boars, reigning predominantly over man, have killed or wounded, and are still killing and wounding, numbers of poor human beings. The Arms Act has combined its full force to complete the human sacrifice with the Forest Administration! Is it worthy of our civilized British Government to allow such human sacrifices, in the 19th century, offered by the Arms Act priest and accepted by the Forest Deity on the altar of their reputed wisdom of ages? Let us now see the subject in hand from a sanitary point of view. The vicinity of a jungle to an inhabited portion of a village always tends considerably towards the increase of various sorts of diseases, and I am ready to prove this, not only under the "Vagbhut" and "Sooshroot" works, but also from the canons of modern medical science.

What is a still worse feature of the Forest Administration remains to be mentioned. Paper demarcation of forests is naturally unknown to cattle which are not, and cannot be, trained at schools and colleges. (*Laughter*). Cattle trespassing into forests are carried to pounds for no fault of theirs or their owners, but from that of the forest preservers, who never fence them as they want to turn their own faults to their own advantage. They are then released on payment of fines. The owners are prosecuted for the cattle trespass and fined as a separate source of income in addition to civil damages which are also recovered without mercy. The pound fee and fine rates have been increased. In one of the talookas of the Nasik District the aggregate amount of fines in 18 such prosecutions was 450 rupees during four months, civil damages and pound fees excluded.

I cannot enter, gentlemen, into any more details, as I think what is said is sufficient for the present purpose. Let me repeat once more with all my power that neither the Forest Law nor its administration are carried out in the interests of the people. The whole thing is treated as a source of revenue, a golden spring for Government. What else can there be under the sun more abominable, more horrible, more cruel, than the sham philanthrophy of the mismanaged administration of forests. (*Loud cheers*).

Mr. V. N. Apte (*Poona, No.* 161, *in list.*)—Amongst the several grievances which this Indian National Congress has made its duty to bring before our rulers for redress those connected with the Forest Laws administration must take a foremost place. These laws may

**Res. XI. Necessity for mitigating the harshness of the practical administration of the Forest Laws.**

have been framed with a benevolent intention, as all laws and regulations presumably are; but the way in which they are enforced on the poor ryot is simply cruel. It must be a strange irony of fate that our rulers should have, I will not say deliberately, but perhaps unwittingly, so enacted laws and regulations that many of the necessaries of life—things which are essential to keep life and soul together—are denied to us, or rather made too dear to be attainable by the poor, such as salt, firewood and corn, while other articles which are detrimental to health, nay, to the very life of the ryot, ruinous to him, body and soul, are, so to say, forced down his throat, for instance, liquor and opium.

Firewood is as great a necessity as food itself. What would you do without it even if you had plenty of corn? Man is said to be a cooking animal. That is one of the characteristics of man distinguishing him from the lower animals. He must cook his food before he can eat it. Then again, he must have firewood to protect himself from the rigour of cold to warm himself with. Again, he has cattle (his sole wealth to feed, and so he must have grass and fodder for them. Then come also his implements and his hut, which require from time to time to be repaired or renewed. Where is the wood to come from for these purposes except from the forest about his village? He has not always the money to buy these materials with, and so he goes into the forest, as his forefathers have done for generations, and hews down a suitable tree. But then he is prosecuted and punished. Is this justice, I ask? Gentlemen, the Forest Laws and Regulations are so stringent and so harshly administered that these necessaries of life are made almost unattainable both to the ryot and his cattle. People living in large towns and cities can have no adequate idea of the hardships to which in the districts the ryot is subjected by these forest rules. The cow movement, which is assuming such proportions, has its origin partly in the stringency of the Forest Laws. The numerous witnesses, who were examined by the late Bombay Forest Commission, gave, as you are already aware, painful details of the effects of these laws.

I need not, therefore, enter into them here especially after the speeches of some of my predecessors. I will therefore only once more make an appeal to our rulers. This appeal is on behalf of the voiceless ryot. It is an appeal on behalf of the masses and not the classes. The demand for the elective principle of representation may be said to come from the educated and enlightened "microscopic minority," but certainly this appeal, which concerns the conditions of life, both of man and animal, comes from the ryot. It must therefore be heard and prompt relief given. (*Cheers*).

MR. K. B. MULLICK (*Serampur, No. 34, in list*)—MR. PRESIDENT, SISTER AND BROTHER DELEGATES,—In asking permission to say a word or two on the resolution before the Congress, I may mention that my brother delegates from Bengal said to me: "What business have you coming from Bengal to take any part in the discussions in regard to Forest Act? Where you are there is no serious trouble about this matter?" I reply that we are proclaiming to the world that we have given up sectional distinctions and have become a united people. Millions are suffering under the Forest Laws, and though I personally am not so suffering, I equally desire their improvement. I wish, however, to propose an amendment. I have very little hope that it will even be seconded; but a sense of duty prompts me to say a word or two in regard to this Act. I wish to substitute for the words in the resolution: "By the practical administration of the Forest Laws," the words, "by the operation of section 41 of the Forest Act." The reason why I want to substitute these words is simply this: I have no knowledge of the operation of the Forest Laws in Bengal, to which I belong, as I have lived in Rajputana for the last twelve years. But I know that in and about Ajmere there is a large class of poor people who earn their livelihood simply by cutting small trees in rocky wastes and bringing them to the market. They have no other means of livelihood, and from generation to generation they have thus subsisted. These poor people, especially many women, who have to support themselves and their children, depend simply on these waste land products derived from lands situated near the frontier of a British possession called Ajmere, a small place in Rajputana, surrounded by a number of Native States. These poor helpless folk have to pay blackmail to the British Forest Department for every twig of fuel they bring in to the market, though this feeble trade is the only means of their subsistence. If it is not the law itself which is in fault I do not know what is. If it is not the oppressive operation of section 41. I do not what it is. The section is an amended section. It makes it criminal for any one to cut down forest trees, not only from these wastes, the ownership of which by the British Government is disputed, but from their own land. Before they can cut the smallest branch of a tree they have to get permission from the Government officials. If they do not, they come under the operation of the law, and are taken before the nearest Magistrate and punished. If this is not the oppresive operation of the Forest Law of India, I do not know how to characterise it. My only object in coming here is to try and save these poor people from the oppressive action of this section.

THE PRESIDENT.—I fear that you have hardly understood the bearing of your so-called amendment. The adoption of this will make that alone to be the grievance. This resolution

**3rd Day.**

**Res. XI. Necessity for mitigating the harshness of the practical administration of the Forest Laws.**

speaks of the practical administration of the Forest Laws, and it therefore covers a much larger area. Is it your object to restrict our protest to complaint against the operation of this particular section and this only?

MR. MULLICK.—No, certainly not.

THE PRESIDENT.—If not, your complaint against the operation of this particular section is already covered by our more general proposition, and ceases to be an amendment. I thought I made that clear when I wrote to you on receipt of your notice of intention to move this amendment.

MR. MULLICK.—Well, if the words "practical administration of the Forest Laws" means or includes the operation of Section 41, my amendment falls to the ground But does it? Is this quite certain?

THE PRESIDENT.—Yes.

MR. MULLICK.—Then I withdraw the amendment.

MR. VIRA RAGHAVA CHARYA (*Madras, No.* 763, *in list*)—GENTLEMEN AND FELLOW DELEGATES,—If I stood here as an advocate on behalf of the people of this country in a technical sense, and if you constituted yourselves a public tribunal, I would charge the Government of India in regard to the administration of the Forest Laws under the following two heads: First, I say that I would charge them with breach of faith or contract; and, secondly, I would charge them with misappropriation. I charge them with breach of faith, because when this Act was introduced in 1877, the Government distinctly assured us that it was introduced not with a view of raising revenue, but in the interests of the people at large. A Commission was sent to some of the European countries, and the experts reported that the periodical famines which ravage this country could probably be minimised by the growth of protected forests. A resolution was consequently passed, and we were distinctly told that the Government would not endeavour to increase its revenue from these forest lands. Now, so far as this Madras Presidency is concerned, in the year 1877 the revenue was 4½. In 1878 it was 6¼ lakhs. In 1879 6½ lakhs. In 1883 it grew to 8 lakhs. In 1884 it was 9 lakhs. In 1887 it went up to 12 lakhs. In 1888 and 1889 it had grown to 13 lakhs. That is only in the Presidency of Madras. Although they assured us that the Act was introduced not to increase the revenue, they have been systematically encroaching upon lands belonging to the public. Then, as to the charge of misappropriation in our own presidency. There are two or three charters of land prevailing. In Chundu and Tungari and other districts, the ownership of the land is with the people, not with the Government. The Government, in violation of the several regulations passed in the times of the East India Company, have been gradually extending their rights over these lands belonging to the people, and reserving large tracts in them to the detriment of the cattle and the general health of the people. Not only are people suffering, but the cattle are also dying in large numbers. The death rate in times of famine has greatly increased. Last year in two or three districts there was an increase of 81,000 deaths among cattle owing to the rigour of the Forest Laws, and in some districts the Collectors themselves have reported that there ought to be some relaxation in the working of these laws. By the Government's short-sighted and immoral policy, as regards forest questions, they are not only making the people still poorer and more helpless, and more liable to succumb in any scarcity, but they are also causing the destruction of cattle in large numbers—cattle which, here in India, as you all know, are the primary requisite of all agriculture. Spade culture in our poor soils is practically impossible; a man *cannot* dig a sufficient area to earn a subsistence. Ploughing is essential, but this without cattle is impossible, and the Government, or its limb, the Forest Department, is gradually but certainly destroying the cattle. It is here, as in the case of the army, as in the case of excise, the Government enter on a course and orginate a policy upon the highest noblest and most unassailable principles, but having got in the end of the wedge, they throw aside all these principles, and thereafter work the scheme for their own profit. They created an army to defend their own territories, they have expanded it so as to enable them to seize the territories of others. They originated the excise to check insobriety and then gradually expanded it so as to spread drunkenness broad cast and increase their own revenue. So they started the Forest Administration to benefit the country and conserve the rights of posterity, and now they work it only to pile up revenue, careless that they are ruining the peasantry and perilling the existence of *any* posterity. Against this misconception by Government of their duty to us, to England and to God, this resolution is a premonetary protest; it will be stronger a good deal next year, and I ask you to carry it unanimously. (*Loud cheers.*)

**3rd Day.**

**Res. XI. Necessity for mitigating the harshness of the practical administration of the Forest Laws.**

THE PRESIDENT.—Shall I now put this question? (*Yes, yes, vote, vote*). Well then our 11th Resolution stands as follows :—

RESOLVED—*That having regard to the very serious discontent created, especially in Peninsular India, by the practical administration of the Forest Laws, the Government of India be most respectfully, but earnestly, entreated to investigate this carefully and endeavour to mitigate its harshness and render it less obnoxious to the poorer classes.*

The Resolution was then put and carried unanimously.

**Res. XII. Thanking British Committee and urging them to extend the scope of their labours.**

MR. K. G. NATU (*Poona, No.* 183, *in list*)—MR. PRESIDENT, BROTHER DELEGATES, LADIES AND GENTLEMEN,—If ever the saying that "art is long and life is short" is anywhere realized, it is realised in this Congress Hall, when the man who stands here to give utterance to his thoughts is allowed five minutes, and no more. But fortunately for myself I am entrusted with a proposition which does not require much argument. It requires only a heart; and is there a soul that lives that is not moved with gratitude to those who are working in England for the protection of India? I need not repeat their names. There is one among us now, Mr. Hume (*prolonged cheers*), whose name will be remembered not only by ourselves but by posterity as one who has brought about the resurrection of the whole country. (*Loud cheers*). Yesterday it was said that what India wants is to pass from death unto life, and that is what is aimed at by those who are so generously working for us. I beg, now to move the following Resolution :—

*That this Congress hereby tenders its most grateful acknowledgments to Sir W. Wedderburn, and the members of the British Congress Committee, for the services rendered by them to India during the past year, and respectfully urges them to widen henceforth the sphere of their usefulness, by interesting them selves not only in those questions dealt with by the Congress here, but in all Indian matters submitted to them, and properly vouched for, in which any principle accepted by the Congress is involved.*

When I look on you, representing as you do every province, every class, every creed, the whole of India is mirrored in the view, and I ask, is India so poor that it has no feelings of gratitude towards those who are working for it? What are the services that they are rendering? They are reiterating your utterances. There are oceans and mountains between us; and your cry perhaps is not heard so far away; but they are standing at the heart of the Empire, repeating your prayers, pressing for a consideration of your grievances and insisting on justice for you, While, on the one hand, they are pleading with Great Britain to do something for India on the other hand they are turning towards us and breathing hope into our hearts, by their support and sympathy. There is the true heart in them bent on doing good to our country. They are not paid servan.ts. Their work is a labour of love. It is not their own advancement but our welfare that they seek. How oh, how can we sufficiently thank them? And yet, such is human nature, while we thank them for all that they are doing and have done, we now ask them to do more. (*Cheers*). We want them henceforth not to restrict their exertions to those special great fundamental questions, which have been discussed and adjudicated on by this Congress, but to interest themselves generally in all Indian matters involving any principle accepted by the Congress, properly vouched representatations in regard to which may be submitted to them from this country. Matters, in the first place, often occur between Congresses, which need immediate action, like that Bombay judicial appointment which is fresh in all your minds, and again, monthly. cases are cropping up, involving no doubt violations of principles that the Congress has insisted on, yet hardly of such national importance as to warrant their discussion in this national assembly, with the very brief space of time it has at its disposal, and yet, for all that, cases involving cruel wrongs and gross injustice, in regard to which immediate public protest in England and in the House of Commons is essential, and we desire that our British Committee should be in a position to deal with all such matters. At present they have only the mandate from us to deal with and press Congress questions. We, as representing the nation, now desire to empower them to deal with all Indian questions on India's behalf, involving violations in letter or in spirit of those great principles, which we have, in our various sessions, affirmed on behalf of our countrymen and constituents; and we are not desirous of restricting the right to seek their intervention to the openly acknowledged members of the Congress party, to the Standing Congress Committees, as was at one time contemplated. No, national as is our movement, and dear as it is to every Indian's heart whether he so acknowledge it or, for fear of the powers that be, conceal his true feelings, we desire that this channel for the redress of grievances should be open to all India, not merely to Standing Congress Committees but to all associations, sabhas and other public bodies that have been, or may be, formed amongst our countrymen.

3rd Day.

Res. XII. Thanking British Committee and urging them to extend the scope of their labours.

Of course we must have definite rules, under which such references will have to be made. We must make sure that all such complaints are, as the resolution says, properly vouched for.

Again, of course, there are multitudes of private grievances, not only not national, but not even public in their nature, which, if put forward in England at all, must be pushed through private agents and not through a public body like our British Committee. Our rules must provide for this and must leave the fullest discretion in all cases to our Committee to move or not to move in any matter. But these are mere details ; it is the principle of this new and important departure that this resolution affirms. and it is one I venture to say that you will all concur in. (*Here the gong sounded*). My time is spent and yet I have only said half of what I wished to say. Never mind, perhaps, I may be allowed to say the other half at the next Congress. (*Laughter and cheers*).

Mr. Girisha Chandra Sett (*Calcutta, No.* 8, *in list*)—Fellow Delegates,—It is with great pleasure that I find myself privileged to second the resolution. I am sure there is no one here who is likely to forget the name of Sir William Wedderburn. If this country can be grateful to any body, it is to that eminent gentleman who has labored so long, not only in India but also in England, for the good of this land, and who is also continuing his labour in its behalf. We are also grateful to all the members of the British Congress Committee who from year to year have been anxiously endeavouring to do their best to ameliorate the condition of this country. Mr. Nathu has so fully and ably expounded the true purport of this measure that I need now only add that I trust you will all carry the resolution by acclamation.

The President.—I shall now formally put to you the 12th Resolution, which runs thus :—

Resolved—*That this Congress hereby tenders its most grateful acknowledgments to Sir W. Wedderburn, and the members of the British Congress Committee, for the services rendered by them to India during the past year, and respectfully urges them to widen henceforth the sphere of their usefulness, by interesting themselves, not only in those questions dealt with by the Congress here, but in all Indian matters submitted to them, and properly vouched for, in which any principle accepted by the Congress is involved.*

The Resolution was then carried by acclamation.

Res. XIII. Universal gratitude for the signal services rendered to India by the late Mr. C. Bradlaugh and grief at his untimely death.

Mr. Pherozshah Mehta (*Bombay, No.* 256, *in list*)—Mr. President and Delegates all,—It is with the most unfeigned reluctance that I have been persuaded—I ought almost to say over persuaded—to undertake the painful task of placing before you the next resolution. For it is a task which I cannot approach without being overcome with the deepest and most sincere emotion. To me human speech has always seemed helpless and impotent in the presence of death, and as I rise to speak of it, the death of Charles Bradlaugh seems to rush upon the mind as fresh in all its terrible and mournful reality, as if it were only yesterday. India had never more reason to lament what the poet has described, with all the force of the old Hellenic conviction, as "the mystery of the cruelty of things," than when it was suddenly and despite the prayers of millions, deprived of the valiant knight who had sworn to do battle for her ; her chosen and trusted champion, her true and tender friend, her wise and sober counsellor, her accredited representative in the great and august counsel of the Empire. It is only two short years ago—nay, not so much, not two—that, plucked from the very jaws of death, snatched, as he himself said, from the blackness of the grave, we greeted him, in the name and at the call of all India, with the simple enthusiasm which his unselfish and untiring devotion to India's cause had already created f om one end of the country to the other. I well remember how our hearts were unutterably stirred within us, at finding him in our midst, restored, as we then fondly, but alas, vainly, hoped, to health and a long career of noble usefulness. I shall never forget, (and who that was present could forget ?) the memorable speech which, his gentle heart moving him almost to tears, he addressed to the vast concourse of people that had assembled to welcome and greet him, and in which he pledged himself, modestly and unostentatiously, but earnestly and feelingly, "to do his best, so far as one man may, for the greater happiness of India's people, the greater peace for Britain's rule, and the greater comfort of the whole of Britain's subjects." Only one short year was given him to redeem his promise. But even in that short year how nobly, how indefatigably, how devotedly he applied himself to the task he had undertaken, with all that large human sympathy which always seemed to me to pervade and direct his fearless, powerful and uncompromising vindication and championship of right and truth and justice. Even during the few months that have elapsed since his death, how often have we missed, on great occasions and small, the ring of his sagacious and powerful advocacy, and how often have we had reason to exclaim.—

> "Oh, for the touch of a vanished hand,
> And the sound of a voice that is still!"

**3rd Day.**

**Res. XIII. Universal gratitude for the signal services rendered to India by the late Mr. C. Bradlaugh and grief at his untimely death.**

Death's heavy hand has indeed fallen heavily upon us in the loss of Charles Bradlaugh. England has lost in him one of her best sons like unto those knight errants of old "who went about redressing human wrong," one of those large-hearted and large-minded Englishmen whose love and sympathy, reared and nurtured in a lofty conception of moral and political duty, does more than is imagined to transform the feeling of gratitude for the material blessings of British rule, inestimable as they are, into a sentiment of earnest, devoted and enlightened loyalty. His name has become a household word in the remotest parts of the country. It is a more eloquent and surer tribute to his worth than monuments of brass and marble. These may be raised to deserving as well as undeserving people. We have a statue in Bombay to Lord Reay, we have another to Sir Richard Temple. But the heart cannot belie itself. Let us then reverently enshrine his memory in our hearts as we have already enshrined those of John Bright and Henry Faucett! (*Cheers*). I beg to propose the following resolution: —

*That this Congress puts on record an expression of the gratitude felt throughout India for the signal services rendered by the late Mr. Charles Bradlaugh to that country's cause, and of the deep and universal sorrow which his untimely death has engendered, and that a copy of this Resolution, signed by the President, be transmitted through the British Committee for presentation to Mrs. Bradlaugh Bonner."*

MR. K. P. KAVYABISHARAD (*Allahabad, No. 89, in list*)—FELLOW DELEGATES,—Fully conscious as I am of my utter unworthiness to stand before this august assembly, I am really grateful to the learned President for permitting me to second this resolution. Although suffering from the disadvantage of coming after that distinguished orator and patriot, Mr. Pherozshah Mehta, I dare to stand up because I yield to none, not even to Mr. Mehta himself, in keenness of appreciation of our late champion's services or of grief at his untimely loss, though I have not his power to give expression in words to what my heart feels. What shall I say of Charles Bradlaugh, a man "the latchet of whose shoes I am not worthy to unlose." Before even he had begun to take an active interest in Indian affairs, I had learned to admire, nay, almost to worship him. An unworthy and insignificant disciple of his, words cannot describe the joy I experienced when he stepped forward to fight my country's battle, or the pain I felt at his irreparable loss. I had, however, the consolation of knowing that my grief was shared by all my countrymen from the Himalayas to Cape Comorin; from the Indus to the Brahmapootra. We all of us know that Charles Bradlaugh was no mealy-mouthed philanthropist. He used no empty words. He was a practical man in every sense of the word. He was slow to promise, but sure to perform. "Thorough" was his motto. What he undertook to do he meant to do thoroughly. He could never be disturbed by the bureaucratic owls hooting their hoots, and misrepresenting this national assembly in every way. But it is not for me to dilate on the merits of Mr. Bradlaugh. You know them full well, and they have been referred to by the honorable gentleman who preceded me with a fulness and pathos to which I can never attain. But as an illustration of Mr. Bradlaugh's universal sympathy for us, permit me to quote from memory a few words of the late lamented member for India—words that have been ringing in my ears from the memorable day of his Bombay speech. Said he: "Born of the people, trusted by the people, for whom shall I work if not for the people? I know no geographical or race limitations." Such was the man to whom we owe a debt of immense and endless gratitude. (*Cheers.*)

MUNSHI SADRUDDIN AHMED (*Allahabad, No. 81, in list*) then spoke in Urdu—

> *"Oh! God thou has't turned my smiles into tears, and added anguish to my sorrow,*
> *Thou hast made the song of my heart mournful as the Nightingale's and hast watered the flowers of my garden with fire."*
>
> (*Verse.*)

The objects of the Indian National Congress are so very straightforward, simple and reasonable, that no one ever thought of antagonism from any one—nay it was hoped that all the Mussalmans as a body (in accordance with the saying that Hindus and Mahomedans have been together for 800 years like the chest piece and the skirt of the same coat) would be of the same mind; and no opposition was feared or expected from the Anglo-Indians, and specially from those of them whose flesh and skins had been nourished with Indian salt; and

3rd Day.

Res. XIII. Universal gratitude for the signal services rendered to India by the late Mr. C. Bradlaugh and grief at his untimely death.

from those officers who, by virtue of India's good name, obtained positions ranging from an Assistantship to Lieutenant-Governmentship ; but—

"*I was wrong in what I thought.*"
(*Verse.*)

Shortly after (the Congress had made some progress) the fire of antagonism was kindled. Those Europeans upon whom we relied as friends turned into enemies. Aligarh and Benares also aimed side blows treacherously. The poor Congresswallas began to grow disappointed so far as Indian Officers were concerned, and they contemplated securing a powerful help and patren in England. The country was in this condition when English papers began to reveal that Mr.Charles Bradlaugh had cast the skirt of mercy upon us helpless Indians, in other words, that the sun of Bradlaugh's sympathy having risen from the West had lighted the East. This news, however, was not believed universally in India and was considered to be the Congresswalla's gossip till at last Mr. Bradlaugh came to the Bombay Congress. His bright face, reverend locks, benign manners, majesty of speech, public sympathy, constancy of mind, vivified the soul of the nation, and all were convinced that that helmsman would steer our ship to the shore of desire. Our countrymen, thus consoled and rejoiced, were taking part in the proceedings of the Calcutta Congress when the ill news of his illness made all anxious, and soon after our return from Calcutta we suddenly heard the sad occurrence of his death.

"*O friends, I pray shed tears of blood for Bradlaugh, for the sake of God. He who in Bombay joined brother-like with all has alas! suddenly left our company. I have learnt the cause of his death, viz., that ever in anxiety for India's freedom that great man has fought to death.*"
(*Verse.*)

It was our desire to make that revered man our leader before the Imperial Throne when our caravan should reach London. But alas he whom we were to place before the Imperial Throne has sunk into the pit of the grave. It was our aspiration to make this patron of the country the consort of the bride, the embodied aspirations of the Congress, to make ready all the requisites of procession and pleasure, so much so as to make, with our thanks and love as it were, garments of brocade for the bridegroom. But alas we had to read the following verse instead.

"*We have seen many a body besmeared with dust; if the friend changed dress we saw a coffin.*"
(*Verse.*)

I will recite now some verses of condolence. The last hemistich gives the date of the deceased's death (*by adding up the numerical values of its letters*).

"*When he who loved our country fell ill my prescription of sorrow was huge. Why may not the inhabitants of Earth cause torrents of blood tears to flow when that high-minded man took abode in heaven?*

*For the cause of justice he acted many parts, some time he was a pleader and some time a physician.*

*The guardian is gone, the patron is gone, the adviser is gone; if you think rightly the Congress is now an orphan. The world of souls is filled with lamentation. Angels weep and Moses himself is grieved. Bradlaugh has not died, but the day of resurrection has come. Alas, a thousand times a heavy calamity has befallen us.*
(*Verse.*)

I support the resolution, a copy of which will be sent to his daughter to prove our sorrow for her father's death as some consolation to her.

Moulvi Abdula Aziz Saheb (*Nagpur, No. 428, in list*) then spoke in Urdu as follows:—

Mr. President, Fellow Delegates, Ladies and Gentlemen,—It is absolutely binding upon us all to be grateful to all those who show us kindness, who try to get our grievances removed, and who do not let an opportunity escape without doing us good. The late lamented Mr. Bradlaugh, who was neither a follower of any of the Indian religions nor an inhabitant of India, was kind enough to shew sympathy to us, took up our cause and promised, though unostentatiously yet most sincerely, to educate British public opinion upon Indian matters to such an extent that our grievances should become dreams of the past, and thereby the union between England and India eternally cemented. We are, therefore, bound to place on record our feelings of deep gratitude towards him. We cannot refrain at the same time from expressing our great sorrow for his untimely severance from us. His untimely death has been an irreparable loss to us, to the whole of India, and every true son of India is conscious of this. Had he been spared to us, Lord Cross's Bill for amending the

Legislative Councils in India would have been never withdrawn, but amended upon the lines laid down by the Indian National Congress and passed into law. I do, therefore, most earnestly beseech you, ladies and gentlemen, never to forget his services, and to hold for-ever engraven in your hearts the sacred memory of him who laboured so much and so unselfishly for us and for India.

**Res. XIII. Universal gratitude for the signal services rendered to India by the late Mr. C. Bradlaugh and grief at his untimely death.**

THE PRESIDENT.—I will now formally put to you our 13th Resolution, and it is only meet and fitting that you should, if you accept it, as accept it you will, pass it in solemn silence, all standing in reverence to the memory of our great champion.

"RESOLVED—*That this Congress puts on record an expression of the gratitude felt throughout India for the signal services rendered by the late Mr. Charles Bradlaugh to that country's cause, and of the deep and universal sorrow which his untimely death has engendered, and that a copy of this Resolution, signed by the President, be transmitted through the British Committee for presentation to Mrs. Bradlaugh Bonner.*"

The Resolution was then put and assented to silently by all, the entire assembly (visitors as well as delegates) standing in solemn silence during the whole time that the Resolution was being read and put, and until the President declared the Resolution to have been unanimously carried.

**Res. XIV. Mr. Dadabhai Naorojee.**

MR. W. C. BONNERJEE (*Calcutta, No. 1, in list*)—(*who was received with loud cheers*) said.—MR. PRESIDENT AND GENTLEMEN,—I am extremely grateful to you for the kindness with which you have received me. I understand the feeling that prompted your kindness, and I assure you I appreciate it heartily. The resolution which I have to propose for your consideration is one which does not require any advocacy on my part to induce you to accept it. It is this :—

*That this Congress hereby puts formally on record its high estimate and deep appreciation of the great services which Mr. Dadabhai Naorojee has rendered, during more than a quarter of a century, to the cause of India, that it expresses its unshaken confidence in him and its earnest hope that he my prove successful, at the coming elections, in his candidature for Central Finsbury, and at the same time tenders, on behalf of the vast population it represents, India's most cordial acknowledgments to all in England, whether in Central Finsbury or elsewhere, who have aided or may aid him to win a seat in the House of Commons.*"

Is there any one amongst you who has not heard the name of Dadabhai Naorojee or, having heard it, does not revere it, does not love it, does not carry it about with him as a household word? From the time when he was an young man to the present day when he is over three score years old, he has devoted himself, his fortune, his talents, his life one may say, to the cause of his country. There is no publicist among us who knows the economical condition of India so well as Mr. Dababhai Naorojee. He has fought, and in my opinion fought successfully, many a tough battle with the adversaries of India. Chief amongst them was that very superior person Sir Mountstuart Elphinstone Grant Duff, who, when he was in India, only corresponded with such high personages as Prince Bismark and the Empress Frederick. (*Laughter*). Now Mr. Dadabhai Naorojee, not for any personal advantage to himself, but only for the sake of his country, has been trying for some years to get into the House of Commons, so that there, in the midst of the representatives of Great Britain herself, he may plead the cause of his native country. You know how difficult it is even for Englishmen to get into the House of Commons. He has failed once, but the spirit which led him to devote his life to his country is still in him and stirring him on to do the best he can to get a seat in the House of Commons. All that I ask you to do by this resolution is to say that you have your old confidence in the old man, and that you will be sincerely grateful to any constituency in Great Britain that will do itself the inestimable honor of sending Mr. Dadabhai Naorojee to the House of Commons. (*Cheers*)

THE HONORABLE MR. SANKARA NAIR (*Madras, No. 807, in list*).—It is only as a matter of form that I rise to second this proposition. Mr. Dadabhai Naorojee took up the question of national reform long before any one of us turned his attention to the subject ; and how well, how ably, and how persistently he has fought for us, has been so well insisted on by Mr. W. C. Bonnerjee, that it is needless for me to add anything to what he has already said. It is only just and proper that to him, and to those in India and in England who have been aiding him, and are still aiding him, whether in Central Finsbury or elsewhere, we should tender our most cordial acknowledgments. With these remarks I leave the resolution in your hands, confident of its unanimous acceptance. (*Cheers*).

THE PRESIDENT.—I now put our 14th Resolution which I really need not read again.

The Resolution was then put and carried by acclamation.

**3rd Day**

**Res. XV. Postponement of the English Session until after the British General election.**

Mr. C. N. Nayadu (Chairman of the Reception Committee) (*Nagpore, No. 432, in list*).—Mr. President, Sister and Brother Delegates,—The proposition that I have to bring before you runs thus :—

*That in view of the General Election, now impending in England, and in accordance with the recommendation of our British Committee, the provisional arrangements set on foot, in pursuance of the Resolution passed at the Calcutta Congress of 1890 for holding, all things being convenient, a Congress of not less than 100 Delegates in England in 1892, be now suspended until after such General Election."*

Gentlemen, this is one of the most important, if not the most important resolution, that has been brought before the Congress. You know that our existence as a Congress is largely based upon the efforts that we may make in England for the recognition of our proceedings. It is a matter of vital importance that we should go to England and try and move the people there and our Mother Empress, and impress upon them the necessity of granting us the reforms that we are praying for. You know well that unless we go there, and knock at the door of the head quarters of the Empire, nothing really satisfactory will come of our movement. We have to move the British nation, and through the nation the British Parliament, through the British Parliament the Secretary of State, and through the Secretary of State and Her Majesty's Ministry our Government in India to grant us the reforms that we advocate, and unless we do so I do not see how we can hope to succeed within any reasonable time.

The system on which the British Government is now administered is this : The Government here complies with the orders of the Secretary of State, the Secretary of State is guided by the sense of the majority of the House of Commons, when this finds an expression ; and the House, as it were, only speaks out when the constituencies press it. So we must go to the fountain head if we wish to get our grievances redressed. Unless we send a strong representative body of Indians to England, I fear we shall not be able to move the constituencies or obtain any reasonable instalment of that which we are longing for. I do not wish to make a long speech on this subject, because the argument was fully gone into at the last Congress by able speakers. The necessity is felt by all of us, and I am sure you will all agree with me and adopt the resolution without any hesitation. (*Cheers*). But there are two things that I have to bring to your notice : First, we asked the several Standing Congress Committees on the last occasion to give us lists of the delegates they desired to be sent to England to represent us there. These lists we do not consider it necessary now to make public—for as the general elections are expected to take place in 1892, and we have been asked by the British Committee to suspend our going to England till after the election is over, many things may occur between now and then to modify these lists. When the elections are over then we shall expect to receive new lists up to date. (*Cheers*). Secondly, you are aware that the British Committee have most generously invited our delegates to England, when we do send our chosen 100, to be their guests for one month. (*Loud cheers*). I am sure that you all appreciate the generosity and kindness of this noble offer of hospitality, and that you all join with me in heart-felt thanks (*Hear, hear*) to these brave English gentlemen, on whom we have only that claim that sufferers from injustice ever have on British hearts, and who are, yet, ready to labour for us as they do, and to receive us as their guests as they promise—and will. (*Long and continued cheering*).

Babu Bhupendra Nath Basu (*Calcutta, No. 6, in list*).—Mr. President, Brother and Sister Delegates,—It is not desirable at this stage of the proceedings to dwell at length on the resolution now before you : nor is it necessary. Fears were entertained by the gentlemen who suggested it at the last Congress that Conservative India, so largely represented in the Congress, might hesitate to accept it. All fears were dispelled, all misgivings swept away, when the resolution was put to the vote and carried with acclamations by all sections of the Congress. Delegates from all parts of India, delegates representing widely divergent views on matters of social usage, delegates of all creeds and castes, Hindus and Mussalmans, Brahmins and Sudras, all stepped on to the platform at the mandate of the Chairman to support the resolution. And you, brother delegates from Bengal, will certainly remember that one of us, always modest and retiring, always reticent and unpretentious, but always a warm supporter of the Congress movement, himself the worthy representative of one of the most ancient and orthodox families of Calcutta, for once in his life, shaking off his habitual reserve, came forward to speak in favour of the resolution. I allude to Maharaj Kumar Neel Krishna (*loud cheers*) who, alas ! for us, is now no more to help and to cheer us. Well, gentlemen, the question has been asked with pertinacious insistance, the cry has been raised, and swelled into volume, by the arts of the enemy. What have been the achievements of the Congress ? What have been the results of these annual gatherings ? Mine is not the creed of easy success. No triumph is worth the achievement unless reached through sacrifice and labour It has taken Ireland, with representatives in the House of Commons, backed by the unselfish patriotism and devotion to duty of thousands of her sons, backed by sacrifices almost superhuman, backed by the indomitable energy and untiring patience of the Irish race, backed by the moral support of civilized Europe and backed by the great liberal party in England, it has taken Ireland nearly a century to bring her programme to the threshold of victory. And we poor Indians, held for ages in foreign yoke, diversified by creeds and castes, distracted by mutual jealousies and internal dissensions, fanned into flame by the breeze of official favour, sleeping for centuries the sleep of petrified Ahalya, and just awakening into life at the magic touch of one, whose memory, we and our sons after us, will cherish with the love and reverence, with which we Hindus have been accustomed to regard the great Rama, of the family of Raghu,—what could we expect to do in the brief space of seven years ? It is a wonder that we have been able to achieve the little that may safely be placed to our credit, something of which was recalled yesterday to our minds by our friend Surendra Nath Bannerjee, but does any man in this great hall, even the most sanguine amongst us, believe for a moment that we shall succeed in winning our battle on the soil of India ? Our officials, " lulled by the langour of the land of the lotus, " are not easy to move. Bureaucratic India has turned a deaf ear to our cry. Come then, friends, gird up your loins, and fight your battle on the soil, where no slave can breathe. Our real masters are the people of England, and to them we must appeal.

We, in Bengal, have made up our minds, and found our men. Reverend Pundits learned in the Shastras have pronounced that there is no harm in a sea-voyage. Long before the question of sea-voyages had become the burning question of the day, the only passage in the Shastras, which the opponents of reform cited in support of their narrow-minded views, was interpreted for other purposes by the late Pundit Taranath Tarka Bachaspati, justly considered in his time the first grammarian of India, and he said that not sea-voyages, but the expiation of sins by drowning oneself in the sea was what was interdicted in the Kaliyuga. Through a wrong interpretation of one single passage in the Shastras, we Hindus had been burning our widows for centuries, and through the wrong interpretation of another passage, we have shut the door on our progress. Well, gentlemen, the question of sea-voyages, so far as Bengal is concerned, has, thanks to the energetic efforts of Maharaj Kumar Benoy Krishna, been practically settled, and orthodox Hindus, hoary with age, and of indisputable authority, have pronounced themselves in their favour. I have no doubt that the other provinces of India will readily find men to espouse our cause in England. The Central Provinces have pronounced their verdict. My friend, Mr. Mudholkar, continues to be the same respected member of Hindu society as he was before he went to England at the mandate of the Congress and in obedience to the call of duty.

THE PRESIDENT.—More respected, more.

Our President says more and I say, yea, with all my heart.

Well, gentlemen, the way being cleared shall we halt in sight of the promised land ? Here in India we ask for bread and they give us stones. Let us now stand before the bar of the British public, pleading our cause, pleading the cause of our country, which is the cause of justice and of freedom, a cause which has never failed, and is not now going to fail for the first time, and success shall be ours.

The misgivings of doubt, the sneers of contempt, the voice of cavil will be drowned for ever and we shall earn for ourselves the gratitude of the voiceless millions of India and of generations yet to come.

MR. A. C. PARTHASARADHI NAIDU (*Madras, No.* 751, *in list.*)—I wish that this resolution did not exist in the Agenda Paper. I wish it were in my power to expunge it now. For, when this resolution was moved last year at Calcutta, I capered with joy and fondly believed that the scheme would soon become an accomplished fact. Deeply regretting therefore the circumstances that have necessitated the postponement of the Congress Session in London, I, however, think it reasonable that the arrangements of the London Congress should be suspended as signified in the resolution in question. I consider the causes that have contributed to the suspension as Providential ; for during the two years that will elapse, Pundits and others might thoroughly investigate the question of the feasibility or otherwise of sea-voyages, so that there might not be any persecution when the band of Congress Delegates returned from England. I have much pleasure in announcing the report that H. H. the Maharajah of Mysore and His Highness the Rajah of Bobbili are contemplating visits to England, and that they have asked the opinion of the Pundits in Southern India and in Benares on the question of sea-voyages. It is almost certain that the result of this investigation will be favourable, and I hope therefore that Delegates from India will be able to go in a body to England and present to the British public their grievances in the most right loyal manner possible. (*Applause.*)

SWAMI ALARAM (*Allahabad, No.* 76, *in list*) spoke in Hindi as follows,—Friends, in the last Congress at Calcutta, it was resolved that the Congress of 1892 should be held

3rd Day.

Res. XV. Postponement of the English Session until after the British General Election.

in London. But anticipating the dissolution of Parliament, the British Committee has recommended the postponement of the Congress in London till after the Elections, for in the time of Election members are too much occupied with their own affairs to attend to anything else. We fully concur with the suggestions of the Indian Political Agency, and say that the Congress Session of 1894 should be held in London. It is heard that Mr. Hume is about to enter Parliament. If this be true, the Congress will soon attain its objects. Friends, may God elevate Mr. Hume to the position of Secretary of State for India, and then and then only the grievances of the 300 millions of the Indians would be redressed. Mr. Hume is not going to separate himself from the Congress as was given out some time ago, but will continue to be its General Secretary, and thus nurture the tree which he has planted. Friends, don't remain inactive like stone statues during this interval, but continue to hold these grand Congresses as usual year after year. In 1894 the Congress should be held in London, and you should be prepared to send your delegates there. The loss of caste, consequent on a sea-voyage, is a pure misconception. Sea-voyage is not an *ekadasi* fast that is broken by eating a grain of gram. There is no harm in a person cooking his own food and eating it anywhere. Here you drink water brought to you through pipes, and there too you have to do the same. This in no way would take away your caste. It is stated in Nannuck Chandrodaya that Guru Nannuck went to Mecca for the good of the people, still he did not lose his caste. How think you, then, that you would lose it by undertaking a sea voyage? Friends, England is a land of angels (*laughter*), then why do you raise unnecessary objections to seeing angels! Though sixty years old and a sanniyasi (hermit) still, if I be alive, certainly I would go to England, and with this view I have commenced studying English. That well known Englishman, Mr. Bradlaugh, died while labouring for your good, then don't you feel ashamed in shrinking from visiting England, his birth-land, his home, which his death has hallowed. A series of Congresses held in India would not be so effective in rousing public attention in Britain as a single Congress in London. Let us, therefore, hold our Congress in 1894 in London before the threshold of our Mother Empress Victoria and pray her to redeem those solemn and sacred pledges given by Parliament in 1833 and by Her Majesty herself in 1858.

Pundit Shyam Narayan Masaldan (*Oudh, No. 123, in list*)—Mr. Chairman, Ladies and Gentlemen,—I have great pleasure in supporting the Resolution which is now before you. It was resolved last year that the London session of the Congress should be held this next spring But now our English friends and members of our British Committee are of opinion that we should hold our session in London after the General Elections which must come before long; and I agree with this opinion, because I think that at present with the near prospects of a General Election the public mind of Great Britain is so much excited that it is hardly possible to divert its attention to any other subject, however interesting and even important that subject may be. If after the assembling of a new Parliament when the present excitement would have ceased, and when (I also hope) the Liberals will have been installed in office, we go to England—and the larger our number the better it would be—and lay our grievances before the English nation, acquaint them with the hardships and injustice of an alien bureaucracy, extenuating nothing, nor setting down aught in malice, but telling them plainly what our sufferings are, and what it is that we want and what those measures are which would mitigate those sufferings and lighten the burden of our political and social sorrows, I have no doubt that the English people, whose love of justice and fair play is proverbial, who having enjoyed themselves the fruits of freedom from time immemorial, have so often helped to nurse the infant liberties of less advanced states, will redress our grievances and free us from those political evils which our own fate (for after all what does it avail to blame the officials who may be but mere instruments of an evil fate?) has brought upon us. Every new Parliament has its own ambitions and aspirations, and the next Parliament, which I trust will be Liberal, will have its own ambitions, not the least of which will be (at least with a large majority of our Liberal friends) to do something for India. Those who are fighting for Irish Home Rule may well be expected to take some interest in the furtherance of a movement, which is beyond doubt the greatest political movement of modern times, and which, while it embodies all the best features of Irish Home Rule, involves none of the drawbacks and dangers, which some, though I am not amongst the number, believe to attach to this latter. If we go out in large numbers to England and appeal to them for help, rest assured that help they will give us, and through their support our cause will form a strong plank in the Liberal platform.

Of course, our critics will not be slow to discredit our movement in their eyes. They will tell them what they have been telling our Government here that we are not fit for what we want, that our chief demand for a moderate measure of representation in the Legislative Councils is premature, and out of place in a country like India, where there are so many sects and creeds, so many discordant elements that would defy all attempts at bringing them together to work harmoniously under a representative system. Now, I will not wait to examine the sincerity of these criticisms. I can only say that if they are not deceiving the Government then they are themselves labouring under a very lamentable self-deception. It may be a rather hard task to cure them of this self-delusion, but it is certainly wisest to take every precaution

3rd Day.

Res. XV. Postponement of the English Session until after the British General Election.

to prevent the contagion of this malady spreading to the people of England. It is one of the noblest traits in the character of Englishmen that, as soon as they are convinced of the existence of any political evil or injustice, they do not rest until that evil has been removed or that injustice redressed. The English are well aware that even in countries where the coexistence of divergent races and creeds was a source of political discontent and instability, the establishment of representative institutions has been the means of restoring public contentment and tranquillity. It is one of the principles of human nature that the highest class of feelings are called into existence and nourished only by exercise and action. Men who are accustomed to take part in public affairs, to make sacrifices, for these are, by mere force of habit and circumstance, raised to a higher level of morality, while those who have no interest in public matters, whose daily actions and aspirations are confined to their own selves, however good and pure-minded they may be, come instinctively to take a narrow view of man's calling, lose their generous sympathies, and become unconsciously selfish and demoralized. There will be sectarianism, class bias, disunion and all the rest of it among a people who are debarred from taking part in public concerns, in things which raise the mind, if even for amoment, above the sordid veil of self and awaken it to wider and more generous sympathies. On the contrary, when a different set of principles prevails, then the results will be far happier, as we see in Switzerland. That country is divided into a number of Cantons each having little in common with the rest. The differences between the Protestants and the Catholics are most marked. Even the nationalities are various. In former times there used to be great feuds among them. But in spite of all this Switzerland is the most democratic country in Europe, and ever since it has become so, feuds and quarrels have, practically, disappeared, differences of race and religion have lost their odious features, and the Swiss people are considered the most peaceful and contented people in Europe. Take another instance, that of Canada. There, too, so long as "British ascendancy" prevailed, the people were on the verge of rebellion. In Canada there are two such discordant elements as the French and the English. At one time it was thought impossible to reconcile the two, and attempts were made to rule Canada, not in accordance with the wishes of the Canadians but according to English ideas. The attempt egregiously failed. Discontent and disaffection rose to the highest pitch, until, fortunately for England, wiser counsels prevailed, and Canada was granted representative institutions which appeased the public mind and have ever since converted that country into one of the most loyal portions of the British Empire.

If differences of race and religion did not stand in the way of representative Government in Canada and Switzerland, I see no reason why they should constitute any argument against the limited representation that we claim for the people of India. If it is not granted to us, it is because the English nation has not yet made up its mind that it shall be granted to us, and it has not made up its mind because it is not yet sufficiently informed upon Indian matters. The moment its information is complete it will do justice to India. It is for us to go to England and inform it.

The President.—I know every one would like to speak on this subject. I think I could myself speak straight off for an hour (*laughter*), but I really must urge you to finish our work. Now shall I put this resolution without further speaking? (*Cries of yes, yes, vote, vote*). Come then, our 15th Resolution will stand thus :—

Resolved—*That in view of the General Election, now impending in England, and in accordance with the recommendation of our British Committee, the provisional arrangements set on foot, in pursuance of the Resolution passed at the Calcutta Congress of 1890 for holding, all things being convenient, a Congress of not less than 100 Delegates in England in 1892, be now suspended until after such General Election.*"

The Resolution was then put and carried *nemine dissentiente*.

Res. XVI. Assignment of funds for British Committee and General Secretary's Office.

Mr. J. Ghosal (*Calcutta, No.* 14, *in list*)—Mr. President and Fellow Delegates,—I have been called upon to move a merely formal resolution. As you have passed the twelfth resolution with acclamation, we have cleared the ground. We have acknowledged gratefully the services rendered to this country by the British Committee, and we expect that they will go on working for the good of this country. But for that purpose we must provide them with funds. They are giving their services gratuitously, time and much time, that to most of them means money, and we must at least provide for actual expenses, printing and the like, incurred on our behalf, and for these expenses we have to allot, as we do every year, a certain sum of money. A calculation has been made as to the amount that will be required to meet the expenses of next year, and this is the resolution which has been framed :—

*That a sum of Rs. 40,000, exclusive of individual donations, is assigned for the expenses of the British Committee of the Congress and Rs. 6,000 for the General Secretary's*

**3rd Day.**

**Res. XVI. Assignment of funds for British Committee and General Secretary's Office.**

*office and establishment, and that the several circles do contribute as arranged in Committee for the year 1892.*

I have no doubt that you will unanimously adopt this resolution. May I also add the suggestion that you should not merely vote the money but do your best to see that it is made promptly available for remission to England. (*Cheers*).

MR. VIRARAGHAVA CHARIAR (*Madras, No. 763, in list*)—This subject has been threshed out by the Subjects Committee whom we appointed to consider it and other questions, and they have come to the conclusion that Rs. 40,000 should be voted to meet the expenses of the British Agency in England and promptly paid in, so as to keep the Committee going with its work. The money is urgently required, and if we forget to discharge our duty the Secretary is frequently bothered in making the necessary payments. I therefore appeal to you not only to order the money now, but to collect it and remit it at once to England. (*Cheer and cries of vote, vote*).

THE PRESIDENT.—By all means, if no one else wishes to speak on this subject ? (*None, none*). Then I put the 16th Resolution in these words :—

RESOLVED —*That a sum of Rs. 40,000, exclusive of individual donations, is assigned for the expenses of the British Committee of the Congress and Rs. 6,000 for the General Secretary's office and establishment, and that the several circles do contribute as arranged in Committee for the year 1892."*

The Resolution was carried unanimously.

**Res. XVII. Re-election of General and Joint General Secretaries**

MR. W. C. BONNERJEE (*Calcutta, No. 1, in list*)—MR. PRESIDENT AND GENTLEMEN,—It has always been my privilege to propose one resolution at the meetings of the Congress—I refer to the re-appointment of Mr. Hume as General Secretary (*loud and continuous cheering*), and of Pandit Ajudhya Nath as Joint General Secretary (*loud cheers*). This resolution does not require any seconding or putting to the vote from the chair. I have always proposed this to the Congress except at the last meeting, and I do it now. There is but one word that I ought to say. You must have all been dismayed by the circular issued by Mr. Hume in which he hinted that perhaps he would not be able to continue our General Secretary ; and you may have heard that the health of Pundit Ajudhya Nath is such that it is with the greatest difficulty that he can retain his post. But Mr. Hume and Pundit Ajudhya Nath have yielded to the persuasion that has been brought to bear upon them. (*Cheers.*) I ask you to carry this resolution with acclamation as usual ; and I think I may say, in conclusion, that we bring you glad tidings of great joy.

*That Mr. A. O. Hume and Pundit Ajudhya Nath are re-elected General and Joint-General Secretaries for the ensuing year.*

The resolution was carried by acclamation, the delegates rising, and crowds of them bestrewing the platform with showers of flowers.

**Res. XVIII. Eighth Congress to be held at Allahabad.**

MR. A. O. HUME (*Punjab, No. 130, in list*) who was received with further long continued bursts of cheers and showers of flowers,—BROTHER DELEGATES,—I also have the privilege of annually submitting one resolution ; but before I ask you to accept it I have one or two little matters to touch upon. In the first place, I would attempt to thank you for the kind manner in which you have received me. It is hopeless for me to find words to express my gratitude for the sympathetic attitude which you always assume in regard to me in return for such small poor sympathy as I have been able to show you. (*Loud cheers*). The first point on which I wish to touch is this. I have been very unwilling to continue in the post of your General Secretary simply because circumstances will prevent my visiting India next year, and I think that if the duties of the General Secretary are to be properly performed he ought to visit the country, and I should be unwilling to continue in an office the duties of which I could not adequately fulfil. That alone is the reason for my hesitation in continuing to hold the office of General Secretary. You know well that my heart is ever with you all ! (*Loud burst of cheers.*) I have hesitated to accept the honor offered to me ; but when I found that my friends here were of opinion that for the good of the Congress it was necessary that I should remain I at once acceded. (*Cheers*). And I am thoroughly pleased at heart that it should have been thought necessary that I should remain. Then I want to allude publicly to one or two little points about which there is a misunderstanding. I came across in the *Gujerati* the other day, and in some other native papers, passages referring to the accounts of the British Committee, and saying that they, the writers, did not know what became of the money that went to England. Now, elaborate and full accounts are sent out every year to this country, and if the Standing Congress Committees do not choose to distribute them, we in England are not to blame. There is nothing secret, every farthing spent at home is accounted for, and you get a regular account audited by professional accountants as auditors. Then I am told that a great number of persons in India do not understand that the newspaper *India* is the property of the Congress. It was started

3rd Day.

Res. XVIII. Eighth Congress to be held at Allahabad.

with your funds by the British Committee. Some people fancy that Mr. Digby is the proprietor. He is nothing of the kind. He is paid £100 a year for editing the paper, in addition to his other salary. It is absolutely your property (*cheers*) and it is your interest to develop its circulation. If you only do your duty in that respect it will be perfectly self-supporting. At present it is rather a drag upon the funds that you send home to the English agency. I hope therefore that in this matter you will all exert yourselves. I have occupied four and a half minutes. Another half minute will suffice to submit the resolution which it has always my been duty to propose.

"RESOLVED—*That the Eighth Indian National Congress do assemble on the 26th December 1892 at Allahabad.*" (*Cheers.*)

To me there is something saddening and something gladdening in this announcement: gladdening, because we have reached the Eighth Congress and are going to have a gathering which I know will be successful; saddening, because, for the first time from the commencement of the Congress, I shall not be present to share your enthusiasm and your labors for the good of the country. But be sure that, though distant from you in body, my spirit will be with you and I shall watch over your progress, and shall be expecting, if still in the land of the living, to receive good tidings and hear that the next Congress is the most successful that you have ever had. Remember that our opponents have been always telling the world—you and I know how false it is—that these Congresses depend entirely upon Mr. Hume. It will be for you to show next year, when Mr. Hume has not been near the country for twelve months, that you can run the Congress yourselves as well as or better than it has ever been run when Mr. Hume was present. I lay this burden upon you. (*Loud cheers*).

HON'BLE PANDIT AJUDHYA NATH (*Allahabad, No.* 74, *in list*).—MR. PRESIDENT AND FELLOW DELEGATES,—On behalf of the N. W. Provinces I cordially invite the Congress to Allahabad. (*Cheers, and three cheers for Pandit Ajudya Nath*). According to the usual practice it would not be necessary to say a word more. But under the special circumstances I ask permission to add a few words. I want those good friends, whether Anglo-Indians or others, who have been saying that this is the beginning of the end to note once for all that there is no lack of enthusiasm for the Congress in the country. (*Cheers*). India means to carry on this movement, or, as our opponents call it, agitation (be it so) as long as our reasonable demands are not granted; and if Government defer the granting of these demands the Government and the British Parliament and the British Nation will be responsible before man and God for this waste of India's time, India's money and India's energy. (*Loud cheers*). We are all sorry that one of the reasons why Mr. Hume will be unable to attend the Congress next year is failing health. At the same time there is some consolation, both to him and to us, in this that, if we hold the Congress in his absence, and if he finds any shortcomings—and shortcomings there must be—he will still be able to teach us how to overcome them. While heartily and sincerely thankful to Mr. Hume for the invaluable assistance he has rendered to us at the time when we most needed it, for all he has done, for all he is doing for us (*cheers*), we are sure that no one will be happier than himself to discover that his political child, the Indian National Congress, has not only learned to walk but is able to work for itself. (*Cheers.*)

THE PRESIDENT.—You will now allow me to put to you formally our 18th and last Resolution.

RESOLVED—*That the Eighth Indian National Congress do assemble on the 26th December 1892 at Allahabad.*

The Resolution was then carried by acclamation amidst a perfect storm of cheers.

Vote of Thanks to the President.

MR. SURENDRA NATH BANNERJEE—(*Calcutta, No.* 11, *in list*)—BROTHER DELEGATES—I have to invite you to join me in the performance of a duty which I am sure will be most welcome and acceptable to you all, and that is to tender our acknowledgments and our most cordial expressions of gratitude to Mr. P. Ananda Charlu for his conduct as President of this great assembly. (*Cheers*). The President of the National Congress has a most responsible, most difficult, and I was going to say most embarrassing, duty to perform. He has, in the first instance, to enforce the rules of debate and also the rule in regard to the limitation of time—a very unpleasant duty at times. I think I express the sense of this great gathering when I say that, having regard to the delicate nature of his duties and the responsible character of his functions, he has nobly merited an expression of our acknowledgments. I hope and trust that this vote will be carried by acclamation.

The vote was then carried by acclamation with a good deal of cheering.

**3rd Day.**

**President's Concluding remarks.**

The President.—Gentlemen,—I am now *functus officio.* I have no right to ask you to listen to me with authority ; this, however, I am entitled to ask, that since I have to address my brethren they will give me a patient and indulgent hearing. My object, first, is to thank you all, the entire body of delegates, for the manner in which you have made it possible for me to discharge the function which you have assigned to me. It is but right that having done me the honor of electing me to this chair, you should assist me in my efforts to deserve that honor ; and, if in the discharge of the duties entrusted to me any measure of success has attended my efforts, it is solely due to you, one and all. But I find it necessary to single out two bodies who are entitled to special praise at my hands. One body is composed of the many gentlemen who spoke in connection with the resolutions. I cannot too highly praise the sense of proportion that marked them generally. If occasionally there was a little trespassing beyond the allotted time, I put it down, and put it down rightly I believe, to the enthusiasm under which the speaker was speaking at the time, not to any oblivion of the rule that I am sure he was determined, in his heart of hearts, to observe strictly. If, therefore, in dealing with any of the speakers I have unwillingly been a little peremptory (*No, no*), I beg of you to excuse me. Then there is another body to whom my thanks are due, consisting of gentlemen who were inclined and qualified to speak, but who, out of respect to the authority you have vested in me, have foregone that pleasure, and have thereby proved in the highest degree their possession of that sense of propriety that should belong to every representative elected to a national assembly. And now, gentlemen, I beg, on your behalf and on my own behalf, to thank the Chairman and the various members of the Reception Committee for all they have done to make this Congress a success. In a work done by a large number of people, the apportionment of praise is an invidious task. I do not therefore propose to bring before you any names as entitled to any special consideration, except to say that Mr. Narayan Swami conducted the Congress car to triumph and victory, as Narayana conducted the Pandavas in their virtuous war to undoubted victory. Mr. Hume in his circular referred to the undoubted fact that this Congress indicates a distinct stage which we have reached. In that we all unquestionably concur. But he suggested that the Congress sessions in India might be suspended for some time. That suggestion was facing me when I came here from Madras, and one of the things that I wanted to incite you to do was to differ from Mr. Hume in that matter. I am glad to find that without my help you have done this and have resolved to continue to hold these annual Congresses without intermission. Now a few words more, by way of completing the remarks which you were kind enough to hear from me when I began. At that time, not knowing how you were going to determine, I could certainly not have given you what, in my mind, ought to be the forecast of the future of this institution. Is it to be reduced in dimensions, and in numbers, and denuded of all demonstration ? Or is it to be a mere demonstration ? Or is it to be an institution coupled with demonstration? Considering that one main object that we have in view is to unify India, and that in that respect we have yet to go a long way, it is desirable that the propagandist character of the Congress should not cease for some time to come. (*Cheers*). Wherever we have a centre in India, promising anything like a good local audience, and giving us the prospect of gathering together a large body of visitors, it is our religious duty to pitch our camp there, and do all that we can to influence those who assemble. Whatever be the method adopted next year, we must, in order to carry out our purpose effectually, go in for a big moveable pavilion of our own, with seats sufficient to accommodate at least four thousand persons ; and over it we must have a banner containing a monogram " I. N. C." (Indian National Congress) inseparably intermingled with the crosses of St. George, St. Andrew and St. Patrick of the British flag. (*Cheers*). If in that way we meet at different stations, we should, I think, in addition to the regular Congress work, devote one day to an important purpose to which no time has yet been allotted at the Congress sittings. We have no doubt on the opening day the Chairman's speech and the President's speech ; but I think it is necessary that we should add to our programme, by proposing in regard to each presidency or important province, an honorable mention, and from every one of those provinces or presidencies some one should give a review of the administration thereof with well attested and calmly stated facts by way of response. If we can devote, say, one day to hearing speakers in that way, the Congress record will contain not merely what takes place in regard to those questions with which Congress is immediately connected, but a good, intelligent and careful review of the administration of the whole country from the closing of one session to the beginning of another. Those, gentlemen, are the thoughts which I should have added to the observations with which I began the meeting, but, as I have said, I could not then do so. The only thing that now remains for me is to thank you again from the bottom of my heart for the manner in which you have received the proposal of thanks to me (*cheers*), and to declare, as I now do, this Seventh Indian National Congress dissolved.

Three cheers, again and again repeated, were then given for Her Majesty the Queen Empress, and then the Congress dissolved.

# APPENDIX I.

## LIST OF DELEGATES

WHO ATTENDED THE

# SEVENTH INDIAN NATIONAL CONGRESS,

## *HELD AT NAGPUR, DECEMBER, 1891*

| Number. | Presidency or Government. | Congress Circle. | Electoral Division. | Names in full of Delegates, with honorary titles, scholastic degrees, etc. | Race, Religious denomination, and Caste, if any, | Occupation and Address. | How and when elected. |
|---|---|---|---|---|---|---|---|
| 1 | Bengal. | Calcutta. | Northern Metropolitan Electoral Division. | Mr. W. C. Bonnerjee ... | Bengali Brahmin. | Barrister-at-Law, Fellow of the Calcutta University, 6, Park Street. | At a Public Meeting held at the Albert Hall, Calcutta, on the 8th December 1891. |
| 2 | " | " | " | Dr. Jagadis Chandra Lahiri. | do. | Medical Practitioner, 101 College Street, Calcutta. | do. |
| 3 | " | " | " | Dr. Mohini Mohun Bose, M.D., L.R.C.P. Edin., etc | Kayastha. | Hony. Magistrate, Zemindar, Physician and Surgeon, 111, College Street, Calcutta. | do. |
| 4 | " | " | " | Babu Pulin Bihari Sircar. | do. | Merchant, 21, Beadon Street, Calcutta. | do. |
| 5 | " | " | " | Babu J. Bose ... | do. | Landowner, 35-1 Raja Naba Kissen's Street, Calcutta. | do. |
| 6 | " | " | " | Babu Bhupendra Nath Basu, M.A., B.L. | do. | Solicitor, High Court, Calcutta. | do. |
| 7 | " | " | " | Babu Preonath Ghosh | do. | Solicitor, 11, Beadon Street, Calcutta. | do. |
| 8 | " | " | " | Babu Girisa Chandra Sett, B.A., B.L. | do. | Solicitor, High Court, Calcutta. | do. |
| 9 | " | " | " | Babu Herambo Chandra Moitra, M.A. | Bengali Brahmo. | Editor, "Indian Messenger," Professor, City College, Calcutta. | do. |
| 10 | " | " | " | Babu Kali Charan Banerji, M.A., B.L. | Bengali Christian. | Vakil, High Court, Fellow of the Calcutta University. | do. |
| 11 | " | " | " | Babu Surendranath Banerjee, B.A. | Bengali Brahmin. | Editor, "Bengalee," Principal and Proprietor, Ripon College, Honorary Presidency Magistrate, Municipal Commissioner, etc. | do. |
| 12 | " | " | " | Babu Amoynath Bose ... | Bengali Kayastha | Landowner, 13, College Square. | do. |
| 13 | " | " | Southern Metropolitan Electoral Division. | Revd. C. N. Banerjea, B.A. | Bengali Christian. | Missionary, Bhowanipore ... | do. |
| 14 | " | " | British Indian Association. | Mr. J. Ghosal ... | Bengali Brahmin. | Zemindar, Merchant, Municipal Commissioner, Honorary Magistrate, Vice-President, Bengal National Chamber of Commerce. | At a Committee Meeting of the British Indian Association held on the 15th December 1891, and Bengal National Chamber of Commerce, 4th December 1891. |
| 15 | " | " | " | Pandit Pran Nath Saraswati, M.A., B.L. | Kashmiri Brahmin. | Vakil, High Court, Bhowanipore. | At a Committee Meeting of the British Indian Association on the 15th December 1891. |

| Number. | Presidency or Government. | Congress Circle. | Electoral Division. | Names in full of Delegates, with honorary titles, scholastic degrees, etc. | Race, Religious denomination, and Caste, if any. | Occupation and Address. | How and when elected. |
|---|---|---|---|---|---|---|---|
| 16 | Bengal. | Calcutta | Bengal National Chamber of Commerce. | Babu Narain Dass ... | Hindu Khetre. | Zemindar, Merchant, and Banker. | At a Meeting of the Members held on the 4th December 1891. |
| 17 | " | " | Indian Association. | Raya Yatindra Nath Chowdhuri, M.A., B.L. | Bengali Kayastha. | Zemindar, Barahanagar ... | At a Meeting of the Committee of the Indian Association held on the 3rd December 1891. |
| 18 | " | " | " | Babu Krishna Kumar Mitra, B.A. | Bengali Brahmo. | Superintendent, City College, Editor, "Sanjivani." | do. |
| 19 | " | " | Nuddea. | Babu Akshoy Kumar Mitra. | Bengali Kayastha. | Municipal Commissioner, Chogdah. | At a Public Meeting held at Chogdah on the 25th October 1891. |
| 20 | " | " | " | Babu Jadu Nath Chatterjee, B.L. | Bengali Brahmin. | Vakeel, Honorary Magistrate, Municipal Commissioner, Zemindar, Krishnaghur. | At a Public Meeting held at Krishnaghur on the 6th December 1891. |
| 21 | " | " | " | Babu Bishwambhar Roy. B.L. | Bengali Kayastha. | Pleader, Member, District Board, Nuddea, Local Board, Kushtea. | do. |
| 22 | " | " | " | Babu Pulin Bihari Lahiri. | Bengali Brahmin. | Pleader, Member, District Board, Vice-Chairman, Local Board, Krishnaghur. | do. |
| 23 | " | " | " | Babu Banku Behari Singha. | Hindu. | Merchant and Talukdar, Vice-Chairman, Local Board, Member, District Board, Hony. Magistrate. | At a Public Meeting held at Nuddea on the 6th December 1891. |
| 24 | " | " | " | Babu Nundo Gopal Bhadury. | do | Merchant and Talukdar ... | do. |
| 25 | " | " | Howrah. | Babu Akshoy Charan Dass B.L. | Bengali Hindu Kaibartta. | Pleader, District Court, Hony. Secretary, Howrah People's Association and Howrah Congress Committee, and Honorary Assistant Secretary, Howrah Pleaders' Association, 3 Lakshman Das's Lane, Howrah. | At a Public Meeting held at the Howrah Town Hall on Saturday, the 26th September 1891. |
| 26 | " | " | Maniram pur (24 Peganahs.) | Babu Surendra Nath Banerjea. | Bengali Brahmin. | Zemindar ... ... | At a Public Meeting held at Manirampur on the 15th November 1891. |
| 27 | " | " | Khulna. | Babu Indu Bhusan Mazumdar, B.A., B.L. | Hindu Kayastha. | Pleader, Landholder, Member, Local Board. | At a Public Meeting held at Khulna on the 15th December 1891. |
| 28 | " | " | " | Babu Jadub Chandra Dass | do. | Pleader and Landholder ... | do. |
| 29 | " | " | Jessore. | Babu Radhika Charan Dutt B.A., B.L. | Hindu Kayastha. | Pleader ... ... | At a Public Meeting held at Jessore on the 22nd December 1891. |
| 30 | " | " | Magurah (Jessore District.) | Babu Ambica Charan Sirkar. | Hindu Baroi. | Pleader, Landholder, Honorary Magistrate, Vice-Chairman, Local Board, Magurah. | At a Public Meeting held at Magurah on the 6th December 1891. |
| 31 | " | " | " | Babu Basanta Cumar Bose. | Hindu Kayastha. | Pleader ... ... | do. |
| 32 | " | " | Midnapur | Rajah Srinarain Pal ... | do. | Zemindar, Dharenda ... | At a Public Meeting held at Midnapur on the 17th November 1891. |
| 33 | " | " | " | Babu Trailokya Nath Pal. | Hindu Satgopa. | Pleader, Member, District Board. | do. |
| 34 | " | " | Serampur (Hooghly District.) | Babu K. B. Mullick ... | Hindu Kayastha | Journalist ... ... | At a Public Meeting held at Serampore on the 3rd December 1891. |
| 35 | " | " | " | Mrs. Amelia Sophia West | Eurasian Christian. | Landowner ... ... | do. |
| 36 | " | " | Murshidabad. | Babu Nafar Dass Roy ... | Hindu Kshatriya | Zemindar ... ... | At a Public Meeting held at Murshidabad on the 7th December 1891. |
| 37 | " | " | Bankura. | Babu Mahesh Chandra Banerjee, B.A., B.L. | Bengali Brahmin. | Vakil, Member, District Board, Honorary Magistrate and Municipal Commissioner. | At a Public Meeting held at Bankura on the 11th December 1891. |
| 38 | " | " | Chittagong | Babu Dhirendra Lall Khastgir, B.L. | Hindu Vaidya. | Pleader and Landholder .. | At a Meeting of the Chittagong Association on the 20th December 1891. |
| 39 | " | " | Assam. | Babu Meghanatha Banerjee. | Hindu Brahmin. | Medical Practitioner, Jaipur, Dibrugarh. | At a Meeting on the 21st December 1891. |
| 40 | " | " | " | Babu Durga Kant Roy, B.A., B.L. | Hindu Baidya. | Pleader, Dhubri, Assam ... | Do. on the 6th December 1891. |
| 41 | " | Dacca | Tangail (Mymensing District) | Babu Frosonno Kumar Bose. | Brahmo. | Talukdar ... ... | At a Public Meeting held at Tangail on the 22nd December 1891. |
| 42 | " | " | Bogra | Babu Jadab Lal Roy ... | Hindu Kayastha. | Talukdar, Honorary Magistrate and Zemindar's Agent. | At a Public Meeting held at Bogra on the 4th December 1891. |

| Number. | Presidency or Government. | Congress Circle | Electoral Division. | Names in full of Delegates, with honorary titles, scholastic degrees, etc. | Race, Religious denomination and Caste, if any. | Occupation and Address. | How and when elected. |
|---|---|---|---|---|---|---|---|
| 43 | Bengal. | Barisal | Backargunge. | Babu Jagadis Mukherjee, B.A. | Hindu Kayastha. | Professor, Beraj Mohan Institution, Barisal. | At a Public Meeting held at Barisal on the 20th December 1891. |
| 44 | ,, | ,, | ,, | Babu Hara Kanta Sen ... | Hindu Vaidya. | Secretary, Barisal Loan Office | do. |
| 45 | ,, | Rajshahye | Dinajepore | Babu Madhava Chandra Chatterjee, M.A., B.L. | Hindu Brahmin. | Pleader, Vice-Chairman, Municipal Board. | At a Public Meeting held on the 30th November 1891, at Dinajepore. |
| 46 | ,, | ,, | ,, | Babu Umesh Chandra Khasnavish. | Hindu Kayastha. | Zemindar, Mukhtear, Municipal Commissioner. | do. |
| 47 | ,, | ,, | ,, | Babu Khetra Nath Banerjee. | Bengali Brahmin. | Zemindar ... ... | do. |
| 48 | ,, | ,, | ,, | Babu Jogesh Chandra Sinha, B.A., B.L. | Hindu Kayastha. | Pleader ... ... | do. |
| 49 | ,, | ,, | Pubna | Babu Mohini Mohan Chakravarti, M.A., B.L. | Bengali Brahmin. | Pleader, District Court, Vice President, Municipality. | At a Public Meeting held on the 8th December 1891, at Pubna. |
| 50 | ,, | ,, | ,, | Babu Mohini Mohan Lahiri, M.A., B.L. | do. | Pleader, District Court, Pubna | do. |
| 51 | ,, | Rampur Beauleah | Rampur Beauleah. | Babu Mukanda Mohun Maitra, B.L. | Hindu Brahmin. | Pleader, District Court ... | At a Public Meeting held at Rampur Beauleah on the 6th December 1891. |
| 52 | ,, | Bhagalpore. | Purneah | Babu Baroda Kanta Banerjee, B.L. | Bengali Brahmin. | Pleader ... ... | At a Public Meeting held at Purneah on the 5th December 1891. |
| 53 | ,, | ,, | ,, | Babu Parbutty Charan Dass, B.L. | Brahmo. | Pleader, Member, District Board. | do. |
| 54 | ,, | ,, | ,, | Babu Jogendra Nath Mukherjee, M.A., B.L. | Hindu Brahmin. | Pleader and Municipal Commissioner. | do. |
| 55 | ,, | ,, | Bhagalpore | Babu Joti Kumar Ghosal, B.L. | do. | Pleader ... ... | At a Public Meeting held at Bhagalpore on the 12th December 1891. |
| 56 | ,, | ,, | ,, | Babu Abinash Chandra Bosu, B.L. | Hindu Kayastha. | do. ... | do. |
| 57 | ,, | ,, | ,, | Babu Khettra Nath Ghosal, B.L. | Hindu Brahmin. | do. ... | do. |
| 58 | ,, | Chota Nagpur. | Ranchi. | Babu Prabhu Narayan... | Hindu Kayastha. | Mukhtear and Zemindar .. | At a Public Meeting held at Ranchi on the 20th December 1891. |
| 59 | ,, | ,, | ,, | Babu Jagatpal Sahay ... | do. | Pleader ... | do. |
| 60 | ,, | ,, | Hazaribagh | Babu Akhoy Kumar Gupta | Hindu Vaidya. | Contractor ... | At a Public Meeting held at Hazaribagh on the 25th October 1891. |
| 61 | ,, | Behar. | Patna. | Babu Guru Prasad Sen, M.A., B.L. | do. | Editor, "Behar Herald," Vakil, Zemindar and Municipal Commissioner. | At a Public Meeting held at Patna on the 18th December 1891. |
| 62 | ,, | ,, | ,, | Babu Bisweswar Singh ... | Hindu Kshetriya | Pleader, Zemindar, Municipal Commissioner, Honorary Magistrate, Member, Local Board, Arrah. | do. |
| 63 | ,, | ,, | ,, | Babu Saligram Singh B.A., B.L. | do. | Vakil, High Court, Zemindar, Honorary Presidency Magistrate, Calcutta. | do. |
| 64 | ,, | ,, | ,, | Babu Purnendu Narayan Singh, M.A., B.L. | Hindu Kayastha. | Pleader, Bankipore ... | do. |
| 65 | ,, | ,, | ,, | Syed Abdul Hamid, B.A. B.L. | Mahomedan. | Pleader, Zemindar, Vice-Chairman, Local Board, Member, District Board, Honorary Magistrate. | At a Public Meeting held at Patna on the 1st December 1891. |
| 66 | ,, | ,, | ,, | Moulvie Amir Hyder ... | do. | Pleader & Zemindar, Bankipur | do. |
| 67 | ,, | ,, | Gya. | Babu Nand Kishore Lall, M.A., B.L. | Hindu Kayastha. | Zemindar and Vakil ... | At a Public Meeting held at Gya on the 20th December 1891. |
| 68 | ,, | ,, | ,, | Babu Siva Sankar Sahoy | do. | Zemindar and Pleader | do. |
| 69 | ,, | Mozufferpur. | Mozufferpur. | Babu Shorashi Charan Mitra, B.L. | do. | Pleader | At a Public Meeting held at Mozufferpur on the 6th December 1891. |
| 70 | ,, | ,, | ,, | Babu Parmeshwar Narain Mahtha. | Hindu Kshatriya. | Zemindar, Banker and Indigo Planter, Honorary Magistrate, Municipal Commissioner and Member, District Board. | do. |
| 71 | ,, | ,, | ,, | Moulvie Syed Ahmed Hossein, B.A., B.L. | Mahomedan Shiah. | Zemindar and Pleader .. | do. |
| 72 | ,, | ,, | ,, | Syed Mahomed Raza .. | do. | Zemindar .. | do. |
| 73 | ,, | ,, | ,, | Mr. Pringle Kennedy, M.A., B.L. | European. Christian | Pleader .. | do. |
| 74 | ,, | N.-W. P | Allahabad. | Pandit Ajudhianath ... | Cashmeri Brahmin. | Pleader, High Court, Landowner, Merchant and Banker, Fellow, Allahabad and Calcutta Universities. | At a Public Meeting held at Allahabad on the 7th November 1891. |

| Number. | Presidency or Government. | Congress Circle. | Electoral Division. | Names in full of Delegates, with honorary titles, scholastic degrees, etc. | Race, Religious denomination, and Caste, if any. | Occupation and Address. | How and when elected. |
|---|---|---|---|---|---|---|---|
| 75 | Bengal. | N.-W. P. | Allahabad. | Babu Charoo Chander Mitter | Hindu Kayastha. | Pleader, Zemindar and Municipal Commissioner. | At a Public Meeting held at Allahabad on the 7th November 1891. |
| 76 | " | " | " | Swami Ala Ram ... | Hindu | Preacher ... | do. |
| 77 | " | " | " | Munshi Kashi Prasad ... | Hindu Kayastha. | Vakil, High Court ... | do. |
| 78 | " | " | " | Pundit Balkrishna Bhatta. | Hindu Brahmin. | Editor, "Hindi Pradip" & Head Pundit, Kayastha Pathshala. | do. |
| 79 | " | " | " | Pandit Madan Mohan Malaviya, B. A., L.L. B. | Malaviya Brahmin. | Pleader and Journalist. | do. |
| 80 | " | " | " | Pandit Baldeo Ram Dave. | Gujrati Nagar Brahmin. | Vakil, High Court, N.-W. P... | do. |
| 81 | " | " | " | Munshi Sadruddeen ... | Mahomedan. | Zemindar ... ... | do. |
| 82 | " | " | " | Pandit Moti Lall Nehru. | Kashmiri Brahmin. | Vakil, High Court, N.-W. P... | do. |
| 83 | " | " | " | Mirza Tufail Ali Beg ... | Mahomedan. | Zemindar ... ... | do. |
| 84 | " | " | " | Syed Anwar Hussain Kazmi. | do. | do. | do. |
| 85 | " | " | " | Meer Hatim Ali ... | do. | do. | do. |
| 86 | " | " | " | Syed Akhtar Hussain ... | do. | do. | do. |
| 87 | " | " | " | Syed Hafiz Abdul Huq... | do. | Physician and Zemindar ... | At a Public Meeting held at Kara on the 5th November 1891. |
| 88 | " | " | " | Sheikh Mahomed Zakrallah. | do. | Zemindar .. ... | do. |
| 89 | " | " | " | Pandit Kaliprasanno Kavyabisharad. | Hindu Bengali. | Editor, "Indian Union and Cosmopolitan," Proprietor, Secular Press, Bhowanipore. | do. |
| 90 | " | " | " | Syed Mahomed Taki ... | Mahomedan. | Zemindar ... ... | do. |
| 91 | " | " | " | Sheik Inayet Ali ... | do. | do. | do. |
| 92 | " | " | " | Syed Sultan Hussain ... | do. | do. | At a Public Meeting held at Sahela on the 4th November 1891. |
| 93 | " | " | " | Syed Aulad Hussain ... | do. | do. | do. |
| 94 | " | " | " | Syed Nazim Hussain ... | do. | do. | do. |
| 95 | " | " | " | Meer Ahmed Hussain ... | do. | do. | do. |
| 96 | " | " | " | Syed Mahomed Hadi ... | do. | Zemindar and Muafidar .. | At a Public Meeting held at Ujhani on the 3rd November 1891. |
| 97 | " | " | " | Meer Mehndi Ali ... | do. | Private Service ... ... | At a Public Meeting held at Janka on the 8th November 1891. |
| 98 | " | " | Cawnpore. | Mahomed Muksoodul Huq. | Mahomedan. | do. | At a Public Meeting held at Cawnpore on the 23rd December 1891. |
| 99 | " | " | " | Pundit Jankinath ... | Kashmiri Brahmin. | Pleader and Zemindar ... | do. |
| 100 | " | " | " | Babu Gulzari Lal ... | Hindu Bunniah. | Banker, Zemindar and Contractor. | do. |
| 101 | " | " | " | Babu Bunsidhar ... | Hindu Mehesri. | Zemindar ... ... | do. |
| 102 | " | " | " | Babu Nundun Lal ... | Hindu Khetri. | Cloth Merchant ... | do. |
| 103 | " | " | " | Hurnam Sing Varma ... | Punjabi Khetri. | Proprietor "Cawnpore Gazette." | do. |
| 104 | " | " | " | Pundit Maharajkishen ... | Kashmiri Brahmin. | Rais ... ... | do. |
| 105 | " | " | " | Pundit Prithinath ... | | Pleader, Zemindar and Municipal Commissioner. | do. |
| 106 | " | " | " | Pundit Hurdeo Narayan Koul. | do | Pleader ... ... | do. |
| 107 | " | " | " | Babu Prayag Chandra Mitra, B.A. | Bengali Kayastha | Vakil High Court ... | do. |
| 108 | " | " | Agra. | Lala Gokul Chand ... | Hindu Vaisya. | ...... | At a Public Meeting held at Agra on the 24th December 1891. |
| 109 | " | " | " | Babu Ram Dass Chathe. | Hindu. | Teacher, Bookseller and Printer. | do. |
| 110 | " | " | " | Babu Jumna Das Biswas. | Hindu Kayastha. | Pleader, Municipal Commissioner and Editor, "Nasim-Agra." | do. |
| 111 | " | " | Kumaon. | Pandit Jwala Dutt Joshi. | Hindu Brahmin. | Vakil, High Court ... | At a Public Meeting held at Almora on the 24th December 1891. |
| 112 | " | " | " | Pandit Badri Dutt Joshi. | do. | Pleader ... ... | do. |

| Number. | Presidency or Government. | Congress Circle. | Electoral Division. | Names in full of Delegates, with honorary titles, scholastic degrees, etc. | Race, Religious denomination, and Caste, if any. | Occupation and Address. | How and when elected. |
|---|---|---|---|---|---|---|---|
| 113 | Bengal. | N.-W. P. | Etawah. | Lala Suraj Prasad Johari. | Hindu Kshatriya | Jeweller ... ... | At a Public Meeting held on the 22nd November 1891, at Etawah. |
| 114 | " | " | Aligarh. | Hafiz Abdurrahim ... | Mahomedan. | Pleader ... ... | At a Public Meeting held at Aligarh on the 20th December 1891. |
| 115 | " | " | " | Pandit Udai Ram ... | Hindu Brahmin. | Private Service ... ... | do. |
| 116 | " | " | Farukhabad. | Mr. Gopal Rao Hari Puntaker. | Mahratta Brahmin. | Secretary, Vaidik Samaj ... | At a Public Meeting held at Farukhabad on the 16th November 1891. |
| 117 | " | " | Azimgarh. | Munshi Basder Sahai ... | Hindu Kayastha. | Second Master, C. M. H. School. | At a Public Meeting held at Azimgarh on the 13th December 1891. |
| 118 | " | " | Dehra Doon. | Lala Baldeo Singh ... | Arya Mahajan. | Zemindar, Banker, and House Proprietor. | At a Public Meeting held at Dehra Doon on the 9th December 1891. |
| 119 | " | " | Muttra. | Babu Radhe Lal Shorma. | Vedic Brahmin. | Vedic Updeshak ... | At a Public Meeting held at Brindabun on the 16th December 1891. |
| 120 | " | Oudh. | Lucknow. | Nawab Hashmat Alikhan. | Mahomedan. | Rais ... ... | At a Public Meeting held at Lucknow on the 17th December 1891. |
| 121 | " | " | " | Babu Bansi Lal Singh ... | Hindu Kshatriya. | Pleader, High Court, and Municipal Commissioner. | do. |
| 122 | " | " | " | Pandit Shri Kishen ... | Kashmiri Brahmin. | Government Pensioner | do. |
| 123 | " | " | " | Pandit Sham Narayan Masladan | do. | Zemindar and Municipal Commissioner. | do. |
| 124 | " | " | " | Pandit Sheo Bihari Lal Misra. | Hindu Brahmin. | Pleader and Secretary Jalsa Tahzib. | do. |
| 125 | " | " | " | Pandit Lakshman Prasad Brahmachari. | Brahmin. | Missionary ... ... | do. |
| 126 | " | " | " | Revd. R. C. Bose, M.A. ... | Christian. | do. ... | do. |
| 127 | " | " | " | Munshi Gunga Pershad Varma. | Hindu Kshatriya. | Editor and Proprietor "Advocate" and "Hindusthani," Municipal Commissioner. | do. |
| 128 | " | " | " | Babu Bhuban Mohan Ray | Bengali Brahmo. | Merchant and Secretary to the Brahmo Samaj at Lucknow. | do. |
| 129 | " | " | " | Babu Heera Lall Sircar. | Bengali Kayastha | Homœopathic Practitioner ... | do. |
| 130 | " | Punjab. | Lahore. | Mr. A. O. Hume, C.B. ... | European | Late Indian Civil Service, Fellow of the Calcutta University. | At a Public Meeting held at Lahore on the 13th December 1891. |
| 131 | " | " | " | Capt. A. T. Banon ... | do. | Late Bengal Staff Corps, Zemindar, Kulu, Kangra. | do. |
| 132 | " | " | " | Lala Murlidhar ... | Hindu Vaishya. | Pleader, Umballa ... | do. |
| 133 | " | " | Amritsar | Baba Narain Singh ... | Sikh Guru. | Pleader ... ... | At a Public Meeting held at Amritsar on the 20th December 1891. |
| 134 | " | " | " | Sodhi Nund Kumar Sing | do. | Preacher ... ... | do. |
| 135 | Bombay | Sindh. | Kurrachi. | Mr. Shewakram Awatrai. | Hindu Amil. | Pleader and Municipal Commissioner. | By a Meeting of the Sindh Sabha. |
| 136 | " | " | Sukkur. | Mr. Pesumul Zowkiram Samit. | do. | Pleader and Vice-President, Sukkur Municipality. | do. |
| 137 | " | Surat. | Surat. | Mr. Hardeoram Nanabhai Haridas. | Valmik Kayastha. | Landowner ... | By a Meeting of the Praja Hit Vardhak Sabha. |
| 138 | " | Sholapur | Sholapur. | Rao Bahadur P. L. Nagpurkar. | Brahmin. | Pleader, Chairman, Local Board, Municipal Commissioner. | At a Public Meeting held at Sholapur on the 21st October 1891. |
| 139 | " | " | " | Rao Saheb S. K. Kirloskar, B.A. | do. | Pleader, High Court, and Municipal Commissioner. | do. |
| 140 | " | " | " | Rao Saheb Goutam Moti Chaund Shaha. | Jain. | Pleader and Municipal Commissioner. | do. |
| 141 | " | " | " | Rao Saheb Anna Anandrao Deshmukh. | Singayat. | Pleader ... | do. |
| 142 | " | " | " | Mr. Ganesh Krishna Autrolkar. | Brahmin. | do. ... | do. |
| 143 | " | " | " | Mr. Vithal Shamrao Katkar. | do. | do. ... | do. |
| 144 | " | " | " | Mr. Bala Saheb Deshmukh. | Mahratta Kunbi. | Inamdar ... ... | do. |
| 145 | " | Belgaum | Belgaum. | Rao Saheb Sadashiv Balkrishna Bhate. | Mahratta Brahmin. | Pleader, District Court, Municipal Commissioner, Member, Local Board, Secretary, District Association. | At a Public Meeting held at Belgaum on the 24th December 1891. |

| Number. | Presidency or Government. | Congress Circle. | Electoral Division. | Names in full of Delegates, with honorary titles, scholastic degrees, etc. | Race, Religious denomination, and Caste, if any. | Occupation and Address. | How and when elected. |
|---|---|---|---|---|---|---|---|
| 146 | Bombay. | Bhusawal. | Bhusawal. | Rao Saheb Chintaman Bapojee Morgankar. | Deccan Brahmin. | Pleader and Vice-Chairman Municipality, Bhusawal. | At a Public Meeting held at Bhusawal on the 4th November 1891. |
| 147 | " | " | " | Mr. Vithal Govind Dastane. | Mahratta Brahmin. | Pleader ... ... | do. |
| 148 | " | " | " | Mr. Kesheo Ballal Sahasra Buddhe. | Deccan Brahmin. | Railway Contractor and Municipal Commissioner. | do. |
| 149 | " | " | " | Mr. Sakharam Ganesh Patankar. | do. | Pleader and Municipal Commissioner. | do. |
| 150 | " | Ahmednagar. | Ahmednagar. | Rao Saheb Hari Ram Chandra Saraph. | Mahratta Brahmin. | Pleader and Municipal Commissioner. | At a Public Meeting held at Ahmednagar on the 21st November 1891. |
| 151 | " | " | " | Sheikh Heyat Saheb ... | Mahomedan. | Inamdar of Akola ... | do. |
| 152 | " | " | " | Mr. Dattatraya Ganesh Gokhale. | Mahratta Brahmin. | School Master ... ... | do. |
| 153 | " | " | " | Mr. Pandhari Nath Bapuji Bhalerao. | do. | Vakil ... ... | do. |
| 154 | " | " | " | Mr. Gobind Bapaji Pawar. | Hindu Mahratta. | School Master ... ... | do. |
| 155 | " | " | " | Mr. K. B. Limaye ... | Mahratta Brahmin. | Editor, "Jagada Darsha" ... | do. |
| 156 | " | " | " | Mr. Shankar Vinayek Vable. | do. | Pleadar ... ... | do. |
| 157 | " | " | " | Mr. Vasudev Vishnu Ketkar. | do. | Pleader and Member, Local Board. | do. |
| 158 | " | " | " | Mr. Bahvant Babaji Deshpande, B. A. | do. | Landholder ... ... | do. |
| 159 | " | " | " | Mr. Ganesh Krishna Dabholkar. | do. | Jaghirdar Akolnir, Member, Local Board. | do. |
| 160 | " | " | " | Mr. Sada Shiv Vyankatesh Jog. | do. | Pleader ... ... | do. |
| 161 | " | Deccan. | Poona. | Mr. Vishnu Narayan Apte. | Mahratta Brahmin. | Assistant Manager and Accountant, Deccan Paper Mills. | At a Public Meeting held at Poona on the 9th December 1891. |
| 162 | " | " | " | Mr. Vinayak Narain Apte. | do. | Merchant ... ... | do. |
| 163 | " | " | " | Mr. Vasudeo Laxaman Athavale. | do. | do. ... ... | do. |
| 164 | " | " | " | Mr. Bal Gungadhur Tilak B.A., L.L.B. | do. | Editor "Mahratta" and "Kedari." | do. |
| 165 | " | " | " | Rao Saheb Mahadeo Ballal Namjoshi. | do. | Municipal Commissioner and Secretary, Reay Museum. | do. |
| 166 | " | " | " | Mr. Shankar Ganesh Deshpande, B.A., L.L.B. | do. | Pleader ... ... | do. |
| 167 | " | " | " | Mr. Ramchandra Keshav Limaye. | do. | do. ... ... | do |
| 168 | " | " | " | Mr. Narayan Babaji Kanit Kar. | do. | Pleader and Trustee, Devasthan. | do. |
| 169 | " | " | " | Mr. Vaman Vishnu Lele | do. | Pleader, Secretary, Indo-American Dye House Company. | do. |
| 170 | " | " | " | Mr. Madhav Krishna Deshmukh. | do. | Merchant and Moneylender | do |
| 171 | " | " | " | Rao Bahadur Vishnu Moreshvar Bhide. | do. | Pensioned, 1st Class Judge. Chairman, Poona Sarvajanik Sabha, Honorary Magistrate. | do. |
| 172 | " | " | " | Mr. Gopal Krishna Gokhale, B.A. | do. | Professor, Fergusson College, Editor, Sarvajanik Sabha's Quarterly Journal. | do. |
| 173 | " | " | " | Rao Saheb Raghunath Ramchandra Avasti. | do. | Banker, Pensioned Sub-Engineer. | do. |
| 174 | " | " | " | Mr. Hari Narain Apte ... | Arya | Journalist and Editor of "Karmanuka." | do. |
| 175 | " | " | " | Mr. Krishnarao Purushottam Bhat, B.A. | Brahmin | ...... | do. |
| 176 | " | " | " | Mr. Pandurang Rangnath Shiralkar. | Mahratta Brahmin. | Merchant ... | do. |
| 177 | " | " | " | Mr. Keshav Pandurang Godbole. | do. | Head Master, City School ... | At a Public Meeting held at Poona on the 18th December 1891. |
| 178 | " | " | " | Mr. Hari Govind Limaye | do. | ...... | do. |
| 179 | " | " | " | Mr. Sitaram Ganesh Deodhar, B.A. | do. | School Master ... | do. |
| 180 | " | " | " | Mr. Ramkrishna Bhikaji Kulkarni. | do. | do. ... ... | do. |
| 181 | " | " | " | Mr. Krishnarao Govind Limaye, B.A. | do. | ...... | do. |
| 182 | " | " | " | Mr. Narayan Sakharam Panse, B.A. | do. | School Master ... ... | do. |

| Number. | Presidency or Government. | Congress Circle. | Electoral Division. | Names in full of Delegates, with honorary titles, scholastic degrees, etc. | Race, Religious denomination, and Caste if any. | Occupation and Address. | How and when elected. |
|---|---|---|---|---|---|---|---|
| 183 | Bombay. | Deccan. | Poona. | Rao Saheb Kashinath Govind Natu. | Mahratta Brahmin. | Pleader and Municipal Commissioner. | At a Public Meeting held at Poona on the 18th December 1891. |
| 184 | " | " | " | Rao Saheb Naro Bhaskar Deodhar. | do. | Member, Local Board, Sirur of Poona Zillah. | do. |
| 185 | " | " | " | Mr. Ganesh Narayan Ghotavdeker. | do. | Merchant, Agriculturist and Editor of "Shet Kari." | do. |
| 186 | " | " | " | Mr. Sydenham Smith ... | European | Pleader ... ... | do. |
| 187 | " | " | Dhulia. | Rao Bahadur Govind Rao Ramchandra Garud. | Brahmin. | do. ... | At a Public Meeting held at Dhulia, on the 6th November 1891. |
| 188 | " | " | " | Mr. Krishnarao Vasudeo Garud. | do. | Merchant ... ... | do. |
| 189 | " | " | Satara. | Mr Dattatraya Balvant Parasnis. | Mahratta Brahmin. | Moneylender and Editor, "Maharasthra Kokil." | At a Public Meeting held at Satara on the 22nd November 1891. |
| 190 | " | " | " | Rao Saheb Govindkrishna Ranade. | do. | Pleader, Inamdar and Municipal Commissioner. | do. |
| 191 | " | " | " | Mr. Ganesh Gopal Kuver. | do. | Pleader ... ... | do. |
| 192 | " | " | " | Mr. Kaikhasru Adarji Ghasvala. | Parsee | Merchant and Contractor ... | do. |
| 193 | " | " | " | Mr. Ganesh Ballal Phausalkar. | Mahratta Brahmin. | Pleader ... ... | do. |
| 194 | " | " | " | Mr. Narhar Govind Ranade. | do. | Inamdar and Moneylender ... | do. |
| 195 | " | " | " | Mr. Ganesh Shridhar Ranade. | do. | Inamdar ... ... | do. |
| 196 | " | " | " | Mr. Sakhram Nilkant Bapu Saheb Kahere. | do. | Inamdar and Moneylender ... | do. |
| 197 | " | " | " | Mr. Raghunath Pandurang Karandikar. | do. | Pleader, High Court ... | do. |
| 198 | " | " | " | Mr. Vasudeo Ramchandra Jolekar, B.A., LL.B. | do. | do. ... | do. |
| 199 | " | " | " | Rao Bahadur Ganesh Pandurang Agte | do. | Inamdar and Honorary Magistrate, Vice-President, Municipality, District and Local Boards. | do. |
| 200 | " | " | " | Rao Saheb Balvant Shridhar Sahasra Buddhe. | do. | Pleader and Municipal Commissioner. | do. |
| 201 | " | " | Wai Taluka. | Rao Saheb Ramchandra Krishna Kothavale. | do. | Inamdar and Moneylender, Chairman, Municipality, Member, District and Local Boards. | At a Public Meeting held at Wai on the 19th November 1891. |
| 202 | " | " | Nasik. | Rao Saheb Janardan Raghunath Nimkar. | Mahratta Brahmin. | Pleader, Municipal Commissioner, and Member, Local Board. | At a Public Meeting held at Nasik on the 22nd November 1891. |
| 203 | " | " | " | Mr. Vamanrao Balkrishna Ranade. | Arya. | Editor, "Duyaw Chakshu ... | do. |
| 204 | " | " | " | Rao Saheb Vamanrao Mahadeo Pradhan. | Mahratta Prabhu. | Pleader, Municipal Commissioner, Member, Local Board. | do. |
| 205 | " | " | " | Mr. Balwant Ganesh Nowle. | Hindu Mahratta. | Private Mukhtear and Vakil Sinuar. | do. |
| 206 | " | " | " | Mr. Sitaram Damodar Bhonde. | Mahratta Brahmin | Banker, Municipal Commissioner and Member, Local Board. | do. |
| 207 | " | " | " | Mr. Sridhar Gopal Pattekar. | do. | Vakil and Mukhtear ... | do. |
| 208 | " | " | " | Rao Saheb Gangadhar Nar-sinah Ketkar. | do. | Pleader, Municipal Commissioner and Member, Local Board. | do. |
| 209 | " | " | " | Mr. Narayan Vishnu Bam. | do. | Preacher ... ... | o. |
| 210 | " | " | " | Rao Saheb Anant Roop Kavale. | do. | Pleader and Municipal Commissioner | do. |
| 211 | " | " | " | Rao Saheb Ganesh Raoji Kshri Sagar. | do. | Pleader, Member of Local and District Boards. | do. |
| 212 | " | " | " | Mr. Keshav Mohadeorao Wadkar | do. | Merchant ... | do. |
| 213 | " | " | " | Rao Saheb Purushotam Sadashiv Matange. | do. | Pleader and Municipal Commissioner. | do. |
| 214 | " | " | Kolhapur. | Mr. Vishnu Govind Kale | do. | Teacher, Mission High School | At a Public Meeting held at Kolhapur on the 20th December 1891. |
| 215 | " | " | " | Mr. Ramchandra Narayan Gokhale. | do. | Pleader ... ... | do. |
| 216 | " | " | " | Mr. Ramchandra Narsingh Kulkarni. | do. | Teacher ... ... | do. |
| 217 | " | " | " | Mr. Ramchandra Baldeo Apte. | do. | Pleader ... ... | do. |

| Number. | Presidency or Government. | Congress Circle. | Electoral Division. | Names in full of Delegates, with honorary titles, scholastic degrees, etc. | Race, Religious denomination, and Caste, if any. | Occupation and Address. | How and when elected. |
|---|---|---|---|---|---|---|---|
| 218 | Bombay. | Deccan. | Kolhapur. | Mr. Chintamon Hari Sohoni. | Mahratta Brahmin. | Pleader, Inamdar ... | At a Public Meeting held at Kolhapur on the 20th December 1891. |
| 219 | " | " | " | Mr. Vishnu Krishna Bashingkar, B.A., LL.B. | do. | Pleader ... ... | do. |
| 220 | " | " | " | Mr. Dattatrya Pandurang Prani. | do. | Teacher, Mission High School | do. |
| 221 | " | " | " | Mr. Krishnaji Dadaji Kulkarni. | do. | Merchant ... ... | do. |
| 222 | " | " | " | Mr. Dattatrya Dadaji Pandit. | do. | Landholder and Merchant ... | do. |
| 223 | " | " | " | Mr. Shankar Raghunath Gokhale | do. | Shastree Manager Vidya Vilass | do. |
| 224 | " | " | " | Mr. Ramchandra Narayan Pinge. | do. | Pleader ... ... | do. |
| 225 | " | " | Walva. | Mr. Ramchandra Vishnu Bhagwat. | do. | Pleader and Village Munsiff, Municipal Commissioner. | At a Public Meeting held at Islampur on the 29th November 1891. |
| 226 | " | " | " | Mr. Kondo Kesheo Sahasrabuddhe. | do. | Pleader and Municipal Commissioner. | do. |
| 227 | " | " | " | Mr. Krishnaji Laxman Desai. | do. | Pleader ... ... | do. |
| 228 | " | " | " | Mr. Hari Narayan Tagore. | do. | Merchant ... ... | do. |
| 229 | " | " | " | Rao Saheb Govind Dhondeo Limaye. | do. | Vakil, Municipal Commissioner, Member, District and Local Boards. | do. |
| 230 | " | " | " | Mr. Dinker Raoji Kuvera. | do. | Pleader ... ... | do. |
| 231 | " | " | Bijapur. | Mr. Pandurang Anant Desai, B.A., L.L.B. | do. | Pleader and Landholder ... | At a Public Meeting held at Bijapur on the 20th December 1891. |
| 232 | " | " | " | Rao Saheb Raghavendra Krishna. | do. | Pleader, Chairman, Municipality, Vice-President, District and Local Boards. | do. |
| 233 | " | " | " | Mr. Krishnaji Ramchandra Kalaindekar. | do. | Pleader, and Chairman, Local Board. | do. |
| 234 | " | " | " | Mr. Datatraya Govind Joshi. | do. | Pleader ... | do. |
| 235 | " | " | " | Mr. Sido Timaji Badami | do. | Pleader and Landholder ... | do. |
| 236 | " | " | Yeola. | Mr. Khemchand Dajiba Guzrathi. | Hindu Guzrathi. | Banker and Cloth Merchant, Municipal Commissioner. | At a Public Meeting held at Yeola on the 22nd December 1891. |
| 237 | " | " | " | Mr. Jagjivan Khemchand Guzrathi. | do. | Banker and Cloth Merchant | do. |
| 238 | " | " | Kanara. | Rao Saheb Pundalik Narayan Pandit. | Mahratta Brahmin. | Pleader ... | At a Public Meeting held at Silsil on the 16th December 1891. |
| 239 | " | Bombay. | Bombay. | Mr. Manickaba Hormusji Nicholson. | Parsee. | Broker ... | At a Meeting of the Presidency Association on the 16th December 1891. |
| 240 | " | " | " | Mr. Goverdhun Dass Soonder Dass. | Bhatia. | Merchant and Mill Agent ... | do. |
| 241 | " | " | " | Mr. Purmanund Dass Jeevun Dass. | do. | Cotton Merchant ... | do. |
| 242 | " | " | " | Mr. Goverdhun Dass Jaithabhoy. | do. | do. ... | do. |
| 243 | " | " | " | Mr. Bhugwan Dass Jaithabhoy. | do. | do. ... | do. |
| 244 | " | " | " | Mr. Mahadeo Vaman Bhat, B.A., L.L.B. | Mahratta Brahmin. | Pleader, High Court ... | do. |
| 245 | " | " | " | Mr. Narayan Gunaji, Welinkar, M. A. | Arya. | Professor, Wilson College ... | do. |
| 246 | " | " | " | Mr. Daji Abaji Khare, B.A., L.L.B. | Prahmin. | Vakil, High Court, Fellow of the Bombay University. | do. |
| 247 | " | " | " | Mr. Purshottam Parsharam Khare, B.A., L.L.B. | Mahratta Brahmin. | Pleader, High Court, and Law Professor. | do. |
| 248 | " | " | " | Mr. Sorabji Kavasji Khambata. | Parsee. | Broker ... | do. |
| 249 | " | " | " | Mr. Shapurshah Hormasji Hodivala | do. | 3, Marine Street ... | do. |
| 250 | " | " | " | Mr. Gangadhur Sadashiv Gokhale. L.C.E. | Mahratta Brahmin. | Architect and Engineer ... | do. |
| 251 | " | " | " | Mr. Jagmohan Dass Vandravan Dass. | Dasa Pervad Bania. | Merchant and Banker, Justice of the Peace, Councillor, Municipal Corporation. | do. |
| 252 | " | " | " | Mr. Mahadev Bhaskar Chanbul, B.A., L L.B. | Kayastha Prabhu. | Pleader, High Court ... | do. |
| 253 | " | " | " | Mr. Sitanath Gopinath Ajinkya. | Arya. | Pleader, High Court, late Subordinate Judge. | do. |
| 254 | " | " | " | Mr. Gonesh R. Kirloskar, M.A., L.L.B. | Mahratta Brahmin. | Justice of the Peace, Fellow of the Bombay University. | do. |

| Number. | Presidency or Government. | Congress Circle. | Electoral Division. | Names in full of Delegates with honorary titles, scholastic degrees, etc. | Race, Religious denomination, and Caste, if any. | Occupation and Address. | How and when elected. |
|---|---|---|---|---|---|---|---|
| 255 | Bombay. | Bombay. | Bombay. | Mr. Balaji Abaji Bhagwat, B.A., L.L.B. | Mahratta, Brahmin. | Pleader, High Court. | At a Meeting of the Presidency Association on the 16th December 1891. |
| 256 | „ | „ | „ | Mr. Pherozeshah M. Mehta, M.A. | Parsee. | Barrister-at-Law. Councillor of the Municipal Corporation, Fellow of the Bombay University. | do. |
| 257 | „ | „ | „ | Mr. Dinshaw Edulji Wacha. | do. | Merchant, Councillor of the Municipal Corporation. | do. |
| 258 | „ | „ | „ | Mr. Sadashiva Waman Kane. | Brahmin. | Medical Practitioner ... | do. |
| 259 | „ | „ | „ | Mr. Hari Sitaram Dikshit. | do. | ...... | do. |
| 260 | „ | „ | „ | Munshi Sheikh Hossein | Mahomedan. | Preacher and Agriculturist ... | do. |
| 261 | „ | „ | Colaba. | Mr. Vinayek Shivarao Dighe Dharkar. | Kayastha Prabhu. | Merchant, Inamdar, Khot, Municipal Commissioner, Member, Local Board, Director, Penkar Spinning and Weaving Company. | At a Public Meeting held at Alibag on the 12th December 1891. |
| 262 | „ | „ | „ | Mr. Waman Bapuji Deva. | Brahmin. | Landholder and Merchant ... | do. |
|  | „ | „ | „ | Rao Saheb Chimnaji Narayan Bhate. | do. | Pleader ... | do. |
| 264 | „ | „ | Bassin. | Munshi Raghunath Moroba Ryker. | Hindu. | Landlord, Pensioner, Municipal Commissioner, Member, Local Board. | At a Public Meeting held at Bassin on the 25th October 1891. |
| 265 | „ | „ | „ | Munshi Bhau Raghunath Thakur. | Brahmin. | Merchant and Landholder ... | do. |
| 266 | „ | „ | Ratnagiri. | Rao Saheb Dhondo Mohadeo Barve. | do. | Pleader, Municipal Commissioner and Member, Local Board. | At a Public Meeting held at Ratnagiri on the 8th November 1891. |
| 267 | „ | „ | „ | Mr. Gangadhar Laxman Oka. | do. | Sowkar and Landholder ... | do. |
| 268 | „ | „ | „ | Mr. Damodar Krishna Karandikar, B.A. | do. | Sub-Editor, "Native Opinion" | do. |
| 269 | „ | „ | Thana. | Mr. Balkrishna Narayan Bhajekar, B.A., L.L.B. | do. | Pleader, High Court ... | At a Public Meeting held at Thana on the 12th December 1891. |
| 270 | „ | „ | „ | Mr. Lakshman Ballal Joglekar. | do. | Pleader ... | do. |
| 271 | „ | „ | „ | Mr. Hari Lakshman Patel. | do. | Pleader and Member, District Board. | do. |
| 272 | Govt. of India. | Berar. | Sarvajanik Sabha. | Mr. Ganesh Shrikrishna Khaparde, B.A., L L B. | Mahratta Brahmin. | Pleader, High Court, Landholder and Malguzar, Municipal Commissioner, Chairman, District Board. | At a Meeting of the Berar Sarvajanik Sabha on the 23rd October 1891. |
| 273 | „ | „ | „ | Mr. Rangnath Narsing Mudholkar, B A., L.L.B. | do. | Pleader, High Court, Landholder and Municipal Commissioner. | do. |
| 274 | „ | „ | „ | Mr. Prahlad Narayan Jog, B.A., L L.B. | do. | Pleader, High Court, and Banker. | do. |
| 275 | „ | „ | „ | Mr. Ganesh Nagesh Sahasrabudhe. | do. | Pleader ... | do. |
| 276 | „ | „ | „ | Mr. Gulam Ahmed Sowdagar. | Mahomedan. | Zemindar, Member, Local Board. | do. |
| 277 | „ | „ | „ | Mr. Balkrishna Hari Karandikar. | Mahratta Brahmin. | Pleader, Municipal Commissioner, and Member, Local Board. | do. |
| 278 | „ | „ | Amraoti. | Mr. Moro Vishwanath Joshi, B.A., L L B. | do. | Pleader, High Court ... | At a Public Meeting held at Amraoti on the 21st October 1891. |
| 279 | „ | „ | „ | Mr. Antaji Govind Keskar. | do. | Pleader and Vice-Chairman, Municipality. | do. |
| 280 | „ | „ | „ | Mr. Yeswant Govind Keskar. | do. | Proprietor and Editor, "Pramad Sindhu." | do. |
| 281 | „ | „ | „ | Mr. Tukaram Padmajee Deshmukh. | Hindu Kshatriya. | Cultivator ... | do. |
| 282 | „ | „ | „ | Mr. Balwant Ramchandra Augal, B.A., L.L.B. | Mahratta Brahmin | Pleader, High Court ... | do. |
| 283 | „ | „ | „ | Dr. Ramchandra Narsinh Mudholkar, L. M.S. | do. | Medical Practitioner | do. |
| 284 | „ | „ | „ | Mr. Dipchand Mangniram. | Jain Marwadi. | Banker and Moneylender ... | do. |
| 285 | „ | „ | „ | Mr. Narhar Bhagwant Deshpande. | Mahratta Brahmin. | Landholder and Inamdar ... | do. |
| 286 | „ | „ | „ | Mr. Madho Laxaman Changde. | do. | Pleader and Landholder ... | do. |
| 287 | „ | „ | „ | Mr. Tukaram Malharao Kale. | Kunbi. | Banker and Sowkar ... | do. |

| Number. | Presidency or Government. | Congress Circle. | Electoral Division. | Name in full of Delegates with honorary titles, scholastic degrees, etc. | Race, Religious denomination, and Caste, if any. | Occupation and Address. | How and when elected. |
|---|---|---|---|---|---|---|---|
| 288 | Govt. of India. | Berar. | Amraoti. | Mr. Dariaji Chenduj Chuke. | Mali. | Banker ... ... | At a Public Meeting held at Amraoti on the 21st October 1891. |
| 289 | " | " | " | Mr. Tukaram Shamras Deshmukh. | Kshatriya | Cultivator ... ... | do. |
| 290 | " | " | " | Mr. Raghwendra Sakharam Kalegiri. | Mahratta Brahmin | Pleader and Inamdar ... | do. |
| 291 | " | " | " | Mr. Chintaman Ramchandra Kelkar. | do. | Editor, "Pramod Sindhu" ... | do. |
| 292 | " | " | " | Mr. Shivapa Gurapa Kapshe. | Singayat | Contractor ... ... | do. |
| 293 | " | " | " | Mr. Mahadev Gangadhar Wamle, B.A., LL.B. | Mahratta. Brahmin. | Pleader, High Court ... | do. |
| 294 | " | " | " | Mr. Vinayek Savlaram Oak. | do. | Pleader ... ... | do. |
| 295 | " | " | " | Mr. Tikamdas Bhivraj ... | Marwadi. | Sowkar ... ... | do. |
| 296 | " | " | " | Mr. Pandurang Govind | Mahratta Brahmin. | Pleader and Landholder ... | do. |
| 297 | " | " | " | Mr. Mahimaji Sonagi Patel. | Kunbi. | ...... ... | do. |
| 298 | " | " | " | Mr. Gopal Narayan Deshpande. | Mahratta Brahmin. | Pleader and Landholder ... | do. |
| 299 | " | " | " | Mr. Krishnaji Bapuji Kide. | do. | Banker and Member, Local Board. | do. |
| 300 | " | " | " | Mr. Bahiraodas Jethmal. | Marwadi. | Banker ... ... | do. |
| 301 | " | " | " | Mr. Bhimrao Bapuji ... | Brahmin. | Pleader and Member, Local Board. | do. |
| 302 | " | " | " | Mr. Vithul Atwaram Bhudang. | Mahratta Brahmin. | Sowkar, Member, Local Board | do. |
| 303 | " | " | " | Mr. Balkrishna Madhab. | do. | Banker, Agriculturist and Member, Local Board. | do. |
| 304 | " | " | " | Mr. Kushal Sing Budhusing. | Rajput. | Banker ... ... | do. |
| 305 | " | " | " | Mr. Nicholas Godfrey ... | European Christian. | Pleader ... ... | do. |
| 306 | " | " | " | Mr. Shivaram Aochutji Patel. | Kunbi. | Agriculturist ... ... | do |
| 307 | " | " | " | Mr. Sakharam Chimnajee Gole. | Mahratta Brahmin. | Landholder and Editor, "Shetkari." | do. |
| 308 | " | " | " | Mr. Vishwanath Kashinath Kale. | do. | Pleader ... ... | do. |
| 309 | " | " | " | Mr. Vasudeo Narayan Jog. | do. | Pleader, Banker, and Municipal Commissioner. | do. |
| 310 | " | " | " | Mr. Lahuram Hiralal ... | Hindu Kalal. | Abkari Contractor ... | do. |
| 311 | " | " | " | Mr. Lakshman Ramkrishna Ghude. | Mahratta Brahmin. | Landholder and Moneylender. | do. |
| 312 | " | " | " | Mr. Ramchandra Ballal Godbole. | Mahratta Brahmin. | Educationalist ... ... | do |
| 313 | " | " | " | Mr. Keshav Balvant Deshpande. | do. | Banker and Landholder ... | do. |
| 314 | " | " | " | Mr. Shitaram Tukaram Patel. | do. | Landholder ... ... | do. |
| 315 | " | " | " | Mr. Sardarshing Umrao Sing. | Rajput. | Banker and Landholder ... | do. |
| 316 | " | " | " | Ramkrishen Sakharam Pethe. | Hindu Kalal. | Landholder ... ... | do. |
| 317 | " | " | " | Mr. Shitaram Govindram Pethe. | do. | do. ... | do. |
| 318 | " | " | " | Mr. Govind Narayen Kane. | Christian. | Pleader ... ... | do. |
| 319 | " | " | " | Mr. Sawlaram Lakshman Oak. | Mahratta Brahmin. | Landholder, Merchant and Moneylender. | do. |
| 320 | " | " | " | Mr. Mahboob Rant Hamja Rant. | Mahomedan. | Landholder ... ... | do. |
| 321 | " | " | " | Mr. Gopal Waman Bapat, B.A. | Mahratta Brahmin | Law Student ... ... | do. |
| 322 | " | " | " | Mr. Ramchandra Renko Dole. | Mahratta Brahmin | Banker, Landholder, and Member, Local Board. | do. |
| 323 | " | " | " | Mr. Balkrishna Jairam Pendke. | do. | Banker and Municipal Commissioner. | do. |
| 324 | " | " | " | Rao Saheb Rambilas Pokarmal. | Marwadi | Banker and Landlord ... | do. |
| 325 | " | " | " | Mr. Srinivas Raghunath | Mahratta Brahmin. | Pleader ... ... | do. |
| 326 | " | " | " | Mr. Kondo Balaji ... | do. | do. ... ... | do. |
| 327 | " | " | " | Mr. Siddesvar Krishna Joshi. | do. | Pleader and Landholder ... | do. |
| 328 | " | " | " | Mr. Padmanabha Raoj Dande. | do. | Pleader ... ... | do. |

| Number. | Presidency or Government. | Congress Circle. | Electoral Division. | Names in full of Delegates, with honorary titles, scholastic degrees, etc. | Race, Religious denomination, and Caste if any. | Occupation and Address. | How and when elected. |
|---|---|---|---|---|---|---|---|
| 329 | Govt. of India. | Berar. | Amraoti. | Mr. Manok Bansi ... | Hindu Chatarpan. | Banker ... ... | At a Public Meeting held at Amraoti on the 21st October 1891. |
| 330 | " | " | " | Mr. Moro Ramchandra Pandit. | Mahratta Brahmin. | Landholder and Moneylender | do. |
| 331 | " | " | Akola | Rao Saheb Deorao Vinayek. | do. | Pleader, Landholder and Municipal Commissioner. | At a Public Meeting held at Akola on the 15th December 1891. |
| 332 | " | " | " | Mr. Shankar Govind ... | do. | Pleader ... ... | do. |
| 333 | " | " | " | Mr. Vyankatesh Ramchandra Mudholkar. | do. | Editor, "Vaidarbha," Honorary Secretary, Municipal Committee. | do. |
| 334 | " | " | " | Mr. Laloo Vithobo Patel | Kunbi | Moneylender and Agriculturist. | do. |
| 335 | " | " | " | Mr. Vishwanath Ramjee | Mahratta Brahmin. | Banker and Agriculturist ... | do. |
| 336 | " | " | " | Mr. Govind Ramrao Deshpande. | do. | ......... | do. |
| 337 | " | " | " | Mr. Hari Ramchandra Anwiker. | Hindu Krishnapachi. | Editor and Proprietor, "Shudha Varadhi," and Municipal Commissioner. | do. |
| 338 | " | " | " | Mr. Dattatraya Vishnu Bhagwat, B.A., LL.B. | Mahratta Brahmin. | Pleader, High Court, Vice-Chairman, District Board. | do. |
| 339 | " | " | " | Mr. Ramchandra Gopalrao Deshpande. | do. | Landed Proprietor ... | do. |
| 340 | " | " | " | Mr. Gopalrao Govind Mote. | do. | Banker ... ... | do. |
| 341 | " | " | " | Mr. Dinanath Gopal ... | do. | Sowkar and Member, Local Board. | do. |
| 342 | " | " | " | Mr. Krishnarao Ganesh | Hindu Parbhu. | Pleader ... ... | do. |
| 343 | " | " | " | Mr. Anant Vishun Bhagwat. | Mahratta Brahmin. | do. ... ... | do. |
| 344 | " | " | " | Mr Renukadas Balvant | do. | Jaghirdar and Merchant ... | do. |
| 345 | " | " | " | Mr. Trimbuck Waman ... | do. | Merchant ... ... | do. |
| 346 | " | " | " | Mr. Anandrao Ambadas Lote. | do. | Banker ... ... | do. |
| 347 | " | " | " | Mr. Martand Laxman Gupte. | do. | Pleader ... ... | do. |
| 348 | " | " | " | Mr. Jaikrishna Bagojee | do. | Banker and Member, Local Board. | do. |
| 349 | " | " | " | Mr. Onkardas Lalchand | Jain Marwari. | Banker ... ... | do. |
| 350 | " | " | " | Mr. Venkatish Krishna Desai. | Mahratta Brahmin. | Pleader and Municipal Commissioner. | do. |
| 351 | " | " | " | Mr. Ramchandra Shastri | do. | Preacher and Physician ... | do. |
| 352 | " | " | " | Mr. Govind Pandharinath. | do. | Banker's Agent ... | do. |
| 353 | " | " | " | Mr. Shivram Anant ... | do | do. ... ... | do. |
| 354 | " | " | " | Mr. Balkrishna Waman Udgirkar. | do. | Pleader ... ... | do. |
| 355 | " | " | " | Mr Shankar Patel ... | Kunbi | Agriculturist, Member of Local Board. | do. |
| 356 | " | " | " | Mr. Surajmul Govindram. | Hindu Agarwalla. | Banker and Municipal Commissioner. | do. |
| 357 | " | " | " | Mr. Balwant Vinayek Digambar. | Mahratta Brahmin. | Banker and Agriculturist ... | do. |
| 358 | " | " | " | Mr. Bhagu Sing Chain Sing. | Rajput | Banker's Agent nd Agriculturist. | do. |
| 359 | " | " | " | Mr. Ramchandra Vinayek. | Hindu | D. P. W. Contractor ... | do. |
| 360 | " | " | " | Mr. Ganesh Hanmant Thombray. | Mahratta Brahmin. | Moneylender and Agriculturist. | do |
| 361 | " | " | " | Mr. Maruti Ganesh Asarkot. | do. | Banker, Agriculturist, Proprietor of Ginning Factory, and Vice-Chairman of the Local Board. | do. |
| 362 | " | " | " | Mr. Popatlal Parasharam. | Jain Shrawak. | Banker ... ... | do. |
| 363 | " | " | " | Mr. Hansilal Panachand. | Hindu Guzerathi. | do. ... ... | do. |
| 364 | " | " | " | Mr. Mesaji Shivaji ... | Kunbi. | Banker and Member, District Board. | do. |
| 365 | " | " | " | Mr. Pandurang Bapuji Rajanderker. | Mahratta Brahmin. | Cultivator ... ... | do. |
| 366 | " | " | Wun. | Mr. Vithul Ganesh Sarmokadam. | do. | Jaghirdar ... ... | At a Public Meeting held at Yeotmal on the 29th November 1891. |
| 367 | " | " | " | Mr. Wasudeo Balvant Sarmokadam. | do. | do. ... ... | do. |

| Number. | Presidency or Government. | Congress Circle. | Electoral Division. | Names in full of Delegates with honorary titles, scholastic degrees, etc. | Race, Religious denomination, and Caste, if any. | Occupation and Address. | How and when elected. |
|---|---|---|---|---|---|---|---|
| 368 | Govt. of India. | Berar. | Wun. | Mr. Waman Balwant Sule. | Parbhu Hindu. | Landowner ... ... | At a Public Meeting held at Yeotmal on the 29th November 1891. |
| 369 | " | " | " | Mr. Ram Chander Gonesh Mundle, B.A., LL.B. | Mahratta Brahmin. | Pleader ... ... | do. |
| 370 | " | " | " | Mr. Laxaman Chintaman Bapal. | do. | do. ... ... | do. |
| 371 | " | " | " | Mr. Gopal Narayan Bhat. | do. | Pleader and Izardar ... | do. |
| 372 | " | " | " | Mr. Baliram Raghav Sastikar. | do. | Pleader ... ... | do. |
| 373 | " | " | " | Mr. Ramchandra Raghonath Bapat. | do. | do. ... ... | do. |
| 374 | " | " | " | Mr. Laxaman Rangrao Dane. | do. | Izardar ... ... | do. |
| 375 | " | " | " | Mr. Daji Ramchandra Halbe. | do. | Landholder ... ... | do. |
| 376 | " | " | " | Mr. Hari Vithul Subhedar. | do. | Izardar ... ... | do. |
| 377 | " | " | " | Mr. Narayn Ganesh Deshpande. | do. | Jaghirdar ... ... | do. |
| 378 | " | " | " | Mr. Narhar Balaji ... | Hindu Kompti. | Izardar ... ... | do. |
| 379 | " | " | " | Mr. Govind Krishna Deshmukh. | Mahratta Brahmin. | Jaghirdar ... ... | do. |
| 380 | " | " | " | Mr. Sadashiva Moreshvar Dev. | do. | Pleader ... ... | do. |
| 381 | " | " | " | Mr. Krishnaji Bhicaji Palintkar. | do. | Landlord ... ... | do. |
| 382 | " | " | " | Mr. Sitaram Bavaraji Patel. | Hindu Kunbi. | Izardar ... ... | do. |
| 383 | " | " | " | Mr. Sono Divakar Deshmukh. | Hindu Vidur. | Mukhtear ... ... | do. |
| 384 | " | " | " | Mr. Ramchandra Govind Ruikar. | Hindu Teli. | Izardar ... ... | do. |
| 385 | " | " | Ellichpur. | Mr. Vasudeva Krishna Donge. | Hindu Vithoor. | Pleader ... ... | At a Public Meeting held at Ellichpur on the 8th November 1891. |
| 386 | " | " | " | Mr. Bapu Mahadeva Pandse. | Mahratta Brahmin. | do. ... ... | do. |
| 387 | " | " | " | Mr. Narayan Ramchandra Gadbikar. | do. | do. ... ... | do. |
| 388 | " | " | " | Mr. Vyankatrao Hanmantrao Deshmukh. | do. | Landlord and Moneylender... | do. |
| 389 | " | " | " | Mr. Mahitobsing Kishansing Jemadar. | Rajput. | Moneylender and Cultivator. | do. |
| 390 | " | " | " | Mr. Ramrao Sadashiva Sadhu. | Brahmin. | Agent ... ... | do. |
| 391 | " | " | " | Mr. Laxman Balkrishna. | Hindu Goldsmith. | Contractor ... ... | do. |
| 392 | " | " | " | Mr. Gangadhar Narayan Jogdale. | Brahmin. | Pleader ... ... | do. |
| 393 | " | " | " | Mr. Sukhusing Babusing Jemadar. | Hindu Lohariya. | Agent and Cultivator ... | do. |
| 394 | " | " | " | Mr. Hiralal Amarchand. | Hindu Mahesri. | Moneylender ... ... | do. |
| 395 | " | " | " | Mr. Padmol Dipraja Sahu. | Hindu. | Moneylender and Cultivator. | do. |
| 396 | " | " | Buldana. | Mr. Bappoosa Tukasa ... | Lod Bunniah. | Sowcar, Landlord and Member Local Board. | At a Public Meeting held at Buldana on the 23rd May, 1891. |
| 397 | " | " | " | Mr. Rawaji Raghav Tagde. | Arya. | Pleader ... ... | do. |
| 398 | " | " | " | Mr. Damodar Hari Ranade. | do. | do. ... ... | do. |
| 399 | " | " | " | Mr. Ganpatrao Sambhogi Patel. | Kunbi. | Contractor ... ... | do. |
| 400 | " | " | " | Mr. Narayansa Chinausa. | Lod Bunniah. | Sowkar and Landlord ... | do. |
| 401 | " | " | " | Mr. Krishnarao Venkatish Deshpande. | Mahratta Brahmin. | Trader and Vatandar ... | do. |
| 402 | " | " | " | Mr. Annaji Ram Chandra Pimprekar. | do. | Pleader ... ... | do. |
| 403 | " | " | " | Mr. Shrikrishna Chimnaji Deshpande. | do. | do. ... ... | do. |
| 404 | " | " | " | Mr. Wasudeo Balaji Pimlikar. | do. | do. ... ... | do. |
| 405 | " | " | Basim. | Mr. Shankar Govind Naik Barve. | do. | Landlord and Moneylender ... | At a Public Meeting held at Basim on the 15th November 1891. |
| 406 | " | " | " | Mr. Seshrao Raghunath... | do. | Pleader and Municipal Commissioner. | do. |

| Number. | Presidency or Government. | Congress Circle. | Electoral Division. | Names in full of Delegates with honorary titles scholastic degrees, etc. | Race, Religious denomination and Caste, if any | Occupation and Address. | How and when elected. |
|---|---|---|---|---|---|---|---|
| 407 | Govt. of India. | Berar. | Basim. | Mr. Luxamon Atmaram, Mahajana. | Mahratta Brahmin. | Merchant, Moneylender, and Vice-President, District Board | At a Public Meeting held at Basim on the 15th November 1891. |
| 408 | " | " | " | Mr. Vinayek Vishnu Gokhale. | do. | Pleader ... ... | do. |
| 409 | " | " | " | Mr. Yeshmant Vaman Dighe. | Kshatriya. | Pleader and Municipal Commissioner. | do. |
| 410 | " | " | " | Mr. Chimnarao Trimbuck | Brahmin. | Landlord and Member, Local Board. | do. |
| 411 | Central Provinces | Nagpur. | Nagpur. | Mr. Atmaram Bhagwant | Mahratta Brahmin. | Pleader, Landed Proprietor and Malguzar. | At a Public Meeting held at Nagpur on the 3rd December 1891. |
| 412 | " | " | " | Mr. Anna Saheb Upadhay | do. | Landlord and Malguzar ... | do. |
| 413 | | " | " | Mr. K. Parigah Naidu | Hindu Telegu. | Contractor ... ... | do. |
| 414 | " | " | " | Mr. Mahomed Ismail Bin Vazir. | Mahomedan Sunni. | Accountant .. ... | do |
| 415 | .. | " | " | Mr. Abdur Rahman ... | do. | Mukhtear ... ... | do. |
| 416 | " | " | " | Mr. Mahomed Ghulam Mohiuddin. | do. | Merchant ... ... | do. |
| 417 | " | " | " | Mr. Mumuji Adamji ... | do. | Contractor ... ... | do. |
| 418 | " | " | " | Mr. Keshavrao Shivram Bhandare. | Mahratta Brahmin. | Writer ... .. | do. |
| 419 | " | " | " | Mr. Balwantrao Govind Mahajan. | do. | Advocate ... .. | do. |
| 420 | " | " | " | Mr. Dattoo Vinayek Gokhalay. | do. | Contractor ... .. | do. |
| 421 | " | " | " | Mr. Anantrao Vinayek Kaptan. | do. | Sowkar and Malguzar ... | do. |
| 422 | .. | " | " | Mr. Vithalrao Vinayek Kalikar. | do. | Rais, Sowkar and Malguzar ... | do. |
| 423 | " | " | " | Mr. Ramchundra Raghunath Bobdey. | do. | Pleader ... ... | do. |
| 424 | " | " | " | Mr. Tara Narayan Roy, L. M. S. | Bengali Vaidya. | Medical Practitioner ... | do. |
| 425 | " | | " | Mr. Gopalrao Madhorao Panditji. | Mahratta Brahmin. | Muafidar, Malguzar and Honorary Magistrate. | do. |
| 426 | " | " | " | Mr. Chunni Lalji ... | Hindu Marwari. | Mukhtear and Honorary Magistrate. | do. |
| 427 | .. | " | " | Mr. Gopalrao Udhoji ... | Mahratta Brahmin. | Malguzar ... ... | do. |
| 428 | " | " | " | Mr. Abdul Aziz ... | Mahomedan. | Pleader and Secretary, Local Board. | do. |
| 429 | " | " | " | Mr. Krishnarao Narayan Karmarkar. | Mahratta Brahmin. | Editor, "Bousla," and Teacher, City School. | do. |
| 430 | " | " | " | Mr. F. W. Dillon. | European. | Barrister-at-Law... ... | do. |
| 431 | " | " | " | Mr. Jadava Wasudeva Dake, B. A. | Marhatta Brahmin. | Teacher ... ... | do. |
| 432 | " | " | " | Mr. C. Narayan Swami Nayadu. | Hindu Kshatriya | Pleader and Landholder, President, Municipality, and Secretary, District Council. | do, |
| 433 | " | " | " | Mr. Bhagiratha Prasada, B. A. | Hindu Kalar. | Professor, Hislop College, and Municipal Commissioner. | do. |
| 434 | " | " | " | Mr. Cottari Venkat Ramana Nayadu. | Kshatriya. | Barrister-at-Law ... | do, |
| 435 | " | " | " | Mr. Cottari Soorya Prokashrao Nayadu, B. A. (Cantab). | Kshatriya. | Barrister-at-Law ... | do. |
| 436 | .. | " | " | Mr. Gopal Mukund Bootee | Brahmin. | Banker, Landlord and House Proprietor. | do. |
| 437 | " | " | " | Mr. P. Vijayarangam Nayadu. | Hindu Telegu. | Merchant, Banker and Landlord. | do. |
| 438 | " | " | " | Mr. Hiralal Rambux ... | Sonar. | Pleader ... ... | do |
| 439 | " | " | " | Rambux Khashiram ... | do. | Merchant and Goldsmith ... | do. |
| 440 | " | " | " | Mr. Balkrishna Dattatriya, Foazdar. | Brahmin. | Banker and Malguzar ... | do. |
| 441 | " | " | " | Rai Doorga Pershad ... | Hindu Kayastha. | Pleader ... ... | do. |
| 442 | " | " | " | Mr. Shridhar Trimbak ... | Mahratta Brahmin. | Pleader, Malguzar, Sowkar and Member, Local Board. | do. |
| 443 | " | " | " | Mr. Martand Bapuji Vaikar. | do. | Pleader, Banker and Malguzar. | do. |
| 444 | " | " | " | Rev. P. Timothy ... | Christian Telegu. | Pastor ... ... | do. |
| 445 | " | " | " | Mr. Dhundiraj Ramkrishna, B.A. | Mahratta Brahmin. | ...... ... | do. |
| 446 | " | " | " | Rev. John Douglas, M.A. | European. | Clergyman .. ... | do. |
| 447 | " | " | " | Mr. Bhaskar Baji Rao Deshpande, F.A. | Mahratta Brahmin. | Landlord and Teacher .. | do. |
| 448 | " | " | " | Mr. [1]Hormusji Dinshaw Panthakey. | Parsi. | Merchant ... ... | do. |

| Number. | Presidency or Government. | Congress Circle. | Electoral Division. | Names in full of Delegates, with honorary titles, scholastic degrees, etc. | Race, Religious denomination, and Caste, if any | Occupation and Address. | How and when elected. |
|---|---|---|---|---|---|---|---|
| 449 | Central Provinces. | Nagpur | Nagpur. | Mr. Mahomed Hamid-ud-deen. | Mahomedan Sunni | Handicraftsman ... | At a Public Meeting held at Nagpur on the 3rd December, 1891. |
| 450 | " | " | " | Mr. Sultan Ali ... | do. | Merchant ... ... | do. |
| 451 | " | " | " | Mr. Hafiz-ud-deen Ahmed | do. | Draftsman ... .. | do. |
| 452 | " | " | " | Mr. MirzaRaza Ali Beg | do. | Conservancy Inspector ... | do. |
| 453 | " | " | " | Mr. Krishnarao Govind Deshpande, M.A., B.L. | Mahratta Brahmin. | Pleader, Malguzar, and Agriculturist. | do. |
| 454 | " | " | " | Mr. Burjorjee Bezonjee | Parsi. | Watchmaker ... ... | do. |
| 455 | " | " | " | Mr. Jamnadas Botdar .. | Marwari. | Sowkar and Mill Agent .. | do. |
| 456 | " | " | " | Mr. Ganpatrao Narayana Gokhale. | Mahratta Brahmin. | Pleader and Malguzar ... | do. |
| 457 | " | " | " | Mr. Gopal Hari Bhide ... | do. | Pleader, Zemindar and Municipal Commissioner. | do. |
| 458 | " | " | " | Bapurao Dada Tinkere, M.A. | do. | Pleader, Malguzar and Municipal Commissioner. | do. |
| 459 | " | " | " | Mr. Shivaram Tanbaji Dobe, B.A. | do. | Teacher, City School ... | do. |
| 460 | " | " | " | Mr. Sadashiv Ganpat Subhedar, B.A. | do. | Rais, Landed Proprietor and Malguzar. | do. |
| 461 | " | " | " | Mr. Murlidhara Amrita Buty. | do. | Banker and Malguzar ... | do. |
| 462 | " | " | " | Mr. Nilkant Damodar Udhoji. | do. | Pleader and Malguzar ... | do. |
| 463 | " | " | " | Mr. Wasudeva Trimbak | do. | Sadar Munim and Landholder | do. |
| 464 | " | " | " | Mr. Hari Mahadeo Pandit. | do. | ...... ... | do. |
| 465 | " | " | " | Mr. Baoji Kashinath Gokhale. | do. | Pleader ... ... | do. |
| 466 | " | " | " | Babu Bipin Krishna Bose, M.A., B.L. | Kayastha. | Advocate ... ... | do. |
| 467 | " | " | " | Mr. Kanhojirao Mohite Amir Rao. | Kshatriya. | Rais and Mokasdar ... | do |
| 468 | " | " | " | Rev. D. Whitton ... | European. | Principal, Hislop College .. | do. |
| 469 | " | " | " | Rev. S. Bhewaji ... | Native Christian. | Licentiate and Teacher ... | do. |
| 470 | " | " | " | Mr. Alexander Robertson, M.B., M.C. | European. | Professor, Hislop College ... | do. |
| 471 | " | " | " | Mr. Madho Moreshvar Jamdar, B.A. | Mahratta Brahmin. | Rais and Landlord ... | do. |
| 472 | " | " | " | Mr. Shrikrishna Shridhar Munshi. | do. | Rais and Malguzar ... | do. |
| 473 | " | " | " | Mr. Narayan Dajiba Wadegaonkar, B.A. | do. | Landed Proprietor ... | do. |
| 474 | " | " | " | Mr. Pandurang Rao Gujar | Mahratta. | Rais, Malguzar and Mokasdar | do. |
| 475 | " | " | " | Rajah Nowlaji Rao Gujar | do. | Rais, Malguzar, Sowkar Mokasdar, Sardar and Hony. Magistrate. | do. |
| 476 | " | " | " | Mr. Keshav Vinayek Joshi, B.A. | Mahratta Brahmin. | Headmaster, City High School. | do. |
| 477 | " | " | " | Mr. Jadava Prabhakar Vatak, B.A. | Mahratta Brahmin. | Malguzar and Landed Proprietor. | do. |
| 478 | " | " | " | Mr. Purushottam Ganesh Parenjpe, B.A. | do. | Landed Proprietor ... | do. |
| 479 | " | " | " | Mr. Ramchandra Amritrao Buty. | do. | Banker and Malguzar ... | do. |
| 480 | " | " | " | Mr. Shivashankar Puriji Guru, Gosai Padampuruj | do. | Sowkar, Malguzar and Merchant. | do. |
| 481 | " | " | " | Mr. Parashram Krishna Hardas, B.A. | do. | Teacher and Mulguzar ... | do. |
| 482 | " | " | " | Mr. Gangadhar Rao Madhaw Chitnavis. | Hindu Probhu. | Rais, Mulguzar, Mokasdar, Municipal Commissioner and President, District Council. | do. |
| 483 | " | " | " | Mr. Gosain Ramkrishna Puriji Guru Padmapuriji | Goswami Brahmin | Merchant, Sowkar and Malguzar. | do. |
| 484 | " | " | " | Mr. Venkoba Jairam Mooley. | Mahratta Brahmin. | Broker, Banker and Malguzar | do. |
| 485 | " | " | " | Mr. James Bremner, M. A | European. | Professor, Hislop College ... | do. |
| 486 | " | " | " | Mr. Shankar Kashinath ... | Kolar. | Sowkar ... ... | do. |
| 487 | " | " | " | Mr. Kashinath Zolbaji Dawray. | Kunbi. | Sowkar, Landholder and Malguzar. | do. |
| 488 | " | " | " | Mr. Ramdhan Paramsukha | Marwadi. | Silk Merchant ... | do. |
| 489 | " | " | " | Mr. Hanmantrao Patel ... | Kunbi. | Malguzar ... ... | do. |
| 490 | " | | " | Mr Chintaman Krishna Duvali. | Brahmin. | Pleader ... ... | do. |

| Number. | Presidency or Government. | Congress Circle. | Electoral Division. | Names in full of Delegates, with honorary titles, scholastic degrees, etc. | Race, Religious denomination, and Caste. if any. | Occupation and Address. | How and when elected. |
|---|---|---|---|---|---|---|---|
| 491 | Central Provinces. | Nagpur. | Nagpur. | Mr. Vinayek Jogeshvar Bute. | Mahratta Brahmin. | Banker ... .. | At a Public Meeting held at Nagpur on the 3rd December 1891. |
| 492 | " | " | " | Mr. Mahmood Khan ... | Mahomedan Sunni. | Malguzar ... ... | do. |
| 493 | " | " | " | Mr. Mahomed Abdulla ... | do. | do. ... ... | do |
| 494 | " | " | " | Mr. Mahomed Hamiduddin. | do. | Clerk ... ... | do. |
| 495 | " | " | " | Munshi Yusuf Ali ... | do. | Merchant ... ... | do. |
| 496 | " | " | " | Mr. Mahomed Kasim ... | do. | do. ... ... | do. |
| 497 | " | " | " | Mr. Abdul Kiyum ... | do. Shiah. | do. ... | do. |
| 498 | " | " | " | Mr. Ghulam Abbas ... | do. | do. ... ... | do. |
| 499 | " | " | " | Mr. Kyder Miyan ... | Mahomedan Sunni. | Kashtkar ... ... | do |
| 500 | " | " | " | Mr. Ganpatrao Gopalrao Ghataley. | Mahratta Brahmin. | Banker, Landed Proprietor and Malguzar. | do. |
| 501 | " | " | " | Mr. Allahuddeen ... | Mahomedan Sunni. | Kazi ... ... | do. |
| 502 | " | " | " | Mr. Abdur Salam Khan | do. | Siladar ... ... | do. |
| 503 | " | " | " | Sheikh Budhun ... | do. | Merchant ... ... | do. |
| 504 | " | " | " | Mr. Amir Miyah ... | do. | Handicraftsman... ... | do. |
| 505 | " | " | " | Mr. Mahomed Vizlul Huq | do. | Malguzar ... ... | do. |
| 506 | " | " | " | Mr. Kayum Ali Khan ... | do. | ...... | do. |
| 507 | " | " | " | Mr. Kareem Ali ... | do. | Kashtkar ... ... | do |
| 508 | " | " | " | Mr. Yawa Meer Khan ... | do. | do. ... ... | do. |
| 509 | " | " | " | Mr. Akbar Mir Khan ... | do. | do. ... ... | do. |
| 510 | " | " | " | Mr. Abdul Jabar Khan... | do. | Malguzar ... ... | do. |
| 511 | " | " | " | Mr. Mumtaz Ali Khan ... | do. | do. ... ... | do. |
| 512 | " | " | " | Mr. Khurshed Husain ... | do. | do. ... ... | do. |
| 513 | " | " | " | Mr. Yakub Ali ... | do. | Muafidar ... ... | do. |
| 514 | " | " | " | Mr. Rafiuddeen ... | do. | Medical Practitioner .. | do. |
| 515 | " | " | " | Mr. Waris Mahomed ... | do. | Mukhtear ... ... | do. |
| 516 | " | " | " | Mr. Abdur Rahman ... | do. | Merchant ... ... | do. |
| 517 | " | " | " | Mr. Mahomed Hussain ... | do. | Hakim ... ... | do. |
| 518 | " | " | " | Mr. Ahmed Ali ... | Mahomedan Shiah. | Malguzar ... ... | do. |
| 519 | " | " | " | Mr. Ghulam Mahomed ... | do Sunni. | Mukhtear ... ... | do. |
| 520 | " | " | " | Mr. Madhow Narayan Patwardhan. | Mahratta Brahmin | Pleader ... ... | do. |
| 521 | " | " | " | Mr. Shrinivas Ramchandra Herdas. | Mahratta Brahmin. | Dharma Shastri ... | do. |
| 522 | " | " | " | Mr. A. Krishna Swami Mudaliar. | Hindu Tamil | Contractor and Landed Proprietor. | do. |
| 523 | " | " | " | Mr. Chhotelal Tulsiram | Modewani Hindu | Contractor and Banker ... | do. |
| 524 | " | " | " | Mr. Biharilalji Kewalaram Dube. | Brahmin. | Banker, Malguzar and Landed Proprietor | do. |
| 525 | " | " | " | Mr. Sethram Narayan Jaduram. | Vaishnava | General Merchant and Contractor, Banker and Landed Proprietor. | do. |
| 526 | " | " | " | Mr. Ramkaran Golchha | Jain Marwari. | Banker ... ... | do. |
| 527 | " | " | " | Mr. Narayana Dass ... | Bunniah | Merchant ... ... | do. |
| 528 | " | " | " | Mr. Tukaram Kashinath | Mahratta Brahmin | Private Service ... | do. |
| 529 | " | " | " | Mr. Ananta Singha ... | Native Christian. | Merchant, Banker and Agriculturist | do. |
| 530 | " | " | " | Mr. Chintaman Dadaji Dharoskar. | Marhatta Brahmin. | Banker and Malguzar ... | do. |

| Number. | Presidency or Government. | Congress Circle. | Electoral Division. | Names in full of Delegates, with honorary titles, scholastic degrees, etc. | Race, Religious denomination, and Caste if any. | Occupation and Address. | How and when elected. |
|---|---|---|---|---|---|---|---|
| 531 | Central Provinces. | Nagpur. | Nagpur. | Mr. Rajaram Sitaram Dikshit. | Marhatta Brahmin. | Contractor ... ... | At a Public Meeting held at Nagpur on the 3rd December 1891. |
| 532 | " | " | " | Mr. Bhansaheb Kaloo ... | do. | Pensioner ... ... | do. |
| 533 | " | " | " | Sheikh Valebhai Suleiman. | Mahomedan Shiah | Merchant ... ... | do. |
| 534 | " | " | " | Mr. Ahlogirao Ginjara ... | Marathi | Malguzar ... ... | do. |
| 535 | " | " | " | Mr. Abasaheba Ginjara | do. | Pensioner ... ... | do. |
| 536 | " | " | " | Mr. Trimbakrao Appaji Dikshit. | Mahratta Brahmin | Pleader and Malguzar ... | do. |
| 537 | " | | " | Sheikh Hassanji ... | Mahomedan Shiah | Merchant ... ... | do. |
| 538 | " | " | " | Mr. Damodar Atmaram Kahte. | Brahmin | Deputy Manager, Swadshi Mills. | do. |
| 539 | " | " | " | Rai Debipershad, B.A., B.L. | Kayastha | Pleader ... ... | do. |
| 540 | " | " | " | Mr. T. Laxmana Swami Nayadu. | Hindu Telegu | Pensioner ... ... | do. |
| 541 | " | " | " | Mr. Govind Mukund Booty. | Hindu Brahmin. | Banker, Landlord and House Proprietor. | do. |
| 542 | " | " | " | Mr. Ram Chandra Ganesh Nareley. | Marhatta Brambin | Pleader, Landed Proprietor and Malguzar. | do. |
| 543 | " | " | Kamptee. | Mr. J. Robinson ... | American. | P. W. D. Contractor ... | At a Public Meeting held at Kamptee on the 6th December 1891. |
| 544 | " | " | " | Mr. Bhundas Naidu ... | Hindu Telegu. | Contractor and Honorary Magistrate. | do. |
| 545 | " | " | " | Syed Abdul Rahiman ... | Mahomedan Sunni. | Clerk ... ... | do. |
| 546 | " | " | " | Mr. Kesheo Ramchandra Kelkar. | Mahratta Brahmin. | Head Clerk ... ... | do |
| 547 | " | " | " | Pandit Gyarasram Sarma | do. | Dharmashastri ... | do. |
| 548 | " | " | " | Mr. L. B. Sitaram ... | Kalal. | Akbari Contractor and Malguzar. | do. |
| 549 | " | " | " | Mr. Hiralal Sukul ... | Brahmin. | Pleader ... ... | do. |
| 550 | " | " | " | Mr. Raghunath Purshottum. | do. | do. ... | do. |
| 551 | " | " | " | Mr. Coopooswamy Naidu | Telegu Hindu. | Medical Practitioner and Landowner. | do. |
| 552 | " | " | " | Mr. Hurnath Seo Balabh | Hindu. | Banker ... ... | do. |
| 553 | " | " | " | Mr. Shankar Lall .. | Baniah. | Malguzar and Cloth Merchant. | do. |
| 554 | " | " | " | Mr. Biharilal Sukul ... | Brahmin. | Landowner and Head Clerk. | do. |
| 555 | " | " | " | Mr. Champalal Sadani | Baniah. | Cloth Merchant ... | do. |
| 556 | " | " | " | Mr. Jaganath Ramchand | do. | Banker and Cloth Merchant. | do. |
| 557 | " | " | " | Mr. Ahmed Khan ... | Mahomedan Sunni. | Medical Practitioner ... | do. |
| 558 | " | " | Wardha | Mr. Keshavarao Mahadeo Kawley. | Mahratta Brahmin. | Pleader ... ... | At a Public Meeting held at Wardha on the 2nd December 1891. |
| 559 | " | " | " | Mr. Balaji Sakharam Gaonde ... | Kunbi. | Malguzar, Cultivator and Member, Local Board. | do. |
| 560 | " | " | " | Mr. Bapuji Fakirji Bobde | do. | Malguzar and Cultivator ... | do. |
| 561 | " | " | " | Mr. Shet Ishwardas Mohta. | Marwadi Vaishnava | Banker, Malguzar, Municipal Commissioner, Director of Hinganghat and Pulgaon Mills. | do. |
| 562 | " | " | " | Mr. Bhargava Govind Karmarkar ... | Mahratta Brahmin. | Malguzar and Banker ... | do. |
| 563 | " | " | " | Mr. Baliram Chanaji Kumdeva. | Hindu Kunbi. | Banker and Malguzar ... | do. |
| 564 | " | " | " | Mr. Balkrishna Pandurang Kalyana. | Mahratta Brahmin. | Malguzar and Banker ... | do. |
| 565 | " | " | " | Mr. Damodar Nilkanta Khare, B.A., LL.B. | do. | Pleader ... | do. |
| 566 | " | " | " | Mr. Hari Balwant Peshkar. | do. | Malguzar and Banker ... | do. |
| 567 | " | " | " | Mr. Bhagwantrao Hurbu Hore. | Kunbi. | do. ... | do. |
| 568 | " | " | " | Mr. Ganpatrao Deskar ... | do. | do. ... | do. |
| 569 | " | " | " | Mr. Abhiman Patel ... | do. | Malguzar ... | do. |
| 570 | " | " | " | Mr. Deorao Rajaram Deshpande. | Mahratta Brahmin. | Banker and Malguzar ... | do. |
| 571 | " | " | " | Mr. Ramkrishna Punzaji | Bhata. | Malguzar ... | do. |
| 572 | " | " | " | Mr. Vasudeo Vittal Vadatkar. | Hindu Vidur. | do. ... | do. |

| Number. | Presidency or Government. | Congress Circle. | Electoral Division. | Names in full of Delegates with honorary titles, scholastic degrees, etc. | Race, Religious denomination, and Caste, if any. | Occupation and Address. | How and when elected. |
|---|---|---|---|---|---|---|---|
| 573 | Central Provinces. | Nagpur. | Wardha. | Mr. R. Shrinivas Naidu | Hindu Telugu. | ...... ... | At a Public Meeting held at Wardha on the 2nd December 1891. |
| 574 | " | " | " | Pandit Hiralal Dube ... | Brahmin. | Malguzar and Cultivator ... | do. |
| 575 | " | " | " | Mr. Laxman Chimnaji ... | Mahratta Brahmin. | Agent .. | do. |
| 576 | " | " | " | Mr. Hari Vaman Kelkar, B.A., L.L.B. | do. | Pleader and Municipal Commissioner. | do. |
| 577 | " | " | " | Mr. Baliram Kashinath... | do. | Pleader, Malguzar and Cultivator. | do. |
| 578 | " | " | " | Mr. Krishnarao Narayan Deshmukh. | do. | Pleader and Landlord ... | do. |
| 579 | " | " | " | Mr. Baliram Narayan Deshmukh, B.A., B.L. | do. | do. ... | do. |
| 580 | " | " | " | Mr. Vaman Vithal Barve | do. | Trader ... | do. |
| 581 | " | " | " | Mr. Shet Bacheraj ... | Marwari. | Banker, Landlord and Mill Agent. | do. |
| 582 | " | " | " | Mr. Pandurang Bapuji ... | Mahratta Brahmin. | Agriculturist ... | do. |
| 583 | " | " | " | Mr. Vasudeo Vinayek Paranjpe. | do. | Pleader and President, Municipal Committee. | do. |
| 584 | " | " | " | Mr. Prahlad Bhashkar Deshpande. | do. | Malguzar ... | do |
| 585 | " | " | " | Rev. Dugald Revie ... | European. | Medical Practitioner and Municipal Commissioner. | do. |
| 586 | " | " | " | Mr. Yadarao Pandurang Kalyani. | Mahratta Brahmin. | Banker and Malguzar ... | do. |
| 587 | " | " | " | Mr. Ganpatrao Patel Meghey. | Kunbi. | do. ... | do. |
| 588 | " | " | " | Mr. Jagannath Gonesh Badhe, L.C.E. | Mahratta Brahmin. | ...... ... | do. |
| 589 | " | " | " | Mr. Narayan Shripat Patel. | Kunbi. | Malguzar ... | do. |
| 590 | " | " | Wadhona and Arvi. | Mr. Anandrao Rangrao | Mahratta Brahmin. | Malguzar, Arvi, Wardha District. | At a Public Meeting held at Arvi on the 2nd November 1891. |
| 591 | " | " | " | Mr. Tukaram Maladia ... | Kunbi. | Private Service ... | At a Public Meeting held at Wadhona on the 13th December 1891. |
| 592 | " | " | " | Mr. Shittaram Lalla ... | Marwadi. | Banker ... | do. |
| 593 | " | " | " | Mathura Das ... | do. | do. ... | do. |
| 594 | " | " | " | Mr. Maruti Raghav ... | Mahratta Brahmin. | Private Service ... | do. |
| 595 | " | " | " | Mr. Ramchandra Vitul | do. | Priest ... | do. |
| 596 | " | " | " | Mr. Tukaram Bapu Gadge. | do. | Private Service ... | do. |
| 597 | " | " | " | Mr. Govinda Patel ... | Kunbi. | Malguzar ... | do. |
| 598 | " | " | " | Mr. Vithul Shittaram ... | Mahratta Brahmin. | do. ... | do. |
| 599 | " | " | " | Mr. Shrawan Patel ... | Kunbi. | do. ... | do. |
| 600 | " | " | " | Mr. Ramsing Mansing ... | Kshatriya | Banker, Malguzar, and Landholder. | do. |
| 601 | " | " | " | Mr. Suryabhan Patel ... | Kunbi. | Malguzar ... | do. |
| 602 | " | " | " | Mr. Dewaji Patel ... | do. | do. ... | do. |
| 603 | " | " | " | Mr. Dulchand ... | Marwadi. | Banker ... | do. |
| 604 | " | " | " | Mr. Yadavrao Gajanan Deshmukh. | Mahratta Brahmin. | Malguzar ... | do. |
| 605 | " | " | " | Mr. Dinaji Ghagre ... | Kunbi. | do. ... | do. |
| 606 | " | " | " | Mr. Ganpatrao Kesheo Deshmukh. | Mahratta Brahmin. | do. ... | do. |
| 607 | " | " | " | Mr. Dadopant Dada ... | do. | do. ... | do. |
| 608 | " | " | " | Mr. Vyankatrao Anantrao. | do. | do. ... | do. |
| 609 | " | " | " | Mr. Madhovrao Vithalrao Deshmukh. | do. | do. ... | do. |
| 610 | " | " | " | Mr. Sheorao Chintaman | do. | do. ... | do. |
| 611 | " | " | " | Mr. Bajirao Dadaji Bhopkar. | Mahratta. | Malguzar and Landed Proprietor. | do. |

| Number. | Presidency or Government. | Congress Circle. | Electoral Division. | Names in full of Delegates, with honorary tittles, scholastic degrees, etc. | Race, Religious denomination, and Caste, if any. | Occupation and Address. | How and when elected. |
|---|---|---|---|---|---|---|---|
| 612 | Central Provinces. | Nagpur. | Bhandara | Mr. Ramchandra Narayan Kardale. | Mahratta Brahmin. | Malguzar and Municipal Commissioner. | At a Public Meeting held at Bhandara on the 16th December 1891. |
| 613 | " | " | " | Mr. Jogeshvar Keshav Pande. | Brahmin | Pleader ... | do. |
| 614 | " | " | " | Mr. Vishvanath Nilkanth Pandit, B.A., L.L.B. | do. | do. ... | do. |
| 615 | " | " | " | Mr. Rangrao Hari ... | Native Christian. | Pleader, Malguzar, Vice-Chairman, Municipality, and Secretary, Local Board. | do. |
| 616 | " | " | " | Mr. Vithoba Laxman Chutake. | Hindu. | Sowkar and Malguzar ... | do. |
| 617 | " | " | " | Mr. Sitaram Lalman Sao | do. | Banker, Malguzar, and Municipal Commissioner. | do |
| 618 | " | " | " | Mr Sakharam Rewaram Kasor. | do. | Banker, Trader and Malguzar | do. |
| 619 | " | " | " | Mr. Pundalik Pandurang Dalalkosti. | do. | Broker and Malguzar ... | do. |
| 620 | " | " | " | Mr. Sheocharan Raghu Pande. | Mahratta Brahmin. | Malguzar and Mukhtear ... | do |
| 621 | " | " | " | Mr. Amant Rangnath Tanksale. | do. | Malguzar and Cultivator ... | do. |
| 622 | " | " | " | Mr. Damodar Vinayek Kaley. | do. | Contractor ... | do. |
| 623 | " | " | " | Mr. Purshottam Madhav Ragalwar. | do. | Malguzar and Contractor ... | do. |
| 624 | " | " | " | Mr. Raghu Krishna Katya. | do. | Landlord and Agent ... | do. |
| 625 | " | " | " | Mr. Sakharam Sitaram Wazalwar. | do. | Pleader, Banker and Malguzar. | do. |
| 626 | " | " | " | Mr. Raghunath Govind Deosant. | do. | Landlord ... ... | do. |
| 627 | " | " | " | Mr. Govind Balwant Pandripandey. | do. | Pleader ... ... | do. |
| 628 | " | " | " | Mr. Govind Vishnath Katre. | do. | Malguzar ... ... | do. |
| 629 | " | " | " | Mr. Narayan Janardhan | Hindu | Contractor ... ... | do. |
| 630 | " | " | " | Mr. Gangadhar Balwant Gokhale, B.A., B L | Mahratta Brahmin. | Pleader ... ... | do. |
| 631 | " | " | " | Mr. Vishnu Rajaram ... | do. | Contractor .. ... | do. |
| 632 | " | " | " | Rev. J. Sandilands, M A., M.B. | European | Missionary ... ... | do. |
| 633 | " | " | Rampaili | Mr. Tulsiram Paika Patel | Hindu Powar. | Banker and Malguzar ... | At a Public Meeting held at Arambha on the 30th November 1891. |
| 634 | " | " | Umrer. | Mr. Vithulrao Mukundrao Deshmukh. | Kunbi | do. ... | At a Public Meeting held at Umrer on the 20th December 1891. |
| 635 | " | " | " | Mr Laksman Wasudeo Deshmukh. | Mahratta Brahmin. | Talukdar, Mokasdar, Malguzar, Banker and Agriculturist. | do. |
| 636 | " | " | " | Mr. Bijichand Ramchandra. | Marwari | Banker and Grain Merchant | do. |
| 637 | " | " | " | Mr. Janardhan Damodar Naik. | Mahratta Brahmin. | Sowkar, Malguzar, Agriculturist, Honorary Magistrate and Municipal Commissioner. | do. |
| 638 | " | " | " | Mr. Vamanrao Vaijnathrao Deshmukh. | do. | Malguzar, Tukumdar, and Agriculturist. | do. |
| 639 | " | " | " | Mr. Narayan Shridhar ... | do. | Sowkar, Malguzar, Honorary Magistrate, Municipal Commissioner and Member, Local Board. | do. |
| 640 | " | " | Balaghat. | Mr. Gopal Bijirao ... | do. | Agent and Municipal Commissioner. | At a Public Meeting held at Balaghat on the 16th December 1891. |
| 641 | " | " | " | Mr. Shamrao Kesheo Mazumdar. | do. | Malguzar and Municipal Commissioner | do. |
| 642 | " | " | " | Mr. Narayan Krishna Kelkar. | do. | Pleader ... ... | do. |
| 643 | " | " | " | Mr. Raghunath Moreshvar Bhawalkar. | do. | Merchant and Contractor ... | do. |
| 644 | " | " | " | Mr. Parmanand Sitaram Sao. | Jain | Moneylender and Jemadar ... | do. |
| 645 | " | " | " | Mr. Asalat Khan ... | Mahomedan. | Malguzar and Moneylender | do. |
| 646 | " | " | " | Mr. Munnaram Tularam | Bania | Mukhtear ... ... | do. |

| Number. | Presidency or Government. | Congress Circle. | Electoral Division. | Names in full of Delegates, with honorary titles, scholastic degrees, etc. | Race, Religious denomination, and Caste, if any. | Occupation and Address. | How and when elected |
|---|---|---|---|---|---|---|---|
| 647 | Central Provinces. | Nagpur. | Balaghat. | Mr. Marreshwar Jaggannath. | Marhatta Brahmin. | Mukhtear, Burha and Member, Municipal Committee. | At a Public Meeting held at Balaghat on the 18th December 1891. |
| 648 | " | " | Bharaswada. | Mr. Jageshwar Pandurang. | do. | Banker ... ... | At a Public Meeting held at Bharaswada on the 23rd November 1891. |
| 649 | " | " | " | Mr. Ramchandra Yeshwant Phushi. | do. | Malguzar ... ... | do. |
| 650 | " | " | " | Mr. Gunpatro Bhiwaji Patel. | Kunbi | Banker and Malguzar ... | do. |
| 651 | " | " | " | Mr. Ghusaji Patel. ... | Hindu | Malguzar ... ... | do. |
| 652 | " | " | " | Mr. Chimnaji Niluji Kale. | Kunbi. | do. ... ... | do. |
| 653 | " | " | " | Rajmalji Nimbaji Kharde | do. | do. ... ... | do. |
| 654 | " | " | Arvi. | Mr. Baswant Sakharam. | Kunbi. | Banker, Malguzar and Landed Proprietor. | At a Public Meeting held at Arvi on the 2nd November 1891. |
| 655 | " | " | " | Mr. Raghunath Narayan Abhiankar. | Hindu. | Merchant, Malguzar and Agriculturist. | do. |
| 656 | " | " | " | Mr. Hari Vithul Gaikard | do. | Malguzar ... ... | do. |
| 657 | " | " | " | Mr. Vasudeva Krishna Abhiankar. | do. | do. ... ... | do. |
| 658 | " | " | " | Gopal Balkrishna Deshpande. | Mahratta Brahmin. | do. ... ... | do. |
| 659 | " | " | " | Mr. Hansraj Dwilal Parwar. | Jain. | Banker and Landholder ... | do. |
| 660 | " | " | " | Mr. Manaji Janoji Mali. | Hindu. | Landlord and Agriculturist ... | do. |
| 661 | " | " | " | Mr. Narayan Chimnaji... | Kunbi. | Banker and Malguzar ... | do. |
| 662 | " | " | " | Mr. Naraynrao Patel ... | do. | Malguzar ... | do. |
| 663 | " | " | " | Mr. Vasudeva Bhaskar. ... | Mahratta Brahmin. | do. ... ... | do. |
| 664 | " | " | " | Mr. Chandulal Ram Chandra Parwar. | Jain. | Banker, Malguzar and Landed Proprietor. | do. |
| 665 | " | " | Ashti. | Mr. Jainarayan Lala ... | Marwari. | Malguzar ... ... | At a Public Meeting held at Ashti on the 3rd December 1891. |
| 666 | " | " | " | Mr. Chintaman Shivaji Dhole. | Hindu Teli. | Sowkar and Agriculturist ... | do. |
| 667 | " | " | " | Mr. Laxman Govind ... | Hindu. | Pleader ... ... | do. |
| 668 | " | " | " | Mr. Keshav Balkrishna Shastri. | Mahratta Brahmin. | Agriculturist ... ... | do. |
| 669 | " | " | " | Mr. Chintamanji Dhabaley Dhole. | Hindu Teli. | Sowkar, Malguzar and Agriculturist. | do. |
| 670 | " | " | " | Mr. Raghunath Keshav Deshpande. | Mahratta Brahmin. | Banker and Malguzar ... | do. |
| 671 | " | " | " | Mr. Ambadas Atmaram Deshpande. | do. | Banker, Malguzar and Member, Local Board. | do. |
| 672 | " | " | " | Mr. Mahadeorao Babuji Mukaddam. | Hindu Teli. | Sowkar and Agriculturist ... | do. |
| 673 | " | " | Rajnandgaon. | Mr. Kashinath Trimback Khare. | Mahratta Brahmin. | Contractor and Trader ... | At a Public Meeting held at Rajnandgaon on the 22nd November 1891. |
| 674 | " | " | " | Pandit Vidhata Prasad ... | do. | Merchant ... ... | do. |
| 675 | " | " | " | Mr. Ganesh Kashinath Khare. | do. | Contractor and Municipal Commissioner. | do. |
| 676 | " | " | " | Pandit Srinivash Rao ... | do. | Pleader ... ... | do. |
| 677 | " | " | " | Mr. V. Sarangapani Moodaliar. | Hindu Vaisya. | Contractor and Municipal Commissioner, Manager, Balram Press and Proprietor, "Rajnandgaon Gazette." | do. |
| 678 | " | " | " | Babu Kedarnath Bagchi. | Hindu Bengali. | Pleader ... .. | do. |
| 679 | " | " | " | Pandit Gajadhar Sukla ... | Brahmin. | Banker and Agent, C. P. Mills. | do. |
| 680 | " | " | " | Pandit Sheoraj Mali ... | do. | Pleader ... ... | do. |
| 681 | " | " | " | Pandit Shankar Prasad Pandey. | do. | Pleader and Municipal Commissioner. | do. |
| 682 | " | " | " | Pandit Gangadhor Odho... | Hindu. | Pleader and Pensioner ... | do. |
| 683 | " | " | " | Pandit Seetaram Raghoonath. | do. | State Advocate ... | do. |
| 684 | " | " | " | Mr. Abdul Husain ... | Mahomed an Shiah. | Shopkeeper ... ... | do. |

| Number. | Presidency or Government | Congress Circle. | Electoral Division. | Names in full of Delegates, with honorary titles, scholastic degrees, etc. | Race, Religious denomination, and Caste if any. | Occupation and Address. | How and when elected. |
|---|---|---|---|---|---|---|---|
| 685 | Central Provinces. | Nagpur. | Bilaspur. | Mr. Sadashiv Asaram Sao. | Bania. | Banker, Malguzar and Landed Proprietor. | At a Public Meeting held at Bilaspur on the 26th October 1891. |
| 686 | " | " | " | Mr. Nagendra Nath De | Hindu Bengali. | Barrister-at-law and Secretary, Municipal Committee. | do. |
| 687 | " | " | " | Mr. Ali Mahomed Bheemjee. | Mahomedan Sunni. | Law Agent ... ... | do. |
| 688 | " | " | " | Sheik Khoda Bux ... | do. | Mukhtear and Zemindar ... | do. |
| 689 | " | " | " | Mr. Manindra Nath Sircar, M.A. B.L. | Kayastha. | Pleader and Municipal Commissioner. | do. |
| 690 | " | " | " | Mr. V. P. Lobo ... | Eurasian Christian. | Merchant and Contractor ... | do. |
| 691 | " | " | " | Mr. Mahomed Akbar Khan. | Mahomedan Sunni | Malguzar ... ... | do. |
| 692 | " | " | " | Mr. Bapurao Sadasiv ... | Brahmin. | Pleader and Municipal Commissioner. | do. |
| 693 | " | " | Raipur. | Mr. Govind Hari Mankeshvar. | Mahratta Brahmin. | Contractor ... | At a Public Meeting held at Raipur on the 22nd November 1891. |
| 694 | " | " | " | Mr. Tukarm Vishnu. | do. | Pleader ... | do. |
| 695 | " | " | " | Mr. Gujaram Ragho Bagchi. | do. | do. | do. |
| 696 | " | " | Katole. | Mr. Sheoram Gonesh. | do. | Malguzar ... | At a Public Meeting held at Katole on the 6th December 1891. |
| 697 | " | " | " | Mr. Baburao Mankar Deshmukh. | Kunbi | Banker, Malguzar and Landed Proprietor. | do. |
| 698 | " | " | " | Mr. Luxman Prabhukar Pachkhede. | Hindu. | Landholder ... | do. |
| 699 | " | " | " | Baliram Mankar Deshmukh. | Kunbi. | Banker, Malguzar and Landed Proprietor. | do. |
| 700 | " | " | " | Mr. Sitaram Anandrao Patel. | do. | Sowkar and Malguzar ... | do. |
| 701 | " | " | " | Mr. Radharam Dewaji Patel. | do. | Malguzar and Landed Proprietor. | do. |
| 702 | " | " | Ramtek. | Mr. Raghunath Sheoram Pandey | Brahmin. | Landlord ... | At a Public Meeting held at Ramtek on the 7th December 1891. |
| 703 | " | " | Hinganghat. | Mr. Rekhchand Mohta. | Marwari Vaishnava | Merchant, Sowkar, Municipal Commissioner and Chairman, Hinganghat Mill Company. | At a Public Meeting held at Hinganghat on the 21st December 1891. |
| 704 | " | " | " | Mr. Sakharam Ashtekar Patel. | Kunbi. | Malguzar ... | do. |
| 705 | " | " | " | Mr. Mohanaji Govindrao Patel. | do. | do. | do. |
| 706 | " | " | " | Mr. Kesheo Sheoram Bhawalkar. | Mahratta Brahmin. | Trader, Banker, Pensioner and Manager, Hinganghat Mills. | do. |
| 707 | " | " | Chanda. | Mr. G. Ramchandra Narayan. | do. | Pleader and Member, District Board. | At a Public Meeting held at Chanda on the 10th November 1891. |
| 708 | " | " | " | Mr. Daji Ganesh Diwekar. | do. | Pleader and Landed Proprietor. | do. |
| 709 | " | " | " | Rev. Israel Jacob ... | Christian Telegu. | Missionary ... | do. |
| 710 | " | " | Pardi. | Mr. Hambirji Patel ... | Hindu. | Malguzar ... | At a Public Meeting held at Pardi on the 20th November 1891. |
| 711 | " | " | " | Mr. Wallaji Patel ... | Kunbi | do. ... | do. |
| 712 | " | " | Saoner. | Mr. Raghoba Ratiram Pali. | Mahratta Brahmin. | Malguzar and Vice-President, Municipal Committee. | At a Public Meeting held at Saoner on the 23rd December 1891. |
| 713 | " | " | " | Mr. Bapu Khem Patel ... | do. | Malguzar ... ... | do. |
| 714 | " | " | " | Mr. Kushal Dhundi Patel. | Lodhi Bunniah. | Banker and Malguzar | do. |
| 715 | " | " | Burha. | Mr. Jiyalal Balaram ... | Kayastha. | Malguzar and Cultivator ... | At a Public Meetting held at Burha on the 18th December 1891. |
| 716 | " | " | " | Mr. Sheodas Anupchand. | Marwari. | Merchant, Malguzar and Member, Local and District Boards. | do. |
| 717 | " | " | Pandharna. | Mr. Balkrishna Ganesh Bandsode. | Mahratta Brahmin. | Banker, Malguzar and Vice President, Municipal Committee. | At a Public Meeting held at Pandharna on the 15th December 1891. |

| Number. | Presidency or Government. | Congress Circle. | Electoral Division. | Names in full of Delegates, with honorary titles, scholastic degrees, etc. | Race, Religious denomination, and Caste, if any. | Occupation and Address. | How and when elected. |
|---|---|---|---|---|---|---|---|
| 718 | Central Provinces. | Jabalpur | Jabalpur. | Mr. D. Raghubar Prasad, B.A. | Brahmin. | Schoolmaster ... ... | At a Public Meeting held at Jabalpur on the 19th December 1891. |
| 719 | " | " | " | Mr. Bapu Waman Joshi. | do. | Landed Proprietor ... | do. |
| 720 | " | " | " | Babu Jogendra Nath Seal B A., B L. | Hindu Bengal. | Pleader and Landholder ... | do. |
| 721 | " | " | " | Mr. Alfred Nundy ... | Native Chistian. | Barrister at Law and Municipal Commissioner. | do. |
| 722 | " | " | Betul. | Babu Krishna Chandra Bannerjee. | Bengali Brahmin. | Landholder ... ... | At a Public Meeting held at Betul on the 10th December 1891. |
| 723 | " | " | " | Babu Ramchandra Bannerjee. | do. | do. | do. |
| 724 | " | " | " | Mr. Mukund Ram Dharmadhikari. | Mahratta Brahmin. | Banker, Multar and Landholder. | do. |
| 725 | " | " | " | Mr. Laxman Bhat Dharmadhikari. | do. | do. | do. |
| 726 | " | " | Saugor. | Babu Kali Prasonno Mukherjee, B.A., B.L. | Bengali Brahmin. | Pleader and Member, District Board. | At a Public Meeting held at Saugor on the 22nd November 1891. |
| 727 | " | " | " | Mr. Indra Prasad Bhandari. | Brahmin. | Banker and Malguzar ... | do. |
| 728 | " | " | " | Mr. Tantiah Naidu ... | Hindu. | Contractor, Malguzar, Honorary Magistrate, Member, District Board. | do. |
| 729 | " | " | " | Pandit Shiv Ram Hardikar. | Mahratta Brahmin. | Banker and Malguzar .. | do. |
| 730 | " | " | " | Mr. Gopal Sakharam Shikhande. | do. | Pleader and Municipal Commissioner. | do. |
| 731 | " | " | Khandwa. | Pandit Vithal Waman Pagay. | do. | Pleader ... ... | At a Public Meeting held at Khandwa on the 25th October 1891. |
| 732 | " | " | " | Mr. Ganpatrao Gangaram. | do. | Contractor ... ... | do. |
| 733 | " | " | " | Pandit Vishnupant Ramkrisna Gudray. | do. | Pleader ... ... | do. |
| 734 | " | " | " | Rao Ramsing Pratap Sing | Hindu Rajput. | Zemindar ... ... | do. |
| 735 | " | " | Harda | Mr. Sadashib Ramchandra Patwardhan. | Mahratta Brahmin. | Pleader, Malguzar, Editor and Proprietor, "Nyasudha." | At a Public Meeting held at Harda on the 28th October 1891. |
| 736 | " | " | " | Mr. Raghunathrao Waman Kekrey. | do. | Banker and Malguzar ... | do. |
| 737 | " | " | " | Mr. Vishnu Damodar Quidarkar. | do. | Banker and Landholder ... | do. |
| 738 | " | " | " | Mr. Krishnarao Narayan Paroolkar. | do. | Banker, Malguzar and Municipal Commissioner. | do. |
| 739 | " | " | " | Mr. Krishnarao Narayan Rogay. | do. | Banker, Jaghirdar and Malguzar. | do. |
| 740 | " | " | " | Mr. Bhikaji Vinayek Nayak. | do. | Banker, Landlord and Malguzar. | do. |
| 741 | " | " | " | Mr. Babuji Sitaram ... | do. | Contractor ... ... | do. |
| 742 | " | " | Chhindwara. | Mr. Vinayek Ganesh Wazalwar. | do. | Pleader ... ... | At a Public Meeting held at Chhindwara on the 14th December 1891. |
| 743 | " | " | Burhanpur. | Mr. Habibullah Kadervhai Makdaiwala. | Mahomedan. | Merchant and Landed Proprietor. | At a Public Meeting held at Burhanpur on the 17th November 1891. |
| 744 | " | " | " | Mr. Deochand Manikchand Shet. | Bania | Moneylender and Malguzar | do. |
| 745 | " | " | " | Mr. Trimbak Narayanrao Mahajan. | Brahmin | do. do. ... | do. |
| 746 | " | " | " | Mr. Vithul Manulal Shet | Hindu Vani Agarwala. | do. do. ... | do. |
| 747 | " | " | " | Mr. Govindrao Ramchandra. | Mahratta Brahmin | Malguzar ... ... | do. |
| 748 | " | " | " | Mr. Ganpat Raoji ... | do. | do. ... ... | do. |
| 749 | Madras. | Madras. | Madras. | Mr. M. P. Narayanswami Nayadu. | Hindu Vishnuvite. | Merchant and Landholder ... | At a Meeting of the Mahajana Sabha on the 11th December 1891. |
| 750 | " | " | " | Rao Saheb T. V. Apparan Naidu. | Hindu. | Merchant and Municipal Commissioner, Treasurer, Southern India Merchants Company. | do. |
| 751 | " | " | " | Mr. Atheepadu Custooree Parthasaradhi Naidu. | Hindu Vaishnava | Editor, "Audhrapraksika" ... | do. |
| 752 | " | " | " | Mr. S. Veeraraghava Charry. | Tamil Brahmin | Merchant ... ... | do. |
| 753 | " | " | " | Mr P. Bala Krishna Pillai. | Hindu Vaishnava | Contractor and Landholder ... | do. |

| Number. | Presidency or Government. | Congress Circle. | Electoral Division. | Names in full of Delegates, with honorary titles, scholastic degrees, etc. | Race, Religious denomination, and Caste, if any. | Occupation and Address. | How and when elected. |
|---|---|---|---|---|---|---|---|
| 754 | Madras. | Madras. | Madras. | Mr. G. Siva Rama Brumhum Sastry. | Brahmin. | Landholder ... ... | At a Meeting of the Mahajana Sabha held on the 11th December 1891. |
| 755 | " | " | " | Mr. Kuttalay Ethiraja Pillay. | Vellala Vaishnava. | Merchant and Contractor ... | do. |
| 756 | " | " | " | Mr. M. S. Narain Swamy Iyer, B.A. | Brahmin. | Zemindar ... ... | do. |
| 757 | " | " | " | Mr. Paul Peter Pillai. | Native Christian. | Agent and Landholder ... | do. |
| 758 | " | " | " | Mr. G. E. Sampathu Chetty. | Hindu. | Merchant and Honorary Secretary, City Club. | At a Meeting of the Mahajana Sabha on the 16th December 1891. |
| 759 | " | " | " | Mr. Krishnama Charriar B.A., B.L. | Hindu Vishnuvite Bramhin. | Vakil, High Court Madras ... | do. |
| 760 | " | " | " | Mr. R. Sreeramulu Sastriyar, B.A., B.L. | do. | do. do. ... | do. |
| 761 | " | " | " | Mr. V. Ranga Charriar, B.A., B.L. | ...... | do. do. ... | do. |
| 762 | " | " | " | Rai Bahadur P. Ananda Charlu, B.L. | Brahmin. | Vakil, High Court and Municipal Commissioner. | do. |
| 763 | " | " | " | Mr. M. Veeraraghava Charriar, B.A. | Hindu Vishnuvite Brahmin. | Joint Editor, "Hindu" ... | do. |
| 764 | " | " | " | Mr. V. Masilamani Pillai B.A., B.L. | Hindu. | Vakil, High Court ... | do. |
| 765 | " | " | " | Mr. M. Venkatrao. | Brahmin. | Merchant and Landholder ... | do. |
| 766 | " | " | Salem. | Rao Saheb C. Venkata Chariar. | do. | Landlord, Malguzar and Member, District Board. | At a Public Meeting held at Salem on the 19th December 1891. |
| 767 | " | " | " | Mr. S. Srinivasa Iyengar, B.A. | do. | Pleader ... ... | do. |
| 768 | " | " | " | Mr. Bhavani Krishnarao, B.A., B.L. | do. | do. ... ... | do. |
| 769 | " | " | " | Mr. C. Vijiaraghava Chariar, B.L. | do. | do. ... ... | do. |
| 770 | " | " | " | Mr. W. Vira Swamy Aiyar. | do. | Pleader and Municipal Commissioner. | do. |
| 771 | " | " | " | Mr. Y. Sesha Chellu Iyer. | do. | Landholder and Member, District Board. | do. |
| 772 | " | " | " | Mr. Narasinha Chary ... | do. | Landholder ... ... | do. |
| 773 | " | " | " | Mr. M. K. Rungasawmi Chetty. | Sudra. | Merchant ... ... | do. |
| 774 | " | " | Cuddapah. | Mr. V. Ramanuja Rao. | Brahmin. | Pleader, District Court, Cuddapah. | At a Public Meeting held at Cudapah in December 1891. |
| 775 | " | " | Bezwada | Mr. Tadanky Venkatanarasa Aiyar. | Brahmin. | Pleader ... ... | At a Public Meeting held at Bezwada on the 14th December 1891. |
| 776 | " | " | " | Devaguptam Seshachalapaty Row. | do. | Schoolmaster and Editor, "Krishna News." | do. |
| 777 | " | " | " | Mr. Singaraza Lingaya | do. | Pleader, Hony. Magistrate & Municipal Commissioner | do. |
| 778 | " | " | " | Mr. Madabhushi Lukshmi Narasinha Charyulu. | Hindu Vaishnava. | Pleader ... ... | do. |
| 779 | " | " | " | Mr. Katuri Narayanaswami Naidu. | Sudra. | Cashier ... ... | do. |
| 780 | " | " | " | Mr. Patri Venkata Subbaran. | Brahmin. | Landholder ... ... | do. |
| 781 | " | " | Trichinopoly. | Mr. A. Krishnaswamy Iyer. | do. | Landholder and Mirasdar ... | At a Public Meeting held at Trichinopoly on the 12th December 1891. |
| 782 | " | " | " | Mr. T. R. Ratnam Ayar, B.A. | do. | Professor, S. P. G. College ... | do. |
| 783 | " | " | Guntur | Mr. Paturi Shrivamulu . | do. | Pleader, Banker and Malguzar | At a Public Meeting held at Guntur on the 29th November 1891. |
| 784 | " | " | " | Mr. Sanagapolli Rama swami Chettiar. | Hindu Vaishya. | Merchant ... ... | do. |
| 785 | " | " | " | Mr. Nyapati Hanumanta Row. | Brahmin. | Teacher and Inamdar ... | do. |
| 786 | " | " | Rajah mundry. | Mr. Kolichena Appaya Dikshitulu, B.A. | do. | Teacher ... ... | do. |
| 787 | " | " | " | Mr. A. Sunderamaya, B.A. | do. | Pleader and Hony. Magistrate. | At a Public Meeting held at Rajamundry on the 5th December, 1891, |
| 788 | " | " | Coconada. | Rao Saheb N. Subbarao Puntulu, B.A., B.L. | do. | Vakil, High Court, Municipal Commissioner, and Member, Local and District Boards. | At a Public Meeting held at Coconada on the 18th December 1891. |
| 789 | " | " | " | Sri Rajah K.R.V. Krishnaram Bahadur. | do. | Zemindar ... ... | do. |

| Number. | Presidency or Government. | Congress Circle. | Electoral Division. | Names in full of Delegates, with honorary titles, scholastic degrees, etc. | Race, Religious denomination, and Caste, if any. | Occupation and Address. | How and when elected. |
|---|---|---|---|---|---|---|---|
| 790 | Madras. | Madras. | Bellary. | Mr. M. Ramanujalu Naidu. | Hindu Vaishnava | Contractor ... ... | At a Public Meeting held at Bellary on the 6th December 1891. |
| 791 | " | " | " | Rao Bahadur A. Sobapatty Mudaliar. | Hindu Valala. | Merchant, Millowner and Chairman, Municipality. | do. |
| 792 | " | " | " | Mr. B. Janardhanan Pillai. | Hindu. | Contractor ... ... | do. |
| 793 | " | " | " | Mr. K. Venkata Row ... | Brahmin. | Pleader, Landholder and Director, Bellary Spinning and Weaving Coy. | do. |
| 794 | " | " | Shrivalipatur. | Mr. R. M. Chittambaram Iyer. | do. | Pleader ... ... | At a Public Meeting held at Shrivalipatur on the 15th December 1891. |
| 795 | " | " | " | Mr. L. P. S. Shunmuga Naidu. | Hindu. | Merchant ... ... | do. |
| 796 | " | " | Gooty. | Rao Saheb P. Kesava Pillai. | Hindu Vaishnava | Pleader, Landholder and Member District Board. | At a Public Meeting held at Gooty on the 10th December 1891. |
| 797 | " | " | " | Mr. Amidala Cheunabasavamai Gand. | Hindu Singayet. | Landholder ... ... | do. |
| 798 | " | " | Madura. | Mr. M. T. Tirimalu Moodaliar. | do. | Mirasidar, Madura ... | At a Public Meeting held on the 2nd December 1891. |
| 799 | " | " | " | Mr. P. N. Muttusawmy Iyer, B.A., B. L, | Hindu Brahmin. | Vakil, High Court, Madura. | do. |
| 800 | " | " | " | Mr. J. M. Nalaswami Pillai, B.A., B.L. | Hindu. | do. do. ... | do. |
| 801 | " | " | North Arcot. | Mr. K. Nalathumby Mudaliar. | Hindu Valala. | Abkari Contractor ... | At a Public Meeting held at Arcot on the 20th December 1891. |
| 802 | " | " | Masulipatam. | Mr. M. Rambhotlu Chetty. | Hindu. | Merchant, Cuddapah ... | At a Public Meeting held in December 1891. |
| 803 | " | " | Mayaveram. | Mr Sivasami Sastrial ... | Brahmin. | Landlord ... ... | At a Public Meeting held at Mayaveram on the 11th December 1891. |
| 804 | " | " | Tinnevelly. | Mr. C. V. Ramanujalu Naidu. | Hindu Vaishnava. | do. | At a Public Meeting held at Tinnevelly on the 12th December 1891. |
| 805 | " | " | Nellore. | Mr. T. V. Venkatarama Aiyar, B.A., B. L. | Tamil Brahmin. | Vakil, High Court, and Member, District Board. | At a Public Meeting held at Nellore on the 18th December 1891. |
| 806 | " | " | " | Mr. Muturaji Vyankatraj Puntulu. | do. | Contractor ... ... | do. |
| 807 | " | " | Calicut. | The Honorable C. Sankaran Nair, B.A., B. L. | Hindu Nair. | Vakil, High Court, and Member, Legislative Council, Madras. | At a Public Meeting held at Calicut on the 4th December 1891. |
| 808 | " | " | " | Mr. C. Kirshnan, B.A., (Cantab.) | Hindu. | Barrister-at-Law ... | do. |
| 809 | " | " | " | Mr. C. Kunhi Raman Menon, B.A. | Nair Hindu. | Editor and Proprietor, "Kerala Patrika" and Member, District Board. | do. |
| 810 | " | " | Secunderabad. | Mr. Arcot Ramanujnm Modaliar. | Hindu. | Pensioner and Zemindar ... | At a Public Meeting held at Secunderabad on the 1st December 1891. |
| 811 | " | " | " | Mr. Pondicheri Ramachandra Pillay. | Hindu. | Pealder, High Court, and Landholder. | do. |
| 812 | " | " | " | Mr. P. Veeraghavalu Naidu. | do. | ...... | do |

DD

# APPENDIX II.

# SUMMARY OF RESOLUTIONS

PASSED AT THE

# FIRST, SECOND, THIRD, FOURTH, FIFTH AND SIXTH CONGRESSES.

## RESOLUTIONS PASSED AT THE FIRST CONGRESS.

### RESOLUTION I.

**Resolved**—That this Congress earnestly recommends that the promised inquiry into the working of the Indian Administration, here and in England, should be entrusted to a Royal Commission, the people of India being adequately represented thereon, and evidence taken both in India and in England.

### RESOLUTION II.

**Resolved**—That this Congress considers the abolition of the Council of the Secretary of State for India, as at present constituted, the necessary preliminary to all other reforms.

### RESOLUTION III.

**Resolved**—That this Congress considers the reform and expansion of the Supreme and existing Local Legislative Councils, by the admission of a considerable proportion of elected members (and the creation of similar Councils for the North-Western Provinces and Oudh, and also for the Punjab) essential; and holds that all Budgets should be referred to these Councils for consideration, their members being moreover empowered to interpellate the Executive in regard to all branches of the administration; and that a Standing Committee of the House of Commons should be constituted to receive and consider any formal protests that may be recorded by majorities of such Councils against the exercise by the Executive of the power which would be vested in it, of overruling the decisions of such majorities.

### RESOLUTION IV.

**Resolved**—That in the opinion of this Congress the competitive examinations now held in England for first appointments in various civil departments of the public service should henceforth, in accordance with the views of the India Office Committee of 1860, "be held simultaneously, one in England and one in India, both being as far as practicable identical in their nature, and those who compete in both countries being finally classified in one list according to merit," and that the successful candidates in India should be sent to England for further study, and subjected there to such further examinations as may seem needful. Further, that all other first appointments (excluding peonships, and the like) should be filled by competitive examinations held in India, under conditions calculated to secure such intellectual, moral, and physical qualifications as may be decided by Government to be necessary. Lastly, that the maximum age of candidates for entrance into the Covenanted Civil Service be raised to not less than 23 years.

### RESOLUTION V.

**Resolved**—That in the opinion of this Congress the proposed increase in the military expenditure of the empire is unnecessary, and, regard being had to the revenues of the empire and the existing circumstances of the country, excessive.

### RESOLUTION VI.

**Resolved**—That in the opinion of this Congress, if the increased demands for military expenditure are not to be, as they ought to be met, by retrenchment, they ought to be met, firstly, by the re-imposition of the Customs duties; and, secondly, by the extension of the license-tax to those classes of the community, official and non-official, at present exempted from it, care being taken that in the case of all classes a sufficiently high taxable minimum be maintained. And, further, that this Congress is of opinion that Great Britain should extend an imperial guarantee to the Indian debt.

### RESOLUTION VII.

**Resolved**—That this Congress deprecates the annexation of Upper Burmah, and considers that if the Government unfortunately decide on annexation, the entire country of Burmah should be separated form the Indian Viceroyalty and constituted a Crown Colony, as distinct in all matters from the Government of the country as is Ceylon.

### RESOLUTION VIII.

**Resolved**—That the resolutions passed by this Congress be communicated to the Political Associations in each province, and that these Associations be requested, with the help of similar bodies and other agencies, within their respective provinces, to adopt such measures as they may consider calculated to advance the settlement of the various questions dealt with in these resolutions.

### RESOLUTION IX.

**Resolved**—That the Indian National Congress re-assemble next year in Calcutta and sit on Tuesday, the 28th of December, 1886, and the next succeeding days.

---

## RESOLUTIONS PASSED AT THE SECOND CONGRESS.

### RESOLUTION I.

**Resolved**—That this Congress of Delegates from all parts of India do humbly offer its dutiful and loyal congratulations to Her Most Gracious Majesty, the Queen-Empress, on the approaching completion of the first half century of her memorable, beneficent and glorious reign, and heartily wish her many, many more, and happy years of rule over the great British Empire.

### RESOLUTION II.

**Resolved**—That this Congress regards with the deepest sympathy, and views with grave apprehension. the increasing poverty of vast numbers of the population of India and (although aware that the Government is not overlooking this matter and is contemplating certain palliatives) desires to record its fixed conviction that the introduction of Representative Institutions will prove one of the most important practical steps towards the amelioration of the condition of the people.

### RESOLUTION III.

**Resolved**—That this Congress do, emphatically, re-affirm the 3rd Resolution of the Congress of 1885, and distinctly declare its belief that the reform and expansion of the Council of the Governor-General for making laws and of the Provincial Legislative Councils, therein suggested, have now become essential alike in the interests of India and England.

### RESOLUTION IV.

**Resolved**—That this Congress is of opinion that, in giving practical effect to this essential reform, regard should be had (subject to such modifications as, on a more detailed examination of the question, may commend themselves to the Government) to the principles embodied in the following tentative suggestions :—

(1.)—The number of persons composing the Legislative Councils, both provincial and of the Governo General, to be materially increased. Not less than one-half the Members of such enlarged Council to be elected. Not more than one-fourth to be officials having seats *ex-officio* in such Councils, and not more than one-fourth to be Members, official or non-official, nominated by Government.

(2.)—The right to elect Members to the Provincial Councils to be conferred only on those classes and members of the community, *primâ facie*, capable of exercising it wisely and independently. In Bengal and Bombay the Councillors may be elected by the Members of Municipalities, District Boards, Chambers of Commerce and the Universities, or an electorate may be constituted of all persons possessing such qualifications, educational and pecuniary, as may be deemed necessary. In Madras the Councillors may be elected either by District Boards, Municipalities, Chambers of Commerce and the University, or by Electoral Colleges composed of Members partly elected by these bodies and partly nominated by Government. In the North-West Provinces and Oudh and in the Punjab Councillors may be elected by an Electoral College composed of Members elected by Municipal and District Boards, and nominated, to an extent not exceeding one-sixth of the total number, by Government, it being understood that the same elective system now in force where Municipal Boards are concerned will be applied to District Boards and the right of electing Members to these latter extended to the cultivating class. But whatever system be adopted (and the details must be worked out separately for each province) care must be taken that all sections of the community and all great interests are adequately represented.

(3.)—The elected Members of the Council of the Governor-General for making laws, to be elected by the elected Members of the several Provincial Councils.

(4.)—No elected or nominated Member of any Council to receive any salary or remuneration in virtue of such Membership, but any such Member, already in receipt of any Government salary or allowance, to continue to draw the same unchanged during Membership, and all Members to be entitled to be reimbursed any expenses incurred in travelling in connection with their Membership.

(5.)—All persons, resident in India, to be eligible for seats in Council, whether as electees or nominees, without distinction of race, creed, caste or colour.

(6.)—All legislative measures and all financial questions, including all budgets, whether these involve new or enhanced taxation or not, to be necessarily submitted to and dealt with by these Councils. In the case of all other branches of the administration, any Member to be at liberty, after due notice, to put any question he sees fit to the *ex-officio* Members (or such one of these as may be especially charged with the supervision of the particular branch concerned) and to be entitled (except as hereinafter provided) to receive a reply to his question, together with copies of any papers requisite for the thorough comprehension of the subject, and on this reply the Council to be at liberty to consider and discuss the question, and record thereon such resolution as may appear fitting to the majority. Provided that, if the subject in regard to which the inquiry is made involves matters of Foreign policy, Military dispositions or strategy, or is otherwise of such a nature that, in the opinion of the Executive, the public interests would be materially imperilled by the communication of the information asked for, it shall be competent for them to instruct the *ex-officio* Members, or one of them, to reply accordingly, and decline to furnish the information asked for.

(7.)—The Executive Government shall possess the power of overruling the decision arrived at by the majority of the Council, in every case in which, in its opinion, the public interests would suffer by the acceptance of such decision; but whenever this power is exercised, a full exposition of the grounds on which this has been considered necessary, shall be published within one month and in the case of local Governments they shall report the circumstances and explain their action to the Government of India, and in the case of this latter, it shall report and explain to the Secretary of State; and in any such case on a representation made through the Government of India and the Secretary of State by the overruled majority, it shall be competent to the Standing Committee of the House of Commons (recommended in the 3rd Resolution of last year's Congress which this present Congress has affirmed) to consider the matter, and call for any and all papers or information, and hear any persons on behalf of such majority or otherwise, and thereafter, if needful, report thereon to the full House.

## RESOLUTION V.

**Resolved**—That this Congress do invite all Public Bodies and all Associations throughout the Country, humbly and earnestly, to entreat His Excellency the Viceroy to obtain the sanction of Her Majesty's Secretary of State for India, to the appointment of a Commission, to enquire exhaustively into the best method of introducing such a tentative form of Representative Institutions into India, as has been indicated in Resolutions III. of the past, and IV. of the present year's Congress.

## RESOLUTION VI.

**Resolved**—That a Committee composed of the gentlemen named in the margin* be appointed to consider the Public Service Question and report thereon to this Congress.

* Hon'ble Dadabhai Naoroji (*Bombay*).
" S. Subramania Iyer (*Madras*).
" Peary Mohun Mookerjee (*Calcutta.*)
Mr. G. Subramania Iyer (*Madras*).
Babu Motilal Ghose (*Calcutta*).
Mr. Surendra Nath Banerjee (*Calcutta*).
" Gungapershad Varma (*Lucknow*).
" Ramkali Chaudhuri (*Benares*).
Mr. Guru Prasad Sen (*Patna*).
Pundit Prannath (*Lucknow*).
Munshi Kashipershad (*Allahabad*).
Nawab Reza Ali Khan (*Lucknow*).
Mr. Hamid Ali (*Lucknow*).
Lala Kanhyalal (*Amritsar*).
Rao Sahib Gungadhar Rao Madhaw Chitnavis (*Nagpur*).
Mr. Rahimatulla M. Sayani (*Bombay*).

## RESOLUTION VII.

**Resolved**—That this Congress approves and adopts the report* submitted by the Committee appointed by Resolution VI.

---

### * REPORT.

We, the Members of the Committee appointed by the Congress to submit a statement in connection with the Public Service Question, have the honor to report that the following resolutions were unanimously adopted by us at a meeting held yesterday:—

1.—That the open Competitive Examination be held simultaneously both in India and in England.

2.—That the simultaneous Examinations thus held be equally open to all classes of Her Majesty's subjects.

3.—That the classified lists be prepared according to merit.

4.—That the Congress express the hope that the Civil Service Commissioners will give fair consideration to Sanskrit and Arabic among the subjects of examination.

5.—That the age of candidates eligible for admission to the open Competitive Examination be not less than 19 nor, as recommended by Sir C. Aitchison, more than 23 years.

6.—That simultaneous examinations being granted, the Statutory Civil Service be closed for first appointments.

7.—That the appointments in the Statutory Civil Service, under the existing rules, be still left open to the Members of the Uncovenanted Service and to professional men of proved merit and ability.

8.—That all appointments requiring educational qualifications, other than covenanted first appointments, be filled by Competitive Examinations held in the different Provinces, and open in each Province to such natural-born subjects of H. M. only as are residents thereof.

These Resolutions, it is hoped, cover the main principles which underlie the questions set by the Public Service Commission. For a more detailed consideration there was no time.

(Sd.) DADABHAI NAOROJI,
*President of the Committee.*

*30th December 1886.*

### RESOLUTION VIII.

**Resolved**—That, in the opinion of this Congress, the time has now arrived when the system of trial by jury may be safely extended into many parts of the country where it is not at present in force.

### RESOLUTION IX.

**Resolved**—That, in the opinion of this Congress, the innovation made in 1872 in the system of trial by jury, depriving the verdicts of juries of all finality, has proved injurious to the country, and that the powers then, for the first time, vested in Sessions Judges and High Courts, of setting aside verdicts of acquittal, should be at once withdrawn.

### RESOLUTION X.

**Resolved**—That, in the opinion of this Congress, a provision, similar to that contained in the Summary Jurisdiction Act of England (under which accused persons in serious cases have the option of demanding a committal to the Sessions Court), should be introduced into the Indian Code of Criminal Procedure, enabling accused persons, in warrant cases, to demand that, instead of being tried by the Magistrate, they be committed to the Court of Sessions.

### RESOLUTION XI.

**Resolved**—That this Congress do place on record an expression of the universal conviction that a complete separation of executive and judicial functions (such that in no case the two functions shall be combined in the same officer) has become an urgent necessity, and that, in its opinion, it behoves the Government to effect this separation without further delay, even though this should, in some Provinces, involve some extra expenditure.

### RESOLUTION XII.

**Resolved**—That, in view of the unsettled state of public affairs in Europe, and the immense assistance that the people of this country, if duly prepared therefor, is capable of rendering to Great Britain in the event of any serious complications arising, this Congress do earnestly appeal to the Government to authorise (under such rules and restrictions as may to it seem fitting) a system of Volunteering for the Indian inhabitants of the country, such as may qualify them to support the Government effectively in any crisis.

### RESOLUTION XIII.

**Resolved**—That Standing Congress Committees be constituted at all important centres.

### RESOLUTION XIV.

**Resolved**—That the Third Indian National Congress assemble at Madras on the 27th of December, 1887.

### RESOLUTION XV.

**Resolved**—That, copies of these Resolutions be forwarded to His Excellency the Viceroy-in-Council, with the humble requests that he will cause the 1st Resolution to be submitted in due course to Her Majesty the Queen-Empress, that he will cause all the Resolutions to be laid before Her Majesty's Secretary of State for India, and that he himself will be graciously pleased, in consultation with his colleagues, to accord them his best consideration.

---

## RESOLUTIONS PASSED AT THE THIRD CONGRESS.

---

### RESOLUTION I.

**Resolved**—That a Committee is appointed, consisting of the gentlemen (marginally enumerated*) to consider what rules, if any, may now be usefully framed in regard to the constitution and working of the Congress, with instructions to report thereon to the Congress, on the 30th instant.

* Messrs. Namjoshi Chandavaker, Mir Humayun Jah Bahadur, Hajee Mahomed Abdul Shakoor Badshaw Sahib, S. Subramania Iyer, W. S. Gantz, Rangiah Naidu, Surendranath Banerjee, Trailokhyanath Mitra, Kali Charan Banerjee, Guru Prasad Sen, Saligram Singh, Ram Kali Chaudhuri, Hafiz Abdul Rahim, Rampal Singh, Pandit Madan Mohun, Ganga Prasad Varma, Bishan Narayen Dar, Hamid Ali, Murlidhur, Satyanand Agnihotri, H. H. Dhruva, W. C. Bonnerjee, Norendranath Sen, Eardley Norton, Joy Govind Shome, Iswari Lal Sircar, G. Subramania Iyer, D. A. Khare, S. A. Saminada Iyer, Sabapathy Mudaliar, A. O. Hume, C. Vigiya Raghava Chariar, Govind Buksh, Karandikar.

### RESOLUTION II.

**Resolved**—That this Congress re-affirms the necessity for the expansion and reform of the Council of the Governor-General for making, Laws, and the Provincial Legislative Councils, already set forth in Resolutions III. of the Congress of 1885 and 1886, and expresses the earnest hope that the Government will no longer delay action in the direction of this essential reform.

### RESOLUTION III.

**Resolved**—That this Congress once again places on record an expression of the universal conviction that a complete separation of the Executive and Judicial functions (such that in no case the two functions shall be combined in the same officer) has become an urgent necessity, and declares that, in its opinion, it behoves the Government to effect this separation, without further delay, even though this should, in some Provinces, involve some extra expenditure.

### RESOLUTION IV.

**Resolved** —That in view of the loyalty of Her Majesty's Indian subjects, this Congress considers it desirable that the Queen's Proclamation should be given effect to ; that the Military Service in its higher grades should be practically opened to the natives of this country ; and that the Government of India should establish Military Colleges in this country, whereat the natives of India, as defined by Statute, may be educated and trained for a military career as officers of the Indian Army.

### RESOLUTION V.

**Resolved**—That, in view of the unsettled state of public affairs in Europe, and the immense assistance that the people of this country, if duly prepared, therefor, are capable of rendering to Great Britain, in the event of any serious complications arising, this Congress once again earnestly appeals to the Government to authorize (under such rules and restrictions as may to it seem fitting,) a system of Volunteering for the Indian inhabitants of the country, such as may qualify them to support the Government, effectively, in any crisis.

### RESOLUTION VI.

**Resolved**—That, as the administration of the Income-Tax, especially as regards incomes below Rs. 1,000, has proved extremely unsatisfactory, it is essential, in the opinion of the Congress, that the taxable minimum be raised to Rs. 1,000, the loss of revenue thus involved being made good, and further financial difficulties, if any, met by reductions in the existing public expenditure, or, should this prove impossible, by the re-imposition of an import duty on the finer classes of cotton goods.

### RESOLUTION VII.

**Resolved**—That, having regard to the poverty of the people, it is desirable that the Government be moved to elaborate a system of Technical Education, suitable to the condition of the country, to encourage indigenous manufactures by a more strict observance of the orders, already existing, in regard to utilizing such manufactures for State purposes, and to employ more extensively, than at present, the skill and talents of the people of the country.

### RESOLUTION VIII.

**Resolved**—That, in view of the loyalty of the people, the hardships which the present Arms' Act (XI of 1878) causes, and the unmerited slur which it casts upon the people of this country, the Government be moved so to modify the provisions of Chapter IV., and, if necessary, other portions of the said Act, as shall enable all persons to possess and wear arms, unless debarred therefrom, either as individuals or members of particular communities or classes, by the orders of the Government of India (or any local authority empowered by the Government of India on that behalf) for reasons to be recorded in writing and duly published.

### RESOLUTION IX.

**Resolved**—That the rules drafted by the Committee appointed under Resolution I. stand over for consideration till next Congress, but that, in the meantime, copies be circulated to all Standing Congress Committees, with the request that they will, during the coming year, act in accordance with these rules, so far as this may seem to them possible and desirable, and report thereon to the next Congress, with such further suggestions as to them may seem meet.

### RESOLUTION X.

**Resolved**—That the Fourth Indian National Congress assemble at Allahabad on the 26th December, 1888.

### RESOLUTION XI.

**Resolved**—That copies of these Resolutions be forwarded to His Excellency the Viceroy-in-Council, with the humble request that he will cause all the Resolutions to be laid before Her Majesty's Secretary of State for India, and that he himself will be graciously pleased, in consultation with his colleagues, to accord them his best consideration.

## RESOLUTIONS PASSED AT THE FOURTH CONGRESS.

### RESOLUTION I.

**Resolved**—That this Congress affirms the necessity for the expansion and reform of the Council of the Governor-General for making laws and regulations, and of the existing Provincial Legislative Councils, already set forth in Resolutions III. of the Congress of 1885 and 1886, and Resolution II. of the Congress of 1887 (a tentative scheme for which expansion and reform was suggested in Resolution IV. of the Congress of 1886); and further urges that a Legislative Council (of the same character as those which have been suggested for Provinces where Legislative Councils already exist) be established for the Punjab.

### RESOLUTION II.

**Resolved**—That this Congress, while appreciating the concessions proposed in the Report of the Public Service Commission, yet feels it necessary to put distinctly on record its opinion that full justice will never be done to the people of this country until the open competitive examination for the Civil Service of India is held simultaneously in England and in India.

### RESOLUTION III.

**Resolved**—That this Congress, having read and considered Resolution XI. of the Congress of 1886, to wit—

> "That this Congress do place on record an expression of the universal conviction that a complete separa-"tion of the executive and judicial functions (such that in no case the two functions shall be "combined in the same officer) has become an urgent necessity; and that, in its opinion, it behoves "the Government to effect this separation without further delay; even though this should, in "some provinces, involve some extra expenditure"—

and Resolution III. of the Congress of 1887, to the same effect, does now, hereby, affirm the same respectively.

### RESOLUTION IV.

**Resolved**—That this Congress, having read and considered Resolution VIII. of the Congress of 1886, to wit—

> "That, in the opinion of this Congress, the time has now arrived when the system of trial by jury "may be safely extended into many parts of the country where it is not at present in force"—

Resolution IX. of the Congress of 1886, to wit—

> "That, in opinion of this Congress, the innovation made in 1872 in the system of trial by jury, de-"priving the verdicts of juries of all finality, has proved injurious to the country, and the powers "then for the first time vested in Sessions Judges and High Courts of setting aside verdicts of "acquittal should be at once withdrawn"—

and Resolution X. of the Congress of 1886, to wit—

> "That in the opinion of this Congress, a provision similar to that contained in the Summary Jurisdic-"tion Act of England (under which accused persons in serious cases have the option of demand-"ing a committal to the Sessions Court) should be introduced into the Indian Code of Criminal Proce-"dure, enabling accused persons, in warrant cases, to demand that, instead of being tried by the "Magistrate, they be committed to the Court of Sessions"—

does now, hereby, affirm the same respectively.

### RESOLUTION V.

**Resolved**—That, as it is the general belief of the people of this country that the existing system of police administration in India is highly unsatisfactory in itself and oppressive to them, the Government be respectfully urged to appoint a commission, consisting of official and non-official members, to investigate the entire question as speedily as possible.

## RESOLUTION VI.

**Resolved**—That this Congress having read and considered Resolution IV. of the Congress of 1887, to wit—

> "That in view of the loyalty of Her Majesty's Indian subjects, the Congress considers it desirable that the "Queen's Proclamation should be given effect to; that the Military services in the higher grades should "be practically opened to the natives of this country; and that the Government should establish "Military Colleges in the country whereat the natives of India, as defined by Statute, may be educated "and trained for a Military career as officers of the Indian Army."

Resolution XII. of the Congress of 1886, and Resolution V. of the Congress of 1887, to wit—

> "That in view of the unsettled state of public affairs in Europe, and the immense assistance that the "people of this country, if duly prepared therefor, are capable of rendering to Great Britain in the "event of any serious complications arising, the Congress once again earnestly appeals to the Government to authorize (under such rules and restrictions as to it may seem fitting) a system of "Volunteering for the Indian inhabitants of the country, such as may qualify them to support the "Government effectually in any crisis:"

and Resolution VIII. of the Congress of 1887, to wit—

> "That in view of the loyalty of the people, the hardships which the present Arms Act (XI of 1878) causes, "and the unmerited slur which it casts upon the people of this country, the Government be moved "so to modify the provisions of Chapter IV., and, if necessary, other portions of the said Act, as shall "enable all persons to possess and wear Arms unless debarred therefrom, either as individuals, or "members of particular communities or classes, by the orders of the Government of India, (or any "local authority empowered by the Government of India on that behalf), for reasons to be recorded "in writing and duly published;"

does now, hereby, affirm the same respectively.

## RESOLUTION VII.

**Resolved**—That, having regard to the fact that a serious increase in the consumption of intoxicants has taken place under the systems of Abkari and Excise now prevailing in India, the Government be respectfully urged to adopt some such improved system as shall tend to discourage insobriety.

## RESOLUTION VIII.

**Resolved**—That, as the administration of the Income-Tax, specially as regards incomes below Rs. 1,000, has proved extremely unsatisfactory, it is essential, in the opinion of the Congress, that the taxable minimum be raised to Rs. 1,000.

## RESOLUTION IX.

**Resolved**—That this Congress being of opinion that it is the first duty of the British Government in India to foster and encourage education, as well general as technical, in all its branches, and that the declaration made in the recent resolution of the Government of India on the subject of education is calculated to encourage the tendency to reduce imperial expenditure on education, and to withdraw from the control of it, respectfully urges upon Government the extreme importance of increasing, or at any rate of not decreasing, the present expenditure on education, and of the Government continuing to control the Educational Institutions of all kinds now existing.

## RESOLUTION X.

**Resolved**—That, having regard to the poverty of the people, the importance of encouraging indigenous manufactures, and the difficulty of practically introducing any general system of technical education with the present imperfect information, Government be moved to delay no longer the appointment of a mixed commission, to inquire into the present industrial condition of the country.

## RESOLUTION XI.

**Resolved**—That the foregoing Resolutions be submitted for the favourable consideration of His Excellency the Viceroy, and for transmission by him to Her Majesty's Government, with the humble request of this Congress that the reforms suggested in the said Resolutions (based as most of these are on Her Gracious Majesty's Proclamation of 1858) may now be effected; and that should it be deemed necessary first to institute any enquiry into any of the matters forming the subjects of these resolutions, such enquiry may be made, as speedily as possible, by a Parliamentary Committee.

## RESOLUTION XII.

**Resolved**—That this Congress, having watched with interest and sympathy the exertions that are being made in England for the total abrogation of laws and rules relating to the regulation of prostitution by the State in India, places on record its appreciation of the services thus rendered to this country, and its desire to co-operate by all means in its power in the attainment of this laudable object.

### RESOLUTION XIII.

**Resolved**—That no subject shall be passed for discussion by the Subject Committee or allowed to be discussed at any Congress by the President thereof, to the introduction of which the Hindu or Mahomedan Delegates as a body object, unanimously or nearly unanimously ; and that if, after the discussion of any subject which has been admitted for discussion, it shall appear that all the Hindu or all the Mahomedan Delegates, as a body, are unanimously, or nearly unanimously, opposed to the Resolution which it is proposed to pass thereon, such Resolution shall be dropped ; provided that this rule shall refer only to subjects in regard to which the Congress has not already definitely pronounced an opinion.

### RESOLUTION XIV.

**Resolved**—That the question of the introduction of a Permanent Settlement of the Land Revenue Demand into the Madras and Bombay Presidencies and other provinces be referred to the several Standing Congress Committees, with instructions to report upon the same, in so far as it affects their respective circles, to the Congress of 1889.

### RESOLUTION XV.

**Resolved**—That this Congress puts on record its disapproval of the recent enhancement of the Salt Tax, as involving a perceptible increase to the burthens of the poorer classes, as also the partial absorption, in a time of peace and plenty, of the only Financial Reserve of the Empire.

### RESOLUTION XVI.

**Resolved**—That the Fifth Indian National Congress do assemble in the Bombay Presidency (either at Bombay itself or at Poona, as may be settled hereafter) on the 26th of December, 1889.

### RESOLUTION XVII.

**Resolved**—That Mr. A. O. Hume be re-appointed General Secretary for the ensuing year.

---

## RESOLUTIONS PASSED AT THE FIFTH CONGRESS.

### RESOLUTION I.

**Resolved**—That an address be presented to Mr. Charles Bradlaugh, M.P., on behalf of this Congress here assembled, and that Messrs. Adam, Pherozshah Mehta, and W. C. Bonnerjee are appointed a Committee to settle the wording of the said address.

### RESOLUTION II.

**Resolved**—That the following skeleton scheme for the reform and reconstitution of the Council of the Governor-General for making Laws and Regulations, and the Provincial Legislative Councils, is adopted, and that the President of this Congress do submit the same to Charles Bradlaugh, Esq., M.P., with the respectful request of this Congress that he may be pleased to cause a Bill to be drafted on the lines indicated in this skeleton scheme and introduce the same in the British House of Commons :—

## SCHEME.

(1) The Imperial and Provincial Legislative Councils to consist respectively of members, not less than one-half of whom are to be elected, not more than one fourth to sit *ex-officio*, and the rest to be nominated by Government.

(2) Revenue districts to constitute ordinarily territorial units, for electoral purposes.

(3) All male British subjects above 21 years of age possessing certain qualifications and not subject to certain disqualifications (both of which will be settled later) to be voters.

(4) Voters in each district to elect representatives to one or more electoral bodies, according to local circumstances at the rate of 12 per million of the total population of the district, such representatives to possess certain qualifications and not to be subject to certain disqualifications, both of which will be settled later.

(5) All the representatives thus elected by all the districts included in the jurisdiction of each electoral body, to elect members to the Imperial Legislature at the rate of 1 per every five millions of the total population of the electoral jurisdiction, and to their own Provincial Legislature at the rate of 1 per million of the said total population, in such wise that whenever the Parsees, Christians, Mahomedans or Hindus are in a minority, the total number of Parsees, Christians, Mahomedans or Hindus, as the case may be, elected to the Provincial Legislature, shall not, so far as may be possible, bear a less proportion to the total number of members elected thereto, than the total number of Parsees, Christians, Hindus or Mahomedans, as the case may be, in such electoral jurisdiction, bears to its total population. Members of both legislatures to possess certain qualifications and not to be subject to certain disqualifications, both of which will be settled later.

(6) All elections to be by ballot.

## RESOLUTION III.

**Resolved**—That this present Congress does hereby ratify and confirm the resolutions passed by previous Congresses as to—

(*a*) the urgent necessity for the complete separation of executive and judicial functions, such that, in no case, shall the two functions be combined in the same officer ;

(*b*) the expediency of extending into many parts of the country, where it is not at present in force, the system of trial by jury ;

(*c*) the necessity of withdrawing from the High Courts, the powers, first vested in them in 1872, of setting aside verdicts of acquittal by juries ;

(*d*) the necessity of introducing, into the Code of Criminal Procedure, a provision enabling accused persons, in warrant cases, to demand that, instead of being tried by the Magistrate, they be committed to the Court of Sessions ;

(*e*) the highly unsatisfactory character of the existing system of Police Administration in India, and the absolute necessity of a fundamental reform therein ;

(*f*) the expediency of both, establishing Military Colleges in India, whereat the Natives of India, as defined by Statute, may be educated and trained for a military career as officers of the Indian Army, and of authorising, under such rules and restrictions as may seem necessary, such a system of volunteering for the Indian inhabitants of the country as may qualify them to support the Government in any crisis ;

(*g*) the extremely unsatisfactory character of the Income Tax Administration, especially as regards incomes below rupees one thousand, and the expediency of raising the taxable minimum to this amount :

(*h*) the extreme importance of increasing, instead of diminishing, as the present tendency ap pears to be, the public expenditure on education in all its branches, and the necessity, in view to the promotion of one of the most essential of these branches, the technical, of the appointment of a mixed commission to enquire into the present industrial condition of the country ;

(*i*) the impolicy and injustice involved in the late increase of the Salt Tax in a time of profound peace, and the urgent necessity for an immediate reduction of this tax, and the reimposition, to balance the deficit thus caused, of light *ad valorem* import duties ;

(*j*) the necessity for the reduction of, instead of the continual increase to, the military expenditure of the country.

## RESOLUTION IV.

**Resolved**—That this Congress hereby tenders its sincere thanks to Messrs. Caine and Smith, and the members who voted with them, in connection with the debate on the Indian Excise Question in the House of Commons ; and, while fully appreciating what has been done by some of the local Governments towards the improvement of their systems of Excise and Abkari, desires to express the earnest hope that no further time may be lost in giving full effect to the Resolution of the House of Commons.

## RESOLUTION V.

**Resolved**—That this Congress, while thanking Her Majesty's Government for raising the age for the Indian Civil Service Competitive Examination from 19 to 23, does hereby put on record an emphatic expression of the universal disappointment which has been created by the rest of that Government's orders in regard to the Public Service Question, (the net result of which orders is to place the people of India in a worse position than they previously held), and reiterates the national conviction that no real justice will be done to India, in this matter, until the simultaneous holding in India, and in England, of all examinations, for all Civil branches of the Public Service in India, at present held only in England, be conceded.

## RESOLUTION VI.

**Resolved**—That, in view of the loyalty of the people, the hardships, that the Arms Act (XI of 1878), as at present administered, entails, and the unmerited slur which it casts upon them, the Government be moved so to modify the rules made under this Act that all restrictions as to the possession and bearing of arms shall apply equally to all persons residing in or visiting India ; that licenses to possess and bear arms shall be liberally and generally distributed wherever wild animals habitually destroy human life, cattle or crops ; and that these and all licenses issued under the rules shall be granted once for all, shall operate throughout the Provincial jurisdiction within which they are issued, be only revocable on proof of misuse, and shall not require yearly or half-yearly renewals.

## RESOLUTION VII.

**Resolved**—That the Government be urged to take the subject of a Permanent Settlement once more under consideration in view to practical action thereon, such that fixity and permanency may be given to the Government Land Revenue demand without further delay, at any rate, in all fully populated and well cultivated tracts of country.

## RESOLUTION VIII.

**Resolved**—That, in view of the fall that has already occurred in the price of silver and in the exchange value of the Indian Rupee, it is impolitic on the part of the British Government to maintain any hindrances whatever to the consumption of silver for manufacturing purposes ; and that this Congress strongly urges upon Her Majesty's Government that, not only as an act of juctice to India (a matter which has been repeatedly brought to the notice of Her Majesty's Ministers), but also as an act of expediency in the interests of Her Majesty's British as well as Indian subjects, the plate duties should be immediately abolished, and Hall-marking be made a voluntary institution.

## RESOLUTION IX.

**Resolved**—That this Congress respectfully expresses the earnest hope that, in the interest of the people of India, the House of Commons will forthwith restore the right, formerly possessed by members of that Honourable House, of stating to Parliament any matter of grievance of the natives of India, before Mr. Speaker leaves the Chair, for the presentation in Committee of the Indian Budget statement, and earnestly trusts that the House of Commons will, in future, take into consideration the Annual Indian Budget statement at such a date as will ensure its full and adequate discussion ; and further authorizes the President, Sir William Wedderburn, Bart., to sign a petition in the name and on behalf of this Congress for presentation to the House of Commons in accordance with the terms of this Resolution.

## RESOLUTION X.

**Resolved**—That, in view to his approaching departure, this Congress puts on record an expression of the high sense entertained, not only in the Bombay Presidency, but throughout India, of the ability integrity and impartiality that have characterised Lord Reay's administration, as also of the gratitude which the whole country feels to be his due for the sympathy that he has ever extended to Indian aspirations and efforts.

## RESOLUTION XI.

**Resolved**—That the Subjects Committee be instructed to settle the question, (left open in the skeleton scheme for the reconstruction of the councils, embodied in Resolution II.), of the qualifications requisite for, and the disqualifications which should debar from, becoming—

(*a*) a Voter ;
(*b*) a Representative ;
(*c*) a Member of a Provincial Legislative Council ; and
(*d*) a Member of the Imperial Legislative Council ;

and to submit their Report thereon to Charles Bradlaugh, Esq., M.P., for the purposes of the Bill which he has been requested to have drawn.

## RESOLUTION XII.

**Resolved**—That Mr. A. O. Hume, C.B., be re-elected General Secretary of the National Indian Congress for the ensuing year.

## RESOLUTION XIII.

**Resolved**—

(*a*) That in view of the large number of delegates this year assembled, and the probability arising from past experience, of their number continuing to increase year by year, henceforth the number of delegates to be allowed from each Congress circle be limited to five per million of the total population of the circle : the Standing Committee of each circle allotting the number which their jurisdiction, as a whole, is entitled to elect, amongst their several electoral divisions, as may seem most expedient.

(*b*) That from the date of Mr. Hume's departure for England, the Hon'ble Pundit Ajoodhianath be appointed Joint General Secretary, and that Rs. 5,000 be assigned for the payment by him of such Assistant Secretaries as he may find it necessary to employ, clerical assistance, postage, telegraphs and printing ; and further that Mr. W. C. Bonnerjee be appointed Standing Counsel for Bengal, Mr. Pherozshah Mehta, Standing Counsel for Bombay, and Mr. Ananda Charlu, Standing Counsel for Madras, to the Joint General Secretary.

(*c*) That the tentative rules for the constitution and working of the Congress, which were first considered at Madras, and in regard to which various addenda have from time to time been circulated, be thoroughly considered during the coming year by the several Standing Congress Committees, and definitely dealt with by the Congress at its next session.

(*d*) That this Congress does hereby confirm the appointment of Sir W. Wedderburn, Bart., and Messrs. W. S. Caine, M.P., W. S. Bright Maclaren, M P., J. E. Ellis, M.P., Dadabhai Naoroji and George Yule, as a Committee (with power to add to their number) to guide and direct the operations and control the expenditure of the National Congress Agency in England, and does further tender its sincere thanks to these gentlemen, and to Mr. W. Digby, C.I.E., the Secretary for the service which they are rendering to India.

(*e*) That this Congress does formally appoint Mr. George Yule, Mr. A. O. Hume, Mr. Adam, Mr. Eardley Norton, Mr. J. E. Howard,* Mr. Pherozshah Mehta, Mr. Surendranath Banerjee, Mr. Mono Mohan Ghose, Mr. Shurfuddin, Mr. R. N. Mudholker, and Mr. W. C. Bonnerjee to represent its views in England and press upon the consideration of the British Public the political reforms which the Congress has advocated.

(*f*) That a sum of Rs. 45,000 be raised for the expenses of the Congress work in this country and in England during the ensuing year, and that the different Standing Committees do send their respective apportioned amounts to the General Secretary, the one half in three, and the balance in six months.

## RESOLUTION XIV.

**Resolved**—That the Sixth Indian National Congress do assemble at some City in Bengal, the exact place to be fixed hereafter, on the 26th of December, 1890.

## RESOLUTION XV.

**Resolved**—That the Fifth Indian National Congress hereby tenders its heart-felt thanks to its President, Sir William Wedderburn, as well for his ready sacrifice of personal and political considerations involved by his journey from England to India, as for that courtesy, impartiality and never-failing sympathy which, characteristics of his long and honourable career as an official of this country, have marked his control of the proceedings of this assembly.

---

* By some oversight, this gentleman's name was omitted, when the Resolution was read to the Congress ; the error has been rectified with the consent of the several Standing Congress Committees.

# RESOLUTIONS PASSED AT THE SIXTH CONGRESS.

## RESOLUTION I.

**Resolved**—That this Congress, having considered the draft Bill recently introduced into Parliament by Mr. Charles Bradlaugh, entitled "an Act to amend the Indian Councils Act of 1861," approves the same as calculated to secure a substantial instalment of that reform, in the Administration of India, for which it has been agitating, and humbly prays the Houses of Parliament of the United Kingdom of Great Britain and Ireland to pass the same into law; and further that its President, Mr. Pherozshah Mehta, is hereby empowered to draw up and sign, on behalf of this assembly, a petition to the House of Commons to the foregoing effect, and to transmit the same to Mr. Charles Bradlaugh for presentation, thereto, in due course.

## RESOLUTION II.

**Resolved**—That this present Congress does hereby ratify and confirm the resolutions passed by previous Congresses as to—

(*a*) the urgent necessity for the complete separation of executive and judicial functions, such that, in no case, shall the two functions be combined in the same officer;

(*b*) the expediency of extending into many parts of the country, where it is not at present in force, the system of trial by jury;

(*c*) the necessity of withdrawing from the High Courts the powers, first vested in them in 1872, of setting aside verdicts of acquittal by juries;

(*1*) the necessity of introducing, into the Code of Criminal Procedure, a provision enabling accused persons, in warrant cases, to demand that instead of being tried by the Magistrate they be committed to the Court of Sessions;

(*e*) the highly unsatisfactory character of the existing system of Police Administration in India, and the absolute necessity of a fundamental reform therein;

(*r*) the expediency of both, establishing Military Colleges in India, whereat the Natives of India, as defined by Statute, may be educated and trained for a military career as officers of the Indian Army, and of authorising, under such rules and restrictions as may seem necessary, such a system of volunteering, for the Indian inhabitants of the country, as may qualify them to support the Government in any crisis;

(*g*) the extremely unsatisfactory character of the Income Tax Administration, especially as regards incomes below rupees one thousand, and the expediency of raising the taxable minimum to this amount;

(*h*) the extreme importance of increasing, instead of diminishing, as the present tendency appears to be, the public expenditure on education in all its branches, and the necessity, in view to the promotion of one of the most essential of these branches, the technical, of the appointment of a mixed commission to enquire into the present industrial condition of the country;

(*i*) the necessity for the reduction of, instead of the continual increase to, the military expenditure of the country;

(*j*) the necessity, if any real justice is to be done to the people of India, of holding, simultaneously in India and England, examinations, at present held only in England, for the Civil branches of the Public Service in India;

(*k*) the expediency of so modifying the rules made under Act XI of 1878 (the Arms Act) that all restrictions as to the possession and bearing of arms shall apply equally to all persons residing in or visiting India; that licenses to possess and bear arms shall be liberally and generally distributed wherever wild animals habitually destroy human life, cattle or crops; and that these and all licenses issued under the rules shall be granted once for all, shall operate throughout the Provincial jurisdiction within which they are issued, be only revocable on proof of misuse, and shall not require yearly or half-yearly renewals.

## RESOLUTION III.

**Resolved**—That this Congress respectfully expresses the earnest hope that in the interest of the people of India, the House of Commons will forthwith restore the right formerly possessed by members of that Honourable House, of stating to Parliament any matter of grievance of the natives of India before Mr. Speaker leaves the chair for the presentation in Committee of the Indian Budget statement, and earnestly trusts that the House of commons will, in future, take into consideration the Annual Indian Budget statement at such a date as will ensure its full and adequate discussion, and further authorizes its President to sign a Petition, in the name and on behalf of this Congress, for presentation to the House of Commons, in accordance with the terms of this Resolution.

## RESOLUTION IV.

**Resolved**—That, while recognizing the action taken, in response to its previous prayers, in the matter of Excise Reform by H. M.'s Secretary of State for India and the Supreme Government here, and noting with pleasure the increase to the import duty on Spirits, the taxation imposed on Indian-brewed malt liquors, the decision of the Bengal Government to abolish the outstill system, and the closing of over 7,000 liquor shops by the Madras Government in 1889-90, this Congress regrets that it is still necessary to urge the Government of India to insist on *all* Provincial administrations carrying out in their integrity the policy in matters of Excise enunciated in paras. 103, 104 and 105 of the despatch published in the *Gazette of India* of March 1st, 1890, especially as to subsection 4 of para. 103, *viz.*—

"That efforts should be made to ascertain the existence of local public sentiment, and that a reasonable amount of deference should be paid to such opinion when ascertained."

## RESOLUTION V.

**Resolved**—That the condition of the Finances of India having materially improved, and those special circumstances on which the Government relied to justify the recent enhancement of the Salt Tax having practically ceased to exist, this Congress considers it essential that the enhancement referred to should be remitted at an early date, and empowers its President to submit a special memorial on the subject in its name and on its behalf to H. E. the Viceroy in Council.

## RESOLUTION VI.

**Resolved**—That having reference to the expectations created throughout the country by the Despatch of Her Majesty's Secretary of State in 1862, the principles of which were re-affirmed in a subsequent Despatch of 1865, promising the extension of a Permanent Settlement to all temporarily settled tracts in which certain conditions were fulfilled, and to the fact that throughout large portions of the country those conditions have long since been fulfilled, this Congress respectfully submits that the Government of India is now in honour bound to take up this question of Permanent Settlement, without further delay, in view to practical action thereon such that fixity and permanency may be given to the Government Land Revenue demand as explicitly promised, by Her Majesty's Secretary of State, more than a quarter of a century ago.

## RESOLUTION VII.

**Resolved**—That this Congress, having observed with surprise a notice, apparently official, in various Calcutta newspapers which runs as follows:—

THE CONGRESS.

"The Bengal Government having learnt that tickets of admission to the visitors' enclosure in the Congress pavilion have been sent to various Government officers residing in Calcutta, has issued a circular to all secretaries, and heads of departments subordinate to it, pointing out that under the orders of the Government of India the presence of Government officials, even as visitors at such meetings, is not advisable, and that their taking part in the proceedings of any such meetings is absolutely prohibited:"

and having also considered a letter addressed by the Private Secretary of His Honor the Lieutenant-Governor of Bengal to the Secretary of the Reception Committee, of which the following is an exact copy:—

BELVEDERE, *26th December* 1890.

"DEAR SIR,—In returning herewith the seven cards of admission to the visitors' enclosure of the Congress pavilion, which were kindly sent by you to my address yesterday afternoon, I am desired to say that the Lieutenant-Governor and the members of his household could not possibly avail themselves of these tickets, since the orders of the Government of India definitely prohibit the presence of Government officials at such meetings.

Yours faithfully,
P. C. LYON,
*Private Secretary.*

"To
J. GHOSAL, ESQ.,
*Secretary, Congress Reception Committee.*"

authorizes and instructs its President to draw the attention of His Excellency the Viceroy to the declaration embodied in these papers that Government servants are prohibited from attending any meetings of this Congress even as spectators, and to enquire, most respectfully, whether His Honor the Lieutenant-Governor of Bengal has, or has not, correctly interpreted the orders of the Government of India.

## RESOLUTION VIII.

**Resolved**—That the best thanks of this Congress be tendered to Mr. Charles Bradlaugh, M.P., for the invaluable services rendered by him during the past year, as also to Sir W. Wedderburn, Mr. W. S. Caine, Mr. J. Bright Maclaren, M.P., Mr. J. Ellis, M.P., Mr. George Yule, and Mr. Dadabhai Naorojee for the unselfish zeal and ability with which they have presided over the British Agency of the Congress; further that they put on record an expression of their high appreciation of the manner in which Mr. Digby, C.I.E., Secretary of the Agency, and Messrs. Surendra Nath Banerjee, R. N. Mudholkar, W. C. Bonnerjee, Eardly Norton, and A. O. Hume, delegates to England, respectively, discharged the onerous duties imposed upon them, and of their gratitude to all those members of the British public who so kindly welcomed and so sympathetically gave audience, in over fifty public and a far larger number of private meetings, to one or more of these delegates.

## RESOLUTION IX.

**Resolved**—That a vote of thanks be recorded to Kumar Debendra Mullick and brothers, proprietors of the Tivoli Gardens, Mr. N. C. Bose and Babu Bhupendra Nath Bose, proprietors of Mohan Bagan Villa, and to the Hon'ble Sir Romesh Chandra Mitra, Mr. T. N. Palit, Babus Janokee Nath Roy, Gopee Mohan Roy, Harendra Nath Roy, Kissory Mohan Roy, Ramanath Ghose, and Jamadar Ghasiram, owners of houses kindly lent for the use of delegates.

## RESOLUTION X.

**Resolved**—That the Seventh Indian National Congress do assemble on the 26th December, 1891. at either Madras or Nagpcre, as may be hereafter settled, in consultation between the Madras, Central Provinces and Berar Committees, and the Joint General Secretary.

## RESOLUTION XI.

**Resolved**—That provisional arrangements be made to hold a Congress, of not less than 100 delegates, in England, all things being convenient, in 1892, and that the several Standing Congress committees be directed to report, at the coming Congress, the names of the delegates that it is proposed to depute from their respective circles.

## RESOLUTION XII.

**Resolved**—That of the Funds now in the Joint General Secretary's hands and about to be received, a further sum of twenty thousand rupees be added to the Permanent Fund and placed in fixed deposits, and that the rest of the funds accruing on account of this current year, 1890, be held by him available for the immediate purposes of the British Committee of the Indian National Congress, but to be replaced as the subscriptions for 1891 are received, and ultimately, also added to the Permanent Fund.

## RESOLUTION XIII.

**Resolved**—That a sum of Rs. 40,000, exclusive of individual donations, is assigned for the expenses of the British Committee of the Congress and Rs. 6,000 for the General Secretary's Office and Establishment, and that the several circles and districts do contribute as arranged in Committee.

## RESOLUTION XIV.

**Resolved**—That Mr. A. O. Hume and Pandit Ajoodhia Nath are re-elected General and Joint-General Secretaries for the ensuing year.

## RESOLUTION XV.

**Resolved**—That this Congress does formally appoint Messrs. G. Yule, Pherozshah Mehta, W. C. Bonnerjee, J. Adam, Mono Mohan Ghose, A. O. Hume, Kali Charan Banerjee, Dadabhai Naorojee, D. A. Khare, and such other gentlemen as may volunteer for the duty with the sanction and approval of the Standing Congress Committees of their respective circles, to represent its views in England, and press upon the consideration of the British Public the political reforms which the Congress has advocated.

CALCUTTA :
*December 31st, 1890.*

PHEROZSHAH MEHTA,
*President of the Sixth Indian National Congress.*

# REPORT

OF THE

# EIGHTH

# Indian

# National Congress,

HELD AT

ALLAHABAD,

*On the 28th, 29th, and 30th of December,*

1892.

# Contents.

# SUMMARY OF RESOLUTIONS

PASSED AT THE

# EIGHTH INDIAN NATIONAL CONGRESS,

**Held at Allahabad on the 28th, 29th and 30th December, 1892.**

---

## Resolution I.

**Resolved**—That this Congress, while accepting in a loyal spirit the Indian Councils Act recently enacted by the Parliament of Great Britain, as explained by the present Prime Minister, with the assent of the then Under-Secretary of State for India,—that it is intended by it to give the people of India *a real living representation* in the Legislative Councils,—regrets that the Act itself does not, in terms, concede to the people the right of electing their own representatives to the Council, and hopes and expects that the rules, now being prepared under the Act, will be framed on the lines of Mr. Gladstone's declaration in the House of Commons, and will do adequate justice to the people of this country; further, that it prays that these rules may be published in the official Gazettes, like other proposed legislative measures, before being finally adopted.

## Resolution II.

**Resolved**—That this Congress hereby places on record its deep regret at the resolution of the Government of India on the report of the Public Service Commission, in that—

(*a*) Whereas, if the recommendations of the Public Service Commission had been carried out in their integrity, the posts proposed to be detached from the schedule of the Statute of 1861 would have formed part of an organised Service, specially reserved for the Natives of India, the resolution of Government leaves these posts altogether isolated, to which appointment can be made only under the Statute of 1870;

(*b*) Whereas, while 108 appointments were recommended by the Public Service Commission for the Provincial Service, 93 such appointments only have actually been thrown open to that Service: the number to be allotted to Assam not having yet been announced;

(*c*) Whereas, while a Membership of the Board of Revenue and a Commissionership of a Division, were recommended for the Province of Bengal and some other Provinces, the Government has not given effect to this resolution;

(*d*) Whereas, while one-third of the Judgeships were recommended to be thrown open to the Provincial Service, only one-fifth have been so thrown open. such

And this Congress, again, distinctly puts on record its opinion, that full justice will ı be done to the people of this country, until the open Competitive Examination for the Service of India is held simultaneously in England and in India.

## Resolution III.

**Resolved**—That this Congress, seeing the serious mischief arising to the the combination of Judicial and Executive functions in the same official, on on record its deliberate and earnest conviction that a complete separation of t has become an urgent necessity, and that, in its opinion, it behoves the Government to effect this separation without further delay, even though this should, in some provinces, involve extra expenditure.

## Resolution IV.

**Resolved**—That having regard to the diversity of opinion that prevails on the Currency Question, and the importance of the question itself, this Congress desires to express its earnest hope, that unless its hands are forced by the action of any Foreign Power, necessitating a change in the currency, or the standard, which might prove injurious to the interests of the country, the Government of India will refrain from taking any steps, until the labors of the Brussels Conference have been completed: and, further, that the Government will lay before the Public, for discussion, the proposals which Lord Herschell's Committee may recommend, before definite action, if any, is resolved upon.

## Resolution V.

**Resolved**—That this Congress concurs with its predecessors in strongly advocating—

(*a*) The reduction of the salt duty by at least the amount of its latest enhancement;

(*b*) The raising of the Income-tax taxable minimum from five-hundred to one thousand;

(*c*) Persistent pressure by the Government of India on all Provincial Administrations, to induce them to carry out, in its integrity, the Excise policy enunciated in paragraphs 103, 104, 105 of the Despatch, published in the Gazette of India of March, 1890, and the introduction of a simple system of local option in the case of all villages;

(*d*) The introduction into the Code of Criminal Procedure of a provision enabling accused persons, in warrant cases, to demand that instead of being tried by the Magistrate they may be committed to the Court of Sessions;

(*e*) The fundamental reform of the Police administration, by a reduction in the numbers and an increase in the salaries and in the qualifications of the lower grades, and their far more careful enlistment; and by the selection for the higher posts of gentlemen of higher capacities, more in touch with the respectable portions of the community, and less addicted to military pretensions, than the majority of existing Deputy Inspectors-General, Superintendents, and Assistant Superintendents of Police are;

(*f*) A modification of the rules under the Arms Act, so as to make them equally applicable to all residents in, or visitors to India, without distinction of creed, caste or colour; to ensure the liberal concession of licences wherever wild animals habitually destroy human life, cattle, or crops; and to make all licences, granted under the revised rules, of life-long tenure, revocable only on proof of misuse, and valid throughout the Provincial jurisdiction in which they are issued;

(*g*) The establishment of Military Colleges in India, whereat natives of India, as defined by statute, may be educated and trained for a military career as Commissioned or Non-commissioned Officers (according to capacity and qualifications) of the Indian army;

(*h*) The organising throughout the more warlike races of the Empire of a system of Militia service; and

(*i*) The authorising and stimulating of a wide-spread system of volunteering, such as obtains in Great Britain, amongst the people of India.

## Resolution VI.

**lved**—That this Congress views with the deepest concern and alarm the recent Government with respect to trial by Jury, and particularly the action of the of Bengal and Assam in withdrawing the right of trial by Jury in the erious offences, and most respectfully, but firmly, protests against such policy and action as retrograde, reactionary, and injurious to the best interests of the country, and prays that the same may be reversed by the Government of India, and failing that, by the Government in England; and that, as prayed for in resolutions of previous Congresses, the right of trial by Jury be extended to those parts of the country where it is not now in force, it being the only safeguard for the people in the present unsatisfactory condition of the administration of Criminal Justice in British India.

## Resolution VII.

**Resolved**—That having regard to the fact that the abnormal increase in the annual Military Expenditure of the Empire since 1885-86 is principally owing to the Military activity going on beyond the natural lines of the defences of the country, in pursuance of the Imperial policy of Great Britain in its relation with some of the Great Powers of Europe, this Congress is of opinion that, in bare justice to India, an equitable portion of that expenditure should be borne by the British Treasury, and that the revenues of India should be proportionately relieved of that burden.

## Resolution VIII.

**Resolved**—That this Congress is emphatically of opinion, that it is highly inexpedient in the present state of Education in the country, that Government grants for High Education should in any way be withdrawn, and, concurring with previous Congresses, affirms in the most emphatic manner, the importance of increasing the public expenditure on all branches of Education, and the expediency, in view to the promotion of one of the most essential of these branches, *i. e.*, the technical, of appointing a mixed Commission to enquire into the present industrial condition of the country.

## Resolution IX.

**Resolved**—That this Congress emphatically re-affirms Resolution III of the Congress of 1891, and having regard to the fact that fully fifty millions of the population, a number yearly increasing, are dragging out a miserable existence on the verge of starvation, and that in every decade several millions actually perish by starvation, deems it imperatively necessary that the cost of administration, especially in the military branch of the Public Service, should be greatly reduced, and that measures should at once be taken to give, as was promised by the British Government over thirty years ago, fixity and permanence to the land revenue demand, and thus permit capital and labour to combine to develop the agriculture of the country, which, under the existing system of temporary settlements, in recent times often lasting for short periods, in some cases only extending to ten and twelve years—is found to be impossible; and to establish Agricultural Banks. And this Congress, again, most earnestly entreats the people of Great Britain and Ireland, not to permit any further sacrifice of life owing to the shortcomings of the existing, doubtless well-intentioned, but none the less unsatisfactory, administration, but to insist, and, that speedily, on the reforms, then and now, so earnestly advocated.

## Resolution X.

**Resolved**—That this Congress entirely adopts Resolution XI of the Congress of 1891, and reiterates its prayer, that having regard to the very serious discontent created, particularly in Peninsular India, by the practical administration of the Forest Laws, the Government of India do investigate this matter carefully, and endeavour to mitigate the harshness of such administration, and render it less obnoxious to the poorer classes.

## Resolution XI.

**Resolved**—That Mr. W. C. Bonnerjee, Mr. P. M. Mehta, Mr. Surendra Nath Banerji, and Rai Bahadur Anunda Charlu, be appointed a Committee to prepare a petition on the line indicated by the petition printed at foot, and that the President be authorised to sign it, on behalf of this Congress, and send it to Mr. Dadabhai Naoroji, M. P., for presentation to the House of Commons.

To

The Hon'ble, The Commons of Great Britain and Ireland, in Parliament assembled.

The humble petition of the President and Members of the Eighth Indian National Congress, held at Allahabad, on the 28th, 29th and 30th of December, 1892;

*Respectfully Showeth,*

(1) That in conformity with a resolution adopted at the Eighth Indian National Congress, your humble petitioners beg to bring to the attention of your Hon'ble House, the deep disappointment which prevails in all parts of Her Majesty's Indian Empire at the orders passed upon the labours of the Public Service Commission.

(2) That the Commission was instructed by the Government of India to submit a scheme which might reasonably be expected to possess the elements of finality and to do full justice to the claims of the Natives of India to higher and more extensive employment in the Public Service. Neither object has been secured by the labours of the Public Service Commission. The Statutory Service, under which appointments had been made, has been abolished, and nothing has been done to secure to the people the full enjoyment of the boon conferred upon them by the Act of 1870. The Government of India, in their resolution appointing the Commission, observed, "that the Statute of 1870 is one of remarkable breadth and liberality, and it empowers the Government of India and the Secretary of State, acting together, to frame rules under which Natives of India may be admitted to any of the offices hitherto reserved for the Covenanted Civil Service." But the result of the Commission's enquiry has been a reduction in the number of offices open to Indians.

(3) That in respect, likewise, to simultaneous examinations in England and in India for appointment in the Civil Service, the Report of the Commission, endorsed by the Government of India, has given no satisfaction whatever. The weight of the evidence taken by the Commissioners was distinctly in favour of simultaneous examinations. Among the witnesses examined, there was a very large preponderance of those who were in favour of simultaneous examinations.

(4) That the disappointment which is everywhere felt at the resolution of the Government of India on the Public Service Commission, is of such a character that this Congress has felt constrained to lay the matter before the Hon'ble House, and to pray that it will direct the Government of India to give full effect to the Act of 1870, in the matter of appointing Natives of India to the Public Service of their country.

## Resolution XII.

**Resolved**—That this Congress, in concurrence with the first Congress held at Bombay in 1885, considers that the creation of a Legislative Council for the Province of the Punjab is an absolute necessity for the good Government of that Province, and, having regard to the fact that a similar Council has been created for the United Provinces, hopes that no time will be lost in creating such a Council.

## Resolution XIII.

**Resolved**—That this Congress hereby tenders its most grateful acknowledgments to Sir W. Wedderburn and the members of the British Congress Committee, for the services rendered by them to India during the past year, and entirely approves and confirms the re-construction of the British Committee of the Congress which has been effected by them, as also the new arrangements which they have made in regard to their office establishment, and the journal "*India*;" and that this Congress also tenders its thanks to Mr. W. Digby, C. I. E., for the services which he rendered to the cause during his tenure of office as Secretary to the British Committee.

## Resolution XIV.

**Resolved**—That this Congress is thankful that the House of Commons is vigilant in regard to the recent purity legislation by the Government in India, and desires, once again, to enter its protest against all State-regulated immorality in India.

## Resolution XV.

**Resolved**—That, regard being had to the present political situation in England, the provisional arrangements set on foot, in pursuance of the resolution passed at the Calcutta Congress, 1890, for holding—all things being convenient—a Congress of not less than hundred delegates in England, in 1892, be now suspended, until after the Session of the Congress in 1893.

## Resolution XVI.

**Resolved**—That this Congress most respectfully and cordially tenders, on behalf of the vast population it represents, India's most heartfelt thanks to the electors of Central Finsbury for electing Mr. Dadabhai Naoroji their member in the House of Commons; and it again puts on record its high estimate and deep appreciation of the services which that gentleman has rendered to this country, reiterates its unshaken confidence in him, and looks upon him as India's representative in the House of Commons.

## Resolution XVII.

**Resolved**—That this Congress hereby empowers the Trustees of the Congress Permanent Fund—now locked up in the "New Oriental Bank Corporation, Ld.," at present in liquidation—to send, at least, five hundred pounds out of it to the British Committee, to be recouped by subscriptions from the Standing Congress Committees.

## Resolution XVIII.

**Resolved**—That, regard being had to the representations received from the British Committee, this Congress is of opinion, that a sum equivalent in Rupees to two thousand eight hundred pounds sterling, be allotted for the expenses of the British Committee, for the year 1892-93; that deducting the money which has been received up to now, the balance be allotted amongst the different Standing Congress Committees, in accordance with the arrangements come to with them; and that the sum be remitted to England as soon as practicable.

## Resolution XIX.

**Resolved**—That this Congress re-appoints Mr. A. O. Hume, C. B., to be its General Secretary, and appoints Rai Bahadur P. Ananda Charlu, to be its Joint-General Secretary for the ensuing year.

## Resolution XX.

**Resolved**—That the Ninth Indian National Congress do assemble on such day after Christmas, 1893, as may be determined upon, at Amritsar.

## Resolution XXI.

**Resolved**—That this Congress hereby tenders its best thanks to His Highness the Maharaja of Darbhanga, for having so kindly lent his Castle and grounds for the holding of this Congress.

## Resolution XXII.

**Resolved**—That this Congress confirms the appointment of Pandit Bishumbhar Nath, in place of the late Pandit Ajudhia Nath, as one of the Trustees of the Congress Permanent Fund.

W. C. BONNERJEE,

*President of the Eighth Indian National Congress.*

# DETAILED
# REPORT OF THE PROCEEDINGS
OF THE
# EIGHTH INDIAN NATIONAL CONGRESS,
HELD AT
# *ALLAHABAD,*
**On the 28th, 29th, and 30th of December, 1892.**

## FIRST DAY'S PROCEEDINGS.

**1st Day.**

The Eighth Indian National Congress assembled on the afternoon of the 28th of December, 1892, in a large octagonal Hall, specially erected for the purpose, on the grounds of Lowther Castle, at the very place at which the Fourth Congress had met four years before. The Castle, which is now the property of His Highness the Maharaja of Darbhanga, had been very generously placed by him at the disposal of the Reception Committee; and its extensive grounds were once more covered with rows upon rows of tents, in which more than 400 delegates were housed, the rest finding accommodation elsewhere.

The Hall measured 150 feet by 150 feet, and afforded room for 3,500 chairs for delegates and visitors. It was a splendid structure,* and admittedly surpassed in elegance and finish, the best of the halls in which the Congress had held its deliberations before.

By about 1 P. M., over 600 delegates and 2,400 visitors had taken their seats within the pavilion. At a quarter past one, came PANDIT BISHUMBHAR NATH, the venerable Chairman of the Reception Committee, and took his seat on the platform. He had been ailing seriously for some months past; but, nerved by his strong sense of duty, he came, at considerable risk to his health, to discharge the duties which appertained to his office, as Chairman, of welcoming the delegates and of opening the proceedings of the Congress.

Precisely at 1-30 P. M., Pandit Bishumbhar Nath, (*Allahabad, No.* 333, *in list*) rose and said:—

**Chairman of Reception Committee's Address.**

MY SISTER AND BROTHER DELEGATES,—Though professing to be a devout votary of Temperance up to this moment, I feel something has just inebriated me. It cannot be alcohol or wine. It is something too cheery and elevating. It is, I fancy, that cordial nectar, the intoxicating pleasure of meeting you all here in this hall of all nations. (*Cheers*). My proper function, on this occasion, I am happy to notice, is a short and sweet one, and equally grateful to my own feelings. I have not to preach a sermon from the pulpit, nor to inflict upon you a long verbose speech with a pyrotechnic display of oratory. My duty is simply to bow to you all, and wish you cordial greetings after my oriental etiquette.

An indifferent speaker, such as I am, might naturally feel nervous on rising to address so grand an assemblage, which, I may say without using any figure of hyperbole, is a miniature imitation of the highest deliberative Council in the world. Should

* The entire credit of this exceedingly effective construction belonged to Lala Ram Charan Das, Rai Bahadur, Senior Vice-Chairman of the Municipal Board, Honorary Magistrate and Banker, of Allahabad, under whose direction and superintendence the Hall was planned and built.

my words fail me in giving expression adequately to my grateful feelings, I am confident you will appreciate the language of my heart, which, I believe, is the proper vehicle for conveying the sense of gratitude and esteem. Permit me then, on behalf and in the name of the Reception Committee, who have done me an honour that I do not deserve, to welcome you here to the Eighth Indian National Congress. (*Cheers*). The welcome, I beg to offer you, is not merely a ceremonious one. It is, I assure you, prompted by that *sanctum sanctorum*, the heart of hearts. There is an Arabic saying which in plain English means "Seldomer, the Welcomer,"—its paraphrase being—add to affection come by alternation. You are, therefore, the more welcome as we have the pleasure of meeting here again after a rather long interval of four years.

You must have observed, I dare say, that there is a certain amount of advantage, combined with convenience, in the situation of this our tabernacle, close as it is to the Government House. Had we been privileged to establish a telephonic communication, between that stately mansion and this cottage of the people, His Honour the Lieutenant-Governor (*Cheers*) would have been able to listen to what we say, and thus to give us a hearing, if it so pleased him. But His Honour proceeded on his winter tour only yesterday.

As I proceed further, I cannot help observing, that in our mundane affairs smiles and tears stand sometimes side by side, and that joy and sorrow are, as it were, born twins, as a Persian phrase goes. You will, therefore, excuse me, if you find me animated or affected by mixed feelings of pleasure and pain. I am exceedingly glad to see so many worthy representatives assembled here from the various parts of this vast peninsula. And your genial presence, while it has brought a cheery sunshine into our midst, proves to demonstration that the keen, abiding interest evinced in our movement, is keeping pace with the steady development of the movement itself. At the same time, I am grievously sad to miss from amongst us that noble patriot of his country, whom alas ! I see only in shadow and not in substance now, and into whose shoes I have been constrained, against my own will, to step by an unfortunate devolution of melancholy succession. Lamentable it is, indeed, that the necrology of our other leading men has swelled out of all proportions, and that we have to mourn deeply their untimely and premature loss. But as survivors left in the field, it behoves us to complete what they unfortunately have not been able to finish. It is our duty to cherish and perpetuate their sacred memory, and in order to attain that object, we must strive to lay stone upon stone, layer upon layer, and storey upon storey, until our Temple of Liberty rears up its proud head and reaches its destined pinnacle of glory, to the utter amazement and confusion of those who have been watching its rise with a degree of unjustifiable suspicion and mistrust. (*Cheers*).

This monument, no doubt, serves as the best living testimony of the blessings of liberty which we happily enjoy under the *Pax Britannica*. And the common platform, upon which we stand hand in hand, has its solid foundation sunk deep in the adamantine rock of true devotion to the august Throne of our beloved Sovereign, the Queen-Empress of India. (*Cheers*). Every true Englishman, with whom the love of Liberty is an instinct, must rejoice in his heart to witness that that proud day in the history of the British occupation of India has come, when the children of the soil have learnt to stand upon their feet, and are now claiming their just rights in a loyal and constitutional manner. Both posterity and the history of our movement when written calmly, will, I am convinced, accord a just appreciation to its legitimate aims and reasonable objects. They not only err but sin, and sin criminally too, who insinuate that this movement is calculated to sap and undermine the foundation of constituted authority. (*Hear, Hear*, and *Cheers*). To be sure, such sappers and miners its supporters are not. Indeed, they are the sentinels in a hopeful band of volunteers, whose watch-word and bugle-call are, "Beware of true enemies in the guise of false friends." And the shibboleth of that band, marching forward with the banner of liberty, is—Peace, Progress, and Political advancement. The movement, instead of being a heap of loose dynamite, as it has been stigmatised, is a useful and necessary safety-valve in the highly complex machinery of the British rule in India. Our position has been well recognised by that eminent statesman, His Excellency Lord Lansdowne, our ruling Viceroy, and we do not now stand in need of any more characters from the minor satellites. (*Cheers*).

**1st Day.**

**Chairman of Reception Committee's Address.**

The late Lord Lytton, one of our distinguished Viceroys, on the occasion of the Delhi Assemblage, was pleased to observe that the polity affecting the well being of the British Indian Empire involved administrative problems left unsolved by Cæsar, unsolved by Charlemagne, and unsolved by Akbar. Of these, a crucial problem, which is, I believe, the burning question of the day, is, what is the possible remedy for ameliorating the condition of the 280,000,000 of souls in this extremely poor country. I would venture to reply, that the remedy is not far to seek. It lies in reducing the enormous military expenditure, in curtailing the "Home charges," and in mitigating the general rigour of taxation (*Cheers*). It is true that the British rule, as regards its intrinsic value, is solid pure gold, and therefore, as costly as that precious metal itself. It is, however, a true axiom of modern political science, that a State must adapt its polity to the good of its people, and that it must govern them not only justly, but cheaply too. Lord Brougham says, somewhere in his *Political Philosophy*, that "the good of the people is the only object to be considered in the arrangements of Government, and that this fundamental doctrine is the test by which every institution must be tried; and every institution is to be supported or condemned according as it is found sufficient to answer its purpose of promoting the common good or wanting in this object." There are various other means that might be resorted to for bettering the condition of the people here, such as utilising indigenous products and materials, and giving a more extended scope to the employment of competent Indians, of proved merit, in the public service, without distinction of colour and creed, which is a great bane of an alien rule. (*Cheers*).

I may, now, as well proceed to observe that our present Session is the *calmy eighth* in contrast to the *stormy fourth*. In 1888, the opposition shewn on the part of the local authorities, lamentably countenanced by the narrow policy of our late Pro-Consul, had naturally roused our enthusiasm to such a pitch that it not only over-powered and crushed down opposition, but frustrated all selfish designs to set one class against another. Happily, however, though there is now a lull in that respect, the movement has acquired a lasting permanency, which it is impossible to shake or disturb. (*Cheers*). Certain incidents, with which we were amused on the occasion of the last session here, and the adverse criticisms, which left a fugitive effect upon our minds, stale and unprofitable as they now are, have all faded out of our view, and been happily relegated to the limbo of oblivion. Raja Shiva Prasad too with all his stars and decorations and historical lore, both sacred and profane, (*Laughter*) has evidently received no inspiration to re-appear on the scene; and a bogus Patriotic Association, started by him and his colleagues, did die a natural death so soon as it was born. Is this not a true touchstone for testing the righteousness or otherwise of a cause? (*Cheers*).

Sir Auckland Colvin, in the midst of an over-crowded programme of his hygienic and humanitarian fads, has left some testamentary relics of a fragmentary nature. One of them is his studied and laboured oration delivered not long ago at the Mahomedan Anglo-Oriental College at Aligarh. He there confessed to having borrowed a great deal of his politics from the political teachings of the venerable sage there. (*Hear, Hear*). It is the repetition of the old story again, that the introduction of a representative system on an expanded basis into our Legislative Councils would not suit the existing condition of our people. We need not now care much for such imbecile platitudes. We have gained a partial victory. (*Cheers*). The India Councils Bill has passed into law. And though we have not got all that we wanted, the day, I hope, is within measurable distance, when the enlightened and benevolent policy of the Liberal statesmen and the intuitively generous instincts of the British nation will prompt them, in the interests of justice, to concede further the privileges claimed by Her Majesty's Indian subjects, who yield to none in their devotion to their Sovereign. (*Cheers*).

Permit me to say a word as to the necessity or otherwise of holding these annual sessions of the Congress. Some of our critics say that it is a sheer waste of money spent upon, what they are pleased to call, "talking Camps," and that the enormous amount wasted already might have been profitably used otherwise, with far better and more practical results. I regret I am unable to share this view. In the good old days some fanciful means and appliances were hit upon, now and then, by the then rulers of this country, for the purpose of enabling their people to make their personal grievances audible. Anang Pal, a distinguished Hindu monarch, and long after him the Emperor Jahangir, had fastened for the purpose, in their palaces at Delhi and Agra respectively 'chains of justice' made of gold. But such chains could scarcely have been of any practical service or use, even in those days, when the wonderful powers of steam and electricity had not been discovered or utilised. We are now at the fag-end of the nineteenth century, and live under the ægis of a rule, which recognises only lawful agitation by constitutional means. Hence the necessity of our resorting to such a course. Whether such agitation is a blessing or a curse of the present civilisation, I do not propose to discuss here. We must go on, and go on vigorously, and not cease to agitate until we reach the goal of our ambition. (*Cheers.*)

The rise and growth of the British Indian Empire, with its great dimensions, enormous population, and vast resources, will stand unparalleled in the annals of the world. And it will remain a marvel for ever how a handful of merchants, trading originally in tea and silk, have carved out for their sovereign an empire, in comparison with which the historical Roman Empire falls into the shade. (*Hear, Hear*). Whether this brightest jewel in the diadem of Britannia has been acquired by a breach or observance of the Ten Commandments is a matter that need not be discussed here. One thing is quite obvious. Its safe preservation in her casket needs an extension of a more considerate and liberal treatment towards those from whose exhausted mines it has found its way into distant shores. (*Cheers*). The Bible of the British Constitution is as Christian as the Gospel of the faith of the British people. And it is to the truths inculcated in that Bible that we appeal most earnestly for the political regeneration of India ; and Her Majesty's Indian subjects, who represent races once great in their own way but now comparatively behind in the race of progress, do crave from Her that humane treatment which the mighty can well afford to vouchsafe to the fallen. (*Cheers*). The Political Emancipation of India will be a landmark in the history of the British civilisation, and when that time comes, and come it must, it will change the relations between the conqueror and the conquered, into those of affectionate ties and intimate friendship. (*Cheers*).

Many speculative persons, I observe, have been exercising their minds, by asking themselves—Why ought England to retain India ? I would say to them—Because India wants to be retained by England, and by no other power on earth. (*Cheers*). If Russia dares to move an inch beyond the line of demarcation, chalked out for her, she must think over twice before she ventures to take such a perilous step. (*Cheers*).

I must now close by being allowed to quote a passage from a useful work. It is :—"That the deep sense of duty, a special heritage of the British nation, handed down to them from the days of their Puritan ancestors, has made them scorn the idea of holding rule over others, solely to benefit themselves. And this feeling, I hope, will retain its strength in upholding her beneficial rule over India for many many generations to come." To this I myself would say thrice—Amen, amen, amen. (*Cheers*).

It only remains for me now to request you to elect a President for this assembly. I crave one word more. I appeal to those who have eyes to see for themselves and not jaundiced eyes as some of our journalistic friends seem to have. Let them judge and say whether the present session is duller than the dullest, or livelier than the liveliest that we ever had before. (*Cheers*).

I beg your pardon for my feeble and tremulous voice which I have lost during my illness. (*Prolonged cheering*).

**Election of President.**

**Mr. Ananda Charlu proposes Mr. W. C. Bonnerjee**

MR. P. ANANDA CHARLU, (*Madras, No.* 1, *in list*).—President of the Seventh Indian National Congress, who on rising was greeted with cheers, said :—GENTLEMEN,—As your cheers have preceded me, so I precede the distinguished gentleman whose name I am going to propose to you for election as your President. It has been said that we have finished one cycle and are beginning another. It is therefore most appropriate that the gentleman who inaugurated the first cycle should be here to attend the opening of the second cycle.

**1st Day.**

**Election of President.**

The first cycle began in a very small way, but to what proportions it rose we all know. (*Cheers*). Let this be the small beginning of another cycle which I hope Mr. W. C. Bonnerjee, whom I propose to be your President, will succeed in making it swell to larger dimensions still. (*Cheers*).

**Mr. Wacha seconds.**

MR. DINSHAW EDULJI WACHA, (*Bombay, No. 39, in list*,).—GENTLEMEN,—I have the honour to second the proposition which has been just proposed. I think my friend is right in saying that this is the beginning of the second cycle of the Congress. The first cycle took its birth in Bombay, and being a Bombay man, I feel a peculiar pride and pleasure in seconding the resolution. Gentlemen, it was intended that this Resolution should have been seconded by Mr. Pherozeshah Mehta, but I regret to say that unfortunately at the last moment he was laid up with fever and has not been able to attend this Congress. With these words I heartily second the proposition which my friend has proposed. In Mr. Bonnerjee you will find the stoutest and most ardent advocate the Congress has, and its strongest pillar too. (*Cheers*).

**Mr. Bonnerjee declared elected.**

PANDIT BISHUMBHAR NATH, (*Allahabad, No.* 333, *in list*).—GENTLEMEN,—It is evident from the manner in which you have received the proposal to elect Mr. W. C. Bonnerjee, as your President, that you heartily approve it. There is no other proposal before you. I take it then that it is your unanimous desire that Mr. W. C. Bonerjee should be your President. (*Cries of yes, yes, and prolonged cheers*). I declare Mr. Bonnerjee to be duly elected President of this Congress, and (*addressing Mr. Bonnerjee*) I request you, Sir, to kindly take the chair.

Mr. W. C. Bonnerjee, (*Calcutta, No.* 178, *in list*,) then took the chair amid deafening cheers. When the ovation had subsided—

**Babu Surendra Nath Banerji reads a message of welcome from H. H. the Maharaja of Durbhanga.**

BABU SURENDRA NATH BANERJI, (*Calcutta, No.* 188, *in list*) rose and said :—GENTLEMEN,—Before we proceed with the business of the day, I have been requested by the President to inform you that he has just received a telegram from His Highness the Maharaja of Durbhanga (*cheers*,) which, I am sure, will afford you the greatest satisfaction to hear.—The telegram runs as follows :—

"As Proprietor of Lowther Castle, I welcome the delegates to the Congress. It is a source of the greatest pleasure to me that the first use of this property, since my acquiring it, has been for Congress purposes."

In response to a call from Babu Surendra Nath Banerji, three hearty cheers were given to His Highness the Maharaja.

**The President's Inaugural Address.**

MR. W. C. BONNERJEE, (*Calcutta, No.* 178, *in list*) who was received with renewed cheers, then rose and addressed the assembly as follows :—

BROTHER DELEGATES, LADIES AND GENTLEMEN,—The position, which, by your unanimous voice, you have called me to fill, is a most distinguished and honourable one. I am proud to fill it, and I trust that, with your help and by your forbearance, I may be able to discharge the duties which will be required of me as the President of the Eighth Indian National Congress adequately and satisfactorily. (*Cheers*). Those duties, as all of you who have attended our Congresses before know, are heavy and onerous in the extreme, and I appeal to you to deal out to me, in the same spirit in which you dealt out to my predecessors, such help and indulgence as may be needed by me.

You have been reminded that I have the honour to be the person, who inaugurated the Congress movement in Bombay, in the year 1885, as its first President. It is a singular coincidence that the Bombay Meeting was held on this very day, the 28th of December. The first cycle of our existence thus commenced on the 28th December, under my humble presidency, and ended with the presidency of my friend Mr. Ananda Charlu, who so kindly proposed my election. The second cycle begins on the same day seven years afterwards, again under my humble presidency. At the first Congress there were only a few of us assembled together, but as I pointed out at the time, there were various causes which prevented a larger muster. Those, however, who assembled there on that occasion, were animated by a sincere desire to make the movement a success and fully determined that it should be so if hard work could effect it. And I appeal to those assembled here to-day to say whether that movement has been a success or not. (*Applause*). Year after year we have met, each meeting vieing with its predecessor in the number of delegates attending it, the sacrifices which the delegates made to attend it, in the energy, zeal and determination with which the business was passed through, and the moderation which throughout characterised the proceedings before the Congress. There can be no doubt—say what those who do not view our proceedings with friendly eyes, may—that the Congress movement has been a success and a conspicuous success. The persons to whom I have referred have been troubling their brains, from almost the very commencement of the movement, to find out how it is that this movement, which they are pleased to call only a "native" movement, has been such a success. And they have hit upon one of the causes, which they have, iterated and reiterated, in season and out of season, as the cause of the success of the Congress; namely, the influence over us of that great man Allan Octavian Hume. (*Loud and prolonged cheers*). That Mr. Hume possesses, and has exercised, a vast amount of influence over the Congress movement, and over each single Congress which has met, is a fact. We are not only not ashamed to acknowledge it, but we acknowledge it with gratitude to that gentleman, and we are proud of his connection with the Congress. (*Cheers*). But the movement is only to some extent, and I may say, only to a limited extent, due to the influence which Mr. Hume has exercised over us. It is not the influence of this man, or of that man, or of any third man that has made the Congress what it is. It is the British Professors who have discoursed eloquently to us on the glorious constitution of their country; it is the British Merchants who have shown to us how well to deal with the commodities of our country; it is the British Engineers who have annihilated distance and enabled us to come together for our deliberation from all parts of the Empire; it is the British Planters who have shown us how best to raise the products of our soil; it is all these, in other words, it is all the influences which emanate from British rule in India that have made the Congress the success it is. (*Cheers*). The Congress is a mere manifestation of the good work that has been done by all those to whom I have referred (and I ought also to have referred to the British missionaries who have worked amongst us); and all that we wish by this movement to do is, to ask the British public, both in this country and in Great Britain, that, without any strain on the connection which exists between Great Britain and this country, such measures may be adopted by the ruling authorities that the grievances under which we labour may be removed, and that we may hereafter have the same facilities of national life that exist in Great Britain herself. How long it will take us to reach the latter end no one can tell; but it is our duty to keep the hope of it before us, and keep reminding our British fellow subjects that this hope shall always be with us. (*Cheers.*)

Some of our critics have been busy in telling us, thinking they knew our affairs better than we know them ourselves, that we ought not to meddle with political matters, but leaving politics aside devote ourselves to social subjects and so improve the social system of our country. I am one of those who have very little faith in the public discussion of social matters; those are things which, I think, ought to be left to the individuals of a community who belong to the same social organisation, to do what they can for its improvement. We know how excited people become when social subjects are discussed in public. Not long ago we had an instance of this when what was called the Age of Consent Bill was introduced into the Viceregal Legislative Council. I do not propose to say one word as to the merits of the controversy that arose over that measure, but I allude to it to illustrate how apt the public mind is to get agitated over these social matters if they are discussed in a hostile and unfriendly spirit in public. But to show to you that those who organised the Congress movement, had not lost sight of the question of social reform, I may state that when we met in Bombay for the first time, the matter was discussed threadbare, with the help of such distinguished social reformers as Dewan Bahadur Raghu Nath Rao of Madras, Mr. Mahadeo Govind Ranade, and Mr. Krishnaji Lakshman

**1st Day.**

**The President's Inaugural Address.**

Nulkar of Poona, Mr. Norendro Nath Sen, and Mr. Janakinath Ghosal of Calcutta, and others. The whole subject was considered from every point of view, and we at last came to the conclusion, with the full consent and concurrence of those distinguished men, that it would not do for the Congress to meddle itself, as a Congress, with questions of social reform. At the same time we also came to the conclusion, that those gentlemen who were anxious, in a friendly spirit, to discuss their own social organisations should have an opportunity of doing so in the Congress Hall, after the business of the Congress should be over. The principal reason which actuated us in coming to that conclusion was that at our gatherings there would attend delegates following different religions, living under different social systems, all more or less interwoven with their respective religions, and we felt it would not be possible for them as a body to discuss social matters. How is it possible for a Hindu gentleman to discuss with a Parsee or a Mahomedan gentleman matters connected with Hindu social questions? How is it possible for a Mahomedan gentleman to discuss with Hindu and Parsee gentlemen matters connected with Mahomedan social questions? And how is it possible for a Parsee gentleman to discuss with Hindu and Mahomedan gentlemen matters connected with Parsee social customs? We thought, and I hope you will agree that we were right, that under the circumstances, all we could do was to leave it to the Hindus and the Mahomedans, Parsees, and other delegates to discuss their respective social matters in a friendly spirit amongst themselves, and arrive at what conclusions they pleased, and if possible, to get the minority to submit to the views of the majority. (*Cheers*). I may point out that we do not all understand in the same sense what is meant by social reform. Some of us are anxious that our daughters should have the same education as our sons, that thay should go to Universities, that they should adopt learned professions; others, who are more timid, would be content with seeing that their children are not given in marriage when very young, and that child widows should not remain widows all the days of their lives. Others, more timid still, would allow social problems to solve themselves. It is impossible to get any common ground, even as regards the members of the same community, be it Hindu, Mahomedan or Parsee with respect to these matters. Thus it was that social questions were left out of the Congress programme; thus it was that the Congress commenced and has since remained, and will, I sincerely trust, always remain as a purely political organisation, devoting its energies to political matters, and political matters only. I am afraid that those, whether belonging to our own country or to any other country, who find fault with us for not making social subjects a part of our work, cherish a secret wish that we might all be set by the ears, as we were all set by the ears by the Age of Consent Bill, and that thus we might come to an ignominious end. They mean us no good, and when we find critics of that description talking of the Congress as only fit to discuss social problems, I think the wider the berth we give them the better. (*Cheers*).

I, for one, have no patience with those who say we shall not be fit for political reform until we reform our social system. I fail to see any connection between the two. Let me take, for instance, one of the political reforms which we have been suggesting year after year, *viz.*, the separation of Judicial from Executive functions in the same officer. What possible connection can there be between this, which is a purely political reform, and Social reform? In the same way, take the Permanent Settlement which we have been advocating, the amendment of the law relating to forests and other such measures;—and I ask again, what have these to do with Social Reforms? Are we not fit for them because our widows remain unmarried and our girls are given in marriage earlier than in other countries? because our wives and daughters do not drive about with us visiting our friends? because we do not send our daughters to Oxford or Cambridge? (*Cheers*).

It is now my sorrowful duty to officially announce to you that death has been busy amongst the ranks of Congressmen during the year just passed. Standing on this platform and speaking in this city, one feels almost an overpowering sense of despair when one finds that the familiar figure and the beloved face of Pandit Ajoodhianath is no more. We mourned for him when he died, we have mourned for him since; and those of us who had the privilege of knowing him intimately, of perceiving his kindly heart, his great energy, his great devotion to the Congress cause, and the sacrifices he made for that cause, will mourn for him to the last. With Pandit Ajudhianath has passed away that other great Congress leader, Mr. George Yule. These were the two most prominent figures in the Congress held in this city in 1888: Pandit Ajudhianath as the Chairman of the Reception Committee; Mr. Yule as the President of the Congress. It was my singular good fortune to have been the means of inducing both these gentlemen to espouse the Congress cause. I was here in April, 1887, and met Pandit Ajudhianath, who had not then expressed his views, one way or another, with regard to Congress matters. I discussed the matter with him. He listened to me with his usual courtesy and urbanity, and he pointed out to me certain defects which he thought existed in our system; and, at last, after a sympathetic hearing of over an hour and a half, he told me he would think of all I had said to him, and that he would consider the matter carefully and thoroughly, and then let me know his views. I never heard any thing from him from that time until on the eve of my departure for Madras to attend the Congress of 1887. I then received a letter from him in which he said I had made a convert of him to the Congress cause, that he had thoroughly made up his mind to join us, that he was anxious to go to Madras himself, but that illness prevented him from doing so, and he sent a message that if it pleased the Congress to hold its next Sessions at Allahabad in 1888, he would do all he could to make the Congress a success. And you know—certainly, those of you who attended know—what a success he did make of it. Our venerable President of the Reception Committee of this present Congress has told us the difficulties which had to be encountered to make that Congress a success, and I do not belittle his services or those of any other worthy Congressman who worked with him at that Congress, when I say that it was owing to Pandit Ajudhianath's exertions that that Congress was the success it was.

When it was time to select a President for recommendation to the Congress of 1888, it was suggested to me, I being then in England, that I might ascertain the views of Mr. George Yule, and ask him to preside. I accordingly saw him at his office in the City, and had the same kind of conversation with him as I had had, the year before, with Pandit Ajudhianath. He also listened to me kindly, courteously and sympathetically, and asked me to give him all the Congress literature I had. I had only the three Reports of the Congress meetings of 1885, 1886 and 1887, and I sent these to him; and to my great joy, and, as it afterwards turned out, to the great benefit of the Congress, Mr. Yule came to see me at my house and told me that he entirely sympathised with the cause, and that, if elected to be the President of the Congress of that year, he would be proud of the position and would do what he could for us. Those who had the good fortune to attend the Congress of 1888, know how manfully and how well he sustained the duties of his position; how he pointed out that the chief plank in the Congress platform—namely, the reform and reconstitution of the Legislative Councils of this country—was by no means an invention on the part of the Congress; that that point had received the attention and had been favourably considered and spoken of by that marvellous English Statesman, Benjamin Disraeli, Earl of Beaconsfield. He told us that we were treading on the footsteps of that great man, and that if we perseveringly stuck to our colours, some time or other we should get what we wanted. From that time to the day of his death, Mr. Yule worked with us, gave us his valuable advice and helped us considerably as regards our working expenses. Pandit Ajudhianath as you know, from the time he joined the Congress, worked early, worked late, worked with the old, worked with the young, never spared any personal sacrifices, so that he might do good to his country and to the Congress, and his lamented death came upon him when he was coming back from Nagpore, after having worked there for the success of the Nagpore Congress of last year. Those who ever so slightly knew Pandit Ajudhianath and Mr. Yule will never be able to forget the great services which those gentlemen rendered to the Congress cause.

From Madras we have the sad news of the death of Salem Rama Swami Moodeliar. He was an earnest worker and did yeoman's service to the cause of his country. In 1885,

1st Day.

The President's Inaugural Address.

he was one of a band of three who were deputed to go to Great Britain during the then general election: his colleagues being Mr. N. G. Chandravarkar of Bombay, and Mr. Monomohun Ghose of Calcutta, and these three devoted men vied with each other as to who could do the most work for the benefit of his country. Salem Rama Swami Moodeliar served on the Public Service Commission, and we all know the bitter disappointment he felt when the Secretary of State for India did not carry out what he had hoped he would; namely, accept the recommendations of the Public Service Commission as a whole. There were some recommendations of the Commission which Salem Rama Swami Moodeliar, and those who worked with him, did not approve; but in order that the recommendations of which they approved might be carried into effect, he and his colleagues gave in their adhesion to them, and all joined in signing the Report. I remember that the Report did not give any satisfaction to the country at large. We had discussions on the subject at the Congress of 1888, and some of us were very anxious that that report should be disavowed, and that we should, by a resolution, tell the Government that the recommendations of the Commission did not come up to our expectations at all. Salem Rama Swami Moodeliar advised us not to agitate the matter then, but wait until the Secretary of State's orders were out. If, he said, the Secretary of State accepted those recommendations the matter might well be allowed to rest for some years to come; but if he did not do so, then he, Rama Swami Moodeliar, would be the first to re-open the question and carry on the agitation to the end of his life, if necessary. He was a sagacious and courageous man, and in him the Congress has lost a leader of eminence and earnestness. In Madras, we have also lost G. Mahadeo Chetty and Ramaswamy Naidu, both earnest Congress workers, and they will be missed by their Congress friends and acquaintances. In Bengal, we have had two heavy losses by the death of Prannath Pandit and Okhoy Coomar Dass. Prannath Pandit was the worthy son of a worthy father, the late Mr. Justice Sumbhoonath Pandit—the first native gentleman who was appointed to the Bench of the High Court;—and though he died young he was of great service to his country and to our cause, and had he been spared he would have done still greater services. Okhoy Coomar Dass was a younger man still, but his energy was great, and as a public man he outshone many of his contemporaries in Lower Bengal. It was due to him that many abuses in our Courts of Justice were exposed, and it was due to him that Howrah owes its Standing Congress Committee. We grieve for all these spirits who have passed away from us, and I would beg leave, on behalf of this Congress, to express to their respective families our respective and reverential condolences in the great loss that has overtaken them. "Sorrow shared is sorrow soothed," says the old adage, and, if that be a fact, I have no doubt that our sympathy will go somewhat towards assuaging the grief of their families.

Gentlemen, I must now proceed to call your attention to subjects more exciting, though, with the exception of a couple of them, I am not in a position to say, they are more cheering. The first piece of cheering news I have is that Lord Cross's India Councils Bill, after delays which seemed to many of us to be endless, has at last passed through the Houses of Parliament and received the Royal assent. From what we have been able to gather from the speeches delivered by the Viceroy during his tour in Madras, it would seem that the Rules under which the Act is to be given effect to, are now under the consideration of the Government of India. We all know that the Act in terms does not profess to give us much, but it is capable, I believe, of infinite expansion under the Rules that are to be framed. If those Rules are framed in the spirit in which the present Prime Minister of England understood the Act was framed, and what he said was assented to by the then Under-Secretary of State for India, namely, that that the people of India were to have real living representation in their Legislative Council,—if those Rules are framed in the spirit of true statesmanship, statesmanship such as one would have confidently expected from Sir Thomas Munro, Mountstuart Elphinstone, Lord William Bentinck and a host of other distinguished Anglo-Indian statesmen who have made British India what she is—I have no doubt we shall all be glad to put away the first plank in our Congress platform, namely, the reform and reconstitution of the Legislative Councils. The spirits that seem to be abroad just now in this country however do not seem to me to give a very hopeful augury as to these Rules. I am afraid that some of our rulers have been possessed with the idea that we have been progressing too fast. It is a great pity that this should be so. But if these rules do not come up to our expectations, gentlemen, we must go on with our agitation and not stop until we get what we all think and we all believe, and, what is more, what our rulers themselves have taught us to believe, we have a right to get (*Cheers*).

Another cheering event to which I have to call attention is the return of our leader, our revered leader, Dadabhai Naoroji (*Three Cheers*) to sit in the House of Commons as member for Central Finsbury. You all know it had been hoped that he would be able to come out from England to occupy the position I am now occupying. We all looked forward to his presence amongst us with hopefulness and trust and with great satisfaction, because, if he had been with us we could have shown to him, face to face, that our confidence in him is just as high as it ever was. We could have told him, by word of mouth, of the great joy which spread throughout the length and breadth of India when the news of his return to the House of Commons was received, of the anxiety with which we watched the fate of the election petition which was presented against his return, and how glad we were that it was at last withdrawn. And he could have carried back with him to England our message of gratitude to the electors of Central Finsbury (*Cheers*), and have shown them that in electing him as their representative they had also elected a representative for the people of India in the House of Commons. (*Cheers*). Unfortunately, his opponent, Captain Penton, had presented that hateful petition, and just at the moment that Mr. Naoroji was to have made his preparations to come out to India, it was fixed to be heard. Mr. Naoroji had to stay. There was a hand to hand struggle, and it was at last found that the number of votes for the two candidates was on a level. Captain Penton must have felt that if he went on any further his number might come down, and then Mr. Naoroji would retain his seat and Captain Penton would have to pay all the costs. He thought discretion the better part of valour, and prudently withdrew his petition, each party paying his own costs, and the seat of Mr. Naoroji is now perfectly safe. And as long as this present Parliament lasts he will remain our member (*Cheers*), and we shall get all the help, it is possible for him to give us, in the cause of Indian reforms. But we must not expect too much from him. He is but one in a House of 670 members, and though he will do for us all that prudence, good sense, vast knowledge and great eloquence can do, yet he is single-handed. To be strong, he must receive all the support he can from this country, and backed by that support he may be able to put our case convincingly before the House. But, what we really want is not that our countrymen generally should sit in the House of Commons. Englishmen themselves find it extremely hard to find seats there, how much more must we who are "blackmen." What we want and have a right to get is that our countrymen should have the opportunity of really representing to the Government the views of the people of this country in this country. What we want is that there should be responsible Government in India. I have always felt that the one great evil of the Indian administration is that our rulers are responsible to no one outside of their own consciences. That they conscientiously endeavour to do what they can for the good Government of our country, may be accepted as an undeniable fact and accepted with gratitude. But it is not enough that our rulers should only be responsible to their own consciences. After all they are human beings, with human frailties, and human imperfections. It is necessary that they should be responsible to those over whom they have been placed by Providence to rule. (*Cheers*). In making these observations I have not lost sight of the fact that the Government of India, in India, is responsible to the Government of India, in Westminster, and that the Government of India in Westminster is responsible to the Cabinet of the day, of which he is invariably one of the members. Nor have I forgotten that the Cabinet of the day is responsible to the House of Commons. But when you come to consider what this responsibility really is, I think, you will all agree with me that I have not overstated the case in the slightest degree. Unless the Secretary of State for India happen to be a personage of exceptional force of character and of great determination, such as the late Prime

Minister proved to be when he was in charge of the India Office, he generally, to use Burke's language, says "ditto" to the Government of India in India. The Cabinet is so troubled with the affairs of the vast British Empire that the members really have no time to devote to India as a body, and leave her to their colleague the Secretary of State for India. When any Indian question comes before the House of Commons, what do we see? The Cabinet of the day has always a majority in the House, and it always finds supporters among its own party, whether they are would be placemen or whether they are country gentlemen who go to the House of Commons as the best club in England. (*Cheers*). And in non-party matters—and they make it a pretence in the House of Commons to regard Indian affairs as matters non-party,—in all non-party matters, the Government of the day can always rely upon a large amount of support from the opposition. (*Hear, Hear*). There are a few members of the House of Commons who make it a point to devote a portion of their time and energies to the consideration of Indian questions. But they are only a few; they have hardly any following; and if they press any matters on the attention of the House, with any degree of zeal, they are voted down as bores by the rest of the House of Commons. (*Hear, Hear*). Of course the case of Mr. Bradlaugh (*Cheers*) was entirely different. He was a most masterful man, and by his mastery over his fellowmen, he attained the position for himself which he occupied in the House of Commons at the time of his death. There are but few in England like Mr. Bradlaugh. I am sorry to say that since the death of that great man we have not been able to find one who possesses his capacity, possesses his knowledge, or posseses the influence which he exercised over the House of Commons. Therefore, when you consider what the responsibility of the Government of India is to the Government of England and the House of Commons, you will not, I think, be able to come to any other conclusion than that it is *nil*. (*Hear, Hear*).

By the reconstitution of the Legislative Councils on lines that would allow representatives of the people to be elected to these Councils, the Government would be face to face with them. They would know, at first hand, what the real feelings and the real grievances of the people are. (*Hear, Hear*). They would then be able to devise measures which would be in consonance with the feelings of the people, and which would get rid of their grievances. At present, the *modus operandi* is this. A Secretary thinks that a particular measure ought to be passed, and it may be taken that he honestly believes that the measure would be for the benefit of the country. He invites two or three Indian gentlemen of eminence, with whom he is acquainted, to see him. He speaks to them in private, and gets their views, which, unfortunately, in the case of these Indian gentlemen, generally coincide with the views he himself holds. (*Laughter*). The measure is passed. There is a great cry of indignation in the country. The answer of the Government is,—"Oh, but we consulted the leaders of your society, and it is with their help this measure has been passed." I hold that the time has passed for this sort of statesmanship. If the Government make a real effort to arrive at what the views of the country and people generally are, I have no doubt that they will be able so to shape their policy as to give satisfaction to all concerned. This, to my mind, is the chief thing that we need. (*Hear, Hear*). In the Councils our representatives will be able to interpellate the Government with regard to their policy and the mode in which that policy is being given effect to. My conviction is, that the weal and woe of our country is not so much dependent upon the Viceroy or the Local Governor, however sympathetic and kind, but upon the officials who have to administer the law and come in contact with the people. Until there is the right of interpellation granted to us in our own Councils, there will be no true reponsibility on the part of our Government. I repeat that those who are placed over us, our Viceroys, Governors, Lieutenant-Governors and others of lesser degree, are more or less actuated by the desire to do us good, both for their own sake as well as for the sake of the people of the country; but the system under which they work is a vicious one, and the result is, no good is really done. (*Cheers*).

Now, Gentlemen, while a Conservative Government has given us this India Councils Bill, and a Radical constituency has sent one of our countrymen to the House of Commons, showing in the first instance some, and in the second, a great amount of liberality, here in this country, we have had in a neighbouring province a policy adopted which has made a painfully profound sensation over the whole of this vast empire—a sensation which it will take a very long time to allay. In the first place, though we, in this Congress, and the country generally, have been pressing and pressing and pressing the Government not to take away the grants for education but to increase those grants, so far as the provinces of Bengal and Bombay are concerned, grants in aid of high education have been doomed. Government require, they say, money for primary education; they do not wish to spend money upon high education. I am not one of those who believe that primary education is not required. I think, it is as much required as high education. But I confess, I do not understand for a moment why it is necessary to starve high education in order that primary education may be provided for and protected. (*Cheers*). Government ought to foster education of all kinds alike; it ought to spend its resources upon every kind of education (*Renewed Cheers*) for the people; not only primary education but technical education of all kinds, and also high education. It is said,—"you who have had, and who appreciate, high education ought to maintain it yourselves." I know of no other country in which such a thing as this has been said by the Government to the people they rule over. It is one of the first duties of the Government to educate the people just as it is their duty to protect them from thieves and robbers. (*Cheers*). If they tell the people to-day—"Go and educate yourselves," why should they not tell them to-morrow—"You are rich and can afford to keep durwans. Go and protect yourselves against thieves and robbers, we will not do so." (*Cheers*).

But the sensation, to which I have referred, is one not so much due to the doings of our Bengal and Bombay Governments as regards high education, as to the notification which the Lieutenant-Governor of Bengal has lately issued, withdrawing trial by Jury in serious cases from the seven Districts in Bengal, where the system of trial by Jury has been in existence for some years. (*Cries of "Shame"*). The plea, upon which this notification has been based, is that trial by Jury has been a failure as a means for the repression of crime. (*Cries of Shame, and no, no*). Can it be said that if a Sessions Judge trying a case with the assistance of Assessors and without the assistance of a Jury acquit a prisoner, that he is a failure as a means for the repression of crime? If that cannot be said with regard to Sessions Judges, with what justice can it be said in regard to Juries? (*Cheers*). Those of us who have had any acquaintance with the subject, have long felt that the administration of Criminal Justice in this country has been extremely unsatisfactory. There has not been much said about it, because it affects people, the majority of whom are poor men—men who cannot make much noise. They submit to what takes place, grumble among their fellows and cry *kismut*. Now let us see how the matter stands. While in Civil cases the evidence is taken down in the language in which the witness gives it, by an officer specially appointed for the purpose, and in appeals the evidence thus taken down is made the basis of the judgment of the Appellate Court where it differs from the notes of the Judge, in Criminal cases the evidence is, as a rule, taken down by the presiding officer in English. Most of these presiding officers are gentlemen who come to us here from Great Britain. They, no doubt, try and learn the languages of the people they are sent out to govern, but the circumstances, in which they are placed, and the circumstances in which the people of this country are placed, are such that they are compelled to live in utter isolation from one another. You may read the books of a country, you may know its literature well, but unless you have a familiar acquaintance with the people of the country, unless you have mixed familiarly with them, it is impossible for you to understand the language these people speak. Why is there so much outcry about what is called "Babu English."? Many Babus, and in this designation I include my countrymen from all parts of India, know English Literature better, I make bold to say, than many educated men in England. (*Cheers*). They know English better and English Literature better than many Continental English scholars. They know English History, as well, if not better, than Englishmen themselves. Why is it then that when they write English, when they speak English, they sometimes make grievous blunders? Why is it then that their composition is called stilted? Because their knowledge is derived from books only and not from contact with the people of England. If an English gentleman were to write a book or write a letter, in the vernacular with which he is supposed to be most familiar, I am afraid his composition would bear a great family likeness to "Babu English." It would be "English Vernacular." It would contain grammatical mistakes which would even shame our average school boy. Let an English gentleman, thoroughly acquainted with the vernacular of a district, speak to a native of that district. His pronunciation would be such that the native, even if educated, would find it difficult to understand him. It is gentlemen of this description who hear country-people, called as witnesses before them, give their evidence in the vernacular. How is it possible for them to understand them correctly? How much do you think of what these witnesses say to the Judge is taken down correctly and finds a place in the Judge's notes? (*Little or nothing*).

——And when an appeal is preferred to the Appellate Court, it is this evidence, and this evidence alone, upon which the Judges of that Court have to act. When the District Judge tries a Civil case, he has the plaint and written statement translated for him into English by his clerk. The evidence given before him is, as a rule, interpreted to him by the pleaders on either side. But when the same District Judge acts in his capacity as Sessions Judge and presides over Criminal trials, he, as a rule, takes down the evidence, without the aid of interpreters, in English, and he charges the Jury, in Jury cases, in the vernacular of the country. (*Laughter*). The Indian Penal Code has been translated into all the vernaculars of the country, and those who know these languages and who know English, I think, are agreed, that it is extremely difficult to make out what the vernacular Penal Code means; and charging the Jury in the vernacular means, that the Judges have to explain the Penal Code to them in the vernacular—a superhuman task almost! Again, while in Civil cases pleaders, and particularly pleaders of position are allowed a free hand as regards cross-examination, in Criminal cases, particularly in cases where the accused is unable to employ pleaders of eminence, but is compelled to have either junior pleaders or mukhtars, the cross-examination of the witnesses may be said almost to be a farce. The presiding officer gets impatient in a very short time, cuts short the cross-examination at his own sweet will and pleasure, and in many cases most important facts are not elicited in consequence. (*Hear, Hear*). While in Civil appeals, you, as a rule, get a patient hearing, the argument sometimes lasting for days, just think, those of you who have any experience of these Courts, what takes place when Criminal appeals are heard by Sessions Judges in the moffassil! They are often taken up at the fag end of the day and listened to with impatience, and then is asked the almost invariable question, as the Judge, after hearing the appeal for a few minutes, is about to rise for the day,—"Have you any thing more to say; I will read the papers for myself and give the decision to-morrow." The Judge rises, and the poor man's appeal is over Some appeals are dismissed and some, though this is more rare, are allowed. Again, while in Civil cases there is hardly any fear of their being decided on facts outside the record, in Criminal cases there is the greatest fear that outside influence is brought to bear upon the presiding officer. The thing is inevitable when you consider that the District Magistrate is the real head of the Police of the district, and that all officers trying Criminal cases, except the Sessions Judge, are subordinate to him and depend on him for promotion; and as regards the Sessions Judges themselves, they may, by the system which has now been introduced of dividing the Civil Service into two branches, find themselves independent of the District Magistrate one day and his subordinate the next, during the time he oscillates as acting Sessions Judge and Joint Magistrate, as not unoften happens. Again, in Civil cases we have the right of appeal as of course, and, if they are of sufficient value of appealing to Her Majesty in Council; in Criminal cases we have to apply for leave, to appeal and have our appeal only from the Sessions Judge to the High Court, and from the inferior judiciary to the Sessions Judge, and in some cases to the District Magistrates. There are many other points to which attention may be called but I think I have said enough to convince those who are not familiar with the matter, that I was right when I said that the administration of Criminal justice in this country was most unsatisfactory. (*Cheers*). The only safeguard which accused persons have against this system in Sessions cases, is trial by jury. (*Hear, Hear*). And now the notification of the Lieutenant-Governor of Bengal withdraws this safeguard from the seven districts in Bengal where it existed, and the whole of India has been threatened with a like withdrawal. (*Cries of "Shame*)". The question is not a provincial but an imperial one, and of the highest importance. I therefore think, it is our duty to take this question up and help our Bengal brethren to the utmost extent of our power to get back what they have lost, and to see that other parts of the country are not overtaken by the same fate. (*Hear, Hear*).

Let us for the moment consider, what is the meaning of "trial by Jury having failed as a means for the repression of crime." One of the learned Judges of the Calcutta High Court who was consulted upon this matter, I refer to Mr. Justice Beverley, said, that he did not think that a person bent upon committing a crime would stop to think whether, if he was detected, he would be tried by a Judge with a Jury or tried by a Judge with the aid of Assessors. (*Loud Cheers*). Judges and Juries do not sit to repress crime but to ascertain if crime has been committed, and if the Jury find that crime has been committed, the Judge punishes the offender. (*Cheers*). It is the duty of the police to see that crime is not committed, and when, in spite of their vigilance, crime is committed, to bring the offender to justice. In this country, where unfortunately the police are not over-scrupulous as to how they get up cases, trial by Jury is the most essential safeguard against injustice. Jurymen being drawn from the people themselves are better able to understand the language in which witnesses give their evidence, better able to understand and appreciate the demeanour of witnesses—the twists and turns in their answers, the rolling of their eyes, the scratching of their heads, and various other contortions of their physiognomy which witnesses go through to avoid giving straight answers to straight questions— than the Judge upon whom, unless he be an officer of exceptional and brilliant talents, they are lost. (*Hear, Hear*). A former Lieutenant-Governor of Bengal, himself a Sessions Judge of large experience, and, therefore, able to speak with authority on the subject—I allude to the late Sir A. Rivers Thompson,—said in regard to Jurymen, that they were more scrupulous in accepting police evidence than the Judges were, and that it was quite right that it should be so. The law allows Sessions Judges to make references to the High Court if they differ from the verdict of a Jury. These references come up before the High Court, and the learned Judges of that Court have before them only the evidence recorded in English by the Sessions Judge, the evidence recorded in the Court of the Committing Magistrate and the Judge's charge. Though they may be men of brilliant talents, men of great experience, men of great conscientiousness, I still venture to think that it is impossible for them—human beings as they are—reading merely the dry bones of the evidence placed before them upon paper, to come to a correct conclusion as to whether the Judge was right or the Jury were right. (*Cheers*). If they heard the evidence given by the witnesses in their presence, their conclusion would no doubt be accepted as more satisfactory, and if they differed from the Jury it might be that the Jury were wrong, but under the present system how can that be done? How can it be said, that when they accept the opinion of the Sessions Judges, the Sessions Judges are right and the Jury wrong? And in many of these references, the High Courts have accepted the verdict of the Jury and differed from the recommendation of the Judge. (*Cheers*). The only ground for saying that the system of trial by Jury has failed is, as I understand, that the High Court has in some instances differed from them, and adopted the recommendation of the Sessions Judge. I have told you, it is impossible—regard being had to the limitation of human nature—to say with confidence, who was right and who was wrong; but assuming that the Jury were wrong in many instances, and that they had given improper verdicts, what is the consequence? A few more persons who would have been in jail are now free men. What then? Has there been any complaint on the part of the people of these seven districts, that they went about in fear of their lives, because by the obstinacy and perversity of Jurymen, accused persons who ought to have been condemned to death had been set free? (*Hear, Hear*). Did any one say, that he or she regarded the system with disfavour or dislike or fear? Had any one suggested, that the system should be abolished? I say emphatically, No! No complaint reached the Government from the people affected, that the system had failed. It is the overflowing desire on the part of the Government to do good to us that has been the cause of the withdrawal of this system! Save us from our well-wishers, say I. (*Loud Cheers*). I could have understood the action of Government if there had been any hue and cry in the country on the subject. I could have understood it, if any representation had come from those affected to the Government; but under the circumstances this bolt from the blue I do not understand and cannot appreciate. (*Loud Applause*). It is said that, trial by Jury is foreign to this country. We who have cherished our Punchayet system for generations to be told that trial by Jury is foreign to us, to be told so at the fag end of the nineteenth century, why it is strange indeed! No, no, gentlemen—it was on our Punchayet system that Lord Cornwallis proceeded when in 1790 he ruled that we should have trial by Jury. It was on that system that Sir Thomas Munro based his regulation which his successor promulgated in 1827. It was on that system that the Bombay regulation on the subject was introduced, and when these regulations were codified in 1861, it was on that system the law was based. We must have the system extended to the whole country and not withdrawn from any part of it, and we must therefore join together and agitate on the subject from one end of India to the other, and say, that this notification, which has given rise to so much discontent, was not required, and that it should be withdrawn, and withdrawn as speedily as possible, and the policy of which it is the outcome reversed. (*Loud Applause*).

I am afraid gentlemen, I have detained you longer than I should have done. (*Cries of, "No, No, and go on"*). I have but a few more words to say, and these I shall say as briefly as I can. I said at the outset, that the Congress movement has been a great success, but it behoved us all to make it even a greater success than it is. During the Jury agitation in Bengal I was greatly pained, more pained than I can describe, by one of the apologists of the Government saying openly in his paper, that the agitation against the Jury notification was of no account because it was only a "native" agitation and that no Europeans had joined it. As a matter of fact, I know from personal knowledge that a great many very respectable and independent gentlemen in Calcutta joined the movement and cordially sympathised with it. But supposing it had been otherwise? This same apologist has, day after day, pointed out that the withdrawal of trial by Jury, in these seven Bengal districts, in serious cases, does not in any way touch Europeans or European British Subjects. If he is right in this, it is a matter of no surprise that Europeans have not joined the movement. But because Europeans have not joined the movement, is a movement of the people of this country to be despised? Is our voice not to be listened to, because, forsooth, to that voice has not been added the voice of our European fellow-subjects? (*Hear, Hear, and Cheers*). We would welcome, welcome with open arms, all the support which we can get from our European fellow-subjects. I believe, that so far as the non-official Europeans are concerned, their interests and ours, in this country, are the same; we all desire that there should be a development of the resources of the country and that there should be enough for all who are here, whether for a time or in perpetuity. (*Hear, Hear*). But apart from that, why is our voice to be despised? It is we who feel the pinch; it is we who have to suffer, and when we cry out, it is said to us, "O! we cannot listen to you; yours is a contemptible and useless and a vile agitation, and we will not listen to you." Time was when we natives of the country agitated about any matter, with the help of non-official Europeans, the apologists of the Government used to say triumphantly, "this agitation is not the agitation of the natives of the country, but has been got up by a few discontented Europeans; don't listen to them, it is not their true voice; it is the voice of these Europeans." But now we are told, "don't listen to them, it is their own voice and not the voice of the Europeans." (*Shame*). It is sad that such reflections should be published by responsible journalists pretending to be in the confidence of our rulers. I hope and confidently trust that these are not the sentiments by which any administration in India is actuated. I hope and trust that when we make respectful representations to the Government, they will be considered on their own merits, whether we are joined in our agitation by our European fellow-subjects or whether we stand by ourselves; and in order that these representations of ours, not only on the Jury question but on other questions which touch us, may succeed, it is necessary that we, in our Congress, should work and work with a will. It is not enough that you should come from long distances and be present at the annual sittings of the Congress. It is necessary, when you go back to your respective Provinces and districts, that you should display the same zeal and interest there. It has been the habit to leave the whole of the Congress work to the Secretary. We go back to our districts and sleep over it and leave the Secretary to do all he can for the business, in the shape of getting money, and then when it is time for the sessions to be held, we put on our best clothes, pack up our trunks and go. But that is not work. Let us all on our parts act zealously and make sacrifices: without money it is impossible to be successful in anything. Let each of us go back and help our respective Secretaries; let us try and get as much money as we can for the success of the cause. (*Hear, hear*).

**1st Day.**

**The President's Inaugural Address.**

You all know that our cause has the support of some distinguished men in England, who form, what is called the Congress Committee in England. They are willing to give us their services unstintingly, ungrudgingly, but you can not expect them to give their services to us at their own expense. You can not expect that the necessary expenses required for the hiring of rooms, for the printing of papers, for the despatch of telegrams and all other things necessary for carrying on the great cause, shall be paid out of their own pockets. We must do our best to support them; we must do our best to support the cause; and if we are true to ourselves, if we are true to our principles, if we are true to our country, be assured that in the fulness of time all that you require from the benign Government of the British nation, all that you seek from them to make you true citizens, will be given to you by that nation. (***Loud and prolonged applause***).

**Election of the Subjects Committee.**

Mr. Surendra Nath Banerji, *Officiating* Joint General Secretary, (*Calcutta*, *No*. 188, *in list*).—I now request the Secretaries of the several Standing Congress Committees to hand in the lists of the names of those gentlemen who have been elected by the delegates of each circle to represent them on the Subjects Committee.

The lists having been given in, they were read out, and approved by the whole assembly.

The following gentlemen were elected to the Subjects Committee:—

| | | | |
|---|---|---|---|
| CALCUTTA CIRCLE. | 1. | MR. J. GHOSAL (No. 187) .. .. | (Calcutta.) |
| | 2. | BABU TARAK NATH PALIT (No. 182) .. | do. |
| | 3. | „ NALIN BEHARI SARKAR (No. 183) .. | do. |
| | 4. | „ HERAMBA CHANDRA MAITRA (No. 179) .. | do. |
| | 5. | „ KALIPRASANNA KAVYAVISHARAD (No. 185) | do. |
| | 6. | „ KHITENDRA NATH TAGORE (No. 180) .. | do. |
| | 7. | RAI YATINDRA NATH CHAUDHRY (No. 189) | (24 Perghanas.) |
| | 8. | BABU MOHIT CHANDRA BASU (No. 194) | do. |
| | 9. | „ ROMESH CHANDRA MANDAL (No. 209) .. | (Hooghly.) |
| | 10. | „ KESHAVA CHANDRA SADHU (No. 208) .. | do. |
| | 11. | MR. K. B. MULLICK (No. 222) .. | do. |
| | 12. | BABU TARAPADA BANERJEE (No. 195) .. | (Nuddea.) |
| | 13. | „ HARI PRASAD CHATTERJEE (No. 196) .. | do. |
| | 14. | „ KALIGOPAL MAZOOMDAR (No. 200) .. | (Jessore.) |
| | 15. | „ BENIBHUSAN ROY (No. 199) .. | (Khulna) |
| | 16. | „ HARDYAL NAG (No. 224) .. | (Tippera.) |
| | 17. | „ CHARUCHANDRA MITRA No 2. (No. 223) | do. |
| | 18. | „ BAIKUNTHA NATH SEN (No. 210) .. | (Berhampore.) |
| | 19. | „ BROJENDRA NATH SEAL (No. 211) .. | do. |
| | 20. | „ NAFAR DAS ROY (No. 214) .. | do. |
| | 21. | „ DHAN KRISHNA GHOSE (No. 220) .. | (Beerbhoom.) |
| | 22. | MR. K. B. DUTT (No. 201) .. | (Midnapore) |
| | 23. | BABU NAVA KUMAR MITRA (No. 204) .. | do. |
| | 24. | „ RADHANATH CHANGKAKOTI, (No. 227) .. | (Debrugarh.) |

**Election of the Subjects Committee.**

| Circle | No. | Name | Place |
|---|---|---|---|
| CALCUTTA CIRCLE—(*contd.*) | 25. | BABU LAKSHMINATH BEZBARUA (No. 226) .. | (Debrugarh.) |
| | 26. | „ BHOLANATH BARUA (No. 225) .. | do. |
| DACCA CIRCLE. | 1. | „ SARAT CHANDRA BASU (No. 239) | (Dacca.) |
| | 2. | „ HEM CHANDRA ROY (No. 191) | do. |
| | 3. | „ ANATHBANDHU GUHA (No. 230) | (Mymensing.) |
| | 4. | „ SRINATH RAI (No. 231) | do. |
| FURREEDPORE CIRCLE. | 1. | BABU GIRIJA SANKAR MAZOOMDAR (No. 240) | (Furreedpore.) |
| | 2. | „ AMBIKA CHANDRA MAZOOMDAR (No. 241) | do. |
| BARISAL CIRCLE. | 1. | BABU HARA KANTA SEN (No. 248) | (Backerganj.) |
| RUNGPORE CIRCLE. | 1. | BABU KRISHNA KUMAR MITRA (No. 190) | (Rungpore.) |
| | 2. | „ SATIS KAMAL SEN (No. 247) | do. |
| DINAJPORE CIRCLE. | 1. | BABU MADHAV CHANDRA CHATTERJEE (No. 245) | (Dinajpore.) |
| PUBNA CIRCLE. | 1. | BABU JNYANA GOVIND CHAKRAVARTI (No. 235) | (Assam.) |
| BHAGALPORE CIRCLE. | 1. | BABU PARVATICHARAN DAS (No. 282) | (Purnea.) |
| | 2. | „ SRIMOHAN THAKUR (No. 278) | (Bhagulpore.) |
| CHOTA NAGPORE CIRCLE. | 1. | BABU RADHAGOVIND CHAUDHRY (No. 255) | (Chota Nagpore.) |
| BEHAR CIRCLE. | 1. | BABU GURU PRASAD SEN (No. 259) | (Bankipore.) |
| | 2. | „ SALIGRAM SING (No. 264) | do. |
| | 3. | „ MAHABIR SAHAY (No. 263) | do. |
| | 4. | MAULVI ABDUL HAMID (No. 257) | do. |
| | 5. | BABU NUNDKISHORE LAL (No. 270) | (Gya.) |
| | 6. | „ GADADHAR PRASAD (No. 261) | do. |
| MOZUFFERPORE CIRCLE. | 1. | BABU SORASICHURAN MITRA (No. 272) | (Mozufferpore.) |
| BENARES CIRCLE. | 1. | HON'BLE RAMKALI CHAUDHRY (No. 283) | (Benares.) |
| | 2. | MR. UPENDRA NATH BASU (No. 288) | do. |
| | 3. | BABU MOKSHADA DAS MITTRA (No. 287) | do. |
| | 4. | „ ANNADA CHARAN DATTA (No. 292) | do. |
| | 5. | PUNDIT CHUNNU LAL (No. 295) | do. |
| | 6. | BABU BHOLANATH RAI (No. 299) | (Ghazipur.) |
| | 7. | „ BENI PRASAD (No. 329) | (Mirzapur.) |
| | 8. | „ SREE RAM (No. 318) | do. |
| | 9. | „ MUKTESHWAR RAI (No. 309) | (Azamgarh.) |
| N. W. P. CIRCLE. | 1. | RAJA RAMPAL SINH (No. 334) | (Allahabad.) |
| | 2. | PANDIT SUNDER LAL (No. 335) | do. |
| | 3. | „ MOTI LAL NEHRU (No. 339) | do. |
| | 4. | MR. D. BANERJI (No. 337) | do. |
| | 5. | PANDIT BALDEV RAM DAVE (No. 340) | do. |
| | 6. | BABU CHAROO CHUNDRA MITTRA (No. 341) | do. |
| | 7. | PANDIT MADAN MOHAN MALAVIYA (No. 346) | do. |
| | 8. | BABU DURGA CHARAN BANERJEE (No. 374) | do. |
| | 9. | SYED ABDUL RAOOF (No. 382) | do. |
| | 10. | MUNSHI SADRA-UD-DIN (No. 430) | do. |
| | 11. | PANDIT PRITHI NATH (No. 473) | (Cawnpore.) |
| | 12. | HAFIZ ABDUL RAHIM (No. 510) | (Aligarh.) |
| | 13. | PANDIT JAGAN NATH (No. 498) | (Agra.) |
| | 14. | MR. ALFRED NUNDY (No. 497) | do. |
| | 15. | BABU PRAHLAD SING (No. 520) | (Meerut.) |
| | 16. | „ BRIJNANDAN PRASAD (No. 604) | (Moradabad.) |
| | 17. | „ NARENDRA CHANDRA BOSE (No. 602) | do. |
| | 18. | „ PREO NATH BANERJEE (No. 595) | (Bareilly.) |
| | 19. | PANDIT JWALA DUTT JOSHI (No. 598) | (Almorah.) |
| | 20. | „ ANAND NARAIN (No. 528) | (Dehra Doon.) |
| | 21. | BABU BAIKUNTHANATH SARKAR (No. 590) | (Shahjahanpur.) |

**Election of the Subjects Committee.**

| Circle | No. | Name | Place |
|---|---|---|---|
| OUDH CIRCLE. | 1. | BABU BANSI LAL SINH (No. 530) | (LUCKNOW.) |
| | 2. | MR. BISHAN NARAIN DAR (No. 532) | do. |
| | 3. | „ HAMID ALI KHAN (No. 533) | do. |
| | 4. | „ BIPIN BEHARI BOSE (No. 545) | do. |
| | 5. | NAWAB ALI MAHOMED KHAN (No. 552) | do. |
| | 6. | BABU GUNGA PRASAD VARMA (No. 531) | do. |
| | 7. | PANDIT JAGAT NARAIN (No. 538) | do. |
| | 8. | BABU GOKUL CHAND (No. 577) | (Fyzabad.) |
| | 9. | „ RAMSARAN DAS (No. 574) | do. |
| | 10. | MUNSHI ALI HOSSEN SAHEB (No. 575) | do. |
| | 11. | „ IMTIAZ ALI (No. 576) | do. |
| | 12. | BABU PITAM RAI (No. 569) | (Sitapur.) |
| | 13. | MUNSHI MURLIDHAR (No. 571) | do. |
| | 14. | PANDIT SITAL PRASAD (No. 588) | (Kalakankar) |
| PUNJAB CIRCLE. | 1. | CAPTAIN A. BANON (No. 609) | (Lahore.) |
| | 2. | LALA RAM CHAND (No. 607) | do. |
| | 3. | MR. N. GUPTA (No. 610) | do. |
| | 4. | LALA MURLI DHAR (No. 612) | (Umballa.) |
| | 5. | „ KANHAYA LAL (No. 615) | (Amritsar.) |
| | 6. | MR. NUND KISHORE (No. 619) | do. |
| | 7. | „ BULAKI RAM (No. 618) | do. |
| | 8. | DR. PARMANAND (No. 611) | do. |
| | 9. | MR. UMA SANKAR (No. 616) | do. |
| | 10. | BABA NARAIN SING (No. 617) | do. |
| | 11. | MAULVI UMRAO MIRZA HAIRAT (No. 621) | (Delhi.) |
| | 12. | MR. RAGHUNATH DAS (No. 623) | do. |
| SHOLAPORE CIRCLE. | 1. | MR. P. L. NAGPURKAR (No. 64) | (SHOLAPORE) |
| | 2. | „ D. B. CHAKRADEO (No. 63) | do. |
| SATARA CIRCLE. | 1. | MR. BULWANT SRIDHARA SAHASRABUDDHE (No. 70) | (Satara) |
| | 2. | „ R. P. KARANDIKAR (No. 69) | do. |
| AHMEDNAGAR CIRCLE. | 1. | MR. B. B. NAGARKAR (No. 61) | (Ahmednagar) |
| DECCAN CIRCLE. | 1. | RAO BAHADUR VISHNU MORESWAR BHIDE (No. 85) | (Poona.) |
| | 2. | MR. GOPAL KRISHNA GOKHALE (No. 82) | do. |
| | 3. | „ KASHINATH GOVIND NATU (No. 93) | do. |
| | 4. | „ MAHADEO BULLAL NAMJOSHI (No. 96) | do. |
| | 5. | „ JANARDAN RAGHUNATH NIMKAR (No. 101) | do. |
| | 6. | „ RAM CHANDRA KESHAV LIMAYE (No. 86) | do. |
| | 7. | „ R. T. KIRTANE (No. 108) | do. |
| BOMBAY CIRCLE. | 1. | MR. D. E. WACHA (No. 39) | (Bombay.) |
| | 2. | „ DAJI ABAJI KHARE (No. 40) | do. |
| | 3. | „ CHIMAN LAL H. SATAVAID (No. 49) | do. |
| | 4. | DR. S. W. KANE (No. 41) | do. |
| | 5. | „ M. G. DESHMUKH (No. 50) | do. |
| | 6. | MR. JAGAMOHAN DAS VRINDAVANDAS (No. 42) | do. |
| | 7. | „ T. DE SOUZA (No. 54) | do. |
| SINDH. | 1. | RAO BAHADUR PISUMAL ZOKEI RAM (No. 60) | (Sindh.) |
| BERAR CIRCLE. | 1. | RAO SAHEB DEVA RAO VINAYAK (No. 134) | (Berar.) |
| | 2. | MR. G. S. KHAPARDE (No. 120) | do. |
| | 3. | „ R. N. MUDHOLKAR (No. 119) | do. |
| NAGPORE CIRCLE. | 1. | MR. NARAYAN SWAMI NAIDU (No. 141) | (Nagpore Dn.) |
| | 2. | „ BHAGIRATH PRASAD (No. 139) | do. |
| | 3. | „ HARI MAHADEO PANDIT (No. 144) | do. |
| | 4. | „ LAXMAN GOBIND DESKARA (No. 169) | do. |

**Election of the Subjects Committee.**

NAGPORE CIRCLE—(*contd.*)

5. Mr. K. V. JOSHI (No. 145) (Nagpore.)
6. „ RAM GULAM AVASTI (No. 138) (Jubbulpore.)
7. „ RAOJI GOVIND KHIRWARKAR (No. 160) (Hoshangabad.)
8. „ N. N. DE (No. 150) (Bilaspur.)
9. „ NUND LAL (No. 153) do.

MADRAS CIRCLE.

1. RAI BAHADUR P. ANANDA CHARLU (No. 1) (Madras.)
2. THE HON'BLE C. SANKARA NAIR (No. 2) do.
3. MR. VIRARAGHAVA CHARIAR (No. 5) do.
4. „ V. RAGHAVACHARY S. (No. 7) do.
5. „ PETER PAUL PILLAY (No. 9) do.
6. „ V. JAGANNADHA SHASTRI (No. 15) (Parvatipur)
7. „ P. VENKAT RAO PANTALU (No. 14) do.
8. „ P. KESAVA PILLAY (No. 37) (Gooty)
9. „ S. VIRARAGHAVA IYER (No. 17) (Palghat)
10. „ C. ANNAMALAI MUDALIAR (No. 31) (Bellary)
11. „ C. VIJIARAGHAVA CHARIAR (No. 22) (Salem)
12. „ C. VENKATA CHARIAR (No. 21) do.
13. „ RAMASWAMY CHETTIAR (No. 26) do.
14. „ S. M. NARAIN SWAMY IYER (No. 10) (Shivaganga)
15. „ D. V. RAJAGOPALA CHARIAR (No. 30) (Chittoor)
16. „ V. VYATHI IYER (No. 27) (Salem)
17. „ NATARAJU IYER (No. 4) (Madras)
18. „ RAGHU RAM RAO (No. 12) (Chingleput)

**Congratulations to Mr. Naoroji and thanks to Central Finsbury.**

THE PRESIDENT:—It has been suggested that you should authorize me to send in your name to Mr. Dadabhai Naoroji, a telegram congratulating him on his being elected a member of the House of Commons, and also thanking the electors of Central Finsbury for having elected him. (*Loud and enthusiastic cheers*). I shall do so in your name this evening. (*Cheers*).

The Congress will stand adjourned till 11 A. M. to-morrow.

The meeting broke up with three cheers for Her Majesty the Empress of India.

The Subjects Committee then met and sat until late in the evening. It met again on the following day, and sat for several hours.

# SECOND DAY'S PROCEEDINGS.

## Thursday, 29th December, 1892.

The Congress reassembled at 1-30 P. M.

**2nd Day.**

**Cheers for Mr. Gladstone.**

The President.—Gentlemen,—This is the 29th of December, 1892. On this day eighty-three years ago, the Grand Old Man of England was born. Let me call for three cheers for Mr. Gladstone.

Three hearty cheers having been given,

The President—As we have done hitherto, I suppose I have your permission to send a telegram to Mr. Gladstone congratulating him on the eighty-third Anniversary of his birthday. (*Yes, Yes, and Cheers*).

The President then read out the following rules for the conduct of business at the sittings of the Congress :—

*Rules for the Conduct of Business.*

**Rules for the conduct of business.**

(*a*)—No one who is not a delegate will be allowed to address the Congress or vote on any matter.

(*b*)—Every delegate must address the assembly from the speaker's platform.

(*c*)—The proposers, seconders, and supporters of each resolution will be selected by the Subjects Committee.

(*d*)—The President will allot the time during which each speaker can speak, and no one should exceed this without the special permission of the President. The President will sound his gong once to warn each speaker when the time allotted to him is drawing to a close, and he will sound it a second time when that period has elapsed ; and should he consider that the speaker ought to cease speaking, the President will touch the gong again, when the speaker must, there and then, close his address.

(*e*)—Any delegate not selected but who may wish to speak on any resolution should send in his name and that of the Congress Circle to which he belongs, legibly written on a piece of paper, to the President, and may speak when called upon by the President to do so.

(*f*)—Any one wishing to propose any amendment to any resolution must send to the President a slip of paper containing the amendment, his own name and that of his seconder, as also the names of the Congress Circles to which they respectively belong ; a similar slip should be handed to the reporter.

(*g*)—Any one who wishes to propose a new subject for discussion by the Congress must give previous notice of it in writing, to the President, at the commencement of the sitting, with a copy of any resolution he wishes to propose, his own name, and the name of the Congress Circle he belongs to.

(*h*)—No other business shall be brought forward before the Congress until the subjects and resolutions approved by the Subjects Committee have been disposed of. But afterwards, if time permits, any delegate who shall have given notice in writing, at the commencement of the sitting, to the President, of his desire to have a particular subject discussed, or a definite resolution, which he sets forth, proposed, shall have a right to,

**2nd Day.**

**Rules for the conduct of business.**

and a delegate who at any time previous to rising shall have given such notice may, with the permission of the President, rise and ask the President to take the sense of the assembly as to whether such subject will be discussed. No speaking at this stage shall be allowed. The President will simply read out the subject and the proposed resolution, and make any such remarks as he considers essential, and take a vote of the assembly as to whether the subject shall or shall not be discussed. If the vote is in the affirmative, the proposer will then set forth the subject and the resolution he therein proposes, with such explanations as he considers necessary, and then, after due discussion, the question will be disposed of in the usual way. If the vote is in the negative, the subject shall be at once dropped.

THE PRESIDENT.—I now call upon Rai Bahadur Ananda Charlu to move the first Resolution :—

**Resolution I.**

**Reform of the Legislative Councils.**

RAI BAHADUR ANANDA CHARLU (*Madras, No. 1 in list*).—MR. PRESIDENT AND GENTLEMEN,—I shall not begin with reading this amply worded proposition, as I fear that, when I finish reading it, I might be out of breath. Proceeding straight to the consideration of the measure to which the proposition relates, I must say that I fully share the profound regret, which is everywhere felt, at the absence in the Act itself of a clause, embodying the principle of representation, meant to be given by it. (*Cheers*). If such a clause existed in it, it would put it out of the power of narrow-minded men to deny the right as years elapse. (*Hear, Hear*). This is all the more to be regretted, because the mover of the Bill, Lord Cross, had himself made his object clear when he said that he meant "not only to give the Governor-General, the Governors and Lieutenant-Governors the sufficient assistance which they might require, but so as they might get the *best representatives of the people of the country.*"

With an intention such as this presumably before him, it is difficult to see how the draftsman of the Bill managed not to insert it, unless he took his cue from the satirist who has said that language was given to man to hide his thoughts and not to express them. When, however, the Bill passed on to the House of Commons, all our hopes were fully revived when Mr. Gladstone spoke on it. A couple of lines from that great man's speech may be usefully cited here. Mr. Gladstone said : "I believe I am justified in looking forward not merely to a *nominal but to a real living representation of the people of India.*" (*Hear, Hear and Cheers*). This declaration as to the scope of the Bill by Mr. Gladstone was assented to by the Under-Secretary who stood sponsor to it in the House of Commons. The words of Lord Salisbury in the House of Lords may be likewise quoted to show how he understood the aims of the Bill which is asked for. He said :—"If we are to do it, and if it has to be done, let us do it systematically......taking care *that the machinery to be provided shall effect the purpose of giving representation, not to accidentally constituted bodies, not to small sections of the people here and there, but to the living strength and vital forces of the whole community of India.*" (*Hear, Hear and cheers*).

When the Bill was passed into an Act, accompanied with these declarations and elucidations, and transmitted to the authorities here, our fears ought to cease ; and the solution of such a course is perhaps this : that the authorities in England meant to give the authorities here an opportunity and a scope to inaugurate a truly liberal measure of reform and thereby earn credit and achieve a reputation. In this reasonable view we might well rest, hoping for the best. But certain utterances of His Excellency the Viceroy during his recent tour, gave cause for some alarm and made it necessary for us to declare ourselves at this meeting of the Congress. (*Hear, Hear*). If the fears I have expressed prove ultimately that I have been an unfounded alarmist, I shall be glad to stand corrected. (*Cheers*). Since coming here I have not been able to speak to the delegates from the different parts of the country to see what particular method should be adopted in each particular place. But I think it right to put to you a test case for your anxious consideration. Take a city with four hundred thousand persons. Suppose, on a certain given standard of individual fitness, there are about four hundred and sixty men there, and thirty-two of them, on the ground of that standard, go into a Municipal Board. Would you hold that, in such a case, the possession of a franchise by only those thirty-two men is a real living representation as regards the four hundred thousand constituting, *ex hypothesi*, the population of the city, or as regards even the four hundred and odd who are on a level of qualification with those thirty-two men? (*No, No.*) Yet such a course is threatened by what His Excellency the Viceroy was pleased to say. I think we have a right to expect that, while the Government is at liberty to fix the standard of fitness ever so high as it thinks proper, after the standard is once set forth and enunciated, all persons on a level of qualification on that score must unquestionably possess the franchise as an *individual or personal* franchise. (*Loud and Prolonged applause*). Any thing short of it will be a perfect farce, if not a sham, and an unjustifiable injustice to the vast majority. (*Renewed cheers*). Another thing we have a right to expect is the denial of the franchise to mere voluntary bodies. When this was submitted to His Excellency, he gave an answer which showed that such a rule would, in his opinion, be an injustice to important special interests. I am afraid that this reply involves a confusion between voluntary bodies and special interests. No one denies or ought to deny that special interests should receive protection. But protection of such interests is one thing, and conferring the franchise on voluntary bodies is quite another thing. The two are not identical. They do not stand together. The former may be fully secured, without having recourse to the latter method. If instances of the kind I have brought to your notice exist—and not a few of them do exist—then I venture to assert that, in all such cases, there is not or cannot be any pretence of a real living representation; and that any scheme which admits of such cases would only prove the World's Grand Old Man to have been a false prophet; and, it would certainly not be in consonance even with Lord Salisbury's view of the situation. (*Loud Cheers*).

With these remarks I shall read the proposition which runs thus:—

*That this Congress, while accepting in a loyal spirit the Indian Councils Act recently enacted by the Parliament of Great Britain, as explained by the present Prime Minister, with the assent of the then Under-Secretary of State for India,—that it is intended by it to give the people of India a real living representation in the Legislative Councils,—regrets that the Act itself does not, in terms, concede to the people the right of electing their own representatives to the Council, and hopes and expects that the rules, now being prepared under the Act, will be framed on the lines of Mr. Gladstone's declaration in the House of Commons, and will do adequate justice to the people of this country; further, that it prays that these rules may be published in the official Gazettes, like other proposed legislative measures, before being finally adopted.* (*Cheers*).

Babu Surendranath Banerjea, (*Calcutta, No.* 188, *in list*).—Mr. President, Sister and Brother Delegates,—In seconding this resolution I am reminded of the words, the memorable words, of the Member for India, Mr. Dadabhai Naoroji. (*Cheers*). In a remarkable communication, which he has addressed to you, Sir, as the Joint-General Secretary and to the President of the Reception Committee, he has made the remark that it is time that a new departure should be made in the Congress programme, and that we should begin a new cycle. To my mind there is nothing which affords a more conspicuous instance of your recognition of the advice, conveyed to you by our distinguished friend, than your election to the office of President, of the gentleman under whose auspices, the work of the first cycle was so happily begun. (*Cheers*). That cycle was a glorious one, fruitful of splendid results. God grant that the promises of the past may be accomplished in the present, and that the new cycle may prepare the way for the fulfilment of those hopes and aspirations which we are accustomed to identify with this grand and magnificent movement. (*Cheers*). But, gentlemen, there is a discordant note sounded in the camp of our opponents. (*Laughter*). We have been told that ours is a discredited movement; that our enthusiasm is on the wane; and a writer, improving on the situation, writing in one of the journals published in this place, was good enough the other day to tell his readers that this feeble and faulty organization was about to disappear, (*laughter*), and if it is at all to be remembered, it would be recalled to mind with a smile of contempt. (*Laughter*). Well, when I was reading that paragraph, a thought occurred to my mind, and I am sure the same thought must be passing through the minds of many of you within the sound of my voice. I said to myself that if our movement was a discredited movement, how came it to pass that so sapient a journalist should devote four columns of his ponderous artillery to the extermination of that which was naught, and to the condemnation of that which was beneath contempt? (*Loud cheers*). Prosecuting the same line of thought, it occurred to me that if our movement was so utterly discredited, so unworthy of mention, how was it that a late Viceroy, one of the astutest that ever sat on the Viceregal throne, honoured us with a great oration, on the eve of his retirement at the memorable St. Andrew's dinner at Calcutta? It also occurred to me as I was reading this passage to ask—how it was that Lord Lansdowne the other day, extended to us, the representatives of this discredited movement, the friendly hand of recognition? (*Cheers*). Our movement to pass away, unhonoured and unmourned ! Much more likely that this miserable rag of a newspaper will vanish into the inane, without a word of sorrow or regret. (*Applause*). This splendid organization to pass away unhonoured and unmourned ! Why, it has left its foot-prints deep upon the fleeting sands of Time. It has become part and parcel of the history of Modern India. Will any body deny that this Indian Councils Act, which we are discussing at the present moment, is the outcome of our labours and of our self-sacrificing efforts? Who ever had heard of the expansion and reconstitution of the Legislative Councils before the Congress started the subject ? (*Applause*). And within the life-time of a generation, we have obtained what may be regarded as the first instalment of reform in this direction, which it has cost other countries centuries of incessant toil and effort. And indeed, we may well be proud of what we have achieved in other directions. You appealed and agitated for the wider employment of your countrymen in the public service of the land ; you prayed that the age for the open competitive examination for the Indian Civil Service be raised; you prayed that simultaneous examinations be held in India as well as in England. You have got the one, but not got the other. The other will come to you in its own good time. (*Cheers*). It is monstrous that our young men should be compelled to travel a distance of over ten thousand miles, and to pass a most difficult competitive examination, forsooth, for the inestimable boon of serving in their own country ! (*Applause*). Did you ever hear of such monstrous injustice? Why, the people of Ceylon which is a Crown colony of England are better off. They have simultaneous examinations there for the higher appointments. But not only so, even Java, a Dutch colony, said to be a most misgoverned country, has this privilege which we in India do not possess. (*Hear, Hear and 'shame'*). Our rulers profess to be guided by the gracious terms of the Queen's Proclamation, which is the Magna Charta of our rights and privileges (*cheers*) ; and in that Proclamation there are these words of gracious promise :—"And it is our further will that so far as may be, our subjects of whatever race, creed or colour, be freely admitted into all offices, the duties of which they may be qualified, by their education, their ability and integrity duly to discharge." (*Hear Hear*) Mark also the memorable words of Lord Ripon in interpreting the Proclamation—words of righteous indignation against the meaning sought to be put upon that document by Sir James Stephen. I desire to commend these words not only to the members of this Congress, but to the enlightened and informed consciences of our rulers. Lord Ripon said upon that occasion : "Our power and influence rests upon the conviction of our good faith more than upon any other foundation, aye, more than upon the valour of our soldiers or the reputation of our arms." (*Cheers.*) What becomes of the Proclamation, what becomes of the generous words of our Sovereign, of the beneficent interpretation put upon them by her Viceroy, when viewed in the light of the proceedings of the Government of India? To tell the people of India that they are freely entitled to fill every office in the gift of the Crown, and that merit is to be the sole qualification, and then to point out to them that London is the only place, a place ten thousand miles distant, where these examinations are to be held, is to be guilty, if it were the case of an ordinary individual, of impudent and impertinent hypocrisy. (*Loud Cheers*). I presume there is to be one code of morality for individuals, another for Governments. I brush aside this cob-web of sophistry as truly unworthy of our rulers. As much for the maintenance of the honour of our Sovereign, and the credit and reputation of the English people, as for our own interests, we ought to agitate for simultaneous examinations being held in this country as well as in England. (*Cheers*).

There has been progress in all respects save one; and this leads me to that very unhappy Notification which has been issued in Bengal restricting the right of trial by Jury. Year after year in your Congresses you have been praying for the extension of the right of trial by Jury: the Government answers your demand by restricting the right in Bengal. At one stroke of the pen, without any warning or explanation of any kind, we find this precious right filched away from us. [*A voice:—Question.*] It is a very important question and one intimately connected with the matter I am discussing, for if we had Representative Councils, I am perfectly certain we should have long before this brought the Government to book through the exercise of the right of interpellation, which our members would enjoy. Is it conceivable that if we had a reconstituted Council with the right of interpellation, the Government of Sir Charles Elliott could have withdrawn the system of trial by Jury without a protest from the Council, without a host of questions being put to him of an exceedingly unpleasant character? I think, therefore, it will be admitted that this is a matter which is relevant to the point I am discussing. I wish to say one word more, and that is this, that though this question concerns the people of Bengal alone, brother-delegates from Madras and Bombay, you must not lay the flattering unction to your souls that you will escape the fate which has overtaken us. If you have read the despatch which has recently been issued, you will find that the Government is at the present moment considering the propriety of withdrawing the trial of murder cases from the cognizance of juries in the Bombay districts, and of restricting the right of trial by Jury in the Madras Presidency, where, as you know, it has been extended to every district. Therefore, this is a question in which we are all deeply interested, the people of Bengal, the people of Madras and the people of Bombay, and we should stand shoulder to shoulder in safe-guarding the rights which have come down to us from the past, consecrated by the labours of those who have gone before us. (*Cheers*).

In the resolution which has been entrusted to me, you express your regret that the Indian Councils Act does not come up to our expectations. Year after year we have been recording resolutions praying for the introduction of the representative element in the Councils and the expansion of their functions. Lord Dufferin despatched a minute to the Secretary of State in which he partly supported the views of the Congress and recommended the reconstitution of the Provincial Councils upon an elective basis. (*Hear, hear*). But what do we find has been done? As a matter of fact the representative element has not been recognized in the Act, but a clause has been inserted which is known as 'the Kimberley clause,' and which provides for the selection, but not the election, of representative members from various bodies. Great was the regret felt on the Liberal side of the House that the Bill did not provide for the recognition of the elective element. There was one gentleman, however, who raised a discordant note, and that was Mr. Maclean, the late member for Oldham. (*Hisses*). I think we may treat even Mr. Maclean with some little consideration. Mr. Maclean was pleased to tell the House that this Bill was nothing more or less than an offer to hand over the Empire to the control of the Baboos of Bengal. (*Laughter*). The Baboos of Bengal have never wanted anything of the kind. Their friends have never urged such a claim on their behalf. Mr. Maclean unfortunately forgot that what was intended for Bengal was intended for the rest of India as well (*cheers*), and he forgot also that in the year 1878, he spoke at a great meeting held in the town of Bombay, and that at that meeting he supported a resolution which provided for the reconstitution and the expansion of the Legislative Councils! Mr. Maclean may have changed his views. Possibly, Mr. Maclean is of the opinion that it is an old-fashioned practice to stick to one's principles. (*Laughter*). He may not think it necessary to be guided by the considerations of such a paltry morality. At any rate, he owes it to the public to offer some explanation with regard to this convenient change of front. But with the exception of Mr. Maclean and of that worthy Baronet, also from the Bombay Presidency, Sir Richard Temple, there was really no sort of opposition worthy of the name in the House of Commons, and the Bill passed amid what might be considered the unanimous approval of the House. But there was one utterance, a remarkable and a statesmanlike utterance, and that was from Mr. Gladstone in which he gave expression to those enlightened views upon which we base our right for a liberal interpretation of the Indian Councils Act. (*Hear, hear and cheers*). My friend has read an extract from Mr. Gladstone's speech, but I desire to quote two more passages in order to emphasize the demand which we now make for a generous construction of the Act. Mr. Gladstone observed:—

2nd Day.

Resolution I.

Reform of the Legislative Councils.

"It is there that we stand upon solid ground, and Her Majesty's Government ought to understand that it will be regarded as a most grave disappointment, if, after all the assurances we have received that an attempt will be made to bring into operation this powerful engine of Government, there should not be some result such as we anticipate from their action. I do not speak of its amount: I speak more of its quality." (*Hear, hear and cheers*).

And again:—

"All these things induce us to look forward hopefully to a great future for India, and to expect that a real success will attend the genuine application, even though it may be a limited one, of the elective principle to the Government of that vast and almost immeasurable community." (*Renewed applause*).

Well, we appeal to Mr. Gladstone, and the illustrious leaders of the Liberal party, for the application of the elective principle to the constitution of the Councils, and I am sure that we will not appeal in vain. (*Prolonged cheers*). A party that is pledged to the principle of Home Rule in Ireland cannot but lend an indulgent ear to the aspirations of the people of India for the wider extension of Self-Government in this country. (*Loud applause*). Self-Government is the ordinance of nature, the dispensation of Divine Providence; it is the leaven of modern society; it is the cement which binds together the most distant families of the human race; it is of universal application; it transcends considerations of race, colour and creed. "Representative institutions," remarked Mr. Gladstone, in a great speech he made in the year 1890, "are consecrated possessions which in the counsels of Providence have been entrusted to the care and the guardianship of the English people." (*Loud applause*). We appeal to Mr. Gladstone, we appeal to his colleagues to admit us into this inestimable legacy of the Anglo-Saxon race. (*Prolonged cheering*). Wherever floats the flag of England, Self-Government is the order of the day. (*Hear, hear*). Wherever Englishmen have gathered together in their colonies, be they in the frigid zones of the north, or amid the blazing heat of the Equator, or in those distant tracts watered by the southern seas, Self-Government again is the order of the day. We are not Englishmen or men of English race or extraction, but we are British subjects, (*hear, hear and cheers*), the citizens of a great and free empire; we live under the protecting shadows of one of the noblest constitutions the world has ever seen. (*Applause*). The rights of Englishmen are ours, their privileges are ours, their constitution is ours. (*Loud applause*). But we are excluded from them. (*Cries of 'shame'*). How long is this exclusion to last? That will depend very much upon ourselves. If we are true to the traditions of the Congress, and loyal to the noble teachings of our great Chief (*loud cheers*), who, though not present in body, is present in spirit with us—if we live up to the exalted standard of his noble life—if we consecrate our efforts by the spirit of self-sacrifice, if we are unsparing in our pecuniary sacrifices, unremitting in our personal efforts, then the great God who presides over the destinies of fallen nations will in his own due time pour down upon us, in plentiful abundance, his choicest blessings; and though we may receive a temporary check, and the flag which we now hold aloft may droop from our sinking hands, I am confident that in the near future there will rise up others, who, more fortunately situated than ourselves, will carry that standard to victory, and establish in this luckless land those principles of liberty, which, while they will serve to weld together the diversified elements of our common nationality, will, at the same time, place the Empire of Britain in this country upon the only unchangeable basis upon which it can rest, viz., the love, the gratitude and the contentment of a vast and immeasurable population. (*Loud and prolonged cheers*).

Raja Ram Pal Sinh, (*Allahabad, No. 334, in list,*) Gentlemen,—After listening to the illustrious gentleman whose eloquent language you have just heard, you will not be at all pleased with a speaker like me who speaks in plain and broken English. But, gentlemen, I am sure that the righteousness and the importance of the cause which I advocate, and in behalf of which I now stand before you, will plead my excuse. I am only going to say what is right and just, and it is for this reason I now venture in all humility to stand before you. You know, Gentlemen, that I have been a traveller in foreign countries, and that I have probed the opinions of foreigners in regard to my country, my countrymen and our real interests; and I am sorry to say that these people,—not only Englishman, but other Europeans and even Americans too, in fact, the world generally—have called you a degenerate race, a nation which cannot be compared to the least civilised community in Europe, because they say you do not show that spirit of independence which European gentlemen, as a rule, have, because the mass of your population do not possess that sturdy sense of self-respect and that love of liberty which would make them resent every wrong and injustice, and boldly claim their rights and privileges. And I must say that there is some truth in this indictment (*A voice "very little"*). But the indications of the growth of a new spirit which are everywhere visible now, will, I am sure, soon take away this reproach from our people. (*Hear, hear*). Then, gentlemen, you have been seeking a voice in the Legislative Councils of your country by loyal and respectful representations, and your critics have said that you will never get it until you express your wishes forcibly. But their views have been proved to be unsound. (*Hear, hear*). The English Government have listened to our prayers, and may the Government be blessed in that they have promised to give us a voice in the Legislative Councils of our country. (*Loud and prolonged cheers*). This right ought certainly to have been conferred upon us long ago in pursuance of Her Majesty's gracious Proclamation. (*Hear, hear*). But there seemed to be no hope of the promises of that Proclamation being fulfilled until the Congress, this happy child of the British administration (*cheers*), now eight years old, came into existence and made its voice heard. (*Renewed applause*). You must insist, gentlemen, still further, on the rights and privileges, which have been promised to you, as subjects of Her Majesty, the Queen of England and the Empress of India, (*Hear, hear and cheers*), being granted to you in their integrity, and you may be sure that they *will* be granted. (*Renewed applause*). Indeed, even Lord Lansdowne said the other day at Poona that your rights will be granted to you.

Gentlemen, the reason of my rising here is to caution you that when you receive the right of representation, you should take care not to return such members as have, as a rule, been hitherto appointed to the Legislative Councils, men who would merely hold up their hands when the Viceroy would hold up his, and keep them down, when the Viceroy would keep down his. (*Hear, hear*). Such men ought ever to be kept away from the Councils. (*Cheers*). But you should elect, gentlemen, men who should be able to think for themselves, and to speak out their minds freely. (*Hear, hear*). The duties of members of Legislative Councils, always responsible, are becoming more and more onerous day by day. The condition of the people is growing from bad to worse. (*Hear, hear*). The resources of the country are being drained week by week and year by year. It is becoming more and more necessary that Government should devise measures to check the growth of poverty, necessary as much for the stability and reputation of the British administration, as for the welfare of the people. (*Hear, hear and cheers*). It is true that we enjoy under this administration, the blessings of a general education; it is true that we enjoy security of life and property; it is true that we have facilities for travelling by rail such as never existed before; it is true that we have excellent postal and telegraph services. For all these, and numerous other similar blessings and benefits, we feel, and shall always feel, sincerely grateful to the British Government. (*Loud cheers*). But, gentlemen, it is also unfortunately too true that vast millions of Her Majesty's subjects in India are living from hand to mouth, and are eking out a most miserable existence on the verge of starvation. (*Cries of "shame," "shame"*).

The causes of this evil are manifest. The practical monopoly of all the high offices in the administration by foreigners, who do not make this country their home, and who spend the greater portion of their pay and pension in foreign lands; the monopoly of the foreign trade by foreign merchants, and the annual drain in the shape of Home charges, coupled with the heavy loss by exchange, must naturally make the country poor and the people miserable. (*Loud and prolonged cheers*). And in order, gentlemen, to press on the attention of Government, the urgent necessity of the reforms which we believe to be necessary to remedy this deplorable state of things, we require the presence in the Legislative Councils, of men who are acquainted with the condition of the country, and who would fearlessly represent the grievances of the people to Government, and plead that they may be considered in a truly earnest and paternal spirit, and, so far as may be possible, remedied. (*Cheers*).

Gentlemen, it has been said, and very well said, that a king who is loved by his subjects is better secured than one of whom they are afraid, like the Emperor of Russia, for instance (*Hear hear*); and therefore I feel certain that if our grievances had been properly represented to Her Majesty, the people of India would long since have been made happy, the gracious promises of Her Majesty's Proclamation would have been fulfilled, and there would have been greater sympathy between the rulers and the ruled. (*Cheers*). In conclusion, I earnestly hope that it will be impressed upon the Government that the reform and reconstitution of the Legislative Councils will be equally beneficial to Her Majesty's Government and to the people of this country. (*Loud applause*).

[Raja Ram Pal Sinh then addressed the meeting in Urdu, much to the same effect.]

Mr. M. B. Namjoshi, (*Poona, No. 96, in list,*).—Gentlemen,—The resolution that I rise to support, you may well take it, is a self-supporting resolution, and one which hardly requires any observations from any one to commend it to your acceptance. However, for the purposes of the few observations that I am going to make, I have divided the resolution into four parts. The first part gives the history of the movement and the outcome of it; the second part expresses our regret, because the Act does not make any provision for the introduction of the elective principle into the re-constituted Legislative Councils; the third part expresses the hope that a liberal interpretation will be put upon the Act in framing rules to give effect to its provisions, and that the wishes of the nation will be fully met in that direction; and the last part makes a prayer, and the prayer is that the Government of India will be pleased to publish these rules before passing them finally, so that the public might have an opportunity of expressing their opinions regarding them, and judging for themselves how far their wishes are met by the rules. These are the four parts into which I divide the resolution for the purposes of the observations I have to address to you.

Now, gentlemen, we express regret, because in the case of permissive legislation, we are always dependent on the good will of the executive. (*Hear, hear.*) This is what we do not want. (*Cheers*). The Bombay Act of 1878 deals with the subject of Local Self-Government, and it remained a dead letter till 1883, (*cries of 'shame,'*) when it pleased the Government to introduce the elective principle into the constitution of the Municipalities. The Local Government did nothing like it until it was pressed to do so by the higher authorities. (*'Shame'*). We wish that this may not be the case here, (*Cheers,*) and we, therefore, regret that the measure which has been passed does not provide for the certain introduction of the elective principle into the constitution of our Councils. (*Cheers.*) However, the thing has been done (and we have hardly time to speak upon it), and we, therefore, dispose of that part of the subject by the expression of our regret, and rely upon the Act as it is, and upon the assurances given by the leading statesmen of the day in the House of Commons, for the fulfilment of our desires. And, gentlemen, I have not the least doubt that if the Government give effect to those assurances, our purpose will be served. (*Hear, hear and cheers*). Statesmen in Parliament have declared that the intentions of the Legislature should be met most liberally by the Government, and we only express the hope that they will be so met. And, lastly, we ask that the Government will publish the rules, which they have been authorised to frame under the Act, before passing them finally. These rules are, as it were, a secondary piece of legislation. The Parliament passed the Act, and has left it to the Local Government to pass rules under the Act. The Parliament thus took the Government here into its confidence, and it is but just and reasonable that the Government, in its turn, should take the public into its confidence, (*Cheers.*) The benefits of such a course are too obvious to require any mention. Under Lord Ripon's Government executive orders were issued requiring that rules framed under a particular Act should be published, so that the public might have an opportunity of making suggestions regarding them. We only require the Government to follow the instructions laid down by Lord Ripon, and as I believe that the sympathies of the present Government are with us, I hope and trust that they will be pleased to grant this our very reasonable prayer. (*Loud Cheers*).

Mr. Narayan Swami Nayadu (*Nagpore, No. 141, in list,*).—Mr. President and Brother Delegates,—In supporting the resolution so ably put forward by my learned friend Mr. Ananda Charlu, and so well supported by my friend Mr. Surendra Nath Banerjee, I think it will be unnecessarily taking up your time to add anything more in the shape of arguments upon the subject. The resolution simply states what we expected and in what we feel disappointed, and it also expresses the hope that the Government of India will do what they ought to do unasked. (*Hear, hear and cheers*). I believe, gentlemen, that it was under the dispensation of a benign Providence that India was placed in such close relationship with the British Empire, the greatest empire that the world has ever seen. (*Hear, hear and cheers*). India was once in the zenith of civilisation, but time and circumstances brought about her downfall. And it seems it was with a view to restore her to her former high position that the Almighty Providence entrusted the destinies of this country to our Aryan brethren of the West. (*Cheers*). I call Englishmen our Aryan brethren, because they belong to the Aryan race. (*Hear, hear*). It behoves Englishmen that they should well discharge the duties so solemnly imposed upon them by the Great Providence. They have educated us, and opened to us the rich stores of the noble literature of their country. The result of that education is that a large number of our brethren here are as enlightened and as well educated as Englishmen are. They are occupying leading positions as lawyers, doctors, engineers, and so on in the different walks of life open to them. (*Hear, hear*). We naturally desire now that our English brethren should enable us to rise to the same position as they occupy by conferring upon us all those inestimable political privileges that they themselves enjoy. (*Cheers*). They ought to see, and see with becoming pride, that India is not now what it was fifty years ago; that, thanks to the fostering influences of their own administration, we have made great progress in education and enlightenment, and have learnt to appreciate what our rights are and what our duties are to our fellowmen, to our sovereign and to our country. (*Hear, hear and cheers*). They ought to give us an opportunity now to exercise those rights and to perform those duties, that we may be able to promote our common welfare. (*Cheers*). Our request is a very moderate and simple one. We say that the people ought to have a voice in the framing of the laws which are to govern them. We say that there should be a real representation of the people in the Legislative Councils of the country, based on the principle of election. We are convinced that this is absolutely necessary in the interests both of the people and the Government. (*Loud cheers*). We had expected that provision would be made for such representation in the Councils Act recently passed by Parliament. And we were very sorry to see that no such provision was made but that the matter was left in the hands of the executive administration. The solemn assurances given by the Under-Secretary of State for India, coupled with the most important utterance of Mr. Gladstone, to which reference has already been made, have inspired us, however, with the hope that an honest and earnest effort will be made to secure by the rules to be framed under the Act, a living representation of the people in the Councils. The Government are indeed bound to frame such rules as will secure that object. This they can only do by recognising the principle of election in those rules, in conformity with the views of Mr. Gladstone and those who agreed with him. And I earnestly hope that the Government will do this, and thereby make the reconstitution of the Legislative Councils a source of real benefit to the country. (*Cheers*). I hope you will all agree with me in thinking that this resolution has been framed in such a manner as to meet with your unanimous approval, and I commend it confidently to your acceptance. (*Loud cheers*).

Mr. Uma Shunkar, (*Lahore, No. 616, in list,*).—Gentlemen,—After hearing so many eloquent speakers who have preceded me, it would have been better for me to keep quiet, as I do not think that anything has been left for me to touch upon. But the request of my fellow delegates of the town I come from, impels me to say a few words to you. I come from Amritsar, the sacred and religious city of the Sikhs. (*Hear, hear*). Now none of you can say that the Sikhs have not proved themselves to be the most loyal subjects of Her Most Gracious Majesty the Queen by their devotion to her. (*Cheers*). And, gentlemen, they desire the reform that you advocate in this resolution as much as others do, because they believe it will conduce to the good both of the Government and the people. (*Loud Cheers.*) Gentlemen, the resolution that I have come here to support is like the request of an intelligent young man who having passed his preliminary examination, goes to his parents and asks for text books of a higher class. One would expect that the parents will be delighted to see the progress the young man has made, and gladly supply him with such books as he requires. But what would be thought of those parents who would refuse to give him the books he needs, and give him instead books of an inferior character, too ill-suited to his advanced mental capacity? (*Cheers.*) Can any one say that the reform that the condition of the country demands, and that we have so long and so persistently been praying for, has been granted to us ? ('*No,*' '*none.*') And is it not a matter of supreme regret that it has not been granted? ('*Yes,*' '*yes,*' *and cheers.*) However, gentlemen, we need not yet despair. Our object can to a great extent be gained if the rules which are to be framed under the Act, be made in the spirit of Mr. Gladstone's declarations in the House of Commons. And I hope, and hope with confidence, that they will be so framed (*loud cheers*), and that the reputation of our Government for desiring and promoting the advancement of the Indian people will not only be maintained but enhanced. (*Renewed applause*). With these few words, I heartily support the resolution, and hope you will all support me. (*Loud Cheers*).

HAFIZ MUHAMMAD ABDUL RAHEEM, (*Aligarh, No.* 510, *in list,*).—GENTLEMEN,—As called upon by our worthy President, I rise to support this resolution with pleasure. I shall first translate it for the sake of those who do not know English. (The speaker, who spoke in Urdu, here stated the purport of the resolution and then proceeded as follows:) Gentlemen, you have heard what the resolution says. It embraces many points. My predecessors have fully dealt with each and all of them. I wish to say a few words in respect of only two of them.

The first point is as to why we express regret at the fact that the Act as passed by Parliament, does not, in terms, concede to the people the right of electing their own representatives to the Councils, but leaves it to the Governor-General in Council, if he so please, to make from time to time regulations as to the conditions under which such nominations, or any of them, shall be made, and to prescribe the manner in which such regulations shall be carried into effect. Gentlemen, the introduction of the elective principle in the constitution of our Councils, was and is the most essential part of the reform we have been contending for for so many years. (*Hear, hear*). We had expected that Parliament would recognise that principle in the Act in clear and unmistakable terms. But instead of doing that, it has left the matter in the hands of the Government of India. We have no guarantee that the discretion so vested in the Government would be wisely and liberally exercised, none even that it will not be abused (*Hear, hear and cheers*). Some of our administrators have no doubt been very liberal and far-seeing statesmen (*Hear, hear*). But there are others among them who are illiberal and short-sighted. A spirit of retrogression seems to have taken possession of their minds and seems to be guiding their actions. Far from desiring to extend liberty and to secure fresh privileges to the people, they seem to delight in curtailing and restricting what little the people enjoy ('*Shame*'). The present Lieutenant-Governor of Bengal affords us an instance. Sir Charles Elliot is a Civilian of these Provinces. He began his career here. There is a great deal of difference between the education and the ideas of liberty which education brings, which prevail in these Provinces and those in Bengal. When Sir Charles Elliot came to be the Lieutenant-Governor of the Lower Provinces, he did not probably like the liberty and the privileges enjoyed by the people there, and consequently commenced attacks on them in various forms and ways. One of the deadliest of such attacks was the one he hurled at the system of trial by jury, which had been in force there for the last thirty years (*Cries of* '*shame,*' '*shame*'), and had been spoken well of by many preceding Lieutenant-Governors! Sir Charles Elliot abolished that system by one stroke of his pen! ('*Shame,*' '*shame*'). Section 269 of the Code of Criminal Procedure gives a discretionary power to the Lieutenant-Governor to extend or withdraw the system of trial by jury wherever and whenever he may think fit to do so. And Sir Charles Elliot has exercised that discretion, *with* the sanction of the Government of

India, in a manner which has shocked the whole thoughtful population of India. (*Cheers*). If the right of trial by jury had been secured to the people by the provision of the law, it would have been beyond the power of a tyrannically disposed Lieutenant-Governor like Sir Charles Elliot to deprive them of it after they had enjoyed it for 30 long years, in the manner in which he has done it (*Hear, hear and cheers*). We regret that the provisions of the Councils Act do not secure to the people the right of electing their representatives to the Council, but merely empower the Governor-General in Council to introduce from time to time such rules as he may think fit for the nomination of members to the Council, because we fear that if there happen to be a Governor-General as despotically inclined as Sir Charles Elliot, he might by one stroke of his pen, at any time abrogate or suspend the regulations that may be in force for the election of members, supposing that such regulations have been introduced. (*Loud and prolonged applause*).

The second point to which I wish to draw your attention is as to why this resolution contains a prayer that the rules that are at present being framed under the Act may be first published as draft rules before being confirmed and enforced. It is the recognised practice of all civilised Governments, and of the British Government in India as well, that they publish the draft of every proposed enactment or rule which is likely to affect the public before it is passed, in order to afford the public an opportunity to offer such suggestions or criticisms upon them as they may deem fit to make. Even Municipal bye-laws which affect only a small local area are laid before the public before they are confirmed. (*Hear, hear*). The rules and regulations relating to the nomination of members to the Legislative Councils will affect the whole of this vast country. Both reason and justice therefore make it all the more necessary that they should be published, and the public invited to express their opinion regarding them, before they are finally sanctioned. (*Loud Cheers*). If this wise course is not adopted, and the rules are flung all of a sudden upon the people, and fail to meet their just demands, we shall have no option left to us but to prefer objections to them both here and in England, and send up petitions to Parliament until we have got them revised and brought into harmony with our reasonable aspirations and desires. (*Cheers*). If for no other reason, I hope the Government of India will publish the draft rules for this one reason alone. (*Cheers*). With these few remarks, I heartily support this resolution. (*Loud cheers*).

Moulvi Wahabuddeen (*Moradabad, No. 606, in list,*).—Gentlemen,—After so many speakers have spoken, it is superfluous for any other person to rise and say anything in support of the resolution now before you. But I have only a few remarks to offer, and I hope you will allow me to do so. You know, gentlemen, that this Councils Act has been passed after thirty years. The first Act was passed in 1861; and it is now in 1891 (1892) that this second Act has been passed, which is no doubt the direct outcome of the agitation of the National Congress. (*Cheers*). In criticising the provisions of this Act, however, we should not forget that the art of administration is a very difficult one. (*Hear, hear*). My predecessors have spoken in a very despairing tone of the possible results of this Act. I agree to some extent with them. But I hope for far better results. (*Hear, hear and cheers*). I base my hope on the fact that the British Government both in this country and in England, pride themselves upon this that they are always open to conviction, and are ever willing to modify their opinions whenever they find that they are mistaken, and also willing to adopt what may be shown to be most acceptable to the nation at large. (*Hear, hear*). The British Empire is the most extensive empire the world has yet seen. (*Hear, hear*). And it is at the same time so powerful that it can most gracefully make concessions to the reasonable wishes of its people, and thereby strengthen the bonds of their attachment to it. (*Loud cheers*). And I fully believe that the Government will concede to us, slowly it may be but most surely, all that is reasonable and feasible in our demands. (*Loud cheers*). Now we have been agitating for the reform of the Legislative Councils for eight years. Throughout the length and breadth of India, in every hamlet and house-hold, we have asked for some reform which will secure to us a voice in our Legislative Councils. And I am glad to find that our prayers have at last been listened to. (*Cheers*).

Resolution I.

Reform of the Legislative Councils.

Lord Lansdowne's speeches at Madras and Poona leave no doubt in my mind that our requests will soon be granted, and I earnestly hope they will be granted. (*Cheers*). For surely nothing could be more injurious to the British administration, than that an impression should go abroad that the promises held out by His Excelleney are not to be carried out, and that the British Government is not willing to concede to the reasonable wishes of its people. (*Cheers*). It would also be deeply to be regretted if the prayers of nearly thirty crores of people who have, with folded hands, been praying that a change should be made in the law in respect of the constitution of the Legislative Councils, should be disregarded by Government. (*Cheers*). I would say that if an impression once goes abroad that the Government deliberately ignore the united wishes of the people, it would not at all be creditable to the British Government. (*Loud cheers*). I therefore hope and trust that the promises held out by Lord Lansdowne will soon be fulfilled and that the wishes of the nation will be fully satisfied. (*Loud cheers*).

The resolution was then put to the vote and carried unanimously.

Mr. G. K. Gokhale (*Poona, No. 82, in list,*).—Mr. President, Ladies and Gentlemen,—The proposition which I have to move for your adoption is as follows:—

Resolution II.

Employment of Indians in the Public Service.

"*That this Congress hereby places on record its deep regret at the resolution of the Government of India on the Report of the Public Service Commission, in that—*

(*a*) *Whereas, if the recommendations of the Public Service Commission had been carried out in their integrity, the posts proposed to be detached from the schedule of the Statute of 1861 would have formed part of an organised Service, specially reserved for the Natives of India, the resolution of Government leaves these posts altogether isolated, to which appointment can be made only under the Statute of 1870;*

(*b*) *Whereas, 108 appointments were recommended by the Public Service Commission for the Provincial Service, 93 such appointments only have actually been thrown open to that Service: the number to be allotted to Assam not having been yet announced;*

(*c*) *Whereas, a membership of the Board of Revenue and a Commissionership of a division were recommended for the Province of Bengal and some other Provinces, the Government has not given effect to this resolution;*

(*d*) *Whereas, one-third of the Judgeships were recommended to be thrown open to the Provincial Service, only one-fifth have been so thrown open.*

*And this Congress, again, distinctly puts on record its opinion that full justice will never be done to the people of this country, until the open competitive examination for the Civil Service of India is held simultaneously in England and in India.*

Really, gentlemen, if ever a mountain was in labor and brought forth a mouse, it was in the present instance of the work of the Public Service Commission. (*Cheers*). Those of you who may remember the loud flourish of trumpets with which this Commission was heralded into being, will easily understand what I say. And we of the Poona Sarvajanik Sabha here especially remember with what tremendous indignation and excitement Lord Dufferin spoke to us at Poona in 1887 about the way in which our Bengal brethren were predicting all sorts of evil from the appointment of the Commission. (*Hear, hear*). We, however, now find that the instinctive manner in which our countrymen of Bengal seemed to shrink from that Commission, has been more than justified. Gentlemen, the Commission was appointed to devise a scheme which might reasonably be expected to possess the necessary elements of finality and to do *full justice* to the claims of the people of this country for their higher and more extensive employment in the public service. But what is the result? Have we been granted higher and more extensive employment? ('*No*,' '*no*'). You will find upon a careful consideration of the subject, that we have not merely not gained anything, but we have been actually put back considerably. (*Cries of 'shame'*). Just consider where we were before the appointment of this Commission. Of course, there was the Statute of 1861, which had reserved certain posts for those alone who would pass the London examination, but under the rules of 1879, *one-sixth of the whole recruitment* was secured to natives of India. Mark, one-sixth of the whole recruitment was secured and not one-sixth of the reserved posts only, as the Government of India and the Commission have tried to assume. (*Hear, hear*). There is much difference between one-sixth of the total recruitment and one-sixth of the reserved schedule posts. There are only about 600 scheduled posts. But over and above these, about 150 other posts are generally held by Covenanted Civilians. Thus there are altogether about 750 posts which are held by Covenanted Civilians in this country. Gentlemen, remember that I am taking the figures which the Government of India themselves have supplied, in their reply to a representation from the Indian Association of Calcutta, and not the higher ones given by the Commission in its report. Well, under the rules of 1879, if full effect had been given to them, we should, in the long run, have had one-sixth of these 750 posts and not merely one-sixth of the 600 reserved by the Act of 1861. (*Hear, hear*). Gentlemen, I grieve to say that in regard to this question of one-sixth, the Commission itself has written in a very misleading manner. In recommending that 108 posts should be detached from the schedule of the Act of 1861, the Commission has gravely stated that the number is greater than the one to which we were entitled under the rules of 1879. Of course, the posts reserved by the Act of 1861 are only 600, and one-sixth of them, *i. e.*, 100 is undoubtedly less than 108. But it is simply astonishing that the Commission should have ignored the fact that the rules of 1879 had secured to us one-sixth of the annual recruitment, and this recruitment takes place, not for the 600 reserved posts only, but for the 750 reserved and unreserved posts which are generally held by Covenanted Civilians. Thus, if full effect had been given to the rules of 1879, about 125 posts, usually held by members of the Covenanted Service, would have, in the long run, been held by Statutory Civilians. And when, therefore, the Commission recommended the setting apart of 108 posts only, it did, beyond a shadow of doubt, recommend a number that was smaller than that which was secured to us by the rules of 1879. (*Hear, hear and cheers*). Thus did the Commission discharge the duty entrusted to it, of doing full justice to the claims of the people of this country to *higher and more extended employment* in the higher grades of the public service! ('*Shame*', '*shame*').

Gentlemen, you now see what our position was before the appointment of the Commission. Next let us look at what the Commission proposed for us. The Commission proposed that in place of the posts secured to us by the rules of 1879, 108 posts from the schedule of the Act of 1861 should be set apart for us. Well, this was giving us 108 in the place of our 125, but there was one good feature about the Commission's recommendation. The Commission had recommended that these 108 posts should be detached from the schedule of the Act of 1861 by Parliamentary legislation, and should then be incorporated into the Provincial Service which the Commission had proposed to create. That service practically was to be exclusively for the natives of this country, while the Imperial service was intended for those who passed the examination in London. If this recommendation of the Commission had been carried out, these 108 posts would have formed part of the Provincial Service. The Secretary of State was, however, afraid of facing Parliament. Lord Cross felt that if he took the matter before the House of Commons, inconvenient questions might be raised, and his own hands, to some extent, forced, because at that time our high-souled and devoted champion, Mr. Charles Bradlaugh (*loud cheers,*) was alive, and he would certainly have seen that some justice at least was done to the people of India. It was necessary, therefore, to avoid Parliamentary legislation, and this choice being made the subsequent course of the Secretary of State was clear. And the position now is this :—Government has retained the Statutes of 1861 and 1870, but the rules of 1879 framed under the Act of 1870, have been abolished, and the 108 posts which the Commission proposed to detach from the schedule of the Statute of 1861 *by Parliamentary legislation* remain in that schedule. And the Government of India now proposes to place instead about 93 or 94, out of the posts reserved in the schedule, on a separate list, and make appointments to them, if it thinks that competent natives are available, under the Act of 1870. (*Cries of 'shame'*). Gentlemen, if the scheme of the Commission had been adopted, the schedule of the Act of 1861 would itself have been curtailed by Parliamentary enactment, and the posts cut off, *i. e.*, 108 in number, would have *formed part of the Provincial Service.* But by avoiding Parliamentary legislation, these posts

**Resolution II.**

**Employment of Indians in the Public Service.**

—and even their number has been reduced from 108 to 93 or 94—have now been left hanging alone and unconnected between the two services, the Civil Service of India and the Provincial Service, and appointments to them would only be special appointments under the Act of 1870. This leaves a large measure of discretion to Government, which, I am not sure, will not be abused. (*Cheers.*) Then, Gentlemen, you have to remember that the Secretary of State has already decided that appointments made under the Act of 1870 are made to single posts only and do not form part of an organized service. Indeed, when the Commission made its recommendation about the 108 posts, one of its chief arguments in favour of its scheme was that by it the natives would be great gainers, inasmuch as the posts detached from the schedule of the Statute of 1861 would form part of an organized service. The distinction between appointments to specific posts and appointments to posts forming part of an organized service was thus stated by the Commission:—"Membership in an organized service ensures a more permanent status and involves more certain prospects than if appointment is made to a particular post only and every step of further promotion requires a fresh exercise of the power of appointment under the Statute. In the former case, the merit and ability required as a condition of first appointment are, in the absence of positive evidence to the contrary, presumed for purposes of subsequent promotions; in the latter case, they have to be proved afresh at each step." When a person is a member of an organized service *Government* has to prove his incapacity before he is passed over; while when he holds a specific appointment only, such as are conferred under the Act of 1870, it is for *him* to prove that he deserves to be promoted. (*Hear, hear*).

Thus if the 108 or rather 93 appointments had been thrown into the Provincial Service, we should have had a right to all those appointments and should have got them all, unless the Government were able to prove that there was not a single individual amongst us natives of India fit for any of them. But now we have ourselves to prove our fitness, in a manner satisfactory to Government, before we get them. Gentlemen, you will thus see that if the scheme of the Commission had been adopted, the Government would have had to prove our incompetency in each case before they could be in a position to appoint a Covenanted Civilian to any of these posts. This means an important difference. The grievance is a very serious one, and it is therefore only proper that it should occupy the foremost position in this resolution. (*Cheers*).

The second part of the resolution is one which you can very easily understand, and I shall not therefore detain you more than a moment in speaking upon it. It states that while the Commission recommended 108 appointments to be given to us, the Government has only given 93, or, including 2 or 3 appointments for Assam, about 96. Thus the number recommended by the Commission has been considerably reduced, and the quality also of the appointments has been lowered, inasmuch as the highest posts recommended by the Commission have been withheld by Government. (*Cries of 'shame'*). To sum up our complaints in this matter, we find that even the retrograde recommendations of the Commission have been deprived by the Government of India of whatever beneficent character they possessed; that the number and quality of the posts proposed to be detached by the Commission from the schedule to the Statute of 1861 have been reduced; and that a large and perilous measure of discretion has been reserved by Government to itself which is almost sure to be abused. And all this as the outcome of the labours of a Commission solemnly appointed to do full justice to our claims for larger and more extensive employment in the higher grades of the public service! (*Cries of 'shame'*).

The last part of the resolution deals with the question of simultaneous examinations. I do not wish to say much on this question, partly because I can say very little on this subject that may appear new to you, and partly because I have been anticipated in my observations by my friend Babu Surendra Nath Banerji, who has stated the case with his usual eloquence and vigour. But I will say this, that, so far back as the year 1860, a Committee of the Indian Office did actually recommend the holding of simultaneous examinations as the only way to adequately fulfil the pledges that have been from time to time given to the people of this country by Government in this matter. (*Hear, hear*):

**Resolution II.**

**Employment of Indians in the Public Service.**

Gentlemen, in those days the consciences of our rulers were not so elastic as they have now become. (*Hear, hear and cheers*). The Committee of the India Office felt that though Government had been repeatedly promising that no distinction would be made among Her Majesty's subjects on the ground of race, colour or creed, yet, practically, for years together they shut us out from the Civil Service of our own country. The Committee therefore unanimously recommended the holding of simultaneous examinations in England and India. (*Hear, hear*). Gentlemen, the value of that recommendation of the Committee was further enhanced by the fact that it was made only three years after that terrible event, the Mutiny of 1857. There is a point in that, for if ever a policy of distrust would have been justified, it would have been so at that time! (*Hear, hear*). And yet what the Committee of the India Office recommended as necessary in 1860, the Public Service Commission of 1886 chose to regard as unsafe and dangerous. ('*Shame*'). Theoretically, of course, there is no inequality, but as pointed out by Babu Surendra Nath Banerji, though we are told that we are at liberty to enter the Civil Service, if we can, when we want to enter, we are asked to seek a door which stands at a distance of ten thousand miles from this country. And thus practically what they give us with one hand they take away by the other. (*Cries of 'shame'*).

Gentlemen, I must not take up more of your time, but I will only say one word in regard to the promises which have so often been made to us in this matter. So far back as 1833, the Parliament of England deliberately declared that as far as admission to the Public Service of India was concerned, no obstacles would be placed in the path of natives on the score of race, creed or color. That declaration was further emphasised in the great Proclamation of 1858. And if these solemn promises are to be fulfilled, there is only one way in which that can be done, and that is by holding simultaneous examinations here and in England. (*Cheers* . We might for the present be prepared even to accept some limitations. We might, for instance, go in for the compromise suggested by Mr. Dadabhai Naoroji in his evidence before the Public Service Commission, that the annual recruitment should be half of natives and half of Europeans. Personally, I may go further and say that natives who pass in India should be compelled to reside for two years at some English University. But, so long as we are not examined here, it is idle to say that because the competitive examination is the same, therefore natives and Europeans are placed on a footing of equality. (*Cheers*). Unfortunately the fact cannot be gainsaid, that of late our rulers have been showing a disposition to regret the promises given us in the past; and I should not be surprised if they one day turned round and said, that these promises were never intended to be carried out. In that case, I say, it would be well for them to openly and publicly fling into flames all these promises and pledges as so much waste paper, and tell us once for all, that after all we are a conquered people and can have no rights or privileges. (*Loud cheers*).

That the Government has, of late, been pursuing a policy of retrogression is clear to every one. Turn whichever way we may, we find that a change, and a change for the worse, is coming over the spirit of the Government. Whether you consider the Jury Notification in Bengal, or the curtailment of educational grants, or the treatment accorded to Municipalities, you cannot help feeling that Government is treating us with increasing jealousy and distrust every day. And unless this regime of distrust is soon changed, unless the policy of Government is inspired by more sympathetic feelings, darker days cannot but be in store for this poor country. (*Cheers*). Gentlemen, it is not difficult to understand why this change of spirit has come upon the Government. Indeed the reason was eloquently given expression to by Mr. Pherozeshah Mehta at the last Bombay Provincial Conference. Mr. Mehta said that it was all very well for the rulers to talk of raising the subject to the level of the ruler, but when the subject began to press close, uncomfortably close, the temptation to kick back a little was irresistible.

Gentlemen, in the midst of this dark and dismal situation, there is only one relieving feature. It is the election of Mr. Dadabhai Naoroji to Parliament. (*Cheers*). You know what Mr. Dadabhai has said in his letter to the President, that he has spent the greater portion of his past life in efforts to secure, on the part of the rulers, a better recognition

**Resolution II.**

**Employment of Indians in the Public Service.**

of the claims of Natives to admission into the higher grades of the public service in India, and in the House of Commons he intends to do what he can in regard to this affair. Let us, therefore, hope that through the exertions of Mr. Dadabhai Naoroji, and through the exertions of English friends, and through our own exertions, a change will soon be brought about in the present unsympathetic policy of the Government of India (*Cheers*); and the Government of India can give us no better earnest of such a change of spirit than a reconsideration and modification of its recent unjust and unsatisfactory orders relating to the Report of the Public Service Commission. (*Loud applause*).

PANDIT MADAN MOHAN MALAVIYA, (*Allahabad, No. 346 in list,*).—Mr. PRESIDENT AND GENTLEMEN,—I rise to second this resolution more as a matter of form than of necessity; because, in the first place, the subject has been discussed very fully in previous Congresses, and, in the second place, the very lucid speech of my esteemed friend Mr. Gokhale, renders it unnecessary for me to offer any further remarks to show the reasonableness of the proposition before you. If you look back at the arguments addressed to you in previous Congresses, you will see that the worst apprehensions which were expressed regarding the results of the Public Service Commission, have been realised, and that very few of the recommendations which tended to our benefit have been accepted. ('*Shame*'). It is really a matter for deep regret that it has been so. It cannot but pain us, people of India, to find that though we have been agitating for the last thirty years for an adequate share of employment in the public service of our country, and though our claims to such share have been repeatedly recognised in the most solemn manner by the Queen and Parliament of Great Britain and Ireland, we are not up to this time allowed a free and fair scope in the matter of that service. (*Cheers*). Acts of Parliament and the Proclamation of the Queen have laid it down that Natives of India will be freely admitted to every post the duties of which they may, by their integrity and ability, be able to discharge. But in actual practice their claims are deliberately and shamelessly ignored, and Europeans are pitchforked into places of emolument which Indians are by their ability and character fully qualified to fill. (*Cries of 'shame' and loud cheers*). This, gentlemen, has become a question of the most serious importance. It is one in which the most vital interests of the people are involved. We are not prompted to ask for a more extensive employment of our countrymen in the public service simply for the pleasure of seeing them there. If our country were not being drained of its money year after year by the inordinate employment of persons whose home it is not, and who would not make it their home, (*hear, hear*), we would never have given such painfully earnest attention to the matter as we are now giving. (*Loud cheers*). But this ceaseless drain is making India every day poorer and poorer, and it is the duty of every well-wisher of the country to endeavour to stop or check it, as best as he can. (*Cheers*).

It is hardly necessary for me to tell you what amount of drain the employment of non-domiciled Europeans causes on this country, but if you permit me, I will give you a few figures taken from a Parliamentary return of the annual salaries of officers employed in India in 1889-90 to give you an idea of what that drain is. The paper I quote from is dated the 31st March, 1892. It shows that among persons drawing salaries ranging from Rs. 5,000 to Rs. 10,000 per annum, there were 1,207 Europeans, 96 Eurasians and 421 Natives of the country, and they drew respectively in the aggregate—Europeans 88 lakhs, Eurasians 6 lakhs, and Natives of this country 29 lakhs per annum. (I leave the fractions out). In posts with salaries ranging from Rs. 10,000 to Rs. 20,000 per annum, there were 713 Europeans, 8 Eurasians and 45 Natives, and the salaries they respectively drew were represented by 97 lakhs for Europeans, 1 lakh for Eurasians, and 5 lakhs for Natives of the country. In posts with salaries varying from Rs. 20,000 to Rs. 30,000 there were 300 Europeans, 2 Eurasians and 4 Natives of India—the total of their salaries being 72 lakhs for Europeans, Rs. 46,000 for Eurasians, and Rs. 95,000 for Natives. These figures relate to the civil department. I need not trouble you with those relating to the military and other departments, though I have got them in my hand. I will give you the total of what was given in the shape of salaries to Europeans and Natives respectively in India in 1889-90. The Europeans numbered 13,178 in all the departments—I am only speaking of posts with salaries of Rs. 1,000 and upwards,—the Eurasians 3,309, and the Natives of the country, 11,554. But the salaries which they respectively drew in the aggregate were—Europeans, Rs. 8,77,14,431, Eurasians, Rs. 72,96,026, and Natives, Rs. 2,55,54,313; that is to say, the Europeans drew 9 crores nearly as against 2½ crores drawn by Natives. (*Hear, hear*).

So far as regards salaries. Consider now the pensions which Europeans, and Natives received respectively. Natives of India received in pensions here Rs. 59,81,824 only, while the amount of pensions drawn in England alone by Europeans came up to £3,710,678. (*Hear, hear*).

I think I need not trouble you with any more figures, as I think those I have given speak sufficiently eloquently. They show there is a great and inordinate drain of India's money because of the inordinate employment of Europeans in the higher ranks of the public service. If you analyse these figures, if you go into the lists of the different departments, and separate the Civil from the Military, you will be further astonished at the result. The greater portion of all the good posts are reserved for Europeans, while the children of the soil get the smaller appointments, carrying small salaries with them. (*Cries of 'shame'*).

This is one of those causes which is at the bottom of the increasing poverty of the people of this country. About that poverty there cannot now be the slightest doubt. Lord Dufferin's Government did doubt the accuracy of the statements made about the poverty of the people, and he, therefore, appointed a committee of enquiry, the result of which was embodied in the now well-known resolution of October 1888. That resolution says that there is evidence to show that there is a great deal of poverty in the country; and with that fact established, and with the knowledge that in this country the average annual income per head is only £2 as against £39 per head in England,—I think, no man can for a moment doubt that the result of the present system of getting out excessively highly paid Europeans for employment in the higher ranks of the Indian Service, must have a most disastrous effect on the prosperity of this country. (*Loud cheers*).

I shall not take up much more of your time. I only hope that this ruinous condition of things will not be allowed to go on much longer (*applause*); but if it is, I do not know what the consequences will be. European officials of Government come here for only a short period of time, say twenty or twenty-five years at the utmost. They feel therefore, as a rule, but a temporary and limited interest in its welfare. But we who live here permanently have to suffer the consequences of good or bad administration for all time. It is, therefore, that we beg of them to govern the country economically and well. And it is as a means to that end, that we ask them to substitute the comparatively cheaper indigenous talent and industry in place of the highly costly imported foreign agency in the administration. (*Cheers*). And I devoutly hope they will not longer refuse to listen to this voice of reason and justice. (*Renewed cheers*).

This question of the services has engaged the attention of Mr. Dadabhai Naoroji ever since the year 1855, and he is anxious that this Congress should re-affirm the resolution that until simultaneous examinations are held in India as well as in England, full justice will not be done to the people of this country. He is so anxious that we should do so, because he intends to bring the matter before Parliament. You know Mr. Dadabhai has fought many a battle in connection with this question. It was through his endeavours that the Act of 1870 was passed by Parliament. He had, of course, hoped for very much better things from that Act, but all the good it was expected to do was nullified by the way the appointments were made under it. We too complained of the Statutory Service, not because it was a Statutory Service, but because the discretion vested in the Government was exercised in a faulty manner. We asked that simultaneous examinations should be held in England and in India, but we did not expect that while that concession would not be given to us, the Statutory Service would be practically abolished. But when we hoped and prayed for better things, the little that we had has been snatched away from us with cruel hands. Such is the justice our rulers have come to administer to us now! (*Cries of 'shame' 'shame'*). However, it is clear that so long as simultaneous examinations are not held in this country and in England, it is idle to expect our countrymen to enter that service in sufficiently large numbers. We only ask for simultaneous examinations here and in England, though, as Mr. Dadabhai said at the first Congress, the right thing would be to hold examinations for

**2nd Day.**

**Resolution II. Employment of Indians in the Public Service.**

admission into the Civil Service of Indiain India only, (*cheers*), because those that want to enter the Civil Service of India should take the trouble to come to India to compete for it. (*Cheers*). It is singularly unjust to compel the people of this country to go ten thousand miles away from their country, to pass an examination to qualify themselves for service in their own country. (*Loud applause*). No other people labour under such an awful disadvantage. Must we alone be subjected to it because we are the subjects of a strong power like England ? (*Loud cheers*). England, we know, has got the strength of a giant, but she should not use it as a giant in enforcing unfair terms and conditions against a people, placed by Providence under her care, but should allow her nobler instincts to guide her in this matter as they have guided her in many others, and see that we are governed practically, and not merely theoretically, in consonance with those noble principles of justice and good government which her honoured Sovereign and her statesmen have laid down for the purpose, and which guide her in the conduct of her own affairs. (*Cheers*). We pray only for a fair field and for no favour. (*Loud and prolonged applause*).

Mr. Janardan Raghu Nath Nimkar, (*Poona, No.* 101, *in list*,).—Gentlemen and Brother Delegates,—It devolves upon me to support the second resolution. I have been desired to speak in English, but I have a great esteem for my vernacular—Marathi—in which I have the liberty of expressing myself more fully and emphatically. However, I will try my best to satisfy the audience by addressing in both.

For the sake of my own convenience and that of the subject under consideration, I may divide the subject into two parts, the first of which consists chiefly of our regret regarding matters mentioned in items *a, b, c* and *d* of the proposition, and the second of a suggestion to be made to our worthy Government. As to the first part, I have but very little to say as that part hardly requires any explanation or argument. But I will cite to you an instance whereby you will come to know at a glance the position we have been put in by the Public Service Commission. No doubt my way of explanation would at first sight seem to you a rural one, but upon consideration—I may say a deeper and impartial consideration —(*laughter*) of the same, the truth will be whispering itself into your ears and hearts.

The nation—our country India—has been long since suffering from a liver complaint in the form of the Civil Service question. It grew weaker and weaker day by day. A doctor— the Civil Service Commission—was brought in. The pulse and every other part of the body was ostensibly examined, and every diagnosis was had. Medicines were prescribed and remedies were suggested, but never administered. (*Laughter and cheers.*) Notwithstanding all the outward, rather external, remedies, the patient could find no cure. Not only were there no hopes of recovery, but the health which commenced to point its way to fate, could by no means be restored to its former state. Is it not, gentlemen, then wonderful to bring in a doctor for the relief of an impatient patient, and more wonderful to find the doctor's skill tending to accelerate the death of the sufferer ? (*Cheers*). Oh, be assured that the patient is suffering from a certainly known disease, but that the doctor pretends not to know what he really does not intend doing, or knowing does not administer the proper remedy, or not administering the proper remedy finds himself in such a position that he feels inclined very naturally to conceal his own mistake, which he may colour otherwise. But you know we are not impatient patients and can patiently watch the movements of our too benevolent doctor. Is it fair and just, I ask, to take away from us that which we specially crave for, and to make us unjustly appear foolish by comparing our former position, when we had made no demand, with our present position ? Can we be called guilty because we invoked the help of a doctor, and should we be made to suffer under the principles of contributary negligence ? It would just be equivalent to the story of the lamb and the wolf, where the latter found pretence to kill the former by advancing a most absurd argument of the current of water going upwards from below, simply because the lamb had touched it for drinking. (*Cheers*). Gentlemen, such being the state of things, it would simply be dangerous and ridiculous to pray for any thing any more, beyond silently praying to the Almighty for a proper justification of things.

There is no use saying anything more on the first part, and so I now turn to the second part, which is really more important and a key to the whole fabric of secrecy. I cannot now continue my speech in English for reasons other than personal, and I must now ride over my vernacular horse which will take me more safely to where I must go before this august assembly. (*A laugh*). Words do mean either this or that, but when they are heated they get in them some spirit by way of conduction. I must mainly support the second part of the proposition, for a part fully supported makes the whole supported by way of a witty system of arguments. Many of us may be under a mistake, the mistake of considering the permission to our children to appear in England for the competitive Civil Service Examination as a boon. I should like to say, it is quite otherwise. I come here from Nasik, a distance of about 700 miles. The journey has caused my voice to cheat me and I cannot prosecute it. (*Laughter*). I had been to Zanzibar in 1876, while in my prime, in a big civil case, and lived there for about a year, following the same profession that I do now. My travel to and from Zanzibar brought on me diseases, the continued ill-effects of which have invalidated me for the whole of my life. So I assure you from a personal experimental point of view that to send our children to England, a place at a distance of thousands of miles, would be to lose them for ever, in many cases though not in all. (*Hear, hear*). I have reason to say that many of our Native Civilians, who have been to England, enjoy a comparatively shorter life. The variety of difficulties in going to England, at all events, on either this or that ground, is insurmountable. I am not going to put forward before you the difficulty from a religious point of view, on which I have no occasion to express my opinion in this assembly.

Would any of you like to send your children away to Brahma Loka, or to Badri Kedar, to study the Yogas under the Himalayan Yogis for even a short term? I think not. It is a misery to have falsehoods covered over with a showy truth. The reason why simultaneous competitive examinations, in England and in India, are not liked by our Government is but an open secret. We are not insensible to the spirit of words or actions or gestures. Why should not English boys come over to India to compete with us here, especially when they would even here have some advantages over us in the matter of the examination? Their training here from the beginning would fit them, besides, much better for their duties, as they have to serve here just after passing the examination. (*Hear, hear*). We know what sort of Civilians they generally are when they first come here, as well as how stagnant some of them remain even after they have long been entrusted with responsible duties. Many of you have always occasions to appear before Civilians in the variety of your duties, and you must find, though you may not say so for reasons plain enough, that some of them are, in common sense and in human dealings, no better than our common people.

We have a natural right to compete here in India, and we have every facility for doing so. Why should we be deprived of it and driven to the forbidding alternative of transporting our children to a distant land, for no fault of theirs, in the very days of their prime, when there is every danger of their falling into the many temptations which would beset them there? (*Cheers*). We have our graduates here from our colleges. We have our lawyers and our doctors too, who have passed here, standing on the same level with the Europeans. What is there, then, more difficult to be accomplished in the Civil Service? Has the English Bishop the power like our ancient Rishis, to make an Indian youth know everything earthly and heavenly by merely placing his holy hand upon his head, and by sprinkling the holy water of the English Ganges—the Thames—upon him? (*Laughter*). I dare say, there is nothing required for success in the Civil Service Examination that cannot be accomplished here in India. (*Hear, hear*). But the notion that the observance of the sacred condition, namely, that of passing the test in England, as the real bestower of universal knowledge upon the brains of the student, must be cast to the ground. (*Cheers*).

As I have already remarked, I do not consider the privilege of competing for the Civil Service in England as a boon at all. Until the examination is held in our own land, it merely purports to be a sham show of a gift which the giver simply holds out in his hands but never intends really to part with. (*Loud cheers*). In short, the condition precedent is virtually the withholding the boon itself. Friends and gentlemen, what earthly reason there is for not holding simultaneous examinations in England

and India, it is difficult to say. But I cannot help thinking that our rulers do not really wish to make us Civil Servants in the sense of European Civil Servants. (*Cheers*). It is not an instalment they have granted but a bit of infected bread thrown at a barking dog. So beware of the danger, and agitate, agitate, and agitate, honestly and most loyally, till you get what you want. (*Cheers*). Appeal to the good sense of the civilized British Public, without whose help we cannot move an inch from the pit we are fallen in. If examinations are held in India, Indian brain will doubtless surpass the European brain in some exceptional cases, it will equal it in ordinary cases, but will be inferior to it in none. (*Hear, hear*). In any case there will be a difficulty in maintaining the white guests of the land, on the field of the Civil Service, the provisions of the host being short of his own appetite. (*Hear, hear and cheers*). New posts cannot under the circumstances be created, having regard to the financial condition of the country, and hence springs the motive for confining the Civil Service examination to London. (*Cheers*).

Gentlemen, examinations in India would result in a thirteenth month in a famine year, for a high-salaried Famine Commissioner swallows up a mountain of food himself, which would otherwise be made use of in a famine year in saving the lives of the dying millions. (*Cheers*). In this way the second part of the proposition is a key to the secrecy and sacredness of the Government policy, and a key to the prosperity and welfare of India. (*Hear, hear*). And now, gentlemen, as I said at the commencement of my speech, I will give you a vernacular illustration and summary of the subject.

An old blind man of eighty having no estate and progeny performed austerities for a long time. God Shiva came down to him to give him a *wara* (gift or blessing). The old man bowed and prayed that he might see a *chhattra* (regal umbrella) on the head of his grandson. And our demand in the second part is to the same effect. (*Hear, hear*). And I hope that by the grace of the Almighty God, under the favorable auspices of the nineteenth century, and by the benevolence of the Liberal party and ministry, we may be given what is ours by natural right. (*Cheers*). Let Englishmen come here and let Indians go to England as they may like, for competitive examinations, and let fair justice be done to India by Britannia, proud of her unselfish and philanthropic benevolence as displayed in liberating millions of Negroes. (*Loud and prolonged applause*).

MOULVI UMRAO MIRZA HAIRAT, (*Delhi, No. 621, in list,*) then spoke in Urdu thus.—MR. PRESIDENT AND GENTLEMEN,—

Yah kis dil-e-ghamdīda ki zarī-o-buka hai Jis se ki ghazab aj zamane men hua hai.
Jo chashm hai khunbar hai jo dil hai wah majrūh, Jo sīna hai wah çhāk ka bhi chāk hua hai.
Kyon āj barastī hai yeh māyusī-o-hirman, Kyon aj zamane men yeh wawaila hua hai,
Yah kaun si mahfil hai nazar ati hai wīran, Sāqi ka nishan hai na surahī ka patā hai.
(*Cheers*).

I am a Mahomedan, but not a Mahomedan whom Anti-Congress men might call a hired Mahomedan (*Laughter and cheers*). I am a Mahomedan who has joined the Congress after full deliberation. I have considered all its aims and objects, pondered over them and fully understood them before coming here to make my speech. (*Hear hear*). I am a Mahomedan who has always had in view the welfare and progress of India. I shall be happy to sacrifice my person and my property for the sake of my countrymen (*cheers*). I am a Mahomedan who desires to cement further the union of Hindus and Musalmans. (*Cheers*). So far as I understand it, the Congress movement is more beneficial to Mahomedans than to other communities, because it aims at the improvement of India's welfare and prosperity, and the Mahomedans being poorer than others must naturally derive greater benefits from it. (*Hear, hear and cheers*). To explain this let us take, for instance, a dining table at which two persons are sitting. The one who is more hungry will naturally and necessarily consume a greater portion of the food than the other. For this reason I consider the Congress to be an extremely good, or rather, I should say, the best movement for our welfare. (*Cheers*).

In the Congress of 1888 which was held on these very dates, in this very city, and nearly on this very spot, I came and delivered a speech. And I wish, Mr. President, with your permission, to enquire as to why some people are against this movement. It is to me quite surprising and inexplicable. It seems that they have not perhaps fully understood the objects of the Congress. Had they properly understood them, it would have been clear to them that what we Congressmen want is only the fulfilment of the solemn pledges held out to us by Her Majesty the Empress of India. (*Cheers*). We ask for the same rights that our gracious mother Queen has so very kindly and generously promised to confer upon us. (*Hear, hear, and cheers*). Should we not, with due respect, implore her to fulfil those promises, and to thereby improve our present miserable condition? To whom shall we go for the redress of our wrongs and the satisfaction of our wants, if we are not to lay them freely before our Government? (*Hear, hear*). Should we ask for them from Russia, or implore France to befriend us, or expect help from any other power? No, that shall never be. (*Loud cheers*). We have the pride of being the subjects of the British Government, and, God willing, we shall not be the subjects of another power. (*Renewed applause*). We regard this Government as our benefactor, and therefore lay our grievances and wants freely before it, and ask it to remedy them. The Anti-Congressists perhaps look up to some other power, and hence they do not wish to bring the needs of the people to the notice of the Government, and try to lull it into the false belief that the people are happy and contented. (*Loud cheers*). They have tried to frighten us also into silence by misrepresenting our objects and our motives. But how can we honestly remain silent, and put on an appearance of content, when our hearts are aching, and increasing poverty is making life more and more burdensome day by day? (*Cheers*). We certainly do not like to cry out for help in any condition, but what shall we do if our suffeings do not allow us to remain silent? (*Cheers*). In our religion prayer is devotion, and he who lays his wants before the Almighty God is His favourite devotee. It rests with him to grant our prayer or not to grant it. It is our duty to lay our wants before him. (*Hear, hear*). Almost all religious systems inculcate prayer to God. Whenever we are in trouble, it comes spontaneously out of our mouth, "O God! deliver us from this affliction." Will He consider us undutiful for doing this, and suspect our good faith? No. Never. Those who do not humble themselves before Him, those who do not lay their wants before His gracious Throne, do not perhaps hold him to be the remover of difficulties. (*Cheers*). This illustrates our position in relation to our Sovereign also. We believe our government to be just, generous and merciful (*cheers*), and we further believe that it will redress all our grievances, and satisfy our just demands, and hence our request to Government. (*Cheers*). Those who do not so appeal to Government, do not probably consider it to be just and strong. Those who charge us with sedition and say that we conspire against Government, are themselves the real traitors. (*Cheers*). Fy! Fy! How can any man in his senses charge us with sedition? Is sedition spoken before a public assembly held in a public place, in a city which is the seat of Government?—before an assembly consisting of Europeans, reporters of newspapers, and thousands of persons of different castes and creeds? O God, save us from such infamous imputations! We merely seek justice, such justice as will promote the prosperity of India, and the glory of England (*loud cheers*),—by which I mean what I am going to say in English, so that you gentlemen may not think that I am ignorant of that language. (*Hear, hear*). I know English very well and can deliver speeches also in it. But being a Mahomedan, both in appearance and at heart, I thought it was incumbent on me to make my speech in my own language on this occasion. Justice may be defined as follows:—"Justice is neither an internal balance of the soul's faculties, nor a rule imposed by the will of the stronger; but a mutual agreement to abstain from aggressions, varying from time to time with the varying interests of society, but always determined by considerations of general utility." (*Hear, hear and cheers*).

The resolution which I stand here to support relates to the Civil Service. Before I proceed to deal with it, I must thank the Government for raising the standard of age for the Civil Service Examination. I should also like to ask the opponents of the Congress why they show such eagerness now to take advantage of that change, which has been brought about by the efforts of the Congress? (*Cheers*). To maintain their position, they ought to have stuck to the old limit of age and refused to derive any benefit from the new one. (*Laughter and cheers*). But no, they would not do so. They may well be compared to a fox who sits closely watching a tiger who is in search of prey. As soon as the tiger has come by it and has satisfied his hunger, and goes away leaving the refuse behind, the fox comes quickly in to feast upon it. But he shows his gratitude to the tiger by denouncing him all the same and warning the animals of the forest to beware of him. (*Laughter*). We have got one of our prayers granted after so many years of labour and expense, and our opponents are now coolly coming in to share the gain with us without any expression of gratitude. We do not grudge them this. (*Hear, hear*). We only say that it is the height of ingratitude on their part to stand in our way and oppose us any longer. (*Cheers*). But they are now silent, and from the fact of their silence, we may well conclude that they have at least half consented to our proposals. (*Cheers*).

The restriction as to the Civil Service examination taking place only in London means practically that Indians should not become Civilians. (*Cheers*). If we cast but a cursory glance at the diverse creeds and religious persuasions prevailing in this country, it would soon become manifest how fettered Indians are with religious restrictions and what their mode of life is. In the first place, Indian boys of 18 or 19 are scarcely in a position to compete for the Civil Service examination. In the second place, even supposing that they are fit, their religious restrictions stand in their way. (*Hear, hear*). Thus they must get over these insurmountable difficulties before they can reach England. And then what would it matter if out of thirty or thirty crores of people only a handful of them succeeded in getting into the Civil Service. Such being the circumstances, we beseech the Government to remove the restriction of the examination being held only in England. And we hope the Government will certainly listen to our prayers, and accede to our request. (*Cheers*). I conclude my speech with this prayer :—"O God! Bless thou our Government still further; incline its heart mercifully to our prayers; ever know us to be loyal and faithful to our Government, and make our Government kind and just towards us." Amen! (*Loud applause*).

Rai Jotindro Nath Choudhry (*Calcutta, No.* 189, *in list,*).—Mr. President and Gentlemen,—After the very eloquent speeches which you have heard on this question, I have very little to add. But as I feel very strongly on the subject, I shall only very briefly give my views on the same.

To serve one's own country is a right inalienable from its people. So in this view I look upon all those appointments which can be safely given to the natives of the soil and which are filled by foreigners, as so many appointments robbed from the people to whom they belong by natural right, specially in India where we Indians are most cruelly debarred from all the higher employments. (*Cheers*). Our claim to the Civil branches of the Public Service rests on double grounds. The greater employment of the natives of this country in the Public Service of their own country can be supported on economic and political grounds also. When Indians will be employed, more largely than hitherto, in the higher branches of the Public Service, it will, I am sure, go a great way to solve the great question of the Indian poverty. On the other hand, the necessary suffering of the people under a foreign or alien rule will, to a large extent, be mitigated by the wider employment of the natives of the country in the higher branches of the Public Service, inasmuch as it will make, as nearly as may be, the Government a National one, and thereby will take away much of the grievances which must otherwise be the fate of the governed. But I do not understand why the Government should hesitate to grant the National prayer, I mean the desire of the Indians to be permitted to be employed in the higher branches of the Public Service of their own country, more largely than has hitherto been the case—a desire, which, as we have seen, is supported by justice and good policy alike. (*Cheers*).

We all know how the recommendations of the Public Service Commission were unsatisfactory in the extreme; but still unsatisfactory were the orders of the Government thereon. It will be impossible for me to describe *seriatim*, all the points of grievances which arise natuarally out of those orders; I shall attempt here only to deal with the salient ones. As for example, we see it recommended by the Commission "that a provision should be inserted in the Statute 24 and 25 Victoria, Cap. 54, enabling the Secretary of State in Council, with the concurrence of a majority of members present at a meeting, to remove appointments or classes of appointments from the schedule, or include them in the schedule, as may seem desirable from time to time, provided that no such order shall take effect until it has, with the reasons for making it, been laid for ninety days before both Houses of Parliament." Now if this concession were granted to the Indians, by a slight change in the Statute of 1861, it would have been a constitutional gain to us of the highest order, and, moreover, it would have been, for the matter of that, an extension and legislative embodiment of the policy which has been adopted by the Government since the days of the Statute of 1793. (*Hear, hear*). I would have liked to have this incorporated in the body of the resolution itself. As regards the necessity and bare justice of holding an examination in India for the Covenanted Civil Service simultaneously with the examination in London, it is unnecessary for me to say much. To deny this would be inconsistent with the liberal Statute of 1833 and the noble words of the Royal Proclamation of 1858. (*Cheers*).

In paragraph 11 of the letter of the Government of India, No. 1838, addressed to the Chief Secretary to the Government of Bengal, which was practically an answer to the memorial submitted by the Indian Association praying for the reconsideration of the resolution containing the orders of the Government regarding the Provincial Service, we find the reasons, or the so-called reasons, for the exclusion of a membership of the Board of Revenue and a Divisional Commissionership from the lists of offices thrown open to the Provincial Service. The so-called reasons are these—I shall quote here the exact words—"that it was not advisable," "that a definite proportion of Commissionerships could not be transferred to the Provincial Service," "that it was dissented from or only agreed to after much hesitation by a strong minority," and "that the mere fact of their being entered in the list could not have been held to give the Provincial Service any right whatever to either of them." All these reasons are perfectly unintelligible, at least to my humble self. (*Cheers*). The paragraph ends by saying "that the Government still retain the power to appoint any Native of India to either of the posts with the sanction of the Secretary of State for India." No body denies the power which the Government have in this connection, but the question is, is there any likelihood of a Native of India being ever appointed to either of these two posts under the present circumstances. ('*None*', '*None*'.) It is for this reason absolutely necessary that we should insist upon having these two appointments, along with other appointments, detached from the scheduled appointments of the Covenanted Civilians, (*cheers*) and upon having them included in the list of appointments to be reserved for the Provincial Service. (*Cheers*). With these words I have much pleasure in supporting the resolution.

MUNSHI ROSHAN LAL (*Allahabad, No.* 348 *in list,*).—MR. PRESIDENT AND GENTLEMEN,—I do not propose to take up much of your time because sufficient has been said already. I shall only briefly say what I have to say on the subject of holding simultaneous examinations in England and in India. The speakers who have already spoken have dwelt more particularly upon the distance of India from England, but none of them have noticed the chief difficulty, and it is an insuperable one, namely, that of caste. (*Hear, hear*). Our Government has known it from the very beginning, because at the impeachment of Warren Hastings it was said that there was not one man from this country to find fault with him in England, and Mr. Burke said that that was owing to the prejudices of the people which prohibited them from going to England. What was the intention, then, in holding the Civil Service examination in England only? The intention was patent and clear; it was because prejudices were in the way of allowing Hindus to compete for these examinations that they were held in England only. (*Cheers*). This prejudice has taken such a strong hold upon the public mind here that even Mahomedans, till lately, thought it contrary to their religion to go to England. (*Hear, hear*). Government who knew full well that this country was possessed of such a prejudice, ought not to have, for one moment, thought of holding these examinations in England alone, and ought from the very beginning to have held the examination simultaneously in England and in India. (*Cheers*). Then, you know how easy it is to compete for an examination in one's own country. English students have the advantage of being in their own country, while those from here have to go so far as ten

**2nd Day.**

**Resolution II. Employment of Indians in the Public Service.**

thousand miles in order to compete for the Civil Service examination. But this is not all. If the Government had passed a resolution that only those persons who paid taxes to the amount of Rs. 3,000 or Rs. 2,000 a year would be allowed to compete, I think I might have been content. This holding of the examination in England, means the shutting out of a mass of Indians from the competition, because it is well known that enormous sums are required to enable Indians to go to England and compete for this examination. This has not hitherto been brought to your notice, and I consequently think it my duty to submit it for your consideration, and for the consideration of a Government which is called just and benevolent, a Government full of good intentions towards those who are under its rule. (*Cheers*). I am not sure that the country is yet reconciled to the idea that Hindus can go to England without loss of caste. If these difficulties are in our way, let our competition with Europeans be equal and just and upon our own grounds. (*Cheers*).

The resolution was then put to the vote and carried unanimously.

**Resolution III. Separation of Judicial & Executive Functions.**

MR. R. N. MUDHOLKAR, (*Berar, No.* 119, *in list*,).—MR. PRESIDENT, LADIES AND GENTLEMEN,—The Resolution with which I am entrusted runs thus :—

*That this Congress, seeing the serious mischief arising to the country from the combination of Judicial and Executive functions in the same official, once again puts on record its deliberate and earnest conviction that a complete separation of these functions has become an urgent necessity, and that, in its opinion, it behoves the Government to effect this separation without further delay, even though this should, in some provinces, involve extra expenditure.*

You all know that in that remarkable post-prandial oration which Lord Dufferin delivered in 1888 and in which he thought it necessary to make an attack upon the Congress, the only thing, he could say about this proposed reform was that it was a counsel of perfection. (*Hear, hear.*) When the armour of irony could not furnish anything except this single phrase to his Lordship, the country naturally felt that this was a demand which the Government had made up its mind could not long be resisted, and that we were within a measurable distance of the accomplishment of one of our wishes at last. (*Hear, hear*). Since that speech was delivered four years have elapsed, and except in Madras where a small beginning has been made, nothing has been done in any other part of the country. On the contrary we find a disposition manifested on the part of the Executive to extend their powers and to encroach upon the province of the judiciary.('*Shame*'). It is therefore no wonder if a change has become necessary, and if the Congress, as representing the people, finds it necessary to pronounce its opinion clearly and in no mistakable manner in regard to a proposition which during the last three years was put along with others in what is called an 'omnibus resolution'. Our demand for the separation of the executive from the judicial functions is based not on any sentiment or mere theoretical grounds, but on grounds of expediency ; because we perceive that the system in existence is productive of hardship and inconvenience to the people. I shall go further and say that it is productive in many cases of actual injustice. (*Cheers*). And after all what is it that we ask. ? We ask for a very simple thing. We see here several functions combined in one individual. We say, "have a division of labour ; assign criminal work and civil work to different officers." And no one would have supposed that this was a matter in which the Government would have thought it necessary to make any resistance or delay. But some excuse or other is put forward and we are obliged over and over again to repeat our demand. (*Shame, shame*).

The present system, I need hardly say, is productive of actual hardship in several cases. (*Cheers*). Those who have any experience of court-life will know what the hardship is and to what extent it proceeds at times. I have practised for the last twelve years in a non-regulation province, where this combination of functions exists in a very aggravated form, and I may take credit for knowing something of the evils of the system. In that province we have a combination not only of executive and judicial functions, but we have there officers who are Civil Judges, Criminal Judges and revenue officers also ; and we there feel the hardship more than you do here. This is the way in which this combination of functions tells on the disposal of cases and so often produces actual injustice. A case is fixed f r trial on a particular day, and the parties and their witnesses are present; but unfortunately some urgent executive business crops up and the trial of the case has to be put off; the parties have then to go away and have thus to incur unnecessarily fresh expense. But that is nothing, for in the meantime there is an opportunity afforded to those who are so inclined to concoct evidence, and those who know anything of the Police know that the opportunity is not rarely taken advantage of. (*Hear, hear*). But there is a great deal more. Most of these officers have to go on circuit, and I know what going on circuit means. People living in the south-eastern or in the southern parts of the district are taken to its far eastern limits inhabited by tigers. The executive work has to be done with tigers (*laughter*), and there not only our officers but a host of attendants and suitors have to find accommodation for themselves under the shadowy trees of the forest. (*Cries of 'shame'*).

Then in criminal cases also great injustice is perpetrated, because when an officer goes on tour the defendant is not seldom driven to sell or mortgage his house in order to raise sufficient money to induce an able man from the Bar to go out to defend him; for otherwise he will have to dispense with all legal assistance and throw himself on the mercy of his Judge, and the mercy of the Judge is a matter of which we can never be sure. If these were the only considerations which I could have urged, I should have said that even upon these considerations, the system is one which stands condemned and should be corrected. (*Cheers*). But there are other things also. Law, in India, as everywhere, has become a science, and it is a very intricate science in India even now. One would expect that those who are to dispense justice should be up to the mark in it. But it is not the fault of the Executive Officers if they possess no such qualities. When they have to write a hundred letters a day and to settle boundary and other disputes, and to attend to multifarious duties of other kinds they cannot be blamed if they have no time to read the Law Reports. (*Hear, hear*). There are many who cannot even find time to read the Acts themselves (*laughter*), and so far as they are concerned we cannot justly blame them, although it means a real hardship to the people. The administration of justice is thus entrusted to persons who, to speak plainly, are not capable of properly discharging their duties, and therefore we have a right to ask that this system should be put an end to. (*Cheers*). Look again at the duties of an executive officer and of a Judge. Are they compatible? Certainly not. The frame of mind necessary for an executive officer and the frame of mind necessary for a Judge are different. Executive officers ought to mix freely with the people, they ought to try to make friends with them, they ought to see this and to see that. A Judge, on the contrary, ought to shut his ears against everything except that which comes before him in Court. But an executive officer has, as such, to learn everything, and to do everything; and when he comes upon the bench, he is expected to divest his mind of whatever he has heard elsewhere. Even the best officer of Government is after all a human being, and no one can blame him much, if, when he has come into contact with different people and has heard all sorts of rumours outside, he cannot divest himself of the bias which he has imbibed. It is not fair to the officials that this system should be allowed to exist, if, under it, Judges in many cases must come to a knowledge of facts from outside information. This objection is fatal to the system. It impairs the efficiency of the system, and makes justice in many cases an impossibility. Upon that ground alone the system ought to be condemned. (*Cheers*).

As the law exists in India, the powers which are given to Magistrates are something tremendous, and the present system is one which has been called dangerous, not by Congressmen only, but also by the most sedate body in the country, I mean the Judges of the Calcutta High Court. This is what they say:—"In India the powers of the police in investigating cases and the powers of the Magistrate in the trial of cases are closely connected, and it frequently happens that it is combined in the same individual. It not unfrequently happens that the Chief Executive Magistrate practically becomes the prosecutor and may frequently become the Judge, though he may have formed a strong opinion on the case behind the back of the accused without having had the opportunity of hearing his explanation or defence." (*Hear, hear*). I suppose no words that I can use can be stronger than the words these Judges of the Calcutta High Court have used. In fact the Government themselves admit the necessity of improving the present system and effecting a real reform. But say they, "where is the money to come from." Where is the money to come from? I should say, from the same treasury which supplies money for the Frontier defences and wars. (*Cheers, and a voice 'or from distilleries'*). I take Mr. Evans' explanation and say, or from distilleries (*Laughter*). I go further. Supposing all this costly military expenditure is absolutely necessary (*a voice, "no",*) supposing, I say, for the sake of argument that it is so—I am decidedly of opinion that it is not necessary—but supposing it is—even then I say that the measure that we advocate is one which is so imperative, the reform is so absolutely essential, that even if it is necessary that additional taxation should be imposed, the administration of justice should be rendered more efficient and more secure even by resorting to additional taxation. (*Cheers*). It is upon these considerations that I commend this proposition for your acceptance. (*Loud cheers*).

MR. AMBICACHARAN MOZUMDAR (*Furreedpore, No. 241, in list,*).—MR. PRESIDENT AND GENTLEMEN,—It has been often said of the other propositions with which we have had to deal, that they are class propositions, but I believe that the proposition with which we are now dealing is not amenable to that sort of observation at all. It is a proposition which affects the nobility, the gentry and the peasantry alike. (*Hear, hear*). It is just four years ago, when, while assembled here, you shared in the regret so touchingly expressed by our distinguished countryman, your well-known omnibus driver, Babu Kally Churan Banerji, (*cheers*) that we had still to reaffirm this resolution. What then, gentlemen, must be our feelings to-day to hear after four years that, it is no longer a question of the separation but the emancipation of the Judiciary from the thraldom of the Executive. (*Hear, hear*).

In every circular order issued, in every notification passed, in every resolution adopted, there is always observable a distinct tendency to under-estimate and override purely judicial functions, and to emphasise the superiority of the executive. In every enactment passed there is always reserved a clause giving power to the local government to frame rules, and this clause is invariably made a loop-hole or pretext for encroachments on the sacred domains of judicial administration. ('*Shame*'). We are ostensibly governed by elaborate codes of Civil Procedure, but our Courts are practically guided by a set of circular orders emanating from the Executive Government. Now, gentlemen, I do not know how you fare under the Civil Procedure Code, but speaking for myself and for the place whence I come, I may tell you that we are in the midst of an awful convulsion in this direction. There we have the Civil Procedure Code, a code which provides a certain procedure for the conduct of civil trials, but there comes forth an edict from the Lieutenant Governor which smashes the procedure altogether, and you find that the latter edict prevails. ('*Shame*'). In criminal cases, too, we have certain modes prescribed for conducting criminal trials, but a fiat comes from the Government that the trial must not be proceeded with further than three adjournments. Now I should like to know whether the Executive Government would be prepared to hold that if after three successful adjournments the culprit succeeds in avoiding arrest, the case should not be proceeded with further. (*Hear, hear*). Now, gentlemen, this is the condition under which we live; and if we are to consider the opposition which the Government has itself displayed, and the attitude which it has assumed towards this movement, I believe you will all be struck with surprise. Of late we have got a Lieutenant Governor in Bengal who seems to be entirely possessed with the mania for wandering and knocking about the country. It was said by an Englishman that it was a characteristic of the Irish people that they were to be found everywhere except in Ireland; similarly our Lieutenant Governor is to be found everywhere except at his head quarters, Belvedere, and he wants all his subordinates to be everywhere except at their legitimate posts, at the head quarters. One of the District Magistrates in my part of the country, who, I know, is one of the ablest and most conscientious men in the Civil Service, had the boldness and courage to oppose this system, and he observed in one of his administration reports that it seriously interfered with his judical duties at head quarters. Now, gentlemen, you will be all surprised to hear what umbrage he gave the Lieutenant Governor by taking such an attitude. Here I will read a resolution on the Administration Report published in the Calcutta Gazette of the 3rd November, 1892. The Magistrate to whom I refer is Mr. Hare, the District

Magistrate of Dacca. The resolution says:—"The Lieutenant Governor is surprised to read that an officer of Mr. Hare's ability and energy should protest againat the length of tour imposed upon him and that the Commissioner of the Division should be inclined to support him. His Honour believes that if a Collector distributes his tour throughout the year, he will not find that it interferes with his work at the *sadar*; but at least the manner in which that work and those duties differ from the calls on the time of Collectors of other important districts should have been fully stated before the orders of Government were impugned; and in future if the period of tour falls short of that prescribed, a full explanation should be submitted." Now you know that man's poor Calendar consists of 365 days 15 minutes and 30 seconds, and no more. We have 52 Sundays and 32 close holidays during which the Criminal Courts never sit. The Lieutenant-Governor, however, wants twenty more days added to these in order that his injunctions may be carried out. There remain five months in the year for the discharge of Civil duties, and the exercise of judicial functions is one of them. (*Hear, hear*).

Now this being the attitude of the Lieutenant-Governor of Bengal in regard to the Criminal side, I will show you how he has also been tampering with Civil justice in the foremost province of the empire. In reviewing the administration of civil justice for the year which has just closed, the Lieutenant-Governor has tried first of all to enunciate a novel measure or standard for judging the judicial capacities and industry of Munsifs and Subordinate Judges. He was anxious first of all to ascertain what he called the 'unit,' of a case. I cannot understand what this unit means, but he was anxious to establish this in order to ascertain the respective merits and demerits of Munsifs and Subordinate Judges. He first of all says that two Small Cause Court suits are equal to one ordinary suit; and three ordinary suits are equal to one appeal suit. (*Laughter*). What kind of weight was this weight? Troy weight it cannot be, nor can it be the Apothecaries' weight; it might be Avoirdupois weight, but for its shortness; nor can it be the N.-W. P. or Assam weight, for we know that Assam has become a successful academy for the training of judicial officers. (*Laughter*). He says the unit of cases must be taken at 1,900 a year, and he goes further and says that as has been done in one district, each Munsif should decide 2,500 cases. Gentlemen, I have the honour, most dishonourable, of belonging to that very district. Now having struck out that average, he goes out of the way of all known administrative reports and passes an encomium upon those Munsifs who have massacred 2,500 cases a piece. In his eagerness, however, he forgot the other figures; you have only to go lower down his report to find what was the result in appeal of these 2,500 cases. We find that in that district more than 53 per cent of these cases were reversed upon appeal, whereas in the neighbouring district the percentage does not come up to even 40 per cent! (*Hear, hear*). Then in regard to the mode in which the Lieutenant-Governor is dealing with this question, you can well understand that violent diseases are often contagious, and this contagion is spreading far and wide and contaminating many of the officials. (*Cries of 'shame'*).

I shall now give you some illustrations of the mischief which has been done by this unholy alliance of the judicial and executive functions. I shall not refer to the Salem riot case, nor the Sham Bazar riot case. But I shall refer you to more recent cases. The first of these cases is the case of the Empress *versus* Mahabut Ali. It was a case under Sections 408 and 463 of the Penal Code for breach of trust and forgery. In that case you will find that the Sessions Judge went out of his way and asked the enquiring Magistrate to commit the case to him. (*Cries of 'shame'*). So you see that this tendency of the Executive officers has permeated the mind of even District Judges. The result of that case is well known to my Patna friends. The jury acquitted the accused, but the Judge referred the case to the High Court, and the High Court, unfortunately for the Judge, confirmed the verdict of the jury. (*Hear, hear*). The second of these cases is the case of the Empress, on the prosecution of Watson and Co. *versus* Brajendronath Chatterjee. This case came from the Nuddea District. The accused was the Principal of a College in the mofussil of Bengal. I will not allude to the details of this case, but it is said that this unfortunate gentleman spoke something against the oppression of Watson and Co's. servants, and he came to grief over it. A case under section 107 was instituted against him, and it was heard before the Sub-divisional

Magistrate. Mr. Fisher was the District Magistrate of Nuddea, and in his supreme anxiety to maintain supervision over the acts of his subordinates, he issued written instructions to the Sub-divisional Officer, which ran as follows:—"Perhaps you are aware that a certain Professor is delivering lectures against Watson and Company. It is necessary that you should bind him down and nip him in the bud." (*Cries of 'shame' 'shame'*). I am sorry that I should have to speak against this Sub-divisional Magistrate, and I offer a sincere apology to any of his relatives who may be here. But the interests of truth and justice make it my duty to say what I am saying here. Brajendronath had not committed any riot or any thing of the kind; he had only delivered some speeches, and he was to be bound down to do—what? Not to make any speeches for the term of one year! (*Laughter*). If that were the law, I am afraid that our esteemed and learned friend the President would have to find life-long security, and I don't think that even the term of one life would suffice for my esteemed friend Babu Surendra Nath Banerji. (*Laughter*).

The last case to which I come is the well known case of Mr. H. A. D. Phillips *versus* Rajah Sooryakant Acharya of Mymensingh. (*Hear, hear*). This nobleman built a town hall in his district at his own expense, and he contributed largely towards the cost of providing an efficient system of water supply for the good of his townsmen as well as for the benefit of the District Magistrate, Mr. H. A. D. Phillips. (*Hisses*). Why do you hiss at Mr. Phillips? You should rather hiss at the vicious system of which he is the outcome. (*Hear, hear*). Well, Raja Sooryakant Acharya was hauled before the Assistant Magistrate, one Mr. Hallifax, but though the case was placed before Mr. Hallifax it was practically in the hands of Mr. Phillips himself. In fact the case, as it was conducted before Mr. Hallifax, was a solemn farce enacted before the public and before two eminent barristers of the Calcutta Bar, and, I may go further and say, within the cognizance of the Lieutenant-Governor of Bengal himself. (*'Shame', 'shame'*). Here was a case in which the possession of nobility, the exercise of public spirit and of private hospitality were not sufficient to protect a man from the terrible consequences of the unjust wrath of the executive head of the district! Rajah Sooryakant Acharya, for reasons best known to Mr. Phillips, was put into the prisoners' dock like an ordinary criminal, and, as if that was not sufficient, it seems that a common felon was introduced into that box at the same time to receive his sentence. (*'Shame', 'shame'*). And to whom do you think all this was due? Not to Mr. Hallifax, the presiding officer, but to the prosecutor Mr. H. A. D. Phillips, who openly and unblushingly declared that Mr. Hallifax was merely his "Post Office and conduit pipe." (*'Shame', 'shame'*). I could have quoted to you many more cases of this nature, but my time is up, and I ought not to abuse the indulgence which I have received from the chair as well as from yourselves.

Now as to the second part of this Resolution which states that the separation of judicial and executive functions should be effected without further delay, even if it should in some Provinces involve extra expenditure. I think I am able to show that so far as the Province of Bengal is concerned no additional expenditure will be needed. You will find from the Government Administration Report that there are in Bengal some forty District and Assistant Superintendents of Police. Now these gentlemen receive between them by way of salary no less a sum than Rs. 2,54,455 annually. But that is not all; they do something more; they travel, though for whose benefit I do not know and they receive in the shape of travelling allowance a sum which amounts to Rs. 22,386. In Behar, we have 17 District and Assistant Superintendents who draw Rs. 1,26,650 as salary, and a further sum of Rs. 18,651 as travelling allowance; and the total sum expended on account of these District and Assistant Superintendents of Police and their establishments amounts to Rs. 6,87,400. In Bengal, there are altogether only 47 Districts, and only 47 Additional officers are required to separate the judicial from the executive functions of the Magistrate, to have Judicial Magistrates as distinguished from and in addition to Executive Magistrates. A first grade Joint Magistrate whose pay is Rs. 900 a month will quite serve the purpose. The pay of 47 such Magistrates would amount to Rs. 5,31,600 per annum, and we would still have a saving of about Rupees 7,000, which according to Sir Charles Elliot's estimate of the proper pay of a clerk, from Rs. 25 to Rs. 30, would sufficiently cover the cost of the necessary establishment. But the Government will ever be short of money for a reform which the people call for, while they have always money available to wage wars amongst mountain fastnesses and to maintain a scientific frontier. (*Shame.*) I submit, however, that in the interests of justice, the reform which we so earnestly pray for by this resolution ought to be carried out without delay. (*Cheers.*) And if the Government remain callous to our prayer, we ought to appeal to the people of England, by whom we may fully expect justice to be done. In doing so, we shall be pleading to a people who have judicial functions entirely separated from the executive in their country; to a people for whom Milton wrote and Sidney died', and by whom the *Magna Charta* was obtained; and I believe we shall not appeal to them in vain. (*Loud cheers*).

MR. HEM CHANDRA RAI, (*Dacca*, No. 191, *in list*,).—MR. PRESIDENT, LADIES AND GENTLEMEN,—It has been pointed out that the administration of criminal justice, at least in one of the provinces, whose moral and material progress it behoves the Congress to watch and safeguard, has undergone such a change for the worse that something more than our ordinary vigilance must be called into requisition, and prompt steps adopted to arrest the further development of the policy of subordinating the judiciary to the executive, which, thanks to the mischievous activity of the ruler of one of the sister provinces, now obtains in Bengal, and coming from there, I cannot help expressing our heartfelt gratitude to our distinguished brethren from the other provinces, happily better circumstanced in this respect, for their determination to make common cause with us in earnestly pressing this suggestion of ours for the complete separation of judicial functions from executive ones, on the notice of the authorities, in the light of certain recent events, some of which it will be my duty briefly to indicate.

Sir, the Local Government in Bengal have, somehow or other, taken it into their head that there are more acquittals than are desirable. The fiat has gone forth, and the District Magistrates have begun to coerce the subordinate Magistracy into convicting persons against the plain dictates of justice. (*Shame, shame*). What with this unwholesome official pressure, what with the persistent Anglo-Indian clamour against the supposed weakness of the Native Magistracy, aided partly by the indifference of the highest court in the land, to which, we cannot, as a fact look up always with hopeful confidence, the situation of our Deputy Magistrates has become anything but enviable. (*Cheers*). Cases are not unfrequently referred to them with almost plain directions as to how they are to be decided, and do you think, gentlemen, that after such a strong expression of opinion from his chief, a Deputy Magistrate, in absolute dependence as he is upon his official superior for his future elevation in service, would have the high judicial probity to arrive at findings justified by legal materials and approved by the dictates of his concience? No wonder, then, that this sneaking habit on the part of some of the District Officers of tampering with the independence of the Subordinate Magistracy has lowered the Criminal Courts in the estimation of the public, and has brought about a widespread feeling of alarm, which it is in the interests of good Government instantly to allay. (*Cheers*).

I have referred to the prevailing mania for conviction. Is it to be at all wondered that when the ruler of a Province publicly approves of the work of and bestows praise upon those of the Magistrates, who are able to show a greater percentage of convictions than their other compeers, without caring to enquire what the nature of the instances have been in which the latter have acquitted persons,—is it to be at all wondered that the administration of criminal justice has arrived at a very bad pass, indeed, and has become a sham altogether? Fancy, the noble principles of justice almost unheeded, the efficiency of the administration of criminal justice gauged by gross arithmetical computation, and officers plainly told to help the police-prosecutions, and cynically ridiculed if they attempt to play the rolê of a Judge! ('*Shame*,' '*shame*'). No, gentlemen, the indignation that prevails in my province in regard to this matter, cannot be adequately described by any words of mine. Cases have been cited to you, showing the pernicious interference of the District Magistrates with the judicial work of their subordinates, and I am not going to tread over the same ground again; but permit me to recount some of the instances of the public

2nd Day.

Resolution III.

Separation of Judicial & Executive Functions.

disapproval by the executive head of the province of purely judicial findings, a course unwarranted by the facts of the cases in point, unseemly in the extreme, and utterly subversive of judicial independence. (*Hear, hear*). You remember the Shambazar Riot Case. Well, there an experienced Civilian Judge, aided by an efficient jury, after a prolonged hearing came to the conclusion that the charge had not been satisfactorily brought home to the accused, and discharged them. The Lieutenant-Governor, on the *ex-parte* representation of the Commissioner of Police, the virtual prosecutor in the case, condemned the Judge in a way that even the *Englishman* newspaper, the sole apologist His Honor has in the press, was not able to approve of Sir Charles Elliott's action, and criticised it severely. (*Shame, shame.*) You have heard of the Dacca Bribery Case. Well, there the best Judge on the Calcutta bench pronounced the accused not guilty, and surely ordinary decency should have induced the Lieutenant-Governor to accept the verdict of the highest Court in the land as final; but he did nothing of the kind; he took an early opportunity of expressing his own belief in regard to the case. (*Shame.*) Therefore it is that I earnestly beg of you to unite with us in renewing our prayer for the separation of judicial and executive functions, and in respectfully praying that the adoption of the suggestion, which even Lord Dufferin was pleased to characterise as "a counsel of perfection", may no longer be deferred, even though it may lead to some extra expenditure. (*Cheers.*) Gentlemen, the system is already in vogue in the Presidency town, where the Magistrates are purely judicial officers, untainted by executive capacities; and it does seem to me anomalous that while the healthier system should prevail in places where we have an intelligent public, a strong bar, and an over-vigilant press to safeguard our liberties, the other arrangement should flourish in the Moffusil, where we have no such wholesome checks upon it. (*Hear, hear.*) I therefore commend the third resolution to your unanimous acceptance. (*Cheers*).

Mr. K. G. Natu, (*Poona, No.* 93, *in list,*).—Mr. President and Gentlemen,—It is said that an error, however small, ought never to be allowed to stand uncorrected, and I must begin at the beginning by saying that my name is not K. A. Natu, as printed in the printed resolution, but K. G. Natu. (*Laughter*). Now without making any apology, I shall at once go to the subject and make one or two remarks. The subject has been exhaustively dealt with by the speakers who have preceded me, and they have left me very little to say. But I wish to notice this fact most prominently: that the tendency of modern legislation here is to subordinate the Judicial to the Executive. You will find that realised, so far as the Bombay Presidency is concerned, in the Land Revenue Code, the Hereditary Offices Act, the Income Tax Act, and a host of other Acts which give you no relief whatever. A small clause is added at the end of these enactments which provides that "no suit shall lie," and there is an end of the matter. You must keep quiet. The tendency in England is otherwise. There they generally subordinate the Executive to the Judiciary. I am really surprised to hear that so great a change takes place when Englishmen come here to India. Here they change their colours and their principles. This is a growing evil and it is therefore to be protested against. There is not the slightest doubt about it.

The second thing to which I wish to refer is the objection that the separation of the judicial from the executive is a transformation which is dangerous in some respects for the collection of revenue. Some are afraid of that, but when they hear that so far south as Tanjore and Madura they have made a beginning without any fear at all, that the Maharajah of Baroda has it under his contemplation to introduce the same reformed system, these critics will not be able to substantiate that objection, because they will find that there is really no danger in it. (*Hear, hear.*) Then as to the importance of the separation. I have, in the course of my practice, come across men who after having been Executive officers have become Judges, but they have still in them a legacy of their former ideas, a legacy of what they were before. On the Bench of Magistrates there are officers who spend their time in forming suspicions and directing arrests. When such an officer is made a Judge, he often sees that there is no evidence against the accused, and that the prisoner has established his innocence. The Pleader has said all he had to say, the Judge admits all his arguments, but still he says "yet there is something at the bottom of it for which the accused must be punished." (*Ironical cheers.*) There is no doubt that some officials would be very sorry to have to make a choice between the two. They think when these two functions are divided all is gone. But it is, I say, for the benefit of all that these two functions should be separated. I will tell you of one case. When an Assistant Collector sanctions the prosetion of a *patel*, what does he do? He sends the papers with a letter to the Collector saying that in his own mind he was perfectly convinced of the man's guilt; so that it comes to be a reference not from Phillip sober to Phillip drunk but from Phillip drunk to Phillip more drunk! (*Cheers.*)

Rao Saheb Deva Rao Venayak, (*Berar, No.* 134, *in list*).—Mr. President, Sister and Brother Delegates,—

It is a curious coincidence in my case that I have to stand before you for the second time at the same place where I have stood once before, for the very same reasons, about the very same grievance, and to speak to the very same resolution; or rather to enter the very same protest against the present judicial administration of our country. When I stood before you on the last occasion, I thought it was the first and last time I should have to protest against the existing practice of combining the judicial with the executive functions in the same individual; but I am sorry that I have been obliged to stand up to speak a second time about it. (*Hear, hear*). On that first occasion, I gave my reasons, and along with my reasons I added my twenty six years' experience, for protesting against the practice. Now I have simply to add four more years of my experience to what I said four years ago. I also gave illustrations to prove what I said, that the system was extremely faulty; and now again I have the misfortune to say the same thing.

You know that I come from the Berars, where we had the pleasure of receiving you as our guests last year. There, as most of you know, we have a Deputy Commissioner, as you have a Collector, who controls the administration of a whole district, and I may be permitted to say that he is all in all. In our province the designation has some special charm about it. For you will see that there he is not only the Magistrate and Collector, but he is also the Civil Judge of the district, though lately some of these civil powers have been taken out of his hands entirely. The powers exercised by other officers are called the powers of a Deputy Commissioner, so that you see there is a peculiar liking in our Province for the term "Deputy Commissioner." In criminal matters we have not made any advance; we are now just where we were four years ago. The system is productive of injustice and unfair results. But I need not dwell upon that part of the subject, because my predecessors have exhausted, or nearly exhausted it, and it is useless for me to take up your time in going over the same ground and giving a few more illustrations to illustrate the same thing. There, as everywhere else, there are noble exceptions, and we have noble exceptions amongst us, I am glad to say. (*Hear, hear.*) But with all our noble exceptions, I mean individual cases of impartial and fair-minded officers who mean to do justice, to be fair and unbiased towards persons going before them in the shape of party over party, the system itself is rotten at the bottom. (*Cheers*). We cannot always rely upon noble exceptions. And I need not say that where people are living under a civilised Government, they expect a civilized method of judicial administration. What we claim is but fair justice; that fair justice ought to be done. (*Cheers*). It is as much, if not more, in the interests of the government as in the interests of the people, that fair and impartial justice should be meted out. By administering justice to the people, the Government will acquire popularity, and the people will then be more loyal, more dutiful and more useful in times of need. (*Cheers*). You have not seen, gentlemen, a more careful and a more astute statesman than Lord Dufferin; and what did Lord Dufferin say in regard to our prayer? He said it was a counsel of perfection. We want that counsel to be acted upon. (*Cheers.*) We want the reform to be introduced. We believe that our Government is a liberal Government and will do us justice. But you must go on agitating constitutionally and loyally, for what is due to you and you are bound to succeed. With these remarks I submit to you the resolution which has been proposed and seconded. (*Loud Cheers*).

Mr. Murli Dhur, (*Umballa, No.* 612, *in list,*).—Mr. President and Gentlemen,—My knowledge of the English language can be compressed into the smallest pill box,

**2nd day.**

**Resolution III. Separation of Judicial & Executive Functions.**

(*laughter,*) and I am really surprised that I should be called upon to support the present Resolution. I thought it was only the old, the infirm, the blind, the deaf and the mute that required the support of any body. The Resolution before the meeting is not deaf, but it falls flat upon deaf ears. (*Hear, hear*). It can see, but others don't see the inside of it. (*Hear, hear*). It is not dumb, it can speak and speak with silent tongue; but others don't hear it, because they are deaf; and really an old man like myself is not a proper person to support a Resolution which is old enough to take care of itself. (*Laughter*). It is 8 years old, but if you think it is a child then I will take it into my hands. (*Laughter*).

Well, gentlemen, the union has not proved a happy one, and therefore it is high time that there should be a judicial separation between the parties. Of course one of the parties desires to bring a case into Court, and as I belong to the side of the complainant, I appear on behalf of *Lady Justitia* before this august tribunal. (*Hear, hear and cheers*). She does not merely want a judicial separation, but she wants a complete divorce, and I hope her prayer will be granted. (*Cheers.*)

But I do not see what is your reason for asking for the separation of the judicial from the executive functions, unless it may be that you seem to think that thousands of innocent persons are now being sent to jail. But have you such a horror of a jail? Why? There all distinctions of caste and creed and colour are done away with; there you all dine at the same table. Brahmos and Theosophists are for universal brotherhood, and there is certainly universal brotherhood within the precincts of the jail. (*Laughter*). Of course there are separate quarters provided in the jail for different kinds of prisoners. Englishmen, for instance, are not quartered in the same place as 'niggers' are kept in. But there should be no distinction whatever, and perhaps they will come to the same level some day. (*Laughter*).

Now I will come to the point, and shall quote some instances of the kind of justice we get in the Punjab. The head of the district is the only officer of the district who combines all the functions in himself. He is the Commissariat Officer, the Chief Commissioner of Police, the Judge, the Magistrate, the Juryman, the Counsel, the Prosecutor and everything. Nothing more is desired to make him more formidable and irresistible. He is perhaps more irresistible than the Czar of Russia himself, (*hear, hear,*) and is it not cruel on your part to desire to deprive the lion of his claws and the tiger of his teeth? Surely you will not be so cruel, gentlemen. A man belonging to the (?) class in the Umballa district was actually *chalanned* to the Magistrate by the Tehsildar for spending more money than was prescribed by the rules of his caste upon the marriage of his son. The man actually came with this *chalan* signed by the Tehsildar. I saw the *chalan* myself and I showed it to the District Judge, and the man actually thought he was to be criminally prosecuted. But it was not so; it was only a sort of threat held out to him. (*Shame.*) The Court, of course, could not hear his case at Amritsar, so the man followed the camp. I do not know what became of this man, but no criminal prosecution was launched against him, and he only had to follow the Magistrate's camp here and there. The spending of less money was all that was wanted; otherwise the reform was done. That is the sort of reform we have got in the Punjab! This is one instance of our reform.

Now I come to the criminal administration of justice. All the functions of the Civil Courts were at one time suspended from the Chief Judge downwards. The Magistrate of the district is a truly conscientious man, and is a gentleman who seeks the welfare of the people. And I tell you, sincerely and honestly, that he is the most sincere well-wisher of the people and devises means for their welfare. (*Hear, hear*). But unfortunately he is guided by the Police, who do not care a fig for the welfare of the people. He established Punchayet Courts throughout the districts and authorised Tehsildars and others to receive petitions on unstamped paper or on paper bearing a stamp of eight annas. They are called Nowsherwani petitions; and what is the nature of these petitions? They are in the nature of mortgage and sale-deeds which formerly used to be cancelled by third-class Magistrates. They had no Civil powers whatever, but they could deal with cases relating to property worth thousands of rupees. (*Cries of 'shame'*). These people used to sit in judgment upon money-lenders, keep them in confinement, examine their books; and in one instance Mr. R. P. Warburton, to whom a similar petition was presented, examined the books, and when the man failed to attend in obedience to verbal orders, he was ordered to be prosecuted. (*Cries of 'shame'*).—(Here the President sounded his gong).—Gentlemen, my knell has sounded; the time of my dissolution is come; now I am a shadow and must disappear. (*Laughter and cheers*).

**2nd Day.**

**Resolution III. Separation of Judicial & Executive Functions.**

The Resolution was then put to the vote and carried unanimously.

**Resolution IV. The Currency Question.**

MR. D. E. WACHA, (*Bombay, No. 39, in list,*).—MR. PRESIDENT, LADIES AND GENTLEMEN,—The Resolution I am going to move for your approval is this—

"*That having regard to the diversity of opinion that prevails on the Currency Question, and the importance of the question itself, this Congress desires to express its earnest hope that, unless its hands are forced by the action of any Foreign Power, necessitating a change in the currency, or the standard, which might prove injurious to the interests of the country, the Government of India will refrain from taking any steps, until the labors of the Brussels Conference have been completed: and, further, that the Government will lay before the Public, for discussion, the proposals which Lord Herschell's Committee may recommend, before definite action, if any, is resolved upon.*"

You are all aware that if at this moment there is a burning problem of the day—a burning problem in the practical and satisfactory solution of which all the great nations of the world—great in strength and great in wealth—are deeply interested, it is the problem of Currency. It looks simple enough how to give tolerable stability to the ratio between silver and gold; but it is superfluous for me to tell you, you who all well understand it, that though simple as the question looks, when you come to consider it seriously, you cannot help acknowledging it to be one of the most difficult and complicated of economic problems which the latter days of the nineteenth century have to deal with. Neither can you help acknowledging that it is one on the correct solution of which entirely depends the economic salvation in the near future of a country so peculiarly circumstanced as ours,—a country, subject to foreign yoke, raising its revenue in silver and paying almost one-fourth of its obligations in gold; a country whose trade is mostly with a powerful and gold using country; a country, in short, suffering at the present moment in an aggravated form all the evils arising partly from the selfish policy of its rulers and partly from a mischievous piece of legislation in States far away but on whose silver mines it is necessarily obliged to depend. (*Hear, hear*).

Some definite idea of the difficulties of the subject may be derived when I say that the ablest experts and the most experienced authorities broadly differ from each other, and that apart from the wide and radical differences of opinion prevailing among the greatest bankers and merchants of the West. Even the experts who were appointed by our gracious Sovereign as a Royal Commission on Currency in 1886, were unable to arrive at a unanimous decision on the subject. There was a majority report and a minority report, besides individual opinions and individual dissents. But the general tendency was to let the problem alone, lest a precipitate jump in the great unknown might lead to graver consequences, of a more far-reaching character than those which were to be witnessed at the date of the drawing up of the Final Report, namely, October 1888.

Such being the difficulties surrounding the problem, I take it for granted that you do not expect me here to descant on the causes of the present evils or to discuss at length the merits and demerits of the remedies proposed, specially those having reference to India, namely, the closing of the mint against the private coinage of silver and the introduction of a gold standard with or without a gold currency. It would be presumptuous for me to speak with anything like dogmatism on a matter on which the ablest experts in England and elsewhere are hopelessly at conflict. (*Hear, hear.*) From the tenor of the resolution just read to you, you will have understood what its sole aim and object is. It is this. We, the delegates in Congress assembled, earnestly desire at this critical juncture, when some action on the part of the Government is reported to be imminent, that it will refrain from

**2nd day**

**Resolution IV. The Currency Question.**

either taking a leap in the dark or adopting precipitately a measure which might eventually prove to be infinitely worse in its consequences than the evils to be witnessed at present. (*Hear, hear.*) In doing so we are not going to commit ourselves to any particular panacea, proposition, or fad. We are not going to tell our rulers that we favour bimetallism or monometallism. Neither are we going to pronounce any decisive opinion on the proposal for a gold standard and gold currency or for closing the mint against private coinage. No. All that we do pray Government to consider is this. That having regard to the great divergence of opinion among experts themselves on the various proposals—one class confidently asserting that nothing but good can be their outcome, while another class asserting with equal confidence that nothing but greater evils can be the result,—having regard to this divergence, as wide asunder as the poles, it would be the part of wise and cautious statesmanship to pause before taking any rash steps which may involve the country in grave consequences from the effects of which it might become a formidable task to extricate it altogether. (*Hear, hear.*) Government cannot deny this wide divergence as revealed by the Royal Currency Commission, and, lately, by the Committee presided over by Lord Herschell, so far as we have been able to learn from the part evidence hitherto taken. Every remedy, when put to the test in the crucible, seems to be defective, that is to say, it presents, its good as well as its bad side. While to add to the gravity of the situation, *none* is able to assert with confidence that there is a preponderance of advantages over disadvantages in the several remedies proposed. (*Hear, hear*).

Gentlemen, I do not speak without the book on this subject. I refer you to the text of the Currency Report itself in verification of my statement. I beg to refer you to the entire Chapter III, of Part I. of that report which is signed by *all* the members of the Commission. Under such circumstances, I am sure you will agree with me when I state that it would be wisdom on the part of a deliberative assembly like ours to refrain from pronouncing any definite opinion on the various remedial proposals and asserting that we approve these and we disapprove these. (*Hear, hear.*) I think there is yet time to exercise the virtue of patience, aye, Job-like patience. I am aware that there are those who say that the Indian Government has preserved patience enough, and that it is the height of folly on our part to counsel further patience as the only counsel of perfection. But, gentlemen, we must all remember that in a matter of such immense import as Currency—whose effects are always far-reaching and last for more than one generation,—it would be considered a want of true economic insight on our part to be impatient. For, after all, what are fifteen or sixteen years in a period of what may be called economic revolution. Surely, nobody denies that all the world over, not India alone, there is passing a great economic wave, the end of which we have not yet seen. As in matters physical, so in matters economical, the ordinances of nature stand good. You seldom have a clear sky while a hurricane is hanging on the horizon or actually brewing. It is only when the hurricane has spent itself, and probably done its worst, that the atmosphere again becomes clear and nature resumes her normal condition. And as there are physical hurricanes which no human ingenuity can avert, so there are economical hurricanes which no human wisdom can enable us to avoid. In my opinion, we have not yet seen the worst of the present economic revolution; and unless the worst which is now looming on the horizon is passed, we will not see the end of our difficulties. Evils of this kind have to be endured. And, I repeat, that it is the part of wisdom so to endure them than to face greater evils under the impulse of momentary alarm and under the delusion created by plausibilities the effects of which are an unknown quantity. (*Hear, hear.*) In the economic life of a nation, as in its political life, fifteen years are as a drop in the ocean. Posterity, in all probability, will condemn our impatience to reform the Currency in the dark, and curse us if we reform or improve it in a way which might entail on it greater evils than those we ourselves are enduring. (*Hear, hear.*)

Gentlemen, when I say that the virtue of patience should be exercised, I am not unaware of what a limited class of Anglo-Indians, mostly servants of the Crown, and a handful of non-officials (though not planters) who support the official classes, speak as to such a waiting policy. A well-known Official in Bombay characterised it as the "gospel of inertia," while another called it the "policy of drift." This limited class, and, I believe, I am right in calling it "a microscopic minority," is no doubt very impatient. It thinks the evils are intolerable and should no longer be borne. It is this class which is too eager to force the hands of Government. Now, I do not deny the existence of the evils complained of. In fact none denies them. But at any rate, so far as my personal knowledge is concerned, I have not yet heard a single individual of that impatient minority boldly telling Government that if certain remedies propounded by it are carried out, it takes upon itself the responsibility of saying that no harm to the general interests of the people of this country, specially the producers, will come of their adoption. (*Hear, hear.*) It seems that each and all shrink from undertaking that responsibility. But if these irresponsible persons shrink, is there not the greater reason for a responsible Government to shrink? (*Hear, hear.*) The fact is, gentlemen, that there is at present only a choice of evils—evils certain and known and evils uncertain and unknown, but, according to all experts, of possibly greater magnitude. What, gentlemen, under such circumstances would practical wisdom suggest? Is it not prudent to prefer the lesser evils in order to avoid the greater and the unknown. (*Hear, hear.*)

The whole question of Currency, you will thus see, hinges on this *one* point, and I appeal to you all to realise the issues which hang on this momentous question. When you have realised their gravity, you will, I dare say, admit at once that it is a question in which precipitate action of any kind is wholly to be deprecated, aye, vigorously resisted.

We, therefore, wish that this Resolution be submitted to Government with the view of postponing action till the results of the final labours of the Brussels Conference (which has now postponed its sittings till May,) are made known, and till the Indian public has had the opportunity of considering the resolution at which Lord Herschell's Committee may arrive. We have full confidence in the wisdom of the Government of India that it will not take any hurried or rash step. Up to date, notwithstanding the agitation of the Indian Currency Association in the Presidential cities, Lord Lansdowne's Government has exercised great prudence and patience. The circumstance is, in my opinion, and I presume in your opinion also, not an unwarrantable assumption of its determination to take no action till it was reasonably satisfied that the proposed changes will in no way be prejudicial to the best interests of this great country. That it has been fully alive to the hardships and other embarrassments arising from the steady decline in the value of silver for years past, goes without saying. For the last sixteen years and upwards it has closely watched the dwindling rupee, and has half a dozen times earnestly drawn the attention of the India Office to the effects of low silver on the sterling remittances to the Secretary of State, and to the fact of the growing difficulty of bringing about an equillibrium in the annual balance sheet of the Empire.

Soon after the demonetisation of silver by Germany in 1873, there was appointed a Departmental Committee, at the instance of our Government, to investigate into the causes of the depreciation of that metal and its diminished exports to India, and to suggest remedies. It carefully went into the whole question, and had, I believe, the benefit of the counsel of the late lamented Professor Fawcett. (*Hear, hear*). The conclusions it came to may be briefly recapitulated here. (1) That the total remittances actually made to India in Government Bills and treasure together, in the ordinary course of business, have declined, but only on a slight scale. (2) That except for other causes, and excluding the extraordinary years of the cotton famine, there is no evidenee to show that the demand for silver would have materially fallen. (3) But that the supply of a different form of remittance, namely, Government Bills, has superseded to a great extent the necessity of remitting bullion. (4) That the effect of this cause has to be measured in very large figures, as the yearly amount payable by India for the disbursements of the Home Government has risen since the Indian Mutiny from £5,000,000 to £15,000,000, a difference of which the magnitude will be appreciated when it is remembered that it is considerably more than half of the total amount of silver annually produced. (5) That the full effect of this substitution has only been recently felt, as that effect was retarded by the construction of Indian Railways, which involved an expenditure in India of money raised in England, counterbalancing, therefore, an equal amount of expenditure in England of money raised in India. (6) That the amount of the disbursements which has just been stated appears to represent the present normal expenditure of the Home Government, and that, therefore, unless by some marked change of policy, no diminution of that amount can be looked for."

I need not wait to inform you, gentlemen, that the Departmental Committee hit the nail on the right head. It is the Home Charges which are such a dreadful source of evils. (*Hear, hear*). The Committee insinuated a change in the policy which has led to those charges, but you all know that those have been increasing instead of diminishing, principally owing to the "forward" policy in frontier matters, which has been in such feverish ascendancy for the last seven years.

Again, in 1878, the identical proposals which are now put forward by the Currency Association, namely, the closing of the mint to private coinage, and a gold standard, were submitted by the Indian Government to the Secretary of State. These were referred for consideration to a Departmental Committee also, who reported that they could not recommend them for adoption. The principal objections urged against them, and reiterated by the Currency Commission (*vide* Part I. of their Final Report—Section 176) were :—

(*a*) That by enacting a gold standard without a gold currency, it would be practically equivalent to the establishment of an inconvertible token currency.

(*b*) That the closing of the only mint now open to the free coinage of silver might have so serious an effect upon the market value of the metal, that it would be impossible to maintain the rate of exchange fixed upon.

(*c*) That it would not meet the real difficulty of the present situation in India, which is, that owing to the fall in all gold prices, a larger amount of produce has to be exported in payment of gold debts; and that consequently any apparent gain to the Government of India would be balanced by a corresponding loss to the people of that country.

(*d*) The danger of illicit coinage which would be greatly increased if the exchange value of the rupee were raised much above its intrinsic value.

An enormous mass of literature on the subject has, however, accumulated since the Currency Commission published their report. But I should not omit to remind you at this stage that that Commission was composed of the ablest experts, with Lord Herschell, than whom a more impartial and capable judge could not be found, as President. Our own able Finance Minister, Sir David Barbour, as well as the late Sir Louis Mallet, permanent Under Secretary to the India Office, were also on the Commission. Thus India's interests were ably represented in that body of experts. It took evidence of every class of witnesses. Anglo-Indian witnesses, official and non-official, were also examined; among the latter, such men as Mr. Bythell, Mr. Comber, Mr. Birkmyre, Mr. Maclean, Mr. Barr Robertson, Sir Evelyn Baring and many others. Mr. Dadabhai Naoroji himself tendered evidence as the Indian representative. (*Applause*). So also Mr. E. Sassoon. Some of you may have read the evidence of some of these gentlemen and be aware of the general tendency of their respective inferences. Again, economists of the highest repute in Europe and the United States were invited to give an expression of their opinion on the general question, men like Professors Marshall and Dr. Soetbeer, Professors Nasse and Lexis, M. Lavelaye, Mr. David Wells, Mr. Dana Horton, and, lastly, Mon. Vandenberg, President of the Java Bank. Thus every variety of opinion and every shade of it was elicited. Those views were closely examined from every conceivable stand-point, and if any person, as President, could have sifted that tangled mass of conflicting evidence, and still more tangled mass of conflicting and imperfect statistics, it was Lord Herschell. How imperfect and conflicting the latter were may be learned from the 5th paragraph of the opening report. The Commissioners observe, "that there is hardly any fact connected with it on which there are not considerable differences of opinion. When we proceed from facts to inferences these differences naturally become more marked." (*Hear, hear*). The majority reported that it was not practical for any nation, *without united action*, to do anything to appreciate silver. They agreed that it was every way desirable and advantageous to the world at large to have an extended use of the metal, but unanimity was absolutely essential for the purpose. But the whole difficulty lies there. How can an extended use of silver be brought about? Great Britain, France, Germany and the United States thought one way because their interests lay in one direction.

Those are diametrically opposed to the interests of other countries, neither powerful nor great, who think another way. But it has been stated since, that inasmuch as the interests of the great nations are conilicting, India should be allowed an unfettered action to regulate her own Currency, apart from the exigencies of British-Indian finance! The interests of India, however, are,in my personal opinion, so indissolubly bound up with those of England that I, for one, fail to perceive how it is possible to treat the question of Indian Currency without reference to India's financial relations with that country. It would be absurd to expect England with her gold currency and her loans and advances to foreign countries, amounting to hundreds of millions sterling, to agree to a change which would bring about an extended use of silver. Neither could the countries of Latin Union do so. Nor for that matter could the United States, though for the present gold is leaving that country. The States are in reality suffering from the evils of their own creation,—I mean the Bland and Sherman legislation. In endeavouring to find market for the production of their silver mines they have really killed the goose that laid the silver eggs. The States sowed the wind and are now reaping the whirlwind, the effects of which are being felt here. (*Hear, hear*).

The Royal Commission carefully considered all the conditions which existed at the time it drew up its report, especially those of Indian exchange, and came to the conclusion that matters should be allowed to remain where they were, till further knowledge and experience were gained. Now Sir David Barbour was upon that Commission. In 1885 he published a book on Bi-metallism and propounded therein certain theories. But the knowledge and experience which he later on derived as a Commissioner must, I presume, have considerably modified his original opinions, and were he to re-edit the book, it would not be a matter of surprise to find him discarding some of those theories. Very few Indians and Anglo-Indians agree with him in the efficacy of the remedies he now advocates. He is, I admit, an excellent Finance Minister, who has consistently fought against the over-grown military expenditure of the empire, and deserves our thanks. (*Applause.*) The bogeyman of General Chesney has done us valuable service, for otherwise our military expenditure might have to-day mounted to even a higher figure than 22 crores, with a corresponding large amount to be paid in the shape of "loss by exchange." But his proposals on the reform of Indian Currency have, I fear, found few followers here or in England.

Matters remained quiet enough till the autumn of 1890, when the ill-fated Sherman Act came into operation empowering the United States' treasury to buy 4½ million oz. of silver per month. The American legislature in its hurry to appreciate silver legislated in a way which has not only defeated its object but produced results the very opposite of those which it fondly anticipated. After a temporary boom it landed the States in difficulties, and the influence of the operations of the legislation of 1890 are having their baneful effect on Indian Currency. But for that legislation, there would, in all probability, have been no occasion for the agitation of the Indian Currency Association. The rapid fall of silver to 39d. alarmed that microscopic minority whose leader is the Hon'ble Mr. Mackay. Now none denies the evils to which he drew public attention some months ago, though, it must be observed, in a spirit of wild exaggeration. Many of his statements were such as could not stand the test of a close examination. In fact they have been successfully combated since. He and his Association were seized with a panic. They sounded the tocsin of false alarm and took a blind jump into the great unknown. They did not retreat from their original position till their mistake was pointed out by the majority of the sober on-lookers. I am only speaking to the naked fact when I say that the Mackay propaganda went up booming like a rocket only to come down like a stick. (*Laughter.*) The Government had till then stood aloof. In Bombay, too, every one who fully understood the complexities of the problem, held themselves aloof. Messrs. Beaufort and Symon, two influential English merchants, had the courage to oppose the agitation. Mr. Mackay, thinking his case was hopeless here, proceeded to England with a light heart to see if Manchester would come to his aid. But that city gave him no encouragement whatever, and judging from what has lately appeared in the English papers, I for one should not be surprised if his propaganda comes to be rejected there wholesale. (*Hear, hear*). Mr. Mackay went to England with the object of giving his evidence before Lord Herschell's Committee and convincing that body. But he returned to India a wiser and more sober man. He found his own level before the experts of the Committee. He was interviewed by the English press in Bombay in which, as you may have read from the papers, he was constrained to counsel his colleagues that they should for the present bear the evils as best they may for some time longer. (*Hear, hear.*)

All these facts, gentlemen, show how difficult it is even under present circumstances to find a safe remedy. No doubt each and every one of us are fully aware of the growing evils and temporary dislocation of trade under an unstable ratio. But we are also aware that these evils, however intolerable, have to be endured, and must be endured, till the hurricane of exchange has blown over. As you cannot stem the advancing tide, so it is not possible to stem the progress of this silver hurricane. (*Hear, hear.*)

Under the circumstances, we have formulated this Resolution asking the Government, in the first instance, not to be led away by the cry of a powerful and interested class and legislate in a hurry so as to create new evils of a greater magnitude. We also trust and hope that it will not be seized with the panic which has seized the Currency Association and its followers; that it will not act precipitately so as to make a change in the Standard or Currency leading to new disasters. Tampering with the Currency is a dangerous thing. The most mature consideration is imperative before a change is resolved upon, especially in a country like India where you have 300 millions of people to deal with, and where the entire revenue is raised in silver, while one-fourth of it has to be remitted in gold, with a foreign trade partly in silver and partly in gold. What the evils of the change may be I will not try to enumerate at this late hour (for I have already been long and our President has been courteously forbearing in allowing me double the time prescribed and more.) I could say a great deal on the subject for the next six hours. But I think I could not give you a more succinct idea of the evils to be apprehended than by reading a paragraph on the subject from the *Statist* of 5th November last, which I now hold in my hands. It really tells you all in a nutshell, so to say.

"Assuming that a gold standard were adopted, the rupee would be degraded in India to the position of the shilling in England, that is to say, the value of the rupee would not be fixed by the value of the silver in it, as at present, but by the manipulation of the Government. Now, it is contrary to all the traditions and all the principles of British Government to give to any official, no matter who he may be, powers so enormous as would be necessary to manipulate the Currency of a vast empire with a view to giving to it a fictitious value. If the Prime Minister were corrupt he would be able to enrich himself by disturbing the money market. If he were unwise he would throw all trade into confusion by his folly or his unskilfulness. That appears to us an unanswerable objection to all proposals for artificially maintaining the value of the rupee. But it is only one amongst a multitude of objections not less forcible. Suppose the rupee were degraded to the rank of one shilling—were made, that is to say, a mere token coin;—prices in future would be determined, not by the intrinsic value of the rupee, but by the value of gold, prices in India, that is to say, would cease to be silver prices, and would at once become gold prices. Let us assume that the advocates of the plan would shrink from attempting to raise the rupee to the value of 2s, that they would be moderate in their aims and would be content, let us say, to raise it to 1s-6d. The rise would amount to about 20 per cent., and there must in consequence be a fall in all prices of about 20 per cent. Between 1873 and 1880 there was a ruinous fall in prices in all gold-using countries of just about that percentage. Producers, manufacturers, and merchants suffered disastrously. Credit was shaken, trade was depressed, and all because the purchasing power of gold rose. India was exempted from the sufferings of the gold-using countries because she had a silver standard and a silver currency. There was no fall in prices in India, no shock to credit, no failures on a vast scale. Trade continued to improve, the resources of the country were developed, and its prosperity has since steadily increased. Now it is seriously proposed to deprive India by the act of her own Government of the immense advantages conferred upon her by her silver standard and her silver currency. We presume that the plan is based upon the mistaken notion that the value of gold is more stable than that of silver. We have seen that between 1873 and 1880 all gold prices fell ruinously. We have also seen that during the same period silver prices did not fall, in other words, while a smaller quantity of gold year after year exchanged for a larger quantity of all other commodities, silver included, the same quantity of silver, or nearly the same, exchanged for the same quantity of all other commodities, gold excluded. Does it not necessarily follow that it was the conditions which determine the value of gold which altered, not the conditions which determine the value of silver; or to put the matter into, perhaps, plainer language, does it not necessarily follow that the value of silver during the past twenty years has been far more stable than the value of gold? The plan, then, is based upon an absolute error, upon a misreading of the history of the past twenty years and having its root in error its fruit cannot fail to be injury and disaster.

"We have seen above that the plan, if adopted and successfully carried out, would deprive India of an inestimable advantage her monetary system now confers upon her and would bring about a disastrous fall in prices. Let us try to realise what a fall in prices in a country like India to the extent, say, of 20 per cent. would actually mean. The land tax, which our readers will recollect is really a rent, is fixed for a term of years in rupees. If the purchasing power of the rupee were raised 20 per cent. or anything like so much, the land tax would be raised in exactly the same proportion, for every rupee would then represent 20 per cent. more of the produce of the ryot's land. Similarly the rents of houses and lands all over India would be raised to the same extent. All the other taxes payable to the Government would likewise be raised. So would all debts due at the time the change was made; in other words, every banker and capitalist, as well as every usurer, would find his property, so far as it had been lent out to others, increased 20 per cent., while every debtor throughout the length and breadth of India would also find his debts augmented by 20 per cent. Of course, likewise, officials' salaries would be enhanced in the same way. The result, therefore, would be that the Government, the official classes, bankers, landlords, and usurers, would all receive 20 per cent. more of the property of the vast population of India. There would be a sweeping transfer of property from the producing working millions who create the wealth and make the prosperity of the Empire to the servants of those millions and to the parasites who prey upon them. We would ask any sane man, whose brain has not been addled by currency disquisitions beyond his capacity, whether this is a project that ought to be listened to for a single moment? Whether it is to be thought of that the whole strength of the British Empire should be used to impoverish the hard-working millions, and to enrich usurers and Government officials? And if it is not, we would urge upon public opinion to reject so monstrous a proposal with contumely. The ordinary man must not think that it is a question for experts alone, which may be left to a hole-and-corner committee. It is one that affects the whole future of the British Empire. Whatever may happen we must defend India to our last shilling and our last man. We are at this moment spending large sums in preparing against a Russian attack. Will it strengthen us if an attack should come to have wide-spread distress and discontent created by the acts of our own Government?" These are the dire evils apprehended, but I may say that the effects of the closing of the mint would be infinitely worse than those above described. (*Hear, hear.*)

I need not inform you, gentlemen, that the *Statist* is a first-class economic journal, and bears a first-class reputation with its twin the *Economist.* The Anglo-Indian agitators say they are monometallists and write all in the interests of the great "gold bugs" of Lombard Street. That may be so. But what we have to see is whether their arguments have been successfully combated. Gentlemen, without being accused of egotism, I may say that I have been a close student of this Currency question for the last 12 years. I have not yet met with a single serious criticism in current Anglo-Indian or English literature on the subject in which the views of the two able journalists, so far as India is concerned, have been controverted. Meanwhile here is one of them, writing at the distance of 6,000 miles, in defence of the Indian ryots and the Indian tax-payers generally. A stronger defence in the interests of the people of this country I have not yet come across. I have seldom perused writings on such a subject so remarkably critical and wholesome in character, and I recommend each and all of you, brother delegates, to read, mark and inwardly digest all that has appeared about Indian Currency and Indian finance in the pages of the *Statist* and

*Economist* for this year. I am sure it will repay perusal and will enable you to acquire a fair idea of the *pros* and *cons* of the whole controversy. You will also learn there how dangerous it is for our Government to legislate in panic or adopt other measures in a hurry and to repent of them afterwards. It is for this reason we earnestly appeal to Government to move cautiously in the matter, so as not to jeopardise the interests of millions of its subjects entrusted to its care. There should be, in the words of the late Mr. Bagehot, a "reasonable apprehensiveness" of the effects of the remedies now in the air and with which it is supposed to be closely identified. It has on its shoulders a solemn responsibility, which, it is to be trusted, it will conscientiously endeavour to discharge in the best interests of the governed. (*Applause.*) With these observations I now commend the resolution to your approval. (*Loud and prolonged applause.*)

Captain Banon (*Lahore, No. 609, in list,*).—Gentlemen,—I am most unfortunate in coming after a speaker like Mr. Wacha, for he has so thoroughly exhausted the subject that he has left me nothing further to say. What we want is that Government should do nothing in a hurry, because the dangers of acting in a hurry, in a matter like this, are very great. (*Hear, hear.*) It is very easy matter for people to talk about the Currency, and there are no end to the fads and nostrums which are supposed to work all manner of miracles; but should they fail, the consequences may be terrible, and may even lead to national bankruptcy. (*Hear, hear.*) We want things to be left very much as they are at present; and it is not only the Congress, but other people also, who want things to be left alone. The greater portion of the non-official European community, to which I have the honor to belong, are desirous that nothing should be done; because if anything is done to increase the gold value of the rupee, it will act fatally on almost all the planting interests in India, as well as most of the manufacturing interests. There are tea and coffee planters, and indigo planters, and others who trade in wheat, rice, and oil-seeds, and if the gold value of the rupee is increased, all the capital which they have sunk in these industries will be depreciated, and these industries, perhaps, may no longer prove remunerative.

I hold in my hand a small pamphlet entitled "*A Gold Standard for India, critically examined,*" by a Mr. Stoker of the Indian Civil Service. He is one of the rising Civilians in these provinces, and is now Commissioner of Excise; and I may here say, that I totally disagree with Mr. Evans' remarks on a former resolution. It is said that the Currency Question is a very hard question to understand, but in this pamphlet Mr. Stoker has gone a long way to make this question simple of comprehension. Of course, he, like many others, as I understand, thinks that the Government ought not to allow everybody to present their silver at the mint to be coined into rupees, and provided the gold value of the rupee falls lower, the free coinage of silver should be stopped, to keep up the gold value of the rupee. (*Hear, hear.*) The question really is this, does the fall in the gold value of the rupee affect the people of this country so much that it has become necessary to take this extreme measure? For, in this pamphlet Mr. Stoker shows that if you make the gold value of the rupee stable, you, at the same time, make the silver value of the rupee unstable, and our trade is not only with countries using a gold currency, but also with countries using a silver currency. Mr. Stoker writes as follows, in this very able pamphlet of his, which I have already brought to your notice. "It is true that the volume of trade with the East is inconsiderable compared with the volume of trade wlth the West. But still it is profitable in itself, and, as will presently appear, serves as a means of adjusting the Home Charges. * * * It appears from these figures that eastern countries pay India for nearly two-thirds of her goods by bills on London, and that these payments almost equal in amount the remittances which the Indian Government has to make to England." (*Hear, hear.*)

If the Indian Government think that in consequence of the failure of the Brussels Monetary Conference there is a danger of the rupee falling from fifteen pence to eight pence, ten pence, or even to a shilling, I think they would be justified in temporarily closing the Indian mints to the free coinage of silver, on the understanding, that they will be again opened when silver has regained its present value. (*Hear, hear.*) But as the depreciation of the rupee is entirely due to the Home Charges, I think a better way would be to render the Indian Government independent of the fluctuations to which the rupee is subject. This can only be done in one way, and that is to collect Customs duties *in gold* at the Indian Ports equal in amount to the Home Charges. (*Hear, hear.*) From fifteen to twenty millions sterling would be required; but the English Government raise more than twenty millions by their Customs duties; and so the people of England can scarcely blame the Indian Government for doing what their own Government does for revenue purposes. (*Cheers.*) As the President has warned me that my time is up, I will, with your permission, resume my seat after having seconded this resolution. (*Cheers*).

PROFESSOR BHAGIRATHA PRASADA, (*Nagpur, No.* 139, *in list,*).—Gentlemen,—I rise to support the resolution which my learned friend Mr. Wacha has proposed and which Captain Banon has seconded. The chief object of this resolution is to request the Government of India not to hurry matters, and to place before the public any proposals which the Government might think proper to carry out, in order to save itself and the country from the disastrous effects of the Currency troubles, with this exception only, that its hands are forced by any foreign power by which it may be compelled to take action. But if it be forced by any association in India it should not do anything without consulting public opinion in India itself. My learned friend Mr. Wacha has told you what the effect of hasty action may be, and he has quoted to you the example of America. You remember the action taken by America on the silver question, and how it led to all the difficulties and disasters. It is absolutely necessary that this country should be consulted before any action is taken, because in case the Government failed to take all circumstances into account, the result might be very disastrous. (*Hear, hear*). The case must be studied by people whose interests are concerned, for, as I have said, if all the circumstances are not considered, the solution of the difficulty may prove to be ruinous. A few years ago there was a special Factory Act passed, and at that time telegrams passed between the Secretary of State and the Indian Government. The Secretary of State said, "you must pass such a clause." The Government said, "we cannot do so because it is against the interest of India." Then the Secretary of State said—"O no! we have it here and you must do it." The Government of India said, "We cannot do it, because the majority of the Council do not agree." The Secretary of State pressed for the insertion of the clause in question, simply because the Lancashire merchants complained that unless the Government of India had the same factory legislation as existed in England, their interests would suffer, as the people of India would then be able to produce better cloth and undersell them. (*Hear, hear.*) For these reasons, it is necessary for us to go to the Government of India and pray that no action be taken until the Brussels Conference has concluded its sittings, and that in case any action is to be taken on the recommendation of Lord Herschell's Committee, it should first be made known to the public, and after public discussion is over and the Government has come to know what the views of the public are, then action should be taken. That being the case I heartily support this proposition and ask you to be good enough to adopt it. (*Cheers*).

The PRESIDENT.—Before I put this resolution to the vote, I think it my duty to tell you that the Congress as a body are in no way bound, and are supposed not in any way to give countenance to the views which have been expressed by Mr. Wacha or by Captain Banon or by the last speaker, Professor Bhagirath Prasad of Nagpore. (*Hear, hear.*) They may be right in their views or they may not; we may agree with them individually or we may not; but the reason why we wish to pass this resolution is that it may not be taken that we are not alive to the importance of the question, and that the Government may know that what we desire them to do is so to act that our country may not in any way be made the loser by any measure which may be undertaken. (*Cheers.*) With these observations I put this resolution to the vote.

The resolution was then put to the vote and passed unanimously.

---

# THIRD DAY'S PROCEEDINGS.

## Friday, December 30th, 1892.

**3rd Day.**

**Resolution V. Reduction of the Salt duty; raising of the Income-tax taxable minimum; reform of the excise administration; Judicial and Police reforms; modification of the Rules under the Arms Act; Military Colleges; Volunteering.**

The Congress re-assembled at 11 A. M.

MR. G. S. KHAPARDE, (*Berar, No.* 120, *in list*).—MR. PRESIDENT, LADIES AND GENTLEMEN —The resolution which I put forward for the favor of your adoption reads as follows :—

*That this Congress concurs with its predecessors in strongly advocating—*

(a) *The reduction of the salt duty by at least the amount of its latest enhancement;*

(b) *The raising of the Income-tax taxable minimum from five-hundred to one thousand ;*

(c) *Persistent pressure by the Government of India on all Provincial administrations, to induce them to carry out, in its integrity, the Excise policy enunciated in paragraphs* 103, 104, 105 *of the Despatch, published in the Gazette of India of March* 1890, *and the introduction of a simple system of local option in the case of all villages ;*

(d) *The introduction into the Code of Criminal Procedure of a provision enabling accused persons, in warrant cases, to demand that instead of being tried by the Magistrate they may be committed to the Court of Sessions ;*

(e) *The fundamental reform of the Police administration, by a reduction in the numbers and an increase in the salaries and in the qualifications of the lower grades, and their far more careful enlistment ; and by the selection for the higher posts of gentlemen of higher capacities, more in touch with the respectable portions of the community, and less addicted to military pretensions, than the majority of existing Deputy Inspectors-General, Superintendents, and Assistant Superintendents of Police are ;*

(f) *A modification of the rules under the Arms Act, so as to make them equally applicable to all residents in, or visitors to India, without distinction of creed, caste, or colour ; to ensure the liberal concession of licences wherever wild animals habitually destroy human life, cattle, or crops ; and to make all licences, granted under the revised rules, of life-long tenure, revocable only on proof of misuse, and valid throughout the Provincial jurisdiction in which they are issued ;*

(g) *The establishment of Military Colleges in India, whereat natives of India, as defined by Statute, may be educated and trained for a military career as Commissioned or Non-commissioned Officers (according to capacity and qualifications) of the Indian army ;*

(h) *The organising throughout the more warlike races of the Empire of a system of Militia service ; and*

(i) *The authorising and stimulating of a wide-spread system of volunteering, such as obtains in Great Britian, amongst the people of India.*

I ask you not to be deterred by the length of this resolution which I propose, and do not imagine you have got a very hard task before you. On the contrary we have got a long bill of fare to-day, and I propose to give you some healthy and solid food in it. They

**3rd Day.**

**Resolution V.**

**Reduction of the Salt duty; raising of the Income-tax taxable minimum; reform of the excise administration; Judicial and Police reforms; modification of the Rules under the Arms Act; Military Colleges; Volunteering.**

are all long resolutions, but they are all familiar to you, and to me many of them are like old friends. I have been dealing with them for the last four years, and I have to deal with them again. They do not all share the character of old friends, and I should have been very glad to drop some of them, only if I had been assured that they had reached their destinations. But as it is, we have to carry them with us year after year.

I wish to give you now a popular version of this long resolution. Imagine a poor man coming to this Congress and talking to you, and then you will see what he wants. Salt is the first and foremost necessity of life. Therefore his prayer is about salt in the first instance. (*Hear, hear.*) This poor man says, "You have taxed salt too much ; you have lately increased the duty by eight annas, and I cannot have enough of salt. So if you cannot remove the duty on it altogether, then do away with at least this extra eight annas lately imposed upon it." (*Hear, hear and cheers*). Then he talks about his income. A man who does not get enough of salt does not get enough of food ; so he says—"I want a little more food and a little better food. (*Hear, hear*). I don't wish to get any luxuries, and I surely don't want drink, so I want you to conduct the Excise administration as rigidly as possible, and to give effect to local option." Though, of course, we would like that there should be no drink at all, if the Government must have its revenue from liquor shops, let us have them only where we want them. (*Cheers*). Having had a little more salt and a little more food, and not desiring any drink at all, he desires something more, and says—"Protect me from the Police. The Police give me a great deal of trouble." (*Hear, hear.*) The poor man cannot complain like the rich. Learned lawyers are very good people but they do not work for nothing. So the poor man cannot engage the services of these people, and he naturally desires to have protection from the police. (*Hear, hear.*) Supposing the Police do protect him. Then he says, now and then mistakes are made by the Police. Therefore he desires that native gentlemen who know him and his wants, should be appointed in the higher ranks of the Police. (*Hear, hear.*) Then he says—"In case I should have the misfortune to be charged with some offence, give me the right to have a jury of good native gentlemen who understand me to try me." (*Hear, hear.*) If you give him all these things, he feels a little hopeful. What does he desire next ? He wants to go into his fields. But there are wild animals about it who come and do injury to his crops and cattle. He wants therefore to have a little rifle with him, (*hear, hear,*)—a smooth-bore will do just as well. Therefore he asks for a modification of the Arms Act. (*Hear, hear.*) He also likes to have bright colours upon him and to serve in the army. Therefore he asks you for a little bit of volunteering. But he cannot always go a long distance. Therefore he asks you to organise a militia. (*Hear, hear and cheers*).

Looked at in this way, you will see that the whole resolution is connected from the beginning to the end. Among these subjects there are one or two which I wish particularly to speak to you about. I have been trained to drive the omnibus under an able master like Kalicharan Banerjee. He got me into it, with a few passengers in the omnibus. Two of these have come under great disfavor. One of them wanted to rule the whole of India, and to obtain supreme authority there, and we tried to introduce him. But what do you think the Government have done ? They have confiscated seven of his large estates. Thus this poor man in endeavouring to extend his sphere to the whole of India has lost nearly all he had. There is another gentleman here amongst you all, of whom you would like to hear something, and that gentleman is POLICE REFORM. We have from time to time been speaking about him, and I suppose no subject comes more home or is understood better than this. (*Hear, hear*). I am not permitted to mention names, but I know certain gentlemen, admirable detectives and Superintendents of Police, and they have always got kudos, but only one of them is an Indian. And what has been the consequence ? He is senior by a year and a half and he has been placed below a junior. This is exceedingly bad. (*Hear, hear*). Moreover detective duties require a knowledge of the languages of the people and their modes and habits of life. A detective should be able to mix with them and disguise himself as one of them. Do you think any English gentleman will be able to pass amongst us as a Brahmin, or a cooli or a koonby ? It is impossible. We have a tremendous cry raised against juries. The Lieutenant-Governor of Bengal wants

**3rd Day.**

**Resolution V.**

**Reduction of the Salt duty; raising of the Income tax taxable minimum; reform of the excise administraton; Judicial and Police reforms; modification of the Rules under the Arms Act; Military Colleges; Volunteering.**

to blame juries for acquitting people. But he has not found out the real culprits. The Police bring up persons who are thoroughly innocent, and what can be the consequence? (*Hear, hear.*) Instead of condemning the jury-system, they should extend it to other districts where it does not at present obtain, and the higher grades of the Police department ought to lose some of their estates, and natives should be allowed to enter into them. Then the whole thing will be carried out properly. I am most anxious that these reforms should be carried out as speedily as possible. (*Hear, hear*). With these remarks I commend this resolution to you. The subject is a large one and I commend it to your best consideration. (*Cheers*).

REV. T. EVANS, (*Lahore, No.* 608, *in list*,).—Gentlemen,—My first pleasant duty is to convey the cordial compliments of my friend and your friend, and the friend of India,—Mr. W. S. Caine—(*cheers*), to the members of this Congress, and especially to that portion of the assembly who are honest *water-drinkers*. (*Applause*).

My attention at present shall be given to the question of Abkari, or more strictly speaking "Shur-ab-kari." (*Laughter*). "Shur" is a Persian word for *evil*, and it is a very appropriate term for the Excise Department in India. (*Hear, hear*). I wish to impress upon this assembly the urgent need of a dual reform in this matter. First and foremost we require a radical reform among the *people* of India. (*Hear, hear.*)

Time was when drinking habits were almost exclusively confined to the lower classes, when indulgence in *shur-ab* was considered a low and a degrading and a vile habit, fit only for the very lowest classes of the people. (*Hear, hear.*) Those days are gone, and it is a sad fact that now all classes of people indulge, and it seems a stern fact that social advancement and English education go hand in hand with indulgence in strong drinks. Some students, I am told, think that they are not, and cannot be, full-fledged "gentlemen" (*laughter*) till they drink English made liquor—and that to be able to indulge in alcohol is "a *sign of culture.*" (*Shame.*) Then we also see that in this matter religious grades are degraded. There was a time when Brahmins held *maddyam* or alcohol in utter abhorrence, and looked upon those who used it with disgust. But now we have Brahmins who not only drink but who traffic in the poison. (*Shame, shame*). This I have found to be the case in a number of stations throughout India. It is true the *Veda* prohibits the use of liquor in strong words—"*Muddyam ma peyam ma deyam ma grahyam*," *i. e.*, intoxicants should not be drunk, given or taken. Among the five mortal sins of the Hindu religion for which there can be no atonement, to indulge in liquor is one. It is said to be a crime equal to that of killing a Brahmin or a cow. And yet none of these sacred prohibitions are regarded. The filthy flood of strong drink overleaps all bounds, social and sacred, and the Brahmin in these degenerate days has come down to the low level of the lowest castes, for all worshippers at the intoxicating altar of Bacchus, high and low, become "hail fellows, well met," as they unite in imbibing alcohol. (*Shame.*)

It is easy to say—"petition Government to shut the liquor shops."—A better plan would be to shut our own mouths and abstain from alcohol. (*Hear, hear*). Some one has said :—"There is a little liquor shop which every man can close. It is that little liquor shop just beneath your nose." (*Cheers*). Then I ask—*Who is to lead?* Is it not the leaders of society? Is it not the leaders of the National Congress? Where are the Brahmins—the Barristers—the graduates of the Universities? Will these not come down to rescue? Let all the noble Bonnerjees, Chatterjees and Mookerjees of Bengal;—all the Chariars, and Iyers and Ayengers of Madras;—all the Cowasjees, the Hormusjees and Naorojees of Bombay; and all Pundits and Purohits of the N. W. P. and Cashmere, with all the Moulvies and Sayyeds of the Mahomedans, come forward to head the battle against the monster demon drink;—yea, and the Sirdars and Gooroos of the Sikhs, and the Missionaries and Ministers of the Christian religion, as well as all the delegates of the Congress, all should join hand to hand and heart to heart to attack the *Rakshas*—*i. e.* the demon of drink, and chase the hydra-headed monster out of the land. (*Cheers*). Remember your responsibilities as men of light and leading. The lower orders look up to us, as we are, so will they be. "*Jas raja tas parja.*" "*Jaisa bap, taisa beta.*" "*Jaisa swami, taisa sevak.*" Gentlemen, you are leaders—see that you lead in the right way and set a proper example to the masses. (*Hear, hear*).

Resolution V.
Reduction of the Salt duty; raising of the Income-tax taxable minimum; reform of the excise administration; Judicial and Police reforms; modification of the Rules under the Arms Act; Military Colleges; Volunteering.

I am hoping to be able to say that we have now over a hundred Associations throughout India in connection with the Anglo-Indian Temperance Association whose head quarters is in London. (*Hear, hear*). I have just been up to the north of the Punjab, where I have in one month organized 8 new societies with over 2,000 new members, and the friends in Lahore are all alive, and are moving to build a large Temperance Hall which is to cost Rs. 20,000, (*hear, hear,*) as well as to start a Temperance Journal in the vernacular. The work is going on, but the flood of drink is also on the increase. This you will see if you look at the leaps and bounds made by the Abkari Revenue. Take a few statistics. In Bengal, the normal rate of the excise revenue for many years was from 50 to 60 lakhs of rupees. Now it is 110 lakhs. (*Shame, shame*). In Madras the excise revenue has thus advanced.—

| | | |
|---|---|---|
| In 1850 | it was .. .. .. | Rs. 21,73,509; |
| in 1860, | .. .. .. .. | „ 29,70,722; |
| in 1870, | .. .. .. .. | „ 59,18,364; |
| in 1880, | .. .. .. .. | „ 61,13,402; |
| in 1887, | .. .. .. .. | „ 91,66,476; |
| in 1888, | .. .. .. .. | „ 97,38,896; |

or an increase since 1880 of no less than 36 lakhs of rupees. (*Shame, shame.*) The increase in Bombay has gone on at an equally rapid rate, and the same is the case in the Central Provinces. As to the N.-W. P., in 1858, the excise revenue here was but 19 lakhs; now, it is over 50 lakhs. (*Shame, shame.*) Above 10 years ago the excise revenue of the Punjab was hardly 10 lakhs, it is now nearly 20. Eighteen years ago the excise revenue of the whole of India was 230 lakhs, it is now about 450 lakhs of rupees. (*Shame, shame*). This may be a grand thing for the Government, but it is most ruinous to the people. (*Cheers*). Therefore I say make a strong stand against the terrible evil before the land is flooded with a deluge of destruction. (*Hear, hear.*) "Charity begins at home," and the people of India must begin this reform by sweeping the curse clean out of their own homes and putting all who drink under the ban of social ostracism. You put those out of caste who drink water from the hands of the low caste people;—why then are they not put out of caste for drinking liquor made and mixed by dirty and degraded "*kalars*"? (*Hear, hear*).

Home reform first, and then we want—*Government reform.* Government has moved a little under pressure;—but we want it to move much more. (*Cheers*). If it be asked what we want the Government to do, I answer—first of all, we want the Government *to be true to its own professed policy and promises,* (*hear, hear and cheers,*) the professed policy of—"a maximum of revenue from a minimum of consumption." Is this carried out? I don't hesitate to say—No. Do you ask for proof? There are many. Take one just now.

If the policy is to supply the public demand only, I ask why does the Government sanction the manufacture of *much more* drink than the contractors with all their greed can sell? I visited last year most of the *Government distilleries* in the N.-W. P. and the Punjab, and without a single exception I found that there are *more* stills sanctioned than are required. Let me now give a few cases. In the Punjab at—

| | | | |
|---|---|---|---|
| Gujranwalla | 10 stills sanctioned | .. .. .. | only 5 at work; |
| Lahore | 18 „ „ | .. .. .. | „ 6 „ |
| Ferozepore | 8 „ „ | .. .. .. | „ 3 „ |
| Amritsar | 15 „ „ | .. .. .. | „ 13 „ |
| Jullundhar | 6 „ „ | .. .. .. | „ 3 „ |
| Umballa | 6 „ „ | .. .. .. | „ 3 „ |
| Ludhiana | 6 „ „ | .. .. .. | „ 4 „ |

In the N. W. P. at Allahabad, 29 stills sanctioned—only 20 taken, and of these only 12 at work. A contractor who has been in the Allahabad distillery for many years, by name *Buddhoo,* told me that though the Government has always sanctioned 29 stills, he never saw more than 18 at work, and as a rule they do not use more than 10 or 12. Does this show that the Government wants "*minimum of consumption*"? No; but the trade is overstocked, and besides the extra stills, there are thousands of gallons of liquor kept in store in the godowns of the distilleries to be used in case of need;—and at the time of the

3rd Day.

Resolution V.

Reduction of the Salt duty; raising of the Income-tax taxable minimum; reform of the excise administration; Judicial and Police reforms; modification of the Rules under the Arms Act; Military Colleges; Volunteering.

"*holee*" festival Government allows the stills to work day and night, and the liquor shops are allowed to be opened for hours later than the demands of the Excise Law. (*Shame, shame*).

Again, why is the "minimum guarantee" system in vogue in Bombay by which the contractor for liquor is bound down to produce so many thousand gallons whether he is able to sell it or not? Why? Because he has to pay a duty on each gallon and the more the gallonage the greater the revenue. Further, why does not Government consult the public in opening grog shops and give effect to the principle of local option? In the *Gazette of India* for the 1st March, 1890, the Viceroy wrote:—"That efforts should be made to ascertain the existence of local public sentiments, and that a reasonable amount of deference should be paid to such opinion when ascertained." On the 29th of March, 1890, Lord Cross, the Secretary of State for India in his Excise Despatch to the Viceroy, said:—

"That while absolute local option in Excise matters is not feasible, yet weight can be, *and should be*, and is given to local option in regard to licensing liquor shops." Now I ask—are these concessions granted? I do not hesitate to say—they are not. Only to-day I got a letter about a petition to remove a grog shop from an objectionable position in the district of Umballa. That petition was sent to the Deputy Commissioner four months ago—but no reply! (*Shame.*) In Madura, in Calicut, in Tanjore, in Sholapur, in Cuddapah, in Fureedpore, in Lahore, in Agra, in Mussooree, and in Dehra Doon, to my own positive knowledge, petitions of this nature have been rejected on paltry excuses, and as to making an effort "to ascertain the existence of local public sentiment" about grog shops, *no such effort is ever made.* (*Shame, shame.*) From pressure brought to bear by the British Parliament promises are made, laws are enacted; but if they tend to diminish the revenue, they are evaded, and the Government of India winks at their evasion for revenue reasons. (*Shame, shame.*)

This is the case not only with the liquor but also with the opium and *chandu*. Sometime ago the opium dens were condemned, and a law was made to shut them up. Now what do we find? Listen to a *Confidential* despatch from the head of the Excise Department in the N.-W. P. Here it is:—

"*Confidential. No. I of* 1892. *D/* 26 *July*, 1892.

*From T. Stoker, Esquire, C. S., Commissioner of Excise, N. W. P. and Oudh,*

*To all Commissioners and Collectors, N. W. P. and Oudh.*

*D/* 26 *July*, 1892.

Sir,—You are already aware that henceforth the *chandu* and *madak* smoking is absolutely prohibited on the premises licensed for the sale of the drug. It is impossible to doubt that this prohibition will be followed by the opening in many places of unlicensed places of resort where smokers can obtain the facilities which they require, and that such places will have to be kept under observation both for general reasons, and also with a view to prevent the use of illicit opium.

As the law now stands, the authorities have no power to suppress consumption on premises where opium or its preparations are not sold. There is nothing in the law to prevent any one opening a saloon for the accommodation of opium-smokers who bring their own *chandu*. He can supply pipes and lamps and service, and charge a fee for their use, and the law cannot touch him unless he is detected selling opium or its preparations, or found in possession of more than the legal quantity. On this point the opinion of the Board of Revenue is that it is not altogether advisable that such places should be suppressed. Collectors should watch such establishments carefully so as to prevent the sale thereat of illicit opium. The known conditions of *chandu* smoking render the maintenance of some common places for the consumption of the drug an almost absolute necessity. No efforts should be made to suppress such places, as it is better that they should be known, and thus be liable to supervision.

I have, &c.,

(Sd.) G. C. HAMPTON,

*Hd. Asst. for Commissioner of Excise.*

Now, I ask, is not this a shameful policy of shabby shuffling to try to evade the law in order to facilitate the sale of extra opium? Is such a condition worthy of the dignity of the British Government? (*Applause*). The *root* of the whole matter is the effort made to *increase the revenue*. But is it politic, is it expedient, is it just to replenish the revenue from the vice and the demoralization of the people?—yea, and to do so by resorting to ways and means that are mean and dishonorable? Let us then send forth floods of petitions to England to show the British public how the Excise administration is conducted here. We have strong friends and patriots there in the persons of Messrs. Caine, S. Smith, Schwaan and others. (*Cheers.*) Supply them with shot and shell to destroy this citadel of iniquity, for the work must be done by the powerful and patriotic vote of the House of Commons—the paladium of English justice and fair-play. (*Loud applause*).

MR. OUDH BEHARI LAL, (*Allahbad, No.* 416 *in list,*)—MR. PRESIDENT AND GENTLEMEN,—I rise to support this resolution. I hold in my hand copy of an extract from instructions of the Court of the Directors of the East India Company issued so long ago as the year 1838. It runs as follows :—

"It cannot be too strongly urged upon Collectors that the object which Government has in view is to restrain and, if possible, to arrest and diminish the total actual consumption of spirituous liquor, whether clandestine or licensed, being fully persuaded that any amount of revenue that may be lost by the efficiency of the system to this end, will be repaid a hundred-fold by preservation and advancement of moral feelings and industrious habits among the people." (*Hear, hear*). These are the noble words of the Directors of the East India Company, used in the year 1838, but what do we *actually* find now? Has this been the policy of the Government since? I say emphatically—no. (*Cheers.*) Instead of being true to their words, they have adopted a policy based only on financial considerations. (*Shame*). They do not seem to recognise that what is morally wrong cannot be politically right. It is certainly wrong on the part of individuals to yield to temptations, but it is no less wrong, especially on the part of the Government, to allow temptations to multiply before the masses of the people of this country. (*Cheers*).

Let it not be understood that we desire to make the people of India moral by means of resolutions of the House of Commons; that is impossible. They must be made moral by influences working at home. What we contend is that the Government ought to see that liquor shops are not forced upon the people in places where they are not wanted, and that distilleries are not established against the wishes and sentiments of the people. (*Hear, hear*). When sometime ago I went on a Temperance tour to Benares, I was sorry to hear in various places that it was generally believed that it was not the intention of the Government officials to close liquor shops, merely on the request of the people, for they think that if they were to yield to the demands of public opinion, it would show their weakness. From what has occurred in various places, I am inclined to think that the belief is not groundless. It is a shame and a scandal that some of the Government officials who come to this country forget their British instincts and become as despotic and autocratic as they can be. They not only defy the voice of the public here but try to ignore even resolutions passed by the House of Commons, and do not consider themselves responsible to anybody. If this is not despotism, I should like to know what it is. The interests of this country and the honor of England alike require that it should not be so, and that an earnest effort ought to be made by all concerned in the welfare of these great countries to stem the tide of drunkenness, which threatens to deluge this land and bring disgrace upon the English people. (*Cheers*).

[Munshi Sheikh Husain *alias* Sheikh Chand Wahid, (*Bombay No.* 52, *in list*),—*This gentleman spoke next in support of the resolution in Urdu, but he has not supplied either a copy of his speech, or a translation thereof. Hence no report of his speech can be given, there having been no reporters for vernacular speeches.*

MR. B. S. SAHASRABUDDHE, (*Poona, No.* 70, *in list,*)—MR. PRESIDENT AND GENTLEMEN,—This resolution combines many propositions. My predecessors have spoken upon many portions of it, and I would confine my attention to those points only which I wish to bring

3rd Day.

Resolution V. Reduction of the Salt duty; raising of the Income-tax taxable minimum; reform of the excise administration; Judicial and Police reforms; modification of the Rules under the Arms Act; Military Colleges; Volunteering.

particularly to your notice. It is proposed to introduce into the Code of Criminal Procedure a provision enabling accused persons in warrant cases to demand that instead of being tried by Magistrates they may be committed to the Court of Sessions. I will give you one instance which will convince you of the real necessity for this provision. A person was accused of committing theft; he was first of all sent before a second class Magistrate, and after evidence had been taken the District Magistrate was moved and thought it was his duty, in exercise of his powers of revision, to send the case to another Magistrate. Charges were then drawn up; and when the Pleader for the accused saw that the Magistrate was bent upon convicting the man, he made a representation to the Magistrate that it would be better in the interests of justice to send up the case to the Court of Sessions. If we had the right asked for here, he could certainly demand that the case should be sent up. Fortunately the case was sent up to the Sessions Court, and there, after careful enquiry by the Sessions Judge, the man was acquitted (*hear, hear*;) and the Judge's remarks show that the case was a false one. If the good sense of the Magistrate had not induced him to commit the case to the Sessions, the man would have been convicted. (*Hear, hear.*) If we have a section introduced in the Criminal Procedure Code, enabling the accused in warrant cases to demand that his case should be sent up to the Sessions, it would be a great advantage. Therefore you see our humble prayer is that there should be a provision introduced into the Code of Criminal Procedure to enable a person to demand that he may, under certain circumstances, be committed to the Court of Sessions. (*Cheers*).

As to the reduction of the salt duty, this is one of the propositions which affects the masses very much, and we may therefore call this the poor man's proposition. (*Hear, hear.*) It is said that we never care for the masses, and that we are never anxious to protect their interests; but here is a case which will show that we have been agitating for years for some relief to the poorest of the poor (*hear, hear,*) and we have to regret that there are no signs yet of that relief coming. All that we see is that the Viceroy has given some attention to the matter, for when he was at Madras he said that this would be the first tax which he would wish to see reduced. But we do not know when the tax will be reduced. (*Hear, hear.*) So that there is every necessity for our repeating this prayer in the interests of the masses; and we earnestly hope that it will be granted before long. (*Cheers*). I hope you will all concur in carrying this proposition with acclamation. (*Loud cheers*).

MUNSHI ABDUL QADIR, (*Punjab, No.* 614 *in list*).—*This gentleman supported the resolution in a speech in Urdu, but he has not supplied either a copy of the speech or a translation of it in English, and hence no report of his speech can be given, there having been no reporters for vernacular speeches.*

THE PRESIDENT.—I have received two other applications from delegates for permission to speak upon this resolution. Is it necessary to have it further discussed?—(*Cries of 'no,' 'no;' 'vote, 'vote.'*)

The motion was then put to the meeting and carried unanimously.

Resolution VI. Demands the withdrawal of the Jury notification and the extension of the system of trial by Jury.

BABU GURU PRASAD SEN, (*Bankipur, No.* 259, *in list*)—MR. PRESIDENT AND GENTLEMEN,—In their letter dated 31st May, 1890, the Government of India asked the Government of Bengal for a report (1) as to 'how the Jury system has worked in the Lower Provinces, (2) what opinion is entertained as to its merits as a means for the repression of crime, (3) what improvements, if any, are called for in its application.' To clear the ground for the adoption of the resolution on the Jury question which I shall presently propose, it shall be necessary for us to examine these questions.

In my humble opinion, no amount of platitudes, or denunciation, but a careful examination of figures comprising the crime statistics for a number of years can alone help us in coming to a right conclusion regarding the matter. We have Jury trials and Non-jury trials in Sessions Court under the Government of Bengal, and the result of trials with jury as compared with the result of Sessions case trials without jury, will show the merit of each. Such a statement I now hold in my hand. It is a comparative statement of the above kind from 1877 to 1891 compiled from the Reports of the Administration

**Resolution VI. Demands the withdrawal of the Jury notification and the extension of the system of trial by Jury.**

of Criminal Justice in the Lower Provinces. It will be tedious to read to you all the figures, even if our 10 minutes' rule will allow. I shall crave your permission to take it as read, and I shall hand over a copy to our Secretary for record as a part of this address. I shall however read to you the summary of the result.

From 1877 to 1891, barring the years 1879, 1880, 1881, and 1882 for which certain figures are not available, the number of trials with jury was 3,567; the number of verdicts agreed to by the Sessions Judges was 2,921; the number of verdicts not agreed to by the Sessions Judges was 632; the number of references disposed of, under Section 307, Criminal Procedure Code was 238; verdicts approved of by the High Court were 90; verdicts set aside by the High Court were 148. The percentage, therefore, of verdicts not agreed to by the Sessions Judges to the whole number of verdicts during these years, was 16·9. The percentage of verdicts actually set aside to the total number of verdicts, was 3·68. While, if all cases in which the Sessions Judges disagreed from the verdict of the jury, had been referred by them under Section 307, Criminal Procedure Code, to the High Court, and the verdicts set aside in the same proportion as in cases referred, the percentage of verdicts which would have been set aside, would be 11·8.

On the other hand, we find that during the same period the total number of Non-jury trials, *i.e.*, trials with Assessors, was 12,141. The number of appeals disposed of by the High Court from the decisions of the Sessions Judges was 8,205; the number of cases in which there were no appeals, was 3,936; of the appeals disposed of, 6,632 were affirmed, and the number reversed, modified and sent back, was 1,603. The percentage of judgment, of Sessions Judges affirmed to the total number of appeals, was 81·6, and the percentage of judgments reversed, modified, and sent back, was 19·4. The percentage of judgments affirmed or not disturbed to the total number of trials was 86·7, while the percentage of judgments that would have to be corrected by the High Court, if there had been appeals in all cases to the total number of trials, would be 13·3.

It would, perhaps, be conceded that the cases not referred were such that if they were before the High Court there would be less chance of their being set aside. Under the present Code (Section 307, Cr. P. C.,) wrong verdicts may be set aside in every instance; it is not, therefore, an irremediable wrong. (*Hear, hear*). Again, there are doubtless cases in which no appeal against the sentence of the Sessions Judge is preferred, because the prisoner has no money or friends to take up his case before the High Court; and if appeals had been preferred in these cases the sentences would not have been affirmed; while, therefore, the mode in which the percentage has been worked out in column 9 of the Statement A. I have in hand, is unfavourable to the Jury, the mode by which the percentage in column 7 of the Statement B. also in hand, has been worked out, is very favourable to the Sessions Judge, and they have been worked out in this way to remove all hesitation in adopting them for the purpose of comparison.

Now, comparing these figures, we find that while the actual percentage of verdicts of juries set aside during these years has been only 3·68; the actual percentage of judgments of Sessions Judges reversed by the High Court in appeal, is 19·4. (*Hear, hear*). While if all disagreed verdicts had been referred to by the Sessions Judges to the High Court, under Section 307 of the Criminal Procedure Code, and these verdicts set aside in the same ratio as those referred, the percentage of verdicts set aside would have been only 11·8, but the percentage of judgments of the Sessions Judges that would have to be corrected by the High Court, to the total number of trials, treating cases not appealed against as affirmed, would be 13·3. (*Hear, hear*). [ The Statement A. referred to above is published as *Appendix II.* ]

These figures, I hold, conclusively prove that the Jury system has worked much better than the Non-jury or the Assessor system. (*Cheers*). Opinions, from whatever source they may come, would be of no weight if not based on facts, and isolated facts can scarcely furnish a correct basis for generalization. (*Hear, hear*).

Elsewhere the opinions on which the action of the Government of Bengal has been based have been sufficiently scrutinized, and it has been very satisfactorily shown that

**3rd Day.**

**Resolution VI.**

**Demands the withdrawal of the Jury notification and the extension of the system of trial by Jury.**

they do not support the conclusion, much less justify the action which the Government of Bengal has chosen to take in this matter. I shall not take time by repeating arguments there used.

It will be seen that the Jury system has been primarily condemned on the opinions of some of the Sessions Judges; but the figures reveal the rather astounding fact that there has been a steady deterioration of late years in the work of these Sessions Judges (*hear, hear*); thus :

| Years. | Percentage of Judgments of Sessions Judges affirmed to the total number of appeals. | Percentage of Judgments of Sessions Judges not disturbed to the total number of trials. |
|---|---|---|
| 1877 | 81·5 | 89·1 |
| 1878 | 83·6 | 91 |
| 1879 | 85·2 | 89·6 |
| 1880 | 80·4 | 87 |
| 1881 | 80·7 | 88·3 |
| 1882 | 82·5 | 89·9 |
| 1883 | 83·8 | 89·1 |
| 1884 | 82·5 | 88·6 |
| 1885 | 79·9 | 84·1 |
| 1886 | 83 | 88·4 |
| 1887 | 80 | 86·3 |
| 1888 | 79·7 | 85·5 |
| 1889 | 78·1 | 85·6 |
| 1890 | 78·6 | 83·7 |
| 1891 | 77·4 | 83·5 |

There is, however, another set of figures which clearly indicates such depreciation, and is enough to excite consternation and alarm. (*Hear, hear.*) These figures are—

| Years. | Total number of sentences of death passed by the Sessions Judges decided on reference by the High Court. | Confirmed. | Commuted or set aside. | Percentage of sentences of death passed by the Sessions Courts, and set aside by the High Court. |
|---|---|---|---|---|
| 1886 | 26 | 16 | 10 | 38·4 |
| 1887 | 34 | 23 | 11 | 28·2 |
| 1888 | 31 | 13 | 18 | 41·9 |
| 1889 | 22 | 11 | 11 | 50 |
| 1890 | 33 | 19 | 14 | 42·4 |
| 1891 | 48 | 32 | 16 | 33·3 |

The Jury system is condemned because of the prejudices of native jurors to convict in murder cases. Elsewhere it has been satisfactorily shown that the supposed reluctance does not exist; but in the face of the figures I have placed before you, the only action that should have been taken was not to take away the safeguard of a Jury trial but to extend it to other places where it does not exist, specially in cases punishable with murder. (*Hear, hear and cheers*).

**3rd Day.**

**Resolution VI. Demands the withdrawal of the Jury notification and the extension of the system of trial by Jury.**

With reference to the second question, Mr. Justice Beverley observes :—"As to the merits of the system as a means for the repression of crime, it seems to me that it is difficult to form an opinion. I should think it extremely improbable that a murderer or a dacoit, before committing the offence, would sit down to consider whether in the event of his being apprehended he would be tried by a Judge sitting with Assessors, or by a Judge and Jury. On the other hand, the employment of juries to try criminal cases does tend to disseminate a knowledge of the criminal law, and such extended knowledge, it may be presumed, must have a tendency to repress crime. A statistical test of the merits or demerits of the Jury system as bearing upon the repression of crime, might be afforded by a comparison of the statistics of human crimes before and after the introduction of the system in 1862, or by a comparison of the statistics of such crime in Jury districts and those districts in which the system has not been introduced. But any such statistical comparison would be by no means conclusive." (*Hear, hear*).

The Statements B. and C. which I hold in hand, have been compiled from Crime Statistics for a series of years, beginning with the year 1878, for the purpose of such comparison :—[These Statements are published as *Appendices III and IV.*]

It will be found at a glance,

(1) That the offences under the Indian Penal Code have not at all increased ;

(2) That all other offences, excepting offences against property, have decreased ;

(3) That the slight increase in offences affecting property can only be traced to the inefficiency of the Police and the poverty of the people ;

(4) That as regards the Jury districts there has been a sensible decrease of all offences under the Indian Penal Code ;

(5) That this sensible decrease is decidedly marked with reference to all offences excepting offences affecting property ;

(6) That the number of offences in the Assessor districts has to a certain extent increased ;

(7) That this increase is marked both in offences affecting property and offences falling under other heads ;

(8) But that it is more marked in offences affecting property than in the other kinds of offences ;

(9) That the number of petty offences under Special Laws (infringement of Bye-laws of Municipalities and such like) have almost doubled from 1880 to 1890.

And the conclusion from the second of these Statements is that while in 1878 the proportion of our criminal population, *i.e.*, persons convicted under the Indian Penal Code to the whole population of Bengal, was one in 958, taking 66 millions as the population of the Lower Provinces, it was one in 1,155 in 1891 taking 66 millions again, as the basis of calculation, without taking into consideration the increase since then. (*Hear, hear*).

I have not at present in hand, figures giving such 'percentages for other countries, but from the comparison of the percentages in the Lower Provinces at two different periods, I ask what was the good of raising all this commotion ? (*Cheers*).

Then as to the last point, it is generally assumed that the Jury system was an exotic institution brought in for the first time in India in 1862. There appears to be some misapprehension on this subject. It may be that we had no institution by this particular name in India previous to that year. It may be that to a certain extent, the spirit of Local Self-Government had been crushed out of us; but that no country was better fitted to receive the institution of Jury, and for the matter of that Local Self-Government of all kinds, than India, and that the institution of Jury came to be planted in a congenial soil in 1862, there cannot be any doubt.—(*Cheers*). The antiquity of the system

**3rd Day.**

**Resolution VI. Demands the withdrawal of the Jury notification and the extension of the system of trial by Jury.**

of Jury trials in England cannot perhaps be traced back to a period anterior to the 11th century of the Christian era. But look to the *Sanhitas*, none of them later than the Christian era, and you shall find that in ancient India, the trials of all cases, Civil and Criminal, used to be in the Court of the King's Council, Assemblies of Townsmen, Companies of Traders, and Families. (*Hear, hear.*) You will find a complete account of it in *Yajnyavalka Sanhita* and its commentaries, the *Mitakshara* and *Viramitrodaya*. The Court of the King in Council used to be presided over, in the absence of the King, by the *Pradvivak* (Chief Justice), and composed of an uneven number of *Sabhasadas* (members of the assembly)—7 and 5 were the usual number—taken from all classes of people, while the other tribunals as their names indicate, were composed of the people themselves. The relic of all these, the *Punchayat*, still attests the vigour, with which Local Self-Government used to be carried on at one time in India. (*Cheers*). And even now the people say '*Punch muh Parmeshwar*'—the voice of the *Punch* is the voice of God. That indicates the kind of reverence and awe, with which our people even now look on the voice of *five* of themselves, and if any reform, short of reforming the Police and the Magistracy, and insisting on a better knowledge in our Sessions Judges of the language of the people, is needed here, it is in the selection of the people's *Punch*. (*Cheers*). Hundreds of such men are available in every town, nay in every important village, if one was to know where to find them out. And in this connection let me make a suggestion. If instead of the Police, the members of the District and Local Boards or Municipalities were to be entrusted with the duty of finding out men for selection, there would be no lack of good, honest and able men to fill up the Jury list. (*Hear, hear.*)

I beg now to propose the resolution, with which I have been entrusted, for your acceptance. It is as follows :—

*That this Congress views with the deepest concern and alarm the recent policy of the Government of India and of the Governments of Bengal and Assam in withdrawing the right of trial by Jury in the majority of serious offences, and most respectfully, but firmly protests against such policy and action as retrograde, reactionary, and injurious to the best interests of the country, and prays that the same may be reversed by the Government of India and failing that, by the Government in England; and that as prayed for in resolutions of previous Congresses, the right of trial by Jury be extended to such parts of the country where it is not now in force, it being the only safeguard for the people in the present unsatisfactory condition of the administration of criminal Justice in British India. (Cheers).*

We have this year separated the Jury question from our Omnibus Resolution because of the importance the question has assumed in Bengal and is likely soon to assume in other parts of India. The reference in the first part of this resolution is in one sense to a local matter affecting even not the whole of Bengal; but no apology is needed to introduce this to you, as you have in past years determined that the extension of the Jury system in criminal trials, wherever it does not prevail at present, lies at the very threshold of any reform in the administration of Criminal Justice in India, and thus any restriction of it in any part of India, in any form, you cannot but hold to be a retardation of a needed reform. (*Cheers*). Trial by jury, as I have shown to you, I hope conclusively, from the Criminal Statistics of Bengal, is a great safeguard for the protection of the life, liberty and property of the people. (*Cheers*). Again, the way in which the restriction on the Jury system has been imposed affects the general policy of good Government in India. (*Hear, hear*). It has certainly created much consternation and alarm; but I venture to hope there is no reason to distrust the motive of Government, and in that hope we pray that the present Jury policy may be reversed by the Government of India, and failing that, by the Government in England, and the Jury system introduced in parts, where it does not exist at present, it being the only safeguard for the people in the present unsatisfactory condition of the administration of Criminal Justice in British India. (*Cheers*).

BABU BAIKUNTHA NATH SEN, (*Murshidabad, No. 210 in list*),—MR. PRESIDENT AND GENTLEMEN,—The subject before you must be looked at from the Congress point of view. The principle underlying the system of trial by jury was introduced in Madras and

Bombay in 1832, and in Bengal, by an Act of the Supreme Council, in 1861, and the Local Government, vested with the authority given by the act, selected 7 districts for the enjoyment of the privilege in respect of certain classes of offences. In 1867, Sir Cecil Beadon was for the extension of the system to other districts. (*Hear, hear*). In 1871, Commissioners recommended withdrawal, but the recommendations were rejected. (*Hear, hear.*) In 1872, the Code of Criminal Procedure provided for a reference to the High Court by the Judge in case of disagreement between the Jury and the Judge. In 1884, there was a discussion of the question by Government, resulting in leaving things *statu quo.* In 1892, came the Jury notification, under consideration, published in Bengal on the 26th of October last, and in Assam, a few days later. No previous notice, no reasons contemporaneously given! but certain correspondence published *after* the notification giving the opinions of some officials! (*Shame.*)

**3rd Day.**

**Resolution VI.**
**Demands the withdrawal of the Jury notification and the extension of the system of trial by Jury.**

Neither the Government of Bengal nor the Administration of Assam have yet published any resolution setting forth the grounds on which their action in withdrawing the trial of heinous offences by Jury is based. (*Hear, hear*). But it can be gathered from the correspondence published that the system has been condemned on the ground of failure of justice, it being borne in mind that the notification can be supported on two grounds only, *viz.*, political considerations and failure of justice. (*Hear, hear*). A privilege once granted and enjoyed for a period of 30 years ought not to be taken away without making out a very strong case for such a measure. (*Cheers*). The Government has therefore to establish clearly the alleged failure of justice in cases decided by the Jury to justify its action. (*Hear, hear*).

The statistics given by the learned mover of this resolution surely do not justify the action of the Government. If it could be shown that there has been a decline in the number of convictions for certain classes of offences, and that crime has increased in consequence, the position of Government would be strengthened; but how does the matter actually stand? Even the best apologists of the notification do not suggest that crime has increased in consequence of acquittals of really guilty persons. (*Cheers.*) It would be interesting in connection with this to compare India with England, and some other European countries. From the statistics available from one of the best authorities, it would be found that the Prison population per one hundred thousand was 90 in England, in 1882; 158 in France, in 1885; 230 in Italy, in 1887; 120 in the United States, in 1886; 160 in Japan, in 1887; and 38 in India, in 1887. (*Hear, hear*). And I may here mention that eminent criminologists of England, of Germany, and of Italy, have expressed their surprise at the small ratio which the prison population bears to the general population in India. (*Hear, hear, and cheers*).

The number of trials, convictions and acquittals ought no doubt to be taken into consideration with reference to this particular point, in anticipation of any argument that might be urged by the supporters of the notification. There were in India in 1881,—11,72,000 trials, and 5,27,000 acquittals; in 1887,—13,77,000, trials, and 7,03,000 acquittals; that is to say, there was an increase in the 6 years of 19 p. c. in the number of cases tried, and of 4.5 p. c. in acquittals. (Population increased 4.5 per cent. in the six years.) This decline of 4.5 per cent. in convictions is not owing to a failure of justice in trials by Jury, but is attributable to many important factors, such as the poverty of the country, the vigorous action, and the unnecessary and unjustifiable action of the Police, the mismanagement of cases before Magistrates, the perfunctory and unsatisfactory commitments of cases to the Sessions Court. (*Hear, hear*).

As regards cases of homicide in England, the ratio of convictions is about 50 per cent., whereas of convictions in respect of other offences, the ratio is about 75 per cent. It becomes a question of grave importance why in England with an efficient Police and an intelligent and educated jury there is a larger percentage of acquittals in cases of homicide than in other cases. (*Hear, hear*). And here I cannot help bringing to your notice the fact that Mr. John Bright, in one of his speeches advocating the abolition of capital sentences, observed that the Jury naturally were over-scrupulous in weighing evidence in cases where the punishment

3rd Day.

Resolution VI. Demands the withdrawal of the Jury notification and the extension of the system of trial by Jury.

might be death. (*Hear, hear.*) Now in India the percentage of acquittals in cases of homicide is far less than what it is in England, notwithstanding that the Indian Jury is supposed to be averse to capital punishment and is over-scrupulous in weighing evidence in cases where such punishment is possible. (*Hear, hear.*) Any decline in convictions in cases of heinous offences, even if assumed for the sake of argument, does not necessarily establish a failure of justice. A reform of the Police ought to precede any attempt to withdraw the system of trial by Jury. (*Cheers*).

If the statistics do not justify the notification, can it be supported by the opinions of Subordinate Officials, or Commissioners of Divisions, Sessions Judges and Magistrates and some of the Judges of the High Court? Irrespective of the merit or demerit of those opinions, it is a fact that the opinions were neither asked for nor given with reference to the question of the withdrawal of the system of trial by Jury. (*Hear, hear.*) In certain cases they were only asked to express how far the system had been successful as a means for the repression of crime and what improvements could be made in it. It is, to say the least, unfair to the Hon'ble Judges of the High Court, unfair to the officials mentioned and unfair to the people at large, to use those opinions obtained ostensibly for one purpose for altgether a different one. (*Cheers*). Sir Charles Elliott is credited with strength of mind and the courage of convictions, which seven Lieutenant-Governors preceding him are alleged to have been wanting in; if so, he ought to have put the question of the withdrawal of the system of trial by Jury in cases of certain heinous offences pointblank to those whom he thought fit to consult, and ought to have published his grounds for issuing the notification to give the public an opportunity to criticise those gounds.—But what did His Honor do? From the summits of the Darjeeling Hills, he suddenly hurled the notification down at the head of the people. The people were quite stunned, and when they recovered consciousness, they found that the notification had, only four days after its publication, come into operation, and that their cherished and valued right of trial by jury in heinous cases, had been taken away by His Honor by one single stroke of the pen in exercise of the authority given him under section 269 of the Criminal Procedure Code. (*Cries of 'shame, shame'*). A few days later, the Assam Administration published a similar notification in the official Gazette, with this difference only that the order is to come into force from the 1st of January next!

Now, gentlemen, at a peaceful time, when political considerations are not even suggested as having any thing to do with the notification, the manner of its publication cannot be too strongly condemned. (*Cheers*). If a bill be introduced for the first time in the Legislative Council, it has to be published in the official Gazette and public criticism is to be considered. *A fortiori* when a vested right, exercised by a large number of Her Majesty's subjects for a period of thirty years, is intended to be taken away by the Governor of a country, the proposal ought to be allowed to be subjected to public criticism, by timely publication. Why this unseemly haste, this precipitancy in sending forth a fiat, which gives rise to so much irritation and excitement, and results in an agitation the like of which has scarcely ever been seen. (*Hear, hear*). Is the expected good likely to counterbalance the discontent and dissatisfaction which has been caused by it among the most loyal of Her Majesty's subjects? No. The notification is the outcome of a policy which is retrograde and reactionary, and which is now being pursued by the Government of Bengal in utter defiance of public opinion. (*Shame*). I won't say that the notification is meant to be a slap to Babudom; but what I do say is that the measure is a deliberate insult to this Congress, which has been year after year recording its resolution for the extension of the system of trial by jury in places where the same is not in vogue. This being so, the Congress must not be content simply with the withdrawal of the notification, but should re-double its efforts for the extension of the system of trial by jury to places where it is not at present in force. And for this purpose, we should move the Government of India, and if necessary, the Government of England. (*Loud cheers*).

Mr. Lakshminath Bezbarua, (*Assam, No. 226 in list*).—Mr. President and Gentlemen.—In supporting this resolution on behalf of the people of Assam, I have this much to say, that the notification came upon the people of Assam in a very evil hour. It cannot be generally known that this privilege was given to the people of Assam long before the Bengal people had the good fortune of getting it. (*Hear, hear*). It is as old as the British rule in Assam, which began sixty years ago. All of a sudden, like a thunderbolt from a blue sky, this notification fell upon them, completely putting them out and surprising them. If there is any province in India which wants trial by jury more than another it is Assam. (*Hear, hear*). You know that Assam is a non-Regulation Province; it is in fact still in darkness, and the people are backward and poor. Education has not there made much progress, and civilisation has made but little advance. And it is also well known that raw and inexperienced Civilians are generally imported into Assam, who not only administer justice in a lawless manner, but tyrannise over the people, and often do things which you will be surprised to hear of, but not nine-tenths of which are ventilated in the columns of newspapers. (*Hear, hear*). We have got no good Barristers or Advocates in Assam to explain things to these young Civilians, who are generally scarcely out of their teens when there. Therefore, it is absolutely necessary for us to have the safeguard which trial by jury affords against miscarriages of justice. (*Cheers*). With these few words, I beg to support the resolution. (*Cheers*).

**3rd Day.**

**Resolution VI.**

**Demands the withdrawal of the Jury notification and the extension of the system of trial by Jury.**

PANDIT SHAM NARAYAN, (*Lucknow, No.* 541 *in list*).—*This gentleman supported the resolution in a speech in Urdu, but as he has not sent either a copy of the speech or its translation in English, and as there were no vernacular reporters, we are unable to give a report of his speech here*).

MR. R. K. LIMAYE, (*Poona, No.* 86, *in list,*).—MR. PRESIDENT AND BROTHER DELEGATES,—In supporting this resolution, I have to observe that the present is one of those instances in which the Government, with an honest desire to improve the administration of justice, thinks, but I believe wrongly, that it ought to mould its conduct by hearing one side of the problem only, *viz.*, the official side. In the present case, if the Government had taken the public into its confidence a little, it would have found reasons, not to curtail the system, but to develop and expend it. (*Hear, hear*). Mind the Panchayat or Jury system has not been imported here from abroad. It is an old institution of ours. (*Hear, hear*). But really we need not go so very far back. Let us examine the law as it stands at this day. The law lays down that the trial (of course, in some grave and serious offences and in some districts chosen by the Local Governments,) should be by jury. In such a trial, the majority of the Jury constitutes one Judge and the District Judge, another Judge. If they disagree, the case is decided by the High Court on a reference. If they agree, the Judge decides the case at once. There is no independent power in the Jury. (*Hear, hear*). If the Judge and the majority of the Jury acquit or convict an accused, you cannot say that the Jury were wrong. If the High Court decide the matter on a reference, justice is done there. Where is the occasion then for a failure of justice which might discredit the system? (*Cheers.*) I say if proper persons are selected to sit on the Jury by responsible officers, (I think the Government officials would not like to be told that they fail in this duty,) then how can the system fail at all? (*Cheers*). The statistics so far as they can be gathered from published reports, point to one conclusion only, viz., that no case has yet been made out by the officials to discredit the system as a whole, but that one-sided and insufficient materials were placed before the Government, which, without pausing to hear the other side, passed erroneous orders. (*Cheers*).

Perhaps it may be said that there is no necessity for assisting a Judge by a Jury. To that the reply is simply this. Where the Sessions Judges as a rule are strangers to the habits, customs, language, &c., of the accused and the witnesses, it is imperatively necessary that they should be assisted by a strong and intelligent Jury, to avoid such appalling mistakes as some of the European Judiciary are found at times to commit. (*Cheers*). All the delegates of the Dekkan, and some from other parts also, full well know by this time the important murder of the meaning of the words *Kâranîbhût* committed at Satara the other day. (*Hear, hear*). कारणीभूत was not understood by the learned Magistrate to mean "cause of" as it should have been, but was interpreted by him, with his great *aya* and *cooly*

3rd Day.

Resolution VI.

Demands the withdrawal of the Jury notification and the extension of the system of trial by Jury.

learning,—(*laughter*), to mean "*causing fiend.*" (*Laughter*). I think I must stop here. I need not cite any more instances as they are too numerous. I heartily support the resolution and commend it to your favourable consideration. (*Cheers*).

MR. RAMANUJA CHARIAR, (*Madras, No.* 568 *in list*).—MR. PRESIDENT AND GENTLEMEN,—The subject of this resolution is one about which I am aware there can hardly be any difference of opinion. My reason for speaking on this occasion is to show that although the presidency of Madras is unaffected by the recent Bengal Notification, yet the people of Madras heartily sympathise with their brethren in Bengal. (*Cheers*). The recent misfortune that has befallen that Presidency is a calamity which may be considered to be common to the whole country. (*Hear, hear*). But the remarks which were made by our President in his inaugural speech as regards the difference in the mode of recording evidence in civil and criminal trials in Bengal, do not apply to the procedure in our country. In civil cases in the Madras presidency the depositions are recorded in the vernacular by a clerk differently from the manner in which the evidence in criminal cases is taken down. Both in civil and criminal cases the Judge is empowered to record the depositions in English in brief, and the decisions are also recorded by the Judge himself in English. But leaving this difference in the mode of recording evidence aside, it cannot be denied that Juries have in the majority of cases rendered good service to the people in the trial of cases. Sometimes Judges display a desire to get rid of Juries, and in entertaining such a desire they have an object in view. There are some cases tried by Sessions Courts in which from the very nature of the offences, it is impossible to get any clear and positive evidence. For instance in cases of bribery, and in cases in which the offence is committed clandestinely and in private. In such cases some Judges, in the absence of strict legal proof, seem determined to convict the accused on the strength of their own moral conviction of the man's guilt, and in such cases it is convenient to get rid of the Jury and base the Judge's conviction on indirect evidence strengthened by his own conviction of the probabilities of the case—which is a very wide term. It is for such reasons that some Judges have evinced a desire to abolish Juries, but that is no reason why we should not insist upon the retention of Juries. Juries in most cases agree with the Judge. In Madras Juries almost invariably follow the lead of the Judge. Therefore the allegation which has been made with regard to Juries being the cause of a failure of justice cannot apply to Madras. These are the reasons which I beg leave to advance against the abolition of trial by Jury in Sessions cases. (*Cheers*).

BABU TARAPADO BANERJEE, (*Nuddea, No.* 195 *in list,*).—BROTHER DELEGATES,—It is with much diffidence that I rise to support this resolution which has been so ably proposed and seconded. I have no intention of figuring in the capacity of a speech-maker to-day. I wish only to say this that in the final decision of this important matter, are involved the interests of a large proportion of the people of India, and that upon it depends the future of our national advancement. (*Cheers*). We have been deprived of a valued right which according to all sound principles of criminal jurisprudence, even the humblest member of a subject race is entitled to claim and possess. It is an admitted principle of law that in accusations of a serious and grave nature, the accused should have the privilege of choosing his own judges. (*Hear, hear*). To be judged by one's own peers is a privilege highly valued as a safeguard against any failure of justice. And our Lieutenant-Governor, Sir Charles Elliott, has deprived us most unceremoniously of this privilege. (*Shame*).

As regards my own district, I am told that the Judges, with only one single exception, have borne testimony to the fact that Native Juries are not only fully competent to perform the duties of Judges of facts, but are above bribery and corruption. (*Cheers*). The facts and figures which have been placed before us to-day show that the Jury system has worked very satisfactorily in all districts in Bengal. I therefore fail to see why this notification should have ever been issued, and why the Government of India should not be able to revoke it. But recent events in connexion with what is called the 'compromise' show that we have very little hope of good from that quarter. I would therefore request you to organise a delegation to England to represent your grievance there. (*Hear, hear*).

**3rd Day.**

**Resolution VI.**
**Demands the withdrawal of the Jury notification and the extension of the system of trial by Jury.**

The matter is of the utmost importance. It is not the concern of a day or an hour, but our perpetual happiness is involved in it, and I ask you all to unite in securing a satisfactory solution of this question. (*Cheers*).

MR. C. V. NAYADU, (*Nagpore, No.* 143 *in list,*).—MR. PRESIDENT AND GENTLEMEN,—I rise to support the sixth resolution, so ably put before you by my learned countryman of Behar. You have heard with regret how in Lower Bengal a single notification emanating from the Government there, has abolished the Jury system that was in vogue there ever since the year 1862. About Bombay and Madras you have heard ere this as to how unsatisfactorily Juries are treated in those Presidencies. I would now request you to hear something of the criminal administration of the Central Provinces. (*Hear, hear*).

It is nearly 40 years since the Criminal Law, as administered in other parts of British India, has been in force in our Provinces. We have a Judicial Commissioner doing the work of a High Court. We have in force in our Provinces all the Criminal Laws that are applicable to other parts of India. In almost every district we have Honorary Magistrates appointed from among the educated class, and there is no lack of educated gentlemen who can weigh the evidence of any criminal case heard by them and come to a correct finding. (*Hear, hear*). Several reforms have been introduced in the administration of our Provinces during the last 15 years, and the people there are not now what they were some years ago. We find a large number of educated gentlemen and graduates of various Universities in almost every district. We have Local Self-Government in our midst. The Municipal Acts are in force amongst us. The members of District Councils and Municipalities are acquitting themselves in such an excellent manner that questions of importance relating to the welfare of the country are very often referred to them for opinion. (*Hear, hear.*) And we the delegates of the Central Provinces are clearly of opinion that the time has come when the system of trial by Jury may be safely extended to many of our districts. (*Cheers.*) The principle involved in this system is simply this :—That an accused person should be tried by his countrymen, who know the customs, manners and the language of the accused. (*Hear, hear*). It cannot be urged by any body that there is a single district in our Provinces which cannot supply such men as can do justice to any criminal case that may be brought before them. (*Hear, hear*). We do not however at present wish that the Jury system be extended to all the districts in the Province, but we wish and pray that it be introduced at least in the districts of the head quarters of the four divisions of our Provinces, namely, Nagpore, Jabbalpore, Hoshangabad and Raipur. (*Hear, hear*).

You have heard this subject urged from the Congress platform again and again. For want of a jury system hundreds of innocent men are sharing the ignoble quarters of a prison house, and hundreds who should have been there are gentlemen at large. (*Loud cheers.*) In order to blot out the evil and to ensure the happiness of millions of our countrymen, the Government should, instead of turning a deaf ear to our representations, come forward, kindled with that fire of duty and with that love of justice that characterize every Englishman, to give us what we want and what we expect of them as our right. The fellow subjects of Windsor Castle will ever be bound together by the bonds of brotherhood ; the proud banner of St. George, St. Andrews and St. Patrick of the British flag will ever wave gloriously in the air, as long as the sun and the moon remain in the firmament. (*Cheers*). The common subjects of one Sovereign, the common children of one fatherland will happily march onwards beating the drum gaily for the glory of our Queen-Empress. (*Cheers*).

MR. S. B. BHATE, (*Belgaum, No.* 72 *in list*).—MR. PRESIDENT AND GENTLEMEN,—In coming to this platform my object is simply to state to you that the policy which has been advocated by the Bengal Government, seems to have found favor with the Government in our Presidency also. There were communications made to many Sessions Judges where the system prevails, and these Judges were asked to report upon the kind of work done by juries. The Sessions Judges have in a hole and corner way reported to the Government that the system is at fault, and that juries have been doing their duties in a way of which the less said the better. But these statements are based upon facts which are not at all capable of proof (*hear, hear,*) and are based upon a one sided view of the matter. Belgaum is one of those districts where

3rd Day.

Resolution VI. Demands the withdrawal of the Jury notification and the extension of the system of trial by Jury.

this system has been working for four or five years, and so far as the work of jurors is concerned, there have not been any flagrant instances of failures of justice. (*Hear, hear.*) Yet the Sessions Judges have ventured to report to Government without consulting the wishes of the people who are most intimately concerned with the matter, that the system has proved an unmitigated failure, and our Local Government seems anxious to follow this notification of Bengal by a similar one in three or four of our districts. (*Shame.*) Poona is one, Belgaum is another, and Surat the third. These three districts are being marked out for being deprived of the system of trial by jury. (*Shame.*) This is a matter against which a most emphatic protest must be entered in the most earnest and unmistakeable language by us all, and I hope our protest will not go in vain. With these few words I commend the resolution to your unanimous acceptance. (*Loud Cheers*).

The resolution was then put to the vote and carried unanimously.

Resolution VII. Claim for an equitable contribution by England towards Indian military expenditure abnormally increased owing principally to the Imperial policy of Great Britain.

Mr. D. E. Wacha, (*Bombay, No.* 39, *in list*).—Mr. President, Ladies and Gentlemen, The resolution I am about to propose to you is one which, I am sure, will not only commend itself to your approval but be carried by acclamation—such is the admitted justice of its demand and such the unanimity on the subject. It is as follows:—

*" That having regard to the fact that the abnormal increase in the annual military expenditnre of the Empire since* 1885-86 *is principally owing to the military activity going on beyond the natural lines of the defences of this country, in pursuance of the Imperial policy of Great Britain in its relation with some of the great Powers of Europe, this Congress is of opinion, that, in bare justice to India, an equitable portion of that expenditure should be borne by the British Treasury, and that the revenues of India should be proportionately relieved of that burden."*

You would no doubt, remember, gentlemen, that at previous Congresses, particularly at the one held last year at Nagpur, I expatiated at length on the enormous growth of the military expenditure since 1884-85. It has risen from 16 to 22 crores in seven years. But it is altogether needless for me on this occasion to tire your patience by referring to its particulars once more. You will, however, have understood from the drift of the resolution just read to you what is it that we now demand of the Home Government. It is acknowledged in all quarters, aye, even by those who are the unmitigated apologists of the " Forward policy" feverishly pursued by the Government of India, that the gross injustice of throwing on this country for years past, the *whole* burden of the military expenditure, a considerable portion of which should, in all fairness, be borne by the British Treasury, ought no longer to be tolerated, past endurance as it is, and entailing as it does oppressively heavy sacrifices on the already over-burdened tax-payers of the land. (*Hear, hear.*) That the demand for the reparation of such injustice should be heard, and loudly heard, in the hall of St. Stephen itself goes without saying. For it is an injustice against which the Indian Government has been protesting vigorously enough for the past fifteen years, but protesting in vain. (*Hear, hear.*) Responsible administrators at Calcutta and at Westminster have not only protested against the shameful injustice, but recorded their deliberate opinion as to the expediency of redressing it, considering that wealthy England partly defends herself at home at the expense of the revenues of impoverished India. (*Shame*). Apart from the long-standing scandal of the charges in connexion with the Home depôts to which I drew pointed attention at the sittings of the First Congress, and apart from other unjust charges, such as those of transport, arrears of pensions, and so forth—apart from these, the Imperial policy of Great Britain in its relations with Russia, and its attitude towards the whole question, known as the Eastern question, (*hear, hear*) have foisted on India the annual permanent charge of 2 crores on account of the 30,000 additional troops maintained since the acquisition of Upper Burmah and the Penjdeh incident. That this additional burden is altogether unjustifiable is well-known. So, too, all the cost of the so-called " Special defences". You would remember my referring to these last year and reading to you a few extracts from the minutes of two of the members of the Government of India on the subject, namely, those of the Hon'ble Mr. C. P. Ilbert and Sir Auckland Colvin. They courageously protested not only against the unfairness of the burden, but against the policy

3rd Day.

Resolution VII. Claim for an equitable contribution by England towards Indian military expenditure abnormally increased owing principally to the Imperial policy of Great Britain.

which led to that addition. I particularly read out to the Congress that part of the joint minute of those members of the Government in which it was observed that the addition of 30,000 troops to the then existing force, under the plea of safe-guarding the Empire against attack from without, was hollow, and that its veiled object was purely the kindling of the faggots of external aggression. That minute is so valuable an one and so remarkably prophetic every way, as subsequent events have demonstrated, that I could not do better than have it inserted as part of my speech for your benefit. And, with the permission of the President, I would place it on the table for the purpose. [*Vide* Appendix V.] Now, I say, that the warning of Mr. Ilbert and Sir Auckland Colvin was prophetic. This must be clear to you from the number of so-called punitive expeditions undertaken by the Government of India, under the mischievous advice of its military advisers (*hear, hear,*) since 1885-86—expeditions which have enabled them to acquire the Zhob valley and that portion of Baluchistan which is now known as British, and such strategical places as Gilgit, Chalt, Hunza and Nagyar, and the probability, later on, of the occupation of Chitral, not to say anything of the continued bullying and baiting attitude adopted towards the Ameer of Afghanistan (*hear, hear,*) with the fixed determination to have a bold "spring forward" on a fitting opportunity. All the places I have alluded to, have been almost forcibly acquired (*shame*) under the plea of checkmating Russia in her nearer advance to India and carrying on a filibustering policy beyond the Hindu Kush. As I informed you, it is the policy of keeping Russia away from the Bosphorus, which is the sole object of Russia's advance nearer the confines of India. But for this Imperial policy of Great Britain, of which Russia's onward march is the logical sequence, all the events that have occurred on the North-West Frontier would have been nowhere, and this incubus of a large standing army, gnawing away the finances of India and eating into the vitals of the tax-payers would have never been known. (*Hear, hear.*)

Members of the Standing Committees of the Congress at various centres would remember that in 1888, Mr. Martin Wood, an honoured gentleman and a veteran, though now retired, Anglo-Indian journalist, who has been fully in sympathy with the legitimate aspirations of the Congress, and who is unostentatiously doing great service to the cause of this country at home, had addressed a most thoughtful letter to the Congress on the subject of this disastrous "Forward policy." Owing, unfortunately, to some technicality it yet remains unrecorded in your proceedings. But most of you are perfectly cognisant of the facts and arguments with which that letter bristles. These have not yet lost their value. If at all, their relevancy is a great deal emphasised and their importance enhanced by the events which have transpired and are transpiring since the date of the inditement of the letter. It must be in your recollection that the cardinal point to which Mr. Wood referred in that correspondence was this forward policy of the Government which is the dominant factor of the chronic embarrassment of Indian finances. It is also the key to the whole material condition of the country. I passingly referred to that cardinal point in my speech last year, but as it bears the closest relation to the subject-matter of the resolution now before you, I deem it advisable to quote the passage at whole length, and afterwards place this letter on the table also, with the permission of the President, as part of this day's proceedings. [*Vide* Appendix VI.] Mr. Wood observed :—

"It is a maxim acknowleged by our statesmen that expenditure depends on policy. In this instance the grievous addition to the unproductive outlay from Indian revenues is wholly due to the revolutionary change entered on in 1876, followed by the disastrous invasion of Afghanistan in 1878-80, and now sought to be perpetuated by the establishment of permanent military posts far beyond the physical boundaries of India on the West, for the maintenance of which the immensely costly railways already referred to, have been constructed. You are well aware that the policy has been adopted, and forced on India under cover of partisan counsels among certain English politicians ; but this does not make it any more worthy of approval or lessen the need for its being checked, or, if possible, reversed." Thus it is *the policy* which is at the root of the expenditure, and all of you will agree with me in thinking that, next to seeing that expenditure controlled or its burden partially relieved by the British treasury, our constant aim should be to nag on at the

3rd Day.

Resolution VII.

Claim for an equitable contribution by England towards Indian military expenditure abnormally increased owing principally to the Imperial policy of Great Britain.

mischievous policy, with a view to its reversal. (*Applause.*) But meanwhile let me further point out to you the broad considerations which we are sometimes apt to overlook or postpone, as Mr. Wood justly observes, amidst the stress of other current topics. These considerations are :

(*a*) "The financial position of India dominates all its other material conditions.

(*b*) "The pressure caused by the absorption of your resources, consequent on the fatal error of thrusting military outposts beyond the natural boundaries of India, transcends in its cramping and distressing effects all other financial and fiscal mistakes put together.

(*c*) "That error, with its concomitant military extravagance, is one of executive policy, and no reform in administration nor in the local Legislative Councils will avail to obtain a reversal of that erroneous policy or security against repetitions of similar sacrifices of India's true interests.

(*d*) "By appealing in respect of the paramount financial peril of India, first, to Her Majesty's Secretary of State as the one directly responsible authority, and, next, to the High Court of Parliament, your Congress will effectually convince independent English politicians of the capacity of your people to understand and deal with those large questions of policy, on the right solution of which depends the present and future welfare of the masses of your people."

Gentlemen, I need not tell you how weighty are these considerations, and what is, therefore, the duty of the Congress in reference to them. I dare say you fully comprehend the drift of the extracts just read and clearly understand the position of Indian finance as dominated by the huge octopus of military expenditure. The Currency question becomes of secondary importance in comparison with it. For though you may remedy your Currency, the financial embarrassments arising from the burdensome military expenditure will continue to prevail until the policy which entails it is absolutely reversed. (*Hear, hear.*)

I am deeply of conviction, and, so too, I believe, you are, that were this policy to be reversed to-morrow, we would see an end to the "prolonged wail" of our Finance Ministers in succession touching the growing difficulty of bringing an equillibrium in the annual balance sheet of the empire. We would then at once see an end to the inspired statements put forth from time to time about the enhancement of old and the imposition of new taxation. (*Hear, hear.*) I am one of those who have long since felt that in the direct proportion that the Home obligations of all character are reduced, will India find greater stability in the ratio between silver and gold. As I stated to you last evening, that was the opinion of the Departmental Committee of experts in 1876. It is idle to say that many of our gold obligations, especially those in connection with guaranteed railways, could not be converted into silver. There are no insurmountable obstacles in the way of the needed conversion. So experienced a Finance Minister as Sir John Strachey was deliberately of opinion, as observed in his book of Indian Finance, that it was practical. It is the powerful vested and most selfish interests, coupled with the tenacious perversity of some of the men at the helm of affairs at Westminster, which are in the way of the solution. (*Hear, hear.*)

But this is somewhat of a digression from the subject proper. What I have to remind you about is this : that the military policy pursued since 1876 by the Government of India, notably since 1885-86, is the real difficulty of India, not the temporary evils arising from Currency. (*Hear, hear.*)

I observed at the outset that not only is the entire Native press but even the Anglo-Indian press in favour of the demand made in the resolution before you. The Government of India itself has, since 1879, more than once bitterly complained in its despatches of the unjust burden saddled on the Indian Treasury in reference to that portion of the military expenditure which in all conscience and equity should be borne by the British Treasury. For it is incurred in consequence of the policy pursued by England towards

**Resolution VII.**

**Claim for an equitable contribution by England towards Indian Military Expenditure abnormally increased owing principally to the Imperial policy of Grent Britain.**

Russia in Europe. Even apart from the charges arising out of that policy, there are others which have been seriously objected to from time to time as being unjust,—charges of a variety of character which I enumerated at length in my speech at the First Congress and in support of which I submitted extracts from State despatches and other official returns of the Government of India itself. I will not, therefore, detain you by again reiterating them on this occasion, because there is an absolute unanimity on the point. The only thing now essential is to formulate our demand as definitely as possible, based on such unanimity. In so doing, we really support the Government of India and strengthen its hands. (*Hear, hear.*)

But, gentlemen, I may further request you to remember that it is not only the Government here that has protested against the injustice of the burden of military expenditure being laid by a rich country like England on so poor a country like India. (*Shame.*) Members of the Council of India too have protested against it. When the entire cost of the unrighteous second Afghan war was at first attempted to be foisted on India, some of those members vigorously recorded their minutes against the scandalous injustice of the attempt. Some went into the broad question we are discussing to-day. These minutes, I believe, are so germane to the substance of the resolution before you that I would be wanting in my task if I did not acquaint you with them. They are all taken from the Blue Books on Afghanistan published by order of the House of Commons in 1879-80-81. The entire cost of the Second Afghan war was, as you are aware, 25 crores of Rupees. And it was after a memorable debate in the House of Commons that India was done paltry justice to by a contribution of 5 crores from the British Treasury at the rate of a crore per annum, though there was not an inconsiderable body of English opinion in favour of England bearing the whole cost.

This is what Sir Erskine Perry, one of the truest and staunchest friends of India in the India Council, whose loss we must for ever deplore, observed: " I deny absolutely that the interest of India demand a war. Lord Lytton has told us more than once that the Central Asian question *is not an Indian but a European question,* that it depends on the policy of the Cabinet. I bow to the reasoning the soundness of which I am not in a position to judge; but as our Indian politics are charged by Parliament with the protection of the revenues of India, I maintain that *it is unjust to throw any of the cost of an Imperial policy on the revenues of that extremely poor country.*" (*Hear, hear.*)

The late Sir Henry Durand, then Military Member of the Council and who was afterwards Lieutenant-Governor of the Punjab, minuted :—

" For the above reasons I should have been disposed to vote against the present charge on the revenues of India, but looking upon it only as an advance to the Imperial Government, feeling also that it is expedient that no time should be lost in providing for a necessity growing out of an actual war, and having been given the power under Section 23 of 21 and 22 Vict., Chapter 106, of recording my opinion, I have voted with my colleagues in the affirmative."

Sir Barrow Ellis recorded the following minute, and I ask you to listen to it most attentively as it has a great bearing on the general question. Sir Barrow Ellis, too, you may know, was a steadfast and true friend of this country and a just and most sympathetic Civilian, the type of whom is getting rare.

" It is not for me to justify the war, nor to seek to determine the causes that have led to it, except in so far as they bear on the question whether the charge ought to be borne by Indian revenues or by the Imperial Treasury. Had the war been undertaken on account of aggression by Shere Ali, or because the Afghans menaced the peace and security of India, then doubtless, at whatever cost, the charge would fairly have been debitable to India, but surely no one will allege these to be the causes of the war. It is not anything that Shere Ali has said or done that *per se* justifies the extreme step of declaring a war that must at least cost much money, and many valuable lives. *The war is clearly the outcome of events in Europe, and the necessity for it has arisen from the action of Russia, which action again was devised as a support to the schemes in Europe. It is thus in the interest of the Empire, and*

**3rd Day.**

**Resolution VII. Claim for an equitable contribution by England towards Indian Military Expenditure abnormally increased owing principally to the Imperial policy of Great Britain.**

*in furtherance of European policy*, *that the war has been brought about*, and it is in these considerations that its justification must be found. I trust, therefore, that it will be borne in mind *that the mere fact of the locale being on the Indian Frontier ought not to be made an excuse for placing a new burthen upon India.* In any case substantial aid will be freely given by India in the supply of war material, and in meeting the ordinary cost of a large portion of the troops engaged ; *the additional charges involved ought to be accepted by the British Nation, and this liability, I doubt not will be generally recognised. The people of India are unrepresented, and it is the more incumbent, therefore, that the British Nation should impose on India no charge of this kind that is not just and beyond challenge.* Taxation is already as heavy in India as it well can be, and the people will feel the more new taxes, which in any case would cause grave dissatisfaction, not to say discontent, when the imposition of such taxes is due to an *expenditure which ought in fairness to be borne by the Imperial Exchequer, and not by the already over-weighted Indian tax-payer.*" (*Hear, hear.*)

Gentlemen, I ask you to consider whether the weighty reasons stated in the minute of Sir Barrow Ellis do not still hold good ? Is it not time we should reiterate them at this juncture with all the strength legitimately at our command, especially, when the expenditure, which stood at 14 crores before the breaking out of the second Afghan war, now stands at 22 crores, and the burden of the additional cost is admitted on all sides to be intolerable ?

But let us pass from the testimony of the Members of the Council of India (there is other evidence which for want of time, I refrain from referring to in this place) to that of another and distinguished official, of purely English training, who occupied the post of Finance Minister during the ever-memorable Viceroyalty of the beloved Lord Ripon, (*Loud applause*), one who by his conspicuous financial ability and appreciation of the real material condition of India, gave the greatest satisfaction to all classes of Her Majesty's subjects here, I mean Sir Evelyn Baring, now Lord Cromer, (*Applause*) whom we should all gladly welcome as Viceroy (*Loud applause*) if, as is rumoured, he is to succeed Lord Lansdowne. Minuting on the question of military expenditure, Sir Evelyn Baring observed (*vide* Blue Books on Afghanistan, 1879-80-81) :—

" I do not think the financial condition of India is free from anxiety whose main source of revenue is derived from payments in silver, either fixed in perpetuity or only capable of increase at long intervals, while at the same time it owes a large sum annually in gold. *The Home charges have of late years been gradually increasing.* In 1881-82 they will amount to no less than 18 millions sterling. The charge is abnormally high, and moreover includes many remittances which are merely in the nature of banking transactions, *but when all reasonable deductions have been made, the amount which India must send home to meet her current wants is still very large.* Obviously under such conditions our essential element of State finance—stability—must be wanting."

Then, after referring to the precariousness of opium receipts and the necessity of keeping down the Salt duty as low as possible, and after reviewing other sources of revenue, Sir Evelyn further observed :—

" Lastly, the pressure of population upon the soil, which year by year increases in intensity, presents an economic difficulty of the first magnitude with which, indeed, I doubt the capability of Government to cope by any direct means, but which renders it imperative upon us to reduce in every possible way the pressure of taxation. *On these grounds I consider not only that it would be in the highest degree unwise to take any steps which could have for the result a large increase of a wholly unproductive nature, but I entertain a strong opinion that the reduction of present Military expenditure is of all others the financial question which most deserves the attention of the Government of India.*" (*Hear, hear.*)

Finance Minister after Finance Minister who succeeded Sir E. Baring has spoken in the same strain, so that I do not at all feel myself called upon to say aught more upon this subject after the authoritative opinions of all such experts and statesmen. I trust, therefore, that this resolution on which all India and even the Council of India are agreed, will be passed by acclamation. (*Loud applause.*)

3rd Day.

Resolution VII. Claim for an equitable contribution by England towards Indian Military Expenditure abnormally increased owing principally to the Imperial policy of Great Britain.

PANDIT MADAN MOHAN MALAVIYA, (*Allahabad, No.* 346 *in list,*)—GENTLEMEN—The resolution which is now before you is one of immense practical importance and deserves your heartest support. While the question of Exchange is troubling the minds of the Indian Government, we connot do better than to lay this resolution before them in the hope that it will receive that attention from the Government in India and in England which it so manifestly deserves. If the Home Charges were reduced, the recruit depôts for India needlessly mantained in England at the expense of the former while actually serving as part of the defensive service of the latter, and if the other charges on account of military expenditure to which Mr. Wacha has referred were brought under the full control of the Government of Indian, I feel Indian treasury will be surely relieved to a considerable extent. England is in all honour bound to contribute her fair share of which she at present is unjustly depriving this poor country. There are no two opinions on the justice of our demand. Mr. Wacha has sufficiently brought the salient points in connection with it under your consideration. I will not, therefore, detain you any longer beyond expressing the hope that the Government in England will give their very best attention to this subject and afford to the finances of India that relief to which she is so equitably entitled. (*Cheers.*)

The Resolution was then put to the vote and carried unanimously.

Resolution VIII. Deprecates diminution of grants for Higher Education and advocates increased expenditure on Education generally, and an inquiry into the industrial condition of the country with a view to promote Technical Education.

MR. BROJENDRANATH SEAL, (*Murshidabad, No.* 211, *in list*).—MR. PRESIDENT AND FELLOW DELEGATES,—Any display of personal modesty on my part, any rhetorical flourish of faltering diffidence, even if I were disposed to go through such graceful or graceless attitudinizing in obedience to custom, is effectually checked by the thought that I have been asked to review a policy which closely touches the vital interests of 220 millions of human beings in not more than a few brief minutes. A national system of education which moulds the minds and destinies of a seventh of the entire human race has something in it of the endless vista, something of the measureless tread of generations that we find in the awful mysteries and dispensations of Providence. A statesman with the creative gift, with the vision and the faculty divine, will find in the unrealised potencies of such a situation the *materia prima*, the unorganised matter, for educing a moral world peopled with the "fair humanities and intelligential essences" of the millenium. Something of the prophetic vision, an inspired sense of the glorious possibilities of an enlightened and puissant Federation of Nations in this dark Eastern Continent, filled the minds of the grea tpioneers of western education in India, among whom we find the illustrious names of Munro and Elphinstone, of Macaulay and Bentinck. (*Cheers*). Excuse me, Sir, if in the presence of this vast national gathering which is the faint beginning of the realisation of their hope and their prophecy, I linger for a moment in fond illusion as with a sense of present reality over the constellated glory of that noble band, before I turn to contemplate the shadows that are now stealthily creeping over the fair vision of India's future enlightenment which fired their imagination and inspired their efforts.

The present educational policy of the Government may be described under the four heads of University, Secondary, Primary and Special (or technical) education. As regards University education, in the words of Sir Raymond West, President of the Indian Section of the last Oriental Congress, "the policy of withdrawal from University education has been steadily pursued" in recent years. In Bengal three State Colleges have been already transferred to private or Municipal management, and "the retrogression has been marked in 1889-90 by reducing the staff of European Professors at the Hoogly College, and by placing the Krishnagar and Rajshaye Colleges under a European Principal of the Subordinate Educational Service assisted by graduates of the Calcutta University." The two last Colleges now exist on sufferance, and their fate would have been sealed ere long had it not been for the large public endowments that led to their foundation and in a manner pledged Government to their maintenance. "The reduction of Collegiate expenditure will appear from the fact that the cost of each student to Government has fallen by 20 per cent." In Bombay the State grant to the University of Rs. 15,000 a year has been threatened, and higher fees will have to be imposed upon the candidates. "In the Punjab, of six Colleges only one remained under Government in 1890-91." In Madras, where, as in Bengal, there are

**3rd Day.**

**Resolution VIII. Deprecates diminution of grants for Higher Education and advocates increased expenditure on Education generally, and an inquiry into the industrial condition of the country with a view to promote Technical Education.**

a number of aided and unaided Colleges, the same policy of withdrawal has been definitely kept in view. Shortly after the Viceroy's last visit, Dr. Duncan, the officiating Director of Public Instruction, Madras, declared that while the State would not abandon the cause of higher education, the people must themselves come forward to found or endow Colleges if they desired the extension of such education. This would be specially necessary as the State funds would be more and more applied to primary education, and as "the missionary societies that now maintain large colleges will in all probability withdraw from the field in India and employ their resources in Africa and other lands." This last remark of the learned Doctor applied to all the provinces of India, and the withdrawal of the missionaries from the field of secular instruction will only aggravate the difficulties of the situation which the retrogressive State policy is fast bringing on. (*Hear, hear*).

With regard to Secondary Education, the education imparted in our high schools, the same policy of withdrawal is everywhere manifest. (*Hear, hear*). The Lieutenant-Governor of Bengal has devised a definite scheme, beautiful in its simplicity and symmetry, for effecting this withdrawal, under which two Zillah Schools would be annually abolished where these exist alongside unaided institutions, and the education service would literally die out in course of time as vacancies would not then have to be filled up. (*Shame*). Indeed there is a probability of the education service being made non-pensionable, and this change will facilitate the abolition of the Government Colleges and Zillah Schools. Gentlemen, these proposals may appear to you very drastic, but you must remember that the evergrowing desire for high education in Bengal has been regarded in some circles as a disease which demands drastic remedies. (*Shame*). There are even desperate devices ingeniously adopted by those who control the State expenditure on Education. The Accountant-General is in the habit of deducting large sums as probable savings from the totals of sanctioned expenditure. In 1889-90 the deductions amounted to about 2 lacs, and in 1890-91, to about Rs. 1,70,000, or about one eleventh of the whole sanctioned expenditure. These large deductions are two-handed engines, they force on a reduction of educational expenditure, and they make a show, in the end, of State liberality, as the actual expenditure, to whatever extent reduced, cannot but exceed the curtailed estimate. "In 1889-90 grants-in-aid were refused to 413 Secondary Schools, and this was followed in 1890-91 by a decline of 2,000 in the number of pupils in these establishments. (*Shame, shame*). In Madras, in 1888-89, there were 147 Upper Secondary Schools of which only 4 remained which were directly supported and controlled by Government." The Municipalities are everywhere told that they must curtail their grants for secondary education, which must be left to take care of itself unsupported by state or local funds.

I now proceeed to consider the attitude of Government towards Primary Education. The partial abandonment of collegiate and secondary education has been professedly made in the name of primary education. Gentlemen, the extension of elementary instruction among the masses is a matter of the highest importance from the politico-administrative as well as the socio-economic point of view. (*Hear, hear*). In India specially, where the machinery and modes of administration, the laws and the polity are not of indigenous growth, and are based on the most enlightened economic, sanitary, juristic and political views, the diffusion of primary education among the masses is a permanent State necessity, if the people and the Government are to be in touch with each other. (*Cheers*). But, gentlemen, I am sorry to find that the Government is desirous here also to shift the burden on the shoulders of others, (*shame,*) I mean the Municipalities and Local Boards. In Bengal we do not hear any longer of the State being compelled to curtail its expenditure on higher education in the interests of primary education; the cry is now different. It is that it is the Municipalities and the District Boards that must provide for the elementary instruction of the masses. The matter has an interesting history. When the reduction of State expenditure on high education was decided upon, the Director of Public Instruction recommended an addition of 10 lacs a year to the primary education funds, and was confident that this would place the State system of elementary instruction on a satisfactory basis. The Government held out hopes of such an expansion, but the 10 lacs exist only in imagination, and there is a talk of the imposition of a local cess. (*Shame*). The matter has now assumed a new

Resolution VIII. Deprecates diminution of grants for Higher Education and advocates increased expenditure on Education generally, and an inquiry into the industrial condition of the country with a view to promote Technical Education.

aspect. In the recent resolution of the Bengal Government on the working of Municipalities outside Calcutta, the Lieutenant-Governor notes that only 29 per cent. of the boys of school-going age receive primary education, and expresses his opinion that less than 50 per cent. cannot be considered satisfactory in the case of Municipal towns. Taking the population in Municipal towns according to the returns of the last Census, and counting the cost at 10 as. per head, the Lieutenant-Governor finds that 3.2 per cent. of the total Municipal income (outside Calcutta) will suffice for the end in view. Expenditure on secondary education does not come in Sir Charles Elliott's view within the legitimate scope of Municipal bodies, at any rate not until the claims of primary education and other paramount interests are fully met. Sir Charles Elliott holds the same views with regard to the responsibilities of District Boards for primary education. In his resolution reviewing the reports on the working of District Boards in Bengal, the Lieutenant-Governor notes that the general average expenditure on education is only 20.5 per cent. on the ordinary income of the Boards, and trusts that the report for next year will show a more liberal expenditure on this object. The state of things in Bombay with regard to primary instruction is best seen from the following extract :—"In the Bombay Presidency where perhaps public education has been the most earnestly pushed forward, one sixteenth of the land-tax is handed over to the Local Boards, and they are required to spend one-third of the amount on elementary education. *(Hear, hear)*. The primary schools are treated as a first charge on the public revenue, whether local or provincial, and secondary schools have in some cases been even suppressed."

Now as regards special (including scientific and technical) training, with the exception of the Faculties of Law, Medicine and Engineering, very little provision is made for imparting Collegiate or secondary instruction of the special or technical kind outside the Bombay Presidency. There is however a general desire on the part of Local Governments that the science courses for the degree examinations should attract more students than the literary course. "In Madras, in 1887-88, there was a transfer of about 30 per cent of candidates from languages to the various optional subjects." In Bengal, the fact that a greater percentage of candidates are plucked year after year at the Philosophy and History examinations than at the science examinations might *prima facie* be expected to make the science course more attractive than the literary one, but the Director reports in 1890-91 that there has been a steady decline in late years in the number of students taking up science in aided and unaided institutions. In 1890-91 the proportion of B. Course to A. Course condidates was in Government Colleges 1 to 2½, in aided Colleges 1 to 18, and in unaided Colleges 1 to 6. The Government however have adopted another method in their commendable zeal for the encouragement of science studies, and have begun to abuse the A. Course men as inferior or third class men. In Sir Charles Elliott's opinion what the country wants most is a diversity of pursuits for its educated youth and not an adherence to the beaten path of literary careers. Personally Sir Charles Elliott has in many ways shown his earnestness in the cause of higher scientific education in this country, and his recent institution of medals for scientific research by a generous donation proves him a friend to scientific education, just as he is a friend to primary education, provided both can be extended and advanced without additional responsibilities being thrown upon Government. Sir Charles Elliott rejoices to see that there is a perceptible movement in all parts of his province in favour of the establishment of industrial schools. We do not hear a word however of the Polytechniques or Technological institutes, or even of the agricultural, commercial and industrial schools of the secondary grade, which among the Continental nations have borne such splendid fruit in equipping them for the struggle for existence all over the globe, and which England is now fast developing for the sake of her own most cherished and vital interests. *(Hear, hear)*. This is a curious trait, gentlemen, of the educational policy of Government all over India. The anxiety and the alarm caused in high places by the overgrowth of literary education, the diversion of the energies and the intellect of the country to practical and technical subjects, and the disinclination to take real scientific or technical training in hand by establishing a net work of industrial, commercial or agricultural schools, are

**3rd Day.**

**Resolution VIII. Deprecates diminution of grants for Higher Education and advocates increased expenditure on Education generally, and an inquiry into the industrial condition of the country with a view to promote Technical Education.**

characteristic symptoms of the Government attitude and policy. (*Hear, hear*). Two good results are however already visible : the standard of University examinations or of admission to them is being materially raised, and this is as it should be ; and in Bombay, Madras and the Punjab practical or non-literary examinations have been instituted by the Government which are not intended to lead up to the University. These examinations are worse than useless in the absence of special schools of the secondary grade. Still these ends are so high and paramount in themselves that every sound educationist would welcome the reduction in the number of University students that may be due to the operation of such causes; but whatever diminution there has been in Madras (and the diminution has been already in course of a year) or may be in Calcutta or Bombay from the raising of the examination fees must be held on all sides to be a source of the most profound regret. (*Cheers*). It is also a matter of painful surprise that in view of the fact that the science course is taught little, if at all, in the aided and unaided Colleges, the Government should not, with all its zeal for the diffusion of scientific knowledge, see the necessity of staying or checking its policy of withdrawal from the State Colleges, which are acknowledged on all hands to be the only properly equipped agencies for the diffusion of such knowledge. (*Cheers*). In England they have a Government Science and Art department for which the Parliament annually votes more than five-hundred thousand pounds sterling. (*Hear, hear*). I should state, however, that in Bombay a large impetus was given to scientific instructions under Lord Reay,—(*cheers*),—and that the expenditure in 1890-91 rose from Rs. 89,000 to Rs. 1,23,000 contributed by Government. The Victoria Jubilee Institute is doing most excellent work in this regard. While higher institutions either of the collegiate or of the secondary grade are, therefore, with the above exceptions, not thought to be within the scope of the State responsibilities in the matter of education, the Government are favorably disposed towards the establishment of lower schools of handicraft and mechanical industry under District Boards and Municipalities.

The recent educational policy may be briefly sketched thus :—Higher education of the University as well as the secondary grade tabooed as regards State or Municipal aid ; the attempted diversion of a large class of students from the academic or literary to practical or professional studies other than law, in the interests of the industrial development of the country, if not also with an ulterior political motive, combined with the non-provision of polytechniques or technological institutes, or even of commercial, industrial or agricultural schools of the secondary grade, to impart that very sound scientific and technical training which the Government is so very anxious to see diffused and extended in the material and economic interests of the country. (*Shame, shame.*) An anxious and watchfnl regard for the intellectual improvement of the masses, combined with a strange apathy to that higher education, which, in the language of Mountstuart Elphinstone, is the light that must touch the mountain tops before it can pierce to the levels and the depths. (*Hear, hear.*) And finally the non-expansion of the State system of elementary education for the masses, not because of the indifference of the people, but because the Government will not undertake the cost of extension, but would fain saddle the Municipal and Local Boards with it ; in one word, the practical denial of the responsibilities of the Government for any sort or degree of education whatever, in contravention of the theory and practice of all civilised states. (*Shame, shame*). This is the position to which we are reduced to-day in India !

Indeed, when in the shadow of the great modern ideas that are stalking abroad, the States of Mysore and Baroda are developing national systems of education ;—when, in the great struggle that has begun among the races of mankind, immobile China has begun to move, and besides adding Mathematics to the Chinese classics for the Civil Service examinations, has opened a great State College of Foreign knowledge, the *Tweng wen-Kwan*, where the English, French, German and Russian languages, the physical, the physico-mathematical and the natural history sciences (including such abstruse sciences as physical astronomy and meteorology) are taught by European and American Professors;—when Japan has provided for a population of 40 millions a full-fledged national system of education after the Prussian pattern, providing a Minister of education and the machinery of State Universities and compulsory instruction, so much so that Tokio can boast of a psychological laboratory such as Cambridge lacks, and a Professor of Psychology who has brought out a great work on this most modern of subjects; when the great post-mediæval European Renaissance is likely to usher in the greater Renaissance of the world;—we in India are confronted to our dismay, our discomfiture, our shame, by this unique spectacle of a civilised Government with the noblest traditions, practically renouncing some of the gravest responsibilities and functions of all civilised Governments, and reversing its own just and enlightened policy of a hundred years, built up and codified by the statesmen who have bequeathed this priceless legacy of an Empire! (*Mournful applause*).

**3rd Day.**

**Resolution VIII. Deprecates diminution of grants for Higher Education and advocates increased expenditure on Education generally, and an inquiry into the industrial condition of the country with a view to promote Technical Education.**

Before I proceed to show how the present policy is a reversal and a violation of our great Educational Charter, allow me, gentlemen, in passing, to notice, with the contempt they deserve, some glaring sophisms which we often meet with now-a-days in a certain class of writings and speeches.

It is often said that high education is a gratuitous state gift to our middle and upper classes,—that students here pay less than they have to do in European Colleges and Universities, and that an eleemosynary high education is a source of danger to the state.

Gentlemen, in reply let me read the evidence of Mr. Wordsworth, late Principal, Elphinstone College, Bombay, and Dr. Duncan, Officiating Director of Public Instruction, Madras, given before the Education Commission of 1882. Here is what Dr. Duncan says:—

"Compare these classes (the classes from which the students of the Madras Presidency College are drawn) and the fees they pay with the classes whose sons attended the Scotch Universities and the fees charged them. A Scotch Arts Student usually pays six or nine guineas a year, according as he attends the lectures of two or three Professors, whereas the Madras student pays Rs. 60, and the Calcutta student Rs. 144, a year. I protest against the practice of singling out the people of this country from those of all other countries in the civilised world as a people who receive an eleemosynary education at the hands of the State. I have compared India with Scotland. If we compare it with Germany it will be still more apparent that India is not so exceptionally dealt with as is commonly supposed. Mr. Lethbridge has recently shewn that the tuition-fees in some of our Government Colleges are high as compared with those of Oxford and Cambridge." (*Hear, hear.*)

Principal Wordsworth's evidence runs thus:—"The fees paid for attendance or lectures at the Elphinstone College amount to Rs. 60 a term. I have a nephew who is a student of the University of Bonn. He is attending 18 lectures weekly this term, and he writes to me that his fees amount to 70 marks for the term, which one may estimate at Rs. 35. Most of the lectures he attends are gratuitous. The fees he is now paying are for lectures in law and Italian literature which are really extras. I fancy that the son of a small official or merchant in Germany enjoys the advantages of academic education at a much cheaper rate than the Hindu or Parsi in Bombay does, and has also, I must regretfully admit, a much superior article for his money. But it is not considered in Germany an injury to the rest of the community or a religious injustice that a superior education should be available at the public cost to the middle classes on whom the stability and improvement of every modern State depend." (*Cheers*).

Another standing ground of alarm is the supposition that the Universities in India are turning out a disproportionately large number of educated young men who find no outlet for their energies and cultivated talents, and in their disappointed ambition sow broadcast the seeds of discontent over the country. A few facts and figures would be here apposite. In England, in 1891, the number of College students, exclusive of evening students and extension classes, was about 22,000 out of a population of 27 millions, or a male population of about 13 millions;—in India, the number was about 15,000 out of a total population of 220 millions, or a male population of about 110 millions. (*Hear, hear*). Look at the matter from another point of view. In British India 21 per cent. of the boys of school-going age attend school; in England 7.2 per cent. of the males were illiterate in 1890, giving certainly more than 93 per cent. of the boys at school; and since the Parliamentary grant of

**3rd Day.**

**Resolution VIII. Deprecates diminution of grants for Higher Education and advocates increased expenditure on Education generally, and an inquiry into the industrial condition of the country with a view to promote Technical Education.**

ten shillings per head to managers of elementary schools, we might put the figure still higher. Now the youths receiving secondary education, in the words of Sir Raymond West, amount after all to only five per cent. of the whole number recorded as under instruction in India, and the students in Colleges amount to no more than one per cent. In England the proportion is twice as great, in a German State four or five times as great,—of youths under secondary education. In a German town, from a third to a half of the children are in the High Schools." Now as the total number under instruction relatively to the male population is five times as great in England and Germany as in India, the proportion of youths receiving secondary instruction relatively to the male population is seen to be ten times as great in England, and twenty or twenty-five times as great in Germany, as in our country. (*Hear, hear*).

The State grants for education in India are threatened with curtailment on the ground that India cannot afford to spend so much on education. Gentlemen, India spends just one per cent. of her revenue on education. No other civilised Government in the world shows a low proportion like this. (*Hear, hear*). In 1889-90 the total expenditure on public education in India was Rx. 2,765,869 of which Rx. 488,403 came from local rates and cesses, Rx. 129,464 from municipal funds, Rx. 581,623 from subscriptions, endowments, &c., and Rx. 767,289 from provincial revenues. We find on the other hand that the annual grants to primary schools alone amounted in the United Kingdom in 1890 to £5,161,471, and the Parliamentary vote for the Government Science and Art department was £530,986. (*Hear, hear.*)

I shall now show, gentlemen, how the present policy is a reversal and a violation of our great Educational Charter, I mean the Court of Directors' Despatch of 1854 with the Revised Code of 1859. Before I describe the provisions of the Charter I shall have briefly to sketch the history of educational policy and organization under the British administration. It was on the occasion of the grant of the Company's Charter in 1813 that a clause was inserted providing that a sum of one lakh of rupees was to be set apart from the surplus revenues and applied to the revival and improvement of literature and the encouragement of the learned natives of India, and for the introduction and promotion of a knowledge of the sciences among the inhabitants of British India." (*Hear, hear*). But for nine years the grant remained a grant on paper. From the evidence of Sir Charles Trevelyan, Mr. W. W. Bird and Mr. C. H. Cameron before a Select Committee of the House of Lords in 1852-53, we learn that the lakh of rupees was not drawn from 1813 to 1821. A Committee of Instruction was appointed in 1823, and "worked on the old lines devoting their energies to the promotion of oriental learning among the literary classes of Mahomedans and Hindus." Munro's minute on indigenous education and Elphinstone's on the encouragement of oriental learning advocating the continuance of the Dakshini grants of the Peshwas, are too well-known to need any but a passing mention. Macaulay's "zeal for useful, practical and scientific knowlege" brought on Lord William Bentinck's Resolution of March, 1835, which "decided in favor of English education to the entire neglect alike of oriental and vernacular instruction." From that time until we come to the Despatch of 1854, the control and supervision of education remained in the hands of bodies variously named Councils of Education, Educational Boards, University or Collegiate Boards in the various provinces. "It was after the reversal of the East India Company's Charter in 1853," I am quoting from a blue-book, "that the Educational Despatch of the Directors, dated 19th July, 1854, came out to India." The object of this great document was large and national. "It marked out the spheres of usefulness of all classes of institutions, Oriental, English and Vernacular, then working in the country, and it cared for the educational interests of the entire community." (*Hear, hear*). The really comprehensive character of the Code is seen in the summary given of it in the 3rd paragraph of the Revised Code of 1859.

The improvement and far wider extension of education, both English and Vernacular, having been the general objects of the Despatch of 1854, the means prescribed for the accomplishment of those objects were (1) the constitution of a separate department of the administration for the work of education; (2) the institution of Universities at the

**Resolution VIII. Deprecates diminution of grants for Higher Education and advocates increased expenditure on Education generally, and an inquiry into the industrial condition of the country with a view to promote Technical Education.**

several Presidency towns; (3) the establishment of training institutions for raising up teachers for the various classes of schools; (4) the maintenance of the existing Government colleges and schools of a higher order, and the increase of their number when necessary; (5) the establishment of additional Zillah or Middle Schools; (6) increased attention to vernacular schools for elementary education, including the indigenous schools already existing throughout the country, and finally, (7) the introduction of a system of grants-in-aid under which the efforts of private individuals and of local communities would be stimulated and encouraged by pecuniary grants from Government, in consideration of a good secular education being afforded in the aided schools." The Blue-Book from which I quote, here adds:—"The objects of this Despatch were thus not one but many, not the limitation of State expenditure and efforts to elementary instruction, but the extension and improvement of education of every class." *(Hear, hear and cheers.)*

Gentlemen, I do not pretend that the Directors' Despatch, any more than the Magna Charta of the English people, is perfect. It laid down a policy that was capable of development. It was in some respects in advance of the English system that then obtained, and in other respects retrograde. It enunciates the responsibilities of the State for all the grades and kinds of education, and hence the State system that has been built upon it has included within its scope Universities, high schools, primary schools as well as technical institutions. In this respect it was an advance on the English system of the day, in other respects it was retrograde. It introduced the grant-in-aid system including in its scope higher education as well as lower and middle, to which last alone it was confined in England. No doubt the grant-in-aid system was intended by the Directors as an "auxiliary to the direct measures of our Government for the extension and improvement of general education." But altogether too much emphasis was placed on the future possibilities of the grant-in-aid system and on its applicability to all grades of education.

As a matter of fact the grant-in-aid system has only a limited applicability. It is totally unsuited to the institutions for the highest University education, whose watchword is centralisation, massive and august, the pomp and circumstance of knowledge enthroned, working through "the interwoven affinities of historic association and human imagination and sentiment," as embodied in venerable foundations and endowments, whether State-managed or State-chartered. The grant-in-aid system is also unsuited to the elementary education of the masses. I am personally of opinion that the Continental system which finds in local rates and cesses the resources for working the machinery of a national system of compulsory education, is the one to which we must ultimately tend in India, but in its earlier stages elementary instruction must not only be managed and supervised but also be maintained by the State, until the Municipalities and Local Boards become fit through the prior fulfilment of their primary responsibilities to undertake the work of popular education. (*Cheers*). The grant-in-aid system is suited and suited very well to secondary education. Under secondary education I include all institutions intermediate between the primary schools and the University Colleges. I have no hesitation in including also under secondary education all Colleges that teach up to the standard of the F. A. or Previous Examinations of the Indian Universities. Here also there are two qualifying principles—(1) superior institutions of the secondary grade must be maintained to serve as a model for the aided institutions; these institutions would answer to the Lyceum and the Gymnasium of the Cotinent; (2) in backward communities and districts the full responsibility for secondary education must be retained by the State. These are the qualifications required to be borne in mind in interpreting the grant-in-aid system of the Despatch of 1854. As a matter of fact the inapplicability of the grant-in-aid system to elementary instruction was soon seen by the Directors and was corrected in the Code of 1859, which ordered that the means of such instruction should be provided by the direct instrumentality of Government Officers" and that the means for the diffusion of such education should be found by the levy of educational rates, if expedient. (*See Paragraphs* 50,51 *and* 52).

**3rd Day.**

**Resolution VIII. Deprecates diminution of grants for Higher Education and advocates increased expenditure on Education generally, and an inquiry into the industrial condition of the country with a view to promote Technical Education.**

The inapplicability of the grant-in-aid system to the University Colleges of higher standing (I do not include the second grade Colleges) has been established above by the most cogent considerations, but this is a point which remains to be embodied in our educational Code. The full and undivided responsibility of Government for the maintenance of an adequate number of such centralised bodies must be provided for by legislation. We want a fresh revision of the Code of 1854 to enforce action in favour of University education such as the revision of 1859 did in favour of elementary education.

But, gentlemen, whatever the defects of the Despatch of 1854, it never denied the responsibility of Government for undertaking any grade or kind of education, high or low. It sets out with the declaration that the education of the Indian people is to be undertaken as "a sacred duty" as a means of "conferring upon the natives of India those vast moral and material blessings which flow from the general diffusion of useful knowledge," (*hear hear,*) and if it introduced grants-in-aid they were intended to be not the sole or sufficient machinery but only an auxiliary one. But what shall we say of the present policy which denies not merely sole responsibility as regards University and secondary education, but would not even go so far as the grant-in-aid system, of a policy, which, not content with withdrawing from higher education, would paralyse it by placing it under the ban, as regards municipal and local aid, in the name of the education of the masses! (*Shame*). The Despatch of 1854, gentlemen, speaks not of the entire withdrawal of Government, but of partial withdrawal by the introduction of grants-in-aid when expedient. Again, the Despatch of 1854 does not stand in the way of municipal aid or aid of local bodies to secondary or higher schools. Indeed para 62 speaks of the future possible transfer of many of the existing institutions to the management of local bodies under the control of and *aided by the State*, and it has been subsequently held that municipalities and local boards come under the definition of local bodies. Neither does the Despatch of 1859 in providing that the funds for the extension of elementary instruction may be drawn from local cesses if expedient, forbid the employment of the funds of bodies like municipalities and local boards on secondary education. Gentlemen, this question of the duties and responsibilities of Government under the Codes of 1854 and 1859, in the matter of making an adequate provision for all grades and kinds of education came up before the Education Commission of 1882-84. Here are the recommendations of the Bengal Provincial Committee.

" We cannot close this report without adding to the recommendations therein put forward an expression of our deliberate opinion that, independently of any efforts which the people may hereafter make for the promotion of education in various directions, increased assistance on the part of Government is necessary, if education in Bengal is to progress at a rate corresponding to the advancing requirements of the country. For the spread and improvement of primary education, for a due increase in the machinery of inspection, for an enhanced provision of scholarships to enable boys to advance to higher stages of instruction, for a far wider spread of University Education, for a more liberal scale of grants-in-aid and for the promotion of education among girls,—for all these objects, more liberal assignments are urgently demanded, if the requirements of the time are to be met, and if a comparison with European standards is to be justified. The amount of any further grants that may be made by Government for the promotion of these objects depends, of course, upon financial and political considerations with which we have no concern; we have merely to express our opinion as to the need that seems to us to exist for an increased allotment. We have no means of knowing accurately what proportion of the State revenue is devoted to education of different classes in European countries and in America; but we have grounds for believing that the educational allotments in these countries are framed on a far more liberal scale than in Bengal. (*Hear, hear*). And we cannot refrain from expressing an earnest hope that means may be found either from Provincial revenues or from additional Imperial assignments, for meeting in a more adequate manner the necessities of this Province." (*Cheers*).

After this wise and weighty expression of opinion, I shall not need to make any further observation on this aspect of the question. With regard to the Commission on technical education prayed for in the resolution I have to move, I have already, gentlemen, explained my views on the question. Briefly put, special or technical education is of three grades, corresponding to the three grades of general education: (1) primary grade, comprising schools of handicraft and mechanical industry introduced by a course of elementary general instruction; (2) secondary grade, comprising among others agricultural, industrial and commercial schools, and led up to by a course of secondary general education; and (3) University or facultative grade, comprising the Faculties of Law, Medicine, Engineering, Technology, and Agricultural Chemistry, &c., and working through colleges, academies, polytechniques or technological institutes and other institutions. The subject is of vast importance, and the best organization of a system of technical instruction suited to the economic needs of India can only be settled by the labours of a Commission of experts. (*Hear, hear*). The urgency of such a Commission cannot be gainsaid. Remember, gentlemen, that in India about 87 per cent. of the population depend for subsistence upon agricultural labour and the produce of the soil, only 13 per cent. being given to industrial and manufacturing pursuits; and that as established by statistical economy, the greater the percentage of agricultural labourers in any old and populous community, the deeper the poverty. (*Hear, hear.*) Remember also the fact of the growing sterility of the soil in India, where throughout vast tracts, from 300 to 500 souls on the average live on the produce direct and indirect of a square mile, including both cultivated and uncultivated areas; and that the only way of staving off sterility and starvation is to relieve the pressure on the soil by means of the industrial and commercial development of the country. (*Cheers.*)

**3rd Day.**

**Resolution VIII. Deprecates diminution of grants for Higher Education and advocates increased expenditure on Education generally, and an inquiry into the industrial condition of the country with a view to promote Technical Education.**

With these words I beg to move the resolution entrusted to me, which runs thus:—

*That this Congress is of opinion, that it is highly inexpedient in the present state of Education in the country, that Government grants for High Education should in any way be withdrawn, and, concurring with previous Congresses, affirms in the most emphatic manner, the importance of increasing the public expenditure on all branches of Education, and the expediency, in view to the promotion of one of the most essential of these branches, i. e., the technical, of appointing a mixed Commission to enquire into the present industrial condition of the country.* (*Cheers.*)

Babu Heramba Chundra Maitra, (*Calcutta, No.* 179, *in list*).—Mr. President, Ladies and Gentlemen,—It was said by an eminent Englishman that in order that a cause might prosper, it must be opposed by the *Times*. Similarly, I think it might almost be said that in order that a political principle may be proved to be sound, it must be violated by the Government of India and upheld by the National Congress. (*Hear, hear*). At the time when the dispute between England and America on the question of taxation was at its height, it was said by Edmund Burke, the greatest of political philosophers, that the American people felt the pulse of their freedom in this: if in the matter of taxation they were free, they considered themselves free; if in that they enjoyed no freedom, then they thought themselves bondsmen. In judging of the enlightenment of a Government, we must feel its pulse in its educational policy. (*Hear, hear*). If there it is going right, then its heart is sound; if there it is going wrong, there is disease and rottenness in the heart. (*Hear, hear.*) Applying this test to the proceedings and policy of the Government of India in the matter of Education, we see from indisputable facts and figures that, however liberal the Government may be in its professions, in its actions it is utterly illiberal. I will here refer to certain figures which I have noted down. In the year 1890, while the total expenditure of the Government of India came up to 82½ crores, its expenditure on education came up only to 76 lakhs or $\frac{11}{12}$ per cent.—not even one per cent. of the whole, and in the same year the military expenditure was 20½ crores, or 25 per cent. of the whole. (*Shame, shame*). Now let us go back to the year 1885. In that year, while the total expenditure was 71 crores 36 lakhs, the expenditure on education was only 79 lakhs or 1⅛ per cent. of the total. But what is the state of things in England? The Government profess to rule us according to English ideas and principles, but I undertake to show that they withhold English principles and sentiments from us when they like, and apply them when they are grievously burden-

**3rd Day.**

**Resolution VIII. Deprecates diminution of grants for Higher Education and advocates increased expenditure on Education generally, and an inquiry into the industrial condition of the country with a view to promote Technical Education.**

some and oppressive to us. (*Hear, hear*). When they talk of the excise revenue, they say—"Oh! the incidence of the taxation in England is much greater than in India, and you ought to be satisfied,"—forgetting that we are a sober people, and that an ounce of liquor in this country means infinitely more shame and wickedness than a gallon in England. But in education they do not compare the state of things here with that in England. We find that in 1891, in the United Kingdom, out of a total expenditure of 89½ millions sterling, 6¼ millions was devoted to education, that is to say, in their own country they spend 7 per cent. of the whole on education. But when they come to our country, they spend not more than 1 per cent. of the revenues in the diffusion of knowledge. (*Shame, shame*). I have already referred to the figures of 1885 and 1890. In the revised estimate of 1891, and in the Budget of 1892 also they give us 1 per cent. of the total expenditure for education. So that in this respect, we are indeed living in paradise, for the fruit of the tree of knowledge is forbidden fruit to us. (*Hear, hear.*) Why is it that in the matter of education the Government of India adopts a policy so different from the course followed in England? Does truth become untruth, justice become injustice when it comes to this country? In this age of Congress and Conferences, I would suggest a Conference of scientists and psychologists sitting together to discuss whether the eternal verities, abstract notions, the moral principles which are our birthrights as the children of a most righteous God,—whether even these undergo climatic variations.

With regard to the relation between primary and high education, I will not waste your time by trying to prove that, though the Government says it is necessary to reduce the expenditure on high education in order to promote primary education, there is really no hostility between the two, but primary education must advance in proportion as high education is advanced. (*Cheers.*)

I must draw your attention to the proportion of military expenditure to the expenditure on education in this country. The former comes up to 25 per cent. and the latter to only 1 per cent. of the total expenditure. In 1891, we find from the revised estimate for that year, out of a total of 82½ crores, 21 crores 41 lakhs were spent on the maintenance of the army and on defensive military works. In the Budget for 1892, out of a total of 85 crores, 21 crores 84 lakhs or nearly 22 crores are allotted to military expenditure. In the face of these facts, what becomes of the glorious prophecy of Victor Hugo, that the pen will kill the sword, and intellectual controversies will banish sword and bloodshed from the earth? As far as we are concerned, we see that the sword is killing the pen, and that military barbarism is going to extinguish culture and refinement. (*Loud cheers*). There never was a bridal day more glorious in its dawn and more vernal in its melodies, than that which witnesses the marriage of the human mind with knowledge,—the marriage of man, made after the image of God, with light, the eldest child of God according to the Hebrew legend. Woe unto the Government which effects a divorce between them, and woe unto the people that silently acquiesces in such a divorce! (*Cheers.*) With these words, I commend the resolution to you, appealing to you to see that its spirit is followed. (*Loud cheers.*)

MR. K. V. JOSHI, (*Nagpur, No.* 145, *in list*).—MR. PRESIDENT, LADIES AND GENTLEMEN,—I rise to support this Resolution. We wish to know why high education is so much at a discount with the Government of India. It is a surprise to us that the Government of India should be acting as they have been acting in the matter of high education. Is it right for the Government of India to say that they shall not allow us to enjoy the blessings of high education? That is the question. Gentlemen, because we are poor, Government should not withdraw its aid from high education but should increase it. (*Cheers*). What progress can you expect of a people who are only half educated? I submit that the claims of high education should not be sacrificed to those of primary education, any more than the manager of a mill should be sacrificed to the claims of the mill hands. The manager must be there before the great engines can be worked properly. (*Hear, hear*). Therefore I submit that the claims of high education should never be subordinated to those of primary education.

There is another point to which I desire to call attention, and that is that only a few years ago, Government expressed its opinion that education should be so regulated as to fit the educated for the pursuit of commercial and industrial undertakings. We ask the Government to carry out that policy, but that cannot be well done without the appointment of a Commission to enquire into the industries and trades of the country. Hence we ask for the appointment of such a Commission. The rebellion of the belly is worse than all other rebellions; and therefore we beseech the Government not to curtail the expenditure upon education, but to increase it, and thereby to fit the people better to earn their living. (*Cheers*).

There is one thing more. We must show the Government how this can be done. Where are the funds to come from? With regard to that, I need only say that where there is a will there is a way. (*Hear, hear and cheers*).

[The President's gong having been here sounded, the speaker, in obedience thereto, stopped speaking.]

BABU HARI PRASAD CHATTERJEE, (*Krishnagore, No.* 196, *in list*).—GENTLEMEN,—I rise to support this resolution, and I support it most heartily on behalf of the community I represent. (*Cheers*).

The Resolution was then put to the vote and carried unanimously.

**3rd Day.**

**Resolution VIII. Deprecates diminution of grants for Higher Education and advocates increased expenditure on Education generally, and an inquiry into the industrial condition of the country with a view to promote Technical Education.**

BABU BAIKUNTH NATH SEN, (*Moorshidabad, No.* 210, *in list*).—MR. PRESIDENT AND GENTLEMEN,—The resolution which I have to propose runs as follows :—

**Resolution IX. Grievous distress amongst the people of India. Urgent necessity for a reduction of the cost of administration, an extension of the system of Permanent Settlement, and the establishment of Agricultural Banks.**

*That this Congress emphatically re-affirms Resolution III of the Congress of* 1891, *and having regard to the fact that fully fifty millions of the population, a number yearly increasing, are dragging out a miserable existence on the verge of starvation, and that in every decade several millions actually perish by starvation, deems it imperatively necessary that the cost of administration, especially in the military branch of the Public Service, should be greatly reduced, and that measures should at once be taken to give, as was promised by the British Government over thirty years ago, fixity and permanence to the land revenue demand, and thus permit capital and labour to combine to develop the agriculture of the country, which, under the existing system of temporary settlements, in recent times often lasting for short periods, in some cases only extending to ten and twelve years—is found to be impossible; and to establish Agricultural Banks. And this Congress, again, most earnestly entreats the people of Great Britain and Ireland, not to permit any further sacrifice of life owing to the shortcomings of the existing, doubtless well-intentioned, but none the less unsatisfactory, administration, but to insist, and that speedily, on the reforms, then and now, so earnestly advocated.*

With a new face, but with a face little powdered, you must have noticed that the main question involved in this proposition is the question of the fixity and permanence of the Government demand upon land. Now in the fifth Congress I had occasion to move, and in the sixth Congress to second a resolution on this very subject, and what I had to say on it, I have already said. I need not take up your time now, because time is very valuable at the present moment, and repeating those arguments will be only wasting time. This much only shall I say, that in referring to the millions of deaths from starvation, we appeal most earnestly to the humanity of our rulers, and entreat them to adopt measures which will prevent these deaths, or at any rate reduce their number. (*Cheers*). We suggest that the Government should reduce the burden of taxation. We also suggest that a certain fund should be set apart to establish banks for the benefit of the agricultural classes, and that fixity and permanence should be given to the land revenue demand in places where it is not so fixed; and we appeal to the people of Great Britain and Ireland not to allow the existing sad state of things to go on any longer, but to insist upon the reforms we advocate being speedily carried out. And I hope that our appeal will not go in vain. (*Cheers.*) With these remarks I place the resolution confidently before you for your acceptance. (*Cheers.*)

**3rd Day**

**Resolution IX.**
**Grievous distress amongst the people of India. Urgent necessity for a reduction of the cost of administration, an extension of the system of Permanent Settlement, and the establishment of Agricultural Banks.**

Mr. Peter Paul Pillay,—(*Madras, No. 9, in list,*)—Mr. President and Gentlemen—In seconding the resolution that has been just read to you I have to make this observation that the agricultural classes of the country, at least as far as the Madras Presidency is concerned, are in great poverty and wretchedness. Those that are well acquainted with their condition will not deny the truth. But certain people would not believe that so much poverty and semi-starvation prevails among the agricultural population. I shall therefore lay before you certain figures which will incontrovertibly prove that the ryot population in the Madras Presidency are deeply sunk in indebtedness, poverty and wretchedness. (*Hear, hear.*) The figures are taken from the Administration Reports of the Department presided over by a gentleman who lately wrote a flattering memorandum to establish that the ryot is materially prospering since forty years.

According to last year's rent roll, the number of ryots, single puttadars, and joint puttadars, is 32,50,000. For these ryots the total number of sales and mortgages of immovable property for the past 10 years, from 1882-1883 to 1891-1892, is 44,95,432. The average for 10 years is thus about 4,50,000. (*Hear, hear.*) Besides the ryots in Government villages, there are ryots or tenants in zamindari and proprietary villages which cover one fifth of the area of the whole Presidency. Immoveable property includes house property the transfer of which by sale or mortgage forms a very small percentage of the proportion of sales and mortgages. Taking all these into consideration, the number of sales and mortgages of immovable property will form not less than 10 per cent. of the number of ryots on an average during the last 10 years. (*Hear, hear.*) The number of sales and mortgages is steadily increasing by leaps and bounds. In the year 1882-1883 there were 3,14,948 sales and mortgages; but in 1891-1892 there were no less than 6,08,907 sales and mortgages. (*Hear, hear.*) Confining myself to the Tinnevelly district to which I belong, and which contains 2,68,000 ryots, I find that there were no less than 74,087 sales and mortgages last year. Considering all circumstances, the number of mortgages and sales is about 25 per cent. of the number of ryots. (*Hear, hear*) During the last year there were no less than 39,83,067 notices of demand. Notices of distraint or attachment numbered 1,82,940, and the number of defaulters was 1,61,871. The figures of sales and mortgages and the coercive measures adopted for recovering land revenue, clearly show that the people are driven to the hardship of selling and mortgaging their immovable property. (*Hear, hear*).

There are several causes that contribute to the growing poverty of the agricultural population. The conditions and circumstances under which the operations of agriculture have to be carried on are growing hard. Even the different influences that work the social revolution resulting in the disturbance of the labor market of the country, are highly injurious to the agricultural prosperity of the land. The excellent resolution of the Poona Industrial Conference that caste should be protected as an industrial institution correctly represents the state of things. By various influences that work at the destruction of the fabric of Indian society labour is disturbed, and the country is losing valuable hardy and skilled labourers whose loss cannot easily be supplied under the present circumstances of Indian society. (*Hear, hear.*) From this cause alone, let alone others for the moment, I fear that Indian agriculture is fast sinking like that of Spain. In addition to this the ryots' difficulty is increasing owing to the rigorous working of the Forest Laws, which are obstructive and injurious to the very materials necessary for agriculture. (*Hear, hear.*) I spoke about this last year.

The rigour of the Government in collecting revenue is also increasing. Twenty or thirty years ago the Collectors of revenue had the patience to wait for the close of the *Fasli* year before they resorted to coercive measures, as the land for which the tax might be due is the best security for the arrears. But since the passing of Act II of 1864, the rigour has increased. Whether the ryot is prepared at the time or not, the collection is cleared for every instalment of the *kistbunds*. If the instalment be not paid within three days after demand, the ryots' property is attached and sold, and the ryot is obliged to sell and mortgage his property, movable or immovable, in order to meet the demand. (*Cries

3rd Day.

Resolution IX.
Grievous distress amongst the people of India.
Urgent necessity for a reduction of the cost of administration, an extension of the system of Permanent Settlement, and the establishment of Agricultural Banks.

*of 'shame.'*) It is a virtue on the part of the Government to observe strict punctuality in the demand of the land revenue. But it is a misfortune to the ryot to be unable to equally exercise the virtue of punctuality in responding to the demand. (*Hear, hear*). I know of instances where even wealthy and respectable land-holders, being unprepared at the nick of time, were unnecessarily subjected to coercive measures by distraint and attachment by low-paid *ameens*. (*Shame.*) A little courtesy in such cases will spare a lot of unnecessary pain of mind and mortification without causing the loss of a single pie to the State. (*Hear, hear.*)

However, as I have said, there is increasing hardship in the growing demand of the land revenue. All the direct and indirect taxation which the ryot has to pay is a direct charge upon the income derived from his land. (*Hear, hear*). The land revenue is increasing as a general rule by periodical settlements. The village and local cesses too are direct enhancements of the land revenue by 12½ per cent. (*Hear, hear*). There is nothing practically to check the settlement officer in enhancing the revenue upon land arbitrarily. This keeps the ryot population in great distress and uneasiness, which prevent the agricultural classes from improving their lands. (*Hear, hear.*) When the land has undergone improvement at great cost and labor, towards which the State has contributed nothing, it is an unreasonable and cruel hardship to saddle the enterprise of a diligent ryot with increased assessment. (*Cheers*). But when high or enhanced assessment is fixed for lands that have not been improved, but have, on the contrary, deteriorated, it becomes a gross absurdity and monstrous injustice. (*Cheers.*) Yet such an absurd and unjust procedure is a very common incident in these periodical settlements. (*Shame.*) The decisions of the Settlement Officer are pracitically final and unappealable. Such being the case, the system is naturally productive of corruption among the Subordinate Officers of Settlement departments, who are entrusted with enormous but practically irresponsible power. (*Hear, hear.*) The Settlement departments are absolutely independent of District Revenue Officers whose local knowledge is not taken into account.

One necessary incident to lands that are not permanently settled is that they are subject to a remission of taxes in bad seasons, which may be due to either insufficiency of rain water or to its excess. Only on extraordinary occasions is any remission given for dry lands, but remissions are given ordinarily for wet lands. When the crops fail remission of taxes for failure of crops is nothing but just. Before 1860 the actually cultivated area only was taxed and the uncultivated portion was untaxed, whether the want of cultivation was owing to the negligence of the ryot or not. The ryot consulted his convenience to cultivate a portion or the whole of his puttah lands. There was no pressure put on the ryot this way, and by allowing a portion of his land to lie fallow, the land was not exhausted and the cattle had some grazing over such lands. (*Hear, hear*). But since 1860 all lands are indiscriminately assessed whether cultivated or not. When a plot of land lies uncultivated the burden of proof to show that the want of cultivation was not owing to the neglect of the ryot lies with him. This is very difficult to prove. As a matter of course all uncultivated puttah lands are taxed in ordinary seasons. Then certain rules regarding the granting of remissions are open to serious objection. According to the Madras Revenue Board standing orders, remission is to be given, when an entire Revenue field is left waste, and when the crops on the entire area have totally failed, and not in portions only of the fields, provided that the excess or deficiency of water has not been occasioned by any neglect of the persons to whom the land belongs, or is not due to the neglect on the part of the ryots concerned to carry out the customary repairs to the irrigation work which forms the source of supply. If any supply of water is received during the year, though the lands may have been irrigated entirely by well water, the full compounded rate will be charged for double crop lands and single wet rate for single crop lands. When no supply of water is received the dry rate is leviable. For remission and for water supply, every thing depends upon the *ex parte*, irresponsible, and generally untrustworthy village accountants. Prohibitory assessments are levied often arbitrarily and upon *ex parte* representations. When nature is unkind to the

**3rd Day.**

**Resolution IX. Grievous distress amongst the people of India. Urgent necessity for a reduction of the cost of administration, an extension of the system of Permanent Settlement, and the establishment of Agricultural Banks.**

ryot, it is only humane and just that the ryots should be exempted from taxation for lands that could not possibly be cultivated in bad seasons and yield large revenue in good seasons. (*Hear, hear*). So many excuses or pretexts are invented to refuse remission. On my way here I heard of an extraordinary instance of the whole District of Sholapore being granted a remission of the magnificent sum of Rs. 23 only last year, when there was a serious drought there, (*shame, shame*), and when the Government found it necessary to open relief works at a large cost for the relief of the sufferers. There is no reason whatever for the rigorous recovery of local cesses on lands, as roads are for the benefit of all classes and particularly for the benefit of trade, which must be taxed always to make up the deficiency during seasons of drought.

Whether in the proposed reform for the permanent settlement of the land revenue there would be room for remission I cannot say, but one thing is certain that small landholders will feel it a great hardship if there be no remission during bad seasons, as they cannot be expected to store the superfluity of the years of plenty for years of scarcity and famine while they are paying land revenue uniformly for good seasons and bad seasons. (*Hear, hear*). The land revenue administration as far as it affects the ryotwari landholders, is conducted in such a way as to be productive of great indebtedness, poverty and ruin, leading to increase of ruinous litigation, the inevitable consequence of abnormal transfers of immoveable property, and to crimes, to which the poor people would resort when fair means of living fail, and to great dissatisfaction throughout the land. (*Hear, hear.*)

With these remarks I would second the resolution praying for reforms in the Land Revenue administration which are so urgently needed. (*Cheers.*)

MR. HARI MAHADEO PUNDIT, (*Nagpore, No. 144, in list*).—MR. PRESIDENT AND GENTLEMEN,—I come to support this resolution which deals with the important subject of a permanent settlement, but as time is very short and the importance of the subject is patent to all, I shall not take up more than three minutes in supporting the resolution. The question is a simple one. A layman can understand it; the agriculturists understand it, and not only do they uuderstand it but they feel the hardships of the present system bitterly to their cost. (*Hear, hear*). And it will be wasting your time and my energies if I were to attempt to enlighten you by entering into a detailed history of the subject. I have only to say one word on behalf of the Central Provinces which are being crushed by the effects of temporary settlements. (*Hear, hear.*) The duration of the settlements has come down there from 30 years to 20 years, from 20 years to 15 years, and from 15 years to 12 years, and God only knows whether it will not come down to 3 years, and perhaps to a few months; though representations have been made on behalf of the dumb millions, those Provinces being inhabited mainly by the aboriginal tribes, yet the Government has turned a deaf ear to those representations. (*Shame, shame.*). And, gentlemen, while on this resolution, I may be allowed to express my regret that at the Nagpore Congress, owing perhaps to the modesty of the delegates of the Provinces, this subject was not given that prominence which it deserved but was placed in what is called the 'Omnibus' Resolution. Gentlemen, the Chief Commissioner of the Central Provinces observed that as the subject was placed in an omnibus Resolution, the Congress did not consider it to be of great importance. But as the subject has now been given a prominent place, I hope the Chief Commissioner will recognise that the Congress considers the subject to be of first rate importance, and I hope he will endeavour to secure to us the boon that we pray for. (*Cheers.*) I have only to add that I thank you heartily on behalf of the people of the Central Provinces for emphasising the necessity and importance of this reform. (*Cheers*).

MR DAJI ABAJI KHARE, (*Bombay, No. 40, in list*).—MR. PRESIDENT AND GENTLEMEN,—I have much pleasure in supporting the resolution. I am here to speak in reference to the Bombay Land Administration. It has been often asserted by different Revenue authorities that the Bombay Land revenue administration is the best of its kind in India. But you will see that the enhancements which have of late been laid upon land on our side

**Resolution IX. Grievous distress amongst the people of India. Urgent necessity for a reduction of the cost of administration, an extension of the system of Permanent settlement, and the establishment of Agricultural Banks.**

have in a great many parts of that Presidency amounted to a confiscation of private property. (*Hear, hear*). In the Rutnagiri district, there is a class of landholders not in the good books of the Government, and the Government tried to remove them from their lands; but having failed to do so they resorted to putting such heavy assessments on their holdings that these holders must be out of pocket to the amount of about 1,000 per annum. (*Shame, shame*). In another part of the same Presidency, the Government has adopted 33 per cent. as the standard of increase which might safely be put upon land assessments, and no one knows how this percentage has been arrived at. But what we do know is that this 33 per cent. is not always stuck to. And it is notorious that in fixing this standard they have not taken into calculation the increased cost of cultivation. Where certain revenue officers were questioned the reply they gave was that no inquiries had been yet entered upon and that the increased cost of cultivation was a thing which need not be taken into consideration. (*Shame.*)

The Bombay system has done mischief in another respect. Though the Government profess not to tax improvements made by the people in their own lands, in every enhancement we find that indirectly improvements and other things are included in the assessment. All these circumstances have effected more injury in Bombay than they have done in any other part of India, and we on our side would be very glad to get the benefit of this proposition if the Government be pleased to adopt it. (*Cheers*). It has been said that if the Government gave up its power of increasing assessments, they will lose their revenue. But as has been suggested, it the Government were now to take twenty years' assessment, and secure the people against any assessment for the future, the money which would now come in would be sufficient to compensate the Government against any loss of the kind that is apprehended. With these observations I support the resolution. (*Cheers.*)

Munshi Sadar-ud-din Ahmad,—(*Allahabad, No.* 430, *in list*).—Supported the resolution in Urdu. He said :—Mr. President and Gentlemen,—It is extremely appropriate to pass a resolution praying for a permanent settlement of the land revenue at a meeting of the Congress at Allahabad, because Allahabad is a district, where owing to the excessive assessment of land made by a *merciful* officer,—whose secred name I dare not utter without performing my ablutions, but for whom I pray God, he may be protected from Captain Hearsey's attacks,—(*laughter*)—many villages have been ruined or have passed into the hands of the money-lenders. Well, gentlemen, this is not the first time that we are considering this question of a permanent settlement of the Land Revenue. At two previous sessions of the Congress, the question has been very fully discussed, and it has been shown by the most cogent of arguments that the well-being of the people, on which depends the prosperity of the Government, (*hear, hear,*) demands that the system of a Permanent Settlement should be extended to those parts of the country where it is not at present in force. The Government itself has long laid it down that whenever in any *Mahal* (parish) eighty per cent. of the whole culturable area has been brought under cultivation, the land revenue of that *mahal* should be settled permanently. In support of this view of mine, I would refer you to the despatches No. 14, dated July 9th, 1862, and No. 11, dated the 24th March, 1865, from the Secretary of State for India to the Governor-General of India in Council ; to the Rules of settlement, prepared by a member of the Viceregal Council and published under date January 22nd, 1865, to Circular No. 24, dated 27th November, 1867, and Circular No. 10, dated 26th July, 1865, of the Board of Revenue of these Provinces, issued in compliance with the orders of the Government of India, dated 19th June, 1865, and the despatch of the Secretary of State, No. 11, of 24th March, 1865. Many more official authorities might be cited in support of the same view. And it is a matter of surprise and regret to us, that notwithstanding these explicit declarations of the opinion of Government regarding the desirability of a Permanent Settlement of the Land Revenue, wherever eighty per cent. of the whole culturable area has been brought under cultivation, the system of permanent settlement is not yet extended to those places which fulfill the above condition. (*Cheers.*) I can find no plausible reason for this, except it may be that an insignificant part of some of the *Mahals* (parishes) remains still uncultivated. If that be the only reason, I do not hesitate to say that it is clearly unjust not to settle the land revenue permanently of places which virtually fulfill

**3rd Day.**

**Resolution IX.**

**Grievous distress amongst the people of India. Urgent necessity for a reduction of the cost of administration, an extension of the system of Permanent settlement, and the establishment of Agricultural Banks.**

the above requirements. Really, if this is the only reason for withholding the benefits of a permanent settlement from the people, the officers of Government seem to me to be acting as wisely as would a dentist who would refuse to affix a new set of teeth until all the old ones have dropped out. *(Hear, hear)*. Of what benefit would a permanent settlement be to the people when the land has been thoroughly deteriorated under the mischievous influences of temporary settlements. (*Cheers.*) The increasing poverty of the agricultural population, which is in no small measure due to this system of temporary settlements, under which the assessments of the revenue are being always increased, should induce the Government to extend the system of Permanent Settlement without any further unnecessary delay. (*Cheers*).

[The speaker closed his speech with a few pathetic verses composed by him in memory of the late Hon'ble Pandit Ajoodhia Nath in Urdu, but he has not supplied us with a copy or an English translation of them, and hence they are not published here.]

MR. BISHAN NARAYAN DAR, (*Lucknow, No. 532 in list,*)—MR. PRESIDENT, LADIES AND GENTLEMEN,—I have much pleasure in supporting the resolution which has just now been proposed. The resolution is composed of two parts. The first part emphasises the question of the poverty of India, and the second part suggests certain remedies for that poverty. Now in regard to this part of the resolution which deals with military expenditure, much has been said in former years, and a good deal has been said on the subjeet to-day also by Mr. Wacha. But I think that before we talk of the remedies, we have to contend with the assertion made by the Government organs that India is not a poor country and therefore needs no remedies. This is not a bare assertion. I will draw your attention to a very important State paper, and by referring to that you will see that the Government in its wisdom has come to the conclusion that whatever we do or do not in regard to this poverty question, we are all wrong ; that India has improved in trade, in manufactures and in the condition of the masses. At least we are told by Sir John Strachey that the present Government of India does not take half as much land revenue from the people as was taken by former rulers. I say that before we go to the remedies for the evil, it is necessary to combat the assertions of those who support the Government view that India is not poor. (*Hear, hear*).

India is an agricultural country, and in order to judge of the prosperity of India, it is of the utmost importance to see what the material condition of the agricultural classes is. I hold in my hand a report of some official enquiries which were held in the year 1888 by the Government of India into the material condition of the masses. The Report is a report issued by the Local Government upon the enquiry to which I have alluded. It will be observed that in all matters of the utmost vital importance to the well being of this country Government carries on things secretly, under the cover of darkness and without the light of public opinion. (*Shame*). This is the way of the Government. Wherever there is any important matter, anything regarding the condition of society or the public, Government manages it secretly and privately. The very results of the inquiry are kept concealed and hermetically sealed. (*Shame*). This Report while discussing the question of the poverty of the agricultural classes and of the masses, generally divides them into four classes. First, the agriculturists having a right of occupancy in the land and holding over five acres. Eight agriculturists of this class were examined by Mr. Cadell, seven of whom were found to have been living for some months upon only one meal a day. The second refers to agriculturists, who having the right of occupancy were holding less than five acres. In regard to them the Report says that the majority of them go on for months and years on one meal a day only; and the Report adds, with great satisfaction, that the people do not mind it. (*Cries of "shame"*). The third class were agricultural laborers. Now in regard to them the Report is almost unanimous in saying that the condition of these labourers is far from being what it should be and that a considerable majority of them live for months and months upon one meal a day. Now when these starved and emaciated people came before these Magistrates and Collectors, when they saw them, they described them as "thin but happy"—(*shame, shame*)—"thin but decent-looking and humorous." (*Laughter.*) Thus the Report is not lacking in humour. I think the time has long past in India when the story of Nero fiddling when Rome was burning should be repeated. (*Hear, hear.*) Here you have English officials who have all the sympathies and affections of men, writing in this way! The man's thinness means that he was pining away, and it has no humourous side about it. I think it was Mr. Irwin who himself got so much disgusted with this official cynicism that he said that being thin and happy was a paradox to him. Unless thinness was the result of some medicines or low diet, it would be a paradox to me also to believe that men looking like these were also happy. In regard to the fourth class, the outside artisan class, it is said that upon the whole they do not suffer from insufficiency of food. These are results stated after an inquiry instituted by the Local Government under the orders of the Government of India; and they bear out the melancholy dictum of Sir W. W. Hunter that forty millions of the people are constantly living upon the verge of starvation.

**3rd Day**

**Resolution IX. Grievous distress amongst the people of India. Urgent necessity for a reduction of the cost of administration, an extension of the system of Permanent settlement, and the establishment of Agricultural Banks.**

I must submit to you the opinions of one or two officials. Mr. Harrington, Commissioner of the capital of the N. W. Provinces and Oudh, admits the woful poverty of the people, and in regard to the question whether it is true or not that a considerable portion of the population of India suffer from an insufficiency of food, he says :—

"The assertion that the greater proportion of the population of India suffer from a daily insufficiency of food is perfectly true as regards a varying but always considerable proportion of the population, for a considerable part of the year in the greater part of India." (*Hear, hear.*) Mr. Irwin, another high authority on the subject and not altogether free from the bias of official optimisn, says in his "*Garden of India.*" "The greal evil of rural Oudh is, as has been already observed, the insufficiency of the produce of the soil to maintain the population in comfort, after defraying their rent and the cost of cultivation. While this is so, of what use is it for Government to devote its energy and its resources to any thing but direct action on the sources of the evil. While the millions suffer from chronic hunger, it would be as easy to make a pyramid stand upon its apex as to regenerate them by ornamental legislation or by anything but putting them beyond the ceaseless pressure of physical want." (*Hear, hear.*)

Now in the face of these opinions the Local Government says in its Report that there is no such habitual insufficiency of food in the case of the majority, or any considerable section of the population. (*Cries of "shame."*) This is the conclusion to which they have come! The Government of India endorses the statement, the Secretary of State probably says ditto, and the Blue book is left to moulder upon the shelf. (*Shame, shame.*)

This is the question before you. Whatever remedy is proposed, whether a reduction of military expenditure or something else, unless you succeed in convincing the English people of the serious character of the problem pressing upon us, unless you succeed in impressing upon them the necessity of finding some satisfactory solution of it, all your resolutions are in vain. This is a resolution which may well be called the people's resolution. (*Cheers*).

The resolution was then put to the vote and carried unanimously.

**Resolution X. Necessity for mitigating the harshness of the practical administration of the Forest Laws.**

Mr. R. P. Karandikar,—(*Satara, No.* 69, *in list*).—Mr. President and Gentlemen,—Having considered all the above questions, I think it is but right and proper that your attention should be directed to the question of the laws relating to the Conservation of Forests. The Resolution which I have the honor to move is this :—

*That this Congress entirely adopts Resolution XI of the Congress of* 1891, *and reiterates its prayer, that having regard to the very serious discontent created, particularly in Peninsular India, by the practical administration of the Forest Laws, the Government of India do investigate this matter carefully, and endeavour to mitigate the harshness of such administration, and render it less obnoxious to the poorer classes.*

In speaking on this subject, I feel the force of the voice of the eight thousand people who have sent me here, (*hear, hear*), urging me to press this subject on the attention of the Congress. Meetings were held, one at Belgaum, where about 6000 persons attended, and the other at Dahe where 3000 people were present, where the desire was expressed that this question should once more receive the attention of the Congress. (*Hear, hear*). This circumstance alone will show you the gravity of the question and the necessity for this resolution.

**3rd Day.**

**Resolution X.**

**Necessity for mitigating the harshness of the practical administration of the Forest Laws.**

On this occasion the people have been specially fortunate in having for their spokesmen the body of the Government itself. This year, in considering the reports submitted by the Forest Officers, the Government passed a resolution containing some strictures on the administration of forests by the Officers of the Department, taking them to task and calling upon them to obey the orders which had been issued by the Government really and without cavil. (*Hear, hear*). That is the wording of the last paragraph of the Resolution submitted by the Bombay Government. Here are spokesmen of the grievances suffered by the people whom the people never expected at all. With this admission of the discontent created by the Forest Administration, I think I shall not be justified in going over the same ground. We did ask the Government of India on the last occasion to investigate this matter carefully and to endeavour to mitigate the hardships which are experienced by the people by the improper administration of the Forest laws. And it is a matter of the purest gratification that unasked the Government of Bombay has taken upon itself the gracious task of enquiring into the grievances of these people. (*Cheers.*) If I were to quote to you certain facts which I have gathered from the recent Administration Report of 1891-92, they would go distinctly to prove the necessity of such an investigation by higher authority. *When this Resolution was passed by the Bombay Government, the Officers of the Depart*ment were not satisfied with it as it was a very bitter pill for them to swallow, and it was taken up by the Press on behalf of the Officers concerned. While this was the attitude of the Bombay Government their Resolution was sent to the Government of India, who in their gracious appreciation of the circumstances of the country were satisfied that what the Bombay Government had placed before them was true and they stigmatised the conduct of the officers charged with the administration of the Forest laws, and at the same time expressed their regret that the matter was not investigated earlier. (*Cheers.*) Therefore in our Resolution we entirely adopt the Resolution of the Congress of 1891, and reiterate our prayer for investigation into these matters. If the grievances of the people had been removed, there would have been no necessity for further enquiry; but those grievances still exist, and therefore we call upon the Government of India to enquire into the matter. I have arranged these grievances under several heads. The first of those grievances is that during the year 1891-92, the number of cattle killed by snakes rose from 1095 to 1187, and the number killed by wild animals and snakes together amounted to 2,820. Having regard to the fact that the habitations of these poor people are begirt on all sides by Forests, it is the duty of the Government to keep the inhabitants of the Forests within their own bounds also. Then what as the number of the cattle impounded?—3,39,296 as against 3,31,491. When I remarked on the last occasion that the Government itself was sometimes helpless against its own officers, I did not think I should have to refer again to the same fact; but the Government was alive to the fact and saw that its officers were growing rather independent. And another fact is that there is a decline in the number of cattle throughout the Presidency except Sindh. The decline has taken place chiefly in Sholapore and Sattara, and the want of fodder is undoubtedly responsible for that decline. In this state of circumstances one would have expected that the Government would have allowed the Forests to be opened, just as we have heard of the Nizam's Government opening its closed Forests to cattle. (*Hear, hear.*) I will give you figures to show how the revenue is rising gradually, and especially in Sattara. In 1873 the revenue was Rs. 11,871; in 1880 it rose to something like Rs. 45,000. These are facts, and I have a number more, which will prove the necessity of strengthening the hands of a benevolent Government and the fallacy of condemning the Government for the acts of its officers. We feel the oppression not on account of the acts of the Government but of its officers. We pray the Government of India to enquire into the matter, and we also congratulate the Bombay Government in having in a straightforward manner taken their officers to task. (*Cheers.*) We hope next year to come out successfully in regard to this matter, and I hope to give you a better account next year if you are pleased to accept this Resolution. (*Cheers.*)

MR. P. KESHAVA PILLAI (*Gooty, No.* 37, *in list*)--MR. PRESIDENT LADIES AND GENTLEMEN.—We are fully alive to the advantages of preserving forests from indiscriminate denudation, but the hardships and harassments the Act and the rules cause to the ryots and the poor may be avoided by some modification of the Act as well as the Rules. (*Hear, hear.*)

**3rd Day.**

**Resolution X. Necessity for mitigating the harshness of the practical administration of the Forest Laws.**

The Officers of the Special Department vie with each other in enhancing taxes on various forest produces but also in adding one after another under the taxable forest produces, thus abolishing gradually almost all the communal rights of the villagers.

Contrary to all the principles of law, that under the Forest Act if a head-load, or hand-load of firewood or other wood, were seized in any place, no matter where, it may be in the midst of a town far away from the precincts of a forest, reserved or unreserved, the presumption is that until the contrary is proved by the defendant, the seized property is forest produce. This provision in the Act has been a source of much oppression and hardship to the people, at the hand of Forest Subordinates.

The High Court of Madras so long ago as 1885 observed in their report on the administration of Criminal Justice in the Presidency as follows:—

"These facts (the increase in offences under the Abkari, Forest, Police and Salt Acts and the decrease in the number of offences under the Hackney Carriages Act and the Municipal Acts) indicate that while sanitary rules have either been less rigorously enforced or less frequently infringed, increased activity has been exhibited in the working of those special Acts—Abkari, Forest and Salt—where care is most necessary, that injudicious zeal should not be permitted to lead to prosecutions which cannot be supported or to harass the people unnecessarily." (*Hear hear.*) So all the excesses committed by the Forest officers are attributed to zeal.

Even His Excellency the Governor of Madras seems to be actuated by zeal in this respect. While His Excellency was touring through the Cudappah District, it would appear he came across a man taking a handful or a little more of *Sunkesa* leaves from a tree, if I may so call it, for the purpose of using it as medicine; and His Excellency was pleased to order that that man should be prosecuted under the Act. (*Shame, shame.*) The man was tried and punished to pay a fine of a few Rupees for mischief. I can quote worse instances if there were time for doing it.

Well, as it is we cannot expect the Departmental officers to be more lenient or generous in the treatment of all such so-called offences when the Governor himself is of such a frame of mind. (*Hear, hear.*)

But I think that it ought to be acknowledged with thankfulness that the Government of Madras was pleased during the last year to withdraw the restriction placed on loose stones, mud, sand, &c. in unreserved forests, if we can call them forests at all. This was done on a reference made by the Honorable Mr. Grose of the Board of Revenue, whose attention was drawn to the subject by the *Hindu* of Madras. The Government was generous enough to acknowledge that the grievances complained of in the *Hindu* were not imaginary, said that certain Collectors misunderstood its intentions, ordered the immediate withdrawal of the orders of the Collectors, and directed the Board of Revenue to frame a new set of rules in consonance with the wishes of the Government. We hope it will be liberal and just enough to justify our expectations raised by the resolution. (*Cheers.*)

The Government and the Board admit in the said resolution that the Revenue Inspectors, village officers and such other people are not to be trusted, and that they would feather their own nests instead of benefiting the Government if powers were invested in them to collect seigniorage in all such articles.

Knowing this as they do, why do they not exempt the necessaries of life for the ryot and the cattle, the green wood for agricultural implements, thatching grass, vegetable manure, and grass from the control of such petty officers and redress a grievous wrong, the poor ryot and the poor man are suffering from in silence and misery? (*Cheers.*)

The policy of reserving *Parumboke* lands near villages when they exceed 100 acres, and in some places even 50, is a great injury done to the cattle. The absurdity of it is that in many so-called reserved forests even shrubs do not grow. It is all then harassment and trouble to the ryot, and the starvation and deterioration of the cattle. There remains very little pasture ground unrestricted for the cattle of the ryot population. The ryots are obliged to exhaust their dry fodder such as straw, cholum, stalk, &c., in feeding

3rd Day.

Resolution X.
Necessity for mitigating the harshness of the practical administration of the Forest Laws.

them even in good seasons, and thus it becomes difficult for them to maintain them in the times of scarcity. Of course he cannot shoot down all the cattle, other than the ploughing cattle, as generously suggested by a Forest Officer ?

The prevention of people from collecting even dried wood in the forests reserved and unreserved, without a pass, gives scope to the forest subordinates to cause annoyance and suffering to the poor, and especially the honor of poor women, who resort to these places for collecting firewood, is not at all times safe at the hands of the ruffianly and low paid class of guards and Tanadars. (*Hear, hear.*)

Even the Departmental Officers were obliged to say in their Report of 1884-85 in this wise—"Forest guards and Tanadars have been strictly warned against interfering with villagers found collecting brushwood, &c., for firewood from unreserved areas."

Further, the prohibition to remove fuel from the forests compels the ryots to make use of such useful manure as cowdung as fuel, and this coupled with the difficulty experienced in getting vegetable manure, tends to impoverish the land. The policy of reserving even cultivated and cultivable land by making forced settlements with the ryots, restricts the area of cultivation which is a danger in the face of growing poverty and increasing population. (*Cheers.*)

The Resolution was then put to the vote and carried unanimously.

Resolution XI.
Appointment of a committee to prepare a petition to Parliament regarding the results of the Public Service Commission.

MR. A. NUNDY (*Agra No.* 497, *in list*).—MR. PRESIDENT LADIES AND GENTLEMEN,—The resolution which I have to propose runs as follows :—

*That Mr. W. C. Bonnerjee, Mr. P. M. Mehta, Mr. Surendra Nath Banerjee, and Rai Bahadur Anunda Charlu, be appointed a Committee to prepare a petition on the lines indicated by the petition printed at foot, and that the President be authorised to sign it, on behalf of this Congress, and send it to Mr. Dadabhai Naoroji, M. P., for presentation to the House of Commons.*

*To*

*The Hon'ble The Commons of Great Britain and Ireland, in Parliament assembled.*

*The humble petition of the President and Members of the Eighth Indian National Congress, held at Allahabad, on the 28th, 29th and 30th of December, 1892,*
*Respectfully Showeth,*

(1). *That in conformity with a resolution adopted at the Eighth Indian National Congress, your humble petitioners beg to bring to the attention of your Hon'ble House, the deep disappointment which prevails in all parts of Her Majesty's Indian Empire at the orders passed upon the labours of the Public Service Commission.*

(2). *That the Commission was instructed by the Government of India to submit a scheme which might reasonably be expected to possess the elements of finality and to do full justice to the claims of the Natives of India to higher and more extensive employment in the Public Service. Neither object has been secured by the labours of the Public Service Commission. The Statutory Service, under which appointments had been made, has been abolished, and nothing has been done to secure to the people the full enjoyment of the boon conferred upon them by the Act of 1870. The Government of India, in their resolution appointing the Commission, observed, " that the Statute of 1870 is one of remarkable breadth and liberality, and it empowers the Government of India and the Secretary of State, acting together, to frame rules, under which Natives of India may be admitted to any of the offices hitherto reserved for the Covenanted Civil Service." But the result of the Commission's enquiry has been a reduction in the number of offices open to Indians.*

(3). *That in respect likewise to Simultaneous Examinations in England and in India for appointment in the Civil Service, the Report of the Commission, endorsed by the Government of India, has given no satisfaction whatever. The weight of the evidence taken by the Commissioners was distinctly in favour of simultaneous exami-*

3rd Day.

**Resolution XI. Appointment of a Committee to prepare a petition to Parliament regarding the results of the Public Service Commission.**

*nations: Among the witnesses examined, there was a very large preponderance of those who were in favour of simultaneous examinations.*

(4). *That the disappointment which is everywhere felt at the resolution of the Government of India on the Public Service Commission, is of such a character that the Congress has felt constrained to lay the matter before the Hon'ble House, and to pray that it will direct the Goverument of India to give full effect to the Act of* 1870, *in the matter of appointing Natives of India to the Public Service of their country.*

*And your petitioners will, as in duty bound, ever pray.*

I must confess it was with a certain amount of hard feeling towards our distinguished President that I left this hall last evening. And it was for having thrust on me a duty I was unwilling to undertake—that of moving this resolution.

But I am glad now the President gave me an opportunity of standing on this platform, for I am thereby enabled to explain a matter which might otherwise give rise to misapprehension. The number of Indian Christian Delegates attending the Congress this year is very small, and the enemies of this National movement might get hold of this fact and say that so far at least as the Indian Christians are concerned their interest is diminishing and they are quietly withdrawing their support from a cause which they had at first warmly espoused. This is not so, the absence of most of the Christian Delegates is due to the fact that they are at the present moment attending a Christian Conference which is now assembled in Bombay and which meets only once in ten years. (*Hear, hear.*) I am glad to avail myself of this opportunity for asserting in emphatic terms that the Christians are still as warmly interested in the Congress movement as they at any time were, that we strongly feel that our fate is bound up with the fate of our fellow countrymen, and that we consider it a privelege to be associated with them in the common cause of agitating in a legitimate manner to remove the disabilities and grievances from which we are all suffering. (*Cheers.*)

The resolution committed to my charge is a necessary corollary to a previous resolution which has been fully discussed and unanimously passed by you—I mean the second resolution. In that resolution you have deplored the fact that the recommendations of the Public Service Commission have not been carried out in their integrity, that the number of appointments for the Provincial Service have been reduced from 108 to 93, that the number of Judgeships have been reduced from one-third to one-fifth, and you have further recorded your opinion in that resolution that full justice will never be done to the people of this country until the competitive examination for the Civil Service of India is held simultaneously in England and in India. It is therefore unnecessary, and indeed it would be beyond my province, to enter into the questions arising from the Report of the Public Service Commission, which have already been discussed and passed. The only point that I have to put before you is whether you think it desirable or not that we should carry our grievances with reference to the admission of the Natives of the country in to the Civil of a Petition to the British House of Commons.

A few weeks ago the late Lieutenant-Governor of these Provinces, in the last public function in which he took part, *i. e.*, the opening of the Benares Water-Works, volunteered a certain amount of paternal and parting advise. Even he had to concede that it was possible for the people living under the benign rule of the British Government to suffer from grievances of which they might reasonably complain. (*Hear, hear.*) But what was the advice Sir Auckland Colvin gave for the redress of these grievances? Ninety-nine out of a hundred Englishmen would have said, agitate, and agitate strongly, till you attain your object. Not so the ex-Lieutenant-Governor. He expressed a pious horror of agitation, and stigmatised in bitter terms what he called the professional agitator, but wound up by advising his hearers if they had a grievance to do what—to lay them before the District Magistrate! (*A laugh.*) Evidently Sir Auckland thought a man had only to go to the District Magistrate with his grievance and it would be immediately redressed, a curious commentary on facts as they really exist. But even he admitted the possibility of people going to a District Magistrate being disappointed, for he went on to add—'if the Magistrate fails

**3rd Day.**

**Resolution XI.**

**Appointment of a Committee to prepare a petition to Parliament regarding the results of the Public Service. Commission.**

you go to the Commissioner.' And here he thought there was almost a certainty of a speedy redress of all grievances. But still he went on—if by any mischance there was a denial of justice by that official, then as a last resource, there was an appeal to the head of the Local Government. The Lieutenant-Governor's advice ended there;—he could not conceive any remedy beyond that. He could not conceive it possible that the Lieutenant-Governor would ever fail to redress any grievance brought before him. He must have said to himself that if a ruler of a sister province, in his tender solicitude for the people under his charge, is actually engaged in redressing a grievance which never existed, and to remove which no one had ever asked, surely it could never happen that a real grievance could be brought before a Local Government without its being immediately redressed.

Well, gentlemen, our experience is unfortunately otherwise, and if I may be permitted to take the liberty of supplementing the profound utterances of a Lieutenant-Governor, I would add—'if you fail to obtain redress from a Lieutenant-Governor go to the Viceroy, and if you fail there go to the Secretary of State, and if you are disappointed there, lay your grievance by means of a petition—before the House of Commons. (*Hear, hear.*) And this is precisely what the resolution before you asks you to do. In doing so you will not only avail yourself of the only remedy now remaining to us, from which we can hope, sooner or later, to obtain a redress of our grievances in this matter, but you will also thereby be carrying out the advice of our venerable and distinguished countryman—Mr. Dadabhai Nowrojee, (*cheers*) who has advised us strongly to support his hands by means of a petition to the British House of Commons. With these remarks I commend the resolution for your acceptance. (*Cheers.*)

Babu Kali Prosanno Kavyavisharada, (*Calcutta No.* 185, *in list*).—Gentlemen,—In seconding the resolution I think the less I say the better it will be for you. Year after year this Congress has passed resolutions, and now in the present session this is only a corollary to the resolutions previously passed. Our only means of redress is to present a petition to the House of Commons, and who can prepare a better petition than those whom we propose to entrust with that duty. (*Hear, hear.*) Such a petition will tend to strengthen the hands of our illustrious country man, Mr. Dadabhai Nowrojee, in Parliament. Not that I am sanguine in my expectations that this petition will have the desired effect, but I fully believe that we cannot appeal in vain to that noble nation who have won renown for themselves for spending thousands of pounds out of their own pockets for the liberation of negro slavery of Africa. (*Cheers.*) It is dangerous to be a prophet, but I see the hand of Heaven laid upon the wheels of time. Despot, thy days are numbered; thy sceptre has been wrested from thy hands and given to nobler statesmen who have a higher sense of duty in conformity with the nationality to which they belong. (*Cheers.*)

The Resolution was then put to the vote and carried unanimously.

**Resolution XII.**

**Legislative Council for the Punjab.**

Mr. Kanhaya Lall, (*Lahore No.* 615 *in list*).—Mr. President and Gentlemen,—The Resolution, that I have to propose runs as follows:—

*That this Congress, in concurrence with the first Congress held at Bombay in 1885, considers that the creation of a Legislative Council for the Province of the Punjab is an absolute necessity for the good Government of that Province, and, having regard to the fact that a similar Council has been created for the United Provinces, hopes that no time will be lost in creating such a Council.*

You have hear this resolution which asks for the creation of a Legislative Council for the Punjab, just as we have in the United Provinces of the N.-W. P. and Oudh. I must say it is with great hesitation that I propose this resolution, because I feel it is a speculation in the present state of things, the Legislative Council being filled by members nominated or selected, whatever you may call it, from the people, but not on the representative principle. People who accept seats notwithstanding their incompetency to hold such a responsible charge, do so simply to aggrandize themselves, and to add another name "honourable"—dishonourable would be more appropriate,—to their titles. So it is a speculation, because if those rules which we expect are not sanctioned for a long time to come and the Council is constituted upon the same lines as the existing Councils, then we

**Resolution XII. Legislative Council for the Punjab**

shall be in a worse position than we are in at present. The present machinery for enacting laws for us is to some extent a reliable one, I mean, the Supreme Legislative Council of India where able men sit. They have some regard for a sense of duty. But if people are selected from our Province without representation, then there will be the danger of harm. Some four or five years ago a Tenancy law and a Revenue law were enacted for the Punjab, and passed in the same year. It was the opinion of the Financial Commissioner and the Board of Revenue that these laws affecting important rights in property, should sweep away the prevailing local practices which were to be excluded altogether. But it was the wisdom of the Legislative Council of the Government of India which prevented their agreeing with the opinion of the Revenue authorities, and a right of appeal was left in these important cases. Therefore I say that I feel hesitation in moving this resolution. But as this Congress has by a resolution in 1885 committed itself to such a resolution and demanded a Council for the Punjab, and because there is the expectation of getting such rules by which real representation may be secured, therefore I propose this resolution. (*Hear, hear.*) I also propose it because it is not a wise thing to say that I shall not acquire property or build a house because it may be occupied by bad tenants. There may be a time when it may be occupied by a good tenant if it exist. For these reasons I commend the resolution to you for your acceptance. (*Cheers.*)

MR. MURLIDHAR (*Umballa, No. 612, in list,*).—MR. PRESIDENT LADIES AND GENTLEMEN,—There are cotton manufactures in Bombay, art industries in Poona, flour mills in Delhi, and if this legislative mill had been like all other mills, then we would not have been under the necessity of working for its reform. For this mill we would have got ordinary laborers to work. But this is not a windmill, because if it had been a windmill we would have found Don Quixotes to work it. These are found in India in large numbers, but such a mill is not to be found in England because there are no Don Quixotes there; these are only to be found in India. (*Laughter.*) If the Councillors are to sit only like dumb creatures, then I say make a statue of Liberty and simply place it upon the Legislative stage, and then you will see what a beautiful spectacle it will be (*Laughter and cheers.*) It will be noble to look at. But as long as these illiterate and dumb people who do not understand a word of English, the language in which the proceedings are conducted, will sit mute and dumb, I do not see the least difference between these honourables and dumb statues (*Cheers.*) It is therefore that you have called these Legislative Councils a sham. Why then do you inflict this sham upon us? Oh! but we have not even the satisfaction of having this sham in our province, and therefore we hunger for it. We hope we shall not have to wait long; that there will be a reformation, and that the time is coming when we shall have a real representation. (*Cheers.*) If I had dared to give utterance to such feelings in regard to honourable members, and if I had been a native of some Native State, then perhaps you would have found my head off my shoulders. I would have been a headless ghost, and you would not have seen my shadow. (*Laughter.*)

The Resolution was then put to the vote and carried unanimously.

**Resolution XIII. Thanking the British Committee and Mr. Digby. Confirming new arrangements about the office of the Committee and the Journal "India."**

MR. D. N. BANERJEE, (*Allahabad, No. 337, in list,*).—GENTLEMEN,—The resolution that I have to propose runs as follows:—

*That this Congress hereby tenders its most grateful acknowledgements to Sir W. Wedderburn and the members of the British Congress Committee, for the service rendered by them to India during the past year, and entirely approves and confirms the re-construction of the British Committee of the Congress which has been effected by them, as also the new arrangements which they have made in regard to their office establishment, and the journal "India;" and that this Congress also tenders its thanks to Mr. W. Digby, C. I. E., for the services which he rendered to the cause during his tenure of office as Secretary to the British Committee.*

I am exceedingly sorry for you all because I feel sure that I am bound to disappoint you. Probably you have seen me very closely associated with Babu Surendro Nath Banerjee during these days here; and probably you think that I have been able to borrow something from him of that inestimable gift which he possesses, or that he has been able

**3rd Day.**

**Resolution XIII. Thanking the British Committee and Mr. Digby. Confirming new arrangements about the office of the Committee and the Journal "India."**

to give me some of it. But he has done nothing of the kind. The fount of eloquence which was in our family, has descended, according to the law of primogeniture, to the eldest branch of which my dear nephew Babu Surendro Nath Banerjee is a worthy member. So pardon me, gentlemen, if I do not come up to your expectations.

But still I have some thing to say and must say in support of this resolution. It is a very simple task to rise and express our gratitude to those who have done something for our benefit ; and it was only that idea which has encouraged me to appear before you.

We have undertaken a very grave cause ; it is admitted that the ultimate success of the great undertaking depends a good deal upon the sympathy and support of the British public. *(Hear, hear)*. It is therefore our duty, I think, to record our gratitude to those men who are now engaged in the British Committee of the Congress, working in England in order to interest the people of England in our behalf. (*Cheers*). Seldom do we find English gentlemen, after having retired from the service, after life-long labour, devote themselves to the cause of the people of the country without private purposes of their own to serve. But that is not the case with the distinguished gentlemen who are now upon that Committee and working there. (*Hear, hear)*. Gentlemen, I think we should be guilty of the highest ingratitude if upon an occasion like this you do not record your deep appreciation of the valuable services these gentlemen are rendering to our cause. I do not think I need single out any one out of the names which are there for any special praise, for, I think even the chief among them would be after all a chief among equals; and with these observations I will retire with a credit of three minutes in my favor which I leave as a start on behalf of the first man who will follow me. (*Cheers*).

Mr. K. B. Mullick, (*Kalna, No. 222, in list,*).—Mr. President and Gentlemen,—The task which has been entrusted to me, you will all concede, is a most gracious and pleasing one. I am called upon to support the vote of thanks which has been proposed to be given to the British Committee. Gentlemen, you are aware that that Committee is a most important adjunct of this Congress. (*Hear, hear*). The European gentlemen who are on that Committee are your mouthpiece, and as such they discharge most important duties connected with this Congress. I have therefore very great pleasure indeed in seconding the resolution moved by my predecessor. In this connection I shall make only one remark with regard to Mr. Digby's services to the Congress. You are aware that his connection has now been severed, not because he did not like to work for you, but it has been owing to circumstances over which he had no control; and I can assure you, gentlemen, that although his connection has been severed, he continues to take the same earnest interest in the Congress as before. (*Hear, hear.*) As Secretary to the Committee he discharged his duties loyally, with spirit and zeal, not to say that he did it to the entire satisfaction of this Congress and the members of the Committee ; and it is therefore that we record this expression of our gratitude. (*Cheers*). With these few remarks I have to express my own great pleasure in being able to second this resolution. (*Cheers*).

The President here stated that the Hon'ble Sunkar Nair, of Madras, was to have moved this resolution, but through an oversight, it had been moved by another speaker. He offered an apology to Mr. Nair for the mistake, and requested him to support the resolution.

The Hon'ble Sunkar Nair, (*Madras, No. 2, in list,*).—who on rising was greeted with cheers, said :—Gentlemen, I suppose I must say something now. You are aware that agitation here in India alone is hardly sufficient for our purposes ; and that it is necessary to educate English public opinion upon the questions at issue between ourselves and our opponents. It was therefore necessary that there should be a committee of European gentlemen like the British Committee at London, to impress upon the English public and upon the House of Commons the necessity of effecting some of the reforms which we have been advocating. And it is only meet therefore that we should return our most cordial and grateful thanks and acknowledgements to the members of the British Committee for the services they have so voluntarily and sincerely been rendering in that direction. (*Cheers*).

My predecessor Mr. Mullick has already referred to Mr. Digby's services; but there is one fact I should like to mention, and that is, the fact of Mr. Digby having resigned the Secretaryship of the Congress Committee. We all know what his labors have been, and what he has done for us. It would indeed be too much to recapitulate them here. (*Cheers*). Consequent upon his resignation we have been called upon to make other arrangements, and I have no doubt that you will agree with me in approving the recommendations which have been made to you. With these few remarks I support this resolution. (*Cheers*).

**3rd Day.**

**Resolution XIII. Thanking the British Committee and Mr. Digby. Confirming new arrangements about the office of the Committee and the Journal "India."**

The Resolution was then put to the vote and carried unanimously.

**Resolution XIV. Protests against State-regulated immorality in India.**

CAPTAIN BANON, (*Punjab, No.* 609, *in list*,)—MR. PRESIDENT AND GENTLEMEN,—The resolution that I have to propose for your acceptance is as follows :—

*That this Congress is thankful that the House of Commons is vigilant in regard to the recent purity legislation by the Government in India, and desires, once again, to enter its protest against all State-regulated immorality in India.*

In moving this resolution it is necessary for me to say only a very few words. When the Congress passed this resolution four years ago at this very place, Allahabad, they supposed that no doubt would ever again be felt as to what view they took of this matter, and so they never troubled to re-affirm this resolution since. But we are now obliged to ask you to once more pass this resolution, for it has been said that the India Office have been hinting that as the Congress have not reaffirmed this resolution, they have since changed their opinion concerning it. Besides this, our reaffirmation of it at the present moment, will very considerably strengthen the hands of the Anti-C. D. Acts party in England, who are about to move in this matter as soon as Parliament reassembles next month. Under these circumstances we again ask you to pass this resolution unanimously. (*Cheers*).

MR. V. N. BHIDE, (*Poona, No.* 85, *in list*,).—MR. PRESIDENT AND GENTLEMEN,—I gladly second the resolution which you know requires very little to be said in support of it. This is a resolution which I think we need not dwell much upon, because to do so would be to suppose that our Government and the Government in England are interested in regulating immorality, which is a thing I cannot believe. (*Hear, hear.*) But sometimes improbabilities happen, and possibly this might be one of them. I second the resolution in the hope that this is the last time we shall have to bring such a resolution before so honourable and respectable a body of delegates as are assembled here from all parts of India. (*Loud Cheers*).

The Resolution was then put to the vote and carried unanimously.

**Resolution XV. Postponement of the English Session until after the Congress of 1893.**

THE PRESIDENT.—GENTLEMEN,—In moving the next resolution one word of explanation is necessary. We have heard from friends in England that Parliament would be so busy in the ensuing Session with domestic legislation, that the Congress would not then be able to get a hearing in England. Therefore it has been considered desirable to postpone the sitting of the Congress which it was proposed to hold in England in 1893, and I consequently move the following resolution :—

*That, regard being had to the present political situation in England, the provisional arrangements set on foot, in pursuance of the resolution passed at the Calcutta Congress,* 1890, *for holding—all things being convenient—a Congress of not less than hundred delegates in England, in* 1892, *be now suspended, until after the Session of the Congress in* 1893.

The Resolution was put to the vote and carried unanimously.

3rd Day.

Resolution XVI. Thanking Central Finsbury, and appointing Mr. Naoroji as India's representative in the House of Commons.

THE PRESIDENT.—I shall now move the sixteenth resolution which runs as follows :—

*That this Congress most respectfully and cordially tenders, on behalf of the vast population it represents, India's most heartfelt thanks to the electors of Central Finsbury for electing Mr. Dadabhai Naoroji their member in the House of Commons; and it again puts on record its high estimate and deep appreciation of the services which that gentleman has rendered to this country, re-iterates its unshaken confidence in him, and looks upon him as India's representative in the House of Commons.*

I do not think it needs seconding, and feel sure you will carry it by acclamation. (*Loud Cheers*).

The Resolution was put and carried by acclamation.

Resolution XVII. Financial arrangements of the Congress.

THE PRESIDENT.—GENTLEMEN,—We have a permanent fund of Rs. 35,000 in the Oriental Bank, and I hope that fund will increase in the course of time. In addition to that we have a sum of Rs. 1,900 and odd also locked up in that Bank. But hopes are held out to us that we shall get 75 per cent. of our money. Sometimes it is not very easy to collect money as it is required, and therefore if you will empower the trustees to send to England not more than £500 out of these sums, it will save a great deal of trouble, and as subscriptions come in, the money will be refunded to the permanent fund, and thus your permanent fund will remain intact. With this explanation I move—

*That this Congress hereby empowers the Trustees of the Congress Permanent Fund—now locked up in the "New Oriental Bank Corporation, Ld.," at present in liquidation—to send at least five hundred pounds out of it to the British Committee, to be recouped by subscriptions from the Standing Congress Committees.*

The Resolution was put to the vote and carried unanimously.

Resolution XVIII. Contributions to the Congress Fund.

BABU SURENDRA NATH BANERJI, (*Calcutta, No. 188, in list.*),—MR. PRESIDENT, LADIES AND GENTLEMEN,—I have been entrusted with what might be called a purely formal resolution, but nevertheless it is a resolution which, affecting as it does the highest and best interests of the Congress, because it affects its financial interests, is of the greatest importance to that body. Let me in the first place read out the words of the resolution :—

*That, regard being had to the representations received from the British Committee, this Congress is of opinion, that a sum equivalent in Rupees to two thousand eight hundred pounds sterling, be allotted for the expenses of the British Committee, for the year 1892-93; that deducting the money which has been received up to now, the balance be allotted amongst the different Standing Congress Committees, in accordance with the arrangements come to with them; and that the sum be remitted to England as soon as practicable.*

I have remarked that this is a purely business resolution, and it needs a word or two of explanation. You know perfectly well that the British Committee have reduced their expenses. I need not offer any explanation in regard to that measure of the British Committee, for it is fully explained in the admirable and lucid note which has been addressed by Sir William Wedderburn to the various Standing Committees of the Congress. Our expenses for the next year will come up to £2,800. If you have read that note which I hold in my hands, you will find that out of this £2,800, £900 represents the unrealised balance due for this year. Therefore, practically, the expenses of next year will be £1,900, or £100, less than the estimate of the British Committee. You will also have noticed, if you have read this memorandum, that this sum of £1,900 includes a very large item of £ 1,100 representing the expenses which have to be met for the purpose of keeping up and maintaining our journal *India*. Well, there will be a balance to our credit, as far as that item is concerned. There will be subscriptions coming forth, and I hope and trust in increasing numbers in future years. I hope and trust it will be our privilege to wipe off this item of expenditure in the not distant future as soon as *India* becomes a self-supporting journal. *India* must be maintained. It is the right hand and the organ of the Congress; it is our foundation, our right arm of strength, to fight the constitutional battle in which we are engaged at the present moment. It is not enough that we should hold a great demonstration here and there once in the course of a year; but it is necessary that we should keep ourselves *in evidence* before the British public, because after all they are the great tribunal to whom we appeal with hope and confidence for the redress of our grievances, for the vindication of our rights, and for the vindication of that gracious Proclamation which we regard as the *Magna Charta* of our rights and privileges. (*Loud applause*).

If it is your wish, if it is your verdict that the British Committee should be maintained, it is necessary also that *India* should be maintained, and maintained in the highest state of efficiency. Well, gentlemen, if you are able to get subscribers to the tune of 5,000 copies, then the journal becomes self-supporting, and not only so, but you yourselves are relieved of a part of the expenses of the British Committee. Five thousand subscribers at the rate of six rupees a year amounts to Rupees thirty thousand per annum, and if you are able to send from this country Rupees thirty thousand as subscriptions for *India*, you will be relieved from further expenses either of *India* or for the British Committee of the National Congress. (*Hear, hear*). How many of us are here—I suppose eight or nine hundred delegates; how many are here as sympathisers and how many as visitors? Expectant India is looking upon the scene which is being enacted within this pavilion, and I hope and trust it will be an easy task not only to procure five thousand subscribers, but if necessary, five times five thousand. (*Loud applause*).

Why, gentlemen, in Bengal to-day I find (my friend opposite shakes his head over there) we have a vernacular journal which shall be nameless at the present moment, whose principles and precepts I for my part hold in perfect abhorrence,—that vernacular journal has a circulation as I am told of twenty thousand, and is it impossible for us, for you assembled delegates with all the vast influence which I am sure you possess over your countrymen, to secure for *India* at least as many subscribers as that nameless journal possesses at the present moment? I hope and trust therefore that efforts will be made by us on our return home to secure this circulation for *India*.

Gentlemen, you will permit me to repeat the hope I have already expressed that there will be no difficulty in raising the sum of forty thousand. Rs. 40,000 spread over a population of 280,000,000 of human beings—why, it does not come to a pie per head. Is there any difficulty in raising a sum like this amongst all this vast, *multitudinous*, in the words of Mr. Gladstone, *community*? I do not think there ought to be any difficulty whatever. It is a matter of arrangement, and partly a matter of organisation, and it is a matter of rational allotments made to the various Standing Committees. I have received an admirable report sent to me by a Bengal delegate, Babu Girja Sunkur Mozumdar, in which he makes certain suggestions in regard to the organisation of Bengal districts and sub-divisions. I commend that note to my friend Mr. Ghosal for the consideration of the Standing Committee of the Congress. It is a note well worthy to be reflected upon and given effect to; and in case effect is given to it, we will not be under the necessity of going to our Rajas and Maharajas to beg of them for donations, and they in their turn of begging of us for God's sake not to allow their names to be published in the newspapers. Therefore if it is a matter of organisation, why should we put ourselves in a position to beg for this money. In Bombay, in response to an appeal which I made, when I had the honor of addressing one of the sittings of the Congress, in the course of a couple of hours the meeting responded to that appeal in a munificent manner and a large subscription of Rs. 65,000 was voted on the spot, and half of that amount was put down there and then. Have that fervour and that enthusiasm dwindled? Are the men of 1893 different from the men of 1889? We are told by a journalist, who of course thrives and prospers in the capital of the N. W. Provinces, that ours is a discredited movement, and that our enthusiasm is on the wane! Brother delegates, I call upon you on behalf of this great Congress, I call upon you for the protection of your honor, for the protection of your own good name, to give the lie direct to our opponents (*loud applause*), to give a practical manifestation of your sincerity in a way which no Englishman can ignore. I was very much interested in reading the other day the vaticinations of another journal also published in this city; truly they are twin journalists, the Castor and Pollux of Allahabad, who seek to enlighten not only this city but the whole of the North-Western Provinces, and who seek to be the spokesmen of

3rd Day.

Resolution XVIII. Contributions to the Congress Fund.

the Government of India and of the Government of the North-Western Provinces. One of the two was good enough to devote half a dozen lines, and no more than half a dozen lines, to that splendid oration which was delivered from the chair upon the opening of the Congress, and in commenting upon that speech, this journal was pleased to say that it was a "colourless speech." Very colourless indeed, when the President denounced in scathing terms the system of the administration of Criminal Justice that prevailed in Bengal! Very colourless indeed, when he condemned in emphatic language the Jury notification issued by Sir Charles Elliot ? Very colourless indeed, when he pointed out the utter absence of responsibility on the part of the Government of India! Forsooth, it was a very colourless speech! And it was this veracious truthful Journalist who after having endeavoured, vainly, I hope and trust, to delude the public, proceeded to observe that it was a colourless speech in keeping with the colourless character of the Congress, and that all life and vitality had departed from this movement. Life and vitality departed from this splendid organisation, this noble Congress which has done us so much valuable service in the past and which, under God's providence, is yet destined to achieve so much more! Let it not be said, however, that we can talk by the yard but that we perform by the inch. This is the particular charge which we bring against the Government. We tell the Government and their officers that the measure of their performances falls infinitesimally short of the measure of their promises. Let that not be said against us, men of the Congress, men of the forward party, men of the progressive party. If we do talk by the yard and are liberal in our promises, then we should return home to act and not to fall asleep like *Kumbhkarno* of old. Bear this fact in mind that if you wish to succeed with Englishmen, you must show that you are in earnest, and the measure of your earnestness will be judged by the measure of your sacrifices. I call upon you, brother delegates, once again to put your hands into your pockets, to unloose your purse strings, to devote your time to the service of the Congress, and to silence the calumnies which are scattered broadcast against us, by practically demonstrating the fervour of your enthusiasm. Show to the world, show to every body, friends and foes alike, that the enthusiasm which inspired us in the early days of the Congress has not abated. If you are true to the principles of this noble institution, if we are firm and loyal in our attachment to the standard of the Congress, then I am perfectly certain that we shall establish our claims to that measure of political rights and liberties which are identified with the name of the Congress and which are identified with the political regeneration of the multitudinous inhabitants of this great Empire. (*Loud applause*). Once again I ask you to come forward, and by your personal sacrifices to show your devotion to the Congress, and to silence the calumnies of its enemies and to make the Congress the great success, which, under the providence of God, it is destined to be in the history of this vast Empire. (*Loud and continued applause*).

SWAMI ALA RAM, (*Allahabad, No.* 386, *in list*).—BROTHER DELEGATES,—In the first instance, I must give ten thousand thanks to the citizens of Allahabad, inasmuch as they have surpassed the past seven Congresses in the amount of work they have accomplished this year. I mean that the last Congresses received the invaluable help of the indefatigable Mr. Hume, and some of them had no inconsiderable amount of encouragement from the presence of Members of Parliament, so that their promoters used to be inspired with hope and confidence in a special manner. In this, the Eighth National Congress however, neither Mr. Hume nor any member of Parliament is present; and the Joint General Secretary of the Congress, the Hon'ble Pandit Ajudhia Nath, has also most unfortunately disappeared from the scene. Such being the case, the residents of Allahabad were not free from misgivings as to its success. But as time rolled on, they girded up their loins with such enthusiastic devotion to the sacred national cause, that they forgot even their food and drink, and made the present Congress outshine its predecessors. (*Cheers*). Subscriptions too, be it said to the credit of the donors, have been liberally contributed.

Now I must address myself to the resolution in hand. I have the greatest pleasure in seconding it. The Indian National Congress is a garden the produce of which 30 crores of the people of India will enjoy to the permanent stability of the British rule for all time to come. (*Cheers*). The British Congress Committee is a fountain built for the purpose of keeping the Congress garden fresh and green (*hear, hear*); and it is the duty of the people of India to see that the streams of subscription continue to flow freely and uninterruptedly, so that the Congress garden may not suffer from want of proper nourishment. (*Cheers*). What is now needed for this purpose is to raise a fund of £2,800, which, I think, is equivalent to Rs. 45,000 and if this amount is realised once for all, there will not be the necessity of repeating similar appeals year after year. Efforts should be made without delay. Mr. Surendranath Banerjee is, in my opinion, the proper person to undertake the task. Money is the most essential requisite. Nothing can be achieved without it. A poet has truly observed:—A mother curses her child who has no pice, a father regards his penniless son as a plague; being without a pice, a person is ignored by his friends; without it, a brother and a sister are no relations; a nephew in need is looked upon as a stranger; "who are you?" says a sister to her own brother in straits; the mother-in-law wishes her daughter to be released from the conjugal ties of an impecunious husband, and the father-in-law disowns an indigent son-in-law; a wife regards her poor husband as dead to her and thinks him to be a burden on her neck". (*Laughter and Cheers*). So you see that the question of funds should receive the first consideration. In a word, for the success of the Congress movement you must effectually set in motion the British Congress Committee water-works by your supplies. The people of India are about 30 crores in number, and if every one pays a pice, it will amount to lacs. (*Cheers*).

**3rd Day.**

**Resolution XVIII. Contributions to the Congress Fund.**

A certain sage has said:—"There are four sharers of our wealth—(1). Religion, (2). thieves, (3). the King, and (4). the fire. If not diverted to religion, it will eventually fall to the lot of the other three. The Indian National Congress is a sacred cause; it is a grand religion by which 30 crores of the people of India are to be benefited; and the wealth of men who neglect their duty towards this religion, will surely prove a curse to them. (*Cheers*). For this reason, you should subscribe heartily for the protection and promotion of the Congress religion. I must now conclude by calling on you to say three times "*Congress ki jay.*" (May the Congress be victorious.) (*Loud applause*).

The appeal was heartily responded to. As the President got up to put the Resolution to the vote, notes, silver and copper coins and promises to pay began to pour in thick and fast from every quarter. For the next half of an hour, the Secretaries on the President's table were busy receiving money and recording names of subscribers to *India* and the Congress Fund. But it had already got late, lights had to be brought in, and some business had still to be gone through before the Congress could dissolve, and, the work of collection had therefore to be stopped. When later on the money came to be counted and the promises classified, it was found that Rs. 906-15-3 had been paid in cash, Rs. 12,515 promised, and 925 new subscribers registered for *India*, making a total contribution of over Rs. 18,000 in support of the Congress Cause.

**Resolution XIX. Re-election of the General Secretary. Appointment of a Joint General Secretary.**

The President.—Gentlemen,—You know that when our lamented friend Pandit Ajoodhia Nath died, it was put upon me to take his place as Joint General Secretary, and I submitted. But it was with the greatest possible difficulty that I was able to carry on the work. In the first place my health is not what it used to be; and in the second place, I have to make frequent visits to England to look after the education of my children. It became necessary for me to go to England in July last and I remained there for some time, and asked permission to place my duties in the hands of Babu Surendra Nath Banerji. He was overwhelmed with work, and it was only his devotion to the Congress cause and his great friendship to me, which induced him to accept the duty. But, gentlemen, we must not work our willing horses too much, we are willing and ready enough to do all that we can, but you must put somebody else in his place, and I don't think you will differ with me when I propose to insert the name of Mr. Anunda Charlu as Joint General Secretary. (*Cheers*). It took a great deal of time to persuade him to accept the office, but I was at him and he could not refuse. The resolution which I have to move is this:—

*That this Congress re-appoints Mr. A. O. Hume, C. B., to be the General Secretary, and appoints Rai Bahadur P. Ananda Charlu, to be the Joint-General Secretary of the Congress for the ensuing year.*

The Resolution was put to the vote and carried by acclamation.

3rd Day.

Resolution XIX.

Mr. Anunda Charlu,—(*Madras, No.* 1, *in list,*).—Gentlemen,—I have submitted to your wish in the full belief that I shall have your valuable assistance—active assistance from every one of you, so as to lighten the labours which I have undertaken at the earnest request of our worthy and learned President. (*Cheers*).

Resolution XX. The Ninth Congress to be held at Amritsar.

The President.—Gentlemen,—I now move—

*That the Ninth Indian National Congress do assemble on such day after Christmas,* 1893, *as may be determined upon, at Amritsar.* (*Cheers*).

Mr. Kanhaiya Lal,—(*Amritsar, No.* 615, *in list,*).—Gentlemen,—After the Congress which was held in 1888, we expressed the desire that the following meeting of the Congress should be held at Lahore. I am glad that we are in a position again to do so, and we now invite the Congress to meet at Amritsar, because we consider it very necessary that they should do so. (*Cheers*). It is a feeble heart that does not beat well and the circulation from which does not go to the extremities. Our Congress has not got a weak heart and its circulation should therefore reach the extremities. We want the help and succour of our brethren in Bengal in matters of education and politics, so that we may have the same high sense of duty which they possess. We invite our brethren in Madras to put us in the way of properly organising practical subjects; and we invite gentlemen from Bombay to give us lessons in political economy so that we may thoroughly utilise our means and our resources; and for these purposes we invite you all to the city of Amritsar, which means the 'Lake of immortality'; as every one individually wants immortality, so the Congress collectively wants immortality, and after the Congress has been held in Amritsar in the Punjab, it will, I hope, gain immortality, not only because the name "Amritsar" denotes immortality, but because it is also the frontier province of India. (*Cheers*).

The Resolution was carried by acclamation and with ringing cheers.

Resolution XXI. Thanking H. H. the Maharaja of Darbhanga

The President.—Gentlemen,—I now move—

*That this Congress hereby tenders its best thanks to His Highness the Maharaja of Darbhanga, for having so kindly lent his Castle and grounds for the holding of this Congress.*

The motion was put to the vote and carried unanimously.

Resolution XXII. Appointment of a Trustee.

The President.—Gentlemen,—The Trustees of the Congress Permanent Fund were the two Joint Secretaries, the three Standing Counsel and the late Pandit Ajoodhya Nath. At his death the remaining Trustees asked Pandit Bishumbher Nath to take the vacant place. Gentlemen, I don't think we could have made a better selection, and I ask you therefore to confirm the action of the Trustees. I therefore move—

*That this Congress confirms the appointment of Pandit Bishambar Nath, in place of the late Pandit Ajudhia Nath, as one of the Trustees of the Congress Permanent Fund.*

The motion was put and carried by unanimously.

The President's concluding address.

The President.—Gentlemen,—My attention has been called to an omission in my address in opening this Congress, namely, that I did not refer to the death of the Revd. R. C. Bose. I fully intended to refer to it. I think the same feeling of regret must be felt by us at his loss as a member of the Congress as must be felt by us individually at the loss of a friend, and I shall include his name in the print of my speech, if it is ever printed. (*Cheers*).

The President.—The last duty which I have to perform is a very pleasant one. It is on your behalf to tender our best thanks to the Reception Committee at Allahabad for the great trouble they have taken on our behalf, and I will ask special thanks to be given ot Pandit Bishamber Nath (*cheers*) who was in such a state of health that I thought he would not be able to open these Congress proceedings; but the spirit of the Congress upon him is such that he left a sick-bed and came here. He is a man of advanced years and he is not a Bengalee. But I wish he had been, because we should have been proud to call him our countryman. But as he happens not to be a Bengalee, I can only say that when a gentleman of his position, of his age and his infirmities, leaves his sick-bed and comes here not only on the first day but day after day, it is wicked to say that we have no life in us. (*Loud Cheers.*) Let us again give three cheers for Pandit Bishambhar Nath. (*Three hearty cheers were here given for Pandit Bishambhar Nath.*)

**3rd day.**

**The President's concluding address.**

Next after him who have worked heart and soul for the sake of this Congress are the gentlemen whose names I shall mention as they have been given to me, not intending by reading one name before another to convey any idea that that gentleman deserves more credit than his fellow. Those names are: Raja Rampal Sinh (*cheers*), Lala Ram Charan Das (*cheers*), Babu Charoo Chandra Mitter (*cheers*), Mr. J. Ghosal (*cheers*), Pandit Moti Lal Nehru (*cheers*), Pandit Baldeo Ram Dave (*cheers*), Munshi Madhava Prasad (*cheers*), Pandit Madan Mohan Malaviya. (*Cheers*).

Now, gentlemen, in this country, try as we may, it is not possible to get on without the assistance of English gentlemen. Mr. Hume is not here but his spirit is here. (*Loud cheers*). But on the Reception Committee there has been a gentleman who was Mr. Hume's co-adjutor for many years, and who has worked in almost every Congress for us. His energy, his devotion and love of this work are well known to you. I need hardly mention the name of Captain Banon. (*Three cheers were given for Captain Banon*). He has helped us with true English determination, and we have to tender him also our most heartfelt thanks. (*Cheers*).

**Vote of thanks to the President.**

THE HON'BLE SANKARA NAIR, (*Madras, No. 2, in list*) then moved a vote of thanks to the President.—The motion was carried by acclamation, and three hearty cheers were given for MR. W. C. BONNERJEE.

**Cheers for Her Majesty the Queen-Empress.**

THE PRESIDENT.—I thank you, gentlemen, for the way in which my name has been received; and now only one thing more. Before we separate, let us unite in giving three deafening cheers for Her Most Gracious Majesty the QUEEN-EMPRESS VICTORIA.

Loud and enthusiastic cheers were given for Her Majesty, and repeated again and again, and then the assembly dissolved rather late in the evening.

# APPENDIX I.

## LIST OF DELEGATES

WHO ATTENDED THE

# EIGHTH INDIAN NATIONAL CONGRESS,

### *HELD AT ALLAHABAD, DECEMBER, 1892.*

| Number. | Presidency or Government. | Congress Circle. | Electoral Division. | Names in full of Delegates, with honorary titles, scholastic degrees, etc. | Race, Religious denomination, and Caste, if any. | Occupation and Address. | How and when elected. |
|---|---|---|---|---|---|---|---|
| 1 | Madras. | Madras. | Madras Mahajana Sabha. | Rai Bahadur P. Ananda Charlu, B.A., B.L. | Hindu Brahmin, Vaishnava. | Vakil, High Court, Madras, Fellow, M. University, Joint Genl. Secy., I. N. Congress. | Public Meeting of the Sabha held on 19th December, 1892. |
| 2 | ,, | ,, | ,, | The Hon'ble C. Sankara Nair, B.A., B.L. | Hindu. | Vakil, High Court, Member, Legislative Council, Madras. | do. |
| 3 | ,, | ,, | ,, | Mr. S. Viraswamy Iyangar. | Hindu Brahmin, Vishnavite. | Landholder. ... | do. |
| 4 | ,, | ,, | ,, | ,, K. Natraju Iyer, B.A. | Hindu Brahmin. | Teacher, Aryan High School. | do. |
| 5 | ,, | ,, | Madras, Triplicane. | ,, M. Viraraghava Chariar, B.A. | Hindu Brahmin, Vaishnava. | Managing Proprietor and Joint Editor "Hindu," Secretary, Standing Congress Committee. | do. |
| 6 | ,, | ,, | ,, | ,, Viraraghava Chary, S. | do. | Merchant, Triplicane ... | Public Meeting on 4th December, 1892. |
| 7 | ,, | ,, | ,, | ,, Viraraghava Chariar, S. | do. | P. W. D. Contractor ... | do. |
| 8 | ,, | ,, | ,, | ,, Krishnamachary, G.... | do. | Merchant, Triplicane ... | do. |
| 9 | ,, | ,, | ,, | ,, Peter Paul Pillay, ... | Vellalu Protestant. | Agent, Landowners' Association, Madras. | do. |
| 10 | ,, | ,, | Shivaganga Madura District. | ,, Narayan Swamy Iyer, S.M. | Brahmin. | Assistant Master, Raja's High School, Shivaganga. | Public Meeting at Shivaganga on 27th November, 1892, and Public Meeting at Dindigal on 19th December, 1892. |
| 11 | ,, | ,, | Kuvanpuch (N. Arcot.) | ,, Narasimha Chary, T. | Hindu Brahmin, Vaishnava. | 2nd Grade Pleader, Ranipet... | Public Meeting on 22nd December, 1892. |
| 12 | ,, | ,, | Chingleput | ,, Raghuram Row, D. | do. | First Grade Pleader. ... | Public Meeting on 16th December, 1892. |
| 13 | ,, | ,, | N. Vizagapatam. | ,, Rao Sahib J. Vizianarasinha Raju. | Hindu Kshatriya. | Landholder, Vizianagram ... | Public Meeting at Vizianagram held on 22nd November, 1892. |
| 14 | ,, | ,, | Parvatipur and the Parvatipur Mahajana Sabha. | ,, P. Venkat Rau Pantulu. | Hindu Brahmin. | Pleader, Parvatipur, Vizagapatam District. | Elected at a Public Meeting on 21st November, 1892. |
| 15 | ,, | ,, | ,, | ,, Venkat Jagannadha Shastri. | do. | First Grade Pleader, Northern Circles, Member, Taluq Board, Parvatipur, Secretary, Mahajana Sabha, Parvatipur. | do. |
| 16 | ,, | ,, | Palghat. | ,, K. A. Vythinatha Iyer Avergal, B.A. | do. | Teacher, Brennen College, Tellicherry. | Public Meeting on 18th December, 1892. |
| 17 | ,, | ,, | ,, | Rao Sahib S. Viraraghava Iyer Avergal. | do. | Landlord and Municipal Commissioner. | do. |
| 18 | ,, | ,, | Rajamahendri Literary Association. | Mr. Ch. Venkatramayah. | do. | Pleader. ... | Association's Meeting on 20th December, 1892. |

| Number. | Presidency or Government. | Congress Circle. | Electoral Division. | Names in full of Delegates, with honorary titles, scholastic degrees, etc. | Race, Religious denomination, and Caste, if any. | Occupation and Address. | How and when elected. |
|---|---|---|---|---|---|---|---|
| 19 | Madras. | Madras. | Salem. | Mr. P. S. V. Chettiar ... | Hindu Shaiva Vaishya. | Mirasidar and Merchant, Jalakantapara. | Public Meeting on 24th December, 1892. |
| 20 | ,, | ,, | ,, | ,, J. Nagalinga Chettiar. | do. | do. ... | do. |
| 21 | ,, | ,, | ,, | ,, C. Venkatachariar. ... | Hindu Vaishnava Brahmin. | Landholder and Member, District Board, Salem. | do. |
| 22 | ,, | ,, | ,, | ,, C. Vijiaraghavachariar, B.A. | do. | Pleader and Municipal Commissioner. | do. |
| 23 | ,, | ,, | ,, | ,, Venkata Row. ... | Hindu Brahmin Shaiva. | Money-lender and Merchant, ... | Public Meeting on 19th December, 1892. |
| 24 | ,, | ,, | ,, | ,, M. Ponnusami Chettiar. | Hindu, Shaiva Vysya. | Shroff, Shivapet, Salem. ... | Public Meeting on 24th December, 1892. |
| 25 | ,, | ,, | ,, | ,, Md. Abdul Qadir Sahib. | Mahomedan, Sunni. | Mirasidar and Merchant. ... | do. |
| 26 | ,, | ,, | ,, | ,, Ramaswami Chettiar. | Hindu Shaiva Vaishya. | Merchant. ... | do. |
| 27 | ,, | ,, | ,, | ,, V. Vyathi Iyer ... | Hindu Brahmin. | Government Pleader. ... | do. |
| 28 | ,, | ,, | Arni (Chittore.) | ,, D. V. Narsinhachary, B.A. | Hindu Brahmin Vaishnava. | Contractor and Landholder, | Public Meeting held on 11th December, 1892. |
| 29 | ,, | ,, | Guntur Town and Tax Payers' Association, Guntur. | ,, S. Ramuswamy Chetty. | Hindu Vaishnava Vaishya. | Merchant and Assistant Secretary, Taxpayers' Association. | Public Meeting on 21st November, 1892. |
| 30 | ,, | ,, | Chittoor. | ,, Damal Willivalum Rajagopal Chariar. | Brahmin, Vaishnava. | First Grade Pleader, Chittore, North Arcot, and Landholder. | Public Meeting on 24th November, 1892. |
| 31 | ,, | ,, | Bellary (Town and District.) | ,, C. Annamalai Mudalliar, Graduate of the College of Agriculture. | Hindu, Shaiva Vithalo. | Agent of Messrs. A. Subhapatty Mudalliar and Co., Merchants and Landholders at Bellary. | Public Meeting on 11th December, 1892. |
| 32 | ,, | ,, | ,, | ,, C. S. Krishnaswamy Iyer. | Hindu Brahmin Shaiva. | Landholder. | do. |
| 33 | ,, | ,, | Wallajahnuggur, Town. | ,, P. Seshachella Pillai. | Hindu Karnama Caste. | Contractor, Wallajahnuggur. | Public Meeting of Wallajahnuggur Association on 20th December, 1892. |
| 34 | ,, | ,, | Vijiavada Sabha. | ,, Devaguptam Sesha Chalapati Row. | Hindu Brahmin. | Commission agent and Merchant and Editor "Krishna News", Anglo-vernacular fortnightly, and Vernacular Secretary Vijiavada Sabha. | Public Meeting under the auspices of the Vijiavadasabha on 23rd. November, 1892. Public Meeting at Rajmandry on 4th December, 1892. |
| 35 | ,, | ,, | ,, | ,, Juhuri Subharayudu Garu. | Hindu Vaishya. | Merchant and Contractor. | Public Meeting under the auspices of the Vijiavadasabha on 23rd November, 1892. |
| 36 | ,, | ,, | Nellore. | ,, P. Balakrishna Pillai. | Hindu Karnama Caste. | Contractor, Nellore. | Public meeting held on 23rd December, 1892. |
| 37 | ,, | ,, | Gooty People's Association, Anantpur. | ,, Rao Saheb P. Kesava Pillai. | Hindu Karnama. | Pleader, Gooty. | Public meeting held at Anantpur Town on 16th December, 1892. |
| 38 | Govt. of India. | ,, | Secundrabad. | Lala Dharama Chandra. | Jain Hindu. | Photographer Artist. | Public Meeting on 14th December, 1892. |
| 39 | Bombay. | Bombay. | Bombay Presidency Association. | Mr. D. E. Wacha. ... | Parsee Zoroastrian | Mill Agent, Journalist, Municipal Commissioner, Honorary Secretary, Presideney Association, &c. | General Meeting of the Bombay Presidency Association held on 15th December, 1892. |
| 40 | ,, | ,, | ,, | ,, Daji Abaji Khare, B.A., LL.B. | Brahmin. | Pleader, High Court, Girgaum, Bombay. | Do., and General Meeting of Nasik Sarvajanik Sabha held on 4th December, 1892. General Meeting held at Ratnagiri on 7th December, 1892. |
| 41 | ,, | ,, | ,, | Dr. S. W. Kane. ... | do. | Medical Practitioner ... | General Meeting of the Bombay Presidency Association held on 15th December, 1892. |
| 42 | ,, | ,, | ,, | Mr. Jagmohan Das Vandravandas. | Hindu. | Merchant ... ... | do. |

| Number. | Presidency or Government. | Congress Circle. | Electoral Division. | Names in full of Delegates, with honorary titles, scholastic degrees, etc. | Race, Religious denomination, and Caste, if any. | Occupation and Address. | How and when elected. |
|---|---|---|---|---|---|---|---|
| 43 | Bombay. | Bombay. | Bombay Presidency Association. | Mr. Ranchordas Vallabhi. | Brahmin. | Merchant ... ... | General Meeting of the Bombay Presidency Association held on 15th December, 1892. |
| 44 | " | " | " | " Mahadeo Vaman Bhat B.A., LL.B. | do. | Pleader, High Court. ... | do. |
| 45 | " | " | " | " Purushottama Parasharama Khare, B.A., LL.B. | do. | Pleader, High Court, Thakurdwar, Bombay. | do. |
| 46 | " | " | " | " Gangadhara S. Gokhale, L.C.E. | do. | Architect and Engineer, Apollo Street, Bombay. | do. |
| 47 | " | " | " | " T. T. Muzumdar. | Nagar Brahmin. | Barrister-at-Law, High Court, Bombay. | do. |
| 48 | " | " | " | " Chunni Lal Lallubhai Parekh. | Hindu Vaishya. | Merchant. ... ... | do. |
| 49 | " | " | " | " Chiman Lal H. Satavaid, B.A., LL.B. | Hindu. | Pleader, High Court, Girgam, Back Road. | do. |
| | | | | | | | Public Meeting Ahmedabad held on 19th December, 1892, and Public Meeting at Ankleswara held on 17th December, 1892. |
| 50 | " | " | " | " Moreshwar Gopal Deshmukh, B.A., B.SC., M.D. | do. | Medical Practitioner, Fellow, Bombay University, Dean of the Faculty of Arts, Girgam, Bombay. | At a General Meeting of the Bombay Presidency Association held on 15th December, 1892. |
| 51 | " | " | " | " Paramananda Jiwan-Das. ... | do. | High Court Vakil; Vice-President Taluqa Local Board; Municipal Commissioner. | do. |
| 52 | " | " | " | Munshi Sheikh Husein Sheikh Chand. | Mahomedan. | Islam Missionary, David Sassoon's Silk Mill, Bombay. | do. |
| 53 | " | " | " | Dr. John de Cunha. | Christian Portuguese. | Medical Practitioner, Bombay. | At a Special Public Meeting of the Association on 21st December, 1892. |
| 54 | " | " | " | Mr. L. DeSouza, B.A., LL.B. | do. | Pleader, High Court, Bombay. | do. |
| 55 | " | " | Mohad. | " Mahadeo Bhikaji Oke. | Brahmin. | Taluqa Mohad, Colaba, District Bombay. | Public Meeting held at Mohad on 22nd December, 1892. |
| 56 | " | " | Dapoli (Ratnagiri District.) | Rao Sahib Dhondo Mahadeo Barve. | do. | Vice-President Taluqa Local Board, Dapoli; Municipal Commissioner, Khot; Pleader, Sub-Judge's Court, Ratnagiri. | Public Meeting held at Dapoli on 20th November, 1892. |
| 57 | " | " | " | Mr. Makund Waman Barve. | do. | Inamdar, Dapoli, District Ratnagiri. | do. |
| 58 | " | " | Bassein. | " Hari Laxman Patel. ... | do. | Pleader, Bassein, Bombay. ... | Public Meeting held at Bassein on 4th December, 1892. |
| 59 | " | " | Chiploon. | " Wasudeo Gopal Chitale. | do. | Pleader, Indore. ... | Do., and General Meeting of the Chiploon Association held on 1st November, 1892. |
| 60 | " | Sindh. | Sindh Sabha. | " Pesumal Zokeiram. ... | Hindu Lodhana. | Pleader, Sukkur, in Shikaba District. | Elected by Sindh Sabha on 17th December, 1892. |
| 61 | " | Ahmednagar. | Ahmednagar. | " Balwant Bhau Nagarkar. | Brahmin. | Editor of "Culture," a religious and social monthly, and Brahmo Preacher, Bombay, Tardeo Road. | Public Meeting of the inhabitants held at Ahmadnagar on 10th December, 1892. |
| 62 | " | " | " | " Krishnaji Wasudeo Joshi. | do. | Vakil, Ahmadnagar. ... | do. |
| 63 | " | Sholapur | Sholapur. | " Dinkar Ballal Chakradeo. | do. | Pleader and landholder, Sholapur. | At a Public Meeting held under the auspices of the Association on 18th October, 1892. |
| 64 | " | " | " | " P. L. Nagpurkar | do. | Pleader, Sholapur. ... | do. |
| 65 | " | Bhusawal. | Jalgaon. | Rao Sahib Sitaram Mahadeo Barve. | do. | Pleader, Member of the District Local Board and also of Jalgaon Municipality. | At a Public Meeting held at Jalgaon on 20th November, 1892. |
| 66 | " | " | " | Mr. Abaji Ragho Mahalas. | do. | Subordinate Government Pleader and Chairman, Jalgaon Municipality. | do. |
| 67 | " | Satara. | Satara. | " Dattatreya Balawant Parasnis. | Brahmin. | Editor and Proprietor "Maharashtra Kokil." | Public Meeting at Satara on 20th November, 1892, Public Meeting at Wai on 27th November, 1892, and Public Meeting at Borgaon on 5th December, 1892. |

| Number. | Presidency or Government. | Congress Circle. | Electoral Division. | Names in full of Delegates, with honorary titles, scholastic degrees, etc. | Race, Religious denomination, and Caste, if any. | Occupation and Address. | How and when elected. |
|---|---|---|---|---|---|---|---|
| 68 | Bombay. | Satara. | Satara. | Rao Sahib Ramchandra Krishna Kothawale. | Brahmin. | Inamdar and landholder, Member of the District Local Board, Satara, and Chairman, Municipal Committee, Wai. | Public Meeting at Borgaon on 5th December, 1892. Public Meeting at Wai on 27th November, 1892. |
| 69 | ,, | ,, | ,, | Mr. Raghunath Pandu-ranga Karandikar. | do. | Pleader, High Court, Satara.... | do. |
| 70 | ,, | ,, | ,, | Rao Sahib Balawanta Shridhara Sahasrabudhe. | do. | District Pleader, and Municipal Commissioner, Satara. | do. |
| 71 | ,, | ,, | ,, | Rao Bahadur Ganesh Pandurang Apte. | do. | Inamdar, Vice-President District Board and Municipality, Satara. | do. |
| 72 | ,, | Belgaum. | Belgaum. | Mr. Sadasiva Balkrishna Bhate. | do. | Pleader, Municipal Commissioner, Member District Local Board; Joint Secretary District Association, Belgaum. | General Meeting held at Belgaum on 18th December, 1892. |
| 73 | ,, | ,, | ,, | ,, Bhim Rao Ramjee Guthkar. | do. | Pleader. | do. |
| 74 | ,, | Ichalkaranji. | Ichalkaranji. | ,, Ramchandra Baladev Apte. | do. | Member of A. V. School Committee, Ichalkaranji, in charge of I. N. Congress Hall of Ichalkaranji, Member of Poona Industrial Conference. | Public Meeting held at Ichalkaranji on 14th December, 1892. |
| 75 | ,, | ,, | ,, | ,, Ramchandra Ballal *alias* Baba Sahib Ranade. | do. | President, Sarvajanik Sabha, Ichalkaranji. | do. |
| 76 | ,, | Deccan. | Poona Sarvajanik Sabha. | ,, Krishnaji Sakharam Joshi. | do. | Pleader, Karandwar State. ... | General Meeting of the Poona Sarvajanik Sabha held on 6th December, 1892. |
| 77 | ,, | ,, | ,, | ,, Naro Bhaskar Deodhar. | do. | Pensioned Deputy Educational Inspector, Member Poona Sarvajanik Sabha and Member Local Board, Taluka Sirur. | Do. and Public Meeting held at Poona on 20th November, 1892. |
| 78 | ,, | ,, | ,, | ,, Ranganatha Bapuji Melay. | do. | Member of the Poona Sarvajanik Sabha and Sowkar, Poona. | do. |
| 79 | ,, | ,, | ,, | ,, Vasudeo Laxman Athavale. | do. | Member of the Poona Sarvajanik Sabha, Joint Secretary Deccan Standing Congress Com., Sowkar, Inamdar, Narayan Peth, Poona. | do. |
| 80 | ,, | ,, | ,, | ,, Raghunath Narayan Pandit. | do. | Member of the Poona Sarvajanik Sabha and Sowkar, Kesava Peth, Poona. | do. |
| 81 | ,, | ,, | ,, | ,, Vinayak Narayana Apte. | do. | Member of the Poona Sarvajanik Sabha and Merchant Shanwarpeth, Poona. | do. |
| 82 | ,, | ,, | ,, | ,, Gopala Krishna Gokhale, B. A. | do. | Professor, Fergusson College; Superintendent New English School, Hon. Secretary and Member, Poona Sarvajanik Sabha, Editor of the "Quarterly Journal" of the Sabha. | do. |
| 83 | ,, | ,, | ,, | ,, Shivarama Hari Sathe. | do. | Member and Hon. Secretary Poona Sarvajanik Sabha, and Editor "Nyayashraya," Mehoonpoora, Poona. | do. |
| 84 | ,, | ,, | ,, | ,, Raghunatha Daji Nagarkar. | do. | Member of the Poona Sarvajanik Sabha, Municipal Commissioner, District Pleader, Budhwar Peth, Poona. | do. |
| 85 | ,, | ,, | ,, | Rao Bahadur Vishnu Moreshwara Bhide. | do. | Pensioned First Class Sub-Judge; Chairman, Poona Sarvajanik Sabha, Sadashiwa Peth, Poona. | do. |
| 86 | ,, | ,, | ,, | Mr. Ramachandra Kesava Limaye. | do. | District Pleader, Sadashiva Peth, Poona. | Public Meeting held at Poona, 20th November, 1892. |
| 87 | ,, | ,, | ,, | ,, Madhusudan Wasudeo Athalye. | do. | Landholder, Poona ... | do. |
| 88 | ,, | ,, | ,, | ,, Raghunatha Ramachandra Agasti. | do. | Pensioned Sub-Engineer, Municipal Commissioner, Member, Arbitration Court; Kalewaver, Poona. | do. |

| Number. | Presidency or Government. | Congress Circle. | Electoral Division. | Names in full of Delegates, with honorary titles, scholastic degrees, etc. | Race, Religious denomination, and Caste, if any. | Occupation and Address. | How and when elected. |
|---|---|---|---|---|---|---|---|
| 89 | Bombay. | Deccan. | Poona. | Mr. Wamana Balakrishna Ranade. | Brahmin. | Member, Poona Sarvajanik Sabha; Member, Nasik Sarvajanik Sabha, Editor of "Dnayan Chakshu," Poona. | Public Meeting at Poona on 20th November, 1892, and General Meeting of the Nasik Sarvajanik Sabha on 4th December, 1892. |
| 90 | ,, | ,, | ,, | ,, Mahadeva Rajarama Bodas, M. A. | do. | Editor of the "Mahratta," English Paper. | Public Meeting held at Poona on 30th November, 1892. |
| 91 | ,, | ,, | ,, | ,, Keshava Rao Chiman Rao Dhole. | do. | Municipal Commissioner, Banker; member, Poona Sarvajanik Sabha. | do. |
| 92 | ,, | ,, | ,, | Shrimant Narhar Balakrishna Paranjpe. | do. | Banker; Proprietor of Fatoor Ginning Press and Secretary and Treasurer Basatkot Spinning and Weaving Co. | do. |
| 93 | ,, | ,, | ,, | Mr. Kashinath Govinda Natu. | do. | Pleader and Secretary, Deccan Standing Congress Committee, Sadashiva Peth, Poona. | do. |
| 94 | ,, | ,, | ,, | ,, Narayana Bapuji Kanitakar. | do. | District Pleader, Municipal Commissioner and joint administrator, Chinchwada Sansuttar. | do. |
| 95 | ,, | ,, | ,, | Shrimant Narhar Rao Trimbaka Rajmukhikara, B. A. | do. | Inamdar and Sirdar; Proprietor of "Nyayashray" Shanwar Peth, Poona. | do. |
| 96 | ,, | ,, | ,, | Rao Saheb Mahadeo Ballal Namjoshi. | do. | Municipal Commissioner; Editor, "Industrial Review"; Secretary, Industrial Conference, Mehoopura, Poona. | do. |
| 97 | ,, | ,, | Poona Arbitration Court. | Mr. Vinayaka Sadashiva Yerawadikar. | do. | District Pleader, Kasba Petta, Poona. | General Meeting of the Arbitration Court held on 12th December, 1892. |
| 98 | ,, | ,, | Sarvajanik Sabha, Nasik. | ,, Krishna Rao Jayrama Gupte. | Parbhoo. | Pleader, Sub-Judge's Court, Malegaun, zilla Nasik. | General Meeting of the Sabha held on 4th December, 1892. |
| 99 | ,, | ,, | ,, | ,, Vaijanatha Jiaji Ratnaprekhe. | Brahmin. | Contractor, Taluka Nandgaon, zilla Nasik. | do. |
| 100 | ,, | ,, | ,, | ,, Trimbaka Sadashiva Gokhale. | do. | Pensioned Government Servant, Malegaun, zilla Nasik. | do. |
| 101 | ,, | ,, | ,, | ,, Janardan Raghu Nath Nimkar. | do. | District Pleader, Member of Nasik Taluka Local Board. | do. |
| 102 | ,, | ,, | ,, | ,, Vishwa Nath Bapuji Pande. | do. | Private Clerk, Srinar, Zilla Nasik. | do. |
| 103 | ,, | ,, | ,, | ,, Anant Raoji Kawle. | do. | Municipal Commissioner of Srinar, Member of Taluka Local Board and Nasik District Local Board; Srinar, zilla Nasik. | do. |
| 104 | ,, | ,, | ,, | ,, Balwant Ganesh Navale. | Hindu Shimpi. | Municipal Commissioner, Srinar, Vakil Srinar, District Nasik. | do. |
| 105 | ,, | ,, | ,, | ,, Gangadhar Narsingha Ketkar. | Brahmin. | District Pleader, elected member of the Nasik District and Taluka Local Board. | do. |
| 106 | ,, | ,, | ,, | ,, Tukarama Hanmant Patel Morare. | Mahratta. | Farmer, Contractor, Mhasrol, Taluka Nasik, District Nasik. | do. |
| 107 | ,, | ,, | Dhulia. | ,, Vinayak Narayana Paranjpe, B.A. | Hindu Brahmin. | Money-lender, Chalisgaon. | Public Meeting presided over by Rao Bahadur G. R. Garud. |
| 108 | ,, | ,, | Dharwar. | ,, Ramachandra Trimbaka Kirtane, B.A., LL. B. | Do. | Pleader, Dharwar. | Public Meeting held, on 11th December, 1892. |
| 109 | ,, | ,, | ,, | ,, Jivan Rao Hanwant Rao Betigiri, B.A., LL. B. | Do. | Pleader and landed proprietor. | do. |
| 110 | ,, | ,, | Hubli (Dharwar District). | ,, T. Swaminath Iyer. | Do. | Railway servant; Locomotive Department, S. M. Ry., Hubli. | do. |
| 111 | ,, | ,, | Gayan Samaj, Poona. | ,, Purushottama Ganesh *alias* Anna Ghorpare. | Do. | Professor of Music, Mehoopoora, Poona. | General Meeting of Gayan Samaj held at Poona, 20th November, 1892. |
| 112 | ,, | ,, | Bhimthudi. | Rao Saheb Bhikaji Ananda Rao Deshpande. | Brahmin. | Pleader of the District Court, Poona, Inamdar; Chairman of the Baramati Municipality and Member of Local Board, Bhimthudi. | At a Public Meeting held at Baramati, 5th December, 1892. |

| Number. | Presidency or Government. | Congress Circle. | Electoral Division. | Names in full of Delegates, with honorary titles, scholastic degrees, etc. | Race, Religious denomination, and Caste if any. | Occupation and Address. | How and when elected. |
|---|---|---|---|---|---|---|---|
| 113 | Bombay. | Deccan. | Rui (Kolhapur.) | Mr. Kashi Nath Ranga Nath Joshi. | Brahmin. | Land-holder, Rui, Kolhapur District. | At a Public Meeting held at Rui, 25th December, 1892. |
| 114 | ,, | ,, | ,, | ,, Appaji Vishnu Kulkarni. | do. | Land-holder, Rui, Kolhapur District. | do. |
| 115 | | ,, | ,, | ,, Krishnaji Dadaji Kulkarni. | do. | do. | do. |
| 116 | Hyderabad Assigned Districts. | Berar. | Amraoti. | ,, Keshav Balwant Deshpande. | Marhatta Brahmin. | Land-holder ... ... | At a Public Meeting held at Amraoti on 6th November, 1892. |
| 117 | ,, | ,, | ,, | ,, Vasudeo Narayn Jog. | do. | Pleader ... ... | do. |
| 118 | ,, | ,, | ,, | ,, Moreshwar Bapuji Marathe. | do. | Pleader ... ... | do. |
| 119 | ,, | ,, | ,, | ,, Ranganath Narsinha Mudholkar, B.A., LL.B. | do. | Pleader, High Court, and Land-holder. | Do. and General Meeting of the Berar Sarvajanik Sabha on 6th November, 1892. |
| 120 | ,, | ,, | ,, | ,, Ganesh Shrikrishna Khaparde. | do. | Vakil, High Court, Malguzar, Vice-chairman Municipal Committee and Chairman District Board. | At a Public Meeting at Amraoti on 6th November, 1892. |
| 121 | ,, | ,, | ,, | ,, Panduranga Govinda. | do. | Vakil, High Court, and Land-holder. | At a Public Meeting held at Amraoti on 6th November, and a Public Meeting at Akola on 11th December, 1892. |
| 122 | ,, | ,, | ,, | ,, Vinayaka Savlaram Oak. | do. | Pleader ... ... | At a Public Meeting held at Amraoti on 6th November, 1892. |
| 123 | ,, | ,, | [illegible]ichpur | ,, Bapu Mahadeo Pandse. | do. | District Court Pleader ... | Public Meeting held at Ellichpore on 13th November, 1892. |
| 124 | ,, | | ,, | ,, Gangadhara Narayana Jagdall. | do. | do. | do. |
| 125 | ,, | ,, | ,, | ,, Vasudeo Krishna Dange. | Hindu Krishna Pakshi | do. | do. |
| 126 | ,, | ,, | ,, | ,, Shripat Mahadeo Keskar. | Hindu Brahman. | District Court Pleader and Land-holder. | do. |
| 127 | ,, | ,, | Akola | ,, V. R. Mudholkar ... | do. | Municipal Commissioner and Editor, "Vaidarbha," Akola. | Public Meeting at Akola, 11th December, 1892. |
| 128 | ,, | ,, | ,, | ,, Ramachandra Vishnu Mahajana. | do. | Agriculturist and Banker ... | do. |
| 129 | ,, | ,, | ,, | ,, Ram Rao Gopal Deshpande. | do. | Deshpande and Land-holder. | do. |
| 130 | ,, | ,, | ,, | ,, Rama Rao Jagirdar ... | do. | Jagirdar of Babulgaon ... | do. |
| 131 | ,, | ,, | ,, | ,, Shankara Govinda ... | do. | Banker ... ... | do. |
| 132 | ,, | ,, | Mangrul Pir Taluq. | ,, Ram Krishna Balirama Kiday. | do. | Savakarkarniya ... | Public Meeting held on 21st November, 1892 |
| 133 | ,, | ,, | Berar Sarvajanik Sabha. | ,, Lakshmana Atmaram Mahajana. | do. | Merchant, Money-lender, and Vice-President, District Board, Bassein. | At a General Meeting of the Sabha held on 5th November, 1892. |
| 134 | ,, | ,, | ,, | Rao Sahib Dev Rao Vinayak. | do. | Vakil, High Court, Land-lord and Municipal Commissioner. | Do. and at a Public Meeting of the Akola people at Akola, held on 11th December, 1892. |
| 135 | ,, | | ,, | Mr. Kondo Balaji Purekar. | do. | Pleader and Municipal Commissioner, Amraoti. | At a General Meeting of the Sabha held on 5th November, 1892, and Public Meeting held at Amraoti on 6th November, 1892. |
| 136 | ,, | ,, | Malkapur Taluq | ,, Vasudeo Balaji Pimplikar. | do. | Pleader, Malkapur | At a Public Meeting held at Malkapur on 24th December, 1892 |
| 137 | ,, | ,, | ,, | ,, Sampat Rao Parwata Rao Deshmukh. | Hindu Marhatta. | Land-lord ... ... | do. |
| 138 | Central Provinces. | Nagpur. | Jabalpore. | ,, Ram Gulam Avasthi. | Hindu Brahmin. | Teacher, Mission School, Jabalpur, Editor of "Shubhachintaka," a weekly Anglo-Hindi paper. | At a Public Meeting held at Jabalpore on 17th December, 1892. |
| 139 | ,, | ,, | Nagpore. | ,, Bhagiratha Prasada, B.A. | Hindu. | Professor of Mathematics, Hislop College, Nagpur; Municipal Commissioner, Nagpur, Secretary, Total Abstinence Association and President of Young Men's Association; Secretary, Reception Committee, 7th Indian National Congress, and Secretary, C. P. Standing Congress Committee, Nagpur. | At a Public Meeting held in the City School, Nagpore, on 20th November, 1892 At a Public Meeting held at Damoh on 22nd December, 1892. |

| Number. | Presidency or Government. | Congress Circle. | Electoral Division. | Names in full of Delegates, with honorary titles, scholastic degrees, etc. | Race, Religious denomination, and Caste, if any. | Occupation and Address. | How and when elected. |
|---|---|---|---|---|---|---|---|
| 140 | Central Provinces. | Nagpur. | Nagpur. | Mr. Mahadeva Sakharam. | Goldsmith. | Contractor, Cash and Pay Office, B. N. R., Nagpur. | At a Public Meeting held in the City School, Nagpur, on 20th November, 1892. |
| 141 | " | " | " | " C. Narain Swamy Nayadu. | Hindu, Madrasi Kshatriya. | Pleader, Central Provinces and Berar, Nagpur; Chairman, Reception Committee, 7th Indian National Congress, Nagpur; Municipal Commissioner and President, Nagpur Municipal Board; Secretary, District Board, Nagpur; President Theosophical Society, Nagpur, &c. | do. |
| 142 | " | " | " | " C. S. Nayadu, B.A., (Cantab.) | do. | Barrister-at-Law, Nagpur ... | do. |
| 143 | " | " | " | " C. V. Nayadu. | do. | Do. | do. |
| 144 | " | " | " | " Hari Mahadeva Pandit. | Maharastra Brahman. | Editor, "Deshasevaka," an Anglo-Marathi weekly. | Public Meeting at Ichal-Karanji on 14th December, 1892. |
| 145 | " | " | " | " Kesava Vinayak Joshi, B.A. | Brahmin. | Head Master, City Aided School, Nagpur. | Public Meeting held at the City School, Nagpur, on 20th November, 1892. |
| 146 | " | " | Raipur. | " Kedarnath Bagchi, M.A. | Bengali Brahmin. | Pleader, Raipur ... ... | General Meeting held at Raipur on 27th November, 1892. |
| 147 | " | " | " | Pandit Nandalal ... | Gujrati Brahmin. | Sanyasi, Raipur ... ... | do. |
| 148 | " | " | " | Mr. Gajaram Ragho Bagchi. | Maharastra Brahmin. | Pleader, Raipur ... ... | do. |
| 149 | " | " | " | " Govind Prasad Dube. | Hindustani Brahmin. | Do. | do. |
| 150 | " | " | Bilaspur. | " Nagendranatha De. | Bengali Kayastha. | Barrister-at-Law, Hon. Magistrate and Municipal Secretary, Bilaspur. | Public Meeting held at Bilaspur on 17th November, 1892. |
| 151 | " | " | " | " Thakur Bisal Singha. | Rajput. | Zamindar, Akalta, Bilaspur. | do. |
| 152 | " | " | " | " Sheikh Qhwaja Bukhsh. | Mahomedan Sunni. | Agent to the Zamindar of Safa, Bilaspur. | do. |
| 153 | " | " | " | Pandit Nandlal Tiwari. | Hindustani Brahmin. | Mukhtar of Champa, Zamindar, Bilaspur. | do. |
| 154 | " | " | Sagor Hita-Sabha. | " Damodara Rao Shrikhande. | Maharastra Brahmin. | Pleader, Damoh ... ... | By a General Meeting of the Hita Sabha, Sagor, held on 20th November, 1892. Public Meeting held at Damoh on 22nd December, 1892. |
| 155 | " | " | " | Mr. Vinayak Ganesa Vaidya. | do. | Pleader, Sagor ... ... | By a General Meeting of the Hita Sabha, Sagor, held on 20th November, 1892. |
| 156 | " | " | Harda. | " Balawant Kashinath Agnihotri. | Arya Vaidic Maharashtra Brahmin. | Malguzar, Harda ... | Public Meeting held at Harda on 8th November, 1892. |
| 157 | " | " | " | " Govinda Rao Narayan Paroolkara. | do. | do. | do. |
| 158 | " | " | " | " Krishna Rao Narayana Rogay. | do. | Jagiradar, Harda ... | do. |
| 159 | " | " | " | " Vishnu Damodar Quidarkar. | do. | Banker, Harda ... ... | do. |
| 160 | " | " | Hoshangabad. | " Raoji Govinda Khirwarkar. | do. | Pleader, Harda ... ... | do. |
| 161 | " | " | Raj Nandgaon. | Pandit Shankara Prasada. | Hindustani Brahmin. | Pleader, Raj Nandgaon ... | Public Meeting held at Raj Nandgaon on 8th November, 1892. |
| 162 | " | " | " | Swami Brahmanand Saraswati. | Hindu Sanyasi. | Hindu Preacher, Raj Nandgaon. | do. on 21st December 1892. |
| 163 | " | " | " | Pandit Shrinivas Rao Modak. | Maharastra Brahmin. | Pleader, Raj Nandgaon ... | Do. on 8th November, 1892. |
| 164 | " | " | " | Mr. V. Sarangpani Mudaliar. | Madrasi Tailanga. | Municipal Commissioner, Manager, "Balram Press," Proprietor of "Raj Nandgaon Gazette" and General Contractor, Raj Nandgaon. | do. |

| Number. | Presidency or Government. | Congress Circle. | Electoral Division. | Names in full of Delegates, with honorary titles, scholastic degrees, etc. | Race, Religious denomination, and Caste, if any. | Occupation and Address. | How and when elected. |
|---|---|---|---|---|---|---|---|
| 165 | Central Provinces. | Nagpur. | Chhindwara. | Mr. Prabhakara Sridhara Raduy. | Brahmin. | Land-owner, Chhindwara ... | By a Public Meeting held at Chhindwara on 20th November, 1892. |
| 166 | ,, | ,, | ,, | ,, Mathuraprasada. | Kayastha. | Pleader and Land-owner, Chhindwara. | do. |
| 167 | ,, | ,, | ,, | ,, Vinayak Rao Ganesha Wazalwara. | Maharashtra Brahman. | do. | do. |
| 168 | ,, | ,, | Wardha. | ,, Keshava Rao Mahadeva Kawlay. | do. | Malguzar, Banker and Pleader, Wardha. | By a Public Meeting held at Wardha on 27th November, 1892. |
| 169 | ,, | ,, | ,, | ,, Laxman Govinda Deskara. | do. | do. | do. |
| 170 | ,, | ,, | ,, | ,, Narayana Shripat Patel. | Hindu Kunbi. | Malguzar and Cultivator of Mouza Takli, Tahsil Wardha. | do. |
| 171 | ,, | ,, | District Association, Wardha. | ,, Balkrishna Panduranga Kalyani. | Hindu Brahman. | Malguzar and Cultivator, Wardha. | At a General Meeting of the Wardha District Association held on 16th November, 1892. |
| 172 | ,, | ,, | ,, | ,, Ganpata Rao Kashinath Meghay. | Hindu Kunbi. | Malguzar and Banker of Tukli, Tahsil Wardha. | do. |
| 173 | ,, | ,, | ,, | ,, Balirama Chanaji ... | do. | Malguzar and Cultivator Takli, Tahsil Wardha. | do. |
| 174 | ,, | ,, | Balaghat. | ,, Sham Rao Keshav Mazumdar. | Maharashtra Brahman. | Municipal Commissioner for the town of Burha, Landholder, Malguzar, Balaghat. | By a Public Meeting held at Balaghat on 20th November, 1892. |
| 175 | ,, | ,, | ,, | ,, Moreswara Jagannatha. | do | Municipal Commissioner for the town of Burha, and Malguzar, Balaghat. | do. |
| 176 | ,, | ,, | ,, | ,, Narayana Krishna Kelkar. | do. | Municipal Commissioner and Secretary for the Town of Burha; Pleader, Balaghat. | do. |
| 177 | ,, | ,, | Burhanpur. | ,, Raghunath Rao Balkrishna Bhide. | do. | Manager, "Arya Baibhava" Press, Burhanpur. | By a Public Meeting held at Burhanpur on 10th December, 1892. |
| 178 | Bengal. | Calcutta. | The Northern Metropolitan Electoral Division. | Mr. W. C. Bonnerjee ... | Bengali Brahmin. | Barrister-at-Law, 6, Park Street, Calcutta. | At a Public Meeting held at the Albert Hall, Calcutta, on 22nd December, 1892. |
| 179 | ,, | ,, | ,, | Babu Heramba Chandra Maitra, M. A. | Bengali Brahmo. | Professor, City College, Calcutta. | do. |
| 180 | ,, | ,, | ,, | ,, Khitendra Nath Tagore. | Bengali Brahmin. | Zamindar, 6, Dwarka Nath Tagore's lane, Calcutta. | do. |
| 181 | ,, | ,, | ,, | ,, Amoy Nath Bose ... | Bengali Kayastha. | Private service, 13, College Square, Calcutta. | do. |
| 182 | ,, | ,, | ,, | ,, Tarak Nath Palit, B. L. | do. | Vakil, High Court, Bechoo Chatterjee's Street, Calcutta. | do. |
| 183 | ,, | ,, | ,, | ,, Nalin Behari Sircar. | do. | Merchant, Municipal Commissioner and Port Commissioner, 21, Beadon Street, Calcutta. | do. |
| 184 | ,, | ,, | ,, | ,, Monmotho Mohan Bose. | do. | Assistant Professor, Physical Science, Metropolitan Institution, 38, Muktaram Babu's Street, Calcutta. | do. |
| 185 | ,, | ,, | The Southern Metropolitan Electoral Division. | Pandit Kali Prasanna Kavyabisharad. | Hindu. | Editor, "Cosmopolitan" and Proprietor "Secular Press," Bhowanipur. | At a Meeting of the Division held on the 8th December, 1892. |
| 186 | ,, | ,, | ,, | Babu Basonto Kumar Bose, M. A., B. L. | Hindu Kayastha. | Vakil, High Court, Calcutta. | do. |
| 187 | ,, | ,, | British Indian Association. | Mr. J. Ghosal ... | Bengali Brahmin. | Zamindar, Merchant, Vice-President, Bengal National Chamber of Commerce, Honorary Magistrate and Municipal Commissioner, Calcutta. | At a Committee Meeting of the British Indian Association. At a Committee Meeting of the Bengal National Chamber of Commerce, and at a Public Meeting held at the Albert Hall on the 22nd December, 1892. |

| Number. | Presidency or Government. | Congress Circle. | Electoral Division. | Names in full of Delegates, with honorary titles, scholastic degrees, etc. | Race, Religious denomination, and Caste, if any. | Occupation and Address. | How and when elected. |
|---|---|---|---|---|---|---|---|
| 188 | Bengal. | Calcutta. | Indian Association, Calcutta. | Babu Surendra Nath Banerjee, B. A. | Bengali Brahmin. | Principal, Ripon College, Hon. Magistrate, Municipal Commissioner, Chairman, North Barackpore Municipality and Editor, "Bengalee." | At a meeting of the Committee held on the 4th of November, 1892. |
| 189 | ,, | ,, | ,, | Rai Jotindra Nath Choudhry, M. A., B. L. | Hindu Kayastha. | Zamindar, and Hon. Magistrate Barahnagar, (24, Parganas) | do. |
| 190 | ,, | ,, | ,, | Babu Krishna Kumar Mitra, B. A. | Bengali Brahmo. | Superintendent, City College and Editor, "Sanjibani." | do. |
| 191 | ,, | ,, | ,, | ,, Hem Chandra Rai, M. A., B. L. | Hindu, Bengali Vaidya. | Pleader, Judge's Court, 24. Parganahs. | do. |
| 192 | ,, | ,, | ,, | Dr. Mohini Mohan Bose, M. D., L. R. C. P. | Bengali, Brahmo. | Zamindar, Hon. Magistrate, Physician and Surgeon 64/1 Mechooa Bazar Street, Calcutta. | do. |
| 193 | ,, | ,, | 24, Parganahs, Barahnagar. | Babu Haridas Mukerjee. | Hindu Brahmin. | Zamindar, Barahnagar (District, 24 Parganahs.) | At a meeting held on the 4th December, 1892, at Barahnagar. |
| 194 | ,, | ,, | ,, | ,, Mohit Chandra Bose, M. A., B. L. | Hindu Kayastha. | Vakil, High Court, Barahnagar, (24 Parganahs.) | Do. |
| 195 | ,, | ,, | Krishnagar (Dt. Nuddea.) | ,, Tarapada Banerjee, B. L. | Bengali Brahmin | Vakil, Judge's Court, and Municipal Commissioner, Nuddea | At a public meeting held on the 1st December 1892. |
| 196 | ,, | ,, | ,, | ,, Hari Prasad Chatterjee, B. L. | Do. | Pleader, Judge's Court, Nuddea | Do. |
| 197 | ,, | ,, | Chakdah (District Nuddea.) | ,, Akshoy Kumar Mitra. | Hindu Kayastha. | Vice-chairman, Municipality, Taluqdar, Chakdah (District Nuddea.) | At a public meeting held at Chakdah Bazar on the 13th November, 1892. |
| 198 | ,, | ,, | Khulna. | ,, Jadab Chandra Das. | Hindu Barui. | Pleader, Land-holder, Khulna. | At a public meeting held at the Khulna Town Hall on the 3rd of December, 1892. |
| 199 | ,, | ,, | ,, | ,, Beni Bhushan Ray, B. L. | Hindu Kayastha. | Pleader. Honorary Secretary, Khulna Loan Office, and Secretary, Khulna Trading Company, Limited. | Do. |
| 200 | ,, | ,, | Jessore Branch Committee. | ,, Kaligopal Mazoomdar | Do. | Taluqdar, Jessore ... | At a meeting of the Jessore Branch Congress Committee held on the 4th December, 1892. |
| 201 | ,, | ,, | Midnapur. | Mr. K. B. Dutt ... | Bengali Kayastha. | Barrister-at-Law, Advocate, Midnapur. | At a Public Meeting at Midnapur held on the 27th of November, 1892. |
| 202 | ,, | ,, | ,, | Babu Jotindra Nath Mallik. | Hindu Tamli. | Zamindar ... ... | do. |
| 203 | ,, | ,, | ,, | ,, Upendra Narayn Pal. | Hindu Kaystha. | Zamindar, Dharinda, (District Midnapur). | do. |
| 204 | ,, | ,, | ,, | ,, Nava Kumar Mitra. | do. | Pleader, Judge's Court and Member of the Local and the District Boards, Midnapur. | do. |
| 205 | ,, | ,, | Bally. | Rai Avinash Chandra Banerjee. | Hindu, Brahmin. | Hardware Merchant, Honorary Magistrate, Chairman Bally Municipality, Secretary Bally Sadharani Sabha, 7 Raja Udmant's Street, Calcutta. | At a Public Meeting held on the 26th November, 1892. |
| 206 | ,, | ,, | Serampur (District Hughly). | Babu Hari Mohan Gossain, B. A. | Bengali Brahmin. | Head Master, Serampur Union Institution. | At a Public Meeting held on the 27th of November, 1892. |
| 207 | ,, | ,, | ,, | Mrs. A. S. West. ... | European Christian. | Land-holder, Serampur, ... | At a Public Meeting held on the 13th November, 1892. |

| Number. | Presidency of Government. | Congress Circle. | Electoral Division. | Names in full of Delegates, with honorary titles, scholastic degrees, etc. | Race, Religious denomination, and Caste, if any. | Occupation and Address. | How and when elected. |
|---|---|---|---|---|---|---|---|
| 208 | Bengla. | Calcutta. | Hughly Chinsurah and Chandernagore. | Babu Keshav Chandra Sadhu. | Bengali Hindu. | Trader, Rai Bagan, British Chandernagore. | At a Public Meeting held at Chinsurah on the 11th December, 1892. |
| 209 | ,, | ,, | ,, | ,, Romesh Chundra Mandal. | Bengali Hindu Subarnabanik. | Zamindar and Municipal Commissioner, Kamarpara Road, Chinsurah. | do. |
| 210 | ,, | ,, | Murshidabad. | ,, Baikuntha Nath Sen B.A., B.L. | Bengali Hindu Vaidya. | Vakil, High Court, Chairman, Barhampur Municipality, President, Murshidabad Association, Honorary Magistrate and Zamindar. | At a Public Meeting of the Murshidabad Association held on the 4th December, 1892. |
| 211 | ,, | ,, | ,, | ,, Brojendra Nath Seal, M.A. | Bengali Brahmo (Sadharan). | Principal, Barhampur College, Bengal. | do. |
| 212 | ,, | ,, | ,, | ,, Mohendra Nath Mukerjee. | Bengali Brahman. | Pleader, Zamindar and Honorary Magistrate. | do. |
| 213 | ,, | ,, | ,, | ,, Gourballabh Sen, M.A. B.L. | Bengali Kayastha Hindu | Pleader and Zamindar ... | do. |
| 214 | ,, | ,, | ,, | ,, Nafardas Roy ... | Bengali Hindu Kshatriya. | Zamindar, Honorary Magistrate, Municipal Commissioner, and Honorary Secretary, Murshidabad Association. | do. |
| 215 | ,, | ,, | ,, | ,, Hemendra Nath Sen, B.A., B.L. | Bengali Hindu Baidya. | Pleader ... ... | do. |
| 216 | ,, | ,, | ,, | Kumar Umesh Chandra Roy. | Bengali Brahman. | Zamindar ... ... | At a Public Meeting of the Murshidabad Association held on the 12th December, 1892. |
| 217 | ,, | ,, | ,, | Babu Harasankar Bhattacharya. | do. | Pleader, Zamindar, Honorary Magistrate and Municipal Commissioner. | do. |
| 218 | ,, | ,, | ,, | ,, Dinabandhu Sanyal. | do. | Retired Deputy Collector ... | do. |
| 219 | ,, | ,, | Bankura. | ,, Ramanand Chatterjee, M.A. | Bengali Brahmo. | Professor, City College, Calcutta. | At a Meeting of the inhabitants held on the 4th December, 1892. |
| 220 | ,, | ,, | Birbhum. | ,, Dhan Kanto Ghose, M.A. B.L. | Bengali Hindu Kayastha. | Pleader, Judge's Court, Zamindar, and late Chairman, Soory Municipality. | At a Meeting held at Soory on the 22nd November, 1892. |
| 221 | ,, | ,, | Kalna. | ,, Jogendro Nath Sen. | Hindu Vaidya. | Land-holder and Physician, Kalna. | At a Public Meeting held on the 27th of November, 1892. |
| 222 | ,, | ,, | ,, | Mr. K. B. Mallick ... | Bengali Kayastha. | Journalist ... ... | do. |
| 223 | ,, | ,, | Comilla. | Babu Charu Chandra Mittra, B.A.B.L. | Hindu Bengali Kayastha. | Pleader, Judge's Court and Land-holder, Tipperah. | At a Public Meeting of the People's Association, Comilla, held on the 4th December, 1892. |
| 224 | ,, | ,, | Tipperah. | ,, Hardayal Nag ... | Bengali Hindu. | Pleader. Land-holder, Vice-Chairman, Local Board, Chandpur, Tipperah. | At a Public Meeting at Chandpur held on the 4th December, 1892. |
| 225 | ,, | ,, | Assam, Gauhati. | ,, Bholanath Baruah ... | Assamese Hindu Kayastha. | Merchant, Gauhati ... | At a Meeting of the Assamese Residents of Calcutta held on the 12th December, 1892. |
| 226 | ,, | ,, | ,, | ,, Lakshmi Nath Bezbarua, B.A. | Assamese Hindu Brahman. | Editor of "Janoki," 18, Savaram Basak's lane, Calcutta. | do. |
| 227 | ,, | ,, | Dibrugarh, Assam. | ,, Radhanath Changkakoti. | Assamese Brahman. | Proprietor "Radhanath" Printing Press, Secretary, Upper Assam Association, Municipal Commissioner and Member Local Board, Dibrugarh, Assam. | At a Public Meeting of the Upper Assam Association held on 7th December, 1892, at Dibrugarh. |
| 228 | ,, | Mymensing. | Mymensing. | ,, Revati Mohan Guha, M.A., B.L. | Hindu Kayastha. | Pleader, Judge's Court, Mymensing. | At a Meeting held on the 3rd December, 1892. |
| 229 | ,, | ,, | ,, | ,, Kailash Chandra Nag. | Hindu. | Taluqdar, Sherpur town, Mymensing. Chairman, Sherpur Town Municipality. | do. |
| 230 | ,, | ,, | ,, | ,, Anath Bandhu Guha, B.L. | do. | Pleader and Taluqdar, Member of the District Board, Honorary Magistrate, Secretary, Mymensing Association. | do. |
| 231 | ,, | ,, | ,, | ,, Srinath Rai, B.L. ... | Bengali Kayastha. | Pleader, Municipal Commissioner, Secretary, Mymensing Association. | do. |

| Number. | Presidency or Government. | Congress Circle. | Electoral Division. | Names in full of Delegates, with honorary titles, scholastic degrees, etc. | Race, Religious denomination, and Caste, if any. | Occupation and Address. | How and when elected. |
|---|---|---|---|---|---|---|---|
| 232 | Bengal. | Mymensing. | Kishoregunj, District Mymensing. | Babu Rajani Kanta Rai. | Hindu Kayastha. | Talukdar, Post Office Joraitola, Kishoregunj, Mymensing. | At a meeting held on the 27th November, 1892, at Kishoregunj. |
| 233 | " | " | Tangail. | " Prasonno Kumar Bose. | Hindu Brahmo. | Talukdar, Alisakandar ... | At a meeting of the inhabitants of Tangail residing at Calcutta held on the 25th December, 1892. |
| 234 | " | Pubna. | Pubna. | " Mahendra Narain Chakravarti, B.A., B. L. | Hindu Brahmin. | Pleader, Judge's Court, Pubna, and Land-holder. | At a public meeting held on the 6th November, 1892, at the local Town Hall. |
| 235 | " | " | " | " Jnyana Gobind Chakravarti, B. A., B. L. | Do. | Pleader, Judge's Court, Pubna, and Honorary Magistrate, Independent Bench, Pubna. | At a public meeting held on the 6th November, 1892, at the local Town Hall. |
| 236 | " | " | " | " Mohini Mohun Lahiri, M. A., B. L. | Do. | Pleader Judge's Court, Pubna, and Land-holder. | At a public meeting held on the 6th November, 1892, at the local Town Hall. |
| 237 | " | Dacca. | Munshigunj. | " Kishori Mohun Bose. | Hindu Kayastha. | Zamindar and Member, Local Board, Munshigunj, Dacca. | At a public meeting held at Munshigunj, on 9th December, 1892. |
| 238 | " | " | " | " Jagat Chandra Roy. | Do. | Pleader and Member, Local Board, Munshigunj. (Dacca). | Do. |
| 239 | " | " | Dacca. | " Sarat Chandra Bose, B. L. | Bengali Brahmo. | Pleader, Judge's Court, Secretary, Dacca Congress Committee. | At a meeting held on 19th December, 1892. |
| 240 | " | Furridpore. | Furridpore Suddur Division. | Mr. Girja Shankar Mozumdar, M. A., B. L. | Hindu Vaidya. | Zamindar and Vakil, High Court, Calcutta. | By the Furridpur Suhrid Sabha; on the 4th December, 1892, and at a public meeting held on the 21st November at Goalundo. |
| 241 | " | " | " | " Ambica Charan Mozumdar, M. A., B. L. | do. | Zamindar and Pleader, District Court, Furridpore. | At a public meeting held at Furridpore, on the 4th December, at Manickdaha on the 11th December, and at Mada ripur, on the 29th November, 1892. |
| 242 | " | " | " | " Amrita Lal Roy Chaudhary. | Hindu Brahman. | Zamindar ... ... | do. |
| 243 | " | " | " | " Nilkanth Chatterjee, M. A., B. L. | do. | Pleader, District Court, Mymensingh. | At a public meeting held at Furridpur, 4th December, and at Madaripur, on 29th December, 1892. |
| 244 | " | " | " | " Prithis Chandra Roy Chaudhury. | Hindu Kayastha. | Zamindar, Olapore, District Furridpore, Sub-Division Gopalgunj. | At a public meeting held at Furridpore, on the 4th December, and at Tangail on the 22nd November, 1892. |
| 245 | " | Dinajpur | Dinajpur. | Babu Madhava Chandra Chatterji, M. A., B. L. | Bengali Hindu Brahman. | Pleader and Vice-Chairman of the Dinajpur Municipality. | At a public meeting held on the 14th November, 1892. |
| 246 | " | " | " | " Umesh Chandra Khasnavis. | Bengali Hindu Kayastha. | Mukhtar, Zamindar and Municipal Commissioner, Dinajpur. | do. |
| 247 | " | Rungpore. | Rungpore. | " Satish Kamal Sen, B. A., B. L. | Baidya Hindu. | Pleader, District Court, Rungpur. | do., and on the 14th December, 1892. |
| 248 | " | Barisal. | Backergunge. | " Harakanta Sen ... | Bengali Hindu Vaidya. | Assistant Secretary, Barisal Peoples' Association, Secretary Loan Office, Barisal. | At a general meeting of the residents of Backergunge, held on the 27th November, 1892, and at a meeting of the Peoples' Association held on the 22nd December, 1892. |
| 249 | " | Chota-Nagpur. | Hazaribagh Giridhi Sub-Division. | Munshi Khublal Peshkar. | Hindu, Kayastha. | Peshkar, Palgunj Raj Estate, (Giridhi.) | At a public meeting held on 19th December, 1892. |
| 250 | " | " | " | Munshi Davi Churn Lal. | " | Pleader, Giridhi ... ... | do. |

| Number. | Presidency or Government. | Congress Circle. | Electoral Division. | Names in full of Delegates, with honorary titles, scholastic degrees, etc. | Race, Religious denomination, and Caste, if any. | Occupation and Address. | How and when elected. |
|---|---|---|---|---|---|---|---|
| 251 | Bengal. | Chota Nagpore | Hazaribagh Sudder Sub-Division. | Babu Hanuman Prasad | Hindu Kayastha. | Government Pensioner, Honorary Magistrate, Hazaribagh. | At a public meeting held at Hazaribagh, on the 26th November, 1892. |
| 252 | „ | „ | „ | Mirza Imdad Ali ... | Mahomedan. | Landholder, Honorary Magistrate and Municipal Commissioner, Hazaribagh ... | do. |
| 253 | „ | „ | Hazaribagh. | Babu Narendra Nath Mukerjee. | Bengali Hindu, Brahman. | Landholder, Hazaribagh ... | At a Committee meeting of the Hazaribagh Association, held on 23rd December, 1892. |
| 254 | „ | „ | Lohardonga. | „ Parbhu Narain ... | Hindu Bihari Kaystha. | Mukhtar and Zamindar Ranchi. | At a public meeting held at Ranchi, on 15th November, 1892. |
| 255 | „ | „ | „ | „ Radha Gobind Chaudhari, M.A., B.L. | Hindu Bengali Vaidya. | Pleader „ „ | do. |
| 256 | „ | Behar. | Patna. | Moulv Basharat Hosain. | Mahomedan. | Zamindar, Bankipur ... | At a General Meeting held at Patna on the 25th November, 1892. |
| 257 | „ | „ | „ | Moulvi Abdul Hamid, B.A., B.L. | do. | Zamindar, Pleader, Secretary, Standing Congress Committee, Hon. Magistrate, and Member, Local Board. | do. |
| 258 | „ | „ | „ | Babu Udit Singh ... | Hindu Brahman. | Zamindar, Sultangunj, Patna City. | do. |
| 259 | „ | „ | „ | „ Guru Prasad Sen, M.A., B.L. | Hindu. | Vakil, High Court, Municipal Commissioner, Zamindar, Secretary, Behar Land-holder's Association and Editor, "Behar Herald." | do. |
| 260 | „ | „ | „ | „ Bisheshar Singh ... | Hindu Kshatriya. | Zamindar, Pleader, Hon. Magistrate, Bankipur, and Member, Local Board. | do. |
| 261 | „ | „ | „ | „ Gadadhar Prasad ... | Hindu Behari Kayastha. | Pleader, Zamindar, Chairman, Local Board, Member, District Board, and President 5th Kayastha Conference. | do. |
| 262 | „ | „ | „ | „ Purnendu Narayn Singh, M.A., B.L. | Hindu Kayastha. | Zamindar and Pleader, and Secretary, Patna Ratepayer's Association. | do. |
| 263 | „ | „ | „ | „ Mahabir Sahay, B.A., B. L. | Hindu Behari Kayastha. | Vakil High Court, Calcutta, and Zamindar. | do. |
| 264 | „ | „ | „ | „ Saligram Singh, B.A. B.L. | Hindu Kshatriya. | Zamindar, and Vakil High Court, 119, Ripon Street, Calcutta. | Do; & by the British Indian Association on the 22nd December, 1892, and the Indian Association on the 4th November, 1892. |
| 265 | „ | „ | Bankipur. | „ Bhagwat Prasad Singh. | Hindu Brahman. | Zamindar ... ... | At a meeting held at Patna on the 25th November, 1892. |
| 266 | „ | „ | Darbhanga | Babu Durga Prasad ... | Hindu Kayastha. | Zamindar, Darbhanga ... | At a Public Meeting held on the 4th December, 1892, at Darbhanga. |
| 267 | „ | „ | „ | , Bhavani Dhar Palit, B.A. | Bengalee Kayastha. | Head Master, E. B. School, Darbhanga. | do. |
| 268 | „ | „ | „ | „ Mewalal Saha ... | Hindu Banya. | Merchant, Darbhanga ... | do. |
| 269 | „ | „ | „ | „ Ameer Singh ... | Hindu Kshatriya. | Proprietor "Hari Prakash Press," Benares. | do. |
| 270 | „ | „ | Gaya. | „ Nand Kishore Lall, M.A., B.L. | Hindu Kayastha. | Vakil and Zamindar, Gaya ... | At a Public Meeting held at Gaya on 15th December, 1892. |
| 271 | „ | „ | „ | Hakim Syed Altaf Hosain. | Mahomedan Sayyed | Hakim (Medical Practitioner) 1st Road, Gaya. | do. |
| 272 | „ | Mozaffarpur. | Mozaffarpur. | Babu Shorashi Charan Mittra, B. L. | Hindu Kayastha. | Pleader, Mozaffarpur .. | At a Public Meeting held in Mozafferpur on the 27th November, 1892. |
| 273 | „ | „ | „ | „ Rameshwara Narayan Mehta. | Kshatriya. | Hon. Magistrate, Zamindar and Banker, Nandipati Road, Mozafferpur. | do. |
| 274 | „ | „ | „ | Syed Afzal Hosein ... | Mahomedan. | Mokhtar, Mozafferpur ... | do. |

| Number. | Presidency or Government. | Congress Circle. | Electoral Division. | Names in full of Delegates, with honorary titles, scholastic degrees, etc. | Race, Religious denomination, and Caste, if any. | Occupation and Address. | How and when elected. |
|---|---|---|---|---|---|---|---|
| 275 | Bengal. | Bhagalpur. | Bhagalpur. | Mr. S. C. Mookerjee ... | Bengalee Brahmin. | Barrister-at-law, 6, Park Street, Calcutta. | At a public meeting held on the 23rd November, 1892. |
| 276 | ,, | ,, | ,, | Babu Siva Shanker Sahay | Hindu Behari Kayastha. | Pleader, Bhagalpur ... | do. |
| 277 | ,, | ,, | ,, | ,, Hira Jha, B. A. | Brahmin. | Cultivator ... ... | do. |
| 278 | ,, | ,, | ,, | ,, Srimohan Thakur ... | do. | Zamindar, Municipal Commissioner, Member, District Board, and Local Board, Hon. Magistrate, Bhagalpur. | do. |
| 279 | ,, | ,, | ,, | ,, Rashbehari Mandal | Hindu Behari Gope. | Zamindar, Hon. Magistrate, Member District Board. | do. |
| 280 | ,, | ,, | Purneah. | ,, Jogendra Nath Mookerjee, M. A., B. L. | Bengalee Brahmin. | Pleader, Judge's Court, Municipal Commissioner, Purnea. | At a public meeting held on the 30th November, 1892. |
| 281 | ,, | ,, | ,, | ,, Kamikha Nath Ghose, L. M. S. | Bengali Satgope. | Medical Practitioner, Municipal Commissioner, and Hon. Magistrate, Purneah. | do. |
| 282 | ,, | ,, | ,, | ,, Parbutty Churn Das, B. A., B. L. | Brahmo, Vaidya. | Pleader, Judge's Court, Purneah, Member of the District Board and Land-holder. | do. |
| 283 | N.-W. P. | Benares. | Benares. | The Hon'ble Babu Ramkali Chaudhri. | Bengali Brahman. | Member, Legislative Council, N.-W. P. and Oudh; Municipal Commissioner, Hon. Magistrate and Retired Judge, Small Cause Court, Benares. | At a public meeting held at Benares, on 23rd October, 1892. |
| 284 | ,, | ,, | ,, | Pandit Uma Shankar Dube. | Hindustani Brahman. | Pensioner, Benares ... | do. |
| 285 | ,, | ,, | ,, | Mr. Raghunath Rao ... | Dakshini Brahman. | Zamindar, Benares ... | do. |
| 286 | ,, | ,, | ,, | Pandit Narain Shastri ... | do. | Acharya in Sanskrit Grammar, late Officiating Professor of Sankhya Philosophy in the Benares College. | do. |
| 287 | ,, | ,, | ,, | Babu Mokshadadas Mitra. | Bengali Kayastha. | Zamindar, Benares ... | do. |
| 288 | ,, | ,, | ,, | ,, Upendranath Basu, B. A., LL. B. | do. | Vakil, High Court, Benares... | do. |
| 289 | ,, | ,, | ,, | ,, Nilratan Banerji ... | Bengali Brahman. | Zamindar, Kodai Chowki, Benares. | do. |
| 290 | ,, | ,, | ,, | Munshi Shankar Lal ... | Gujrati Nagar Brahman. | Rais, Zamindar, Hon. Treasurer, Union Club, Benares. | do. |
| 291 | ,, | ,, | ,, | Babu Chintamani Mukerji, B. A. | Bengali Brahman. | School Master, Benares ... | do. |
| 292 | ,, | ,, | ,, | ,, Annada Charan Datta, B. A. | Bengali Kayastha. | Pleader, Benares ... | do. |
| 293 | ,, | ,, | ,, | Babu Narsingh Das ... | Hindu. | Vakil, Benares ... | do. |
| 294 | ,, | ,, | Sujan Samaj, Benares. | ,, Satish Chander Muzumdar. | Bengali Brahman. | Pleader, Judge's Court, Benares. | At a general meeting of the Sujan Samaj, Benares, held on 17th December, 1892. |
| 295 | ,, | ,, | ,, | Pandit Chhannu Lal Joshi | Brahman. | Pleader, Benares ... | do. |
| 296 | ,, | ,, | ,, | Goswami Janga Bahadur Puri. | Hindu Gosain. | Zamindar and Banker, Benares | do. and public meeting at Nagpur held in City School, Nagpur, on 20th November, 1892. |
| 297 | ,, | ,, | ,, | Goswami Ramacharan Puri. | do. | do. ... | At a general meeting of the Sujan Samaj, Benares, held on 17th December, 1892. |
| 298 | ,, | ,, | ,, | Babu Mathura Das ... | Gujrati Baniya. | Banker, Allahabad ... | do. |
| 299 | ,, | ,, | Ghazipur. | ,, Bholanath Ray, B.A., B. L. | Brahman. | Zamindar, Pleader High Court, Member and Secretary Municipal Board, Ghazipur. | At a public meeting held at Ghazipur, on 13th November, 1892. |
| 300 | ,, | ,, | ,, | ,, Damri Rai ... | do. | Zamindar and Pleader, Ghazipur. | do. |
| 301 | ,, | ,, | ,, | ,, Kuber Nath ... | Kayastha. | do. ... | do. |
| 302 | ,, | ,, | ,, | ,, Khudi Rai ... | Bhuinhar Brahman. | do. ... | do. |
| 303 | ,, | ,, | ,, | Munshi Udit Narain Lal | Hindustani Kayastha. | do. ... | do. |

| Number. | Presidency or Government. | Congress Circle. | Electoral Division. | Names in full of Delegates, with honorary titles, scholastic degrees, etc. | Race, Religious denomination, and Caste, if any. | Occupation and Address. | How and when elected. |
|---|---|---|---|---|---|---|---|
| 304 | N.-W.P. | Benares. | Ghazipur. | Babu Shrinath Deva ... | Hindustani Brahman. | Zamindar, Ghazipur ... | Public meeting held at Ghazipur, on 13th November, 1892. |
| 305 | ,, | ,, | ,, | Babu Govind Narain Singh. | do. | Talukdar, Ghazipur ... | do. |
| 306 | ,, | ,, | ,, | Moulvi M. Usman Khan | Mahomedan. | Zamindar and Pleader, Ghazipur. | do. |
| 307 | ,, | ,, | ,, | Babu Bishwanath Singh | Hindustani Brahman. | Zamindar, Ghazipur ... | do. |
| 308 | ,, | ,, | ,, | Munshi Aditya Prasad ... | Hindustani Kayastha. | Zamindar and Pleader, Ghazipur | do. |
| 309 | ,, | ,, | Azamgarh. | Babu Mukteshwar Ray... | Bhuinhar Brahman. | Pleader, Member, Municipal Board, and Secretary Standing Congress Committee, Azamgarh. | Public meeting held at Azamgarh, on 4th December, 1892. |
| 310 | ,, | ,, | ,, | ,, Brij Bihari Lal ... | Sunar. | Pleader, Azamgarh ... | do. |
| 311 | ,, | ,, | ,, | ,, Sunder Das ... | Agarwala Baniya. | General Merchant and Zamindar. | do. |
| 312 | ,, | ,, | ,, | ,, Gouri Shankar Singh | Hindu. | Pleader, Municipal Commissioner and Zamindar. | do. |
| 313 | ,, | ,, | ,, | Munshi Basudeo Sahai ... | Hindu Kayastha. | Teacher, Church Mission High School. | do. |
| 314 | ,, | ,, | ,, | Moulvi Muhammad Zain-ul-Abdin. | Mahomedan. | Pleader and Member, District Board. | do. |
| 315 | ,, | ,, | ,, | Mirza Muhammad Naim, | Mahomedan. | Pleader and zamindar ... | do. |
| 316 | ,, | ,, | Gorakhpur. | Thakur Ghumai Ram ... | Hindu. | Pleader ... ... | Public meeting held at Gorakhpur, on 5th December, 1892. |
| 317 | ,, | ,, | ,, | Pandit Bindeshwari Prasad. | Brahman. | Pleader and zamindar ... | do. |
| 318 | ,, | ,, | Mirzapur. | Babu Sree Ram ... | Hindu Khatri. | Zamindar, Banker, Pleader, Member, Municipal and District Boards, and Secretary, Arya Samaj. | Public meeting held at Mirzapur, on 25th December, 1892. |
| 319 | ,, | ,, | ,, | Babu Mahadeo Prasad Sinha. | Hindu Brahman. | Rais, Zamindar, pargana Kerait. | do. |
| 320 | ,, | ,, | ,, | Setha Laduram Poddar, | Hindustani Marwari Agarwala | Banker ... ... | do. |
| 321 | ,, | ,, | ,, | Babu Badrinath Setha ... | Hindustani Kshatriya. | Stone-contractor and Honorary Secretary, Saraswat Kshatriya Hit Karini Sabha. | do. |
| 322 | ,, | ,, | ,, | ,, Jadu Nath Sinha ... | Hindu Kshatriya. | Zamindar and Banker, Gopiganj, pargana Bhadohi. | do. |
| 323 | ,, | ,, | ,, | ,, Nanhu Lal ... | Hindu Khatri. | Service, President Arya Samaja. | do. |
| 324 | ,, | ,, | ,, | ,, Kedarnath Bhattacharji, B. A. | Brahman. | Vakil, High Court, and Municipal Commissioner. | do. |
| 325 | ,, | ,, | ,, | Chowdhari Wasudeva Sharma. | Hindu Brahman. | Zamindar ... ... | do. |
| 326 | ,, | ,, | ,, | Pandit Ghanshiam Sharma. | do. | Panditai ... ... | do. |
| 327 | ,, | ,, | ,, | Pandit Ram Prakash Sharma. | do. | Preacher ... ... | do. |
| 328 | ,, | ,, | ,, | Babu Kedarnath Muzumdar. | do. | Medical Practitioner ... | do. |
| 329 | ,, | ,, | ,, | Babu Beni Prasad ... | Bhargava. | Honorary Magistrate, Merchant, Zamindar, and Member, Municipal and District Boards. | do. |
| 330 | ,, | ,, | ,, | Chowdhari Badri Narain Sharma. | Hindu Brahman. | Zamindar ... ... | do. |
| 331 | ,, | ,, | ,, | Setha Bihari Lal ... | Agarwala Marwari. | Banker ... ... | do. |
| 332 | ,, | ,, | Ballia. | Babu Yamuna Prasad ... | Mahajan Kandu. | Mahajani, Ballia ... | By a public meeting held at Ballia, on 2nd December, 1892. |

| Number. | Presidency or Government. | Congress Circle. | Electoral Division. | Names in full of Delegates, with honorary titles, scholastic degrees, etc. | Race, Religious denomination, and Caste, if any. | Occupation and Address. | How and when elected. |
|---|---|---|---|---|---|---|---|
| 333 | N.-W.P. | Allahabad. | Allahabad. | Pandit Bishumbhar Nath | Hindu Brahman. | Vakil, High Court, President, Vakils' Association, Fellow, Allahabad University, and Chairman, Reception Committee of the 8th I. N. Congress, Allahabad. | At a Public Meeting held at the Kayastha Pathsala on 29th October, 1892. |
| 334 | " | " | " | Raja Rampal Sinh ... | Hindu Kshatriya. | Taluqdar of Rampore, Oudh, Honorary Magistrate, Member, District Board; Vice-President, Reception Committee. | do. |
| 335 | " | " | " | Pandit Sundar Lal, B.A. | Hindu Guzrati Nagar Brahman. | Vakil, High Court, Fellow, Allahabad University, and Member of the Council of Law Reporting, N.-W. P., Allahabad. | do. |
| 336 | " | " | " | Lala Ram Charan Das, Rai Bahadur. | Hindu Khatri. | Banker, Land-holder, Honorary Magistrate, Senior Vice-Chairman, Municipal Board, Allahabad, and Member, Reception Committee. | do. |
| 337 | " | " | " | Mr. D. Banerji ... | Hindu Brahman. | Barrister-at-Law, Canning Road, Allahabad. | do. |
| 338 | " | " | " | Mr. T. P. Crowley ... | European Christian. | Of the firm of Messrs. Crowley and Co. Mechanical Engineers and Contractors, Member, Municipal Board. | do. |
| 339 | " | " | " | Pandit Moti Lal Nehru... | Hindu Brahman. | Vakil, High Court, Hon. Secretary, Reception Committee, Elgin Road, Allahabad. | do. |
| 340 | " | " | " | Pandit Baldev Ram Dave. | Guzrati Nagar Brahman. | Vakil, High Court, N.-W.P., Allahabad. | do. |
| 341 | " | " | " | Babu Charoo Chandra Mitter. | Hindu Bengali Kayastha. | Zamindar, Municipal Commissioner, Hon. Secretary, Reception Committee, Mitrasram, Lowther Road, Allahabad. | do. |
| 342 | " | " | " | Pandit Lakshmi Narayan Vyasa. | Hindu Brahman. | Vaidya, President, Hindu Samaj, Allahabad. | do. |
| 343 | " | " | " | Munshi Madhava Prasad, | Hindu Kayesth. | Vakil, High Court, Hon. Magistrate. | do. |
| 344 | " | " | " | Munshi Jwala Prasad ... | do. | Vakil High Court, N.-W. P. | do. |
| 345 | " | " | " | Munshi Kashi Prasad ... | do. | Vakil High Court, and Secretary. Hindu Samaj, Mootheegunge, Allahabad. | do. |
| 346 | " | " | " | Pandit Madan Mohan Malaviya. | Hindu Brahman. | Vakil High Court, N.-W. P., Hon. Secretary Reception Committee, Allahabad. | do. |
| 347 | " | " | " | Babu Parbati Charan Chatterji, C.E. | Bengali Brahman. | Vakil, High Court, N.-W.P., Kidgunge, Allahabad. | do. |
| 348 | " | " | " | Munshi Roshan Lal ... | Arya Samajist. | Barrister-at-Law, Stanley Road, Allahabad. | do. |
| 349 | " | " | " | Babu Khettara Mohan Bose. | Hindu Kayastha. | Tradesman, Allahabad ... | do. |
| 350 | " | " | " | Babu Preonath Chatterji. | Hindu Brahman. | Vakil, High Court, Allahabad, | do. |
| 351 | " | " | " | Munshi Mathura Prasad. | Hindu Kayastha. | Pleader, Allahabad ... | do. |
| 352 | " | " | " | Babu Abinash Chandra Banerji, L.M.S. | Bengali Hindu Brahman. | Medical Practitioner, Allahabad. | do. |

| Number. | Presidency or Government. | Congress Circle. | Electoral Division. | Names in full of Delegates, with honorary titles, scholastic degrees, etc. | Race, Religious denomination, and Caste, if any. | Occupation and Address. | How and when elected. |
|---|---|---|---|---|---|---|---|
| 353 | N.-W.P. | Allahabad. | Allahabad. | Babu Dattee Lal, B.A. ... | Hindu Khatri. | Vakil, High Court, Mahajanitola, Allahabad. | At a Public Meeting held at the Kayastha Pathshala, Allahabad, on 29th October, 1892. |
| 354 | ,, | ,, | ,, | Babu Lal Behari Lal ... | do. | Trader, Guzrati Mohullah. Allahabad. | do. |
| 355 | ,, | ,, | ,, | Lala Sheo Churan Lal, B. A., LL. B. | Jain. | Vakil, High Court, Allahabad. | do. |
| 356 | ,, | ,, | ,, | Lala Badri Prasad ... | Hindu Agarwala. | Pleader Jouhuritola, Allahabad. | do. |
| 357 | ,, | ,, | ,, | Lala Ram Lal Jouhuri ... | do. | Mahajan, Jouhuritola, Allahabad. | do. |
| 358 | ,, | ,, | ,, | Mr. M. Corbett ... | European Christian. | Merchant, Municipal, Commissioner, Canning Road, Allahabad. | do. |
| 359 | ,, | ,, | ,, | Lala Kanhya Lal ... | Hindu Agarwala. | Mahajan, Mirganj, Allahabad. | do. |
| 360 | ,, | ,, | ,, | Munshi Mahesh Prasad... | Hindu Kayastha. | Pleader, Allahabad ... | do. |
| 361 | ,, | ,, | ,, | Lala Ganesh Das ... | Hindu Marwaree. | Banker and Municipal Commissioner, Katra, Allahabad. | do. |
| 362 | ,, | ,, | ,, | Pandit Govind Rao Goray | Hindu Brahman. | Pensioner, Daraganj, Allahabad. | do. |
| 363 | ,, | ,, | ,, | Munshi Sheombhar Lal... | Hindu Kayastha. | Pleader, Allahabad ... | do. |
| 364 | ,, | ,, | ,, | Babu Raghubar Dyal ... | do. | do. ... | do. |
| 365 | ,, | ,, | ,, | Pandit Jay Krishna Vyas | Hindu Brahman. | Medical Practitioner, Ahiyapur, Allahabad. | do. |
| 366 | ,, | ,, | ,, | B. Tinkuri Mukerji, L. M S. | do. | Medical Practitioner, Allahabad. | do. |
| 367 | ,, | ,, | ,, | Pandit Jagannath Sarma. | do. | Vaid, Editor, Prayag Samachar, Allahabad. | do. |
| 368 | ,, | ,, | ,, | Babu Beni Madhub Rai Chaudhri. | do. | Zamindar, Kidganj, Allahabad. | do. |
| 369 | ,, | ,, | ,, | Pandit Beni Madhub Bhattacharji. | do. | Government Pensioner, Municipal Commissioner and Honorary Magistrate, Daraganj, Allahabad. | do. |
| 370 | ,, | ,, | ,, | Pandit Deoki Nandan Tiwari. | do. | Proprietor. Rampataka, Ahiyapur, Allahabad. | do. |
| 371 | ,, | ,, | ,, | Lala Ramdhan Lal ... | Hindu Kayastha. | Makhtar, Allahabad ... | do. |
| 372 | ,, | ,, | ,, | Babu Nitai Charan Mittra. | do. | Druggist, Johnstonganj Road, Allahabad. | do. |
| 373 | ,, | ,, | ,, | B. Govind Chandra Basu, M. B. | do. | Medical Practitioner, Ranikimandi, Allahabad. | do. |
| 374 | ,, | ,, | ,, | Babu Durga Charan Banerjee, B. A. | Hindu Brahman. | Vakil, High Court, Allahabad. | do. |
| 375 | ,, | ,, | ,, | ,, Rajaram Bhargava | Hindu. | Zamindar and Municipal Commissioner. Allahabad. | do. |
| 376 | ,, | ,, | ,, | ,, Mahesh Prasad ... | Hindu Kayastha. | Pleader, Karelabagh Road, Allahabad. | do. |
| 377 | ,, | ,, | ,, | Lala Bhawani Prasad ... | Hindu Khattri. | Banker, Allahabad ... | do. |
| 378 | ,, | ,, | ,, | ,, Brij Mohan Lal ... | do. | do. ... | do. |
| 379 | ,, | ,, | ,, | Pundit Kedar Nath Choubay. | Hindu Brahman. | Vaidya, Ahiyapur, Allahabad. | do. |
| 380 | ,, | ,, | ,, | ,, Balkrishna Bhutta | do. | Editor, "Hindi Pradip," Allahabad. | do. |
| 381 | ,, | ,, | ,, | Babu Shama Churan Mukerji. | do. | Pleader and Mill-owner, Karbala, Allahabad. | do. |
| 382 | ,, | ,, | ,, | Syed Abdul Raoof ... | Mahomedan. | Barrister-at-Law, Elgin Road, Allahabad. | do. |
| 383 | ,, | ,, | ,, | Dr. S. P. Roy, M. B. ... M. R. C. S. | Hindu Brahman. | Medical Practitioner and Municipal Analyst, Muthiganj, Allahabad. | Do. and at a Public Meeting of the Rajshahi Association held on 3rd December, 1892. |
| 384 | ,, | ,, | ,, | Mr. Fateh Chand ... | Jain. | Barrister-at-Law, Johnstonganj, Allahabad. | At a Public Meeting held at the Kayastha Patshala Allahabad on 29th October, 1892. |
| 385 | ,, | ,, | ,, | Lala Mohan Lal ... | Hindu Khatri. | Contractor, Allahabad ... | do. |
| 386 | ,, | ,, | ,, | Swami Alaram ... | Hindu. | Preacher, Allahabad ... | do. |
| 387 | ,, | ,, | ,, | Pundit Shivaram Panday | Hindu Brahman. | Vaidya, Mahajanitola, Allahabad. | do. |

| Number. | Presidency or Government. | Congress Circle. | Electoral Division. | Names in full of Delegates, with honorary titles, scholastic degrees, etc. | Race, Religious denomination, and Caste, if any. | Occupation and Address. | How and when elected. |
|---|---|---|---|---|---|---|---|
| 388 | N.-W.P. | Allahabad. | Allahabad. | Lala Baboo Lal ... | Hindu Khatri. | Banker, Allahabad ... | At a Public Meeting held at Kayastha Pathshala, Allahabad, on 29th October, 1892. |
| 389 | ,, | ,, | ,, | Pandit Brij Mohun Doobay. | Hindu Brahman. | Trader, Ahiyapur, Allahabad. | do. |
| 390 | ,, | ,, | ,, | Mr. Madan Mohun Pragwal. | do. | Pragwal, Allahabad. ... | At a Public Meeting held, at Tej Pal Gokul Das Dharamsala, Allahabad, on 20th December, 1892. |
| 391 | ,, | ,, | ,, | Mr. Amritakrishna Bose. | Hindu Kayastha. | Medical Practitioner, Land-holder, Calcutta, Allahabad. | Do. and at a General Meeting of the Metropolitan Union held on 17th December, 1892. |
| 392 | ,, | ,, | ,, | Lala Mewa Lal ... | Hindu | Banker & Zemindar, Mootheegunge, Allahabad. | At a Public Meetiug held at Tej Pal Gokul Das' Dharamsala Allahabad on 20th December, 1892. |
| 393 | ,, | ,, | ,, | Babu Hari Mohun Roy B. A. | Hindu. Brahman. | Vakil, High Court, Allahabad. | do. |
| 394 | ,, | ,, | ,, | Lala Ganesh Prashad ... | Hindu Agarwala | Banker and Zemindar, Allahabad. | do. |
| 395 | ,, | ,, | ,, | Mr. Ajodhia Prashad Pragwal. | Hindu Brahman. | Pragwal, Allahabad ... | do. |
| 396 | ,, | ,, | ,, | ,, Behary Lal Pragwal ... | do. | do. | do. |
| 397 | ,, | ,, | ,, | ,, Brij Nath Pachbhaia ... | do. | do. | do. |
| 398 | ,, | ,, | ,, | ,, Sitaldeen Panday | do. | do. | do. |
| 399 | ,, | ,, | ,, | ,, Sitaram Pragwal ... | do. | do. | do. |
| 400 | ,, | ,, | ,, | Babu Jogendra Nath Mukerjee. | do. | Pleader, Kidgunge, Allahabad. | do. |
| 401 | ,, | ,, | ,, | Pandit Luchmi Narain Choubay. | do. | Trader, Allahabad ... | do. |
| 402 | ,, | ,, | ,, | ,, Sree Gobind Choubay. | do. | Contractor, do. ... | do. |
| 403 | ,, | ,, | ,, | Babu Jagadish Narain ... | Hindu Kshatriya. | Zemindar, do. ... | At a Public Meeting held in Gunga Das ka Chouk on 6th December, 1892. |
| 404 | ,, | ,, | ,, | Lala Madari Lal ... | Khatri. | Zemindar, Gangadas ka Chauk | do. |
| 405 | ,, | ,, | ,, | ,, Mahadeo Prasad Kapur. | do. | Banker, Allahabad ... | do. |
| 406 | ,, | ,, | ,, | Pandit Ram Narayan Proha. | Brahman. | Prohitai, Allahabad ... | do. |
| 407 | ,, | ,, | ,, | Lala Govind Prasad ... | Khatri. | Trader Allahabad ... | do. |
| 408 | ,, | ,, | ,, | ,, Choonilal ... | do. | Banker & Zamindar, Allahabad. | do. |
| 409 | ,, | ,, | ,, | ,, Durga Prasad ... | do. | Merchant, Allahabad ... | do. |
| 410 | ,, | ,, | ,, | Chaube Gobind Deo ... | Brahman. | ,, ,, ... | do. |
| 411 | ,, | ,, | Allahabad. Hindu Samaj. | Babu Vaidya Nath Das... | Agarwala Bania. | Banker ... | At a General Meeting of the Samaj held on 27th December, 1892. |
| 412 | ,, | ,, | ,, | ,, Hem Chandra Chatterjee. | Bengali Brahman. | Pleader, Allahabad ... | do. |
| 413 | ,, | ,, | ,, | ,, Nityaranjan Mukerjee. | Hindu Brahman. | Land-holder, Allahabad ... | do. |
| 414 | ,, | ,, | ,, | Rai Bahadur Niranjan Mukerjee. | do. | do. | do. |
| 415 | ,, | ,, | ,, | Pandit Sarju Prasad ... | do. | Teacher, Divinity School, Allahabad. | do. |
| 416 | ,, | ,, | ,, | Mr. Oudh Behari Lal, M.A. | Hindu Kayesth. | Teacher, Allahabad ... | do. |
| 417 | ,, | ,, | ,, | Pandit Brij Nath ... | Hindu. Brahman. | Preacher, Allahabad ... | do. |
| 418 | ,, | ,, | ,, | Swami Purushottama Gir. | do. | Hindu Ascetic ... | do. |
| 419 | ,, | ,, | ,, | Pandit Sheo Ram Chundra Tewary. | Hindu | Mahajan, Allahabad ... | do. |
| 420 | ,, | ,, | Allahabad. | Hakim Mahomed Hossein | Mahomedan Sunni. | Zamindar, Allahabad ... | At a Public Meeting held at Allahabad on 24th December, 1892. |
| 421 | ,, | ,, | ,, | Syad Meerjan ... | do. Shia. | do. | do. |
| 422 | ,, | ,, | ,, | Meer Akhtar Hossein ... | do. | do. | do. |
| 423 | ,, | ,, | ,, | Hakim Mahomed Anwar. | do. Sunni. | do. | do. |
| 424 | ,, | ,, | ,, | Mirza Kulb Ali Beg ... | do. Shia. | do. | do. |
| 425 | ,, | ,, | ,, | Moulvi Ameer Ali ... | do. | do. | do. |
| 426 | ,, | ,, | ,, | Meer Anwar Hossain ... | do. | do. | do. |
| 427 | ,, | ,, | ,, | Mirza Tufel Ali Beg ... | do. Sunni. | do. | do. |
| 428 | ,, | ,, | ,, | Hafiz Kurimbux ... | do. | do. | do. |
| 429 | ,, | ,, | ,, | Mr. Bhagwan Das, B.A.... | Hindu. | Head Master, Colonelgunge School, Allahabad | do. |

| Number. | Presidency or Government. | Congress Circle. | Electoral Division. | Names in full of Delegates, with honorary titles, scholastic degrees, etc. | Race, Religious denomination, and Caste, if any. | Occupation and Address. | How and when elected. |
|---|---|---|---|---|---|---|---|
| 430 | N.-W.P. | Allahabad. | Allahabad. | Munshi Sadruddin ... | Mahomedan. | Zamindar ... ... | At a Public Meeting held at the Kayastha Patshala on 29th October, 1892. |
| 431 | " | " | Kara. | Mir Mohammed Taqi ... | Mahomedan, Sunni. | Zamindar, Kara ... | At a Public Meeting held at Kara, on 17th December, 1892. |
| 432 | " | " | " | Mir Munauwar Ali ... | do. | do. | do. |
| 433 | " | " | Ujahini. | Mir Mahomed Hadi ... | do. | Zamindar, Ujahini ... | At a Public Meeting held on 22nd December, 1892. |
| 434 | " | " | " | Sheikh Abdul Rahman ... | do. | do. | do. |
| 435 | " | " | Manjhanpur. | Syad Tawangar Ali ... | Mahomedan, Sunni. | Zamindar, Manjhanpur ... | At a Public Meeting held in Manjhanpur on 19th December, 1892. |
| 436 | " | " | " | Syad Mubaraq Husain ... | do. | Zamindar, do. | do. |
| 437 | " | " | " | Syad Ahmed Husain ... | do. Shia. | do. | do. |
| 438 | " | " | " | Syad Karim Buksh ... | do. Sunni. | do. | do. |
| 439 | " | " | Karari. | Syad Ikbal Husain ... | Mahomedan. | Zamindar, Karari ... | At a Public Meeting held at Karari, on 31st December, 1892. |
| 440 | " | " | " | Syad Zafar Husain ... | do. Sunni. | do. | do. |
| 441 | " | " | " | Syad Ibni Husain ... | do. | do. | do. |
| 442 | " | " | " | Syad Fida Husain ... | do. Shia. | do. | do. |
| 443 | " | " | " | Syad Munawar Ali ... | do. Sunni. | do. | do. |
| 444 | " | " | " | Syad Fyaz Husain ... | do. | do. | do. |
| 445 | " | " | " | Syad Nadir Husain ... | do. Shia. | do. | do. |
| 446 | " | " | Sohila. | Syad Amir Husain ... | Mahomedan, Sunni. | Zamindar, Sohila ... | At a Public Meeting held on 20th December, 1892. |
| 447 | " | " | " | Syad Shamshad Husain... | do. Shia. | do. | do. |
| 448 | " | " | " | Mir Aulad Husain ... | do. do. | do. | do. |
| 449 | " | " | " | Mir Nazim Husain ... | do. do. | | do. |
| 450 | " | " | Kanihar. | Mir Ghulam Mahomed ... | Mahomedan Shia. | Zamindar, Kanihar ... | At a Public Meeting held at Kanihar on 21st December, 1892. |
| 451 | " | " | Cawnpore. | Pundit Munna Lal ... | Hindu Brahmin. | Agent of the Firm of Gobind Prasad and Co., Cawnpore. | At a Public Meeting held on 22nd December, 1892. |
| 452 | " | " | " | Lala Govind Prasad Mihrotra. | Khuttree. | Merchant and Contractor, Cawnpore. | do. |
| 453 | " | " | " | Maharaj Doorgaprasad Bajpai. | Brahman. | Zamindar and Rais, Cawnpore. | do. |
| 454 | " | " | " | Hakim Asgar Hossain ... | Mahomedan. | Physician, Cawnpore ... | do. |
| 455 | " | " | " | Babu Manmath Nath Mukerji, B. A., B. L. | Bengali. Brahman. | Vakeel, High Court, Cawnpore. | do. |
| 456 | " | " | " | Babu Ganga Dayal ... | Hindu Kayastha. | Pleader, Cawnpore ... | do. |
| 457 | " | " | " | Aga Abdul Qasim Shirazi, | Mahomedan. | Arab Horse dealer ... | do. |
| 458 | " | " | " | Mr. Sidh Gopal Misra ... | Brahman. | Zamindar, Honorary Magistrate, and Vice-Chairman, Municipal Board. | do. |
| 459 | " | " | " | Lala Gopi Nath ... | Khuttree. | Export and Import Agent ... | do. |
| 460 | " | " | " | Babu Nabin Chundra Bose. | Bengali Kayasth. | Pleader, Cawnpore ... | At a Public Meeting held at Cawnpore on 11th December, 1892. |
| 461 | " | " | " | Rai Devi Prasad, B. A., B. L. | Hindu Kayasth. | Vakeel, High Court, and Zamindar, Cawnpore. | do. |
| 462 | " | " | " | Babu Sheo Narain ... | Arya Samajist. | Banker and Member, Municipal Board, Cawnpore. | do. |
| 463 | " | " | " | Babu Srish Chandra Gupta. | Bengali Vaidya. | Merchant ... ... | do. |
| 464 | " | " | " | Mr. Janki Nath ... | Arya Samajist. | Zamindar, Cawnpore ... | do. |
| 465 | " | " | " | Lala Ram Dhun ... | Hindu Vaishya. | Zamindar, " ... | do. |
| 466 | " | " | " | Lala Narayan Das ... | do. | Merchant, " ... | do. |
| 467 | " | " | " | Lala Debi Das ... | Hindu Khuttree. | " " ... | do. |
| 468 | " | " | " | Lala Chundika Prasad ... | Hindu Vaishya. | Cloth Merchant, Cawnpore ... | do. |
| 469 | " | " | " | Lala Madan Chand Khunna. | do. | Merchant and Contractor ... | do. |
| 470 | " | " | " | Babu Trailokya Nath Banerji. | Hindu Brahman. | Pleader and Municipal Commissioner, Cawnpore. | do. |

| Number. | Presidency or Government. | Congress Circle. | Electoral Division. | Names in full of Delegates, with honorary titles, scholastic degrees, etc. | Race, Religious denomination, and Caste, if any. | Occupation and Address. | How and when elected. |
|---|---|---|---|---|---|---|---|
| 471 | N.-W.P. | Allahabad. | Cawnpore. | Babu Gopal Chandra Banerji. | Bengali Brahman. | Chemist, Manager of the Kaisar Soap Manufacturing Company, Cawnpore. | At a Public Meeting held at Cawnpore on 11th December, 1892. |
| 472 | " | " | " | Pandit Hriday Narayan Koul. | Kashmiri Brahman. | Pleader, Joint Secretary, Reform Association and Divisional Congress Committee, Cawnpore. | do. |
| 473 | " | " | " | Pandit Pirthi Nath ... | do. | Pleader, Secretary, Divisional Congress Committee, Reform Association, and Temperance Association, and Municipal Commissioner, Cawnpore. | do. |
| 474 | " | " | " | Babu Bansidhar ... | Arya Samajist. | Banker and Zemindar ... | do. |
| 475 | " | " | " | Pandit Janki Nath ... | Kashmiri Brahman. | Pleader ... ... | do. |
| 476 | " | " | " | Bhai Hurnam Singh Varma. | Panjabi Khatri. | Late Government Military Sowar, Proprietor of the "Cawnpore Gazette." | do. |
| 477 | " | " | " | Lala Kedarnath Kerya ... | Hindu Vaishya. | Merchant ... ... | do. |
| 478 | " | " | " | Lala Suntokh Chand Bhandari. | Jain. | Banker and Merchant ... | do. |
| 479 | " | " | Farrukhabad. | Pandit Gopal Rao Hari... | Arya, Maharashtra Brahman. | Secretary, Vedic Samaj and Divisional Congress Committee, Farrukhabad. | At a Public Meeting held at Furrukhabad on 20th November, 1892. |
| 480 | " | " | " | Chowbay Harsevak Lal... | Brahman. | Vakil and Zamindar ... | do. |
| 481 | " | " | " | Mr. S. P. Mukerji ... | Bengali Brahman. | Service, Camp Fatehgarh ... | do. |
| 482 | " | " | " | Mr. Sarup Narain ... | Kayastha. | Pleader, Farukhabad ... | do. |
| 483 | " | " | " | Seth Mina Mall ... | Buneah. | Merchant, do. ... | do. |
| 484 | " | " | " | Mahomed Yakub Ali ... | Mahomedan. | Zamindar, do. ... | do. |
| 485 | " | " | " | Mr. Akbar Hossein ... | do. | do. ... | do. |
| 486 | " | " | " | " Hifazat Hossein ... | do. | " and Member of the District Board, Farrukhabad. | do. |
| 487 | " | " | Banda. | Lala Raghubar Dayal ... | Hindu Kayasth. | Legal Practitioner and Secretary Kayasth Sabha. | At a Public Meeting held on 6th November, 1892. |
| 488 | " | " | " | Munshi Mata Prasad ... | Kayasth. | Legal Practitioner and Zamindar and President, Kayasth Sabha, Banda. | do. |
| 489 | " | " | Jhansi. | Babu Shiva Pada Ghosh. | Bengali Kayasth. | Pleader, Jhansi ... ... | At a Public Meeting held at Jhansi on 10th November, 1892. |
| 490 | " | " | " | " Kali Prasanna Biswas. | Bengali Vaishya. | Medical Practitioner, Progressive Medical Hall, Jhansi. | do. |
| 491 | " | " | " | " Basant Kumar Sanyal. | Bengali Brahman. | Pleader, Jhansi ... ... | do. |
| 492 | " | " | " | Pandit Prag Das ... | Arya Brahman. | do. | do. |
| 493 | " | " | " | Mr. Kesho Das, B. A. ... | Hindu. | Pleader and Zamindar, Jhansi. | do. |
| 494 | " | " | Agra. | Pandit Mohan Krishna Dar. | Hindu Kashmiri Brahman. | Trader, Agra ... ... | At a public meeting held at Agra on the 15th November, 1892. |
| 495 | " | " | " | Mr. V. Subrahmanya Aiyar, B. A. | Hindu Madrasi Brahman. | Professor of Mathematics, St. John's College, Agra. | do. |
| 496 | " | " | " | Mr. N. B. Wadekar ... | Hindu Brahman. | Merchant, Agra ... ... | |
| 497 | " | " | " | Mr. A. Nundy ... | Christian. | Barrister-at-Law, Agra | do. |
| 498 | " | " | " | Pandit Jagannath ... | Hindu Kashmiri. | Rais and Pleader, Agra ... | do. |
| 499 | " | " | " | Pundit Tulsiram Misra, M. A. | Hindu Brahman. | Professor, St. John's College, Agra. | do. |
| 500 | " | " | " | Lala Dwarka Das ... | Hindu Vaishya. | Pleader and Municipal Commissioner, Agra. | do. |
| 501 | " | " | " | Pandit Kamta Prasad ... | Kashmiri Brahman. | Rais and Pleader, Agra ... | do. |
| 502 | " | " | " | Babu Kedarnath, B.A., B. L. | Hindu Vaishya. | Vakil, High Court, Agra ... | do. |
| 503 | " | " | Muttra. | Pandit Radha Charan Goswami. | Brahman. | Priest, Radharaman Street, Brindaban, District Muttra. | At a Public Meeting held at Muttra on 17th November, 1892. |
| 504 | " | " | " | Mr. Chote Lal ... | Hindu Kayasth. | Municipal Commissioner and Member of Kayesth Samaj, Pleader, Holigate, Muttra. | do. |
| 505 | " | " | " | Babu Jagannath Prasad... | Bhargava. | Pleader, Merchant and Member, Municipal Board, Ghi ki mandi, Muttra. | Do. and at a meeting o the Vaishnav Dharma-f pracharak Sabha on 3rd December, 1892. |

| Number. | Presidency or Government. | Congress Circle. | Electoral Division. | Names in full of Delegates with honorary titles, scholastic degrees, etc. | Race, Religious denomination, and Caste, if any. | Occupation and Address. | How and when elected. |
|---|---|---|---|---|---|---|---|
| 506 | N.-W.P. | Allahabad. | Muttra. | Kuar Hukam Singh ... | Jat. | Resaldar of Angai, Member of the Local Board and General Treasurer of the Jat Sabha of India. | At a Public Meeting held at Muttra on 17th November, 1892. |
| 507 | " | " | " | Mr. Radhe Lal Sharma... | Arya Brahmin. | Vedic Upadeshak ... | do. |
| 508 | " | " | Aligarh. | Babu Kishori Lal ... | Hindu, Vaishya. | Pleader and Zamindar ... | At a Public Meeting held at Aligarh on 18th December, 1892. |
| 509 | " | " | " | Thakur Kalyan Singh ... | Hindu, Rajput. | do. | do. |
| 510 | " | " | " | Hafiz Abdul Rahim ... | Mahomedan. | do. | do. |
| 511 | " | " | " | Babu Ram Narayan ... | Hindu Vaishya. | Zamindar and Banker ... | do. |
| 512 | " | " | " | M. Mahomed Mustajaba-ul-la Khan. | Mahomedan. | Zamindar, Aligarh ... | do. |
| 513 | " | " | " | Pandit Udai Ram | Brahmin. | Service, Aligarh ... | do. |
| 514 | " | " | " | M. Mahomed Amanat-Ulla Khan. | Mahomedan. | Zamindar, Aligarh ... | do. |
| 515 | " | " | " | Syad Mushtak Ali ... | Mahomedan. | do. | do. |
| 516 | " | " | " | Sheikh Mushtak Ali ... | Mahomedan. | do. | do. |
| 517 | " | " | " | Muhammad Sarfaraz Khan. | Mahomedan. | Pleader, Aligarh ... | do. |
| 518 | " | " | " | M. Muhammad Zafar Ali Khan | do. | Pleader, Aligarh ... | do. |
| 519 | " | " | " | M. Umrao Khan ... | do. | Zamindar, Aligarh ... | do. |
| 520 | " | " | Meerut. | Babu Prahlad Singh ... | Hindu Vaishya. | Vakil, High Court, and Zamindar, Meerut. | At a Public Meeting held at Meerut on 16th December, 1892. |
| 521 | " | " | " | Lala Baburam ... | Hindu, Vaishya. | Pleader, Meerut ... | do. |
| 522 | " | " | " | Babu Hira Lal ... | do. | do. | do. |
| 523 | " | " | " | Pandit Ram Prasad, M.A. | Hindu Kayasth. | Vakil, High Court, N.-W. P., Meerut. | do. |
| 524 | " | " | " | Lala Ghansayam Das ... | Vaishya. Agarwal. | Pleader and Zamindar, Meerut. | do. |
| 525 | " | " | " | Babu Abhayapada Bose, B. A. | Bengali. Kayasth. | Budhana Gate, Meerut City... | do. |
| 526 | " | " | " | Babu Dindayal ... | do. | Banker ... ... | do. |
| 527 | " | " | Saharunpur. | Mr. Madan Mohan Lal, B. A., LL. B. | Hindu, Vaishya. | Vakil, High Court, Saharanpur. | At a Public Meeting held at Saharanpur on 17th December, 1892. |
| 528 | " | " | Dehra Dun | Pandit Anunda Narain ... | Kashmiri Brahman. | Pleader, Municipal Commissioner and Landholder. | At a Public Meeting held on 18th December, 1892, at Dehra Dun. |
| 529 | " | " | " | Captain A. W. Hearsey. | European Christian. | Retired list, H. M. S. ... | do. |
| 530 | " | Oudh. | Lucknow. | Babu Bansilal Singh ... | Hindu Khatri. | Vakil, High Court, N.-W. P., Lucknow. | At a Public Meeting held at Lucknow on 9th December, 1892. |
| 531 | " | " | " | Munshi Ganga Prasad Varma. | do. | Editor and Proprietor of the "Advocate" and the "Hindustani," Lucknow. | do. |
| 532 | " | " | " | Pandit Bishan Narayan Dar. | Hindu Brahmin. | Barrister-at-Law, Lucknow ... | do. |
| 533 | " | " | " | Mr. Hamid Ali Khan ... | Mohomedan. | Barrister-at-Law, Lucknow ... | do. |
| 534 | " | " | " | Prince Mirza Faraidon Qadir Bahadur, of the Royal Family of Delhi. | Mahomedan. | Wasiqadar, Lucknow. ... | At a General Meeting of the Anjuman-i-Muhammadi held at Lucknow on 23rd December, 1892. |
| 535 | " | " | " | Prince Yunus Qudr Bahadur, of the Royal Family of Delhi. | do. | do. | do. |
| 536 | " | " | " | Nawab Zaighamuddaula Bahadur. | Mahomedan. | Rais and Wasiqadar, Lucknow. | At a Public Meeting held at Lucknow on 9th December, 1892. |
| 537 | " | " | " | Pandit Lachman Prasad | Brahman. | Brahmo Missionary, Lucknow, | do. |
| 538 | " | " | " | Pandit Jagat Narain ... | Brahman. Hindu. | Pleader, Lucknow ... | do. |
| 539 | " | " | " | Babu Bhuban Mohon Rai, | do. | Merchant, Aminabad, Lucknow. | do. |
| 540 | " | " | " | Hakim Syed Husain Jafar. | Mahomedan. | Editor "Jubilee Paper," Lucknow. | At a Public Meeting held at Lucknow on 9th December, 1892. |
| 541 | " | " | " | Pandit Shyam Narain Muslacan. | Kashmiri Brahman | Land-holder and Municipal Commissioner, Lucknow. | At a Public Meeting held at Lucknow on 9th December, 1892. |

| Number. | Presidency or Government. | Congress Circle. | Electoral Division. | Names in full of Delegates, with honorary titles, scholastic degrees, etc. | Race, Religious denomination, and Caste, if any. | Occupation and Address. | How and when elected. |
|---|---|---|---|---|---|---|---|
| 542 | N.-W. P. & Oudh. | Lucknow. | Lucknow. | M. Abdul Basir Hazur ... | Mahomedan. | Service, Lucknow ... | Public Meeting, 9th December, 1892. |
| 543 | ,, | ,, | ,, | Nawab Hashmat Hussain. | do. | Wasiqadar, Lucknow. ... | do |
| 544 | ,, | ,, | ,, | Babu Kedarnath. ... | Hindu Kshtriya | Vakil, Lucknow ... | do |
| 545 | ,, | ,, | ,, | Babu Bipin Behari Bose, M. A. ... | Bengali Kayastha. | Vakil, High Court, and Secretary, Rifah-i-am-Association, Lucknow. | At a Meeting of the Association held on 3rd December, 1892. |
| 546 | ,, | ,, | ,, | Rai Suraj Narain Bahadur, B.A. | Kashmiri Brahman. | Vakil, High Court, Lucknow. | At a Public Meeting held at Lucknow on 9th December, 1892. |
| 547 | | ,, | Lucknow. Anjuman-i-Muhammadi. | Syed Kazim Hussein ... | Mahomedan. | Service, Lucknow. | At a General Meeting of the Anjuman-i-Muhammadi held at Lucknow 23rd December, 1892. |
| 548 | ,, | ,, | ,, | Nawab Muhammad Hasan. | do. | Govt. Pensioner, Lucknow ... | do |
| 549 | ,, | ,, | ,, | Syed Ashiq Hossein ... | do. | Secretary, Anjuman-i-Muhammadi Mansurbag, Lucknow and Editor of the "Qaul." | do |
| 550 | ,, | ,, | ,, | Mirza Muhammad Husein, | do. | Service, Lucknow ... | do |
| 551 | ,, | ,, | ,, | Maulvi Syed Murtaza Husein. | do. | do. ... | do |
| 552 | ,, | ,, | ,, | Nawab Ali Mumammad Khan. | do. | Late President Anjuman-i-Muhammadi, Govt. Pensionholder and Wasiqadar, Lucknow. | do |
| 553 | ,, | ,, | ,, | Maulvi Faqarud-din ... | do. | Merchant, Lucknow. | do |
| 554 | ,, | ,, | ,, | M. Muhammad Taqi Khan. | do. | Head Munshi, C. M. School, Lucknow. | do |
| 555 | ,, | ,, | ,, | Mirza Raza Husein. | do. | Merchant, Lucknow ... | do |
| 556 | ,, | ,, | ,, | Baqur Mirza Sahib ... | do. | Wasiqadar, Lucknow. ... | do |
| 557 | ,, | ,, | ,, | M. Aga Syed Ali Khan. | do. | do. | do |
| 558 | ,, | ,, | ,, | M. Aga Ahmed Ali Khan. | do. | do. | do |
| 559 | ,, | ,, | ,, | M. Baqar Mirza Khan. | do. | do. | |
| 560 | ,, | ,, | ,, | M. Mirza Muhammad Ali Khan. | do. | do. | do |
| 561 | ,, | ,, | ,, | Syed Husein *alias* Syed. | do. | Service, Lucknow. | do |
| 562 | ,, | ,, | ,, | Syed Muhammad Naqi ... | do. | do. | do |
| 563 | ,, | ,, | ,, | Syed Muhammad Mehdi. | do. | Pensioner, Lucknow ... | do |
| 564 | ,, | ,, | ,, | Mirza Aga Husain Sahib. | do. | Nawab and Rais, Lucknow ... | do |
| 565 | ,, | ,, | ,, | M. Aga Sajjad Ali Khan. | do. | Wasiqadar, Lucknow ... | do |
| 566 | ,, | ,, | ,, | Aga Muhammad Husein Sahib. | do. | Service, Lucknow ... | do |
| 567 | ,, | ,, | ,, | Syed Baqar Ali Khan ... | do. | do. | do |
| 568 | Madras. | Madras. | Madras. | Ramanuja Chary ... | Hindu Brahman. | Pleader, Member District Board, Chingleput. | At a Public Meeting. |
| 569 | N.-W.P. & Oudh. | Lucknow. | Sitapur. | Babu Pitam Rai ... | Hindu Kayasth. | Pleader, Judicial Commissioner's Court, Sitapur, Municipal Commissioner, Hon. Magistrate and Zamindar, Sitapur. | At a Public Meeting held on 9th December, 1892. |
| 570 | ,, | ,, | ,, | Babu Chail Behari Lal, B.A. | Hindu Kayastha. | Vakil, Sitapur ... | do. |
| 571 | ,, | ,, | ,, | Munshi Murli Dhar ... | do. | Pleader and Zamindar, Sitapur. | do. |
| 572 | ,, | ,, | ,, | Babu Sitaram Thetha ... | Hindu Kshatriya. | Banker, Sitapur. ... | do. |
| 573 | ,, | ,, | Fyzabad. | Babu Baldeo Prasad .. | Hindu Kshatriya. | Vakil and Honorary Secretary to the Municipal Board, Fyzabad. | At a Public Meeting of the residents of Fyzabad and Ajudhia held at Fyzabad, on 20th November, 1892. |
| 574 | ,, | ,, | ,, | Babu Ram Saran Das, M.A., F.A.U. | Hindu Kayasth. | Secretary and Manager of the Oudh Commercial Bank, Limited; Zamindar, and Honorary Magistrate, Fyzabad. | do |
| 575 | ,, | ,, | ,, | Munshi Ali Hussein ... | Mahomedan. | Zamindar, Vakil and Secretary District Board, Fyzabad | do. |
| 576 | ,, | ,, | ,, | ,, Imtiaz Ali, B. A. | do. | Vakil, Fyzabad. | do. |
| 577 | ,, | ,, | ,, | Babu Gokul Chand ... | Hindu Kshatriya | Vakil, Zamindar, Honorary Magistrate and Chairman of the Municipal Board, Fyzabad. | do. |
| 578 | ,, | ,, | ,, | Pandit Radha Kishen ... | Hindu Kashmiri Brahman. | Vakil and Zamindar, Fyzabad. | do. |
| 579 | ,, | ,, | ,, | Munshi Sarfaraz Ali ... | Mahomedan. | Zamindar and Rais, Fyzabad. | do. |
| 580 | ,, | ,, | ,, | ,, Balak Ram ... | Hindu Kayasth. | Vakil and Land-holder, Fyzabad. | do. |

| Number. | Presidency or Government. | Congress Circle. | Electoral Division. | Names in full of Delegates, with honorary titles, scholastic degrees, etc. | Race, Religious denomination, and Caste, if any. | Occupation and Address. | How and when elected. |
|---|---|---|---|---|---|---|---|
| 581 | N.-W. P. & Oudh. | Lucknow. | Sultanpur. | Babu Shambhunath ... | Hindu. | Vakil, Sultanpur ... | At a Public Meeting held on 10th December, 1892. |
| 582 | " | " | Partabgarh | Munshi Ramchandra, M.A. | Hindu. Kayasth. | Vakil, High Court, N.-W. P., Partabgarh. | At a Public Meeting held at Partabgarh on 4th December, 1892. |
| 583 | " | " | " | Pandit Kirpa Shankar ... | Hindu Nagar Brahman. | Pleader Partabgarh ... | do. |
| 584 | " | " | " | Pandit Balraj Sahai Upadhia. | Hindu Brahman. | Pleader and Zamindar, Partabgarh. | do. |
| 585 | " | " | Bahraich | Pandit Sitala Prasad Misra. | do. | Vakil, Bahraich ... | At a Public Meeting of the residents of Bahraich held on 19th December, 1892. |
| 586 | " | " | " | Munshi Jugul Kishore ... | Hindu Kayastha. | do | do. |
| 587 | " | " | Kalakankar | Pandit Bisheshar Dayal Sukul | Hindu. Brahman | Pleader, land-holder and banker, Kalakankar. | At a Public Meeting held at Kalakankar on 27th December, 1892. |
| 588 | " | " | " | P. Sital Prasad Upadhya, | do. | Landholder and Joint Manager of the "Hindustan" Kalakankar. | do. |
| 589 | " | " | " | Thakur Basant Singha ... | Hindu Khsatriya. | Land holder, Kalakankar ... | do. |
| 590 | " | Rohilkhand. | Shahjahanpur. | Babu Baikunth Nath Sirkar. | Hindu | Pleader, Shajahanpur ... | At a Public Meeting held at Shahjahanpur on 20th December, 1892. |
| 591 | " | " | " | Munshi Bakhtawar Singh, | Arya Agarwal. | Editor and Proprietor of "Arya Darpan." | do. |
| 592 | " | " | " | Lala Saligram Sheth ... | Hindu Kahatry | Zeminder, Banker ... | do. |
| 593 | " | " | " | Babu Radha Krishna ... | Hindu. | Pleader and Municipal Commissioner. | do. |
| 594 | " | " | Bareilly. | Mr. Ram Sarup, B. A., LL. B. | Hindu, Khatri | Vakil, High Court, N.W.P., Bareilly. | At a public meeting held at Bareilly on 9th December 1892. |
| 595 | " | " | " | Babu Preonath Banerji. | Hindu Brahman | Vakil, High Court, and Municipal Commissioner, Bareilly. | do. |
| 596 | " | " | " | Lala Kalka Prasad ... | Hindu. Kayasth | Pleader, Bareilly. ... | do. |
| 597 | " | " | " | Lala Janki Prasad, M.A. | do | do. | do. |
| 598 | " | " | Almora. | Pundit Jwaladatta Joshi. | Brahman | Vakil, High Court, Almora... | do. |
| 599 | " | " | " | Pundit Badridatta Joshi, LL. B. | Brahman. | Vakil, High Court, Almora ... | At a Public Meeting held at Almora on 10th November, 1892. |
| 600 | " | " | " | Pandit Kamalapati Joshi. | do. | Pleader, Dt. Court, Almora... | do. |
| 601 | " | " | " | Sheikh Manulla ... | Mahomedan. | Trader and Merchant, Almora. | do. |
| 602 | " | " | Moradabad. | Babu Narendra Chandra Bose, B. L. | Hindu Kayasth | Vakil, High Court, and Zamindar, Moradabad. | At a Public Meeting held at Moradabad on 17th December, 1892. |
| 603 | " | " | " | Babu Sundar Lal ... | Hindu Kayasth | Pleader, Moradabad ... | do. |
| 604 | " | " | " | Babu Brijnandan Prasad, M.A., LL. B. | Hindu, Khatri | Vakil, High Court, Moradabad. | do. |
| 605 | " | " | " | M, Mohammad Nabi Khan. | Mahomedan, Pathan. | Service. ... | do. |
| 606 | " | " | " | Sheikh Wahabuddeen ... | Mahomedan. | Pleader and Zamindar ... | do. |
| 607 | Punjab. | Lahore. | Lahore. | Lala Ram Chandra ... | Panjabi Hindu. | Proprietor, "Anglo-Sanskrit" Press. | Public Meeting held at Lahore on 4th December, 1892. |
| 608 | " | " | " | The Rev. T. Evans ... | European Christian. | Missionary and Temperance Preacher. | do. |
| 609 | " | " | " | Captain A. T. Banon ... | European. | Late Bengal Staff Corps, Zamindar Kulu-Kangra. ... | do. |
| 610 | " | " | " | Mr. N. Gupta ... | Bengali Vaidya. | Editor of the "Tribune." ... | do. |
| 611 | " | " | " | Dr. Parmanand ... | Panjabi Hindu. | Surgeon Dentist, Lahore ... | do. |
| 612 | " | " | Umballa. | Lala Murlidhar ... | Hindu Vaishya. | Pleader, Umballa ... | Public Meeting held at Umballa, 17th December, 1892. |
| 613 | " | " | " | Bhai Mahar Singh Chaubay. | Panjabi Sikh. | General Merchant, Lahore ... | Public Meeting held at Lahore on 4th December, 1892. |

| Number. | Presidency or Government. | Congress Circle. | Electoral Division. | Names in full of Delegates, with honorary titles, scholastic degrees, etc. | Race, Religious denomination, and Caste, if any. | Occupation and Address. | How and when elected. |
|---|---|---|---|---|---|---|---|
| 614 | Punjab. | Lahore. | Umballa. | Munshi Abdul Qadir Taib. | Muhamadan. | Manager, "Barrin Gazette." | At a Public Meeting held at Umballa on 17th December, 1892. |
| 615 | " | " | Amritsar. | Lala Kanhaiya Lal ... | Hindu Bhatia. | Pleader, Chief Court, Punjab. | Public Meeting held at Amritsar on 11th December, 1892. |
| 616 | " | " | " | Mr. Uma Shankar ... | Hindu. | Barrister-at-Law, Amritsar ... | do. |
| 617 | " | " | " | Baba Narain Singh ... | Sikh. | Pleader, Amritsar ... | do. |
| 618 | " | " | " | Mr. Bulaki Ram ... | Hindu. | Barrister-at-Law, Amritsar ... | do. |
| 619 | " | " | " | Babu Nandkishore Kakker. | Hindu Khatri. | Head Master, Hindu High School. | do. |
| 620 | " | Delhi. | Delhi. | Lala Sultan Singh ... | Jain. | Rais and Banker ... | Public Meeting held at Delhi on 21st December, 1892. |
| 621 | " | " | " | Moulvi Mirza Umrao Hairat. | Mahomedan. | Literary pursuit, Delhi ... | do. |
| 622 | " | " | " | Mr. Balawant Singh ... | Hindu Khattree. | Medical College, Lahore ... | do. |
| 623 | " | " | " | Mr. Raghunath Dass ... | Hindu Vaishya. | Barrister-at-Law, Delhi. ... | do. |
| 624 | " | " | " | Lala Gokul Chand ... | Hindu Khattri. | Banker, Delhi ... | do. |
| 625 | " | " | " | Lala Girdhari Lal ... | do. | Pleader, Chief Court, Punjab, Delhi. | do. |

# APPENDIX II.

1. The following statements have been drawn from the figures given in the Reports of the Administration of Crimiual Justice in the Lower Provinces of Bengal. The percentages are not in all cases given in the Reports, but have been worked out :—

*Statement (A.)*

| Years. | 1. Number of trials with Jury. | 2. Number of verdicts agreed to by the Sessions Judges. | 3. Number of verdicts not agreed to by the Sessions Judges. | 4. References disposed of under Sec. 307 Cr. P. C. | 5. Verdicts approved of by the High Court. | 6. Verdicts set aside by the High Court. | 7. Percentage of verdicts not agreed to by the Sessions Judges to the whole number of verdicts. | 8. Percentage of verdicts set aside by the High Court to total verdicts. | 9. Percentage of verdicts which would have been set aside if all cases in which the Sessions Judges had disagreed had been referred by them to the High Court and the verdicts set aside in the same proportion as in cases referred. | Remarks |
|---|---|---|---|---|---|---|---|---|---|---|
| 1877 | 342 | 285 | 57 | 25 | 8 | 17 | 16.6 | 4.9 | 11.3 | |
| 1878 | 399 | 352 | 47 | 25 | 10 | 15 | 11.8 | 3.7 | 7 | |
| 1879 | | | | | | | | | | In these years the Administration Reports do not give the number of cases of which reference was made to the High Court, and the number in which the verdicts were set aside or approved; but give the number of persons in respect of whom the verdicts were approved or set aside. They are therefore useless for the purpose of comparison. |
| 1880 | | | | | | | | | | |
| 1881 | | | | | | | | | | |
| 1882 | | | | | | | | | | |
| 1883 | 344 | 292 | 52 | 16 | 3 | 13 | 15.1 | 3.7 | 12.2 | |
| 1884 | 346 | 263 | 69* | 27 | 12 | 15 | 19.9 | 4.3 | 11 | In 14 cases tried by the Sessions Judge of Patna neither the Sessions statements nor the records of cases shew whether the Judge agreed with the verdict or not. |
| 1885 | 348 | 282 | 66 | 25 | 4 | 21 | 18.9 | 6 | 15.9 | |
| 1886 | 284 | 239 | 45 | 24 | 9 | 15 | 15.8 | 5.2 | 9.9 | |
| 1887 | 339 | 263 | 76 | 19 | 10 | 9 | 22.4 | 2.6 | 10.6 | |
| 1888 | 305 | 240 | 65 | 25 | 11 | 14 | 21.3 | 4.6 | 11.9 | |
| 1889 | 285 | 235 | 50 | 13 | 7 | 6 | 17.5 | 2.1 | 8.1 | |
| 1890 | 285 | 230 | 55 | 19 | 6 | 13 | 19.2 | 4 5 | 13.2 | |
| 1892 | 290 | 240 | 50 | 20 | 10 | 10 | 17.2 | 3.4 | 8.6 | |
| Total .. | 3567 | 2921 | 632 | 238 | 90 | 148 | 16.9 | 83.1 | | |

*N.B.*—Average of Jury verdicts that would have been set aside in 11 years (1877, 1878 and 1883 to 1891) if reference had been made in cases of all verdicts dissented from by the Sessions Judge and the verdicts set aside in the same ratio, as in cases referred, is 11.8.
Average percentage of verdicts actually set aside to the total number of verdicts in 11 years is 3.68.

## Statement—(B.)

| Years. | 1 | 2 | 3 | 4 | 5 | 6 | 7 | 8 |
|---|---|---|---|---|---|---|---|---|
| | Number of trials with assessors. | Number of appeals disposed of.* | Number of cases not appealed against. | Affirmed. | Reversed, modified and sent back. | Percentage of judgments of Sessions Judges affirmed to the total number of appeals. | Percentage of judgments affirmed or not disturbed to the total number of trials with assessors. | Percentage of judgments corrected by the High Court to the total number of trials. |
| 1877 | 1087 | 640 | 447 | 522 | 118 | 81.5 | 89.1 | 10.9 |
| 1878 | 1165 | 635 | 528 | 533 | 104 | 83.6 | 91 | 9 |
| 1879 | .. | .. | .. | .. | .. | 85.2 | 89.6 | 10.4 |
| 1880 | .. | .. | .. | .. | .. | 80.4 | 87 | 13 |
| 1881 | .. | .. | .. | .. | .. | 80.7 | 88.3 | 11.7 |
| 1882 | .. | .. | .. | .. | .. | 82.5 | 89.9 | 10.1 |
| 1883 | 766 | 667 | 329 | 559 | 108 | 83.8 | 89.1 | 10.9 |
| 1884 | 1075 | 692 | 383 | 571 | 121 | 82.5 | 88.6 | 11.4 |
| 1885 | 1047 | 796 | 251 | 626 | 170 | 79.9 | 84.1 | 15.9 |
| 1886 | 1046 | 696 | 350 | 578 | 118 | 83 | 88.4 | 11.6 |
| 1887 | 1064 | 725 | 339 | 580 | 145 | 80 | 86.3 | 13.7 |
| 1888 | 1157 | 833 | 324 | 664 | 169 | 79.7 | 85.5 | 14.5 |
| 1889 | 1171 | 770 | 401 | 602 | 168 | 78.1 | 85.6 | 14.4 |
| 1890 | 1100 | 838 | 262 | 659 | 179 | 78.6 | 83.7 | 16.3 |
| 1891 | 1283 | 911 | 322 | 708 | 203 | 77.4 | 83.5 | 16.5 |
| Total.. | 8205 | 3936 | 6602 | 1603 | 81.6 | 19.4 | 86.7 | 13.3 |

* A few of the appeals under this column, are also appeals from the sessions trial in jury cases; but as these appeals could only be made on a point of law, or on account of a misdirection by the Judge, the result favourable or otherwise affects the merit of the decision of Sessions Judges alone—and as separate figures are not available, they may very well be taken for the purpose of comparison.

*N.B.*—Average percentage of judgments that would be reversed in 11 years (1877, 1878 and 1883 to 1891) if all judgment not appealed from were treated as affirmed is 13.3.

Average percentage of judgments reversed notified and sent back to the total number of appeals during the 11 years (1877, 1878 and 1884 to 1891) is 19.6.

Explanation of Statement (A):—Figures in columns 1 to 6 are from the Reports. Figures in column 7 show the percentage of verdicts not agreed to by the Sessions Judge to the total number of verdicts of Juries. Figures in column 8 show the percentage of verdicts of Juries set aside by the High Court to the total number of verdicts. Figures in column 9 show the percentage of verdicts that would have been set aside, if all the cases in which the Sessions Judges had differed from the Jury, had been referred by them under Section 307 Cr. P. C., to the High Court, and the verdicts set aside in the same ratio as in the cases referred. It would perhaps be conceded that the cases not referred were such that if they were before the High Court there would be less chance of their being set aside. Under the present Code (Section 307 Cr. P. C.) wrong verdicts may be set aside in every instance; it is not therefore an irremediable wrong.

Explanation of Statement (A) :—Figures in columns 1, 2, 4 and 5 are form the Reports. Figures in column 3 give the difference between columns 1 and 2, and show cases in which no appeals have been preferred. The percentage in column 6 has been worked out from the figures in columns 2 and 4. In column 7 the percentage of judgments of Sessions Judges with the aid of Assessors not disturbed to the full number of trials has been worked out ; the Sessions Judges being credited with result "affirmed" or "not disturbed," for cases not appealed against *plus* cases actually in appeal and affirmed by the High Court. There are doubtless cases in which no appeal against the sentenee of the Sessions Judge is preferred, because the prisoner has no money or friends to take up his case before the High Court ; and if appeals had been prefeired in these cases the sentences would not have been affirmed : while therefore, the mode in which the percentage has been worked out in column 9 of Statement A is unfavourable to the Jury, the mode by which the percentage in column 7 of the Statement B. has been worked out is very favourable to the Sessions Judges, and they have been worked out in this way to remove all hesitation in adopting them for the purpose of comparison. The figures in column 8 shew the percentage of verdicts set aside or corrected by the High Court to the total number of trials.

The inferences are :—

First.—There is a gradual and distinct falling off in the quality of the decisions of the Sessions Judges as the following table will show.

| Years. | Percentage of judgments of Sessions Judges affirmed to the total number of appeals. | Percentage of judgments of Sessions Judges not disturbed to the total number of trials. |
|---|---|---|
| 1877 | 81·5 | 89·1 |
| 1878 | 83·6 | 91 |
| 1879 | 85·2 | 89·6 |
| 1880 | 80·4 | 87 |
| 1881 | 80·7 | 88·3 |
| 1882 | 82·5 | 89·9 |
| 1883 | 83·8 | 89·1 |
| 1884 | 82·5 | 88·6 |
| 1885 | 79·9 | 84·1 |
| 1886 | 83 | 88·4 |
| 1887 | 80 | 86·3 |
| 1888 | 79·7 | 85·5 |
| 1889 | 78·1 | 85·6 |
| 1890 | 78·6 | 83·7 |
| 1891 | 77·4 | 83·5 |

Secondly.—The result of trials by Jury has been much better than that of trials by the Sessions Judge with the aid of Assessors.

| Years. | Percentage of verdicts not agreed to by the Sessions Judge to the whole number of verdicts. | Percentage of verdicts set aside to the total number of verdicts. | Percentage of verdicts which would have been set aside, if all the cases in which the Sessions Judge had disagreed had been referred by him to the High Court and verdicts set aside in the same ratio as in cases referred, |
|---|---|---|---|
| 1877 | 16·7 | 4·9 | 11·3 |
| 1878 | 11·8 | 3·7 | 7 |
| 1879 | 14·1 | " | " |
| 1880 | 16·8 | " | " |
| 1881 | 15·8 | " | " |
| 1182 | 16·7 | " | " |
| 1883 | 15·1 | 3·7 | 12·2 |
| 1884 | 19·9 | 4·3 | 11 |
| 1885 | 18·9 | 6 | 15·9 |
| 1886 | 15·8 | 5·2 | 9·9 |
| 1887 | 22·4 | 2·6 | 10·6 |
| 1888 | 21·3 | 4·7 | 11·9 |
| 1889 | 17·5 | 2·1 | 8·1 |
| 1890 | 19·2 | 4·5 | 13·2 |
| 1891 | 17·2 | 3·4 | 8·6 |

Comparing the two tables, it will appear that the High Court would have corrected the following percentage of total number of judgments of Sessions Judge with the aid of Assessors, if cases not appealed against were to be treated as affirmed along with the cases actually affirmed on appeal.

| 1877 | 1878 | 1879 | 1880 | 1881 | 1882 | 1883 | 1884 | 1885 | 1886 | 1887 | 1888 | 1889 | 1890 | 1891 |
|---|---|---|---|---|---|---|---|---|---|---|---|---|---|---|
| 10·9 | 9 | 10·4 | 13 | 11·7 | 10·1 | 10·9 | 11·4 | 15·9 | 11·6 | 13·7 | 14·5 | 14·4 | 13·2 | 16·5 |

While, if reference had been made in all cases and verdicts set aside in the same ratio as in cases referred, the High Court would have had to correct the verdict of the Juries as per following percentage to all verdicts :—

| 1877 | 1878 | 1879 | 1880 | 1881 | 1882 | 1883 | 1884 | 1885 | 1886 | 1887 | 1888 | 1889 | 1890 | 1891 |
|---|---|---|---|---|---|---|---|---|---|---|---|---|---|---|
| 11·3 | 7 | " | " | " | " | 11.8 | 11 | 15·9 | 9.9 | 10·6 | 11·9 | 8·1 | 16·3 | 8.6 |

That is to say the percentage of the interference of the High Court that would be needed in all Jury trials in case all disagreed verdicts have been referred to and the ratio of reversals, have been the same as in cases referred, as compared with the Sessions Judge trials with the aid of Assessors in case all cases not appealed from were to be treated as "affirmed," would be as follows.

| 1877 | 1878 | 1879 | 1880 | 1881 | 1882 | 1883 | 1884 | 1885 | 1886 | 1887 | 1888 | 1889 | 1890 | 1891 |
|---|---|---|---|---|---|---|---|---|---|---|---|---|---|---|
| + ·4 | – ·2 | " | " | " | " | + ·9 | – ·4 | 0 | – 1·7 | –3·1 | –2·6 | –6·3 | –3·1 | –7·9 |

2. The following table will show the percentage of sentences of death passed by the Sessions Judge and reversed by the High Court. If it be true that native Jurors show reluctance to convict persons of murder because they are afraid of extreme sentences of death by Sessions Judges, the Sessions Judges show a tendency to pass capital sentences where people should have been absolutely acquitted or sentenced in other ways. The figures of the earlier years are not available.

| Years. | Total number of sentences of death by the Sessions Judges decided on reference by the High Court. | Confirmed. | Commuted or set aside | Percentage of sentences of death passed by the Sessions Courts and set aside by the High Court. |
|---|---|---|---|---|
| 1886 | 26 | 16 | 10 | 38·4 |
| 1887 | 39 | 28 | 11 | 28·2 |
| 1888 | 31 | 18 | 13 | 41·9 |
| 1889 | 22 | 11 | 11 | 50 |
| 1890 | 33 | 19 | 14 | 42·4 |
| 1891 | 48 | 32 | 16 | 33·3 |

# APPENDIX III.

| Years. | Total number of offences under the Indian Penal Code reported as true. | Total number of offences affecting property. | Total number of other offences under the Indian Penal Code. | Total number of offences in the Jury districts. | Total number of offences in the Jury districts affecting property. | Total number of other offences under the Penal Code. | Total number of offences in the Assessor districts. | Total number of offences in the Assessor districts affecting property. | Total number of other offences under the Penal Code. | Total number of offences under Special Laws. |
|---|---|---|---|---|---|---|---|---|---|---|
| 1890 | 1,36,611 | 68,294 | 68,317 | 34,050 | 14,416 | 19,634 | 102,561 | 53,878 | 48,683 | 75,686 |
| 1889 | 1,41,254 | 72,950 | 68,304 | 34,604 | 14,669 | 19,935 | 106,650 | 58,281 | 48,369 | 69,603 |
| 1888 | 1,34,746 | 65,757 | 68,989 | 33,703 | 12,781 | 20,920 | 101,043 | 52,876 | 48,067 | 62,502 |
| 1887 | 1,34,498 | 63,704 | 70,794 | 34,379 | 12,798 | 21,581 | 100,119 | 50,906 | 49,213 | 53,595 |
| 1886 | 1,40,263 | 67,291 | 72,972 | 37,631 | 15,020 | 22,611 | 102,632 | 52,271 | 50,361 | 53,843 |
| 1885 | 1,38,032 | 69,025 | 69,007 | 37,487 | 15,893 | 21,594 | 100,545 | 53,132 | 47,413 | 47,908 |
| 1884 | 1,39,139 | 69,852 | 69,287 | 36,858 | 15,913 | 20,945 | 102,281 | 53,939 | 48,342 | 51,876 |
| 1883 | 1,30,701 | 60,750 | 69,951 | 35,692 | 13,936 | 21,756 | 96,009 | 46,814 | 48,195 | 55,247 |
| 1882 | 1,33,628 | 59,254 | 74,374 | 36,070 | 13,806 | 22,264 | 97,558 | 45,448 | 52,110 | 51,638 |
| 1881 | 1,31,908 | 58,673 | 73,235 | 36,249 | 14,214 | 22,031 | 95,663 | 44,459 | 51,204 | 39,028 |
| 1880 | 1,35,557 | 61,415 | 74,147 | 38,396 | 15,315 | 23,083 | 97,161 | 46,102 | 51,059 | 47,539 |
| 1879 | 1,34,452 | 67,871 | 66,481 | 42,552 | 19,218 | 23,334 | 91,900 | 48,653 | 43,247 | 37,204 |
| 1878 | 1,39,382 | 70,691 | 68,691 | 43,447 | 18,465 | 24,982 | 95,935 | 52,226 | 43,709 | 33,200 |

# APPENDIX IV.

| Years. | Total number of persons convicted for offences under the I. P. C. | Total number of persons convicted under the I. P. C. for offences against property. | Total number of persons convicted under the I. P. C. for offences against the public tranquillity. | Total number of persons convicted under the I. P. C. for other offences. | Total number of persons convicted under the I. P. C. for offences in the Jury Districts. | Total number of persons convicted for offences against property in the Jury Districts. | Total unmber of persons convicted for offences against the public tranquillity in the Jury Districts. | Total number of persons convicted for other offences in the Jury Districts. | Total number of persons convicted for offences under the I. P. C. in Assessor Districts. | Total uumber of persons convicted for offences against property in assessor Districts. | Total number of persons convicted for offences against the public tranquillity in assessor Districts | Total number of persons convicted for other offences under the I. P. C. in Assessor Districts. |
|---|---|---|---|---|---|---|---|---|---|---|---|---|
| 1878 | 68,836 | 30,733 | 6,027 | 32,076 | 21,094 | 8,037 | 1,630 | 11,427 | 47,742 | 22,696 | 4,397 | 20,649 |
| 1879 | 65,283 | 28,532 | 6,034 | 30,717 | 20,545 | 8,374 | 1,620 | 10,551 | 44,738 | 20,158 | 4,414 | 20,166 |
| 1880 | 64,043 | 25,012 | 5,902 | 33,129 | 18,985 | 6,878 | 1,579 | 10,528 | 45,058 | 18,134 | 4,323 | 22,601 |
| 1881 | 59,916 | 23,008 | 6,002 | 30,906 | 16,958 | 6,059 | 1,437 | 9,462 | 42,958 | 16,949 | 4,565 | 21,444 |
| 1882 | 60,312 | 23,301 | 5,495 | 31,516 | 17,159 | 5,934 | 1,274 | 9,951 | 43,153 | 17,367 | 4,221 | 21,565 |
| 1883 | 58,679 | 23,107 | 5,842 | 29,730 | 16,306 | 5,470 | 1,545 | 9,291 | 42,373 | 17,637 | 4,297 | 20,439 |
| 1884 | 60,093 | 27,003 | 6,039 | 26,951 | 15,629 | 6,220 | 1,444 | 7,965 | 44,464 | 20,883 | 4,595 | 18,986 |
| 1885 | 59,705 | 26,773 | 6,451 | 26,481 | 15,883 | 6,459 | 1,506 | 7,918 | 43,822 | 20,314 | 4,945 | 18,563 |
| 1886 | 58,219 | 24,404 | 6,667 | 27,148 | 15,244 | 6,008 | 1,440 | 7,796 | 42,975 | 18,396 | 5,227 | 19,352 |
| 1887 | 55,416 | 21,846 | 7,007 | 26,563 | 13,756 | 4,986 | 1,445 | 7,325 | 41,660 | 16,860 | 5,562 | 19,238 |
| 1888 | 56,731 | 23,063 | 7,257 | 26,411 | 13,811 | 4,663 | 1,311 | 7,837 | 42,920 | 18,400 | 5,946 | 18,574 |
| 1889 | 59,400 | 25,649 | 7,420 | 26,331 | 14,136 | 5,528 | 1,418 | 7,190 | 45,264 | 20,121 | 6,002 | 19,141 |
| 1890 | 57,188 | 23,696 | 8,224 | 25,268 | 14,007 | 5,449 | 1,465 | 7,093 | 43,181 | 18,247 | 6,795 | 18,175 |
| 1891 | 58,856 | 24,362 | 7,896 | 26,598 | 14,355 | 5,448 | 1,489 | 7,418 | 44,501 | 18,914 | 6,407 | 19,180 |

# APPENDIX V.

*Minute by the Honourable Sir A. Colvin and the Honourable Mr. C. P. Ilbert on the proposed permanent increase in the strength of the Indian Army.*

[From Return. East India (Army). Ordered, by the House of Commons, to be printed, 16th September, 1887.]

1. Whilst fully agreeing in the proposals of our colleagues for a better organisation of the Indian Army, we regret that we are unable, for the reasons given in this Minute, to concur in the recommendations of the Despatch which it accompanies, regarding a permanent increase in the numerical strength of that army. We have no desire to dispute the claim of our military colleagues to speak on the point with greater authority than any to which we can pretend; but we perceive that there is great divergence of opinion on the subject among military men ; and we think that, in the consideration which has been now given to the subject, the obligation af the English Government to contribute towards the safety of its Indian Empire has been unduly minimised.

2. The Indian Army Commission, who were appointed by and reported to Lord Lytton's Government, who wrote with perfect knowledge of the rapidity and the direction of the Russian advance in Central Asia, and on whose recommendations are based some of the most important proposals of the Despatch, summarised as follows, in their Report of November 1879, the purposes for which the Army of India must be maintained:—

"(*a*) Preventing and repelling attacks, or threatened aggression, from foreign enemies beyond the border.

"(*b*) Making successful armed disturbance or rebellion within British India or its feudatory states impossible.

"(*c*) Watching and overawing the armies of Native feudatory states." (Report Paragraph 17.)

3. It appears indisputable from the Report that, in their enumeration of these purposes, the Commission contemplated the contingency of operations beyond the frontier, not merely against Russia with Afghanistan as our ally, but against Russia assisted by Afghanistan.

They say: "The external foes which the Indian Army may have to meet on its land frontier are Russia and Afghanistan on the north-west. . . . . . For operations against Russia, or Afghanistan assisted by Russia, a force of two army corps, or 50,000 to 60,000 fighting men, might possibly be necessary. No one has ever suggested that the Army of India should be maintained at a strength necessary to put into the field a larger force than this." (Report, Paragraph 17.)

4. They were of opinion that the Army of India, if properly organised, was sufficient to provide for the purposes thus enumerated, without any addition to its numerical strength.

5 They expressly made the reserve that, in making this estimate, thy did not take into consideration the contingency of a permanent or lengthened military occupation of Afghanistan.

"We have not considered," they say, "the question of the future military occupation of Afghanistan proper, or any part of it not embraced in the conditions of the Treaty of Gandamak. We are well aware that, if there is to be a permanent, or even a lengthened, military occupation of Afghanistan, it can no more be provided from the Army, or the distribution of the Army that we propose, than it could be from the Army as it now is. There can be no doubt that the duty of garrisoning Afghanistan will not be popular with the regular Native troops, and that if the occupation of the country is of any duration, constant relief of regiments will be called for, which will involve the maintenance in India of a number of regiments extra to the present establishment. We presume, therefore, that if Afghanistan is to be occupied for any great length of time—a matter on which, as far as we know at present, no decision has been arrived at—regiments will be specially raised in India, and perhaps to some extent in Afghanistan itself for local service in that country, thus obviating the necessity for a system of constant relief from the regular Native Army."

6. The data on which the Army Commission based their estimates have not, so far as we have been able to learn, been proved insufficient. Nor is it suggested that, in consequence of any changes which have been made since the Commission's Report was presented, the fighting power of the Indian Army is less than it then was. On the contrary our honourable military colleague, in a Minute dated 10th September 1884, which was forwarded to the Secretary of State under cover of a Despatch dated the 10th of March last, expresses himself as follows in respect of these points: "Until she (Russia) is much further consolidated on the Herat frontier, she will, I believe, make no further attempt to advance towards India; and then her task is gigantic." (Paragraph 45). He considered a small increase in the strength of the Army necessary, which should not exceed 10,000 in all, of whom 4,000 would be Europeans; neither was he disposed to say that this increase should take place immediately. He wrote further:—

"Thus the general result of what was effected in 1882 has been that the strength of the Native and Britsh troops remains what it was before the changes were made; but the Army is organised on a more enconomical, efficient, and useful basis, better adapted to war and the general requirements of the country, and, from the increased strength of the battalions, more in accordance with the recommendations of some of our most experieneed officers. Thus, in considering the present strength of the Army, it must be prominently kept in view that the result of the changes carried into effect in 1882 did not bring about a reduction in the total strength of our fighting power in India." (Paragraph 34).

The contingency which the Army Commisson, when it submitted its Report, thought possible has now become more possible; but this furnishes no ground for believing that the precautions then recommended as sufficient, in the event of such a danger overtaking us are insufficient now. It is necessary, on the contrary, to remember that since the Commission wrote, a large scheme of strategical frontier railways has been sanctioned, and is being vigorously pushed on; while an elaborate plan of frontier defensive works is also about to be put into execution. Apart altogether from the immediate purpose which they are expected to serve, these works will add indirectly, but not inconsiderably, to the mobility and the fighting strength of our forces.

7. The frontier fortification to which we refer cannot require, for their occupation, an increase to the India Army of 27,000 men. We fail to see why any force needed for this purpose should not be obtained in the mode contemplated by Lord Lytton's Government, that is to say by withdrawing the necessary troops from other parts of India. [*See* Paragraph 13 of the Despatch of 22nd. May, 1879; Blue Book on East India Army System p.3.]

8. If the above reasoning is correct, there seems to us every reason to apprehend that the increase of our forces beyond the needs enumerated by the Army Commission may prove a weapon less of defence than of aggression. The presence in India of so strong a force as is desired may even suggest the permanent occupation of some part of Afghanistan. Against the policy of extending to a point beyond Kandahar, the frontier, formal or practical, of British India, and the area which must be permanently held by British troops, weighty arguments, moral, political, and financial, have been and may still be urged. But, whatever may be the merits of such a proposal, it forms no part of the grounds on which an increase to our Army is now advocated; and is foreign, we have every reason to believe, to the desires or intentions of our colleagues.

9. We are thus of opinion that as no circumstances have arisen which, from a military point of view, have not been already foreseen and guarded against, the proposal to increase the strength of the Army by 27,000 men should be negatived. We are further of opinion that the proposal is open to the objection that it may lead to the advocacy, and possibly to

the adoption, of projects for the extension of our present frontier. The question then narrows itself to this: Is it the duty of the Government of India to maintain and charge to Indian revenues a permanent addition to its forces, not required for India, but available for the purpose of extending and securing its dominion beyond India?

10. We are wholly unable to admit that the Indian Government is under any obligation to maintain a standing army beyond the numbers indicated by the Army Commission, or for purposes other than those enumerated by them. They can draw on England, as in practice they always draw, should necessity arise for a temporary increase to the forces in India; obtaining what is required, paying for it so long as it is needed, and dismissing it when the need is over.

11. Where is the line to be drawn if India admits its liability to maintain a force strong enough, not only to fulfil the purposes which have been enumerated in this Minute, but to acquire and maintain against all comers positions in Afghanistan, or elsewhere? It is desired, apparently, to have a force for home use, and a force for exterior use. The necessary strength of the former can be measured; but where is a measure to be found for the latter? It has to deal with that unknown quantity, the assumed military possibilities of the Russians in Central Asia and Afghanistan. If the principle is admitted that an army is to be maintained from Indian revenues for exterior use, it is difficult to see how its numbers are to be controlled, or why we shall not presently be told that 100,000 men are as necessary as 10,000. It has been already pointed out that the existence of such a force would be no mean agent in bringing about the very risk which it is meant to obviate. A standing army which is larger than is necessary for home requirements will be a tempting, and almost an irresistible, weapon of offence beyond the border.

12. It is asked how provision is to be made for an increase of native troops should a merely temporary addition to the English force in India in the event of war be advocated. We reply that, unless our frontier is to be extended, we are unable to see the necessity for any such increase. If, on the other hand, the frontier is to be extended, the new territory acquired must, we believe, be held by the aid of local levies. Experience, it is agreed on all sides, has shown that Indians will not enlist for service beyond the frontier. It must be further remembered that a system of reserves such as it is proposed to initiate, will gradually furnish us with the power of increasing our native forces to a considerable extent.

13. It can hardly be contended that the mere establishment of a reserve necessitates, of itself, an increase in the English force, and that the latter must be proportioned, not only to the native force actually under arms, but to that force *plus* the reserve.

The Appendices to the Despatch prove how large a number of young men trained to arms annually leave the army, and are scattered about the country. These men, though unavailable for the purpose of increasing our military strength, are as much an element of danger as the proposed reserve will be. No count has been hitherto taken of their existence, we believe, in fixing the strength of British troops in India. Nor, whatever, may be urged as to English troops, can the existence of a Native reserve possibly furnish arguments for an addition to the number of our Native Army.

14. Finally, it is stated that, even were all we have urged to be admitted, we cannot depend on England for reinforcements, and that we must not risk the Indian Empire on the ability of the English Gevernment to furnish us with troops at the moment we may happen to want them. The alternative appears to us unquestionable; if India is to maintain troops additional to those needed for her own requirements, solely because England cannot be trusted to supply them, our military financial arrangements with the English Treasury should be so altered as to set free a sum equivalent to that required for the addition to our forces in India.

15. So far we have dealt with general considerations. The financial effect of the proposals makes the case against them, in our opinion, more cogent. It is not contended even by those who desire to add no more than 10,000 to our English and 17,000 to our Native

troops, that the total ultimate cost will be less than about 1,500,000 *l.* a year. There can be no doubt that, to meet this cost, we shall be compelled to resort to taxation of a considerable amount, and seriously to burden our finances. So far, on the other hand, as we effect our object without taxation, it can only be by charging to loans the very costly unproductive military works in which we are at present engaged, the execution of which, at least in part, we believe to form an obligatory charge upon our revenue.

16. On the subject of taxation, we desire to draw attention to paragraphs 9 to 14 of the late Viceroy's Minute of 22nd September, 1884. We agree entirely with the opinion of those who hold that, as an alien people, our best claim to the regard of the natives of the country, and therefore one of our main sources of security lies in the fact that taxation is light. We believe that this is a principle which has been admitted by all Governments foreign to their subjects, and that it has been uniformly recognised and adopted by our predecessors in the administration of British India. It seems an axiom which at the present time it is singularly incumbent on the Government of India to bear in mind. If it was important when India had no European neighbour, it becomes much more so when she has at her frontier a power whose agents will make the most of all our mistakes, and bid against us by every means at their disposal, for popularity. We are aware that it is easy to push this consideration too far, and that the Indian Government must be prepared to risk a certain unpopularity if it is convinced that the measures which it has in view, and for which the imposition of burdens is required, are of so urgent a character as to necessitate their adoption, all drawbacks notwithstanding. But we have given in this Minute our reasons for holding that in the present instance no sufficient case is made out for departing from the policy above indicated.

17. There is considerable probability of our being called upon after a term of years during which our precautions have proved uncalled for, and our taxation has appeared vexatious, to relax our precautionary measures, and of our then being tempted to pass from the extreme of precaution to the extreme of negligence.

18. We do not deny that there may be force in the contention to which we have alluded, that, if we look to England for reinforcements in the event of war, we may find the English Government incapable, when called upon, of meeting our requirements. But there is at least an equal risk that if we accept from such an apprehension burdens which do not belong to us, we shall find ourselves keeping up, at the cost of the Indian revenues, a reserve which, in the event of circumstances arising that necessitate the action of troops, for extra Indian purposes, as in the case of Egypt, Abyssinia, and the Soudan, will be drawn upon by the English Government.

19. To sum up: Regarding, for the reasons we have given, the proposed increase of the Indian Army as unnecessary, we adhere to what are described by the late Army Commission as "the principles so strongly enunciated by Lord Mayo, and reiterated by his successors, that the people of India ought not to be called upon to support or pay for one single unnecessary soldier." (Paragraph 575). We cannot admit that it is the business of the Government of India, under the apprehension that reliance cannot be placed on the Government in England, to assume more than its hitherto recognised share of the common obligation. We would not accept as a charge upon Indian revenues any single item of expenditure which should be undertaken by the Government at home.

A. COLVIN,
C. P. ILBERT.

*Simla, 14th August, 1885.*

---

## THE INDIAN MILITARY AND TRANS-FRONTIER EXPENDITURE QUESTION.

A Letter by W. MARTIN WOOD, Esq., (late Editor, "*Times of India.*")

NOTE.—*The letter, copy of which is reprinted below, was forwarded to the Managing Committee of the National Congress held at Allahabad, December* 1888, *with the hope of its being serviceable in the deliberations of that representative assembly.*

*Owing, probably, to the late date at which it as received it does not seem to have been duly placed before the final Sub-Committee: it is now published in order that the considerations embodied therein may receive due attention from the constituents of the Congress with a view to the suggestions it contains being dealt with by the next Congress, so far as may be deemed desirable and expedient.*

Having for the past five and twenty years been familiar with Indian affairs I may be permitted to tender my congratulations on the holding of the fourth of these National Congresses which have already done so much, and must yet do more, in securing co-operation amongst those of diverse races, creeds, and provinces of the Indian Continent, in dealing with those broad questions of public interest that concern all the Indian peoples living under the benign sway of Her Majesty, the Queen-Empress. In common with many others of your friends I have rejoiced to watch the rise and prospect of this remarkable popular movement, in which has been manifested a just appreciation of those constitutional principles that are cherished by British statesmen of all parties; also, by its managers' tact and discretion in applying those principles to the present political conditions of India. Your movement exemplifies unity in diversity. On one hand it is a sign, amongst many others, of the rapid progress made, during a comparatively short period, in the removal of race antipathies and provincial antagonisms that had long separated the several Indian peoples; on the other, by your judicious method of securing representation from each province and race, you are cherishing that principle of local management and administration so essential under the diverse, physical and climatic conditions of India, and which, in modern political phrase, is described as federal union.

2. Amidst the large number of leading and pressing questions that demand your attention, your managers do well in not attempting to deal with too many at once; and observers, such as myself, must be satisfied to leave to your choice the final selection of those subjects that you deem most pressing in order of practical importance. This choice has, on the whole, been so wisely exercised that it is with diffidence that I venture to make two or three suggestions that may prove serviceable for your forthcoming meeting. It would be manifestly unprofitable for me to repeat or revive those topics that the several Congresses have already taken in hand, and the draft programme for your forthcoming meeting is not yet before me.

3. Looking at Indian affairs from an outside and independent standpoint, it seems to me desirable that I should speak of two or three large questions which, because of their preponderant financial influence, really dominate the material condition of India and its possibilities of future progress. These may, for the present, be classed under three main heads:—

*a.* The rapid addition to Indian military expenditure and the increasing expensiveness of its character:

*b.* The Trans-frontier policy since 1875, which has been the chief cause of that increase:

*c.* The Financial arrangements between England and India.

4. Let us briefly review the first of these. In 1863-4 your army expenditure was only 14½ millions; and so recently as 1874-5, under Lord Northbrook, the estimate was again about the same, though the account shewed 15½ millions. Since 1876, when Quetta was first occupied, the advance in your military expenditure has been by leaps and bounds, until the Budget for the current year shews an estimate of over nineteen millions sterling. Nor is this all. The strategical railways beyond the natural boundaries of India have cost im-

mense sums (estimated in the Financial Statement of 1886-7 at twelve millions sterling) while the interest thereon and the working charges—which cannot be met by any returns those lines will yield—constitute a heavy debit against the commercial railways of India; therefore that loss on working must be reckoned as a direct addition to current military charges. Then it must be remembered that the modern palatial barracks erected during the last twenty years in every part of India have cost ten or twelve millions, the greater part of which was defrayed out of current revenues, thus adding heavily to the burdens of the people. More recently these burdens have been directly increased; that is by the decision come to in 1885—no one knows at whose advice or on whose authority—to add permanently 10,000 to the British troops on the Indian establishment as well as increasing the Native army. These changes it was estimated would add two millions sterling to your annual military expenditure; but I believe, it will be found that the cost of these charges—referred to with evident anxiety in the Financial Statement for 1886-7—amounts to nearly three millions. These increases were also in directions which specially add to the amounts of home charges, thereby enhancing the heavy "losses by exchange."

5. It is a maxim acknowledged by our statesmen that expenditure depends on policy. In this instance the grievous addition to the unproductive outlay from Indian revenues is wholly due to the revolutionary change entered on in 1876; followed by the disastrous invasion of Afghanistan in 1877-80; and now sought to be perpetuated by the establishment of permanent military posts far beyond the physical boundaries of India on the West, for the maintenance of which the immensely costly railways already referred to have been construced. You are well aware that this policy has been adopted and forced on India under cover of partisan counsels amongst certain English politicians; but this does not make it any more worthy of approval or lessen the need for its being checked and, if possible, reversed. Irrefutable arguments against this new trans-frontier policy are embodied in the series of Minutes on Central Asia placed on record in 1867-9 by Sir John Lawrence and the strong men of his Executive Council; those arguments were afterwards confirmed by Lord Lawrence and other truly Conservative Anglo-Indian statesmen in 1878-9, when raising their protest against the Afghan War of that period, which was contrived in secret, entered upon suddenly with scarcely a pretence of public justification, and in flagrant defiance of those constitutional restraints prescribed in Sections 55 and 56 of the Government of India Act of 1858. For convenience of reference I may remind you that a permanent record of the protests against, and exposure of the unsoundness of the new frontier policy is contained in the volume, issued by Lord Lawrence and his co-adjutors, entitled *Causes of the Afghan War* (Chatto and Windus, 1879). The results of this fatal departure from the better traditions of Anglo-Indian statesmanship have been traced out, and applied to an elucidation of the present adverse financial condition of India, in a pamphlet by Mr. John Da Costa (copy of which I send) entitled *The Financial Situation in India as exposed in the Budget Statements of* 1886-7. (P. S. King and Sons, 1887).

6. The question then arises, what can be done by your Congresses in regard to this subject? The first condition is that its magnitude should be realised. It seems to me that it would be well, through some carefully selected committee, to ascertain and sum up the amount of the enormous burden that has been thrust on India by this new trans-frontier policy since 1876. Such computation should include the cost of the invasion and annexaiton of Upper Burmah; also the continuous addition to that cost entailed by the egregious political error of destroying the Native dynasty of Mandalay. If I do not dwell on the question of Burmah it is because that is fresh in your minds, and does not require for its elucidation that retrospective research which is needed for replacing the Western-Frontier question on its right basis. Then having placed before yourselves and the public the monstrous cost of these departures from the settled policy of Lord Lawrence, Mayo, and Northbrook, the way will be open to you to proceed to such protest and remonstrance as may seem expedient.

7. In connection with these subjects I desire to draw your attention to certain broad considerations that may be overlooked or postponed amidst the current topics of detail

that necessarily occupy the foreground of your programme and to which you are already committed. These considerations may be thus enumerated:—

*a.* The financial position of India dominates all its other material conditions.

*b.* The pressure caused by the absorption of your resources, consequent on the fatal error of thrusting military outposts beyond the natural boundaries of India, transcends in its cramping and distressing effects, all other financial and fiscal mistakes put together.

*c.* That error, with its concomitant military extravagance, is one of executive policy, and no reform in administration nor in the Local Legislative Councils will avail to obtain either reversal of that erroneous policy or security against repetitions of similar sacrifices of India's true interests.

*d.* By appealing in respect of the paramount financial peril of India, first, to Her Majesty's Secretary of State as the one directly responsible authority, and next, to the High Court of Parliament, your Congress will effectually convince independent English politicians of the capacity of your people to understand and deal with those large questions of policy, on the right solution of which depends the present and future welfare of the masses of your people.

8. The subject of the financial relations between India and the British Treasury is one that demands closer and more continuous attention than it has yet received from your leaders—with one or two notable exceptions who are so conspicuous that they need not here be named. It is not practicable in this communication to do more than indicate the course of investigation and effort required in this direction. From the very beginning of British sway over India the whole cost of maintaining that control has been thrust on the weaker power and the dependent country. By her possession of India this United Kingdom has derived power, prestige, and an incalculable amount of pecuniary profit. Yet every shilling of administrative and military expenditure incurred in maintaining the connection between the two countries has been sustained by India. It is high time that something was done to revise this unequal relation, the onesided terms of which have been settled and maintained by the stronger party alone. Your-Congress can scarcely do less than ask for some remission or redress of this hard bargain. For instance, your people have had no say in the transactions that have gone to make up your public debt of nearly 200 millions, (besides the railway debt.) Why should not an Imperial guarantee of that debt be granted? This would involve no outlay by the British taxpayer, who is really ultimately responsible, while such a course would be an immense relief to India. Then, why should not the cost of the home Indian administration be borne by the British Treasury; as that of the Colonies always has been—as also the whole of the military and naval charges incurred in acquiring our Colonial Empire? There are cogent reasons, also, why the home military charges now debited to India should be sustained, or, at least, shared by our Treasury. Most obvious arguments of political justice indicate that something should be done in this direction; and the financial relief that would be thereby afforded to India would also result in real advantage to England itself by improving the material condition of your people. But the political gain would be still greater. One of the chief causes of the comparative neglect of Indian interests in Parliament is due to the feeling, unconfessed but always present, that the British taxpayer has no direct interest in the economical administration of your finances. If only a moderate proportion of the Indian home charges were defrayed by England, say a couple of millions per annum, this would secure for your country an effective representation in our Parliamentary proceedings. If your Congress were to formulate and put forward an appeal to this effect, it would meet with response from several of our fair-minded politicians, in both parties, who are sincerely desirous of doing justice to your people.

9. In thus venturing to make these few suggestions—which pressure on my time prevents being put into more complete shape—I do not, by any means, forget those other subjects that are already engaging your attention; but the topics to which I have briefly

referred comprise, as you will perceive, some that are of the *greatest relative importance.* They pertain to a class of questions which have been too much left to be dealt with by executive authorities who are virtually irresponsible, but who really control all the fortunes of India. As British subjects, you are also British *citizens* in the true constitutional meaning of that term. As such you have the obvious right of making your voice heard in the Executive Councils of the Empire. Trusting that this high patriotic function will be performed by the forthcoming Congress in the spirit of moderation and intelligent loyalty manifested in the proceedings of its predecessors.

I am, Gentlemen,
Your sincere well-wisher,
W. MARTIN WOOD.

*West Kensington,*
*November 23rd,* 1888.

# APPENDIX VI.

## SUMMARY OF RESOLUTIONS.

PASSED AT THE

## FIRST, SECOND, THIRD, FOURTH, FIFTH, SIXTH AND SEVENTH CONGRESSES.

### RESOLUTIONS PASSED AT THE FIRST CONGRESS.

#### RESOLUTION I.

**Resolved**—That this Congress earnestly recommends that the promised inquire into the working of the Indian Administration, here and in England, should be entrusted to a Royal Commission, the people of India being adequately represented thereon, and evidence taken both in India and in England.

#### RESOLUTION II.

**Resolved**—That this Congress considers the abolition of the Council of the Secretary of State for India, as at present constituted, the necessary preliminary to all other reforms.

#### RESOLUTION III.

**Resolved**—That this Congress considers the reform and expansion of the Supreme and existing Local Legislative Councils, by the admission of a considerable proportion of elected members (and the creation of similar Councils for the North-Western Provinces and Oudh, and also for the Punjab) essential; and holds that all Budgets should be referred to these Councils for consideration, their members being moreover empowered to interpellate the Executive in regard to all branches of the administration; and that a Standing Committee of the House of Commons should be constituted to receive and consider any formal protests that may be recorded by majorities of such Councils against the exercise by the Executive of the power which would be vested in it, of overruling the decisions of such majorities

#### RESOLUTION IV.

**Resolved**—That in the opinion of this Congress the competitive examinations now held in England for first appointments in various civil departments of the public service should henceforth, in accordance with the views of the India Office Committee of 1860, "be held simultaneously, one in England and one in India, both being as far as practicable identical in their nature, and those who compete in both countries being finally classified in one list according to merit," and that the successful candidates in India should be sent to England for further study, and subjected there to such further examinations as may seem needful. Further, that all other first appointments (excluding peonships, and the like) should be filled by competitive examinations held in India, under conditions calculated to secure such intellectual, moral, and physical qualifications as may be decided by Government to be necessary. Lastly, that the maximum age of candidates for entrance into the Covenanted Civil Service be raised to not less than 23 years.

### RESOLUTION V.

**Resolved**—That in the opinion of this Congress the proposed increas in the military expenditure of the empire is unnecessary, and, regard being had to the revenues of the empire and the existing circumstances of the country, excessive.

### RESOLUTION VI.

**Resolved**—That in the opinion of this Congress, if the increased demands for military expenditure are not to be, as they ought to be met, by retrenchment, they ought to be met, firstly, by the re-imposition of the Customs duties ; and, secondly, by the extension of the license-tax to those classes of the community, official and non-official, at present exempted from it, care being taken that in the case of all clsses a sufficiently high taxable minimum be maintained. And, further, that this Congress is of opinion that Great Britain should extend an imperial guarantee to the Indian debt.

### RESOLUTION VII.

**Resolved**—That this Congress deprecates the annexation of Upper Burmah, and considers that if the Government unfortunately decide on annexation, the entire country of Burmah should be separated from the Indian Viceroyalty and constituted a Crown Colony, as distinct in all matters from the Government of the country as is Ceylon.

### RESOLUTION VIII.

**Resolved**—That the resolutions passed by this Congress be communicated to the Political Associations in each province, and that these Associations be requested, with the help of similar bodies and other agencies, within their respective provinces, to adopt such measures as they may consider calculated to advance the settlement of the various questions dealt with in these resolutions.

### RESOLUTION IX.

**Resolved**—That the Indian National Congress re-assemble next year in Calcutta and sit on Tuesday, the 28th of December, 1886, and the next succeeding days.

---

## RESOLUTIONS PASSED AT THE SECOND CONGRESS.

### RESOLUTION I.

**Resolved**—That this Congress of Delegates from all parts of India do humbly offer its dutiful and loyal congratulations to Her Most Gracious Majesty, the Queen-Empress, on the approaching completion of the first half century of her memorable, beneficent and glorious reign, and heartily wish her many, many more, and hapyy years of rule over the great British Empire.

### RESOLUTION II.

**Resolved**—That this Congress regards with the deepest sympathy, and views with grave apprehension, the increasing proverty of vast numbers of the population of India and (although aware that the Government is not overlooking this matter and is contemplating certain palliatives) desires to record its fixed conviction that the introduction of Representative Intsitutions will, prove one of the most important practical steps towards the amelioration of the condition of the people.

## RESOLUTION III.

**Resolved**—That this Congress do, emphatically, re-affirm the 3rd Resolution of the Congress of 1885, and distinctly declare its belief that the reform and expansion of the Council of the Governor-General for making laws and of the Provincial Legislative Councils therein suggested, have now become essential alike in the interests of India and England.

## RESOLUTION IV.

**Resolved**—That this Congress is of opinion that, in giving practical effect to this essential reform, regard should be had (subject to such modifications as, on a more detailed examination of the question may commend themselves to the Government) to the principles embodied in the following tentative suggestions :—

(1.)—The number of persons composing the Legislative Councils, both provincial and of the Governor-General, to be materially increased. Not less than one-half the Members of such enlarged Council to be elected. Not more than one-fourth to be officials having seats *ex-officio* in such Councils, and not more than one-fourth to be Members, official or non official, nominated by Government.

(2)—The right to elect Members to the Provincial Councils to be conferred only on those classes and members of the community, *primâ facie*, capable of exercising it wisely and independently. In Bengal and Bombay the Councillors may be elected by the Members of Municipalities, District Boards, Chambers of Commerce and the Universities, or an electorate may be constituted of all persons possessing such qualifications, educational and pecuniary, as may be deemed necessary. In Madras the Councillors may be elected either by District Boards, Municipalities, Chambers of Commerce and the University, or by Electoral Colleges composed of Members partly elected by these bodies and partly nominated by Government. In the North-West Provinces and Oudh and in the Punjab Councillors may be elected by an Electoral College composed of Members elected by Municipal and District Boards, and nominated, to an extent not exceeding one-sixth of the total number, by Government, it being understood that the same elective system now in force where Municipal Boards are concerned will be applied to District Boards and the right of electing Members to these latter extended to the cultivating class. But whatever system be adopted (and the details must be worked out separately for each province) care must be taken that all sections of the Community and all great interests are adequately represented.

(3.)—The elected Members of the Council of the Governor-General for making laws, to be elected by the elected Members of the several Provincial Councils.

(4.)—No elected or nominated Member of any Council to receive any salary or remuneration in virtue of such Membership, but any such Member, already in receipt of any Government salary or allowance, to continue to draw the same unchanged during Membership, and all Members to be entitled to be reimbursed any expenses incurred in travelling in connection with their Membership.

(5.)—All persons resident in India, to be eligible for seats in Council, whether as electees or nominees, without distinction of race, creed, caste or colour.

(6.)—All legislative measures and all financial questions, including all budgets, whether these involve new or enhanced taxation or not, to be necessarily submitted to and dealt with by these Councils. In the case of all other branches of the administration any Member to be at liberty, after due notice, to put any question he sees fit to the *ex-officio* Members (or such one of these as may be especially charged with the supervision of the particular branch concerned) and to be entitled (except as hereinafter provided) to receive a reply to his question, together with copies of any papers requisite for the thorough comprehension of the subject, and on this reply the Council to be at liberty to consider and discuss the question, and record thereon such resolution as may appear fitting to the majority. Provided that, if the subject in regard to which the inquiry is made involves matters of Foreign policy, Military dispositions or strategy, or is otherwise of such a nature that, in the opinion of the Executive, the public interests would be materially imperilled by the communication of the information asked for, it shall be competent for them to instruct the *ex-officio* Members, or one of them, to reply accordingly, and decline to furnish the information asked for.

(7.)—The Executive Government shall possess the power of overruling the decision arrived at by the majority of the Council, in every case in which, in its opinon, the public interests would suffer the acceptance of such decision ; but whenever this power is exercised, a full exposition of the grounds on which this has been considered necessary, shall be published within one month and in the case of local Governments they shall report the circumstances and explain their action to the Government of India, and in the case of this latter, it shall report and explain to the Secretary of State ; and in any such case on a representation made through the Government of India and the Secretary of State by the overruled majority, it shall be competent to the Standing Committee of the House of Commons (recommended in the 3rd Resolution of last year's Congress which this present Congress has affirmed) to consider the matter, and call for any and all papers or information, and hear any persons on behalf of such majority or otherwise, and thereafter, if needful, report thereon to the full House.

## RESOLUTOIN V.

**Resolved**—That this Congress do invite all Public Bodies and all Associations throughout the Country, humbly and earnestly, to entreat His Excellency the Viceroy to obtain the sanction of Her Majesty's Secretary of State for India, to the appointment of a Commission, to enquire exhaustively into the best method of introducing such a tentative form of Representative Institutions into India, as has been indicated in Resolutions III. of the past, and IV. of the present year's Congress.

## RESOLUTION VI.

**Resolved**—That a Committee composed of the gentlemen named in the margin* be appointed to consider the Public Service Question and report thereon to this Congress.

*Hon'ble Dadabhai Naoroji (*Bombay*).
,, S. Subramania Iyer (*Madras*).
,, Peary Mohun Mookerjee (*Calcutta*).
Mr. G. Subramania Iyer (*Madras*).
Babu Motilal Ghose (*Calcutta*).
Mr. Surendra Nath Banerjee (*Calcutta*).
,, Gungapershad Varma (*Lucknow*).
,, Ramkali Chaudhuri (*Benares*).
Mr. Guru Prasad Sen (*Patna*).
Pundit Prannath (*Lucknow*),
Munshi Kashipershad (*Allahabad*).
Nawab Reza Ali Khan (*Lucknow*).
Mr. Hamid Ali (*Lucknow*).
Lala Kanhyalal (*Amritsar*).
Rao Sahib Gangadhar Rao Madhaw Chitnavis (*Nagpur*).
Mr. Rahimatulla M. Sayani (*Bombay*).

## RESOLUTION VII.

**Resolved**—That this Congress approves and adopts the report* submitted by the Committee appointed by Resolution VI.

## RESOLUTION VIII.

**Resolved**—That, in the opinion of this Congress, the time has now arrived when the system of trial by jury may be safely extended into many parts of the country where it is not at present in force.

---

## *REPORT.

We, the Members of the Committee appointed by the Congress to submit a statement in connection with the Public Service Question, have the honor to report that the following resolutions were unanimously adopted by us at a meeting held yesterday :—

1.—That the open Competitive Examination be held simultaneously both in India and in England.

2.—That the Simultaneous Examinations thus held be equally open to all classes of Her Majesty's subjects.

3.—That the Cassified lists be prepared according to merit.

4.—That the Congress express the hope that the Civil Service Commissioners will give fair consideration to Sanskrit and Arabic among the subjects of examination.

5.—That the age of candidates eligible for admission to the open Competitive Examination be not less than 19, nor, as recommended by Sir C. Aitchison, more than 23 years.

6.—That Simultaneous Examinations being granted, the Statutory Civil Service be closed for first appointments.

7.—That the appointments in the Statutory Civil Service, under the existing rules, be still left open to the Members of the Uncovenanted Service and to professional men of proved merit and ability.

8.—That all appointments requiring educational qualifications, other than covenanted first appointments, be filled by Competitive Examinations held in the different Provinces, and open in each Province to such natural-born subjects of H. M. only as are residents thereof.

These Resolutions, it is hoped, cover the main principles which underlie the questions set by the Public Service Commission. For a more detailed consideration there was no time.

(Sd.) DADABHAI NAOROJI,
*President of the Committee.*

*30th December, 1886.*

## RESOLUTION IX.

**Resolved**—That, in the opinion of this Congress, the innovation made in 1872 in the system of trial by jury, depriving the verdicts of juries of all finality, has proved injurious to the country, and that the powers then, for the first time, vested in Sessions Judges and High Courts, of setting aside verdicts of acquittal, should be at once withdrawn.

## RESOLUTION X.

**Resolved**—That, in the opinion of this Congress, a provision, similar to that contained in the Summary Jurisdiction Act of England (under which accused persons in serious cases have the option of demanding a committal to the Sessions Court), should be introduced into the Indian Code of Criminal Procedure, enabling accused persons, in warrant cases, to demand that, instead of being tried by the Magistrate, they be committed to the Court of Sessions.

## RESOLUTION XI.

**Resolved**—That this Congress do place on record an expression of the universal conviction that a complete separation of executive and judicial functions (such that in no case the two functions shall be combined in the same officer) has become an urgent necessity, and that, in its opinion, it behoves the Government to effect this separation without further delay, even though this should, in some Provinces, involve some extra expenditure.

## RESOLUTION XII.

**Resolved**—That, in view of the unsettled state of public affairs in Europe, and the immense assistance that the people of this country, if duly prepared therefor, is capable of rendering to Great Britain in the event of any serious complications arising, this Congress do earnestly appeal to the Government to authorise (under such rules and restrictions as may to it seem fitting) a system of Volunteering for the Indian inhabitants of the country, such as may qualify them to support the Government effectively in any crisis.

## RESOLUTION XIII.

**Resolved**—That Standing Congress Committees be constituted at all important centres

## RESOLUTION XIV.

**Resolved**—That the Third Indian National Congress assemble at Madras on the 27th of December, 1887.

## RESOLUTION XV.

**Resolved**—That, copies of these Resolutions be forwarded to His Excellency the Viceroy-in-Council, with the humble requests that he will cause the 1st Resolution to be submitted in due course to Her Majesty the Queen-Empress, that he will cause all the Resolutions to be laid before Her Majesty's Secretary of State for India, and that he himself will be graciously pleased, in consultation with his colleagues, to accord them his best consideration.

# RESOLUTIONS PASSED AT THE THIRD CONGRESS

## RESOLUTION I.

**Resovlved**—That a Committee is appointed, consisting of the gentlemen (marginally enumerated*) to consider what rules, if any, may now be usefully framed in regard of the constitution and working of the Congress, with instructions to report thereon to the Congress, on the 30th instant.

* Messrs. Namjoshi, Chandravaker, Mir Humayun Jah Bahadur, Hajee Mahomed Abdul Shakoor Badshaw Sahit, S. Subramania Iyer, W. S. Gantz, Rangiah Naidu, Surendranath Banerjee, Trailokhyanath Mitra, Kali Charan Banerjee, Guru Prasad Sen, Saligram Singh, Ram Kali Chaudhuri, Hafiz Abdul Rahim, Rampal Singh, Pandit Madan Mohun, Ganga Prasad Varma, Bishan Narayen Dar, Hamid Ali, Murlidhur, Satyanand Agnihotri, H. H. Dhruva, W. C. Bonnerjee, Norendranath Sen, Eardley Norton, Joy Govind Shome, Iswari Lal Sircar, G. Subramania Iyer, D. A. Khare, S. A. Saminada Iyer, Sabapathy Mudaliar, A. O. Hume, C. Vigiya Raghava Chariar, Govind Buksh, Karandikar.

## RESOLUTION II.

**Resolved**—That this Congress re-affirms the necessity for the expansion and reform of the Council of the Governor-General for making Laws, and the Provincial Legislative Councils, already set forth in Resolutions III. of the Congress of 1885, and 1886, and expresses the earnest hope that the Government will no longer delay action in the direction of this essential reform.

## RESOLUTION III.

**Resolved**—That this Congress once again places on record an expression of the universal conviction that a complete separation of the Executive and Judicial functions (such that in no case the two functions shall be combined in the same officer) has become an urgent necessity, and declares that, in its opinion, it behoves the Government to effect this separation, without further delay, even though this should, in some Provinces, involve some extra expenditure.

## RESOLUTION. IV.

**Resolved**—That, in view of the loyalty of Her Majesty's Indian subjects, this Congress considers it desirable that the Queen's Proclamation should be given effect to; that the Military Service in its higher grades should be practically opened to the natives of this country; and that the Government of India should establish Military Colleges in this country, whereat the natives of India, as defined by Statute, may be educated and trained for a military career as officers of the Indian Army.

## RESOLUTION V.

**Resolved**—That, in view of the unsettled state of public affairs in Europe, and the immense assistance that the people of this country, if duly prepared, therefor, are capable of rendering to Great Britain, in the event of any serious complications arising, this Congress once again earnestly appeals to the Government to authorize (under such rules and restrictions as may to it seem fitting,) a system of Volunteering for the Indian inhabitants of the country, such as may qualify them to support the Government, effectively, in any crisis.

## RESOLUTION VI.

**Resolved**—That, as the administration of the Income-Tax, especially as regards incomes below Rs. 1,000, has proved extremely unsatisfactory, it is essential, in the opinion of the Congress, that the taxable minimum be raised to Rs. 1,000, the loss of revenue thus involved being made good, and further financial difficulties, if any, met by reductions in the existing public expenditure, or, should this prove impossible, by the re-imposition of an import duty on the finer classes of cotton goods.

### RESOLUTION VII.

**Resolved**—That, having regard to the poverty of the people, it is desirable that the Government be moved to elaborate a system of Technical Education, suitable to the condition of the country, to encourage indigenous manufactures by a more strict observance of the orders, already existing, in regard to utilizing such manufactures for State purposes, and to employ more extensively, than at present, the skill and talents of the people of the country.

### RESOLUTION VIII.

**Resolved**—That, in view of the loyalty of the people, the hardships which the present Arms' Act (XI of 1878) causes, and the unmerited slur which it casts upon the people of this country, the Government be moved so to modify the provisions of Chapter IV., and, if necessary, other portions of the said Act, as shall enable all persons to possess and wear arms, unless debarred therefrom, either as individuals or members of particular communities or classes, by the orders of the Government of India (or any local authority empowered by the Government of India on that behalf) for reasons to be recorded in writing and duly published.

### RESOLUTION IX.

**Resolved**—That the rules drafted by the Committee appointed under Resolution I. stand over for consideration till next Congress, but that, in the meantime, copies be circu ltated to all Standing Congress Committees, with the request that they will, during the coming year, act in accordance with these rules, so far as this may seem to them possible and desirable, and report thereon to the next Congress, with such further suggestions as to them may seem meet.

### RESOLUTION X.

**Resolved**—That the Fourth Indian National Congress assemble at Allahabad on the 26th December, 1888.

### RESOLUTION XI.

**Resolved**—That copies of these Resolutions be forwarded to His Excellency the Viceroy-in-Council, with the humble request that he will cause all the Resolutions to be laid before Her Majesty's Secretary of State for India, and that he himself will be graciously pleased, in consultation with his colleagues, to accord them his best consideration.

## RESOLUTOINS PASSED AT THE FOURTH CONGRESS.

### RESOLUTION I.

**Resolved**—That this Congress affirms the necessity for the expansion and reform of the Council of the Governor-General for making laws and regulations, and of the existing Provincial Legislative Councils, already set forth in Resolutions III. of the Congress of 1885 and 1886, and Resolution II. of the Congress of 1887 (a tentative scheme for which expansion and reform was suggested in Resolution IV. of the Congress of 1886); and further urges that a Legislative Council (of the same character as those which have been suggested for Provinces where Legislative Councils already exist) be established for the Punjab.

### RESOLUTION II.

**Resolved**—That this Congress, while appreciating the concessions proposed in the Report of the Public Service Commission, yet feels it necessary to put distinctly on record its opinion that full justice will never be done to the people of this country until the open competitive examination for the Civil Service of India is held simultaneously in England and in India.

## RESOLUTION III.

**Resolved**—That this Congress, having read and considered Resolution XI. of the Congress of 1886, to wit—

"That this Congress do place on record an expression of the universal conviction that a complete separa-"tion of the eexcutive and judicial functions (such that in no case the two functions shall be "combined in the same officer) has become an urgent necessity; and that, in its opinion, it behoves "the Government to effect this separation without further delay; even though this should, in "some provinces, involve some extra expenditure"—

and Resolution III. of the Congress of 1887, to the same effect, does now, hereby, affirm the same respectively.

## RESOLUTION IV.

**Resolved**—That this Congress, having read and considered Resolution VIII. of the Congress of 1886, to wit—

"That in the opinion of this Congress, the time has now arrived when the system of trial by jury "may be safely extended into many parts of the country where it is not at present in force"—

Resolution IX. of the Congress of 1886, to wit—

"That, in opinion of this Congress, the innovation made in 1872 in the system of trial by jury, de-"priving the verdicts of juries of all finality, has proved injurious to the country, and the powers "then for the first time vested in Sessions Judges and High Courts of setting aside verdicts of "acquittal should be at once withdrawn"—

and Resolution X. of the Congress of 1886, to wit—

"That in the opinion of this Congress, a provision similar to that contained in the Summary Jurisdic-"tion Act of England (under which accused persons in serious cases have the option of demand-"ing a committal to the Sessions Court) should be introduced into the Indian Code of Criminal Pro-"cedure, enabling accused persons, in warrant cases, to demand that, instead of being tried by the "Magistrate, they be committed to the Court of Sessions"—

does now, hereby, affirm the same respectively.

## RESOLUTION V.

**Resolved**—That, as it is the general belief of the people of this country that the existing system of police administration in India is highly unsatisfactory in itself and oppressive to them, the Government be respectfully urged to appoint a commission, consisting of official and non-official members, to investigate the entire question as speedily as possible.

## RESOLUTION VI.

**Resolved**—That this Congress having read and considered Resolution IV. of the Congress of 1887, to wit—

"That in view of the loyalty of Her Majesty's Indian Subjects, the Congress considers it desirable that the "Queen's Proclamation should be given effect to; that the Military services in the higher grades "should be practically opened to the natives of this country; and that the Government should esta-"blish Military Colleges in the country whereat the natives of India, as defined by Statute, may be "educated and trained for a Military career as officers of the Indian Army."

Resolution XII. of the Congress of 1886, and Resolution V. of the Congress of 1887, to wit—

"That in view of the unsettled state of public affairs in Europe, and the immense assistance that the "people of this country, if duly prepared therefor, are capable of rendering to Great Britain in the "event of any serious complications arising, the Congress once again earnestly appeals to the Govern-"ment to authorize (under such rules and restrictions as to it may seem fitting) a system of "Volunteering for the Indian inhabitants of the country, such as may qualify them to support the "Government effectually in any crisis;"

and Resolution VIII. of the Congress of 1887, to wit—

> "That in view of the loyalty of the people, the hardships which the present Arms Act (XI of 1878) causes, "and the unmerited slur which it casts upon the people of this country, the Government be moved "so to modify the provisions of Chapter IV., and, if necessary, other portions of the said Act, as shall "enable all persons to possess and wear Arms unless debarred therefrom, either as individuals, or "members of particular communities or classes, by the orders of the Government of India, (or any "local authority empowered by the Government of India on that behalf), for reasons to be recorded "in writing and duly published;"

does now, hereby, affirm the same respectively.

## RESOLUTION VII.

**Resolved**—That, having regard to the fact that a serious increase in the consumption of intoxicants has taken place under the systems of Abkari and Excise now prevailing in India, the Government be respectfully urged to adopt some such improved system as shall tend to discourage insobriety.

## RESOLUTION VIII.

**Resolved**—That, as the administration of the Income-Tax, specially as regards incomes below Rs. 1,000, has proved extremely unsatisfactory, it is essential, in the opinion of the Congress, that the taxable minimum be raised to Rs. 1,000.

## RESOLUTION IX.

**Resolved**—That this Congress being of opinion that it is the first duty of the British Government in India to foster and encourage education, as well general as technical, in all its branches, and that the declaration made in the recent resolution of the Government of India on the subject of education is calculated to encourage the tendency to reduce imperial expenditure on education, and to withdraw from the control of it, respectfully urges upon Government the extreme importance of increasing, or at any rate of not decreasing, the present expenditure on education, and of the Government continuing to control the Educational Institutions of all kinds now existing.

## RESOLUTION X.

**Resolved**—That, having regard to the poverty of the people, the importance of encouraging indigenous manufactures, and the difficulty of practically introducing any general system of technical education with the present imperfect information, Government be moved to delay no longer the appointment of a mixed commission, to inquire into the present industrial condition of the country.

## RESOLUTION XI.

**Resolved**—That the foregoing Resolutions be submitted for the favourable consideration of His Excellency the Viceroy, and for transmission by him to Her Majesty's Government, with the humble request of this Congress that the reforms suggested in the said Resolutions (based as most of these are on Her Gracious Majesty's Proclamation of 1858) may now be effected; and that should it be deemed necessary first to institute any enquiry into any of the matters forming the subjects of these resolutions, such enquiry may be made, as speedily as possible, by a Parliamentary Committee.

## RESOLUTION XII.

**Resolved**—That this Congress, having watched with interest and sympathy the exertions that are being made in England for the total abrogation of laws and rules relating to the regulation of prostitution by the State in India, places on record its appreciation of the services thus rendered to this country, and its desire to co-operate by all means in its power in the attainment of this laudable object.

### RESOLUTION XIII.

**Resolved**—That no subject shall be passed for discussion by the Subject Committee or allowed to be discussed at any Congress by the President thereof, to the introduction of which the Hindu or Mahomedan Delegates as a body object, unanimously or nearly unanimously; and that if, after the discussion of any subject which has been admitted for discussion, it shall appear that all the Hindu or all the Mahomedan Delegates, as a body, are unanimously, or nearly unanimously, opposed to the Resolution which it is proposed to pass thereon, such Resolution shall be dropped; provided that this rule shall refer only to subjects in regard to which the Congress has not already definitely pronounced an opinion.

### RESOLUTION XIV.

**Resolved**—That the question of the introduction of a Permanent Settlement of the Land Revenue Demand into the Madras and Bombay Presidencies and other provinces be referred to the several Standing Congress Committees, with instructions to report upon the same, in so far as it affects their respective circles, to the Congress of 1889.

### RESOLUTION XV.

**Resolved**—That this Congress puts on record its disapproval of the recent enhancement of the Salt Tax, as involving a perceptible increase to the burthens of the poorer classes, as also the partial absorption, in a time of peace and plenty, of the only Financial Reserve of the Empire.

### RESOLUTION XVI.

**Resolved**—That the Fifth Indian National Congress do assemble in the Bombay Presidency (either at Bombay itself or at Poona, as may be settled hereafter) on the 26th of December, 1889.

### RESOLUTION XVII.

**Resolved**—That Mr. A. O. Hume be re-appointed General Secretary for the ensuing year.

---

## RESOLUTIONS PASSED AT THE FIFTH CONGRESS.

### RESOLUTION I.

**Resolved**.—That an address be presented to Mr. Charles Bradlaugh, M. P., on behalf of this Congress here assembled, and that Messrs. Adam, Pherozshah Mehta, and W. C. Bonnerjee are appointed a Committee to settle the wording of the said address.

### RESOLUTION II.

**Resolved**—That the following skeleton scheme for the reform and reconstitution of the Council of the Governor-General for making Laws and Regulations, and the Provincial Legislative Councils, is adopted, and that the President of this Congress do submit the same to Charles Bradlaugh, Esq., M. P., with the respectful request of this Congress that he may be pleased to cause a Bill to be drafted on the lines indicated in this skeleton scheme and introduce the same in the BritishHouse of Commons :—

### SCHEME.

(1) The Imperial and Provincial Legislative Councils to consist respectively of members, not less than one-half of whom are to be elected, not more than one-fourth to sit *ex-officio*, and the rest to be nominated by Government.

(2) Revenue districts to constitute ordinarily territorial units, for electoral purposes.

(3) All male British subjects above 21 years of age possessing certain qualifications and not subject to certain disqualifications (both of which will be settled later) to be voters.

(4) Voters in each district to elect representatives to one or more electoral bodies, according to local circumstances at the rate of 12 per million of the total population of the district, such representatives to possess certain qualifications and not to be subject to certain disqualifications, both of which will be settled later.

(5) All the representatives thus elected by all the districts included in the jurisdiction of each electoral body, to elect members to the Imperial Legislature at the rate of 1 per every five millions of the total populations of the electoral jurisdiction, and to their own Provincial Legislature at the rate of 1 per million of the said total population, in such wise that whenever the Parsees, Christians, Mahomedans or Hindus are in a minority, the total number of Parsees, Christians, Mahomedans or Hindus, as the case may be, elected to the Provincial Legislature, shall not, so far as may be possible, bear a less proportion to the total number of members elected thereto, than the total number of Parsees, Christians, Hindus or Mahomedans, as the case may be, in such electoral jurisdiction, bears to its total population. Members of both Legislatures to possess certain qualifications and not to be subject to certain disqualifications, both of which will be settled later.

(6) All elections to be by ballot.

## RESOLUTION III.

**Resolved**—That this present Congress does hereby ratify and confirm the resolutions passed by previous Congresses as to—

(a) the urgent necessity for the complete separation of executive and judicial functions, such that, in no case, shall the two functions be combined in the same officer;

(b) the expediency of extending into many parts of the country, where it is not at present in force, the system of trial by jury;

(c) the necessity of withdrawing from the High Courts, the powers, first vested in them in 1872, of setting aside verdicts of acquittal by juries;

(d) the necessity of introducing, into the Code of Criminal Procedure, a provision enabling accused person, in warrant cases, to demand that, instead of being tried by the Magistrate, they be committed to the Court of Sessions;

(e) the highly unsatisfactory character of the exsting system of Police Administration in India, and the bsolute necessity of a fundamental reform therein;

(f) the expediency of both, establishing Military Colleges in India, where at the Natives of India, as defined by Statute, may be educated and trained for a military career as officers of the Indian Army, and of authorising, under such rules and restrictions as may seem necessary, such a system of volunteering for the Indian inhabitants of the country as may qualify them to support the Government in any crisis;

(g) the extremely unsatisfactory character of the Income Tax Administration, especially as regards incomes below rupees one thousand, and the expediency of raising the taxable minimum to this amount:

(h) the extreme importance of increasing, instead of diminishing, as the present tendency appears to be, the public expenditure on education in all its branches, and the necessity, in view to the promotion of one of the most essential of these branches, the technical, of the appointment of a mixed commission to enquire into the present industrial condition of the country;

(i) the impolicy and injustice involved in the late increase of the Salt Tax in a time of profound peace, and the urgent necessity for an immediate reduction of this tax, and the reimposition, to balance the deficit thus caused, of light *ad valorem* import duties;

(j) the necessity for the reduction of, instead of the continual increase to, the military expenditure of the country,

## RESOLUTION IV.

**Resolved**—That this Congress hereby tenders its sincere thanks to Messrs. Caine and Smith, and the members who voted with them, in connection with the debate on the Indian Excise Question in the House of Commons; and, while fully appreciating what has been done by some of the local Governments towards the improvement of their systems of Excise and Abkari, desires to express the earnest hope that no further time may be lost in giving full effect to the Resolution of the House of Commons.

## RESOLUTION V.

**Resolved**—That this Congress, while thanking Her Majesty's Government for raising the age for the Indian Civil Service Competitive Examination from 19 to 23, does hereby put on record an emphatic expression of the universal disappointment which has been created by the rest of that Government's orders in regard to the Public Service Question, (the net result of which orders is to place the people of India in a worse position than they previously held), and reiterates the national conviction that no real justice will be done to India, in this matter, until the simultaneous holding in India, and in England, of all examinations, for all Civil branches of the Public Service in India, at present held only in England, be conceded.

## RESOLUTION VI.

**Resolved**—That, in view of the loyalty of the people, the hardships, that the Arms Act (XI of 1878), as at present administered, entails, and the unmerited slur which it casts upon them, the Government be moved so to modify the rules made under this Act that all restrictions as to the possession and bearing of arms shall apply equally to all persons residing in or visiting India; that licenses to possess and bear arms shall be liberally and generally distributed wherever wild animals habitually destroy human life, cattle or crops; and that these and all licenses issued under the rules shall be granted once for all, shall operate throughtout the Provincial jurisdiction within which they are issued, be only revocable on proof of misuse, and shall not require yearly or half-yearly renewals.

## RESOLUTION VII.

**Resolved**—That the Government be urged to take the subject of a Permanent Settlement once more under consideration in view to practical action thereon, such that fixity and permanency may be given to the Government Land Revenue demand without further delay, at any rate, in all fully populated and well cultivated tracts of country.

## RESOLUTION VIII.

**Resolved**—That, in view of the fall that has already occurred in the price of silver and in the exchange value of the Indian Rupee, it is impolitic on the part of the British Government to maintain any hindrances whatever to the consumption of silver for manufacturing purposes; and that this Congress strongly urges upon Her Majesty's Government that, not only as an act of juctice to India (a matter which has been repeatedly brought to the notice of Her Majesty's Ministers), but also as an act of expediency in the interests of Her Majesty's British as well as Indian subjects, the plate duties should be immediately abolished, and Hall-marking be made a voluntary institution.

## RESOLUTION IX.

**Resolved**—That this Congress respectfully expresses the earnest hope that, in the interest of the people of India, the House of Commons will forthwith restore the right, formerly possessed by members of that Honourable House of stating to Parliament any matter of grievance of the natives of India, before Mr. Speaker leaves the Chair, for the presentation in Committee of the Indian Budget statement, and earnestly trusts that the House of Commons will, in future, take into consideration the Annual Indian Budget statement at such a date as will ensure its full and adequate discussion; and further authorizes the President, Sir William Wedderburn, Bart., to sign a petition in the name and on behalf of this Congress for presentation to the House of Commons in accordance with the terms of this Resolution.

## RESOLUTION X.

**Resolved**—That, in view to his approaching departure, this Congress puts on record an expression of the high sense entertained, not only in the Bombay Presidency, hut throughout India, of the ability, integrity and impartiality that have characterised Lord Reay's administration, as also of the gratitude which the whole country feels to be his due for the sympathy that he has ever extended to Indian aspirations and efforts.

## RESOLUTION XI.

**Resolved**—That the Subjects Committee be instructed to settle the question, (left open in the skeleton scheme for the reconstruction of the councils, embodied in Resolution II.), of the qualifications requisite for, and the disqualifications which should debar from, becoming—

(*a*) a Voter;

(*b*) a Representative;

(*c*) a Member of a Provincial Legislative Council; and

(*d*) a Member of the Imperial Legislative Council;

and to submit their Report thereon to Charles Bradlaugh, Esq., M.P., for the purpose of the Bill which he has been requested to have drawn.

## RESOLUTION XII.

**Resolved**—That Mr. A. O. Hume, C.B., be re-elected General Secretary of the National Congress for the ensuing years.

## RESOLUTION XIII.

**Resolved**—

(*a*) That in view of the large number of delegates this year assembled and the probability arising from past experience, of their number continuing to increase year by year, henceforth the number of delegates to be allowed from each Congress circle be limited to five per million of the total population of the circle: the Standing Committee of each circle allotting the number which their jurisdiction, as a whole, is entitled to elect, amongst their several electoral divisions, as may seem most expedient.

(*b*) That from the date of Mr. Hume's departure for England, the Hon'ble Pundit Ajoodhianath be appointed Joint General Secretary, and that Rs. 5,000 be assigned for the payment by him of such Assistant Secretaries as he may find it necessary to employ, clerical assistance, postage, telegraphs and printing; and further that Mr. W. C. Bonnerjee be appointed Standing Counsel for Bengal, Mr. Pherozshah Mehta, Standing Counsel for Bombay, and Mr. Ananda Charlu, Standing Counsel for Madras, to the Joint General Secretary.

(*c*) That the tentative rules for the constitution and working of the Congress, which were first considered at Madras, and in regard to which various addenda have from time to time been circulated, be thoroughly considered during the coming year by the several Standing Congress Committees, and definitely dealt with by the Congress at its next session.

(*d*) That this Congress does hereby confirm the appointment of Sir W. Wedderburn, Bart., and Messrs. W. S. Caine, M.P., W. S. Bright Maclaren, M. P., J. E. Ellis, M. P., Dadabhai Naoroji and George Yule, as a Committee (with power to add to their number) to guide and direct the operations and control the expenditure of the National Congress Agency in England, and does further tender its sincere thanks to these gentlemen, and to Mr. W. Digby, C.I.E., the Secretary for the service which they are rendering to India.

(*e*) That this Congress does formally appoint Mr. George Yule, Mr. A. O. Hume, Mr. Adam, Mr. Eardley Norton, Mr. J. E. Howard,* Mr, Pherozshah Mehta, Mr. Surendranath Banerjee, Mr. Mono Mohan Ghose, Mr. Shurfuddin, Mr. R. N. Mudholker, and Mr. W. C. Bonnerjee to represent its views in England and press upon the consideration of the British Public the political reforms which the Congress has advocated.

(*f*) That a sum of Rs. 45,000 be raised for the expenses of the Congress work in this country and in England during the ensuing year, and that the different Standing Committees do send their res-

* By some oversight, this gentleman's name was omitted, when the Resolution was read to the Congress; the error has been rectified with the consent of the several Standing Congress Committees.

pective apportioned amounts to the General Secretary, the one half in three, and the balance in six months.

### RESOLUTION XIV.

**Resolved**—That the Sixth Indian National Congress do assemble at some City in Bengal, the exact place to be fixed hereafter, on the 26th of December, 1890.

### RESOLUTION XV.

**Resolved**—That the Fifth Indian National Congress hereby tenders its heart-felt thanks to its President, Sir William Wedderburn, as well for his ready sacrifice of personal and political considerations involved by his journey from England to India, as for that courtesy, impartiality and never-failing sympathy which, characteristics of his long and honourable career as an official of this country, have marked his control of the proceedings of this assembly.

---

## RESOLUTIONS PASSED AT THE SIXTH CONGRESS.

### RESOLUTION I.

**Resolved**— That this Congress, having considered the draft Bill recently introduced into Parliament by Mr. Charles Bradlaugh, entitled " an Act to amend the Indian Councils Act of 1861," approves the same as calculated to secure a substantial instalment of that reform, in the Administration of India, for which it has been agitating, and humbly prays the Houses of Parliament of the United Kingdom of Great Britain and Ireland to pass the same into law; and further that its President, Mr. Pherozshah Mehta, is hereby empowered to draw up and sign, on behalf of this assembly, a petition to the House of Commons to the foregoing effect, and to transmit the same to Mr. Charles Bradlaugh for presentation, thereto, in due course.

### RESOLUTION II.

**Resolved**—That this present Congress does hereby ratify and confirm the resolutions passed by previous Congresses as to—

(*a*) the urgent necessity for the complete separation of executive and judicial functions, such that, in no case, shall the two functions be combined in the same officer;

(*b*) the expediency of extending into many parts of the country, where it is not at present in force, the system of trial by jury;

(*c*) the necessity of withdrawing from the High Courts the powers, first vested in them in 1872, of setting aside verdicts of acquittal by juries;

(*d*) the necessity of introducing, into the Code of Criminal Procedure, a provision enabling accused persons, in warrant cases, to demand that instead of being tried by the Magistrate they be committed to the Court of Sessions;

(*e*) the highly unsatisfactory character of the existing system of Police Administration in India, and the absolute necessity of a fundamental reform therein;

(*f*) the expediency of both, establishing Military Colleges in India, whereat the Natives of India, as defined by Statute, may be educated and trained for a military career as officers of the Indian Army, and of authorising, under such rules and restrictions as may seem necessary, such a system of volunteering, for the Indian inhabitants of the country, as may qualify them to support the Government in any crisis;

(*g*) the extremely unsatisfactory character of the Income Tax Administration, especially as regards incomes below rupees one thousand, and the expediency of raising the taxable minimum to this amount;

(*h*) the extreme importance of increasing, instead of diminishing, as the present tendency appears to be, the public expenditure on education in all its branches, and the necessity, in view to the promotion of one of the most essential of these branches, the technical, of the appointment of a mixed commission to enquire into the present industrial condition of the country;

(*i*) the necessity for the reduction of, instead of the continual increase to, the military expenditure of the country;

(*j*) the necessity, if any real justice is to be done to the people of India, of holding, simultaneously in India and England, examinations, at present held only in England, for the Civil branches of the Public Service in India;

(*k*) the expediency of so modifying the rules made under Act XI of 1878 (the Arms Act) that all restrictions as to the possession and bearing of arms shall apply equally to all persons residing in or visiting India; that licenses to possess and bear arms shall be liberally and generally distributed wherever wild animals habitually destroy human life, cattle or crops; and that these and all licenses issued under the rules shall be granted once for all, shall operate throughout the Provincial jurisdiction within which they are issued, be only revocable on proof of misuse, and shall not require yearly or half-yearly renewals.

## RESOLUTION III.

**Resolved**—That this Congress respectfully expresses the earnest hope that in the interest of the people of India, the House of Commons will forthwith restore the right formerly possessed by members of that Honourable House, of stating to Parliament any matter of grievance of the natives of India before Mr. Speaker leaves the chair, for the presentation in Committee of the Indian Budget statement, and earnestly trusts that the House of Commons will, in future, take into consideration the Annual Indian Budget statement at such a date as will ensure its full and adequate discussion, and further authorizes its President to sign a Petition, in the name and on behalf of this Congress, for presentation to the House of Commons, in accordance with the terms of this Resolution.

## RESOLUTION IV.

**Resolved**—That, while recognizing the action taken, in response to its previous prayers, in the matter of Excise Reform by H. M.'s Secretary of State for India and the Supreme Government here, and noting with pleasure the increase to the import duty on Spirits, the taxation imposed on Indian-brewed malt liquors, the decision of the Bengal Government to abolish the outstill system, and the closing of over 7,000 liquor shops by the Madras Government in 1889-90, this Congress regrets that it is still necessary to urge the Government of India to insist on *all* Provincial Administrations carrying out in their integrity the policy in matters of Excise enunciated in paras. 103, 104 and 105 of the despatch published in the *Gazette of India* of March 1st, 1890, especially as to sub-section 4 of para. 103, *viz.*—

"That efforts should be made to ascertain the existence of local public sentiment, and that a reasonable amount of deference should be paid to such opinion when ascertained."

## RESOLUTION V.

**Resolved**—That the condition of the Finances of India having materially improved; and those special circumstances on which the Government relied to justify the recent enhancement of the Salt Tax having practically ceased to exist, this Congress considers it essential that the enhancement referred to should be remitted at an early date, and empowers its President to submit a special memorial on the subject in its name and on its behalf to H. E. the Viceroy in Council.

## RESOLUTION VI.

**Resolved**—That having reference to the expectations created throughout the country by the Despatch of Her Majesty's Secretary of State in 1862, the principles of which were re-affirmed in a subsequent Despatch of 1865, promising the extension of a Permanent Settlement to all temporarily settled tracts in which certain conditions were fulfilled, and to the fact that throughout large portions of the country those conditions have long since been fulfilled, this Congress respectfully submits that the Government of India is now in honour bound to take up this question of Permanent Settlement, without further delay, in view to practical action thereon such that fixity and permanency may be given to the Government Land Revenue demand as explicitly promised, by Her Majesty's Secretary of State, more than a quarter of a century ago.

## RESOLUTION VII.

**Resolved**—That this Congress, having observed with surprise a notice, apparently official, in various Calcutta newspapers which runs as follows :—

THE CONGRESS.

"The Bengal Government having learnt that tickets of admission to the visitors' enclosure in the Congress pavilion have been sent to various Government officers residing in Calcutta, has issued a circular to all secretaries, and heads of departments subordinate to it, pointing out that under the orders of the Government of India the presence of Government officials, even as visitors at such meetings, is not advisable, and that their taking part in the proceedings of any such meetings is absolutely prohibited :"

and having also considered a letter addressed by the Private Secretary of His Honor the Lieutenant-Governor of Bengal to the Secretary of the Reception Committee, of which the following is an exact copy :—

BELVEDERE, *26th December*, 1890.

"DEAR SIR,—In returning herewith the seven cards of admission to the visitors' enclosure of the Congress pavilion, which were kindly sent by you to my address yesterday afternoon, I am desired to say that the Lieutenant-Governor and the members of his household could not possibly avail themselves of these tickets, since the orders of the Government of India definitely prohibit the presence of Government officials at such meetings.

"To
J. GHOSAL Esq.,
*Secretary, Congress Reception Committee.*"

Yours faithfully,
P. C. LYON,
*Private Secretary.*

authorizes and instructs its President to draw the attention of His Excellency the Viceroy to the declaration embodied in these papers that Government servants are prohibited from attending any meetings of this Congress even as spectators, and to enquire, most respectfully, whether His Honor the Lieutenant-Governor of Bengal has, or has not, correctly interpreted the orders of the Government of India.

## RESOLUTION VIII.

**Resolved**—That the best thanks of this Congress be tendered to Mr. Charles Bradlaugh, M. P., for the invaluable services rendered by him during the past year, as also to Sir W. Wedderburn, Mr. W. S. Caine, Mr. J. Bright Maclaren, M. P., Mr. J. Ellis, M. P., Mr. George Yule, and Mr. Dadabhai Naoroji for the unselfish zeal and ability with which they have presided over the British Agency of the Congress; further that they put on record an expression of their high appreciation of the manner in which Mr. Digby, C. I. E., Secretary of the Agency, and Messrs. Surendra Nath Banerjee, R. N. Mudholkar, W. C. Bonnerjee, Eardley Norton, and A. O. Hume, delegates to England, respectively, discharged the onerous duties imposed upon them, and of their gratitude to all those members of the British public who so kindly welcomed and so sympathetically gave audience, in over fifty public and a far larger number of private meetings, to one or more of these delegates.

## RESOLUTION IX.

**Resolved**—That a vote of thanks be recorded to Kumar Debendra Mullick and brothers, proprietors of the Tivoli Gardens, Mr. N. C. Bose and Babu Bhupendra Nath Bose, proprietors of Mohan Bagan Villa, and to the Hon'ble Sir Romesh Chandra Mitra, Mr. T. N. Palit, Babus Janokee Nath Roy, Gopee Mohan Roy, Harendra Nath Roy, Kissory Mohan Roy, Ramanath Ghose, and Jamadar Ghasiram, owners of houses kindly lent for the use of delegates.

## RESOLUTION X.

**Resolved**—That the Seventh Indian National Congress do assemble on the 26th December, 1891, at either Madras or Nagpore, as may be hereafter settled, in consultation between the Madras, Central Provinces and Berar Committees, and the Joint General Secretary.

## RESOLUTION XI.

**Resolved**—That provisional arrangements be made to hold a Congress, of not less than 100 delegates, in England, all things being convenient, in 1892, and that the several Standing Congress Committees be directed to report, at the coming Congress, the names of the delegates that it is proposed to depute from their respective circles.

## RESOLUTION XII.

**Resolved**—That of the Funds now in the Joint General Secretary's hands and about to be received, a further sum of twenty thousand rupees be added to the Permanent Fund and placed in fixed deposits, and that the rest of the funds accruing on account of this current year, 1890, be held by him available for the immediate purposes of the British Committee of the Indian National Congress, but to be replaced as the subscriptions for 1891 are received, and ultimately, also added to the Permanent Fund.

## RESOLUTION XIII.

**Resolved**—That a sum of Rs. 40,000, exclusive of individual donations, is assigned for the expenses of the British Committee of the Congress and Rs. 6,000 for the General Secretary's Office and Establishment, and that the several circles and districts do contribute as arranged in Committee.

## RESOLUTION XIV.

**Resoved**—That Mr. A. O. Hume and Pandit Ajoodhia Nath are re-elected General and Joint-General Secretaries for the ensuing year.

## RESOLUTION XV.

**Resoved**—That this Congress does formally appoint Messrs. G. Yule, Pherozshah Mehta, W. C. Bonnerjee, J. Adam, Mono Mohan Ghose, A. O. Hume, Kali Charan Banerjee, Dadabhai Naorojee, D. A. Khare, and such other gentlemen as may volunteer for the duty with the sanction and approval of the Standing Congress Committees of their respective circles, to represent its views in England, and press upon the consideration of the British Public the political reforms which the Congress has advocated.

## RESOLUTIONS PASSED AT THE SEVENTH CONGRESS.

### RESOLUTION I.

**Resolved**—That a Committee be appointed to consider and report, on or before the morning of the 30th instant, whether, or not, it is advisable to discontinue the Annual Sessions of the Indian National Congress until after the British Session, and, if not, under what regulations, as to numbers of delegates, localities for assemblage, and the like, future Congresses shall be held. The Committee to be composed as follows:—

EX-OFFICIO MEMBERS:

The President.

The Chairman of the Reception Committee.

The General Secretary.

The Joint General Secretary.

The Standing Counsels to the Congress.

ORDINARY MEMBERS:

Messrs. Surendranath Bannerjee.
Viraraghava Chariar.
Hafiz Abdul Raheem.
Gangapersad Varma
Pringle Kennedy.
Guruprasad Sen.
D. E. Watcha.
M. B. Namjoshi.
Hamid Ali Khan.
Vishnu Moreshwar Bhide.

Messrs. Murlidhar.
Mudholkar.
Deo Rao Vinayak.
Gopal Rao Bhide.
Bipin Krishna Bose.
Dajee Abajee Khare.
Madan Mohan Malaviya.
Saligram Singh.
Sankara Nair.

### RESOLUTION II.

**Resolved**—That this Congress re-affirms the conclusion arrived at by all previous Congresses, *viz.*, that India can never be well or justly governed, nor her people prosperous or contented, until they are allowed, through their elected representatives, a potential voice in the Legislatures of their own country, and respectfully urges the people of Great Britain and Ireland, whose good will towards India it gratefully recognizes, to permit no further delay in the concession of this just and necessary reform.

### RESOLUTION III.

**Resolved**—That this Congress, concurring in the views set forth in previous Congresses affirms—

That fully fifty millions of the population, a number yearly increasing, are dragging out a miserable existence on the verge of starvation, and that, in every decade, several millions actually perish by starvation.

That this unhappy condition of affairs is largely due to—

(*a*) the exclusion of the people of India from a due participation in the administration, and all control over the finances, of their own country, the remedy for which has been set forth in Resolution II;

(*b*) the extravagant cost of the present administration, Militray and Civil, but especially the former; and to

(*c*) a short-sighted system of Land Revenue Administration, whereby not only is all improvement in the agriculture of the country, on which nine-tenths of the population depend for subsistence, rendered impossible, but the gradual deterioration of that agriculture assured.

That hence it has become imperatively necessary—

that the cost of the administration be greatly reduced; in the military branch, by a substantial reduction of the standing army, by the substitution of long term local European troops like those of the Hon. E .I. Company, for the present short term Imperial regiments with their heavy cost of recruitment in England, in transport and of excessive mortality amongst non-acclimatized youths; by the cessation of the gigantic waste of money that has gone on now for several years, on so-called Frontier Defences, and by a strict economy in the Commissariat, Ordnance and Store Departments; and in the Civil branch, by the wide substitution of a cheaper indigenous agency for the extremely costly imported Staff; and

that measures be at once taken at give, as was promised by the British Government thirty years ago, fixity and permanence to the Land Revenue demand and thus permit capital and labour to combine to develop the agriculture of the country, which, under the existing system of temporary settlements, in recent times often lasting for short periods, in some cases only extending to 10 and 12 years, is found to be impossible; and to establish agricultural banks.

That this Congress does most earnestly entreat the people of Great Britain and Ireland not to permit any further sacrifice of life by the shortcomings of the existing, doubtless well-intentioned, but none the less unsatisfactory, administration, but to insist, and speedily, on these reforms.

## RESOLUTION IV.

**Resolved**—That this Congress, concurring with previous Congresses, is of opinion that, to ensure the adequate protection and efficient defence of the country, it is desirable that the Government should conciliate Indian public opinion and encourage and qualify the Indians to defend their homes and their Government—

(*a*) by so modifying the rules under the Arms Act, as to make them equally applicable to all residents in, or visitors to, India, without distinction of creed, class or colour; to ensure the liberal concession of licenses wherever wild animals habitually destroy human life, cattle or crops, and to make all licenses granted under the revised rules, of life-long tenure, revocable only on proof of misuse and valid throughout the Provincial Jurisdiction in which they are issued;

(*b*) by establishing Military Colleges in India, whereat natives of India, as defined by Statute, may be educated and trained for a military career, as *commissioned or non-commissioned* officers (according to capacity and qualifications) of the Indian army;

(*c*) by organising, throughout the more warlike races of the Empire, a system of militia service; and

(*d*) by authorizing and stimulating a widespread system of volunteering, such as obtains in Great Britain, amongst the people of India.

## RESOLUTION V.

**Resolved**—That as one step towards ensuring the wider employment of Indians in the administration of the country, and as a matter of simple justice to the people of India, this Congress, agreeing with previous Congresses, declares it to be essential that all examinations for any and all of the Civil Branches of the Public Service in India, which at present are held only in England, should henceforth be also held simultaneously in India.

## RESOLUTION VI.

**Resolved**—That this Congress concurs with its predecessors in strongly advocating—

(*a*) the reduction of the salt tax, by at least the amount of its latest enhancement;

(*b*) the raising of the income tax taxable minimum from Rs. 500 to Rs. 1,000;

(*c*) persistent pressure by the Government of India on all Provincial Administrations, to induce them to carry out, in its integrity, the excise policy enunciated in paras. 103, 104 and 105 of the despatch, published in the *Gazette of India*, of March 1st, 1890, and the introduction of a simple system of local option in the case of all villages.

## RESOLUTION VII.

**Resolved**—That having regard to the unsatisfactory character, in many respects, of the Judicial and Police Administration, this Congress concurs with its predecessors in strongly advocating—

(*a*) the complete separation of Executive and Judicial functions such that in no case shall the two functions be combined in the same officer;

(*b*) the extension into many parts of the country, where it is not at present in force, of the system of trial by jury;

(*c*) the withdrawal from High Courts of the powers, first vested in them in 1872, of setting aside verdicts of acquittals by juries;

(*d*) the introduction, into the Code of Criminal Procedure, of a provision enabling accused persons, in warrant cases, to demand that instead of being tried by the Magistrate they be committed to the Court of Sessions;

(*e*) the fundamental reform of the Police Administration, by a reduction in the numbers and an increase in the salaries, and in the qualifications of the lower grades, and their far more careful enlistment, and by the selection for the higher posts of gentlemen of higher capacities, more in touch with the respectable portions of the community, and less addicated to military pretensions, than the majority of the existing Deputy Inspectors General, Superintendents and Assistant Superintendents of Police.

## RESOLUTION VIII.

**Resolved**—That this Congress, concurring with previous Congresses, affirms the importance of increasing (instead of diminishing, as appears to be the present policy of the Government) the public ependiture on all branches of edncation, and the expeportance of increasing (instead of diminishing, as appears to be the present policy of the diency, in view to the promotion of one of the most essential of these branches, the techni cal, of appointing a mixed Commission to enquire into the present industrial condition of the country.

## RESOLUTION IX.

*Read the following telegram from General Booth:—*

> "May I be allowed to commend, to the attention of the Congress, the claims of the millions of India's starving poor and to urge the consideration of some scheme by which these destitute multitudes can be placed upon the waste lands of the country, in such an organised and befriended manner, as will enable them to gain, for themselves, those necessaries of a healthy existence which, in their present circumstances, are denied; praying for the blessing of God upon the labours of the Congress, yours in sympathy with every effort for the amelioration of the miseries of mankind."

**Resolved**—That the following telegram be despatched in reply to General Booth:—

> "The Congress having received and considered your kindly message thank you cordially for the same. No possible scheme of internal immigration can perceptibly relieve the fifty to sixty millions of half-starving paupers, whose sad condition constitutes the primary *raison d'être* of the Congress. It is only by modifying the adverse conditions out of which this widespread misery arises, and by raising the moral standard of the people, that any real relief is possible. As regards the first, the Congress programme now embodies all primarily essential reforms; as regards the second, in every province and in every caste, associations, public or private, are working with a yearly increasing earnestness. Many good missionaries are labouring in same field, and we have to thank you that your army too is now engaged in the good work of elevating our masses. May your efforts and ours, in both directions, be crowned with success. Congress, including men of many creeds, welcomes cordially all who seek to benefit our suffering brethren."

## RESOLUTION X.

*Read the Report of the Committee appointed, under Resolution (I.), which runs as follows:—*

> "Your Committee have considered the matter referred to them and have also consulted, informally, various members of the Subjects Committee and other delegates. They are clearly of opinion that it is not advisable to discontinue the Annual Session of the Indian National Congress until after the British Session, and that future Congresses should be held under the same regulations as heretofore."

**Resolved**—That the Annual Sessions of the Congress in India continue to be held until all necessary reforms have been secured.

## RESOLUTION XI.

**Resolved**—That having regard to the very serious discontent created, especially in Peninsular India, by the practical administration of the Forest Laws, the Government of India be most respectfully, but earnestly, entreated to investigate this carefully, and endeavour to mitigate its harshness and render it less obnoxious to the poorer classes.

## RESOLUTION XII.

**Resolved**—That this Congress hereby tenders its most grateful acknowledgments to Sir W. Wedderburn, and the members of the British Congress Committee, for the services rendered by them to India during the past year, and respectfully urges them to widen henceforth the sphere of their usefulness, by interesting themselves, not only in those questions dealt with by the Congress here, but in all Indian matters submitted to them, and properly vouched for, in which any principle accepted by the Congress is involved.

## RESOLUTION XIII.

**Resolved**—That this Congress puts on record an expression of the gratitude felt, throughout India, for the signal services rendered by the late Mr. Charles Bradlaugh to that couutry's cause, and of the deep and universal sorrow which his untimely death has engeddered; and that a copy of this Resolution, signed by the President, be transmitted through the British Committee for presentation to Mrs. Bradlaugh Bonner,

## RESOLUTION XIV.

**Resolved**—That this Congress, hereby, puts formally on record its high estimate and deep appreciation of the great services which Mr. Dadabhai Naoroji has rendered, during more than a quarter of a century, to the cause of India; that it expresses its unshaken confidence in him and its earnest hope that he may prove successful, at the coming elections, in his candidature for Central Finsbury, and, at the same time, tenders, on :half of the vast population it represents, India's most cordial acknowledgments to all ın England, whether in Central Finsbury or elsewhere, who have aided, or may aid him, to win a seat in the House of Commons.

## RESOLUTION XV.

**Resolved**—That in view of the General Election now impending in England, and in accordance with the recommendation of our British Committee, the provisional arrangements, set on foot in pursuance of the Resolution passed at the Calcutta Congress of 1890, for holding, all things being convenient, a Congress of not less than 100 Delegates in England in 1892, be now suspended until after such General Election.

## RESOLUTION XVI.

**Resolved**—That a sum of Rs. 40,000, exclusive of individual donations, is assigned for the expenses of the British Committee of the Congress, and Rs. 6,000 for the General Secretary's office and establishment, and that the several circles do contribute as arranged ın Committee for the year 1892.

## RESOLUTION XVII.

**Resolved**—That Mr. A. O. Hume and Pandit Ajoodhianath are re-elected General and Joint-General Secretaries for the ensuing year.

## RESOLUTION XVIII.

**Resolved**—That the Eighth Indian National Congress do assemble on the 26th December, 1892, at Allahabad.

# REPORT

OF

THE NINTH

# Indian National Congress,

HELD AT

# LAHORE,

**the 27th, 28th, 20th and 30th December**

# 1893.

# CONTENTS.

# SUMMARY OF RESOLUTIONS

PASSED AT THE

# NINTH INDIAN NATIONAL CONGRESS

HELD AT LAHORE ON THE 27TH, 28TH, 29TH, AND 30TH, DECEMBER, 1893.

## RESOLUTION I.

**Resolved**—That this Congress while tendering its most sincere thanks to His Excellency the Viceroy for the liberal spirit in which he has endeavoured to give effect to the Indian Councils' Act of 1892, regrets to have to put on record the facts, that alike in the Rules of the Government of India and in the practice of most of the Local Governments, notably in that of the Government of Bombay, material alterations are necessary if real effect is to be given to the spirit of this act, and, that the Punjab, one of the most important Provinces in the Empire, is still denied the right to be represented, either in the Viceroy's or in any Local Council.

## *RESOLUTION II.*

**Resolved**—That this Congress, in concurrence with the first Congress held at Bombay in 1885 and other subsequent Congresses, considers that the creation of a Legislative Council for the Province of the Punjab is an absolute necessity for the good Government of that Province, and, having regard to the fact that a similar Council has been created for the United Provinces, hopes that no time will be lost in creating such a Council.

## RESOLUTION III.

**Resolved**—That this Congress concurs with its predecessors in strongly advocating—

(*a*) The reduction of the salt duty by at least the amount of its latest enhancement;

(*b*) The raising of the Income-tax taxable minimum from five-hundred to one thousand Rupees;

(*c*) Persistent pressure by the Government of India on all Provincial Administrations, to induce them to carry out, in its integrity, the Excise policy enunciated in paragraphs 103, 104, 105 of the Despatch, published in the Gazette of India of March, 1890, and the introduction of a simple system of local option in the case of all villages.

(*d*) The introduction into the Code of Criminal Procedure of a provision enabling accused persons, in warrant cases, to demand that instead of being tried by the Magistrate they may be committed to the Court of Sessions;

(*e*) The fundamental reform of the Police administration, by a reduction in the numbers and an increase in the salaries and in the qualifications of the lower grades, and their far more careful enlistment; and by the selection for the higher posts of gentlemen of higher capacities, more in touch with the respectable portions of the community, and less addicted to military pretensions than the majority of existing Deputy Inspectors-General Superintendents, and Assistant Superintendents of Police are;

(*f*) A modification of the rules under the Arms Act, so as to make them equally applicable to all residents in, or visitors to India without distinction of creed, caste or colour; to ensure the liberal concession of licences wherever wild animals habitually destroy human life, cattle or crops; and to make all licences, granted under the revised rules, of life-long tenure, revocable only on proof of misuse, and valid throughout the Provincial jurisdiction in which they are issued;

(*g*) The establishment of Military Colleges in India, whereat natives of India, as defined by statute, may be educated and trained for a military career as Commissioned or Non-commissioned Officers (according to capacity and qualifications) of the Indian army.

(*h*) The organising throughout the more warlike races of the Empire of a system of Militia service; and

(*i*) The authorising and stimulating a wide-spread system of volunteering such as obtains in Great Britain, amongst the people of India.

## RESOLUTION IV.

**Resolved**—That this Congress is of opinion that the time has arrived when, in the interest of public medical education and the advancement of medical science and of scientific work in this country, as also in the cause of economic administration, the Civil medical service of India should be reconstructed on the basis of such services in other civilised countries, wholly detached from and independent of the Military service, so as to give full effect to the educational policy of Government, which is to encourage education for its own sake in every branch, and to raise a scientific medical profession in India by throwing open fields for medical and scientific work to the best talent available and indigenous talent in particular.

## RESOLUTION V.

**Resolved**—That this Congress desires to thank the British House of Commons for their just and wise vote in regard to Simultaneous Examinations in England and in India, and most earnestly prays that august body to insist upon their orders being given prompt effect to by the Secretary of State for India and the Government of India.

## RESOLUTION VI.

**Resolved**—That this Congress having now for many successive years vainly appealed to the Government of India to remove one of the graves stigmas on British rule in India, one fraught with incalculable oppression to all classes of the community throughout the country, now hopeless of any other redress, humbly entreats the Secretary of State for India to order the immediate appointment, in each province, of a Committee (one half at least, of whose members shall be non-official natives of India, qualified by education and experience in the workings of the various courts to deal with the question) to prepare each a scheme for the complete separation of all Judicial and Executive functions in their own province with as little additional cost to the State as may be practicable, and the submission of such schemes, with the comments of the several Indian Governments thereon, to himself, at some early date which he may be pleased to fix.

## RESOLUTION VII.

**Resolved**—That this Congress having considered the report of the Parliamentary members of the India Office Committee on the subject of the Rules, Orders and Practices in Indian Cantonments with regard to prostitution and contagious disease, hereby endorses their conclusions :

1. That the system and incidental practices described in that report and the statutory rules, so far as they authorized or permitted the same, did not accord with the plain meaning and intention of the resolution of the House of Commons of June 5th 1888 ; and

2. That the only effective method of preventing these systematic malpractices is by express legislation.

## RESOLUTION VIII.

**Resolved**—That this Congress, concurring in the views set forth in previous Congresses, affirms :

That fully fifty millions of the population, a number yearly increasing, are dragging out a miserable existence on the verge of starvation, and that in every decade, several millions actually perish by starvation.

And humbly urges, once more, that immediate steps be taken to remedy this calamitous state of affairs.

## RESOLUTION IX.

**Resolved**—That having regard to the very serious discontent created, especially in Peninsular India and in certain hilly tracts in the Punjab, by the practical administration of the Forest Laws, the Government of India be most respectfully, but earnestly, entreated to investigate this carefully and endeavour to mitigate its harshness and render it less obnoxious to the poorer classes.

## RESOLUTION X.

**Resolved**—That this Congress having on many previous occasions urged on the Government of India, the necessity for giving, as was promised by the British Government over thirty years ago, fixity and permanence to the Land Revenue demand, wherever this has not already been conceded, desires now to reiterate emphatically this recommendation and to call attention to the profound alarm which has been created by the action of Government in interfering with the existing permanent settlement in Bengal and Behar (in the matter of the survey and other cesses ) and with the terms of the sanads of the permanently settled estates in Madras, and deeming such tampering with solemn public pledges no matter under what pretences, a national calamity, hereby pledges itself to oppose, in all possible regitimate ways, any and all such reactionary attacks on permanent settlements and their holders.

## RESOLUTION XI.

**Resolved**—That this Congress regrets extremely that the Government of India have not only failed to carry out the pledges for a permanent settlement in the Provinces in which it does not exist ( given by the Secretary of State in his despatches of 1862 and 1865 ) but have also failed to give effect to the policy of granting a modified fixity of tenure and immunity from enhancements, laid down in 1882 and 1884 by the Government of India, and approved by the Secretary of State.

## RESOLUTION XII.

**Resolved**—That this Congress is of opinion that it is inexpedient in the present state of Education in the country, that Government grants for High Education should in any way be withdrawn, and concurring with previous Congresses, affirms in the most emphatic manner, the importance of increasing the public expenditure on all branches of Education, and the expediency (in view to the promotion of one of the most essential of those branches *i. e.* the technical,) of appointing a mixed Commission to enquire into the present industrial condition of the country ; and, looking to the great poverty of many classes of the community, strongly recommends, that in all classes of Government or Municipal Schools and Colleges, all fees shall be reduced in proportion to the means of parents and relations and remitted wholly in the case of very poor students ; and, focussing the universal opinion of the Indian Community that undue stress is being laid at present upon mere mental development, this Congress earnestly recommends that henceforth, in all grades and classes of Schools and colleges, at least equal attention should be devoted to the physical development of the students.

## RESOLUTION XIII.

**Resolved**—That this Congress regrets to notice that the Secretary of State for India in his recent despatch to the Government of India has enunciated the doctrine that occasions may arise in which it may be the duty of the Executive Government to criticise Judicial errors, the Congress being of opinion that such criticism is calculated to shake the confidence of the people in the independence of Judicial tribunals.

## RESOLUTION XIV.

**Resolved**—That this Congress places on record its deep regret at the recent hasty legislation of the Government of India closing the Indian mints against the private coinage of silver, whereby the people of this country have been subjected to further indirect taxation of a burdensome and indefinite character, and some of the most important trades and industries, notably the Mill industry, have been seriously disorganized and injured.

## RESOLUTION XV.

**Resolved**—That this Congress records its emphatic protest against the Exchange Compensation Allowance granted to the undomiciled European and Eurasian *employés* of Government, involving an annual expenditure of over a crore of Rupees, and to the Banks, to the extent of £138,000, at a time when the financial situation of the country is far from satisfactory and the country is threatened with additional taxation.

## RESOLUTION XVI.

**Resolved**—That the Government of India be moved, once for all, to put a stop, by new and express legislation, (the existing provisions of the Penal Code having proved inoperative) to the existing oppressive system of forced labor (known as *Begar*) and forced contributions of supplies (known as *Rasad*) which, despite numerous Resolutions of the Government of India, are still prevalent throughout India.

## RESOLUTION XVII.

**Resolved**—That this Congress tenders its most sincere thanks to Lord Northbrook for his powerful advocacy of India's claim to have her burden of Home Charges reduced, and respectfully entreats the House of Commons to appoint at an early date a Committee of their Honourable House to arrive at some equitable settlement of the matter.

## RESOLUTION XVIII.

**Resolved**—That in the opinion of this Congress, the time has now come to raise the status of the Chief Court of the Punjab to that of a Chartered High Court in the interest of the administration of Justice in that Province.

## RESOLUTION XIX.

**Resolved**—That this Congress tenders its best thanks to the Electors of Central Finsbury, both for their kindly sympathy in its objects and for having so generously accorded to it the valuable services of their honoured member Mr. Naoroji, who is destined, the Congress hopes, long to represent both Centra Finsbury and India in the British House of Parliament.

## RESOLUTION XX.

**Resolved**—That a sum of Rs. 60,000 be assigned for the expenses of the British Committee and the cost of the Congress Publication, "India," and that the several circles do contribute as arranged either now, or hereafter in Committee, for the year 1894.

## RESOLUTION XXI.

**Resolved**—That this Congress hereby tenders its most grateful acknowledgments to Sir W. Wedderburn and the members of the British Congress Committee for the services rendered by them to India during the past year.

## RESOLUTION XXII.

**Resolved**—That this Congress re-appoints Mr. A. O. Hume, C.B., to be its General Secretary for the ensuing year.

## RESOLUTION XXIII.

**Resolved**—That the Tenth Indian National Congress do assemble on such day after Christmas Day 1894, as may be later determined upon, at Madras.

LAHORE,
*December 31st, 1893,*

DADABHAI NAOROJI,
*President of the Ninth Indian National Congress.*

# DETAILED
## REPORT OF THE PROCEEDINGS
OF THE
# NINTH INDIAN NATIONAL CONGRESS,
HELD AT
# LAHORE,
### On the 27th, 28th, 29th, and 30th of December, 1893.

---

## FIRST DAY'S PROCEEDINGS.

First Day.

FOR THE ASSEMBLAGE of the NINTH INDIAN NATIONAL CONGRESS, a very spacious and beautiful octagonal Pavilion was erected in the Capital of the Punjab on a large piece of ground in the vicinity of the Lahore Railway Station. The Union Jack floating at its top, visible from a great distance, and numerous flags and buntings of various devices made up a grand and imposing spectacle. The inside of the Pavilion was tastefully decorated and provided room for 4,000 seats. On each of the four days over which the sittings of the Congress extended, nearly all the chairs were occupied by the Delegates and Visitors. The attendance on the first day was so large that the late arrivals had to content themselves with standing room. The grounds, laid out with gravelled walks and beds of flower, looked like a well-kept garden picturesquely dotted over with neat little structures for the accommodation of the different Congress offices and a temporary Post and Telegraph Office.

This being the first meeting of the National Congress in the Punjab a very large number of applications for Visitor's Tickets were received long before the day fixed for the first sitting. Tickets for firstclass seats at Rs. 50 each were eagerly purchased, not a single one remaining unsold.

The first sitting of the Congress commenced at 2 P.M. on Wednesday, the 27th December, 1893, when Sirdar Dayal Sing Majithia, the Chairman of the Reception Committee of the Congress, whose duty it was to open the proceedings by welcoming the delegates and calling upon them to elect their President said :—

"I am in so much pain that I am sorry I shall have to deny myself the pleasure of addressing you this afternoon. I am suffering much from rheumatic pains and cannot stand ; so with your permission I will ask Mr. Harkishen Lal to read my address."

Mr. Harkishen Lal immediately took up his place on the tribune at the rear of the President's seat and read out the following address on behalf of the Chairman of the Reception Committee.

First Day.

Chairman of Reception Committee's Address.

LADIES, GENTLEMEN AND FELLOW-DELEGATES,—It has fallen to me on behalf of the Reception Committee of the Ninth Indian National Congress to accord a cordial welcome to the delegates of the Ninth Indian National Congress to the capital of our Province and in doing so I cannot help feeling an overpowering sense of glory and pride such as I have never before experienced in my life. It is our peculiar good fortune to live under a Government which, by the spread of liberal education and the annihilation of distances, has made it practicable for us—the inhabitants of the remote parts of this vast empire—to meet every year at different centres to discuss those great problems so intimately connected with the advancement and prosperity of our fatherland. We have a glorious past of course of which we need not be proud, and we clearly see the prospect of a hopeful future before us under the benign influence of British rule and I think most of us present here believe that the kingdom of heaven is not behind but before. The darkness that enshrouded the land for so many centuries has begun to be dispelled, and the streaks are already visible above the horizon that herald the approach of a glorious dawn. A hundred years ago when Lord Cornwallis was laying the foundations of the empire on a solid basis the country, as a whole, was still in a state of disorder and anarchy. Two generations later witnessed the advent of that illustrious nobleman, Lord William Bentinck, who first sowed the seeds which fell fast on the fertile soil and germinated vigorously, and watered by the generous hand of Lord Hallifax, and warmed by the establishment of universities sprouted forth into luxuriant growth. The crisis that followed in 1857 enveloped the empire in momentary gloom, but this speedily passed away and the car of progress began once more to glide smoothly and rapidly along, propelled by the genial force imparted by that great statesman who in a moment of imminent peril, safely guided the vessel of State to her moorings—the immortal Canning. A generation later appeared on the scene that liberal-minded ruler, that candid friend, that cordial sympathiser, that suppressor of wrong and supporter of the weak and the down-trodden, the best and the most illustrious of Viceroys, the righteous Ripon to whom we owe the amalgam that united the scattered units of the Indian nation and stimulated those national sentiments and aspirations of which the Indian National Congress is the direct outcome. The National Congress—the greatest glory of the British rule in this country—thus started, has had its sittings at the principal centres of Indian intelligence and progress. But this is its first session in this Province and it rouses our deepest emotions and stirs up our innermost feelings to be able to give it a hearty greeting and to have an opportunity to show the rites of hospitality to those who at considerable personal risk and sacrifice have undertaken distant journeys and assembled under this roof for furthering the cause of their country. This is the second attempt that has been made towards holding the Congress in the Punjab. The first attempt was made at Allahabad in 1888 when the delegates from this Province offered to invite the next Congress to Lahore but that attempt was infructuous because some of our leaders having recently had experience of the opposition that the Congress had met in the North-Western Provinces entertained apprehensions of greater and more serious difficulties being thrown in our way in this Province. We are glad, however, to say that no such apprehensions have visited us on the present occasion. We now live under the strong regime of a wise and dispassionate ruler who as an ex-Judge of one of the highest tribunals in this country takes a judicious view of questions, and does not allow himself to be carried away by executive impulses or administrative theories. It gives us much pleasure to express our sense of obligation to Sir Dennis Fitzpatrick personally in spite of the resolution of the Punjab Government on the now famous circular letter of our Director of Public Instruction for his fair attitude toward the Congress, to tender our thanks to local officials who taking their cue from their Chief have offered no opposition but have rather treated us with courtesy during the time that preparations were going on for the Congress Comparison is odious and I shall, therefore, avoid it as far as possible but all those who were present at Allahabad

**First Day.**

**Chairman of Reception Committee's Address.**

in 1888 and heard the speech of the late lamented Pandit Ajudhia Nath in his capacity of President of the Reception Committee will be able to form a contrast in their minds as to the circumstances under which the fourth Congress was held and the ninth Congress has now assembled here. The fact that this is a frontier and younger province only lends additional vigour to the contrast and reflects greater credit on the head of the local administration. It has been asserted that the Congress is a Babu-movement and the martial races of India have no sympathy with it. This great assembly is a living refutation of all assertions of that description. The Congress has already had two sittings at Allahabad and on each occasion the hearty and active adherence which the people of the N.-W. Provinces and Oudh have shown to the cause speaks for itself. It is true that the Congress has never been held here previous to this occasion but it was not because the people of this Province did not feel any interest in this National Movement and appreciated it duly but on account of the apprehended difficulties I have alluded to before. It is impossible and quite unnatural that in the midst of the general national reawakening the Punjab alone should lie steeped in torpor. The east gave light to the west in old antiquity but the light so given has come back reflected in greater brightness and its revivifying influence is felt from the Himalayas to Cape Comorin. To suppose that the Punjab has held aloof from the Congress is absurd. Is it possible that those credited with possessing most fire in their blood should be the least susceptible to this influence ?

No, the wand of the magician has touched our eyes. The history and literature of England have permeated our minds, the great heritage of our western Aryan brethren has descended on us collaterally as it were, and we are allowed at times, grudgingly it may be, to have a share in it. We happily live under a constitution whose watchword is freedom and whose main pillar is toleration. We look back complacently on our past history and glory in it. Can we then in the midst of this national upheaval remain quiescent and indifferent ? The same generous causes that are at work elsewhere have been operating here also and any difference in the results hitherto obtained is attributable mainly to the fact that these causes reached here last in point of time. We may naturally be somewhat behmd the other provinces in the race of progress but we are not idle and if we be true to the traditions with which our past records are replete we should try hard to make up our deficiencies and take our proper place in the march of national advancement.

It would be superfluous now to meet the stale old charge of disloyalty and sedition brought against the Congress. It has been discussed threadbare and the Congress has come triumphant out of the discussion. The highest authority in the land—the head of the Government of India—has been pleased to characterize the Congress as a "perfectly legitimate" movement "representing in India what in Europe would be called the more advanced liberal party." No endeavour was spared to traduce the Congressmen, to call them by all manner of harsh and disreputable names, to attribute to them selfish and other motives, to misrepresent their aims and objects, and to discredit them before the public in India and in England. But we are happy to be able to say that not only have the Congressmen survived all the desperate endeavours of their opponents but have actually grown so influential that when a short time ago an attempt was made to get up an anti-Congress demonstration in one of the important cities of this province not far from the capital, the all-powerful district officer actually discouraged the attempt on the ground that such a demonstration even though backed by all the official influence of that place would prove perfectly abortive and quite inadequate for the purpose of stemming the tide of educated public opinion in favour of the national movement. The district officer was right. The hand of the clock cannot be put back. The country has been advancing rapidly under the banner which floats and flutters in the air proudly from Peshawar to Calcutta. The arbiter of the destiny of nations has not placed the people

First Day.

Chairman of Reception Committee's Address.

of this vast country under the *ægis* of British rule for no purpose. The ancient mother of art and science, of religion and philosophy, rent and torn by internal dissension and trampled under the oppressor's relentless foot was to be rescued from her woful fate, and lo! a body of obscure merchants was sent out to trade in the East, and how this magnificent empire was built up subsequently is known to the readers of history. But these merchants from the far West were only the means to an end. Flushed with success, exultant man often arrogates to himself what he could have never dreamt to accomplish without the help of the Almighty, the causer of causes. "There is a divinity that shapes our ends." It is this divinity that shaped the ends of the body of obscure merchants, instilled patience and wisdom in their breast, expanded their views, enabled them to overcome their older and more powerful competitors, diverted their attention from commerce to conquest, taught them to form a mature organization out of raw materials, inspired them with the principles of righteous toleration and led them along the career of splendid achievements which are now the wonder and admiration of the whole civilized world. Verily there is a deeper meaning in all this than that a handful of Englishmen should grow rich at the expense and miseries of the countless millions that inhabit this woe-worn land. England's mission in India would remain unfulfilled if she failed to raise a once great but now fallen country from her present degraded position to place her on the path of moral, material and political advancement and prosperity.

It is this mission which the Indian National Congress calls upon England to perform. It is for this that we are knocking at her door. Happily for both England and India the genius of the English people is eminently fitted for the performance of this mission. Their views and sympathies are as liberal as their possessions are world-wide and it is therefore that they have been able to establish an Empire over which the sun never sets. In the economy of providence there is always a fitness of things, an adaptation of means to ends; and if at this moment England heads the great powers of the world it is because she has eminently deserved her exalted position. And that position she will continue to occupy and to maintain as long as she does not descend from her high moral pedestal, and governs the people committed to her care by providence not in the interests of the rulers but of the ruled. For ourselves we are fully sensible of the numerous boons we have received at her hands and our hearts overflow with gratitude Those who call us ungrateful either do not understand us or misrepresent us. The Indian mind still connects Royalty with Divinity and considers it a meritorious act to have a sight of the royal person. It has not yet been divested of the notion that the king is the vicegerent of God on earth, not that law is superior even to a king. This makes Indians the most loyal and law-abiding people on the face of earth. What the Congress contends is not that the country should be transferred from English to Indian hands, no,—not the change of hands, for it would be entirely suicidal, but that the people should be governed on those broad and liberal principles which have been held by eminent British statesmen and administrators themselves to be most conducive to the interests of the both the rulers and the subjects.

The constitution of all civilized Governments allows appeal to the highest authorities. British India is no exception to this rule. The laws in force here permit appeal in almost every branch of administration. The judgment of an inferior officer is open to examination by his superior. Why should then the exercise of this privilege in matters constitutional be looked on with any disfavour at all? The Congress has been called seditious and disloyal—not because it aims at overturning the foundations of British rule in India, for it is patent that its attempts are, on the contrary, directed towards consolidating those foundations—but because it petitions for the rights of the people guaranteed by repeated declaration of the highest authorities, and proposes in case of ill success in this country to lay their case before Her Majesty's Government in England, before the British Parliament and before the British nation, the ultimate Courts of appeal in whose probity and sense of justice and fairplay they have unbounded confidence. To do this effectually the Congress has to discuss questions vitally connected with the well-being of the Indian people and to lay their grievances before the bar of English public opinion which otherwise cannot know, or understand those grievances, or grant any redress. Is there anything wrong or unnatural in this procedure ?

It is the law of supply and demand which is a recognized principle in political economy. It is said that it is demand that brings in the supply. Man is so constituted that want is natural to him. When the want is felt the supply comes. Providence thus meets all demands. Even the man of religion has said that there can be no supply without demand. Did not the greatest teacher, the prince of prophets, say "ask and it shall be given unto you, seek and ye shall find, knock and it shall be opened unto you ?" Of course that is the law of prayer and inspiration in the world of spirit but the same interpreted in the language of flesh means the law of demand and supply. Now, gentlemen, imagine if it is not the law of our Anglo-Indian opponents, the utterances of their acknowledged saviour ? Is it not strange that they should object to our following the footsteps of their own great matter ? Is it not unwise and impolitic as well as unchristian of them to oppose the behaviour which "the beloved son of God" commands us to adopt ? Besides this there is a common saying that "the mother does not give milk till the child weeps." What wrong are we doing ? Where is our crime ? We are simply knocking at the door of the great British and Christian nation. We are crying for milk, say even for water before mother England. Is it improper on her part to give us a suckle ? The hungry and thirsty children and hergreat, the people of India, the weeping children of mother England, expect nourishment from that great English nation ? We might be alien in race and creed, in manners and customs, ideas and thoughts, but without asking, seeking and knocking hard at the door of our paternal Government we cannot find redress. We should be foremost to admit that in times past, before we could lisp, we received precious gifts from the hands of the Government, which we still possess and enjoy, but now that we have learnt to articulate it, we are not precluded from praying for better gifts beneficial alike to ourselves and our rulers and also essential for the good government of the country.

The Congress has passed eight years of its existence but what are eight years in the life of a nation ? Yet within this brief period it has succeeded in obtaining a few concessions which we highly prize, and these concessions should open the eyes of the wary and suspicious amongst us and encourage us all to persevere in the cause we have taken up for the amelioration of the condition of our country. These concessions prove the generosity of which the British nation is capable and they establish the consolation that if we apply to it for succour in our need, our appeal will not be futile or abortive. Let us then keep steadily the object we have in view, work strenuously in "faith, hope and charity," perfect our organization, strive with all our might to lift our nation from the despondency in which it is immersed and respectfully but firmly approach our rulers for the great good that it is always in their power to confer on us. And let us trust that our rulers will not misunderstand our utterances, nor misjudge our actions but will be considerate and charitable towards us. Give us our just rights, concede our reasonable demands, govern us on principles of equity and good conscience and strengthen the foundations of the empire by broadbasing it upon the people's will.

The distinguished President of the first and eighth Congresses in his inaugural address at Allahabad last year declared that the second cycle of the Congress began under his presidency. It is a happy coincidence that the second Congress of the second cycle

First Day.

Chairman of Reception Committee's Address.

should have been proposed to be held under the leadership of the same illustrious countryman of ours who guided the deliberations of the second Congress of the first cycle. I shall not anticipate your proceedings but nevertheless I cannot help congratulating ourselves on having in our midst one who has devoted all the talents and energies of a lifetime, with a supreme singleness of purpose, to promoting our cause, and who, by dint of ability, indomitable courage and perseverance, has forced his way to the highest deliberative assembly in the British empire, the Imperial Parliament of Great Britain and Ireland. I am referring, I need scarcely tell you, to Mr. Dadabhai Naoroji, who has inaugurated a new era in Indian political life and whose name now is a household word throughout the length and breadth of this land.

Those who assert that he does not represent the people of Indian in the House of Commons err greivously. The glorious receptions he has been accorded since his landing at Bombay should suffice to remove their error. All India with one heart accepts his representation, and hopes that immeasurable good will flow from it at no distant date. We must heartily congratulate ourselves on having also in our midst him who first directed our aims and aspirations, guided and controlled our counsels, cheered us in our difficulties, spent large sums of money, abandoned rest and comfort to promote our tottering cause and laid the foundation stone of that grand fabric which now proudly rears its lofty head—I mean our kind, noble, and affectionate friend Mr. Hume, the Father of the Indian National Congress. He has undertaken a long voyage to benefit us, to call us to our sense of duty, to rouse our flagging zeal, to stir up our drooping spirits, to encourage us with his presence and we are particularly fortunate in having the advantage of his guidance, advice and active co-operation at this the first session of the Congress in this province. May he and Mr. Dadabhai Naoroji both be spared long to work on behalf of suffering humanity in general and this country in particular !

The business before us this session is fairly large and I have carefully refrained from touching upon any of the subjects included in it for fear of needlessly encroaching upon your time. Before, however, I conclude, I must ask you to conceive the joy, because it is beyond all power of expression, which fills my heart at the sight of this great assembly—an assembly consisting of the cream of the Indian community. And I accord you once more a most hearty and cordial welcome to our old historic city.

When the address was over Sirdar Dayal Singh requested the delegates to elect a President and to proceed with the business before them.

Election of President.

Rai Bahadur Ananda Charlu Proposes Mr. Dadabhai Naoroji, M. P.

Rai Bahadur Ananda Charlu, ( *Mrdras, No. 838, in list.* ) said :—Brother Delegates, for presiding over your deliberations I have been privileged to have the honour of proposing one, who has achieved a foremost place in the ranks of our worthiest men, (*Hear hear.*) one, who is the embodiment of all that resolute perseverance can make, who is distinguished for unselfish devotion to the public cause, *(applause.)* and one, who, at the same time, is a model of winning simplicity and kindliness of manner ; one who has been accepted by all classes and creeds in this land as a matchless leader ; one who has been careering to this city amid ovations unexampled for enthusiasm and their universality ; *(applause.)* one whom we never need, under any circumstances, consent to exchange for five millions even of Chesneys ; one who has immortalised himself by his good works and one who has shed the greatest lustre upon the family and the country to which he belongs—I mean Mr. Dadabhai Naoroji. *(Loud and prolonged applause.)*

Moulvie Mohurrem Ali Chiste Seconds.

Moulvie Mohurrem Ali chiste, ( *Lahore, No. 266, in list.* ) in seconding the motion in Urdu said :

"Gentlemen,—I feel myself proud in seconding the proposal of my Madrasi brother

I think it is a proposal laid before you only in a formal manner, otherwise there was no necessity of proposing and seconding a Resolution which has been already passed by the unanimous voice of our countrymen long before the present Session of the Congress. (*Cheers.*) The enthusiastic welcome which you all have given him in the capital of the Punjab, the thundering cheers with which you have received him in this hall, and the successive applause you have given to the proposal of the first speaker, clearly shows the esteem and love which the "Grand old man of India" possesses among all sects of the Indian community. (*Cheers.*)

**First Day.**

**Election of President.**

**Moulvie Mohurrem Ali Chiste Seconds.**

"Gentlemen, you all know that I am a true and orthodox Mahomedan (*Cheers*) and Mr. Dadabhai Naoroji is a Parsi, but, still, I shall be wanting in my duty if I do not bear testimony to the great regard and esteem which this distinguished Indian statesman possesses even among my co-religionists for his genius, tact, zeal, perseverence, high statesman-like character and for his devotion to the cause of India. (*Cheers.*) In religious matters we of course differ, and I am so much devoted to the cause of my religion that it is my hearty desire that true Islam may extend from one end of the world to the other, and then extend its greatest blessing *i. e.* to remove the different nationalities of the world and unite them all in one tie of brotherhood. But, still, there is nothing in our sacred religion which prevents us from uniting with the non.-Moslem element of the world, from showing sympathy to and working in harmony with the followers of other religions and at least from taking part with our other countrymen in those worldly matters in which we have a common-cause and in which we are equally interested. (*Cheers.*) It is my hearty desire that not only the different sects in India should become united in worldly matters, but also that all the subjects of Her Majesty may join together as one nation under the British flag to improve the prosperity of all of them and to loyally defend the British Crown. (*Cheers.*) There ought to be no term like a "native subject" or a "European subject" but there ought to be the only one term of "Kaisri Riyaya" for all Her Majesty's subjects. (*Cheers.*) If we all throw away our nonsensical prejudices and show our sympathies towards each other, not only by words but also by deeds, there is every probability of this hope being fulfilled. The regard shown by our countrymen to the philanthropic Englishmen who have shown brotherly affection towards India, is a clear proof of the theory that Indians are second to none in showing gratitude and affection, if anybody cares for them. There is now present among us one Englishman, and I challenge anybody to tell me the name of any Indian who is more respected by our countrymen than that gentleman—I mean Mr. Hume. (*Loud cheers.*) It clearly shows that no religious differences are allowed to create differences in respect of worldly and national matters which are proposed for the welfare of mankind in general. We always think that we are honoring ourselves in honoring a philanthropic man. (*Cheers.*) It is therefore that I have been requested by my friends, and, especially, by the Mahomedan delegates present here, to formally second the proposal. With these words, gentlemen, I second the proposal for electing Mr. Naoroji as President of the Ninth Indian National Congress. (*Loud cheers.*)

The motion was then put to the Assembly by the Chairman of the Reception Committee and Mr. Dadabhai Naoroji declared duly elected president of the Ninth Indian National Congress.

Mr. Dadabhai Naoroji, M. P., who was received with a perfect storm of cheers and applause, the whole assembly rising to its feet, then took the chair. The newly elected President in addressing the Congress said:

**The President's Inaugural Address.**

LADIES AND GENTLEMEN,

I need not say how deeply I feel the honour you have done me, by electing me a second time to preside over your deliberations. I thank you sincerely for this honour In the performance of the onerous duties of this high position I shall need your great indulgence and support, and I have no doubt that I shall receive them. (*Applause.*)

### PLEASURE OF PRESIDING AT THE FIRST CONGRESS IN PUNJAB.

I am much pleased that I have the privilege of presiding at the very first Congress held in Punjab, as I had at Calcutta in 1886. I have taken, as you may be aware, some interest in the material condition of Punjab. In my first letter to the Secretary of State for India in 1880 on the material condition of India I took Punjab for my illustration, and worked out in detail its total annual income and the absolute wants of its common labourer. As to the loyalty of the Punjabis—Hindus, Sikhs, or Muhammadans—it has proved true through the most fiery ordeal on a most trying and critical occasion. (*applause.*)

### PECULIAR FEATURES OF THIS CONGRESS.

The occasion of this session of the Congress in Punjab has been a most happy coincidence. On Punjab rests a double responsibility—one external and one internal. If ever that hated threatened invasion of the Russians comes on, Punjab will have to bear the first brunt of the battle, and contented under British rule, as I hope India will be, Punjab will fight to her last man in loyalty and patriotism—loyalty to the British power, and patriotism to protect the hearths and homes of her beloved country of India. (*Loud applause.*)

### INTERNAL RESPONSIBILITY.

The internal responsibility which at present rests upon the Punjabis and other warrior races of India is this I have always understood and believed that manliness was associated with love of justice, generosity and intellect. So our British tutors have always taught us and have always claimed for themselves such character. And I cannot understand how any one could or should deny to your and other manly races of India the same characteristics of human nature. But yet we are gravely told that on the contrary the manliness of these races of India is associated with meanness, unpatriotic selfishness, and inferiority of intellect, and that therefore, like the dog in the manger, you and the other warrior races will be mean enough to oppose the resolution about Simultaneous Examinations, and unpatriotic and selfish enough to prevent the general progress of all India. ("*shame.*")

Can offence and insult to a people, and that people admitted to be a manly people, go any further? Look at the numbers of Punjabis studying in England. Now this happy coincidence of this meeting in Punjab you, considering every son of India as an Indian and a compatriot, have invited me—not a Punjabi, not a Muhammadan, nor a Sikh—from a distance of thousands of miles to enjoy the honour of presiding over this Congress, and with this gathering from all parts of India as the guests of the Punjabis, you conclusively, once for all and for ever, set the matter at rest that the Punjabis with all other Indians do earnestly desire the Simultaneous Examinations as the only method in which justice can be done to all the people of India, as this Congress has repeatedly resolved. And, moreover, Punjab has the credit of holding the very first public meeting in favour of the Resolution passed by the House of Commons for Simultaneous Examinations. (*cheers.*)

### THE PEOPLES OF THE UNITED KINGDOM.

When I use the words English or British, I mean all the peoples of the United Kingdom.

### MR. JUSTICE TELANG.

It is our melancholy duty to record the loss of one of our greatest patriots, Justice

Kasinath Trimbak Telang. It is a heavy loss to India; you all know what a high place he held in our estimation for his great ability, learning, eloquence, sound judgment, wise counsel and leadership. I have known him and worked with him for many years, and I have not known any one more earnest and devoted to the cause of our country's welfare. He was one of the most active founders of this Congress, and was its first hard-working Secretary in Bombay. From the very first he had taken a warm interest and active part in our work, and even after he became a Judge his sound advice was always at our disposal.

### APPOINTMENT OF MR. RANADE.

I am glad Mr. Mahadhev Govind Ranade is appointed in his place. (*cheers.*) It does much credit indeed to Lord Harris for the selection, and I am sure Mr. Ranade will prove himself worthy of the post. I have known him long, and his ability and learning are well known. (*applause.*) His sound judgment and earnest work in various ways have done valuable services to the cause of India. (*applause.*)

I am also much pleased that an Indian, Mr. Pramada Charan Bannerji, succeeds Mr. Justice Mahmud at Allahabad. (*cheers.*)

### THANKS TO LORD KIMBERLEY.

I feel thankful to the Local Governments and the Indian Government for such appointments, and to Lord Kimberley for his sanction of them, among which I may include also the decision about the Sanscrit Chair at Madras. (*applause.*) I feel the more thankful to Lord Kimberley, for I am afraid, and I hope I may be wrong, that there has been a tendency of not only not loyally carrying out the rule about situations of Rs. 200 and upwards to be given to Indians, but that even such posts as have been already given to them are being snatched away from their hands. Lord Kimberley's firmness in not allowing this is therefore so much the more worthy of praise and our thankfulness.

Lord Kimberley also took prompt action to prevent the retrograde step in connection with the Jury system in Bengal for which Mr. Paul and other friends interested themselves in Parliament; and also to prevent the retrograde interference with the Chairmanship of Municipalities, at the instance of our British Committee in London. I do hope that in the same spirit Lord Kimberley will consider our representations about the extension of the Jury system.

### MESSAGE OF GOODWILL FROM CENTRAL FINSBURY.

Before proceeding further, let me perform the gratifying task of communicating to you a message of sympathy and goodwill which I have brought for you from Central Finsbury. (*Loud applause and three cheers for the electors of Central Finsbury.*) On learning that I had accepted your invitation to preside, the Council of the Central Finsbury United Liberal and Radical Association passed a Resolution, which I have now the pleasure of placing before you, signed by Mr. Joseph Walton, the Chairman, and forwarded to me, by the Honorary Secretary, Mr. R. M. H. Griffith, one of my best friends and supporters :—

*The Central Finsbury United Liberal and Radical Association send a Greeting to the forthcoming Indian National Gongress.*

The Central Finsbury United Liberal and Radical Association, in view of Mr. Naoroji's visit to India at the end of November next, have passed the following Resolution :—

"1. That the General Council of the Central Finsbury United Liberal and Radical Association desire to record their high appreciation of the admirable and most exemplary manner in which Mr. Dadabhai Naoroji has performed his duties as representative of this constituency in the House of Commons, and, learning that he is, in the course of a few months, to visit India to preside over the Ninth Session of the Indian National Congress, request him to communicate to that body an expression of their full sympathy alike with all the efforts of that Congress for the welfare of India, and with the Resolution which has been recently passed by the House of Commons (in the adoption of which Mr. Dadabhai Naoroji has been so largely instrumental) in favour of holding Simultaneous Examinations in India and in Britain of candidates for all the Indian Civil Services; and further express the earnest hope that full effect will, as speedily as possible, be given by the Government to this measure of justice which has been already too long delayed. *(applause.)*

"2. That a copy of this resolution be forwarded to Mr. Dadabhai Naoroji.

"(Signed) JOSEPH WALTON,
"*Chairman of Meeting.*"

The Resolution has been sent to Mr. Naoroji with an accompanying letter, which says:

"Central Finsbury United Liberal and Radical Association,
"20, St. John Street Road, Clerkenwell,
London, E.C.

"DEAR SIR,—I have been directed to forward to you the enclosed copy of Resolution passed at the last meeting of the Council of this Association.

"Joining in the hope of my colleagues that the result of our efforts may be of material and lasting good, and wishing you a fruitful journey, with a speedy return to us, the constituents you so worthily represent in Parliament,

"I am, yours faithfully,
"R. M. H. GRIFFITHS,
"*Honorary Secretary.*

"The Honourable DADABHAI NAOROJI, M. P.,
"House of Commons, Westminster.
"*August 7th*, 1893."

## HAS THE CONGRESS JUSTIFIED ITS EXISTENCE?
## THE BRIGHT SIDE OF BRITISH RULE.

It has been my good fortune and happy privilege of being present at the first Session in 1885 with about eighty delegates. Eight years have since passed away, and we meet to-day for the ninth time. The first question which naturally now arises is—Has the Congress justified its existence? Has it borne any good fruit? I say that it has done both. But it is more. Its existence is also the justification and the best proof of the bright side of the British Rule. *(cheers.)* If any proof were wanted that British Rule has not been altogether without good results, the British people may well point with pride and satisfaction to the unique phenomenon of this Congress as the result of the beneficent part of their work in this country. *(applause.)*

## ITS JUSTIFICATION.

Dealing with its own justification of itself, we may look back to the Resolutions which were formulated at its first session and see what has been accomplished therefrom.

## THE LEGISLATIVE COUNCILS.

The Legislative Councils have been reformed, if not even to the moderate extent and in the manner in which we desired, still some advance has been made in their constitution and mode of work. Representation, though small and very imperfect, is, even as it is, a vital step for our future progress and for the consolidation of British Power. The right of interpellation will enable us, with much advantage and relief to Government itself, to ask some explanations directly and immediately without having to wait for the circuitous process of questions in the House of Commons.

### REPRESENTATIVE CHARACTER OF THE CONGRESS.

These small reforms in the Legislative Councils have, by their operation, indirectly brought out prominently, and undeniably proved, the truly representative character of our Congress. Most of those who have found admission as representatives are members of this Congress. (*cheers.*) In the Viceroy's Council we have the Hon. Mr. Pherozeshah M. Mehta, (*applause.*) the Hon. the Maharaja of Durbhanga, and the Hon. Mr. G. M. Chitnavis, and in the Provincial Councils the Hon. Messrs. W. C. Bonnerjee, Surendranath Bannerjea, Lalmohun Ghose, Maharaja Jagadindranath Roy (of Bengal), the Hon. Messrs. Rangia Naidu, Kalyansundram Iyer, Vashyam Iynger (of Madras), Hon. Messrs. P. M. Mehta and Chimunlal H. Setalvad (of Bombay), and the Hon. Raja Rampal Singh and the Hon. Charu Chunder Mitter (of Allahabad). In the late Hon. Mir Humayun Jah, C.I.E., of Madras, we have lost one of our most distinguished representatives and staunch supporters. Hon. Mr. Vishnu Raghunath Natu, B.A., LL.B., Pleader, High Court, Bombay (Bombay Legislative-Council), elected by District Local Boards of Southern Division.

### ELECTORS' NATIONAL FEELING.

It has also proved to us the gratifying and encouraging feature that the Electors have made no differences of creed, but have voted on the only right principle of fitness and of common Indian nationality and welfare. (*Hear, hear.*)

### THE EDUCATED ARE THE NATURAL LEADERS.

The fact is, and it stands to reason, that the thinking portion and the educated, whether in English or in their own learning, of all classes and creeds, in their common nationality as Indians, are naturally becoming the leaders of the people. Those Indians, specially, who have received a good English education, have the double advantage of knowing their own countrymen as well as understanding and appreciating the merits of British men and British rule, with the result, as Sir Bartle Frere has well put it: "And now wherever I go I find the best exponents of the policy of the English Government, and the most able co-adjutors in adjusting that policy to the peculiarities of the Natives of India, among the ranks of the educated Natives." (*applause.*)

Or as the Government of India has said: "To the minds of at least the educated among the people of India—and the number is rapidly increasing—any idea of the subversion of the British power is abhorent." (*Hear, hear.*)

Government of India's Despatch, dated 8th June, 1880, to Secretary of State for India.

And as Lord Dufferin, as Viceroy of India, has said in his Jubilee Speech: "We are surrounded on all sides by Native gentlemen of great attainments and intelligence, from whose hearty, loyal and honest co-operation we may hope to derive the greatest benefit." (*applause.*)

It would be the height of unwisdom, after themselves creating this great new force, "which is rapidly increasing" as "the best exponents and co-adjutors," as "abhoring the subversion of the British power," and from whose "hearty, loyal and honest co-operation the greatest benefit can arise," that the Ruling authorities should drive this force into opposition instead of drawing it to their own side by taking it into confidence and

First Day.

The President's Inaugural Address

thereby strengthening their own foundation. This Congress represents the Aristocracy of intellect and the New Political Life, created by themselves, which is at present deeply grateful to its Creator. Common sense tells you—have it with you, instead of against you.

### SIMULTANEOUS EXAMINATIONS—ASSURANCE BY THE UNDER-SECRETARY OF STATE FOR INDIA.

With regard to your other most important Resolution, to hold examinations simultaneously both in India and England for all the Civil Services, it would not have become a practical fact by the Resolution of the House of Commons of 2nd June last had it not been to a large extent for your persevering but constitutional demand for it made with moderation during all the years of your existence. (*applause.*) I am glad that in the last Budget debate the Under-Secretary of State for India has given us this assurance.

Debates. Vol. XVII., 1893, p. 1835.

"It may be in the recollection of the House that, in my official capacity, it was my duty earlier in the Session to oppose a Resolution in favour of Simultaneous Examinations, but the House of Commons thought differently from the Government. That once done, I need hardly say that there is no disposition on the part of the Secretary of State for India or myself to attempt to thwart or defeat the effect of the vote of the House of Commons on that resolution. (*Hear, hear and applause.*)

We all cannot but feel thankful to the Secretary of State, Lord Kimberley, and the Under-Secretary of State, Mr. George Russell, for this satisfactory assurance.

### CIVIL, MEDICAL AND ENGINEERING SERVICES.

I may just remark here in passing that I am not able to understand why the higher Civil and Educational Medical Services are handed over to Military Medical Officers, instead of there being a separate Civil Medical Service, dealt with by Simultaneous Examinations in India and England, as we expect to have for the other Civil Services. I also may ask why some higher Civil Engineering posts are given to Military Engineers.

### BRITISH INTEREST IN INDIAN AFFAIRS, AND DESIRE TO DO JUSTICE.

One thing more I may say: Your efforts have succeeded not only in creating an interest in Indian affairs, but also a desire among the people of the United Kingdom to promote our true welfare. (*Hear, hear.*) Had you achieved in the course of the past eight years only this much and no more, you would have amply justified your existence (*cheers.*) You have proved two things—that you are moderate and reasonable in what you ask, and that the British people are willing to grant what is shown to be reasonable.

### PAST RESOLUTIONS ADVANCING.

It is not necessary for me to enlarge upon the subject of your justification further than this, that all the Resolutions you have formulated have more or less advanced; that they are receiving attentive consideration is testified by the continuous discussions that have been going on in the press and on the platform both here and in England. In England itself many a cause, great or small, has to agitate long before making an impression. What struggles have there been in Parliament itself and out of Parliament for the Corn Laws, Slavery Laws, Factory Laws, Parliamentary Reforms, and many others, in short, in every important Legislation? We must keep courage, persevere, and "never say die." (*Loud applause.*)

### RETURN OF AN INDIAN TO THE HOUSE OF COMMONS.

One more result, though not the least, of your labours, I shall briefly touch upon. The effect which your labours produced on the minds of the people of the United Kingdom has helped largely an Indian to find his way into the Great Imperial Parliament, and in confirmation of this, I need not go further than remind you of the generous action of Central Finsbury and the words of the Resolution of the Council of its United Liberal and Radical Association which I have already placed before you. (*applause.*)

### FIRST ATTEMPT BY THE HON. MR. LAL MOHAN GHOSE

As you are all aware, though it was long my wish, my friend the Hon. Mr. Lal Mohan Ghose made the first attempt, and twice contested Deptford, with no little chances of success, but adverse circumstances proved too strong for him. We owe a debt of gratitude to Deptford, and also to Holborn, which gave me the first lift, and in my contest there, though a forlorn hope, the Liberal electors exerted their utmost, and gave me a very satisfactory poll. (*cheers.*)

### FRIENDS IN UNITED KINGDOM.

My mind also turns to those good friends of India—Bright, Fawcett, Bradlaugh and others, (*applause*)—who pioneered for us, prepared for the coming of this result, and helped us when we were helpless.

### RECEPTION IN THE HOUSE OF COMMONS.

This naturally would make you desire and lead me to say a few words about the character of the reception given to the Indian Member in the House of Commons. It was everything that could be desired. (*cheers.*) The welcome was general from all sides, as the interest in Indian affairs has been much increasing, and there is a desire to do justice to India. (*Renewed cheering.*) Mr. Gladstone on two occasions not only expressed his satisfaction to me at finding an Indian in the House, but expressed also a strong wish to see several more.

### INDIAN QUESTIONS IN THE HOUSE.

The attendance on Indian questions has been good, and what is still better, the interest in the Indian debates has been earnest, and with a desire to understand and judge rightly. India has indeed fared well this Session, notwithstanding its other unprecedentedly heavy work.

### THE FRIENDS IN THE HOUSE.

Thankful as we are to many Members of all sides, I am bound to express our special thanks to the Irish, Labour and Radical Members. (*Loud cheers.*) I heard from Mr. Davitt, two days before my departure, "Don't forget to tell your colleagues at the Congress that every one of Ireland's Home Rule Members in Parliament is at your back in the cause of the Indian People," (*Prolonged cheering.*) All our friends who had been working for us before are not only as zealous and staunch as ever, but more active and earnest. I cannot do better than to record in this place with thankfulness the names of all those Members from all parties who voted for the Resolution of 2nd June last in favour of Simultaneous Examinations in England and India for all the Indian Civil Services.

As the ballot fell to Mr. Herbert Paul, (*Three cheers for Mr. Paul.*) he, as you are aware, moved the Resolution, and you know also how well and ably he advocated the cause, and has ever since kept up a watchful interest in and eye on it. I may mention here that I had sent a whip or notice to every Member of the House of Commons for this debate.

**First Day.**

**The President's Inaugural Address.**

*2nd June 1893.*

11h. 55m. B. M.

Numb. 111.

Supply,—Order for Committee read ;

Motion made, and Question proposed, "That Mr. Speaker do now leave the Chair :"—

Amendment proposed, to leave out from the word "That" to the end of the Question, in order to add the words "all open Competitive Examinations heretofore held in England alone for appointments to the Civil Services of India shall henceforth be held simultaneously both in India and England, such Examinations in both Countries being identical in their nature, and all who compete being finally classified in one list according to merit :—(*Mr. Paul* :)—

Question put, "That the words proposed to be left out stand part of the Question :"—

The House *divided* ; Ayes 76, Noes 84.

NOES.

Allan, William (Gateshead)
Arch, Joseph
Baker, John
Barry, E. (Cork, S.)
5 Barry. John (Wexford, S.)
Beith, Gilbert
Bennet, Joseph
Birrell, Augustine
Bodkin, Matthias M.
10 Bright, Jacob (Manchester)
Burnie, Robert John Dickson
Burns, John
Byles, William Pollard
Caine, William Sproston
15 Cameron, Charles
Clark, Dr. G. B. (Caithness-sh.)
Clough, Walter Owen
Crean, Eugene
Cremer, William Randal
20 Crombie, John William
Crosfield, William
Curran, Thomas B. (Kilkenny)
Dalziel, James Henry
Dodd, Cyril Joseph Settle
25 Donelan, Captain A.
Evans, Samuel T. (Glamorgan)
Everett, Robert Lacey
Farquharson, Dr. R. (Aberd'sh)
Fenwick, Charles (Northumb.)
30 Field, William (Dublin)
Finucane, John
Flynn, James Christopher
Frye, Fred. C. (Kensington, N.)
Gane, Lawrence
35 Gibney, James
Hardie, J. Keir (West Ham, S.)
Healy, Maurice (Cork)
Hogan, James Francis
Holden, Angus (Yorkshire)
40 Holden, Isaac (Keighley)
Holland, William H.
Hunter, William Alexander
Jordan, Jeremiah
Keah, John Seymour
45 Kennedy, Patrick James
Lambert, George
Lawson, Sir Wilfred (Cumb'lnd)
Leese, Joseph Francis
Leng, John
50 Lennox, Rt. Hon. Lord W. C. G.
Luttrell, Hugh Fownes
McGregor, Dr. Donald
M'Cartan, Michael
M'Carthy, Justin
55 M'Hugh, Patrick A. (Leitrim)
M'Laren, Walter S. B. (Cheshire)
Maden, John Henry
Morton, Alpheus C. (Peterboro')
Morton, E. J. C. (Devonport)
60 O'Brien, P. J. (Tipperary)
O'Keeffe, Francis Arthur
Palmer, George Wm. (Reading)
Pease, Henry Fell (Yorks, N. R.)
Pickersgill, Edward Hare
65 Pryce-Jones, Sir Pryce
Richardson, Joseph
Robinson, Thomas (Gloucester)
Schwann, Charles E.

Sexton, Thomas
70 Shaw, Charles Edw. (Stafford)
Shaw, William Rawson (Halifax)
Smith, Harry (Falkirk)
Smith, Samuel (Flint)
Snape, Thomas
75 Spicer, Albert
Sullivan, Donal (Westmeath)
Sullivan, T. D. (Donegal, W.)
Tanner, Charles Kearns
Tuite, James
80 Wallace, J. Stewart (Limehouse)
Wason, Eugene
Webb, Alfred
Wedderburn Sir William
Wilson, John (Lanark)

Tellers for the Noes, Mr. Paul and Mr. Naoroji.

### OUR POSITION IN THE HOUSE.

#### *The Indian Parliamentary Committee.*

I may say here a few words about the progress we are making in our Parliamentary position. By the exertions of Sir William Wedderburn, (*applause.*) Mr. Caine, (*applause.*) and other friends, an Indian Parliamentary Committee has been formed, of which Sir William Wedderburn is the Chairman and Mr. Herbert Roberts is the Secretary. (*applause.*) The Committee is not yet fully formed. It will, we hope, be a larger General Committee of our supporters with a small Executive Committee, like other similar Committees that exist in the House for other causes. I give the names of the Members now fully enrolled in this Committee :—

Mr. Jacob Bright
" Caine
" John E. Ellis
Dr. W. A. Hunter
Mr. Illingworth
Sir Wilfred Lawson
Mr. Walter B. McLaren
" Swift MacNeill
" Dadabhai Naoroji
Mr. H. Paul
Sir Joseph Pease
Mr. T. H. Roberts
" R. T. Reid
" Samuel Smith
" C. E. Schwann
" Eugene Wason
" Webb
Sir W. Wedderburn

Besides these, there are a large number of Members (exclusive of the 70 or 80 Irish Members already referred to) whom we count as supporters and hope to see fully enrolled Members on our Indian Parliamentary Committee before long.

### GOD-SPEED AND WISHING SUCCESS TO ME.

On the eve of my departure, the committee invited me to a private dinner at the House, and gave me a hearty God-speed and wishes of success, with an expression of their earnest desire to see justice done to India. (*applause.*)

### THANKS TO MR. GEORGE RUSSELL, UNDER-SECRETARY OF STATE FOR INDIA.

Before leaving this subject of Parliament, let me offer to Mr. George Russell, the Under-Secretary of State for India, my sincere thanks for his sympathetic and cordial treatment of me in all I had to do with him, and for his personal good feeling and kindness towards me. (*applause.*)

### MUCH FUTURE WORK TO DO.

With all that has been done by the Congress, we have only begun our work. We have yet much and very much more work to do till that political, moral and material condition is attained by us which will raise us really to the level of our British fellow-citizens in prosperity and political elevation, and thereby consolidate the British power on the imperishable foundation of justice, mutual benefit and the contentment and loyalty of the people.

### FUTURE HOPEFUL

The reason why I have dwelt upon our past life is that it shows that our future is promising and hopeful, that our faith in the instinctive love of justice and fair play of the people of the United Kingdom is not misplaced, and that if we are true to ourselves and learn from the British character the self-sacrifice and perseverance which the British so largely possess, we need never despair of obtaining every justice and reform which we may reasonably claim as our birthrights as British citizens. (*cheers.*)

### OUR FUTURE WORK.

What then is to be our future work? We have yet to surmount much prejudice, prepossessions, and misapprehension of our true, material and political condition. But our course is clear and straight before us. On the one hand we need not despair or quarrel with those who are against us; we should on the other hand go on steadily, perseveringly and moderately with the representation of our grievances and just rights.

### LEGISLATIVE COUNCILS.

In connection with the question of our Legislative Councils we have yet very much work before us. Not only are the present rules unsatisfactory even for the fulfilment of the present Act itself as interpreted in the House by Mr. Gladstone, not only have we yet to obtain the full "living representation" of the people of India in these Councils, but also much further extension of their present extremely restricted powers which render the Councils almost a mere name. By the Act of 1861 (19), without the permission of the Governor General no member can introduce any measure (which virtually amounts to exclusion) about matters affecting the public debt or public revenues or for imposing any charge on such revenue, or the discipline and maintenance of any part of Her Majesty's Military or Naval forces. This means that, as far as the spending of our money is concerned, the Legislative Council is simply as if it did not exist at all. (*Cries of "shame, shame."*) No motion can be made by any member unless such motion be for leave to introduce some measure or have reference to some measure actually introduced thereunto. Thus there is no opportunity of calling any Department or Government to account for their acts (sec. 52). All things which shall be done by the Secretary of State shall have the same force and validity as if this Act (1861) had not been passed. Here is full arbitrary power. By the Act (1892, sec. 52) no member shall have power to submit or propose any resolution or to divide the Council in respect of any such financial discussion or the answer to any question asked under the authority of this Act or the rules made under this Act. Such is the poor character of the extent of concession made to discuss finances or to put questions. Rules made under this Act (1892) shall not be subject to alteration or amendment at meetings for the purpose of making Laws and Regulations. Also (Act 1861, sec. 22) the Secretary of State for India can by an Act of Parliament raise any money in the United Kingdom for the Government of India, and thus pile up any amount of burden on the Indian taxpayer, without his having a word to say upon it We are to all intents and purposes under an arbitrary rule, and are just only about at the threshold of a true Legislative Council.

### THE BUDGET DISCUSSION.

Amongst the most important work of the Councils is the Budget. What is the condition of the Budget debate both here and in England? The House of Commons devotes week after week for supply of the English Budget, when every item of expenditure is discussed or may be altered; and not only that, but the conduct of the department during the year is brought under review, which becomes an important check to any arbitrary, unjust or illegal action. But what is the Indian Budget debate or procepure? Here the Financial Statement is made by the Finance Ministe . Then a week or so after, a few speeches are made to no practical effect, no practical motion or resolution, and the whole thing is over. (" *Shame.*") Somewhat similar is the fate of the Indian Budget in the House of Commons, with the advantage of proposing any amendments and, at least, of having one amendment with practical effect of a division or vote. But there is also the important advantage of bringing in any Indian measure or motion in the course of the Session in accordance with the rules and orders of the House like any other measure or motion. I felt thankful that at the last Budget debate, though there was the usual additional agony of the last day of the Session, yet there was not also the agony of scanty attendance, thanks to the increasing interest in the House in Indian matters and to the friends of India. *(applause.)* In both places no practical check on any waste, extravagant or unnecessary expenditure. I am not at present discussing the merits of such Councils and restriction of powers, but that such matters will require your attention and consideration, that even in this one matter of Legislative Councils you have yet to secure Mr. Gladstone's "real living representative voice of the people" being heard upon every detail of the Government of British India. (*Hear, hear.*)

### DIRECT INDIAN REPRESENTATION IN PARLIAMENT.

There is, however, another important matter—I mean the direct representation from India in the Imperial Parliament. (*applause.*) As all our Imperial questions and relations between India and the United Kingdom, all amendments of Parliamentary Acts already passed and existing, or all important Acts that may be and can be only passed hereafter in Parliament, and all our ultimate appeals can be settled in Parliament alone, it is of extreme importance that there should be some reasonable direct representation from India in the House of Commons, and the representatives may be Indians or Europeans as long as they are the choice directly of Indian Constituencies, just as you have delegates to this Congress of Indians or Europeans.

Central Finsbury has been generous to us; other constituencies may also extend to us such generous consideration and help, but it is not fair that we should be left to depend upon the generosity of English Constituencies. (*Hear, hear.*) Under present circumstances we have a right to have direct representation. I hope the time is not very distant when we may successfully appeal to Parliament to grant us the true status of British political citizenship. (*Cheers.*) I do not overlook that several matters will have to be considered, and I am not at present placing before you a cut-and-dry scheme. My only object is to draw your attention to this vital subject.

### POVERTY OF INDIA.—WANT OF CALM JUDGMENT AMONG ANGLO-INDIANS.

But the greatest question before you, the question of all questions, is the Poverty of India. (*Hear, hear.*) This will be, I am much afraid, the great future trouble both of the Indian people and of the British Rulers. It is the rock ahead. In this matter we are labouring under one great disadvantage. This poverty we attribute to the system, and not to the officials who administer that system. (*Hear, hear and applause.*) But, unfortunately for us, for themselves and the British people, the officials (with clear-sighted exceptions of course) make the matter personal, and do not consider impartially and with calmness of judgment this all-important subject. The present Duke of Devonshire has well put this state of the official mind, which is peculiarly applicable in connection with this subject. He said: "The Anglo-Indian, whatever may be his merits, and no doubt they are just, is not a person who is distinguished by an exceptionally calm judgment.

Speech, H. of C., 23rd August 1883.

### THE PERSONAL VIEW HE TAKES OF THE QUESTION OF POVERTY WARPS HIS JUDGMENT.

Mr. Gladstone also lately, in the Opium debate, remarked :—"That it was a sad thing to say, but unquestionably it happens not infrequently in human affairs, that those who ought from their situation to know the most and the best, yet from prejudice and prepossessions knew the least and the worst." (*Hear, hear.*)

This has been our misfortune with officials. But there have been and are some thoughtful officials who know the truth, like Lord Lawrence and others in the past, and in the present times like the latest Finance Ministers, Lord Cromer, Sir Auckland Colvin and Sir David Barbour, who have perceived and stated the terrible truth that British India is extremely poor. Among other officials, several have testified to the sad fact, in "Confidential Reports," which Government do not publish—and this after a hundred years of the work of these officials under the present unnatural system. The system being unnatural, were the officials the very angels themselves, or as many Gladstones, they cannot prevent the evils of the system and cannot do much good. When Mr. Bayley and I moved for a Royal Commission of Inquiry, it was said that I had not produced evidence of poverty. It was not so; but it is difficult to make those see who would not see. (*Laughter and applause.*) To every member of the House I had previously sent my papers of all necessary evidence on the annual income and absolute wants of the people of India. I do not know whether any of those who opposed us had taken the trouble to read this, and it was unfair to expect that in making out a *prima facie* case for our motion, I should reiterate, with the unnecessary waste of some hours of the precious time of the House, all the evidence already in their hands.

RETURNS WANTED.

You remember my papers on the Poverty of India, and I have asked for Returns to bring up information to date, so that a fair comparison of the present with the past may enable the House to come to a correct judgment. I am sorry the Government of India refuses to make a return of a Note prepared so late as 1881 by Sir David Barbour, upon which the then Finance Minister (Lord Cromer) based his statement in his speech in 1882 about the extreme poverty of the mass of the people. I do not see why the Government of India should refuse. The Note, I am told, is an important document. Government for its own sake should be ready to give it. In 1880, the present Duke of Devonshire, then Secretary of State for India, readily gave me some statistics and information prepared by Mr. F. Danvers, though I did not know of their existence. This enabled me to point out some errors and to explain some points which had been misunderstood. Such information is extremely necessary, not merely for the sake of the exceedingly poor masses of the people, but for the very stability of the British power itself.

The question of the Poverty of India should be fully raised, grappled with and settled. The Government ought to deal boldly and broadly with it. Let there be a return in detail, correctly calculated, made every year of the *total* annual income of *all* British India, per head of population, and of the requirements of a labourer to live in working health, and not as a starved beast of burden. Unless such complete and accurate information is given every year in detail, it is idle and useless to make mere unfounded assertions that India is prospering.

THE AVERAGE INCOME OF THE MASS OF THE PEOPLE MUCH SMALLER THAN RS. 27.

It must also be remembered that Lord Cromer's annual average of not more than Rs. 27 per head is for the whole population, including the rich and all classes, and not what the great mass of the population can or do actually get. Out of the total annual income of British India all that portion must be deducted which belongs to European Planters, Manufacturers and Mineowners, and not to the people of British India, excepting the poor wages they receive, to drudge to give away their own country's wealth, to the benefit of a foreign people. Another portion is enjoyed in and carried out from the country on a far larger share per head by many who are not the children of the soil—official and non-official. Then the upper and middle classes of the Indians themselves receive much more than their average share. The great mass of the poor people therefore have a much lower average than even the wretched "not more than Rs. 27" per head.

### MY CALCULATION.

You know that I had calculated the average of the income as being Rs. 20 per head per annum, and when Lord Cromer's statement of Rs. 27 appeared, I requested him to give me his calculations but he refused. However, Rs. 20 or "not more than Rs. 27"—how wretched is the condition of a country of such income, after a hundred years of the most costly administration, and can such a thing last? (*cries of "no, no"*.)

### SIR JOHN SHORE'S PREDICTION IN 1787.

It is remarkable that there is no phase of the Indian problem which clear-headed and fair-minded Anglo-Indians have not already seen and indicated. More than a hundred years ago, in 1787, Sir John Shore wrote these remarkable, far-seeing, and prophetic words :—

"Whatever allowance we may make for the increased industry of the subjects of the State, owing to the enhanced demand for the produce of it (supposing the demand to be enhanced), there is reason to conclude that the benefits are more than counter-balanced by evils inseparable from the system of a remote foreign dominion."

(Parl. Ret. 377 of 1812.)

### PREDICTION CONFIRMED BY SECRETARY OF STATE FOR INDIA IN 1886 AFTER ONE HUNDRED YEARS.

And these words of prophecy are true to the present day. I pass over what has been said by other European Officials at different times during the hundred years. I come to 1886, and here is a curious and complete response after a hundred years by the Secretary of State for India. In a despatch (26th January, 1886) to the Treasury, he makes a significant admission about the consequences of the character of the Government of the foreign rule of Britain. He says :—

"The position of India in relation to taxation and the sources of the public revenues is very peculiar, not merely from the habits of the people and their strong aversion to change which is more specially exhibited to new forms of taxation, but likewise from the character of the government, which is in the hands of foreigners, who hold all the principal administrative offices and form so large a part of the Army. The imposition of new taxation which would have to be borne wholly as a consequence of the foreign rule imposed on the country and virtually to meet additions to charges arising outside of the country would constitute a political danger, the real magnitude of which, it is to be feared, is not at all appreciated by persons who have no knowledge of or concern in the Government of India, but which those responsible for that government have long regarded as of the most serious order

What a strange conformation fulfillment and explanation of the reason of the prophecy of a hundred years ago and admission now that because the character of the present government is such that it is in the hands *foreigners who hold all the principal administrative offices and from so large a part of the army* the consequence of it is a "*political danger*," the real magnitude of which is "*of the most serious order*."

Need I, after this declaration even, despair that some of our Anglo-Indian friends would not take a lesson from the Secretary of State and understand the evil of the system under which India is suffering? Have I ever said anything clearer or stronger than this despatch has done? It gives my whole fear of the future perils to the people of India, and political danger to the British Power, in a nutshell. This shows that some of our Anglo-Indian authorities have not been, nor are, so dull and blind as not to have seen before or see now the whole peril of the position, and the unnatural and suicidal system of administration.

## FIGURES QUOTED WITHOUT UNDERSTANDING THEM, AND INCORRECT CALCULATIONS OF AVERAGES.

Yes, figures are quoted by some of what they call "increase of trade," "balance of trade in favour of India," "increase of industry," "hoarding of treasure in British India," etc., etc.; but our misfortune is that these people, with bias and prejudices and prepossessions, and apparently having not very clear ideas of the principles, processes, and details of commercial and banking operations and transactions, and of the perturbations of what Sir John Shore called "the evils of a distant foreign dominion," are not able to understand and read aright these facts and figures of the commercial and economic conditions of British India. These people do not realise or seem to understand that what are called "the trade returns of British India" are misleading, and are *not* the trade returns of *British India.* A good portion of both the imports and exports of both merchandise and treasure belong to the Native States and to countries beyond the borders, and not to British India. A separate return must be made of the imports and exports of the non-British territories, so that a correct account of the true trade of British India may be given by itself—and then there should be some statement of the exports which are not trade exports at all, but only political and private European remittances; and then only will it be seen how wretched this British Indian true trade is, and how fallacious and misleading the present returns are. A return is made every year called "The Material and Moral Progress of India." But that part regarding "Material Progress" to which I am confining my observations is very imperfect and misleading. As I have already said, nothing short of a return every year of the average annual income per head of population of British India, and of the absolute necessaries of life for a healthy labourer, in detailed calculation can give any correct idea of the progress or otherwise of the material condition of the people of British India. I ask for "detailed calculation" in the returns, because some of the officials seem to have rather vague notions of the Arithmetic of Averages, and though the foundation figures may be correct, they bring out results far from truth. I have pointed out this with instances in my papers. I have communicated with the Secretary of State for India, and he has communicated with the Governments in India. But I do not know how far this correction has been attended to by those who calculate averages.

## A NATURAL SYSTEM WOULD BENEFIT BOTH COUNTRIES.

What is grievous is that the present unnatural system, as predicted by Sir John Shore, is destructive to us, with a partial benefit to the United Kingdom with our curse upon it. But were a natural system to prevail, the commercial and industrial benefits aided by perfect free trade that exists between India and the United Kingdom, will be to both countries of an extent of which we can at present form no conception. Englishmen

## HANKER AFTER NEW MARKETS.

But here is an inexhaustible market of 221,000,000 of their own civilized fellow-citizens with some 66,000,000 more of the people of the Native States, and what a great trade would arise with such an enormous market, and the United Kingdom would not for a long time hear any thing about her "unemployed." It is only some people of the United Kingdom of the higher classes that at present draw all the benefit from India. The great mass of the people do not derive that benefit from the connection with India which they ought to get with benefit to both countries. On the other hand, it is with the Native States that there is some comparatively decent trade. With British India, as compared with its population, the trade of the United Kingdom is wretched indeed after a century of a very costly administration paid for by the poverty-stricken ryots.

### BETTER TO TRADE WITH THAN HOLD PEOPLE AS SLAVES.

Truly has Macaulay said emphatically: "To trade with civilised man is infinitely more profitable than to govern savages; that would indeed be a doting wisdom, which in order that India might remain a dependency, would make it a useless and costly dependency which would keep a hundred millions (now really 221,000,000) of men from being our customers in order that they might continue to be our slaves." Should this doting wisdom continue?

### MY VIEWS ON POVERTY RIDICULED AT FIRST.

It is impossible for me to explain in this address all the misapprehensions. I have already explained my views as fully as possible in my papers. These views were at first ridiculed and pooh-poohed till the highest financial authorities, the latest Finance Ministers themselves, admitted the extreme poverty of India. Lord Cromer summed up the situation in these remarkable words in 1882: "It has been calculated that the average income per head of population in India is not more than Rs. 27 a year." "In England the average income per year per head of population was £33; in France it was £23; in Turkey, which was the poorest country in Europe, it was £4 a head." Comment is unnecessary. Let us and the Government

### NOT LIVE IN A FOOL'S PARADISE.

Or time may bring disasters to both when it is too late to stop them. This poverty is the greatest danger both to us and the rulers. In what hapes and varieties of forms the disease of poverty may attack the body-politic, and bring out and aggravate other evils, it is difficult to tell or foresee, but that there is danger of "most serious order," as the Secretary of State declares, nobody can deny.

### BRITAIN MAY DEFY HALF A DOZEN RUSSIAS.

Were the people of British India allowed to enjoy the fruits of their own labour and resources, and were fair relations established between the British and Indian peoples, with India contented and prosperous, Britain may defy half a dozen Russias. *(Loud cheers.)* Indians will then fight to the last man and to the last rupee for their share, as patriots and not as mercenaries. The rulers will have only to stamp their foot, and millions will spring up to defend the British power and their own hearths and homes. *(Renewed Cheering.)*

### THE DESIRE OF THE CONGRESS TO SUPPORT GOVERNMENT.

We, the Congress, are only desirous of supporting Government, and having this important matter of poverty grappled with and settled, we are anxious to prevent "the Political danger" of the "most serious order," declared to exist by the Secretary of State himself. We desire that the British connection should endure for a long time to come for the sake of our material and political elevation among the civilised nations of the world. It is no pleasure or profit to us to complain unnecessarily or wantonly about this poverty.

### NOT ENEMIES OF BRITISH RULE.

Were we enemies of British rule, our best course would be, not to cry out, but remain silent, and let the mischief take its course till it ends in disaster as it must. But we do not want that disaster, and we therefore cry out, both for our own sake and for the sake of the rulers. *This evil of poverty must be boldly faced and remedied.*

**First Day.**

**The President's Inaugural Address.**

This is the question to which we shall have to devote our best energies. We have, no doubt, to contend against many difficulties, but they must be surmounted for everybody's sake..

### THE UNITED KINGDOM SHOULD SHARE IN THE EXPENDITURE OF THE EUROPEAN SERVICES.

The next subject to which I desire to draw your attention is this. We have a large costly European Army and European Civil Services. It is not to be supposed that in these remarks I accept the necessity for them. I take at present the situation as it is. I now submit to the calm consideration of the British people and Government these questions. Is all this European service entirely for the sole benefit of India? Has the United Kingdom no interest or benefit in it?. Does not the greatness of, and the greatest benefit to the United Kingdom arise from its connection with India? Should not the cost of such greatness and great benefits be shared by the United Kingdom in proportion of its means and benefit? Are not these European services especially imposed upon us on the clearly admitted and declared ground of maintaining the British power? Let us see what our rulers themselves say.

Lord Beaconsfield said:—

"We had to decide what was the best step to counteract the efforts Russia was then making, for though war had not been declared, her movements had commenced in Central Asia, and the struggle has commenced which was to decide for ever which power should possess the great gates of India, and that the real question at issue was whether England should possess the gates of her own great Empire in India, and whether the time had not arrived when we could no longer delay that the problem should be solved and in a manner as it has been solved by Her Majesty's Government."

Hansard, Vol. 250, p. 1094. 25th February, 1880

Again he says:—

"We resolved that the time has come when this country should acquire the complete command and possession of the gates of the Indian Empire. Let me at least believe that the Peers of England are still determined to uphold not only the Empire but the honour of this country."

Can any words be more emphatic to show the vast and most vital stakes, honour and interests of the United Kingdom?

Lord Kimberley, the Secretary of State for India, tells us:—

"We are resolutely determined to maintain our supremacy over our Indian Empire . . . . that among other things," he says, "that supremacy rests upon the maintenance of our European Civil Service," that "we rest also upon the magnificent European Force which we maintain in that country."

*Times*, 13th June, 1893. Mans'n House Dinner to Lord Roberts.

This again is another emphatic declaration of the vast stakes and interest of the United Kingdom for which the European Services are maintained entirely at our expense.

I shall give one more autnority only:—

See what a man like Lord Roberts, the symbol of physical force admits. He says to the London Chamber of Commerce: "I rejoice to learn that you recognise how indissolubly the prosperity of the United Kingdom is bound up with the retention of that vast Eastern Empire," and again he says at Glasgow: "That the retention of our Eastern Empire is essential to the greatness and prosperity of the United Kingdom." Now, I ask again, that with all such deep, vast and great interests, and the greatness

*Times*, 25 May, 1893. Dinner by the London Chamber of Commerce.

*Times*, 29th July, 1893.

and prosperity of the United Kingdom, essentially depending on the Eastern Empire, and indissolubly bound up with it, is it reasonable, is it just and fair, is it British that *all* the cost of such greatness, glory, and prosperity of the United Kingdom should be entirely, to the last farthing, thrown upon the wretched Indians, as if the only relations existing between the United Kingdom and India were not of mutual benefit, but of mere masters and slaves as Macaulay pointed out to be deprecated. (*Applause and cries of "no, no".*)

### THE PRESENT NAVY REQUIRED FOR THE VERY EXISTENCE OF BRITAIN.

As for the navy, the *Times* regards and it is generally admitted that the very existence of Britain itself depends upon the command of the sea. The *Times* says: "They will never forgive the Minister or the Ministry that leaves them weaker at sea than any possible combination of France and another power."

By a telegram I read at Aden I found Mr. Gladstone "re-affirmed the necessity of British supremacy."

For any war vessels that may be stationed in India for the protection of the interests of both, the expenditure may be fairly shared.

### RELATIONS WITH IRELAND COMPARED.

In the Bill for the better Government of Ireland there are provisions by which Ireland is required to pay a certain share of the Imperial expenditure according to its means, and when necessary to pay a similar share of anv extraordinary expenditure, Ireland having all its resources at its own command. Now see how vastly different is our position. Not only will Ireland have all her internal services, Irish or under Irish rules, causing no foreign drain from her, but she will also, as she has always enjoyed, continue to enjoy her share in all the gain and glory of the British Empire. Irishmen can be Viceroys, Governors, and have any of the appointments in the military or civil services of the Empire, with the additional advantage of a large number of members in Parliament. The Indians, on the other hand, have not only no such share at all in the gains and glory of the British Empire, but are excluded even from the Services of their own country, with the consequences of an exhausting foreign drain, of the deplorable evils foretold by Sir John Shore and subjected to the imposition of every farthing of the expenditure. Nor has India any votes in Parliament. And we have now the additional misfortune that the British Cabinet, since the transfer to the Crown, is no longer the independent tribunal to judge between us and the Indian authorities, and this adds heavily to our difficulties for obtaining justice and redress, except so far as the sense of justice of the non-official members of the Parliament helps us.

### MISAPPREHENSION ABOUT THE BURDEN OF EXPENDITURE—UNITED KINGDOM HAS SPENT NOTHING.

There is a strange general misapprehension among the people of the United Kingdom. They do not seem to know that they have not spent a single shilling either in the formation of the British Indian Empire or in its maintenance, and that, as far as I know, every farthing is taken from the Indians, with the only exception in my knowledge that Mr. Gladstone with his sense of justice allowed £5,000,000 towards the last Afghan War, which, without having any voice in it, cost India £21,000,000. (*Loud cries of "Shame."*) I cannot blame the people of the United Kingdom generally for this mistake, when even well-informed papers give utterances to this most unfortunate fallacy. As for instance a paper like the *Statist*, in the extract which my friend Mr. Dinshaw. E. Wacha gave you last year, says: "Whatever may happen, we must defend India to our last shilling and our last man," while the fact is that they have not spent even their first shilling or any shilling at all; (*Laughter.*) but on the contrary derived benefits in various ways from India of millions on millions every year. ("*Shame*".) Nor have the fighters in creating and maintaining the British Indian Empire been only the British soldier to" the last man." Indian soldiers have done the main work, and if India can be made prosperous and contented as it can be by true statesmanship, the Indian soldier will be ready to fight to " the last man " to defend British power. (*Loud cheers.*)

Britain in fact cannot send to India "to its last man." The very idea is absurd ; on the contrary she can draw from India for her European purpose an inexhaustible strength.

Again, the *Statist* says :—" We are at this moment spending large sums of money in preparing against a Russian attack." Not a farthing of the British money ? Every farthing of these " large sums," and which are crushing us, is " imposed " upon the people of British India. Such misleading statements are often made in the English press to our great injury. (*"Shame."*)

### APPEAL TO THE BRITISH PEOPLE AND PARLIAMENT FOR JUST RELATIONS.

I repeat, then, that we must submit to the just consideration of the British people and parliament whether it is just and right that they should not pay a fair share, according to their stakes and means, towards all such expenditure as is incurred for the benefit of both India and the United Kingdom, such expenditure, and the respective share of each, being settled on a peace footing, any extraordinary expenditure against any foreign invasion being also further fairly shared.

### WEAKNESS FROM EUROPEAN SERVICES.

Before closing this subject, I may just remark that while leaving necessarily the highest offices of power and control, such as Viceroys and Governors to Europeans, I regard the enormous European Services as a great political and imperial weakness, in critical political times to the British power, as well as the cause, as the present Duke of Devonshire pointed out, of the insufficiency of an efficient administration of the country ; and also the main cause of the evils feretold by Sir John Shore, and admitted by the Secretary of State for India, after a hundred years, as a political danger of " a most serious order " ; and of the poverty of India.

### ADMITTED UNFAIRNESS OF SOME HOME CHARGES.

I would not say much upon the next subject, as you have had only lately the highest testimonies of two Viceroys and three Secretaries of State for India—of Lord Northbrook and Lord Ripon, and of the Duke of Argyll, Lord Cross, and Lord Kimberley. You remember the debate raised by Lord Northbrook in the House of Lords a few months ago that the Home Military Charges were unfair and unjust, and all the authorities I have named endorsed the complaint. But even the heads of the Indian authorities are so much in terror of the Treasury that Lord Kimberley said :—" The India Office has no particular desire that the question should be re-opened and discussed anew, for bitter experience has taught the department that the re-opening of a question of this kind generally results in the imposition of additional charges." Is this one other disadvantage of the transfer to the Crown ? Lord Kimberley hit the nail on the head why India was so unfairly treated (and the same may be applied to such other treatment of India by the Indian authorities themselves) when he said :—" The reasons why proposals that must throw fresh burdens on the Government of India are so frequently made in the House of Commons is that those who make them know that their own pockets will not suffer in the desire to make things agreeable and comfortable. *(Laughter.)* The taxpayers of the country exercise no check upon such proposals, and the consequence is that charges are sometimes imposed upon the Government of India which that Government thinks unjust and unnecessary." It must be borne in mind that charges "imposed on the Government of India" means the suffering party is the poor tax-payer of India.

The Duke of Argyll characterises these charges as "unjust and illegal tribute to England." But mark the words of Lord Cross :—"I am certain that in the course of a few years the Indian people will force us to do them justice." This is just the feature "to be forced to do justice" which I always deplore. We desire that all necessary reforms and acts of justice should be spontaneous on the part of Britain, in good grace and in good time as gifts claiming our gratitude, and not to wait till "*forced*," with loss of grace from the giver and the loss of gratitude from the receiver. *(Hear, hear.)*

I offer my thanks to Lord Northbrook and other Lords for that debate, though yet barren of any result. But we may fairly hope that such debate must sooner or later produce good results. It is like a good seed sown and will fructify.

### SOME SMALLER ITEMS OF COMPLAINT.

Here are some smaller items : The cost of the India Office Building of about half a million, of the Royal Engineering College of £134,000, and of other buildings is all cast on India. The cost of the Colonial Office Building, £100,000, is paid from the British Exchequer. The India Office Establishment, etc., about £230,000 a year, is all imposed on India, while the £41000 of the Colonial Office and £168,000 for Colonial Services are paid from the British Exchequer. The Public Debt of India (excluding Railway and Productive Works) is incurred in creating and preserving the British power, but all our cries to give us at least the benefit of a British guarantee have been in vain, with the curious suicidal effort of showing to the world that the British Government itself has no confidence in the stability of its own power in India. *(Hear, hear.)*

### INCREASE OF BURDENS ALREADY TOO MUCH IN 1870.

In 1870 Mr. Gladstone declared India to be "too much burdened," when the Annual Expenditure was £39,000,000; and what expression can be used now when, with an extremely poor income, the burden now is nearly 75 per cent. heavier, or Rx 68,000,000 this year.

### OTHER SUBJECTS OF THE CONGRESS.

Passing on to other subjects, I hope the separation of Executive and Judicial functions will receive attention as its necessity has been recognised. We have to persevere for this as well as for other parts of our programme, bearing in mind one great difficulty we have to contend with. Unfortunately the Indian authorities when they determine to do or not to do a thing under the notion of preserving prestige and strength, as if any false prestige can be a strength, disregard even Resolutions or Acts of Parliament itself and resort to every device to carry their own point or view. *(Loud cries of "Shame.")* We cannot expect Parliament to watch Indian affairs from day to day, and therein lies the impunity and immunity of the Indian Administration.

### THE STATUTORY SERVICE.

I shall refer to only two instances : First, the case of the misleadingly called "The Statutory Service," and what in reality was created out of, and as a part and parcel of, the Covenanted Civil Service. I can speak with some authority, for I was the very proposer of the Memorial of the East India Association to Sir Stafford Northcote which resulted in the Clause of the Act of 1870. But the Indian authorities would not have it.

They moved heaven and earth to thwart it; it is a long and a sad story for the good name of Britain, and they never rested till they made the Statute a dead letter, though it still stands on the Statute Book of the Imperial Parliament. ("*Shame.*") However, I hearwith pleasure, and I hope it is true, that a disposition has arisen, for which I understand Lord Kimberley is to be thanked, to redress this glaring and unfortunate wrong—unfortunate for British prestige, for British honour and British good faith, and I do hope that the Government would do this redress ungrudgingly, with good grace, completeness and generosity. This instance illustrates another unfortunate phase of the Administration.

### CONTRAST OF THE FOREST SERVICE FOR EUROPEANS.

The Forest Department is recruited by examinations in England and by selection in India. Such selection is not based upon a Resolution or Act of Parliament, but upon the will of the authorities and consisting of Europeans. The Government of India in Resolution No. 18 F, of 29th July, 1891, have described them as untrained and uncovenanted officers, who have been unconditionally appointed in past years, and yet they are ordered in the regular Indian Forest Service; while those Native Civilians, created and backed by an Act of Parliament, as distinctly belonging to the Covenanted Civil Service, are excluded from that Civil Service to which the Act distinctly appointed them. Can such difference of treatment of Europeans and Indians preserve British prestige for honour and justice, and would it increase or diminish the existing attachment of the Indians to British rule?

### THE CANTONMENT ACT.

The second instance was the practical disregard of the Resolution of the House of Commons about the State regulation of vice. But in this case there were vigilant watchers like Mrs. Butler, Mr. Stansfeld, M. P., Mr. Stuart, M. P., and others, and they did not allow the Resolution to become a dead letter. In this case also I am glad to find that the Indian authorities now mean to give loyal effect to the Resolution, and well may they do so, for the sake of the British good name, fame, and prestige for morality of every kind upon which mainly British strength and influence rest.

### THE CURRENCY QUESTION.

On the Currency Question I need not dwell much. My views are known to you. Now that the Sherman Law is repealed by the United States, we may hope to see a settled condition in time. No amount of currency jugglery or devices in this country could have any influence (except that of creating troubles in the country itself, as has happened) on the loss in the remittances to England for Home Charges, which must be paid in gold, and will fluctuate with the rise or fall of gold in the United Kingdom. As if this crushing loss was not enough for the wretched taxpayers, further burdens were laid to make things agreeable and comfortable with other people's money, as Lord Kimberley would say, of high exchange to the European officials, and the further most unwarranted payment of £138,000 to the banks, with whose transactions in profits or loss the taxpayer has no connection whatever. ("*Shame, shame.*") Some strange precedents are made in this matter to silence opposition and to support banks at the expense of the taxpayers, which will lead to serious troubles in the future. Should not the millowners and other concerns also claim compensation for the dislocation of their industry or transactions by the currency action of the Government, as Government itself admits to have caused such dislocation? Would the British Exchequer have paid any such money to the British banks? Such a thing would never have been thought of The utmost that is done in any crisis is allowing the Bank of England to issue more notes under strong restrictions. Had the banks made profits instead of loss, would they have handed them to the taxpayer? Then it would have been called the reward of shrewdness, foresight, enterprise, etc., etc.

The whole currency troubles from which India is suffering, and which are so peculiar to India and so deplorable to the Indian taxpayer, and from which no other silver-using country suffers, is one of the best illustrations and object lessons, and proof of the soundness of Sir John Shore's prophecy about the evil consequences of the present unnatural system of a remote foreign dominion, or as the Secretary of State called the danger of "a most serious order."

ADDITIONAL TAXATION.

The currency muddle will necessitate new taxation. The usual easy and unchecked resource of putting off the evil day by borrowing is already resorted to, and in the spirit of keeping things agreeable and comfortable to those who have votes in Parliament, there is danger of increase in the salt tax. I do hope that Government will have some moral courage and some mercy upon the wretched taxpayer, and reduce even the salt tax by reimposing the cotton duties. Not that by this means India will be saved a pie from the addition of burdens, but that a little better able shoulders will have to bear them, or, as Lord Salisbury once coolly put it, that as India must be bled, the lancet should be directed to the parts where there was at least sufficient blood, not to those which are already feeble from the want of it.

THE RELATIONS WITH NATIVE STATES.

Another subject of our future work to which I need only touch now is the relations of the Government with the Native States. There is much unnecessary irritation and dissatisfaction where there ought to be the pleasantest harmony with much greater devoted loyalty than what even now really exists. And it is also a great mistake for a foreign power not to draw the military capacity and spirit of the country to their own side by giving it a fair career and interest in their own service. Make the military races feel it to their advantage and interest to be loyal to the British rule instead of keeping them alienated from the Government.

RESOLUTIONS TO BE DISCUSSED WITH MODERATION.

I need not say more upon our future work, as various Resolutions of importance will be placed before you for your consideration, and I am sure you will deliberate with that moderation and fairness for which you have already distinguished yourselves and acquired just credit, and for which I offer you my hearty congratulations. You recognise, I have no doubt, that at every turn you have yet serious questions to grapple with and much work to do

GOOD FEELING AMONG ALL MY COUNTRYMEN.

Anyone who has watched my public career must have seen that my main underlying principle and the desire of my heart is to promote, as far as I can, good fellow-feeling among all my countrymen. (*Loud applause.*) And I have no doubt that all the educated and thinking men and all true friends of our own country will continue to do all that lies in their power to bring about stronger and stronger friendly ties of commont nationality, fellow-feeling, and due deference to each other's views and feelings amongs the whole people of our country.

Government must be firm and just in case of any unfortunate differences; as far as Government are concerned, their duty is clearly to put down with a strong hand any lawlessness or disturbance of the peace, no matter who the parties concerned may be. They can only stand, as they ought, on the only sure and right foundation of even-handed justice to all, and cannot allow anyone to take the law into his own hands; the only wise policy is to adhere to their declared policy of strict neutrality and equal protection and justice to all creeds. (*Hear, hear.*)

## CORDIAL CONFERENCES BETWEEN HINDUS AND MUHAMMADANS.

I was much pleased to read in the papers that cordial conferences had been held between Muhammadans and Hindus in various places to devise means to prevent any deplorable occurrences happening in the future.

## CORDIAL NATIONAL RELATIONS BETWEEN THE TWO COMMUNITIES.

Looking back to the past as my own personal experience of my life, and as far back as I know of earlier days, at least on my side of India, I feel a congratulation that all associations and societies of members of all creeds have worked together in harmony and union, without any consideration of class or creed in all matters concerning our common national public and political interests. No doubt, latterly, even in such common matters, differences of views have arisen and will arise, but such differences of views, when genuine, are healthy, just as is the case in the United Kingdom itself with its two political parties. (*Hear, hear.*)

## THE HARMONY IN THE CONGRESS.

What makes me still more gratified and look forward hopefully in the future is that our Congress has not only worked so far in the union and concord of all classes and creeds, but has taken care to provide that such harmony should continue in the future. As early as in the Congress at Allahabad of 1888 you passed this Resolution (XIII):—

> "That no subject shall be passed for discussion by the Subject Commitee, or allowed to be discussed at any Congress by the President thereof, to the introduction of which the Hindu or Muhammadan delegates as a body object unanimously or nearly unanimously, and that if, after the discussion of any subject which has been admitted for discussion, it shall appear that all the Hindu or all the Muhammadan delegates as a body are unanimously or nearly unanimously opposed to the Resolution which it is proposed to pass thereon, such Resolution shall be dropped; provided that this rule shall refer only to subjects in regard to which the Congress has not already definitely pronounced an opinion."

As I have already said, the highest wish of my heart is that all the people of India should regard and treat each other as fellow-countrymen, with fellow-feeling for the good of all. (*Applause.*)

## INTERESTS OF ALL INDIANS ARE IDENTICAL.

We may, I am convinced, rest fully assured that whatever political or national benefit we may acquire will in one or other way benefit all classes, (*Hear, hear.*) the benefit of each taking various forms. The interests of us all are the same. We are all in the same boat. We must sink or swim together. Government cannot but treat us all alike. It is unreasonable for us to expect from them, and unjust and unwise for them to show, any undue favour to any particular class or community. The only solid foundation for them is justice and impartiality, and the only just demand from us also can only be justice and impartiality. (*Loud applause.*)

## PROSPEROUS COUNTRY IS GOOD FOR ALL.

If the country is prosperous, then if one gets scope in one walk of life, another will have in another walk of life. As our Indian saying goes: "If there is water in the well it will come to the cistern." If we have the well of prosperity we shall be able to draw each our share from it. But if the well is dry we must all go without any at all.

First Day.

The President's Inaugural Address.

## MORAL FORCE THE TRUE BASIS OF BRITISH STRENGTH IN INDIA.

A word for the basis upon which the strength of British power stands. Britain can hold India, or any one country can hold another, by moral force only. You can build up an empire by arms or ephemeral brute physical force, but you can preserve it by the eternal moral forces only. Brute force will, some time or other, break down ; righteousness alone is everlasting. *(Cheers).* Well and truly has Lord Ripon said "that the British power and influence rests upon the conviction of our good faith more than upon the valour of our soldiers or the reputation of our arms." *(Applause.)* Mr. Gladstone says: " It is the predominance of that moral force for which I heartily pray in the deliberations of this House and the conduct of our whole public policy, for I am convinced that upon that predominance depends that which should be the first object of all our desires, as it is of all our daily official prayers, namely, that union of heart and sentiment which constitutes the truest basis of strength at home, and therefore both of strength and good fame throughout the civilised world." *(Applause.)*

Debates, 9th August, 1892, p. 1892.

And here is a remarkable instance cited by Mr. Gladstone of a people of a different race becoming attached even to the much despised Turkish rule. How much more will the people of India, if contented and prosperous, become attached to the rule of such a people as the British? Referring to Lebanon, Mr. Gladstone said: "Owing to the wise efforts of Lord Dufferin and others about thirty years ago local management was established, since which the province has become contented and attached to the Turkish empire."

Lord Roberts, the apostle of British strong arm to maintain British power, and though much imbued with many of the prejudices against the progress of the Indians, as a true soldier admits without hesitation what he considers as the only solid foundation upon which British strength must for ever rest. He says: "But however efficient and well equipped the army of India may be, were it indeed absolute perfection and were its numbers considerably more than they are at present, our greatest strength must ever rest on the firm base of a united and contented India."

Truer and more statesmanlike words could not be uttered. Permit me to give one more extract. Mr. Gladstone, referring to Irish Home Rule, said: "There can be no nobler spectacle than that which we think is now drawing upon us, the spectacle of a nation deliberately set on the removal of injustice, deliberately determined to break, not through terror and not in haste, but under the sole influence of duty and honour, determined to break with whatever remains still existing of an evil tradition, and determined in that way at once to pay a debt of justice and to consult by a bold, wise, and good act its own interests and its own honour."

Am I at all unreasonable in hoping that such noble statesmanship, honour, and good faith of the British people will, in fulness of time, also extend to India similar justice? I shall hope as long as I live.

## INDIANS ABOVE EVERYTHING.

Let us always remember that we are all children of our mother country. Indeed, I have never worked in any other spirit than that I am an Indian, *(cheers.)* and owe duty to my country and all any countrymen. Whether I am a Hindu, a Muhammadan, a Parsi, a Christian, or any other creed, I am above all an Indian. Our couatry is India; our nationality is Indian. *(Loud cheers.)*

First Day.

The President's Inangural Address.

### OUR DUTY.

The question for us, especially a body like this, who have received the blessings of education, is How are we to perform our duty to our country? Certainly no one requires to be taught that no great cause or object can ever be accomplished without great sacrifices—personal and pecuniary. We can never succeed with the British people by mere declamations. We must show that we believe in the justice of our cause by our earnestness and self-sacrifice. (*Hear, hear.*)

### SELF-SACRIFICE—EXAMPLE OF BRITISH PEOPLE.

I desire now to impress upon my countrymen with all the earnestness I am capable of to prepare themselves for sacrifices. We observe every day what sacrifices the British people make for attaining any object, great or small, and how persistently they stick to it; and among the lessons which we are learning from them let us learn this particular one, with the double advantage and effect of showing that Indians have public spirit and love of their country, and also proving that they are earnest in what they are asking. (*applause.*)

### WORK WILL GO ON INCREASING—NECESSITY OF PERFECT ORGANISATION.

Our work for the amelioration of our country and for obtaining all the rights and benefits of British citizenship will go on increasing, and it is absolutely necessary that our organisation, both here and in the United Kingdom, should be much improved and made complete. Without good organisation no important work can be successfully done; and that means much pecuniary and personal sacrifice. We must remember the Congress meets once a year. The general secretaries and the Standing Committees have to carry out the details and inform the circles of the work and resolutions of the Congress.

### THE PROVINCIAL CONFERENCES WILL DO THEIR PROVINCIAL WORK.

But the most important and national work formulated by the Congress has to be done with watchfulness, day after day, in London by your British Committee. (*cheers.*) And, further, by your Resolution XII. of the seventh Session, you "urged them (the Committee) to widen henceforth

### THE SPHERE OF THEIR USEFULNESS

by interesting themselves not only in those questions dealt with by the Congress, but in all Indian matters submitted to them and properly vouched for in which any principle accepted by the Congress is involved." (*Renewed cheering.*)

Fancy what this means. Why, it is another India Office! You have put all India's every-day work upon the shoulders of the Committee. It becomes exceedingly necessary for efficient and good work to have some paid person or persons to devote time to study the merits of all the representations which pour in with every mail, or by telegrams, before any action can be taken on them. It is in the United Kingdom that all our great fights are to be fought, all our national and imperial questions are to be settled, and it is to our British Committee in London that we have to look for the performance of all this responsible and arduous work, with the unfortunate feature that we have to contend against many adverse influences, prepossessions and misunderstandings. We have to make the British people unlearn a good deal.

### MANY BRITISH FRIENDS AND ANGLO-INDIANS WILLING TO WORK.

On the other hand, we have this hopeful feature also—that we have not only many British friends, but also Anglo-Indians, who, in the true spirit of justice and of the gratitude to the country to which they owe their past career and future provision, appreciate the duty they owe to India, and are desirous to help us, and to preserve the British Empire by the only certain means of justice, the honour and righteousness of the British people, and by the contentment and prosperity of India.

### THE FRIENDS WHO ARE NOW WORKING.

You know well how much we owe to the present English members of our Committee, Sir William Wedderburn, (*Three cheers for Sir William Wedderburn.*) Mr. Hume, Mr. Reynolds, Mr. Adam, Mr. Schwann, M. P., and Mr. McLaren, M. P. If we want all such help at the fountain head of power and without which we cannot do much good, we must take care to supply them always, promptly and accurately, all necessary sinews of war. (*Hear, hear and applause.*)

### "INDIA."

Then there is the journal "INDIA," without which our work will not be half as efficient as with it. It is an absolute necessity as an instrument and part of the organisation. Every possible effort must be made to give it the widest circulation possible both here and in the United Kingdom. I wish it could be made weekly instead of monthly.

With proper effort ten thousand copies should be easily disposed of here as a beginning, and we *must* do this.

### MY THANKS.

This is the first opportunity I have of meeting you after the Congress of 1886, over which I had the honour to preside at Calcutta. Let me now thank you personally for your constant remembrance of me, for your unceasing encouragement, and for your two most kind and gratifying Resolutions passed at the last two Sessions as representatives of every class and creed, and almost wholly consisting of Hindu and Muhammadan delegates, and each delegate being elected by and representative of the whole mixed community of the place he represents, on the basis of common interest and nationality. I must beg your indulgence to record those Resolutions in this address. The first Resolution (XIV) passed by the Seventh Congress in 1891, while I was a candidate, is this :—

> " Resolved, that this Congress hereby puts formally on record its high esteem and deep appreciation of the great services which Mr. Dadabhai Naoroji has rendered, during more than a quarter of a century, to the cause of India, and it expresses its unshaken confidence in him, and its earnest hope that he may prove successful at the coming election, in his candidature for Central Finsbury ; and at the same time tenders, on behalf of the vast population it represents, India's most cordial acknowledgments to all in England, whether in Central Finsbury or elsewhere, who have aided or may aid him to win a seat in the House of Commons."

I need not say how right earnestly Central Finsbury listened to your appeal and fulfilled your hope, for which we owe them our most unstinted thanks, and to all those who helped in or out of Central Finsbury. (*Loud applause.*)

I may here once more express my hearty thanks to many ladies and gentlemen who worked hard for my election. After I was elected, you passed the second Resolution (XVI.) in the last Session. I may point here to the significant incident that in that Congress there was, I think, only one Parsi delegate, and he even not the delegate of Parsis, but of all classes of the people. This Resolution was :—

> "Resolved that this Congress most respectfully and cordially tenders, on behalf of the vast population it represents, India's most heartfelt thanks to the Electors of

Central Finsbury for electing Mr. Dadabhai Naoroji their Member in the House of Commons; and it again puts on record its high esteem and deep appreciation of the services which that gentleman has rendered to this country, reiterates its unshaken confidence in him, and looks upon him as India's representative in the House of Commons."

Let me also now take this opportunity, on Indian soil, to tender my most heartfelt thanks for the telegrams, letters, and addresses of congratulation which I received from all parts and classes of India—literally I may say from the prince to the peasant, from members of all creeds, from Hindus, Muhammadans, Christians, Parsis, from Ceylon, from the High Priest of Budhists, and Budhists, and other residents from the Cape, British Guiana, Australia, and in short from every part of the British Empire where there were Indian residents. Ladies and Gentlemen, put aside my personality and let me join in your rejoicings as an Indian in the great event in Indian annals of an Indian finding his way in the Imperial Parliament. (*Loud and Prolonged Cheering.*)

And lastly, beginning from the distant Western Gate of India, where the Indian residents of Aden, of all creeds, gave me a most hearty reception ; then the great portal of India, the dear old City of my birth, gave me a most magnificent welcome with its never-ceasing kindness towards me, Poona doing her best to vie with Bombay, and through Punjab so splendidly ; and this series of welcome now ending in your extraordinary one which I am utterly unable to describe. Is there any reward more grand and more gratifying than the esteem, the joy with my joy, the sorrow with my sorrow, and above all the "unshaken confidence" of my fellow-countrymen and country-women of our grand, old, beloved country.

## CONGRATULATIONS IN THE UNITED KINGDOM.

I may refer to an incident which, as it is satisfactory, is also very significant of the real desire of the British people to do justice to India. The congratulations on my election from all parts of the United Kingdom also were as hearty and warm as we could desire, and expressing satisfaction that an Indian would be able to voice the wants and aspirations of India in the House of Commons.

I can assure the Congress that, as I hope and wish, if you will pay an early visit to the United Kingdom and hold a Session there, you will obtain a kind and warm reception from its peoples. And you will, by such direct and personal appeal to the British Nation, accomplish a vast amount of good. (*Hear, hear.*)

## OUR FATE AND OUR FUTURE,

Our fate and our future are in our own hands. If we are true to ourselves and to out country and make all the necessary sacrifices for our elevation and amelioration, I, for one have not the shadow of a doubt that in dealing with such justice-loving, fair-minded people as the British, we may rest fully assured that we shall not work in vain. It is this conviction which has supported me against all difficulties. I have never faltered in my faith in the British character and have always believed that the time will come when the sentiments of the British Nation and our Gracious Sovereign proclaimed to us in our Great Charter of the Proclamation of 1858 will be realised, (*applause*) viz., "In their prosperity will be our strength, in their contentment our best reward." And let us join in the prayer that followed this hopeful declaration of our Sovereign : "May the God of all power grant to us and to those in authority under us strength to carry out these our wishes for the good ot our people."

My last prayer and exhortation to the Congress and to all my countrymen is—Go on united and earnest, in concord and harmony, with moderation, with loyalty to the British rule and patriotism towards our country, and success is sure to attend our efforts for our just demands, and the day I hope is not distant when the World will see the noblest spectacle of a great nation like the British holding out the hand of true fellow-citizenship and of justice to the vast mass of humanity of this great and ancient land of India with benefits and blessings to the human race. (*Loud and Prolonged Cheering.*)

**First Day.**

**The President's Inaugural Address.**

Syed Nazir Hussain Nazim, Persian Poet, (*Lahore, No. 268, in list*) read an Urdu poem specially composed in honour of the occasion. The poet was applauded several times while reading the poem.

**Election of a Subjects Committee.**

The President: The next business I have to do, is to call upon you to appoint your Subjets Committee.

Mr. Hume, (*Calcutta, No. 1, in list*): It is my duty to read out the names of the gentlemen proposed, but as I have been suffering from inflamation of the lungs I must ask Mr. Mudholkar to perform that duty.

The following are the names of the Delegates proposed to serve on the Subjects Committee:—

| Circle | | Name | | No. | Place |
|---|---|---|---|---|---|
| CALCUTTA CIRCLE. (Includes the Presidency and Burdwan Divisions, Orissa, Assam, Sylhet, and Cachar.) | 1 | THE HON'BLE SURENDRA NATH BANERJI | ... | No. 8, | (CALCUTTA.) |
| | 2 | KALI CHARAN BANERJI, ESQ. | ... | „ 10, | do. |
| | 3 | J. GHOSAL, ESQ. | ... | „ 5, | do. |
| | 4 | REV. C. N. BANERJI | ... | „ 11, | do. |
| | 5 | DR. JAGADISH CHANDRA LAHIRI. | | „ 9, | do. |
| | 6 | PUNDIT KALI PRASANNA KAVYA-BISHARAD | ... | „ 12, | do. |
| | 7 | DR. MOHINI MOHUN BOSE | ... | „ 6, | do. |
| | 8 | BABU BENODE BEHARY BOSE | ... | „ 4, | do. |
| | 9 | RAI JOTINDRA NATH CHAUDHURY. | | „ 7, | do. |
| | 10 | BABU UPENDRA NATH SEN | ... | „ 13, | do. |
| | 11 | „ PRAFULLA CHANDRA GHOSE. | | „ 14, | (24-Perghanas.) |
| | 12 | „ BAIKUNTHA NATH SEN | ... | „ 16, | (Murshidabad.) |
| | 13 | „ MOTI LAL BANERJI | ... | „ 17, | do. |
| | 14 | „ RAMANI MOHUN MULLIK | ... | „ 23, | (Nuddea.) |
| | 15 | „ AMBICA CHARAN MOITRA | ... | „ 26, | do. |
| | 16 | „ VENI BHUSAN ROY | ... | „ 28, | (Khulna.) |
| | 17 | „ AKSHOY KUMAR MITRA | ... | „ 27, | (Jessore.) |
| | 18 | „ KRISHNA KUMAR MITRA | ... | „ 29, | (Mymeasingh.) |
| | 19 | „ PRASANNA KUMAR BOSE | ... | „ 30, | do. |
| | 20 | „ DINA NATH BISWAS | ... | „ 31, | do. |
| DACCA CIRCLE. (Includes the District of Dacca.) | 1 | BABU JAGAT CHANDRA ROY | ... | „ 32, | (Dacca.) |
| | 2 | „ SARAT CHANDRA BOSE | ... | „ 33, | do. |
| | 3 | „ SARAT CHUNDER GUPTA | ... | „ 34, | do. |
| FURRIDPORE CIRCLE. (Includes the District of Furridpore.) | 1 | BABU AMBICA CHARAN MOZOOMDAR. | | „ 35, | (Furridpore.) |
| | 2 | „ PRITHVIS CHANDRA ROY CHAUDHURY. | ... | „ 36, | do. |
| | 3 | „ GORA CHAND DAS | ... | „ 37, | do. |

**First Day.**

**Election of a Subjects Committee.**

| Circle | | Name | | No. | Place |
|---|---|---|---|---|---|
| BARISAL CIRCLE. (Includes the District of Barisal.) | 1 | BABU NIBARAN CHANDRA DAS ... | No. | 38, | (Barisal.) |
| RUNGPORE CIRCLE. (Includes the District of Rungpore.) | 1 | BABU RAM KUMAR BOSE ... | „ | 39, | (Rungpore.) |
| PUBNA CIRCLE. (Includes the District of Pubna.) | 1 | BABU MOHINI MOHAN CHAKRAVARTY. ... | „ | 40, | (Pubna.) |
| | 2 | „ MOHENDRA NARAIN CHAKRAVARTY. ... | „ | 41, | do. |
| JALPAIGURI CIRCLE. (Includes the District of Jalpaiguri.) | 1 | BABU UMAGATI ROY ... | „ | 42, | (Jalpaiguri.) |
| RAMPORE BEAULEAH CIRCLE. (Includes the District of Rajshahye.) | 1 | DR. AKSHOY KUMAR BHADURI ... | „ | 43, | (Rampore Beauleah.) |
| | 2 | BABU RAMA PRASAD MULLIK ... | „ | 44, | (Maldah.) |
| BHAGALPORE CIRCLE. (Includes the entire Bhagalpore Division.) | 1 | BABU JOGENDRA NATH MUKERJEE. | „ | 45, | (Purneah.) |
| | 2 | „ PARVATI CHARAN DAS ... | „ | 46, | do. |
| | 3 | „ UGRA MOHUN THAKOOR ... | „ | 47, | (Bhagalpore.) |
| CHOTA NAGPUR CIRCLE. (includes the entire Chota Nagpur Division.) | 1 | RAI JADU NATH MUKERJEE ... | „ | 49, | (Hazaribagh.) |
| | 2 | MUNSHI MATHURA PRASAD ... | „ | 53, | (Giridih.) |
| | 3 | BABU SAKTI KANTA BHATTACHARYYA. | „ | 54, | do. |
| BEHAR CIRCLE. (includes the Patna Division, except the Mozufferpur District.) | 1 | BABU GURU PRASAD SEN ... | „ | 57, | (Bankipore.) |
| | 2 | RADHIKA PRASAD GHOSE, ESQ ... | „ | 59, | (Chupra.) |
| BENARES CIRCLE. (includes the Benares Division.) | 1 | BABU JAGAT NARAIN SINHA ... | „ | 60, | (Benares.) |
| | 2 | PUNDIT SRINATH DEVA ... | „ | 62, | do. |
| | 3 | BABU SRIRAM ... | „ | 67, | (Mirzapur.) |
| | 4 | „ BENI PRASAD ... | „ | 69, | do. |
| | 5 | ALFRED NUNDY, ESQ. ... | „ | 169, | (Gorakhpur.) |
| N. W. PCES CIRCLE. (includes whole N. W. Pces. except the Benares Division.) | 1 | HON'BLE RAJA RAMPAL SING ... | „ | 70, | (Allahabad.) |
| | 2 | „ CHAROO CHUNDRA MITTRA. | „ | 71, | do. |
| | 3 | PUNDIT MADAN MOHAN MALAVYA. | „ | 73, | do. |
| | 4 | „ SUNDER LAL ... | „ | 75, | do. |
| | 5 | „ PRITHVI NATH ... | „ | 93, | (Cawnpore.) |
| | 6 | BABU KEDAR NATH ... | „ | 101, | (Agra.) |
| | 7 | CHOWBEY DAMMI LAL ... | „ | 113, | (Mainpuri.) |
| | 8 | HAFIZ MAHOMED ABDUR RAHIM. | „ | 128, | (Aligarh.) |
| | 9 | BABU JYOTI PRASAD ... | „ | 138, | (Shaharanpur.) |
| | 10 | PUNDIT RAM PRASAD ... | „ | 143, | (Meerut.) |
| | 11 | MUNSHI BHAKTAWAR SINGH ... | „ | 153, | (Shajehanpur.) |

First Day.

Election of a Subjeets Committee.

| Circle | No. | Name | | Reg. No. | Place |
|---|---|---|---|---|---|
| OUDH CIRCLE. (Includes the entire Province of Oudh.) | 1 | BABU BANSI LAL SINGH | ... | No. 173, | (Lucknow.) |
| | 2 | MUNSHI GUNGA PRASAD VARMA. | | „ 175, | do. |
| | 3 | MR. MAHOMED NASIM | ... | „ 179, | do. |
| | 4 | MR. HAMID ALI KHAN | ... | „ 181, | do. |
| | 5 | BABU GOKUL CHAND | ... | „ 188, | (Fyzabad.) |
| DELHI CIRCLE. (Includes the Delhi Division.) | 1 | ABUL AL MONSUR | ... | „ 193, | (Delhi.) |
| | 2 | BABU KEDAR NATH | ... | „ 198, | do. |
| | 3 | LALA GIRDHARI LAL | ... | „ 200, | do. |
| | 4 | BABU PYARI LAL | ... | „ 204, | do. |
| | 5 | LALA GIRDHARI LAL | ... | „ 218, | do. |
| PUNJAB CIRCLE. (Includes the whole Punjab except the Delhi Division.) | 1 | E. C. JASSAWALA, ESQ. | ... | „ 227, | (Lahore,) |
| | 2 | LALA HARKISHEN LAL, B.A. | ... | „ 228, | do. |
| | 3 | BABU JOGENDRA CHUNDER BOSE. | | „ 231, | do. |
| | 4 | LALA MADAN GOPAL, M.A. | ... | „ 232, | do. |
| | 5 | „ DHANPAT RAI, B.A., L.L.B. | ... | „ 235, | do. |
| | 6 | „ LAJPAT RAI | ... | „ 237, | do. |
| | 7 | BAKSHI JAISHI RAM | ... | „ 243, | do. |
| | 8 | LALA LAL CHAND | ... | „ 247, | do. |
| | 9 | „ SADANAND | ... | „ 253, | do. |
| | 10 | MUNSHI NABI BUKSH KHAN | ... | „ 264, | do. |
| | 11 | MOULVIE MOHURREM ALI CHISTE. | | „ 266, | do. |
| | 12 | MIR NISARALI SHOHRAT | ... | „ 267, | do. |
| | 13 | SYED NAZIR HUSSAIN NAZIM | ... | „ 268, | do. |
| | 14 | MOULVIE WALLIULLAH | ... | „ 272, | do. |
| | 15 | MUNSHI GOLAM MAHOMED | ... | „ 273, | do. |
| | 16 | LALA DHARAMDAS SURI | ... | „ 275, | do. |
| | 17 | „ GANPAT RAI | ... | „ 278, | do. |
| | 18 | CHARLES GOLOKNATH, ESQ. | ... | „ 280, | do. |
| | 19 | RAI BAHADUR P. C. CHATTERJEE. | | „ 283, | do. |
| | 20 | LALA BALMUKUND | ... | „ 298, | do. |
| | 21 | DR. PARMANAND | ... | „ 302, | do. |
| | 22 | K. P. ROY, ESQ. | ... | „ 304, | do. |
| | 23 | LALA SANGAM LAL | ... | „ 313, | do. |
| | 24 | LALA CHETAN ANAND | ... | „ 360, | (Mooltan.) |
| | 25 | „ HARBHAGWAN DAS | ... | „ 374, | (Jhelum.) |
| | 26 | SIRDIR GAJJAN SINGH | ... | „ 392, | (Ludhiana.) |
| | 27 | LALA JIVAN KISHEN | ... | „ 410, | (Gujranwalla.) |
| | 28 | PUNDIT SHEO NARAIN | ... | „ 441, | (Jullundur.) |
| | 29 | RAIZADA BHAGAT RAM | ... | „ 442, | do. |
| | 30 | LALA HANSRAJ SEWHNEY | ... | „ 452, | (Shahpur Bhera.) |
| | 31 | SIRDIR CHANDA SINGH BHIND | ... | „ 502, | (Ferozepur.) |
| | 32 | SHEIKH UMAR BUKSH | ... | „ 522, | (Hoshiarpur.) |
| | 33 | „ NABI BUKSH | ... | „ 568, | (Gurdaspur.) |
| | 34 | LALA DWARKA DAS | ... | „ 589, | (Umballa) |
| | 35 | „ MURLIDHAR | ... | „ 591, | do. |
| | 36 | „ KANAHYE LAL | ... | „ 636, | (Amritsar.) |
| SINDH CIRCLE. (Includes the entire province of Sindh.) | 1 | SHIVANDAS NOOMAL, ESQ. | ... | „ 674, | (Kurrachee.) |
| | 2 | TAHILRAM KHEM CHAND, ESQ. | ... | „ 675, | do. |
| | 3 | HIRANAND KHEM SINGH, ESQ. | ... | „ 696, | do. |

| First Day. — Election of a Subjects Committee. | | | | |
|---|---|---|---|---|
| SINDH CIRCLE.—(contd:) | 4 MUTHRADAS RAM CHAND, ESQ. ... | No. 697, | (Kurrachee.) |
| | 5 HEMATSINGH GAJSINGH ADVANI, ESQ. ... | „ 700, | (Shikarpur.) |
| | 6 R. B. PESUMAL ZOKIRAM, ESQ. ... | „ 718, | (Sukkur.) |
| AHMEDABAD CIRCLE. (Includes the Ahmedabad District, Cutch and Kattiwar, Rajcot.) | 1 RUNCHHODLAL VANDRAWANDAS PATWARI, ESQ. ... | „ 722, | (Ahmedabad.) |
| | 2 SETH PURSHOTTAMBHAI MAGHANBAI HATTISING ... | „ 728, | do. |
| SURAT CIRCLE. (Includes Surat and Broach.) | 1 HARDEORAM NANABHAI HARIDAS, ESQ. ... | „ 729, | (Surat.) |
| SHOLAPUR CIRCLE. (Includes only the Sholapur District.) | 1 SHRIDHAR NARAYAN SATHAYE, ESQ. | No. 730, | (Sholapur.) |
| BELGAUM CIRCLE. (Includes only the Belgaum District.) | 1 SADASIVA BALKRISHNA BHATE, ESQ. | „ 733, | (Belgaum.) |
| | 2 HON'BLE VISHNU RAGHUNATH NATU ... | „ 734, | do. |
| BHUSAWAL CIRCLE. (Includes only the Bhusawal District.) | 1 RAO SAHEB VITHAL GOVIND DASTANE ... | „ 736, | (Bhusawal.) |
| | 2 ABAJI RAGHU MAHALAS, ESQ. ... | „ 737, | (Jalgaon.) |
| SATARA CIRCLE. (Includes only the Satara District.) | 1 BALVANT SHRIDHAR SAHASRABUDHE, ESQ. ... | „ 738, | (Satara.) |
| | 2 RAGHUNATH PANDURANG KARANDIKAR, ESQ. ... | „ 741, | do. |
| | 3 DATTATRAYA BALVANT PARAMES, ESQ. ... | „ 742, | do. |
| DECCAN CIRCLE. (Includes the Deccan except the Sholapur, Belgaum and Nugger Districts; and Khandesh except the Bhusawal District.) | 1 KASHINATH GOVIND NATU, ESQ. ... | „ 745, | (Poona.) |
| | 2 PROFESSOR GOPAL KRISHNA GOKHALE ... | „ 749, | do. |
| | 3 RAGHUNATH DAJI NAGARKAR, ESQ. | „ 756, | do. |
| | 4 RAO BAHADUR VISHNU MORESHWAR BHIDE ... | „ 758, | do. |
| | 5 BALGANGADHAR TILAK, ESQ. ... | „ 760, | do. |
| | 6 RAJARAM YESHWANT RAJE, ESQ. ... | „ 770, | (Nasik.) |
| ICHALKERANJI CIRCLE. (Includes the Southern Marhatta Country.) | 1 DATTATRAYA GANESH TIKAKAR, ESQ. ... | „ 773, | (Ichalkeranji.) |
| BOMBAY CIRCLE. (Includes the Bombay island, Colaba, Thana and Ratnagiri Districts.) | 1 DAJI ABAJI KHARE, ESQ. ... | „ 779, | (Bombay.) |
| | 2 DR. K. N. BHADURJI ... | „ 780, | do. |
| | 3 W. A. CHAMBERS, ESQ. ... | „ 781, | do. |
| | 4 DINSHAW EDULJI WACHA, ESQ. ... | „ 782, | do. |
| | 5 HARI SITARAM DIXIT, ESQ. ... | „ 784, | do. |
| | 6 DR. BHALCHANDRA KRISHNA ... | „ 786, | do. |
| | 7 DR. MORESHWAR GOPAL DESHMUKH ... | „ 790, | do. |

| | | | | |
|---|---|---|---|---|
| BOMBAY CIRCLE.—<br>*(contd.)* | 8 SITARAM BALLAL JOGLEKAR, ESQ. | No. 794, | (Thana.) | **First Day.**<br>**Election of a Subjects Committee.** |
| BERAR. CIRCLE.<br>(Includes the whole of Berar.) | 1 RAGNATH NARSING MUDHOLKAR, ESQ. ... | „ 798, | (Amraoti.) | |
| | 2 GANESH SRIKRISHNA KHAPARDE, ESQ. ... | „ 800, | do. | |
| | 3 RAO SAHEB DEORAO VINAYEK ... | „ 804, | do. | |
| NAGPUR CIRCLE.<br>(Includes the whole of the C. Pces.) | 1 KESHAV VINAYEK JOSHI, ESQ. ... | „ 815, | (Nagpur.) | |
| | 2 C. V. NAIDU, ESQ, ... | „ 816, | do. | |
| | 3 DR. ADHAR SING GOUR ... | „ 817, | do. | |
| | 4 R. SRINIVASARAO NAIDU, ESQ. ... | „ 818, | do. | |
| | 5 GANPATRAO NARAYAN GOKHALE, ESQ. ... | „ 819, | do. | |
| | 6 HARI MAHADEO PUNDIT, ESQ. ... | „ 820, | do. | |
| | 7 BALIRAM NARAYAN DESHMUKH, ESQ. ... | „ 830, | (Chhindwara.) | |
| | 8 ALI MAHOMED BHIMJI, ESQ. ... | „ 834, | (Harda.) | |
| | 9 KESHAVRAO MAHADEO KOULE, ESQ. | „ 836, | (Wardha.) | |
| MADRAS CIRCLE.<br>(Includes the entire Madras Presidency.) | 1 G. SUBRAMANIA IYER, ESQ. ... | „ 837, | (Madras.) | |
| | 2 RAI BAHADUR P. ANAND CHARLU. | „ 838, | do. | |
| | 3 PETER PAUL PILLAY, ESQ. ... | „ 839, | do. | |
| | 4 C. VENKATA CHARIAR, ESQ. ... | „ 841, | (Salem.) | |
| | 5 W. VIRASWAMY IYER, ESQ. ... | „ 843, | do. | |
| | 6 K. P. ACHHUTHA MENON, ESQ ... | „ 846, | (Palghat.) | |
| | 7 HON'BLE C. SANKARAN NAIR ... | „ 849, | (Calicut.) | |
| | 8 K. P. RAMAN MENON, ESQ. ... | „ 850, | do. | |
| | 9 C. K. RAMAN MENON; ESQ. ... | „ 851, | do. | |
| | 10 RAO BAHADUR C. JAMBULINGAM MUDALIAR ... | „ 852, | (Cuddapah. | |
| | 11 N. S. RAJARAM, ESQ. ... | „ 853, | (Tanjore.) | |
| | 12 HON'BLE N. SUBBARAO PANTULU GARU ... | „ 856, | (Rajahmundry.) | |
| | 13 O. V. JAGANNADHA SHASTRI, ESQ. | „ 860, | (Vizagapatam.) | |
| | 14 HANUMANTH GOND, ESQ. ... | „ 861, | (Bellary.) | |
| | 15 T. CHIDAMBARA ROW, ESQ. ... | „ 865, | (Kurnool.) | |
| | 16 K. V. SUBRAMANIA IYER, ESQ. ... | „ 866, | (Sivaganga.) | |
| | 17 S.M.NARAYAN SWAMY IYER, ESQ. | „ 867, | do. | |

**Adjournment of the Assembly.**

The President: you have heard the names of the gentlemen proposed, read to you, do you approve of them as read?

Adopted unanimously.

The President: The Subjects Committee will meet in half an hour, at the adjoining hotel where Mr. Hume and a few of us are residing, whilst this assembly adjourns until to-morrow (Thursday) at 2 o'clock.

# SECOND DAY'S PROCEEDINGS.

## Thursday, 28th December, 1893.

THE Delegates and Visitors assembled to-day at 2 P. M.

**Second day.**

The President said: Ladies and Gentlemen, we now begin our business and I have no doubt that in the arduous task of regulating our deliberations I shall have every support and indulgence from the audience. I need not waste more words, for time is precious and I now call upon Mr. R. N. Mudholkar to move the first resolution. *(Loud applause.)*

**Resolution I.**

**Reformed and Enlarged Legislative Councils.**

Mr. R. N. Mudholkar *(Berar, No. 798, in list)* who was received with applause said: Mr. President, ladies and gentlemen, the first motion which I have the honour of submiting for your consideration runs as follows :—

*That this Congress while tendering its most sincere thanks to His Excellency the Viceroy for the liberal spirit in which he has endeavoured to give effect to the Indian Councils' Act of 1892, regrets to have to put on record the facts, that alike in the Rules of the Government of India and in the practice of most of the Local Governments, notably in that of the Government of Bombay, material alterations are necessary if real effect is to be given to the spirit of this act, and, that the Punjab, one of the most important Provinces in the Empire, is still denied the right to be represented, either in the Viceroy's or in any Local Council*

Sheikh Umar Buksh, *(Lahore, No. 522, in list)* translated the motion into Urdu.

Mr. Mudholkar said: This motion, gentlemen, consists of several parts; I shall not deal with every part of it, but confine my remarks to such general considerations as are necessary and refer in special to the rules issued by the Viceroy for his own Council, and leave to others, who come after me, the consideration of the rules framed with regard to Local Councils. Gentlemen, you know that the reform and enlargement of the Legislative Councils has been always the main plank in the platform of the Congress. From the time of the first Congress this has been considered as the subject which deserved before all others a place in the forefront of matters for our consideration, and it is a matter of congratulation to be able to say that in this important matter we have obtained a measure of success. *(Applause.)* The success certainly is not as great as we wished, but there is some measure of success. The demand for the enlargement and reform of the Legislative Councils has indeed been made for many years, long before the Congress came into existence, but it has been from the time that the Congress took the subject earnestly in hand that the Government have felt themselves constrained to take the matter into consideration. *(Hear, hear.)*

In 1887 Lord Dufferin sent a despatch to the Secretary of State asking for the enlargement and reform of the Legislative Council. After his departure, and when Lord Lansdowne took the reins of Government, the subject was referred to him and he made a report similar to that of his predecessor. In three sessions of Parliament, Bills were brought in for carrying out this object, but it was only, however, last year, 1892, that an Act was passed. The Conservative Government was in almost the last year of its existence when the Bill was first placed before Parliament and it saw signs sufficient to make it careful that if it did not pass the Act, a measure of a much more liberal kind would be

Second day.

Resolution I.

Reformed and Enlarged Legislative Councils.

enacted. They therefore passed the Act of 1892. It did not give to us exactly what we wanted or in the manner we wanted, but it gave us this much. In the Act there is permission, so to say, granted to the Viceroy to select or elect persons for nomination to his Council. By the Act there is no right of election as such granted, but in the nominations the Viceroy has to make, he is empowered to make rules with the sanction of the Secretary of State, and in making those rules a wide discretion is left to him. Last year when the Act was passed, we took this matter into consideration and this was the resolution we passed. "That this Congress while accepting in a loyal spirit the Indian Councils' Act recently enacted by the Parliament of Great Britain, as explained by the present Prime Minister, with the assent of the then Under-Secretary of State for India—that it is intended by it to give the people of India *a real living representation* in the Legislative Councils,—regrets that the Act itself does not in terms concede to the people the right of electing their own representatives to the Council, and hopes and expects that the rules, now being prepared under the Act, will be framed on the lines of Mr. Gladstone's declaration in the House of Commons, and will do adequate justice to the people of this country; further, that it prays that these rules may be published in the official Gazettes like other proposed Legislative measures, before being finally adopted." Our demand with regard to the Legislative Council was four-fold. We wanted an increase of the number of members and wanted that a portion of the members should be elected, we wanted that the budget and all financial matters should be placed before the Legislative Councils for consideration and discussion and lastly, we wanted the right of nterpellation. Now the Act is merely permissive in all these matters, but though permissive it must be thankfully accepted and it must be thankfully acknowledged, that the permission which is given, is given in such a way and with such guarantees that we have every reason to look forward to a bright and happy future. Statesmen of both parties, when the Bill came on for discussion, pledged themselves that there should be a real living representation. Although the Act does not contain anything about election, the Viceroy has to frame such rules as will enable him to obtain the opinions of representative classes and communities and on those opinions he is to base his nominations. Mr. Gladstone on the side of the Liberal Party once announced views which ought to infuse hopefulness in us. The Act after it was passed was sent to India and H. E. the Viceroy had to frame rules and it is a matter of satisfaction to us that when the Viceroy announced his intention with regard to these matters, his announcement was very satisfactory. He said that the budget will be annually and regularly submitted to the Legislative Council and he also stated that the right of interpellation would be granted and he further announced that the number of members would be increased. He also announced that rules would be Issued for giving a sort of a right of election. What he has done in the matter of the increase of members is this. With regard to the Viceregal Council he has announced his intention that as many as ten persons will be appointed from the non-official communities. With respect to the right of electing these persons, he has announced that four of them will be selected by the four Local Legislative Councils, one from Bengal, one from the North-west Provinces, one from Bombay and one from Madras. Each of the Legislative Councils of these Presidencies will elect a member to represent them and he shall be a non-official. Then with regard to the other provinces, which have not got any Legislative Councils, he said that though at that time he could not exactly formulate his policy he would, however, arrange so that those Provinces should be represented in a manner similar to the four Presidencies. Well, as I said, gentlemen, we have not got as many members in the Legislative Council as we wished and asked for, but there is some increase. Then again, though the right of election itself is not granted by the act there is some kind of election granted. So far we may say, good. With reference to the Local Legislative Councils, the number has also been increased. In Bengal and the North-West Provinces the maximum limit has been allowed to be reached and in Bombay and Madras also a considerable advance has been made. As to the Budget, as I have already said, H. E. the Viceroy announced that it would be annually placed before the Legislative Council, and he also said that the right of interpellation would be granted with certain restrictions. As to these points I should like to address a few remarks to you. About the Budget the rules run only to this extent, that the Annual Budget will be printed and circulated, so to say, amongst the members, and on that day on which it is to come up, such members as have any remarks to offer may then offer them. There may be some discussion but there is to be no vote. Now as I said in the beginning, we are thankful to the Viceroy for what he has done. He loyally accepted the Act with the declaration with which it was accompanied and he has not tried to take away what the Act gave us. So far we are thankful to him; but with regard to these matters, in my own opinion, and I believe in saying so I reflect the opinion of the majority of my brother delegates, His Excellency has not gone so far as he could have gone without danger to the Government. On the Budget there is to be no vote—a mere discussion followed by no expression of opinion or without ascertaining the views of those present. A mere discussion without any expression of opinion or without ascertaining the views of those present will not be of much value; it might, perhaps, enable Government to explain their own views, but it will not enable Government or the outside public, or the English public, to ascertain what were the views of the country with regard to these financial proposals. If there is one matter in regard to which we are most vitally interested, it is the financial question. (*Hear, hear.*) In the House of Commons, to which as a last resource, we have to appeal, we find the Indian Budget night is a night on which the House is almost empty. Fortunately this year it was not so but it is generally the case. The control of Indian finance is weak and if it is to be properly kept in hand then there should be effective control in India itself and that control cannot be exercised if in the Viceregal or in the Local Legislative Councils there is not to be any ascertainment of opinion. In that matter the Viceroy has not gone as far as he could. Then as to the right of interpellation the restrictions imposed are still greater. Questions are to be permitted and answers are to be given to them but after the answers are given there is to be no discussion. Now, without discussion it is useless to have any interpellation. I know that the viceroy has said that in the House of Commons interpellation is not allowed to be followed by any discussion, but then in that assembly they have got the right that we have not got in India, which is that of bringing forward motions. Here in India no motions can be brought forward, no divisions taken, or any proper ventilation of a grievance allowed and therefore with regard to this right of interpellation there could have been, with safety, a departure from the English practice to suit the Indian circumstances. These are the remarks I wish to offer on these two main points. There are other matters I should like to touch on, but in obedience to the order from the chair, I must certainly leave the platform, but before going I would only say this much, that we have made a beginning and although it is not as great as we wanted, it is still a beginning, and if the future is to be great it can only be great if we strive with might and main for it; if we strive with our heart and soul we shall get what we want, though we way have to wait for some years. In the meantime let us do our best to achieve success in what we have got.

PROFESSOR G. K. GOKHALE (*Poona, No. 749, in list*) seconded the motion and said:— MR. PRESIDENT, LADIES AND GENTLEMEN,—I have been asked to second the resolution which has been just now put before you by Mr. Mudholkar. The instructions of the Subjects Committee to me are that I should confine myself only to the Bombay Presidency, and I will, therefore, straight way proceed to a consideration of the rules that have been framed for that Presidency. Gentlemen, in regard to these rules, I will not say that they have been deliberately so framed as to defeat the object of the Act of 1892, but I will say this, that if the officer who drafted them had been asked to sit down with the deliberate purpose of framing a scheme to defeat that object, he could not have done better. (*Laughter and applause.*) Let me briefly explain what I mean. There are eight seats that have been thrown open to election in the Bombay Presidency. Of these, two are specifically assigned by the Government of India in their rules, namely, one to the Bombay University and one to the Bombay Municipal Corporation. This leaves six seats, and they have to be disposed of by the Bombay Government at their own discretion. It is in regard to these six seats that we have every reason to complain; for the Bombay Government have distributed them in such a manner that it will for all practical purposes have four of the seats at its own disposal. I must tell you that there are four divisions in the Bombay Presidency; there is, first of all, Sind, then the Northern Division, then the Central Division and then the Southern Division. With these four divisions I think the most natural thing for the Bombay Government to do was to assign one seat to each division, by allowing one to the Municipal and Local Boards alternately and so on, and the remaining two seats to the interests of trade and agriculture. Instead of doing that what Government has done is this. It has given two of the six seats to the European Mercantile Community, it has given one to the Sirdars of the Deccan, one to the Zemindars of Siad and only two seats go to the general public of the Presidency. In this matter Government appears to have entirely subverted the right principles of representation and put minorities above the general public, whereas what Government should always do is, first of all, to safeguard the interests of the general public and then take care of the interests of the minorities. (*Hear, hear and applause.*) I will now proceed to a more detailed consideration of the whole thing. There are three complaints we have to make. In the first place the European Mercantile community has got much more than it has a right to, whilst the Native Mercantile community of Bombay has been entirely ignored. The Bombay Chamber of Commerce gets one member and the Kurrachi Chamber gets one member. Lord Harris said in one of his speeches that a member was given to Kurrachi because the Chamber there represented trade interest to the extent of about fifteen crores, but you must remember that the Native Mercantile Community of Bombay has in its own hands trade to the extent of about 50 crores, but in spite of that fact the Native Mercantile Community has not got a single member. (*Shame.*) Then there is another complaint, and that is that the Central Division which is the most important division of the Presidency has been left absolutely unrepresented. (*Shame.*) This division is larger in area, larger in population and larger in the spread of education—generally larger in every respect, than the other three divisions of the Presidency; but in spite of this the Central Division has not been allowed a single seat, This Central Division has within its limits, Poona, Satara, and other places which are the home of the Marhatta population. With all these interests the division has not been allowed a single representative. Then it will be found if you examine Lord Harris's answers to the various memorials on the subject, that Government takes its stand upon very falacious principles. Lord Harris said he had to safe-guard the interest of a certain class, but he should have remembered that the intentions of the Legislative Act were such that the interests of the general public should be first represented because ninety-nine out of every hundred acts of legislation affect the interests of the general population. The Bombay Council passes laws like the Forest Act, Police Act, and the Abkari Act, all of which affected the interests of the general public and not of the Chamber of Commerce. (*Laughter and hear, hear.*) There was another thing that Lord Harris said in order to justify the representation he had given to the Sirdars and Zemindars and it was that these persons were supposed to be representatives of the ancient landed aristocracy, but in regard to these two classes we know that there is practically no education and that they are more or less under the thumb of the Political Officers and, therefore, election by these classes does not mean the samething as election by the Municipalities and Local Boards. (*Hear, hear.*) What Government say is this:—that these two classes have got representation because they represent the agricultural interest. I think a greater misrepresentation—I don't mean intentional misrepresentation—of the real state of things could not have been made by His Excellency, because if any class deserves to have its interests safeguarded, it is the peasant class and not the landlords, and the Sirdars and Zemindars represent the landlords and not peasants. The interests of the latter can only be represented through the Local Boards whose members are elected by the agriculturalists. I believe I have now pointed out the principal defects in the Bombay scheme and I cannot take more time—("*Go on*")—I must conform to the rules and stop, but in conclusion I should like to say that this expression of opinion on behalf of this Congress must show the Bombay Government and the Government of India what their failing is and I trust they will take an early opportunity to set matters right *(Loud applause.)*

PUNDIT BISHEN NARAYN DAR ( *Oudh, No. 184, in list* ) said :—MR. PRESIDENT, LADIES AND GENTLEMEN,—I have much pleasure in supporting the resolution now before you. I understand that to that resolution a rider has been suggested to be added by our friends who come from the North-West and Oudl to the effect that the North West and Oudh are in the same boat so far as the regulations are concerned as Bombay and if you have no objection to the addition of that rider then I will speak upon it as forming part of the resolution.

Mr. Hume: I must call your attention to the fact that this proposal was brought before the Subjects Committee and negatived and consequently if it is to be brought forward now it must be formally moved as an amendment.

Mr. Dar: I was told that it had only just been sent up to the President and I therefore mentioned it. Now, gentlemen, we too in the N. W. and Oudh have rules and regulations which have been framed under the Councils' Act and which are not very different from those to which reference has already been made by the gentleman from Bombay. We too have similar grievances with regard to the representation which has been accorded us under the new reform, and I will just point out to you one or two things in the rules framed under the Act for the N. W. and Oudh to show you how faulty and defective they are, and how they frustrate the very object of the Councils' Act; an object which was well expressed by Mr. Gladstone when he said that it was to give real, living representation to the people of India. *(Hear, hear.)* The first question that arises with regard to the regulations for my Province is, and I think I may here speak for other provinces who have got the new franchise,—Who are the constituents who elect members now? Under these regulations it is the District Boards, Municipal Boards, the Senates of the Universities and such Associations as the Chambers of Commerce and the British Indian Association. This is the new electorate that has been formed to return members to the Legislative Councils. Now I should like to make one or two general remarks upon the character of this new electorate formed under the new rules. In the first place it seems perfectly incomprehensible on what principle of territorial arrangement these rules have been framed. In the N. W. and Oudh we have, for instance, two elective groups; one composed of the ten municipalities divided into two groups and the other of District Boards that form also two groups in themselves. Now with regard to territorial arrangement I have only to mention that Meerut is linkcd with Lucknow and Fyzabad is connected with another town at the Western extremity of the same Province. I cannot understand this ; there may be some

Second day.

Resolution I.

Reformed and Enlarged Legislative Councils.

solution of the problem but at present it passes my comprehension, and I am sure it passes the comprehension of most of you to explain the anomaly and the rules. (*Hear, hear.*) Then with regard to the larger representation it has been given, at any rate in our part of the country to the district boards; that is another arrangement perfectly incomprehensible to me. To go no further I will only refer to administration Reports of the Government of the N. W. to show what they think of the District Boards in their Province. In the Administration Report for 1890-91, it is stated on page 53, that to the District Officer, entrusted as he is with the extensive powers of a magistrate and collector, are turned the eyes of all residents in the district and it is not to be wondered at if the District Board in its present as in its former shape remains much of an honorary body content in a considerable measure to register the Magistrate's order and carry out such instructions as he confides to the members. I think this is enough to show that the Government themselves do not think much of the capacity for local self-government of these Distrtct Boards and I cannot understand on what principle, out of the 108 Municipal Boards, six only have not the elective principle. All the rest have it, and Municipal Boards, from their nature, are more advanced bodies representing, as they do, more advanced views of public opinion. Out of these ten only come under the franchise. Of these very District Boards, said to be incompetent bodies from the local self-government point of view, why forty-four have been selected for this purpose, is perfectly incomprehensible to me. (*Hear, hear.*) Then there is another thing. In every country where representative institutions exist, property and intelligence are amongst the principal qualifications of voters. Now here I cannot understand how it is that only a few Municipalities and a few District Boards have been arbitrarily selected for this new franchise. If, for instance, the same property be the qualification of a voter for the Legislative Council as it is for every member of your Municipal or District Boards, then I cannot understand why those possessing this qualification should not be given this right. I do not understand why out of our many District and Municipal Boards, only a certain number are selected for this purpose. Then there is another side of the question. Another name for representative Government is that it is responsible Government, a Government that is responsible to the people in whose interest it exists. Anything that weakens this principle of responsibility in the minds of those who carry on the Government should be eliminated (*Hear, hear.*) Where in the present arrangament, where in the new electorate is the feeling of responsibility located? The member of the Council may feel himself responsible to four or five gentlemen who meet together by chance and elect him and perhaps never meet again, but I cannot understand how that member can feel himself responsible to the people between whom and himself there is no real constitutional relationship. Now, gentlemen, the people are not his electors; they are not even the electors of his electors; he cannot feel himself bound by any obligation towards those whose representative he is supposed to be. Then there is another point; it is with regard to the condition of residence. It seems to me that the sixth rule of the rules and regulations framed for the N. W. is to the effect that a person can only be eligible for the Council who is a resident within one of the Municipalities whose delegates form a group and elect him. Now, this is a perfectly incomprehensible arrangement to me. The simple principle on which the condition of repr sentation exists in every other country where representative Government exists, is that a man will be more interested in the welfare of the place in which he lives. On the same basis a man with property is supposed to be interested in the welfare of his country. A man who is returned to the Council does not come as the representative of the particular Municipality that returned him, but as the representative of his Province. I cannot understand how the same question of residence can apply to him. And if there is another man whom this group of electors, these delegates, want to elect, and if his only disqualification happens to be that he is not a resident within the Municipality whose

Second day.

Resolution I.

Reformed and Enlarged Legislative Councils.

delegates they are, I don't see on what principle the Government can set aside that election. Now, gentlemen, there is another point which has very often been stirred up in the N. W. P. It is with regard to the eligibility of officials for election to the Council. I am sorry that the Secretary of State, upon this matter, differed from the Government of India and over-ruled them, and omitted a rule which was certain to have been a very useful one; but perhaps he thought the officials would have, with their own good sense refrained from thrusting themselves too much in the field and would not do anything to hamper or to retard the progress of the new reform. Evidently he did not know he had to deal with a peculiar set of men. I can only refer to the experience we have had in Lucknow at the election about which most of you may have heard. Well, in June last the election to the membership of the Legislative Council took place. There were two rival candidates; one was our esteemed friend Mr. Hamid Ali Khan, (*Applause.*) and another was a well known official, Babu Sriram. There was a difference in the party to which the latter belonged and the District Magistrate who happened to be the Chairman of the Municipal Board thought the best way to make up that difference was to persuade the Municipal Commissioners to vote for him. They voted for him and made him their delegate and from the beginning it was known he was going to vote for somebody who would be a sort of nonentity in the Council. Five delegates met, three of them were quite sure to vote for the non-official and very popular candidate as one had been elected by the Barielly Municipal Board on that condition, and he had accepted it, promising that he would vote for Hamid Ali Khan. He came to Lucknow and some official pressure having had been brought to bear on him he most reluctantly changed his mind. He came to us with tears in his eyes and said he was compelled to go against his conscience because pressure had been brought to bear on him (*Shame.*) We referred this to the Deputy Commissioner, our District Magistrate and his superior, but no notice was taken (*Shame.*) of this communication until after the election and then he, Mr. Mulock, did not answer the question as he should have done if only to vindicate his character. The result was, Mr. Khan was defeated and the other gentleman elected. This is what the Officials have done and what they certainly will do in the future, now that they have got the privilege of getting themselves elected as delegates or even contesting the seats on the Legislative Councils. I regret the decision of the Secretary of State on three grounds. First, it seems to me perfectly inconsistent that while to the Imperial Legislative Council, non-official members alone should be elected by the local Legislative Councils and that by the votes only of the non-official members, a member of the Local Legislative Council can, under the present rules, be returned by the vote of the official members also, and this is an inconsistency I cannot understand. Then it seems to me a very regrettable thing that these officials on one side, and the people on the other should be dragged from time to time into electoral contests and placed in opposite camps, for, by reason of of this, a feeling arises which ought not to be created. These are some of the prominent defects in the regulations which mar and stultify the good promises of the New Councils' Act. Let us hope that Government will soon see these defects as plainly as we do and that they will deal with us fairly and honestly and now that the magnificent boon has been conferred upon us, such as no conquering nation ever conferred on its conquered people, they will see that the boon comes to us not in any grudging spirit but as a measure of hope and a pledge of peace—something to forge new bonds of affection between the rulers and ourselves, and if I may use the words of the Irish patriot, "something which may remove the dark clouds which hitherto rested upon a noble race and dimmed the glory of a mighty empire. (*Loud applause.*)

MOULVIE MOHURREM ALI CHISTI. (*Lahore, No, 266, in list.*) supported in Urdu.*

* As there were no Reporters for the vernacular speeches and neither copies nor English translations of them have been supplied by any but one or two of the speakers, reports of most of the vernacular speeches cannot be given. It is a great pity to omit them as many of the vernacular speeches were of a superior order and a few were the best of all the speeches made at the 9th I. N. Congress.

BABOO BAIKUNTHA NATH SEN (*Bengal, No. 16, in list.*) said:—MR. PRESIDENT, BROTHER DELEGATES, LADIES AND GENTLEMEN—As you know, I am a Bengal delegate and I will confine myself in supporting this resolution to Bengal only. In the first place, I thank Government and express our gratitude to them for what has been done, although undoubtedly a homeopathic dose of the elective principle of a thousandth degree has been administered to us, yet we must receive it with gratitude and good grace with the hope that better things are in store for us in the future. (*Hear, hear.*) Then, gentlemen, we must thank the Bengal Government for which it has actually done. As at present constituted, the Council consists of 20 members and of these the maximum official number is ten. Now you will no doubt hear with satisfaction that the procedure adopted and the appointments made, make the official number in the Bengal Council, nine and the non-official number eleven, so that, if the non-officials combine they can out-vote the Government. This is a good and hopeful feature and one for which we must thank the Government; but at the same time we have still the same grievances to represent and the same complaints to make as those of Bombay and N. W. P. If the rules framed by the Indian Government as well as those framed by the Bengal Government, be taken together, it will be seen that the Corporation of Calcutta has to recommend one member, the Calcutta University one, the associations of the Merchants and Manufacturers one and one to be returned by the European Tradesmen and then two are to be returned by the Municipal Corporations and two by the District Boards. These are the eight members who have to be recommended by these bodies for the acceptance of Government. The landed interest here has not been properly considered. Considering the landed interest from the quantitative as well as the qualitative point of view, it is not an interest which should have been ignored, as apparently the rules do ignore it. Although I must say there is this redeeming feature that at the present moment we have two big Zemindars in the Councils who indirectly represent the landed interest, being Zemindars themselves, namely the Maharajah of Durbhanga and the Maharajah Jagadindra Nath Roy Bahadur of Natore. It happens that the representatives of two big houses have been returned, not by anybody representing the Zemindary interests, but by other electoral bodies. The question of the principle, however, remains untouched, that the landed interest has not been recognized as a body to be entitled to rocommend a member. The British Indian Association is a very strong Association in every part of the country and during the discussions about the Councils Bill in both Houses of Parliament, this Association was particularly mentioned as a fit and proper body to have the franchise and it is to be regretted that that Association or similar Associations have not been considered as qualified to recommend one member. (*Hear, hear.*) Now leaving this question, I have to offer some observations with regard to the recommendations which are to be made and have been made by the Municipal Corporations and District Boards. Now, hear what the Government has done. It is this ; Municipal and District Boards are to form certain groups and they are to recommend by rotation. There are nine divisions, each division being administered and presided over by a Commissioner. The divisions are : The Presidency Division, Rajshahye, Burdwan, Orissa, Chota Nagpur, Patna, Chittagong, Dacca and Bhagulpore Divisions. The question is whether from a theoretical as well as practical point of view the principle is sound. All human institutions are liable to errors. I don't say Government has done it intentionally or that Government has not done, what it has done, with the best of intentions and I will place before you what justified Government in following this procedure. My contention is that the principle is not sound. A geographical distribution of certain areas for the purpose of election is not a sound one, for the choice is limited within a certain defined space and that necessarily cannot make the choice as desirable. An expansion of the arena of choice should, I think be preferred to diminution or contraction. In the next place, it is only a particular portion of the community that takes an interest at the time of the so-called election. We are passing through a stage of education in such matters, and in this geographical distribution a certain portion is interested in elections and receives education and the other portion does not. I would, therefore, suggest that the District Boards as well as Municipal Corporations should be linked together and that they should be jointly allowed to elect Now it might be said in justification of the move taken by Government that they wanted to secure a greater chance of men being returned from the Mofussil Districts. They wanted to safeguard against a monopoly, as it were, of men from more enlightened or educated divisions such as the Presidency Division. It must be supposed that that would be safeguarded against if there was a limitation to the effect that no division would be entitled to return more than one member. In that there would, I submit, be avoided one difficulty. It would minimise the difficulty of the question of residence. In Bengal there was a contect regarding the residence clause in respect of one election which had to be set aside and in his place the Maharajah of Natore was returned. If what I have suggested is accepted then there would be a true representation in the sense of representing the whole province and not a certain group of Municipalities or District Boards. The gong has gone and I cannot say much more, but I would only add with regard to the landed interest that while the Bengal European Chamber of Commerce has got one and while the British Indian Association of Oudh enjoys the same privilege, being something like a branch Association, the main Association has not been given these privileges. (*Hear, hear.*)

MR. TAHILRAM KHEMCHAND *(Sindh, No. 675, in list.)* said :—MR. PRESIDENT AND GENTLEMEN,—I will take you back to the Bombay Presidency so far as it concerns Sindh. Although Sindh forms part of the Presidency of Bombay it is separate in more senses than one. You have learned that two out of the eight seats have been allotted to Sindh, but you should not run away with the impression that on that account Sindh is better represented in the Council than any other part of the Presidency. Though two seats have been allotted and as regards the number of seats we have no grievance to lay before you, in the matter of distribution we are in the same boat as other Presidencies. Of the two seats, one is allotted to the Jaghirdars and Zemindars on an assessment of Rs. 1,000. They constitute the landed interest and do not represent the agricultural population or rural interest which is represented in the Local Boards of Sindh. Next, the second seat has been allotted to the Chamber of Commerce of Kurrachee which body, most of you know, is composed of only 31 houses and of these by far the greate majority of them, namely 17, are merely branches of corresponding firms in Bombay and elsewhere (*Hear, hear.*) Now what does this come to? it is practically giving a second representation to the Bombay Chamber of Commerce. In justification of that seat it is urged that a member for the Chamber of Commerce would represent the trade of Sindh, as if no other member, say, a member of the city Municipality, would ever advocate the trade interest of a growing and increasing city like Kurrachee. I think an argument like this cannot possibly carry weight, because any man connected with Sindh would advocate the interest of the Port which is giving such importance to the whole of Sindh. From the distribution of the seats you will find that not only the agricultural interests are not properly represented but the urban interests are altogether ignored, and the wealth and intelligence of the city are completely unrepresented just in the same way as in other parts of the Bombay Presidency. (*Loud applause.*)

MR. KESHAV VINYEK JOSHI (*Nagpore, No. 815, in list.*) said :—MR. PRESIDENT AND GENTLEMEN,—As a gentleman invited to a party would be thankful to the host, so this Congress would be thankful to the Government of India and the Secretary of State for the concession which has been made to the people of India and for the confidence reposed in the Public of India. But as a gentleman invited to such a party would feel a peculiar discomfort if only the meals were served and no water was provided for quenching his thirst, so I say we are disappointed with the Government in the matter of Legislative Council elections. (*Laughter and applause.*) The Central Provinces, which I have been called upon to represent, have been peculiarly unfortunate. What Government promised on the one hand it took away with the other. Whilst there are over fifty Municipalities, only six are permitted the right of voting which has made it quite impossible for many men, capable and intelligent citizens, to vote in a matter which affects them most. Again, while the whole of the Central Provinces have to return only one member to the Viceroy's Council, four electoral communities have been constituted and the result has been most unfortunate. A process of elimination has been enjoined which I will explain to you. Take for example a province with four divisions. Imagine that eaeh division is entitled to return 12 members from the district Councils and Municipal bodies together. Fancy A secures 5 votes in each of the four divisions; fancy also, that B obtains 7 votes in one of them; and that C., D, and E, obtain seven votes each in the remaining divisions. By the process of elimination A's name would be struck off in each of the four divisions because whoever happens to get the lowest number of votes in a particular division has his name struck off. B meets with a similar fate not having got any votes in 3 divisions. That being so the Government appoints one of the three, namely, C, D, or E, with the result that the gentleman who secured not more than 7 votes in the Province is returned, while the gentleman who had secured 20 votes not in one but in all the divisions, is not sent up. I would put it to you—Is this representation? (*Cries of "No, no."*) Then the next thing is that Government has added other difficulties, and one of those by reserving entirely to itself the right of sending any one it chooses irrespective of the number of votes he may have secured. A gentleman who at the last election secured 12 votes has not been returned, but a gentleman from the Nagpur Division who obtained 6 votes has been returned. I would submit with your kind permission that if there had only been one elective body Mr. A who got 20 votes would have been at once returned; the people's man would have been where he should have been and the object of real representation would have been gained. This is our situation and I will put it to you—Is this representation? I would put it simply—Is this proper treatment to a Province which has no local Legislative Council of its own? I would further ask you whether there could be found a people or a single man in the desert of Sahara who would consider that representation? if not, then I would say we are equally disappointed with those who have not the right of representation. Therefore, I heartily support the proposal of my friend Mr. Mudlolkar and I also thank you very much for the patience with which you have listened to me.

SIRDIR GAJJAN SINGH (*Punjab, No. 392, in list*) supported the motion in Urdu.

RAO BAHADUR C. JAMBULINGAM MUDALIAR (*Madras, No. 852, in list.*) said:—MR. PRESIDENT AND FELLOW DELEGATES,—I have also to join in the chorus of gratitude which has been raised by my predecessors for the very generous manner in which the Government of India has worked out the Indian Council's Act so far as that Government is concerned, but we in Madras have also grievances to relate and to get redressed and we pray that this Congress will pass a resolution on them. Our gnevances, however, are not of so extensive a magnitude as those of our Bombay bre hren, but still they are grievances and deserve your careful consideration. Coming to the subject directly, a very brief explanation of our Madras system will be necessary for the purpose of understanding our grievances. According to the Madras arrangements there are seven non-official members who are to be elected by the various bodies as prescribed by the rules of the Government of India and the Local Government. Of

Second day.

Resolution I.

Reformed and Enlarged Legislative Councils.

these seven members four have to be elected by the Municipalities and the District Boards of our Presidency and the remaining three members are to be elected by the various associations and public bodies and the Presidency City. The arrangement for the election of these four members by the District Boards and Municipalities is that the Presidency is divided geographically into two divisions, Northern and Southern and each division is to elect for its own Municipalities a member, and for its District Boards another member, so that we have two members elected by the 55 Municipalities of the Presidency and two members, by the 21 District Boards. We do not grumble at that arrangement, but our special concern is the manner of division. Whatever may be the reasons for irrationally dividing the parts of other Presidencies, Madras offers a convenient means of division. The Government of India in its various reasons which have been given for justifying the election by Municipalities and District Boards, states that *vast areas and territories cannot be adequately represented* by the few members given by the Act, and, therefore, though a territorial representation is a very desirable thing, it could not, under the present state of things, be carried out and that, therefore, the principle of representation recognized by the Government of India is a representation of class interest, the class interest being the rural interest as represented by the District Boards, the civic interests, as represented by the Municipalities, and so forth. But in our Presidency we could carry out a very complete territorial arrangement, satisfactory to all concerned. Our Presidency has just four branches or divisions which have four distinct languages and these four divisions have physical features peculiar to each; therefore the most rational division would be to divide the Presidency according to these natural features and according to these languages; for example Malabar and Cannary, they form a small part of the Presidency and are unique in themselves so far as their natural features and their laws and customs are concerned. No other parts of the Presidency sympathise with these customs, therefore, it stands to reason that these two districts and others nearly allied to them must have a member. So with the Tamil and Telegu districts a natural division should have been made. This division would carry out in a most efficient manner a proper representation for the country. Another grievance, and a very important one, is that of the representation of the Zemindars and landholders. As we are assembled in this Congress, probably there are not many Zemindars present, but it does not necessarily follow that we should not advocate their interests. The rules provide that in the Council there should be a representation of Zemindars paying a *peshka* of Rs. 20,000. Some special Legislation now going on in the Madras Legislative Council has shown unmistakably that the person who is called the representative of the Zemindars and who is nominated by the Government is no representative whatever and his position has been repudiated by every zemindar in the Presidency, and has been told in so many words that he has betrayed the interests of his class in a very suicidal manner. *(Loud applause.)*

The President then put the motion to the vote and it was unanimously adopted.

Resolution II.

Creation of a Legislative Council for the Punjab.

LALA HARBHAGWAN DAS —*(Punjab, No. 374, in list)*—moved:

*That this Congress, in concurrence with the first Congress held at Bombay in 1885 and other subsequent Congresses, considers that the creation of a Legislative Council for the Province of the Punjab is an absolute necessity for the good Government of that Province, and, having regard to the fact that a similar Council has been created for the United Provinces, hopes that no time will be lost in creating such a Council.*

Sheikh Umar Buksh translated the motion in Urdu, as he did in all subsequent cases.

MR. BHAGWAN DAS said—MR. PRESIDENT AND BROTHER DELEGATES,—In submitting this motion for your adoption, I need not say that were it my duty simply to

Second day.

Resolution II.

Creation of a Legislative Council for the Punjab.

convince you, delegates from other Provinces, and get your concurrence in this resolution, no argument would be necessary, because none of you from other Provinces can with any justification say that whereas you are enjoying the benefit of your Local Councils and have even obtained a share of representation in the Supreme Legislative Council, that we should be denied in the Punjab the benefit of having a local Council. There is a greater person whom we have to convince that we are in need of a local Council, than the brother Delegates and people of other Provinces, and that person is our paternal Government who holds her sons of the Punjab dearer than her sons of any other Province. And in appealing to you and putting this resolution before you, I would only ask your testi mony and to give your opinion so as to assure our paternal Government that the constitution of the people of the Punjab is as strong as that of the people of other Provinces and we are quite capable of swallowing the pill of Legislative Council and will survive it as others have survived. *(Hear, hear.)* I will put before you one thing which may be said by the Government in reply to our request, and it is this. Government can very well say, while the people of the Punjab are called upon to do all the fighting work for the whole of India, therefore, in good grace the people of other Provinces should do the Legislative work for the Punjabis. *(Laughter.)* But let me assure you that the Punjabis, while continuing to do the fighting for the whole of India, can find members to do the Legislative work for themselves. *(Hear, hear.)* In this matter we require very little help from the outside members of other Provinces. I submit that lots of reasons can be adduced to show that the creation of a local Legislative Council is necessary for the Punjab and in doing so I need not repeat the reasons why local Legislative Councils are necessary for the different Provinces in such a large country as India. Such reasons might have sounded very well in 1801 or 1802 when the country was first brought under the British sway and when there were no Legislative Councils, but to repeat those arguments now would be useless. There is one thing I may submit for your consideration which is this. That if there are no reasons or causes which make it necessary that besides a Supreme Legislative Council for the whole of India there should be separate Local Legislative Councils for the N. W. Provinces, Bombay, Bengal and Madras, there are strong reasons why there should be a local Legislative Council for the Punjab. All of you know that the Punjab is practically the gateway of the whole of India, and its population consists of the remnants of every race that has from time to time invaded India and left some settlers here. These people have so affected the social customs an d laws of the country that it would be a very interesting study for a specialist if he were to devote his whole life to the study of the different customs that obtain amongst the people of the Punjab. There is a distinct confession in section 5 of the Punjab Laws Act, which is in force in this country that in matters of succession, inheritance, marriage divorce and adoption and many other things the people shall be governed by the customs obtaining in the communities to which they belong. This section considered by itself shows that the Government of India practically acknowledges its ignorance of the customs and institutions of the people of the Punjab and this section makes every Judge and every Court before whom an individual case may be brought, not only a Court of Justice but really a Legislature. Therefore, we submit, that when the work of legislation for our Province is left, as it sometimes is in the hands of an inexperienced judge imported from Europe, the result is not satisfactory. I think if a local Legislative Council is granted to us we would do its work at least as creditably, if not more creditably than the people of other provinces have done and to the satisfaction of the Government and of the people themselves. With these remarks I place the motion before you for your kind approval and acceptance.

Lala Murlidhur (*Punjab, No. 591, in list*) seconded the motion addressing the meeting in Urdu,

Second day.

Resolution II.

Creation of a Legislative Council for the Punjab.

SHEIKH UMAR BUKSH (*Punjab, No. 522, in list*) in supporting the motion said:—Gentlemen, I feel great pleasure in supporting this resolution. It is a resolution which the Congress has discussed from the very beginning of its existence. We repeat it at every Congress. I beg to submit that the principle involved is one recognized by the Indian Government as well as by the British Government from 1861 when the Indian Councils Act was first passed. The principle which is involved in this resolution is the principle of local legislation. As you know every Province in this country has its local Legislative Council, but it is only the Punjab which has been deprived of this boon. Notwithstanding that the principle has been recognised I beg to submit that the Government of India has not done anything in regard to the matter. The Congress has passed several resolutions but they have not been given effect to. A promise was once made in 1882 or 1883 when Sir James Lyall was Lieutenant Governor here. The first year he came here the Indian Acssociation of this Province gave him an address in which this point was referred to and in reply the Lieutenant Governor promised that he would try his best to have local legislation for the Province as soon as possible. He remained here for 5 years but nothing was done to realize that promise. After he left the Province the present Lieutenant Governor came and a similar address was presented to him and a similar request was made. Of course I cannot say he made the same promise as was made by Sir James Lyall, but he did not retract that promise and as a successor of Sir James Lyall I think he is bound to try his best to see that that promise is carried out. (*Applause.*)

LALA THAKURDAS (*Punjab, No. 394. in list*) supported in Urdu.

MIR NISAR ALI SHOHRAT (*Punjab, No. 267, in list*) also supported in the vernacular.

LALA KANAHYE LAL (*Punjab, No. 636, in list*) signified his intention of opposing.

THE PRESIDENT :—Any one wishing to propose an amendment must send to the President a slip of paper containing the amendment, his own name and that of his seconder and the names of the Congress Circles to which they respectively belong and a similar slip should be handed to the Reporters. Do I understand, Mr. Kanahye Lal that you wish to propose an amendment or do you simply oppose the motion ?

Lala Kanahye Lal having stated that he simply wished to oppose it, the President pointed out that he would attain his object by voting against the original proposition.

Lala Kanahye Lal was then allowed to address the meeting. He said :—My voice is weak but I cannot allow myself to let the opportunity pass of raising an objection to the cuicidal policy which is going on with reference to this resolution. If this resolution is passed and if a Legislative Council is given here under the present circumstances without any guarantee as to representation and selection and election it would be a suicidal policy. I myself moved the resolution last year with great hesitation; now that great hesitation instead of being relaxed has assumed a stronger aspect, and now I am dead against it. I have seen a Lieutenant Governor, in whom we could confide appointing a person admittedly his friend; without any respect to the friendship of the subjects, he has sent up a man, his own friend, and no friend of the people. It might be said that he represents the Sikh community, but you might just as well say that the Golden Temple at Amritsar represents the Sikh community. As an educated man I am in favour of a forward policy, but gentlemen of my province don't support this proposal without a full consideration of the matter. If a Legislative Council is given you will find such multifarious laws and so many snares for your feet that there will be no guarantee which now exists in the Acts and Laws which come from Higher Tribunals and noble personages such as compose the Council of the Viceroy. Therefore, if a Council is given there is every likelihood of the nomination of inferior personages under the thumb of officials, and there will be a multiplicity of snares for your feet—so take care.

**Second day.**

**Resolution II.**

**Creation of a Legislative Council for the Punjab.**

The motion was then put to the vote and carried.

THE PRESIDENT: The next resolution has been repeatedly put and is called the omnibus resolution and therefore I hope the speakers will satisfy themselves with a few remarks as all the questions have been well discussed. I will read the resolution which is a speech in itself.

The following resolution was then read.

**Resolution III.**

**Confirmation of Resolutions previously passed *In re* Salt duty reduction, Raising the Income tax taxable minimum; Excise administration and Police reform, Arms Act modification, Military Colleges; Vounteering.**

*Resolved—That this Congress concurs with its predecessors in strongly advocating—*

(a) *The reduction of the salt duty by at least the amount of its latest enhancement;*

(b) *The raising of the Income-tax taxable minimum from five-hundred to one thousand rupees;*

(c) *Persistent pressure by the Government of India on all Provincial Administrations to induce them to carry out, in its integrity, the Excise policy enunciated in paragraphs 103, 104, 105, of the Despatch published in the Gazette of India of March, 1890, and the introduction of a simple system of local option in the case of all villages;*

(d) *The introduction into the Code of Criminal Prosedure of a provision enabling accused persons, in warrant cases, to demand that instead of being tried by the Magistrate they may be committed to the Court of Sessions;*

(e) *The fundamental reform of the Police administration, by a reduction in the numbers and an increase in the salaries and in the qualifications of the lower grades, and their far more careful enlistment; and by the selection, for the higher posts, of gentlemen of higher capacities, more in touch with the respectable portions of the community, and less addicted to military pretensions than the majority of existing Deputy Inspectors-General, Superintendents, and Assistant Superintendents of Police are;*

(f) *A modification of the rules under the Arms Act, so as to make them equally applicable to all residents in, or visitors to, India without distinction of creed, caste or colour; to ensure the liberal concession of licenses wherever wild animals habitually destroy human life, cattle or crops; and to make all licenses granted under the revised rules, of life-long tenure, revocable only on proof of misuse, and valid throughout the Provincial jurisdiction in which they are issued;*

(g) *The establishment of Military Colleges in India, whereat natives of India, as defined by statute, may be educated and trained for a military career as Commissioned or Non-commissioned Officers (according to capacity and qualifications) of the Indian army;*

(h) *The organising throughout the more warlike races of the Empire of a system of Militia service; and*

Second day,

Resolution III.

Confirmation of Resolutions previously passed *In re* Salt duty reduction, Raising the Income tax taxable minimum; Excise administration and Police reform, Arms Act modification, Military Colleges; Volunteering.

(i) *The authorising and stimulating of a wide-spread system of volunteering such as obtains in Great Britain, amongst the people of India.*

THE HON'BLE VISHNU RAGHUNATH NATU (*Belgaum, No. 734, in list*) said:—MR. PRESIDENT, LADIES AND GENTLEMEN,—I must in the first place thank the President for reading out the corrected form of the present resolution, because I consider this omnibus resolution to include our standing grievances and through a mistake of the Printer, myself and my friends have been included in those standing grievances (*Laughter.*) I do not wish now to be a standing grievance to you, therefore I will merely touch on a few points of the resolution. This resolution contains nine propositions and that number nine coincides with our ninth session of the Congress. It shows for certain that the Government of India does not listen to our very necessary requests which are to meet the wants and wishes of the masses and the number of our ordinary standing grievances is increasing year after year although we are persistently asking Government to reduce the number. ("*Shame.*") In the first place I have to point out that the reduction of the Salt duty is a question of very great importance to the masses whose interests of all others must be at our heart. We have been promised a reduction of the Salt duty from time to time by Viceroys but it has never been carried out and I am afraid under those so-called financial difficulties under which the Government of India are now feeling awkward, it will not be very convenient for the Government to reduce the Salt tax. We must nevertheless from year to year insist on Government reducing it. It is a duty upon a necessary of life and which, if reduced, would conduce to the welfare of the masses. With regard to the Abkari Department I have simply to say it is for the elected members of Local Councils to take up the matter, as we have done in Bombay with the Abkari Policy, bringing it forward every year for discussion when we discuss the Budget. We shall dun Government until the grievance is removed. As regards these nine propositions I say they can be considered under three heads: the first set under the head of taxation; and the second set under that of the army. I think the increase in the army which is going on from year to year involves the Government in great expenditure and makes them raise the taxes. Both these sets of questions are inter-dependent and can only be solved if, as pointed out by our President, Government trusts us as very loyal subjects of Her Majesty and employs us more in the army: the expenditure will be reduced and thereby the taxation will also be reduced. The one question of the army is naturally dependent on the question of taxation and if Government takes into consideration the last three propositions and goes upon the principle laid down then surely the Government will be able to reduce the tax on salt and the income tax. With regard to the Arms Act, I come from a Province in which the Forest grievance is a great one and the rules at present are so very hard that it has become necessary for the people to place the matter before Government. Every year the number of wild beasts is increasing and the licenses every year are curtailed and if there be any wild game, as sportive officers are fond of killing it, it must be left for them and although the wild beasts kill the people they are not allowed to kill them. I will point out a concrete instance. There was a case of a man who had a license for "personal safety" and that man happened to be in a village which was close to a dense forest and when he wanted to shoot a wild animal—a tiger, the whole of the District Officers were down upon him and said that he was using the weapon against his license. ("*Shame.*") This question has to be considered in connection with the Forest policy of Government and must also be discussed every year. With regard to the police I have to say one word. There is one satisfactory thing which I cannot but mention. We have to admit what is done for us, and admit what is attempted by Government. I believe the Government of India and some Local Governments have admitted that the Police, as at present constituted, is not a proper department and

Second day.

Resolution III.

Confirmation of Resolutions previously passed *In re* Salt duty reduction, Raising the Income tax taxable minimum; Excise administration and Police reform, Arms Act modification, Military Colleges; Volunteering.

there are many defects which ought to be eliminated. In the Presidency of Bombay when there was a discussion this year on police improvement in the Province of Sindh, Lord Harris promised that he would see that a better class of men were employed in the service; but as regards the other Provinces I cannot say anything safely, but I insist on all those gentlemen who take an interest in the matter to make this a point for discussion every year before the Council and urge upon the Government to do all they can to improve the character and status of the lower grades of police. At present, we find many of the constables are simply the scum of Society. They are unfit to do their duty, and not only that but they are simply troubling and injuring and interfering with the administration of justice everywhere. Therefore in the interest of the masses, in the interest of the people and also in the interest of the Government it is necessary to raise the character of the police. With these few remarks and as the President at the outset said the speakers must confine themselves to very short speeches, I will take my seat. (*applause.*)

MR. G. S. KHAPARDE (*Berar, No. 800, in list*) in seconding the motion said:—Because this proposition has been put to you every year and because you have been in the habit of seeing me here generally in connection with this proposition, I beg of you not to look upon it as a trifling or an unimportant proposition. Standing here in the Punjab as I do you will see that there is great propriety in this proposition. It really follows on the two which have gone before. In the first proposition the grievance was that there was no right conceded to the Punjab to be represented on the Councils and secondly there is a demand for a Council itself and thirdly you come to the last proposition, namely, a demand for arms. You have been told and everyone has acknowledged that the Punjab represents the manhood of the whole of your country. It has been defending us and fighting our battles against all invaders and it is likely that it may have to fight these battles again within a very short time, therefore what is more natural for these loyal people to ask for?—arms. (*applause.*) You remember that somebody told you, and it is an acknowledged fact that the Sikh warrior has been foremost in all battles. He has fought as a sepoy, now I say let him fight as an officer—as a Colonel or as a General if you please. (*applause.*) This is a very natural and a very straight and forward demand. Then if you concede this and grant them these rights you need not tell me afterwards that we cannot reduce the Salt Tax because there will be a deficiency of revenue, we cannot touch the Excise, we cannot give you more arms because we shall have to employ many more police to look after you. All these things will disappear. We have got the arms and the fighting power and we are all loyal. Therefore you can directly take away a number of the objections on the score of there being financial difficulty, or if you please, financial embarassment. They find the people loyal, equal to fighting and capable of bearing arms and they don't know what reason to assign for not granting them these arms. (*applause.*) I am as anxious as the Subjects Committee to make the speeches as short as possible, therefore I will close my remarks.

PUNDIT KALI PRASANNA KAVYABISHARAD (*Calcutta, No. 12, in list*) said:—LADIES AND GENTLEMEN,—The omnibus is before you. You have heard the conductor and the driver and now the mule makes its appearance. (*Laughter.*) Well, he has to drag it on and it is no business of the mule to look at the passengers but you will excuse me if he casts a side-glance at one of the passengers, namely, the fundamental reform of the police administration. All of us know that we have an ill-paid and corrupt police and instances of that are too well known to be repeated. The latest glaring instance comes from Allahabad. Before the High Court a case recently came up in which a man stood sentenced to be hanged for murdering his wife but his wife afterwards made her

**Second day.**

**Resolution III.**

**Confirmation of Resolutions previously passed** *In re* **Salt duty reduction, Raising the Income tax taxable minimum; Excise administration and Police reform, Arms Act modification, Military Colleges; Volunteering.**

appearance; the police, however did not let him go; they charged him with killing a woman under his protection who might not be his wife and after a good deal of bother the man was dismissed without further penalty. Similar cases have occurred before that and you know that full well in Bengal. The Issur Napit of Howrah case is too well known in Bengal. He was sentenced to death for the murder of his daughter but that daughter made her apparance afterwards and by that accident he had his life saved. In Allahabad a woman was imprisoned by the grace of this ill-paid and mighty police for committing the crime of abortion and while in jail the woman was found to be with child. Instances like these can be multiplied but I do not wish to multiply them. I simply wish to say that all the passengers are well known to you and I have the simple duty of dragging them on before you and I know you will pass them.

HAFEEZ MAHOMED ABDUR RAHIM (*N. W. Provinces, No. 128, in list*) supported in Urdu.

The motion was then carried unanimously.

DR. K. N. BHADURJI (*Bombay, No. 780, in list*) proposed:

**Resolution IV.**

**Reconstruction of the Civil Medical Service in India.**

*That this Congress is of opinion that the time has arrived when, in the interest of public medical education, and the advancement of medical science and of scientific work in this country, as also in the cause of economic administration, the civil medical service of India should be reconstructed on the basis of such services in other civilised countries, wholly detached from, and independent of, the Military Serviee, so as to give full effect to the educational policy of Government, which is to encourage education for its own sake in every branch, and to raise a scientific medical profession in India by throwing open fields for medical and scientific work to the best talent available and indigenous talent in particular.*

DR. BHADURJI said:—MR. PRESIDENT AND GENTLEMEN,—My task is considerably lightened by the pointed reference made in the President's address to the subject of the resolution and the manner in which you received it. The proposition it is my privilege to submit to you is one which I am sure will readily commend itself to you, from whatever point of view it may be considered. It refers primarily to the administration of an important department of the State service, but it also embraces questions of very wide interest. There are the general questions of efficiency and economy, of the rights and privileges of the sons of the country, of higher education, of the advancement of medical and sanitary sciences, which advancements have come to be recognized as a measure—and perhaps a large measure—of the civilisation and material progress of a country. (*Hear, hear.*) Thus the subject I have the privilege to introduce to you is one which might be considered co-extensive in importance with the Civil Service question, and has interest, of not only for the medical profession, but for all workers for the good of the country and its people, and, as such, demands the anxious consideration of our Government. Government are no less concerned with it than our men of light and leading, for it is the pride and glory of the British rule that it aims not only to work the amelioration of the condition of the people of this country, but to raise the Indian nation in the scale of civilisation and intellectual and scientific advancement. Education and Western methods have been the means employed by the humane rule of our gracious sovereign for the noble purpose of carrying enlightenment to her Indian subjects to fit them to take part in the administration of the country according to British methods. And it has been over and over again declared that in every department of the State the principles of justice and equity shall have full play and merit, will enable sons of the soil to rise to high administrative offices; and later on, as the maturing influences of education began to bear fruit, and talent was capable of being reared in India

Second day.

Resolution IV.

Reconstruction of the Civil Medical Service in India.

as well as in England, some of the highest offices which were formerly reserved for the competition-wallahs were opened to the best products of English education in India. Our Arts Colleges and Law Schools have furnished high grade Revenue Officers and High Court Judges, Standing Counsels and Registrars. Our Engineering Colleges have given high grade officers in the P. W. D. and Executive Engineers, and all with a purely Indian education on British methods and without any finishing touches from British Universities—events which speak to the efficiency and excellence of the institutions that have produced such material and so gloriously discharged their duty by the people and Government of the country. But it is a most lamentable fact, that though medical education on British methods and by British teachers has been growing in the country for upwards of half a century, our Medical Colleges, which cost us a third more than the sister Colleges, have not yet supplied us, with a purely Indian College career, anything better than an Assistant Surgeon on Rs. 100 —200 a month, or the ordinary general practitioner ! ("*Shame.*") Surely it cannot be that it is the poorest intellect that is drawn to our medical schools, either as pupils or as teachers, the other Colleges having produced such brilliant results. What, then, is the cause of such dwarfed growth of the products of our medical schools ? In answering this question it is necessary to remember that they are denied all fair play, and the opportunity, let alone the encouragement, which are so essential to the growth and development of talent, and that they are refused admission to all the fields for the cultivation and growth of medical science. Is not the answer to be found in thc fact of the slave trade which the department of the Surgeon-General is allowed to carry on and this department having refused all emancipation to the pupils of our medical schools ? The Arts and Engineering Colleges have long enjoyed emancipation from the regrettable serfdom of the medical schools, and, strange to say, that when the Public Service Commission further enfranchised the *alumni* of the sister Colleges, the *alumni* of the Medical Colleges were not so much as even thought of by them, as if the medical service was not a public service or a service in which the public and the Government were at all interested ; and this, perhaps, because the Commission did not take within their purview the state of a bondsmen class. The Assistant Surgeons may represent their grievances individually, but like serfs they dare not do so collectively, and it is a question if their grievances ever get a hearing, for years have gone by but no response has come. But the evils of this monopoly of the Indian Medical Service are of much wider significance, and affect the people and the Government alike, and it is time they were carefully looked into. Let us study them in their different aspects for a while. The medical service of the country is both military and civil. The military medical service includes the military, which is by far the larger branch of the Indian Medical Service, which is open to all British subjects holding the ordinary practising diplomas of Great Britain by open competitive examinations held in London. Its graded salaries range according to military rank from Rs. 300 odd to Rs. 1,800 odd. Its officers, about 269 in number, are under the control of the head of the sister military service, called the Army Medical Service of the British Army, (ii) The military Apothecary, or the warrant military officer class recruited in India, and to which pure natives of India are admissible or not according to circumstances. The members of this class have a lower standard of preliminary education and a shorter course of professional study than is required of the Assistant Surgeon. But all the same, though they begin with a somewhat lower figure than the Assistant Surgeons, the warrant medical officers rise to twice as much as the Assistant Surgeons, and are even promoted to the uncovenanted grade and put in charge of civil stations, though they are enlisted for military purposes. The Civil Medical Service consists of three divisions : (i) the civil branch of the military Indian Medical Service, which exceeds the military branch by over a hundred members. These are supposed to be officers lent to the civil department, the Indian Medical Service being purely a military

Second day.

Resolution IV.

Reconstruction of the Civil Medical Service in India.

enlistment with a military covenant. Their salaries vary from Rs. 500 to Rs. 2,500 according to the civil appointments and the military rank of the incumbents. Thus in many cases the salaries are not the regular salaries attached to the post, but they represent the military rank of the incumbent. This branch of the Indian Medical Service, a military service by enlistment like the sister Army and Naval Service, has the monopoly of all high grade civil appointments connected with the science of medicine, and has the sole charge of medical education and state sanitation. (ii) The Assistant Surgeon class are open to University graduates only. They rise from Rs. 100 to Rs. 200. They are in charge of civil dispensaries and hold minor appointments in hospitals. They have gone through a thoroughly British education and under British teachers, and have passed examinations " quite as stringent as those for British diplomas" (as reported to the Government of India by a special committee of Indian Medical Service men), and thus their qualifications are as high as those of most members of the Indian Medical Service, which many of our graduates have entered by open competition in England. They have often acted as Civil Surgeons to the full satisfaction of Government, as was naturally to be expected from their qualifications. But they can never be full or *pucca* Civil Surgeons. ("*Shame*") They may be Analytical Chemists and conduct the whole duties of Chemical Analyser to Government, but in spite of their long experience and approved work they are always to be under young Surgeon Captains whose knowledge and experience of Chemical Analysis is thus described by Dr. Voelcker in his official report to the Government of India. Although the Assistant Surgeons may be quite competent and qualified to hold Civil Surgeoncies and the Professorship of Chemistry, they cannot aspire to such places but must remain content with Rs. 150 to Rs. 200 a month. The salary of the Chemical Analyser to Government is Rs. 1,000 or Rs. 1,700 or more according to his military rank. With what ease our University graduates secure the ordinary British diplomas is known to us all, and our graduates had only to pay their passage to England to secure both the ordinary English diplomas and a commission in the Indian Medical Service. But unfortunately, for reasons not very plain, the getting of the commissions became more difficult than securing the diplomas. Alarmed at the great inrush of natives into the Indian Medical Service, at one time the authorities seriously thought of either closing the service to the natives or imposing some fresh restrictions. Is it that the standard of teaching in our medical schools has lowered, or is it that the competition has got heener ? Assurance, however, is often given to the public that the teaching at our medical schools is on a level with British teaching in British schools, for here also it is done by British teachers ; and complaints have often been made that the competition is less fierce than it used to be. Then there is the Uncovenanted Medical Service open to all Univeisity graduates with Indian or British degrees or diplomas. This service was specially instituted in 1867 for the encouragement and utilisation of the best products of our Indian Medical Schools and at the same time to lessen the expense of the Medical Department. It is like the Provincial Civil Service with similar rules of pay and pension, and some of the high grade appointments of the Indian Medical Service incorporated therewith. To this service Assistant Surgeons are also eligible. But, strange as it may appear, it is nevertheless true, that whilst graduates of other faculties have been elected to high posts in the judicial and revenue branches of the public service, and High Court Judges have had no objection to colleagues of pure Indian training, and the Engineering Colleges have been giving a first-class man every year for higher service in the P. W. D., the Medical Colleges have not given even two graduates in twenty years worthy to be recommended by the Surgeon-General for admission into the Uncovenanted Medical Service—a fact which hardly reflects credit on the teaching of the Professors supplied by the Surgeon-General's Department. Is it not a fact that the Surgeon-General has not only not recommended an outsider or an Assistant Surgeon for admission to this Service, but actually opposed

Second day.

Resolution IV.

Reconstruction of the Civil Medical Service in India.

such admission of high class Assistant Surgeons whose claims were urged by distinguished executive officers of Government in their districts from their personal knowledge of the meritorious work done by their Assistant Surgeons? And is it not a fact also that the only appointment held by an outsider was recently wrested from the non-official profession and slipped into the hands of an Indian Medical Service man? Such have been the predatory instincts of the monopolist department. Thus in spite of the Government having made special provision for the recognition and encouragement of the non-official profession, the monopolists have been allowed for nearly a quarter of a century to come in the way of Government carrying out their declared policy of justice and fair play to the profession in India. (*applause.*) This military service monopoly of the fields, of work in the hospitals, and *post mortem* rooms, and teaching institutions, which has a large share in the rearing of a scientific and progressive profession and the advancement of the medical sciences themselves, have resulted in an unjust keeping back and actual degradation of the profession in India. The monopoly is against all manner of work by the local profession in the local hospitals. Even honorary work by members of the local profession is again and again wrecked on the shibboleth of that indefinable and unscrutable thing called "discipline," which rides roughshod over all rules and regulations which govern the relations of professional men and professors in the West. Specialists are not believed here to know their own requirements, and have to submit, as regards the methods of their work and the conduct of their classes, to the orders of the College Principal who is reckoned here to be an universal specialist. A non-military medical officer of an institution of actually higher and longer standing as regards his professional qualifications and connection with his hospital is always to be considered junior to his military colleagues of lower professional status and of much shorter connection with the institution. But the evil influences of the monopoly of the Indian Medical Service are not without their recoil on the service itself and the institutions it is connected with. For, as Dr. Carter said, it is hardly to be expected that the body of medical officers in India (from whom the staff of Professors is drawn) can always offer a wide enough field for selection. Moreover, owing to the service rules having for their basis the providing of places for men, and not finding men for places, a shuffling of cards takes place to suit the requirements, not of the special posts, but the office requirements of the Surgeon-General's Department, and it has not been possible even for the Service men to put forth as much work in upwards of fifty years as is put forth in as many months by some of the provincial schools of Europe. It is by no means cheerful to have to reflect that with India's vast opportunities and material the only professional service paper requires a State subsidy for its subsistence and boasts of no more than 128 subscribers, when even provincial medical journals in England have been flourishing both in wealth of scientific contributions and paying subscriptions. By circumstances the service men are led to look forward to a rise more in their service than in their profession, for to be even a Surgeon-General one has to rise in the service and not in the profession, and the Surgeon-General is taken as a universal professional expert, for he is the referee of Government in all matters medical and scientific, not because of his professional work and fame, but because he wears the badge of that office into which he must tumble in his turn. It is thus that it is possible for a Surgeon-General to advise Government even in the full light of our advanced times that experimental physiology and pathology require no vivisection, a pieco of information that would create laughter and surprise in a class of beginners in a British medical school! Again, the Service monopoly of the educational and the allied institutions is subversive of all principles which govern the cultivation and development of medical education and medical science. Nowhere else in the world is the selection of educationists and votaries of science confined to a graded service in which men try their hands at different subjects as they advance in their grades. Nowhere else is a doctor, even a military doctor, regarded as a potential professor of various medical and sister sciences. Nowhere else could be found records of such feats and transformations on lecture pulpits as that of a military doctor appearing as a Physician and Professor of Medicine in the spring months, as Professor of Midwifery and an Obstetric Physician in the summer months, as Professor of Ophthalmology and Zoology—as if every oculist was a born naturalist—in the autumn, and as an expert in lunacy in the winter months of the same year. What other medical schools in the world could boast of such *tableaux vivants* on their lecture pulpits? (*Laughter and applause.*) Where else in the world could be found schools in which not a single session passes by without a change in the several professorships? That such a state of affairs is against the very intentions of all educational institutions requires no argument to establish. What happens is that the professors before they have any time to pick up some knowledge of the subject they are "ordered" by their Surgeon-General to teach in the Colleges, suddenly receive an order to teach quite another subject! This unnatural system and its manifest evils were often protested against by the service professors themselves, but as service men they nave only to obey the orders of their Surgeon-General. Only recently the Director of Public Instruction of Madras has after a careful inquiry into the system advised Government that this state of affairs must mend or end. He lays down that the appointment of Professors in the medical schools should not, as heretofore, rest with the Surgeon-General, and that selections thereto must be on the basis of merit and capacity alone, or that the Professors should be selected by the Secretary of State as for the other Colleges, and that no transfer should be allowed, in case the Professor is a service man, at the will and convenience of the Surgeon-General. Our other Colleges do not exist for any special service, but the services of specially qualified men are requisitioned straight from the Universities. Even military Germany will not sacrifice her medicial education and Colleges to the interests and conveniences of her military medical service. And where else would it be accepted that a military service for two years and a little experience of general practice as a Civil Surgeon and guarder of jail birds is a necessary training and qualification for a medical Professorship, or that such training is a touchstone wherewith to transform every military doctor into a potential Professor of everything that is taught in a Medical School, or a potential Sanitary Commissioner or Analytical Chemist? Nowhere else in the world is the imperial service of the medical profession and its sciences forced to recognise any other covenant for their cultivation and advancement than that of faithful work, nor has the covenant any limitations of caste, colour, or creed, but is open to recruits from all ranks and conditions of men, the only standard of admission being capacity and merit Nowhere else in the woild are medical men told that if they did not wear military uniform they would be excluded from the covenant of working for the advancement of the sciences and contributing to the glory and welfare of their profession. But the service monopoly of the College appointments reduces our medical schools to the status of mere trade manufactories or unions. The pupils of our medical schools are made to take leave of their *alma mater* with this silent blessing from their masters. "You were here to pick up enough knowledge to enable you to earn a livelihood as an Anglicised hakim: it is not your business to come here again. You can never be fit to take part in or continue our work as professors. Perhaps we may not mind your coming in with us provided you purchase a right to wear our uniform." Whilst in every other country the Colleges make it their pride to bring up a generation of pupils who continue the work of their masters, and masters and pupils reflect credit on, and take pride in each other, and have common feelings and aspirations and pleasures of work for the advancement of the science, and the several *alma maters* show particular regard for their own sons, out here all these best traditions of renowned schools have been annihilated since the creation of the service monopoly. And there can be no attachment of pupils to masters who wish not to see them again except by the bedside of patients for consultations, and who block their every avenue of a scientific or even a high professional career. This in itself is a lamentable state of things and wants speedy mending in the interest of education and for the good name of our medical schools and the dignity of the profession in India. It is melancholy to reflect, that though our medical schools have existed for upwards of fifty years, and India has offered the widest opportunities to the privileged workers, she has no scientists of her own, and has to beg of other countries to solve her scientific questions, and can boast of no Harley-street men of her own in whose hands even our European friends could place themselves, and be thus saved the necessity of a hasty flight to the Harley street in London, directly their ailments get above the stage of mere trifles! (*Applause*) Then there is the important question of economy.

At this point the President intimated that Dr. Bhadurjee's time allotted to him in which to bring forward his motion had expired.

THE PRESIDNT:—We must stick to the rules. There may be special occasion when an extension of the time is necessary and I think I have allowed that extension and have taken into account that this is a new proposition. (*Cries of " Go on."*)

DR. BHADURJEE:—I am sorry to be going against the rules of the Congress, but I know you will excuse me for I do so in bringing forward a new subject of which the people are ignorant. Men of light and leading have not yet thoroughly grasped the subject, and I ask you, whether are you going to vote on this matter in ignorance?

THE PRESIDENT:—The chair must be obeyed. I anticipated this and I gave you a much longer time than is properly allowed. But as the speaker pleads for a further extension and as this is a new subject I put it to the Congress whether they wish to hear Dr. Bhardurjee further. (*Cries of " Yes."*)

THE PRESIDENT:—Then you may take five minutes more.

Dr. Bhadurjee continuing said:—It is a familiar fact that a military article is a costly one, and whenever military men are borrowed for civil duty the borrowing departments have to pay them not only the regular salaries of the appointments but also their rank allowances. Look at the difference in the salaries of the College professors. In the Educational Department the grade service scale is Rs. 500 to Rs. 1, 500, the latter being the Principal's salary, and the sister Colleges have had first-rate men on such a scale without the further emoluments of private practice which the medical professors indulge in. And though the medical professors are by no means chosen on the recognised principles of educational appointments, they never begin under Rs. 700, and may rise to Rs. 1,800, or more, *i. e.* they require a third more than the professors of the other Colleges for their military rank allowances. Again, these allowances are proportionate to the rank of the officers, so that a Professorship may cost Rs. 700 or Rs. 1,200, according as the incumbent is a Captain or a Major. Thus our medical schools are costlier by a third than the sister institutions. And looked at from the point of view of Government themselves, they are still more expensive. At one of our medical schools Government have appointed a professor of the same race and the same qualifications as his military colleagues and at almost half their salary scale. The reason Government gives is that the other professors are paid at a higher rate because they are military men! Thus this non-military professor has to work on a scale of Rs. 350 to Rs. 750 side by side with his military colleagues, whose scale runs from Rs. 700 to Rs. 1,800! The laws of demand and supply will operate in regard to our medical schools as well, and

Second day.

Resolution IV.

Reconstruction of the Civil Medical Service in India.

like the sister Colleges they also may be sure of getting good men, especially with the further emoluments of private practice. Good men would gladly come out to India if they were sure of a straight road to the professorships of their special subjects. It is the circuitous roate of military service and general practice and guardianship of jail birds, and what is not at all an inconsiderable factor, interest and smiles of the Surgeon-General, which deters really good men from seeking a scientific career in India. Taking the Presidency College appointments alone, the saving is some Rs. 36,000 a year But this is only on eight appointments. There are some 361 military men in civil employ, and with many of their appointments the ratio is much higher. Even at the ratio of one-third, the saving comes to 15 lakhs on 361 appoinfments. The grade scale pay only of 361 of these military officers comes to over 35 lakhs. Add to this the allowances, which amount to at least 25 per cent. Thus the total saving per year is nearly 20 lakhs. The civil medical service, with a strength of 361 members, that is, a hundred more than the military requirements, has grown to be a distinct service by itself, and there can be no justification for a military detachment of military doctors being any more quartered on a medical school and civil hospitals and on the taxpayer. Time was when military doctors, they being the only exponents of Western medical science to be found in the country and at the disposal of Government, were called in by Government to start their medical schools and look after their civil medical relief work. All honour to the noble pioneers of medical education in India, members of the Indian Medical School, who helped Government in their noble and humanising work of sowing the seed of Western medical education, and they deserve our highest gratitude, for it never occurred to them to monopolise College and hospital fields as reserve pasture ground for themselves or for their service. They considered themselves men of science and medicine first and service men afterwards, and not allowing the instincts of their liberal profession and training to be swamped by any ideas of service or monopoly interest, they stoutly opposed the closing of the fields of work in medicine and the allied sciences against anybody, and pleaded for their being kept open for all comers straight through the recognised avenues of special qualification and training. If such was the necessity in 1867, when the medical schools were only 25 years in existence, how much more so now, with the rapid advance of the special sciences since 1867! It appears that the idea of scheduling these appointments originated with a Surgeon-General, and it is the Surgeon-General's Department that docked the appointments for his Service, the Indian Government not realising that such an indulgence to a military department meant total subversion of their noble intentions and policy, and little expecting that the Surgeon-General's Department would knock their Uncovenanted Medical Service into a dead letter. The Colleges were founded not for "any governmental or executive wants," said a mouthpiece of Government, but for the cultivation and diffusion of Western medical science to promote the happiness of the people of India. The monopoly of the civil medical appointments forms no article of the covenant of the Indian Medical Service, and surely the medical Colleges do not exist for quartering supernumerary military men. If England herself will not allow her army doctors to be billeted on her civil hospitals and educational institutions, will she allow such an extraordinary and unjust procedure in India? And if the War Office will not allow army doctors of the British army to be kept in civil employ, if at all, for longer than three years—for it would be against the discipline and the very intentions of the army system—will it allow the Indian Government any longer to disregard these principles in the case of the Indian army? But this "reserve" argument is really a delusion and a snare. The actual strength of the military Indian Medical Service is some 269 men, but some 361 members of what is really military service have crept into what is called the civil reserve. To have 361 reserves for 268, regulars, or to lend 361 from a capital of 268 is a novel idea indeed. The proposal aims at a natural disposition of things, and some suggestions have been made in my memorandum on the subject as regards the lines on which the scheme of reform may be adapted to existing circumstances. By the institution of a purely civil medical service for India medical education and the profession will rise with their enfranchisement and science will advance, and India will also take her place with other countries in scientific and medical progress, and there will be no more need of indenting on other countries for their scientists to solve Indian questions. Again the experience and knowledge that the sons of the country will gain with free and fair play to their talent will remain in the country and for the country's good. At present the Indian experience of the army doctors, who alone have every means of developing talent and gaining knowledge and experience, is lost to India, for it is all carried away from the country with the pensions in sterling. Indian experience is gained at India's expense, but not for her good. And last, but not least, England will have the satisfaction of carrying out her noble mission and policy towards India, and add to her honour and glory by raising India as a nation with a full measure of material and scientific progress in the department of medicine and sanitation which are so intimately connected with the progress of civilisation amongst the advanced people (*loud applause.*)

DR. M. M. BOSE (*Calcutta, No. 6 in list*) seconded the motion and said :—I need only add a few words to what Dr. Bhadurjee has said. I shall first take up the question of public medical education. We know that in England and other places the Professor has to devote his whole time to the subject in which he teaches. Here we find a surgeon coming from outstation duties for a year or two and then he is transferred to a surgeonship in the Districts and then he is not only called upon to perform the duties of a Professor but of surgeon to a hospital and also has to fill many other appointments. You cannot expect to produce good scientific men unless you have at the head of the institution in the professorial chair a man who devotes his whole time and energy to his work. We have got a class of Assistant Surgeons, and why not encourage them? They work for 12, 20 or 24 years and after 24 year's service they get the same pay as that upon which an Englishman begins. If we employ these men who know the social customs and manners of the people, causes of disease, and they can really do the duty more efficiently than the Surgeons who are often inexperienced people, matters will improve. For instance the Secretary of State has power to appoint Professors to the Presidency College, directly from England without any class examination. Why should not men directly from Oxford and Cambridge be imported here and placed on the teaching staff of the medical classes of the Presidency Colleges? We should not mind taking them from England if they were appointed as teachers in the medical classes. The mover has dealt with the question from various points of view and I only hope our brethren will take it up earnestly. No doubt if this is put before the English public and the Indian public we shall in time have the Indian Madical Service reconstituted. (*Applause.*)

DR. BHALCHANDRA KRISHNA (*Bombay, No. 786, in list*) said :—MR. PRESIDENT, BROTHER DELEGATES, LADIES AND GENTLEMEN,—I have very great pleasure in supporting the resolution which has been so eloquently and lucidly proposed by my esteemed friend, Dr. Bhadurjee. He has done full justice to it. I need not, therefore, reiterate the sentiments which he has expressed to the Congress. I will, however, dwell upon two or three most important points bearing on the subject. The separation of the Military and Civil Medical Services is as important a subject as that of the Civil Service, and I trust it will receive from you the same measure of attention as the subject of the Simultaneous Examination in England and India. Apart from the fact that this separation will encourage scientific medical education for its own sake, it will also

**Second day.**

**Resolution IV.**

**Reconstruction of the Civil Medical Service in India.**

improve the status of the medical profession and of the subordinate medical service—I mean the class of Assistant Surgeons, who, although generally very capable men, have to rot on Rs. 100 to Rs. 150 or Rs. 200 per mensem all their life, while their compeers by spending the passage money to England and passing an ordinary examination in the Covenanted Medical Service, commence from Rs. 350 and rise to Rs. 1,500, or even to Rs. 1,800 per mensem. The Apothecary class can rise to Rs. 400 and even to Rs. 800 per mensem, and occupy the post of Honorary Surgeons and House-Surgeons; but all these are denied to the Assistant Surgeons. If this separation and reconstitution is effected, it will entirely change the present state of things. It will enable the Assistant Surgeons to rise higher in their service as regards pay, and encourage them to improve their medical and scientific knowledge. Along with this there will have to be effected a change in the appointments to the professorial chairs in the Medical College. The haphazard manner of appointing a military medical officer to any and every chair in the Medical College has been the bane of medical education and the advancement of medical science in India. These appointments must be thrown open to the best available talent either in England or here by free competition. (*Hear, hear.*) It is only by adopting this course that the best specially trained men will be available instead of confining the selection to the charmed circle of military medical men. Such men will encourage the study of the medical science in all its branches, and will ultimately create a taste for original research. But the most important advantage will be economic administration. From the recent issue of the *Quarterly Indian Army List*, it is found that the total expenditure on all the 361 appointments of military medical officers in civil employ comes to about Rs. 43 lakhs. The military medical officers like every military article are very dear, and I believe they are one-third dearer than others who do not belong to the Military Medical Service. If the reconstitution be effected with one-third of the salaries of the present scale, there would be a reduction of Rs. 12 lakhs. (*applause.*) All civil appointments carry other allowances, and on an average they come to at least one-fourth of the grade salaries, that is about eight lakhs, so that there will be a total saving of twenty-three lakhs annually. Will this not be a source of relief to the general taxpayer? The monopoly of scheduled appointments which has existed for some years past was intended by a Surgeon-General who looked more to the interest of the service men than to that of the people or the tax-payer. Its introduction was generously and strenuously opposed by men like Sir W. G. Hunter and Sir George Birdwood, but without any avail. They fought for the principle that the College and other important appointments should be thrown open to the best talent wherever available. This monopoly has grown so strong that the military medical officers consider these appointments as a preserve or as a birthright, and even the slightest encroachment on this sacred preserve is most bitterly opposed and resented. ("*Shame.*") It has given rise to a feeling of intense jealousy. I will not further take up your time, but will give you two concrete instances of this feeling of intense jealousy which prevails in the service. I have not come here with the object of airing the grievance of any individual person, but I am compelled to mention an instance to illustrate what I am striving to put before you. The eminent gentleman who addressed you just now has fallen a victim to the service jealousy. ("*Shame.*") That noble and liberal statesman, who presided over the destinies of Bombay some years ago—I mean Lord Reay (*applause.*) created a new professorship for Pharmacological research. His Highness the Gaekwar of Baroda was generous enough to endow a chair for the purpose of investigating native drugs, and my friend was chosen to fill that chair. He is the only native M. D. of the London University and holds excellent certificates from eminent scientists in Europe. He filled the chair with great credit to himself. But from the moment of his appointment to the moment of the urgent abolition of that chair, he was persecuted, opposed, and annoyed by that clique of the army medical men at the Grant Medical College. Another instance is that of my distinguished friend, Dr. Deshmukh, M. D., of the Bombay University He was an Assistant Surgeon and filled the appointment of Assistant Chemical Analyser to the Government of Bombay for thirteen years with great ability and satisfaction to the Government. But when the Chemical Analysership to the Government fell temporarily vacant, he was distinctly told that it was a scheduled appointment, and he could never hope to get it in the face of the fact that such appointments were conferred temporarily on deserving of uncovenanted servants of Government. He was disgusted with the treatment and resigned the service in despair, while a young surgeon who never knew anything of analysis was pitchforked into it. I will not further take up your time, but will heartily support the motion, and commend it to your unanimous and cordial acceptance. (*Loud applause.*)

DR. BHUGATRAM SAWHUY (*Punjab, No. 487, in list*) said :—MR. PRESIDENT, BROTHER DELEGATES, LADIES AND GENTLEMEN,—After having heard my predecessors, I don't think there is much left for me to say on the subject. I just want to add that this proposition has my entire sympathy and support, and that as far as I can judge I deem it absolutely necessary, in the interests of the medical science and of original scientific research in this country that the Civil Medical Service should be separated from the Military Medical Service and that appointments in the Civil Medical Service should be thrown open to the best talent available. At present the only service open to the natives of India educated in the Indian Medical Colleges is the subordinate Medical Service carrying poor emoluments. viz, beginning with a handsome salary of Rs. 100, and rising to Rs. 200 a month after going through the ordeal of a curriculum of 5 years with stiff examinations to pass and two septenneal examinations to qualify them for promotion. It should be remembered that an Assistant Surgeon has not only to do the main portion of the Civil Medical work but that he has generally to perform the most difficult part of it, *e.g.* the most important surgical operations and treating all sorts of medical cases and doing any kind of Medico-legal work. In fact he is expected to be almost as efficient as a specialist in any branch of Medical Science as far as the septenneal examinations are concerned. But the injustice does not stop there. Even if an Assistant Surgeon has the means and pluck to go to Europe and obtain English degrees, on his return he is treated no better than an ordinary Assistant Surgeon while a military medical man with similar qualifications has a chance of aspiring to the highest appointment in the Civil ; not only that but even an apothecary with no experience whatever of the Civil Medical duties can at once be transferred from a Military Apothecary into a Civil Surgeon superseding men possessing far superior professional knowledge and great experience of the Civil Medical work. We do not at all wish ill of our Eurasian brethren of the Military Subordinate Medical Service but it will be undoubtedly more just if their prospects were improved in their own department and those of Assistant Surgeons in the Civil. The only remedy for the redress of the grievances of the Indian Medical profession including all creeds and classes *i. e.* Hindus, Mahomedans, Parsis, Eurasians, Native Christians &c &c is to give all a fair play and no favour in filling up appointments as Civil Surgeons by holding simultaneous open competition examination in England and India while chairs in the Indian Medical Colleges should be filled up by selection from the pick of the profession in both countries instead of making them a monopoly of the Military Medical Service as is at present done. A Professor of Physology being by a single stroke of the pen transformed into a Chemical Analyser and a Chemical Analyser into a Professor of Surgery to the great detriment of the interests of the students and discouragement of the profession generally.

The motion was carried and the Congress adjourned till one o'clock the next day Friday.

---

# THIRD DAY'S PROCEEDINGS.

## Friday, 29th December, 1893.

The Congress re-assembled at one o'clock on Friday afternoon.

**Third day.**

**Cheers and Telegram to Mr. Gladstone on his birthday.**

THE PRESIDENT :— The fifth resolution will be proposed by the Hon'ble Mr. Surendra Nath Banerji of Bengal but before he proceeds with it I have to communicate to you that I have received a document signed by one hundred and twenty five gentlemen from Jullunder in favour of Simultaneous Examinations which is the subject of this resolution Further, before we proceed with that resolution I beg to propose that we give three cheers for Mr. Gladstone on this, his birthday and I propose also that a telegram be sent from the Congress congratulating him and wishing him many more birthdays. (Three hearty cheers were then given for Mr. Gladstone by the delegates and visitors all rising from their seats). And the President was authorised to send a telegram to Mr. Gladstone as suggested by him.

The Hon'ble Mr. Surendra Nath Banerji (*Calcutta, No. 8, in list*)—moved :—

**Resolution V.**

**Indian Civil Service Simultaneous Examinations in England and in India.**

*That this Congress desires to thank the British House of Commons for their just and wise vote in regard to Simultaneous Examinations in England and in India, and most earnestly prays that august body to insist upon their orders being given prompt effect to by the Secretary of State for India and the Government of India.*

MR. PRESIDENT, BROTHER-DELEGATES, LADIES AND GENTLEMEN :—In moving this resolution it is impossible not to advert for a moment or two to the great and momentous changes which have taken place within the last few months in the constitution of the Government of this country. The year 1893 will be memorable in the annals of British India, memorable in the glorious record of the undying achievements of the British people in this country. It will be remembered not for the battles that have been fought and won, not for the treaties that have been concluded, nor even for that last accession to our treaties, concluded by Sir Mortimer Durand with the Amir of Afghanistan, by which the Indian tax-payer has been burdened with a further burden of six lakhs of rupees a year. But it will be remembered as the year which witnessed the birth of representative institutions in this country, *(applause)* and the formal, the clear, the emphatic recognition, by the British House of Commons, of the principle that the natives of this country shall enjoy the same practical facilities with their European fellow-subjects, in regard to that examination which constitutes the passport to high appointments in the land of their birth *(applause).* Nor will the year be less memorable for the reversal, at any rate the partial reversal, of that policy which had culminated in the issue of the Jury Notification. Last year about this time, in Congress assembled, we were deploring the fact that a British Government, wedded to the traditions of popular liberty, should have so far forgotten those traditions as to have issued a notification restricting the right of trial by jury. *(Shame).* This year it is our proud privilege to be able to offer our congratulations to the Government of India on having reverted to the paths of returning wisdom and sound sense. *(applause.)* Last year we had hoped—with some it was a dstant hope—that representative institutions would be established in this country. This ear the enlarged Councils with their enlarged functions are an accomplished fact *Loud applause*). Last year in our wildest dreams, in the most rapturous moments of prophetic inspiration, when the mind travels out of itself into the world of the unknown and the unseen, we could not anticipate that the Parliament of Great Britain would affirm the principle of Simultaneous Examinations (*Hear, hear.*) And yet the unexpected has come to pass ; and to you, Sir, (here the speaker turned to Mr. Dadabhai Naoroji) it must be the crowning satisfaction of your life to be able to feel that you are a chosen instrument in the hands of Almighty Providence for the good of the people (*Applause*)—to know that you have by your efforts brought within measurable distance of success a question, to the satisfactory solution of which you have dedicated the energies of a life-time. I think I express the sense of this Congress, and I may add, of the educated community throughout the Empire, when I say that it is our earnest hope and our ardent prayer that you may long be spared to devote yourself to the good of your country, and to present to us the men of a younger generation that lofty ideal of public duty which we can never hope to attain to, but which we may hope to follow, at a measurable distance from you the great pattern of our race. (*Applause.*)

The resolution, with which I have been charged, records the gratitude of this Congress to the British House of Commons for its vote in connection with the question of Simultaneous Examinations. It has been said—I will assume that it has been said in ignorance—that the vocabulary of the Indian languages does not contain the word gratitude. (*Laughter.*) I am not here to discuss that question. Whether we have the word or not, the feeling is there, deep, passionate and profound. But if the word does not find a place in our vocabularies, I think I can find a rational explanation for it. The feeling is so strong and so intense that human language which is only a human contrivance, a vehicle for our thoughts and feelings, fails to give adequate expression to the deepseated sentiment of gratitude which finds a lodgement in the breast of every true-born Indian. (*Loud applause.*) However that may be, Mr. Paul and his friends are entitled to our deepest gratitude. (*Loud applause.*) There is one aspect of the question which is not to be overlooked. Not only have they done a great service to the people of India, they have done a memorable service to their own country. They have vindicated the honour of their Sovereign and our Sovereign ; they have redeemed the plighted faith of the British nation, and by adding to the contentment of the people they have added to the stability of the Throne in India. (*Applause.*) For after all upon what does the permanence of British rule depend in India ? Not upon its army, not upon its navy, not upon its impregnable fortresses, not upon its wonderful lines of strategic railway, wonderful alike for its strength and its expensiveness, nor even upon the subsidising of the Ameer. These are adventitious aids to power which may fail us in the sorest day of trial. (*Hear, hear.*) The permanence of British rule depends upon the contentment, the happiness, the willing allegiance of the vast and the multitudinous population (*applause*) who in the ordering of Divine Providence have been committed to the care and guardianship of the British Government in India. (*Hear, hear.*) But how can you hope to conciliate a people or win their gratitude, when you degrade them by employing them in subordinate positions, and when you show your contempt for them by breaking faith with them. ("*No, no.*") I know it is a very serious charge to bring against the Government of this country, but the words have not escaped me. I make use of them deliberately and advisedly with a full sense of my responsibility for every word I utter. I desire to arraign the Government of India before the Bar of British and Indian public opinion—before the Bar of civilised humanity in all parts of the globe ; for the history of the Civil Service question is one unbroken record of broken promises. (*Applause.*) Bear with me for a few moments as I carry you through this dismal record of broken pledges. In 1853 a Select Committee of the House of Commons sat on the renewal of the Company's Charter. Mr. Hay Cameron gave evidence before that Committee. Mr. Cameron was an Anglo-Indian ex-official and he had

Third day.

Resolution V.

Indian Civil Service Simultaneous Examinations in England and in India.

been a Member of the Supreme Legislative Council. Now mark the evidence which Mr. Cameron with all the weight of his official authority gave before the Committee. He said that not a single native of India had been appointed to any high office within the twenty years that had elapsed since the enactment of the Charter Act to which he might not have been appointed before the passing of that Act ; in other words the Charter Act had remained a dead-letter. That was in 1853. But let us pass on to more recent times. In 1869 the Duke of Argyle, not the reactionary Conservative Duke of 1893, but the Liberal and Radical Duke of 1869, speaking from his place in Parliament as Secretary of State for India said " we have broken our promises and have not kept our engagements with the people of India." In 1875 Lord Lytton speaking as Vice-chancellor of the University of Calcutta said " The promises of the Queen remain inadequately redeemed." But Lord Lytton had something more to say about the matter in language still more emphatic. He sent a secret despatch home to which our President referred from his place in the House of Commons,—a secret despatch in which he unburdened his soul and disclosed his innermost thoughts. The secret despatch has found its way into publicity, and what do we find there ? Lord Lytton says " we have cheated the people of India," *(Shame.)* " we have broken to the hope the words of promise we had uttered to the ear." Let us now proceed from opinions to facts. In 1870 a Parliamentary Statute was passed for the purpose of conferring upon natives of India some of those high appointments which had hitherto been reserved to members of the covenanted service. These appointments were to be made subject to rules to be framed by the Government of India. The Statute was passed in 1870. When were the rules passed, may I enquire. ? The Government of India overburdened with its multitudinous work was able to pass six rules in six years' time *(Laughter.)* and then exhausted by the effort—*(Laughter)*—it needed breathing time, and there was another pause for six years before the rules were given effect to. *(Shame.)* Then came the Public Service Commission, and here we have again an illustration of the old remark "a mountain was in labour and a mouse was produced." *(Laughter.)* The Public Service Commission recommended the abolition of the statutory service, and that part of the recommendation, I need hardly say, has been promptly given effect to. Then the Public Service Commission recommended the reduction—not in so many words but the practical effect of their recommendations came to that—of the number of high appointments hitherto open to natives of India, and finally they voted against Simultaneous Examinations, in spite of the weight of evidence to the contrary. Unsatisfactory as were the results of the labours of the Public Service Commission, the Resolution of the Government of India was still more unsatisfactory. The Public Service Commission had offered us one hundred and eight appointments, hitherto reserved for the Covenanted Service, but the Government of India in the abundance of their good-will to the people reduced the number to 93. *(Laughter and cries of Shame.)* The Public Service Commission had recommended that a Divisional Commissionership and a membership of the Board of Revenue should be assigned to the Provincial service, but for reasons which we are not able to follow, the Government of India thought fit to dispense with this part of their recommendation. The other day I was having a talk with a high official who wanted to know, I quote his words, " the reason why you gentlemen are so persistent in pressing for Simultaneous Examinations." I said if he wanted me to state my views frankly, I would gladly do so. On receiving an assurance that he wished to know my views about the matter, I said " we have lost all faith in the bureaucracy in the matter of the bestowal of high offices on our countrymen. Our interests and their interests are in conflict. Whatever appointments will be given to us will have to be taken away from them ; officials are after all men, not angelic creatures, emanations of the all-beauteous mind, they are swayed by influences and feelings to which all flesh is heir. We feel therefore that we should fall back on a test which shall be independent of the exercise of personal discretion on the part of the members of the bureaucracy."

In pressing for Simultaneous Examinations we take our stand upon the Proclamation of the Queen, (*Hear, hear.*) the Magna Charta of our rights and liberties. (*Applause.*) The Proclamation, the whole Proclamation, and nothing but the Proclamation, is our watch-word, our battle cry, the Gospel of our political deliverance. I have heard it said that to grant Simultaneous Examinations would be to expose the Empire to wreck and ruin. Is it not written in a book—one of the noblest in the literature of mankind, a book which in the judgment of our rulers contains the inspired writings of prophets and sages—that "Righteousness exalteth a nation?" I have yet to learn that any Government or any institution has suffered by adapting its policy to the dictates of justice and morality. Statesmanship divorced from morality is a mean, contemptible thing: it is not worth the name. Statesmanship divorced from morality is political jugglery. I hope I have not tired out your patience. (*No, no.*) You know perfectly well that the Government of India have gone against us, and the Council of the Secretary of State—the old gentlemen of the India Council—they too have gone against us. Will any one in this Congress or outside the Congress tell me what useful purpose the India Council serves? (*Cries of "none."*) It is said to be a consultative body, but it is a body which the Secretary of State need not consult at all. He may, if he chose, ignore his Council. It is the asylum, the haven of refuge for retired Anglo-Indian officials, who having by reason of their age been declared disqualified for service in India, are by reason of their age declared qualified for service in England. What is a disqualification here is a qualification in England. (*Shame.*) I am disposed to make use in this connection of the words which Milton applies to a being whose name shall not be mentioned:—"Evil be thou my good." I do not wish to enter into the various objections which have been raised against Simultaneous Examinations, but there are one or two which call for some remark. It is said that the martial races are opposed to Simultaneous Examinations (*No, no*). I see before me the representatives of the martial races, men whose brothers, relations and friends have fought, and bled in the defence of the Empire, in Burma, in the distant Soudan, and amid the defiles of Afghanistan, men who constitute the bulwark of the Empire,—I appeal to them to say whether they are in favour or against Simultaneous Examinations (*Cries of "in favour."*) I was quite prepared for that response. You have indeed given the lie direct to the allegation by holding the first public meeting in support of Simultaneous Examinations in the Capital of the Punjab; and by whom was that meeting presided over? Not by a Bengalee Babu, but by Sirdar Dyal Singh Majithia, the scion of one of the most illustrious of the Sikh houses in the Punjab. (*Cries of three cheers for Sirdir Dyal Singh.*)

**Third day.**

**Resolution V.**

**Indian Civil Service Simultaneous Examinations in England and in India.**

The Hon'ble Mr. Banerji here called for three cheers for the Hon'ble Mr. Ranade and the Maharajah of Kupurthala who entered the hall at this stage of the proceedings.

The Hon'ble Mr. Banerji continuing his speech said:—Let us travel from the Punjab to the North-West Provinces. You must have followed with some interest the recent elections to the Council of the North-West Provinces. And what is there so noticeable in the elections? We find that the Allahabad group of Municipalities returned my esteemed friend Babu Charoo Chunder Mitter, a Bengali gentleman, as their representative to the Legislative Council. I am perfectly convinced that even the Government itself does not attach the smallest credence to this hollow delusion. If they did, would they have appointed a Bengali gentleman to be a Judge of the High Court of the North West Provinces in succession to Mr. Justice Syed Mahmood? It is too late to raise this question. It is a question involving racial considerations which have been set at rest by the Statute of 1833 and the Proclamation of the Queen, We are further told that the successful candidates must be trained in the highest forms of English education, and that the Examination should be the test for English qualifications. I have not the slightest objection to make the examination as stiff as you like—make it as English as you

Third day.

Resolution V.

Indian Civil Service Simultaneous Examinations in England and in India.

may—but do not delude us with the hollow promise that you will place Englishmen and Indians on the same footing, as regards facilities for admission to these examinations, when you do not mean to do so, when your promises are fettered with conditions, which involve the taking away with the one hand what is conferred with the other. Then we are confornted with difficulties as to the holding of the examination in this country. We are told that a *viva voce* examination cannot be held here. The London University however have agreed to hold Simultaneous Examinations as regards their B.A., and Matriculation standard, and *vivu voce* forms part of the London University Examinations. The London University are a body of experts who must have considered all the difficulties in their way, and must have been convinced that they were not insurmountable in their character. Why should the Government of India be startled out of its wits by the product of its own affrighted imagination? Let them try the experiment in an honest manner, and these obstacles and difficulties, I am convinced, will disappear. There is one of the controversialists in regard to this question whom I have purposely kept in the back ground: he is no other than General Chesney. (*Hissses.*) The Congress possesses such magnanimity that even he may be treated with some little courtesy at our hands. General Chesney was pleased to tell the House of Commons that the competitive test however suitable to English men was unsuitable to the natives of this country, and that the Indian gentlemen who have found their way by competition into the Indian Civil Service have not proved themselves to be able and efficient administrators. I want to read to you two extracts in this connection—one from the pen of Lord Macaulay who holds that the competitive test, although purely intellectual in its character, is also a moral test, and the other extract will be from the report of the Public Service Commission which bears unequivocal testimony to the efficiency as administrators of those Indian gentlemen who have made their way into the Civil Service through the open door of competition. This is what Lord Macaulay says :—"Early superiority in the Sciences and Literature generally indicates the existence of some qualities which are securities against vice—industry, selfdenial, a taste for pleasures not sensual, a laudable desire of honourable distinction, a still more laudable desire to obtain the approbation of friends and relatives. We therefore believe that the intellectual test which is about to be established will be found in practice to be the best moral test that can be devised." Then with reference to the charge against the Indian Civilians who have entered the Service through competition, the Public Service Commission make these remarks :—"The results generally when considered in connection with the positions attained by European officers of similar standing in the service appear to support the view that although on the one hand there may not have been any instances of exceptional success in the official careers of the native gentlemen who have entered the service through the English competition, on the other hand they have not fallen short of the position which Civil Servants with the same length of service ordinarily attain. The Commission is able to add its own testimony that the majority of the Native Covenanted Civilians who were examined as witnesses displayed intelligence and ability in the manner in which they gave their evidence."

I need not detain you at any further length. We are within measurable distance of success. I may say that in one sense we are in view of the promised land. The positon, however, is one that is not free from anxiety and embarrassment. The forces of the bureaucracy are arrayed against us; we are in dire conflict with them; but I have no doubts, or misgivings as to the ultimate issue of this conflict. Where have you heard of a cause, founded upon the highest justice, ennobled by the spirit of liberty, sanctified by the genius of self-sacrifice, has been worsted in the long run? In this conflict we shall be aided by the moral forces of humanity, and the sympathies of the good and the true in all parts of the civilised world will be with us. The banner which so proudly floats over this Congress, and which under God's Providence, I hope and trust, will in a measurable distance of time become the banner of an emancipated people, promises us the victory that is in store for us. (*Loud applause.*) The past fills us with hope. Our record has been a brilliant one. Where is the Vernacular Press Act, where are our sham Councils, where is the Jury Notification? They have all disappeared before the irresistible and the triumphant advance of public opinion (*applause.*) As in the past so in the future, our hopes will be centred in the British House of Commons, the Palladium of liberty, the sanctuary of the free; and to the British Parliament we appeal for enforcing that mandate which is the product of their own spontaneous generosity—to the British Parliament we appeal for justice and liberty, to the British Parliament we appeal for admission to the rights of British citizenship, and to them we appeal to perform towards India the noblest and the most onerous duty that has yet devolved on any nation, ancient or modern, and under God's blessing we are confident that our appeal will not have fallen on heedless ears, but that it will elicit a response worthy of the greatest representative assembly that the world has yet seen. (*Loud and prolonged cheering.*)

MR. HAMID ALI KHAN (*Oudh, No. 181, in list*) in seconding the motion said:—I suffer from two difficulties at the present moment, the first is that notice was just given to me a moment ago and I have had barely time to clear my thoughts when I was called upon to speak, and the second is that I have the pleasure of following the greatest orator of the day whose eloquence is still ringing in our ears. (*Hear, hear.*) I shall consider myself as one of the greatest orators if I do not make a fool of myself before you. (*Laughter.*) Every question as you know has two sides, but the question now engaging the attention of the Congress has only one side. Viewed from another point, it has three sides, a Mahomedan, a Hindu, and an Anglo-Indian side. To the latter it is a question of bread, pure and simple, and as they have been enjoying it the whole of their lives, it is but natural that they should look upon one who endeavours to deprive them of a portion of it as big as the eye of a fly, with anything but affection. (*Laughter.*) But there is every reason to hope that their appetite will give way to a better feeling. I have done with the Anglo-Indians, now one word as to the Hindoo side of the question before I proceed to touch the third side. If simultaneous examinations are allowed and the condition of stopping two years in England after passing is removed, such of the Hindoos as have religious scruples and object to proceed to England will not be required to go there. Then let us look to the third side of the question upon which I wish to dwell fully two minutes. When the news of the passing of simultaneous examinations by the House of Commons reached this country, our Anglo-Indian friends exhibited grave symptoms of affection towards the Mahomedans and the assertion was made that the Mahomedans were preparing a Petition to Parliament against the proposed change. I rejoice to say that the good sense of the Mahomedans has prevailed (*Hear, hear.*) They have refused to listen to the advice of the *Pioneer* and those it represents. Repeated efforts were made in the Provinces by those whose business it is to please the officials to get up a petition, but it failed, and I am sure I represent the views of the Mahomedans, at least of those in my part of the country, when I say without fear of contradiction that the majority are decidedly in favour of holding the examinations in India. As for myself I thoroughly believe that the Mahomedans will, if we succeed in getting the boon, be ever so much better off. Want of means deters many promising young Mahomedans from proceeding to England to prosecute his studies. (*Hear, hear.*) There are I believe twenty four Indian gentlemen who have passed the competetive examination in England and out of those only two are Mahomedans. If we had the simultaneous examinations in India, I am sure that the number of Mahomedans would be much greater and if we succeed in getting this boon I am sure the country will have the pleasure of seeing many Mahomedans

Third day.

Resolution V.

Indian Civil Service Simultaneous Examinations in England and in India.

coming out successful in this country. Supposing I prove to be a false prophet and the Mahomedans do not succeed then it can be safely predicted they will not be in a worse position. But I look at my watch and find the time has nearly gone. I will conclude these remarks by saying, let us one and all, the representatives of every community, creed and sect assembled is this Congress, unanimously pass this resolution of our Grand Old Man (*applause*) who enjoys the confidence and respect of the House of Commons and who commands the admiration and affection of the people to a degree which could be better imagined than described. Mr. Hume is our father and a tower of strength to the Indian Government and a monument of eternal pride and glory to the British Rule. (*Hear, hear.*)

THE HON'BLE RAJA RAMPAL SINGH *(Allahabad, No. 70, in list)* in supporting the resolution said :—After hearing the eloquent speech of my friend the Hon'ble Mr.Surendra Nath Banerji, I have resolved to adopt another method of supporting the resolution, and it is this, my eloquent friend began by praising the generous and liberal Englishmen who supported this motion, I wlll praise the subject itself. The righteousness of this cause is ringing in the ear of every Indian, but does not find any echo in official quarters. It travelled over land and water into the capital of Great Britain and there it touched the hearts of the liberal-minded M. Ps. of England and prepared them to fight the battle. *(Hear, hear.)* A battle was fought and the glory was theirs, but the righteousness of this cause does not rest here. It so impressed the minds of the great party that the Secretary of State through his Lieutenant stated in the Lower House that they had no intention of thwarting the Resolution. That is a proof of the righteousness of the cause in itself. I have shown you the good quality of the cause itself, I should like now to enter into the details and show you the good service it will do to this country if it is accepted by the Government ; both in England and in India. Firstly, it will take away the stigma which has been cast upon Government of practically closing the doors of the Civil Service Examination to Indians. Gentlemen, you know that more than thirty years ago the privilege of passing our examination in England, or in other words of competing for the Civil Service was given us and some of our Bengali friends went there and gained success, of whom Baboo Surendranath Benerji is one. Their success frightened the Indian Government and the consequence was that obstacles began to be put in the way of any more of our countrymen getting admission into that Service by various devices, devices which are not creditable to the high officials who were their authors. One instance of that was the reduction of the age and they held out a sop by opening a new Service in this country called the Statutory Civil Service. It was intended for gentlemen of true merit and ability, but I should say unfortunately it was given to gentlemen of disproved merit and disa bility. (*Hear, hear and laughter.*) If examinations were held in this country it would do an immense deal of good to the people of this country because even with the increase of age it is surely not easy for our candidates to properly compete with the Engligh people in their own language. I will quote one instance to you and you will imagine what difficulties one labours under when he goes to England. I was over 25 years of age when I went to Europe for the first time and though I was accompanied by a number of my Indian servants yet I did not for sometime find it easy to get myself settled there and to manage everything smoothly. Imagine for a boy, a hobbledehoy of 15 to go to England to find everything for himself from laundresses to the landlady. How difficult for him to go and compete in this examination. (*Hear, hear and laughter.*) So, gentlemen, if this concession is granted it will induce our English friends to settle down in this country and if it fails to do that, I am sure it will. be very serviceable to the Hindus, domiciled Christians, Mahomedans and every body. That is one of the blessings it will confer. Another is this that it will create a better feeling between the rulers and the ruled and you know a thing is better secured by being loved than by being feared, and by establishing these examinations in India,

Third day.

Resolution V.

Indian Civil Service Simultaneous Examinations in England and in India.

Her Majesty's Government will please the people so much that they will be doubly prepared to fight against Russia and her enemies if they get this concession. It will check the draining of Indian resources to a certain extent and will stimulate higher education in India. (*Hear, hear.*) Gentlemen, whilst the Indian resoarces are drained away by free trade, I am a liberal, but I should like to see the protectionist policy in India especially for English goods and the English things Maharajahs have. I should have been pleased if our nobles of this country like Peter the Great went to England and learnt shipmaking and learnt to do something. (*Hear, hear.*) If a Maharajah is fond of English articles he would be quite welcome to them if he taught his workmen to make them. (*Hear, hear.*) Foreign articles of luxury are ruining our country. However, gentlemen, Eng lish Civilians have made India their happy hunting ground; they come here and return to England with our money, but were they replaced by Iadians the money would remain in the country. I may now be allowed a little digression which I will finish in a couple of minutes. I belong to the Imperial Club in England. One day I was asked by a member "Rajah, which Government do you praise, English or Mahomedan ?" I said. "So far as the security of life and the security of property is concerned, so far as education is concerned, so far as the facility of communication is concerned I praise yours, but so far as the safety of the riches of India is concerned I praise the Mahomedan Government." (*Hear, hear.*) He then asked what proof I had, and I said :—"You go there and earn and return to your country to spend, but the Mahomedans when they conquered the country became Indians and if they deprived the rajah of his raj, they created a Nawab and if they pulled down a temple they put up a mosque and therefore the riches of the country remained there. But you take the resources of the country away." Don't you, gentlemen think it a shame that all these 35 years we have had the privilege of entering the Civil Service, there are only 20 Indians in it, whilst of Europeans there are between 900 and 1000. If examinations were established in this country, every one who wished to educate his children for it would give them higher education. If you aim high you are sure to hit at least low, but if you don't aim at all you don't kill. The second bell is gone and I finish. I say in conclusion, allow me to assure you, we are members of martial races, but if a man intellectually distinguishes himself, his ablities will be respected by us as well as by Her Majesty's Government irrespective of his race or nationality. (*Loud applause.*)

MUNSHI RASHAN LAL (*Allahabad, No. 78, in list*) said :—MR. PRESIDENT AND BROTHER-DELEGATES,—At the last session of the Congress I ventured to say a few words on the subject of the injustice and injury done to India by not holding simultaneously examinations for the Indian Civil Service both in England and in India. I rejoice to find, gentlemen, that the subject has more prominently come since before the British public and Parliament. Of course we are indebted for this great benefit as for oother political advantages to our worthy Chairman (*Hear, hear.*) All our warmest thanks are also due to Mr. Paul for the sympathy he has shown by successfully moving a resolution in the House of Commons on the subject. (*Hear, hear.*) (*Three cheers were here given for Mr. Paul*) As might have been expected and anticipated this was a great surprise to the Anglo-Indian community. Of course they were bound to raise some sort of objection to it although I was unable to follow many of their arguments. With the greatest difficulty I could make out one thing. They say that if simultaneous examinations were allowed both in England and in India, the Indian Civil Service would become the monopoly of the Bengali Babu. I fail to see how this, in view of Her Most Gracious Majesty's Proclamation, could be an objection. The Proclamation is our pride and hope and you will find it says "We hold ourselves bound to the natives of our Indian territories by the same obligations and duties which bind us to all our other subjects. With the blessing of Almighty God, we shall faithfully and conscientiously fulfil those duties" And it goes on further to say, "And it is our further will, so far as can be, our subiects of whatever race or creed may be freely and impartially admitted to offices in our services to the duties

Third day.

Resolution V.

Indian Civil Service Simultaneous Examinations in England and in India.

of which they may be qualified by their education, ability and integrity fully to discharge. I say, gentlemen, if the Bengali Babus prove by their education and ability and integrity they are able to discharge those duties why should they not do so. But I am prepared to refute the objection as baseless, groundless and utterly untrue. I don't admit that the martial races of the Punjab or the people of the N.W.P. are intellectually inferior to any race in the whole world. (*Hear, hear.*) I will give you one example from Barielly College. Lal Bhedur stood first in the Calcutta University and there are many other examples that the youths of the Punjab and N.W.P. have often outshone our Bengali friends. I don't wish to make any invidious distinctions between races, but I wish to say the objection is baseless. I say if the examinations are held in this country the Bengalis will have only a fair chance with the Hindus, Mahomedans, Punjabis and N.W.P. men. Many a flower in the Punjab is born to bloom unseen and cast its scent on the desert air The men of the Punjab will, when they have the chance, show themselves fitted by ability and integrity to act as Indian Civil Servants. They now bemoan their sad lots and feel that the mere accident of birth, being born in this land, prevents them from entering the service, whereas if they were born in England they would have every chance of coming out to rule over their own country. The law is very unjust and we cannot get it easily amended, but are we to be hopeless? The way has been cleared before us and we believe the British public and Parliament will at no distant date do us justice (*applause.*) When the rules for the Civil Service were passed, India was entirely forgotten and also Her Majesty's Proclamation. These faults will soon be removed and our just rights accorded (*Loud applause.*)

COTARI VENKATA RAMAN NAIDU (*Nagpur, No. 816, in list*) said :—After the orator of India it would be presumptuous for me to venture on any further remarks, so ably has he dealt with the resolution which he has placed before you. The time allowed by the President of this Tribunal, in his wisdom, Is so short that one cannot possibly exhaust the subject either to the satisfaction of the speaker or of the hearers. However, it will suffice if I say as the supporter of this resolution on behalf of the Central Provinces, that it is very essential in the interests of the rulers and the ruled that the examinations for the highest service in the country should be held simultaneously in England and in India. Gentlemen, this is a proposition which is but just and fair and perfectly in accord with the several declarations and proclamations of Her Majesty the Queen of England and Empress of India. It is a subject on which there can possibly be no two opinions and it is hardly worth while my further dilating on the subject. I hope that the motion may be carried unanimously and without a single dissentient voice (*applause.*)

The resolution was then put to the meeting and carried unanimously.

THE PRESIDENT :—I have also to mention that a petition containing eight or nine thousand signatures has been received from the Punjab, which is to go to the House of Commons in connection with the Simultaneus Examinations.

Resolution VI.

Separation of Judicial and Executive functions.

MR. KALI CHARAN BANERJI (*Calcutta, No. 10, in list*) said :—MR. PRESIDENT AND BROTHER-DELEGATES,—The terms of the resolution I have the honour to present are these :—

*'That this Congress having now for many successive years vainly appealed to the Government of India to remove one of the gravest stigmas on British rule in India, one fraught with incalculable oppression to all classes of the community throughout the country, now hopeless of any other redress, humbly entreats the Secretary of State for India to order the immediate appointment, in each province, of a Committee (one half at least, of whose members shall be non-official natives of India, qualified by education and experience in the workings of the various courts to deal with the question) to prepare each a scheme for the complete separation of all Judicial and Executive functions in their own provinces with as*

*little additional cost to the State as may be practicable, and the submission of such schemes, with the comments of the several Indian Governments thereon, to himself, at some early date which he may be pleased to fix.*

Third day.

Resolution VI.

Separation of Judicial and Executive functions.

Brother Delegates, it is not necessary to argue the principle of the resolution, the principle has never been challenged even by the most ardent advocate of the plurality question. We have at the present moment something like an articulate concensus all round in regard to the principle. Refuge from the demand for the practical enforcement of it has been sought in the plea that compliance with it would involve financial insolvency. It will not take you long to be satisfied that that plea is not tenable. I believe that the Department of Finance is not outside the scope of the adage that where there is a will there is a way. (*Hear, hear.*) We have had an illustration, a notable illustration, of the inclusion of the Department of Finance within the scope of this adage; we have had a notable illustration of it in those quarters in which it has been considered that justice demands compensation allowances and there financial insolvency has not been pleaded for one moment. ("*Shame.*") But further, if judicial and executive functions, combined as they are at present, for the most part have been overtaken by a certain body of officers, it is not at any rate an arithmetical improbability that if the functions were separated, and along with such separation there was a division among the officers as well, that the problem might be solved. At any rate we are not left to deal with the question on the basis of *apriori* possibilities. We have to thank an eminent member of that very body of whom as a nation we may justly be proud, an eminent member who has not laid the passion for power to sacrifice within him that feeling for the good of his country and the interests of justice. An eminent member of that very body has given a practical scheme and shows that it is possible without very much additional cost to the State to separate judicial from executive functions and in fact give effect to the resolution. That scheme has been submitted to the inspection of those who have a right to pronounce on the merits of it and, as we know, it has had the approval of the highest authorities. If the principle is acknowledged, if again we are in a position to place before Government a scheme for giving effect to the principle what means this inertia on the part of the Government to give effect to a principle which must be given effect to if justice is to be done in this country. The inertia is inexplicable in this country, and as if to move an inert Government we have had a visitation of late in our part of the country, a visitation in connection with which we have witnessed the focussing of all the evils of this combination. That visitation has been overruled by that same providence by which I believe it was permitted. But yet it is for us to move on the basis of it, so that Government may not be allowed to exalt of the inertia which characterises it in this respect. I refer to the Balladhun murder case, recently disposed of by the High Court in Calcutta. You will allow me to say that whereas the object of this resolution is to prevent in the first place anything like a league, consciously or unconsciously, being entered into between the Magistracy and the Police or the union of the prosecutor and the judge in one and the same person and thus interfere with the administration of the law, and that a young Magistrate should not possess influences of a most unwholesome type which adhere to him even when he passes out of the Executive Department, whereas it is our object to prevent the judges coming into contact with the contagion which attaches to those in the Courts of the Magistrates, I say all these evils have been focussed in this typical case of which we had a practical experience in our part of the country. Let me place before you one after the other the different evils illustrated by that case and as you consider those points you should be in a position to declare, with one voice, that there shall no longer be anything like inertia on the part of Government. (*Hear, hear.*) The case is one in which seven persons, six Manipuris and one Goorkha, were charged with the offence of docoity with murder. About one month after the occurrence, during which time the

Third day.

Resolution VI.

Separation of Judicial and Executive functions.

inference was that not Manipuris but Kukis had committed the offence, the case was taken up by an Inspector of Police and, would you believe it, the men were in the custody of the police for three months before being sent up to the Magistrate and for more than a month, after the police applied before the Magistrate for leave to detain the men as the case had not been completed and the Magistrate always granted an extension of time. (*Shame.*) It so happened that on one particular occasion the police applied for 8 days' time, and what do you fancy was the order of the Magistrate? Why, 10 days instead of 8. Nor is that all. The police managed to extract something like a confession which had to be recorded, but they did not take the men before the Magistrate.

The High Court found on this point there was time enough for the prisoners to have been sent to the Magistrate, who was to try them to record the confession. The way in which the police managed, the way in which it was possible for them to manage, to have the confessions of the prisoners recorded, was that they got two Magistrates to do it who had nothing to do, and would have nothing to do with the trial of these prisoners. They got the Magistrates to travel all the way to where the prisoners were in police custody, there to record their confessions. I have said we aim in this motion to prevent anything like a league between the Magistrates and the police. There ought to be a check on the police, but here we find that the Magistracy showed themselves obsequious to the demands of the police and as if both had one and the same object in view. Then we come to the Magistrate himself; the Magistrate who committed these prisoners to take their trial at the Sessions. Prosecutor and judge as he was, let us consider how he went about the business. When the prisoners were placed before him for trial, application was made that they should be allowed to consult their pleader. Will you believe it, that application was refused. ("*Shame.*") Then again when the witnesses for the prosecution were examined in chief, an application was made on behalf of the prisoners that they should be allowed to exercise the right of cross-examination. Will you believe it, brother delegates, that application was also refused. ("*Disgraceful*") Nor was that all. There was a witness in the box and whilst being examined he gave evidence of a certain kind. The Investigating Police Officer was there and he told the Magistrate that the witness had told a different story to him and he, the Magistrate, declared that he was a hostile witness, although there was nothing before him to determine or even to infer why he should do so beyond the whispered insinuation of the Police officer. There was no justification for this as the High Court has found. And on the basis of this whisper not only did the Magistrate declare the witness a hostile witness, but he called upon him to find bail to the extent of Rs. 200, in order that he might appear to answer a charge of perjury that might be brought against him. ("*Shame, shame*".) And so the prosecutor and judge behaved after that style. I have referred to a third evil, how the Magistrates who pass through this training when they grow to be Judges cannot get over the influence which dominates them whilst Magistrates. Consider how the Sessions Judge behaved. When before the Sessions Judge it was pointed out that a great deal of pressure—which need not be characterised—had been used on these prisoners to extort confessions from them, the judge said he could not believe tutoring because he considered the Inspector of police was incapable of tutoring. Nor was that all; some of the witnesses examined before him, had a different story to tell to that given before the Magistrate, and although when examined before the Magistrate the test of cross-examination had been denied to the prisoners, nevertheless the Sessions Judge received the depositions made before the Magistrate's Court in order to contradict the evidence given before him, a procedure with which the High Court has found fault. And to crown all there was a document in the case which, if admitted in evidence, would have destroyed the case for the prosecution and completely smashed it up. It was the dying dclaration of a woman found to have been mortally wounded. The Sessions Judge would not allow the document to be received in evidence. He said it was a statement which had been made not in the presence of the accused persons and consequently when the accused persons wanted to have the benefit of it, they were denied it. ("*Most shameful.*") An application was made on behalf of the prisoners, that the Magistrate before whom the statement was made, should be examined at the Sessions trial in order that any difficulty might be got over. "Now," says the Sessions judge, "I have read through the dying declaration and I say it is an incoherent and unreliable statement and it is no use sending for the Magistrate." For a time he passed no order but eventually refused the application. So while denying to the accused the benefit of the declaration, he, in his executive capacity, looked into the document and pronounced judgment on it, and absolutely refused to call the Magistrate, before whom the statement had been recorded. You will see how this God-given Police, Committing Magistrate, and Sessions Judge, at every stage exhibited the evils of this combination of judicial and executive functions ; and if nothing else would move the Government, I say this case ought to have moved the Government, for you know that the result of the Sessions Judge's trial was that four of the prisoners were sentenced to death and three to transportation for life. If you have any consideration for these persons who passed through an ordeal which must challenge all description,—men who had this sentence of death hanging on them for such a time—if you have any sympathy for them you will pass this motion, and go to the Secretary of State and demand that the Government of India shall no longer be allowed to exhibit a culpable inertia in this matter. (*Loud applause.*)

THE HON'BLE N. SUBBARAO PANTULU GARU *(Madras, No. 856, in list)* in seconding the motion said :—MR. PRESIDENT, BROTHER-DELEGATES, LADIES AND GENTLEMEN,—After what has so eloquently fallen from the mover of this proposition, it is hardly necessary for me to place before you any further arguments. However, it is but right in this connection that I should state that the Madras Government have initialled a scheme, though of a small and limited extent, for separating the judiciary in the lower ranks and divesting it of its executive functions. That scheme has been in work for a week or two, but I say that so long as the higher ranks of the Magistracy are not divorced from the executive functions, no substantial justice can be done to the people of the country. As an instance, I will bring to your notice a case from a district in my Province, namely, Salem. There a merchant was assessed with an income tax for the year 1892-93 and he preferred an appeal to the Deputy Collector who is also the Deputy Magistrate. That appeal was in due course rejected and he paid the tax. Sometime in November 1892, two months later, the Deputy Magistrate was deputed by Government to investigate a case against a subordinate official and one day, on the 6th February 1893, he took it into his head to summon that same merchant whose business had all been settled, to produce his account books before him (the Deputy Collector and Deputy-Magistrate) at eleven o'clock that very morning. The summons which was sent out that morning reached him at half past ten and the merchant arrived a little after twelve noon. I may here mention that in the printed summons form, the hour had been put down at 12, but had been changed to 11 for reasons best known to the Deputy Collector himself. When the merchant arrived he was asked why he had disobeyed the summons, and why he had not come at 11. o'clock as stated in the summons. He replied that the summons had only reached him at 10. 30 and he had made all haste to obey the call of the Deputy collector. A statement explanatory of his conduct was taken down and then the Deputy Magistrate went on to take a statement in connection with the conduct of the official into whose case he had been ordered to enquire. Apparently, the answers of the merchant were not satisfactory ; there was something more he might have stated which would have supported the case against the official in question. A few days later, proceedings were issued by the same Deputy Magistrate and Collector, ordering the

Third day.

Resolution VI.

Separation of Judicial and Executive functions.

prosecution of the merchant for disobedience of the summons in respect of which he had already given his explanation, and the case was transferred to the Subordinate Magistrate who was divested altogether of all executive functions. He took the case in his file, entered it in his diary, gave it a number and ordered processes to be issued. But there came an oral message from the Deputy Magistrate and Collector that the case should be stopped ; so the Subordinate Magistrate scored out the entry and substituted in its place another case the number of which should properly have been 53. He changed there to 45 and scored out the 45 from the records so as to make it appear that there had been no case against this merchant before. A day or two later the Deputy Magistrate and Collector issued an order that the proceedings should be stayed for the present. That order was issued sometime in February 1893 ; and up to date the proceedings have been stayed for the present and I don't know when that present will become the past. (*Laughter.*) This illustrates my contention that although there is a partial separation in the lower grades,there can be no substantial justice and good to the country until the judicial and executive functions are completely divorced. Well, we are thankful to the Government for giving us a concession in connection with the Legislative Councils, but it is with the deepest regret that we see the Government are apathetic with regard to most necessary reforms touching alike the poor and the rich and we hope and trust that this appeal to the Secretary of State will be productive of good and in due course committees will be arranged for which will submit schemes. I am sure that any additional cost with which each or any Provincial Fund might be saddled in this connection will be amply compensated by the closer attention which the Revenue officials will be able to pay to that branch and which will bring additional revenue to the Exchequer of the country. (*applause.*)

BABU AMBICA CHURN MAZOOMDAR (*Bengal, No. 35, in list*) said:—MR. PRESIDENT, BROTHER DELEGATES, LADIES AND GENTLEMEN,—Although the question of the separation of the judicial and executive functions has prominently engaged the attention of this assembly for the last seven or eight years, its history is as old as the days of the permanent settlement. In those days the civil, the criminal and the fiscal functions were all united in the same person generally known as the Collector of the district, and it is exactly 100 years to-day that Lord Cornwallis whose administration is distinguished for the many reforms it introduced in the judicial system of this country, was the first to effect a disrupture in this tripple alliance by separating the Dewani from the *Mal Adwalats.* Gentlemen, it was Section 1 of Reg II of 1793 which introduced this great change. But although the civil powers were thus wrested away from the hands of the Collector, the Criminal functions still remained vested in him. It appears, gentlemen, that it is not we who have suddenly grown restless agitators, but it seems, our grandfathers even were ill-content with this anomalous system. For, that great Indian reformer, politician and philanthropist—that giant agitator, Rajah Ram Mohun Roy, over and over again bore testimony to the general feeling of his age. Gentlemen, my time is limited and I can only refer you to the remarkable evidence which he gave before a Committee of the House of Commons in 1831. Ram Mohun Roy did not live to see the result of this enquiry ; but you all know, how in 1833 a regulation was passed (I mean Reg IX of that year) by which Deputy Collectors and assistants were provided exclusively for revenue work, and how in 1839 the judicial and executive functions of the Magistrate-Collector were separated, the Collector's salary being fixed at Rs. 23,000 and that of the Magistrate at Rs. 12,000 a year. And seven years after, Act XV of 1843 created the class of officers known as Deputy Magistrates for relieving the District Magistrates. But alas! the eventful year 1858, among other changes, witnessed after 20 years the unhappy reunion of the judicial and the executive functions. The Collector was reinvested with Magisterial powers, and the Deputy Collectors and the Deputy Magistrates were amalgamated into what is now known as the subordinate executive service.

Since the question has been taken up by this Congress, one Viceroy at least has openly declared himself in favour of our proposal. Latterly, the subject has engaged also the attention of the British public and Parliament, chiefly through the exertions of our British Committee in London and the generous labours of Sir Richard Garth, the late Chief Justice of Bengal; and recently two successive Secretaries of State have admitted the desirability of our proposal. Lord Cross said, that he thought the subject to be so important that he was anxious to deal with it himself; and Lord Kimberley has admitted that the fusion is, to use his Lordship's own language, "contrary to right and good principle." Sometime in April last in the House of Lords, Lord Stanley of Alderley asked, "Whether in view of the unsatisfactory state of criminal administration in India, Government was prepared to effect a separation between the Judicial and the executive functions." In reply to this the Earl of Kimberley said:—"though the proposal was most desirable, yet Government was unable to entertain it, as it would require double the staff at present to do so."

What a grim mockery! with one-sixth of the entire population of the country living in a state of chronic starvation, and the most industrious people of the most fertile parts of the largest province in the empire passing through an actual famine, and an embarrassed treasury, according to Sir David Barbour, threatened with an apalling deficit of nearly two crores of rupees, Government was able to entertain the proposal for compensation allowance and with one stroke of the pen grant over 100 lakhs of rupees for the *savings* of the most *extravgantly* paid officers in the world; but alas! it was unable to entertain a proposal for the reform of its judicial administration at a probable cost of even less than one-eighth of that amount!

As to this cost, gentlemen, you are aware that various schemes have been suggested from different quarters, all of which clearly tend to shew that the proposal is quite feasible and that Lord Kimberley's assertion is based upon either misconception or misrepresentation. In May last, at the invitation of the Indian Association, I had the honour of proposing one of these schemes which I now submit to your judgment, particularly as I have been emboldened to do so on account of the support it has materially found in the scheme subsequently prepared and published by Mr. R. C. Dutt of the Indian Civil Service. Gentlemen, Messrs. Dutt and B. De, who have both clearly pointed out the feasibility of the proposal are District Magistrates of very high reputation and, as such, their opinions are entitled to very great weight. The scheme which I now beg to submit to this house is as follows:—

The primary idea involved in this question is the establishment of two parallel lines of service without any point of contact with each other; one of these lines embracing the executive, and the other the purely judicial functions of criminal administration. Any scheme that may be devised for the establishment of such a system must proceed upon a fair consideration of the strength requisite for each branch of the service, and of the nature of control and supervision necessary for its proper maintenance, regard being always had to the paramount consideration of the financial position of the State and the economic condition of the people. I propose to discuss the question under four different heads.

### I.—DISTRIBUTION OF OFFICERS.

2. Considering the position and strength of the present combined service, it will be found that there are 47 districts in Bengal, Behar, Orissa, and Chota Nagpore. These are divided into 135 executive sub-divisions, including the *sudder*. These 135 sub-divisions are manned by 434 officers in the subordinate judicial and executive service. They are classed as follows:—

**Third day.**

**Resolution VI.**

**Separation of Judicial and Executive functions.**

| | | |
|---|---|---|
| Dy. Magistrate and Dy. Collectors | ... ... | 294 |
| Probationary Dy. Magistrates | ... ... ... | 20 |
| Special Dy. Collectors | ... ... ... | 23 |
| Sub-Deputy Magistrates and Sub-Deputy Collectors | ... | 97 |
| | Total ... | 434 |

If the 23 special Deputy Collectors be taken out of this number, there remain 411 officers who are employed in the performance of the subordinate judicial and executive work in the Lower Provinces. Now, upon a proper comparison of the different kinds of work usually performed by these officers, it will be found that the amount of executive business done by them nowhere bears an even proportion to their judicial work. At the head-quarter stations two-thirds of their time are usually devoted to criminal cases, and only one-third to revenue, settlement, excise, income-tax, land registration, certificate, chowkidari, and other miscellaneous business of an executive nature. At the sub-divisions where executive work is very light, nearly three-fourths of the time of the sub-divisional officers are generally given to the disposal of criminal cases.

3. From the above it would at once appear that the practical difficulty, as far as the actual working of the proposed system is concerned, arises in dealing with the sub-divisions, where generally there is but one officer for both kinds of work. This difficulty is further enhanced from a consideration of the fact that it is not even possible to entertain another whole-time officer for most of these places. The judicial officer would no doubt find his hands fairly full, but the executive officer would not. To obviate this state of things I would first of all propose to effect a partial readjustment of executive work according to territorial limits. It may be necessary to have certain classes of these works centralized at the district head-quarters; but I do not understand why the land registration, income-tax and the certificates for each sub-division may not be, with considerable advantage, transferred to their respective sub-divisions. Such an arrangement would greatly relieve the congested head-quarters, and add vastly to the convenience of the people. This being done, it seems easy enough to have a fair distribution of officers for the two functions separately. This I shall illustrate by the following process.

4. There are, as shewn above, 135 sub-divisions *i.e.*, 47 head quarter or *sudder* and 88 rural sub-divisions. Having regard to the proportion of the works appertaining to the two functions as noticed above, 3 judicial and 2 executive officers for each of the 47 sudder sub-divisions, and 1 judicial and 1 executive officer for each of the 88 rural sub-divisions, would be a fair adequate distribution for the entire province; and it is a singular coincidence that the result would be found exactly to tally with the present strength of the subordinate service. Thus—

| | | |
|---|---|---|
| Judicial | ... ... | 47×3=141 |
| | | 88×1= 88 |
| | | 229 |
| Executive | ... ... | 47×2=94 |
| | | 88×1=88 |
| | | 182 |
| Total | ... | 411 |

Third day.

Resolution VI.

Separation of Judicial and Executive functions.

For the sake of convenience the 229 judicial officers may be designated Deputy Magistrates, and the 182 executive officers Deputy Collectors. It will be observed that the 23 special Deputy Collectors who may be required for special duties have been kept out of this calculation.

5. It may be noticed here that there was a time, when almost every important sub-division used to be manned with two officers, and it is only recently that the secret tendency of centralization, so deeply ingrained in Indian administration, has drawn more officers to the head-quarters. The effect of this narrow policy is observable in the actual outturn of work in the sub-divisions, as compared with the sudder stations. The sub-divisional officers, unable to cope with their work single-handed, manage to cut down the number of criminal institutions by summarily dismissing a large percentage of these cases under Section 203 of the Criminal Procedure Code; whereas at the head-quarters where complaints are usually received by the District Magistrate, the file is always three times as heavy as in a sub-division. When a sub-divisional magistrate is complimented in the administration report as having successfully put down crime within his jurisdiction, it has virtually no other meaning than that he has used this process of simplification more largely than usual. These *clever* officers are not certainly abler than the District Magistrates or their fellows at the head-quarters. What they really do is to discourage litigation, rather than repress crime. Hence beneath the even surface of official reports there is always an under-current of wide-spread popular discontent. Much of the abuses in our criminal administration may be traced to this source, though popular indignation is often-times mistakenly directed against either the helpless officers concerned, or the controlling Magistrate who is sometimes forced to be a party to these unseemly proceedings. A fair distribution of officers and of work would also largely improve the tone of the present criminal administration all over the country.

6. I do not pretend to maintain that, after all, it may not still be found necessary to increase the present strength of the service by the addition of a few more officers to meet the exigencies of this or that place, or the occasional necessities of the one or the other branch of the service. Such additional provisions are not at times avoidable, even under the existing system, and may not, I presume, be found too much to bear under the proposed separation. The statement of the Earl of Kimberley in reply to the question put by Lord Stanley of Alderley in the House of Lords, that it would require *double the staff* to effect a separation of the two functions is clearly based upon a misapprehension of facts. Given the total amount of consolidated work and the number of officers who conjointly perform the same, it is rather difficult to conceive how by resolving the former into its component parts, it is rendered impossible to meet the requirements of each part by a proportionate distribution of the latter without *doubling* its strength As has been already pointed out, some slight increase might be found necessary; but to say that it would necessitate an enormous increase by one-half, or even one-fourth the present number, is surely an exaggeration.

## II.—ESTABLISHMENT.

7. As regards the establishment of ministerial officers, it seems hardly necessary to point out that the scheme herein proposed nearly does away with additional expenditure on this head. There is at present provision for 4 such officers to each Deputy Magistrate and Deputy Collector, and if a separation is effected by a redistribution of the latter the establishments must necessarily go with their superior officers. No doubt some incidental and initial expenses will be required. The question of expenditure will, however, be separately considered as bearing upon the whole question.

Third day.

Resolution VI.

Separation of Judicial and Executive functions.

III.—CONTROL.

8. Now comes the rather difficult question of control and supervision. On the executive side, the collector, by which I would purpose to designate the chief executive head of a district, may no doubt, as at present, have the entire management and control of the subordinate executive branch ; and the only question is how to deal with the judicial branch cut off from the present amalgamated service. Is it to be placed solely and exclusively under the Sessions Judge ? Or is it to be managed by a district officer, independent of the latter and exercising functions similar to those of the present District Magistrate ? The latter alternative is open to the serious objection of having the effect of practically not *separating the two* functions but of *splitting up the administration into three* parts ; and the working of such a system would, in all probability, result in the creation of two instead of one autocratic functionary for each district. Much of the criminal law of the country, for obvious reasons, has a distinct tendency to relapse towards arbitrary exercise of authority, and an independent officer at the head of a number of Magisterial subordinates will necessarily become as meddlesome and obstructive, as the district magistrates are supposed to be at present. On the other hand by placing the subordinate magistrates entirely under the sessions judge, the work of that officer would be increased to an extent where it would be impossible to expect adequate supervision and proper discharge of business, without serious detriment to his other legitimate duties. Not to speak of purely administrative work incidental to every department of administration, there would be such a heavy file of appeals and references as to completely over-master a single officer, however high his abilities may be. These and other considerations induce me to reject either of the above proposals, and to suggest the following arrangement as being least open to any serious objection.

9. The judicial branch in question may be safely placed under the sessions judge with a joint-magistrate under him with the power of hearing appeals from subordinate magistrates. This officer, whether he be called an additional or an assistant or a subordinate sessions judge will occupy pretty nearly the same position under the court of sessions as the subordinate judge on the civil side now holds under the district judge. All appeals from the decisions of subordinate magistrates should be preferrable to the judge of sessions, and by him as in civil cases transferred to this additional officer for disposal. He should besides be able to assist the judge in matters of account and inspection, as also in such other business as may be delegated to him. As to original institutions at the head quarters, complaints may be received by officers, and then distributed among the several deputy magistrates according to their respective jurisdiction. More than the present district magistrate, he will also be in a position to dispose of a large number of original cases. Thus, there will be established one complete system of judicial administration, with two branches, civil and criminal, diverging from a common point, the former including the subordinate civil judge and the munsiffs, and the latter the subordinate sessions judge, and the deputy magistrates. The Collector will thenceforth be left in undisturbed control over the purely executive service, consisting of the deputy collectors, the police, the registration and other departments. He will then be in a position also to attend more properly to the growing business of the district and local boards, and to attend to sundry other works of all of which he may be now called the jack though the master of none. There seem to be another distinct advantage in this proposal. The additional officers proposed to be recruited from the rank of Joint Magistrates who in time are to succeed as District and Sessions Judges, will have a special training under this system, and are therefore likely to prove infinitely superior to those raw half-trained Joint-Magistrates, who are now unfortunately pitchforked to the very responsible position of District Judges without, however, the requisite training and experience that alone can ensure success in judicial trials, and compensate for the natural shortcomings of a foreign judge.

Third day.

Resolution VI.

Separation of Judicial and Executive functions.

IV.—COST.

10. As to the additional cost involved in these charges, various suggestions have from time to time been made for the curtailment of expenses in other directions. The cost of the often-talked of exodus of Governments to the hills is an unnecessary and cruel burden on the people. The military and home charges might afford not a small field for a strong Government to secure proper economy. The disestablishment of the Indian church or a reduction thereof might also be pointed out as one of the available sources. But each and all of these suggestions involve questions of very grave difficulty In fact some of these may be found almost impracticable under the present state of affairs. I would, therefore, confine my proposals nearer home and within the range of practical economy.

11. At the last Congress at Allahabad I had occasion to point out, though very cursorily, that over 6 *lakhs* of rupees are annually spent for mere supervision and control of the police department. It has to be noted that this large sum is absorbed simply in the pay and travelling allowances of the district and assistant superintendents of Police It was there shown that there were no less than 57 of such officers in Bengal and Behar. It would appear that the strength for the entire Presidency, including Orissa and Chota Nagpore, consisted of 50 district superintendents, 36 assistant superintendents and 15 *probationers!* By a strange irony of fate, a recent Resolution of the local Government sanctioned by the Government of India and the Secretary of State, has changed this already heavy list into one of 55 district superintendents, 29 assistant superintendents, and 8 probationers, giving a grand total of 93 officers maintained on a salary of Rs. 50,350 *per mensem.* It would thus appear that while the pay and travelling allowances of these officers together amounted in 1885 to Rs. 6,01,974, their pay alone would now amount to Rs. 6,04,200 a year. This is the order of progress and economy in our Indian administration! It is quite apparent that with the exception of a few appointments for the Hill Tracts and one or two military out-posts, the services of most of these officers could be safely dispensed with, when the present district magistrates would be left free to superintend the Police department more closely and efficiently than at present. In fact, it would be simply monstrous, after the proposed separation, to retain two heads for a simple department. There was time when probably the commissioner of the division was known also as the superintendent of the police, and the same designation might hereafter be transferred to the collector. Subsequent enquiries have only confirmed me in the opinion then expressed by me, and my present conviction is that the practical difficulty in that direction lies only in the sweeping nature of the proposal. At all events it may be found quite practicable to abolish the post of the 29 Assistant Superintendents who are merely sinecures kept only as a reserve for leave vacancies, and a considerable saving may thus be effected without prejudice to any department. These assistant superintendents, be it noted, alone cost us Rs. 1,21,000 a year, besides travelling allowances.

12. But the principle source from which the necessary fund may properly be drawn is the large surplus receipt from the judicial administration. The figures are contained in Government's own annual reports of successive years. Take, for instance, the account for 1890. It stands thus :—

| Heads. | | Receipts. | Expenditure. |
|---|---|---|---|
| | | Rs. | Rs. |
| Civil | ... | 85,61,519 | 49,89,686 |
| Criminal | ... | 13,92,088 | 25,97,558 |
| Total | ... | 99,53,607 | 75,87,244 |

So, in that year there was a clear surplus of over 230 *lakhs* of rupees after meeting a deficit of more than 12 *lakhs* on the criminal side. Pretty nearly the same state of things may be predicated of every year of our judicial administration. This enormous saving ought legitimately to be spent on the improvement of that administration. The people have oftentimes complained of this unjust saving, and Sir Richard Garth, C.J, once urged it as a ground for a considerable reduction in the court-fess. If the money will now be diverted to its proper channel and spent in carrying out a much-desired reform in the judicial administration of the country, the people may be expected to be satisfied with their money's worth.

13. As to the 47 new appointments required to be opened under the proposed arrangement, it must be remembered that there exist even at present several joint-magistrates in some of the largest and most important districts. Even supposing that their full number were all to be new creations, the cost of maintaining these 47 officers, taking the salary of each, at Rs. 900, (the pay of a first grade joint-magistrate) would be found to be only little over 5 *lakhs* of rupees a year. The extra deputy magistrates that may possibly be required according to the varying circumstances of some of the most criminal and the largest districts cannot be in all more than 20 in number, and these, together with their establishments, would not involve a further outlay of more than another 1½ *lakhs* a year. Surely it would not be difficult to meet a demand of 7 *lakhs* of rupees out of the sources just mentioned.

V.—HONORARY MAGISTRATES.

14. To minimise the demand for additional subordinate magistrates, I would suggest for further extension and development of the system of trial by honorary magistrates. Pleaders, as a rule, are now almost wholly excluded from participation in this branch of honorary service. I fail to perceive the logic of this exclusion, particularly in the case of those members of the profession who carry on little or no business in the subordinate criminal courts. The number of these magistrates, as well as of the benches composed of them, might therefore be largely increased. A system of promotion might also be introduced so as to invest them with higher and more extended powers as they either gain in experience, or prove their efficiency in administration. The benches already established in the mofussil are found to perform not an inconsiderable amount of work though they usually sit only once or twice a week. If their number be increased, it would be possible to have daily sittings of these magistrates by the process of rotation. In that case a large amount of work might be disposed of by such magistrates, who would thus prove very useful and substantial adjuncts to the general administration.

From the scheme as detailed above it will appear, that with a slight redistribution of work, the proposed separation may easily be effected, and that even if the reform were to be carried out throughout the whole of the Bengal Presidency, including Behar, Orissa and Chota Nagpur, the total additional cost would not exceed more than 6 *lakhs* of rupees at a liberal calculation.

In Madras a partial separation has already been effected by separating the subordinate judicial and the executive branches. It is gratifying to observe, that in the last administration report for Madras, the Government ungrudgingly admits, that the separation, as partially effected, has worked satisfactorily. It is satisfactory also to note, that so much has been done there at little or no additional cost. But the district head still continues to be the same there as it is in other provinces. A separation in this may be effected at a very small cost, as there are only 21 districts in that Presidency and the additional expenditure under this head cannot probably exceed two *lakhs* of rupees a year.

In Bombay the Hon'ble Pherozshah Mehta has suggested a scheme which seems to be eminently adapted to the state of the Western Presidency. Lately in the Bombay

Third day.

Resolution VI.

Separation of Judicial and Executive functions.

Council he said :—Increase the number of Sub-judges and invest them with Magisterial powers, and curtail the number of Assistant Collectors and Mamlatdars. He would fix the salary of the new Sub-Judges at Rs. 300/—and by working out this scheme the Hon'ble member for the Bombay University has distinctly pointed out that there would be a saving of over one lakh of rupees in that Presideney. Gentlemen, joking is no argument, and yet all the argument advanced from the side of Government against this fair proposal was but an unseemly joke used at the expense of a poor old woman! The Hon'ble Mr. Nugent said :—"The Mamlatdars were perhaps the hardest worked officers under Government and the most deserving. The present system worked very well, although they might occasionally hear of an asthmatic old lady being fined Rs. 15 for making salt." This, gentlemen, I take to be the first official note of opposition to our proposal. But how true it is that shafts at random sent often find marks the archer little meant. Yes, if the Mamlatdars are the hardest worked officers under Government, why not relieve them of their criminal duties? If they are the most deserving, why not make the best of them the additional Sub-Judges? The present system does not bring them either relief or reward. Then the Hon'ble member says *the present system worked very well.* Very well indeed! But very well for whom that is the question. Yes, it is very well for some person to be able to chase and belabour with impunity a tender boy of 11 years of age for the grave offence of saying Good morning" to a European and then to have his complaint dismissed, because the beating did not leave any mark on his person. It is very well indeed for a Deputy Commissioner to be able to tear off documentary evidence against him from the records of a Court of Justice and enjoy greater immunity than a Duchess in England. How very well it is to have an unfortunate gentleman tried thrice over for the same alleged offence, because each time the order of discharge failed to recommend itself to the District Magistrate and then to have him ultimately convicted by a subordinate Magistrate. It is of course very well for a settlement officer to be able to go armed with gun and force open into the Zenana of a respectable Zemindar and thence drag him in illness a distance of 30 miles, and after all this to be sure to get the support and sympathies of the district and the divisional authorities. How very well it is for an Assistant Magistrate to be able to set at naught the order of a Sessions Judge for bail and keep a poor stamp vendor in jail at his own sweet pleasure; and how supremely well it is for a magistrate to have the fancy to drive quietly through the crowded streets of one of the busiest cities in the country and finding a slow moving heavy laden cart in his way, to come down and flog the unfortunate driver down to the ground and then have the poor man's complaint compromised in the court of a Subordinate Magistrate. Sir, it may be some satisfaction to you to learn that since you left us in 1887, we have made some progress in our act of proseletysing to our faith. A Magistrate of Patna has accepted the first commandment of our creed and ruled that the time for the cross-examination of witnesses for the prosecution should be always cut down to 5 minutes. May the time be not far distant when the entire propaganda of this Congress will be accepted by the services in their entirety.

But gentlemen, we are perhaps forgetting the "asthmatic old lady." Poor Aka Bhujanga was fined 15 rupees for boiling a little salt-earth for medicinal purposes! But does the Hon'ble gentleman know that the average income of an Indian hardly exceeds Rs. 20 a year? Indian salt seems to have no strength in these days; or as salt now comes from Liverpool, probably no one need now owe any obligation to the Indian tax payer.

But it is no use enumerating concrete cases of injustice and hardship arising from the fusion of these two functions. Every year such instances are increasing in amazing number. So long, however, as these cases were referrable to mere individual idioscyncracies there could not be perhaps much danger. But when Governments and administrations

**Third day.**

**Resolution VI.**

**Separation of Judicial and Executive functions.**

begin openly to countenance and encourage such practices, the matter necessarily wears a different aspect and becomes one of gravest apprehensions to the people ; for then it becomes a part of the settled policy of the administration. From individual cases to generalizations and from generalizations to theories and principles—this is the order of all human institutions ; and, gentlemen, we are at the present moment brought face to face with such a grave crisis. After numberless instances of improper interference with the judicial independence of our magistrates, we now find Governments and administrations boldly enunciating the principle in their public resolutions. The first enunciation is contained in the Government of Bengal's resolution dated the 28th November, 1891, on the Report of the Police Commission of that year which strongly recommended, that for the better administration of criminal justice, the best local legal practitioners should be engaged to advise the police and assist the Magistrates. On this the Government said:—"Sir Charles Elliot doubts if cases would be much improved by legal advice given to the Police. If advice is required the District or the Sub-divisional Magistrate is the proper person to apply to. The Lieutenant-Governor is, however, of opinion that more attention should be devoted to the prosecution of Police Cases." And again in para 10 of the resolution :—"The District Magistrates are to assist their Subordinate Magistrates by judicious advice and criticism." Here, gentlemen, probably lies the root of those astounding revelations which came to light in the well-known Backergunge case and which subsequently formed the subject of a serious dispute between the Chief Justice and the Lieutenant-Governor of Bengal.

Then, the same Government in the administration report for the last year quotes with approbation the opinion of the Commissioner of the Rajshahye Division that "no magistrate should pass any decision without consulting the District Magistrate." Again the very same Government says, "they (the magistrates) prefer to consider themselves *Judges* and to assign to the Police the functions of committing Magistrates." Yes, to the eternal glory of Indian magistrates be it ever recorded that they prefer to consider themselves as judges. So much for original trials. Then as to commitments to the Court of Sessions. Sir Charles Elliot in his resolution on the administration report for Tipperah says, "As regards sessions trials the magistrate has adopted, not unknown to me, of allowing no commitment till he is consulted and till the record is inspected by him. Mr. Macpherson practically followed this course."

Gentlemen, it is no wonder that with plain directions such as these emanating from the Government itself, the Judicial independence of subordinate magistrates should stand completely paralysed. And truly has Justice Trevelyan observed in the disgraceful case of Pullup Singh Vs. Perry—"Of course every subordinate Magistrate is liable to some extent to be influenced by observations made by the district magistrates ; but the arrangements for the administration of justice in this country are responsible for the danger."

Gentlemen, how fast doth contagion spread ! From Calcutta to Madras, over 900 miles across the sea, and not long ago we find there the Magistrate of Bellary issuing the following circular published in the Hindu of Sep. 6. last, which has unmistakably a strong family likeness to the circulars of the Lower Provinces. The circular says :—"The magistrates ought to support the police and they ought not to consider that their duty is to sit and hear cases as the High Court and Sessions Judges do and decide on evidence ; but they should remember, that they are there for repressing crimes." Are Sessions Judges and High Courts, we ask, for encouraging crimes ?

Then from Madras to the Punjab, a distance of over 1200 miles, and there we find the Cantonment Magistrate of Jullunder in forwarding two cases to Deputy Commissioner

Third day.

Resolution VI.

Separation of Judicial and Executive functions.

Colonel Roberts, writing the following pleasant epistle which surpasses all comments. "My dear Roberts, in forwarding these two cases I had been particularly asked by Colonel Pennington to ask you to try the case yourself, or to send to an European Magistrate. As you will be busy packing &c. prior to going home, and the case is likely to be a long one, you would kindly transfer it to Rowe. We are very anxious that a searching enquiry be made and an exemplary punishment be given. Colonel Pennington and I have both been vilified by these men who are the cats-paws of some big men among the sudder agitators."

But, gentlemen, the climax of this ludicrous farce is probably reached in the North Western Provinces where even an Inspector of Jails can, it seems, sit in judgment over judicial officers. "The list of such criminals," writes this august functionary, "who, in my opinion, have been treated with exceptional leniency by the convicting courts, contains several instances indicating either a pussilanimity on the part of courts in dealing effectively with criminals of this class, or a deplorable indifference to the repression of crimes by omitting to award deterrent sentences. In this connection I desire to invite attention to the pertinent comments of Government contained in para 10 of the review of the Police Report for 1891, wherein it is observed that inefficient Magistrates who are habitually incapable of appreciating the relative heinousness of crime, of apportioning the punishment to the offences, or of exercising discrimination in the examination of evidence, shall not be allowed to exercise their powers unchecked." Alas! what an impertinence on the one hand and a degradation on the other! I am sure the Government which issued the original edict will itself be sorry to find, that its declarations should have led to such travesty of administration. How truly did Sir John Peter Grant writing in 1856 observe,—"The smoothness and silence with which public affairs go on when all power in all departments is centred in one train of officials cannot be regarded as good for the people, however agreeable they may be for the administration. The existing system of criminal procedure, to speak in moderate language, is not like the system of a country administered by rational beings." These, gentlemen, are not the words of any Congress man, but of an English administrator uttered 30 years before the birth of this Congress.

In the name of justice and humanity we appeal to the noble instincts of the great Anglo-Saxon race and beseech them to preserve in this country those lofty traditions of their own which are associated with the mighty progress of the world. To Whigs and Tories, to Liberals and Conservatives, to Radicals and Unionists, we appeal to all; for they are all Britons, whose ancestors in days gone by have judged kings and princes, peers and commons with evenhanded justice, and before whose august tribunal, in our own day, even the heir-apparent to the throne bows as low as the lowest subject in the realm. Such is the glory of the British constitution, and may that glory shine with undiminished splendour in the East as it is doing in the West. The most extravagant arrangements are being every year made for the maintenance of what is called "a scientific frontier", and we ask only for the establishment of a rational interior. And as loyal subjects of the crown we would remind our rulers, that the hugest structures have often-times the largest cracks, and therefore the best edifices are those which are surest at the foundations.

MR. RAGHUNATH PANDURANG KARANDIKAR (*Satara, No. 741, in list*) said:— This was a subjeet discussed at the Bombay Provincial Conference held under the presidency of Mr. Sayani, a distinguished Mahomedai gentleman. There the scheme of the distinguished Counsel Mr. Mehta was discussed, which scheme is published in pamphlet form and has just been adverted to by the learned supporter Mr. Mazoomdar. The Conference appointed a Committee to report their opinion on the scheme and we are asked now by this motion to place the matter before the Secretary of State and ask him to request the Government of India to give their own opinion on the report that

Third day.

Resolution VI.

Separation of Judicial and Executive functions.

might be made by a Committee that may be appointed. As for myself, I am not so sanguine about the work of such a Committee, but you must know that it is necessary to move that large and cumberous machinery, the Government of India, and that cannot be better done than through the Secretary of State. (*applause.*) You will expect me, coming as I do from Bombay, to give you instances where there have been failures of jusitce or an attempt on the part of some to cause a failure of justice. Well, I may say that in the district of Satara we pull on very well, and there I may say the fault is not of the officials, but that of the system. I will quote to you an instance of a collector, who, you know, is always the District Magistrate, an assistant collector, and also that of a mamlatdar, both of whom had something to do with Magisterial functions. Under the Guardians and Wards Act, you know, it is possible for a collector to administer the property of a minor. The Collector in the exercise of the powers conferred upon him prefers a complaint to himself as District Magistrate and he, as the District Magistrate, then proceeds to take action upon it. One instance occurred in which there was likely to be an abuse of power and on the matter being brought to his notice it was dropped. I now quote the instance of an Assistant Collector who had the powers of a Magistrate and was also in charge of a taluka presided over by a mamlatdar. He was passing along a road one day when he noticed some men working in a field and he thought that they had committed an offence. He took the initiative of asking the mamlatdar to commit the accused persons to the Court of Sessions. These orders were carried out, but the Sessions Judge, who happened to be a man of sense and mature experience, discovered that there could be no law which authorised such action on the part of a Collector and therefore the case was quashed. The third case is that referred to by Mr. Mazoomdar in supporting this proposition ; there a poor old woman was fined fifteen rupees for making a little salt and this matter was reported by the Collector of the District who happened to be a man with sympathies. The High Court looked into the matter and reduced the fine. You will be able to see by these instances that it is not so much the fault of the officers as the fault of the system itself. It is the system which is to be remedied and that remedy must be sought in the aid which might be derived from asking the Secretary of State to appoint committees to enquire into the matter. The greatest obstacle is said to be the financial difficulty, but as has been pointed out, the Government would do much better if it asked the people to contribute towards the expense of removing this evil, rather than imposing additional taxation for the compensation allowance. (*applause.*) There is sufficient data for us to pass the proposition and I would heartily join in supporting it. (*Hear, hear.*)

LALA LAJPAT RAI (*Punjab, No. 237, in list.*) said:—MR. PRESIDENT, BROTHER DELEGATES, LADIES AND GENTLEMEN,—The question involved in the resolution now before you is of such vital importance that the stronger the case we make out the better for us. After trying the Government of India and the Local Government for eight years, now we are taking our case to the Secretary of State for India and we hope to make the strongest case possible. You know that it is necessary for the peace and progress of a country that its people should have a voice in the Legislative Councils but it is much more essential for the security of life and property that the laws, when once made in those Councils, should be faithfully carried out. It is, I say, much more essential for the peace and prosperity of the country that the people should have full confidence in the courts of justice which administer justice to them. It is most essential for the peace of the country and the security of property that people should believe that the administration of justice is complete and effectual and a more dire misfortune cannot be imagined than the discontent that results from the people losing faith in the impartiality of the courts of justice. (*Hear, hear.*) Gentlemen, the evil is the greatest possible in the Punjab and therefore I will ask for your indulgence to put a concrete case before you. Here is another short case. The functions of the Government.

**Third day.**

**Resolution VI.**

**Separation of Judicial and Executive functions.**

are not only administration but also trading. The Government has got certain traffics into its hands, the opium and liquor traffics being amongst the number ; and who is the head of these traffics? who is the representative of Her Majesty in these trades in every district? It is the Deputy Commissioner of the district and do you know who is the head of the courts? it is the Deputy Commissioner himself—a trader, administrator of justice, a Revenue Collector, Forest Officer, Opium officer and what not: All these functions are embodied in one person here in the Punjab. Added to this is the difficulty that in many districts this officer is a military officer taken away from Her Majesty's army and we know what legal knowledge such an officer possesses. In one case a Colonel in charge of a district tried summarily a case whch was not triable summarily and the conviction had to be quashed by the Chief Court. In the Punjab the opium traffic is divided, for in many districts different sorts of opium are sold, and do you know what the Government does for the protection of the opium traffic? The order goes to the district officer that one particular sort of opium will be sold which the people don't like and which Government perhaps gets cheaper, and the other is to be put down. The order is communicated to the Subordinate Excise officers who take out warrants and bring people before the District Officers and they are sentenced to different terms of imprisonment, varying from one month to six months. I hold in my hands copies of several judgments in which these oppressions could be seen. In one of these cases the District Magistrate admits that a travelling *jogi* brought a few *masha*s into the district while passing through it. The District Magistrate said the man had not committed an offence but the excise must be protected and sentenced him to a month's imprisonment. One of the richest bankers in the district had his house searched and a few rupees worth of opium was found and the District Magistrate imposed the full sentence of three months' rigorous impisonment. Such cases could be multiplied by hundreds. Now let us look at the Forest Department. In some districts the Deputy Commissioner is the head of the Forest Department. Sometimes the people are starving and go to the forest and take certain berries and thus save themselves from death by starvation, but they are brought up for trespass and sentenced to different terms of imprisonment, because the Forest Laws must be vigorously administered. It is these evils which are undermining the safety of the Empire and which, it is high time, should be put down both in the interest of Government and for our own safety. These are not the only cases ; all those who read newspapers know the judicial vagaries that were committed in the Umballa District in the name of friendship to the agricultural class. Lots of people to whom money was due by the agricultural classes were ordered by the District Magistrate either to give full receipts to their debtors without receiving any payment or to compromise their cases according to the wishes and proposals of the debtors and for their not obeying these most unreasonable orders they were first ordered to give securities for good behaviour. When they had signed these documents the District Magistrate found that they had placed themselves entirely at his mercy and he showed them his mercy by compelling them to grant receipts to their debtors for all their dues without receiving a single pice in payment from any one of them. There are numberless cases on record where you can see that the District Magistrate in making his awards has compelled the people to file receipts or compromise their suits. These cases can be enumerated by thousands in the Punjab, because the Government in its benignity, in its beneficence thinks that the military officers alone can govern the Punjab. These things are only possible in the Punjab because unfortunately we are not sufficiently educated to have the moral courage to put our cases before the public. We are afraid of the District Magistrate, the Assistant Commissioner and the Extra Assistant Commissioner and all these cases never see the light of the day. For want of education we have not sufficient boldness to expose them. The District Magistrate is the District Judge also in many cases and in consequence civil justice suffer too. The Deputy Commissioner often writes, "in

Third day.

Resolution VI.

Separation of Judicial and Executive functions.

case of conviction a sentence of imprisonment should be awarded," and you can percieve the effect of this upon the Subordinate Magistrates whose promotion depends on the opinion of that Deputy Commissioner. There are some men who will not kill their conscience in this way but what is their fate ? They are doomed : their promotion is stopped and they are put back in the list. This is the effect of their independence ! It is the system I condemn and not the people who administer it. The judgments, the copies of which I hold in my hand, were written by an officer for whom I have the greatest respect but he was helpless. He had to give the accused persons different terms of imprisonment because he did not like to injure the chance of his own promotion. It is the system I condemn and it is high time that you, my brothers from the other Provinces, should come to the rescue of the Punjab. Separation to some extent has been carried out in some Province but here to no extent whatever. And this is what we call a question of principle. We are told that the greatest difficulty comes from a financial point of view, but I will show you that the taxation from justice gives a net profit to Government. From the official reports you will find that the net profit to Government from the administration of civil justice is twenty five lakhs of rupees, while the expenditure on civil justice does not exceed twelve lakhs, so that there is a net profit to Government, so far as civil justic is concerned, of over twelve lakhs. From the sale of process-serving stamps there is a net profit of two and a half lakhs. It is in the Punjab alone that the taxation on justice has reached its limit, and it is in the Punjab alone that civil refunds are levied. The Judges refuse to interfere, because the law does not allow them to interfere although the cases may be of the grossest possible injustice. I say, taking all these things into consideration, if the scheme of separation is carried into effect in the Punjab, Government will not have to incur any additional expenditure. But even if additional expenditure had to be incurred, I submit it would be better to incur it here than incur an expenditure of several crores on the frontier. If the people of the Rowalpindi, Peshawar and Kohat districts are discontented, I challenge the Government to say whether these fortresses on which they are spending so much money, will protect the interests of the country. Let these people have justice, for it is justice alone that brings home to them the potentialities of a Government. They simply know the men who administer justice to them and if these Judges do not carry out their duties honestly and properly, I challenge any Government to keep secure on its own foundations. Government undermines its own foundations. by not completely separating the Judicial from the Executive. It is high time that we should remind Government that the Punjab is no longer that infant province requiring to be governed by military officers who come here without any legal training, as Deputy Commissioners and preside over courts of which they are unable to uphold the prestige. It is under these circumstances that I, from the Punjab, heartily support this resolution and appeal to the gentleman presiding over this Congress that he will specially relate the hardships of the Punjab in the House of Commons. It is there alone that we can get redress. We, Punjabis, have not the moral courage and education to come forward as we should and therefore it is that our case suffers and we appeal to you to have the case taken before the highest tribunal, namely, the British House of Commons. (*Applause.*)

SIRDIR CHANDA SING BHIND (*Punjab, No. 502, in list*) said:—MR. PRESIDENT, LADIES AND GENTLEMEN,—It is with feelings of pride and pleasure that I rise to support the Resolution moved by our worthy friend Mr. K. N. Bannerji of Bengal. The resolution, as you have all heard, is to separate the two functions of the Judiciary and the Executive, now resting in one and the same officer, and indeed the resolution is a noble one and worthy of the consideration of this august assembly. The two functions, gentlemen, in order to be performed faithfully and conscientiously require men of two different frames of mind. The mind of one, in order to be faithful to his duties as a Judge, ought

**Third day.**

**Resolution VI.**

**Separation of Judicial and Executive functions.**

not to romain biassed by any administrative feelings or feelings of selfish aim, in fact it ought not to feel itself subordinate to any earthly power whatever, but to that Almighty Father Who out of the same elements has made both him and the one upon whom he sits in judgment, while on the other hand, the mind of the Executive, in order to be an able administrator, a competent collector and a perfect master of management, should be quite different, with ready resources and means, not always strictly fair, whereby to please his superior officers. In fact, gentlemen, you place the Bible in the hands of the one and ask him always to be just, and arm the other with a sword and ask him always to make conquests. How can, therefore, gentlemen, one and the same person, the Bible in one hand and sword in the other, be presumed to remain faithful both to his Maker on High and to his own master and motives here in this world of selfish aims. The evils of the combination of the two functions, as shown by our national gathering, have been admitted by the Government, but the difficulty with them in effecting the separation has always been a question of money. This year, gentlemen, the Secretary of State for India seems to have found some immense treasure, buried under the ground floor of his office wherefrom he has been enabled to be so merciful to the Amir of Kabul as to increase his stipend by six lakhs of rupees a year, and from the same source perhaps, he has been enabled to become so kind a brother to his own countrymen here in charge of the destinies of 280 millions of his fellow beings, as to grant them compensation allowance from the first of April 1893. Therefore, gentlemen, you may safely entertain a fervent hope that when this prayer of ours reaches him next, it will move his merciful and paternal heart to take compassion upon the voiceless millions whose destinies the Judge on High has been pleased to place under his charge. And if under these circumstances even, he remains deaf to our humble prayers, let him know that he and we all have one day to stand before the Tribunal, in whose dock the prince and the peasant are made to stand side by side. Here perhaps, I may have spoken a little harshly ; but gentlemen, you all see that I am blind, as blind as Justice is always represented to be, which makes no distinction between a king and a clown.

The evils of the combination of the two functions are, gentlemen, known more to us, the legal practitioners, than to others. During my long experience as a pleader, I have met with instances which, if told, will not fail to boil the blood of any just-minded man. Once, not long ago, a Sahukar who was coming home from his father-in-law's house with his bride, was on a moon lit night attacked and looted by two particular *badmashes*. The report of the fact was given to the police at the nearest station by the Sahukar who gave to them a full description of his two assailants. The Police at once came to the scene of occurrence and arrested a dozen youngsters of the surrounding villages including, of course, the two really guilty, perhaps already known to them as their intimate friends ; but upon those two presenting their quota of the booty to the police they were released. But gentlemen, hear of the fate of the remaining ten. Eight of them were heavily fined in private by the guardians of the peace and property and protectors of life and limb—I mean the police—and the remaining two, who had been previously convicted of a similar offence were chalaned and sent before the District Magistrate, to appear before him as two sacrificial goats with a lot of concocted evidence against them. They engaged me as their pleader, the evidence for the prosecution was taken, and on argument shown to be false, the Magistrate admitted the innocence of the accused ; but the District superintendent of Police who stood there as public prosecutor represented that the discharge of the two accused who were great *badmashes* in the district, would go materially to the detriment of the administration of the district. On hearing this argument there came the magisterial inspiration that a *prima facie* case had been made out against the accused, the charge was framed, alibi pleaded and proved, but as you all know, this plea is now a days always held to be an usual one and seldom believed to be true. The Magistrate treated both the accused with the full dose of his magisterial powers; 4 years rigorous imprisonment and 30 stripes each. Their appeal was also dismissed and now those two really innocent persons are in a felon's jail suffering the penalties for what they, in fact, never did, tasting the bitter fruits of this unnatural and highly pernicious system. This punishment alone is not sufficient for them, there is more in store for them; when they come out of the jail, that engine of oppression placed in the hands of the police, chapter VIII of the criminal procedure code 1882, that theoretically useful but practically pernicious, that well-meant but ill used law, will enable the Police to send the two victims before the District Magistrate to furnish security for good behaviour or in default to return to the quarters they so recently left, for another term of 3 years.

Again, gentlemen, this system is pernicious in many other ways. The Magistrates, who are often collectors of revenue for the Government, are always inclined to take the side of the Government, their employer, rather than to take the side of justice they are paid to administer. In administering the Opium and Excise laws specially, they shut their eyes towards justice and often convict innocent persons on the most insignificant and trifling evidence and when in such cases appeals are lodged, the cases are not infrequently argued exparte at Mess-tables by the administrators of the district and such arguments remain unrebutted by the accused or his counsel.

MR. JHIND RAM (*Punjab, No. 402, in list*) said:—MR. PRESIDENT AND BROTHER DELEGATES,—I will tell you how justice is administered in the Punjab and you will see that this is one of the most essential reforms of the administration. In my part we have Frontier regulations for the suppression of crime in the Frontier districts. Under these regulations, a Deputy Commissioner, not a Magistrate, is empowered to sentence a man to undergo rigorous imprisonment for seven years and there is no appeal at all. My friend yesterday was complaining that there was no appeal for a sentence of one month, but I come from that part of the country where there is no appeal even in cases where a sentence of seven years is passed. There is another satisfaction, and that is, there is no botheration of trial, the rules of procedure are simple and go straight and send the accused to jail. There is no need to quote High Court authorities, neither is the accused called upon to pay for pleaders because under the rules he has no right to be defended by Counsel. A Deputy Commissioner appoints a council of three or four persons whom he thinks fit to appoint. He can appoint any one he likes. The *Jirga* is not bound to record any evidence, it has simply to give an opinion and if the opinion is for a conviction, the Deputy Commissioner sends the accused then and there to jail. Look how simple the procedure is, no botheration of any sort. (*Laughter.*) It is provided in the regulations that the Deputy Commissioner can make over a case to the *Jirga* in which he thinks there is not sufficient evidence for a conviction. As the Deputy Commissioner is the District Officer he generally contrives to make over all cases in which he thinks there is not sufficient evidence for a conviction. He can withdraw any criminal case from the ordinary criminal tribunal before conviction is pronounced and make it over to the honorable court of *Jirga*. Look at the hardship to the accused, for before the *Jirga* he has either to clear himself or be sentenced to a long term of imprisonment. I am told that a Deputy Commissioner in one of the frontier districts has passed a standing order directing his subordinates to send over every case of murder after enquiry for his perusal. If he thinks the evidence sufficient he orders the trial to proceed, if he sees it is doubtful, it is made over for trial to the *Jirga*. So that any one who by chance gets into the clutches of the police has every opportunity afforded him of trying the healthy and bracing cliamate of a jail. In other parts of the country and in all civilised countries it is a principle of law to presume that an accused person sent up for trial should be considered innocent until proved to be guilty, but in our part an accused is presumed to be guilty until he proves the contrary. I must now disappear or I may be made over to the *Jirga* for making these remarks. I therefore support the resolution heartily on behalf of the people of the frontier whom I represent. (*Applause.*)

The resolution was then put to the meeting and carried unanimously.

**Third day.**

**Resolution VI.**

**Separation of Judicial and Executive functions.**

**Resolution VII.**

**Protests against State-regulated immorality in India.**

Mr. D. E. WACHA (*Bombay, No. 782, in list,*) proposed :—

" *That this Congress having considered the report of the Parliamentary members of the India office Committee on the subject of the Rules, Orders and practices in Indian Cantonments with regard to prostitution and contagious diseases, hereby endorses their conclusions* :—

*1. That the system and incidental practices described in that report and the Statutory rules so far as they authorized or permitted the same, did not accord with the plain meaning and intention of the resolution of the House of Commons of June 5th, 1888 ; and*

*2. That the only effective method of preventing these systematic malpractices is by express legislation.*"

He said : MR. PRESIDENT, LADIES AND GENTLEMEN :—The Resolution which I have just read to you requires little or no recommendation from me. I am confident that it will meet with your cordial approval, represents as it does the almost unanimous sentiment of all our countrymen in different parts of the country on the subject of the odious Acts. I take it for granted that most of you, if not all, are more or less aware of the history of the C. D. Acts, and that you expect no lengthy speech from me to acquaint you with the circumstances which led in 1888 to the adoption by the House of Commons Mr. Maclaren's resolution for their immediate repeal. Suffice to say here that the objectionable and degrading system which was in vogue about the time was sanctioned and administered under certain Acts and Statutory rules scheduled to the then existing Cantonment Acts, and numerous official orders and regulations which may be said to have culminated in a Circular Memorandum issued from the Army head quarters at Simla, dated 17th June 1886, in the name of the Commander-in-Chief (Lord Roberts) and with the signature (by order) of Major General Chapman as Quarter-Master-General in India. That Circular, and certain other papers, became the following year (July 1887) the subject of questions in the House of Lords and of action by the India Office, and subsequently formed an important element in the discussion in the House of Commons on 5th June 1888 upon the Resolution which was then moved by Mr. MacLaren and passed *nem con.*

Now, gentlemen, so intensely hostile was the feeling agaist these hated Acts throughout the country that the people with one voice welcomed that Resolution as a great relief. (*Hear, hear.*) They breathed more freely in the hopeful belief that at last the first deliberative assembly in the civilised world had risen to the height of the occasion, condemned legalised vice in the terms it deserved, and interposed its supreme authority with a view to arresting the inroads which State regulated incontinence was fast making in the land—inroads which, it was seriously apprehended, might loosen those sacred bonds which had kept a simple society like that of the Indians in its almost pristine purity for ages, and preserved their national morality. I will at once give credit to the Government of India that at the time of the passing of the Resolution, it was prepared to obey the mandate of the House of Commons as conveyed to it in the Despatch of the Secretary of State for India, dated 15th October 1888. But it was soon drawn away from its righteous purpose by the deplorable phariseeism of the Military hierarchy which had determined, as was made plain by subsequent events, to defeat the object of the Resolution. A spirit of rebellion seemed to have prevailed among that hierarchy. It was thought

Third day.

Resolution VII.

Protests against State-regulated immorality in India.

that the mandate of the House was more honoured in the breach than in the observance (*Shame*). The organs of the services bellowed forth in their respective columns the same views almost in the same strain. No doubt steps were taken to amend the then existing Acts. But the new Acts and the rules and regulations which were enacted under them scandalised those who had been most instrumental and active in the House of Commons in passing Mr. MacLaren's resolution. (*Hear, hear.*) The new measure was passed in October 1889 and was called " The Cantonment Act, 1889," and on the 21st December following the draft rules which had been settled after considerable correspondence between the Secretary of State and the Government of India were published " for the information of persons likely to be affected thereby with an intimation that they would be taken into consideration on the expiry of three months." The publication of the rules aroused the attention of various newspapers and religious organisations, both here and in England. A number of protests were submitted to the authorities, notably one by the Revd. Allen Rees, Secretary of the Weslyan Conference Social Purity Committee. This protest and others elicited a reply from Lord Cross. But correspondence still went on till, on 21st October 1891, the Government of India requested the Commander-in-Chief to cause careful inquiry to be made "whether the Military authorities are keeping strictly within the terms of the Cantonment Act and the Rules approved by the Secretary of State; and whether there is reason to believe that compulsion in excess of that which is authorised under the rules (Nos. 4 and 5) is resorted to." It would be clear to you, gentlemen, from the tenor of the above extract I have quoted, that the rules of the Cantonment Act were being evaded and the evils complained of under the old system were in no way abated. In fact the Cantonment authorities winked at the rules, specially in the Punjab. But if the officials, responsible for the faithful administration of the Act were blind on purpose there were other eyes keen enough to watch their actions. (*Hear, hear.*)

You are no doubt aware of the existence in England for a number of years past of a Society consisting of many a noble lady and gentleman, called the British Committee for the abolition of State Regulation of Vice in India and throughout the British dominion," whose anxious care is to see that the national morality undergoes no deterioration or is undermined. The morality of a nation is what the chastity of its mothers makes it (*applause*). Inspired by this altruistic instinct it is doing most excellent work in this direction, specially under the indefatigable exertions of Mrs. Josephine Butler, Professor Steuart and Mr Stansfield, its three noblest and strongest pillars. (*Loud cheers.*) I regret to say that it is a reflection on us Indians that we have not yet among us such a Society for the protection of Indian women. (*Hear, hear.*) But we are a young nation and should make it a point to learn from our parents, the British, their good traits of character and establish wide among us Purity Societies of the kind described. Meanwhile we owe a deep debt of gratitude to Mrs. Butler and her colleagues that they are not only watching the morals of English but of Indian women also. (*Applause.*)

Now, no sooner was the Cantonment Act of 1889 passed than the Society began obtaining through its authorised and trusty delegates all information as to the way in which the Act and the Rules were being carried out. Among them were two American ladies, Mrs. Andrew and Miss Bushnell. These went obtrusively but honestly about their mission and were able to collect a mass of unimpeachable information as regards ten Cantonments in the Upper Provinces which tended to demonstrate most conclusively that the rules were being scandalously ignored and their object ruthlessly defeated. Under the circumstances, Mr. Stansfield and other Members of Parliament made in the early part of 1893 strong representations to the Secretary of State for India that they were in possession of trustworthy information that at certain stations the Resolution of the House of Commons had been practically disregarded, and that it was imperative a Select Committee of the House be nominated to immediately inquire into the matter.

The ultimate result of those negotiations was the appointment of a Special Commission by the Government of India to investigate into the truth of the allegations made by the two lady agents of the Purity Society and to report whether in their opinion they were correct. Having taken evidence at Umballa, Meerut and Lucknow, the Commission considered that on the whole the allegations were unfounded. The service oragns re-echoed the opinion and the two American ladies were denounced for the untrustworthiness of the information they had collected. In fact, they were roundly abused and accused of aspersing the fair character of the service consisting of officers and gentlemen ! Thus a cloud of dust was raised to conceal the Truth. But Truth cried out from the bottom of the well, and with such irresistible vigour, that eventually the facts as originally communicated by the two ladies were demonstrated to be absolutely correct. The Secretary of State's Departmental Committee, which was appointed to independently investigate the matter and of which Mr. Stansfield was a member, took oral evidence of the ladies, but the most searching cross-examination failed to shake the original allegations made by them regarding the practices under the Cantonment Acts at the ten stations which they personally visited. (*Loud cheers.*) This evidence was fully supported by that of Mr. Hyslop Bell who was also deputed to visit India for the same purpose by the same Society. All the minutes of their evidence might be read in the massive Parliamentary Blue Book published about four months ago. The evidence of Mrs. Andrew and Miss Bushnell was so overpowering that Lord Roberts, who when first examined before the Departmental Committee stoutly repudiated the allegations, was obliged at the conclusion of the inquiry to offer his most unqualified apology to the two ladies which indeed was very creditable to his character for honesty as a distinguished soldier and gentleman (*applause*). You have all read that apology and it is therefore superfluous for me to quote it here. Thus, gentlemen, the net result of the investigation of the English Committee was this. It unmasked the organised official hypocrisy of those in India who had so long successfully misled the British public. We Indians, therefore, owe, I repeat, a deep debt of gratitude not only to the two ladies but to Mrs. Josephine Butler and her colleagues, male and female, for their strenuous and disinterested agitation for the removal of the objectionable practices both under the old and the new Cantonment Acts. (*Applause.*)

But, gentlemen, this evidence and the circumstances that have transpired since Lord Roberts offered his apology, lead us naturally to enquire as to the broad inference to be drawn therefrom ? What lesson this incident teaches us and our rulers ? I believe, gentlemen, that the evidence now collected in the Blue Book is a remarkable object lesson of the highest value to the administrators of this country. It teaches us that no implicit reliance can be placed on official statements, even when those statements are made by Special Commissions consisting of officials themselves. In the present case, it is plain, that the authorities who were concerned in the administration of the Cantonment Acts successfully humbugged (I am sorry I cannot find a more expressive word than that) Lord Roberts and the Government of India who all along had vigorously maintained their view that there was no infringement of the Acts and the rules framed under them, and that the mandate of the House of Commons was being loyally obeyed. I dare say most of you have perused the very admirable article in the last number of *India* by Professor Steuart referring to this unpleasant exposure by the two American ladies, and trenchantly commenting on the conduct of the Cantonment officers and the authorities at head quarters. The observations ought to open the eyes of the Government of India if it has not already done so. If that Government and Lord Roberts were so long kept in dense ignorance

Third day.

Resolution VII.

Protests against State-regulated immorality in India.

of the true situation as regards the Cantonment Acts, what are we to infer regarding the conduct of the Military administration generally? Is there no valid reason to doubt the extreme want of strict supervision and control over the appalling Military expenditure which is a source of such chronic embarrassment to Indian finances? (*Hear, hear.*) On the Congress platform it has been my privilege more than once to refer to this expenditure. And after a careful perusal of the Blue Book on these odious Acts, I need not say, I am strongly confirmed in my doubts as to the fallacious character of official reports generatly. The object lesson taught to us by the evidence of the two ladies is therefore extremely valuable, I repeat. It teaches us that if we have hard facts to submit to Government in reference to any grievous questions connected with any branch of the Imperial or Provincial administration, it is our bounden duty to submit them without fear or hesitation For facts which may be incontrovertible can never be assailed howsoever strenuous the efforts to contradict them. (*Hear, hear.*) Year after year many of us have the opportunity to read the administration reports of the different provinces of the empire, besides many an important Blue Book on grave affairs, home and foreign ; but it is more than doubtful whether these contain a correct record of facts. So far as my own impression goes, I do not hesitate to say that I make a large reservation when perusing such reports Their chief defect seems to be that extraordinary tendency to suggest something which is opposed to fact. Official mendacity, I am afraid, is on the increase. It is a vice which so veteran a publicist as the late lamented Mr. Knight (*cheers*) deeply deplored and was not slow to denounce in withering terms. (*Hear, hear.*) We are having our annual Provincial Conferences. In my humble opinion we cannot perform a better duty towards ourselves and our rulers than that of contradicting such official information as we may have unimpeachable grounds to believe is incorrect. We should be thus performing a most useful function. We may go even further and publish our own unofficial Blue Book (or black book if you like) on the administration as a counterblast to the official and present it to Parliament. Hard facts are always appreciated by that deliberative assembly. And if our unofficial Blue Books contain incontrovertible facts you may depend on it that they will be highly valued. The good that such publications might do would be incalculable—good to ourselves and to our rulers. Let us therefore follow the excellent example of the two noble ladies (*eheers*) whose faithful version was so instrumental in scattering to the wind all the official claptrap in which the Military authorities at head quarters indulged in reference to the Cantonment Act. This is the moral which the evidence teaches us. (*Hear, hear.*) Gentlenen, I will not now detain you any longer but exhort you to adopt the resolution by acclamation. Let us all earnestly hope that for the better purity of our Indian sisters of all caste and creed, we may soon witness a healthy reform in the matter. *(Loud applause.)*

THE HON'BLE CHAROO CHUNDER MITTER—(*Allahabad, No. 71, in list*) in seconding the motion said :—This subject was discussed in 1888 in the Congress at Allahabad for the first time and was again taken up by the Congress in 1892 at the same place and it has again fallen to the lot of an Allahabad delegate to second the resolution in the Punjab. But I hope that this will be the last time that we shall have to deal with a subject of such a delicate nature as this. I think the less said on the question the better and therefore without further remarks I beg to second the resolution which I hope you will carry unanimously. *(Hear, hear)*

The motion was then carried unanimously.

THE PRESIDENT : It was intended that the next resolution should be proposed by Mr. Seymour Keay, but unfortunatey he has been laid up these two or three days with his old complaint and is unable to attend. He had made the subject a special study The motion will be presented by Pundit Madan Mohun Malaviya.

Third day.

Resolution VIII.

Grievous distress amongst people of India.

PUNDIT MADAN MOHUN MALAVIYA *(Allahabad, No. 73, in list)* moved.

*That this Congress, concurring in the views set forth in previous Congresses, affirms :*

*That fully fifty millions of the population, a number yearly increasing, are dragging out a miserable existence on the verge of starvation, and that in every decade, several millions actually perish by starvation.*

*And humbly urges once more that immediate steps be taken to remedy this calamitous state of affairs.*

MR. PRESIDENT AND BROTHER DELEGATES,—It is with a heaving heart I rise to propose this motion. It is a matter of very great regret that a resolution of this character should have to be passed year after year without our having the consolation of recording that the Government had paid earnest attention to the matter. I say, it is a matter of very great regret because of all the grievances under which our people are suffering, of all the troubles that they have to undergo, this question of poverty is the greatest, and as such, one would expect that the Government would devote its attention to remedy the grievance which year after year the best intelligence of India has put forward for its consideration. Gentlemen, as I have said, it is a matter of deep regret that we should have to use the words of this resolution once more. This subject was brought to the attention of Government as early as 1885, when the first Congress met in Bombay. Again in 1886, when we met at Calcutta for the first time, the subject was, if anything, more emphatically dwelt upon and we urged Government to institute enquiries and to take steps to remedy the spread of poverty which we complained of. Though nine years have rolled by, the Government have not yet taken any step to remedy the state of affairs. All they did was to institute a hole and corner enquiry in 1888, not with a view to remedy the greivance, but to silence the complaints, if possible, by saying that the poverty complained of existed not so much in reality as in imagination and the reports published by Government and the Resolution of the 24th October, 1888, was directly meant to serve that end. But if Government make these hole and corner enquiries and evidence not sought and evidence not received, and reports and resolutions are hurled at the heads of the people, with a view to throw dust into their eyes, who is to blame if the people don't believe them, and if we complain of the cruel indifference of the Government; who is to blame if we have to appeal again and again to the Englishmen who have come to govern the country and those who have taken the responsibility of guiding our destinies in England; who is to blame if we have to appeal again and again for justice in this country? When a proposal was put forward recently in the House of Commons, asking that a Royal Commission might be appointed to enquire into the complaint, it was said by those who did not care to have such an enquiry, that the honorable gentleman who presides over this assembly, had not supplied sufficient evidence of poverty, but, as the President well remarked, you cannot make people see if they aro not inclined to see. Facts and figures have been supplied both this year and in previous years which leave no room for doubt that poverty has been increasing, goes on increasing and will go on increasing, unless something is done to remedy it. If they choose to ignore all that is said to them they cannot tell us with decency that we have not given them evidence. They talk of the sense of solemn responsibility in having undertaken the task of guiding the destinies of the millions of this land. When you come to think of the small attention they bestow on Indian questions and the light-heartedness with which they deal with the most solemn questions, you begin to suspect, they do not realise their responsibility to God and man; for injustice, oppression and suffering, are going on under their rule. They have asked us to supply evidence of the poverty. Will they kindly come and see.? If they believe in God and believe they will have to render an account of their stewardship in this country, let them come ont to this country once in their lives

**Third day.**

**Resolution VIII.**

**Grievous distress amongst people of India.**

and go from village to village and town to town and see in what misery the people live. Let them come out and ask the people what the country was, say, before the mutiny. Where are the weavers, where are those men who lived by different industries and manufactures, and where are the manufactures which were sent to England and other European countries in very large quantities year after year? All that has become a thing of the past; every one sitting here is clothed in cloth of British make, almost every one—and wherever you go you find British manufactures and British goods staring you in the face. All that is left to the people is to drag out a miserable existence by agricultural operations and make infinitesimal profit out of the little trade left to them. In the matter of the services, in the matter of trade, our people are not enjoying one hundredth part of the profit and gain which they used to enjoy fifty years ago. How then is it possible for the country to be happy? how is it surprising that the country is not more poor than it is? There are only two kinds of evidence we can offer to our critics, one is the direct evidenc of the eyes, and we invite them to acquire that for themselves the other is the indirect evidence supplied by the experience of those who have lived in this country and know the way in which the people live. Any such evidence I am ready to place before you, the evidence of men in the veracity and accuracy of whose statements no man dare utter a doubt. I will first call attention to what Mr. John Bright said in 1853, in the House of Commons. Speaking of India he said, "what is it that the people of India, if they spoke by my mouth, have to complain of? They would tell the House that, as a rule, throughout almost all the Presidencies, and throughout those Presidencies most which have been longest under British rule, the cultivators of the soil, the great body of the population of India, are in a condition of great impoverishment, of great dejection and of great suffering" Later on Lord Lawrence in 1864 said, "India is on the whole a very poor country. The mass of the population enjoy only a scanty subsistence." Speaking in 1873, he again said, "The mass of the people were so miserably poor that they had barley the means of subsistence." In 1868-69 Mr. W. R. Robertson, then the head of the Agricultural Department in Madras said. "The condition of the agricultural labourer in India is a disgrace to any country calling itself civilised." Sir Auckland Colvin speaking in 1885 in connection with the License Tax Amendment Bill remarked, "The masses of the people are men whose income at the best is barely sufficient to afford them the sustenance necessary to support life, living as they do on the barest necessaries of life." In 1882 Sir Evelyn Baring said, speaking as the Finance Minister of this country, "It has been calculated that the average income per head of the population in India is not more than Rs. 27 a year, and though I am not prepared to pledge myself to the absolute accuracy of a calculation of this sort, it is sufficiently accurate to justify the conclusion that the tax paying community is exceedingly poor. To derive any very large increase of revenue from so poor a population as this, is obviously impossible, and if it were possible, would be unjustifiable." Again in the discussion on the budget after repeating the above statement regarding the income of Rs. 27 per head per annum, he said: "But he thought it was quite sufficient to show the extreme poverty of the masses of the people. In England the average income per head of the population is £33, (*it is now £41*) in France it was £23, in Turkey which was the poorest country in Europe it was £4 per head. He would ask honourable members to think what Rs. 27 per annum was to support a person and then he would ask whether a few annas was nothing to such poor people." Again if you come to 1888 you find that the Government of India admit indirectly that there was a great and increasing poverty, for what did they say in their white washing resolution? they said, "There is evidence to show that in all parts of India there is a numerous population which lives from hand to mouth, is always in debt, does not save and has little or nothing to fall back upon in bad seasons." It is unnecessary for me to multiply these quotations; any man who cares to know the real facts can read the valuable papers of our illustrious chairman and the paper issued by the Poona

Third day.

Resolution VIII.

Grievous distress amongst people of India.

*Sarvajanik Sabha* in which the condition of the country is graphicly and truly depicted. There was no shadow of fact in the excuse that our illustrious chairman did not supply facts, for by official papers the fact is proved that there is great poverty and that Government is doing nothing or precious little to remove that poverty or check its growth. I ask you to say by this resolution that there are fully fifty millions of the population dragging out a miserable existence on the verge of starvation. It is a serious statement to make, yet I am emboldened to ask you to give consent to this motion, because, if anything, it does not fully express the poverty of the land; it falls short because I think the numbers are not correct, it underrates the numbers. You might ask me to give my authority for saying this. I appeal to your own experience, but if you want indirect authority there is that of Sir Charles Elliot and Sir Willian Hunter. The latter says. "The remaining fifth, or forty millions, go through life on insufficient food," whilst Sir Charles Elliot says, " I do not hesitate to say that half our agricultural population never know from year's end to year's end what it is to have their hunger fully satisfied." Let the rulers think over those words and ask themselves what they will have to say to God when they go before Him. I accept all these statements of officials of Government and ask, why does not Government do something to remedy the evil? We say that several millions perish by starvation. It is unnecessary to tire you with many figures but I will say this to prove that statement. The loss of life by war from 1793 to 1890 in the whole world was 4,500,000, the loss of life in eight years by fever alone in India was 4,349,922. Does that not prove conclusively that several millions of our people die from sheer starvation, and are we not justified in asking our rulers to earnestly give this matter their most earnest consideration before the danger developes into a danger of serious character? (*Loud applause.*)

PUNDIT GOPINATH, (*Punjab, No. 255, in list*) seconded the motion addressing the Congress in Urdu.

BABU AMBICA CHARN MOITRA (*Bengal No. 26, in list*) in supporting the motion said:—MR. PRESIDENT, BROTHER-DELEGATES, LADIES AND GENTLFMEN,—I have much pleasure in supporting the resolution which has been so ably moved and seconded and I thank the members of the subjects committee for allowing me the sacred privelege of addressing the cream of our Indian society assembled at this national tribunal. The subject matter of this resolution may now be taken as admitted, as it has been proved to mathematical demonstration by eminent authorities both here and in England. The problem to be solved now is how to cope successfully with such a curse as the poverty of India. We must like a good physician feel well the national pulse and scrutinize the signs of the times and strike at the very root of the disease. The flow of the Indian money from the national exchequer to a foreign land should be stopped as far as possible; there must be retrenchment too, right round in India. The financial minister to the Government of India must make bold to scrape out all useless items of expenditures from the Indian Budget as unmercifully as the British surgeon so cleverly deals with the sloughs in a carbuncle. These are the roots of the disease. But so that we might induce the Indian Government to pay due attention to our just and legitimate prayers, we must let them know, that it is the voice of the people and not that of a microscopic minority that speaks through us. Improve the individual units in a nation and you will have a happy, contented and loyal set of people. My countrymen, we must urge on the several Governments, both local and supreme, to take a little more practical interest in the cause of mass and technical education as they are unhappily and unsuccessfully now trying to put down high education. I make bold to say that no power in the land can now check the onward march of high education in India as Providence has ordained otherwise. High and mass education are twin sisters, and they must walk on

Third day.

Resolution VIII.

Grievous distress amongst people of India.

together along the path of progress and we will then have no discordant tune ever marring the marvellous effects of the harmonious unity as we hope one day to have here

One point more and I have done. I should like to see the early foundation of a national industrial and commercial conference to hold its annual sittings at the Congress times and consist of delegates and others who might interest themselves in the question. I would wish such a conference, if so advised for making arrangements, or such of its members as might so desire, to raise the necessary funds for the due develpment of the immense natural resources, and mineral resources in particular, of the country all through India, by opening up banks, arts and industrial schools and establishing factories and the like at suitable centres all through this vast country, so as to cope successfully with the unjust and almost exclusive invasion and monopoly of foreign industry which is sucking as if it were the very life blood of all India and replacing indigenous industry, thereby making many a poor family in India homeless and famished. I should like to see more of industrial and commercial life in my fellow countrymen, than I see at present so that we might settle once for all this great problem which is a stumbling block alike to the Government and to our Indian patriots.

Let it not be supposed for a moment that I yield to any here in my loyalty to the British Raj. We are all conscious of the manifold blessings of the costly but otherwise fair and just government under which we now live. It is as just and fair as a foreign Government can be. Having regard to the present position of the country we could not possibly have a better form of foreign Government than we have now, and I for myself have great faith in the deep sense of justice which is the birthright of every true born Briton. We must go on and on with loyal agitation as the Congress has so ably carried on in the past and that too, constitutionally and with moderation and I can safely predict, the day is not far distant when all our legitimate and just prayers will undoubtedly be granted by the Government. (*Loud applause.*)

MR. MAHOMED ALI BHIMJI (*Central Provinces, No. 834, in list*) said :—MR. PRESIDENT, BROTHER-DELEGATES, LADIES AND GENTLEMEN,—Before I proceed further I would ask you not to cry out "louder, louder," because if you do that you damp the spirit of the speaker and he becomes slower and slower instead of louder and louder. (*Laughter.*) When a man rises to propose, second, or support a motion he generally says, "I have great pleasure," but in this instance I am sorry to say I cannot support this resolution with great pleasure. And why? Because it is a resolution referring to the poverty of India and no man has been found to feel pleasure in the poverty of his own country. (*applause.*) There is an additional reason to feel pain in the fact that it is necessary to bring forward such a resolution. I honestly tell you before Almighty God that in this world I dont believe there is any rule better than the British rule. (*Hear, hear.*) But yet under this British rule, the best of all rules, we are compelled to bring this resolution on the poverty of India. We have got laws, we have got peace, we have got police, we have got rail ways, tram ways, telegraphs, every thing that civilization can desire, but yet with all that the country is poverty stricken, the first and fundamental principle is wanting. The first test of good Government is that the country should be prosperous and not poverty stricken. In that first test it is our misfortune to say that the Government, owing to the peculiar system under which it is carried out, has failed and miserably failed. You may have been surprised to hear from my friend opinions expressed by high officials from 1878. If you like I will give you dates and years and the names of British officials who have said that the reason of the poverty in India is the British rule. In a paper written by our honorable president, it is most conclusively shown to exist, and if you have time to go through it, I would recommend you all to read it most thoughtfully and carefully, and say what conclusion you come to. It is not the men who carry out the system, but the system they have to carry out that is to be blamed. If we had not such conscientious rulers over us we would not have been able to gather the information which they supply and have done for the past hundred years and we would not have been able to say that a great many officials have been crying out against this system since 1787. It must be told to the credit of Englishmen, that although they carry out the system they do their duty, but still if the system is bad, what other results can be expected? It is our bounden duty to press our demands for a reform of the system. We have during nine long years been crying out for reform, yet our cry has not been answered and this very necessary reform is still withheld from us. A few months ago our respected President brought forward a motion in the House of Commons for an enquiry into the administration of India. That motion was defeated, but we must not be disappointed, we must go on persistently knocking at the door of the British House of Commons and we may rest assured that it will be opened to us. It is not that Government is not aware of this poverty; Government knows that povorty is prevalent in India, but they are also aware that they cannot find means to romove the poverty. There are people who say that the people themselves are to blame for the poverty. Such is not the case. Mr. John Bright in 1858, said that when a country is rich, and the people of that country are poor, there must be something fundamentally wrong in the Government of that country. If it is our misfortune to be poor, how have we become poor? It is because we have lost our industries. It is no fault of ours, we are willing to take up the industries but then the Manchester people come in and interfere and our industry is not assisted or encouraged. Therefore, the best plan is to go on knocking at the door of the House of Commons and ask for redress. I have, therefore, the melancholy pleasure of asking you to carry this resolution unanimously. *(Applause.)*

**Third day.**

**Resolution VIII.**

**Grievous distress amongst people of India.**

MOULVIE MOHURREM ALI CHISTI, (*Panjab, No. 266, in list*) supported in Urdu.

The motion was unanimously adopted.

MR. C. VENKATA, CHARIAR (*Madras No. 841, in list*) moved:

*That having regard to the very serious discontent created, especially in Peninsular India and in certain hilly tracts in the Punjab, by the practical administration of the Forest Laws, the Government of India be most respectfully but earnestly entreated to investigate this carefully and endeavour to mitigate its harshness, and render it less obnoxious to the poorer classes.*

**Resolution IX.**

**Necessity for mitigating the harshness of the practical administration of the Forest Laws.**

He said: This is a proposition which has been discussed by this national assembly year arter year and it has been discussed from various points. Now, I shall only point out to you a few practical defects that have been experienced in the Madras Presidency. I will first request your permission to state the difficulties in obtaining the land for agricultural purposes. The practice that has been obtaining in Madras is that, if a ryot wanted land for the purpose of cultivation, he has to make his application to the Revenue officials. That application is not disposed of either by the Tahsildar, or Divisional officers and has to go to the Forest Department, that is to say, to the District Forest Officer, then the same application is forwarded to the Ranger officer who has again to send it to the Forest Guard. You will note that these Forest officers, called guards, or servants, who are paid from eight to twelve rupees a month, have the discretion of either granting or withholding land for the purposes of cultivation. Practically the power is entirely vested in these lower officials. If the land mentioned in the application adjoins a Forest Reserve, or reserved land, which in area is less than 300 acres or so, (generally more than that is set aside for the purpose of reservation) his application is rejected and the piece of land is thenceforth a Forest Reserve. So you will see that year after year

Third day.

Resolution IX.

Necessity for mitigating the harshness of the practical administration of the Forest Laws

the number of reservations has been increasing and that the quantities of waste lands valuable for cultivation are decreasing. The consequence is that, it is extremely difficult to get land for the purposes of agriculture. The next point to which I call your attention is that the immemorial rights of grazing cattle and cutting and collecting fuel have been completely ignored under the Forest rules. The Government say that although the ryots have been utilising the forests for a number of years as cattle-grazing grounds and for fuel cutting, it was a privilege and not a right and was at the sweet will and pleasure of Government and could be withdrawn at any moment. The difficulty in the matter of grazing and fodder for cattle is so great that it resulted in the death of thousands of cattle in the year of 1891-92. According to the administration report of the Forest Department of the Madras Government and in the Report of the operations of the Departments of Land records and Agriculture for 1891-92, the number of cattle dying from various diseases was given as 87,349. The number of cattle dying from snake bite and by wild animals and poisoning comes to 99,307. The deaths by poisoning come to 18, the deaths by snake bite to 1171, deaths by wild animals to 10,189. I must tell you that these numbers do not include the sheep. The death of sheep from all diseases comes to 31,448. The death of sheep by snake bite was 153, and by wild animals it came to 5,953. Again from the Forest Administration Report you will see what was the unmber of cattle decreased in 1891-92. *(Cries of "time")* As I have been warned I shall pass on to other subjects which are more important. In respect to cattle found trespassing into Forests which have been extended on both sides of the public roads, as well as on all sides of villages, the fines recovered on account of those that were impounded during the year 1890-91, amounted to Rs. 1,50,015, and the sum during 1891-92, came to Rs. 1,83,722. In respect of these cattle which trespassed upon Forests and in respect of which fines were levied under the Cattle Trespass Act, there was also a second punishment under the amended Forest Laws, but two years ago there was no such second conviction. The Forest Officers were satisfied with impounding cattle. Now the practice in our Presidency and especially in Salem, is to prosecute the owners of cattle before Magistrates, and there have been convictions and heavy fines in some cases and the third way of dealing with offenders is by taking compensation according to the will and pleasure of the Forest Officer. *(Renewed cries of "time.")*

The speaker continuing said: In conclusion I would like to read to you the following extract from a minute of the Madras Government on Forest administration: "His Excellency the Governor-in-council cannot too strongly condemn any tendency to unnecessarily harass the people of the country by the application of the penal clauses of the Forest Law and desires that the Board will issue direct orders to the Collectors of the districts above mentioned with a view to remedying the unsatisfactory state of things which appears to exist. There has been a marked increase during the year, particularly in the districts of Sâlem, North Arcot, Trichinopoly and North Malabar in the number of cases compounded, and the amount realised in compensation fees has almost doubled as compared with 1890-91. The Board is unable to account for this large increase owing to the want of satisfactory explanations from the Collectors concerned. It would be instructive to know whether the power of impounding has been properly exercised and the Board should obtain and submit further information on this point. It should be borne in mind that the power of compounding should not be used in cases where the evidence is not sufficiently strong to secure convictions, but is intended to meet those cases where the evidence is clear; but there are circumstances, such as the petty nature of the offence and ignorance of the law on the part of an offender, or distance of the place of offence from a Magistrate's Court, which render it inadvisable to institute a conviction. The number of cases pending disposal at the close of the year was considerably larger than at the end of the previous year but Collectors have not furnished sufficient information under this head to enable the Board to judge how far the delay in the disposal of cases was due to the Officers of the Department and how far to the Magistracy. There is some inconsistency between the Board's statement at paragraph 40 of the Administration Report, for the increase in the number of forest offences in Kistna was due to the fact that the people were compelled to resort to injurious lopping of branches for fodder, and the statement at paragraph 50 to the effect that the ryots in Kistna were allowed as a special case to remove the leaves of certain fodder trees from the forests." (*Applause.*)

**Third day.**

**Resolution IX.**

**Necessity for mitigating the harshness of the practical administration of the Forest Laws**

MR. K. G. NATU, (*Poona, No. 745, in list*) in seconding the motion said:— MR. PRESIDENT, AND BROTHER-DELEGATES,—This resolution has been repeated and the arguments on it have been reiterated from year to year, but still we must repeat it until we attain our end. Gentlemen, bad laws are instruments of oppression. When lawlessness prevails and the law does not resent it, where can we find a remedy. (*Applause.*) Here lawlessness is legalised, laws are made to prevent oppression, but what will prevent it when the laws themselves sanction that oppression? The noble lords who pass the laws scarcely know any thing about the effects which they will have upon the people for whom they are made. Our worthy President has told you of the great poverty of India, and if you take into consideration all the bad laws and their effects, you will find the spectacle of poverty more shocking than it has been hitherto. A poor man who perhaps lives on one meal a day, goes to the forest and he perhaps happens to pick up a few dry sticks. Directly he does it, the guard of the forest pounces upon the poor fellow, and sends him up for trial. (*Hear, hear.*) His trial begins and the Forest Officer is the witness, the prosecutor, the judge and every thing; he is fined and the spoil is divided between the Treasury and the Forest guard. If there is a magistrate who is inclined to take a lenient view, he is warned not to do the like of that again. Now, let us see how the Forest Laws deal with this man's cattle. There are villages in which there is no pastural land and the cattle have to exist on thorns, thistles and brambles. The cattle stray upon the forest land and the man is fined, and being impatient to get out of the clutches of the Forest guard he manages to pay the fine. But that is not sufficient. As soon as he gets down the steps of the Court house, he is called up again and told, he has paid a fine for trespass, he must now pay for the damage. With what difficulty the man pays the fine you can easily imagine. Then again you have to consider how the Forest Act deals with the trees that grow upon the lands which are undoubtedly yours and the property of no one else. But you are told they are not yours, you have to pay if you want wood, and you are astonished to find that what was once yours is no longer yours. If you cut the trees even on your own land, you have to pay for them or be punished. ("*Shame.*") In the Konkan the land has to be burnt before crops can be sown, and theie the ryots are not allowed to take the material to burn their land, they must either steal or starve. One word more; the British Government is anxious to advance the interests of peasants, the marrow and bone of the country. It is not denied in any quarter that the peasant is the strength of the country. I ask, if Government is sincere in its intentions and proposals, are these the means employed which are calculated to advance the prosperity of the country? I pause for a reply. (*Applause.*)

PUNDIT MEGHAN RAM (*Punjab, No. 556, in list*) in supporting the motion said:— MR. PRESIDENT, BROTHER-DELEGATES, LADIES AND GENTLEMEN,—The resolution which I have been called upon to support, has been before the Congress for many years, but the severity of the rules in force in the hilly districts of the Punjab has not, before this, attracted the attention of this Congress. It is to the severity of these rules that I rise to direct your attention for the first time. The rules, as you will see, are very arbitrary and unworthy of a civilized Government. These rules were framed by the

**Necessity for mitigating the harshness of the practical administration of the Forest Laws**

Punjab Government and recieved the sanction of the Governor General-in-Council on 21st May, 1855; and by the provisions of the Punjab Laws Act IV of 1872, they acquired the force of law in the hill districts. By rule 1, the civil authorities are empowered to declare any area wheresoever situated, a Reserved Forest, and the people, under rule VI, have no right to object either on the score of proprietary or manorial rights. By these rules the Government has despotically and unreasonably sanctioned the illegality of the action of the civil officers whenever they like to do so. It is a well established rule of law, that no person will be convicted under the provisions of any penal law or rule so long as guilt is not, by clear and reliable evidence, brought home to him; but in order to protect their own rights, so unlawfully obtained, or acquired, the Government in the highest amount of unwisdom and despotism has enacted rule IX which runs as follows :—

"The villagers, the owners and occupants of the land may be rendered responsible for conflagrations occurring within their bounds, whether accidental or not, or by whomsoever caused, and such owner, occupant or villager may in this case be treated as if he had been guilty of the infraction of the rules."

Now Gentlemen, supposing an owner of the land, in which a Reserved Forest is situate, is at Calcutta, and in his absence some grass, brushwood or any part of a tree takes fire he, under the wording of the rule, is as much liable to punishment, provided in Rule XII, which is a fine of Rs. 100, or in default thereof to imprisonment not exceeding three months. Will any of you who are members of the legal profession tell me after considering the law, wherein does his defence lie, for he is guilty, not for any wilful neglect, but even for an accident which is beyond his power and knowledge. Will the defenders of Government come forward to tell me, wherein the justice of these rules consist? Those who accuse the Ameer of Kabul for monopolising the trade of fruits &c. in Afghanistan, will come forward to advise the Government to repeal these rules and leave the timber trade of the country in the hands of those who according to their natural and ancient rights are the owners of the land now included in the Reserve Forests and trees growing upon it.

Gentlemen! those of you who have not been to the hills and seen the hill-men and have not learnt their customs, manners and the way of their living, do not know what the wood and grass means to these men. It is their life and the life of their cattle; their chief property and important means of subsistence. The people of the hills live in thatched houses which are built and roofed mainly by bamboos, brushwood and grass &c. They have to live in a climate where in the winter season no one can expect to protect himself against the severe cold without fire which remain burnt day and night in their rooms; but now according to the Forest Law they cannot cut trees even though they may be in their very fields under their own cultivation or situate in their compounds, without the sanction of Forest Officers. Do you know the trouble and tediousness which an ignorant hill-man, standing in a great need of wood, is required to undergo in order to obtain it? He must apply to the head of the Forest Department. His application must, according to the practice, go to the guards and other officers. If by good fortune report is made in his favour, the order will be issued to the guard in charge to allow him to cut and remove a specified tree &c. Supposing he stands in need of repairing his house which he must do every now and then, the delay which is the necessary consequence of this practice is not injurious to him alone but to all the members of his family.

Those of you who are acquainted with the customs and religious belief of the hill-men will understand that the hill-men who are in the habit of appeasing *Khetarpal* (god of field) by offering homages, how they must now try to appease the living god of Forests in order to attain his object easily ; but gentlemen ! the hill-men offer to the *Khetrapal* only twice in a year *i. e.* on each harvest, or on the occasion of marriage of a son, or daughter, and it is very easy to appease an invisible being if such there be, and it is very difficult to offer homage to a living god of Forests, whose assistance is required every now and then. I have forgotten to tell you that the trees, shrubs, or brushwood, growing on lands called the village commons or other joint holdings, are declared to be the property of the Government, though the land belongs to the proprietary body who are responsible for the payment of the Government revenue assessed on the whole estate. I will not detain you any longer with the details at this time, but hope to do so on some other occasion. The Forest Law in fact, in the hills of the Punjab, like the swollen limb of a camel, cannot be called sound and satisfactory and requires the special attention of our benign Government to which I request you to refer the matter for consideration and enquiry.



The motion was unanimously adopted.

The Congress then adjourned till 12 o'clock the following day (Saturday.)

---

# FOURTH DAY'S PROCEEDINGS.

## Saturday, 30th December, 1893.

**Fourth day.**

The Congress reassembled at 12 o'clock on Saturday.

THE PRESIDENT at the outset of the proceedings said: We have to-day a long list of resolutions and unless I am very strict in the matter of the time to be allowed to each speaker, there is no chance of getting through all the business. Therefore I warn every one of the speakers, that I shall most strictly strike the first gong at etght minutes and the second at ten for proposers, and for every body else, the first gong will be sounded at four minutes, and the second at five minutes, and I hope every speaker will use his capacity to convey his speech in telegraphie language, as concise and as mathematical as possible, for I was a Professor of Mathematics and I like it.

**Resolution X.**

**Permanent Settlement and the creation of alarm by Government interference with it.**

MR. PETER PAUL PILLAY (*Madras, No. 839, in list*) said: MR. PRESIDENT, LADIES AND GENTLEMEN,—It is exactly one hundred years since the introduction of Permanent Settlement by the East India Company in 1793. Instead of celebrating its centenary amid rejoicings and demonstrations of loyalty, we have to express our deep sorrow and alarm at the threatened national calamity in the extinction of permanent settled estates. The Resolution is in these terms.

*That this Congress, having on many previous occasions urged on the Government of India the necessity for giving, as was promised by the British Government over thirty years ago, fixity and permanence to the Land Revenue demand wherever this has not already been conceded, desires now to reiterate emphatically this recommendation and to call attention to the profound alarm which has been created by the action of Government in interfering with the existing permanent settlement in Bengal and Behar (in the matter of the survey and other cesses) and with the terms of the sanads of the permanently settled estates in Madras, and deeming such tampering with solemn public pledges, no matter under what pretences, a national calamity, hereby pledges itself to oppose in all possible legitimate ways, any and all such reactionary attacks on permanent settlements and their holders.*

Continuing Mr. Pillay said:—The Congress has been praying for Permanent Settlement for lands that are subject to periodical settlement. Instead of granting the request the Government is trying to undo the Permanent Settlement for lands that have had the benefit of the Permanent Settlement. What we would construct the Government would destroy. This destructive agency must be protested against in a business-like manner. In 1793 Permanent Settlement was introduced, exactly 100 years ago. Instead of celebrating the centennial anniversary with all demonstrations of joy and loyalty, we have the mournful task of expressing alarm at the destructive agencies at work against the boon, and of disapproving the action of the Government in tampering with the settlement with all the unhappy consequences. The Government is guilty of acts of omission and commission which, if allowed to go on unchecked, would ultimately result in the extinction of the Zemindari system. For instance, in the Madras Presidency, the Zemindars Association petitioned the Government to regulate the succession of zemindaries, as in the case of the Taluqdars of Oudh, by legislation. The Government positively refused to do so, though the legislative reform is demanded by justice and expediency. I shall read one passage from the Government order to illustrate the narrow-minded policy of the

Permanent Settlement and the creation of alarm by Government interference with it.

Government. It is as follows:—"In coming to the above conclusion in regard to the requests contained in the memorial, the Government is not unmindful of the fact that, in the absence of check on alienations, the existing large estates may in process of time get broken up into smaller estates which may be purchased by persons who may look on the lands they have acquired merely as speculative investments and who may, therefore, devote their energies solely to the enhancement of their rent roll."

Here the inaction of the Government, inspite of the prayer of the zemindars, shows the complaisance with which the Government views the ruin of proprietary. It is the Government that drives the proprietary estates to sale. The same Government order contains the proceedings of the Board of Revenue, according to which the Revenue Officers are recommended to purchase them at auction sale, with all the advantages of the Government holding the anomalous position of both a seller and a buyer. This is a very convenient and summary way of extinguishing the zemindary system.

There are several instances where the Government recently purchased zemindaries. Here we have settled estates which are being unsettled in a summary way, instead of the unsettled estates, being settled according to the prayer of the Congress. There is another very serious grievance regarding the manner in which the Government violates the terms of Permanent Settlement by the Proprietary Village Service Bill, which is being pushed through with culpable haste simply on account of the retirement of the officer in charge of the Bill ten days hence. It is to be passed next Friday, the 5th January, in the face of the protest from the press, the zemindars, and all the members of the Council who love fair play and justice. This is a most disgraceful action by an official clique, supported by the supposed representative of the zemindars themselves to whose suicidal advocacy my friend, Mr. Jambulingam Moodaliar, alluded to the other day, and by a non-official member whom the Madras Government considers as its legal luminary and who has the audacity to discover efficiency and improvement inspite of the contrary having been shown by the opinions of the zemindars and others interested in the Bill.

By the Bill new cess is to be levied and the village servants are to be placed under the control of Revenue officers, except in the nominal power of appointment, subject to appeal from dissatisfied parties and to veto by the officers even without appeal. The Zemindars contend that this is a sheer violation of the terms of the Permanent Sanads which I shall read from the Regulation Book. It is as follows:—"Wherefore the British Government impressed with a deep sense of the injuries arising to the State and to its subjects from the operation of such principles has resolved to remove from its administration so fruitful a source of uncertainty and disquietude, and to grant to Zemindars and other landlords, their heirs and successors, a permanent property in their land in all time to come and to fix for ever a moderate assessment of public revenue on such lands; the amount of which shall never be liable to be increased under any circumstances." This is the solemn pledge contained in these regulations. Then again with regard to another point, there is a violation of the terms of Permanent Sanads. It is section 11, and as it is rather a long one I will read a portion of it. "Where a zemindar, or his under farmer tenants, ryots, may have cause of complaint against a Curnum for breach of his duty, such zemindar shall be free to institute a suit in the adwalut of the zillah for the purpose of bringing such Curnun to trial and punishment; but where a zemindar may deprive a Curnun of his office, without such previous regular process, the zemindar shall be liable to make such satisfaction for the injury as the adwalut of the zillah may decree."

In the original Bill the framers were candid enough to insert the clause "The terms of Sanad Milkyat Issimrar notwithstanding." We now find that clause is struck out.

Fourth day.

Resolution X.

Permanent Settlement and the creation of alarm by Government interference with it.

Though the justifying clause of the unjustifiable legislation is removed, the Bill is kept up. The Hon'ble mover of the Bill now boldly says that the Bill is not opposed to the terms of Permanent Sanad. What are his reasons? This cess is no violation because of the local cess being no violation, according to the Despatch to the Government of India by the Secretary of State. The Secretary of State's Despatch to the Government of India, dated 10th May, 1870, says: "In view therefore of these facts and considerations, Her Majesty's Government have now to intimate to your Excellency the conclusion to which they have come, after a careful consideration of a controversy which has now been going on for a long course of years This conclusion is that rating or local expenditure is to be regarded—as it has hitherto been regarded, in all the Provinces of the Empire—as taxation separate and distinct from the ordinary land revenues; that the levying of such rates upon the holders of land, irrespective of the amount of their land assessment, involves no breach of faith on the part of the Government, whether as regards the holders of permanent or o temporary tenures; and that when such rates are levied at all, they ought, so far as may be possible, to be levied equally, without distinction and without exemption, upon all the holders of property accessible to the rate." Here the Government is the judge of its own action. The road-cess is a direct charge upon lands payable in good or bad seasons, whether the tenant's portion is recoverable or not, with all the permanency and rigour of permanent *perihcush*. Call it by any name you like. It is a direct and unjustifiable enhancement of land revenue contrary to the solemn pledges. The Zemindars contend that two wrongs cannot make one right. Simply because they bore patiently one violation, it is no reason that there should be another violation. With regard to the control over servants also, the proposed Bill is a violation, because the only restriction in the exercise of control was that the Rumums or Village accountants should be removed by Civil Courts. Beyond this, every kind of interference with the power of Zemindars is a violation. Though the Revenue officers consulted opposed the Bill, it is forced on the Zemindars on the pretext of improving the Police administration. The occasion for the introduction of the Bill was the complaint of certain ryotwari villagers against exaction and terrorem by the village watchers under the Village Service Act, which has been said to be a chief cause of increase of crimes. Very strongly the Government has deduced arguments for the extension of the Act to proprietary villages with all the wisdom of a quack who would poison A in order to cure the poison of B. thus poisoning both. In the original statement of Objects and Reasons, the false plea was set up that the village servants of proprietary estates are notoriously guilty of crimes. When facts were shown to the contrary, the framers struck out the false premises but retained the false conclusion of the Bill, that it is necessary for the improvement of Police administration. The Government should cast out the beam from its own eyes before it ventures to remove the mote from that of its neighbours.

The trifling object of securing due submission of agricultural and vital statistics can be secured well without the Bill enforcing a new cess in addition to the old ones against which there has been no complaint. (*Applause.*)

BABU BAIKUNTHA NATH SEN (*Bengal, No. 1c, in list*) in seconding the resolution said:—This motion is composed of three parts, first it contains a reiteration of the recommendations made on previous occasions for the extension of the concession to provinces and tracts of land where Permanent Settlement does not prevail, the second portion consists of an expression of alarm on the part of the Congress in consequence of the attitude which the Government has taken in respect of the permanently settled provinces and regrets the tampering with its pledges. With regard to the second question it appears that the Government, instead of showing indications of extending the privilege of permanent settlement to tracts where it does not prevail, its attitude goes rather to interforc

**Fourth day.**

**Resolution X.**

**Permanent Settlement and the creation of alarm by Government interference with it.**

with Permanent Settlement where it exists. I will confine my remarks to Bengal. At present Behar is about to be subjected to a Cadastral survey. Whatever the merits of such a survey may be, it is not my object to discuss; I will speak of the cesses to be imposed on account of that survey. Government undertakes to pay one eighth of the expenses of that survey, the remaining seven eighths being borne by the land owning interests. So, that is a fresh imposition on permanently settled estates, practically interfering with their permanent settlement. When this resolution was first brought before the Congress, we hoped for a favourable order from Government, but not only have our endeavours been abortive but we are threatened with a monstrosity and the Congress has taken timely note of it. It has become the duty of the Congress to express its alarm, but does the duty of the Congress cease here? No, something ought to be done to take protective measures, and therefore the Congress pledges itself to oppose by all legitimate means and in a thoroughly constitutional manner, to oppose all measures which are attacks on Permanent Settlement. We may indulge in a hope that our attempts will not fail and assure others that this is not an impotent threat on the part of the Congress. We know the history of the Jury Resolution. *(Applause.)* We had resolved to ask for an extension of the jury system and the extension of the system with reference to crimes which are now not tried by juries, but we know that a notification was issued for restriction. Now in the same way we are threatened with regard to settlements and by a strong combination we may succeed in averting the danger threatening us and frustrate the object; the unjust attempt of Government to interfere with permanently settled lands and placing on landowners fresh impositions. *(Hear, hear.)* Gentlemen, my time is up and so I must stop here in obedience to our worthy President's rule, though I had more to say.

SHEIKH WAHAB-UD-DIN, (*N. W. Provinces, No. 155, in list*) said: MR. PRESIDENT AND GENTLEMEN,—Government has spent twenty crores of rupees over a scientific frontier and if the present fiscal policy of the present administrators is allowed to continue, it will break the very backbone of the Empire. It is rightly said in all quarters that the peasantry and landed gentry are the backbone of a nation, and this is not the first instance in which Bengal and Madras have had to complain of a breach of faith. When the settlement promises were given to the people of this country, the state of things which prevailed, was very different; but now all India, from one end to the other, is surely attached to the British Crown, and their loyalty and devotion to the British Crown has been rewarded in the manner explained in the Resolution. The rulers are not to be found strong everywhere and I am sorry to say that Bengal is not presided over by such a strong Governor as the Punjab, and so, nearly the maximum limit of taxation has been reached. We cruel tyrannical Mahomedans in the past days never took thirtytwo crores of rupees from the country in all shapes, but the British Government, notwithstanding its claim to civilisation, humanity, and christianity, is realising no less than twentyfive crores in the shape of land revenue. But this is not the fault of the British Government at home, or the British Public at home. The British Government have sent out a number of agents to govern this country on behalf of the Queen and the English nation, and it is our duty that we should inform them from time to time, how those agents behave and how they are carrying out the behests of their masters. This very Province in which I am standing, the capital of which is Lahore, was forty three years ago annexed to the British Empire. What was the condition of the country at that time? We were fiscally stronger, we were physically much more strong than at present, but the Forest Laws and taxations have deteriorated the condition of every man. The people have become poorer and poorer and there is scarcely left any margin for the peasant and for the landed gentry to make any provision for the future or even to support themselves and their families. Agricultural experts have said from time to

Fourth day.

Resolution X.

Permanent Settlement and the creation of alarm by Government interference with it.

time, that there is not a single nation on the face of the earth which is so industrious and so diligent in cultivating the land as the Indian peasantry, but notwithstanding this we find periodically, to quote the words of Sir Roper Lethbridge, that "the modern legalised armies of the Pindaris are let loose: I refer to the periodical settlements." Time is up, so I will say no more (*applause.*)

MR. B. G. TILAK (*Bombay, No 760, in list*) said:—MR. PRESIDENT, AND BROTHER DELEGATES,—I have great pleasure in supporting the proposition, and in doing so I shall point out first, that this is one of those resolutions which furnishes a complete answer to the charge brought against the Congress that it exists for the benefit of the educated classes of this country. (*applause.*) We are not seeking to benefit that class, but the poor classes, and I shall point out that coming as I do from Bombay, I don't plead for the Zemindars, but the ryots of Bombay. There the necessity of Permanent Settlement is keenly felt by all classes of the community. The resolution before us shows the necessity of fixity and permanence of the Land Revenue demand without reference to the method of assessing the settlement or the Government revenue. That is, whether the Government be dealing with the landlords, or with the owners of the villages, or with the ryots directly as in Madras and Bombay, we find that the present inconvenience of the revised revenue settlement is caused by the increase; the enhancement is so great that the agriculturalists in Bombay and Madras feel the necessity of a Permanent Settlement. I am not going to anticipate my friend Mr. Abaji Khare, who is going to lay before you the inconveniences of a revised settlement every 20 or 30 years. So far as Bombay is concerned, we have experienced the evils of revised settlements to such an extent, that we all very cordially support the proposition placed before you. I may mention one case of revised settlements carried out every 30 years. The increase sometimes amounts to as much as 700 per cent. Government has recognized the necessity of remedying this evil and in a resolution, Government says that the enhancement is not to be more than 33 per cent Notwithstanding that resolution, the Survey authorities have increased the assessment by 700 per cent and the wonder is that, it is sanctioned by the Government of Bombay, the Government of India, and the Secretary of State. After all, it would not be possible to remedy all these evils without the boon of Permanent Settlement. I would, with these remarks, support the proposition. (*Applause.*)

SIRDIR GURU CHARN SING (*Punjaw, No. 310, in list*) It is my pleasant duty to stand before you and support that part of the resolution which urges, that Permanent Settlement of Land Revenue be granted to those provinces which do not already enjoy that privilege. Had it not been for the fact that the Secretary of State for India that omnipotent gentleman who rules India from Downing Street, has condemned the principle of Permanent Settlement of Land Revenue, I would have contented myself by simply saying that, because Bengal and some other Provinces have been permanently settled, therefore that principle is sound in policy, useful to the State, advantageous to the landlord, and beneficial to the tenant. But unfortunately for us, the authorities seem to think, that they have made a mistake by giving Permanent Settlements to Bengal and to some other Provinces. They assign their reasons for it, the soundness or unsoundness of which I leave to you to decide. They say that when Land Revenue was permanently settled in Bengal, it was done on the supposition,

Vide Baden Powell Land system of India Vol. I. P. 290.

(1) That the landlord would improve the lands and will treat the tenants leniently and benevolently.

(2) That as both classes grow rich, though the Land Revenue would not alter, other Revenues would increase; for wealthy people want more and more in way of foreign imports and artisles of luxury, and the custom house would reap the benefit in the shape of duty.

All these expectations have been rudely disappointed with rare exceptions. The Zemindars, as a class, did nothing for the tenants, but rack rent them or hand them over to the patnidars or rent farmers who did so still more. Gentlemen, mark the argument. Supposing all these statements to be true (about the truth of which I have grave doubts) I ask, are the tenants in places, where Permanent Settlements have been effected, not better off than in our parts of the country? The landlord may be exacting, but surely he will not be so exhorbitant in his demands as the landlord in a temporary settled place is compelled to be.

**Fourth day.**

**Resolution X.**

**Permanent Settlement and the creation of alarm by Government interference with it.**

Each new settlement brings with it its own evils and raises the assessment by about 50 per cent., after every 20 years or so. At least such is the case in Punjab. And when the landlord has to pay so much more, he throws the whole burden upon the tenant by raising the rent by about 100 per cent. This is the hardship from which tenants suffer under temporary settlements. The other argument advanced by the noble Secretary of State requires no refutation, for it is an undisputed fact that both the landlord and the tenants now spend more money on foreign goods than they did in 1793, when Land Revenue was permanently settled in Bengal. But gentlemen, it is not enough that we should prove to our rulers that the system of Permanent Settlement is beneficial but they also want us to tell them how the changes are to be effected. Their argument is, that there are no big Zemindars like Bengal in the Punjab and with whom are they to settle the Revenue ?

I humbly ask the question, with whom do the Government settle Revenue in cases of temporary settlements ? Separate estates are marked out as assessment circles, and the Revenue is settled with the holders of these estates. These men and their representatives are responsible to the Government for the assessed Revenue, and the same method can be adopted in case of Permanent Settlements. Of course the system of collecting Land Revenue will not be so simple as you have in other Provinces, but that is a difficulty which is not insurmountable and ought not to delay justice because, to use the words of that eminent jurist, Jeremy Bentham, "Justice delayed is justice denied."

The system of temporary settlements is detrimental to the interests of the landlord as well as to those of the tenant. The landlord suffers for he dare not improve or reclaim the land, because the dread of the new settlement and the increased assessment is always hanging over his head. The more he improves his land the higher will be the assessment he shall be burdened with. The tenant suffers still more. As with each settlement the assessment increases, the landlord arbitrarily multiplies the rent. As regards this poor class of people, the produce is the same but the rent is raised higher. They have large families to support and other worldly expenses to incur. I hope I am not exaggerating the facts when I say that more than 90 per cent of these people, who work in their fields and brave the freezing colds of December nights and the scorching heat of June days, hardly get their bare subsistence.

The margin of profit in cultivation has grown so narrow that you find these poor people always in debt, and they have to borrow money from the money lender at something like 30 per cent interest. What is the result if the crop fails? They are ruined and ruined with no fault of their own; ruined not through their extravagance or imprudence but simply because they are unfortunately so circumstanced that no amount of honest labour on their part can save them from the hands of poverty. In vain they try to make the two ends meet, the calamity comes like death. The family is broken up, their cattle are sold for debts, the bread winner of the family either dies of a broken heart or lingers in the dark recesses of a Civil Jail under the decree of the money lender. If he has any son, the poor youth leaves home in despair and joins the army where he ends his

Fourth day.

Resolution X.

Permanent Settlement and the creation of alarm by Government interference with it

days at a handsome salary of 7 rupees a month. I have said enough to move your hearts, if you have any. The well known saying "That we have nothing to do with the taxes but to pay them, and nothing to do with the laws but to obey them," applies to us. Yes. we do pay the taxes and obey the laws without a murmur but we humbly ask, that the taxes be reasonable, and the laws be just. That is our position. I therefore ask for Permanent Settlement in the interests of the landlord, but much more in the interests of the tenant, a class which is dumb, a class which is poor and a class which is helpless. And I, for one, though pessimistic in other matters, feel certain that our demands will be conceded. When I look round, I feel no hesitation in saying, and I proudly say, that ours are the demands of a nation and to use the words of Sir W. Hunter, they may be delayed, they may be modified but cannot be ignored.

MR. KESHAV VINAYEK JOSHI (*Nagpur, No. 815, in list*) said :—MR. PRESIDENT, AND BROTHER-DELEGATES,—There is a saying that a ghost is one who has his feet turned backwards, and we have a Government with its feet turned backwards. (*Laughter.*) In the Central Provinces the Government is pursuing a retrograde policy and the settlement which was granted 30 years ago is now about to be interfered with. The Settlement operations now in progress are modified and are only to stand for twelve years or ten years and at the end of that time, Government will be able to enhance rents again. In some cases, the enhancement has been 200 per cent and 300 per cent. I will say one word about the Province which is being subjected to this cruel experiment. I have travelled through all the villages and I can bear testimony that the people are so poor that they live on *mowra* flowers and seed of tamarinds, and these are the people who are to be subjected to this experiment. ("*Shame.*") In the Central Provinces, we suffer from something which is not to be found anywhere else. We have a close relationship with both the Government of India and the Government of Bombay. On the one hand, we are told that an Act passed for Bengal is binding on the Central Provinces, and on the other hand, in the matter of Educational policy we are bound to the Bombay University. Therefore, we are bound, I cannot say why, by the *Rewari* system as well as the Permanent Settlement. We suffer from the evils of both. I put it to you and ask you, whether you think such evils should continue from year to year with the poverty of the people increasing. I speak from experience and conviction. (*applause.*)

The President intimated that Mr. Laksnman Prasad of Lucknow had an amendment to bring forward.

PUNDIT LAKSHMAN PRASAD (*Oudh, No. 171, in list*) : Before bringing forward my amendment, I wish to ask if this resolution goes against the Cadastral Survey.

THE PRESIDENT : No.

PUNDIT LAKSHMAN PRASAD : Then I withdraw my amendment.

The Seconder of the amendment having also agreed to withdraw, the motion was unanimously adopted.

Resolution XI.

Government failure in granting its promised modified fixity of tenure.

MR. DAJI ABAJI KHARE (*Bombay, No. 779, in list*) proposed :

*That this Congress regrets extremely that the Government of India have not only failed to carry out the pledges for a permanent settlement in the Provinces in which it does not exist (given by the Secretary of State in his despatches of 1862 and 1865), but have also failed to give effect to the policy of granting a modified fixity of tenure and immunity from enhancements, laid down in 1882 and 1884 by the Government of India and approved by the Secretary of State.*

He said : MR. PRESIDENT AND GENTLEMEN,—You will have observed from the wording of this resolution that it is not only not inconsistent with the previous resolution which has been passed, but affords a strong argument why Government should accede

**Fourth day.**

**Resolution XI.**

**Government failure in granting its Promised modified fixity of tenure.**

to the request you have already preferred to them. I propose this resolution and I hope you will accept it, for half a loaf is better than no bread. In this Province where Permanent Settlement does not prevail, there exists an institution by which every twenty five, or thirty years, the assessment of land is revised, and after that revision, the assessment is almost always increased, and my complaint is that that increase has at times been so unreasonable as to have amounted, in particular instances, almost to the confiscation of private property, and in others, it has greatly discouraged the improvement of land. In increasing these assessments Government have laid down, for themselves, a limit and they have issued a resolution in which they have said that the increased assessment should not exceed the limit of thirty three per cent. Now, there is no data by which we can judge of the justness of this limit, nor have Government taken into account the increased population of the country and the increased cost of production to the cultivators, but have arbitrarily said, that the profits of the cultivator may be taken as the standard and Government may take their share of the profits on that reckoning. Granted for the sake of argument, that the increased profits are represented by thirty three per cent, let us see how the system has operated in some instances. Government in their resolution said, that no assessment on an individual holding could be increased by more than one hundred per cent; but we find that in a recent survey settlement in the Bombay Presidency, an assessment was increased by seven hundred per cent. I may cite some particular instances from which you will see how unjustly these increases have worked out. In a taluka holding which paid four rupees as assessment, the amount has now been increased, under the revised settlement, to forty five rupees; another holding which formerly paid nine rupees, now pays thirty and another which paid three, now pays fifteen rupees. These are three instances out of several where actually Government have increased the assessments more than the hundred per cent to which it pledged itself in a solemn resolution. Another instance of confiscation and double enhancement is that relating to full eighty villages in the Ratnagiri District. In that taluka there exists no pretence for saying that the holders of the villages have increased their profits. Their profits have remained the same, but the increase in the assessment has been so much, that the holders who used to pay a hundred or two hundred, now pay two thousand rupees to Government Then there is another instance in the same category which I may cite to you for your consideration. The way this thirty three per cent. is collected is at times very queer There is a taluka in the Khandesh Division where, when the settlement was made in 1852-55, a prospective railway was taken into consideration and the lands were assessed on the prospective profits. In 1890, when the assessment was revised, the same railway was taken as an argument for increasing the assessment over thirty three per cent. Then I would come to the question of the discouragement of improvements. I need not tell you that the ordinary landholders are terribly afraid of improving their lands and you may get an instance of this when I tell you that the late Mr. Telang, himself as a tenant, was afraid of improving his land. In the Bombay Council in 1886, he strongly asked Government for a pledge that improved land would not be taxed, and then Lord Reay made a solemn promise, that no improvements carried out by the holder himself would be taxed by the Government. The same principle has been clearly laid down in a resolution issued by Lord Ripon, but notwithstanding this we have to record a breach of those pledges in the recent settlement in the Panwell taluka. There some land which the holder had converted into rice land has been taxed, not on the previous arrangement but on the new lines for rice-lands. In this matter you have not only the ignorance of the ryots to deal with, but there is also the strong significant fact that such taxation on improvements has discouraged the people, from one end of the Presidency to the other, from putting their money into land. But you have also to see how Government behave with regard to the petitions submitted by the people. In the Ratnagiri district we got a petition prepared and submitted against the assessment. That was in 1892, but as yet we have received

Fourth day.

Resolution XI.

Government failure in granting its Promised modified fixity of tenure.

no reply. Gentlemen, you will observe from this how well one may bring his grievance before Government, when a petition is sent from a district in 1892, and has not yet been replied to by the Commissioner to whom it was sent. Having got no answer an appeal was preferred to the Government of Bombay who returned the petition forsooth, for want of a copy of the order of the authority against whom that petition was presented. But the authority against whom that appeal was preferred had made no order whatever, therefore the petitioners were unable to put forward any order. In these circumstances I would ask you to support the proposition. Although it does not so much concern Bengal, but in Bombay and in some parts of Madras, the Central Provinces and in the Punjab also, great grievances exist and if this request goes from the Congress it will have assisted a great many poor agriculturists in their daily toil. This is precisely a question of importance to the agriculturists who are a large majority of the population. You all know that they are a comparatively voiceless majority and I would appeal to you to give them the benefit of your voice and carry these grievances from this country even to England, if necessary, in order to get some redress in the matter. With these words I beg to propose the motion which I have already read out to you. *(Applause.)*

MR. G S. KHAPARDE (*Berar, No. 800, in list.*) in seconding the motion said: MR. PRESIDENT, AND BROTHER-DELEGATES,—You probably all know the old saying "Unto him that hath, much shall be given and from him that hath not, even that which he hath, it shall be taken away." I will give you a few reasons why the proposition should be accepted by all here. The first is that, every few years a fresh settlement comes on and these re-settlements involve a great deal of expenditure. Government may pay some of the expense, but the ryots have to bear the most of it. What Government usually does is to say it costs very little; it only cost Re. 1 per acre, but as a matter of fact, it costs more, for it costs their forced labour of which you will hear later on. Letting alone that, it unsettles periodically the relations between the money lender and the people. The peasant knows that to-day he can borrow at Re. 1 per cent, but his holding might increase in rent whilst the land itself might deteriorate in value or become worthless. So the relations between the money lender and the poor peasant become unsettled every twenty or thirty years. But that is not all; the relations between the superior holder and the inferior holder become disturbed. Supposing I own 2000 acres of land. I let it out to other people. When I know the period is approaching when the land will be re-assessed and re-surveyed, I naturally want to cover the loss that might be incurred. I say to the tenant, you used to pay me Rs. 20 before, you must now pay me Rs. 25, part of which is to go as expenses of re-settlement, something for myself of course—well you know all about that. *(Laughter.)* This trouble is now going on in my own Province of Berar, but I am glad to tell you that Colonel Mackenzie, and the Resident Mr. Plowden, are both inclined to hear our complaints, and we got up a memorial to show, there was no necessity for a re-survey. It was said that prices had increased, we showed that they had not; they said that the railways had not been taken into consideration, we showed that they had. I think I need go no further. There may be other Provinces where the circumstances may be similar and I would advice you to bring forward your reasons. I have said enough to recommend the proposition, and I hope you will carry it. *(Applause.)*

MIR. NISAR ALI SHOHRAT (*Punjvb, No. 267, in list*) supported in Urdu.

The motion was unanimously adopted.

Fourth day.

Resolution XII.

Protests against withdrawal of Government grant for High Education, recommends increased expenditure on general and technical education, advocates students' physical development, prays for reduction of the poor students' fees and asks for an enquiry regarding industrial condition.

MR. M. B. NAMJOSHI, (*Poona, No, 761, in list.*) said:—MR. PRESIDENT AND BROTHER-DELEGATES,—The motion I have to place before you has grown since it was first presented to you four years ago, and I consider it a matter of regret that new grievances have arisen every year. The motion is as follows.

*That this Congress is of opinion that it is inexpedient in the present state of Education in the country, that Government grants for High Education should in any way be withdrawn, and concurring with previous Congresses, affirms in the most emphatic manner, the importance of increasing the public expenditure on all branches of Education, and the expediency (in view to the promotion of one of the most essential of those branches, i.e. the technical) of appointing a mixed Commission to enquire into the present industrial condition of the country; and looking to the great poverty of many classes of the community, strongly recommends, that in all classes of Government or Municipal Schools and Colleges, all fees shall be reduced in proportion to the means of parents and relations and remitted wholly in the case of very poor students; and, focussing the universal opinion of the Indian Community that undue stress is being laid at present upon mere mental development, this Congress earnestly recommends that henceforth, in all grades of schools and colleges, at least equal attention should be devoted to the physical development of the students.*

Four years ago, or rather five years, the local Government, acting under the direction of the Government of India, were thinking of withdrawing their support to higher education. It was then that we took up this question for discussion and our prayer was that, Government should not withdraw its support to higher education. A year after that, Government thought of introducing technical education into several Provinces, but it was without proper attention to the wants of the nation and generally done in a haphazard way. We asked for a commission of enquiry to get full knowledge of the industrial wants of the people. Now we have two additional requests to make; one relates to fees. We think, fees should be remitted to some extent, and that greater attention should be paid to physical education in schools and colleges. On the first part of the resolution, we need not say anything more than has already been said. As to the reduction and remission of fees, I think it is necessary so far as primary education is concerned. Although Municipalities and Local Boards have the fullest freedom in other matters, the Government have reserved certain rights. Naturally they claim they have the right of saying what fees should be levied in schools, but Government does not allow that and even goes further and prescribes that the number of free studentships held in a school shall be so many, and still went a step further and said that they would not only prescribe the number but the castes and communities they should be held by. Although the Municipalities are the spending bodies, they have not the power to levy the fees, or distribute the studentships according to the wants of the communities. As to physical education, the number of deaths amongst the educated classes has forced this subject on our attention. We consider it is necessary that greater attention should be given to physical education. I say greater, because in most Provinces, Schools and Colleges have made a beginning in physicial education, but what they are doing is, according to our thinking and this motion, not enough and we say that greater attention might be given. Having proceeded thus far, I will say a few words with regard to the actual state of things. The present state of education in this country you know. In higher education not 1 per cent of the whole population have gone through the entire course. In primary education we have not many schools. Hundreds and thousands of people receive no education at all and the Gaekwar has given us a lesson in this matter. If primary education is made free and compulsory, then our wants will be satisfied. As to higher education in our Province and, I believe, in Bengal not only are they not establishing more schools of the second grade, but they are withdrawing grants on one pretence

**Fourth day.**

**Resolution XII.**

**Protests against withdrawal of Government grant for High Education, recommends increased expenditure on general and technical education, advocates students' physical development, prays for reduction of the poor students' fees and asks for an enquiry regarding industrial condition.**

or another from institutions for secondary education and that is a state of things which is not satisfactory. And although we refer in terms and words to higher education, we thereby not only mean college education but secondary education. As to primary education, the burden of providing a larger number of schools has been thrown on the Municipalities and Local Boards. The Government agreed in the first place to bear a certain proportion of the expenditure but now after seven or eight years, Government is doing all it can not to act up to its promise. That is the present state of education; and if Government should withdraw from primary, and college or secondary education, there would be felt a greater want. So long as the people are unable to stand on their own legs, Government ought not to follow the policy of withdrawal. The second part of the resolution refers to an enquiry by a mixed Commission. It is admitted by the Government of India that such an enquiry is necessary and you will be glad to know that in most Provinces this enquiry has been made. It was ordered in 1886, and except in Bombay, such enquiry has been made and our prayer is that, instead of making the enquiry there a departmental one, it ought to be by a mixed Commission. The reason for this prayer is, that officials have to conduct the affairs of their Department and are not in touch with the people. It is necessary that the representatives of the people should be associated with the Commission. *(Applause.)* Our President has put before you the great question of the poverty of the people. That is the question of the day. Many schemes have been thought of to do away with that poverty, but primary education has been acknowledged by all economists as the best, and if free education is given we may have hope. Our hopes are in the spread of education; and therefore we pray that the Municipalities may be allowed to levy fees according to their own convictions and not those of Government. Our last prayer is, as I have told you, in consequence of the large number of deaths amongst the educated classes. We trust that Government will give us more physical education in our schools and colleges. *(Hear, hear and applause.)*

BABU NIBARAN CHANDRA DAS (*Bengal, No. 38, in list*) said:—MR. PRESIDENT, LADIES AND GENTLEMEN,—The resolution looks very big on paper but upon analysis you will find it is a very simple one. We want a continuation of high education, we want for poorer classes cheaper education, and we want a promise of physical education That is all the resolution places before you. Now, with regard to higher education I have a few words to put before you. It is said that we are under a civilised Goverment and so we are, but I do not think any Government has a right to be called civilised if it does not place facilities at the door of the very poorest to educate themselves. Universities have been founded, colleges opened and schools established all over the country and so far the Government has redeemed its character as a civilised Government. But now colleges are being abolished, schools are to be disorganised and educational institutions pulled down. *("Shame.")* Government is now pursuing a reactionary policy and this policy is suicidal in the extreme. I tell you emphatically, this policy will cast a slur upon the Government in the history of the world. With regard to higher education I ask you to bear one thing in mind, that the Government spends only one per cent of its revenue on education whereas the Government is not ashamed to spend twenty five per cent of its revenue upon expenditure. (*"Shame."*) Government is very economical in matters of education; retrenchment is the order of the day. The financial bugbear looks nowhere more terrific than in the department of education. (*Hear, hear*). Now you are going to give exchange compensation to the Government European officials, yet there is no money for higher education. I should like to draw your attention to one fact in connection with the Punjab. There is only one college and not a single *Zilla* school maintained by the Government. That is all the Punjabis receive in the way of education from Government and I hear that the fees which the students in this Province have to pay are very high, and the poorer classes can hardly afford to go to the colleges and receive the benefits of education. When we were living under Mahomedan and Hindoo rulers, we used to receive education free. Now we have to pay for it and yet we are under a civilised Government. (*Hear, hear.*) With regard to physical education I have a few words to say. I am a graduate of the Calcutta University. I have passed almost all the Examinations of the University and I am also a graduate in Law and you may fancy, I am a very clever fellow but I am not. (*Laughter.*) I point out myself as a very peculiar piece of humanity. What a weak figure I present to you! To the business of the world I am hardly equal, because my physical education has been lamentably neglected. I am the victim of a bad system. The strain upon my system has been a great deal too much for me; I am a dyspeptic, care worn man, hardly equal to the duties of life. Do you like to have creatures like myself, or would you like to have an illiterate man physically able to bear all the turmoils and troubles of life? True it is, as the last speaker said, that something is being done for physical education in Colleges and Schools, but I should like to tell you that it is very, very little. If you want education in the proper sense, you must look to your body as well as to your mind. We must pay attetion to our physical development as well as to our intellectual culture. As the lease of life accorded me by the President is very short I cannot expatiate more upon the subject. He is not willing to extend the lease and so I must retire (*Laughter and applause.*)

**Fourth day.**

**Resolution XII.**

**Protests against withdrawal of Government grant for higher education, recommends increased expenditure on general and technical education, advocates students physical development, prays for reduction of the poor students' fees and asks for an enquiry regarding industrial condition.**

BAKHSHI RAM LABHAVE (*Punjab, No. 454, in list*) supported the motion in Urdu.

LALA LAJPAT RAI (*Punjab, No. 237, in list*) said: MR. PRESIDENT, BROTHER-DELEGATES, LADIES AND GENTLEMEN,—The first two portions of the subject have been thoroughly threshed out in previous congresses and suffice it for me to say that in discouraging higher education and in reducing the expenditure upon it, the Government is laying itself open to a charge of forgetting its noble mission and work in India, and of forgetting the high ideal chalked out for it by the founders of the Empire. While other civilised countries, like Europe and America, are spending large sums of money on education it is a matter of regret that the Government of India is reducing that expenditue. As to the question of technical education I beg to submit that it is of still greater importance. While civilised countries, like Europe and America, are devising national systems of technical education in order to fit their citizens to compete with other civilised countries in the arts and industries, India, with its growing poverty and starving population and its embarrassed exchequer, is sleeping. No care has been taken of the industries of the country. The students are not taught to live independently of Government employment and still it is said, the people of India do not like learning for learning's sake and hanker after Government employment; but how can a nation with an average income of Rs. 22 per head pursue learning for learning's sake? (*Applause.*) How are we to fill our stomachs, if the education of the country means only to fit ourselves for Government clerkships, or law Professorships, neither of which can improve the material prosperity of the country itself? Therefore, it is essential for the material progress of the country, that Government should look into and provide technical instruction in Schools and Colleges and enable us to earn our livelihood independently of Government employment and become useful citizens of the Empire. This leads me to the third and fourth portions of the resolution with which we, Punjabis, are particularly concerned. It is forty four years since the Punjab came under British sway and it is thirty or thirty five years that the Department of Public Instruction has been started here; but do you know what progress has been made since then? One of the two Government colleges has been abolished: I mean the Delhi Government college. The fees in Government colleges have been this year raised from Rs. 2, to Rs. 12, per mensem and they have also been raised in schools. The bravery of the Punjabis, the Sikhs, and the Rajpoots on the fields of Egypt, Abysinia, and Afghanistan has been

(This portion of text not available)

technical education. Coming, as I do, from the Madras Presidency, I say not a farthing has been spent on technical education. We have got a number of graduates all over the bazaars in Madras who are walking about with no bread to eat and is it a wonder when they have not been given any sort of practical education which would enable them to win their bread? It is high time that we, most unanimously, like loyal subjects of the Queen, directed the attention of the Government of India with a view to get them to take immediate steps with regard to technical education. Let us not consider this to be a joke, for having regard to the poverty of India, it is the question of all the imperial questions and one that we ask Government to solve with the least possible delay. Let us appeal to the Government; we are not appealing as aliens. It was England who went to the assistance of the Italians in their struggle for liberty, and it was England who extended her hand when Greece wanted to establish herself as a nationality. We are neither Italians nor Greeks, but the legitimately adopted children of Englishmen and have a right to claim indulgence at the hands of our rulers. With these words I support the resolution moved by Mr. Namjoshi who has every right to speak on this economic question. (*Applause.*)

**Fourth day.**

**Resolution XII.**

**Protests against withdrawal of Government grant for High Education, recommends increased expenditure on general and technical education, advocates students' physical development, prays for reduction of the poor students' fees and asks for an enquiry regarding industrial condition.**

The motion was unanimously adopted.

RAI BAHADUR. P. ANANDA CHARLU (*Madras, No. 838, in list*) moved:

*That this Congress regrets to notice that the Secretary of State for India in his recent despatch to the Government of India has enunciated the doctrine that occasions may arise in which it may be the duty of the Executive Government to criticise Judicial errors, the Congress being of opinion that such criticism is calculated to shake the confidence of the people in the independence of Judicial tribunals.*

**Resolution XIII.**

**Expression of regret regarding the Executive interference with Judicial decisions and the Secretary of State's despatch on the Subject.**

He said: MR. PRESIDENT, BROTHER-DELEGATES, LADIES AND GENTLEMEN,—It seems to me that the mere announcement of the doctrine ought to secure its downright condemnation. I cannot conceive how a case may occur which would necessitate the dangerous power of the Executive Government being called forth for the correction of what the Secretary of State has chosen to call judicial errors. In the face of the numerous facilities that exist for the redress of wrongs on behalf of the aggrieved, in the face of a carefully elaborated system of appeals, in the face of a goodly contingent of well trained judges, in the face of an almost limitless power of revision possessed by the High Courts of the several Provinces and Presidences, it is beyond my comprehension to conceive, how a case or an action, escaping all these for correction, would require the Executive Government in its superior wisdom to criticise. Well, I cannot conceive of a case which would arise for the exercise of this dangerous power in the hands of the Executive Government. I should deplore the existence of this doctrine on the record, because the retention of this doctrine on the record cannot but be, as stated in the resolution itself, a shock to the confidenec of the people in the independence of the judicial tribunals. It will also be a standing menace to the judicial independence on the part of the tribunals. Thus it will be an unwarrantable detraction of the supremacy of the law, the non-recognition of which is characteristic of barbarous deeds and the recognition of which is the first fundamental principle of an enlightened Government.

MR. KALI CHARAN BANERJI (*Calcutta, No. 10, in list*) in seconding the motion said:—MR. PRESIDENT, BROTHER-DELEGATES, LADIES AND GENTLEMEN,—Yesterday you passed a resolution appealing to the Secretary of State for the immediate separation all around of judicial from executive functions. If the association of these two functions in one and the same person is fraught with evil, surely the subordination—the moral—I

Fourth day.

Resolution XIII.

Expression of regret regarding the Executive interference with Judicial decisions and the Secretary of State's despatch on the Subject.

had almost said the immoral subordination—for judicial purposes of the judiciary, must be absolutely disastrous. It is the old controversy between might and right and I take it that one of the outstanding triumphs of modern civilisation is the subordination of might to right. Our Courts are the bulwarks of our rights and the Executive unfortunately are not above the weakness of encroaching, and sometimes wantonly, on our rights. It is to be regretted therefore, that the despatch of the Secretary of State should articulate a concession calculated to stimulate many a privileged contempt of Court. All the more dangerous because of the proviso in the despatch, that publicity is not to be given to it All honour to the judicial independence of the Bengal officer whose action has been the occasion for bringing this controversy to a head and you may be interested in knowing that that officer is a close relation of one of your most foremost citizens. At the same time judicial independence may not always be proof against the prospect of executive censorship, when that censorship is material in more senses than one and even if such independence were impervious to such censorship we may take that the people realise the possibility of the executive interfering with it. So then their confidence in our tribunals shall be rudely shaken and so they shall be deprived of one of the comforts they have, when their rights are encorached upon. Any way many a subordinate judiciary, to secure the golden opinion of those who are their material superiors, may be tempted to disregard the pronounced views and directions of superior tribunals to the prejudice of many a suffering member of the community. In seconding this resolution I ask you to focus the voice of the Congress on the side of the independence of our judicial tribunals.

RAI JOTINDRA NATH CHAUDHURY (*Bengal, No. 7, in list*) in supporting the motion said:—MR. PRESIDENT, BROTHER-DELEGATES, LADIES AND GENTLEMEN,—The present resolution, I take it, can be characterised as a corollary to the one which you adopted yesterday. I mean the one relating to the separation of the Judicial and the Executive functions, because the subject matter of the present resolution has reference to the interference, by way of criticism of the administrative officers, with the judicial dicisions of the magistracy in the country. Many of you at least know the history of the quarrel between the High Court of Calcutta on the one hand and the Bengal Government on the other; therefore I shall give you a short statement, dealing with the salient features only, how the quarrel had begun and how it ended. Babu Atul Chandra Chatterji, a Deputy Magistrate in one of the Sub-divisions of Barisal District, was, a few months ago, not only found fault with, because he had not shown satisfactory percentages of convictions but he was threatened by the Commissioner of the Division, that unless he would convict more men in future, his promotion should be stopped; or in other words, Babu Atul Chandra was told point blank that if he expected promotion in his service, he should convict those whose only fault would be to appear as accused men in any case before his court. Under a fiat like this, emanating from such a quarter, we can well understand what would be the fate of many accused men before the subordinate magistracy. Now gentlemen, I ask you to ponder over and weigh fully, the principle which underlies this new doctrine of the Commissioner of the division. The principle is nothing more than the total subversion of that noble principle which has made the administration of criminal justice by the English nation a glory to them and a blessing to the ruled—I mean the principle of letting even 99 guilty men go unpunished but of not allowing an innocent man being punished. I think, gentlemen, you are surprised how an English High Official can enunciate, for the guidance of his subordinate officers, a principle so very repugnant to the British sense of justice; but I hope your sense of surprise will vanish when you will hear that the Commissioner in question was acting under, and perhaps was taking his cue from our Lieutenant Governor of Bengal, whose sense of justice is well llustrated in his now famous speech at Purulia wherein he said, "that when a riot has been committed, somebody should have been punished." Thanks to Mr. Stanley, the Sessions

**Fourth day.**

**Resolution XIII.**

**Expression of regret regarding the Executive interference with Judicial decisions and the Secretary of State's despatch on the Subject.**

Judge of Barisal, to whom we all owe a heavy debt of gratitude, who had brought the whole matter to the notice of the High Court, Calcutta ; and the honourable judges sent to the Secretary of State for India a strong protest against this interference of the Lieutenant-Governor of Bengal with the judicial works of the subordinate magistrates. A similar case had also occurred long before this Barisal case. In that still more unfortunate case, the Lieutenant-Governor had not only criticised the judicial proceedings of another subordinate Magistrate but also had caused his reflections to be published in the Local Government Gazette. The Honourable Judges resented also this interference. These protects were sent to the Secretary of State for India through the Government of India, which I regret to say not only sided with the Lieutenant-Governor of Bengal, but also impressed upon the Secretary of State, the necessity and expediency of the Executive Officers in India being empowered to interfere with the decisions of the judicial officers. From its action in connection with the Jury Notification in Bengal, we were convinced that the Government of Lord Lansdowne was very effeminate and miserably weak ; but I am sure no one will be able to put forth this weakness as one of the excuses why we should spare the Government of India from our criticism. If the Government of India do not vigilantly watch the doings of the Local Governments and check their vagaries, when necessary in the cause of justice to the people of India, we can pertinently ask, what is the use of having such a costly, supreme controlling Government? The matter ultimately coming before the Secretary of State for India, he in his despatch on the subject gave utterance to the following which gives occasion to the resolution which has been placed before you. The words of the Secretary of State were as follow:—"While therefore I am not prepared to admit that cases may not occasionally arise in which it is the duty of a Government in India to criticise judicial errors, I think it necessary in the interests of the community that the administrative officers of whatever rank should abstain from publishing officially reflections upon the dicisions and judicial acts of Magistrates and Courts of Law. Now gentlemen, if you ponder over these words, which I have just now quoted, I have no doubt that you will concur with me in thinking that our position in reference to the subject matter of the quarrel between the Local Governments and the High Courts is not a whit better even after the order of the Secretary of State than it was before his recent order. We expected from him a statesmanlike and straightforward reply indicating the wise policy of not allowing administrative officers, either publicly or privately, to criticise the judicial acts of the Subordinate Magistracy in this country, and not a reply couched in a language which, if it means anything, means only a clever attempt to satisfy both parties in the quarrel, without facing the problem directly which was before him for his decision. Taking such a view of the letter as I do, I can not but press upon you that we, Congress-men, should try our utmost to have the principle, as enunciated in the letter of the Secretary of State, revised. We are told that under the British rule we have been enjoying a superior administration of justice both civil and criminal. I, for myself, do not subscribe wholly to this opinion, because the costliness of the administration of justice during the British rule is a great stigma on the administration. Notwithstanding its defects, however, we are thankful to the British nation for the system of administration of justice which they have introduced into this country. Now this boon is at stake, because we see the administrative officers are allowed, even though privately, to criticise the judicial acts of the Magistrates. It is therefore we pray, that the Secretary of State will, at his earliest opportunity, undo the effects, it may be his unintentional effects, of his ill-advised letter and set at rest finally the question at issue. We say in the resolution that the confidence of our countrymen in our courts will be shaken, if such policy is allowed to be continued. This policy of criticism, by the administrative officers, of the judicial acts of our judicial officers, is to be condemned both on account of the magistrates themselves and on that of the peoples of this country. The officers,

**Fourth day.**

**Resolution XIII.**

**Expression of regret regarding the Executive interference with Judicial decisions and the Secretary of State's despatch on the Subject.**

thus hampered in their judicial acts, will have two paths open to them, namely, either to resign the service or to sacrifice their conscience for the success and promotion in the service. The officers, certainly not angels themselves, but as men, liable to be influenced by selfish considerations will, under the present state of things, in many cases at least, be compelled to subordinate their sense of duty to the prospects of their own aggrandisements which means, in innumerable cases, injustice and hardship to the people of this country. What we want to have is, that the administrative officers will not be allowed in any case to interfere with the judicial acts of the Magistrates and Judges and to let the latter have their mind and conscience free in the discharge of their judicial duty, so that there should be no occasion, either for the officers to be compelled to do their duty under the Damocles' sword, as it were, and to sacrifice their conscience in the discharge of their judicial functions, or for the pepole of India to complain that the judicial decisions of our courts of law are dictated by hints which our judicial officers receive from their administrative superiors and not by considerations of justice. The principle for which we contend requires no elaborate argument and I therefore hope that you will adopt this resolution with perfect unanimity.

PUNDIT MOHAN LAL (*N.W. Provinces, No. 135, in list*) in supporting the resolution said :—MR. PRESIDENT, LADIES AND GENTLEMEN,—I beg to support the motion, and I dare say it is one of the most important propositions because the matter complained of is one which encroaches on the liberties of the people ; because it hampers the independence and the impartiality of the Courts of Justice. Sir, it is a recognized principle of law, that courts of justice should be untampered with by any external interference. That is the only safeguard for the people—the courts of justice ought not to be intimidated, ought not to be brought under undue influence. I say, the existence of such a despatch here in India would amount sometimes perhaps to an intimidation to our judges and chief justices, and perhaps it might bring undue influence upon them, because it would be a good chance for the executive to criticise their judgments. It is not a wonder that this august body could not keep quiet when it found that the independence of the people is at stake and what is more, the independence of the judiciary is at stake. Sir, this is not a new thing we have to face. The people of England have had to face it, for the same conflict arose between the House of Commons and the Crown on the one side and the Courts of Justice on the other. I would remind all students of constitutional history of the action of James.I. who asked the King's Bench, when Lord Coke was Chief Justice, to legalise proclamations. The Chief Justice and the three judges declined and history says: "They also formally declared that the king had no prerogative but what the law of the land allowed him. By their firmness on this occasion, the judges rendered an important service to their country. A check was given to the exercise of arbitrary power in this direction and for some time no proclamation imposing fines and imprisonment was issued." Here we see the spirit of the English Judges and how they faced their King and Government. In another case the King asked the Attorney General, then Lord Bacon, to ask the Lord Chief Justice to consult the King before he pronounced judgment in a certain case. This is what is written of that incident,"Hereupon James directed the Attorney General, Bacon to write to the Chief Justice ordering him and the rest of the judges not to proceed to judgment until they had spoken with the King. Coke shortly replied that if it was wished that the other judges should receive the information just given to him Bacon had better write to them himself. This was done, but the next day the judges as if nothing had happened, proceeded with their argument. The day following they despatched a letter to the King signed by all the twelve, informing His Majesty that as they were unanimously of opinion, that the Attorney General's letter was contrary to the law, they felt bound by their oaths to pay no attention to it and they accordingly proceeded with the case on the appointed day." In fact they did not pay the least attention to the order of the King. You remember when the House of Commons had a conflict with the Queen's Bench Division in that famous case of Stockdale *v. s.* Hansard. There the House of Commons wanted the Queen's Bench Division to proclaim, that the passages in the pamphlet were not libelous. The words of Lord Denman were very cogent on the point, and showed the independence and steadfastness of the Judges. Here we have to face the same thing but the difference is this; there in England the Judges fought for the people and vindicated their own independence, but here we have to fight for ourselves and advocate for the judges. Before I resume my seat I would only say that the existence of such a despatch here in India would bring great hardship on our people and a stigma of disgrace on our administration, and I say that such a despatch is unconstitutional, contrary to law and against the principles of justice and good conscience.

**Fourth day.**

**Resolution XIII.**

**Expression of regret regarding the Executive interference with Judicial decisions and the Secretary of State's despatch on the Subject.**

The motion was unanimously adopted.

MR. D. E. WACHA (*Bombay, No. 782, in list*) said: MR. PRESIDENT, LADIES AND GENTLEMEN,—The Resolution I have been entrusted with is as follows:—

**Resolution XIV.**

**Protests against the stoppage of silver coinage in Mints and thereby subjecting Mill and other industries to an indirect burdensome taxation.**

*That this Congress places on record its deep regret at the recent hasty legislation of the Government of India closing the Indian Mints against the private coinage of silver, whereby the people of this country have been subjected to a further indirect taxation of a burdensome and indefinite character, and some of the most important trades and industries, notably the Mill industry, have been seriously disorganised and injured.*

It would be in your recollection, gentlemen, that I had the privilege of moving the resolution on the burning question of currency which was unanimously adopted by the Congress at its sitting last year at Allahabad. But at the time the Government of India, as you are aware, had neither disclosed its ultimate intentions nor taken any measures whatever in reference thereto. Consequently, the Congrees contented itself with what was called a resolution of caution. We respectfully observed to the Government of India that on a subject so important as the reform of the currency of the empire, which in its permanent effects would be far reaching for many a year to come, it would be a part of wisdom and statesmanship to exercise all necessary caution and circumspection, and proceed to take all practical steps with such deliberation as to cause little or no injury to the vast and divers interests at stake in this country. (*Hear, hear.*) In fact, we prayed to Government that it would not legislate in panic—panic created by the steady decline in the value of silver measured by gold and by the contemplated repeal or modification of the Sherman Act. It is, therefore, a matter of profound regret to have to notice on this occasion that notwithstanding the warning, not only from the Congress but from other influential quarters, barring the Anglo-Indian Currency Association which created so much artificial agitation about two years ago, the Government of India suddenly sprung a mine on the public by passing at Simla within half an hour what is now known as the Indian Coinage Amendment Act. No opportunity was allowed to the public to discuss the merits of the measure. (*Hear, hear.*) And what is indeed worse still is the fact that no non-official member was summoned to attend the deliberations of the Viceregal Legislative Council and give the benefit of his counsel! (*Shame*) Of course, the indispensable Mr. (now Sir James) Mackay was there; but the reason of his presence need not be explained. It would have been a scandal had the amended piece of legislation been jockeyed through the Council without the presence of even *one* mercantile member! Moreover, it was notorious that he had acted throughout as the most active non-official spokesman of the Government of India.

But it is superfluous to refer at greater length to the circumstances under which

**Fourth day.**

**Resolution XIV.**

**Protests against the stoppage of silver coinage in Mints and thereby subjecting Mill and other industries to an indirect burdensome taxation.**

the Act was passed, and to the great evil which followed immediately on its heel Almost all the disastrous consequences which were foretold began to be slowly realised Perhaps, the depth of the trade depression and of the general distrust of the nostrum put into practice by Government, could not have reached a lower depth than at the present moment. And there are old and experienced men who even now ominously shake their heads as if to say we might anticipate a lower deep still which would devour everything (*Hear, hear.*) But let us hope that the prophecies of our Cassandras may remain unrealised, and that with the advent of the new year we may witness a slow but gradual revival; though, for my part, I would not hesitate to declare that it would be futile for even the most sanguine to see exchange going back even to *15d.* at the end of the next twelve months, unless altogether new and unexpected factors, which it is impossible to foresee now, contribute to that consummation. (*Hear, hear.*)

It was generally apprehended that the closing of the Mints would usher evils of a character the magnitude of which it would not be easy to forecast. None can deny after the experience of well nigh six months that the evils have indeed turned out of a magnitude more colossal than before. In the speech I made at Allahabad on the subject twelve months ago, you would remember that I had foreshadowed, on the authority of the *Statist*, what evils the tinkering of currency may usher in for the ryot and the intermediary, for the banker and the merchant, for the taxpayer and the State. There is not a single class who is not suffering at the present moment from the fictitious value of the Rupee. For, gentlemen, please remember that the value of that coin does not at present represent anything like the value of the silver contained in it. The Rupee is artificially increased in value beyond its intrinsic worth. There is, in short, as a result of the tinkering, an immense transfer of property from the teeming millions of toilers who create wealth and a corresponding prosperity to the creditor class and Government servants. The hard-working labourers, mostly the overtaxed peasantry, is being impoverished in order that Government officials, and usurers may fatten at their expense (*Hear, hear.*)

But it may be useful at this stage to enquire whether there was any imperative necessity on the 26th June last to take that fatal jump in the dark unknown whereby all India has been engulfed in losses the amount of which it is impossible to estimate except in millions? We have, of course, heard the Government point of view which is this. That it was absolutely imperative in anticipation of the contemplated repeal of the Sherman Act to take the precautionary step of closing the Mints and thus check the inflow of the white metal and give some stability to exchange. The Government observed that its sole object was to prevent the Rupee from dwindling to a shilling or even ten pence! Thus the closing of the mints was considered a sort of preventive measure against the possible deluge of silver with which India might be overwhelmed in the dread contingency of the repeal of the Sherman Act! The Government further declared that it was justified in embarking on the legislative measure on the strength of the report of Lord Herschell's Committee. But, gentlemen, what are the actual facts? The Sherman Act ceased to be the law in the United States two months ago. But has its repeal in the slightest way assisted the Government in its object? On the contrary, is it not the case that it has made the previous confusion, wrought by the Amended Coinage Act, worse confounded as all India knows to its cost. In this matter it should not be forgotten, gentlemen, that were it not for the undue haste with which the Government of India moved, the repeal of the American Act might in all probability have never taken place or delayed to an indefinite period. Had counsel in the first instance been taken by our Government with that of the United States, prior to legislation, it is the belief of many that the Government of India would have acted wisely. In all probability a joint action might have been the means of averting the crisis in silver then apprehended and saved the people both here and in the United States from the heavy losses which we all now so sincerely deplore. The paralysis of trade which still prevails might have been obviated to a large extent and generally a more hopeful turn of events might have been fairly anticipated. The immediate repeal of the Sherman Act is in fact the *direct* consequence of the sudden closing of the Mints by the Indian Government. The latter has proved a curse instead of a blessing. (*Hear, hear.*)

**Fourth day.**

**Resolution XIV.**

**Protests against the stoppage of silver coinage in Mints and thereby subjecting Mill and other industries to an indirect burdensome taxation.**

Then as to the other plea, namely, that the action of our Government was based on the report of the Herschell Committee I may say this. I have the highest respect for the eminent persons who composed the Committee and for the distinguished Lord High Chancellor who presided over it. They were all undoubtedly men conversant with the pros and cons of the Silver question. But it appears to me that that Committee came to a conclusion which was altogether unwarranted by the weight of the evidence collected. Gentlemen, I do not make this statement carelessly or with a light heart. No. I make it on the strength of a careful perusal of the evidence itself. No unbiassed individual who cares to study that evidence can fail to arise from its perusal without being satisfied at the one sided character of the conclusion. In fact, it simply registers the previous decision of the Government of India as recorded in the minute of Sir David Barbour, the Finance Minister, dated 26th June 1892. I have already observed that the conclusion of the Committee is not borne out by the weight of the evidence. I will give facts in corroboration of that opinion. In all twenty-four gentlemen were called as witnesses. Of these one was Dr. Giffen, of the Board of Trade. But as his evidence was confined to certain statistics of production of the two metals it may be ommitted from our computation. Of the remaining twenty three, ten were for and thirteen against the closing of the Mints. Of those in favour, four were Anglo-Indian officials whose qualifications to pronounce an opinion may be more than doubted, namely, Sir J. Lyall, Mr. Bliss, Mr. J. Baines and Sir Charles Bernard. Among the non-officials Mr. J. Mackay was most conspicuous, of course. Of the thirteen who were against the proposed measure, two were Anglo-Indian officials, Sir T. Hope and Sir Raymond West, both of whom have paid considerable attention to currency questions. Of the rest, four were eminent Eastern bankers and seven were merchants, the most notable of whom was Mr. Stephen Ralli, of the eminent house of Messrs. Ralli Brothers, who have branches all over the civilised world. Our worthy President was also one of the thirteen who was against the closing of the Mints. (*Applause.*) I might quote, gentlemen, many a pertinent extract from the evidence of these, but that would detain you so long that I would rigidly refrain myself from that temptation, especially when our President has already shewn his indulgence towards me by allowing me to speak on this subject for a little more than the orthodox ten minutes. I must, therefore, ask you to read the evidence yourselves to be fully satisfied as to my statement that the report of the Committee is against the weight of the evidence. The opinion of men of eminence and varied banking and mercantile experience was set at naught, while that of the ten witnesses, four of whom were officials of no experience whatever, was accepted as conclusive because it chimed in with the view entertained by the Government of India. For that matter the Secretary of State might as well have forebore to call into existence the Committee and directed the Indian Government to act on the lines of Sir David Barbour's Minute of 26th June, 1892. (*Hear, hear.*) For, I repeat, that practically the report of the Committee is simply a paraphrase of that Minute.

If, gentlemen, the whole country, save the official classes, who have been liberally allowed the iniquitous exchange compensation allowance at the expense of the overburdened taxpayer, is suffering from the evil consequences of the Amended Coinage

**Fourth day.**

**Resolution XIV.**

**Protests against the stoppage of silver coinage in Mints and thereby subjecting Mill and other industries to an indirect burdensome taxation.**

Act, we have to thank Lord Herschell's Committee for it. The Committee, it is apparent, was simply a blind to enable the Government to carry out its ill considered proiect—a project which was never allowed to be freely discussed by an enlightened public but which, on the contrary, was passed within half an hour into law without most of the representatives of the public in the Council being invited. No other Act affecting the permanent interests of millions of people was passed so precipitately in recent time save the Vernacular Press or Black Act of unhappy memory. (*Shame).* Thus, not only was injustice rendered to the people but to injustice was added injury of an irreparable character. I will not go so far as to say with Mr. Chaplin that it was a "Crime." But that it was a huge and inexcusable blunder I would unhesitatingly assert. For its whole tendency has been, as I said at the outset of my speech, to rob one large class of people to pay another. It robs the ryots ; it entails an additional burden on them in order to actually compensate a microscopic minority already in receipt of salaries which find no parallel in any part of the civilised globe ! (*Hear*, *hear.*)

I do not believe, gentlemen, that save the members of the Anglo-Indian Currency Association and their adherents, there is to be found anywhere, either here or in England, an approval of the currency measure adopted by the Government. Sir William Houldsworth, a staunch advocate of Bimetallism and an active supporter of Sir David Barbour condemns the report of the Herschell Committee and calls it one sided. Again Professor Foxwell in his article *in the Nineteenth Century* condemns it. So do many experienced men qualified to pass an opinion—Mr. Barr Robertson among them. Again, almost all the leading financial journals condemn it, such as the *Economist*, the *Statist*, and so on. Thus there is a consensus of opinion that the Act is a huge blunder and entails heavy sacrifices on the masses, specially the impoverished peasantry who will now have to produce more and part with the fruit of their labours at a lower price to meet the State demand for land revenue. (*Shame.*) I shall refrain from dilating on this part of the subiect as the gentleman who will second this resolution will refer to it at greater length. I shall therefore briefly touch on the effects of the Act on the trade and industries of the country. As to the trade in general there was a dead lock. Imports and Exports fell off at once within three months of the date of the closing of the Mints. The trade with silver using counries received a violent shock, specially with China. The cotton industry suffered most. At Bombay, which is the principal centre of that industry, there are 70 cotton Mills at work. Most of the product of these is exported to China and Japan. The monthly average shipment, which has gone on steadily rising by leaps and bounds since 1882-3, equalled 25,000 bales before the date of the closing of the Mints. According to the latest trade returns, I find that it has fallen off to *16,250 bales.* I give the statistics of the triennul period from June to October, which is the latest month for which data are available, which will inform you at once how serious is the fall in the exports of this one article of our local industry.

| | 1891 | | 1892 | | 1893 | |
|---|---|---|---|---|---|---|
| | In Crores of lbs. | In Lakhs of Rupees. | In Crores of lbs. | In Lakhs of Rupees. | In Crores of lbs. | In Lakhs of Rupees. |
| **June.........** | **1·34** | **50·94** | **1·46** | **47·89** | **0·98** | **35·41** |
| July.......... | 1·50 | 58·38 | 1·57 | 52·09 | 0·33 | 12·38 |
| August...... | 0·98 | 35·34 | 2·02 | 69·20 | 1·05 | 38·17 |
| September . | 1·53 | 54·92 | 1·51 | 52·55 | 0·79 | 27·87 |
| October..... | 1·24 | 43·71 | 1·31 | 46·39 | 0·91 | 32·84 |

On the day the Act was passed remittances for bales sold at Hongknog and Shanghai

**Fourth day.**

**Resolution XIV.**

**Protests against the stoppage of silver coinage in Mints and thereby subjecting Mill and other industries to an indirect burdensome taxation.**

were estimated at lakhs of Rupees. Exchange on Hongking and Shanghai was 220 Dollars and 312 Taels respectively. But there was an immediate fall to 180 in the former, equivalent to 18 per cent. To that extent the mill companies suffered on their remittances at the date the Act was passed. The same was the case with remittances expected from Shanghai where exchange diminished about 15 per cent. But these were not the only losses. To these have to be added the serious check the mills received in their shipments and on shipments on the way—not to say aught of the contraction of the monthly exports. I leave you to realise the extent of the loss. It cannot but be roughly estimated at many a hundred lakh for which the Government has failed to make any reparation ! For the moment the industry is seriously crippled, though by prudent economies it is not improbable it may improve gradually as adjustment takes place. (*Hear, hear.*)

Again, the trade in general in all its branches has been dislocated which it will take months to revive. The national loss on this account it is not possible to estimate with anything like accuracy. A proper census alone might tell us roughly what it may have come to.

There is, however, a further aspect of this currency reform which it is needful to point out. I mean its effect on India's balance of trade with the principal silver using countries. It bears close connexion with the annual sterling remittances to the Secretary of State. At present we have to remit on an average 17 millions sterling per annum or say 27 crores of Rupees at the current rate of exchange. Probably, if exchange goes to a shilling, as there is every probability of its doing so, the equivalent in Rupees may reach 34 crores. But be the amount of remittance in Rupees what it may, it is an unquestionable fact that a greater portion of it is discharged from the balance of our trade with China and other silver using countries. The currency legislation has by one stroke crippled, if not destroyed, that favourable balance. And in the proportion that it is unfavourable in the immediate future our remittances will prove more burdensome. (*Hear, hear.*) I dare say some of you have noticed the statistics which appeared on this subject in the *Economist.* That leading financial journal showed that while India's trade with gold using countries gave an annual balance in her favour of 19 lakhs, that with silver using countries, gave a balance of 22 crores per year. (*Hear, hear.*) I leave it to you, gentlemen to realise the significance of these broad statistics. The contingency, I may say, was clearly perceived by bankers and merchants. Some of the gentlemen connected with banking and commerce who were examined before the Herschell Committee plainly forecast the evil consequences which we are now experiencing. But their mature warning was set at naught and the Act was passed in the teeth of it. Under the circumstances, I regret to have to say that it is impossible to acquit Government of its deliberate error in this respect. The Act is a huge blunder and I believe that this is the proper occasion, when the representatives of the different parts of the country have met together on a common platform, to ventilate their common grievance and to enter our emphatic protest against that precipitate piece of legislation. In spite of its transparent evils I extremely regret to observe the Viceroy and Governor General attempting to defend this measure and even going to the length of saying in his Despatch to the Secretary of State that it had the approval of almost the whole of the communities of India ! I protest and say that it is absolutely fallacious and inaccurate for Lord Lansdowne to say so. (*Hear, hear.*) Save the interested clique, who call themselves the Anglo-Indian Currency Association, and their blind adherents and advocates, the community as a whole has viewed with the greatest disfavour the legislation of June 26th. (*Hear, hear.*) By all means let the Government of India defend its action. It is at perfect liberty to do so. But let it not mislead the British public.

**Fourth day.**

**Resolution XIV.**

**Protests against the stoppage of silver coinage in Mints and thereby subjecting Mill and other industries to an indirect burdensome taxation.**

Let it not conceal the truth that in no part of India any considerable majority of the people have approved of its currency nostrum. In the interest of truth let us declare with our unanimous voice from this platform that the statement made by the Viceroy and Governor General that his currency policy has met with general approval is absolutely incorrect. Let it be proclaimed on the housetop. Let it be published in the four corners of the world so that they may not be misled by the words of Lord Lansdowne. (*Hear, hear.*) Let us at the same time respectfully inform the Government that the currency legislation is an error and that the sooner it acknowledges the error and returns to the state of affairs which existed before 26th June the better for the trade and the country at large, and specially for the impoverished peasantry who are the backbone of its finance. (*Loud applause.*)

MR. R. P. KARANDIKAR (*Satara, No. 741, in list*) in seconding the motion said: MR. PRESIDENT, LADIES AND GENTLEMEN,—We have called this enactment "hasty," and hasty it was because you must know that the standing orders were suspended by the Viceroy at the suggestion of the gentleman who took charge of this scheme from the beginning. Sir David Barbour said at the beginning of the proceedings, that he had an important bill to introduce which affected the monetary standard and they would see that it was essential that it should be passed at that present sitting of the Council, and in consequence it was necessary to suspend the standing orders. Therefore, and I think with good reason, we call it a hasty enactment. I recall the year 1878 as the year in which several enactments were passed which now form the bulwarks of the omnibus resolution you pass every year. It was in 1878 that the Abkari, Opium, and Forests Acts were passed, and also the gagging act, I mean the Newspapers Act. We have it from the Viceroy that in that year the closing of the mints was pressed, but it was reserved for the present Viceroy to carry that proposition into effect. The Viceroy in speaking of the measure at the United Service Club dinner remarked that it was idle to suppose that the mere passing of the Act for the closing of the mints would at once lead to a scarcity of coined silver. The problem would work itself out in due time and those who were best able to judge were by no means prepared to admit that the great experiment had failed, or was destined to failure. Continuing the Viceroy said "I believe it has been described as the crime of June 26th. It is a crime for which I am still unrepentant, a crime which, although no doubt it has created a good deal of alarm, will, I still believe, prove to be a turning point in the commercial and fiscal history of this country." That is still to be judged. Lower down he says. "I say that so long as there was a chance that the Brussels Conference would bring about some concerted action for the rehabilitation of silver, we were excusable if we waited upon events, but when it became clear that the Conference would be abortive, and that even our own Government was not prepared to co-operate effectually in rehabilitating the white metal, one course and one course only, was open to us: the course which we adopted when we perpetrated the crime of June 26th." Well, he goes a little further and says. "Since then we have no doubt had a disturbance of values and a temporary dislocation of our business with silver using countries." Here is a distinct admission by the Viceroy that the Act has acted in such a manner as to dislocate the mass of our trades and industries. With regard to agriculture, it is a matter of the gravest concern to us all that the agricultural population which is the backbone of the country and 82 per cent of the population should be indirectly burdened with this additional taxation It is prepared to fight face to face with an evil, but this is a side thrust. If you stop the free coinage of silver, you naturally increase the burden on the tax payer. The agricultural population have to bear the cost of this increased expenditure. On the Bombay side they pay their taxes in the months of January and March and you all know that when the time comes for him to pay the assessments he is in a fix to find the money.

They have to sell their corn and if the price of silver is enhanced by such an Act as this, he has to sell more in, order to get the rupee than he did previously. That is the indirect taxation he will suffer under. This is the grievance which the agricultural population has placed before you in a constitutional manner. I hope, therefore, you will approach Government with a strong protest. Your protest last year was unaviling. I hope you will convey to Government that there is a conviction in the minds of people that the enactment has had the effect of increasing the taxation generally. In the evidence given by our learned President before the Commitee he was asked this question, "Do you not deprecate any stoppage of the free coinage in India?" He answered, "yes," and went on to say that if free coinage was stopped the result would be, that the rupee would be artificially raised in value on account of being made scarce. And first of all, beginning with the poor cultivator, in order to pay Rs. 10, he would have to part with more produce in order to satisfy the demands of Government. One and all these reasons will convince you that this proposition must be carried. *(Loud applause.)*

**Fourth day.**

**Resolution XIV.**

**Protests against the stoppage of silver coinage in Mints and thereby subjecting Mill and other industries to an indirect burdensome taxation.**

THE HON'BLE RAJA RAMPAL SINGH *(Allahabad, No. 70, in list)* intimated that he was not in favour of the proposition, and favoured a gold standard. He wished to prepare the minds of those present for a series of articles he was shortly going to write on the subject.

The motion was then carried.

THE HON'BLE SURENDRA NATH BANERJI *(Calcutta, No. 8, in list)* said: MR. PRESIDENT AND BROTHER-DELEGATES,—The resolution I have the honour to propose runs as follows :—

*That this Congress records its emphatic protest against the Exchange Compensation Allowance granted to the undomiciled European and Eurasian employes of Government, involving an annual expenditure of over a crore of Rupees, and to the Banks, to the extent of £1,38,000 at a time when the financial situation of the country is far from satisfactory, and the country is threatened with additional taxation.*

**Resolution XV.**

**Protests against granting Exchange Compensation Allowance to European and Eurasian Government servants.**

He said: In moving this proposition I am reminded of the felicitous words of His Excellency the Viceroy to which reference has already been made by the previous speakers. In a recent speech which he delivered and from which extracts have been read before this Congress, Lord Lansdowne described the Currency Act and the Exchange Compensation Allowance which is a further development of the Act as the "crime of the 26th of June." That is the verdict of contemporary opinion and if I may venture to take a forecast of the future, I will say this : that it will be the deliberate judgment of history that it is a crime and worse than a crime, it is a political blunder of the gravest magnitude, the consequences of which it would be difficult to exaggerate or over-estimate. You are familiar with the name of Sir James Fitz Stephen ; he was a member of the Viceregal council ; he is no friend to the people of India and no friend of the human race. *(Laughter and applause.)* He was an advocate of the doctrine of force against the doctrine of moral persuasion in the Government of India. You remember the remarkable interpretation he put upon the gracious terms of the Queen's Proclamation. That interpretation was quoted with an air of jubilant triumph by the *Pioneer* and *Civil and Military Gazette*. (*Loud Cries of "Shame"*.) What was that interpretation? He said that the Queen's Proclamation was a mere ceremonial document ("*Shame*") ; that it enjoined no command, that it laid no mandate, and imposed no obligation upon the Government of this country. Well, Sir James Fitz Stephen, such as he was and such as he is, was compelled in his place in the Viceregal Council to make a remark to which I

Fourth day.

Resolution XV.

Protests against granting Exchange Compensation Allowance to European and Eurasian Government servants.

wish to draw the attention of this Congress. He was compelled to observe that a single act of injustice done by the Government of this country was more disastrous to its prestige and influence than a great military disaster upon an Asiatic battle field It is not for us to pronounce punishment on the Government of this country, for we members of the educated community, are more deeply interested than we can find words to express, in the prosperity of the country and in the maintenance in an undiminished measure of the influence and prestige of the British Government in India. We know that Government has done great things in the past and we know that Government is destined to achieve still greater things in the future : for we know that Government is imbued with the spirit of progress. It has its aberrations but even the Heavenly bodies have their eccentricities over which no control can be exercised. But whatever may be our views, the forces—the moral forces—march to their destined consummation without reference to human will or human judgment and it is written in characters of light in the awful and sublime pages of history, that injustice avenges itself with compound interest. I charge the Government of India with trifling with the interests of the people and having been guilty of injustice to the interests committed to its care by granting this absurd allowance to its non-domiciled Europeans. It is a grave charge but I make it deliberately. What is the justification set forth ? It is this : that the rupee, that unfortunate coin, has been so depreciated in its value that many Europeans who have to make remittances to England suffer loss in consequence and it is a great hardship to them. No doubt it is so to those who draw three or four thousand rupees a month. (*Laughter.*) But there are many Europeans who have no remittances to make Why should they be included in this act of beneficence ? It is also given to non-domiciled Eurasians. May I inquire who are these non-domiciled Eurasians ? I suppose it means the Eurasians who have no domicile in this country. But have they a domicile anywhere ? They are, perhaps like the wandering Jews of the middle ages, homeless and houseless. They too must have an increase given to their salary. Let me put this case to the Government of India, let me put this to the Anglo Indian advocates of Exchange Compensation Allowances, if instead of the rupee having been depreciated it had been appreciated, if instead of our having to pay Rs. 15 or Rs. 16 for a sovereign we had to pay Rs. 5 or Rs. 6, would there have been an abatement or reduction of their pay ? Would they have submitted to such a reduction ? Would not there have been a fearful outcry and would not we all have joined that outcry because it would have been a gross and deliberate injustice to a deserving class of public officials ? (*Applause.*) If the interests of the officials need to be protected, the interests of the people also should be protected ; their interests should be protected in preference to the interests of the officials. The Government of India in their reply which was sent to the Indian Association who protested against this outrage, for such it is, admitted that the European officials had no legal claim upon the Government but that they had a moral claim upon the Government. It is refreshing to find Government taking its stand upon the high ground of morality. (*Laughter and applause.*) These moral considerations, mind you, were never present to their minds when they were discussing the question of Simultaneous Examinations and when they had to consider the claims of the natives of the soil to the indefensible right they possessed to the high offices under the Government of their own country. But when it comes to questions of a frontier war, of the building of impregnable fortresses, the subsidising of the Amir, or of granting Compensation Allowances to the European officials, then we are treated to these homilies about moral considerations and obligations. I will take my stand on the same ground as the Government of India has taken its stand. I will give battle to the Government on its own chosen ground and I will be prepared to show that the Government has no justification to grant Compensation Allowances even upon the principle by which it professes to be guided. For whose sake does this country exist ? For the sake of the services, or do the services

**Protests against granting Exchange Compensation Allowance to European and Eurasian Government servants.**

exist for our sake? This is the crucial question. If the services exist for our sake, and the Government have said more than once that the services should exist for the benefit of the country, it is very obvious that the interests of the country must have the preference and that they cannot be sacrificed for the benefit of the services. Let us see how the interest of the country have been served. You will find that the interests of the country have been deliberately sacrificed. The commonest domestic matters have been starved on the ground that the money has not been forthcoming. It is admitted by Lord Dufferin that the reform of the Police is a counsel of perfection, but when the Congress pressed this home on the Government, the Government came forward with the pleas that, "We have not got any funds for the improvement of the Police." It is admitted that the fusion of the Judicial and Executive functions is contrary to the principle admitted by Lord Cross, but the reform cannot be carried out because there are no funds. Local bodies press upon the Provincial bodies the urgency of sanitary improvements, and the Provincial Governments urge upon the Supreme Government the urgency of these matters, but there again it is the eternal want of pence. But when it comes to a question of granting Compensation to the services, then Government is as rich as the richest Government in the world, and from whom is this money taken? You heard yesterday the story of India's poverty related in graphic and earnest language by Pundit Madan Mohan; you heard on the highest official authority that 20,000,000 of people had died of starvation in the last few years; you heard that 40,000,000 live on one meal a day and now these 40,000,000 people will be burdened with additional taxation. They will be stinted of their food, of their rice and of their salt, in order that the highly paid officials of the Government must be provided with their usual brandy, beef and champagne. (*Shame.*) I think it is an unutterable shame. One can scarcely repress the sense of indignation one feels when he has to discuss a matter like this Call this a civilised, a Christian and a Righteous administration! They say that in the most sacred of their books it is written that "Righteousness exalteth a nation." But, is this civilisation, is this Christianity, is this consistent with the tenets of the principles of Righteousness? I feel that language fails me to describe what I consider to be the iniquity of the Government in this matter of Compensation, (*Applause.*) and those allowances have been granted at a time when you are threatened with fresh taxation. If you read through the Budgets of the last few years, you will find that from 1888 to 1893 there have been constantly recurring deficits and these deficits have come to the large sum of eleven crores of rupees and this year, 1893-94 is threatened with a deficiency of nearly two crores of rupees. I think we may take it that additional taxation will be necessary and judging from the suggestions which have found their way into the official organs, Government leaves us no doubt as to the manner in which the taxation will be levied. Here again the unjustness of the measure is apparent: it is proposed to enhance the salt duty for the sake of these highly paid officials. (*"Shame."*) I do not think I need detain you at any further length. I invite you not to submit to this; I invite you not to submit to this gross act of injustice, and not to submit to this deliberate affront to the public opinion of the country. The issue is plainly before us. It is this: the country exists for the people and the officials exist for us. This Exchange resolution is the embodiment of a principle which Government has persistently followed and what is that principle? We are the children of the soil; we are the helots of the land, the hewers of wood and the drawers of water and we exist for the services, the Gods of the bureaucracy. Illustrious men of Bombay, men of the Punjab, men of northern India, men of Bengal, let us combine, let us take a firm stand, and let us not rest until we have succeeded in convincing these Gods of their iniquities; (*Applause*) let us not rest till we have disenchanted them of the illusion under which they labour, namely, that the country is theirs and not ours. The country is ours and theirs and India is for England and also for India; primarily for India and secondarily for England and

Fourth day.

Resolution XV.

Protests against granting Exchange Compensation Allowance to European and Eurasian Government servants.

the officials ought to understand, and they will understand that, when they harmonise their interests with ours, and when they are animated by that lofty love, that deep and fervent sympathy for the people which characterised the early founders of the British Empire. Where are the Bentincks, the Cannings and the Ripons of Indian administration? They are gone for ever. Let there be no misconception of my attitude or that of the Congress. We have no antipathy towards the officials and no feeling of conflict between them and ourselves. Was not our venerated and illustrious leader Mr. Hume an official? (*Cries of "three cheers for Mr. Hume."*) Where shall we find an official like him to cement the bonds of sympathy between the official and non-official Europeans and Indians? But, gentlemen, we have fallen on evil times and our hope and prayer is that the giver of all good may come to the rescue of this luckless land and may instil into the hearts of our rulers a sense of their responsibility so that they may rise to their high station and do their duty to the unrepresented millions of this great country (*Loud and prolonged applause.*)

MR. W. A CHAMBERS (*Bombay, No. 781, in list*) said in seconding the resolution: MR. PRESIDENT, LADIES AND GENTLEMEN,—The previous speaker asked you if the granting of compensations to some Europeans and Eurasians domiciled in this country was a Christian or righteous act. I say, it is neither Christian, it is neither righteous, nor is it————(*Loud Applause.*)

The fact that such a resolution, as the one which I am about to second, is necessary, almost makes us despair of the Government of India. The Government is notoriously poor it is with the greatest difficulty that it can meet its liabilities and yet upon the most flimsy grounds, it gives to its already overpaid servants an annual present of one crore of rupees. Were the Government able to afford it we might not grumble, but they cannot afford it, and to raise the money, they must further squeeze the unfortunate tax-payers of this country. Whenever native opinion requests a favour of the Government the answer offered is, "we have no funds for such a purpose," but the moment the European Civilians approach it and ask for an increase of salary, it is given. As an Englishman and one who has been sitting in this Congress a long time, listening to your speech, I say, I was almost ashamed I was an Englishman. (*Applause.*) Now as an Englishman, who sincerely believes that there is a great mission in this land for his countrymen to perform, this is a most melancholy spectacle because it is likely to convey a bad impression to the minds of the natives of India. (*Hear, hear.*) Why should a certain class of Europeans be favoured? Most Englishmen suffer by the loss in exchange. We have to bear it; it is one of the disadvantages of living in India. We have enjoyments and privileges which balance this disadvantage. I can assure you that the life which an European leads here is much more luxurious, much more pleasurable than that which he leads at home. (*Hear, hear.*) You may have noticed that some of them are constantly alluding to their stay in this country as a time of exile. Do not believe these statements! I tell you that they find, inspite of the fall of the rupee, India to be a very pleasant place of abode. (*Applause.*)

Let us examine the grounds upon which the Civil Servants base their claim. They state that twenty years ago the rupee was worth two shillings but that it is now worth only a little more than one shilling. This is so, and no doubt it is very hard that their emoluments should have suffered in this fashion. It is unsatisfactory that a man should have been better off when a bachelor twenty years ago than he is now with a growing and expensive family. Yet this is no fault of the Indian Government and as protectors of the tax-payers of India, it was their duty to have insisted, as Lord Kimberley on one occasion did, that a contract is a contract. The Government engaged

**Fourth day.**

**Resolution XV.**

**Protests against granting Exchange Compensation Allowance to European and Eurasian Government servants.**

to pay so many rupees for their services and this they were doing. It may appear cruel to state this ; it may be said we are a Congress of Shylocks, but in this particular instance they are the Shylocks who wish to get as much out of the Indian people as possible. (*Loud applause.*) Just one word here to the Anglo Indian papers which have supported the Civilians in their agitation. I should like them to state the case thus ; for Government of India insert Coal Owners of England and for Civilians insert Miners. What then is their position ? It is that the miners are a set of good for nothing fellows who are never contented and that the coal owners are giving them as much wages as it is in their power to pay and as much as they deserve. We will not be so severe as this, but simply say that you are getting as much as you deserve and as much as the Government of India can afford. (*Hear, hear.*) Compare the position of an English Civilian with that of his colleague here. In England there are two divisions of the Civil Service, the higher and the lower. In the lower a boy starts at £70 per annum and the maximum is £250. We must however, for a proper comparison, take the higher division ; the examination is of a very severe character and the men attracted to it are equal in position to those who compete for the Indian Civil Service. A boy in the higher division begins on a salary of £100 a year and may reach £600. Now, take the Indian Service and examine its remuneration. A boy starts upon Rs. 400 a month, say, (with the rupee at one shilling) £240 per year and he may reach £2000, or more. He has also a handsome pension at the end of his service. We therefore see, that even with the rupee at one shilling, the remuneration is still sufficient for any reasonable man. The cry of the Indian Civilian brings to my mind the conduct of some of my native friends. In the course of business I have much to do with native Contractors. They often come to me at the end of their works and say, "Sahib, I have lost Rs. 5,000 or Rs. 10,000 on that contract," meaning thereby that they have not made Rs. 5,000 or Rs. 10,000 so much as they expected. The Civilian has not lost but he has set an artificial value upon his rupee and he is disappointed, because it does not come up to his expectations. I, therefore, think that as, after all, this compensation allowance only effects some 6000 persons and that as you speak on behalf of the tax-payers of this country, it is your duty to protest against the recent action of the Indian Government in increasing the salary of the Civilian at this juncture. (*Loud Applause and three cheers for Mr. Chambers.*)

MR. D. E. WACHA (*Bombay, No. 782, in list*) in supporting the Resolution, observed : I am not going to detain you, gentlemen for more than a minute. But I think it my duty at this stage to submit to you certain statistics in reference to the gold prices of many an article of domestic consumption in an ordinary English home. It has been loudly alleged that the English Civilian or Military officer in India has to convert his Rupees into gold, and that owing to low exchange he now obtains for those Rupees a smaller equivalent in gold than before or say ten years ago. That this smaller equivalent does not suffice to buy the necessary comforts for his wife and children at home, and that so far the low exchange is entailing extreme hardship on him. We may admit at once that the equivalent in sterling is smaller than before. But the question we have to inquire into is this. Whether the smaller equivalent does not represent in reality an equal purchasing power as before. It is notorious that gold prices of articles of daily consumption have fallen considerably in England. All competent experts place the average fall at 20 per cent. I shall therefore demonstrate to your satisfaction from the statistics of prices I have collected from the Statistical Abstract of the United Kingdom that the fall in the gold price of various articles—from 1882 to 1892—ranged from 3 to 47 per cent. As an ounce of fact is worth a pound of theory, I shall at once proceed to read to you the prices of each of the 60 articles I have selected for comparison and leave you to judge how far the contention of the Anglo-Indian officials is borne out by facts. I emphatically say that the facts are dead against them and therefore their cry

**Fourth day.**

**Resolution XV.**

**Protests against granting Exchange Compensation Allowance to European and Eurasian Government servants.**

as to hardship and so forth is hollow and the exchange compensation allowed is therefore most iniquitous. (*Loud applause.*)

Statement contrasting average price of the undermentioned Articles in the United Kingdom in 1882 and 1892, with percentage of Increase or Decrease. (Vide Statistical Abstract Untited Kingdom 40th No. p.p. 140-143.)

| Articles. | Per. | 1882. | 1892. | Percentage. + or — | Articles. | Per. | 1882. | 1892. | Percentage + or — |
|---|---|---|---|---|---|---|---|---|---|
| Wheat ......... | Cwt. | 10·67s. | 7·66s. | —30 | Barley ......... | Cwt. | 7·12s. | 6·04 | —15 |
| Do. Flour...... | " | 16·33s. | 11·10s. | —47 | Oats ............ | " | 6·75s. | 6·40s. | —5 |
| Other Flour .... | " | 10·09s. | 8·27 | —18 | Maize ........... | " | 7·15s. | 5·33 | —25 |
| Bacon ........... | " | 53·04s. | 40·86s. | —23 | Brandy ......... | Gallon | 9·02s. | 9·02s. | * |
| Hams............ | " | 55·56s. | 47·30s. | —15 | Wine............ | " | 6·95s. | 6·95s. | * |
| Beef ............ | " | 51·57s. | 40·78s. | —21 | Cigars ......... | ℔. | 14·21s. | 9·20s. | —35 |
| Butter........... | " | 5·23£ | 5·48£ | +5 | Tobacco ...... | " | 10·06d. | 9.98d. | —08 |
| Margarine...... | " | 3·60£ | 2·84£ | —21 | Candles......... | Doz. ℔. | 67·36d. | 53·30s. | —21 |
| Cheese ......... | " | 2·80£ | 2·43£ | —15 | Paraffin......... | Cwt. | 1·76£ | 1·36£ | —22 |
| Coffee........... | Cwt. | 3·81£ | 4·65£ | +22 | Almonds ...... | Cwt. | 3·4£ | 3·36£ | —1 |
| Eggs ............ | Doz. | 8·44d. | 8·18d. | —3 | Apples ......... | Bush. | 6·57s. | 6·00 | --8 |
| Fish............. | Cwt. | 33·56s. | 21·64s. | —35 | Currants ...... | Cwt. | 26·72d. | 23·14 | —13 |
| Lard ............ | " | 55·95s. | 35·88s. | —34 | Raisins......... | " | 37·45d. | 30·23 | —19 |
| Saltad Meat ... | " | 3·35£ | 2·65£ | —32 | Oranges, &c. . | Bush. | 7·86d. | 6·07s. | —22 |
| Preserved do. . | " | 3·02£ | 2·44£ | —19 | Buttons......... | Gross. | 2·21d. | 1·76s. | —20 |
| Olive Oil ...... | Ton | 40·39£ | 37·24£ | —7·80 | Cotton Yarn... | ℔. | 1·08d. | 1·05d. | —3 |
| Onions ......... | Basket. | 3·39s. | 3·28s. | —3 24 | Feathers ...... | " | 68·83s. | 22·71s. | —70 |
| Potatoes......... | Cwt. | 6·67s. | 6·32s. | —5·54 | Boots & Shoes. | Doz. Pair | 3·98£ | 3·15£ | —26 |
| Pork ........... | " | 40·18s. | 34·20s. | —15 | Gloves ......... | Pair | 23·87d. | 21·38d. | —10 |
| Rice ............ | Cwt. | 7·98s. | 6·89s. | —13 | Linen Yarn ... | ℔. | 10·76d. | 9·27d. | —16 |
| Spices .......... | ℔. | 13·49d. | 7·75d. | —42 | Silk Raw ...... | " | 16·54d. | 13·09s. | —26 |
| Sugar........... | Cwt. | 28·67s. | 17·06s. | —40 | Woolens ...... | " | 42·53d. | 40·80d. | —40 |
| Tea.............. | ℔. | 12·58d. | 10·07d. | —20 | Paperwriting.. | Cwt. | 35·29d. | 23·44s. | —43 |

The motion was unanimously adopted.

LALA DHARM DASS SURI (*Punjab, No, 275, in list,*) moved :—

**Resolution XVI.**

**Praying the Indian Government for removing by express legislation the oppressions caused by forced labour and forced Supply.**

*That the Government of India be moved, once for all, to put a stop, by new and express legislation, (the existing provisions of the penal code having proved inoperative) to the existing oppressive system of forced labour (known as Begar) and forced contributions of supplies (known as Rasad) which, despite numerous Resolutions of the Government of India, are still prevalent throughout India.*

This speaker made a very impressive speech giving several instances of oppression and received applause more than once. Parts of his speech were, however, written and were read out. The report of the speech was not complete and that incomplete report was taken away by him on the understanding, that it would be soon returned with his corrections, but as he has not done so and to avoid any further delay in printing this Report, the speech is reluctantly ommitted.

LALA KANAHYE LAL (*Punjab, No. 636, in list*) in seconding said : MR. PRESIDENT, LADIES AND GENTLEMEN,—We are the Punjabis who live near the Black and the White Mountains. An officer with an expedition comes along and sends to us his requisition which may contain a list of so many carts and so many mules &c. just as if so many quails were to be got. He impounds human souls in hundreds, takes the father from his children, separates the husband from the embraces of the wife, just to equip his forces and make them up to the standard of requirement of the Transport Department It was at my request that the Subjects Committee brought this matter forward. The people have been begging me to bring it forward, because they feel the consequences of

Praying the Indian Government for removing by express legislation the oppressionsed caused by forced labour and forced Supply.

it whilst you do not, for you are barristers, pleaders, and merchants and you have never been seized in that way to perform something against your will. Are we always to depend on those who live outside to redress the evils of our administration ? Ladies have to come from America and outside and we dare not take up a subject where humanity is concerned. It is the spectacle of these human souls being taken away by the *chuprassies* which is just like what I have seen in the London Graphic. There you see the slave hunter going to the different villages taking the people away at night and taking slaves away with a rope round their necks and bringing them to the markets for sale. A portion of Her Majesty's Navy is engaged in suppressing this slave trade, but here Her Majesty's Officers are employed in making slaves. (*Applause.*)

BABU MOHINI MOHUN CHAKRAVARTY (*Bengal, No. 40, in list*) in supporting said: MR. PRESIDENT, LADIES AND GENTLEMEN,—The resolution which I have to support has already been read to you. It deals with a standing complaint which is not only prevalent in our part of the country, but throughout the whole of India. In those districts it prevails most where by reason of the backward state of education and intelligence of the people and by reason of those places being distant from the centre of public opinion these things cannot be remedied by the people themselves. It exists in those districts because the people cannot bring forward their complants to the public authorities and be heard. I shall, however, bring to your notice instances where complaints have been made to the authorities but they were not remedied by the authorities. Gentlemen, the resolution says that there is a provision of the Penal Code to the effect that such labour is illegal. Notwithstanding the existence of such a provision in the Penal Code, this forced labour is in existence and has, I regret to say, been brought to the notice of public authorities without being remedied, and without the cases having been brought to the notice of those who are willing to do justice to the people. This system of labour is even adopted by high officials of Government and they are not amenable to justice because they are supposed to do no wrong. It was to a certain extent true that lower officials adopted this system and were greatly to blame, but the higher officials were sometimes none the less guilty. Here is an instance I will lay before you. In this case certain Manipuris had been forced to labour. They complained to the Chief Commissioner in 1891. Up to this time they have not had a reply to their petition. In consequence we have memorialised Government. I advise my brother delegates also to memorialise on this point. (*Applause.*)

MR. RATIRAM DURGARAM DAVE (*Bombay, No. 778, in list*) said :—MR. PRESIDENT AND BROTHER-DELEGATES,—I have great pleasure in supporting this Resolution. I come from Gujrat in the Bombay Presrdency and it will, I trust, be some relief to this Congress to learn that on our side this evil of Veth (as we call it) is not so great a Zoolum as would appear to be the case in the Punjab. I need hardly say to this learned assembly that Veth is a well known ancient Indian prerogative of the State and of Inamdars and grantees from the state. But the British Government cannot officially recognise or allow any iniquity or Zoolum, even if sanctioned by antiquity and an early local usage and from an early period. The Government of Bombay has pronounced itself strongly against *Veth* of any kind.

However, in spite of the Government resolution, in rural parts the evil still largely obtains. Sometimes there are *Jolnukani Sahebs* who always impose this Veth and oppress the ryot. More commonly great Zoolum is done by officious native subordinates such as Mamlutdars and Police Patels who, to please their Sabs, override the standing orders of the Government, drag away the cartmen from their hearths and homes, force supplies and sometimes do not even pay a pice to the poor men.

**Fourth day**

**Resolution XVI.**

**Praying the Indian Government for removing by express legislation the oppressions caused by forced lobour and forced Supply.**

There are also, I must add, some noble District officers who strictly obey the orders of Government and pay for everything they want on our side.

In the Military Department matters I fear, are worse and require the strong hand of Legislation fof the removal of the evil.

The Government of Bombay, however, as a Government, has done much to put down this evil. Only about two months ago, H. E. Lord Harris while conferring a C.I.E on a Bombay native Chief specially complimented him for his abolishing pressed labour in his State, again by a recent Government Resolution all Political agents and their assistants in our part have been directed to buy their own supplies and not to use a Rajans carriage even if offered. Thus the evil is not equally great on our side and a little more free use of the right of interpellation will equally put down the evil in other places.

LALA HARBHAGWAN DASS (*Punjab, No. 374, in list*) said :—The resolution says in so many words that the existing laws passed by the Government of India have proved quite ineffectual. Do you know the reason ? It is this : as injustices are done by the higher officials because the Judicial and Executive functions are combined together, so in this case there is so much oppression because the functions of the robber and the Policeman are combined in one individual. The persons who are the greatest offenders in this respect are the persons who have got the duty and right to administer the laws against this evil. I support this resolution, for unless Government takes very special measures against this, there is no hope of any remedy being effected. I shall not be doing justice to both sides of the question if I omit to give the reasons which might be given by the Executive for levying *begar* from the people. Some of the authorities say that the people of India are so much after the right of volunteering and though we are not at present prepared to grant that right yet in the meantime we shall be gratifying their wishes by training them to be volunteers by bringing them up as coolies and *dooli* bearers. To show you the hardship of the law, I may mention a certain instance which came under my notice. Once happening to follow the camp of a District Magistrate, I saw a certain shop keeper brought before the Deputy Collector because he refused to supply milk to a regiment on the march which had halted near the village, and he was called upon to furnish Rs. 100 to another shop keeper who was to be asked to supply the regiment with milk. And in my presence he agreed to pay Rs. 60 only to be excused from opening a milk shop where the regiment was halted for two days. If this is a tax it has got no name. With these remarks I support the resolution.

SWAMY ALA RAM (*Allahabad No, 82, in list,*) supported the motion addressing the Meeting in Hindi :

The proposition was then carried.

**Resolution XVII.**

**Tenders thanks to Lord Northbrook for his endeavouring to reduce the Home Charges and prays the House of Commons to appoint a committe to settle the matter.**

PROFESSOR G. K. GOKHALE (*Poona No. 748, in list.*) said : MR. PRESIDENT, LADIES AND GENTLEMEN,—The resolution I have to propose is as follows :—

*That this Congress tenders its most sincere thanks to Lord Northbrook for his powerful advocacy of India's claim to have her burden of Home Charges reduced, and respectfully entreats the House of Commons to appoint at an early date a Committee of their Honourable House to arrive at some equitable settlement of the matter.*

He said : Many of you may be aware that in the month of May last a very important dehate on this question took place in the House of Lords on a motion brought forward by Lord Northbrook and in the course of that debate many serious

**Fourth day.**

**Resolution XVII.**

**Tenders thanks to Lord Northbrook for his endeavouring to reduce the Home Charges and prays the House of Commons to appoint a committe to settle the matter.**

and damaging statements were made by responsible statesmen on both sides ; so much indeed that if ever the Government of the country were put on its trial I should be content to frame the indictment on those admissions. It was admitted during that debate that year after year, in spite of the protests from Secretaries of State and Viceroys of India, burdens were thrown on the Indian exchequer which properly belonged to England. It was admitted by Lord Kimberley that this was because the India Office was powerless against the combined forces of the Treasury and the War Office. Another important statement was made by the Duke of Argyle. His Grace said in a low tone, possibly because he wanted to say it in a whisper, that the people of the country should not hesitate in the matter and that the grievance should be remedied before the impression got abroad in India that there was such a grievance. But the Duke of Argyle does not seem to know that from this very Congress platform Mr. Wacha has year after year protested against the Home Charges and that long before this Mr. Power, Mr. Nowrojee Furdonjee and other gentlemen raised their powerful voices against this unjust burden. If you look at the Home Charges particularly during the last thirty years, you will see that the figures have increased from £7,000,000 to £16,000,000, and if you calculate the value in rupees, they have risen from seven to twenty or twenty six crores. At the same time it is only fair to state that a large part of this increase is of such a nature that we cannot claim any sort of redress from the House of Commons in regard to it, because there have been loans taken by the Government of India in England and the interest on these must be paid. There are particularly two items in regard to which we have a right to ask for redress and these are the expenditure incurred in connection with the India Office and that in connection with the Indian Army in England. I will pass over the expenditure in connection with the India Office because although that office pays, and liberally pays, their respectable and at the same time useless and mischievous old gentlemen, it is comparatively a small matter and may be left for the present. In regard to the Home Military Charges, if you look at the figures for the last thirty years you will find they have risen from £2,000,000 to over £5,000,000 or if you calculate the value in rupees, it is a rise from two crores to eight crores or just four fold. The Recruiting Charges are a heavy item. The men cost the War Office £19 per head but India is charged £105 a man. It has been said by no less an authority than Sir Charles Dilke that the whole sum which is about seventy five lakhs of rupees may be saved if the Indian Government are allowed a free hand and have the right to recruit for themselves. The Stores Charges is a varying quantity. It is never less than about fifty lakhs of rupees and last year it was nearly a crore. It is very discreditable that the War Office charges not merely an extravagant price but it tries to make a profit out of the contracts. As to the Indian trooping services, there are a certain number of ships built at India's expense to bring the soldiers here and to take them back again and the expenditure on them is very great. Now my point is that the British troops might be brought and taken away like private passengers in other steamers instead of these big ships, which are five months in the year lying idle and means a very large and useless expenditure. Another item is the payment made to the War Office for pensions to the troops which is about a third of a million. Last year Lord Northbrook raised his powerful voice against it and showed that during the last twenty years England had taken more than four millions beyond what it was entitled to take. There are other items which might be mentioned but I may say that any one who closely studies the subject will arrive at the conclusion that about a million pounds or one and a half crores of rupees per annum can be saved to the Indian Treasury if there is a more reasonable and more equitable adjustment of the charges. There is a sort of partnership between India and England which strongly reminds me of the dwarf and the giant in Goldsmith's *Vicar of Wakefield*. There have been occasions on which England borrowed troops from India and there have also been occasions when India had to borrow troops from England. Whenever England borrowed

**Fourth day.**

**Resolution XVII.**

**Tenders thanks to Lord Northbrook for his endeavouring to reduce the Home Charges and prays the House of Commons to appoint a committe to settle the matter.**

troops she forgot to pay but when India borrowed them she had to pay all the ordinary and the extraordinary expenses ; and in some cases even the charges for recruiting the soldiers had been extorted from India. In regard to all these matters it is but just and right that we should complain and Lord Northbrook is entitled to our best thanks for his powerful services. In the first place the resolution proposes to express our best thanks to him for his powerful advocacy of India's just claims and in the second place it entreats the House of Commons that it will listen to us in an attentive manner and appoint a committee in order to consider the whole question so that ultimately a fair adjustment of the charges may be arrived at. With these remarks I leave the resolution before you for your unanimous adoption. (*Applause.*)

MR. D. B. CHAKRADEV (*Sholapur, No. 731, in list*) seconded the motion addressing the meeting in Urdu. He said :—MR. PRESIDENT AND GENTLEMEN,—I am much obliged to you for having permitted me to address in *Urdu*. I am all the more thankful for the indulgence, for it is the *liugua franca* of united India—the common speech of the Indian nation united in heart and sympathy—in aims and aspirations.

The resolution on the subject of the Home Charges which has just been proposed by my friend Professor Gokhale will, I have no doubt, commend itself to your acceptance, and does not seem to require any lengthened argument on my part. The justice of our grievance in this matter is now admitted on all sides ; some of the burdens at present thrown on India are condemned as simply inequitable and unfair. The one crore or so, for instance, which we have to pay from year to year for the mere privilege of employing British troops, is a charge which is regarded as a monstrous piece of injustice. But there is no need to go into details. The whole subject demands a thorough, impartial enquiry and examination, and it is matter for satisfaction that it is being pressed on the attention of the British Parliament and the British public by our friends in England ; and the ability, and the earnestness with which Lord Northbrook is pleading on our behalf for a juster adjustment of these burdens, he is entitled to our warmest thanks. We are, of course, proud of our position in the imperial system of Great Britain, and are cheerfully willing to loyally bear our proper share in the responsibilities of that position. But we contend that charges are at present thrown upon India which she ought not, in fairness and equity, to be called upon to bear, and our demand is a demand for a fairer apportionment of these charges. Our worthy and revered President, of whom and of whose work we are all so proud and who so thoroughly enjoys the confidence of all India will, on his return to England, press this demand upon the consideration of Parliament with an authority to which no one else can pretend, and I think it adds in no small degree to the strength of this demand that it goes forth from the National Congress assembled at the Capital of the Punjab and with the full sanction and approval of the representatives of the martial people of Northern India. It is clear that it is not the Babus of Bengal or the Brahmins of the Deccan alone who are urging these demands, but that the men of the Punjab and the men of the North-West Provinces join heartily with their brethren of Bengal, Madras and Bombay in submitting this demand for the favourable consideration of Parliament ; and let us trust that it will be impartially and in a spirit of just sympathy considered by the authorities in England. With these few remarks I beg to support the resolution moved by Professor Gokhale and submit it for your approval. Thanking you for the patience with which you have kindly listened to my observations I beg to resume my seat.

The motion was then carried unanimously.

Fourth day.

Resolution XVIII.

Raising the status of the Chief Court in the Punjab to that [illegible] High Court.

LALA DWARKADASS *(Punjab, No. 589, in list)* said :—MR. PRESIDENT, LADIES AND GENTLEMEN,—The proposition which I have been commissioned to lay before you runs thus :

*That in the opinion of this Congress, the time has now come to raise the status of the Chief Court of the Punjab to that of a Chartered High Court in the interest of the administration of Justice in this Province.*

It is a well known fact that the Executive machinery of the British administration of this country is very delicate and the wheels by which that machinery is set in motion are so hidden from the public sight, that the people never know or see them and the people at large don't understand this refined apparatus and at times the hypocritical grounds upon which the British administration is carried on. And when they don't understand these things, you cannot expect them to appreciate that Government. But if, for example, you ask a poor villager or trader what he thinks of the British Government., you will discover that all his notions are clearly traceable to what he sees of that Government in the Courts they have established for the people. He sees the British Courts and sees their effect for good or evil. It is, therefore, of the highest importance alike in the interests of the British Government and the attachment which should exist amongst the people, that the Courts which are constituted by the Government should inspire confidence amongst the people and become powers of unmixed good. Gentlemen, you had read to you yesterday the resolution with regard to the separation of Judicial and Executive services. That was one way of remedying the evil which at present attaches to the Courts. But there is another way in which you can effect the independence of the Courts. This second remedy is by giving a High Court to this Province, a status by means of which it will be able not only to acquire independence itself, but also be able to support the Subordinate Courts especially when they come into conflict with the whimsical policy of any Executive officer of the Government. It will be just like the remedy you proposed by another resolution to make it imposible for your Judicial Officers to be afterwards put under Executive influences and so enable them to carry on their Judicial works independently and without any powerful interference (*Applause.*) By the operation of the one scheme you take it out of the range of possibilities for justice to be tampered with by Executive functions, by the other you make it possible for Judicial officers to have nothing to do with political matters. One remedy is by way of discouraging the combination of Executive influences with the impartial administration of justice, the other scheme is to enable Judicial officers to administer justice by being free from political influences. One scheme is a negative method whilst the other scheme is a positive method of bringing about the same end. In the Punjab the officers of the Chief Court hold their appointments during the pleasure of the Governor General. Their appointments and removals rest with him and as he is guided by the Council of the Lieutenant Governor the Judges of the Chief Court, therefore, hold their high offices at the pleasure of the Lieutenant Governor. What Judge has his judicial instinct so high that he, with all his hopes and prospects depending on the Lieutenant Governor, would care to go against the policy of that Official ? If the Court is raised to the status of a High Court the Judges will hold their offices during the pleasure of the Queen. It will not be possible for the Government to dismiss them because they did not agree to follow the policy of the Executive officials. They would be able to exercise proper independence and act with strict impartiality in the administration of justice, and the High Court would not only be able to secure independence for itself but also be able to support the independence of the Subordinate Courts. In this Province the decisions of the Judiciary are arrived at according to the rules and regulations which the Chief Court frames under Statutory powers. For example, one of the most vexed questions in this Province is the indebtedness

Fourth day.

Resolution XVIII.

Raising the status of the Chief Court in the Punjab to that of a Chartered High Court

of the ryot. Of course it is admitted that the ryot is indebted and Government thinks that the only way to relieve the ryot and get him out of his present difficulty is to support him against the claims of the money lender. We would not have had much cause of complaint in that, but this admission of the Local Government has gone so far as to contaminate the decisions of not only the Subordinate Courts but those of the Chief Court itself. In cases between money lenders and the royt, only written contracts are the basis of claims and the terms of the contracts when they have not even been brought into question by either parties our philanthropic Government have thought fit to substitute and place upon them an interpretation entirely foreign to the claim. Such judgments are often upset by the Highest Appellate Court. But sometimes the Highest Appellate Court endorses the views of the Government and it comes about, that the Chief Court is also not found to be independent of the policy which guides the Government. Sometimes our Court is so weak that even in minor matters it cannot make its voice felt. If I multiplied these cases of weakness I would encroach on your time, but I cannot pass over the subject without alluding to one or two. There is one important district in which a Magistrate established a number of *Panchayets* to settle claims between the money lender and the ryot. The object of the *Panchayet* was to always settle the claim of the money lender in favour of the ryot. The ryots themselves composed the *Panchayet* and you can very well understand what their decisions were. This state of things went on for several months and claims were settled by the *Panchayet* without any legal authority. When the matter was brought to the notice of the Chief Court, not by the public or the press, but by the judicial authorities of that district, the Chief Court sent a report to the Local Government and it felt itself bound to interfere in this matter. The Magistrate was told to put down the *Panchayet* but he was not censured, at least so far as is known, by the Chief Court or the Government. I remember a case which came before the Chief Court and before the Senior Judge of that Court. In that case the same District Magistrate had been called upon to send in the records of the case. The file of the record was evidently so ugly that he did not think fit to submit it. For three months he did not forward it and the Chief Court had ultimately to decide the matter without consulting the records. But there was nothing said about the conduct of the District Magistrate. That very District Magistrate, in that very district which had been unfortunate in other respects, no sooner he had taken charge of the District began to hold his Court in his own house. The matter was brought to the notice of the Chief Court and the Lieutenant Governor, and they requested that gentleman to hold his Court at the Kutchery, at least for judicial purposes. The Lieutenant Governor, however, did not condescend to answer the memorial presented to him on the matter. This order was passed in August last and to this day that District Magistrate holds his Court at his own private house. Such cases are not to be met with under the High Courts of other Provinces and the reason is that the Judges are not subordinate to the Local Authority or the Supreme Government. (*Applause.*) I may refer in one word to the difference in the revisional powers. It is impossible that our Judges can be so impartial or independent of the declared views of Government on certain matters as they should be and as it is necessary they should strive to be. Just see what a difference there is between the revisional powers of the Chief Court and the High Court. Revisions in the High Court lie on three grounds, illegality, material irregularity, and on the ground of a subordinate Court not having exercised the jurisdiction vested in it, or having exercised jurisdiction not vested in it. The Punjab Courts Act has prescribed a diffirent procedure. The word "illegality" has been taken out of the enactment. In other Provinces you find most of the applications rest on the point of illegality, but here that has been cut down by one fiat legislature. (*Applause and cries of "Time.*

LALA MUNSHI RAM (*Punjab, No. 440, in list*) in seconding the motion said: It would be cruel to you and disrespectful to the chair if at this late hour I proceeded to inflict a speech on you. My predecessor has dealt fully with the subject before you. He has laid before you the points which go to prove the necessity of a High Court instead of a Chief Court for this Province and in view of all the other Provinces having got High Courts it would be needless for me to try and impress upon you the sore need of such a Court here. I will simply confine myself to giving you the chief points which speak for themselves. In the first place we have not got efficient Judges on account of having only a Chief Court here. Some four or five years ago, and perhaps my friends will bear me out in this, the Chief Court was in such a state that an able Judge could not be found in the Punjab and a Small Causes Court Judge of Bombay was offered the seat and would you believe it, that Small Causes Court Judge refused it. This shows the respect in which our Chief Court is held. The Judges here and even the Small Causes Court Judge of Bombay think it an indignity to sit on a Bench which has such a reputation throughout India. I will put it to you, brother delegates from other Provinces who enjoy the benefits of a High Court, whether you do not think that Judges appointed by the Crown direct are more independent than those Judges appointed by the Government here. I certainly do think that if the Judges are made more independent than they are, the cause of justice will gain a great deal. I do not mean to insinuate that there have not been cases of efficient Judges in this Province and I am proud to acknowledge that there has been a Judge in this Chief Court who has had the independence to set every tradition of the service at defiance in pronouncing his judgments upon the misdoing and misdeeds of his subordinates ; but this is an exceptional case. If we had all our Judges of such an independent character our lives and properties would be much safer than now. I think quite enough has been said to show you that a High Court for the Punjab is a necessity and with these remarks I heartily second the proposition.

**Fourth day.**

**Resolution XVIII.**

**Raising the status of the Chief Court in the Punjab to that of a chartered High Court**

The motion was then adopted.

**Resolution XIX.**

**Thanks to the Electors of Central Finsbury.**

MR. G. SUBRAMANIA IYER (*Madras, No. 837, in list*) proposed :

*That this Congress tenders its best thanks to the Electors of Central Finsbury, both for their kindly sympathy in its objects and for having so generously accorded to it the valuable services of their honoured member Mr. Naoroji, who is destined, the Congress hopes, long to represent both Central Finsoury and India in the British House of Parliament.*

He said : This resolution does not require any speech or any argument to commend itself to you. You know very well how during recent Elections which brought the Radical Government into power, the people of Central Finsbury did us the favour of returning one of our own men to the House of Commons as their representative. Not only have they done this but they have done us the further favour in permitting their representative in the House of Commons to divide his time between protecting their own exclusive interests and advocating those of this country ; and again, they have conferred another favour by not insisting on his staying in their own country while Parliament is in session, but allowing him to come here and preside over our deliberations. Furthermore, they also record with satisfaction that their representative had the entire confidence of the people there and they record also their approval of the aims and objects of this Congress. These considerations have earned for the Electors of Central Finsbury our lasting gratitude—(*Applause.*)—and in recording in this Congress assembled our gratitude to them for the favours which they have shown to us we are only doing our duty. (*Loud Applause*).

**Fourth day.**

**Resolution XIX.**

**Thanks to the Electors of Central Finsbury.**

MR. R. N. MUDHOLKAR (*Berar, No. 798 in list*) in seconding the proposition said :—There are times when the language of man fails to afford an adequate measure of the strength or depth of his feelings. As the great poet of the Victorian era has said : "Words like language half reveal and half conceal the soul within." This is an occasion on which I find that words fail me to express the feeling which I and, I have no doubt, all of you entertain towards the Electors of Central Finsbury. By the inscrutable decree of Providence the destinies of England and India are closely bound together. We know, the whole main spring of action lies in England, in Westminster Hall and although there is our administration in India, if we want to obtain justice we must appeal to that august assembly of which Bright, Fawcett and Bradlaugh were such distinguished members. The last named gentleman earned the title of "member for India," but what is more natural for us to wish, that there should be one of us in that great assembly. It rested with the people of England to grant our wishes and to satisfy our aspirations and it reflects the greatest lustre on the noble character of the English that they set aside all race feeling and with a free and open mind appreciated the great qualities which characterises our illustrious and revered President. In doing honour to him and in doing honour to us they have done honour not only to themselves, not only to the people of England but to the whole of humanity. For a portion of what is called a race of conquerors, to have thus chosen one of the conquered to represent them in their Parliament, (and this is what the people of Central Finsbury have done,) is a great reason for rejoicing and by their act they have earned our eternal gratitude and we hope they will be able to secure our gratitude for a long time to come. (*Loud Applause.*)

LALA FATEHCHAND (*Punjab, No. 395, in list*) in supporting the motion said :—Last year when the Congress passed a resolution thanking Central Finsbury for the election of our distinguished President to the House of Commons, that resolution was passed in a way which showed that our gratitude was as deep and as intense as any sincere gratitute could be. A year has passed since then and many things have happened and we have reason to be even more grateful to them and to congratulate ourselves on what has been accomplished during that year. The career of our distinguished President in the House of Commons during the last session has been one which will be memorable in the annals of India and when we remember that the Electors of Central Finsbury on the eve of his departure for this country passed a resolution approving of his conduct in the House of Commons we have especial reason to congratulate ourselves as well as to be grateful to the Electors of Central Finsbury. They have set an example to the rest of the constituencies in England and have shown that they are above those racial prejudices which may guide more narrow minded people. I hope the Electors of Central Finsbury will know what they have done for us is not forgotten here and I hope that our distinguished President may long be spared to serve them first and then India. I also hope sincerely that he may long be spared so that that relationship which has been brought about by the generosity of Central Finsbury Electors may continue between him and them. (*Loud Applause.*)

PUNDIT GOPINATH (*Punjab, No. 255, in list*) having supported the motion in Urdu and "three cheers" having been given for the Electors of Central Finsbury the proposition was adopted.

**Resolution XX.**

**Assignment of Funds for the British Congress Committee.**

THE HON'BLE MR. SURENDRA NATH BANERJI (*Çalcutta, No. 8, in list*) moved :—

*That the sum of Rs. 60,000 be assigned for the expenses of the British Committee and the cost of the Congress publication, "India;" and that the several circles do contribute, as arranged, either now or hereafter in Committee, for the year 1894.*

He said :—MR. PRESIDENT AND GENTLEMEN,—A word of apology is necessary from me for being on this platform a second time to-day. (*Cries of "no, no"*). I am here, I may say, in obedience to the mandate of our venerable leader Mr. Hume

Fourth day.

Resolution XX.

Assignment of Funds for the British Congress Committee.

who, you will be sorry to hear, is indisposed. That is the reason I have the honour to lay this resolution before and invite you to accept it with that enthusiosm which the Congress has always been able to display when a critical occasion arises. It is a practical resolution and it has reference to your work in England. You will see that we make a demand upon you for the sum of Rs. 60,000 during the year 1894. You will at once ask me the question as to why instead of Rs. 47,000, as was demanded last year, we should raise the sum this time to Rs. 60,000, and you are entitled to an explanation which you shall have at my hands forthwith. The Rs. 60,000 includes private subscriptions and donations which the Rs. 47,000 did not include. Therefore you will see at once that we do not ask you to subscribe more for 1894 than for 1893. So let there be no sense of alarm in the minds of the delegates in connection with this matter. What is this money wanted for? It is wanted for *India* our publication and it is wanted for the British Committee. Gentlemen, we may cry here at the top of our voices and we have been doing so for the last two or three days and yet our grievances will go unredressed unless and until we can make ourselves heard before the Bar of British Public opinion. We must voice our grievances in the columns of the English newspapers and from the platforms of English public meetings, and from the floor of the British House of Commons. *India* and the British Committee constitute the right arm of our strength; they are the musket to the soldiers and they must be kept in the highest state of efficiency; and as far as *India* is concerned we must secure to it the largest possible measure of circulation. The English people must be persuaded to take an interest and feel a concern in the affairs of their great dependency. You must agitate! agitate!! agitate!!! and incur a vast measure of self-sacrifice before you can obtain a footing on the platform of British politics. You have made large sacrifices and I recognise the measure of your self-sacrifices, but you have yet to make much larger sacrifices before you can accomplish the enfranchisement of your nation. Look at the heroic acts of self-sacrifice of the Irish people, not for one day, not for one year, but for the greater part of a century; and it is because of these acts of self-sacrifice that the Home Rule question has come within a measurable distance of satisfactory solution. As it has been with Ireland so will it be with us. We must rise to the height of our situation and if we can do this, then and then only, will the Congress programme be accomplished to the full measure. I do not wish to make an appeal: I will not call upon you to come forward with your subscriptions at this meeting but I hope and trust that when we meet next year at Madras—(*Applause*)—it will be possible for us to say that we have fulfilled the promises we make to-day; that it will be possible for us to say that we have redeemed the vote that we shall presently record. Our greatest charge against the Government of this country is that it does not fulfil or redeem the pledges it makes. Let not that charge be brought against the Congress that it does not know how to redeem the promises it so solemnly makes. Therefore, men of Bombay, men of Bengal, men of the North-West Provinces, men of the Punjab, men of Madras, let us all return to our homes, and let us work energetically and persistently to raise this money, so that when we meet next year it will be our glorious privilege and pride to be able to tell the Congress that we have redeemed the vote of to-day and that we have paid the full amount for the maintenance of the British Committee and our newspaper "India." (*Loud Applause.*)

MR. K. P. ROY (*Punjab, No. 304, in list*) in seconding the motion said: MR. PRESIDENT, LADIES AND GENTLEMEN,—My determination throughout this Congress has been not to appear before you as a speaker, and against my will I have come up here However, I have to support the appeal to you to enable the Congress to pay the cost of the publication "India" and the expenses of the British Committee. Without my knowledge or consent I have been selected for this object, but as the Congress is sitting in the Punjab and I am one of the humble workers of the Reception Committee, I had to appear. (*Applause.*) I appeal to all of you, and particularly the young men of the Punjab. You must not overlook the fact that the British Committee require sinews of war, and unless you fight the battle where the grievances are to be relieved you never will succeed. Where Government is, there our grievances must be made known (*Applause.*) If we have to be governed in Downing Street and by the House of Commons and House of Lords, there the grievances have to be laid. We have had to establish a British Committee and go there and spend our money and energy in order to secure the aims of the Congress and that success which the Congress labours for and deserves Therefore, I ask you to take this matter into serious consideration. Don't be frightened because the battle is to be fought in England. I know a good many Indians feel apprehension about the foundations of the Congress which they think are being removed to England, and they ask, is it wise and proper ? What is wanted is only to support the superstructure in England which is necessary for the preservation and continuance of the Congress. Therefore, it should be done. (*Applause.*) I say that the foundation of the Congress remains in India, it is in no way removed ; it is secure, but we must have subordinate Divisions and one of the most important is the British Committee in England, which must be supported at any cost. Unless you do it, all your labours here will go for nothing. If you wish to be heard, and heard you must be, and if you are determined to secure success, go and shout it forth at the top of your voice to the British Public and the House of Commons where it will be heard and you will gain success. I, therefore, second the motion. (*Loud applause.*)

Pundit Madan Mohun Malavya (*Allahabad, No. 73, in list*) said :—I rise, Mr. President, to support this resolution because I feel it is necessary that something more should be said in regard to this matter than what has already fallen from the previous speakers. Gentlemen, we have to recognise the necessity of voting Rs. 60,000 for the expenses of the British Committee and the organ "India" which is rendering valuable service to the cause. Although we seem to show by our cheers and applause that we appreciate the fact fully, the moment we turn homewards we seem to forget that we have to carry out a promise made in this Hall. A long correspondence has to be gone through to bring in a portion of the subscriptions which have been promised year after year. I must protest against that practice and I must ask every one to go away from this hall with a stern resolution to give effect to this vote by bringing in money as early as possible. (*Applause.*) We have been speaking of the poverty of the people ; we believe they are suffering from starvation and injustice. We are anxious that these should be removed ; find the means and enable our friends in England to remove it (*Hear, hear.*) I am reminded of what the poet has beautifully said in speaking of what one desires. He says "you love the roses and so do I, and I wish the sky would rain roses down ; for see Queen, will it rain roses ? No, my pretty Prattler, it never will rain roses, if we want more roses we must plant more trees." If you want, gentlemen, that the British Committee should be maintained in a state of efficiency and able to bring you that justice you have been crying for so earnestly, you should keep it in a state in which it will be able to kill that demon of tyranny which denies you justice in the matter of Home Charges, and to demonstrate the real poverty of the people of this country and bring some relief. You must make up your minds to work from day to day and week to week to make up the money. When you have done that, then alone you will have done your duty by your country. An objection has been raised that the money for the purpose of *India* and the Committee is so much money sent out of the country ; but gentlemen, you must not forget that for all litigation you have to incur expense. Every Privy Council case incurs expense, but these are cases in which the interests not of one man, not of half a dozen families, but of vast millions are concerned. Therefore, you must not grudge this Rs. 60,000. It is all wanted to enable that noble band of English gentlemen, who are giving their service and time, energy and attention so courageously and unselfishly to carry on the work. If we don't back up their efforts and don't send money in proper time we expose ourselves to the censure that we are not prepared to do our duty to our country. (*Applause.*)

Fourth day.

Resolution XX.

Assignment of Funds for the British Congress Committee.

THE PRESIDENT:—I have to say one word. What we in the British Committee have to urge upon you is to be prompt in your payments. You do ultimately pay, but we are very much worried when we have not the money in time. I appeal to you and trust that what you propose to contribute you will contribute promptly and therefore, we shall receive it gratefully. (*Loud applause.*)

The motion was then unanimously carried.

Resolution XXI.

Thanks to Sir William Wedderburn and to the members of the British Congress Committee.

THE PRESIDENT:—As we are very much pressed for time let me move the next resolution. The resolution is :—

*That this Congress hereby tenders its most grateful acknowledgments to Sir W. Wedderburn and the members of the British Congress Committee for the services rendered by them to India during the past year.*

I think so highly, ladies and gentlemen, of the services of these gentlemen that I will not make a speech. (*Three cheers were then given for the British committee.*)

The motion was then unanimously adopted.

Resolution XXII.

Re-appointment of Mr. A. O. Hume as General Secretary.

THE PRESIDENT : In the absence of our esteemed friend the Hon'ble Mr. W. C. Bonnerjee who almost always moves the resolution which is to follow, it will be moved by our esteemed and indefatigable Secretary Mr. J. Ghosal.

MR. J. GHOSAL (*Calcutta, No. 5, in list.*) who on rising was received with loud applause said :—MR. PRESIDENT AND GENTLEMEN,—The resolution which I have been unexpectedly called upon to propose is in one sense a very formal one, but in another sense it is a most important one, as it is very closely connected with most of the Congress works to be done between its one sitting and another ; for the period of one whole year and taking all the necessary steps for giving proper effect to the resolutions we are now passing. But for all that it does not require from any one any speech or words to commend it to your acceptance. It will suffice if the resolution is only read out to you. Unfortunately, however, this year there is a little difference in the circumstances connected with the matter which I am about to submit to you. The resolution is for the re-appointment of our revered General Secretary, Mr. A. O. Hume, and the little difference that I mentioned is this: Mr. Hume is unwilling to accept the office this year, not that he is unwilling to work for the Congress, or for us, as he has hitherto done ; you may rest assured that he will work for us as hard as possible till he takes his last breath in this world. He is unwilling because he thinks that his failing health will not permit him to work as much as would be necessary to do justice to the office and also because he does not expect to be able to spend even a portion of the ensuing year in this country. But I can assure you, gentlemen, that there is no reason to apprehend that our works will suffer in his hands on account of his ill health. It has been my privilege and good fortune to know him very intimately, perhaps more intimately than any one present in this hall. I worked with him before the National Congress came into existence and excepting at the last Congress when he was absent from India, I worked under him at every Congress from the very first, living together and working together for weeks, both before and after each Congress sitting and I have never seen him shirk or

Fourth day.

Resolution XXII.

Re-appointment of Mr. A. O. Hume as General Secretary.

neglect any work nor to allow a single day's delay in doing what, though important, could, without any harm, be delayed for days and that even when suffering from fever or such other complaint. (*Hear, hear.*) On one occasion at the time of a Congress Session, I saw him work day after day till past midnight, when he had been getting attacks of fever every evening, in order to keep everything ready for the day following. He is an indefatigable worker and loves work, particularly work for the good of our country. Whether in good or bad health, or whether residing in or out of India, I have no doubt that he will do more work for us than any other Secretary we could appoint in his stead. (*Applause.*)

Allow me gentlemen to ask you one question; can you concieve the idea of our revered leader, the father of the Congress, being separated from us and from his infant child, the Congress itself, before he is separated from or leaves this world. To me personally, and I dare say to several others present in this hall, the very idea would be really painful. May the Supreme Being grant him long life and health to continue and complete the noble work he has so disinterestedly, so earnestly and so well begun for the amelioration of the miserable condition of the helpless people (ourselves) of this country. You know very well how helpless we all Indians are without the help of Englishmen of position. Whether Mr. Hume can work or not, so long as he lives we cannot think of severing his connection with us, or with the Congress; and so far as I know, he too never contemplates the adoption of such a course, I mean to cut off his connection with India, its people or with the Congress altogether and even if he ever thinks of doing so, we who are looked upon by him as his children should personally approach and entreat him to give up the idea and I am sure that we shall not approach and entreat him in vain. (*Applause*). I have already spoken much more than I had intended and I belive that there is no need of my saying anything further for the adoption of this resolution by you which runs thus :

*That this Congress re-appoints Mr. A. O. Hume, C. B., to be its General Secretary for the ensuing year.*

This resolution never required a seconder and I hope that this time, as in the former years, you will carry it by acclamation. (*Loud applause and three cheers for Mr. Hume.*)

The resolution was carried by acclamation.

Resolution XXIII.

Tenth Congress to be held at Madras.

MR. G. SUBRAMANIA IYER (*Madras, No. 837, in list*) said :—MR. PRESIDENT, LADIES AND GENTLEMEN,—I have the pleasant duty to make a formal proposal to you in the way of an invitation that this Congress will do us the honour of meeting in the capital of our Province, Madras. It is a poor country and cannot boast of any great traditions or great natural scenery. But if you accept the invitation, Madras will not yield to any Province in the heartiness of its welcome. On the strength of our devotion to the Congress we invite you to the capital of our Province. (*Applause.*) The resolution I move is in these words :

*That the Tenth Indian National Congress do assemble on such day after Christmas Day 1894, as may be later determined upon, at Madras.*

MR. H. MORGAN BROWNE (*Calcutta, No. 2, in list*) seconded the motion and said : MR. PRESIDENT, LADIES AND GENTLEMEN,—In one sense I am sorry to be here, because, gentlemen, if Mr. Hume were not unable to speak on this resolution you would not be listening to a humble lieutenant. But as I have to second the resolution I am

Fourth day.

Resolution XXIII.

Tenth Congress to be held at Madras.

glad to do so, and I am happy to think that the Congress next year will meet in Madras. I will take this opportunity of saying a few words which I trust you will not take amis from so young a worker in the cause of India. I have now travelled many thousand miles in India and I have seen a great deal of the country for the short time I have been here and I have seen a good many Committees, and I have noticed amongst the Indian people unparalleled and well sustained enthusiasm for the cause of their country's enfranchisement. But I have noticed a serious tendency to allow your enthusiasm to detract somewhat from the value of solid hard work and I wish to impress on you that your enthusiasm should be diverted into more profitable channels. If you wish to obtain your great country's freedom, I say you will not obtain it by great mass meetings or by giving Mr. Hume a torch light procession, by waving banners and shouting cheers and by the other components of an Indian *tamasha*. I say you will not in that way achieve your country's freedom. You have got to take a leaf out of the political book of your English friends in this matter. There the stress of public life is enormous and a cause can only succeed by the individual efforts of every individual interested in it. I wish to point out what has been done in England by one of the most successful political organizations in existence. It is the Fabian Society—a little society which does not contain more than 1000 members, but it has done more in the last ten years to revolutionize political life than all the other societies have done in the last century. (*Hear, hear.*) How was that done? By every man being a worker. No one waited to see what his friend was going to do or what they were going to think about him; there was no question of personal dignity entered into, and these men, each one regardless of what any one else might say, irrespective of what any one might think, went on doing his work in his own way and in his own time. He would work without thinking whether it was his duty to lead or follow. That is what I would have you, Indian people, do throaghout the length and breadh of the land. You must forget some of your old customs, you must learn something higher than the dignity which is to be associated with ancient customs. Good solid hard work performed in an honest cause is wnat is wanted for the welfare of the country and I would have everyone remember that you cannot achieve your country's good except by individual work and that good is only won by each one doing his utmost to achieve that good. (*Hear, hear.*) Englishmen who hold the political faith, I hold, will always be willing to help you. We are always ready, we of the Radical faith, to stretch out a helping hand to India's toiling millions. To those painfully treading on the path which England has already trod we are willing to extend help, but, I say, if it was in our power to grant to you all those reforms you are endeavouring to obtain, it would be wrong to grant them. You will only achieve the real good if you win them for yourselves as others have done. (*Applause.*) No man can give you political salvation, you must win it. You have had within this year the first fruits of victory, you stand at the parting of the ways; on the one side you are leaving behind the old bureaucratic institutions of a despotic Government, and entering on the path of representative institutions. (*Applause.*) Along that path you have only advanced some little way and you have got to fight hard and long before you reach the goal; but it is now within your sight, the prize is within your grasp and if each will strive manfully without thinking what others may do, and if you will all do that, you will, in the words of our Scripture "acquit yourselves like men and be strong." Believe me, success is not very far distant. (*Loud applause.*)

THE PRESIDENT:—There is another invitation from Belgaum but if you do not wish it I will not read the letter itself which has been received from there. It is an invitation to hold the next session of the Congress in that town. I mention it now because those who prefer to see the next Congress meet at Belgaum would be able to carry out their wishes by voting against this proposition and if it is rejected, by moving

Fourth day.

Resolution XXIII.

Tenth Congress to be held at Madras.

another resolution for holding the next Congress at Belgaum which, however, would no be needed if this one is carried out. The motion is :

*That the Tenth Indian National Congress do assemble on such day after Christmas Day 1894, as may be later determined upon, at Madras.*

The motion was then put to the vote and carried.

THE PRESIDENT :—On your behalf I thank the inhabitants of the Belgaum District for sending us this invitation for it shows clearly that there is an earnestness abroad and that the people of the country are willing to have both political education and to mix with their fellow countrymen as much as possible. I offer, therefore, to the delegates who brought this invitation our sincere thanks for it. (*Loud applause.*)

Vote of thanks to the President.

LALA LAJPAT RAI (*Punjab, No. 237, in list*) said :—There would be no justification for my appearing on this platform a second time this day but for the fact that I am going to perform the duty of proposing a hearty vote of thanks to our learned President (*Loud applause and three cheers for Mr. Dadabhai Naoroji.*) It is not an easy task to preside over the deliberations of such a large assembly as the Indian National Congress, but the manner in which our President has performed that duty has been most pleasing and impartial and he is entitled to the heartiest thanks we can possibly give him. By doing this we shall be showing that we really feel grateful for the services he has done for the country. I have just one word to say to my brother delegates from other Provinces and it is this : that I hope you will excuse all our shortcomings for we have already told you we are not sufficiently advanced either in education or riches—(*Cries of* "*no, no.*") and if we have not been able to give you a sufficiently splendid reception we hope you will excuse us. (*Loud applause.*)

MR. J. GHOSAL (*Calcutta, No. 5, in list*) :—As the motion refers personally to the illustrious occupant of the chair he cannot put it to the vote and therefore I have been asked to perform that pleasant duty. Let me tell you that the motion has not been seconded nor I wish that it should be seconded. It should be carried by acclamation and I beg to call upon my brother delegates to do so and I am sure you will carry it by acclamation. (*Loud applause and* "*three cheers for Mr. Dadabhai Naoroji.*")

The motion was then carried by acclamation.

President's concluding address.

Two poems in the vernacular were then recited. At the conclusion of the recitations the President rose and was most enthusiastically received. He said :—I have first to announce to the Subjects Committee that they should send their delegates here at eleven o'clock tomorrow for the purpose of finishing the financial part of our business. The next thing I have to announce is that I am sorry to hear from Mr. Seymour Keay that he has not been in a condition to come here and help us as he expected to do. He sends his best wishes for the Congress and hopes that he will be able to be present at its meetings next year. Again, we have received many telegrams and letters containing good wishes for the success of the Congress and expressing the regret of many persons who have not been able to attend. I may mention that the Maharajah of Durbhanga expresses his regret at not being able to attend and wishes us every success. The Prince of Palegang has sent a telegram and we have received a number of letters and telegrams of a very encourag ing character, wishing us every success. Then there is also a letter from the Hon'ble the Maharajah Pratap Narayan Singh. He sends a letter acknowledging with thanks

Fourth day.

President's concluding address.

the invitation we sent him and expresses his best wishes for our success : private business prevented him coming here. Now, gentlemen, I do not know how to thank you for the very kind and cordial vote of thanks you have tendered me. As I have said repeatedly, I am one of you and it is my duty to do individually what I can for, as Mr. Morgan Browne advised us, every one and cach of us must do the best he can, for it is only by these means that the good of all will be accomplished. I have done my duty and it is a great gratification to me that the invitation to attend this Congress was sent to me so many thousands of miles away and that you had not forgotten me. I was able, with pleasure, to accept that invitation and when I came here I found myself, as it has often been said, the idol of my country. (*Loud Applause.*) I am overpowered by your kindly and splendid reception and the only way in which I can express my deep sense of appreciation of it is by using the simplest word possible and saying "I thank you." I must acknowledge my obligations to the Reception Committee who have done everything in their power to make me comfortable and to make me feel that I am amongst my own family, in my own country. I therefore return my most sincere thanks to the committee. The one name I will mention in connection with the Reception Committee in making this acknowledgment will be that of Sirdir Dyal Singh, the President of that Committee. (*Loud applause.*) Then as a delegate of all the delegates here I offer my thanks on behalf of the delegates to Sirdir Dyal Singh and to the members of the Reception Committee for the admirable manner in which they have attended to the wants of the delegates and making their stay as comfortable as possible. I have to offer also thanks on behalf of the Congress to the Volunteers who have, from all I have observed, done good and useful work. (*Applause.*) It was not a mercenary service but a service of the heart and a feeling towards their own country to contribute what they could in their position towards the success of the Congress. And lastly, I have to say one word to the Congress itself. During the time I have had the honour of presiding here, whether in the Subjects Committee or in this Congress Hall, you have done everything you could to show that you were prepared to work cordially and sympathetically with me. You have attended to all my wishes and you have not given me the slightest trouble in the conduct of the deliberations of this Congress and to maintain perfect order. I say it reflects on you the highest credit and demands from me my sincere gratitude which I offer with every pleasure. Before I conclude I will ask you to give three sterling cheers for the Queen Empress of India.

Loud and enthusiastic cheers were then given for Her Majesty and were followed by equally hearty cheers for "the people of the United Kingdom," for "Central Finsbury," for "British rule," for "the Congress" and for "the Lieutenant Governor of the Punjab."

Dissolution of the Congress.

THE PRESIDENT :—Well gentlemen, I now declare your deliberations at an end, trusting that you will meet at Madras next year with some work done and some reforms achieved. I bid you farewell and declare the Congress dissolved.

The delegates and visitors dispersed at about a quarter past six and as they left the Hall repeatedly cheered " the Grand Old Man of India.

# APPENDIX I

# LIST OF DELEGATES

WHO ATTENDED THE

# NINTH INDIAN NATIONAL CONGRESS,

*HELD AT LAHORE, DECEMBER, 1893.*

| Number. | Presidency or Government. | Congress Circle. | Electoral Division. | Names in full of Delegates, with Honorary Titles, Scholastic Degrees, etc. | Race, Religious denomination, and Caste, if any. | Occupation and Address. | How and when elected. |
|---|---|---|---|---|---|---|---|
| 1 | Bengal. | Calcutta. | Northern Metropolitan Electoral Division. | Mr. A. O. Hume, C.B. ... | European Christian. | Retired Civil Servant. | At a Committee Meeting held at No. 3, Hastings Street, Calcutta, on the 19th December, 1893. |
| 2 | " | " | " | Mr. H. Morgan Browne. | do. | Secretary, British Congress Committee. | do. |
| 3 | " | " | " | Babu Amoy Nath Bose. | Hindu Kayastha. | Teacher, E. School, 13, College Square, Calcutta. | do. |
| 4 | " | " | " | " Binode Behari Bose, B.A. | do. | Zemindar, 65, Bagbazar Street, Calcutta. | do. |
| 5 | " | " | British Indian Association. | Mr. J. Ghosal ... | Hindu Brahmin. | Zemindar, Merchant, Secretary, Congress Committee, Honorary. Presidency Magistrate and Municipal Commissioner, Calcutta. | At a Committee Meeting of the British Indian Association on the 12th December, 1893. |
| 6 | " | " | Indian Association. | Dr. Mohini Mohun Bose, M.D., L.R.C.P. EDIN, &c. | Brahmo. | Zemindar, Hony. Magistrate, Physician and Surgeon. | At a Meeting of the Indian Association held on the 1st December, 1893. |
| 7 | " | " | " | Rai Jotindra Nath Chaudhury, M.A., B.I. | Hindu Kayastha. | Zemindar, Baranagore. | do. |
| 8 | " | " | " | Hon'ble Surendra Nath Banerji, B.A. | Hindu Brahmin. | Secretary, Indian Association, Editor, "Bengalee," Proprietor, Ripon College, Honorary Presidency Magistrate, Member, Bengal Legislative Council and Chairman, North Barrackpore Municipality. | do. |
| 9 | " | " | " | Dr. Jagadish Chandra Lahiri. | do. | Medical Practitioner, 101, College Street, Calcutta. | do. |
| 10 | " | " | Bengali Christian Conference. | Mr. Kali Charan Banerji, M.A., B.L. | Bengali Christian. | Vakil, High Court, Fellow of the University of Calcutta, 81, Baranasi Ghose's Street, Calcutta. | At a Meeting of the Bengali Christian Conference held on the 8th December, 1893. |

| Number. | Presidency or Government. | Congress Circle. | Electoral Division. | Names in full of Delegates, with Honorary Titles, Scholastic Degrees, etc. | Race, Religious denomination, and Caste, if any. | Occupation and Address. | How and when elected. |
|---|---|---|---|---|---|---|---|
| 11 | Bengal. | Calcutta. | Bengali Christian Conference. | Revd. C. N. Banerji, B.A. | Bengali Christian. | Missionary, L. M. Society, Bhowanipur, Calcutta. | At a Meeting of the Bengali Christian Conference held on the 8th December, 1893. |
| 12 | " | " | Southern Metropolitan Electoral Division. | Pandit Kali Prasanna Kavyabisharad. | Agnostic. | Journalist and Proprietor, "Secular Press," 33, Balaram Bose's Ghat Road, Bhowanipore, Calcutta. | At a Public Meeting of the inhabitants of the Southern Metropolitan Electoral Division held on the 17th December, 1893. |
| 13 | " | " | " | Babu Upendra Nath Sen. | Hindu Vaidya. | Kaviraj and Zemindar, 29, Colootola Street, Calcutta. | do. |
| 14 | " | " | 24 Perghs. Taki. | " Prafulla Chandra Ghose. | Hindu Kayastha. | Zemindar and Honorary Magistrate, Taki. | At a Committee Meeting of the Branch Indian Association, Taki. |
| 15 | " | " | Katwa. | " Aghore Nath Barat. | Hindu Vaidya. | Private Service, Alampur. (Katwa.) | At a Public Meeting held at Katwa on the 10th December, 1893. |
| 16 | " | " | Murshidabad. | Babu Baikuntha Nath Sen, B.A., B.L. | do. | Vakil, High Court, Chairman, Berhampur Municipality, President, Murshidabad Association, Zemindar and Honorary Magistrate. | At a Meeting of the Murshidabad Association on the 29th November, 1893. |
| 17 | " | " | " | " Moti Lal Banerji. | Hindu Brahmin. | Pleader and Zemindar. | do. |
| 18 | " | " | " | " Bhowani Kishore Chakravarty. | do. | Pleader, Judge's Court, Berhampore. | do. |
| 19 | " | " | " | " Hemendra Nath Sen, B.A., B.L. | Hindu Vaidya. | do. | do. |
| 20 | " | " | " | " Hem Lal Banerji. | Hindu Brahmin. | Zemindar, Berhampore. | At a meeting of the Murshidabad Association on the 20th December 1893 |
| 21 | " | " | " | " Janoki Nath Singh. | Hindu Kayastha. | do. | do. |
| 22 | " | " | Nuddea. | " Nanda Gopal Bhaduri. | Hindu Brahmin. | Landholder, Kishengunge. | At a Public Meeting held at Krishnaghur on the 26th November, 1893 |
| 23 | " | " | " | " Ramani Mohun Mullick. | Hindu Vaidya. | Zemindar, Hony. Magistrate, Chairman, Meherpore Local Board, and Member Nuddea District Board. | do. |
| 24 | " | " | Katdaha. (District Nuddea.) | " Chuni Lal Bose ... | Hindu Kayastha. | Zemindar, Katdah, Poradah. | At a Public Meeting held at Katdaha on the 20th December, 1893 |
| 25 | " | " | Chogda. (Nuddea District.) | " Hari Nath Singha. | Tamuli Vaishnava. | Teacher, Chogda M. E. School. | At a Meeting held at the Local School Premises on the 26th November, 1893. |
| 26 | " | " | Kushtea. (Nuddea District.) | " Ambica Charan Moitra, B.L. | Hindu Brahmin. | Pleader, Municipal Commissioner, Hony. Magistrate and Landholder. | At a meeting held at the Kushtea Bar Library on the 8th December 1893. |
| 27 | " | " | Jessore. | " Akshoy Kumar Mitra, | Hindu Kayastha. | Hony. Magistrate, Municipal Commissioner and Talukdar, Jessore. | At a Meeting of the Jessore Branch Congress Committee held on the 9th December, 1893. |
| 28 | " | " | Khulna. | " Veni Bhusan Roy, B.A., B.L. | do. | Pleader, Judge's Court, Khulna. | At a Public Meeting held at Khulna on the 4th December, 1893. |

| Number. | Presidency or Government. | Congress Circle. | Electoral Division. | Names in full of Delegates, with Honorary Titles, Scholastic Degrees, etc. | Race, Religious denomination, and Caste, if any. | Occupation and Address. | How and when elected. |
|---|---|---|---|---|---|---|---|
| 29 | Bengal. | Calcutta. | Kishoreganj. (Mymensingh.) | Babu Krishna Kumar Mitra. | Brahmo. | Lecturer, City College, and Editor, "Sanjibanee" 6, College Square, Calcutta. | At a meeting held on the 8th December, 1893. |
| 30 | " | " | Tangail. (Mymensingh.) | " Prasanna Kumar Bose. | do. | Talukdar and Superintendent, Sanjibanee Office. | At a Meeting of the inhabitants of Tangail residing in Calcutta, held on the 23rd December, 1893, at 6, College Square, Calcutta. |
| 31 | " | " | " | " Dina Nath Biswas, B.L. | do. | Pleader, Judge's Court, Pubna. | do. |
| 32 | " | Dacca. | Munshiganj (Dacca District.) | " Jagat Chandra Roy. | Hindu | Pleader, Hony. magistrate, and Vice-Chairman, Local Board, Munshiganj. | At a Public Meeting held on the 12th December, 1893. |
| 33 | " | " | Dacca. | " Sarat Chandra Bose, B.A., B.L | Hindu Theist. | Pleader, Judge's Court, and Secretary, Congress Committee, Dacca. | At a General Meeting of the Local Bar-Association held on the 12th December, 1893. |
| 34 | " | " | " | " Sarat Chunder Gupta. | Hindu Vaidya. | Pleader, Municipal Commissioner, Hony. Magistrate, Member, Dacca District Board and Chairman, Narainganj Local Board. | At a General Meeting of the Local Bar-Association held on the 12th December, 1893. |
| 35 | " | Furridpore. | Furridpore. | " Ambica Charan Mazoomdar, M.A., B.L. | do. | Pleader, Zemindar, Municipal Commissioner and Member, District Board. | At a Public Meeting held on the 21st December, 1893. |
| 36 | " | " | " | " Prithvis Chandra Roy Chaudhury. | Hindu Kayastha. | Zemindar, 35/2 Beadon Street, Calcutta. | do. |
| 37 | " | " | Manikdaha. | " Gorachand Das, B.A., B.L. | Hindu Napit. | Pleader, Judge's Court, Barisal. | At a meeting of the Manikdaha Hitashadhini Sabha held on the 21st December, 1893. |
| 38 | " | Barisal. | Backerganj. | " Nibaran Chandra Das, M.A., B.L. | Hindu Vaidya. | Pleader, Judge's Court, Barisal. | At a Public Meeting of the inhabitants of Backerganj held on the 20th December, 1893. |
| 39 | " | Rungpore. | Rungpore. | " Ram Kumar Bose. | Hindu Kayastha. | Mukhtar, Rungpore. | At a Public Meeting held at Rungpore on the 19th December, 1893. |
| 40 | " | Pubna. | Pubna. | " Mohini Mohun Chakravarty, M.A. B.L. | Hindu Brahmin. | Pleader and Vice-Chairman, Municipality, Pubna. | At a Public Meeting held on the 27th November, 1893. |
| 41 | " | " | " | " Mohendra Narain Chakravarty, | do. | Zemindar, Pubna. | do. |
| 42 | " | Jalpaiguri. | Jalpaiguri. | " Umagati Roy, B.L. | do. | Pleader and Hony. Secretary to the Branch Indian Association and Standing Congress Committee. | At a meeting of the Branch Indian Association held on the 19th November, 1893. |
| 43 | " | Rampore Beauleah. | Rampore-Beauleah. | Dr. Akshoy Kumar Bhaduri, L.M.S. | do. | Medical Practitioner. | At a Meeting of the Rajshahye Association on the 19th December, 1893. |
| 44 | " | " | Maldah. | Babu Rama Prasad Mullick. | Hindu Vaidya. | Zemindar, Banker and Indigo Planter. | At a Public Meeting of the Merchants held at Nawabgunge on the 29th November, 1893. |

| Number. | Presidency or Government. | Congress Circle. | Electoral Division. | Names in full of Delegates, with Honorary Titles, Scholastic Degrees, etc. | Race, Religious denomination, and Caste, if any. | Occupation and Address. | How and when elected. |
|---|---|---|---|---|---|---|---|
| 45 | Bengal. | Bhagalpore. | Purneah. | Babu Jogendra Nath Mukerjee, M.A., B.L. | Hindu Brahmin. | Pleader, Judge's Court and Municipal Commissioner, Purneah. | At a Public Meeting held at Purneah on the 19th December, 1803. |
| 46 | " | " | " | " Parvati Charan Das, B.L. | Brahmo. | Pleader, Judge's Court and Member, District Board, Purneah. | do. |
| 47 | " | " | Bhagalpore- | " Ugra Mohun Thakoor. | Hindu Brahmin. | Zemindar. | At a Public Meeting held on the 14th November, 1893. |
| 48 | " | " | " | " Tariny Prasad Dobay. | do. | Manager, Barari Estate. | do. |
| 49 | " | Chota Nagpur. | Hazaribagh. | Rai Jadu Nath Mukerjee B.L. | do. | Zemindar, Vakil, Hony. Magistrate, Vice-Chairman, Hazaribagh Municipality and Director, Chota Nagpur Banking Association Ld. &c. | At a Public Meeting held at Hazaribagh on the 3rd December, 1893. |
| 50 | " | " | " | Mr. M. L. Mitter, | Bengali Christian. | Hony. Magistrate, and House and land-owner. | do. |
| 51 | " | " | " | Babu Narendra Nath Mukerjee. | Hindu Brahmin. | Landholder. | do. |
| 52 | " | " | Giridih. | Pandit Deo Datta Bharati. | do. | ...... | At a Public Meeting held at Giridih on the 18th December, 1893. |
| 53 | " | " | " | Munshi Mathura Prasad. | Hindu Kayastha. | Zemindari Service, Peshkar, Palgunge Raj Estate, Giridih. | do. |
| 54 | " | " | " | Babu Sakti Kanta Bhattacharyya, B.L. | Hindu Brahmin. | Pleader, Giridih. | do. |
| 55 | " | " | Manbhoom. | " Ananga Mohun Bhattacharyya, B.L. | do. | Pleader, Landholder, Municipal Commissioner and Member, District Board. | At a Public Meeting held on the 9th December, 1893. |
| 56 | " | " | " | " Srish Chunder Tewari, B.L. | do. | Pleader and Landholder, Purulia. | do. |
| 57 | " | Behar. | Bankipore. | Babu Guru Prasad Sen. | Hindu Vaidya. | Pleader, Municipal Commissioner, Zemindar and Banker. | At a Public Meeting held at Bankipur on the 6th December, 1893. |
| 58 | " | " | Darbhanga. | Pundit Bishnu Dutt Chowbey. | Hindu Brahmin. | Teacher, Dalton Institution, Darbhanga. | At a Public Meeting held on the 18th December, 1893. |
| 59 | " | " | Chupra. | Mr. Radhika Prasad Ghose. | Hindu Kayastha. | Barrister-at-Law, Chairman, Chupra Municipality, Vice-Chairman of the Local Board, Member, District Board and Honorary Magistrate, Chupra. | At a Public Meeting held on the 23rd December, 1893. |
| 60 | N. W. P. | Benares. | Benares. | Babu Jagat Narain Sinha. | Sarasvat Brahmin. | Zemindar, Rais, Municipal Commissioner and Member, District Board, Ghazipur. | At a Public Meeting held at Benares on the 10th December, 1893. |
| 61 | " | " | " | " Bhowani Prasad. | Hindu Khettri. | Zemindar, Kachourigali, Benares. | do. |
| 62 | " | " | " | Pundit Srinath Deva. | Hindu Brahmin | Talukdar of Devakali and Member District Board, Ghazipur. | do. |

| Number. | Presidency or Government. | Congress Circle. | Electoral Division. | Names in full of Delegates, with Honorary Titles, Scholastic Degrees, etc. | Race, Religious denomination, and Caste, if any. | Occupation and Address. | How and when elected. |
|---|---|---|---|---|---|---|---|
| 63 | N.W.P. | Benares. | Benares. | Munshi Shankar Lal Desai. | Hindu Brahmin. | Rais, Banker, Zemindar, Treasurer 'Union Club' and "Carmichæl Library," Nandan Sahi Street, Benares. | At a Public Meeting held at Benares on the 10th December, 1893. |
| 64 | „ | „ | „ | „ Basudeo Sahai. | Hindu Kayastha. | Teacher, C. M. High School, Azamgarh. | do. |
| 65 | „ | „ | Kashi Sujan Samaj. | Lala Durga Prasad. | Hindu Khettri. | Banker, Sidhesvari Mahalla, Benares. | At a General Meeting of the Sujan Samaj held on the 16th December, 1893. |
| 66 | „ | „ | „ | Munshi Sankatha Prasad. | do. | do. | do. |
| 67 | „ | „ | Mirzapur. | Babu Sriram. | do. | Pleader, Zemindar and Banker; Member, District and Municipal Boards. | At a Public Meeting held on the 21st December, 1893. |
| 68 | „ | „ | „ | Pundit Ram Prakash Sarma. | Hindu Brahmin. | Priest ... ... | do. |
| 69 | „ | „ | „ | Babu Beni Prasad. | Hindu Bhargava. | Zemindar, Merchant, Hony. Magistrate, Vice-President, Municipal Board and Member, District Board. | do. |
| 70 | „ | Allahabad. | Allahabad. | The Hon'ble Raja Rampai Singh. ... | Hindu Rajpoot | Talukdar, Vice-President, Pratapgarh District-Board and Member, Legislative Council, N. W. P. and Oudh. | At a Public Meeting held at the Kayastha Pathasala, Allahabad, on the 6th December, 1893. |
| 71 | „ | „ | „ | The Hon'ble Charoo Chundra Mittra. | Hindu Kayastha. | Zemindar, Municipal Commissioner and Member, Legislative Council N. W.P. and Oudh. | do. |
| 72 | „ | „ | „ | Dr. Abinash Chunder Banerjee, L.M.S. | Hindu Brahmin. | Medical Practitioner, Allahabad. | do. |
| 73 | „ | „ | „ | Pundit Madan Mohun Malavya, BA., LLB. | do. | Vakil, High Court, N.W.P. and Hony. Secretary, Standing Congress Committee, Allahabad. | do. |
| 74 | „ | „ | „ | „ Jwala Dutt Joshi. | do. | Vakil, High Court, N.W.P. Johnstonganj, Allahabad. | do. |
| 75 | „ | „ | „ | „ Sunder Lal, B.A. | do. | Vakil, High Court, N.W.P. Fellow of the University of Allahabad and Member of the Council of law Reporting, N.W.P. | do. |
| 76 | „ | „ | „ | „ Buldeo Ram Dave. | do. | Vakil, High Court, N.W.P. Allahabad. | do. |
| 77 | „ | „ | „ | Babu Durga Charan Banerjee, B.A. | do. | do. | do. |
| 78 | „ | „ | „ | Munshi Rashan Lal, B.A. | Arya Samajist. | Barrister-at-Law, Stanley Road, Allahabad. | do. |
| 79 | „ | „ | „ | Pundit Deoki Nandan Tewari. | Hindu Brahmin. | Editor and Proprietor "Rampataka" Ahiyapur, Allahabad. | do. |
| 80 | „ | „ | „ | „ Balkrishna Bhatta. | do. | Editor and Proprietor, "Hindi Pradip" | do. |

| Number. | Presidency or Government. | Congress Circle. | Electoral Division. | Names in full of Delegates, with Honorary Titles, Scholastic Degrees, etc. | Race, Religious denomination, and Caste, if any. | Occupation and Address. | How and when elected. |
|---|---|---|---|---|---|---|---|
| 81 | N.W.P. | Allahabad. | Allahabad. | Lala Brij Mohun Lal. | Hindu Khatri. | Zemindar and Banker, Allahabad. | At a Public Meeting held on the 16th December, 1893. |
| 82 | " | " | " | Swamy Alaram. | Sanyasi. | Ascetic, Hindu Sabha, Allahabad. | At a Meeting of the Hindu Sabha held on the 6th December, 1893. |
| 83 | " | " | Cawnpore. | Babu Ramsing Bhargava. | Hindu Bhargava. | Pleader and Municipal Commissioner, Cawnpore. | At a Public Meeting held at Cawnpore on the 17th December, 1893. |
| 84 | " | " | " | " Bunsidhur. | Arya Samajist. | Zemindar and Banker. | do. |
| 85 | " | " | " | " Madan Chand Khannah. | Hindu Khatri. | Merchant and Contractor. | do. |
| 86 | " | " | " | Pundit Bhaktanund Sarma. | Hindu Brahmin. | Priest and Journalist. | do. |
| 87 | " | " | " | Lala Govind Prasad Mirhotra. | Hindu Khatri | Merchant and Contractor. | do. |
| 88 | " | " | " | Bhai Hurnam Singh Varma. | do. | Proprietor, "Cawnpore Gazette," Late Govt. Military Sowar and now a Pensioner. | do. |
| 89 | " | " | " | Babu Ganga Dyal ... | Hindu Kayastha. | Pleader ... | do. |
| 90 | " | " | " | Lala Devi Dass ... | Hindu Khettri. | Merchant ... | do. |
| 91 | " | " | " | " Hukum Chand ... | Hindu Vaisya. | General Merchant and Banker. | do. |
| 92 | " | " | " | " Ram Swaroop ... | Hindu Agarwala. | Banker ... | do. |
| 93 | " | " | " | Pundit Prithvi Nath ... | Hindu Brahmin. | Pleader, Municipal Commissioner, Secretary, Divisional Congress Committee and Reform and Temperance Association. | do. |
| 94 | " | " | " | Lala Chandika Prasad. | Hindu Vaisya. | Merchant ... | do. |
| 95 | " | " | " | Babu Shew Narain ... | Arya Samajist. | Banker and Municipal Commissioner. | do. |
| 96 | " | " | " | " Mahendra Nath Ganguly. | Hindu Brahmin. | Medical Practitioner and Municipal Commissioner. | do. |
| 97 | " | " | " | Lala Santokh Chand Bhandari. | Jain. | Merchant and Banker ... | do. |
| 98 | " | " | " | Pundit Hirdey Narain Kaul. | Cashmere Brahmin. | Pleader, Zemindar, Merchant, Joint Secretary, Divisional Congress Committee and Reform and Temperance Association, Cawanpore. | do. |
| 99 | " | " | Agra. | Pundit Tulsi Ram Misra. M.A., M.B.S., F.T.S. | Hindu Brahmin. | Professor of Sanskrit and Philosophy, St. John's College, and Joint Secretary Divisional Congres Committee, Agra. | at a Public Meeting held at Agra on the 17th December, 1893. |

| Number. | Presidency or Government. | Congress Circle. | Electoral Division. | Names in full of Delegates, with Honorary Titles, Scholastic Degrees, etc. | Race, Religious denomination, and Caste, if any. | Occupation and Address. | How and when elected. |
|---|---|---|---|---|---|---|---|
| 100 | N.W.P. | Allahabad. | Agra. | Pundit Kampta Prasad. | Hindu Brahmin. | Rais and Pleader District Court, Agra. | At a Public Meeting held at Agra on the 17th December, 1893. |
| 101 | " | " | " | Babu Kedar Nath, B.A., B.L. | Hindu Vaisya. | Vakil, High Court and Law Lecturer, St. John's College, Agra and Secretary, Divisional Congress Committee. | do. |
| 102 | " | " | " | " Ram Chandra, B.A. | Hindu Vaisya. | Teacher, Agra College. | do. |
| 103 | " | " | " | " Beni Madhab Sirkir, M.A. | Hindu Kayastha. | Professor of Mathematics, St. John's College, Agra. | do. |
| 104 | " | " | " | Chowbey Chhakkan Lal. | Hindu Brahmin. | Pleader, District Court and Zemindar. | do. |
| 105 | " | " | " | Babu Jumna Das Biswas. | Hindu Kayastha. | Pleader and Editor, "Nassim" Agra. | do. |
| 106 | " | " | " | Pundit Mohun Kishen Dar. | Hindu Brahmin. | Rais and Manager, Stewart Tanning Factory, Agra. | do. |
| 107 | " | " | " | Babu Beni Kanta Dutt B.A. | Hindu Kayastha. | Professor, St. John's College, Agra. | do. |
| 108 | " | " | " | Babu Bireshwar Sanyal. | Hindu Brahmin. | Legal Practitioner, District Court, Agra. | do. |
| 109 | " | " | " | Pundit Jagannath ... | do. | Pleader, Zemindar and Vice-President, Divisional Congress Committee, Agra. | do. |
| 110 | " | " | " | M. Rahimuddin ... | Mahomedan. | Pleader, District Court, Agra. | do. |
| 111 | " | " | " | M. Rahim Buksh ... | do. | Rais and Mukhtear, Agra. | do. |
| 112 | " | " | " | Sheik Khwaj Buksh ... | do. | Rais, Agra ... | do. |
| 113 | " | " | Mainpuri. | Chowbey Dammi Lal B.A. | Hindu Brahmin. | Vakil, High Court, N. W. P. Practising at Mainpuri. | At a Public Meeting held at Mainpuri on the 22nd December, 1893. |
| 114 | " | " | Muttra. (Brindaban.) | Radha Churn Goswami Vidyavagisha. | do. | Priest, Radharaman Street, Brindaban. | At a Public Meeting held at Brindaban on the 22nd December, 1893. |
| 115 | " | " | " | Babu Baij Nath ... | Hindu Bhargava. | Zemindar and Indigo Merchant. | do. |
| 116 | " | " | " | " Jagannath Prasad. | do. | Rais, Zemindar, Pleader, and Municipal Commissioner Ghiamundi, Muttra. | do. |
| 117 | " | " | " | Kumar Hukum Singh ... | Arya, Jat. | Reosatdar, Zemindar and Member, Local Board, Po. Baldeo, District Muttra. | do. |
| 118 | " | " | " | Mani Lal Goswami ... | Hindu Brahmin. | Priest, Radharaman Street, Brindaban. | do. |
| 119 | " | " | Dehra Doon. | Pundit Braj Lall ... | Arya Brahmin. | Chemist ... | At a representativ Meeting held at Dehr Doon on the 20th December, 1893. |
| 120 | " | " | " | Pundit Anand Narain ... | Hindu Brahmin. | Landholder, Pleader and Municipal Commissioner. | do. |

| Number. | Presidency or Government. | Congress Circle. | Electoral Division. | Names in full of Delegates, with Honorary Titles, Scholastic Degrees, etc. | Race, Religious denomination, and Caste, if any. | Occupation and Address. | How and when elected. |
|---|---|---|---|---|---|---|---|
| 121 | N.W.P. | Allahabad. | Dehra Doon. | Lala Lachhmi Chand ... | Hindu Arya Mahajan. | Banker. ... | At a representative Meeting held at Dehra Doon on the 20th December, 1893. |
| 122 | " | " | Jhansi. | Babu Shiva Pada Ghose. | Hindu Kayastha. | Pleader ... | At a Public Meeting held at Jhansi on the 20th December, 1893. |
| 123 | " | " | " | " Prasanna Coomer Chatterji. | Hindu Brahmin. | do. ... | do. |
| 124 | " | " | " | Mr. Shunker Sahai Varma. | Arya Kayastha. | do. ... | do. |
| 125 | " | " | " | Babu Keshava Das Chowdhury, B.A. | Arya Vedic. | Pleader and Zêmindar ... | do. |
| 126 | " | " | " | Pundit Prag Das ... | Arya Brahmin. | Mukhtear and Zemindar. | do. |
| 127 | " | " | " | Babu Basanta Coomer Sanyal. | Hindu Brahmin. | Pleader ... | do. |
| 128 | " | " | Aligarh. | Hafeez Mahomed Abdur Rahim. | Sheikh Mahomedan. | Pleader and Zemindar ... | At a Public Meeting held at Aligarh on the 17th December, 1893. |
| 129 | " | " | " | Pundit Udai Ram ... | Hindu Brahmin. | Service, Karchuaganj, Aligarh. | do. |
| 130 | " | " | " | Babu Jogendra Nath Chatterji. | do. | Vakil ... | do. |
| 131 | " | " | " | Mahomed Zafar Yali Khan. | Mahomedan Pathan. | Pleader and Zemindar ... | do. |
| 132 | " | " | " | Mahomed Sarfaraz Khan. | do. | do. | do. |
| 133 | " | " | " | Syed Sarfaraz Ali ... | Mahomedan Syed. | do. | do. |
| 134 | " | " | " | Mahomed Shahbaz Khan. | Mahomedan Pathan. | Service ... | do. |
| 135 | " | " | Shaharanpur. | Pundit Mohun Lal ... | Hindu Brahmin. | Advocate, N. W. P. High Court. | At a Public Meeting held at Shaharanpur on the 22nd December, 1893. |
| 136 | " | " | " | Mr. Madan Mohun Lal, B.A., L.L.B. | Vaisya Agarwal. | Vakil, High Court, N.W.P. | do. |
| 137 | " | " | " | Lala Narain Das ... | Hindu. | Pleader ... | do. |
| 138 | " | " | " | Babu Jyoti Prasad ... | Hindu Bhargava. | Pleader, Shaharanpur ... | do. |
| 139 | " | " | " | Dr. Jnanendra Nath Roy Chowdhury. | Hindu. | Medical Practitioner ... | do. |
| 140 | " | " | " | Pundit Maharaj Narain. | Hindu Brahmin. | Pleader, High Court, Allahabad. | do. |
| 141 | " | " | " | Mr. Bulant Rai ... | Hindu Arya. | Pleader, Shaharanpur ... | do. |
| 142 | " | " | Meerut. | Babu Prahlad Singh ... | Hindu Vaisya. | Pleader, Zemindar and Municipal Commissioner. | At a Public Meeting held at Meerut on the 17th December, 1893. |
| 143 | " | " | " | Pundit Ram Prasad, M.A. | Hindu Kayastha. | Pleader, Meerut ... | do. |

| Number. | Presidency or Government. | Congress Circle. | Electoral Division. | Names in full of Delegates, with Honorary Titles, Scholastic Degrees, etc. | Race, Religious denomination, and Caste, if any. | Occupation and Address. | How and when elected. |
|---|---|---|---|---|---|---|---|
| 144 | N.W.P. | Allahabad. | Meerut. | Lala Babu Ram ... | Hindu Vaisya. | Pleader, Meerut ... | At a Public Meeting held at Meerut on the 17th December, 1893. |
| 145 | " | " | " | Babu Ghansham Dass ... | do. | do. ... | do. |
| 146 | " | " | " | Lala Babu Lal, B.A. ... | do. | do. ... | do. |
| 147 | " | " | " | Babu Kishen Dyal ... | do. | do. ... | do. |
| 148 | " | " | " | Chowbey Radhe Lal ... | Hindu Brahmin. | do. ... | do. |
| 149 | " | " | " | Babu Raghubir Sarun ... | Hindu Vaisya. | Rais, Pleader and Municipal Commissioner. | do. |
| 150 | " | " | " | " Dungar Mal ... | Hindu Khettri. | Vakil, Notary Public and Landholder, Meerut. | do. |
| 151 | " | " | Farrukhabad. | Pundit Gopal Rao Hari Bakhashi | Maharashtri Brahmin. | Late Educational Sub-Deputy Inspector and Secretary, Vaidic Samaj and Divisional Congress Committee. | At a Public Meeting held on the 3rd December, 1893. |
| 152 | " | " | " | Lala Durga Prasad ... | Hindu Khettri. | Merchant and Member, Local Board. | do. |
| 153 | " | " | Shajehanpur. | Munshi Bhaktawar Singh. | Arya Agarwal. | Editor & Proprietor of the "Arya Darpan" a Hindi and Urdu monthly. | At a Public Meeting held at Shajehanpur on the 22nd December, 1893. |
| 154 | " | " | " | Babu Kalka Prasad, B.A. | Hindu Kayastha. | Pleader ... | do. |
| 155 | " | " | Moradabad. | Sheikh Wahab Uddin ... | Mahomedan. | Pleader and Zemindar, Moradabad. | At a Public Meeting held at Moradabad on the 19th December, 1893. |
| 156 | " | " | " | Babu Madan Mohun Das. | Hindu Vaisya. | Pleader ... | do. |
| 157 | " | " | " | Mr. Brij Nandan Prasad, M.A., L.L.B. | Hindu Khettri. | Vakil and Zemindar ... | do. |
| 158 | " | " | " | Pundit Bishwambhar Nath Aga. | Hindu Brahmin. | Zemindar ... | do. |
| 159 | " | " | " | Babu Narendra Chunder Bose. | Hindu Kayastha. | Pleader, Moradabad ... | do. |
| 160 | " | " | " | Pundit Avatar Krishna Aga. | Hindu Brahmin. | Proprietor, of "Najmul Hind" Urdu Newspaper. | do. |
| 161 | " | " | " | Puadit Bishwambhar Nath. | do. | Landholder ... | At a Public Meeting held at Moradabad on the 21st December, 1893. |
| 162 | " | " | " | Babu Brijnath ... | Hindu Vaisya. | Service ... | At a Public Meeting held at Moradabad on the 23rd December, 1893. |
| 163 | " | " | " | Pundit Hari Har Nath. | Hindu Brahmin. | Wasigdar, C/o Mr. Brij Nandan Prasad, Vakil. | do. |
| 164 | " | " | " | Lala Damodar Das ... | Hindu Vaish. | Merchant and Banker ... | do. |
| 165 | " | " | " | Babu Sunder Lal ... | do. | Pleader, District Court. | do. |
| 166 | " | " | Bulandshahar. | Lala Bishen Lal ... | Hindu Bania. | Zemindar ... | At a General Meeting held on the 24th December, 1893. |
| 167 | " | " | " | " Kanahya Lal ... | do. | do. ... | do. |

| Number. | Presidency or Government. | Congress Circle. | Electoral Division. | Names in full of Delegates, with Honorary Titles, Scholastic Degrees, etc. | Race, Religious denomination, and Caste, if any. | Occupation and Address. | How and when elected. |
|---|---|---|---|---|---|---|---|
| 168 | N.W.P. | Allahabad. | Barielly. | Babu Ram Swarup, B.A., L.L.B. | Hindu Khettri. | Vakil, Barielly. ... | At a Meeting of the Vakil's Association held on the 23rd December 1893. |
| 169 | " | " | Gorakhpur. | Mr. Alfred Nundy ... | Bengali Christian. | Barrister-at-Law ... | At a Public Meeting held at Gorakhpur on the 23rd December, 1893. |
| 170 | " | " | Azamgarh. | Munshi Vasudeo Shahai. | Hindu Kayastha. | Teacher, C. M. High School, Azamgarh. | At a Public Meeting held on the 19th December 1893. |
| 171 | Oudh. | Lucknow. | Lucknow. | Pundit Lakshman Prasad. | Brahmo. | Brahmo Missionary ... | At a Public Meeting held at Lucknow on the 22nd December, 1893. |
| 172 | " | " | " | Swami Brahmanund Sarasvati. | Arya Sanyasi. | Missionary ... | do. |
| 173 | " | " | " | Babu Bansi Lal Singh ... | Hindu. | Vakil and Zemindar ... | do. |
| 174 | " | " | " | " Kedar Nath ... | Hindu Khatri. | Vakil and Municipal Commissioner. | do. |
| 175 | " | " | " | Munshi Gunga Prasad Varma. | do. | Editor and Proprietor of the "Advocate" and the "Hindustani" and Municipal Commissioner. | do. |
| 176 | " | " | " | Pundit Ikbal Shunker Kachak. | Hindu. | Pleader, Lucknow ... | do. |
| 177 | " | " | " | Pundit Juggat Narain ... | do. | Vakil, Lucknow ... | do. |
| 178 | " | " | " | Seth Sitaram ... | Hindu Khatri. | Merchant ... | do. |
| 179 | " | " | " | Mr. Mahomed Nasim ... | Mahomedan. | Vakil ... | do. |
| 180 | " | " | " | Babu Khetra Nath Mookerjee. | Hindu Brahmin. | Agriculturist ... | do. |
| 181 | " | " | " | Mr. Hamid Ali Khan ... | Mahomedan. | Barrister-at-Law, Muffidar and Municipal Commissioner. | do. |
| 182 | " | " | " | Rai Pitam Singh ... | Hindu. | Zemindar ... | do. |
| 183 | " | " | " | Pundit Sham Narain Masuldan. | Hindu Brahmin. | Zemindar and Municipal Commissioner. | do. |
| 184 | " | " | " | Pundit Bishen Narain Dar. | do. | Barrister-at-Law. ... | do. |
| 185 | " | " | " | Babu Bhuban Mohun Roy. | Brahmo. | Trader ... | do. |
| 186 | " | " | Fyzabad. | Babu Charu Chunder Ghose. | Hindu Kayastha. | Medical Practitioner ... | At a Public Meeting held at Fyzabad on the 17th December, 1893. |
| 187 | " | " | " | Pundit Radha Kishen ... | Cashmiri Brahmin. | Vakil and Zemindar ... | do. |
| 188 | " | " | " | Babu Gokul Chand ... | Hindu Khettri. | Vakil, Zemindar, Hony. Magistrate, Chairman, Municipal Board and Vice-Chairman, District Board, Fyzabad. | do. |
| 189 | " | " | Pertabgarh. | " Ram Chandra, M.A. | Hindu Kayastha. | Vakil ... ... | At a Public Meeting held at Pertabgarh on the 14th December, 1893. |

| Number. | Presidency or Government. | Congress Circle. | Electoral Division. | Names in full of Delegates, with Honorary Titles, Scholastic Degrees, etc. | Race, Religious denomination, and Caste, if any. | Occupation and Address. | How and when elected. |
|---|---|---|---|---|---|---|---|
| 190 | Oudh. | Lucknow. | Pertabgarh. | Mr. Mir Ali Sha ... | Mahomedan, Syed. | Zemindar ... ... | At a Public Meeting held at Pertabgarh on the 14th December, 1893. |
| 191 | " | " | Kala Kankar. | Pundit Deo Datta Sarma. | Hindu Brahmin. | Private Service ... | At a Public Meeting held at Kala Kankar on the 18th December, 1893. |
| 192 | " | " | " | " Mahadeo Prasad Upadhya. | do. | Zemindar ... ... | do. |
| 193 | Punjab. | Delhi. | Delhi. | Abul Al Monsur ... | Mahomedan. | Merchant, Delhi ... | By a Public Meeting held at Delhi on the 16th December, 1893. |
| 194 | " | " | " | Nisar Hussain ... | do. | do. | do. |
| 195 | " | " | " | Lala Sanwal Das ... | Hindu Vaisya. | do. | do. |
| 196 | " | " | " | " Ganeshi La ... | Hindu Khettri. | Merchant, Chandney Chauk, Delhi. | do. |
| 197 | " | " | " | " Madhow Prasad ... | Hindu | Merchant, Banker and Landholder, Allahabad. | do. |
| 198 | " | " | " | Babu Kedar Nath ... | Hindu Vaisya. | Pleader ... | do. |
| 199 | " | " | " | Mr. Raghunath Das Gorga. | do. | Barrister-at-law, Delhi. | do. |
| 200 | " | " | " | Lala Girdhari Lal ... | Hindu Vaisya. | Pleader and Municipal Commissioner, Delhi. | At a Public Meeting held on the 17th December, 1893. |
| 201 | " | " | " | " Jugal Kishore ... | Hindu Kayastha. | Pleader ... | do. |
| 202 | " | " | " | " Shadi Ram ... | Oswal Jain. | Merchant and Jeweller. | do. |
| 203 | " | " | " | " Gokul Chand ... | do. | do. | do. |
| 204 | " | " | " | Babu Pyari Lal ... | Hindu Jain. | Pleader, Delhi ... | do. |
| 205 | " | " | " | Lala Bunsidhur Seth ... | Hindu Khettri. | Merchant ... | do. |
| 206 | " | " | " | " Banarasi Das ... | Hindu Vaisya. | Private Service, Chooriwalla Mahalla, Delhi. | do. |
| 207 | " | " | " | " Bunsidhur ... | Arya Khettri. | Banker and Commission Agent. | do. |
| 208 | " | " | " | Sirdir Ram Singh ... | Sikh. | Rais, Delhi | do. |
| 209 | " | " | " | Lala Ram Chand ... | Arya Vaisya. | Banker, Merchant and Commission Agent, Mori Gate, Delhi. | do. |
| 210 | " | " | " | " Gokul Chand, B.A. | Hindu Arya-Khettri. | Merchant and Banker, Nil-Ka-Katri, Delhi. | do. |
| 211 | " | " | " | " Bhajan Lal ... | Hindu Khettri. | Banker, Daruba Bazar, Amarki Gate, Delhi. | do. |
| 212 | " | " | " | " Sanwal Das ... | do. | Banker and Landholder. | do. |
| 213 | " | " | " | " Sunder Lal Khanna. | do. | General Merchant and Commission Agent. | do. |
| 214 | " | " | " | " Sultan Singh ... | Hindu Jain. | Banker and Landowner. | do. |

| Number. | Presidency or Government. | Congress Circle. | Electoral Division. | Names in full of Delegates, with Honorary Titles, Scholastic Degrees, etc. | Race, Religious denomination, and Caste, if any. | Occupation and Address. | How and when elected. |
|---|---|---|---|---|---|---|---|
| 215 | Punjab. | Delhi. | Delhi. | Lala Gur Sahayak ... | Hindu. | Government Pensioner. | At a Public Meeting held on the 17th December, 1893. |
| 216 | „ | „ | „ | „ Balmukund ... | Hindu Khettri. | Merchant ... | do. |
| 217 | „ | „ | „ | „ Brindaban ... | do. | do. ... | do. |
| 218 | „ | „ | „ | „ Gridhari Lal ... | do. | Pleader, Chief Court, Lahore. | do. |
| 219 | „ | „ | „ | „ Lal Chand ... | do. | Cloth Merchant, Daruba Bazar Gali. | do. |
| 220 | „ | „ | Industrial and Commercial association of Upper India, Delh | Babu Puran Chand ... | Hindu. | Merchant ... | At a Public Meeting held on the 22nd December, 1893. |
| 221 | „ | „ | „ | „ Raj Rajeshwar Mukerjee. | Hindu Brahmin. | do. ... | do. |
| 222 | „ | Lahore. | Lahore. | Lala Sarab Dyal ... | Hindu Khettri. | Government Pensioner. | At a Public Meeting held at Lahore on the 10th December, 1893. |
| 223 | „ | „ | „ | „ Naranjan Das ... | Hindu Agarwal. | Pleader, Chief Court, Lahore. | do. |
| 224 | „ | „ | „ | „ Bhagwan Das ... | Hindu Khettri. | do. | do. |
| 225 | „ | „ | „ | „ Saligram ... | Hindu Arora. | Proprietor, "Aror Bans" Press, Lahore. | do. |
| 226 | „ | „ | „ | „ Prabhu Dyal, B.A., L.L.B. | Hindu. | Pleader, Lahore. ... | do. |
| 227 | „ | „ | „ | Mr. E. C. Jassawala ... | Parsi. | Merchant and House-Proprietor, "Rose Cottage," Lahore. | do. |
| 228 | „ | „ | „ | Lala Har Kishen Lal, B.A. | Hindu Arora. | Barrister-at-Law, Chief Court, Lahore. | do. |
| 229 | „ | „ | „ | „ Gopal Das ... | Hindu Khettri. | Cloth Merchant, Lahore. | do. |
| 230 | „ | „ | „ | Dr. Jai Singh, L.M.S. ... | Sikh. | Medical Practitioner, Lahore. | do. |
| 231 | „ | „ | „ | Babu Jogendra Chunder Bose, M.A., B.L. | Hindu Kayastha. | Pleader, Chief Court, Lahore. | do. |
| 232 | „ | „ | „ | Lala Madan Gopal, M.A. | Hindu Khettri. | Barrister-at-Law, Lahore. | do. |
| 233 | „ | „ | „ | „ Ishwar Das, M.A. ... | Hindu. | Pleader, Chief Court, Lahore. | do. |
| 234 | „ | „ | „ | „ Beni Prasad ... | Hindu Khettri. | Retired Sub-Engineer, P. W. D. Lahore. | do. |
| 235 | „ | „ | „ | „ Dhanpat Rai, B.A., L.L.B. | do. | Pleader, Chief Court, Lahore. | do. |
| 236 | „ | „ | „ | Rai Bahadur Babu Mall. | Hindu Kayastha. | Government Pensioner. | do. |
| 237 | „ | „ | „ | Lala Lajpat Rai ... | Hindu Agarwal. | Pleader, Chief Court, Lahore. | do. |
| 238 | „ | , | „ | Bhai Sorchal Singh ... | Sikh. | House Proprietor ... | do. |

| Number. | Presidency or Government. | Congress Circle. | Electoral Division. | Names in full of Delegates, with Honorary Titles, Scholastic Degrees, etc. | Race, Religious denomination, and Caste, if any. | Occupation and Address. | How and when elected. |
|---|---|---|---|---|---|---|---|
| 239 | Punjab. | Lahore. | Lahore. | Sirdir Mehr Sing Chowala. | Sikh. | Merchant ... | At a Public Meeting held at Lahore on the 10th December, 1893. |
| 240 | " | " | " | Sheikh Ata Mahomed ... | Mahomedan. | Private Service ... | do. |
| 241 | " | " | " | Lala Kahin Chand ... | Hindu Khettri. | do. ... | do. |
| 242 | " | " | " | " Bulakiram Shastri. | Hindu Chopra. | Barrister-at-Law, Chief Court, Lahore. | do. |
| 243 | " | " | " | Bakshi Jaishi Ram ... | Hindu Mahajan. | Pleader, Lahore. ... | do. |
| 244 | " | " | " | Babu Amrita Lal Rai, B.A., B.L. | Hindu Brahmin. | do. ... | do. |
| 245 | " | " | " | Munshi Khairuddin ... | Mahomedan. | Zemindar ... | do. |
| 246 | " | " | " | Dewan Maya Das ... | Hindu Khettri. | Mukhtear ... | do. |
| 247 | " | " | " | Lala Lal Chand, M.A. ... | Arya. | Pleader, Chief Court, Lahore. | do. |
| 248 | " | " | " | Dr. Thakur Das ... | Hindu Khettri. | Viceroy's Chemist, Lahore and Simla. | do. |
| 249 | " | " | " | Lala Nehal Chand ... | Hindu. | Contractor ... | do. |
| 250 | " | " | " | " Barkat Ram ... | do. | do. ... | do. |
| 251 | " | " | " | Bhai Pertap Singh ... | Sikh. | do. ... | do. |
| 252 | " | " | " | Lala Beli Ram ... | Hindu. | do. ... | do. |
| 253 | " | " | " | " Sadanand ... | Hindu Arora. | General Merchant ... | do. |
| 254 | " | " | " | Munshi Shams-Ud-Din S. Shaiq. | Mahomedan. | Proprietor, "Shams Hind" Press, Lahore. | do. |
| 255 | " | " | " | Pundit Gopi Nath ... | Hindu Brahmin. | Secretary, "Sanatan Dharma Sabha," Lahore. | do. |
| 256 | " | " | " | Mr. B. B. Ghose ... | Hindu Kayastha. | Merchant and Proprietor, Empress Medical Hall, Lahore. | do. |
| 257 | " | " | " | Sirdir Dayal Singh Majithia. | Sikh. | Jagirdar ... | do. |
| 258 | " | " | " | Moulvie Haji Ahmed Sahib. | Mahomedan. | Hakim-i-Haziq ... | do. |
| 259 | " | " | " | Lala Tara Chand Sahib. | Hindu. | Rais, Lahore ... | do. |
| 260 | " | " | " | Mr. Feroz Din ... | Mahomedan. | Draftsman ... | do. |
| 261 | " | " | " | Lala Maya Das ... | Hindu. | Private Service ... | do. |
| 262 | " | " | " | Pundit Mankameshwar Nath. | do. | Rais, Lahore ... | do. |
| 263 | " | " | " | Mirza Aziz Beg ... | Mahomedan. | Hakim ... | do. |
| 264 | " | " | " | Munshi Nabi Buksh Khan. | do. | Editor, "Koh-i-noor" Lahore. | do. |
| 265 | " | " | " | Moulvie Amir Buksh Sahib. | do. | Imam ... | do. |

| | Presidency or Government. | Congress Circle. | Electoral Division. | Names in full of Delegates, with Honorary Titles, Scholastic Degrees, etc. | Race, Religious denomination, and Caste, if any. | Occupation and Address. | How and when elected. |
|---|---|---|---|---|---|---|---|
| 266 | Punjab. | Lahore. | Lahore. | Moulvie Mohurrem Ali Chisti. | Mahomedan. | Editor and Proprietor, "Rafiq-Hind" Lahore. | At a Public Meeting held at Lahore on the 10th December, 1893. |
| 267 | " | " | " | Mir Nisar Ali Shohrat. | do. | Journalist ... | do. |
| 268 | " | " | " | Syed Nazir Hussain Nazim. | do. | Poet, Lahore ... | do. |
| 269 | " | " | " | Mirza Golam Mahomed Sahib. | do. | Landholder ... | do. |
| 270 | " | " | " | Chowdhury Khoda Bux Sahib. | do. | Zemindar ... | do. |
| 271 | " | " | " | Moulvie Seraj-ud-Din ... | do. | Imam, Chauhatta Musjid, Lahore. | do. |
| 272 | " | " | " | " Waliulla ... | do. | Proprietor, "Siddiqi Press" Lahore. | do. |
| 273 | " | " | " | Munshi Golam Mahomed | do. | Rais ... | do. |
| 274 | " | " | " | Mian Serajuddin ... | do. | Merchant ... | do. |
| 275 | " | " | " | Lala Dharam Das Suri. | Hindu Khettri. | Vakil, High Court, Allahabad. | do. |
| 276 | " | " | " | Babu Harish Chandra ... | Hindu Brahmin | Contractor ... | do. |
| 277 | " | " | " | " Ram Krishna ... | Hindu Arora. | Merchant ... | do. |
| 278 | " | " | " | Lala Ganpat Rai ... | do. | Barrister-at-Law, Chief Court, Lahore. | do. |
| 279 | " | " | " | " Shib Das ... | Hindu Khettri | Pleader ... | do. |
| 280 | " | " | " | Mr. Charles Goloknath, B.A., L.L.B. | Christian. | Barrister-at-Law, Lahore. | do. |
| 281 | " | " | " | Lala Ram Das ... | Hindu Khettri. | Cloth Merchant, Dabi Bazar, Lahore. | do. |
| 282 | " | " | " | Bawa Surmukh Das ... | Sadhu. | Hindu Missionary ... | do. |
| 283 | " | " | " | Rai Bahadur Protul Chunder Chatterjee, M.A., B.L. | Hindu Brahmin. | Pleader, Chief Court, Lahore and Fellow of the Punjab University. | do. |
| 284 | " | " | " | Lala Ram Chand Manoktele. | Hindu Arora. | Proprietor, "Anglo-Sanskrit Press," Lahore. | do. |
| 285 | " | " | " | Lala Roshan Lal ... | Hindu Kayastha. | Pleader, Lahore ... | do. |
| 286 | " | " | " | " Ram Chand ... | Hindu Agarwal. | Manager, "Tribune," Lahore. | do. |
| 287 | " | " | " | " Hira Lal ... | Hindu Khettri. | Proprietor, "Ærated water Manufactory," Anarkali, Lahore. | do. |
| 288 | " | " | " | " Palaram Khannah. | do. | Proprietor "Khannah Brothers, Tailoring Company," Lahori-Gate, Lahore. | do. |
| 289 | " | " | " | Mr. Nogendra Nath Gupta. | Hindu Vaidya. | Editor, "Tribune," Lahore. | do. |
| 290 | " | " | " | Syed Safdar Ali ... | Mahomedan. | Munshi ... | do. |
| 291 | " | " | " | Munshi Kurim Buksh Khakar. | do. | do. ... | do. |

| Number. | Presidency or Government. | Congress Circle. | Electoral Division. | Names in full of Delegates, with Honorary Titles, Scholastic Degrees, etc. | Race, Religious denomination, and Caste, if any. | Occupation and Address. | How and when elected. |
|---|---|---|---|---|---|---|---|
| 292 | Punjab. | Lahore. | Lahore. | Moulvie Kutub-ud-Din. | Mahomedan. | Late of Settlement Office and at present Private service. | At a Public meeting held at Lahore on the 10th December, 1893. |
| 293 | " | " | " | Lala Lajpat Rai ... | Hindu Khettri. | Physician ... | do. |
| 294 | " | " | " | " Kashi Nath Mehra. | do. | Proprietor, "Gold & Silver Manufactory," Lahore. | do. |
| 295 | " | " | " | " Manohur Lal ... | do. | Banker and Contractor. | do. |
| 296 | " | " | " | " Daya Ram ... | Hindu Arora. | Editor, "Aror Bans Prokash," Lahore. | do. |
| 297 | " | " | " | Babu Sarat Chandra Mukerjee, M.A. | Hindu Brahmin. | Professor, D.A.V. College, Lahore. | do. |
| 298 | " | " | " | Lala Balmkund ... | Hindu Khettri. | Banker, Landowner and Merchant. | do. |
| 299 | " | " | " | Seth Ram Dass ... | Hindu. | Contractor ... | do. |
| 300 | " | " | " | Lala Govind Ram ... | Hindu Khettri. | Pleader, Chief Court, Lahore. | do. |
| 301 | " | " | " | Mr. M. C. Mukerji ... | Bengali Christian. | Professor, Mission College, Lahore. | do. |
| 302 | " | " | " | Dr. Parmanand ... | Arya Khettri. | Surgeon and Dentist ... | do. |
| 303 | " | " | " | Lala Khem Chand ... | Hindu Bhatiya. | Druggist ... | do. |
| 304 | " | " | " | Mr. K. P. Roy, M.A., B.L. | Hindu Brahmin. | Pleader, Chief Court, Lahore. | do. |
| 305 | " | " | " | Babu Bama Pada Roy ... | do. | Rais ... | do. |
| 306 | " | " | " | " Shama Pada Roy ... | do. | do. ... | do. |
| 307 | " | " | " | " Megh Nath Banerjee. | do. | do. ... | do. |
| 308 | " | " | " | " Jai Gopal Sahib ... | Hindu. | Editor, Atab-i-Punjab ... | do. |
| 309 | " | " | " | Lala Hira Lal Kapur ... | do. | Proprietor, "Khettri Samachar." | do. |
| 310 | " | " | " | Sirdir Guru Charan Sing, B.A., L.L.B. | Hindu Sikh. | Barrister-at-Law, Lahore. | do. |
| 311 | " | " | " | Pundit Sham Lal, M.R.A.S. | Hindu. | do. | do. |
| 312 | " | " | " | Lala Nursing Das ... | Hindu Khettri. | Banker ... | do. |
| 313 | " | " | " | " Sangam Lal ... | Hindu. | Pleader, Chief Court, Lahore. | do. |
| 314 | " | " | " | Babu Hari Ram Sahokar. | Hindu Arora. | Banker ... | do. |
| 315 | " | " | " | Lala Amir Chand ... | Hindu. | Contractor ... | At a Public Meeting held at Lahore on the 24th December, 1893. |
| 316 | " | " | " | " Shankar Das ... | Hindu Khettri. | General Contractor, Lakkar Mandi, Wadda Werra, Lahore. | do. |
| 317 | " | " | " | Mian Abdul Karim ... | Mahomedan Pathan. | General Contractor, Campbellpur, District Rowalpindi. | do. |

| Number. | Presidency or Government. | Congress Circle. | Electoral Division. | Names in full of Delegates, with Honorary Titles, Scholastic Degrees, etc. | Race, Religious denomination, and Caste, if any. | Occupation and Address. | How and when elected. |
|---|---|---|---|---|---|---|---|
| 318 | Punjab. | Lahore. | Lahore. | Syed Mahomed Shah ... | Mahomedan, Syed. | General Contractor, Campbellpur, District Rowalpindi. | At a Public Meeting held at Lahore on the 4th December, 1893. |
| 319 | " | " | " | Pundit Ichra Chand ... | Hindu Brahmin. | Mukhtear ... | do. |
| 320 | " | " | " | Lala Ram Dyal ... | Hindu Khettri. | Banker ... | do. |
| 321 | " | " | " | " Gobardhan Das ... | Hindu Bania. | do. ... | do. |
| 322 | " | " | " | Munshi Imamdin ... | Mahomedan. | Zemindar ... | do. |
| 323 | " | " | " | Lala Ganda Mal ... | Hindu Khettri. | Pensioner ... | do. |
| 324 | " | " | " | Munshi Fukhiruddin ... | Mahomedan. | Draftsman ... | do. |
| 325 | " | " | " | Lala Hakim Rai ... | Hindu Khettr | Merchant ... | do. |
| 326 | " | " | " | " Dewan Chand ... | do. | Cloth Merchant, Anarkali, Lahore. | do. |
| 327 | " | " | " | Sheikh Amiruddin ... | Mahomedan. | Mukhtear ... | do. |
| 328 | " | " | " | Mian Mahomed Koushauddin. | do. | Bookseller ... | do. |
| 329 | " | " | " | Mirza Golam Hussain ... | do. | Contractor ... | do. |
| 330 | " | " | " | Moulvie Ferozuddin ... | do. | Zemindar ... | do. |
| 331 | " | " | " | Mahomed Abdulla ... | do. | do. ... | do. |
| 332 | " | " | " | Munshi Serajuddin ... | do. | Khashnavis ... | do. |
| 333 | " | " | " | Sheikh Fateh Mahomed. | do. | Merchant ... | do. |
| 334 | " | " | " | Mian Fazaldin ... | do. | do. ... | do. |
| 335 | " | " | " | Munshi Ali Buksh ... | do. | Proprietor of a Tailor Shop. | do. |
| 336 | " | " | " | Mian Hakimdin ... | do. | Merchant ... | do. |
| 337 | " | " | " | Hakim Mahomed Sherif. | do. | Medical Practitioner ... | do. |
| 338 | " | " | " | Lala Kaushi Ram ... | Hindu Khettri. | Shawl Merchant ... | do. |
| 339 | " | " | " | Mr. Beheman H. Khurshed. | Parsi. | Late Manager of Messrs Jahangir and Co., Lahore. | do. |
| 340 | " | " | " | Munshi Wali Mahomed. | Mahomedan. | Preacher ... | do. |
| 341 | " | " | " | Mr. Nagina Singh, B.A. | Sikh. | Tutor ... | do. |
| 342 | " | " | " | Lala Harbhagwan Das. | Hindu Khettri. | Mukhtear ... | do. |
| 343 | " | " | " | Syed Abdulla Shah ... | Mahomedan. | Zemindar ... | do. |
| 344 | " | " | " | Dave Lachman Das Nagar. | Nagar Brahmin. | Rais and Zemindar, Mouza Thakoordwar, District Moradabad. | At a Meeting of the Nagar Brahmins at Lahore on the 25th December, 1893. |

| Number. | Presidency or Government. | Congress Circle. | Electoral Division. | Names in full of Delegates, with Honorary Titles, Scholastic Degrees, etc. | Race, Religious denomination, and Caste, if any. | Occupation and Address. | How and when elected. |
|---|---|---|---|---|---|---|---|
| 345 | Punjab. | Lahore. | Lahore. | Lala Nand Lal ... | Hindu. | Merchant ... | At a Public Meeting held at Lahore on the 26th December, 1893. |
| 346 | " | " | " | Pundit Basant Lal ... | Hindu Brahmin. | Pleader ... | do. |
| 347 | " | " | " | Babu Hari Krishna ... | Hindu. | Merchant ... | do. |
| 348 | " | " | " | Hazi Ahmed ... | Mahomedan. | Hakim ... | do. |
| 349 | " | " | " | Sirdir Anand Singh ... | Sikh. | Contractor ... | do. |
| 350 | " | " | " | Mr. M. E. Jassawalla ... | Parsee. | Merchant ... | do. |
| 351 | " | " | " | Lala Beni Prasad B. A. | Hindu Khettri. | Pleader ... | do. |
| 352 | " | " | " | " Jowala Prasad ... | Hindu Kayastha. | Mukhtear ... | do. |
| 353 | " | " | " | Sirdir Maya Sing Ahluwalya. | Sikh. | Professor ... | do. |
| 354 | " | " | " | Lala Totaram ... | Hindu Khettri. | Landholder ... | do. |
| 355 | " | " | Mooltan. | Mr. Ganesh Das ... | Hindu Arora. | Contractor, Mooltan ... | At a Public Meeting of the Residents of Mooltan held on the 18th December, 1893. |
| 356 | " | " | " | Pundit Ram Bowa Sarma. | Hindu Brahmin. | Purohit and Pundit ... | do. |
| 357 | " | " | " | Swami Brahmanundji ... | Hindu Mohunt. | President, "Dharma Sabha" Mooltan. | do. |
| 358 | " | " | " | Chaudhury Kriparam ... | Hindu Arora. | Halwai, Mar Subzi Mundi, Lahore. | do. |
| 359 | " | " | " | Pundit Thakurdat Sarma. | Hindu Brahmin. | Priest, Astrologer and Municipal Commissioner. | do. |
| 360 | " | " | " | Lala Chetan Anand, B. A. | Hindu Arora. | Pleader and Municipal Commissioner, Mooltan. | do. |
| 361 | " | " | " | " Ishwar Das B. A. ... | do. | Mukhtear, Mooltan ... | do. |
| 362 | " | " | " | Mr. Rustomji Dadabhai. | Parsee. | Merchant ... | do. |
| 363 | " | " | " | Lala Parmanand ... | Arya Arora. | Pleader, Mooltan ... | do. |
| 364 | " | " | " | Babu Mohendra Nath Banerjee B. A., B. L. | Hindu Brahmin. | do. do. ... | do. |
| 365 | " | " | " | Lala Vir Bhan ... | Hindu. | Pensioner and Secretary, "Sonatan Dharma Sabha" Mooltan. | do. |
| 366 | " | " | " | Mr. Praduman Singh ... | Hindu Sikh. | Pleader, Mooltan ... | do. |
| 367 | " | " | " | Lala Kishen Chand ... | Hindu. | Shopkeeper ... | At a Public Meeting held at Mooltan on the 22nd December, 1893. |
| 368 | " | " | " | " Hotoo Ram ... | do. | Contractor, Mooltan ... | do. |
| 369 | " | " | Abotabad. | Chowdhuri Thakur Das | Arya Khettri. | Shopkeeper, Abotabad, Hazara. | At a Public Meeting held at Abotabad on the 8th December, 1893. |

| Number. | Presidency or Government. | Congress Circle. | Electoral Division. | Names in full of Delegates, with Honorary Titles, Scholastic Degrees, etc. | Race, Religious denomination, and Caste, if any. | Occupation and Address. | How and when elected. |
|---|---|---|---|---|---|---|---|
| 370 | Punjab. | Lahore. | Abotabad. | Lala Dhani Ram ... | Vedic Khettri. | Merchant, Abotabad, Hazara. | At a Public Meeting held at Abotabad on the 8th December, 1893. |
| 371 | " | " | " | " Uttam Chand ... | Hindu Khettri. | Abotabad, Hazara ... | do. |
| 372 | " | " | " | Bukshi Bishen Dass F.T. | Vedic Muhyal. | Head Master, "Albert Victor Anglo-Sanskrit School, Abotabad. | do. |
| 373 | " | " | " | Lala Nathu Ram ... | Hindu Khettri. | Mookhtari Adalot, Abotabad, Hazara. | do. |
| 374 | " | " | Jhelum. | " Harbhagwan Das, L. L. | Hindu Arya Khettri. | Pleader, Jhelum ... | By a Public Meeting held at Jhelum on the 21st December, 1893. |
| 375 | " | " | " | Mr. Bishen Das ... | Hindu Arya. | Mukhtear and Member, Municipal Board, Jhelum. | do. |
| 376 | " | " | " | Lala Fateh Chand ... | Hindu Ubrai Khettri. | Pleader, Jhelum ... | do. |
| 377 | " | " | Pind Dadan Khan. | Mr. Ram Saran ... | Hindu Brahmin. | Mukhtear ... | Elected by the people of the place on the 24th December, 1893. |
| 378 | " | " | Ludhiana. | Lala Labhoo Ram Nagar | Arya Khettri. | Sugar Merchant and Assistant Secretary, Arya Samaj and Temperance Society, Ludhiana. | By a Public Meeting held at Ludhiana on the 8th December, 1893. |
| 379 | " | " | " | " Sanwan Mall Sahib | Hindu Khettri. | Trader and Landowner | do. |
| 380 | " | " | " | " Shib Dyal ... | do. | do. ... | do. |
| 381 | " | " | " | " Chint Ram Mohindar. | Arya Sudra. | Cloth Merchant ... | do. |
| 382 | " | " | " | " Mansa Ram ... | Arya Bania Agarwal. | Pleader and Member, "Theosophical Society," Ludhiana. | do. |
| 383 | " | " | " | " Kishori Lal | Hindu Khettri. | Banker and Proprietor of the Firm of Messrs Banka Rai Chandoo Lal and K. L. M. Rai Company, Ludhiana. | do. |
| 384 | " | " | " | " Nathu Mall ... | do. | Pensioner, Rahoon, District Jullunder. | do. |
| 385 | " | " | " | " Khusi Ram ... | Hindu Bhabru. | Pansari (Drug Seller) ... | do. |
| 386 | " | " | " | Babu Ram Nath ... | Hindu Khettri. | Proprietor of the Firm of Messrs R. N. Choopra Brothers, Ludhiana. | do. |
| 387 | " | " | " | Lala Umrao Singh ... | Arya Khettri. | Banker, Landholder and Secretary, Arya Samaj and Temperance Society, Ludhiana. | do. |
| 388 | " | " | " | Mian Abdul Guffar Khan | Mahomedan Pathan. | General Army Contractor and Proprietor, Punjab Manufacturing Co., Ludhiana. | do. |
| 389 | " | " | " | Lala Ram Rattan ... | Hindu Bania Agarwal. | Pleader and Vice-President, Arya Samaj, Ludhiana. | do. |

| Number. | Presidency or Government. | Congress Circle. | Electoral Division. | Names in full of Delegates, with Honorary Titles, Scholastic Degrees, etc. | Race, Religious denomination, and Caste, if any. | Occupation and Address. | How and when elected. |
|---|---|---|---|---|---|---|---|
| 390 | Punjab. | Lahore. | Ludhiana. | Lala Gopi Mall ... | Hindu Khettri. | Merchant ... | By a Public Meeting held at Ludhiana on the 8th December, 1893. |
| 391 | " | " | " | Babu Shib Saran Das ... | Hindu Arya. | Rais, Contractor and Municipal Commissioner. | do. |
| 392 | " | " | " | Sirdir Gajjan Singh ... | Sikh. | Pleader, Chief Court, Lahore and Secretary, Funeral and Marriage Committee and District Congress Committee; Member, Khalsa College Committee and Vice-President, Goordnara Committee &c. | do. |
| 393 | " | " | " | Lala Durga Dutt ... | Hindu Bania Agarwal. | Pleader, President District Congress Committee and Vice-President, Temperance Society &c. | do. |
| 394 | " | " | " | " Thakurdas ... | Hindu Khettri. | Writer ... | At a Public Meeting held at Ludhiana on the 20th December, 1893. |
| 395 | " | " | " | " Fateh Chand B.A., L.L.B., Cambridge. | Hindu. | Barrister-at-Law, Ajmere. | do. |
| 396 | " | " | " | " Shadi Ram ... | Hindu, Khettri. | Banker ... | do. |
| 397 | " | " | " | " Lajpat Rai ... | Hindu. | Contractor ... | do. |
| 398 | " | " | " | Babu Amar Nath Sahib | do. | Rais and Contractor ... | do. |
| 399 | " | " | " | Lala Lahouri Mal ... | Hindu. | Landowner and Proprietor of Workshops. | do. |
| 400 | " | " | " | " Ama Dutt ... | Hindu Agarwal. | Rais, Amritsar ... | do. |
| 401 | " | " | Dera Ismail Khan. | Mian Sahara ... | Mahomedan. | Physician and Druggist, Dera Ismail Khan. | At a Public Meeting held at Dera Ismail Khan on the 14th December 1893. |
| 402 | " | " | " | Mr. Jhind Ram ... | Arya Khettri. | Pleader, Chief Court, Lahore and Secretary, Divisional Congress Committee, Dera Ismail Khan. | do. |
| 403 | " | " | " | Lala Hira Nand Saibgal | do. | Mukhtear and Vice-President, "Bhratri Sabha," Dera Ismail Khan. | do. |
| 404 | " | " | " | Malik Bhagwan Das Kapur. | do. | Zemindar, Pleader and President, "Bhratri Sabha," Dera Ismail Khan. | do. |
| 405 | " | " | " | Malik Kaura Khan ... | Mahomedan Biloch. | Zemindar, Kulochi. District Dera Ismail Khan. | do. |
| 406 | " | " | " | Lala Chiman Lal ... | Arya Arora. | Physician, Druggist and Proprietor of "the Medical Hall," Dera Ismail Khan. | do. |

| Number. | Presidency or Government. | Congress Circle. | Electoral Division. | Names in full of Delegates, with Honorary Titles, Scholastic Degrees, etc. | Race, Religious denomination, and Caste, if any. | Occupation and Address. | How and when elected. |
|---|---|---|---|---|---|---|---|
| 407 | Punjab. | Lahore. | Dera Ismail Khan. | Lala Lilaram Nandwani. | Arya Arora. | Zemindar, and late Editor, "Bhratri Risala." | At a Public Meeting held at Dera Ismail Khan on the 14th December, 1893. |
| 408 | " | " | " | Bhagat Shivdyal ... | Hindu Bhatia. | Guru, (Ecclasiastic) ... | do. |
| 409 | " | " | Gujranwalla. | Lala Dhani Ram B.A., L.L.B., | Hindu Khettri. | Pleader, Gujranwalla ... | At a Public Meeting held at Gujranwalla on the 17th December, 1893. |
| 410 | " | " | " | Lala Jivan Kishen ... | Hindu Kayastha. | Pleader and Vice-President, Municipal Board, Gujranwalla. | do. |
| 411 | " | " | " | " Sunder Lal ... | Hindu Khettri. | Mukhtear ... | do. |
| 412 | " | " | " | " Gokul Chand ... | do. | Contractor, Jandiala, Sherkhan, Gujranwalla District. | do. |
| 413 | " | " | " | Sirdir Harsa Singh ... | Sikh. | do. ... | do. |
| 414 | " | " | " | " Chet Singh ... | do. | Merchant, Jandiala, Sherkhan, Gujranwalla District. | do. |
| 415 | " | " | " | Lala Gunga Ram ... | Hindu Khettri. | Pleader, Gujranwalla ... | do. |
| 416 | " | " | " | Mr. B. C. Chatterjee, B.A. | Bengali Christian. | Head Master, Mission Higlh School, Gujranwalla. | do. |
| 417 | " | " | " | Lala Mela Ram Talwar | Hindu Khettri. | Rais and Zemindar ... | do. |
| 418 | " | " | " | " Gian Chand Chopra | do. | Rais and Municipal Commissioner. | do. |
| 419 | " | " | " | " Kahan Chand ... | Hindu Arora. | Pleader, Municipal Commissioner and Secretary, "Aror Bans Sabha," Gujranwalla. | do. |
| 420 | " | " | Montgomery. | Pundit Saligram ... | Hindu Kashmiri Pundit. | Pleader, Montgomery ... | At a Public Meeting held at Montgomery on the 22nd December, 1893. |
| 421 | " | " | " | Lala Shib Das ... | Hindu Khettri. | do. ... | do. |
| 422 | " | " | " | Sett Ram Ditta ... | do. | Banker ... | do. |
| 423 | " | " | Jhang. | Munshi Amir Chand Trikha. | Hindu Brahmin. | Mukhtear, Jhang ... | By a Public Meeting held at Jhang on the 12th December, 1893. |
| 424 | " | " | " | Munshi Devi Dyal ... | Hindu Arora. | Zemindar and Banker ... | do. |
| 425 | " | " | " | Mian Golam Hussain ... | Mahomedan. | Manager of the Estate of late Nowab Ismail Khan. | do. |
| 426 | " | " | " | Lala Kashi Ram ... | Hindu Khettri | Pleader and Member, Municipal Board, Mooltan. | do. |
| 427 | " | " | " | Lala Lal Chand ... | Hindu Arora. | Pleader, Meghiana ... | do. |
| 428 | " | " | " | Chowdhury Ramlal ... | do. | Zemindar and Merchant | do. |

| Number. | Presidency or Government. | Congress Circle. | Electoral Division. | Names in full of Delegates, with Honorary Titles, Scholastic Degrees, etc. | Race, Religious denomination, and Caste, if any. | Occupation and Address. | How and when elected. |
|---|---|---|---|---|---|---|---|
| 429 | Punjab. | Lahore. | Jullundur. | Lala Ram Kishen ... | Hindu Khettri. | Pleader, Jullundur ... | By a Public Meeting held at Jullundur on the 9th December, 1893. |
| 430 | „ | „ | „ | Pundit Chhugga Ram ... | Hindu Brahmin. | do. ... | do. |
| 431 | „ | „ | „ | Sirdir Surjan Singh ... | Sikh. | Munshi, Kharkat Kalan | do. |
| 432 | „ | „ | „ | Lala Mohun Lal ... | Hindu Khettri. | Banker and Zemindar, Basti Shaikh, Jullundur. | do. |
| 433 | „ | „ | „ | Mr. Kali Prasanna Chatterjee. | Hindu Brahmin. | Sub-Editor, "Tribune" Lahore. | do. |
| 434 | „ | „ | „ | Sirdir Kishen Singh ... | Sikh. | Mukhtear, Jullundur ... | do. |
| 435 | „ | „ | „ | Bawa Salamat Rai ... | Hindu Khettri. | Pleader, do. ... | do. |
| 436 | „ | „ | „ | Syed Najib Ali Shah ... | Mahomedan Syed. | Zemindar, Basti Shaikh, Jullundur District. | do |
| 437 | „ | „ | „ | Rai Saligram ... | Hindu Khettri. | Rais, Municipal Commissioner, Hony. Magistrate and Landholder, Jullundur. | do. |
| 438 | „ | „ | „ | Pundit Devi Chand ... | Hindu Brahmin. | Pleader and Municipal Commissioner. | do. |
| 439 | „ | „ | „ | Lala Dev Raj ... | Arya Khettri. | Zemindar, Jullundur City | do. |
| 440 | „ | „ | „ | „ Munshi Ram ... | do. | Pleader and Editor, "Satdharma Pracharak" and President, "Arya Pratinidhi Sabha." | do. |
| 441 | „ | „ | „ | Pundit Sheo Narain ... | Hindu Brahmin. | Pleader, Jullundur City | do. |
| 442 | „ | „ | „ | Raizada Bhagat Ram ... | Arya Khettri. | Barrister-at-Law, Jullundur City. | do. |
| 443 | „ | „ | „ | Sirdir Uttam Singh ... | Sikh. | Pleader ... | do. |
| 444 | „ | „ | „ | Mr. Madan Gopal ... | Hindu Khettri. | do. ... | do. |
| 445 | „ | „ | „ | Lala Gajjar Mal ... | do. | Banker and Editor of the "Bharat Sewak" and Secretary, Purity Association, Jullundur. | do. |
| 446 | „ | „ | „ | „ Gokul Chand ... | do. | Mukhtear, Jullundur City | do. |
| 447 | „ | „ | „ | „ Ram Nath ... | Hindu. | Pleader ... | By a Public Meeting held at Jullundur on the 24th December, 1893. |
| 448 | „ | „ | „ | „ Narain Das B.A. L.L.B. | Hindu Bania. | Pleader, Jullundur Cantonment. | do. |
| 449 | „ | „ | Shahpur Bhera. | Babu Brij Lal ... | Hindu Khettri. | Pleader, Shahpur ... | By a Public Meeting held at Shahpur on the 17th December, 1893. |
| 450 | „ | „ | „ | Lala Shankar Das Sahib | do. | do. ... | do. |
| 451 | „ | „ | „ | „ Gandat Mal ... | do. | Teacher, English School and Secretary, Arya Samaj, Bhera. | do. |

| Number. | Presidency or Government. | Congress Circle. | Electoral Division. | Names in full of Delegates, with Honorary Titles, Scholastic Degrees, etc. | Race, Religious denomination, and Caste, if any. | Occupation and Address. | How and when elected. |
|---|---|---|---|---|---|---|---|
| 452 | Punjab. | Lahore. | Shahpur Bhera. | Lala Hans Raj Sewhney | Hindu Khettri. | Pleader, Rawalpindi and Secretary, Managing Committee, A. S. High School, Bhera. | By a Public Meeting held at Shahpur on the 17th December, 1893. |
| 453 | „ | „ | „ | „ Parmeshwari Sahai | Thiest Kayastha. | Teacher, A. S. High School, Bhera. | do. |
| 454 | „ | „ | „ | Bakshi Ram Labhaye ... | Hindu Khettri. | Proprietor, "Dost Hind" and "Wilson Press," Bhera and late P. Secretary to H. H. The Maharaja of Kashmir. | do. |
| 455 | „ | „ | „ | Malik Ram Das Anand | Arya Khettri. | Contractor, Bhera ... | do. |
| 456 | „ | „ | „ | Lala Bhagwan Das ... | Hindu Khettri. | do. ... | By a Public Meeting held at Shahpur on the 18th December, 1893. |
| 457 | „ | „ | „ | Sant Prabhu Dyal ... | Hindu Brahmin. | Pleader, Jammu and Kashmir. | do. |
| 458 | „ | „ | „ | Lala Jivan Mal ... | Hindu Khettri. | Banker and Contractor, Bhera. | do. |
| 459 | „ | „ | „ | Lala Bhagat Ram Seth | do. | Merchant ... | do. |
| 460 | „ | „ | „ | „ Hari Ram Chopra | do. | Banker ... | do. |
| 461 | „ | „ | „ | „ Lal Chand Mehra ... | do. | Mukhtear, Bhera ... | do. |
| 462 | „ | „ | „ | „ Beliram ... | Hindu. | Petition Writer, 1st grade | do. |
| 463 | „ | „ | „ | „ Muthra Das ... | do. | Late Munsiff, now a Pensioner, Bhera. | do. |
| 464 | „ | „ | Peshwar. | Babu Sheo Shahai | Arya Khettri. | Continental Agent ... | By a Public Meeting held at Peshwar on the 22nd December, 1893. |
| 465 | „ | „ | „ | Pundit Mul Chand ... | Vedic Brahmin. | Pleader, Peshwar ... | do. |
| 466 | „ | „ | „ | Sirdir Sunder Singh ... | Sikh. | do. ... | do. |
| 467 | „ | „ | „ | Lala Mulchand Lomba ... | Vedic Khettri. | Rais and Landholder ... | do. |
| 468 | „ | „ | „ | Dr. Sitaram ... | Vedic Brahmin. | Medical Practitioner ... | do. |
| 469 | „ | „ | „ | Mr. B. M. Amoria ... | Parsi. | Merchant, Rawalpindi ... | do. |
| 470 | „ | „ | „ | Mr. Boga ... | do. | do. ... | do. |
| 471 | „ | „ | „ | Lala Mahesh Das ... | Hindu Khettri. | Banker, Rais and Municipal Commissioner. | do. |
| 472 | „ | „ | „ | „ Harji Mall ... | do. | Banker ... | do. |
| 473 | „ | „ | „ | Mr. Dadabhai ... | Parsi. | Merchant ... | do. |
| 474 | „ | „ | Gujrat. | Lala Ganesh Das ... | Hindu Arya. | General Contractor and Money-lender. | At a Public Meeting held at Gujrat on the 11th December, 1893. |
| 475 | „ | „ | „ | „ Bishwambhar Das. | do. | Pleader, Gujrat ... | do. |
| 476 | „ | „ | „ | Bawa Shiv Dyal ... | Sikh. | Mukhtear ... | do. |

| Number. | Presidency or Government. | Congress Circle. | Electoral Division. | Names in full of Delegates, with Honorary Titles, Scholastic Degrees, etc. | Race, Religious denomination, and Caste, if any. | Occupation and Address. | How and when elected. |
|---|---|---|---|---|---|---|---|
| 477 | Punjab. | Lahore. | Gujrat. | Lala Niranjan Dar ... | Hindu Vedic. | Pleader, Gujrat ... | At a Public Meeting held at Gujrat on the 11th December, 1893. |
| 478 | " | " | " | " Thakur Das ... | Hindu. | Mukhtear ... | do. |
| 479 | " | " | " | Sirdir Meher Singh ... | Sikh. | Government Pensioner | do. |
| 480 | " | " | Rawalpindi. | Lala Devi Ditta Mall ... | Hindu Khettri. | Merchant, City Rawalpindi. | By a Public Meeting held at Rawalpindi on the 10th December, 1893. |
| 481 | " | " | " | " Bhagat Ram Sahai. | do. | Zemindar of Bhera, (Shahpur District.) | do. |
| 482 | " | " | " | Hakim Nand Lal Sethi. | Arya. Khettri | Munshi, Rawalpindi ... | do. |
| 483 | " | " | " | Lala Maya Das Sawhuy. | do. | Pleader, Municipal Commissioner and Zemindar. | do. |
| 484 | " | " | " | Pundit Shivram Jhingan. | Hindu Brahmin. | Pleader's Agent, Rawalpindi City. | do. |
| 485 | " | " | " | Mehta Kripa Ram ... | Arya Khettri. | Proprietor of the "Himalaya Press," City Rawalpindi. | do. |
| 486 | " | " | " | Mr. Bhagat Kishen Chand | Kalal. | Pensioner and Rais ... | do. |
| 487 | " | " | " | Dr. B. R. Sawhuy, M.B., B.S., L.R.C.P., M.R.C.S. | Hindu Khettri. | Medical Practitioner, Rawalpindi City. | do. |
| 488 | " | " | " | Mr. G. R. Sawhuy ... | do. | Barrister-at-Law ... | do. |
| 489 | " | " | " | Lala Ganes Das Sethi ... | do. | Sowkar ... | do. |
| 490 | " | " | " | Mr. Pestonji Dadabhai ... | Parsi. | Pleader, Rawalpindi Cantonment. | do. |
| 491 | " | " | " | Chowdhuri Batamal Anand | Hindu Khettri. | Proprietor of the "Gulshan Punjab Press." | do. |
| 492 | " | " | " | Lala Gurdas Ram Chudda. | Hindu Arya. | Sowkar ... | do. |
| 493 | " | " | " | Lala Jagannath Sethi ... | do. | Contractor ... | do. |
| 494 | " | " | " | " Govind Ram Sethi. | do. | Iron Merchant ... | do. |
| 495 | " | " | " | " Hari Ram Sethi ... | do. | Showkar ... | do. |
| 496 | " | " | " | " Radha Kishen Sethi. | do. | Merchant and Contractor | do. |
| 497 | " | " | " | " Prabhu Dyal Kali ... | Hindu Khettri. | Rais and Munshi ... | do. |
| 498 | " | " | " | " Hari Ram Puri ... | do. | Contractor ... | do. |
| 499 | " | " | " | " Jivaram Thakur ... | do. | Merchant and Proprietor of the "Agerton Press," "The Punjab Times" and the "Taj-ul-Akbar" Cantonment, Rawalpindi. | do |
| 500 | " | " | " | Mr. Hem Chunder Mukerjee, L.L. | Bengali Christian. | Pleader, Rawalpindi City. | do. |
| 501 | " | " | Ferozepur. | Sirdir Gurmukh Sing, B.A. | Jat, Sikh. | Pleader, Ferozepur City. | At a Public Meeting held at Ferozepur City on the 17th December, 1893. |
| 502 | " | " | " | " Chanda Singh Bhind | do. | do. | do. |
| 503 | " | " | " | Lala Mukunda Lal Sandhi, B.A. | Hindu Khettri. | do. | do. |

| Number. | Presidency or Government. | Congress Circle. | Electoral Division. | Names in full of Delegates, with Honorary Titles, Scholastic Degrees, etc. | Race, Religious denomination, and Caste, if any. | Occupation and Address. | How and when elected. |
|---|---|---|---|---|---|---|---|
| 504 | Punjab. | Lahore. | Ferozepur. | Mr. Nathaniel Prem Das. | Christian. | Missionary, American Mission, Ferozepur City. | At a Public Meeting held at Ferozepur City on the 17th December, 1893. |
| 505 | " | " | " | Lala Kashi Ram, B.A. ... | Hindu Khettri | Pleader ... | do. |
| 506 | " | " | " | " Bhava Ram, B.A. ... | Hindu Agarwal. | Mukhtear ... | do. |
| 507 | " | " | " | " Behari Lal ... | Hindu Khettri. | Merchant and Contractor | do. |
| 508 | " | " | " | " Kishen Lal ... | Hindu Agarwal. | do. | do. |
| 509 | " | " | " | " Jethu Mal ... | Hindu Vaisya. | do. | do. |
| 510 | " | " | " | Sirdir Atma Singh ... | Sikh. | Contractor, Flour Mills, Ferozepur. | do. |
| 511 | " | " | " | Lala Durga Das ... | Hindu Khettri. | Manager, Ginning Factory, Kasur. | do. |
| 512 | " | " | " | Lala Kashi Ram ... | do. | Pleader, and Proprietor of Ginning Factories at Kasur, Okara and Housi; Member and Hony. Secretary, Municipal Committee, Ferozepur City. | do. |
| 513 | " | " | " | " Gridhari Lal ... | do. | Sowkar, Ferozepur City. | do. |
| 514 | " | " | " | " Shankar Das ... | do. | Sowkar and Municipal Commissioner, Ferozepur City. | do. |
| 515 | " | " | " | " Ram Nath ... | do. | Pleader ... | do. |
| 516 | " | " | " | " Ram Sukh Das ... | Hindu Agarwal. | Pleader and Landowner. | do. |
| 517 | " | " | " | " Din Dyal ... | Hindu Kayastha. | Pleader ... | do. |
| 518 | " | " | " | " Harzi Ram ... | Hindu. | do. ... | do. |
| 519 | " | " | " | " Nanak Chand ... | Hindu Agarwal. | Sub-Agent, Messrs Bryan Durant & Co's Agency, Ferozepur City. | do. |
| 520 | " | " | Hoshiarpur. | Babu Hira Ram, L.L. ... | Hindu Khettri. | Pleader and Zemindar ... | By a Public Meeting held at Hoshiarpur on the 10th December, 1893. |
| 521 | " | " | " | Lala Thakur Das Varma. | Arya. | do. ... | do. |
| 522 | " | " | " | Sheikh Umar Buksh, B.A. | Mahomedan. | Pleader, Zemindar, Municipal Commissioner and Vice-President, Anjuman Islamia, Hoshiarpur. | do. |
| 523 | " | " | " | Lala Bir Bal Vaid ... | Hindu | Zemindar, Money-lender and President, Hoshiarpur Peoples' Association. | do. |
| 524 | " | " | " | Lala Amar Chand, L.L. | Hindu Khettri. | Pleader ... | do. |
| 525 | " | " | " | Pundit Jagannath, L.L. | Hindu Brahmin. | do. ... | do. |
| 526 | " | " | " | Lala Thakur Das ... | Hindu Khettri. | Zemindar and Money-lender. | do. |

| Number. | Presidency or Government. | Congress Circle. | Electoral Division. | Names in full of Delegates, with Honorary Titles, Scholastic Degrees, etc. | Race, Religious denomination, and Caste, if any. | Occupation and Address. | How and when elected. |
|---|---|---|---|---|---|---|---|
| 527 | Punjab. | Lahore. | Hoshiarpur. | Mr. Ram Chand Sarma. | Arya Brahmin. | Merchant ... | By a Public Meeting held at Hoshiarpur on the 10th December, 1893. |
| 528 | " | " | " | Lala Fateh Chand ... | Hindu Khettri. | Zemindar and Money-lender. | do. |
| 529 | " | " | " | " Puran Chand ... | Hindu. | Grain Merchant, Hoshiarpur. | do. |
| 530 | " | " | " | Pundit Tulsi Ram ... | Arya. | Mukhtear and Zemindar. | do. |
| 531 | " | " | " | Sadhu Tulsi Ram ... | Hindu Brahmin. | Preacher ... | do. |
| 532 | " | " | " | Lala Gajjar Mal ... | Hindu. | Banker and Zemindar ... | do. |
| 533 | " | " | " | " Narain Das, L.L. ... | Hindu Kalal. | Pleader, Merchant and Zemindar. | do. |
| 534 | " | " | " | " Sham Das, L.L. ... | Hindu Agarwal. | Pleader and Municipal Commissioner. | do. |
| 535 | " | " | " | Seth Suraj Mall ... | do. | Merchant ... | do. |
| 536 | " | " | " | Pundit Budri Nath ... | Kashmiri Brahmin. | Mukhtear, Hoshiarpur ... | do. |
| 537 | " | " | Sialkote. | Lala Labha Mall ... | Arya Bhatia. | Pleader and Public Prosecutor, Sialkote. | By a Public Meeting held at Sialkote on the 13th December, 1893. |
| 538 | " | " | " | " Charan Das ... | Hindu. | Mukhtear, Sialkote ... | do. |
| 539 | " | " | " | " Balmukund ... | do. | Teacher, American Mission School, Sialkote. | do. |
| 540 | " | " | " | Bhai Hazra Singh ... | Sikh. | Banker, Sialkote ... | do. |
| 541 | " | " | " | Lala Bhim Sen ... | Hindu Kayastha. | Pleader, Sialkote ... | do. |
| 542 | " | " | " | Sirdir Ganda Singh Uberoi. | Sikh. | Proprietor "Punjab Sports Works," Sialkote. | do. |
| 543 | " | " | " | Lala Sawan Mal ... | Jain. | Banker ... | do. |
| 544 | " | " | " | Pundit Mul Rai ... | Hindu Brahmin. | Editor and Proprietor "Sanatan Dharma Gazette." | do. |
| 545 | " | " | " | Bhai Ludha Singh ... | Sikh. | Teacher, American Mission School, Sialkote. | do. |
| 546 | " | " | " | Lala Karta Kishen ... | Arya Kayastha. | Pleader ... | do. |
| 547 | " | " | " | Pundit Shankar Das ... | Hindu. Brahmin | do. ... | do. |
| 548 | " | " | Hissar | Lala Gouri Shankar ... | Hindu | Banker ... | By a Public Meeting held on the 13th December, 1893. |
| 549 | " | " | " | " Ram Chandra ... | do. | do. ... | do. |
| 550 | " | " | " | Pundit Deo Dutt Sarma. | do. | Teacher, Sanskrit Pathasala, Hissar. | do. |
| 551 | " | " | " | Mr. Churamani, L.L. ... | Arya Vaisya. Agarwal. | Pleader ... | do. |
| 552 | " | " | Dharamsala. | Bukshi Sohun Lal ... | Arya Mahajan. | Pleader, Landholder and Member, Dharamsala Municipality. | At a Public Meeting held at Dharamsala on the 5th December, 1893. |

| Number. | Presidency or Government. | Congress Circle. | Electoral Division. | Names in full of Delegates, with Honorary Titles, Scholastic Degrees, etc. | Race, Religious denomination, and Caste, if any. | Occupation and Address. | How and when elected. |
|---|---|---|---|---|---|---|---|
| 553 | Punjab. | Lahore. | Dharamsala. | Lala Sukh Dayal, L.L. ... | Arya Mahajan. | Pleader, Landholder and Vice-President, Dharamsala Municipality. | At a Public Meeting held at Dharamsala on he 5th December, 1893. |
| 554 | " | " | Kangra. | " Brij Lal, B.A. ... | do. | Mukhtear ... | At a Public Meeting held at Kangra on the 17th December, 1893. |
| 555 | " | " | Gurdaspur. | " Guru Charan Das ... | Hindu Khettri. | Pleader, Zemindar and President, Municipal Committee, Gurdaspur. | At a Public Meeting held at Gurdaspur on the 9th December, 1893. |
| 556 | " | " | " | Pundit Meghan Ram ... | Hindu Brahmin. | Pleader and Municipal Commissioner. | do. |
| 557 | " | " | " | Mr. Ranji Shah ... | Hindu Shewalia | Sowkar, Gurdaspur ... | do. |
| 558 | " | " | " | Chowdhuri Nathu Mal ... | Hindu Brahmin. | Sowkar and Landholder. | do. |
| 559 | " | " | " | " Jivan Mal ... | Hindu Joshi Brahmin. | Chowdhuri Bazar, Gurdaspur. | do. |
| 560 | " | " | " | Lala Vir Bhan ... | Hindu Khettri. | Landholder ... | do. |
| 561 | " | " | " | " Mohun Lal ... | Hindu. | Munshi ... | do. |
| 562 | " | " | " | " Muta Mal ... | Hindu Saini. | Mukhtear and Landholder. | do. |
| 563 | " | " | " | Bawa Sunder Singh ... | Sikh. | Pleader ... | do. |
| 564 | " | " | " | Dewan Rallia Ram Bali. | Hindu Brahmin. | do. | do. |
| 565 | " | " | " | Lala Ram Saran Das ... | Hindu Arya. | Pleader and Landholder. | do. |
| 566 | " | " | " | " Das Mal Mehta ... | Hindu Khettri. | Contractor, Dinanagore, District Gurdaspur. | do. |
| 567 | " | " | " | " Nathuram Sowkar. | Hindu Arya Alawalia. | Sowkar, Pandori, Banisan, Gurdaspur. | do. |
| 568 | " | " | " | Sheikh Nabi Buksh ... | Mahomedan Sheikh. | Pleader and Municipal Commissioner. | do. |
| 569 | " | " | " | Mr. Nanak Chand ... | Hindu Khettri. | Merchant, Dinanagore, District Gurdaspur. | At a Public Meeting held at Gurdaspur on the 10th December, 1893. |
| 570 | " | " | " | Lala Bhava Mal ... | Hindu Mahajan. | Merchant and Municipal Commissioner, Dinanagore. | do. |
| 571 | " | " | " | " Shib Dyal Talwar ... | Hindu Khettri. | Mukhtear and Revenue Agent, Gurdaspur. | do. |
| 572 | " | " | " | " Kashmira Mal ... | do. | Merchant, Dinanagore ... | do. |
| 573 | " | " | Umballa. | Lala Ramsaran Das ... | Hindu Vaisya Agarwal. | Mukhtear, Umballa ... | At a Public Meeting held at Umballa on the 19th December 1893 |
| 574 | " | " | " | " Than Singh ... | do. | Contractor and Proprietor of "Upper India Steam Flour Mills," Umballa. | do. |
| 575 | " | " | " | " Hari Singh ... | do. | Contractor, Banker, Zemindar and Municipal Commissioner, Fyzabad. | do. |

| Number. | Presidency or Government. | Congress Circle. | Electoral Division. | Names in full of Delegates, with Honorary Titles, Scholastic Degrees, etc. | Race, Religious denomination, and Caste, if any. | Occupation and Address. | How and when elected. |
|---|---|---|---|---|---|---|---|
| 576 | Punjab. | Lahore. | Umballa. | Lala Karam Chand ... | Hindu Arya Agarwal. | Contractor, Umballa ... | At a Public Meeting held at Umballa on the 19th December, 1893. |
| 577 | " | " | " | " Tilak Chand ... | do. | Pleader, Umballa ... | do. |
| 578 | " | " | " | " Lachmi Ram ... | do. | Municipal Commissioner, Umballa. | do. |
| 579 | " | " | " | Pundit Brij Mohun Dattatriya. | Kashmiri Brahmin. | Journalist ... | do. |
| 580 | " | " | " | Babu Durga Churn Mookerjee. | Hindu Brahmin. | Medical practitioner ... | do. |
| 581 | " | " | " | Babu Shyama Churn Mookerjee. | do. | Merchant ... | do. |
| 582 | " | " | " | Lala Janki Prasad ... | Hindu Vaisya Agarwal. | Co-proprietor, "Upper India Steam Flour Mills" Umballa. | do. |
| 583 | " | " | " | Mr. G. Law ... | Christian | Retired Medical Service | do. |
| 584 | " | " | " | Mahomed Fazil ... | Mahomedan | Assistant, "Upper India Steam Flour Mills," Umballa. | do. |
| 585 | " | " | " | Babu Khirode Chunder Chatterjee B.A. B.L. | Hindu Brahmin. | Pleader, Umballa City ... | At a Public Meeting held at Umballa on the 20th December, 1893. |
| 586 | " | " | " | Munshi Abdul Kadir Tayaf. | Mahomedan. | Journalist ... | do. |
| 587 | " | " | " | Lala Gopal Das, B.A. ... | Hindu Agarwal. | Pleader, Umballa ... | do. |
| 588 | " | " | " | Pundit Shahzada Ram ... | Hindu. Brahmin. | do. | do. |
| 589 | " | " | " | Lala Dwarka Das, M.A. | Hindu Vaisya Agarwal | do. | do. |
| 590 | " | " | " | Pundit Madhuram, B.A. | Hindu Brahmin. | do. | do. |
| 591 | " | " | " | Lala Murlidhar ... | Hindu Agarwal. | do. | do. |
| 592 | " | " | Amritsar | " Gopaldas Sahib .... | Hindu. | Pleader, Chief Court, Punjab. | At a General Meeting held at Amritsar on the 10th December, 1893. |
| 593 | " | " | " | " Nathu Mal Khalsa. | Hindu Khettri. | Zemindar and Quanango. | do. |
| 594 | " | " | " | Pundit Kashmira Mal Sahib. | Kashmiri Brahmin. | Pleader ... | do. |
| 595 | " | " | " | Lala Ram Nath ... | Hindu Khettri. | Sowkar ... | do. |
| 596 | " | " | " | Pundit Behari Lal ... | Hindu Brahmin. | Pleader, Chief Court, Punjab. | do. |
| 597 | " | " | " | Lala Shib Churn Das, B.A. | Hindu Khettri. | Pleader ... | do. |
| 598 | " | " | " | Roy Baldeo Das ... | Hindu Bania. | Shawl Merchant ... | do. |
| 599 | " | " | " | Lala Sadhu Ram ... | Hindu Arya. | do. | do. |

| Number. | Presidency or Government. | Congress Circle. | Electoral Division. | Names in full of Delegates, with Honorary Titles, Scholastic Degrees, etc. | Race, Religious denomination, and Caste, if any. | Occupation and Address. | How and when elected. |
|---|---|---|---|---|---|---|---|
| 600 | Punjab. | Lahore. | Amritsar. | Pundit Ram Rattan Sahib. | Hindu Brahmin. | Jagirdar and Sowkar ... | At a General Meeting held at Amritsar on the 10th December, 1893. |
| 601 | " | " | " | Lala Dina Nath ... | Hindu Khettri. | Mukhtear ... | do. |
| 602 | " | " | " | " Gyan Chand ... | do. | Zemindar ... | do. |
| 603 | " | " | " | Babu Jagannath ... | do. | Contractor ... | do. |
| 604 | " | " | " | " Shibdas Kapur, B.A. | Hindu Kapur. | Banker, Bazar Harising, Amritsar. | do. |
| 605 | " | " | " | " Murlidhar ... | Hindu Agarwal. | Lawyer and Secretary, Bar Room, Amritsar. | do. |
| 606 | " | " | " | Chowdhury Ghasita Mal. | Hindu Khettri. | Merchant ... | do. |
| 607 | " | " | " | Bawa Basant Singh ... | Sikh. | Mukhtear, Amritsar ... | do. |
| 608 | " | " | " | Babu Chatturbhuj Sahib. | Hindu Meheshin. | Pleader ... | do. |
| 609 | " | " | " | Lala Asar Das ... | Hindu Khettri. | Zemindar ... | do. |
| 610 | " | " | " | Babu Radharam Sahib ... | Hindu Arora. | Lawyer ... | do. |
| 611 | " | " | " | Lala Nandlal ... | Hindu Khettri. | Hakim ... | do. |
| 612 | " | " | " | " Sunder Das Sahib ... | do. | Merchant ... | do. |
| 613 | " | " | " | Bhai Dinga Singh ... | Sikh. | Mukhtear, Amritsar ... | do. |
| 614 | " | " | " | Sirdir Pertap Singh ... | do. | Timber Merchant ... | do. |
| 615 | " | " | " | Mr. B. Harnum Singh ... | Sikh. | Merchant and Contractor. | do. |
| 616 | " | " | " | Lala Shib Das Mal ... | Hindu Khettri. | Sowkar ... | do. |
| 617 | " | " | " | Bawa Makhan Singh ... | Sikh. | Pleader ... | do. |
| 618 | " | " | " | Lala Ram Chand Sahib. | Hindu Khettri. | Pleader, Amritsar ... | do. |
| 619 | " | " | " | Babu Gossain Lal ... | do. | Mukhtear ... | do. |
| 620 | " | " | " | Lala Shib Dyal ... | do. | do. ... | do. |
| 621 | " | " | " | Bhai Mahatab Singh Sahib. | Hindu Arora. | Banker, Vice-President, "Trade Association" and Secretary, "Aror Bans Sabha", Amritsar. | do. |
| 622 | " | " | " | Bhai Govind Singh ... | Sikh. | Merchant and President, "Trade Association," Amritsar. | do. |
| 623 | " | " | " | Lala Sukh Dyal ... | Hindu Khettri. | Merchant ... | do. |
| 624 | " | " | " | " Dewan Chand ... | do. | Banker ... | do |
| 625 | " | " | " | " Gunga Bishen ... | do. | Merchant ... | do. |
| 626 | " | " | " | Babu Balmukund ... | do. | Proprietor, Soap Factory, Amritsar. | do. |
| 627 | " | " | " | Lala Ram Chand Sarup. | do. | Banker ... | do. |
| 628 | " | " | " | Bawa Narain Singh ... | Sikh. | Pleader ... | do. |

| Number. | Presidency or Government. | Congress Circle. | Electoral Division. | Names in full of Delegates, with Honorary Titles, Scholastic Degrees, etc. | Race, Religious denomination, and Caste, if any. | Occupation and Address. | How and when elected. |
|---|---|---|---|---|---|---|---|
| 629 | Punjab. | Lahore. | Amritsar. | Lala Joy Kishen Das ... | Hindu Khettri. | Merchant ... | At a General Meeting held at Amritsar on the 10th December, 1893. |
| 630 | " | " | " | Pundit Mulraj ... | Hindu. Brahmin. | Barrister-at-Law .. | do. |
| 631 | " | " | " | Mr. Todar Mal ... | Hindu Khettri. | do. ... | do. |
| 632 | " | " | " | Lala Rela Mal ... | do. | Cloth Merchant ... | do. |
| 633 | " | " | " | Lala Ram Chand ... | do. | Banker ... | do. |
| 634 | " | " | " | " Bishen Das ... | do. | Hakim ... | do. |
| 635 | " | " | " | " Amolak Ram ... | do. | Banker, Bazar Sirki Bandan, Harbhaj Rai's Temple, Amritsar. | do. |
| 636 | " | " | " | " Kanahye Lal ... | do. | Pleader ... | do. |
| 637 | " | " | " | " Jwalanund ... | do. | ...... | do. |
| 638 | " | " | " | " Hardyal Sitiwala ... | do. | Trader ... | do. |
| 639 | " | " | " | Sirdir Golab Singh ... | Sikh. | Jagirdar ... | do. |
| 640 | " | " | " | " Shib Nath Roy Sahib. | Hindu Brahmin. | Jagirdar of Shib Nath Roy Pura. | do. |
| 641 | " | " | " | Mohunt Harnum Singh. | Sikh | Mohunt, Amritsar ... | do. |
| 642 | " | " | " | Lala Devi Dyal ... | Hindu Khettri. | Mukhtear ... | do. |
| 643 | " | " | " | Sirdir Rachpal Singh Pandariwala. | Sikh. | Jagirdar and Zemindar ... | do. |
| 644 | " | " | " | Lala Nehal Chand ... | Hindu Bania. | Banker and Municipal Commissioner. | do. |
| 645 | " | " | " | Mr. Mohun Lal ... | Hindu Brahmin. | Barrister-at-Law ... | do. |
| 646 | " | " | " | Pundit Ruplal ... | do. | Pleader ... | do. |
| 647 | " | " | " | Lala Ralya Ram ... | Hindu Khettri. | Contractor ... | At a Public Meeting held at Amritsar on the 15th December, 1893. |
| 648 | " | " | " | Moulvie Niazali Khan ... | Mahomedan. | Editor of the "Amritsar Gazette," and "Wakil Punjab," Proprietor of the "Wakil-Punjab Press" and Bookseller. | do. |
| 649 | " | " | " | Lala Dooney Chand, M.A. | Hindu Arora. | Mukhtear, Amritsar ... | At a General Meeting held at Amritsar on the 23rd December, 1893. |
| 650 | " | " | " | Mr. Nathu Singh ... | Sikh. | Trader ... | do. |
| 651 | " | " | " | Mr. Mody. B. Hormusji. | Parsi. | Merchant ... | do. |
| 652 | " | " | " | Mrs. Mody. B. Hormusji. | do. | ...... | do. |
| 653 | " | " | " | Mr. Ram Rattan ... | Hindu Khettri. | Commission Agent ... | do. |
| 654 | " | " | " | Mr. Guruditta Mal ... | do. | ...... | do. |
| 655 | " | " | " | Lala Bhagat Ram ... | do. | Merchant ... | do. |
| 656 | " | " | " | Mr. Kripa Ram ... | do. | Broker ... | do. |

| Number. | Presidency or Government. | Congress Circle. | Electoral Division. | Names in full of Delegates, with Honorary Titles, Scholastic Degrees, etc. | Race, Religious denomination, and Caste, if any. | Occupation and Address. | How and when elected. |
|---|---|---|---|---|---|---|---|
| 657 | Punjab. | Lahore. | Amritsar. | Babu Karam Chand ... | Hindu Khettri. | Merchant ... | At a General Meeting held at Amritsar on the 23rd December, 1893. |
| 658 | " | " | " | " Prithvi Chand ... | do. | Contractor ... | do. |
| 659 | " | " | " | Lala Jaswant Rai ... | Hindu. | Private Service ... | do. |
| 660 | " | " | " | Bhai Ontam Singh ... | Arora. | Banker and Merchant ... | do. |
| 661 | " | " | " | Lala Mul Chand ... | Hindu Khettri. | Banker, Phulanwala Chauk, Amritsar. | do. |
| 662 | " | " | " | Pundit Devi Das ... | Hindu Brahmin. | Physician, Amritsar ... | do. |
| 663 | " | " | " | Mr. Mangu Mal ... | Hindu Bania. | Banker and Shawl Merchant. | do. |
| 664 | " | " | Kasur. | Lala Bhowani Shankar ... | Hindu. | Pleader ... | At a Public Meeting held on the 20th December, 1893. |
| 665 | " | " | " | " Banki Mal ... | do. | Sowkar ... | do. |
| 666 | " | " | " | " Chunni Lal | Hindu Khettri. | Sowkar and Zemindar ... | do. |
| 667 | " | " | Quetta (Beluchistan.) | Sirdir Hukum Singh ... | Sikh. | Contractor ... | At a Public Meeting held at Quetta on the 24th December, 1893. |
| 668 | " | " | " | Mr. Jamsetji Edulji Captain. | Parsi. | Merchant ... | do. |
| 669 | " | " | " | Mirza Niaz Mahomed ... | Mahomedan. | do. ... | do. |
| 670 | " | " | " | Mr. Jamsetji Sorabji Vania. | Parsi. | Contractor ... | do. |
| 671 | " | " | " | Mr. Ardeshere Ruttanji Garwalla. | do. | Contractor and Merchant. | do. |
| 672 | " | " | " | Sirdir Amrit Singh ... | Sikh. | do. ... | do. |
| 673 | " | " | " | " Harnum Singh ... | do. | Merchant ... | do. |
| 674 | Bombay. | Sindh. | Kurrachee. | Mr. Shivandas Noomal, B.A. | Hindu Lohana. | Merchant, Kurrachee ... | Elected at a Meeting of the Congress Committee held at Kurrachee on the 21st December, 1893. |
| 675 | " | " | " | Mr. Tahilram Khemchand, B.A., L.L.B. | Hindu Amil. | Pleader and Municipal Commissioner, Kurrachee. | do. |
| 676 | " | " | " | Mr. Asanund Tejbhandas, B.A. | Hindu Brahmin. | Pleader, Kurrachee ... | do. |
| 677 | " | " | " | Mr. Lalchand Hasamal, B.A., L.L.B. | Hindu Amil. | do. ... | do. |
| 678 | " | " | " | Mr. Lalchand Pahlagrai. | Hindu. | Cashier, Agra Bank, Kurrachee. | At a meeting of the Sindh Sabha held at Kurrachee on the 20th December, 1893. |
| 679 | " | " | " | Mr. Revachand Ramrukhmal. | do. | Merchant, Kurrachee ... | do. |
| 680 | " | " | " | Mr. Basarmal Tarachand. | do. | do. ... | do. |
| 681 | " | " | " | Mr. Deolmal Dowlagram, B.A. | do. | ...... | do. |

| Number. | Presidency or Government. | Congress Circle. | Electoral Division. | Names in full of Delegates, with Honorary Titles, Scholastic Degrees, etc. | Race, Religious denomination, and Caste, if any. | Occupation and Address. | How and when elected. |
|---|---|---|---|---|---|---|---|
| 682 | Bombay. | Sindh. | Kurrachee. | Professor Naik ... | Hindu. | Professor, D. J. Sindh College, Kurrachee. | At a meeting of the Sindh Sabha held at Kurrachee on the 20th December, 1893. |
| 683 | " | " | " | Professor Bejwade ... | do. | do. ... | do. |
| 684 | " | " | " | Mr. Boolchand Doyaram, B.A. | do. | Landlord, Capitalist, Former Fellow, Wilson College and Editor, "Sindh Times." | do. |
| 685 | " | " | " | Mr. Sahib Singh Chandsingh Shahani, M.A. | do. | Professor, Wilson College, Bombay. | do. |
| 686 | " | " | " | Mr. Chatur Singh Ailmal. | Hindu Amil. | Pleader, Hyderabad, (Sindh.) | do. |
| 687 | " | " | " | Mr. Pribhdas Shewakram Adrani. | Hindu. | Manager, "Hiranand Academy" Hyderabad (Sindh.) | do. |
| 688 | " | " | " | Mr. Wadhamal Bellaram. | Hindu Amil. | Pleader, Hyderabad (Sindh.) | do. |
| 689 | " | " | " | Mr. Manjhanmal Kundanmal. | do. | Pleader and Municipal Commissioner, Hyderabad (Sindh.) | do. |
| 690 | " | " | " | Mr. Lekhraj Tilakchand. | Hindu. | Editor, "Prabhat", Hyderabad (Sindh.) | do. |
| 691 | " | " | " | Mr. Jhamatmal Vasanmal. | do. | Pleader, Hyderabad (Sindh.) | do. |
| 692 | " | " | " | Mr. Lilaram Jethmal, B.A., L.L.B. | do. | do. ... | do. |
| 693 | " | " | " | Mr. Thakurdas Khemchand. | do. | Municipal Commissioner and Merchant, Hyderabad (Sindh.) | do. |
| 694 | " | " | " | Mr. Atmaram Thannwardas. | Hindu Amil. | Contractor, Hyderabad, (Sindh.) | do. |
| 695 | " | " | " | Mr. Thawerdas Ramchand- | do. | Pleader, and Municipal Commissioner, Hyderabad, (Sindh.) | do. |
| 696 | " | " | " | Mr. Hiranand Khem Singh, B.A., L.L.B. | do. | Pleader and President of the Municipality, Hyderabad, (Sindh.) | do. |
| 697 | " | " | " | Mr. Muthradas Ramchand B.A., L.L.B. | Hindu Bhatia. | Pleader and Municipal Commissioner, Hyderabad, (Sindh.) | do. |
| 698 | " | " | " | Mr. Jevatram Alimchand, L.M.S. | Hindu Amil. | Medical Practitioner, Hyderabad, (Sindh.) | do. |
| 699 | " | " | " | Seth Chuharsingh Depsing Lala. | Hindu. | Contractor, Shikarpur, (Sindh.) | do. |
| 700 | " | " | Shikarpur (Sindh.) | Mr. Hematsingh Gojsingh Advani, B.A., L.L.B. | Hindu Lohana. | Pleader, Shikarpur ... | At a representative Public Meeting held at Shikarpur on the 17th December, 1893. |
| 701 | " | " | " | Mr. Shivaldas Mulchand. | Hindu Mandari. | do. ... | do. |
| 702 | " | " | " | Seth Hemraj Girdharidas. | Hindu Bhatia. | Merchant, Shikarpur ... | do. |
| 703 | " | " | " | Mr. Chandumal Khemchand. | Arya Bhatia. | Pleader, Shikarpur ... | do. |

| Number. | Presidency or Government. | Congress Circle. | Electoral Division. | Names in full of Delegates, with Honorary Titles, Scholastic Degrees, etc. | Race, Religious denomination, and Caste, if any. | Occupation and Address. | How and when elected. |
|---|---|---|---|---|---|---|---|
| 704 | Bombay. | Sindh. | Shikarpur (Sindh). | Mr. Jhamrai Uttamchand | Hindu Bhatia. | Pleader and Municipal Commissioner, Shikarpur. | At a representative Public Meeting held at Shikarpur on the 17th December, 1893. |
| 705 | " | " | " | Bhai Menghraj Motoomal. | Hindu. | Merchant | do. |
| 706 | " | " | " | Bhai Bhocharmal Kimatrai. | Hindu Bhobjia. | Contractor ... | do. |
| 707 | " | " | " | Mr. Murlidhar Jeramdas. | Hindu. | Zemindar ... | do. |
| 708 | " | " | " | Mr. Kalumal Tikumdas. | do. | Zemindar and Pleader ... | do. |
| 709 | " | " | " | Mr. Lokram Jowmal ... | do. | do. ... | do. |
| 710 | " | " | " | R. S. Bhai Hiranand Gangaram. | Masand. | Zemindar and Member of the Local Board. | do. |
| 711 | " | " | " | Bhai Tirthsing Ramsing. | Hindu Chabia. | Merchant and Zemindar. | do. |
| 712 | " | " | Sukkur (Sindh.) | R. S. Dewan Chetanram A.M. | Hindu Khettri Amil. | Pleader and Municipal Commissioner, Sukkur. | At a Public Meeting held at Sukkur on the 11th December, 1893. |
| 713 | " | " | " | Mr. Cowasji Framji Malkar. | Parsi. | Merchant and Landlord, Sukkur. | do. |
| 714 | " | " | " | R S. Mookai Dewan das. | Hindu Lohana. | Merchant, Sukkur ... | do. |
| 715 | " | " | " | R. S. Dewan Tindan Mal. | do. | Pleader, Zemindar, Municipal Commissioner and Member, District Board, Rohri, Sindh. | do. |
| 716 | " | " | " | Mr. Dosabhai Cowasji ... | Parsi. | Contractor, Sukkur, Sindh. | do. |
| 717 | " | " | " | R. S. Fatehchand Wahyamal. | Hindu Lohana. | Pleader and Municipal Commissioner, Sukkur. | do. |
| 718 | " | " | " | R. B. Pesumal Zokiram. | do. | Pleader and Vice-President, District Local Board, Sukkur. | do. |
| 719 | " | , | " | Lala Dhanrajmal Lakhomal. | Hindu Khettri. | Pleader, Sukkur ... | do. |
| 720 | " | " | " | Mr. Rochaldas, F. ... | Hindu Lohana. | do. ... | do |
| 721 | " | Ahmedabad. | Panchmahals. | Mr. Ganpatrao Sitaram Mukadam. | Hindu Brahmin. | Member and Senior Treasurer, Temperance association, Baroda; Member, Social Reform association and Telang Memorial Committee, Godhra, Panchmahals. | By a Public Meeting held on the 15th November, 1893. |
| 722 | " | " | Ahmedabad. | Mr. Runchhodlal Vandrawandas Patwari B.A., L.L.B. | Hindu Bania. | Pleader, Ahmedabad ... | At a Public Meeting held at Ahmedabad on the 18th December, 1893 |
| 723 | " | " | " | Mr. Ganesh Gopal Pundit, B.A. | Hindu Daxni Brahmin. | Agriculturist, Ahmedabad. | do. |
| 724 | " | " | " | Mandal Harilal Vakil B.A., L.L.B. | Hindu Bania. | Secretary, Bombay University Union, Ahmedabad. | do. |

| Number. | Presidency or Government. | Congress Circle. | Electoral Division. | Names in full of Delegates, with Honorary Titles, Scholastic Degrees, etc. | Race, Religious denomination, and Caste, if any. | Occupation and Address. | How and when elected. |
|---|---|---|---|---|---|---|---|
| 725 | Bombay. | Ahmedabad. | Ahmedabad. | Mr. Jatashankar Latadhar Vaid. | Hindu Brahmin. | Medical practitioner, Ahmedabad. | At a Public Meeting held at Ahmedabad on the 18th December, 1893. |
| 726 | " | " | " | Mr. Vanmalidas Ladhabai Modi. | do. | Editor and Proprietor of the "Hindustan," Ahmedabad. | do. |
| 727 | " | " | " | Mr. Maniklal Harilal ... | Hindu Bania. | Vakil, Ahmedabad ... | do. |
| 728 | " | " | " | Seth Purshottambhai Maghanbhai Hattising. | Hindu Jain. | Merchant, Ahmedabad. | do. |
| 729 | " | Surat. | Surat. | Mr. Hardeoram Nanabhai Haridas. | Hindu Kayastha. | Landowner, 161, Malabar Hill, Bombay. | By a Public Meeting held at Surat on the 17th December, 1893. |
| 730 | " | Sholapur. | Sholapur. | Mr. Shridhar Narayan Sathaye, B.A., L.L.B. | Deccan Brahmin. | Pleader, Sholapur Bijapur. | At a Public Meeting held under the auspices of the Sholapur people's association on the 30th November, 1893. |
| 731 | " | " | " | Mr. Dinker Ballal Chakradev. | Hindu Brahmin. | Pleader and Municipal Commissioner. | do. |
| 732 | " | " | " | Mr. J. Seymour Keay, M.P. | European Christian. | Member of the House of Commons, England, and Agent and Secretary, Hyderabad Deccan Spinning and Weaving Co. | do. |
| 733 | " | Belgaum. | Belgaum. | Mr. Sadasiva Balkrishna Bhate. | Hindu. Brahmin. | Pleader, Municipal Chairman and Member, District Local Board. | At a Public Meeting held at Belgaum on the 14th December, 1893. |
| 734 | " | " | " | The Hon'ble Vishnu Raghunath Natu, B.A., L.L.B. | do. | High Court Pleader, Belgaum, and additional Member, Bombay Legilative Council. | do. |
| 735 | " | Bhusawal. | Bhusawal. | Rao Saheb Chintaman Bapuji Morgankar. | do. | Pleader and Vice-President, Bhusawal Municipality. | At a Public Meeting held at Bhusawal on the 2nd December, 1893. |
| 736 | " | " | " | RaoSaheb Vithal Govind Dastane. | do. | Pleader and Vice-President, Local Board, Bhusawal. | do. |
| 737 | " | " | Jalgaon (Khandesh.) | Mr. Abaji Raghu Mahalas. | do. | Subordinate Government Pleader and Municipal Chairman, Jalgaon. | At a Public Meeting held at Jalgaon on the 2nd December, 1893. |
| 738 | " | Satara | Satara. | Mr. Balvant Shridhar Sahasrabudhe. | do. | Pleader and Municipal Commissioner, Satara. | By a Public Meeting held at Satara on the 13th December, 1893. |
| 739 | " | " | " | Mr. Vasudeo Ram Chandra Joglekar, B.A., L.L.B. | do. | High Court Vakil, Satara. | do. |
| 740 | " | " | " | Mr. Ganesh Hari Hardikar, B.A. | do. | Sowkar, Money-lender and Agriculturist, Satara. | do. |
| 741 | " | " | " | Mr. Raghunath Pandurang Karandikar. | do. | Pleader and Editor of "Vidropak," Satara. | do. |
| 742 | " | " | " | Mr. Dattatraya Balvant Parames. | do. | Editor of the Monthly Magazine "Maharashtra Kokil" | do. |
| 743 | " | Deccan | Poona. | Mr. Girirow Madhav Ghate. | do. | Pleader, Gulburga, (Deccan.) | By a Public Meeting held at Poona on the 10th December, 1893. |

| Number. | Presidency or Government. | Congress Circle. | Electoral Division. | Names in full of Delegates, with Honorary Titles, Scholastic Degrees, etc. | Race, Religious denomination, and Caste, if any. | Occupation and Address. | How and when elected. |
|---|---|---|---|---|---|---|---|
| 744 | Bombay. | Deccan. | Poona. | Mr. Madhavrow Jatkar. | Hindu Brahmin. | Merchant, Satara ... | By a Public Meeting held at Poona on the 10th December, 1893 |
| 745 | " | " | " | Mr. Kashinath Govind Natu. | Hindu. | Pleader, District Court, Poona. | do. |
| 746 | " | " | " | Mr. Rungnath Bapuji Melag. | Hindu Brahmin. | Member, "Sarvajanik Sabha" and Sowkar, Poona. | do. |
| 747 | " | " | " | Mr. Ramkrishna Bhikaji Kulkarni. | do. | Teacher, "Nutan Marathi Vidyalaya" and Editor "Dyan Prakash," Poona. | do. |
| 748 | " | " | " | Mr. Shivaram Hari Sathe. | do. | Editor of "Nyashraya" and Honorary Secretary, "Sarvajanik Sabha," Poona. | do. |
| 749 | " | " | " | Mr. Gopal Krishna Gokhale, B.A. | do. | Professor, Ferguson College and Honorary Secretary and Editor of the Quarterly Journal of the "Sarvajanik Sabha," Poona. | do. |
| 750 | | " | " | Mr. Ramchandra Keshav Limaye. | do. | Pleader, District Court, Sadashiv Peth, Poona. | do. |
| 751 | " | " | " | Shreemant Shankarrao Narayan Natu. | do. | Municipal Commissioner, Sowkar and Inamdar, Shanwar Peth, Poona. | do. |
| 752 | " | " | " | Mr. Vinayek Narayan Apte. | do. | Manager, "Dyan Prakash," Grain dealer and Agent of the "Mercantile Bank Limited," Poona. | do. |
| 753 | " | " | " | Mr. Naro Bhaskar Deodhar. | do. | Inamdar, Retired Deputy Educational Inspector and Member, "Sarvajanik Sabha." | do. |
| 754 | " | " | " | Shreemant Moreshwarrao Vishvanath Natu. | do. | Inamdar, 1st Class Sirdir and Jagirdar, Poona. | do. |
| 755 | " | " | " | Mr. Ramchandra More shwar Sane. | do. | Pleader, District Court, Narayan Peth, Poona. | do. |
| 756 | " | " | " | Mr. Raghunath Daji Nagarkar. | do. | Pleader, Municipal Commissioner and Inamdar, Budhwar Peth, Poona. | do |
| 757 | " | " | " | Shreemant Narharrao Trimbak Rajinachikar, B A. | do. | Inamdar, Mehenpura, Poona. | do. |
| 758 | " | " | " | Rao Bahadur Vishnu Moreshwar Bhide. | do. | Retired 1st Class Sub-Judge; 1st Grade Honorary Magistrate and Chairman, "Sarvajanik Sabha," Poona. | do. |
| 759 | " | " | " | Mr. Vaman Balkrishna Ranade. | do. | Editor "Dyan Chakshu," a Marathi Weekly. | do. |
| 760 | " | " | " | Mr. Bal Gangadhar Tilak, B.A., L.L.B. | do. | Law Lecturer, Ferguson College, and Editor of the "Kesari" a Marathi Weekly and the "Marhatta" English Weekly. | do. |

| Number. | Presidency or Government. | Congress Circle. | Electoral Division. | Names in full of Delegates, with Honorary Titles, Scholastic Degrees, etc. | Race, Religious denomination, and Caste, if any. | Occupation and Address. | How and when elected. |
|---|---|---|---|---|---|---|---|
| 761 | Bombay. | Deccan. | Poona. | Mr. Mahadeo Ballal Namjoshi. | Hindu Brahmin. | Editor, "Quarterly Journal of the Industrial Association of Western India," Secretary Metal Manufactory and Municipal Commissioner. | By a Public Meeting held at Poona on the 10th December, 1893. |
| 762 | " | " | " | Mr. Vasudeo Ganesh Joshi. | do. | Manager, "Chitrasala Printing Press," Poona. | do. |
| 763 | " | " | " | Mr. Hari Mahadeo Paranjpai. | do. | Editor and proprietor, "Native Opinion" Girgaon, Bombay. | By a Meeting of the Committee of the Poona "Sarvajanik Sabha" held on the 8th December 1893. |
| 764 | " | " | Barawali. | Rao Saheb Bhikaji Anandrao Deshpande. | do. | Pleader and Chairman of the Barawali Municipality and Member, Local Board, Poona. | At a Public Meeting held at Barawali on the 15th December, 1893. |
| 765 | " | " | Nasik. | Mr. Gangadhar Narsing Ketkar. | do. | Pleader, District Court, Nasik. | At a General Meeting of the Nasik "Sarvajanik Sabha" held on the 9th December, 1893. |
| 766 | " | " | " | Mr. Shridhar Gopal Putekar. | do. | Pleader and Municipal Commissioner. | do. |
| 767 | " | " | " | Mr. Eknath Shamlal ... | Hindu Gujrati Kadwa. | Merchant, Yeola ... | do. |
| 768 | " | " | " | Mr. Jagjivan Khemchand. | Hindu Gujratj. | Banker, Yeola ... | do. |
| 769 | " | " | " | Mr. Anant Raoji Kavale. | Hindu Brahmin. | Pleader, Municipal Commissioner and Member, District Local Board, Nasik. | do. |
| 770 | " | " | " | Mr. Rajaram Yeshwant Raje. | Hindu Parbhu. | Pleader, Sub-Judge's Court, Sinnar, District Nasik. | do. |
| 771 | " | " | " | Mr. Namadeva Tukaram Simpi. | Hindu Simpi. | Merchant, Yeola ... | do |
| 772 | " | Ichalkeranji. | Ichalkeranji. | Mr. Vishnu Moreshwar Limaye. | Hindu Brahmin. | Pleader, Ichalkeranji State. | At a Public Meeting held at Ichalkeranji on the 9th December, 1893. |
| 773 | " | " | " | Mr. Dattatraya Ganesh Tikakar. | Hindu. | Municipal Commissioner. | do. |
| 774 | " | " | Kagal. | Mr. Krishnaji Dadaji Kulkarni. | Hindu. Brahmin. | Landholder, Village Rui, Halkalanjab P.O. Kolhapore. | At a Public Meeting held at Rui on the 23rd December, 1893. |
| 775 | " | Bombay. | Bombay. | Mr. Dadabhai Naoroji, M.P. | Parsi. | Member of British Parliament. | At a Meeting of the Bombay Presidency Association held on the 18th December, 1893. |
| 776 | " | " | " | Dr. John. D. Cunha, L.M.S. | Portuguese Christian. | Medical Practitioner ... | do. |
| 777 | " | " | " | Mr. Gangadhar Sadasheo Gokhale. | Hindu Brahmin. | Engineer ... | do. |
| 778 | " | " | " | Mr. Ratiram Durgaram Dave, B.A. | Hindu Gujrati. | Fellow of the University of Bombay and Articled Clerk, Messrs Payne Gilbert and Logani, Solicitors, Bombay. | do. |
| 779 | " | " | " | Mr. Daji Abaji Khare, B.A., L.L.B. | Deccan Hindu. | Pleader, High Court, Bombay. | do. |

| Number. | Presidency or Government. | Congress Circle. | Electoral Division. | Names in full of Delegates, with Honorary Titles, Scholastic Degrees, etc. | Race, Religious denomination, and Caste, if any. | Occupation and Address. | How and when elected |
|---|---|---|---|---|---|---|---|
| 780 | Bombay. | Bombay. | Bombay. | Dr. K. N. Bhadurji, M.D. | Parsi. | Medical Practitioner ... | At a Meeting of the Bombay Presidency Association held on the 18th December, 1893. |
| 781 | " | " | " | Mr. W. A. Chambers ... | European Christian. | Civil Engineer ... | do. |
| 782 | " | " | " | Mr. Dinshaw Edulji Wacha. | Parsi. | Mill Agent, Member, Municipal Corporation and and Secretary, Presidency Association, Bombay. | do. |
| 783 | " | " | " | Dr. M. R. Setna L.M.S., J.P. | do. | Medical Practitioner ... | do. |
| 784 | " | " | " | Mr. Hari Sitaram Dixit. | Hindu Gujrati. | Solicitor, High Court, Bombay. | do. |
| 785 | " | " | " | Mr. Sadashiv Vaman Kane, L.M.S. | Deccan Hindu. | Medical Practitioner ... | do. |
| 786 | " | " | " | Dr Bhal Chandra Krishna, L.M.S. | do. | Medical Practitioner and Member of the Municipal Corporation, Bombay. | do. |
| 787 | " | " | " | Mr. B. N. Bhajikar, B.A., L.L.B. | do. | Vakil and Inamdar, Girgaon, (Bombay.) | do. |
| 788 | " | " | " | Mr. Pranalal. K. Joshipara | Gujrati Hindu. | Civil Engineer ... | do. |
| 789 | " | " | " | Mr. Narsingrao Sayaboo. | Deccan Hindu. | Contractor ... | do. |
| 790 | " | " | " | Mr. Moreshwar Gopal Deshmukh, B.A., B.S.C., M.D. | do. | Medical Practitioner, Syndic in Arts and Justice of the Peace, Bombay. | do. |
| 791 | " | " | " | Mr. Madasadmi Vasudeo Athalye, B.A. | do. | Landholder ... | do. |
| 792 | " | " | " | Rao Bahadur. Nil Kantha Bhagwant. | Hindu. | Pensioned Deputy Collector. | do. |
| 793 | " | " | Thana. | Mr. Ardeshere Cursetji Pallonji. | Parsi. | Merchant, Thana ... | At a Public Meeting held at Thana on the 21st December, 1893. |
| 794 | " | " | " | Mr. Sitaram Ballal Joglekar. | Hindu Brahmin. | Pleader, Thana ... | do. |
| 795 | " | " | " | Mr. Mangaldas Devidas. | Hindu Bania. | Merchant, Thana ... | do. |
| 796 | " | " | " | Mr. Mahadeo Ganesh Pundit. | Hindu Brahmin. | Pleader, Thana ... | do. |
| 797 | " | " | Colaba. | Mr. Waman Bapuji Deva. | do. | Landholder and Merchant, Pen, District Colaba. | At a Public Meeting held at Colaba on the 21st December, 1893. |
| 798 | Govt. of India. | Berar. | Amraoti. | Mr. Rangnath Narsing Mudholkar, B.A., L.L.B. | Hindu Maharshtra Brahmin. | Pleader, Landholder and Municipal Commissioner, Amraoti. | At a Public Meeting held at Amraoti on the 22nd November, 1893. |
| 799 | " | " | " | Mr. Moreshwar Bapuji Marathi. | do. | Pleader, Amraoti ... | do. |
| 800 | " | " | " | Mr. Ganesh Srikrishna Khaparde, B.A., L.L.B. | do. | Pleader, Landholder, Malguzar, Vice-Chairman, Town Municipality and Chairman, District Board, Amraoti. | do. |

| Number. | Presidency or Government. | Congress Circle. | Electoral Division. | Names in full of Delegates, with Honorary Titles, Scholastic Degrees, etc. | Race, Religious denomination, and Caste, if any. | Occupation and Address. | How and when elected. |
|---|---|---|---|---|---|---|---|
| 801 | Govt. of India. | Berar. | Amraoti. | Mr. Wasudeo Narayan Jog. | Hindu Brahmin. | Pleader, Banker and Municipal Commissioner. | At a Public Meeting held at Amraoti on the 22nd November, 1893. |
| 802 | " | " | " | Mr. Keshav Balwant Deshpande. | do. | Banker and Landholder. | do. |
| 803 | " | " | " | Mr. Vinayek Sowlaram Oke | do. | Pleader ... | do. |
| 804 | " | " | " | Rao Saheb Deorao Vinayek. | do. | Pleader, Landholder and Municipal Commissioner. | At a Meeting of the Berar "Sarvajanik Sabha" held on the 10th December, 1893. |
| 805 | " | " | " | Mr. Golam Ahmed Khan. | Mahomedan. | Landholder, Merchant and Member, Local Board, Mulkhapur. | do. |
| 806 | " | " | Ellichpur. | Mr. Gangadhar Narayan Jagadale. | Hindu Brahmin. | Pleader, Ellichpur ... | At a Public Meeting held at Ellichpur on the 7th December, 1893. |
| 807 | " | " | Akola. | Mr. Hari Ram Chandra Amikar. | Hindu Krishnapakshi. | Editor of the "Shadh Varhadi." | At a Public Meeting held at Akola on the 10th December, 1893. |
| 808 | " | " | " | Mr. W. Venkatesh Ramchandra Mudholkar. | Hindu Brahmin. | Editor, "Vaidarbha," and Honorary Secretary, Municipal Committee. | do. |
| 809 | " | " | Basim. | Mr. Govind Kasheo Chavak. | Hindu Kayastha Prabhd. | Pleader, Basim ... | At a Public Meeting held at Basim on the 3rd December, 1893. |
| 810 | " | " | " | Mr. Lakshman Atmaram Mahajan. | Hindu Brahmin. | Merchant, Member, District Board, Basim; Vice-Chairman, Taluq Board, Mangrulpir, Basim District. | do. |
| 811 | " | " | Wun. | Mr. Gopal Narayan Bhat. | do. | Pleader and Municipal Commissioner, Yeotmal, Berar. | At a Public Meeting held on the 9th December, 1893. |
| 812 | " | " | " | Mr. Baliram Raghu Sastikar. | do. | Pleader, Yeotmal ... | do. |
| 813 | " | " | " | Mr. Lakshman Chintaman Bapat. | do. | Pleader and Municipal Commissioner, Yeotmal. | do. |
| 814 | " | " | " | Mr. Ramchandra Ganesh Mundle, B.A., L.L.B. | do. | do. ... | do. |
| 815 | Central Provinces. | Nagpur. | Nagpur. | Mr. Keshav Vinayek Joshi, B.A. | Hindu Maharashtri Brahmin. | Head Master, Neill City High School, Nagpur. | At a Public Meeting held at Nagpur on the 22nd November, 1893. |
| 816 | " | " | " | Cotari Venkata Raman Naidu. | Hindu Khettri. | Barrister-at-law ... | do. |
| 817 | " | " | " | Dr. Adharsing Gour, M.A., (Dublin) L.L.D., L.L.M., F.R.A.S., F.R.S. &c. &c. | do. | Barrister-at-law, Hoshangabad. | do. |
| 818 | " | " | " | Mr. R. Srinivasarao Naidu. | do. | Agent to the Zemindars of Chanda (Wardha District.) | do |
| 819 | " | " | " | Mr. Ganpatrao Narayan Gokhale. | Hindu. Brahmin. | Pleader and Landholder, Nagpur. | do. |
| 820 | " | " | " | Mr. Hari Mahadeo Pundit. | do. | Editor and Proprietor of "Desha-Sewaka," Chitnavispura, Nagpur. | do. |

| Number. | Presidency or Government. | Congress Circle. | Electoral Division. | Names in full of Delegates, with Honorary Titles, Scholastic Degrees, etc. | Race, Religious denomination, and Caste, if any. | Occupation and Address. | How and when elected. |
|---|---|---|---|---|---|---|---|
| 821 | Central Provinces. | Nagpur. | Saugor. | Mr. Vinayekrao Vaidya. | Hindu. Brahmin. | Pleader ... | At a Meeting ot the "Hit Sabha" held on the 3rd December, 1893. |
| 822 | " | " | " | Mr. Damodar Ramchandra Srikhande. | do. | do. ... | do. |
| 823 | " | " | " | Mr. Lakshman Anant Mahatkar. | do. | do. ... | do. |
| 824 | " | " | Damoh. | Mr. Gopal Das Sarma. | do. | Contractor, Damoh ... | By a Meeting of the Damoh "Sukh Karni Sabha held on the 19th December, 1893. |
| 825 | " | " | Balaghat. | Mr. Narayan Krishna Kelkar. | do. | Pleader and Secretary, Municipal Committee, Balaghat. | At a Public Meeting held at Balaghat on the 1st December, 1893. |
| 826 | " | " | Rajnand gaon State. | Pundit Bhagwan Datta Seratia. | do. | Landholder and Editor, "Rajnandgaon." | At a Public Meeting held at Rajnandgaon on the 18th December, 1893. |
| 827 | " | " | Jubbulpur. | Mr. Ganesh Wasudeo Saney. | do. | Merchant and Contractor. | At a Special Meeting of the Literary and Scientific Association of Jubbulpur on the 17th December, 1893. |
| 828 | " | " | Hoshangabad. | Mr. Vishnu Ram Krishna Gudrey. | do. | Pleader, Hoshangabad ... | At a Meeting of the townspeople of Hoshangabad held on the 20th December, 1893. |
| 829 | " | " | Chhindwara. | Mr. Muthra Prasad ... | Hindu Kayastha. | Pleader and Landowner, Chhindwara. | By a Public Meeting held at Chhindwara on the 3rd December, 1893. |
| 830 | " | " | " | Mr. Baliram Narayan Deshmukh, B.A., B.L. | Hindu Brahmin. | do. ... | do. |
| 831 | " | " | " | Mr. Vinayek Ganesh Wazalwar. | do. | do. ... | do. |
| 832 | " | " | " | Pundit Prabhakar Shastri. | Hindu Brahmin. | Landowner ... | do. |
| 833 | " | " | Burhanpur. | Mr. Raghunath Balkrishna Bhide. | do. | Proprietor of the "Arya Vai Bhaw" Press, Burhanpur. | At a Public Meeting held at Burhanpur on the 15th December, 1893. |
| 834 | " | " | Harda. | Mr. Ali Mahomed Bhimji. | Mahomedan. | Agent, Cotton Presses and Cotton Ginning Factories, Indore and Bombay. | At a Public Meeting held at Harda on the 18th December, 1893. |
| 835 | " | " | " | Mr. Trimbak Jaywant Sabnis. | Hindu Saraswat | Clerk to the Jagirdar of Ajanas Anapura, Post Harda, C. P. | do. |
| 836 | " | " | Wardha. | Mr. Keshavrao Mahadeo Kaule. | Hindu Brahmin. | Pleader, Banker, Malguzar and Municipal Commissioner, Wardha. | At a Meeting of the District Association of Wardha held on the 19th December, 1893. |
| 837 | Madras. | Madras. | Madras. | Mr. Ganapathy Subramania Iyer. | do. | Editor of the Hindu" and Municipal Commissioner. | At a Meeting of the "Mahajan Sabha" held on the 18th December, 1893. |
| 838 | " | | " | Rai Bahadur. P. Ananda Charlu. | do. | Vakil, High Court and Joint General Secretary, Indian National Congress. | do. |

| Number. | Presidency or Government. | Congress Circle. | Electoral Division. | Names in full of Delegates, with Honorary Titles, Scholastic Degrees, etc. | Race, Religious denomination, and Caste, if any. | Occupation and Address. | How and when elected. |
|---|---|---|---|---|---|---|---|
| 839 | Madras. | Madras. | Madras. | Mr. Peter Paul Pillai ... | Nativie Christian. | Agent, and Landholder. | At a Meeting of the "Mahajan Sabha" held on the 18th December, 1893. |
| 840 | " | " | " | Mr. K. Ethiraja Pillai ... | Hindu Vaisya. | Merchant and Contractor. | do. |
| 841 | " | " | Salem. | Mr. C. Venkata Chariar. | Hindu Brahmin. | Landholder and Member, District Board, Salem. | At a Public Meeting held at Salem on the 14th December, 1893. |
| 842 | " | " | " | Mr. B. Krishna Ram, B.A., B.L. | do. | Pleader, Salem ... | do. |
| 843 | " | " | " | Mr. W. Viraswamy Iyer. | do. | Pleader and Chairman, Salem Municipality. | do. |
| 844 | " | " | " | Mr. U. Venkata Ram, B.A., B.L. | do. | Pleader, Salem ... | do. |
| 845 | " | " | " | Mr N. Ramswamy Iyer, B.A., B.L. | do. | do. ... | do. |
| 846 | " | " | Palghat (Malabar.) | Mr. K. P. Achhutha Menon. | Hindu Nair. | Pleader, Municipal Commissioner and Honorary Magistrate, Palghat. | At a Public Meeting held at Palghat on the 23rd December, 1893. |
| 847 | " | " | " | Mr. S. Kutton Nair ... | do. | Landholder ... | do. |
| 848 | " | " | Tellicherry. | Mr. M. Gopal Menon, B.A., B.L. | do. | Apprentice-at-Law, Madras. | At a Public Meeting held at Tellicherry on the 20th December, 1893. |
| 849 | " | " | Calicut. | The Hon'ble C. Sankaran Nair, B.A., B.L. | do. | Vakil, High Court, Member, Legislative Council and Fellow of the University, Madras. | At a Public Meeting held at Calicut on the 16th December, 1893. |
| 850 | " | " | " | Mr. K. P. Raman Menon. | do. | Pleader, Calicut ... | do. |
| 851 | " | " | " | Mr. C. K. Raman Menon. | do. | Editor and Proprietor, "Kerala Patrika," Calicut. | do. |
| 852 | " | " | Cuddapah. | Rao Bahadur C. Jambulingam Mudaliar, B.A., | Hindu Velala. | Pleader, Cuddapah ... | At a Public Meeting held at Cuddapah on the 16th December, 1893. |
| 853 | " | " | Tanjore. | Mr. N. S. Rajaram ... | Hindu Brahmin. | Banker and Landholder, Negapatum. | By a Public Meeting held at Tanjore on the 16th December, 1893. |
| 854 | " | " | Bezwada (Kristna District.) | Sri Raja Kocherlakota Ramchandra Venkata Kristna Row Pantulu Bahadur. | do. | Zemindar ... | Elected at a Meeting of the "Viziavada Sabha" of Bezwada on the 17th December, 1893. |
| 855 | " | " | " | Mr. D. Seshachalapati Row. | do. | Editor, "Kristna News" and Vernacular Secretary, "Viziavada Sabha," Bezwada. | do. |
| 856 | " | " | Rajahmundry. | The Hon'ble N. Subbarao Pantulu Garu, B.A., B.L. | do. | Vakil, High Court, Member, Legislative Council, Madras; Member, District Board and Municipal Commissioner, Rajahmundry. | At a Public Meeting held at Rajahmundry on the 13th December, 1893. |
| 857 | " | " | " | Mr. N. Subramanya ... | Hindu. | Inamdar ... | do. |
| 858 | " | " | " | Mr. S. Lakshmipaty ... | Hindu Brahmin. | Banker and Landholder. | do. |

| Number. | Presidency or Government. | Congress Circle. | Electoral Division. | Names in full of Delegates, with Honorary Titles, Scholastic Degrees, etc. | Race, Religious denomination, and Caste, if any. | Occupation and Address. | How and when elected. |
|---|---|---|---|---|---|---|---|
| 859 | Madras. | Madras. | Ellore. | Mr. A. Kanakarajee, B.A. | Hindu. | 1st Grade Vakil, Godavary. | By a Public Meeting held at Ellore on the 19th November, 1893. |
| 860 | " | " | Vizagapatam. | Mr. O. V. Jagannadha Shastri. | Hindu Brahmin. | Pleader, Member, Taluq Board, Parvatipur, District Board, Vizagapatam and Secretary, Mahajan Sabha. | By a Public Meeting held at Vizagapatam on the 20th December, 1893. |
| 861 | " | " | Bellary. | Mr. C. Hanumanthi Gond. | Hindu. | Hony. Magistrate, Member, District and Taluq Boards and Mirasidar, Hospet. | Elected at a Meeting held by the people of the place on the 13th December, 1893. |
| 862 | " | " | " | Mr. D. Gopala Charlu ... | do. | Pleader, Bellary ... | do. |
| 863 | " | " | " | Mr. B. Subba Sastrulu ... | do. | Inamdar, Bellary ... | do. |
| 864 | " | " | " | Mr. B. Madhava Row ... | do. | do. ... | do. |
| 865 | " | " | Kurnool. | Mr. T. Chidambara Row, B.A. | Hindu Brahmin. | Pleader, Landholder and Member, District Board, Kurnool. | At a Public Meeting held at Kurnool on the 21st December, 1893. |
| 866 | " | Madura. | Sivaganga. | Mr. K. V. Subramania Iyer, B.A., B.L. | do. | Vakil, Madura ... | At a Public Meeting held at Madura on the 16th December, 1893. |
| 867 | " | " | " | Mr. S. M. Narayana Swamy Iyer, B.A. | do. | Teachar, Raja's High School, Sivaganga, Madura District. | do. |

# APPENDIX II.

## SUMMARY OF RESOLUTIONS.

PASSED AT THE

## First, Second, Third, Fourth, Fifth, Sixth, Seventh and Eighth Congresses.

## RESOLUTIONS PASSED AT THE FIRST CONGRESS.

### RESOLUTION I.

**Resolved**—That this Congress earnestly recommends that the promised inquiry into the working of the Indian Administration, here and in England, should be entrusted to a Royal Commission, the people of India being adequately represented thereon, and evidence taken both in India and in England.

### RESOLUTION II.

**Resolved**—That this Congress considers the abolition of the Council of the Secretary of State for India, as at present constituted, the necessary preliminary to all other reforms.

### RESOLUTION III.

**Resolved**—That this Congress considers the reform and expansion of the Supreme and existing Local Legislative Councils, by the admission of a considerable proportion of elected members (and the creation of similar Councils for the North-Western Provinces and Oudh, and also for the Punjab) essential; and holds that all Budgets should be referred to these Councils for consideration their members being moreover empowered to interpellate the Executive in regard to all branches of the administration; and that a Standing Committee of the House of Commons should be constituted to receive and consider any formal protests that may be recorded by majorities of such Councils against the exercise by the Executive of the power which would be vested in it, of overruling the decisions of such majorities.

### RESOLUTION IV.

**Resolved**—That in the opinion of this Congress the competitive examinations now held in England for first appointments in various civil departments of the Public service should henceforth, in accordance with the views of the India Office Committee of 1860, "be held simultaneously, one in England and one in India, both being as far as practicable identical in their nature, and those who compete in both countries being finally classified in one list according to merit," and that the successful candidates in India should be sent to England for further study, and subjected there to such further examinations as may seem needful. Further, that all other first appointments (excluding peonships, and the like) should be filled by competitive examinations held in India, under conditions calculated to secure such intellectual, moral, and physical qualifications as may be decided by Government to be necessary. Lastly, that the maximum age of candidates for entrance into the Covenanted Civil Service be raised to not less than 23 years.

### RESOLUTION V.

**Resolved**—That in the opinion of this Congress the proposed increase in the military expenditure of the empire is unnecessary, and, regard being had to the revenues of the empire and the existing circumstances of the country, excessive.

### RESOLUTION VI.

**Resolved**— That in the opinion of this Congress, if the increased demands for military expenditure are not to be, as they ought to be, met by retrenchment, they ought to be met, firstly, by the re-imposition of the Customs duties; and, secondly, by the extension of the license-tax to those classes of the community, official and non-official, at present exempted from it, care being taken that in the case of all clssses a sufficiently high taxable minimum be maintained. And, further, that this Congress is of opinion that Great Britain should extend an imperial guarantee to the Indian debt.

### RESOLUTION VII.

**Resolved**—That this Congress deprecates the annexation of Upper Burmah, and considers that if the Government unfortunately decide on annexation, the entire country of Burmah should be separated from the Indian Viceroyalty and constituted a Crown Colony, as distinct in all matters from the Government of the country as is Ceylon.

### RESOLUTION VIII.

**Resolved**—That the resolutions passed by this Congress be communicated to the Political Associations in each province, and that these Associations be requested, with the help of similar bodies and other agencies within their respective provinces, to adopt such measures as they may consider calculated to advance the settlement of the various questions dealt with in these resolutions.

### RESOLUTION IX.

**Resolved**—That the Indian National Congress re-assemble next year in Calcutt and sit on Tuesday, the 28th of December, 1886, and the next succeeding days.

---

## RESOLUTIONS PASSED AT THE SECOND CONGRESS.

---

### RESOLUTION I.

**Resolved**—That this Congress of Delegates from all parts of India do humbly offer its dutiful and loyal congratulations to Her Most Gracious Majesty, the Queen-Empress, on the approaching completion of the first half century of her memorable, beneficent and glorious reign, and heartily wish her many, many more, and happy years of rule over the great British Empire.

### RESOLUTION II.

**Resolved**—That this Congress regards with the deepest sympathy, and views with grave apprehension, the increasing poverty of vast numbers of the population of India, and (although aware that the Government is not overlooking this matter and is contemplating certain palliatives) desires to record its fixed conviction that the introduction of Representative Institutions will prove one of the most important practical steps towards the amelioration of the condition of the people.

### RESOLUTION III.

**Resolved**—That this Congress do, emphatically, re-affirm the 3rd Resolution of the Congress of 1885, and distinctly declare its belief that the reform and expansion of the

Council of the Governor-General for making laws and of the Provincial Legislative Councils, therein suggested, have now become essential alike in the interests of India and England.

### RESOLUTION IV.

**Resolved**—That this Congress is of opinion that, in giving practical effect to this essential reform, regard should be had (subject to such modifications as, on a more detailed examination of the question, may commend themselves to the Government) to the principles embodied in the following tentative suggestions:—

(1)—The number of persons composing the Legislative Councils, both provincial and of the Governor-General, to be materially increased. Not less than one-half the Members of such enlarged Councils to be elected. Not more than one-fourth to be officials having seats *ex-officio* in such Councils, and not more than one-fourth to be Members, official or non-official, nominated by Government.

(2)—The right to elect Members to the Provincial Councils to be conferred only on those classes and members of the community, *prima facie*, capable of exercising it wisely and independently. In Bengal and Bombay the Councillors may be elected by the Members of Municipalities, District Boards, Chambers of Commerce and the Universities, or an electorate may be constituted of all persons possessing such qualifications, educational and pecuniary as may be deemed necessary. In Madras the Councillors may be elected either by District Boards, Municipalities, Chambers of Commerce and the University, or by Electoral Colleges composed of Members partly elected by these bodies and partly nominated by Government. In the North-West Provinces and Oudh and in the Punjab Councillors may be elected by an Electoral College composed of Members elected by Municipal and District Boards, and nominated, to an extent not exceeding one-sixth of the total number, by Government, it being understood that the same elective system now in force where Municipal Boards are concerned will be applied to District Boards and the right of electing Members to these latter extended to the cultivating class. But whatever system be adopted (and the details must be worked out separately for each province) care must be taken that all sections of the Community and all great interests are adequately represented.

(3)—The elected Members of the Council of the Governor-General for making laws, to be elected by the elected Members of the several Provincial Councils.

(4)—No elected or nominated Member of any Council to receive any salary or remuneration in virtue of such Membership, but any such Member, already in receipt of any Government salary or allowance, to continue to draw the same unchanged during Membership, and all Members to be entitled to be reimbursed any expenses incurred in travelling in connection with their Membership.

(5)—All persons, resident in India, to be eligible for seats in Council, whether as electees or nominees, without distinction of race, creed, caste or colour.

(6)—All legislative measures and all financial questions, including all budgets, whether these involve new or enhanced taxation or not, to be necessarily submitted to and dealt with by these Councils. In the case of all other branches of the administration, any Member to be at liberty, after due notice, to put any question he sees fit to the *ex-officio* Members (or such one of these as may be especially charged with the supervision of the particular branch concerned) and to be entitled (except as hereinafter provided) to receive a reply to his question, together with copies of any papers requisite for the thorough comprehension of the subject, and on this reply the Council to be at liberty to consider and discuss the question, and record thereon such resolution as may appear fitting to the majority. Provided that, if the subject in regard to which the inquiry is made involves matters of Foreign policy, Military dispositions or strategy, or is otherwise of such a nature that, in the opinion of the Executive, the public interests would be materially imperilled by the communication of the information asked for, it shall be competent for them to instruct the *ex-officio* Members, or one of them, to reply accordingly, and decline to furnish the information asked for.

(7)—The Executive Government shall possess the power of overruling the decision arrived at by the majority of the Council, in every case in which, in its opinion, the public interests would suffer by the acceptance of such decision; but whenever this power is exercised, a full exposition of the grounds on which this has been considered necessary, shall be published within one month, and in the case of local Governments they shall report the circumstances and explain their action to the Government of India, and, in the case of this latter, it shall report and explain to the Secretary of State; and in any such case on a representation made through the Government of India and the Secretary of State by the overruled majority, it shall be competent to the Standing Committee of the House of Commons (recommended in the 3rd Resolution of last year's Congress which this present Congress has affirmed) to consider the matter, and call for any and all papers or information, and hear any persons on behalf of such majority or otherwise, and thereafter, if needful, report thereon to the full House.

### RESOLUTION V.

**Resolved**—That this Congress do invite all Public Bodies and all Associations throughout the Country, humbly and earnestly, to entreat His Excellency the Viceroy to obtain the sanction of Her Majesty's Secretary of State for India, to the appointment of a Commission, to enquire exhaustively into the best method of introducing such a tentative form of Representative Institutions into India, as has been indicated in Resolutions III. of the past, and IV. of the present year's Congress.

### RESOUTION VI.*

**Resolved**—That a Committee composed of the gentlemen named in the margin* be appointed to consider the Public Service Question and report thereon to this Congress.

*Hon'ble Dadabhai Naoroji (*Bombay.*)
" S. Subramania Iyer (*Madras.*)
" Peary Mohun Mukerjee (*Calcutta.*)
Mr. G. Subramania Iyer (*Madras.*)
Babu Motilal Ghose (*Calcutta.*)
Mr. Surendra Nath Banerjee (*Calcutta.*)
" Gungapershad Varma (*Lucknow.*)
" Ramkali Ghaudhuri (*Benares.*)
Mr. Guru Prasad Sen (*Patna.*)
Pundit Prannath (*Lucknow.*)
Munshi Kashipershad (*Allahabad.*)
Nowab Reza Ali Khan (*Lucknow.*)
Mr. Hamid Ali (*Lucknow.*)
Lala Kanhyalal (*Amritsar.*)
Rao Sahib Gangadhar Rao
Madhaw Chitnavis (*Nagpur.*)
Mr. Rahimatulla M. Sayani (*Bombay.*)

### RESOLUTION VII.

**Resolved**—That this Congress approves and adopts the report* submitted by the Committee appointed by Resolution VI.

### RESOLUTION VIII.

**Resolved**—That, in the opinion of this Congress, the time has now arrived when the system of trial by jury may be safely extended into many parts of the country where it is not at present in force.

---

### *REPORT.

We, the Members of the Committee appointed by the Congress to submit a statement in connection with the Public Service Question, have the honor to report that the following resolutions were unanimously adopted by us at a meeting held yesterday :—

1.—That the open Competitive Examination be held simultaneously both in India and in England.

2.—That the Simultaneous Examinations thus held be equally open to all classes of Her Majesty's subjects.

3.—That the Classified lists be prepared according to merit.

4.—That the Congress express the hope that the Civil Service Commissioners will give fair consideration to Sanskrit and Arabic among the subjects of examination.

5.—That the age of candidates eligible for admission to the open Competitive Examination be not less than 19, nor, as recommended by Sir C. Aitchison, more than 23 years.

6.—That Simultaneous Examinations being granted, the Statutory Civil Service be closed for first appointments.

7.—That the appointments in the Statutory Civil Service, under the existing rules, be still left open to the Members of the Uncovenanted Service and to professional men of proved merit and ability

8.—That all appointments requiring educational qualifications, other than covenanted first appointments, be filled by competitive Examinations held in the different Provinces, and open in each Province to such natural-born subjects of H. M. only as are residents thereof.

These Resolutions, it is hoped, cover the main principles which underlie the questions set by the Public Service Commission. For a more detailed consideration there was no time.

(Sd.) DADABHAI NAOROJI,
*President of the Committee.*

*30th December, 1886.*

### RESOLUTION IX.

**Resolved**—That, in the opinion of this Congress, the innovation made in 1872 in the system of trial by jury, depriving the verdicts of juries of all finality, has proved injurious to the country, and that the powers then, for the first time, vested in Sessions Judges and High Courts, of setting aside verdicts of acquittal, should be at once withdrawn.

### RESOLUTION X.

**Resolved**—That, in the opinion of this Congress, a provision, similar to that contained in the Summary Jurisdiction Act of England (under which accused persons in serious cases have the option of demanding a committal to the Sessions Court), should be introduced into the Indian Code of Criminal Procedure, enabling accused persons, in warrant cases, to demand that, instead of being tried by the Magistrate, they be committed to the Court of Sessions.

### RESOLUTION XI.

**Resolved**—That this Congress do place on record an expression of the universal conviction, that a complete separation of executive and judicial functions (such that in no case the two functions shall be combined in the same officer) has become an urgent necessity, and that, in its opinion, it behoves the Government to effect this separation without further delay, even though this should, in some Provinces, involve some extra expenditure.

### RESOLUTION XII.

**Resolved**—That, in view of the unsettled state of public affairs in Europe, and the immense assistance that the people of this country, if duly prepared therefor, is capable of rendering to Great Britain in the event of any serious complications arising, this Congress do earnestly appeal to the Government to authorise (under such rules and restrictions, as may to it seem fitting) a system of Volunteering for the Indian inhabitants of the country, such as may qualify them to support the Government effectively in any crises.

### RESOLUTION XIII.

**Resolved**—That Standing Congress Committees be constituted at all important centres.

### RESOLUTION XIV.

**Resolved**—That the Third Indian National Congress assemble at Madras on the 27th of December, 1887.

### RESOLUTION XV.

**Resolved**—That, copies of these Resolutions be forwarded to His Excellency the Viceroy-in-Council, with the humble requests that he will cause the 1st Resolution to be submitted in due course to Her Majesty the Queen-Empress, that he will cause all the Resolutions to be laid before Her Majesty's Secretary of State for India, and that he himself will be graciously pleased, in consultation with his colleagues, to accord them his best consideration.

# RESOLUTIONS PASSED AT THE THIRD CONGRESS

### RESOLUTION I.

**Resolved**—That a Committee is appointed, consisting of the gentlemen (marginally enumerated*), to consider what rules, if any, may now be usefully framed in regard to the constitution and working of the Congress, with instructions to report thereon to the Congress, on the 30th instant.

* Messrs. Namjoshi, Chandravarker, Mir Humayun Jah Bahadur, Hajee Mahomed Abdul Shakoor Badshaw Sahib, S. Subramania Iyer, W. S. Gantz, Rangiah Naidu, Surendranath Banerjee, Trailokhyanath Mitra, Kali Charan Banerjee, Guru Prasad Sen, Saligram Singh, Ram Kali Chaudhuri, Hafiz Abdul Rahim, Rampal Singh, Pandit Madan Mohun, Ganga Prasad Varma, Bishen Narayen Dar, Hamid Ali, Murlidhar, Satyanand Agnihotri, H. H. Dhruva, W. C. Bonnerjee, Norendranath Sen, Eardley Norton, Joy Govind Shome, Iswari Lal Sircar, G. Subramania Iyer, D. A. Khare, S. A. Saminada Iyer, Sabapathy Mudaliar, A. O. Hume, C. Vigiya Raghava Chariar, Govind Buksh, Karandikar.

### RESOLUTION II.

**Resolved**—That this Congress re-affirms the necessity for the expansion and reform of the Council of the Governor-General for making Laws, and the Provincial Legislative Councils, already set forth in Resolutions III. of the Congress of, 1885, and 1886, and expresses the earnest hope that the Government will no longer delay action in the direction of this essential reform.

### RESOLUTION III.

**Resolved**—That this Congress once again places on record an expression of the universal conviction, that a complete separation of the Executive and Judicial functions (such that in no case the two functions shall be combined in the same officer) has become an urgent necessity, and declares that, in its opinion, it behoves the Government to effect this separation, without further delay, even though this should, in some Provinces, involve some extra expenditure.

### RESOLUTION IV.

**Resolved**—That, in view of the loyalty of Her Majesty's Indian subjects, this Congress considers it desirable that the Queen's Proclamation should be given effect to; that the Military Service in its higher grades should be practically opened to the natives of this country; and that the Government of India should establish Military Colleges in this country, whereat the natives of India, as defined by Statute, may be educated and trained for a military career as officers of the Indian Army.

### RESOLUTION V.

**Resolved**—That, in view of the unsettled state of Public affairs in Europe, and the immense assistance that the people of this country, if duly prepared therefor, are capable of rendering to Great Britain, in the event of any serious complications arising, this Congress once again earnestly appeals to the Government to authorize (under such rules and restrictions as may to it seem fitting,) a system of Volunteering for the Indian inhabitants of the country, such as may qualify them to support the Government, effectively, in any crises,

### RESOLUTION VI.

**Resolved**—That, as the administration of the Income-Tax, especially, as regards incomes below Rs. 1,000, has proved extremely unsatisfactory, it is essential, in the opinion of the Congress, that the taxable minimum be raised to Rs. 1,000, the loss of revenues thus involved being made good, and further financial difficulties, if any, met, by reductions in the existing publc expenditure, or, should this prove impossible, by the re-imposition of an import duty on the finer classes of cotton goods.

### RESOLUTION VII.

**Resolved**—That, having regard to the poverty of the people, it is desirable that the Government be moved to elaborate a system of Technical Education, suitable to the condition of the country, to encourage indigenous manufactures by a more strict observance of the orders, already existing, in regard to utilizing such manufactures for State purposes, and to employ more extensively, than at present, the skill and talents of the people of the country.

### RESOLUTION VIII.

**Resolved**—That in view of the loyalty of the people, the hardships which the present Arms' Act (XI of 1878) causes, and the unmerited slur which it casts upon the people of this country, the Government be moved so to modify the provisions of Chapter IV., and if necessary, other portions of the said Act, as shall enable all persons to possess and wear arms, unless debarred therefrom, either as individuals or members of particular communities or classes, by the orders of the Government of India (or any local authority empowered by the Government of India on that behalf) for reasons to be recorded in writing and duly published.

### RESOLUTION IX.

**Resolved**—That the rules drafted by the Committee appointed under Resolution I., stand over for consideration till next Congress, but that, in the meantime, copies be circulated to all Standing Congress Committees, with the request that they will, during the coming year, act in accordance with these rules, so far as this may seem to them possible and desirable, and report thereon to the next Congress, with such further suggestions as to them may seem meet.

### RESOLUTION X.

**Resolved**—That the Fourth Indian National Congress assemble at Allahabad on the 26th December, 1888.

### RESOLUTION XI.

**Resolved**—That copies of these Resolutions be forwarded to His Excellency the Viceroy-in-Council, with the humble request that he will cause all the Resolutions to be laid before Her Majesty's Secretary of State for India, and that he himself will be graciously pleased, in consultation with his colleagues, to accord them his best consideration.

## RESOLUTIONS PASSED AT THE FOURTH CONGRESS.

### RESOLUTION I.

**Resolved**—That this Congress affirms the necessity for the expansion and reform of the Council of the Governor-General for making laws and regulations, and of the existing Provincial Legislative Councils, already set forth in Resolutions III. of the Congress of 1885 and 1886, and Resolution II. of the Congress of 1887 (a tentative scheme for which expansion and reform was suggested in Resolution IV. of the Congress of 1886) and further urges that a Legislative Council (of the same character as those which have been suggested for Provinces where Legislative Councils already exist) be established for the Punjab.

### RESOLUTION II.

**Resolved**—That this Congress, while appreciating the concessions proposed in the Report of the Public Service Commission, yet feels it necessary to put distinctly on record its opinion that full justice will never be done to the people of this country until the open competitive examination for the Civil Service of India is held simultaneously in England and in India.

### RESOLUTION III.

**Resolved**—That this Congress, having read and considered Resolution XI of the Congress of 1886, to wit—

"That this Congress do place on record an expression of the universal conviction that a complete se-
" paration of the executive and judicial functions (such that in no case the two functions hall be
" combined in the same officer) has become an urgent necessity; and that, in its opinion, it
" behoves the Government to effect this separation without further delay, even though this
" should, in some provinces, involve some extra expenditure"—

and Resolution III. of the Congress of 1887, to the same effect, does now, hereby, affirm the same respectively.

### RESOLUTION IV.

**Resolved**—That this Congress, having read and considered Resolution VIII. of the Congress of 1886, to wit—

"That in the opinion of this Congress, the time has now arrived when the system of trial by jury "may be safely extended into many parts of the country where it is not at present in force"—

Resolution IX. of the Congress of 1886, to wit—

"That in the opinion of this Congress, the innovation made in 1872 in the system of trial by jury, "depriving the verdicts of juries of all finality, has proved injurious to the country, and the pow- "ers then, for the first time, vested in Sessions Judges and High Courts, of setting aside verdicts "of acquittal should be at once withdrawn"—

and Resolution X. of the Congress of 1886, to wit—

"That in the opinion of this Congress, a provision similar to that contained in the Summary Juris- "diction Act of Englad (under which accused persons in serious cases have the option of "demanding a committal to the Sessions Court) should be introduced into the Indian Code of Criminal Procedure, enabling accused persons, in warrant cases, to demand that, instead of "being tried by the Magistrate, they be committed to the Court of Sessions"—

does now, hereby, affirm the same respectively.

### RESOLUTION V.

**Resolved**—That, as it is the general belief of the people of this country that the existing system of police administration in India is highly unsatisfactory in itself and oppressive to them the Government be respectfully urged to appoint a commission, consisting of official and non-official members, to investigate the entire question as speedily as possible.

### RESOLUTION VI.

**Resolved**—That this Congress having read and considered Resolution IV. of the Congress of 1887, to wit—

"That in view of the loyalty of Her Majesty's Indian subjects, the Congress considers it desirable "that the Queen's Proclamation should be given effect to; that the Military services in the "higher grades should be practically opened to the natives of this country, and that the "Government should establish Military Colleges in the country whereat the natives of India, "as defined by Statute, may be educated and trained for a Military career as officers of the "Indian Army;"

Resolution XII. of the Congress of 1886, and Resolution V. of the Congress of 1887, to wit—

"That in view of the unsettled state of public affairs in Europe, and the immense assistance that "the people of this country, if duly prepared therefor, are capable of rendering to Great Bri- "tain in the event of any serious complications arising, the Congress once again earnestly "appeals to the Government to authorize (under such rules and restrictions as to it may seem "fitting) a system of Volunteering for the Indian inhabitants of the country, such as may "qualify them to support the Government effectually in any crises;"

and Resolution VIII. of the Congress of 1887, to wit—

> "That in view of the loyalty of the people, the hardships which the present Arms Act (XI of 1878) "causes, and the unmerited slur which it casts upon the people of this country, the Government "be moved so to modify the provisions of Chapter IV., and, if necessary, other portions of the "said Act, as shall enable all persons to possess and wear Arms unless debarred therefrom, "either as individuals, or members of particular communities or classes, by the orders of the "Government of India, (or any local authority empowered by the Government of India on "that behalf), for reasons to be recorded in writing and duly published ;"

does now, hereby, affirm the same respectively.

### RESOLUTION VII.

**Resolved**—That, having regard to the fact that a serious increase in the consumption of intoxicants has taken place under the systems of Abkari and Excise now prevailing in India, the Government be respectfully urged to adopt some such improved system as shall tend to discourage insobriety.

### RESOLUTION VIII.

**Resolved**—That, as the administration of the Income-Tax, specially as regards incomes below Rs. 1,000, has proved extremely unsatisfactory, it is essential, in the opinion of the Congress, that the taxable minimum be raised to Rs. 1,000.

### RESOLUTION IX.

**Resolved**—That this Congress being of opinion that it is the first duty of the British Government in India to foster and encourage education, as well general as technical, in all its branches, and that the declaration made in the recent resolution of the Government of India on the subject of education is calculated to encourage the tendency to reduce imperial expenditure on education, and to withdraw from the control of it, respectfully urges upon Government the extreme importance of increasing, or at any rate of not decreasing, the present expenditure on education and of the Government continuing to control the Educational Institutions of all kinds now existing.

### RESOLUTION X.

**Resolved**—That, having regard to the poverty of the people, the importance of encouraging indigenous manufactures, and the difficulty of practically introducing any general system of technical education with the present imperfect information, Government be moved to delay no longer the appointment of a mixed commission, to inquire into the present industrial condition of the country.

### RESOLUTION XI.

**Resolved**—That the foregoing Resolutions be submitted for the favourable consideration of His Excellency the Viceroy, and for transmission by him to Her Majesty's Government, with the humble request of this Congress that the reforms suggested in the said Resolutions (based as most of these are on Her Gracious Majesty's Proclamation of 1858) may now be effected ; and that should it be deemed necessary first to institute any enquiry into any of the matters forming the subjects of these resolutions, such enquiry may be made, as speedily as possible, by a Parliamentary Committee.

### RESOLUTION XII.

**Resolved**—That this Congress, having watched with interest and sympathy the exertions that are being made in England for the total abrogation of laws and rules relating to the regulation of prostitution by the State in India, places on record its appreciation of the services thus rendered to this country, and its desire to co-operate by all means in its power in the attainment of this laudable object.

### RESOLUTION XIII.

**Resolved**—That no subject shall be passed for discussion by the Subject Committee or allowed to be discussed at any Congress by the President thereof, to the introduction of which the Hindu or Mahomedan Delegates as a body object, unanimously or nearly unanimously; and that if, after the discussion of any subject which has been admitted for discussion, it shall appear that all the Hindu or all the Mahomedan Delegates, as a body, are unanimousiy, or nearly unanimously, opposed to the Resolution which it is proposed to pass thereon, such Resolution shall be dropped ; provided that this rule shall refer only to subjects in regard to which the Congress has not already definitely pronounced an opinion.

### RESOLUTION XIV.

**Resolved**—That the question of the introduction of a Permanent Settlement of the Land Revenue Demand into the Madras and Bombay Presidencies and other provinces be referred to the several Standing Congress Committees, with instructions to report upon the same, in so far as it affects their respective circles, to the Congress of 1889.

### RESOLUTION XV.

**Resolved**—That this Congress puts on record its disapproval of the recent enhancement of the Salt Tax, as involving a perceptible increase to the burthens of the poorer classes, as also the partial absorption, in a time of peace and plenty, of the only Financial Reserve of the Empire.

### RESOLUTION XVI.

**Resolved**—That the Fifth Indian National Congress do assemble in the Bombay Presidency (either at Bombay itself or at Poona, as may be settled hereafter) on the 26th of December, 1889.

### RESOLUTION XVII.

**Resolved**—That Mr. A. O. Hume be re-appointed General Secretary for the en-suing year.

---

## RESOLUTIONS PASSED AT THE FIFTH CONGRESS.

---

### RESOLUTION I.

**Resolved**—That an address be presented to Mr. Charles Bradlaugh, M. P. on behalf of this Congress here assembled, and that Messrs. Adam, Pherozshah Mehta, and W. C. Bonnerjee are appointed a Committee to settle the wording of the said address.

### RESOLUTION II.

**Resolved**—That the following skeleton scheme for the reform and reconstitution of the Council of the Governor-General for making Laws and Regulations, and the Provincial Legislative Councils, is adopted, and that the President of this Congress do submit the same to Charles Bradlaugh, Esq., M. P., with the respectful request of this Congress that he may be pleased to cause a Bill to be drafted on the lines indicated in this skeleton scheme and introduce the same in the British House of Commons :—

### SCHEME.

(1) The Imperial and Provincial Legislative Councils to consist respectively of members, not less than one-half of whom are to be elected, not more than one-fourth to sit *ex-officio*, and the rest to be nominated by Government.

(2) Revenue districts to constitute ordinarily territorial units, for electoral purposes.

(3) All male British subjects above 21 years of age possessing certain qualifications and not subject to certain disqualifications (both of which will be settled later) to be voters.

(4) Voters in each district to elect representatives to one or more electoral bodies, according to local circumstances at the rate of 12 per million of the total population of the district, such representatives to possess certain qualifications and not to be subject to certain disqualifications, both of which will be settled later.

(5) All the representatives thus elected by all the districts included in the jurisdiction of each electoral body, to elect members to the Imperial Legislature at the rate of 1 per every five millions of the total population of the electoral jurisdiction, and to their own Provincial Legislature at the rate of 1 per million of the said total population, in such wise that whenever the Parsees, Christians, Mahomedans or Hindus are in a minority, the total number of Parsees, Christians, Mahomedans or Hindus, as the case may be, elected to the Provincial Legislature, shall not, so far as may be possible, bear a ress proportion to the total number of members elected thereto, than the total number of Parsees, Christians, Hindus or Mahomedans, as the case may be, in such electoral jurisdiction, bears to its total population. Members of both Legislatures to possess certain qualifications and not to be subject to certain disqualifications, both of which will be settled later.

(6) All elections to be by ballot.

## RESOLUTION III.

**Resolved**—That this present Congress does hereby ratify and confirm the resolutions passed by previous Congresses as to—

(*a*) the urgent necessity for the complete separation of executive and judicial functions, such that, in no case, shall the two functions be combined in the same officer;

(*b*) the expediency of extending into many parts of the country, where it is not at present in force, the system of trial by jury;

(*c*) the necessity of withdrawing from the High Courts, the powers, first vested in them in 1872, of setting aside verdicts of acquittal by juries;

(*d*) the necessity of introducing, into the Code of Criminal Procedure, a provision enabling accused persons, in warrant cases, to demand that, instead of being tried by the Magistrate, they be committed to the Court of Sessions;

(*e*) the highly unsatisfactory character of the existing system of Police Administration in India, and the absolute necessity of a fundamental reform therein;

(*f*) the expediency of both, establishing Military Colleges in India, whereat the Natives of India, as defined by Statute, may be educated and trained for a military career as officers of the Indian Army, and of authorising, under such rules and restrictions as may seem necessary, such a system of volunteering for the Indian inhabitants of the country as may qualify them to support the Government in any crises;

(*g*) the extremely unsatisfactory character of the Income Tax Administration, especially as regards incomes below rupees one thousand, and the expediency of raising the taxable minimum to this amount;

(*h*) the extreme importance of increasing, instead of diminishing, as the present tendency appears to be, the public expenditure on education in all its branches, and the necessity, in view to the promotion of one of the most essential of these branches, the technical, of the appointment of a mixed commission to enquire into the present industrial condition of the country;

(*i*) the impolicy and injustice involved in the late increase of the Salt Tax in a time of profound peace, and the urgent necessity for an immediate reduction of this tax, and the re-imposition, to balance the deficit thus caused, of light *ad valorem* import duties;

(*j*) the necessity for the reduction of, instead of the continual increase to, the military expenditure of the country.

## RESOLUTION IV.

**Resolved**—That this Congress hereby tenders its sincere thanks to Messrs. Caine and Smith, and the members who voted with them, in connection with the debate on the Indian Excise Question in the House of Commons; and, while fully appreciating what has been done by some of the local Governments towards the improvement of their systems of Excise and Abkari, desires to express the earnest hope that no further time may be lost in giving full effect to the Resolution of the House of Commons.

### RESOLUTION V.

**Resolved**—That this Congress, while thanking Her Majesty's Government for raising the age for the Indian Civil Service Competitive Examination from 19 to 23 does hereby put on record an emphatic expression of the universal disappointment which has been created by the rest of that Government's orders in regard to the Public Service Question, (the net result of which orders is to place the people of India in a worse position than they previously held), and reiterates the national conviction that no real justice will be done to India, in this matter, until the simultaneous holding in India, and in England, of all examinations, for all Civil branches of the Public Service in India at present held only in England, be conceded.

### RESOLUTION VI.

**Resolved**—That, in view of the loyalty of the people, the hardships, that the Arms Act (XI of 1878), as at present administered, entails, and the unmerited slur which it casts upon them, the Government be moved so to modify the rules made under this Act that all restrictions as to the possession and bearing of arms shall apply equally to all persons residing in or visiting India; that licenses to possess and bear arms shall be liberally and generally distributed wherever wild animals habitually destroy human life, cattle or crops; and that these and all licenses issued under the rules shall be granted once for all, shall operate throughout the Provincial jurisdiction within which they are issued, be only revocable on proof of misuse, and shall not require yearly or half-yearly renewals.

### RESOLUTION VII.

**Resolved**—That the Government be urged to take the subject of a Permanent Settlement once more under consideration in view to practical action thereon, such that fixity and permanency may be given to the Government Land Revenue demand without further delay, at any rate, in all fully populated and well cultivated tracts of country.

### RESOLUTION VIII.

**Resolved**—That, in view of the fall that has already occurred in the price of silver and in the exchange value of the Indian Rupee, it is impolitic on the part of the British Government to maintain any hindrances whatever to the consumption of silver for manufacturing purposes; and that this Congress strongly urges upon Her Majesty's Government that, not only as an act of justice to India (a matter which has been repeatedly brought to the notice of Her Majesty's Ministers), but also as an act of expediency in the interests of Her Majesty's British as well as Indian subjects, the plate duties should be immediately abolished, and Hall-marking be made a voluntary institution.

### RESOLUTION IX.

**Resolved**—That this Congress respectfully expresses the earnest hope that, in the interest of the people of India, the House of Commons will forthwith restore the right, formerly possessed by members of that Honourable House, of stating to Parliament any matter of grievance of the natives of India, before Mr. Speaker leaves the Chair, for the presentation in Committee of the Indian Budget statement, and earnestly trusts that the House of Commons will, in future take into consideration the Annual Indian Budget statement at such a date as will ensure its full and adequate discussion; and further authorizes the President, Sir William Wedderburn, Bart., to sign a petition in the name and on behalf of this Congress for presentation to the House of Commons in accordance with the terms of this Resolution.

### RESOLUTION X.

**Resolved**—That, in view to his approaching departure, this Congress puts on record an expression of the high sense entertained, not only in the Bombay Presidency, but throughout India, of the ability, integrity and impartiality that have characterised Lord Reay's administration, as also of the gratitude which the whole country feels to be his due for the sympathy that he has ever extended to Indian aspirations and efforts.

### RESOLUTION XI.

**Resolved**—That the Subjects Committee be instructed to settle the question, (left open in the skeleton scheme for the reconstruction of the councils, embodied in Resolution II.), of the qualifications requisite for, and the disqualifications which should debar from, becoming.—

*(a)* a Voter ;
*(b)* a Representative ;
*(c)* a Member of a Provincial Legislative Council ; and
*(d)* a Member of the Imperial Legislative Council ;

and to submit their Report thereon to Charles Bradlaugh, Esq., M. P., for the purpose of the Bill which he has been requested to have drawn.

### RESOLUTION XII.

**Resolved**—That Mr. A. O. Hume, C. B., be re-elected General Secretary of the National Congress for the ensuing year.

### RESOLUTION XIII.

**Resolved**—

*(a)* That in view of the large number of delegates this year assembled and the probability arising from past experience, of their number continuing to increaso year by year, henceforth the number of delegates to be allowed from each Congress circle be limited to five per million of the total population of the circle: the Standing Committee of each circle allotting the number which their jurisdiction, as a whole, is entitled to elect, amongst their severa electoral divisions, as may seem most expedient.

*(b)* That from the date of Mr. Hume's departure for England, the Hon'ble Pundit Ajoodhianath be appointed Joint General Secretary, and that Rs. 5,000 be assigned for the payment by him of such Assistant Secretaries as he may find it necessary to employ, clerical assistance, postage, telegraphs and printing; and further that Mr. W. C. Bonnerjee be appointed Standing Counsel for Bengal, Mr. Pherozshah Mehta, Standing Counsel for Bombay, and Mr. Ananda Charlu, Standing Counsel for Madras, to the Joint General Secretary.

*(c)* That the tentative rules for the constitution and working of the Congress, which were first considered at Madras, and in regard to which various addenda have from time to time been circulated, be thoroughly considered during the coming year by the several Standing Congress Committees, and definitely dealt with by the Congress at its next session.

*(d)* That this Congress does hereby confirm the appointment of Sir W. Wedderburn, Bart., and Messrs. W. S. Caine, M. P., W. S. Bright Maclaren, M. P., J.E. Ellis, M.P., Dadabhai Naoroji and George Yule, as a Committee (with power to add to their number) to guide and direct the operations and control the expenditure of the National Congress Agency in England, and does further tender its sincere thanks to these gentlemen, and to Mr. W. Digby, C. I. E., the Secretary, for the service which they are rendering to India.

*(e)* That this Congress does formally appoint Mr. George Yule, Mr. A. O. Hume, Mr. Adam, Mr. Eardley Norton, Mr. J. E. Howard,* Mr. Pherozshah Mehta, Mr. Surendranath Banerjee, Mr. Mono Mohan Ghose, Mr. Shurfuddin, Mr R. N. Mudholker, and Mr. W.C. Bonnerjee to represent its views in England and press upon the consideration of the British Public the political reforms which the Congress has advocated.

---

* By some oversight, this gentleman's name was omitted, when the Resolution was read to the Congress; the error has been rectified with the consent of the several Standing Congress Committees.

(f) That a sum of Rs. 45,000 be raised for the expenses of the Congress work in this country and in England during the ensuing year, and that the different Standing Committees do send their respective apportioned amounts to the General Secretary, the one half in three, and the balance in six months..

### RESOLUTION XIV.

**Resolved**—That the Sixth Indian National Congress do assemble at some City in Bengal, and exact place to be fixed hereafter, on the 26th of December, 1890.

### EESOLUTION XV.

**Resolved**—That the Fifth Indian National Congress hereby tenders its heart-felt thanks to its President, Sir William Wedderburn, as well for his ready sacrifice of personal and political considerations involved by his journey from England to India, as for that courtesy, impartiality and never-failing sympathy which, characteristics of his long and honourable career as an official of this country, have marked his control of the proceedings of this assembly.

## RESOLUTIONS PASSED AT THE SIXTH CONGRESS.

### RESOLUTION I.

**Resolved**—That.this Congress, having considered the draft Bill recently introduced into Parliament by Mr. Charles Bradlaugh, entitled" an Act to amend the Indian Councils' Act of 1861," approves the same as calculated to secure a substantial instalment of that reform, in the Administration of India, for which it has been agitating, and humbly prays the Houses of Parliament of the United Kingdom of Great Britain and Ireland to pass the same into law; and further that its President, Mr. Pherozshah Mehta, is hereby empowered to draw up and sign, on behalf of this assembly, a petition to the House of Commons to the foregoing effect, and to transmit the same to Mr. Charles Bradlaugh for presentation, thereto, in due course.

### RESOLUTION II.

**Resolved**—That this present Congress does hereby ratify and confirm the resolutions passed by previous Congresses as to—

(a) the urgent necessity for the complete separation of executive and judicial functions, such that, in no case, shall the two functions be combined in the same officer ;

(b) the expediency of extending into many parts of the country, where it is not at present in force, the system of trial by jury ;

(c) the necessity of withdrawing from the High Courts the powers, first vested in them in 1872, of setting aside verdicts of acquittal by juries ;

(d) the necessity of introducing, into the Code of Criminal Procedure, a provision enabling accused persons, in warrant cases, to demand that instead of being tried by the Magistrate they be committed to the Court of Sessions ;

(e) the highly unsatisfactory character of the existing system of Police Administration in India, and the absolute necessity of a fundamental reform therein ;

(*f*) the expediency of both, establishing Military Colleges in India, whereat the Natives of India, as defined by Statute, may be educated and trained for a military career as officers of the Indian Army, and of authorising, under such rules and restrictions as may seem necessary, such a system of volunteering, for the Indian inhabitants of the country, as may qualify them to support the Government in any crisis ;

(*g*) the extremely unsatisfactory character of the Income Tax Administration, especially as regards incomes below rupees one thousand, and the expediency of raising the taxable minimum to this amount;

(*h*) the extreme importance of increasing, instead of diminishing, as the present tendency appears to be, the public expenditure on education in all its branches, and the necessity, in view to the promotion of one of the most essential of these branches, the technical, of the appointment of a mixed commission to enquire into the present industrial condition of the country;

(*i*) the necessity for the reduction of, instead of the continual increase to, the military expenditure of the country;

(*j*) the necessity, if any real justice is to be done to the people of India, of holding, simultaneously in India and England, examinations, at present held only in England, for the Civil branches of the Public Service in India;

(*k*) the expediency of so modifying the rules made under Act XI of 1878 (the Arms Act) that all restrictions as to the possession and bearing of arms shall apply equally to all persons residing in or visiting India; that licenses to possess and bear arms shall be liberally and generally distributed wherever wild animals habitually destroy human life, cattle or crops; and that these and all licenses issued under the rules shall be granted once for all, shall operate throughout the Provincial jurisdiction within which they are issued, be only revocable on proof of misuse, and shall not require yearly or half-yearly renewals,

## RESOLUTION III.

**Resolved**—That this Congress respectfully expresses the earnest hope that in the interest of the people of India, the House of Commons will forthwith restore the right formerly possessed by members of that Honourable House, of stating to Parliament any matter of grievance of the natives of India before Mr. Speaker leaves the chair, for the presentation in Committee of the Indian Budget statement, and earnestly trusts that the House of Commons will, in future, take into consideration the Annual Indian Budget statement at such a date as will ensure its full and adequate discussion, and further authorizes its President to sign a Petition, in the name and on behalf of this Congress, for presentation to the House of Commons, in accordance with the terms of this Resolution.

## RESOLUTION IV.

**Resolved**—That, while recognizing the action taken, in response to its previous prayers, in the matter of Excise Reform by H. M.'s Secretary of State for India and the Supreme Government here, and noting with pleasure the increase to the import duty on Spirits, the taxation imposed on Indian-brewed malt liquors, the decision of the Bengal Government to abolish the outstill system, and the closing of over 7,000 liquor shops by the Madras Government in 1889-90, this Congress regrets that it is still necessary to urge the Government of India to insist on *all* Provincial Administrations carrying out in their integrity the policy in matters of Excise enunciated in paras. 103, 104 and 105 of the despatch published in the *Gazette of India* of March 1st, 1890, especially as to sub section 4 of para. 103, *viz.*—

"That efforts should be made to ascertain the existence of local public sentiment, and that a reasonable amount of deference should be paid to such opinion when ascertained

**RESOLUTION V.**

**Resolved**—That the condition of the Finances of India having materially improved, and those special circumstances on which the Government relied to justify the recent enhancement of the Salt Tax having practically ceased to exist, this Congress considers it essential that the enhancement referred to should be remitted at an early date, and empowers its President to submit a special memorial on the subject in its name and on its behalf to H. E. the Viceroy in Council.

**RESOLUTION VI.**

**Resolved**—That having reference to the expectations created throughout the country by the Despatch of Her Majesty's Secretary of State in 1862, the principles of which were re-affirmed in a subsequent Despatch of 1865, promising the extension of a Permanent Settlement to all temporarily settled tracts in which certain conditions were fulfilled, and to the fact that throughout large portions of the country those conditions have long since been fulfilled, this Congress respectfully submits that the Government of India is now in honour bound to take up this question of Permanent Settlement, without further delay, in view to practical action thereon such that fixity and permanency may be given to the Government Land Revenue demand as explicitly promised, by Her Majesty's Secretary of State, more than a quarter of a century ago.

**RESOLUTION VII.**

**Resolved**—That this Congress, having observed with surprise a notice, apparently official, in various Calcutta newspapers which runs as follows :—

THE CONGRESS.

"The Bengal Government having learnt that tickets of admission to the visitors' enclosure in the Congress pavilion have been sent to various Government officers residing in Calcutta, has issued a circular to all secretaries, and heads of departments subordinate to it, pointing out that under the orders of the Government of India the presence of Government officials, even as visitors at such meetings, is not advisable, and that their taking part in the proceedings of any such meetings is absolutely prohibited :

and having also considered a letter addressed by the Private Secretary of His Honor the Lieutenant-Governor of Bengal to the Secretary of the Reception Committee, of which the following is an exact copy :—

BELVEDERE, *26th December, 1890.*

"DEAR SIR,—In returning herewith the seven cards of admission to the visitors' enclosure of the Congress pavilion, which were kindly sent by you to my address yesterday afternoon, I am desired to say that the Lieutenant-Governor and the members of his household could not possibly avail themselves of these tickets, since the orders of the Government of India definitely prohibit the presence of Government officials at such meetings.

"To<br>J. GHOSAL ESQ.,<br>*Secretary, Congress Reception Committee.*"

Yours faithfully,<br>P. C. LYON,<br>*Private Secretary.*

authorizes and instructs its President to draw the attention of His Excellency the Viceroy to the declaration embodied in these papers that Government servants are prohibited from attending any meetings of this Congress even as spectators, and to enquire, most respectfully, whether His Honor the Lieutenant-Governor of Bengal has, or has not correctly interpreted the orders of the Government of India.

### RESOLUTION VIII.

**Resolved**—That the best thanks of this Congress be tendered to Mr. Charles Bradlaugh, M. P., for the invaluable services rendered by him during the past year, as also to Sir W. Wedderburn, Mr. W. S. Caine, Mr. J. Bright Maclaren, M. P., Mr. J. Ellis, M. P., Mr. George Yule, and Mr. Dadabhai Naoroji for the unselfish zeal and ability with which they have presided over the British Agency of the Congress; further that they put on record an expression of their high appreciation of the manner in which Mr. Digby, C. I. E., Secretary of the Agency, and Messrs. Surendra Nath Banerjee, R. N. Mudholkar, W. C. Bonnerjee, Eardley Norton, and A. O. Hume, delegates to England, respectively, discharged the onerous duties imposed upon them, and of their gratitude to all those members of the British public who so kindly welcomed and so sympathetically gave audience, in over fifty public and a far larger number of private meetings, to one or more of these delegates.

### RESOLUTION IX.

**Resolved**—That a vote of thanks be recorded to Kumar Debendra Mullick and brothers, proprietors of the Tivoli Gardens, Mr. N.C. Bose and Babu Bhupendra Nath Bose, proprietors of Mohan Bagan Villa, and to the Hon'ble Sir Romesh Chandra Mitra, Mr. T. N. Palit, Babus Janokee Nath Roy, Gopee Mohan Roy, Harendra Nath Roy, Kissory Mohan Roy, Ramanath Ghose, and Jamadar Ghasiram, owners of houses kindly lent for the use of delegates.

### RESOLUTION X.

**Resolved**—That the Seventh Indian National Congress do assemble on the 26th December, 1891, at either Madras or Nagpur, as may be hereafter settled, in consultation between the Madras, Central Provinces and Berar Committees, and the Joint General Secretary.

### RESOLUTION XI.

**Resolved**—That provisional arrangements be made to hold a Congress, of not less than 100 delegates, in England, all things being convenient, in 1892, and that the several Standing Congress Committees be directed to report, at the coming Congress, the names of the delegates that it is proposed to depute from their respective circles.

### RESOLUTION XII.

**Resolved**—That of the Funds now in the Joint General Secretary's hands and about to be received, a further sum of twenty thousand rupees be added to the Permanent Fund and placed in fixed deposits, and that the rest of the funds accruing on account of this current year, 1890, be held by him available for the immediate purposes of the British Committee of the Indian National Congress, but to be replaced as the subscriptions for 1891 are received, and ultimately, also added to the Permanent Fund.

### RESOLUTION XIII.

**Resolved**—That a sum of Rs. 40,000, exclusive of individual donations, is assigned for the expenses of the British Committee of the Congress and Rs. 6,000 for the General Secretary's Office and Establishment, and that the several circles and districts do contribute as arranged in Commitee.

### RESOLUTION XIV.

**Resolved**—That Mr. A. O. Hume and Pandit Ajoodhia Nath are re-elected General and Joint-General Secretaries for the ensuing year.

### RESOLUTION XV.

**Resolved**—That this Congress does formally appoint Messrs. G. Yule, Pherozshah Mehta, W. C. Bonnerjee, J. Adam, Mono Mohan Ghose, A. O. Hume, Kali Charan Banerjee, Dadabhai Naorojee, D. A. Khare, and such other gentlemen as may volunteer for the duty with the sanction and approval of the Standing Congress Committees o their respective circles, to represent its views in England, and press upon the considera-tion of the British Public the political reforms which the Congress has advocated.

---

## RESOLUTIONS PASSED AT THE SEVENTH CONGRESS.

---

### RESOLUTION I.

**Resolved**—That a Committee be appointed to consider and report, on or before the morning of the 30th instant, whether, or not, it is advisable to discontinue the Annua Sessions of the Indian National Congress until after the British Session, and, if not, undei what regulations, as to numbers of delegates, localities for assemblage, and the like, future Congresses shall be held. The Committee to be composed as follows :—

EX-OFFICIO MEMBERS :

The President.
The Chairman of the Reception Committee.
The General Secretary.
The Joint General Secretary.
The Standing Counsels to the Congress.

ORDINARY MEMBERS :

Messrs. Surendranath Bannerjee.
Viraraghava Chariar.
Hafiz Abdul Raheem.
Gangapersad Varma.
Pringle Kennedy.
Guruprasad Sen.
D. E. Wacha.
M. B. Namjoshi.
Hamid Ali Khan.
Vishnu Moreshwar Bhide.

Messrs. Murlidhar.
Mudholkar.
Deo Rao Vinayak.
Gopal Rao Bhide.
Bipin Krishna Bose.
Dajee Abajee Khare.
Madan Mohan Malaviya.
Saligram Singh.
Sankara Nair.

### RESOLUTION II.

**Resolved**—That this Congress re-affirms the conclusion arrived at by all previous Congresses, *viz*, that India can never be well or justly governed, nor her people prosperous or contented, until they are allowed, through their elected representatives, a potential voice in the Legislatures of their own country, and respectfully urges the people of Great Britain and Ireland, whose good will towards India it gratefully recognizes, to permit no further delay in the concession of this just and necessary reform.

### RESOLUTION III.

**Resolved**—That this Congress, concurring in the views set forth in previous Congresses affirms—

That fully fifty millions of this population, a number yearly increasing, are dragging out a miserable existence on the verge of starvation, and that, in every decade, several millions actually perish by starvation.

That this unhappy condition of affairs is largely due to—

(*a*) the exclusion of the people of India from a due participation in the administration, and all control over the finances, of their own country; the remedy for which has been set forth in Resolution II;

(*b*) the extravagant cost of the present administration, Military and Civil, but especially the former ; and to

(*c*) a short-sighted system of Land Revenue Administration, whereby not only is all improvement in the agriculture of the country, on which ninetenths of the population depend for subsistence, rendered impossible, but the gradual deterioration of that agriculture assured.

That hence it has become imperatively necessary—

that the cost of the administration be greatly reduced; in the military branch, by a substantial reduction of the standing army, by the substitution of long term local European troops like those of the Hon. E. I. Company, for the present short term Imperial regiments with their heavy cost of recruitment in England, in transport and of excessive mortality amongst non-acclimatized youths ; by the cessation of the gigantic waste of money that has gone on, now for several years, on so-called Frontier Defences, and by a strict economy in the Commissariat, Ordnance and Store Departments ; and in the Civil branch, by the wide substitution of a cheaper indigenous agency for the extremely costly imported Staff; and

that measures be at once taken to give, as was promised by the British Government thirty years ago, fixity and permanence to the Land Revenue demand and thus permit capital and labour to combine to develop the agriculture of the country, which under the existing system of temporary settlements, in recent times often lasting for short periods, in some cases only extending to 10 and 12 years, is found to be impossible ; and to establish agricultural banks.

That this Congress does most earnestly entreat the people of Great Britain and Ireland not to permit any further sacrifice of life by the shortcomings of the existing, doubtless well-intentioned, but none the less unsatisfactory, administration, but to insist, and speedily, on these reforms.

## RESOLUTION IV.

**Resolved**—That this Congress, concurring with previous Congresses, is of opinion that, to ensure the adequate protection and efficient defence of the country, it is desirable that the Government should conciliate Indian public opinion and encourage and qualify the Indians to defend their homes and their Government—

(*a*) by so modifying the rules under the Arms Act, as to make them equally applicable to all residents in, or visitors to, India, without distinction of creed, class or colour ; to ensure the liberal concession of licenses wherever wild animals habitually destroy human life, cattle or crops, and to make all licenses granted under the revised rules, of life-long tenure, revocable only on proof of misuse and valid throughout the Provincial Jurisdiction in which they are issued ;

(*b*) by establishing Military Colleges in India, whereat natives of India, as defined by Statute, may be educated and trained for a military career, as *commissioned or non-commissioned* officers (according to capacity and qualifications) of the Indian army;

(*c*) by organising, throughout the more warlike races of the Empire, a system of militia service; and

(*d*) by authorizing and stimulating a widespread system of volunteering, such as obtains in Great Britain, amongst the people of India.

### RESOLUTION V.

**Resolved**—That as one step towards ensuring the wider employment of Indians in the administration of the country, and as a matter of simple justice to the people of India, this Congress, agreeing with previous Congresses, declares it to be essential that all examinations for any and all of the Civil Branches of the Public Service in India, which at present are held only in England, should henceforth be also held simultaneously in India.

### RESOLUTION VI.

**Resolved**—That this Congress concurs with its predecessors in strongly advocating—

(*a*) the reduction of the salt tax by at least the amount of its latest enhancement;

(*b*) the raising of the income tax taxable minimum from Rs. 500 to Rs. 1,000;

(*c*) persistent pressure by the Government of India on all Provincial Administrations, to induce them to carry out, in its integrity, the excise policy enunciated in paras. 103, 104 and 105 of the despatch, published in the *Gazette of India*, of March 1st, 1890, and the introduction of a simple system of local option in the case of all villages.

### RESOLUTION VII.

**Resolved**—That having regard to the unsatisfactory character, in many respects, of the Judicial and Police Administration, this Congress concurs with its predecessors in strongly advocating—

(*a*) the complete separation of Executive and Judicial functions such that in no case shall the two functions be combined in the same officer;

(*b*) the extension into many parts of the country, where it is not at present in force, of the system of trial by jury;

(*c*) the withdrawal from High Courts of the powers, first vested in them in 1872 of setting aside verdicts of acquittals by juries;

(*d*) the introduction, into the Code of Criminal Procedure, of a provision enabling accused persons, in warrant cases, to demand that instead of being tried by the Magistrate they be committed to the Court of Sessions;

(*e*) the fundamental reform of the Police Administration, by a reduction in the numbers and an increase in the salaries, and in the qualifications of the lower grades, and their far more careful enlistment, and by the selection for the higher posts of gentlemen of higher capacities, more in touch with the respectable portions of the community, and less addicted to militan pretensions, than the majority of the existing Deputy Inspectors General, Superintendents and Assistant Superintendents of Police.

### RESOLUTION VIII.

**Resolved**—That this Congress, concurring with previous Congresses, affirms the importance of increasing (instead of diminishing, as appears to be the present policy of the Government) the public expenditure on all branches of education, and the expediency, in view to the promotion of one of the most essential of these branches, the technical, of appointing a mixed Commission to enquire into the present industrial condition of the country.

### RESOLUTION IX.

*Read the following telegram from General Booth :—*

"May I be allowed to commend, to the attention of the Congress, the claims of the millions of India's starving poor and to urge the consideration of some scheme by which these destitute multitudes can be placed upon the waste lands of the country, in such an organised and befriended manner, as will enable them to gain, for themselves, those necessaries of a healthy existence which, in their present circumstances, are denied ; praying for the blessing of God upon the labours of the Congress, yours in sympathy with every effort for the amelioration of the miseries of mankind."

**Resolved**—That the following telegram be despatched in reply to General Booth :—

"The Congress having received and considered your kindly message thank you cordially for the same. No possible scheme of internal immigration can perceptibly relieve the fifty to sixty millions of half-starving paupers, whose sad condition constitutes the primary *raison d'être* of the Congress. It is only by modifying the adverse conditions out of which this widespread misery arises, and by raising the moral standard of the people, that any real relief is possible. As regards the first, the Congress programme now embodies all primarily essential reforms ; as regards the second, in every province and in every caste, associations, public or private, are working with a yearly increasing earnestness. Many good missionaries are labouring in same field, and we have to thank you that your army too is now engaged in the good work of elevating our masses. May your efforts and ours, in both directions, be crowned with success. Congress, including men of many creeds, welcomes cordially all who seek to benefit our suffering brethren."

### RESOLUTION X.

*Read the Report of the Committee appointed, under Resolution (I.), which runs as follows :—*

"Your Committee have considered the matter referred to them and have also consulted, informally, various members of the Subjects Committee and other delegates. They are clearly of opinion that it is not advisable to discontinue the Annual Session of the Indian National Congress until after the British Session, and that future Congresses should be held under the same regulations as heretofore."

**Resolved**—That the Annual Sessions of the Congress in India continue to be held until all necessary reforms have been secured.

### RESOLUTION XI.

**Resolved**—That having regard to the very serious discontent created, especially in Peninsular India, by the practical administration of the Forest Laws, the Government of India be most respectfully, but earnestly, entreated to investigate this carefully, and endeavour to mitigate its harshness and render it less obnoxious to the poorer classes.

### RESOLUTION XII.

**Resolved**—That this Congress hereby tenders its most graetful acknowledgments to Sir W. Wedderburn, and the members of the British Congress Committee, for the services rendered by them to India during the past year, and respectfully urges them to widen henceforth the sphere of their usefulness, by interesting themselves, not only in those questions dealt with by the Congress here, but in all Indian matters submitted to them and properly vouched for in which any principle accepted by the Congress is involved.

### RESOLUTION XIII.

**Resolved**—That this Congress puts on record an expression of the gratitude felt throughout India, for the signal services rendered by the late Mr. Charles Bradlaugh to that country's cause, and of the deep and universal sorrow which his untimely death has engendered; and that a copy of this Resolution, signed by the President, be transmitted through the British Committee for presentation to Mrs. Bradlaugh Bonner.

### RESOLUTION XIV.

**Resolved**—That this Congress, hereby, puts formally on record its high estimate and deep appreciation of the great services which Mr. Dadabhai Naoroji has rendered, during more than a quarter of a century, to the cause of India; that it expresses its unshaken confidence in him and its earnest hope that he may prove successful, at the coming elections, in his candidature for Central Finsbury, and, at the same time, tenders, on behalf of the vast population it represents, India's most cordial acknowledgments to all in England, whether in Central Finsbury or elsewhere, who have aided, or may aid him, to win a seat in the House of Commons.

### RESOLUTION XV

**Resolved**—That in view of the General Election now impending in England, and in accordance with the recommendation of our British Committee, the provisional arrangements, set on foot in pursuance of the Resolution passed at the Calcutta Congress of 1890, for holding, all things being convenient, a Congress of not less than 100 Delegates in England in 1892, be now suspended until after such General Election.

### RESOLUTION XVI.

**Resolved**—That a sum of Rs. 40.000, exclusive of individual donations, is assigned for the expenses of the British Committee of the Congress, and Rs. 6,000 for the General Secretary's office and establishment, and that the several circles do contribute as arranged in Committee for the year 1892.

### RESOLUTION XVII.

**Resolved**—That Mr. A. O. Hume and Pandit Ajoodhianath are re-elected General and Joint-General Secretaries for the ensuing year.

### RESOLUTION XVIII

**Resolved**—That the Eighth Indian National Congress do assemble on the 26th December, 1892, at Allahabad.

# RESOLUTIONS PASSED AT THE EIGHTH CONGRESS.

### RESOLUTION I.

**Resolved**—That this Congress, while accepting in a loyal spirit the Indian Councils' Act recently enacted by the Parliament of Great Britain, as explained by the present Prime Minister, with the assent of the then Under-Secretary of State for India,—that it is intended by it to give the people of India *a real living representation* in the Legislative Councils,—regrets that the Act itself does not, in terms, concede to the people the right of electing their own representatives to the Council, and hopes and expects that the rules, now being prepared under the Act, will be framed on the lines of Mr. Gladstone's declaration in the House of Commons, and will do adequate justice to the people of this country; further, that it prays that these rules may be published in the official Gazettes, like other proposed legislative measures, before being finally adopted.

### RESOLUTION II.

**Resolved**—That this Congress hereby places on record its deep regret at the resolution of the Government of India on the report of the Public Service Commission, in that—

*(a)* Whereas, if the recommendations of the Public Service Commission had been carried out in their integrity, the posts proposed to be detached from the schedule of the Statute of 1861 would have formed part of an organised Service, specially reserved for the Natives of India, the resolution of Government leaves these posts altogether isolated, to which appointment can be made only under the Statute of 1870;

*(b)* Whereas, while 108 appointments were recommended by the Public Service Commission for the Provincial Service, 93 such appointments only have actually been thrown open to that Service: the number to be allotted to Assam not having yet been announced;

*(c)* Whereas, while a Membershin of the Board of Revenue and a Commissionership of a Division, were recommended for the Province of Bengal and some other Provinces, the Government has not given effect to this resolution;

*(d)* Whereas, while one-third of the Judgeships were recommended to be thrown open to the Provincial Service, only one-fifth have been so thrown open.

And this Congress, again, distinctly puts on record its opinion, that full justice will never be done to the people of this country, until the open Competitive Examination for the Civil Service of India is held simultaneously in England and in India.

### RESOLUTION III.

**Resolved**—That this Congress, seeing the serious mischief arising to the country from the combination of Judicial and Executive functions in the same official, once again puts on record its deliberate and earnest conviction that a complete separation of these functions has become an urgent necessity, and that, in its opinion, it behoves the Government to effect this separation without further delay, even though this should, in some provinces, involve extra expenditure.

### RESOLUTION IV.

**Resolved**—That having regard to the diversity of opinion that prevails on the Currency Question, and the importance of the question itself, this Congress desires to express its earnest hope, that unless its hands are forced by the action of any Foreign Power, necessitating a change in the currency, or the standard, which might prove injurious to the interests of the country, the Government of India will refrain from taking any steps, until the labors of the Brussels Conference have been completed: and, further that the Government will lay before the Public, for discussion, the proposals which Lord Herschell's Committee may recommend, before definite action, if any, is resolved upon.

### RESOLUTION V.

**Resolved**—That this Congress concurs with its predecessors in strongly advocating—

(*a*) The reduction of the salt duty by at least the amount of its latest enhancement

(*b*) The raising of the Income-tax taxable minimum from five-hundred to one thousand;

(*c*) Persistent pressure by the Government of India on all Provincial Administrations, to induce them to carry out, in its integrity, the Excise policy enunciated in paragraphs 103, 104, and 105 of the Despatch published in the Gazette of India of March, 1890, and the introduction of a simple system of local option in the case of all villages;

(*d*) The introduction into the Code of Criminal Procedure of a provision enabling accused persons, in warrant cases, to demand that instead of being tried by the Magistrate they may be committed to the Court of Sessions;

(*e*) The fundamental reform of the Police administration, by a reduction in the numbers and an increase in the salaries and in the qualifications of the lower grades, and their far more careful enlistment; and by the selection for the higher posts of gentlemen of higher capacities, more in touch with the respectable portions of the community, and less addicted to military pretensions, than the majority of existing Deputy Inspectors-General Superintendents, and Assistant Superintendents of Police are;

(*f*) A modification of the rules under the Arms Act, so as to make them equally applicable to all residents in, or visitors to India, without distinction of creed, caste or colour; to ensure the liberal concession of licenses wherever wild animals habitually destroy human life, cattle or crops and to make all licenses, granted under the revised rules, of life-long tenure, revocable only on proof of misuse, and valid throughout the Provincial jurisdiction in which they are issued;

(*g*) The establishment of Military Colleges in India, whereat natives of India as defined by Statute, may be educated and trained for a military can as Commissioned or Non-commissioned Officers (according to capacity and qualifications) of the Indian army;

(*h*) The organising throughout the more warlike races of the Empire of a system of Militia service; and

(*i*) The authorising and stimulating of a wide-spread system of volunteering such as obtains in Great Britain, amongst the people of India.

**RESOLUTION VI.**

**Resolved**—That this Congress views with the deepest concern and alarm the recent policy of Government with respect to trial by Jury, and particularly the action of the Governments of Bengal and Assam in withdrawing the right of trial by Jury in the majority of serious offences and most respectfully, but firmly, protests against such policy and action as retrograde, reactionary, and injurious to the best interests of the country, and prays that the same may be reversed by the Government of India, and failing that, by the Government in England; and that, as prayed for in resolutions of previous Congresses, the right of trial by Jury be extended to those parts of the country where it is not now in force, it being the only safeguard for the people in the present unsatisfactory condition of the administration of Criminal Justice in British India.

**RESOLUTION VII.**

**Resolved**—That having regard to the fact that the abnormal increase in the annual Military Expenditure of the Empire since 1885-86 is principally owing to the Military activity going on beyond the natural lines of the defences of the country, in pursuance of the Imperial policy of Great Britain in its relation with some of the Great Powers of Europe, this Congress is of opinion that, in bare justice to India, an equitable portion of that expenditure should be borne by the British Treasury, and that the revenues of India should be proportionately relieved of that burden.

**RESOLUTION VIII.**

**Resolved**—That this Congress is emphatically of opinion, that it is highly inexpedient in the present state of Education in the country, that Government grants for High Education should in any way be withdrawn, and, concurring with previous Congresses, affirms in the most emphatic manner, the importance of increasing the public expenditure on all branches of Education, and the expediency, in view to the promotion of one of the most essential of these branches, *i. e.*, the technical, of appointing a mixed Commission to enquire into the present industrial condition of the country.

**RESOLUTION IX.**

**Resolved**—That this Congress emphatically re-affirms Resolution III of the Congress of 1891, and having regard to the fact that fully fifty millions of the population, a number yearly increasing, are dragging out a miserable existence on the verge of starvation, and that in every decade several millions actually perish by starvation, deems it imperatively necessary that the cost of administration, especially in the military branch of the Public Service, should be greatly reduced, and that measures should at once be taken to give, as was promised by the British Government over thirty years ago, fixity and permanence to the land revenue demand, and thus permit capital and labour to combine to develop the agriculture of the country, which, under the existing system of temporary settlements, in recent times often lasting for short periods, in some cases only extending to ten and twelve years—is found to be impossible; and to establish Agricultural Banks. And this Congress, again, most earnestly entreats the people of Great Britain and Ireland, not to permit any further sacrifice of life owing to the shortcomings of the existing, doubtless well-intentioned, but none the less unsatisfactory, administration, but to insist, and, that needily, on the reforms, then and now, so earnestly advocated.

**RESOLUTION X.**

**Resolved**—That this Congress entirely adopts Resolution XI of the Congress of 1891, and reiterates its prayer, that having regard to the very serious discontent created, particularly in Peninsular India, by the practical administration of the Forest Laws, the Government of India do investigate this matter carefully and endeavour to mitigate the harshness of such administration, and render it less obnoxious to the poorer classes.

**RESOLUTION XI.**

**Resolved**—That Mr. W. C. Bonnerjee, Mr. P. M. Mehta, Mr. Surendra Nath Banerji, and Rai Bahadur Ananda Charlu, be appointed a Committee to prepare a petition on the line indicated by the petition printed at foot, and that the President be authorised to sign it, on behalf of this Congress, and send it to Mr. Dadabhai Naoroji, M. P, for presentation to the House of Commons.

To

The Hon'ble, The Commons of Great Britain and Ireland, in Parliament assembled.

The humble petition of the President and Members of the Eighth Indian National Congress, held at Allahabad, on the 28th, 29th, and 30th of December, 1892,
*Respectfully Showeth,*

(1) That in conformity with a resolution adopted at the Eighth Indian National Congress, your humble petitioners beg to bring to the attention of your Hon'ble House, the deep disappointment which prevails in all parts of Her Majesty's Indian Empire at the orders passed upon the labours of the Public Service Commission.

(2) That the Commission was instructed by the Government of India to submit a scheme which might reasonably be expected to possess the elements of finality and to do full justice to the claims of the Natives of India to higher and more extensive employment in the Public Service. Neither object has been secured by the labours of the Public Service Commission. The Statutory Service, under which appointments had been made, has been abolished, and nothing has been done to secure to the people the full enjoyment of the boon conferred upon them by the Act of 1870. The Government of India, in their resolution appointing the Commission, observed, "that the Statute of 1870 is one of remarkable breadth and liberality, and it empowers the Government of India and the Secretary of State, acting together, to frame rules under which Natives of India may be admitted to any of the offices hitherto reserved for the Covenanted Civil Service." But the result of the Commission's enquiry has been a reduction in the number of offices open to Indians.

(3) That in respect, likewise, to simultaneous examinations in England and in India for appointment in the Civil Service, the Report of the Commission, endorsed by the Government of India, has given no satisfaction whatever. The weight of the evidence taken by the Commissioners was distinctly in favour of simultaneous examinations. Among the witnesses examined, there was a very large preponderance of those who were in fovour of simultaneous examinations.

(4) That the disappointment which is everywhere felt at the resolution of the Government of India on the Public Service Commission, is of such a character that this Congress has felt constrained to lay the matter before the Hon'ble House, and to pray that it will direct the Government of India to give full effect to the Act of 1870 in the matter of appointing Natives of India to the Public Service of their country.

**RESOLUTION XII.**

**Resolved**—That this Congress, in concurrence with the first Congress held at Bombay in 1885, considers that the creation of a Legislative Council for the Province of the Punjab is an absolute necessity for the good Government of that Province and having regard to the fact that a similar Council has been created for the United Provinces, hopes that no time will be lost in creating such a Council.

### RESOLUTION XIII.

**Resolved**—That this Congress hereby tenders its most grateful acknowledgments to Sir W. Wedderburn and the members of the British Congress Committee, for the services rendered by them to India during the past year, and entirely approves and confirms the re-construction of the British Committee of the Congress which has been effected by them, as also the new arrangements which they have made in regard to their office establishment, and the journal "*India* ;" and that this Congress also tenders its thanks to Mr. W. Digby, C. I. E., for the services with he rendered to the cause during his tenure of office as Secretary to the British Committee.

### RESOLUTION XIV.

**Resolved**—That this Congress is thankful that the House of Commons is vigilant in regard to the recent purity legislation by the Government in India, and desires, once again, to enter its protest against all State-regulated immorality in India.

### RESOLUTION XV.

**Resolved**—That, regard being had to the present political situation in England, the provisional arrangements set on foot, in pursuance of the resolution passed at the Calcutta Congress, 1890, for holding—all things being convenient—a Congress of not less than hundred delegates in England, in 1892, be now suspended, until after the Session of the Congress in 1893.

### RESOLUTION XVI.

**Resolved**—That this Congress most respectfully and cordially tenders, on behalf of the vast population it represents, India's most hearfelt thanks to the electors of Central Finsbury for electing Mr. Dadabhai Naoroji their member in the House of Commons ; and it again puts on record its high estimate and deep appreciation of the services which that gentleman has rendered to this country, reiterates its unshaken confidence in him, and looks upon him as India's representative in the House of Commons.

### RESOLUTION XVII.

**Resolved**—That this Congress hereby empowers the Trustees of the Congress Permanent Fund—now locked up in the "New Oriental Bank Corporation, Ld.," at present in liquidation—to send, at least, five hundred pounds out of it to the British Committee, to be recouped by subscriptions from the Standing Congress Committees.

### RESOLUTION XVIII.

**Resolved**—That, regard being had to the representations received from the British Committee, this Congress is of opinion, that a sum equivalent in Rupees to two thousand eight hundred pounds sterling, be allotted for the expenses of the British Committee, for the year 1892-93 ; that deducting the money which has been received up to now, the balance be allotted amongst the different Standing Congress Committees, in accordance with the arrangements come to with them ; and that the sum be remitted to England as soon as practicable.

### RESOLUTION XIX.

**Resolved**—That this Congress re-appoints Mr. A. O. Hume, C. B., to be its General Secretary, and appoints Rai Bahadur P. Ananda Charlu, to be its Joint-General Secretary for the ensuing year.

### RESOLUTION XX.

**Resolved**—That the Ninth Indian National Congress do assemble on such day after Christmas, 1893, as may be determined upon, at Amritsar.

## RESOLUTION XXI.

**Resolved**—That this Congress hereby tenders Its best thanks to His Highness the Maharaja of Darbhanga, for having so kindly lent his Castle and grounds for the holding of this Congress.

## RESOLUTION XXII.

**Resolved**—That this Congress confirms the appointment of Pandit Bishumbhar Nath, in place of the late Pandit Ajudhia Nath, as one of the Trustees of the Congress Permanent Fund.

# REPORT

OF

# THE TENTH

# Indian

# National Congress

HELD AT

# MADRAS,

**On the 26th, 27th, 28th, and 29th December,**

**1894.**

---

## CONTENTS.

# INTRODUCTION.

The Tenth Congress.

AMID scenes of enthusiasm which only belong to a great and popular Cause, the Tenth Indian National Congress successfully accomplished the yearly task of placing before an increasingly attentiye public the need for Reform and the need for redress of grievances in the Indian Empire. In four days of exemplary application to the work in hand much sound common-sense, much political sagacity, much eloquence of a high order was brought to bear upon the pressing problems of modern India. If the proceedings towards the close of the Session were somewhat subdued in the recent shadow of a public sorrow—the sudden death of the young Maharajah of Mysore—none the less did the work of clear enunciation of popular rights go forward with unabated zeal to its appointed completion.

The Congress Hall was a large building capable of holding nearly 5,000 persons and throughout the four days during which the deliberations lasted was at all times full to overflowing It stood in a large compound of several acres in extent plentifully supplied with fine trees Innumerable tents and offices with their occupants hurrying to and fro, and the large house set apart for the President and some of the delegates, with the frequent arrival and departure of visitors some distinguished and some the reverse, for all had access to the Congress Headquarters—all these made up a scene of intense animation and interest. If absence of friction and perfection of results are tests of efficient organization then the arrangements of the Reception Committee must have been as well-nigh perfect as it is possible for human arrangements to be Not only in this busy camp, but in the stressful moments of Committee meetings, everything worked with a regularity and a smoothness which is not often met with.

A word must be said about the Volunteer Corps—one of the remarkable features of these Indian Congresses. During the Congress week some 200 young men of good family thought it an honour, and by their helpfulness, tact and discretion made it an honour, to be in constant attendance upon the delegates to the National Parliament. Never obtrusive, but always at hand, and always willing to take messages, to receive orders and to get things done, these young men under a genial captain and efficient lieutenants contributed in no small measure to the amenities of that strenuous political life. Mr. Webb was especially struck with their bearing and efficiency and many a hard-pressed delegate had good reasons to be grateful for their unselfish and untiring services.

Chairman of Reception Committee's Address

The First Day's Proceedings opened with the address of the Chairman of the Reception Committee. In a telling and eloquent address the Hon. Mr. P. Rungiah Naidu welcomed the 1,200 delegates of the Tenth Indian Congress to Madras, reminding them in the words of the late Rajah Sir T. Madhava Row, K.C.S.I., that the Congress is the "soundest triumph of British Administration and a crown of glory to the British Nation." He pointed out that the Congress was steadily increasing in power and influence and gradually penetrating all classes and sections of the people. "The political horizon of the educated Indian citizen is no longer his village or district, not even the capital city of his province, but it is now the whole Indian Continent."

After referring to the Charter of Indian liberties, the Queen's Proclamation of 1858, and to attempts which have been made from time to time to explain away the obvious meaning of that historic document, Mr. Rungiah Naidu declared fairly and squarely that the Indian Bureaucracy were selfish. "I say that most deliberately" he added "and the history of the last 35 years is my justification for saying so." The two following paragraphs taken from his address illustrate well that strong and effective criticism of the defects of Anglo-Indian rule coupled with a generous recognition of its advantages, which has always marked the utterances of the Congress leaders.

"We are at present, more than we ever were, in need of the support of British public opinion, because in proportion as our agitation acquires prestige and grows in influence, so does the opposition in this country grow strong. Of this opposition you have seen a remarkable proof in the latest official contribution to the literature on the Simultaneous Examinations Question. The Parliamentary Blue Book on that question marks, I fear, a further straining of the relations between educated Indians and the officials, from which latter nothing but abuse, misrepresentation and determined opposition are, it would seem, hereafter to be expected even in our most moderate attempts at self-improvement. They would seem to have persuaded themselves into the belief that to have established English Schools and Colleges is the greatest mistake of British rule in India, and that inasmuch as their abolition is out of the question, the next best thing, from their point of view, is to cry down the men educated in these institutions, call them names, and characterise them as a class of disloyal men, devoid of influence with their own countrymen, and incapable of discharging any responsible public duty. Our Anglo-Indian friends speak as if nothing good can come out of the people for whose education the State expends as much as a crore of rupees every year. They seem to be almost ashamed of their own literature, of the teachers and professors of their own nationality, and enamoured of ignorance and superstition as the best mental state of the Indian people. I have no doubt that this Blue Book, so disappointing and so retrograde and so unworthy of the Englishman's reputation for fair dealing, will be subjected to severe criticism in the course of our proceedings. And I merely refer to it here to show what amount and what kind of opposition we should be prepared for in this country before our objects are attained."

"To abuse the opponent is a favourite form of argument with a certain description of people, and failing to meet us with fair reasoning or on the ground of justice or political wisdom, the opponents of the Congress, that is, of educated Indians, call us disloyal, and attribute to us revolutionary designs. Gentlemen, with mad men and with people who talk wildly under the exciting sense of losing interests, we have no concern. If there be any reasonable persons amongst our opponents, I should like to take them into my confidence and ask them why they think we are disloyal If a rule which has established peace, order and security in the country, which administers justice as impartially as human tribunals can do, which constantly stimulates material prosperity, which has conferred on the people the inestimable blessing of Education, liberty of conscience and freedom of discussion, and of which, indeed the possibilities for future good are even greater than what has actually been done in the past—if such a rule cannot excite the loyal attachment of the people, I am at a loss to know what kind of rule may be expected to excite their loyalty Gentlemen, the fact is, the persons that charge us with disloyalty are the victims of their own guilty conscience, of some evil thought concealed in their minds, and it is only such persons that see disloyalty everywhere, and, like Macbeth, perceive a dagger in the air. Nor is it anything but the most ludicrous absurdity to see disloyalty in political agitation conducted on strictly constitutional lines and in a spirit of confidence in the rulers. What is the gaod of the education and freedom that have been vouchsafed to us if we do not make use of them for our own improvement. We have no desire but to live on terms of the utmost amity and regard with our Anglo-Indian fellow-subjects. We feel we want their guidance and their sympathy which, whenever shown, we have most sincerely and unstintingly reciprocated."

Chairman of Reception Committee's Address.

Speaking of the enthusiasm which this Congress has evoked in Southern India Mr. Rungiah Naidu said "Thore can be no doubt that, although after the first few years the Congress as a great patriotic enterprise lost the attractions of novelty, it has lost no portion of its influence on the intelligent classes of the community as the only institution calling into play what resources of public spirit exist in the country and imparting weight and dignity to such non-official, Indian opinion as gives itself expression from time to time. Nothing proves this fact better than the unprecedented outburst of enthusiasm throughout Southern India when the preparations for this Congress were set on foot in the middle of the year." * * * The most remarkable feature in the work of our organization this time was the system of raising the necessary funds by appealing for help to every house and every place of business in the locality, a system which, first started in the city of Madras, was immediately adopted in every centre of Congress activity in all the districts of the province. The Reception Committee has collected till now nearly 40,000 rupees, of which nearly if not more than half was collected in exceedingly small amounts, in the shape of single rupees, of annas and pies."

In the concluding paragraphs of this address a reference to the Mahomedan community exhibits again that firm but temperate and conciliatory attitude which as we have said before characterizes the Congress on the questions of the day. "We do not conceal from ourselves the fact that an important section of our Mahomedan fellow countrymen have stood aloof from our movement under the mistaken impression that it is disliked by the powers-that-be, and that not to join such a movement, to denounce it, and to actually oppose it, is the surest passport to Government's favour and official advancement. But the time is gone, altogether gone, when subserviency to official power can play the role of real merit and win admission to the public service, and our deluded fellow country-men are just

**Chairman of Reception Committee's Address.**

now discovering that the game is after all not paying, and that in these days no community gets a hearing for its representations, especially when the governing power is vested in the hands of foreigners, unless those representations are backed up by a powerful and organized agitation. Educational Conferences are accordingly being organized, political societies are being established, and whispers of discontent are being heard—all showing that soon our Mahomedan fellow countrymen, though they may not all join the Congress, will press their claims by public agitation on lines parallel to our own. They are quite welcome to this method and we shall most cordially wish them success. They cannot have claims different from our own or claims with which we of the Indian National Congress do not fully and warmly sympathize."

**President's Address.**

The formal election of the President was the next business and being quickly over Mr. Alfred Webb, M.P., for West Waterford began his inaugural address as President of the Tenth Indian National Congress. The distinguishing characteristic of a very thoughtful and sympathetic address was a moderation and a sweet reasonableness which has proved extremely disconcerting not to say irritating to that hostile chorus of unofficial officialdom—the Anglo-Indian Press. In vain would the most uncompromising opponent ransack Mr. Webb's opening address for any vestige of sentiments which overstepped the bounds of sober and legitimate criticism. The address should be read in its entirety, but the following noteworthy pafagraphs may be quoted here.

"The ends you have in view are similar to those of politicians in other quarters of the globe. The difficulties before you are, however, greater. Else where politicians have to deal principally with homogeneous populations, to whom, at least in theory, equal political rights may at once be accorded you have largely to work for those who have yet to pass through a long process of assimilation and elevation. All the greater necessity that in assemblages such as this you shoul set yourselves to the task. All the greater necessity that a deaf ear should be turned to doctrines of despair. The question is not concerning the difficulties, but whether or not the difficulties are to be faced; and if to be faced, the sooner the better. And it is alone by and through organizations such as yours that they can be faced."

"It is at the same time necessary to bear in mind that you stand at the most critical period of a people's history. Your populations, heretofore supine, are awakening to consciousness and new hopes, whilst they may not fully as yet have acquired habits of self-restraint and sentiments of responsibility. Mistakes are certain to be made and are sure to be attributed by opponents, not to their true source—former conditions, but to the awakening, the ennobling process itself. We must be prepared to meet misrepresentations and calumny. We must take heed that in our leading we give no just cause for accusation."

"Nothing in what I have said or intend to say must however be taken to imply a want of appreciation of the character and services of numbers of my fellow-citizens, whose lives have been and are being given to the administration and government of India. They were doubtless at first attracted to the service solely as a career in life. But residence here, sympathy with your people, and a sense of duty, rapidly impel to higher motives. They become sincerely anxious for your welfare and devoted to what they believe your highest good. Never has more conscience been brought to the government of a conquered country. We here are not set against them, unless, indeed, they are determined to set themselves against us. The services of men of their training, temper, and turn of mind may, perhaps for generations to come, be necessary. They are to be honoured and respected in their sphere. But they must not impede or prevent the gradual application to the government of this country of principles other than those laid down by statesmen of the first rank fully half a century ago. I might perhaps have been more affected than I have been by the attitude and language of many of them regarding your country and your people, were it not that it is such as I have been accustomed to hear from the same class in Ireland regarding my country and my people. If the anticipations of the former regarding your capacities and your future are as fully belied as have been the anticipations of the latter regarding our capacities and our future, you may rest satisfied. Closely allied, in blood and religion, as this class in Ireland has been to us, their efforts to govern independently of Irish opinion have resulted in failure. How much less likely is it that they can succeed here without availing themselves of your assistance more largely than heretofore."

"While most anxious not to implicate your cause with Irish politics, or the relations between Great Britain and Ireland, I may occasionally illustrate your affairs by reference to my own country. Your interests are in fact closely involved in some effectual settlement of the Irish question. One of your principal and most just complaints is that no sufficient attention is given to your affairs in Parliament. Whilst months are allotted to the consideration of the British budget, a few hours are grudged to yours. Parliament is paralysed with work. It has undertaken functions it cannot perform. Three separate Parliaments had enough to do to manage the affairs of England, Scotland, and Ireland. They were merged into one when the population of the United Kingdom was only fifteen millions. That population has now risen to thirty-eight millions. Parliament has, moreover, undertaken to care for your two hundred and eighty millions. The sphere of law is becoming both wider and more minute. Surely Parliament ought to be more of an Imperial, less of a local, assembly! For generations to come, England, the heart of the Empire, must have the preponderating influence in Imperial councils. That we grant. You, who are Indian, and I, who am Irish, trust that our Imperial rights will not suffer from that preponderating English influence. But at present the Imperial Parliament is occupied largely with the affairs of under five millions of people, and ministries rise and fall with reference to the question of Ireland, and not in connection with great Imperial interests. The entire Empire is concerned in the speedy settlement of the Irish question."

After referring in some detail to various items in the Congress programme Mr. Webb concluded an address which had been listened to with profound attention in these words:—"Apart from those family and national ties, which to each one of us are the first of life's blessings—the choicest gifts of God—I regard this

President's Address

visit to India, and permission to take part in the proceedings of this great assemblage, as the highest privilege, and one that cannot but profoundly influence my remaining years. So far, two convictions before all others, press themselves upon me. The one: the greatness, apart from its inception and much of its history, of the mission of the United Kingdom in this land—the other: that this Congress movement is the necessary and logical outcome, the richest fruit of that noble mission, of which we citizens of the United Kingdom should be proud. You yourselves are taking up the work--the work which you and you alone can ultimately perfect—'the eradication by direct friendly intercourse of all possible race, creed, or national prejudices amongst all lovers of your country.' This is in truth the greatest combined peaceful effort for the good of the largest number of the human race that history has recorded."

Election of Subjects Committee.

The President's address finished, there was one of those little incidents which are the envy and despair of opponents of the national movement—namely, the reading of a letter announcing a gift of Rs. 10,000 to the Congress Cause from the young Rajah of Ramnad. 'How can we stop a movement to which—as if popular euthusiasm were not enough—inconvenient Rajahs contribute their thousands of Rupees?' say opponents. How indeed? How much more suitable, think retiring Governors, if that money had been contributed to the raising of some fitting memorial with which to mark our beneficent rule! The election of the Subjects Committee, whose function it is to arrange the agenda paper for each day and to select the speakers for the different resolutions, concludes the first day's proceedings. But the work of the day is by no means over—the Subjects Committee has to meet to discuss the substance and the wording of the Resolutions to be brought forward—one hundred keen-witted politicians, themselves a small parliament, delegated by the Congress itself, will hold debate far into the night so that no hasty or ill-considered proposition may be put forward at to-morrow's meeting. Truly a prudent and hard-working body this Congress!

Resolution I. Cotton Excise Duty.

The Second Day's Proceedings begin with the reading of the Rules of Debate, the reading over of the Standing Orders as it were, and then the Congress settles down to formulate by the utterances of its chosen spokesmen and the words of its written resolutions, its perpetual programme of retrenchment and reform. A resolution condemning the imposition of Excise Duty on Indian manufactured cottons on grounds of urgency is given precedence of debate and becomes Resolution I. This day the Excise Duty Bill is down for third reading in the Viceroy's Council. Therefore it is deemed advisable that the protest of India's Parliament should be in the hands of India's Legislators before the Bill actually becomes law—which by means of the telegraph may be done, and is done after an exhaustive speech from that old Congress-wallah Mr. D. E. Wacha, and after the motion has been neatly seconded by the Hon. Mr. A. Sabapathy Mudeliar.

Mr. Wacha after saying amid cheers that the Government of India deserved their warm gratitude for having at last been able to extort from the Secretary of State for India the concession to impose an import duty on cotton goods, proceeded to show that this act of tardy justice reluctantly accorded by the autocrat at Westminster was accompanied by two disadvantages. Firstly, a large revenue—a crore and a half rupees—had been needlessly sacrificed during the last twelve months; and secondly there was the countervailing excise. The excise duty failed to satisfy the three tests of a sound and successful tax, namely, productiveness, economy and equity. In no case could the excise bring in more than 8½ lakhs of revenue, which would probably be eaten up by the heavy cost of collection. "It will then be reasonably asked why is the Bill brought forward. To that we have a reply from the Financial member himself. Because the Secretary of State deems it opportune to please the Philistines of Manchester" Loud cries of "Shame!" showed that the speaker had expressed what was in the minds of his hearers, and what every one there and many elsewhere knew to be strictly true.

Resolution I. Cotton Excise Duty.

The following sentences put the matter succinctly and clearly. "I daresay most of you, if not all, have perused the very able and exhaustive memorial on the subject submitted some time ago to the Government of India by the Bombay Mill Owners' Association; also the minute of the Hon. Mr. Westland, dated 14th July last, which accompanied the despatch of the Government of India to the Secretary of State, dated 7th August, recommending that, if any excise duty was to be levied, it should be on all counts of yarn above "twenty-fours." The former body collected statistics from 105 mills in the country, 70 of which are in Bombay, the centre of the industry, and conclusively demonstrated that of the total manufactures counts between "twenty-fours" and "thirties" only come to 6 per cent., and that the total value of exports of Indian manufactured cottons above "twenties" does not exceed 86 lakhs of rupees. On the other hand out of the bulk of all descriptions of cotton fabrics imported into India from the United Kingdom only 2 per cent. are of counts under "twenties." Virtually, then, Lancashire does not compete with this country in the coarser kinds, and India does not compete with Lancashire in the finer kinds. Thus statistics completely disprove the cry of protection. Absolutely nothing is protected by the import duty, which, therefore, in no way acts as a bounty on home-made cottons. This being the exact economic condition of the indigenous industry, can it be reasonably urged that the excise duty is justifiable? And if it be not justifiable, can we not characterise it as unjust? For of what use imposing a duty for which there exists no justification? Again, as Mr. Westland observed in his speech, revenue is not the consideration. That simply emphasizes the injustice. For if there be no necessity to levy it for purposes of revenue and if it is not even for purposes of counter-balancing the import duty, what is it imposed for? The Honorable the Finance Minister gives a reply to the query. It is to please the Secretary of State on behalf of those good and pious people of Manchester."

Resolution II. Land Question.

Resolution II deals with the Land Question and was entrusted in the first place to the able hands of Mr. Boikunta Nath Sen, a native of Bengal, the province of the Permanent Settlement. The Resolution was a protest against interference by Government with the existing Permanent Settlement in Bengal and Behar (*e.g.*, the Behar Cadastral Survey) and with certain permanently settled estates in Madras: the Resolution also reminded Government

Resolution II.
Land Question.

of certain pledges that had been given to extend the Permanent Settlement, and suggested in a spirit of extreme conciliation that if more permanent settlements were out of the question, there should be at any rate a modified fixity of tenure and immunity from enhancement of land revenue for a period of say 60 years so as to secure to landholders the benefit of their improvements. In fact this second clause of the Resolution is a demand for an Agricultural Improvements Act—very necessary where an impecunious Government is the landlord !

Mr. Boikunta Nath Sen pointed out—an easy task—that the Government were not fulfilling their pledges with regard to the land : and then, turned aside to meet the modern objections about "unearned increment" in the following sentences :– "These despatches laid down certain rules for the extension of the permanent settlement. There were certain conditions precedent, *viz.*, the bringing under cultivation of a certain portion of the area. Four-fifths of the entire area was fixed as the amount to be brought under cultivation in order that the permanant settlement might be accorded to such local area. Now in some tracts, with the object of getting that privilege, the conditions have been fulfilled, in some other parts the conditions have been partially fulfilled; and if time will allow they will also surely be fulfilled. The fulfilment of these conditions is not an easy thing; it requires the investing of money. Here comes in the question of unearned increment. It is not the unearned increment which these land-owners are trying to get ; they are investing their money, they are bestowing their labour, and they ask for a return. So you see, these persons who now hold under temporary settlement, are not at all asking for the unearned increment. They wish to have the fruits of their own labour and a return for the capital they have invested. Before the despatch of 1862 there was no stimulus whatsoever for investing money, because there was no knowing when the property might be remeasured, when there might be interference by Government again, and when the property would be snatched away from their hands. There was no security, no value, and therefore no stimulus for investing money. But the despatch of Government emboldened the people, it induced them to invest their money to improve the land. They have fulfilled their part of the contract, and if it had been, Gentlemen, a question between individual and individual, perhaps one would be inclined to ask 'Why not sue?'"

The Hon. Mr. V. R. Natu then took up the question from the Bombay point of view, asserting strongly that all India, Ryots as well as Zemindars were interested in the maintenance of existing Permanent Settlements. He then proceeded to show how necessary was the second clause of the Resolution giving striking instances of the outrageous demands of Government. The matter is very simple. Government have laid it down that on a new Revision of Survey in the Bombay Presidency, the assessment in the case of any given group of villages shall not be increased by more than 33 per cent. Yet Mr. Natu was able to quote unquestioned instances where there had been increases; in 3 Taluqs in the Ratnagiri District and 3 Taluqs in the Albag District, an extremely poor district, there had been the enormous increase of 1,200 per cent. ! In concluding he said "We say that whenever you introduce Revision Surveys you should simply adhere

**Resolution II. Land Question.**

to your own terms, that you should simply limit your demand to 33 per cent. That is the only limited demand. We do not want a permanent settlement in the sense in which it is understood in Bengal. Foreigners, including the President who comes from a foreign country, should not be misled into supposing that the bulk of the population in India requires a permanent settlement in the sense in which it is understood in Bengal. It is a limited demand, a demand accepted by Government as proper and just and followed for some years."

Here came an amendment. Captain Banon—a very old friend of the Congress and, as he himself said, a ryotwar of the Punjab—suggests that Congress should propose a permanent settlement for all India, bringing the land under the Permanent Settlement of Lord Cornwallis into the general settlement—of course Bengal losing something by the arrangement, but the rest of India—at least that is Captain Banon's view—gaining largely. The following paragraph from his speech, which was very short and very much to the point, shows clearly his standpoint.

I may begin by saying that I am very desirous of a permanent settlement for all India, because I myself am a ryotwar in the Punjab; but the only difficulty that I can see to our getting this permanent settlement is the permanent settlement at present existing in Bengal. Government say that they lose quite enough money already by this permanent settlement in Bengal, and that as long as it exists they cannot give a permanent settlement to the rest of India. I live amongst the ryotwars, as I am one of them, and I know that they consider it very unfair to them that they should pay twice as much land revenue as they would pay but for this permanent settlement in Bengal. I would also direct your attention to another question. It has always been alleged against this Congress that it favours the interests of the richer classes as against those of the poorer classes. That I do not believe, but I think if you support this Resolution, you will add a good deal of colour to the accusations against us."

The Amendment is not supported—although it struck a note which may sound louder in the future—and the Hon. Mr. K. Kalyanasundram Iyer, proceeded to unfold the grievances of Tanjore. Very real grievances they appear to be as the speaker showed well. " Now, Gentlemen, what do these constant re-settlements mean ? You have an excellent illustration in the methods adopted in the re-settlement of the district of Tanjore. The Government, being fully alive to the evils attendant on settlement operations generally, determined that the average out-turn of land should, first and once for all, be estimated upon scientific principles, and that in future revisions the rise in prices alone should be taken into account. The procedure adopted was this: the average yield of land was ordered to be estimated by a scientific classification of soil, but not to be checked and tested by actual experiments in harvesting; apparently this scientific classification of soil is so finely graded that the officers of the settlement department have often, with reference to one and the same soil, been obliged to differ from themselves and each other, while with regard to the actual experiment made the result has been by no means more satisfactory. A small plot of land, the tenth part of an acre, was selected by the settlement department itself for the experiment in har-

Resolution II.
Land Question.

vesting, and upon the result of this single experiment hundreds of acres, nay thousands of acres, were settled as being able to produce a particular out-turn. The Mirasidars of the district naturally objected to such a course; they loudly complained that the actual yield of the land in their possession was a great deal less than the estimate fixed by the department, and they clamourously demanded an *Amani* management for a reasonable period, for the purpose of determining the average yielding capacity of the land; but their complaints and their demands were alike rejected and they were in fact told that if the actual facts were not consistent with the theory evolved by the settlement department it was so much the worse for their facts. Now, Gentlemen, the utter unreliability of this theoretical settlement is clearly shown by the action of the authorities themselves The gentleman who was appointed the settlement officer of the district, after a classification of the soil, reported to Government that the re-settlement of the district would involve an increase of eighteen and a half lakhs of rupees, the assessment under the old settiement being about forty-one lakhs; but he added, that if the district were to be treated upon scientific principles an increase of twenty-eight lakhs would not be too much. Apparently to the great loss of Government, he finally recommended an increase of only fourteen and a half lakhs. This was reduced by the Board of Revenue by two lakhs, and finally by Government to eleven and a half lakhs. Thus you see the final decision of the Government imposed an increase of assessment representing only forty per cent. on what should have been the increase according to the accurate scientific theory."

Mana Vikrama Raja follows with the complaint of Malabar, another district in Madras, where Revenue Settlement operations are in " full swing." The whole speech gives a clear consecutive account of the history of the land revenue in Malabar and must be read as a whole To show that the present scheme of government affords ground for complaint the following short quotation from this very able speech will suffice. " In the face of the pledge already made, Government has determined to revise the existing assessment in spite of the repeated protests and representations of the people, and a scheme of settlement is at the present moment awaiting the orders of the local Government. I may add that according to this scheme, the existing revenue in three typical Taluqs of the District under wet, dry, and garden lands will be increased by 95 per cent., 49 per cent. and 335 per cent. respectively, resulting in an aggregate increase of over 15 lakhs whilst their present revenue is only 10½ lakhs."

Mr. Peter Paul Pillai a well-known figure at successive Congresses, and others continued to press the case against the Government and then the Resolution on the Land Question was passed unanimously. Mr. Seymour Keay, M.P., then came forward amidst enthusiastic cheers to move Resolution III dealing with the poverty of India. In a speech which was frequently cheered to the echo, Mr. Seymour Keay marshalled in a telling manner a great deal of statistical material. A few quotations must be given to show the nature of the argument, but the whole speech is deserving of careful study.

# INTRODUCTION.

The Tenth Congress.

AMID scenes of enthusiasm which only belong to a great and popular Cause, the Tenth Indian National Congress successfully accomplished the yearly task of placing before an increasingly attentiye public the need for Reform and the need for redress of grievances in the Indian Empire. In four days of exemplary application to the work in hand much sound common-sense, much political sagacity, much eloquence of a high order was brought to bear upon the pressing problems of modern India. If the proceedings towards the close of the Session were somewhat subdued in the recent shadow of a public sorrow—the sudden death of the young Maharajah of Mysore—none the less did the work of clear enunciation of popular rights go forward with unabated zeal to its appointed completion.

The Congress Hall was a large building capable of holding nearly 5,000 persons and throughout the four days during which the deliberations lasted was at all times full to overflowing It stood in a large compound of several acres in extent plentifully supplied with fine trees Innumerable tents and offices with their occupants hurrying to and fro, and the large house set apart for the President and some of the delegates, with the frequent arrival and departure of visitors some distinguished and some the reverse, for all had access to the Congress Headquarters—all these made up a scene of intense animation and interest. If absence of friction and perfection of results are tests of efficient organization then the arrangements of the Reception Committee must have been as well-nigh perfect as it is possible for human arrangements to be Not only in this busy camp, but in the stressful moments of Committee meetings, everything worked with a regularity and a smoothness which is not often met with.

A word must be said about the Volunteer Corps—one of the remarkable features of these Indian Congresses. During the Congress week some 200 young men of good family thought it an honour, and by their helpfulness, tact and discretion made it an honour, to be in constant attendance upon the delegates to the National Parliament. Never obtrusive, but always at hand, and always willing to take messages, to receive orders and to get things done, these young men under a genial captain and efficient lieutenants contributed in no small measure to the amenities of that strenuous political life. Mr. Webb was especially struck with their bearing and efficiency and many a hard-pressed delegate had good reasons to be grateful for their unselfish and untiring services.

Chairman of Reception Committee's Address.

The First Day's Proceedings opened with the address of the Chairman of the Reception Committee. In a telling and eloquent address the Hon. Mr. P. Rungiah Naidu welcomed the 1,200 delegates of the Tenth Indian Congress to Madras, reminding them in the words of the late Rajah Sir T. Madhava Row, K.C.S.I., that the Congress is the "soundest triumph of British Administration and a crown of glory to the British Nation." He pointed out that the Congress was steadily increasing in power and influence and gradually penetrating all classes and sections

Resolution III. Poverty of India.

173 persons, man, woman and child had each an amount of 6½ rupees a year for their support !"

This Resolution was supported among others by Lala Murlidhar, in an amusing speech which kept the whole Congress in a perpetual roar of laughter. The speech, which is short should be read as a whole; quotations would give no correct idea of the effect produced.

Resolution IV. Secretary of State's Council.

The Secretary of State's Council and the need for its abolition formed the subject matter of Resolution IV, which was moved by Mr. Eardley Norton in a brilliant and powerful speech. A severe, and at times witty, indictment of both the theory and the practise of the India Council. Why do we object to the India Council? Let Mr. Norton answer. "We object for this simple reason: that although its members are, possibly, imbued with the very best of intentions—mere intentions are not sufficient for practical politics—these same members are swayed by the same official interest, trained in the same official career, steeped in the same official prejudices, as the men cut here who, also with the best of intentions, are resolutely endeavouring to thwart and obstruct your moral, material and political reforms. Unless and until you sweep away the powerful association which, through all the intervening stretch of land and sea, is ever ready to help its fellow officials in this country, to condone their faults, to pander to their extravagance, to restrict your privileges, and to deny you your prerogatives, the re-constitution of tho Legislative Councils must remain practically a sham."

The speaker then proceeded to deal in a masterly manner with the constitution and powers of the Council. Of the Council's commercial incapacity here is what he said :—"Although Lord Canning in 1858 sent an urgent despatch to the Secretary of State strongly protesting against his contemplated action, that particular Secretary of State in Council sanctioned the construction of the Calcutta and South Eastern Railway, and guaranteed interest at the rate of 5 per cent. This was done after eleven years experience had taught that such concessions were irreconcilable with the true interests of India. The result of this was that the whole thing practically became bankrupt, and the Secretary of State had to purchase the railway at the cost of half a million sterling ! Not content with this purchase of 1858, in 1859 the Council granted another concession, this time, by way of strict impartiality, in my own particular Presidency of Madras, to the Madras Irrigation Company upon substantially the same basis guaranteeing to pay in perpetuity interest at 5 per cent. upon one million pounds sterling Soon after this it was found the calculations were all wrong. The work never paid its expenses. What did the Secretary of State in Council do ? He promptly advanced an additional £6,000 without security, with the result that eventually India had to buy this concern at par. I have dealt with Calcutta and Madras. Let us see what is done in the Presidency to which Mr. Wacha belongs. I find in Bombay that in 1869 the India Council sanctioned the purchase of the Elphinstone Land and Press Company for Rs. 1,000 per share while the selling price was only Rs. 339. These illustrations show that the commercial capa-

Resolution IV.

Secretary of State's Council.

city of the gentlemen who receive handsome salaries and pensions from us is not so great as to entitle them to retain our confidence or our admiration."

"Now let us look at some interesting figures illustrative of the licentious and criminal extravagance of these twelve or fourteen gentlemen at home. India has been charged—and has had to pay—£821,100 for the erection of certain buildings in England. Of this £540,000 has been absorbed in the construction and furniture of the India Office, a place not unfrequently devoted to giving, at the expense of India, costly entertainments to visitors to England unconnected with this country. I find that £70,000 have been spent on the erection of a library, £68,000 upon our old friend the Store Depot, and £100,000 upon the Indian Engineering College for the manufacture of experts who after importation find themselves shelved in favour of Royal Engineers. Now I come to the most extraordinary and alarming of all the items, namely, £38,000 which have been spent, Sir, on the construction of a Lunatic Asylum at Ealing." The manner in which Mr. Norton dealt with the famous institution at Ealing must be read in the full report.

Concluding, the speaker accurately voiced the feelings of all present in the following sentences. "With me there is no mending that Council. It must be ending. Let it be decapitated and its head decently buried in another continent to that in which lies interred its trunk, lest the two baneful things re-unite and the monster be resuscitated. For a worse system than the present could not be invented by the ingenuity of man. The Council is a secret body; its discussions are not public; its conclusions do not see the light of day; it is not open to the influence of outside criticism; it is not responsible to Parliament; it cannot be affected by public opinion. You cannot have a worse body than that to rule or to misrule you."

Mr. Mudholkar in support emphasized the utter uselessness of the India Council and related the following striking instance of a grievance against this Council. "You know, Gentlemen—particularly those of you who come from Bombay—what the *Inam* commission is. When the *Inam* Commission was let loose in certain provinces, which need not be mentioned here, certain *Inams* were attached and the proceeds taken to the Government treasury pending investigation, which in some cases went on for a period of 25 years. At last it was found that the *Inamdars* were entitled and their claims were allowed. But during all this time Government had received the profits. The *Inamdars* asked for arrears. The Government of India disallowed the claim. There was an appeal to the Secretary or State and his Council. Well, one would have expected that if the claim was just, Government would have taken time to verify the thing. No! Claims of right and justice like this would most certainly hamper the hands of our Council, and these claims were summarily rejected. This is the justice which is received from the highest executive authority." With the passing of this Resolution the business of the Second day came to an end.

The Third Day's Proceedings opened with Resolution V relating to the promised Financial Enquiry. Mr. Mudalier in moving the Resolution well expressed the opinion of educated Indians on the scope of this promised enquiry in the following words "I think I can make you understand our position by a brief illustration, which may not be elegant, but at the same time expresses our ideas briefly and in a short compass. The action of the Government—if the promise of the Secretary of State results in action in the terms of that promise—seems to me like the conduct of a stupid cartman who loads or overloads his cart without considering and measuring the strength of his bullocks. The Government idea of making an enquiry into the expenditure only without making corresponding enquiries as to the capacity of the Indian tax-payer to bear the present burdens seems to be based on foregone conclusions. It postulates that the Indian people are very happy and contented under the present fiscal burdens, that they have nothing whatever to complain of, and that the present taxation can be continued without any diminution."

He was followed by Mr. Morgan-Browne in a speech containing several suggestive facts and figures. Here are one or two extracts. "When I was travelling in the Punjab I met an Anglo-Indian, himself an officer of Government, who told me this little story. Somewhere here in Madras there was a man who helped a Colonel, a man of some influence, in a matter of some importance. This Colonel out of gratitude offered this man an appointment and wrote to him saying 'I can get you an appointment as an Inspector of Stores in London at £250 a year. He replied 'I am very much obliged to you for your kind offer, but unfortunately I have a wife and family, and I cannot afford to take up the post on such a low salary.' And so, Gentlemen, the post went elsewhere. Afterwards the Colonel wrote to this man and said, 'I am very sorry to hear that you have declined the appointment, for it is worth £1,250 a year.' What does that mean? It means £1,000 a year in the shape of bribes."

Dealing with the financial methods of the Government of India, Mr Morgan-Browne said :—"There was published quite recently a return on Indian Military Expenditure. Now this is an instructive return because it show you although late in the day, some of the financial methods of this Government. The return is headed "East India (Military Expenditure)." The first thing you notice on opening the return is that the items of "Military Works" and "Special Defence Works" have been absolutely ignored. Now we put a question to Mr Fowler, the Secretary of State for India, as to why in a return of Military Expenditure such an important part of Military Expenditure as that of "Military Works was left out. He replied that the Return only dealt with Army Expenditure, and that "Military Expenditure" was the ordinary heading under which this is placed in the accounts. Well, Gentlemen, we turn up the Accounts of the Government of India, and we find no such heading as "Military Expenditure." In those accounts Military Expenditure figures under three heads, "Army Services "Military Works" and "Special Defence Works." I do not see how we can exonerate the Government of India from either being extremely ignorant of their own accounts or else deliberately deceiving the public in England with the heading of Military Expenditure, which, while suggesting the whole, was meant to cover only a portion.

Resolution V

Financial Enquiry.

And finally, referring to the cry of Anglo-Indian Officialism that the fall in Exchange has been the sole cause of the financial embarrassment of the Government of India, the speaker made the following significant statement, founded as he had previously explained on the published accounts of the Government of India. "Gentlemen, the increase in the Revenues in this country exceeded the increase in the cost of exchange by 2½ crores, and by that same amount, namely, 2½ crores, the increase in Military and Civil expenditure exceeded the increase in the Revenues. I want you to appreciate these facts which I am giving you on the figures of the Government of India. I want you to realize that these facts give the lie direct to the assertion of the Government of India that the fall in the rupee has accounted for the deficit and has been the sole cause of it."

Mr. G. Subramania Iyer, the able Editor of the *Hindu* Newspaper. brought further damaging evidence against the financial methods of the Government of India, quoting no less an authority than Sir W Hunter. Here is what he said:—"Sir William Hunter writing in the columns of the *Times* has gone to the extent of accusing the Government of India of want of honesty generally. When he criticised Mr. Westland's budget, in which Exchange was taken at 14d. per Rupee, although everybody knew that that rate was excessively high, Sir W. Hunter even said that Mr. Westland did that in order to mitigate the scandal of sacrificing 14 millions of Rupees of potential Indian Revenue to party exigencies in England; in other words, he asserted that this high rate of exchange was assumed in order to allay the public feeling against the exclusion of Manchester goods from the Tariff Act. Such being the case, Sir, it will not be said that we are presumptuous in asking for this enquiry into the ability of the Indian people to bear their existing financial burdens."

The same speaker neatly summed up the financial history of India during the last ten years in a couple of sentences. "Mr. Westland said in his budget speech that within the last ten years, four new taxes had been imposed and the surpluses of the Provincial Governments swept off into the Imperial coffers. Still the financial difficulties have not disappeared, for the very sufficient reason that all the further proceeds of this taxation have been spent upon wars and upon Compensation Allowance to the European Employes of Government."

And Mr. Nagarkar from Poona reminded his hearers of the abortive Fawcett Committee on this question of finance, and made a practical suggestion by which its lost labours might be recovered and utilized. "You are all aware that as far back as the year 1870 or thereabouts, the British Parliament appointed a similar Committee of Enquiry which was popularly styled the Fawcett Committee because Mr. Fawcett, whose immortal name stands indelibly engraved on the hearts of the whole Indian nation, was one of its members. This Committee, having continued its labours for four full years, recorded a huge mass of evidence, but had no time to give a Report or to summarise the evidence it had collected, because by the time the labours of this Committee had been nearly completed, the British Parliament was dissolved, and along with it this Committee also was dissolved. If the scope of the enquiry of the present Committee is extended, and an

**Resolution V.**

**Financial Enquiry.**

examination of the Revenue side of the administration included in it, the work on this Committee will have been much simplified. They have only to fill up the gap which the last Committee left at the end of 1882, and to examine half-a-dozen witnesses, the heads of each department, with a view to ascertaining the change that has taken place during the last 20 years ; and when this is done the enquiry will not occupy a very large portion of the Committee's time."

**Resolution VI.**

**Simultaneous Examinations.**

The next Resolution was only like the last, of considerable present interest. It was the opportunity for educated and thinking India to give its answer to Mr. Fowler's despatch on the question of Simultaneous Examinations, and a very significant and weighty answer it is. This was Resolution VI. on the question of Simultaneous Examinations, protesting against the way in which the Secretary of State and the Government of India had set aside the vote of the House of Commons on this subject. The occasion was one to call forth all the gifts of an orator and Mr. Surendra Nath Banerjea acquitted himself in a manner worthy of the occasion and of his own high reputation. Here is India's reply by the lips of her favourite orator to the Secretary of State's despatch on Simultaneous Examinations.

Mr. Surendra Nath Banerjea begins by expressing the disappointment which had been experienced. "Gentlemen, last year about this time, we were rejoicing that the House of Commons had definitely affirmed the principle of Simultaneous Examinations. Last year about this time, in Congress assembled, we expressed the hope—I was somewhat sceptical about the matter—that the Government of India would see its way to give effect to the resolution of the House and fulfil the just and legitimate aspirations of the people of India Those hopes have now been blasted. We meet to-day under the shadow of a great disappointment." He then proceeds to describe Mr. Fowler's despatch in terms which arouse enthusiastic assent from the 1,200 delegates there assembled.

"Our Sovereign has passed round the word of emancipation, she has declared that we are to be free ; that we are to be eligible to the highest offices in the State ; Parliament has endorsed the mandate ; and we shall see to it that no minister of the Crown, however highly placed he may be, that no Government, however influential it may be, is permitted to nullify the gracious pledges of our Sovereign and the authoritative declaration of Parliament. Gentlemen, last year about this time, I have already remarked, we were rejoicing about the resolution of the House of Commons. These rejoicings have given place to disappointment. I do not know what view you take of the despatch of the Secretary of State. I regard it in the light of a deliberate affront offered to the public opinion of this country."

The speaker then turned to the despatch itself and literally riddled it with his destructive criticism, denouncing in no measured terms the spectre of racial disability which this despatch had conjured up from a dead past. This is what India thinks of the Secretary of State's despatch. "The Secretary of State in that document invites the Government of India to state the conditions subject to which, in the opinion of the Government, the resolution may be given effect to.

Resolution VI. Simultaneous Examinations.

Mark the loyalty of the Secretary of State to his masters, the House of Commons. It is evident from the words of the despatch which I have just quoted that, in the opinion of the Secretary of State, the resolution of the House of Commons cannot be given effect to in its entirety, for he wants an expression of opinion from the Government of India, as to the modifications subject to which the resolution may be carried out. The views of the Secretary of State—the sinister views I was going to add—become more apparent in the second paragraph of the despatch. The Secretary of State openly invites the Government of India to open the battery of its hostile criticism upon the doomed resolution of the House. The Secretary of State says, in the language of diplomacy which is usual on such occasions, that he has no desire to fetter the discretion of the Government of India with regard to any remark which the Government may think fit to make upon the resolution of the House of Commons. I should like to know what the Secretary of State himself would think if the Government of India were to send round a despatch, which it had received from the Secretary of State, and invite the various subordinate Governments to treat it in the spirit of hostile criticism; but, perhaps, that is only an error in form, a mistake in procedure. We come to something which is a great deal worse in the third paragraph. He says that it is to be an indispensable condition on the part of any recommendation which the Government of India may make, that an adequate number of appointments should be held by Europeans. The Secretary of State need not have taken the trouble to say so. It was a mere work of supererogation. At the present moment the Civil Service is the monopoly of Europeans."

And here is laid bare the true meaning of this official document. "Gentlemen, when the Secretary of State lays down this recommendation in this naked form, in this undisguised fashion, he invites a protest and a remonstrance; for the Secretary of State now, for the first time, introduces the element of racial disability into a question from which considerations of racial disability have been eliminated for a period of more than thirty years; for what does the order of the Secretary of State amount to? It comes to this that if Simultaneous Examinations were granted, and, say, that fifty appointments were competed for, and the first fifty candidates were Natives of India, all of them would not get the appointments —some of them would be disqualified by reason of their race; they would suffer for the crime of colour. Would the Secretary of State venture to introduce a condition like this just now? If not, why should he be permitted to conjure up into existence the dead, buried and forgotten spectre of racial disability."

Finally after showing with inexorable logic that the spirit of the Queen's Proclamation of 1858 was being shamelessly violated—a Proclamation which the worst Government India ever had (that of Lord Lytton) concurred with the best Government she ever had (that of Lord Ripon) in regarding as peculiarly sacred and binding upon all—Mr. Surendra Nath Banerjea concluded in these noble words. "But, Gentlemen, it is open to us in the meantime to prove by our loyalty, our devotion, and self-sacrifice that we are qualified for the boon we pray for. So let the moral victory prepare the way for that political emancipation to which our

Resolution VI. Simultaneous Examinations.

fondest aspirations tend. The promised land is full in view but an untoward fate prevents us from entering it; nevertheless, from the Sinai of faith and hope, lik Moses of old, we may obtain a prospective view of the glories of the land of Canaan the destined inheritance of our children and our children's children. I am con fident that in the fulness of time, under the Providence of God and the auspices of British Rule, they will take possession of this land of promise where their fetters will fall off, their badge of political slavery will disappear; where, being British subjects in name, they will be British subjects in reality, and where, under the fostering influence of free political institutions, they will develop a civilisation the noblest which the world has ever seen, the emblem of indissoluble union between England and India, a civilisation fraught with unspeakable blessings to the people of India and unspeakable renown to the English name. That is the future which with the eye of faith we see awaits us; that is the future which looms in the distance; that is the future which inspires us with an enthusiasm of which the Anglo-Indian bureaucracy can have no conception; that is the future for which we work, and for which some of us, at any rate, are prepared to lay down our liyes; it is the future of an emancipated people, ennobled by the spirit of liberty consecrated by the genius of self-sacrifice and consolidated by fervent loyalty to the British connection."

After the great orator many more press home the heavy charges against the Government in this particular. Rajah Rampal Singh, an old and staunch worker in the Congress, awakens inextinguishable laughter by his quaint way of exposing the clumsy eiforts of an ex-Secretary of State to cancel the Queen's Proclamation by a flank attack. Speaking of the doctrine of equality which breathes throughout that Proclamation he said:—" As we did not appreciate these blessings, no objection was thrown in our way, but when a few of our Bengali friends passed their Examinations successfully in Eugland then Lord Lytton's Government began to meditate, and he wrote a letter, a private letter, after consulting all the Governors and Eieutenant-Governors, to Lord Cranbrook, and in this he proposed that the systems of the Military and Civil Service should be identical, and the Examination for the Civil Service should be closed for Indians. To this Lord Cranbrook replied that shutting up the Board of the Civil Service would require the sanction of Parliament, which he said 'he did not like to undertake because he did not expect success.' "

Mr. Venkata Subba Row, of Madras, puts the merits of the case very clearly thus :—" What is our case ? Gentlemen, there are competitive examinations held, at which candidates are selected for the Civil Service of India. Well, if it was declared that there examinations are not open to the natives of this country I should not be standing here to argue this particular question. But our rulers do not say that They say that these examinations are open both to Englishmen and Indians They say that they proceed only upon considerations of merit as determined by these competitive examinations. They do not object even if all the successful candidates at these competitive examinations should turn out to be Indians; they would raise no objection whatever. But with all this fairness of

Resolution VI. Simultaneous Examinations.

principle, with all this love of even-nandedness, with all this good feeling for Indians, our rulers do one thing which practically nullifies their benevolent intentions. They hold their examinations in London, and in London alone, near the homes of Englishmen and far away from here, far off from the native place of those who are directly interested in those examinations."

Mr. Hafiz Abdul Rahim—a Mahomedan from that centre of Mahomedan exclusiveness and opposition, Aligarh—voices the approval of enlightened and educated Mahomedan opinion with the claims which the Congress puts forward. "Gentlemen, there is no doubt that Mahomedans have become poorer in comparison with their former state; it is alleged, and it is not denied, that they are poorer than other communities at present. You know that it is not the richer and wealthier classes that take to the Service all over the world; it is generally the middle class that desires to join the public service of the land. But it is beyond the means and power unfortunately of the Indian middle classes to send their youth to England. If the Civil Service Examinations were held in India it is my sincere conviction that Mahomedan youths would derive greater benefits than they can ever derive if the Examination continues to be held in London only."

Finally Mr. Joshi and Professor Gokhale criticise still further but always effectively this spectre of racial disability which has been resuscitated by the Secretary of State in his ill-conceived despatch. Mr. Joshi says. "The evil that has been done in the despatch of the Secretary of State is this: that the Secretary of State has introduced a new principle by way of racial distinction I say, Gentlemen, that this is a monstrous principle to introduce in the case of this country, for this reason: that if you once admit the principle that a certain minimum number of Europeans is necessary in the Civil Service of this country, there will be a time not very distant when you can imagine the Anglo-Indian bureaucracy stopping you from going even to England and competing through the channel that is open to you at present."

And Prof. Gokhale from Poona—that home of learned men and able politicians, *pace* the cricketing Governor's different opinion—clinches the matter in a few sober and dignified sentences. "The Government of India and the Secretary of State have now authoritatively laid down that a certain minimum humber of posts, and those the highest, must always and for all time to come be held by Europeans; and most of the local Governments have supplied a key to this proposition by saying in their despatches that that minimum has now been reached. The doctrine of the Government of India and the Secretary of State, therefore, means that the present arrangements should be perpetuated, and is, in fact, an attempt to keep us always under as a subject race. Gentlemen, is it not plainly our duty as men not to allow this barefaced attempt to succeed? Some of our opponents often say:—'But you are a subject race.' Now all that I would say to such men is this, 'We know we are a subject race, and the consciousness is humiliating enough; and they are not good friends of the Empire who indulge in the pastime of needlessly reminding us of the fact.'

Resolution VI. Simultaneous. Examinations.

It is true that England has come here as a conqueror, but she has of her own accord solemnly pledged herself not to hold the country as a conqueror. Let our opponents put themselves into our position, and then say what they would feel. I believe they will allow that it is not wrong to love one's country. I believe they will allow that it is not wrong to have a high ideal for one's country And then I believe they will allow that it is not wrong for us to be dissatisfied with our present condition. Well, Gentlemen, the pledges of equal treatment which England has given us have suppliod us with a high and worthy ideal for our nation; and if these pledges are repudiated, one of the strongest claims of British rule to our attachment will disappear."

Resolution VII. Judicial Service.

The next Resolution deals with the Judicial Service and is rather technical, but in the hands of able speakers discloses a very real grievance. The Resolution urges that the Judicial Service should be more largely recruited from the legal profession than is now the case The obvious need for this is well stated in the words of Sir Charles Paul. Advocate-General of Calcutta, quoted by one of the speakers. Here is what the leader of the Calcutta Bar has said on this subject. " It is a mistake in these advanced days to appoint Civilians to high judicial posts which ought to be filled properly by thoroughly trained and thoroughly experienced Barristers and Pleaders. What can an ordinary Civil Servant, however intelligent and well edncated he may be, know of the tremendous complications and the innumerable technicalities of a mixture of English and Mahomedan laws? We have a number of codes; all of a strictly technical character, based principally on English Law. Now, it often happens that Sectional orders issued by Government do not clearly and expressly state the law on the points to which they refer. It is taken for granted that the Administrator, Judge or Magistrate, knows the law; but he frequently, being a Civilian, does not know it. It is absolutely necessary, therefore, for men who have to construe these Sections to be acquainted with the principles on which they are founded. It is hopeless to expect men merely by the light of nature to arrive at a proper interpretation of the Sections. Many years of extensive practice, and a long familiarity with principles and cases, will alone fit a man for so great a task. I would here particularise the frequent unfamiliarity of all non-professional Judges with the law of evidence. Points of law which arise in the course of the examination of witnesses require to be readily decided. I do not think that under our present system there is sufficient ability or enlightenment for that purpose."

Resolution VIII. Medical Service.

Resolution VIII relates to the Medical Service, and prays for a complete separation of the Civil Medical Service from the Military Service, at whose triumphant chariot-wheels the Civil Medical Officer in India is ignominiously dragged. The gross injustice of the present system and the evil which it works were eloquently put forward by Dr. Bahadurji of Bombay, in a speech which contains an extremely cogent and lucid account of the whole position. After dealing exhaustively with the higher Medical Service. Dr. Bahadurji turns to the subordinate service and there discloses a perfectly infamous state of things. " To turn to the second part of the resolution, *viz.*, the subject of the Subordinate Medical Service.

It has three branches. First, the Assistant Surgeons. These are our graduates in medicine, who have passed both educational and professional tests higher than those required for the I. M. S., and being Assistant Surgeons on Rs. 100 a month, rise to be old Assistant Surgeons on Rs. 200 a month, and retire on the grand pension of Rs. 100, whilst members of the Military Service who sponge on the Civil Department rise from Rs. 500 to Rs. 2,500. The Assistant Surgeons do, and have done, all the work, even field work as Volunteers in the Afghan and other campaigns, of the Civil Military. Surgeons, but without their pay or their position."

**Resolution VIII. Medical Service.**

And again:—"Then there are two other enlistments for the sabordinate service—one military and the other civil—the former being open to Christians only. But see what difference the element of religion makes in the treatment accorded to the two classes. John, the Christian, and Pandu, the non-Christian, both seek admission to their respective services. John, the Christian, need not know more than the High School fourth standard, reading, writing, and sums, but Pandu, the non-Christian, must pass a much higher test. They both go through the same professional course and examination. John, the Christian, then begins as a Military Apothecary, and works under the regimental Surgeons. His salary ranges from Rs. 50 to Rs. 450. He may, however, be promoted to the uncovenanted grade and given even Rs. 750 by being found a post in the Civil Department. His new designation is Assistant Surgeon, I. M. S., and he rises from the rank of Lieutenant to that of Major. But Pandu, the non-Christian, begins as a Hospital Assistant and dies a Hospital Assistant. His work is as vast as it is responsible. He practises medicine, surgery and midwifery He it is who really dispels the ignorance and prejudice of the masses in regard to the western system of medicine. He treats a thousand times more cases in a month than the highest officer of a hospital does in a year On his judgment, intelligence and integrity depend the lives of his fellow citizens in the mofussil, questions of life and death turning upon the nature of his evidence in medico-legal cases. But, alas! the respectability and responsibility of this most important servant of the State are in an inverse ratio and that too in very abnormal proportions. One feels almost ashamed to say that the non-Christian Pandu who does such responsible and excellent work for the Government is paid no higher salary than is paid to a senior *punka-wallah* in the hospital, or a cook or a coachman The scale of his pay is Rs. 16 to Rs. 80 odd."

**Resolution IX. Legislative Councils.**

Other speakers press the matter home; and we pass on to the IXth Resolution relating to the Legislative Councils. It must always be a matter of regret that the Government of India and the various Provincial Governments in the various Rules framed under the Indian Councils Act of 1892 gave so niggardly an interpretation of the rights conferred by the Statute. The authorities in India have unfortunately succeeded in thwarting to no inconsiderable extent the expressed purpose and plain intentions of Parliament in this respect. Pandit Madan Mohan Malaviya of Allahabad—a welcome speaker at the Congress—had no difficulty in showing how far the actual facts fell short of

**Resolution IX. Legislative Councils.**

Mr. Gladstone's anticipation of "a real living representation of the people or of Lord Salisbury's strongly expressed hope that representation would be given "to the living strength and vital forces of the whole community of India." Mr Bhagiratha Prasad, of Nagpur, showed in a very clear and well-reasoned speech the peculiar folly of the arrangements which had been made with regard to the Central Provinces. While complaints rrom the Punjab, who have been ignored altogether, Bombay, Madras and Bengal, proved how wide is the dissatisfaction with the present rules.

At the close of the day's proceedings a very sad piece of intelligence became known and was communicated from the Chair at the time of adjournment. The evening papers had announced the sudden death from Diphtheria of the young Maharajah of Mysore, whose progressive reign had long excited universal feelings of admiration and respect.

**Resolution X. Vote of sympathy with Royal Family of Mysore.**

At the beginning of the Fourth Day's Proceedings there was brought home to everyone the consciousness of the *lacrimæ rerum.* Very quietly in the presence of a public sorrow did the delegates assemble: and then the President in a few simple but eloquent words moved in the name of the whole Congress a vote of sympathy with the Royal Family of Mysore in their sad bereavement. The Indian Congress pointed with keen regret, touched with a sense of patriotic pride, to the loss which the Indian Peoples had sustained by the premature close of a constitutional reign which was at once "a vindication of their political capacity, an example for their active emulation, and an earnest of their future political liberties."

**Resolution XI. Trial by Jury.**

In the next resolution Congress asked for an extension of the jury system, but late so wantonly invaded by Sir Charles Elliot; that finality should be given to verdicts of acquittal passed by a jury; and that in any case the power at present possessed by Government to appeal against acquittal should be taken away. The reasonableness of the demand for an extension of the system of trial by jury was forcibly put by the Hon. Mr. C. H. Sitalvad of Bombay. "Suffice it to say that the agitation that followed that Notification, and the Report of the Commission that was appointed by Government to consider that matter, fully established, once for all, that the system of trial by jury, instead of being a failure, as was sought to be made out by the officials, was a complete success; while some of the members of the Commission recommended its further extension Gentlemen, if trial by jury is a necessity in England, I maintain that it is a greater necessity in India where the majority of the Judges, unacquainted with the manners and customs of the people, are not in a proper position, as a jury selected by the people themselves would be, to deal with questions of fact."

Alluding to Government's power of appealing against acquittals, the same speaker brought out the glaring injustice of this proceeding in a manner it does not seem easy to refute. "Under this provision of the law, Government have the power of appealling against any order of acquittal, appellate and original; and the Limitation Act allows them the long period of six months within which they can do it. Contrast this with the privilege accorded to an accused appealing against conviction. If an accused is sent to jail for a period of one month, or is sentenced to a fine of Rs. 50, or is committed to the Sessions, he has no power to appeal, while in the case of summary trials he has no power of appeal at all. Even in cases where he has the power to appeal he must exercise that power within 30 days, in the case of convictions by Magistrates, and within 60 days, in the case of convictions by Sessions Courts. Thus, Gentlemen, while an accused person—I ought to say a native accused person, because the Criminal Procedure Code most shamelessly violates the fundamental principles of law, that the law is no respecter of persons, and exempts European British subjects from these Rules—must appeal within 30 or 60 days, as the case may be, when he is sentenced to undergo rigorous imprisonment for 3 months, or must make up his mind to sit still and bear it, your august Government with all their resources at their back have the proud privilege of hanging the sword of Damocles over the head of acquitted persons for 6 months."

Mr K. N. Desmuki put in a strong plea for the Central Provinces, who are certainly very hardly used in most things by a paternal Government—in fact they are the ugly duckling of our Indian Administration. Here is the short list of their grievances. Mr. K. N. Desmuki says, "I am from the Central Provinces, the non-regulated provinces ; the provinces having no Legislative Council ; the provinces having no Chartered High Court ; the provinces having no jury system. So you see, Gentlemen, we want many things. But be not afraid, please ; we do not want them all at once and at one and the same time. Our Indian people are well known to the civilised world for their patience. Among other things that we want is the jury system."

And again, he shows that the demand is no revolutionary request. "We do not want anything which is new to us ; we do not want anything which is an innovation to us ; but we want a thing which was the right and privilege of our forefathers, we want a thing which was enjoyed by our worthy forefathers, and enjoyed without any disturbance, without any interference. And what was that ? It was the jury system, but fortunately or unfortunately it had a very different name, a name known to all of you here, and that was the "*Panchayet*" system."

Mr. Ambica C. Mozumdar in a powerful speech, carries vigorous war into the camp of the opposition. He opens with the following eloquent sentences. "Sir, the almost proverbial immobility of Indian reform is probably nowhere so conspicuous as in the slow and imperceptible development of the system of trial by Jury. Here it seems to have moved in cycles even larger than those of the great orb which is the centre of the mighty planetary system under which we live Decades passed away after the British conquest before the system of trial by jury was properly secured to Her Majesty's Indian subjects living within the Presidency towns. It then took three decades more to reach a few favoured spots in the regions of the Western and the Eastern Ghats and the Assam Valleys ; and then another cycle of full thirty years rolled away before seven districts in the Gangetic Provinces came to receive its blessings. There it has ever since stood as if fossilized beyond all possibility of further growth. But now that the country

Resolution XI
Trial by jury

has completed another revolution of thirty years more, has not the usual period of probation passed and the time fully arrived for doling out another measure of this reform to the suffering millions of this vast empire ? If the privilege is still to be withheld Anglo-Indian bureaucracy must be false to its own established tradition."

Then, after placing some carefully prepared statistics before his hearers he sums up their results thus :—" From these it would appear that while the Magistrates were found wrong in 30 per cent. of cases in which there was an appeal from their decisions, Sessions Judges sitting with assessors were found wrong in about 28 per cent., while juries were found wrong only in 4½ per cent. with the barest possibility of 11 per cent. It follows, therefore, that as regards perversity of judgment, Judges left to themselves are at least 2½ times as perverse as Judges kept straight by jurors, while the Magistrate's perversity is 2 degrees in excess of that of the Sessions Judges."

Finally he draws a vivid picture of the arbitrary and anomalous administration of the criminal law in British India, as between district and district. " Gentlemen " he says " a murder is a murder, with the gallows for its destined goal, whether it is committed in Dacca or in Faridpur, and yet the merest accident of its being committed on this or that side of an almost imaginary line, sometimes drawn through restless waters, may determine whether the same man shall be dealt with as a true citizen or as a bondsman. Sir, where is the clause in the great testament of the Queen-Mother that, while imposing upon my head the liabilities of her Government deprives me of an equal share in the privileges of her rule ? Why should I day by day and year after year, standing on one bank of a river, gaze mournfully on the other bank, and have to say to myself that it is over there that the shackles fall off and true citizenship begins ?"

Resolution XII.
Separation of
Judicial and
Executive
Functions.

Resolution XII deals with that important question, long over-ripe for solution, of the separation of judicial and executive functions. The three or four short speeches on this subject, of such vital interest to the poorer classes of the people who are at the mercy of a corrupt police, should be carefully read. A single quotation from one of them must here suffice. Mr. K. Srinivasa Row says :—" I will give you one example in which the combination of the executive and judicial functions has been a failure. In the Bellary district, (my own district) a confidential circular was sent round by the District Magistrate to the effect that the Magistrates who hear and decide cases should remember that they are responsible for the detection and suppression of crime. They were told that the duty which we thought was entirely the duty of the Police was to be undertaken by them. The Magistrates are asked to support and assist the Police. And I will tell you why this was done. Government found that when the last Administration Report was published the number of convictions was not quite as large as they desired, and our Editors—whom we have either to thank or curse, I do not know which—sat upon the Administration Report and said that poor convictions showed poor detection. Government therefore wanted to show to the Editors a larger number of convictions, as being synonymous with greater efficiency in Criminal Administration. Accordingly this Circular was issued which means in effect that the District Magistrate should ask his subordinates to make friends with the Police, and that if fault is found with the Police, they should excuse them."

**Resolution XIII. The Punjab Chief Court.**

On Resolution XIII praying for the establishment of a Chartered High Court in the Punjab, Bakshi Jaishi Ram, of Lahore, spoke with authority. "We want equal treatment with other subjects of Her Majesty the Queen. As there is such a large surplus under the head of Law and Justice, I do not see why the people of the Punjab should not have a High Court when the people of the North-West Provinces and Oudh have one. The law which is in force in the Punjab is the same as that which is in force in Bengal, Madras, Bombay and the North-West Provinces. The Highest tribunal is the High Court, and it is only that Court that can give final decisions in important matters connected with the welfare of the people. Another ground for the establishment of a High Court is that there is an anomaly in reference to Appeal cases in our Province. There is no right of Appeal in the case of suits the value of which is within Rs. 1,000, when the judgment of the Appellate Court agrees with the judgment of the Original Court." The people of Sindh also are deeply interested in this question—as at present their highest appellate court, short of the Privy Council, is a Judicial Commissioner, a covenanted civilian, who may be a good officer, but very bad Judge. A High Court for the Punjab might well have jurisdiction over Sindh—in easy railway communication with Lahore—pending better arrangements for litigants in Sindh.

**Resolution XIV Military and Civil Expenditure.**

Resolution XIV on Military and Civil expenditure was necessarily of interest because of the growing attention which the abnormal growth of Indian expenditure is attracting to all financial questions connected with India. Mr. Wacha—an old authority on this and all financial questions—had no difficulty in strengthening the assertion of all persons having knowledge of the subject (with the not unnatural exception of the Government of India and India Office officials) that not exchange but excessive and ruinously extravagant expenditure on the Military and Civil Services is the true cause of India's financial distress. His speech, which bristles with statistics, must be read *in extenso* as it defies quotation.

**Resolution XVI. Omnibus Resolution.**

Passing over a short resolution on Public Education we come to Resolution XVI—the Omnibus Resolution—the Resolution which sets forth the standing grievances of the Indian Empire. Pandit Bishan Narain Dar in an able speech made the following brief and emphatic assertion, which was loudly cheered. "Gentlemen, if I were asked to point out any action or any measures of the Government of India to show that the policy of the Government in this country has of late been that India is not for Indians or for Englishmen but solely and wholly for Anglo-Indians, I should point to two measures; I should point to the rejection of our demands for Simultaneous Examinations, and I should point to the granting of Exchange Compensation Allowance. India is at present governed in the interests of a particular class. Now, Gentlemen, I look upon these two actions of Government as two crimes—grave crimes committed against the just aspirations of the people of this country, against the honour of England and against the

**Resolution XVII. Proposed further powers of District Magistrates.**

Resolution XVII is very important It deals with proposed amendments to Section 15 of the Police Act of 1861. A serious wrong is about to be perpetrated —has already been perpetrated—and prompt action ought to be taken in England and India to bring the Indian Government back into the ordinary paths of equity and common sense. Let Messrs Mudholkar, of the Berars, and Namjoshi, of Poona, explain. Says Mr. Mudholkar "There is a section in the Police Act by which, if it is found that any part of the country is in a disturbed condition, Government have the power of imposing what is called a punitive police there, that is, a police specially so employed, and the cost of that police is defrayed not from the general revenue of the country but from a tax specially raised for that purpose. The tax is levied in the locality where the police have to be quartered. It was suggested to Government that this measure—which has been in existenee from 1861—is not a just one; that it is desirable to make some changes, and that it is only persons who have really committed any disturbance who should defray those expenses. At first sight this looks very just and proper, but look at the insidious manner in which this principle is sought to be worked out. The way in which the Government proposes to proceed is this; whenever such a Police has to be employed the cost of such additional police force shall be borne as the Magistrate of the District may direct. Now let us understand what this means. It means that such community or classes as the Magistrate thinks has committed the offence is to be taxed with the whole thing; but not only that, his power of differentiation extends to that community as a whole. He may say that only five or six men who are responsible shall be called on to pay; such persons in such manner and to such extent as he thinks fit. If there is a man against whom he has a grudge, that man may be singled out, and from that man the whole cost can be claimed."

"Then there is this dangerous procedure existing, not only with regard to the imposition of the tax, but also with regard to another thing in which the same powers are given If any damage to property is caused, if any person has received grievous hurt, or any person is killed, power is given to the District Magistrate to give compensation for the loss or for the destruction of property, or for the injury caused to the person. That compensation he has got the power of levying from such classes of the community as he thinks proper, or from such individuals, in such manner, and to such extent, as he thinks proper."

Mr. Namjoshi after alluding to various defects in the proposed legislation. points out that "in section 30 or 31 it proposes to entrust to the Police, to the Inspector, or the officers of the Police, the novel power of stopping, controlling and regulating processions or assemblies not only in public places, but also in private places." Such a power he adds, is "dangerous" and "unprecedented." "It is unprecedented in that it un-makes the blessings, that it un-makes the good that written law guarantees to the subjects of foreign rule, inasmuch as it leaves not only large powers but large powers of discretion, not only to District Magistrates but to Superintendents of Police, and not only to Superintendents of Police, but, as this Bill seems to indicate, to the Assistant Superintendents of Police, and some lower grades of Police Officers also."

Then we come to numerous Resolutions of great, though minor, importance. On Forest Management, which the subordinates of the Forest Department make to press heavily on the poor people within their jurisdiction. On the Liberty of the Press, relating to a gross violation of this principle of rudimentary justice, in British territory within the boundaries of native States—rather late in the day, pertinently remarks one of the speakers, to plead for the liberty of the Press! On the arbitrary character of the imposition for Water-cess, one of those side-attacks on existing rights by which governments not infrequently cancel long-established concessions. Finally to formal Resolutions and a few last words by the President spoken simply from an honest heart and sympathetic understanding. Then amid hearty cheers for Her Gracious Majesty the Queen-Empress, for India's old and valued friend Mr. A. O. Hume, and for India's distinguished son and trusted representative in the British Parliament, Mr. Dadabhai Naoroji, the Tenth Indian National Congress brought its arduous labours to a successful and appropriate termination.

## GLOSSARY OF INDIAN TERMS USED IN THE REPORT.

*Abkari* ... ... Excise of spirits.

*Agraharamdar* ... ... A landholder under a particular tenure.

*Amani* ... ... Management of Land-Revenue direct under Government.

*Candy* ... ... A measure (Madras)=500 lbs.

*Crore* ... ... A numeral=ten millions.

*Durbar* ... ... A ceremonial assembly.

*Fasli* ... ... Of or belonging to a harvest; the agricultural year, beginning about April or May.

*Gaurakshani* ... ... Cow-protection. There is a widespread movement in India for protecting and preserving cows, the sacred animal of the Hindu.

*Inam* ... ... A gift, grant of land (lit. a reward)

*Inamdar* ... ... Inam-holder, grantee of land; land-owner.

*Janmi* ... ... Landlord (Malabar).

*Kons=Khots* ... ... Landholders under a particular tenure—landlords.

*Kotwal* ... ... Police officer, administrative officer generally.

*Lakh* ... ... A numeral=100,000 When denoting sums of Rupees by figures the arrangement of the commas is determined by the number of crores or lakhs and not by the thousands. Thus Rs. 317,94,62,000=317 crores 94 lakhs and 62 thousand rupees.

*Malguzar* ... ... Payer of Revenue, landlord (Central Provinces).

*Marwadi, Marwari* ... One of the banker caste, a banker.

*Mirasdar, Mirasidar* ... A landholder.

*Mofussil* ... ... Country districts as opposed to capital towns.

*Munsiff* ... ... A judicial officer.

*Paddy* ... ... Unhusked rice.

*Pandal* ... ... Shed, pavilion.

*Pandit* ... ... A learned man—professor.

*Pasi* ... ... A low-caste man, a servant.

*Peishcush* ... ... A tribute or ffering, land revenue

*Pukka* ... ... Perfect (*lit.* baked, cooked) used of Government posts, &c., it signifies the *permanent* as distinguished from the *acting* appointment.

*Punkah-wallah* ... ... Punkah-man, the servant who pulls the punkah.

*Putti* ... ... A measure=500 lbs.

*Pymash* ... ... Measurement, survey.

*Ryot, ryotwar* ... ... Tenant, occupant of land not under any landlord or middleman.

*Ryotwari* ... ... Tenant right—the system of individual holdings direct from the State.

*Sabha* ... ... A society, association.

*Sanyasi* ... ... An ascetic.

*Sarvajanik Sabha* ... An influential political association at Poona.

*Shastras* ... ... Scriptural code of law.

*Shikar* ... ... Hunting; a day's shikar=a day's shooting.

*Shikart* .. ... A hunter.

*Sowcar* ... ... A money-lender.

*Sudra* ... .. The lowest of the four great castes, Brahmin (priest), Kshattrya (warrior), Vaysya (merchant), Sudra (servant).

*Sunnad* ... ... A title-deed.

*Taluq, Taluqa* ... ... An administrative area.

*Taluqdar* ... ... A Taluq-holder, an estate holder, big landlord, &c.

*Thannah* ... ... An administrative area for purposes of police.

*Topee* ... ... A Sun-hat.

*Wallah* ... ... A fellow, a man, Congress-wallah=a Congress-man.

*Zemindar* ... ... A landholder, landowner.

# RESOLUTIONS

PASSED AT THE

# TENTH INDIAN NATIONAL CONGRESS

## HELD AT MADRAS

## On the 26th, 27th, 28th and 29th December, 1894.

### RESOLUTION I.

Cotton Excise Duty.

**Resolved**—(*a*) That this Congress respectfully enters its emphatic protest against the injustice and impolicy of imposing excise duty on Cottons manufactured in British India as such excise is calculated to cripple seriously the infant Mill Industry of this country.

(*b*) That this Congress puts on record its firm conviction that in proposing this excise the interests of India have been sacrificed to those of Lancashire, and it strongly deprecates any such surrender of Indian interests by the Secretary of State.

(*c*) That in case the Excise Bill becomes law this Congress earnestly prays that the Government of India will without delay seek the sanction of the Secretary of State to exercise the powers which the Bill confers on Government to exempt all Cottons from "twenties" to "twenty-fours" from the operation of the Act.

(*d*) That the President be authorized to telegraph the above Resolution to the Government of India and to the Secretary of State.

### RESOLUTION II.

Land Question.

**Resolved**—(*a*) That this Congress desires to express the profound alarm which has been created by the action of Government in interfering with the existing Permanent Settlement in Bengal and Behar (in the matter of Survey and other cesses) and with the terms of sunnads of permanently settled estates in Madras; and, deeming such interference with solemn pledges a national calamity, hereby pledges itself to oppose in all possible legitimate ways all such re-actionary attacks on permanent settlements and their holders, and resolves to petition Parliament in that behalf.

(*b*) That this Congress regrets extremely that the Government of India have not only failed to carry out the pledges (given by the Secretary of State in his despatches of 1862 and 1865) for permanent settlement in the Provinces in which it does not exist, but have also failed to give effect to the policy of granting modified fixity of tenure and immunity from enhancements laid down in 1882 and 1884 by the Government of India and approved by the Secretary of State; and this Congress hereby entreats the Government of India to grant a modified fixity of tenure and immunity from enhancement of land-tax for a sufficiently long period of not less than sixty years so as to secure to landholders the full benefits of their own improvements.

## RESOLUTION III.

Poverty of India.

**Resolved**—That this Congress, concurring in the views set forth in previous Congresses, affirms:

That fully fifty millions of the population, a number yearly increasing, are dragging out a miserable existence on the verge of starvation, and that in every decade, several millions actually perish by starvation.

And humbly urges, once more, that immediate steps be taken to remedy this calamitous state of affairs.

## RESOLUTION IV.

Secretary of State's Council.

**Resolved**—That this Congress considers the Abolition of the Council of the Secretary of State for India, as at present constituted, the necessary preliminary to all other reforms; and suggests that in its place a Standing Committee of Members of the House of Commons be appointed.

## RESOLUTION V.

Financial Enquiry.

**Resolved**—That this Congress while thanking Her Majesty's Government for the promise they have made to appoint a Select Committee of Members of Parliament to enquire into the financial expenditure of India, regards an enquiry with so limited a scope as inadequate, and is of opinion that if the enquiry is to bear any practical fruit it must include an enquiry into the ability of the Indian people to bear their existing financial burdens and into the financial relations between India and the United Kingdom.

## RESOLUTION VI.

Simultaneous Examinations

**Resolved**—(*a*) That this Congress expresses its deep sense of disappointment at the despatch of the Secretary of State supporting the views of the Government of India on the question of Simultaneous Examinations, and this Congress hereby places on record its respectful but firm protest against the despatch, as, among other things, introducing a new principle inconsistent with the Charter Act of 1833 and the Proclamation of the Queen of 1st November 1858 (the solemn pledges contained in which the Secretary of State and the Government of India now seek to repudiate) by creating a disability founded upon race, for the despatch lays down that a minimum of European officials in the Covenanted Service is indispensable

(*b*) That in the opinion of this Congress the creation of the Provincial service is no satisfactory or permanent solution of the problem, as this service, constituted as it is at present, falls short of the legitimate aspirations of the people, and the interests of the subordinate service will not suffer by the concession of Simultaneous Examinations.

(*c*) That no attempt has been made to make out a case against the holding of Simultaneous Examinations for the recruitment of the Engineering, Forest, Telegraph and the higher Police Service Examinations, and the

Congress regrets to notice that the despatches of the Secretary of State, the Government of India, and the various local Governments are absolutely silent with regard to this aspect of the Resolution of the House of Commons.

(*d*) That this Congress respectfully urges on Her Majesty's Government that the Resolution of the House of Commons of 2nd June 1893 on the question of Simultaneous Examinations should be speedily carried out as an act of justice to the Indian people.

## RESOLUTION VII.

**Judicial Service.**

**Resolved**—That this Congress views with great dissatisfaction the system of recruiting the higher Judicial Service of the country, and is of opinion that provision should be made for proper Judicial training being given to persons who are appointed to the post of District and Sessions Judge, and that the higher Judicial Service in Bengal, the N. W. P. and Oudh, Bombay and Madras, and the Judicial Service generally in other parts of the country, should be more largely recruited from the legal profession than is now the case.

## RESOLUTION VIII.

**Medical Service.**

**Resolved**—(*a*) That this Congress is of opinion that the present constitution of the Higher Civil Medical Service is anomalous, indefensible in principle, injurious in its working, and unnecessarily costly; that the time has arrived when in the interests of Public Medical Education, and the advancement of Medical Service and of scientific work in the country, as also in the cause of economic administration, the Civil Medical Service of India should be reconstructed on the basis of such service in other civilized countries, wholly detached from and independent of the Military Service.

(*b*) That the very unsatisfactory position and prospects of Members of the Subordinate Civil Medical Service (Assistant-Surgeons and Civil Hospital Assistants) compared with members of similar standing in other departments of the Public Service, require thorough investigation and redress, and pray that Government will grant for the purpose an open enquiry by a mixed Commission of official and non-official members

(*c*) That whilst this Congress views with satisfaction the desire of the Imperial Government to reorganise the Chemical Analyser's department with a view to its administration as an independent scientific department it earnestly hopes that Government will not fail to recognise the responsible and meritorious work of Assistant, or as they in reality are, Government Chemical Analysers, and place them on the footing of Specialists

## RESOLUTION IX.

**Legislative Councils.**

**Resolved**—(*a*) That this Congress, in concurrence with the preceding Congresses, considers that the creation of a Legislative Council for the Province of the Punjab is an absolute necessity for the good Government of that Province, and having regard to the fact that a Legislative Council has been created for the N.-W. Provinces, urges that no time be lost in creating such a Council for the Punjab.

(*b*) That this Congress, in concurrence with the preceding Congress, is of opinion that the rules now in force under the Indian Councils Act of 1892 are materially defective, and prays that His Excellency the Viceroy in Council will be pleased to have fresh rules framed in a liberal spirit, with a view to a better working of the Act, and suited to the conditions and requirements of each Province.

## RESOLUTION X.

Vote of Sympathy with Royal Family of Mysore.

**Resolved.**—That this Congress wishes to express its respectful condolence and sympathy with the Royal family of Mysore in their recent sad and sudden bereavement, and at the same time to testify to its deep sense of the loss which has been sustained in the death of the Maharajah of Mysore, not only by the State over which he ruled with such wisdom, ability and beneficence, but also by all the Indian peoples, to whom his constitutional reign was at once a vindication of their political capacity, an example for their active emulation, and an earnest of their future political liberties.

## RESOLUTION XI.

Trial by Jury.

**Resolved**—(*a*) That, in the opinion of this Congress, the time has now arrived when the system of trial by Jury may be safely extended, in cases triable by Sessions Courts, to many parts of the country where it is not at present in force.

(*b*) That, in the opinion of this Congress, the innovation made in 1872 in the system of trial by Jury, depriving the verdicts of Juries of all finality, has proved injurious to the country, and that the powers, then, for the first time, vested in Sessions Judges and High Courts, of setting aside verdicts of acquittal, should be at once withdrawn.

(*c*) That in the opinion of this Congress it is extremely desirable that the power at present vested in Government to appeal against acquittals be taken away.

## RESOLUTION XII.

Separation of Judicial and Executive Functions.

**Resolved**—That this Congress having till now vainly appealed for many successive years to the Government of India, and also to the Secretary of State, to remove one of the gravest defects in the system of administration and one fraught with incalculable oppression to all classes of people throughout the country, and having noted with satisfaction the admission of the evil by two former Secretaries of State (Lord Kimberley and Lord Cross), and being of opinion that the reform is thoroughly practicable, as has been shown by Messrs. R. C. Dutt, M. M. Ghose and P. M. Mehta, entreats the Government of India to direct the immediate appointment in each province of a Committee (one-half at least of whose members shall be non-official natives of India, qualified by education and experience in the workings of various Courts to deal with the question) to prepare a scheme for the complete separation of all Judicial and Executive functions in their own province with as little additional cost to the State as may be practicable, and the submission of such schemes, with the opinions of the several Governments thereon, at an early date.

## RESOLUTION XIII.

The Punjab Chief Court.

**Resolved**—That this Congress re-affirms the opinion of the preceding Congress that the time has now come to raise the status of the Chief Court of the Punjab to that of a Chartered High Court in the interests of the administration of justice in this Province.

## RESOLUTION XIV.

Military and Civil Expenditure.

**Resolved**—That having regard to the fact that the embarrassed condition of the finances of the country has been giving cause for grave anxiety for some years past, this Congress records its firm conviction that the only remedy for the present state of things is a material curtailment in the expenditure on the Army Services and other Military Expenditure, Home Charges, and the cost of Civil Administration, and in view of the proposed appointment of a Parliamentary Committee to investigate the subject this Congress strongly recommends that the Standing Congress Committees of the several Presidencies and Provinces should, so far as practicable, make arrangements to send to England at least one well qualified delegate from each Presidency or Province to urge such reduction before the Committee.

## RESOLUTION XV.

Public Education.

**Resolved**—That this Congress is emphatically of opinion that it is inexpedient in the present state of education in the country that Government grants for higher education should in any way be withdrawn, and, concurring with previous Congresses, affirms in the most emphatic manner the importance of increasing public expenditure on all branches of education and the expediency of establishing Technical Schools and Colleges.

## RESOLUTION XVI.

Omnibus Resolution.

**Resolved**—That this Congress concurs with its predecessors in strongly advocating:—

(*a*) The reduction of the Salt duty by at least the amount of its latest enhancement;

(*b*) The raising of the Income-Tax taxable minimum from five hundred to one thousand Rupees;

(*c*) The persistent pressure by the Government of India on all Provincial administrations to induce them to carry out in its integrity the excise policy enunciated in paragraphs 103, 104, 105, of the Despatch published in the *Gazette of India* of March 1890, and the introduction of a simple system of local option in the case of all villages;

(*d*) The introduction into the Code of Criminal Procedure of a provision enabling accused persons in warrant cases to demand that instead of being tried by the Magistrate they may be committed to the Court of Sessions;

(*e*) The fundamental reform of the Police Administration by a reduction in the numbers and an increase in the salaries and the qualifications of the lower grades, and their far more careful enlistment; and by the selection for the higher posts of gentlemen of higher capacities, more in touch with the respectable portions of the community, and less addicted to military pretensions, than the majority of existing Deputy Inspectors-General, Superintendents and Assistant Superintendents of Police are at present;

(*f*) A modification of the rules under the Arms Act so as to make them equally applicable to all residents in, or visitors to, India without distinction of creed, caste, or colour; to ensure the liberal concession of licences wherever wild animals habitually destroy human life, cattle, or crops; and to make all licences, granted under the revised rules, of life-long tenure, revocable only on proof of misuse, and valid throughout the Provincial jurisdiction in which they are issued;

(*g*) The establishment of Military Colleges in India, whereat, natives of India, as defined by statute, may be educated and trained for a military career, as

Commissioned or non Commissioned officers (according to capacity and qualifications) in the Indian army ;

(*h*) The organizing throughout the more warlike races of the empire of a system of militia service ;

(*i*) The authorizing and stimulating of a widespread system of volunteering, such as obtains in Great Britain, amongst the people of India ;

(*j*) The discontinuance of the Exchange Compensation allowance granted to undomiciled European and Eurasian employees of Government, involving an annual expenditure of over a crore of rupees while the Exchequer is in a condition of chronic embarrassment ;

(*k*) The giving effect to the Report of the Parliamentary members of the India Office Committee on the subject of the Rules, Orders, and Practices in Indian Cantonments, with regard to Prostitution and contagious disease, and the endorsing of their conclusions ;—

(i) That the system and incidental practices described in that Report, and the statutory rules, so far as they authorized or permitted the same, did not accord with the plain meaning and intention of the Resolution of the House of Commons of June 5th, 1888 ; and

(ii) That the only effective method of preventing these systematic malpractices is by express legislation.

## RESOLUTION XVII.

Proposed further powers of District Magistrates.

**Resolved**—That this Congress hereby empowers its President to convey to the Government of India its opinion that the powers proposed to be conferred on District Magistrates, by amendments and additions to section 15 of Police Act V of 1861, with respect to the levy of the costs of punitive police and of granting compensation, are of a most arbitrary, dangerous, and unprecedented character.

## RESOLUTION XVIII.

Forest Management.

**Resolved**—That this Congress records its deep-felt gratitude to the Government of India for its circular resolution No. 22/F, published in the Supplement to the *Gazette of India*, dated 20th October 1894, and its high appreciation of the generous principle, which it enunciates, of subordinating fiscal interests to the needs and agricultural interests of the ryot population in the management of forests.

And would further represent that in forests falling under classes 3 and 4 of the said resolutions, fuel, grazing concessions, fodder, small timber for building houses and making agricultural implements, edible forest products, &c., may be granted free of charge in all cases, under such restrictions as to quantity, &c., as the Government may deem proper ; and that wherever hardship may be felt, under present conditions, the policy of the said Resolution may be carried out with reference to existing Forest areas, and the existing Reserve boundaries so adjusted as to leave a sufficiently large margin to facilitate the enjoyment by the agricultural population of their communal rights without molestation and annoyance by the minor subordinates of the Department.

## RESOLUTION XIX.

Liberty of the Press.

**Resolved**—That this Congress, being of opinion that the Government of India Notification of 25th June 1891 in the Foreign Department, gagging the Press in territories under British administration in Native States, is retrograde, arbitrary, and mischievous in its nature and opposed to sound statesmanship and to the liberty of the people, most respectfully enters its emphatic protest against the same and entreats its cancellation without delay.

## RESOLUTION XX.

Water-cess.

**Resolved**—That this Congress views with apprehension the arbitrary policy of the Government of India with regard to the imposition of water-cess, introducing as it does a disturbing element in taxation, and suggests that the imposition of the said cess be regulated by certain defined principles affording security to the rights of landowners and of persons investing money in land.

## RESOLUTION XXI.

Indian Colonists in South Africa.

**Resolved**—That this Corgress earnestly entreats Her Majesty's Government to grant the prayer of Her Majesty's Indian subjects, resident in the South African Colonies, by vetoing the Bill of the Colonial Government disenfranchising them

## RESOLUTION XXII.

Deputations to Lord Elgin and Mr. Fowler.

**Resolved**—That a deputation consisting of the following gentlemen be appointed for the purpose of presenting Resolutions numbered 1, 2, 3, 6, 7, 8, 9, 11, 12, 13, 14, 15, 16, 17, 18, 19, 20 and 21 to His Excellency Lord Elgin ; and that the British Committee of the National Congress be requested to arrange a similar deputation to wait upon the Secretary of State for India in London.

*From Bengal and Behar*:—His Highness the Maharajah Bahadur of Durbhanga, Sir Romesh Chunder Mitter, *Kt.*, The Honorable Mr. W. C. Bonnerjee, The Honorable Mr. Surrendra Nath Banerjea, Mr. J. Ghosal, Babu Saligram Sing, Mr. Shurefuddin, Rai Jotendranath Chaudhuri and Babu Boikunt Nath Sen.

*From the North-West Provinces*:—The Honorable Rajah Rampal Singh and The Honorable Baboo Charoo Chandra Mitter.

*From Oudh*:—Sheikh Rajah Hussein Khan, Mr. Hamid Ali Khan and Baboo Gokal Chand.

*From the Punjab*:—Sirdar Dayal Sing Majithia, Baboo Kali Presonno Roy, Mr. Jussawala, Shaik Umar Buksh, Lala Murlidhar and Bakshi Jaishi Ram.

*From Bombay*:—The Honorable Mr. P. M. Mehta, C.I.E.

*From the Central Provinces*:—The Honorable Mr. G. M. Chitnavis and Rai Bahadur C. Narainswami Naidu.

*From Poona*:—Rao Bahadur V. M. Bhide, Mr. S. B. Bhate, Mr. N. B. Mule and Mr. P. L. Nagpurkar.

*From Berar*:—Rao Saheb Deorao Vinayek.

*From Madras*:—Manivikram Rajah of Calicut, The Honorable Mr. Sabapathy Mudaliar, Rai Bahadur P. Ananda Charlu and Mr. G. Subramania Iyer."

## RESOLUTION XXIII.

British Committee Grant.

**Resolved**—That a sum of Rs. 60,000 be assigned for the expenses of the British Committee and the cost of the Congress publication, "India," and that the several circles do contribute as arranged, either now, or hereafter in Committee, for the year 1895.

## RESOLUTION XXIV.

Vote of Thanks to British Committee.

**Resolved**—That this Congress hereby tenders its most grateful thanks to Sir W Wedderburn and the other members of the British Congress Committee for the services rendered by them to India during the present year.

## RESOLUTION XXV.

Appointment of General Secretary.

**Resolved**—That this Congress reappoints Mr. A O. Hume, C. B., to be its General Secretary for the ensuing year.

## RESOLUTION XXVI.

Meeting Place of XIth Congress.

**Resolved**—That the Eleventh Indian National Congress do assemble on such day after Christmas day, 1895, as may be later determined upon, at Poona.

## RESOLUTION XXVII.

Constitution of Congress.

**Resolved**—That this Congress is of opinion that the time has come when the constitution of the Congress should be settled, and rules and regulations laid down as to the number of Delegates, their qualifications, the localities for assemblage, and the like, and with this view the Congress requests the Standing Congress Committee of Poona to draw up draft rules and circulate them among the different Standing Congress Committees for their report; these reports, together with the draft rules and the report thereon to be laid before the next Congress for its consideration.

ALFRED WEBB,
*President of the Tenth Indian National Congress.*

MADRAS,
*29th December*, 1894.

# DETAILED
# REPORT OF THE PROCEEDINGS
OF THE
# TENTH INDIAN NATIONAL CONGRESS,
HELD AT
# MADRAS,
## *On the 26th, 27th, 28th, and 29th of December, 1894.*

## FIRST DAY'S PROCEEDINGS.

The first sitting of the Congress commenced at 2-30 P.M. on Wednesday, the 26th December, 1894, when the Honorable Mr. P. Rungiah Naidu, the Chairman of the Reception Committee, in welcoming the delegates, said:— **First Day.**

MY BROTHER DELEGATES AND GENTLEMEN,

**Chairman of Reception Committee's Address.**

On behalf of the Reception Committee of the Tenth Indian National Congress and on behalf of the Indian community of Southern India generally, I offer you my most cordial greetings and welcome you to our city.

Seven years ago when Madras had the privilege of witnessing the third Session of the Congress, the position that I now so unworthily fill was filled by that illustrious Indian Statesman, the late Rajah Sir T. Madhava Row, K.C.S.I., who described the Congress as the "soundest triumph of British administration and a crown of glory to the British nation" and whose death and that of Pandit Ayodhyanath and other conspicuous figures in our ranks have vacated places not yet adequately filled. But patriots and statesmen have to pay the debt of nature, and what we have lost in individual strength we hope we have been able to make good by increased intensity and extent of national feeling. Our organization in every part of the country has improved in influence and solidarity; it has extended to orders of society below the middle class; has roused the attention of our British fellow subjects; and, what is more significant of its influence, has provoked the envy and anger of a certain section of the Anglo-Indian community.

In the vast concourse of people which we behold assembled under this beautiful pavilion, in the thousand and more delegates of position and rank come from the North and South and East and West of this great Continent, in the festive joy that the celebration of this national occasion communicates at this moment to almost every house in this city, in the hundreds of meetings attended by thousands of people that have been held all over South India during the last six months, held not in cities and towns merely but even in villages and hamlets, to further the national cause, and in the numberless small and big channels through which money has flowed into the Congress coffers, a system of collection from house to house having been universally adopted by our Committees, by which the prince and peasant, the merchant and trader, the petty artizan and labourer, have been brought under contribution—

**First Day.**

**Chairman of Reception Committee's Address.**

you will see in all these, Gentlemen, the complete falsification of malicious predictions and the frustration of impotent envy, as well as the gradual maturing of the consummation of the forces which this movement embodies and attests, and which bind us all together in common fellow-feeling and in common devotion to our revered sovereign.

The political horizon of the educated Indian citizen is no longer his village or district, not even the capital city of his province, but it is now the whole Indian continent, a substitution which is so favourable to the growth of enlightened patriotism. Whether this process of the enlargement of our political vision will lead at length to a welding into a united and unified whole of the different sections of the population, as we hope and believe it will, or whether the consummation will be, as some of our well-wishers assert, a federal and peaceful association of them all, is a question which must be left to the future to solve. As a practical body, as a movement having certain tangible and immediate ends in view and striving to supply wants actually felt, and as an enterprise carefully steering clear of all visionary and merely sentimental objects, it is not the business of the Congress to devote itself to aims which are not within its reach and which will more properly engage the efforts of posterity. Nor is it our object to disregard the law of continuity in evolution, to break from old moorings, and to launch into a work of destruction and reconstruction. We most emphatically repudiate therefore that visionary and revolutionary character with which our enemies have endowed our movement, and claim for it a thoroughly practical and legitimate character, and a character sincerely loyal to all those elements in the British rule which are conservative as well as progressive.

We take our stand on the Proclamation of 1858, which we hold is the charter of our political liberties and is binding for all time to come on the representatives of the British sovereignty in this country to the same extent and in the same sense as those charters that the English nation, by their intense love of freedom and robust political spirit, have wrung from time to time from their unwilling and tyrannical sovereigns. Aye, Gentlemen, our charter is even more binding—if indeed there can be any difference of degree in the obligation of pledges given—because, while the concessions to the British nation were made under circumstances of a more or less coercive character, Her Majesty gave her pledges voluntarily and of her own accord, and under circumstances which, if Her Majesty had represented political principles and traditions different from those of England, would have furnished justification for less calmness, generosity and wisdom than so graciously inspired that immortal document. Gentlemen, we have been told recently by the highest official authorities that the Proclamation conveyed no pledges whatever to the people of this country, and that political expediency, as understood by the men in power for the time being, was the only criterion determining the obligations of the rulers to the ruled. Well, all I can say is, that this is a most unfair and perverse view to take, a view that would certainly sully the honour of the Empress and her responsible servants, would contradict the noblest traditions of British rule, and injure the best and the most abiding interests of the whole Indian Empire. You may remember, Gentlemen, what Her Majesty told Lord Derby when the Proclamation was being drafted. The noble lady that she is, the paragon of all feminine and royal virtues—may God prolong her life, and may her rule in India last as long as do the sun and moon—she exhorted him to remember that "it was a female sovereign who spoke to more than a hundred millions of Eastern people on assuming the direct Government over them and after a bloody civil war, giving them *pledges* (mark the words, Gentlemen!) *which her future reign was to redeem, and explaining the principles of her Government.*" Knowing thus the true meaning of the Proclamation, let those who will, deny it, but until the Proclamation is formally withdrawn and the sovereign of Great Britain and India formally announces that neither Justice, nor Truth, nor Integrity is the dominant guiding principle of British Indian rule, but that this principle is expediency, and expediency alone, as may be understood by the Viceroy or the Secretary of State for India for the time being—until then the people of this country will take their stand on that most cherished charter of theirs and demand with confidence and determination the fulfilment of their legitimate, loyal and honourable aspirations.

We may derive satisfaction however from the belief that this attempt to belittle the importance of the Proclamation is confined to those Englishmen who are interested in the perpetuation of the present administrative system, and that the English nation, as a whole, including the responsible guardians of their imperial interests, will strongly disapprove of the attempt to uphold the ascendancy of a limited class of Her Majesty's subjects in disregard of her own deliberate and repeated pledges and of the contentment and prosperity of the Indian people so truly and dearly loved by her. But to convince the English people that such an attempt is being made and that the selfishness of the bureaucracy is the most dangerous enemy of the British Indian Empire, is our chief difficulty. Yes, Gentlemen, the Indian bureaucracy is selfish. I say that most deliberately, and the history of the last 35 years is my justification for saying so. It is for this reason that we have thought it necessary to strengthen our organization in England and to educate public opinion there, as well as to continue with unabated vigour and enthusiasm our work in this country. As was to be expected, this policy has borne fruit. We have secured the sympathy of a large number of Members of Parliament, while the English press no longer affects silent contempt, although misrepresentation as well as sympathy distinguishes its criticisms. It behoves us therefore, Gentlemen, to strengthen as much as possible the hands of the British Congress Committee and of our other friends. We are very anxious to draw closer the tie of sympathy between us and our English friends and rouse greater interest in that country on behalf of our movement. It was this aspect of the situation that induced us to invite a member of Parliament to preside over our deliberations, and on our having been able to secure you, Sir—Mr. Alfred Webb, through your truly patriotic and condescending fellow feeling, we have every reason to congratulate ourselves. Through you we are confident of enlisting the sympathy of a very important section of the House of Commons as well as of those true sons of Britain whose generosity and sense of justice are, like their love of freedom, of world-wide celebrity.

We are at present, more than we ever were, in need of the support of British public opinion, because in proportion as our agitation acquires prestige and grows in influence, so does the opposition in this country grow strong Of this opposition you have seen a remarkable proof in the latest official contribution to the literature on the Simultaneous Examinations Question. The Parliamentary Blue Book on that question marks, I fear, a further straining of the relations between educated Indians and the officials, from which latter nothing but abuse, misrepresentation and determined opposition are, it would seem, hereafter to be expected even in our most moderate attempts at self-improvement. They would seem to have persuaded themselves into the belief that to have established English Schools and Colleges is the greatest mistake of British rule in India, and that inasmuch as their abolition is out of the question, the next best thing, from their point of view, is to cry down the men educated in these institutions, call them names, and characterise them as a class of disloyal men, devoid of influence with their own countrymen, and incapable of discharging any responsible public duty. Our Anglo-Indian friends speak as if nothing good can come out of the people for whose education the State expends as much as a crore of rupees every year. They seem to be almost ashamed of their own literature, of the teachers and professors of their own nationality, and enamoured of ignorance and superstition as the best mental state of the Indian people. I have no doubt that this Blue Book, so disappointing and so retrograde and so unworthy of the Englishman's reputation for fair dealing, will be subjected to severe criticism in the course of our proceedings. And I merely refer to it here to show what amount and what kind of opposition we should be prepared for in this country before our objects are attained.

First Day.

Chairman of Reception Committee's Address.

To abuse the opponent is a favourite form of argument with a certain description of people, and failing to meet us with fair reasoning or on the ground of justice or political wisdom, the opponents of the Congress, that is, of educated Indians, call us disloyal, and attribute to us revolutionary designs. Gentlemen, with mad men and with people who talk wildly under the exciting sense of losing interests, we have no concern. If there be any reasonable persons amongst our opponents, I should like to take them into my confidence and ask them why they think we are disloyal. If a rule which has establishod peace, order and security in the country, which administers justice as impartially as human tribunals can do, which constantly stimulates material prosperity, which has conferred on the people the inestimable blessing of Education, liberty of conscience and freedom of discussion, and of which, indeed, the possibilities for future good are even greater than what has actually been done in the past—if such a rule cannot excite the loyal attachment of the people, I am at a loss know what kind of rule may be expected to excite their loyalty. Gentlemen, the fact is, the persons that charge us with disloyalty are the victims of their own guilty conscience, of some evil thought concealed in their minds, and it is only such persons that see disloyalty everywhere, and, like Macbeth, perceive a dagger in the air. Nor is it anything but the most ludicrous absurdity to see disloyalty in political agitation conducted on strictly constitutional lines and in a spirit of confidence in the rulers. What is the good of the education and freedom that have been vouchsafed to us if we do not make use of them for our own improvement. We have no desire but to live on terms of the utmost amity and regard with our Anglo-Indian fellow-subjects. We feel we want their guidance and their sympathy which, whenever shown, we have most sincerely and unstintingly reciprocated.

At no time were our best efforts more needed than they are now. Our country is passing through a period of crisis, which crisis will endure, I am afraid, in a more or less acute form, until India survives her present transition state and finds its fit place in the international system of the world. Not only the principles of Government, but the system of trade and industry, the provision for the security of the country, and the burden of the taxpayer himself, no longer depend on the needs and capacity of the country, but on the politics of Europe, and, regard being had to India's inability to bear the strain of this anomalous relation and to her limited resources, it behoves all responsible for her well-being to exercise the utmost care to husband and develop carefully those resources and save the country from possible disaster. An absentee Government involves a frightful drain on the country's financial resources, an overgrown military system absorbs one-third of the net revenue, the free trade principles thrust upon us have destroyed the old industries, the population has grown in advance of the food supply, and poverty is increasing from year to year. This is not all. There is a growing reluctance on the part of the Government to grapple with the problems arising from these evils, to do strict justice to the people whenever their interests clash with those of the ruling country, and to meet public opinion in a spirit of sympathy and confidence. We have also to reckon with a new evil that is rapidly coming to the front and threatens serious results, I mean, the evil of a hostile Anglo-Indian opinion which, powerful as it must always be, is ceasing more and more to represent that of the responsible official class, but echoes to an increasing extent the self-interest, the prejudices and passing feelings of those Englishmen who come here merely to earn their livelihood, who have no permanent stake in the country, and whose opinions on Indian matters do not always possess, for their soundness, the guarantee of education, enlightened patriotism, or past tradition and future fame. I need not say that this change in the constitution of Anglo-Indian opinion has made itself rather inconveniently manifest of late, and I am not sure that it has not controlled the decisions even of the Government. Consequently, discontent, irritation and a certain restlessness have seized the people, and the feeling between the ruling and ruled communities is not all that is desirable. Gentlemen, these are some of the evils of the present situation, and I am confident that the issue of our deliberations will show a due estimate of these evils and will suggest adequate and practical remedies.

There has been, indeed, a good deal of disappointment. The decision of the Secretary of State for India on the Simultaneous Examinations Question and the extraordinary grounds on which that decision is based, have shaken our confidence in the liberal professions of the party in power. Indeed nothing can be more disheartening than that a Resolution of the House of Commons should be contemptuously set aside by the Indian bureaucracy. The scheme of the Provincial Civil Service has proved an extremely unsatisfactory measure. The reformed Legislative Councils have failed to furnish an effective and adequate means of obtaining official recognition for non-official public opinion. The system of criminal administration has not been improved. Our demand for a Parliamentary inquiry into the affairs of our country, though it was about to be granted in 1884, has since been rejected as unpractical and undesirable. No steps have been taken to reduce the excessive military and civil expenditure of Government. And, lastly, Indian public opinion has failed to prevent the appropriation of over a crore of Rupees for a virtual increase in the salaries of the Government's European employees.

Still, by the side of these disappointments is the encouraging fact that our aims and demands are now known and approved to a wider extent by public opinion in the United Kingdom as well as in India, and that in regard to some particular matters the Government have moved sympathetically. An influential party of members of Parliament pledged to sympathy with our aspirations—if not to an actual support of our particular demands—has been organized. Our British Committee has been strengthened and has been able to do better and more work. And even such a typical bureaucrat as Sir Auckland Colvin, not to speak of Sir David Barbour and Mr. Samuel Laing, has admitted that the chief cause of all the financial woes of the Indian Government is to be traced more to the system of Government than to a depreciated currency, or to the other temporary causes, in which official timidity, in the face of large and inconvenient problems, is apt to take shelter. How is it, may I ask, Gentlemen, that it took nine years of ceaseless agitation by the Congress before the financial advisers of our Government could muster up courage to admit this fact—a fact which was but too patent to all disinterested minds! Let all who will affect contempt for us—it is enough if we are able to convert our officials as we have been able to convert Sir Auckland Colvin and Sir David Barbour.

Another important victory in our campaign is the admission we have obtained from Lord Cross and Lord Kimberley, besides other eminent authorities, that the combination of executive and judicial functions in the same officer is a serious evil and that it is only the want of necessary funds that stands in the way of the evil being remedied. In the administration of the Forest department a policy of regard for the interests of the agricultural population has been enunciated, though whether such a policy will be given effect to by local officers will depend on the watchfulness of our press and our public bodies as well as on the local Governments. In the Police department measures for the promotion of native Inspectors to higher offices, till now reserved for Europeans, are being matured. I am hopeful that other reforms will follow in due course on the lines of the Congress!

There can be no doubt that, although after the first few years the Congress as a great patriotic enterprise lost the attractions of novelty, it has lost no portion of its influence on the intelligent classes of the community as the only institution calling into play what resources of public spirit exist in the country and imparting weight and dignity to such non-official Indian opinion as gives itself expression from time to time Nothing proves this fact better than the unprecedented outburst of enthusiasm throughout Southern India when the preparations for this Congress were set on foot in the middle of the year. The Reception

First Day.

Chairman of Reception Committee's Address.

Committee was formed in the month of August, and immediately our energetic Secretaries sent forth their shafts of circulars to pierce the pent-up enthusiasm of our mofussil friends, with the result that a degree of activity and disinterested co-operation sprang up everywhere, every nook and corner was permeated with the Congress enthusiasm, meetings were held, committees were formed, old organizations were revived, apathetic places were shamed into activity, private grudges were forgotten jealousies disappeared, a very salutary spirit of emulation came upon every little community, and at length what appeared to be a colossal and burdensome task, the task of arranging or your satisfactory reception and for the conduct of business by the Congress itself, has been gone through with astonishing ease, with absence of friction, and with that most wholesome of all pleasures, the pleasure of excitement in the discharge of a serious public duty. The most remarkable feature in the work of our organization this time was the system of raising the necessary funds by appealing for help to every house and every place of business in the locality, a system which, first started in the city of Madras, was immediately adopted in every centre of Congress activity in all the districts of the province. The Reception Committee has collected till now nearly 40,000 rupees, of which nearly if not more than half was collected in exceedingly small amounts, in the shape of single rupees, of annas and pies. It is by no means an uncommendable spirit, I may observe, for men of respectable position, accustomed to command and brought up in the comforts of comparative affluence, to go about the streets every day, both morning and evening, entering and quitting house after house, explaining the objects and advantages of the Congress movement and its claim on the help of the masses however small, and doing all this without feeling their pride wounded or dignity compromised, and it is a spirit in strange contrast to that of individuals, not touched by the quality of self-sacrifice fostered by the Congress activity. What is singularly encouraging, the uneducated poor man gave as willingly as the educated man of the middle class. If there are persons amongst our own countrymen who cannot comprehend the educative influence, in the highest sense, of such a movement, not to speak of the demands for political concession that it directly makes, we can only pity their short-sightedness and pray that it may soon be replaced be good sense and far-seeing patriotism.

We do not conceal from ourselves the fact that an important section of our Mahomedan fellow countrymen have stood aloof from our movement under the mistaken impression that it is disliked by the power that-be, and that not to join such a movement, to denounce it, and to actually oppose it, is the surest passport to Government's favour and official advancement. But the time is gone, altogether gone, when subserviency to official power can play the role of real merit and win admission to the public service, and our deluded fellow countrymen are just now discovering that the game is after all not paying, and that in these days no community gets a hearing for its representations, especially when the governing power is vested in the hands of foreigners, unless those representations are backed up by a powerful and organized agitation. Educational Conferences are accordingly being organized, political societies are being established, and whispers of discontent are being heard—all showing that soon our Mahomedan fellow countrymen, though they may not all join the Congress, will press their claims by public agitation on lines parallel to our own. They are quite welcome to this method and we shall most cordially wish them success. They cannot have claims different from our own or claims with which we of the Indian National Congress do not fully and warmly sympathize. Only, let every community in India, the Mahomedan as well as the Hindu, the Parsee and the Native Christian, which wants to perpetuate itself, to preserve its national vitality in a healthy and unimpaired state, and to prevent seeds of decay from lodging themselves in the core and eventually poisoning the whole body politic, read aright the lessons of the past and of contemporaneous history. The nation that understands the change in the spirit of the age, and, quickened with the inspiration of national unity and greatness, adapts its institutions and appliances to the new conditions, beats in the struggle the rival, who, cherishing with strange fatality his stolid conservatism and uninspiring recollections of the past, refuses to change, neglects national consolidation and rejects the suggestions of modern needs, and whose leaders are men regarding individual fortunes as of greater account than the interests and honour of the commonwealth.

First Day.

Chairman of Reception Committee's Address

Gentlemen, I have detained you too long. But before concluding I should like to take this opportunity of tendering, on behalf of the Reception Committee, my most heartfelt thanks to Colonel G. M. J. Moore, C.I.E., the President of the Madras Municipality, for the readiness with which he has rendered help to our Committee in providing the necessary comforts for the delegates, in making the required sanitary arrangements in the various camps, and in securing their convenience in various other ways, and, in short, for his not having been content with doing what a President of the local corporation might be ordinarily expected to do.

Gentlemen, this is a moment when we all feel that a great dream, a dream which in other times and places rulers and statesmen have dreamed in vain—the dream of the Unity of the Indian people—is about to be realized. At such a moment nothing but good ideas and pure aspirations occupy our minds, and the heart overflows with genuine goodwill and brotherly feeling. In the name of those who have co-operated in the organization of this Congress, in the name of the people of Madras and Southern India generally, I once more offer you my most cordial greetings. We receive you with open arms and extend to you the right hand of fellowship for having so kindly and so condescendingly responded to our invitation. *(Loud Cheers)*

The Honorable Mr. P. Rungiah Naidu, again rising :—Now, Gentlemen, it is left for you to select your President and proceed with the business of the Congress.

Election of President.

Raja Sir Savalai Ramasawmi Mudelliar :—Gentlemen, it gives me immense pleasure to move the first proposition for your acceptance ; it is one that needs no discussion or debate. This vast concourse of the Indian people, assembled from all parts of this great empire to deliberate on questions of the deepest interest to its welfare and happiness, requires the guidance of mature experience and vast knowledge for the successful termination of its proceedings. The methods of deliberation and representation adopted by the people of this country are those most familiar to our rulers, and it is but meet and proper that we should from time to time place ourselves under the guidance of eminent men versed in the methods and procedure of that august assembly which is pre-eminently the model for imitation by all the nations of the world, the British Parliament. *(Cheers)*

In our choice of a President to rule this great assembly we shall also be giving practical testimony of our anxious desire to unite in the closest bonds of union and fellowship with our western brethren, under whose benign guidance an all-wise and beneficent Providence has placed us. *(Cheers)*

I have therefore to propose the name of one who has evinced a very deep concern for the welfare of the people of this country, and has always made the cause of the masses the chief aim of his life, and who, in his own words, is "the soldier in political warfare ready to go to any land whenever ordered." *(Cheers)*

With the firm conviction that my proposal will be accorded a very warm and enthusiastic reception by men assembled from all corners of this great empire representing the diverse castes and creeds that inhabit this land, I propose for your unanimous acceptance the quiet and unostentatious member for West Waterford, Mr. Alfred Webb. *(Cheers)*

Three hearty Cheers were then given for Mr Alfred Webb, M.P.

Raja Rampal Singh :—Gentlemen, I have much pleasure in seconding this proposition and I have in doing so, to point out to you two very momentous and noteworthy things. They are these : the Congress, which showed such weakness in its beginning, has

First Day

Election of President.

been slowly and surely progressing so as to enter into the sympathy of English gentlemen. (*Hear, hear, and Cheers.*) Up to this time we have had ten sittings, inclusive of the one in which we are met here, and we see that if half the number of meetings has been presided over by Indians, the other half has been presided over by Englishmen (*Cheers*), including my learned friend Mr Dadabhai Naoroji, (*Loud and continued Cheers*) because he is naturalised and a member of Parliament. The other point I should like to bring to your notice is this: Our "microscopic minority" has now so grown that it rules India from Cape Comorin up to the range of the Himalayas. (*Cheers*)

If Lord Dufferin had been a witness here to-day, he would have withdrawn his words on the spot. I have to say nothing more, but to second the resolution, which is a very pleasant duty for me to perform. (*Cheers*)

The Honorable Mr P. Rungiah Naidu :—Gentlemen, it is my duty to put it to the vote, and I hope all of you will vote for it by acclamation.

The motion was carried with enthusiastic cheering.

Mr. Alfred Webb, who was received with loud and prolonged cheers, the whole assembly rising to their feet, then took the Chair.

The President :—

President's Address.

Friends and Fellow-Subjects,—You call me to the presidency of the tenth meeting of the Indian National Congress. Thanking you for the honour, I proceed to discharge the duties of the post under a sense of its privileges and responsibilities.

The objects of these Congresses cannot be better stated than in the words of your first President :—"The promotion of personal intimacy and friendship amongst all the more earnest workers in [your] country's cause in all parts of the Empire; the eradication, by direct friendly intercourse, of all possible race, creed, or national prejudices amongst all lovers of [your] country; and the fuller development and consolidation of those sentiments of national unity that had their origin in [your] Lord Ripon's ever-memorable reign; the authoritative record, after this has been carefully elicited by the fullest discussion, of the matured opinions of the educated classes in India on some of the more important and pressing of the social questions of the day; the determination of the lines upon and the methods by which, during the next twelve months, it is desirable for native politicians to labour in the public interests."

The ends you have in view are similar to those of politicians in other quarters of the globe. The difficulties before you are, however, greater. Elsewhere politicians have to deal principally with homogeneous populations, to whom, at least in theory, equal political rights may at once be accorded; you have largely to work for those who have yet to pass through a long process of assimilation and elevation. All the greater necessity that in assemblages such as this you should set yourselves to the task. All the greater necessity that a deaf ear should be turned to doctrines of despair. The question is not concerning the difficulties, but whether or not the difficulties are to be faced; and if to be faced, the sooner the better. And it is alone by and through organizations such as yours that they can be faced.

It is at the same time necessary to bear in mind that you stand at the most critical period of a people's history. Your populations, heretofore supine, are awakening to conscious ness and new hopes, whilst they may not fully as yet have acquired habits of self-restraint and sentiments of responsibility. Mistakes are certain to be made, and are sure to be attributed by opponents, not to their true source—former conditions, but to the awakening, the ennobling process itself. We must be prepared to meet misrepresentations and calumny We must take heed that in our leading we give no just cause for accusation.

First Day.

President's Address.

You have met at Bombay twice, at Calcutta twice, at Allahabad twice, at Nagpur, at Lahore you now meet at Madras for the second time. But seventy-two representatives attended your first assembly. The numbers gradually increased to over 1,800 at Bombay, since which meeting they have, on your own motion, for concentration of effectiveness, been restricted to about 1,000. Your proceedings have been conducted with dignity, fairness, courtesy, and tact.

Your Presidents hitherto have been distinguished men, mainly, as was right, from amongst your own people, and representing, as they should, some of the principal races and religions of India. Most eminent amongst these Presidents was Dadabhai Naoroji, not only because of his great abilities and his life long services to his country, but because of the position he occupies as your only Native representative in the Imperial Parliament. The electors of Finsbury have done themselves honour in returning him. As to your other native Presidents, the ability of their addresses, and the manner in which they conducted you proceedings, showed their fitness for the trusts confided to them. The lamented George Yule of Calcutta, almost one of yourselves, presided at your Fourth Congress. Sir William Wedderburn conducted the fifth. I have styled Mr. Naoroji your only *Native* representative in the Imperial Parliament. In Sir William Wedderburn you have another representative equally zealous and devoted—one of the faithful few whose clear conceptions of equality and justice have been unobscured by long official service. There is another name which, although not on the list of your Presidents, cannot be omitted in recalling, however slightly, your past proceedings—that of Charles Bradlaugh, "the friend and champion of India." He attended and addressed your Fifth Congress. The report of the Sixth is formally dedicated to his memory. You never lost a better or an abler friend. Few men were ever so sincerely mourned by a larger proportion of the human race.

Having already placed in the chair two Scotchmen, you have now chosen an Irishman. Doubtless, after a becoming interval with native Presidents, you will call an Englishman. My nationality is the principal ground for my having been selected. I have none of the brilliant qualifications of my predecessors. On your invitation I take the position that was intended for a great fellow-countryman of my own. However, I do not question the fitness of your choice, for I am representative in several respects. I was nurtured in the conflict against American slavery. In the words of William Lloyd Garrison, the founder of that movement, "My country is the world; my countrymen are all mankind." To aid in the elevation of my native land has been the endeavour of my riper years. In the words of Daniel O'Connell. "My sympathies are not confined to my own green island. I am a friend to civil and religious liberty all over the world." I hate tyranny and oppression wherever practised, more especially if practised by my own Government, for then I am in a measure responsible. I have felt the bitterness of subjection in my own country. I am a member of the Irish Parliamentary Party. I am one of the Indian Parliamentary Committee. I am a Dissenter, proud of the struggles of my Quaker forefathers for freedom of thought and action: a Protestant returned by a Catholic constituency—a Protestant living in a Catholic country, testifying against craven fears of a return to obsolete religious bitterness and intolerance—fears in your country and in mine worked upon to impede the progress of liberty.

To be placed in this chair is the highest honour to which I can ever aspire.

That I have not resided in India is no disqualification. Free peoples are within their own borders the best judges of their own affairs. But where are concerned the interests of a large population governed by a dominant class, the members of that class, whose apparent interests lie in a continuance of that domination, cannot as a rule judge fairly. There are rare exceptions, such as Sir William Wedderburn, but generally speaking their vision is obscured by prejudices. West Indian slavery would never have been abolished by West Indian planters, nor American slavery by Southern Whites. Catholics would never have

First Day.

President's Address.

been emancipated in Ireland, the Church would not have been disestablished, or the franchise extended, by that class which was directly interested in the continuance of existing institutions.

Nothing in what I have said or intend to say must however be taken to imply a want of appreciation of the character and services of numbers of my fellow-citizens, whose lives have been and are being given to the administration and government of India. They were doubtless at first attracted to the service solely as a career in life. But residence here, sympathy with your people, and a sense of duty, rapidly impel to higher motives. They become sincerely anxious for your welfare and devoted to what they believe your highest good. Never has more conscience been brought to the government of a conquered country. We here are not set against them, unless, indeed, they are determined to set themselves against us. The services of men of their training, temper, and turn of mind may, perhaps for generations to come, be necessary. They are to be honoured and respected in their sphere. But they must not impede or prevent the gradual application to the government of this country of principles other than those laid down by statesmen of the first rank fully half a century ago. I might perhaps have been more affected than I have been by the attitude and language of many of them regarding your country and your people, were it not that it is such as I have been accustomed to hear from the same class in Ireland regarding my country and my people. If the anticipations of the former regarding your capacities and your future are as fully belied as have been the anticipations of the latter regarding our capacities and our future, you may rest satisfied. Closely allied, in blood and religion, as this class in Ireland has been to us, their efforts to govern independently of Irish opinion have resulted in failure. How much less likely is it that they can succeed here without availing themselves of your assistance more largely than heretofore.

In our efforts for reform and constitutional liberty, much will depend upon individual character and training ; upon the extent to which we wisely administer the powers we have. The English are not naturally better or braver than other peoples. They owe their success partly to high average reliability and a high sense of duty. What they personally undertake they usually perform. Like others, they are moved by selfish considerations ; but having, in politics or administrative office once engaged for the public weal, they are not apt to neglect it for private interests ; they can rely upon each other. Let us take pattern by them in these respects.

While most anxious not to implicate your cause with Irish politics, or the relations between Great Britain and Ireland, I may occasionally illustrate your affairs by reference to my own country. Your interests are in fact closely involved in some effectual settlement of the Irish question. One of your principal and most just complaints is that no sufficient attention is given to your affairs in Parliament. Whilst months are allotted to the consideration of the British budget, a few hours are grudged to yours. Parliament is paralysed with work It has undertaken functions it cannot perform. Three separate Parliaments had enough to do to manage the affairs of England, Scotland, and Ireland. They were merged into one when the population of the United Kingdom was only fifteen millions. That population has now risen to thirty-eight millions Parliament has moreover, undertaken to care for your two hundred and eighty millions. The sphere of law is becoming both wider and more minute. Surely Parliament ought to be more of an Imperial, less of a local, assembly ! For generations to come, England, the heart of the Empire, must have the preponderating influence in Imperial councils. That we grant. You, who are Indian, and I, who am Irish, trust that our Imperial rights will not suffer from that preponderating English influence. But at present the Imperial Parliament is occupied largely with the affairs of under five millions of people, and ministries rise and fall with reference to the question of Ireland, and not in connection with great Imperial interests. The entire Empire is concerned in the speedy settlement of the Irish question.

We hold to Imperial unity undisputed and intact. To question this would be idle; we do not question it, nor do we desire to question it. We believe that the period of small states—too often a burden alike to themselves and to the world, with their dissensions and wars—is rapidly passing away, and that a better era is dawning, when, under the ægis of immensely powerful states, the peoples can rest secure and enjoy real liberty. The series of events by which this change has been wrought is sufficiently painful, often unutterably shocking. We may well turn with horror from the record. I for one would rather be descended from those who rest in the graves of the conquered than from those who rode with victors. There is no true glory in mere domination. In public places and museums I turn with shame from the pitiful trophies torn from subject peoples. We must however accept the conditions of these changes. Let us enjoy their benefits, which are many. After all, the external prestige of nationality is not the important consideration. Individual liberty, the wise administration of local affairs, the educating of a responsible population—these are of far greater consequence. And imperial unity cannot realize its full strength and will not fulfil its true functions until all are trained to enjoy these benefits, and these benefits are extended to all. What man of ordinary intelligence could prefer Russian despotism to British freedom? British power in India will remain invulnerable against foreign aggrandisement so long as you believe that with the spread of modern ideas and education, which are largely due to British rule, will come an extension of English liberty.

There is no possibility of turning back. Once imbue nations with aspirations after progress and enlightenment, and they must go forward towards liberty. For fifty years the Anglo-Indian Government has been urging you to educate yourselves, to imbibe principles of constitutional liberty, to obliterate old divisions, to break down caste prejudices, to rise to the level of British citizenship, and to unite for the good of a common country. Taking up Sir William Hunter's *History of the Indian Peoples*, the first sentence that riveted my attention was one in which the hope is expressed that the Anglo-Indian schools would "become the nurseries of a self-respecting nation." The towers of a university were the first object that met my gaze the morning after my arrival in India. Nationality has well been defined in your debates as "The aggregate of those who are citizens of one country," [one definite geographical unit] "subordinate to one power, subject to one supreme legislature, taxed by one authority, influenced for weal or woe by one system of administration, urged by like impulses to secure like rights and to be relieved of like burdens. * * It has for its central stock, like the trunk of a tree, the people who have for ages and generations settled and domiciled in a country with more or less ethnic identity at the bottom, and more or less unified by being continually subjected to identical environments and to the inevitable process of assimilation." Those who accept any such definition circle in narrow grooves of thought if they believe that such nationality is inimical to Imperial strength and unity. It may in truth be its outcome and its crown.

Politics are amongst the most ennobling, most comprehensive spheres of human activity, and none should eventually be excluded from their exercise. There is much that is ludicrous, much that is sad, much that is deplorable about them. Yet they remain, and ever will remain, the most effective field upon which to work for the good of our fellows. The political atmosphere, that which we here hope to breathe, is one into which no thought of "greed, or lust, or low ambition" should enter. We desire the good of all. We work for all. No class, however lowly, however despised, must be shut out from our sympathies and our endeavours—from the expectations of that great future towards which we all yearn. We desire not alone the brotherhood of man, but the brotherhood and sisterhood of men and women. For in proportion as men and women sympathise with each other, take part in each other's pursuits, and strive for the common weal, in such proportion is public life elevated and purified. Amongst women are to be found some of your best and most earnest friends in the United Kingdom.

Admitting the paramount necessity for the maintenance of the unity of the Empire we know that all questions relating to arms and the armed forces of the Crown must be treated with circumspection. We must weigh well our words and the difficulties of the situation.

In Ireland during most of my lifetime it has been a penal offence to carry arms without a licence, and licences are strictly guarded. In India you rest under closer restrictions Some modification of the rules under the Arms Act is necessary, "so as to make them equally applicable to all residents in, or visitors to, India, without distinction of creed, caste, or colour; to ensure the liberal concession of licences wherever wild animals habitually destroy human life, cattle, or crops; and to make all licences, granted under the revised rules, of life-long tenure, revocable only on proof of misuse, and valid throughout the provincial jurisdiction in which they are issued." With us the prohibitions are an insult to the soil; with you, to the race.

Nothing is more striking in considering the condition of India than its poverty compared with the wealth of the Western world, especially compared with that of the United Kingdom. (The riches of Great Britain are so enormous that the poverty of Ireland scarcely affects the general average.) The mean annual income of the inhabitants of the United Kingdom has been estimated at £33 14*s.*; that of the people of India, at from Rs. 20 to Rs. 27. Mr. Fowler, in his ministerial statement this year, dwelt upon the comparative lightness of the burthen of Indian taxation contrasted with that of the United Kingdom, forgetting that 5 per cent. on an income of Rs. 20 is a much heavier burthen than 7½ per cent. on £33. It is impossible, upon any basis of fair play to justify debiting you with so many large items, such as the India Office and India Office expenses, recruiting depots, loss on exchange, and the like, which really form a portion of the British home charges. If the maintenance of the Indian Empire is so essential to British prestige and greatness, if the honour and glory are to be Britain's, surely she, not you, should bear the heavy burthens. She does not attempt to collect similar charges from the Colonies.

The aggregate *annual savings* of the United Kingdom in the years between 1840 and 1888 have been estimated at £ 10,000,000, or over £300,000 a day. Such accumulations of wealth, combined with parsimonious dealings with poorer peoples, are irreconcilable with real belief in the precepts of righteousness.

The expenditure upon the Army in India, which in 1882-83 stood at Rx. 18,359,000 (including Rx. 17,000 for Afghanistan and Rx. 1,308,000 for Egypt), had in 1893 risen by 27 per cent. to Rx. 23,877,000. Any advantages to be derived from this increased expenditure have not been shared in alike by British and by native troops. The pensions of European officers have been raised 37 per cent., of native officers only 11 per cent. Thirteen per cent. more per man is spent upon the British rank and file; 4 per cent. less per man upon the native rank and file.

Your taxes spent abroad have risen from Rx. 17,369,000 in 1882, by 31 per cent to Rx. 22,911,000 in 1892. In the former year they amounted to 23 per cent., in the latter to 25 per cent. of your total expenditure. No country could permanently afford such a drain. These increases are not by any means entirely due to alterations in the rate of exchange.

These startling facts demand grave consideration east and west of Suez. Apart from a reference to the daily deteriorating condition of agriculture generally, I am not competent to speak on the state of your peasantry, but so far as all accounts go, official included, there are strong grounds to apprehend danger from the agricultural condition of the country. I am aware that this problem constantly engages the attention of the Supreme Government, and it is to be hoped that it will take a new departure in its policy of land revenue. Mere palliatives will never do. A judicious and statesmanlike survey of the existing situation should enable it to devise a satisfactory remedy. Whatever action may be taken to free the impoverished peasantry from the hands of the money-lenders will go a great way to ameliorate their condition. And Government itself should modify its cast-iron system of exacting revenue at dates at which the cultivators are least prepared to discharge the State dues.

We must, however, not take a gloomy view of the situation. If you have greater difficulties to contend with than we in Ireland, you will remember that your population has been increasing, whilst ours has been reduced by over 40 per cent. within the past half century. Whilst you have lee-way to make up in education and material advancement, your relative progress has been and is out of all proportion to ours.

The justice or, and necessity for, adequate representation in your superior and local Councils is apparent, and naturally claims much of your attention. The administrative mutilation of the manifest intentions of Parliament in framing the Indian Councils Act is much to be deplored. I see that complaints have been made in every province where the enlarged Councils are established, that the distribution of seats for representation of the people is most unsatisfactory; and that, while some interests are over-represented, other important interests are not represented at all. This is not in accordance with the expressed views of British statesmen on both sides of the House when the Bill was discussed. Mr. Gladstone said: "I believe I am justified in looking forward, not merely to a nominal, but to a real living representation of the people of India." Lord Salisbury was no less emphatic: "If we are to do it, and if it has to be done, let us do it systematically * * taking care that the machinery to be provided shall effect the purpose of giving representation, not to accidentally constituted bodies, not to small sections of the people here and there, but to the living strength and vital forces of the whole community of India." How little have these anticipations been realized! We have here a striking instance of the extent to which administration can defeat the intentions of legislation.

It is indeed almost more necessary for the contentment of a people that they should have the administration rather than the enactment of the laws in their own hands. It is moreover desirable that judicial should, as far as possible, be separated from executive functions, and that civil and military employments in medical and other departments should not be held by the same persons. The average military officer, supreme in his own sphere, is of all others least suited by his training to administer civil affairs in a sympathetic and conciliatory spirit. And it has been well said "The frame of mind necessary for an executive officer and the frame of mind necessary for a judge are different. Executive officers ought to mix freely with the people, they ought to try to make friends with them, they ought to see this, and they ought to see that. A judge, on the contrary, ought to shut his ears against everything except that which comes before him in court. But an executive officer has, as such, to learn everything and to do everything, and when he comes upon the bench, he is expected to divest his mind of whatever he has heard elsewhere. Even the best officer of Government is after all a human being."

You have properly protested against the curtailment of your rights regarding trial by jury. Whether we compare the number of convictions before and since the institution of the system thirty years ago, or the state of affairs in districts where it was not established with that where it was established, there appears nothing to justify recent changes. Officials sometimes forget that the general attitude of the people towards the law is of more consequence than the number of malefactors sentenced. It is an old principle of English jurisprudence that it is better that many guilty should escape than that one innocent man should suffer. Love of law, the conception that it is for the good of all—so deeply implanted in the hearts of sovereign peoples, who have been able to mould it to their will—is naturally a plant of slow growth with peoples less favoured.

Regarding criminal procedure in India, the public conscience at home has been from time to time outraged by instances that have reached us of what appeared to be undue partiality towards Europeans. A number of such cases have been well summed up in a book by Ram Gopal Sanyal recently published in Calcutta. The Dum Dum and the Guntakal cases appeared to many of us in Parliament disastrous miscarriages of justice, detrimental to British prestige, the outcome of that brutal contempt for your people which is unhappily still characteristic of many ignorant and prejudiced Europeans, and the product of that race hatred which it ought to be the Government's first care to stamp out. Even the appearance or suspicion of judging the efficiency of magistrates and police by their success in securing convictions should be avoided. We all hope that the Government of India, whose desire for impartiality and justice we all admit, is keenly alive to these evils, and will try its best to consider favourably your representations on the subject. I trust that ere long they may be removed.

Meanwhile let us not embitter our lives, or weaken our energies for practical work Human justice is after all fallible justice. We all fall short where our own interests are concerned! Let what we believe to be injustice by others impel us to higher standards, to nobler ideals of life, to wider charity and forgiveness, to deeper trust in an Omniscience that will yet right every wrong and wipe the tear from every eye.

We rejoiced at the adoption of Mr. Paul's motion regarding Simultaneous Examinations; still more at the frank spirit in which it appeared to have been accepted by the Government. We thought it a great step forward—a solid advantage gained. We have been correspondingly disappointed by the extent to which official counsels have since prevailed, even to the reversal by a Liberal Cabinet of the solemn decision then arrived at. Such vacillation tends to weaken the power of the House of Commons. We have lately seen it instanced as a reason why the Upper Chamber should properly set at naught the resolution of the Lower. When public opinion has secured the acceptance by the House of such a great principle, it has a right to consider its work accomplished. I but voice the pain which this proceeding has caused to many of the most ardent supporters of the Government.

Upon the other hand few actions of the present Government are more indicative of the progress of liberal ideas than the recent convention with Japan for the abolition of consular jurisdiction. This convention may not be without hopeful significance regarding your future. How comes it that powers over British citizens which it is considered inexpedient to accord to Indian judges trained in British law, have freely, and almost without comment, been granted to judges in Japan?

The education of the people claims the first attention of Government now-a-days. I regret that in your case the expenditure thereupon bears such a small proportion to that for military purposes. We must, however, individually bear in mind—at least with us in the United Kingdom there is need to bear in mind—that education in itself confers no special claim to employment by the State. Education fits us for life and enables us the better to use and to enjoy life. It widens our horizon. But we must not expect too much from it. It should be a blessing to all; it might easily be a curse to some, if it spoiled them for the proper discharge of the simple duties that come nearest to them.

I desire now to refer to three subjects—Drink, the Regulation of Vice, and Opium—which have more particularly interested many British friends of India. In this connection I must confess that, as a member of a professedly Christian land, I am almost ashamed to stand before you. Christians claim to carry a message of love and enlightenment to the world. You and we have come together; and what have been the consequences? Have you wronged us, or have we wronged you? Have you for individual gain forced ruin and demoralization upon us, or have we forced them upon you? These questions carry their own answers. We owe our highest civilization and culture originally to the East. In return we have handed back some benefits, but also some of the lowest products of Western civilization.

As to the Drink curse (largely introduced and widely extended by us), there have been repeated denunciations in your debates. It has formed the subject of a resolution at more than one Congress. The spread in India of this evil is fully discussed in the debate on the "Reform in excise administration" at your Sixth and Eighth Congresses. It is deplorable to hear that "people have become more addicted to drink, because it has been thought to be an adjunct of Western civilization;" that "It has been left for [your] Christian rulers to love it, stimulate it, and pet it, and make money by millions of pounds out of it." In this Presidency the excise licences appear to have increased fivefold within forty years. I understand that in India as a whole they have doubled within twenty years. The East India Company, ostensibly at least, strove to reduce consumption. Can we believe that such is the object of Government at the present day? There is scarcely a family in the United Kingdom that has not suffered from the ravages of drink. I am one of those who believe that safety only lies in complete abstinence. To many peoples our introduction of it has meant annihilation. You cannot be too much upon your guard against its insidious advances. I rejoice that the attention you have given to the subject has already contributed in the Madras Presidency alone to the closure of thousands of liquor shops. In such respects as these I have long been of the opinion that the crimes committed by society through Government against the people, are often greater and less excusable, and more disgraceful to character, than the worst crimes ever committed by the people against society and against Government. The former are deliberate and far-reaching. In a certain sense they are without justification, and every citizen is responsible. The latter have generally been committed by the irresponsible few in moments of excitement.

With regard to the odious Cantonment Acts, your testimony has been clear and true. At Allahabad in 1888 you unanimously resolved "That this Congress, having watched with interest and sympathy the exertions that are being made in England for the total abrogation of laws and rules relating to the regulation of prostitution by the State in India, places on record its appreciation of the services thus rendered to this country, and its desire to co-operate by all means in its power in the attainment of this laudable object." This must have had considerable influence with the Home Government in the changes which it has prescribed and which the Government in India is now so tardily carrying out. The history of this question is most significant from the 9th July 1887, when Lord Cross telegraphed to the Viceroy: "I apprehend system is indefensible and must be condemned," till 11th August 1893, when Lord Roberts had the manliness to apologize to Mrs. Andrews and Dr. Kate Bushnell for having denied the accuracy of their revelations upon the subject. But for the ability and devotion of these American ladies, officials would still conceal the truth from the British public, as they managed to conceal it even from the responsible head of a responsible department. What a commentary upon Indian administration! What an argument for local representation! That system of administration is indeed faulty which admits of simply docketing, without obeying, instructions that do not meet the approval of officials. It is easy, but cannot be permanent. For the first time—I say it without meaning offence—the methods of the Indian administration have been fully exposed; and since they have been detected in one particular, we at home must beware of too blindly trusting them in others.

To Opium I find little reference in your proceedings. It is a subject which engages the attention of many of the more thoughtful and conscientious of your friends. There are difficulties surrounding it. No doubt, we in the United Kingdom for our own purposes encouraged the use of the drug, spread its cultivation, and forced it upon China. How are we to retrace our steps? Certianly not at your expense. The decrease of the revenue from this source by 16 per cent. within the past ten years is a warning that such revenue cannot permanently be depended upon. Consideration for the rights of your Independent States complicates the problem. I cannot here initiate discussion upon it. Your business for this session is already planned and cannot be altered. However at some time, your knowledge and

First Day.

President's Address.

advice would be helpful to those of us in the United Kingdom, who desire to do our duty in this matter.

The reforms we desire are not likely to be accomplished, your cause cannot be effectually pleaded, until you are satisfactorily represented alike in your Provincial Councils and in the Imperial Parliament. In proportion as each class and each interest within the United Kingdom has been enabled to make its voice heard in the Imperial Parliament, in just such proportion has that assembly been strengthened and dignified. That strength and that dignity will undoubtedly at some period be increased by representation from the component parts of the Empire. If the Empire is, as we believe it to be, one and indivisible, one indivisible spirit of liberty must pervade every portion of it. If all cannot eventually be raised to one level, all may equally be lowered. If absolutism is necessary here, absolutism will certainly taint and ultimately undermine the fabric of English liberty. Already the workings of ascendancy in India have not been without their influence in retarding steady liberal progress in the United Kingdom.

I have thus ventured, within the short time at my disposal, to lay before you my views regarding the questions that have most engaged your attention and are likely again to come up for discussion. You may the better appreciate the spirit in which I landed upon your shores and in which I shall follow your debates.

We may proceed to our task with hope and confidence. Within the lifetime of a generation you have obtained what may be regarded as the first instalment of reform, in the direction of the expansion and reconstruction of the Legislative Councils, which has cost other countries centuries of toil and effort. You have every reason to be proud of what you have achieved in other directions. You must not be cooled by temporary discouragements, by the unfaithfulness of some, the want of faith of the many. Reform progresses like the steady rise of the tide through many an ebb and flow of the waves. Confident are we that through all storm and cloud, the sun of constitutional liberty will yet shine with pure and beneficent effulgence upon your country. Let it be your individual care to carry back from these Congresses, into every day life and every-day occupations, true elevation of mind, belief in your future, and your own power to mould your future. This future depends more upon yourselves than upon any political or financial changes. Before all you must cultivate a spirit of generous toleration and of charity between class and class and creed and creed.

Considering the general advancement of the world, from which no portion of its surface can be permanently excluded, we have every cause for encouragement, every incentive to press forward, setting no limits to the possible material and spiritual advancement of mankind. Never before were men and women so alive to their capabilities and to their responsibilities towards each other. Let us advance together in ever-widening combinations with ever-broadening hopes, labouring for the good of all.

"For oh! it were a gallant deed
To show before mankind,
How every race and every creed
Might be by love combined—
Might be combined, yet not forget
The fountains whence they rose
As, filled by many a rivulet,
The stately " Ganges " flows."

One of your sages has compared the soul of man to a bird, and earthly existence to the period marked by its flight through a room—out of the illimitable into the illimitable By devoting ourselves to the good of others, we can best occupy that brief space. The wish assertion of common rights is enlightened altruism.

First Day.

President's Address.

Here I brought to a conclusion this address, as, with the exception of a few sentences, I had prepared it in Ireland and on the ocean. Since then I have landed in India, have seen some of your schools and colleges, have lingered in the crowded streets of your cities, have listened to the hum of your manufactories, have talked with your leaders, have watched the sun rise and set on the plains where such a large proportion of your population hardly wring their living from the soil. I now somewhat realize the surpassing beauty of your land. I have met you here face to face. How faint and weak, how inadequate to the expression of my inmost feelings is what I have written and spoken. Apart from those family and national ties, which to each one of us are the first of life's blessings—the choicest gifts of God—I regard this visit to India, and permission to take part in the proceedings of this great assemblage, as the highest privilege, and one that cannot but profoundly influence my remaining years. So far, two convictions before all others, press themselves upon me. The one: the greatness, apart from its inception and much of its history, of the mission of the United Kingdom in this land—the other that this Congress movement is the necessary and logical outcome, the richest fruit of that noble mission, of which we citizens of the United Kingdom should be proud. You yourselves are taking up the work—the work which you and you alone can ultimately perfect—"the eradication by direct friendly intercourse of all possible race, creed or national prejudices amongst all lovers of your country.' This is in truth the greatest combined peaceful effort for the good of the largest number of the human race that history has recorded. (*Loud and long continued Cheers.*)

The President:—My first duty is a pleasing one; it is to ask Mr Surendra Nath Banerjea to read a letter, which was placed in my hands just before the meeting commenced.

The Honorable Mr Surendra Nath Banerjea, who on rising was received with enthusiastic cheers, said:—

I may say you will be gratified with the pleasing announcement which the letter that the President has asked me to read contains. It is the announcement of a munificent and princely gift by one of the great men of your Presidency on behalf of the Congress cause. (*Cheers.*) The letter, which is from the Rajah of Ramnad, is as follows:—

"I have the honor to inform you that I have remitted a sum of Rs. 10,000 in aid of the funds of the Indian National Congress, as a small token of the sympathy which I feel for the movement, which is throughly loyal in its character and is fraught with unspeakable blessings to the people of India. I trust that my donation will be received by the Committee of the National Congress."

Three cheers were then given for the Rajah of Ramnad.

Election of Subjects Committee.

The President:— I now call upon the delegates of the different Congress Circles to elect the members of the Subjects Committee. Let the Secretaries of the various Congress Circles send up the list of the Members.

Mr. Ghosal:—The following are proposed as members of the Subjects Committee:—

## MADRAS.

| | | |
|---|---|---|
| 1. | The Hon'ble P. Rungiah Naidu Garu ... .. ... | Madras. |
| 2. | „ C. Sunkaran Nair ... ... ... ... | do. |
| 3. | G. Parameswaram Pillai, Esq. ... ... ... ... | do. |
| 4. | M. Viraraghavachariyar, Esq. ... ... ... ... | do. |
| 5. | Rai Bahadur P. Ananda Charlu ... ... ... ... | do. |
| 6. | Eardley Norton, Esq. ... ... ... ... ... | do. |
| 7. | Hubert Morgan-Browne, Esq. ... ... ... ... | do. |
| 8. | Dewan Bahadur S. Subramania Iyer, C. I. E.... ... ... | do. |
| 9. | Peter Paul Pillai, Esq. ... ... ... ... ... | do. |

First Day.

Election of Subjects Committee.

10. Syed Mahomed Bahadur ... ... ... ... ... Madras.
11. G. Subramania Iyer, Esq. ... ... ... ... ... do.
12. M. R. Ramakrishna Iyer, Esq. ... ... ... ... do.
13. R. Venkata Subba Rao, Esq. ... ... ... ... do.
14. V. Arunagiri Naidu, Esq. ... ... ... ... ... do.
15. The Honorable Mr. Kaliana Sundaram Iyer ... ... Tanjore.
16. S. A. Saminatha Iyer, Esq. ... ... ... ... do.
17. K. Vasudeva Iyengar, Esq... ... ... ... ... Trichinopoly.
18. The Honorable N Subba Rao Pantulu ... ... ... Godavery.
19. G. Venkata Ratnam, Esq. ... ... ... ... ... do.
20. V. V. Avadani Pantulu. ... ... ... ... ... Masulipatam.
21. Syama Sundara Rao, Esq. ... ... .. ... ... Vizianagaram.
22. Ł. Krishnasawmi Iyer, Esq. ... ... ... ... Tinnevelly.
23. K. R. Gurusami Iyer, Esq. ... ... ... ... do.
24. W. Vierasami Iyer, Esq. ... ... ... ... ... Salem.
25. T. S. Balakrishna Iyer, Esq. .. ... ... ... Coimbatore.
26. K. Srinivasa Row, Esq. ... ... ... ... ... do.
27. The Honorable A. Sabapathy Mudaliyar ... ... ... Bellary.
28. Rev. Stephenson... ... ... ... ... ... Gooty
29. Rai Bahadur C. Jambulinga Mudaliyar ... ... ... Cuddapah.
30. K. R. Ramasami Iyer, Esq... ... ... ... Malabar and Canara.
31. V. Ryru Nambiar, Esq. ... .. ... ... ... do.
32. Achuta Menon, Esq. ... ... ... ... ... do.
33. J. Seymour Keay, Esq., M. P. ... ... ... ... Secunderabad.
34. P. Ramachandra Pillai, Esq. ... ... ... ... do.

## BOMBAY.

1. D E. Wacha, Esq. ... ... ... ... ... Bombay.
2. The Honorable C. H. Sitalvad ... ... ... do.
3. Dr. K. N. Bhadurji ... ... ... ... ... do.
4. W. A. Chambers, Esq. ... ... ... ... ... do.
5. Dr. M. G. Deshmock ... ... ... ... ... do.
6. A. Dev, Esq. ... ... ... ... ... .. do.
7. Jag Mohan Das Vasidra Vandas, Esq. ... ... ... do.
8. Mulraj Khatao, Esq. ... ... ... ... do.
9. Gokuldas Dwarkadass Talatu, Esq. ... ... ... Ahmedabad.
10. Govind Apaji Patil, Esq. ... ... ... ... do.
11. Govindarao Apaji Patil, Esq. ... ... ... ... do.
12. G. S. Mukhadam, Esq. ... ... ... .. ... do.
13. Dayabhai Ijutram, Esq. .. ... ... ... ... do.
14. S. R. Kirloskar, Esq. ... ... ... ... ... Sholapur.
15. S. N. Sathayee, Esq. ... ... ... ... ... do.
16. N. B. Moolay, Esq. ... ... ... ... Ahmednugar.
17. Balakrishna Ramachandra Kotwal ... ... ... Dhulia.
18. Vasudeva Bapuje Akat, Esq. ... ... ... ... do.
19. The Honorable V. R. Natu, B.A., LL.D. ... ... ... Belgaum.
20. S. A. Chhatre, Esq. ... ... ... ... ... do
21. S. B. Bhate, Esq. ... ... ... ... ... do.
22. Rai Bahadur V. M. Bhide ... ... ... ... Deccan Circle.
23. K. P. Gadgil, Esq. ... ... ... ... ... do.

| | | | |
|---|---|---|---|
| 24. | K. G. Natu, Esq. ... ... ... .. ... | Deccan Circle. | **First Day.** |
| 25. | M. B. Namjoshi, Esq. ... ... ... ... ... | do. | **Election of Subjects Committee.** |
| 26. | Prof. G. K. Gokhale ... ... ... ... ... | do. | |
| 27. | R. D. Nagarkar, Esq. ... ... ... ... ... | do. | |
| 28. | Rajaram Yeshwant Raja, Esq. ... ... .. ... | Nasik. | |
| 29. | R. P. Karandikar, Esq. ... ... ... ... ... | Satara. | |
| 30. | G. B. Phansalkar, Esq. ... ... ... ... ... | do. | |
| 31. | V. S. Sahasrabudhi, Esq. ... ... ... ... | do. | |
| 32. | D. B. Parasnis, Esq. .... ... ... ... ... | do. | |
| 33. | Dowlat Ram Jetumal, Esq. ... ... ... ... | Sind. | |
| 34. | G. Pesumal, Esq. ... ... ... ... | do. | |

## BERAR.

1. R. N. Mudholkar, Esq.
2. G. N Kane, Esq.
3. L. C. Bapat, Esq.

## CENTRAL PROVINCES.

1. Rao Saheb Balananda Rao Mahajana.
2. C. V. Naidu, Esq.
3. Dr. Adarasingha Gour, M.A., LL.D.
4. K. N. Desmukhi, Esq.
5. N. K. Kelakara, Esq.
6. K. V. Joshi, Esq.
7. Rao Saheb Kasinath Rao Vaidya.
8. Baghirath Prasad, Esq.
9. Lekshmana Rao.

## N. W. P. & OUDH.

1. The Honorable Raja Rampal Singh.
2. The Honorable Charoo Chunder Mitter.
3. Pandit Madan Mohan Malaviya, B.A., LL.B.
4. A. Nundy, Esq.
5. Pandit Toolsiram Misra.
6. Haviz Abdul Rahim, Esq.
7. Ganga Prasad Varma, Esq.
8. Pandit Bishan Narain Dar.
9. Pandit Sham Narain.

## PUNJAB.

1. Lala Murlidhar.
2. Bakshi Jaishiram.
3. Captain Banon.

## BENGAL.

| | | |
|---|---|---|
| 1. | J. Goshal, Esq. ... ... ... ... ... ... | Calcutta. |
| 2. | The Hon'ble Babu Surendra Nath Banerjea ... ... | do. |
| 3. | Babu Kalicharan Banerji ... ... ... ... | do. |
| 4. | Rev. C. N. Banerjee. ... ... ... ... ... | do. |
| 5. | Babu Meher Mitter. ... ... ... ... ... | do. |
| 6. | Babu Heramba Chandra Moitra ... ... ... ... | do. |
| 7. | Babu Krishna Kumar Mitter ... ... ... ... | do. |
| 8. | Babu Nibran Chandra Datta ... ... ... ... | do. |

First Day.

Election of Subjects Committee.

| | | |
|---|---|---|
| 9. | Pasupathi Nath Basu, Esq. ... ... ... ... | Calcutta. |
| 10. | Babu Promath Nath Mittra ... ... ... ... | do. |
| 11. | P. N. Mitter, Esq. ... ... ... ... ... | do. |
| 12. | Pandit Kali Prasanna Kabya Bisharad ... ... ... | do. |
| 13. | Babu Bishnu Pada Chatterjee ... ... ... ... | Hooghly. |
| 14. | Babu Kedar Nath Banerjee .. ... ... ... | do. |
| 15. | Babu Sarat Chandra Chakravarti ... ... ... | Dacca. |
| 16. | Babu Jotindra Nath Roy Chowdhri ... ... ... | 24 Purgannahs |
| 17. | Kali Prasanna Acharya, Esq. ... ... ... ... | Rajshahye. |
| 18. | Babu Madeb Chandra Chatterjee ... ... ... ... | Dinajpur. |
| 19. | Babu Rakhal Das Sen ... ... ... ... ... | do. |
| 20. | Babu Amarchandra Datta ... ... ... ... | Mymensing. |
| 21. | Babu Sasanka Kumar Ghosh ... ... ... ... | do. |
| 22. | Babu Boikanta Nath Sen ... ... ... ... | Moorshidabad. |
| 23. | Babu Hemendra Nath Sen ... ... .. ... | do. |
| 24. | Babu Ambica Charan Mozumdar ... ... ... ... | Faridpur. |
| 25. | Babu Prithish Chandra Roy ... ... ... ... | do. |
| 26. | Babu Sarat Chandra Sen ... ... ... ... | Chota Nagpur. |
| 27. | Hara Kanta Sen, Esq. .. ... ... ... ... | Bakerganj. |
| 28. | Babu Jadav Lal Roy ... .. ... ... ... | Bogra. |
| 29. | Kunja Lal Shaha, Esq. . ... ... ... | Pabna. |
| 30. | Babu Mohini Mohan Chakravarti ... ... ... | do. |
| 31. | Babu Sasanka Mohan Sen ... ... ... ... | Chittagong. |

The President :—Is it the pleasure of the Congress that these names should be confirmed ? (*Voices*, Yes ! Yes !)

Mr. R. Venkataratnam :—I have an amendment to move.

The President :—What is the nature of your amendment ?

Mr. Venkataratnam :—If you will allow me to speak, I will tell you.

The President :—You must state the terms of your amendment from your place.

Mr. Venkataratnam :—I move that a certain name be omitted from the Subjects Committee. (*Cries of*, No ! No ! )

The President :—Give me the grounds of your objection. Has he not been properly put forward by his district ?

Mr. Venkataratnam :—My objection is that a gentleman of that nature (*Interruption*)

The President :—Your amendment is entirely out of order. I cannot consider any such amendment (*Cheers*). Gentlemen, let those that are in favour of confirming these names say " Aye" (*Voices*, All ! All !) I declare these gentlemen duly elected. The Subjects Committee will meet in one hour at 5-30 p.m., and the Congress itself adjourns till 12 o'clock tomorrow.

# SECOND DAY'S PROCEEDINGS.

**Thursday, the 27th December, 1894.**

The Congress met at 12 noon.

THE PRESIDENT :—Mr. Ghosal will now read out the rules for the conduct of business.

Second Day.

Reading of Rules for conduct of business.

MR. GHOSAL :—Gentlemon, these are the rules for the conduct of business. Please hear them attentively, as the business of the Congress will be conducted according to these rules :—

TENTH INDIAN NATIONAL CONGRESS, 1894.

RULES FOR THE CONDUCT OF BUSINESS.

No one who is not a Delegate will be allowed to address the Congress or vote on any matter.

Every Delegate must address the assembly from the speaker's platform.

The proposers, seconders, and supporters of each resolution will be selected by the Subjects Committee.

The President will allot the time during which each speaker can speak, and no one should exceed this without the special permission of the President. The President will sound his gong once to warn each speaker when the time allotted to him is drawing to a close; he will sound it a second time when that period has elapsed; and should he consider that the speaker ought to cease speaking, the President will touch the gong again when the speaker must, there and then, close his address.

Any Delegate not selected but who may wish to speak on any resolution should send in his name and that of the Congress Circle to which he belongs, legibly written on a piece of paper, to the President, and may speak when called upon by the President to do so.

Any one wishing to propose any amendment to any resolution must send to the President a slip of paper containing the amendment, his own name and that of his seconder, as also the names of the Congress Circles to which they respectively belong; a similar slip should be handed to the Reporter.

Any one who wishes to propose a new subject for discussion by the Congress must give previous notice of it in writing to the President at the commencement of the sitting, with a copy of any resolution he wishes to propose, his own name, and the name of the Congress Circle he belongs to.

No other business shall be brought forward before the Congress until the subjects and resolutions approved by the Subjects Committee have been disposed of.

But afterwards, if time permits, any Delegate who shall have given notice in writing, at the commencement of the sitting, to the President of his desire to have a particular subject discussed, or a definite resolution, which he sets forth, proposed, shall have a right to move, but any delegate who at any time previous to rising shall have given the necessary notice may, with the permission of the President, rise and ask the President to take the sense of the assembly as to whether such subject shall be discussed. No speaking at this stage shall be

Second Day.

Rules for conduct of business.

allowed. The President will simply read out the subject and the proposed resolution and make any such remarks as he considers essential and take a vote of the assembly as to whether the subject shall or shall not be discussed. If the vote is in the affirmative the proposer shall then set forth the subject and the resolution he proposes with such explanations as he considers necessary, and then after due discussion the question shall be disposed of in the usual way. If the vote is in the negative, the subject shall be at once dropped.

The President :—Mr. Morgan-Browne has a short statement to make to you.

Mr. Morgan-Browne :—Gentlemen, your British Committee has published a Report and a statement of accounts for the current year. The delegates will be furnished with a copy of this Report upon application to Mr. Parameswaram Pillai, one of the Secretaries of the Reception Committee. I also wish to state that for the convenience of the delegates and the secretaries of the various Congress Committees, there is put up in this compound an office where subscriptions to "*India*" will be received, and the names and addresses of the people subscribing for next year will be taken down. I trust that many will take the opportunity of registering their names as subscribers to the Congress organ "*India*" and paying their subscriptions. Let me just remind you, Gentlemen, that this is a cash office—no credit (*Laughter*)

The President :—I desire to say that the letters I have received, as President of the Congress, are quite too numerous for me to answer. I have to thank the different writers. The letters have been handed over to the Secretaries and will be properly dealt with by them. Mr. Wacha, of Bombay, will now move the first resolution.

Mr. D. E. Wacha, who on rising was received with Cheers, said :—Mr. President, Ladies and Gentlemen, the resolution that has been entrusted to me runs as follows :—

Resolution I. Cotton Excise Duty.

Mr. D. E. Wacha.

(*a*) That this Congress respectfully enters its emphatic protest against the injustice and impolicy of imposing excise duty on cottons manufactured in British India, as such excise is calculated to cripple seriously the infant mill industry of this country.

(*b*) That this Congress puts on record its firm conviction that in proposing this excise the interests of India have been sacrificed to those of Lancashire, and strongly deprecates any such surrender of Indian interests by the Secretary of State.

(*c*) That in case the Excise Bill becomes law this Congress earnestly prays that the Government of India will, without delay, seek the sanction of the Secretary of State to exercise the powers which the Bill confers on Government to exempt all cottons from "twenties" to "twenty-fours" from the operation of the Act.

(*d*) That the President be authorised to telegraph the above Resolution to the Government of India and to the Secretary of State.

You will observe, Gentlemen, that the Resolution is divided into four parts, but, before I dwell on each of these, I may as well explain to you why it has been judged necessary by the Subjects Committee to give this Resolution precedence over all others. It is the urgency of the occasion which demands it. As you are all aware, the Excise Duty Bill will be read for the third time and passed into law this day. And this is the earliest opportunity which is offered to the Congress to make its voice, as the exponent of enlightened native public opinion, heard in the Council of the empire at Calcutta. We must therefore be prompt and speedy in our action. (*Hear, hear.*) Coming now to the subject matter of the Resolution, I may say it will not require any very lengthened observations from me to commend its adoption to you, for the question has been very ably and intelligently threshed out, not only by enlightened Native and English public opinion, as represented by the Press, but by experts such as the Mill Owners' Association and the Government of India. Thus all India, so to speak, has exhausted the discussion on the merits and demerits of the piece of legislation which is now on the anvil. (*Cheers.*) Now, before I specifically refer to the different sections of the Resolution, let me say one word as to the Government of India itself. It deserves our warm gratitude for having at last been able to extort from the Secretary of State for India the concession to impose an import duty of five per cent. on all the finer classes of cotton goods. In this instance, I may mention, the Government of India has really voiced the needs of the people and nobly advocated their true interests. (*Cheers.*) It is to be sincerely hoped that, in all other matters affecting our permanent welfare, the advocacy of the Government will be of a similarly gratifying character. (*Loud Cheers.*) In such an event, I have not the least doubt in my own mind, and I daresay you will agree with me in that opinion, that our progress will be quicker and a great deal more satisfactory than hitherto. (*Loud Cheers.*) For, Gentlemen, remember that the Government, or rather the State, and the People are the same. We cannot be in opposition to it. For our interests are identical. (*Applause.*) The interests of the people are the interests of the State, and *vice versâ.* But while we rejoice at the tardy justice which the Government has been able to secure from the autocrat at Westminster, it is at the same time a matter of regret that it should be accompanied by some disadvantages. These are of a two-fold character. Firstly, a large revenue has been needlessly sacrificed during the last twelve months; and secondly, it has been unfortunately deemed expedient to have a countervailing excise. As to the sacrifice of the revenue it may be observed that had the cotton manufactures of Lancashire been included in the Tariff Bill which was passed just twelve months ago, the Government treasury would have been richer to-day by well nigh a crore-and-a-half. (*Hear, hear.*) To that extent the sacrifice was needless. We have, as it were, made a present of it to the importers, when we might have stemmed the additional deficit expected at the close of the financial year and altogether obviated the necessity of so iniquitous a Bill as is now before the Supreme Legislative Council. (*Hear, hear.*) It is notorious that during the year the imports of finer goods, the value of which averages between 26 and 30 crores per annum, have been abnormal. At the very least they are 2 crores in excess of that average. The importers took time by the forelock and were shrewd enough to forestall Government in anticipation of the impending duty. So much then for the refusal of the Secretary of State to impose the duty at the proper time. The other and the more important disadvantage is the countervailing excise—of course, as a counterblast to the import duty. I shall directly show how it it is uncalled for. Nay, not only uncalled for, but how unjust and impolitic. But before I dilate on that injustice and impolicy, I would detain you a while on what economists consider to be the principles of a sound and successful excise. These are three in number. Firstly, its productiveness; secondly, its economy; and thirdly, its equity. As to productiveness, we have it on the authority of the Financial Member of the Government of India himself that the revenue to be derived from the excise is not the reason for its imposition. But if then there is to be no productiveness, where is the *raison d'être* of the measure? Tested by the first principle, it fails to command our approval. Coming to the next principle, we are again told that the receipts will be barely commensurate with the cost of collection. The cost of establishment is large, while according to Mr. Westland, the revenue at the most may reach 7 lakhs, if all yarns between "twenties" and "twenty-fours" are taxed, and only 1½ lakhs if yarns between "twenty-fours" and "thirties" are taxed. Here again the test is not fulfilled. Then, as to the equity of the excise. It is, I presume, superfluous for me to observe that the equity is simply in the air. (*Laughter.*) Thus, tested in the crucible of the economists the measure miserably fails. Nay, it commands universal disapproval. I will go a step further and say that it has not even the merit which primitive methods of excise possess, namely, the exigency of the revenue. It will then be reasonably asked why is the Bill brought forward. To that we have a reply from the Financial Member himself. Because the Secretary of State deems it opportune to please the Philistines of Manchester. (*Shame!*)

Now, Gentlemen, in the first clause of the Resolution we say that the Excise Bill is unjust and impolitic. I shall endeavour to justify the two statements. Firstly, because no

**Second Day.**

Resolution I.
Cotton Excise Duty.

MR. D. E. WACHA.

case whatever has been made out to show that the import duty on cotton goods will be protective in its character or act as a beunty on our home manufactures. I daresay most of you. if not all, have perused the very able and exhaustive memorial on the subject submitted some time ago to the Government of India by the Bombay Mill Owners' Association; also the minute of the Hon. Mr. Westland, dated 14th July last, which accompanied the despatch of the Government of India to the Secretary of State, dated 7th August, recommending that, if any excise duty was to be levied, it should be on all counts of yarn above "twenty-fours." The former body collected statistics from 105 mills in the country, 70 of which are in Bombay, the centre of the industry, and conclusively demonstrated that of the total manufactures counts between "twenty-fours" and "thirties" only come to 6 per cent.; and that the total value of exports of Indian manufactured cottons above "twenties" does not exceed 86 lakhs of rupees. On the other hand, out of the bulk of all descriptions of cotton fabrics imported into India from the United Kingdom only 2 per cent. are of counts under "twenties." Virtually, then, Lancashire does not compete with this country in the coarser kinds, and India does not compete with Lancashire in the finer kinds. Thus statistics completely disprove the cry of protection. Absolutely nothing is protected by the import duty, which, therefore, in no way acts as a bounty on home-made cottons. This being the exact economic condition of the indigenous industry, can it be reasonably urged that the excise duty is justifiable? And if it be not justifiable, can we not characterise it as unjust? (*Hear, hear.*) For of what use imposing a duty for which there exists no justification? Again, as Mr. Westland observed in his speech, revenue is not the consideration. That simply emphasises the injustice. For if there be no necessity to levy it for purposes of revenue and if it is not even for purposes of counterbalancing the import duty, what is it imposed for? The Honorable the Finance Minister gives a reply to the query. It is to please the Secretary of State on behalf of those good and pious people of Manchester (*Laughter.*) I have, I trust, demonstrated to you the injustice of the levy. Let me for a moment refer to the impolicy of it. I say, and so do all who are keenly interested in the natural growth and development of the industry, that it is impolitic from the economic point of view. The flourishing cotton trade, I fear, is liable to be seriously hampered, though the Secretary of State seems to regard this contingency with a light heart. My belief is that not only will our future industrial development be retarded, but that the prosperity which has hitherto attended our manufactures will receive a rude shock, especially in Africa and Arabia. It is indeed most unfortunate. While the Government of India is sincerely desirous of witnessing a further development of the country's cotton manufactures, it is constrained under the arbitrary instructions of a superior authority to do the very thing which will arrest that development. (*Hear, hear.*) Are we not all aware that the future material progress of this country will depend on the advance it may make in its manufactures of all kinds of raw products? Do we not desire to become as far as possible independent of foreign countries for the finer class of cloths we now require—cloths of all descriptions, whose imports average about 28 to 30 crores per annum? I have great faith, Gentlemen, in the industrial revolution of India. She underwent one--a most mischievous one about a century ago. What with heavy export duties on indigenous cottons on the one hand, and light import duties on foreign fabrics on the other, our rulers actually killed the thriving cloth trade (*Shame*)—a state of things from which we have but recently emerged. Our material salvation, therefore, rests upon our making progress with the spinning of finer counts, (*Hear, hear*), and so long as artificial restraints of the character of this unjustifiable excise duty are put upon our industry it is vain to hope that we shall ever get the chance we want, and bring about that peaceful industrial revolution which would lead to our prosperity. On these economic grounds the measure will no doubt be considered extremely impolitic. (*Hear, hear.*)

I now pass on to the second clause of the Resolution, which records, and justly, the unanimous opinion of all India that in levying the excise duty her interests have been sacri-

*Second Day.* Resolution I. Cotton Excise Duty. MR. D. E. WACHA.

ficed. Surrendering in the fashion the Government of India has surrendered in the present case is a policy fraught with danger to the empire, for it is impossible to say how the authorities here may go on surrendering and surrendering. (*Hear, hear*) I have noticed with profound regret the extremely lame defence which Mr. Westland made in the Council Chamber the other day in reference to this surrender. The Government, he said, were powerless in the matter. The authority of the Secretary of State was supreme. Virtually, it would signify this, that the Government is simply the registrar of the ukases of the great autocrat for the time being at Westminster! In that case administration in India must cease to exist. Let it be conducted from the other end of the world. Gentlemen, we all feel humiliated at this spectacle—at this open declaration of its helplessness by the Indian Government! (*Hear, hear*) Surely, the *Englishman* is not far wrong when it severely criticises this attitude of our rulers here. Whatever be its views, and those of the *Pioneer* on other problems of the administration, none can deny that in this instance they are a correct echo of the feeling and sentiments of Anglo-Indians and Indians alike. Such helplessness not to call it by a stronger word, is indeed most undesirable. Gentlemen, if I were Viceroy and Governor-General (*Laughter*) I would rather resign my post than be such a silent, humble and obedient servant to the Secretary of State. (*Loud Applause*) I would ten times advocate the cause of India and defend it to the last hour rather than surrender myself in the fashion the Government seems to have done. (*Loud Cheers*) I repeat there is a great political danger in surrenders of such character, but I will refrain from dilating on the point as not germane to the resolution. I therefore pass on to the third clause, which prays that Government may be pleased to obtain, as soon as possible, the sanction of the Secretary of State to exempt all yarns above "twenties" and under "twenty-fours." Were such an exemption speedily granted, I am sure that all India would be pleased, while the industrial developments which we are now witnessing would continue on their onward natural course, leading to greater material prosperity to our people in the near future. Let us all devoutly wish that our prayer, which by the fourth clause of the Resolution we authorise our President to communicate forthwith to the Government of India, may be favourably considered. With these observations I cordially commend the Resolution to your approval. (*Loud Cheers.*)

HON. A. SABAPATHY MOODELLIAR.

THE HON. MR. A. SABAPATHY MOODELLIAR, in seconding the Resolution, said:—Brother Delegates,—I think I have a very easy task to perform, after what has been said so eloquently and so exhaustively by my friend Mr. D. E. Wacha, of Bombay, so please, Gentlemen, do not expect from me any more remarks on the point. I will, however, take this opportunity of pointing out to you, Gentlemen, that this measure will cripple the industries of Madras as well as of Bombay, in fact of India generally. They say that the object of imposing this duty on our Indian manufactures is to satisfy the demands of the Lancashire people. You have all read the statement made by the Financial Secretary that the Government of India is quite powerless to exempt the Indian manufacturer from this excise duty, as it has been stipulated by the Secretary of State that the import duties cannot be collected, cannot be imposed, unless the Indian Government makes it a point to agree to the collection of the excise duty. Under these circumstances I think we have no other alternative but to bring to the notice of Government that all yarns ranging up to "twenty-fours" should at least be exempted; otherwise, not only will Indian industry be crippled in its infancy, but facilities will certainly be given to Japan and other countries, which are now taking up this industry very extensively, to compete and be independent of Bombay and other centres, from which at present they draw very large supplies. So, my dear brethren, all we can now do is to protest as strongly as we possibly can and ask our President to telegraph this Resolution without any delay, as I hear that the sitting of the Council will take place soon to decide this question. I have therefore great pleasure in seconding this proposition, and I hope you will accord your assent with one unanimous voice. (*Cheers.*)

**Second Day.**

Resolution I.

THE PRESIDENT :— The first Resolution has been properly proposed and seconded. Those of you who are of opinion that it should be passed please say "Aye." The Resolution was carried with acclamation.

THE PRESIDENT :—Mr. Boikunta Nath Sen will propose the second Resolution.

Resolution II. Land Question.

MR. BOIKUNTA NATH SEN.

MR. BOIKUNTA NATH SEN :—Mr. President, Fellow-Delegates and Gentlemen,—I have been entrusted with the second Resolution, which is to this effect :—

(*a*) That this Congress desires to express the profound alarm which has been created by the action of the Government in interfering with the existing permanent settlement in Bengal and Behar (in the matter of survey and other cesses) and with the terms of Sunnads of permanently settled estates in Madras; and deeming such interference with solemn pledges a national calamity, hereby pledges itself to oppose in all possible legitimate ways all such reactionary attacks on permanent settlements and their holders, and resolves to petition Parliament in that behalf.

(*b*) That this Congress regrets extremely that the Government of India have not only failed to carry out the pledges (given by the Secretary of State in his Despatches of 1862 and 1865) for permanent settlement in the provinces in which it does not exist, but have also failed to give effect to the policy of granting modified fixity of tenure and immunity from enhancement laid down in 1882 and 1884 by the Government of India and approved by the Secretary of State; and this Congress hereby entreats the Government of India to grant a modified fixity of tenure and immunity from enhancement of land-tax for a sufficiently long period of not less than sixty years so as to secure to landholders the full benefits of their own improvements.

Now this Resolution may be called the Resolution regarding the land we live on. The whole of the Indian population is interested in the solution of this question : and I may say directly interested. Bengal enjoys certain privileges which the other sister provinces do not enjoy. But the vested rights of Bengal have been threatened, therefore Bengal too is directly concerned. The importance of the question is fully appreciated by all, and it has gradually in the course of five or six years secured for itself a certain amount of prominence. Now this question was first mooted in the fourth Congress. In the fifth Congress the Resolution was to this effect—I mean the Resolution on this subject :—" That the Government be " urged to take the subject of a permanent settlement once more under consideration in view to " practical action thereon, such that fixity and permanency may be given to the settlement of " the Government Land Revenue demand without further delay, at any rate in all fully " populated and well cultivated tracts of the country" Now after this Resolution was adopted by the Congress, year after year Resolutions have been recorded from this Congress platform repeating the prayer for fixity and permanency of Government land revenue demand. Year after year it has been requested that practical effect might be given to the principles laid down in the Secretary of State's despatch of 1862, which has been approved by subsequent despatches, and that effect might also be given to the line of action indicated in those despatches. Now in the despatch of 1862, amongst other things, you will find this, that " after the most careful review of all these considerations Her Majesty's Govern- " ment are of opinion that the advantages which may be reasonably expected to accrue, not " only to those immediately concerned with the land but to the community generally, are " sufficiently great to justify them in incurring the risk of some prospective loss of revenue " in order to attain them, and that a settlement in perpetuity in the districts in which the " conditions required are or may hereafter be fulfilled is a measure dictated by sound policy " and calculated to accelerate the development of the resources of India, and to insure in the " highest degree the welfare and contentment of all classes of Her Majesty's subjects." Now with this despatch before us, and with the noble and the liberal principle formulated in the despatch, we had, of course, good reasons to hope ; but the question is—have our expectations been fulfilled ? The successive measures adopted by Government are not evolutions of forward progress, but they are re-actionary and retrograde in their nature, and it is in

Second Day.

Resolution II. Land Question.

Mr. Boikunta Nath Sen.

view of this that last year on this subject Resolutions were adopted by Congress similar to the one which is now being placed before you for your acceptance. In this there is only the addition that the Congress resolves to petition Parliament in that behalf. Last year there was the alarm noted. Now, Gentlemen, the imposition of cesses in Bengal—I mean the Road cess and the Public Works cess—was an infringement of the terms of the permanent settlement. It was in direct violation of the pledge that was given. (*Hear, hear*) It was not sufficient to threaten those who had been enjoying the benefits of a permanent settlement, but, over and above that, in Behar, which is included in Bengal, a cadastral survey was introduced (*Hear, hear*) That was the third blow that was given. The fourth is yet in contemplation,—I mean another cess for the maintenance of tho Records of this Survey. Now this Cadastral Survey has been commenced, and the area of survey has been selected by Government, and I must say a very bad selection has been made. You know, Gentlemen, the Maharajah of Durbhanga (*Cheers*), who is the premier Zemindar of Bengal, (he was once a ward of Court, that is, the Government held the property in trust for him during his minority). During the Stewardship of Government, while the Government was holding or managing this property as Trustee, a cadastral survey entailing an expenditure of lakhs of rupees was held. His estates then, ought to have been the last selected by Government for the purpose of re-survey (*Hear, hear*) The landholder does not want it, no other tenure-holders of subordinate interest require it, the agriculturists do not require it; but the Government says against all these voices, "We require it." Why? Is it for fiscal purposes? Or is it for statistical purposes? Or is it for the creation of disunion between agriculturists, tenure-holders and Zemindars. I hope it is not the last. If it is for fiscal purposes, then it is patent, that the permanent settlement will be brutally assailed again. (*Hear, hear*) If it is for statistical purposes, the Government has no right to call upon the Zemindars or the agriculturists to make any contribution towards the expenses (*Cheers*), so that from all possible stand-points of view, from the different aspects of the case, the whole measure is unjustifiable. Now this Congress pledges itself to oppose by all legitimate ways and means such reactionary attacks on the part of the Government; and here I cannot help again mentioning the name of the Maharajah of Durbhanga (*Hear, hear*), in consequence of the bold attitude he has taken, the noble and magnanimous way in which, at considerable sacrifice, and I may say even risk, he has been trying to maintain the integrity of the permanent settlement. (*Cheers*) We ought to be thankful to him. This Congress is following a line which he single handed has been following, and now that these things are going on, what are we to do? Last year we resolved that we should oppose the illegal interference of the Government by all legitimate means, but no definite method was pointed out. our legitimate ways and means were not definitely pointed out; this time you have it, *viz.*, that we propose to petition Parliament in that behalf. Our perspective must be adjusted according to the altered circumstances; that is the only remedy left for the present. This is a grievance for which we ask redress, and this is the only legitimate way in which we can approach the fountain head of justice; at the same time I must say that the diminution of the discharge from the channels of the fountain-head, caused by Executive intervention, is not a very hopeful sign for us There might be tampering with the orders and mandates and Resolutions of Parliament; for our sad experience shows, as you will have occasion to hear from other speakers, that these mandates from Parliament are not always given effect to. (*Shame!*) Still we must persist. and I think you will all accept this part of the Resolution. I believe I ought not to take up your time any longer as regards the first part. I do not know whether I have exceeded my time, Mr. President. (*Cries of* "No, No".) (The President here intimated to the speaker that his time had not yet expired.)

Now I come to the second part. (*Cheers*) Gentlemen, with regard to this second part, you see there is a sort of concession on our part. I say concession on our part,

Second Day.

Resolution II.
Land Question.

Mr. Boikunta
Nath Sen.

because hitherto we have been asking for and demanding permanent settlement in the Government Land Revenue demand; that is we have been asking for fixity in perpetuity as it were But you will see that to a certain extent we recede from that position. It cannot be expected —perhaps that is the opinion of the majorfty—that we should get that sort of permanent settlement which has been accorded to Bengal. But we can get it in a modified form. Now when the permanent settlement in Bengal was completed, that is in the year 1793, a contemporaneous minute from the Board of Revenue of Fort Saint George, recorded by Mr. White, was sent up and was approved by the Commission that was appointed for enquiring into the state of affairs of the late East India Company. It was in 1812 that that Commission placed on record its approval of the scheme proposing to extend the permanent settlement to this Presidency also. Thus from 1812 full fifty years passed away, and it was not until 1862 that we come to the despatch of the Secretery of State for India in which the Government lay down certain rules for the extension of the permanent settlement. The despatch of 1862 was again approved by that of 1865, and then there was a despatch by the Viceroy in 1882, which was also approved in 1885.

These despatches laid down certain rules for the extension of the permanent settlement. There were certain conditions precedent, *viz.*, the bringing under cultivation of a certain portion of the area. Four-fifths of the entire area was fixed as the amount to be brought under cultivation in order that the permanent settlement might be accorded to such local area. Now in some tracts, with the object of getting that privilege, the conditions have been fulfilled; in some other parts the conditions have been partially fulfilled; and if time will allow they will also surely be fulfilled. The fulfilment of these conditions is not an easy thing; it requires the investing of money. Here comes in the question of unearned increment. It is not the unearned increment which these land-owners are trying to get; they are investing their money, they are bestowing their labour, and they ask for a return. So you see, these persons who now hold under temporary settlement, are not at all asking for the unearned increment. They wish to have the fruits of their own labour and a return for the capital they have invested. Before the despatch of 1862 there was no stimulus whatsoever for investing money, because there was no knowing when the property might be re-measured, when there might be interference by Government again, and when the property would be snatched away from their hands. There was no security, no value, and therefore no stimulus for investing money. But the despatch of Government emboldened the people, it induced them to invest their money to improve the land. They have fulfilled their part of the contract, and if it had been, Gentlemen, a question between individual and individual, perhaps one would be inclined to ask "Why not sue?" (*Cheers*) Why not bring a suit for damages? (*Hear, hear*) Why not sue for specific performance of the contract? (*Cheers*) And the issue would have been a veiy simple one for a Civil Court of Justice to decide. But here you have Royal prerogatives. Here the Municipal Laws would not affect the party concerned. In the case of individuals there is what you would call a breach of faith, liability to damages, liability to perform specifically the contract agreed upon, for which you could bring a suit in Court; but with regard to the Crown, we supplicate, we entreat. You see this in the words of the Resolution, that this Congress hereby "entreats" the Government. (*Cheers*) We do not demand whatwe are entitled to get as a matter of right in the Civil Court, but we supplicate and entreat. Then again, we do not ask the Government to part with its entire control over the property; for we do not ask for settlement in perpetuity, as I call it in contradistinction to temporary settlement. Let a sufficiently long period be given to us with a certain amount of assurance—in fact, it is a microscopic demand that we make after all. What we say is—let there be some sort of assurance given to us so that we may be willing to invest money, and so that we may expect to get a sufficient return for the money that we invest and for the labour that we bestow. Now the Government will still have the power to make a fresh settlement; we say let the settlement be for sixty years, and let no enchancement be made for sixty years. This, I submit, is a very fair and modest request, and the Government—at least for its own sake in order to get out of the difficulty, or at least to show an appearance of keeping its pledge—ought to accede to our prayer and our request. With these remarks I ask you to accept the Resolution. (*Loud Cheers.*)

**Second Day.**

**Resolution II. Land Question.**

THE PRESIDENT:—This Resolution will be seconded by the Honorable Mr. Natu, of Bombay.

**HON. MR. V. R. NATU.**

THE HONORABLE MR. NATU:—Mr. President, Ladies and Gentiemen—After the eloquent and able address of my predecessor it would not be proper for me to take up your time but for one very important thing, and that thing concerns the masses of the Presidencies of Madras and Bombay. The gentleman who preceded me represents the Presidency of Bengal, and our opponents are likely to say that his interests coincide with the interests of the Bengal Zemindars; that he simply sheds crocodile tears; and that he himself, being a Zemindar, does not take an interest in the welfare of the masses. I think it necessary, therefore, to take up your time for a few minutes while I explain to you how the Resolution before you affects, to the greatest extent, the interests of the masses of this country. You know that in India 80 per cent. of the population is an agricultural population, and that the bulk of the Revenue derived by Government comes from land. So this question is not only a question for the people but also a question for the Government; it is the duty of the people to watch the increasing demands of Government carefully, and it is the duty of Government, or at least it is to the interest of Government, to take as much as possible from the people. In this conflict of interests it is always a most important thing for us to see how far Government is carrying out the pledges which it has solemnly made from time to time. So far as our Presidency is concerned I would simply point to two Resolutions which were passed by the Government of India in 1882 and in 1884. Those Resolutions were very useful to the people because they placed certain limits or checks upon the enhancement which was to be made on Revision Survey. There is the Resolution on a new revision of Survey in the Bombay Presidency. The Assessment was not to be increased in the case of a group of villages by more than 33 per cent. Now, even in spite of this Resolution, and even in spite of the promises made from time to time by well-known men like Lord Ripon, the present Government of Bombay have taken a retrograde step in unduly enhancing the assessment; and in that connection I will simply refer you to the instance of the Konkan Taluqs. The assessment on these villages has already been considered, and the Revenue from this group of villages has been increased by 44 per cent. In the case of Assam you know that last year the same Resolutions which were applied to the Presidency of Bombay were to a certain extent applied to other Provinces of India Assam is an instance before us. There the increase of assessment was enormous. And what was the enormous increase? It was simply 100 per cent. And what was the increase in the Presidency of Bombay? It was 1,200 per cent. in the case of three Taluqs in the Ratnagiri District, and of three Taluqs in the Albag District, the poorest district. The limit put down was simply in the case of individual holdings; but the change from 100 per cent. to 1,200 per cent. is certainly a very great leap, and the question is certainly of such vital importance to the masses that from year to year we must bring it before the Congress, and year after year we must urge upon the attention of Government the necessity of redeeming the pledges given to us; for the whole peace and prosperity of this country depends upon the good-will of the masses, consisting, as they do, chiefly of the agricultural population. In India you will find that the Government, as has already been explained by my predecessor, not only failed to act up to the despatches of 1862 and 1865, but also failed to carry out the little promises which were made, and the little concessions which were accepted as Rules in the Presidency of Bombay and other parts of India. Those Rules have been over-ridden, and Government is not willing to carry out even those small concessions. Our country is not an industrial country; it is a country of agri-

Second Day.

Resolution II. Land Question.

Hon. Mr. V. R. Natu.

culturists; and every day the Government is putting a burden upon the agriculturists Gentlemen, the support which you should accord to this Resolution will further show that this Congress does not wish it to be understood that it represents the classes only but also the masses of India. I would point out one instance from the Presidency of Bombay where the entire assessment of the land was increased by 12 lakhs. When we consider these facts we see that the question is one of immense importance to every one of us, requiring to be studied from all points of view. One word before I take my seat, and that is this. In discussing the question of pormanent settlement we must always draw a line of demarcation between the permanent settlement which exists in the Presidency of Bengal and the little concessions that we ask for in the Presidencies of Madras and Bombay. In the case of the permanent settlement in Bengal the State has to deal with the middle-men, the Zemindars In the case of Madras and Bombay the State has to deal directly with the agriculturists, the Talukdars and Ryots. Even in that case Government is so charitable in taking care of the interests of the Ryots that it has put checks upon the demands of the Kons; but at the same time it is not charitable enough towards the Kons themselves. Government is increasing its demands upon the Kons while it does not allow the Kons to increase their demands upon the Ryots. But there is another thing which I want to point out, and it is this, that while Government has enacted the Bengal Tenancy Act in the interests of the tenants it does not carry out that principle in its own case when it has to deal directly with the millions and millions of ryots in India. Government always says that the masses must be kindly treated, it also further states that the agricultural interests must be watched. There is a Bill before the Legislative Council—that is, the Deccan Agriculturists' Indebtedness Act. The Bill is so short that it has entirely disappointed all men in the Presidency of Bombay. As the Agricultural Committee suggested, their poverty is not due entirely to the Sowcars, but is much more due to the demands which have been made from time to time by the Government. So it must be noted that while the Bill is pretty useful so far as the Sowcars are concerned, the Government shelves the most important question so far as the Ryots of the Deccan are concerned, and it is sure not to take up this question because Mr. Lee Warner does not like it. (*Shame*) There is one other point. In the case of the Deccan Agriculturists' Act the Government was requested by the Poona Sarvajanik Sabha to take up the question of the demand, namely, that the demand should not be made in times of scarcity, and that Government should make concessions from time to time to the Ryots in times of famine; but that question has been entirely dropped. We say that whenever you introduce Revision Surveys you should simply adhere to your own terms, that you should simply limit your demand to 33 per cent. That is the only limited demand. We do not want a permanent settlement in the sense in which it is understood in Bengal. Foreigners, including the President who comes from a foreign country, should not be misled into supposing that the bulk of the population in India requires a permanent settlement in the sense in which it is understood in Bengal. It is a limited demand, a demand accepted by Government as proper and just and followed for some years. When the Government is hard pressed for money they should not commit a breach of faith, so Gentlemen, I request that this great and important proposition may always be brought before this Congress until we find that Government is pledged in the interest of these classes to fully redeem those pledges, and thus secure to us the benefits of pledges so solemnly given by men who really understood the case of the poverty of our people. With these few remarks I request that you will accept this Resolution without a voice of dissension. (*Cheers.*)

The President:—An amendment has been placed in my hands. The course I propose to follow is to let the proposer and seconder of the amendment speak, and then to call upon other gentlemen to speak. I have to remind the proposer and seconder of the amendment that they have only five minutes each. Captain Banon will now move the amendment.

**Second Day.**

**Resolution II. Land Question.**

Capt. Banon.

Captain Banon :—Mr. President and Gentlemen, I have an amendment to propose and it is in the following terms :—

"That this Congress desires to urge upon the Government of India the policy and expediency of granting the fixity and permanency of the Land Revenue, and that if the only obstacle to the grant of a permanent settlement to all India be the former permanent settlement of Lord Cornwallis, this Congress, being solely actuated for the common good of all India, and not of one portion only, will, in the interests of the agricultural and labouring classes, offer no opposition to. nor make any protest against, the re-assessment, by the Government of India, of the land under the Permanent Settlement of Lord Cornwallis."

I may begin by saying that I am very desirous of a permanent settlement for all India, because I myself am a ryotwa in the Panjab; but the only difficulty that I can see to our getting this permanent settlement is the permanent settlement at present existing in Bengal. Government say that they lose quite enough money already by this permanent settlement in Bengal, and that as long as it exists they cannot give a permanent settlement to the rest of India. I live amongst the ryotwars, as I am one of them, and I know that they consider it very unfair to them that they should pay twice as much land revenue as they would pay but for this permanent settlement in Bengal. I would also direct your attention to another question. It has always been alleged against this Congress that it favours the interests of the richer classes as against those of the poorer classes. That I do not believe, but I think if you support this Resolution, you will add a good deal of colour to the accusations against us.

There is another matter also that I should like to bring to your notice. By passing this resolution regarding this permanent settlement, you alienate from you the support of the radical party in England who are against landlordism and the unearned increment. There is one last point that I want to bring to your notice and that is, the Budget Speech of Mr. Westland last year. He asserts that Congress brings forward many resolutions, but that all these resolutions cost money. "Will the Congress bring forward any resolution whereby money may come into the Government coffers?" he says, and he holds out a sort of condition or stipulation to us that if we find him money he is quite ready to grant our resolutions—any resolution that is at all reasonable. I have no doubt that if we do find him the money, we shall get several things that we are asking for, such as, a lighter Salt Tax, some reduction of Income Tax, less harsh Forest Laws, better organization of the police, and the separation of judicial and executive functions. Gentlemen, I have only five minutes, I cannot say any more; but I think you should bear all this in mind in considering the fermer resolution, and now with your permission I will sit down. *(Hear, hear.)*

The President :—The amendment will be seconded by Mr Parthasarady, of Madras. (No one however came forward to second the amendment). There appears to be no seconder to this amendment; it therefore falls to the ground. I now call upon the Honorable Mr. K. Kalyanasundram Iyer to speak on the original Resolution.

Hon. Mr. K. Kalyanasundram Iyep

The Hon. Mr. K. Kalyanasundram Iyer :—Mr. Chairman and Gentlemen, in my humble opinion a permanent settlement of the land revenue due to Government is the only proper settlement suitable to the condition of this country. The main objection against a permanent settlement is that the nation as a whole is entitled to what is termed the unearned increment—that is, when the value of the land and its produce has increased in consequence of the increase of population and wealth and not by any exertions on the part of the land owner, then the State, as representing the community, may justly claim this increase; but however sound this claim may be in countries where lands have accumulated in the hands of a few, it loses its force in a country like India where the agricultural population forms the majority, nearly eighty per cent., and is almost identical with the community itself. If to

**Second Day.**

**Resolution II. Land Question.**

**Hon. Mr. K. Kalyanasundram Iyer.**

this fact be added the consideration that about fifty millions of people depending on agriculture for their maintenance and support are on the verge of starvation, then it would be a fair demand on Government to ask that the agriculturalists be allowed to retain in their hands whatever increase they can get, so that the condition of these poor people might be bettered by direct and indirect means. (*Cheers*) While such are the arguments in favour of a permanent settlement, Gentlemen, the policy that is being pursued by Government seems to be one of a very opposite nature. There are already loud complaints that with respect to estates which have been once permanently settled the ryots and the holders are being encroached upon by Government. With regard to settlements which are most common in this Presidency, namely, Ryotwar Settlements, it used at one time to be held that a period of thirty years was the shortest interval within which a re-settlement might be made. But recently, in connection with one of the most important districts in this Presidency, this period was reduced by the Governor to twenty years. (*Shame*) Now, Gentlemen what do these constant re-settlements mean? You have an excellent illustration in the methods adopted in the re-settlement of the district of Tanjore. The Government, being fully alive to the evils attendant on settlement operations generally, determined that the average out-turn of land should, first and once for all, be estimated upon scientific principles, and that in future revisions the rise in prices alone should be taken into account. The procedure adopted was this: the average yield of land was ordered to be estimated by a scientific classification of soil but not to be checked and tested by actual experiments in harvesting; apparently this scientific classification of soil is so finely graded that the officers of the settlement department have often, with reference to one and the same soil, been obliged to differ from themselves and each other (*Cheers*); and with regard to the actual experiment made the result has been by no means more satisfactory. A small plot of land, the tenth part of an acre, was selected by the settlement department itself for the experiment in harvesting, and upon the result of this single experiment hundreds of acres, nay thousands of acres, were settled as being able to produce a particular out-turn. The Mirasdars of the district naturally objected to such a course; they loudly complained that the actual yield of the land in their possession was a great deal less than the estimate fixed by the department, and they clamourously demanded an *Amani* management for a reasonable period, for the purpose of determining the average yielding capacity of the land; but their complaints and their demands were alike rejected (*Shame*) and they were in fact told that if the actual facts were not consistent with the theory evolved by the settlement department it was so much the worse for their facts. Now, Gentlemen, the utter unreliability of this theoretical settlement is clearly shown by the action of the authorities themselves. The gentleman who was appointed the settlement officer of the district, after a classification of the soil, reported to Government that the re-settlement of the district would involve an increase of eighteen and a half lakhs of rupees, the assessment under the old settlement being about forty-one lakhs; but he added, that if the district were to be treated upon scientific principles an increase of twenty-eight lakhs would not be too much. (*Shame.*) Apparently to the great loss of Government, he finally recommended an increase of only fourteen and a half lakhs. This was reduced by the Board of Revenue by two lakhs, and finally by Government to eleven and a half lakhs. Thus you see the final decision of the Government imposed an increase of assessment representing only forty per cent. of what should have been the increase according to the accurate scientific theory. (*Cheers*) This shows that the authorities themselves have no confidence in their scientific methods. (*Cheers*) Well, Gentlemen, these are the difficulties attending a re-settlement, but apart from these difficulties there is the fact that on occasions like these Government are very apt strangely to forget their recognised obligations. With respect to Tanjore the Board of Revenue reported that if the full additional assessment had to be imposed upon the district, it would become the duty of Government to lay out very considerable sums of money, for an equitable and economical distribution of water Government was generous enough to recognise this obligation, but, Gentlemen, nothing has yet been done in this latter direction, and, so far as the Mirasdars can see, there does not seem to be a prospect of anything being done in the near future. Yet the additional assessment has not only been imposed but actually collected. (*Shame*) . This should be sufficient to convince you that the permanent settlement is the only proper settlement to be applied to India, but, if it is impossible for us to get from Government a permanent settlement, we ought to be content with the next best thing, namely, the period of sixty years which is referred to in the resolution and which is certainly not too long. I submit, therefore, that the resolution as worded is most moderate, and I hope that you will all unanimously adopt it. (*Cheers.*)

**Second Day.**

**Resolution II. Land Question.**

**Hon. Mr. K. Kalyanasundram Iyer.**

**Mana Vikrama Raja.**

Mana Vikrama Raja :—Mr. President, Brother Delegates, Ladies and Gentlemen : I have much pleasure in giving my cordial support to this proposition, the more so as I come from a district (Malabar) where Revenue Settlement operations are now in full swing, and where the question of assessment has been seriously engaging the attention of my countrymen for some time past. You have doubtless learned from the able speakers who have just preceded me, how a land-tax in perpetuity was ever obtained or was ever attempted to be introduced into this country and how conducive it is to agricultural prosperity. They have told you in common with the worthy speakers at the fifth and sixth Congresses held at Bombay and Calcutta that an agricultural crisis alone obtained for them the boon of this system, and that Government has by its own action distinctly and unmistakably admitted that in its opinion the fixing in perpetuity of the Government demand is an unfailing, if not the only, remedy against all agricultural depression and therefore promotes the agricultural prospects of a country. Be it noted that this admission on the part of Government is very material, as a sound administrative principle is involved therein, which is best shown by the action of Government itself. Now, Gentlemen, having stated this much, it only remains for me to explain how far this policy has been adopted with respect to my district. (*Hear, hear.*)

Before proceeding further, I must tell you, Gentlemen, that the time allotted to a speaker under the rules does not allow me to do full justice to this subject, though no one will deny that it is one of vital interest and admits of a thorough and argumentative discussion. I shall therefore simply lay before you, as briefly as possible, certain facts and considerations which will show you the justice of our demand and our right to claim it. (*Hear, hear*).

Perhaps few of you, Gentlemen, know that unlike other districts, lands in Malabar are purely private property and that this has been so since the time of the colonisation of the district. The Hindu Rulers, despotic though some of them were, did not interfere with the integrity of this private ownership; these Rulers merely claimed Military Service from the landed proprietors in the exercise of their Sovereign rights the State revenue being chiefly derived from customs and other excise dues. Consequently when the country passed out of the hands of the Hindu Sovereigns into those of their conquerors, all that the latter obtained were the rights and privileges which the former enjoyed. The Government having recognized the unique existence of this private ownership in lands, the question whether it can adopt the same principles of Settlement as have been adopted in other districts with respect to our district seems to me a debatable one. To make the whole thing clear I shall briefly indicate to you the various steps taken from time to time by successive conquerors in the Revenue Settlement of Malabar, and you will, when you have heard them, doubtless agree with me that the Government cannot, with any show of justice, revise the existing assessment, much less carry out the revision on the lines proposed by the local authorities. Now, Gentlemen, prior to the British rule, the Province was administered by Hindu Rulers who did not introduce any kind of land taxation. It was subsequently invaded by Hyder Ali, and even under him and his son Tippu, no definite and organized system of land assessment was introduced, though attempts were made now and then to introduce the same. In 1792 the district was formally ceded to the East India Company. On the cession of the district in 1792, Joint Commissioners were

Second Day.

Resolution II. Land Question.

MANA VIKRAMA RAJA.

appointed for the management of the affairs of Malabar and Canara which were administered by the Bombay Government till 1801, when they were transferred to the Govermnent of Fort St. George. The Commission was then abolished and the district subjected to the contro and superintendence of collectors.

Even before this transfer, the Court of Directors and the Supreme Govermnent of Bengal instructed the Bombay Government to consider the expediency of extending the system of Permanent Settlement to our district; while even subsequent to the transfer steps were taken by the Madras Government for the introduction of this system into a number of districts, among which was included Malabar. It has also been amply demonstrated that the tendency of the authorities was to grant Permanent Settlements—that is to fix unalterable assessments in perpetuity- whenever there was a crisis. It now remains for me to show you, Gentlemen, that there was a serious crisis in Malabar about this time and that the authoritie were obliged to resort to the expediency of guaranteeing the permanency of our land-tax. (*Hear, hear*)

Simultaneously with the transfer of our district to this Presidency, it was placed, as I have already told you, in charge of a principal Collector, Major MacLeod being the first officer so appointed. One of his first acts was to effect certain changes in the land assessments and in the exchange values of the current coins, with the result that the inhabitants rose up in arms *en masse*. He was unable to quell the stir and insurrection he had himself roused by his ill-advised innovations, and was obliged to resign and quit the country, handing over charge of the district to his successor, Mr. R. Rickards. This new officer's first act was to allay the exasperated public feeling by notifying that the old exchange prices would be revived, and that all complaints relating to land assessments would be carefully attended to and investigated. Later on in June 1803, Mr. Rickards called together all the leading *Janmis* and explained that, subject to the approbation of the Board of Revenue, he proposed to have a new *pymash* and adopt certain new principles for a permanent taxation. (*Cheers*)

These principles, which were fully explained to them, were approved by all the landed proprietors in the district who unanimously concurred in them and duly declared their acquiescence, praying that they might be permanently applied to all lands then under cultivation as also to waste lands which might thereafter be reclaimed. An agreement was thereupon formally signed and executed by all the *Janmis* in the district. These facts were duly reported to the Government of Madras which formally and finally notified the same, ordering their adoption as the basis of a permanent and unalteraole Settlement. (*Loud Cheers*) A Proclamation on the above lines and fully setting forth these principles and facts was issued on the 21st July 1805 following the instructions already issued to all Collectors in 1802.

Now, Gentlemen, you can clearly see from the above account that the Proclamation was issued with the sole object of conciliating a people who had become disaffected on account of the innovations in the assessment brought about by Major MacLeod. This Proclamation and the agreement I have referred to plainly indicate that what the people wished for, and obtained, was a reasonable and permanent Assessment. These documents are not capable of any other interpretation than that the principles and money rates already agreed upon and fixed between the Collector on behalf of Government and the *Janmis* of the district were to be permanent and unalterable. (*Loud Cheers*)

Now, Gentlemen, I ask you to remember that the Permanent Settlement of Bengal was granted in 1793 when there was a famine; that that of the N.-W. Provinces was also granted when there was a similar crisis; and that inferentially the tendency of Government has been to fix the land assessment in perpetuity when the exigencies of the circumstances necessitated such a step. You will also remember, Gentlemen, as I have just told you, that Government was in a similar predicament about this time. There was an insurrection in the district caused by the ill advised innovations of a Collector. People rose up in arms *en masse*, and the only expedient which it was possible for his successor to adopt in order to restore peace and tranquility in the district was to guarantee fixity of tenure by a Permanent assessment of the land. This was accordingly done by the issue of the Notification of 1803 and the Proclamation of 1805, which may justly be described as our Magna Charta. (*Cheers*) It is thus amply demonstrated, Gentlemen, that what was intended to be granted, and what was granted, was a Permanent Settlement fixing the principles and rates of assessment in perpetuity and for ever. Nay, the assessment then fixed still continues unaltered according to the letter and spirit of the pledge, and the rates then fixed are applied even at the present day when waste lands are newly brought under cultivation, even though prices have since risen high at varying periods. This is accounted for by the fact that in fixing the commutation value in 1805 a very wide margin was left for any probable rise in prices for some succeeding years. Nevertheless, and in the face of the pledge already made, Government has determined to revise the existing assessment in spite of the repeated protests and representations of the people and a scheme of settlement is at the present moment awaiting the orders of the local Government. I may add that according to this scheme, the existing revenue in three typical Taluqs of the District under wet, dry, and garden lands will be increased by 95 per cent., 49 per cent. and 335 pei cent. respectively, resulting in an aggregate increase of over 15 lakhs whilst their present revenue is only 10½ lakhs. (*Shame*)

It is also noteworthy that Government has adopted these rates of assessment as the basis of calculation in permanently disposing of lands escheated to the State, and that several capitalists have, relying on the said Proclamation, invested large sums of money in effecting improvements on lands which at the time of revision it is intended to tax in violation of all rules on the subject.

Under such circumstances, I have no hesitation in characterizing the present attempt to revise the existing taxes as a gross breach of faith, and an illegal and unwarrantod interference with the rights of private property. (*Cheers*) You will thus see, Gentlemen, that so far as my own district is concerned, Government, in the first instance, is not only guilty of the charge of not extending the concession so humanely granted by the Supreme Government fully a generation ago, even though all the conditions have been satisfactorily fulfilled, but is committing a sadder breach of faith in revoking a Permanent Settlement already granted. (*Shame*)

Gentlemen, let us grant for a moment for the sake of argument that the Settlement already made in 1805 is not a permanent and unalterable one Then the question arises whether the time has not arrived for extending to our district the concession of a permanent fixture of land-tax in pursuance of the policy adopted in the Despatches of 1862 and 1865. I can emphatically assert that the Malabar district satisfies all the conditions necessary to justify the introduction of a Settlement in perpetuity. More than four-fifths of the cultivable area is under cultivation, as the latest statistics prove, and all the main Railway lines and feeders have been completed or are under construction with every prospect of completion before the settlement of the district becomes an accomplished fact. There are no Government Irrigation Works in the district nor will there ever be any such works. (*Hear, hear*)

I fear that most of what I have told you now refers particularly to my district, Malabar, and my only explanation for so doing is, as I have conclusively shown, that in this particular case Government is revoking a Permanent Settlement already granted. I have already told you, in common with the previous speakers on the subject, how beneficial it is to fix the land tax in perpetuity and forever No one can deny that it is calculated to accelerate

Second Day.

Resolution II.
Land Question.

Mana Vikrama Raja.

the development of the resources of India and to ensure in the highest degree the welfare and contentment of all classes of Her Majesty's subjects. Its advantages have without doubt been considered sufficiently important to have justified incurring the risk, if any, of the loss of a prospective revenue, to say nothing of the security to property which it unquestionably affords. *(Cheers)*

For these reasons I have much pleasure in supporting the important proposition now before you, which I trust you will unanimously adopt. *(Loud Cheers)*

Mr. C. V. Naidu.

Mr. C. V. Naidu :—Mr. President and Brother Delegates, following my learned predecessors in the matter of this Resolution, the proposer, the seconder and the supporters of this sadly needed Resolution it would be superfluous on my part to venture any further remarks advocating its enthusiastic adoption. The heart strongly beats in every bosom, and urges every one to at least open his lips and utter such few words, as may prove commendable to your kindest appreciation. I hail from the Central Provinces, and as duty demands it I ought to speak at least a few words to show to you, Gentlemen, how badly we are really treated in the Central Provinces in respect of this Resolution. In the Central Provinces within the past four decades there have been three settlements. Invariably we have had during the last two settlements a fixity of duration that was 30 years at a time ; but most sadly during the present settlement, most astonishingly, and, I must say most unwarrantably they are going shamefully to reduce the fixity of tenure from thirty years. *(Shame)* They are going backwards to twenty and fifteen, instead of progressing ; when according to the time of civilisation we ought to be going onwards rather than backwards. Probably there are a few of the sister Provinces represented here who are in the same category as my own province—that is even if the assessment and the tax had surpassed the human conception because the Government does not think it its honorable duty to pry into the secrets of the resources of this country ; yet, at a most haphazard step, it goes on to assess according to its whims. My province is taxed at the rate of 65 per cent., though you know and you fully know according to Lord Ripon's despatches, that whenever there must be a permanent Settlement, it must not be more than fifty per cent. ; but in our backward province, our tax comes to 65 or 70 per cent. So it is also a shameful undertaking on the part of Government not to consult the comforts or the convenience of each. A word or two, if I am within my limits, I wish to say in regard to the amendment of my friend Capt. Banon. *(Hear, hear)*

The President :—That is out of order as the amendment has fallen through.

Mr. Naidu :—I have been specially asked by my friends to express on their behalf the views of the rest of the Presidency in regard to the amendment.

The President :—No, no. You must not deal with that.

Mr. Naidu :—I yield to your dictum and proceed. Gentlemen, I have nothing further to add than to recommend the Resolution to your unanimous acceptance. *(Cheers)*

Mr. Peter Paul Pillai.

Mr. Peter Paul Pillai :— Mr. President and Brother Delegates, I had the honour of moving this very resolution at the Congress held at Lahore last year, and to be the seconder of the same resolution concerning the same question of permanent settlement in the Congress held at Allahabad the year before last. Without repeating the remarks that I made on the previous occasions, I would confine myself to the consideration of the arguments adduced by the opponents of the permanant Settlement. Among the opponents, we have that conspicuous personage. Sir William Hunter. There are three important arguments adduced by the opponents of the Permanent Settlement and by those who would undo the Settlement already granted to certain estates in the Madras Presidency and the estates in Bengal. Here I would correct the misapprehension of some of the previous speakers who spoke as if there were no Permanent Settlement in this part of India ; on the contrary, there are estates whose area is somewhere about thirty thousand square miles under a Permanent Settlement granted in

1802. The three arguments adduced by the opponents of the Permanent Settlement are, firstly, that it is unjust to tax one part of the Presidency more than the others; secondly—and on this point we have a note by Mr. Dadabhai Naoroji (*Cheers*)—that a permanency of tenure which deprives the State, that is the community, of the benefit of the unearned increment caused by the action of the community and not by any action of the landlord, is now being most energetically contested; and, thirdly—as was urged upon the introduction of the Proprietary Estates Village Service Bill into the Madras Legislative Council—that Government is justified in imposing laws for the good of the country, which the Zemindars are bouud to accept even to the extent of paying the taxation introduced in addition to the taxation fixed at the time of the Permanent Settlement. These are the three important arguments, that I would consider. With regard to the rate of taxation, according to the correct statements of the Court of Wards who have the accurate and correct accounts of the estates under their management, the average income of an estate under the management of the Court of Wards is 31·8 per cent. of the gross income. Now we find that the collection of rent or revenue while the estates are under the management of the Court of Wards is much larger than when the estates are managed by the proprietors themselves without the advantage of having the Officials to collect the revenue; again we find that the local cess is levied to the extent of 6¼ per cent. to enhance the land revenue—you may call it local cess or any other cess, but it is a direct enchancement of land revenue—and so we find that on the whole the land revenue paid by Zemindars in this Presidency may be put down at 50 per cent. of the gross income. In Bengal, from what I hear, the average *peishcush* in proportion to the gross income is 22 per cent., and with local and Public Works cesses, and arrears of uncollected rents the percentage may be 40; and so we find that the permanently settled estates after all are not lightly taxed. At the time of the Permanent Settlement, the Bengal Estates were assessed at the rate of 90 per cent. of the gross income, whereas in Madras the percentage is 66 per cent. of the net income; on these estates the rate of assessment was very enormous at the beginning of the century, so much so that on account of the inability of the Zemindars to pay a large proportion of the revenue, several Zemindaris were sold or resumed; and so we find that these were not lightly assessed. In maintaining the contrary Sir William Hunter is not quite consistent. In reading his famous work "What England has done for India," I met with the statement that the rate of taxation of the ryot is 7 per cent. on his income. Being a small ryot myself, I was astonished to find the data upon which Sir W. Hunter came to this monstrous conclusion. From my experience as a ryot, I paid 50 per cent. for some years and in others more than cent. per cent. of the income I derived. I had lately to write to the Tahsildar of my place regarding certain difficulties owing to which for the past five years I had not been able to derive a single grain out of my lands. Difficulties have been created in the cultivation of my land, so that after all, the rate of assessment of Zemindari estates is not so light as it is misrepresented to be. Are the ryots of the other provinces complaining of the comparatively light taxation of the Bengal and Madras Zemindars? I have never come across any complaint made by the ryot population. On the contrary, they find it a calamity and a national grievance of the gravest character that large proprietors should become extinct and ruined; and not only that, but that the Zemindars, Landlords, and Native Princes should become the refuges or asylums of the distressed population in British territories by a large patronage and by liberal charity. With these remarks I resume my seat. (*Hear, hear*)

Mr. S. A. Saminatha Iyer.

Mr. S. A. Saminatha Iyer:—Mr. President, Gentlemen and Brother Delegates—I am now called upon to support the proposition which has been moved so ably, and seconded so exhaustively, by gentlemen from Bengal and Bombay, and supported by my honorable friend Mr. K. Kalyanasundram Iyer, of Tanjore. I come from the same district, and I have the same grievance to complain of—namely, the recent Settlement that has been introduced into the district of Tanjore. The ground has been traversed so ably and so exhaustively by my friend, that I shall be tiring you by going over that same ground; so I shall content myself by referring to a few facts which have not been touched upon by him. I lave been, from the very commencement of the settlement operations in that district, connected with the movement of the people objecting to the mode of operation carried on by the Settlement Department. (*Cheers*) From time to time the Tanjore People's Association was watching the manner in which the Settlement operations were carried on by the Settlement Department. The defects were pointed out, but the gentlemen who pointed out those defects, because they happened in a manner to be connected with the Government Department, were, in fact, found fault with for pointing out the real defects in the operation of that department. (*Shame*) Because they aie Government Officials, surely they do not lose the right which a ryot possesses—to object to the mode of operation of the Settlement Department. (*Hear, hear*) They have two capacities, one the official capacity and the other the capacity of Mirasidars. When there is a real grievance why should their mouth be shut? Why should they not honestly complain of the way in which their lands are being assessed by the Settlement Depaitment? (*Cheers*) Wher the Settlement Commissioner recommended an increase of nearly 18½ lakhs of Rupees over the 41 lakhs now levied from the people of Tanjore, loud complaints were made. And what was the result? The Settlement Commissioner himself had to revise his figures, had to reduce the amount by 4 lakhs. Not satisfied with this, not satisfied with the way in which this 14½ lakhs was arrived at, memorials were prepared and submitted for consideration to Government, with the result that the Board of Revenue who had to consider the proposals of the Commissioner thought it advisable to cut down the figure by 2 lakhs. They arbitrarily cut it down by 2 lakhs, and no consideration was paid to our representation—I say so advisably, because had all our representations been fully considered, instead of 2 lakhs they must have cut down 7 lakhs. (*Hear, hear*)

We do not at all grudge an increase of revenue to Government; we are loyal subjects of Her Gracious Majesty; we are willing to come forward and help Government by contributing our mite when there is really a demand for increase of taxation. (*Cheers*) Gentlemen, you will find that, not satisfied with the Board's decision, we waited upon His Excellency Lord Wenlock in a deputation, and a most gracious and kind hearing was granted to us by His Excellency. Our grievances were listened to with an amount of patience which almost surprised us. Many of our complaints were considered, not only by his Excellency, but also by the first member of Council, Mr. H. E. Stokes, to be well founded, and our expectations were raised. We thought that the 14½ lakhs recommended by the Board of Revenue would be cut down by 7 lakhs, as we were justly entitled to expect such a reduction. Hopes were created in us and not vainly, because they fully realised that all our recommendations were founded upon solid facts; and if a decision had been given then and there, the result would have been favourable to us. Time was taken; a month elapsed; and Settlement and other officers had a conference with His Excellency (*Shame*); with the result that instead of giving us what we were justly expecting at the hands of Government, we were given a lakh (*Shame*), a mere pittance, not sufficient to alleviate the misery of millions of people that were subjected to it. (*Shame*) That is the way we are dealt with, under the Government of His Excellency Lord Wenlock, whom we expected to deal with agricultural matters in a liberal spirit, judging from the address which he delivered when he was appointed Governor of Madras. Another point I wish to touch upon in this connection is this: One argument advanced in favour of the increase now imposed upon the Tanjore Mirasidars is, that the price of land in the Tanjore district has risen, and is rising; while the fact that the people are even now willing, with the increase that the Government has imposed upon land revenue, to pay a high price for the lands in their district is said to be an indication of the productiveness of the soil of their district. I say "No!", emphatically "No!". Tanjorians as a class are a home-loving people, a people who are almost all of them agriculturalists; they have no other means of investing their capital; they cannot

Resolution II. Land Question.

Mr. S. A. Saminatha Iyer.

take, and will not take, to other modes of investment; they have a predilection for investing their money in landed property; and though the profit they derive from landed property is very small, they are still prepared to pay high prices for the land in their district. That is the only reason why high prices are still kept up notwithstanding the prohibitive assessment that Government has imposed on that district. If, therefore, the Permanent Settlement were to be introduced all through India, and if Tanjore should be one of those favoured districts to which this would be extended, it will be a great blessing which will be conferred not only on the Tanjorians but also on the other districts subject to this same Ryotwari Settlement. It is not Tanjore alone that has been subjected to this revision of assessment. Government having found that they have made a profit, and a very great profit indeed, by the revision of assessment in the Tanjore district, have extended their Settlement Operations to the unfortunate people of Trichinopoly, and from Trichinopoly they intend to proceed to Malabar, and then to Godavery and Kristna, and then to Madura and Tinnevelly. We fully sympathise with the inhabitants of those districts. Because Tanjore was first settled, and a large increase has been derived, it is not right that Government should think that the other districts are equally capable of bearing the increase which Tanjore has been thought capable of bearing. Under these circumstances, I most heartily support the proposition that has now been brought before you for your acceptance, and I trust that with one unanimous voice, you will accept this Resolution. (*Cheers*)

Mr. Sarvakuttikay then addressed the meeting in Malayalam, his remarks meeting with frequent applause.

The President:—The second resolution has been properly moved, seconded and supported. I now put it to the meeting. Those in favour of this Resolution say "Aye." (*Voices*, All! All!)

The Resolution was passed unanimously.

The President:—I now call upon Mr. Seymour Keay to move the next Resolution.

Resolution III. Poverty of India.

Mr. Seymour Keay.

Mr. Seymour Keay, M.P., who was received with enthusiastic cheers, said:—Mr. President, Fellow-Delegates, Ladies and Gentlemen, I do not think that there is any apology necessary on my part in coming before you to-day for the purpose of moving a resolution which I must say, from my own point of view, and after the large amount of study which I have devoted to the subject, I consider to be not of less importance than any other resolution which is on the programme of this vast assembly. (*Cheers*) The resolution which I have to propose is as follows:—

> "That this Congress, concurring in the views set forth in previous Congresses, affirms:—That fully fifty millions of the population, a number yearly increasing, are dragging out a miserable existence on the verge of starvation, and that in every decade, several millions actually perish by starvation; and humbly urges, once more, that immediate steps be taken to remedy this calamitous state of affairs."

I have said, Gentlemen, that I think no apology is necessary, and I think that you will all admit that this is the case when it is remembered that we are at this moment speaking on behalf of the people of an Empire consisting of no less than two hundred and eighty seven millions of human beings, that that Empire's population actually consists of no less than $\frac{4}{5}$ths of the inhabitants of the whole British Empire, and that the population with which we are now dealing constitutes no less than $\frac{1}{6}$th part of the entire human race itself. (*Hear, hear*) I say that during 32 years of close personal intercourse with the masses of the people in this country, the conviction has long ago been forced upon me that, although, as we know, we have in the Government of India a great Government, which has done much good, and which no doubt desires to do a great deal more, yet at the same time it is at this

**Second Day.**

Resolution III. Poverty of India.

Mr. Seymour Keay.

enormous disadvantage, that it is, and from its nature, must be, an alien Government, and that it must, as an alien Government, have this enormous drawback, namely, that it must be tremendously expensive as compared with the cost of any indigenous Government. (*Hear, hear*) What I hold is this, and what I ask you, with the vast knowledge which you, the delegates here present, bring to bear upon this question, to support me in saying, is this:—that this enormous drawback of expensiveness has caused, and is now causing, the people not to get richer and richer as they ought to do, but the great masses of them to become poorer and poorer every year (*Shame*), until at this moment there is a very large section of the population which is actually continually verging upon the point of starvation even in the midst of years of plenty. Now, Gentlemen, it was for this reason and with these convictions that we made a strong effort in the closing hours of our last session of Parliament, and brought forward a Resolution in the sense of the remarks which I have now addressed to you. We brought forward a Resolution demanding that an enquiry should be instituted into the condition and the wants of the people of India, and their ability to sustain the present enormous cost of Government. (*Cheers*) Well, Gentlemen, what was the result? We were met on the floor of the House of Commons by the official apologists in their usual strong phalanx of opposition to all enquiry whatsoever. I will give you a few words presently from the mouth of one of these official apologists, but at this stage and in now moving before you this resolution, I will at once proceed to give you a few of the hard and miserable facts on which our present action is founded. I hope that in doing so, we may be able to prove to ourselves and to the English Parliament and people also, that there is positive danger to the frame-work of the Government of India itself (*Cheers*), not from our speaking out as I am speaking to you to day, but from our own and their silence (*Cheers*), if they continue to insist upon burking all enquiry as they are attempting to do at the present moment (*Hear, hear*). In the first place, Gentlemen, allow me to give you a general summary of a Parliamentary return which I was able to obtain on my motion three years ago. It is a return showing respectively the number and emoluments of the European and the Native officers employed in the Indian Government, receiving pay of Rs. 1,000 a year and upwards. That return shows that while, if you exclude the rank and file of the European soldiers, there are only 70,000 Europeans in the whole of this vast country yet, of these 70,000 Europeans no less than 28,000 hold Government posts worth over Rs. 1,000 a year. What is the total of their pay? These 28,000 Europeans draw as pay the enormous sum of no less than 15½ crores of Rupees a year! Worse still Gentlemen, the return shows that of these 28,000 Europeans, no less than 33 per cent. that is to say ⅓rd part of the whole, although they are quartered upon your revenues, reside not in India but in England (*Hear, hear*)! In other words, they are absolutely non-effective for your Government. And the amount of pay or rather pension which these absentees receive comes actually to 6 crores of Rupees at this moment every year (*Shame*); and it is growing still! What country can go on standing that? On the other hand, we have the other page of the Return. We have there got a statement as to the Natives who receive pay from the Government of India exceeding Rs. 1,000 a year. Well I have already mentioned that there are only 70,000 Europeans, but there are not only 70,000 of you. There are 287 millions of you the natives of India. Yet of the whole 287 millions of Natives, there are only 17,000 persons employed in the whole Empire at a pay of over Rs. 1,000 a year (*Shame*). What do these 17,000 draw? These 17,000 draw actually only 3 crores of Rupees amongst the whole of them. In other words, what you have got is this:—the absentee Europeans actually draw from the revenues of your country more than double the whole amount of the whole salary of the whole of the Natives who are allowed to enter into the administration of their own country (*Shame*)! Now, Gentlemen, let us turn to the other side of the medal, and let us contemplate for a little the condition of those people who have to pay the enormous sums which I have just described. The other day, in August last, in the House of Commons, the Government officers were put up to say that any such enquiry into the condition of the people as we wanted was impossi-

Second Day.

Resolution III.
Poverty of India.

Mr. Seymour Keay.

ble. We met them in this wise. We pointed out that seven years ago the Government of India themselves of their motion and for their own purposes actually took upon themselves to make just such an enquiry as we asked for. But how was that enquiry carried out? It was actually done in the Secret Department (*Shame*!) I do not know why the starvation of scores of millions of people should be supposed to be an official secret. (*Laughter*). Anyhow, what did the Government of India do on that occasion? At one time a very high and distinguished officer of the Government of India, Sir William Hunter, then Director-General of Statistics at Calcutta, had published a little book called "England's Work in India". In that book he had made a statement to the effect that 40 millions of the people of India go through life upon insufficient food even in years of plenty. This statement went abroad. It was circulated extensively in England, and commented upon largely in the public press and in the House of Commons. The Government of India thought that it was desirable that, if possible, they should get statistics and reports from their own subordinate officers, with the object of enabling them to deny the truth of that statement. They did this, as I have said in the Secret Department. They issued a confidential circular to all the Local Governments and Administrations; and if it were not for the responsibility which lies on me to tell you the truth, I would be ashamed to go on and tell you the next step which the Government of India took (*Laughter*). The next step that the Government of India took, in order to get Reports from their officers in favour of their view, was to deliberately vitiate the whole case by absolutely misquoting Sir W. Hunter in this confidential circular. (*Shame*) Sir William Hunter had said that 40 millions, that is about $\frac{1}{6}$th part of the population, go through life upon insufficient food. What did the Government of India ask of their Governors and Lieutenant-Governors and Administrators? They asked whether it was true, or only partially true, that the greater part of the population of India go through life on insufficient food. Comment is needless, Gentlemen. You know what this would be called, if it were done in private life. You know that no one would have dared to do it, except in the Secret Department, of the Government of India. (*Shame*) Furthermore, each Government was told by the Government of India in the official circular that to get evidence in the matter, they should carefully select for the enquiry officers of judgment and discretion. (*Laughter*) They did appoint officers of judgment and discretion, and, of course, they got a great many replies tinged with the roseate hue which is always visible on the surface of all official records which are compiled by the orders of the Government of India. But what I have to say to you is, that, even in spite of all this careful warning, even in spite of all this careful misleading, the truth actually found its way even into these confidential replies. (*Cheers*) I will only give you three or four pictures drawn from this official, though confidential source, the confidential nature of which we were enabled with the greatest difficulty to break through by threatening the late Under-Secretary of State for India, Sir John Gorst, with untold difficulties and opposition unless he put the Blue Books into our hands. (*Cheers*) He put them into our hands as a means of keeping us quiet because if he had not done so, he knew that he would have fared worse. (*Shame*) You will observe from this, that I have every title to use these facts now, as I did last August in the House of Commons. (*Hear, hear*).

The first picture that I shall lay before you is a Census taken of twelve villages in the district of Rampore. In these twelve villages the population was found to consist of 2,000 persons. Of these, 1,600 were cultivators and the remaining 400 were labourers. What did the Deputy Commissioner, a high Officer of the Government of India, find on the most careful examination, and on an Industrial Survey of the whole of these twelve villages scattered in different parts of Rampore? He found that, after laying aside the rent and cost of cultivation, the whole amount left for the support of the people came only to Rs. 16 a year for the cultivator and Rs. 13 a year for the labourer. The next case is from the Report of the Commissioner of Rai Bareily, with a population of 1,000,000 souls. This officer took

13

**Second Day.**

Resolution III.
Poverty of India.

Mr. Seymour Keay.

a census of thirty average families scattered throughout the whole of that populous district and he found that these thirty families consisted of 173 persons. He found that the gross crop amounted to the value of Rs. 2,800. He also found that for seed and for hired labour and for 25 per cent. interest to the usurer, there had been paid by these 173 persons the amount of Rs. 600, and that the rent which they had to pay amounted to Rs. 1,080. The result was that deducting this Rs. 1,680 from the Rs. 2,800, the balance for the sustenance of these villagers and their families amounted to Rs. 1,120. In other words these 173 persons, man, woman and child had each an amount of 6½ rupees a year for their support! (*Shame*). Well then, it may be asked, how did these people live at all? I shall not need to answer that question to you. (*Hear, hear*).

You well know that the capital of the country is being eaten into, and that the usurer is being applied to, because the ground will not give sufficient sustenance; and now the usurer's merciless demands have to be satisfied in addition to the demands of Government. But there was another small item to add to the Rs. 6½ per head a year. This pains-taking and zealous officer goes further, and gives us particulars showing how this additional item was made up. It was due to the fact that these 173 persons had been able to get work outside the land, and by that and other means had earned a sum of Rs. 750 amongst them altogether. This officer actually showed how this Rs. 750 was made up, and here are some of the items recorded in his report, which you delegates from India generally will well under stand. It is actually from sources such as these that the revenues of a great Government are collected.

| | Rs. | A. | P. |
|---|---|---|---|
| Weaving 5 pieces of cloth... ... ... ... ... | 1 | 0 | 0 |
| Salary paid to the village watchman ... ... ... | 4 | 0 | 0 |
| Sold the skin of a dead bullock ... ... ... ... | 2 | 0 | 0 |
| Sold butter during the year ... ... ... ... | 3 | 0 | 0 |
| Made 10 woollen blankets ... ... ... ... | 10 | 0 | 0 |
| Received a present from his brother ... ... ... | 50 | 0 | 0 |
| Earned by carrying palanquins ... ... ... ... | 3 | 0 | 0 |
| Thatching houses during the year ... ... ... ... | 7 | 0 | 0 |
| A boy eleven years old receives for his labour (per day) ... | 0 | 1 | 0 |
| Wife acts as midwife to the village, and brings the husband (per annum) .. ... ... ... ... ... | 6 | 0 | 0 |

The result was that, besides the Rs. 6½ each earned on the land they were able scrape together another Rs. 4 each from sources off the land; and from these two combined sources of income they were actually able to obtain as much for their sustenance as Rs. 10½ every year. And this was only after pouring into the Government treasury every earning which had been made by every man, woman and child in the whole of the villages.

The next picture which I have to offer for your view relates to a part of the Fyzabad district, with a population of 1,000 000. Major Anson was the Deputy Commissioner of that district. I do not know where he is now. Somebody may tell us that (*A voice*, "Korandumpore"), I should be glad to hear that he has not been sent to some pestilential climate (*Laughter*) This zealous officer went deeper still into the matter. He actually made out with the greatest pains and care a regular tabular statement of the different degrees of starvation of the inhabitants of his district. He divided for that purpose the whole population into six classes. We are not talking now of 173 persons, not of 2,000 persons, we are not talking merely of a census of twelve villages, but we are talking of the best estimate which Major Anson could form of the condition of the whole population of his district put together He divides the population, as I have said, into six classes, and the classes are these. Of course, first of all there is the cultivator or farmer, then the farm labourer, the petty dealer, the village artisan, the domestic servant, and the corn dealer. Major Anson puts down in this table of his, the amount of sustenance that each of these classes gets during the year. In the first place he starts from what is the official basis of calculation. He starts on the datum that 2 lbs. weight of dry grain or pulse daily is the minimum required for the healthy life of an adult engaged in agricultural pursuits—the famous 2 lbs. ration in fact (*Laughter*). The cultivator, he proves, gets $\frac{5}{8}$ths of 2 lbs.; that is, he is at the top of the tree. The cultivator himself does not get 2 lbs., but he gets only $\frac{5}{8}$ths thereof in the whole year, even during years of plenty. The farm labourer gets $\frac{3}{8}$ths of 2 lbs.—that is, in other words, he has to carry on his laborious calling upon less than half of the 2 lbs ration. The day labourer is better off, he gets $\frac{2}{3}$rds of 2 lbs. The petty dealer is a little richer still and gets $\frac{3}{4}$ths of 2 lbs. The village artisan and the domestic servant actually revel in luxury upon 2 lbs. of dry grain a day (*Laughter*). The corn dealer who is a single person is actually the only living individual in the whole district who gets more than 2 lbs of dry grain a day. All the others are actually maintaining bare life upon 2 lbs. or wasting away in slow starvation upon less than 2 lbs. And even this result is shown to have been arrived at after throwing into the gulf every earning of every man, woman and child who lives upon the soil.

The last picture which I shall give you consists of a most important piece of evidence furnished by the Chief Commissioner of the Fyzabad district, with a population as I have said of 1,000,000. That officer refers the Government to their own Education Reports. They had been talking about educating the people, and he refers them to their own Education Report to shew that education is absolutely impossible in any shape or form amongst these cultivators or their families, for the simple reason that every child, from the time it begins to toddle, has to be sent out to work in the fields, for the purpose of adding to the attenuated incomes of the parents, in the manner I have described. (*Shame*). He declares that if a cultivator in his district were to send his child to school, he would simply lose 30 per cent. of the whole of the little income on which he manages to keep himself and his family from the verge of starvation. The Commissioner then adds his own opinion. He says "It has been "calculated that about 60 per cent.—mark, 60 per cent.—of the entire population are sunk in "such abject poverty that, unless the small earnings of child labour are added to the general "stock by which the family is kept alive, some members of the family must starve." Then he sums up in these words. "With the bulk of these people education would be synonymous with starvation." This outspoken officer goes still further, and refers the Government of India to a published work of reference, the Oudh Gazetteer. He shews from that work that no less than one half of the population of those districts are compelled to sell themselves into a sort of slavery, merely for the purpose of getting food. I think the bond slave contract is called "Sewuk." No doubt the Delegates from Oudh will be able to understand it. I will quote to you the words of this distinguished officer on this woeful subject. He says "As every bond slave is a bankrupt, and as the bond slaves form a large proportion of "the whole, it may be gathered that the agricultural classes are now deeply embarrassed. "The only motive for entering into the bond slave contract is want of food and that "this is an increasing motive is shewn by the increasing number of bond slaves." He then adds, "every second man met with in the fertile plains of Hisampur is now a bond slave" What then does this outspoken officer proceed to do? At the close of his letter to the Government, he calls upon them to do exactly what we in the House of Commons last August called upon the Government to do, and what I hope this Congress will now call upon the Government to do. This Commissioner of Fyzabad closes, I say, by begging and praying of the Government of India to appoint strong Commissions so that further enquiries may be made and a prompt line of action mapped out. How did the Government of India receive these statements from these Officers, which I have been giving to you? How did they receive the recommendation to appoint Commissions and to map out a line of action which was so earnestly

**Second Day.**

Resolution III.
Poverty of India.

Mr. Seymour Keay.

put before them by their own distinguished officer? Did they proceed to appoint strong Commissions to investigate the state of the affairs of these suffering millions? No; they collected all these papers together; they labelled them "confidential" in red letters, and they buried them in the cellars under the Government Offices in Calcutta. (*Shame*) in the hopes that they would never be heard of more. I have shewn you, therefore, that the Government first tried to mislead these officers, and that when they failed in doing so and when they got replies which they did not want, they absolutely refused to carry out the recommendations of their own officers and burked the whole thing in the most dishonest manner. Is it not scandalous that in this country, with the publicity which is enjoyed in regard to official matters generally the misery of millions of our fellow subjects should be held to be an official secret at all? I want to know why it should not rather be proclaimed upon the housetops, for the very purpose of ensuring that effective steps should be taken to remove the cause and to remedy the evil. Yet what happens? Simple terror seizes them whenever they hear us in Parliament standing up and demanding a Parliamentary or any other kind of enquiry. I shall prove this most conclusively, I think, by giving you what I consider to be a most damning indictment of this whole system of suppression of evidence by one of their own leading officials, no less a man than Sir Louis Malet who was then permanent Under Secretary of State for India. What did he say about this question of an enquiry into the economic wants of India? In an official minute, which is published in an appendix to the Famine Blue Books, you will find a quotation in which he makes this most extraordinary revelation against his own fellows in the Secretary of State's Council. He says "If there is any one thing which is wanting in any "investigation of Indian problems, it is an approach to trustworthy and generally accepted "facts. Now I am compelled to say that since I have been connected with the India Office I "have found a strong repugnance to the adoption of any adequate measures for the collection "of a comprehensive and well digested set of facts." Then he concludes with this remarkable statement—"The only occasion on which I had the misfortune of encountering the vehement "opposition of some members of the Council was in my advocacy of Dr. Forbes Watson's "proposals for an Industrial Survey of India." Why was it, I ask, that Sir Louis Malet found that all his colleagues joined together against him in the India Council for the purpose of resisting an Industrial Survey of India? Why, I ask, do they resist it still? There is only one answer. It is simply this:—They well know that such an Industrial Survey would show such an appalling picture of poverty and misery now existing under their administration, that upon the revelation of the heart-rending suffering of scores of millions of helpless human beings the British nation would rise up as one man and overturn their entire system. (*Loud Cheers*) Well, Gentlemen, as I have already said, I quoted some of these facts last August in the House of Commons. It was obvious that Sir Richard Temple, who was sitting opposite me, intended to follow me in the debate. Accordingly, I challenged him directly to traverse these terrible facts, and I said that when I sat down if he got up and gave even any colourable reply, or any fair or reasonable reply, to the facts which I had adduced, he would do the most unusual thing that an official apologist had done. I challenged him to do this, but I at the same time added that I knew that he would not (*Laughter*). Well, thus conjured, he followed me in the debate; but what did he say? I call your special attention to this, because I think it proves, at all events, that in the House of Commons on that occasion we did score one considerable point against men who, like him, used to be trusted by the House of Commons, because forsooth! they had worn their official spectacles so long that they never failed to carry them about with them in their pockets. I will tell you what Sir Richard Temple was driven to say, and I will give you his precise words. He said, in direct and immediate answer to the statements that I had made, "Those sorts of calculations are not worth the paper they are written "on, or even the breath with which they are uttered. The officials put an arbitrary figure for "the supposed produce of land and then put their own value upon it." Mark the word "officials." They are all high officers of Government who served along with him as his own colleagues. He further says "The whole data are all supposititious, and then they draw out "deductions which are impossible; what is the use of my detaining the House by going into "such ridiculous figures as these? These supposed facts are not facts at all. All that the "Honorable Gentleman can possibly know is that there are so many people and that there are "so many acres of ground. These figures are simply tabular statements of particular theories. "I should say they are in fact shams, delusions, and snares which are presented to the House." (*Shame*)

Here indeed was a curious rôle that I had to take up I fear, Gentlemen, that the Chairman will be sounding his gong (*Voices* "Go on," "Go on,") I would not detain you a minute but for the fact that I have a few important things yet to tell you. However I shall be very brief. Here was I coming forward as I now come forward in defence of the characters of these honorable men, these high European officials of the Government of India. I came forward and said then what I say now; I denied then, and I deny now, that there is anything of the character of exceptional dishonesty among any class of European servants of Government. (*Cheers*) My belief is, and I distinctly say as I said then, that Indian officers are neither better nor worse than ordinary human beings. (*Laughter*) When an ordinary human being has no check upon him, there is no doubt that that human being will not always show the best side of his character. But here was an official apologist, Sir Richard Temple, actually coming forward on the floor of the House of Commons itself, and saying that these his own colleagues and fellow servants were nothing but "Frauds" and "Cheats" and "Shams." I utterly repudiate such an outrageous doctrine. I make every allowance for the shortcomings of our Indian officials. Their position is one of great responsibility but with little check, as I have said, and it being such, they are not likely always to shew the better side of their nature. But you must remember their temptations. They have no inducement to turn aside and investigate as independent men, like you or I may have. They have the temptation to do the contrary. Their position is this; their official table groans under pleasant and costly viands, and as they sit there at the feast, they have no inducement to look aside to see whether or not there is a skeleton presiding at the banquet; they have no temptation to see if there is any mystic handwriting on the wall; on the contrary they look only at the dishes that are before them and they go on enjoying them to the best of their hearts' content. (*Cheers*) But in all this what I want to point out to you is this, that there is no exceptional dishonesty whatever. It is true that the mass of optimist officers do deceive their own Government, but that is only because they are themselves first thoroughly deceived. They are, as you know, transcendent optimists by their training in the Service from their youth up, and as such they are inclined to close their eyes to the despair and to the disaster which we, and all independent observers, see in perhaps the not far off future Gentlemen, I speak in a most responsible position in the presence of all you delegates, and I say from close personal observation of the agricultural classes in India that it is useless for anyone to deny, that biting adversity is now eating into the heart of the great mass of the agricultural population. As the struggle for life becomes harder and harder, a deep and sullen sense of wrong is stealing throughout the length and breadth of the land. It is not the result of any single incident. I can certify with all sureness that it is nothing of the nature of race hatred or antagonism of any kind whatsoever. What is it then? It is the noiseless but ever increasing growth of gradually accumulating pangs. It is the embitterment caused by the steady advance of pinching poverty; when the daily toil becomes more incessant and yet the out-turn becomes less and less every year from the over-cropped fields; when the little savings, hoarded perhaps for two generations, have to be dug up from the floor of the mud hut and handed over to the Revenue officer; when the scanty meal becomes scantier; when the little condiment eaten with the rice or the pulse has to be intermitted; when the bangle on the arm of wife or baby has to be taken off and sold, and its proceeds paid over to the Revenue Officer (*Shame*); when the marriage of the daughter has to be postponed until the

Second Day.

Resolution III.
Poverty of India.

Mr. Seymour Keay.

money-lender can be induced to advance the wherewithal. It is the sense of wrong and injustice felt, when the bread-winner is taken away from his home and imprisoned in the Civil Jail. It is the exasperation of a ruined family when the holding is confiscated for arrears of land tax, and when its occupant from that hour descends in the social scale, and ceasing to be a farmer, becomes a landless labourer. Gentlemen I will only add one word in conclusion. The only hope for India lies in bringing the real facts of this position before the English Parliament and people (*Hear, hear, and Cheers*), who, I assure you, have not at this moment the slightest conception of the real state of things. Once inform them of the truth, and I say, and I say it with all assurance, that the great heart of the English nation will grant you both speedy and effective remedy. (*Loud and long continued Cheers*)

The President :—We shall now adjourn for half an hour.

The Congress re-assembled at 3-45 p.m.

The President :—The third resolution will be seconded by Mr. Nundy.

Mr. Nundy.

Mr. Nundy :—Mr. President and Brother Delegates, after the able and exhaustive manner in which the honorable member who had charge of this resolution has dealt with this subject, I am sure you will not require a lengthy speech from me to commend the resolution to your acceptance. Such an array of facts and figures has been placed before you that I am sure they will carry conviction to your minds, that the condition of the rural population of India is indeed desperate, and that it is high time that something be done for them by the Government of India. I shall not trouble you with any further statistics, but I shall confine myself to a few facts having special reference to the provinces I come from, namely, the North-West Provinces. I am sorry I have not got the last Administration Report of the Government of the North-West Provinces. I tried my best to get it, but I could not. I would have read a few passages from it. From that you would have come to the conclusion either that the speaker who has just addressed you was romancing, or that the Administration Report considerably indulged in romance itself. Here of course I do not profess to give the very words. The purport of the Report was this :—That the condition of the rural population of the North-West Provinces had of late years considerably improved. Sir Charles Crosthwaite, who began his career in the North-West Provinces, and after a service of considerable length left for the Central Provinces, and then for Burmah, returned to his Province about a year and a half ago. In the first Report that he issued he congratulated the people in very strong and unmistakable terms that, during his absence of twelve years or so, their condition had considerably improved. Now, Gentlemen, you might ask how it is that statements relating to the same people should differ so strangely as does the account furnished to you by the previous speaker and that of the Administration report of the Government of the North-West Provinces. I submit that it is not that the Lieutenant-Governor has deliberately placed on record facts or opinions which he does not believe, but that his opportunity for ascertaining the real state of things, is very scanty indeed, and not very often availed of. There are two sources from which he can obtain information—one, from personal observation, and the other, from reports submitted to him by his subordinate officers, Collectors and Commissioners. When he is on tour, if he likes, he has certainly an opportunity for ascertaining what the position of the people is But you know, Gentlemen, what the tour of the Governor of a Province is. Surrounded as he is by officials, from the Commissioner down to a *Pasi*, it is almost impossible for him to come in contact with any of the people. It is very seldom indeed that he is able to make a personal visit to the villages and make a personal enquiry. He is entirely in the hands and under the guidance of officials. Certainly in some places where he goes he has addresses given to him, by members of the District Board or by members of the Municipal Committees. But what do these contain ? They are drawn up under the inspiration and under the direction of the official chairman, and simply set out the views of the officials themselves. (*Cheers*) My friends and myself from the North West Provinces were rather amused when we heard the previous speaker quote the remarks of the Commissioner of Fyzabad. Well, within the last year and a half Sir Charles Crosthwaite has been making a tour in certain portions of Oudh. He visited several places in the Fyzabad division, and in all those places addresses were given to him drawn up by members of the District Board, and by members of the Municipal Committees. Every one of these officials set out in glowing terms the fact that the country was becoming daily more and more prosperous, and that there was absolutely no ground whatever for grievances of any kind. The Lieutenant-Governor on several occasions made a reply congratulating the people upon the fact that the country was growing prosperous and that they were able to appreciate and recognise the real improvement in the condition of the country was becoming more and more prosperous every day.

Another source of information of which Governors can avail themselves is the reports furnished to them by the Collectors and Commissioners. Now, Gentlemen, you know there are District Officers and District Officers. There are some of them, especially those of seven or eight years' standing, as unfortunately most of our Collectors are, who are, as we may call them, more or less *shikaris*. So long as they can get their *shikar*, they are absolutely indifferent to, and they will not trouble themselves about, any other matter. There is also what is called the easy-going Collector, who thinks life too short for him to think of any thing beyond the daily routine of business. There is the ever-calculating Collector who has his eyes on the Commissionership. He makes it a point as far as possible to give such an account of the people as he thinks will coincide with the views of the Government under which he is serving, and you know very well that any Government would look with great distrust upon any of its officers who tried to make out a state of things which did not coincide with their own views. Those of my friends that come from the North-West Provinces will know of a case which occurred in the time of Sir John Cooper, where one of the District Officers persistently, and for a period of two years, I believe, submitted a series of reports commenting strongly on the administration of the country, and on the condition of the people. What was the result? The result was that he was sent away from the North-West Provinces to the Central Provinces! (*Shame! Shame!*) with a stigma on his name, and with a distinct understanding that he was never to become a Commissioner, although, I think, he was one of the cleverest European officers that ever came to this country. So the District Officer never became *pukka* Commissioner. Then again, Gentlemen, there are some officers who I am glad to say, are conscientious officers, and it is from the material offered by those officers that the previous speaker has quoted very largely. Gentlemen, I am not going to quote any further statistics. But there are one or two quotations I should like to give—they are very short ones—relating to the North-West Provinces, which will bear out the statement made by Sir William Hunter that nearly 40 millions of the people are on the verge of starvation and daily pass their lives with insufficient food. These reports sent by the Collectors were, thanks to the previous speaker, allowed to be published by the Government of India. As they were sent in response to a confidential circular, for a long time they did not see the light of day. I will just quote to you two paragraphs. One is about the province of Oudh which is now under the administration of the Lieutenant-Governor of the North-West Provinces. Speaking of Oudh, Mr. H. C. Irwin of the Bengal Civil Service says "The "great evil of rural Oudh is * * * the insufficiency of the produce of the land to main-"tain the population in comfort, after defraying rent and cost of cultivation. While this "is so, of what use is it for Government to devote its energy and its resources to anything "but direct action on the sources of the evil. While the millions suffer from chronic hunger it "would be as easy to make a pyramid stand upon its apex as to regenerate them by orna-"mental legislation or by anything but putting them beyond the ceaseless pressure of "physical want." And then Mr. Irwin winds up with the warning, "Let not the latter end

Second Day.

Resolution III. Poverty of India.

Mr. A. Nundy.

"of our rule in Oudh so wholly forget the beginning as to perpetuate and stereotype the "degradation of the cultivators, to remedy which we professedly annexed the country. The "Mutiny should have been treated as an interruption of our policy, charged indeed with grave "lessons worthy of being laid to heart, but not as a new revolution changing its aims and "objects. Let it not be said of us by the future historian, that with all the means in our hands "of raising the peasantry of Oudh from the squalid poverty and debasement which for centu-"ries past have been their lot, we ignobly suffered them to perish for mere want of enactment "that they should be saved".

Then the Collector of Shajahanpur writes to this effect :—

"The poorer classes eat only the coarsest and cheapest grains, and can eke out a "subsistence so long as these are procurable at not less than 14 seers to the Rupee"

Mr. Holderness writing of the Pilibhit District says :—

"That the landless labourer's condition is not all that could be desired. The united "earnings of a man, his wife and two children cannot be put at more than three Rupees "per month. When prices of food grains are moderate, work regular, and the health of the "household good, this income will enable the family to have one good meal a day, to keep a "thatched roof over their head, to buy cheap cotton clothing and occasionally a thin "blanket. The small cultivator is slightly better off but he has not always enough to cat or "sufficiently warm clothes."

"Mr. Harrington, Commissioner of Fyzabad, maintains that the assertion that a "large proportion of India suffers from a daily insufficiency of food is perfectly true as "regards a varying but always considerable proportion of the population for a considerable "part of the year in the greater part of India".

I think, Gentlemen, these quotations, coupled with those which we have already heard from the previous speaker, show from official lips what the actual condition of the rural population of India is. But it might be said that these reports were submitted in the year 1882, and that since then perhaps there has really been a change for the better. I will just state some facts which will show that it could not possibly be that their condition has improved since 1882. The settlement is now going on in the North-West Provinces. I do not desire to say anything on the question of the settlement, but what I say is this :—that the re-assessment has in some cases taken the form of an increase in the revenue from 50 to 100 per cent. I know this from my own personal experience of the district in which I live, where it has been increased from 75 to 100 per cent. This has naturally been followed by the Zemindars trying to increase the rents of the tenants. It would be impossible even for them to meet the Government demands if they did not increase the rent ; and many of them have asserted that, were it not that Zemindaris were ancestral property, they would rather give them up than pay the present rate of assessment. It cannot be said that within the last five years the settlement has contributed to the improvement of the condition of the rural population of the North-West Provinces. Then again, fifteen years ago, only in the large towns were there octroi duties, but now, under the orders of the Lieutenant-Governor, in almost every city with a population of from four to five thousand, cesses have commenced to be levied, and the cesses have been increased by 15 per cent. I do not know what is the case in other Provinces, but I must say it is simply scandalous as regards the nature of the articles on which this cess is levied. Fuel that is brought in, grass, vegetables and all other things that are articles of consumption of the poor are made subject to these cesses. That surely cannot contribute to any improvement in the condition of the poor. Another fact—(here the President struck the gong). One minute more and I shall have finished. This matter will form one of the subjects of discussion later on. The forest laws have been enacted in such a form that whereas ten or fifteen years back the Zemindars and the Villagers were allowed to graze their cattle in the forests, now these have become close preserves. I now hear from the villagers that it is very difficult indeed to get pasture for their cattle. These laws within the last five years have contributed to make the position of the people more difficult Then again, as you know, there is such a large export of corn from this country that of late years the prices have risen so high, especially in some districts of the North-West Provinces, that whereas thirty years ago grain was being sold at 2 maunds per Rupee, it is now sold at 22 seers per Rupee, while wheat which was sold at [illegible] maunds per Rupee, is now sold at 14 or 15 seers a Rupee. Thus, while, on the one hand, the income of the people is being considerably diminished, on the other hand, there is a considerable rise in the price of the articles of consumption. I am warned that it is time for me to stop and so I shall stop here. (*Hear, hear*)

Second Day.

Resolution III. Poverty of India.

MR. A. NUNDY

LALA MURLIDHAR.

LALA MURLIDHAR.—Mr. President, Ladies and Gentlemen—During the five minutes that are at my disposal I will make my last will and testament. (*Laughter*) The question of the poverty of India has been discussed. (*Voices, "Louder, Turn this side."*) Gentlemen, I am not going to distribute sweets. I am crying like an old man for bread. (*Laughter*) The poverty of my English language entitles me I think to speak on the poverty of India. (*Laughter*) "It is easier for a camel to pass through the eye of a needle than for a rich man to enter into the Kingdom of Heaven." If that precept were to be taken in its literal sense and accepted as Gospel truth, then I submit there is no happier country than India (*Laughter*) and no happier people than the Indians. (*Applause*) You should pity the rich people of England for the vast treasures of wealth they have hoarded and the numerous troops they have kept, and you should thank heaven that you have been placed in this desirable position, so that the doors of heaven have been opened to you while they have been shut against all the people of Europe. (*Laughter and Applause*) Why should you complain of the poverty of India? If you are to be possessed of riches and wealth there would be fear of being robbed by thieves and robbers. (*Laughter*) You have been saved the trouble and anxiety of hoarding riches, and you should lead the life of anchorites in the jungle as prescribed by the Shastras, and you should be content and happy with leading that life. (*Laughter and Cheers*) I deny that India is poor; on the contrary, I believe it is growing richer and richer every day. In support of my contention I will cite authorities which will be convincing, and which will silence the authority of the honourable Member of Parliament, the mover of this Resolution. Gentlemen, I cite the authority of the great and mighty Rajah of Benares, Rajah Siva Prasad (*Laughter and Cheers*), the authority of the mighty Rajah of Bhinga (*Laughter*) the authority of the ex-Nabob of Hyderabad. (*Laughter*) When India abounds with Patriots like these (*Laughter*) how can you say that India is growing poorer? You will see innumerable huts in place of a few palaces, you will see people crying by hundreds and thousands and millions. Then what more do you want? (*Laughter*) You are rich in the immensity of your poverty. (*Laughter and Cheers*) As for facts and figures why do you go to Sir William Hunter or any other authority? Go and see those figures in houses and see their squalid condition, pale and miserable, (*Hear, hear*) with no food to eat, and with no drink to take, and with no salt. Well then, is not that the condition of anchorites and holy people? What do you want more? Why do you ask Government for this or that? (*Laughter and Cheers*

Does this all really represent the poverty of India? With all the delegates in their gala dress, dressed in European style and having every article of clothing, can you possibly think that it lies in their mouths to say that their country is poor? Have not the officials undergone a considerable amount of sacrifice by throwing open the doors of heaven to you, compensating themselves therefore by the so-called Exchange Compensation Allowance? (*Loud and continued Cheers*) Then they have disencumbered you of the heavier burdens, they have taken away the troubles from you, they have asked you to lead a quiet life, to have no concern in public affairs nor to be bothered about them in any way. You can sit at home and do your work. They have left their castles in England and are here as sojourners.

Why should you complain when you lead such a happy and contented life? (*Laughter*) What! You are an ungrateful people. (*Laughter and Cheers*) Really you are. (*Laughter*) You ask to be admitted to the Government of your country? Why should you have all this bother-ation? (*Laughter*) Numerous troops have been employed to protect you and your lives. Numerous civil officials have taken the care off your shoulders. Then what do you want more? Litigation, which is a curse to the country, is eating into the [illegible]; you want the Government to do this and that; you want to reduce taxation; you cry that India is poor. Have you done your share of the work; have you contributed anything towards reducing the poverty of the country; have you established any manufactories; have you discarded European clothing; have you shown to the world that you are really feeling and working for the poor? If you go to their houses and partake of their wretched food and live as they do, shivering with cold at midnight in those miserable huts with naked bodies; then you will feel the pinching poverty; then you will really feel the suffering of the people. Until you place yourselves in the position of the poverty-stricken people you will not be able to say that India is your mother-land, that the people are poor, and that you advocate their cause. Do advocate their cause sincerely. Pledge yourselves to squat rather on the bare ground than to send for chairs from Austria, three thousand miles away, which cost you Rs. 5,000 Act as practical patriots and show by your life that you truly and sincerely feel for the poor; then, the sympathy of all the poor and the rulers of the land shall be yours, and your names shall be placed in history, and God will be immensely pleased with you for having done your work. (*Cheers*)

Gentlemen, the time for my dissolution is at hand. (*Laughter: Voices*, Go on, Go on) One practical suggestion I would like to make to the delegates assembled in this august hall, and that is, act zealously, sincerely and loyally in the most respectful manner; strive day and night to remove the dark portion that is eating into the vitals of the nation; feel sincerely for the poor, treat them as your brethren, and discard all luxury. For luxury is not the share of the poverty-stricken people; it is only the share of the people cursed because they cannot afford to give anything in charity; because they cannot build hospitals; because they cannot even worship God without wealth and riches—so say our Shastras, so say all the wise men both of the East and West. Acquire wealth by all honest means; spend it on charity and on the poor, and show by your words and deeds that you do really feel for the poor. (*Loud and long continued Cheers*)

Babu Bishnupada Chatterji.

Babu Bishnupada Chatterji:—Mr. President, Delegates and Gentlemen,—We all of us complain of the shortness of our lives, but the five minutes' life allotted to the supporter of a Congress resolution after the illustrious speakers who have preceded me seems to me to be unusually long. Gentlemen, in rising to support this resolution I do not offer any apology for the hoarseness of my voice, for has not a Congress delegate had to cry himself hoarse over this very same subject from year to year since the first Congress met in Bombay in 1885? But the language of the prayer is the same, and we all know that we have got to repeat our prayers every day of the year consisting of 365 days. What then is the great question The great question is, is India really impoverished? I answer the question in the affirmative, and to do so I rely upon the testimony of great men who have cared to open their lips and give us a bit of their minds. First of all, then, the idea was in the mind of Sir John Shore. The next man who got the idea was Mr. John Bright. The next man was Lord Lawrence, and then two ministers of the Government of India, Sir Evelyn Baring and Sir Auckland Colvin. Then we also have the testimony of men like Sir William Hunter, Sir William Wedderburn, and Sir Charles Elliott of Bengal; we also note that the Secretary of State for India, who may be styled the Czar of all the Indies, has himself admitted in 1886 that there is poverty among the people of India. I need hardly mention, Gentlemen, the name of Mr. Dadabhai Naoroji. (*Cheers*) The Government of India have stated in so many words that "there is evidence to show that in all parts of India there is a numerous population "which lives from hand to mouth (*Hear, hear*), is always in debt, does not save, and has little "or nothing to fall back upon in bad seasons." Sir Charles Elliott of Bengal says;—"I do not "hesitate to say that half of our agricultural population never know from year's end to year's "end what it is to have their hunger fully satisfied." Now, Gentlemen, this is direct evidence, and I might say, in the case of the Bengal Government direct evidence coupled with the local investigation of what are officially called "tours." Gentlemen, it is said that a confession, a voluntary confession, can bring home the guilt to an accused person. This is the evidence, Gentlemen, of hostile witnesses and most unwilling witnesses. But this is not all. The last remark comes from the head of a Government whose Commissioners can swallow their words as glibly as they swallow ice cream on a hot summer's day. (*Laughter*) I refer to Mr. Luttman Johnson and also to Mr. Tuite. But even this is not all. There is corroboration. Have we not been told times without number that the annual average income per head of the population of England is now £41, and that of Turkey £4? Lord Cromer's calculation, including the rich as well as the poor, however incorrectly, sets it down in India at Rs. 27, and Mr. Dadabhai Naoroji's sets it down at Rs. 20. The Honorable Member of Parliament, Mr. Seymour Keay, has stated to you that the average annual income of certain men of Rampore and Rai Bareily is Rs. 6. I will confine my remarks to a certain portion of Bengal, and will show by a rough calculation a similar result. The average labourer in Bengal (and I will confine my remarks to a certain quarter only, having nothing to do with any interests inland) gets work for seven months of the year. Taking his wages to be 3 annas per diem he gets annually, say, Rs. 42. Taking rice at Rs. 4 per maund, and taking his consumption to be a seer of rice a day, we have Rs. 36. If you deduct 36 from 42 the result is Rs. 6, which is what was shewn by Mr. Seymour Keay. And this is in reference to a single man. Just fancy to yourselves if he has a wife, and children, the doctor's bill, the thatch to repair, and other necessaries of life to provide for! Bengal is not a garden of Eden, and the labourers are not so many walking Adams. (*Laughter*) He has to pay the cost of clothing too. Now, Gentlemen, we all know that many families in India have literally got to live upon one meal a day, and this, in a country where the land yields anything which can be desired. Is it too much, Gentlemen, after this, to say that fully 50 millions of the people of India are on the very verge of starvation? Yesterday the President told you, if I remember right, that some years back the population of England was 15 millions and that now it is 38 millions; while fully 40 million Indians (let me take the number of Sir W. Hunter not to mention that of Sir Charles Elliott) live on the very verge of starvation. You have heard of the recurring famines of Behar, of Central India, of Madras, and last though not least, of Faridpur. Gentlemen, is it, then, a wonder that there should be such famines, when so many people are literally living on the very verge of starvation? Everything was ready. The spark of a bad season was wanted, and the whole thing burst into flame, and the whole country put on the weird aspect of conflagration and of famine. Gentlemen, now let us see what are the causes. Well, it is not for me to narrate to you all the causes, but I should say that the first cause is stationary income and increase of expenditure by leaps and bounds. Under this head, by way of illustration, I would only mention Exchange Compensation, Military Expenditure, and adventitious shows to keep up the prestige of the British lion by such pageants as the Delhi Durbar and the Lahore Durbar. It seems to me it is the spectacle of a consumptive man in purple. Then I would mention other causes, namely, the natural decay of indigenous manufactures; the abolition of the caste system, or the division of industries; then the poverty of the soil, the visitation of floods and famine, giving rise to eternal indebtedness and law suits; and then the costly system of foreign Government, which has been mentioned to you by other speakers. Last year when supporting the resolution for the separation of the executive and judicial functions of a Magistrate, Mr. Mozumdar showed to you as clearly as possible that out of a saving of 230 lakhs (in a certain year), separation of these functions would, at the most, cost only some 7 lakhs. And that has not been done for Bengal, as we are told that it is not neces-

Second Day.

Resolution III.
Poverty of India.

sary to seek any such remedy, for does hot Sir Charles Elliott tell us that Ganja and Opium are a highly concentrated food, and that the people should supply themselves with Kesur (*Laughter and Cheers*)

The President struck the gong, and the speaker ceased speaking.

THE PRESIDENT :—I now call upon Mr. A. C. Parthasarathy Naidu, of Madras, to address the meeting in Telugu. Permit me, Gentlemen, to apologise to you for not understanding the vernaculars of this country. It is not the fault of my parents, for if they had had the least idea that I should one day be called upon to occupy this position, I am sure they would have given me quite a good education in the vernaculars. (*Laughter*)

Mr. Parthasarathy Naidu then spoke in Telugu amid frequent bursts of applause.

THE PRESIDENT :—The resolution has now been properly moved, seconded and supported; let those who are in favour of it hold up their hands (*Voices* All, All).

The Resolution was carried unanimously.

THE PRESIDENT :—Mr. Norton will move the next resolution. An amendment has been put into my hands, but it is out of order.

Mr. Eardley Norton then came forward amid a perfect storm of applause. At this point Miss Muller (a Madras delegate, and the proposer of the amendment ruled out of order) who had taken up a position on the platform, while the audience were cheering Mr. Norton, attempted to address the assembly in disobedience to the President's ruling.

MISS MULLFR :—I should like to know upon what grounds my amendment is ruled out of order. (*Interruption*) I have a right to ask the Chairman to inform me upon what grounds he has ruled my amendment out of order. (*Cries of* No! No! Chair! Chair!) I move an amendment—(*Interruption*).

THE PRESIDENT :—The amendment is out of order. Go on, Mr. Norton, please.

MISS MULLER :—My brothers, I should like to know how my amendment is out of order (*Voices* "Sit down, Sit down" Chair! Chair!)

THE PRESIDENT :—Gentlemen, sit down, please.

MR. E. NORTON :—I do trust, Gentlemen, you will obey the Chair.

Miss Muller then retired from the platform and the audience resumed their seats.

Resolution IV.
Secretary of
State's Council.

MR. EARDLEY
NORTON.

MR. EARDLEY NORTON:—Mr. President, the Resolution which I am asked to move runs as follows :—

That this Congress considers the abolition of the Council of the Secretary of State for India, as at present constituted, the necessary preliminary to all other reforms; and suggests that in its place a standing committee of members of the House of Commons be appointed.

It is quite impossible for me, Sir, within the time at my disposal to pretend to deal adequately with the resolution which has been entrusted to my care. I shall, therefore, confine myself to enunciating a few only of those principles which I assume will commend themselves to those assembled here, quoting by way of illustration a few instances to support those principles and my arguments. It is impossible for me to-day to do more than touch lightly upon the merits of the needed reform and illustrate by a few significant instances India's present unfortunate plight and the necessity for the concession she demands. Now, Sir, this particular reform, the abolition of the Council of the Secretary of State for India, is the natural and necessary consequence of the re-constitution of the Legislative Councils which has given to the people of this country the first taste of a true though far off freedom; which has recognised, partially and with many jealous limitations, their right to elect their own representatives; and which has thereby conferred upon them the initial instalment of

Second Day.

Resolution IV. Secretary of State's Council.

Mr. Eardley Norton.

a freer and a greater self-government in the future which I trust, by their conduct of public affairs, they will justifythe right to exercise and extend for the benefit of all mankind (*Cheers*). It is impossible now that there has been conceded to them—dimly perhaps and only partially, limited by restrictions which in my opinion are both foolish and unfair—the first fruits of their perseverance and self-denial, it is impossible for them to stand where they are, unless mdeed they are prepared to surrender all those present and prospective privileges which invest living with dignity, and make life itself something more noble, more worth having, than the mere patient existence of the brute creation. Do you wish to go back upon these eight years' struggles, and do you wish to give up all that we have fought for and won? Or do you wish to press forward to the light, believing that you yourselves, like most other sentient human beings, and like all other subjects of Her Majesty the Queen, are endowed with the right of making yourselves heard by the men of your own choice? If this, indeed, be your wish, as I believe, my friends, it is, and if you are not content to rest idle and indifferent where you are; if you are earnest in your resolve to make yourselves more and more fit for that greater and more generous franchise which must come to you in time, then you will agree with me that hand in hand with the re-constitution of the Legislative Councils must come the abolition of the Council of the Secretary of State for India. (*Cheers*) At present we stand sandwiched between officials in India and officials in England. (*Cheers*) I know not which are worse. (*Laughter*) We are asphyxiated by the air in which we live, which permits us only with difficulty to think, or do, or say. (*Cheers*) Until you get rid of that asphyxiating medium, until you break the last link which stands between you and your right freely to elect your own representatives, and to clothe them with the power, which the elected own in England and elsewhere, to make themselves heard effectively as your representatives in the Councils of the nation, and to regulate your taxation (*Cheers*) as well as your legislation, so long will you remain only partially enfranchised and only partially worthy either of the life which is yours by gift of God, or of the models which Great Britain has so long been training you to study, to imitate, to admire. Surely you must agree with me—I venture, of course, to speak only for Madras with which I am personally connected—that hitherto the re-constitution of the Legislative Councils has been followed by not unsuccessful attempts, on the part of the Government which administers the rules under which these Councils sit, to limit unfairly the rights, the privileges and the utility of the members whom the people have nominated. They are not yet endowed with sufficient freedom of speech or of debate, and it is in the hope that you will insist upon having these greater and necessary rights conferred upon them, that I ask you to vote for this proposition. I speak with personal interest on this point, because when I was last year at home I was in constant communication with Sir William Wedderburn and our old friend Mr. Hume; and both these gentlemen have commissioned me to tell you, that unless and until you strengthen their hands by sending them the resolution which I propose, you will not be doing what in you lies to give energy and vitality to the popular movement on the road to self-government. Why do we object, Sir to the India Council? We object for this simple reason: that although its members are, possibly, imbued with the very best of intentions—mere intentions are not sufficient for practical politics—these same members are swayed by the same official interest, trained in the same official career steeped in the same official prejudices, as the men out here who, also with the best of intentions, are resolutely endeavouring to thwart and obstruct your moral, material and political reforms. Unless and until you sweep away the powerful association which, through all the intervening stretch of land and sea, is ever ready to help its fellow officials in this country, to condone their faults, to pander to their extravagance, to restrict your privileges, and to deny you your prerogatives, the re-constitution of the Legislative Councils must remain practically a sham. In speaking of Madras let me give one or two illustrations only—time will not permit me to do more—of the methods adopted by persons in whose hands the destiny of the local Legislative Council lies. It seems to me—and I have followed the debates with considerable scrutiny and interest—that the Government of Madras has been seeking with some success to solve the problem of how best to thwart the efforts of our representatives to elicit information or to undo wrong. For this purpose the Government has arranged a system whereby, by a sub-division of labour, nothing useful shall follow the action of the elected members. (*Laughter*) In the first place we have the senior member of Council who, whenever a pertinent question is addressed to the Government, is put forward to assume the position of a nineteenth century Delphic Oracle and to make himself even more unintelligible than usual. (*Laughter*) When this gentleman has succeeded in this not over-difficult task we have the junior member of Council, with his reputation for honesty, pushed forward to give a point-blank denial to statements which on investigation are discovered to be true. (*Laughter*) We have the flat contradiction followed up by the admission of the truth in the interval betwen that meeting and the next, in other words, we have the flat contradictions followed up by an admission of their own inaccuracy. (*Laughter*) So far as I have seen, however, there is never any official apology tendered to the gentleman whose question has been met with a point-blank denial. However, the object of this particular illustration is this. What do you suppose is the real meaning of what I may designate as there local impertinences? They would not exist if the gentlemen who gave the answers, or rather did not give the answers, (*Laughter*) were not quite sure of the cordial approval and support of the members of the Secretary of State's Council in England. Let us look for one second at the constitution of that Council. I go back to the year 1884—as a matter of fact the condition of things has not much changed since then—and I find that of the fourteen members, seven are members of the Civil Service, five of the Army, one a Barrister and one an English Banker. Now, Sir, this particular Council is a Council the reason for whose existence lies in the fact that it is supposed to consist of members peculiarly qualified by long personal enperience of India to know what the wants and desires of India really are; what are its ambitions and what its capabilities. The first thing that would strike a critic is the extraordinary fact that since 1858 when the Council came into existence, until to-day not one Indian subject of Her Majesty the Queen has been offered a place on that Board. (*Shame*) Another point which seems to me singular is this: that not one single gentleman who pays us the compliment of accepting a seat on that Council, and who does us the honour of drawing £1,200 a year in addition to his pension for doing nothing that we want done, not one of these gentlemen contributes by way of taxes to the Indian Government. (*Shame*) Let me suggest that the constitution of the Council requires something more than mere mending. Look at the term of office of its members. Under the old Act of Parliament, its members were originally placed on it during good behaviour. That was found, I presume, to be rather a precarious tenure (*Laughter*) because it has been changed into an appointment for ten years, subject to recommendation on the part of the Secretary of State, who may at pleasure extend it from ten years to fifteen. Is not that somewhat of the nature of a permanent settlement with fixity of tenure (*Laughter*), modified, of course, by the benevolent interposition of a Secretary, kindly moved by his personal whims and caprices? Next, what with regard to the jurisdiction of the Council? I find that there seems to be some doubt as to what the Council can do and what it cannot do. The Duke of Argyll seconded by his Lord Chancellor, Lord Selborne, was strongly of opinion that the Secretary of State's Council had no right to do anything whatever except to offer mere opinions. A little later, and I find that the Marquis of Salisbury seconded by his Lord Chanceller, Lord Cairns, was as strongly of opinion that on all questions affecting the financial arrangements of this country the voice of the majority of the Council is entitled to carry its full weight. In this conflict of opinion, it seems to me the time has come when we should interfere and put an end to the doubts raised by putting an end to the Council itself. (*Laughter* and *Cheers*) Then Sir, I find that Henry Fawcett, a name which ought to commend itself to every Indian who recognises the worth of a true and generous patriotism, publicly announced his mature opinion that with regard to all questions of frontier policy all Secretaries of State carried out their views, without reference to, and without the consultation of, this particular Council. Then, what on earth is the use of this Council? (*Cheers*) If the Secretary of State is to be controlled by the Council, then abolish the Secretary of State. If the Council is to be controlled by the Secretary of State, then abolish the Council. The dual existence is useless, dangerous, expensive, obstructive. (*Cheers*)

Who can help being struck with the fact that, during the first ten years of its life the Secretary of State interfered to overrule it only eight times? I find each time he so interfered and overruled, it was with regard to some question of the Indian services. That is not a very important matter, and I fail to see why we should pay twelve gentlemen or more £1,200 each for settling the local disagreements of the officials in this country. Let me mention, Sir, by way of illustration, what the commercial capacity of the members of this Council appears to be. I will give you three instances as to the way in which they deal with commercial matters. To those more particularly who are so enthusiastic over the poverty of India and the question of trying to rearrange her finances, I need scarcely say that good commercial instincts and good commercial habits are matters of primary importance for the due regulation of this country's affairs. Yet I find commercial incapacity apportioned by the Council with admirable impartiality to its dealings with all three Presidencies. Thus: although Lord Canning in 1858 sent an urgent despatch to the Secretary of State strongly protesting against his contemplated action, that particular Secretary of State in Council sanctioned the construction of the Calcutta and South-Eastern Railway, and guaranteed interest at the rate of 5 per cent. This was done after eleven yoars experience had taught that such concessions were irreconcilable with the true interests of India. The result of this was that the whole thing practically became bankrupt, and the Secretary of State had to purchase the railway at the cost of half a million sterling! Not content with this purchase of 1858, in 1859 the Council granted another concession, this time, by way of strict impartiality, (*Laughter*) in my own particular Presidency of Madras, to the Madras Irrigation Company upon substantially the same basis, guaranteeing to pay in perpetuity interest at 5 per cent. upon one million pounds sterling. Soon after this it was found the calculations were all wrong. The work never paid its expenses. What did the Secretary of State in Council do? He promptly advanced an additional £6,000 without security, with the result that eventually India had to buy this concern at par. (*Shame*) I have dealt with Calcutta and Madras. Let us see what is done in the Presidency to which Mr. Wacha belongs. I find in Bombay that in 1869 the India Council sanctioned the purchase of the Elphinstone Land and Press Company for Rs. 1,000 per share while the selling price was only Rs. 339. (*Shame*) These illustrations show that the commercial capacity of the gentlemen who receive handsome salaries and pensions from us is not so great as to entitle them to retain our confidence or our admiration. (*Cheers*) I will not enter upon more recent financial transgressions illustrative of the Council's commercial incapacity. We are all only too familiar with its proved incompetency on matters of finance. Now with regard to the Council's method of legislation, let me quote a single instance, by way of accent, from the speech of a person no less capable than our former Premier, Mr. Gladstone. Emphasising the fashion in which Indian legislation is carried on, this is what he said: "Suddenly in the dark, in the "privacy of the Council chamber, I believe in answer to a telegram, without the knowledge "of Parliament, without the knowledge of the country, a law was passed totally extinguishing "the freedom of the native press. I think a law such as that is a disgrace to the British "Empire." So do I. (*Loud Cheers*) Yet this is what the expensive anachronism of the Indian Council does not blush to effect. (*Cheers*) Now let us look at some interesting figures illustrative of the licentious and criminal extravagance of these twelve or fourteen gentlemen at home. India has been charged—and has had to pay—£821,100 for the erection of certain buildings in England. Of this £540,000 has been absorbed in the construction and furniture of the India Office, a place not unfrequently devoted to giving, at the expense of India, costly entertain ments to visitors to England unconnected with this country. (*Laughter*) I find that £70,000 have been spent on the erection of a library, £68,000 upon our old friend the Store Depôt

Second Day

Resolution IV. Secretary of State's Council.

Mr. Eardley Norton.

and £100,000 upon the Indian Engineering College for the manufacture of experts who after importation find themselves shelved in favour of Royal Engineers. (*Laughter*) Now I come to the most extraordinary and alarming of all the items, namely, £38,000 which have been spent, Sir, on the construction of a Lunatic Asylum at Ealing. (*Laughter and cries of "Shame"*) Without wishing to be even inferentially discourteous, I admit I have a very intense curiosity to know who these Lunatics are. (*Laughter*) I want to know who are their fathers; (*Laughter*) and for what purpose they are bred to be nurtured at our expense. (*Laughter*) In England if a man has the advantage or the disadvantage, I do not know which, of having a lunatic father or son (*Laughter*), the cost of the lunatic is a charge either on his private family or on the parish rates. But when we in India send home our official lunatics manufactured locally (*Laughter*), or when we find them sprinkled up and down the country-side, manufactured in England possibly by parents who find time hanging heavy on their hands (*Laughter*), we are called upon to meet an annual expenditure of £9,663. (*Shame*) That surely is an exorbitant demand on the part of those who place their private trade-mark on their offspring without the State's consent. (*Laughter*) India spends £136,588 on the salaries of her officials in England, and we find that this sum under the head of General Administration is swollen into a sum of £229,262. Five ships for the transport of soldiers have been built at a cost of £1,118,787 sterling. The annual upkeep of these ships was £277,072. I find another singular thing. I find that if a soldier in the service of the Queen, in quest of honour and glory, has won a distinguished service pension for valour in the field, whether it be in Afghanistan or Canada, in New Zealand or South Africa, if this distinguished soldier once comes within the confines of India the whole of his pension during the remainder of his official career in India is paid by the Indian tax-payer. (*Shame*) I find further that £192,227-12-10 are spent annually by way of absentee allowance to the highly salaried staff of your civil and military departments, who are enjoying themselves at your cost on privilege leave at home. I find, by way of contrast, that the Council of the Secretary of State for India was good enough to spend upon the natives of India, who are primarily entitled to the relief and the charities of the tax-payers of this country, the munificent sum of £218-14-8. (*Laughter and Shame*) India pays £74,470 annually on pensions, including a remarkable item of £10,033 which covers the pension of officers who were pensioned between the years 1834 and 1877, instead of being transferred to other offices in which they could have given India value for their annuities. (*Shame*) But this is not all. We pay, Sir, for an establishment in China. I should like to know why? We pay for a mission to the Court of Persia. I should like to know why? We pay our proportionate share of the Consulate at Jeddah? Where is Jeddah (*Laughter*) and what has India to do with the Consulate there? (*Cheers*) I find that for these items we are charged £25,366 per year. On the other hand the Colonies are called upon to pay nothing. When I say Colonies, I mean all those Colonies which can fight their own battles; for instance, Australia, Africa, or Canada. These are "invited" to subscribe by the Secretary of State for the Colonies But Hongkong, Colombo, Shanghai and Singapur are mulcted, like India, whether they like it or not. The great difference between the Colonies and India is that the Colonies are not at the mercy of the British Empire, because they have physical force, and India is at its mercy, because India has not physical force. This essential difference the India Council remembers and trades upon, and the difference accounts for the difference in treatment. (*Shame*) One would have supposed that it was sufficient to deal with large items like those I have mentioned, but it is impossible, in the review of the meanness of the Secretary of State and his Council at India's expense, to pass over in silence a very remarkable item. I find here, Sir, at page 56 of the Home Accounts of the Government of India 1893, amongst other things which the Indian tax-payer is called upon to pay and does pay, that he pays an annual sum of £1,329 for the annual up-keep and refreshment of 32 servants consisting of 28 housemaids not entitled to pension, (*Laughter*) one house keeper, and three charwomen. (*Loud laughter*) If you will divide 32 by 12, each member of Council, excluding the President, that is the Secretary of State, but including the Vice-President, has about 2⅔rds of a housemaid all to himself. (*Laughter*) For that we are made to pay. (*Laughter*) By way of illustration of the absolutely illimitable extravagance of the India Office, let me mention two more items. First of all when a prince—his name need not be mentioned—came out to India some time ago India had to pay and did pay his expenses. But when the same prince went to Australia, Australia did not pay his expenses (*Shame*). I find also that it was discovered absolutely necessary for the imperial grandeur of Calcutta that the picture of a Viceroy and the picture of a Prince should be painted and hung up in the Council Chamber of that Capital. The pictures were provided and the tax-payer of India was fleeced to the extent of £812 for their cost. (*Shame*) I turn to lighter topics. I do not myself lay much emphasis upon, or feel much respect for, orders, garters, titles, ribbons, medals, and similar rubbish. (*Laughter*) But other people do, and it is a matter of taste. But I fail to see, Sir, why the extension of the Order of the Star of India should have cost us during the last five years £13,769 sterling. (*Shame*) One point more and I have done. We are prone to hail the advent of a new Viceroy with enthusiasm because we believe he will inaugurate a new departure and try to be fair and just as a ruler. But in the majority of cases I think we all hail his departure with unfeigned pleasure (*Laughter*), because we find at the end of five years that in the main we have been grievously disappointed. The golden vessel has degenerated into an earthy vase. Most of us are old enough to recollect when Lord Lytton came to this country and when he went away. It was quite right that he should go away. The great regret was that he did not go away sooner. (*Cheers*) For transporting him and his family from Calcutta to England this country had to pay the enormous sum of £5,280. (*Shame*) Now, some time ago —with this I will close—a man whose name like Fawcett's ought to conjure up in you a sensation of lasting gratitude—that great Quaker demagogue of the people, John Bright, (*Cheers*) said, when he opposed the formation of this particular Council with a deeper statesmanlike penetration than is possessed by those who call themselves statesmen in India, "These 15 gentlemen "with handsome salaries, fair retiring allowances, and a good deal of patronage at their dispos-"al, and whose work would be so easy that nobody was able to say exactly why th y were "appointed, would be the last persons to complain of the Act under which they were created, "and they would find that their friends in that House and out of it, and in the Press, would say "that nothing was so admirable as the Act passed in 1858, and the result would be that little "or no concern would be felt in the affairs of India, and its interests would be to a great extent "neglected; that complaints might be made of such neglect, but these fifteen gentlemen would "still assert with the most unblushing countenances, that nothing could be better than their "administration of India." It is because we realize that that prophecy, unlike most prophecies, has come true; it is because we desire to put an end to the evils which John Bright so graphically described, that I ask you to-day to adopt this resolution which will strengthen the hands of your British Committee at Home, working with marvellous devotion and unselfishness, unpaid, in the cause of Indian Reform. (*Cheers*) I trust, Sir, no man in India will, for one moment, shut his eyes to the real facts of the situation, nor suppose that this particular attack upon the India Council is likely to be successful at its first onslaught. It was not so we won the recognition of the elective principle. (*Cheers*) It would be folly not to recognise that we shall find arrayed against us in the future, as we found arrayod against us in the past, all that racial jealousy, all that personal dislike, all that individual antipathy, all that malice and envy and hatred and uncharitableness can summon to join and weld together in one obstructive whole, to impede our wishes, to repel our crusade, to crush our ambitions, and to drain our purses. (*Cheers*) But, my friends, as you have vanquished in the past so shall you be victorious in the future if as in the past, you be true to yourselves, your country and your cause. (*Cheers*) I have delivered the message which our friends in England have asked me to give you. There has already been drafted a Bill which I hope will be brought forward in the next

Second Day.

Resolution IV. Secretary of State's Council.

Mr. Eardley Norton.

or in the immediately succeeding Parliament; and when we have this particular institution swept out of the way, then we shall breathe freely; then our taxes will be spent on our own wants (*Cheers*), then we shall be able to impose those taxes ourselves. (*Cheers*) Personally I am not very much enamoured of the suggestion that in lieu of the Secretary of State and his Council, we should have a standing Committee of Parliament at home, because I feel that the Standing Committee may in the course of years become the monopoly of the retired Anglo-Indian official who trickles into Parliament. (*Hear, hear from Mr. Seymour Keay*) But, like most selections in life, it is a choice between two evils. Some of us may prefer to abide by the evil we know of than fly to the evil of which we do not know. But, personally. I would sooner embark on any venture; sooner trust to any new tribunal sooner pin my faith on any proposed combination, than entrust anything in which I felt a personal interest to the clutches or the carelessness of the India Council. (*Cheers*) With me there is no mending that Council. It must be ending. Let it be decapitated and its head decently buried in another continent to that in which lies interred its trunk, lest the two baneful things re-unite and the monster be resuscitated. (*Laughter and Cheers*) For a worse system than the present could not be invented by the ingenuity of man. The Council is a secret body; its discussions are not public; its conclusions do not see the light of day; it is not open to the influence of outside criticism; it is not responsible to Parliament; it cannot be affected by public opinion. You cannot have a worse body than that to rule or to misrule you. (*Cheers*) The standing Committee of the House of Commons will have at any rate this advantage: in the first place it will be very much less expensive, because it will sweep away the £1,200 a year of these gentlemen, and in the second place, you will have the advantage of its members speaking in public, subject to public opinion, subject to debate and subject to criticism. (*Cheers*) So far as I am concerned this part of the resolution is only tentative. I shall be open to discuss and consider any better substitute for the Council whose execution we all desire so heartily to attend. (*Laughter*)

To you, Sir, (*turning to the President*) the President of this Congress and a member of the mother of all Parliaments, we Englishmen and Indians here assembled alike turn for comfort any relief; to you, who at this holy season of the year, have come among us bringing from your own united party a message of hope, of good will, of perseverance (*Cheers*); to you, who like us have graduated and are graduating still in the school of political persecution and political duress (*Cheers*); to you, whose life-long connection with the struggles of your own countrymen for liberty and for self-government must necessarily teach you to be in reverent sympathy with all men, who like ourselves are facing odds in our struggle for our rights (*Cheers*) We believe that when you leave us, you will not forget us. (*Cheers*) Your closer contact and touch with the peoples of this country and with their aims and methods, since you have moved among them, will show you that there is much that is good and lovable in their character. (*Cheers*) And we are certain that, impelled alike by sympathy and conviction towards the unrepresented millions of Her Majesty's Indian subjects, you will give them the assistance as well of your voice as of your vote, when next they appeal for hearing and relief to the Imperial and United Parliament of Great Britain and Ireland (*Loud and long continued Cheers*)

The President:—This resolution will be seconded by Mr. R. N. Mudholkar of Berar.

Mr. R. N. Mudholkar.

Mr. R. N. Mudholkar:—Mr. President, Ladies and Gentlemen—The resolution which has been moved in such eloquent terms and with such an array of facts and figures by my friend Mr. Norton may appear to some to be worded in rather a strong manner But I am sure that when you have heard his facts and when you bestow your attention on the reason of the thing, you will be convinced that it is not as strong as it should be. We say in that Resolution that this Congress considers the abolition of the Council of the Secretary of State for India as at present constituted to be a necessary preliminary to all reforms.

**Second Day.**

**Resolution IV. Secretary of State's Council.**

**Mr. R. N. Mudholkar.**

What we mean by this is that all that we have asked for will not be granted to us unless this body is removed from our path. It has been said very often in England, with regard to other things and other objects, that Ireland blocks the way. Here in India we might well say with another meaning that the Council of the Secretary of State blocks the way. (*Hear, hear*) You say that all your people are miserably poor, that you are overtaxed, that the burdens of the country ought to be lightened. It is the Secretary of State in London who governs you. He has a Council there, and it is his Council which stops the way, and obstructs the path of reform. You have been for years asking for the Permanent Settlement; in fact, several Secretaries of State have seen the necessity of granting a Permanent Settlement. Again, it is his Council that blocks the way. You have asked for that small modicum of reform, namely, granting a representative element with regard to the Legislative Councils. It again came in the way. It was the Secretary of State's Council. There is the Simultaneous Examinations Question. Who comes between you and the attainment of your wishes? Again, the Council of the Secretary of State. It is these gentlemen who, holding a high position in England, exercise that power, not for your good, not for the purpose for which they are appointed, but to frustrate the very object for which they were called into existence. I say advisedly that they violate the very principle for which the Law called them into existence. (*Cheers*) When in 1857-1858 it was proposed to take the Government of India from the Company, it was proposed that the late Board of Directors should be abolished, and that the old Board of Control should be abolished, and that India should be taken over by the Crown and be directly managed through a Secretary of State. It was objected by persons who were friendly to the old "John Company," that there would be no protection of Indian interests. Various measures were suggested. It was suggested that certain cities should have representatives. That was abandoned, and several other projects also were abandoned, and at last this Council was created. And for what purpose? For protecting the interests of this country. So this Council was created for protecting our interests. It was conceived that a body of experts was necessary to consult with the Secretary of State, because the man who would be called upon to fill the position of Secretary of State would often be utterly ignorant of the duties of the office, and therefore it was resolved that for protecting the interest of the people of India there should be a body of experts. Now that body consists for the most part of members of the Indian Services. It is these gentlemen occupying this position who are supposed to protect our interests! And they are supposed to protect our interests in two ways; firstly, as the final executive authority, and, secondly, as directing the policy of the Government of India from England. I say in regard to both these matters that they have failed, and failed egregiously. (*Cheers*) As executive authorities those who have held high positions naturally by their predilections, by the bias natural to their minds, view things as the officials here; and finally when the decision is passed here by the Government it is very difficult to get the Secretary of State or his Council to reverse it;—that is the final executive authority. And whether you look to high matters like those I have referred to, or to individual grievances, or cases like those of Crawford or Wilson Russell, the Secretary of State's Council does not fulfil its function, namely, that of protecting the interests of India. (*Shame*)

I shall mention to you only one particular instance of individual grievances. You know, Gentlemen—particularly those of you who come from Bombay—what the *Inam* commission is. When the *Inam* Commission was let loose in certain provinces, which need not be mentioned here, certain *Inams* were attached and the proceeds taken to the Government treasury pending investigation, which in some cases went on for a period of 25 years. At last it was found that the *Inamdars* were entitled and their claims were allowed. But during all this time Government had received the profits. The *Inamdars* asked for arrears. The Government of India disallowed the claim. (*Shame*) There was an appeal to the Secretary of State and his Council. Well, one would have expected that if the claim was just, Government would have taken time to verify the thing. No! Claims of right and justice like this would most

**Second Day.**

Resolution IV. Secretary of State's Council.

Mr. R. N. Mudholkar.

certainly hamper the hands of our Council, and these claims were summarily rejected. (*Shame*) This is the justice which is received from the highest executive authority. Well, then, abandoning these individual instances, and abandoning also other matters, we find the Secretary of State's Council not serving its purpose in another way. When the law was passed, it was believed that in regard to financial matters at least the Council would be able to control and check the action of the Secretary of State. The Duke of Argyll had other views and in several instances the Secretary of State over-ruled his Council. and carried things with a high hand. Now, then, has the Council fulfilled its purpose ? (*Cries of* No ! No ! *and Cheers*)

But you must not blame the Council ; it is not the man or the Council, but the system which we are attacking. (*Hear, hear*) You also find that in several matters affecting most vital questions between England and India they are over-ruled and cannot enforce their action. That means that it is a Council which is utterly useless, and as it does not serve any useful purpose it ought to be abolished. On both these grounds, therefore, the Secretary of State's Council should be abolished. (*Hear, hear*) Then it may be asked, " What shall be put in its place? There must be some consultative body " Speaking for myself, I should much prefer an elective Council. That is a demand, however, which we may enunciate hereafter. For the present what we may verily ask is that there should be a Standing Committee of the House of Commons. (*Cheers*) Under the present system the Secretary of State is a perfect autocrat, because even if the Council were to push their views to the extreme and carry matters to Parliament, the Secretary of State, with a Parliamentary Majority behind his back, can easily over-ride the decisions of the Council. But if you have a Standing Committee of the House of Commons, chosen as that body would be from all sides, it would carry a weight and have a prestige which a Council like the Secretary of State's cannot have. It would carry far greater weight, and enforce its opinions with far greater authority than the present body, and on these grounds, therefore, Gentlemen, I second this Resolution for your acceptance. (*Loud Cheers*)

The President :--The fourth resolution has been properly moved and seconded. Let those who are in favour of it hold up their hands (*Voices,* " All " " All ".)

The Resolution was carried unanimously.

The President.

The President :—This brings us to the close of our business for the day ; but there are some important matters to be brought before you. First of all, there is an announcement to be made by Mr. P. Ananda Charlu ; next I am going to announce the business for to-morrow ; and then I will read a letter received by me impugning my conduct in the Chair, as to which I shall ask for your opinion.

Rai Bahadur P. Ananda Charlu.

Rai Bahadur P. Ananda Charlu :—Gentlemen, on a former occasion the delegates had an invitation from the Cosmopolitan Club, and that Club has made up its mind to invite you all heartily on this occasion also. On the last occasion the delegates accepted the invitation, and I hope that you will follow the same course. The invitation will be for the 29th instant at 7 P.M. (*Cheers*)

The President.

The President :—The Members of the Subjects Committee will please remain here, as we mean to conclude our business now as soon as the meeting rises. Refreshments will be provided here for the members of the Subjects Committee. To-morrow the Congress will meet at 12 o'clock and sit continuously till four. We think that a more convenient arrangement than breaking up the business during the day. I have now to read a letter which I have received. It is my duty to read it to you. It is signed by three members of the Congress, but I do not intend to give their names :—

" To the President of the National Congress. Sir,—We feel that you have not complied " with the rules of fair play by refusing to grant a hearing to Miss Muller, and by further refusing to

Second Day.

Resolution IV Secretary of State's Council.

The President.

"give any reasons for your summary action. We protest against your action, and shall take steps to "make public the indignation that we feel at your conduct." (*Shame, Shame*)

Now, I don't intend in future to give any explanation of my rulings. If you are not satisfied with my rulings in future, you can put me out of the Chair. But, seeing the extremely painful character of this incident, seeing the fact that the only lady in the place was engaged in it, and that she was the only English-woman here, and also that she is a relative of a dear friend of mine, I think I am entitled to give some explanation. According to the rules the Subjects Committee arranges the business here. It arranges the Resolutions, and it arranges the list of speakers. Miss Muller was not on the list of speakers; the amendment which she handed to me had nothing whatever to do with the Resolution before the meeting, and also, apart from that, would have been entirely out of order at any time in these meetings. I should have ruled it out of Order at any time. Now I desire to know whether after hearing this explanation, you think that I have complied with the rules of fair play? (*Cries of* You have! You have! *Three cheers were here called for* Mr. Webb *and given most heartily, the audience standing.*) I am quite sure that you will support me in my future rulings, and I now consider that this most painful incident is entirely at an end, and buried in our recollections. The Congress now adjourns till 12 o'clock to-morrow (*Prolonged Cheers*).

---

# THIRD DAY'S PROCEEDINGS.

**Friday, the 28th December, 1894.**

The Congress assembled at 12 o'clock.

Third Day.

THE PRESIDENT.

THE PRESIDENT:—Gentlemen, in commencing the proceedings for this day, it is necessary that I should remark that the amount of business that we have to get through is very great. I was rather lenient yesterday, it being the first day, but I must be a little more strict to-day. I am willing to stop here till 10 o'clock but I doubt whether everybody would do the same. I must restrict the speakers to the recognised time. I have now to call upon Mr. C. Jambulingam Mudalier, to propose the fifth resolution.

Resolution V. Financial Enquiry.

RAI BAHADUR C. JAMBULINGAM MUDALIER.

RAI BAHADUR C. JAMBULINGAM MUDALIER:—Mr. President and Brother Delegates— The resolution which has been placed in my charge and which I move runs thus:—

This Congress, while thanking Her Majesty's Government for the promise they have made to appoint a Select Committee of Members of Parliament to enquire into the financial expenditure of India, regards the enquiry with so limited a scope as inadequate, and is of opinion that if the enquiry is to bear any practical fruit it must include an enquiry into the ability of the Indian people to bear their existing financial burthens and into the financial relations between India and the United Kingdom.

Gentlemen, it is necessary that before I begin to explain the several component parts of this Resolution I should state briefly the occasion for the introduction of this Resolution at this Congress. You remember that about four months ago the Indian Budget Statement was introduced into the House of Commons, and that the proceedings at that introduction showed a marked contrast to the proceedings on similar occasions in former years. It gave rise to an enormous amount of animated and interesting discussion regarding several points concerning the welfare of India. We must express our gratitude to that Committee of India's true and trusted friends (*Hear, hear*), presided over by Sir William Wedderburn (*Cheers*) for the interest it has created among the members of the British House of Commons, in matters concerning the welfare of this vast Empire. (*Hear, hear*) We must express our gratitude in an equal degree to that band of 153 philanthropic members of the House of Commons (*Cheers*) who have promised to interest themselves in the impartial consideration of the questions relating to this great Empire, (*Hear, hear*) But, Gentlemen, we have also to express our gratitude and thanks to an official holding a high position in India, particularly in connection with the matter before you—I mean Mr. Westland, the Financial Secretary with the Government of India, to whose sophistry and bad logic is to be ascribed the fact that this year's Indian Budget aroused such unusual interest and attention. To him also we shall render our thanks without stint or reserve, because, but for his statement that exchange is the principal cause of the terrible deficit in the Indian finances of this year, it is probable that our eminent brethren of Bombay, the eminent economists of the Bombay Presidency Association, would not have been stirred up to immediate action, and probable also that the British Committee of the Indian National Congress would not have felt the need of publishing a note on Mr. Westland's Budget. Now, Gentlemen, on the motion to go into Committee on the East India Revenue Accounts our friend Mr. Samuel Smith moved an amendment in these terms. "That in the opinion of this House a full and independent

"Parliamentary enquiry should take place into the condition and wants of the Indian people, "their ability to bear the existing financial burdens, the nature of the Revenue system "and the possibility of reduction in the expenditure, also the financial relations between "India and the United Kingdom, and generally the system of Government in India."

Now, Gentlemen, this amendment of Mr. Samuel Smith's was seconded by no less an expert in Indian Economy than our illustrious countryman Dadabhai Naoroji (*Cheers*) and supported by one whose voice you have heard, and who having come from England is sitting before us as a delegate in this National Congress (*Cheers*)—I mean Mr. Seymour Keay. (*Cheers*) The Secretary of State, denying the premises put forward by the Indian party, granted, or at least promised to grant, at the very beginning of the next Session of Parliament a Select Committee. For what purpose? To inquire into the financial expenditure—expenditure only—of India, and nothing more. Gentlemen, we must render our thanks to the Secretary of State for this concession, though we may differ in our views as to the scope of the enquiry. The clock has been placed before me and I shall not be very long; but on this proposition I must ask your indulgence and also the kind permission of the President because I feel it incumbent to pass in review the statements made in the House of Commons by certain members of the Opposition, against which it is necessary that we should enter our most solemn and emphatic protest and send that message to England for the edification of those Members. (*Hear, hear*) Now, Gentlemen, I shall go into the subject. I think I can make you understand our position by a brief illustration, which may not be elegant, but at the same time expresses our ideas briefly and in a short compass. The action of the Government—if the promise of the Secretary of State results in action in the terms of that promise—seems to me like the conduct of a stupid cartman who loads or overloads his cart without considering and measuring the strength of his bullocks. The Government idea of making an enquiry into the expenditure only without making corresponding enquiries as to the capacity of the Indian tax-payer to bear the present burdens seems to be based on foregone conclusions. It postulates that the Indian people are very happy and contented under the present fiscal burdens, that they have nothing whatever to complain of, and that the present axation can be continued without any diminution. Gentlemen, this ignores several points and several matters about which authorities have expressed themselves in no unmistakable language; it ignores the fact that the Salt tax is a most oppressive and galling tax touching the poor; it ignores the fact that eminent authorities have pronounced that there ought to be a reduction of the Salt tax at the earliest possible opportunity, at least to its former limits; it ignores the fact that the Income Tax as assessed at present is an extremely burdensome tax, especially on the poor of this country, because the taxable minimum is placed at Rs. 500, and it ignores also the fact that this Congress year after year on behalf of the poor of this country has been resolving, and sending out its resolutions, to raise the minimum at least to Rs. 1,000 (if not to the limit prescribed for the English tax payer, *viz.*, £150); it ignores also the fact that the opium revenue is at best a most uncertain revenue, and that it threatens to vanish so soon as China can produce its own indigenous article; it ignores further the tendency of the present temperance movement, which has found very valuable and strong support in the House of Commons; lastly, it ignores the grinding poverty of India, about which statisticians of eminence have pronounced and spoken in no doubtful language. That subject of poverty has been dealt with by a master, and it is impossible for me to add anything to that. But, Gentlemen, I shall only mention one circumstance which Mr. Seymour Keay omitted probably out of modesty—I mean the enquiries made by himself, the things which he mentioned before the British House of Commons. Five villages of the Bombay Presidency were selected by him for investigation, and he pointed out that the income of the inhabitants of these villages was not enough to meet the maintenance of the cattle and the starvation rates of the ryots and also the payment of the Government taxes. Gentlemen, Sir Richard Temple, about whom I shall have to speak much, with a self-sufficiency peculiar to himself, thought that he had

**Third Day**

**Resolution V. Financial Enquiry.**

RAI BAHADUR C. JAMBULINGAM MUDALIER.

demolished and pulverised Mr. Seymour Keay when he said "How then do these people pay the taxes?", conveniently forgetting for the moment that the chronic indebtedness of the Indian ryot is a proverb that could find place in dictionaries and books of proverbs, conveniently forgetting also that the cry for Agricultural Banks in this country to relieve the ryot from the strong grip of the money-lender is not a false cry, and that the Government is also anxious about it. But, Gentlemen, Mr. Seymour Keay has survived this pulverising process and has returned to us, and we congratulate him for that. (*Hear, hear*) I shall say only a few words on the second point in this Resolution, *viz.*, the financial relations between India and the United Kingdom, considering it superfluous and unnecessary for me to add anything to the speech of Mr. Seymour Keay relating to the poverty of India. The simple fact about this is that upwards of 20 millions of pounds are annually remitted to England for the purpose of meeting necessary and unnecessary expenditure in that country ; and all this money is completely lost to this country. Mr. Eardley Norton my friend, (*Cheers*) yesterday gave details very accurately from Blue Books about the need for this expenditure. I shall only add one item which he probably omitted in the long list and catalogue of figures he had. He mentioned that for a Lunatic Asylum in England £3,000 were spent for construction, but he omitted to say that the sum of £2,300 per annum is also spent for pay and pensions—of whom? I do not know. It is incomprehensible to minds that have not yet attained that maturity of understanding which is possessed by those inmates of the famous institution at Ealing. (*Laughter*) I shall not trouble you any more because my time is limited, but I must ask for your indulgence in this particular matter because it was on the identical proposition before the House of Commons that the opponents to this Resolution made speeches to which we have the strongest objection, and I do believe that this Congress will enter its most emphatic protest against those statsments. For the present, Gentlemen, I begin with Sir Andrew Scoble, formerly legislative member of the Government of India. As to his views with reference to the necessity for enquiry into Indian affairs his objection, and a strong objection it must be so far as he is concerned, is that this will be a very tedious and costly procedure; as to the poverty of India he does not wage war with the statistics of the world. He conceives that the result of the enquiries which statisticians have made on the subject is that about Rs. 25 per head is the average income of the native of India. We find here an admission from an opponent of the calculations made more or less by Dadabhai Naoroji (*Cheers*) and Lord Cromer. But, Gentlemen, Sir Andrew Scoble finds a mysterious method by which the Indian population, in spite of their income of Rs. 25 per annum, get rich, healthy, happy, and contented. It is impossible for me to put in my own words what that explanation is and therefore I shall simply read his words and read them for your edification. This is what he says :—

"The only result of the enquiries which statisticians have made on the subject is "that about 25 Rupees per head is the average income of the natives of India. As far as "money transactions are concerned, this may be a fair representation, but as far as the "necessaries of life and the conditions which make up the difference between poverty "and wealth are concerned, these depend upon matters which are not purchased by "money, and into the provision of which money does not enter at all. The poverty of India "is relative."

I am sure, Gentlemen, that you are all greatly edified, and are informed as to the manner in which India gets happy and contended in spite of the 25 Rupees per annum. I now come, Gentlemen, to the only personage with whom I am concerned—Sir Richard Temple. Mr. Seymour Keay read two passages yesterday, and I shall not trouble you with them now, but I can simply say that he has got a sovereign contempt for all the statisticians of the world, and is not without resources to substitute something else for the figures of the statisticians, and that is his own knowledge of 25 years in India. He says "At the time I was in India the poorest labouring man could earn 5 Rupees in the month, that is Rs 60 a year." That is a statement from his general knowledge of 25 years' experience in this country which he would boldly put forward against the statements of statisticians, who have laboured in the field of politics and Indian economy for years. This is with reference to official statisticians. With reference to unofficial statisticians he has got a very respectable phrase in calling Dadabhai Naoroji an "amateur statistician." Then, Gentlemen, this is a matter which you must seriously consider and tell me if that is really the state of things. With reference to the Civil Service Examinations he states :—" Certainly we are most undoubtedly afraid lest men "who have passed the Examination should not be qualified for the great Civil Service, and " we are certainly afraid of the greater number of places being won by men of Bengal who are " absolute aliens to many of the people of India, and who would not be acceptable to the " rest of India. Madras is a peculiar case. Madras is quite the quietest, the safest part of " India, and then the people who must enter the Civil Service are quite homogeneous with the " natives of Madras. There, if anywhere, the plan might answer. But to have these Simul-" taneous Examinations is a danger which the Madras people foresaw and objected to. It is " not Madrasis who would get in but Bengalis, and they begged the Government that they " might be governed by Englishmen rather than by Bengalis"

I do not know, Gentlemen, which blockhead in Madras gave expression to that sentiment, but he has another delicious passage here about Dadabhai Naoroji himself :—

" I desire to speak with peculiar respect of the race from which the honorable " member springs. It is one of the most ancient and noble races in this world ; and among it " are many of the best friends I have anywhere. But 1 do say that they are not natives of " India, and the Honorable member when he spoke on behalf of the natives of India, did not " do so in the sense of being himself a native of India"

Do you say, Gentlemen, that Dadabhai Naoroji is not recognised as a native of India (*Cries of* No, No), to represent our case before the House of Commons. I conclude, Gentlemen, as I hear the call of the President that my time is out. (*Cheers*)

Mr. H. Morgan-Browne.

Mr. H. Morgan-Browne :—Mr. President and Fellow-Delegates—You have all heard the Resolution, therefore I will not repeat it ; but I want you to notice at once the form of the enquiry which has been granted us by the House of Commons. That enquiry is a purely financial one, moreover it is a one-sided one—what you may call a one-legged enquiry ! (*Laughter*) It is only going to deal with the financial expenditure, and is not going to deal with revenue. What I want you to keep clearly in your minds is that this so called financial enquiry is no part or portion of the larger enquiry which we have been asking for, and which we will continue to demand until it is granted us. I do not want you to consider that this enquiry is in any way a concession to the demand which India has made, namely, that the whole system of Government in this country shall be brought to the bar of public opinion in England (*Cheers*), and that there shall be such a stock-taking as was customary at the renewal of the old Company's charters. I want you to keep this enquiry entirely separate in your minds from that larger enquiry we are demanding, and I ask you to do so for this reason ;—they will endeavour, when this enquiry has been held, and when they have succeeded, as they probably will succeed, in making this enquiry abortive—they will endeavour to put you off from that larger enquiry by saying " We have granted you all that you have asked for." (*Hear, hear*) Remember also this ; the whole weight of the Government of India and the whole weight of that India Council will be brought to bear in order to make this enquiry in the nature of an audit. Now, Gentlemen, there is one thing we do not want in this world, and that is an audit of the Government of India's Accounts. The Government of India keep excellent Accounts. Their Accounts are admirably displayed—when you can understand them. (*Laughter*) We do not want an audit of the Government of India's Accounts. (*Hear, hear*) Now I want, if I can, to suggest a few points for your consideration

Third Day.

Resolution V. Financial Enquiry.

Mr. H. Morgan-Browne.

with regard to that enquiry—I want to put before you a few of the methods of the Government of India's Finance. I first of all come to that question about the Famine Insurance Fund. Gentlemen, you all know that although there has been a Famine Insurance Fund in existence for something like 16 years, there is only one person or body of persons who never heard of that fund, namely, the Government of India. (*Laughter*) Thus the Government of this country have proved to their own satisfaction that they are at perfect liberty to appropriate the funds raised for that special purpose to any other purpose; and they have scoffed at the accusation we made that they have broken the pledge they gave to this country. I believe that in all matters of complaint against a Government, we should, as far as possible, found our case, not on the utterances and statements of the people of the country, but upon the statements and utterances of the Government itself; therefore for all these figures which I propose to place before you I have gone to one source and one source alone—the public figures and the public documents of the Government of India. (*Hear, hear*) Well, in 1878, the Government of India created a Licence Tax, afterwards changed into the Income Tax, and a certain local Cess to provide against the danger of recurring famines. What was it they told you at the time they imposed these additional taxes? Here is one of the pledges they made. This was said by Sir John Strachey himself. "I feel confident that I shall be "able to satisfy the Council and the public that the resolution which the Government has "proclaimed will be faithfully carried out, and that the proceeds of these new taxes will be "expended for the purpose of providing what I have called an insurance against famine, and "for no other purpose whatever." Well. Gentlemen, the Government of India must forgive us if we have learnt not to put implicit reliance even in their most solemn pledges. At the time these assurances were made with that *ore rotundo* which the officials of Government know so well how to assume, at that very time public doubt grew strong, and a great many requests were made to the Government of India to define and re-define and re-define their position in this matter. At length the matter reached the ears of the Viceroy, that eminent personage who sits upon the Simla Hills, (*Laughter*) and a deputation came to him and suggested that the people were not yet satisfied with the repeated pledges given by Government; and then this peroration was addressed to them. "As the representative of the Sovereign in India I "regret that such language should have been held to me by you. The sole purpose of the "additional taxation you complain of was the preservation of the lives of the people of India "from the effects of Famine; whatever may be the faults or shortcomings of this Government," (A strange admission, Gentlemen! There are it seems faults and shortcomings even in the Government of India!) "its action in the matter to which your address makes reference was "dictated by the sincerest and most anxious desire to give the people of India the greatest "protection that could practically be provided for them against the calamities of future "famine. To insinuate the contrary is to insinuate a calumny." Gentlemen, we are now in a position not to insinuate a calumny but to make and register a very strong accusation in this matter. (*Cheers*)

What has been done with these taxes? In 1878 they produced something like Rx. 900,000; in the last year for which there are accounts I believe they are estimated to produce Rx. 1,730,300. During the last 16 years, for the sole purpose of providing the people of India with a Famine Insurance fund, taxes amounting in all to Rx. 17,429,592 were collected, out of which the Government of India promised to spend every year a sum of not less than 1½ Millions Sterling. Now let us see how they have kept their promises. For the 16 years the total expenditure on Famine Relief and Insurance amounted roughly to 16 crores of Rupees, that is to say, accepting the statement of the Government of India, we find, on the most liberal computation which we can make, only 16 crores of Rupees have been paid by the Government of India for this purpose 24 crores of Rupees promised, and 16 crores paid; discount off the promises of the Government of India 8 crores of Rupees, or 33 per cent. (*Cheers*) This, Gentlemen, is a very large discount to make on the promises of a big Government. I pass from the Famine Insurance Fund to the question of the Exchange Compensation allowance. It is proposed to take a million sterling from this Revenue, that is to say, to appropriate one milion sterling of the Famine fund for the deficiencies of the Government of India. Now where is that million going? That million which is taken from the pockets of the Indian Tax-payer by breaking one of the most solemn of pledges, *viz.*, the pledge to protect them from the possibility of famine, that money is going into the pockets of 900 comfortable Civil Servants of the Crown in India (*Shame*); that is going to pay the so-called Exchange Compensation allowance. (*Shame*) But Gentlemen, we are reasonable men we do not object to Exchange Compensation allowance altogether, but we object to it when given, as it is. What is this Exchange Compensation allowance? At present it is in most cases an indiscriminate increase of the salaries of certain officials out here; and those officials are often the youngest as well as the most inexperienced. Every man, whether he came here twenty years ago when the Rupee was 2*s.*, or whether he came yesterday when the Rupee was at 1*s.* 2*d.*, is to be allowed to remit half his pay to England at 1*s.* 6*d.*, so that the youngest servants of the State are paid for their untried services more than the course of exchange can ever have led them to expect. We object, and I think rightly, to indiscriminate Exchange Compensation allowance of this nature, and to these financial methods of the Government of India. (*Hear, hear*)

Now I come to another point—the question of stores. This again, I would suggest, is one of the points which should be rammed home at the Financial Enquiry. It does not matter that these matters which I am bringing before you are old stories, the public have not heard them often enough, and we want to bring them before the public and the House of Commons. Here is an entry in "Stores," "Law and Justice; Engine and Tea-Roller" £426-8-2. What does that mean? (*Laughter*) There are many other strange entries, but my time is short, so I will pause for a moment over this entry:—"Political; Presentation Articles" £327-5-5. This entry re-calls to my mind several little meannesses of the Government of India. Do you remember the present that was made to the Sultan of Zanzibar by the British Ambassador? That was debited to the Revenues of India. *Shame*) Do you remember the ball at Constantinople, which was also charged—some £8,000 Sterling—on the Revenues of the Government of India? (*Shame*) Do you know why that was charged? It was said that it was an excellent thing for India that England should be on good terms with the Sultan of Turkey. (*Laughter*) Then I mention to pass over "Stationery and Printing." "Telegraph Lines in India," "Stamps," "Post Offices," "Special Defence Works" that expensive theory of the Government of India the "Scientific Frontier"—and I ask "Why cannot you encourage home industries here in India instead of spending money on the falling rupee?" (*Hear, hear*) Last of all, Gentlemen, this question of stores reminds me of another thing and that is this: this Store Department, which spends 1½ millions of pounds every year, which, including capital expenditure, spent 4 million pounds of the Indian tax-payers' money in 1892-93 (4 million pounds means 7 crores of rupees!) is one of the most corrupt Government departments that the world has ever seen. (*Cheers*) Let me tell you a little incident about this Department. When I was travelling in the Punjab I met an Anglo-Indian, himself an officer of Government, who told me this little story. Somewhere here in Madras there was a man who had helped a Colonel, a man of some influence, in a matter of some importance. This Colonel out of gratitude offered this man an appointment and wrote to him saying "I can get you an appointment as an Inspector of Stores in London at £250 a year." He replied "I am very much obliged to you for your kind offer, but unfortunately I have a wife and family, and I cannot afford to take up the post on such a low salary," and so, Gentlemen, the post went elsewhere. Afterwards the Colonel wrote to this man and said, "I am very sorry to hear you have declined the appointment, for it was worth £1,250 a year." What does that mean? It means £1,000 a year in the shape of bribes. (*Shame*) Gentlemen, this is only one story there are many more; but I must pass on to a very important matter, and that is, to the Military expenditure of the Government of India, or rather to the methods of the Government of India in dealing with it. (*Hear, hear*)

There was published quite recently a return on Indian Military Expenditure. Now this is an instructive return because it shows you, although late in the day, some of the financial methods of this Government. The return is headed "East India (Military Expenditure)." The first thing you notice on opening the return is that the items of "Military Works" and "Special Defence Works" have been absolutely ignored. Now we put a question to Mr. Fowler, the Secretary of State for India, as to why in a return of Military Expenditure such an important part of Military Expenditure as that of "Military Works" was left out. He replied that the Return only dealt with Army Expenditure, and that "Military Expenditure" was the ordinary heading under which this is placed in the accounts. Well, Gentlemen, we turn up the Accounts of the Government of India, and we find no such heading as "Military Expenditure." In those accounts Military Expenditure figures under three heads, "Army Services", "Military Works" and "Special Defence Works." I do not see how we can exonerate the Government of India from either being extremely ignorant of their own accounts or else deliberately deceiving the public in England with the heading of Military Expenditure, which, while suggesting the whole, was meant to cover only a portion. (*Shame*) I am afraid that I have already exceeded my time allowance, (*Cries of* Go on, Go on) and so I must conclude: but before I do so, I must really bring to your notice one important matter, and that is the statement that the fall in the rupee is the sole cause of all the misfortunes of the Government of India. Now, Gentlemen, I am going to give you a few more figures, and I have done. We take the last decade, a period when there was no war and no famine—I speak under correction. No war expenditure was shown in the accounts, but in this instructive little Return to which I have been referring, it is shown that the war expenditure amounted to £11,000,000 during eight years; although that expenditure had been concealed and smothered amongst the general heads of expenditure of the Army. I am not speaking without the book, Gentlemen; there is literally in the accounts of the Government of India no mention of all this Military Expenditure on the frontier, which, in the return, is called exceptional war expenses. (*Shame*) During that decade there was nothing to disturb the finances of the Government of India. During those years the income of this country increased by 9½ crores of Rupees while the increase in the cost of exchange was only 7 crores of Rupees. During that same period Military and Civil Expenditure increased by no less than 12 crores of Rupees. (*Shame*) Gentlemen, the increase in the Revenues of this country exceeded the increase in the cost of exchange by 2½ crores, and by that same amount, namely, 2½ crores, the increase in Military and Civil expenditure exceeded the increase in the Revenues. I want you to appreciate these facts, which I am giving you on the figures of the Government of India. I want you to realize that these facts give the lie direct to the assertion of the Government of India that the fall in the rupee has accounted for the deficit and has been the solo cause of it. These figures show that the statement of Mr. Westland is an absolutely false statement, (*Shame*) and that that speech of Mr. Fowler's, for which he has been so much admired in the *Times* and the *St. James's Gazette* is founded on a fallacy, which contradicts the accounts of the Government of India and conceals the true state of affairs. (*Loud Cheers*)

MR. G. SUBRAMANIA IYER.

MR. G. SUBRAMANIA IYER:—Mr. Chairman and Gentlemen, Mr. Morgan-Browne has said that the object of the enquiry for which we ask is not in the nature of an audit on a big scale. We do not want an enquiry of that kind, but the enquiry we want, and which we ask for, must be such as will embrace not only the various items of expenditure but also the general financial policy, the general results of the financial administration, and the general financial condition of the Government of India. We have tried to ask for an enquiry of that kind, although Her Majesty's Government has been willing to grant an enquiry of a limited nature. But what is the object? Why should we ask for an enquiry at all? Are there no

Third Day.

Resolution V. Financial Enquiry.

Mr. G. Subramania Iyer.

responsible authorities who will do that of their own accord ? If there be defects and shortcomings in the financial administration of this country, will they not try to rectify them of their own accord ? Well, Gentlemen, our belief is that they have failed to do that, and that, unless we bring to bear upon them the pressure of public opinion, the pressure of Parliament, those authorities responsible for the good administration of this country will not do that. Gentlemen, this is not a statement made without authority; this is not an irresponsible statement made by us Congress-Wallahs. As a fact, Gentlemen, such of you as have watched current politics in this country must be aware of the very general complaint that has been made with regard to the financial difficulties that exist in the system of the great machinery of the Indian Government, that there is no centre which bears the burden of responsibility. There is no place where responsibility can be spotted. There is neither an individual nor an authority whose business it is to control the administration of the country and to set right any defect—any departures from sound doctrines that might take place. The Government of India has not done it. The India Council has failed to rectify our financial errors. Parliament has failed to do it. The speakers yesterday and our Chairman himself have drawn your attention to the fact that amidst the enormous imperial and local business that Parliament has to discharge it most unfortunately forgets and ignores the almost boundless interests of this great country. It is unfortunate that it should be so, but still it is a fact that, although the constitution of the Indian Government vests the final contnol and authority in Parliament, Parliament from the very nature of the case fails to give sufficient attention to the interests of this country. Then, with regard to the Council of Her Majesty's Secretary of State, a good deal was said about the utter uselessness of that institution and I do not want to say anything more to-day; but all of you are aware that while the Council is often very powerful to obstruct progress and reform in this country, it is entirely powerless to effect any good against policies, fancies, or whims, or against any vested interests in Parliament. Then, coming to the Government of India, what has it done ? I do not want to say a word in disparagement of the Government of India. The Viceroy and his Councillors are great and conscientious men. The Government of India has ben managed and officered by men who hold the very highest places in the list of statesmen of the world; the history of no country contains, nay, can present a more glorious array of statesmen celebrated for the highest statesmanship and broad principles; and to the Government of no country in the world have been brought to a greater extent than to the Government of India the great principles of civilised Government in modern days. We admit all that, but, unfortunately, since the Government was transferred to Her Majesty directly, there seems to be a slackness come over the Government of India, and the interests of this country have been more or less neglected. Well, such being the case, the necessity arises for the people of this country and for their friends in England to ask for a proper enquiry. We have seen that this request of ours has been supported recently by some eminent Anglo-Indian authorities, amongst whom are, I may tell you, Sir David Barbour, Sir Auckland Colvin and others, while even the *London Times* has said—all these authorities have said—that the greatest defect in the system of the Government of India is that there is no place in which the responsibility for the proper Government of this country can be fixed. Sir William Hunter writing in the columns of the *Times* has gone to the extent of accusing the Government of India of want of honesty generally. When he criticised Mr. Westland's budget, in which Exchange was taken at 14d. per Rupee, although everybody knew that that rate was excessively high, Sir W. Hunter even said that Mr. Westland did that in order to mitigate the scandal of sacrificing 14 millions of Rupees of potential Indian Revenue to party exigencies in England ; in other words, he asserted that this high rate of exchange was assumed in order to allay the public feeling against the exclusion of Manchester goods from the Tariff Act. Such being the case, Sir, it will not be said that we are presumptuous in asking for this enquiry into the ability of the Indian people to bear their

MR. G. SUBRAMANIA IYER.

existing financial burdens. It may also from experience be said of this Government : that during the last 30 years, the Government of India and those authorities who are responsible for the Government have had absolutely no policy in guiding the administration of this country. Well this complaint of the financial distress in India is not a new complaint. Eighteen years ago Sir John Strachey made it, and then it is also known that conscientious Viceroys, eminent Viceroys, like Lord Mayo and Lord Lawrence, have made the same complaint, that the finances of the country require particular looking after. Yet all these warnings and all these experiences have been useless, and what is the guarantee, Gentlemen, that, whilst in the past experience has gone for nothing, in the future the constituted authorities of the Indian Government will take care that the financial policy of this country shall be definitely and properly controlled? Mr. Westland said in his budget speech that within the last 10 years, four new taxes had been imposed and the surpluses of the Provincial Governments swept off into the Imperial coffers. Still the financial difficulties have not disappeared, for the very sufficient reason that all the further proceeds of this taxation have been spent upon wars and upon Compensation Allowance to the European Employés of Government. (*Shame*) The *London Times* pointed out recently that there were three duties which the Government of India were bound to bear in mind. One of these duties was to enforce the strictest economy in the administration of the public funds. But how can the strictest economy be expected when the authorities in England ask the Government of India to contribute for all sorts of purposes? (*Cheers*) And then, another duty of the Government of India was to manage the financial affairs with greater forethought and prudence. But what inducement is there for the Government of India or for those gentlemen who constitute the Government to administer the finances with greater forethought and prudence? (*The President at this juncture struck the gong*) I shall conclude presently. The third duty is to avoid at all hazards any increase in Home charges, or sterling liabilities of any kind. That also is impossible because the Indian payments in England in whole or in part are met by fresh issues of sterling loans. Well, all these considerations point to the fact that unless pressure is brought to bear upon the authorities, and unless we request Parliament to institute an enquiry, there is no chance of the financial affairs of this country being properly controlled. I, therefore, most heartily support the Resolution that has been placed before you. (*Cheers*)

MR. R. D. NAGARKAR.

MR. R. D. NAGARKAR :—Mr. President, Brother Delegates, Ladies and Gentlemen, I have great pleasure in supporting the Resolution which has been so ably proposed, seconded, and supported by the speakers who have preceded me.

The Resolution, as you will see, presents a twofold character. In the first place it embodies the expression of thanks to the Imperial Parliament of Great Britain for the Committee which it has given us, and in the second place it embodies a prayer to the effect that the scope of the enquiry which has been assigned to this Committee should be so far extended as to include within its operation an enquiry into the ability of the people of India to bear the present financial burdens, and into the financial relations between India and the United Kingdom; for it is perfectly clear that if the enquiry is to be conducted on the lines and within the limits which have been assigned to this Committee, such an enquiry will not bear practical fruit. All know that the scope which has been assigned to this Enquiry is limited to an examinatien of the Expenditure side only, and that on grounds of policy all examination of the Revenue side has been taken away from its cognizance. Our life-long cry against British Administration is that it has been increasing the expenditure beyond all reasonable bounds, and has actually driven the people of India and the Indian Administration to the verge of starvation and poverty. (*Shame, Shame*) You all know that when we speak of Expenditure we do so in reference to the Revenue aspect of the question, and if you give a moment's thought to the consideration of the subject, you will be able to realise fully that, with regard to many important heads of administration,

Mr. R. D. Nagarkar.

Revenue and Expenditure are indissolubly bound up together, that they cannot be considered independently of each other, and that one cannot be separated from the other. You might spend fifty times more money, but if you are able to show that increased expenditure is calculated to bring in a proportionate increase in the Revenue without causing any additional hardship upon the people, then the increased expenditure, far from being condemned would rather be welcomed; but, on the other hand, if the increased expenditure does not bring in a proportionate increase in the Revenue, then such a situation of affairs becomes a matter for serious anxiety, and involves considerations of the soundness or otherwise of the policy of the British Administration towards India. (*Cheers*) A mere increase in expenditure is not necessarily to be condemned, nor is a mere decrease in expenditure necessarily to be applauded, but condemnation or applause is to be applied only when one branch of the administration has been examined in the light thrown upon it by another branch of the administration. (*Hear, hear*) All this, Gentlemen, I have stated by way of illustration, to show that in most important heads of administration questions of Revenue and Expenditure are entirely dependent upon one another, and that it is absolutely impossible to do adequate justice to the one without taking cognizance of the other. (*Hear, hear*) The proposal for including the examination of the Revenue side of the administration within the scope of the enquiry which has been assigned to this committee being a matter of absolute necessity, it can also be supported on other important grounds. You are all aware that as far back as the year 1870 or thereabouts, the British Parliament appointed a similar Committee of Enquiry which was popularly styled the Fawcett Committee because Mr. Fawcett, whose immortal name stands indelibly engraved on the hearts of the whole Indian nation, was one of its members. (*Cheers*) This Committee, having continued its labours for four full years, recorded a huge mass of evidence, but had no time to give a Report or to summarise the evidence it had collected, because by the time the labours of this Committee had been nearly completed, the British Parliament was dissolved, and along with it this Committee also was dissolved. If the scope of the enquiry of the present Committee is extended, and an examination of the Revenue side of the administration included in it, the work of this Committee will have been much simplified. They have only to fill up the gap which the last Committee left at the end of 1882, and to examine half a dozen witnesses, the heads of each department, with a view to ascertaining the change that has taken place during the last 20 years; and when this is done the enquiry will not occupy a very large portion of the Committee's time. From this you will be satisfied, Gentlemen, that the inclusion of an enquiry into the Revenue side of the question is an absolute necessity, and that unless it is conducted hand in hand with an enquiry into the Expenditure side, no Enquiry will ever be complete. If the Secretary of State or the Parliament of England are not pleased to allow that, then they had better save themselves the trouble of appointing any Committee at all, because we are of the firm conviction that unless the Committee is constituted on the lines which we have indicated in our Resolution, the result of the present Committee would eventually be to create a feeling of general discontent and dissatisfaction throughout the whole Indian Nations. (*Cheers*) With these remarks I most heartily commend the proposition to your acceptance. (*Cheers*)

Mr. A. C. Parthasarady Naidu.

Mr. A. C. Parthasarady Naidu then addressed the Meeting in Tamil amid frequent bursts of applause.

The President:—The fifth resolution has been properly moved, seconded, and supported. Let those who are in favour of it hold up their hands. (*Voices, All, All.*)

The Resolution was carried unanimously.

The President:—The next resolution will be moved by the Hon. Surendra Nath Banerjea.

**Third Day.**

Resolution VI.
Simultaneous
Examinations.

Hon. Surendra
Nath Banerjea.

The Hon. Surendra Nath Banerjea, who on rising was greeted with tremendous cheering, moved the following resolution :—

That this Congress expresses its deep sense of disappointment at the despatch of the Secretary of State supporting the views of the Government of India on the question of Simultaneous Examinations, and this Congress hereby places on record its respectful but firm protest against the despatch as, among other things, introducing a new principle inconsistent with the Charter Act of 1833 and the Proclamation of the Queen of 1st November 1858 (the solemn pledges contained in which the Secretary of State and the Government of India now seek to repudiate) by creating a disability, founded upon race, for the despatch lays down that a minimum of European officials in the Covenanted Service is indispensable.

That in the opinion of this Congress the creation of the Provincial service is no satisfactory or permanent solution of the problem, as this service, constituted as it is at present, falls short of the legitimate aspirations of the people, and that the interests of the subordinate service will not suffer by the concession of Simultaneous Examinations.

That no attempt has been made to make out a case against the holding of Simultaneous Examination for the recruitment of the Engineering, Forest, Telegraph, and the higher Police Service Examinations, and the Congress regrets to notice that the despatches of the Secretary of State, the Government of India, and the various local Governments are absolutely silent with regard to this aspect of the Resolution of the House of Commons.

That this Congress respectfully urges on Her Majesty's Government that the resolution of the House of Commons of 2nd June 1893, on the question of Simultaneous Examinations should be speedily carried out as an act of justice to the Indian people.

Mr. President, Brother Delegates, Ladies and Gentlemen,—I thank you most cordially for the kind greeting which you have accorded me. I do not take it in the light of a personal compliment, but as the expression of your enthusiasm—I was going to add of your unabated enthusiasm for the Congress cause. (*Cheers*) I have heard it said that our enthusiasm is on the wane, that the first forvour of the early days of the Congress movement is fast disappearing. I desire those sceptics who indulge in sentiments such as these, to witness the grand and imposing spectacle of to-day (*Cheers*), and to be convinced of the error of their ways. Oh, No! our enthusiasm is not on the wane. It continues to glow as brightly as ever (*Hear, hear*), and so far as some of us are concerned, it will centinue to glow until the vital spark of life itself has been extinguished (*Loud Cheers*), and then we shall bequeath it, as a sacred legacy, to those who, coming after us, will bear our names, will profit by our labours, and seek to extend the ever-widening sphere of our political rights, and to hasten forward the accomplishment of the perfected destiny of an emancipated people. (*Cheers*) Gentlemen, last year about this time, we were rejoicing that the House of Commons had definitely affirmed the principle of Simultaneous Examinations. Last year about this time, in Congress assembled, we expressed the hope—I was somewhat sceptical about the matter—that the Government of India would see its way to give effect to the resolution of the House and fulfil the just and legitimate aspirations of the people of India. Those hopes have now been blasted. We meet to-day under the shadow of a great disappointment; but we need not despair. More than once before this have we led a forlorn hope to victory. More than once before this have we triumphed against vituperation and scorn and ridicule, and I hope and trust it may yet be possible for us to shatter to pieces the stronghold in which Anglo-Indian prejudice has found a safe and a last asylum. (*Cheers*) It would not be the least memorable of the many achievements of the Congress. It would be the crowning triumph of this generation. (*Cheers*)

Gentlemen, speaking at Madras from this platform, speaking for myself, I say that it is impossible to withhold the tribute of our gratitude and admiration from the only Govern-

Third Day

Resolution VI. Simultaneous Examinations.

Hon. Surendra Nath Banerjea

ment in India, the Government of Madras, (*Cheers*) which supported the resolution of the House of Commons. I know that since then a chahge has come across the spirit of Lord Wenlock's dreams. I remember his Vizagapatam speech. *Scriptum manet.* What has been written remains and that despatch will continue to be regarded, at any rate for the time being as a monument of the disinterested philanthrophy, which is only another name for far-sighted statesmanship, of the Government of Madras. (*Cheers*) I know not how it is, but the conduct of Madras officials has often appeared to me in the light of a riddle, which I have not been able to solve. (*Laughter*) You gentlemen of Madras may be more fortunately situated in this respect (*Cries of* No, No), and may possibly be able to give me an answer (*No, No*), Madras officials, in their own country and under the wholesome influence of Madras opinion, have often been known to be the champions of progressive ideas and of liberal Government. Transferred to Bengal, placed under unhealthy influences and unholy associations, they become the apostles of reactionary measures. (*Laughter*) When the Vernacular Press Act was imposed upon every other province in India, Madras escaped the scourge, because the Duke of Buckingham, the Governor of Madras, would not have it. (*Cheers*) When every other Government voted against the resolution of the House of Commons the Madras Government voted in favour of it. (*Cheers*) But strangely enough it was a Madras official, Sir Alexander Arbuthnot, who from his place in the Supreme Council, stood as sponsor to the Vernacular Press Act. And, again, it was a Madras official, Sir Philip Hutchins, who was the author of the jury notification (*Hisses*), the inspirer and the malignant genius of the policy of Lord Lansdowne. (*Cheers*) Gentlemen, one word more about Lord Wenlock. He has asked us to wait and watch and to submit to the orders of the Secretary of State. We desire to tell Lord Wenlock and all else whom it may concern, that we cannot submit to a decision which will have the effect of stereotyping our political servitude. (*Hear, hear and Cheers*) We cannot afford to palter with our birthright, nor sell it for a mess of potage. Our Sovereign has passed round the word of emancipation, she has declared that we are to be free; that we are to be eligiblo to the highest offices in the State; Parliament has endorsed the mandate; and we shall see to it that no minister of the Crown, however highly placed he may be, that no Government, however influential it may be, is permitted to nullify the gracious pledges of our Sovereign and the authoritative declaration of Parliament. Gentlemen, last year about this time, I have already remarked, we were rejoicing about the resolution of the House of Commons. These rejoicings have given place to disappointment. I do not know what view you take of the despatch of the Secretary of State. I regard it in the light of a deliberate affront offered to the public opinion of this country. We prayed in Congress, we prayed in our public meetings, we deluged the House of Commons with petitions in favour of Simultaneous Examinations. I must not omit to mention the one solitary protest which was sent to the House of Commons—it emanated from this city. (*Laughter*) Half a dozen nobodies (*Laughter*), whose names I do not remember—I do not care to remember their names—met in the back slums of your city, concocted a bit of paper which they called a petition to Parliament, and sent it to the House of Commons. (*Shame, disgraceful*) I think their conduct was very disgraceful. Whom was it presented by? It was presented by no other person than General Sir George Chesney. (*Hisses*) Who is General Sir George Chesney! He was the late Military Member of the Viceregal Council, and, what is more significant, the father of the editor of the *Pioneer* newspaper. (*Laughter*) Well this solitary protest, emanating from the back slums of your city, signed by half a dozen nobodies, was presented to the House of Commons, by the late Military Member of the Viceregal Council. (*Laughter*) It was indeed a desperate cause which needed such an upholding. Baron Reuter—I think I ought to call him Baron and give him all his honours—thought the event to be of such great political importance that he flashed the intelligence from Europe across to Asia for the edification of the two hundred and fifty millions of the people of India.

Third Day.

Resolution VI.
Simultaneous Examinations.

Hon. Surendra Nath Banerjea.

Well, Gentlemen, we though we had made some impression on the Ministry for the late Under Secretary of State Mr. George Russell, from his place in the House of Commons, declared—I think it was in connection with the budget speech—that the Government, having offered its opposition to the resolution, would not throw further difficulties in the way of its being given effect to. How did the Ministry proceed to carry out this part of their promise. They proceeded to carry it out in the same way in which they generally carry out their promises. (*Laughter*) They addressed a despatch to the Government of India. The Government of India in its turn solicited the opinion of the local Governments. Mark you, the *modus operandi* followed by these various Governments; they consulted in secret; they deliberated in secret; they wrote their despatches in secret; they submitted them in secret; nobody heard a word about the matter; they did not take the opinions of those public bodies whose opinions they are accustomed to solicit in regard to questions of public importance; and they were wise in their reticence (*Laughter*), because they knew perfectly well that, if they had followed the usual procedure, consulted the various local bodies—Hindu and Mahomedan—for I refuse to believe that any conscientious Mahomedan (barring, of course, the celebrated half-a-dozen nobodies of your town) that any conscientious Mahomedan could have voted against the resolution of the House of Commons (*Cheers*)—I am perfectly convinced that, if they had consulted the public bodies and followed the usual procedure, there would have been an overwhelming consensus of opinion in favour of the resolution of the House of Commons. Well, Gentlemen, the Secretary of State based his orders upon these various despatches which that high functionary received. The despatch of the Secretary of State is an extraordinary document. It contains three paragraphs extending over thirteen lines. (*Laughter*) I desire to call your attention to the number "three" which is unlucky with us Hindus (*Laughter*), and the number "thirteen" which is unlucky with Christians. (*Laughter*) The despatch is short and sweet; brevity they say is the soul of wit; brevity is the essence of this document; but I must confess its wit is not apparent. The Secretary of State in that document invites the Government of India to state the conditions subject to which, in the opinion of the Government, the resolution may be given effect to. Mark the loyalty of the Secretary of State to his masters, the House of Commons. It is evident from the words of the despatch which I have just quoted that, in the opinion of the Secretary of State, the resolution of the House of Commons cannot be given effect to in its entirety for he wants an expression of opinion from the Government of India, as to the modifications subject to which the resolution may be carried out. The views of the Secretary of State—the sinister views I was going to add—become more apparent in the second paragraph of the despatch. The Secretary of State openly invites the Government of India to open the battery of its hostile criticism upon the doomed resolution of the House. The Secretary of State says, in the language of diplomacy which is usual on such occasions, that he has no desire to fetter the discretion of the Government of India with regard to any remark which the Government may think fit to make upon the resolution of the House of Commons. I should like to know what the Secretary of State himself would think if the Government of India were to send round a despatch, which it had received from the Secretary of State and invite the various subordinate Governments to treat it in the spirit of hostile criticism; but, perhaps, that is only an error in form, a mistake in procedure. We come to something which is a great deal worse in the third paragraph. He says that it is to be an indispensable condition on the part of any recommendation which the Government of India may make, that an adequate number of appointments should be held by Europeans. The Secretary of State need not have taken the trouble to say so. It was a mere work of supererogation. At the present moment the Civil Service is the monopoly of Europeans. I don't quarrol with them for it. It is their monopoly, and we are trying to break through the monopoly. There are about 940 appointments in the Civil Service, and how many, do you think, are filled by Natives of India? About 40. What is the native population of India? It is two hundred millions. The European population consists of seventy thousand souls, exclusive of the Army. Out of two hundred millions, forty persons only are deemed qualified to hold appointments in the Covenanted Civil Service. (*Shame*) Out of seventy thousand, nearly a thousand are deemed to be qualified for appointments in the Civil Service. (*Shame*) These figures involve the greatest slur upon the Government of this country, for these figures, if they mean anything, mean this—that, after a century of British rule, after a century of enlightened administration and liberal education, only forty of our countrymen have been qualified for service in the higher appointments under the Government of this country. (*Cheers*) Well, Gentlemen, if Simultaneous Examinations were conceded, I am quite sure that for many years to come the ratio would not be sensibly diminished for, as the Madras Government very properly observed in their despatch, the immediate effect of Simultaneous Examinations would be an accession in the number of candidates competing at the Examination, but not necessarily an accession in the number of successful candidates. But, Gentlemen, when the Secretary of State lays down this recommendation in this naked form, in this undisguised fashion, he invites a protest and a remonstrance; for the Secretary of State now, for the first time, introduces the element of racial disability into a question from which considerations of racial disability have been eliminated for a period of more than thirty years; for what does the order of the Secretary of State amount to? It comes to this that if Simultaneous Examinations were granted, and, say, that fifty appointments were competed for, and the first fifty candidates were Natives of India, all of them would not get the appointments—some of them would be disqualified by reason of their race; they would suffer for the crime of colour. (*Shame*) Would the Secretary of State venture to introduce a condition like this just now? If not, why should he be permitted to conjure up into existence the dead, buried and forgotten spectre of racial disability? (*Cheers*)

Gentlemen, I say that the despatch is inconsistent with the Charter Act of 1833. You remember the eighty-seventh section of the Charter Act. It lays down:—"That "no Native of India nor any natural born subject of His Majesty, resident therein, shall "by reason only of his religion, place of birth, descent, colour, or any of them. be dis-"abled from holding any place, office or employment under the said Company." The point was carried a little further by the terms of the Queen's proclamation. Let us repeat the Queen's proclamation; let this great assembly stand up in reverential awe of that great proclamation, which we have come here to vindicate, to uphold and to maintain. (*Here the whole audience stood up.*) "It is our further will that so far as may be our subjects of "whatever race or creed be freely and impartially admitted to all offices in our service the "duties of which they may be qualified by their education, their ability and their integrity "duly to discharge." Gentlemen, we take our stand upon this proclamation; the proclamation is our watchword, our battle cry, our Magna Charta, not a Magna Charta wrung by Barons in open revolt against their king, but the spontaneous gift of a beneficent sovereign. (*Cheers*) It heralds the dawn of a new epoch in the history of this country: it represents the establishment of a closer relationship between the Queen of England and the people of India; it is the starting point of modern Indian history; it was given on a great and historic occasion; it is a sacred document, and to mark its solemn character Her Majesty was pleased to invoke the blessing of Almighty God upon it, "and may the God of all power, she exclaimed, "grant unto us and those in authority under us strength to carry out these our wishes for the "good of our people." Yet a document of this character, of this magnitude, of this solemnity, of this sacred nature, is sought to be repudiated by the Government of Lord Lansdowne. (*Shame*) I feel myself as a loyal subject of the Crown overwhelmed with a sense of shame and humiliation at the action of our Rulers who pretend to be the ministers, the faithful, the loyal, the devoted agents of our Sovereign; the proclamation is repudiated, its solemn character is called in question, for this is precisely what the Government of India does in the despatch to which I have called your attention. The Government of India says it is not necessary to make the concession for the fulfilment of the so-called pledges, upon which the claim is founded; and these so-called pledges were given by our Sovereign on a great and historic occasion invoking the aid of Divine Providence to enable her to carry them out. Gentlemen, if I can show you that the worst Government that we ever had and the best Government that we ever had both unite in testifying to the solemnity of these pledges, we shall have made out a strong case in favour of our contention. Undoubtedly the worst Government that we ever had—it is a matter of history, it is a matter of public notoriety, a matter of general accord– was the Government of Lord Lytton—it was the Government of the Vernacular Press Act, the Government of the Arms Act, the Government which initiated the policy of aggression beyond the frontiers, a policy which has been fraught with that reckless military expenditure which our friend Mr. Wacha deplores from year to year in vain from his place in this Congress. What does Lord Lytton say about this matter? I hope I am not tiring your patience. (*No, No*) In a speech that he delivered in March, 1877, as Chancellor of the Calcutta University, he said that the proclamation of the Queen (I quote his words) contains solemn pledges spontaneously given and founded upon the highest justice. He went on to observe that these pledges have not yet been adequately redeemed. Then in that secret despatch which has more than once been quoted in our discussions, in that secret despatch which he wrote to the Secretary of State, he said, "We have cheated the people of India." (*Shame*) The word "cheated" is his own word, not a paraphrase of my own. "We have cheated the people of India, we have broken to the hope, the words of promise which we have uttered to the ear." That was what was said by Lord Lytton. The best Government that we have ever had was undoubtedly the Government of Lord Ripon (*Enthusiastic* (*Cheers*), the Government which repealed the Vernacular Press Act, the Government which conferred upon us the inestimable boon of local self-Government, the Government which introduced a higher tone, a higher and nobler moral ideal into the Administration and placed that Administration for the first time in touch with popular sympathies. Well, Gentlemen, during the height of the Ilbert Bill discussion this matter of the proclamation of the Queen engaged the attention of the Viceregal Council There was a gentleman of the name of Mr. Thomas. I think you gentlemen of Madras may know him; he hailed from this Presidency. He was Member of the Supreme Council at that time. He had read a little work issued at that time by Sir James FitzStephen; he was well grounded in that work, and he was an apt disciple of Sir James FitzStephen. He observed in the course of a speech that he made from his place in the Supreme Council that the proclamation enjoined no duty, imposed no obligation, laid no mandate on the Government of India. (*Shame*) Against this solemn and public repudiation of the proclamation Lord Ripon raised his voice in indignant protest. Let me read those words which have been read a hundred times in the past—they will be read a hundred times in the future—they will be read by generations to come until the terms of that Proclamation have been vindicated and fulfilled to the letter.

"To me it seems" exclaimed Lord Ripon, "a very serious thing to put forth to the " people of India a doctrine which renders worthless the solemn words of their Sovereign and " which converts her gracious promises, which her Indian subjects have cherished for a quarter " of a century, into a hollow mockery as meaningless as the compliments which form the " invariable opening of an oriental letter. The document is not a treaty—it is not a diplo- " matic instrument—it is a declaration of principles of Government which, if it is obligatory " at all, is obligatory in respect to all to whom it is addressed. The document, therefore, to " which Sir FitzJames Stephen has given the sanction of his authority, I feel bound to repu- " diate to the utmost of my power. It seems to me to be inconsistent with the character of my " Sovereign and with the honour of my country, and if it were once to be received and acted " upon by the Government of England it would do more than anything else could possibly do to " strike at the root of our power and to destroy our just influence. I have read in a book, the "authority of which the Hon'ble Mr. Thomas will admit, that righteousness exalteth a nation, "and my study of history, which has not been limited, has led me to the conclusion that it is not "by force of her armies or by the might of her soldiery that a great empire is permanently "maintained, but that it is by the righteousness of her laws, by her respect for the principles "of justice. To believe otherwise appears to me to assume that there is not a God in Heaven "who rules over the affairs of men, and who can punish injustice and iniquity in nations as "surely as he can in the individuals of which they are composed."

But, Gentlemen, I have yet a higher authority than the authority of Lord Ripon in support of my view; that is the authority of Her Majesty the Queen herself. I hope that is an authority which will be accepted by Lord Lansdowne and his quondam councillor Sir Philip Hutchins. Her Majesty, when the proclamation was being discussed, wrote a letter to Earl Derby, at that time Prime Minister, requesting him that he would be good enough, to write the Proclamation in his own language, in terms which would be worthy of a female sovereign addressing a vast and a distant population, and for the first time in their history giving them solemn pledges. But, Gentlemen, the Government of India relies upon a saving clause—"So far as may be." The saving clause won't save the Government. (*Laughter*) That is perfectly true. The saving clause must be interpreted in connection with the context. What is the character and the scope of the proclamation? It is a noble declaration of a beneficent policy; it is a royal proclamation, and must be interpreted in the spirit of queenly beneficence. Those who have recourse to tactics of this description seem to me not to understand the slur and humiliation which they involve upon the honour of their country and Sovereign. To say, as Lord Ripon puts it, that a proclamation has been issued purporting to make solemn promises when, as a matter of fact, no such promises are made, is to be guilty of an unheard of piece of hyprocrisy. It is a proceeding which may recommend itself to the approving judgment of official experts, but, if accepted, it would represent a piece of diplomatic mendacity unworthy of those who have recourse to it.

Gentlemen, there are one or two other matters which I wish to touch upon very briefly. The Government of India tells us that if Simultaneous Examinations were granted the Provincial Service would suffer. I should like to know since when the Government of India has developed this wonderful concern for the well-being of the Provincial Service. I remember the years 1870, 1880, and 1890. Through the space of twenty years there was not the smallest manifestation of this anxiety for the betterment of the prospects of the Provincial Service—it has probably been stimulated by our agitation in connection with Simultaneous Examinations. What the Government of India really says is this, that the Covenanted Service is not intended for you gentlemen of India, it is meant for Europeans. But here is, another service. You may enter it and we will improve it for you, but really this is the service that you must confine your ambition to. You may remember that in 1870 the Parliamentary Statute was passed. Under that Statute rules were to be framed by the Government of India subject to which rules, members of the Uncovenanted Service were to be promoted to appointments hitherto reserved for the Covenanted Service. The Government framed half-a-dozen rules in as many years, then it paused for another six years, and then appointed a member of the Uncovenanted Service to an appointment hitherto reserved for the Covenanted Service. If the Government is really so anxious about the well-being of the Provincial Service, might I be permitted to ask how was it that the Government did not accept that part of the recommendation of the Public Service Commission which provided that the appointment of a Divisional Commissioner and a member of the Board of Revenue should be reserved for the Provincial Service, or how was it that the Government of India did not, in accordance with the recommendations of the Public Service Commission, alter the schedule attached to the Act of 1861 for the betterment of the Provincial Service?

I have been told that the martial races would resent the holding of Simultaneous Examinations. Why the martial races should resent it is a thing which I cannot understand.

Third Day.

Resolution VI. Simultaneous Examinations.

Hon. Surendra Nath Banerjea.

They do not care for civil appointments. Their ambition lies in a different direction altogether. They want to be the captains of our army, the leaders of our battalions. They say that the Central Asian subjects of the Czar are admitted into the commissioned ranks of the Russian army; they pray that they may be placed on the same footing with the Mahomedan subjects of the Czar. The Government will not gratify their ambition in this respect and ascribe to them fancied grievances which they never feel, and make them the pretext for denying us that justice to which we are entitled. Then again it is said that an Indian official is placed at a disadvantage in comparison with a European, if he is called upon to deal with those unhappy riots and disturbances between Hindus and Mahomedans which have taken place in recent years. I think, Sir, I speak the sense of this great Congress and of every educated Indian, be he a Hindu or Mahomedan when I say that we deplore these differences and these disturbances (*Hear, hear*), and we go a step further and observe that the Government of India is directly responsible for these disturbances by following a policy of "Divide and rule." (*Shame*) I think it is very shameful that the Government of India, which is responsible for this state of things, should take advantage of it to deprive us of our legitimate claims and aspirations. I am sure that tactics so discreditable would not recommend themselves to the judgment of the British public or to members of Parliament, two of whom we have on this platform. (*Cheers*)

One point more and I shall be done. It is said that the masses do not wish that we should fill the higher appointments. It is a monstrous proposition to bring forward that the masses would prefer foreign Magistrates and Judges to Magistrates of their own race and colour. This represents a perversity in human nature, a miracle in human disposition which I am not prepared to accept upon the *ipse dixit* of the Government of India. Gentlemen, if the Government is really so careful and so solicitous of the interests of the masses, might I be permitted to inquire why it does not reduce the Salt Tax, which presses so heavily upon the masses? (*Laughter*) Might I be permitted to enquire why it does not abandon the opium revenue which demoralises the masses; might I be permitted to ask why it does not raise the taxable minimum for the Income Tax which would afford sensible relief to the masses? These are things which the Government will not do; but when it wants to defeat (the legitimate aspirations of the educated classes then forsooth it becomes the champion of the masses. (*Laughter*)

Gentlemen, there can be no question that we have sustained a great defeat, and I think we owe it to ourselves that we should convert this defeat into a victory. We should consecrate our efforts by that spirit of lofty self-denial and patriotic devotion which, by making men divine, renders human endeavour irresistible. We are bound to win the fight in which we are engaged;—

"For Freedom's battle once begun,
Bequeathed from bleeding Sire to Son,
Though often lost, is ever won."

In a conflict between the Government and popular rights the popular side has always triumphed. (*Hear, hear*) The victory has always remained with the People so long as they have manfully stuck to their guns. I cannot persuade myself to think that the sacrifices which we have been able to make in this connection have at all been commensurate with the greatness of the occasion or the urgency of the crisis. Where is the universal protest against Mr. Fowler's despatch? The whole country should ring with the voice of indignation. It is no use recording a resolution like this and then going to sleep over it. It is no use recording a resolution like this unless we are in a position to make every town, every hamlet, every province, every district ring with the cry of indignant protest against Mr. Fowler's despatch. Gentlemen, it is possible for each one of us assembled here to do something according to the measure of our capacities and the measure of our opportunities. There are more than 1,000 delegates before me; may we not resolve before the year 1895 has closed, to send each one of us to Parliament a petition containing at least 1,000 signatures? Then we shall have before the year 1895 has expired at least 1,000 petitions laid before Parliament with a million signatures. Our numbers will make an impression upon the House of Commons, they will make an impression even on that fossilised institution, the India Council. (*Laughter*) I am sure if Mr. Dadabhai Naoroji were here (*Cheers*) he would make this appeal to you, only with much greater force and emphasi than I can command. Gentlemen, it may be that notwithstanding all these efforts we may not succeed; it may be that success may not crown our efforts on this occasion; it may be that the flag which we hold aloft, the emblem of battle and the emblem of victory, may droop from our sinking hands; but we may be quite sure that others will rise up in more fortunate times who, working under happier conditions, will carry that flag triumphantly to victory. (*Cheers*) It is this hope which sustains, animates, cheers, and comforts us. I am confident that twenty years hence when the dust and heat of this controversy will have been allayed, English statesmen will wonder how their predecessors in office could have refused so reasonable a measure of concession to the just aspirations of the people of India. But so it has always been with the rulers of men who decked in brief authority, too frequently forget the terrible responsibility which, under the Providence of God, devolves upon them in respect to those who are placed under their care.

But, Gentlemen, it is open to us in the meantime to prove by our loyalty, our devotion, and self-sacrifice that we are qualified for the boon we pray for. So let the moral victory prepare the way for that political emancipation to which our fondest aspirations tend. The promised land is full in view but an untoward fate prevents us from entering it; nevertheless, from the Sinai of faith and hope, like Moses of old we may obtain a prospective view of the glories of the land of Canaan, the destined inheritance of our children and our children's children. I am confident that in the fulness of time, under the Providence of God and the auspices of British Rule, they will take possession of this land of promise where their fetters will fall off, their badge of political slavery will disappear; where, being British subjects in name, they will be British subjects in reality, and, where under the fostering influence of free political institutions, they will develop a civilisation the noblest which the world has ever seen, the emblem of indissoluble union between England and India, a civilisation fraught with unspeakable blessings to the people of India and unspeakable renown to the English name. That is the future which with the eye of faith we see awaits us; that is the future which looms in the distance; that is the future which inspires us with an enthusiasm of which the Anglo-Indian bureaucracy can have no conception; that is the future for which we work, and for which some of us, at any rate, are prepared to lay down our lives; it is the future of an emancipated people, ennobled by the spirit of liberty, consecrated by the genius of self-sacrifice and consolidated by fervent loyalty to the British connection. (*Loud and long continued Cheers*)

Hon. Rajah Rampal Singh.

The Hon. Rajah Rampal Singh:—Mr. President, Brother Delegates, Ladies and Gentlemen,—When I rise on this occasion after my able friend the Hon. Babu Surendra Nath Banerjea, I do not rise with the empty ambition to speak before you or distinguish myself by my speech, but I simply rise according to the English saying, that Nelson said, 'that every Englishman should do his duty.' I simply rise to express my sentiments on this occasion, but not to inflict a speech upon you. Speaking on this occasion, Gentlemen, first I should like to read to you the promises which have been made to us by the Queen and her predecessor, then I will try to show you how by the representatives of Her Majesty some steps have commenced to be taken to violate these pledges, and then I will bring before you the circumstances of India which urgently require some conciliatory measure to enable us to keep our place as a nation, because the best riches of the country consisting in the produce of the soil do not profit us as they should do, as I will show you later on.

The next thing for retaining the riches of the country is to engage in trade, and even that is not entirely in our hands. The monopoly of the Indian trade is in the hands of alien merchants. The third and last resource to keep the country in its proper position is Government service. Even that is at hazard. I am coming gradually to these points, but you will allow me first to begin with Her Majesty's promise, and then I will show you how that promise has been defeated. This is from the letter of the Governor of the Punjab, who has been so well praised for his conclusive letter which he has written against this Resolution of Parliament. In order to understand our present position with regard to this question, it is necessary at starting to look back to its past history. That history, so far as regards what we deal with here, began with Section 87, cap. 3 & 4, William IV., which runs thus: "Be it enacted that no native of the said territories nor any natural born subject of Her Majesty resident therein shall by reason only of his religion, place of birth, descent, colour, or any of them, be disabled from holding any place of office or employment under the said Company". I may be allowed to point out to you what this meant. I may be permitted to read a little further by which you will see that not only the Civil Service but the Military Service appointments also were opened to us. (*The President struck the gong*). I must submit to the chair, but I hope I shall be allowed to go on for a little time more. Lord Ellenborough, in the debate of the 5th of July, 1833, charged the Government with proposing to place the political and military powers in India in the hands of the natives of India. Then comes Her Majesty's Proclamation which you have all heard. As we did not appreciate these blessings, no objection was thrown in our way, but when a few of our Bengali friends passed their Examinations successfully in England then Lord Lytton's Government began to meditate, and he wrote a letter, a private letter, after consulting all the Governors and Lieutenant-Governors, to Lord Cranbrook, and in this he proposed that the systems of the Military and Civil Service should be identical, and the Examination for the Civil Service should be closed for Indians. (*Shame*) To this Lord Cranbrook replied that shutting up the Board of the Civil Service would require the sanction of Parliament, which he said " he did not like to undertake because he did not expect success " (*Laughter*) He asked Lord Lytton to propose some other scheme, and the other scheme proposed was to reduce the age of the candidates from 21 to 19. These promises were made. I have got two other letters, but I need not read them, because the gong is gone. There is a letter which Her Majesty wrote to Lord Derby and which our able proposer has already mentioned here. Well, Gentlemen, when the authorities saw that we were not ready to avail ourselves of the gracious promises of the Sovereign, they were silent; now that they perceive that we crave the fulfilment of those promises the Government are endeavouring to nullify the pledges of the Crown. (*Cheers*) It seems to me that the promises or, as they have been called by the late Viceroy, "so called pledges," were not intended to be redeemed. They were simply made to satisfy us, but were never intended to be fulfilled. I have told you, that the circumstances of India are in a most deplorable state; to prove this, I must quote you one instance. I cannot help doing it because it is a triumph for India. There is an Urdu proverb which says that " There is no beauty if a man of the party cries out for justice and " brings forward his claim; but there is a glory if the members of the Government themselves " come forwand and admit the righteousness of our claims." (*Hear, hear*) Gentlemen, when this Congress was going on for the first time at Allahabad I incurred the great odium of Sir Auckland Colvin. I had been the only Taluqdar favourably disposed to the Congress. I was advised by his Honour, and urged not to have anything to do with this movement. I was told that it was a movement hostile to Government, and every means was adopted to persuade me to give it up, but of late I see that his Honour is himself favourably inclined to it. The first quotation I will read to you is this: His Honour says: " Unless exchange materially " rises without the Rupee appreciating in India, either the growth of Military and Political " expenditure must at least be put an end to, or the English Tax-Payer must contribute per- " manently towards the defence of India. The only remaining alternative is bankruptcy. If " we enter on a course of successive measures of fresh taxation Russia without moving a man " or a gun needs only to bide her time." The fact of India's poverty has been admitted, and

HON. RAJAH RAMPAL SINGH.

the monopoly of trade is in the hands of alien merchants; the cultivation of the soil, the mines, the mineral wealth, and the forest products of the country are being heavily taxed; we do not derive that profit that other countries receive from the lands; the mines of this country being worked by alien merchants, we do not derive benefit. The only thing we can look to for our support is at present the Civil Service. The Civil Service costs nearly 13 crores and some lakhs to the country; the Military Service costs the country 23 crores and 75 lakhs. We cannot ask for Military Service. We have only to depend on the Civil Service. If a Simultaneous Examination is not held in this country, we cannot properly compete with our brethren in English. English candidates are in their own country amongst their own people, taught by their own tutors; whereas we have to go over land and water to a place quite unknown to us, there to be taught by alien tutors, while we have to live amongst foreign people, and then to prepare our lessons. Therefore it would be highly unjust and unfair to us if a Simultaneous Examination is not held in this country. (*Cheers*)

MR. R. VENKATA SUBBA ROW.

MR. R. VENKATA SUBBA ROW:—Brother Delegates, Ladies and Gentlemen—In coming forward to support this Resolution, which has been so ably and so eloquently moved and seconded, I find myself in a very unenviable situation. I find that much that I wished to say upon this subject has already been anticipated, and, what is worse, I have to speak with the words of one of our greatest orators ringing not only in my ears but in your ears. (*Applause*) Nevertheless I proceed to speak; the importance of the subject inspires me with courage, and the indulgence which I hope to meet with at your hands arms me with strength. I will not, however, scrutinise the despatch of the Secretary of State against which Mr. Surendra Nath Banerjea entered his most emphatic protest. (*Applause*) That is unnecessary. That document is beautifully transparent. It cannot stand the light of reason, and I do not like to compromise before this large assembly the authors of that document. Remember, Gentlemen, that, with all their faults, our Secretary of State, our Viceroys, and our Governors are all big men with big titles, drawing big salaries; and that the only good they can do to us is to deny, and, when that is not possible, to delay, our rights and our privileges. (*Hear, hear and Laughter*) They are still entitled to our esteem and regard and perhaps also to our thanks, because they stimulate us to work and win battles with greater speed though not with greater ease. I will not, therefore, undertake the unpleasant and uninteresting work of dissection but I will proceed to make a few anatomical observations upon that wonderful production, so that you may not be misled by the high parentage it claims, both on the maternal and the paternal side in the Council of the Secretary of State for India and in the Council of the Viceroy in this country.

Gentlemen, this is not a mere figure of speech. It is something more than that. It has a very strong, if strange, foundation in fact. The history of this wonderful despatch commences on the 22nd of June last year; when the Right Honorable the Secretary of State, in obedience to the mandate of the House of Commons, with much reluctance and amidst the protests of kith and kin resolves and proceeds upon a communication with the Viceroy. The event is announced; we hail it with hope, and we jump with joy. The Under Secretary and others give us the assurance. As to the result of that event, Lo! on the 19th of April of this year, nearly ten months afterwards—nine months and 10 or 12 days after the communication reached the Viceroy—after this full period of gestation the birth of a monster is announced with glee and satisfaction. (*Loud Laughter*) Our Anglo-Indian friends sing lullabies. Shall we cry or laugh? Gentlemen, the event is too serious not to kindle our indignation, too serious not to make us resent the mockery involved in it; for what is it but the most serious matter affecting the welfare of three hundred millions of Her Majesty's loyal subjects. To hold out hope and keep everybody on the tiptoe of expectation; and then at the end of ten months to tell us coolly to go on and chew the bitter cud of disappointment after the sweet hopes we entertained—what is it but a mockery of the most childish type unworthy of the dignity and honour of Her Majesty's Ministers; unworthy of the English character; unworthy of the prestige of Britain, undeserved by the loyal sons of Hindustan? When, on the 19th April Mr. Fowler accepted the recommendation of the Viceroy, it does not seem to have flashed across his brain that he was bound at all events to give some effect to the Resolution of the House of Commons, at least out of respect to the despatch of his predecessor Lord Kimberley, or in consideration of the assurance given by the Under Secretary, Mr. George Russell, or at least on account of the respect due to the great body that passed the Resolution, and the source from which it emanated. Gentlemen, Mr. Fowler failed in the discharge of a most important duty, and has violated the most solemn pledges and promises given to the people of this land by Her Most Gracious Majesty to the people of India, and repeated over and over again by Her Majesty's Ministers and representatives. (*Hear, hear and Cheers*) Gentlemen, I will not go into these pledges and promises, Mr. Surendra Nath Banerjea has quoted them all to you and he has also explained them to you, how these pledges and promises for so many years remained unfulfilled. I will, therefore, put the case simply before you, to see how the case stands and how the despatch of the Secretary of State has done us a very great injustice. What is our case? Gentlemen, there are competitive examinations held, at which candidates are selected for the Civil Service of India. Well, if it was declared that these examinations are not open to the natives of this country I should not be standing here to argue this particular question. But our rulers do not say that. They say that these examinations are open both to Englishmen and Indians. They say that they proceed only upon considerations of merit as determined by these competitive examinations. They do not object even if all the successful candidates at these competitive examinations should turn out to be Indians; they would raise no objection whatever. But with all this fairness of principle, with all this love of even-handedness, with all this good feeling for Indians, our rulers do one thing which practically nullifies their benevolent intentions. They hold their examinations in London, and in London alone, near the homes of Englishmen and far away from here, far off from the native place of those who are directly interested in those examinations. Now, Gentlemen, what did Mr. Paul's resolution wish to effect? He simply proposed an additional examination centre. He never wished to augment the Statutory service for Indians, he never proposed to abolish London as the place of examination, even though he would have been justified if he had done that, because the examination for the Civil Service of this country ought to be held in this country—(*Here the President struck the gong. Voices*, Go on, Go on)

The President :—Gentlemen, I must really claim your indulgence. I am trying to conduct the proceedings of the Congress as well as I can. If you go on at the present rate, the business will not be done till 12 o'clock. I must ask you when I strike the gong not to say "Go on, Go on." You have done it in every case, and there must be a limit to everything.

Mr. Venkata Subba Row :—I do not know how to proceed. It is an important thing, and I am the only Madras speaker to speak upon it. Unless the President is a little more indulgent, I had better not proceed at all. (*Voices*, Time, Time *and* Go on, Go on) I am perfectly willing to obey the chair, and I do not wish to go on for a minute unless that is your desire.

The President :—I will give three minutes' time to the speaker.

Mr. Venkata Subba Row :—Well, Gentlemen, I do not wish to enter into the objections raised against this resolution in the despatch of the Secretary of State for India. I will simply urge upon you that we must protest against it, and pray for Simultaneous Examinations; we must appeal to the Government of India once more, and if we find once more, as before, that no good can come out of it, let us appeal to the House of Commons, the great representative assembly. Let us appeal to that and ask that honourable house to re-affirm its resolution which has been set at naught by the Secretary of State. (*Cheers*)

Let us not despair of success. With justice on our side, with right on our side, the sanctity of self-sacrifice, with the sympathy of nations on our side, who can doubt that victory will be on our side? Who can doubt that the blessing of God will be on our side? Who can doubt that the force of opposition will melt away before our march? Who can doubt that ere long we shall wave the triumphant banner of the Congress in this second campaign of our political deliverance? May we not hope that we shall meet with that victory? Gather courage from our enlarged councils; gather hope from the presence on this occasion of two distinguished gentlemen who did themselves the honour and us the justice of voting in favour of Mr. Paul's Resolution. (*Applause*) May we not hope that the presence of these two distinguished gentlemen, our illustrious President and Mr. Seymour Keay, will help to win the sympathies of other members? May we not hope that the life-work of our Grand Old Man will be crowned with fruit even in his lifetime, and that the gracious Proclamation of our noble Queen will be vindicated and fulfilled, to the eternal glory of her reign, to the undying fame of England and the everlasting happiness of India? (*Cheers*)

Moulvie Hafiz Abdul Rahim.

Moulvie Hafiz Abdul Rahim:—Mr. President, Brother Delegates and Gentlemen, I have risen to support this Resolution, and I support it very strongly and most heartily. Gentlemen, you have heard all the reasons in support of this Resolution, adduced by previous speakers. I am going to particularize only one with a somewhat sectional motive—as distinguished from a selfish one. Gentlemen, there is no doubt that Mahomedans have become poorer in comparison with their former state; it is alleged, and it is not denied, that they are poorer than other communities at present. Certainly in former times they were predominant in every branch of the Public Service, but unfortunately their numbers have gradually so thinned that they are now few and far between. This fact I am sorry to say is owing to their own apathy and indifference in obtaining the English education provided by the British Government equally and alike for all. But now, after losing all that they had, they have become wiser, and are trying to obtain that English education, and I am glad to say that the percentage of the English educated Mahomedan boys is on the increase. I have the sad experience to relate that a friend of mine who had every hope of coming out successful, and who was fully expected by all who knew him to pass that severe examination for admission to the Covenanted Civil Service, could not go to England, merely for want of funds. Thus all his hopes of becoming a Civil Servant and of serving his country in that way have been damped. And I suppose there will be found a good many similar cases among Mahomedans all over India. Gentlemen, you know that it is not the richer and wealthier classes that take to the service all over the world; it is generally the middle class that desires to join the public service of the land. But it is beyond the means and power unfortunately of the Indian middle classes to send their youth to England. (*Hear, hear*) If the Civil Service Examinations were held in India it is my sincere conviction that Mahomedan youths would derive greater benefits than they can ever derive if the Examination continues to be held in London only. Of course, Gentlemen, their share in the service cannot be expected to be more than what is proportionate to their population, and those of my Mahomedan brethren who oppose Simultaneous Examinations base their opposition on the fear that Mahomedans would be nowhere in Competitive Examinations. This very plausible ground has been accepted by some of the local Governments. But, Gentlemen, considering the progress that Mahomedan youths are now making in education, and the fact that in University Examinations also some of them have obtained the highest distinction, I think there is not much reason for entertaining any such fear. (*Hear, hear*) And, supposing they are not prepared to derive sufficient benefit from the institution of Simultaneous Examinations, Gentlemen, is in right that for the sake of one out of five boys, the four remaining should be stayed for an indefinite time from getting their hopes realised? In my opinion the best remedy for Mahomedans under the circumstances, is to support rather than to oppose this beneficial resolution, which will undoubtedly confer blessings upon them as upon others. With these remarks I support this resolution, and I commend it to your acceptance. (*Cheers*)

Third Day.

Resolution VI. Simultaneous Examinations.

MR. M. V. JOSHI.

MR. M. V. JOSHI :—Mr. President and Brother Delegates, you have heard the eloquent address of our friend Babu Surendra Nath Banerjea. All that is to be said on this subject has been already said, and it leaves me, or any other speaker in fact, very little to saw on this topic; but still I would put before this assembly for its consideration certain points which to me seem to require a certain amount of handling. The points are these: In looking to the history of the Resolution of the House of Commons passed in June, 1893, we have to consider the painful fact that after all, our efforts, or rather, the efforts of our allies and supporters in the House of Commons, were not crowned with success. But what has been done? The evil that has been done in the despatch of the Secretary of State is this: that the Secretary of State has introduced a new principle by way of racial distinction. (*Hear, hear*) I say, Gentlemen, that this is a monstrous principle to introduee in the case of this country for this reason: that if you once admitethe principle that a certain minimum number of Europeans is necessary in the Civil Service of this country, there will be a time not very distant when you can imagine the Anglo-Indian bureaucracy stopping you from going even to England and competing through the channel that is open to you at present. Once accept the principle that a certain minimum number of Europeans is necessary in the Civil Service of this country, and I say that the day will not be far distant when they will try their best to cut our number down and not allow us even to go through the Competitive Examination in England. Well, Gentlemen, another feature which has been altogether lost sight of is this, that this setting aside of the will of the Imperial Parliament by the Executive, by the responsible ministers of the Crown, involves a constitutional principle of far-reaching importance. (*Hear, hear*) I beseech you, Gentlemen, consider well this point, and see that this subversive doctrine is not allowed to remain unchallenged. (*Applause*) This resolution when it was passed by the House of Commons caused great rejoicings throughout the length and breadth of the country. But when you find the House of Commons itself defied and baffled in this way by the responsible ministers of the Crown, I say that this is all the hope now left to us. But let us not despair. The constitutional principle and the violation of it are matters of consideration to the English public, as well as the public in India. But to us out here at any rate, and to the whole world if you please, there is the ludicrous spectacle of an Imperial Parliament sitting and its behests defied by the ministers of the Crown. I say there never was such an occasion in the record of Parliament or of Indian history before. (*Hear, hear*) That is a point which must needs be well considered As I say, Sir, this point cannot fail to affect the prestige of the British Government in India, and that is a point well worth being considered by the responsible ministers of the Crown, including the Secretary of State for India. Well, Gentlemen, the prospect before us is not a brilliant one. Our enemies are strong in the strength of Anglo-Indian bureaucracy (*Hear, hear*) our capacities are very limited indeed, our weapons are few, our allies and supporters in the House of Commons are only very few. They form a small minority: they are a devoted minority no doubt, but still they are a very small minority, and do not identify themselves with any of the political parties in England. That makes this struggle very difficult; but at the same time I would ask you not to lose hope and courage, because unless we fight this battle as manfully as suggested by our friend Mr. Banerjea, unless we fight this battle, I say, on the lines laid down for us before, unless we make the sound of this country, the voice of this country, din into the ears of the British public, until then we stand no chance of getting any of the grievances redressed which are referred to in this Resolution. Then the task before us is this; we have to create a public opinion, not only here, but, as I say, we have to take our complaint to England by such ways and means as may be considered sufficient by this august assembly. I commend this proposition to you with these few remarks. (*Cheers*)

PROFESSOR G. K. GOKHALE.

PROFESSOR G. K. GOKHALE :—Mr. President and Gentlemen, after listening to so many speeches on this subject, I should not be surprised if you were disposed to revolt against the infliction of yet another at this late hour. All I can say by way of apology is that it is not of my owu choice that I come before you to attempt the infliction. Gentlemen, during the last year and a half, this subject of Simultaneous Examinations has been so prominently before us that it has thrown into the shade almost all other questions of current politics, and we might well say about it what Edmund Burke once said of the American question. We have had this question in every shape. We have examined it from every point of view. Our invention has been exhausted. Reason is fatigued. Experience has given judgment. But Anglo-Indian obstinacy is not yet conquered. (*Cheers*) And remember, Gentlemen, this that we have to conquer is perhaps the worst kind of obstinacy; for it is not based so much on wrong judgment; it is not based even so much on prejudice; it is obstinacy based on the strong foundations of self interest and love of domination. (*Hear, hear*) Well, Gentlemen, I have no wish to take you over familiar ground, but there are two or three points connected with this controversy which suggest some rather serious considerations, and with your permission I will make an observation or two about them. And the first point to which I would invite your attention is that to which such prominence has been given in the resolution which we are considering, namely, that about an irreducible minimum of Europeans in the service. Gentlemen, when we speak on this point let there be no mistake and no misunderstanding. Those who may have read the literature on this subject must have been struck by the fact that till recently British Statesmen, however anxious to lay down some such principle as that now enunciated, have always felt that they could not do so openly, and have always therefore thrown a politic veil over the whole thing. Those scruples however, have now disappeared, that veil has been torn off, and it is this circumstance which fills us perhaps as much as any other, not only with disappointment, but with alarm. (*Cheers*) The Government of India and the Secretary of State have now authoritatively laid down that a certain minimum number of posts, and those the highest, must always and for all time to come be held by Europeans; and most of the local Governments have supplied a key to this proposition by saying in their despatches that that minimum has now been reached. The doctrine of the Government of India and the Secretary of State, therefore, means that the present arrangements should be perpetuated, and is, in fact, an attempt to keep us always under us a subject race. Gentlemen, is it not plainly our duty as men not to allow this barefaced attempt to succeed? Some of our opponents often say :—"But you are a subject race." Now all that I would say to such men is this, "We know we are a subject race, and the consciousness is humiliating enough; "and they are not good friends of the Empire who indulge in the pastime of needlessly remind- "ing us of the fact." It is true that England has come here as a conqueror, but she has of her own accord solemnly pledged herself not to hold the country as a conqueror. (*Hear, hear*) Let our opponents put themselves into our position, and then say what they would feel. I believe they will allow that it is not wrong to love one's country. I believe they will allow that it is not wrong to have a high ideal for one's country. And then I believe they will allow that it is not wrong for us to be dissatisfied with our present condition. Well, Gentlemen, the pledges of equal treatment which England has given us have supplied us with a high and worthy ideal for our nation; and if these pledges are repudiated, one of the strongest claims of British rule to our attachment will disappear. (*Cheers*)

Another point to which I would invite your attention is this. It is often stated that if Simultaneous Examinations were granted, the Bengalis would swamp the entire service, and that this result would be resented by the people of the other parts of the country. Now, Gentlemen, in the first place this assertion does grave injustice to the people of other parts. I believe most of us can hold our own even against Bengalis. But assuming for the sake of argument that that would be the result, what then? Are not the Bengalis nearer to us than the Europeans who have at present a monopoly of the service? We have at present in the Bombay Presidency a Bengali gentleman as a Sessions Judge. Now, there may be abler men in the service, but one more respected by the people, or regarded with greater feelings of affection, is nowhere to be found. (*Cheers*) Then, Gentlemen, our opponents often say that the relations

Third Day.

Resolution VI. Simultaneous Examinations.

Professor G. K. Gokhale.

between Hindus and Mahomedans in this country are such that Hindus will not submit to the authority of Mahomedans, or Mahomedans to the authority of Hindu Collectors and Judges But let those who rashly encourage such feelings beware of what they do. For if once such feelings were to prevail generally what would there be to stand in the way of their application to the case of smaller officers also, such as Tahsildars, Subordinate Judges and Police Officers? And then the task of Government would be impossible, unless indeed the country were cut up into two camps and the Hindus shut up in one and the Mahomedans in the other Then, Gentlemen, it is often urged that the Provincial Service has been specially constituted for us and that we should be satisfied with it. Well, all I can say in regard to Provincial and Statutory Services is that they can never satisfy the people. Take, for instance, the Bombay Provincial Service. I have paid some close attention to this subject, and I have no hesitation in saying that as at present constituted it is a disgrace to the Government and an insult to the people. There is not a single redeeming feature in it. I will give you only one illustration. Take the standard that the Bombay Government has prescribed for the competitive examination for this service. Remember, Gentlemen, these members of the Provincial Service are one day to be appointed to the posts detached from the Covenanted Service and thus placed on a level with men who have passed the London Civil Service examination, which is perhaps the stiffest examination of any that we know of. And yet what is the standard of education that the Government of Bombay has proposed for the competitive test? The Government of Bombay proposed that these men should know English sufficiently to understand official Reports. (*Laughter and Cries of "Shame"*) This is all they want. As regards the second language there is no classical language, Sanskrit, Persian, or Greek. All that is expected of these men is that they should show a moderate acquaintance with one of the vernaculars of the Presidency. Perhaps you may say if the literary side is defective the mathematical side is strong. These men are probably required to pass an examination in differential and integral calculus. No! nothing of the kind. These men have to pass an examination in Arithmetic up to simple interest (*Laughter*) not compound interest, Algebra up to simple equations (*Laughter*) not Quadratic Equations, and the first two books of Euclid. This is all the Mathematical test. These men are one day to take their places by the side of men who have passed the London examination one of the stiffest and severest examinations, which is equivalent to the M. A. examination. When these men come to be appointed to these posts, is it possible for them to command respect? Is it possible for them to respect themselves? The whole of the Provincial scheme of the Bombay Government is so utterly ludicrous that it is impossible to believe that it emanated from a responsible Government. All that we say therefore is that no solution of the question based on a Provincial Service will ever satisfy us. (*Cheers*) Taking a dispassionate view of the whole situation, we have every right to urge that Simultaneous Examinations ought to be granted to us, and so I am glad to say that, taking the whole thing into account, there are good grounds for hope. It may be that for a moment we have been cast down by defeat, but the circumstances to-day are more encouraging than they were several years before, when our leaders fought single-handed for the Indian people to get the concession we have been praying for. Whatever may be said of the Madras Government, and in whatever way the officials of that Government may now act, the despatch of that Government remains a document of which the Madras people may well be proud. We have the resolution of the House of Commons. Lastly we have a strong public opinion becoming stronger and stronger every day, which may inspire us to continue the fight which is bound to be a long and arduous one, in behalf of generations yet unborn. (*Loud Cheers*)

Mr. Ghulam Ahmed Khan, of Berar, addressed the meeting in Hindustani.

Mr. Seymour Keay.

Mr. Seymour Keay:—Mr. President, Fellow-delegates, Ladies and Gentlemen, at this ate hour I only venture to say that I have one claim to come forward and to detain you for a few moments, and that claim consists in the fact that I was privileged to do something towards the carrying of the successful division in Parliament with regard to these Simultaneous Examinations; (*Cheers*) and that division was made successful, I may say, entirely because of the solid phalanx of devotion to India which we, who whipped up that division, found in the ranks of the Irish Parliamentary Party, (*Cheers*) of which your President is such a worthy and an honoured member. Well, Gentlemen, I also have the honour to be the member of the House of Commons to whom Mr. Gladstone gave (in answer to a question of mine) the promise which was the foundation of all the subsequent proceedings. The promise as you know was very fairly worded. The promise was that the Government of India would be addressed at once and that they were to be asked to say "In what mode and under what conditions and limitations the Resolution of the House could be carried out." Now, Gentlemen, we at once said that that was a satisfactory statement. There was no statement whatever that the Government of India was to be asked whether or not the Resolution of the House of Commons was to be carried out. There was nothing of the kind. It was only in what mode and under what conditions or limitations the Resolution of the House could be carried out. (*Hear, hear*) Well then, in this form the matter went to the India Office. What happened then? The India Office in the first place waited for twenty days, and did nothing, as was quite characteristic of them in such cases. (*Laughter*) They then wrote to the Government of India a brief letter, which has been well described by the mover of this Resolution. They certainly put into that letter the very words which Mr. Gladstone had promised to me should be used; but they added at the tail-end of the letter a scorpion-like sting. That sting was that they added the so-called "essential condition" of which you have heard to day, namely, that there should be an irreducible minimum of Europeans in the service for ever, and for all time to come. (*Hear, hear*) Now, it is very seldom that I have any occasion to come forward as an apologist for the doings of the Government of India. But I must say that on this occasion justice should be done to them by putting the boot upon the proper leg, and the proper leg to put the boot upon is the leg of the Secretary of State and his Council in London. (*Laughter*) Because what he did was to append this condition for the consideration of the Government of India along with and in opposition to Mr. Gladstone's promise. He did this simply for the purpose of rendering it impossible for the Government of India to reply in any other terms than that they could not carry out the Resolution. I will do the Goverment of India justice to say that they told this to the Secretary of State to his face. You must allow me to quote from their reply to the despatch. They could not speak clearer and they could not say in plainer words that he, and not they, was responsible for the adverse reply. They said to the Secretary of State, "in referring the matter for our consideration, your Lordship has pointed out that it is indispensable that an adequate number of the members of the Civil Service should be Europeans, and that no scheme would be admissible which does not fulfil that essential condition." They go on to say, "But it appears to us (the Government of India) that this condition, if conceded, is itself destructive of the Resolution, which requires that all who compete should be finally classed in one list according to their merit." They then conclude as follows:—" We are therefore compelled to the conclusion that to give effect to the Resolution in its entirety is wholly incompatible with the essential condition on which your Lordship has so strongly insisted." (*Cheers*) Well, Gentlemen, I have cleared the Government of India from a part of the odium, at all events, but not from all. I fear I must admit that they were only too willing to find the essential and impossible condition in the Secretary of State's letter.

They then proceeded with the solemn farce of sending out the letter to their subordinates, and what did they do then? They then ventured to super-impose even more impossible conditions, in order further to secure a reply in the negative. That is how the farce went on. In the few moments which I have, I will only call your attention to one or two of the most extraordinary arguments which have been used against Simultaneous Examina-

Third Day.

Resolution VI. Simultaneous Examinations.

Mr. Seymour Keay.

tions in the Blue Book, and which have not been adverted to on this platform to-day. What are we told in the first place? The Bombay Government was good enough to come forward and say that they recognised that the desire on the part of the natives of India to enter their own Civil Service is quite a natural aspiration. But what do they immediately add? They say that though it may be quite a natural aspiration, "we cannot suppose that this aspiration could be a ground for serious political action." The Lieutenant-Governor of the Punjab goes farther still. He also admits the aspirations of the natives for employment in the administration of their country but declares, in so many words, that they shonld not be given the weight of a feather, (*Shame*) if they conflict with British ideas of what they think best for the benefit of the people. Gentlemen, the benefit of the people fills these papers like a flowing river. Nothing whatever is said about the loss of European appointments. Oh no! On the contrary, what is the chief reason given by the Government of India themselves and adopted by the Secretary of State for refusing these Examinations? It is not that there would be a single European shut out of the service. Nothing of that sort. Never for a moment. The reason is stated to be their burning fear that the Sikhs and Mahomedans of the North would possibly be excluded from public employment. (*Cheers*) Then there is the question which was mentioned by a previous speaker. It had been alleged that the Bengalis would monopolise the service. A previous speaker well said that the Bengalis are after all nearer to the other nations than Europeans. But the Government of India just places that upside-down, and declare in unmeasured terms that the greatest possible and the crowning advantage of the European is that he is an absolute alien both by religion and by race. Why? Because in consequence of his absolute non-connection with the people he is perfectly certain not to take sides in local quarrels. You cannot fail to see the absolute dishonesty of that argument, because if it were an argument at all. I need not say that it would apply to England just as well as to India; and it would be just as true to say that for that reason it would be for the benefit of England, and that England would be much better off, if her Civil Service were to be peopled by Russians instead of by Englishmen. (*Cheers*)

Well, Gentlemen, I don't think I need go further in showing the absolute insincerity and hypocrisy which obtains throughout these despatches. I want to know why there is only one thing which is not found in the whole of the hundred and ten pages of that Blue Book. There is not a hint or whisper in it of any admission that the natives of India have even the faintest right to live on their own soil, much less that they have any preferential claim over the other subjects of the British Empire to administer in their own country. On the contrary there is the direct opposite of such an admission, and there is a deliberate denial of this written on the face of these papers by responsible Governors, and by Mr. Garstin of Madras. They actually set forth this glaringly absurd argument;—that if you were to allow the Indians to hold examinations in India it would be nothing less than a scandalous injustice to the inhabitants of other parts of the British Empire, such as New Zealand, Australia and even far-off Canada. Why did not they put into the Blue Book another thing which they have omitted. Why didn't they come forward plumply and honestly and say "We have a great many comfortable appointments and we want to keep them for ourselves"? Why, I can respect a class of officials who come forward with honest truth in their mouths like that, but I repel the suggestion that any of the arguments to be found in any of these papers can be treated as having the faintest tinge of honesty or statesmanship. On the contrary, they are crammed with phrases of Pecksniffian hypocrisy. I will now close, as the gong has already sounded, with one sentence which, on careful examination and perusal, defines what has been done in these papers. I say that the decision which has been passed upon them is in the first place a frightful injustice perpetrated on the Indian people; in the second place it is a gross unfairness committed against the Government of India's own officers, to whom this matter was pretended to be referred for their impartial opinion, and in the third place I say that it is a breach of faith with the House of Commons. Yes, Gentlemen, we will be prepared to stand by what we say, that it is nothing more nor less than a positive breach of faith with the British Parliament, (*Cheers*) and I join with other speakers and with you in trusting that we are very far from finished yet with this matter of Simultaneous Examinations. We have once defeated our own Government for your sakes and we are perfectly prepared to defeat them again. (*Cheers*) If the fortune of the ballot gives us only a fair chance, we will have another Resolution this session. (*Hear, hear*). We will go on in the hope that we may at last be able to secure the performance of what after all is nothing but the simplest act of ordinary justice to the Indian people. (*Cheers*)

The President :—Let those who are in favour of this Resolution hold up their hands. (*Voices* All, All).

The Resolution was carried unanimously.

Resolution VII.
Judicial Service.

Hon. Mr. N.
Subba Row.

The President :—The next resolution will be moved by the Honorable Mr. N. Subba Row.

The Hon. Mr. N. Subba Row :—Mr. President, Fellow-delegates, Ladies and Gentlemen, it is in the fitness of things that this Resolution should come at the fag end of the day, for you know the announcement made by the President that we are to disperse at 4 o'clock.

The President :—No, no.

The Hon. Mr. N. Subba Row :—I am corrected by the President that we shall go on up to a late hour. However, in the fitness of things it comes as it were at the fag end of the day because this fact illustrates the manner in which the work is done in our Mofussil District and Sessions Courts. The resolution which I have the honour to place before you is a very simple and a very short resolution. The resolution is this :—

"This Congress views with great dissatisfaction the system of recruiting the higher Judicial Service of the country, and is of opinion that provision should be made for proper Judicial training being given to persons who are appointed to the post of District and Sessions Judge, and that the higher Judicial Service in Bengal, the North-West Provinces and Oudh, Bombay and Madras, and the Judicial Service generally in other parts of the country, should be more largely recruited from the legal profession than is now the case."

I shall simply state a few facts in support of the resolution just now placed before you, and I shall confine myself briefly to the Province to which I belong, namely, the Madras Presidency. In this Presidency the office of the District Judge is recruited from the ranks of Sub-Collectors, officers who have spent the greater portion of their official life in executive work, and who by the time they come to be appointed as District Judges are well imbued, as it were, with an executive frame of mind, not with a judicial frame of mind. It is these gentlemen that are called upon to discharge the responsible and important duties of presiding over the highest Court in each district. Now, these officers of the Sub-Collector's grade—are they men who have distinguished themselves in the service, who have shown, in the course even of their executive work, their comprehensive grasp of the matters placed before them? Are they men who have the highest ability, the highest talehts? I regret to say that generally it is not so. The department of the Judicial service has not earned the reputation of being recruited from men who have distinguished themselves by their ability, or whose services have earned the reward of a seat on the bench. However, even granting that these officers are men of ordinary average service, we shall see how this selection is further made. These officers when they are once appointed are not allowed to continue to discharge the duties of the new office. Once a Sub-Collector is appointed to the grade of a District Judge, there is no guarantee that he will be retained in that office; to-day a Sub-Collector, to-morrow an acting District Judge, the third day an acting District Collector, and back

Third Day.

Resolution VII. Judicial Service.

Hon. Mr. N. Subba Row.

again the fourth day an acting District Judge, forwards and backwards till by some chance or it may be by some specially meritorious bad act, (*Laughter*) he is finally fixed to the District Judge's place. (*Shame*) Such is the mode in which the judicial service in this Presidency—I say it without any fear of contradiction—is recruited: and when it is so recruited do you wonder that the judicial service has become to be regarded as the inferior service, and that it is not generally coveted by members of the Civil Service? Gentlemen, the result of the present system is seen in the kind of work turned out by our District Judges; and the kind of work turned out is noticed year after year in our administration reports and is viewed with dissatisfaction. I have been connected with mofussil district courts for the last fifteen years, and I must say I concur with the wording of this resolution very strongly. Even though our District Judges are of some years' standing some of them, I may say most of them, cannot write judgments according to the Code of Civil Procedure—the A.B.C. of the Law which they are called upon to administer. (*Shame*) I know of specific judgments which have been returned for this reason to a District Judge of some years' standing in the Service. It is no wonder, therefore, if these officers, saturated with the executive training which they have previously received, should not consider it of the first importance to hear the pleaders engaged in cases fully, thoroughly, and with the greatest patience; and we need not be surprised even if a District Judge should come to the bench with a written judgment before hearing the arguments of the Bar. (*Shame*) These are the District Judges who have got appellate jurisdiction over experienced subordinate Judges and District Munsiffs in our Presidency. These are the District Judges who are the final arbiters in all regular appeals, who are the final arbiters in all small cause suits, and who have unlimited jurisdiction in all property cases. Now with the improvement in character, and advancement in knowledge of law on the part of these subordinate Judges and District Munsiffs, and with a progressive Bar at each centre of the district the inferiority of the District Judges is becoming day by day more and more apparent. I shall trouble you only with a short quotation from the Administration Report of this year. It says, "It is impossible to view the results of the "year with entire approval, and in certain cases they can only be described as eminently "unsatisfactory." Yet it is these Judges who preside over the highest Court in the district and have Appellate jurisdiction over experienced Subordinate Judges. You will believe me when I say that one District Judge heard eight appeals from the Subordinate Judge and reversed every one of them, though that Subordinate Judge was a very experienced man and had been in service for several years as a District Munsiff, and as a pleader for a good many years more and received very different treatment at the hands of the High Court in certain other judgments which came up on appeal. (*Hear, hear*)

Now, in thus drawing a gloomy picture of our halls of justice, let me not be understood as finding fault with the Government officers who are called upon to preside over the Court. They are men of high culture. It is not their fault, but it is the fault of the system which calls upon them without sufficient training to fill the high and responsible position of dispensing justice beween man and man. This is not their fault, it is the fault of the system to which we have all to submit, and, besides, there is one other important circumstance which adds, as it were, to the inferiority of the District Judges That is the canons of judging the efficiency of the judicial officers. The canon is not to judge by the quality of work but by the quantity of work turned out by them—not by the soundness or justice of their decisions but the number of the decisions delivered. That is the canon that prevails throughout all the Courts in the Madras Presidency It is that canon which is responsible for the deterioration of this class of officers· and with large number of decisions and reports and text books flooding us every day, we have no reason to find fault with District Judges for not being posted in these decisions. They have no time to read them. They have no previous training to follow them with interest; it is no congenial task with them, and, therefore, you should not blame them if they are driven mor and more to brush aside all artificial law, and to rely on their own unadulterated common sense. (*Laughter*) For the reason I have stated, we ought not to be surprised if our District Judges come to consider that "sufficient unto the day is the evil thereof"; and that this expiatory period of judgeship must somehow or other be gone through in order to earn their pension of £1,000 a year for the work they have done in this country. (*Hear, hear*)

Of course, I must not be understood as saying that in this large class of Judicial officers we do not stumble now and then on some really good and efficient District Judges. What is the feeling of these good District Judges—men who have taken congenially to the task and distinguished themselves in the service? I may tell you that I had recently a conversation with one of the most eminent and satisfactory District Judges of this Presidency. I had a talk with him on this subject, and he said "You know I was specially qualified, you know I passed an examination in Law, I have been a Registrar in the High Court; "and will you believe me," he added, "when I first took my seat as a District Judge, my heart "sank within me at the thought of my responsibility in administering law." That was the feeling which that eminent and most satisfactory Judge expressed to me only recently, and he requested me to press the matter strongly upon Government and see that the present mode of recruitment is bettered. (*Cheers*) Gentlemen, if the evil stopped here, there might be some satisfaction. Unfortunately, the evil does not stop here. According to our rules, according to our Charter, one-third of our High Court Judges should be recruited from this class, the class about which we are speaking, that is to say, two judges of the High Court should be recruited from this class. What is the result of this system of recruitment? You have only to ask any of the lawyers practising in the High Court and Mofussil Courts. No eminent lawyer will care to predict what turn any case may take in any particular Court. I must say this system is responsible for a substantial increase in litigation; in fact, litigation has become a question of gambling, a question of toss up, and no one can be sure, notwithstanding he has a good case, that that would be the view which would prevail in the Courts. (*Shame*)

I am glad to think that there is some hope that this state of things may come to an end at no distant future. For when the unsatisfactory state of recruitment of our Judges, was brought to the notice of His Excellency Lord Wenlock, His Excellency said that the present condition of affairs was not so satisfactory as it might be, and that the subject was receiving the careful consideration of Government. I am sure you will join me in the hope that before Lord Wenlock leaves these shores, His Excellency will see that this necessary reform is given effect to, and will leave behind him a permanent mark of his good intentions and broad sympathies. (*Hear, hear*) I am encouraged to indulge this hope, because it is during his tenure of office that the first instalment of reform, the separation of judicial from executive functions, has been carried into effect. This is the first Presidency in which that reform has been carried into effect in the subordinate ranks of the Magistracy, and the result of that reform has been a great success, and has given great satisfaction to all the people of this country. We thank the Madras Government, not simply for the reform which is of immediate benefit to us, but for the example which it has set to other Governments showing that the question of separating executive from judicial functions can be solved without difficulty. (*Cheers*) Therefore, I say we have very good reasons for viewing with dissatisfaction the system of recruiting the higher judicial service in this country. The remedy which we suggest is that it should be more largely recruited from the legal profession than is now the case. Now on that point I have only to draw your attention to the remarks of Sir Charles Paul, Advocate General of Calcutta, in an interview which he had with Sir Raymond Blathwayte. These remarks are of very great significance in connection with this subject. He says, "It is "a mistake in these advanced days to appoint Civilians to high judicial posts which ought to "be filled properly by thoroughly trained and thoroughly experienced Barristers and Pleaders. "What can an ordinary Civil Servant, however intelligent and well educated he may be,

**Third Day.**

Resolution VII
Judicial Service.

Hon. Mr. N.
Subba Row.

"know of the tremendous complications and the innumerable technicalities of a mixture "of English and Mahomedan laws? W have a number of codes; all of a strictly technical "character, based principally on English Law. Now, it often happens that Sectional "orders issued by Government do not clearly and expressly state the law on the points to "which they refer. It is taken for granted that the Administrator, Judge or Magistrate "knows the law; but he frequently being a Civilian, does not know it. It is absolutely "necessary, therefore, for men who have to construe these Sections to be acquainted with the "principles on which they are founded. It is hopeless to expect men merely by the light of "nature to arrive at a proper interpretation of the Sections. Many years of extensive practice, "and a long familiarity with principles and cases, will alone fit a man for so great a task. I "would here particularise the frequent unfamiliarity of all non-professional Judges with the "law of evidence. Points of law which arise in the course of the examination of witnesses "require to be readily decided. I do not think that under our present system there is sufficient "ability or enlightenment for that purpose." This is the conception which Mr. Paul, the Advocate General, formed. I am sure every one who has got any knowledge of the working of our Courts will agree with him that the main source from which the judiciary should be recruited should be the Bar. (*Hear, hear*) You will note that we do not go so far as Mr. Paul's remarks. He says the judiciary should almost exclusively be recruited from the Bar. What we say is that it should be more largely recruited from the legal profession than it is now. So far as the Madras Presidency is concerned, this is not at all done. Therefore, we ask that at least some attempt should be made in that direction. So far as the scheme of recruiting the service is concerned, it is a large scheme which has to be worked out. So far as I am concerned I have thought it out but it is unnecessary to place those things before you. Seeing that British Justice is the stronghold on which we rely we ask that those who preside over these Courts should be able to dispense justice between man and man, which is the point on which British prestige is so much founded. (*Cheers*)

Mr. K. G. Natu.

Mr. K. G. Natu:—Mr. President, Brother Delegates and Gentlemen, in seconding this resolution I have much pleasure in testifying that the subject matter of this resolution forms the marrowbone of British justice and British administration. Time was when justice trembled when it had to deal with a powerful man. The aggrieved party, if weak, saw hardly any hopes of getting redress when he had to contend with a millionaire. In fact, Might and Right went hand in hand. They were synonymous terms. But there was a dawn of better things; British light and British power came into this country, and with it also British justice. You have observed how at times even the greatest men have been brought to justice before the bar of Parliament. I am saying this, simply because I want to impress upon you the importance of justice, and to show what sort of men are sent out here in order to administer noble justice. Civilians are sent out to this country by Government. Very well! But as soon as they have come, as soon as they have spent a few months in getting a smattering of the language of the district, they are placed in charge of three or four taluqs, with powers magisterial and over the revenue; and you know that a Magistrate is as much a Judge as any. Frequently justice mis-carries owing to ignorance of the language. How often have you heard of violent hands being laid on poor syces by their angry masters owing to ignorance of the language. For instance the expressions घोडासुयोंतनांध and नाकात थडीवागते are literal translations of the corresponding English phrases "Tie the horse in the sun," and "I have got a cold in the nose." (*Laughter*) But what Mahratha is there who pretends to understand the meaning conveyed by them? I remember a well-known Judge who laid claim to being a thorough Mahratha scholar, and who for many years presided at the Zilla sessions. In a case tried by him, one of the witnesses happened to say रुण्याचातांब्या. The judge got out of temper and said to the witness. "You are a down right liar. How the devil can you change silver into copper?" (*Laughter*) After his first fury was over, he was told that *Tambay* means a vessel of any metal and not necessarily of copper. This was the case with a man who laid pre-

Third Day.

Resolution VII. Judicial Service.

Mr. K. G. Natu.

tensions to scholarship. You may easily judge of those who come to India and pass in the Vernaculars of the country in about a couple of months. (*Hear, hear*) Therefore the requisite in the course of judicial training is a thorough knowledge of the language and habits of the people; and the next thing is a knowledge of the law of the land. The Civil Service Examination held in England prepares a kind of general groundwork, but it does not qualify the student for any special branch. This has to be studied as a speciality. He comes here as a Collector, occupies that position for a few months, then he is transferred to the office of Assistant Judge, with appellate powers, both in civil and criminal cases. Now, I can understand the sudden change of status. But I cannot understand that a sudden change of status is commensurate with a consistent change of character. It is not possible that the change is sufficient to introduce into the mind of the man a thorough knowledge of the Hindu or Mahomedan laws, or of the Civil Procedure, as soon as he is transferred from the place of Collector to the place of Judge. It is impossible. The worst of it is not come; it is yet to come. Government has of late created a number of Judges called the benches of Magistrates. I have every regard for the system; the system is not to be found fault with; it is the men that fill the posts, who are placed as Magistrates to govern us. They can send a man to prison for two years. They are a class of Magistrates sent out to us who have spent their lives in counting figures, men who had to find levels and to construct bridges men who knew nothing but to live on ancestral property, who had nothing to do but to gossip, men who are perfectly innocent of law or procedure. These men are made to sit in judgment, to decide upon the arguments adduced before them. They are the men who are to draw the line of demarcation as to where the criminal ends and the civil begins; (*Laughter*) and yet they sit in judgment upon us; they are to decide most important questions of life and liberty, and I may say, with sheer disregard to the cause of justice. This creation of Judges, this mode of administering justice, really lowers in the eyes of the people that deep respect and profound veneration with which the surrounding nations have looked upon British administration and justice. I would therefore humbly pray to Government "Train your Judges and let them judge." With these few remarks I second the proposition. (*Cheers*)

The President:—A representative fron Tinnevelly, Mr. A. R. Krishna Iyer, has expressed a wish to speak on this resolution. I now call upon him to speak.

Mr. A. R. Krishna Iyer.

Mr. A. R. Krishna Iyer:—Brother Delegates and Gentlemen, the proposition that I have the honour to support is a proposition that has already been proposed by Mr. Subba Row. Coming to my arguments immediately, we all know what an important part practice plays in the development of theory in all sciences. Theory and practice are so related to one another that the one assists the other in various ways. The inter-relation between theory and practice is so great that nothing need be said about the inter-relation between the two; and Law being a highly complex science, the plea of practice upon theory is here illustrated to a greater extent than in any other department of knowledge. It is only when theory is put into practice that theory is better understood, and this is pre-eminently so in the highly complex department of the science of Law. Therefore Gentlemen, we see what trained legal practitioners can do towards administering justice as Judges. The sphere of an executive officer is entirely separate from the sphere of a judicial officer; the frame of mind calculated to make a good Judge is different from the frame of mind which makes a good Collector. One is an executive officer, the other is a judicial officer. The District Judge or any other Judge will be praised if he takes time to write a judgment, even in a small and simple suit; whereas a Collector will be blamed if he hesitates, even if the hesitation be properly grounded, even for five minutes, with reference to a quarrel or an affray. What is wanted for one frame of mind is the power of grappling with difficulties. There is not time enough for the Collector to grapple with difficulties. But the Judge is more calm; he is better fitted to exercise his

Third Day.

Resolution VII.
Judicial Service.

Mr. A. R. Krishna Iyer.

duties as a judicial officer. Such being the vast difference between the frame of mind calculated to fill the responsible position of a Collector and that required for filling the responsible position of a District Judge or any other Judge, we must take care that such officers alone are appointed for filling the post of Collector and for filling the post of Judge as have the necessary qualifications; while to transplant an officer from one department to another will be a serious absurdity (*Voices* Time, Time). Therefore on other grounds also I heartily support the Resolution that has already been seconded. (*Cheers*)

The Resolution was carried unanimously.

The President:—The next resolution will be moved by Dr. Bahadurji of Bombay.

Resolution VIII.
Medical Service.

Dr. Bahadurji.

Dr. Bahadurji:—Mr. President, Brother Delegates and Gentlemen: the Resolution that has been entrusted to my care reads as follows:—

(*a*) That this Congress is of opinion that the present constitution of the Higher Civil Medical Service is anomalous, indefensible in principle, injurious in its working, and unnecessarily costly; that the time has arrived when in the interests of Public Medical Education, and the advancement of Medical Service and of scientific work in the country, as also in the cause of economic administration, the Civil Medical Service of India should be reconstructed on the basis of such service in other civilized countries, wholly detached from and independent of the Military Service.

(*b*) That the very unsatisfactory position and prospects of Members of the Subordinate Civil Medical Service (Assistant Surgeons and Civil Hospital Assistants) compared with members of similar standing in other departments of the Public Service, require thorough investigation and redress, and prays that Government will grant for the purpose an open enquiry by a mixed Commission of official and non-official members.

(*c*) That whilst this Congress views with satisfaction the desire of the Imperial Government to re-organise the Chemical Analyser's department with a view to its administration as an independent scientific department, it earnestly hopes that Government will not fail to recognise the responsible and meritorious work of Assistants, or as they in reality are, Government Chemical Analysers, and place them on the footing of Specialists.

The subject of the resolution I have just read to you has engaged such a considerable share of public attention since it was first spoken to from the Congress platform last year that I need hardly enter into details again. The question of Simultaneous Examinations is, no doubt, of great importance to the public, but you will agree with me that the subject of the medical service of the country is of equal, if not greater, public importance, and that it is a matter of surprise and regret that it should have so long remained unnoticed by our popular leaders. They would seem not to have noticed that, in the very matter of Simultaneous Examinations, the Covenanted Civil Medical Service of India most directly demonstrates that the opponents of Simultaneous Examinations have rather overstated their case and drawn on their imagination as regards the *sine quâ non* of a long residence in England for the acquiring of that mental, moral and magnetic equipment which alone can impart the necessary administrative ability and courage, and social adaptability to Indian youths as members of the I. C. S. For, indeed, many an Indian member of the Covenanted I. M. S. had only to voyage to England to pass the Burlington House Examination to obtain his commission, and this accomplished (in a few weeks after arrival in England), he had only to put in his regulation six months at Netley before he returned to India as a member of the I. M. S. What, then, have the opponents of Simultaneous Examinations to say to the fact that Indian Members of the Covenanted I. M. S. acquired administrative ability, courage and social adaptability, qualities required in no smaller degree in the military than in the civil department, but also imbibed martial spirit by a mere effort of a trip across the sea to obtain a commission in Her Majesty's army? (*Laughter*)

To examine briefly the subject of the Resolution, let us study the different parts separately. I shall deal mainly with the first two sections, leaving the last to my friends who will follow me. The first part says that the constitution of the higher Civil Medical Service is anomalous, indefensible in principle, injurious in its working, and very costly, and prays that the constitution be revised and remodelled on the basis of what obtains in other civilised countries. To realise the absurdity and the mischief of the present constitution of our higher Civil Medical Service, let us contrast it with what it is all the world over. The Civil Medical Service of any country is concerned with the several departments of education, of sanitation, of special scientific and expert work, as of chemical analysis and of civil medical relief. The practice outside India is to recruit the service from the open profession of medicine and science, the necessary qualifications being a special training and ability, and no mere ordinary practising license or degree: men are found for posts and not posts for men. But in India it is far otherwise. The selection is restricted to a small class of men who form the stock in trade, so to say, of a military depôt, called the Indian Medical Service. The competition for this service is open to any one who possesses a British qualification in medicine, surgery and midwifery. Many of our graduates, and even plucked students, who could afford a trip to England, scored such easy victories in the competition some years ago that their overwhelming numbers raised an alarm and led to the closing of the service against them for the time being. It was thrown open again, but some agency or mystic force has since prevented the Indian candidates from regaining their old position in the pass list. This covenanted military service requires for its own military purposes—the purposes for which the enlistment is intended—some 170 men; but, like all depôts which have a large stock of articles lying idle, this service depôt has more than twice that number of men for whom the Military Department has no room or work, and it is for these military men that work is found in the Civil Department as posts become available, and they are trotted out in plain clothes as professors or political agents, guardians of jail-birds, or Civil Surgeons, Sanitary Commissioners or Chemical Analysers, etc., etc., under orders from the Civil Surgeon-General, also a *médecin militaire* in plain clothes. Scientific and expert advisers to all others civilised Governments are individuals who have worked at special and scientific subjects and possess special qualifications. But in India it is a single individual who advises Government on all matters connected with the science of medicine. He is the Civil Military Surgeon-General, *i.e.*, the Surgeon-General in plain clothes. He rises to that position not by virtue of any scientific work or merit, but by a special process of development through the grades of Captaincy, Majorship, Major-Generalship to which he must gravitate by the mere weight of years. And the mere fact of his donning the hat of the Surgeon-General is taken by Government to infuse into his head the expert knowledge not in one branch but in all the different departments of science and medicine. (*Laughter*)

Again, the genesis of a medical profession in India is equally peculiar. All the civilised world over it is by a special training in a special subject after graduation that one becomes a professor. But in India the course of training requires at the outset two years' shooting and messing with a regiment, and then the experience, perhaps, of a general practitioner as a Civil Surgeon, or of a guardian of jail-birds, or of some such other work : after this special process of development or rather degeneration a *medecin militaire* may be electroplated as a professor, should he happen to possess the special connections where with to excite the electric fluid in the Surgeon-General's Office. (*Laughter*) But this is a wonderful fluid; it has the power to make a Professor of Pathology, for instance, disappear from the chair of Pathology only to reappear as a Professor of Midwifery! That this is all anomalous and indefensible in principle needs no argument to establish. That such a constitution of a Civil Medical Service must be very inferior in its working will be readily accepted and can be easily demonstrated by a few actual examples within one's personal knowledge. Examples are illustrations of the evils of a system of which the special cases are themselves the victims, and it would be only narrow-mindedness to construe the citations as personal attacks. Under this absurd system a Professor who has never had any training in Biology—has not even looked into the inside of a frog—becomes gifted with the audacity, not to say confidence, to pretend to examine our Arts and Science Graduates in Comparative Anatomy. Under this absurd and mischievous system the Professor of Zoology has to be a born Ophthalmologist and *vice versa*. What does the teaching in Biology consist of? Some two dozen readings from text-books from a pulpit decorated with bottled pickles of zoological specimens; the readings over, the class repairs to a museum where a single personally conducted tour by some obliging curator begins and completes the course of practical zoology! Is this not a fraud both on the University and on the public? Under this unnatural system, a Chemical Examiner who has not a day's experience of his work to boast of, and whilst he is still learning his work from his assistant, considers it a very natural thing to report on the work of his assistant from the superior place into which he finds himself pitchforked. Again, the teaching of Physiology, for instance, may continue to be of the most primitive kind, till an outsider exposes it, works violent changes in the College, and causes the teaching of this very important subject to be intrusted to capable and proper hands. Undef this system again, Government themselves, by attempting to extort all possible knowledge from a medical head which they cover with the Surgeon-General's *topee,* as a matter of course, when the individual arrives at the age of investiture, make themselves the laughing-stock of the thinking world by the novel ideas extracted from some Surgeon-General. Not so long ago a Surgeon-General deliberately declared that experimental physiology had nothing to do with vivisection. It does not require much technical knowledge to understand that the very contrary is the case, for physiology deals with the phenomena of life, and experimental physiology deals with experiments on living beings. Again, Government medical advisers may not know the ordinary requirements of scientific research. Three laboratories in the Bombay Presidency have been rendered useless for the purposes for which they were built. One has been turned into a carcase incinerator, another into a go-down, and the third one Lord Harris assured us the other day would be put to some useful purpose, and he further assured us that after all the expenditure on these was not a matter of lakhs but only thousands Not only this: the *Times of India* remarked the other day that for scientific purposes a pound of ice or a pice worth of kerosine oil would give a bacteriologist any desired temperature for his cultivation purposes. This knowledge was unfortunately not in the possession of the highly paid scientific advisers of Government, who were compelled to vote further sums of money for the removal of their scientists and their baggage to more shady regions. But one need not multiply these instances. The monopoly of the I. M. S. not only recoils thus on the heads of the monopolists themselves, but what is more important from the point of view of the interests of the country itself, it prevents all growth of talent in the country, degrades the profession of India, as we shall see presently. (*Applause*)

It has been urged that the appointments must be so reserved for the Imperial purposes of a Military reserve. To begin with, a reserve of nearly 400 men for an effective service of less than half that number is an absurdity in which the military department alone can revel. But the reserve argument accuses the Government of hypocrisy and dishonesty. The Government have publicly declared that the medical schools were founded for the cultivation of the medical science of the West, for the benefit and happiness of the Indian people, and "not for any Governmental or Executive wants," and that they fostered the growth of science and higher education for their own sake. If these then be no longer their intentions, or rather the intentions of our latter-day Government, let them say so honestly, and not keep posing as honest patrons of science and education. The conditions under which the growth of science and medical education has suffered so long carry their own condemnation, and it is time the Indian people and not only the profession, rose as one man to appeal to the authorities to emancipate medical education and science from the thraldom of an aggressive Military Department, which has no moral or legal right to the monopoly it has built up for itself (for their covenant is purely a military covenant, and has no reference whatever to any right—much less extraordinary right—to civil appointments). It is only by such emancipation of medical education and science, by throwing open their fields of work to the best talent available in Europe or in India, that India can hope to advance to a forward place in the march of civilisation in the matter of scientific assimilation and growth. (*Loud Applause*)

Scientific Congresses in a land where science is allowed no fair play, and where there is no such thing as a scientific profession, are but false emblems of scientific progress. I was asked to join the Calcutta Medical Congress. I should have been delighted to take part in any proper Medical Congress. But I did not join this Calcutta Congress for the simple reason that it is no genuine Congress of a homogeneous liberal profession. Compared with genuine Congresses it had the elements of sham and hypocrisy in its very constitution. For, look the facts straight in the face. Here is a group of men—the monopolists—asking their bondsmen to rub shoulders with them just for the parposes of a good gathering. Men who have been looked upon as an inferior lot, incapable to rise to the position of their teachers in their own *alma mater*, unfit to take part in the work of scientific medicine, are now suddenly considered fit to discuss scientific works with masters and superior persons. A mere Congress gathering gives no unity to the profession in India, and removes not the unjustifiable limitations placed on its Indian members. The question of economy having been fully discussed on previous occasions need not be again taken up now. Only recently some military scenes have occurred in the matter of some dozen appointments which have increased the military expenditure by thousands, and it was time the whole question was gone into by an open public inquiry. (*Cheers*)

To turn to the second part of the resolution, *viz.*, the subject of the Subordinate Medical Service. It has three branches. First, the Assistant Surgeons. These are our graduates in medicine, who have passed both educational and professional tests higher than those required for the I. M. S., and being Assistant Surgeons on Rs. 100 a month rise to be old Assistant Surgeons on Rs. 200 a month, and retire on the grand pension of Rs. 100, (*Shame*) whilst members of the Military Service who sponge on the Civil Department rise from Rs. 500 to Rs. 2,500. The Assistant Surgeons do, and have done, all the work, even field work as Volunteers in the Afghan and other campaigns, of the Civil Military Surgeons, but without their pay or their position. The highest career is open to members of every other faculty of our Universities, but altogether closed to members of the Medical faculty. It is surprising that members of the sister faculties did not perceive for so long the unjust treatment accorded to their fellow graduates. A special service, the Uncovenanted Medical Service, on the lines of the uncovenanted counterpart of the I. C. S., was specially created more than twenty-five years ago for the employment of Indian graduates, but the Military Surgeon-General has contrived to make it a complete dead-letter by absorbing all the appointments into his military schedule. If, indeed, in twenty years the medical school of Bombay for instance, can not turn out a fit enough graduate for the Uncovenanted Medical Service, it is high time the College constitution was overhauled. (*Hear, hear and Applause*) The Assistant Surgeons have often complained. Instead of redress they have received nothing but threats from the domineering Military Surgeon-General, who contrived to keep out all evidence before the Public Service Commission in the matter of the wrongs they all along inflicted on their victims—the subordinate service. It is time the public moved in the matter and demanded an open public inquiry. (*Cheers*)

Then there are two other enlistments for the subordinate service—one military and the other civil—the former being open to Christians only. But see what difference the element of religion makes in the treatment accorded to the two classes. John, the Christian, and Pandu, the non-Christian, both seek admission to their respective services. John the Christian need not know more than the High School fourth standard, reading, writing, and sums,

Third Day.

Resolution VIII. Medical Service.

Dr. Bahadurji.

but Pandu, the non-Christian, must pass a much higher test. They both go through the same professional course and examination. If anything, Pandu has to undergo a severer examination. John, the Christian, then begins as a Military Apothecary, and works under the regimental Surgeons. His salary ranges from Rs. 50 to Rs. 450. He may, however, be promoted to the uncovenanted grade and given even Rs. 750 by being found a post in the Civil Department. His new designation is Assistant Surgeon, I. M. S., and he rises from the rank of Lieutenant to that of Major. But Pandu, the non-Christian, begins as a Hospital Assistant and dies a Hospital Assistant. (*Shame*) His work is as vast as it is responsible. He practises medicine, surgery and midwifery. He it is who really dispels the ignorance and prejudice of the masses in regard to the western system of medicine. He treats a thousand times more cases in a month than the highest officer of a hospital does in a year. On his judgment, intelligence and integrity depend the lives of his fellow citizens in the mofussil, questions of life and death turning upon the nature of his evidence in medico-legal cases. But alas! the respectability and responsibility of this most important servant of the State are in an inverse ratio, and that too in very abnormal proportions. One feels almost ashamed to say that the non-Christian Pandu who does such responsible and excellent work for the Government is paid no higher salary than is paid to a senior *punka-wallah* in the hospital, or a cook or a coachman. The scale of his pay is Rs. 16 to Rs. 80 odd. (*Shame*) Can there be any other reason for this great difference in treatment between the Christian Apothecary and the graduate Assistant Surgeon and Hospital Assistant, in every way his superior, and superior in many respects and equal in others to his Christian brethren generally, than that the specially favoured class belongs to the Christian race? (*Loud cries of Shame*) Is this religious tolerance or religious persecution by the polished methods of modern times? It is hard to believe that the responsible representatives of Her Majesty in India can be at all aware of this incredibly unfair treatment meted out to their most responsible, patient and faithful servants. There is not a department of State administered by civilians pure and simple, where any such horrible system of slavery is practised on its minor officers, as has been so atrociously done by military usurpers of the Civil Medical Department. Will the public stand this any longer? Now that it has been familiarised with these manifest wrongs which scandalise the fair fame of British justice and fair play it is its bounden duty to appeal to the authorities for immediate redress. Let every presidency town hold public meetings to memorialise Government for a public inquiry such as the Congress prays for, and let the leaders of the people do their duty by the people and work for this public cause—a cause so intimately bound up with the material progress of the country. (*Loud and long continued Cheers*)

Rai Bahadur P. Ananda Charlu.

Rai Bahadur P. Ananda Charlu:—Mr. President, Delegates, Ladies and Gentlemen, my appearance before you is due to a strong sense of duty in me to tell you all, that the proposition which has just been placed before you is not the embodiment of a grievance on the part of medical men only. It is a question which is entitled to as serious a consideration as any other we have yet discussed or may yet discuss. Dr. Bahadurji has attempted, and has succeeded in his attempt, to open our eyes to a stupendous wrong that is in our midst; he has given you a great deal of information, and he has given you all that information with an eloquence which might have carried you away from the facts; he spoke so eloquently that I have some fear that in your admiration for his eloquence you may not have noticed certain contrasts to which attention is due. I shall therefore—without eloquence—contrast those facts for your consideration. He called your attention to the Medical Service which consists of a higher and a lower grade. In the higher grade there are two states—one military and the other civil. Enlistment for the military takes place in England, enlistment for the Civil takes place in India. It is necessary to note that geographical peculiarity, because it will enable you to find out certain differences existing, to which I shall presently call your attention. Now, to those who are enlisted in England the starting pay is Rs. 500, to those who are enlisted here the starting pay is Rs. 100. To those

RAI BAHADUR P. ANANDA CHARLU.

that belong to the Military Service enlisted in England the goal in hope is Rs. 2,500; to those that enter the Civil Military Service of this country the highest hope is Rs. 200—not a question of thousands at all. (*Shame*) Another important feature that deserves to be noticed is this: To enter into the service recruited in India, those who wish to qualify for medical education have to be either Matriculates, First Arts men, or Graduates, whereas for qualifying in England for the other highly paid Service the educational qualification is that they need not be even Under-graduates. Now, there is another important circumstance worth noticing, which is this. Under the Indian Medical Service you can rise up to what is called Assistant Civil Surgeon; you can never become a District Surgeon. A comparison has been instituted between the Covenanted Civil Service and this. In connection with that I may point out to you that although there is a covenant on the part of the Government with the persons who enter the Covenanted Civil Service, that certain appointments should be given to them—although some of those appointments are taken away or attempted to be taken away, yet here, without there being any such binding covenant, not a single District-Surgeonship is open to be given to the person who graduates in this country. If you want to become a District Surgeon go you must across the waters, go you must to pass the examination which shall give you an entrance into that service which I have described. In the lower, again, there are two classes. The facts have been mentioned; I shall simply call your attention to the contrast that exists. The "Apothecary" was the former name; "Hospital Assistant" is the name bestowed on the less favoured gentlemen. The apothecary's place is now taken by the more high-sounding title of "Assistant Surgeon." He indeed, is recruited in this country, but is attached to Military Service; he begins with a pay of Rs. 56, and may rise to Rs. 450, whereas the other gentleman, the Hospital Assistant, having nearly the same medical training and education, has to begin with Rs. 16 and can never rise beyond Rs. 80. The educational qualification apart from the medical training possessed by these gentlemen is also worthy of contrast. The Fifth Standard is enough for the more highly paid man while the Seventh Standard is necessary for the less paid man. Gentlemen, one further point of distinction I shall notice, and that is, the apothecary—the military apothecary or the Assistant Surgeon—must be Christian; the Hospital Assistant, be he ever so clever, can never enter that Service. Now, that is the main and the only distinction, and it carries with it that the one man who is a Christian begins with Rs. 50 and rises to Rs. 450, but the other man, not being Christian, has to begin with Rs. 16 and concludes with Rs. 80. (*Shame*)

DR. M. G. DESHMOOK.

DR. M. G. DESHMOOK:—Mr. President and Gentlemen You must have seen by this time that what we ask for is nothing more than to do away with the monopoly of all Civil Medical and Scientific appointments in this land by the Military Medical Service. We do not ask that the higher appointments in the Civil Medical and Scientific Service be given to one class or to another. What we ask is that these appointments shall be thrown open to all classes alike. Gentlemen, monopoly of every kind has its own peculiar evils, but in the case of filling appointments of a scientific nature, appointments which require scientific training and special qualifications, restriction in the selection of these appointments is productive of great evils and is most unsuitable. Monopoly, Gentlemen, of this kind should have no place in the case of appointments relating to the scientific and medical services; for the greater and wider the field of selection that is thrown open to such appointments, the better and the more qualified are the men who can be obtained for these services. No political exigency can be called into requisition to support this monopoly, no bureaucrat of the deepest dye can cry out danger to the State, even if the highest scientific and medical appointments are filled by men not belonging to the ruling class. (*Cheers*) Therefore monopoly by the ruling class alone is unsuitable and undesirable in this case. Monopoly again is unsuitable in this case because the monopoly was first created at a time, when probably there was in this country no scientific medical profession existing; but now it is almost more than a third of a century that medical education and scientific education have been given in different centres of this country, and there is enough

Third Day.

Resolution VIII. Medical Service.

Dr. M. C. Deshmook.

indigenous material produced from these centres It is, therefore, high time that this monopoly should be broken, and this indigenous material utilised in filling up the higher appointments of the scientific and medical service. There is again one advantage in using this material of indigenous character; there is a financial advantage; and therefore both in the interests of fair play and justice, as well as of efficiency of service and economy of administration, the sooner the monopoly is broken the better. (*Hear, hear*)

With regard to the third point of this resolution, what I have to say is, that this is the apt time when our Congress should witn one voice protest, and call the attention of Government to tbe desirability of removing the disability under which the assistants of the Chemical Analyser's Department labour, a disability by which these gentlemen, these hard-worked servants of Government, are rendered ineligible to attain the higher ranks of that same department. Gentlemen, the assistants in reality do all the work, the work of a scientific nature and of special requirement. They do all the work of this department, while they are compelled to work under superiors who have very little special training, and who have no experience. I speak on this subject from my own personal experience. Gentlemen, I may tell you in speaking of this personal experience that I am not standing here to air my own personal grievances, for although after serving for thirteen years in the Government service I was compelled to resign that service, yet, I have nothing to gain, by airing my grievances here, as I do not seek re-entrance into the service; but still the experience which I have gained, the disgust which is occasioned in my mind at the treatment accorded me are well worth citing here, so that this Congress may with one voice draw the attention of Government to the fact that the disability in the Chemical Analyser's department should be forthwith removed. This is the proper time for the Congress to take up this question, because it is understood that the Government of India intends to re-constitute this department on a better basis. This re-constitution has come to pass in this wise:—only two years ago after the resignation of my service as Assistant to the Chemical Analyser, the Medical profession of Bombay and Calcutta took up that case. They were impressed with the glaring injustice of that case, so they started an agitation, which continued from month to month, until two years had elapsed, and the attention of Government was directed to the impropriety, and to the most glaring injustice that is done to the Chemical Analyser class; and now in consequence of this agitation, the Government of India has made up its mind to re-constitute this department. It is, therefore, useful for this Congress at this moment to draw the attention of Government to the fact, that the condition and status of the Assistants in this Department and the disability under which they labour should be taken into consideration while these rules are being framed. For, Gentlemen, when I was serving as Chemical Analyser to Government, on one or two occasions it so happened that acting Cnemical Analysers were appointed who had no knowledge, no special training in that department, but who nevertheless were placed at the head of that department. I thought that I might as well put in my claim to be acting Chemical Analyser; but, Gentlemen, the Surgeon-General thought fit not to comply with my request, seeing that this was not allowed by the rules. (*Shame*) If such a thing is not allowed by rules, let us now approach Government and say that as they are now re-constituting the department, let them change the rules and let them make better provision for these Assistants. (*Hear, hear*)

The President :—The eighth resolution has been duly proposed, seconded, and supported. Let all those who are in favour hold up their hands. (*Voices*, All, All.)

The Resolution was carried unanimously.

Resolution IX Legislative Councils.

Pandit Madan Mohan Malaviya.

The President :—I now call upon Pandit Madan Mohan Malaviya to move the next resolution.

Pandit Madan Mohan Malaviya :—Mr. Chairman, Ladies and Gentlemen, it has fallen to my lot to move the next Resolution which runs thus :—

(*a*) That this Congress, in concurrence with the preceding Congress, considers that the creation of a Legislative Council for the Province of the Punjab is an absolute necessity for the good government of that Province, and having regard to the fact that a Legislative Council has been created for the N. W. Provinces, requests that no time should be lost in creating such a Council for the Punjab.

(*b*) That this Congress, in concurrence with the preceding Congress, is of opinion that the rules now in force under the Indian Councils Act of 1892 are materially defective and prays that His Excellency the Viceroy in Council will be pleased to have fresh rules framed in a liberal spirit with a view to a better working of the Act and suited to the conditions and requirements of each Province.

Now, Gentlemen, this question concerns the Legislative Councils, which are practically the bodies which decide what taxation shall be imposed upon the people and how the revenues raised shall be spent, and in fact all questions which affect the weal and woe of the two hundred and odd millions of this country in the most important respect. You remember, Gentlemen, that for years past the Congress laboured to bring about the reform of the Legislative Councils. We laboured earnestly to bring about a reform of these Councils by having an increase in the number of members who form those Councils, and by having a right of discussing the Budget, &c. Our request was conceded, but in a very partial and limited manner. The Indian Councils Act of 1892 was passed, by which the number of our members was partially increased and certain powers were conferred upon us. We might then have hoped that the Councils as now constituted, or rather reformed, would be something better than the Councils which existed before these reformed Councils. But, Gentlemen, I will invite your attention only to some points, to some facts, which have happened within the last 12 months, and ask you to say whether you consider that with all the reform that has been brought to you in these Councils, the Legislative Councils of India, including that of the Governor-General in Council, are anything but shams, so far as the real and true interests of the people of India are concerned. (*Cheers*) Gentlemen, you will remember the debate on the Indian Tariff Bill, you will remember the debate on the Indian Councils Bill; you will remember how while there was a strong desire on the part of the members of the Councils, including, so far as one could see, His Excellency the Viceroy himself, to levy, to re-impose, the cotton duties, the Council felt their hands fully restrained by a dictum of the Secretary of State for India; you will remember the piteous wailings of some of the members of the Council, the piteous tones in which some of the official members of the Councils tried to excuse their conduct by saying that they were bound, being official members, to vote in obedience to the orders of the Secretary of State for India. (*Shame, Shame*) Gentlemen if there is one characteristic of Englishmen which distinguishes them above all other people, which entitles them to the respect of nations more than anything else, it is their sense of duty. (*Cheers*) We thought we were under the impression that an Englishman taking up any position of responsibility would lay aside all other considerations except those which should govern his conduct in relation to those, for the betterment of whose condition and for the protection of whose interests he was appointed. But, Gentlemen, here we have a sad confession of the weakness—shall I say something worse? No, Gentlemen, I will only say weakness, or let me say the powerlessness—of the official members, as confessed by themselves so far as the protecting of the interests of India is concerned. When the question of re-imposing the cotton duties comes up again, the permission which the Secretary of State has granted is accompanied by the mandate that this duty so urgently needed by the distressed condition of Indian finance cannot be re-imposed unless a countervailing excise duty is imposed upon Indian manufactures. (*Hear, hear*) Gentlemen, what does it show? It fully demonstrates this sad fact, that the Government of India is powerless to protect the interests of Indians. Unfortunately, they are not equally powerless when doing mischief to the people of India. (*Cheers*) You will remember, Gentlemen, how the Exchange Compensation Allowance was granted. At that time the Government of India and the Secretary of State agreed together that Exchange Compensation should be allowed, and it was allowed. Therefore as matters stand now you find that the Government of India, as at present constituted, is powerless for the good of the

Third Day.

Resolution IX. Legislative Councils.

Pandit Madan Mohan Malaviya.

Indians in all matters affecting the finances of India, and is potent for mischief in relation to matters affecting those interests. (*Cheers*)

Gentlemen, I have not referred to this without an object; I only wish to point out to you the extreme necessity of having a further reform of these Councils, by means of which we might have a larger number of non-official members in the Councils, armed with greater and more substantial powers to protect the interests of the people of this country. I was going to refer you to the division on the Indian Tariff Bill, simply to show you that so far as I see, every official member supported that measure which every non-official member of the Viceroy's Council opposed. Here are the proceedings recorded; you have only this satisfaction, to see that the "Ayes" and the "Noes" are recorded, but beyond that they were powerless to protect you against the injustice wrought upon you. Therefore, Gentlemen, it is a matter of extreme necessity, finding that the Official members of the Government of India are bound by the dictum of the Secretary of State, and finding also to our great regret that the Secretary of State, that high State dignitary is not guided by his own reasonings. by his own wishes, by his own convictions, so far as one could judge them, but that he is guided by paltry party considerations, by a desire to please a few persons in Lancashire—it becomes extremely necessary tnat you should unite in a body to pray to Her Majesty to grant further reform of the Councils (*Cheers*), in order tnat our interests may be protected. And now, Gentlemen, that is, no doubt, not before the Congress at this moment, but all that I have brought it in for is to show you how very little, how very small, is the measure of reform that we seek of the Government in asking them to give us all that could be given, that can be liberally given, justly given, under the Councils Act of 1892. If with the entire Council standing as it does against us, our interests cannot be fully protected, is there not the greatest reason why that should be conceded in the most liberal spirit, so that we might derive the greatest benefit we can from it? Has it been so conceded and has the Indian Councils Act of 1892 been so worked? You will remember your esteemed Chairman of the Reception Committee inviting your attention to the assertions of Mr. Gladstone and Lord Salisbury in that connection. With your permission I should like to read those words again, to shew what hopes we were allowed to entertain, what promises were made to us. Mr. Gladstone speaking as the head of the Liberal party said, "I believe I am justified in looking forward not merely to a nominal but "to a real living representation of the people." Lord Salisbury, on his side, speaking on the same subject, said in the House of Lords, "If we are to do it, and if it has to be done, of course "accepting that it must be done, let us do it systematically, taking care that the machinery "provided shall effect the purpose of giving representation, not to accidentally constituted "bodies, not to small sections of the people here and there, but to the living strength "and vital forces of the whole community of India." (*Cheers*) Gentlemen, if the persons entrusted with the framing of the rules under the Act here had been good enough to carry out the promises given by these responsible statesmen, given by the Under Secretary of State for India and the Secretary of State for India in that connection, we should have had little reason to complain so far as the rules of the Councils Act are concerned. But, Gentlemen, while there is an extreme solicitousness to bring in the latest improvements of western science into India, where the interests of the people of India are not directly concerned, there is an extreme unwillingness on the part of some of our Anglo-Indian Administrators to introduce reforms in the political administration of the country, which centuries ago were pronounced to be beneficent, and which centuries ago were adopted in England. You must have read, Gentlemen, most of you, that before the Reform Bill of 1832, there were what was called "rotten boroughs" in England. What has become of those boroughs? I am sorry I am not able to lay my hands upon the book in which I read of them; and cannot therefore quote it in detail, but as far as I remember, it was simply this, that there were half-a-dozen seats in Parliament owned sometimes by one rich man, ten seats owned by another rich man, and I believe there was one gentleman, a large landowner so far as I can remember, who had eleven seats in Parliament under his thumb. (*Laughter*) Gentlemen, we thought that those times had gone by, that the constitutional battles which the English people had fought, that the agitation which they had carried on, had established the principle that "in the multitude of councillors there is wisdom"—that the greater the number of men who are admitted to a voice in the administration of the country, the greater is the chance of the administration being best conducted. Therefore, Gentlemen, what we expected in every way was that the franchise would be conferred under the present Act—the Indian Councils Act of 1892—in as liberal a spirit as it could be. (*Cheers*)

I will refer you to what has happened chiefly in Bombay and in the North-West Provinces. I should not trespass upon the ground which will be taken up by my Bombay friends. I will only briefly refer to it, and then I will say a few words with reference to the North-West Provinces. In Bombay, Gentlemen, eight seats have been thrown open to the non-officials, of these eight seats two have been given to the Bombay Corporation and Senate of the Bombay University, of the remaining six seats two together have been given to the Zemindars of Sind and the Chamber of Commerce at Kurrachee, one has been given to the Bombay Chamber of Commerce, and two only to the general public. A very important division, the Central division, which includes Poona and Satara, has been excluded. (*Shame, Shame*) Now, Gentlemen, I will only say this, that a system which leaves out a historical and well known place, a place which has been noted for the keenness of the intellect of its Brahmins and its other people, (*Cheers*) a place which is regarded by the people of the Deccan as the seat of learning and piety—a system which leaves out such a place, is a system which stands condemned by itself. (*Hear, hear*) A few words with regard to the North-West Provinces. There it has been our lot to have the greatest share of this illiberal dispensation of the franchise. Gentlemen, there are 103 Municipalities in the North-West Provinces and Oudh; and there are 44 District Boards. While this privilege of electing members has been conferred upon all these 44 District Boards, they being grouped together in two groups and having the right to send one member from each group, only 10 out of the 103 Municipalities in the entire Provinces have been thought fit to be entrusted with this privilege. Now, you will please consider that, in the first place, this system which requires representative delegates to be elected, not by the people directly but by their elected representatives, is in itself a very objectionable system; we want the people themselves to be allowed to elect; (*Hear, hear*) and we do not see any reason why they should not. In England, when the organisation and the system of administration had not attained half that perfection, which I may say for administrative purposes, the administration has attained in India, they extended the franchise to people enjoying a certain property qualification; while persons enjoying in this country a certain income it may be a hundred rupees a month or two hundred rupees a month, are considered to be fit to be elected Municipal Commissioners or members of the District Board. If the Government do not see their way to conferring this privilege upon all the electors who elect members for the Municipality and District Boards, where on earth is the difficulty, where is the justification for not allowing those persons who are entitled by reason of their property qualification to sit as members of the District Boards and Municipalities to elect members for the Councils directly? (*Hear, hear*) However, if this is not done, Gentlemen, let at least the members composing the Municipalities and District Boards meet at one central place—the railway makes the journey very easy—and vote for the men directly. (*Cheers*) What is at present required is that the various District Boards and Municipalities hold meetings at their respective places and nominate one representative to vote at a central place. Out of a population of 40 millions, you find ten persons meeting together in the province to return two members to the Council. What could be more unsatisfactory than that? Gentlemen, I am very much afraid of the President's gong, and I do not wish to disobey the authority of the chair; so I will not take up any more time. I will only say this: that if the different administrators in this country really and honestly desire to give effect to the provisions of the Indian Councils Act, as explained by the Secretary of State, and the Under Secretary of State, and by Mr. Gladstone and Lord Salisbury, they should extend the franchise to all those persons who are entitled to sit as members of the Local and Municipal Boards; or at least if they cannot venture on such a scheme as that so soon, let them confer this power at least on all the members of the District and Local Boards, and, instead of having a distilled representation, let the people elect the members themselves. Gentlemen, I will not take up more of your time, but I hope that the Government may yet see the urgency and the necessity of this reform, and that it may grant it before long. (*Loud Cheers*)

BAKSHI JAISHI RAM.

BAKSHI JAISHI RAM :—Gentlemen, we meet at Madras again after seven years. It has been said that during this period the people of India have succeeded in securing the right of selection in the constitution of the Legislative Councils. It is also maintained that the right of interpellation has been granted, and that the privilege of discussing the budget has been allowed. Gentlemen, however valuable and enviable these privileges may be, we Panjabis have really shared in none of them. We have no Legislative Council, and we have no right of returning a representative to the Supreme Legislative Council. Gentlemen, I trust you will all agree with me in endorsing a vote of deep regret that during this period of seven years our Province has noticed what we may call a retrograde progress. Gentlemen, at the time when we met last at Madras the proprietors in our villages did exercise certain rights which they do not exercise to-day. The villages in our province formed what we may describe as small republics, the villagers appointed the village officers for themselves, and at the same time they used to decide all questions in the internal administration of the village by themselves. The only concern they used to have was to pay the land revenues. What was going to happen outside the boundaries of their village they did not care about. They did not care even for the bloody wars or political revolutions that used to take place. These small republics, as they have been described by such an eminent jurist as Sir Henry Maine, were not as to-day. Before 1888 nobody could be appointed as village headman who had rendered himself obnoxious to the village community. The village accountant was appointed by the village headman or the village proprietors, and the village watchman was appointed by the village headman; the Zemindar was a representative on behalf of the Government: still the District officers were bound to consider the opinion of the village headman. Gentlemen, the year 1888 brought a very different epoch into our province. All the powers which the village proprietors used to exercise have been taken away, and at the present day all the village officers, whether they be the village accountant or the village watchman, are all appointed by the will of the District Officer. (*Shame*) The opinion of the village proprietors is no more of concern, and any person may be forced on the village proprietors by the District Officer. But this is not all, Gentlemen. The scheme regarding local self-government was laid down by Sir Charles Aitcheson, and was also brought into force by the same officer, but Sir Charles Aitcheson had to vacate office, and in his absence the scheme brought into force ceased to have its real character, and now the District Officer is the sole proprietor of the District Boards as of the Municipalities. So, Gentlemen, I submit it is retrograde progress which our Province has been making, and I hope that you will all express deep regret on this subject. (*Hear, hear*) Gentlemen, no reason is known why the privileges that are exercised by the sister provinces are not allowed to the Punjab. What reason exists why the people of the N.-W. Provinces should have a Legislative Council, while the people of the Punjab have not? Is it because the people of the Punjab shed their blood in 1859 against their own people, and secured the glory of the British Crown by fighting in the fields of Abyssinia or other foreign countries? Or is it because for the present the fighting tribes are supplied in a great measure by the Punjab? Or is it because the frontier crisis is some day to be decided by the people of the Punjab? Gentlemen, with these remarks I second the resolution. (*Cheers*)

MR. W. A. CHAMBERS.

MR. W. A. CHAMBERS :—Mr. Chairman and Delegates, we in Bombay feel particularly aggrieved upon this matter of the Councils Act. We were led to believe with the rest of the people of India, in reading the discussions in the House of Commons, that the Act which

Third Day

Resolution IX. Legislative Councils.

Mr. W. A. Chambers.

was to be then presented to the people of India, in answer to their agitation, was something worth having. We have unfortunately discovered in Bombay that, in consequence of having at our head His Excellency Lord Harris, a man who belongs to a reactionary party, the boon is scarcely worth the receiving. Now, as has already been said by the gentleman who moved this resolution, there have been eight seats given to the people of Bombay, but the great grievance we have, and here I speak as a Bombay man on behalf of those people who are called Poona Brahmins, is that the Poona Brahmins have been absolutely forgotten, and left altogether in the cold. (*Shame*) Lord Harris has discovered that the Poona Brahmins, in consequence of being left out of the scheme, are not in the best of tempers; he tells us when they complain that they are a set of fellows who are absolutely without common sense. (*Shame*) It is, as has already been said "a shame", but unfortunately it is true. Lord Harris has discovered that the Poona Brahmins, in consequence of the fact that they resent this stricture upon them, and are not willing to sit down under it, are men he cannot trust. Lord Harris may be, and possibly is, a very able cricketer. (*Laughter*) Lord Harris may be very skilful in the cricket field; but as an English politician, and I think your President will bear me out, as a statesman Lord Harris's reputation in England is very small indeed. (*Hear, hear*)

Now we are not only aggrieved in consequence of the way we have been treated with reference to our Poona friends, but we are disgusted at the way in which His Excellency has conducted the proceedings of the Council. We have certainly had interpellations put under his Presidentship; I will tell you of one or two of them, and I will then ask you your opinion as to his conduct. The first thing I want to draw your attention to is this. There is a Municipality near Bombay called Bandora; it had as its president a non-official European; this gentleman ceased to be President, and it was suggested that a native gentleman should be appointed in his place. This suggestion was not carried out, and in answer to the question whether this was not so, and why an official was appointed, the member was calmly told that the Government thought it was best. Now, Gentlemen, I say it again seriously, as a responsible politician, this is not the way in which the English House of Commons intended that this Act should be used. The intention of the Act was that you should have some influence given you, and one of the privileges given you was that you should be able to ask questions; and to give such ansanswer as that is an insult to the Bombay people. (*Hear, hear*) Now, in regard to another matter, another question was put to Lord Harris. The Municipality of Ahmedabad was opposed to some drainage scheme, and the Government was anxious that this drainage scheme should be carried out. They could not carry it out with the Board as then constituted, so a number of Government Commissioners were nominated, and the scheme was then, of course, at the mercy of Government. A question was put by another popular representative as regards this particular method of getting Government sanction, and he was told again that the Government thought it best Again, a question that has been alluded to by our dear friend was put—and I am glad to see that these questions are put—a question was put in the Council asking if it was true that the senior Chemical Analyser was not doing his work, that his assistant was doing it, and that he was getting all the honour and glory of it—but of course not in those exact terms, they would not be so vulgar nor so truthful as we are on a Congress platform; (*Laughter*) and the answer was given that they thought that was the proper sort of thing to do. Then the gentleman who put the question pressed the matter—I was glad to see that, as pertinacity of this kind shows the country has some vitality in it—the question was put again, and again the answer was given by this reactionary Governor of ours, that the Government did not think it was expedient to present the Report. (*Shame*) Unfortunately the Government do not think it expedient to present many reports, but fortunately for us there are now growing up among the people of India English people who wish to be here as your friends. (*Cheers*) Fortunately there is a spirit growing up which will necessitate that the Government's action, whether they think it expedient or not, shall be shown up to public criticism. Now, another question was put by one of our Councillors—again the popular member. I am simply bringing this question before you to show you how

Third Day.

Resolution IX.
Legislative Councils.

Mr. W. A. Chambers.

we have been absolutely "jockeyed"—you understand that expression—jockeyed out of our rights altogether by the Bombay Government, and out of the privileges which were given to us by the House of Commons. A gentleman on the Bombay Council asked some question about Exchange Compensation. Exchange Compensation is a very delicate matter indeed. The answer given to him was that it was out of order, (*Laughter*) that it could not be discussed, that it was an Imperial matter. (*Shame*) What is the use of such an answer in such a matter? I think it is a shameful answer, indeed. Another question was asked by some gentleman in reference to the land revenue in Bombay and increased assessment, and he wished to discuss the matter on the budget motion. The member—a popularly elected representative—was ruled out of order. (*Shame*) This is what is taking place in Bombay at the present moment, and Lord Harris wonders that the Deccan is in a state of revolt. I say that if it is not in a state of revolt then the Deccan deserves the treatment it has received. It does not deserve a representation by the popular party. I read the debates in the House of Commons on this matter, and am certain that the House of Commons meant you well in it. I am certain that the meaning of that Act was that, so far as practicable, representative institutions should be given to you. I believe other Governments have acted fairly, that is moderately fairly. In Bombay unfortunately we are men who think we have a very great grievance. We come to you here, as citizens of other parts of India, to lay these grievances before you, and to ask your opinion, and if your opinion coincides with ours (Yes, Yes), that Bombay has not been fairly treated, it is your duty—nay it is your privilege—to support us by passing this resolution with acclamation. (*Loud Cheers*)

Mr Bhagiratha Prasad.

Mr. Bhagiratha Prasad :—Mr. President, Brother Delegates and Gentlemen, the proposition before us consists of two parts. In the first part we repeat what we have done so often, that a Legislative Council should be, without any further loss of time, created for the Punjab. I am one of those who hold that no reform is of any use unless we find in it harmonious development of the whole. Such being the case I have great pleasure in supporting this part of the resolution, and I assure my Punjab friends that the people of the Central Provinces would heartily congratulate them, the moment they know that the request has been granted. (*Cheers*)

In the second part we complain that the rules now in force under the Indian Councils Act of 1892 are materially defective, and pray that His Excellency the Viceroy in Council will be so pleased as to have fresh rules framed, in a liberal spirit with a view to a better working of the Act, and suited to the conditions and requirements of each Province. In this respect the Central Provinces have, Gentlemen, grievances of a graver nature than any other province, I believe, has, and this you will presently see. Our Government often accuses us of being merely theoretical people, and of never submitting any practical scheme. This accusation cannot however, be brought against the Central Provinces people in this instance at least, as they formulated a scheme and submitted it for the favourable consideration of the Government: the Government did not, however, condescend to vouchsafe us any reply. And what did it do? It created four electoral Colleges one for each division. Were the people to return members to these? No; nothing of the sort. Municipal Committes and District Councils elected members for these. Did all the Municipal bodies and District Councils do so? (*A voice*, Yes) No, Gentlemen, nothing of the sort. You are greatly mistaken. Only six Municipalities out of some 56 got this right. Is it not now clear that by leaving out some 50 Municipalities, a large number of well qualified and intelligent citizens was left out (*Voices*, Yes, Yes, *and cries of* Shame). Let us, however, proceed still further. The members returned by these constituted themselves as stated above into four electoral colleges, one for each division. Each Commissioner is required to send in the name of the only gentleman who should happen to get the highest number of votes—not by ballot—in the electoral college for the division of the Commissioner, and the Chief Commissioner will know officially nothing whatsoever regarding any other candidates. According to this system, a gentleman who really gets the highest number of votes in the whole of the province may be altogether left out. I shall illustrate this by taking a hypothetical case. Let us suppose each of these electoral colleges consist of 11 gentlemen, and that a candidate gets five votes in each of them and hence 20 in the whole; but his name is not officially before the Chief Commissioner, as his defeat in each of the colleges prevents the Commissioners sending up his name. Then of the names before the Government: a gentleman getting only six votes and that only in one division and in no other, is selected. Is now, Gentlemen, this latter gentleman the real representative or the former? (*Voices,* Former). But how can the former be secured, his name being not at all officially before the Government? Is not now this a grievance? (*Voices,* Yes, Yes). But let me go still further on. The rules do not make it obligatory upon the Government to make a selection from out of the candidates returned by the colleges; the Government may reject all these and may recommend one from outside. Such a power, I believe, other Governments have not got; they simply confirm the elections. Is not, Gentlemen, the election in the Central Provinces a greater farce than in any other province? It is not due so much to the rules as to the help given by Sir A. P. MacDonnell and the Hon'ble Mr. J. Woodburn, that we got the Hon'ble Mr. G. M. Chitnavis as our representative, and for this help the whole of the Central Provinces has been laid under deep obligation by these two truly liberal officers. (*Cheers*) Now, Gentlemen, when it is clear that the Government may reject the candidates returned by the electoral colleges, is the gentleman appointed to represent us, the Central Provinces people, a representative of the people or of the Government? (*Voices:* Government). Truly so. And is not this awkward? Will he not, under ordinary circumstances, take only such steps in the Council as may not displease the Government? To do otherwise requires a really strong back-bone. Is not, Gentlemen, our grievance of a graver nature than that in any other Province? (*Voices:* It is, It is). Thank you, Gentlemen, it is for these reasons that I commend the whole proposition for your favourable consideration, and hope that the Government will soon see its way to grant the whole of our prayer, and thus give us, in the words of Mr. Gladstone, a really living representation. (*Loud Cheers*)

Mr. Kaliprasanna Acharya.

Mr. Kaliprasanna Acharya:—Mr. President and Brother Delegates, I come from the district of Rajshahye in Bengal. It is one of the several districts forming the Rajshahye division. Last year some of the Municipalities of this Division, according to their respective incomes, jointly received the privilege of electing or selecting, as you may choose to call it, a member for our local Legislative Council. In connection with this election, I had the misfortune personally to witness some of the evil effects of a defective rule, known technically as the "Residential clause." There were several gentlemen contesting the seat; and a gentleman of education and position got the absolute majority. But the gentleman who got the next largest number of votes, objected to the election, and filed a regular election petition with the Commissioner of the Rajshahye Division. The ground of objection was that the elected gentleman was not a resident of the division. There were affidavits and counter-affidavits filed and eminent counsel brought from Calcutta to Darjeeling, a distance of about 400 miles. After a hard fight on both sides, which entailed heavy expenditure and much trouble to the parties concerned, the whole thing ended in a *fiasco*; the election was set aside and a fresh one ordered. (*Shame*) Now, Gentlemen, the gentleman who obtained the absolute majority had, and has yet, his paternal residence and some landed property in the Rajshahye division; and these facts were not denied by his opponent. His only disqualification was that he finished his education in England, and being a very able man, chose for his profession a wider and better field in Calcutta than in his own division. Gentlemen, the Government is, I think, willing to have the best men in the Council. If so why should the "Residential clause" intervene and debar us from electing a Calcutta gentleman? It may be that a person who habitually lives in the metropolis may not know the ins and outs of the mofussil; but I fail to see the harm in electing such a person. I am myself a pleader, and my duty is to plead the cause of others, mofussil people, in the Sadar courts. I habitually reside in the Sadar station of my district and seldom go to the interior, to my clients' houses, to look after their cases. My clients, by letters, or by agents, or personally, instruct me. Why could we

Third Day

Resolution IX. Legislative Councils.

Mr. Kaliprasanna Acharya.

not do the same thing in the case of our representative in the Council? This "Residential clause," Gentlemen, is a great evil and should no longer remain in force. Although in our subsequent election we had the good fortune to find an educated young nobleman willing to take the responsible duties of a Councillor on his shoulders, yet I am afraid, we may sometimes be put to difficulty to get hold of a really fit and able man. His Honour the Lieutenant-Governor of our Province perhaps anticipated the difficulty, and meant to give a liberal interpretation to the clause; but in our case the Indian Government willed otherwise. So I ask you, Gentlemen, to pray His Excellency the Viceroy in Council to cancel this rule altogether, and allow us the free discretion of choosing our own man. (*Hear, hear*)

Mr. Peter Paul Pillai.

Mr. Peter Paul Pillai:—Mr. Chairman and Brother Delegates, you have heard the grievance of the North-West Provinces and of the Bombay Presidency, but the Madrasis have reason to envy our friends in the two Provinces in one particular point; that is to say, with regard to the landholders of the North-West Provinces, they have the privilege of sending two elected members, and in the Bombay Presidency also they have some privilege, but in the Madras Presidency we are not given the privilege of an elective seat for the landholders. In this respect we are in a much worse position than before the Act of 1892. Formerly the landowner was one member out of eleven, now he is one out of twenty-one, and so the position is worse. Moreover, we find that out of the eleven seats for non-officials five are assigned to local Boards and Municipalities, and two seats are allowed, one for the University, and one for the Chamber of Commerce, while four seats are not assigned to any constituency at all, so we have one great grievance in this respect. We have been representing our grievance first to the Local Government and then to the Supreme Government but we have had no satisfactory reply to our prayer. The first reply was that it was not in the power of the Local Government to grant our request, while the Supreme Government replied that it was in the power of the Local Government. We had to go to the Secretary of State for India complaining against this. A nominated member is useless, and even worse than useless, as he has not the power of making independent criticism on the Government in regard to a Bill brought before the Council affecting the interests of the landowning community. We have a very strong instance in point. The same member that is nominated by Government, if elected by the landowners, would be a valuable and even-minded representative of the landowners. Instead of being so, we find that he is the supporter of the Government measures at the sacrifice of his own interests and those of his brethren. Thus we bring before the Congress this matter hoping that measures will be adopted to rectify the grievances complained of. The worst difficulty that will befall the landholding community as a consequence of the measure now passed will be the confiscation of property. The landowners form the most influential community in the Presidency, and have landed interests in more than 80 per cent. of the country, but we find that they are not only very inadequately represented but are not represented at all. With these remarks I support the resolution. (*Hear, hear*)

The President:—Is Mr. Karandikar here? (*Voices* No, No.) The Resolution was put to the vote and carried.

Rai Bahadur P. Ananda Charlu.

Rai Bahadur P. Ananda Charlu:—I have to make certain announcements under the orders of the President. The Subjects Committee will meet in quarter of an hour. The President asks me to announce that the Congress meets at 11 o'clock to-morrow.

The President.

The President:—There is a most important notice that I regret to be the mouthpiece of announcing to the Congress, a piece of news sadder than almost any that we could have received. It is the death of the Maharajah of Mysore. The newspaper states "His Highness the Maharajah of Mysore died this morning at 7 o'clock, of Diphtheria. His remains will be cremated at Benares." That renders it impossible for us to make any announcements regarding entertainments.

# FOURTH DAY'S PROCEEDINGS

**Saturday, the 29th December, 1894.**

Fourth Day.

The Congress assembled at 11 o'clock.

Resolution X. Vote of Sympathy with the Royal Family of Mysore.

THE PRESIDENT

THE PRESIDENT :—Friends and Fellow Delegates, you all feel the heavy cloud, you all feel the dark cloud, under which we meet to-day. The bright sunshine and the blue sky outside ill accord with the feelings of oppression and sadness that dwell in all our hearts. There is no occasion that I should mention the reason. We all know, we have all felt, since last night when we heard the terrible news of the death of the Maharajah of Mysore, that this Congress could not end in the joyful manner in which it had commenced. There is no need that I should say anything regarding the character of the services, the patriotism, and the life of the deceased Maharajah. That, of course, will be properly spoken to upon other occasions by men who have known him all their lives, and who are fully aware of his services to his country and to his race. It just remains for me to move the following Resolution which, of course, will be received by you standing, and which will be passed by you with raised arms in silence :—

> That this Congress wishes to express its respectful condolence and sympathy with the Royal Family of Mysore in their recent sad and sudden bereavement and at the same time to testify to its deep sense of the loss which has been sustained in the death of the Maharajah of Mysore not only by the State over which he ruled with such wisdom, ability and beneficence, but also by all the Indian peoples, to whom his constitutional reign was at once a vindication of their political capacity, an example for their active emulation, and an earnest of their future political liberties.

The Resolution was carried in deep silence, the audience standing with right arms raised.

THE PRESIDENT :—Now it is my duty to announce that in consequence of this bereavement and out of respect to the memory of the Maharajah, the entertainment to the Delegates has been abandoned. I have to announce to the Delegates that the entertainment to be given by Mr. Krishnadass to-morrow evening has also been abandoned ; and might I express my personal desire that for the rest of the time I shall be here we may have no music or demonstration of any kind. The eleventh Resolution will be moved by the Hon. Mr. Sitalvad, of Bombay.

Resolution XI. Trial by Jury

HON. C. H. SITALVAD.

THE HON. MR. C. H. SITALVAD :—Mr. President and Gentlemen, the Resolution that I have the honour to lay before you runs thus :—

> (*a*) That, in the opinion of this Congress, the time has now arrived when the system of trial by Jury may be safely extended, in cases triable by Sessions Courts, to many parts of the country where it is not at present in force.
>
> (*b*) That, in the opinion of this Congress, the innovation made in 1872 in the system of trial by Jury, depriving the verdicts of Juries of all finality has proved injurious to the country, and that the powers, then, for the first time, vested in Sessions Judges and High Courts, of setting aside verdicts of acquittal, should be at once withdrawn.
>
> (*c*) That, in the opinion of this Congress, it is extremely desirable that the power at present vested in Government to appeal against acquittals be taken away.

You will see, Gentlemen, that part (*a*) of the resolution asks that the system of trial by jury may be extended to those parts of the country where it is at present not in force. At the Congress Session of 1892, held at Allahabad, when we entered our most emphatic protest against that most arbitrary and reactionary measure of Sir Charles Elliot known as the "Jury Notification," this matter was so fully discussed that I think it is now idle for me to trouble you again with the facts and figures that were placed before you on that occasion. Suffice it to say that the agitation that followed that Notification, and the Report of the Commission that was appointed by Government to consider that matter, fully established, once for all, that the system of trial by jury, instead of being a failure, as was sought to be made out by the officials, was a complete success; while some of the members of the Commission recommended its further extension. Gentlemen, if trial by jury is a necessity in England, I maintain that it is a greater necessity in India whore the majority of the Judges, unacquainted with the manners and customs of the people, are not in a proper position, as a jury selected by the people themselves would be, to deal with questions of fact. (*Cheers*) That being so, Gentlemen, I do not think any further argument is required to induce you to press again your prayer for the further extension of the jury system to other parts of the country.

Paragraph (*b*) asks that finality be given to the verdicts of juries. As the law stands at present, Gentlemen, after the jury has delivered its verdict, if the Judge does not agree with it, he has power to make a reference to the High Court, who can dispose of the case in such manner as they may deem proper. You will agree with me, Gentlemen, that this proceeding is, on the face of it, very anomalous. Juries are constituted judges of facts, and it is certainly anomalous that where five gentlemen admittedly better qualified than the judge himself, better qualified because of their intimate knowledge of the customs and manners of the people, to deal with questions of fact, that where these five gentlemen are agreed upon a particular view of a case, the Judge should still have the power of over-riding their decision and referring the case to the higher authorities. Gentlemen, I can conceive of no greater condemnation of the present system than the fact that the various High Courts, notably that of Bombay, have practically refused to give full effect to this provision of the law. They have laid down from time to time that, although according to the strict letter of the law the whole case is opened up by a reference, they will not disturb the verdict of the jury simply because they think it wrong, but will only interfere when the conclusion arrived at on the record is so patently and manifestly perverse that no reasonable man could arrive at it. And, Gentlemen, one of the reasons that induced the High Court to lay down these rulings is pregnant with great wisdom and foresight, and it is this, If you once disturb the finality of the verdicts of juries you will be taking away the sense of responsibility of jurymen. You will agree with me that it is desirable that there should be some errors committed by juries rather than that anything should be done to take away from them their sense of responsibility. (*Cheers*)

The last paragraph of the Resolution for which I, in the Subjects Committee, was mainly responsible, deals with the power vested in local Governments to appeal against acquittals. Gentlemen, comprehensive as I think a great many provisions of the present Criminal Procedure Code are, I cannot conceive anything more illiberal in spirit and more mischievous, than the provisions on appeals in acquittals. Consider for a moment, Gentlemen, the wide powers vested in Government. Under this provision of the law, Government have the power of appealing against any order of acquittal, appellate and original; and the Limitation Act allows them the long period of six months within which they can do it. Contrast this with the privilege accorded to an accused appealing against conviction. If an accused is sent to jail for a period of one month, or is sentenced to a fine of Rs. 50, or is committed to the Sessions, he has no power to appeal, while in the case of summary trials he has no power of appeal at all. Even in cases where he has the power to appeal, he must exercise that power within 30 days, in the case of convictions by Magistrates, and within 60 days, in the case of convictions by Sessions Courts. Thus, Gentlemen, while an accused person—I ought to say a native accused person, because the Criminal Procedure Code most shamelessly violates the fundamental principles of law, that the law is no respecter of persons, and exempts European British subjects from these Rules (*Shame*)—must appeal

Fourth Day.

Resolution XI.
Trial by Jury.

HON. C. H.
SITALVAD.

within 30 or 60 days, as the case may be, when he is sentenced to undergo rigorous imprisonment for 3 months, or must make up his mind to sit still and bear it, your august Government with all their resources at their back have the proud privilege of hanging the sword of Damocles over the head of acquitted persons for 6 months. (*Shame*) Then, Gentlemen, we have to consider the actual way in which this provision is worded. Generally, when an acquittal is recorded in a Sessions Court, it may be even with the concurrence of a jury, it is ordinarily the District Magistrate, who is often a junior Collector, who sits in judgment on that order of acquittal, and thus deals with it. If he thinks the Sessions Judge is wrong he moves Government to appeal; and Government, on the recommendation of the District Magistrate, sanctions the appeal. It is a fact well known, Gentlemen, that when these appeals against acquittal come before the High Court, a large majority of them are certainly fruitless; but that only shows the wisdom of the High Court in acquitting, not that of the Government in preferring the appeals. (*Hear, hear*) True, Gentlemen, that a large majority of the appeals are fruitless, but what of the trouble, expense, and mental anxiety to which the poor accused is put? (*Hear, hear*) Then, again, I think, Gentlemen, that this power is very dangerous when left in the hands of the Local Governments, and I would illustrate this to you by recent events in my own Presidency. After the unhappy disturbances between Hindus and Mahomedans in Poona, a few months back, thirteen innocent people were hauled up by order of the Government before the Sessions Judge; and after an elaborate trial, the costs of which exceeded Rs. 10,000, the Sessions Judge, agreeing with the jury that all the Police evidence was hopelessly perjured and unreliable, acquitted the accused. Gentlemen, it is most confidently said in my part of that Presidency that Government seriously contemplate appealing against the acquittal. (*Shame*) Knowing the facts, I cannot conceive how any reasonable human being can think of appealing against that acquittal. Gentlemen, bearing in mind as I do the unimpeachable character that the present ruler of the Presidency has established for want of tact, for want of statesmanship, and for illiberal principles, I shall not be surprised if it turns out to be true; (*Shame*) and if it turns out to be true, then the thirteen poor people who have been falsely accused, who have spent Rs. 10,000, who have been put to such mental anxiety for three or four months, and who have been unnecessarily incarcerated for a period of two months, wih again have the anxiety and trouble put upon them of appearing before the High Court and defending themselves once more. Gentlemen, I think I have sufficiently shown you that this power is a very dangerous one to be kept in the hands of the Government, and that it should be speedily done away with. With these words I will commend the Resolution for your acceptance. (*Loud Cheers*)

MR. K. N.
DESMUKI.

MR. K. N. DESMUKI:—Mr. President, Brother Delegates, and Gentlemen, I am from the Central Provinces, the non-regulated provinces; the provinces having no Legislative Council; the provinces having no Chartered High Court; the provinces having no jury system. So you see, Gentlemen, we want many things. But be not afraid, please; we do not want them all at once and at one and the same time. Our Indian people are well known to the civilised world for their patience. Among other things that we want is the jury system. I do not wish to deal with the matters that have already been so ably and so exhaustively treated by my learned and eminent friend, simply because I cannot express them in better words. I cannot, however, Gentlemen, induce myself to be content without saying a very few words regarding my own provinces. The jury system is not extended to our provinces. We have not tasted the sweets of the jury system. Our humble prayer is for the extension of the jury system. Gentlemen, believe me, we Central Provinces persons, we people coming from the Central Provinces are not Khonds, are not Santals, are not men who have no touch of the present civilization. We are educated men; we are indeed highly obliged to the English Government for the clear education and enlightenment we have received. It has opened a new era in the history of the Central Provinces. During the last twenty years, English education has made very rapid progress; the existence of three Colleges in the

Fourth Day.

Resolution XI. Trial by Jury.

Mr. K N. Desmuki.

Central Provinces, the enterprising spirit shown by the educated men and trading classes in starting cotton factories, fully bear testimony to what I say before this responsible and august assembly here. It may appear, Gentlemen, surprising to you, nevertheless it is a fact, and an admitted fact, as disclosed by the Report of the Education Commission, that even primary education in the Central Provinces has been far in advance of what it has been in other provinces. Regarding the spread of higher education both the Administration and Educational Reports speak for themselves. The scheme of Local Self-Government which has made the Government of Lord Ripon so very popular, so very dear to the Indian people, has proved a complete success in our provinces. (*Hear, hear*) The interest the people take in the public affairs of the Central Provinces is evident from the fact that the Municipal Committees and the District Councils elect their own Chairmen. And whom do they elect, Gentlemen? Not official men but non-official members for that body. Gentlemen, all these facts will show clearly that we are fit for the boon of the jury system; they will convince you, Gentlemen, here that we have got sufficient material in our provinces from which juries can be selected. Gentlemen, if the natives of the Central Provinces are actually found, after serious trial and sufficiently long experience, to be fit to hold independent charge of the District—in plain words to be in the post of Deputy Commissioners—if they are thought, and wisely thought, to be competent to hold a seat on the Supreme Legislative Council of Calcutta, then, Gentlemen, is it not absurd, is it not unsound, is it not impolitic, to say that we are not yet fit to enjoy the jury system? (*Cheers*)

Gentlemen, I protest, and protest very strongly, with the greatest possible emphasis and force, that undoubtedly the time has come when the jury system should be extended to the Central Provinces. We do not want anything which is new to us; we do not want anything which is an innovation to us; but we want a thing which was the right and privilege of our forefathers, we want a thing which was enjoyed by our worthy forefathers, and enjoyed without any disturbance, without any interference. And what was that? It was the jury system, but fortunately or unfortunately it had a very different name, a name known to all of you here, and that was the "Panchayet" system. (*Hear, hear*) We ask for it, Gentlemen, with great courage and with great boldness, which certainly we should never have had courage or boldness to do under any other Government either native or foreign, because we know, and know full well, that we are living under the beneficent rule of Her Gracious Majesty, that we have got the most gracious, the most noble, the most worthy Charter, the solemn Proclamation of Her Majesty, that we are supported, and indeed very staunchly and very sincerely, by the British Committee; and not only by that Committee, but by almost all members of Parliament; and not only that, Gentlemen, but by all noble-minded and liberal-hearted gentlemen at home, (*Cheers*) whose motive in life, Gentlemen, is "Righteousness exalteth a nation," whose aim and object in life, Gentlemen, is to uphold the strong, and help the weak in the righteous cause. With these few remarks, and not to trouble the learned President, and not to take up your valuable time, I conclude, and have great pleasure in seconding the Resolution which has been so ably put forward by my learned friend. (*Cheers*)

The President.

The President:—I am going to take a somewhat unusual course, which I do not intend to adopt again. There are a couple of very important speakers who have to be heard on this Resolution but who have not yet arrived. So I shall take the liberty of going on with Resolution XII and then coming back to Resolution XI. Resolution XII will be proposed by Rai Bahadur P. Ananda Charlu, of Madras.

Resolution XII. Separation of Judicial and Executive Functions.

Rai Bahadur P. Ananda Charlu.

Rai Bahadur P. Ananda Charlu:—Mr. President and Brother Delegates, the proposition I have to place before you runs as follows:—

That this Congress having till now vainly appealed for many successive years to the Government of India, and also to the Secretary of State, to remove one of the gravest defects in the system of administration and one fraught with incalculable oppression to all classes of people throughout the country, and having noted with satisfaction the admission of the evil by two former Secretaries of State (Lord Kimberley and Lord Cross), and being of opinion that the reform is thoroughly practicable, as has been shown by Messrs. R. C. Dutt, M. M. Ghose and P. M. Mehta, entreats the Government of India to direct the immediate appointment in each province of a Committee (one-half at least of whose members shall be non-official natives of India, qualified by education and experience in the workings of various Courts to deal with the question) to prepare a scheme for the complete separation of all Judicial and Executive functions in their own province with as little additional cost to the State as may be practicable, and the submission of such schemes, with the opinions of the several Governments thereon, at an early date.

**Fourth Day.**

**Resolution XII. Separation of Judicial and Executive Functions.**

**Rai Bahadur P. Ananda Charlu.**

That, Gentlemen, is a proposition that explains itself. It is a speech in itself; every word that has to be said in favour of that proposition has been said so often that it is needless to say it again. The only thing that remains to be done after having said every thing that one should say, and after having put before the authorities schemes worked out with great elaboration, is, to ask them to appoint a committee and try whether they cannot see their way to carry out by their own men what is admitted on all hands ought to be carried out. That is the proposition, and I recommend it to your consideration. *(Cheers)*

**Mr. S. B. Bhate.**

Mr. S. B. Bhate:—Mr. Chairman and Brother Delegates, the Resolution which has been placed before you by Rai Bahadur P. Ananda Charlu is, as he has stated to you, one which speaks for itself. The importance of the principles involved in it is so great that it can never be over-estimated. The two functions are so inconsistent with each other that it is impossible that one and the same individual should rise to the satisfactory discharge of both. *(Hear, hear)* The Executive Officer is an officer who is expected to have his eyes about him, whilst the judicial officer is one who is obliged, by the nature and reason of the functions which he has to perform, to shut his eyes to everything except that which is placed before him by those who are concerned in the cases which come up for solution before him. Now, then, in the one case the officer is required to maintain a system of *espionage* to collect each and every bit of information that he can have access to in or out of office, whilst a judicial officer is, by the necessity of his position as Judge or as Magistrate, required to go straight to the point and see that his ears are not poisoned by anything that might be whispered into them by parties or by advocates of parties interested in those cases. Now how on earth is one and the same man to educate himself up to the level of a satisfactory discharge of these two incompatible functions? It is in the nature and reason of things that such an officer must be a failure—an unmitigated failure. We know that in each and every man each and every organ is fitted to perform one particular function with characteristic efficiency, and although that organ may be turned to a purpose other than that for which it is fitted, such misuse involves a waste of energy which under the circumstances is to be deprecated. I may direct your attention to the organ of locomotion. You find that our legs which are given us to walk with, are the proper organs for locomotion. Cases have been known in which hands have been used for locomotion with some effect; but you find that the waste of energy involved in this application of the instruments of prehension to the purpose of locomotion is simply absurd. Here, then, is an illustration to which I ask your attention in order that you may see how very incompatible is the position which is thrust upon an officer when he is asked to be a Magistrate and a Judge and an Executive officer rolled up into one. Therefore, as Rai Bahadur Ananda Charlu has very ably said in putting this Resolution before you, it does not need anything more than the barest mention that it may commend itself to your universal acceptance. With these words I leave it to you to pass it. *(Cheers)*

The President:—This Resolution will be supported by Mr. K. Srinivasa Row, of Coimbatore.

Fourth Day.

Resolution XII. Separation of Judicial and Executive Functions.

Mr. K. Srinivasa Row.

Mr. K. Srinivasa Row:—Brother Delegates, the mover of this proposition has set an example of brevity, and I would follow him; but it seems to me that, strongly worded as the proposition is, the Government is still not convinced of the necessity for the separation of the executive and judicial functions. While we are saying year after year, that the separation of executive and judicial functions is necessary, Government turns a deaf ear to our cries, and we cannot go on year after year asking for the same thing when Government seems to have faith in combination. I will give you one example in which the combination of the executive and judicial functions has been a failure. In the Bellary district, (my own district) a confidential circular was sent round by the District Magistrate to the effect that the Magistrates who hear and decide cases should remember that they are responsible for the detection and suppression of crime. They were told that the duty which we thought was entirely the duty of the Police was to be undertaken by them. Now what follows from this, Gentlemen? It follows that the District Magistrate thinks not as we are thinking, that the separation of executive and judicial functions is necessary in the interests of justice, but that combination is necessary for the detection and suppression of crime. What is the effect of the circular, Gentlemen? It is this. The Magistrates are asked to support and assist the Police. And I will tell you why this was done. Government found that when the last Administration Report was published the number of convictions was not quite as large as they desired, and our Editors—whom we have either to thank or curse, I do not know which—sat upon the Administration Report and said that poor convictions showed poor detection. Government therefore wanted to show to the Editors a larger number of convictions, as being synonymous with greater efficiency in Criminal Administration. Accordingly this Circular was issued which means in effect that the District Magistrate should ask his subordinates to make friends with the Police, and that if fault is found with the Police, they should excuse them. (*Shame, Shame*) That is what it has come to really. We are advocating year after year the separation of executive and judicial functions, but the Government does not seem to have faith in separation. It wants to show a cleaner Administration Report. Now, a question was put in the Legislative Council asking why this confidential circular was issued, and the answer was given by the Honorable Mr. Bliss, who gives answers to these questions in the Council in the shape of riddles and conundrums. And what did he say? He took shelter, not under any principle of law or under any Act or any Section of the Procedure Code (which now rules, and which is a Code of every day reference in Court), but he went to an Act called the Police Act of 1869, and referred to the preamble of that Act, and said that the preamble of the Police Act justified the issue of the circular. The preamble says that Magistrates are responsible and must be helped by the Police in the detection and suppression of crime. Nothing more, Gentlemen. That preamble says nothing more than this; it refers to the Police as being subordinate to the Magistrate in the detection and suppression of crime. It does not say that the Magistrates should assist the police in the detection of crime. Now, I will tell you that in my own district the state of things has come to be this. I have heard from experienced men that twenty years ago our Magistrates were much more independent of the Police than they are now of the Station House officers. They are bound to work well with the Police, because they are very often under the influence of the Police Superintendent; the promotion of the Magistrates lies entirely in the hands of the District Magistrate, who is also an executive officer and the Collector of the District, who issues confidential circulars and demi-officials, who asks that people may be committed, and asks practically that people may be convicted because he wants them to be convicted. (*Shame*) That is really the state of things, Gentlemen. Now unless the Magistrates are removed from this executive influence, we cannot hope to better the state of things. Unless and until we remove these drawbacks from the Subordinate Magistrates and have it laid down that District Magistrates must not be Collectors, or that they ought not to be District Magistrates and Collectors together, we cannot better matters. (*Cheers*)

Fourth Day.

Resolution XII. Separation of Judicial and Executive Functions.

Mr. V. S. Sahasrabudhi.

Mr. V. S. Sahasrabudhi :—Mr. President, Brother Delegates and Gentlemen, am called upon to support this proposition which has been ably put by Rai Bahadur P. Ananda Charlu. Well, you know, Gentlemen, this is a propo ition the principle of which has already been accepted by the authorities and, as is set forth in the proposition, has been accepted as it were by Lord Kimberley and Lord Cross. You know, Gentlemen, the plea put forward is that there is want of funds. But, Gentlemen, you know the adage that "where there is a will there is a way ;" and if this maxim is borne in mind, and if the authorities take that view, and if they really and honestly attempt to find money for it we are sure they will be able to find it. They have been able to find money for Exchange Compensation, and yet they say they have no money to carry out this essential reform of the seperation of executive and judicial functions. This separation which is asked for by all people has not been granted to us. They say there is a want of money; but that plea cannot avail them. We have men in the position of Messrs. P. C. Dutt, M. M. Ghose and Pherozeshah Mehta, who have already put forward schemes which ought to commend themselves to Government and which will shew them that the cost will not be extra to a large amount; and even if it involves a cost of extra amount, I am sure the Government of India could find out means to have this essential reform established and carried out. I come from the Satara District, and I will give you one illustration where the combination of executive and judicial functions vested in one officer resulted in failure of justice. I refer to the well known "Wai case" against thirteen gentlemen in that District, which was really a police case. That case was tried by a Magistrate who is in executive charge of that Taluka. I say there was a failure of justice in it. Near the Magistrate's camp there was the camp of the Police Superintendent, and the latter used to come and sit occasionally in Court while the Police witnesses were being examined. (*Shame*) Thus, Gentlemen if there had been an independent authority not connected with the executive functions, the result would certainly have been that those thirteen innocent persons would never have been incarcerated and would never have suffered the agonies and miseries which they were put to, since they were sent from Wai to Satara; and the magistrate having given an unappealable sentence all attempts to get them free were of no effect. This was on account of the combination of the functions in the same executive officer. If this Magistrate had had nothing to do with executive functions certainly these men would never have been incarcerated, and if we find failure of justice in such cases it is necessary that Government should take in hand this reform and have a complete separation of executive and judicial functions. Then only shall we have those essential reforms for which for many years we have been crying out. I hope, Gentlemen, you will join with me in asking that this Resolution be passed with acclamation. (*Cheers*)

Mr. Mohini Mohan Chakravarti.

Mr. Mohini Mohan Chakravarti :—This resolution embodies a very simple demand on the part of the people of India. It wants a mixed commission to be appointed for framing the rules and for framing a scheme for the separation of executive and judicial functions which are now bound up in one and the same person, and as such, I say it is a very moderate demand. The desirability of this separation has already been considered not only in this country but also in England, and two ex-Secretaries of State for India have expressed their opinion that this separation should be carried out. (*Hear, hear*) But what their lordships say is tantamount simply to this: 'We know that this reform is needed for your country, but the difficulty is that we have no funds in hand, and therefore, notwithstanding that this scheme is necessary for the welfare of England and India, still, not having sufficient funds in our hands, we cannot carry out this scheme at present.' We think the plea on the part of the Government is—I will not say unjust, but an unrighteous one. You know, Gentlemen, that crores of Rupees have been spent on what is called the scientific frontier. In the face of all this squandering of public money I do not know how it can lie with the Government to say that this reform which is needed for us cannot be granted because

**Fourth Day.**

**Resolution XII. Separation of Judicial and Executive Functions.**

MR. MOHINI MOHAN CHAKRAVARTI.

there are not sufficient funds in their hands. Well, Gentlemen, I say that this plea on the part of the Government is quite unjust; for what justification have the Government to turn insolvent at the moment when a much needed reform is to be carried out. That insolvency if any, is entirely due to their squandering propensity in other directions which are not at all necessary, is due to their indulging in luxury at the cost of our poor mother land. Well Gentlemen, this being the state of things you can take this matter into consideration Schemes have been propounded from time to time, of which mention has been made in this resolution, as for instance the scheme by my countrymen, Mr. R. C. Dutt, Mr. Ghose and that well-known citizen of Bombay Mr. Mehta. All these schemes say that these reforms can be carried out by Government with the least possible cost to the State. Even if the matter is costly, and if the Government is not in a position to find funds for carrying it out an attempt should be made in order to meet this desire on our part for reforming this particular state of things which casts a slur as it were on the civilised Government under whose surveillance we live. (*Hear, hear*)

Gentlemen, I do not quote to you other examples of the oppression wrought by the system which is at present in vogue, because instances are rife on all hands, and every one of you I think is acquainted with one or two. The thing is this, there is no question that the present system is calculated to do mischief. But there is one necessary preliminary for carrying out this reform, and that necessity is to collect instances in which the present state of things is calculated to work mischief. Well, so far as the collection of statistics, is concerned, I should say that the work is already over. What is now wanting, is the inauguration of the reform, and for the purpose of the inauguration, our demand is very moderate—the appointment of a commission to enquire into the possibility of introducing this reform with the least possible cost to the State, because the Government say they have no funds, and because it is absolutely necessary for the good of the country. With these remarks, Gentlemen, I would commend this resolution to your acceptance. (*Cheers*)

The Resolution was then put to the vote and carried.

THE PRESIDENT:—We now go back to resolution XI. I now call upon Mr. Mozumdar, of Faridpur, to support that resolution.

**Resolution XI. Trial by Jury.**

MR. AMBICA C. MOZUMDAR.

MR. AMBICA C. MOZUMDAR:—Sir, the almost proverbial immobility of Indian reform is probably nowhere so conspicuous as in the slow and imperceptible development of the system of trial by Jury. Here it seems to have moved in cycles even larger than those of the great orb which is the centre of the mighty planetary system under which we live. Decades passed away after the British conquest before the system of trial by jury was properly secured to Her Majesty's Indian subjects living within the Presidency towns. It then took three decades more to reach a few favoured spots in the regions of the Western and the Eastern Ghats and the Assam Valleys; and then another cycle of full thirty years rolled away before seven districts in the Gangetic Provinces came to receive its blessings. There it has ever since stood as if fossilized beyond all possibility of further growth. But now that the country has completed another revolution of thirty years more, has not the usual period of probation passed and the time fully arrived for doling out another measure of this reform to the suffering millions of this vast empire? If the privilege is still to be withheld Anglo-Indian bureaucracy must be false to its own established tradition. (*Cheers*)

Gentlemen, you may remember, that in 1867, Sir Cecil Beadon, as Lieutenant-Governor of Bengal, was for extending the system to other districts of the Lower Provinces, and you must be aware how a chorus of opposition from the district officers thwarted his noble purpose. Again, in 1884, the Government of Lord Ripon launched the question, and again the tide of opposition flowed from the lower depths of the service, and the question was thrown back. It is a strange arrangement peculiar to Anglo-Indian administration, that no reform can be effected without the consent and concurrence of those whose colliding interest it always is to oppose such improvements. Gentlemen, it is the Services, and not the Government, that have throughout mainly blocked our way. (*Cheers*) And what, after all, is the justification for this stolid immobility of the Government? The plea of impecuniosity does not arise here, as it does in the case of the separation of judicial from executive functions; nor is there here the shadow of any political bugbear such as is said to haunt the question of Simultaneous Examinations. This is not one of those problems upen which India can be either lost or ruined. This is a question of pure administrative justice between India and Indians. Justice in this country is sold and not administered, and should not the purchaser, even when he pays a fancy price for it, have some choice in the selection of his article of purchase? (*Cheers*) Then where is the difficulty? It is generally urged that the difficulty lies in the ingrained perversity of Indian jurors in returning wrong verdicts, or, in other words, verdicts which fail to commend themselves to the infallible opinions of English Judges. Instead of indulging in dogmatism let us tread upon solid ground of facts and figures. Thanks to Sir Charles Elliot and his hobby, the Jury Notification has opened men's eyes to the insecurity in which they live, and has also unearthed a mass of valuable information which reveals the true state of things. (*Cheers*)

I shall begin with a statement of figures supplied by the Bengal Administration Reports showing how the matter stands. I shall begin with the Magistrates.

| Year. | Number of Convictions appealed against. | Number set aside by Sessions Court. | Percentage of Reversals. |
|---|---|---|---|
| 1884-85 ... ... ... | 8,296 | 2,416 | 29·25 |
| 1885-86 ... ... ... | 9,067 | 2,556 | 28·35 |
| 1886-87 ... ... ... | 9,279 | 2,680 | 29·35 |
| 1887-88 ... ... ... | 9,459 | 2,972 | 31·41 |
| 1888-89 ... ... ... | 10,415 | 3,137 | 30·15 |

Now Sessions Judges are not Indian jurors, and yet whence arose this perversity in them to set aside such a large percentage of convictions? Were the Magistrates wrong or the Judges in error? We, the people, should be perfectly willing to accept either of the alternatives. Let us then ascend a step higher, and consider the state of things in the Courts of those Sessions Judges whose work is not hampered by irresponsible jury men.

| Year. | Number of Convictions appealed against. | Number set aside by High Court. | Percentage of Reversals. |
|---|---|---|---|
| 1884-85 ... ... ... | — | — | 29 |
| 1885-86 ... ... ... | — | — | 28 |
| 1886-87 ... ... ... | 2,879 | 842 | 28 |
| 1887-88 ... ... ... | 3,246 | 975 | 30 |
| 1888-89 ... ... ... | 3,322 | 887 | 27 |

If the sentences of death passed by these Judges were alone taken into account it would appear that on an average fully 38 per cent. of the sentences appealed against were reversed by the High Court. So much for the infallibility of Judges trying cases with the aid of assessors! So much for the infallibility of a system which prevails in $\frac{5}{6}$ths of the largest province of the Empire! (*Cheers*)

Against this, compare the following statement showing the results of trial by jury. I take the figures from Babu Guru Pershad Sen's valuable statement to be found at page 26 of the Appendix to the Congress Report for 1892.

| Year. | Percentage of Verdicts not agreed to by Sessions Judges. | Percentage of Verdicts set aside by High Court. | Percentage of Verdicts which would have been set aside if all the verdicts dissented from had been referred to High Court. |
|---|---|---|---|
| 1884-85 ... ... ... | 19·9 | 4·3 | 11 |
| 1885-86 ... ... ... | 18·9 | 6 | 15·9 |
| 1886-87 ... ... ... | 15·8 | 5·2 | 9·9 |
| 1887-88 ... ... ... | 22·4 | 2·6 | 10·6 |
| 1888-89 ... ... ... | 21·3 | 4·7 | 11·9 |

**Fourth Day.**

**Resolution XI.**
**Trial by Jury.**

MR. AMBICA C. MOZUMDAR.

From these it would appear that while the Magistrates were found wrong in 30 per cent. of cases in which there was an appeal from their decisions, Sessions Judges sitting with assessors were found wrong in about 28 per cent., while juries were found wrong only in 4½ per cent. with the barest possibility of 11 per cent. (*Cheers*) It follows, therefore, that as regards perversity of judgment, Judges left to themselves are at least 2½ times as perveres as Judges kept straight by jurors, while the Magistrate's perversity is 2 degrees in excess of that of the Sessions Judges. (*Loud Cheers*)

The other objection specially urged against the proposed extension is the alleged incompetency of the present non-jury districts to meet the requirements of the privilege Gentlemen, I should have attached some importarce to the converse proposition that there are not many competent and trained Judges in the service fit to deal with jurors in this country (*Laughter*) To begin with, I should like to know if all the shires and counties in England and Scotland were equally advanced at any time, and if the difference in their qualifications was ever made the ground for a difference of administrative rights and privileges among them Then, are we to understand that ever since 1861 the people have made no progress in education, in independence of judgment and decision of character ? And will any one affirm that there are not now some at least among the non-jury districts whose position at the present day might compare favourably with those of the few favoured districts thirty to sixty years back It cannot be ; it is impossible. (*Hear, hear*) To assert the contrary would be a gross libel on British rule in India. There have sprung up in most of these districts Colleges and High Schools, self-governing Municipal and Local Boards, which the people are managing with commendable success. There are independent Benches of Honorary Magistrates in almost every thannah and, above all, there is established in all these places a strong public opinion the force of which is not infrequently felt even by Government. And if further evidence is needed I would refer to the admissions of the oppcsite side. (*Hear, hear*)

In the abortive discussion of 1884 to which I have already referred, we find that the unbiassed opinion of no less than seven of the veteran officers of Government who were consulted on the subject, namely, Mr. Campbell of Rajshahye, Judge Worgan of Cuttack Mr. Cornish of Midnapore, Mr. Bignold of Chittagong, Commissioners Wilson of Burdwan and Lowis of Chittagong, were all in favour of the proposed extension. Mr. Campbell remarked—"The limited experience which I have had of the jury system in the 24 Pergunnahs and "Nuddeah has strongly impressed me in favour of its extension throughout the Regulation "Districts. I cannot say that I attach much importance to the argument from prejudice and "class feeling in exceptional cases." Judge Worgan said—"If men can be found to this "number (*i.e.*, 225) of the same amount of fitness that is possessed by the present assessors, I "think that satisfactory juries could always be formed. I have found the assessors as a rule "take an intelligent interest in the proceedings, in which I have always endeavoured to "make them feel that they occupy an important and practical position ; and though I think "them in some cases prone to acquit, I have frequently found where I have over-ruled that "their doubts were endorsed by the High Court on Appeal." Gentlemen, the Census Report for Bengal in 1891 shews there is hardly a district in Bengal where two to three thousand educated men could not be found to form a jury list. (*Hear, hear*) Then Mr. Cornish of Midnapore frankly observed—"I am quite convinced that the decisions of our criminal Courts "will never command the confidence of the people till some system of trial by jury is estab "lished. As a Magistrate, either trying a case, or committing it for trial, I have often felt "that no judgment that I could give would satisfy myself. How then could I expect it to "satisfy others ?" (*Hear, hear*)

Commissioner Larminie, though opposing the introduction on principle, yet candidly observed—"As far as my experience goes—and I have had a good many opportunities of "judging of the character of the men who would probably have to serve on a jury—it would be

"nearly as easy to obtain an intelligent jury here (i.e., the backward district of Cuttack) as in "Burdwan, and I am not at all sure that the Cuttack verdict would not generally be a more "honest one." If, as was actually contended by Commissioner Larminie, "the existence of the "institution is due more to political reasons than to its intrinsic merits from a judicial point "of view," and if its object be "to secure the liberty of the subject from the risk of being "unjustly interfered with by Judges who are removable at the pleasure of the paramount power," Gentlemen, all I can say is, that, having regard to foreign domination, to diversities of race, and to the diversities of customs, manners, and feelings, under which the people live and die, and, above all, to the difficulties that exist in estimating Indian evidence, the universal adoption of trial by jury is nowhere so urgently needed as in India. (*Loud Cheers*)

Gentlemen, if I should ever be asked to point out the chief defect of British rule in India, I would thrice repeat—it is its administrative anomalies, and then unhesitatingly add that of all such anomalies there are none so anomalous as the anomalies of its administration of criminal justice. Apart from the irrational union of the judicial and the executive functions, it has to be observed that though all the people are living in the same country and under the same sovereign, and are apparently protected by the same punitive laws, the criminal procedure of the country is one huge, cumbrous and complex machine comprising about half-a-dozen different modes of trial, varying from the most primitive to the most highly civilized method of administration. By a strange fatality it has broken up the entire population into divisions of political castes at the head of which the European Brahmins have one kind of criminal Shastras, while the Indian Sudras have quite another. (*Hear, hear*) Then among these latter there are, like oases in a desert, a patch here and a patch there where the people enjoy greater security of life, liberty, and property than the multitudinous population who inhabit the vast arid expanse all round. Gentlemen, a murder is a murder, with the gallows for its destined goal, whether it is committed in Dacca or in Faridpur, and yet the merest accident of its being committed on this or that side of an almost imaginary line, sometimes drawn through restless waters, may determine whether the same man shall be dealt with as a true citizen or as a bondsman. Sir, where is the clause in the great testament of the Queen-Mother that, while imposing upon my head the liabilities of her Government deprives me of an equal share in the privileges of her rule? (*Cheers*) Why should I day by day and year after year, standing on one bank of a river, gaze mournfully on the other bank, and have to say to myself that it is over there that the shackles fall off and true citizenship begins? (*Loud Cheers*

Sir, we are judged without evidence, and condemned without trial! Alas, we seem to be nobody's care. Even the Viceroy, whom we loyally welcome as an hereditary ruler, in his anxiety to accentuate the invidious distinction of colour, has lost no time in issuing on his own motion confidential circulars to protect the rights of those who virtually need no protection. But though the people have been long crying for help in this and other connections, the gods are asleep, and there is no response to their call Is the race of British philanthropists extinct? And have the mighty builders of this vast empire left no heritage of broad and noble ideals of justice for their successors? We are not appealing to Jews or Cossacks; but to those for whom they proudly say Milton wrote and Sydney died and for whom the Magna Charta was obtained; and, in making our present appeal, we are asking not only for the protection of our life, liberty, and property, but also for the vindication of the honour and dignity of the great British Constitution. (*Loud and long continued Cheers*)

Mr. K. Srinivasa Row

Mr. K. Srinivasa Row:—I would ask your attention to clauses B and C of the Resolution. I am not in favour of clauses B and C. Now as regards clause B, it seems to me that the present state of the law in respect of B and C, at least in the district from which I come, is satisfactory. I do not see my way therefore to accepting B and C; because at present the verdict of a jury is held to be sufficiently reasonable, and, if it is sufficiently reasonable

Fourth Day.

Resolution XI
Trial by Jury.

to secure justice to the people, it is accepted by the Judge. If it is not, what does the Judge do after the verdict is given? It is only in exceptional cases that he takes care to differ from them. The law lays down that he has simply to report his views to the High Court. Thus, the cases in which he differs are few, and he takes good care to show good grounds when he differs. Then the case is referred to the High Court, and if the High Court do not agree with the Judge's views they call for the records and go into the case. I do not think there is anything unjust in it. Then I come to clause ... anything unjust in that either, because a reference is made by the District Magistrate and the Government ... The District Magistrate does not make a reference in each and every case, he does so only in exceptional cases. I do not of course wish you, Gentlemen, to think I am supporting the officials; and, if my views do not meet with your approval, do not support them. Well then, the reference is made by the District Magistrate to Government, Government refers it to the High Court, and the High Court has got the final decision in its hands. This is in a case in which a man has been unjustly acquitted. Unless the High Court says there is reason to interfere with the verdict, the verdict is final. It seems to me, therefore, that in the working of the clause, there is no difficulty, and there is nothing unreasonable about it. We have always got the High Court, the highest authority and the palladium of our rights and liberties, to see that justice is done and to decide matters as the final authority.

The Resolution was then put to the vote and carried.

THE PRESIDENT:—The thirteenth Resolution will be moved by Lala Murlidhar, of Umballa.

Resolution XIII.
The Punjab Chief Court.

LALA MURLIDHAR.

LALA MURLIDHAR:—Mr. President and Brother Delegates, this is neither the time nor the occasion for exchanging mutual greetings. This is a day not of rejoicing, but of national mourning. I am grieved to hear of the death of the Maharajah of Mysore, and so every Indian feels the shaft in his heart, every eye is moistened and the loss will be felt greater by Mother India, who has become old in her old age, because she is not likely to get her son again. But I tell you that the thing is not true, it is false, because a righteous and great prince never dies but always lives in the memory of a grateful nation. (*Cheers*) I tell you he is happy in his eternal home, from which there is no return to the terrestrial globe.

Now, Gentlemen, I come to the resolution. It is as follows:—

That this Congress re-affirms the opinion of the preceding Congress that the time has now come to raise the status of the Chief Court of the Punjab to that of Chartered High Court in the interests of the administration of justice in this Province.

We want a High Court in the Punjab. We want a High Court not so high as the tower of Babel. (*Laughter*) so as to be beyond the reach of ordinary suitors, nor so low as to be within the reach of the impious hands of calumny We want a High Court just as high as this lighthouse of yours, to be a torchlight to the erring officials, and a beacon of light to suffering humanity. Gentlemen, we have got a Chief Court in the Punjab, but as we have not got a sea-shore there, we are without a light-house and, therefore, we want our Chief Court to be converted into a real light-house to shed light and lustre over the Province and to soothe sorrowing hearts. We want Judges to be impartial, just and honest. We, Gentlemen, do not want unadulterated justice; we want justice tempered with mercy, we do not want justice alone to be administered to Indians and all the mercy to Anglo-Indians. (*Laughter*) You know, perhaps the case of Pandit Gopinath. I will give only one instance. He filed an action for defamation in the Court of the Magistrate of Lahore against a very influential member of the Supreme Council. What was the fate of this case? As soon as he filed the action, he was examined on oath, but was not believed and he was required to produce evidence of good behaviour before issuing process on the defendant, and at last he was compelled to seek for justice in the High Court of Calcutta, where the case was compromised, and judgment given for the plaintiff, on the

Fourth Day.

Resolution XIII. The Punjab Chief Court.

Lala Morlidhar.

confession of the defendant. Who but the High Court of Madras could have passed a decree for damages of Rs. 100 against its own Governor Sir M. Grant Duff? It was only the High Court that could do it—the bulwark of the liberty of the people. This palladium of justice we want; we want men of the calibre of Sir Barnes Peacock Mr. Justice Ranade, Pandit Shumbhu Nath, Babu Dwarkanath Mitter, Sir Richard Garth; we want men like Mr. Justice Straight, to be "straight" and honest, and to be independent of the opinion of friends or foes, we want them to be appointed directly by the Crown, and not to be subordinate to Indian authority, so as to be free from any chance of bias or prejudice. With these few words I beg leave to move the resolution. (*Cheers*)

Bakshi Jaishi Ram.

Bakshi Jaishi Ram:—Mr. President, Brother Delegates and Gentlemen, we Punjabis are expected to live on air. When the Government has to hold a Durbar or any other big state function, the choice falls on the Punjab, but when a demand is made on behalf of the people, which tends to result in material good for the people, deaf ears are turned by Government towards the people of the Punjab. It is not necessary for me to say anything of the Resolution regarding the establishment of the High Court in the Punjab which is passed in the Congress year after year, but suffice it to point out that last year, on behalf of an Association in the Punjab, a representation was sent to Government. You will be surprised to learn that up to the present time no answer has been received. Though it is more than one year that the Memorial has been sent to Government, yet that Memorial remains quite unanswered. Gentlemen, I will place certain statistics before you to show that we are not in any way behind the people of the North-West Provinces, and as the North-West Provinces have a High Court there is no reason why we should not have one. If the question is to be determined on the area of the Provinces, the area of the North-West Provinces is 107,503 square miles while the area of the Punjab is 110,660 square miles. The area under cultivation in the North-West Provinces is 57,026,042 acres, while in the Punjab the area is 96,103,936 acres. The area assessed and surveyed in the North-West Provinces amounts to 12,856,608 acres while, in the Punjab it is 17,168,021 acres. In order to determine whether there is a necessity for this demand, we may take the number of suits instituted In the year 1891 the number of suits instituted in the North-West Provinces and Oudh including the three taluqs, was 307,282, while in the Punjab alone it was 301,662. The value of the Civil Suits that were instituted in the North-West Provinces and Oudh was Rs 2,44,08,016, while in the Punjab it was Rs. 2,32,24,141. The number of Criminal Appeals and Revisions in 1892 in the North-West Provinces and Oudh was 28,339, while in the Punjab it was 27,472. If, Gentlemen, the spread of education is to be considered with a view to the establishment of a High Court, even then I tell you we are not inferior to the people of the North-West Provinces. The number of candidates who passed the entrance examination in 1892 and 1893 in the Allahabad University was 749, and in the Punjab 789 The expenditure which is incurred by the Government on education in the North-West Provinces amounts to Rs. 5,58,802, while in the Punjab it amounts to Rs. 9,39,256. Then, Gentlemen, the income which the Government make under the head of Law and Justice in this Province leaves a great surplus after defraying all expenses under the same head. In the year 1891-92 the income to Government by the sale of Court-fee and other stamps was Rs, 40,69,000, while the expenditure under the head of Law and Justice in the same year was Rs. 29,66,000. Gentlemen, after deducting the sale of stamps, &c., there is a surplus of ten lakhs every year. So, Gentlemen, with the figures which are laid before you, I submit I have made a sufficiently strong case for the establishment of a High Court in the Province of the Punjab. (*Cheers*)

We want equal treatment with other subjects of Her Majesty the Queen. As there is such a large surplus under the head of Law and Justice, I do not see why the people of the Punjab should not have a High Court when the people of the North-West Provinces and Oudh have one. The law which is in force in the Punjab is the same as that which is in force in Bengal, Madras, Bombay and the North-West Provinces. The highest tribunal is the High

Fourth Day.

Resolution XIII. The Punjab Chief Court.

Bakshi Jaishi Ram.

Court, and it is only that Court that can give final decisions in important matters connected with the welfare of the people. Another ground for the establishment of a High Court is the there is an anomaly in reference to Appeal cases in our Province. There is no right of Appeal in the case of suits the value of which is within Rs. 1,000, when the judgment of the Appellate Court agrees with the judgment of the Original Court. The establishment of High Court will result in the removal of this anomaly. Then, Gentlemen, the Chief Court has also to exercise certain *quasi* legislative powers in regard to a good many questions relating to alienation and inheritance, and many othen points that ought all to be determined by custom But these things, as well as custom, can only properly be decided by a High Court; and I would therefore ask you to consider, Gentlemen, would it not be better for us to have a High Court for the purpose of expounding Custom and dociding intricate questions of Law. With these remarks I second the Resolution which has been proposed by my friend, Mr. Murlidhar. (*Cheers*)

The Resolution was put to the vote and carriod.

Resolution XIV. Military and Civil Expenditure.

Hon. Mr. C. Sankaran Nair.

The President :—The fourteenth Resolution will be moved by the Hon'ble Mr. C Sankaran Nair

The Hon. Mr. C. Sankaran Nair :—Mr. President, Delegates, Ladies and Gentlemen, the proposition that I have to move is this :—

That having regard to the fact that the embarrassed condition of the finances of the country has been giving cause for grave anxiety for some years past, this Congress records its firm conviction that the only remedy for the present state of things is a material curtailment in the expenditure on the Army Services and other Military Expenditure, Home Gharges, and the cost of Civil Administration, and in view of the proposed appointment of a Pacliamentary Committee to investigate the subject, this Congress strongly recommends that the Standing Congress Committees of the several Presidencies and Provirces should, so far as practicable, make arrangements to send to England at least one well qualified delegate from each Presidency or Province to urge such reduction before the Committee.

Gentlemen, the first part of this proposition is really the same as Pesolution V which we passed yesterday. That resolution demands a full enquiry by the Parliamentary Committee which has been promised to us. Now, I would ask you for a moment to consider the gravity of the situation. We have brought forward charges, heavy charges, against the Government of India; we have complained, that the Civil Service of India refuses to remedy our grievances on account of selfish motives. We have complained also that the military expenditure has become so heavy that we would rather live comfortably now and suffer in a remote future all the horrors of a Russian invasion, than be slowly starved to death before that time comes, if it ever does. (*Laughter*) These are heavy charges, and there is not the slightest doubt that the Government of India will bring forward skilled witnesses and experts before the Parliamentary Committee to show that no reduction of expenditure is possible, to show that we are a set of discontented men, and to show that the reforms for which we pray are impracticable. Now, in order to meet that body of evidence, any written statement is useless. It is impossible to anticipate all the doubts and difficulties which may arise, and which will arise in the minds of the members of the Parliamentary Committee when they hear the statements that will be made before them by skilled witnesses sent up for examination by the Government of India. Now, the only way of meeting that evidence is by sending our own delegates, men who will represent our views, men who will explain the facts apparently adverse to us which may be placed before the Committee by the Government of India, men who will carry conviction into the minds of the members of the Parliamentary Committee by the information which they will be able to place before them. Unless we do that, it is suicidal to ask for a Parliamentary Committee The same feelings of justice and fair-play to which we all appeal, will be invoked by the Government of India in their favour, and if we do not place the Parliamentary Committee in a favourable situation to pronounce a decision on all the questions that will be presented to them for solution, the result will be that that Parliamentary Committee will have to hold, and the British House of Commons and the British public will have to accept, that our allegations are unfounded, and that the serious charges which we bring against the Government of India are not worth any attention. That will be the result. In order to avoid that, as I stated, the only course that we can adopt is to send our own delegates who will be able to convince them. If we succeed in satisfying the Parliamentary Committee of the justice of our claims, then you may depend upon it that British justice will not be appealed to in vain. (*Loud and continued Applause*) It has not been appealed to in vain in the past, (*Applause*) and history shows, in India, in England, and in the Colonies, that the sense of British justice will not be appealed to in vain if we urge our demands properly and persistently. Therefore I would say that we are bound to strain every nerve, to spare no pains, to make every effort to supply this condition of success—that is, to depute a competent body of repeesentative Indians to place before the Committee such information as will persuade them to grant us those rights and privileges for the attainment of which we must be prepared to sacrifice our time, our money and our unremitting labour. With these remarks I place the proposition before you. (*Cheers*)



Mr. D. E. Wacha :—The Honorable Mr. Sankaran Nair, the mover of the Resolution, has stated the reason why it is incumbent on us to submit evidence before the Parliamentary Committee of Enquiry which is about to be granted to us next session. No doubt it is necessary for us to verify the allegations we have been bringing against Government for some years past, and I have no hesitation in saying that if half-a-dozen Indians of knowledge and experience could be found to proceed to England and give evidence in support of those allegations before the Committee, we should be fully able to establish our case. For the facts to which we endeavour to draw the attention of the authorities from time to time are there. They cannot be gain-said. They are on record in the many official publications of the various provincial administrations and of the Government of India. What those facts are I will endeavour to bring before you as briefly as possible within the extremely limited time at my command. They all have reference to finance. Now, Gentlemen, you know the well-known saying that a good Government cannot exist with bad finances and that a bad Government can exist with good finances. (*Hear, hear*) It is bad finance, then, which is at the root of our complaint. You have often heard it said that if India is ever lost, it will be lost on the floor of the House of Commons. Gentlemen, for my part, I say I do not believe it. (*Hear, hear*) It is simply cant to say so. It is the cant of the official classes, and the cry is taken up parrot-like. No, I am firmly of belief that so long as the House of Commons is alive to its serious responsibilities India can never be lost. On the contrary, India will gain by the interference of the Houes of Commons in Indian matters. (*Cheers*) But I have great fears that if India is lost to the British, it will be on account of its miserable finances. (*Hear, hear*) It is the mismanagement of our finances which is at the root of the chronic embarrassment of the Indian Treasury. Now, Gentlemen, let me tell you that it is a maxim of state-craft that expenditure is regulated by policy. It is the policy of the Government of India which is the greatest disturbing element of its finances. For the last ten years it is the military policy of the empire which has dominated the whole domain of Indian finance. It is that hollow plea of "preparedness," preparedness to meet England's enemies on the frontiers east and west of India, which has entailed enormous expenditure on the army services in all its branches. Its oppressive effects have been evident in the difficulty which the Government has found during the last few years in balancing the annual income and expenditure. This transcends all other causes put together But for this fatal policy, which has such powerful advocates in the Viceregal Council, India would not be to-day in the financial strait it is—a strait which finds Government at its wits' ends to meet the many deficits. For the permanent interests of India it is imperative that we should demand a material departure from, if not a complete reversal of, that mischievous policy. The Secretary of State is in the first instance the responsible authority who should be appealed

**Fourth Day**

**Resolution XIV Military and Civil Expenditure.**

**Mr. D. E. Wacha.**

to; but in the second instance the High Court of Parliament. (*Cheers*) I assert, Gentlemen that in order to produce a healthy condition in our finances, so essential for the cause of good Government, the Military policy of the Government must be vigorously attacked. (*Hear, hear*)

As to the facts in reference to the military expenditure, it would be superfluous for us to refer to them here at any length. I may say, speaking for myself, that I have been a sort of wandering minstrel on more than one platform. (*Laughter*) On this subject I have raised a wail, and a "prolonged wail" chanting to one tune in divers tones. (*More Laughter*) From the day of the very first Congress, held at Bombay, I have descanted on the many facts and figures in connection with the ever growing military expenditure—facts and figures which are now acknowledged to be correct. (*Cheers*) In March last, in my capacity of Honorary Secretary of the Bombay-Presidency Association, I prepared a memorial embodying facts and figures which our Association submitted to the Viceroy in Council. The Hon'ble Mr. Westland steered clear of them, but took the opportunity to fling gibes and jeers at the Congress. On the lines chalked out in that memorial, the British Committee of the Congress launched a Memorandum, which was circulated among Members of Parliament at or about the time of the debate on the Indian budget. Mr. Fowler had absolutely nothing to say to the figures embodied there. He took shelter for his failure to challenge them under the plea that he had no time to go into them. Gentlemen, do you believe thet had those figures been inaccurate, Mr. Fowler, well-coached by the permanent officials of the India Office, would have been slow to prove their fallacy? (*Hear, hear*) Well, then, I say that I have no inclination to go into all the details of military expenditure which since 1885 has mounted up from 16 to 23 crores. I shall only submit to you the broad features of that growth, dealing also with civil expenditure; in addition I will put before you a table of the growth of revenue during the same period, and ask you to judge for yourselves. For further enlightenment, I can only refer you to the more elaborate and comprehensive Memorandum of Sir William Wedderburn's Committee to which I have just referred—a Memorandum, which as you know, even an ex-Finance Minister, no other than the redoubtable Sir Auckland Colvin—is constrained to confess is quite conclusive. (*Hear, hear*) Here then, Gentlemen, I submit to you the following three tables: first, **A**, which shows the total growth of net military expenditure, civil salaries and establishments, and miscellaneous charges during the decade, secondly **B**, which shows the total increase during the same period of the Home Charges, as discharged by what are called "sterling remittances," and, lastly, **C**, which exhibits the growth of the principal heads of revenue.

## A

***Statement showing Total Growth of net Military Expenditure, Civil Salaries and Establishments and Miscellaneous Charges from 1884-85 to 1892-93.****

| Particulars. | In Crores of Rupees. | | |
|---|---|---|---|
| | 1884-85. | Annual Average, 1885-86 to 1892-93. | Total growth in 8 years. |
| Net Army Services (exclusive of Exchange) ... ... ... ... | 15·20 | 18·28 | 3·08 |
| „ Military Roads ... ... ... ... ... ... | 0·95 | 1·14 | 0·19 |
| „ Special Defences ... ... ... ... ... | ... | 0·51 | 0·51 |
| Total Military Expenditure ... | 16·15 | 19·89 | 3·78 |
| Civil Salaries and Establishment ... ... ... ... ... | 10·37 | 11·65 | 1·28 |
| Miscellaneous Civil charges ... ... ... ... ... | 3·59 | 3·73 | 0·14 |
| Total Civil Expenditure ... | 13·96 | 15·38 | 1·42 |
| Total Military and Civil ... | 30·11 | 35·27 | 5·20 |

*Revised Estimates.

## B

*Statement showing the Total Growth of Sterling Remittances and Loss by Exchange from 1884-85 to 1892-93.**

| Particulars. | | In Millions. | | |
|---|---|---|---|---|
| | | 1884-85. | Average Annual growth, 1885-86 to 1892-93. | Total growth in 8 years. |
| Sterling Remittances ... ... ... ... ... ... | £ | 13·75 | 14·59 | 0·84 |
| Total Loss, by Exchange ... ... ... ... ... | Rx | 3·35 | 6·30 | 2·95 |
| Loss by Exchange on Army Services only ... ... ... | Rx | 0·94 | 1·74 | 0·80 |

## C.

*Statement showing Total Growth of net Revenue from 1884-85 to 1892-93.**

| Heads of Revenue. | In Crores of Rupees. | | |
|---|---|---|---|
| | 1884-85. | Average annual growth, 1885-86 to 1892-93. | Total growth in 8 years. |
| Land ... ... ... ... ... ... | 18·42 | 19·90 | 1·48 |
| Opium ... ... ... ... ... .. | 5·84 | 6·16 | 0·32 |
| Salt ... ... ... ... ... .. | 6·02 | 7·19 | 1·17 |
| Stamps ... ... ... ... ... .. | 3·42 | 3·82 | 0·40 |
| Excise ... ... ... ... ... ... | 3·88 | 4·55 | 0·67 |
| Provincial Rates ... ... ... ... ... ... | 2·73 | 3·19 | 0·46 |
| Customs ... ... ... ... ... ... | 0·86 | 1·28 | 0·42 |
| Assessed Taxes ... ... ... ... ... ... | 0·48 | 1·36 | 0·89 |
| Forests ... ... ... ... ... ... | 0·30 | 0·55 | 0·25 |
| Registration ... ... ... ... ... ... | 0·10 | 0·15 | 0·25 |
| Tributes ... ... ... ... ... ... | 0·70 | 0·74 | 0·04 |
| Total... | 42·75 | 48·89 | 6·14 |
| Net Total, less Assignments, &c. ... | 41·52 | 47·49 | 5·97 |

Now, Gentlemen, you will have noticed from the figures just read out to you, how much more oppressive is the burden of Military and Civil expenditure than the whole burden of Exchange, which was hitherto fallaciously considered to be the sole factor of the embarassment of our finances. (*Cheers*) The fallacy has been exploded, and it is to be hoped that the Finance Department will not again use it to throw dust in the public eye. (*Cheers*) I repeat, then, that as far as this expenditure and the expenditure in connection with a part of what are called Home Charges, is concerned, our representatives, if they only go about it in the right way, will be able to make out an extremely good case, not from their own facts and figures, but from facts and figures contained in numberless official publications, especially those ponderous blue and yellow books called the "Finance and Revenue Accounts of the Government of India." Similarly, other subjects, such as those of land revenue enhancements, could be properly represented to the Parliamentary Committee to prove the correctness of our grievance in that matter. But I will not detain you further. Before, however, I resumo my seat, I beg to refer to three important recommendations which we should bring to the notice of the Committee. Firstly, revision of the unequal and one-sided apportionment of the charges in connection

*Revised Estimates.

Fourth Day.

Resolution XIV Military and Civil Expenditure.

MR. D. E. WACHA.

with the army services which is insisted upon by the British Treasury. As you are aware, India is a joint sharer in the cost of all changes which from time to time are made in the British army under that fatal scheme known as the Army Amalgamation Scheme of 1859, on which I descanted sufficiently at the first Congress. Professor Fawcett called it a joint partnership in which the wealthy and strong partner (England) unjustly demanded more than her fair share from the weaker, and the poorer one (India). As usual the weaker vessel has gone to the wall. (*Shame*) This unequal and one-sided way of sharing the cost requires to be modified. There is ample evidence to prove our case and enforce the suggestion I have just referred to. Secondly, there should be some statutory declaration for a fixed contribution by England to India towards the increased military expenditure, which is solely brought about by England's continental policy, of checkmating Russia on the Bosphoros. I said enough on this subject at the Congress at Nagpore and must desist from reiterating my views here. Thirdly, it is time that we agitated for the guarantee of India's debt by the Imperial Government. The first Congress at Bombay laid great stress on this, but since then the subject has been put aside. For, Gentlemen, remember, John Bull is thoroughly alive when he feels that he is being mulcted in his pocket. (*Laughter*) It is only when the shoe pinches him that he is awake, and endeavours to find out in what part of the shoe it is that he feels the pinch. When he finds that in his own budget he has to pay annually to India a certain sum as his imperial contribution, he would soon begin to take a keen interest in the budget. Our Indian budget, in that contingency you may rely upon it, would be well attended and well debated. (*Hear, hear*) It will not be such a solemn mockery, snare, and delusion, as it is now. (*Hear, hear*) This is a consummation devoutly to be wished in our own permanent interest. Political justice demands it, and I need not dwell upon the many political advantages attending on such a condition of our financial affairs. In short, India's interests, instead of being neglected as they are now, would be most watchfully and carefully attended to. Let us therefore all work together and make one united effort to achieve that result. And one way of achieving it is to put it before the proposed Parliamentary Committee. Our case, I repeat, is an unimpeachable case, and we are bound to succeed in the end if it is properly represented by those whom we may depute to represent it. (*Loud and long continued Cheers*)

MR. A. B. NAKHRE.

MR. A. B. NAKHRE :—Mr. Chairman, Ladies and Gentlemen, and Fellow Delegates; I have great pleasure in supporting the Resolution which is now before the house. Indeed, I have not much to say after what has been said by the last speaker. I have come from a small district called Saugar in the Central Provinces. It was lately affected by a great famine. In our district wheat is the staple food, and that crop completely failed this year. The failure was to such an extent that we did not reap even a one-anna crop and our condition was reduced to such an extent that every *Malguzar* in the district was utterly ruined. Every one of them became a debtor. When we represented the matter to Government, the Government first of all refused to admit that there was anything like a famine, but when we showed them by facts and figures that there was a famine they said, "see for yourselves what you can do, we cannot help you." When we said to the Government, "We shall not be able to give you any money this time," and when the Government saw that that was really the case, then they came forward with a small sum of three lakhs as a loan to the people for seed grain. You know it is a district with a large area, where more than eighty per cent. of the population is agricultural. Three lakhs of rupees were nothing; but when we showed this to Government, and asked for more, they would not give it; then our poor people were driven to starvation. (*Shame*) We asked Government to open relief works. They did open relief works, but to a small extent; the poor people were given only the now famous ration of one-anna per man as fixed by Sir Richard Temple; and that was given to men required to work from early morning till evening. It was only given for work done, and not to those who could not work. Subscriptions had to be raised and a private relief fund was formed for those who could not work.

In 1878, after the great famine of Madras, the Government, in order to insure us against famine, levied a tax called an additional tax for famine insurance, and promised to save us from these famines in future; but when the famine came they said, "We never promised any such thing as that," and the whole money was appropriated. The Central Provinces have paid more than twenty-two lakhs of rupees into the treasury on account of this famine insurance fund, and had the Government come forward with only a small amount, the two districts would have been saved; but the Government said "we have no money, we have not promised to insure you against famine." I do not know why the additional tax was taken. There is a great deal of extravagance on the part of the Government, and it is necessary that steps should be taken to check such extravagance, and it is, therefore, necessary to substantiate our case before the British nation, so that it may exercise a check over this extravagance on the part of the Government and save our peasantry from being ruined. If the peasantry are ruined, it will be difficult to replace it. Our Government must not break its promises and act so dishonestly every time. (*Cheers*)

Fourth Day.

Resolution XIV. Military and Civil Expenditure.

Mr. A.B.Nakhre.

The Resolution was then put to the vote and carried.

The President:—Mr. Master will move the next resolution.

Resolution XV. Public Education.

Mr. Master.

Mr. Master:—Mr. President and Delegates, Ladies and Gentlemen, it gives me immense pleasure to move the following Resolution:—

That this Congress is emphatically of opinion that it is inexpedient in the present state of education in the country that Government grants for higher education should in any way be withdrawn, and concurring with previous Congresses, affirms in the most emphatic manner the importance of increasing public expenditure on all branches of education and the expediency of establishing Technical schools and Colleges.

Leaving the other part of the Resolution to the gentleman who is to follow, I shall say a few words on that portion which relates to technical education, in the sense of industrial education. The subject of technical education is the subject in which I am specially interested. Simply with a view to show you that I am not a theorist, I, with your permission, will say a word or two with respect to myself. Leaving Government service and going to England, I studied in a Technical College for a number of years, and it is as a result of that education that I started an Industry which I have been carrying on for the last eight years. (*Applause*) I have written papers and pamphlets on the subject, and am more or less familiar with the question of technical education. Gentlemen, the age we are living in is the age of Science; Science is the factor of a revolution in the industrial world. India was once known for her arts and industries. She taught the whole world the art of weaving, but, in consequence of her failure to keep pace with the advancement of science, she has suffered and suffered very cruelly from industrial paralysis. We look with immense satisfaction to the growth of the export trade of this country, but the true salvation of this country is in the development of arts and industries. An eminent man has said that for development we must expect envelopment, and in the shape of envelopment I ask where are the technical schools and colleges? In Calcutta we have none. I say, in the sense of Industrial Colleges, and not in the sense of Engineering Colleges, in Calcutta we have none. In Madras we have none In Bombay we have one; but I am sorry to say that for want of funds it has been starving. There is no chair of Chemistry, no chair of Physics Poverty of means brings poverty of results. (*Hear, hear*)

The British Commissioners in their Report on Technical Education say: "Technical "High Schools now exist in nearly every continental State. Our Commissioners believe that "the success which has attended the foundation of extensive manufacturing establishments, "engineering shops, and other works on the continent could not have been achieved to its full "extent, in the face of many retarding influences, had it not been for the system of high "technical instruction in these schools. * * * * With the exception of one school in Paris, "all these schools have been created, and are maintained, almost at the expense of several

Fourth Day

Resolution XV. Public Fducation.

Mr. Master.

"States." What more can I say, Gentlemen. All these schools on the continent, according to the information supplied by the gentlemen or by the jury appointed by the English Government, are maintained, at the expense of the State. "The buildings are palatial, the laboratories and Museums are costly and extensive, and the staff of Professors, who are well paid "according to the continental standard, is so numerous as to admit of the utmost sub-division "of the subjects taught." An eminent authority, while dealing with the subject in respect of Great Britain, said: "We may be justified in hoping * * * * that the Legislature and "the State will more and more recognise the claims of Science to their attention, so that it "may no longer require the begging box" but may "speak to the State like a favoured "child to its parent, sure of parental solicitude for its welfare; that the State will recognise "in Science its elements of strength and prosperity, to foster which the clearest dictates of self "interest demand." Both on account of prosperity, and strength, according to this authority, I hope the Government will come forward to give a liberal support to the cause of Science (*Hear, hear*)

Gentlemen, technical education does not at all mean simply familiarity with the tools or implements of handicraft; the solution of the problem is not to be found in teaching carpentry, fitting, or the like, as understood by some, for we have no dfficulty whatever in finding workmen here who could do their work to our entire satisfaction. What we really want is Captains of industry who by their superior and advanced scentific knowledge can carry on research work in departments of Chemistry and Physics, and understand the *rationale* which means the "reason why" of a process adopted in manufacture. It is absolutely necessary for us to follow the same lines which other countries have followed for the purposes of improving the industrial position. With all the raw material at our very door, with all the evidence of skill the Indians have shown in arts and manufacture, the sight of the country depending upon other countries for almost all manufactured articles is to me, I say, somewhat dreadful. Technical education is a part and parcel of higher education, and should lead Industry to carry on a successful war in the market where mere elementary knowledge will not suffice (*Cheers*)

Mr. Tulsi Ram.

Mr. Tulsi Ram:—Mr. Chairman, Ladies and Gentlemen, and Fellow Delegates coming as a Delegate for the Weavers of Southern India, I beg to lay before you the present unhappy condition of the weavers. Weaving is declining rapidly and threatening to disappear very soon if remedial measures are not at once adopted. Most of the weavers have become agriculturalists: some are employed in keeping carts and bulls, in collecting sand from rivers for building purposes. Is that the condition of a weaver? Benares and Madura are the only two great centres of the weaving industry, and if Government do not foster technical education, it will be a great death-blow to the cause of industry in this part of India

I feel proud to tell you that we have at this time in our midst that most distinguished educationalist, the Hon'ble and Rev. Dr. Miller; (*Cheers*) for this is a proposition which concerns the education of the masses, the education of the people of India. Brethren, the weavers as a class do not know how to read and write. If they appear before a Registrar, without enquiring of them whether they know how to read and write, he asks them to touch the pen. He anticipates thoroughly that they are ignorant, and that the Government are not caring for the education of the masses. At present the people are devoting their attention to primary education only. While Europe and America, not satisfied with the power of steam, are trying to introduce electricity as a prime factor in the automatic operations of cotton printing and other things, we are doing our work in the most primitive fashion with the shuttle and the loom Government should encourage in every way, and give help to, labourers and artisans They will soon disappear if no help is given, for the prosperity of a nation only depends on the skilfulness and dexterity and the economical habits of the industrial portion of the community. (*Cheers*)

Fourth Day.

Resolution XVI. Omnibus Resolution.

Pandit Bishan Narain Dar.

The Resolution was put to the vote and carried.

The President :—The next resolution will be moved by Pandit Bishan Narain Dar.

Pandit Bishan Narain Dar :—Mr. President and Gentlemen ; the Resolution which I have the honour to move runs thus :—

That this Congress concurs with its predecessors in strongly advocating :—

(a) The reduction of the Salt duty by at least the amount of its latest enhancement ;

(b) The raising of the Income-Tax taxable minimum from five hundred to one thousand Rupees ;

(c) The persistent pressure by the Government of India on all Provincial administrations to induce them to carry out in its integrity the excise policy enunciated in paragraphs 103, 104, 105, of the Despatch published in the *Gazette of India* of March 1890, and the introduction of a simple system of local option in the case of all villages ;

(d) The introduction into the Code of Criminal Procedure of a provision enabling accused persons in warrant cases to demand that instead of being tried by the Magistrate they may be committed to the Court of Sessions ;

(e) The fundamental reform of the Police Administration by a reduction in the numbers and an increase in the salaries and in the qualifications of the lower grades, and their far more careful enlistment ; and by the selection for the higher posts of gentlemen of higher capacities, more in touch with the respectable portions of the community, and less addicted to military pretensions, than the majority of existing Deputy Inspectors-General, Superintendents and Assistant Superintendents of Police, are at present ;

(f) A modification of the rules under the Arms Act so as to make them equally applicable to all residents in, or visitors to, India without distinction of creed, caste, or colour ; to ensure the liberal concession of licences wherever wild animals habitually destroy human life, cattle, or crops ; and to make all licences, granted under the revised rules, of life-long tenure, revocable only on proof of misuse, and valid throughout the Provincial jurisdiction in which they are issued ;

(g) The establishment of Military Colleges in India, whereat, natives of India, as defined by statute, may be educated and trained for a military career, as Commissioned or Non-Commissioned officers (according to capacity and qualifications) in the Indian army ;

(h) The organizing throughout the more warlike races of the empire of a system of militia service ;

(i) The authorizing and stimulating of a widespread system of volunteering, such as obtains in Great Britain, amongst the people of India ;

(j) The discontinuance of the Exchange Compensation allowance granted to undomiciled European and Eurasian employees of Government, involving an annual expenditure of over a crore of rupees while the Exchequer is in a condition of chronic embarrassment ;

(k) The giving effect to the report of the Parliamentary members of the India Office Committee on the subject of the Rules Orders, and Practices in Indian Cantonments, with regard to Prostitution and contagious disease, and the endorsing of their conclusions :—

(i) That the system and incidental practices described in that Report, and the statutory rules, so far as they authorized or permitted the same did not accord with the plain meaning and intention of the resolution of the House of Commons of June 5th, 1888 ; and

(ii) That the only effective method of preventing these systematic malpractices is by express legislation.

Fourth Day.

Resolution XVI. Omnibus Resolution.

Pandit Bishan Narain Dar.

Gentlemen, it is not necessary for me to speak much in support of a Resolution which contains demands, multifarious no doubt, but of the most vital importance to the various sections of the Indian community, with regard to which there exists no difference of opinion whatever. The demands that are included in this Resolution have been urged from the very beginning of the Congress, upon the attention of the Government of this country and the Government of England. Their importance is the same as it was ten years ago; their urgency is the same, and be it remembered that the obstinacy of our Government in refusing to grant them is also the same. Gentlemen, it is impossible for me within the time at my disposal to give you even a brief review of the various demands that are included in this Resolution, but in touching upon a few of the most important ones I take up first of all the very first thing which is put in the Resolution with regard to the reduction of Salt Duty. If there is any demand which is made by the Congress in the name of the poorer masses of this country, it is the demand which is included in the first portion of this Resolution. It touches not the richer class, nor those who are called the higher class, but it touches the vast masses of the country. (*Cheers*) When you consider how heavy is the Salt Duty which the Indian masses have to pay, as compared with what is paid by other countries, you will have some idea as to what effect the present system must have upon the fortunes of this country. The average income per head in Europe is £15 4*s*., and the salt duty per head 1*s*. 11*d*. The average income per head in India is calculated at £2, and the salt duty 6*d*. In Europe the salt duty is two-thirds per cent. on the income and in India it is about one and a quarter per cent. (*Hear, hear*)

Now, Gentlemen, coming to the Police Reform, which you urge, if there is anything which has a most important bearing with regard to the question of the popularity or unpopularity of the Government of India, so far as the masses of the people are concerned, it is their relations with the Police of this country. If they know the Government, they know it through the Police or the Collector; and if the Police system is vicious and oppressive, as at present it is undoubtedly, then whatever may be the virtue in the Government, what ever their intentions, so far as the mass of the people are concerned, the Government will and must remain unpopular. The two principal things which we urge with regard to this Police reform are, that there should be sufficient inducement in the Police Department for men of the higher class, for men of higher social standing, to seek service in this Department, and also that the higher posts should be thrown open to the natives of this country. The practice that at present obtains under that system is that the posts of District Superintendent of Police and other higher posts are almost invariably filled by Europeans, or, in fact, by such Europeans as are not thought to be fit for anything else. They are given those posts. I submit that this is a reform most urgently needed, not in the interests of that class which this Congress is particularly supposed to represent by our critics, but in the interests of the masses at large. (*Cheers*)

Now I come to the Rules under the Arms Act. If I support this part of the Resolution, it is because I look upon the present rules, the present system, under which the Arms Act exists as a brand of racial disqualification, a badge of servitude which we have never borne under the worst despot. Even in Mahomedan times, whatever may be the merits or demerits of their *regime*, the distinction which is stereotyped by such laws as the Arms Act did not exist, and I am sure it does not speak to the credit of the English Government in this country that after 150 years of British rule a badge of racial distinction should be allowed in this country. (*Cheers*) Another very important demand which is included in this Resolution is as regards the Military career of the people of this country. I should have thought that those people who have of late evinced such keen interest in the welfare of the martial races of this country, when the question of Simultaneous Examinations was before them, would have done something for the career of these martial races. I think that this is a demand which the martial races are perfectly justified in making, not only upon the ground of their own personal interest, but upon the very high ground of patriotism and loyalty—patriotism to their own country and loyalty to their sovereign. (*Cheers*) They make this demand because they think that the time has come when on financial considerations there should be more natives of this country following the military career, in order to cut down the foreign agency which at present eats up our money, because they think that it is loyal to their Sovereign to be prepared, should any critical occasion arise, to defend the honour of their Sovereign, and also because they think it patriotic, should any emergency arise, to fight for the ashes of their fathers and the temples of their gods. It is upon these high principles that these demands are urged upon the attention of the Governments of India and of England. (*Cheers*)

Gentlemen, another most important subject which is included in this list with which I have to deal is that dealing with the Exchange Compensation Allowance. Gentlemen, if I were asked to point out any action or any measures of the Government of India to show that the policy of the Government in this country has of late been that India is not for Indians on for Englishmen but solely and wholly for Anglo Indians, I should point to two measures; I should point to the rejection of our demands for Simultaneous Examinations, and I should point to the granting of Exchange Compensation Allowance. (*Loud Cheers*) India is at present governed in the interests of a particular class. Now, Gentlemen, I look upon these two actions of Government as two crimes—grave crimes committed against the just aspirations of the people of this country, against the honour of England and against the noblest instincts of humanity. About the poverty of India you have heard a good deal. Mr. Seymour Keay spoke with great authority upon this point, and we all listened to him with the deepest earnestness when he went into the miserable and impoverished condition of the people of this country. We have also heard the figures and facts cited, in support of the charge we bring against Government, by Mr. Wacha, who has lately spoken. Mr. Seymour Keay is, after all, an Englishman, and is a member of the Radical party. He is one of those Lord Salisbury called the one-legged rulers of the House of Commons; Mr. Wacha is a Parsee, and, therefore, in the ethnology of Anglo-Indians, he is not a native of India; but let us hear what one of their trusted officials has to say on this point. (*Hear, hear*)

A very remarkable article appeared some months ago in an English Magazine, by the late Lieutenant-Governor of our Provinces, Sir Auckland Colvin. He writes on the perilous growth of military expenditure in this country. He says that if the expenditure of the Indian Government goes on increasing, then Russia need not move troops, she has only to bide her time, discontent will do its work, and the retribution will come. Now, Gentlemen, when such is the impoverished condition of this country, Exchange Compensation has been granted to Anglo-Indians, in spite of the critical condition of Indian finances. (*Shame*) The poor taxpayer is burdened with an additional tax. The man who cannot properly afford to pay for salt, has that commodity taxed. The poor man is taxed so that the rich man may be pampered. It is a very sad reflection that under God's providence, under British rule in this 19th century, and in the time of one of the noblest sovereigns that has ever ruled the children of men, under such conditions of Indian finances it should come to pass that to those "who have much, more should be given, and from those who have little even that little should be takea away." (*Cheers*) Now, Gentlemen, for this measure it is not only the Government of India, but I must say it is also the Home Government, that is responsible. We can never expect the Anglo-Indians to support us in a measure like that; it was to their interest to urge their claims and to get as much as they possibly could. Upon all such occasions the House of Commons, the British Parliament, has been the main pillar of Hope. From the Anglo-Indians we can never expect much, and we do not expect much; but we have always thought, and do still think, although I am afraid with great misgivings, that the moment (whatever the Anglo-Indian may do here) we appeal to the House of Commons and bring the injustice and the anomaly of the arrangement to their notice, that anomaly and that injustice is sure to be removed and

Fourth Day.

Resolution XVI. Omnibus Resolution.

Pandit Bishan Narain Dar.

redressed. (*Hear, hear*) But upon this measure, and upon other measures lately, the conduct of the Liberal Government in the House of Commons (I heard it with sorrow and I utter it with reluctance) has been anything but worthy of their past traditions. I am sorry that Parliament has made itself so conspicuous in this manner. I am sorry that on the question of Exchange Compensation it has thought it right to reject the just demands of a weak race in order to maintain the unjust demands of a strong race. Gentlemen, it is a verv sad thing that the fair fame of England and of her Parliament for justice and integrity—a fame which rests upon the solid foundation of History; a fame which has been our Pole star, and has guided our course over the troubled sea of Anglo-Indian oppression—that that fame at present seems surrounded by mists and fogs of low party consideration and class interests, and is obscured and dimmed, and that round us and about us there is nothing but the blackness and darkness of despair. (*Cheers*)

Our great friend and leader, Mr. Hume (*Cheers*) has sent us through the pages of *India* a message of hope. He is ever hopeful, and is never daunted by difficulties and troubles We have seen in critical times and on many occasions that Hope shone in his breast like a sacred pillar of fire, whence it went out into the breasts of others. I shall be very happy indeed if my countrymen will draw as much consolation as possible from that message of hope, because something is needed to console the people of India in their hour of trouble and grief. Things are going from bad to worse; discontent is spreading; it is coming over the Indian mind like the shadow of some great eclipse; but in the midst of darkness and despair there is only one ray of hope in this political agitation, and that is the presence of two individuals who are India's best friends in the House of Commons. (*Hear, hear*) There are few spectacles more noble under the sun and more liked by the gods than that of a good man fighting hard against adversity for the interests of the people. (*Cheers*) Gentlemen, I trust that through the exertions of these gentlemen, the English Parliament may come to realise the justice and expediency and the necessity of our demands, as well as the discontent which their rejection is sure to create in the people's mind, and the serious consequences which always follow in the train of popular discontent. I am sure that, if they once realise this, it will not be long before they turn their steps towards the direction wherein lies the peace and permanence and prosperity of the Empire. (*Loud and long continued Cheers*)

Mr. Ranga Chari.

Mr. Ranga Chari:—Mr. President, Ladies and Gentlemen, the proposition I have the honour to second contains the budget of our standing grievances. Unfortunately for us, this has formed no small part of the deliberations of this august body, year after year I justify my selection for seconding this resolution, not on the ground that I have the necessary ability and experience to deal with all the multifarious questions of importance therein contained, but that I have the honour to be the Captain of the Volunteer Corps of the Tenth National Congress. I will, therefore, confine my remarks only to clauses (*g*), (*h*) and (*i*) of the resolution. Before proceeding in detail with the clauses themselves, I take it for granted, and you will all concur with me in so doing, that whatever national traits we are beginning to lose, we still retain in us the martial spirit that adorned our ancestors of old. For the proof of this I do not wish to take you back and call your attention to the many deeds of valour and victory recorded in the pages of your history. Gentlemen, the very simple fact that the Government of this country has been throwing every kind of obstacle in the way of the admission of the natives of this country to offices in the military department is a patent, nay irrefutable proof, of the existence of a latent martial capacity in the nation. (*Hear, hear*)

The short-sighted policy pursued by Government in respect of recruitment for military service is objectionable on two broad and important grounds;—on the ground of expenditure, and on the ground of justice and expediency. Looking at the statistics of 1880 as to the comparative cost per head of a soldier in different countries, we find that in France with an army of 900,000 it is Rs. 185; in Germany with an army of 1,200,000, Rs. 145; in

England, Rs. 277; and in India, Rs. 775. By the establishment of military colleges the cost per head will be diminished, and the number of imported soldiers might also be reduced. (*Hear, hear*) Looking again at the prospects of native officers in the British army we find a native of India cannot even after 30 years' service rise beyond a Subadar Major, on the paltry sum of Rs. 200 per month, but a young Sub-Lieutenant, on his arrival here, gets Rs. 300 per mensem on the ground of justice and expediency. (*Shame*)

**Fourth Day.**

**Resolution XVI. Omnibus Resolution.**

**Mr. Ranga Chari.**

Let me refer you to the pledges given by the British Government with reference to this matter:—The Act of 1833 enacts that "No native of the said territories, nor any natural "born subject of Her Majesty, shall by reason only of his religion, place of birth, descent or "colour, be disabled from holding any place, office, or employment under the said Govern- "ment." The Secretary of State in a despatch, dated the 26th January 1886, in referring to the incidence of new taxation in India, refers to the causes of danger resulting from the "character of the Government which is in the hands of foreigners, who hold all the principal "administrative offices and form so large a part of the army." This he says would "constitute "a political danger"

The expedient of admitting a few noblemen and feudatory chiefs as honorary officers of the Indian Army, such as the Maharajahs of Gwalior, Kashmir, Mysore, Kooch-Behar, and others, is not alone sufficient to cure the evil. The loyalty, devotion, the bravery and heroism of native soldiers are well known, and have been often recognised by Government. The native soldiery is the ultimate bulwark and the main support of the Empire. Sir G. Greaves, late Commander-in-Chief or Bombay, speaking on the military policy of India said, "We rely upon you, and you depend upon us" (*Cheers*) About volunteering, let me call your attention to the fact that H. R. H. The Duke of Connaught attested the expediency of establishing Military Colleges. Mr. Justice Bailey, who was Commandant of the Bombay Volunteer Corps, said that natives might be admitted as Volunteers. Gentlemen, let me not be misunderstood in asking for these concessions; we do not thereby mean that every office in the army should be thrown open to us, that every one of us should have free licence to use arms and ammunition, that admission to military colleges should be free and unrestricted; but what we want, Gentlemen, is to ask Government to instruct us in all that is noble, to teach us how to defend the Government and ourselves against foreign aggression, to protect us from the raids of wild animals, in short, practically to teach us the inestimable boon of self-help, bearing in mind that "God helps those that help themselves." (*Loud Cheers*)

**Pandit Kaliprasana Kabya Bisharad.**

Pandit Kaliprasana Kabya Bisharad:—Gentlemen, the "Omnibus" is before you, and a man has to drag it on once again. A kind printer or some kind friend was disposed to give him some rest, but the President goads him to drag it on, and so he drags it on without inflicting a speech upon you, and he retires after supporting the Resolution. (*Laughter*)

**Munshi Shaik Husein.**

Munshi Shaik Husein supported the Resolution in Hindustani amid frequent bursts of applause.

**Mr. Bissanath Chandik.**

Mr. Bissanath Chandik:—As an humble representative of the Marwari community, amongst whom, as you are aware, education has not spread to the extent that it has in other communities, I rise to support the resolution that has just been proposed and seconded. You will concede that there is a fitness of things in a professional banker, who is ever busy with his calculation of rupees, annas and pies, coming forward to speak on that part of the "Omnibus" Resolution, regarding the raising of the taxable minimum of income-tax from Rs. 500 to Rs. 1,000. The speakers that preceded me have, however, urged such convincing reasons, and so ably too, that very little remains to be done on my part. Gentlemen, it might be said by our opponents that, like little children, we do not know what we clamour for. They might say that a benign Government has by devotion to the people's interests,

Fourth Day.

Resolution XVI.

Omnibus Resolution.

MR. BISSANATH CHANDIK.

involved itself in almost hopeless bankruptcy, and that it ill becomes us "saucy children to add to the troubles of such a loving parent. (*Laughter and Cheers*) To ensure our safety, our Indian rulers have increased the British force and swelled our military expenditure to keep us from war; they have generously given an allowance to a neighbour to add to our glory; they have been conquering and annexing to strengthen our administration; they have been manning all ranks of the Services with British talent at a much greater expense, excluding, utterly excluding the children of the soil; to help our progress, they have been passing liberal measures to break our industries and cripple our commerce. (*Laughter and Cheers*)

And what is the result, Gentlemen, of this humane and self-sacrificing policy of Anglo Indian rule? The administration is growing more and more expensive, and the tax-payer poorer and poorer. We are now so tax-ridden that the next straw will crush our backs; and yet the Government of India presents an annual deficit of three crores and a half. Shall we not be grateful for its good intention and its beneficent rule? To pray at this moment for any even slight lightening of any public burden would be cruel to such a paternal Government. Still, ungrateful Indians that we are, our earnest appeal to Britain and to British justice shall only be "Save us from our friends, our Anglo-Indian friends!" (*Laughter and Cheers*) In days when war was feared and it was felt that our military force was not sufficient to meet the contingency of the war the income-tax was introduced. The income-tax, Gentlemen, strictly speaking, is not a duty levied on commerce or manufacture, not a tax on land or agriculture, it is an impost that is levied on money every time that it changes hands. It is, we admit, not so heavy as our land tax, nor quite so iniquiteus as our salt tax. (*Laughter*) We are alive to the financial embarrassments of the Government; but the Government must cut its coat according to its cloth. We call for retrenchment; we want a cheaper administration, and along with it we ask for a proportionate lightening of our burdens. (*Cheers*) We have been saddled with an income tax. Every man who succeeds in barely keeping body and soul together is required to pay the Government a benevolence of 2 per cent. on his little earnings. A family with an annual income of Rs. 500 cannot command more than the barest necessaries of life. How long will an uneconomical Government continue to extort, from a class of people on the brink of starvation, such a heavy duty, and that too on no properly taxable commodity? We demand that at least the minimum of taxable income be raised, so that the burden may fall only on such shoulders as can be expected to bear it. Gentlemen, I therefore beg to support the proposition that the minimum be raised to Rs. 1,000 per annum. (*Loud Cheers*)

The Resolution was put to the vote and carried.

THE PRESIDENT.

THE PRESIDENT:—In connection with this "Omnibus" Resolution I should like to say that Mr. Bannerji has handed over a petition to the Congress, signed by 26 missionaries, relating to clause (*k*) of this Resolution, and urging upon us the question of temperance and social purity.

I should like to say that this day, the 29th of December, eighty-five years ago, the "Grand Old Man" of England was born. Let me call for three cheers to him. (*Three hearty Cheers were given for Mr. Gladstone*) As we have done hitherto, Gentlemen, I suppose with your permission, I may send a telegram to Mr. Gladstone, congratulating him on the eighty-fifth aniversary of his birthday, I am particularly glad that I, an Irishman, should have the opportunity of appending my name to it. (*Hear, hear and Cheers*) I suppose we may also send a telegram to India's Grand Old Man, Mr. A. O. Hume, expressing our thanks in behalf of the cause with which he had so much to do in starting. (*Loud Cheers*)

Three enthusiastic cheers were then given for Mr. A. O. Hume.

THE PRESIDENT:—The next Resolution will be moved by Mr. R. N. Mudholkar, o the Berars.

Resolution XVII. Proposed further powers of District Magistrates.

MR. R. N. MUDHOLKAR.

MR. R. N. MUDHOLKAR :—Mr President, Ladies and Gentlemen, the Resolution which I move is as follows :—

That this Congress hereby empowers its President to convey to the Government of India its opinion that the powers proposed to be conferred on District Magistrates, by amendments and additons to section 15 of Police Act of 1861, with respect to the levy of the costs of punitive police and of granting compensation, are of a most arbitrary, dangerous, and unprecedented character.

This may appear to some rather as a lawyer's resolution, as a matter with which the general public have nothing to do, but which concerns only the lawyers. Allow me, my friends, to tell you that it is a matter which concerns not the lawyer so much as the public and the country. There is a very great danger looming in the distance, not a very great distance, but a distance which is quite measurable. In October last there was a Bill introduced, nominally for the purpose of introducing some slight amendments in the Police Act. In the shape and under the guise of this amendment, a revolution is sought to be effected in the administration of this country, a revolution which will place not your liberties certainly, but your property in every sense of the term, entirely at the mercy of one man in the district. (*Cheers*) There is a section in the Police Act by which, if it is found that any part of the country is in a disturbed condition, Government have the power of imposing what is called a punitive police there, that is, a police specially so employed, and the cost of that police is defrayed not from the general revenue of the country but from a tax specially raised for that purpose. The tax is levied in the locality where the police have to be quartered. It was suggested to Government that this measure—which has been in existence from 1861—is not a just one; that it is desirable to make some changes, and that it is only persons who have really committed any disturbance who should defray those expenses. At first sight this looks very just and proper, but look at the insidious manner in which this principle is sought to be worked out. One would think that there should be an enquiry to find out who are the men who have committed the offence, and that it should be only those who would be called upon to pay. (*Hear, hear*) But no, that is not the way in which the Government proposes to work. The way in which the Government proposes to proceed is this; whenever such a Police has to be employed the cost of such additional police force shall be borne as the Magistrate of the District may direct. In the words of the proposed law—

(*a*) By the inhabitants of, or persons having interests in land, in the local area described in the notification ; or by both.

(*b*) By any such inhabitants or persons or class or classes of such inhabitants or persons, or both, as aforesaid, as in the opinion of the Magistrate have caused or contributed to the disturbance or other cause which led to the quartering of the additional police force, and no portion of such cost shall be payable by any person or class of persons who, in the opinion of the Magistrate, have been free from blame ;

(*c*) And such Magistrate, after enquiry, if necessary, shall apportion such cost according to his judgment of their respective means among the inhabitants and other persons who are, as aforesaid, liable to bear the same.

Now let us understand what this means. It means that such community or classes as the Magistrate thinks has committed the offence is to be taxed with the whole thing ; but not only that, his power of differentiation extends to that community as a whole. He may say that only five or six men who are responsible shall be called on to pay ; such persons in such manner and to such extent as he thinks fit. (*Loud cries of Shame*) If there is a man against whom he has a grudge, that man may be singled out, and from that man the whole cost can be claimed. Then there is also a further thing. The evil does not iest there. You may ask, why ? Because there will be an enquiry. It is to be remembered that in doing these things,

**Fourth Day.**

**Resolution XVII. Proposed further powers of District Magistrates.**

**Mr. R. N. Mudholkar.**

the Magistrate will be acting, not in a judicial capacity, but in an executive capacity. There is the District Magistrate, it is true, but the District Magistrate and the Police act in all criminal matters as two different persons. He is defined to be the Chief Executive Officer of the District, and as such he is not at all amenable to the High Court proceedings; and, as the law does not give any right of appeal, you cannot go to the Sessions Court, nor can a High Court send for the case under its powers of Extraordinary Jurisdiction. So in that way the door of the High Court, which is often resorted to when there is an injustice, is closed to you. (*Hear, hear*)

Then there is this dangerous procedure existing, not only with regard to the imposition of the tax, but also with regard to another thing in which the same powers are given. If any damage to property is caused, if any person has received grievous hurt, or any person is killed, power is given to the District Magistrate to give compensation for the loss or for the destruction of property, or for the injury caused to the person. That compensation he has got the power of levying from such classes of the community as he thinks proper, or from such individuals, in such manner, and to such extent, as he thinks proper. (*Shame*) I should certainly say there is at present in India not one officer who possesses powers like these. In the British Isles there is no body of persons, much less an individual person, who possesses powers like these, and it is these powers which are sought to be conferred. upon persons who live, as you know, far away from public opinion, in what are called distant Mofussil districts. (*Hear, hear*) Gentlemen, it is not necessary to suppose that these gentlemen would be in any way actuated by malice in what they do. We shall assume the most charitable case, the case of a man who, with the best of motives, always tries to do the thing which he considers just. How many cases are there in which even with the best of motives there have been failures of justice? Have there not been cases in which even honest judges have passed convictions, and those convictions have been upset on appeal? Do we not know of cases where persons, with the best of motives, have been biassed by interested persons to take a particular view of things. Now, under these circumstances, at a time when public excitement must be very strong on account of the disturbances, is it too much to suppose that one party or the other may gain his ear, and that the District Magistrate may be induced to take that party's view of things? (*Cheers*) As I say, we shall give him credit for the best of motives. We need not say that he is actuated by any ill-feeling or ill-will; but any Magistrate, even the District Magistrate, is only a human being, and he has got all the frailties and all the weaknesses of a human being. Looking to the fact as I have already pointed out, that this law would be put into force in times of great excitement, it is more than likely that the District Magistrate may take sides; and, taking sides, as he would do, would there be any justice at all? Therefore, as this proposal is entirely subversive of all our ideas of justice, of fair play, it behoves us to protest against it, as a violation of the very first principles of fair play and justice. (*Cheers*) Such powers are utterly unprecedented, such powers are most arbitrary, and such powers are most dangerous; and we, who are sitting in Congress, ought to protest against it. One word more it is necessary to say, Gentlemen, and it is this. We have confined our attention to one section only, for this reason, not that we consider that the other amendments are faultless, but because this amendment violates the very first principles of fair play and justice, and violates all principles of constitutional administration. It is necessary that we should enter our emphatic protest against it, and I believe if we here in Congress do our duty, and if we go out each to our district, and send our protestations, they will be listened to. (*Loud Cheers*)

**Mr. M. B. Namjoshi.**

Mr. M. B. Namjoshi:—Mr. President and Brother Delegates, Mr. Mudholkar has referred to section XV, and particularly to two features of it. I shall refer to a third feature, and then I will give you an idea of those additions and alterations and dangerous features which they have introduced into every place. The section that Mr. Mudholkar refers to, not only makes people within the Police District liable to the taxes, but it also makes non-residents, the absentee landlords, liable to pay the taxes; and this power also is left to the District Magistrate. (*Shame*) Those of you who have been reading the newspaper accounts of the recent riots between the Hindus and the Mahomedans in the different parts of the country will, perhaps, remember one of the speeches of the satrap of the North-West Provinces, in which he, in a large public durbar, referred to the conduct of the large landlords in his province, and tried to implicate them, and to connect them both directly and indirectly with the *Gaurakshani* riots which had taken place in the different provinces. I believe, Sir, that is the spirit, that is the inspiring deity of this Bill; and I say it advisedly, because I find that the Government of India, is framing this act on the advice of the North-West Provinces Government alone. (*Shame*) The other provinces have not been consulted, their opinions have not been obtained, and it is on the recommendation of the satrap of that province that this Bill is being undertaken now.

**Fourth Day.**

**Resolution XVII. Proposed further powers of District Magistrates.**

**Mr. M. B. Namjoshi.**

With reference to the other two sections, beyond the other additions or alterations that are being made, I think this Bill suffers, not only from the fault of omission, but also from the fault of commission. Faults of omission during the limited time that I have before me I will not go on to illustrate, but I will simply give the points to which I object. It suffers from the fault of omission, because it has not taken note of the circumstances that are developed in different provinces and that require special treatment. (*Hear, hear*) All of you friends from Madras and other provinces know what happened at Masulipatam. You know the circumstances under which the powers of declaring or enlisting what are called honorary constables were used; you also know how the conduct of the District Magistrates was arbitrary. No notice has been taken of that. You also know what has happened in other provinces with reference to rules about music and the granting of a licence. It suffers from the fault of commission; because in section 30 or 31 it proposes to entrust to the Police, to the Inspector, or the officers of the Police, the novel power of stopping, controlling and regulating processions or assemblies not only in public places, but also in private places. (*Shame*) That is, as the resolution says, dangerous. (*Shame*)

The fourth point is that the Bill is rather unprecedented in some features; its unprecedented nature lies, you will see, in the fact that while it gives very large powers to the District Magistrates, it makes no provision in the Bill to see that these powers are properly exercised. In the Bombay Police Act the same principle prevails, and though there is a laxity in the supervision to be exercised, the Act at least provides that the large powers which the Police and the Magistrates will enjoy under that Act shall be properly supervised, not only by the heads of Government, but by Courts also; but this feature is wanting in this Bill. It is unprecedented in another respect, in that it un-makes the blessings, that it un-makes the good that written law guarantees to the subjects of foreign rule, inasmuch as it leaves not only large powers but large powers of discretion, not only to District Magistrates but to Superintendents of Police, and not only to Superintendents of Police, but, as this Bill seems to indicate, to the Assistant Superintendents of Police, and some lower grades of Police Officers also; this is quite unprecedented. On all these points I have instances to give, but during the short time at my disposal I cannot do it. (*Cheers*)

The resolution was put to the vote and carried

**Resolution XVIII. Forest Management.**

**Mr. R. P. Karandikar.**

Mr. R. P. Karandikar:—Mr. President and Brother Delegates, the resolution that I have the honour to propose runs as follows:—

That this Congress records its deep-felt gratitude to the Government of India for its circular resolution No. 22/F, published in the Supplement to the *Gazette of India*, dated 20th October 1894, and its high appreciation of the generous principle, which it enunciates, of subordinating fiscal interests to the needs and agricultural interests of the ryot population in the management of forests.

And would further represent that in forests falling under classes 3 and 4 of the said resolutions, fuel, grazing concessions, fodder, small timber for building houses and making agricultural

**Fourth Day.**

Resolution XVIII. Forest Management.

MR. R. P. KARANDIKAR.

implements, edible forest products, &c., may be granted free of charge in all cases, under such restrictions as to quantity, &c., as the Government may deem proper; and that wherever hardship may be felt, under present conditions, the policy of the said Resolution may be carried out with reference to existing Forest areas, and the existing Reserve boundaries so adjusted as to leave a sufficiently large margin to facilitate the enjoyment by the agricultural population of their communal rights without molestation and annoyance by the minor subordinates of the Department.

This is the Resolution that we have now before us, and I am glad that I am enabled at this stage to put it before you. I am glad, because we have been for three successive years pressing this matter on the attention of the Government of India. You remember, Gentlemen, those of you that were present at Nagpore, the Resolution that was placed before the Congress there was number 11, of 1891, which said that it was necessary that Government should investigate this matter more carefully and do all in its power to mitigate its hardship. The next Resolution on this subject was number 10 of 1892 Those were the Resolutions which were passed by the Congress unanimously, on the first two occasions by the delegates in the one case from Bombay, and in the other from Madras, and on the third occasion by delegates from the Punjab. You will thus perceive the intensity of the feeling of dissatisfaction and discontent that is likely to accrue from a foolish administration of the law. It seems to me, therefore, that we are perfectly justified in thanking the Government of India for the circular which it has been pleased to issue in this matter. (*Cheers*) It may be said that the very object of the Forest Law was to conserve such forests as were over and above the wants of the people. You remember these were the words of the honorable gentleman that was in charge of this Bill before it was passed. But you see, things have come to such a pass that Government is powerless against its own officers, that Government is now come to be complimented for having issued the circular which is objected to in the same breath.

Now, I think Gentlemen, there is reason to thank this Government, not because it has enunciated the same principle that was the object of the law, but because it is very difficult in these days even for Government officers to acknowledge a good and sound principle against the conduct and action of their own subordinates. It is on this ground that I claim your attention to this proposition and claim that the Government of India is entitled to our heart-felt gratitude for the circular issued by it. Following the vote of grateful thanks we offer, we have something to add to it; we cannot stop here, for what is pointed out in the circular needs amendment, and what is that? It consists of six elements, which those that have followed the Resolutions will be able to observe consist of these things:—First, things which concern food, then cattle, then housing, then the general agricultural prosperity of the country, then the communal rights of the agriculturists and their boundaries, and lastly come the minor subordinates of the Forest Department. We called upon Government to pay particular attention to these six heads, and called also upon Government to point out to their subordinates that they were responsible for the hardships created by the Forest administration. In this particular, I might well say that we might ask the Government to say take care of the shillings, the pounds will take care of themselves It is these subordinate officers that run the risk of entailing upon the head of Government censure which in some measure they do not merit. It is these officers that have to be warned and we ask the Government to warn these officers. With these words I beg to commend this resolution to your acceptance. (*Cheers*)

MR. C. NARASIMHULU NAIDU, of Madras, seconded the Resolution in Tamil.

REV. W. W. STEPHENSON.

REV. W. W. STEPHENSON :—Mr. President and Fellow Members, I have much pleasure in supporting this resolution, and I say this on the ground that I sympathise very thoroughly in the main with this Congress. (*Hear, hear*) I think that this resolution has been very well drawn. It contains pretty well all that is required at the present

Resolution XVIII. Forest Management.

REV. W. W. STEPHENSON.

time, and it expresses it clearly, and there are several sentences of which, if time allowed, one could point out the wisdom. I should like to say that the two important points are the hardships which the people suffer under the present rules, and the still greater hardships which the people suffer by reason of the way in which they are carried out. Now, with regard to the hardships of the present rules, the Government has said that fiscal interests are not of the first importance. Then why on every stone taken away from the field, on every particle of salt-earth taken by the washerman, on every possible thing that can be gathered up in that way should a tax be payable? A few weeks ago in my district I came across an old man with a few sheep and goats on his right hand and a very bad pasture to the left. But a few yards away there was magnificent green grass in a reserve, yet the poor animals were not allowed to nibble a single blade, and the poor man cried out, "Why has God made all these creatures, while the Forest Department will not allow the cattle to graze?" What is the other question? Even supposing we can get no relaxation of rules, there is the carrying out of the present rules which I believe is almost entirely left in the hands of subordinates of the Forest Department. I maintain that there ought not to be the almost constant friction between the villagers and the subordinates of the Forest Department that there exists to-day; I maintain that, and that there is no department of Government that comes so closely in touch with the people, that pinches them more keenly than these two departments, *viz.*, the Salt and the Forest, which I have sometimes called the Irritation Departments. (*Laughter*) Now I maintain that Government ought to watch their subordinates exceedingly keenly, and that every District Forest Officer, or rather every District Magistrate (who is really the forest officer, because the forest officer is his subordinate), ought to be instructed most carefully that every source of irritation and annoyance by the minor subordinates of the department ought to be abolished for ever. (*Cheers*)

MR. NIZAMUDDIN KUMRUDDIN.

MR. NIZAMUDDIN KUMRUDDIN, of Satara, supported the proposition in Hindustani.

The Resolution was put to the vote and carried.

THE PRESIDENT:—The next Resolution will be moved by Mr. P. Ramachandra Pillai of Secunderabad.

Resolution XIX. Liberty of the Press.

MR. P. RAMACHANDRA PILLAI.

MR. P. RAMACHANDRA PILLAI:—Fellow Delegates, Ladies and Gentlemen, the Resolution that I have been entrusted with runs thus:—

That this Congress, being of opinion that the Government of India Notification of 25th June 1891, in the Foreign Department, gagging the Press in territories under British administration in Native States, is retrograde, arbitrary and mischievous in its nature, and opposed to sound statesmanship and to the liberty of the people, most respectfully enters its emphatic protest against the same and entreats its cancellation without delay.

Gentlemen, before I say a few words upon this Resolution I must express my thanks to the gentlemen of the Subjects Committee for taking up this subject upon the programme of this Congress, because this is a new subject which the people of Secunderabad and people similarly situated in the territory of Hyderabad were very anxious that this Congress should take up as being an important subject. so that there be no more gagging of the press in a territory subject to the Government of India, but unfortunately situated out of British India. (*Hear, hear*) I therefore express my deep gratitude to the gentlemen of the Subjects Committee, and, in doing so, I not only express my own thanks but also those of my constituents. Gentlemen, the Notification referred to in this Resolution appears in the Government of India Notification under date 25th June, of 1891, which I shall read for your information:—

"Whereas some misapprehension has hitherto existed as to the regulations in force in territory under the administration of the Governor-General in Council, but beyond the limits of British India, with reference to newspapers published within such territory, the Governor-General in Council has been pleased to make the following order:—

1. No newspaper or other printed work, whether periodical or other, containing public news or comments on public news shall, without the written permission for the time being in force of the Political Agent, be edited, printed, or published, after the 1st day of August 1891, in any local area administered by the Governor-General in Council but not forming part of British India.

2. If after the day aforesaid any person shall without such permission as aforesaid edit, print, or publish any such newspaper or other work as aforesaid in any such local area as aforesaid the Political Agent may by order in writing;

    (*a*) require him to leave such local area within seven days from the date of such order

    (*b*) and prohibit him from re-entering such local area without the written permission of the Political Agent.

3. If any such order as is mentioned in the last foregoing paragraph be disobeyed, the offender shall be liable to forcible expulsion from such local area in pursuance of an order to be made in writing by the Political Agent.

Now, Gentlemen, from the language of this Notification it is clear that the Political Agent of the Court of the Native State is clothed with the authority of granting permission as he may choose; and he can refuse permission without any grounds, and he can also revoke the permission once granted without grounds; and any offender can be deported after a week s notice, and if he disobeys he can be oxpelled by physical force. (*Shame*) Yes, Gentlemen, it is a downright shame. Now the worst part of it is this, that the Editor of a newspaper, publishing it in the territories not subject to the Native State but in the territory subject to the British laws, can be condemned unheard. He has no chance of being heard. No accusation need be made. It is left to the whim and caprice of the Political Agent for the time being. Gentlemen, those who are acquainted with Native States are aware that they are full of intrigues and corruption and what-not, notwithstanding the best intentions of the rulers themselves. The Political Agent, notwithstanding his ability, his shrewdness and his sense of justice, must, as an Englishman, see things as they take place in Native States through blue spectacles. He is the last man to know the real state of things in Native States, for the simple reason that the Political Agent, who is called the "Bara Sahib" or the "great Sahib" cannot see small things, while the few people that are privileged to approach misrepresent things for their own ends. It is impossible for him to see the real state of affairs, and it is therefore all the more necessary that there should be a free press to ventilate the grievances of the people and to bring to the prompt attention of the public and the Government the short-comings prevailing in those Native States. (*Cheers*)

Gentlemen, I think that the policy by which the Government of India was actuated in issuing this notification was a most suicidal one, because the Government of India, as the paramount power, naturally expects the Native State to be administered properly To be administered properly it is necessary that the Government of India and the local Government should be accurately informed of the real state of affairs in those States. The only means of obtaining reliable information is by means of a free press, and, if that is gagged, the outlet for the available information is shut out. Now, if there is any thing rotten in the Native States it must affect the paramount power of the Government of India, and I will, therefore, ask you to enter your emphatic protest against this, and to pass this Resolution. (*Cheers*)

Gentlemen, by way of illustration, take up the case of Hyderabad, the first Native State in India. It has a population of 10 millions (*Hear, hear*) of whom $\frac{9}{10}$ths are Hindus and $\frac{1}{10}$th Mahomedans and other nationalities. It has a ruler who is very just, and there is a Prime Minister who is a very amicable man; and there are some Secretaries able and honest, but unfortunately the general administration of Hyderabad is anything but satisfactory. The Police Administration is something disgraceful; you must havo read in the papers only recently that there have been two instances of high-handedness by the Kotwal, Akbar Jung. (*Hear, hear*)

**Fourth Day.**

**Resolution XIX. Liberty of the Press.**

**Mr. P. Ramachandra Pillai.**

One was the case of a Marwadi who was forcibly turned out of the house with his wife at the instance of his landlord, without an order of a Court of justice, and his property, which was worth Rs. 50,000, taken and sold For the last six or eight months the man has been petitioning the various Secretaries and the Minister, but nothing has been done. That is one instance. There is another which is a more disgraceful one. Two learned Sanyasis belonging to the Arya Samaj, who are now seated on the dais, were lecturing in Hyderabad. This man Akbar Jung had the audacity to send for these gentlemen and tell them that they were preaching against the Moslem religion and that they must leave Hyderabad. (*Shame*) Their lectures were listened to with attention by all people, Mahomedans, Parsees, and Christians, and not a man said that there was any thing in their lectures which was objectionable; and what was the result? These Sanyasis had to leave Hyderabad and come to Secunderabad where they delivered their lectures, and immediately after, their paid preacher and Pandit was kept in confinement and eventually deported from Hyderabad without any inquiry. (*Shame*) Petitions poured into the Government, but no redress has yet been granted. I quote these two instances by way of illustration to show with what arbitrary power the Police is exercising its functions in Hyderabad, and thus it is, therefore, all the more necessary that there should be a press to ventilate these grievances. Gentlemen, you know the reason why I asked some of my friends to take up this subject,—in order that, perhaps, the matter might be more forcibly placed before you by persons like Babu Surendra Nath Banerjea or some other person of commanding eloquence; but I was confident that this august body, consisting, as it does of gentlemen of culture and experience, did not require eloquence or particular social position to commend the arguments to their judgment. I therefore feel confident, Gentlemen, that you will pass the Resolution with acclamation. (*Cheers*)

**Mr. G. Subramania Aiyer.**

Mr. G. Subramania Aiyer:—Mr. Chairman and Brother Delegates, I have great pleasure in seconding this proposition. Mr. Ramachandra Pillai seems to regret that he was not able to secure an eloquent speaker to commend this proposition to you. But I do not think any very great eloquence is wanted to secure your approbation on behalf of this proposition. Well, Gentlemen, it is rather late in the day to plead for the liberty of the Press. I do not believe the British Indian Government is prepared to contend that under any circumstances a free press can be anything but a blessing to the people, and it seems to me to be a peculiar inconsistency on the part of the British Government in India, that while it tolerates a free press in its own dominions it should place it under any restraint in those parts of the land which are under its direct administration in the Native States. Gentlemen, oftentimes these small spots of land are the places of refuge to those who are victims of misgovernment in Native States, and glad and thankful as I am to acknowledge that in many Native States great improvement has taken place on all lines of administration, yet there are still a few important, though small, Native States which are scandalous for misgovernment and maladministration. (*Hear, hear*) Nowhere is the light of criticism more needed than in some of these Natives States; and we of the Congress and the educated community generally of India have often been found fault with for not taking up and criticising matters relating to the Native States. But, Gentlemen, how is it possible under the policy which is pursued in regard to native states by the British Government? And, even supposing that all these Native States become paragons of good government, even supposing that no maladministration prevails, does it follow that a free Press will be anything but an advantage? It may be said that this retrograde and absurd policy has been adopted at the suggestion and request of the rulers of these Native States. But we have always been under the impression that it was the duty of the paramount Government to discourage all these senseless and foolish eccentricities on the part of those rulers, because if a native ruler

Fourth Day.

Resolution XIX. Liberty of the Press.

Mr. G Subramania Aiyer.

makes an absurd request it does not follow that the British Government should grant it especially when the granting of that request tends to perpetuate maladministration. There fore, Sir, I think that a long speech to commend this proposition to you is not wanted. It is inconsistent with the principle of the British Government and with their traditions; and I think it only requires the matter to be brought to the notice of the Government for its being annulled immediately. (*Cheers*)

The Resolution was put to the vote and carried.

Resolution XX. Water-cess.

Mr. G. Venkataratnam.

Mr. G. Venkataratnam:—Mr. President and Brother Delegates, the Resolution that I have the honour to submit for your acceptance runs as follows:—

"That this Congress views with apprehension the arbitrary policy of the Government of India with regard to the imposition of water-cess, introducing as it does a disturbing element in taxation, and suggests that the imposition of the said cess be regulated by certain defined principles affording security to the rights of landowners and of persons investing money in land'

This subject of Water-cess comes for the first time before the Congress. It is one of very great importance, as it affects not only the Madras Presidency, but also the North-West Provinces and the Punjab. wherever State irrigation works exist. Any measure aiming at fixity of tenure and permanence of land assessment would be practically useless in the case of irrigated lands, unless there be also fixity of water-cess demand. The charge for water forms in such cases the larger portion of the payment made to Government. The landowner gains therefore little or nothing by a permanent settlement of merely land assessment, so long as the water-cess is liable to fluctuations at the pleasure of Government. Whether the lands are ryotwari lands subject to periodical evisions of settlement, or enfranchised Inams, or permanently settled estates, they are alike subject to the payment of water-cess, if they take water for irrigation purposes from Government Works. The policy of the Government of India in regard to water-cess is, to quote its own words "that a fair commercial value should "be put upon all water supplied, provided that the price charged is not so great as to bar its "use on lands which really derive benefit from canal irrigation." This policy is applicable to the whole of India. In this Presidency this policy is embodied in the provisions of Act VII, of 1865, known as the Madras Water Cess Act. The so-called principle underlying the Act is that the Government should derive "a fit return" on the outlay incurred on irrigation works by the imposition of water-cess on lands irrigated thereby. The Government has power to levy the cess at such rates as it thinks fit, to enhance them at pleasure, to frame such rules as it thinks fit, and to alter or amend the same at pleasure.

This policy, the commercial policy, has in its practical application failed in giving security to rights of property in land and in causing any very material alteration for the better in the general condition of the agricultural population, for whose benefit these irrigation works were primarily intended. This element of uncertainty is fully illustrated by the recent action of the Government of Madras in the Districts of Tanjore, Godavery and Kistna. What in fact the Government gives the cultivator with one hand it apparently takes away from him with the other. In Tanjore, the Government raised the water rates by about 50 per cent In the Godavery and Kistna Deltas, the rates were suddenly raised by a stroke of the pen by 25 per cent. in the case of all lands irrigated for five years consecutively. This was done in the midst of the current agricultural year, without any inquiry, without any notice to the parties concerned, and without even consulting the local officer of the District (*Shame*) And what is worse, the notification enhancing the cess was issued after the time prescribed for filing applications for discontinuance of water had expired, after the sowing and transplanting season had advanced, and after the ryots had taken water in the full confidence that they would have to pay for it only at such rates as had been prevailing at the commencement of the Fasli. To crown all this, the Government tried to give a colour of legality to this procedure by issuing another notification, nearly a month afterwards, that is, on the 13th September, extending the time for relinquishment of water till the 15th September. The Government probably overlooked the fact that it was a physical impossibility for the Gazette containing this notification to reach the hundreds of villages in the Districts within 24 hours! From the very nature of things the extension granted was only an extension in name, as none of the cultivators could avail themselves of it, inasmuch as the cultivation season had advanced too far. When the Government was interpellated on this subject at the last meeting of the Legislative Council, the Government found itself unable to justify its action in enhancing the cess during the course of the year, and had to invoke the aid of rules, superseded more than twelve years ago, denying to the ryots the option, the full option, allowed under the rules in force at the commencement of the Fasli (*Cheers*)

Another significant circumstance is that the capital outlay on the irrigation works in question has long since been amply repaid. The Government has been making a clear profit on the transaction. The Godavery Delta, according to the latest Administration Report available, after paying an interest of 4 lakhs and odd, gave, in 1892-93, a surplus revenue of 13 lakhs and odd and a total surplus revenue of 271 lakhs and odd up to 1892-93, after paying interest on the capital amount The Kistna Delta is similarly a paying concern, the surplus revenue therefrom being 134 lakhs and odd, and the net return being 8·87 per cent. The value of irrigation works cannot be measured merely by the amount of revenue realised by Government on account of water-cess. The large increase in land revenue, customs, income-tax and other taxes in the said Districts is in a great measure due to the construction of these irrigation works. (*Hear, hear*)

While, therefore, the Government has been making such large direct profit and participating also in the indirect benefits of these irrigation works, it is preposterous to say that it has not been receiving "a fit return" for its outlay, even assuming the soundness of the principle of treating works of this kind as an independent source of revenue. The arbitrary enhancement of the cess under such circumstances, and that too with retrospective effect, as the Government has practically done in the present instance, cannot be defended either on any known commercial principles or on considerations of fiscal justice. This, coupled with the extraordinary position taken by the Government in upholding its action even after its attention was called to the illegality thereof by means of memorials and interpellations, has created a sense of insecurity, and the Government has to thank itself if the public have come to think that its water-cess policy is above all regulations and rules. (*Cheers*)

While revisions of settlement are presumed to proceed upon some defined principles, the water-cess seems to recognise no such principle; "fair commercial value" and "fit return" are very vague expressions. What is the limitation to the so-called "fit return"? The Government does not care whether the cess-payer receiyes a fair return for the cess he pays, nor does it trouble itself as to whether its demand is not actually trenching upon the cess-payer's share of the produce Irrigated lands suffer from over-assessment of both land tax and water-coss. If it was the policy of the old District officers, so to regulate their assessment as to make the people regard their individual holdings as their own, and to stimulate their industry, and if, in fact, they attached greater importance to remote rather than to proximate consequences, and acted on the principle that Government revenue would increase as the people advanced in prosperity, their successors have been unfortunately pursuing quite a different policy, in which the commercial principle seems to be in the ascendant. (*Cheers*) This policy is fully explained by Sir Charles Aitchison in the following words:—

"In these days when money is sorely needed to meet on every hand the growing demand for improvements, not to speak of the Military Sink into which so much of it is poured, there is a strong temptation to force up the assessment. It is a dangerous policy. The mischief of over-assessment is insidious. The millions of India are as yet voiceless. It

Fourth Day.

Resolution XX. Water-cess.

Mr. G. Venkataratnam.

is not the cry of the tillers of the soil that is borne on the Press. They suffer in silence, and their sorrows reach the ear of authority only when the mischief is done, when the wells get out of gear, when the cultivation grows slowly, when the transfers of land to the moneyed classes are so frequent as to attract official notice, when men begin to leave their ancestral homes, when perhaps the seeds of revolution have been sown. Great as the development of India has been it is much retarded by the want of agricultural capital. In spite of all her material improvements, and new industries, unexampled growth of trade, and great addition to the general wealth, India is almost a purely agricultural country. But she is no longer the sole consumer of her own produce. She is coming every day into wider competition with other agricultural countries in the markets of the world. If she is to succeed, old methods must give way to better, and capital must be accumulated to provide the improvements. For this a margin of profit must always be left to the landowner. A system of assessment which periodically dips into every increase requires to be carefully supervised at all times. One injudicious turn of the screw may do mischief to a district which cannot be repaired in one or two generations." (*Cheers*)

These are weighty words, coming as they do from one of the ablest Lieutenant Governors that ever ruled in this country. It is high time that we should enter our emphatic protest against the present retrograde policy—a policy not only highly detrimental to the best interests of the people, but also opposed to the traditions of good Government. This Government is not a commercial speculator, but a Government to whose care is committed the well-being of a numerous population. Its policy in respect of land assessment or water cess should stand on a higher footing, and, while not retarding the progress of agriculture and industry, should be so shaped as to afford security to the rights of landowners and persons investing money in land. (*Cheers*)

Mr. V. V. Avadani.

Mr. V. V. Avadani:—Mr. President and Brother Delegates, I rise to second the proposition so ably and exhaustively moved by my predecessor. He has placed before you the arbitrary policy of the Government, and has shown you how it is arbitrary in its character and how it is proving injurious in its practical working. He has also told you the circumstances under which the enhancement of water-cess by 25 per cent., on the existing amount of water-cess, was raised in the deltas of the Kistna and the Godavery Rivers by the local Government, undor the direction of the Government of India. The class of subjects that are directly interested in the matter of the payment of the water-cess have not even been so much as consulted. There are several thousands of landholders, ryots, mirasidars and agraharamdars in the Districts who are affected by the imposition of this new burden. There are several public bodies like the Kistna District Association in several centres of these two Districts, whose opinion has not been asked for on this vital question. Not one of the thousands of persons directly affected by the Government Notification ever knew anything of the imposition before the publication of the unwelcome news in the official *Gazette*. It came upon them, Gentlemen, like a thunderbolt. Sir, is this state of things possible in any other dependency of the British Empire than dumb India? Is there any other country where taxation is resorted to without consulting the wishes of the tax-payer? Is this state of things possible in Ireland, Canada, or Australia? Is this not proof positive that the Government is arbitrary, and means to be arbitrary? The case of the Kistna and Godavery Districts is much worse than that of Tanjore, to which reference has been made. Before the re-settlement opefations commenced in that District, its people had been heard. His Excellency, Lord Wenlock heard them and tried, though inadequately, to redress their grievances. But in the case of the Kistna and Godavery deltas, in the matter of the enhancement of water-cess, the Government has not thought well to hear the people or their accredited agents. (*Shame*)

Although the Government of Madras is said to have written to the Imperial Government not to raise the water-cess before the re-settlement of the land revenue. which will be

**Fourth Day.**

**Resolution XX. Water-cess.**

**Mr. V. V. Avadani.**

made in the near future, its word has not been heeded. A peremptory mandate has been issued. Why, it may be asked, why this precipitate urgency? The answer is simple. The Imperial Exchequer must find new sources of income to meet the deficit caused by the growing demands of the compensation allowance, home charges, and military expenditure. In reply to the question put by the Hon'ble Mr. N. Subba Rao, to the local Government on the subject, it was stated that the rise in the price of grain was the main reason for enhancing the water-cess. The argument seems plausible on the face of it. But examine it with a little scrutiny and you will see its speciousness. In the Kistna District an acre of land yields a putti, or candy, of paddy a year on an average. The price of a putti to the ryot at the time of the harvest is but Rs. 20 on an average. But you will have to deduct from this the necessary expenses incident to wet cultivation, *viz.*, cost of manuring the field, the cost of transplanting, the cost of cultivation, the cost of reaping the crop, the land revenue, the water-cess, the road-fund, the local and other cesses; and these will hardly leave Rs. 2 per acre as a margin to the over-worked ryot. But the Government of Madras in its reply has taken into account not what the paddy fetches to the ryot at the time of the harvest, when he usually sells it to meet the payment of Government dues, but the average of the price of paddy throughout the year in the general market. This then is the error which brings about those imaginary higher prices which have led the Government to believe that the ryot is growing richer than ever. The Government of Madras further thinks that the ryots will not relinquish their holdings by reason of this enhancement, and therefore feels itself safe in raising the tax. Is this the policy that a Government should adopt? (*Cries of* No, No) The Government ought to bear in mind that within the deltas in question the staple produce is paddy, and the bulk of the people are engaged from morning till evening in its cultivation, and are unfit for any other walk of life by force of habit. Hence is the dire necessity for them to fight against odds, to contract debt after debt, and drag on a famished existence. In conclusion, Gentlemen, if it is not desirable to give cause for discontent and disaffection to a large section of British subjects, who are agriculturists by profession, as well as that still larger portion of subjects, the consumers of rice; if it is not desirable to follow the purely mercantile policy of screwing out every pie from the hard pressed and hard-pushed, long enduring ryot; if it is desirable to lend the hand of timely succour to the agriculturists of the benighted parts of this Presidency in their unavailing efforts to relieve themselves of the weighty burden of over 14 lakhs of rupees, I call upon you—I beseech you—and others—delegates of this noble Congress, to sympathise with the distressing situation of your brethren in the delta tracts by passing this resolution. (*Cheers*)

**Mr. S. B. Sankaram.**

Mr. S. B. Sankaram:—I have only three minutes before me, Gentlomen, and my voice is hoarse, so you must excuse me if I do not do justice to the subject in hand. Five years ago, about this time, I appeared in the Bombay Congress, adorned with the presence of the late lamented Charles Bradlaugh, (*Cheers*) to bring my humble self, then a member of the Vizagapatam Volunteer Rifles forward, as a proof in flesh and blood that we Indians are fit for Volunteer service. To-day I stand before you to show that we are not the representatives of ourselves but the representatives of a people, for I am here before you to-day elected by 23 villages of the Ellore Taluq in the Godavery District. (*Heav, hear*) The interest that is evinced by those ryots is shown wnen I tell you that some of those very ryots are to-day in this pandal as delegates. Gentlemen, although I am not chosen by any scientific mode of election, to quote Mr. Pherozeshah Mehta, I am a representative of those 23 villages. Now, it is not right for me to tell you a long tale of the sufferings of the ryots, after you have already heard the two speakers who have gone before me. Well, I briefly tell you that our ryots are endowed with brains, and they put these sorts of questions to those that are in authority:—When you say that the revenues of one department are to be utilised for that department alone, and there is such a surplus of the water revenue, why impose this tax unexpectedly? You tell us that the Water Cess Act contains words that

Fourth Day.

Resolution XX. Water-cess.

Mr. S. B. Sankaram.

show that it can be increased at pleasure; but never had we believed before the date of imposition of this cess that the pleasure mentioned in the Act would be the pleasure of anybody but a Russian autocrat; we always believed that it would not be the pleasure of a constitutional Government. Now, Gentlemen, they ask the Government if it is not for such a purpose, as the improvement of water works, but for an imperial purpose, how is it that all the burden is thrown upon the shoulders of the ryot, and especially upon the ryots of the Godavery and Kistna Districts, the ryots cultivating wet land for the past five years? Then as to the procedure adopted in raising this tax, I tell you that no time was allowed them It came at a time when it would be impossible for the ryot to reject the water tax levied on the 15th September for water that had been taken in the months of June and July Now, Gentlemen, with these supplications they approach those who are responsible for the imposition of these additional and unjust taxes. (*Cheers*)

The Resolution was put to the vote and carried.

Resolution XXI. Indian Colonists in South Africa.

The President:—I have received an important letter from the Gooty Association through Mr. Kesava Pillai, drawing our attention to a subject which in the pressure of business has been lost sight of by us, *viz.*, the position of our fellow countrymen in the African Colonies. I now move.

That this Congress earnestly entreats Her Majesty's Government to grant the prayer of Her Majesty's Indian subjects, resident in the South African Colonies, by vetoing the Bill of the Colonial Government disenfranchising them.

This Resolution was put to the vote and carried.

The President:—I would now ask Mr. Ghosal to read the Twenty-second Resolution, which will also be moved from the Chair.

Resolution XXII.

Deputations to Lord Elgin and Mr. Fowler.

Mr. Ghosal —The twenty-first resolution on the agenda now becomes the twenty-second resolution which runs as follows:—

That a deputation consisting of the following gentlemen be appointed for the purpose of presenting Resolutions numbered 1, 2, 3, 6, 7, 8, 9, 11, 12, 13, 14, 15, 16, 17, 18, 19, 20 and 21 to His Excellency Lord Elgin; and that the British Committee of the National Congress be requested to arrange a similar deputation to wait upon the Secretary of State for India in London.

*From Bengal and Behar*:—His Highness the Maharajah Bahadur of Durbhanga, Sir Romesh Chunder Mitter, *Kt.*, The Honorable Mr. W. C. Bonnerjee, The Honorable Mr. Surendra Nath Banerjea, Mr. J. Ghosal, Babu Saligram Sing, Mr. Shurefuddin, Rai Jotendranath Chaudhuri and Babu Boikunt Nath Sen.

*From the North-West Provinces*:—The Honorable Rajah Rampal Singh and The Honorable Baboo Charoo Chandra Mittra.

*From Oudh*:—Sheikh Rajah Hussein Khan, Mr. Hamid Ali Khan and Baboo Gokal Chand,

*From the Punjab*:—Sirdar Dayal Singh Majithia, Baboo Kali Prosonno Roy, Mr. Jussawala Shaik Umar Buksh, Lala Murlidhar and Bakshi Jaishi Ram.

*From Bombay*:—The Honorable Mr. P. M. Mehta, C.I.E.

*From the Central Provinces*:—The Honorable Mr. G. M. Chitnavis and Rai Bahadur C. Narainswami Naidu.

*From Poona*:—Rao Bahadur V. M. Bhide, Mr. S. B. Bhate, Mr. N. B. Mule and Mr. P, L. Nagpurkar.

*From Berar*:—Rao Saheb Deorao Vinayek.

*From Madras*:—Manivikram Rajah of Calicut, The Honorable Mr. Sabapathy Mudaliar, Rao Bahadur P. Ananda Charlu and Mr. G. Subramania Iyer."

The President will, of course, head the deputation.

The President:—I beg to move this Resolution. Let those who are in favour of it hold up their hands (*Voices, All, All*)

The Resolution was carried unanimously.

Fourth Day.

Resolution XXIII. British Committee Grant.

Hon. Mr. Surendra Nath Banerjea.

The President :—The Twenty-third Resolution will be moved by the Hon'ble Babu Surendra Nath Banerjea

The Hon Mr. Surendra Nath Banerjea :—Mr. President and Brother Delegates, the Resolution, which is intrusted to me, runs as follows :—

That a sum of Bs. 60,000 be assigned for the expenses of the British Committee and the cost of the Congress publication, "*India*," and that the several circles do contribute as arranged, either now, or hereafter in Committee, for the year 1895.

Gentlemen, this is a business resolution, and it will not require many words from me to recommend it to your earnest and enthusiastic acceptance. This resolution was substantially the resolution which you accepted last year. This was the resolution which you substantially accepted the year before. In 1892 you provided a sum of Rs. 60,000 for the purpose of meeting the expenses of the British Committee and of our organ, *India*. Last year you also provided a sum of Rs. 60,000 for the same purpose. I hope, therefore, no difficulty will be raised in the way of the unanimous acceptance of this resolution. Gentlemen, you will remember that, in the beginning of this year, we initiated a departure—I was going to observe a memorable departure—in our financial programme. Hitherto we had relied solely and exclusively, at any rate very largely, upon subscriptions and donations. Subscriptions and donations come in fitfully and capriciously. They are a weak reed to rely upon. You cannot rest upon so slender a foundation, and it was therefore thought necessary that we should make a departure. Human nature demands a *quid pro quo*, and we were resolved to satisfy this immutable law of nature. The *quid pro quo* that we wanted to give was our organ, *India*. We resolved last year to raise the circulation of *India*, to 10,000 copies. Ten thousand copies would mean Rs. 60,000. Rs. 60,000 would cover the expenses of the British Committee and of *India*. I may perhaps, with your permission, enter somewhat into the details of the calculations. You spend about £2,000 a year for the maintenance of *India* £1,000 for the support of the British Committee. Your expenses, therefore, really come up to about £3,000. But in these days of the depreciated rupee and with no one to grant us exchange compensation allowance, (*Cheers*) we are compelled to provide a sum of Rs. 60,000. Well, Gentlemen, it must not, for one moment, be imagined that we discard subscriptions and donations. I am a Brahmin, and I may claim for myself that I am a Brahmin of Brahmins. My hereditary profession is to beg, not to borrow or steal. (*Laughter*) I am prepared to stretch out the right hand of a Brahmin to receive any subscription or donation that any gentleman may be prepared to give me at the present moment. We do not theiefore discard subscriptions or donations. We thankfully receive them whenever they are offered. We thankfully received Rs. 10,000 from my noble friend, the Rajah of Ramnad, who, I am glad to say, was present on the platform the other day. But, at the same time, as I have already remarked, we cannot always be expecting these subscriptions and donations. An institution which depends wholly and solely upon them depends upon very weak foundations indeed. Gentlemen, we initiated this departure, and what was the amount that you budgeted last year? You budgeted a sum of Rs. 60,000 (At this stage a cheque for Rs. 600 was handed in to the speaker) I have just received from the Hon'ble Mr. Sabapathy Mudaliar Rs. 600 on account of subscription for a hundred copies of *India* for 1894 for the Bellary public. Are there not gentlemen assembled in this Congress ready and valiant enough to follow the noble example (*Cheers*) of this distinguished countryman of ours? Well, Gentlemen, we provided a sum of Rs. 60,000, and how much did we realise? I am told, by my friend, Mr. Morgan-Browne, that we have realised only two-thirds of the amount subscribed, and, when Madras pays in the arrears (I am quite confident that Madras will pay up the arrears before we separate), then the amount will possibly be raised to three-fourths of the sum that was subscribed. The charge that we bring in season and out of season against the Government of this country

**Fourth Day.**

Resolution **XXIII.**

British Committee Grant.

HON. MR. SURENDRA NATH BANERJEA.

is that it makes solemn promises and sacred pledges, and that these promises and pledges are broken. Let not the same charge be brought against the delegates of the National Congress. Let it not be said that we make pubhc and ostentatious professions of self-sacrifice, but that, when the hour of performance comes, we are not equal to the occasion. I am anxious for your honour. If you have a particle of self-respect, if you care aught for your chartered rights, if you feel the smallest concern for the political advancement of your children and your children's children, then I ask you to subscribe whatever is possible for you to pay down for the promotion of those interests, which are identified with the Congress movement. (*Cheers*) I think we are about 3,000 of us here assembled, including the spectators—I say sympathetic spectators—and I take it that Englishmen must sympathise with us in our struggles for political liberty. (*Cheers*) We are about 3,000 of us assembled here. Well, if the 1,500 delegates were each to undertake to procure subscribers for at least 10 copies of *India*, the number would amount to 15,000 copies. We should be in a position to raise Rs. 90,000, *i.e.*, Rs. 30,000 in excess of the demands of the British Committee. This is not a difficult task, this is not an impossible task. What is Rs. 60,000 when rateably divided amongst a population of 200 millions of human beings? What is Rs. 60,000 when we take into consideration the vast sums of money that our Rajahs and our Princes and our great men expend for the entertainment of big officials. (*Cheers*) Well, Gentlemen, the other day they had no difficulty in raising I think it was Rs. 75,000 for a statue for Lord Lansdowne. You gentlemen of Bombay are deploring the fact that there are people in that Presidency so lost to all considerations of patriotism that they have interested themselves in the movement for the purpose of erecting what purports to be a national memorial in honour of Lord Harris. (*Shame*) A shameful procedure it is, and, I think, as a protest against these dishonourable demonstrations, we, the men of the Congress, ought to be able to show that we are prepared to pay at least as much for the sake of the Congress as these men are prepared to pay for the gods of their worship. Gentlemen, I think, the outlook is very hopeful. We have got in England our own organisation in the British Committee. We have our own organ, *India*. We have a Parliamentary Committee ready to supplement the efforts of the British Committee, and we have this vast gathering of this National Congress which serves to communicate the impetus to the movement along the entire line. It seems to me that the outlook is an exceedingly hopeful one. The prospect before us is bright and it is becoming brighter and brighter day by day. I ask you, brother delegates, standing here facing those distant generations who are to come after us, is it not our duty, the highest that we owe to ourselves, the highest that we owe to our families, the highest that we owe to our Maker, to improve this golden opportunity, to plant those seeds which, when they fructify, will be fraught with unspeakable blessings to the people of this country? (*Cheers*) I feel that at this critical time in the history of India anybody who fails to do his duty to the National Congress stands condemned before the eyes of God and man. I can conceive of no holier duty, no more sanctified trust, than that we should improve the golden opportunity before us. Make it the occasion of a splendid future for generations yet unborn. (*Cheers*) I ask you, brother delegates, to rise to the height of the occasion, to the solemnity of our mission. Do your duty to the National Congress by unloosing your purse strings. Do the duty that is yours, pay what you have to give; it will be fruitful to the giver, it will be helpful to after-generations. (*Cheers*) I desire that this motion may be carried with acclamation. (*Cheers*)

The Resolution was carried by acclamation.

Resolution **XXIV**

Vote of Thanks to British Committee.

THE PRESIDENT :—I now put the next resolution to the vote which is as follows :—

That this Congress hereby tenders its most grateful thanks to Sir W. Wedderburn and the other members of the British Congress Committee for the services rendered by them to India during the present year.

The Resolution was carried by acclamation.

Fourth Day.

THE PRESIDENT:—I now put the next resolution to the meeting, *viz:*—

Resolution XXV Appointment of General Secretary.

That this Congress re-appoints Mr. A. O. Hume, C.B., to be its General Secretary for the ensuing year. (*Cheers*)

The Resolution was carried by acclamation.

MR. V. M. BHIDE, then moved the following resolution:—

Resolution XXVI. Meeting Place of XIth Congress.

That the Eleventh Indian National Congress do assemble on such day after Christmas day, 1895, as may be later determined upon, at Poona.

It is proposed to hold this Congress next year at Poona. My duty on this occasion is very simple. I am an inhabitant of Poona, and I come to invite all my brother delegates to the Congress to be held at Poona in the next Christmas holidays, and I hope that you will all come. We shall be very happy to receive you and do all we can to suit your convenience and pleasure. (*Hear, hear*)

MR. JUGMOHANDAS VRANDRAVANDAS:—On behalf of Bombay, I most cordially welcome you to the city of Poona next year.

The Resolution was carried with acclamation.

THE PRESIDENT:—We shall now go to the Twenty-seventh Resolution, which runs as follows:—

Resolution XXVII. Constitution of Congress.

THE PRESIDENT.

That this Congress is of opinion that the time has come when the constitution of the Congress should be settled, and rules and regulations laid down as to the number of Delegates, their qualifications, the localities for assemblage, and the like, and in this view the Congress requests the Standing Congress Committee of Poona to draw up draft rules and circulate them among the different Standing Congress Committees for their reports; these reports together with the draft rules and the report thereon to be laid before the next Congress for its consideration.

Let as many of you as are of opinion it should be passed hold up their hands (*Voices, All, All*) That closes the business of the Congress. But there are one or two formal matters. There is a notification which states that if the meeting closes before sunset, the photographer wants to take a group consisting of the President, members of the Subjects Committee, and as many delegates as may wish to attend.

Vote of Thanks to the Chair.

MR. P. SOMASUNDRAM CHETTIAR:—Mr. President and Gentlemen, I rise with the greatest happiness and pleasure to express, on behalf of the Delegates of the National Congress now here assembled, as well as on behalf of the inhabitants of this Presidency, of which I am an old inhabitant, our warm and grateful thanks to you from the bottom of our hearts for having kindly presided as President of this Assembly, and for your leaving your country for this laudable purpose, and we hope that you and Mr. Seymour Keay as members of the House of Commons, will endeavour as far as you can to alleviate all the grievances which we have now laid before you.

RAI BAHADUR P. ANANDA CHARLU:—The proposition placed before you is one concerning the President. Therefore as he cannot put it to the vote, it devolves upon me to do so.

The proposition was carried with Cheers.

President's Reply

THE PRESIDENT:—Friends and fellow subjects,—I address you in the same terms with which I commenced my opening address a few days ago, but I would add now dear friends and dear fellow subjects, I have felt quite overpowered by your kindness and consideration since I came to this country, and I feel additionally overpowered by this renewed mark of your kind feelings towards me. At this late hour of the evening it is quite impossible for me to do justice to such a Resolution as that which has now been passed. In so far as my

**Fourth Day.**

**President's Reply.**

efforts to conduct this Congress in a proper and dignified manner have been successful, in so far it has been owing to your good feeling and to the help and consideration that I have received from you. I has been particularly due to the kind friends that have sat round this table and to whom I have been constantly able to appeal for advice and assistance. In returning thanks I may surely, on behalf of the delegates, return thanks to the Madras Reception Committee, the chairman and the members—for their reception and entertainment of us all. Whilst it would be impossible to name all those to whom we are under obligations, I cannot, on my own account, refrain from referring to a few. I should like to name Messrs. P. Rungiah Naidu, Ananda Charlu, Sankara Nair, G. Parameswaram Pillai, Viraraghava Chariar, and J. Goshal; and, in addition to these gentlemen, I desire to thank the Volunteers for the help that they have given. (*Hear, hear*) In remarking upon the splendid arrangements made here, I am sure they are largely due to the Volunteeus, and on my own account—an old man who has come amongst you—I feel as if they had treated me with almost filial attention and kindness I feel it very deeply, and I shall never forget their kindness to me here. In so far, Gentlemen, as there has been any friction here, in so far as any one may feel hurt by my hastiness in the chair, or cutting them short, (*No, no!*)—anything of that kind is entirely due to myself; I alone am responsible for it, and I am sure you will make every allowance. What I have particularly admired in this assemblage has been the manly spirit—the manly spirit of your delegates—the spirit in which you have spoken out for your country, the manly and loyal spirit which cannot but in the end prevail. I should like to urge this upon you—the keeping down of all class or local differences. These have not indeed been apparent in my private conversations with members of every class and from all districts. In the house, as well as here, I have never found an inkling of that, and I would beg of you, if ever a shade or a shadow of such suspicions enter your hearts, put them from you. Everyone here has been actuated by a sincere desire to serve not party, or caste, or district, but your common and beloved country. (*Loud Cheers*)

There is one other request—prayer I might almost say—that I would desire to urge upon you, that you should put from you the demon of personality. Never in your sittings let the question of personality enter into your proceedings. Everyone here has common rights, and is entitled to take part in the proceedings of the Congress. No one has a higher idea than myself of the necessity that there is of entering upon political objects in a high and pure spirit—that great objects are best obtained by good men. I cannot refrain from repeating the lines of an Irish poet, referring to the spirit of nationality. He says:—

> It whisper'd too, that Freedom's ark,
> A service high and holy,
> Should not be marr d by passions dark,
> And feelings vain and lowly.
>
> For Freedom comes from God's right hand,
> And needs a goodly train;
> And righteous men must make our land
> A nation once again.

True, Gentlemen, but we cannot judge anyone here. It is for districts and for the constituencies to judge as to the proper men to send up, but once here they must be received on a footing of equality. (*Cheers*) Gentlemen, I do entreat that you should press forward. Do not so much consider how soon you are going to obtain your objects. You have already obtained an absolute good in holding these Congresses. Were the whole of this Congress movement to be swept away, it would leave memories that would never die. You have already attained a great good; this movement can never die. You yourselves are scarcely aware how much you have gained in advancing the spirit of unity and love. Press forward! Keep up your movement! (*Loud Cheers*)

Gentlemen, perhaps now I might say a few words in reference to myself. Might I make a confession, I never felt so lonely the last thirty or forty years of my life as I did on the steamer coming here. But the moment I touched the shore at Bombay those feelings vanished. and the moment I reached the station here, all misgivings faded away, and I felt renewed with a strong spirit. I felt no misgivings as to my ability to take this chair. (*Cheers*)

Now, Gentlemen, it is with a feeling of intense sadness that I here bid you good bye. You are all young and hearty, and you will meet again and again in these Congresses ; but I am an old man (*No, no*), and in a very few days the heavy curtain of 6,000 miles will pass down between us. My earnest hope is that I shall see you again, and again take part in your proceedings. (*Hear, hear*) But, however this may be, Gentlemen, I shall always regard this as one of the greatest—I may say one of the happiest—experiences of my life. It has doubled my responsibilities, and with feelings that I cannot properly give expression to, I beg to thank you most heartily for the kind resolution you have passed to-day. (*Loud and enthusiastic Cheers*)

Three cheers were then given for Her Majesty the Queen-Empress, for Mr. A. O. Hume, for the British Committee, and for Mr. Dadabhai Naoroji, M. P. and the Tenth Indian National Congress dissolved.

# APPENDIX

# LIST OF DELEGATES

WHO ATTENDED THE

# Tenth Indian National Congress,

## HELD AT MADRAS, DECEMBER, 1894.

| Number. | Presidency or Government. | Congress Circle. | Electoral Division. | Names in full of Delegates, with Honorary Titles, Scholastic Degrees, etc. | Race, Religious denomination, and caste, if any. | Occupation and Address. | How, and when elected. |
|---|---|---|---|---|---|---|---|
| 1 | Madras | Madras | IV, V, VI. Municipal Divisions. | Hon. Mr. P. Rungaya Naidu Caru. | Vysya. | Zemindar, Vakil, High Court; President, Mahajana Sabha; Member, Madras Legislative Council. | By a Public Meeting held on the 18th December 1894. |
| 2 | „ | „ | „ | Rajah Sir Savalai Ramasawmy Mudaliar, K.C.I.E. | Hindu. | Dubash, Ashburnham and Co. | do |
| 3 | „ | „ | „ | Dr. S. Pulney Andy... | Christian. | Medical Practitioner. | do |
| 4 | „ | „ | „ | Mr. M. Doraisamy Pattar. | Hindu Sudra. | Partner in Messrs Arulanadum & Sons. | do |
| 5 | „ | „ | „ | „ N. Krishnaswami Naidu, B.A., B.L. | Hindu Vysya. | Vakil, High Court ... | do |
| 6 | „ | „ | „ | „ C. Krishnan ... | Hindu Malayali. | Barrister-at-Law ... | do |
| 7 | „ | „ | „ | „ K. Rajagopaula Chariar, B.A., B.L. | Hindu Brahmin. | Vakil, High Court ... | do |
| 8 | „ | „ | „ | „ C S. Theagaraja Mudliar | Hindu. | Merchant ... | do |
| 9 | „ | „ | „ | „ V. Arunagiri Naidu | do | do ... | do |
| 10 | „ | „ | „ | Rai Bahadur A. Danaketi Mudliar | do | Landed Proprietor ... | do |
| 11 | „ | „ | „ | Mr. C. Ranganadam Naidu | do | do | do |
| 12 | „ | „ | „ | „ G. Paramaswaram Pillai, B.A. | do | Editor. *Madras Standard.* | Do. also by Students Meeting, Triplicane, the Kerala Mahajana Sabha, by the I and II Municipal Divisions and at Calicut and Palghat, Malabar. |

| Number. | Presidency or Government. | Congress Circle. | Electoral Division. | Names in full of Delegates, with Honorary Titles, Scholastic Degrees, etc. | Race, Religious denomination, and caste, if any. | Occupation and Address. | How and when elected. |
|---|---|---|---|---|---|---|---|
| 13 | Madras | Madras | IV, V, VI. Municipal Divisions. | Mr. K. Ramanuja Chariar | Hindu Brahmin. | Teacher ... | By a Public Meeting held on the 18th December 1894. |
| 14 | " | " | " | " Iyaswamy Pillai... | Hindu. | Banker ... | do |
| 15 | " | " | " | " K. Narayana Rao, B.A., B.L. | Brahmin. | Vakil, High Court ... | do |
| 16 | " | " | " | " S. K. Nayar ... | Hindu Nayar. | Staff of the *Madras Standard.* | do |
| 17 | " | " | " | Rev. T. B. Pandian. . | Indian Christian. | Minister ... | do |
| 18 | " | " | " | Mr. S. Subraya Chariar, B.C.E. | Brahmin. | Retired Executive Engineer. | do |
| 19 | " | " | " | " V. Thirumalai Pillai | Hindu Sudra. | Attorney-at-Law ... | do |
| 20 | " | " | " | " T. S. Muthusawamy Sastriar | Hindu Brahmin. | Tutor Madras Christian College. | do |
| 21 | " | " | " | " T. Runga Chariar, B.A., B.L. | Hindu Brahmin Vishnavite. | High Court Vakil, Ananda Bagh, Egmore. | do |
| 22 | " | " | " | " T. Streenivas ... | Hindu. | Barrister-at-Law, Egmore. | do |
| 23 | " | " | " | " M. Thirumala Chariar. | Brahmin. | Banker and Money Lender. | do |
| 24 | " | " | " | " T. V. Arogiasawmy Pillai, M.A., B.L. | Christian. | Assistant Professor, Pachhiappa College. | do |
| 25 | " | " | " | " W. Raju Naidu ... | do | Editor, *Eastern Star.* | do |
| 26 | " | " | " | " D. J. Melchizedek. | do | Apothecary ... | do |
| 27 | " | " | " | Rai Bahadur P. Ananda Charlu, B.A., B.L. | Hindu Brahmin. | Vakil, High Court ... | do |
| 28 | " | " | " | Mr. J. C. Ganesh Sivaraja Jogi | " | 335 Thambu Chetty Street. | do |
| 29 | " | " | " | " V. Ethirajulu Naidu | Hindu Sudra. | Secretary, Vannekula Sangham; Merchant, Pudupet. | do |
| 30 | " | " | " | Moulvie Hajee Ziya-ud-deen Mahamad | Masalman | Skin Merchant ... | do |
| 31 | " | " | " | Haji Sheikh Fursat Sahib | do | Skin Merchant and Mirasidar | do |
| 32 | " | " | " | Mr. V. Ryru Nambiar, B.A., B.L. | Hindu Nayar | Vakil, High Court ... | do |
| 33 | " | " | " | " P. Aiyasawmy Mudliar, M.A., B.L. | Hindu Sudra | do ... | do |
| 34 | " | " | " | V. Masilamoney Pillai, B.A., B.L. | Hindu. | Vakil, High Court, Pursewaukum | do |

| Number. | Presidency or Government. | Congress Circle. | Electoral Division. | Names in full of Delegate with Honorary Titles, Scholastic Degrees, etc. | Race, Religious denomination, and caste, if any. | Occupation and Address. | How and when elected. |
|---|---|---|---|---|---|---|---|
| 35 | Madras | Madras | I, III, Municipal Divisions. | Mr. P. Subrahmania Chetty | Hindu Sudra. | Merchant ... | By a Public Meeting held on the 12th December 1894. |
| 36 | ,, | ,, | ,, | ,, C. B. Samuja Chetty | Vysya, Syvite. | do ... | do |
| 37 | ,, | ,, | ,, | ,, P. N. Muthusawmy Naidu | Hindu. | do ... | do |
| 38 | ,, | ,, | ,, | ,, P. Murugesa Chetty | do | Landholder ... | do |
| 39 | ,, | ,, | ,, | ,, Sreeramulier Naidu | do | Merchant ... | do |
| 40 | ,, | ,, | ,, | ,, C. Subbau Rao Saheb | do | Jaghirdar ... | do |
| 41 | ,, | ,, | ,, | ,, C. G. Mursalim Rowthar | Masalman. | Merchant ... | do |
| 42 | ,, | ,, | ,, | ,, P. M. Mahamad Makdum Rowthar. | do | do ... | do |
| 43 | ,, | ,, | ,, | ,, V. Jagannadhan Naidu | Hindu Sudra | Manager, City P. and P. Co., Seven Wells Street | do |
| 44 | ,, | ,, | ,, | ,, T. S. Theagaraja Iyer, B.A., B.L. | Brahmin. | Vakil, High Court, Black Town | do |
| 45 | ,, | ,, | ,, | ,, A. Subramania Iyer | do | Teacher, Christian College, Madras | do |
| 46 | ,, | ,, | ,, | ,, N. Lakshmanasawmy Mudliar, B.A. | Hindu Sudra. | Tutor, Christian College | do |
| 47 | ,, | ,, | ,, | ,, B. Parthasarathy Naidu | do | Merchant, 34 Subraya Mudali Street, Black Town | do |
| 48 | ,, | ,, | ,, | ,, B. Ramasawmy Naidu | do | do | do |
| 49 | ,, | ,, | ,, | ,, P. Doraisawmy Mudliar, B.A, B.L. | do | Vakil, High Court; Secretary, People's Club | do |
| 50 | ,, | ,, | ,, | ,, N. R. Adipuranam Pillai | do | Dubash, Binny & Co., Madras | do |
| 51 | ,, | ,, | ,, | ,, K. M. M. S. T. Somasundaram Chetty | do | Merchant, Coral Merchant Street | do |
| 52 | ,, | ,, | ,, | ,, M. Varada Chetty | Hindu Vysya. | Vakil, High Court ... | do |
| 53 | ,, | ,, | ,, | ,, P. V. Krishnaswami Chetty, B.A., B.L. | do | do ... | do |
| 54 | ,, | ,, | ,, | ,, C. Ramanuja Chetty | do | Government Pensioner, Trivettur High Road | do |

| Number. | Presidency or Government. | Congress Circle. | Electeral Division. | Names in full of Delegates, with Honorary Titles, Scholastic Degrees, etc. | Race, Religious denomination, and caste, if any. | Occupation and Address. | How and when elected. |
|---|---|---|---|---|---|---|---|
| 55 | Madras | Madras | I, III Municipal Divisions. | Mr. C. V. Sundram Sastriyar | Hindu Brahmin. | Vakil, High Court ... | By a Public Meeting held on the 12th December 1894. |
| 56 | " | " | " | " C. V. Kumaraswamy Sastriar | do | do ... | do |
| 57 | " | " | " | " C. V. Visvanada Sastriar | do | Apprentice-at-Law... | do |
| 58 | " | " | " | " B. Punchapa Kesa Sastriar, B.A., B.L. | do | Vakil, High Court ... | do |
| 59 | " | " | " | " P. B. Krishnasawmy Naidu | Sudra | Dubash, Agents, Spencer & Co. | do |
| 60 | " | " | " | " P.B. Moonasawmy Chetty | Hindu | Merchant ... | do |
| 61 | " | " | " | " G. Subrayulu Chettiyar | Vysya | Merchant, Coral Merchant Street | do |
| 62 | " | " | " | " A. Balajee Sing... | Mahratta | Contractor ... | do |
| 63 | " | " | " | " M. M. Rajagopala Chariar | Brahmin | do ... | do |
| 64 | " | " | " | " C. S. Rajaratnam Mudliar | Sudra | Merchant ... | do |
| 65 | " | " | " | " P. Krishnasawmy Mudliar | do | Broker, Eales & Co... | do |
| 66 | " | " | " | " Sankara Narayana Shastriar | Brahmin | Vakil, High Court ... | do |
| 67 | " | " | " | Miss Müller, B.A., Cam.. | European | House Proprietor, London and Member, London School Board | do |
| 68 | " | " | " | Mr. T. Venkata Subbiar, B.A., B.L. | Brahmin | Vakil, High Court ... | do |
| 69 | " | " | " | " T. S. Narayana Shastriar, B.A. | do | Law Student | do |
| 70 | " | " | " | " S. Subbiah Chettiar | Vysya | Attorney-at-Law ... | do |
| 71 | " | " | " | " A. V. Subramania Iyer, B.A., B.L. | Brahmin. | Vakil, High Court ... | do |
| 72 | " | " | " | " T. V. Apparao Naidu | Hindu. Andi. Vellama | Merchant and Special Magistrate, Sembiam | do |
| 73 | " | " | " | " T. Krishnasawmy Chetty | Hindu. | Merchant, 8 Guruwappen Street | do |
| 74 | " | " | " | " S. Annu Chetty.... | do | do ... | do |
| 75 | " | " | II Municipal Division. | " P. Somasundram Chettiar | Hindu Sudra | Merchant ... | By a Public Meeting held on the 16th December 1894. |
| 76 | " | " | " | " K. Ramanuja Chariar, B.A. | Brahmin | Tutor, Pachhiappa's College | do |

| Number. | Presidency or Government. | Congress Circle. | Electoral Division. | Names in full of Delegates, with Honorary Titles, Scholastic Degrees, etc. | Race, Religious denomination, and caste, if any. | Occupation and Address. | How and when elected. |
|---|---|---|---|---|---|---|---|
| 77 | Madras | Madras | II. Municipal Division. | Mr. Bisesarnath Chaudik | Kshattrya | Merchant ... | By a Public Meeting held on the 16th December 1894. |
| 78 | „ | „ | „ | „ P. Desikachari, B.A. | Brahmin | Teacher, Pachhiappa's College. | do |
| 79 | „ | „ | „ | „ N. Balasubramania Mudliar, M A. | Hindu Sudra | Pachhiappa's College. | do |
| 80 | „ | „ | „ | „ T. Sitarama Chetti. | Vysya | Merchant, Moses & Co., Mount Road | do |
| 81 | „ | „ | „ | „ P. M. Sivagnana Mudliar, B.A., B.L. | Hindu | Vakil, High Court ... | do |
| 82 | „ | „ | „ | „ T. Ethiraju Mudliar | do | do ... | do |
| 83 | „ | „ | „ | „ C. Venkata Subramania Iyer, B.A., B.L. | Brahmin | do ... | do |
| 84 | „ | „ | „ | V. Chengalya Vardappa | do | do ... | do |
| 85 | „ | „ | „ | „ K. Venkata Lingam Chetti | Hindu. | do ... | do |
| 86 | „ | „ | „ | „ M. Venkata Rao... | Brahmin. | Merchant ... | do |
| 87 | „ | „ | „ | „ S. Gurusawmy Chettiar, B.A., B.L. | Vysya. | Vakil, High Court, Black Town | do |
| 88 | „ | „ | „ | „ S. Thirumalaisawmy Chettior, B.A., B.L. | do | do ... | do |
| 89 | „ | „ | „ | „ Bysani Rungiah Chetty | do | Merchant ... | do |
| 90 | „ | „ | „ | „ S. Nathusawmy Chetty | do | Vakil, High Court ... | do |
| 91 | „ | „ | „ | „ S. Varadarajulu Chetty, B.A., B.L. | do | do ... | do |
| 92 | „ | „ | „ | „ N. S. Rajaram Iyer | Brahmin. | Landholder and Merchant | do |
| 93 | „ | „ | „ | „ S. P. Ramakrishna Naidu | Hindu. | Landholder, 24, Krishna Street, Muthialpett | do |
| 94 | „ | „ | „ | „ C. Ethirajulu Chettiar | Vysya. | Merchant ... | do |
| 95 | „ | „ | „ | „ T. Doraisawmy Iyer | Brahmin. | Cashkeeper, Messrs. Parry & Co. | do |
| 96 | „ | „ | „ | „ A. Kondiah Chettiar | Vysya. | Merchant, Armenian Street | do |
| 97 | „ | „ | „ | „ Venkata Krishnama Chetty | do | Merchant ... | do |
| 98 | „ | „ | „ | „ G. T. Alwar Chettiar | do | Merchant and Landholder | do |

| Number. | Presidency or Government. | Congress Circle. | Electoral Division. | Names in full of Delegates, with Honorary Titles, Scholastic Degrees, etc. | Race, Religious denomination, and caste, if any. | Occupation and Address. | How and when elected. |
|---|---|---|---|---|---|---|---|
| 99 | Madras | Madras | VII. Municipal Division. | Mr. P. S. Raghava Charriar, B.A. | Brahmin. | Teacher, Pachhiappa's College | By a Public Meeting held on the 16th December 1894. |
| 100 | ,, | ,, | ,, | ,, R. Sriramulu Shastriar, B.A., B.L. | do | Vakil, High Court, Adiapa Naicker Street, Black Town | do |
| 101 | ,, | ,, | ,, | ,, Krishnama Charriar, B.A., B.L. | do | Vakil, High Court, Mint Street | do |
| 102 | ,, | ,, | ,, | ,, S. P. Venkata Ramanajulu Naidu | Hindu. | Ship Dubash ... | do |
| 103 | ,, | ,, | ,, | ,, P. Venkatachella Mudliar B.A. | do | Teacher, Christian College. | do |
| 104 | ,, | ,, | ,, | ,, W. A. Krishnasawmy Iyer | Brahmin. | Medical Practitioner, Triplicane | do |
| 105 | ,, | ,, | ,, | ,, C. Gopala Row ... | do | Teacher, Pachhiappa's College. | do |
| 106 | ,, | ,, | ,, | ,, Trikutam Subba Row | do | Landholder (Gooty), now at Summer House, Triplicane. | Do. & by a Special Meeting of the Hindu Progressive Union, Triplicane, held on the 18th November 1894. |
| 107 | ,, | ,, | ,, | ,, M. K. Lakshmana Charriar | do | Agent, Life Insurance Company, Bombay. | By a Public Meeting held on the 16th December 1894. |
| 108 | ,, | ,, | ,, | ,, T. Ruplal ... | Hindu Gujerati. | Landlord & Merchant. | do |
| 109 | ,, | ,, | ,, | ,, T. Balakrishna Doss | do | do ... | do |
| 110 | ,, | ,, | ,, | ,, W. Uttam Chand. | do | do ... | do |
| 111 | ,, | ,, | ,, | ,, C. Thirumalai Naidu | Hindu. | Landlord ... | do |
| 112 | ,, | ,, | ,, | ,, B. V. Krishna Rao | Brahmin. | Superintendent, Bellary Bank | do |
| 113 | ,, | ,, | ,, | ,, A. C. Parthasarathy Naidu | Hindu. | Editor, *Andra Prakashika* | do |
| 114 | ,, | ,, | ,, | ,, P. K. Kothandurama Iyer, B.A., B.L. | Brahmin. | Vakil, High Court ... | do |
| 115 | ,, | ,, | ,, | ,, M. A. Singra Chariar | do | Cashier, Madras Bank | do |
| 116 | ,, | ,, | ,, | ,, M. A. Gopala Chari, B.A., B.L. | do | Vakil, High Court ... | do |
| 117 | ,, | ,, | ,, | ,, M. A. Parthasarathy Iyengar, B.A., B.L. | do | do ... | do |
| 118 | ,, | ,, | ,, | ,, A. Bhimasena Rao. | do | Manager, *Janopakarani* Office | do |

| Number. | Presidency or Goverment. | Congress Circle. | Electoral Division. | Names in full of Delegates, with Honorary Titles, Scholastic Degrees, etc. | Race, Religious denomination, and caste, if any. | Occupation and Address. | How and when elected. |
|---|---|---|---|---|---|---|---|
| 119 | Madras | Madras | VII Municipal Division. | Mr. C. Kamalanatham Naidu | Hindu. | Coach Builder, Mount Road | By a Public Meeting held on the 16th December 1894. |
| 120 | " | " | " | " G. Sivarama Brahmagnyanam | Brahmin. | Joint Editor, *Andra Prakashika* | do |
| 121 | " | " | " | " Peter Paul Pillai... | Christian Velala. | Agent, Landholders' Association | do |
| 122 | " | " | " | " V. Krishnasawmy Iyengar, B.A., B.L. | Brahmin. | Merchant, 8 Guruwappa Street | do |
| 123 | " | " | " | " C. N. Kalyanasundara Mudliar | Sudra. | Clerk, Madras Bank... | do |
| 124 | " | " | " | G. Varada Naidu... | do | Shrotriamdar, Chintadripet | do |
| 125 | " | " | " | " T. Ganshyam Singh | Rajput. | Proprietor, City Stables | do |
| 126 | " | " | " | " K. Srinivasa Raghava Iyengar, B.A., B.L. | Brahmin. | Vakil, High Court ... | do |
| 127 | " | " | " | " S. Samana, B.A. ... | do | Landlord, Mill Owner | Do., also by a Public Meeting of the Students of Madras on the 21st December 1894. |
| 128 | " | " | " | " Bashyam Iyengar, B.A. | do | Chemists and Druggists, Tilplicane | By a Public Meeting held on the 16th December 1894. |
| 129 | " | " | " | " A. Viraraghava Chariar | do | Clerk, Madras Bank | do |
| 130 | " | " | " | " S. Raghava Chariar | do | Contractor ... | do |
| 131 | " | " | " | " M. Viraraghava Chariar | do | Manager, *The Hindu.* | do |
| 132 | " | " | " | " A. Krishnaswamy Iyer | do | Yogi ... | do |
| 133 | " | " | " | " P. Krishna Rao, L.M.S. | do | Surgeon, 117 Viraraghava Mudali Street. | do |
| 134 | " | " | " | " D. R. Balaji Rao, B.A., B.L. | do | Vakil, High Court ... | do |
| 135 | " | " | " | " A. Sankaran Iyer, B.A., F.M.U. | do | Retired Dewan Peshkar, Cochin, 21 Nallatambi Street, Triplicane. | do |
| 136 | " | " | " | " G. Subramania Aiyar, B.A. | do | Editor, *The Hindu* ... | do |
| 137 | " | " | " | " S. Varada Chari ... | do | Partner, Messrs. Srinivasa Varadachari & Co. | do |

| Number. | Presidency or Government. | Congress Circle. | Electoral Division. | Name in full of Delegates, with Honorary Titles, Scholastic Degrees, etc. | Race, Religious denomiuation, and caste, if any. | Occupation and Address. | How and when elected. |
|---|---|---|---|---|---|---|---|
| 138 | Madras | Madras | VII Municipal Division. | Mr. S. Srinivasa Chari. | Brahmin | Partner, Messrs. Srinivasa Varadachari & Co. | By a Public Meeting held on the 9th December 1894. |
| 139 | „ | „ | „ | „ Parathasarathy Iyengar | do | Yogi ... | do |
| 140 | „ | „ | VIII Municipal Division. | „ P. R. Sundram Iyer, B.A., B.L. | do | Vakil, High Court ... | do |
| 141 | „ | „ | „ | „ S. Gopalaswamy Aiyengar | do | do ... | do |
| 142 | „ | „ | „ | „ T. Raja Gopalachari, M.A., B.L. | do | Head Master, Wesleyan Mission College, Royapettah | do |
| 143 | „ | „ | „ | „ T. R. Ramanatha Iyer, B.A., B.L. | do | Vernacular Superintendent, Pachhiappa's College | do |
| 144 | „ | „ | „ | „ K. P. Sankara Menon, B.A., B.L. | Hindu Malayali Sudra | Vakil, High Court, Mylapore | do |
| 145 | „ | „ | „ | „ K. Srinivasa Iyengar, B.A., B.L. | Brahmin | do ... | do |
| 146 | „ | „ | „ | „ R. Kuppusawmy Iyer, B.A., B.L. | do | do ... | do |
| 147 | „ | „ | „ | „ M. Punithavelu Mudliar, B.A. | Hindu Sudra | Land Owner, Mylapore | do |
| 148 | „ | „ | „ | „ M. Manikam Mudliar. | do | Contractor ... | do |
| 149 | „ | „ | „ | „ P. Subramania Iyer, B.A., B.L. | Brahmin | Attorney-at-Law, Mylapore | do |
| 150 | „ | „ | „ | „ R.. Subramania Iyer, B.A., B.L. | do | Vakil, High Court, Mylapore | do |
| 151 | „ | „ | „ | „ A. Ramamurthi Mudliar. | Hindu Sudra | Vakil's Clerk, Mylapore | do |
| 152 | „ | „ | „ | „ M. Venugopal Pillai. | do | Banker and Government Pensioner | do |
| 153 | „ | „ | „ | „ M. Swaminada Mudliar. | do | Landholder, Mylapore | do |
| 154 | „ | „ | „ | „ V. R. Kuppusamy Iyer, B.A., B.L. | Brahmin | Vakil, High Court ... | do |
| 155 | „ | „ | „ | „ Eardley Norton. | European | Barrister-at-Law, Dunmore House, Mylapore | Do., also by Mylapore and Triplicane Municipal Divisions, the Students of Madras the Triplicane Literary Union, and the Hindu Progessive Union. |

| Number. | Presidency or Government. | Congress Circle. | Electoral Division. | Names in full of Delegates, with Honorery Titles, Scholastic Degrees, etc. | Race, Religious denomination, and caste, if any. | Occupation and Address. | How and when elected. |
|---|---|---|---|---|---|---|---|
| 156 | Madras | Madras | VIII. Municipal Division. | Mr. R. Runga Row, B.A., B.L. | Mahratta Brahmin | Vakil, High Court, Mylapore | By a Public Meeting held on the 9th December 1894. |
| 157 | " | " | " | " V. C. Sesha Chariar, B.A., B.L. | Brahmin | do ... | do |
| 158 | " | " | " | " T. V. Vaidyanada Iyer, M.A. | do | Professor, San Thome College | do |
| 159 | " | " | " | " T. Jivaji Row, B.A., B.L. | do | Vakil, High Court ... | do |
| 160 | " | " | " | " C. S. Raja Gopala Chariar | do | Landlord, Mylapore | do |
| 161 | " | " | " | " Venkata Mahapathi Naidu | Sudra | Landlord ... | do |
| 162 | " | " | " | " M. R. Ramakrishna Iyer, B.A., B.L. | Brahmin | Vakil, High Court ... | do |
| 163 | " | " | " | " T. Rangaramanuja Chariar, B.A., B.L. | do | do ... | do |
| 164 | " | " | " | " E. Venkatarama Sarma, B.A., B.L. | do | do ... | do |
| 165 | " | " | " | " C. R. Tiruvenkata Chariar, B.A., B.L. | do | do ... | do |
| 166 | " | " | " | " V. Suryanarayana Rao, B.A., B.L. | do | do ... | do |
| 167 | " | " | " | " R. Venkata Subba Rao, B.A., B.L. | do | do ... | do |
| 168 | " | " | " | " V. Krishnasawmy Iyer, B.A., B.L. | do | do ... | do |
| 169 | " | " | " | Syed Mahamad Sahib Bahadur | Masalman | Landlord, Adyar ... | do |
| 170 | " | " | " | Mr. V. Runga Chariar, B.A., B.L. | Brahmin | Vakil, High Court ... | do |
| 171 | " | " | " | " V. C. Desika Chariar, B.A., B.L. | do | do ... | do |
| 172 | " | " | " | " Kasthuriranga Iyengar B.A., B.L., | do | do ... | do |
| 173 | " | " | " | Dewan Bahadur S. Soobramanya Iyer, C.I.E., B.A., B.L. | do | Vakil, High Court, The Luz, Mylapore | do |
| 174 | " | " | " | Mr. R. Balajie Row, B.L. | do | Vakil, High Court, Mylapore | do |
| 175 | " | Tanjore. | Mayavaram | " M. S. Natesa Aiyar | do | Mirasidar, Mayavaram | By a Public Meeting held on the 24th November 1894. |
| 176 | " | " | " | " N. P. Krishnaswamy Iyer | do | Schoolmaster, Municipal High School. | do |

| Number. | Presidency or Goverment. | Congress Circle. | Electoral Division. | Names in full of Delegates, with Honorary Titles, Scholastic Degrees, etc. | Race, Religious denomination and caste, if any. | Occupation and Address. | How and when elected. |
|---|---|---|---|---|---|---|---|
| 177 | Madras. | Tanjore | Mayavaram | Mr. N. P. Srinivasa Iyer, B.A., L.T. | Brahmin | Asst. Master, Municipal High School. | By a Public Meeting held on the 24th November 1894. |
| 178 | " | " | " | " S. Narayanaswamy Iyer, B.A. | do | Head Master, Municipal High School. | do |
| 179 | " | " | " | " S. Vaidyanathier. | do | Pleader ... | do |
| 180 | " | " | " | " A. V. Subramania Iyer | do | Mirasidar and Municipal Councillor | do |
| 181 | " | " | " | " I. Kodandaramier. | do | Mirasidar ... | do |
| 182 | " | " | " | " Swamiada Pillai | Hindu Velala | do ... | do |
| 183 | " | " | " | " M. Sivaswamy Shastriar | Brahmin | 1st Grade Pleader ... | do |
| 184 | " | " | " | " K. Latchmana Iyer | do | Municipal Councillor and Honorary Magistrate | do |
| 185 | " | " | Negapatam. | " S. Kuppusawmy Iyer, B.A., B.L. | do | Vakil, High Court, Negapatam. | By Public Meetings held on the 27th November and 5th September 1894. |
| 186 | " | " | " | " T. B. Panchapakesa Chettiar | Hindu Sudra | Landholder .. | do |
| 187 | " | " | " | " R. Srinivasa Iyengar, B.A. | Brahmin | Landholder, Pleader, Member District and Taluq Boards, Tanjore and Negapatam | do |
| 188 | " | " | " | " P. Rathnasabhapathi Pillai, B.A. | Hindu Velala | Vakil, District Court | do |
| 189 | " | " | " | " G. S. Ramasawmy Iyer | Brahmin | Professor, Wesleyan Mission College | do |
| 190 | " | " | " | " R. Vahideva Naidu | Hindu Sudra | Schoolmaster ... | do |
| 191 | " | " | " | " Kunjithapatham Iyer, B.A., B.L. | Brahmin | Pleader ... | do |
| 192 | " | " | " | " T. S. Sivavadinahi Udayar | Hindu | Landlord .. | do |
| 193 | " | " | " | " K. Krishna Row. | Brahmin | Pleader ... | do |
| 194 | " | " | " | " C. A. Subramania Iyer, B.A. | do | do ... | do |
| 195 | " | " | " | " P. T. Tincaninatha Shastri. | do | do ... | do |
| 196 | " | " | " | " B. S. Nataraja Snastri, B.A., B.L. | do | do ... | do |
| 197 | " | " | " | " S. A. Balakrishna, B.A., B.L. | do | do ... | do |

| Number. | Presidency or Government. | Congress Circle. | Electoral Division. | Names in full of Delegates, with Honorary Titles, Scholastic Degrees, etc. | Race, Religious denomination, and caste, if any. | Occupation and Address. | How and when elected. |
|---|---|---|---|---|---|---|---|
| 198 | Madras | Tanjore | Patukota. | Mr. Vijaya Raghunatha Thirumalai Singupuliar | Hindu Sudra | Zemindar, Kollarkota. | By a Public Meeting held on the 15th December 1894. |
| 199 | ,, | ,, | ,, | ,, P. V. Ramachandra Iyer | Brahmin | Journalist, Tanjore ... | do |
| 200 | ,, | ,, | ,, | ,, T. S. Govindaswamy Pillai | Hindu | Mirasidar ... | do |
| 201 | ,, | ,, | ,, | ,, K. F. N. Naina Mahamad Lavvai Marakayar Avergal. | Masalman. | Merchant ... | do |
| 202 | ,, | ,, | ,, | ,, S. Ramaswamy Iyer | Brahmin | Pleader ... | do |
| 203 | ,, | ,, | Mannargudi. | ,, Gopalasawmy Iyengar | do | School Manager, Mannargudi | By a Public Meeting held on the 11th November 1894. |
| 204 | ,, | ,, | ,, | ,, Sadagopa Mudliar | Hindu Velala | Mirasidar, Kottur ... | do |
| 205 | ,, | ,, | ,, | ,, K. G. Srinivasa Mudliar | do | Mirasidar, Municipal Councillor, Mannargudi | do |
| 206 | ,, | ,, | ,, | ,, D. Kuppusawmy Iyer | Brahmin | Mirasidar ... | do |
| 207 | ,, | ,, | ,, | ,, V. Anantharaman Iyer | do | Merchant | do |
| 208 | ,, | ,, | ,, | ,, R. Rajappier ... | do | Municipal Councillor and Member, Taluq Board | do |
| 209 | ,, | ,, | ,, | ,, S. Venkataramier. | do | Mirasidar ... | do |
| 210 | ,, | ,, | ,, | ,, Dasaratha Rama Iyer | do | do ... | do |
| 211 | ,, | ,, | ,, | ,, A. J. Doraiswamy Mudliar | Hindu Sudra | Landholder ... | do |
| 212 | ,, | ,, | ,, | ,, S. Ramadurai Iyer | Brahmin | Mirasidar | do |
| 213 | ,, | ,, | Nannilam. | ,, G. S. Subramania Iyer | do | Pleader, Negapatam. | By a Public Meeting held on the 1st November 1894 |
| 214 | ,, | ,, | ,, | ,, S. Srinivasa Raghava Chariar | do | Vakil, District Court. | do |
| 215 | ,, | ,, | ,, | ,, M. Chidambaram Pillai | Hindu Velala | Vakil, High Court ... | do |
| 216 | ,, | ,, | ,, | ,, P. Sabhapathi Iyer | Brahmin | Mirasidar ... | do |
| 217 | ,, | ,, | ,, | ,, G. Sambasiva Aiyar Avergal. | do | Mirasidar and Pleader | do |

| Number. | Presidency or Government. | Congress Circle. | Electoral Division. | Names in full of Delegates, with Honorary Titles. Scholastic Degrees, etc. | Race, Religious denomination, and caste, if any. | Occupation and Address. | How and when elected. |
|---|---|---|---|---|---|---|---|
| 218 | Madras | Tanjore | Mannargudi | Mr. A. Thiagaraja Iyer | Brahmin | Landholder ... | By a Public Meeting held on the 1st November 1894 |
| 219 | ,, | ,, | ,, | ,, S. Krishnasawmy Iyengar | do | Mirasidar ... | do |
| 220 | ,, | ,, | ,, | ,, Ramchandra Naidu | Hindu | Landholder, Member, District and Taluq Boards | do |
| 221 | ,, | ,, | ,, | ,, Govindaswamy Iyer | do | Landholder and Member, District Board | do |
| 222 | ,, | ,, | ,, | Rai Bahadur S. A. Swaminada Iyer | Brahmin | Government Pleader, Tanjore; Landholder and Member, District Board and Devasthanam Committee | By a Public Meeting held on the 2nd December 1894. |
| 223 | ,, | ,, | ,, | Mr. S. A. Ananthanarayana Iyer, B.A., B.L. | do | Vakil, High Court ... | do |
| 224 | ,, | ,, | ,, | ,, S. Ramachandra Iyer, B.A., B.L. | do | do ... | do |
| 225 | ,, | ,, | ,, | ,, C. Gopal Row, B.A., B.L. | do | Mirasidar ... | do |
| 226 | ,, | ,, | ,, | ,, C. Rajagopal Pillai | Hindu Velala | do ... | do |
| 227 | ,, | ,, | ,, | ,, T. V. Kuppusawmy Shastriar, B.A. | Brahmin | Pleader and Landholder | do |
| 228 | ,, | ,, | Tanjore. | ,, T. N. Ramier, B.A., B.L. | do | Pleader ... | do |
| 229 | ,, | ,, | ,, | ,, T. Sadasiva Row, B.A., B.L. | do | Vakil, High Court and Mirasidar | do |
| 230 | ,, | ,, | ,, | ,, S. Venkatasubbier. | do | Pleader ... | do |
| 231 | ,, | ,, | ,, | Hon. Mr. K. Kalayanasundaram Iyer, B.A., B.L. | do | Vakil, High Court and Landholder, Member, Madras Legislative Council | do |
| 232 | ,, | ,, | ,, | ,, K. S. Srinivasa Pillai. | Hindu Velala. | Pleader and Municipal Councillor | do |
| 233 | ,, | ,, | ,, | ,, G. P. Subramania Pillai, B.A., B.L. | Brahmin. | Vakil, High Court ... | do |
| 234 | ,, | ,, | ,, | ,, Bucharam Sahib Sirdar | Kshattriya. | Tanjore Royal Family. | do |
| 235 | ,, | ,, | ,, | ,, Raghunatha Jadava Rao Sahib | do | do ... | do |
| 236 | ,, | ,, | Tiruvalur. | ,, M. Ramanada Iyer, B.A. | Brahmin. | Pleader ... | By a Public Meeting held on the 25th November 1894. |

| Number. | Presidency or Government. | Congress Circle. | Electoral Division. | Names in full of Delegates, with Honorary Titles, Scholastic Degrees, etc. | Race, Religious denomination and caste, if any. | Occupation and Address. | How and when elected. |
|---|---|---|---|---|---|---|---|
| 237 | Madras | Tanjore | Tiruvalur | Mr. K. Virasawmy Iyer | Brahmin | Second Grade Pleader and Union Chairman. | By a Public Meeting held on the 24th November 1894. |
| 238 | ,, | ,, | ,, | ,, T. K. Ramaswamy Iyer | do | Pleader ... | do |
| 239 | ,, | ,, | ,, | ,, N. Vaithinada Aiyar | do | do ... | do |
| 240 | ,, | ,, | ,, | ,, T. R. Vaithinada Aiyar | do | do ... | do |
| 241 | ,, | ,, | ,, | ,, K. S. Krishnaswamy Iyengar | do | Vakil, District Court. | do |
| 242 | ,, | ,, | ,, | ,, K. Ramaswami Shastrial | do | Pleader and Landholder | do |
| 243 | ,, | ,, | ,, | ,, T. Somasundaram Mudliar | Sudra. | Mirasidar ... | do |
| 244 | ,, | ,, | ,, | ,, K. Sesha Iyer ... | Brahmin. | Landholder and Retired Magistrate | do |
| 245 | ,, | ,, | ,, | ,, A. Varadaraja Iyengar | do | Landlord ... | do |
| 246 | ,, | ,, | Combaconum. | ,, S. Krishnasamy Iyer, B.A. | do | Head Master, Town High School | do |
| 247 | ,, | ,, | ,, | ,, N. Krishnasawmy Iyengar, B.A., B.L. | do | Vakil, High Court and Mirasidar | do |
| 248 | ,, | ,, | ,, | ,, T. S. Sivaswamy Iyengar | do | Honorary Magistrate and Municipal Councillor | do |
| 249 | ,, | ,, | ,, | ,, A. L. Thiruvengadam Pillai | Hindu Velala. | Mirasidar and Municipal Councillor | do |
| 250 | ,, | ,, | ,, | ,, P. Thambisawmy Mudliar | Indian Christian. | Mirasidar and Municipal Councillor | do |
| 251 | ,, | ,, | Kuttalam. | ,, M. R Ramanadier, B.A. | Brahmin. | Pleader ... | By a Public Meeting held on the 16th November 1894. |
| 252 | ,, | ,, | Shiyali. | ,, N. Natesa Iyer ... | do | Mirasidar ... | By a Public Meeting held on the 24th November 1894. |
| 253 | ,, | ,, | ,, | ,, C. Sabanayaga Mudliar | Hindu Velala. | do ... | do |
| 254 | ,, | ,, | Tiruvadi. | ,, N. C. Srinivasa Chari | Brahmin | Mirasidar and Pleader | By a Public Meeting held on the 26th November 1894. |
| 255 | ,, | ,, | ,, | ,, K. K. Ramier, B.A. | do | Head Master, High School | do |
| 256 | ,, | ,, | Tiruturaipundi. | ,, G. Venkatarenga Chariar | do | Pleader and Member Union | By a Public Meeting held on the 22nd November 1894. |

| Number. | Presidency or Government. | Congress Circle. | Electoral Division. | Names in full of Delegates, with Honorary Titles, Scholastic Degrees, etc. | Race, Religious denomination and caste, if any. | Occupation and Address. | How and when elected. |
|---|---|---|---|---|---|---|---|
| 257 | Madras | Tanjore | Tiruturaipundi | Mr. Ramalinga Mudliar | Hindu Velala. | Mirasidar ... | By a Public Meeting held on the 22nd November 1894. |
| 258 | „ | Trichinopoly. | Srirangam, | „ K. S. Kuppusawmy Aiyengar | Brahmin. | do ... | By a Public Meeting held on the 4th December 1894. |
| 259 | „ | „ | „ | „ Sadarasanam Chakram Aiyangar | do | Jewel Merchant ... | do |
| 260 | „ | „ | „ | „ Kovalagudi Rengaswamy Iyengar | do | Mirasidar and Municipal Councillor | do |
| 261 | „ | „ | „ | „ S. Ramanujam Iyengar | do | Pleader and Municipal Councillor | do |
| 262 | „ | „ | Lalgudi. | „ T. Kanagasabasa Pillai | Hindu | Mirasidar, Kuhur ... | By a Public Meeting held on the 25th November 1894. |
| 263 | „ | „ | „ | „ A. Chidambara Iyer | Brahmin. | Mirasidar ... | do |
| 264 | „ | „ | „ | „ A. K. Narayanaswamy Iyer, B.A., B.L. | do | Valuer and Contractor | do |
| 265 | „ | „ | „ | „ Annaswamy Iyer. | do | Mirasdar, Lalgudi ... | do |
| 266 | „ | „ | Trichinopoly | „ Vyasa Row, B.A. ... | do | Assistant Professor of Science, S. P. G. College | By a Public Meeting held on the 4th December 1894. |
| 267 | „ | „ | „ | „ T. Sadasiva Tawker | do | Merchant ... | do |
| 268 | „ | „ | „ | „ Umamabeswara Iyer | do | Mirasidar and Municipal Councillor | do |
| 269 | „ | „ | „ | „ T. S. Palaniswamy Pillay, B.A., B.L. | Hindu Velala | Vakil, High Court ... | do |
| 270 | „ | „ | „ | „ S. R. Rengaswamy Aiyengar, B.A., B.L. | Brahmin | Landholder and Vakil | do |
| 271 | „ | „ | „ | „ S. Kuppusawmy Sarma, B.A., B.L. | do | Vakil, High Court and Member, District Board | do |
| 272 | „ | „ | „ | „ S. R. Krishnaswamy Iyengar | do | Mirasidar, Srirangam | do |
| 273 | „ | „ | „ | „ K. Vasudeva Iyengar | do | Mirasidar and Municipal Commissioner, Srirangam | do |
| 274 | „ | „ | „ | „ T. R. Kuppuswamy Iyengar | do | Pleader, Municipal Commissioner and Member, District Board | do |
| 275 | „ | „ | „ | „ R. Kuppuswamy Iyengar | do | Pleader ... | do |

| Number. | Presidency or Government. | Congress Circle. | Electoral Division. | Names in full of Delegates, with Honorary Titles, Scholastic Degrees, etc. | Race, Religious denomination, and caste, if any. | Occupation and Address. | How and when elected. |
|---|---|---|---|---|---|---|---|
| 276 | Madras | Trichinopoly | Trichinopoly | Mr. K. Srinivasa Raghava Iyengar | Brahmin | Mirasidar ... | By a Public Meeting held on the 4th December 1894. |
| 277 | ,, | ,, | ,, | ,, L. S. Ramachandra Iyer B.A., B.L. | do | Vakil, High Court and Member, District Board | do |
| 278 | ,, | ,, | ,, | ,, P. G. Sundaresa Shastriar, B.A. | do | Manager, National High School | do |
| 279 | ,, | ,, | ,, | ,, M. A. Tirunarayana Achari, B.A., B.L. | do | Vakil, High Court ... | do |
| 280 | ,, | ,, | ,, | ,, R. M. P. Venkatesa Row | do | Mirasidar, Peranur... | do |
| 281 | ,, | ,, | ,, | ,, M. S. Anantharatnam Iyer | do | Mirasidar and Honorable Magistrate | do |
| 282 | ,, | ,, | ,, | ,, C. Chellappa Chettiar | Hindu | Vakil and Municipal Councillor | do |
| 283 | ,, | ,, | ,, | ,, Tulagaram Tawker | Brahmin. | Merchant ... | do |
| 284 | ,, | ,, | ,, | ,, T. V. Sanjeeva Rao | do | Pleader ... | do |
| 285 | ,, | ,, | ,, | ,, P. Olagappa Pillai | Hindu Sudra | Proprietor of the *Southern Star Press* | do |
| 286 | ,, | ,, | Kulitalai. | ,, R. V. Renga Row... | do | Mirasidar, Vice-President, Taluq Board and Member, District Board | By a Public Meeting held on the 3rd December 1894. |
| 287 | ,, | ,, | ,, | ,, M. S. Narayanaswamy Iyer | Brahmin. | Pleader, Chairman, Union; Member, Taluq and District Boards, and Devasthan Committee | do |
| 288 | ,, | ,, | ,, | ,, P. T. Rengaswamy Iyengar | do | Pleader and Mirasidar | do |
| 289 | ,, | ,, | ,, | ,, V. V. Narayanaswamy Iyer | do | Pleader ... | do |
| 290 | ,, | ,, | ,, | ,, M. K. Ramaswamy Iyer | do | Pleader and Mirasidar | do |
| 291 | ,, | ,, | ,, | ,, N. Swamy Iyer, B.A. | do | Pleader ... | do |
| 292 | ,, | ,, | ,, | ,, K. T. Chandrasekara Row | do | Pleader and Mirasidar | do |
| 293 | ,, | ,, | ,, | ,, P. T. Varada Iyengar | do | do ... | do |
| 294 | ,, | ,, | ,, | ,, M. M. Venkatramier | do | Pleader, Mirasidar and Member, Punchayet | do |
| 295 | ,, | ,, | ,, | ,, V. K. Seshatayee Iyer. | do | Mirasidar ... | do |

| Number. | Presidency or Government. | Congress Circle. | Electoral Division. | Names in full of Delegates, with Honorary Titles, Scholastic Degrees, etc. | Race, Religious denomination, and caste, if any. | Occupation and Address. | How and when elected. |
|---|---|---|---|---|---|---|---|
| 296 | Madras | Coimbatore. | Coimbatore. | Mr. V. Kuppusawmy Iyer | Brahmin | Pleader, Coimbatore... | By a Public Meeting held on the 1st December 1894. |
| 297 | " | " | " | " R. Venga Iyer ... | do | Pleader and Landholder | do |
| 298 | " | " | " | J. Krishna Iyengar | do | Pleader ... | do |
| 299 | " | " | " | " C. V. Venkataramana Iyengar, B.A. | do | Land Owner, Coimbatore | Do., also by the Hindu Progressive Union. |
| 300 | " | " | " | " K. V. Srinivasa Shastri | do | Mirasidar and Merchant | By a Public Meeting held on the 1st December 1894. |
| 301 | " | " | " | " P. M. Chakrapani Chetty, B.A. | Vysya. | 1st Grade Pleader ... | do |
| 302 | " | " | " | " C. C. Venkataramana Iyer | Brahmin. | do ... | do |
| 303 | " | " | " | " T. S. Balakrishnier, B.A., B.L. | do | Vakil, High Court and Member, Local Board | do |
| 304 | " | " | " | " K. Narayana Sastri. | do | do ... | do |
| 305 | " | " | " | " N. V. Varadachari. | do | Vakil, High Court ... | do |
| 306 | " | " | " | " K. Sesha Iyer ... | do | Landholder and Member, District Board | do |
| 307 | " | " | " | " B. Vencatachala Mudliar, B.A., B.L. | Hindu Sudra. | 1st Grade Pleader ... | do |
| 308 | " | " | " | " C. A. Vencatakrishna Iyer. | Brahmin. | Pleader and Municipal Councillor | do |
| 309 | " | " | " | " S. P. Narasimhalu Naidu | Hindu Velala. | Editor, *The Crescent*; Honorary Magistrate, Member, District and Taluq Boards | do |
| 310 | " | " | " | " N. Kolandavelu Pillai | do | Merchant, Proprietor, Joseph and Co.; Municipal Councillor, Joint Secretary, Brahmo Samaj, Coimbatore | do |
| 311 | " | " | " | " V. A. Kulasekara Mudliar | do | Banker, Mettupalayam. | do |
| 312 | " | " | " | " Girija Chettiar ... | Hindu. | Merchant, Director, Janopakaranidhi Sugar Manufactory | do |
| 313 | " | " | " | " V. T. Seshachalam Mudliar | Velala. | Secretary, Sugar Manufactory, Director, Cotton Mill | do |
| 314 | " | " | " | " C. Sadasiva Mudliar | do | Banker, Honorary Magistrate, Municipal Commissioner | do |

| Number. | Presidency or Government. | Congress Circle. | Electoral Division. | Names in full of Delegates, with Honorary Titles, Scholastic Degrees, etc. | Race, Religious denomination, and caste, if any. | Occupation and Address. | How and when elected. |
|---|---|---|---|---|---|---|---|
| 315 | Madras. | Coimbatore. | Coimbatore | Mr. C. M. Padmanabha Chariar, B.A., B.L. | Brahmin. | Vakil, High Court ... | By a Public Meeting held on the 1st December 1894. |
| 316 | ,, | ,, | ,, | ,, M. Sambandha Mudliar, B.A. | Hindu. | Landholder and Merchant | do |
| 317 | ,, | ,, | ,, | ,, Vittaldas Salt ... | do | Merchant, Tiruppur . | do |
| 318 | ,, | ,, | ,, | ,, A. T. Thiruvencataswamy Mudliar | Sudra. | Abkari Contractor ... | do |
| 319 | ,, | ,, | ,, | ,, V. R. Krishna Iyer, B.A., B.L. | Brahmin. | Vakil, High Court ... | do |
| 320 | ,, | ,, | ,, | ,, G. Kasturi Iyengar. | do | Assistant Master, College | do |
| 321 | ,, | ,, | ,, | ,, K. Chavadappier, B.A., B.L. | do | do ... | do |
| 322 | ,, | ,, | ,, | ,, S. Kadar Khan ... | Masalman. | Merchant and Landholder, Udamalpett | do |
| 323 | ,, | ,, | Erode. | ,, M. Govinda Row... | Brahmin. | Pleader, Erode ... | do |
| 324 | ,, | ,, | ,, | ,, G. Kasthuri Aiyengar. | do | Assistant Master ... | do |
| 325 | ,, | ,, | Karathur. | ,, V. Krishnier ... | do | Landholder ... | do |
| 326 | ,, | ,, | ,, | ,, Eswara Iyer ... | do | Editor, *Haladam Am.* | do |
| 327 | ,, | ,, | Dharapuram. | ,, D. Alagirisawmy Naidu | Hindu Sudra | Sowkar and Landed Proprietor | By a Public Meeting held on the 2nd December 1894. |
| 328 | ,, | ,, | ,, | ,, R. Ramachandra Naidu | do | Landholder ... | do |
| 329 | ,, | ,, | Kanyur. | ,, N. V. Desikachariar, M.A., B.L. | Brahmin | Vakil, High Court, Coimbatore | By the Amravathi Mahajana Sabha on the 28th October 1894 |
| 330 | ,, | ,, | ,, | ,, V. S. Ramaswamy Shastriar | do | Pleader ... | do |
| 331 | ,, | ,, | ,, | ,, N. C. Narasimha Chariar, B.A., B.L. | do | Vakil, District Court | do |
| 332 | ,, | ,, | ,, | ,, C. Nageswarier ... | do | Pleader ... | do |
| 333 | ,, | ,, | ,, | ,, K. N. Venkataraman Iyer | do | Secretary, Mahajana Sabha | do |
| 334 | ,, | ,, | ,, | ,, C. K. Vencatagiri Shastri | do | Landlord ... | do |
| 335 | ,, | ,, | ,, | ,, C. Krishnier ... | do | do ... | do |
| 336 | ,, | ,, | ,, | ,, C. N. Ramaswamy Iyer | do | do ... | do |

| Number. | Presidency or Government. | Congress Circle. | Electoral Division. | Names in full of Delegates, with Honorary Titles, Scholastic Degrees etc. | Race, Religious denomination, and caste, if any. | Occupation and Address. | How and when elected. |
|---|---|---|---|---|---|---|---|
| 337 | Madras. | Coimbatore | Kanyur | Mr. C. S. Anantha Krishnier | Brahmin | Landlord ... | By a Public Meeting held on the 11th November 1894 |
| 338 | ,, | ,, | ,, | ,, S. Visvanathier | do | do ... | do |
| 339 | ,, | ,, | ,, | S. Balakrishna Shastri | do | Banker ... | do |
| 340 | ,, | ,, | ,, | ,, S. Ramaswamy Iyer | do | Landlord ... | do |
| 341 | ,, | ,, | Satyamangalam, | ,, P. S. Srinivasa Iyer | do | Vakil ... | By a Public Meeting held on the 26th November 1894 |
| 342 | ,, | ,, | ,, | ,, Ramakrishna Shastri | do | Mirasidar ... | do |
| 343 | ,, | ,, | ,, | ,, S. S. Sivaswamy Shastriar | do | do ... | do |
| 344 | ,, | ,, | Udamalpet. | ,, A. Srinavasa Iyer | do | Pleader ... | By a Public Meeting held on the 11th November 1894 |
| 345 | ,, | ,, | ,, | ,, T. S. Ramaswamy Shastri | do | do ... | do |
| 346 | ,, | ,, | Karur. | ,, T. R. Ramachandra Iyer | do | do ... | By a Public Meeting held on the 1st December 1894 |
| 347 | ,, | ,, | Kollegal. | ,, A. S. Narayana Row | do | do ... | By a Public Meeting held on the 6th December 1894 |
| 348 | ,, | ,, | Bhavani. | ,, Venkatarenga Chetty | Vysya | Landlord ... | By a Public Meeting held on the 1st December 1894 |
| 349 | ,, | South Arcot. | Tindivanam. | ,, P. S. Venkataramier | Brahmin | Pleader, Tindivanam.. | By a Public Meeting held on the 3rd December 1894 |
| 350 | ,, | ,, | ,, | ,, V. Muthusawmy Aiyar | do | do ... | do |
| 351 | ,, | ,, | ,, | ,, H. Raghavendra Rao | do | do ... | do |
| 352 | ,, | ,, | ,, | ,, C. Ramanujachari | do | do ... | do |
| 353 | ,, | ,, | ,, | ,, T. A. Subiaswamy Chetty | Hindu Sudra | do ... | do |
| 354 | ,, | ,, | ,, | ,, T. Sundararama Iyer | Brahmin | do ... | do |
| 355 | ,, | ,, | ,, | ,, T. K. Venkatarama Iyer | do | 2nd Grade Pleader... | do |
| 356 | ,, | ,, | ,, | ,, Agaram Sundara Iyer | do | 1st Grade Pleader and Assistant Public Prosecutor | do |

| Number. | Presidency or Government. | Congress Circle. | Electoral Division. | Names in full of Delegates, with Honorary Titles, Scholastic Degrees, etc. | Race, Religious denomination, and caste, if any. | Occupation and Address. | How and when elected. |
|---|---|---|---|---|---|---|---|
| 357 | Madras | South Arcot | Tindivanam | Mr. P. Narasimha Chari | Brahmin | Pleader ... | By a Public Meeting held on the 3rd December 1894. |
| 358 | „ | „ | Cuddalore. | „ Thiruvenkata Chariar | do | 1st Grade Pleader and Municipal Councillor | By a Public Meeting held on the 4th December. 1894. |
| 359 | „ | „ | „ | „ Lakshminarayana Reddiar | Hindu Sudra | Landholder, Kullapattam | do |
| 360 | „ | „ | „ | „ P. Sama Rau Garu | Brahmin | 1st Grade Pleader and Municipal Councillor, Thirupapuliyur. | do |
| 361 | „ | „ | „ | „ S. Rajagopala Chari, B.A., B.L. | do | Pleader ... | do |
| 362 | „ | „ | „ | „ R. Srinivasa Iyengar | do | do ... | do |
| 363 | „ | „ | „ | „ A. Raghava Chariar | do | Landholder ... | do |
| 364 | „ | „ | „ | „ V. Krishnamurthy Row | do | Pleader ... | do |
| 365 | „ | „ | „ | „ M. Appaji Reddiar | Hindu | Landholder ... | do |
| 366 | „ | „ | „ | „ P. S. Arumugha Pillai | do | Assistant, Messrs. Joseph & Sons. | do |
| 367 | „ | „ | „ | „ S. Subramanya Reddiar, B.A., B.L. | do | Vakil, High Court ... | do |
| 368 | „ | „ | „ | „ T. Subbraya Chettiar | do | Merchant ... | do |
| 369 | „ | „ | „ | „ A. Rama Row ... | Brahmin. | Pleader ... | do |
| 370 | „ | „ | „ | „ N. S. Natesa Iyer, B.A., B.L. | do | 1st Grade Pleader ... | do |
| 371 | „ | „ | „ | „ C. Subramaniah. | do | Mirasidar ... | do |
| 372 | „ | „ | „ | „ S. Lakshminarasimha Iyer | do | Landholder ... | do |
| 373 | „ | „ | „ | „ S. Angappa Chetty | Vysya. | Merchant | do |
| 374 | „ | „ | Villupuram. | „ K. N. Ramanuja Chari | Brahmin. | Pleader ... | By a Public Meeting held on the 26th November 1894. |
| 375 | „ | „ | „ | „ T. Sankara Aiyar | do | do ... | do |
| 376 | „ | „ | „ | „ Arunachella Mudliar | Hindu-Velala | Headmaster, Hindu Primary School | By a Public Meeting held on the 11th November 1894. |
| 377 | „ | „ | Chidambaram. | „ M. C. Ramaswamy Iyer | Brahmin. | Mirasidar, Pleader, and Municipal Councillor | By a Public Meeting held on the 5th December 1894. |
| 378 | „ | „ | „ | „ T. N. Desika Chariar | do | Pleader and Landholder. | do |

| Number. | Presidency or Government. | Congress Circle. | Electoral Division. | Names in full of Delegates, with Honorary Titles, Scholastic Degrees, etc. | Race, Religious denomination, and caste, if any. | Occupation and Address. | How and when elected. |
|---|---|---|---|---|---|---|---|
| 379 | Madras | South Arcot. | Chidambaram. | Mr. A. Rengaswamy Pillai | Hindu Velala. | Mirasidar and Pleader | By a Public Meeting held on the 5th December 1894 |
| 380 | „ | „ | „ | „ Tillai Nayagam Pillai | do | Mirasidar ... | do |
| 381 | „ | „ | „ | „ Nagabhushanam Pillai | do | do ... | do |
| 382 | „ | „ | „ | „ Kuppu Pillai ... | do | do ... | do |
| 383 | „ | „ | „ | „ H. Muthusawmy Mudliar | do | Merchant ... | do |
| 384 | „ | „ | „ | „ K. Varada Chariar. | Brahmin. | Pleader and Mirasidar | do |
| 385 | „ | „ | „ | „ T. H. Jaganatha Iyer | do | Landholder & Schoolmaster | do |
| 386 | „ | „ | „ | „ V. Swaminatha Jetavalabha, B.A. | do | Mirasidar and Head Master Pachhiappa's High School and Municipal Councillor | do |
| 387 | „ | „ | „ | „ V. Desika Chariar. | do | Pleader ... | do |
| 388 | „ | „ | „ | „ C. Rengasawmy Iyengar | do | Pleader and Mirasidar | do |
| 389 | „ | „ | „ | „ B. Appa Rao ... | do | Landlord ... | do |
| 390 | „ | „ | Nellikuppam. | Moy-ud-deen Ibrahim-Sahib. | Masalman. | Merchant ... | do |
| 391 | „ | „ | Porto Novo. | Mr. T. A. Thetha Mudliar | Hindu Sudra. | do ... | do |
| 302 | „ | „ | Tirukoilur. | „ C. V. Narayanasawmy Iyer | Brahmin. | Pleader ... | do |
| 393 | „ | „ | Thiruvendipuram. | „ T. Sankara Iyer... | do | do ... | do |
| 394 | „ | Malabar | Palghaut | „ P. S. Sesha Iyer... | do | Vakil, High Court ... | By a Public Meeting held on the 25th November 1894. |
| 395 | „ | „ | „ | „ K. P. Achyutha Menon. | Hindu Nair | 1st Grade Pleader, and Honorary Magistrate Municipal Councillor, Palghat | do |
| 396 | „ | „ | „ | „ S. Viraraghava Iyer. | Brahmin | Landed Proprietor ... | do |
| 397 | „ | „ | „ | „ K. Govinda Menon. | Hindu Nair | 2nd Grade Pleader, Ottapatam | do |
| 398 | „ | „ | „ | „ T. L. Viraraghava Pathar. | Brahmin | Banker and Landed Proprietor and Municipal Councillor | do |
| 399 | „ | „ | „ | Hon. C. Sankara Nair, B.A., B.L. | Hindu Nair | Vakil, High Court and Member, Madras Legislative Council | do |

| Number. | Presidency or Government. | Congress Circle. | Electoral Division. | Names in full of Delegates, with Honorary Titles, Scholastic Degrees, etc. | Race, Religious denomination, and caste, if any. | Occupation and Address. | How and when elected. |
|---|---|---|---|---|---|---|---|
| 400 | Madras | Malabar | Palghaut | Mr. P. S. Chinnaswamy Pillai | Velala | Landholder, Member, District Board and Chairman, Municipal Council | By a Public Meeting held on the 25th November 1894. |
| 401 | „ | „ | „ | „ P. A. Ramaswamy Iyer | Brahmin | Landholder and Pleader | do |
| 402 | „ | „ | „ | „ Kunnathal Madampil Raman Unni Muppil Nair of Manargal | Hindu Nair | Landlord ... | do |
| 403 | „ | „ | „ | Dr. A. Theyzumu Menon | do | Medical Practitioner | do |
| 404 | „ | „ | „ | Mr. V. P. Venkata Chariar | Brahmin | Pleader and Municipal Councillor | do |
| 405 | „ | „ | „ | „ T. R. Viraraghavam Pattar. | do | Landlord and Merchant | do |
| 406 | „ | „ | „ | „ V. Raman Nair, B.A., B.L. | Hindu Nair | Vakil, High Court ... | do |
| 407 | „ | „ | „ | „ V. Venga Iyer ... | Brahmin | Pleader ... | do |
| 408 | „ | „ | Calicut | „ K. U. Narayana Menon. | Hindu Nair | Editor, *Malabar and Travancore Spectator* | By a Public Meeting held on the 3rd December 1894. |
| 409 | „ | „ | „ | „ P. C. Amman Raja | do | Landlord and Member of the Zamorin's Family at Calicut | do |
| 410 | „ | „ | „ | „ C. Sankurri Menon | do | Assistant Secretary, Kerala Mahajana Sabha | do |
| 411 | „ | „ | „ | „ K. Ramanurri Nair | do | Landlord ... | do |
| 412 | „ | „ | „ | „ K. C. Manavikraman Raja | Hindu Samantha | Landlord and Member, Zamorin's Family; Secretary, Karala Mahajana Sabha | do |
| 413 | „ | „ | „ | „ Chanthroth Valia C. Nambiar | Hindu Nair | Landlord and Member, District Board | do |
| 414 | „ | „ | „ | „ P. A. Krishna Menon | do | 1st Grade Pleader and Municipal Councillor | do |
| 415 | „ | „ | „ | „ K. R. Subramania Shastri | Brahmin | Vakil, High Court ... | do |
| 416 | „ | „ | „ | „ R. Devaraja Iyer | do | Assistant Master, High School | do |
| 417 | „ | „ | „ | „ L. R. Subramania Iyer | do | Merchant ... | do |
| 418 | „ | „ | „ | „ M. Krishna Nair, B.A., B.L. | Hindu Nair | Vakil, High Court ... | do |
| 419 | „ | „ | „ | „ N. Subramania Iyer | Brahmin | Pleader and Municipal Councillor | do |

| Number. | Presidency or Government. | Congress Circle. | Electoral Division. | Names in full of Delegates, with Honorary Titles, Scholastic Degrees, etc | Race, Religious denomination, and caste, if any. | Occupation and Address. | How and when elected. |
|---|---|---|---|---|---|---|---|
| 420 | Madras | Malabar | Calicut | Mr. S. Kadri Kutty Keyi | Masalman | Landholder ... | By a Public Meeting held on the 3rd December 1894. |
| 421 | " | " | " | " M. Gopala Menon. | Hindu Nair | Vakil, High Court ... | do |
| 422 | " | " | " | " C. M. Rarichan ... | Hindu Tier | Landholder ... | do |
| 423 | " | " | " | " C. Karunakara Menon | Hindu Nair | Assistant Manager, *The Hindu* | do |
| 424 | " | " | " | " C. Adinarayana Nair | do | Pleader ... | do |
| 425 | " | " | " | " K. R. Ramaswami Iyer | Brahmin | do ... | By a Public Meeting of the Kerala Mahajan Sabha on the 3rd December 1894 |
| 426 | " | " | Cannanore | " C. Kuntri Kannan Vaidhya | Hindu | Dewan to H. H. Sultan Ali, Rajah of Cannanore | By a Public Meeting held on the 18th November 1894. |
| 427 | " | " | " | " V Kuntri Raman Nair | do | Landlord and Member, District Board | do |
| 428 | " | " | Tellicherry | " T. S. Narayana Kurup, B.A., B.L. | Hindu Nair | Vakil, High Court and Municipal Councillor | By a Public Meeting held on the 5th December 1894. |
| 429 | " | " | " | " M. Gopala Menon | do | Pleader ... | do |
| 430 | " | " | " | " P. K. Kelappa Kurup, B.A., B.L. | do | Vakil, High Court ... | do |
| 431 | " | " | Mangalore | " C. Krishna Batta | Brahmin | do ... | By a Public Meeting held on the 2nd December 1894. |
| 432 | " | Tinnevelly. | Ambasamudram. | " Sadhu Ramasubbier | do | General Secretary, Mahajana Sabha, Ambasamudram | By a Public Meeting held on the 5th November 1894. |
| 433 | " | " | " | " T. V. Lakshmana Iyengar | do | Pleader and Secretary, Mahajana Sabha, Ambasamudram | By a Public Meeting held on the 9th December 1894. |
| 434 | " | " | " | " R. Subbier ... | do | do ... | do |
| 435 | " | " | " | " H. T. Subbasami Iyer | do | do ... | do |
| 436 | " | " | " | " A. S. Rama Subbier | do | Landholder ... | do |
| 437 | " | " | " | " Thenatha Puly Nalla Kutti Siva Subramania Thever | Hindu Sudra. | Zemindar, Singapatti | do |
| 438 | " | " | " | " Sankarasubbiah Iyer | Brahmin. | Landlord & Merchant. | By a Public Meeting held on the 22nd November 1894. |

| Nnmber. | Presidency or Government. | Congress Circle • | Electoral Division. | Names in full of Delegates, with Honorary Titles, Scholastic Degrees, etc. | Race, Religious denomination and caste, if any. | Occupation and Address. | How and when elected. |
|---|---|---|---|---|---|---|---|
| 439 | Madras | Tinnevelly | Ambasamudram | Mr. Sundara Karayalam Pillai | Sudra. | Landlord ... | By a Public Meeting held on the 22nd November 1894. |
| 440 | " | " | " | " Devanayagain Pillai | Velala. | Contractor ... | do |
| 441 | " | " | Tinnevelly | " S. Kalyanarama Iyer | Brahmin | Vakil, High Court and Landholder | do |
| 442 | " | " | " | " K. R. Guruswamy Iyer, B.A., B.L. | do | Landholder & Pleader | do |
| 443 | " | " | " | " T. R. Sulochanam Mudliar | Hindu. | Landlord, Vennarpet | do |
| 444 | " | " | " | " P. N. Venkatachala Iyer, B.A. | Brahmin | Pleader and Landholder, Member, Taluq Board. | do |
| 445 | " | " | " | " S. Palaniandi Mudliar | Velala. | Pleader and Municipal Councillor. | do |
| 446 | " | " | " | " V. M. Syed Rowther | Masalman. | Merchant and Director, Cotton Factory | do |
| 447 | " | " | " | " V. Chinnasawmy Iyer | Brahmin | Vakil ... | do |
| 448 | " | " | " | " V. Subbasawmy Iyer | do | do ... | do |
| 449 | " | " | " | " K. G Krishnasawmy Iyer | do | Pleader ... | do |
| 450 | " | " | " | " T. K. Thirumalayappa Pillai | Hindu. | Landholder, Merchant and Temple Trustee | do |
| 451 | " | " | " | " T. S. Subramania Pillai | Velala. | Landholder & Pleader | do |
| 452 | " | " | " | " P. M. Kailasam Pillai | do | Landholder, Pleader, and Secretary, Hindu College Committee | do |
| 453 | " | " | " | " S. Varadarajier ... | Brahmin. | Vakil ... | do |
| 454 | " | " | " | " A. R. Krishnier ... | do | Vakil and Landholder | do |
| 455 | " | " | " | " P. Muthukumarasawmy Pillai | Velala. | Mittadar ... | do |
| 456 | " | " | " | " G. Ramabadrier .. | Brahmin. | Vakil and Landlord... | do |
| 457 | " | " | " | " Kanthimathinatha Pillai | Velala. | Mittadar and Devasthanam Trustee | do |
| 458 | " | " | " | " A. V. Thirumalayappa Pillai | Hindu Sudra. | Member, Devasthanam Committee | do |
| 459 | " | " | " | " K. Raghunatha Iyer | Brahmin. | Zemindar, Puthur ... | do |
| 460 | " | " | " | " C. R. Kanthimathinatha Pillai | Hindu Velala. | Mittadar and 1st Grade Pleader | do |

| Number. | Presidency or Government. | Congress Circle | Electoral Division. | Names in full of Delegates, with Honorary Titles, Scholastic Degrees etc. | Race, Religious denomination, and caste, if any. | Occupation and address. | How and when elected. |
|---|---|---|---|---|---|---|---|
| 461 | Madras | Tinnevelly | Tinnevelly | Mr. J. T. Srinivasagam Pillai | Hindu Velala | Vakil, High Court, Palamcottah | By a Public Meeting held on the 22nd November 1894. |
| 462 | „ | „ | Gopalasamudrum. | „ G. R. Sankarier ... | Brahmin. | Head Master, H. L. S. School, Gopalasamudram | By a Public Meeting held on the 28th November 1894. |
| 463 | „ | „ | Srivaikuntham. | „ K. V. Srinivasa Iyer Avergal | do | Landholder & Pleader | By a Public Meeting held on the 22nd November 1894. |
| 464 | „ | „ | „ | „ P. Joseph Nadar Avergal | Sudra. | Pleader & Landholder | By a Public Meeting held on the 3rd December 1894. |
| 465 | „ | „ | „ | „ S. Ponnaiah Nadar Avergal | Hindu. | President, Kayalp Salt Company | do |
| 466 | „ | „ | Virudupati. | „ G. P. S. Shanmuga Nadar | Hindu Sudra | Merchant ... | By a Public Meeting held on the 17th November 1894. |
| 467 | „ | „ | „ | „ S. P. Poomappu Nadar | do | do ... | do |
| 468 | „ | „ | „ | „ K. S. Manikkavasabha Nadar | do | Head Master, Hindu Middle School | do |
| 469 | „ | „ | Srivilliputur. | „ S. Pamiengar ... | Brahmin. | Pleader ... | By a Public Meeting held on the 25th November 1894. |
| 470 | „ | „ | „ | „ S. Raghaviengar... | do | do | do |
| 471 | „ | „ | „ | „ K. A. Gopalasawmy Shastriar | do | Inamdar of Chettikolam | do |
| 472 | „ | „ | Satur. | „ C. Annamalai Mudliar | Hindu. | Agent, Sabhapathi Mudliar & Co. | By a Public Meeting held on the 17th November 1894. |
| 473 | „ | Madura. | Sivagunga. | „ S. R. S. Chidambaram Chetty | Hindu Sudra. | Merchant, Sivagunga | By a Public Meeting held on the 9th December 1894. |
| 474 | „ | „ | „ | „ M. G. Govinda Varada Iyengar | Brahmin. | Pleader & Landholder | do |
| 475 | „ | „ | „ | „ Mahamu Sundara Pandya Theva | Hindu. | Sub-division Zemindar, Sivagunga, Member, Union and Landlord—Royal Family | do |
| 476 | „ | „ | „ | „ S. M. Narayanaswamy Iyer, B.A. | Brahmin. | Head Master, Rajra High School, Sivagunga | do |
| 477 | „ | „ | „ | „ K. V. Subramania Iyer, B.A., B.L. | do | Pleader, Sivagunga... | do |
| 478 | „ | „ | „ | „ P. S. Anantha Narayana Shastriar | do | do ... | do |
| 479 | „ | „ | „ | „ P. N. Ramaswamy Iyer | do | Merchant ... | do |

| Number. | Presidency or Government. | Congress Circle. | Electoral Division. | Names in full of Delegates, with Honorary Titles, Scholastic Degrees, etc. | Race, Religious denomination, and caste, if any. | Occupation and Address. | How and when elected. |
|---|---|---|---|---|---|---|---|
| 480 | Madras. | Madura | Sivagunga. | Mr. P. Anantha Narayana Iyer | Brahmin | Pleader ... | By a Public Meeting held on the 9th December 1894. |
| 481 | „ | „ | „ | „ P. S. Ramaswamy Iyer | do | do ... | do |
| 482 | „ | „ | „ | „ P. S. Hari Hari Iyer | do | do ... | do |
| 483 | „ | „ | „ | „ V. Vasvanathier... | do | do ... | do |
| 484 | „ | „ | „ | „ B. Narayanaswamy Iyer | do | Teacher ... | do |
| 485 | „ | „ | „ | „ A. K. Subbaramier | do | School Master ... | do |
| 486 | „ | „ | Mana Madura. | „ U. G. Sankara Narayana Aiyar | do | 2nd Grade Pleader, Mana Madura | By a Public Meeting held on the 16th December 1894. |
| 487 | „ | „ | Madura. | „ P. N. Muthuswamy Iyer, B.A., B.L. | do | Vakil, High Court ... | By a Public Meeting held on the 17th November 1894. |
| 488 | „ | „ | „ | „ P. Narayana Iyer | do | Vakil, High Court; Member, District and Taluq Boards | do |
| 489 | „ | „ | „ | „ M. Vencataramier, B.A., B.L. | do | Member, Taluq Board, Editor, *Madura Mail* | do |
| 490 | „ | „ | „ | „ V. Bhashyachariar | do | Vakil, High Court ... | do |
| 491 | „ | „ | „ | „ G. Srinivasa Row | do | 1st Grade Pleader and Landholder | do |
| 492 | „ | „ | „ | „ P. S. Subramania | do | Pleader ... | do |
| 493 | „ | „ | „ | „ T. R. Seshier ... | do | do ... | do |
| 494 | „ | „ | „ | „ M. Madhu Iyer, B.A., B.L. | do | Vakil, High Court ... | do |
| 495 | „ | „ | „ | „ G. Subbarajulu Naidu | Hindu Sudra | Landholder, Sowcar, and Municipal Councillor | By a Public Meeting held on the 23rd September 1894. |
| 496 | „ | „ | „ | „ V. C. Sriraman Chettyar | Vysya | Merchant and Municipal Councillor | do |
| 497 | „ | „ | „ | „ C. K. Veeraswamy Naidu | Velala | Proprietor, Soap Manufactory | do |
| 498 | „ | „ | „ | „ Allu Seetharamier | Brahmin | Merchant and Municipal Councillor | do |
| 499 | „ | „ | „ | „ K. Ramiah Bhaga Nathar | do | Merchant ... | do |
| 500 | „ | „ | „ | „ V. S. Krishnaswamy Iyer | do | do ... | do |
| 501 | „ | „ | „ | „ R. Muthuswamy Pillai | Sudra | Pleader and Municipal Councillor | do |

| Number. | Presidency or Government. | Congress Circle. | Electoral Division. | Names in full of Delegates, with Honorary Titles, Scholastic Degrees, etc. | Race, Religious denomination, and caste, if any. | Occupation and Address. | How and when elected. |
|---|---|---|---|---|---|---|---|
| 502 | Madras | Madura | Madura. | Mr. E. S. Subramania Iyer | Brahmin | Pleader .. | By a Public Meeting held on the 23rd September 1894. |
| 503 | " | " | " | " P. Sankarasubbiar | do | do ... | do |
| 504 | " | " | " | " D. Saundra Rajiengar | do | do ... | do |
| 505 | " | " | " | " Perianna Nadar... | Sudra | Merchant & Member, Taluq Board | do |
| 506 | " | " | " | " M. Nagalingam Pillai | Velala | Pleader ... | do |
| 507 | " | " | " | " Seshadri Aiyengar | Brahmin | Sub-divisional Zemindar, Thiruthervalai | do |
| 508 | " | " | " | " C. Srinivasa Iyer, B.A., B.L. | do | Vakil, High Court ... | do |
| 509 | " | " | " | " V. Narayanaswamy Iyer | do | Mirasidar ... | do |
| 510 | " | " | " | " K. M. Ramaswamy Iyer | do | Pleader ... | do |
| 511 | " | " | " | " N. M. Sundaramier | do | Merchant ... | do |
| 512 | " | " | " | " M. K. Sankaranarayana Iyer | do | do ... | do |
| 513 | " | " | " | " L. K. Tholasi Row, B.A. | do | Editor, *Janamanoranjan* | do |
| 514 | " | " | " | " S. Krishnaswamy Iyer | do | Merchant ... | do |
| 515 | " | " | " | " M. V. Subramanier | do | Manager, *Madura Mail* | do |
| 516 | " | " | " | " K. Krishnaswamy Naidu | Hindu | Editor, *Indian Chronicle* | do |
| 517 | " | " | Uttamapalayam | " M. T. Thirumalai Mudliar | Hindu Velala | Mirasidar, Uttamapalayam and Member, Taluq Board | By a Public Meeting held on the 25th November 1894 |
| 518 | " | " | " | " P. Naraniyer ... | Brahmin | Mirasidar ... | do |
| 519 | " | " | Solavandam | " Gopala Iyengar... | do | 1st Grade Pleader ... | do |
| 520 | " | " | " | " V. Komatchiappa Mudliar | Velala | Landholder ... | do |
| 521 | " | " | Periyakulam | " V. P. Rajanaier... | Brahmin | Pleader ... | By a Public Meeting held on the 17th December 1894. |
| 522 | " | " | " | " S. Muthuswamy Iyer | do | Landholder, Member, District and Taluq Boards | do |

| Number. | Presidency or Government. | Congress Circle. | Electoral Division. | Names in full of Delegates, with Honorary Titles, Scholastic Degrees, etc | Race, Religious denomination, and caste, if any. | Occupation and Address. | How and when elected. |
|---|---|---|---|---|---|---|---|
| 523 | Madras. | Madura. | Periyakulam | Mr. J. R. Muthusawmy Iyer | Brahmin | Schoolmaster, Municipal Councillor and Member, District and Taluq Boards | By a Public Meeting held on the 5th December 1894. |
| 524 | " | " | Paramakudi | " T. V. Kothanda Rama Iyengar | do | Pleader, Landlord, and Member, Union | By a Fublic Meeting held on the 26th November 1894. |
| 525 | " | " | " | " S. Vendantham Iyengar | do | Pleader and Landlord | do |
| 526 | " | " | " | " S. Venkatarama Iyengar | do | do ... | do |
| 527 | " | " | " | " P. S. Santhanakrishnam Pillai | Velala | Pleader ... | do |
| 528 | " | " | Dindigul. | " T. Rajagopala Naidu | Hindu Vishnavite | Pleader, Dindigul Municipal Councillor | By a Public Meeting held on the 25th November 1894. |
| 529 | " | " | " | " Sneharajanulu Naidu | do | Sowcar and Landholder | do |
| 530 | " | " | " | " N. A. Subbia Chettyar | Hindu Vysya | Sowcar and Merchant | do |
| 531 | " | " | " | " N. Ramaswamy Chettyar | do | Sowcar and Money Lender | do |
| 532 | " | " | " | " R. Venkatesa Naidu | Hindu Sudra | Landholder and Municipal Councillor | do |
| 533 | " | " | " | " L. A. Vengasawmy Iyer | Brahmin | Pleader ... | do |
| 534 | " | " | " | " A. R. Seetharamier | do | do ... | do |
| 535 | " | " | " | " P. R. Narayana Shastriar | do | Pleader and Municipal Councillor | do |
| 536 | " | " | " | " S. Srinivasa Iyer | do | Pleader ... | do |
| 537 | " | " | " | " A. S. Parasuramier | do | Pleader and Honorary Magistrate | do |
| 538 | " | " | Sholavandam | " Ponnambha Mudliar | Hindu Velala | Landholder ... | By a Public Meeting held on the 8th December 1894. |
| 539 | " | Salem. | Salem. | " W. Virasawmy Iyer | Brahmin | Pleader, Salem ... | By a Public Meeting held on the 26th November 1894. |
| 540 | " | " | " | " E. S. Ramasamy Iyer, B.A., B.L, | do | Vakil, High Court... | do |
| 541 | " | " | " | " S. Ramasawmy Iyer, B.A., B.L. | do | Pleader ... | do |
| 542 | " | " | " | " S. Krishna Row | do | do ... | do |
| 543 | " | " | " | " D. A. Balakrishnier | do | Pleader and Municipal Councillor | do |

| Number. | Presidency or Government. | Congress Circle. | Electoral Division. | Names in full of Delegates, with Honorary Titles, Scholastic Degrees, etc | Race, Religious denomination, and caste, if any. | Occupation and Address. | How and when elected. |
|---|---|---|---|---|---|---|---|
| 544 | Madras | Salem | Salem | Mr. C. Venkataramier | Brahmin | Landholder ... | By a Public Meeting held on the 26th November 1894. |
| 545 | ,, | ,, | ,, | ,, T. Ramaswamy Iyengar | do | Pleader and Landholder, Namakal | do |
| 546 | ,, | ,, | ,, | ,, S. Srinivasa Iyengar, B.A. | do | Pleader, Salem ... | do |
| 547 | ,, | ,, | ,, | ,, A. L. Arunachalam Chettiar | Hindu Sudra | Banker ... | By a Public Meeting held on the 8th December 1894. |
| 548 | ,, | ,, | ,, | ,, U. Vencata Row, B.A., B.L. | Brahmin | Pleader ... | do |
| 549 | ,, | ,, | ,, | ,, C Vijiaraghava Chariar, B.A. | do | Pleader and Municipal Councillor | do |
| 550 | ,, | ,, | ,, | ,, V. S. Srinivasa Shastri, B.A., L.T. | do | Schoolmaster ... | By a Public Meeting held on the 9th December 1894. |
| 551 | ,, | ,, | ,, | ,, M. Rathamanabha Chetty | Hindu Vysya | Mittadar ... | do |
| 552 | ,, | ,, | ,, | ,, S M. Mahamad Sahib | Masalman | Merchant and Municipal Councillor | do |
| 553 | ,, | ,, | ,, | ,, Chanda Mea Sahib | do | Merchant ... | do |
| 554 | ,, | ,, | ,, | ,, D. Seshagiri Iyer | Brahmin | Pleader and Member, District Board | do |
| 555 | ,, | ,, | ,, | ,, P. Raja Row ... | do | Pleader ... | do |
| 556 | ,, | ,, | ,, | ,, R. Shanmuga Mudliar | Velala | Landlord and Merchant | do |
| 557 | ,, | ,, | ,, | ,, T. Narasinga Row | Brahmin | Municipal Councillor, Shotriam Pensioner | do |
| 558 | ,, | ,, | ,, | ,, S. Kanaka Sabbai Mudliar, B.A. | Velala | Mittadar .. | do |
| 559 | ,, | ,, | ,, | ,, C. Varada Chariar | Brahmin | Landholder ... | do |
| 560 | ,, | ,, | ,, | ,, N. Ramaswamy Iyer | do | Pleader ... | do |
| 561 | ,, | ,, | ,, | ,, D. B. Narasier | do | do ... | do |
| 562 | ,, | ,, | ,, | ,, T. Subramania Iyer, B.A., B.L. | do | Vakil, High Court; Member. District Board | do |
| 563 | ,, | ,, | ,, | ,, C. Vencatachari ... | do | Landlord and Member, District Board | By a Public Meeting held on the 8th December 1894 |
| 564 | ,, | ,, | ,, | ,, Abdul Karim Sahib | Masalman | Priest ... | do |
| 565 | ,, | ,, | ,, | ,, Hassan Mian Gulam Sahib | do | do | do |

| Number. | Presidency or Government. | Congress Circle. | Electoral Division. | Names in full of Delegates, with Honorary Titles, Scholastic Degrees, etc. | Race, Religious denomination, and caste, if any. | Occupation and Address. | How and when elected. |
|---|---|---|---|---|---|---|---|
| 566 | Madras | Salem | Salem | Mr. Venkatachallapathi Iyer | Brahmin | Merchant ... | By a Public Meeting held on the 8th December 1894. |
| 567 | ,, | ,, | ,, | ,, C. Vencataramanier B.A., B.L. | do | Vakil, High Court ... | do |
| 568 | ,, | ,, | ,, | ,, T. N. Subrama Shastriar | do | 2nd Grade Pleader and Landholder | do |
| 569 | ,, | ,, | ,, | ,, V. R. Vencataramana Iyer | do | Landholder ... | do |
| 570 | ,, | ,, | ,, | ,, N. Narasinga Row | do | do ... | do |
| 571 | ,, | ,, | ,, | ,, V. Kasturi Chetty | Hindu Sudra | Pleader and Honorary Magistrate | do |
| 572 | ,, | ,, | ,, | ,, Paramasiva Kanudar | do | Zemindar ... | do |
| 573 | ,, | ,, | ,, | ,, Rangaya Kanudar | do | do | do |
| 574 | ,, | ,, | ,, | T. Venkata Row | Brahmin | Pleader ... | do |
| 575 | ,, | ,, | ,, | ,, Venkatarama Reddiar | Hindu Sudra | Zemindar ... | do |
| 576 | ,, | ,, | Namakal | ,, Doraiswamy Reddiar | do | do ... | By a Public Meeting held on the 9th December 1894. |
| 577 | ,, | ,, | Thirupathur. | ,, D. Venkataramanier | Brahmin | Pleader ... | By a Public Meeting held on the 3rd December 1894. |
| 578 | ,, | ,, | ,, | ,, B. Venkataramanier | do | 1st Grade Pleader . | do |
| 579 | ,, | ,, | ,, | ,, S. A Venkataramanier | do | Pleader ... | do |
| 580 | ,, | ,, | ,, | ,, C. Kalayanasundar Nadar | Hindu | Mittadar and Member, Taluq Board | do |
| 581 | ,, | ,, | ,, | ,, T. Gangadharam Pillai | Hindu Sudra | Pleader ... | do |
| 582 | ,, | ,, | ,, | ,, C. Ranganadar Mudliar | do | Pleader and Municipal Councillor, Vice-President, Taluq Board Member, District Board | do |
| 583 | ,, | ,, | ,, | ,, T. M. Lakshmana Iyer | Brahmin | Pleader ... | do |
| 584 | ,, | ,, | ,, | ,, R. T. Ramaswamy Iyer | do | do ... | do |
| 585 | ,, | ,, | Trichengudi. | ,, S. Manika Mudliar | Hindu Sudra | 2nd Grade Pleader ... | By a Public Meeting held on the 2nd December 1894. |
| 586 | ,, | ,, | Royacotah. | ,, T. Muthukrishna Mudliar | Velala | Mitta Zemindar, Sanitary President, Member, Taluq Board | By a Public Meeting held on the 3rd December 1894. |

| Number. | Presidency or Government. | Congress Circle. | Electoral Division. | Names in full of Delegates, with Honorary Titles, Scholastic Degrees, etc. | Race, Religious denomination, and caste, if any. | Occupation and Address. | How and whan elected. |
|---|---|---|---|---|---|---|---|
| 587 | Madras. | Salem | Dharmapuri | Mr. M. Ramaswamy Naidu | Hindu Sudra | Mittadar and Member, District Board | By a Public Meeting held on the 13th December 1894. |
| 588 | ,, | Chingleput. | Chingleput | ,, M. N. Vencatachari | Brahmin | Pleader ... | By a Public Meeting held on the 8th December 1894. |
| 589 | ,, | ,, | ,, | ,, Y. M. Ramanuja Chari | do | do ... | do |
| 590 | ,, | ,, | ,, | ,, Samarapuri Pandaram | Sudra | Merchant ... | do |
| 591 | ,, | ,, | ,, | ,, Doraiswamy Mudliar | Velala | Trader and Hindu Preacher | do |
| 592 | ,, | ,, | ,, | ,, Vedagiri Chetty ... | Sudra | Merchant ... | do |
| 593 | ,, | ,, | ,, | ,, I. Alasingara Chari | Brahmin | Pleader ... | do |
| 594 | ,, | ,, | ,, | ,, C. Kesava Raghava Mudliar | Velala | Zemindar of Manali... | do |
| 595 | ,, | ,, | ,, | ,, C. Rajagopala Chari | Brahmin | 1st Grade Pleader ... | do |
| 596 | ,, | ,, | ,, | ,, Ramanuja Chari ... | do | Vakil, High Court ... | By a Public Meeting held on the 13th December 1894. |
| 597 | ,, | ,, | ,, | ,, Vedachalla Mudliar | Hindu Vellala | Pleader & Landholder | do |
| 598 | ,, | ,, | ,, | ,, Shumgaroya Mudliar | do | Zemindar of Nalathur | do |
| 599 | ,, | ,, | ,, | ,, T. M. Srinivasa Chari | Brahmin | Pleader ... | do |
| 600 | ,, | ,, | Conjeeveram. | ,, V. Perumal Mudliar | Hindu Velala | Merchant and Municipal Councillor | By a Public Meeting held on the 9th December 1894. |
| 601 | ,, | ,, | ,, | ,, T. K. S Ramakrishna Iyer | Brahmin | Pleader & Landholder | do |
| 602 | ,, | ,, | ,, | ,, V. Vencata Chari | do | do ... | do |
| 603 | ,, | ,, | ,, | ,, C.P. VencataCharlu | do | Landholder ... | do |
| 604 | ,, | ,, | ,, | ,, E. K. N. Appau Iyengar | do | Shrothriamdar and Commission Agent | do |
| 605 | ,, | ,, | ,, | ,, D. A. Ramanuja Chari | do | Landholder and Member, District Board | do |
| 606 | ,, | ,, | ,, | ,, N. S. Bhashyam Iyer | do | Merchant and School Master | do |
| 607 | ,, | ,, | ,, | ,, A. Krishnaswamy Iyer | do | Merchant ... | do |
| 608 | ,, | ,, | ,, | ,, C. S. Vencataramier | do | Pleader ... | By a Public Meeting held on the 13th December 1894. |

| Number. | Presidency or Government | Congress Circle. | Electoral Division. | Names in full of Delegates, with Honorary Titles, Scholastic Degrees, etc. | Race, Religious denomination, and caste, if any. | Occupation and Address. | How and when elected. |
|---|---|---|---|---|---|---|---|
| 609 | Madras | Chingleput | Conjeeveram | Mr. T. K. N. Srinivasa Chari | Brahmin | Pleader ... | By a Public Meeting held on the 13th December 1894. |
| 610 | ,, | ,, | ,, | ,, C. Raghava Chari. | do | do ... | do |
| 611 | ,, | ,, | ,, | ,, C. A. Krishnama Chari | do | do ... | do |
| 612 | ,, | ,, | ,, | ,, T. E. Kumaravenkata Chari | do | Pleader and Municipal Councillor | do |
| 613 | ,, | ,, | ,, | ,, P. Ramachandra Shastri | do | Pleader ... | do |
| 614 | ,, | ,, | ,, | ,, M. K. Ramanathasarma | do | Merchant ... | do |
| 615 | ,, | ,, | ,, | ,, V. S. Varadaraja Mudliar | Velala | Merchant and Municipal Councillor | do |
| 616 | ,, | ,, | ,, | ,, A Nagamia Chettiar | Hindu | Sowcar ... | do |
| 617 | ,, | ,, | ,, | ,, N. Vencataraghavier | Brahmin | 2nd Grade Pleader and Landlord | do |
| 618 | ,, | ,, | ,, | ,, W. Sivachidambara Mudliar | Velala | Merchant ... | do |
| 619 | ,, | ,, | ,, | ,, A. Valayudu Chetty | Vysya | Sowcar ... | do |
| 620 | ,, | ,, | Siruvallur | ,, P. Sanjeeviah Garoo | Brahmin | Mirasidar and Member, Sembiam Union | By a Public Meeting held on the 1st December 1894. |
| 621 | ,, | ,, | ,, | ,, V. P. Thiruvencata Chari | do | Pleader and Landholder | By a Public Meeting held on the 18th December 1894. |
| 622 | ,, | ,, | ,, | ,, S. Ramiah Chetty. | Vysya | Merchant ... | do |
| 623 | ,, | ,, | Peralur | ,, P. Parthasarathy Naidu | Velala | Mirasidar and Member, Taluq and District Boards | By a Public Meeting held on the 6th December 1894. |
| 624 | ,, | ,, | Sriperam | ,, Vencataraghava Reddiar | Hindu Sudra | Mirasidar ... | By a Public Meeting held on the 13th Decembe 1894. |
| 625 | ,, | ,, | Chetramnur | ,, C. Vedachalla Mudliar | do | do ... | By a Public Meeting held on the 21st December 1894 |
| 626 | ,, | ,, | Kalattur | ,, C. Ramabhagra Naidu | do | do ... | do |
| 627 | ,, | ,, | Trivallore | ,, A. Krishnama Chariar | Brahmin | Pleader and Shrotriyamdar | By a Public Meeting held on the 26th November 1894. |
| 628 | ,, | ,, | Madurantakam | ,, A. Krishnamachary | do | 2nd Grade Pleader ... | do |

| Number. | Presidency or Government. | Congress Circle. | Electoral Division. | Names in full of Delegates, with Honorary Titles, Scholastic Degrees, etc. | Race, Religious denomination, and caste, if any. | Occupation and Address. | How and when elected. |
|---|---|---|---|---|---|---|---|
| 629 | Madras | Chingleput. | Madurantakam | Mr. A. Seshadri Iyengar | Brahmin | Mirasidar ... | By a Public Meeting held on the 23rd November 1894. |
| 630 | " | " | " | " M. P. Rangachari. | do | do ... | do |
| 631 | " | " | " | " M. Vijiaraghava Chari | do | do .. | do |
| 632 | " | Cuddapah | Cuddapah. | " C. Chellaiya Pillai, B.A., B.L. | Indian Christian | Vakil, High Court ... | By a Public Meeting held on the 25th October 1894. |
| 633 | " | " | " | Rai Bahadur C. Jambulingam Mudliar, B.A., M.L. | Hindu Volala | do ... | do |
| 634 | " | " | " | Mr. Venkadari Rangaya Chetty Garu | Hindu Vysya | Commission Agent and Landholder | do |
| 635 | " | " | " | " V. Ramaswamy Reddy | Sudra. | Landholder ... | do |
| 636 | " | " | " | " Y. Pappayya Chetty | Vysya. | Merchant ... | do |
| 637 | " | " | " | " Krishnam Venkata Subbayya Chetty | Hindu Vysya | Pleader ... | do |
| 638 | " | " | " | " Murti Vencata Subbia | Balja. | Cloth Merchant ... | do |
| 639 | " | " | Madanapalle | " T. Narayana Shastri | Brahmin. | Headmaster, High School | By a Public Meeting held on the 7th October 1894. |
| 640 | " | " | " | " R. Giri Row, B.A.... | do | First Grade Pleader and Member, Punchayet-Union | do |
| 641 | " | " | " | " M. K. Subba Row. | do | Pleader and Manager, High School, Madanapalle | do |
| 642 | " | " | " | " O. Lakshmana Sarma | do | Pleader ... | do |
| 643 | " | " | " | " Gunti Sriramanuja Chetty | Hindu Vysya | Trader ... | do |
| 644 | " | " | " | " G. Gopalakrishnaiyar | Brahmin. | Pleader and Landed Proprietor | By a Public Meeting held on the 2nd December 1894. |
| 645 | " | " | " | " R. Seshagiri Row | do | Pleader and Landholder | do |
| 646 | " | " | " | " N. Venkataramana Row, B.A. | do | do ... | do |
| 647 | " | " | " | " Y. Sabapathi Iyer | do | Pleader ... | do |
| 648 | " | " | " | " R. Madhava Row | do | do ... | do |
| 649 | " | " | " | " P. Andhinarayana Iyer | do | do ... | do |

| Number. | Presidency or Government. | Congress Circle. | Electoral Division. | Name in full of Delegates, with Honorary Titles, Scholastic Degrees, etc. | Race, Religious denomination, and caste, if any. | Occupation and Address. | How and when elected. |
|---|---|---|---|---|---|---|---|
| 650 | Madras. | Cuddapah. | Madanapalle. | Mr. M. K. Srinavasa Iyer | Brahmin | First Assistant, High School | By a Public Meeting held on the 2nd December 1894. |
| 651 | „ | „ | Proddutur. | „ Paramahamsa Bala Subramania Ramasawmy | do | Hindu Priest ... | By a Public Meeting held on the 25th October 1894. |
| 652 | „ | „ | „ | „ H. Ranga Row Garu | do | Pleader ... | By a Public Meeting held on the 3rd December 1894. |
| 653 | „ | „ | „ | „ C. S. Srinivasa Iyer Garu | do | do ... | do |
| 654 | „ | „ | „ | „ H. Kuppu Row ... | do | do ... | do |
| 655 | „ | „ | „ | „ Y. Venkatanarayana Reddy | Sudra. | Landholder ... | do |
| 656 | „ | „ | „ | „ D. Narasiah Chetty Garu | Vysya. | Merchant and Sowcar | do |
| 657 | „ | „ | „ | „ A. Ramacharlu ... | Brahmin. | Pleader ... | do |
| 658 | „ | „ | „ | „ C. Sundaracharlu | do | do ... | do |
| 659 | „ | „ | „ | „ K. Chinnakondiah Chetty | Vysya. | Merchant ... | do |
| 660 | „ | „ | „ | „ K. Seshiah Chetty | do | do ... | do |
| 661 | „ | „ | „ | „ Parigi Barasaib Garu | Masalman. | Merchant and Agent, Bellary Cotton Press | do |
| 662 | „ | „ | „ | „ Gajyala Vencata Ramayyer | Brahmin. | Pleader ... | do |
| 663 | „ | „ | „ | „ J. B. H. Venkoba Iyengar | do | Pleader and Landholder | do |
| 664 | „ | „ | „ | „ V. Narasinga Row, B.A. | do | Pleader ... | do |
| 665 | „ | „ | „ | „ Y. Nagayya Garu.. | do | Pleader and Landholder | do |
| 666 | „ | „ | „ | „ K. Balasubbiah Chetty | Vysya. | Merchant and Sowcar | do |
| 667 | „ | „ | Piler. | „ B. Rangayya Row.. | Brahmin. | Miracidar, Landlord, Chairman, Union | By a Public Meeting held on the 4th November 1894. |
| 668 | „ | „ | Voyalpad. | „ Volipalli Venkata Ramiah Chetty | Hindu Vysya. | Landlord and Sowcar | By a Public Meeting held on the 20th November 1894. |
| 669 | „ | „ | „ | „ G. Sambu Row Garu | Mahratta Brahmin. | Landholder ... | do |
| 670 | „ | „ | „ | „ S. V. Narasimha Chari | Brahmin. | Pleader ... | do |

| Number. | Presidency or Government. | Congress Circle. | Electoral Division. | Names in full of Delegates, with Honorary Titles, Scholastic Degrees, etc. | Race, Religious denomination, and caste, if any. | Occupation and Address. | How and when elected. |
|---|---|---|---|---|---|---|---|
| 671 | Madras | Cuddapah | Nandalur. | Mr. C. V. Seshagiri Row | Brahmin | Pleader and Shotriamdar | By a Public Meeting held on the 18th December 1894. |
| 672 | ,, | ,, | ,, | ,, V. Srinivasa Chari | do | Pleader ... | do |
| 673 | ,, | ,, | ,, | ,, C. Seshiah Shastri | do | do ... | do |
| 674 | ,, | ,, | ,, | ,, C. P. Guru Murty Shastri | do | do ... | do |
| 675 | ,, | ,, | ,, | ,, C. P. Guru Murty Shastri | do | Pleader and Landholder | do |
| 676 | ,, | ,, | ,, | C. Sesha Challi Iyer | do | Pleader ... | do |
| 677 | ,, | Godavery | Cocanada | ,, B. Venkata Row Pantulu Garu, B.A., B.L. | do | Vakil, High Court and Member, District Board | By a Public Meeting held on the 21st November 1894. |
| 678 | ,, | ,, | ,, | ,, Ganjam Venkataratnam Pantulu Garu | do | Pleader and Member, District Board | do |
| 679 | ,, | ,, | ,, | ,, D. Seshagiri Row Pantulu Garu, B.A, B.L. | do | Vakil, High Court, Member, District Board; Secretary, Rajah's College | do |
| 680 | ,, | ,, | ,, | ,, P. Pamrikal Row, B.A. | do | Assistant Professor, Rajah's College | do |
| 681 | ,, | ,, | ,, | ,, K. Pera Razu ... | do | Pleader ... | do |
| 682 | ,, | ,, | ,, | ,, D Subramanyam Garu | do | do ... | do |
| 683 | ,, | ,, | ,, | ,, A. Rama Murti Garu | do | Merchant ... | do |
| 684 | ,, | ,, | ,, | ,, D. V. Hanumantha Row Garu | do | Inamdar ... | do |
| 685 | ,, | ,, | ,, | ,, B. Venkataratnam Garu | Vysya. | Merchant, Municipal Councillor, Member, District and Taluq Boards; Chairman, Native Chamber of Commerce | do |
| 686 | ,, | ,, | ,, | ,, P. C. Venkataratnam Garu | do | Merchant ... | do |
| 687 | ,, | ,, | ,, | ,, V. Padmanabham. | do | Merchant and Member, District Board | do |
| 688 | ,, | ,, | ,, | ,, P. Ramalingesa Sarma | Brahmin | Pleader ... | do |
| 689 | ,, | ,, | ,, | ,, C. Sivayanarayana Murti Naidu Garu | Telegu Hindu | Merchant ... | do |
| 690 | ,, | ,, | ,, | ,, T. Krishnaswamy Naidu Garu | Sudra. | do ... | do |

| Number. | Presidency or Government. | Congress Circle. | Electoral Division. | Names in full of Delegates, with Honorary Titles, Scholastic Degrees, etc. | Race, Religious denomination, and caste, if any. | Occupation and Address. | How and when elected. |
|---|---|---|---|---|---|---|---|
| 691 | Madras. | Godavari | Ellore. | Mr. T. V. Srinivasa Iyer, B.A, | Brahmin | Schoolmaster, C.M.S. High School | By a Public Meeting held on the 25th November 1894. |
| 692 | „ | „ | „ | „ V. Rama Row ... | do | Pleader ... | do |
| 693 | „ | „ | „ | „ K. Raghunatha Chary | do | Inamdar ... | do |
| 694 | „ | „ | „ | „ S. Sundararama Shastri | do | Pleader ... | do |
| 695 | „ | „ | „ | „ S. B. Sankaram ... | do | do ... | do |
| 696 | „ | „ | „ | „ Sitaramayar ... | do | Editor, *Desopakari* ... | do |
| 697 | „ | „ | „ | „ A. Kanaka Raju, B.A. | do | Pleader ... | do |
| 698 | „ | „ | „ | „ G. V. Siva Row ... | do | do ... | do |
| 699 | „ | „ | „ | „ Venkata Krishna Iyer | do | do ... | do |
| 700 | „ | „ | „ | „ M. Lakshmana Das | Hindu | Landholder ... | do |
| 701 | „ | „ | „ | „ M. Seetayar Garu | do | do ... | do |
| 702 | „ | „ | „ | „ W. Gopalratnam .. | Vysya | Pleader ... | do |
| 703 | „ | „ | „ | „ P. Gopalam, B.A. ... | Hindu | do ... | do |
| 704 | „ | „ | Rajahmundry. | „ N. Krishna Row Pantulu Garu, B.A., B.L, | Brahmin | do ... | By a Public Meeting held on the 2nd December 1894. |
| 705 | „ | „ | „ | „ S. Bhimasankar Row | do | do ... | do |
| 706 | „ | „ | „ | „ R. Krishna Row ... | do | do ... | do |
| 707 | „ | „ | „ | „ K. Venkataratnam Garu | do | Head Master, A. E. L. M. School | do |
| 708 | „ | „ | „ | „ Shree Raja K. R. V. Krishna Row | do | Zemindar of Polavaram | do |
| 709 | „ | „ | „ | „ Ramachandra Row Pantulu Garu B.A., B. L. | do | Vakil, High Court ... | do |
| 710 | „ | „ | „ | „ C. H. Venkataramayar Garu | do | Pleader ... | do |
| 711 | „ | „ | „ | „ C. Venkatachellum Garu, B.A., B.L. | do | Vakil, High Court ... | do |
| 712 | „ | „ | „ | „ A. Sundraramiah Garu | do | Pleader and Honorary Magistrate | do |
| 713 | „ | „ | „ | „ S. Sambasiva Row Garu | do | Pleader ... | do |
| 714 | „ | „ | „ | „ K. Streeramulu Garu | do | do ... | do |

| Number. | Presidency or Government. | Congress Circle. | Electoral Division. | Names in full of Delegates, with Honorary Titles, Scholastic Degrees, etc. | Race, Religious denomination, and caste, if any. | Occupation and Address. | How and when elected. |
|---|---|---|---|---|---|---|---|
| 715 | Madras | Godavery | Peddapuram. | Mr. M. C. Venkataraghava Iyengar. | Brahmin | Pleader ... | By a Public Meeting held on the 1st December 1894. |
| 716 | „ | „ | „ | „ C. H. Seshiah Garu | do | do ... | do |
| 717 | „ | „ | „ | „ A. Venkataramiah Garu | do | do ... | do |
| 718 | „ | „ | „ | „ V. Virayya Garu... | do | Inamdar, Agent to Jagampet Zemindary | do |
| 719 | „ | „ | „ | „ Lakshmanapathi Shastri Garu | do | Schoolmaster ... | do |
| 720 | „ | „ | „ | „ Namali Subba Row Garu. | do | do ... | ... |
| 721 | „ | „ | Narsapur. | „ A. Subba Row Pantulu Garu | do | Inamdar ... | By a Public Meeting held on the 27th October 1894. |
| 722 | „ | „ | „ | „ M. Venkatalutchi Narasimha Charlu Garu | do | Pleader ... | do |
| 723 | „ | „ | „ | „ Orugunty Kantayya Guru, B.A. | do | do ... | do |
| 724 | „ | „ | Bhimavaram. | „ T. Sambasiva Row, B.A. | do | Inamdar ... | By a Public Meeting held on the 14th October 1894. |
| 725 | „ | „ | Tanuku. | „ K. Bhima Raza Garu | Kshattriya. | do ... | By a Public Meeting held on the 2nd November 1894. |
| 720 | „ | „ | „ | „ Y. Venkatachellam Garu | Brahmin. | Pleader ... | do |
| 727 | „ | „ | „ | „ P. Subba Row Garu | do | Inamdar, Chairman, Landholders' Association, Alamur ... | do |
| 728 | „ | „ | „ | „ Y. Venkatachellum Garu | do | Pleader and Assistant Secretary, People's Association ... | do |
| 729 | „ | Vizagapatam. | Vizianagaram. | „ J. Syamasundara Row Pantulu Garu, B.A. | do | Landholder ... | By a Public Meeting held on the 23rd November 1894. |
| 730 | „ | „ | „ | „ N. V. Chellapathi Shastri Garu | do | Asst. Master, Maharajah's College and Secretary, Merchants Association | do |
| 731 | „ | „ | „ | „ P. Suryanarayana Shastri, B.A. | do | Schoolmaster ... | do |
| 732 | „ | „ | „ | „ P. Krishna Murti Pantulu Garu | do | Pleader ... | do |
| 733 | „ | „ | „ | „ K. L. Narasimha Pantulu Garu | do | do ... | do |

| Number. | Presidency or Government. | Congress Circle. | Electoral Division. | Names in full of Delegates, with Honorary Titles, Scholastic Degrees, etc. | Race, Religious denomination, and caste, if any. | Occupation and Address. | How and when elected. |
|---|---|---|---|---|---|---|---|
| 734 | Madras | Vizagapatam | Vizagapatam | Mr. M. Surya Narayana | Brahmin. | Pleader ... | By a Public Meeting held on the 1st December 1894. |
| 735 | | ,, | ,, | ,, H. Ramadas Naidu | Telugu. | Landlord ... | do |
| 736 | ,, | ,, | ,, | ,, D. V. Narasinga Row, B.A., B.L. | Brahmin. | Pleader ... | do |
| 737 | ,, | ,, | Parvatipur | ,, T. Venkata Row Pantulu | do | do ... | By a Public Meeting held on the 11th December 1894. |
| 738 | ,, | ,, | ,, | ,, Ati Appadu ... | do | Pleader, Member District and Taluq Boards | do |
| 739 | ,, | ,, | ,, | ,, Ati Krishnaiah ... Pantulu | do | Pleader ... | do |
| 740 | ,, | ,, | ,, | ,, O. V. Jagannadha Shastri | do | Pleader and Member, Taluq and District Boards | do |
| 741 | ,, | ,, | Marangi | ,, Banderu Surya Narayanaswamier Pantulu | do | Pleader and Landholder | By a Public Meeting held on the 20th December 1894. |
| 742 | ,, | ,, | Masulipatam. | ,, V. Abhirama Iyer, B.A., B.L. | do | First Grade Pleader... | By a Public Meeting held on the 25th November 1894. |
| 743 | ,, | ,, | ,, | ,, R. Venkataratnam Naidu, M.A. | Hindu. Sudra. | Assistant Professor, Noble College | do |
| 744 | ,, | ,, | ,, | ,, V. Venkataramah Pantulu | Brahmin. | Landed Proprietor ... | do |
| 745 | ,, | ,, | ,, | ,, Vemiru Subba Row Pantulu, B.A. | do | Landholder, Godugupet | do |
| 746 | ,, | ,, | ,, | ,, K. Seethapathi Row, B.A. | do | do | do |
| 747 | ,, | ,, | ,, | ,, V. V. S. Avadhani Garu | do | Pleader and Municipal Councillor | do |
| 748 | ,, | ,, | ,, | ,, V. Ramaswamy Iyer, B.A., B.L. | do | Lecturer, Noble College | do |
| 749 | ,, | ,, | ,, | ,, T. Venkatapayya Garu | do | Pleader ... | do |
| 750 | ,, | ,, | ,, | ,, T. Nagabhushanam, M.A. | do | Landholder ... | do |
| 751 | ,, | ,, | ,, | ,, P. T. Narasimha Chari, B.A., B.L. | do | Vakil, High Court ... | do |
| 752 | ,, | Kistna | Bezvada. | Rao Bahadur M. Ethurajulu Pillai Garu | Sudra Vaishnava. | Merchant and Landed Proprietor | By a Public Meeting held on the 27th October 1894. |
| 753 | ,, | ,, | ,, | Mr. K. Gangarazu Garu | Brahmin. | Landholder ... | do |

| Number. | Presidency or Government. | Congress Circle. | Electoral Division. | Names in full of Delegates, with Honorary Titles, Scholastic Degrees, etc. | Race, Religious denomination, and caste, if any. | Occupation and Address. | How and when elected |
|---|---|---|---|---|---|---|---|
| 754 | Madras. | Kistna | Bezvada | Rao Bahadur S. Lingayya Pantulu Garu | Brahmin | Pleader, Landholder, Honorary Magistrate and Municipal Chairman | By a Public Meeting held on the 27th October 1894. |
| 755 | „ | „ | „ | MrV. Ramidas Pantulu | do | Landholder ... | do |
| 756 | „ | „ | „ | „ Vinakota Kodanda Ramayya | do | Pleader ... | do |
| 757 | „ | „ | „ | „ Vinnakota Lakshmi Narasimham | do | Secretary, Vijiamandla Sabha | do |
| 758 | „ | „ | „ | „ M. Arunachellaiyar. | do | Landholder ... | do |
| 759 | „ | „ | „ | „ T. Venkataramaniah Pantulu Garu | do | Pleader and Landholder | do |
| 760 | „ | „ | „ | „ M. Venkateswara Row | do | Dewan, Senwarapet Estate | do |
| 761 | „ | „ | „ | „ M. Subbiah ... | do | Pleader ... | do |
| 762 | „ | „ | „ | „ M. Pranakusa Pillai | Vysya. | Landholder ... | do |
| 763 | „ | „ | „ | „ M. Gajapathi Row Pillai Garu | do | do ... | do |
| 764 | „ | „ | „ | „ D. Seshachellapathi Row | Brahmin. | Editor, *Kistna News*; Municipal Councillor, Manager, Tiruvier Zemindari; Assistant Secretary, Vijiavada Sabha | do |
| 765 | „ | „ | „ | „ Kosairaju Subbiah Garu | do | Landholder ... | do |
| 766 | „ | „ | Guntur. | „ Purushotam ... | Vysya. | Pleader ... | By a Public Meeting held on the 26th November 1894 |
| 767 | „ | „ | „ | „ P. Venkata Reddy. | do | Teacher, A. E. M. College | do |
| 768 | „ | „ | „ | „ C. V. Subramanya Shastri | Brahmin. | Pleader and Honorary Magistrate | do |
| 769 | „ | „ | „ | „ S. Ramaswamy Gupta | Vysya. | Merchant ... | do |
| 770 | „ | „ | „ | „ K. Appiah Dikshathulu, B.A. | Brahmin. | Landholder ... | do |
| 771 | „ | „ | Guntur | Hon. Mr. N. Subba Row Pantulu Garu, B.A., B.L. | do | Vakil, High Court and Member, Madras Legislative Council | By a Public Meeting held on the 26th November 1894. |
| 772 | „ | „ | „ | Mr. V. Bhavana Charlu, | do | Landholder, Chairman, Municipality; President, Pleaders' Association | do |
| 773 | „ | „ | „ | „ A. M. Sundara Siva | do | Principal, Sanscrit Teachers' Association; Chairman, Taxpayer's Association | do |

| Number. | Presidency or Government. | Congress Circle. | Electoral Division. | Names in full of Delegates, with Honorary Titles, Scholastic Degrees, etc. | Race, Religious denomination, and caste, if any. | Occupation and Address. | How and when elected. |
|---|---|---|---|---|---|---|---|
| 774 | Madras | Kistna | Guntur | Mr. K. Lakshmininarasimha, B.A. | Brahmin | Landholder ... | By a Public Meeting held on the 26th November 1894. |
| 775 | " | " | " | " V. Jayaramaiyar. | do | 1st Assistant, Sanscrit High School | do |
| 776 | " | " | Cherala | " Jagarlu Mudi Naidu | Hindu Vysya | Merchant and Landed Proprietor | By a Public Meeting held on the 17th November 1894. |
| 777 | " | " | " | " J. Pundareekashadu Naidu Garu | do | do ... | do |
| 778 | " | " | Gudivada | " T. Gopalakrishna Murty | Brahmin | Pleader and Landholder | By a Public Meeting held on the 5th December 1894. |
| 779 | " | " | " | " P. Ananda Row ... | do | do ... | do |
| 780 | " | " | " | " M. Bhapi Razu ... | do | do ... | do |
| 781 | " | " | " | " G. Venkatarayudu | do | Pleader ... | do |
| 782 | " | " | " | " V. Krishna Row... | do | Landholder and School Master | do |
| 783 | " | " | " | " T. Purushotam Pantulu | do | Pleader and Landholder | do |
| 784 | " | " | " | " C. Anvaduriah ... | do | Landholder ... | do |
| 785 | " | " | " | " R. Parthasarthi Iyer | do | do ... | do |
| 786 | " | " | " | " P. Venkatachellum Garu | do | do ... | do |
| 787 | " | " | " | " Patri Vencata Subba Row | do | Landholder, Secretary, Brahma Samaj, Bezvada | do |
| 788 | " | " | " | " N. Pullayya Garu., | Sudra | Ryot ... | do |
| 789 | " | " | Narsaravupet | " V. Seshavataram Garu | Vysya | Pleader and Secretary, People's Association | By a Public Meeting held on the 3rd December 1894. |
| 790 | " | " | " | " U. Anjanayalu Garu | do | Pleader and Joint Secretary, Taluq Association | do |
| 791 | " | " | " | " M. Sriramlu Garu | do | Merchant, Contractor, Member, Union Punchayet and Medical Board | do |
| 792 | " | " | Bapatla | " C. Venkatadri, B.A. | Brahmin | Pleader ... | By a Public Meeting held on the 18th November 1894. |
| 793 | " | Nellore | Venkatagiri | " Kuruwada Raghaviah Garu | do | Landholder, Secretary, H. L. S. School | By a Public Meeting held on the 18th December 1894. |

| Number. | Presidency or Government. | Congress Circle. | Electoral Division | Names in full of Delegates, with Honorary Titles, Scholastic Degrees, etc. | Race, Religious denomination, and caste, if any. | Occupation and Address. | How and when elected. |
|---|---|---|---|---|---|---|---|
| 794 | Madras | Nellore | Kanigiri | Mr. A. V. Ramaniya Charlu | Brahmin | Pleader ... | By a Public Meeting held on the 16th December 1894. |
| 795 | ,, | ,, | ,, | ,, M. Vencata Subba Row | do | do ... | do |
| 796 | ,, | ,, | ,, | ,, M. Vencatachella Mayya Garu | do | do ... | do |
| 797 | ,, | ,, | Nellore. | ,, M. Venkatasubba Chetty | Hindu Vysya | Merchant and Contractor | By a Public Meeting held on the 1st December 1894. |
| 798 | ,, | ,, | ,, | ,, D. N. Venkataramanaier, B.A., B.L. | Brahmin | Pleader and Municipal Councillor | do |
| 799 | ,, | ,, | ,, | ,, P. Subbiah Chetty. | Vysya | Merchant ... | do |
| 800 | ,, | ,, | ,, | ,, T. V. Venkataramaier, B.A., B.L. | Brahmin | Vakil, High Court; Government Pleader and Member, District Boards | do |
| 801 | ,, | ,, | ,, | ,, V. Venkatachallam Iyer, B.A., B.L. | do | Pleader ... | do |
| 802 | ,, | ,, | ,, | ,, Sugaram Subba Row Pantulu | do | Landowner ... | do |
| 803 | ,, | ,, | ,, | ,, B. Balakristna Reddy | Hindu | Landholder ... | do |
| 804 | ,, | ,, | ,, | ,, D. Venkatarama Reddy | do | Zemindar ... | do |
| 805 | ,, | ,, | ,, | ,, A. Venkayya Pantulu | Brahmin | Vakil, District Court and Municipal Councillor | do |
| 806 | ,, | ,, | ,, | ,, N. Suryanarayana Row | do | do ... | do |
| 807 | ,, | ,, | ,, | ,, A. R. Arunachella Iyer, B.A., B.L. | do | Pleader ... | do |
| 808 | ,, | ,, | ,, | ,, N. Seshadri Iyergar, B.A. | do | do ... | do |
| 809 | ,, | ,, | ,, | ,, Sultan Mohideen Sahib | Masalman | Landlord ... | do |
| 810 | ,, | ,, | ,, | ,, P. Balakrishna Pillai | Hindu Vysya | Contractor and Landed Proprietor | do |
| 811 | ,, | ,, | Ongole. | ,, C. Lakshminarasimha Row Garu. | Brahmin | Pleader and Municipal Councillor | By a Public Meeting held on the 13th November 1894. |
| 812 | ,, | ,, | ,, | ,, K. Mannara Krishna Row, B.A. | do | Pleader ... | do |
| 813 | ,, | ,, | ,, | ,, G. Ramanadhaiya Garu | do | do ... | do |

| Number. | Presidency or Government. | Congress Circle. | Electoral Divisional | Names in full of Delegates, with Honorary Titles, Scholastic Degrees, etc. | Race, Religious denomination, and caste, if any. | Occupation and Address. | How and when elected. |
|---|---|---|---|---|---|---|---|
| 814 | Madras | Nellore | Ongole | Mr. D. Markandiah Sastri Garu | Brahmin | Municipal Councillor and Member, District Board | By a Public Meeting held on the 13th November 1894. |
| 815 | ,, | | ,, | ,, P. Venkatarangiah Garu | do | Landholder & Banker | do |
| 816 | ,, | Ganjam. | Chicacole. | ,, B. Viyanna Pantulu Garu B.A. | do | Landholder, Pleader and Member, Taluq Board | By a Public Meeting held on the 22nd November 1894. |
| 817 | ,, | ,, | ,, | ,, J. Ramaseshayyah Shastri | do | Inamdar ... | do |
| 818 | ,, | ,, | ,, | ,, K. Ramaswamy Iyer, B.A. | do | Assistant Master, M. H. School | By a Public Meeting held on the 4th November 1894. |
| 819 | ,, | ,, | ,, | ,, Ippili Venkama Chetty | Hindu Vysya | Pleader ... | do |
| 820 | ,, | ,, | ,, | ,, V. Guraviah Sastri | Brahmin | Pleader, Municipal Councillor and Member, Taluq and District Boards | do |
| 821 | ,, | ,, | ,, | ,, S. Baupi Razu Pantulu | do | Pleader, Secretary, Town Hall Committee | do |
| 822 | ,, | ,, | ,, | ,, T. Venkatasiva Row | do | Proprietor, Sowdam Estate, Municipal Councillor, Member, District and Taluq Boards | do |
| 823 | ,, | ,, | ,, | ,, K. Venkatanarasiah Naidu | Hindu Vaishnava | Inamdar ... | do |
| 824 | ,, | ,, | Sompet. | ,, N. Venkata Rangadam Pantulu | do | Proprietor of Talasamudram Estate | By a Public Meeting held on the 1st December 1894. |
| 825 | ,, | ,, | ,, | ,, N. Ramanujasawmy Pantulu, B.A., B.L. | Brahmin | Pleader ... | do |
| 826 | ,, | ,, | ,, | ,, Gajana Kodanda Ramayya Garu | do | do ... | do |
| 827 | ,, | ,, | Berhampur | ,, P. Venkanna Panthulu | do | Pleader and Municipal Commissioner | By a Public Meeting held on the 17th November 1894. |
| 828 | ,, | ,, | ,, | ,, K. S. Kodandaramaiyer, B.A., B.L. | do | Pleader and Chairman, Municipal Council | do |
| 829 | ,, | ,, | ,, | ,, Maralla Venkatachellapattu Row Panthulu | do | Pleader, Landed Proprietor and Municipal Councillor | do |
| 830 | ,, | ,, | ,, | ,, V. Venkatajogayya Pantulu | do | Pleader ... | do |
| 831 | ,, | ,, | ,, | ,, P. Venkateswarier Pantulu | do | do ... | do |

| Number. | Presidency or Government. | Congress Circle. | Electoral Division. | Names in full of Delegates, with Honorary Titles, Scholastic Degrees, etc | Race, Religious denomination, and caste, if any. | Occupation and Address. | How and when elected. |
|---|---|---|---|---|---|---|---|
| 832 | Madras | Ganjam | Berhampur | Mr. Byculli Raja Garu | Brahmin | Dewan to the Rajah of Kallicota | By a Public Meeting held on the 17th November 1894. |
| 833 | " | " | " | " Sadasiva Misri ... | do | Landholder ... | do |
| 834 | " | " | " | " G. Raghava Row-Panthulu Garu, B.A., B.L. | do | Vakil, High Court and Municipal Councillor | do |
| 835 | " | " | Ganjam | " K. S. Rama Murti Panthulu Garu | do | Assistant Teacher, Kallicota College | do |
| 836 | " | " | Parla Kimedi | " Appanna Ponda ... | Urya Brahmin | Assistant Master, Maharajah's High School | By a Public Meeting held on the 18th December 1894. |
| 837 | " | " | " | " S. S. Raja Guru, B.A. | do | Tutor to the 2nd Prince of Parla Kimedi | do |
| 838 | " | " | " | " B. K. Dwipayana Row | Madwa Brahmin | Municipal Chairman | do |
| 839 | " | " | " | " G. Khadanga ... | Urya Brahmin | Landholder ... | do |
| 840 | " | Anantapur | Gooty | The Rev. William Wilson Stephenson | European Christian | Missionary ... | By a Public Meeting held on the 5th December 1894. |
| 841 | " | " | " | Mr. P. Kassava Pillai | Hindu Vysya | Pleader and Member, District Board | do |
| 842 | " | " | " | Syed Shah Ishmael Pir Husain Sharvardiy 'ul Kadri | Masalman Syed | Priest, Landholder and Member, Taluq Board | do |
| 843 | " | " | " | Mr. Junginucota Seshagiri Row | Brahmin | Landholder ... | do |
| 844 | " | " | " | " M. Nagesa Row ... | do | Pleader and Landholder | do |
| 845 | " | " | " | " O. Madha Row ... | do | Pleader ... | do |
| 846 | " | " | " | " M. Subba Row ... | do | 2nd Grade Pleader ... | do |
| 847 | " | " | " | " Chenna Busavanna Garu | Lingayet | Landholder and Ryot | do |
| 848 | " | " | Anantapur | " C. N. Muthusawmy Iyer | Brahmin | Contractor and Municipal Councillor | By a Public Meeting held on the 18th December 1894. |
| 849 | " | " | " | " P. Anathmurti Row | do | Pleader, Landholder and Municipal Councillor | do |
| 850 | " | " | " | " K. Timma Reddy | Sudra | Pleader and Landholder | do |
| 851 | " | " | " | " S. Vedajee Row ... | Brahmin | Pleader, Municipal Councillor and Member, District Board | do |

| Number. | Presidency or Government | Congress Circle. | Electoral Division. | Names in full of Delegates, with Honorary Titles, Scholastic Degrees, etc. | Race, Religious denomination, and caste, if any. | Occupation and Address. | How and when elected. |
|---|---|---|---|---|---|---|---|
| 852 | Madras. | Anantapur | Penukonda | Mr. S. Sesha Shastri, B.A., B.L. | Brahmin | Pleader and Landholder | By a Public Meeting held on the 19th October 1894. |
| 853 | „ | | „ | „ V. R. Chakravarti Iyengar | do | Pleader, Jaghirdar, Chairman, Temple Committee | do |
| 854 | „ | „ | Tadpatri | „ M. Lakshmina Narasimha Shastri Garu | do | Pleader and Shotriamdar | By a Public Meeting held on the 21st October 1894. |
| 855 | „ | Kurnool | Kurnool | „ T. Chidambara Row, B.A. | do | Pleader, Landholder, Chairman, Municipality and Member, District and Taluq Boards and Temple Committee | By a Public Meeting held on the 3rd September 1894. |
| 856 | „ | „ | „ | „ A. Subba Row ... | do | Pleader ... | do |
| 857 | „ | „ | „ | „ Allur Tirumal Row Garu | do | Pleader and Landholder | By a Public Meeting held on the 23rd September 1894. |
| 858 | „ | „ | „ | „ P Seshiah Chetty | Vysya. | Sowcar ... | do |
| 859 | „ | „ | „ | „ C. Subramania Iyer | Brahmin. | Pleader and Landholder | do |
| 860 | „ | „ | „ | „ C. Kristappa ... | Vysya. | Merchant ... | do |
| 861 | „ | Bellary. | Bellary. | „ C. S. Subramania Iyer, B.A., B.L. | Brahmin. | Vakil, High Court ... | By a Public Meeting held on the 28th November 1894. |
| 862 | „ | „ | „ | „ Vitta Seshappa Chetty | Vysya. | Secretary, Stock and Loan Transacting Company | do |
| 863 | „ | „ | „ | „ M. Ramanajulu Naidu | do | Contractor ... | do |
| 864 | „ | „ | „ | „ Yadavendram Pillai | do | do ... | do |
| 865 | „ | „ | „ | „ F. Seshachella Row B.A. | Brahmin. | Pleader ... | do |
| 866 | „ | „ | „ | „ C. Krishtappa ... | Hindu. | Merchant ... | do |
| 867 | „ | „ | „ | „ M. Nagesa Row ... | Brahmin. | Pleader and Landholder | do |
| 868 | „ | „ | „ | „ G. Virabhadrappa Naidu | Lingite. | Merchant and Proprietor, Liquor Distillery. | do |
| 869 | „ | „ | „ | „ K. Srinivasa Row, B.A. | Brahmin. | Pleader ... | do |
| 870 | „ | „ | „ | „ D. Gopala Charlu | do | do ... | do |
| 871 | „ | „ | „ | „ W. H. Ranga Row | do | do ... | do |
| 872 | „ | „ | „ | „ D. Venkatakrishnama Charlu | do | Inamdar ... | do |

| Number. | Presidency or Government. | Congress Circle | Electoral Division. | Names in full of Delegates, with Honorary Titles, Scholastic Degrees, etc. | Race, Religious denomination, and caste, if any. | Occupation and Address | How and when elected. |
|---|---|---|---|---|---|---|---|
| 873 | Madras | Bellary | Bellary | Mr. W. Krishnama Charlu | Brahmin. | Pleader ... | By a Public Meeting held on the 28th November 1894. |
| 874 | " | " | " | " T. Purushotama Row | do | do ... | do |
| 875 | " | " | " | " C Seetharam Chetty | Vysya. | Abkari Contractor ... | do |
| 876 | " | " | " | " B. Streenivasa Row | Brahmin. | Merchant ... | do |
| 877 | " | " | " | " P. Krishnamurti Achari | do | Pleader ... | do |
| 878 | " | " | " | " V. Krishna Row .. | do | Sowcar ... | do |
| 879 | " | " | " | " Madani Seshama Chetty | Vysya. | Merchant and Proprietor, Weaving and Cotton Mill | do |
| 880 | " | " | " | " S. G. Venkataraman Iyer, B.A., B.L. | Brahmin. | Pleader ... | do |
| 881 | " | " | " | " G. Latchman Row | do | Pleader, Landholder, and Municipal Councillor | do |
| 882 | " | " | " | " T. V. Chellaperumal Pillai | Velala. | Merchant ... | do |
| 883 | " | " | " | " V. Rungasawmy Naidu | do | Secretary, Bellary Civil Society | do |
| 884 | " | " | " | " T. M. Arunagan Pillai | do | Merchant ... | do |
| 885 | " | " | " | Hon. Mr. Sabhapathi Mudliar | do | Merchant and Member, Madras Legislative Council | do |
| 886 | " | " | " | Mr. S. Marisidappah | Lingayite. | Merchant ... | do |
| 887 | " | " | " | " Olahanda Kistappah | Vysya. | Merchant, Honorary Magistrate and Municipal Councillor | do |
| 888 | " | " | " | " K. Venkata Row | Brahmin. | Pleader ... | do |
| 889 | " | " | Narain Devaikare. | " A. Bhima Row ... | do | do ... | By a Public Meeting held on the 4th December 1894. |
| 890 | " | " | " | " S. Krishtacharlu . | do | do ... | do |
| 891 | " | " | " | " W. Sitarama Row. | do | do ... | do |
| 892 | " | " | " | " K. Viswanadha Row | do | do ... | do |
| 893 | " | " | Hospet. | " B. Sitarama Row ... | do | Inamdar ... | do |
| 894 | " | " | " | " B. Subbha Shastri | do | Manager, Humpy Temple | do |
| 895 | " | " | Adoni. | " C. Hanumantha Gond | do | Merchant and Landholder | By a Public Meeting held on the 30th November 1894. |

| Number. | Presidency or Government. | Congress Circle. | Electoral Division. | Names in full of Delegates, with Honorary Titles, Scholastic Degrees, etc. | Race, Religious denomination, and caste, if any. | Occupation and Address. | How and when elected. |
|---|---|---|---|---|---|---|---|
| 896 | Madras | Bellary | Adoni | Mr. T. Ranga Row... | Brahmin | Merchant and Municipal Councillor | By a Public Meeting held on the 30th November 1894. |
| 897 | " | " | " | " P. Sabhapachi Mudliar | Velala. | Agent, Messrs. Sabhapathi Mudliar & Co. | do |
| 898 | " | " | " | " Gindanoor Bhima Row | Brahmin. | Pleader and Municipal Councillor | do |
| 899 | " | " | " | " Naiothy Venkoba Row | do | Merchant and Municipal Councillor | do |
| 900 | " | North Arcot. | Vellore. | " V. C. Seshachariar | do | Pleader and Secretary, Vellore Rate Payers' Association. | By a Public Meeting held on the 3rd December 1895. |
| 901 | " | " | " | " N. Krishnama Charlu | do | Landholder ... | do |
| 902 | " | " | " | " P. Thangavelu Mudliar | Vysya. | Proprietor, V. N. Press and Vice-President, R. P. Association. | do |
| 903 | " | " | " | " M. Govindasawmy Naidu | Balija | Merchant ... | do |
| 904 | " | " | Palmaner. | " R. Swaminadha Row | Brahmin. | Mirasidar ... | By a Public Meeting held on the 10th December 1894. |
| 905 | " | " | " | " T. R. Swaminadhayer | do | Pleader ... | do |
| 906 | " | " | " | " A. Swami Iyer ... | do | Pleader and President, Ratepayers' Association | do |
| 907 | " | " | " | " V. Umamabeswara Iyer | do | Pleader ... | do |
| 908 | " | " | " | " C. Varadacharlu... | do | do | do |
| 909 | " | " | " | " B. Rangayya Chetty | Vysya. | Merchant ... | do |
| 910 | " | " | " | " M. Krishnaswamy Iyer | Brahmin. | Pleader ... | do |
| 911 | " | " | " | " A. Venkayya Sarma F. T. S. | do | Landholder ... | do |
| 912 | " | " | " | " N. Srinivasa Varada Chariar | do | Pleader and Landholder | do |
| 913 | " | " | " | " V. Krishnaswamy Iyer | do | do ... | do |
| 914 | " | " | Chittoor. | " B. C. Raghavier, B.A., B.L. | do | Pleader ... | By a Public Meeting held on the 2nd December 1894. |
| 915 | " | " | " | " L. A. Govinda Raghaviah, B.A., B.L. | do | do ... | do |
| 916 | " | " | " | " Narasimhaiyar ... | do | Member, District and Taluq Boards | do |

| Number. | Presidency or Government. | Congress Circle. | Electoral Division. | Names in full of Delegates, with Honorary Titles, Scholastic Degrees, etc. | Race, Religious denomination, and caste, if any | Occupation and Address. | How and when elected. |
|---|---|---|---|---|---|---|---|
| 917 | Madras. | North Arcot | Chittoor | Mr. V. D. Arunachella Mudliar, B.A. | Velala. | Honorary Magistrate and Member, District and Taluq Boards | By a Public Meeting held on the 2nd December 1894. |
| 918 | „ | „ | | „ G. Srinivasa Chariar, B.A. | Brahmin. | Pleader ... | do |
| 919 | „ | „ | „ | „ D. V. Rajagopala Chariar | do | Pleader and Landholder | do |
| 920 | „ | „ | „ | „ Seshama Nayanu Varu | Hindu. | Zemindar of Burgam. | do |
| 921 | „ | „ | „ | „ T. T. Viraraghava Chariar | Brahmin. | Pleader ... | do |
| 922 | „ | „ | „ | „ V. V. Gopala Chariar, B.A. | do | do ... | do |
| 923 | „ | „ | „ | „ C. V. Srinivasa Chariar | do | Pleader and Honorary Magistrate | do |
| 924 | „ | „ | „ | „ C. Subramania Reddy | Hindu Kammavar | Pleader and Landholder | do |
| 925 | „ | „ | Kaveripak | „ C. Sadasiva Mudliar | Velala | Contractor ... | By a Public Meeting held on the 16th December 1894. |
| 926 | „ | „ | „ | „ Bapathy Jagannatha Raja | Vysya | Merchant and Landed Proprietor | do |
| 927 | „ | „ | „ | K. Amin Chettiar. | do | Merchant and Mirasidar | do |
| 928 | „ | „ | „ | „ K. Veerasawmy Mudliar | Velala | Merchant and Landed Proprietor | do |
| 929 | „ | „ | „ | „ K. Thendavareya Pillai | Hindu Karivan | Mirasidar and Landed Proprietor | do |
| 930 | „ | „ | „ | „ K. Devu Mudliar. | Velala | Merchant and Landed Proprietor | do |
| 931 | „ | „ | „ | „ V. Latchmana Mudliar | do | do ... | do |
| 932 | „ | „ | Ranipettai | „ V. S. Sadasiva Mudliar | do | Pleader ... | By a Public Meeting held on the 9th December 1894. |
| 933 | „ | „ | „ | „ W. Vijiaragha a Mudliar | do | Pleader, Landholder and Municipal Councillor | do |
| 934 | „ | „ | „ | „ A. Subramania Iyer | Brahmin | Pleader and Member, District Board | do |
| 935 | „ | „ | Sholinghur | „ Vencatarama Iyer | do | Pleader ... | By a Public Meeting held on the 4th November 1894. |
| 936 | „ | „ | „ | S. A. Shadagopa Charry | do | do ... | do |

| Number. | Presidency or Government. | Congress Circle. | Electoral Divison. | Names in full of Delegates, with Honorary Titles, Scholastic Degrees, etc. | Race, Religious denomination, and caste, if any. | Occupation and Address. | How and when elected. |
|---|---|---|---|---|---|---|---|
| 937 | Madras | North Arcot | Sholinghur | Mr. T. Varadiah Garu. | Brahmin | Pleader and Secretary, Pleaders' Association | By a Public Meeting held on the 4th November 1894. |
| 938 | „ | „ | „ | „ L. Srinivasa Raghavayah | do | Secretary, Branch Theosophical Society | do |
| 939 | „ | „ | „ | „ T. Swaminadhaiyer | do | Pleader ... | do |
| 940 | „ | „ | Tirupati | „ Sheikh Hussain Sahibgin | Masalman | Merchant and Municipal Commissioner | By a Public Meeting held on the 18th December 1894. |
| 941 | „ | „ | „ | „ V. Anantachariar... | Brahmin | Vakil and Municipal Councillor | do |
| 942 | „ | „ | „ | „ M. Sundarachariar | do | Vakil ... | do |
| 943 | „ | „ | „ | „ V. Sundramier ... | do | Schoolmaster ... | do |
| 944 | „ | „ | „ | „ C. Krishnamachariar | do | Vakil and Municipal Councillor | do |
| 945 | „ | „ | „ | „ C. Krishnaswamy Iyer | do | do ... | do |
| 946 | „ | „ | „ | „ T. Krishnayya ... | do | do ... | do |
| 947 | „ | Travancore | Kadayalvedu | „ K. Narayana Nambiar | do | Editor, *Iana Paiyin* | By a Public Meeting held on the 29th November 1894. |
| 948 | Govt. of India | Hyderabad | Secundrabad | „ G. Krishnama Chariar, B.A., B.L. | do | Vakil, High Court and Landholder | By a Public Meeting held on the 4th December 1894. |
| 949 | „ | „ | „ | „ G. Sriramlu Naidu | Hindu | Contractor and Landholder | do |
| 950 | „ | „ | „ | „ B. Krishnaiyangar | Brahmin | Solicitor ... | do |
| 951 | „ | „ | „ | „ P. Ramachandra Pillai | Vysya | Pleader, High Court. | do |
| 952 | „ | „ | „ | „ J. Seymour Keay, M. P. | European | House of Commons... | do |
| 953 | „ | „ | „ | „ Dindigul Kissanna | Vysya | Sowcar ... | do |
| 954 | „ | „ | „ | „ Mir Ali | Masalman | Solicitor, Madras High Court | do |
| 955 | Bombay | Bombay | Bombay | „ Atmaram N. Phansalkar | Hindu. | Teacher, Tardeo ... | By a Meeting of the Bombay Presidency Association held on the 10th December 1894. |
| 956 | „ | „ | „ | „ Jagmohandass Vandravandass | do | Justice of the Peace and Member, Municipal Corporation | do |
| 957 | „ | „ | „ | „ Pestonji Dorabji Panday | Parsi. | ... ... | do |

| Number. | Presidency or Goverment. | Congress Circle. | Electoral Division. | Names in full of Delegates, with Honorary Titles, Scholastic Degrees, etc. | Race, Religous denomination, and caste, if any. | Occupation and Address. | How and when elected. |
|---|---|---|---|---|---|---|---|
| 958 | Bombay | Bombay | Bombay | Mr. Janordhan Sakaram Gadgal, B.A., LL.B. | Hindu. | ... ... | By a Meeting of the Bombay Presilency Association held on the 10th December 1895. |
| 959 | " | " | " | " Dharamsey Sunderdas | do | Mill owner and Justice of the Peace | do |
| 960 | " | " | " | " P. J. Swami ... | do | Medical Practitioner, Bazaar Road, Kamatipura, Byculla | do |
| 961 | " | " | " | " Ardeshir Burjorji. | Parsi. | Tutor to H. H the Prince of Jalwar | do |
| 962 | " | " | " | " M. V. Bhat ... | Brahmin. | Pleader High Court. | do |
| 963 | " | " | " | " Prabhakar Luxumon Nagpurkar | Hindu. | Pleader, Sholapur ... | do |
| 964 | " | " | " | " G. S. Mukhadam. | Brahmin. | Pleader ... | do |
| 965 | " | " | " | " Lalji Ramji ... | Hindu Lohana. | Tobacco Merchant ... | do |
| 966 | " | " | " | " Hari Bhickoo ... | do | do ... | do |
| 967 | " | " | " | " Govind Dasarath... | do | do ... | do |
| 968 | " | " | " | " Gokaldas Gordhandas | do | do ... | do |
| 969 | " | " | " | " D. E. Wacha ... | Parsi. | Mill Agent and Joint Secretary, Presidency Association | do |
| 970 | " | " | " | " Vandravandas Purushottamdas | Hindu. Bhansali. | Merchant, Justice of the Peace and Member, Municipal Corporation, Wardour Road, Breach Candy. | do |
| 971 | " | " | " | " Praulal Kaptandas Soshipara, L.C.E., M.S.A. | Hindu. | Architect and Consulting Surveyor | do |
| 972 | " | " | " | " Mulraj Khata ... | do | Merchant ... | do |
| 973 | " | " | " | " Damodar Laksmidas | do | Mill owner ... | do |
| 974 | " | " | " | " Vardraj Govind Naidu | Hindu Telugu. | Merchant ... | do |
| 975 | " | " | " | " Wanagir Rajoogir. | Hindu Mahratta. | Landlord ... | do |
| 976 | " | " | " | " Ranchordas Tribhuvandas | Hindu. | Merchant, Gowala Tank Road | do |
| 977 | " | " | " | " John daCunha ... | Portuguese Christian. | Medical Practitioner. | do |

| Number. | Presidency or Government. | Congress Circle. | Electoral Division. | Names in full of Delegates, with Honorary Titles, Scholastic Degrees, etc. | Race, Religious denomination, and caste, if any. | Occupation and Address. | How and when elected. |
|---|---|---|---|---|---|---|---|
| 978 | Bombay | Bombay | Bombay | The Hon. V. R. Natu, B.A., LL.B. | Brahmin. | Vakil, High Court and Member, Bombay Legislative Council | By a Meeting of the Bombay Presidency Association held on the 10th December 1894. |
| 979 | „ | „ | „ | Dr. M. G. Deshmukh, M.D., B.SC., B.A. | do | Private Practitioner, Member, Municipal Corporation and Fellow of the University, Girgaum | do |
| 980 | „ | „ | „ | The Hon. C. H. Setalvad, B.A., LL.B. | do | Vakil, High Court and Member, Legislative Council, Bombay, Girgaum | do |
| 981 | „ | „ | „ | Mr. A.M. Dinbandhu... | Hindu. | Merchant ... | do |
| 982 | „ | „ | „ | „ Jiwandas Dayaldas. | do | Broker ... | do |
| 983 | „ | „ | „ | „ Meghji Vallabhadas | do | Merchant ... | do |
| 984 | „ | „ | „ | „ Abaji Viswanath Kolutkar | do | do ... | do |
| 985 | „ | „ | „ | „ W. A. Chambers... | European. | Engineer ... | do |
| 986 | „ | „ | „ | „ Shripata A. Chatri | Brahmin | Pleader, District Court, Belgaum | do |
| 987 | „ | „ | „ | „ Jivanrao H. Betrgiri, B.A., B.L. | do | Pleader, Dharwar ... | do |
| 988 | „ | „ | „ | „ K. G. Agrekar, B.A., B.L. | do | Pleader, Belgaum ... | do |
| 989 | „ | „ | „ | „ V. K. Marathi ... | do | do ... | do |
| 990 | „ | „ | „ | „ K. R. Jahbal, B.A., B.L. | do | do ... | do |
| 991 | „ | „ | „ | „ B. V. Harolekar... | do | do ... | do |
| 992 | „ | „ | „ | T. V. Athnikar ... | do | General Agent, Belgaum | do |
| 993 | „ | „ | „ | „ Gangadhar T. Gokhale | do | Civil Engineer ... | do |
| 994 | „ | „ | „ | „ N. B. Moolay .. | do | Pensioned Deputy Collector, Honorary Magistrate and Member, District and Local Boards | do |
| 995 | „ | „ | „ | „ S. W. Kane ... | do | Medical Practitioner. | do |
| 996 | „ | „ | „ | „ Haji Moulvi Shekh Hussain Shekh-Chand | Musalman | Preacher Islam ... | do |
| 997 | „ | „ | „ | Dr. K. H. Bahadurji | Parsi. | Physician, Malabar Hill | do |

| Number. | Presidency or Government. | Congress Circle. | Electoral Division | Names in full of Delegates, with Honorary Titles, Scholastic Degrees, etc. | Race, Religious denomination, and caste, if any. | Occupation and Address. | How and when elected. |
|---|---|---|---|---|---|---|---|
| 998 | Bombay | Bombay | Colaba. | Mr. Vaman Bapuji Dev. | Parsi | Landed Proprietor and Salt Merchant | By a Public Meeting held on the 12th December 1894 |
| 999 | " | Deccan. | Nasik. | " V. B. Ranade ... | Brahmin | Editor, *Dnyanchakshus* | By a Meeting of the Nasik Sarvajanik Sabha on the 2nd December 1894. |
| 1000 | " | " | " | " R. B. Tholte ... | do | District Pleader, Yeola | do |
| 1001 | " | " | " | " V. B. Akut ... | do | District Pleader, Nasik | do |
| 1002 | " | " | " | " R. Y. Rage ... | Hindu Prabhu | do ... | do |
| 1003 | " | " | " | " A. R. Kawle ... | Brahmin | Vakil, Member, Sinnar Local and District Boards | do |
| 1004 | " | " | " | " G. R. Kshirsagar. | do | Pleader and Member, District and Local Boards | do |
| 1005 | " | " | " | " H. K. Ketkar ... | do | do ... | do |
| 1006 | " | " | " | " G. Narasimha Ketkar | do | District Pleader, Member, District Board and Secretary, Sarvajanik Sabha | do |
| 1007 | " | " | " | " K. S. Deshpande. | do | Member, Municipality, Taluq and Local Boards | do |
| 1008 | " | " | " | " Krishnarao Jayaram Gupti. | do | District Pleader ... | do |
| 1009 | " | " | " | " Ramachandra Mahadeva Paranjape | do | do ... | do |
| 1010 | " | Deccan. | " | " Krishnajee Dhondo Pange | do | Inami Jaghirdar, Konay | do |
| 1011 | " | " | Wai. | " Sadashiv Ramachandra Khale, B.A., LL.B. | do | Pleader, High Court | By a Public Meeting held on the 9th December 1894. |
| 1012 | " | " | Poona. | " G. D. Patwardhan | do | Merchant ... | By a Public Meeting held on the 25th November 1894. |
| 1013 | " | " | " | " Hari Naraen Apte | do | Manager, Anandasram Budhwarpet, Editor, *Konook* | do |
| 1014 | " | " | " | " S. B. Joglekar ... | do | Pleader, Thana ... | do |
| 1015 | " | " | " | " S. K. Bhagavat B.A., LL.B. | do | do ... | do |
| 1016 | " | " | " | " V. K. Satvakar ... | do | Manager, Annapurnagraha Merchant, Budhavarpet | do |

| Number. | Presidency or Government. | Congress Circle. | Electoral Division. | Names in full of Delegates, with Honorary Titles, Scholastic Degrees, etc. | Race, Religious denomination, and caste, if any. | Occupation and Address. | How and when elected. |
|---|---|---|---|---|---|---|---|
| 1017 | Bombay | Deccan | Poona | Mr. R. R. Agasthi ... | Brahmin | Municipal Commissioner and Honorary Magistrate | By a Public Meeting held on the 25th November 1894. |
| 1018 | ,, | ,, | ,, | ,, Shreemant Shankarao Narayan Satya Sahib Watu | do | Ardarand Jaghirdar, Municipal Commissioner | do |
| 1019 | ,, | ,, | ,, | ,, R. S. Mahadev Balal Namjoshi | do | Journalist, Secretary, Industrial Association and Municipal Commissioner | do |
| 1020 | ,, | ,, | ,, | ,, Vinayek Narayan Apte | do | Secretary, Merchants' Bank | do |
| 1021 | ,, | ,, | ,, | ,, Balwant Babaji Godbole | do | Medical Practitioner. | do |
| 1022 | ,, | ,, | ,, | ,, R. S. Kashinath Purusham Gadgil | do | Barrister-at-Law ... | do |
| 1023 | ,, | ,, | ,, | ,, Govind Ballal Deval | do | Author, Dramatic Works, Haripur | do |
| 1024 | ,, | ,, | ,, | ,, Kashinath G. Nathu | do | Pleader, Sadashivapet | do |
| 1025 | ,, | ,, | ,, | ,, Krishnaji Keshav Gokhale | do | Pleader ... | do |
| 1026 | ,, | ,, | ,, | ,, Vishvanath Gangadhar Shapkar | do | Proprietor, *Dnyanachakshus* | do |
| 1027 | ,, | ,, | ,, | ,, Raghunath Daji Nagarkar | do | Pleader and Municipal Commissioner | do |
| 1028 | ,, | ,, | ,, | ,, Vishnu Hari Karandikar | do | Assistant Secretary, Sarvajanik Sabha | do |
| 1029 | ,, | ,, | ,, | ,, Shivram Hari Sathe | do | Editor, *Nyayashraya.* | do |
| 1030 | ,, | ,, | ,, | Rao Saheb Vishnu Moresh Bhide | do | Pensioner, 1st Class Sub-Judge | do |
| 1031 | ,, | ,, | ,, | Mr. Gopalakrishna Gokhale, B.A. | do | Professor, Fergusson College | do |
| 1032 | ,, | ,, | ,, | ,, Sitaram Ganesh Devdhar | do | Teacher, New English School; Editor, *Sudharak* | do |
| 1033 | ,, | ,, | ,, | ,, Narharao Vinayek. | do | Merchant ... | do |
| 1034 | ,, | ,, | Satara. | Rao Saheb B. S. Sahasrabudhi | do | Pleader ... | By a Public Meeting held on the 2nd December 1894. |
| 1035 | ,, | ,, | ,, | Mr. Shreemant L. M. Kanahare | do | Landholder ... | do |
| 1036 | ,, | ,, | ,, | ,, G. B. Phansalkar.. | do | Pleader, High Court. | do |
| 1037 | ,, | ,, | ,, | ,, D. B. Parasnis ... | do | Editor, *Maharashtra Kokil* | do |

| Number. | Presidency or Government. | Congress Circle. | Electoral Division. | Names in full of Delegates with Honorary Titles, Scholastic Degree, etc. | Race, Religious denomination, and caste, if any. | Occupation and Address. | How and when elected. |
|---|---|---|---|---|---|---|---|
| 1038 | Bombay | Deccan | Satara | Mr. R. P. Karandikar | Brahmin | Pleader, High Court. | By a Public Meeting held on the 2nd December 1894. |
| 1039 | „ | „ | „ | „ Nagabudhi Boharu. | Masalman. | Trader | do |
| 1040 | „ | „ | Ahmednagar. | „ Waman Visvanath Mahajan | Brahmin. | Medical Practitioner. | By a Public Meeting held on the 4th December 1894. |
| 1041 | „ | „ | Bhimthadi. | Rao Sahib B. A. Deshpande | do | Pleader, DistrictCourt, Inamdar, Chairman, Municipality, Member, Local Board | do |
| 1042 | „ | „ | Bagalkot Bijapur. | Mr. Siddo Timaji Badami | do | Pleader and Landholder | By a Public Meeting held on the 2nd December 1894. |
| 1043 | „ | Bhusawal. | Jalgaon Khandesh. | „ Abaji Ragho Mhalas | do | Subordinate Government Pleader and Municipal Chairman, Jalgaon | By a Public Meeting held on the 3rd December 1894. |
| 1044 | „ | „ | Dhulia. | „ Balakrishna Ramachandra Kotwal | do | Pleader ... | By a Public Meeting held on the 9th December 1894. |
| 1045 | „ | „ | Bhusaval. | Rao Saheb Chintaman Bapuji Morgankar | do | Pleader and Vice-President, Municipality | do |
| 1046 | „ | „ | „ | Mr. Sakharam Ganesh Patankar | do | Pleader ... | do |
| 1047 | „ | | „ | „ Bapooji Gopal Tapasvi | do | Pleader, Bhadgaon ... | ... |
| 1048 | „ | Sholapur | Sholapur. | „ P. L. Nagpurkar... | do | Pleader ... | ... |
| 1049 | „ | „ | „ | „ Dinkar Balal Chakradev | do | Pleader and Landlord | ... |
| 1050 | „ | „ | „ | „ Dhondo Keshav Kane, B.A. | do | Professor, Mathematics, Fergusson College | ... |
| 1051 | „ | „ | „ | „ Shridhar Narayan Sathaye, B.A., LL.B. | do | Pleader ... | .. |
| 1052 | „ | „ | „ | „ Narayan Sakharam Punche, B.A. | do | Professor, Sanscrit, Fergusson College | ... |
| 1053 | „ | „ | „ | „ Vithal Luxmon ... | do | Pleader, Gulburga ... | ... |
| 1054 | „ | „ | „ | „ Gopal Vithal ... | do | do ... | ... |
| 1055 | „ | „ | „ | „ S. R. Kirloskar ... | do | Pleader, High Court. | ... |
| 1056 | „ | „ | „ | „ Govind Tatyaji ... | do | Merchant and Landholder | ... |
| 1057 | „ | Dharwar | Dharwar | „ D. Y. Athawale ... | do | Landlord ... | By a Public Meeting held on the 3rd December 1894. |

| Number. | Presidency or Government. | Congress Circle. | Electoral Division. | Names in full of Delegates, with Honorary Titles, Scholastic Degrees, etc. | Race, Religious denomination, and caste, if any. | Occupation and Address. | How and when elected. |
|---|---|---|---|---|---|---|---|
| 1058 | Bombay | Sholapur | Sholapur. | Mr. D. H. Palande ... | Brahmin | Landlord ... | By a Public Meeting held on the 3rd December 1894. |
| 1059 | " | " | " | " G. H. Vibhuti ... | Lingayat | Pleader, District Court | do |
| 1060 | " | " | " | " B. S. Joshi ... | Brahmin | Artisan ... | do |
| 1061 | " | " | " | " Datta Ramachandra Patwankar | do | Pleader, Haveri District | do |
| 1062 | " | " | " | " Ramachandra Mahadev | do | Pleader and Zemindar, Vice-President, Haveri Municipality | do |
| 1063 | " | " | Hubli. | " R. A. Sule ... | do | Zamindar ... | By a Public Meeting held on the 2nd December 1894. |
| 1064 | " | " | " | " V. B. Godbole ... | do | do ... | do |
| 1065 | " | Belgaum | Kagnoli. | " Ganesh Daji Shahade | do | Pleader, Sub-Court, Chikodi | By a Public Meeting held on the 1st November 1894. |
| 1066 | " | " | " | " Vinayekrao D. Bhila Wadikar | do | Editor, *Shikshak*, Chikodi | do |
| 1067 | " | " | " | " Krishnaji Khando Kulkarni | do | Merchant, Chikodi ... | do |
| 1068 | " | " | " | " B. A. Mahajan ... | do | Pleader, Sub-Judge Court | do |
| 1069 | " | " | Belgaum | " S. B. Bhate ... | do | Pleader ... | By a Public Meeting held on the 28th November 1894. |
| 1070 | " | " | " | " D. V. Belvi, B.A., LL.B. | do | do ... | do |
| 1071 | " | " | " | " Govind Sreenivas Velati | do | Photographer ... | do |
| 1072 | " | Gujerat. | Kaira Panch Mahals | " Manilal Pranalal Setalvad | do | Pleader ... | By a Public Meeting held on the 4th December 1894. |
| 1073 | " | " | " | " Gokuldas Dwarkadas Talati, B.A., LL.B. | do | do .. | do |
| 1074 | " | " | Ahmedabad. | " Dahyabai Izatram | do | Pleader, District Court | do |
| 1075 | " | " | " | " Govinda Apaji Patel, B.A., LL.B. | do | do ... | do |
| 1076 | " | Ratnagiri | Ratnagiri. | " Madhusudana Wasudev Athalye, B.A. | do | Landlord and Merchant | By a Public Meeting held on the 3rd December 1894. |
| 1077 | " | " | Dapoli. | " A. H. Modak ... | do | Deshmukh Dapoli .. | do |

| Number. | Presidency or Government. | Congress Circle. | Electoral Division. | Names in full of Delegates, with Honorary Titles, Scholastic Degree, etc. | Race, Religious denomination, and caste, if any. | Occupation and Address. | How and when elected. |
|---|---|---|---|---|---|---|---|
| 1078 | Bombay | Surat. | Surat. | Mr. Bezonji Maneckji, B.A. LL.B. | Parsi | Legal Profession, Rustrampura, Surat | By a Public Meeting held on the 12th October 1894. |
| 1079 | " | " | " | " Nanalal Khevlal ... | Hindu | Insurance Agent ... | do |
| 1080 | " | Ichalkaranji | Ichalkaranji. | " R. B. Apte ... | Brahmin | Pleader and Municipal Commissioner | By a Public Meeting held on the 2nd December 1894. |
| 1081 | " | " | Kolhapur. | " L. S. Diga Vedekar. | do | Pleader, Kolhapur ... | By a Public Meeting held on the 21st December 1894. |
| 1082 | " | " | " | Rai Bahadur B. S. Kirtane | do | Pensioner ... | do |
| 1083 | Central Provinces. | Nagpur. | Nagpur. | Rao Saheb Kashinath Rao Vaidhya | do | Pensioned Superintendent, Controller's Office | By a Public Meeting held on the 11th November 1894. |
| 1084 | " | " | " | Mr. Bhagirath Prasad. | Hindu Kalar | Professor, Hyslop College; Municipal Commissioner, Landlord, Damoh | do |
| 1085 | " | " | " | " Ambodasa Krishna Deshpande | Brahmin | Private Secretary to H. H. Kakur Sahib, Piploda, Malguzar | do |
| 1086 | " | " | " | Rao Saheb Keshavrao Bhowalkar | do | Pensioned Extra Assistant Commissioner | do |
| 1087 | " | " | " | Mr. Balwantrao Goyindrao Mahajan | do | Malguzar and Advocate, Judicial Commissioner's Court | do |
| 1088 | " | " | " | " Cotari Venkata Ramana Nayudu | Hindu Khetri. | Barrister-at-Law ... | do |
| 1089 | " | " | " | " Ramjiwan Jogi Nayudu | do | Headmaster, Andhra Sabha School | do |
| 1090 | " | " | " | " Keshav Vinayak Joshi, B.A. | Brahmin. | Headmaster, Neill City High School | do |
| 1091 | " | " | " | " G. W. Sane .. | do | Contractor, G. I. P. Railway and Cloth Merchant | do |
| 1092 | " | " | " | " M. Luxmon Suridhar Jog | do | Teacher, Niell City High School | do |
| 1093 | " | " | " | " V. D. Wadhonikar. | do | Malguzar and Banker. | do |
| 1094 | " | " | " | " K. N. Deshmukh... | do | Pleader, Warda ... | do |
| 1095 | " | " | " | Dr. Adhar Sing Gour, M.A., LL.M., S.C., (Cam.) | Kshattraya | Barrister-at-Law, Hoshungabad | do |
| 1096 | " | " | Balaghat. | Mr. Narayana Kelakar | Brahmin. | Pleader, Balaghat ... | By a Public Meeting held on the 15th November 1894. |

| Number. | Presidency or Government. | Congress Circle. | Electoral Division. | Names in full of Delegates, with Honorary Titles, Scholastic Degrees, etc. | Race, Religious denomination, and caste, if any. | Occupation and Address. | How and when elected. |
|---|---|---|---|---|---|---|---|
| 1097 | Central Provinces. | Nagpur | Rajanandgaon. | Mr. V. Sarangapani Mudliar | Hindu Sudra. | General Contractor and Landlord, Manager, Bulram Press and Municipal Commissioner | By a Public Meeting held on the 25th November 1894. |
| 1098 | „ | „ | Saugor. | „ Narayana Balakrishna Nakhre | Brahmin. | Proprietor, Olcott Press, Saugor | By a Public Meeting held on the 20th December 1894. |
| 1099 | „ | „ | Wardha. | „ Keshavarao Mahadeo Kavale | do | Pleader and Banker, Municipal Commissioner and Member, District Board | By a Public Meeting held on the 6th December 1894. |
| 1100 | Government of India. | Berars. | Akola. | „ V. R. Mudholkar... | do | Editor, "*Vaidharabha*" | By a Public Meeting held on the 17th December 1894. |
| 1101 | „ | „ | Ellichpur. | „ Ganesh Mahesh Sahasrabuddhe | do | Pleader, District Court; Secretary, Municipality, Ellichpur | By a Public Meeting held on the 9th December 1894. |
| 1102 | „ | „ | Amraoti. | „ G. N. Kane ... | do | Pleader ... | By a Meeting of the Berars Sarvajanik Sabha held on the 2d December 1894. |
| 1103 | „ | „ | „ | „ Ghulam Ahmed Khan | Musalman. | Zemindar and Member, District Board | do |
| 1104 | „ | „ | „ | „ Rangnath Narsingn Madholkar, B.A., LL.B. | Brahmin. | Pleader, High Court; Landholder, Vice, Chairman, Municipality. | do |
| 1105 | „ | „ | „ | „ Moro Vishvanath Joshi, B.A., LL.B. | do | Pleader, High Court. | do |
| 1106 | „ | „ | „ | „ Babaji Mahadev Dikshit | Hindu. Prabhu. | Pleader ... | do |
| 1107 | „ | „ | „ | „ Keshav Bulwant Deshpande | Brahmin. | Banker ... | do |
| 1108 | „ | „ | „ | „ Vinayak Sarvadharam Oke | do | Pleader ... | do |
| 1109 | „ | „ | Wun. | „ L. C. Bapat ... | do | Pleader, Yeotmal ... | By a Public Meeting held on the 31st October 1894. |
| 1110 | „ | „ | „ | „ S. M. Deva ... | do | do | do |
| 1111 | „ | „ | „ | „ R. R. Bapat ... | do | do | do |
| 1112 | „ | „ | Bassim. | „ L. A. Mahajan ... | do | Merchant, Mongrul Pir | do |
| 1113 | Bombay. | Scinde. | Karachi. | „ Daulatram Jethumal ... | Hindu. | Pleader ... | By a Meeting of the Scinde Sabha held on the 19th December 1894. |
| 1114 | „ | „ | Sukkur. | Rao Bahadur Peshumal | do | do | do |

| Numbes. | Presidency or Government | Congress Circle. | Electoral Division. | Names in full of Delegates, with Honorary Titles, Scholastic Degrees, etc. | Race, Religious denomination, and caste, if any. | Occupation and Address. | How and when elected. |
|---|---|---|---|---|---|---|---|
| 1115 | Bombay | Scinde | Shikarpur. | Seth Gohindram Khatan Mal | Hindu | Merchant, Shikarpur. | By a Meeting of the Scinde Sabha held on the 10th December 1894. |
| 1116 | " | " | " | Seth Balchand Sitaram | | do | do |
| 1117 | N. W. I | Allahabad. | Allahabad. | Hon. Raja Rampal Singh | Kshattrya | Talukdar and Member, N. W. P. Legislative Council | By a Public Meeting held on the 30th November 1894. |
| 1118 | " | " | " | Hon. Babu Charoo Chander Mitter | Kayesth. | Merchant, Pleader and Member, N. W. P. Legislative Council. | do |
| 1119 | " | " | " | Pandit, Madan Mohan Malaviya, B.A., LL.B. | Brahmin. | Vakil, High Court... | do |
| 1120 | " | " | Alighar. | Hafiz Mahamad Abdur Rahim | Masalman. | Pleader, Aligarh ... | By a Public Meeting held on the 20th December 1894. |
| 1121 | " | " | Agra. | Pandit Tulsi Ram Misr, M.A., F.T.S. | Brahmin. | Professor, St. John's College, Agra | By a Public Meeting held on the 9th December 1894. |
| 1122 | " | Benares. | Benares. | Mr. Raghunath Dass... | do | Pleader ... | By a Public Meeting held on the 20th December 1894. |
| 1123 | " | " | Gorakhpur. | " Alfred Nundy ... | Bengali. Christian. | Barrister-at-Law ... | do |
| 1124 | " | Oudh. | Lucknow | Munshi Gunga Pershad Varma | Hindu. | Editor, *Advocate* ... | By a Public Meeting held on the 17th December 1894. |
| 1125 | " | " | " | Pandit Bishen Narayen Dar | Brahmin. | Barrister-at-Law ... | do |
| 1126 | " | " | " | " Narayan Masladhar | do | Pleader ... | do |
| 1127 | " | " | " | " Ratannath ... | do | do ... | do |
| 1128 | " | " | " | Dr. C. C. Ghose ... | do | ... ... | do |
| 1129 | " " | " | Kalakankar. | Thakur Ramprasad Singh | Kshattraya | Sub-Editor, *Hindustan* | do |
| 1130 | Punjab. | Lahore. | Lahore. | Captain A. T. Banon | European. | Zemindar, Kulu (late) Bengal Staff Corps | By a Public Meeting held at Lahore on the 9th December 1894. |
| 1131 | " | " | " | Mr. H. Morgan-Browne | do | Barrister-at-Law, London | Do. also at Calcutta, Gaya, Madras and other places. |
| 1132 | " | " | " | Lala Murlidhar ... | Katri. | Pleader, Chief Court, Amballa | By a Public Meeting held at Lahore on the 9th December 1894. |

| Number. | Presidency or Government. | Congress Circle. | Electoral Division. | Names in full of Delegates, with Honorary Titles, Scholastic Degrees, etc. | Race, Religious denomination and caste, if any. | Occupation and Address. | How and when elected. |
|---|---|---|---|---|---|---|---|
| 1133 | Punjab | Lahore | Lahore | Mr. Jaishiram | Katri | Pleader, Chief Court, Lahore | By a Public Meeting held at Lahore on the 9th December 1894. |
| 1134 | Bengal. | Calcutta. | Calcutta. | „ J. Ghosa ... | Brahmin. | Zemindar, Merchant, Honorary Presidency Magistrate & Municipal Commissioner | By a Meeting of the British Indian Association on the 21st December 1894. |
| 1135 | „ | „ | „ | Babu Bipin Bihari Mi ra | Kayastha. | Landlord, Upper Circular Road, Sham Bazar | By the Northern Metropolitan Division on the 14th December 1894.<br>By th Noakhali Bar Association on the 27th December 1894.<br>By the Northern Metropolitan Division. |
| 1136 | „ | „ | „ | „ Nibaran Chandra Dutt | do | Merchant | do |
| 1137 | „ | „ | „ | „ Pashupati Nath Basu | do | Landlord, 65, Bagh Bazaar Street | By the Northern Metropolitan Division on the 14th December 1894. |
| 1138 | „ | „ | „ | „ Bomoko Nath Mitter | do | Zamindar | do |
| 1139 | „ | „ | „ | Hon. Surendra Nath Banerjea | Brahmin. | Member, Legislative Council Bengal, and Calcutta Municipality | By the Indian Association on the 7th December 1894. |
| 1140 | „ | „ | „ | Babu Kalicharn Bannerjee, M.A | Bengali. Christian | Pleader ... | do |
| 1141 | „ | „ | „ | Mr. P. N. Mitter ... | Hindu. | Merchant, and Landlord | do |
| 1142 | „ | „ | „ | Babu Kedarnath Banerjee | Brahmin. | do | do |
| 1143 | „ | „ | „ | „ Krishna Kumar Mitter | Kayesth. | Editor, *Sanjibani* ... | do |
| 1144 | „ | „ | „ | „ Herambo Chander Maitro, M.A. | do | Professor, City College | do |
| 1145 | „ | „ | „ | Pandit Kaliprosonno Bisharad | Bengali Atheist | Editor, *Hita bindhi*... | By the Southern Metropolitan Division on the 19th December 1894 |
| 1146 | „ | „ | Baranagore | „ Yalinder Nath Choudry, M.A., B.L. | do | Zamindar ... | By the Indian Association on the 7th December 1894. |
| 1147 | „ | „ | Mymensing | Babu Amarchand Dutt | Kayesth. | Teacher and Editor, *Charu Mihir* | do |

| Number. | Presidency or Government. | Congress Circle. | Electoral Division. | Names in full of Delegates, with Honorary Titles, Scholastic Degrees, etc. | Race, Religious denomination, and caste, if any. | Occupation and Address. | How and when elected. |
|---|---|---|---|---|---|---|---|
| 1148 | Bengal. | Calcutta. | Mymensing. | Babu Sasankar Kumar Ghosh, B.A., B.L. | Kayesth. | Head Master, Muktagacha School | By a Public Meeting held on the 7th December 1894. |
| 1149 | ,, | ,, | Pabna. | ,, Kunjlal Shaba ... | Hindu. | Medical Practitioner | By a Public Meeting held on the 3rd December 1894. |
| 1150 | ,, | ,, | ,, | ,, Mohini Mohan Chakravarti, M.A., B.L. | Brahmin. | Pleader and Municipal Commissoner | do |
| 1151 | ,, | ,, | Hooghly. | ,, Vishnu Pada Chatterjee, M.A., B.L. | do | Pleader ... | do |
| 1152 | ,, | ,, | Backerganj | ,, Harakanta Sen ... | Vaidhya. | Secretary, Bengal Loan Office | By a Public Meeting held on the 11th December 1894. |
| 1153 | ,, | ,, | Murshidabad. | ,, Boykuntha Nath Sen, B.L. | do | Vakil, High Court and Honorary Magistrate | do |
| 1154 | ,, | ,, | ,, | ,, Hemendra Nath Sen B.L. | do | Zemindar and Pleader | do |
| 1155 | ,, | Faridpur. | Faridpur. | ,, Ambica Charan Mozumdar | Brahmin. | Zemindar, Pleader, and Chairman, Municipality | do |
| 1156 | ,, | ,, | ,, | ,, Prithvi Chandra Roy | Hindu. | Zemindar Chutnapur | do |
| 1157 | ,, | Dacca. | Dacca. | ,, Sarat Chandra Chakravarti, B.L. | Brahmin. | Pleader ... | By a Public Meeting held on the 17th December 1894. |
| 1158 | ,, | Chittagong. | Chittagong. | ,, Basanta Mohan Sen, B.A. | Vaidhya. | Landholder ... | By a Public Meeting held on the 19th December 1894. |
| 1159 | ,, | Rajshahye. | Bogra. | ,, Jadublal Roy ... | Kayastha. | Agent to K.B. Estate; Honorary Magistrate | By a Public Meeting held on the 29th December 1894. |
| 1160 | ,, | ,, | Rajshahye | ,, Kali Prosonno Acharya, B.L. | Hindu. | Pleader ... | By a Public Meeting held on the 18th December 1894. |
| 1161 | ,, | Chota Nagpur | Purulia. | ,, Sarat Chandra Sen | Vaidhya. | Vakil, Manbhum ... | do |
| 1162 | ,, | Behar. | Dinapore. | ,, Madhob Chunder Chatterjee, M.A., B.L. | Brahmin. | Pleader ... | By a Public Meeting held on the 23rd November 1894. |
| 1163 | ,, | ,, | ,, | ,, Rakhaldas Sen ... | Vaidhya. | do ... | do |

*The following translations of Speeches delivered in Vernacular were forwarded to the Editor too late for insertion in the body of the Report and are consequently appended here.*

## THE POVERTY OF INDIA.

The following is as near a translation as can be made of the speech delivered by A. C. Parthasaradhi Naidu, in supporting the 3rd Resolution (Poverty of India) of the Tenth Indian National Congress:—

It is needless for me here to dilate on the importance of this resolution as affecting the interests of the teeming millions who inhabit this great land. It is next in importance only to the question of the reform and reconstitution of our Legislative Councils, in which, thanks to the labours of noble Englislimen, we have partially succeeded. It is emphatically the poor man's resolution, and a resolution, too, which we shall be wanting in our duty if we did not again and again press on the attention, the generous attention, of our rulers. H s-torians and travellers in the past have given us a glorious picture of the plenty and prosperity with which India had been blessed, when she was yet a 'barbarous' country, that is to say, when it had not yet been brought under the sphere of influence" of England I am not concerned here to dwell on that picture of a bygone age, except for the purpose of contrasting it with the stern realities of the India we know and see. That is in every say a fascinating picture; indeed, it is so facinating a picture that the majority of Englishman and English women who derive all their notions of India from the books they read, tric themselves into the belief, the preposterous belief, that they can find in the India of to-day, a counterpart to that picture which glows with living colours on the canvas of history. To the great majority of stay at home Englishmen nothing can be more impressive than the stories they hear of the exploits of their countrymen in India, of the stupendous salaries received, of colossal fortunes made, of splendid receptions, balls, fetes which are intended to relieve the monotony of dreadful work in the plains and on the hills; of furloughs cheapry earned, of compensation allowance, &c., &c., &c. But what is the condition of India as we know it,—as imoartial officials like Hunter have described it—as non-official Englishmen like Seymour Keay have found it? A great agricultural class living on the verge of starvation unable to cope with the pressure of population, and the intolerable tyranny of the tax grinding machinery which the Government know so well how to manipulate. Add to this the difficulty of carrying on agricultural operations, the benign regulations of the Forest code, and the declared policy of the Government to carry on Forest administration without reference to the needs of the agriculturist in regard to grazing, implements, &c. Reduced as the ryots are to this pitiable plight, the pressure of oppressive taxation forces them to either sell or mortgage their lands. To the political economist this enormous transfer of property may furnish proof of increasing prosperity; but to *practical economists* like the people of India it is a sign of anything but prosperity! Instead of contributing to their prosperity, these transfers land the ryots in litigation, which again is responsible for the state of chronic indebtedness in which they live. Litigation means ruin in these days,—at least so far as the poor ryots are concerned. Independent of the above causes for the poverty of our country, the extinction, through European competition, of the indigenous manufactures, presents no mean obstacles to the satisfactory solution of the problem of poverty in India. Though of late several new industries have sprung up, they are unable to cope with foreign competition. And even where they show signs of vigorous growth, they are handicapped by an excise duty. While our countrymen are labouring under so many disadvantages, by reason of the monopoly of trade which Europeans enjoy, the resources of India are developing and fructifying their pockets

In fact, it is a case of monopoly all round, whether in the public service or in mercantile concerns. Gentlemen, I must now invite your attention to the Book I hold in my hand. It is called "Forty years Progress in the Madras Presidency," written by Dewan Bahadur Srinivasa Ragava Iyengar, C.I.E. It is no wonder that the people in England should think that we are rolling in riches. God grant such a state to us once more. But I do not know what to say when we find Dewan Bahadur Srinivasa Ragava Iyengar could bring himself to say in this book that so far as this Presidency is concerned, the transfer by sale or mortgage of land by ryots is proof positive of prosperity. That it is not so, needs no further demonstration. Speaking of the cost of food in this country, Dewan Bahadur Srinivasa Ragava Iyengar says that two annas per diem to a Brahmin and one anna to a non-Brahmin are quite sufficient. How valuable are these figures, Gentlemen, it is for you to decide. For my own part I am inclined to think that it is an absurd statement. Much less would have been necessary in bygone days when Brahmins had nothing to do but practice austerities, and lead ascetic lives. In these days of Western civilisation and anglicised notions even in the remotest parts of the rural tracts, and with the ever awaiting *famine*, and the consequent enhanced market rates, coupled with the pressure of taxation of all sorts, how is it possible for Brahmin and non-Brahmin alike to live upon such a starvation allowance! There were days when there were timely rains, there were days when people had free access to forests, there were days when there was no legislature in India to make the commonest necessities of life such as salt, bear taxation, and above all there were days when tastes were simple and the necessaries of life exceedingly cheap; now that those days are gone for ever, is it not a pitiful joke to tell us that what was good enough *then* will be good enough *now?* It passes my wit how the Dewa Bahadur brought himself to perpetrate so egregious a blunder. Though our benign Government may value his opinion on this point, I am sure you gentlemen will not. I will presently show how his opinion is valueless. Behold, gentlemen, the book I hold in my hand. It is a Government publication, which you can have for the modest sum of Re. 1. But the materials which go to make up the book, namely, the calico, the morocco, the superior glazed paper, and all that sort of thing separately valued would cost more than a rupee.

[Here the President sounded the Gong, but encouraged by the vigorous cries of "Go on, the speaker concluded with an impassioned appeal to the President to represent to his countrymen "at home" the true facts of the situation in India, which, instead of teeming with plenty, is at present groaning under the intolerable burden of the oppressive Salt, Forest, and a host of other taxes, local and imperial.]

---

## FINANCIAL INQUIRY.

In supporting the fifth Resolution (Financial Inquiry) Mr. A. C. Parthasaradhi Naidu, of Madras, spoke as follows:—

Our prayer for parliamentary inquiry is not a new one. Upwards of 50 years ago, the now defunct Native Association of Madras, consisting of eminent men like the Honorable Gajula Lakshmi Narasimhulu Chetty Garu, and others, in a memorial extending over 122 paras submitted to Parliament, amongst other things, prayed for an inquiry into Indian affairs at least once in 3 or 5 years. In the good old days of the East India Company of green and pious memory, an inquiry was made once in 20 years; but with the good old Company, that practice has been given up. Such being the case, the appointment of a Parliamentary Committee, which is promised by Her Majesty's Government and which is to inquire only into the expenditure of India, ought to be welcomed, on the principle that half a loaf is better than no loaf. But a partial and defective inquiry conducted in a haphazard fashion may be productive of more harm than good. An inquiry which embraces both revenue and expenditure, the ability of the tax-payer in India to bear the burden of taxation imposed on him, and the unsatisfactory financial relations at present existing between India and England is just what we require. I suspect the Government labours under the delusion that there is practically no limit to the tax paying capacity of the country, and that therefore an inquiry into the sources of income of the country need not be held. We Indians don't and won't grumble to pay reasonable taxes. Far from it. But our only grievance is that the money we pay leaves this country in the shape of big salaries to Europeans, war expenses, and exchange compensation allowances, &c. Although the old Hindu Rajahs were despotic sovereigns and oppressive in their demand of taxes, we derived consolation from the fact that the money did not leave this country in the form of tribute to a foreign and paramount power. Under these circumstances, it is to be earnestly hoped that a thorough and searching inquiry will be held into the financial condition of the country, and that the labours of the Committee, the appointment of which we anxiously look forward to, will pave the way for much needed and long-delayed reforms.